D1302831

GLENCOE LITERATURE

The Reader's Choice

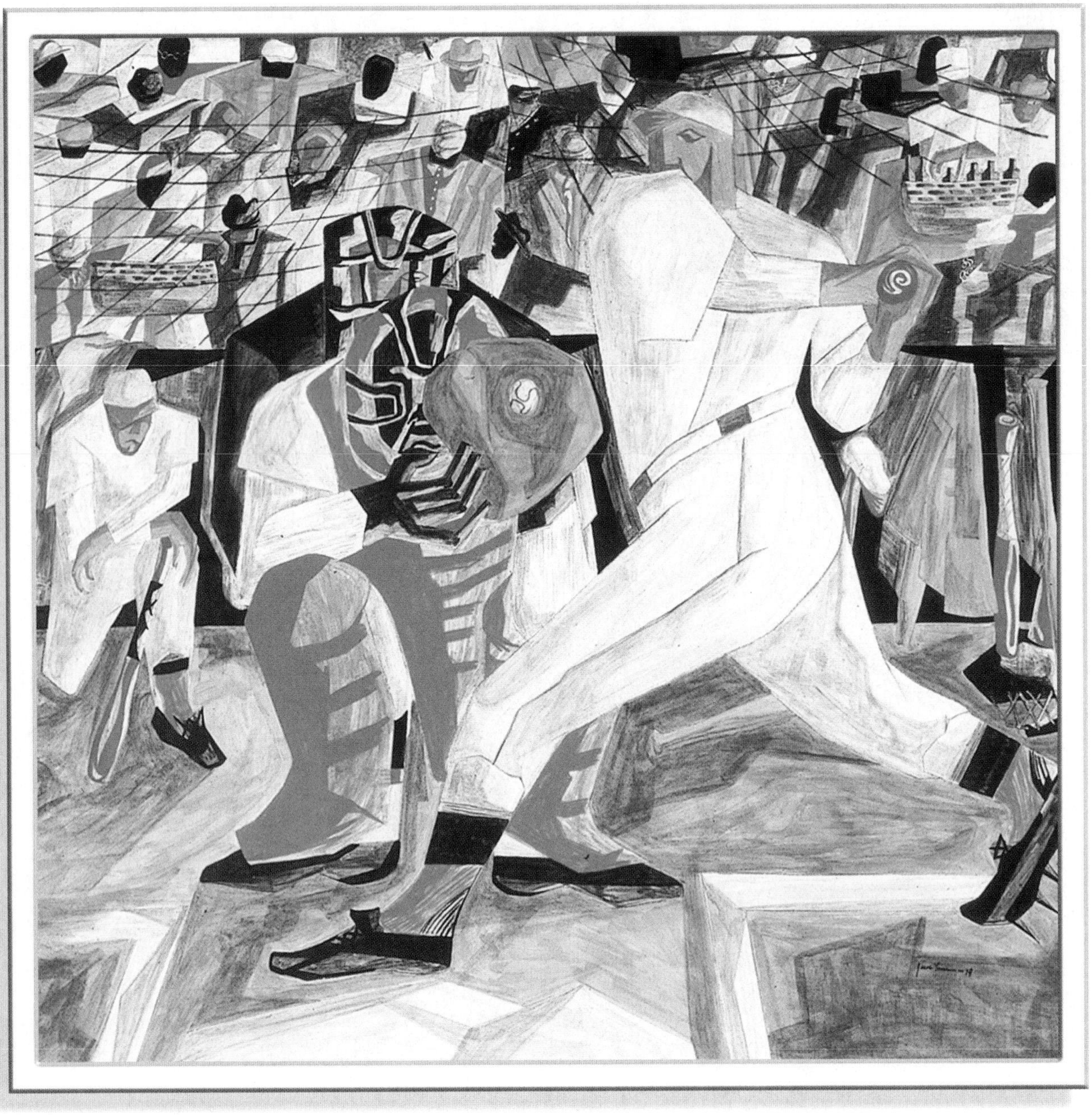

Teacher Wraparound Edition

GLENCOE LITERATURE

The Reader's Choice

Program Consultants

Beverly Ann Chin
Denny Wolfe
Jeffrey Copeland
Mary Ann Dudzinski
William Ray
Jacqueline Jones Royster
Jeffrey Wilhelm

Course 3

Glencoe McGraw-Hill

New York, New York Columbus, Ohio Woodland Hills, California Peoria, Illinois

Acknowledgments

Grateful acknowledgment is given authors, publishers, photographers, museums, and agents for permission to reprint the following copyrighted material. Every effort has been made to determine copyright owners. In case of any omissions, the Publisher will be pleased to make suitable acknowledgments in future editions.

Acknowledgments continued on page R167.

The Princeton Review

The Standardized Test Practice pages in this book were written by The Princeton Review, the nation's leader in test preparation. Through its association with McGraw-Hill, The Princeton Review offers the best way to help students excel on standardized assessments.

The Princeton Review is not affiliated with Princeton University or Educational Testing Service.

Glencoe/McGraw-Hill

A Division of The ***McGraw-Hill*** *Companies*

Copyright © 2002 by The McGraw-Hill Companies, Inc. All rights reserved. Except as permitted under the United States Copyright Act of 1976, no part of this publication may be reproduced or distributed in any form or means, or stored in a database or retrieval system, without the prior written permission of the publisher.

Printed in the United States of America

Send all inquiries to:
Glencoe/McGraw-Hill
8787 Orion Place
Columbus, OH 43240-4027

ISBN 0-07-825107-9
(Student Edition)

ISBN 0-07-825138-9
(Teacher Wraparound Edition)

2 3 4 5 6 7 8 9 10 071/043 05 04 03 02

dg-TxT
SmH Gr8
2002

Senior Program Consultants

Beverly Ann Chin is Professor of English, Director of the English Teaching Program, Director of the Montana Writing Project, and former Director of Composition at the University of Montana in Missoula. In 1995–1996, Dr. Chin served as President of the National Council of Teachers of English. She currently serves as a Member of the Board of Directors of the National Board for Professional Teaching Standards. Dr. Chin is a nationally recognized leader in English language arts standards, curriculum, and assessment. Formerly a high school English teacher and adult education reading teacher, Dr. Chin has taught in English language arts education at several universities and has received awards for her teaching and service.

Denny Wolfe, a former high school English teacher and department chair, is Professor of English Education, Director of the Tidewater Virginia Writing Project, and Director of the Center for Urban Education at Old Dominion University in Norfolk, Virginia. For the National Council of Teachers of English, he has served as Chairperson of the Standing Committee on Teacher Preparation, President of the International Assembly, member of the Executive Committee of the Council on English Education, and editor of the SLATE Newsletter. Author of more than seventy-five articles and books on teaching English, Dr. Wolfe is a frequent consultant to schools and colleges on the teaching of English language arts.

Program Consultants

Jeffrey S. Copeland is Professor and Head of the Department of English Language and Literature at the University of Northern Iowa, where he teaches children's and young adult literature courses and a variety of courses in English education. A former public school teacher, he has published many articles in the professional journals in the language arts. The twelve books he has written or edited include *Speaking of Poets: Interviews with Poets Who Write for Children and Young Adults* and *Young Adult Literature: A Contemporary Reader.*

Mary Ann Dudzinski is a former high school English teacher and recipient of the Ross Perot Award for Teaching Excellence. She also has served as a member of the core faculty for the National Endowment for the Humanities Summer Institute for Teachers of Secondary School English and History at the University of North Texas. After fifteen years of classroom experience in grades 9–12, she currently is a language arts consultant.

William Ray has taught English in the Boston Public Schools; at Lowell University; University of Wroclaw, Poland; and, for the last fourteen years, at Lincoln-Sudbury Regional High School in Sudbury, Massachusetts. He specializes in world literature. He has worked on a variety of educational texts, as editor, consultant, and contributing writer.

Jacqueline Jones Royster is Professor of English and Associate Dean of the College of Humanities at The Ohio State University. She is also on the faculty of the Bread Loaf School of English at Middlebury College in Middlebury, Vermont. In addition to the teaching of writing, Dr. Royster's professional interests include the rhetorical history of African American women and the social and cultural implications of literate practices.

Jeffrey Wilhelm, a former English and reading teacher, is currently an assistant professor at the University of Maine where he teaches courses in middle and secondary level literacy. He is the author and co-author of several books and articles on the teaching of reading and literacy, including *You Gotta BE the Book* and *Boys and Books*. He also works with local schools as part of the fledgling Adolescent Literacy Project and is the director of two annual summer institutes: the Maine Writing Project and Technology as a Learning Tool.

25866

Teacher Reviewers

Bill Beyer
General Wayne Middle School
Malvern, Pennsylvania

Sister Marian Christi
St. Matthew School
Philadelphia, Pennsylvania

Christine Ferguson
North Buncombe Middle School
Asheville, North Carolina

Elizabeth Fischer
Tower Heights Middle School
Centerville, Ohio

Diane Gerrety
Bridgetown Junior High
Cincinnati, Ohio

Susan Giddings
Marble Falls Middle School
Marble Falls, Texas

Denise Goeckel
Magsig Middle School
Centerville, Ohio

Debbie Hampton
Central Davidson Middle School
Lexington, North Carolina

Tammy Harris
Walnut Springs Middle School
Columbus, Ohio

Marlene Henry
Northwood Elementary
Troy, Ohio

Brian Hinders
Tower Heights Middle School
Centerville, Ohio

Cheryl Keffer
Fayette County Schools Gifted Program
Oak Hill, West Virginia

Sheryl Kelso
Oldtown School
Oldtown, Maryland

Gail Kidd
Center Middle School
Azusa, California

Karen Mantia
Northmont City Schools
Clayton, Ohio

Nancy Mast
Hobart Middle School
Hobart, Indiana

Chiyo Masuda
Albany Middle School
Albany, California

Kim Mistler
Delhi Junior High School
Cincinnati, Ohio

Wilma Jean Nix
Baldwin Junior High School
Montgomery, Alabama

Joe Olague
Alder Junior High
Fontana, California

Bonita Rephann
Musselman Middle School
Bunker Hill, West Virginia

Marie Rinaudo
St. John Berchman's Cathedral School
Shreveport, Louisiana

Carol Schowalter
El Roble Intermediate School
Claremont, California

Karen Shannon
Davis Drive Middle School
Apex, North Carolina

Joan Slater
Strack Intermediate
Klein, Texas

Joyce Stakem
St. Catherine of Siena School
Wilmington, Delaware

Elizabeth Struckman
Bridgetown Junior High School
Centerville, Ohio

Debbie Trepanier
Jenkins Middle School
Chewelah, Washington

Sarah Vick
Central Davidson Middle School
Lexington, North Carolina

Erin Watts
Albright Middle School
Houston, Texas

Anne Welch
Huntsville Middle School
Huntsville, Alabama

James Zartler
Centennial Middle School
Portland, Oregon

Book Overview

Contents

THEME ONE

indicates world literature

THEME TWO

THEME ❧ THREE

Which Way to Go?

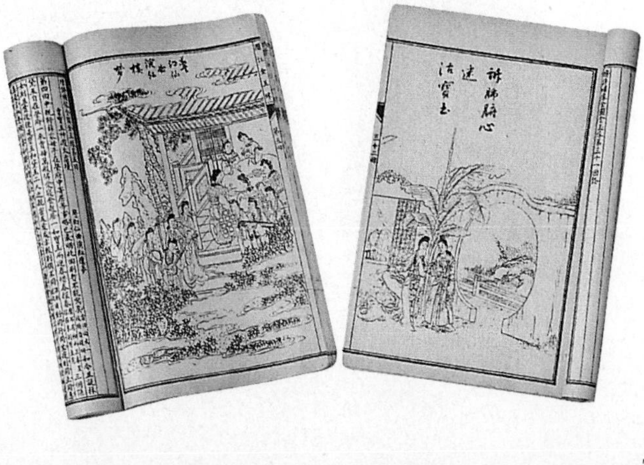

THEME FOUR

CONTENTS

THEME FIVE

Free to Be

THEME SIX

THEME SEVEN

Faces of Dignity

THEME ❧ EIGHT

Hair-Raising Tales

Reference Section

Features

MEDIA Connection

COMPARING SELECTIONS

GENRE FOCUS

Active Reading Strategies

Interdisciplinary Connection

Writing WORKSHOP

Skills

Grammar Link

Listening, Speaking, and Viewing

Reading and Thinking Skills

Technology Skills

Vocabulary Skills

Writing Skills

Skill Minilessons

GRAMMAR AND LANGUAGE

READING AND THINKING

VOCABULARY

Selections by Genre

Fiction

Nonfiction

Poetry

Myths, Legends, Folktales

Drama

Songs

Electronic Media

Comic Strips

Program Philosophy

What are the goals of *Glencoe Literature?*

by Denny Wolfe

Glencoe Literature was inspired by the belief that all students—from all cultures, of all abilities—can benefit from reading rewarding literature. We recognize, however, that in order for students to be well read in today's information society, they need also to read well. With diverse and visually appealing anthologies and instructive resources, ***Glencoe Literature*** helps students meet both goals.

Presenting quality literature for all students To reflect our increasingly diverse society, each book presents as wide an array of selections as possible. A rich mix of classic and contemporary selections unites old voices with new. Authors from many cultures address a wide range of topics and themes. And through informed exposure to a variety of reading material—from creative genres, such as poems, songs, stories, plays, myths, and folktales, to expository texts, such as biographies, oral histories, letters, essays, magazine articles, and editorials—students learn to recognize the purpose and structural features of different kinds of text. ***Glencoe Literature*** enables teachers and students to share a wealth of literary experiences and to explore together the many voices of modern society.

Improving reading skills of all students ***Glencoe Literature*** fosters universal access to the language arts curriculum. Average students, advanced learners, students with special needs, English language learners (ELL)—all can be successful in meeting or exceeding state and local teaching objectives. In the following ways, ***Glencoe Literature*** helps all students develop skills as readers, writers, listeners, speakers, and viewers:

- **Three-Part Instructional Format**
  A well-organized and logical teaching strategy promotes reading comprehension and language development for each selection in ***Glencoe Literature***. The **Before You Read** section sparks interest, builds background knowledge, and previews key vocabulary words from the selection. Next, the **selection pages** include definitions and pronunciation guides for vocabulary words, footnotes for unfamiliar words or concepts, and visual illustrations of other terms mentioned in the text. Finally, the **Responding to Literature** section asks questions that encourage comprehension and higher-order thinking, then follows up with listening, speaking, and writing activities that develop students' comprehension and skills.

- **Systematic Language Instruction**
  To complement instruction of the reading selections, ***Glencoe Literature*** provides several resources to systematically teach and assess spelling, vocabulary, and conventions of language:
  - ***Spelling Power***
  - ***Vocabulary Power***
  - ***Grammar and Composition Handbook***

  These resources allow teachers to move methodically through instruction in skills and strategies.

- **English Language Learners and Students with Special Needs/Strategic Intervention**
  The **Teacher Wraparound Edition,** as well as a wide assortment of print and electronic resources, provides further reading support and activities for ELL students and students with special needs. Every selection is accompanied by specific strategies to make the basic program of instruction accessible to all. Activities for advanced learners are also included to challenge these students to perform to their potential.

- **Striking Design and Considerate Text**
  The engaging design of the text and resources helps students focus attention and read. Clear labels, colored headings, and numbered and bulleted lists frame ideas and highlight key points. Photos and fine art in many styles and from many cultures enhance text and allow students to make connections to the selections. Maps, charts, and graphic organizers make information visual and easy to grasp.

Through its varied and active instructional strategies, ***Glencoe Literature*** welcomes all students to learn the power of literacy and to develop a lifelong love of reading.

How do we honor diverse voices in the classroom?

by William Ray

The classroom in which a diverse group of students meets a diverse curriculum is perhaps the happiest of all, but all students need to be exposed to a culturally diverse literature program. Even in the most homogeneous school, hearing a rich mixture of literary voices is crucial not only to a literary education but also to a democratic society. In the following statement, Sandra Cisneros describes her participation in a discussion of "the house of the imagination" at the University of Iowa; reading these words to students can be a lesson in both metaphor and democracy:

> Everyone seemed to have some communal knowledge which I did not have—and then I realized that the metaphor of house was totally wrong for me. Suddenly I was homeless. There were no attics and cellars and crannies. I had no such house in my memories. As a child I had read of such things in books, and my family had promised such a house, but the best they could do was offer the miserable bungalow I was embarrassed with all my life. This caused me to question myself, to become defensive. What did I, Sandra Cisneros, know? My classmates were from the best schools in the country. They had been bred as fine hothouse flowers. I was a yellow weed among the city's cracks.

Literature as a cultural mirror Many of us are fortunate enough to teach students of diverse backgrounds and so have witnessed some of our students experiencing special moments of recognition when they see their culture reflected in a piece of literature. As a student of mine, some years ago, put it, "I like this book—it feels like home." Using literature of many cultures not only can be a revelation for students who are not of the dominant culture but also can be a springboard for students who wish to share their own experiences. Here are two examples from my classroom:

- One of my urban African-American students, during a discussion of Sandra Cisneros's *House on Mango Street,* educated her white, suburban classmates out of their stereotypical views of urban life.
- A student of Nigerian descent explained to his classmates how Igbo customs have been maintained or changed since the time of Chinua Achebe's novel *Things Fall Apart.*

Cultural awareness and global respect Democracy demands that the voices of everyone be heard. ***Glencoe Literature: The Reader's Choice*** includes representative voices from many corners of the world and from many cultures. For students to develop their own voices, views, and values—grounded in families and communities that schools serve—they must hear and consider the voices of others. Through students' own responses and their classmates' responses to literature contained in these pages, students extend their own world views and take important steps toward becoming responsible thinkers and citizens.

Resources for the Teacher

- *Theme Planning Guide*
- *Interactive Reading Sourcebook*
- *Interactive Lesson Planner*
- *Interactive Teacher's Edition*
- *Presentation Plus!*
- *Testmaker: ExamView Pro*
- *Literature Classics CD-ROM*
- *Block Scheduling Guide*
- *Vocabulary PuzzleMaker*

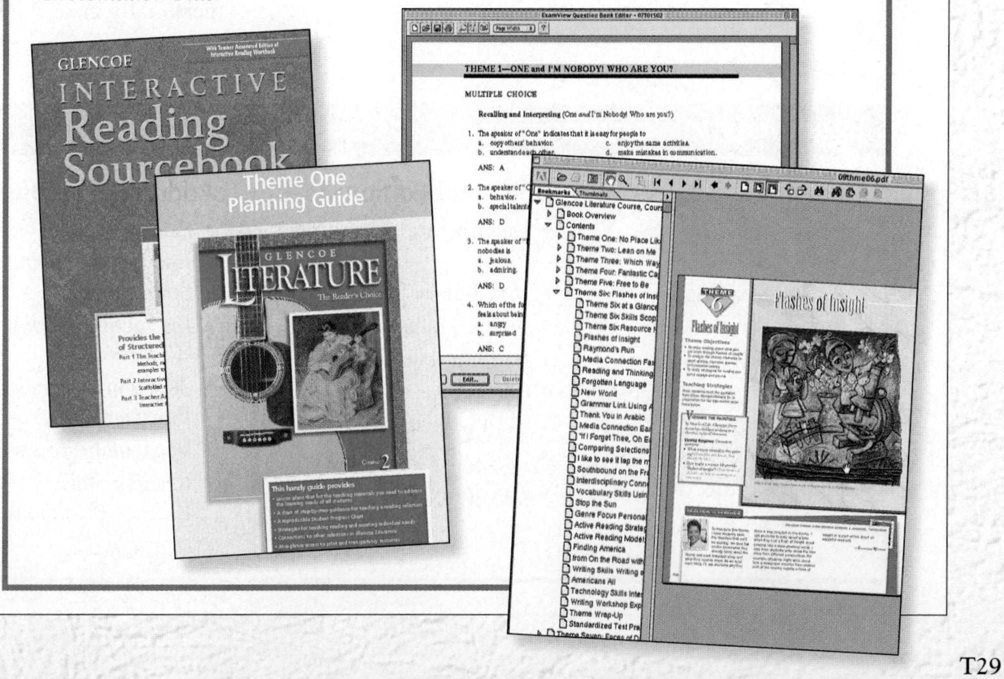

Reading

How do we engage students through critical and creative reading?

by Jeffrey Wilhelm

Reading is a very complex act, and its complexity is largely invisible. When I studied how young readers became engaged with text, I found that proficient readers flexibly used a variety of strategies depending on the text and the reading purpose. Yet less involved readers did not understand that they were supposed to "do" anything at all beyond decoding words. When I asked one student what he saw when he read, he replied, "Words, man. I see nothing but words!" The best readers, on the other hand, could richly describe characters, settings, and situations—often including details that went far beyond the implied meanings of the text.

Active reading In ***Glencoe Literature: The Reader's Choice,*** we base instructional activities on the notion that reading is interactive—that is, a conversation between a reader and a text that results in the creation of meaning. We also base our activities on knowledge of engagement—that is, that readers use a wide range of strategic reading behaviors to personally connect to text and to creatively and critically reflect upon their reading experiences. Key research tells us that visualizing a text enhances comprehension. So the first order of business in assisting reading performance is to carefully model for students our own visualizing process and then to encourage students in their own efforts to "see" and "relate" to characters, forces, and ideas. ***Glencoe Literture: The Reader's Choice*** guides students to use response journals, art, drama, and other creative activities to support this level of reading.

Higher-level thinking skills Once students have visualized and related to text, they can then begin to make inferences, draw conclusions, and evaluate critically the selections they read. Far from being extras, these higher-level thinking skills are essential to synthesizing ideas and to connecting larger ideas and themes across selections. Because students are better able to understand, interpret, and evaluate topics, ideas, and themes that they have related to their own prior knowledge and experiences, ***Glencoe Literature: The Reader's Choice*** introduces critical reading after a rich experiential reading has been supported.

Reading for comprehension Crucial to teaching readers is the notion of reading for meaning. In ***Glencoe Literature: The Reader's Choice,*** students

- consider how the structure of each text supports its meaning
- learn how literary conventions, vocabulary knowledge, and comprehension strategies aid understanding
- develop and practice specific, strategic reading behaviors
- receive direct instruction in how to read in creative and critical ways and through a variety of response dimensions

Our goal is to help students not only develop a powerful repertoire of reading strategies but also consider reading a personally meaningful social pursuit.

Resources for Reading

Student Edition/Teacher Wraparound Edition:

- Active Reading Strategies
- Active Reading Models
- Before You Read
- Reading the Selection
- Responding to Literature
- Comparing Selections
- Media Connections
- Reading and Thinking Skills
- Vocabulary Skills
- Genre Focus
- Reading Handbook
- Glossary
- Skill Minilessons
- Critical Thinking
- Author's Craft

Additional resources:

- *Active Reading Guide*
- *Interactive Reading Sourcebook*
- *Interactive Reading Workbook*
- *Selection Vocabulary Practice*
- *Vocabulary Power*
- *Reading Skills Practice Workbook*
- *Inclusion Strategies Sourcebook*
- *inTIME* magazine
- *Glencoe Literature Library*
- *Five-Star Stories*
- *The Contemporary Readers*
- *Literature Classics CD-ROM*
- Glencoe Literature Web Site (http://www.lit.glencoe.com)

How do we effectively teach literacy?

by Jane Fell Greene

As educators we know a lot more about how students learn to read than we did in the days of *Dick and Jane*. Reading research has informed us that the complex act of reading is neither automatic nor passive, but is rather a highly interactive process in which students must rapidly, fluently, and automatically process print, and then bring their own experiences and knowledge of the world to construct meaning from text.

We know that the following are the common critical elements of all good reading instruction:

- **Word Analysis** Students need to acquire phonemic awareness and to learn sound-symbol correspondence (phonics) as they practice decoding (word identification) and encoding (spelling). The ***Interactive Reading Sourcebook*** provides guidance for the teacher and practice for the student working to acquire these skills. ***Spelling Power*** provides systematic spelling instruction, practice, and assessment.
- **Vocabulary Development** Students need opportunities to develop their knowledge of individual words and morphologic relationships as well as larger concepts. *Glencoe Literature* offers many opportunities for rich classroom discussions and for practice using context clues, figurative language, and other language devices (such as idioms and analogies) to help develop students' vocabulary. ***Vocabulary Practice*** provides additional practice and assessment of in-text vocabulary. In addition, ***Vocabulary Power*** provides systematic instruction, practice, and assessment.
- **Comprehension Skills and Strategies** Students need to bolster comprehension skills and strategies. The **Student Edition,** the ***Active Reading Guide,*** and other resources teach and model essential reading and thinking skills (including summarizing, clarifying, questioning, and predicting) and give students opportunities to practice, re-apply, and connect these skills to other tasks both in and out of the classroom.
- **Independent Reading** Students need to read independently. There is no greater way to develop comprehension, vocabulary, writing, and spelling than to encourage students to read widely and voraciously. *Glencoe Literature* offers an abundance of appropriate and engaging materials for outside reading. See page T94 for a comprehensive list of titles.
- **Assessment Tools** Students need to be met where they are. Because assessment informs instruction, we know it is important for teachers to have access to assessment tools that can be administered quickly and easily and that will provide an ongoing picture of students' reading growth. The ***Initial Screening and Fluency Assessment*** book provides tools to help you gauge your students' proficiency and progress. For more about screening and placement, see page T39 in this book. For more about assessment, see page T36.

Universal access *Glencoe Literature* and its ancillary resources provide universal access to the reading selections and deliver solid, research-based literacy instruction. For example, the ***English Language Learners Sourcebook*** and other program components provide reading support for students learning English. ***The Interactive Reading Sourcebook,*** the ***Inclusion Strategies Sourcebook,*** and other materials offer additional help for students with diverse special needs or who need strategic intervention.

For those students functioning two or more years below grade level, or those functioning below the thirtieth percentile on SAT-9 and other standardized tests, **LANGUAGE!,** our comprehensive literacy intervention curriculum, puts struggling readers back on track. In addition, ***Speaking and Listening to the English LANGUAGE!,*** a teachers' book of 270 sequential, cummulative lessons for English Learners, provides scripted daily lessons and practice in producing sentences in spoken English.

Please see **The Teaching of Reading** beginning on page T84 of this book and the ***Interactive Reading Sourcebook*** for strategic intervention instruction and activities.

Writing

How does writing enhance learning in the language arts classroom?

by Jacqueline Jones Royster

We think of the language arts classroom as a language-rich environment, made all the richer by the collection of texts and activities in ***Glencoe Literature.*** As both art and artifact, writing is a flexible tool that can work dynamically with other elements of instruction to enhance both learning and performance. From this point of view, writing activities are generously incorporated throughout each thematic unit for a variety of purposes.

Writing to make personal connections with reading selections Through journaling and other writing activities, students have a mechanism for responding to whatever they read and making sense of the details. Writing can help students express personal connections with ideas, images, and experiences; see ways to go beyond their own connections toward broader implications; and note critical distinctions between their own experiences and the content of the reading selections.

Writing to experiment as creative thinkers We as teachers accomplish an important cultural task when we help students move from viewing themselves as just consumers of other people's writing to seeing themselves also as producers of writing. The creative writing activities in ***Glencoe Literature*** encourage students to write in many genres and to compose and present their work through various media. With these writing activities, students can explore varied roles and diverse points of view as a way to think seriously about what it means to produce literature.

Writing to understand form and function Through the **Writing Workshops** in ***Glencoe Literature,*** students gain direct experience producing various forms and genres of writing. The genre knowledge students build helps them to see writing as having structure and organization as shaped by audience, purpose, and context. Throughout ***Glencoe Literature*** writing activities reinforce students' understanding of form and function by asking them to try their own hand at writing essays, sonnets, narratives, autobiographical sketches, business documents, satires, parodies, soliloquies, and other distinctive forms.

Writing to develop higher order thinking skills Writing helps students think about what a text says and does and whether it is successful. Students can sort through ideas, weigh the impact and consequences of language choices, and use these assessments to make informed judgments about what works in written expression and why.

The writing activities in ***Glencoe Literature*** foster students' ability to think like literary critics. Through writing, students can express what appeals to them as readers and explain how authors achieve particular effects, justifying their interpretations by providing examples and evidence from the text. Students may also investigate broader meaning of texts through research and writing. By gathering and synthesizing information from primary and secondary sources, students can discover the historical, political, or cultural context of a literary work.

Writing to communicate effectively The act of writing itself—writing frequently for many purposes and in various genres—hones students' abilities as writers and communicators. Through activities, workshops, and assessments, ***Glencoe Literature*** provides ample practice for developing writing skills. For example, **Writing Workshops** at the end of each thematic unit guide students recursively through the writing process, focusing on particular moments of engagement—prewriting, drafting, revising, editing/proofreading, and publishing/presenting.

In addition, complete annotated **Writing Workshop Models** of student writing help teachers and students focus on the **6+1 Traits™** of effective writing:

- **Ideas:** Focused, coherent message with relevant supporting details
- **Organization:** Clear, logical arrangement of main points and supporting details
- **Voice**: Writer's distinctive expression of individuality and sense of audience
- **Word Choice:** Vivid, precise diction appropriate to the writing purpose
- **Sentence Fluency:** Well-structured sentences of varying lengths
- **Conventions:** Correct spelling, grammar, usage, and mechanics
- **Presentation:** Engaging visual layout of words and design elements

Writing to master standard English conventions ***Glencoe Literature*** provides two paths for achieving mastery of grammar, usage, and mechanics:

- **Point-of-Use Approach** In both the Student and Teacher Wraparound editions, **Grammar and Language Minilessons** help teachers review or reteach a skill in grammar, usage, or mechanics while linking that skill to an author's application of it in a literary work, thus giving students a "real-world" example from which to learn.
- **Systematic Approach** Teachers may use the ***Grammar and Composition Handbook*** to study systematically English language conventions, moving methodically through instruction in such skills as identifying parts of speech, using modifiers correctly, and enhancing sentence fluency through sentence combining.

Writing to prepare for the world of work Many writing activities in ***Glencoe Literature*** ask students to draft career-related documents in response to the reading selections. For example, students might write a fictional character's résumé or application letter. In addition, at least one **Writing Workshop** focuses on a business or technical document, such as a business letter or problem-solution report. These kinds of writing help to sharpen students' understanding of audience and purpose, and to enhance their abilities to write clearly and coherently for the world of work.

With such varied purposes for using writing in the company of the other language arts, we believe that students will be well prepared to perform at high levels of quality and excellence.

Resources for Writing

Student Edition/Teacher Wraparound Edition:

- Personal Writing
- Creative Writing
- Writing About Literature
- Comparing Selections
- Writing Skills
- Grammar Links
- Writing Workshops
- Theme Assessments
- Writing Workshop Models with annotations
- Writing Minilessons
- Grammar and Language Minilessons

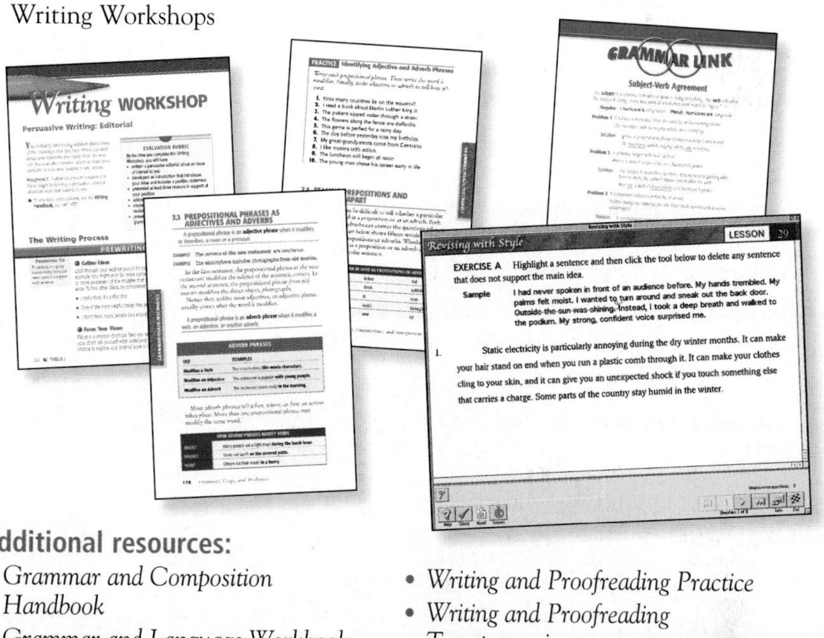

Additional resources:

- *Grammar and Composition Handbook*
- *Grammar and Language Workbook*
- *Interactive Grammar and Language Workbook*
- *Grammar and Language Transparencies*
- *Writing and Proofreading Practice*
- *Writing and Proofreading Transparencies*
- *Research and Report Writing*
- *Writer's Assistant* CD-ROM
- *Revising with Style*

Integrated Language Arts

What are the benefits of an integrated language arts program, such as *Glencoe Literature: The Reader's Choice*?

by Beverly Ann Chin

Current research confirms that integrating the English language arts is an effective way to help students improve their comprehension as well as their communication and thinking skills. Reading, writing, listening, speaking, viewing, and representing—when taught in conjunction and through a variety of classroom and home-based activities—enhance students' critical and creative thinking abilities, and allow real learning to occur. In addition, integrating language arts instruction respects students' individual interests and strengths.

The following discussion outlines the ways in which the ***Glencoe Literature: The Reader's Choice*** anthology and its additional resources effectively and imaginatively integrate the related and reciprocal processes of reading, writing, listening, speaking, viewing, and representing.

Reading and writing Students' reading and writing skills develop when they

- read, analyze, and respond to a wide array of texts—high-quality literature in various genres as well as engaging informational materials
- engage in a variety of writing activities before and after reading, such as writing journal entries and developing graphic organizers; answering questions about the selection; and writing analytical, personal, or creative responses to a variety of prompts
- write and revise for different purposes and audiences and in a variety of modes by completing **Writing Workshops**

For more information on reading and writing, see pages T30–T33.

Listening and speaking Students' listening and speaking skills develop when they

- participate in class discussions, give oral responses to literature, make presentations, and respectfully listen and respond to other viewpoints
- participate in role playing, readers' theater, choral reading, storytelling, and other creative drama activities as an avenue for understanding and interpreting reading selections

Viewing and representing Students' viewing and representing skills develop when they

- complete graphic organizers as well as art and multimedia projects, visually and graphically representing their opinions, ideas, and responses to the reading
- examine the fine art and photographs within selections by responding to viewing questions
- respond to **Selection Focus Transparencies,** which provide visual cues that activate personal associations to the reading selections
- use design principles to format writing assignments and display information on charts, maps, and graphs for written reports and oral presentations

Each language arts skill depends on another for its full expression. How can you know, for example, that students have comprehended what they have read if they do not share their responses to the text through talking, writing, or representing their ideas visually? The language arts skills have been woven together into the fabric of ***Glencoe Literature: The Reader's Choice***. As a result, you can better meet the needs of all the students in your classroom by encouraging the development of their learning styles and multiple modes of expression.

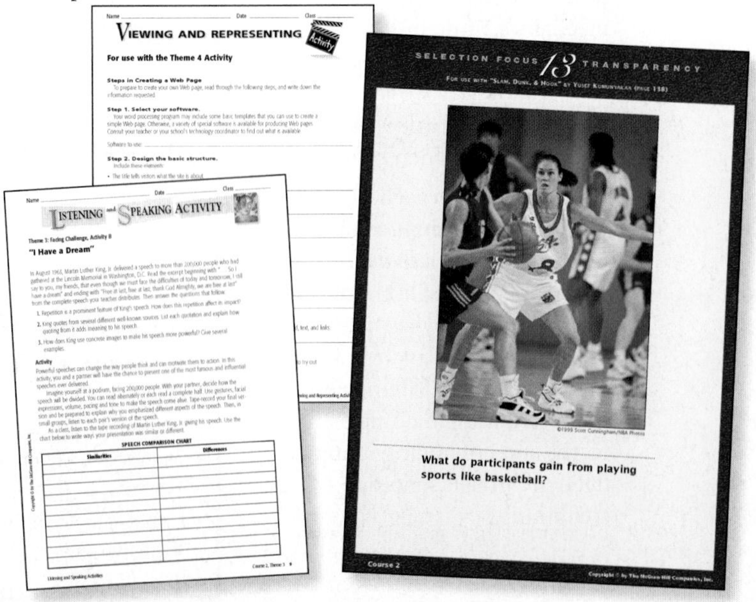

Technology & Media Literacy

What roles do technology and media literacy play in the language arts classroom?

by Jeffrey Wilhelm

Technology is a tool that extends human abilities. The technology components of the ***Glencoe Literature*** program can be integrated into your language arts instruction and used to extend students' abilities to read, write, and think critically and express themselves creatively. The program's wide variety of technology tools includes videos; audiotapes; software; the Glencoe Literature Web site (http://www.lit.glencoe.com); and various technology features, exercises, and activities that are integral to the **Student Edition** and the **Teacher Wraparound Edition.**

Technology as a reading, writing, and research tool

Students may use technology to develop their reading, writing, and research skills. For example, the ***Glencoe Literature*** program includes

- **Technology Skills** features, which offer instruction in such skills as formatting documents, drafting e-mail messages, and creating spreadsheets
- **Internet Connections** activities, which prompt students to conduct research on the selections' authors, themes, or subject matter, using a search engine on the Internet
- **Multimedia projects,** which encourage students to express themselves using a variety of non-print media
- **Writing Workshops,** which encourage students to use word processors to draft their work and provide technology tips for greater success
- ***Writer's Assistant*** and ***Revising with Style*** CD-ROMs and other software programs, which enhance reading, writing, and other language arts skills

You may find that students with special needs are particularly excited by and responsive to the use of technology in the classroom and at home.

Teaching media literacy

When students learn to interpret, analyze, and evaluate media messages as well as create their own, they can exert some control over the way such messages shape their thinking and their lives. Students who are media savvy understand the variety of ways in which different technologies organize and represent information.

Because of the growing importance of media literacy, ***Glencoe Literature*** integrates the study of media into its language arts instruction. Students are asked to

- study various literary genres and informational text types and to consider how the medium affects the message
- apply knowledge gleaned from the study of various media (e.g., television and radio advertisements and interviews) to verbal and visual responses to literary selections
- analyze how opinions, biases, and agendas may be communicated through various media forms

The ***Glencoe Literature*** **Student Edition** includes **Media Connection** activities and **Listening, Speaking, and Viewing** features to enhance students' media literacy. Additional program resources include ***Media Connections Activities, inTIME*** magazine, and ***Humanities Across TIME.*** These tools can help students understand the nature and techniques of mass media and critique various media messages. In addition, they help students learn to produce their own media messages in a variety of aural, visual, and textual formats.

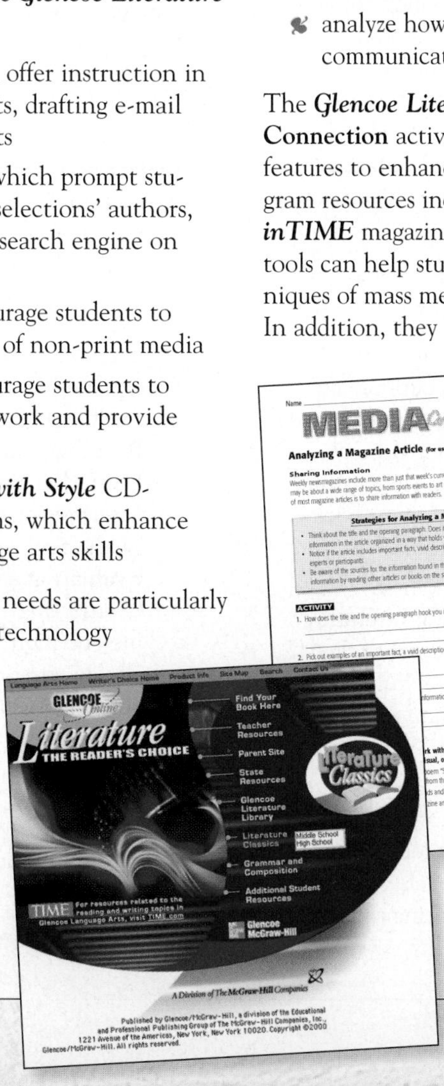

Assessment

How can we use assessment to enhance instruction?

by Beverly Ann Chin

Assessment is an essential part of the teaching and learning process. Assessments, both formal and informal, enable you to reflect on the way you teach and on the way your students learn. When used frequently and effectively, assessment tools provide you and your students with feedback and opportunities to set goals for the future and to modify instruction.

When you use assessment not only as an evaluation of students' knowledge and skills but also as an opportunity for communication—both with students and their parents or guardians—you can enhance and improve the quality of your instruction and curriculum.

Integrating instruction and assessment with *Glencoe Literature* Assessment tools for ***Glencoe Literature*** support the belief that the most effective way to monitor and assess students' progress in a language arts classroom is to use a variety of approaches and procedures: formal tests, informal assessments, writing assessments, performance assessments, and portfolios. All of these types of assessments are designed to be used throughout the school year to help you document students' progress and assess the effectiveness of instruction.

On-going and summative assessment The following components, found in the **Student Edition (SE),** are integral parts of your assessment program:

- **Theme Projects** The **Theme Projects** outlined at the beginning of each thematic unit allow students to develop their understanding of the theme through structured performance-based activities. The projects are reprinted in the ***Performance Assessment*** book along with guidelines and rubrics for evaluation.
- **Responding to Literature** The Responding to Literature activities, including **Analyzing Literature, Literary Elements, Extending Your Response,** and **Skill Minilessons,** provide a varied set of tasks for students to complete. Sample answers and rubrics for evaluation are available in the **Teacher Wraparound Edition (TWE).**
- **Writing Workshops** Near the end of each thematic unit, the **Writing Workshop** engages students in creating an extended piece of writing. Models, strategies, and tips help students develop their writing through the recursive stages of prewriting, drafting, revising, editing/proofreading, and publishing/presenting. A complete **student model** for each workshop appears in the SE, and annotations and **6+1™ evaluation guidelines** are provided in the TWE. In addition, detailed rubrics for the workshops can be found in ***Writing Assessment and Portfolio Management.*** These rubrics can help you evaluate students' command of ideas, organization, voice, word choice, sentence fluency, conventions, and presentation.
- **Theme Assessment** At the conclusion of each thematic unit, the **Theme Assessment** enables students to evaluate their own work and to set goals for future learning. The Theme Assessment also provides an opportunity for portfolio-building. ***Writing Assessment and Portfolio Management*** provides guidelines to evaluate students' portfolios.

In addition to these on-going in-text assessments, ***Glencoe Literature*** provides the following assessment tools:

- **Selection Quick Checks** Each **Selection Quick Check** quiz provides three to five short-answer questions, enabling you to quickly and easily assess basic reading comprehension.
- **Selection and Theme Assessment**
    - **Selection Tests** are formal one- or two-page tests designed to assess students' comprehension of the reading selections. Each test has up to four parts—**Recalling and Interpreting, Using Vocabulary, Interpreting and Evaluating,** and **Evaluating and Connecting**—which include multiple-choice questions, graphic organizers, and essay questions.

- The **Theme Test** is a two-page summative assessment with short-answer and essay questions designed to evaluate students' summative understanding of the selections in a thematic unit.

For your convenience, these selection tests and summative assessments are also available on the ***Testmaker: ExamView Pro* CD-ROM.** This CD-ROM allows you to modify the order, content, and number of questions to meet the particular needs of all your students.

- ***Performance Assessment*** The ***Performance Assessment*** book provides an alternative means for evaluating students' comprehension of each literature selection and each theme as a whole. The book includes an **Assessment Checklist** for most types of speaking and listening or other performance-based activities, as well as detailed rubrics for evaluating specific kinds of student activities.
- ***Grammar and Composition Handbook*** This handbook provides extensive instruction, practice, and assessment for the systematic teaching of oral and written language conventions. The handbook can also be used as a supplement to writing instruction.
- ***Vocabulary Power*** and ***Spelling Power*** These workbooks provide systematic teaching, practice, and assessment of vocabulary and spelling. Reviews, tests, and oral quizzes offer a means for frequent assessment, and an annotated teacher's edition is provided for each level.

Using *Initial Screening and Fluency Assessment* At the start of the school year, you may want to administer the entry-level assessment available in the ***Initial Screening and Fluency Assessment*** book. This quick and informal screening tool for basic reading proficiency will help you determine whether ***Glencoe Literature*** is appropriate for your students or whether certain students would be better served by the intensive intervention program ***LANGUAGE!*** Oral reading fluency assessments may be administered once per theme to monitor students' oral reading proficiency. (For more about entry-level screening and placement, see page T39 in this book.)

Charting student progress and communicating with parents As you work through a thematic unit, you can photocopy the **Student Progress Chart,** found in the ***Theme Planning Guide,*** and use copies to record scores or grades and comments on each student's progress. As you meet regularly with students and their parents or guardians, you can share this information and set goals for future learning. Also see page T44 in this book for more information about how to use the **Student Progress Chart.**

Resources for Assessment

Student Edition/Teacher Wraparound Edition:

- Theme Projects
- Responding to Literature
- Comparing Selections
- Writing Workshops
- Theme Assessments
- Skill Minilessons

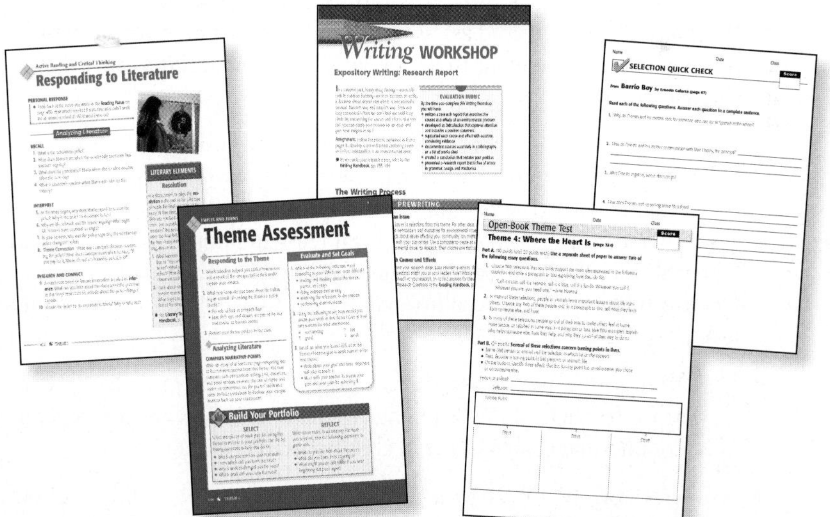

Additional resources:

- *Selection Quick Checks*
- *Selection and Theme Assessment*
- *Performance Assessment*
- *Grammar and Composition Handbook*
- *Vocabulary Power*
- *Spelling Power*
- *Writing Assessment and Portfolio Management*
- *Interactive Tutor: Self-Assessment*
- *MindJogger Videoquizzes*
- *Testmaker: ExamView Pro*
- *Initial Screening and Fluency Assessment*

Instructional Planning and Support

Road Map to Success

The materials in the following pages provide a clear road map for you to follow when planning instruction.

- **Screening and Placement** This feature explains how to determine whether your students are ready to work with the ***Glencoe Literature: The Reader's Choice*** program—or whether they might need an intervention reading program, help in developing English language skills, or special needs instruction. (p. T39)
- **How to Manage a Classroom** These pages suggest various useful ways to group students in a classroom setting to meet the instructional needs of each student. (p. T40)
- **How to Teach a Lesson** These pages provide step-by-step guidance for how to teach a typical reading selection in ***Glencoe Literature: The Reader's Choice,*** using the materials available in the **Student Edition, Teacher Wraparound Edition,** and other resources. (p. T42)
- **Monitoring Student Progress** This segment explains how to use the **Student Progress Chart** to record assessment results and to monitor students' progress through each of the eight thematic units of ***Glencoe Literature: The Reader's Choice.*** (p. T44)
- **Pacing Chart** This extensive chart breaks instruction into a detailed day-by-day plan, showing you what to teach and when to teach it. The chart highlights the components of the program that are essential for helping all students successfully meet or exceed state and local teaching objectives. The chart also lists materials for extra instructional time for English Language Learners and Special Needs students as well as additional resources available to you as you teach each lesson. (p. T46)
- **Teaching English Language Learners** This feature provides background support for teachers of English Language Learners and contrasts several of the most common languages heard in classrooms today. (p. T76)
- **The Teaching of Reading & Strategic Intervention** This section provides instruction, guidelines, and suggested activities for teaching reading. A bibliography of current confirmed research in the teaching of reading concludes this section. (p. T84)
- **Glencoe Resources for Independent Reading** This feature lists the program resources available to support independent reading. (p. T94)

Screening and Placement

Determining whether students are ready to work with the *Glencoe Literature* program—or whether they might need an intervention reading program, help in developing English language skills, or special needs instruction—is your first and most important order of business at the beginning of the school year.

Screen First, Teach Later Academic history and test results can be used as measures of readiness. For example, if a student's SAT 9 score is below the 30–35th percentile, he or she may benefit from the literacy intervention curriculum ***LANGUAGE!***

You may wish to administer the screening assessment in Glencoe's ***Initial Screening and Fluency Assessment*** book to help you determine students' proficiency in reading English. See that book for information on how to administer the screening assessment and how to interpret the results. If students are performing two or more grade levels below where they should be, administer the ***LANGUAGE!*** placement test to further refine the results and to ensure that students get the proper strategic intervention they need.

Teaching English Language Learners Students who are reading one or two grades below level and whose first language is not English would benefit from the ELL support offered as part of the *Glencoe Literature* program. The **Lesson Plan and Resource Managers,** located in each ***Theme Planning Guide,*** include lists of selection-specific resources you can use to provide an additional 30–45 minutes of daily instruction for English Language Learners. In addition, the feature ***Teaching English Language Learners,*** beginning on page T76 contrasts English with several of the most common languages heard in classrooms today and provides background for working with the students who speak those languages. Lastly, the introduction to the ***English Language Learners Sourcebook*** has teaching ideas and suggestions for how to assist those who are struggling to learn English while also learning language arts content. You can also use Glencoe's ***English, Yes!*** program in conjunction with ***Glencoe Literature.***

Teaching Special Needs and Providing Strategic Intervention When analyzing academic history and the results of your initial screenings, you may discover that some of your students have special needs or are at-risk learners. The *Glencoe Literature* program has a number of resources, including the ***Interactive Reading Sourcebook*** and the ***Interactive Reading Workbook,*** that have been developed with special needs and at-risk learners in mind. These materials and other resources listed in the **Lesson Plan and Resource Managers** in the ***Theme Planning Guide*** can help you provide the extra daily instruction that these special populations require.

Teaching Advanced Learners Use materials that will challenge advanced learners and provide them with a rich learning environment. The *Glencoe Literature* program provides a variety of activities and resources that will help you meet their particular needs. In the **Teacher Wraparound Edition (TWE),** for example, activities best suited for advanced learners are labeled L3.

Ensuring Universal Access The *Glencoe Literature* program is committed to helping teachers ensure that every student has access to high-quality literature content and language arts instruction. To meet that goal, learning activities and various instructional notes in the TWE are labeled L1, L2, and L3 for Basic, Average, and Advanced learners. In addition, in the TWE interleaf pages preceding each thematic unit, all reading selections are labeled with DRP® (Degrees of Reading Power) and Lexile® readability measures. These measures can assist you in determining which selections are developmentally suited to your students' reading abilities.

How to Manage a Classroom

As a teacher, your primary focus will likely be on the content and quality of your instruction. But you will also want to consider how to organize your classroom to best meet the needs of your students. The Consortium on Reading Excellence (CORE) recommends ***instructional grouping*** *to manage your classroom more effectively. As you teach* **Glencoe Literature: The Reader's Choice,** *you may find it helpful to use the CORE Flexible-Grouping Model below. The model describes several strategies for organizing students into an assortment of groups to address different learning needs. Implementing the model can help your students make great strides toward meeting or exceeding state and local teaching objectives.*

CORE Flexible-Grouping Model

(Adapted and reprinted with permission from CORE *Teaching Reading Sourcebook*)

Whole Class

Whole-class instruction is most beneficial when the instructional objectives are appropriate for the entire mixed-level group. For example, all students may profit when you have the whole class together to read and discuss a short story.

As a pre-reading activity you might discuss the ***Reading Focus*** *with the whole class, or you might have the class view a short* **Literature Launchers** *video segment.*

Individual or Partner

Individual or partner arrangements provide practice and independent application of an acquired skill. Partners may be at different learning levels, as in a peer-tutoring relationship, or at the same level working on a commonly needed skill.

The ***Responding to Literature*** *section provides opportunities for individual and paired learning. You might also choose to have students act as peer reviewers as they work through each* ***Writing Workshop.***

Teacher-Directed Small Groups

Teacher-directed small groups provide direct instruction to students who share commonly needed skills. During such small-group time, the teacher can closely monitor students and provide structured feedback.

Refer to the **Literature Groups Sourcebook** *for reproducible student activities and strategies for scheduling, forming, managing, and assessing literature discussion groups. In addition, the* **Inclusion Strategies Sourcebook** *provides a broad range of strategies and small group activities designed for strategic intervention.*

Independent Small Groups or Learning Centers

Independent small groups or learning centers are appropriate for interest-based and theme-organized instruction, as well as for cooperative-learning experiences. Learning centers free the teacher to work directly with students who need special attention. Learning center activities should be aligned with specific instructional outcomes. The group composition may be either heterogeneous, representing mixed skill levels and instructional needs, or homogenous, in which students share common skill levels and instructional needs. Homogeneous (same-level) groupings, sometimes termed *needs-based groups*, are used to meet individual needs identified by formal and informal assessment. In order to keep the groups flexible, frequent assessment is necessary.

Theme Projects *or various subject-area activities described in the* **Interdisciplinary Activities** *booklet are especially appropriate for independent small groups or learning center work.*

CORE Flexible-Grouping Model *(continued)*

Cross-Class Regrouping

In some schools, students may be scheduled into another class for skill-based (homogeneous) instruction. This model is often termed *regrouping and replacement* because the regular mixed class is reconstituted into several other classes for targeted instruction. In this regrouping model, teachers in a given grade or even across grades divide up the students based on assessment information and deploy them among groups of teachers. Such grouping maximizes the teacher's ability to focus instruction on a group of students who share common learning needs. Students then return to their heterogeneous home classes for literature-based instruction.

You might divide students into groups to focus on specific areas such as English language conventions, spelling, and vocabulary before gathering in the main classroom for literature-based learning.

Dedicated Reading Classes

An effective method for meeting students' needs in middle school is to enhance the regular, mixed-group literature class with a dedicated reading class that focuses on reading instruction at various skill levels. It is important that students in dedicated reading classes are also scheduled into regular, heterogeneous literature classes. In this way, students receive the skills they need to catch up while also getting the literature they need to develop grade-level concepts and vocabulary.

Use the **Interactive Reading Sourcebook** *and the* **Interactive Reading Workbook** *for dedicated reading skills instruction.*

How to Teach a Lesson

With the *Glencoe Literature* Student Edition (SE), Teacher Wraparound Edition (TWE), and print, transparency, and technology resources in hand, you will be equipped with the tools you need to teach reading and other language arts skills to meet state and local teaching objectives and the learning needs of all your students. The chart below provides step-by-step guidance for how to teach a typical reading selection in *Glencoe Literature,* using the materials available in the SE, TWE, and other resources.

Step One: BEFORE READING

SE	TWE	OTHER RESOURCES
• Read and discuss the author biography. • Work through the **Reading Focus** to help students connect with the selection. • Discuss the information in **Building Background.** • Preteach vocabulary with the **Vocabulary Preview.**	• Set goals using the lesson-specific objectives and skills listed in the side column. • Refer to the **Resource Manager** box in the bottom channel for a list of print, transparency, and technology resources to use in teaching the lesson.	• Motivate your students by viewing and discussing the **Selection Focus Transparency** or, for some selections, the **Literature Launcher.**

Step Two: READING THE SELECTION

SE	TWE	OTHER RESOURCES
• Have students read the selection silently or aloud. You may also assign the selection as homework. • Teach vocabulary words at their point of use and discuss footnotes and **Did You Know?** features.	• Utilize the point-of-use notes and **Active Reading Strategies** in the side column and the extending features in the bottom channel. • Model active reading strategies and critical thinking skills at every opportunity.	• Have students work through the **Active Reading Guide** as they read. • Refer to the **Lesson Plan and Resource Manager** in the ***Theme Planning Guide*** for a list of resources that support, reteach, and enhance the TWE activities.

Step Three: RESPONDING TO THE SELECTION

SE	TWE	OTHER RESOURCES
• Have students answer the **Personal Response** and **Analyzing Literature** questions. • Read and discuss the **Literary Elements** feature. • From the **Literature and Writing** and **Extending Your Response** sections, assign at least one writing and one discussion activity, as well as an alternate activity that meets your students' needs. All students should complete the **Skill Minilesson(s).**	• The **Analyzing Literature** items are scaffolded to provide reading and critical thinking support. TWE annotations make this scaffolding clear. Sample answers may be shared with students. • Make use of the teaching tips for the **Extending Your Response** activities. • Use the rubrics for writing and the answer keys for the **Skill Minilesson(s)** to monitor students' progress.	• Assess students' understanding and skills development by using a variety of assessment resources, including ***Selection Quick Checks, Selection and Theme Assessment, Performance Assessment,*** and ***Testmaker: ExamView Pro.*** • Refer to the **Lesson Plan and Resource Manager** for additional resources for extending and enriching instruction.

Systematic Language Instruction *Vocabulary Power* and *Spelling Power* workbooks and the *Grammar and Composition Handbook* provide for the systematic teaching of vocabulary, spelling, and English language conventions. The Pacing Chart and *Theme Planning Guide* show how to schedule the instruction and assessment of skills and strategies covered in these materials.

Universal Access

Your classroom is a miniature community that includes special populations of students. The **Lesson Plan and Resource Manager** for each selection (found in the ***Theme Planning Guide***) will help you plan your instruction to best serve the needs of all your students and to help them meet or exceed state and local teaching objectives.

Various teaching strategies and student activities found at point-of-use throughout the **Teacher Wraparound Edition** help make the text accessible to all students during the course of regular classroom study. In addition, a comprehensive assortment of print and electronic resources provide the additional instructional support needed to devote specific attention to individual students beyond the regular classroom time to foster their optimal achievement.

English Language Learners (ELL) Do some of your students need more extensive instruction in vocabulary or other English language skills? The **Lesson Plan and Resource Manager** for each selection includes a list of materials specifically created for English Language Learners. These materials may be used daily to provide additional instruction.

- The ***English Language Learners Sourcebook*** provides general teaching strategies for English Language Learners and blackline masters with selection-specific teaching strategies.
- The **Audio Library** includes an oral reading in English of nearly every selection. (Also available in Spanish.)
- Each volume of ***English, Yes!*** contains adaptations of contemporary and classic short stories followed by a comprehensive three-part skills check; it is especially suited for students who need help improving basic English skills.
- The ***Performance Assessment*** booklet may provide the best means of assessment for your ELL students.
- **Spanish Summaries** and **Spanish Translations** are available for nearly every selection.

Special Needs/Strategic Intervention Do some of your students have reading or learning difficulties? The **Lesson Plan and Resource Manager** for each selection also includes a list of materials designed especially for strategic intervention with special needs learners. These materials may be used daily to provide additional instruction.

- The ***Interactive Reading Sourcebook*** provides reading lessons and strategies for teaching reading, and the ***Interactive Reading Workbook*** offers skills practice and opportunities for students to interact with text.
- The ***Inclusion Strategies Sourcebook*** includes general teaching strategies for less-proficient readers and learning disabled and special needs students, along with reproducible student pages with teaching options for meeting individual needs.
- The **Audio Library** includes an oral reading in English of nearly every selection.
- The ***Performance Assessment*** booklet may provide the best means of assessment for your special needs students.

Advanced Learners Do some of your students need acceleration or enrichment activities? Assign these students the challenging activities presented in the TWE and additional resources.

- TWE activities labeled **L3** and point-of-use notes labeled **Advanced Learners** provide opportunities for enrichment.
- The ***Interdisciplinary Activities*** booklet offers ways to explore a topic in more depth and to reinforce content-area standards in mathematics, science, and social studies.
- You may assign additional readings, such as works in the ***Glencoe Literature Library,*** to encourage your students to broaden their study of a particular author, theme, or concept. See page T94 in this book for a list of Glencoe resources for independent reading.

Student Progress As you work through a thematic unit, use photocopies of the **Student Progress Chart** found in the ***Theme Planning Guide*** to record scores or grades and comments on each student's progress and performance. Meet regularly with students and their parents or guardians to share this information and to set goals for future learning.

Monitoring Student Progress

To monitor a student's progress through each thematic unit of *Glencoe Literature,* use the **Student Progress Chart** found in the front of each ***Theme Planning Guide.*** This reproducible chart allows you to

- record letter grades, checkmarks for completed tasks, or scores transferred directly from various assessment tools
- see at a glance how a student has performed on various ongoing and summative assessments of essential reading and language arts skills
- use the information recorded on the chart in judging whether to review material, provide additional practice, or adjust the pace of instruction
- generate a holistic grade that meets the needs of your school system
- conference with parents or guardians regularly to share information about the student's progress and to set goals for the future

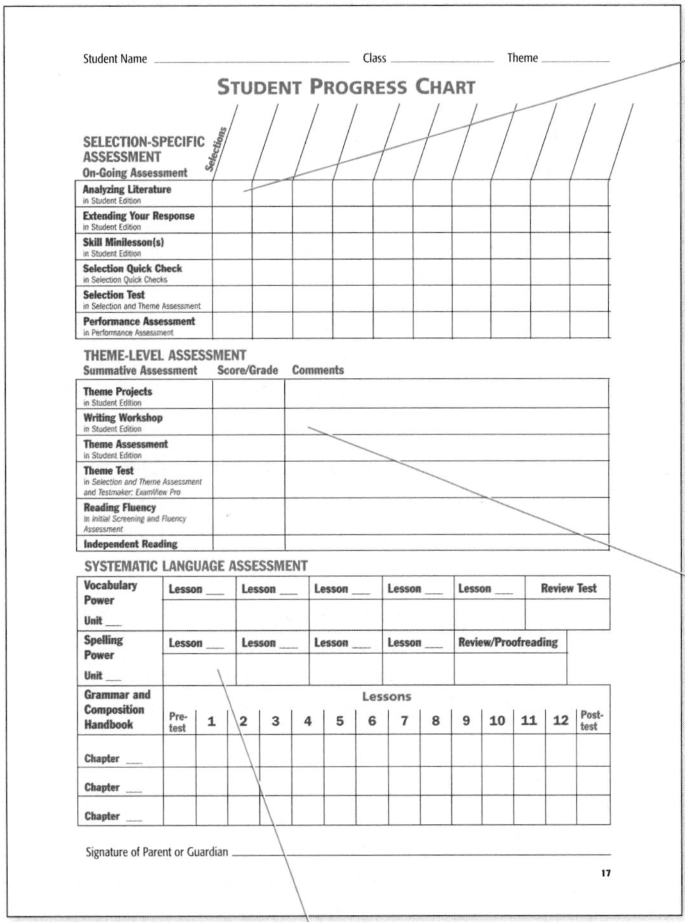

Student Name ______ Class ______ Theme ______

STUDENT PROGRESS CHART

SELECTION-SPECIFIC ASSESSMENT On-Going Assessment	Selections									
Analyzing Literature in Student Edition										
Extending Your Response in Student Edition										
Skill Minilesson(s) in Student Edition										
Selection Quick Check in Selection Quick Checks										
Selection Test in Selection and Theme Assessment										
Performance Assessment in Performance Assessment										

THEME-LEVEL ASSESSMENT

Summative Assessment	Score/Grade	Comments
Theme Projects in Student Edition		
Writing Workshop in Student Edition		
Theme Assessment in Student Edition		
Theme Test in *Selection and Theme Assessment* and *Testmaker: ExamView Pro*		
Reading Fluency in *Initial Screening and Fluency Assessment*		
Independent Reading		

SYSTEMATIC LANGUAGE ASSESSMENT

Vocabulary Power Unit ___	Lesson ___	Lesson ___	Lesson ___	Lesson ___	Lesson ___	Review Test
Spelling Power Unit ___	Lesson ___	Lesson ___	Lesson ___	Lesson ___	Review/Proofreading	

Grammar and Composition Handbook	Lessons												
	Pre-test	1	2	3	4	5	6	7	8	9	10	11	12	Post-test
Chapter ___														
Chapter ___														
Chapter ___														

Signature of Parent or Guardian ______

17

SELECTION-SPECIFIC ASSESSMENT TOOLS

These tools help you evaluate students' understanding of individual reading selections or groups of selections. Analyzing Literature, Extending Your Response, and Skill Minilessons are all found in the **Responding to Literature** section of ***Glencoe Literature.*** The remaining assessment tools are found in the following print resources:

- *Selection Quick Checks*
- *Selection and Theme Assessment*
- *Testmaker: ExamView Pro*
- *Performance Assessment*

THEME-LEVEL ASSESSMENT TOOLS

These tools help you evaluate reading, writing, and critical thinking skills developed over the course of one thematic unit.

- **Theme Projects** can be found at the beginning of each thematic unit in ***Glencoe Literature.*** They are also reprinted in the ***Performance Assessment*** book along with rubrics for evaluation.
- A **Writing Workshop** and **Theme Assessment** appear at the end of each thematic unit. For scoring Writing Workshops and for evaluating students' writing portfolios as part of each Theme Assessment, use the rubrics and guidelines found in ***Writing Assessment and Portfolio Management.***
- Monitor students' **reading fluency** with the fluency assessments in ***Initial Screening and Fluency Assessment.***
- To track students' **independent reading,** you may want to use the resources described on pages T94–T95.

SYSTEMATIC LANGUAGE ASSESSMENT TOOLS

The ***Vocabulary Power*** and ***Spelling Power*** workbooks and the ***Grammar and Composition Handbook*** systematically guide students through a sequence of lessons in vocabulary, spelling, and conventions of language. Pretests, posttests, and reviews help you determine whether students are successfully building on skills they have already learned.

Using the Pacing Chart

The **Pacing Chart** on pages T46–T77 suggests a timetable for teaching lessons in ***Glencoe Literature: The Reader's Choice.*** Designed for a 175-day school year where one-and-a-half to two hours a day are devoted to reading and language arts instruction, the pacing chart offers a manageable schedule for teaching all students all the essential reading and language arts skills. It also lists all the instructional materials you need to help all students meet or exceed state and local teaching objectives.

Pacing Essential Instruction and Assessment for All Students In addition to the many teaching notes, activities, and minilessons within the **Student Edition (SE)** and **Teacher Wraparound Edition (TWE),** the following resources are essential for all students, including average and advanced learners. The **lesson-specific resources** provide point-of-use support and assessment to help you introduce or reteach reading and language arts skills germane to each reading lesson. The **systematic resources** provide a sequence of lessons in vocabulary, spelling, and English language conventions that help you assist your students in learning specific skills and in building on skills they have already learned. These resources include tests to help you assess students' progress.

ESSENTIAL LESSON SUPPORT AND ASSESSMENT

Lesson-Specific Instruction

- *Selection Focus Transparencies*
- *Active Reading Guide**
- *Literary Elements Transparencies*
- *Selection Vocabulary Practice*
- *Selection Quick Checks**
- *Selection and Theme Assessment*
- *Testmaker: ExamView Pro CD-ROM*
- *Performance Assessment*
- *Writing Assessment and Portfolio Management*
- *Initial Screening and Fluency Assessment*
- *inTIME* magazine

Systematic Language Instruction

- *Grammar and Composition Handbook*
- *Vocabulary Power*
- *Spelling Power*

SE: Student Edition TWE: Teacher Wraparound Edition
*Also available in Spanish

Pacing for English Language Learners and Special-Needs Students For English Language Learners and for students with special needs, you may want to offer more intensive instruction. Use the following additional instructional materials.

ENGLISH LANGUAGE LEARNERS

- English Language Learners (TWE)
- *English Language Learners Sourcebook*
- *Theme Planning Guide*
- *Spanish Summaries*
- *Spanish Translations*
- *Audio Library**
- *English, Yes!*

SPECIAL NEEDS/STRATEGIC INTERVENTION

- *Interactive Reading Sourcebook*
- *Interactive Reading Workbook*
- Special Needs (TWE)
- *Inclusion Strategies Sourcebook*
- *Theme Planning Guide*
- *Audio Library**

Pacing with Essential Teaching Tools With every lesson on the pacing chart, you will want to use the following essential teaching tools and resources to help you organize lessons, activities, and assessment.

ESSENTIAL TEACHING TOOLS AND RESOURCES

- *Theme Planning Guide*
  provides detailed lesson plans for each lesson, strategies to teach reading and to meet individual needs, connections to other selections, and facsimiles of all related print and transparency resource pages
- *Literature Groups Sourcebook*
  includes reproducible student activity sheets and strategies for directing and managing literature groups
- *Interactive Lesson Planner CD-ROM*
  allows you to see a day-by-day breakdown of all instructional activities, create your own plan of instruction, and print lesson plans
- *Interactive Teacher Edition CD-ROM*
  gives you point-and-click access to teaching resources and the convenience of editing and printing to suit your needs

Pacing Chart

Note: The pacing of the lesson schedule is only a recommendation. Use the *Interactive Lesson Planner* to customize the pace for your instructional needs.

Lesson Schedule	Essential Lesson Support and Assessment
Theme 1: No Place Like Home Day 1 Lesson and lesson support on SE/TWE pp. 1–3	• *Theme One Planning Guide*, pp. 1–3 • *Performance Assessment*, p. 64
Days 2–4 The Treasure of Lemon Brown Three-part instruction and selection support on SE/TWE pp. 4–16 **Interdisciplinary Connection** Music, SE/TWE p. 17	**Lesson-Specific Instruction** • *Theme One Planning Guide*, pp. 4–11 • *Selection Focus Transparency 1* • *Active Reading Guide*,* p. 1 • *Literary Elements Transparency 1* • *Selection Vocabulary Practice*, p. 7 • *Selection Quick Checks*,* p. 1 • *Selection and Theme Assessment*, pp. 1–2 • *Testmaker: ExamView Pro* • *Performance Assessment*, p. 1 **Systematic Language Instruction** • *Grammar and Composition Handbook*, Lessons 1.1–1.2 • *Vocabulary Power*, Lesson 1 • *Spelling Power*, Lesson 1
Day 5 My Two Dads Three-part instruction and selection support on SE/TWE pp. 18–24	**Lesson-Specific Instruction** • *Theme One Planning Guide*, pp. 12–19 • *Selection Focus Transparency 2* • *Active Reading Guide*,* p. 2 • *Literary Elements Transparency 2* • *Selection Vocabulary Practice*, p. 8 • *Selection Quick Checks*,* p. 2 • *Selection and Theme Assessment*, pp. 3–4 • *Testmaker: ExamView Pro* • *Performance Assessment*, p. 2 • *in*TIME magazine, p. 32 **Systematic Language Instruction** • *Grammar and Composition Handbook*, Lessons 1.3–1.4 • *Vocabulary Power*, Lesson 2
Days 6–7 A Dictionary of Japanese-American Terms Three-part instruction and selection support on SE/TWE pp. 26–37 **Reading and Thinking Skills** Previewing, SE/TWE p. 25	**Lesson-Specific Instruction** • *Theme One Planning Guide*, pp. 20–27 • *Selection Focus Transparency 3* • *Active Reading Guide*,* p. 3 • *Literary Elements Transparency 3* • *Selection Vocabulary Practice*, p. 9 • *Selection Quick Checks*,* p. 3 • *Selection and Theme Assessment*, pp. 5–6 • *Testmaker: ExamView Pro* • *Performance Assessment*, p. 3 • *in*TIME magazine, p. 32 **Systematic Language Instruction** • *Grammar and Composition Handbook*, Lesson 1.5
Days 8–9 Homeless Three-part instruction and selection support on SE/TWE pp. 38–43 **Media Connection** Radio Transcript, SE/TWE p. 44 **Grammar Link** Avoiding Sentence Fragments, SE/TWE p. 45	**Lesson-Specific Instruction** • *Theme One Planning Guide*, pp. 28–35 • *Selection Focus Transparency 4* • *Active Reading Guide*,* p. 4 • *Literary Elements Transparency 4* • *Selection Vocabulary Practice*, p. 10 • *Selection Quick Checks*,* p. 4 • *Selection and Theme Assessment*, pp. 7–8 • *Testmaker: ExamView Pro* • *Performance Assessment*, p. 4 **Systematic Language Instruction** • *Grammar and Composition Handbook*, Lesson 1.6 • *Vocabulary Power*, Lesson 3 • *Spelling Power*, Lesson 2
Days 10–11 Golden Glass Three-part instruction and selection support on SE/TWE pp. 50–57 **Genre Focus** Fiction, SE/TWE pp. 46–47	**Lesson-Specific Instruction** • *Theme One Planning Guide*, pp. 36–43 • *Selection Focus Transparency 5* • *Active Reading Guide*,* p. 5 • *Literary Elements Transparency 5* • *Selection Vocabulary Practice*, p. 11 • *Selection Quick Checks*,* p. 5 • *Selection and Theme Assessment*, pp. 9–10 • *Testmaker: ExamView Pro* • *Performance Assessment*, p. 5 **Systematic Language Instruction** • *Grammar and Composition Handbook*, Lesson 2.1

SE: Student Edition TWE: Teacher Wraparound Edition *Also available in Spanish

English Language Learners (Add 30–45 Minutes a Day)	Special Needs/Strategic Intervention (Add 30–45 Minutes a Day)
• *English Language Learners Sourcebook*, pp. 1–13 • *English, Yes!*	• *Inclusion Strategies Sourcebook*, pp. vii–xii
• Verb Tenses and "If" Clauses, TWE p. 6 • *English Language Learners Sourcebook*, pp. 17, 18 • *Spanish Summaries*, p. 1 • *Spanish Translations*, pp. 1–7 • *Audio Library** • *English, Yes!*	• *Interactive Reading Sourcebook*, pp. T47–T49 • *Interactive Reading Workbook*, pp. 1–2 • Less-Proficient Readers, TWE p. 8 • *Inclusion Strategies Sourcebook*, pp. 71–72 • *Theme One Planning Guide*, p. 6 • *Audio Library**
• Cultural Identities, TWE p. 20 • *English Language Learners Sourcebook*, p. 19 • *Theme One Planning Guide*, p. 14 • *Spanish Summaries*, p. 2 • *Spanish Translations*, pp. 8–10 • *Audio Library** • *English, Yes!*	• *Interactive Reading Sourcebook*, pp. T49–T51 • *Interactive Reading Workbook*, pp. 3–4 • *Inclusion Strategies Sourcebook*, pp. 5–6 • *Theme One Planning Guide*, p. 14 • *Audio Library**
• Suffixes: *-less*, TWE p. 28 • *English Language Learners Sourcebook*, p. 20 • *Spanish Summaries*, p. 3 • *Audio Library** • *English, Yes!*	• *Interactive Reading Sourcebook*, pp. T52–T54 • *Interactive Reading Workbook*, pp. 5–8 • Less-Proficient Readers, TWE pp. 25, 30 • *Inclusion Strategies Sourcebook*, pp. 3–4 • *Theme One Planning Guide*, p. 22 • *Audio Library**
• Favorite Stories, TWE p. 40 • *English Language Learners Sourcebook*, p. 21 • *Spanish Summaries*, p. 4 • *Audio Library** • *English, Yes!*	• *Interactive Reading Sourcebook*, pp. T55–T57 • *Interactive Reading Workbook*, pp. 9–10 • *Theme One Planning Guide*, p. 30 • *Audio Library**
• Working with a Partner, TWE p. 52 • *English Language Learners Sourcebook*, pp. 22, 23 • *Spanish Summaries*, p. 5 • *Spanish Translations*, pp. 11–14 • *Audio Library** • *English, Yes!*	• *Interactive Reading Sourcebook*, pp. T57–T59 • *Interactive Reading Workbook*, pp. 11–12 • Learning Disabled, TWE p. 46 • Emotional, TWE p. 59 • *Inclusion Strategies Sourcebook*, pp. 1–2 • *Theme One Planning Guide*, p. 38

Lesson Schedule	Essential Lesson Support and Assessment
Days 10–11 (continued) **Active Reading Strategies** Strategies for Reading Fiction, SE/TWE pp. 48–49 **Technology Skills** E-Mail, SE/TWE pp. 58–59	
Days 12–13 Mother and Daughter Three-part instruction and selection support on SE/TWE pp. 61–69 **Writing Skills** Using Examples, SE/TWE p. 60	**Lesson-Specific Instruction** • *Theme One Planning Guide*, pp. 44–51 • *Selection Focus Transparency 6* • *Active Reading Guide*,* p. 6 • *Literary Elements Transparency 6* • *Selection Vocabulary Practice*, p. 12 • *Selection Quick Checks*,* p. 6 • *Selection and Theme Assessment*, pp. 11–12 • *Testmaker: ExamView Pro* • *Performance Assessment*, p. 6 **Systematic Language Instruction** • *Grammar and Composition Handbook*, Lesson 2.2 • *Vocabulary Power*, Lesson 4 • *Spelling Power*, Lesson 3
Day 14 Chanclas Three-part instruction and selection support on SE/TWE pp. 70–73 **Comparing Selections** SE/TWE p. 74 **Vocabulary Skills** Using Context Skills, SE/TWE p. 75	**Lesson-Specific Instruction** • *Theme One Planning Guide*, pp. 52–59 • *Selection Focus Transparency 7* • *Active Reading Guide*,* p. 7 • *Literary Elements Transparency 7* • *Selection Quick Checks*,* p. 7 • *Selection and Theme Assessment*, pp. 11–12 • *Testmaker: ExamView Pro* • *Performance Assessment*, p. 6 **Systematic Language Instruction** • *Grammar and Composition Handbook*, Lessons 2.3–2.4 • *Vocabulary Power*, Lesson 5 • *Spelling Power*, Lesson 4
Days 15–16 The Medicine Bag Three-part instruction and selection support on SE/TWE pp. 77–89 **Media Connection** Magazine Article, SE/TWE p. 76	**Lesson-Specific Instruction** • *Theme One Planning Guide*, pp. 60–67 • *Selection Focus Transparency 8* • *Active Reading Guide*,* p. 8 • *Literary Elements Transparency 8* • *Selection Vocabulary Practice*, p. 7 • *Selection Quick Checks*,* p. 8 • *Selection and Theme Assessment*, pp. 13–14 • *Testmaker: ExamView Pro* • *Performance Assessment*, p. 7 **Systematic Language Instruction** • *Grammar and Composition Handbook*, Lesson 2.5 • *Vocabulary Power*, Unit 1 Review/Test • *Spelling Power*, Unit 1 Review/Proofreading
Days 17–18 Writing Workshop Descriptive Writing: Personal Essay Lesson and lesson support on SE/TWE pp. 90–93	• *Writing Assessment and Portfolio Management*, pp. 1–13, 14–16, 41–48
Day 19 Theme Assessment Lesson and lesson support on SE/TWE pp. 94–95	• *Selection and Theme Assessment*, pp. 125–126 • *Testmaker: ExamView Pro* • *Performance Assessment*, p. 91 • *Writing Assessment and Portfolio Management*, pp. 1–12, 41–48 • *Initial Screening and Fluency Assessment*, Theme One Reading Fluency
Theme 2: Lean on Me Day 20 Lesson and lesson support on SE/TWE pp. 98–101	• *Theme Two Planning Guide*, pp. 1–3 • *Performance Assessment*, p. 65

SE: Student Edition TWE: Teacher Wraparound Edition *Also available in Spanish

English Language Learners (Add 30–45 Minutes a Day)	Special Needs/Strategic Intervention (Add 30–45 Minutes a Day)
	• *Audio Library**
• Parents and Daughters, TWE p. 63 • *English Language Learners Sourcebook*, p. 24 • *Spanish Summaries*, p. 6 • *Spanish Translations*, pp. 15–19 • *Audio Library** • *English, Yes!*	• *Interactive Reading Sourcebook*, pp. T60–T62 • *Interactive Reading Workbook*, pp. 13–14 • Emotional, TWE pp. 64 • *Inclusion Strategies Sourcebook*, pp. 73–74 • *Audio Library**
• Word Roots, TWE p. 75 • *English Language Learners Sourcebook*, pp. 25, 26 • *Theme One Planning Guide*, p. 54 • *Spanish Summaries*, p. 7 • *Spanish Translations*, pp. 20–21 • *Audio Library** • *English, Yes!*	• *Interactive Reading Sourcebook*, pp. T62–T65 • *Interactive Reading Workbook*, pp. 15–16 • *Inclusion Strategies Sourcebook*, pp. 9–10 • *Theme One Planning Guide*, p. 54 • *Audio Library**
• Understanding Vocabulary, TWE p. 79 • *English Language Learners Sourcebook*, p. 27 • *Theme One Planning Guide*, p. 62 • *Spanish Summaries*, p. 8 • *Spanish Translations*, pp. 22–28 • *Audio Library** • *English, Yes!*	• *Interactive Reading Sourcebook*, pp. T65–T67 • *Interactive Reading Workbook*, pp. 17–18 • *Theme One Planning Guide*, p. 62 • *Audio Library**
• *English Language Learners Sourcebook*, p. 9 • *English, Yes!*	• *Inclusion Strategies Sourcebook*, pp. 69–70
• *English Language Learners Sourcebook*, pp. 1–13 • *English, Yes!*	• Special Needs, TWE p. 95 • *Inclusion Strategies Sourcebook*, p. xii
• *English Language Learners Sourcebook*, pp. 1–13 • *English, Yes!*	• *Inclusion Strategies Sourcebook*, pp. vii–xii

Lesson Schedule	Essential Lesson Support and Assessment
Days 21–22 from **All Things Bright and Beautiful** Three-part instruction and selection support on SE/TWE pp. 102–111	**Lesson-Specific Instruction** • *Theme Two Planning Guide*, pp. 4–11 • *Selection Focus Transparency* 9 • *Active Reading Guide*,* p. 9 • *Literary Elements Transparency* 9 • *Selection Vocabulary Practice*, p. 9 • *Selection Quick Checks*,* p. 9 • *Selection and Theme Assessment*, pp. 15–16 • *Testmaker: ExamView Pro* • *Performance Assessment*, p. 8 **Systematic Language Instruction** • *Grammar and Composition Handbook*, Lesson 3.1 • *Vocabulary Power*, Lesson 6 • *Spelling Power*, Lesson 5
Days 23–27 **Flowers for Algernon** Three-part instruction and selection support on SE/TWE pp. 112–143 **Reading and Thinking Skills** Making Inferences, SE/TWE p. 144	**Lesson-Specific Instruction** • *Theme Two Planning Guide*, pp. 12–20 • *Selection Focus Transparency 10* • *Active Reading Guide*,* pp. 10–11 • *Literary Elements Transparencies 10, 11* • *Selection Vocabulary Practice*, p. 10 • *Selection Quick Checks*,* pp. 10–11 • *Selection and Theme Assessment*, pp. 17–20 • *Testmaker: ExamView Pro* • *Performance Assessment*, pp. 9–10 **Systematic Language Instruction** • *Grammar and Composition Handbook*, Lesson 3.2
Days 28–30 **The Kid Nobody Could Handle** Three-part instruction and selection support on SE/TWE pp. 145–158 **Media Connection** Song Lyrics, SE/TWE p. 159	**Lesson-Specific Instruction** • *Theme Two Planning Guide*, pp. 21–28 • *Selection Focus Transparency 11* • *Active Reading Guide*,* p. 12 • *Literary Elements Transparency 12* • *Selection Vocabulary Practice*, p. 11 • *Selection Quick Checks*,* p. 12 • *Selection and Theme Assessment*, pp. 21–22 • *Testmaker: ExamView Pro* • *Performance Assessment*, p. 11 • *inTIME* magazine, p. 2 **Systematic Language Instruction** • *Grammar and Composition Handbook*, Lesson 3.3 • *Vocabulary Power*, Lesson 7 • *Spelling Power*, Lesson 6
Days 31–32 **Thank You, M'am** Three-part instruction and selection support on SE/TWE pp. 160–165 **Comparing Selections** SE/TWE p. 166 **Grammar Link** Avoiding Run-on Sentences, SE/TWE p. 167	**Lesson-Specific Instruction** • *Theme Two Planning Guide*, pp. 29–36 • *Selection Focus Transparency 12* • *Active Reading Guide*,* p. 13 • *Literary Elements Transparency 13* • *Selection Vocabulary Practice*, p. 12 • *Selection Quick Checks*,* p. 13 • *Selection and Theme Assessment*, p. 23 • *Testmaker: ExamView Pro* • *Performance Assessment*, p. 12 • *inTIME* magazine, p. 29 **Systematic Language Instruction** • *Grammar and Composition Handbook*, Lesson 3.4
Days 33–34 **The Journey** Three-part instruction and selection support on SE/TWE pp. 168–177 **Technology Skills** Word Processing, SE/TWE pp. 178–179	**Lesson-Specific Instruction** • *Theme Two Planning Guide*, pp. 37–44 • *Selection Focus Transparency 13* • *Active Reading Guide*,* p. 14 • *Literary Elements Transparency 14* • *Selection Vocabulary Practice*, p. 13 • *Selection Quick Checks*,* p. 14 • *Selection and Theme Assessment*, p. 24 • *Testmaker: ExamView Pro* • *Performance Assessment*, p. 13 **Systematic Language Instruction** • *Grammar and Composition Handbook*, Lesson 3.5
Day 35 **Knoxville, Tennessee** and **Legacies** Three-part instruction and selection support on SE/TWE pp. 180–183	**Lesson-Specific Instruction** • *Theme Two Planning Guide*, pp. 45–50 • *Selection Focus Transparency 14* • *Active Reading Guide*,* p. 15 • *Literary Elements Transparency 15* • *Selection Quick Checks*,* p. 15 • *Selection and Theme Assessment*, pp. 25–26 • *Testmaker: ExamView Pro* • *Performance Assessment*, p. 14 **Systematic Language Instruction** • *Grammar and Composition Handbook*, Lessons 3.6–3.7 • *Vocabulary Power*, Lesson 8 • *Spelling Power*, Lesson 7

SE: Student Edition   TWE: Teacher Wraparound Edition   *Also available in Spanish

English Language Learners (Add 30–45 Minutes a Day)	Special Needs/Strategic Intervention (Add 30–45 Minutes a Day)
• Building Background, TWE p. 104 • *English Language Learners Sourcebook*, p. 28 • *Spanish Summaries*, p. 9 • *Spanish Audio Library* • *English, Yes!*	• *Interactive Reading Sourcebook*, pp. T68–T70 • *Interactive Reading Workbook*, pp. 19–20 • Emotional, TWE p. 105 • *Inclusion Strategies Sourcebook*, pp. 25–26, 95–96 • *Theme Two Planning Guide*, p. 6
• Author's Technique, TWE p. 114 • Using the Past Tense of Verbs, TWE p. 125 • *English Language Learners Sourcebook*, pp. 29, 30 • *Spanish Summaries*, p. 10 • *Spanish Translations*, pp. 29–52 • *Audio Library** • *English, Yes!*	• *Interactive Reading Sourcebook*, pp. T70–T73 • *Interactive Reading Workbook*, pp. 21–24 • Less-Proficient Readers, TWE pp. 116, 144 • Visually Impaired, TWE p. 132 • Learning Disabled, TWE p. 138 • *Inclusion Strategies Sourcebook*, pp. 43–44 • *Audio Library**
• Idioms, TWE p. 147 • *English Language Learners Sourcebook*, p. 31 • *Spanish Summaries*, p. 11 • *Audio Library** • *English, Yes!*	• *Interactive Reading Sourcebook*, pp. T73–T76 • *Interactive Reading Workbook*, pp. 25–28 • Emotional, TWE p. 151 • *Inclusion Strategies Sourcebook*, pp. 11–12, 23–24 • *Theme Two Planning Guide*, p. 23 • *Audio Library**
• Pronoun Reference, TWE p. 162 • *English Language Learners Sourcebook*, p. 32 • *Spanish Summaries*, p. 12 • *Audio Library** • *English, Yes!*	• *Interactive Reading Sourcebook*, pp. T76–T78 • *Interactive Reading Workbook*, pp. 29–30 • *Inclusion Strategies Sourcebook*, pp. 39–40 • *Theme Two Planning Guide*, p. 31 • *Audio Library**
• Hispanic Heritage, TWE p. 170 • *English Language Learners Sourcebook*, p. 33 • *Spanish Summaries*, p. 13 • *Spanish Translations*, pp. 53–56 • *Audio Library** • *English, Yes!*	• *Interactive Reading Sourcebook*, pp. T78–T81 • *Interactive Reading Workbook*, pp. 31–32 • Learning Disabled, TWE p. 172 • *Theme Two Planning Guide*, p. 39 • *Audio Library**
• Southern Summer, TWE p. 181 • *English Language Learners Sourcebook*, p. 34 • *Spanish Summaries*, p. 14 • *Audio Library** • *English, Yes!*	• *Interactive Reading Sourcebook*, pp. T81–T83 • *Interactive Reading Workbook*, p. 33 • *Audio Library**

Lesson Schedule	Essential Lesson Support and Assessment
Days 36–37 A Mother in Mannville Three-part instruction and selection support on SE/TWE pp. 184–195	**Lesson-Specific Instruction** • *Theme Two Planning Guide*, pp. 51–58 • *Selection Focus Transparency 15* • *Active Reading Guide*,* p. 16 • *Literary Elements Transparency 16* • *Selection Vocabulary Practice*, p. 14 • *Selection Quick Checks*,* p. 16 • *Selection and Theme Assessment*, pp. 27–28 • *Testmaker: ExamView Pro* • *Performance Assessment*, p. 15 **Systematic Language Instruction** • *Grammar and Composition Handbook*, Lessons 3.8–3.9
Days 38–40 from I Know Why the Caged Bird Sings Three-part instruction and selection support on SE/TWE pp. 198–209 **Genre Focus** Autobiography, SE/TWE p. 196 **Active Reading Strategies** Tips for Reading an Autobiography, SE/TWE p. 197 **Media Connection** Newspaper Article, SE/TWE p. 210 **Writing Skills** Describing a Person, SE/TWE p. 211	**Lesson-Specific Instruction** • *Theme Two Planning Guide*, pp. 59–66 • *Selection Focus Transparency 16* • *Active Reading Guide*,* p. 17 • *Literary Elements Transparency 17* • *Selection Vocabulary Practice*, p. 15 • *Selection Quick Checks*,* p. 17 • *Selection and Theme Assessment*, pp. 29–30 • *Testmaker: ExamView Pro* • *Performance Assessment*, p. 16 **Systematic Language Instruction** • *Grammar and Composition Handbook*, Lesson 3.10 • *Vocabulary Power*, Lesson 9 • *Spelling Power*, Lesson 8
Days 41–43 from Sound-Shadows of the New World Three-part instruction and selection support on SE/TWE pp. 212–223 **Interdisciplinary Connection** Social Studies SE/TWE p. 224 **Vocabulary Skills** Using Familiar Words to Understand New Words, SE/TWE p. 225	**Lesson-Specific Instruction** • *Theme Two Planning Guide*, pp. 67–74 • *Selection Focus Transparency 17* • *Active Reading Guide*,* p. 18 • *Literary Elements Transparency 18* • *Selection Vocabulary Practice*, p. 16 • *Selection Quick Checks*,* p. 18 • *Selection and Theme Assessment*, pp. 31–32 • *Testmaker: ExamView Pro* • *Performance Assessment*, p. 17 **Systematic Language Instruction** • *Grammar and Composition Handbook*, Lessons 3.11–3.12 • *Vocabulary Power*, Unit 3 Review/Test • *Spelling Power*, Unit 3 Review/Proofreading
Days 44–45 Writing Workshop Narrative Writing: Biographical Sketch Lesson and lesson support on SE/TWE pp. 226–229	• *Writing Assessment and Portfolio Management*, pp. 1–13, 17–19, 41–48
Day 46 Theme Assessment Lesson and lesson support on SE/TWE pp. 230–231	• *Selection and Theme Assessment*, pp. 127–128 • *Testmaker: ExamView Pro* • *Performance Assessment*, pp. 91–92 • *Writing Assessment and Portfolio Management*, pp. 1–12, 41–48 • *Initial Screening and Fluency Assessment*, Theme Two Reading Fluency
Theme 3: Which Way to Go? Day 47 Lesson and lesson support on SE/TWE pp. 234–237	• *Theme Three Planning Guide*, pp. 1–3 • *Performance Assessment*, p. 66

SE: Student Edition TWE: Teacher Wraparound Edition *Also available in Spanish

English Language Learners (Add 30–45 Minutes a Day)	Special Needs/Strategic Intervention (Add 30–45 Minutes a Day)
• Compound Words, TWE p. 186 • *English Language Learners Sourcebook*, p. 35 • *Spanish Summaries*, p. 15 • *Spanish Translations*, pp. 57–62 • *Audio Library** • *English, Yes!*	• *Interactive Reading Sourcebook*, pp. T84–T86 • *Interactive Reading Workbook*, pp. 34–35 • Less-Proficient Readers, TWE p. 190 • *Inclusion Strategies Sourcebook*, pp. 25–26, 53–54 • *Audio Library**
• Dialect, TWE p. 200 • *English Language Learners Sourcebook*, p. 36 • *Spanish Summaries*, p. 16 • *Spanish Translations*, pp. 63–68 • *Audio Library** • *English, Yes!*	• *Interactive Reading Sourcebook*, pp. T87–T89 • *Interactive Reading Workbook*, pp. 36–37 • Less-Proficient Readers/Learning Disabled, TWE p. 202 • *Inclusion Strategies Sourcebook*, pp. 7–8 • *Audio Library**
• Immigration Experiences, TWE p. 214 • Vocabulary Acquisition, TWE p. 225 • *English Language Learners Sourcebook*, pp. 37, 38 • *Spanish Summaries*, p. 17 • *Audio Library** • *English, Yes!*	• *Interactive Reading Sourcebook*, pp. T89–T92 • *Interactive Reading Workbook*, pp. 38–39 • Learning Disabled, TWE p. 216 • *Theme Two Planning Guide*, p. 69 • *Audio Library**
• Prewriting in the First Language, TWE p. 226 • *English Language Learners Sourcebook*, p. 9 • *English, Yes!*	
• *English Language Learners Sourcebook*, pp. 1–13 • *English, Yes!*	• Special Needs, TWE p. 231 • *Inclusion Strategies Sourcebook*, p. xii
• *English Language Learners Sourcebook*, pp. 1–13 • *English, Yes!*	• *Inclusion Strategies Sourcebook*, pp. vii–xii

Lesson Schedule	Essential Lesson Support and Assessment	
Days 48–49 **In the Middle of a Pitch** Three-part instruction and selection support on SE/TWE pp. 238–249 **Media Connection** Comic Strip, SE/TWE p. 250	**Lesson-Specific Instruction** • *Theme Three Planning Guide*, pp. 4–11 • *Selection Focus Transparency 18* • *Active Reading Guide*,* p. 19 • *Literary Elements Transparency 19* • *Selection Vocabulary Practice*, p. 17 • *Selection Quick Checks*,* p. 19 • *Selection and Theme Assessment*, p. 33	• *Testmaker: ExamView Pro* • *Performance Assessment*, p. 18 **Systematic Language Instruction** • *Grammar and Composition Handbook*, Lesson 4.1 • *Vocabulary Power*, Lesson 10 • *Spelling Power*, Lesson 9
Days 50–51 **Casey at the Bat** Three-part instruction and selection support on SE/TWE pp. 251–255 **Comparing Selections** SE/TWE p. 256 **Interdisciplinary Connection** Social Studies, SE/TWE p. 257	**Lesson-Specific Instruction** • *Theme Three Planning Guide*, pp. 12–18 • *Selection Focus Transparency 19* • *Active Reading Guide*,* p. 20 • *Literary Elements Transparency 20* • *Selection Quick Checks*,* p. 20 • *Selection and Theme Assessment*, p. 34	• *Testmaker: ExamView Pro* • *Performance Assessment*, p. 19 **Systematic Language Instruction** • *Grammar and Composition Handbook*, Lessons 4.2–4.3
Days 52–53 **The Wise Old Woman** Three-part instruction and selection support on SE/TWE pp. 258–265 **Technology Skills** Multimedia, SE/TWE pp. 266–267	**Lesson-Specific Instruction** • *Theme Three Planning Guide*, pp. 19–26 • *Selection Focus Transparency 20* • *Active Reading Guide*,* p. 21 • *Literary Elements Transparency 21* • *Selection Vocabulary Practice*, p. 18 • *Selection Quick Checks*,* p. 21 • *Selection and Theme Assessment*, pp. 35–36	• *Testmaker: ExamView Pro* • *Performance Assessment*, p. 20 **Systematic Language Instruction** • *Grammar and Composition Handbook*, Lessons 4.4–4.5 • *Vocabulary Power*, Lesson 11 • *Spelling Power*, Lesson 10
Days 54–55 **Bagged Wolf** Three-part instruction and selection support on SE/TWE pp. 268–279 **Reading and Thinking Skills** Monitoring Comprehension, SE/TWE p. 280	**Lesson-Specific Instruction** • *Theme Three Planning Guide*, pp. 27–34 • *Selection Focus Transparency 21* • *Active Reading Guide*,* p. 22 • *Literary Elements Transparency 22* • *Selection Vocabulary Practice*, p. 19 • *Selection Quick Checks*,* p. 22	• *Selection and Theme Assessment*, pp. 37–38 • *Testmaker: ExamView Pro* • *Performance Assessment*, p. 21 **Systematic Language Instruction** • *Grammar and Composition Handbook*, Lessons 4.6–4.7
Days 56–57 **The Moustache** Three-part instruction and selection support on SE/TWE pp. 281–293	**Lesson-Specific Instruction** • *Theme Three Planning Guide*, pp. 35–42 • *Selection Focus Transparency 22* • *Active Reading Guide*,* p. 23 • *Literary Elements Transparency 23* • *Selection Vocabulary Practice*, p. 20 • *Selection Quick Checks*,* p. 23	• *Selection and Theme Assessment*, pp. 39–40 • *Testmaker: ExamView Pro* • *Performance Assessment*, p. 22 **Systematic Language Instruction** • *Grammar and Composition Handbook*, Lesson 5.1 • *Vocabulary Power*, Lesson 12
Day 58 **The Black Walnut Tree** Three-part instruction and selection support on SE/TWE pp. 298–301 **Genre Focus** Poetry, SE/TWE pp. 294–295 **Active Reading Strategies** Active Reading Strategies for Poetry, SE/TWE pp. 296–297	**Lesson-Specific Instruction** • *Theme Three Planning Guide*, pp. 43–47 • *Selection Focus Transparency 23* • *Active Reading Guide*,* p. 24 • *Literary Elements Transparency 24* • *Selection Quick Checks*,* p. 24 • *Selection and Theme Assessment*, pp. 41–42	• *Testmaker: ExamView Pro* • *Performance Assessment*, p. 23 **Systematic Language Instruction** • *Grammar and Composition Handbook*, Lesson 5.2 • *Vocabulary Power*, Lesson 13 • *Spelling Power*, Lesson 11

SE: Student Edition **TWE: Teacher Wraparound Edition** ***Also available in Spanish**

English Language Learners (Add 30–45 Minutes a Day)	**Special Needs/Strategic Intervention** (Add 30–45 Minutes a Day)
• Multiple-Meaning Words, TWE p. 240 • *English Language Learners Sourcebook*, p. 39 • *Spanish Summaries*, p. 18 • *Audio Library** • *English, Yes!*	• *Interactive Reading Sourcebook*, pp. T93–T95 • *Interactive Reading Workbook*, pp. 40–41 • Learning Disabled, TWE p. 242 • Less-Proficient Readers, TWE p. 248 • *Inclusion Strategies Sourcebook*, pp. 17–18 • *Theme Three Planning Guide*, p. 6 • *Audio Library**
• Vocabulary, TWE p. 25 • *English Language Learners Sourcebook*, p. 40 • *Spanish Summaries*, p. 19 • *Spanish Translations*, pp. 69–70 • *Audio Library** • *English, Yes!*	• *Interactive Reading Sourcebook*, pp. T96–T98 • *Interactive Reading Workbook*, pp. 42–43 • *Inclusion Strategies Sourcebook*, pp. 79–80 • *Theme Three Planning Guide*, p. 14 • *Audio Library**
• Verb Tenses, TWE p. 260 • *English Language Learners Sourcebook*, p. 41 • *Spanish Summaries*, p. 20 • *Audio Library** • *English, Yes!*	• *Interactive Reading Sourcebook*, pp. T98–T101 • *Interactive Reading Workbook*, pp. 44–45 • Emotional, TWE p. 266 • *Inclusion Strategies Sourcebook*, pp. 19–20, 93–94 • *Theme Three Planning Guide*, p. 21 • *Audio Library**
• *-ing* Forms, TWE p. 270 • *English Language Learners Sourcebook*, p. 42 • *Spanish Summaries*, p. 21 • *Audio Library** • *English, Yes!*	• *Interactive Reading Sourcebook*, pp. T101–T103 • *Interactive Reading Workbook*, pp. 46–47 • Less-Proficient Readers, TWE p. 280 • *Inclusion Strategies Sourcebook*, pp. 13–14 • *Theme Three Planning Guide*, p. 29 • *Audio Library**
• Cultural References, TWE p. 283 • *English Language Learners Sourcebook*, p. 43 • *Spanish Summaries*, p. 22 • *Spanish Translations*, pp. 71–77 • *Audio Library** • *English, Yes!*.	• *Interactive Reading Sourcebook*, pp. T103–T105 • *Interactive Reading Workbook*, pp. 48–49 • Learning Disabled, TWE p. 285 • *Inclusion Strategies Sourcebook*, pp. 53–54 • *Audio Library**
• *Spanish Summaries*, p. 23 • *Audio Library** • *English, Yes!*	• *Interactive Reading Sourcebook*, pp. T106–T108 • *Interactive Reading Workbook*, p. 50 • Forms of Poetry, TWE p. 294 • *Inclusion Strategies Sourcebook*, pp. 15–16 • *Theme Three Planning Guide*, p. 45 • *Audio Library**

Lesson Schedule	Essential Lesson Support and Assessment
Days 59–60 A Time to Talk, Fire and Ice, and Dust and Snow Three-part instruction and selection support on SE/TWE pp. 302–307 **Vocabulary Skills** Dictionary Skills, SE/TWE p. 308	**Lesson-Specific Instruction** • *Theme Three Planning Guide*, pp. 48–53 • *Selection Focus Transparency 24* • *Active Reading Guide*,* p. 25 • *Literary Elements Transparency 25* • *Selection Quick Checks*,* p. 25 • *Selection and Theme Assessment*, pp. 43–44 • *Testmaker: ExamView Pro* • *Performance Assessment*, p. 24 **Systematic Language Instruction** • *Grammar and Composition Handbook*, Lessons 5.3–5.4 • *Vocabulary Power*, Lesson 14 • *Spelling Power*, Lesson 12
Day 61 Between What I See and What I Say . . . / Entre Lo Que Veo y Digo . . . Three-part instruction and selection support on SE/TWE pp. 309–313 **Grammar Link** Subject-Verb Agreement, SE/TWE p. 314 **Listening, Speaking, and Viewing** Effective Listening Techniques, SE/TWE p. 315	**Lesson-Specific Instruction** • *Theme Three Planning Guide*, pp. 54–59 • *Selection Focus Transparency 25* • *Active Reading Guide*,* p. 26 • *Literary Elements Transparency 26* • *Selection Quick Checks*,* p. 26 • *Selection and Theme Assessment*, pp. 45–46 • *Testmaker: ExamView Pro* • *Performance Assessment*, p. 25 **Systematic Language Instruction** • *Grammar and Composition Handbook*, Lesson 6.1 • *Vocabulary Power*, Unit 3 Review/Test • *Spelling Power*, Unit 3 Review/Proofreading
Days 62–63 Identity and The Lesson of the Moth Three-part instruction and selection support on SE/TWE pp. 316–321 **Media Connection** Newspaper Article, SE/TWE pp. 322–323	**Lesson-Specific Instruction** • *Theme Three Planning Guide*, pp. 60–65 • *Selection Focus Transparency 26* • *Active Reading Guide*,* p. 27 • *Literary Elements Transparency 27* • *Selection Quick Checks*,* p. 27 • *Selection and Theme Assessment*, pp. 47–48 • *Testmaker: ExamView Pro* • *Performance Assessment*, p. 26 • *inTIME* magazine, p. 24 **Systematic Language Instruction** • *Grammar and Composition Handbook*, Lesson 6.2
Days 64–65 Writing Workshop Expository Writing: Writing an Evaluation Lesson and lesson support on SE/TWE pp. 324–327	• *Writing Assessment and Portfolio Management*, pp. 1–13, 20–22, 41–48
Day 66 Theme Assessment Lesson and lesson support on SE/TWE pp. 328–329	• *Selection and Theme Assessment*, pp. 129–130 • *Testmaker: ExamView Pro* • *Performance Assessment*, p. 92 • *Writing Assessment and Portfolio Management*, pp. 1–12, 41–48 • *Initial Screening and Fluency Assessment*, Theme Three Reading Fluency
Theme 4: Fantastic Capers and Mischief Makers Day 67 Lesson and lesson support on SE/TWE pp. 332–335	• *Theme Four Planning Guide*, pp. 1–3 • *Performance Assessment*, p. 67
Days 68–69 The Ransom of Red Chief Three-part instruction and selection support on SE/TWE pp. 337–349	**Lesson-Specific Instruction** • *Theme Four Planning Guide*, pp. 4–11 • *Selection Focus Transparency 27* • *Active Reading Guide*,* p. 28 • *Literary Elements Transparency 28* • *Selection Vocabulary Practice*, p. 21 • *Selection Quick Checks*,* p. 28 • *Selection and Theme Assessment*, pp. 49–50 • *Testmaker: ExamView Pro* • *Performance Assessment*, p. 27

SE: Student Edition   TWE: Teacher Wraparound Edition   *Also available in Spanish

English Language Learners (Add 30–45 Minutes a Day)	Special Needs/Strategic Intervention (Add 30–45 Minutes a Day)
• Unfamiliar Meanings, TWE p. 303 • Personalized Pronunciation Keys, TWE p. 308 • *English Language Learners Sourcebook*, pp. 44, 45 • *Spanish Summaries*, p. 24 • *Audio Library** • *English, Yes!*	• *Interactive Reading Sourcebook*, pp. T108–T110 • *Interactive Reading Workbook*, p. 51 • *Theme Three Planning Guide*, p. 50 • *Audio Library**
• Read Along, TWE p. 315 • *English Language Learners Sourcebook*, pp. 46, 47 • *Theme Three Planning Guide*, p. 56 • *Spanish Summaries*, p. 25 • *Spanish Translations*, p. 78 • *Audio Library** • *English, Yes!*	• *Interactive Reading Sourcebook*, pp. T111–T113 • *Interactive Reading Workbook*, p. 52 • *Theme Three Planning Guide*, p. 56 • *Audio Library**
• Contractions, TWE p. 317 • *English Language Learners Sourcebook*, p. 48 • *Spanish Summaries*, p. 26 • *Spanish Translations*, pp. 79–80 • *Audio Library** • *English, Yes!*	• *Interactive Reading Sourcebook*, pp. T113–T115 • *Interactive Reading Workbook*, p. 53 • *Inclusion Strategies Sourcebook*, pp. 39–40 • *Audio Library**
• Organizing, TWE p. 324 • *English Language Learners Sourcebook*, p. 9 • *English, Yes!*	
• *English Language Learners Sourcebook*, p. xii • *English, Yes!*	• Special Needs, TWE p. 329 • *Inclusion Strategies Sourcebook*, p. xii
• *English Language Learners Sourcebook*, pp. 1–13 • *English, Yes!*	• *Inclusion Strategies Sourcebook*, pp. vii–xii
• Games of Cowboys and Indians, TWE p. 339 • *English Language Learners Sourcebook*, p. 49 • *Spanish Summaries*, p. 27 • *Audio Library** • *English, Yes!*	• *Interactive Reading Sourcebook*, pp. T116–T118 • *Interactive Reading Workbook*, pp. 54–55 • Less-Proficient Readers, TWE pp. 344, 348 • *Inclusion Strategies Sourcebook*, pp. 29–30 • *Theme Four Planning Guide*, p. 6 • *Audio Library**

Lesson Schedule	Essential Lesson Support and Assessment
Days 68–69 (continued) **Media Connection** Comic Strip, SE/TWE p. 336	**Systematic Language Instruction** • *Grammar and Composition Handbook*, Lessons 6.3–6.4 • *Vocabulary Power*, Lesson 15 • *Spelling Power*, Lesson 13
Days 70–71 **John Henry** and from **The People, Yes** Three-part instruction and selection support on SE/TWE pp. 350–357	**Lesson-Specific Instruction** • *Theme Four Planning Guide*, pp. 12–17 • *Selection Focus Transparency* 28 • *Active Reading Guide*,* p. 29 • *Literary Elements Transparency* 29 • *Selection Quick Checks*,* p. 29 • *Selection and Theme Assessment*, pp. 51–52 • *Testmaker: ExamView Pro* • *Performance Assessment*, p. 28 **Systematic Language Instruction** • *Grammar and Composition Handbook*, Lesson 6.5
Days 72–73 **Sally Ann Thunder Ann Whirlwind** Three-part instruction and selection support on SE/TWE pp. 360–368 **Genre Focus** Folktale, SE/TWE p. 358 **Active Reading Strategies** Tips for Reading Folktales, SE/TWE p. 359 **Grammar Link** Using Irregular Verbs Correctly, SE/TWE p. 369	**Lesson-Specific Instruction** • *Theme Four Planning Guide*, pp. 18–25 • *Selection Focus Transparency* 29 • *Active Reading Guide*,* p. 30 • *Literary Elements Transparency* 30 • *Selection Vocabulary Practice*, p. 22 • *Selection Quick Checks*,* p. 30 • *Selection and Theme Assessment*, pp. 53–54 • *Testmaker: ExamView Pro* • *Performance Assessment*, p. 29 • *inTIME* magazine, pp. 30–31 **Systematic Language Instruction** • *Grammar and Composition Handbook*, Lessons 7.1–7.2 • *Vocabulary Power*, Lesson 16 • *Spelling Power*, Lesson 14
Day 74 **Lazy Peter and His Three-Cornered Hat** Three-part instruction and selection support on SE/TWE pp. 370–375 **Listening, Speaking, and Viewing** Storytelling, SE/TWE p. 376	**Lesson-Specific Instruction** • *Theme Four Planning Guide*, pp. 26–33 • *Selection Focus Transparency* 30 • *Active Reading Guide*,* p. 31 • *Literary Elements Transparency* 31 • *Selection Vocabulary Practice*, p. 23 • *Selection Quick Checks*,* p. 31 • *Selection and Theme Assessment*, pp. 55–56 • *Testmaker: ExamView Pro* • *Performance Assessment*, p. 30 **Systematic Language Instruction** • *Grammar and Composition Handbook*, Lesson 7.3 • *Vocabulary Power*, Lesson 17 • *Spelling Power*, Lesson 15
Day 75 **M'su Carencro and Mangeur de Poulet** Three-part instruction and selection support on SE/TWE pp. 377–381	**Lesson-Specific Instruction** • *Theme Four Planning Guide*, pp. 34–41 • *Selection Focus Transparency* 31 • *Active Reading Guide*,* p. 32 • *Literary Elements Transparency* 32 • *Selection Quick Checks*,* p. 32 • *Selection and Theme Assessment*, pp. 57–58 • *Testmaker: ExamView Pro* • *Performance Assessment*, p. 31 **Systematic Language Instruction** • *Grammar and Composition Handbook*, Lesson 7.4
Day 76 **Talk** Three-part instruction and selection support on SE/TWE pp. 382–385 **Comparing Selections** SE/TWE p. 386 **Vocabulary Skills** Using Roots, SE/TWE p. 387	**Lesson-Specific Instruction** • *Theme Four Planning Guide*, pp. 42–48 • *Selection Focus Transparency* 32 • *Active Reading Guide*,* p. 33 • *Literary Elements Transparency* 33 • *Selection Vocabulary Practice*, p. 24 • *Selection Quick Checks*,* p. 33 • *Selection and Theme Assessment*, pp. 57–58 • *Testmaker: ExamView Pro* • *Performance Assessment*, p. 31 **Systematic Language Instruction** • *Grammar and Composition Handbook*, Lessons 7.5–7.7
Days 77–78 **The People Could Fly** Three-part instruction and selection support on SE/TWE pp. 388–394 **Reading and Thinking Skills** Setting a Purpose for Reading, SE/TWE p. 395 **Technology Skills** Photography, SE/TWE pp. 396–397	**Lesson-Specific Instruction** • *Theme Four Planning Guide*, pp. 49–56 • *Selection Focus Transparency* 33 • *Active Reading Guide*,* p. 34 • *Literary Elements Transparency* 34 • *Selection Quick Checks*,* p. 34 • *Selection and Theme Assessment*, pp. 59–60 • *Testmaker: ExamView Pro* • *Performance Assessment*, p. 32 **Systematic Language Instruction** • *Grammar and Composition Handbook*, Lessons 8.1–8.2 • *Vocabulary Power*, Lesson 18 • *Spelling Power*, Lesson 16

SE: Student Edition TWE: Teacher Wraparound Edition *Also available in Spanish

English Language Learners (Add 30–45 Minutes a Day)	Special Needs/Strategic Intervention (Add 30–45 Minutes a Day)
• Multicultural Songs, TWE p. 351 • *English Language Learners Sourcebook*, p. 50 • *Spanish Summaries*, p. 28 • *Audio Library** • *English, Yes!*	• *Interactive Reading Sourcebook*, pp. T119–T121 • *Interactive Reading Workbook*, p. 56 • Learning Disabled, TWE p. 355 • *Theme Four Planning Guide*, p. 14 • *Audio Library**
• Regionalism and Slang, TWE p. 358 • The Prefix *Out-*, TWE p. 362 • *English Language Learners Sourcebook*, p. 51 • *Spanish Summaries*, p. 29 • *Audio Library** • *English, Yes!*	• *Interactive Reading Sourcebook*, pp. T121–T123 • *Interactive Reading Workbook*, pp. 57–58 • Emotional, TWE p. 363 • *Inclusion Strategies Sourcebook*, pp. 35–36 • *Audio Library**
• The Prefix *un-*, TWE p. 372 • Storytelling in Two Languages, TWE p. 376 • *English Language Learners Sourcebook*, pp. 52–53 • *Spanish Summaries*, p. 30 • *Spanish Translations*, pp. 81–84 • *Audio Library** • *English, Yes!*	• *Interactive Reading Sourcebook*, pp. T124–T126 • *Interactive Reading Workbook*, pp. 59–60 • *Inclusion Strategies Sourcebook*, pp. 81–82 • *Theme Four Planning Guide*, p. 28 • *Audio Library**
• *Theme Four Planning Guide*, p. 36 • *Spanish Summaries*, p. 31 • *Audio Library** • *English, Yes!*	• *Interactive Reading Sourcebook*, pp. T126–T128 • *Interactive Reading Workbook*, p. 61 • *Theme Four Planning Guide*, p. 36 • *Audio Library**
• Extending Roots, TWE p. 387 • *English Language Learners Sourcebook*, p. 54 • *Theme Four Planning Guide*, p. 44 • *Spanish Summaries*, p. 32 • *Audio Library** • *English, Yes!*	• *Interactive Reading Sourcebook*, pp. T129–T131 • *Interactive Reading Workbook*, pp. 62–63 • *Inclusion Strategies Sourcebook*, pp. 59–60 • *Audio Library**
• Storytelling Techniques, TWE p. 390 • *English Language Learners Sourcebook*, p. 55 • *Spanish Summaries*, p. 33 • *Spanish Translations*, pp. 85–87 • *Audio Library** • *English, Yes!*	• *Interactive Reading Sourcebook*, pp. T132–T134 • *Interactive Reading Workbook*, pp. 64–65 • Less-Proficient Readers, TWE p. 395 • *Theme Four Planning Guide*, p. 51 • *Audio Library**

Lesson Schedule	Essential Lesson Support and Assessment	
Days 79–80 The Souls in Purgatory Three-part instruction and selection support on SE/TWE pp. 398–406 **Interdisciplinary Connection** Art and Culture, SE/TWE p. 407	**Lesson-Specific Instruction** • *Theme Four Planning Guide*, pp. 57–64 • *Selection Focus Transparency 34* • *Active Reading Guide*,* p. 35 • *Literary Elements Transparency 35* • *Selection Vocabulary Practice*, p. 25 • *Selection Quick Checks*,* p. 35	• *Selection and Theme Assessment*, pp. 61–62 • *Testmaker: ExamView Pro* • *Performance Assessment*, p. 33 **Systematic Language Instruction** • *Grammar and Composition Handbook*, Lesson 8.3
Days 81–82 Spotted Eagle and Black Crow and The Siege of Courthouse Rock Three-part instruction and selection support on SE/TWE pp. 408–417	**Lesson-Specific Instruction** • *Theme Four Planning Guide*, pp. 65–70 • *Selection Focus Transparency 35* • *Active Reading Guide*,* p. 36 • *Literary Elements Transparency 36* • *Selection Vocabulary Practice*, p. 26 • *Selection Quick Checks*,* p. 36 • *Selection and Theme Assessment*, pp. 63–64	• *Testmaker: ExamView Pro* • *Performance Assessment*, p. 34 **Systematic Language Instruction** • *Grammar and Composition Handbook*, Lessons 8.4–8.5 • *Vocabulary Power*, Unit 4 Review/Test • *Spelling Power*, Unit 4 Review/Proofreading
Days 83–84 Chicoria and Coyote and Wasichu Three-part instruction and selection support on SE/TWE pp. 418–424 **Media Connection** Newspaper Article, SE/TWE p. 425	**Lesson-Specific Instruction** • *Theme Four Planning Guide*, pp. 71–76 • *Selection Focus Transparency 36* • *Active Reading Guide*,* p. 37 • *Literary Elements Transparency 37* • *Selection Quick Checks*,* p. 37 • *Selection and Theme Assessment*, pp. 65–66	• *Testmaker: ExamView Pro* • *Performance Assessment*, p. 35 **Systematic Language Instruction** • *Grammar and Composition Handbook*, Lesson 8.6
Days 85–86 Writing Workshop Narrative Writing: Trickster Tale Lesson and lesson support on SE/TWE pp. 426–429	• *Writing Assessment and Portfolio Management*, pp. 1–13, 23–25, 41–48	
Day 87 Theme Assessment Lesson and lesson support on SE/TWE pp. 430–431	• *Selection and Theme Assessment*, pp. 131–132 • *Testmaker: ExamView Pro* • *Performance Assessment*, pp. 92–93	• *Writing Assessment and Portfolio Management*, pp. 1–12, 41–48 • *Initial Screening and Fluency Assessment*, Theme Four Reading Fluency
Theme 5: Free to Be Day 88 Lesson and lesson support on SE/TWE pp. 434–437	• *Theme Five Planning Guide*, pp. 1–3 • *Performance Assessment*, p. 68	
Days 89–90 The Drummer Boy of Shiloh Three-part instruction and selection support on SE/TWE pp. 438–446 **Vocabulary Skills** Using Homophones, SE/TWE p. 447	**Lesson-Specific Instruction** • *Theme Five Planning Guide*, pp. 4–11 • *Selection Focus Transparency 37* • *Active Reading Guide*,* p. 38 • *Literary Elements Transparency 38* • *Selection Vocabulary Practice*, p. 27 • *Selection Quick Checks*,* p. 38 • *Selection and Theme Assessment*, pp. 67–68	• *Testmaker: ExamView Pro* • *Performance Assessment*, p. 36 **Systematic Language Instruction** • *Grammar and Composition Handbook*, Lesson 9.1 • *Vocabulary Power*, Lesson 19 • *Spelling Power*, Lesson 17

SE: Student Edition   TWE: Teacher Wraparound Edition   *Also available in Spanish

English Language Learners (Add 30–45 Minutes a Day)	Special Needs/Strategic Intervention (Add 30–45 Minutes a Day)
• Idiomatic Expressions, TWE p. 400 • *English Language Learners Sourcebook*, p. 56 • *Spanish Summaries*, p. 34 • *Spanish Translations*, pp. 88–91 • *Audio Library** • *English, Yes!*	• *Interactive Reading Sourcebook*, pp. T134–T136 • *Interactive Reading Workbook*, pp. 66–67 • Learning Disabled, TWE p. 403 • *Inclusion Strategies Sourcebook*, pp. 21–22 • *Audio Library**
• Native American Cultures, TWE p. 409 • *English Language Learners Sourcebook*, p. 57 • *Spanish Summaries*, p. 35 • *Audio Library** • *English, Yes!*	• *Interactive Reading Sourcebook*, pp. T137–T139 • *Interactive Reading Workbook*, pp. 68–69 • Less-Proficient Readers, TWE p. 412 • *Inclusion Strategies Sourcebook*, pp. 43–44 • *Theme Four Planning Guide*, p. 67 • *Audio Library**
• Pronoun Reference, TWE p. 419 • *English Language Learners Sourcebook*, p. 58 • *Spanish Summaries*, p. 36 • *Spanish Translations*, pp. 92–94 • *Audio Library** • *English, Yes!*	• *Interactive Reading Sourcebook*, pp. T140–T142 • *Interactive Reading Workbook*, pp. 70–71 • *Theme Four Planning Guide*, p. 73 • *Audio Library**
• Planning a Trickster Tale, TWE p. 426 • *English Language Learners Sourcebook*, p. 9 • *English, Yes!*	• *Inclusion Strategies Sourcebook*, pp. 73–74
• *English Language Learners Sourcebook*, pp. 1–13 • *English, Yes*	• Special Needs, TWE p. 431 • *Inclusion Strategies Sourcebook*, p. xii
• *English Language Learners Sourcebook*, pp. 1–13 • *English, Yes!*	• *Inclusion Strategies Sourcebook*, pp. vii–xii
• Multiple-Meaning Words, TWE p. 440 • *English Language Learners Sourcebook*, pp. 59–60 • *Theme Five Planning Guide*, p. 6 • *Spanish Summaries*, p. 37 • *Spanish Translations*, pp. 95–99 • *Audio Library** • *English, Yes!*	• *Interactive Reading Sourcebook*, pp. T143–T145 • *Interactive Reading Workbook*, pp. 72–73 • *Inclusion Strategies Sourcebook*, pp. 31–32 • *Theme Five Planning Guide*, p. 6 • *Audio Library**

Lesson Schedule	Essential Lesson Support and Assessment	
Days 91–92 **Paul Revere's Ride** Three-part instruction and selection support on SE/TWE pp. 448–456 **Media Connection** Radio Transcript, SE/TWE p. 457	**Lesson-Specific Instruction** • *Theme Five Planning Guide*, pp. 12–19 • *Selection Focus Transparency* 38 • *Active Reading Guide*,* p. 39 • *Literary Elements Transparency* 39 • *Selection Quick Checks*,* p. 39 • *Selection and Theme Assessment*, pp. 69–70	• *Testmaker: ExamView Pro* • *Performance Assessment*, p. 37 **Systematic Language Instruction** • *Grammar and Composition Handbook*, Lesson 9.2
Days 93–94 **Barbara Frietchie** Three-part instruction and selection support on SE/TWE pp. 458–462 **Comparing Selections** SE/TWE p. 463 **Technology Skills** Database, SE/TWE pp. 464–465	**Lesson-Specific Instruction** • *Theme Five Planning Guide*, pp. 20–26 • *Selection Focus Transparency* 39 • *Active Reading Guide*,* p. 40 • *Literary Elements Transparency* 40 • *Selection Quick Checks*,* p. 40	• *Selection and Theme Assessment*, pp. 69–70 • *Testmaker: ExamView Pro* • *Performance Assessment*, p. 37 **Systematic Language Instruction** • *Grammar and Composition Handbook*, Lesson 9.3
Day 95 **The Pinta, the Nina and the Santa Maria; and many other cargoes of Light** and **The Other Pioneers** Three-part instruction and selection support on SE/TWE pp. 466–471	**Lesson-Specific Instruction** • *Theme Five Planning Guide*, pp. 27–32 • *Selection Focus Transparency* 40 • *Active Reading Guide*,* p. 41 • *Literary Elements Transparency* 41 • *Selection Quick Checks*,* p. 41 • *Selection and Theme Assessment*, pp. 71–72	• *Testmaker: ExamView Pro* • *Performance Assessment*, p. 38 **Systematic Language Instruction** • *Grammar and Composition Handbook*, Lessons 10.1–10.2 • *Vocabulary Power*, Lesson 20 • *Spelling Power*, Lesson 18
Day 96 **The Gettysburg Address** and **O Captain! My Captain!** Three-part instruction and selection support on SE/TWE pp. 472–477	**Lesson-Specific Instruction** • *Theme Five Planning Guide*, pp. 33–38 • *Selection Focus Transparency* 41 • *Active Reading Guide*,* p. 42 • *Literary Elements Transparency* 42 • *Selection Vocabulary Practice*, p. 28 • *Selection Quick Checks*,* p. 42	• *Selection and Theme Assessment*, pp. 73–74 • *Testmaker: ExamView Pro* • *Performance Assessment*, p. 39 **Systematic Language Instruction** • *Grammar and Composition Handbook*, Lessons 10.3–10.4
Days 97–98 from **Harriet Tubman: Conductor on the Underground Railroad** Three-part instruction and selection support on SE/TWE pp. 479–491 **Media Connection** Magazine Article, SE/TWE p. 478	**Lesson-Specific Instruction** • *Theme Five Planning Guide*, pp. 39–46 • *Selection Focus Transparency* 42 • *Active Reading Guide*,* p. 43 • *Literary Elements Transparency* 43 • *Selection Vocabulary Practice*, p. 29 • *Selection Quick Checks*,* p. 43 • *Selection and Theme Assessment*, pp. 75–76	• *Testmaker: ExamView Pro* • *Performance Assessment*, p. 40 **Systematic Language Instruction** • *Grammar and Composition Handbook*, Lesson 10.5 • *Vocabulary Power*, Lesson 21 • *Spelling Power*, Lesson 19
Days 99–100 **I Have a Dream** Three-part instruction and selection support on SE/TWE pp. 493–501 **Interdisciplinary Connection** Social Studies, SE/TWE p. 492 **Listening, Speaking, and Viewing** Reaching Your Audience, SE/TWE p. 502	**Lesson-Specific Instruction** • *Theme Five Planning Guide*, pp. 47–54 • *Selection Focus Transparency* 43 • *Active Reading Guide*,* p. 44 • *Literary Elements Transparency* 44 • *Selection Vocabulary Practice*, p. 30 • *Selection Quick Checks*,* p. 44 • *Selection and Theme Assessment*, pp. 77–78	• *Testmaker: ExamView Pro* • *Performance Assessment*, p. 41 **Systematic Language Instruction** • *Grammar and Composition Handbook*, Lesson 11.1 • *Vocabulary Power*, Lesson 22 • *Spelling Power*, Lesson 20

SE: Student Edition **TWE: Teacher Wraparound Edition** ***Also available in Spanish**

English Language Learners (Add 30–45 Minutes a Day)	Special Needs/Strategic Intervention (Add 30–45 Minutes a Day)
• Syntax, TWE p. 450 • *English Language Learners Sourcebook*, p. 61 • *Spanish Summaries*, p. 38 • *Audio Library** • *English, Yes!*	• *Interactive Reading Sourcebook*, pp. T146–T148 • *Interactive Reading Workbook*, pp. 74–75 • *Theme Five Planning Guide*, p. 14 • *Audio Library**
• *Theme Five Planning Guide*, p. 22 • *Spanish Summaries*, p. 39 • *Audio Library** • *English, Yes!*	• *Interactive Reading Sourcebook*, pp. T149–T151 • *Interactive Reading Workbook*, pp. 76–77 • *Inclusion Strategies Sourcebook*, pp. 77–78 • *Theme Five Planning Guide*, p. 22 • *Audio Library**
• Completing Sentences, TWE p. 467 • *English Language Learners Sourcebook*, p. 62 • *Theme Five Planning Guide*, p. 29 • *Spanish Summaries*, p. 40 • *Audio Library** • *English, Yes!*	• *Interactive Reading Sourcebook*, pp. T151–T154 • *Interactive Reading Workbook*, p. 78 • *Audio Library**
• Paraphrasing, TWE p. 473 • *English Language Learners Sourcebook*, p. 63 • *Spanish Summaries*, p. 41 • *Spanish Translations*, pp. 100–101 • *Audio Library** • *English, Yes!*	• *Interactive Reading Sourcebook*, pp. T154–T157 • *Interactive Reading Workbook*, pp. 79–80 • *Inclusion Strategies Sourcebook*, pp. 45–46, 77–78 • *Theme Five Planning Guide*, p. 35 • *Audio Library**
• Noun Suffixes *–ment* and *–ness*, TWE p. 481 • Connotation and Denotation, TWE p. 490 • *English Language Learners Sourcebook*, p. 64 • *Spanish Summaries*, p. 42 • *Spanish Translations*, pp. 102–108 • *Audio Library** • *English, Yes!*	• *Interactive Reading Sourcebook*, pp. T157–T159 • *Interactive Reading Workbook*, pp. 81–82 • *Inclusion Strategies Sourcebook*, pp. 63–64 • *Theme Five Planning Guide*, p. 41 • *Audio Library**
• Root Words, TWE p. 495 • Public Speaking Practice, TWE p. 502 • *English Language Learners Sourcebook*, pp. 65, 66 • *Spanish Summaries*, p. 43 • *Spanish Translations*, pp. 109–112 • *Audio Library** • *English, Yes!*	• *Interactive Reading Sourcebook*, pp. T160–162 • *Interactive Reading Workbook*, pp. 83–84 • *Inclusion Strategies Sourcebook*, pp. 65–66 • *Theme Five Planning Guide*, p. 49 • *Audio Library**

Lesson Schedule	Essential Lesson Support and Assessment	
Day 101 **Sorrow Home** and **Sit-Ins** Three-part instruction and selection support on SE/TWE pp. 503–507	**Lesson-Specific Instruction** • *Theme Five Planning Guide*, pp. 55–60 • *Selection Focus Transparency* 44 • *Active Reading Guide*,* p. 45 • *Literary Elements Transparency* 45 • *Selection Quick Checks*,* p. 45 • *Selection and Theme Assessment*, pp. 79–80	• *Testmaker: ExamView Pro* • *Performance Assessment*, p. 42 **Systematic Language Instruction** • *Grammar and Composition Handbook*, Lesson 11.2 • *Vocabulary Power*, Lesson 23
Days 102–104 **The Battleground** Three-part instruction and selection support on SE/TWE pp. 510–524 **Genre Focus** Historical Fiction, SE/TWE p. 508 **Active Reading Strategies** Tips for Reading Historical Fiction, SE/TWE p. 509 **Reading and Thinking Skills** Identifying Persuasive Techniques, SE/TWE p. 525	**Lesson-Specific Instruction** • *Theme Five Planning Guide*, pp. 61–68 • *Selection Focus Transparency* 45 • *Active Reading Guide*,* p. 46 • *Literary Elements Transparency* 46 • *Selection Vocabulary Practice*, p. 31 • *Selection Quick Checks*,* p. 46 • *Selection and Theme Assessment*, pp. 81–82	• *Testmaker: ExamView Pro* • *Performance Assessment*, p. 43 **Systematic Language Instruction** • *Grammar and Composition Handbook*, Lesson 11.3
Days 105–107 from **Letters from Rifka** Three-part instruction and selection support on SE/TWE pp. 526–538 **Grammar Link** Using Pronouns Correctly, SE/TWE p. 539	**Lesson-Specific Instruction** • *Theme Five Planning Guide*, pp. 69–76 • *Selection Focus Transparency* 46 • *Active Reading Guide*,* p. 47 • *Literary Elements Transparency* 47 • *Selection Vocabulary Practice*, p. 32 • *Selection Quick Checks*,* p. 47 • *Selection and Theme Assessment*, pp. 83–84	• *Testmaker: ExamView Pro* • *Performance Assessment*, p. 44 **Systematic Language Instruction** • *Grammar and Composition Handbook*, Lesson 11.4 • *Vocabulary Power*, Unit 5 Review/Test • *Spelling Power*, Unit 5 Review/Proofreading
Days 108–109 **Writing Workshop** Persuasive Writing: Speech Lesson and lesson support on SE/TWE pp. 540–543	• *Writing Assessment and Portfolio Management*, pp. 1–13, 26–28, 41–48	
Day 110 **Theme Assessment** Lesson and lesson support on SE/TWE pp. 544–545	• *Selection and Theme Assessment*, pp. 133–134 • *Testmaker: ExamView Pro* • *Performance Assessment*, p. 93	• *Writing Assessment and Portfolio Management*, pp. 1–12, 41–48 • *Initial Screening and Fluency Assessment*, Theme Five Reading Fluency
Theme 6: Flashes of Insight Day 111 Lesson and lesson support on SE/TWE pp. 548–551	• *Theme Six Planning Guide*, pp. 1–3 • *Performance Assessment*, p. 69	
Days 112–113 **Raymond's Run** Three-part instruction and selection support on SE/TWE pp. 552–563 **Media Connection** Magazine Article, SE/TWE p. 564	**Lesson-Specific Instruction** • *Theme Six Planning Guide*, pp. 4–11 • *Selection Focus Transparency* 47 • *Active Reading Guide*,* p. 48 • *Literary Elements Transparency* 48 • *Selection Vocabulary Practice*, p. 33 • *Selection Quick Checks*,* p. 48	• *Selection and Theme Assessment*, pp. 85–86 • *Testmaker: ExamView Pro* • *Performance Assessment*, p. 45 **Systematic Language Instruction** • *Grammar and Composition Handbook*, Lesson 11.5

SE: Student Edition TWE: Teacher Wraparound Edition *Also available in Spanish

English Language Learners (Add 30–45 Minutes a Day)	Special Needs/Strategic Intervention (Add 30–45 Minutes a Day)
• *English Language Learners Sourcebook*, p. 67 • *Spanish Summaries*, p. 44 • *Audio Library** • *English, Yes!*	• *Interactive Reading Sourcebook*, pp. T163–T164 • *Interactive Reading Workbook*, p. 85 • *Theme Five Planning Guide*, p. 57 • *Audio Library**
• Historical Fiction, TWE p. 508 • Prefixes, TWE p. 512 • *English Language Learners Sourcebook*, p. 68 • *Spanish Summaries*, p. 45 • *Audio Library** • *English, Yes!*	• *Interactive Reading Sourcebook*, pp. T165–T167 • *Interactive Reading Workbook*, pp. 86–87 • Emotional/Learning Disabled, TWE p. 519 • Less-Proficient Readers, TWE p. 525 • *Theme Five Planning Guide*, p. 63 • *Audio Library**
• Social Adjustment, TWE p. 528 • *English Language Learners Sourcebook*, p. 69 • *Spanish Summaries*, p. 46 • *Spanish Translations*, pp. 113–120 • *Audio Library** • *English, Yes!*	• *Interactive Reading Sourcebook*, pp. T167–T169 • *Interactive Reading Workbook*, pp. 88–89 • Emotional, TWE p. 529 • *Inclusion Strategies Sourcebook*, pp. 69–70 • *Theme Five Planning Guide*, p. 71 • *Audio Library**
• Speaking Before Writing, TWE p. 540 • *English Language Learners Sourcebook*, p. 9 • *English, Yes!*	
• *English Language Learners Sourcebook*, pp. 1–13 • *English, Yes!*	• *Inclusion Strategies Sourcebook*, p. xii
• *English Language Learners Sourcebook*, pp. 1–13 • *English, Yes!*	• *Inclusion Strategies Sourcebook*, pp. vii–xii
• Colloquial English, TWE p. 554 • *English Language Learners Sourcebook*, p. 70 • *Spanish Summaries*, p. 47 • *Audio Library** • *English, Yes!*	• *Interactive Reading Sourcebook*, pp. T170–T172 • *Interactive Reading Workbook*, pp. 90–91 • Learning Disabled, TWE p. 565 • *Inclusion Strategies Sourcebook*, pp. 51–52 • *Theme Six Planning Guide*, p. 6 • *Audio Library**

Lesson Schedule	Essential Lesson Support and Assessment	
Days 112–113 (continued) **Reading and Thinking Skills** Strategies for Reading Informational Text, SE/TWE p. 565	• *Vocabulary Power*, Lesson 24 • *Spelling Power*, Lesson 21	
Day 114 Forgotten Language and New World Three-part instruction and selection support on SE/TWE pp. 566–571 **Grammar Link** Using Adjectives Correctly, SE/TWE p. 572	**Lesson-Specific Instruction** • *Theme Six Planning Guide*, pp. 12–17 • *Selection Focus Transparency* 48 • *Active Reading Guide*,* p. 49 • *Literary Elements Transparency* 49 • *Selection Quick Checks*,* p. 49 • *Selection and Theme Assessment*, pp. 87–88	• *Testmaker: ExamView Pro* • *Performance Assessment*, p. 46 **Systematic Language Instruction** • *Grammar and Composition Handbook*, Lesson 11.6
Days 115–117 Thank You in Arabic Three-part instruction and selection support on SE/TWE pp. 573–588	**Lesson-Specific Instruction** • *Theme Six Planning Guide*, pp. 18–25 • *Selection Focus Transparency* 49 • *Active Reading Guide*,* p. 50 • *Literary Elements Transparency* 50 • *Selection Vocabulary Practice*, p. 34 • *Selection Quick Checks*,* p. 50	• *Selection and Theme Assessment*, pp. 89–90 • *Testmaker: ExamView Pro* • *Performance Assessment*, p. 47 • *inTIME* magazine, pp. 14–15 **Systematic Language Instruction** • *Grammar and Composition Handbook*, Lesson 11.7
Days 118–119 "If I Forget Thee, Oh Earth . . ." Three-part instruction and selection support on SE/TWE pp. 590–596 **Media Connection** Opinion Poll, SE/TWE p. 589 **Comparing Selections** SE/TWE p. 597	**Lesson-Specific Instruction** • *Theme Six Planning Guide*, pp. 26–33 • *Selection Focus Transparency* 50 • *Active Reading Guide*,* p. 51 • *Literary Elements Transparency* 51 • *Selection Vocabulary Practice*, p. 35 • *Selection Quick Checks*,* p. 51 • *Selection and Theme Assessment*, pp. 91–92	• *Testmaker: ExamView Pro* • *Performance Assessment*, p. 48 • *inTIME* magazine, pp. 3–5 **Systematic Language Instruction** • *Grammar and Composition Handbook*, Lesson 11.8 • *Vocabulary Power*, Lesson 25 • *Spelling Power*, Lesson 22
Day 120 Southbound on the Freeway and I Like to See it Lap the Miles Three-part instruction and selection support on SE/TWE pp. 598–603	**Lesson-Specific Instruction** • *Theme Six Planning Guide*, pp. 34–39 • *Selection Focus Transparency* 51 • *Active Reading Guide*,* p. 52 • *Literary Elements Transparency* 52 • *Selection Quick Checks*,* p. 52	• *Selection and Theme Assessment*, pp. 93–94 • *Testmaker: ExamView Pro* • *Performance Assessment*, p. 49 **Systematic Language Instruction** • *Grammar and Composition Handbook*, Lesson 11.9
Days 121–122 Stop the Sun Three-part instruction and selection support on SE/TWE pp. 606–617 **Interdisciplinary Connection** History, SE/TWE p. 604 **Vocabulary Skills** Using Idioms, SE/TWE p. 605	**Lesson-Specific Instruction** • *Theme Six Planning Guide*, pp. 40–47 • *Selection Focus Transparency* 52 • *Active Reading Guide*,* p. 53 • *Literary Elements Transparency* 53 • *Selection Vocabulary Practice*, p. 36 • *Selection Quick Checks*,* p. 53 • *Selection and Theme Assessment*, pp. 95–96	• *Testmaker: ExamView Pro* • *Performance Assessment*, p. 50 **Systematic Language Instruction** • *Grammar and Composition Handbook*, Lesson 12.1 • *Vocabulary Power*, Lesson 26 • *Spelling Power*, Lesson 23
Days 123–124 The Summer of Vietnam Three-part instruction and selection support on SE/TWE pp. 622–627	**Lesson-Specific Instruction** • *Theme Six Planning Guide*, pp. 48–55 • *Selection Focus Transparency* 53 • *Active Reading Guide*,* p. 54 • *Literary Elements Transparency* 54	• *Selection Vocabulary Practice*, p. 37 • *Selection Quick Checks*,* p. 54 • *Selection and Theme Assessment*, pp. 97–98 • *Testmaker: ExamView Pro* • *Performance Assessment*, p. 51

SE: Student Edition **TWE: Teacher Wraparound Edition** ***Also available in Spanish**

English Language Learners (Add 30–45 Minutes a Day)	Special Needs/Strategic Intervention (Add 30–45 Minutes a Day)
• Visualizing, TWE p. 567 • *English Language Learners Sourcebook*, p. 71 • *Spanish Summaries*, p. 48 • *Audio Library** • *English, Yes!*	• *Interactive Reading Sourcebook*, pp. T172–T174 • *Interactive Reading Workbook*, p. 92 • *Theme Six Planning Guide*, p. 14 • *Audio Library**
• Sharing Languages, TWE p. 575 • Idioms, TWE p. 583 • *English Language Learners Sourcebook*, pp. 72, 73 • *Spanish Summaries*, p. 49 • *Spanish Translations*, pp. 121–131 • *Audio Library** • *English, Yes!*	• *Interactive Reading Sourcebook*, pp. T175–T177 • *Interactive Reading Workbook*, pp. 93–94 • Learning Disabled, TWE p. 582 • Less-Proficient Readers, TWE p. 587 • *Inclusion Strategies Sourcebook*, pp. 57–58 • *Theme Six Planning Guide*, p. 20 • *Audio Library**
• Listening and Note-Taking, TWE p. 592 • *English Language Learners Sourcebook*, p. 74 • *Spanish Summaries*, p. 50 • *Spanish Translations*, pp. 132–135 • *Audio Library** • *English, Yes!*	• *Interactive Reading Sourcebook*, pp. T177–T179 • *Interactive Reading Workbook*, pp. 95–96 • Learning Disabled, TWE p. 593 • *Inclusion Strategies Sourcebook*, pp. 49–50 • *Audio Library**
• Vocabulary, TWE p. 599 • *English Language Learners Sourcebook*, p. 75 • *Spanish Summaries*, p. 51 • *Audio Library** • *English, Yes!*	• *Interactive Reading Sourcebook*, pp. T180–T182 • *Interactive Reading Workbook*, p. 97 • *Theme Six Planning Guide*, p. 36 • *Audio Library**
• Idioms, TWE p. 605 • Identifying with the Character, TWE p. 608 • *English Language Learners Sourcebook*, pp. 76, 77 • *Spanish Summaries*, p. 52 • *Spanish Translations*, pp. 136–141 • *Audio Library** • *English, Yes!*	• *Interactive Reading Sourcebook*, pp. T182–T184 • *Interactive Reading Workbook*, pp. 98–99 • Emotional, TWE p. 610 • *Inclusion Strategies Sourcebook*, pp. 47–48 • *Theme Six Planning Guide*, p. 42 • *Audio Library**
• Borrowed Words, TWE p. 624 • *English Language Learners Sourcebook*, p. 78 • *Spanish Summaries*, p. 53 • *Spanish Translations*, pp. 142–143 • *Audio Library** • *English, Yes!*	• *Interactive Reading Sourcebook*, pp. T184–T186 • *Interactive Reading Workbook*, pp. 100–101 • *Inclusion Strategies Sourcebook*, pp. 29–30, 87–88 • *Theme Six Planning Guide*, p. 50 • *Audio Library**

Lesson Schedule	Essential Lesson Support and Assessment
Days 123–124 (continued) **Genre Focus** Personal Essay, SE/TWE pp. 618–619 **Active Reading Strategies** Tips for Reading a Personal Essay, SE/TWE pp. 620–621	**Systematic Language Instruction** • *Grammar and Composition Handbook*, Lesson 12.2
Day 125 Finding America Three-part instruction and selection support on SE/TWE pp. 628–633	**Lesson-Specific Instruction** • *Theme Six Planning Guide*, pp. 56–63 • *Selection Focus Transparency* 54 • *Active Reading Guide*,* p. 55 • *Literary Elements Transparency* 55 • *Selection Vocabulary Practice*, p. 38 • *Selection Quick Checks*,* p. 55 • *Selection and Theme Assessment*, pp. 99–100 • *Testmaker: ExamView Pro* • *Performance Assessment*, p. 52 **Systematic Language Instruction** • *Grammar and Composition Handbook*, Lessons 12.3–12.4 • *Vocabulary Power*, Lesson 27 • *Spelling Power*, Lesson 24
Days 126–127 from On the Road with Charles Kuralt Three-part instruction and selection support on SE/TWE pp. 634–640 **Writing Skills** Writing an Effective Introduction, SE/TWE p. 641	**Lesson-Specific Instruction** • *Theme Six Planning Guide*, pp. 64–71 • *Selection Focus Transparency* 55 • *Active Reading Guide*,* p. 56 • *Literary Elements Transparency* 56 • *Selection Vocabulary Practice*, p. 39 • *Selection Quick Checks*,* p. 56 • *Selection and Theme Assessment*, pp. 101–102 • *Testmaker: ExamView Pro* • *Performance Assessment*, p. 53 • *inTIME* magazine, pp. 6–8 **Systematic Language Instruction** • *Grammar and Composition Handbook*, Lesson 13.1 • *Vocabulary Power*, Lesson 28
Days 128–129 Americans All Three-part instruction and selection support on SE/TWE pp. 642–647 **Technology Skills** Internet, SE/TWE pp. 648–649	**Lesson-Specific Instruction** • *Theme Six Planning Guide*, pp. 72–79 • *Selection Focus Transparency* 56 • *Active Reading Guide*,* p. 57 • *Literary Elements Transparency* 57 • *Selection Vocabulary Practice*, p. 40 • *Selection Quick Checks*,* p. 57 • *Selection and Theme Assessment*, pp. 103–104 • *Testmaker: ExamView Pro* • *Performance Assessment*, p. 54 • *inTIME* magazine, pp. 10–11 **Systematic Language Instruction** • *Grammar and Composition Handbook*, Lessons 13.2–13.3 • *Vocabulary Power*, Unit 6 Review/Test • *Spelling Power*, Unit 6 Review/Proofreading
Days 130–131 Writing Workshop Technical Writing: Bylaws of an Organization Lesson and lesson support on SE/TWE pp. 650–653	• *Writing Assessment and Portfolio Management*, pp. 1–13, 29–33, 41–48
Day 133 Theme Assessment Lesson and lesson support on SE/TWE pp. 654–655	• *Selection and Theme Assessment*, pp. 135–136 • *Testmaker: ExamView Pro* • *Performance Assessment*, pp. 93–94 • *Writing Assessment and Portfolio Management*, pp. 1–12, 41–48 • *Initial Screening and Fluency Assessment*, Theme Six Reading Fluency
Theme 7: Faces of Dignity Day 133 Lesson and lesson support on SE/TWE pp. 658–661	• *Theme Seven Planning Guide*, pp. 1–3 • *Performance Assessment*, p. 70

SE: Student Edition **TWE: Teacher Wraparound Edition** ***Also available in Spanish**

English Language Learners (Add 30–45 Minutes a Day)	Special Needs/Strategic Intervention (Add 30–45 Minutes a Day)
• *English Language Learners Sourcebook*, p. 79 • *Spanish Summaries*, p. 54 • *Spanish Translations*, pp. 144–145 • *Audio Library** • *English, Yes!*	• *Interactive Reading Sourcebook*, pp. T187–T189 • *Interactive Reading Workbook*, pp. 102–103 • *Inclusion Strategies Sourcebook*, pp. 75–76 • *Audio Library**
• Place Names, TWE p. 636 • *English Language Learners Sourcebook*, p. 80 • *Spanish Summaries*, p. 56 • *Audio Library** • *English, Yes!*	• *Interactive Reading Sourcebook*, pp. T189–T191 • *Interactive Reading Workbook*, pp. 104–105 • *Inclusion Strategies Sourcebook*, pp. 41–42 • *Theme Six Planning Guide*, p. 66 • *Audio Library**
• *English Language Learners Sourcebook*, p. 81 • *Spanish Summaries*, p. 56 • *Spanish Translations*, pp. 146–147 • *Audio Library** • *English, Yes!*	• *Interactive Reading Sourcebook*, pp. T192–T194 • *Interactive Reading Workbook*, pp. 106–107 • *Inclusion Strategies Sourcebook*, pp. 91–92 • *Theme Six Planning Guide*, p. 74 • *Audio Library**
• *English Language Learners Sourcebook*, p. 9 • *English, Yes!*	
• *English Language Learners Sourcebook*, pp. 1–13 • *English, Yes!*	• Special Needs, TWE p. 655 • *Inclusion Strategies Sourcebook*, p. xii
• *English Language Learners Sourcebook*, pp. 1–13 • *English, Yes!*	• *Inclusion Strategies Sourcebook*, pp. vii–xii

Lesson Schedule	Essential Lesson Support and Assessment	
Days 134–135 from **All But My Life** Three-part instruction and selection support on SE/TWE pp. 662–671 **Interdisciplinary Connection** Geography, SE/TWE p. 672 **Reading and Thinking Skills** Activating Prior Knowledge, SE/TWE p. 673	**Lesson-Specific Instruction** • *Theme Seven Planning Guide*, pp. 4–11 • *Selection Focus Transparency* 57 • *Active Reading Guide*,* p. 58 • *Literary Elements Transparency* 58 • *Selection Vocabulary Practice*, p. 41 • *Selection Quick Checks*,* p. 58 • *Selection and Theme Assessment*, pp. 105–106	• *Testmaker: ExamView Pro* • *Performance Assessment*, p. 55 • *inTIME* magazine, p. 17 **Systematic Language Instruction** • *Grammar and Composition Handbook*, Lesson 13.4 • *Vocabulary Power*, Lesson 29 • *Spelling Power*, Lesson 25
Days 136–137 from **Anne Frank: The Diary of a Young Girl** Three-part instruction and selection support on SE/TWE pp. 674–683 **Media Connection** Web Site, SE/TWE p. 684–685	**Lesson-Specific Instruction** • *Theme Seven Planning Guide*, pp. 12–19 • *Selection Focus Transparency* 58 • *Active Reading Guide*,* p. 59 • *Literary Elements Transparency* 59 • *Selection Vocabulary Practice*, p. 42 • *Selection Quick Checks*,* p. 59 • *Selection and Theme Assessment*, pp. 107–108	• *Testmaker: ExamView Pro* • *Performance Assessment*, p. 56 **Systematic Language Instruction** • *Grammar and Composition Handbook*, Lesson 14.5 • *Vocabulary Power*, Lesson 30 • *Spelling Power*, Lesson 26
Days 138–139 **The Anne Frank House: Amsterdam** Three-part instruction and selection support on SE/TWE pp. 686–688 **Comparing Selections** SE/TWE p. 689 **Grammar Link** Using Commas Correctly, SE/TWE p. 690 **Writing Skills** Using Transitions in Cause-Effect Relationships, SE/TWE p. 691	**Lesson-Specific Instruction** • *Theme Seven Planning Guide*, pp. 20–25 • *Selection Focus Transparency* 59 • *Active Reading Guide*,* p. 60 • *Literary Elements Transparency* 60 • *Selection Vocabulary Practice*, p. 689 • *Selection Quick Checks*,* p. 60 • *Selection and Theme Assessment*, pp. 107–108 • *Testmaker: ExamView Pro* • *Performance Assessment*, p. 56	**Systematic Language Instruction** • *Grammar and Composition Handbook*, Lesson 13.6 • *Vocabulary Power*, Lesson 31 • *Spelling Power*, Lesson 27
Days 140–142 **The Diary of Anne Frank** Act 1, Scenes 1–2 Three-part instruction and selection support on SE/TWE pp. 696–710 **Genre Focus** Drama, SE/TWE pp. 692–693 **Active Reading Strategies** Tips for Reading Drama, SE/TWE pp. 694–695	**Lesson-Specific Instruction** • *Theme Seven Planning Guide*, pp. 26–39 • *Selection Focus Transparency* 60 • *Active Reading Guide*,* p. 61 • *Literary Elements Transparency* 61 • *Selection Vocabulary Practice*, p. 43 • *Selection Quick Checks*,* p. 61	**Systematic Language Instruction** • *Grammar and Composition Handbook*, Lesson 13.7
Days 143–145 **The Diary of Anne Frank** Act 1, Scene 3 Instruction and selection support on SE/TWE pp. 711–728	**Lesson-Specific Instruction** • *Theme Seven Planning Guide*, pp. 26–39 • *Active Reading Guide*,* p. 62 • *Literary Elements Transparency* 62 • *Selection Vocabulary Practice*, p. 43	• *Selection Quick Checks*,* p. 62 **Systematic Language Instruction** • *Vocabulary Power*, Lesson 32
Days 146–147 **The Diary of Anne Frank** Act 1, Scenes 4–5 Instruction and selection support on SE/TWE pp. 729–743	**Lesson-Specific Instruction** • *Theme Seven Planning Guide*, pp. 26–39 • *Active Reading Guide*,* p. 63 • *Literary Elements Transparency* 63 • *Selection Vocabulary Practice*, p. 43	• *Selection Quick Checks*,* p. 63 • *Selection and Theme Assessment*, pp. 109–110 • *Testmaker: ExamView Pro* **Systematic Language Instruction** • *Spelling Power*, Lesson 28

SE: Student Edition **TWE: Teacher Wraparound Edition** ***Also available in Spanish**

English Language Learners (Add 30–45 Minutes a Day)	Special Needs/Strategic Intervention (Add 30–45 Minutes a Day)
• Vocabulary: Connotation, TWE p. 664 • *English Language Learners Sourcebook*, p. 82 • *Spanish Summaries*, p. 57 • *Audio Library**	• *Interactive Reading Sourcebook*, pp. T195–T197 • *Interactive Reading Workbook*, pp. 108–109 • Less-Proficient Readers, TWE pp. 670, 673 • *Audio Library**
• Articles, TWE p. 676 • *English Language Learners Sourcebook*, p. 83 • *Spanish Summaries*, p. 58 • *Spanish Translations*, pp. 148–152 • *Audio Library** • *English, Yes!*	• *Interactive Reading Sourcebook*, pp. T198–T200 • *Interactive Reading Workbook*, pp. 110–111 • Less-Proficient Readers, TWE p. 678 • *Inclusion Strategies Sourcebook*, pp. 97–98 • *Audio Library**
• *Spanish Summaries*, p. 59 • *Spanish Translations*, p. 153 • *Audio Library** • *English, Yes!*	• *Interactive Reading Sourcebook*, pp. T200–T203 • *Interactive Reading Workbook*, p. 112 • *Theme Seven Planning Guide*, p. 22 • *Audio Library**
• Drama Across Cultures, TWE p. 692 • Dialogue, TWE p. 698 • *English Language Learners Sourcebook*, pp. 84 • *Spanish Summaries*, p. 60 • *Spanish Translations*, pp. 154–164 • *Audio Library** • *English, Yes!*	• *Interactive Reading Sourcebook*, pp. T203–T208 • *Interactive Reading Workbook*, pp. 113–114 • Visually Impaired, TWE p. 704 • *Inclusion Strategies Sourcebook*, pp. 71–72 • *Theme Seven Planning Guide*, p. 31 • *Audio Library**
• Directional Words, TWE p. 712 • *English Language Learners Sourcebook*, p. 85 • *Spanish Translations*, pp. 165–181 • *Spanish Audio Library* • *English, Yes!*	• *Interactive Reading Workbook*, p. 115 • Learning Disabled, TWE p. 727
• Understanding Print Conventions, TWE p. 730 • *English Language Learners Sourcebook*, p. 86 • *Spanish Translations*, pp. 182–195 • *Audio Library** • *English, Yes!*	• *Interactive Reading Workbook*, p. 116 • Emotional, TWE p. 733 • Less-Proficient Readers, TWE p. 739 • *Audio Library**

Lesson Schedule	Essential Lesson Support and Assessment	
Days 148–149 **The Diary of Anne Frank** Act 2, Scenes 1–2 Three-part instruction and selection support on SE/TWE pp. 743–761	**Lesson-Specific Instruction** • *Theme Seven Planning Guide*, pp. 26–39 • *Active Reading Guide*,* p. 64 • *Literary Elements Transparency* 64 • *Selection Vocabulary Practice*, p. 44 • *Selection Quick Checks*,* p. 64	**Systematic Language Instruction** • *Vocabulary Power*, Unit 7 Review/Test
Days 150–153 **The Diary of Anne Frank** Act 2, Scenes 3–5 Instruction and selection support on SE/TWE pp. 762–775 **Media Connection** Song Lyrics, SE/TWE p. 776 **Vocabulary Skills** Analyzing Words, SE/TWE p. 777	**Lesson-Specific Instruction** • *Theme Seven Planning Guide*, pp. 26–39 • *Active Reading Guide*,* p. 65 • *Literary Elements Transparency* 65 • *Selection Vocabulary Practice*, p. 44 • *Selection Quick Checks*,* p. 65 • *Selection and Theme Assessment*, pp. 111–112	• *Testmaker: ExamView Pro* • *Performance Assessment*, p. 57 **Systematic Language Instruction** • *Spelling Power*, Unit 7 Review/Proofreading
Days 154–155 **Writing Workshop** Expository Writing: Historical Research Report Lesson and lesson support on SE/TWE pp. 778–781	• *Writing Assessment and Portfolio Management*, pp. 1–13, 34–37, 41–48	
Day 156 **Theme Assessment** Lesson and lesson support on SE/TWE pp. 782–783	• *Selection and Theme Assessment*, pp. 137–138 • *Testmaker: ExamView Pro* • *Performance Assessment*, p. 94	• *Writing Assessment and Portfolio Management*, pp. 1–12, 41–48 • *Initial Screening and Fluency Assessment*, Theme Seven Reading Fluency
Theme 8: Hair-Raising Tales **Day 157** Lesson and lesson support on SE/TWE pp. 786–789	• *Theme Eight Planning Guide*, pp. 1–3 • *Performance Assessment*, p. 71	
Days 158–161 **Sorry, Right Number** Three-part instruction and selection support on SE/TWE pp. 790–811 **Media Connection** Television Transcript, SE/TWE p. 812 **Listening, Speaking, and Viewing** Critical Viewing, SE/TWE p. 813 **Vocabulary Skills** Using Base Words, SE/TWE p. 814	**Lesson-Specific Instruction** • *Theme Eight Planning Guide*, pp. 4–11 • *Selection Focus Transparency* 61 • *Active Reading Guide*,* p. 66 • *Literary Elements Transparency* 66 • *Selection Vocabulary Practice*, p. 45 • *Selection Quick Checks*,* p. 66 • *Selection and Theme Assessment*, pp. 113–114	• *Testmaker: ExamView Pro* • *Performance Assessment*, p. 58 **Systematic Language Instruction** • *Grammar and Composition Handbook*, Lesson 13.8 • *Vocabulary Power*, Lesson 33 • *Spelling Power*, Lesson 29
Days 162–163 **The Legend of Sleepy Hollow** Three-part instruction and selection support on SE/TWE pp. 815–831	**Lesson-Specific Instruction** • *Theme Eight Planning Guide*, pp. 12–19 • *Selection Focus Transparency* 62 • *Active Reading Guide*,* p. 67 • *Literary Elements Transparency* 67 • *Selection Vocabulary Practice*, p. 46 • *Selection Quick Checks*,* p. 67 • *Selection and Theme Assessment*, pp. 115–116	• *Testmaker: ExamView Pro* • *Performance Assessment*, p. 59 **Systematic Language Instruction** • *Grammar and Composition Handbook*, Lessons 13.9–13.10 • *Vocabulary Power*, Lesson 34 • *Spelling Power*, Lesson 30

SE: Student Edition **TWE: Teacher Wraparound Edition** ***Also available in Spanish**

English Language Learners (Add 30–45 Minutes a Day)	Special Needs/Strategic Intervention (Add 30–45 Minutes a Day)
• Prepositions, TWE p. 744 • *English Language Learners Sourcebook*, p. 87 • *Spanish Translations*, pp. 196–211 • *Spanish Audio Library* • *English, Yes!*	• *Interactive Reading Workbook*, p. 117 • Learning Disabled, TWE pp. 746, 755 • Less-Proficient Readers, TWE p. 752 • *Inclusion Strategies Sourcebook*, pp. 83–84
• Homophones, TWE p. 762 • Latin Word Parts, TWE p. 777 • *English Language Learners Sourcebook*, pp. 88, 89 • *Spanish Translations*, pp. 211–221 • *Audio Library** • *English, Yes!*	• *Interactive Reading Workbook*, pp. 118–120 • Less-Proficient Readers, TWE p. 763 • *Audio Library**
• *English Language Learners Sourcebook*, p. 9 • *English, Yes!*	• Learning Disabled, TWE p. 779 • *Inclusion Strategies Sourcebook*, pp. 75–76
• *English Language Learners Sourcebook*, pp. 1–13 • *English, Yes!*	• Special Needs, TWE p. 783 • *Inclusion Strategies Sourcebook*, p. xii
• *English Language Learners Sourcebook*, pp. 1–13 • *English, Yes!*	• *Inclusion Strategies Sourcebook*, pp. vii–xii
• Print Conventions, TWE p. 792 • Colloquial English, TWE p. 796 • Understanding Critical Viewing, TWE p. 813 • Base Words, TWE p. 814 • *Spanish Summaries*, p. 61 • *Spanish Audio Library* • *English, Yes!*	• *Interactive Reading Sourcebook*, pp. T209–T212 • *Interactive Reading Workbook*, pp. 121–124 • Less-Proficient Readers, TWE p. 795 • Emotional, TWE p. 797 • *Inclusion Strategies Sourcebook*, pp. 99–100 • *Theme Eight Planning Guide*, p. 6 • *Spanish Audio Library*
• Visualizing, TWE p. 817 • *English Language Learners Sourcebook*, p. 94 • *Spanish Summaries*, p. 62 • *Audio Library** • *English, Yes!*	• *Interactive Reading Sourcebook*, pp. T212–T215 • *Interactive Reading Workbook*, pp. 125–128 • Less-Proficient Readers, TWE p. 818 • Learning Disabled, TWE p. 827 • *Inclusion Strategies Sourcebook*, pp. 33–34, 85–86 • *Audio Library**

Lesson Schedule	Essential Lesson Support and Assessment	
Days 164–165 **The Tell-Tale Heart** Three-part instruction and selection support on SE/TWE pp. 834–843 **Genre Focus** Suspense Story, SE/TWE p. 832 **Active Reading Strategies** Tips for Reading a Suspense Story, SE/TWE p. 833 **Media Connection** Web Site, SE/TWE pp. 844–845	**Lesson-Specific Instruction** • *Theme Eight Planning Guide*, pp. 20–27 • *Selection Focus Transparency* 63 • *Active Reading Guide*,* p. 68 • *Literary Elements Transparency* 68 • *Selection Vocabulary Practice*, p. 47 • *Selection Quick Checks*,* p. 68	• *Selection and Theme Assessment*, pp. 117–118 • *Testmaker: ExamView Pro* • *Performance Assessment*, p. 60 • *inTIME* magazine, pp. 22–23 **Systematic Language Instruction** • *Grammar and Composition Handbook*, Lessons 14.1–14.2
Days 166–168 **The Raven** Three-part instruction and selection support on SE/TWE pp. 846–853 **Comparing Selections** SE/TWE p. 854 **Interdisciplinary Connection** Science, SE/TWE p. 855	**Lesson-Specific Instruction** • *Theme Eight Planning Guide*, pp. 28–33 • *Selection Focus Transparency* 64 • *Active Reading Guide*,* p. 69 • *Literary Elements Transparency* 69 • *Selection Quick Checks*,* p. 69 • *Selection and Theme Assessment*, pp. 119–120	• *Testmaker: ExamView Pro* • *Performance Assessment*, p. 61 **Systematic Language Instruction** • *Grammar and Composition Handbook*, Lesson 14.3 • *Vocabulary Power*, Lesson 35 • *Spelling Power*, Lesson 31
Days 169–170 **The Woman in the Snow** Three-part instruction and selection support on SE/TWE pp. 856–866 **Reading and Thinking Skills** Making and Verifying Predictions, SE/TWE p. 867 **Grammar Link** Using Apostrophes to Show Possession, SE/TWE p. 868	**Lesson-Specific Instruction** • *Theme Eight Planning Guide*, pp. 34–41 • *Selection Focus Transparency* 65 • *Active Reading Guide*,* p. 70 • *Literary Elements Transparency* 70 • *Selection Vocabulary Practice*, p. 48 • *Selection Quick Checks*,* p. 70 • *Selection and Theme Assessment*, pp. 121–122	• *Testmaker: ExamView Pro* • *Performance Assessment*, p. 62 **Systematic Language Instruction** • *Grammar and Composition Handbook*, Lesson 14.4 • *Vocabulary Power*, Lesson 36 • *Spelling Power*, Lesson 32
Days 171–172 **The Dinner Party** Three-part instruction and selection support on SE/TWE pp. 869–873	**Lesson-Specific Instruction** • *Theme Eight Planning Guide*, pp. 42–49 • *Selection Focus Transparency* 66 • *Active Reading Guide*,* p. 71 • *Literary Elements Transparency* 71 • *Selection Vocabulary Practice*, p. 49 • *Selection Quick Checks*,* p. 71 • *Selection and Theme Assessment*, pp. 123–124	• *Testmaker: ExamView Pro* • *Performance Assessment*, p. 63 • *inTIME* magazine, pp. 12–13 **Systematic Language Instruction** • *Grammar and Composition Handbook*, Lesson 14.5 • *Vocabulary Power*, Unit 8 Review/Test • *Spelling Power*, Unit 8 Review/Proofreading
Days 173–174 **Writing Workshop** Expository Writing: A Mystery Story Lesson and lesson support on SE/TWE pp. 874–877	• *Writing Assessment and Portfolio Management*, pp. 1–13, 38–40, 41–48	
Day 175 **Theme Assessment** Lesson and lesson support on SE/TWE pp. 878–879	• *Selection and Theme Assessment*, pp. 139–140 • *Testmaker: ExamView Pro* • *Performance Assessment*, pp. 94–95	• *Writing Assessment and Portfolio Management*, pp. 1–12, 41–48 • *Initial Screening and Fluency Assessment*, Theme Eight Reading Fluency

SE: Student Edition **TWE: Teacher Wraparound Edition** ***Also available in Spanish**

English Language Learners (Add 30–45 Minutes a Day)	Special Needs/Strategic Intervention (Add 30–45 Minutes a Day)
• Building Background, TWE p. 836 • *English Language Learners Sourcebook*, p. 95 • *Spanish Summaries*, p. 63 • *Spanish Translations*, pp. 222–226 • *Audio Library** • *English, Yes!*	• *Interactive Reading Sourcebook*, pp. T215–T218 • *Interactive Reading Workbook*, pp. 129–130 • Less-Proficient Readers, TWE p. 839 • *Inclusion Strategies Sourcebook*, pp. 41–42 • *Theme Eight Planning Guide*, p. 22 • *Audio Library**
• Compound Words, TWE p. 847 • *English Language Learners Sourcebook*, p. 96 • *Spanish Summaries*, p. 64 • *Spanish Translations*, pp. 227–232 • *Audio Library** • *English, Yes!*	• *Interactive Reading Sourcebook*, pp. T218–T220 • *Interactive Reading Workbook*, pp. 131–132 • Less-Proficient Readers, TWE p. 848 • *Inclusion Strategies Sourcebook*, pp. 45–46 • *Theme Eight Planning Guide*, p. 30 • *Audio Library**
• Understanding Setting, TWE p. 858 • *English Language Learners Sourcebook*, p. 97 • *Spanish Summaries*, p. 65 • *Spanish Translations*, pp. 233–238 • *Audio Library** • *English, Yes!*	• *Interactive Reading Sourcebook*, pp. T221–T224 • *Interactive Reading Workbook*, pp. 133–134 • Less-Proficient Readers, TWE p. 861 • Learning Disabled, TWE p. 867 • *Inclusion Strategies Sourcebook*, pp. 49–50 • *Theme Eight Planning Guide*, p. 36 • *Audio Library**
• *Theme Eight Planning Guide*, p. 44 • *Spanish Summaries*, p. 66 • *Audio Library** • *English, Yes!*	• *Interactive Reading Sourcebook*, p. T224–T226 • *Interactive Reading Workbook*, p. 135 • *Inclusion Strategies Sourcebook*, pp. 25–26 • *Audio Library**
• Mysteries from Other Cultures, TWE p. 874 • *English Language Learners Sourcebook*, p. 9 • *English, Yes!*	• Less-Proficient Readers, TWE p. 876 • *Inclusion Strategies Sourcebook*, pp. 73–74
• *English Language Learners Sourcebook*, pp. 1–13 • *English, Yes!*	• Special Needs, TWE p. 879 • *Inclusion Strategies Sourcebook*, p. xii

Teaching English Language Learners

by Dr. Jane Fell Greene

Helping English language learners succeed in your language arts classroom requires an understanding of the problems and roadblocks they face, as well as a knowledge of strategies that can help such students gain competence and confidence in using English. The following material is provided as background support for you as you work with your students who are learning English.

Language/Dialect

Nearly 7,500 distinct languages are known to be spoken in the 191 countries of the world. Fewer than 2,000 of those languages have invented orthographic (writing) systems. Linguists have identified distinct families of languages from which modern languages have emerged. Some languages are technically not distinct languages since they are mutually intelligible. These languages are categorized as different languages based on their countries' geographic boundaries, but linguists would say that such languages are really dialects of the same language. Other languages have dialects that are so distinct that they are not mutually intelligible.

Every speaker speaks a dialect, or a particular version of a language. Dialects may be ethnic or regional. In the United States, speakers of English are almost always able to code-switch; that is, they are able to change from one dialect to another. The English dialect that is most widely used by educated speakers and writers is called Standard English.

Phonology

Phonology is the study of sounds produced in spoken language. In each language, each isolated speech sound is called a phoneme. Phonology examines how phonemes interact with each other. Phonology explains the phonological processes in a language as they are related to the rules of production.

Orthography

Orthography is the study of writing systems. The English writing system is alphabetic, so its orthographic system is spelling, a sound-to-symbol code. Speakers of various languages have invented various orthographic systems to map speech to print. Most of the world's spoken languages have no orthographic systems; that is, they have no written forms.

Morphology

Morphology is the study of word formation and structure. In each language, the smallest units of meaning are called morphemes. Morphology studies how words are put together from their smaller parts and the rules governing this process. The English word *cats,* for example, contains the free morpheme *cat* and the bound morpheme for plural, *-s.* Students whose languages do not have these kinds of suffixes can be predicted to have difficulty conceptualizing them linguistically. They will need to understand the linguistic process of adding or altering meaning via morphology before they can be expected to understand and apply the meanings of English morphemes.

Syntax

Syntax is the study of sentence structure. All languages are rule-governed; sentence structure rules differ among languages. Syntax describes how sentences may be grammatically structured in a particular language. In some languages, the rules of syntax are simple; only a few possibilities exist. In English, syntax is complex. For example, while English typically has a subject-verb-object sentence order (e.g., *Juan threw the ball.*), the transformational process permits alteration of word order to produce sentences with similar meanings (e.g., *The ball was thrown by Juan.*) or to ask questions (e.g., *Did Juan throw the ball?*). In each transformation, the word order is altered.

INSTRUCTIONAL SUPPORT AND STRATEGIES

The following resources provide instructional support for teaching students who are learning English.

- ***English Language Learners Sourcebook*** This book provides strategies for teachers to use in helping English language learners, as well as student worksheets that relate to specific selections in ***Glencoe Literature: The Reader's Choice.*** The worksheets are designed for students from all language backgrounds who have had some instruction in English. In addition, suggestions are included for ways to adapt the materials for use with less-proficient students.
- ***English, Yes!*** This literature-based program is for readers who need help improving their basic English skills. Each book offers readability-controlled stories by famous writers, and the stories are presented with illustrations and other features that assist readers in understanding the selection.
- ***Speaking and Listening to the English LANGUAGE!*** This book, by Dr. Jane Fell Greene, provides spiraled lessons in English language structure and functions that are essential for students learning English.

In addition to the resources listed above, the charts that follow can help you grasp the main differences between the English language and the first languages spoken by many of your students. To be sensitive to your students' needs, you will want to understand the challenges they face as they study reading, writing, listening, and speaking in the English language.

Contrastive Analysis of English Learners' First Languages

(Used with permission of Dr. Jane Fell Greene)

English contrasts with CANTONESE		
Phonology	**Orthography**	**Morphology/Syntax**
Cantonese is one of the most widely spoken dialects of Chinese, behind Mandarin. Differences in phonology and vocabulary make oral communication between speakers of Cantonese, Mandarin, and other Chinese dialects difficult. Even within the Cantonese dialect, such varieties as those spoken in Hong Kong and Guangzhou (Canton City) have different phonologies. Nevertheless, the language is mutually intelligible through a common written language. English phonemes that do not exist in Cantonese include /b/, /ch/, /d/, /j/, /g/, /sh/, /th/, /v/, and /z/. English phonemes that can be projected to be difficult for native speakers of Cantonese are /b/, /ch/, /d/, /f/, /g/, /j/, /l/, /m/, /n/, /ng/, /o/, /sh/, /th/, /v/, /z/, *l*-clusters, and *r*-clusters.	People from different regions of China speak different dialects of Chinese. But as the hundreds of Chinese dialects look the same when written, written communication is possible between speakers of different dialects. The Chinese orthographic system is based on image (form), sound, and meaning. Its thousands of distinctive characters, called ideographs, have six symbol types: pictographs, indicatives, ideatives, harmonics, transmissives, and borrowed words.	Cantonese words are single-syllable. Each word carries at least one meaning, but meaning can change based upon the four *tones* in which the words are uttered. Each tone may provide a large number of homonyms. Cantonese has no inflectional suffixes (such as English *-s*, *-ed*, *-ing*, and *-est*) that can add to or modify a word's meaning

For more detailed information about strategies for teaching English language learners, see ***Speaking and Listening to the English LANGUAGE!***

English contrasts with HMONG

Phonology	Orthography	Morphology/Syntax
The Hmong language has 13 vowels and 56 consonants. Like Cantonese and Vietnamese, Hmong is a tonal language, one in which the same word can be produced with various tones which give the word several different meanings. Production of phonemes is complex.	Hmong has an alphabetic orthographic system. In the sense that phoneme-grapheme associations determine production, Hmong's orthography is like that of English. Hmong consonant letters related to English include the following: *m* Bilabial nasal *n* Dental-alveolar nasal *ng* Velar nasal *ny* Alveo-palatal nasal *p* Bilabial stop *b* Implosive *p/b* *ph* *p* with aspiration *t* Dental-alveolar stop *d* Implosive *t/d.* *th* Aspirated *t* *k* Velar stop *kh* Aspirated *k* *7* Glottal stop *c* Alveo-palatal affricate *ch* Aspirated *c* *s* Dental-alveolar fricative *sh* Voiceless alveolar-palatal fricative *h* Laryngeal fricative *l* Dental-alveolar lateral approximate *r* Dental-alveolar central flap	Because Hmong has been so recently coded, and because of the difficult recent history of its speakers, relatively little has been written regarding the grammar, morphology, and syntax rules of Hmong. Hmong is an isolating language; that is, it has no inflection in its nouns or verbs, no endings such as *-ed* or *-ing* to indicate verb tense, and no endings such as *-s* or *-'s* to extend meanings of nouns. In Hmong, each syllable carries a meaning of its own. In speech, however, some syllables are produced more closely than others. Each syllable has a tone that is represented by a consonant letter written at the close of the syllable. This causes no confusion to Hmong speakers, since the only consonant permitted at the end of a syllable is *ng*. The ordinary syllable pattern is CV (consonant-vowel). However, the consonant may be represented by two, three, or even four consonant letters, and the vowel by one or two letters. Hmong's basic sentence structure is SVO (subject-verb-object).

English contrasts with KHMER (CAMBODIAN)		
Phonology	**Orthography**	**Morphology/Syntax**
The Khmer language, native language of Cambodia, is related to Vietnamese. A major difference in sound is that Khmer is nontonal. Khmer has 33 consonants, 24 dependent vowels, 12 independent vowels, and several diacritical markings to assist in pronunciation of its phonemes.	The orthographic system of Khmer has its origin in southern India. The letters, which originated in southern India and were derived from Pali, are unlike those of the Roman alphabet used for English. The Khmer alphabet represents the phonemes of Khmer consonants, dependent vowels, and independent vowels.	Khmer is an uninflected language, but it has a rich system of affixes, including infixes, for derivation. Khmer has nouns, verbs, adverbs, and particles. The usual sentence structure is SVO (subject-verb-object). Khmer uses roots from Sanskrit and Pali to derive new words, much as English uses roots from Latin and Greek. Khmer also borrows words from Chinese, French, and English—most recently to name items of modern Western technology.

English contrasts with KOREAN		
Phonology	**Orthography**	**Morphology/Syntax**
Korean has ten simple vowels and three series of stops and affricates: plain, aspirated, and glottalized. This complicates the task of Romanization (relating their alphabetic system to ours), since more than one Roman letter may represent a single Korean phoneme.	The Korean orthographic system is alphabetic, but it is written top-to-bottom, with spaces between words. The alphabetic system illustrates the CVC (consonant-vowel-consonant) syllabic grouping structure of Korean. Each of the alphabet's 25 letters represents a single consonant or vowel. Vowels are represented by 11 letters, of which there are three basic forms. Korean has borrowed many Chinese characters over the centuries, but since the end of World War II this practice has been gradually phased out. The written language symbols of South Korea comprises Han-Ja (Chinese characters), On-Mun (Korean characters), and Mi-Ahl'bet-gul (Romanization).	Korean words may consist of more than one morpheme. For example, the compound word *nun* + *mul* (eye + water) means "tear." While Korean has borrowed many Chinese words, the language is unrelated to Chinese. The grammar and syntax of Korean are similar to Japanese. Korean, an agglutinative language, adds suffixes to nominal and verbal stems in derivation and inflection. Changing vowels to make a morphologic distinction (such as present/past in verbs) does not exist in Korean. SOV (subject-object-verb) is the usual sentence order, but while the verb is always the last constituent of a sentence, other constituents can be placed anywhere in the sentence.

English contrasts with PILIPINO (TAGALOG)		
Phonology	**Orthography**	**Morphology/Syntax**
Tagalog has 15 consonants, 5 vowels, and 5 diphthongs (vowel glides). Syllable stress distinguishes sounds in words that are otherwise similar. A highly phonetic language, the only sound in Tagalog that is not written is the glottal stop.	Pilipino, the name given to Tagalog when it was made the national language of the Philippines in 1962, has an alphabetic orthographic system based on the Roman alphabet. It is punctuated much like English.	Hundreds of Spanish words were incorporated during three centuries of Spanish rule. Many of its words are multisyllabic, and its morpheme structures work in much the same way as those of English.

English contrasts with RUSSIAN		
Phonology	**Orthography**	**Morphology/Syntax**
Russian consists of 21 consonant sounds and 5 vowel sounds. Most consonants have both a soft and hard pronunciation, which is determined by the vowel that follows it. Consonant blends and clusters occur frequently. Often one of the consonants is omitted in the pronunciation of clusters. When unstressed, vowel sounds are reduced to a sound similar to the English schwa.	The Russian orthographic system is alphabetic. The Cyrillic alphabet differs significantly from English's Roman alphabet.	This highly inflected language has six cases affecting the forms of nouns, adjectives, and pronouns. Verbs also have specific endings dependent on person and number. Russian has no present tense form of the verb *to be*, so this concept may be difficult for native Russian speakers. Word order within a sentence is less strict than in English because case endings help determine the function of words within the sentence. Verb phrases are not used per se; rather, verbs occur in pairs with different aspects (perfective and imperfective) to convey subtleties in meaning. Russian does not use articles, either definite or indefinite, so the concept of article use is difficult for Russian speakers who are learning English. One phenomenon related to Russian vocabulary is its families of words which are derived from a single root by addition of prefixes and suffixes.

English contrasts with SPANISH		
Phonology	**Orthography**	**Morphology/Syntax**
Spanish has five vowels which are consistently produced. Stress, too, is consistent. It is placed on the next to final syllable in words ending in a vowel, *n*, or *s*; and it is placed on the final syllable in words ending in other consonants. The complex vowel system of English is difficult for native Spanish speakers. Until the English vowels are differentiated via phonemic awareness and phoneme-grapheme correspondence rules, speakers may experience difficulty learning to read English. Symbol-sound correspondences differ slightly with Spanish consonants as well. It is important to teach the English code to automaticity, if Spanish speakers are to become literate in English. Basic accent rules of Spanish include these three: (1) Words ending in a vowel, or *n* or *s*, the next to last syllable is stressed. (2) For words ending in a consonant other than *n* or *s*, stress falls on the last syllable. (3) If the word has an accent mark, then that syllable is stressed, ignoring the rules above. Spanish has a one-to-one symbol-sound orthographic system. Its alphabet differs slightly from that of English, as shown below: A (a), B (be), C (ce), CH (che), D (de), E (e), F (efe), G (ge), H (hache), I (i), J (jota), K (ka), L (ele), LL (elle), M (eme), N (ene), Ñ (eñe), O (o), P (p), Q (cu), R (erre), S (ese), T (te),	Like English, Spanish has an alphabetic orthographic system. Vowel letters represent these phonemes: *a*—as the *a* in father *e*—for a syllable ending in a vowel, as the *e* in *they*; for a syllable ending in a consonant, as the *e* in *met* *i*—as the *i* in *machine* *o*—for a syllable ending in a vowel, like the *o* in *vote;* for a syllable ending in a consonant, like the *o* in *pot* *u*—as the *u* in *rule;* silent after *q* and in the groups *gue* and *gui* *y*—When used as a vowel, such as in the words *y* and *voy*, it is pronounced like the Spanish *i.* Diphthongs (vowel glides) represent these phonemes: *ai, ay*—as the *i* in *side* *au*—as the *ou* in *found* *ei, ey*—as the *ey* in *they* *eu*—as the vowel sounds in *may-you* *oi, oy*—as the *oy* in *boy* Semiconsonants represent these phonemes: *i, y*—as the *y* in *yes*. Examples: *bien, hielo* *u*—as with *w* in *well*. Examples: *fuente, agua* Consonants represent these phonemes: *b, v*—When found at the beginning of a word or following a consonant, these are pronounced like a *b*. Otherwise, the phoneme falls between	Spanish has a morphologic system typical of Romance languages, and not dissimilar to English. Modifiers follow the words they modify in Spanish. For example, adjectives follow nouns. A Spanish speaker would refer to the "house red" rather than to the "red house" as in English.

English contrasts with SPANISH *(continued)*	
Phonology	**Orthography**
U (u), V (ve), W (dobla ve), X (equís), Y (i griega), Z (ceta). English sounds not used in Spanish include /j/, /sh/, /th/, and /z/. Problem English phonemes for Spanish speakers can be predicted to include /b/, /d/, /dg/, /h/, /j/, /m/, /n/, /ng/, /r/, /sh/, /t/, /th/, /v/, /w/, /y/, /z/, *s*-clusters, and end-clusters	English's /b/ and /v/ phonemes. *c*—before a consonant or *a, o,* or *u,* as the *c* in *cat;* before *e* or *i* as an *s* *ch*—as the *ch* in *church.* *d*—as the English *d* except between vowels and following *l* or *n* where pronounced as the *th* in *this* *f*—as the *f* in *for* *g*—before *e* or *i,* like the Spanish *j;* otherwise as the *g* in *get* *h*—silent *j*—as an *h* but stronger; silent when at the end of a word *k*—as a *k* *l*—as an *l* *ll*—as the *y* in *you* *m*—as an *m* *n*—as an *n;* except where it appears before a *v,* as an *m* *ñ*—as the *n* in *onion* *p*—as a *p* *q*—as a *k;* always followed by a silent *u* *r*—pronounced with a strong trill at beginning of a word and following an *l, n,* or *s;* little trill when at the end of a word; and medium trill in other positions rr—strongly trilled s—before consonants *b, d, g, l, m, n,* like a *z;* otherwise as an *s* t—like a *t* v—see *b, v* w—usually like a *v* x—when between vowels, like the *x* in *box;* before a consonant, like an *s* y—as the *y* in *yes* z—as an *s*

English contrasts with VIETNAMESE		
Phonology	**Orthography**	**Morphology/Syntax**
Vietnamese phonology is complicated by its series of six tones, which affect not only production, but also meaning. Vietnamese uses a large number of vowels and groups of vowels to create different phonemes. While the system is complex, context helps to simplify them. In modern Vietnamese, there is a trend to pronounce consonant blends and clusters as single phonemes. Consonants located at ends of words are not pronounced at all.	Vietnamese has an alphabetic orthographic system which was devised by seventeenth-century Catholic missionaries to encode the language. Diacritical marks indicate tone and some vowel sounds; a letter may have two diacritical marks. The system creates a one-to-one symbol-sound correspondence code.	Vietnamese words are single-syllable. Nearly half its alphabet is borrowed from Chinese. Each word carries at least one meaning, but meaning can change based upon the tone in which the word is uttered. Vietnamese has no inflectional suffixes (as in English *-s, -ed, -ing,* and *-est*), which can add to or modify a word's meaning.

The Teaching of Reading & Strategic Intervention

Working with struggling readers *How do you ensure that your students have the basic skills needed to be proficient readers? What methods are most effective for teaching reading? What intervention strategies will help your students meet or exceed your teaching objectives? The following information will help you fill the gaps in your students' reading competence. For extra help, use the* **Interactive Reading Sourcebook** *for additional teaching strategies and reading lessons and the* **Interactive Reading Workbook** *for skills practice and opportunities for students to interact with text.*

Effective Teaching Methods

Modeling

Modeling is a means for demonstrating a thinking process. To practice modeling in your classroom, read aloud a segment of text as students follow along in their books. Then, in everyday language, reason aloud. Modeling illustrates for students the steps that competent readers follow to solve a reading problem or to analyze a text. The goal is to have students apply similar reasoning procedures during their own reading processes. The following is an example of modeling that demonstrates how using context clues helps a reader to understand an unfamiliar word.

Model *I wonder what the word* vacant *means. From the first sentence in the passage, it seems that* vacant *describes a seat on a bus. The narrator goes on to say that she "took" the vacant seat. To* take a seat *means "to sit down." The narrator would most likely sit only in an empty seat. So* vacant *probably means "empty."*

To complete the modeling cycle, ask individual students to think aloud, demonstrating their own thinking processes as they employ a reading strategy or skill. Reasoning aloud will make students more aware of what they actually do as they read. Listening to a student think aloud can show you whether the student's abilities are developing and where the student needs support and guidance in applying the strategy (Duffy, Roehler, Herrmann, 1988).

Reciprocal Teaching

Reciprocal teaching (Palinscar and Brown, 1984) is a method of checking understanding during reading that actively engages students, creating in them a feeling of investment in their own learning process. To implement reciprocal teaching in your classroom, you will guide a group of students to apply four reading strategies in a prescribed way with the goal of achieving comprehension of a segment of text. As students become familiar with the process, your role will gradually change from leader to facilitator, and your students will take over the process themselves, alternating in the role of group leader. The order of the strategies may vary depending on your preference. However, students should learn and use the strategies in a consistent order. Following is a brief description of the reciprocal teaching process.

Questioning

After students have read a portion of text, the leader asks the group questions about what they have just read. To formulate such questions, student leaders must consider what the important ideas were in the text. To answer, students in the group must review what they have learned.

Clarifying

The leader points out places in the text that he or she found difficult and invites group members to do the same. Students discuss these troublesome sections and use information in the text and their own knowledge to resolve issues.

Summarizing

The leader summarizes the segment of text. To summarize, student leaders must actively evaluate ideas in the text and determine the key ideas that should be included in the summary. Members of the group respond by suggesting additions or alterations to the summary that the leader has proposed.

Predicting

The leader makes predictions about what will happen next on the basis of what the group has already read. Group members participate by suggesting changes to the predictions or by proposing new predictions. Students use their predictions to prepare themselves to read the next segment of text.

Exploring Expository Texts

Analyzing text structures Noticing the way ideas are organized in a piece of writing helps students anticipate the types of ideas they are likely to encounter and prepares them to comprehend a text (Armbruster, Anderson, and Ostertag, 1989). Most students are familiar with narrative **text structures,** but some may be less familiar with expository text structures. **Expository writing** is nonfiction writing that explains, informs, or persuades. Essays, articles, reports, and manuals are examples of expository writing. Expository writing whose primary purpose is to provide specific or technical information about a topic or event is sometimes called **informational text.** Examples include textbooks, Web resources, reports, proposals, brochures, and manuals.

The most common text structures are time order, compare-contrast, description, cause-effect, and problem-solution. While an expository selection may make use of a variety of text structures, one overriding text structure almost always applies to the whole piece of writing. For example, an author may compare and contrast two ideas within an essay that has an overall cause-and-effect text structure.

Sometimes **signal words** can help a reader determine the text structure. Share the following signal words for common text structures your students are likely to encounter.

TEXT STRUCTURES	SIGNAL WORDS
time order	on, before, during, after, first, last, now, when, then, next, finally
compare-contrast	in contrast to, in comparison with, on the other hand, similarly, both, like, unlike, different, too, not only
description	for example, characteristics of, a feature of, such as, above, near, beside, in front of, first, most important
cause-effect	because, as a result, as a consequence, the effect was, since, due to, therefore, thus
problem-solution	because, if/then, as a result, therefore

As students read expository text, they can also use various **graphic organizers** to help them deconstruct and analyze a text's structure. These graphic organizers not only teach students to expect certain types of ideas and organizations in various types of text but also serve as a way to increase retention of what has been read, providing a kind of map or outline that can be used for reviewing the selection.

Considerate text Some expository texts are easier to comprehend than others, not because the concept load is lighter but simply because the organization is clear and the flow of ideas is cohesive. Such text is called **considerate text.** Considerate text is "text that facilitates understanding, learning, and remembering" (Armbruster and Anderson, 1985). Such a text has certain characteristics that make it well organized overall and also well organized within the paragraphs and sentences. Ideas are developed logically, and connective words such as *however, and, thus,* and *as a result* are embedded to help the reader understand the relationship between ideas. Text features can also contribute to considerate text. Examples of characteristics and text features that can be found in considerate text are shown below.

CHARACTERISTICS	TEXT FEATURES
clearly stated main ideas	headings and subheadings that reveal the hierarchy of ideas
specialized vocabulary defined at the point of use	boldfacing of key vocabulary and concepts
unified paragraphs	footnotes, captioned illustrations, and graphics
introductions and summaries that pull together main ideas	a logical layout

Text that does not contain the above named features can be difficult to navigate and comprehend. Such text is called **inconsiderate text.**

Skills and Strategies for Reading Expository Texts

In the past, reading has been described as more of a skill than an active mental process. We now know that reading is neither automatic nor passive. Reading is a highly interactive process in which students construct meaning from text (Anderson and Pearson, 1984).

We know that students learn what they are directly taught and what they have an opportunity to practice (Tierney, 1982). The ***Interactive Reading Sourcebook*** provides carefully scaffolded, unified lessons that develop students' strategic reading behaviors. While all the active reading strategies discussed in the ***Interactive Reading Sourcebook*** are important for reading both narrative and expository texts, several strategies are especially helpful for exploring expository writing. Among them are the skills and strategies listed below.

- **Previewing** Have students preview the text's structure. Noticing the organization of ideas prepares them for the types of information they will encounter. Have students preview the concepts in the text by looking over text features such as headings and subheadings, charted information, illustrations, captions, and graphics. Have students preview boldfaced terms and footnotes to become familiar with specialized vocabulary.
- **Activating prior knowledge and building background** Prepare students to grasp new knowledge by helping them bring to mind what they already know. Use key concepts and terms in the text to frame general questions that encourage students to think about the topic and to share ideas. Then bolster their background knowledge by providing specific information that will enhance their understanding of the subject.
- **Setting a purpose for reading** Guide students as they set a purpose for reading. For example, if a heading in the text is "What Happened to the Dinosaurs?" ask students what they would like to know related to this topic, such as whether what happened to the dinosaurs could happen again in modern times.
- **Varying reading rate** Teach students to adjust their reading rate. They should slow down when they encounter difficult concepts, connections to previous ideas, new vocabulary, or text that contains a great deal of information.
- **Monitoring comprehension** Encourage students to be aware of their own reading processes and to notice when they have missed something. They can monitor comprehension by questioning themselves as they read. If they do not understand an important idea, they should reread, review, or read on for clarification.
- **Identifying main ideas** Tell students to identify main ideas as they read. Text features such as headings, subheadings, boldfaced terms, and graphics are good indicators of main ideas.
- **Tracking information** Direct students to keep track of key ideas in the text by listing these ideas as they read. They may make an actual list of ideas, create an outline, or write a series of notes. Graphic organizers such as Venn diagrams, problem-solution charts, or concept webs can also be effective organizational tools to aid students' comprehension and retention.
- **Reviewing** Guide students in pulling together and processing key ideas. Students can use their lists, outlines, notes, or graphic organizers, or the text features in the text itself, to review the critical ideas in what they have read. Through discussion, students can summarize, analyze, and evaluate ideas to process and retain what they have read.

Effective Classroom Procedures —

Reading Arrangements

Offer varied classroom reading arrangements to provide support and guidance for struggling readers. For example, reading with partners gives students one-on-one assistance, while participating in choral reading allows students to gain confidence. Use a variety of the reading arrangements suggested below to serve the various needs of your students.

- reading aloud to partners who can help with difficult words
- reading silently with partners, having partners "on-call" to help with difficult sections of the text.
- reading silently to themselves
- taking turns reading aloud in small groups
- following along in their books as you, a volunteer, or a designated group of students reads
- reading silently as they listen to a taped reading
- taking turns reading in a whole-class activity
- participating in choral reading

Independent Reading

Encourage your students to read independently by implementing some of the following suggestions in your classroom.

- Set up a classroom library of books of special interest to your students.
- Assign time in the library for groups or individuals.
- Establish in-class discussion groups (literature groups) where students can work together to focus on topics connected to the literature they are reading.
- Assign independent reading of at least thirty minutes a day, to be done outside of class.
- Have students create products to express and share what they have learned. These products may include reports, posters, collages, multigenre writing, or multimedia presentations.
- Via newsletters, suggest that parents or guardians read aloud with their children. Encourage parents to call attention to items in newspapers and magazines that are of special interest to the family.

Teaching Word Analysis

Decoding and Encoding

Phonemic awareness is the awareness of the distinct sounds of language. **Decoding** is using the knowledge of sounds, and the letters and letter groupings that represent those sounds, to pronounce a word. When students decode, they read printed words by calling to mind the sounds associated with letters. They then blend these sounds together to say the word. **Encoding** is using the knowledge of the correspondence of sounds and letters to spell words.

Phonics and multisyllabic word attack strategies make students aware of predictable connections between sounds and letters. By knowing the sounds to associate with various letters and letter patterns, students have the tools to attack a word they do not know. They know how to sound out a word, where feasible. They know how to break a larger word into syllables and morphemic units and apply their knowledge of sound-letter correspondence to figure out how to say each word part. By saying a word using the correctly associated sounds, they may recognize the word and find that they already know its meaning.

Most students should have had phonics instruction when they first learned to read, but there may be gaps in their skills. For strategic intervention for students who have gaps in their skills, set aside a period of time each day to review multisyllabic, morphemic, and complex phonic elements. There are many ways to teach phonics and word attack strategies and to progress through phonics skills. The list shown here presents a logical progression through these skills and gives several examples for each term. For more detailed information and comprehensive examples, see the ***Interactive Reading Sourcebook.***

1. **Initial Consonants:** A consonant or consonants that appear at the beginning of a word (/s/ secret, /n/ number, /fl/ flush).
2. **Final Consonants:** A consonant or consonants that appear at the end of a word (/r/ fear, /d/ head, /ft/ tuft).
3. **Short Vowels:** Vowel sounds of relatively brief duration (/a/ snack, /e/ pet, /i/ drift).
4. **Long Vowels:** Vowel sounds of relatively long duration (/ā/ bake, /ē/ cede, /ī/ shine).
5. **Consonant Blends:** Consonant groupings in which each letter retains its own sound. These blends may occur at the beginnings or middle of words (/br/ brown, /fl/ fly, /st/ rooster) or at the ends of words (/kt/ fact, /lf/ self, /nt/ rent).
6. **Consonant Digraphs:** Two consonants that together make one sound (/ch/ church, /th/ cloth, /TH/ this, /hw/ wheel; /f/ phone).
7. **Phonograms:** A core group of ending letters that is used to make different words by simply changing the initial consonant or consonants. Also called **word families,** they are useful for phonemic awareness activities using substitution and blending (*cat, rat, hat, sat, chat, flat, gnat, scat*).
8. **Vowel Digraphs:** Pairs that make one sound (/ā/ remain, day; /ē/ sleep, east; /ō/ cloak, bowl).
9. **Vowel Diphthongs:** A vowel sound that glides from one vowel sound to another in the same syllable (/oi/ oil, joy; /ow/ down, amount).
10. **R-Controlled Vowels:** The unique sound of a vowel followed by the letter *r* (/är/ tardy; /ur/ clerk, shirt, turn; /ôr/ storm).
11. **Silent Letters:** Two consonants in which one consonant is not sounded, or is "silent" (/n/ gnat, knowledge; /r/ wrestle, rhyme; /m/ comb).
12. **Syllabication and Morphemic Analysis:** A *syllable* is a spoken part of a word that contains a vowel sound. Breaking a word in syllables or morphemic units helps students decode longer words by sounding out each part (bat/ter, spo/ken, ca/ble, joy/ous, class/room). See the ***Interactive Reading Sourcebook*** for syllabication rules.

Activities to Reinforce Word Analysis

- Have students find words with the targeted sound-spelling correspondence in a paragraph or in a segment of a literature selection and read these words aloud to their partners.
- Have students generate a list of words based on the example words and the targeted sound-spelling correspondence; have students discuss these words in a group.
- Have students in a group review a list of words to determine which words demonstrate a specific sound-spelling correspondence.
- Have students make flashcards of words that teach the appropriate phonics principle; have partners quiz each other on the words.
- Have small groups create cloze sentences that can be completed with words containing the targeted phonics elements. For example, if you are reviewing the *gr* blend, students might construct the following cloze sentence: Everyone had a gr______ time at the party.
- Have students write sentences, paragraphs, poems, or riddles that make use of words that illustrate a particular phonics element.

Effective Vocabulary Instruction

Research tells us that general vocabulary knowledge is a critical component in determining how well readers understand text (Anderson and Freebody, 1981). As students build both oral and print vocabulary knowledge, they increase their comprehension skills and their ability to read strategically.

The ***Interactive Reading Sourcebook*** and the ***Interactive Reading Workbook*** provide vocabulary lessons and activities to develop students' knowledge of larger concepts as well as their understanding of individual words. The vocabulary instruction provides both direct and indirect ways for students to interact with words before, during, and after reading and encourages an ongoing curiosity about language.

Because of the clear connection between readers' vocabulary knowledge and their ability to understand what they read, vocabulary instruction is essential to developing interactive, strategic readers. Vocabulary learning is not a singular, isolated activity. Rather, students build vocabulary through repeated encounters with words in rich oral and written contexts (Nagy, 1988). Teachers reinforce listening, speaking, writing, and reading vocabulary skills by encouraging active classroom discussions, reading aloud to students and having students read aloud, encouraging wide reading across content areas, and encouraging students to use dictionaries and other word references to support meaning and usage. Each encounter with a word provides new clues to its meaning. Students' understandings of those meanings build and deepen over time. The strategies presented here provide ways for you to offer students a variety of interactive opportunities to become involved in the process of building vocabulary.

Using Context Clues

Encourage students to determine the meaning of a word they don't know by using **context**—the words and sentences that surround the unknown word. The following chart shows specific context clues for students to use as they read.

TYPE OF CONTEXT CLUE	EXAMPLES
Synonym Look for a clue (such as *just as*, *like*, or *also*) that shows a word is similar to the unknown word.	The service at this restaurant is *quick*. Is the service at that restaurant just as **expeditious**?
Antonym Look for a clue (such as *but*, *not*, or *rather than*) that shows a word is the opposite of the unknown word.	Yesterday Sam was **despondent,** but today he's *cheerful*.
Definition Look for a phrase that defines or describes the unknown word. Commas, dashes, or parentheses often surround this type of clue.	Mark is interested in **herpetology**—*the study of snakes*.
Example Look for examples that reveal the meaning of the unknown word. Commas, dashes, or parentheses often surround this type of clue.	He can't decide which one of the **martial arts** to study—*karate*, *judo*, or *tae kwon do*.
General Context Sometimes the general context contains clues. Study the main idea of a passage to see if it unlocks the meaning of an unknown word.	Since this was the boy's first **infraction** of the rules, the principal let him go with just a warning. (*infraction:* breaking or violating the rules)

Using Words Parts

Many words can be divided into parts: *prefix*, *root*, and *suffix*. Knowing the meanings of common word parts can help readers unlock the meanings of unknown words. Refer to the ***Grammar and Composition Handbook*** for a thorough discussion of word parts and activities for your students.

Using Language Structure Clues

Have students look for passages that contain **parallel** structures—words arranged in similar ways. Words that have parallel functions often contain clues to unknown words.

At the zoo, we saw a *herd* of zebras, a ***pride*** of lions, and a *pack* of wolves in free-roaming environments. (*Herd, pride*, and *pack* all define groups of animals.)

Using Classifying and Categorizing

Current research indicates that the brain is a pattern detector (Caine and Caine, 1994). Students enjoy sorting and grouping items by similarities or separating items by differences. Introduce word sorts, including open sorts (where students choose how to label categories) and closed sorts (where teachers provide the categories), to give students opportunities to organize ideas. When students see how words fit into a larger category, they expand their vocabulary knowledge.

Using Word Maps

Word maps are wonderful tools for teaching vocabulary. A commonly used word map or concept web shows a central bubble containing a key word or idea. Bubbles that surround the center bubble may be used to show semantic relationships or explain structure.

Using a Concept-Definition Map

As a group activity, completing a concept-definition map can be a powerful tool for building background. A concept-definition map (Schwartz and Raphael, 1985) is a way to define a word visually. The top section of the graphic asks, "What is it?"; the next section asks, "What is it like?"; and the last section asks, "What are some examples?" Direct students to use their prior knowledge about words and concepts to complete the map.

Using a Semantic-Features Chart

Use semantic-features charts (Anders, Bos, and Filip, 1982; Johnson, Toms-Bronowski, and Pittleman, 1982) to help students focus on the discriminating features of items in a group. Ask students to complete the grids with marks to indicate a positive (+), negative (–), or possible (?) correlation.

ANIMALS	FUR	FEATHERS	FOUR LEGS	TWO LEGS
dog	+	–	+	–
fish	–	–	–	–
seal	?	–	?	?

Using Possible Sentences

To encourage students to speculate about word meanings, use "possible sentences" (Beck and McKeown, 1983; Moore and Moore, 1986). Choose approximately ten key vocabulary terms and write them on the board. Then use the words either correctly or incorrectly in sentences. Ask students to comment on whether the sentences are "possible." Alternatively, before students read a selection, they may use five key words in sentences, taking educated guesses about the meaning of the unfamiliar words or phrases. As students encounter the key vocabulary, they should note each term's usage in the selection's context. After reading, students should return to their possible sentences to discuss meanings and to adjust or rewrite as necessary.

Teaching Reading and Thinking Skills

To become competent readers, students need to acquire critical reading and thinking skills and to understand why those skills are important. Use the following information and techniques for teaching these critical skills.

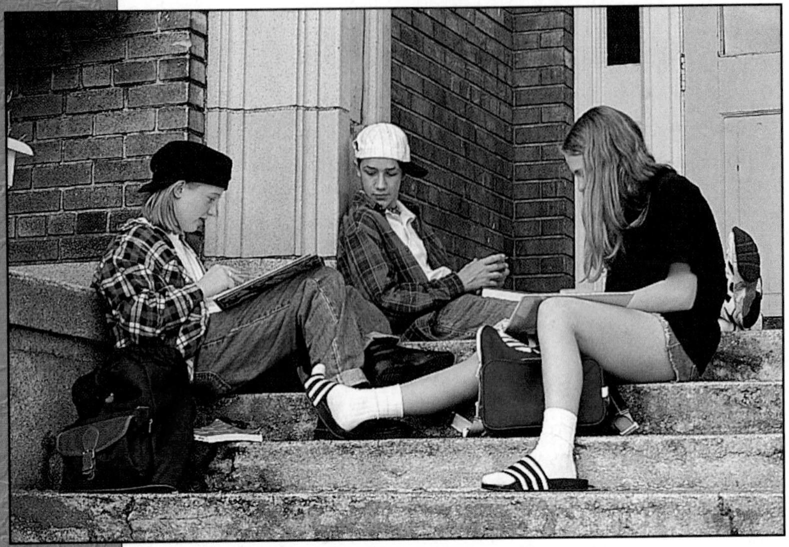

Identifying Main Idea and Supporting Details

Guide students in identifying main ideas and supporting details before, during, and after reading. By activating prior knowledge and previewing text before reading, students learn to anticipate the main ideas they will find. Identifying main ideas and supporting details during and after reading helps students prepare to summarize.

- Ask students to share prior knowledge about an author or a topic.
- Guide students to anticipate what might be important in a selection.
- Look at the text structure of a selection to see how the author organizes ideas.
- Invite students to read one paragraph of text and ask questions such as the following: What one idea are all the sentences in this paragraph about? How does that idea fit in with what I know about this topic? About this author? About the organization of this selection? What sentences add information to the most important idea?
- Remind students to look for headings, captions, illustrations, and other text features to help them determine main ideas.

Summarizing

Summarizing teaches students to reduce information and allows them to rethink what they have read. As students summarize, they learn material more thoroughly; later when they attempt other academic tasks, they will be more easily able to retrieve what they have learned. Students should summarize as often as necessary to monitor their understanding of a selection. Encourage students to summarize more frequently when text material is difficult.

- Ask students: What is this passage about?
- Invite students to begin their summaries by answering *who, what, where, when, why,* and *how*.
- Remind students that only main ideas should be included in a summary and that all the main ideas should be included.
- To determine if students have included all main ideas, ask: Can your summary be easily understood by someone who has not read the selection?
- To help students determine if they have included unnecessary information, ask: If this information were excluded, would your summary still sound complete?

Making Inferences

Making inferences requires that students use their reasoning skills and their experience to take educated guesses about what an author implies or suggests. Because writers often do not directly state what they want readers to know, making inferences is essential to constructing meaning in a selection.

- Guide students to look for text clues. Encourage them to notice descriptions, dialogue, events, or relationships that might signal information a writer is suggesting.
- Ask students to think about what they already know —either from prior text clues or from their own experiences.
- As students read, ask questions that require them to think beyond the literal events of a selection.
- Model your own process of inferring when you read aloud.

Drawing Conclusions

Drawing conclusions helps students to see connections between ideas and events. This strategy is useful in constructing meaning in both fiction and nonfiction and in analyzing and interpreting ideas.

- Ask students to notice specific details about characters, ideas, and information as they read.
- Invite students to use the information they have and their own prior knowledge to think about a larger or more general statement that might be made.

- Caution students not to overgeneralize and not to draw unsound conclusions based on insufficient or inaccurate information.

Understanding Sequence

The order in which thoughts are arranged is called **sequence.** One of the best ways for teachers to help students recognize sequence in a selection is to teach them to look for signal words that indicate chronological order, steps in a process, or order of importance.

SEQUENCE	SIGNAL WORDS
chronological order	first, second, next, then, earlier, later, eventually, finally, last
steps in a process	first, then, add, proceed, finally
order of importance	most important, least important, most significant, the chief reason, most meaningful

- Have students preview the selection. Does the author intend to tell a story? To explain how something works? To present information?
- Ask students to consider what sequence might most logically serve the writer's purpose.
- Direct students to look for clues, or signal words, to help them determine sequence.
- Have students restate the sequence in their own words.

Determining Fact and Opinion

The ability to distinguish fact from opinion has never been more important than it is today. Internet sites and other online resources provide a vast amount of information that is not always accurate. Whenever students read expository texts, guide them in distinguishing fact from opinion.

- Ask students what information is presented.
- Have students determine the source or sources of the information. How is the information supported? Can it be proved? How reliable are the sources cited?
- Is the author or source of information qualified to speak with authority? What are his or her credentials?
- Invite students to evaluate the motivation of the writer. Sometimes writers slant information to convince readers to agree with them.

Analyzing Cause-and-Effect Relationships

Students who can determine why something occurred and what happened as a result are better able to see relationships that allow them to interpret, analyze, and evaluate ideas in a selection.

- To help students find the cause in a passage, ask the question *Why?*
- To help students find the effect, ask the question *What is the result?*
- Ask students to look for clue words that signal cause-and-effect relationships, such as *because, since, as a result, so, the reason that,* and *consequently.*
- Caution students that just because one event precedes another, causality is not necessarily established.

Comparing and Contrasting

Students who are able to see similarities and differences in events, people, and ideas in text are better able to construct meaning from a selection. When writers compare items, they frequently use signal words such as *both, same, alike, like, also,* and *similarly* to provide clues. Signal words such as *unlike, but, although, yet, however, on the other hand, instead,* and *even though* provide clues to contrasting items.

- Ask students to look carefully at the descriptions and other details an author includes in a selection.
- Have them look for clue words that signal that the author is comparing or contrasting items.
- Invite students to think about why a writer might compare or contrast things or people. Is there a larger purpose or idea the author may wish to convey?
- Tell students that sometimes there are no signal words to indicate comparison or contrast. Students must use descriptive details in those instances to infer similarities or differences between items.

Analyzing Problem and Solution

Helping students identify and analyze a problem in a selection enables them to see the complexity of an issue or idea that a writer presents. Asking them to define, evaluate, or even determine a solution to a given problem gives students practice in thinking logically and systematically.

- Have students look for clue words that signal a problem-solution text structure, such as *because, if/then, as a result,* and *therefore.*

- Ask students to identify through their reading the main problem in a passage or selection.
- Ask students how that problem is defined. Is the problem part of an academic task (such as a math problem) or the beginning of the explanation of a process (such as a science experiment)?
- What logical steps or actions may be taken to solve the problem? What possible or partial solutions are presented?
- What happens as a result of the steps or actions taken?
- What other actions may be taken to provide a final solution?
- Ask students to evaluate why a solution did or did not work. How might they have solved the problem differently?

Additional Professional Resources

For more information about the topics, skills, and strategies discussed here, consult the following resources. You may also refer to the additional resources listed in the ***Interactive Reading Sourcebook.***

Anders, P., C. Bos, and D. Filip. 1984. The effect of semantic feature analysis on the reading comprehension of learning-disabled students. In J. A. Niles and L. A. Harris (eds.), *Changing perspectives on research in reading/language processing and instruction*. Rochester, NY: National Reading Conference.

Anderson, R. C., and P. Freebody. 1981. Vocabulary knowledge. In J. T. Guthrie (ed.), *Comprehension and teaching: Research reviews* (pp. 77–117). Newark, DE: International Reading Association.

Anderson, R. C., and P. D. Pearson. 1984. A schema-theoretic view of basic processes in teaching comprehension. In P. D. Pearson (ed.) *Handbook of reading research* (pp. 225–353). New York: Longman.

Armbruster, B., and T. H. Anderson. 1985. Producing "considerate" expository text: Or easy reading is damned hard writing. *Journal of Curriculum Studies* 17(3), pp. 247–252.

Armbruster, B. B., T. H. Anderson, and J. Ostertag. 1989. Teaching text structure to improve reading and writing. *The Reading Teacher* (1989, November), pp. 130–158.

Bear, D., M. Invernizzi, S. Templeton, and F. Johnston. 2000. *Words their way: Word study for phonics, vocabulary, and spelling instruction*. Upper Saddle River, NJ: Prentice Hall.

Beck, I. L., and M. G. McKeown. 1983. Learning words well—A program to enhance vocabulary and comprehension. *The Reading Teacher* 36, pp. 622–625.

Brown, A. L., A. S. Palincsar, and B. B. Armbruster. 1984. Instructing comprehension-fostering activities in interactive learning situations. In R. B. Ruddell, M. R. Ruddell, and H. Singer (eds.), *Theoretical models and processes of reading* (4th ed.). Newark, DE: International Reading Association.

Caine. R. and G. Caine. 1994. *Making connections: Teaching and the human brain*. Menlo Park, CA: Addison-Wesley.

Coté, N., S. R. Goldman, and E. U. Saul. 1998. Students making sense of informational text: Relations between processing and representation. *Discourse Processes* 25(1), pp. 1–53.

Duffy, G. G., L. Roehler, and B. A. Herrmann. 1988. Modeling mental processes helps poor readers become strategic readers. In R. L. Allington (ed.), *Teaching struggling readers: Articles from* The Reading Teacher. International Reading Association.

Fry, E., J. Kress, and D. Fountoukidis. 1993. *The reading teacher's book of lists*. Paramus, NJ: Prentice Hall.

Heller, M. F. 1986. Modeling critical thinking in the English classroom. *Highway One* (1986, Spring), pp. 87–90.

Honig, B., L. Diamond, L. Gutlohn, and J. Mahler. 2000. *CORE: Teaching reading sourcebook*. Novato, CA: Arena Press.

Marks, M., M. Pressley, J. D. Coley, S. Craig, R. Gardner, T. DePinto, and W. Rose. 1993. Three teachers' adaptations of reciprocal teaching in comparison to traditional reciprocal teaching. *Elementary School Journal* 94(2), pp. 267–283.

Meyer, B. J. F., and R. O. Freedle. 1984. Effects of discourse type on recall. *American Educational Research Journal* 21(1), pp. 121–143.

Nagy, W. E. 1988. *Teaching vocabulary to improve reading comprehension*. Newark, DE: International Reading Association.

Ogle, D. 1986. K-W-L: A teaching model that develops active reading of expository text. *The Reading Teacher* 39, pp. 564–570.

Palincsar, A. S., and A. L. Brown. 1984. Reciprocal teaching of comprehension-fostering and comprehension-monitoring activities. *Cognition and Instruction* 1, pp. 117–175.

Pinnell, G., and I. Fountas. 1998. *Word matters: Teaching phonics and spelling in the reading/writing classroom*. Portsmouth, NH: Heinemann.

Richards, J. C., and J. P. Gipe. 1995. What's the structure? A game to help middle school students recognize common writing patterns. *Journal of Reading* 38(8), pp. 667–669.

Rosenblatt, L. 1994. The transactional theory of reading and writing. In R. Ruddell, M. R. Ruddell, and H. Singer (eds.), *Theoretical models and processes of reading* (4th ed., pp. 996–1056). Newark, DE: International Reading Association.

Schumm, J. S., D. S. Haager, and A. G. Leavell. 1991. Considerate and inconsiderate text instruction in postsecondary developmental reading textbooks: A content analysis. *Reading Research and Instruction* 30(4), pp. 42–51.

Schwartz, R. M., and T. E. Raphael. 1985. Concept of definition: A key to improving students' vocabulary. *The Reading Teacher* 39, pp. 198–205.

Guide to Text Readability: DRP® and Lexile® Measures

The **Degrees of Reading Power®** (DRP) program for reading provides a measure for determining the readability of texts. Throughout the teacher materials in your **Teacher Wraparound Edition,** you will encounter DRP readability measures assigned to the reading selections in ***Glencoe Literature: The Reader's Choice*** as well as the readability measures for additional works offered to your students. You will also find readability scores based on the Lexile Framework® for Reading. You can use these to effectively inform your classroom instruction by identifying reading materials that are suitable for individual students. You may also find these readability measures on the ***Glencoe BookLink*** CD-ROM.

Degrees of Reading Power® (DRP)

DRP values indicate the readability of prose text. The higher the value, the more difficult the text. The scale ranges from 0 to 100; commonly encountered English text tends to fall somewhere between 25 and 85. Although middle school texts have an average difficulty of 56 and high school texts have an average difficulty of 62, no single readability level is appropriate for each grade level. Rather, a typical classrom has materials with a range of readability levels available for use—some intended for less-proficient readers, some for average readers, and some for stronger readers. The following chart shows the average DRP readability range for materials widely available for use at each grade. Some materials you might use, however, will certainly fall outside of the range for your particular grade.

Grade	DRP Readability Ranges
6	51–61
7	52–62
8	53–64
9	53–65
10	51–68
11	56–67
12	57–68

The Lexile® Framework

A Lexile measure assigned to a text is the specific number that describes the reading demands of the text. The typical Lexile Scale ranges from 200 to 1700 Lexiles. As with the DRP measures, there is not a direct translation from a specific Lexile measure to a specific grade level. Within any classroom, there will be a range of readers and a range of materials to be read. The levels shown on the following chart indicate the approximate range of Lexile scores for 50 percent of the materials found in a typical grade-level classroom. For example, the middle half of the instructional materials typically found in a sixth-grade classroom range in difficulty from about 850L to 1050L.

Grade	Text Measures (from Lexile Framework Map)
6	850L to 1050L
7	950L to 1075L
8	1000L to 1100L
9	1050L to 1150L
10	1100L to 1200L
11 and 12	1100L to 1300L

*Degrees of Reading Power, DRP, and TASA are registered trademarks of Touchstone Applied Science Associates, Inc. (TASA). Lexile is a registered trademark of MetaMetrics, Inc.

Glencoe Resources for Independent Reading

Foster a lifelong love of reading by encouraging your students to read independently. The resources below can help students improve their critical thinking skills, vocabulary, and ability to connect with literature. Have your students maintain reading lists to keep track of their progress. Parents or guardians can review the lists to help students set manageable goals.

Glencoe Literature Library

This collection of hardcover books includes full-length novels, novellas, plays, and works of nonfiction. Each *Glencoe Literature Library* volume consists of at least one complete extended-length reading accompanied by several related readings from a broad range of genres, such as short stories, poems, essays, or informational articles. In addition, a separate **Study Guide** for each *Glencoe Literature Library* book provides teaching notes and reproducible activity pages for students. Students may also find these activity pages on the **Glencoe Literature Web site** <http://www.lit.glencoe.com>.

Across Five Aprils by Irene Hunt DRP[1] 59
The Adventures of Tom Sawyer by Mark Twain DRP 55
Anne Frank Remembered: The Story of the Woman Who Helped to Hide the Frank Family by Miep Gies and Alison Leslie Gold DRP 57
Bearstone by Will Hobbs DRP 51
Bridge to Terabithia by Katherine Paterson DRP 50
The Call of the Wild by Jack London DRP 62
Cezanne Pinto by Mary Stoltz DRP 54
A Christmas Carol by Charles Dickens DRP 60
The Clay Marble by Minfong Ho DRP 49
Dandelion Wine by Ray Bradbury DRP 56
Dogsong by Gary Paulsen DRP 51
Dragonwings by Lawrence Yep DRP 54
The Friends by Rosa Guy DRP 51
A Gathering of Days: A New England Girl's Journal 1830–1832 by Joan W. Blos DRP 56
The Glory Field by Walter Dean Myers DRP 51
Hatchet by Gary Paulsen DRP 54
High Elk's Treasure by Virginia Driving Hawk Sneve
Homecoming by Cynthia Voigt DRP 48
The House of Dies Drear by Virginia Hamilton DRP 49
I, Juan de Pareja by Elizabeth Borton de Treviño DRP 58
Island of the Blue Dolphins by Scott O'Dell DRP 53
Jacob Have I Loved by Katherine Paterson DRP 52
Johnny Tremain by Esther Forbes DRP 55
Journey to Jo'burg by Beverly Naidoo DRP 50
Julie of the Wolves by Jean Craighead George DRP 55
Letters from a Slave Girl by Mary E. Lyons DRP 51
Letters from Rifka by Karen Hesse DRP 49
Little Women by Louisa May Alcott DRP 60
Lupita Mañana by Patricia Beatty DRP 53
Missing May by Cynthia Rylant DRP 53
Mrs. Frisby and the Rats of NIMH by Robert O'Brien DRP 52
Number the Stars by Lois Lowry DRP 52
The Pigman by Paul Zindel DRP 55
Shabanu: Daughter of the Wind by Suzanne Fisher Staples DRP 54
Shiloh by Phyllis Reynolds Naylor DRP 50
The Slave Dancer by Paula Fox DRP 55
So Far from the Bamboo Grove by Yoko Kawashima Watkins DRP 50
Sounder by William H. Armstrong DRP 53
The Summer of the Swans by Betsy Byars DRP 50
Taking Sides by Gary Soto DRP 52
There's a Girl in My Hammerlock by Jerry Spinelli DRP 46
Treasure Island by Robert Louis Stevenson DRP 56
The True Confessions of Charlotte Doyle by Avi DRP 52
Tuck Everlasting by Natalie Babbitt DRP 56
The View from Saturday by E. L. Konigsburg DRP 53
Walk Two Moons by Sharon Creech DRP 49
Where the Red Fern Grows by Wilson Rawls DRP 47
Winter Thunder and *The Christmas of the Phonograph Records* by Mari Sandoz
The Witch of Blackbird Pond by Elizabeth George Speare DRP 57
A Wrinkle in Time by Madeleine L'Engle DRP 51

inTIME magazine

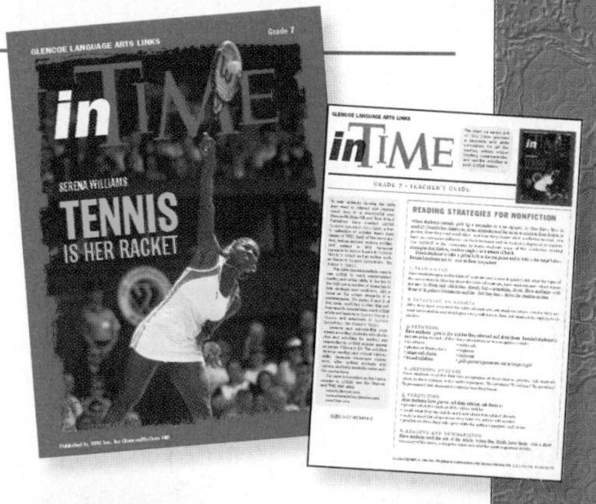

This lively collection of articles drawn from issues of *TIME* helps students develop the skills they need to interact with informational text in a meaningful way. Each of the news stories, feature articles, reviews, profiles, and essays in the magazine connects to an author, work, or theme in ***Glencoe Literature: The Reader's Choice*** as well as to a lesson in ***Glencoe Writer's Choice***. In addition, a separate **Teacher's Guide,** including lessons and reproducible student worksheets designed to develop students' reading and critical thinking skills, accompanies each magazine.

Five-Star Stories

This collection of anthologies features well-known short stories organized by theme and adapted and abridged for a variety of reading levels. You may use the ***Glencoe BookLink*** CD-ROM to identify the exact readability level for each selection. Exercises included in the anthologies help to increase students' vocabulary and improve their reading comprehension, critical thinking, and understanding of literary elements. Themes include the following:

- Travels
- Adventures
- Chills
- Surprises
- Shocks
- Twists
- Encounters
- Conflicts

The Contemporary Readers

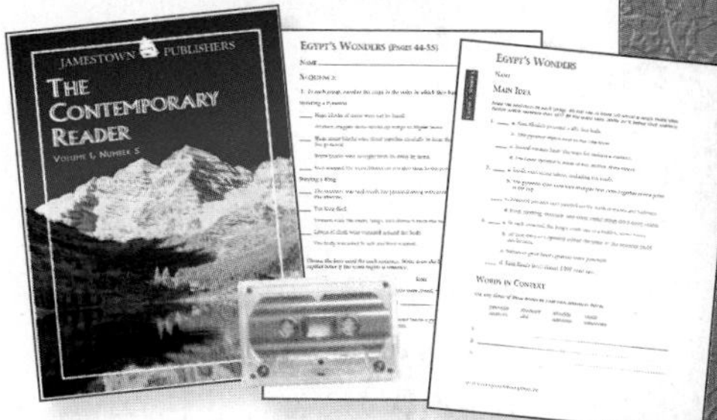

Each volume of ***The Contemporary Readers*** consists of six nonfiction books designed for developing readers from a wide range of backgrounds. The selections included in each book range from eight hundred to twelve hundred words and are linked to such themes as human interest, science and nature, or current issues. A set of audiocassettes and a ***Teacher's Resource Book,*** comprised of a Teacher's Guide and reproducible activity pages, complement each volume. You may use the ***Glencoe BookLink*** CD-ROM to identify the exact readability level for each selection in ***The Contemporary Readers.***

Glencoe BookLink CD-ROM

This CD-ROM provides a database that you can use to identify specific readings for students. The software shows **Degrees of Reading Power® (DRP)** readability scores for all the prose fiction and nonfiction selections in ***Glencoe Literature: The Reader's Choice,*** as well as for the ***Five-Star Stories, The Contemporary Readers,*** books in the ***Glencoe Literature Library***, and a number of other titles. Using ***Glencoe BookLink*** CD-ROM, you can search for specific selections by author and title or create reading lists sorted by range, genre (fiction, nonfiction, poetry, or drama), Glencoe theme, or special areas of interest. To further help you guide students to readings that interest them, ***Glencoe BookLink*** CD-ROM provides brief summaries of reading selections as well as **Lexile®** measures of readability.

Literature Classics CD-ROM

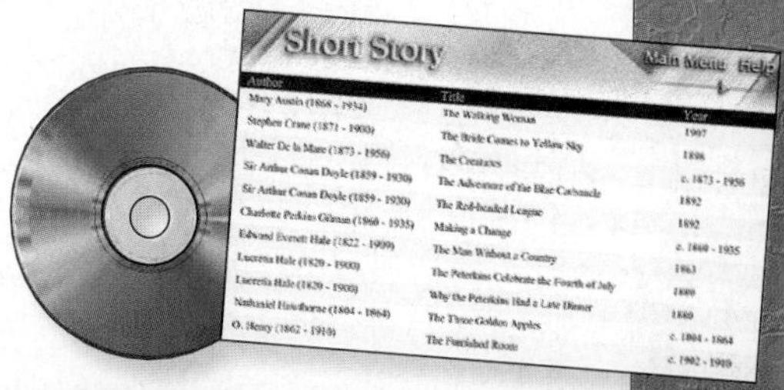

This interactive CD-ROM collects over four hundred assorted classic literature selections that may be used to extend students' reading. You may access selections on the CD-ROM by author, title, date, genre, theme, country, and course/grade level. The **Genre Focus Lesson Plans** and **blackline masters** included with the CD-ROM may be used to monitor students' reading.

---

[1] **Degrees of Reading Power® DRP** values indicate the readability of prose text. The higher the value, the more difficult the text. Though the scale ranges from 0 to 100, texts widely available for use at grades six through eight typically range from 51 to 64. Some materials, however, may certainly fall outside of this range.

Theme 1 At a Glance
No Place Like Home

THEME OPENING

Theme 1: NO PLACE LIKE HOME

SELECTIONS

SKILL FEATURES

WRITING WORKSHOP

THEME ASSESSMENT

- **Responding to the Theme, Analyzing Literature, Evaluate and Set Goals** (p. 94)
- **Build Your Portfolio** (p. 94)
- **Reading on Your Own** (p. 95)
  A Day No Pigs Would Die by Robert Newton Peck
  Walker of Time by Helen Hughes Vick
  Tree by Leaf by Cynthia Voigt
  Missing May by Cynthia Rylant
- **Standardized Test Practice** (pp. 96–97)

KEYS TO LITERARY CONNECTIONS

Comparing Selections

The **Comparing Selections** feature in this theme provides opportunities for addressing diverse aspects of the reading and literature curriculum.

For example, in Comparing Selections on page 74, students compare solutions in Gary Soto's "Mother and Daughter" and Sandra Cisneros's "Chanclas." Through this comparison, students learn ways to deal with everyday problems

World Literature

The Student Edition contains a variety of literature that represents cultures from around the world. World literature selections are highlighted with the icon above.

TEACHING SUPPORT

The Teaching Support offers a wealth of interactive instructional support:

Meeting Individual Needs
- Special Needs
- English Language Learners
- Multiple Modes of Expression
- Advanced Learners

Internet Connection

Assessment

Portfolio Options

Minilessons
- Grammar and Language
- Reading
- Writing
- Listening and Speaking

Connecting to Other Selections

Real-World Connection

Interdisciplinary Connection

Life Skills Connection

Family and Community Activity

Key to Ability Levels

The activities throughout this theme have been coded for students of various abilities.

L1 BASIC activities for all students

L2 AVERAGE activities for average to above-average students

L3 ADVANCED LEARNERS activities for above-average students

Block Scheduling

Activities that are particularly suited to use within a block scheduling framework are identified with this icon.

Teaching Today

The Glencoe *Teaching Today* professional development Web site at www.teachingtoday.glencoe.com features daily teaching tips, free downloads, annotated Web resources, educational news, and a wealth of information on a wide range of topics.

Reading Skills in this theme

Variety of Texts

In addition to short stories, this theme includes the following:

- cartoon
- autobiographical essay
- personal essay
- radio transcript

Comprehension Skills

The following instructional support for comprehension skills appears in this theme of the Student Edition:

- **Active Reading Strategies and Model** (pp. 48–55)
- **Previewing** (p. 25)
- **Reading and Thinking Minilessons** (pp. 16, 37, 89)

See also the **Reading Minilessons** throughout the theme in this Teacher Wraparound Edition.

For strategies for reading longer works, such as novels and novellas, see "Tips for Independent Reading" on page 95.

Reading Resources

Active Reading Guide The ***Active Reading Guide*** provides graphic organizers and study guide questions to support students' reading of each selection (***Active Reading Guide***, pp. 1–18).

Interactive Reading Sourcebook and **Interactive Reading Workbook** The ***Interactive Reading Sourcebook*** and ***Interactive Reading Workbook*** offer focused comprehension strategies and lessons on critical thinking skills as well as fluency practice and activities to teach and support phonics, decoding, spelling, and vocabulary development.

Vocabulary Power The ***Vocabulary Power*** workbook (Lessons 1–5) provides systematic teaching, practice, and assessment of vocabulary for better reading comprehension.

Audio Library Available on audiocassette and on CD, the ***Audio Library*** provides valuable comprehension support.

Glencoe Literature Library Each title in the ***Glencoe Literature Library*** includes a full-length work plus related readings. A separate Study Guide is available for each title.

Five-Star Stories These anthologies of familiar short stories adapted and abridged for a variety of reading levels include exercises to help increase students' vocabulary and improve their reading comprehension.

The Contemporary Readers ***The Contemporary Readers*** are nonfiction books linked to various themes and designed for developing readers from a wide range of backgrounds.

Literature Classics CD-ROM The selections on this CD-ROM can be searched by author, theme, or genre.

inTIME and Humanities Across TIME Coproductions of Glencoe and Time, Inc., these resources include a wealth of high-interest nonfiction related to the selections in this theme.

Assessment in this theme

Glencoe's Assessment Advantage

Assessment Options in the Student Edition

This program offers a number of diverse ways to evaluate student understanding and skill proficiency. In the Student Edition, use the following:

- **Responding to Literature**
  Following each selection, students are asked to recall facts, interpret ideas, and evaluate concepts as they answer a variety of questions and complete activities to extend their understanding.
- **Theme Assessment (pp. 94–95)**
  Here students respond to the selections on personal and analytical levels. They also assume ownership of their learning by setting and evaluating goals and by selecting work for their portfolios.

See also the many **Assessment Resources** listed on the facing page.

The Princeton Review

Standardized Test Practice

The Princeton Review has developed the Standardized Test Practice pages found at the end of this thematic unit (pp. 96–97). For additional practice, direct students to the following resources:

- ITBS Preparation and Practice
- SAT-9 Preparation and Practice
- TerraNova Preparation and Practice

Writing Skills in this theme

Writing Skills

The Student Edition of Theme 1 offers strong instructional support for writing skills:

In Extending Your Response, which follows each selection:

- **Writing About Literature**
- **Personal/Creative Writing**

See also the **Writing Minilessons** throughout the theme in this Teacher Wraparound Edition.

Writing Workshops

Theme 1 concludes with a Writing Workshop that guides students through the process for writing a personal essay (pp. 90–93).

Writing Resources

Writer's Assistant CD-ROM Each **Writing Workshop** is supplemented by an interactive writing guide on the ***Writer's Assistant*** CD-ROM. This easy- to-use writing guide provides prompts, templates, and other tools that lead students through the writing process.

Grammar and Composition Handbook The ***Grammar and Composition Handbook*** (Lessons 1.1–2.5) provides systematic instruction in English language conventions.

Spelling Power The ***Spelling Power*** workbook (Lessons 1–4) provides systematic teaching, practice, and assessment of spelling to help students become better spellers and thus enhance their writing.

Writing and Proofreading Practice Blackline masters present in-depth instruction and practice on a specific step in the writing process and proofreading (pp. 1–6, 7–13).

Writing and Proofreading Transparencies Transparencies provide graphic organizers and proofreading exercises for whole-class instruction (pp. 1–6, 7–8).

Research and Report Writing Guide This resource provides extensive tips and activities to guide students in their writing projects in the literature classroom as well as in classes across the curriculum.

Style and Documentation Sourcebook for Writers This sourcebook is a combination reference and workbook, giving students the most up-to-date information and guidance regarding traditional as well as technological research strategies and documentation.

Revising with Style This resource offers instruction and exercises focusing on the revision process and covering topics from proofreading and correcting common grammatical errors to sentence combining and reordering.

Assessment Resources

Selection Quick Checks For each selection, a **Quick Check** of three to five short-answer questions measures students' literal comprehension.

Selection and Theme Assessment The ***Selection and Theme Assessment*** instrument tests students' abilities to recall, interpret, and evaluate what they've read. The tests consist of multiple-choice, short answer, and essay questions.

Performance Assessment Alternative assessment instruments and rubrics for Theme 1 are found in the ***Performance Assessment*** ancillary.

Writing Assessment and Portfolio Management These notes and strategies, student models, and assessment tools assist with the task of measuring students' progress as writers and as monitors of their own writing.

Testmaker: ExamView Pro Teachers can customize selection and Theme 1 tests by accessing the ***Testmaker*** database.

Interactive Tutor: Self-Assessment The ***Interactive Tutor: Self-Assessment*** software provides multiple-choice tests with immediate feedback to help students evaluate their knowledge and understanding of each literature selection.

MindJogger Videoquizzes Using a popular game show format, ***MindJogger Videoquizzes*** on videocassettes enable teachers to evaluate student understanding of Theme 1 in a quick and fun manner.

Theme 1 SKILLS SCOPE AND SEQUENCE

Lessons	Literary Elements	Reading and Thinking	Writing
The Treasure of Lemon Brown WALTER DEAN MYERS DRP: 56 Lexile: 650	Theme, SE p. 14 *Flashback,* TWE p. 5 *Characterization,* TWE pp. 6, 8, 10, 11 *Simile,* TWE p. 6 *Description,* TWE p. 6 *Suspense,* TWE p. 8 *Theme,* TWE pp. 9, 12, 13 *Personification,* TWE p. 12 *Setting,* TWE p. 13	Text Structures, SE p. 16 *Identify Bias,* TWE p. 6 SN *Less-Proficient Readers,* TWE p. 8 *Identify Bias,* TWE p. 6 *Author's Purpose,* TWE p. 10 *Infer,* TWE p. 13	Character Analysis, SE p. 15 Letter, SE p. 15 Discovering the Blues, SE p. 17 *Description,* TWE p. 6
My Two Dads MARIE G. LEE DRP: 65 Lexile: 1150	Character, SE p. 23 *Character,* TWE p. 20 *Characterization,* TWE p. 21 *Connotation and Denotation,* TWE p. 22	Previewing, SE p. 25 *Summarize,* TWE p. 21 *Evaluate,* TWE p. 22 SN *Less-Proficient Readers,* TWE p. 8	Letter, SE p. 24
A Dictionary of Japanese-American Terms R. A. SASAKI DRP: 54 Lexile: 870	Essay, SE p. 35 *Narrator,* TWE p. 28 *Symbolism,* TWE pp. 29, 30 *Diction,* TWE p. 30 *Style, Simile,* TWE p. 31 *Imagery,* TWE p. 33 *Symbol,* TWE p. 34	Elaborating, SE p. 37 *Analyze Arguments,* TWE p. 30 SN *Learning Disabled,* TWE p. 30 *Use Text Structures,* TWE p. 31 *Infer,* TWE p. 31	Analogy, SE p. 36 Letter, SE p. 36
Homeless ANNA QUINDLEN DRP: 57 Lexile: 920	Stereotype, SE p. 42 *Stereotype,* TWE p. 40 *Diction,* TWE p. 40	Radio Transcript, SE p. 44 *Elaborate,* TWE p. 40 *Author's Purpose,* TWE p. 44 ELL *Favorite Stories,* TWE p. 40	Analyze Details, SE p. 43 Interview Questions, SE p. 43 *Sentence Variety,* TWE p. 45
Golden Glass ALMA LUZ VILLANUEVA DRP: 55 Lexile: 910	Fiction, SE pp. 46 Setting, SE pp. 56 *Setting,* TWE p. 53	Fiction, SE p. 48 SN *Less-Proficient Readers,* TWE p. 46 *Drawing Conclusions,* TWE p. 52 *Identify Cause-and-Effect,* TWE p. 54 ELL *Working with a Partner,* TWE p. 52	Character Analysis, SE p. 57 Personal Writing, SE p. 57
Mother and Daughter GARY SOTO DRP: 55 Lexile: 720	Tone, SE p. 68 *Tone,* TWE pp. 63, 64 *Characterization,* TWE pp. 64, 66, 67 *Foreshadowing,* TWE p. 65	*Evaluate,* TWE p. 63 *Visualize,* TWE p. 65 *Make Critical Judgments,* TWE p. 66 SN *Emotional,* TWE p. 64 ELL *Parents and Daughters,* TWE p. 63	Using Examples, SE p. 60 Compare/Contrast, SE p. 69 Description of a Person, SE p. 69
Chanclas SANDRA CISNEROS DRP: 54 Lexile: 1080	Style, SE p. 73 *Style,* TWE p. 72	Comparing Selections, SE p. 74 *Infer,* TWE p. 72 *Connecting,* TWE p. 72	Diary Entry, SE p. 73
The Medicine Bag VIRGINIA DRIVING HAWK SNEVE DRP: 54 Lexile: 820	Symbol, SE p. 87 *Characterization,* TWE pp. 80, 84 *Diction,* TWE pp. 80, 85 *Symbol,* TWE pp. 81, 83, 85, 86 *Dialogue,* TWE p. 83 *Tone,* TWE p. 84 *Theme,* TWE p. 86	Magazine Article, SE p. 76 Author's Purpose, SE p. 89 *Infer,* TWE p. 80 *Drawing Conclusions,* TWE p. 81 *Compare/Contrast,* TWE pp. 76, 84	Narrator, SE p. 88 Journal Entry, SE p. 88
Writing WORKSHOP Descriptive Writing: Personal Essay			*Concrete Details,* TWE p. 92

Key: Student material is in roman. Teacher material is in italic. Technology ELL English Language Learners

Vocabulary and Spelling	Grammar and Language	Listening, Speaking, and Viewing	Life Skills; Study and Research; Technology
Etymology, SE p. 16 *Word History, TWE p. 15*	Punctuating Dialogue, SE p. 16 ELL *Verb Tenses and "If" Clauses, TWE p. 6* *Double Negatives, TWE p. 12*	Literature Groups, SE p. 15 Reach a Consensus, SE p. 15	Reach a Consensus, SE p. 15 Music Presentation, SE p. 15 Interdisciplinary Connection: Music, SE p. 17 *Internet Connection, TWE pp. 7, 10, 13*
Analogies, SE p. 24	*Adjective Clauses, TWE p. 22*	Literature Groups, SE p. 24	A Heritage Map, SE p. 15 Internet Connection, SE p. 24 ELL *Cultural Identities, TWE p. 20*
Compound Words, SE p. 37	Personal Pronouns, SE p. 37 ELL *Suffixes: -less, TWE p. 28* *Titles, TWE p. 34*	Literature Groups, SE p. 36 Interview, SE p. 36 Present Yourself, SE p. 36	*History Research, TWE p. 32* *Video, TWE p. 32* *Researching, TWE p. 33*
The Prefix *en-*, SE p. 43	Avoiding Sentence Fragments, SE p. 45 *Adjectives, TWE p. 41*	Literature Groups, SE p. 43	Social Studies Research, SE p. 43 Create an Ad Campaign, SE p. 43
Latin Roots, SE p. 57	*Dashes, TWE p. 55*	Literature Groups, SE p. 57	Internet Connection, SE p. 57 E-mail: Mailing, SE p. 58 Lists, SE p. 58 SN *Emotional, TWE p. 59*
Synonyms, SE p. 65 *Etymology, TWE p. 65*	*Adjectives, TWE p. 60* *Compound Adjectives, TWE p. 66*	Literature Groups, SE p. 69	Medical Careers, SE p. 69 *Reading Labels, TWE p. 67*
Using Context Clues, SE p. 75 ELL *Word Roots, TWE p. 75*		Literature Groups, SE p. 73	
Word Origins, SE p. 89 ELL *Understanding Vocabulary, TWE p. 79*	Levels of Usage, SE p. 89 *Adjectives, TWE p. 86*	Literature Groups, SE p. 88 *Storytelling, TWE p. 80*	Geography/Culture Research, SE p. 88 *Internet Connection, TWE p. 76* *Social Studies Research, TWE p. 83* *Real-World Connection, TWE p. 85*
			Decision Making, TWE p. 90

SN **Special Needs and At-Risk Learners**

Theme 1 RESOURCE MANAGER

Lessons	Essential Resources		English Language Learners
The Treasure of Lemon Brown Walter Dean Myers Pacing: 3 Days	**Lesson-Specific Instruction** Selection Focus Transp. 1 * Active Reading Guide, p. 1 Literary Elements Transp. 1 Vocabulary Practice, p. 7 * Quick Checks, p. 1 Selection and Theme Assessment, pp. 1–2	Testmaker: ExamView Pro Performance Assessment, p. 1 **Systematic Language Instruction** Grammar and Comp. Hbk., L. 1.1–1.2 Vocabulary Power, Lesson 1 Spelling Power, Lesson 1	English Language Learners Sourcebook, pp. 17, 18 Spanish Summaries, p. 1 Spanish Translations, pp. 1–7 * Audio Library English, Yes!
My Two Dads Marie G. Lee Pacing: 1 Day	**Lesson-Specific Instruction** Selection Focus Transp. 2 * Active Reading Guide, p. 2 Literary Elements Transp. 2 Vocabulary Practice, p. 8 * Quick Checks, p. 2 Selection and Theme Assessment, pp. 3–4	Testmaker: ExamView Pro Performance Assessment, p. 2 TIME *inTIME* magazine, p. 32 **Systematic Language Instruction** Grammar and Comp. Hbk., L. 1.3–1.4 Vocabulary Power, Lesson 2	English Language Learners Sourcebook, p. 19 Theme One Planning Guide, p. 14 Spanish Summaries, p. 2 Spanish Translations, pp. 8–10 * Audio Library English, Yes!
A Dictionary of Japanese-American Terms R. A. Sasaki Pacing: 2 Days	**Lesson-Specific Instruction** Selection Focus Transp. 3 * Active Reading Guide, p. 3 Literary Elements Transp. 3 Vocabulary Practice, p. 9 * Quick Checks, p. 3 Selection and Theme Assessment, pp. 5–6	Testmaker: ExamView Pro Performance Assessment, p. 3 TIME *inTIME* magazine, p. 32 **Systematic Language Instruction** Grammar and Comp. Hbk., L. 1.5	English Language Learners Sourcebook, p. 20 Spanish Summaries, p. 3 * Audio Library English, Yes!
Homeless Anna Quindlen Pacing: 2 Days	**Lesson-Specific Instruction** Selection Focus Transp. 4 * Active Reading Guide, p. 4 Literary Elements Transp. 4 Vocabulary Practice, p. 10 * Quick Checks, p. 4 Selection and Theme Assessment, pp. 7–8	Testmaker: ExamView Pro Performance Assessment, p. 4 **Systematic Language Instruction** Grammar and Comp. Hbk., L. 1.6 Vocabulary Power, Lesson 3 Spelling Power, Lesson 2	English Language Learners Sourcebook, p. 21 Spanish Summaries, p. 4 * Audio Library English, Yes!
Golden Glass Alma Luz Villanueva Pacing: 2 Days	**Lesson-Specific Instruction** Selection Focus Transp. 5 * Active Reading Guide, p. 5 Literary Elements Transp. 5 Vocabulary Practice, p. 11 * Quick Checks, p. 5 Selection and Theme Assessment, pp. 9–10	Testmaker: ExamView Pro Performance Assessment, p. 5 **Systematic Language Instruction** Grammar and Comp. Hbk., L. 2.1	English Language Learners Sourcebook, pp. 22, 23 Spanish Summaries, p. 5 Spanish Translations, pp. 11–14 * Audio Library English, Yes!

Key: Workbook · Blackline Masters · Textbook · Transparency · CD-ROM · Videodisk (also available in videocassette)

Special Needs/ Strategic Intervention	Reteaching and Enrichment
Interactive Reading Sourcebook, pp. T47–T49 Interactive Reading Workbook, pp. 1–2 Inclusion Strategies Sourcebook, pp. 71–72 Theme One Planning Guide, p. 6 * Audio Library	Literature Launchers, Side A, Segment 1 Fine Art Transparency 7 Reading Skills Practice Workbook pp. 1–2 Grammar and Language Transp., 1 Gr. and Lang. Wkbk., pp. 135, 267 Grammar and Comp. Hbk., L. 6.5, 13.6 TIME *Humanities Across TIME*, Cover 3 Interactive Tutor: Self-Assessment Vocabulary PuzzleMaker Web Site (lit.glencoe.com)
Interactive Reading Sourcebook, pp. T49–T51 Interactive Reading Workbook, pp. 3–4 Inclusion Strategies Sourcebook, pp. 5–6 Theme One Planning Guide, p. 14 * Audio Library	Reading Skills Practice Workbook pp. 3–4 Grammar and Language Transp., 2 Gr. and Lang. Wkbk., p. 159 Grammar and Comp. Hbk., L. 8.3 Interactive Tutor: Self-Assessment Vocabulary PuzzleMaker Web Site (lit.glencoe.com)
Interactive Reading Sourcebook, pp. T52–T54 Interactive Reading Workbook, pp. 5–8 Inclusion Strategies Sourcebook, pp. 3–4 Theme One Planning Guide, p. 22 * Audio Library	Reading Skills Practice Workbook pp. 5–6 Grammar and Language Transp., 3 Gr. and Lang. Wkbk., p. 249 Grammar and Comp. Hbk., L. 4.1, 13.6 TIME *Humanities Across TIME*, Cover 16 Interactive Tutor: Self-Assessment Vocabulary PuzzleMaker Web Site (lit.glencoe.com)
Interactive Reading Sourcebook, pp. T55–T57 Interactive Reading Workbook, pp. 9–10 Inclusion Strategies Sourcebook, p. 32 Theme One Planning Guide, p. 30 * Audio Library	Reading Skills Practice Workbook pp. 7–8 Grammar and Language Transp., 4 Gr. and Lang. Wkbk., p. 121 Grammar and Comp. Hbk., L. 5.1 Media Connection Activities, p. 1 Interactive Tutor: Self-Assessment Vocabulary PuzzleMaker Web Site (lit.glencoe.com)
Interactive Reading Sourcebook, pp. T57–T59 Interactive Reading Workbook, pp. 11–12 Inclusion Strategies Sourcebook, pp. 1–2 Theme One Planning Guide, p. 38 * Audio Library	Fine Art Transparency 10 Reading Skills Practice Wbk., pp. 9–10 Grammar and Language Transp. 5 Gr. and Lang. Wkbk., p. 271 Grammar and Comp. Hbk., L. 13.8 Interactive Tutor: Self-Assessment Vocabulary PuzzleMaker Web Site (lit.glencoe.com)

Web   Audiocassette   Diskette   *Also available in Spanish

Independent Reading

Encourage students to spend thirty minutes each day in independent reading. The following Glencoe components and outside resources provide opportunities for reading related to this theme.

The Glencoe Literature Library

You may want to assign one or more of these titles for independent reading. For a complete listing of titles available in the Glencoe Literature Library, see page T94 of this book

- *Missing May* by Cynthia Rylant
- *Bearstone* by Will Hobbs
- *So Far From the Bamboo Grove* by Yoko Kawashima
- *Homecoming* by Cynthia Voigt
- *High Elk's Treasure* by Virginia Driving Hawk Sneve

inTIME Magazine News stories, feature articles, reviews, profiles, and essays in the magazine connect to an author, work, or theme in *the Student Edition.* See the **in*TIME* Teacher's Guide** for specific connections to this theme.

Resources for Less-Proficient Readers

For reading especially created for less-proficient readers, suggest

- *Five-Star Stories*
- *The Contemporary Readers*

Additional Resources for Independent Reading

The following titles are listed with specific reading selections throughout this theme. You may want to suggest that students look for these in your local or school library.

- *Adam of the Road* by Elizabeth Janet Gray
- *My Side of the Mountain* by Jean Craighead George
- *The Island* by Gary Paulsen
- *A Day No Pigs Would Die* by Robert Newton Peck
- *Walker of Time* by Helen Hughes Vick
- *Tree by Leaf* by Cynthia Voigt

RESOURCE MANAGER (continued)

Lessons	Essential Resources		English Language Learners
Mother and Daughter GARY SOTO PACING: 2 DAYS	**Lesson-Specific Instruction** Selection Focus Transp. 6 * Active Reading Guide, p. 6 Literary Elements Transp. 6 Vocabulary Practice, p. 12 * Quick Checks, p. 6 Selection and Theme Assessment, pp. 11–12 Testmaker: ExamView Pro Performance Assessment, p. 6	**Systematic Language Instruction** Grammar and Comp. Hbk., L. 2.2 Vocabulary Power, Lesson 4 Spelling Power, Lesson 3	English Language Learners Sourcebook, p. 24 Spanish Summaries, p. 6 Spanish Translations, pp. 15-19 * Audio Library English, Yes!
Chanclas SANDRA CISNEROS PACING: 1 DAY	**Lesson-Specific Instruction** Selection Focus Transp. 7 * Active Reading Guide, p. 7 Literary Elements Transp. 7 * Quick Checks, p. 7 Selection and Theme Assessment, pp. 11–12 Testmaker: ExamView Pro Performance Assessment, p. 6	**Systematic Language Instruction** Grammar and Comp. Hbk., L. 2.3-2.4 Vocabulary Power, Lesson 5 Spelling Power, Lesson 4	English Language Learners Sourcebook, pp. 25, 26 Theme One Planning Guide, p. 54 Spanish Summaries, p. 7 Spanish Translations, pp. 20–21 * Audio Library English, Yes!
The Medicine Bag VIRGINIA DRIVING HAWK SNEVE PACING: 2 DAYS	**Lesson-Specific Instruction** Selection Focus Transp. 8 * Active Reading Guide, p. 8 Literary Elements Transp. 8 Vocabulary Practice, p. 7 * Quick Checks, p. 8 Selection and Theme Assessment, pp. 13–14 Testmaker: ExamView Pro Performance Assessment, p. 7	**Systematic Language Instruction** Grammar and Comp. Hbk., L. 2.5 Vocabulary Power, Unit 1 Review/Test Spelling Power, Unit 1 Review/Proofreading	English Language Learners Sourcebook, p. 27 Theme One Planning Guide, p. 62 Spanish Summaries, p. 8 Spanish Translations, pp. 22–28 * Audio Library English, Yes!
Writing WORKSHOP Descriptive Writing: Personal Essay PACING: 2 DAYS	Writing Assessment and Portfolio Management, pp. 1–13, 14–16, 41–48		English Language Learners Sourcebook, p. 9 English, Yes!

Key: Workbook · Blackline Masters · Textbook · Transparency · CD-ROM · Videodisk (also available in videocassette)

Special Needs/ Strategic Intervention	Reteaching and Enrichment
Interactive Reading Sourcebook, pp. T60–T62 Interactive Reading Workbook, pp. 13–14 Inclusion Strategies Sourcebook, pp. 73–74 * Audio Library	Fine Art Transparency 2 Reading Skills Practice Workbook, pp. 11–12 Grammar and Language Transp. 6 Gr. and Lang. Wkbk., p. 121 Grammar and Comp. Hbk., L. 5.1, 13.8 Interactive Tutor: Self-Assessment Vocabulary PuzzleMaker Web Site (lit.glencoe.com)
Interactive Reading Sourcebook, pp. T62–T65 Interactive Reading Workbook, pp. 15–16 Inclusion Strategies Sourcebook, pp. 9–10 Theme One Planning Guide, p. 54 * Audio Library	Literature Launchers, Side A, Segment 3 Reading Skills Practice Workbook, pp. 13–14 Interactive Tutor: Self-Assessment Vocabulary PuzzleMaker Web Site (lit.glencoe.com)
Interactive Reading Sourcebook, pp. T65–T67 Interactive Reading Workbook, pp. 17–18 Theme One Planning Guide, p. 62 * Audio Library	Literature Launchers, Side A, Segment 2 Fine Art Transparency 14 Reading Skills Practice Workbook, pp. 15–16 Grammar and Language Transp. 7 Gr. and Lang. Wkbk., p. 133 Grammar and Comp. Hbk., L. 5.1 Media Connection Activities, p. 2 TIME *Humanities Across TIME*, Cover 8 Interactive Tutor: Self-Assessment Vocabulary PuzzleMaker Web Site (lit.glencoe.com)
Inclusion Strategies Sourcebook, pp. 69–70	Writing and Proofreading Practice, pp. 1–6, 7–13 Writing and Proofreading Transparencies 1–6, 7–8, 25–26 Revising with Style Writer's Assistant

Web Audiocassette Diskette *Also available in Spanish

Theme RESOURCES

To explore the theme further, you may want to use these resources:

- Listening and Speaking Activities (pp. 1–3)
- Viewing and Representing Activities (pp. 1–9)
- Critical Thinking Skills (pp. 2–3)
- Media Connection Activities, (pp. 1–2)
- Interdisciplinary Activities (pp. 2–5)
- Family and Community Activities (p. 20)
- Selection and Theme Assessment (pp. 1–14, 125–126)
- Performance Assessment (pp. 64, 91)

TIME Humanities Across TIME

See also these additional theme planning resources:

- Theme One Planning Guide
- Interactive Reading Sourcebook
- Literature Groups Sourcebook
- Interactive Lesson Planner
- Interactive Teacher Edition
- Glencoe Web Site (lit.glencoe.com)

PRESENTATION Plus!

Use Glencoe's ***Presentation Plus!*** This multimedia teaching tool lets you present dynamic lessons that will engage your students. Using Microsoft PowerPoint®, you can customize the presentation to create your own personalized lessons.

THEME 1

No Place Like Home

Theme Objectives

- To enjoy reading about what "home" means to different people
- To analyze the literary elements in short stories and personal essays
- To apply strategies for reading short stories

Teaching Strategies

Have students read the quotation by Robert Frost and study the art in preparation for the questions below.

VIEWING THE PHOTOGRAPH

Award-winning photojournalist Peter Menzel (b. 1948) tells stories with his pictures.

Responding to the Photograph This photograph is from *Material World,* a book about an average family's life in each of thirty countries. Discussion questions:

- What does the scene convey about life in Iceland? *(It is snowy and has navigable rivers or canals.)*
- What do the family members' possessions reveal about them? *(This family is musical.)*
- What kind of family life does the picture suggest? *(They share several interests, despite the age range.)*

No Place Like Home

"Home is the place where, when you have to go there, they have to take you in."

–Robert Frost

Fire and Ice, 1993. Peter Menzel. From the book *Material World: A Global Family Portrait.*

TEACHER to TEACHER

LAKE PARK ELEMENTARY • LAKE PARK, GEORGIA

To introduce this theme, I make a four column chart on a large roll of paper, labeling each column with one of the words *No Place Like Home.* Then I read a poem to the students that reflects the theme. After reading, we discuss what home means to them, other stories they have read about home, and what home may mean to other people. From the discussion, students add words to the four original columns, plus they add new columns. They may add columns such as *country, homeless people, family.* Students then choose one of the columns and write a story about the ideas presented in it. I provide an "author's chair" for students to read their stories to the class.

—VALLYE BLANTON

THEME 1

THEME CONTENTS

RESOURCE MANAGER

See the *Theme One Planning Guide* (pp. 1–5) for additional teaching notes, strategies, and resources for introducing the theme "No Place Like Home."

Introducing Theme 1

Direct your students' attention to the **Theme Contents.** Ask them to read through the list of selections. Present these discussion questions:

- Which of the titles seem to relate most directly to the theme? *(Students may see a direct link to "My Two Dads," "Homeless," and "Mother and Daughter.")*
- What do you think of when you read the other titles? *(Students may have a variety of associations. "The Treasure of Lemon Brown" and "Golden Glass" could both be titles of adventure stories. Students may ask for a translation of the word* chanclas, *which means "scruffy old shoes.")*
- Just from the titles, which story do you think you will enjoy most? Least?

LITERATURE & HUMANITIES

Have students examine the photo "From Generation to Generation" (National Museum of Women in the Arts) and discuss the significance of the title. Ask them to consider what kinds of things are passed from generation to generation while reading and discussing these stories relating to home and family.

GLENCOE TECHNOLOGY

LITERATURE CLASSICS CD-ROM

Search for other selections related to the theme of "No Place Like Home."

Exploring the Theme

No Place Like Home

- Students may note that "home" is a rather complicated concept; it is more than a place or people. Its meaning may be broad *(as in "homeland")* or narrow *(as in "the place I live now").*
- Students may mention the foods they like, their hobbies and interests, their values and lifestyles. All are influenced by where and with whom they live. Point out that of all the places in which people spend their lives, only *home* has its own word for the pain people feel when they're away—*homesick.* People don't get *schoolsick* during the summer, or *worksick* when they're on vacation. Why is there a special word for the feeling people have when they're away from home?

Starting Points

Humor at Home

Draw your students' attention to Gary Larson's *The Far Side* cartoon. Invite students to explain what is happening in the cartoon. Ask what makes the cartoon humorous.

1. Before they draw their cartoons, ask students to jot down some of the funniest situations they can remember in their own families and then to select one they think has the best potential as a cartoon. Remind students that a cartoon can focus on what people say, what they do, or both. Not every cartoon has words.
2. Point out that cartoons can have one or several panels. Bring in examples of cartoon strips that deal with family situations—such as *For Better or for Worse, Family Circus, Peanuts,* or *Blondie*—to help stimulate ideas.

Family Ties

Students may focus on how being away from home for a period of time changed their attitudes and feelings about home. Even visiting a friend's home and noticing how differently another family lives can change one's perspective.

Exploring the Theme

No Place Like Home

What is home? To some, it is the place where we grew up. To others, it's the family members who shaped us. For still others, it's simply a place where we feel comfortable and loved. In this theme, you will explore how our homes influence us, and how one's understanding of home can change over time.

Starting Points

HUMOR AT HOME

Cartoonists often turn to families as a source of ideas for their work. What family situations can you think of that could make funny cartoons?

- Jot down ideas for cartoons about funny family situations.
- Choose one idea to sketch out. If needed, include dialogue or a caption.

FAMILY TIES

Relationships and events at home prepare us for life on our own. Think of a conversation, argument, or situation that changed the way you think about home.

- How did the experience affect you? Write a few paragraphs to explain what you learned about home, family, and yourself.

The Far Side by Gary Larson

"I love the desert."

The Far Side © 1986 FARWORKS INC. All rights reserved.

Family and Community Activity

Home Life Journal Have students write about their home lives in a journal each day for two weeks. Have them imagine that they are writing to give an accurate picture of American home life as it is today for a future generation. Entries should include specific descriptions, dialogue, and events. At the end of two weeks, students should reread their entries and write a paragraph summarizing home life in the 2000s. Students who are reluctant to share details of their home lives should be encouraged to write about their community instead. What sights, sounds, and events are typical of students' neighborhoods?

Additional Resources

Family and Community Activities, p. 20

Theme Projects

Choose one of the projects below to complete as you read the selections in this theme. Work on your own, with a partner, or with a group.

CRITICAL VIEWING

Visions of Home

1. Create a collage to show what home means to you. Search through magazines, photographs, and newspapers for pictures that say "home."
2. Interview other people about their definitions of home. Write down their observations.
3. Paste your pictures and quotations onto poster board. Write a caption under each picture to explain its significance to you. Label each quote with the speaker's name.

MULTIMEDIA PROJECT

Create a Web Page

1. Collect favorite stories from relatives and close friends for a Web page. Use a Web publishing program that will allow you to create and edit text, graphics, and sound.
2. Gather souvenirs, family photographs, and tape recordings of stories. Write introductions, headings, and comments.
3. Follow the directions in the software to complete your page.

interNET CONNECTION

Visit lit.glencoe.com for more about the authors and ideas in this theme.

LEARNING FOR LIFE

Donate Your Time

1. Research homelessness in your community, and collect donations for a local homeless shelter. Try to get specific data, if possible. Ask what types of donations are needed (clothing, blankets, canned goods, household items).
2. Create posters inviting people to bring items to a central location. Use data from your research to create compelling charts or graphs.
3. Have an adult help you deliver the items.
4. Report to the class about your experience.

interNET CONNECTION

Glencoe Literature Web Site

For other ideas related to "No Place Like Home," suggest that students type the keywords *family tree maker* or *history* and the name of your community.

Theme Projects

Teaching Strategies

The following suggestions may help your students plan and carry out their theme projects.

Critical Viewing

- Before students collect items, present a few of yours. Ask students to note common threads in the pictures and objects. What images of home do the items suggest?
- Suggest that students write a few questions to ask, such as *Where do you feel most at home?* or *Have you ever felt homesick?*
- Have students present their collages to the class.

Multimedia Project

- Ask students to think of stories in terms of "sound bites"—brief responses to a question.
- Suggest that students sketch their page layout before logging onto the computer.

Learning For Life

- Before students begin, ask them how people may become homeless. *(Disasters, unemployment, and illnesses can be causes.)*
- The class may want to work together to develop a slogan for the campaign.
- Suggest that students focus their reports on how their experience has affected their attitudes toward homelessness.

Additional Resources

- ***Interdisciplinary Activities,*** pp. 2–5
- ***Viewing and Representing Activities,*** pp. 1–9
- ***Listening and Speaking Activities,*** pp. 1–3
- ***Critical Thinking Skills,*** pp. 2–3
- ***Selection and Theme Assessment,*** pp. 125–126
- ***Performance Assessment,*** p. 64

Before Reading

Objectives

- To read and analyze a short story
- To identify the theme, or central message, in a short story
- To write a paragraph analyzing a literary character

Skills

Reading/Thinking: Identifying Bias; Identifying Author's Purpose; Inferring; Using Text Structures; Problem and Solution
Writing: Personal Letter
Vocabulary: Etymology
Grammar/Language: Punctuating Dialogue; Double Negatives
Collaboration: Literature Groups

Motivating STUDENTS

Literature Launchers: "Playing the Blues"

Videodisc Side A, Segment 1

Also available in VHS.

Selection Focus Transparency 1: Before presenting the quotation, have students discuss what they value most in life.

Reading Focus: As an extension of the Reading Focus, have each student develop a brief oral presentation describing a treasured object and explaining why the object is important. Students should then present their work to a small group using precise language and sensory details.

Before You Read

The Treasure of Lemon Brown

MEET WALTER DEAN MYERS

Walter Dean Myers was ten years old when he started filling up notebooks with his stories and poems. Yet he never expected that his childhood hobby would blossom into a successful career. "I wrote for years without getting published," he remembers. "I never thought about having [anything] published outside of school publications." Myers later discovered that he could make a living at writing when he won a contest for picture book writers. Today he is an award-winning author, recognized especially for young-adult fiction.

Walter Dean Myers was born in 1937. This story was published in Boys' Life *in 1983.*

READING FOCUS

Think of the objects you treasure most. Perhaps they include a letter, a ring, a picture, or a baseball.

Diagram It!
Using a word web like the one below, brainstorm several objects and personal belongings that you value.

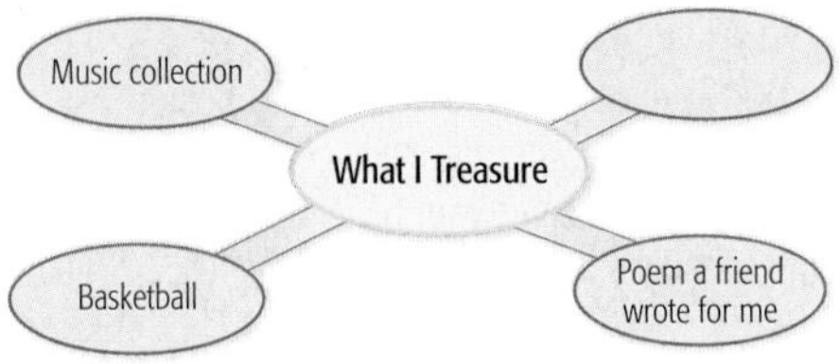

Setting a Purpose
Read to find out how one object can represent a person's life.

BUILDING BACKGROUND

The Time and Place This contemporary story is set in an abandoned Harlem tenement in New York City.

Did You Know? The blues is a type of music that evolved from the experiences of African Americans over the last three centuries. More than just a beat or melody, the blues is a state of mind. The blues express sorrow and hardship.

VOCABULARY PREVIEW

impromptu (im promp′ to͞o) *adj.* made or done on the spur of the moment, without preparation; p. 6
tentatively (ten′ tə tiv lē) *adv.* hesitantly; uncertainly; p. 6
intently (in tent′ lē) *adv.* in a firmly focused way; with concentration; p. 8
involuntary (in vol′ ən ter′ ē) *adj.* not done willingly; p. 8
tremor (trem′ ər) *n.* a shaking or trembling movement; p. 8
commence (kə mens′) *v.* to begin; start; p. 9
eerie (ēr′ ē) *adj.* weird, especially in a frightening way; p. 10
ominous (om′ ə nəs) *adj.* threatening harm or evil; p. 11

RESOURCE MANAGER

Teaching Tools and Resources
- Theme One Planning Guide,
- Literature Groups Sourcebook

Essential Lesson Support

Lesson-Specific Instruction
- Selection Focus Transparency 1
- Literary Elements Transparency 1
- Active Reading Guide,* p. 1
- Selection Vocabulary Practice, p. 7

Assessment
- Selection Quick Checks,* p. 1
- Sel. and Theme Assmt., pp. 1–2

- Testmaker: ExamView Pro
- Performance Assessment, p. 1

Systematic Language Instruction
- Gr. & Comp. Hbk., Lessons 1.1, 1.2
- Vocabulary Power, Lesson 1
- Spelling Power, Lesson 1

English Language Learners
- ELL Sourcebook, p. 17, 18
- Spanish Summaries, p. 1
- Spanish Translations, pp. 1–7
- Audio Library*

- English, Yes!

Spec. Needs/Strat. Interven.
- Interactive Rdg. Sbk., pp. T47–T49
- Interactive Rdg. Wbk., pp. 1–2
- Inclusion Strat. Sbk., pp. 71–72
- Audio Library*

* Also available in Spanish

The Treasure of Lemon Brown

Walter Dean Myers

The dark sky, filled with angry swirling clouds, reflected Greg Ridley's mood as he sat on the stoop[1] of his building. His father's voice came to him again, first reading the letter the principal had sent to the house, then lecturing endlessly about his poor efforts in math. A

B "I had to leave school when I was 13," his father had said, "that's a year younger than you are now. If I'd had half the chances that you have, I'd. . . ."

Greg had sat in the small, pale green kitchen listening, knowing the lecture would end with his father saying he couldn't play ball with the Scorpions. He had asked his father the week before, and his father had said it depended on his next report card. It wasn't often the Scorpions took on new players, especially 14-year-olds, and this was a chance of a lifetime for Greg. He hadn't been allowed to play high school ball, which he had really wanted to do, but playing for the Community Center team was the next best thing.

1. A *stoop* is one or more steps at the entrance of a building that lead up to a raised platform.

Reading the Selection

SUMMARY

Greg Ridley's father has forbidden him to play basketball until his math grades improve. Greg leaves the house and seeks shelter in the "home" of vagrant Lemon Brown, who shares his treasures and memories with Greg. As a result of this encounter, Greg comes to a better understanding of his father's wishes for him.

Spanish Summaries, p. 1

A Active Reading Strategies

PREDICT After students have read the first paragraph, ask them what they think the plot of the story will be.

VOCABULARY If you haven't previewed the selection vocabulary with students, stop and remind them to use context clues to unlock the meanings of new vocabulary words.

Additional Resources

Active Reading Guide, p. 1
Audio Library
Spanish Audio Library

B Literary Elements

FLASHBACK Ask what the shift in verb tenses from the first to the third paragraph indicates. *(Greg's conversation with his father is a flashback.)*

Teaching Support

CONNECTING TO OTHER SELECTIONS

The chart at the right shows three ways to connect "The Treasure of Lemon Brown" to other selections in this book.

For specific teaching strategies, see the ***Theme One Planning Guide,*** pages 9–10.

Connection	Title
Life Skills: Interpersonal Teaching and Mentoring →	from I *Know Why the Caged Bird Sings,* p. 199
Thematic: Understanding Family →	"The Moustache," p. 282
Literary: Dialect →	from *All Things Bright and Beautiful,* p. 103

C Critical Thinking

IDENTIFY BIAS Ask students to describe Greg's problem from his point of view and then from his father's point of view. Explain that since the story is told from Greg's perspective, bias will be present.

D Literary Elements

CHARACTERIZATION Ask students what sort of person they think Greg's father is. Ask whether they like him. *(Most will say that they dislike him because he seems so stern.)*

E Literary Elements

SIMILE Explain to students that a simile compares two unlike things using the words *like* or *as.* Point out the comparison between Greg's father's voice and the "distant thunder" and ask students whether they think using this figure of speech is more effective than simply saying, "He spoke loudly."

F Author's Craft

DESCRIPTION Ask students to list the concrete details the author uses to characterize Greg's street *(the stoop, the abandoned tenement, the boarded-up doors, the graffiti).*

Report cards were due in a week, and Greg had been hoping for the best. But the principal had ended the suspense early when she sent that letter saying Greg would probably fail math if he didn't spend more time studying.

"And you want to play *basketball?*" His father's brows knitted over deep brown eyes. "That must be some kind of a joke. Now you just get into your room and hit those books."

That had been two nights before. His father's words, like the distant thunder that now echoed through the streets of Harlem,[2] still rumbled softly in his ears.

It was beginning to cool. Gusts of wind made bits of paper dance between the parked cars. There was a flash of nearby lightning, and soon large drops of rain splashed onto his jeans. He stood to go upstairs, thought of the lecture that probably awaited him if he did anything except shut himself in his room with his math book, and started walking down the street instead. Down the block there was an old tenement that had been abandoned for some months. Some of the guys had held an impromptu checker tournament there the week before, and Greg had noticed that the door, once boarded over, had been slightly ajar.

Pulling his collar up as high as he could, he checked for traffic and made a dash across the street. He reached the house just as another flash of lightning changed the night to day for an instant, then returned the graffiti-scarred building to the grim shadows. He vaulted[3] over the outer stairs and pushed tentatively on the door. It was open, and he let himself in.

The inside of the building was dark except for the dim light that filtered through the dirty windows from the streetlamps. There was a room a few feet from the door, and from where he stood at the entrance, Greg could see a squarish patch of light on the floor. He entered the room, frowning at the musty[4] smell. It was a large room that might have been someone's parlor at one time. Squinting, Greg could see an old table on its side against one wall, what looked like a pile of rags or a torn mattress in the corner, and a couch, with one side broken, in front of the window.

He went to the couch. The side that wasn't broken was comfortable enough, though a little creaky. From this spot he could see the blinking neon sign over the bodega[5] on the corner. He sat awhile, watching the sign blink first green then red, allowing his mind to drift to the Scorpions, then to his father. His father had been a postal worker for all Greg's life, and was proud of it, often telling Greg how hard he had worked to pass the test. Greg had heard the story too many times to be interested now.

For a moment Greg thought he heard something that sounded like a scraping

2. *Harlem* is a section of Manhattan in New York City inhabited mostly by Puerto Ricans and African Americans.

3. Here, as a verb, *vaulted* means "jumped."
4. A *musty* smell is stale or moldy.
5. The Spanish word *bodega* (bō dā′ gä) can refer to a bar, a restaurant, a shop, or a pantry.

Vocabulary

impromptu (im promp′ to͞o) *adj.* made or done on the spur of the moment, without preparation
tentatively (ten′ tə tiv lē) *adv.* hesitantly; uncertainly

Teaching Support

MEETING INDIVIDUAL NEEDS — ENGLISH LANGUAGE LEARNERS

Verb Tenses and "If" Clauses Write the following sentence on the board: *If I'd had half the chances that you have, I'd . . .* Have students identify the verbs. On page 5, Greg's father uses the past perfect and the conditional when he talks about how his life might have been different. Explain that a sentence beginning with an *if* clause requires a conditional verb.

Activity Pair English speakers with English language learners and have students take turns filling in the following sentence: *If I [   ], I [   ].* Explain that completions show what might happen in the future or might have happened in the past but did not. **COLLAB. LEARN.**

Additional Resources

English Language Learners Sourcebook, pp. 17–18

Jim, 1930. William H. Johnson. Oil on canvas, 21⅝ x 18¼ in. National Museum of American Art, Washington, DC.
Viewing the painting: In what ways might the boy in the painting be similar to Greg?

VIEWING THE PAINTING

William Henry Johnson (1901–1970) was an African American artist whose folk-inspired paintings reflect his humble origins in South Carolina as well as a sophistication acquired in travels from New York to Paris and Scandinavia.

Viewing Response *Like Greg, the boy in the picture seems pensive, serious—perhaps even lonely. Greg enjoys checkers and basketball—simple pursuits. One could hardly imagine him or the boy in the picture involved with rough or tough people or activities.*

interNET CONNECTION

Music Have students search for information about the blues at the Delta Blues Museum online. **L1**

G Literary Elements

SUSPENSE Draw students' attention to the way Myers heightens the suspense with word choice and description as Greg begins to suspect that he's not alone in the building. *(Wind picks up, rain rattles the windowpanes, his stomach tightening, sound of breathing, lightning.)*

H Active Reading Strategies

PREDICT Ask students to predict what will happen to Greg in the meeting with Lemon Brown. Do they think Greg will be harmed?

I Literary Elements

CHARACTERIZATION Discuss the elaborate physical description of Brown. How does Myers use concrete details and descriptive language to help readers visualize Brown as the kind of person who stereotypically would not have a treasure? *(He paints a picture of a homeless, penniless man with such descriptions as "old man," "dirty clothes," "old shoes," and "rags.")*

against the wall. He listened carefully, but it was gone.

Outside the wind had picked up, sending the rain against the window with a force that shook the glass in its frame. A car passed, its tires hissing over the wet street and its red tail lights glowing in the darkness.

Greg thought he heard the noise again. His stomach tightened as he held himself still and listened intently. There weren't any more scraping noises, but he was sure he had heard something in the darkness—something breathing!

He tried to figure out just where the breathing was coming from; he knew it was in the room with him. Slowly he stood, tensing. As he turned, a flash of lightning lit up the room, frightening him with its sudden brilliance. He saw nothing, just the overturned table, the pile of rags and an old newspaper on the floor. Could he have been imagining the sounds? He continued listening, but heard nothing and thought that it might have just been rats. Still, he thought, as soon as the rain let up he would leave. He went to the window and was about to look out when he heard a voice behind him.

"Don't try nothin' 'cause I got a razor here sharp enough to cut a week into nine days!"

Greg, except for an involuntary tremor in his knees, stood stock still. The voice was high and brittle, like dry twigs being broken, surely not one he had ever heard before. There was a shuffling sound as the person who had been speaking moved a step closer. Greg turned, holding his breath, his eyes straining to see in the dark room.

The upper part of the figure before him was still in darkness. The lower half was in the dim rectangle of light that fell unevenly from the window. There were two feet, in cracked, dirty shoes from which rose legs that were wrapped in rags.

"Who are you?" Greg hardly recognized his own voice.

"I'm Lemon Brown," came the answer. "Who're you?"

"Greg Ridley."

"What you doing here?" The figure shuffled forward again, and Greg took a small step backward.

"It's raining," Greg said.

"I can see that," the figure said.

The person who called himself Lemon Brown peered forward, and Greg could see him clearly. He was an old man. His black, heavily wrinkled face was surrounded by a halo of crinkly white hair and whiskers that seemed to separate his head from the layers of dirty coats piled on his smallish frame. His pants were bagged to the knee, where they were met with rags that went down to the old shoes. The rags were held on with strings, and there was a rope around his middle. Greg relaxed. He had seen the man before, picking through the trash on the corner and pulling clothes out of a Salvation Army box. There was no sign of the razor that could "cut a week into nine days."

"What are you doing here?" Greg asked.

"This is where I'm staying," Lemon Brown said. "What you here for?"

Vocabulary

intently (in tent′ lē) *adv.* in a firmly focused way; with concentration
involuntary (in vol′ ən ter′ ē) *adj.* not done willingly
tremor (trem′ ər) *n.* a shaking or trembling movement

Teaching Support

Literature & Humanities

World History and Art
Transparency 33, "The Banjo Lesson" Discuss what else the boy may be learning as he learns to play the banjo.

Meeting Individual Needs: Special Needs

Less-Proficient Readers It is often difficult for less-proficient readers to visualize the information they are reading. For example, if students are struggling with vocabulary or literary devices, they may not comprehend what is happening in the story.

Activity Group less-proficient readers with students with higher reading-skill levels. Have the groups reread page 8 together, focusing on the specific details of Greg's emotions, the setting, and the character of Lemon Brown. Encourage the groups to help each other understand the broader picture. In pairs, the students can then act out a favorite scene. **L1** COLLAB. LEARN.

Additional Resources
Inclusion Strategies

"Told you it was raining out," Greg said, leaning against the back of the couch until he felt it give slightly.

J "Ain't you got no home?"

"I got a home," Greg answered.

"You ain't one of them bad boys looking for my treasure, is you?" Lemon Brown cocked his head to one side and squinted one eye. "Because I told you I got me a razor."

"I'm not looking for your treasure," Greg answered, smiling. "*If* you have one."

K "What you mean, *if* I have one," Lemon Brown said. "Every man got a treasure. You don't know that, you must be a fool!"

"Sure," Greg said as he sat on the sofa and put one leg over the back. "What do you have, gold coins?"

L "Don't worry none about what I got," Lemon Brown said. "You know who I am?"

"You told me your name was orange or lemon or something like that."

"Lemon Brown," the old man said, pulling back his shoulders as he did so, "they used to call me Sweet Lemon Brown."

"Sweet Lemon?" Greg asked.

"Yessir. Sweet Lemon Brown. They used to say I sung the blues so sweet that if I sang at a funeral, the dead would commence to rocking with the beat. Used to travel all over Mississippi and as far as Monroe, Louisiana, and east on over to Macon, Georgia. You mean you ain't never heard of Sweet Lemon Brown?"

"Afraid not," Greg said. "What . . . what happened to you?"

"Hard times, boy. Hard times always after a poor man. One day I got tired, sat down to rest a spell and felt a tap on my shoulder. Hard times caught up with me."

"Sorry about that."

"What you doing here? How come you didn't go home when the rain come. Rain don't bother you young folks none."

"Just didn't," Greg looked away.

"I used to have a knotty-headed boy just like you." Lemon Brown had half walked, half shuffled back to the corner and sat down against the wall. "Had them big eyes like you got. I used to call them moon eyes. Look into them moon eyes and see anything you want."

"How come you gave up singing the blues?" Greg asked.

"Didn't give it up," Lemon Brown said. "You don't give up the blues; they give you up. After a while you do good for yourself, and it ain't nothing but foolishness singing about how hard you got it. Ain't that right?"

"I guess so."

"What's that noise?" Lemon Brown asked, suddenly sitting upright.

Greg listened, and he heard a noise outside. He looked at Lemon Brown and saw the old man was pointing toward the window.

Greg went to the window and saw three men, neighborhood thugs, on the stoop. One was carrying a length of pipe. Greg looked back toward Lemon Brown, who moved quietly across the room to the window. The old man looked out, then beckoned frantically for Greg to follow him. For a moment Greg couldn't move. Then he found himself following Lemon Brown into the hallway and up darkened stairs. Greg followed as closely as he could. They

Vocabulary
commence (kə mens′) *v.* to begin; start

J Active Reading Strategies

QUESTION Ask students why Brown assumes Greg does not have a home. Might it be that he feels only someone with nowhere else to go would come into an abandoned tenement?

K Literary Elements

THEME Point out that Brown's statement "Every man has a treasure" presents an element of the theme of the story. Discuss Greg's assumption that a treasure must have monetary value.

L Active Reading Strategies

QUESTION Ask students why Lemon Brown asks Greg, "You know who I am?" *(To contradict the impression that someone who looks like Brown could not have a treasure or a past worth knowing about.)*

FYI

Thugs The word *thug* comes from a Hindi word that means "thief." British writers introduced the word into English in the nineteenth century.

Language Note

The blues is sorrowful music about hard times. The term *blues* comes from the phrase *blue devils,* a slang reference to the depression that accompanies withdrawal from alcohol addiction.

MEETING INDIVIDUAL NEEDS — MULTIPLE MODES OF EXPRESSION

Linguistic One charming character trait of Lemon Brown is his colorful language. Write this boast on the board: "I sung the blues so sweet that if I sang at a funeral, the dead would commence to rocking with the beat." Show students the basic structure of the brag: I did [what] so [how] that [exaggerated consequence]. Give the following example: *I dance so gracefully that butterflies learn from me.*

Activity Ask students to list some of the things they do well, and have them write some "brags," following Lemon Brown's formula. Have students share some of their brags in small groups.
L2 COLLAB. LEARN.

NO PLACE LIKE HOME 9

M Literary Elements

CHARACTERIZATION Ask students to identify the ways the author provides characterizations of the three thugs. *(The author provides characterizations through Brown's description, through dialogue, and through the narration.)*

N Active Reading Strategies

QUESTION Ask students why they think Brown comes out of hiding and stands at the top of the stairs. *(Some students may think he intends to fight for his treasure. Others may suggest that he intends to protect Greg by diverting the thugs' attention away from the boy.)*

FINE ART TRANSPARENCY 7

You may want to use ***Fine Art Transparency 7*** to spark a discussion of musical instruments and of the mood suggested in the painting.

reached the top of the stairs, and Greg felt Lemon Brown's hand first lying on his shoulder, then probing down his arm until he finally took Greg's hand into his own as they crouched in the darkness.

"They's bad men," Lemon Brown whispered. His breath was warm against Greg's skin.

"Hey! Rag man!" A voice called. "We know you in here. What you got up under them rags? You got any money?"

Silence.

"We don't want to have to come in and hurt you, old man, but we don't mind if we have to."

Lemon Brown squeezed Greg's hand in his own hard, gnarled[6] fist.

There was a banging downstairs and a light as the men entered. They banged around noisily, calling for the rag man.

"We heard you talking about your treasure," the voice was slurred. "We just want to see it, that's all."

"You sure he's here?" One voice seemed to come from the room with the sofa.

"Yeah, he stays here every night."

"There's another room over there; I'm going to take a look. You got that flashlight?"

"Yeah, here, take the pipe too."

Greg opened his mouth to quiet the sound of his breath as he sucked it in uneasily. A beam of light hit the wall a few feet opposite him, then went out.

"Ain't nobody in that room," a voice said. "You think he's gone or something?"

"I don't know," came the answer. "All I know is that I heard him talking about some kind of treasure. You know they found that shopping bag lady with that money in her bags."

"Yeah. You think he's upstairs?"

"HEY, OLD MAN, ARE YOU UP THERE?"

Silence.

"Watch my back, I'm going up."

There was a footstep on the stairs, and the beam from the flashlight danced crazily along the peeling wallpaper. Greg held his breath. There was another step and a loud crashing noise as the man banged the pipe against the wooden banister. Greg could feel his temples throb as the man slowly neared them. Greg thought about the pipe, wondering what he would do when the man reached them—what he *could* do.

Then Lemon Brown released his hand and moved toward the top of the stairs. Greg looked around and saw stairs going up to the next floor. He tried waving to Lemon Brown, hoping the old man would see him in the dim light and follow him to the next floor. Maybe, Greg thought, the man wouldn't follow them up there. Suddenly, though, Lemon Brown stood at the top of the stairs, both arms raised high above his head.

"There he is!" A voice cried from below.

"Throw down your money, old man, so I won't have to bash your head in!"

Lemon Brown didn't move. Greg felt himself near panic. The steps came closer, and still Lemon Brown didn't move. He was an eerie sight, a bundle of rags standing at the top of the stairs, his shadow on

6. Lemon Brown's fist is rough, twisted, and knotted *(gnarled),* like a tree branch. (And, as in most words that start with *gn,* such as *gnaw,* the *g* is silent.)

Vocabulary
eerie (ēr′ ē) *adj.* weird, especially in a frightening way

Teaching Support

interNET CONNECTION

Have students search the Internet for instructions on how to play the harmonica. The students should teach themselves the basics, then prepare a lesson for the class, demonstrating what they've learned. Their presentation should concentrate on a sequence of activities that will help the class learn to play the harmonica.

Reading Minilesson

Author's Purpose Mention that authors usually identify who is speaking when they write dialogue. Note, however, that Myers does not identify the three thugs when they speak. Ask students to discuss possible reasons Myers doesn't clearly identify the speakers. Explain that Myers is probably trying to put the reader in Greg's shoes: he can't see the thugs—he can only hear their voices.

Activity Ask students to work in pairs to rewrite the thugs' dialogue, adding *the first thug said, the second thug mumbled,* and so on. What effect does this have on the passage? Students may note that the rewritten passage is slower and less menacing than the original. **L2** **COLLAB. LEARN.**

Additional Resources

Reading Skills Practice Workbook

Jazz Messenger III, 1994. Gil Mayers. Mixed media, 16 x 10 in. Private collection.

Viewing the painting: How do you think the painting might reflect Lemon Brown's experiences as a blues musician?

the wall looming over him. Maybe, the thought came to Greg, the scene could be even eerier.

Greg wet his lips, put his hands to his mouth and tried to make a sound. Nothing came out. He swallowed hard, wet his lips once more and howled as evenly as he could.

"What's that?"

As Greg howled, the light moved away from Lemon Brown, but not before Greg saw him hurl his body down the stairs at the men who had come to take his treasure. There was a crashing noise, and then footsteps. A rush of warm air came in as the downstairs door opened, then there was only an ominous silence.

Greg stood on the landing. He listened, and after a while there was another sound on the staircase.

"Mr. Brown?" he called.

"Yeah, it's me," came the answer. "I got their flashlight."

Greg exhaled in relief as Lemon Brown made his way slowly back up the stairs.

"You O.K.?"

"Few bumps and bruises," Lemon Brown said.

"I think I'd better be going," Greg said, his breath returning to normal. "You'd better leave, too, before they come back."

"They may hang around outside for a while," Lemon Brown said, "but they ain't getting their nerve up to come in here again. Not with crazy old rag men and howling spooks. Best you stay awhile till

Vocabulary

ominous (om′ ə nəs) *adj.* threatening harm or evil

VIEWING THE PAINTING

Viewing Response *The flames coming out of the saxophone suggest music that's "hot." The contrast of light and dark gives the impression that jazz expresses intense emotions. The shapes are strong and colorful, suggesting a bold and powerful sound. All of these may be a reflection of Lemon Brown's experience as a musician. He seems just the kind of intense, expressive person to fit into the group in the painting.*

O Literary Elements

CHARACTERIZATION Discuss how the encounter with the thugs changes the relationship between Lemon Brown and Greg Ridley. Ask students whether they have had an experience in which they developed a friendship, with a stranger or someone they disliked, while facing an "enemy." *(Such changes often occur in team sports.)*

INTERDISCIPLINARY CONNECTION

"Visual" Music Point out that the painting on page 11 is an attempt to portray sound visually. Explain to students that different forms of art often overlap and connect.

Activity Present a piece of music to the class, preferably one that expresses intense emotion through volume and tempo changes. Divide students into groups and have them discuss what colors and shapes come to mind when they hear the music. Then have them construct drawings that capture the feeling of the music. Ask groups to present their drawings to the rest of the class. **L3**

COLLAB. LEARN.

P Literary Elements

PERSONIFICATION Explain to students that by saying "Mr. Pain," Brown attributes a human quality to an abstract feeling. By using personification, an author can make nonhuman things "come to life" for readers.

Q Literary Elements

THEME Ask students what Brown means when he says, "If you know your pappy did something, you know you can do something too." *(To Brown, his treasure is his message to his son about his hopes and his son's potential. Relate this to the theme of a treasure's sentimental value being more important than its monetary value.)*

R Active Reading Strategies

QUESTION Ask students why they think Greg doesn't understand what Lemon means when he says he didn't perform as well "without somebody to make it worth the while." *(Greg at this point doesn't really appreciate that hard work and the benefits received from it are a father's gift of love to his child.)*

S Literary Elements

THEME Ask students to articulate exactly what Brown treasures, supporting their ideas with details from the text. *(What is important to him is his son's appreciation for how hard Brown worked. The fact that Jesse carried Brown's gift into battle shows that he valued what his father had done for him.)*

Teaching Support

O the coast is clear. I'm heading out West tomorrow, out to east St. Louis."

"They were talking about treasures," Greg said. "You *really* have a treasure?"

"What I tell you? Didn't I tell you every man got a treasure?" Lemon Brown said. "You want to see mine?"

"If you want to show it to me," Greg shrugged.

"Let's look out the window first, see what them scoundrels be doing," Lemon Brown said.

They followed the oval beam of the flashlight into one of the rooms and looked out the window. They saw the men who had tried to take the treasure sitting on the curb near the corner. One of them had his pants leg up, looking at his knee.

"You sure you're not hurt?" Greg asked Lemon Brown.

P "Nothing that ain't been hurt before," Lemon Brown said. When you get as old as me all you say when something hurts is, 'Howdy, Mr. Pain, sees you back again.' Then when Mr. Pain see he can't worry you none, he go on mess with somebody else."

Greg smiled.

"Here, you hold this." Lemon Brown gave Greg the flashlight.

He sat on the floor near Greg and carefully untied the strings that held the rags on his right leg. When he took the rags away, Greg saw a piece of plastic. The old man carefully took off the plastic and unfolded it. He revealed some yellowed newspaper clippings and a battered harmonica.

"There it be," he said, nodding his head. "There it be."

Greg looked at the old man, saw the distant look in his eye, then turned to the clippings. They told of Sweet Lemon Brown, a blues singer and harmonica player who was appearing at different theaters in the South. One of the clippings said he had been the hit of the show, although not the headliner. All of the clippings were reviews of shows Lemon Brown had been in more than 50 years ago. Greg looked at the harmonica. It was dented badly on one side, with the reed holes on one end nearly closed.

"I used to travel around and make money for to feed my wife and Jesse—that's my boy's name. Used to feed them good, too. Then his mama died, and he stayed with his mama's sister. He growed up to be a man, and when the war come he saw fit to go off and fight in it. I didn't have nothing to give him except these things that told him who I was, and what he come from. If you know your pappy did something, you know you can do something too. Q

"Anyway, he went off to war, and I went off still playing and singing. 'Course by then I wasn't as much as I used to be, not without somebody to make it worth the while. You know what I mean?" R

"Yeah," Greg nodded, not quite really knowing.

"I traveled around, and one time I come home, and there was this letter saying Jesse got killed in the war. Broke my heart, it truly did.

"They sent back what he had with him over there, and what it was is this old mouth fiddle and these clippings. Him carrying it around with him like that told me it meant something to him. That was my treasure, and when I give it to him he treated it just like that, a treasure. Ain't that something?" S

"Yeah, I guess so," Greg said.

"You *guess* so?" Lemon Brown's voice rose an octave as he started to put his

Grammar and Language *Minilesson*

Double Negatives Write the following sentence from the story on the board: "I didn't have nothing to give him except these things. . . ." Explain to students that this sentence is grammatically incorrect. It contains a double negative, *didn't* and *nothing;* one negative cancels out, or "negates" the other. Also tell students that authors often use nonstandard English to make characters seem like those in real life.

Activity Write the following sentences on the board and have volunteers suggest corrections:

1. I didn't never go there.
2. I haven't got none.
3. I have never been to no place like that.

(Possible answers: I didn't go there. I haven't got any. I have never been to any place like that.) **L2**

Additional Resources

- ***Grammar and Language Transparency 1***
- ***Grammar and Language Workbook,*** p. 135
- ***Grammar and Composition Handbook,*** Lesson 6.5
- ***Writer's Choice,*** Lesson 12.8

treasure back into the plastic. "Well, you got to guess 'cause you sure don't know nothing. Don't know enough to get home when it's raining."

"I guess . . . I mean, you're right."

"You O.K. for a youngster," the old man said as he tied the strings around his leg, "better than those scalawags what come here looking for my treasure. That's for sure."

"You really think that treasure of yours was worth fighting for?" Greg asked. "Against a pipe?"

"What else a man got 'cepting what he can pass on to his son, or his daughter, if she be his oldest?" Lemon Brown said. "For a big-headed boy you sure do ask the foolishest questions."

Lemon Brown got up after patting his rags in place and looked out the window again.

"Looks like they're gone. You get on out of here and get yourself home. I'll be watching from the window so you'll be all right."

Lemon Brown went down the stairs behind Greg. When they reached the front door the old man looked out first, saw the street was clear and told Greg to scoot on home.

"You sure you'll be O.K.?" Greg asked.

"Now didn't I tell you I was going to east St. Louis in the morning?" Lemon Brown asked. "Don't that sound O.K. to you."

"Sure it does," Greg said. "Sure it does. And you take care of that treasure of yours."

"That I'll do," Lemon said, the wrinkles about his eyes suggesting a smile. "That I'll do."

The night had warmed and the rain had stopped, leaving puddles at the curbs. Greg didn't even want to think how late it was. He thought ahead of what his father would say and wondered if he should tell him about Lemon Brown. He thought about it until he reached his stoop, and decided against it. Lemon Brown would be O.K., Greg thought, with his memories and his treasure.

Greg pushed the button over the bell marked Ridley, thought of the lecture he knew his father would give him, and smiled.

T Literary Elements

THEME Help the students see that Brown's real treasure was what he could give to his child. Explain to students that each person has a different thing he or she treasures.

U Literary Elements

SETTING Ask students to analyze how the weather at the beginning and end of the story reflects Greg's mood. Point out that authors can use setting to enhance the overall atmosphere, or feeling, of a story.

V Critical Thinking

INFER Greg thinks he knows how his father will react to his late arrival. Ask students to infer how Greg will respond to his father's lecture. Share the following model to demonstrate the process involved in inferring:

Model: I noticed that in the past, Greg has not shown much interest in his father's lectures. Now he smiles at the thought of one. I think he smiles because he understands why his father is lecturing. I think he will probably pay more respectful attention.

Thematic Focus

No Place Like Home Ask students whether they think home has become a treasure to Greg. Have students support their answers with references to the selection.

ASSESSMENT

Quick Checks, p. 1

Real-World Connection

Music Reviews Provide students with magazines and newspapers that contain reviews of contemporary jazz or blues musicians. Ask each student to choose one review and then to listen to some of that artist's music (CDs and tapes are available at most public libraries). Have students discuss, in small groups, whether they agree with the reviewer's opinion. **L2** COLLAB. LEARN.

interNET CONNECTION

Students can build their own music libraries by ordering CDs through a music club. Encourage students to access the Web sites of two or more music clubs, such as Columbia House or BMG. Have students study and compare the service contracts from each club to see which one they would rather join.

Responding to the Selection

PERSONAL RESPONSE

There is no one perfect ending to the story, but those students who agree with Lemon Brown's message will most likely find the ending satisfying.

Analyzing Literature

1. Greg is upset because his father won't let him play basketball.
2. Lemon Brown stopped singing the blues because he was comfortable and had no troubles to sing about.
3. Lemon's treasure is a collection of newspaper clippings and an old harmonica.
4. Greg knows that Lemon will be all right. Also, Greg doesn't want his father to know where he has been.
5. Answers should include specific examples from the story.
6. Lemon's life in recent years has had its share of troubles; his wife and his son have died, his career is over, and he has nowhere to live.
7. The treasure recalls the best times of his life and his professional success.
8. Some students may note that Lemon seems to be a survivor. His optimistic spirit and wisdom should carry him through.
9. To Lemon's son the treasure may symbolize his father's love; to Lemon it may symbolize both happier times and his son's love and respect for him; to Greg it may symbolize the importance of father-son relationships.
10. Some students may argue that they have important treasures, such as memories, that remain valuable whether passed on or not.

Responding to Literature

PERSONAL RESPONSE

- Are you satisfied with the ending of the story? Why or why not? What other ending can you imagine?

Brackets connect questions that are paired to develop higher-level thinking skills.

Analyzing Literature

RECALL

1. Why is Greg upset at the beginning of the story?
2. Why did Lemon Brown stop singing the blues?
3. What does Lemon keep as his treasure?
4. Why doesn't Greg tell his father about Lemon?

INTERPRET

5. People "sing the blues" when they suffer difficult or sorrowful times. In your opinion, does Greg have a good reason to sing the blues? Support your answer with examples from the story.
6. In your opinion, does Lemon have good reason to sing the blues over his life? Explain.
7. How does the treasure reflect Lemon's life?
8. In your opinion, will Lemon be okay after Greg leaves him? Why or why not?

EVALUATE AND CONNECT

9. Lemon's treasure is a **symbol** in this story. It stands for things that have value beyond their physical attributes. What might the treasure symbolize to Lemon's son? to Lemon? to Greg?
10. Theme Connection When speaking of his treasure, Lemon says, "What else a man got 'cepting what he can pass on to his son, or his daughter, if she be his oldest?" Do you agree with this statement? Why or why not? Give examples to explain your position.

LITERARY ELEMENTS

Theme

The **theme** of a story is its central message. To find the theme you might ask, "What message is the author trying to tell the readers?" Sometimes a theme is stated directly by the narrator or by a character. Sometimes, however, the reader must figure it out by examining the characters, the plot, and literary devices such as symbolism and mood.

1. What, do you think, is the theme in "The Treasure of Lemon Brown"?
2. In your opinion, does the theme of this story apply to most people? Explain.

• See **Literary Terms Handbook,** p. R10.

LITERARY ELEMENTS

1. *Theme:* Every person has a treasure, and parents' hopes and expectations for, and pride in, their children are a kind of treasure.
2. Many students will agree that most people have something that is precious to them, if only memories of happy times.

Additional Resources

Literary Elements Transparency 1

Literature and Writing

Writing About Literature

Character Analysis When Greg questions whether Lemon really has a treasure, Lemon suggests that Greg might be a fool. Another time he tells Greg "you sure don't know nothing." Why might Lemon say this about Greg? What does Greg say or do that suggests Lemon might be right? In a paragraph, explain why you agree or disagree with Lemon.

Personal Writing

Family Treasure If you had to choose three possessions to pass on to a family member, what would they be? Look back over the items you brainstormed for the **Reading Focus** on page 4. Choose three items you value most. Then write a brief letter to the person who would inherit your three possessions and explain why you are passing them on.

Extending Your Response

Literature Groups

Draw the Mood The setting of a story influences the **mood,** or general feeling, of a selection. Work in a small group to explore the mood and **setting** of "The Treasure of Lemon Brown." One group member can read aloud the description of the first room Greg enters in the tenement, while every other member listens and draws a picture of the room. After the exercise, compare the pictures. Discuss how the atmosphere in each picture influences your feelings about what takes place in the story.

Learning for Life

Reach a Consensus Greg asks Lemon Brown, "You really think that treasure of yours was worth fighting for?" How would you answer this question? Think about what the treasure *is* and what it *symbolizes.* As a group, list the reasons why Lemon should defend his treasure. Then list the reasons why he shouldn't. Discuss the pros and cons, then come to a group consensus. Present your group's opinion to the class.

Interdisciplinary Activity

Music Create a musical presentation of a blues performer for your class. You might play audiotapes, show videotapes, or play an instrument yourself. Include a brief report describing the performer's career and contribution to the blues. Use the World Wide Web, the library, interviews, and other research sources.

The Jazz Singer, 1916. Charles Demuth. Pencil and watercolor, 12¾ x 7¾ in. Private collection.

Reading Further

For other stories of people who need a home and security, read:

Adam of the Road by Elizabeth Janet Gray

Amistad by Walter Dean Myers

Save your work for your portfolio.

Literature and Writing

Writing About Literature

Students' paragraphs should

- clearly state their opinions about Greg's character
- use specific examples from the text to support their opinions

Personal Writing

Students' letters should

- describe the treasures
- explain why the recipient has been chosen to receive the treasures
- take the form of personal correspondence

Extending Your Response

Literature Groups Remind students to focus on the *atmosphere* of the room they sketch. The specific details (the bareness and shabbiness of the "furnishings") should reinforce the mood. **COLLAB. LEARN.**

Learning for Life Explain that consensus is achieved only through open discussion in which everyone's point of view is heard. **COLLAB. LEARN.**

Interdisciplinary Activity Encourage students to be creative in their presentations and to use a variety of media if available.

Teaching Support

MEETING INDIVIDUAL NEEDS: MULTIPLE MODES OF EXPRESSION

Less-Proficient Readers Explain to students that every word has a history, called its etymology. Knowing something about the history of a word can help less-proficient readers better understand how the word is used today. Invite students to read the section on etymology in their dictionary. Then examine a few dictionary entries with students and help them to read the etymological information in each entry.

Activity Ask students to research the word origins of five of the following words: *involuntary, tremor, commence, ominous, gnarled,* and *treasure.* Encourage them to share interesting or surprising facts with the class. **L2**

NO PLACE LIKE HOME 15

Skill Minilessons

GRAMMAR AND LANGUAGE
PUNCTUATING DIALOGUE

1. "Do you read a lot?" I asked the boy sitting next to me on the bus.
2. "I read books about basketball," he said.
3. "Have you read any stories by Walter Dean Myers?" I asked him.
4. Correct
5. Correct

READING AND THINKING
PROBLEM AND SOLUTION

1. His father won't let him play basketball because of his grades.
2. Lemon Brown helps Greg see that his father's "treasure" is his hope that his son will succeed.
3. Greg decides to go home and listen to his father's lecture. He may study math to show that he cares about his father's treasure.

VOCABULARY
ETYMOLOGY

1. When something is tentative, someone tries it hesitantly to see whether it will work.
2. An intent is a goal or an aim.
3. Something eerie makes a person feel timid.

Additional Resources

- ***Grammar and Language Workbook,*** p. 267
- ***Grammar and Composition Handbook,*** Lesson 13.6
- ***Writer's Choice,*** Lesson 20.6
- ***Reading Skills Practice Workbook***
- ***Vocabulary Practice,*** p. 1

RETEACH • REVIEW

Skill Minilessons

GRAMMAR AND LANGUAGE • PUNCTUATING DIALOGUE

Good writers follow these punctuation rules to make quotations and dialogue clear for readers:

- Quotation marks are used before and after the exact words of a speaker.
- A comma sets off the parts of a sentence that come before, between, or after a direct quotation. A comma at the end of a quotation goes inside the quotation marks.
- If a quotation ends with a question mark or an exclamation point, no comma is needed.

"What you mean, if I have one," Lemon Brown said. "Every man got a treasure. You don't know that, you must be a fool!"

PRACTICE Correct mistakes in the use of quotation marks and commas. Write *correct* if a sentence does not contain errors.

1. "Do you read a lot? I asked the boy sitting next to me on the bus.
2. "I read books about basketball", he said.
3. "Have you read any stories by Walter Dean Myers?," I asked him.
4. "Sure," he said, "and I liked them a lot."
5. I agreed. "I like his stories, too."

● For more about punctuating dialogue, see **Language Handbook,** pp. R40–R41.

READING AND THINKING • TEXT STRUCTURES

Writers structure their text in many different ways. One structure you may find when you read is problem/solution. In "The Treasure of Lemon Brown," Greg helped Lemon Brown solve a problem when he howled and scared away the thieves who wanted the old man's treasure.

● For more about text structures, see **Reading Handbook,** p. R97.

PRACTICE Answer these questions about another problem and solution in "The Treasure of Lemon Brown."

1. What problem does Greg have at the beginning of the story?
2. How does Lemon Brown help Greg look at this problem in a different way?
3. What solution does Greg come to at the end of the story?

VOCABULARY • ETYMOLOGY

Etymology is the study of word origins. Many English words come from other languages. For example, the word *impromptu* comes from a Latin phrase that means "ready now." An *impromptu* reply, party, or speech is one that isn't prepared ahead of time. The origins of some words, such as *impromptu,* are very clearly related to their present-day meaning. For other words, a little imagination is needed to make the connection.

PRACTICE Each word below appeared in the story "The Treasure of Lemon Brown." Explain how the origin of each word is tied to its present-day meaning.

1. tentative: from the Latin word *tentare,* meaning "to try."
2. intent: from the Latin word *intendere,* meaning "to aim at."
3. eerie: from the Old English word *earg,* meaning "timid."

ASSESSMENT

- ***Quick Checks,*** p. 1
- ***Selection and Theme Assessment,*** pp. 1–2
- ***Performance Assessment,*** p. 1
- ***Testmaker ExamView Pro***
- ***Interactive Tutor: Self-Assessment***

16 THEME 1

Interdisciplinary Connection

music

Discovering the Blues

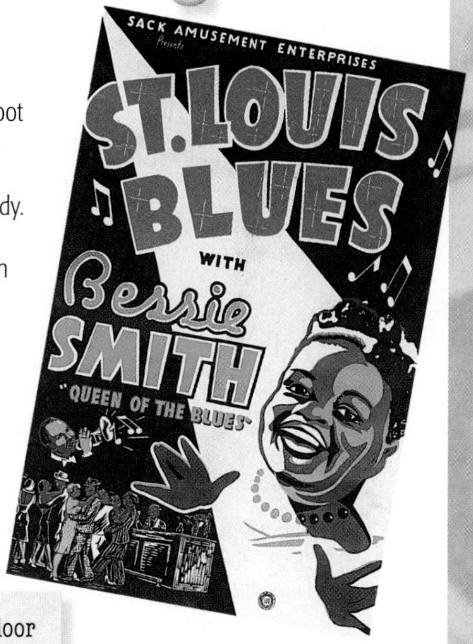

Listen to a blues song, and you're likely to tap a hand or foot to the music before you hum a tune. That's because blues music, which swept the southern United States in the late 1800s and early 1900s, focuses on rhythm instead of melody. Rhythm is a steady beat—a regular pattern of notes that is usually emphasized by drums or stringed instruments, such as guitars. The driving rhythm you hear in jazz and rock songs is borrowed from blues music.

The Origin of Blues Blues music grew out of the "field hollers" that enslaved people used to call out while they labored in the fields. One worker would sing out a call, and the other workers would echo it. Blues musician Bessie Smith used the call-and-response form in these lines from her song "Back Water Blues":

> I woke up this mornin', can't even get out of my door
> I woke up this mornin', can't even get out of my door
> There's enough trouble to make a poor girl wonder
> where she wanna go.

The verse shown above is an example of the twelve-bar blues, a type of rhythm developed by Bessie Smith and other blues musicians. The verse has three lines of music. Each line is divided into four bars—groups of musical notes, rests, and lyrics. A song can have several verses, but each verse must follow the same rhythm.

Experiment With one hand, tap a steady rhythm of four beats. You've just counted out a bar, or measure, in 4/4 time, using four quarter notes. Just as in math, 4/4 can equal many combinations of fractions. So, for variety, a musician will fill a bar with combinations of fast notes, slow notes, and rests. Tap out your four-beat rhythm again, but substitute two quick notes (eighth notes) for one of the quarter notes.

ACTIVITY

Listen to a few blues recordings. Then write two or three verses for a blues song of your own, using the three-line call-and-response form. Work out a rhythm to accompany your lyrics. Recite the lyrics or sing the song to the class.

Interdisciplinary Connection

Objective

- To understand the origin of blues music and to learn the characteristic sounds and rhythms of the blues

Teaching Strategies

Contrast music that is particularly melodic (perhaps a piece from Grieg's *Peer Gynt Suite* or Saint-Saëns's *Carnival of the Animals)* with some blues to ensure that students can tell the difference between music that focuses on melody and music that focuses on rhythm.

Activity

Choose several blues songs to play for students. You may want to have students work in pairs as they compose songs. One student can be responsible for the rhythm and the other for the lyrics. After they have had time to rehearse, have students perform their blues songs.

Teaching Support

MEETING INDIVIDUAL NEEDS — MULTIPLE MODES OF EXPRESSION

Musical Students who are musically inclined may be particularly sensitive to the fact that music is often the cement that binds generations, as well as the wedge that separates one generation from another. People of about the same age tend to like the same music; and one of the most certain signs of aging is that a person begins to dislike the popular music of the day.

Activity Ask students to form small groups to discuss why music is such a powerful force in defining various generations. Which styles of music do they associate with which generations? How does liking the same music bring people together? How does music create difficulties between members of different generations? Are there kinds of music that transcend generational differences? **L2**

Before Reading

Objectives

- To read and analyze a personal essay about a girl who comes to see her father in a new light when she learns about her heritage
- To identify major and minor characters and their roles in the development of a story
- To write a personal letter comparing and contrasting American and Korean cultures

Skills

Reading/Thinking: Summarizing; Evaluating
Writing: Personal Letter
Vocabulary: Analogies
Grammar/Language: Adjective Clauses
Life Skills: Planning a Trip
Collaboration: Literature Groups

Motivating STUDENTS

Selection Focus Transparency 2: Before presenting the quotation, ask students to name something they like about the United States.

Reading Focus: As an extension of the Reading Focus, have students discuss aspects of American culture with which a foreigner would be unfamiliar, such as celebrating Thanksgiving.

Before You Read

My Two Dads

MEET MARIE G. LEE

Marie G. Lee says that writing a book is a lot like maintaining a friendship: "It requires perseverance, it can have its ugly patches, but it is always ultimately fulfilling and worthwhile." Lee, who has written several books for young people, published her first essay in *Seventeen* magazine when she was sixteen years old. Besides writing, Lee enjoys in-line skating, skiing, and tae kwon do.

Marie G. Lee grew up in Minnesota and now lives in New York City. This essay was first published in 1989.

READING FOCUS

How is your family's heritage evident? Is it difficult to maintain one's culture?

Round-robin
In a group, take turns describing a way in which each of you carries on your own culture.

Setting a Purpose
Read this selection to see how the author comes to understand her father and his culture.

BUILDING BACKGROUND

The Time and Place A young Korean American woman joins her family as they visit her parents' birthplace–Korea.

Did You Know? North Korea is governed by a communist regime. South Korea, on the other hand, has a representative form of government. For three years in the 1950s, the two sides fought for control of the country, with the United States sending economic and military aid to South Korea. The war ended in a truce.

VOCABULARY PREVIEW

indifference (in dif′ ər əns) *n.* a lack of feeling, concern, or care; p. 20
smug (smug) *adj.* overly pleased with oneself; too self-satisfied; p. 20
simultaneously (sī′ məl tā′ nē əs lē) *adv.* at the same time; p. 20
blithely (blīth′ lē) *adv.* in a lighthearted way; cheerfully; p. 20
brazenly (brā′ zən lē) *adv.* in a boldly rude manner; p. 21
joviality (jō′ vē al′ ə tē) *n.* hearty, good-natured humor; p. 21
subsequently (sub′ sə kwənt lē) *adv.* at a later time; p. 21
aggression (ə gresh′ ən) *n.* the habit or practice of launching attacks; p. 21
discern (di surn′) *v.* to detect or recognize; identify; p. 21

RESOURCE MANAGER

Teaching Tools and Resources
- Theme One Planning Guide
- Literature Groups Sourcebook

Essential Lesson Support

Lesson-Specific Instruction
- Selection Focus Transparency 2
- Literary Elements Transparency 2
- Active Reading Guide,* p. 2
- Selection Vocabulary Practice, p. 8

Assessment
- Selection Quick Checks,* p. 2
- Sel. and Theme Assmt., pp. 3–4
- Testmaker: ExamView Pro
- Performance Assessment, p. 2

Systematic Language Instruction
- Gr. & Comp. Hbk., Lessons 1.3, 1.4
- Vocabulary Power, Lesson 2

English Language Learners
- ELL Sourcebook, p. 19
- Spanish Summaries, p. 2
- Spanish Translations, pp. 8–10
- Audio Library*
- English, Yes!

Spec. Needs/Strat. Interven.
- Interactive Rdg. Sbk., pp. T49–T51
- Interactive Rdg. Wbk., pp. 3–4
- Inclusion Strat. Sbk., pp. 5–6
- Audio Library*

* Also available in Spanish

두명의 내 아빠

My Two Dads

Marie G. Lee

I am a first-generation Korean-American. On my first trip to Korea at age twenty-six, I found that I had two fathers. One was the Dad I'd always known, but the second was a Korean father I'd never seen before—one surprising and familiar at the same time, like my homeland. A

I was born and raised in the Midwest, and to me, my Dad was like anyone else's. He taught my brothers to play baseball, fixed the garage door, and pushed the snowblower on chilly February mornings. If there was anything different about him, to my child's eyes, it was that he was a doctor.

Growing up, my siblings[1] and I rarely came into contact with our Korean heritage. Mom and Dad spoke Korean only when they didn't want us to know what they were saying. We didn't observe Korean customs, except for not wearing shoes in the house, which I always assumed was plain common sense. I'd once seen a photograph of Dad in a traditional Korean costume, and I remember thinking how odd those clothes made him look.

1. *Siblings* are brothers and sisters.

Reading the Selection

SUMMARY

Author Marie G. Lee writes about how a trip to Korea changed her perception of her father and her cultural heritage. Lee is a first-generation Korean American, who has been brought up in a typically American environment with little exposure to her Korean heritage. When the family takes a vacation to Korea, Lee begins to see a different side of her father, as she learns more about her heritage.

Spanish Summaries, p. 2

A Active Reading Strategies

QUESTION Ask students whether they find it strange that the narrator was twenty-six years old the first time she visited Korea.

VOCABULARY If you haven't pre-viewed the selection vocabulary with students, stop and remind them to use context clues to unlock the meanings of new vocabulary words.

Additional Resources

Active Reading Guide, p. 2
Audio Library
Spanish Audio Library

Teaching Support

CONNECTING TO OTHER SELECTIONS

The chart at the right shows three other ways to connect "My Two Dads" to selections in this book.

For specific teaching strategies, see the ***Theme One Planning Guide,*** pages 17–18.

Connection		Title
Life Skills: Lifelong Learning	→	"The Wise Old Woman," p. 259
Thematic: Discoveries	→	"A Mother in Mannville," p. 185
Literary: Memoir	→	from *Anne Frank: The Diary of a Young Girl,* p. 675

NO PLACE LIKE HOME 19

B Active Reading Strategies

EVALUATE Ask students to evaluate the examples Lee chooses to show that she "forgot" she was Korean. *(She mentions food, friends, and politics.)* Ask students how effective they think these examples are in showing that Lee is more American than Korean. Make sure students give explanations for their opinions.

C Active Reading Strategies

QUESTION Ask students why they think Lee feels "smug" about the prospect of learning Korean. *(Evidently, she expects her skill in learning languages closely related to English to transfer automatically into skill in learning a non-Western language.)*

D Literary Elements

CHARACTER Explain to students that even though the title of the essay indicates that Lee's father is the main character, Lee as the narrator takes that role. Ask students to describe Lee's character on the basis of the first two pages of the essay. *(She is interested in American politics and is good at languages. She seems intelligent, friendly, and popular. Perhaps she is even a little impatient, because she wishes she could breeze through customs as quickly as the flight attendants do.)*

Teaching Support

With my parents' tacit[2] encouragement, I "forgot" that I was Korean. I loved pizza and macaroni and cheese, but I had never so much as touched a slice of kimchi.[3] All my friends, including my boyfriend, were Caucasian.[4] And while I could explain in detail everything I thought was wrong with Ronald Reagan's policies, I had to strain to remember the name of Korea's president.

Attempting to learn the Korean language, *hangukmal*,[5] a few years ago was a first step in atoning[6] for my past indifference. I went into it feeling smug because of my fluency in French and German, but learning Korean knocked me for a loop. This was a language shaped by Confucian rules of reverence,[7] where the speaker states her position (humble, equal, superior) in relation to the person she is addressing. Simultaneously humbling myself and revering the person with whom I was speaking seemed like a painful game of verbal Twister. To further complicate the process, I found there are myriad[8] titles of reverence, starting with the highest, *sansengnim*, which loosely means "teacher/doctor," down to the ultra-specific, such as *waysukmo*,[9] "wife of mother's brother."

Armed, then, with a year's worth of extension-school classes, a list of polite phrases and titles, and a Berlitz tape in my Walkman, I was as ready as I'd ever be to travel with my family to Korea last year.

When we arrived at Kimpo Airport in Seoul, smiling relatives funneled us into the customs line for *wayguksalam*, "foreigners." I was almost jealous watching our Korean flight attendants breeze through the line for *hanguksalam*,[10] "Korean nationals." With whom did I identify more—the flight attendants or the retired white couple behind us, with their Bermuda shorts and Midwestern accents? My American passport stamped me as an alien in a land where everyone looked like me.

I got my first glimpse of my second father when we began trying to hail cabs in downtown Seoul. Because the government enforces low taxi fares, the drivers have developed their own system of picking up only individual passengers, then packing more in, to increase the per-trip profit. The streets are clogged not only with traffic but also with desperately gesticulating pedestrians and empty taxis.

Even my mother was stymied[11] by the cab-hailing competition. When Mom and I traveled alone, cabs zoomed blithely

2. *Tacit* means "understood without words or speech."
3. *Kimchi* is a Korean food made from pickled vegetables.
4. *Caucasian* refers to the group of people who make up what is loosely known as the white race.
5. *hangukmal* (hän gook mäl)
6. *Atoning* is making up for (something).
7. *Confucian* refers to Confucius (kən fū′ shəs), a Chinese teacher who taught that one could maintain peace, harmony, and justice by following certain rules of behavior. *Reverence* (rev′ ər əns) means "deep honor and affection."
8. *Myriad* means "a great number of."
9. *sansengnim* (sun sông nēm); *waysukmo* (wā sook mō)
10. *wayguksalam* (wā gook sə läm); *hanguksalam* (hän gook sə läm)
11. To be *stymied* is to be defeated or blocked.

Vocabulary

indifference (in dif′ ər əns) *n.* a lack of feeling, concern, or care
smug (smug) *adj.* overly pleased with oneself; too self-satisfied
simultaneously (sī′ məl tā′ nē əs lē) *adv.* at the same time
blithely (blīth′ lē) *adv.* in a lighthearted way; cheerfully

20 THEME 1

MEETING INDIVIDUAL NEEDS — ENGLISH LANGUAGE LEARNERS

Cultural Identities Ask English language learners to relate the story of a family member to the class. Have they observed a difference in the family member when among people of his or her own culture? How would students describe these differences? What do they think might be the reasons for these changes?

Activity Encourage students to have family members compare how they feel when they communicate with people from their own culture with when they talk to English-speaking people. Also ask students to use well-chosen details to relate how they feel in these situations.

Additional Resources

English Language Learners Sourcebook, p. 19

past us. When we finally got one, the driver would shut off his meter, brazenly charge us triple the usual fare and ignominiously[12] dump us somewhere not very close to our destination.

But traveling with Dad was different. He would somehow stop a taxi with ease, chitchat with the driver (using very polite language), then shovel us all in. Not only would the cabbie take us where we wanted to go, but some of the usually taciturn drivers would turn into garrulous[13] philosophers.

I began to perceive[14] the transformation of my father from American dad to functioning urban Korean. When we met with relatives, I noticed how Dad's conversational Korean moved easily between the respect he gave his older sister to the joviality with which he addressed Mom's younger cousin. My brother Len and I and our Korean cousins, however, stared shyly and mutely at each other.

Keeping company with relatives eased my disorientation, but not my alienation. Korea is the world's most racially and culturally homogeneous country,[15] and although I was of the right race, I felt culturally shut out. It seemed to me that Koreans were pushy, even in church. When they ate, they slurped and inhaled their food so violently that at least once during every meal, someone would have a sputtering fit of coughing.

Watching my father "turn Korean" helped me as I tried to embrace the culture. Drinking *soju*[16] in a restaurant in the somewhat seedy Namdaemun area, he suddenly lit into a story of the time when Communists from North Korea confiscated his parents' assets.[17] Subsequently, he became a medical student in Seoul, where each day he ate a sparse breakfast at his sister's house, trekked across towering Namsan Mountain (visible from our room in the Hilton), and studied at Seoul National University until night, when he would grab a few hours of sleep in the borrowed bed of a friend who worked the night shift.

I have always lived in nice houses, gone on trips, and never lacked for pizza money. But as my father talked, I could almost taste the millet-and-water gruel[18] he subsisted on while hiding for months in cellars during the North Korean invasion of Seoul. Suddenly, I was able to feel the pain of the Korean people, enduring one hardship after another: Japanese colonial rule, North Korean aggression, and dependence on American military force. For a brief moment, I discerned the origins of the

12. *Ignominiously* means simply "shamefully; disgracefully."
13. *Taciturn* means "not inclined to speak much"; *garrulous* means "talking a lot, especially about unimportant matters."
14. When you *perceive* something, you notice it.
15. The writer's *disorientation* is a feeling of being lost. Her *alienation* is her sense of being different from her relatives. *Homogeneous* (hō′ mə jē′ nē əs) means "of the same kind."
16. *Soju* is a liquor made from rice.
17. The North Koreans seized *(confiscated)* his parents' property and valuables *(assets)*.
18. *Gruel* is a thin porridge.

Vocabulary

brazenly (brā′ zən lē) *adv.* in a boldly rude manner
joviality (jō′ vē al′ ə tē) *n.* hearty, good-natured humor
subsequently (sub′ sə kwənt lē) *adv.* at a later time
aggression (ə gresh′ ən) *n.* the habit or practice of launching attacks
discern (di surn′) *v.* to detect or recognize; identify

E Active Reading Strategies

QUESTION Ask students why they think the Korean cab drivers speak freely to Lee's father. *(Her father relates to them as one Korean to another. Perhaps his command of the language and its nuances may signal his respect for the drivers and his familiarity with the culture.)*

F Literary Elements

CHARACTERIZATION Ask students to describe how Lee's Korean father differs from her American dad. Have students identify the details Lee chooses to portray her Korean father. *(Her Korean father is more formal than her American dad. Lee focuses on his mastery of the language and his ease in the culture that is so strange to her.)*

G Active Reading Strategies

CONNECT Explain to students that Lee's description of Korea as the most racially and culturally homogeneous country in the world is based on the fact that most people living there are of Korean heritage and can trace their ancestry back many generations. Most Koreans speak the same language and share the same customs. Have students compare Korea with the United States, which is probably the most culturally and racially diverse country in the world. Then ask students to think about some of the elements of American culture that people of different ethnic backgrounds have contributed. *(Examples: music, architecture, customs, food, words, place names.)*

Reading Minilesson

Summarize Point out to students that the ability to summarize certain aspects of a story is an important skill, especially if one has to write about a work. Summarizing generally involves rereading the selection to identify the essential items of information and, thus, is an important study skill.

Activity Have students reread page 21 and write a brief paragraph summarizing what Lee says she discovers about her father while in Korea. Ask students to trade papers and compare their summaries with the original section of the story. Students should evaluate their classmates work on the basis of how accurately they summarized the main ideas and critical details **L2**

Additional Resources

Reading Skills Practice Workbook

H Critical Thinking

EVALUATE Ask students why Lee feels she will "never fully know" Korean culture. Discuss with students whether they agree.

Model: I think that Lee feels alienated in Korea because she doesn't understand the language or culture. Although she has learned much about her heritage, there is much more that she has not learned. She has not lived as a Korean so she concludes that she can never fit in. I think this is a fair assumption because she will return to her American life.

I Author's Craft

CONNOTATION AND DENOTATION
Explain that denotation is a word's actual meaning and connotation is what a word implies. The words *dad* and *father* have the same denotation but different connotations. Ask how the two connotations relate to what Lee is saying in her essay. *(Father is a more formal, respectful term, which signifies how she feels about her* dad *in Korea.)*

Thematic Focus

No Place Like Home Ask students how they think Lee's idea of "home" changed as a result of her trip.

ASSESSMENT

Quick Checks, p. 2

noble, sometimes harsh, Korean character. Those wizened[19] women who pushed past me at church were there only because they had fought their way to old age. The noises people made while eating began to sound more celebratory than rude.

And there were other things I saw and was proud of. When we visited a cemetery, I noticed that the headstones were small and unadorned,[20] except for a few with small, pagoda-shaped "hats" on them. The hats *(chinsa)*, Dad told me, were from a time when the country's leaders awarded "national Ph.D.'s,"[21] the highest civilian honor.

Did You Know?
A *pagoda* is a temple, two or more stories high. Each level has its own partial roof and is a little smaller than the level below it.

"Your great-grandfather has one of those on his grave," Dad mentioned casually. I began to admire a people who place such high value on hard work and scholarship. Even television commercials generally don't promote leisure pursuits, such as vacations or Nintendo, but instead proclaim[22] the merits of "super duper vitamin pills" to help you study longer and work harder.

After two weeks, as we prepared to return to the U.S., I still in many ways felt like a stranger in Korea. While I looked the part of a native, my textbook Korean was robotic, and the phrases I was taught—such as, "Don't take me for a five-won[23] plane ride"—were apparently very dated. I tried to tell my Korean cousins an amusing anecdote:[24] in the Lotte department store in Seoul, I asked for directions to the restroom and was directed instead to the stereo section. But the story, related once in English and once in halting Korean, became hopelessly lost in the translation.

Dad decided he would spend an extra week in Korea, savoring[25] a culture I would never fully know, even if I took every Berlitz course I could afford. When I said goodbye to him, I saw my Korean father; but I knew that come February, my American dad would be back out in our driveway, stirring up a froth of snow with his big yellow snowblower.

19. The *wizened* women were shriveled.
20. *Unadorned* means "not decorated."
21. The highest academic degree awarded to graduates in non-science areas of study is the Doctor of Philosophy, or *Ph.D.*
22. To *proclaim* means "to announce."
23. The *won* is a unit of money in both North and South Korea.
24. An *anecdote* is a short account of some incident or event.
25. *Savoring* means "taking great delight in."

Teaching Support

Grammar and Language *Minilesson*

Adjective Clauses Show the grammar transparency or write these sentences from page 22 on the board: "Those wizened women who pushed past me at church were there only because they had fought their way to old age." "I began to admire a people who place such high value on hard work and scholarship." Explain to students that the underlined clauses are adjective clauses. An adjective clause is a subordinate clause that modifies a noun or a pronoun in the main clause of the sentence. Besides *who,* adjective clauses can be introduced by the following words: *which, that, whom, whose, when,* or *where.*

Activity Have pairs of students find three additional adjective clauses in the selection. Have each pair read to the class the sentences in which the clauses appear. **L2**

Additional Resources

- ***Grammar and Language Transparency 2***
- ***Grammar and Language Workbook,*** p. 159
- ***Grammar and Composition Handbook,*** Lesson 8.3
- ***Writer's Choice,*** Lesson 14.3

Responding to Literature

PERSONAL RESPONSE

- What do you think about the author's belief that she can never fully be a part of Korean culture?

Brackets connect questions that are paired to develop higher-level thinking skills.

Analyzing Literature

RECALL

1. Where did Marie G. Lee grow up?
2. What did she know about her father's past?
3. How did the author's childhood differ from her father's?
4. According to Lee, what has influenced the character of the South Korean people?

Seoul, South Korea

INTERPRET

5. Why might Lee's parents have encouraged her to forget her Korean background?
6. Why does the author emphasize the ease with which her father speaks Korean and his effective use of taxis?
7. How does Lee's growing knowledge of Korea affect the way she sees her father?
8. Theme Connection Explain why Lee feels she will never fully understand Korean culture.

EVALUATE AND CONNECT

9. This personal essay presents a **theme,** a main idea or message. What is this theme, and do you agree with it? Use examples to support your answer.
10. How might Lee's essay encourage others to learn more about the culture of their parents or grandparents?

LITERARY ELEMENTS

Character

A **character** is a person, animal, or other creature that appears in a literary work. Characters can be real or imaginary. Usually a story or other work is built around one **main character.** This character is often described in detail, and he or she may change as a result of events that occur. There are also **minor characters** who move the action along by interacting with the main character and providing background information.

1. Who is the main character in "My Two Dads"? How does the main character change or develop from the beginning of the selection to the end?
2. Who are the minor characters? How do they affect the main character?

- See **Literary Terms Handbook,** p. R2.

Responding to the Selection

PERSONAL RESPONSE

Some students may agree that it is very hard to learn to relate to another culture as an adult.

Analyzing Literature

1. Lee grew up in the Midwest.
2. Lee knew only that her father was born in Korea and once wore Korean clothes.
3. The author had a comfortable childhood, whereas her father had to struggle for everything, including food.
4. Koreans are a people who have suffered much pain and hardship and have had to fight for what they have.
5. Many immigrant parents feel that their children will be more successful if they fit in with the dominant culture.
6. Lee shows that her father is as comfortable in Korea as in the United States.
7. Lee grows to admire her father more and more. She sees how well he speaks the language, and she learns how he triumphed over hardship.
8. She seems to suggest that Korean culture is based on the endurance of hardship and pain, with which she has had little experience.
9. One of Lee's themes is that learning about a new culture is very difficult but that if a person tries to learn about his or her ethnic heritage, a better understanding of self and family will result.
10. Lee clearly feels more connected to her father and to her past as a result of her trip to Korea.

LITERARY ELEMENTS

1. **Main character:** Lee. She changes from an "all-American" girl to one who perceives two heritages.
2. **Minor characters:** Lee's mother, Korean relatives, brother, and others. They change Lee's perception of her heritage and herself.

Additional Resources

Literary Elements Transparency 2

Extending Your Response

Creative Writing

Students' letters should

- take the form of personal correspondence
- include both comparisons of and contrasts between American and Korean cultures

Literature Groups Remind students that a debate has formal rules, the most important of which is taking turns. Do not interrupt other speakers. COLLAB. LEARN.

Learning for Life Explain that an itinerary is a list of dates and times that shows where the traveler will be at each stage of a trip.

Skill Minilesson

VOCABULARY • ANALOGIES

1. a
2. b
3. b
4. c

Additional Resources

Vocabulary Practice, p. 2

RETEACH • REVIEW

Extending Your Response

Creative Writing

Writing Home Imagine that you are Marie G. Lee and are just completing your Korean visit. Write to a friend comparing American culture with what you have learned about Korean culture.

interNET CONNECTION

Type the name *Korean Overseas Information Service* into a search engine to find information about Korean culture, language, art, or history.

Literature Groups

A Culture Debate Although her father embraces two cultures, the writer feels she will never be able to do the same. Debate whether people growing up outside of their ancestral culture can ever return to it and feel part of it. As you debate, consider your response to the **Reading Focus** on page 18.

Learning for Life

A Heritage Map Plan a trip to explore a heritage that interests you. You might focus on a group of Asian Americans, a specific Native American culture, a group of European settlers in the United States, or your own heritage. Create a map of the regions and cities to explore, as well as an itinerary that includes the people and specific places you would like to visit.

Save your work for your portfolio.

Skill Minilesson

VOCABULARY • ANALOGIES

An **analogy** is a type of comparison based on the relationships between things or ideas. An analogy is written this way:

virus : illness :: collision : injury

Notice that just as a *virus* can cause an *illness*, a *collision* can cause an *injury.* So, *virus* is to *illness* as *collision* is to *injury.* To understand an analogy, you must first figure out the relationship between the first pair of words.

PRACTICE Choose the word that best completes each analogy.

1. fist : violence :: dove :
   a. peace b. bird c. fear
2. wearily : trudge :: happily :
   a. plod b. skip c. stamp
3. friendly : unfriendly :: smug :
   a. mean b. insecure c. conceited
4. shrug : indifference :: nod :
   a. fear b. joy c. agreement

ASSESSMENT

- ***Quick Checks,*** p. 2
- ***Selection and Theme Assessment,*** pp. 3–4
- ***Performance Assessment,*** p. 2
- ***Testmaker ExamView Pro***
- ***Interactive Tutor: Self-Assessment***

Reading and Thinking Skills

Previewing

Titles, headings, illustrations, and opening paragraphs—like "Coming Attractions" posters at the movies—alert you to what you are about to see. Using these features to learn about a reading selection is called **previewing.**

Preview this opening paragraph from "A Dictionary of Japanese-American Terms" by R. A. Sasaki.

> *Nihonjin* (nē′ hon′ jē-n′)
> At the age of six, I thought "Americans" and "English" meant the same thing—"white people." After all, Americans spoke English. You have to understand, this was at an age when I also wondered why "onion" was spelled with an "o." It seemed to me that it should be spelled with a "u," except that would make it "union," which was a different word altogether.

Note that the heading at the start of the paragraph looks like a dictionary entry. That heading and the title of the selection are clues that the writer may define *Nihonjin.* You learn that the author was confused about word meanings and that she wondered why English spelling was not logical. This information helps you predict the content and tone of the selection.

- For more about previewing, see **Reading Handbook,** p. R93.

ACTIVITY

Preview your next history, social studies, or science reading assignment, using the following suggestions.

1. List the title, headings, subheadings, illustrations, captions, charts, and photographs in the text.
2. Read the assignment. Write a sentence telling why you think previewing did or did not help you to understand the assignment.

Reading & Thinking Skills

Objective

- To use titles, headings, illustrations, opening paragraphs, and structure to preview a selection

Teaching Strategies

After the students have read the explanation, try this previewing exercise. Make up a transparency with thirty words listed in three columns; fifteen of them should be the names of vegetables, randomly distributed throughout. Project the slide for ten seconds. Then ask students to write the words they remember. Prepare a similar transparency, with the names of fifteen fruits. This time preview the activity. Tell students that you will project a slide for ten seconds and that there will be thirty words, fifteen of which are the names of fruits. Explain that after ten seconds you'll remove the slide and ask them to write down the words they remember. After completing, compare the results. How did previewing affect performance?

Activities

1. Students' lists should include all elements mentioned.
2. Answers should indicate that knowing what to expect improved comprehension.

Additional Resources

Reading Skills Practice Workbook

Teaching Support

MEETING INDIVIDUAL NEEDS — SPECIAL NEEDS

Less-Proficient Readers Paragraphs often have the most important information, the main idea, in the first sentence. The opening sentence of a news article usually does this by telling *who, what, when, where, why,* and *how* something happened. The first sentence of each subsequent paragraph usually contains the most important information in that paragraph.

Activity Have students skim a news story (not a feature article) by reading the headline, first paragraph, and first sentence of each paragraph. Discuss the main idea of each paragraph. Then ask students to read the entire article to see if they missed any key ideas when skimming. **L1**

Additional Resources

Inclusion Strategies

Before Reading

Objectives

- To read and analyze an essay by a Japanese American woman who is trying to come to terms with her ethnic identity
- To identify and analyze the relationship between the narrative voice and the central message of an essay
- To write an essay about an author's use of analogy

Skills

Reading/Thinking: Analyzing Arguments; Inferring; Using Text Structures; Elaborating
Writing: Personal Letter
Grammar/Language: Titles; Personal Pronouns
Vocabulary: Compound Words
Listening/Speaking: Interviewing; Oral Presentation
Collaboration: Literature Groups

Motivating STUDENTS

Selection Focus Transparency 3: Before presenting the photograph, have students write in their journals about a time when they experienced or saw others experience discrimination.

Reading Focus: As an extension of the Reading Focus, have students turn their drawings over and discuss whether there are parts of themselves that they don't show others. Examples: dreams, fears, and disappointments.

Before You Read

A Dictionary of Japanese-American Terms

MEET R. A. SASAKI

According to R. A. Sasaki (sä sä′ kē), "History disappears if the stories are not told." As a child in the 1950s, Sasaki didn't study the history of Japanese people in America. It wasn't until the 1970s that she began to explore and understand her heritage. "Gradually I uncovered my world, buried like a treasure, or a lost civilization," she said. She began writing about the Japanese American experience, and one of her stories, "The Loom," won the American Japanese National Literary Award in 1983.

R. A. Sasaki was born in 1952. This selection was published in 1996.

READING FOCUS

When you look into a mirror, what do you see? How would you describe yourself, inside and outside?

Reflect It!
Draw the outline of your head as it would appear in a mirror. Add pictures, words, and symbols to show the person you see reflected in the mirror.

Setting a Purpose
Read to meet a writer who discovers a new side of herself.

BUILDING BACKGROUND

The Time and Place R. A. Sasaki writes about growing up in the 1950s as a third-generation Japanese American.

Did You Know? During World War II, some Americans feared that Japanese Americans might aid the armies of Japan that had bombed Hawaii. In 1942, about 110,000 Japanese and Japanese American residents were sent to live in internment camps in the western United States. At the same time, Japanese Americans were serving in the armed forces and many returned home to the United States as decorated war heroes. Not one case of espionage by Japanese Americans was reported.

VOCABULARY PREVIEW

emulate (em′ yə lāt′) *v.* to imitate; p. 28
convey (kən vā′) *v.* to express; communicate; p. 30
painstakingly (pānz′ tā′ king lē) *adv.* in a way requiring close, careful labor or attention; p. 30
incur (in kur′) *v.* to acquire (something undesirable); bring upon oneself; p. 31
intricate (in′ tri kit) *adj.* full of complicated detail; p. 31
humility (hū mil′ ə tē) *n.* the quality of being humble or modest; p. 32
naive (nä ēv′) *adj.* innocent to the ways of the world; p. 32
inflict (in flikt′) *v.* to force (something unwelcome) on someone; p. 33

RESOURCE MANAGER

Teaching Tools and Resources
- Theme One Planning Guide
- Literature Groups Sourcebook

Essential Lesson Support

Lesson-Specific Instruction
- Selection Focus Transparency 3
- Literary Elements Transparency 3
- Active Reading Guide,* p. 3
- Selection Vocabulary Practice, p. 9

Assessment
- Selection Quick Checks,* p. 3
- Sel. and Theme Assmt., pp. 5-6
- Testmaker: ExamView Pro
- Performance Assessment, p. 3

Systematic Language Instruction
- Gr. & Comp. Hbk., Lessons 1.5

English Language Learners
- ELL Sourcebook, p. 20
- Spanish Summaries, p. 3
- Audio Library*
- English, Yes!

Spec. Needs/Strat. Interven.
- Interactive Rdg. Sbk., pp. T52–T54
- Interactive Rdg. Wbk., pp. 5-8
- Inclusion Strat. Sbk., pp. 3-4
- Audio Library*

* Also available in Spanish

A Dictionary of Japanese-American Terms

R. A. Sasaki

San Francisco Bay, 1936. Erle Loran. Watercolor and gouache on paper, 15 x 19 in.

Nihonjin (nē′ hon′ jē-n′)

At the age of six, I thought "Americans" and "English" meant the same thing—"white people." After all, Americans spoke English. You have to understand, this was at an age when I also wondered why "onion" was spelled with an "o." It seemed to me that it should be spelled with a "u," except that would make it "union," which was a different word altogether.

Reading the Selection

SUMMARY

R. A. Sasaki presents five expressions as dictionary entries and then defines them according to her own life experiences. Her list includes *Nihonjin* ("Japanese"), *Jiichan* ("grandfather"), *osewa ni natta* ("reciprocation"), *Japanese-American,* and *the story of when I was born.* Each word or phrase introduces an autobiographical passage, as Sasaki struggles to resolve the contradictions in her identity as a woman, both Japanese and American. Sasaki ends the essay by describing her trip to Japan, which helps her gain perspective on her heritage.

Spanish Summaries, p. 3

A Active Reading Strategies

RESPOND Encourage students to discuss the author's confusion about *Americans* and *English.* Do they think her misconception is common?

VOCABULARY If you haven't previewed the selection vocabulary with students, stop and remind them to use context clues to unlock the meanings of new vocabulary words.

Additional Resources

Active Reading Guide, p. 3

Audio Library

Spanish Audio Library

Teaching Support

CONNECTING TO OTHER SELECTIONS

The chart at the right shows three other ways to connect "A Dictionary of Japanese-American Terms" to selections in this book.

For specific teaching strategies, see the ***Theme One Planning Guide,*** pages 25–26.

Connection	Title
Life Skills: Lifelong Learning	→ "Americans All," p. 643
Thematic: Cultural Identity	→ "Legacies," p. 182
Literary: First-Person Narrator	→ from *On the Road with Charles Kuralt,* p. 635

B Literary Elements

NARRATOR Ask students which word in the first sentence on page 28 tells the reader that Sasaki is the narrator. *(The word I tells the reader that Sasaki is the narrator.)*

C Active Reading Strategies

CONNECT Explain to students that Sasaki implies a contrast between Kimiko and herself. If Sasaki sees herself as exactly the opposite of Kimiko, what does that tell us about Sasaki? *(She seldom wears dresses, laughs out loud, plays rough games, and fights back if insulted.)*

D Active Reading Strategies

QUESTION Ask students why Sasaki chooses to tell us about emulating her "favorite Western heroes" with Kimiko. How does this particular incident highlight the contrast between the two girls? *(A western hero is a typically American figure—usually rough and male.)*

E Active Reading Strategies

CONNECT Ask students what Sasaki means when she says "there must be different kinds of *Nihonjin,* too." *(Sasaki concludes that people within cultures should not be stereotyped; they have different personalities.)*

Teaching Support

B I never thought about what I was. My parents referred to us as "*Nihonjin*"—Japanese. "*Nihonjin*" meant us. "*Hakujin*" (white people) meant them. Being *Nihonjin* meant having straight black hair and a certain kind of last name. The Chinese kids looked like us, but had one-syllable last names.

When I was in the first grade I got into a fight with Lucinda Lee because she claimed that she was American. "You're Chinese," I accused her. She started to cry. Later, I told my mother about the disagreement, and, to my outrage, she sided with Lucinda. It had never occurred to me that Lucinda was American. That I, too, was American. Other kids never asked me if I was American. It was always, "Are you Chinese or Japanese?"

That's how I found out that I was American—one kind of American. I still wasn't sure how I could be both American and *Nihonjin* (was I English, too? I wondered).

> ***I still wasn't sure how I could be both American and* Nihonjin *(was I English, too? I wondered).***

C Then a little girl who was REALLY *Nihonjin* moved in next door. Her father worked for a Japanese company, and the family had moved to San Francisco straight from Tokyo. Kimiko wore dresses all the time, even when she didn't have to. She covered her mouth with her hand when she laughed, and sounded like a little bird. When I stuck the nose of my wooden six-shooter in her back and called her a "low-down, dirty tinhorn," emulating my heroes on television westerns, my father, sitting in the next room, shot me a dark, warning look that made me quake in my boots. C D It was no good insulting Kimiko, anyway, because she wouldn't get mad and fight back. If Kimiko and I were both *Nihonjin*, well then, all I could say was that there must be different kinds of *Nihonjin*, too. E

Jiichan (jē chăn)

I don't remember my grandfather. *Jiichan* died when I was too young to remember him, but old enough to be afraid of death. He haunted my childhood by appearing in a nightmare so disturbing that I used to force myself to recall it every night before going to sleep so that I wouldn't dream it again. I believed that terrors could only get you when you were least expecting them.

In my dream, there was a large pile of laundry, mainly sheets, on the floor of the dining room in our house on 23rd Avenue. I was sifting through it with my sister, playing in the mountainous folds suddenly dropped into the midst of the usually neat order of my mother's house. We climbed

Vocabulary
emulate (em′ yə lāt′) *v.* to imitate

MEETING INDIVIDUAL NEEDS — ENGLISH LANGUAGE LEARNERS

Suffixes: *-less* Write these words from page 30 on the board: *meaningless, hopeless.* Tell students that the suffix *-less* means *without.* Provide students with other examples: *homeless, childless, heartless.* Not every noun takes this suffix. We usually don't say *dogless* or *liverless.*

Activity Ask students to look for other constructions that follow this pattern. Have students write the root word and then explain how the suffix changes the meaning. Encourage students to record the words and their definitions in their vocabulary notebooks.

Additional Resources

English Language Learners Sourcebook, **p. 20**

the mountain; our feet sank into the soft mass. Suddenly I clutched a stiff hand. I screamed, and the dream ended abruptly; but I knew, without seeing the rest, that it was *Jiichan's* corpse in there.

My sisters, being older, had known *Jiichan* and did not have such dreams. They were not afraid of him. They remembered his quiet presence watching over them as they played in the backyard

Elderly Japanese man with warblers and silvereyes. Courtesy Allen Say.

Viewing the painting: Do you think the man in the painting more closely resembles the narrator's or her sisters' memories of Jiichan?

F Literary Elements

SYMBOLISM Ensure that students understand the symbolism of the dream. Tell them that underneath all the "layers," deep down inside, Sasaki is still Japanese. Her grandfather reaches out to hold her so that she doesn't lose her heritage—and when she knows nothing about the hand, the grip of the past on her is frightening.

VIEWING THE PAINTING

Allen Say (b. 1937) is a Japanese-born American artist. This painting is from his Caldecott Award-winning children's book *Grandfather's Journey*.

Viewing Response *The serene man contemplating the birds seems much like the man remembered by the narrator's sisters. They recall his quietness and the way he watched over them as they played. The narrator never knew her grandfather and has nightmares about him that in no way resemble the reserved dignity of the man in this picture.*

INTERDISCIPLINARY CONNECTION

Compare Paintings Provide students with an example of Western art that depicts a single person contemplating or thinking, to provide a contrast with the painting on page 29. *(Possibilities include self-portraits by Rembrandt or Van Gogh, Whistler's* Arrangement in Black and Gray *[Whistler's Mother], or a photograph of Rodin's statue* The Thinker.*)*

Activity Ask students to work in small groups to list the differences they see between the two works of art. Have them share their insights with the entire class in the form of a brief oral presentation.
L3 COLLAB. LEARN.

G Critical Thinking

ANALYZE ARGUMENTS Sasaki argues that language, labels, and facts can be misleading and inaccurate. Ask students to summarize how she contrasts "facts" with "knowing." *(Facts can be confirmed in a reference work. Knowing comes only through life experience.)*

Model: I think that labels describe only a small part of a person or object. I think Sasaki is saying that when you know something or someone you are aware of the many sides of that person and are no longer content with mere labels.

H Literary Elements

SYMBOLISM Ask how Sasaki further clarifies the symbolism of her dream. *(Her grandfather's hand symbolizes her Japanese heritage, only terrifying if forgotten or unknown. If she knows her heritage, she will recognize her grandfather's hand as her link to the past, and she will not be afraid.)*

I Author's Craft

DICTION Ask students to find the pun on the word *face* and describe how it reflects Sasaki's dilemma. *(Sasaki says she cannot be accepted at "face value" in American society because of her "Asian face." Because of her "Asian face" she can't "forge ahead"; she must "look back" to her grandfather and her homeland to understand her heritage.)*

of the house on Pine Street. They remembered him tending his beloved cherry tree. I was the only one who needed to reconstruct him. I tried to do it by collecting facts—his name, for example, where he was born, that he had left Japan and come to San Francisco sometime around 1897.

G But a part of me has always distrusted language, especially facts. We are so often deceived by them into thinking that we know something. Language is applied after the fact. It is a way of labeling an experience, and if we have never been to Wakayama, Japan, it means nothing that our grandfather was born there. Or if we were not alive in 1897, how can we understand what it meant to leave Japan at that time to come to America?

In 1975 I went to Japan to teach English. I didn't really know why I was going. Finding one's roots at that time was an expression which had been rendered[1] meaningless by overuse. It was just that part of me that distrusts language, wanting to trade facts for knowing.

H Other people don't seem to be haunted by the need to bring their grandfathers alive. Perhaps they remember their grandfathers, spoke the same language and heard their stories. If you know who you are and where you come from, or if you are accepted in American society at face value, you can forge ahead and never look back.[2] My Asian face doesn't let me forget my origins. Everytime I start to forget, I will come upon that stiff hand, which will remind me. And if I don't know who my grandfather was, who I am, I will scream with terror. But if I know, then I will know that it is my grandfather's hand that I hold; and I need not be afraid.

osewa ni natta (o-sĕ′ wă nē năt′ tă)

I decided early on that it was hopeless; I would never be Japanese, so why try? There was too much to know, too much to be understood that could not be conveyed by the spoken English word. I would rather be forward-looking—American.

But much as I tried, I could never leave it behind. Someone would die. We always seemed most Japanese when someone died.

"We should go to the funeral," my mother would say. "Iwashita-san[3] came to Pop's funeral." If someone had sent flowers, we would send flowers. If they had visited the house and brought food, we would do the same. *Koden*, funeral money, was carefully recorded and returned when the occasion arose. It seemed there was a giant ledger that existed in my mother's head that painstakingly noted every kindness ever rendered or received.[4] How could I ever know or remember its contents? I I couldn't keep track of my own life. A friend of mine was hurt once because I didn't remember staying at his sister's house in Minnesota. I felt awful about not remembering. It seems that there

1. Here, *rendered* means simply "made; caused to be."
2. The phrase *face value* refers to value or significance based on outward appearance. The word *forge,* in this context, means "to advance or progress."
3. *Iwashita-san* (ē wäsh tä sän). In Japanese, the suffix *-san* is added to a person's name to show courtesy.
4. A *ledger* is a book in which income and expenses are recorded. *Rendered,* in this case, means "given or paid."

Vocabulary

convey (kən vā′) *v.* to express; communicate

painstakingly (pānz′ tā′ king lē) *adv.* in a way requiring close, careful labor or attention

Teaching Support

MEETING INDIVIDUAL NEEDS — SPECIAL NEEDS

Learning Disabled Students with learning disabilities may not understand Sasaki's statement that "Language is applied after the fact. It is a way of labeling an experience." Explain that experience comes before language.

Activity Ask students to close their eyes and recall *in detail* the tastes, smells, sounds, and sights of a special day. Invite them to share a two-minute summary of the day with a partner. Then, ask students whether they think that partner knows what their day was *really* like. Help students relate this activiy to Sasaki's statement. **L1**

Additional Resources

Inclusion Strategies

are whole periods of my life that have simply dropped from memory. Sensory overload.[5] Am I busier than my mother was, or is there a Japanese gene that weakens in succeeding generations with increased Americanization?

J Perhaps I was simply born too late. The youngest of four girls, I was the only one who didn't remember living in the old Victorian in Japantown[6] where my mother grew up and my grandparents lived until they died. I was the only one who couldn't understand what my grandmother was saying, even when she was speaking English. When someone talked about what a family acquaintance had done for us, I was the only one who didn't know who the person was.

This record-keeping and reciprocation[7] did not revolve only around death. My mother would tell me one day on the phone, "The Noguchis are coming up from Los Angeles. They want to take Kiyo and me out to lunch."

I had never heard of the Noguchis, but it turned out that sixty years before, *Bachan* (my grandmother) had let them stay at Pine for a month after Noguchi-san lost his job. Noguchi-san had recently undergone surgery for cancer. "*Osewa ni narimashita*,"[8] he had said. He had incurred debt. He wanted to repay it before it was too late.

The repayment of debt, then, apparently passes down from generation to generation. What will happen when my mother and my aunt Kiyo are no longer around? The ledger will be gone. How will I know to whom I am obligated, what debts to repay? One day in the future will I open the door to find a total stranger bringing me home-made sushi because of some kind act my grandmother did in 1946? Probably not. When I meet the grandsons and great-granddaughters of my grandparents' friends, who among us will know that our families were once connected? K We will have lost the intricate web of obligation and reciprocation. The people who remember. This community.

Did You Know?
Many people of all nationalities have warmed to the taste of cold Japanese *sushi* (soo′ shē). Small cakes of rice wrapped in seaweed and topped with vinegar are garnished with raw or cooked fish, egg, or vegetables.

Japanese-American
(ja-pə-nēz′ ə-mĕ′-rĭ-kən)

L A Japanese-American is someone who has been trained in the Japanese ways of ultimate courtesy, but who has a quite independent and secret American sensibility locked into that pleasant and self-effacing[9] exterior—like a *bonsai.* A tree trying to grow, but forced, through clipped roots and

5. The phrase *sensory overload* refers to being overwhelmed by too much information or experience.
6. A *Victorian* is a house built in a style of architecture developed during the reign of Great Britain's Queen Victoria (1837–1901). *Japantown* is an area inhabited chiefly by people of Japanese descent.
7. When two people give each other gifts or trade favors, that's *reciprocation.*
8. *Osewa ni narimashita* (ō sē wä nē nä rē mäsh tä)
9. Here, *sensibility* refers to feelings of what is decent and proper. To *efface* is to make less obvious, and *self-effacing* means "tending to stay in the background."

Vocabulary
incur (in kur′) *v.* to acquire (something undesirable); bring upon oneself
intricate (in′ tri kit) *adj.* full of complicated detail

J Author's Craft

STYLE In this paragraph Sasaki stresses that because of her place in the family, she feels even less Japanese than her sisters. She emphasizes her point by saying the phrase, "I was the only one who . . ." three times. This repetition serves to reinforce her idea.

K Critical Thinking

INFER Ask students to use evidence from the text to show the narrator's feelings about losing "the intricate web of obligation and reciprocation. The people who remember. This community." *(By the end of the selection, once she is at peace with her heritage, she is probably sad about losing this "web of obligation and reciprocation.")*

L Literary Elements

SIMILE Sasaki compares Japanese Americans to bonsai trees by using a simile. Explain to students that a simile is a comparison that uses the word *like* or *as.* Discuss the two connections Sasaki makes between Japanese Americans and bonsai trees. *(First, to be both Japanese and American is like being forced into an artificial shape through "clipped roots" and "wired branches"; the brash American spirit is trapped in the courteous humble Japanese exterior. Second, she likens the Japanese, who were interned in camps, to bonsai in that they were shaped, perhaps "deformed," by their experience.)*

Reading Minilesson

Use Text Structures Use the paragraph beginning "Perhaps I was simply born too late" to show students how Sasaki uses repetition to structure her paragraph and to emphasize her point. Point out that the first and third sentences start with a modifier followed by "I was the only one" and the second sentence starts with "I was the only one."

Activity Have students list three ways in which they are "the only one who . . ." in their families. Then ask them to write this information in sentences, which they share in small groups. Discuss how repeating a sequence of words reinforces the point made. **L2** **COLLAB. LEARN.**

Additional Resources

Reading Skills Practice Workbook

Active Reading Strategies

CLARIFY Ask students to explain the connection that Sasaki makes between the nisei, "whose psyches were wired like Japanese baby pines," and their children, who grew up "American, like redwoods." *(Those who were interned feared that discussing their experiences or their Japanese heritage might stunt the growth of their children. By drawing attention to the differences between their children and other American children, they felt they might hurt their chances for success. Sasaki understands their motives—they want their children to be redwoods, not bonsai—but she feels that she missed an important opportunity by not learning more about her heritage.)*

A&E HOME VIDEO® *The following videotape program is available from Glencoe:*

Be sure to preview the video for appropriateness for your class:

- **From a Different Shore: The Japanese-American Experience***

*Also available in the Glencoe Literature *Video Library*

Teaching Support

Did You Know?
Bonsai (bôn sī′) is the art of growing miniature trees in shallow pots or trays. Most bonsai trees are from two inches to three feet tall.

wired branches, into an expected shape. Like *bonsai*, a Japanese-American can be considered warped or deformed, or an object of uncanny[10] beauty.

A Japanese-American is someone who, after a lifetime of being asked if she's Japanese or Chinese, or how long she's been in the States, or where she learned her English, will laugh when some white guy who has taken two semesters of Beginning Japanese tells her that she's mispronouncing her own family name.

Being Japanese-American means being imbued with certain values treasured by Japanese culture—values such as consideration, loyalty, humility, restraint. Values which, when exercised by white Americans, seem civilized; but they make Japanese-Americans seem unassertive, not willing to take risks, lacking confidence and leadership qualities.

Some sansei are like brash young redwoods, so new and naive. It's so clear why the nisei[11] didn't talk. The nisei, whose psyches[12] were wired like Japanese baby pines by the internment. They wanted the third generation to grow up American, like redwoods. They wanted them to shoot for the sky, tall and straight, to walk ahead like gods. To free themselves of the past like a rocket that discards its used stages as it shoots into space. Let go of the past; if you carry your spent burden with you, you will never reach the moon.

the story of when I was born
(thə sto′ rē əv wĕn′ ī wəz born′)

When I was a little girl, and my mother put me to bed, she did not tell me stories about enchanted forests or beautiful princesses. I had seen "Sleeping Beauty." I knew "The Three Bears." These were not the stories I wanted to hear from my mother.

"Tell me the story of when I was born," I would say, mummified[13] up to my chin by bedcovers. There were no magic wands or fairy godmothers in this story. No poisoned apples or pumpkins that turned into coaches. It was a simple story, a sequence of mundane[14] events, barely connected and sparingly described, peopled not by bad wolves or evil stepmothers, but sisters, my father, my mother of course, and friends of the family. The reason I wanted to hear that story, the reason I liked it so much, was because I was in it. It was real.

Life for me began just eleven short years after the Japanese dropped bombs on Pearl Harbor, precipitating[15] events that would

10. If it's *uncanny*, it's so strange and extraordinary as to seem supernatural.
11. *Nisei* (nē sā′) are the U.S.-born children of Japanese immigrants, and *sansei* (sän′ sā) are the grandchildren.
12. The effect of internment on the *psyches* (sī′ kēz)—the souls or minds—of the *nisei* was to make them like bonsai trees, forced to grow into desired shapes and sizes.
13. Here, *mummified* means "covered up like a mummy."
14. Common, ordinary events are *mundane* ones.
15. In this context, *precipitating* means "causing or bringing on."

Vocabulary
humility (hū mil′ ə tē) *n.* the quality of being humble or modest
naive (nä ēv′) *adj.* innocent to the ways of the world

Interdisciplinary Connection

History Sasaki refers to the internment camps for Japanese Americans set up during World War II. For years, many Americans outside California did not know about these camps.

Activity Have students work in small groups to research the Japanese American internment during World War II. Each group should prepare a three- to five-minute oral presentation on one item of interest. Suggest that groups use visual aids, such as photographs or charts, to enhance their presentations (the cramped living space, bathroom facilities, dining arrangements). Some students may want to focus on the physical setup of the camps themselves; some on the daily life; some on education, police force, social activities; some on what happened to the homes, personal belongings, and businesses of people in the camps; and some on how individuals survived. **L2**

Richmond–San Rafael Ferry Arch, c. 1935. John Haley. Watercolor and gouache on paper, 15 x 22¾ in.

Viewing the painting: Does the sky in this painting relate to the author's memories of growing up in the San Francisco Bay area? Explain.

<u>inflict</u> on my family a kind of willed amnesia that would last for forty years.

As soon as he could after the war, my father moved us out of Japantown, into an orderly and integrated neighborhood where we had an Armenian grocery, a Russian delicatessen, an Italian piano teacher, and kind *hakujin* neighbors named the Freemans. The Richmond District of San Francisco, where I grew up, was always foggy. The fog would come in off the Pacific during the night, and when I woke up, I would hear the mournful dialogue of fog horns warning ships in the Golden Gate. Sometimes the fog would burn off by noon, and we would get a glimpse of the blue sky that California is supposed to be so famous for. But often the fog remained all day, or came back in the afternoon, so thick and low that it seemed like a white smoke. If we went anywhere else in the city, we must have looked like foreigners, just come in from Siberia, in our sweaters and coats and knee-high socks. We probably had an intensity, too, that outside people, people who lived in the sun, lacked. A seriousness. An introspection,[16] come from too many days spent inside the house reading, or a range of options that did not include barbecues and lying on the beach.

In school we learned about the explorers, the *Mayflower*, the American Revolution.

16. An *introspection* is an examination of one's own thoughts and feelings.

Vocabulary

inflict (in flikt′) *v.* to force (something unwelcome) on someone

VIEWING THE PAINTING

John Haley

Viewing Response *The sky pictured here might well resemble the one remembered by the narrator. Only "a glimpse of the blue sky" is visible through the thick white fog.*

N Literary Elements

IMAGERY Sasaki emphasizes how foggy her neighborhood was. Ask students to discuss the significance of the fog. *(She says that the fog had the effect of cutting people in her neighborhood off from the rest of San Francisco and making them seem different.)* Point out to students that the image of the veil of fog also suggests that Sasaki's father chose a place that set his family apart from their heritage.

REAL-WORLD CONNECTION

Fear of the Unknown Explain to students that the U.S. government interned American citizens of Japanese descent out of fear that they would show more loyalty to Japan than to the United States. This fear proved to be completely unfounded (whole units of Japanese Americans distinguished themselves heroically during the war), but mistrust of one ethnic group by another is evident in many parts of the world today.

Activity Have students clip a newspaper or magazine article that discusses "ethnic cleansing" or religious hatred. Have students meet in small groups to relate a specific incident and to analyze the role that "fear of the unknown" plays in this cruelty and fighting.

L2 COLLAB. LEARN.

O Literary Elements

SYMBOL Ask students how Sasaki continues—and even expands—the image of the fog. *(As she leaves San Francisco for Japan, she emerges from the fog. Suddenly she discovers the clear blue sky and "pure sunlight" hidden from her sight during her childhood.)* What message does this image convey? *(Her parents' fear, symbolized by the fog, was brought about by the shame of internment. This fear kept Sasaki from knowing her Japanese heritage, symbolized by the sun—an image that appears on the Japanese flag.)*

P Active Reading Strategies

CONNECT As we grow older, we sometimes discover we have confused memories of events, just as Sasaki learns that the house she imagined when she heard the story of her birth was not where she was actually born. Ask volunteers to relate similar experiences.

Thematic Focus

No Place Like Home Ask students to discuss where they think Sasaki would call "home" at the end of the essay—the United States or Japan. Have them use evidence from the essay to support their responses.

ASSESSMENT

Quick Checks, p. 3

When we studied California history, we learned about Father Junipero Serra[17] and the California missions. History, it seemed, focused on the conquerors, never the conquered.

The first time I went to Japan, I was twenty-two. My plane lifted off from San Francisco International, gaining altitude as it banked over the Golden Gate. Down below I could see the Richmond District, the geometrical avenues where I had spent my childhood. Then the plane entered the fog, and for a few seconds there was nothing but whiteness outside my window. For a few seconds, there was no east or west, no time. No memory. Suddenly, we were through. Above the floor of clouds, the sky was blue. The wing of the plane reflected pure sunlight. It was like all the time I was growing up, I thought. We were down there, under the fog, going to school and church and piano lessons—and all that time there was this blue sky, this glorious sun. And suddenly I hated that fog. I'm out of it, I thought, my heart leaping. I'm on this side now.

We were down there, under the fog, going to school and church and piano lessons—and all that time there was this blue sky, this glorious sun.

Going to Japan was like that for me—like breaking through the fog and seeing, for the first time, in full light, where I had come from. What my grandparents had left behind. What they had intended to return to, until circumstances intervened and they ended up staying in America. Until I went to Japan, I was a person without a past; I looked into a mirror and saw no reflection. All I knew was the little white house on 23rd Avenue, in the Richmond District.

It wasn't until I was much older that I realized that the house my mother returned to from the hospital, after she had me, wasn't that house. The school where my sisters had a Halloween parade that day wasn't the school that was just up the hill from that house. All those years, I had imagined the story, my story, in the wrong place.

Living in that fog-shrouded[18] world perhaps made it easier for my mother and father to forget the past—America's lack of faith, the internment, the shame. To forget a heritage that cast suspicion on their loyalty. I didn't have to forget—I never knew.

In wartime, one must choose sides. But the price for doing so can be paid for generations.

17. *Serra* founded the first Spanish mission of the Roman Catholic Church in California, as well as eight others.

18. *Shrouded* means "covered or concealed."

Teaching Support

Grammar and Language Minilesson

Titles Write "Sleeping Beauty" and "The Three Bears" on the board. Then write "The Lady or the Tiger?," Hamlet, Time, New York Times, and Star Wars. Explain that titles of longer works (those published *alone*, as books or monographs) are italicized or underlined, and titles of shorter works (parts of books, magazines, or anthologies) are placed in quotes.

Activity Give students several more titles, identifying their length, and have students punctuate them. **L1**

Additional Resources

Grammar and Language Transparency 3

Grammar and Language Workbook, p. 267

Grammar and Composition Handbook, Lesson 13.6

Writer's Choice, Lesson 20.6

Responding to Literature

PERSONAL RESPONSE

- What advice do you have for the narrator of this essay? Write a quick note to her explaining your ideas.

Brackets connect questions that are paired to develop higher-level thinking skills.

Analyzing Literature

RECALL

1. How did Sasaki learn she was both Japanese and American?
2. According to Sasaki, when can a person "forge ahead" without thinking of the past?
3. What does the ledger in her mother's head contain?
4. How does Sasaki define Japanese American?

INTERPRET

5. Why would the narrator wonder if she is English as well as Japanese and American?
6. Which of Sasaki's actions and words show that she is trying to "forge ahead"?
7. How does Sasaki's attitude toward paying off debt affect her life?
8. Why is a *bonsai* tree, both deformed and beautiful, a good image to represent the narrator's life?

EVALUATE AND CONNECT

9. Why does the author call this essay "A Dictionary of Japanese-American Terms"? How does the title relate to the structure of the selection?
10. How are Sasaki's concerns about being American like the concerns of other Americans? How are they different?

LITERARY ELEMENTS

Essay

An **essay** is a short piece of writing about a single subject. Essays are a type of **nonfiction,** writing that tells about real events and people. The writer of an essay uses facts, examples, and reasons to express an idea or an opinion. "A Dictionary of Japanese-American Terms" is a **personal essay,** an informal essay in which the writer reflects on his or her opinions and personal experiences. In contrast, a **formal essay** is a piece of writing that is serious, highly organized, and carefully researched.

1. What main idea or opinion does R. A. Sasaki express in her essay?
2. Find several facts, examples, or reasons that Sasaki uses to support her main idea.

- See **Literary Terms Handbook,** p. R3.

Responding to the Selection

PERSONAL RESPONSE

Some students may advise Sasaki to be sure that her own children learn about their heritage.

Analyzing Literature

1. Sasaki's parents told her she was *Nihonjin* (Japanese). She learned that she was also American after her argument with the Chinese American girl.
2. A person who knows who he or she is, or is accepted at face value, can forge ahead.
3. The ledger records every kindness given or received.
4. She says a Japanese American is someone who has been trained in Japanese courtesy but has a secret American sensibility locked inside.
5. She wonders whether she is English because she speaks English.
6. An example is "I would never be Japanese, so why try?"
7. At least one friend was hurt because Sasaki didn't remember having stayed at his sister's house.
8. A bonsai tree adjusts to its environment, but its growth is restricted.
9. Sasaki calls her essay "A Dictionary of Japanese-American Terms" because each section begins with a definition.
10. Like many other Americans, she questions language, values facts and her family background, and is "forward-looking." However, her value systems have been influenced by those of her family—even though her heritage has been hidden from her, as if it were something to be ashamed of. Also, her features identify her as "foreign," making assimilation more difficult.

LITERARY ELEMENTS

1. Sasaki expresses confusion and ambivalence.
2. As a child, she didn't realize that she was Japanese *and* American; she never knew her grandfather; and she was overwhelmed at the notion of absorbing Japanese culture.

Additional Resources

Literary Elements Transparency 3

Literature and Writing

Writing About Literature

Students' paragraphs should

- take a stand regarding the appropriateness of the fog-mind analogy.
- include at least two specific examples to support the position.

Personal Writing

Students' letters should

- clearly state the characteristics of the person in the mirror.
- follow the format and tone of personal correspondence.

Extending Your Response

Literature Groups Point out to students that Sasaki has chosen words that help her understand herself. Encourage students to choose words that make them think about who they really are. **COLLAB. LEARN.**

Listening and Speaking Encourage students to prepare several specific, open-ended questions before conducting the interview. Point out that "Please tell me about" is a good way to ask a question.

Performing Encourage students to consider all the senses before confining their performances to the expression of one or two.

Literature and Writing

Writing About Literature

Analogy An **analogy** is a comparison between two things to show how one thing is like the other. Sasaki uses an analogy when she writes that visiting Japan was like "breaking through the fog." Think about the similarities between a fog that hangs over the ground and a fog that might cloud a person's mind. In your opinion, is Sasaki's analogy appropriate? Explain your answer in a paragraph or two, and support it with examples from the selection or your own experience.

Personal Writing

Reflection Sasaki says, "Until I went to Japan, I was a person without a past; I looked into a mirror and saw no reflection." Look back at the reflection you created for the **Reading Focus** on page 26. Write a letter to Sasaki, telling her what type of person you see reflected when you look into a mirror. You might also point out some similarities and differences between the two of you.

Extending Your Response

Literature Groups

Words for Your Life Sasaki defined several words and phrases in her essay. In your group, discuss why you think she chose each one. What has she learned about life and herself from each word? Then take turns describing words or phrases you might choose in writing a narration of your own life. Be prepared to explain your choices.

Listening and Speaking

Interview The *nisei* wanted their children to be confident and to "shoot for the sky." Interview someone who lived through World War II. Record the person's experience and his or her wishes for the children of today. Share your interview with the class.

Performing

Present Yourself Sasaki says she'd never be Japanese because "there was too much to know, too much to be understood that could not be conveyed by the spoken English word." If this is true, how might we explain who we are without words? Present yourself to your class using the five senses (sight, touch, taste, smell, and sound). Bring in photos, music, videos, favorite foods, and other items to represent who you are—but don't speak!

Save your work for your portfolio.

Skill Minilessons

RETEACH • REVIEW

GRAMMAR AND LANGUAGE • PERSONAL PRONOUNS

A **personal pronoun** names a person or thing. A personal pronoun may be the subject or the object of a sentence.

Subjects:	singular	I, you, he, she, it
	plural	we, you, they
Examples:	*I* accused her. *She* started to cry.	
Objects:	singular	me, you, him, her, it
	plural	us, you, them
Examples:	Other kids never asked *me*. I didn't talk to *them*.	

PRACTICE Choose the correct pronouns (subject or object) to complete each sentence.

1. Going to Japan was like that for (I, me).
2. My father moved (we, us) out of Japantown.
3. (She, Her) wore dresses all the time.
4. *Jiichan* died when (I, me) was too young to remember (he, him).
5. (They, them) remembered (he, him) tending his beloved cherry tree.

● For more about personal pronouns, see **Language Handbook**, p. R32.

READING AND THINKING • ELABORATING

Elaborating is adding details and examples to support a statement or idea. Most paragraphs contain a main idea backed up with elaboration that illustrates the idea for the reader. Sasaki says that her neighbor Kimiko is a *Nihonjin* and then elaborates with examples of Kimiko's *Nihonjin* background, habits, and appearance. Good readers learn to recognize main ideas, and the details that follow add to their understanding of the ideas.

PRACTICE Find examples and details in "A Dictionary of Japanese-American Terms" that elaborate on each sentence below.

1. At the age of six, I thought "Americans" and "English" meant the same thing—"white people."
2. *Jiichan* died when I was too young to remember him, but old enough to be afraid of death.
3. Perhaps I was simply born too late.
4. A Japanese American is . . . like a *bonsai*.

● For more about main idea and supporting details, see **Reading Handbook**, pp. R98–R99.

VOCABULARY • COMPOUND WORDS

Compound words are combinations of two words. The meaning of the new word combines the meanings of the original ones. If you see an unfamiliar word made from words you know, use your imagination to get at the meaning of the new word.

painstakingly

The words *pains* and *take* appear in the phrase "to take pains with" something, which means to give careful attention to doing it right. *Painstakingly* means "in a way requiring close, careful labor or attention."

PRACTICE Think about each compound word, then match it with the best definition on the right.

1. pacesetter	a. important or interesting
2. outdistance	b. leave behind; get ahead of
3. overseer	c. a result or consequence
4. newsworthy	d. one whose speed others must match
5. outgrowth	e. one who watches over and directs work

Skill Minilessons

GRAMMAR AND LANGUAGE
PERSONAL PRONOUNS

1. me *(object)*
2. us *(object)*
3. She *(subject)*
4. I/him *(subject/object)*
5. They/him *(subject/object)*

READING AND THINKING
ELABORATING

1. ". . . Americans spoke English."
2. "He haunted my childhood by appearing in a nightmare. . . ."
3. *One possible answer:* "I was the only one who didn't remember living in the old Victorian in Japantown. . . ."
4. *One possible answer:* "A Japanese American is someone who has been trained in the Japanese ways of ultimate courtesy, but who has an independent and secret American sensibility locked into that pleasant "exterior. . . ."

VOCABULARY
COMPOUND WORDS

1. d 2. b 3. e 4. a 5. c

Additional Resources

- ***Grammar and Language Workbook,*** p. 107
- ***Grammar and Composition Handbook,*** Lesson 14.1
- ***Writer's Choice,*** Lesson 11.1
- ***Reading Skills Practice Workbook***
- ***Vocabulary Practice,*** p. 3

ASSESSMENT

- ***Quick Checks,*** p. 3
- ***Selection and Theme Assessment,*** pp. 5–6
- ***Performance Assessment,*** p. 3
- ***Testmaker: ExamView Pro***
- ***Interactive Tutor: Self-Assessment***

Before Reading

Objectives

- To read and analyze an essay about homelessness
- To identify and analyze a stereotype and to learn how stereotypes may lead to unfair judgments
- To write about an author's use of imagery

Skills

Reading/Thinking: Elaborating
Writing: Interview Questions
Vocabulary: The Prefix *En-*
Life Skills: Supporting and Contributing
Grammar/Language: Adjectives
Collaboration: Literature Groups

Motivating STUDENTS

Selection Focus Transparency 4: Before presenting the chart, ask students to discuss their ideas about homeless people.

Reading Focus: As an extension of the Reading Focus, have students follow Quindlen's lead and describe three "dumb things" they love about their homes.

Before You Read

Homeless

MEET ANNA QUINDLEN

Real life," says Anna Quindlen, "is in the dishes." Much of Quindlen's writing follows this belief that the best stories about the world focus on everyday activities and struggles. Quindlen began her writing career as a newspaper reporter, then went on to write columns for *The New York Times*, which at times dealt with politics, current events, and family life. Quindlen won a Pulitzer Prize for commentary in 1992. In addition, she has written a children's book, *The Tree That Came to Stay*, and two highly acclaimed novels about families.

Anna Quindlen was born in 1953. This essay was first published in 1989 in Living Out Loud.

READING FOCUS

How many places have you called "home" in your life? Which "home" is most special to you, and why?

Sharing Ideas
With your group, discuss how your ideas, likes, and dislikes have been shaped by where you have lived.

Setting a Purpose
Read to discover how some people carry their "home" with them.

BUILDING BACKGROUND

The Time and Place It is the mid- to late 1980s, and the writer is reflecting on her encounter with a homeless woman.

Did You Know? There may be as many as three million people in the United States who are homeless—that is, without a permanent address—according to estimates from the late 1990s. Some people are without a home for a short time. For others, being homeless is a way of life. Homeless people include families, patients released from psychiatric hospitals, and single men and women who are unemployed and poor. Many homeless people work but don't earn enough money to afford places to live.

VOCABULARY PREVIEW

anonymous (ə non′ ə məs) *adj.* having no known name or origin; lacking qualities that make one different; p. 40
legacy (leg′ ə sē) *n.* anything handed down from an ancestor or from the past; p. 40
enfeebled (en fē′ bəld) *adj.* lacking force, strength, or effectiveness; weakened; p. 40
crux (kruks) *n.* the most important point or part; p. 41

38 THEME 1

RESOURCE MANAGER

Teaching Tools and Resources
- Theme One Planning Guide
- Literature Groups Sourcebook

Essential Lesson Support
Lesson-Specific Instruction
- Selection Focus Transparency 4
- Literary Elements Transparency 4
- Active Reading Guide,* p. 4
- Selection Vocabulary Practice, p. 10

Assessment
- Selection Quick Checks,* p. 4
- Sel. and Theme Assmt., pp. 7–8
- Testmaker: ExamView Pro
- Performance Assessment, p. 4

Systematic Language Instruction
- Gr. & Comp. Hbk., Lessons 1.6
- Vocabulary Power, Lesson 3
- Spelling Power, Lesson 2

English Language Learners
- ELL Sourcebook, p. 21
- Spanish Summaries, p. 4
- Audio Library*
- English, Yes!

Spec. Needs/Strat. Interven.
- Interactive Rdg. Sbk., pp. T55–T57
- Interactive Rdg. Wbk., pp. 9–10
- Audio Library*

* Also available in Spanish

Homeless

Anna Quindlen

Her name was Ann, and we met in the Port Authority[1] Bus Terminal several Januarys ago. I was doing a story on homeless people. She said I was wasting my time talking to her; she was just passing through, although she'd been passing through for more than two weeks. To prove to me that this was true, she rummaged through a tote bag and a manila envelope and finally unfolded a sheet of typing paper and brought out her photographs.

1. In the New York City area, the *Port Authority* operates all of the major bus and train terminals, airports, harbors, bridges, and tunnels.

Reading the Selection

SUMMARY

Anna Quindlen tries to make homelessness less abstract and more concrete by focusing on individual homeless people and what these people miss by not having a home. She wants the reader to understand that the homeless are not just faceless numbers but individuals who don't have items that we consider basic—such as "curtains, a couch, a stove, potholders."

Spanish Summaries, p. 4

Active Reading Strategies

QUESTION Ask students why they think the narrator is "doing a story on homeless people." *(Students might guess she is working for a newspaper or a local charity.)*

VOCABULARY If you haven't previewed the selection vocabulary with students, stop and remind them to use context clues to unlock the meaning of new vocabulary words.

Additional Resources

- ***Active Reading Guide,*** p. 4
- ***Audio Library***
- ***Spanish Audio Library***

Teaching Support

CONNECTING TO OTHER SELECTIONS

The chart at the right shows three other ways to connect "Homeless" to selections in this book.

For specific teaching strategies, see the ***Theme One Planning Guide,*** pages 33–34.

Connection		Title
Life Skills: Problem Solving	→	"The Siege of Courthouse Rock," p. 414
Thematic: Personal Identity	→	"Identity," p. 317
Literary: Author's Purpose	→	*Flowers for Algernon,* p. 113

NO PLACE LIKE HOME 39

B Literary Elements

STEREOTYPE Have students provide details from the text to show how Quindlen debunks the stereotype of a homeless person. *(She gives Ann a distinctive personality. Ann says that she's "just passing through" and shows pictures of her home.)* Ask how students feel about Ann.

C Active Reading Strategies

QUESTION Ask students what they think Quindlen means when she says "I've never been very good at looking at the big picture." *(She means that she is a detail-oriented person. If she were seeing the"big picture," she would see Ann as a part of the large social problem of "homelessness.")*

D Author's Craft

DICTION Point out the way Quindlen uses concrete language—describing her hot water heater and dish rack, for example, to make her point. Ask students to find instances of concrete language. How does this affect their ideas about homelessness?

E Critical Thinking

ELABORATE Ask students to think about the kind of life Quindlen says we have "edged away from."

Model: I wonder whether there might be a lot less homelessness if people lived in the same place all their lives. No one would be anonymous then, and maybe people would help others more.

Teaching Support

Homeless

B They were not pictures of family, or friends, or even a dog or cat, its eyes brown-red in the flashbulb's light. They were pictures of a house. It was like a thousand houses in a hundred towns, not suburb, not city, but somewhere in between, with aluminum siding and a chain-link fence, a narrow driveway running up to a one-car garage and a patch of backyard. The house was yellow. I looked on the back for a date or a name, but neither was there. There was no need for discussion. I knew what she was trying to tell me, for it was something I had often felt. She was not adrift, alone, anonymous, although her bags and her raincoat with the grime shadowing its creases had made me believe she was. She had a house, or at least once upon a time had had one. Inside were curtains, a couch, a stove, potholders. You are where you live. She was somebody.

C I've never been very good at looking at the big picture, taking the global view, and I've always been a person with an overactive sense of place, the legacy of an Irish grandfather. So it is natural that the thing that seems most wrong with the world to me right now is that there are so many people with no homes. I'm not simply talking about shelter from the elements,[2] or three square meals a day or a mailing address to which the welfare people can send the check—although I know that all these are important for survival. I'm talking about a home, about precisely those kinds of feelings that have wound up in cross-stitch and French knots on samplers over the years.

Did You Know?
Cross-stitch is a needlework stitch that forms an *x*. A *sampler* is a piece of decorative needlework with embroidered letters in various stitches.

D Home is where the heart is. There's no place like it. I love my home with a ferocity totally out of proportion to its appearance or location. I love dumb things about it: the hot-water heater, the plastic rack you drain dishes in, the roof over my head, which occasionally leaks. And yet it is precisely those dumb things that make it what it is—a place of certainty, stability, predictability, privacy, for me and for my family. It is where I live. What more can you say about a place than that? That is everything.

E Yet it is something that we have been edging away from gradually during my lifetime and the lifetimes of my parents and grandparents. There was a time when where you lived often was where you worked and where you grew the food you ate and even where you were buried. When that era passed, where you lived at least was where your parents had lived and where you would live with your children when you became enfeebled. Then, suddenly, where you lived was where you lived for three years, until you could move on to something else and something else again.

And so we have come to something else again, to children who do not understand

2. Here, *elements* means "the forces of nature; weather."

Vocabulary
anonymous (ə non′ ə məs) *adj.* having no known name or origin; lacking qualities that make one different
legacy (leg′ ə sē) *n.* anything handed down from an ancestor or from the past
enfeebled (en fē′ bəld) *adj.* lacking force, strength, or effectiveness; weakened

MEETING INDIVIDUAL NEEDS — ENGLISH LANGUAGE LEARNERS

Favorite Stories Note that the elements of stories are the same in any language. Ask students to tell about some favorite stories in their native languages (ideally having to do with the importance of home) and to identify some of the elements. Who is their favorite character in stories they know in their native language?

Activity Have students describe a favorite setting for a story from their native language, perhaps one characteristic of their native country. Ask how knowing such stories helps them understand the selection.

Additional Resources

English Language Learners Sourcebook, p. 21

what it means to go to their rooms because they have never had a room, to men and women whose fantasy is a wall they can paint a color of their own choosing, to old people reduced to sitting on molded plastic chairs, their skin blue-white in the lights of a bus station, who pull pictures of houses out of their bags. Homes have stopped being homes. Now they are real estate.

F People find it curious that those without homes would rather sleep sitting up on benches or huddled in doorways than go to shelters. Certainly some prefer to do so because they are emotionally ill, because they have been locked in before and they are damned if they will be locked in again. Others are afraid of the violence and trouble they may find there. But some seem to want something that is not available in shelters, and they will not compromise,[3] not for a cot, or oatmeal, or a shower with special soap that kills the bugs. "One room," a woman with a baby who was sleeping on her sister's floor, once told me, "painted blue." That was the crux of it; not size or location, but pride of ownership. Painted blue. F

This is a difficult problem, and some wise and compassionate[4] people are working hard at it. But in the main I think we work around it, just as we walk around it when it is lying on the sidewalk or sitting in the bus terminal—the problem, that is. G It has been customary to take people's pain and lessen our own participation in it by turning it into an issue, not a collection of human beings. We turn an adjective into a noun: the poor, not poor people; the homeless, not Ann or the man who lives in the box or the woman who sleeps on the subway grate.

Sometimes I think we would be better off if we forgot about the broad strokes and concentrated on the details. Here is a woman without a bureau. There is a man with no mirror, no wall to hang it on. H They are not the homeless. They are people who have no homes. No drawer that holds the spoons. No window to look out upon the world. My God. That is everything.

3. In this context, *compromise* suggests being forced to make adjustments that might threaten one's independence or other personal interests.

4. A *compassionate* person sympathizes with the misfortune of others.

Vocabulary

crux (kruks) *n.* the most important point or part

F Active Reading Strategies

QUESTION According to Quindlen, why don't homeless people want to go to shelters? *(Some are emotionally ill and afraid of being locked up. Others fear violence.)*

G Active Reading Strategies

VISUALIZE Ask students what they picture when Quindlen says, ". . . we walk around it when it is lying on the sidewalk or sitting in the bus terminal. . . ." *(Quindlen is speaking about people figuratively avoiding the problem of homelessness as well as literally stepping around homeless people.)*

H Active Reading Strategies

EVALUATE In her last paragraph, Quindlen tries to destroy the stereotype of the homeless once and for all by focusing on small details: "There is a man with no mirror, no wall to hang it on." Ask students how successful they think she has been in debunking stereotypes about homeless people.

Thematic Focus

No Place Like Home Have students discuss Quindlen's definition of home. To what extent does she see a home as an essential part of who a person is? Ask them to cite examples from the text.

ASSESSMENT

Quick Checks, p. 4

Grammar and Language Minilesson

Adjectives Write this sentence from Quindlen's essay on the board: "We turn an adjective into a noun: the poor, not poor people; the homeless, not Ann or the man who lives in the box or the woman who sleeps on the subway grate." Explain that an adjective describes a noun. Tell students that substituting an adjective for a person is defining the person by only one of his or her characteristics.

Activity Have each student choose an object (not a person) in full view in the room and describe it with ten adjectives. As each adjective is read, encourage guesses about what is being described. Point out that objects usually cannot accurately be described by one adjective. **L2**

Additional Resources

- ***Grammar and Language Transparency 4***
- ***Grammar and Language Workbook,*** p. 121
- ***Grammar and Composition Handbook,*** Lesson 5.1
- ***Writer's Choice,*** Lessons 3.3, 12.1

Responding to the Selection

PERSONAL RESPONSE

Some students may suggest that a person's sense of identity would be diminished without a home because one relates what one does at home to who one is.

Analyzing Literature

1. Ann, a homeless woman, is carrying several bags and wearing a dirty raincoat.
2. The picture is of a house, which may have once belonged to Ann.
3. The author cherishes such "dumb" things as the water heater, the dish drainer, and the roof.
4. Homeless people can go to shelters or sleep in doorways, bus stations, and other public places.
5. Quindlen opened her essay with Ann's name to reinforce the idea that Ann is not just an anonymous homeless person.
6. Ann probably felt that having a home meant having an identity. By showing the picture to Quindlen, she could prove she was "somebody."
7. Quindlen describes household objects because she wants her readers to think in detail about what the homeless do without.
8. Some homeless people want a bed, food, and a shower but fear being locked up; others are afraid of violence at the shelters.
9. Quindlen evokes images of everyday objects, the things most people take for granted. These images involve the reader emotionally in the plight of homeless people.
10. Many students will feel that the essay has made homelessness more real to them through the use of details.

Active Reading and Critical Thinking

Responding to Literature

PERSONAL RESPONSE

- Think back to your discussion for the **Reading Focus** on page 38. In your opinion, how can not having a home affect a person's sense of identity?

Brackets connect questions that are paired to develop higher-level thinking skills.

Analyzing Literature

RECALL

1. Describe Ann, the woman in Quindlen's essay.
2. What was the subject of the picture that Ann showed the author?
3. What household objects does the author cherish?
4. According to the essay, what options for shelter exist for people without homes?

INTERPRET

5. Why, do you think, did Quindlen choose to open her essay with Ann's name?
6. What, in your opinion, was the significance of the picture for Ann?
7. **Theme Connection** Why, do you think, does the author describe the importance of household objects in her essay?
8. What conflict do some homeless people face when considering shelter options?

EVALUATE AND CONNECT

9. What images does Quindlen evoke in her essay? How do these images contribute to the effectiveness of the piece?
10. How does the essay reflect or enhance your understanding of the problem of homelessness? Cite specific writer's techniques.

LITERARY ELEMENTS

Stereotype

A **stereotype** is a generalization about a group of people in which individual differences are overlooked. Stereotypes might lead to unfair judgments because of a person's race, ethnic background, or physical appearance.

1. Quindlen's essay might be considered an attempt to break down the stereotype of "homeless people." What are some of the stereotypes Quindlen refers to?
2. What, according to the essay, is the effect of stereotyping on people without homes?

- See **Literary Terms Handbook,** p. R9.

LITERARY ELEMENTS

1. Quindlen points out that not all the homeless are emotionally ill; not all homeless people want to be homeless.
2. Stereotyping of the homeless leads people to think of the problem as an "issue," not something that is happening to real people.

Additional Resources

Literary Elements Transparency 4

Extending Your Response

Writing About Literature

Analyze Details Quindlen's essay uses details about the ordinary contents of people's homes, including her own, to make her point. What details can you visualize about Quindlen's home? about Ann's former home? Write a paragraph that explains how Quindlen's imagery contributes to the effectiveness of her essay.

Creative Writing

Interview Ann Quindlen wrote her essay after writing a newspaper article about homeless people. What interview questions do you suppose Quindlen asked Ann? Write ten questions you would ask Ann if you were to interview her.

Literature Groups

Words to Think About The essay "Homeless" is full of thought-provoking quotations about home and family. In your group, pick the quotation that you think best summarizes Quindlen's point of view. List your reasons and share them with the class.

Interdisciplinary Activity

Social Studies Research the problems of people without shelter in your community. How many people are considered homeless? What are some of the measures being taken to help people without homes? Gather information from agencies that offer food and shelter to needy people. Then write a one-page report to share with the class.

Learning for Life

Create an Ad Campaign Use photographs and information from newspapers, magazines, and government agencies to create an advertising campaign to make people aware of homelessness in your community.

Reading Further

For a story about a family of homeless children, read:
Homecoming by Cynthia Voigt

Save your work for your portfolio.

Skill Minilesson

RETEACH • REVIEW

VOCABULARY • THE PREFIX *en-*

A common meaning of the prefix *en-* is "to make or cause to be." For example, to *enfeeble* someone is to cause that person to become feeble. The prefix *en-* is spelled *em-* when it comes in front of *p, b,* or *m.* So, if bad luck *embitters* you, it makes you bitter.

PRACTICE Match each word on the left with the correct meaning on the right.

1. embolden	a. to give physical form to
2. enfold	b. to give authority to
3. embody	c. to cause to be more energetic
4. enliven	d. to wrap up
5. empower	e. to make brave

Extending Your Response

Writing About Literature

Students' paragraphs should
- include specific details from the essay
- analyze how the imagery contributes to the effectiveness of the essay

Creative Writing

Students' questions should
- explore different aspects of homelessness
- show sensitivity for Ann as a human being

Literature Groups Remind students to consider every group member's viewpoint before choosing a quotation. COLLAB. LEARN.

Interdisciplinary Activity Urge students to try to follow Quindlen's lead by looking beyond mere statistics as they do their research.

Learning for Life Encourage students to find creative ways to share their campaign with as many people as possible.

Skill Minilesson

VOCABULARY • THE PREFIX *EN-*

1. e
2. d
3. a
4. c
5. b

Additional Resources

Vocabulary Practice, p. 4

ASSESSMENT

- ***Quick Checks,*** p. 4
- ***Selection and Theme Assessment,*** pp. 7–8
- ***Performance Assessment,*** p. 4
- ***Testmaker: ExamView Pro***
- ***Interactive Tutor: Self-Assessment***

MEDIA Connection

Objective

- To read and understand the transcript of a radio broadcast

Literature LINK

Homeless Point out to students that this NPR broadcast has an effect similar to Quindlen's article. It, too, puts its audience in touch with real homeless people, and challenges some stereotypes we may have about them.

Analyzing Media

1. Some students may not have realized that children as well as adults are homeless.
2. Some students will agree that coverage by NPR implies that the message is being heard. Others may feel that coverage by major networks is the only real index of success.

Informational Text

inTIME For more examples of informational text, direct students to the articles in the *inTIME* magazine.

Additional Resources

Media Connections, p. 1

MEDIA Connection

RADIO TRANSCRIPT

What can anyone do about homelessness? A group of teens enlisted help from an imaginary bear.

Homeless Children Write Book About Homelessness

From *Weekend Edition Saturday*–National Public Radio, December 25, 1993

STACEY BESS, Teacher [reading]: In the winter, the Wasatch Mountains above Salt Lake City are made of snow. In the city below, tall, glassy buildings reflect street lights and car headlights that shine like the Milky Way. From the mountains, signs and buildings look like clouds and rocky slopes. Even smart animals could get lost here. That's what happened to a bear cub named Frankie.

HOWARD BERKES, Reporter: "Even smart animals could get lost here. Anyone can become homeless." That's the first message sent by the forty-four young authors of *The Homeless Hibernating Bear*, a story they set here in Salt Lake City on busy downtown streets because this is where they were homeless and poor. Most of the kids lived for a time at the city's homeless shelter—a bright, brick, renovated building on a block framed by railroad tracks. Some were part of a peer support group made up of homeless and low-income kids.

BERKES [to students]: Does this book have a happy ending ? In your minds?

WHOLE GROUP: Yes, I think it does.

BERKES: Does it happen that way in real life?

ANNIE [one of the students]: Unfortunately not. I mean, if it did, there wouldn't be homelessness.

BERKES: Are you trying to get people to change the way they behave?

ANNIE: We want the pity stopped, you know, "all these little poor homeless people." You know, it's easy to say something like that, and give money, but it's a different thing to try to work at it, and get it so that it ends, you know.

BERKES: At the School With No Name, a dozen kids autograph their books. And there's talk of movie and cartoon deals, and network television appearances.

ANNIE: I feel like my voice is being heard, giving this message to people. I know it's working, because you're here asking these questions, and I mean, all these people. . . . It just kind of blows them away to think that kids can be thinking, you know, like this.

Analyzing Media

1. What did you learn about homelessness from this part of the NPR broadcast?
2. Do you agree with Annie when she says: "I know it's working, because you're here asking these questions"? Explain your answer.

44 THEME 1

Teaching Support

interNET CONNECTION

Homelessness Have students use a search engine to look for additional information about homeless people.

Reading Minilesson

Identify Author's Purpose Point out that both Quindlen's article and the NPR interview try to give a "human face" to homelessness. Tell students that, as readers, their job is to evaluate the effectiveness of the presentation.

Activity Have groups discuss the various purposes that authors have for writing about a social problem, such as homelessness or illiteracy. Create a class list of reasons, including to draw attention, to persuade, and to inform. Lead a discussion of social causes, and how people feel more inclined to support one if they know someone affected by it. **L3** COLLAB. LEARN.

Additional Resources

Reading Skils Practice Workbook

GRAMMAR LINK

Avoiding Sentence Fragments

A complete sentence contains a subject and a verb. A **sentence fragment** leaves out the subject or the verb. People often speak in sentence fragments, but writers must be more careful.

Problem 1 The subject is missing.
Was born in West Virginia but grew up in Harlem.

Solution Add a subject.
Myers was born in West Virginia but grew up in Harlem.

Problem 2 The subject and verb are missing.
As a child, he read comic books. Even during class.

Solution A Combine the fragment with another sentence.
As a child, he read comic books, even during class.

Solution B Rewrite the fragment as a complete sentence.
As a child, he read comic books. He even read them during class.

Problem 3 The verb is missing.
After high school, Myers faced a problem. No money for college.

Solution A *After high school, Myers faced a problem–no money for college.* [Combine the fragment with another sentence.]

Solution B *After high school, Myers faced a problem. No money was available for college.* [Add a verb to the fragment.]

- For more about sentence fragments, see **Language Handbook**, p. R11.

ACTIVITY

Rewrite the following paragraph to correct the sentence fragments.

When she was twenty-two. R. A. Sasaki flew to Japan. The fog of San Francisco became a symbol. For her confusion. And hidden truth about her roots.

GRAMMAR LINK

Objective

- To recognize and correct sentence fragments

Teaching Strategies

After students read the explanation in the book, reiterate that there are two basic strategies for correcting sentence fragments: (1) **Add** a subject or verb and (2) **Combine** the fragment with another sentence by inserting a conjunction, adverb, preposition, or semicolon. Present the following example, and ask students to apply the combining strategy: *After dinner Mary had a stomach ache. Ate too much food.*

Activity

One acceptable solution: When she was twenty-two, R. A. Sasaki flew to Japan. The fog of San Francisco became a symbol for her confusion and the hidden truth about her roots.

Additional Resources

- ***Grammar and Language Workbook,*** p. 51
- ***Grammar and Composition Handbook,*** Lesson 1.2

Teaching Support

Writing Minilesson

Sentence Variety Ask students to reread a paragraph from Quindlen's article "Homeless," looking at the length of each sentence. Point out that good writers vary the length of their sentences. This technique helps hold the reader's attention and makes an essay or story sound smoother and more rhythmical. Tell students that they should try to vary the length of their own sentences.

Activity Have students choose one piece of writing from their portfolio. Ask them to rewrite one or two paragraphs, paying special attention to the length of their sentences. Suggest that students include their revised paragraphs in their portfolios. **L2**

Additional Resources

- ***Writer's Choice,*** Lesson 2.6

Objective

- To understand the elements of a short story

Teaching Strategies

Explain that these four elements are found in all short stories, although with different emphases.

Characters Invite students to think about what they have read in Theme One. Who are the most memorable characters?

Plot Ask students to review "The Treasure of Lemon Brown" and to identify each plot element. *(**Exposition:** Greg's dilemma and his relationship with his father; **Rising action:** begins when the thugs try to steal Brown's treasure; **Climax:** when Greg learns what Brown's treasure is; **Falling action:** Greg's walk home; **Resolution:** when Greg thinks of the lecture he will get.)* If students have not read this selection, choose another.

Teaching Support

GENRE FOCUS

FICTION

Many of the selections in this book are **short stories**, brief works of prose fiction. **Fiction** is writing about imaginary people and events. **Novels**, the longest type of fiction, are at least a hundred pages long and have more complex plots and characters than short stories. They also have a greater variety of settings. **Novellas** are shorter than novels but longer than short stories. All three types of fiction are unique, but most have the same basic features. The following examples from "The Farmer and His Sons," a fable by Aesop, explain how each element of fiction works.

WHO IS THE STORY ABOUT?

CHARACTERS are the actors, usually people, in a story. The main character is the **protagonist**. The person or force opposing the protagonist is the **antagonist**. A short story or novella usually has one protagonist. A novel may include more than one.

MODEL

In "The Farmer and His Sons," the characters are the father and several brothers. The father is the protagonist.

WHAT HAPPENS TO THE CHARACTERS?

PLOT is the series of events showing how a conflict or problem is resolved. The conflict may be between characters; between a character and an idea (such as *right* or *wrong*); or between a character and a force, such as *nature*. A plot usually unfolds in five steps:

1. **Exposition** introduces the story's setting and characters and sets up the conflict.
2. **Rising Action** develops the story's conflict or problem and builds suspense.
3. **Climax** is the moment of greatest suspense, emotion, and interest.
4. **Falling Action** reveals what happens to the characters after the climax and moves toward a conclusion.
5. **Resolution** completes the falling action and reveals the final outcome of the conflict.

MODEL

The conflict is between characters—the quarrelsome brothers who cannot succeed because they cannot get along.

MEETING INDIVIDUAL NEEDS — SPECIAL NEEDS

Less-Proficient Readers The short story is a form that requires skill because the author must create characters, situations, and settings using as few words as possible. Some writers specialize in the very short story, a form that may be particularly appealing to less-proficient readers.

Activity Assemble a collection of very short stories. Discuss the special characteristics of these brief tales? *(They depend primarily on plot and dialogue. Often they have surprise endings.)* Then assign each student a story to read and report on, focusing on the plot, dialogue, and the surprise ending. **L1**

Most plots contain five steps.

The Farmer and His Sons

A certain farmer had several sons who were always quarreling with one another, and, try as he might, he could not get them to live together in harmony. So he made up his mind to convince them of their foolishness by the following means: First, he asked them to fetch a bundle of sticks, and challenged each in turn to break it across his knee. All tried and all failed.

Then he undid the bundle and handed them sticks one by one. This time they had no trouble at all in breaking them. "There, my sons," said he. "You can see that when you are united you will be more than a match for your enemies, but if you quarrel and separate, your weakness will put you at the mercy of those who would attack you."

Union is strength.

1 EXPOSITION The farmer's problem is the quarreling between his sons.

2 RISING ACTION The farmer devises a plan for helping his sons to get along.

3 CLIMAX The farmer's plan is about to be revealed when he distributes the individual sticks.

4 FALLING ACTION The sons break the sticks easily.

5 RESOLUTION The farmer explains the lesson he has just taught his sons.

WHO IS TELLING THE STORY?

POINT OF VIEW is the vantage point from which a piece of fiction is told. The person relating the events is the **narrator**. In **first-person point of view**, the narrator is a character in the story. In **third-person point of view**, the narrator is outside the story.

MODEL

"The Farmer and His Sons" is told from the third-person point of view by a narrator outside the story.

WHEN AND WHERE DOES THE STORY TAKE PLACE?

SETTING is the time and place in which the story events occur. Short stories and novellas usually have a limited setting. A novel may stretch across different locations and a long period of time.

MODEL

This fable takes place on a farm a long time ago.

WHAT IS THE MEANING OF THE STORY?

THEME is the important message—or meaning—of the story. Sometimes the author states the theme directly, as in a fable. But often the reader has to figure it out.

MODEL

The theme of "The Farmer and His Sons" is that there is strength in unity.

Point of View Explain that a first-person narrator can describe only what he or she sees, hears, or knows. A third-person narrator outside the story is not limited in this way. A third-person narrator can describe the thoughts and feelings of all the characters in the story.

Setting Explain that setting includes such elements as weather, time, place, culture, and season of the year. Invite students to share examples of ways that the setting has enhanced the mood, the plot, and the characters in a story they have read.

Theme Explain that the theme is the central message or meaning of a story or narrative and that stories can have more than one theme. Ask them which theme in Theme One had the greatest impact on them.

Technology

Graphic Aids

Have students use a word-processing program to produce a graph to aid in their note taking.

Use a computer to make a chart that graphically depicts the four elements of a short story. If your computer does not have graphic capabilities, insert a two-row, two-column chart and label each box with a short story element. Fill in the cells with your notes on each element.

Short Story Elements

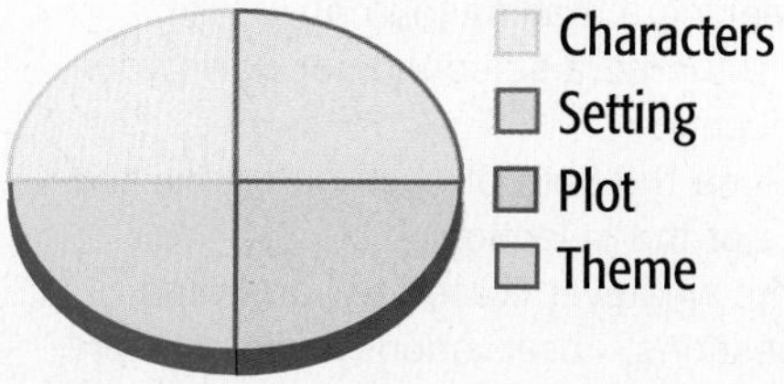

Students can use their charts as study guides or for information for writing.

Active Reading Strategies

Objective

- To understand and apply strategies for reading and understanding short stories

Teach the Strategies

Ask each student to identify something that he or she does well. Then ask each student to write the steps involved in mastering the skill. Invite one or more students to share their lists. Discuss how these skills were acquired. Explain that the acquisition of a skill in reading, as with most other skills, requires involvement. Good readers ask questions, make connections and predictions, and respond to the ideas and emotions they encounter.

Question

Explain to students that good readers are constantly asking and answering questions about the story. They ask questions such as *Why did he do that?* and *What does she mean?*

Connect

Point out that readers should always be on the lookout for links among elements in the story and between the story and real life.

Teaching Support

ACTIVE READING MODEL

Active Reading Strategies

Active Reading Strategies for Fiction

Active readers of fiction talk back to writers. They ask questions and compare writers' ideas with their own experiences. Use the strategies below as you discover ways several writers relate to the saying that there is "no place like home."

- For more about these and other reading strategies, see **Reading Handbook,** pp. R93–R108.

QUESTION

Questioning as you read helps you make sure you are getting to know the characters.

Ask Yourself . . .

- Why do characters behave as they do?
- Do people I know behave this way?
- Did I miss anything I need to know about the characters and the reasons for their actions?

CONNECT

Connecting helps you discover ways that stories reflect real lives.

Ask Yourself . . .

- What does "home" mean in this story?
- How does the selection fit my idea of "home"?

Reading Journal

Getting Started

Students will use their reading journals to record their thoughts and responses while reading. At times, students will be responding to questions incorporated in the selections, but they should also be encouraged to record their ideas and questions whenever they read independently.

Activity Share with students these tips for keeping a reading journal:

- As you read a selection, jot down your thoughts.
- Include the date of each entry and the title of the selection.
- Write whatever comes to your mind. Questions, observations, opinions, predictions, and strong reactions all make for good reading journal entries.
- Remember that you are writing for yourself. A reading journal is a record of your own thought process.

PREDICT

Predicting helps you put details together logically and make educated guesses about what characters will do.

Ask Yourself . . .

- What do I think the characters may do next?
- How will their ideas about home affect the way they act and react to events in the story?

RESPOND

Respond to the characters and events. Think about how they make you feel.

Ask Yourself . . .

- What does this selection say to me?
- How do I feel about the way the plot wraps up?
- What does the theme of the selection say about "home"?

APPLYING THE STRATEGIES

As you read "Golden Glass," follow the Active Reading Model in the margins to get more out of the story.

Predict

One of the best ways to get involved in reading is by predicting what will happen next or what the character will do or say. Emphasize that it is impossible to read passively if one is making predictions. Point out that, as they learn more about the characters or the situation, they may want to change a prediction.

Respond

Explain that active reading involves responding—deciding what the story means to you and what you think about it. Whereas the other three strategies require you to jump into the selection, responding involves stepping back from the selection and seeing where you've been and how the experience has affected you.

Before Reading

Objectives

- To read and analyze a short story about a boy who spends a summer "away" from home, living in a tree house
- To analyze the relationship of the setting of a story to its theme
- To write a character analysis

Skills

Reading/Thinking: Drawing Conclusions; Identifying Cause-and-Effect Relationships
Writing: Journal Entry
Vocabulary: Latin Roots
Grammar/Language: Dashes
Listening/Speaking: Brainstorming
Collaboration: Literature Groups

Motivating STUDENTS

Selection Focus Transparency 5: Before presenting the photograph, ask students which kinds of art they find most beautiful and why.

Reading Focus: As an extension of the Reading Focus, ask students to draw or make a word picture of a place where they would like to spend a summer.

ACTIVE READING MODEL

Before You Read

Golden Glass

MEET
ALMA LUZ VILLANUEVA

What's the most important quality a writer should have? According to poet and fiction writer Alma Luz Villanueva, it's courage. "Writing takes all your courage—to stand by your work and see it through to publication—courage and luck (and discipline, discipline, discipline)," Villanueva says. Those qualities have helped Villanueva earn prizes for her poetry and novels, including a PEN award for fiction in 1994. Some of her work focuses on the search for personal identity, which Villanueva explores in the story "Golden Glass."

Alma Luz Villanueva was born in California in 1944. This story was first published in 1982.

READING FOCUS

In what sort of place would you most like to spend a summer?

Web It!
Make a word web showing a kind of place where you would like to spend a summer.

Setting a Purpose
Read to find out how one teenager spends a summer away from home.

BUILDING BACKGROUND

The Time and Place The setting of this contemporary story is the western part of the United States, but a similar story might be set anywhere there is a parent and a fourteen-year-old.

Did You Know? Many European churches constructed after the year A.D. 900 have magnificent windows of colorful stained glass. Smaller stained-glass objects, such as chandeliers and lamp shades, were introduced much later, in the nineteenth century.

VOCABULARY PREVIEW

angular (ang′ gyə lər) *adj.* bony and lean; p. 51
communion (kə mūn′ yən) *n.* closeness to, and sympathy with, another through sharing feelings or thoughts; p. 52
vividly (viv′ id lē) *adv.* clearly; intensely; p. 52
slither (slith′ ər) *v.* to move along with a sliding or gliding motion, as a snake; p. 52
concoct (kon kokt′) *v.* to make or put together, using skill and intelligence; p. 53
sheathe (shēth) *v.* to enclose in a case or covering; p. 54
hysteria (his ter′ ē ə) *n.* great, uncontrollable terror, panic, or other strong emotion; p. 54
meticulous (mi tik′ yə ləs) *adj.* showing great concern about details; p. 55

50 THEME 1

RESOURCE MANAGER

Teaching Tools and Resources
- Theme One Planning Guide
- Literature Groups Sourcebook

Essential Lesson Support

Lesson-Specific Instruction
- Selection Focus Transparency 5
- Literary Elements Transparency 5
- Active Reading Guide,* p. 5
- Selection Vocabulary Practice, p. 11

Assessment
- Selection Quick Checks,* p. 5
- Sel. and Theme Assmt., pp. 9–10
- Testmaker: ExamView Pro
- Performance Assessment, p. 5

Systematic Language Instruction
- Gr. & Comp. Hbk., Lessons 2.1

English Language Learners
- ELL Sourcebook, p. 22, 23
- Spanish Summaries, p. 5
- Spanish Translations, pp. 11–14

- Audio Library*
- English, Yes!

Spec. Needs/Strat. Interven.
- Interactive Rdg. Sbk., pp. T57–T59
- Interactive Rdg. Wbk., pp. 11–12
- Inclusion Strat. Sbk., pp. 1–2
- Audio Library*

* Also available in Spanish

Golden Glass

Alma Luz Villanueva

It was his fourteenth summer. He was thinning out, becoming <u>angular</u> and clumsy, but the cautiousness, the old-man seriousness he'd had as a baby, kept him contained, ageless and safe. His humor, always dry and to the bone[1] since a small child, let you know he was watching everything.

ACTIVE READING MODEL

A

1. Ted's humor is *dry and to the bone,* which means it is witty, but also sarcastic and sharp, as if it can cut through one's flesh.

Vocabulary

angular (ang′ gyə lər) *adj.* bony and lean

Reading the Selection

SUMMARY

Ted asks his mother whether he may build a fort in the backyard and live there for the entire summer. As Ted builds, he thinks about his father, whom he has not seen in four years. Eventually, Ted constructs a two-story house, the top story nestled in a cypress tree. As the summer progresses, Ted grows more cheerful and more at peace. He also takes a course in stained-glass making. When his window is complete, he installs it in his tree house. As fall arrives, Ted is ready to move back inside.

Spanish Summaries, p. 5

A Active Reading Strategies

EVALUATE Students should evaluate the description of Ted. Does the author's word choice paint a vivid picture of Ted's personality?

VOCABULARY If you haven't previewed the selection vocabulary with students, stop and remind them to use context clues to unlock the meanings of new vocabulary words.

Additional Resources

- ***Active Reading Guide,*** p. 5
- ***Audio Library***
- ***Spanish Audio Library***

Teaching Support

CONNECTING TO OTHER SELECTIONS

The chart at the right shows three other ways to connect "Golden Glass" to selections in this book.

For specific teaching strategies, see the ***Theme One Planning Guide,*** pages 41–42.

Connection		Title
Life Skills: Implementing and Performing	→	"I Have a Dream," p. 494
Thematic: Recognition	→	"The Other Pioneers," p. 468
Literary: Characterization	→	"The Kid Nobody Could Handle," p. 146

B Active Reading Strategies

QUESTION *(It means that a person is self-absorbed or self-centered.)* How do students think their family would react to the plan?

C Active Reading Strategies

CONNECT *(Although Ted's plan seems difficult, it can be carried out.)* Ask students how they would feel about spending the summer alone in a fort.

D Active Reading Strategies

RESPOND *(He seems to have thought out the plan carefully.)* Ask students what information about Ted's character they have gathered thus far. *(Possible responses: He is self-absorbed, he wants his independence from his mother, he is a careful planner.)*

E Critical Thinking

DRAWING CONCLUSIONS Why do Ted's eyes "flash" when his mother mentions his dinner night? *(He has probably assumed he will be exempted from household duties because of living outside.)*

F Active Reading Strategies

CONNECT Why, do you think, is Ted having second thoughts about living outside? *(He is fearful about being alone in the dark; he may also be feeling lonely.)*

Teaching Support

QUESTION

B What does it mean to be at the center of your own universe?

CONNECT

C Is Ted's plan realistic? Could teens you know carry it out?

RESPOND

D What do you think of Ted's plan so far?

He seemed always to be at the center of his own universe, so it was no surprise to his mother to hear Ted say: "I'm building a fort and sleeping out in it all summer, and I won't come in for anything, not even food. Okay?"

This had been their silent communion, the steady presence of love that flowed regularly, daily—food. The presence of his mother preparing it, his great appetite and obvious enjoyment of it—his nose smelling everything, seeing his mother more vividly than with his eyes.

He watched her now for signs of offense, alarm, and only saw interest. "Where will you put the fort?" Vida asked.

She trusted him to build well and not ruin things, but of course she had to know where. She looked at his dark, contained face and her eyes turned in and saw him when he was small, with curly golden hair, when he wrapped his arms around her neck. Their quiet times—undemanding—he could be let down, and a small toy could delight him for hours. She thought of the year he began kissing her elbow in passing, the way he preferred. Vida would touch his hair, his forehead, his shoulders—the body breathing out at the touch, his stillness. Then the explosion out the door told her he needed her touch, still.

"I'll build it by the redwoods, in the cypress trees. Okay?"

"Make sure you keep your nails together and don't dig into the trees. I'll be checking. If the trees get damaged, it'll have to come down."

"Jason already said he'd bring my food and stuff."

"Where do you plan to shower and go to the bathroom?" Vida wondered.

"With the hose when it's hot and I'll dig holes behind the barn," Ted said so quietly as to seem unspoken. He knew how to slither under her, smoothly, like silk.

E "Sounds interesting, but it better stay clean—this place isn't that big. Also, on your dinner night, you can cook outdoors."

His eyes flashed, but he said, "Okay."

F He began to gather wood from various stacks, drying it patiently from the long rains. He kept one of the hammers and a supply of nails that he bought in his room. It was early June and the seasonal creek was still running. It was pretty dark out there and he wondered if he'd meant what he'd said.

Ted hadn't seen his father in nearly four years, and he didn't miss him like you should a regular father, he thought. His father's image

Vocabulary

communion (kə mūn′ yən) *n.* closeness to, and sympathy with, another through sharing feelings or thoughts

vividly (viv′ id lē) *adv.* clearly; intensely

slither (slith′ ər) *v.* to move along with a sliding or gliding motion, as a snake

MEETING INDIVIDUAL NEEDS

ENGLISH LANGUAGE LEARNERS

Working with a Partner English language learners may find it helpful to work with a proficient English speaker to answer active reading questions. Help these students understand the nature of these questions by working with them to answer the first question on page 52: "What does it mean to be at the center of your own universe?" After students feel comfortable with the meaning of the phrase, encourage them to use examples from their own lives.

Activity Have students pair with a native English speaker to discuss the questions in the margins.

Additional Resources

English Language Learners Sourcebook, pp. 22–23

blurred with the memory of a football hitting him too hard, pointed (a bullet), right in the stomach, and the punishment for the penny candies—a test his father had set up for him to fail. His stomach hardened at the thought of his father, and he found he didn't miss him at all.

G He began to look at the shapes of the trees, where the limbs were solid, where a space was provided (he knew his mother really would make him tear down the fort if he hurt the trees). The cypress was right next to the redwoods, making it seem very remote. Redwoods do that—they suck up sound and time and smell like another place. So he counted the footsteps, when no one was looking, from the fort to the house. He couldn't believe it was so close, it seemed so separate, alone—especially in the dark, when the only safe way of travel seemed flight (invisible at best).

The Dream Tree, 1993. Daniel Nevins. Oil & acrylic on wood, 48 x 40 in. Courtesy Williams Collection.

Viewing the painting: How might the boy in the painting feel about Ted's fort? How might Ted feel about this tree?

Ted had seen his mother walk out to the bridge at night with a glass of wine, looking into the water, listening to it. He knew she loved to see the moon's reflection in the water. She'd pointed it out to him once by a river where they camped, her face full of longing—too naked somehow, he thought. Then, she swam out into the water, at night, as though trying to touch the moon. He wouldn't look at her. He sat and glared at the fire and roasted another marshmallow the way he liked it: bubbly, soft and brown (maybe six if he could get away with it). Then she'd be back, chilled and bright, and he was glad she went. Maybe I like the moon too, he thought, involuntarily, as though the thought weren't his own—but it was.

RESPOND H

When is a look "too naked"?

He built the ground floor directly on the earth, with a cover of old plywood, then scattered remnant rugs that he'd asked Vida to get for him. He concocted a latch and a door, with his hand ax over it, just in case.

Vocabulary

concoct (kon kokt′) *v.* to make or put together, using skill and intelligence

Viewing the Painting

Daniel Nevins, born in 1963, lives and works in Gainesville, Florida. He is known for creating paintings with floating and flying figures.

Viewing Response *The lone boy dozing in a tree would probably feel comfortable in Ted's fort. Ted, too, would probably enjoy losing himself in the broad tree.*

Cultural Note

Many cultures have adolescent initiation rites in which young men are isolated from their families to perform certain acts (such as hunting) before they are considered adults. Ask students to name familiar cultural rites that mark the transition to adulthood.

G Literary Elements

SETTING Point out to students the words that Villanueva uses to describe the setting *("very remote"; "it seemed so separate, alone").* Explain that these words also effectively describe how Ted is feeling.

H Active Reading Strategies

RESPOND *(A look is too naked when it reveals a person's innermost thoughts.)* Ask students why they think Ted responds to his mother's "too naked" look by avoiding her. *(Possible answer: He is not mature enough to deal with the idea that his mother is lonely.)*

Meeting Individual Needs: Multiple Modes of Expression

Spatial/Linguistic Young people often dream of a place of their own—a tree house or even an apartment over the garage, separate from, yet connected to, the family. Spatial learners may be able to draw such a place, while linguistic learners may be able to use words to describe a home away from home.

Activity Ask students to suppose they might do as Ted has done and construct a shelter on their parents' property out of readily available materials. Ask students to complete a detailed drawing or write a detailed description of a hideout they could realistically construct on their own in their yards. Where would they build? What materials would they use? How would they furnish the space? What would they do about food? **L2**

Active Reading Strategies (I)

CONNECT Ask students what Ted is thinking about before he remembers his father. Based on what the reader already knows about Ted's father, why might these thoughts lead Ted to think of him? *(Ted is thinking about being afraid [he sleeps with a knife and a pellet gun] and about being lonely ["he missed someone"]. His father had a mean streak and left his family, so Ted may both fear and miss his father.)*

Active Reading Strategies (J)

PREDICT *(Students may suggest that he will stick to his plans because he has spent so much time preparing the fort. He is also becoming more comfortable in his new surroundings.)* Ask students whether they think the separation from his mother will be beneficial to Ted and why. *(Some students may say that the separation will allow Ted to mature because he will have to face his fears alone.*

Active Reading Strategies (K)

CONNECT *(Possible responses: He wants independence from his mother; he enjoys his privacy; he is excited at the prospect of doing things he enjoys.)* Ask students how Ted shows his independence *(Possible responses: He is brave enough to sleep outside alone; he is a careful planner.)*

Golden Glass

He brought his sleeping bag, some pillows, a transistor radio, some clothes, and moved in for the summer. The first week he slept with his buck knife open in his hand and his pellet gun loaded on the same side, his right. The second week Ted sheathed the knife and put it under his head, but kept the pellet gun loaded at all times. He missed no one in the house but the dog, so he brought him in the cramped little space, enduring dog breath because he missed *someone*.

PREDICT (J) Does Ted seem to be the type of person who will stick to his plans for the entire summer?

Ted thought of when his father left, when they lived in the city, with forty kids on one side of the block and forty on the other. He remembered that one little kid with the funny sores on his body who chose an apple over candy every time. He worried they would starve or something worse. That time he woke up screaming in his room (he forgot why), and his sister began crying at the same time, "Someone's in here," as though they were having the same terrible dream. Vida ran in with a chair in one hand and a kitchen knife in the other, which frightened them even more. But when their mother realized it was only their hysteria she became angry and left. Later they all laughed about this till they cried, including Vida, and things felt safer.

He began to build the top floor now but he had to prune some limbs out of the way. Well, that was okay as long as he was careful. So he stacked them to one side for kindling and began to brace things in place. It felt weird going up into the tree, not as safe as his small, contained place on the ground. He began to build it, thinking of light. He could bring his comic books, new ones, sit up straight, and eat snacks in the daytime. He would put in a side window facing the house to watch them, if he wanted, and a tunnel from the bottom floor to the top. Also, a ladder he'd found and repaired—he could pull it up and place it on hooks, out of reach. A hatch at the top of the ceiling for leaving or entering, tied down inside with a rope. He began to sleep up here, without the dog, with the tunnel closed off.

CONNECT (K) In what ways is Ted like you?

Vida noticed Ted had become cheerful and would stand next to her, to her left side, talking sometimes. But she realized she musn't face him or he'd become silent and wander away. So she stood listening, in the same even breath and heartbeat she kept when she spotted the wild pheasants with their long, lush tails trailing the grape arbor,[2]

2. An *arbor* is a shady area covered over and partly enclosed by trees, shrubs, or vines. Here, the arbor is formed by grape vines, probably growing on an arch-like wooden frame called a trellis.

Vocabulary

sheathe (shēth) *v.* to enclose in a case or covering

hysteria (his ter′ ē ə) *n.* great, uncontrollable terror, panic, or other strong emotion

Teaching Support

Reading Minilesson

Identify Cause-and-Effect Relationships Explain to students that Villanueva uses a flashback to explain why Ted is fearful. Instead of saying directly, "Ted is afraid because his father left the family alone in the city," she hints at the reason by having Ted remember his earlier fear. She lets the reader know he is afraid by emphasizing that he sleeps with weapons and then portrays him remembering the nightmares he had when his father left. Villanueva leaves it to the reader to make the direct link between effect and cause.

Activity Have students work in pairs to find other instances in the story in which Villanueva suggests, but does not directly explain, why something happens. *(You may want to provide some hints: Why has Dad left? Why does Mom seem lonely? Why does Ted build a fort? Does living outside cheer Ted up?)* Have them fill in the following chart with their answers. **L2**

CAUSE	EFFECT

Additional Resources

Reading Skills Practice Workbook

picking delicately and greedily at the unpicked grapes in the early autumn light. So sharp, so perfect, so rare to see a wild thing at peace.

She knew he ate well—his brother brought out a half gallon of milk that never came back, waiting to be asked to join him, but never daring to ask. His sister made him an extra piece of ham for his four eggs; most always he ate cold cereal and fruit or got a hot chocolate on the way to summer school. They treated Ted somewhat like a stranger, because he was.

Ted was taking a make-up course and one in stained glass. There, he talked and acted relaxed, like a boy; no one expected any more or less. The colors of the stained glass were deep and beautiful, and special—you couldn't waste this glass. The sides were sharp, the cuts were slow and meticulous with a steady pressure. The design's plan had to be absolutely followed or the beautiful glass would go to waste, and he'd curse himself.

It was late August and Ted hadn't gone inside the house once. He liked waking up, hearing nothing but birds—not his mother's voice or his sister's or his brother's. He could tell the various bird calls and liked the soft brown quail call the best. He imagined their taste and wondered if their flesh was as soft as their song. Quail would've been okay to kill, as long as he ate it, his mother said. Instead, he killed jays because they irritated him so much with their shrill cries. Besides, a neighbor paid Ted per bird because he didn't want them in his garden. But that was last summer and he didn't do that anymore, and the quail were proud and plump and swift, and Ted was glad.

The stained glass was finished and he decided to place it in his fort facing the back fields. In fact, it looked like the back fields—trees and the sun in a dark sky. During the day the glass sun shimmered a beautiful yellow, the blue a much better color than the sky outside: deeper, like night.

He was so used to sleeping outside now he didn't wake up during the night, just like in the house. One night, toward the end when he'd have to move back with everyone (school was starting, frost was coming and the rains), Ted woke up to see the stained glass full of light. The little sun was a golden moon and the inside glass sky and the outside sky matched.

In a few days he'd be inside, and he wouldn't mind at all.

❖

ACTIVE READING MODEL

RESPOND

What do you think about Ted's attention to details? **L**

RESPOND

What are the things about Ted's family that you like? What things don't you understand about his family? **M**

Vocabulary

meticulous (mi tik′ yə ləs) *adj.* showing great concern about details

L Active Reading Strategies

RESPOND *(Some students may connect this attention to his careful planning of the fort. Students may say that it is an admirable quality.)* Ask students whether they would be interested in taking a similar class and why.

M Active Reading Strategies

RESPOND *(Students may say they like Ted's mother because she is understanding. They may not fully understand the conflict with Ted's father.)* What qualities of Ted's would make him a good friend? *(He is caring and fun and talented.)*

Thematic Focus

No Place Like Home Ted creates a setting, a space that belongs to him alone. Discuss how his home reflects his personality and how it helps him become more comfortable with himself and his situation.

ASSESSMENT

Quick Checks, p. 5

FINE ART TRANSPARENCY 10

You may want to use ***Fine Art Transparency 10*** to discuss ways in which building and creating are important to students.

Grammar and Language *Minilesson*

Dashes Write the following sentence on the board: *Maybe I like the moon too, he thought, involuntarily, as if the thought weren't his own—but it was.* Explain that the dash shows a sudden change in thought or speech.

Activity Ask groups to read the sentences on page 52 containing dashes. Have students discuss how and why the thought or speech is "broken."

Additional Resources

- ***Grammar and Language Transparency 5***
- ***Grammar and Language Workbook,*** p. 271
- ***Grammar and Composition Handbook,*** Lesson 13.8
- ***Writer's Choice,*** Lesson 20.8

Responding to the Selection

Personal Response

Some students may not have pictured a solitary place.

Active Reading Response

Students should support their responses with detailed examples.

Analyzing Literature

1. Ted proposes to live in a fort and not enter the house all summer.
2. Vida asks that he not damage any trees and that he still cook when it is his turn, but he may do so outside.
3. Vida watches the reflection of the moon on the water. Ted sees longing on her face.
4. He hangs up a hand ax.
5. She shows no signs of "offense" or "alarm"; she leaves him alone; but she recalls the images of him, much younger and dependent on her.
6. Villanueva shows the relationship between mother and son through their sensitivity to each other's feelings. Ted watches Vida for her feelings, and she is careful not to invade Ted's feelings or his space.
7. Ted realizes that he can like what his mother likes without liking it *because* she likes it.
8. The stained glass represents his meticulousness; the ax, the pellet gun, and the knife represent his concern with safety; the fort represents his desire to be alone.
9. This story primarily focuses on the development of Ted's character. He seems to become a contented, assured young man in one short summer.
10. The care he takes in making the stained-glass window shows his love of precision and his dislike of waste. The window is assembled from cut pieces of glass, in much the way Ted builds his fort and puts himself back together again. The light passing through it seems to reflect his passage into maturity and self-sufficiency.

ACTIVE READING MODEL

Active Reading and Critical Thinking

Responding to Literature

PERSONAL RESPONSE

- Look back at the web you made for the **Reading Focus** on page 50. How do your ideas of a good place to be compare with Ted's plan?

Active Reading Response

Which of your **Active Reading** questions was most helpful in understanding Ted? Why?

Brackets connect questions that are paired to develop higher-level thinking skills.

Analyzing Literature

RECALL

1. What summer plan does Ted propose?
2. What demands does Vida make regarding Ted's plan?
3. What does Vida watch as she stands on the bridge? What emotion does Ted see in her face?
4. What object does Ted hang above the fort door?

INTERPRET

5. Do you think Vida is bothered by Ted's desire to separate himself from his family? Support your opinion with examples from the story.
6. In what ways does the author make clear the relationship between Vida and Ted?
7. Explain what the author means in the sentence, "Maybe I like the moon too, he thought, involuntarily, as though the thought weren't his own–but it was."
8. What objects do you see in the story that symbolize Ted's personality? What does each object tell the reader about Ted?

EVALUATE AND CONNECT

9. In some stories, the writer focuses on a **conflict,** or central problem. In others, characters and their development receive a strong emphasis. Which type of story do you prefer? In your opinion, which type of story is "Golden Glass"? Explain.
10. How does Villanueva use the stained glass to develop the character of Ted?

LITERARY ELEMENTS

Setting

The time and place in which a story takes place is its **setting.** The setting includes any elements in which the action occurs: the historical period; geographic region; season; weather; and spaces, such as buildings, rooms, and landscapes. The culture in which the characters develop is also part of the setting.

1. Which details describe the geographical setting of "Golden Glass"? In what way is this setting important to the story?
2. Are the spaces in which Ted lives important to him? How do you know?

- See **Literary Terms Handbook,** p. R9.

LITERARY ELEMENTS

1. The most important details in terms of the geographical setting may be the trees. The redwood leads to Ted's feelings of isolation and loneliness.
2. Ted's feelings change with his surroundings; for example, the house is a source of conflict for him, but the fort offers him comfort.

Additional Resources

Literary Elements Transparency 5

Extending Your Response

Writing About Literature

Character Analysis Alma Luz Villanueva characterizes Vida and Ted by letting them speak and act in ways that reveal their personalities. Select an important trait of one character. Describe a scene in which that trait is displayed.

Personal Writing

Looking Back Think of a time when you felt a need for a change in your surroundings, or recall a story about someone who wanted such a change. Write a journal entry about the event. Explain how elements of the setting are important to you or the character about whom you are writing.

interNET CONNECTION

Aren't sure exactly which setting you'd prefer to visit? Discover some of the possibilities by finding the home pages of the fifty states. Study the information, follow the links, and examine the many beautiful and interesting places you may someday see.

Literature Groups

Did Ted achieve real independence during his fourteenth summer? Are people interdependent? Look up the two words in a dictionary. Then, with a group, consider the meanings of *independence* and *interdependence.* Brainstorm names of characters you have met in other stories, in movies, and on television. How is each character dependent, independent, and interdependent?

Reading Further

These books are about other teens who find personal spaces:
The Island by Gary Paulsen
A Solitary Blue by Cynthia Voigt
My Side of the Mountain by Jean Craighead George

Save your work for your portfolio.

Skill Minilesson

RETEACH • REVIEW

VOCABULARY • LATIN ROOTS

If you describe something *vividly,* you provide such a clear picture of it that you bring it to life. The word *vivo* in Latin means "live" and *vita* means "life." *Viv* and *vit* are roots, or basic word parts, that have to do with life or liveliness.

PRACTICE Use what you know about the roots *vit* and *viv* to answer each question.

1. How might a *vivacious* person behave?
2. Name one *vital* need that people have.
3. Who needs to be *revived?*

Extending Your Response

Writing About Literature

Students' character analyses should

- focus on one trait of one character
- describe a scene that displays the character trait selected

Personal Writing

Students' journal entries should

- specifically describe both settings—the original one as well as the new one
- clearly show how setting affects the character

Internet Connection To complete this project in a limited amount of time, divide the class into groups, and have each group visit several sites. Ask each group to share the highlights of its "tour" with the class.

Literature Groups As an extension of this activity, ask students to consider whether, and how, it is possible to be both independent and interdependent. COLLAB. LEARN.

Skill Minilesson

VOCABULARY • LATIN ROOTS

1. In a lively manner
2. The need for food or water
3. Someone who has fainted or been near death.

Additional Resources

Vocabulary Practice, p. 5

ASSESSMENT

- ***Quick Checks,*** p. 5
- ***Selection and Theme Assessment,*** pp. 9–10
- ***Performance Assessment,*** p. 5
- ***Testmaker: ExamView Pro***
- ***Interactive Tutor: Self-Assessment***

Technology Skills

Objectives

- To understand and use electronic mailing lists
- To practice subscribing to mailing lists
- To subscribe to and participate in mailing lists

Teaching Strategies

To pique students' interest in mailing lists, have them search for keywords *listserv* and *majordomo.* Explain that these are mailing list servers formed by groups with common interests or concerns. Have students browse the lists to find topics of interest.

Technology Skills

E-mail: Mailing Lists

Mailing lists are like clubs whose members are brought together by a common interest and electronic mail. To join the "club," you subscribe to the e-mail list. It doesn't cost anything to subscribe to a mailing list, and you can find a list on just about any topic that interests you. Once you sign up for a list, you'll receive e-mail relating to its subject. For instance, suppose you enjoy science fiction, and you want to find out what others think of your favorite writers, movies, or TV shows. You can subscribe to a mailing list that features discussion about science fiction. As a subscriber, you can read what other subscribers write and add your own contributions.

Information Overload

When you subscribe to a mailing list, you may find yourself—and your hard drive—overwhelmed with messages. Much of it could be electronic junk mail, also known as *spam.* This junk e-mail is a lot like the advertising delivered by post office mail.

The most common form of spam is the ad that masquerades as a message. Often, the subject line gives away its true identity. For instance, suppose you've subscribed to a mailing list for skateboarders. You browse through messages and come across one with a subject line that reads "The best board available!" Chances are, you've run across an ad.

Other spam can be eliminated by skimming your e-mail. If the subject line doesn't tell you enough, just run your eye quickly over the first few paragraphs of the message to see what you can discover about it. If it looks like something that doesn't interest you, delete it and go on to the next message.

Digests are another tool to help you avoid information overload. Many mailing lists offer a digest option. Instead of sending you dozens of messages daily, they will send a single e-mail with a brief summary of each new message. If a summary of a message looks interesting, you can request the entire message. Mailing lists that offer a digest usually eliminate spam as well.

Teaching Support

interNET CONNECTION

Using E-mail Wisely Suggest that students access a connection such as www.safeteens.com to learn methods of using e-mail and the Internet safely.

Interdisciplinary Connection

History Some students may be interested in learning about the origins of the Internet. Explain to students that the Internet began as a government-funded project and required users to know computer languages, such as COBOL.

Activity Have students log on to the Internet and investigate the history of a particular aspect of online communication, such as search engines or real-time interaction. Have students share their findings with the class. Then encourage students to evaluate their research and raise additional, unanswered questions about the Internet for further investigation. **L2**

Practice

- Access a search engine on the World Wide Web and do a keyword search for "list of lists." The search should lead you to a number of sites with searchable databases of mailing lists.
- Select one of the sites and do a search for literature, a specific author, or other keywords relating to your study in this class. The site's search engine will sift through the database looking for the keywords you specified. If it finds a match, a subscription address will be displayed. Copy it.
- Open your e-mail software. Send a message to the subscription address you copied earlier. Leave the subject line blank. Generally, the format to follow for your message is: subscribe, mailing list name, your name–for example: *subscribe scifi linda sanchez.* In some cases, you may be asked to use a slightly different format or procedure to subscribe. Follow the directions.
- A day or two after you subscribe, you should receive a confirmation message in your electronic mailbox. This message includes important information about the mailing list, the availability of a digest, and instructions for unsubscribing if you want to stop receiving messages.

TECHNOLOGY TIP

The first site you visit may not contain the list you're looking for. Check out several sites and search their databases until you find a few lists that seem promising. Also, read the terms of agreement before you subscribe to a list. Look for lists that have strict policies limiting spam.

ACTIVITIES

1. Find and subscribe to two or three mailing lists that focus on a particular hobby or pastime. In your journal, critique each mailing list. Do you find the information helpful? Are the discussions relevant? How does participation on the mailing list add to or detract from your interest in the topic?
2. Create your own List of Lists for students at your school to use or for your school's Web site. Focus on lists that will interest other students.

Activities

1. You may want to monitor the mailing lists the students choose or suggest they subscribe only to moderated mailing lists.
2. Have students compare lists to avoid repetition.

FYI

Netiquette Present the following rules for using mailing lists to students.

1. Do not "flame," or use offensive or harsh language.
2. Do not type in all capital letters. In cyberspace, typing in all capitals is equivalent to screaming.
3. Keep messages short and to the point.

MEETING INDIVIDUAL NEEDS — SPECIAL NEEDS

Emotional

Subscribing to mailing lists provides students with the opportunity to interact with others as they learn more about topics that interest them.

Activity Have students choose a topic that interests them, such as sports, movies, or comic books. Then have them search for and subscribe to mailing lists devoted to these topics. With practice, students will become familiar with mailing lists and will be able to apply their knowledge to research of all kinds. **L1**

Additional Resources

Inclusion Strategies

Writing Skills

Objective

- To use vivid examples to support generalizations in writing

Teaching Strategies

Narrate one of Aesop's fables to illustrate the importance of using examples. Point out that the fable could be summed up in the moral, but for hundreds of years people have preferred to arrive at the moral by reading the story. Stories are more interesting and often easier to understand than generalizations.

Activities

1. *One acceptable solution:* I love the funny dinosaur theme of the children's play area and the irresistible aroma of french fries at my favorite fast-food place.
2. Students' paragraphs should include one or two general statements, each supported by an example.

Additional Resources

Writer's Choice, Lesson 3.1

Teaching Support

Writing Skills

Using Examples: Pictures, Sounds, and Action

Early in the story "Mother and Daughter," author Gary Soto says that Mrs. Moreno, Yollie's mother, has a strange sense of humor. Then he uses this **example**:

> "Mom, wake me up when the movie's over so I can go to bed," mumbled Yollie.
>
> "OK, Yollie, I wake you," said her mother through a mouthful of popcorn.
>
> But after the movie ended, instead of waking her daughter, Mrs. Moreno laughed under her breath, turned the TV and lights off, and tiptoed to bed. Yollie woke up in the middle of the night and didn't know where she was. . . . She blinked her sleepy eyes, looked around at the darkness, and called, "Mom? Mom, where are you?" But there was no answer, just the throbbing hum of the refrigerator.

The phrase "a strange sense of humor" gives a general description of Mrs. Moreno's personality. The example turns the description into pictures, sounds, and action.

When you add examples to your writing, you can create images in readers' minds.

General Statement	Example
I hate to dress up.	My fanciest clothes are a T-shirt and clean jeans with no holes.

ACTIVITIES

Use examples to illustrate and strengthen your own writing.

1. Write one or more examples to bring the following statement to life: *My favorite fast food place is terrific.*
2. Write a short paragraph about one of your personality traits. Include several examples of your habits or actions to illustrate the trait.

Grammar and Language Minilesson

Adjectives Write on the board, "She blinked her <u>sleepy</u> eyes." *Sleepy* is an adjective modifying *eyes.* Point out that adjectives can come before the noun they modify or they can be predicate adjectives, which follow a linking verb and modify the subject of the sentence. Write on the board, "She was smart." Explain that *smart* is an adjective modifying *she.*

Activity Have students copy three sentences containing adjectives and three containing predicate adjectives from "Mother and Daughter." Have them underline the word each adjective modifies. **L2**

Additional Resources

Grammar and Language Workbook, p. 121

Grammar and Composition Handbook, Lesson 5.1

Writer's Choice, Lesson 12.1

Before You Read

Mother and Daughter

MEET GARY SOTO

Gary Soto grew up in a poor Mexican American neighborhood in California. His father died in a factory accident when Gary was only five. As a child, Soto didn't dream of being a writer, but his life changed in college when he came across a book titled *The New American Poetry.* "I discovered this poetry and thought, 'This is terrific: I'd like to do something like this.'" Soto is now the author of more than thirty books.

Gary Soto was born in 1952. This story was first published in 1990.

READING FOCUS

Think of a time when you couldn't get something you needed.

FreeWrite

Write in your journal about how you reacted to the disappointment of not getting what you needed or wanted.

Setting a Purpose

Read to understand what two people mean by "need."

BUILDING BACKGROUND

The Time and Place This story takes place in a Mexican American neighborhood after World War II.

Did You Know? Education makes a difference—inside or outside the classroom. High school graduates make more money than their peers who haven't graduated. College graduates earn even more. Many employers screen job applicants for reading and writing skills. Good readers learn a job more quickly than those who can't read well.

VOCABULARY PREVIEW

gloat (glōt) *v.* to feel or express pleasure or satisfaction in one's own success or achievement, especially in a triumphant or slightly nasty way; p. 63

meager (mē′ gər) *adj.* not enough in amount or quantity; insufficient; p. 64

taunt (tônt) *v.* to make fun of in a scornful, insulting way; p. 64

sophisticated (sə fis′ tə kā′ tid) *adj.* having or showing knowledge or experience of the world; p. 65

tirade (tī rād′) *n.* a long, angry or scolding speech; p. 67

lurch (lurch) *v.* to move suddenly in a jerky and uneven manner; p. 67

Before Reading

Objectives

- To read and analyze a short story about the relationship between a mother and daughter
- To identify tone, or the attitude an author takes toward his or her subject
- To write a character analysis, using comparison and contrast

Skills

Reading/Thinking: Evaluating; Visualizing; Making Critical Judgments
Writing: Description of a Person
Vocabulary: Etymology; Synonyms
Grammar/Language: Compound Adjectives
Life Skills: Decision Making
Collaboration: Literature Groups

Motivating STUDENTS

Selection Focus Transparency 6: Before presenting the cartoon, have students discuss humorous situations that can arise in a family.

Reading Focus: As an extension of the Reading Focus, have students discuss reactions to disappointment.

RESOURCE MANAGER

Teaching Tools and Resources
- Theme One Planning Guide
- Literature Groups Sourcebook

Essential Lesson Support

Lesson-Specific Instruction
- Selection Focus Transparency 6
- Literary Elements Transparency 6
- Active Reading Guide,* p. 6
- Selection Vocabulary Practice, p. 12

Assessment
- Selection Quick Checks,* p. 6
- Sel. and Theme Assmt., pp. 11–12
- Testmaker: ExamView Pro
- Performance Assessment, p. 6

Systematic Language Instruction
- Gr. & Comp. Hbk., Lessons 2.2
- Vocabulary Power, Lesson 4
- Spelling Power, Lesson 3

English Language Learners
- ELL Sourcebook, p. 24
- Spanish Summaries, p. 6
- Spanish Translations, pp. 15–16
- Audio Library*
- English, Yes!

Spec. Needs/Strat. Interven.
- Interactive Rdg. Sbk., pp. T60–T62
- Interactive Rdg. Wbk., pp. 13–14
- Inclusion Strat. Sbk., pp. 73–74
- Audio Library*

* Also available in Spanish

Reading the Selection

SUMMARY

Mrs. Moreno can't afford to buy her daughter a new dress for her dance, so she dyes an old one black. When it rains at the outdoor dance, the dye runs. Humiliated, Yollie leaves, runs home, and throws the dress at her mother. By morning, Yollie realizes she can't blame her mother. Mrs. Moreno uses some of Yollie's college fund to buy her new clothes for a date.

Spanish Summaries, p. 6

A Active Reading Strategies

PREDICT Ask students how the painting might influence their expectations of the characters.

Additional Resources

Active Reading Guide, p. 6

Audio Library

Spanish Audio Library

VIEWING THE PAINTING

Yreina D. Cervantes is a California artist and social activist whose work has appeared here and in Mexico. Women's, children's, and Chicano issues are represented in her own paintings and the murals she has created jointly with fellow artists.

De la Corazón (From the Heart), 1973. Yreina D. Cervantes. Watercolor, 16 x 12 in. Collection of the artist.

Teaching Support

CONNECTING TO OTHER SELECTIONS

COMPARING selections

This selection is paired with "Chanclas," on pages 71–72. A lesson for teaching a comparison of the two selections appears on page 74.

The chart at the right shows three other ways to connect "Mother and Daughter" to selections in this book.

For specific teaching strategies, see the ***Theme One Planning Guide,*** pages 49–50.

Connection		Title
Life Skills: Problem Solving	→	"The Black Walnut Tree," p. 299
Thematic: Life's Priorities	→	"Dust of Snow," p. 305
Literary: Third-person Limited Point of View	→	"The Drummer Boy of Shiloh," p. 439

Mother and Daughter

Gary Soto

Yollie's mother, Mrs. Moreno, was a large woman who wore a muumuu[1] and butterfly-shaped glasses. She liked to water her lawn in the evening and wave at low-riders, who would stare at her behind their smoky sunglasses and laugh. Now and then a low-rider from Belmont Avenue would make his car jump and shout "Mamacita!"[2] But most of the time they just stared and wondered how she got so large.

B Mrs. Moreno had a strange sense of humor. Once, Yollie and her mother were watching a late-night movie called "They Came to Look." It was about creatures from the underworld who had climbed through molten lava to walk the earth. But Yollie, who had played soccer all day with the kids next door, was too tired to be scared. Her eyes closed but sprang open when her mother screamed, "Look, Yollie! Oh, you missed a scary part. The guy's face was all ugly!"

But Yollie couldn't keep her eyes open. They fell shut again and stayed shut, even when her mother screamed and slammed a heavy palm on the arm of her chair.

"Mom, wake me up when the movie's over so I can go to bed," mumbled Yollie.

"OK, Yollie, I wake you," said her mother through a mouthful of popcorn.

C But after the movie ended, instead of waking her daughter, Mrs. Moreno laughed under her breath, turned the TV and lights off, and tiptoed to bed. Yollie woke up in the middle of the night and didn't know where she was. For a moment she thought she was dead. Maybe something from the underworld had lifted her from her house and carried her into the earth's belly. She blinked her sleepy eyes, looked around at the darkness, and called, "Mom? Mom, where are you?" But there was no answer, just the throbbing hum of the refrigerator.

Finally, Yollie's grogginess cleared and she realized her mother had gone to bed, leaving her on the couch. Another of her little jokes.

D But Yollie wasn't laughing. She tiptoed into her mother's bedroom with a glass of water and set it on the nightstand next to the alarm clock. The next morning, Yollie woke to screams. When her mother reached to turn off the alarm, she had overturned the glass of water.

Yollie burned her mother's morning toast and gloated. "Ha! Ha! I got you

1. A *muumuu* (a Hawaiian word) is a long, loose dress, usually in a brightly colored pattern.
2. Here, the *low-riders* are the drivers of cars that have been customized so that they ride close to the ground. In Spanish, *mamacita* (mä′ mä sē′ tä) means "little momma."

Vocabulary

gloat (glōt) *v.* to feel or express pleasure or satisfaction in one's own success or achievement, especially in a triumphant or slightly nasty way

B Active Reading Strategies

EVALUATE Ask students to discuss their impressions of Mrs. Moreno's sense of humor. Soto describes it as strange and gives an example to support his judgment. Do students agree with his assessment? Discuss how students would react if their mothers played this sort of joke on them. *(Some would be angry; some would find it funny; some would think their mothers were being thoughtful in not disturbing them.)*

C Literary Elements

TONE Explain to students that the way they interpret the paragraph that begins "But after the movie ended . . ." will depend on how they interpret the author's tone. To demonstrate tone, read the entire paragraph aloud twice, using a different tone of voice each time. First read it as if Mrs. Moreno laughed a wicked laugh, and emphasize Yollie's fear. Then read the passage in an upbeat tone to emphasize the humor in the situation. Explain that the difference in the two readings is in tone—how the reader interprets the passage. Taken out of context, the passage could be read either way. Considering how much Mrs. Moreno loves her daughter, however, it seems more likely that the passage is intended to be funny.

D Critical Thinking

EVALUATE Ask students what they think of Yollie's revenge on her mother. Is it funny? Is it appropriate? How do they think their own parents would react in this situation?

MEETING INDIVIDUAL NEEDS — ENGLISH LANGUAGE LEARNERS

Parents and Daughters Invite English language learners to comment on typical relationships between mothers and daughters in their cultures. Do daughters typically ask their mothers' advice and confide in them? How affectionate are they? Invite students to compare and contrast these relationships with that of Mrs. Moreno and Yollie. Encourage the class to join the discussion.

Activity Ask English language learners to write a brief summary of the discussion. Encourage each to work with a partner to compose their summaries and to edit each other's work.

Additional Resources

English Language Learners Sourcebook, p. 24

E Literary Elements

TONE Point out that Soto begins the story by using comic events and a humorous tone. On page 64, however, he shifts to a more serious tone. Ask students what elements give the reader a different perspective on the two characters. *(He explains that, despite jokes, mother and daughter get along. He highlights Mrs. Moreno's hopes for Yollie, Yollie's abilities and talents, and the hardships Mrs. Moreno faced in immigrating to the United States and in her own childhood.)*

F Literary Elements

CHARACTERIZATION Soto says that Yollie responds without sympathy to her mother to avoid hearing the stories of Mrs. Moreno's hardship. Ask students what Yollie's strategy tells us about her character. *(Some students may think that Yollie ought to be more sympathetic and be willing to listen to her mother. Many will identify with Yollie's not wanting to hear the story again and may like her method of avoidance. Others may think that not listening protects Yollie from dealing with the sadness the stories arouse.)*

G Literary Elements

CHARACTERIZATION Point out that Mrs. Moreno's sense of humor may spring from her wish to remain optimistic in the face of difficulties.

back. Why did you leave me on the couch when I told you to wake me up?"

Despite their jokes, mother and daughter usually got along. They watched bargain matinees together, and played croquet in the summer and checkers in the winter. Mrs. Moreno encouraged Yollie to study hard because she wanted her daughter to be a doctor. She bought Yollie a desk, a typewriter, and a lamp that cut glare so her eyes would not grow tired from hours of studying.

Yollie was slender as a tulip, pretty, and one of the smartest kids at Saint Theresa's. She was captain of crossing guards, an altar girl, and a whiz in the school's monthly spelling bees.

"*Tienes que estudiar mucho*,"[3] Mrs. Moreno said every time she propped her work-weary feet on the hassock. "You have to study a lot, then you can get a good job and take care of me."

"Yes, Mama," Yollie would respond, her face buried in a book. If she gave her mother any sympathy, she would begin her stories about how she had come with her family from Mexico with nothing on her back but a sack with three skirts, all of which were too large by the time she crossed the border because she had lost weight from not having enough to eat.

Everyone thought Yollie's mother was a riot. Even the nuns laughed at her antics. Her brother Raul, a nightclub owner, thought she was funny enough to go into show business.

But there was nothing funny about Yollie needing a new outfit for the eighth-grade fall dance. They couldn't afford one. It was late October, with Christmas around the corner, and their dented Chevy Nova had gobbled up almost one hundred dollars in repairs.

"We don't have the money," said her mother, genuinely sad because they couldn't buy the outfit, even though there was a little money stashed away for college. Mrs. Moreno remembered her teenage years and her hardworking parents, who picked grapes and oranges, and chopped beets and cotton for meager pay around Kerman. Those were the days when "new clothes" meant limp and out-of-style dresses from Saint Vincent de Paul.[4]

The best Mrs. Moreno could do was buy Yollie a pair of black shoes with velvet bows and fabric dye to color her white summer dress black.

"We can color your dress so it will look brand-new," her mother said brightly, shaking the bottle of dye as she ran hot water into a plastic dish tub. She poured the black liquid into the tub and stirred it with a pencil. Then, slowly and carefully, she lowered the dress into the tub.

Yollie couldn't stand to watch. She *knew* it wouldn't work. It would be like the time her mother stirred up a batch of molasses for candy apples on Yollie's birthday. She'd dipped the apples into the goo and swirled them and seemed to taunt Yollie by singing

3. *Tienes que estudiar mucho* (tye′ nes kā es to͞o′ dē är mo͞o′ chō)

4. The dresses come from a Catholic organization (named for *Saint Vincent de Paul*) that runs stores selling inexpensive secondhand goods.

Vocabulary
meager (mē′ gər) *adj.* not enough in amount or quantity; insufficient
taunt (tônt) *v.* to make fun of in a scornful, insulting way

Teaching Support

LITERATURE & HUMANITIES

National Women in the Arts Collection
"You've Tried to Break My Heart." [CD]

MEETING INDIVIDUAL NEEDS — SPECIAL NEEDS

Emotional Students with emotional difficulties can benefit from carefully examining the consequences of actions. Ask students how Mrs. Moreno reacts to Yollie's outburst of anger after the dance. Tell them that some people might not have responded so calmly. Discuss other ways Mrs. Moreno might have reacted. Ask them, "How might these different reactions have worsened the situation?"

Activity Have students write a brief paragraph describing the consequences of Yollie's anger when she returns from the dance. Have students identify better ways for Yollie to deal with her disappointment. **L1**

Additional Resources
Inclusion Strategies, p. 24

H

"Las Mañanitas"[5] to her. When she was through, she set the apples on wax paper. They were hard as rocks and hurt the kids' teeth. Finally they had a contest to see who could break the apples open by throwing them against the side of the house. The apples shattered like grenades, sending the kids scurrying for cover, and in an odd way the birthday party turned out to be a success. At least everyone went home happy.

To Yollie's surprise, the dress came out shiny black. It looked brand-new and sophisticated, like what people in New York wear. She beamed at her mother, who hugged Yollie and said, "See, what did I tell you?"

The dance was important to Yollie because she was in love with Ernie Castillo, the third-best speller in the class. She bathed, dressed, did her hair and nails, and primped until her mother yelled, "All right already." Yollie sprayed her neck and wrists with Mrs. Moreno's Avon perfume and bounced into the car.

Mrs. Moreno let Yollie out in front of the school. She waved and told her to have a good time but behave herself, then roared off, blue smoke trailing from the tail pipe of the old Nova.

Yollie ran into her best friend, Janice. They didn't say it, but each thought the other was the most beautiful girl at the dance; the boys would fall over themselves asking them to dance.

I

The evening was warm but thick with clouds. Gusts of wind picked up the paper lanterns hanging in the trees and swung them, blurring the night with reds and yellows. The lanterns made the evening seem romantic, like a scene from a movie. Everyone danced, sipped punch, and stood in knots of threes and fours, talking. Sister Kelly got up and jitterbugged[6] with some kid's father. When the record ended, students broke into applause.

Janice had her eye on Frankie Ledesma, and Yollie, who kept smoothing her dress down when the wind picked up, had her eye on Ernie. It turned out that Ernie had his mind on Yollie, too. He ate a handful of cookies nervously, then asked her for a dance.

"Sure," she said, nearly throwing herself into his arms.

I

They danced two fast ones before they got a slow one. As they circled under the lanterns, rain began falling, lightly at first. Yollie loved the sound of the raindrops ticking against the leaves. She leaned her head on Ernie's shoulder, though his sweater was scratchy. He felt warm and tender. Yollie could tell that he was in love, and with her, of course. The dance continued successfully, romantically, until it began to pour.

"Everyone, let's go inside—and, boys, carry in the table and the record player," Sister Kelly commanded.

J

The girls and boys raced into the cafeteria. Inside, the girls, drenched to the bone, hurried to the restrooms to brush their hair and dry themselves. One girl cried because her velvet dress was ruined. Yollie felt sorry for her and helped her dry the dress off with paper towels, but it was no use. The dress was ruined.

5. *"Las Mañanitas"* (läs män′ yä nē′ täs) is a birthday song.

6. The *jitterbug* is a lively, acrobatic dance that was popular in the 1940s and 1950s.

Vocabulary

sophisticated (sə fis′ tə kā′ tid) *adj.* having or showing knowledge or experience of the world

H Literary Elements

FORESHADOWING Ask students how they think this passage foreshadows the ending of the story. *(Although Yollie's birthday did not turn out exactly as she had planned, everything worked out in the end.)*

I Active Reading Strategies

PREDICT Note that Soto refers three times to the weather. The last time he says, "It began to pour." Ask students to predict what will happen as a result of the rain.

Vocabulary Skills

Etymology The word *sophisticated* is derived from the Greek word sophistes, meaning "expert" or "wise." Someone who is *sophisticated* is wise in the ways of the world. After World War II *sophisticated* also came to mean "refined and elaborate," as in "sophisticated automobile design." Have students look up the following words in a dictionary. Ask them to write the word as it was formed in Old or Middle English and indicate which language the word was borrowed from.

city (Middle English)
ugly (Middle English)
school (Old English)
altar (Old English)

J Literary Elements

FORESHADOWING Explain that Yollie feels sorry for the girl in the velvet dress. This foreshadows Yollie's discovery about her own dress.

Reading Minilesson

Visualize The ability to picture a scene described in a work of literature is an important aid to understanding. Note that Soto paints a detailed picture of the dance, including the people, the setting, and the weather. Ask why students think he devotes so much space to this part of the story. *(Perhaps he wants readers to see the dance through Yollie's dazzled eyes so as to share her disappointment when things go wrong.)*

Activity Ask students to reread page 65, jotting down all the visual elements. Then have them imagine the scene. Encourage students who enjoy drawing to reproduce the scene as they visualize it and discuss how well the drawings match what others imagined. **L2**

Additional Resources

Reading Skills Practice Workbook

K Critical Thinking

MAKE CRITICAL JUDGMENTS Ask students to think about Yollie's reaction to her dress's fading. Note that Yollie feels sorry for the girl in the velvet dress, yet she is convinced that everyone will laugh at her dress. How reasonable is Yollie's reaction?

Model: If Yollie feels sorry for the girl in the velvet dress, I wonder why she thinks people will laugh at her. She assumes people will know that she couldn't afford a new dress and dyed an old one, but they might also assume the dress was defective. I think I'd be embarrassed in either situation, so I think her expectation is normal, even if exaggerated.

L Literary Elements

CHARACTERIZATION Ask students what they think of Yollie's behavior toward Mrs. Moreno after the dance. What motivates her behavior?

M Active Reading Strategies

QUESTION Ask students to discuss Mrs. Moreno's reaction to Yollie's anger. Why does she decide not to say she's sorry? Why does she cry?

VIEWING THE PAINTING

Viewing Response *Students may base their response on the features and/or the expression in the painting and in their understanding of Yollie.*

Mother and Daughter

Yollie went to a mirror. She looked a little gray now that her mother's makeup had washed away but not as bad as some of the other girls. She combed her damp hair, careful not to pull too hard. She couldn't wait to get back to Ernie.

Yollie bent over to pick up a bobby pin, and shame spread across her face. A black puddle was forming at her feet. Drip, black drip. Drip, black drip. The dye was falling from her dress like black tears. Yollie stood up. Her dress was now the color of ash. She looked around the room. The other girls, unaware of Yollie's problem, were busy grooming themselves. What could she do? Everyone would laugh. They would know she dyed an old dress because she couldn't afford a new one. She hurried from the restroom with her head down, across the cafeteria floor and out the door. She raced through the storm, crying as the rain mixed with her tears and ran into twig-choked gutters.

When she arrived home, her mother was on the couch eating cookies and watching TV.

"How was the dance, *m'ija?*[7] Come watch the show with me. It's really good."

Yollie stomped, head down, to her bedroom. She undressed and threw the dress on the floor.

Her mother came into the room. "What's going on? What's all the racket, baby?"

"The dress. It's cheap! It's no good!" Yollie kicked the dress at her mother and watched it land in her hands. Mrs. Moreno studied it closely but couldn't see what was wrong. "What's the matter? It's just a bit wet."

"The dye came out, that's what."

Mrs. Moreno looked at her hands and saw the grayish dye puddling in the shallow lines of her palms. Poor baby, she thought, her brow darkening as she made a sad face. She wanted to tell her daughter how sorry she was, but she knew it wouldn't help. She walked back to the living room and cried.

The next morning, mother and daughter stayed away from each other. Yollie sat in her room turning the pages of an old *Seventeen,* while her mother watered her plants with a Pepsi bottle.

Portrait, 1972. Eloy Blanco. Collection of El Museo del Barrio, New York.

Viewing the painting: What do you see in this young woman's face that reminds you of Yollie?

7. *M'ija* is a shortened form of *mi hija* (mē ē′ hä), meaning "my daughter."

Teaching Support

Grammar and Language *Minilesson*

Compound Adjectives Write the following from pages 64 and 65 on the board: *eighth-grade fall dance, third-best speller.* Note that these expressions contain compound modifiers, which are hyphenated when they precede a noun, showing that they are considered one term. Two questions can help students determine whether a pair of words is a compound modifier (and not just a random pair of adjectives): Does the first word modify the second, and if taken together, do both words modify the noun? *(*Eighth-grade student *does not describe an eighth or a grade student but an eighth-grade student. In the phrase* tall, thin boy, *however, the boy is tall and thin. In the latter instance one would use a comma, not a hyphen.)*

Activity Ask students to find other instances of this hyphen use in the story.

Additional Resources

- ***Grammar and Language Transparency 6***
- ***Grammar and Language Workbook,*** p. 121
- ***Grammar and Composition Handbook,*** Lesson 13.8
- ***Writer's Choice,*** Lesson 12.1

"Drink, my children," she said loud enough for Yollie to hear. She let the water slurp into pots of coleus and cacti. "Water is all you need. My daughter needs clothes, but I don't have no money."

N

Yollie tossed her *Seventeen* on her bed. She was embarrassed at last night's tirade. It wasn't her mother's fault that they were poor.

When they sat down together for lunch, they felt awkward about the night before. But Mrs. Moreno had made a fresh stack of tortillas and cooked up a pan of *chile verde*,[8] and that broke the ice. She licked her thumb and smacked her lips.

"You know, honey, we gotta figure a way to make money," Yollie's mother said. "You and me. We don't have to be poor. Remember the Garcias. They made this stupid little tool that fixes cars. They moved away because they're rich. That's why we don't see them no more."

"What can we make?" asked Yollie. She took another tortilla and tore it in half.

"Maybe a screwdriver that works on both ends? Something like that." The mother looked around the room for ideas, but then shrugged. "Let's forget it. It's better to get an education. If you get a good job and have spare time then maybe you can invent something." She rolled her tongue over her lips and cleared her throat. "The county fair hires people. We can get a job there. It will be here next week."

Yollie hated the idea. What would Ernie say if he saw her pitching hay at the cows? How could she go to school smelling like an armful of chickens? "No, they wouldn't hire us," she said.

The phone rang. Yollie lurched from her chair to answer it, thinking it would be Janice wanting to know why she had left. But it was Ernie wondering the same thing. When he found out she wasn't mad at him, he asked if she would like to go to a movie.

"I'll ask," Yollie said, smiling. She covered the phone with her hand and counted to ten. She uncovered the receiver and said, "My mom says it's OK. What are we going to see?"

O

After Yollie hung up, her mother climbed, grunting, onto a chair to reach the top shelf in the hall closet. She wondered why she hadn't done it earlier. She reached behind a stack of towels and pushed her chubby hand into the cigar box where she kept her secret stash of money.

"I've been saving a little money every month," said Mrs. Moreno. "For you, *m'ija*." Her mother held up five twenties, a blossom of green that smelled sweeter than flowers on that Saturday. They drove to Macy's and bought a blouse, shoes, and a skirt that would not bleed in rain or any other kind of weather.

P

❖

8. *Tortillas* (tôr tē′ yäs) are made from corn or wheat meal and baked on a griddle so that they resemble very flat pancakes, and *chile verde* (chē′ lā vär′ dā) is a spicy sauce made with green chile peppers.

Vocabulary

tirade (tī rād′) *n.* a long, angry or scolding speech
lurch (lurch) *v.* to move suddenly in a jerky and uneven manner

N Active Reading Strategies

QUESTION Why do Yollie and Mrs. Moreno avoid one another the next day? *(Mrs. Moreno isn't sure what to do, and Yollie is probably ashamed of her outburst.)* What leads Yollie to conclude that "it wasn't her mother's fault that they were poor"? *(Yollie overhears her mother's "Water is all you need. My daughter needs clothes, but I don't have no money.")*

O Active Reading Strategies

QUESTION Why doesn't Yollie ask her mother for permission to go out with Eddie? *(Yollie may know her mother will allow her to go, may fear that her mother will punish her for her outburst by not allowing her to go, may be embarrassed to ask anything after having spoken so angrily.)*

P Literary Elements

CHARACTERIZATION Ask students what Mrs. Moreno's gift says about the kind of person she is. *(She can relate to pain and feels that sometimes future goals are less important than morale.)*

Thematic Focus

No Place Like Home Mrs. Moreno and Yollie go through the ups and downs characteristic of families. Ask students how Mrs. Moreno and Yollie would respond to the statement *There's no place like home.*

ASSESSMENT

Quick Checks, p. 6

Real-World Connection

Reading labels Have students research the labels on clothing to see how the care instructions differ. What temperatures should certain materials be washed in? Why should white clothes be separated from darker clothes? What effect do dryers have on clothes? What do the students know about treating stains? Have students come up with ideas for making a white dress permanently black and share these ideas with the class.

Fine Art

TRANSPARENCY 2

You may want to use ***Fine Art Transparency 2*** in a discussion of the ways in which parents' lives and values affect their children.

Responding to the Selection

PERSONAL RESPONSE

Some students may note that, although the details of their disappointments were different from Yollie's, their emotions were very similar.

Analyzing Literature

1. Mrs. Moreno turns off the lights and television set and leaves Yollie sleeping on the couch. Yollie puts a glass of water beside her mother's alarm clock so that her mother will spill it when she awakens.
2. Mrs. Moreno can't afford a new dress. Instead, she buys Yollie new shoes and dyes her white summer dress black.
3. It rains, and the dye on the dress bleeds.
4. Both Yollie and her mother feel unhappy after the dance.
5. Mrs. Moreno is a loving, cheerful mother who works hard to provide for her daughter. Yollie appreciates her mother, but she is sometimes embarrassed and annoyed by her.
6. Yollie doesn't have nice clothes like those of some of the girls at her school. She also has to study hard to succeed so she can provide for her mother in her old age. If Mrs. Moreno had more money, Yollie's life might be easier.
7. What happened at the dance was both humorous and sad. Although Yollie was unhappy, she will probably look back on the evening one day and laugh.
8. Although Yollie and her mother have an emotional relationship, they appreciate one another's point of view and feelings.
9. Humor is very important. Mrs. Moreno, despite what she has suffered in her life, is a cheerful and positive person. Her upbeat personality helps Yollie keep life in perspective.
10. Mrs. Moreno's humor and her love for her daughter help Yollie compensate for the difficult circumstances of her life.

Active Reading and Critical Thinking

Responding to Literature

PERSONAL RESPONSE

- Look back at the notes you made for the **Reading Focus** on page 61. Compare your situation with Yollie's reaction to not being able to buy a new dress. How are the experiences similar and different?

Brackets connect questions that are paired to develop higher-level thinking skills.

Analyzing Literature

RECALL

1. Describe the tricks that Yollie and Mrs. Moreno play on each other after the late-night movie.
2. Why doesn't Mrs. Moreno let Yollie buy a new dress for the dance? What does she do for her instead?
3. What happens at the dance?
4. How do Yollie and her mother feel after the dance?

INTERPRET

5. What kind of mother is Mrs. Moreno? Does Yollie appreciate her? How can you tell?
6. What effect does being poor have on Yollie's life? How might her life be different if her mother had more money?
7. Were the things that happened at the dance humorous, sad, or both? Explain.
8. Describe the ongoing relationship between Yollie and Mrs. Moreno.

EVALUATE AND CONNECT

9. How important, in your opinion, is humor in the lives of the characters? Explain, using examples from this story, other works, or your own experience.
10. Theme Connection What helps Yollie to compensate for the difficult circumstances of her life?

LITERARY ELEMENTS

Tone

Tone is the attitude taken by a writer toward a subject. The tone can vary from gloomy and threatening to cheerful and hopeful. For example, when Gary Soto describes the tricks that Yollie and her mother play on each other in the story opening, his tone is humorous.

1. What is the author's tone when he describes what happens at the party?
2. In your opinion, is the overall tone of the story hopeful? Explain.
3. How might the author be using tone to suggest something about the characters' lives?

• See **Literary Terms Handbook**, p. R10.

LITERARY ELEMENTS

1. Soto's tone is humorous and sad.
2. The overall tone is hopeful. Mrs. Moreno is a survivor, and she has taught Yollie to be a survivor, too.
3. By using a humorous tone to describe a serious subject, Soto may be suggesting that however poor one is, one can always find something to smile about.

Additional Resources

Literary Elements Transparency 6

Extending Your Response

Writing About Literature

Like Mother, Like Daughter? Write one or two paragraphs in which you compare and contrast Yollie and Mrs. Moreno. Use the following questions to help you organize your ideas:

- What do you think are outstanding characteristics of the mother and of the daughter?
- How does each character react to problems?
- What is the overall attitude of each toward life?

Creative Writing

Mom Award Suppose that Yollie wrote about her mother for a school assignment on "The Person I Admire Most." What would she say? Would she include anything negative? Write the assignment in Yollie's words.

Literature Groups

Paths to Success To Mrs. Moreno, studying hard is a path to success. Do you agree that education is the best way to prepare for a successful future? Why or why not? What other routes to success might Yollie consider? Are they equally likely to be effective? Explain. Be prepared to share your ideas with the class.

Learning for Life

Medical Careers Mrs. Moreno wants Yollie to be a doctor one day. But she doesn't specify what kind. Ophthalmologist? Pediatrician? Psychiatrist? Research a career in the field of medicine. Write a brief report. Include answers to the following questions: What is the specialty you chose? What kinds of problems does the specialist take care of? How many years of schooling are required to become such a specialist?

Save your work for your portfolio.

Skill Minilesson

RETEACH • REVIEW

VOCABULARY • SYNONYMS

Synonyms are words with nearly the same meaning. For example, *taunt* and *insult* are synonyms. However, you could *insult* someone accidentally, but you could not *taunt* someone accidentally. Taunting is a deliberate effort to make someone feel ashamed or ridiculous.

PRACTICE For each numbered word, write the letter of its synonym.

1. **gloat**
   a. praise b. boast c. scowl
2. **meager**
   a. scarce b. useless c. smart
3. **lurch**
   a. hurry b. stagger c. spin
4. **taunt**
   a. flirt b. criticize c. ridicule

Extending Your Response

Writing About Literature

Students' paragraphs should

- include both comparisons and contrasts
- answer all three questions posed in the assignment

Creative Writing

Students' essays should

- present Mrs. Moreno from Yollie's perspective
- use specific examples from the story

Literature Groups Point out to students that they don't have to form a consensus about this issue—they may simply "agree to disagree." Different points of view may be equally valid. COLLAB. LEARN.

Learning for Life Remind students that their reports should address all the specific questions indicated in the assignment and focus on one speciality.

Skill Minilesson

VOCABULARY • SYNONYMS

1. b
2. a
3. b
4. c

Additional Resources

Vocabulary Practice, p. 6

ASSESSMENT

- ***Quick Checks,*** p. 6
- ***Selection and Theme Assessment,*** pp. 11–12
- ***Performance Assessment,*** p. 6
- ***Testmaker: ExamView Pro***
- ***Interactive Tutor: Self-Assessment***

Before Reading

Objectives

- To read and analyze a story about a young girl at a party who is self-conscious about her *chanclas,* or old shoes
- To identify a writer's style—his or her individual way of writing and using language
- To write a diary entry

Skills

Reading/Thinking: Inferring; Connecting
Writing: Diary Entry
Collaboration: Literature Groups

Motivating STUDENTS

Literature Launchers: "Getting to Know Sandra Cisneros"

Videodisc Side A, Segment 3

Also available in VHS.

Selection Focus Transparency 7: Before presenting the quotation, have students discuss how important physical appearance is to them.

Reading Focus: As an extension of the Reading Focus, have students discuss how they have overcome embarrassment in the past.

Before You Read

Chanclas

MEET SANDRA CISNEROS

Sandra Cisneros (sis nā′ rōs′) is the only daughter in a family of seven children, and her brothers often made her feel like she had "seven fathers," she recalls. Her family was poor and moved frequently between the United States and Mexico, where her father's parents lived. Later, she wrote stories based on her early experiences "of third-floor flats, and fear of rats." As Cisneros put it, "They're all stories I lived, or witnessed, or heard; stories that were told to me." One of her best-known works is *The House on Mango Street.*

Sandra Cisneros was born in 1954. This story was published in 1983.

READING FOCUS

Think about a time in the past when you felt awkward or embarrassed.

Sharing Ideas
Discuss things that you can do, or that friends can help you do, to feel more comfortable in an embarrassing situation.

Setting a Purpose
As you read, concentrate on the emotions of the characters.

BUILDING BACKGROUND

The Time and Place This story takes place in a poor neighborhood where many Latinos live.

Did You Know? With a population of more than 22 million, Latinos are the fastest-growing minority in the United States. More than 60 percent of Latinos have roots in Mexico. Other places of origin include countries in South and Central America, Puerto Rico, and Cuba. Latinos work in virtually every sector of the U.S. economy.

VOCABULARY PREVIEW

baptism (bap′ tiz′ əm) *n.* a ceremony in which a person becomes a member of a Christian religion; p. 71
tamale (tə mä′ lē) *n.* cornmeal, meat, and red peppers in corn husks, cooked by steaming or roasting; p. 71

RESOURCE MANAGER

Teaching Tools and Resources
- Theme One Planning Guide
- Literature Groups Sourcebook

Essential Lesson Support

Lesson-Specific Instruction
- Selection Focus Transparency 7
- Literary Elements Transparency 7
- Active Reading Guide,* p. 7

Assessment
- Selection Quick Checks,* p. 7
- Sel. and Theme Assmt., pp. 11–12
- Testmaker: ExamView Pro
- Performance Assessment, p. 6

Systematic Language Instruction
- Gr. & Comp. Hbk., Lessons 2.3, 2.4
- Vocabulary Power, Lesson 5
- Spelling Power, Lesson 4

English Language Learners
- ELL Sourcebook, pp. 25, 26
- Spanish Summaries, p. 7
- Spanish Translations, pp. 20–21
- Audio Library*
- English, Yes!

Spec. Needs/Strat. Interven.
- Interactive Rdg. Sbk., pp. T62–T65
- Interactive Rdg. Wbk., pp. 15–16
- Inclusion Strat. Sbk., pp. 9–10
- Audio Library*

* Also available in Spanish

Reading the Selection

Chanclas

Sandra Cisneros

It's me—Mama, Mama said. I open up and she's there with bags and big boxes, the new clothes and, yes, she's got the socks and a new slip with a little rose on it and a pink and white striped dress. What about the shoes? I forgot. Too late now. I'm tired. Whew! [A]

Six-thirty already and my little cousin's baptism is over. All day waiting, the door locked, don't open up for nobody, and I don't till Mama gets back and buys everything except the shoes.

Now Uncle Nacho is coming in his car, and we have to hurry and get to Precious Blood Church quick because that's where the baptism party is, in the basement rented for today for dancing and tamales and everyone's kids running all over the place.

Vocabulary

baptism (bap′ tiz′ əm) *n.* a ceremony in which a person becomes a member of a Christian religion

tamale (tə mä′ lē) *n.* cornmeal, meat, and red peppers in corn husks, cooked by steaming or roasting

SUMMARY

A young girl, excited about a family party, waits eagerly all day for her mother to return from shopping for a new outfit for her. When her mother returns, she has everything the girl has hoped for—except new shoes. Horribly self-conscious in her old shoes, the girl feels as if her feet are the center of attention. Her uncle Nacho insists that she dance with him. Amid the applause of her family and the attention of a boy, she forgets about her old shoes.

Spanish Summaries, p. 7

[A] Active Reading Strategies

EVALUATE Ask students to consider the lack of quotation marks. Do they think this effectively portrays the mood of the conversation? *(Yes. Thoughts or conversations with oneself are not quoted. Not using quotation marks helps the reader see things through the girl's eyes.)*

VOCABULARY Remind students to use context clues to unlock the meanings of new vocabulary words.

Additional Resources

- ***Active Reading Guide,*** p. 7
- ***Audio Library***
- ***Spanish Audio Library***

Teaching Support

CONNECTING TO OTHER SELECTIONS

COMPARING *selections*

This selection can be paired with "Mother and Daughter" on pages 62–67. A lesson for teaching a comparison of the two selections appears on page 74.

The chart at the right shows three other ways to connect "Chanclas" to selections in this book.

For specific teaching strategies, see the ***Theme One Planning Guide,*** pages 57–58.

Connection	Title
Life Skills: Lifelong Learning	→ "The Lesson of the Moth," p. 318
Thematic: Seize the Moment	→ "A Time to Talk," p. 303
Literary: Conflict	→ from *Sound-Shadows of the New World,* p. 213

B Literary Elements

STYLE Ask students why they think that author Cisneros uses grammatically incorrect sentences in this selection. *(to capture the thoughts of the character in a real-life way)*

C Critical Thinking

INFER Ask students to explain how the girl feels when she says, "My feet growing bigger and bigger." Have they ever had a similar feeling?

Model: I can imagine having to kick up my heels while wearing shabby "clunkers"! I think that being asked to dance makes her focus on her old shoes. She must feel as though everyone is staring at her feet.

D Active Reading Strategies

QUESTION Ask students how dancing with Uncle Nacho changes the girl. What allows her to forget her shoes? *(Pride in her ability to dance—in her talent rather than her looks—overcomes her embarrassment about the shoes.)*

Thematic Focus

No Place Like Home Ask students how the girl's attitude toward home and family changes in this story. *(She learns to appreciate her family for what they do for her.)*

ASSESSMENT

Quick Checks, p. 7

Teaching Support

Mama dances, laughs, dances. All of a sudden, Mama is sick. I fan her hot face with a paper plate. Too many tamales, but Uncle Nacho says too many this and tilts his thumb to his lips.

Everybody laughing except me, because I'm wearing the new dress, pink and white with stripes, and new underclothes and new socks and the old saddle shoes[1] I wear to school, brown and white, the kind I get every September because they last long and they do. My feet scuffed and round, and the heels all crooked that look dumb with this dress, so I just sit.

Meanwhile that boy who is my cousin by first communion[2] or something, asks me to dance and I can't. Just stuff my feet under the metal folding chair stamped Precious Blood and pick on a wad of brown gum that's stuck beneath the seat. I shake my head no. My feet growing bigger and bigger.

Then Uncle Nacho is pulling and pulling my arm and it doesn't matter how new the dress Mama bought is because my feet are ugly until my uncle who is a liar says, You are the prettiest girl here, will you dance, but I believe him, and yes, we are dancing, my Uncle Nacho and me, only I don't want to at first. My feet swell big and heavy like plungers, but I drag them across the linoleum floor straight center where Uncle wants to show off the new dance we learned. And Uncle spins me, and my skinny arms bend the way he taught me, and my mother watches, and my little cousins watch, and the boy who is my cousin by first communion watches, and everyone says, wow, who are those two who dance like in the movies, until I forget that I am wearing only ordinary shoes, brown and white, the kind my mother buys each year for school.

And all I hear is the clapping when the music stops. My uncle and me bow and he walks me back in my thick shoes to my mother who is proud to be my mother. All night the boy who is a man watches me dance. He watched me dance.

1. *Saddle shoes* tie with laces and rise to just below the ankle. What makes a saddle shoe unusual is the band, or "saddle," of color across the middle that contrasts with the color of the rest of the shoe.
2. In the Roman Catholic Church, children of a similar age often receive their first communion as a group. The writer's *cousin by first communion* is someone who was in the same group when she had her first communion.

Reading Minilesson

Connecting Explain to students that the style and structure of this brief story is designed to elicit an emotional response. The lack of conventional punctuation, the run-on sentences, and the conversational style combine to convey both the self-consciousness of the girl as she worries about her shoes and the breathless delight she feels as she dances.

Activity Ask students to recall a time when they felt one or both of the emotions the girl experiences (delight or self-consciousness). Have them jot down their answers to these questions: *What caused the feeling? What did you learn from the experience? To what extent was your experience similar to the girl's?* **L2**

Additional Resources

Reading Skills Practice Workbook

Responding to Literature

PERSONAL RESPONSE

- Do you sympathize with the narrator's self-consciousness about her shoes? Why or why not?
- Think back to your discussion for the **Reading Focus** on page 70. What might you say to make the girl feel better?

Analyzing Literature

RECALL AND INTERPRET

1. Describe the girl's shoes. Explain how the shoes add humor to the story.
2. Explain how Uncle Nacho "rescued" the girl, and tell why you think his tactics worked.
3. How do the narrator's emotions change during the course of the story? What causes these changes?

EVALUATE AND CONNECT

4. The title of the story, "Chanclas," means "old, worn-out shoes." In your opinion, is the title fitting? Explain.
5. How would the story be different if it had been told without humor?
6. Consider the importance of old shoes in the story. Explain why clothing is or is not important in a social setting today.

LITERARY ELEMENTS

Style

An author's **style** is the way he or she chooses and arranges words. In "Chanclas," Sandra Cisneros sometimes runs sentences together without punctuation. Her purpose is to quicken the pace of the story, build suspense, and make the words sound like spoken language.

1. Cisneros sometimes treats sentence fragments like complete sentences or leaves out part of a verb phrase. Find an example of this style.
2. What other rule of punctuation does the author break? What effect does she create?

- See **Literary Terms Handbook**, pp. R9–R10.

Extending Your Response

Literature Groups

Family Theme In a group, discuss how the idea of family closeness is important to the story "Chanclas." Address these questions: What details give the reader a feeling for the girl's family? What might the author be saying about the value of the family in Latino culture? What does *family* mean to the girl? Use a word web with *family* in the center to show your answers.

Writing About Literature

Secret Admirer The girl makes several allusions to a boy who watched her dance. What do you think the boy was like? How did he feel about the girl? Write an entry in the boy's diary from the night of the dance.

Responding to the Selection

PERSONAL RESPONSE

Most students will empathize with a young adolescent's feelings of awkwardness at parties. Students' advice should be encouraging and helpful.

Analyzing Literature

1. Her shoes are old and worn. Her exaggerated descriptions of the shoes add humor to the story.
2. Uncle Nacho rescued the girl by insisting she dance and telling her she was pretty. His tactics worked because he understood what was bothering her.
3. The narrator starts out excited about her new outfit. When she realizes she will be wearing her old shoes, she is disappointed. She is able to enjoy herself though, because she shifts her focus to the attention paid her.
4. The title is fitting because it aptly names the major focus in the story—the girl's old shoes.
5. It might have been a sad story about a girl who had an awful time at a party.
6. Students may note that people still judge other people by appearances.

Extending Your Response

Literature Groups After groups have finished, have them share their work with the class. COLLAB. LEARN.

Writing About Literature

Students' diary entries should

- be written in the boy's voice.
- include specific details from the story.

LITERARY ELEMENTS

1. Possible answer: "My feet scuffed and round, and the heels all crooked that look dumb with this dress, so I just sit."
2. Cisneros substitutes commas for periods, heightening the effect of confusion and self-consciousness. She also does not use quotation marks, so the ideas seem like personal thoughts.

Additional Resources

Literary Elements Transparency 7

ASSESSMENT

- ***Quick Checks,*** p. 7
- ***Selection and Theme Assessment,*** pp. 11–12
- ***Performance Assessment,*** p. 6
- ***Testmaker: ExamView Pro***
- ***Interactive Tutor: Self-Assessment***

NO PLACE LIKE HOME 73

COMPARING selections

Objective

- To compare two short stories that deal with the theme of the family as an essential support system

COMPARE **SOLUTIONS**

1. Yollie has her mother in "Mother and Daughter," and the narrator in "Chanclas" has her uncle. Both girls seek male approval, so some students may see the uncle's admiration as more effective.
2. Both girls are sensitive, self-conscious, and emotional. Some will prefer the outgoing girl in "Chanclas."

COMPARE **RESPONSES**

1. In "Mother and Daughter," the dance starts out happily and ends unhappily. In "Chanclas," the reverse in true.
2. Yollie would probably choose a low number. The girl in "Chanclas" had a wonderful time and might choose 9 or 10. **COLLAB. LEARN.**

Additional Resources

Literature Groups Sourcebook

COMPARE **EXPERIENCES**

Students' paragraphs should

- present a stand on each issue.
- include specific details from the stories to support opinions.

Teaching Support

Critical Thinking

COMPARING SELECTIONS

Mother and Daughter and *Chanclas*

COMPARE **SOLUTIONS**

In both stories, a girl overcomes an embarrassing situation with the help of a family member. With a partner, think of other ways the girls are similar.

1. Each girl has a "cheerleader," someone who pushes her to set goals and to dream. How does each one boost the girl's self-confidence? Which character do you think makes the better cheerleader? Why?
2. What kind of friends do you think the girls from "Chanclas" and "Mother and Daughter" would be? Would you choose either one for a best friend? Why?

COMPARE **RESPONSES**

A dance party is crucial to the plots of both stories. With a partner, discuss the following questions about the dances.

1. How did each dance start and end?
2. On a scale of one to ten, with ten being the highest, how do you think each girl would rate the dance? Why?

Portrait, 1972. Eloy Blanco. Collection of El Museo del Barrio, New York.

COMPARE **EXPERIENCES**

The writers of both stories have messages to communicate, but they do so in different ways.

1. Write a few paragraphs comparing the humor and the serious messages of each story. Consider these questions: What contributed most to the humor of each story–the characters or the situations? How?
2. "Some things are more important than money." Do you agree or disagree with this statement? What would the main characters of each story say? What is most important to them, money or something else? Write a brief explanation.

PORTFOLIO OPTIONS

Select and Reflect Have students reflect on the paragraphs they wrote for the activity by asking themselves these questions:

- Have I given enough reasons to support my stand?
- Have I been careful to distinguish my opinion from those of the characters?

Students should attach their comments to their paragraphs and place them in their portfolios. At a later time, they might consider using their answers to these questions to revise their paragraphs as portfolio showcase pieces. **L2**

Additional Resources

Writing Assessment and Portfolio Management, pp. 7–12, 14–16, 38–44

Vo•cab•u•lar•y Skills

Using Context Clues

What do you think *obdurate* means in the following sentence?

Some people react in an obdurate way to certain situations but not to others.

The sentence provides no clues about the meaning of *obdurate,* except that the word is an adjective. Sometimes you can find information about an unfamiliar word by looking at its **context,** the sentence or group of sentences in which the word appears. The context often provides **context clues** that help readers figure out what an unfamiliar word means. There are many kinds of context clues, and the amount of help they provide varies. Study the examples below.

A. Our obdurate boss insisted that we finish the job on schedule, even though we were missing half our workers.

- This example provides only a little help. Being *obdurate* is a flaw of some kind, but what does it mean?

B. A stubborn person may become more obdurate if nagged.

- This example has several context clues. The words *stubborn* and *more* make it clear that *stubborn* and *obdurate* are synonyms.

C. Lisa was too obdurate to follow the coach's suggestions.

- Several clues are provided here. Lisa will not follow the advice of her coach, a more experienced person. She must be stubborn in a determined way.

D. It's hard to reason with an obdurate person–someone who simply won't give in.

- This example provides a definition.

EXERCISE

Use context clues to figure out what the underlined words mean. Write a synonym or a short definition for each word.

1. Yollie thinks the dyed dress will look ugly or tacky, but she is surprised when it comes out shiny black and sophisticated looking.
2. The black puddle at Yollie's feet is a conspicuous sign that her dress had been dyed.
3. In Korea, people follow rules of reverence and use titles of respect when they speak to others.
4. Lemon Brown seems to be a menacing figure at first, but he turns out to be a harmless old man who only wants to protect his memories.

Vo•cab•u•lar•y Skills

Objective

- To learn to use context clues to determine word meanings

Teaching Strategies

After students read the explanation in their books, point out that context and knowledge of root words, particularly Latin and Greek roots, is an unbeatable combination for improving vocabulary. The Latin verb *obdurare* means "to harden." *Obdurate* suggests those who have hardened into immovability. Think of *durable, endure, duress*—all of these connote something that is hard to ruin, to tolerate, to change, or to move.

Exercises

1. *Sophisticated* describes something that isn't tasteless, that is grown-up and pretty.
2. *Conspicuous* means obvious, easy to see.
3. To have *reverence* is to show respect or admiration.
4. Someone who is *menacing* seems threatening.

Additional Resources

Vocabulary Power

Teaching Support

MEETING INDIVIDUAL NEEDS

ENGLISH LANGUAGE LEARNERS

Word Roots Point out to speakers of Romance languages that there may be a connection between their native language and English through Latin roots. For example, in Spanish the root *dur* has a meaning similar to that in Latin (hard).

Activity Have students maintain a list of Latin and Greek roots to use as an aid in figuring out the meanings of unfamiliar words.

Additional Resources

English Language Learners Sourcebook, p. 26

MEDIA *Connection*

Objective

- To understand and apply strategies for reading a magazine article

Literature LINK

The Medicine Bag This magazine article connects to "The Medicine Bag"—the literature selection that immediately follows this lesson. Point out the connection by noting that Martin, like the narrator of the article, is not deeply affected by his Native American heritage until his Lakota Sioux grandfather comes to visit.

Analyzing Media

Some students may say that the narrator is neutral about her roots and prefers to think of herself in the present instead of the past. Other students may agree with Granny that people shouldn't think more about who they are as individuals than about their ethnic backgrounds. Others will disagree and point out that who they are has a lot to do with their heritage.

Additional Resources

Media Connections, p. 2

in TIME ***magazine***

Teaching Support

MEDIA *Connection*

MAGAZINE ARTICLE

Where we come from shapes who we are. Or does it?

Real Indians Eat Jell-O and other things my Granny taught me

by Laurie Carlson—*Northern Lights*, Spring 1993

I don't get it. I've read every book about Indians that Mrs. Corigliano has in the school library, and they're all the same.

Indian kids are supposed to live in wide open spaces, in deserts or forests. They have horses and coyotes and wise grandparents. They get messages from nature and have visions.

I wait here, in our mobile home that has no axles, crowded next to other mobile homes without axles. I watch the television for messages, like everyone else. I wonder if I am the right kind of Indian.

My Granny doesn't have interesting tales about life and stuff. She only wants to talk about Esther Herbert's daughter, who she thinks is too wild.

Granny always makes Jell-O salads for fancy occasions, so I asked her, "What about fry bread?" She laughed and told me her fry bread could be used for shoulder pads.

"Granny," I ask, as she sits and strums her fingertips on the tabletop along with the radio's tune. Her "Primrose Passion" nail tips are the pride of Wanda's Nail Palace. "Aren't you supposed to be teaching me about beadwork and tales about coyotes? What about Indian wisdom? That's what Indian grandmothers in books and movies do."

My Granny snaps her gum and grins at me.

"Honey, be yourself."

She always says that.

That's all my Granny can give me.

I trust her.

"Want me to give you a perm?" she asks.

Analyzing Media

How do you think the narrator feels about her Native American roots? Do you agree with Granny's advice to "be yourself"? Write a brief explanation for each answer including details from the article.

interNET CONNECTION

Native Americans Have students use a search engine to find Web sites maintained by Native Americans. Suggest they try entering key words such as *Sioux* and *Native American.*

Reading *Minilesson*

Compare and Contrast The author bases the structure of this article on comparing and contrasting her Native American grandmother to grandmothers she reads about and sees on TV.

Activity Have students complete the following chart to illustrate how the author structured her article. **L2**

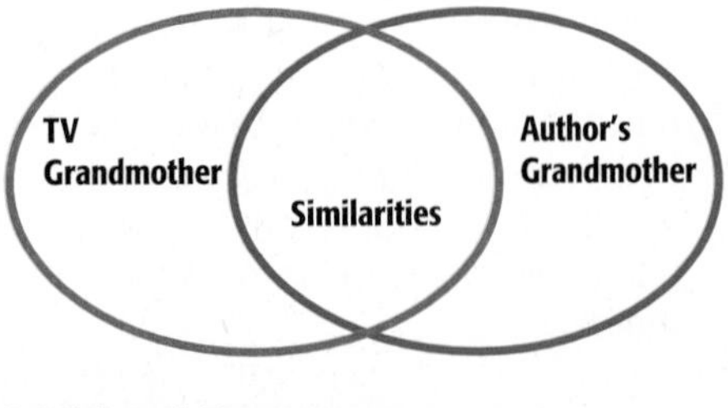

Additional Resources

Reading Skills Practice Workbook

Before You Read

The Medicine Bag

MEET VIRGINIA DRIVING HAWK SNEVE

The Rosebud Reservation in South Dakota was Virginia Driving Hawk Sneve's (snē′ vē) childhood home until she left to attend a boarding high school. She later went on to college and then began her work as a teacher. Sneve is a member of the Rosebud Sioux Tribe, and, as a writer, her goals are linked with her Native American roots. She says, "I try to present an accurate portrayal of American Indian life as I have known it. I also attempt to interpret history from the viewpoint of the American Indian."

Virginia Driving Hawk Sneve was born in 1933. This story was first published in 1975.

READING FOCUS

Name an item you cherish because you received it from someone who means a lot to you.

QuickWrite
Make some notes about the item you cherish and its importance to you.

Setting a Purpose
As you read, think of why two characters have very different attitudes toward the same object.

BUILDING BACKGROUND

The Time and Place This story takes place in a modern American neighborhood.

Did You Know?
"Sioux" is a name for groups of Native Americans also called *Ogallala, Dakota,* or *Lakota.* They farmed, hunted, and fished in the forests and lakes of the north-central part of what is now the United States between the Mississippi River and the Rocky Mountains.

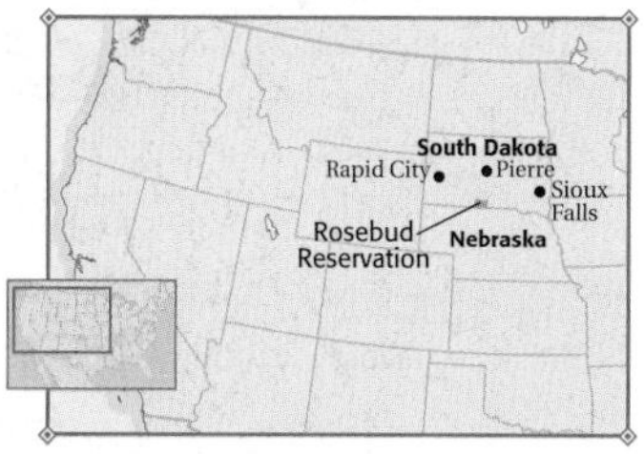

VOCABULARY PREVIEW

stately (stāt′ lē) *adv.* noble; dignified; majestic; p. 79
unseemly (un sēm′ lē) *adj.* not proper to the time or place; not in good taste; p. 80
sheepishly (shē′ pish lē) *adv.* in an awkwardly embarrassed way; bashfully; p. 81
awed (ôd) *adj.* filled with wonder combined with respect; p. 84
sacred (sā′ krid) *adj.* holy; deserving of great respect; p. 85

Before Reading

Objectives

- To read and analyze a short story about the relationship between a boy and his Sioux grandfather
- To identify and analyze symbols
- To write a paragraph analyzing point of view

Skills

Reading/Thinking: Inferring; Drawing Conclusions; Comparing and Contrasting; Identifying Author's Purpose
Writing: Journal Entry
Grammar/Language: Adjectives; Levels of Usage
Vocabulary: Word Origins
Listening/Speaking: Storytelling
Collaboration: Literature Groups

Motivating STUDENTS

Literature Launchers: "Preserving Native American Traditions"

Videodisc Side A, Segment 2

Also available in VHS.

Selection Focus Transparency 8: Before presenting the photograph, ask students to share their perceptions of medicine bags.

Reading Focus: As an extension of the Reading Focus, ask pairs of students to discuss why each object is cherished.

RESOURCE MANAGER

Teaching Tools and Resources
- Theme One Planning Guide
- Literature Groups Sourcebook

Essential Lesson Support

Lesson-Specific Instruction
- Selection Focus Transparency 8
- Literary Elements Transparency 8
- Active Reading Guide,* p. 8
- Selection Vocabulary Practice, p. 7

Assessment
- Selection Quick Checks,* p. 8
- Sel. and Theme Assmt., pp. 13–14

- Testmaker: ExamView Pro
- Performance Assessment, p. 7

Systematic Language Instruction
- Gr. & Comp. Hbk., Lesson 2.5
- Vocabulary Power, Unit 1 Review/Test
- Spelling Power, Unit 1 Review/Proofreading

English Language Learners
- ELL Sourcebook, p. 27
- Spanish Summaries, p. 8
- Spanish Translations, pp. 22–28

- Audio Library*
- English, Yes!

Spec. Needs/Strat. Interven.
- Interactive Rdg. Sbk., pp. T65–T67
- Interactive Rdg. Wbk., pp. 17–18
- Audio Library*

* Also available in Spanish

Reading the Selection

SUMMARY

Martin's Sioux great-grandfather, who is old and ill, comes to stay with Martin and his family. Grandpa tells Martin that he wants him to have his medicine bag, a pouch he wears around his neck and which he received from his father. Martin finds the prospect less than appealing at first, but he ultimately comes to terms with the object's personal and cultural significance.

Spanish Summaries, p. 8

A Active Reading Strategies

QUESTION Where do Martin's friends get their ideas of how Native Americans should look and act? *(from movies and television)*

VOCABULARY If you haven't previewed the selection vocabulary with students, stop and remind them to use context clues to unlock the meanings of new vocabulary words.

Additional Resources

- ***Active Reading Guide,*** p. 8
- ***Audio Library***
- ***Spanish Audio Library***

The Medicine Bag

Virginia Driving Hawk Sneve

A My kid sister Cheryl and I always bragged about our Sioux grandpa, Joe Iron Shell. Our friends, who had always lived in the city and only knew about Indians from movies and TV, were impressed by our stories. Maybe we exaggerated and made Grandpa and the reservation sound glamorous, but when we'd return home to Iowa after our yearly summer visit to Grandpa we always had some exciting tale to tell.

Teaching Support

CONNECTING TO OTHER SELECTIONS

The chart at the right shows three other ways to connect "The Medicine Bag" to selections in this book.

For specific teaching strategies, see the ***Theme One Planning Guide,*** pages 65–66.

Connection	Title
Life Skills: Decision Making	→ "Thank You, M'am," p. 161
Thematic: Native American Culture	→ "Spotted Eagle and Black Crow," p. 409
Literary: Narrator	→ "Thank You in Arabic," p. 574

We always had some authentic Sioux article to show our listeners. One year Cheryl had new moccasins that Grandpa had made. On another visit he gave me a small, round, flat, rawhide drum which was decorated with a painting of a warrior riding a horse. He taught me a real Sioux chant[1] to sing while I beat the drum with a leather-covered stick that had a feather on the end. Man, that really made an impression.

B We never showed our friends Grandpa's picture. Not that we were ashamed of him, but because we knew that the glamorous tales we told didn't go with the real thing. Our friends would have laughed at the picture, because Grandpa wasn't tall and stately like TV Indians. His hair wasn't in braids, but hung in stringy, gray strands on his neck and he was old. He was our great-grandfather, and he didn't live in a tipi,[2] but all by himself in a part log, part tar-paper shack on the Rosebud Reservation in South Dakota. So when Grandpa came to visit us, I was so ashamed and embarrassed I could've died.

There are a lot of yippy poodles and other fancy little dogs in our neighborhood, but they usually barked singly at the mailman from the safety of their own yards. Now it sounded as if a whole pack of mutts were barking together in one place.

I got up and walked to the curb to see what the commotion was. About a block

1. A *chant* is a short, simple melody in which a number of syllables or words are sung to the same note.
2. A *tipi* or tepee is a cone-shaped tent, usually of animal skins, used especially by the Plains Indians. In the Sioux language, tipi is a combination of *ti,* "to dwell," and *pi,* "for use."

Boy on Edge of Chasm, 1993 (detail). Kam Mak. Oil on panels, 14 x 10½ in. Collection of the artist.

Vocabulary
stately (stāt′ lē) *adv.* noble; dignified; majestic

B Active Reading Strategies

VISUALIZE Have students picture Grandpa from the description given in the second paragraph of this page.

MEETING INDIVIDUAL NEEDS — ENGLISH LANGUAGE LEARNERS

Understanding Vocabulary Point out that many words in this selection are often associated with Native Americans, sometimes mistakenly so. Encourage students to help English language learners by visually representing the words—or, if possible, bring in drawings or photos that relate to the selection. Make sure students understand what a reservation is.

Activity Pair English language learners with English speakers. As students read, they should list words that relate to Native Americans. Ask students to put a check mark next to words that describe Joe Iron Shell.

Additional Resources

English Language Learners Sourcebook, p. 27

C Literary Elements

CHARACTERIZATION Grandpa's first words are described as formal. What does his speech say about the kind of person he is? *(Grandpa is someone who believes in the old ways and in the religion and ritual of the Sioux people.)*

D Author's Craft

DICTION Notice the specific details Sneve uses to characterize Grandpa. How does his appearance contrast with what Martin's friends consider proper Native American attire? *(Martin's friends are probably expecting someone who looks like the Indian on the drum that Martin describes. Instead, Grandpa wears a rumpled black suit, a red satin shirt, a bolo tie, and a tall black hat.)*

E Critical Thinking

INFER Martin says, "I was ashamed of how I felt," when he sees his sister's delight at Grandpa's arrival. Then, on page 79, he says, "I was so ashamed and embarrassed I could've died." What causes Martin to feel so strongly?

Model: Martin is wondering about what his friends would think if they saw Grandpa. He looks so different from the Native Americans they imagine. Still, I know he loves the old man and doesn't want anyone to laugh at his grandfather.

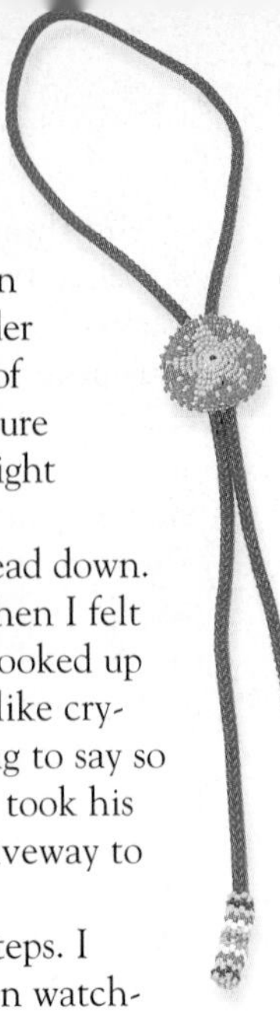

away I saw a crowd of little kids yelling, with the dogs yipping and growling around someone who was walking down the middle of the street.

I watched the group as it slowly came closer and saw that in the center of the strange procession was a man wearing a tall black hat. He'd pause now and then to peer at something in his hand and then at the houses on either side of the street. I felt cold and hot at the same time as I recognized the man. "Oh, no!" I whispered. "It's Grandpa!"

I stood on the curb, unable to move even though I wanted to run and hide. Then I got mad when I saw how the yippy dogs were growling and nipping at the old man's baggy pant legs and how wearily he poked them away with his cane. "Stupid mutts," I said as I ran to rescue Grandpa.

When I kicked and hollered at the dogs to get away, they put their tails between their legs and scattered. The kids ran to the curb where they watched me and the old man.

"Grandpa," I said and felt pretty dumb when my voice cracked. I reached for his beat-up old tin suitcase, which was tied shut with a rope. But he set it down right in the street and shook my hand.

C "*Hau, Takoza,* Grandchild," he greeted me formally in Sioux.

D All I could do was stand there with the whole neighborhood watching and shake the hand of the leather-brown old man. I saw how his gray hair straggled from under his big black hat, which had a drooping feather in its crown. His rumpled black suit hung like a sack over his stooped frame. As he shook my hand, his coat fell open to expose a bright-red, satin shirt with a beaded bolo tie[3] under the collar. His getup wasn't out of place on the reservation, but it sure was here, and I wanted to sink right through the pavement.

"Hi," I muttered with my head down. I tried to pull my hand away when I felt his bony hand trembling, and looked up to see fatigue in his face. I felt like crying. I couldn't think of anything to say so I picked up Grandpa's suitcase, took his arm, and guided him up the driveway to our house.

Mom was standing on the steps. I don't know how long she'd been watching, but her hand was over her mouth and she looked as if she couldn't believe what she saw. Then she ran to us.

"Grandpa," she gasped. "How in the world did you get here?"

She checked her move to embrace Grandpa and I remembered that such a display of affection is unseemly to the Sioux and would embarrass him.

"*Hau,* Marie," he said as he shook Mom's hand. She smiled and took his other arm.

As we supported him up the steps the door banged open and Cheryl came bursting out of the house. She was all smiles and was so obviously glad to see Grandpa that I was ashamed of how I felt. E

"Grandpa!" she yelled happily. "You came to see us!"

3. A *bolo tie* is a piece of cord (often leather) fastened at the neck with an ornamental bar or clasp.

Vocabulary

unseemly (un sēm′ lē) *adj.* not proper to the time or place; not in good taste

Teaching Support

LITERATURE & HUMANITIES

Ask students to consider how the painting "Sun Vow," on page 389 of *American Art History and Culture*, might be seen as a challenge similar to Martin's challenge.

Listening and Speaking Minilesson

Storytelling Reading Grandpa's story doesn't quite convey the mood that hearing it the way Martin did conveys it.

Activity Have students work in groups to prepare a presentation of the story Grandpa tells on pages 85–86. Each student should have the opportunity to read the story aloud, striving for clarity and fluency. The groups should select the most effective reader. The groups should also try to create an appropriate atmosphere for the telling of the story. They may include drums, costume, scenery, and whatever else they think will make the story come to life. **L2**

Grandpa smiled and Mom and I let go of him as he stretched out his arms to my ten-year-old sister, who was still young enough to be hugged.

"*Wicincala*, little girl," he greeted her and then collapsed.

He had fainted. Mom and I carried him into her sewing room, where we had a spare bed.

After we had Grandpa on the bed Mom stood there helplessly patting his shoulder.

"Shouldn't we call the doctor, Mom?" I suggested, since she didn't seem to know what to do.

"Yes," she agreed with a sigh. "You make Grandpa comfortable, Martin."

F I reluctantly moved to the bed. I knew Grandpa wouldn't want to have Mom undress him, but I didn't want to, either. He was so skinny and frail that his coat slipped off easily. When I loosened his tie and opened his shirt collar, I felt a small leather pouch that hung from a thong[4] around his neck. I left it alone and moved to remove his boots. The scuffed old cowboy boots were tight and he moaned as I put pressure on his legs to jerk them off.

I put the boots on the floor and saw why they fit so tight. Each one was stuffed with money. I looked at the bills that lined the boots and started to ask about them, but Grandpa's eyes were closed again.

Mom came back with a basin of water. "The doctor thinks Grandpa is suffering from heat exhaustion," she explained as she bathed Grandpa's face. Mom gave a big sigh, "*Oh hinh*, Martin. How do you suppose he got here?"

G We found out after the doctor's visit. Grandpa was angrily sitting up in bed while Mom tried to feed him some soup.

"Tonight you let Marie feed you, Grandpa," spoke my dad, who had gotten home from work just as the doctor was leaving. "You're not really sick," he said as he gently pushed Grandpa back against the pillows. "The doctor said you just got too tired and hot after your long trip."

Grandpa relaxed, and between sips of soup he told us of his journey. Soon after our visit to him Grandpa decided that he would like to see where his only living descendants lived and what our home was like. Besides, he admitted sheepishly, he was lonesome after we left.

H I knew everybody felt as guilty as I did—especially Mom. Mom was all Grandpa had left. So even after she married my dad, who's a white man and teaches in the college in our city, and after Cheryl and I were born, Mom made sure that every summer we spent a week with Grandpa.

I never thought that Grandpa would be lonely after our visits, and none of us noticed how old and weak he had become. But Grandpa knew and so he came to us. He had ridden on buses for two and a half days. When he arrived in the city, tired and stiff from sitting for so long, he set out, walking, to find us.

He had stopped to rest on the steps of some building downtown and a policeman found him. The cop, according to Grandpa, was a good man who took him

4. Here, a *thong* is a narrow strip of leather or similar material.

Vocabulary

sheepishly (shē′ pish lē) *adv.* in an awkwardly embarrassed way; bashfully

F Literary Elements

SYMBOL Ask students what they think that Martin's leaving the pouch on his grandfather represents. *(It symbolizes his respect for the Sioux tradition.)*

G Active Reading Strategies

CLARIFY Make sure students understand why Grandpa is angry and how Martin's dad is able to calm him. *(Grandpa has probably been protesting that there is nothing wrong with him and that he can feed himself. He will listen to Martin's dad because Martin's dad assures Grandpa that he is not really sick. He does not allow him to feel helpless and dependent, which would diminish the old man's dignity.)*

H Critical Thinking

DRAWING CONCLUSIONS Ask students why Martin and his mother feel guilty when they hear Grandpa's reason for coming to visit. Ask also whether they think Grandpa is telling the whole reason for his visiting. *(The family probably feels guilty because they have not realized that Grandpa is lonely and have not thought to invite him to stay with them. They also have not noticed how old and weak he has become. Even though he doesn't say so, Grandpa probably knows he is going to die, and he wishes to be with his family so that he can give his grandson the medicine bag.)*

MEETING INDIVIDUAL NEEDS — ADVANCED LEARNERS

Native American Mythology Joseph Bruchac, a writer who is part Abenaki, has spent many years collecting and retelling Native American legends, stories, and myths. Among his collections are *Return of the Sun: Tales from the Northeastern Woodlands; Iroquois Stories; The Faithful Hunter and Other Abenaki Stories; Native American Stories;* and *Native American Animal Stories.*

Activity Have students work in small groups, and assign each group several of Bruchac's retellings to read. Have students select one of the retellings to dramatize for the class. If the story has a message or moral, students should end the performance with a clear statement of the message they feel the story conveys. **L3**

VIEWING THE PAINTING

Walter Ufer (1876–1936) is known for his paintings of Native Americans engaged in everyday activities.

Viewing Response *The beadwork, drum, and blankets reflect Native American crafts. In the story, Grandpa is identified as a Sioux when he states that he has come because "it was the right time." The medicine bag also identifies his heritage.*

A Singing Indian. W. Ufer. Oil on canvas, 30 x 25¼ in.

Viewing the painting: What items in this painting reflect the man's Native American heritage? What details about Grandpa reveal his identity as a Sioux?

Teaching Support

MEETING INDIVIDUAL NEEDS: MULTIPLE MODES OF EXPRESSION

Spatial Spatial learners often respond well to assignments involving drawing. They may enjoy analyzing and duplicating some of the special characteristics of this painting.

Activity This painting is primarily made up of geometric patterns. Have students do a drawing or painting that uses bold patterns and colors reminiscent of Native American design. You may wish to suggest that they create a design for a blanket, pottery, jewelry, or tapestry. **L2**

to the bus stop and waited until the bus came and told the driver to let Grandpa out at Bell View Drive. After Grandpa got off the bus, he started walking again. But he couldn't see the house numbers on the other side when he walked on the sidewalk so he walked in the middle of the street. That's when all the little kids and dogs followed him.

I I knew everybody felt as bad as I did. Yet I was proud of this 86-year-old man, who had never been away from the reservation, having the courage to travel so far alone.

"You found the money in my boots?" he asked Mom.

"Martin did," she answered, and roused herself to scold. "Grandpa, you shouldn't have carried so much money. What if someone had stolen it from you?"

Grandpa laughed. "I would've known if anyone tried to take the boots off my feet. The money is what I've saved for a long time—a hundred dollars—for my funeral. But you take it now to buy groceries so that I won't be a burden to you while I am here."

J "That won't be necessary, Grandpa," Dad said. "We are honored to have you with us and you will never be a burden. I am only sorry that we never thought to bring you home with us this summer and spare you the discomfort of a long trip."

Grandpa was pleased. "Thank you," he answered. "But do not feel bad that you didn't bring me with you for I would not have come then. It was not time." He said this in such a way that no one could argue with him. To Grandpa and the Sioux, he once told me, a thing would be done when it was the right time to do it and that's the way it was.

"Also," Grandpa went on, looking at me, "I have come because it is soon time for Martin to have the medicine bag."

K We all knew what that meant. Grandpa thought he was going to die and he had to follow the tradition of his family to pass the medicine bag, along with its history, to the oldest male child.

"Even though the boy," he said still looking at me, "bears a white man's name, the medicine bag will be his."

I didn't know what to say. I had the same hot and cold feeling that I had when I first saw Grandpa in the street. The medicine bag was the dirty leather pouch I had found around his neck. "I could never wear such a thing," I almost said aloud. I thought of having my friends see it in gym class, at the swimming pool, and could imagine the smart things they would say. But I just swallowed hard and took a step toward the bed. I knew I would have to take it.

But Grandpa was tired. "Not now, Martin," he said, waving his hand in dismissal, "it is not time. Now I will sleep."

L So that's how Grandpa came to be with us for two months. My friends kept asking to come see the old man, but I put them off. I told myself that I didn't want them laughing at Grandpa. But even as I made excuses I knew it wasn't Grandpa that I was afraid they'd laugh at.

Nothing bothered Cheryl about bringing her friends to see Grandpa. Every day after school started there'd be a crew of giggling little girls or round-eyed little boys crowded around the old man on the patio, where he'd gotten in the habit of sitting every afternoon.

Grandpa would smile in his gentle way and patiently answer their questions, or

I Active Reading Strategies

QUESTION At first Martin is ashamed of his Grandfather. Ask students what he discovers that begins to make him feel proud. *(He realizes that the 86-year-old man has had the courage to travel so far by himself.)*

J Literary Elements

DIALOGUE Point out that Martin's dad uses the same sort of formal language that Grandpa uses. What do students think of his choice of the word *honored*? *(Martin's father knows how to make Grandpa feel respected.)* What happens when he is careful to match his tone and his words with his guest's? *(Grandpa responds readily.)*

K Literary Elements

SYMBOL What symbolism makes the little leather pouch a valuable item to Grandpa and Martin? *(The medicine bag symbolizes Martin's heritage and the family's history.)*

L Active Reading Strategies

CONNECT Martin says he told himself he didn't invite his friends over because he didn't want them to laugh at Grandpa, but then he says, "I knew it wasn't Grandpa I was afraid they'd laugh at." Ask students whether they have ever exaggerated a description of someone or something and feared that the exaggeration might be discovered.

Interdisciplinary Connection

Social Studies Grandpa is a member of the Sioux tribe. Knowing more about Sioux life will help students better understand Grandpa's love of the old ways.

Activity Have students work in small groups, with each group assigned to research a different aspect of Sioux culture: housing, art, music, religion, etc. Suggest that students use library and Internet resources and, if possible, conduct interviews with someone familiar with Sioux tradition. Each group should prepare a brief presentation, including visual aids. Students should strive for clarity, rearranging words and sentences as necessary. Point out that they should be prepared to modify their organizational plan to respond to the questions and reactions of the audience. **L2**

M Literary Elements

TONE Ask students to read aloud the paragraph that begins, "Finally . . ." Discuss the right tone to use in reading "the great Indian of Bell View Drive" and "Hank, who was supposed to be my best friend." *(sarcastic tone)*

N Active Reading Strategies

QUESTION Ask students how they think Grandpa knows that Martin was embarrassed to bring his friends over. *(He realizes that he is being avoided, and his life experience gives him insight into why Martin is acting this way.)*

O Literary Elements

CHARACTERIZATION How does Grandpa's way of speaking and his uncanny insights make him seem like a prophet or an oracle? *(The fact that he so easily mesmerizes the children adds to the aura that surrounds him.)* What other things do students learn about him?

Sioux vest, Plains Indian. British Museum, London.

he'd tell them stories of brave warriors, ghosts, animals, and the kids listened in awed silence. Those little guys thought Grandpa was great.

Finally, one day after school, my friends came home with me because nothing I said stopped them. "We're going to see the great Indian of Bell View Drive," said Hank, who was supposed to be my best friend. "My brother has seen him three times so he oughta be well enough to see us."

When we got to my house Grandpa was sitting on the patio. He had on his red shirt, but today he also wore a fringed leather vest that was decorated with beads. Instead of his usual cowboy boots he had solidly beaded moccasins on his feet that stuck out of his black trousers. Of course, he had his old black hat on—he was seldom without it. But it had been brushed and the feather in the beaded headband was proudly erect, its tip a brighter white. His hair lay in silver strands over the red shirt collar.

I stared just as my friends did and I heard one of them murmur, "Wow!"

Grandpa looked up and when his eyes met mine they twinkled as if he were laughing inside. He nodded to me and my face got all hot. I could tell that he had known all along I was afraid he'd embarrass me in front of my friends.

"*Hau, hoksilas*, boys," he greeted and held out his hand.

My buddies passed in a single file and shook his hand as I introduced them. They were so polite I almost laughed. "How, there, Grandpa," and even a "How-do-you-do, sir."

"You look fine, Grandpa," I said as the guys sat on the lawn chairs or on the patio floor.

"*Hanh*, yes," he agreed. "When I woke up this morning it seemed the right time to dress in the good clothes. I knew that my grandson would be bringing his friends."

"You guys want some lemonade or something?" I offered. No one answered. They were listening to Grandpa as he started telling how he'd killed the deer from which his vest was made.

Grandpa did most of the talking while my friends were there. I was so proud of him and amazed at how respectfully quiet my buddies were. Mom had to chase them home at supper time. As they left they shook Grandpa's hand again and said to me:

"Martin, he's really great!"

"Yeah, man! Don't blame you for keeping him to yourself."

"Can we come back?"

But after they left, Mom said, "No more visitors for a while, Martin. Grandpa won't

Vocabulary
awed (ôd) *adj.* filled with wonder combined with respect

Teaching Support

Reading *Minilesson*

Compare and Contrast The ability to note an implied contrast is an important reading skill. When Martin's friends come to visit, Grandpa looks completely different from the frail old man who walked down the middle of Martin's street. Sneve describes Grandpa on the day Martin's friends visit by contrasting specific details of his appearance with how he looked earlier.

Activity Have students list the specific differences in Grandpa's appearance. Discuss the overall effect of the changes on Martin and his friends. **L2**

Additional Resources

Reading Skills Practice Workbook

admit it, but his strength hasn't returned. He likes having company, but it tires him."

That evening Grandpa called me to his room before he went to sleep. "Tomorrow," he said, "when you come home, it will be time to give you the medicine bag."

I felt a hard squeeze from where my heart is supposed to be and was scared, but I answered, "OK, Grandpa."

All night I had weird dreams about thunder and lightning on a high hill. From a distance I heard the slow beat of a drum. When I woke up in the morning I felt as if I hadn't slept at all. At school it seemed as if the day would never end and, when it finally did, I ran home.

Grandpa was in his room, sitting on the bed. The shades were down and the place was dim and cool. I sat on the floor in front of Grandpa, but he didn't even look at me. After what seemed a long time he spoke.

"I sent your mother and sister away. What you will hear today is only for a man's ears. What you will receive is only for a man's hands." He fell silent and I felt shivers down my back.

"My father in his early manhood," Grandpa began, "made a vision quest[5] to find a spirit guide for his life. You cannot understand how it was in that time, when the great Teton Sioux[6] were first made to stay on the reservation. There was a strong need for guidance from *Wakantanka,* the Great Spirit. But too many of the young men were filled with despair and hatred. They thought it was hopeless to search for a vision when the glorious life was gone and only the hated confines of a reservation lay ahead. But my father held to the old ways.

"He carefully prepared for his quest with a purifying sweat bath and then he went alone to a high butte top to fast and pray. After three days he received his sacred dream—in which he found, after long searching, the white man's iron. He did not understand his vision of finding something belonging to the white people, for in that time they were the enemy. When he came down from the butte to cleanse himself at the stream below, he found the remains of a campfire and the broken shell of an iron kettle. This was a sign which reinforced his dream. He took a piece of the iron for his medicine bag, which he had made of elk skin years before, to prepare for his quest.

Did You Know?
A *butte* (būt) is an isolated, flat-topped land formation created by the erosion of all but a portion of a hill or plateau.

"He returned to his village, where he told his dream to the wise old men of the tribe. They gave him the name *Iron Shell,* but neither did they understand the meaning of the dream. This first Iron Shell kept the piece of iron with him at all times and believed it gave him protection from the evils of those unhappy days.

5. Traditionally, a Sioux boy became a man by going on a *vision quest.* After purifying himself in a sweat lodge (a steam-heated hut), he stayed alone on a hilltop until he received a vision that showed him his purpose in life.
6. The *Teton* (tē′ ton) *Sioux* were the largest and westernmost group of the Sioux peoples; they're also known as the Lakota. In the 1860s, their hunting grounds in the western Dakotas and Nebraska were overrun by white settlers, and the Teton were forced onto reservations.

Vocabulary
sacred (sā′ krid) *adj.* holy; deserving of great respect

P Active Reading Strategies

QUESTION Why is Martin fearful when Grandpa says that he will give him the medicine bag the next day? *(He may fear the unknown—he is not sure what Grandpa will expect of him. He also probably knows that Grandpa is nearing death.)*

Q Literary Elements

SYMBOL Discuss the content of Martin's dream. Ask students what they think it means. *(Martin's dream reflects his fears and confusion. His emotions are in a "storm." The hill and the drums probably represent the reservation and Martin's Sioux heritage. The dream suggests his ambivalence about his heritage. It seems to be Martin's sacred dream, similar to the one his great-great-grandfather had. It foreshadows his acceptance of his Native American heritage.)*

R Literary Elements

DICTION Point out that Grandpa's speech becomes even more formal. Note the repetition "only for a man's ears" and "only for a man's hands." This is a clear signal that Grandpa is conducting what is for him a sacred ritual.

FYI

Sweat Lodges The Sioux people use sweat lodges, which are somewhat similar to steam baths. People take "sweat baths" in the sweat lodges as part of a ritual to purify both body and spirit.

Real-World Connection

Native American Reservations
Have students research life on Sioux (or other) reservations today. Are the old ways being revived, or are they dying out? Is the language still alive? Do children tend to stay on the reservation or leave? Ask students to record important ideas, concepts, and direct quotations from significant sources. Have them present their findings in a brief oral presentation. **L2**

Fine Art
TRANSPARENCY 14

You may want to use ***Fine Art Transparency 14*** to give students a chance to think about differences between their home and another community.

FYI

Boarding Schools The U.S. and Canadian governments created boarding schools for Native American children that in large part eradicated their culture. Children were taken from their parents and forbidden to speak their native languages to "help them assimilate."

S Active Reading Strategies

QUESTION Ask why Martin looks away when Grandpa cries. *(He is conscious of Grandpa's need for dignity.)*

T Literary Elements

THEME Discuss why Grandpa cries. *(He weeps for the loss of his culture, his father, his son, and perhaps his own impending death.)*

U Literary Elements

SYMBOL When Grandpa opens the bag, the dust that falls out is the old prairie sage. Martin's sage will replace Grandpa's. What does this herb symbolize? *(Grandpa's spirit leaving this earth)*

Thematic Focus

No Place Like Home Discuss the concept of "home" as it applies to Native Americans.

ASSESSMENT

Quick Checks, p. 8

Teaching Support

"Then a terrible thing happened to Iron Shell. He and several other young men were taken from their homes by the soldiers and sent far away to a white man's boarding school. He was angry and lonesome for his parents and the young girl he had wed before he was taken away. At first Iron Shell resisted the teachers' attempts to change him and he did not try to learn. One day it was his turn to work in the school's blacksmith shop. As he walked into the place he knew that his medicine had brought him there to learn and work with the white man's iron.

"Iron Shell became a blacksmith and worked at the trade when he returned to the reservation. All of his life he treasured the medicine bag. When he was old, and I was a man, he gave it to me, for no one made the vision quest any more."

S Grandpa quit talking and I stared in disbelief as he covered his face with his hands. His shoulders were shaking with quiet sobs and I looked away until he began to speak again.

"I kept the bag until my son, your mother's father, was a man and had to leave us to fight in the war across the ocean. I gave him the bag, for I believed it would protect him in battle, but he did not take it with him. He was afraid that he would lose it. He died in a faraway place."

Again Grandpa was still and I felt his grief around me.

"My son," he went on after clearing his throat, "had only a daughter and it is not proper for her to know of these things."

He unbuttoned his shirt, pulled out the leather pouch, and lifted it over his head. He held it in his hand, turning it over and over as if memorizing how it looked.

"In the bag," he said as he opened it and removed two objects, "is the broken shell of the iron kettle, a pebble from the butte, and a piece of the sacred sage." He held the pouch upside down and dust drifted down. U

"After the bag is yours you must put a piece of prairie sage within and never open it again until you pass it on to your son." He replaced the pebble and the piece of iron, and tied the bag.

I stood up, somehow knowing I should. Grandpa slowly rose from the bed and stood upright in front of me holding the bag before my face. I closed my eyes and waited for him to slip it over my head. But he spoke.

T "No, you need not wear it." He placed the soft leather bag in my right hand and closed my other hand over it. "It would not be right to wear it in this time and place where no one will understand. Put it safely away until you are again on the reservation. Wear it then, when you replace the sacred sage."

Grandpa turned and sat again on the bed. Wearily he leaned his head against the pillow. "Go," he said, "I will sleep now."

"Thank you, Grandpa," I said softly and left with the bag in my hands.

That night Mom and Dad took Grandpa to the hospital. Two weeks later I stood alone on the lonely prairie of the reservation and put the sacred sage in my medicine bag.

Grammar and Language *Minilesson*

Adjectives Write the following words on the board: *good, bad, pretty, ugly*. Explain to students that these words are common adjectives, words that describe nouns. Tell students that writers use adjectives to add liveliness to their work.

Activity Have students review page 86, listing some of the precise adjectives Sneve uses. **L1**

Additional Resources

- ***Grammar and Language Transparency 7***
- ***Grammar and Language Workbook,*** p. 133
- ***Grammar and Composition Handbook,*** Lesson 5.1
- ***Writer's Choice,*** Lesson 12.1

Responding to Literature

PERSONAL RESPONSE

- Would your reaction to Grandpa have been different from Martin's? Explain.
- Look at the notes you made for the **Reading Focus** on page 77. How is Martin's response to receiving the medicine bag like your reaction to receiving a cherished gift? How is it different?

Brackets connect questions that are paired to develop higher-level thinking skills.

Analyzing Literature

RECALL

1. What happened during Grandpa's trip from the reservation to the door of his family's home?
2. Explain how Grandpa's appearance differs from that of "TV Indians."
3. What happens when Grandpa gives the medicine bag to Martin?
4. What does Grandpa understand about Martin without being told?

INTERPRET

5. What does Grandpa mean when he tells his family that he has come now, and not earlier, because now is the right time?
6. Why is Martin concerned about introducing his friends to Grandpa? Do his parents, in your opinion, share any of Martin's feelings? Explain.
7. Why do you think Grandpa cries after he tells Martin about how Iron Shell gave him the medicine bag?
8. Explain two or three ways that Martin changes during the story.

EVALUATE AND CONNECT

9. Theme Connection What, in your opinion, does the medicine bag mean to Martin? Does it have the same meaning to Grandpa?
10. At the end of the story, Martin puts the sacred sage–an aromatic plant–in his medicine bag. Explain why this is a strong or weak ending for the story.

LITERARY ELEMENTS

Symbol

A **symbol** is an object, person, place, or experience that stands for something more than what it is. For example, the medicine bag is a leather pouch that holds several items. It is also a symbol of Grandpa's and Martin's identity as Sioux.

1. What other meaning does the medicine bag have?
2. Identify another symbol used in the story.

- See **Literary Terms Handbook,** p. R10.

Responding to the Selection

PERSONAL RESPONSE

Some students may admit to feeling like Martin; perhaps their grandparents' behavior embarrasses them occasionally. Some students may have received a gift that they did not appreciate at first. Others may have respected the spirit in which a gift was given even though the gift itself was not desirable.

Analyzing Literature

1. Grandpa rode on buses for two days and then started walking to find his family. He stopped to rest at a downtown building, and a policeman helped him find the right local bus. When he got to Martin's street, he walked down the middle so he could see the house numbers.
2. Grandpa is old, stooped, gray, and unkempt—not tall, strong, and noble looking.
3. Shortly after giving the bag to Martin, Grandpa dies.
4. Grandpa understands that Martin is embarrassed by him. He also understands that Martin does not want to wear the medicine bag.
5. Grandpa knows he is near death.
6. He has painted a picture of his grandfather as a "TV Indian" for his friends. There's no evidence that Martin's parents are embarrassed by Grandpa, but they do feel guilt for not having invited Grandpa to stay earlier.
7. Grandpa cries because Native American culture has died, and his father and son are dead. He may also be mourning his own impending death.
8. Martin learns to appreciate his great-grandfather more. He also learns that his Sioux heritage is not something on the surface, like the feathers on a "TV Indian." It is a culture that is all but lost.
9. To Martin, the medicine bag is proof that he is a Sioux. To Grandpa, the medicine bag represents his cultural heritage, his father, and his son.
10. Some students may see the ending as strong because it fulfills Grandpa's wish. It seems to reflect Martin's coming to respectful terms with his heritage and traditions.

LITERARY ELEMENTS

1. The medicine bag is a symbol of the old religion and the old culture—and of Grandpa's hopes for Martin. It also symbolizes Martin's attaining manhood.
2. The iron kettle that Grandpa's father found was a symbol of his destiny.

Additional Resources

Literary Elements Transparency 8

Literature and Writing

Writing About Literature

Students' paragraphs should

- answer both questions posed
- support generalizations with details from the story

Creative Writing

Students' journal entries should

- be written from Martin's point of view
- express Martin's feelings

Extending Your Response

Literature Groups Mention that people sometimes go on spiritual retreats, during which time they think about their lives, goals, feelings, and values. Students will not all agree about the value of spiritual journeys. Call for support of their positions. COLLAB. LEARN.

Interdisciplinary Activity Mention that many Web sites provide information about specific tribes. Students should be able to find a significant amount of good information online.

Literature and Writing

Writing About Literature

Narrator Write a paragraph or two explaining why having Martin as narrator makes the story meaningful for the reader. What special information or feelings does Martin bring to the story? Would the story touch the reader's feelings as much if Grandpa were the narrator?

Creative Writing

Journal Entry Write an entry from Martin's journal describing a visit he makes to the reservation after Grandpa's death.

Extending Your Response

Literature Groups

Journeys of Self-Discovery Compare the three journeys that are described in "The Medicine Bag." Consider the following questions: Which characters went on a journey? Did their experiences have anything in common? How is the vision quest a journey? What did each character learn or achieve from his journey? How did each journey help the character to move from one passage of life to the next? Would such a journey, in your opinion, be valuable to you and your friends? Explain.

Interdisciplinary Activity

Geography and Culture When European settlers arrived in America, about four million Native Americans lived in what is now the United States and Canada. What tribal groups lived in your area? Research to find out about these groups. Then create a booklet that covers the following topics: How did native people survive on the land? What was their diet? What kind of homes did they build? What were their beliefs about the land? What types of art and crafts are they known for? What happened to Native Americans once settlers arrived?

Reading Further

If you enjoyed this story by Virginia Driving Hawk Sneve, try these books:

High Elk's Treasure

When Thunders Spoke

Save your work for your portfolio.

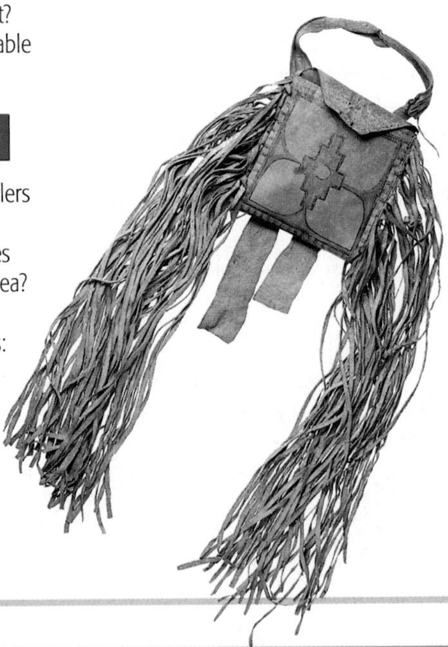

interNET CONNECTION

Sioux Dictionary Students who are interested in Native American culture may enjoy learning additional Sioux words. Invite them to use the keywords *Sioux* and *dictionary* to search for Web sites that contain lists of vocabulary words, written pronunciations, and audio pronunciations. Encourage students to share their findings with the class.

Skill Minilessons

RETEACH • REVIEW

GRAMMAR AND LANGUAGE • LEVELS OF USAGE

Levels of usage refers to the different ways that words are used in written and spoken language–from formal to informal. Formal is the strictest level of usage, and word definitions and grammar standards are carefully observed. By contrast, informal usage is more casual and conversational.

PRACTICE If a sentence below is formal, write *formal.* If it is informal, write *informal* and then rewrite it as a formal sentence.

1. "How-do-you-do, sir."
2. "You guys want some lemonade or something?"
3. "I . . . felt pretty dumb . . ."
4. "Martin, he's really great!"
5. "I will sleep now."

READING AND THINKING • AUTHOR'S PURPOSE

The **author's purpose** is his or her reason for writing the selection. The purpose might be to describe, to inform, to persuade, or simply to entertain. Identifying the author's purpose can help a reader to understand important story ideas.

PRACTICE Write a paragraph or two identifying the author's purpose in "The Medicine Bag." As you write, consider these questions: Is the story entertaining? What does the reader learn about Native Americans in this story? Does the author have more than one purpose?

- For more about the author's purpose, see **Reading Handbook,** p. R107.

VOCABULARY • WORD ORIGINS

The origin of the word *sheepish* is–you guessed it–*sheep.* Even though sheep are not particularly easy to embarrass, they are quite meek and mild, and so is a sheepish reaction. It is easy to see a connection for many words that come from names of animals. A path that *snakes* is one that twists. Other words are not as immediately clear because their meaning comes from a less obvious trait of an animal. To do something *doggedly* is to keep at it without giving up.

PRACTICE Each italicized word comes from the name of an animal. Think about the traits that people associate with the animal and use that knowledge to answer the question.

1. Is a person who behaves *mulishly* someone who is brave, mean, or stubborn?
2. If you *wolf* your food, do you eat it slowly, quickly and greedily, or in a picky way?
3. Is a *foxy* plan a sly and clever one, a dangerous one, or a careless and foolish one?
4. Is a *waspish* remark funny, bad-tempered, or highly intelligent?
5. If you *lionize* someone, do you treat that person as if he or she is worthless, amusing, or important and respectable?

Skill Minilessons

GRAMMAR AND LANGUAGE
LEVELS OF USAGE

1. formal
2. informal; *May I offer you some lemonade or something else to drink?*
3. informal; *I felt foolish.*
4. informal; *Martin, your grandfather is fascinating.*
5. formal

READING AND THINKING
AUTHOR'S PURPOSE

Students' paragraphs should
- identify the central theme of the story.
- follow a clear plan of organization.

VOCABULARY
WORD ORIGINS

1. stubborn
2. quickly and greedily
3. sly and clever
4. bad-tempered
5. important and respectable

Additional Resources

- ***Grammar and Language Workbook,*** p. 227
- ***Reading Skills Practice Workbook***
- ***Vocabulary Practice,*** p. 8

ASSESSMENT

- ***Quick Checks,*** p. 8
- ***Selection and Theme Assessment,*** pp. 13–14
- ***Performance Assessment,*** p. 7
- ***Testmaker: ExamView Pro***
- ***Interactive Tutor: Self-Assessment***

Objectives

- To write a personal essay of approximately 500 to 700 words
- To plan, draft, revise, edit, and present a personal essay
- To reflect on and assess one's essay

GLENCOE TECHNOLOGY

WRITER'S ASSISTANT CD-ROM

Students can use Glencoe's templates and guidelines software for narrative writing to aid them in working through the steps in the writing process for this lesson.

Teaching Strategies

PREWRITING

Gather details Ask students to come up with as many details as possible. It is better to have too much to start with than too few.

Choose your purpose and audience Explain to students that the best writing always keeps the audience clearly in mind. Have students draw a simple picture or write a word at the top of their first page to remind them for whom they are writing.

Teaching Support

Writing WORKSHOP

Descriptive Writing: Personal Essay

You've explored links between home and identity in this theme. Now think about your *own* identity. What makes you who you are? What likes and dislikes, habits, and hopes combine to make you unique?

Assignment: Write a personal essay describing yourself. Follow the process on these pages to create this "self-portrait in words."

- As you write your personal essay, refer to the **Writing Handbook,** pp. R50–R55.

EVALUATION RUBRIC

By the time you complete this Writing Workshop, you will have

- created a thesis statement that presents the main idea of your essay
- described your physical traits, inner qualities, and favorite activities
- written coherent paragraphs using writing techniques such as effective transitions and parallel structure
- ended with a clear and well-supported conclusion
- presented an essay that is free of errors in grammar, usage, and mechanics

The Writing Process

PREWRITING

PREWRITING TIP

Look through photos from your childhood or jot down a few memories. The images and notes may reveal qualities about your personality.

Gather Details

You know yourself better than anyone else does, so you already have a wealth of material for this essay. To tap into it, try these strategies:

- Use a brainstorm board like the one below. Fill each section with as many details as possible.

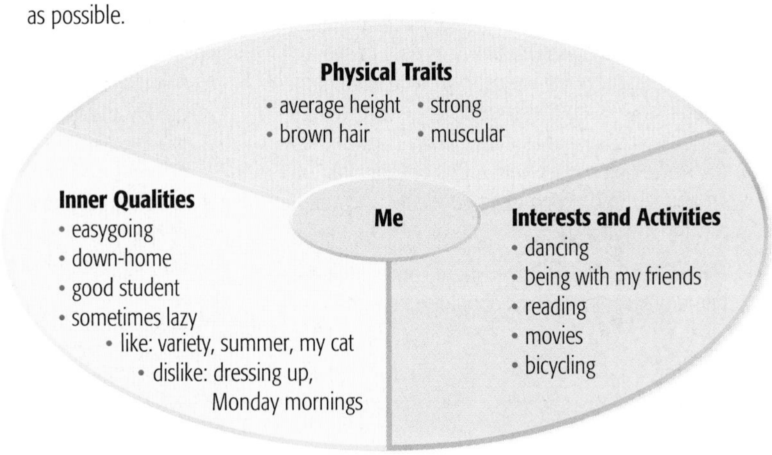

LIFE SKILLS CONNECTION

Decision Making Point out that good writers are good decision makers. Sometimes a writer's most important skill is knowing what to omit from a story or essay. When students begin to list their traits, they are likely to find they have more traits than they can cover in a brief essay. Students will have to decide which traits to include and which to leave out.

Activity Have students chart the traits they have listed in at least two ways. They may use categories such as *Positive Characteristics* versus *Negative Characteristics*, or they may choose to cluster traits around a central characteristic. Using these charts or clusters will help students decide on the information they will include. **L2**

- For a different approach to who you are, try completing sentences like these:

If I were an animal I'd be a(n) ____.	If I were punctuation, I'd be a(n) ____.
If I were a kind of music, I'd be ____.	If I were a machine, I'd be a(n) ____.
If I were a food, I'd be ____.	If I were a place, I'd be ____.

Choose Your Purpose and Audience

You can decide your own purpose and audience for this assignment. You might write to entertain classmates, to preserve memories for the future, or to inform someone who is interviewing or auditioning you. Keep your intended audience in mind as you write.

Find a Focus

Your essay needs a coherent **thesis**–a main idea–to tie it together. You might make a point about your identity. Or you might sum up the overall impression that you want to give your audience. State your thesis in a sentence or two to guide you as you draft.

Sketch Your Plan

A graphic can help you organize your essay. Will you plan one paragraph for physical traits, another for inner qualities, and another for activities and interests? Or will you blend types of characteristics in each paragraph, as you make points that illustrate your thesis?

Introduction: If I were a an animal . . .
Thesis/Main Impression: Contradictions make me who I am.

↓

Body: Favorite Activities

↓

Physical Traits and Inner Qualities

↓

Hopes and Dreams

↓

Conclusion: In twenty years . . .

Find a focus Explain to students that one good way to find a focus is to review their notes and look for an idea that is repeated several times.

Sketch your plan Explain to students that once the sketch is completed, they should think about the logical connections between parts of the essay. One good way to do this is by asking questions. For example, a student might look at the graphic on this page and ask, "How will I make the transition from my favorite activities to physical traits and inner qualities?" A person whose favorite activity is roller-skating might develop the transition this way: *I've loved roller-skating ever since I got my first pair when I was seven. I seemed to be going so fast! I guess that appealed to me especially because I wasn't much of a runner. Skates really changed that—I felt as if I could go anywhere. That appealed to my sense of freedom, which is important to me.* These sentences show how a favorite activity can be logically linked to physical traits and inner qualities.

Additional Resources

- ***Writing and Proofreading Practice,*** pp. 1–6, 7–13
- ***Writing and Proofreading Transparencies 1–6, 7–8***
- ***Writer's Choice,*** Lesson 5.9

MEETING INDIVIDUAL NEEDS — MULTIPLE MODES OF EXPRESSION

Bodily-Kinesthetic There are several good graphic methods to organize an essay. One method that might appeal to kinesthetic learners is "storyboarding." Have students prewrite on stick-on notes one idea per note. Then they can arrange and rearrange their notes on a board or a piece of paper until they have an organization that appeals to them.

Activity Have students organize their essays by storyboarding the ideas they listed when brainstorming. Have them write each of their ideas on a stick-on note and place the notes randomly on the board. Then have students read each note and arrange together notes containing similar ideas. **L2**

DRAFTING

Jump right in If students are having difficulty writing their introductions, suggest that they write the body of the essay first and add the first paragraph and conclusion later.

Make your description clear Emphasize that three elements lead to clear writing:

1. having a clear vision of what you want to describe
2. saying it in simple language
3. including specific details

REVISING

Make adjustments Suggest that students set aside their essays before revising. Then encourage them to read their essays aloud to listen for words and phrases that sound awkward or confusing. Encourage students to use precise words that communicate exactly what they want to say. Suggest they use a thesaurus, a synonym finder, a dictionary, or word processing software that contains an electronic dictionary.

GLENCOE TECHNOLOGY

REVISING WITH STYLE CD-ROM

Invite students to use the *Revising with Style* CD-ROM, which offers instructions and exercises to help students improve their writing skills.

Teaching Support

DRAFTING

DRAFTING TIP
For your personal essay, write in the first person, using the pronouns *I* and *me.* Offer your own views and observations.

Jump Right In

Your introduction needn't be long. A surprising statement to get readers interested and another sentence or two to state your thesis can do the trick. Finish with a sentence that leads into your first body paragraph.

STUDENT MODEL • DRAFTING

When I look at my cat, Tig, I can see myself. Like Tig, I'm athletic and focused, but also lazy and easily distracted. Like Tig, I am independent, but I also like to be with people. These contradictions make me who I am.

Complete Student Model on p. R119.

Make Your Description Clear

Use details from your prewriting notes. For every quality you mention, include examples, as shown in the **Writing Skills** activity on page 60. In your concluding paragraph, you might look toward your future. In what ways do you expect to change as you grow older? Which parts of your identity will never change?

REVISING

REVISING TIP
Transitions such as *for instance, for example,* or *to show what I mean,* will help readers follow your essay.

Make Adjustments

The **Rubric for Revising** can help you strengthen your draft. After your first revisions, you might have a classmate read your draft. Ask him or her which parts of it work best. Then go over the **Rubric for Revising** once more with your classmate and look for additional ways to improve your work.

RUBRIC FOR REVISING

Your revised essay should have

- an introduction that gets your readers interested
- descriptions of your characteristics that are elaborated with examples, anecdotes, and other details
- an appropriate organization with a consistent point of view
- sentence variety to make your personal writing style lively and effective
- effective transitions between paragraphs, passages, and ideas
- a conclusion that summarizes your main points and looks toward the future

Your revised essay should be free of

- confusing or irrelevant details
- errors in grammar, usage, and mechanics

Writing *Minilesson*

Concrete Details Write the following sentence on the board: *I have always been a little superstitious.* Then write and underline the following passage: <u>I carry a rabbit's foot and a four-leaf clover. I never walk under ladders or across the paths of black cats. I stay in bed all day on Friday the thirteenth.</u> Explain that the underlined sentences, which elaborate on or support the first sentence, add color to writing. Discuss the importance of using specific, concrete examples and details.

Activity Give students these sentences and ask them to elaborate on them, using interesting, concrete examples: *I love sports. I read a lot. I'm a picky eater.* Have students share their revisions. **L2**

Additional Resources

Writer's Choice, Lesson 3.5

EDITING/PROOFREADING

For the final copy of your essay, use the **Proofreading Checklist** to help you spot and correct errors, especially sentence fragments, as shown in the **Grammar Link** on page 45.

Grammar Hint

Check each sentence to be sure it has a subject and a verb. Make sure that every verb agrees in person and number with its subject.

Tig is my cat. We have many things in common.

PROOFREADING CHECKLIST

- There are no run-on sentences.
- There are no sentence fragments.
- Each sentence has the correct end punctuation.
- All words are spelled correctly.

STUDENT MODEL • EDITING/PROOFREADING

Another great quality about Tig ^is^ that she is very loving.

Complete Student Model on p. R119.

Complete Student Model

For a complete version of the model developed in this Workshop, refer to **Writing Workshop Models**, p. R119.

PUBLISHING/PRESENTING

If you wrote to entertain classmates, friends, or family, try delivering your essay as a monologue. Plan your monologue so it clearly communicates what you want to say about yourself. Also, keep your audience in mind as you plan the way you will use your voice to express yourself. For example, if you will be speaking to very young children, you might try varying your voice a bit more than usual to hold the children's attention.

PRESENTING TIP

For a monologue, practice your pacing. Ask a friend to help you decide when to pause and when to speed up.

Reflecting

Consider the following questions and then answer them in writing:

- Which aspects of you does your essay show most accurately? Which aspects does your essay leave out?
- What other topics might you like to explore in personal essays?

Save your work for your portfolio.

EDITING/PROOFREADING

Tell students that proofreaders often find that after they spot an error, they tend to relax a little. As a result, they sometimes overlook the next mistake. Suggest that students check for one type of mistake at a time to avoid being distracted and to maintain their focus.

PUBLISHING/PRESENTING

Remind students that they are writing for a particular audience. One good test of the success of an essay is audience reaction. Ask students, "Did your audience respond as you had hoped it would?" Paying attention to the audience's response can help students discover ways to improve their writing.

Reflecting

Portfolio Encourage students to share what they learned about themselves in the process of writing a personal essay.

6+1 TRAITS™ OF WRITING

See the annotated **Writing Workshop Models** on pp. R119–R130 for additional help in evaluating student writing and in teaching the **6+1 Traits™ of effective writing.** Annotations and minilessons address and reinforce the **6+1 Traits™**: Ideas, Organization, Voice, Word Choice, Sentence Fluency, Conventions, and Presentation.

ASSESSMENT

Writing Assessment and Portfolio Management

- Writing Assessment, pp. 1–12, 14–16
- Portfolio Management, pp. 41–48

Theme Assessment

Objectives

- To give a personal response to the stories, discussions, and activities in this theme
- To compare and contrast two characters' definitions of "home"
- To complete a self-evaluation, set a goal, and devise a plan for achieving this goal

Personal Response

1. Students should provide valid reasons for their choices.
2. Accept all reasonable responses.
3. Students' projects should
   - demonstrate a clear relationship to the theme "No Place Like Home."
   - clearly fulfill the requirements outlined on page 3.

Analyzing Literature

Students' writing should

- have an introductory paragraph that identifies the two stories and the two characters to be discussed
- include details from the stories to support conclusions

Evaluate and Set Goals

Evaluate

Have students write a brief description of what they found most enjoyable and most difficult in this theme.

To help students formulate valid reasons for their ratings, you may wish to suggest that they develop a class rubric.

Set Goals

Have students jot down in a chart their goals, the steps they will take to achieve them, and checkpoints. Discuss students' plans in individual conferences.

Theme Assessment

Personal Response

1. Which story, poem, or essay in the theme most helped you to understand the meaning of "No Place Like Home"?
2. What new ideas do you have about the following as a result of your reading this theme?
   - Memories of home can be joyful as well as tragic.
   - Family traditions help form the foundations of home life.
   - Home can be a place, a group of people, or a set of conditions.
3. Present your theme project to the class.

Analyzing Literature

In "Golden Glass" and "My Two Dads," Alma Luz Villanueva and Marie G. Lee describe characters who feel out of place in what some people might consider their homes. Choose these two stories or two others from the theme to compare and contrast how two different characters define home.

Evaluate and Set Goals

1. Which of the following was most enjoyable to you? Which was the most difficult?
   - reading and thinking about the stories
   - doing independent writing
   - analyzing the stories in discussions
   - making presentations
   - doing research
2. How would you assess your work in this theme, using the following scale? Give at least two reasons for your assessment.

   4 = outstanding　　2 = fair
   3 = good　　1 = weak
3. Based on what you found difficult in this theme, choose a goal to work toward in the next theme.
   - Write down your goal and three steps you will take to help you reach it.
   - Meet with your teacher to review your goal and your plan for achieving it.

Build Your Portfolio

SELECT

Choose two of your favorite pieces of work from this theme to include in your portfolio. The following questions can help you decide.

- Which pieces do you consider your best work?
- Which turned out to be more challenging than you thought?
- Which did you learn the most from?

REFLECT

Write some notes to accompany the pieces you selected. Use the following questions to guide you.

- What do you like best about the piece?
- What did you learn from creating it?
- What might you do differently if you were beginning this piece again?

ASSESSMENT

Writing Assessment and Portfolio Management
- Writing Assessment, pp. 1–12
- Portfolio Management, pp. 41–48

GLENCOE TECHNOLOGY

MINDJOGGER VIDEOQUIZZES VIDEODISC

Use *MindJogger* to review the Theme 1 content.

Theme 1
Side A

Also available in VHS.

Reading on Your Own

If you have enjoyed the literature in this theme, you might also be interested in the following books.

A Day No Pigs Would Die
by Robert Newton Peck A boy in rural Vermont, whose father slaughters pigs, develops a new understanding of family and home.

Walker of Time
by Helen Hughes Vick A fifteen-year-old Hopi boy and his funny, sympathetic Anglo friend travel seven hundred years back in time. Here they help a dying civilization to begin the move to a new home.

Tree by Leaf
by Cynthia Voigt Clothilde's family problems are multiplied when her father returns from World War I alive, but disfigured and depressed.

Missing May
by Cynthia Rylant Summer has had many homes, but when she joins her aunt and uncle, she is welcomed and shares in their deep love for one another. When Aunt May dies, Summer and Uncle Ob must come to terms with their loss.

Reading on Your Own

Tips for Independent Reading

Stress the imprtance of each student's spending at least a half-hour a day in independent reading and supply a list of readings related to the theme under study.

Reading the Novel As students read novels associated with the theme "No Place Like Home," encourage them to pay attention to how the author describes the setting. Explain that the setting of a novel can strongly influence the attitudes and actions of the characters.

Practice Present the following discussion questions after students have read a few chapters of their novels: How does the author describe the setting? Of what importance is the setting to the main characters? Can you imagine the characters in a different setting? How might the plot develop differently if the story were set in another time or place?

Glencoe Literature Library

Missing May by Cynthia Rylant is available in the *Glencoe Literature Library*. For a complete listing of the titles, see the **Glencoe Resources for Independent Reading** in the front of this book.

The *Glencoe Literature Library Study Guide* provides instructional support and student activities for works in the *Glencoe Literature Library*.

At the MOVIES

Be sure to preview the following videos for appropriateness for your class:

- In *Homeward Bound*, a dog and a cat face many perils to return to the safety and love they found at home. [G]
- In *Babe: Pig in the City*, Babe and some traveling companions venture far from home and discover an unsettling side of life. [G]

MEETING INDIVIDUAL NEEDS — SPECIAL NEEDS

You may wish to recommend Cynthia Rylant's *Missing May* to your less-proficient readers. The subject matter and style make this book particularly appropriate for these students. **L1**

The books listed at the right are rated for average readers **(L2)** or for students who need more challenging reading material **(L3)**:

- *A Day No Pigs Would Die* by Robert Newton Peck **L2**
- *Walker of Time* by Helen Hughes Vick **L2**
- *Tree by Leaf* by Cynthia Voigt **L3**

Standardized Test Practice

Answers and Analyses

1. A This question requires students to draw a conclusion based on a comparison of the two letters. Students should review each passage for those sections that express the writers' opinions on the funding of the new school. M. Woodrow believes that 23.5 million dollars is "a reasonable price to pay," while T. Martinez believes that the "cost is exorbitant."

The Princeton Review TEST-TAKING TIP

Students do not have to answer the questions in the order in which they are presented. They should answer the questions in the order with which they feel most comfortable. If a student is having trouble with the first question, he or she should skip it and come back to it later. Often a difficult question will seem easier to answer after a student has completed the easier questions.

The Princeton Review TEST-TAKING TIP

Sometimes the "best" answer is simply the "least bad." Advise students that sometimes none of the answer choices will seem right. In these cases, they should use the process of elimination and eliminate the worst choices. The choice they have left, the "least bad," is the one they should pick.

The Princeton Review

Standardized Test Practice

Read the following passages. Then read each question on page 97. Decide which is the best answer to each question. Mark the letter for that answer on your paper.

A New and Improved Smith Middle School

The *Windham Times* newspaper published an editorial opposing the construction of a new middle school. These letters to the editor were responses to that editorial.

LETTER 1

To the Editor:

I am writing about yesterday's editorial opposing a new middle school in Windham. I am dismayed that the *Times* opposes this project. It is time for Windham to take a step into the next millenium and give our children the type of educational institution that they deserve.

When was the last time this town spent a significant amount of money on education? If we want our children to compete with other students in the region and in the world, then we need to give them the tools they need. I strongly believe that 23.5 million dollars is a reasonable price to pay to build a school that will last for decades.

As the parent of a child who will be graduating from the current middle school, and also of a child entering the sixth grade next fall, I feel personally invested in this project. I hope that my eleven-year-old will have more opportunities in a brand new middle school than my fourteen-year-old had. The time is now, Windham. Say YES to a new middle school!

M. Woodrow

LETTER 2

To the Editor:

Thank you for your fair and well-written editorial about the proposed Windham Middle School. Clearly, the cost is exorbitant, especially for a small town. I strongly disagree with those who think that Windham needs such an extravagant new school.

My two children attended the middle school and they received fine educations. They did not have computers in every classroom, or an auditorium large enough to hold an entire school, but they had dedicated and caring teachers. If more money were spent on teachers' salaries, we would see vast improvements in the quality of education without having to spend nearly 23.5 million dollars.

Let's put more money into the existing school. By offering higher salaries, we can make sure that our talented teachers stay, and we can attract qualified new teachers. We can purchase supplies and textbooks and have more money for field trips. These suggestions are more practical and cost-efficient than the plan to build a new school.

T. Martinez

MEETING INDIVIDUAL NEEDS

ENGLISH LANGUAGE LEARNERS

Verb Tense Read the passage aloud to the class. Explain that verbs are the words that we use to understand when a particular action happened, is happening, or will happen. Ask students to look back at the passage and circle as many verbs as they can. Then, go through each verb as a class and identify what tense each particular verb is in. Since this activity could potentially take a lot of time, you might want to assign a different paragraph to each student. Note that many tenses of verbs appear throughout the passages.

1 Compared with the writer of the second letter, the writer of the first letter —

A is less concerned with the amount of money needed to fund the new school.

B has written more letters to the editor about this issue and plans to continue writing.

C is more involved in the community.

D does not believe that the teachers earn their salaries.

2 Both letters are attempting to —

J persuade the reader.

K frighten the reader.

L amuse the reader.

M inform the reader.

3 Both letters give you reason to believe that —

A the newspaper's editorial was unfair to all readers.

B it is old-fashioned to believe that schools should be remodeled.

C building schools is more important than paying teachers well.

D construction of a new school has not begun.

4 The second letter writer states that building a new school is not really necessary because —

J the writer's kids don't want a new school to go to.

K money should not be spent on supplies and materials or on a new building.

L the middle school has excellent teachers.

M the school budget doesn't have enough money.

5 In this passage, the word exorbitant means —

A too small.

B too important.

C too great.

D too clean.

6 What is the main idea of the second letter?

J A new school and updated technology are needed and Windham should invest in them this year.

K A new school is unnecessary and the money could be better spent on teachers and supplies.

L The writer's children each received a fine education at the existing middle school.

M Many people agree that a new school is very important.

STOP

Answers and Analyses

2. J This question is best solved using the process of elimination (POE). There is nothing in either of the letters that attempts to frighten or to amuse. Therefore, choices K and L can both be eliminated. While choice M is a possibility, there are many indications in both letters that the writers are attempting to persuade their readers of their points of view. Therefore, choice J is the best answer.
3. D Remind students that the question requires them to choose the answer that applies to *both* letters. In this case, there is no information in either letter to support choices A, B, or C. Since both letters are arguing over the *proposed* construction of the new school, choice D is the best possible answer.
4. L There is nothing in the second letter to support choices J, K, or M. However, the second letter's writer states that her children "had dedicated and caring teachers," and she wants to make sure "that our talented teachers stay." Choice L reflects this opinion.
5. C Students can determine the best answer by carefully considering the context of the word *exorbitant*. The second letter states that the cost is "exorbitant, especially for a small town." In the following sentence, the cost is referred to as "extravagant". These clues indicate the cost is something big, or great. Therefore, choice C is the best answer.
6. K Choice K best summarizes the second letter. While choice L is true, it is not the main idea of the letter.

Tested Objectives

Item	Reading Objective
1, 2, 3,	Find similarities and differences among texts in the treatment, scope, or organization of ideas
4	Analyze text which uses proposition-and-support patterns
5	Use word meanings within the appropriate context and be able to verify those meanings by definiton, restatement, example, comparison, or contrast
6	Compare original text to a summary for accuracy of the main ideas, inclusion of critical details, and the extent to which it conveys the underlying meaning of the original text

MORE PRACTICE

For additional practice, assign pages from one of the following standardized test resources available as part of Glencoe Literature.

Additional Resources

ITBS Preparation and Practice
SAT-9 Preparation and Practice
TerraNova Preparation and Practice

Theme 2 At a Glance
Lean on Me

THEME OPENING

- **Introducing the Theme** (p. 99)
- **Exploring the Theme** (p. 100)
- **Theme Projects** (p. 101)

Theme 2: LEAN ON ME

SELECTIONS

from **All Things Bright and Beautiful** (p. 102)

Flowers for Algernon (p. 112)

The Kid Nobody Could Handle (p. 145)

Media Connection: You Gotta Be (p. 159)

Thank You, M'am (p. 160)

The Journey (p. 168)

Knoxville, Tennessee (p. 180)

Legacies (p. 180)

A Mother in Mannville (p. 184)

Active Reading Model: *from* **I Know Why the Caged Bird Sings** (p. 198)

Media Connection: Maya's Way (p. 210)

from **Sound-Shadows of the New World** (p. 212)

SKILL FEATURES

Reading and Thinking Skills (p. 144)

Grammar Link (p. 167)

Technology Skills (pp. 178–179)

Genre Focus: Autobiography (p. 196)

Active Reading Strategies (p. 197)

Writing Skills (p. 211)

Interdisciplinary Connection: Social Studies (p. 224)

Vocabulary Skills (p. 225)

WRITING WORKSHOP

Narrative Writing: Biographical Sketch (pp. 226–229)

THEME ASSESSMENT

- **Responding to the Theme, Analyzing Literature, Evaluate and Set Goals** (p. 230)
- **Build Your Portfolio** (p. 230)
- **Reading on Your Own** (p. 231)
  - *Cezanne Pinto* by Mary Stolz
  - *Timothy of the Cay* by Theodore Taylor
  - *Walk Two Moons* by Sharon Creech
  - *Far North* by Will Hobbs
- **Standardized Test Practice** (pp. 232–233)

KEYS TO LITERARY CONNECTIONS

Comparing Selections

The **Comparing Selections** feature in this theme provides opportunities for addressing diverse aspects of the reading and literature curriculum.

For example, in Comparing Selections on page 166, students compare symbols in Langston Hughes's "Thank You, M'am" and Kurt Vonnegut's "The Kid Nobody Could Handle." Through this comparison, students gain insight into the value of mentoring relationships and the importance that some people place on material possessions..

World Literature

The Student Edition contains a variety of literature that represents cultures from around the world. World literature selections are highlighted with the icon above.

TEACHING SUPPORT

The Teaching Support offers a wealth of interactive instructional support:

Meeting Individual Needs
- Special Needs
- English Language Learners
- Multiple Modes of Expression
- Advanced Learners

Internet Connection

Assessment

Portfolio Options

Minilessons
- Grammar and Language
- Reading
- Writing
- Listening and Speaking

Connecting to Other Selections

Real-World Connection

Interdisciplinary Connection

Life Skills Connection

Family and Community Activity

Key to Ability Levels

The activities throughout this theme have been coded for students of various abilities.

L1 BASIC activities for all students

L2 AVERAGE activities for average to above-average students

L3 ADVANCED LEARNERS activities for above-average students

Teaching Today

The Glencoe *Teaching Today* professional development Web site at www.teachingtoday.glencoe.com features daily teaching tips, free downloads, annotated Web resources, educational news, and a wealth of information on a wide range of topics.

Theme 2 At a Glance
Lean on Me

Reading Skills in this theme

Variety of Texts
In addition to personal essays, this theme includes the following:
- cartoon
- short stories
- magazine article
- opinion poll
- poetry

Comprehension Skills
The following instructional support for comprehension skills appears in this theme of the Student Edition:
- **Active Reading Strategies and Model** (pp. 197–206)
- **Making Inferences** (p. 144)
- **Reading and Thinking Minilessons** (pp. 111, 143, 177, 195, 209, 223)

See also the **Reading Minilessons** throughout the theme in this Teacher Wraparound Edition.

For strategies for reading longer works, such as novels and novellas, see "Tips for Independent Reading" on page 231.

Reading Resources

Active Reading Guide The ***Active Reading Guide*** provides graphic organizers and study guide questions to support students' reading of each selection (***Active Reading Guide***, pp. 9–18).

Interactive Reading Sourcebook and **Interactive Reading Workbook** The ***Interactive Reading Sourcebook*** and ***Interactive Reading Workbook*** offer focused comprehension strategies and lessons on critical thinking skills as well as fluency practice and activities to teach and support phonics, decoding, spelling, and vocabulary development.

Vocabulary Power The ***Vocabulary Power*** workbook (Lessons 6–9) provides systematic teaching, practice, and assessment of vocabulary for better reading comprehension.

Audio Library Available on audiocassette and on CD, the ***Audio Library*** provides valuable comprehension support.

Glencoe Literature Library Each title in the ***Glencoe Literature Library*** includes a full-length work plus related readings. A separate Study Guide is available for each title.

Five–Star Stories These anthologies of familiar short stories adapted and abridged for a variety of reading levels include exercises to help increase students' vocabulary and improve their reading comprehension.

The Contemporary Readers ***The Contemporary Readers*** are nonfiction books linked to various themes and designed for developing readers from a wide range of backgrounds.

Literature Classics CD-ROM The selections on this CD-ROM can be searched by author, theme, or genre.

inTIME and Humanities Across TIME Coproductions of Glencoe and Time, Inc., these resources include a wealth of high-interest nonfiction related to the selections in this theme.

Assessment in this theme

Glencoe's Assessment Advantage

Assessment Options in the Student Edition
This program offers a number of diverse ways to evaluate student understanding and skill proficiency. In the Student Edition, use the following:
- **Responding to Literature**
  Following each selection, students are asked to recall facts, interpret ideas, and evaluate concepts as they answer a variety of questions and complete activities to extend their understanding.
- **Theme Assessment (pp. 230–231)**
  Here students respond to the selections on personal and analytical levels. They also assume ownership of their learning by setting and evaluating goals and by selecting work for their portfolios.

See also the many **Assessment Resources** listed on the facing page.

The Princeton Review

Standardized Test Practice
The Princeton Review has developed the Standardized Test Practice pages found at the end of this theme (pp. 232–233). For additional practice, direct students to the following resources:
- ITBS Preparation and Practice
- SAT-9 Preparation and Practice
- Terra Nova Preparation and Practice

Writing Skills in this theme

Writing Skills

The Student Edition of Theme 2 offers strong instructional support for writing skills:

In **Extending Your Response**, which follows each selection:
- **Writing About Literature**
- **Personal/Creative Writing**

In **Writing Skills** Lessons:
- **Writing an Effective Introduction** (p. 211)

See also the **Writing Minilessons** throughout the theme in this Teacher's Wraparound Edition.

Writing Workshops

Theme 2 concludes with a **Writing Workshop** that guides students through the process for writing a biographical sketch (pp. 226–229).

Writing Resources

Writer's Assistant CD-ROM Each **Writing Workshop** is supplemented by an interactive writing guide on the ***Writer's Assistant*** CD-ROM. This easy-to-use writing guide provides prompts, templates, and other tools that lead students through the writing process.

Grammar and Composition Handbook The ***Grammar and Composition Handbook*** (Lessons 3.1–3.12) provides systematic instruction in English language conventions.

Spelling Power The ***Spelling Power*** workbook (Lessons 5–8) provides systematic teaching, practice, and assessment of spelling to help students become better spellers and thus enhance their writing.

Writing and Proofreading Practice Blackline masters present in-depth instruction and practice on a specific step in the writing process and proofreading (pp. 1–6, 14–20).

Writing and Proofreading Transparencies Transparencies provide graphic organizers and proofreading exercises for whole-class instruction (pp. 1–6, 9–10).

Research and Report Writing Guide This resource provides extensive tips and activities to guide students in their writing projects in the literature classroom as well as in classes across the curriculum.

Style and Documentation Sourcebook for Writers This sourcebook is a combination reference and workbook, giving students the most up-to-date information and guidance regarding traditional as well as technological research strategies and documentation.

Revising with Style This resource offers instruction and exercises focusing on the revision process and covering topics from proofreading and correcting common grammatical errors to sentence combining and reordering.

Assessment Resources

Selection Quick Checks For each selection, a **Quick Check** of three to five short-answer questions measures students' literal comprehension.

Selection and Theme Assessment The ***Selection and Theme Assessment*** instrument tests students' abilities to recall, interpret, and evaluate what they've read. The tests consist of multiple-choice, short answer, and essay questions.

Performance Assessment Alternative assessment instruments and rubrics for Theme 2 are found in the ***Performance Assessment*** ancillary.

Writing Assessment and Portfolio Management These notes and strategies, student models, and assessment tools assist with the task of measuring students' progress as writers and as monitors of their own writing.

Testmaker: ExamView Pro Teachers can customize selection and Theme 2 tests by accessing the ***Testmaker*** database.

Interactive Tutor: Self-Assessment The ***Interactive Tutor: Self-Assessment*** software provides multiple-choice tests with immediate feedback to help students evaluate their knowledge and understanding of each literature selection.

MindJogger Videoquizzes Using a popular game show format, ***MindJogger Videoquizzes*** on videocassettes enable teachers to evaluate student understanding of Theme 2 in a quick and fun manner.

Theme 2 SKILLS SCOPE AND SEQUENCE

Lessons	Literary Elements	Reading and Thinking	Writing
from All Things Bright and Beautiful JAMES HERRIOT DRP: 56 Lexile: 720	Imagery, SE p. 109 *Sensory Language, TWE pp. 104, 105* *Oxymoron, TWE p. 105* *Characterization, TWE p. 107* *Suspense, TWE p. 108*	Sequence, SE p. 111 ELL *Building Background, TWE p. 104* *Evaluating, TWE p. 106* *Inferring, TWE p. 107*	Character, SE p. 110 Feature Story, SE p. 110
Flowers for Algernon DANIEL KEYES DRP: 49 Lexile: 850	Irony, SE p. 124 Foreshadowing, SE p. 141 *Irony, TWE pp. 115, 120, 137* *Author's Purpose, TWE, pp. 117, 136* *Allusion, TWE p. 123* *Characterization, TWE p. 130* *Flashback, TWE p. 137*	Cause and Effect, SE p. 143 Making Inferences, SE p. 144 ELL *Author's Technique, TWE p. 114* SN *Learning Disabled, TWE p. 116* *Comparison and Contrast, TWE p. 118* *Evaluating, TWE pp. 125, 128, 138, 140* *Inferring, TWE pp. 126, 132* *Predicting, TWE p. 128* *Paraphrasing, TWE p 134* SN *Less-Proficient Readers, TWE p. 144*	Explaining Author's Style, SE p. 142 Letter, SE p. 142 *Point of View, TWE p. 120* *Explaining Connections, TWE p. 129*
The Kid Nobody Could Handle KURT VONNEGUT DRP: 51 Lexile: 550	Dialogue, SE p. 157 *Word Choice, TWE p. 147* *Dialogue, TWE pp. 148, 150* *Resolution, TWE p. 156*	Song Lyrics, SE p. 159 *Inferring, TWE pp. 150, 153* *Evaluating, TWE p. 153* *Problem and Solution, TWE p. 154* *Questioning, TWE p. 159*	Contrasting Characters, SE p. 158 Job Description, SE p. 158 Journal Entry, SE p. 158 *Dialogue, TWE p. 148*
Thank You, M'am DRP: 47 Lexile: 680 LANGSTON HUGHES	Characterization, SE p. 165 *Characterization, TWE pp. 162, 163, 164* *Word Choice, TWE p. 162*	Comparing Selections, SE p. 166 *Cause and Effect, TWE p. 163* *Evaluating, TWE p. 163*	Setting, SE p. 165 *Creating a Convincing Character, TWE p. 167*
The Journey PATRICIA PRECIADO MARTIN DRP: 54 Lexile: 410	Narration, SE p. 175 *Narration, TWE pp. 170, 171* *Theme, TWE p. 174*	Visualizing, SE p. 177 *Inferring, TWE pp. 170, 173* *Sequence, TWE p. 171* SN *Learning Disabled, TWE p. 172*	Setting, SE p. 176 Dialogue, SE p. 176 Letter, SE p. 176
Knoxville, Tennessee *and* Legacies NIKKI GIOVANNI	Mood, SE p. 183 *Mood, TWE p. 181*	*Inferring, TWE p. 182*	
A Mother in Mannville MARJORIE KINNAN RAWLINGS DRP: 52 Lexile: 670	Narrator, SE p. 193 *First-Person Point of View, TWE pp. 186, 187, 188* *Figurative Language, TWE p. 189*	Understanding Details, SE p. 195 *Inferring, TWE pp. 187, 190* *Using Text Structures, TWE p. 188*	Definition, SE p. 194 Personal Writing, SE p. 194 *Defining a Quality, TWE p. 187*
from I Know Why the Caged Bird Sings MAYA ANGELOU DRP: 56 Lexile: 770	Autobiography, SE p. 196 Dialect, SE p. 207 *Allusion, TWE p. 201* *Word Choice, TWE pp. 202, 203*	Autobiography, SE p. 197 Evaluating, SE p. 209 Newspaper Article, SE p. 210 *Monitoring Comprehension, TWE p. 203* *Drawing Conclusions, TWE p. 205* *Distinguishing Fact from Opinion, TWE p. 208* *Summarizing, TWE p. 210*	Characterization, SE p. 208 Letter, SE p. 208
from Sound-Shadows of the New World VED MEHTA DRP: 56 Lexile: 730	Point of View, SE p. 221 *Sensory Detail, TWE p. 215* *Characterization, TWE p. 216* *Plot, TWE p. 220*	Avoiding Hasty Generalizations, SE p. 223 *Inferring, TWE pp. 216, 219* *Evaluating, TWE p. 218* *Predicting, TWE p. 217*	Evaluation, SE p. 222 Journal Entry, SE p. 222 Letter, SE p. 222 *Combining Sentences for Variety, TWE p. 215* SN *Learning Disabled, TWE p. 216*
Writing WORKSHOP Narrative Writing: Biographical Sketch			*Sentence Structure, TWE p. 228*

Key: Student material is in roman. Teacher material is in italic. Technology ELL English Language Learners

Vocabulary and Spelling	Grammar and Language	Listening, Speaking, and Viewing	Life Skills; Study and Research; Technology
Analogies, SE p. 111 *Word Usage, TWE p. 105* *Multiple-Meaning Words, TWE p. 106*	Precise Verbs, SE p. 111 *Gerunds and Participles, TWE p. 108*	Literature Groups, SE p. 110 Role-Play, SE p. 110 SN *Emotional, TWE p. 105*	Interdisciplinary Activity, SE p. 110 *Real-Word Connection, TWE p. 106* *Internet Connection, TWE p. 106* *Video, TWE p. 108*
Etymology, SE p. 143 *Word Origins, TWE pp. 115, 133*	Spelling, SE p. 143 *Punctuation, TWE p. 122* ELL *Using the Past Tense of Verbs, TWE p. 125* *Contractions, TWE p. 140*	Literature Groups, SE p. 142 *Debating, TWE p. 121* *Adjusting to the Audience, TWE p. 131* SN *Emotional, TWE p. 138*	Internet Connection, SE p. 142 *Science Research, TWE pp. 115, 123, 126, 132, 136* *Decision Making, TWE p. 119* *Internet Connection, TWE p. 130* SN *Visually Impaired, TWE p. 132* *Keeping a Journal, TWE p. 137*
Antonyms, SE p. 158 Synonyms, TWE p. 147	ELL *Idioms, TWE p. 147* *Commas, TWE p. 156* SN *Emotional, TWE p. 151*	Literature Groups, SE p. 158 *Debating, TWE p. 153*	Job Description, SE p. 158 *Music Research, TWE pp. 150, 152* *Social Studies Research, TWE p. 155*
	Run-on Sentences, SE p. 167 ELL *Pronoun Reference, TWE p. 147* *End Punctuation & Quotation Marks, TWE p. 164*	Literature Groups, SE p. 165	
The Prefix *co-*, SE p. 177	Words Ending in *-ly*, SE p. 177 *Sentence Fragments, TWE p. 174*	Literature Groups, SE p. 176 ELL *Hispanic Heritage, TWE p. 170*	Internet Connection, SE p. 176 Letter to the Editor, SE p. 176 Word Processing, SE p. 178 *History Research, TWE p. 173*
	Pronouns and Antecedents, TWE p. 182	Literature Groups, SE p. 182 Reading Poetry, SE p. 182 ELL *Southern Summer, TWE p. 181*	
Analogies, SE p. 195 ELL *Compound Words, TWE p. 186* SN *Less-Proficient Readers, TWE p. 190*	Capitalization, SE p. 195 *Commas and Compound Sentences, TWE p. 192*	Literature Groups, SE p. 194 Role-Play, SE p. 194	Researching Community Resources, SE p. 194 *Social Studies Research, TWE p. 191* *Video, TWE p. 194*
Negating Prefixes, SE p. 209	Subject-Verb Agreement, SE p. 209 ELL *Dialect, TWE p. 200* *Parentheses, TWE p. 206* *Commas with Items in a Series, TWE p. 211*	Literature Groups, SE p. 208 Oral Interpretation, SE p. 208 SN *Less-Proficient Readers, TWE p. 202* *Oral Presentation, TWE p. 205*	Everyday Lessons, SE p. 208 *Author Research, TWE p. 201* *Science Research, TWE p. 204*
Words Ending in *-y*, SE p. 223 Prefixes and Suffixes, SE p. 223 Using Familiar Words to Understand New Words, SE p. 225 ELL *Vocabulary Acquisition, TWE p. 225*	*Capitalization of Compass Points, TWE p. 220*	Literature Groups, SE p. 222 ELL *Immigration Experiences, TWE p. 214* *Describing Sounds, TWE p. 218*	Internet Connection, SE p. 222 Seeking Admission, SE p. 222 Social Studies, SE p. 224 *Real-World Connection, TWE p. 219*
		ELL *Prewriting in the First Language, TWE p. 226*	

SN **Special Needs/Strategic Intervention**

Theme 2 RESOURCE MANAGER

Lessons	Essential Resources		English Language Learners
from All Things Bright and Beautiful JAMES HERRIOT PACING: 2 DAYS	**Lesson-Specific Instruction** Selection Focus Transp. 9 * Active Reading Guide, p. 9 Literary Elements Transp. 9 Vocabulary Practice, p. 9 * Quick Checks, p. 9 Selection and Theme Assessment, pp. 15–16	Testmaker: ExamView Pro Performance Assessment, p. 8 **Systematic Language Instruction** Grammar and Comp. Hbk., L. 3.1 Vocabulary Power, Lesson 6 Spelling Power, Lesson 5	English Language Learners Sourcebook, p. 28 Spanish Summaries, p. 9 * Audio Library English, Yes!
Flowers for Algernon DANIEL KEYES PACING: 5 DAYS	**Lesson-Specific Instruction** Selection Focus Transp. 10 * Active Reading Guide, pp. 10–11 Literary Elements Transparencies 10, 11 Vocabulary Practice, p. 10 * Quick Checks, pp. 10–11 Selection and Theme Assessment, pp. 17–20	Testmaker: ExamView Pro Performance Assessment, pp. 9–10 **Systematic Language Instruction** Grammar and Comp. Hbk., L. 3.2	English Language Learners Sourcebook, pp. 29, 30 Spanish Summaries, p. 14 Spanish Translations, pp. 29–52 * Audio Library English, Yes!
The Kid Nobody Could Handle KURT VONNEGUT PACING: 3 DAYS	**Lesson-Specific Instruction** Selection Focus Transp. 11 * Active Reading Guide, p. 12 Literary Elements Transp. 12 Vocabulary Practice, p. 11 * Quick Checks, p. 12 Selection and Theme Assessment, pp. 21–22 Testmaker: ExamView Pro Performance Assessment, p. 11 TIME *inTIME* magazine, p. 2	**Systematic Language Instruction** Grammar and Comp. Hbk., L. 3.3 Vocabulary Power, Lesson 7 Spelling Power, Lesson 6	English Language Learners Sourcebook, p. 31 Spanish Summaries, p. 11 * Audio Library English, Yes!
Thank You, M'am LANGSTON HUGHES PACING: 2 DAYS	**Lesson-Specific Instruction** Selection Focus Transp. 12 * Active Reading Guide, p. 13 Literary Elements Transp. 13 Vocabulary Practice, p. 12 * Quick Checks, p. 13 Selection and Theme Assessment, p. 23	Testmaker: ExamView Pro Performance Assessment, p. 12 TIME *inTIME* magazine, p. 29 **Systematic Language Instruction** Grammar and Comp. Hbk., L. 3.4	English Language Learners Sourcebook, p. 32 Spanish Summaries, p. 12 * Audio Library English, Yes!
The Journey PATRICIA PRECIADO MARTIN PACING: 2 DAYS	**Lesson-Specific Instruction** Selection Focus Transp. 13 * Active Reading Guide, p. 14 Literary Elements Transp. 14 Vocabulary Practice, p. 13 * Quick Checks, p. 14 Selection and Theme Assessment, p. 24	Testmaker: ExamView Pro Performance Assessment, p. 13 **Systematic Language Instruction** Grammar and Comp. Hbk., L. 3.5	English Language Learners Sourcebook, p. 33 Spanish Summaries, p. 13 Spanish Translations, pp. 53–56 * Audio Library English, Yes!

Key: Workbook · Blackline Masters · Textbook · Transparency · CD-ROM · Videodisk (also available in videocassette)

Special Needs/ Strategic Intervention	Reteaching and Enrichment
Interactive Reading Sourcebook, pp. T68–T70 Interactive Reading Workbook, pp. 19–20 Inclusion Strategies Sourcebook, pp. 25–26, 95–96 Theme Two Planning Guide, p. 8	Reading Skills Practice Workbook pp. 17–18 Grammar and Language Transp. 8 Gr. and Lang. Wkbk., p. 75, 171–178 Grammar and Comp. Hbk., L. 9.1, 9.2 TIME *Humanities Across TIME*, Cover 10 Interactive Tutor: Self-Assessment Vocabulary PuzzleMaker Web Site (lit.glencoe.com)
Interactive Reading Sourcebook, pp. T70–T73 Interactive Reading Workbook, pp. 21–24 Inclusion Strategies Sourcebook, pp. 43–44 * Audio Library	Literature Launchers, Side A, Segment 5 Reading Skills Practice Workbook pp. 19–22 Grammar and Language Transparencies 9, 10 Gr. and Lang. Wkbk., pp. 255–274, 291–292 Grammar and Comp. Hbk., L. 13, 15.1 TIME *Humanities Across TIME*, Cover 17 Interactive Tutor: Self-Assessment Vocabulary PuzzleMaker Web Site (lit.glencoe.com)
Interactive Reading Sourcebook, pp. T73–T76 Interactive Reading Workbook, pp. 25–28 Inclusion Strategies Sourcebook, pp. 11–12, 23–24 Theme Two Planning Guide, p. 25 * Audio Library	Literature Launchers, Side A, Segment 6 Fine Art Transparency 32 Reading Skills Practice Workbook pp. 23–24 Grammar and Language Transp. 11 Gr. and Lang. Wkbk., pp. 257–264 Grammar and Comp. Hbk., L. 13.2 Media Connection Activities, p. 3 TIME *inTIME* magazine, pp. 26–28 TIME *Humanities Across TIME*, Cover 13 Interactive Tutor: Self-Assessment Vocabulary PuzzleMaker Web Site (lit.glencoe.com)
Interactive Reading Sourcebook, pp. T76–T78 Interactive Reading Workbook, pp. 29–30 Inclusion Strategies Sourcebook, pp. 39–40 Theme Two Planning Guide, p. 33 * Audio Library	Literature Launchers, Side A, Segment 4 Reading Skills Practice Workbook pp. 25–26 Grammar and Language Transp., 12 Gr. and Lang. Wkbk., pp. 26–27, 57–58, 267–268 Grammar and Comp. Hbk., L. 1.6, 13.1, 13.6 Interactive Tutor: Self-Assessment Vocabulary PuzzleMaker Web Site (lit.glencoe.com)
Interactive Reading Sourcebook, pp. T78–T81 Interactive Reading Workbook, pp. 31–32 Theme Two Planning Guide, p. 41 * Audio Library	Fine Art Transparency 9 Reading Skills Practice Workbook, pp. 27–28 Grammar and Language Transp. 13 Gr. and Lang. Wkbk., pp. 24–25, 129–130 Grammar and Comp. Hbk., L. 1.2, 6.1, 6.2 Interactive Tutor: Self-Assessment Vocabulary PuzzleMaker Web Site (lit.glencoe.com)

Web   Audiocassette   Diskette   *Also available in Spanish

Independent Reading

Encourage students to spend thirty minutes each day in independent reading. The following Glencoe components and outside resources provide opportunities for reading related to this theme.

The Glencoe Literature Library

You may want to assign one or more of these titles for independent reading. For a complete listing of titles available in the Glencoe Literature Library, see page T94 of this book

- *Walk Two Moons* by Sharon Creech
- *The Friends* by Rosa Guy
- *Cezanne Pinto* by Mary Stolz
- *A Gathering of Days: A New England Girl's Journal 1830–1832* by Joan W. Blos
- *Bridge to Terabithia* by Katherine Paterson

inTIME Magazine News stories, feature articles, reviews, profiles, and essays in the magazine connect to an author, work, or theme in *the Student Edition.* See the **in*TIME* Teacher's Guide** for specific connections to this theme.

Resources for Less-Proficient Readers

For reading especially created for less-proficient readers, suggest

- *Five-Star Stories*
- *The Contemporary Readers*

Additional Resources for Independent Reading

The following titles are listed with specific reading selections throughout this theme. You may want to suggest that students look for these in your local or school library.

- *All Creatures Great and Small* by James Harriot
- *Mrs. Frisby and the Rats of NIMH* by Robert O'Brien
- *Rescue Josh McGuire* by Benjamin Mikaelsen
- *After the Dancing Days* by Margaret Rostkowski
- *Something for Joey* by Robert Peck
- *The Red Pony* by John Steinbeck
- *Portrait of India* by Ved Mehta
- *An Episode of Sparrows* by Rumer Goden
- *Far North* by Will Hobbs
- *Timothy of the Cay* by Theodore Taylor

Theme 2 RESOURCE MANAGER (continued)

Lessons	Essential Resources		English Language Learners
Knoxville, Tennessee *and* **Legacies** NIKKI GIOVANNI PACING: 1 DAY	**Lesson-Specific Instruction** Selection Focus Transp. 14 * Active Reading Guide, p. 15 Literary Elements Transp. 15 * Quick Checks, p. 6 Selection and Theme Assessment, pp. 25–26 Testmaker: ExamView Pro Performance Assessment, p. 14	**Systematic Language Instruction** Grammar and Comp. Hbk., L. 3.6–3.7 Vocabulary Power, Lesson 8 Spelling Power, Lesson 7	English Language Learners Sourcebook, p. 34 Spanish Summaries, p. 14 * Audio Library English, Yes!
A Mother in Mannville MARJORIE KINNAN RAWLINGS PACING: 2 DAYS	**Lesson-Specific Instruction** Selection Focus Transp. 15 * Active Reading Guide, p. 16 Literary Elements Transp. 16 Vocabulary Practice, p. 14 * Quick Checks, p. 16 Selection and Theme Assessment, pp. 27–28	Testmaker: ExamView Pro Performance Assessment, p. 15 **Systematic Language Instruction** Grammar and Comp. Hbk., L. 3.8–3.9	English Language Learners Sourcebook, p. 35 Spanish Summaries, p. 15 Spanish Translations, pp. 57–62 * Audio Library English, Yes!
from **I Know Why the Caged Bird Sings** MAYA ANGELOU PACING: 3 DAYS	**Lesson-Specific Instruction** Selection Focus Transp. 16 * Active Reading Guide, p. 17 Literary Elements Transp. 17 Vocabulary Practice, p. 15 * Quick Checks, p. 17 Selection and Theme Assessment, pp. 29–30 Testmaker: ExamView Pro Performance Assessment, p. 16	**Systematic Language Instruction** Grammar and Comp. Hbk., L. 3.10 Vocabulary Power, Lesson 9 Spelling Power., Lesson 8	English Language Learners Sourcebook, p. 36 Spanish Summaries, p. 16 Spanish Translations, pp. 63–68 * Audio Library English, Yes!
from **Sound-Shadows of the New World** VED MEHTA PACING: 3 DAYS	**Lesson-Specific Instruction** Selection Focus Transp. 17 * Active Reading Guide, p. 18 Literary Elements Transp. 18 Vocabulary Practice, p. 16 * Quick Checks, p. 18 Selection and Theme Assessment, pp. 31–32 Testmaker: ExamView Pro Performance Assessment, p. 17	**Systematic Language Instruction** Grammar and Comp. Hbk., L. 3.11–3.12 Vocabulary Power, Unit 3 Review/Test Spelling Power., Unit 3 Review/Proofreading	English Language Learners Sourcebook, pp. 37, 38 Spanish Summaries, p. 17 * Audio Library English, Yes!
Writing WORKSHOP Narrative Writing: Biographical Sketch PACING: 2 DAYS	Writing Assessment and Portfolio Management, pp. 1–13, 17–19, 41–48		English Language Learners Sourcebook, p. 9 English, Yes!

Key: Workbook · Blackline Masters · Textbook · Transparency · CD-ROM · Videodisk (also available in videocassette)

Special Needs/ Strategic Intervention	Reteaching and Enrichment
Interactive Reading Sourcebook, pp. T81–T83 Interactive Reading Workbook, p. 33 * Audio Library	Grammar and Language Transp. 14 Gr. and Lang. Wkbk., pp. 109–110 Grammar and Comp. Hbk., L. 4.3 Interactive Tutor: Self-Assessment Vocabulary PuzzleMaker Web Site (lit.glencoe.com)
Interactive Reading Sourcebook, pp. T84–T86 Interactive Reading Workbook, pp. 34–35 Inclusion Strategies Sourcebook, pp. 25–26, 53–54 * Audio Library	Fine Art Transparency 6 Reading Skills Practice Workbook, pp. 29–30 Grammar and Language Transp. 15 Gr. and Lang. Wkbk., pp. 243–250, 259–260 Grammar and Comp. Hbk., L. 12, 13.3 Interactive Tutor: Self-Assessment Vocabulary PuzzleMaker Web Site (lit.glencoe.com)
Interactive Reading Sourcebook, pp. T87–T89 Interactive Reading Workbook, pp. 36–37 Inclusion Strategies Sourcebook, pp. 7–8 * Audio Library	Fine Art Transparency 3 Reading Skills Practice Workbook, pp. 31–32 Grammar and Language Transparencies 16, 17 Gr. and Lang. Wkbk., pp. 187–188, 271–272 Grammar and Comp. Hbk., L. 10.1, 13.8 Media Connection Activities, p. 4 Interactive Tutor: Self-Assessment Vocabulary PuzzleMaker Web Site (lit.glencoe.com)
Interactive Reading Sourcebook, pp. T89–T92 Interactive Reading Workbook, pp. 38–39 Theme Two Planning Guide., p. 71 * Audio Library	Reading Skills Practice Workbook, pp. 33–34 Grammar and Language Transp. 18 Gr. and Lang. Wkbk., pp. 249–250, 293–294 Grammar and Comp. Hbk., L. 12.4, 15.1 TIME *Humanities Across TIME*, Cover 14 Interactive Tutor: Self-Assessment Vocabulary PuzzleMaker Web Site (lit.glencoe.com)
	Writing and Proofreading Practice, pp. 1–6, 14–20 Writing and Proofreading Transparencies 1–6, 9–10, 27–28 Revising with Style Writer's Assistant

Web Audiocassette Diskette *Also available in Spanish

Theme RESOURCES

To explore the theme further, you may want to use these resources:

- Listening and Speaking Activities (pp. 4–6)
- Viewing and Representing Activities (pp. 1–6, 10–12)
- Critical Thinking Skills (pp. 4–6)
- Media Connection Activities, (pp. 3–4)
- Interdisciplinary Activities (pp. 6-9)
- Family and Community Activities (pp. 21–22)
- Selection and Theme Assessment (pp. 15–32, 127–128)
- Performance Assessment (pp. 65, 91)

TIME Humanities Across TIME

See also these additional theme planning resources:

- Theme Two Planning Guide
- Interactive Reading Sourcebook
- Literature Groups Sourcebook
- Interactive Lesson Planner
- Interactive Teacher Edition
- Glencoe Web Site (lit.glencoe.com)

PRESENTATION Plus!

Use Glencoe's ***Presentation Plus!*** This multi-media teaching tool lets you present dynamic lessons that will engage your students. Using Microsoft PowerPoint®, you can customize the presentation to create your own personalized lessons.

THEME 2

Lean on Me

Theme Objectives

- To enjoy reading about people who lean on one another for love and support
- To analyze the literary elements in short stories, poetry, and auto-biographical essays
- To apply strategies for reading autobiographical works

Teaching Strategies

Have students read the quotation from *I Know Why the Caged Bird Sings* by Maya Angelou in preparation for the discussion questions below.

VIEWING THE PHOTOGRAPH

Responding to the Photograph

Discussion questions:

- What does the photograph suggest about how it feels to be liked? Do you think it matches real life?
- What does the quotation imply about the speaker?

TEACHER *to* TEACHER

BELLCREEK ELEMENTARY • BELLBROOK, OH

A few days before beginning this theme, I play music students aren’t familiar with, such as the songs “Lean On Me,” “Put a Little Love in Your Heart,” and “You’ve Got a Friend.” I compile and distribute songbooks to introduce the lyrics to students. Students can then describe or draw images that the songs elicit and add them to their books. We then discuss the lyrics and images students have created in the context of the theme. I explain that it is important to work together and figure out how to help those who are having trouble. We also have a collage titled “Lean On Me” divided into three categories: Nations Helping Nations, Communities Helping Communities, and Individuals Helping Individuals. Students research and bring in clippings to add to the collage as we work through the literature in the theme.

—DAVID HERICK

THEME 2

THEME CONTENTS

GENRE FOCUS *AUTOBIOGRAPHY*

Introducing Theme 2

Direct your students' attention to the **Theme Contents.** Ask them to read through the list of selections.

Present these items for discussion:

- Point out to students that several selections in this theme are autobiographical. Ask students what they think the relationship is between autobiography and the theme. *(Students may note that autobiography often deals with the influence of family and friends on the author.)*
- Point out that the stories deal with various kinds of relationships. Ask students to guess, from the titles, what kind of relationship each story deals with.
- Which title captures your interest the most? Why?

LITERATURE & HUMANITIES

As you introduce this theme about relationships among people from diverse backgrounds, you may want to include material from *American Music: Cultural Traditions CD* set, volume 2, track 9, "Talking Dustbowl."

GLENCOE TECHNOLOGY

LITERATURE CLASSICS CD-ROM

Search for other selections related to the theme "Lean on Me."

RESOURCE MANAGER

See the ***Theme Two Planning Guide*** for additional teaching notes, strategies, and resources for introducing the theme "Lean on Me."

LEAN ON ME 99

Exploring the Theme

Lean on Me

- Students may think that life would be easier without some of the people they depend on, such as their parents, but often they fail to consider the loneliness and responsibility independence brings along with freedom.
- Ask students how one can learn by accepting responsibility for hurting someone.
- Ask students to think about all the people they depend on, including people they may not even know personally (such as the farm worker who picks the fruits and vegetables they eat). Challenge students to come up with a list of people who depend on them.

Starting Points

Focus on Friendship

Draw your students' attention to Gary Larson's *The Far Side* cartoon. Invite students to explain what is happening in the cartoon. Ask why the cartoon is humorous. *(Two men are alone on a deserted tropical island. Yet the one thanks the other "for being my friend." The humor comes from the idea that Wayne doesn't really have much choice.)*

- Encourage students to consider life on a deserted island with someone who is not a friend.
- Before students write their messages, encourage them to think about how they define friendship. What does a friend do? How does a friend behave?

Extending a Hand

Students might like to share their experiences with the rest of the class. Suggest that they first describe how they were helped. Then have them describe what they would be willing to do for the other person.

Exploring the Theme

Lean on Me

What would the world be like without the people we depend on? In this theme, you will explore how we help–and sometimes hurt–others and what we learn from such experiences.

Starting Points

FOCUS ON FRIENDSHIP

One of the reasons Gary Larson started drawing cartoons was to make his friends laugh. His strip "The Far Side" has earned chuckles around the world for its absurd, offbeat, and sometimes disturbing ideas. What, do you think, is the point of the Larson cartoon shown here? Write a brief message about friendship based on the cartoon.

EXTENDING A HAND

Think about a time when a friend or family member did something special for you or helped you through a hard time.

- Now imagine the situation is reversed. Write a few notes on what you would do for this person in the same circumstances. Would you do the same thing for someone you knew less well? Explain.

The Far Side by Gary Larson

"Thanks for being my friend, Wayne."

The Far Side © 1993, FARWORKS, INC. Used by permission, all rights reserved.

Family and Community Activity

Volunteer Opportunities Ask students to research volunteer opportunities in their communities. They might check the Internet for information, as well as public documents such as brochures put out by volunteer organizations. What organizations depend on volunteers? What sort of work is available for volunteers? How many volunteers are needed locally, and where is the greatest need? Who is helped by volunteers? What can young people do to help the community? Have students prepare an oral presentation designed to persuade their fellow students to volunteer for a program that accepts teen volunteers.

Additional Resources

Family and Community Activities, pp. 21–22

Theme Projects

Look over the project ideas below. Then, as you read the selections, choose a project to complete. Work on your own, with a partner, or in a group.

LEARNING FOR LIFE

Lend a Hand

1. Volunteer to assist classes with younger children at your school or community center. Talk with your teacher to find out what you can do (teach a sport or craft, help with homework).
2. Keep a journal of your experiences as you work with the children.
3. After two weeks, report to the class on what you learned about yourself and others.

LISTENING AND SPEAKING

Interview

1. Interview someone who works with teenagers, such as a minister or a school counselor.
2. Ask questions like the ones that follow.
   - Why did you choose to work with teens?
   - What is the most important part of your work?
   - When a teenager is not accepted by a group, how do you help that person?
   - How do you encourage teens to help each other?
3. Type your interview questions and answers.

interNET CONNECTION

Visit lit.glencoe.com for additional information about the writers and selections featured in "Lean on Me."

VISUAL LEARNING

Create a Support Web

1. Create a visual web of the influential people in your life: friends, teachers, family, and others. Use poster board or any family-tree software to create your web.
2. Group people in categories: friends in one, family in another. If possible, gather photos of the people in your web.
3. Under each name, jot down how long you have known the person. Also, briefly describe how the person has influenced you, and list the qualities you value in him or her.

Theme Projects

Teaching Strategies

The following suggestions may help your students plan and carry out their theme projects.

Learning for Life

- Before students volunteer, have them think about what skills and knowledge they have to offer.
- Encourage students to keep a journal of feelings, not merely one of events.
- Remind students to include what they learned about themselves through helping others.

Listening and Speaking

- Before students begin this activity, stress that a good interviewer does background research before the interview.
- Suggest that students focus additional questions on the topic of belonging. Why is being accepted so important to teens? How may teens react if they are ostracized?
- Encourage students to avoid questions that require one-word responses.

Visual Learning

- This project is best done individually.
- Suggest that students imagine that they have become famous and must write autobiographies. Whom will they include as important influences on the people they became?
- Remind students that influence may be indirect; role models, for example, influence us merely by being who they are.

interNET CONNECTION

Glencoe Literature Web Site

To further investigate ideas related to the theme "Lean on Me," have students type the keyword *volunteer* into a search engine.

Additional Resources

- ***Interdisciplinary Activities,*** pp. 6–9
- ***Viewing and Representing Activities,*** pp. 1–6, 10–12
- ***Listening and Speaking Activities,*** pp. 4–6
- ***Critical Thinking Skills,*** pp. 4–6
- ***Selection and Theme Assessment,*** pp. 127–128
- ***Performance Assessment,*** p. 65

Before Reading

Objectives

- To read and analyze a story about an unlucky day in the life of a country veterinarian
- To explore the impact of sensory language on a story
- To write a character analysis

Skills

Reading/Thinking: Evaluating; Inferring; Sequencing
Writing: Character Analysis; Feature Story
Vocabulary: Word Usage; Multiple-Meaning Words; Analogies
Grammar/Language: Gerunds and Participles; Precise Verbs
Listening/Speaking: Performing; Literature Groups
Collaboration: Performing; Literature Groups

Motivating STUDENTS

Selection Focus Transparency 9: Before presenting the photograph, discuss with students the various aspects of a veteranarian's job.

Reading Focus: As an extension of the Reading Focus, write the word *empathy* on the board and ask students to define it. Then ask students if they would include *empathy* on their lists. Have students look through the story for examples of empathetic behavior.

Before You Read

from *All Things Bright and Beautiful*

MEET JAMES HERRIOT

For years, James Alfred Wight had told his wife that he was going to write a book about his life as a veterinarian. Finally one day she replied, "Who are you kidding? Vets of fifty don't write first books." Over the next twenty years, the British animal doctor answered his wife's challenge by writing and publishing more than twenty books. Wight used the pen name James Herriot because he didn't want it to seem that he was advertising his veterinary practice.

James Herriot was born in 1916 and died in 1995. All Things Bright and Beautiful *was first published in 1973.*

READING FOCUS

What makes a visit to the doctor a pleasant or unpleasant experience for you?

List Ideas
Jot down some qualities you would want your pet's doctor to have. Share your ideas and experiences with a partner.

Setting a Purpose
Read to find out how one veterinarian gets along with the animals he takes care of—and their owners.

BUILDING BACKGROUND

The Time and Place It is the 1940s in Yorkshire, a rural area in England.

Did You Know? A veterinarian is a doctor who treats animals. James Herriot cared for pets as well as large farm animals during his half century as a country veterinarian. It was a job, he once said, that was like "holidays with pay."

VOCABULARY PREVIEW

docile (dos′ əl) *adj.* easily managed, trained, or taught; p. 103
malice (mal′ is) *n.* a desire to harm another; ill will; p. 104
catastrophic (kat′ əs trof′ ik) *adj.* disastrous; p. 104
inhibition (in′ hə bish′ ən) *n.* a restraint on one's urges; p. 105
infinite (in′ fə nit) *adj.* boundless; limitless; extremely great; p. 105
uncomprehendingly (un kom′ pri hend′ ing lē) *adv.* without understanding; p. 106
alternative (ôl tur′ nə tiv) *n.* another choice; p. 106
placid (plas′ id) *adj.* calm or peaceful; p. 106
frustration (frus trā′ shən) *n.* disappointment or irritation at being kept from doing or achieving something; p. 107

RESOURCE MANAGER

Teaching Tools and Resources
- Theme Two Planning Guide
- Literature Groups Sourcebook

Essential Lesson Support

Lesson-Specific Instruction
- Selection Focus Transparency 9
- Literary Elements Transparency 9
- Active Reading Guide,* p. 9
- Selection Vocabulary Practice, p. 9

Assessment
- Selection Quick Checks,* p. 9
- Sel. and Theme Assmt., pp. 15–16
- Testmaker: ExamView Pro
- Performance Assessment, p. 8

Systematic Language Instruction
- Gr. & Comp. Hbk., L. 3.1
- Vocabulary Power, Lesson 6
- Spelling Power, Lesson 5

English Language Learners
- ELL Sourcebook, p. 28
- Spanish Summaries, p. 9
- Audio Library*
- English, Yes!

Spec. Needs/Strat. Interven.
- Interactive Rdg. Sbk., pp. T68–T70
- Interactive Rdg. Wbk., pp. 19–20
- Inclusion Strat. Sbk., pp. 25-26, 95–96
- Theme Two Planning Guide
- Audio Library*

* Also available in Spanish

from

All Things Bright and Beautiful

James Herriot

Rhos Hilly Down. Sir Cedric Morris (1889–1982). Oil on canvas, 22 x 27 in.

"Move over, Bill!" Mr. Dacre cried some time later as he tweaked the big bull's tail.

Nearly every farmer kept a bull in those days and they were all called Billy or Bill. I suppose it was because this was a very mature animal that he received the adult version. Being a docile beast he responded to the touch on his tail by shuffling his great bulk to one side, leaving me enough space to push in between him and the wooden partition against which he was tied by a chain. A

Vocabulary

docile (dos′ əl) *adj.* easily managed, trained, or taught

Reading the Selection

SUMMARY

A day in the life of a country veterinarian definitely includes "both great and small." On Dr. Herriot's first house call, he tends to the health needs of a farmer's bull; on the second he addresses those of an elderly woman's tiny bird. The veterinarian's life is endangered at the former visit—his patient's in the latter. The veterinarian's job description obviously goes beyond caring for patients' physical needs. It includes retaining composure and a sense of humor and preventing emotional trauma to a patient's owner.

Spanish Summaries, p. 9

A Active Reading Strategies

PREDICT Ask students what they think will happen to Herriot, given the description of the bull and the author's position.

VOCABULARY If you haven't previewed the selection vocabulary with students, stop and remind them to use context clues to unlock the meanings of new vocabulary words.

Additional Resources

- ***Active Reading Guide,*** p. 9
- ***Audio Library***
- ***Spanish Audio Library***

Teaching Support

CONNECTING TO OTHER SELECTIONS

The chart at the right shows three ways to connect this excerpt from *All Things Bright and Beautiful* to other selections in this book.

For specific teaching strategies, see the ***Theme Two Planning Guide***

Connection		Title
Life Skills: Decision Making	→	"Bagged Wolf," p. 269
Thematic: Personal Interaction	→	"A Time to Talk," p. 303
Literary: Characterization	→	"Raymond's Run," p. 553

B Active Reading Strategies

QUESTION Ask students what tone they think the author is trying to convey with the description of himself that he presents. *(Students should note the humor in his tone.)*

FYI

All Things Bright and Beautiful Herriot's title comes from a Thanksgiving song whose words, written by Mrs. Cecil Frances Alexander in 1848, are based on Genesis 1:31. The words have been set to different tunes, including one from the seventeenth-century English melody "Royal Oak." Students may see the words and hear this melody on the Internet. Have them search for *All Things Bright and Beautiful*.

C Literary Elements

SENSORY LANGUAGE Point out to students Herriot's choice of words as he describes what it feels like to be crushed. Ask students which words or images particularly appealed to their senses. *(Possible answers: pop-eyed, life crushed out of me, scarcely able to breathe.)*

Teaching Support

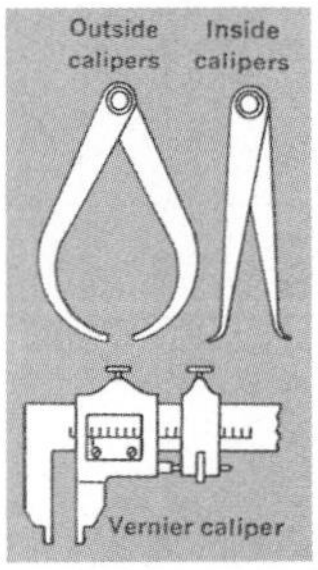

Did You Know?
A pair of *calipers* (kal′ ə pərz′) is a hinged instrument resembling a pair of tongs that is used to measure small objects.

I was reading a tuberculin test and all I wanted to do was to measure the intradermal reaction.[1] I had to open my calipers very wide to take in the thickness of the skin on the enormous neck.

"Thirty," I called out to the farmer.

He wrote the figure down on the testing book and laughed.

"By heck, he's got some pelt on 'im."

"Yes," I said, beginning to squeeze my way out. "But he's a big fellow, isn't he?"

Just how big he was was brought home to me immediately because the bull suddenly swung round, pinning me against the partition. Cows did this regularly and I moved them by bracing my back against whatever was behind me and pushing them away. But it was different with Bill.

Gasping, I pushed with all my strength against the rolls of fat which covered the vast roan-colored flank, but I might as well have tried to shift a house.

The farmer dropped his book and seized the tail again but this time the bull showed no response. There was no malice in his behavior—he was simply having a comfortable lean against the boards and I don't suppose he even noticed the morsel of puny humanity wriggling frantically against his rib cage. **B**

Still, whether he meant it or not, the end result was the same; I was having the life crushed out of me. Pop-eyed, groaning, scarcely able to breathe, I struggled with everything I had, but I couldn't move an inch. And just when I thought things couldn't get any worse, Bill started to rub himself up and down against the partition. So that was what he had come round for; he had an itch and he just wanted to scratch it. **C**

The effect on me was catastrophic. I was certain my internal organs were being steadily ground to pulp and as I thrashed about in complete panic the huge animal leaned even more heavily.

I don't like to think what would have happened if the wood behind me had not

1. The *tuberculin test* is used to diagnose the disease tuberculosis (TB). The narrator has injected the bull with a tiny amount of TB bacteria. An *intradermal* (or inside-the-skin) *reaction* is an allergic reaction that shows up as a thickening of the skin and can indicate whether a bull has TB.

Vocabulary
malice (mal′ is) *n.* a desire to harm another; ill will
catastrophic (kat′ əs trof′ ik) *adj.* disastrous

MEETING INDIVIDUAL NEEDS — ENGLISH LANGUAGE LEARNERS

Building Background In many parts of the world, livestock and pets receive little or no medical care, so some English language learners may not be familiar with the work of a veterinarian. Write *veterinary medicine, veterinarian,* and *vet* on the board. Ask volunteers to explain what a vet does and what title and type of degree a vet has.

Activity Encourage English language learners to interview classmates who have pets, livestock, or horses about some of the things they take their pets to the vet for and about some of the differences between the medical treatment of large and small animals.

Additional Resources

English Language Learners Sourcebook, p. 28

D been old and rotten, but just as I felt my senses leaving me there was a cracking and splintering and I fell through into the next stall. Lying there like a stranded fish on a bed of shattered timbers I looked up at Mr. Dacre, waiting till my lungs started to work again.

The farmer, having got over his first alarm, was rubbing his upper lip vigorously in a polite attempt to stop himself laughing. His little girl who had watched the whole thing from her vantage point[2] in one of the hay racks had no such inhibitions. Screaming with delight, she pointed at me.

"Ooo, Dad, Dad, look at that man! Did you see him, Dad, did you see him? Ooo what a funny man!" She went into helpless convulsions. She was only about five but I had a feeling she would remember my performance all her life.

E At length I picked myself up and managed to brush the matter off lightly, but after I had driven a mile or so from the farm I stopped the car and looked myself over. My ribs ached pretty uniformly as though a light road roller had passed over them and there was a tender area on my left buttock where I had landed on my calipers but otherwise I seemed to have escaped damage. I removed a few spicules[3] of wood from my trousers, got back into the car and consulted my list of visits.

And when I read my next call a gentle smile of relief spread over my face. "Mrs. Tompkin, 14, Jasmine Terrace. Clip budgie's beak."

Thank heaven for the infinite variety of veterinary practice. After that bull I needed something small and weak and harmless and really you can't ask for much better in that line than a budgie.

Number 14 was one of a row of small mean houses built of the cheap bricks so beloved of the jerry builders[4] after the first world war. I armed myself with a pair of clippers and stepped on to the narrow strip of pavement which separated the door from the road. A pleasant looking red haired woman answered my knock.

"I'm Mrs. Dodds from next door," she said. "I keep an eye on t'old lady. She's over eighty and lives alone. I've just been out gettin' her pension for her."

She led me into the cramped little room. "Here y'are, love," she said to the old woman who sat in a corner. She put the pension book and money on the mantelpiece. "And here's Mr. Herriot come to see Peter for you."

Mrs. Tompkin nodded and smiled. "Oh that's good. Poor little feller can't hardly eat with 'is long beak and I'm worried about him. He's me only companion, you know."

"Yes, I understand, Mrs. Tompkin." I looked at the cage by the window with the green budgie perched inside. "These little birds can be wonderful company when they start chattering."

2. A *vantage point* is a position that allows a clear view.
3. *Spicules* (spik′ ūlz) are small, needlelike points.
4. Here, the *mean* houses are humble or modest in appearance. *Jerry builders* were construction companies that often used poor-quality materials to construct houses quickly for returning soldiers and their families after the war.

Vocabulary
inhibition (in′ hə bish′ ən) *n.* a restraint on one's urges
infinite (in′ fə nit) *adj.* boundless; limitless; extremely great

D Literary Elements

SENSORY LANGUAGE Point out that much of the humor of the moment comes from Herriot's image of himself lying "like a stranded fish." Ask students what sort of picture these words suggest. *(The image is particularly apt not only because Herriot is flopping around on his back but also because he has had the wind knocked out of him. Thus, like the stranded fish, he can't breathe.)*

Vocabulary Skills

Word Usage Point out to students that people still refer to something shoddily constructed as "jerrybuilt" or "jerry-rigged."

E Author's Craft

OXYMORON Explain that an *oxymoron* is a figure of speech in which two opposite terms are combined (*pretty ugly,* for example). A *light road roller* is an oxymoron—a road roller is by definition heavy. Herriot is saying something like *I was knocked down by a petite linebacker*.

MEETING INDIVIDUAL NEEDS — SPECIAL NEEDS

Emotional Help students relate to this selection by explaining the importance of having a sense of humor. Read aloud the description of Herriot lying helplessly on the ground, and point out that Herriot's word choice makes the passage comic. Perhaps the event did *seem* comic after the passage of time, but at the moment, Herriot felt completely helpless.

Activity Have students write a journal entry describing an unexpected challenge they faced that now seems humorous. Encourage groups of students to share their stories and discuss why their perspectives changed.
L1 COLLAB. LEARN.

Additional Resources
Inclusion Strategies

Vo•cab•u•lar•y Skills

Multiple-Meaning Words Point out that *owt* is a dialect version of the word *aught*, meaning "zero" or "nothing." It may also mean "anything." For example, "Have I done aught to offend you?"

F Active Reading Strategies

QUESTION Ask students how they think the incident with the bull affected Herriot's feelings about clipping the budgie's beak. *(He feels that he can do something to help the bird, but this simple task is all he feels up to after the fiasco with the bull.)*

G Active Reading Strategies

RESPOND Point out that although Herriot expects a simple house call, it becomes complicated when the bird dies. Ask students how they would feel in Herriot's situation.

H Critical Thinking

EVALUATING Discuss Herriot's decision to replace the bird. Is this the right thing to do? Has concern for Mrs. Tompkin or a desire to save his reputation motivated him? Share the following model:

Model: Judging by Herriot's initial reaction, I think that he was motivated mainly by a desire to save himself. However, he seems to truly care about his patients and their owners. In my opinion, he is doing the right thing by sparing Mrs. Tompkin pain.

Teaching Support

She laughed. "Aye, but it's a funny thing. Peter never has said owt much. I think he's lazy! But I just like havin' him with me."

"Of course you do," I said. "But he certainly needs attention now."

The beak was greatly overgrown, curving away down till it touched the feathers of the breast. I would be able to revolutionize his life with one quick snip from my clippers. The way I was feeling this job was right up my street.

I opened the cage door and slowly inserted my hand.

"Come on, Peter," I wheedled as the bird fluttered away from me. And I soon cornered him and enclosed him gently in my fingers. As I lifted him out I felt in my pocket with the other hand for the clippers, but as I poised them I stopped.

The tiny head was no longer poking cheekily from my fingers but had fallen loosely to one side. The eyes were closed. I stared at the bird uncomprehendingly for a moment then opened my hand. He lay quite motionless on my palm. He was dead.

Did You Know?
The bird's feathers *(plumage)* shimmer with shifting rainbow colors *(iridescence)*.

Dry mouthed, I continued to stare; at the beautiful iridescence of the plumage, the long beak which I didn't have to cut now, but mostly at the head dropping down over my forefinger. I hadn't squeezed him or been rough with him in any way but he was dead. It must have been sheer fright.

Mrs. Dodds and I looked at each other in horror and I hardly dared turn my head towards Mrs. Tompkin. When I did, I was surprised to see that she was still nodding and smiling.

I drew her neighbor to one side. "Mrs. Dodds, how much does she see?"

"Oh she's very shortsighted but she's right vain despite her age. Never would wear glasses. She's hard of hearin', too."

"Well look," I said. My heart was still pounding. "I just don't know what to do. If I tell her about this the shock will be terrible. Anything could happen."

Mrs. Dodds nodded, stricken-faced. "Aye, you're right. She's that attached to the little thing."

"I can only think of one alternative," I whispered. "Do you know where I can get another budgie?"

Mrs. Dodds thought for a moment. "You could try Jack Almond at t'town end. I think he keeps birds."

I cleared my throat but even then my voice came out in a dry croak. "Mrs. Tompkin, I'm just going to take Peter along to the surgery to do this job. I won't be long."

I left her still nodding and smiling and, cage in hand, fled into the street. I was at the town end and knocking at Jack Almond's door within three minutes.

"Mr. Almond?" I asked of the stout, shirt-sleeved man who answered.

"That's right, young man." He gave me a slow, placid smile.

Vocabulary
uncomprehendingly (un kom′ pri hend′ ing lē) *adv.* without understanding
alternative (ôl tur′ nə tiv) *n.* another choice
placid (plas′ id) *adj.* calm or peaceful

Real-World Connection

Veterinary Medicine Herriot is writing about the life of a veterinarian in England during the 1930s. Have students gather information about veterinary medicine today. How has veterinary medicine changed over the years? Students should address issues such as house calls for a domestic pet, technology, and personal relationships between veterinarians and animal owners. Ask students to present their findings in a brief essay. **L2**

interNET CONNECTION

Encourage students to use a search engine to gather information about veterinary medicine today. They might try such key words as *domestic pets, veterinarians,* and *animal owners.*

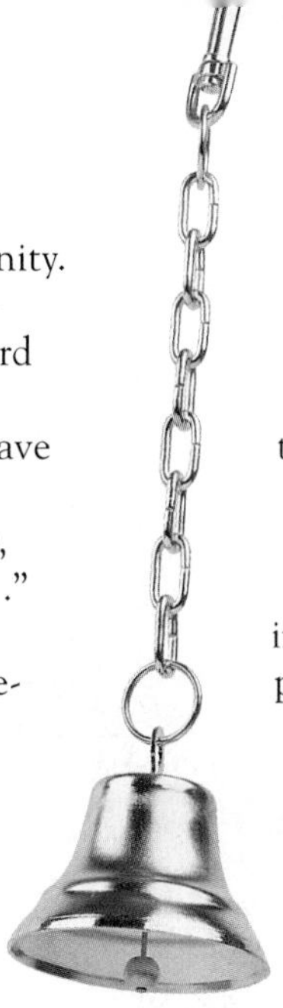

"Do you keep birds?"

He drew himself up with dignity. "I do, and I'm t'president of the Darrowby and Houlton Cage Bird Society."

"Fine," I said breathlessly. "Have you got a green budgie?"

"Ah've got Canaries, Budgies, Parrots, Parakeets. Cockatoos . . ."

"I just want a budgie."

"Well ah've got Albinos, Blue-greens, Barreds, Lutinos . . ."

"I just want a green one."

A slightly pained expression flitted across the man's face as though he found my attitude of haste somewhat unseemly.[5]

"Aye . . . well, we'll go and have a look," he said.

I followed him as he paced unhurriedly through the house into the back yard which was largely given over to a long shed containing a bewildering variety of birds.

Mr. Almond gazed at them with gentle pride and his mouth opened as though he was about to launch into a dissertation[6] then he seemed to remember that he had an impatient chap to deal with and dragged himself back to the job in hand.

"There's a nice little green 'un here. But he's a bit older than t'others. Matter of fact I've got 'im talkin'."

"All the better, just the thing. How much do you want for him?"

"But . . . there's some nice 'uns along here. Just let me show you . . ."

I put a hand on his arm. "I want that one. How much?"

He pursed his lips in frustration then shrugged his shoulders.

"Ten bob."[7]

"Right. Bung[8] him in this cage."

As I sped back up the road I looked in the driving mirror and could see the poor man regarding me sadly from his doorway.

Mrs. Dodds was waiting for me back at Jasmine Terrace.

"Do you think I'm doing the right thing?" I asked her in a whisper.

"I'm sure you are," she replied. "Poor awd thing, she hasn't much to think about and I'm sure she'd fret over Peter."

"That's what I thought." I made my way into the living room.

Mrs. Tompkin smiled at me as I went in. "That wasn't a long job, Mr. Herriot."

"No," I said, hanging the cage with the new bird up in its place by the window. "I think you'll find all is well now."

It was months before I had the courage to put my hand into a budgie's cage again. In fact to this day I prefer it if the owners will lift the birds out for me. People look at me strangely when I ask them to do this; I believe they think I am scared the little things might bite me.

5. Something *unseemly* is not proper or appropriate to the time or place.

6. Here, *dissertation* means "a long speech."

7. In informal British, a *bob* is a shilling, a coin formerly used in the United Kingdom, equal to about twenty cents.

8. *Bung* means "throw" or "toss."

Vocabulary

frustration (frus trā′ shən) *n.* disappointment or irritation at being kept from doing or achieving something

I Literary Elements

CHARACTERIZATION What kind of person is Jack Almond? Ask students how they would describe his attitude toward his birds and toward Herriot. How does he feel when Herriot tells him to "bung" the bird in the cage? *(Almond is clearly proud of his birds and is very knowledgeable. He wants Herriot to slow down and pay attention. He's probably reluctant to sell one of his birds to someone as indifferent as Herriot.)*

J Active Reading Strategies

PREDICT Ask students to predict Mrs. Tompkin's reaction to the new bird. Will she be fooled? Ask students to back up their predictions with reasons.

Reading Minilesson

Inferring Herriot does not say directly what Jack Almond is feeling, but a number of statements about Almond allow the careful reader to infer what he is thinking and how he is feeling.

Activity Have students make a list of the descriptive comments Herriot makes about Almond. Then have them write what each detail or bit of dialogue reveals about Almond. **L2**

Additional Resources

Reading Skills Practice Workbook

K Active Reading Strategies

QUESTION Ask students why they think Herriot is afraid to go back to Mrs. Tomkin's house. *(He probably fears Mrs. Tompkin will figure out the switch he's made. He may think that she will be upset.)*

L Literary Elements

SUSPENSE Ask students to discuss how Herriot heightens the suspense in the final scene. *(He shows the bird acting differently from the original Peter but waits until the last line to reveal Mrs. Tompkin's reaction.)*

Thematic Focus

Lean on Me Ask students how the theme relates to Herriot's story. *(His patients can depend on him; but don't let students miss the fact that the bull literally leans on him. Herriot also leans on others for advice and assistance.)*

ASSESSMENT

Quick Checks, p. 9

A&E HOME VIDEO.® *The following videotape programs are available from Glencoe:*

Be sure to preview the videos for appropriateness for your class:

- A&E's Incredible World of Cats *and* The Incredible Story of Dogs

Teaching Support

K It was a long time, too, before I dared go back to Mrs. Tompkin's but I was driving down Jasmine Terrace one day and on an impulse I stopped outside Number 14.

The old lady herself came to the door.

"How . . ." I said, "How is . . . er . . . ?"

She peered at me closely for a moment then laughed. "Oh I see who it is now. You mean Peter, don't you, Mr. Herriot. Oh 'e's just grand. Come in and see 'im."

In the little room the cage still hung by the window and Peter the Second took a quick look at me then put on a little act for my benefit; he hopped around the bars of the cage, ran up and down his ladder and rang his little bell a couple of times before returning to his perch.

His mistress reached up, tapped the metal and looked lovingly at him.

L "You know, you wouldn't believe it," she said. "He's like a different bird."

I swallowed. "Is that so? In what way?"

"Well he's so active now. Lively as can be. You know 'e chatters to me all day long. It's wonderful what cuttin' a beak can do."

❖

Grammar and Language *Minilesson*

Gerunds and Participles Write these phrases from the story on the board: "Gasping, I pushed with all my strength," "groaning . . . I struggled," "a cracking and splintering." Point out to students that the *-ing* words are participles and gerunds. A gerund is a verb form that ends in *-ing* and is used as a noun. A participle is a verb form that ends in *-ing* or *-ed* and may be used as a part of a verb phrase or as an adjective. Confusing gerunds and participles used as adjectives with verbs is a frequent cause of writing sentence fragments.

Activity Have students go through the story to find five additional phrases that contain *-ing* words. In each instance, students should identify the word as part of a verb, as a gerund, or as a participle used as an adjective. **L2**

Additional Resources

- ***Grammar and Language Transparency 8***
- ***Grammar and Language Workbook,*** pp. 171–178
- ***Grammar and Composition Handbook,*** Lessons 9.1–9.2
- ***Writer's Choice,*** Lessons 15.1, 15.2

Responding to Literature

PERSONAL RESPONSE

- What do you think about Mr. Herriot's replacing the budgie?
- Would you have done the same thing in his position? Why or why not?

Brackets connect questions that are paired to develop higher-level thinking skills.

Analyzing Literature

RECALL

1. What happens to the veterinarian when he starts to leave the bull's pen?
2. Why is the veterinarian relieved when he realizes his next visit is to clip a budgie's beak?
3. How is the outcome of the veterinarian's visit to Mrs. Tompkin's home different from what he expected?
4. Describe what happens when the veterinarian returns to Mrs. Tompkin's home much later.

INTERPRET

5. What does the account of the narrator's accident with the bull show about the life of a veterinarian?
6. What does the author reveal about the veterinarian's character through each of his two visits?
7. How is the vet's visit with Mrs. Tompkin similar to his earlier visit with Mr. Dacre?
8. The story has a "happily ever after" ending. Or does it? What do you think? Explain.

EVALUATE

9. This story is based on Mr. Herriot's actual experience as a country veterinarian, but does the story seem realistic to you? Why or why not?
10. What part does humor play in the story? How would the story be different without humor?

LITERARY ELEMENTS

Imagery

Imagery is the use of words and phrases that appeal to our senses of sight, touch, hearing, smell, and taste. James Herriot uses imagery when he describes how the narrator struggles to push the bull away. ". . . I might as well have tried to shift a house," he writes. This image helps us feel the bull's power.

1. To what sense do these images appeal? Explain how each image adds humor to the situation.
   - "Lying there like a stranded fish on a bed of shattered timbers . . ."
   - "My ribs ached pretty uniformly as though a light road roller had passed over them."
2. To which sense does the following image appeal? What does the image tell you about Mr. Almond, who is described here? "His mouth opened as though he was about to launch into a dissertation."

● See **Literary Terms Handbook,** p. R5.

Responding to the Selection

PERSONAL RESPONSE

Some students may say that if lying can ever be defended, it must be for sparing the feelings of another person, so Herriot did the right thing.

Analyzing Literature

1. The bull leans on Herriot, crushing him against the wall.
2. The veterinarian is relieved because he thinks that visit will be easy.
3. The veterinarian has expected his visit to Mrs. Tompkin to be uneventful but when he takes the bird out of the cage, it dies of fright.
4. She has noticed that the bird is quite different but doesn't suspect that the budgie isn't Peter.
5. The encounter with the bull suggests that the life of a veterinarian can be dangerous.
6. The veterinarian is a kind-hearted man, but he also strives to keep the respect of his clients.
7. Something goes wrong during both visits to clients.
8. Most students will say that the story does end happily; Mrs. Tompkin seems to realize that the bird is different, but she is happy believing that her Peter has suddenly become much more lively.
9. Some students may wonder whether both incidents really happened on the same day.
10. Humor plays an important part in the story. Without humor, the first incident could be sad, and the second incident might cause readers to question the vet's ethics.

LITERARY ELEMENTS

1. The fish image appeals to sight; it evokes a ridiculous picture of the veterinarian. The road-roller image appeals to the sense of touch; it combines antithetical elements (lightness and road roller) into one image.
2. The visual image of Mr. Almond suggests that he hoped for a captive audience.

Additional Resources

Literary Elements Transparency 9

Literature and Writing

Writing About Literature

Students' paragraphs should

- have a clear thesis statement
- include specific examples from the story that support all character traits

Creative Writing

Students' newspaper feature stories should

- answer the questions *who? what? when? where? why?* and *how?* in the opening
- include quotations from the people involved

Extending Your Response

Literature Groups Encourage students to focus on areas of agreement before looking at differences in the qualities they listed. COLLAB. LEARN.

Performing Select two or three different scenarios to perform for the entire class. COLLAB. LEARN.

Interdisciplinary Activity Encourage students to look for pictures to add to their reports.

Literature and Writing

Writing About Literature

Character Write a paragraph or two explaining how the author creates real, flesh-and-blood characters in very few lines. Focus on one of the characters *other than the narrator.* As you write, think about these questions: What do you learn about the character from what he or she says? What do the character's actions tell you about him or her? What does the character contribute to the story?

Creative Writing

Feature Story Suppose you write for a newspaper. You have followed Mr. Herriot, the veterinarian, for the day. Write a short newspaper story about at least one of the events in the selection from *All Things Bright and Beautiful.*

Extending Your Response

Literature Groups

A Perfect Pet Doctor Compare the list you made in the **Reading Focus** on page 102 with the lists of students in your group. Which qualities in a veterinarian do you agree are most important? Which skills does Mr. Herriot possess? Which does he lack? Does he have qualities that you'd like to add to your lists?

Performing

The Secret Is Out Suppose that Mrs. Tompkin discovers that Mr. Herriot has replaced her bird with another one. With a partner, discuss what might happen if she confronted Mr. Herriot about the deception. Consider the following questions: What factors did Mr. Herriot consider before making the decision? What other decisions could he have made? Then role-play a conversation between the two characters. Be sure to use appropriate grammar, word choice, enunciation, and pacing for each character.

Interdisciplinary Activity

Science The first Peter never said "owt much," but the second Peter is a talker. Investigate budgies, parrots, cockatoos, or other talking birds. Take notes on the natural habitat, eating habits, life expectancy, appearance, and other information about each type of bird. Then prepare a brief written report.

Reading Further

You might enjoy reading the rest of *All Things Bright and Beautiful* and these other works by James Herriot:

All Creatures Great and Small
All Things Wise and Wonderful
The Lord God Made Them All

Save your work for your portfolio.

interNET CONNECTION

Animal Sites Discovery Channel and the Public Broadcasting System operate Web sites that have feature stories and current events about animals all over the world. Invite students to explore these sites and to enjoy learning more about the animal world.

Skill Minilessons

RETEACH • REVIEW

GRAMMAR AND LANGUAGE • PRECISE VERBS

Good writers use precise, or exact, verbs to make their writing fresh and believable. Many verbs have synonyms, so writers must choose the verb that most precisely describes a particular character, setting, or action. For example, James Herriot writes, "I left [Mrs. Tompkin] still nodding and smiling and, cage in hand, fled into the street." *Fled* expresses the action and emotion better than *walked* or *ran* might.

- For more about verbs, see **Language Handbook,** pp. R33–R34.

PRACTICE Revise the following sentences by substituting a precise verb for each underlined word or phrase.

1. The bull pushed Mr. Herriot against the wood partition.
2. The bird moved away as Mr. Herriot reached for it.
3. Mr. Herriot left the house to get another bird.
4. Mr. Almond was frustrated with Mr. Herriot.
5. After a day of close calls, Mr. Herriot's head hurt.

READING AND THINKING • SEQUENCE

Several events occur in the selection from *All Things Bright and Beautiful.* The order in which events occur–first, next, and last–is called **sequence.** Author James Herriot maps the story sequence with words and phrases, such as *my next call, after that, within three minutes, back at Jasmine Terrace,* and *it was a long time.*

PRACTICE Write a paragraph that shows the sequence of four important events in the story. Use the author's word clues to help you. Include sequence words, such as *first, next,* and *last,* to clarify the order of events.

- For more about sequencing, see **Reading Handbook,** p. R99.

VOCABULARY • ANALOGIES

An **analogy** is a type of comparison that is based on the relationships between things or ideas. Some analogies, like the one below, are based on a relationship that could be called "degree of intensity."

warm : hot :: attractive : gorgeous

You could describe the degree of intensity in the example like this: "Something very warm is hot, just as something very attractive is gorgeous."

PRACTICE Figure out the relationship between the first pair of words. Then complete the analogy by choosing a second pair that has the same relationship.

1. unfortunate : catastrophic ::
   a. lucky : unlucky
   b. cheerful : pleasant
   c. afraid : terrified
   d. embarrassed : quiet
   e. large : heavy
2. vast : infinite ::
   a. good : perfect
   b. spacious : roomy
   c. tiny : huge
   d. necessary : sufficient
   e. old : wise

- For more about analogies, see **Communications Skills Handbook,** p. R73.

Skill Minilessons

GRAMMAR AND LANGUAGE
PRECISE VERBS

Possible substitutions:

1. squashed, squeezed
2. fluttered, edged
3. dashed from, rushed
4. annoyed, exasperated
5. throbbed, ached

READING AND THINKING
SEQUENCE

Students' paragraphs should

- include four events in sequence
- use transition words from the story

VOCABULARY
ANALOGIES

1. c
2. a

Additional Resources

- ***Grammar and Language Workbook,*** p. 75
- ***Writer's Choice,*** Lesson 3.3
- ***Reading Skills Practice Workbook***
- ***Vocabulary Practice,*** p. 9

ASSESSMENT

- ***Quick Checks,*** p. 9
- ***Selection and Theme Assessment,*** pp. 15–16
- ***Performance Assessment,*** p. 8
- ***Testmaker: ExamView Pro***
- ***Interactive Tutor: Self-Assessment***

Before Reading

Objectives

- To read and analyze a short story about a scientific experiment involving human intelligence
- To examine the functions of irony and foreshadowing in a story
- To write an essay about an author's style

Skills

Reading/Thinking: Comparison and Contrast; Evaluating; Inferring; Predicting; Paraphrasing; Text Structures; Cause and Effect
Writing: Point of View; Explaining Connections; Letter
Vocabulary: Word Origins; Etymology
Grammar/Language: Punctuation; Contractions; Spelling: Homophones
Listening/Speaking: Debating; Adjusting to the Audience
Life Skills: Decision Making; Keeping a Journal
Collaboration: Literature Groups; Discussion and Analysis

Motivating STUDENTS

Literature Launchers: "Meet Daniel Keyes"

Videodisc Side A, Segment 5

Also available in VHS.

Selection Focus Transparency 10: Before presenting this quotation, have students list in their journals some of the things they like most about themselves.

Reading Focus: As an extension of the Reading Focus, discuss ways in which people become more intelligent.

Before You Read

Flowers for Algernon

MEET DANIEL KEYES

Daniel Keyes loves to explore the "complexities of the human mind." Writing allows him to ask questions about personality, intelligence, and the pros and cons of scientific progress. As a photographer, editor, teacher, and merchant seaman, Keyes has met and observed a wide range of people. This experience shows in writings such as "Flowers for Algernon," which Keyes turned into a best-selling novel, a drama, and a movie, "Charly."

Daniel Keyes was born in 1927. "Flowers for Algernon" was first published in 1959 in The Magazine of Fantasy and Science Fiction.

READING FOCUS

Imagine that one day you begin changing. You get smarter and more talented with each passing day.

QuickWrite

List three or four advantages of becoming smarter and more talented. What disadvantages do you see?

Setting a Purpose

Read to discover what happens when a simple person becomes a genius.

BUILDING BACKGROUND

The Time and Place It is 1965 in New York City.

Did You Know? Several kinds of scientists study the brain and the mind:

- A neurosurgeon studies and operates on the brain.
- A psychiatrist studies the workings of the mind.
- A psychologist studies behavior, including thoughts, feelings, and learning abilities. There are many tests to measure human intelligence. The Intelligence Quotient, or I.Q., is one such measure. In recent years, scientists have come to think that people have "multiple intelligences"—special abilities for language, music, physical coordination, and other areas.

VOCABULARY PREVIEW

opportunist (op′ ər tōō′ nist) *n.* one who takes advantage of every opportunity, regardless of consequences; p. 127
tangible (tan′ jə bəl) *adj.* able to be seen, touched, or felt; real; p. 129
intellectual (int′ əl ek′ chōō əl) *adj.* appealing to or involving intelligence or mental ability; p. 130
invariably (in vār′ ē ə blē) *adv.* constantly; always; p. 131
cower (kou′ ər) *v.* to shrink away, as in fear or shame; p. 131
obscure (əb skyoor′) *v.* to hide; p. 134
impaired (im pārd′) *adj.* lessened in quality; damaged; p. 134
stimulus (stim′ yə ləs) *n.* something that causes a response; p. 135

RESOURCE MANAGER

Teaching Tools and Resources
- Theme Two Planning Guide
- Literature Groups Sourcebook

Essential Lesson Support

Lesson-Specific Instruction
- Selection Focus Transparency 10
- Literary Elements Transparency 10, 11
- Active Reading Guide,* pp. 10–11
- Selection Vocabulary Practice, p. 10

Assessment
- Selection Quick Checks,* pp. 10–11
- Sel. and Theme Assmt., pp. 17–20
- Testmaker: ExamView Pro
- Performance Assessment, pp. 9–10

Systematic Language Instruction
- Gr. & Comp. Hbk., Lessons 3.2

English Language Learners
- ELL Sourcebook, pp. 29–30
- Spanish Summaries, p. 10
- Spanish Translations, pp. 29–52
- Audio Library*
- English, Yes!

Spec. Needs/Strat. Interven.
- Interactive Rdg. Sbk., pp. T70–T73
- Interactive Rdg. Wbk., pp. 21–24
- Inclusion Strat. Sbk., pp. 43–44
- Audio Library*

* Also available in Spanish

Flowers for Algernon

Daniel Keyes

progris riport 1—martch 5 1965

Dr. Strauss says I shud rite down what I think and evrey thing that happins to me from now on. I dont know why but he says its importint so they will see if they will use me. I hope they use me. Miss Kinnian says maybe they can make me smart. I want to be smart. My name is Charlie Gordon. I am 37 years old and 2 weeks ago was my birthday. I have nuthing more to rite now so I will close for today. A

Reading the Selection

SUMMARY

Mentally handicapped Charlie Gordon has been selected to participate in an experiment to triple his intelligence. Before the operation, Charlie is pitted against a laboratory mouse named Algernon to see which of them can complete a maze more rapidly. Algernon, who has already undergone the operation, beats Charlie every time. After the surgery, Charlie's intelligence increases rapidly. At the peak of his genius, Charlie observes Algernon and determines that the mouse is declining. Step by step, Charlie regresses; tragically, he loses all the knowledge he gained.

Spanish Summaries, p. 10

A Active Reading Strategies

EVALUATE Ask students to evaluate Charlie from this first entry. What kind of person is he? How do they know?

VOCABULARY Remind students to use context clues to unlock the meanings of new vocabulary words.

Additional Resources

Active Reading Guide, p. 10
Audio Library
Spanish Audio Library

Teaching Support

CONNECTING TO OTHER SELECTIONS

The chart at the right shows three ways to connect "Flowers for Algernon" to other selections in this book.

For specific teaching strategies, see the ***Theme Two Planning Guide.***

Connection		Title
Life Skills: Lifelong Learning	→	"The Lesson of the Moth," p. 318
Thematic: Perspectives	→	"Dust of Snow," p. 305
Literary: Characterization	→	"The Ransom of Red Chief," p. 338

B Active Reading Strategies

QUESTION Ask students what Charlie's carrying a rabbit's foot tells them about his character. *(Charlie is superstitious.)*

FYI

Rorschach Results
Charlie's failure to see anything in the Rorschach test indicates that he lacks the ability to imagine or to project his personality.

C Active Reading Strategies

REVIEW Have students review page 114 looking for the qualities, positive and negative, they see in Charlie. *(He is learning disabled, lacking in imagination, and superstitious. Frequently he feels frightened and tries very hard to please those in authority. The best student in night school, Charlie tries hard and wants to learn.)*

Teaching Support

progris riport 2—martch 6

B I had a test today. I think I faled it. and I think that maybe now they wont use me. What happind is a nice young man was in the room and he had some white cards with ink spillled all over them. He sed Charlie what do you see on this card. I was very skared even tho I had my rabits foot in my pockit because when I was a kid I always faled tests in school and I spillled ink to.

I told him I saw a inkblot. He said yes and it made me feel good. I thot that was all but when I got up to go he stopped me. He said now sit down Charlie we are not thru yet. Then I dont remember so good but he wantid me to say what was in the ink. I dint see nuthing in the ink but he said there was picturs there other pepul saw some picturs. I coudnt see any picturs. I C reely tryed to see. I held the card close up and then far away. Then I said if I had my glases I coud see better I usally only ware my glases in the movies or TV but I said they are in the closit in the hall. I got them. Then I said let me see that card agen I bet Ill find it now.

I tryed hard but I still coudnt find the picturs I only saw the ink. I told him maybe I need new glases. He rote somthing down on a paper and I got skared of faling the test. I told him it was a very nice inkblot with littel points al around the eges. He looked very sad so that wasnt it. I said please let me try agen. Ill get it in a few minits becaus Im not so fast somtimes. Im a slow reeder too in Miss Kinnians class for slow adults but I'm trying very hard.

He gave me a chance with another card that had 2 kinds of ink spillled on it red and blue.

He was very nice and talked slow like Miss Kinnian does and he explaned it to me that it was a *raw shok.*[1] He said pepul see things in the ink. I said show me where. He said think. I told him I think a inkblot but that wasnt rite eather. He said what does it remind you—pretend something. I closd my eyes for a long time to pretend. I told him I pretned a fowntan pen with ink leeking all over a table cloth. Then he got up and went out.

I dont think I passd the *raw shok* test.

progris report 3—martch 7

Dr Strauss and Dr Nemur say it dont matter about the inkblots. I told them I dint spill the ink on the cards and I coudnt see anything in the ink. They said that maybe they will still use me. I said Miss Kinnian never gave me tests like that one only spelling and reading. They said Miss Kinnian told that I was her bestist pupil in the adult nite scool becaus I tryed the hardist and I reely wantid to lern. They said how come you went to the adult nite scool all by yourself Charlie. How did you find it. I said I askd pepul and sumbody told me where I shud go to lern to read and spell good. They said why did you want to. I told them becaus all my life I wantid to be

1. When Charlie says *raw shok,* he is referring to the *Rorschach* (rôr′ shäk) test that gathers information about personality and intelligence from the images people see in inkblot designs.

MEETING INDIVIDUAL NEEDS — ENGLISH LANGUAGE LEARNERS

Author's Technique English language learners may find this fictional story challenging. Write *fiction* and *nonfiction* on the board and ask which type of writing is true and which is not true. Write the term *progress report* on the board and discuss what this means. Tell students that this story contains intentional misspellings and punctuation and capitalization errors.

Activity Read the story aloud or have students listen to it on tape as they follow along in their books. Pause at the end of each progress report to discuss the changes not only in spelling and punctuation but in sentence structure as Charlie's treatment progresses.

Additional Resources

English Language Learners Sourcebook, p. 29

D smart and not dumb. But its very hard to be smart. They said you know it will probly be tempirery. I said yes. Miss Kinnian told me. I dont care if it herts.

Later I had more crazy tests today. The nice lady who gave it me told me the name and I asked her how do you spellit so I can rite it in my progris riport. THEMATIC APPERCEPTION TEST.[2] I dont know the frist 2 words but I know what *test* means. You got to pass it or you get bad marks. This test lookd easy becaus I coud see the picturs. Only this time she dint want me to tell her the picturs. That mixd me up. I said the man yesterday said I shoud tell him what I saw in the ink she said that dont make no difrence. She said make up storys about the pepul in the picturs.

I told her how can you tell storys about pepul you never met. I said why shud I make up lies. I never tell lies any more becaus I always get caut.

She told me this test and the other one the raw-shok was for getting personalty. I laffed so hard. I said how can you get that thing from inkblots and fotos. She got sore and put her picturs away. I dont care. It was sily. I gess I faled that test too.

E Later some men in white coats took me to a difernt part of the hospitil and gave me a game to play. It was like a race with a white mouse. They called the mouse Algernon. Algernon was in a box with a lot of twists and turns like all kinds of walls and they gave me a pencil and a paper with lines and lots of boxes. On one side it said START and on the other end it said FINISH. They said it was *amazed*[3] and that Algernon and me had the same *amazed* to do. I dint see how we could have the same *amazed* if Algernon had a box and I had a paper but I dint say nothing. Anyway there wasnt time because the race started.

One of the men had a watch he was trying to hide so I woudnt see it so I tryed not to look and that made me nervus.

Anyway that test made me feel worser than all the others because they did it over 10 times with difernt *amazeds* and Algernon won every time. I dint know that mice were so smart. Maybe thats because Algernon is a white mouse. Maybe white mice are smarter then other mice.

progris riport 4—Mar 8

F Their going to use me! Im so exited I can hardly write. Dr Nemur and Dr Strauss had a argament about it first. Dr Nemur was in the office when Dr Strauss brot me in. Dr Nemur was worryed about using me but Dr Strauss told him Miss Kinnian rekemmended me the best from all the people

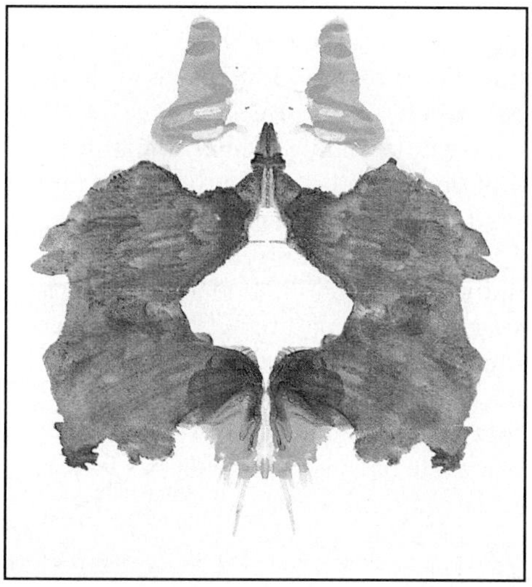

Inkblot design.

2. A *Thematic Apperception* (thē mat′ ik ap′ ər sep′ shən) *Test* asks people to make up stories based on a series of pictures.
3. Charlie writes *amazed,* but he means *a maze.*

D Active Reading Strategies

QUESTION Ask students whether they think Charlie understands what "tempirery" means. How do they know what he thinks it means? *(He thinks it means it might hurt; we know because he says, "I don't care if it hurts.")*

Vocabulary Skills

Word Origins The name *Algernon* comes from an old French word meaning "whiskered."

E Active Reading Strategies

RESPOND Ask students what they think of pitting Charlie against a mouse in this manner. Can they imagine how it must feel to lose over and over again?

F Literary Elements

IRONY When Charlie says, "Their going to use me," he is pleased, but the reader can sense the other meaning of the phrase, as in "to take advantage of." Ask students how this use of irony makes them feel about what he is about to go through.

Interdisciplinary Connection

Psychology Students may be interested in finding out more about the Thematic Aperception Test. The Thematic Aperception Test is based on the idea that one can learn a great deal about people from how they interpret events and from the stories they tell. For example, a person who is people-oriented may look at a picture and be prompted to talk about the relationships of the characters in the drawing. A person who is more data-oriented may focus on objects, numbers, and spatial relationships. The Thematic Aperception Test works almost like a mirror: It reflects the personality of the viewer.

Activity Have students research and write brief reports on the test—what it is and how it is analyzed. Students also may be interested in developing and testing their own versions of the test. **L2**

Charly, 1967. Selmur Productions. Movie still.
Viewing the photograph: How does this scene from the film show Charlie's attitude toward reading?

who she was teaching. I like Miss Kinnian becaus shes a very smart teacher. And she said Charlie your going to have a second chance. If you volenteer for this experament you mite get smart. They dont know if it will be perminint but theirs a chance. Thats why I said ok even when I was scared because she said it was an operashun. She said dont be scared Charlie you done so much with so litle I think you deserv it most of all.

So I got scaird when Dr Nemur and Dr Strauss argud about it. Dr Strauss said I had something that was very good. He said I had a good *motor-vation.*[4] I never even knew I had that. I felt proud when he said that not every body with an eye-q[5] of 68 had that thing. I dont know what it is or where I got it but he said Algernon had it too. Algernons *motor-vation* is the cheese they put in his box. But it cant be that because I didnt eat any cheese this week.

Then he told Dr Nemur something I dint understand so while they were talking I wrote down some of the words.

He said Dr Nemur I know Charlie is not what you had in mind as the first of your new brede of intelek** (coudnt get the word) superman. But most people of his low ment** are host** and uncoop** they are usualy dull apath** and hard to reach. He has a good natcher hes intristed and eager to please.

Dr Nemur said remember he will be the first human beeng ever to have his intelijence trippled by surgicle meens.

Dr Strauss said exakly. Look at how well hes lerned to read and write for his low mentel age its as grate an acheve** as you and I lerning einstines therey of **vity[6] without help. That shows the intenss motor-vation. Its comparat** a tremen** achev** I say we use Charlie.

I dint get all the words and they were talking to fast but it sounded like Dr Strauss was on my side and like the other one wasnt.

Then Dr Nemur nodded he said all right maybe your right. We will use Charlie. When he said that I got so exited

4. Charlie means *motivation* (mō′ tə vā′ shən), the urge or internal need to take action or to make an effort.
5. Charlie is referring to *IQ,* or Intelligence Quotient.
6. *[einstines therey of **vity]* Charlie is referring to the theory of relativity developed by the scientist Albert Einstein.

VIEWING THE PHOTOGRAPH

This still photo is from the film *Charly* starring Cliff Robertson and Claire Bloom and directed by Ralph Nelson. Robertson won the 1968 Best-Actor Oscar for his performance.

Viewing Response *Charlie obviously has a great desire to read.*

FYI

Intelligence Quotient
Also known as IQ, this number is used to estimate a person's rate of mental growth. It is obtained by dividing a person's tested mental age by the chronological age and multiplying by 100. A person with an IQ below 80 is considered intellectually challenged; one of 100 to 115, average; and 200 or above, a genius.

G Active Reading Strategies

CONNECT Ask students to discuss the importance of motivation in their experience. What impact does motivation have on a person's ability to achieve? *(Motivation is the most important factor in achievement; ability is less important.)*

H Literary Elements

IRONY The fact that Charlie doesn't understand the doctors but the reader does is an example of dramatic irony. Ask how Charlie's ignorance makes students feel toward him.

Teaching Support

MEETING INDIVIDUAL NEEDS SPECIAL NEEDS

Learning Disabled Editing another person's writing can be a good drill to improve comprehension. Less-proficient readers may find themselves skimming over some of Charlie's early writing because it takes extra effort to read. Having them edit it by correcting spelling errors and adding missing punctuation and capital letters will aid their comprehension.

Activity Have students work in small groups to edit Charlie's journal from "Then he told Dr Nemur something I dint understand" to "like the other one wasn't." Refer students to the proofreading checklist and proofreader's symbols on the inside back cover of this textbook. **L1**

Additional Resources
Inclusion Strategies

I jumped up and shook his hand for being so good to me. I told him thank you doc you wont be sorry for giving me a second chance. And I mean it like I told him. After the operashun Im gonna try to be smart. Im gonna try awful hard.

progris ript 5—Mar 10

Im skared. Lots of people who work here and the nurses and the people who gave me the tests came to bring me candy and wish me luck. I hope I have luck. I got my rabits foot and my lucky penny and my horse shoe. Only a black cat crossed me when I was comming to the hospitil. Dr Strauss says dont be supersitis Charlie this is sience. Anyway Im keeping my rabits foot with me.

I I asked Dr Strauss if Ill beat Algernon in the race after the operashun and he said maybe. If the operashun works Ill show that mouse I can be as smart as he is. Maybe smarter. Then Ill be abel to read better and spell the words good and know lots of things and be like other people. I want to be smart like other people. If it works perminint they will make everybody smart all over the wurld.

They dint give me anything to eat this morning. I dont know what that eating has to do with getting smart. Im very hungry and Dr Nemur took away my box of candy. That Dr Nemur is a grouch. Dr Strauss says I can have it back after the operashun. You cant eat befor a operashun . . .

Progress Report 6—Mar 15

The operashun dint hurt. He did it while I was sleeping. They took off the bandijis from my eyes and my head today so I can make a PROGRESS REPORT. Dr Nemur who looked at some of my other ones says I spell PROGRESS wrong and he told me how to spell it and REPORT too. I got to try and remember that.

I have a very bad memary for spelling. Dr Strauss says its ok to tell about all the things that happin to me but he says I shoud tell more about what I feel and what I think. When I told him I dont know how to think he said try. All the time when the bandijis were on my eyes I tryed to think. Nothing happened. I dont know what to think about. Maybe if I ask him he will tell me how I can think now that Im suppose to get smart. What do smart people think about. Fancy things I suppose. I wish I knew some fancy things alredy.

Progress Report 7—mar 19

K J Nothing is happining. I had lots of tests and different kinds of races with Algernon. I hate that mouse. He always beats me. Dr Strauss said I got to play those games. And he said some time I got to take those tests over again. Thse inkblots are stupid. And those pictures are stupid too. I like to draw a picture of a man and a woman but I wont make up lies about people.

I got a headache from trying to think so much. I thot Dr Strauss was my frend but he dont help me. He dont tell me what to think or when Ill get smart. Miss Kinnian dint come to see me. I think writing these progress reports are stupid too.

Progress Report 8—Mar 23

Im going back to work at the factery. They said it was better I shud go back to work but I cant tell anyone what the operashun was for and I have to come to the hospitil

I Literary Elements

IRONY Ask students whether they think Charlie will get his wish. With an IQ of over 200, will he be "like other people"? Might Charlie be as lonely when he's smart as he has been up to now? *(Charlie may be happier in that he understands more, but he may be just as lonely because he is too smart.)*

J Active Reading Strategies

REVIEW Ask students what changes in Charlie's personality become apparent immediately after his surgery. *(He becomes frustrated and impatient with his progress and in his relationships with people.)* Is this what they expected to happen?

K Author's Craft

AUTHOR'S PURPOSE Many authors would choose to give the details of Dr. Nemur's discovery. It is probably significant that Keyes chooses not to. Why do students think the author has taken this approach? *(His focus is on the psychology of Charlie, not on the science fiction.)*

MEETING INDIVIDUAL NEEDS — ADVANCED LEARNERS

Measuring Intelligence Encourage students to learn more about IQ and the concept of intelligence. Note that the tests were developed to measure a person's capacity to learn. In recent years, there has been a great deal of controversy about the validity of such tests. Some people think they do not measure ability because they are culturally biased. Others note that there are many different kinds of intelligence but that the tests measure only one kind.

Activity Assign students various topics having to do with the measurement of intelligence. Have them research and present such topics as the validity of intelligence tests, the concept of multiple intelligences, and the success of early-intervention strategies for learning disabled children. **L3**

L Active Reading Strategies

REVIEW The reader already sees that Charlie's writing is changing substantially. Ask students what specific differences they notice in the way Charlie writes and what he writes about. *(Charlie's spelling and grammar are improved. He notices more, interprets more, and analyzes what happens around him.)*

M Literary Elements

IRONY There is clearly a difference between Charlie's perception of his friends and what the reader sees. Ask students to explore the dramatic irony that emerges here. *(Charlie sees his friends as merely joking with him, but, of course, they are making fun of him.)*

N Active Reading Strategies

QUESTION Ask students what Dr. Strauss is doing in giving Charlie the "little television." Be sure that they understand the concept of *sleep learning,* in which people listen to tapes, using the subconscious mind to learn.

for an hour evry night after work. They are gonna pay me mony every month for lerning to be smart.

Im glad Im going back to work because I miss my job and all my frends and all the fun we have there.

L Dr Strauss says I shud keep writing things down but I dont have to do it every day just when I think of something or something speshul happins. He says dont get discoridged because it takes time and it happins slow. He says it took a long time with Algernon before he got 3 times smarter than he was before. Thats why Algernon beats me all the time because he had that operashun too. That makes me feel better. I coud probly do that *amazed* faster than a reglar mouse. Maybe some day Ill beat Algernon. Boy that would be something. So far Algernon looks like he mite be smart perminent.

Mar 25 (I dont have to write PROGRESS REPORT on top any more just when I hand it in once a week for Dr Nemur to read. I just have to put the date on. That saves time)

M We had a lot of fun at the factery today. Joe Carp said hey look where Charlie had his operashun what did they do Charlie put some brains in. I was going to tell him but I remembered Dr Strauss said no. Then Frank Reilly said what did you do Charlie forget your key and open your door the hard way. That made me laff. Their really my friends and they like me.

Sometimes somebody will say hey look at Joe or Frank or George he really pulled a Charlie Gordon. I dont know why they say that but they always laff. This morning Amos Borg who is the 4 man at Donnegans used my name when he shouted at Ernie the office boy. Ernie lost a packige. He said Ernie for godsake what are you trying to be a Charlie Gordon. I dont understand why he said that. I never lost any packiges.

Mar 28 Dr Strauss came to my room tonight to see why I dint come in like I was suppose to. I told him I dont like to race with Algernon any more. He said I dont have to for a while but I shud come in. He had a present for me only it wasnt a present but just for lend. I thot it was a little television but it wasnt. He said I got to turn it on when I go to sleep. I said your kidding why shud I turn it on when Im going to sleep. Who ever herd of a thing like that. But he said if I want to get smart I got to do what he says. I told him I dint think I was going to get smart and he put his hand on my sholder and said Charlie you dont know it yet but your getting smarter all the time. You wont notice for a while. I think he was just being nice to make me feel good because I dont look any smarter. N

Oh yes I almost forgot. I asked him when I can go back to the class at Miss Kinnians school. He said I wont go their. He said that soon Miss Kinnian will come to the hospitil to start and teach me speshul. I was mad at her for not comming to see me when I got the operashun but I like her so maybe we will be frends again.

Mar 29 That crazy TV kept me up all night. How can I sleep with something yelling crazy things all night in my ears. And the nutty pictures. Wow. I dont know

Teaching Support

Reading Minilesson

Comparison and Contrast Explain that writers often use comparison and contrast to develop characters, to move the plot along, or as part of a system of images in a story. In "Flowers for Algernon," Keyes compares and contrasts the old Charlie with the new Charlie. Keeping track of how the old Charlie compares with the new one may help students gain a greater understanding of the theme of the story.

Activity Have students work in small groups to keep a running list of Charlie's behavioral and personality traits. Students can fill in the following chart as they read.

Before the Operation	After the Operation

When students have finished reading, have them answer such questions as *How does the learning disabled Charlie compare with the superintellectual Charlie? How are they different?* Ask groups to report on the major similarities and differences they find. **L2** COLLAB. LEARN.

Additional Resources

Reading Skills Practice Workbook

what it says when Im up so how am I going to know when Im sleeping.

Dr Strauss says its ok. He says my brains are lerning when I sleep and that will help me when Miss Kinnian starts my lessons in the hospitl (only I found out it isnt a hospitil its a labatory). I think its all crazy. If you can get smart when your sleeping why do people go to school. That thing I dont think will work. I use to watch the late show and the late late show on TV all the time and it never made me smart. Maybe you have to sleep while you watch it.

PROGRESS REPORT 9—April 3

Dr Strauss showed me how to keep the TV turned low so now I can sleep. I dont hear a thing. And I still dont understand what it says. A few times I play it over in the morning to find out what I lerned when I was sleeping and I dont think so. Miss Kinnian says Maybe its another langwidge or something. But most times it sounds american. It talks so fast faster then even Miss Gold who was my teacher in 6 grade and I remember she talked so fast I coudnt understand her.

Charly, 1967, Selmur Productions. Movie still.
Viewing the photograph: What may Charlie be thinking as he arranges the puzzle pieces?

VIEWING THE PHOTOGRAPH

From the motion picture *Charly*

Viewing Response *Charlie is clearly puzzled; it is quite difficult for him to figure out what to do.*

O Active Reading Strategies

QUESTION Ask students how they think Charlie is changing. *(Charlie is beginning to think for himself and to question authority.)*

LIFE SKILLS CONNECTION

Decision Making As Charlie becomes more intelligent, he begins to make decisions and ask questions. Adolescence is also a time for independent decision making. As young people mature, they want to be allowed to think and choose for themselves. Sometimes, however, adolescents don't think things through carefully or they are strident in their demands for independence. This behavior tends to make adults react by limiting independence.

Activity Have students work in groups to role-play situations in which they request the right to more independent decision making from parents or teachers. Students should be prepared to backup their arguments with details, reasons, and examples. Have the students who play the authority figures give feedback to the students who play adolescents.
L2 **COLLAB. LEARN.**

P Literary Elements

IRONY Again, dramatic irony is used when Charlie gives his version of his night out. Even though the story is told from Charlie's point of view, readers realize what is happening. Ask students how the story might differ if it were told from an objective point of view.

I told Dr Strauss what good is it to get smart in my sleep. I want to be smart when Im awake. He says its the same thing and I have two minds. Theres the *subconscious* and the *conscious* (thats how you spell it). And one dont tell the other one what its doing. They dont even talk to each other. Thats why I dream. And boy have I been having crazy dreams. Wow. Ever since that night TV. The late late late late late show.

I forgot to ask him if it was only me or if everybody had those two minds.

(I just looked up the word in the dictionary Dr Strauss gave me. The word is *subconscious. adj. Of the nature of mental operations yet not present in consciousness; as, subconscious conflict of desires.)* Theres more but I still don't know what it means. This isnt a very good dictionary for dumb people like me.

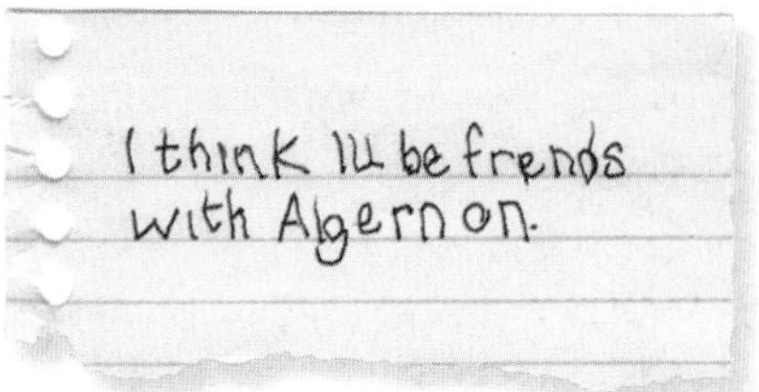

P

Anyway the headache is from the party. My frends from the factery Joe Carp and Frank Reilly invited me to go with them to Muggsys Saloon for some drinks. I dont like to drink but they said we will have lots of fun. I had a good time.

Joe Carp said I shoud show the girls how I mop out the toilet in the factory and he got me a mop. I showed them and everyone laffed when I told that Mr Donnegan said I was the best janiter he ever had because I like my job and do it good and never come late or miss a day except for my operashun.

I said Miss Kinnian always said Charlie be proud of your job because you do it good.

Everybody laffed and we had a good time and they gave me lots of drinks and Joe said Charlie is a card when hes potted.[7] I dont know what that means but everybody likes me and we have fun. I cant wait to be smart like my best frends Joe Carp and Frank Reilly.

I dont remember how the party was over but I think I went out to buy a newspaper and coffe for Joe and Frank and when I came back there was no one their. I looked for them all over till late. Then I dont remember so good but I think I got sleepy or sick. A nice cop brot me back home. Thats what my landlady Mrs Flynn says.

But I got a headache and a big lump on my head and black and blue all over. I think maybe I fell but Joe Carp says it was the cop they beat up drunks some times. I don't think so. Miss Kinnian says cops are to help people. Anyway I got a bad headache and Im sick and hurt all over. I dont think Ill drink anymore.

April 6 I beat Algernon! I dint even know I beat him until Burt the tester told me. Then the second time I lost because I got so exited I fell off the chair before I finished. But after that I beat him 8 more times. I must be getting smart to beat a smart mouse like Algernon. But I dont *feel* smarter.

I wanted to race Algernon some more but Burt said thats enough for one day. They let me hold him for a minit. Hes not so bad.

7. *Charlie is a card when hes potted* means "Charlie is funny when he's had too much to drink."

Teaching Support

Writing Minilesson

Point of View Telling a story from another point of view can result in a very different story. Illustrate this by having students role play. Take the student's part in a typical student-teacher or student-parent conflict. Ask students to play parents' or teachers' roles. (Try asking students, "Why do I have to do home work? I hate homework.") Practice role shifting in a written exercise.

Activity Have students rewrite Charlie's journal entry about the party from "Anyway the headache is from the party" to "I don't think I'll drink anymore" from another viewpoint. They may take the viewpoint of one of Charlie's so-called friends or of someone observing the situation. **L2**

Additional Resources

Writer's Choice, Lesson 4.3

Charly, 1967. Selmur Productions. Movie still.

Viewing the photograph: What does Charlie's smile reveal about his personality?

Hes soft like a ball of cotton. He blinks and when he opens his eyes their black and pink on the eges.

I said can I feed him because I felt bad to beat him and I wanted to be nice and make frends. Burt said no Algernon is a very specshul mouse with an operashun like mine, and he was the first of all the animals to stay smart so long. He told me Algernon is so smart that every day he has to solve a test to get his food. Its a thing like a lock on a door that changes every time Algernon goes in to eat so he has to lern something new to get his food. That made me sad because if he coudnt lern he woud be hungry.

I dont think its right to make you pass a test to eat. How woud Dr Nemur like it to have to pass a test every time he wants to eat. I think Ill be frends with Algernon.

April 9 Tonight after work Miss Kinnian was at the laboratory. She looked like she was glad to see me but scared. I told her dont worry Miss Kinnian Im not smart yet and she laffed. She said I have confidence in you Charlie the way you struggled so hard to read and right better than all the others. At werst you will have it for a littel wile and your doing somthing for sience.

We are reading a very hard book. I never read such a hard book before. Its called *Robinson Crusoe* about a man who gets merooned on a dessert Iland. Hes smart and figers out all kinds of things so he can have a house and food and hes a good swimmer. Only I feel sorry because hes all alone and has no frends. But I think their must be somebody else on the iland because theres a picture with his funny umbrella looking at footprints. I hope he gets a frend and not be lonly.

April 10 Miss Kinnian teaches me to spell better. She says look at a word and close your eyes and say it over and over until you remember. I have lots of truble with *through* that you say *threw* and *enough* and *tough* that you dont say *enew* and *tew*. You got to say *enuff* and *tuff*. Thats how

VIEWING THE PHOTOGRAPH

From the motion picture *Charly*

Viewing Response *Charlie's smile shows his good nature.*

Q Literary Elements

FORESHADOWING Since Algernon is the first of the animals to stay smart for so long, the implication is that all the others were smart for only a short period. What does this suggest about Charlie? *(What happens to Algernon foreshadows what will happen to Charlie.)*

R Active Reading Strategies

REVIEW Explain to students that in writing about *Robinson Crusoe,* Charlie is able to do what he could not do in the psychological tests he took in the beginning of the story. He can now project his feelings (onto Crusoe), draw conclusions, and imagine a person he doesn't know.

Listening and Speaking *Minilesson*

Debating Students may take opposing positions on the subject of the experiment performed on Charlie. Post some basic principles of debate:

1. Debaters are expected to take a stand for or against an issue.
2. Debaters are expected to be able to argue a position effectively and logically even if they don't personally agree with it.
3. Debaters' presentations are strictly timed.

Activity Assign students to opposing positions and have them prepare to debate this question: Is it acceptable to perform risky surgery on someone who is not able to understand the risks completely as long as there is the possibility of a benefit?
L2 **COLLAB. LEARN.**

LEAN ON ME 121

S Literary Elements

IRONY Ask students to explain what is going on with Miss Kinnian when she warns Charlie and then runs to the ladies' room. *(She clearly has read about what Charlie's friends did to him; she goes to the restroom because she is crying.)* Point out the dramatic irony In the way Charlie sees the situation.

T Active Reading Strategies

QUESTION Why is Charlie suddenly self-conscious about his writing? *(He is getting smarter and understands punctuation. Now he sees his old self vividly and is embarrassed.)*

I use to write it before I started to get smart. Im confused but Miss Kinnian says theres no reason in spelling.

April 14 Finished *Robinson Crusoe*. I want to find out more about what happens to him but Miss Kinnian says thats all there is. *Why*

April 15 Miss Kinnian says Im lerning fast. She read some of the Progress Reports and she looked at me kind of funny. She says Im a fine person and Ill show them all. I asked her why. She said never mind but I shoudnt feel bad if I find out that everybody isnt nice like I think. She said for a person who god gave so little to you done more then a lot of people with brains they never even used. I said all my frends are smart people but there good. They like me and they never did anything that wasnt nice. Then she got something in her eye and she had to run out to the ladys room.

April 16 Today, I lerned, the *comma*, this is a comma (,) a period, with a tail, Miss Kinnian, says its importent, because, it makes writing, better, she said, sombeody, could lose, a lot of money, if a comma, isnt, in the, right place, I dont have, any money, and I dont see, how a comma, keeps you, from losing it,

But she says, everybody, uses commas, so Ill use, them too,

April 17 I used the comma wrong. Its punctuation. Miss Kinnian told me to look up long words in the dictionary to lern to spell them. I said whats the difference if you can read it anyway. She said its part of your education so now on Ill look up all the words Im not sure how to spell. It takes a long time to write that way but I think Im remembering. I only have to look up once and after that I get it right. Anyway thats how come I got the word *punctuation* right. (Its that way in the dictionary). Miss Kinnian says a period is punctuation too, and there are lots of other marks to lern. I told her I thot all the periods had to have tails but she said no.

You got to mix them up, she showed? me" how. to mix! them(up,. and now; I can! mix up all kinds" of punctuation, in! my writing? There, are lots! of rules? to lern; but Im gettin'g them in my head.

One thing I? like about, Dear Miss Kinnian: (thats the way it goes in a business letter if I ever go into business) is she, always gives me' a reason" when—I ask. She's a gen'ius! I wish! I cou'd be smart" like, her;

(Punctuation, is; fun!)

April 18 What a dope I am! I didn't even understand what she was talking about. I read the grammar book last night and it explanes the whole thing. Then I saw it was the same way as Miss Kinnian was trying to tell me, but I didn't get it. I got up in the middle of the night, and the whole thing straightened out in my mind.

Miss Kinnian said that the TV working in my sleep helped out. She said I reached a plateau. Thats like the flat top of a hill.

After I figgered out how punctuation worked, I read over all my old Progress Reports from the beginning. Boy, did I have crazy spelling and punctuation! I

Teaching Support

Grammar and Language Minilesson

Punctuation Point out that it is common to make judgments about others based on their grammar. Note that when Keyes wants to show the reader that Charlie is learning disabled, he uses grammar and usage errors to make the point. Mention that people are often judged in just this way. Job applications and résumés are examples of "real world" writing in which grammar and usage play a significant role.

Activity Have students copy and punctuate properly the journal entry dated April 16 and the last three paragraphs of the entry dated April 17. Review students' work for accuracy. **L2**

Additional Resources

- ***Grammar and Language Transparency 9***
- ***Grammar and Language Workbook,*** pp. 255–274
- ***Grammar and Composition Handbook,*** Lesson 13
- ***Writer's Choice,*** Lesson 20

told Miss Kinnian I ought to go over the pages and fix all the mistakes but she said, "No, Charlie, Dr. Nemur wants them just as they are. That's why he let you keep them after they were photostated,[8] to see your own progress. You're coming along fast, Charlie."

U That made me feel good. After the lesson I went down and played with Algernon. We don't race any more.

April 20 I feel sick inside. Not sick like for a doctor, but inside my chest it feels empty like getting punched and a heartburn at the same time.

I wasn't going to write about it, but I guess I got to, because it's important. Today was the first time I ever stayed home from work.

V Last night Joe Carp and Frank Reilly invited me to a party. There were lots of girls and some men from the factory. I remembered how sick I got last time I drank too much, so I told Joe I didn't want anything to drink. He gave me a plain Coke instead. It tasted funny, but I thought it was just a bad taste in my mouth.

We had a lot of fun for a while. Joe said I should dance with Ellen and she would teach me the steps. I fell a few times and I couldn't understand why because no one else was dancing besides Ellen and me. And all the time I was tripping because somebody's foot was always sticking out.

Then when I got up I saw the look on Joe's face and it gave me a funny feeling in my stomack. "He's a scream," one of the girls said. Everybody was laughing.

Frank said, "I ain't laughed so much since we sent him off for the newspaper that night at Muggsy's and ditched him."

"Look at him. His face is red."

"He's blushing. Charlie is blushing."

"Hey, Ellen, what'd you do to Charlie? I never saw him act like that before."

I didn't know what to do or where to turn. Everyone was looking at me and laughing and I felt naked. I wanted to hide myself. I ran out into the street and I threw up. Then I walked home. It's a funny thing I never knew that Joe and Frank and the others liked to have me around all the time to make fun of me. W

Now I know what it means when they say "to pull a Charlie Gordon."

I'm ashamed.

8. A *photostat* is a type of photocopy made on specially treated paper.

U Active Reading Strategies

QUESTION Why doesn't Charlie race Algernon any more? *(Charlie consistently beats him now.)*

V Active Reading Strategies

QUESTION Ask students how Charlie's revelation about punctuation parallels his revelation about his friends. *(Just as he understands how to punctuate and is ashamed of his previous writing, so too he suddenly realizes what his friends are doing and is sickened by his new awareness.)*

W Literary Elements

ALLUSION Point out that Charlie's feeling naked alludes to the story of Adam and Eve in the Bible. After eating from the Tree of Knowledge, they suddenly become self-conscious and want to cover their nakedness.

Thematic Focus

Lean on Me Ask students what links they see between the theme and this story. *(Though Charlie can and does lean on Miss Kinnian, he is truly very much alone, especially as he grows in intelligence. Still, there is a sad interdependence between Charlie and Algernon.)*

ASSESSMENT

Quick Checks, p. 10

Real-World Connection

Genetic Engineering There have been many articles written about genetic engineering. Some articles celebrate the advances of science; others voice concerns about how these discoveries should be used and question whether humankind really knows enough to tamper with the building blocks of life.

Activity Have students gather information from a variety of primary and secondary sources on various aspects of genetic engineering. Each student should report briefly on what he or she finds. Ask students to evaluate their research and relate what they learned to "Flowers for Algernon." **L2**

Responding to the Selection

PERSONAL RESPONSE

Some students may say that they sympathized with Charlie's pain and sense of betrayal. Some will say they would have chosen Charlie as a friend because of his kind nature.

Analyzing Literature

1. Charlie believes that smart people can read and spell and learn easily. He does not realize that these people lack his goodness and kind nature.
2. Charlie is chosen for the project because of his intense desire to learn and because of his willingness to do what is expected of him. His ability to get along with others indicates that he possesses interpersonal intelligence.
3. Charlie becomes more self-conscious; he no longer wants to race with Algernon. He also begins to question authority and realizes his friends have been making fun of him.
4. This is an especially effective way to tell this story since Charlie's intellectual level is shown clearly with each entry. One can see almost daily changes.
5. In his journal entries, Charlie says he both wants and fears the operation.
6. Students' responses should consider the positive and the negative sides of the fulfillment of the wish.

Active Reading and Critical Thinking

Responding to Literature

PERSONAL RESPONSE

- How did you react when Charlie discovered the truth about his friends?
- If you met Charlie before the operation, would you have chosen him as a friend? Why or why not?

Analyzing Literature

RECALL AND INTERPRET

1. What does Charlie think is the difference between himself and smart people? What does Charlie fail to see about the "smart" people around him? Explain.
2. Why is Charlie chosen for the project, even though he fails all the tests? Reread the information about intelligence on page 112. What types of intelligence might Charlie have? Explain.
3. What incidents in the first part of the story indicate Charlie is changing? When he realizes the meaning of "to pull a Charlie Gordon," what new understanding does Charlie have about himself and others?

EVALUATE AND CONNECT

4. The author presents "Flowers for Algernon" as a series of progress reports or journal entries. Is this style an effective way to tell the story? Why or why not? Support your opinion with examples.
5. **Internal conflict** is a struggle within a character. How does the writer show Charlie's internal conflict about the operation?
6. Suppose you wanted to change something about yourself. Someone offers you a risky operation to grant your wish, but the change will last only a few months. Describe the internal conflict you might have when faced with this decision.

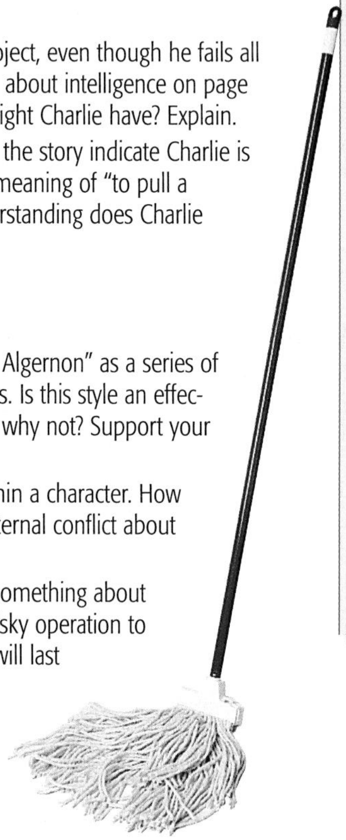

LITERARY ELEMENTS

Irony

Irony is the difference between the way things seem to be and the way they really are. In a story like "Flowers for Algernon," the writer uses irony in two ways. In **dramatic irony,** readers have important knowledge that the character does not (Charlie thinks Frank and Joe like him a lot, but they are cruel to him). In **situational irony,** the outcome of a situation is the opposite of what the character expects (Charlie expects that being smart will help him fit in, but instead he sees how people laugh at him).

1. Reread the progress reports for March 6 to March 8. How does the writer use irony to show Charlie's personality and intelligence?
2. How would the story be different if the writer had simply reported Charlie's scores and not used irony?

- See **Literary Terms Handbook,** p. R5.

LITERARY ELEMENTS

1. Keyes presents information that the reader can understand but that Charlie cannot.
2. The humor inherent in Charlie's common-sense view of the tests would be lost if the results were presented objectively.

Additional Resources

Literary Elements Transparency 10

Flowers for Algernon (Continued)

PROGRESS REPORT 11

A *April 21* Still didn't go into the factory. I told Mrs. Flynn my landlady to call and tell Mr. Donnegan I was sick. Mrs. Flynn looks at me very funny lately like she's scared of me.

B I think it's a good thing about finding out how everybody laughs at me. I thought about it a lot. It's because I'm so dumb and I don't even know when I'm doing something dumb. People think it's funny when a dumb person can't do things the same way they can.

Anyway, now I know I'm getting smarter every day. I know punctuation and I can spell good. I like to look up all the hard words in the dictionary and I remember them. I'm reading a lot now, and Miss Kinnian says I read very fast. Sometimes I even understand what I'm reading about, and it stays in my mind. There are times when I can close my eyes and think of a page and it all comes back like a picture.

C Besides history, geography, and arithmetic, Miss Kinnian said I should start to learn a few foreign languages. Dr. Strauss gave me some more tapes to play while I sleep. I still don't understand how that conscious and unconscious mind works, but Dr. Strauss says not to worry yet. He asked me to promise that when I start learning college subjects next week I wouldn't read any books on psychology—that is, until he gives me permission.

D I feel a lot better today, but I guess I'm still a little angry that all the time people were laughing and making fun of me because I wasn't so smart. When I become intelligent like Dr. Strauss says, with three times my I.Q. of 68, then maybe I'll be like everyone else and people will like me and be friendly.

I'm not sure what an I.Q. is. Dr. Nemur said it was something that measured how intelligent you were—like a scale in the drugstore weighs pounds. But Dr. Strauss had a big argument with him and said an I.Q. didn't weigh intelligence at all. He said an I.Q. showed how much intelligence you could get, like the numbers on the outside of a measuring cup. You still had to fill the cup up with stuff.

Then when I asked Burt, who gives me my intelligence tests and works with Algernon, he said that both of them were wrong (only I had to promise not to tell

A Active Reading Strategies

QUESTION Ask students why they think Mrs. Flynn appears to be frightened of Charlie. *(She doesn't understand what has happened to Charlie to change him so much.)*

Additional Resources

- ***Active Reading Guide,*** p. 11
- ***Audio Library***
- ***Spanish Audio Library***

B Critical Thinking

EVALUATING Discuss Charlie's conclusion with students. Is it good that he now understands why people laugh at him? Is he truly better off? *(Some students may suggest that Charlie is lonelier now because he knows how alone he is.)*

C Active Reading Strategies

QUESTION Ask students why they think Dr. Strauss doesn't want Charlie to read psychology texts. *(He wants to study Charlie's reaction to his increasing intelligence without interference. If Charlie understands psychology, his knowledge may cause him to worry about or question the experiment.)*

D Active Reading Strategies

PREDICT Ask students to predict what will happen to Charlie when his IQ climbs above 200. Will he, in fact, have more friends? Why or why not?

Teaching Support

MEETING INDIVIDUAL NEEDS — ENGLISH LANGUAGE LEARNERS

Using the Past Tense of Verbs
Invite English language learners to discuss what has happened in the story up to this point. Guide students in writing a three- to five-sentence group summary of the first part of the story. Explain to students that because they are writing about what has happened so far, they should be consistent in using the past tense of verbs. Point out the variety of past tenses used in the group summary.

Activity After students have read the rest of the story, have them work individually or with partners to write a one- or two-sentence summary of each progress report. Remind students to use past tenses to summarize.

Additional Resources

- ***English Language Learners Sourcebook,*** p. 30

E Critical Thinking

INFERRING Note, as Charlie becomes increasingly intelligent, he is much quicker to anger. Ask students why they think this occurs. *(He is more self-aware and is thus more defensive and self-protective.)*

F Active Reading Strategies

CONNECT Charlie is shocked at the gap between his former self and his current self. Ask students whether they can relate to Charlie's feelings. Have they ever suddenly understood something and felt different from the person they used to be?

Teaching Support

them he said so). Burt says that the I.Q. measures a lot of different things including some of the things you learned already, and it really isn't any good at all.

So I still don't know what I.Q. is except that mine is going to be over 200 soon. I didn't want to say anything, but I don't see how if they don't know *what* it is, or *where* it is—I don't see how they know *how much* of it you've got.

Dr. Nemur says I have to take a *Rorshach Test* tomorrow. I wonder what *that* is.

April 22 I found out what a *Rorshach* is. It's the test I took before the operation—the one with the inkblots on the pieces of cardboard. The man who gave me the test was the same one.

The test still doesn't make sense to me. It seems to me that anyone could make up lies about things that they didn't really see.

I was scared to death of those inkblots. I knew he was going to ask me to find the pictures and I knew I wouldn't be able to. I was thinking to myself, if only there was some way of knowing what kind of pictures were hidden there. Maybe there weren't any pictures at all. Maybe it was just a trick to see if I was dumb enough to look for something that wasn't there. Just thinking about that made me sore at him.

"All right, Charlie," he said, "you've seen these cards before, remember?"

E "Of course I remember."

The way I said it, he knew I was angry, and he looked surprised. "Yes, of course. Now I want you to look at this one. What might this be? What do you see on this card? People see all sorts of things in these inkblots. Tell me what it might be for you—what it makes you think of."

I was shocked. That wasn't what I had expected him to say at all. "You mean there are no pictures hidden in those inkblots?"

He frowned and took off his glasses. "What?"

"Pictures. Hidden in the inkblots. Last time you told me that everyone could see them and you wanted me to find them too."

He explained to me that the last time he had used almost the exact same words he was using now. I didn't believe it, and I still have the suspicion that he misled me at the time just for the fun of it. Unless—I don't know any more—could I have been *that* feebleminded? F

We went through the cards slowly. One of them looked like a pair of bats tugging at something. Another one looked like two men fencing with swords. I imagined all sorts of things. I guess I got carried away. But I didn't trust him any more, and I kept turning them around and even looking on the back to see if there was anything there I was supposed to catch. While he was making his notes, I peeked out of the corner of my eye to read it. But it was all in code that looked like this:

WF+A DdF-Ad orig. WF-A SF+obj

MEETING INDIVIDUAL NEEDS

ADVANCED LEARNERS

Ink Blots The Rorshach test analyzes personality by classifying and evaluating what people project onto a series of black ink blots on white paper. The inkblots in themselves are meaningless. The Rorshach test, like the thematic apperception test, is relevant only insofar as it encourages people to reveal their perceptions.

Activity Have students research the history and validity of the Rorshach test and report to the class about how the test is used. Remind the students that since their reports will be read aloud, enunciation and fluency are important. Students should observe the reactions of their classmates and modify their reports to respond to the interest and attention span of listeners. **L3**

The test still doesn't make sense to me. It seems to me that anyone could make up lies about things that they didn't really see. How could he know I wasn't making a fool of him by mentioning things that I didn't really imagine? Maybe I'll understand it when Dr. Strauss lets me read up on psychology.

April 25 I figured out a new way to line up the machines in the factory, and Mr. Donnegan says it will save him ten thousand dollars a year in labor and increased production. He gave me a twenty-five-dollar bonus.

I wanted to take Joe Carp and Frank Reilly out to lunch to celebrate, but Joe said he had to buy some things for his wife, and Frank said he was meeting his cousin for lunch. I guess it'll take a little time for them to get used to the changes in me. Everybody seems to be frightened of me. When I went over to Amos Borg and tapped him on the shoulder, he jumped up in the air.

G People don't talk to me much any more or kid around the way they used to. It makes the job kind of lonely.

April 27 I got up the nerve today to ask Miss Kinnian to have dinner with me tomorrow night to celebrate my bonus.

H At first she wasn't sure it was right, but I asked Dr. Strauss and he said it was okay. Dr. Strauss and Dr. Nemur don't seem to be getting along so well. They're arguing all the time. This evening when I came in to ask Dr. Strauss about having dinner with Miss Kinnian, I heard them shouting. Dr. Nemur was saying that it was *his* experiment and *his* research, and Dr. Strauss was shouting back that he contributed just as much, because he found me through Miss Kinnian and he performed the operation. Dr. Strauss said that someday thousands of neurosurgeons[9] might be using his technique all over the world.

Dr. Nemur wanted to publish the results of the experiment at the end of this month. Dr. Strauss wanted to wait a while longer to be sure. Dr. Strauss said that Dr. Nemur was more interested in the Chair of Psychology at Princeton[10] than he was in the experiment. Dr. Nemur said that Dr. Strauss was nothing but an opportunist who was trying to ride to glory on *his* coattails.

When I left afterwards, I found myself trembling. I don't know why for sure, but it was as if I'd seen both men clearly for the first time. I remember hearing Burt say that Dr. Nemur had a shrew[11] of a wife who was pushing him all the time to get things published so that he could become famous. Burt said that the dream of her life was to have a big-shot husband.

Was Dr. Strauss really trying to ride on his coattails?

April 28 I don't understand why I never noticed how beautiful Miss Kinnian really is. She has brown eyes and feathery brown hair that comes to the top of her neck. She's only thirty-four! I think from the

9. The prefix *neuro-* means "nerve," and a *neurosurgeon* (noor′ ō sur′ jən) performs surgery on part of the body's nervous system.
10. The *Chair of Psychology* is the chairperson of the Psychology Department. *Princeton* is a university in New Jersey.
11. Here, *shrew* means "a bad-tempered, nagging woman."

Vocabulary

opportunist (op′ ər to͞o′ nist) *n.* one who takes advantage of every opportunity, regardless of consequences

G Literary Elements

IRONY Note the irony here. Charlie is just as much ostracized as a genius as he was as a learning disabled person. Why do students think this is so? *(Either way, Charlie is exceptional, not part of the mainstream.)*

H Literary Elements

FORESHADOWING Ask what this exchange reveals about the characters of the two doctors. Have students guess how this hints at what is to come. *(Of course, neither one cares about what happens to Charlie. Both are opportunists concerned with their own reputations.)*

MEETING INDIVIDUAL NEEDS: MULTIPLE MODES OF EXPRESSION

Linguistic Linguistic learners learn through language and by reading. These students may be able to add to others' interpretations of "Flowers for Algernon" by comparing it to Mary Shelley's *Frankenstein*. This novel, of course, focuses on the excesses of scientists in their quest for knowledge.

Activity Have students read *Frankenstein* and report on the similar themes between the two stories. Alternatively, allow students to watch a film version of the novel. Tell them to pay particular attention to the theme of tampering with natural law and to compare the motivations of the characters in the two stories. **L2**

I Active Reading Strategies

EVALUATE Discuss Miss Kinnian's definition of intelligence. She says intelligence is not only facts and figures, but experience and the ability to make connections. Ask students what they think of this definition. Is it adequate? Does it help to explain some of Charlie's frustrations?

J Literary Elements

FORESHADOWING Make sure that students understand what Charlie and Miss Kinnian are concerned about. Note that they are both referring to the idea that Charlie may lose all the intelligence he has gained.

K Critical Thinking

EVALUATING Ask students which they think is worse: never having superior intelligence or having once had it, losing it.

Model: I think when Charlie was learning disabled, he envied people who learned and read easily, but he was otherwise contented with his life. Now that he has gained intelligence, he may also have to experience losing it, which would be like dying. So it seems that it is worse to have intelligence and then lose it than never to have had it.

beginning I had the feeling that she was an unreachable genius—and very, very old. Now, every time I see her she grows younger and more lovely.

We had dinner and a long talk. When she said that I was coming along so fast that soon I'd be leaving her behind, I laughed.

"It's true, Charlie. You're already a better reader than I am. You can read a whole page at a glance while I can take in only a few lines at a time. And you remember every single thing you read. I'm lucky if I can recall the main thoughts and the general meaning."

"I don't feel intelligent. There are so many things I don't understand."

She took out a cigarette and I lit it for her. "You've got to be a *little* patient. You're accomplishing in days and weeks what it takes normal people to do in half a lifetime. That's what makes it so amazing. You're like a giant sponge now, soaking things in. Facts, figures, general knowledge. And soon you'll begin to connect them, too. You'll see how the different branches of learning are related. There are many levels, Charlie, like steps on a giant ladder that take you up higher and higher to see more and more of the world around you.

"I can see only a little bit of that, Charlie, and I won't go much higher than I am now, but you'll keep climbing up and up, and see more and more, and each step will open new worlds that you never even knew existed." She frowned. "I hope . . . I just hope to God—"

"What?"

"Never mind, Charles. I just hope I wasn't wrong to advise you to go into this in the first place."

I laughed. "How could that be? It worked, didn't it? Even Algernon is still smart."

We sat there silently for a while and I knew what she was thinking about as she watched me toying with the chain of my rabbit's foot and my keys. I didn't want to think of that possibility any more than elderly people want to think of death. I *knew* that this was only the beginning. I knew what she meant about levels because I'd seen some of them already. The thought of leaving her behind made me sad.

I'm in love with Miss Kinnian.

PROGRESS REPORT 12

April 30 I've quit my job with Donnegan's Plastic Box Company. Mr. Donnegan insisted that it would be better for all concerned if I left. What did I do to make them hate me so?

The first I knew of it was when Mr. Donnegan showed me the petition. Eight hundred and forty names, everyone connected with the factory, except Fanny Girden. Scanning the list quickly, I saw at once that hers was the only missing name. All the rest demanded that I be fired.

Joe Carp and Frank Reilly wouldn't talk to me about it. No one else would either, except Fanny. She was one of the few people I'd known who set her mind to something and believed it no matter what the rest of the world proved, said, or did—and Fanny did not believe that I should have been fired. She had been against the

Teaching Support

Reading Minilesson

Predicting Direct students' attention to the passage on page 128 that begins "We sat there silently," and in which Charlie thinks about the possibility of leaving Miss Kinnian behind. At this point in the story, everything seems to be going well for Charlie, yet the author includes this passage, which mentions loss and death.

Activity Ask students to read through the passage carefully and to discuss in small groups what it seems to suggest will happen to Charlie. What possibilities is he thinking of? Why might he have to leave Miss Kinnian behind? Do the keys and rabbit's foot provide hints as to the significance of this passage? Have each group report briefly on its conclusion. **L2** COLLAB. LEARN.

Additional Resources

Reading Skills Practice Workbook

petition on principle and despite the pressure and threats she'd held out.

"Which don't mean to say," she remarked, "that I don't think there's something mighty strange about you, Charlie. Them changes. I don't know. You used to be a good, dependable, ordinary man—not too bright maybe, but honest. Who knows what you done to yourself to get so smart all of a sudden. Like everybody around here's been saying, Charlie, it's not right."

"But how can you say that, Fanny? What's wrong with a man becoming intelligent and wanting to acquire knowledge and understanding of the world around him?"

L She stared down at her work and I turned to leave. Without looking at me, she said: "It was evil when Eve listened to the snake and ate from the tree of knowledge. It was evil when she saw that she was naked. If not for that none of us would ever have to grow old and sick, and die."

Once again now I have the feeling of shame burning inside me. This intelligence has driven a wedge between me and all the people I once knew and loved. Before, they laughed at me and despised me for my ignorance and dullness; now, they hate me for my knowledge and understanding. What in God's name do they want of me?

M They've driven me out of the factory. Now I'm more alone than ever before . . .

May 15 Dr. Strauss is very angry at me for not having written any progress reports in two weeks. He's justified because the lab is now paying me a regular salary. I told him I was too busy thinking and reading. When I pointed out that writing was such a slow process that it made me impatient with my poor handwriting, he suggested that I learn to type. It's much easier to write now because I can type nearly seventy-five words a minute. Dr. Strauss continually reminds me of the need to speak and write simply so that people will be able to understand me.

I'll try to review all the things that happened to me during the last two weeks. Algernon and I were presented to the American Psychological Association sitting in convention with the World Psychological Association last Tuesday. We created quite a sensation. Dr. Nemur and Dr. Strauss were proud of us.

I suspect that Dr. Nemur, who is sixty—ten years older than Dr. Strauss—finds it necessary to see tangible results of his work. Undoubtedly the result of pressure by Mrs. Nemur.

Contrary to my earlier impressions of him, I realize that Dr. Nemur is not at all a genius. He has a very good mind, but it struggles under the spectre[12] of self-doubt. He

12. A *spectre* is anything that haunts or troubles the mind.

Vocabulary

tangible (tan′ jə bəl) *adj.* able to be seen, touched, or felt; real

L Active Reading Strategies

CONNECT Be sure that students understand the meaning and significance of Fanny's comments. She is specifically comparing what has happened to Charlie to the consequences of Eve's original sin of seeking forbidden knowledge. Ask students how both characters' motivations and the consequences of their actions are similar. *(Both wanted greater knowledge. Eve's sin brought death into the world, just as Charlie's desire for knowledge brings tragedy to him.)*

M Literary Elements

IRONY Point out that the fact that Charlie is "more alone than ever before" is situational irony.

Writing Minilesson

Explaining Connections Write this sentence on the board: *Be careful what you wish for—you just may get it.* This popular saying warns that there may be negative consequences of getting the things we wish for. Neither Charlie nor the doctors conducting the experiment thoroughly considered all the consequences.

Activity Have students each write a paragraph about the possible negative consequences of getting something he or she always wished for. Students should write about what they hoped for and what they failed to consider, exploring the connection between their wishes and the negative consequences. **L2**

Additional Resources

Writer's Choice, Lesson 5.5

wants people to take him for a genius. Therefore, it is important for him to feel that his work is accepted by the world. I believe that Dr. Nemur was afraid of further delay because he worried that someone else might make a discovery along these lines and take the credit from him.

N

Dr. Strauss on the other hand might be called a genius, although I feel that his areas of knowledge are too limited. He was educated in the tradition of narrow specialization; the broader aspects of background were neglected far more than necessary—even for a neurosurgeon.

I was shocked to learn that the only ancient languages he could read were Latin, Greek, and Hebrew, and that he knows almost nothing of mathematics beyond the elementary levels of the calculus of variations.[13] When he admitted this to me, I found myself almost annoyed. It was as if he'd hidden this part of himself in order to deceive me, pretending—as do many people I've discovered—to be what he is not. No one I've ever known is what he appears to be on the surface.

O

Dr. Nemur appears to be uncomfortable around me. Sometimes when I try to talk to him, he just looks at me strangely and turns away. I was angry at first when Dr. Strauss told me I was giving Dr. Nemur an inferiority complex. I thought he was mocking me and I'm oversensitive at being made fun of.

How was I to know that a highly respected psychoexperimentalist like Nemur was unacquainted with Hindustani[14] and Chinese? It's absurd when you consider the work that is being done in India and China today in the very field of this study.

I asked Dr. Strauss how Nemur could refute[15] Rahajamati's attack on his method and results if Nemur couldn't even read them in the first place. That strange look on Dr. Strauss' face can mean only one of two things. Either he doesn't want to tell Nemur what they're saying in India, or else—and this worries me—Dr. Strauss doesn't know either. I must be careful to speak and write clearly and simply so that people won't laugh.

May 18 I am very disturbed. I saw Miss Kinnian last night for the first time in over a week. I tried to avoid all discussions of intellectual concepts and to keep the conversation on a simple, everyday level, but she just stared at me blankly and asked me what I meant about the mathematical variance equivalent in Dorbermann's *Fifth Concerto*.

When I tried to explain she stopped me and laughed. I guess I got angry, but I suspect I'm approaching her on the wrong level. No matter what I try to discuss with her, I am unable to communicate. I must review Vrostadt's equations on *Levels of Semantic Progression*. I find that I don't communicate with people much any more. Thank God for books and music and things I can think about. I am alone

13. The *calculus of variations* is an advanced mathematical system.

14. *Hindustani* is a language spoken in India.

15. To *refute* the attack would be to prove that the criticism is false or incorrect.

Vocabulary

intellectual (int′ əl ek′ cho͞o əl) *adj.* appealing to or involving intelligence or mental ability

N Literary Elements

CHARACTERIZATION Ask students to look carefully at Charlie's criticism of Drs. Nemur and Strauss. What does his criticism say about how he has changed? *(Initially, he accepted whatever any authority figure said without question.)*

O Active Reading Strategies

QUESTION What aspects of the "old" Charlie are still evident, even though he is a different person? *(He still has a sensitive, caring side.)*

Teaching Support

interNET CONNECTION

Multiple Intelligences Have students plan and conduct a multiple-step computer information search to find out more about the concept of multiple intelligences. They can enter that term or the name *Howard Gardner.* They should find out as much as they can about Gardner's ideas, then determine what kinds of intelligence Charlie had before and after the operation. **L2**

in my apartment at Mrs. Flynn's boarding-house most of the time and seldom speak to anyone.

May 20 I would not have noticed the new dishwasher, a boy of about sixteen, at the corner diner where I take my evening meals if not for the incident of the broken dishes.

They crashed to the floor, shattering and sending bits of white china under the tables. The boy stood there, dazed and frightened, holding the empty tray in his hand. The whistles and catcalls from the customers (the cries of "hey, there go the profits!" . . . "*Mazeltov!*"[16] . . . and "well, *he* didn't work here very long . . ." which invariably seem to follow the breaking of glass or dishware in a public restaurant) all seemed to confuse him.

When the owner came to see what the excitement was about, the boy cowered as if he expected to be struck and threw up his arms as if to ward off the blow.

"All right! All right, you dope," shouted the owner, "don't just stand there! Get the broom and sweep that mess up. A broom . . . a broom, you idiot! It's in the kitchen. Sweep up all the pieces."

The boy saw that he was not going to be punished. His frightened expression disappeared and he smiled and hummed as he came back with the broom to sweep the floor. A few of the rowdier customers kept up the remarks, amusing themselves at his expense.

"Here, sonny, over here there's a nice piece behind you . . ."

"C'mon, do it again . . ."

"He's not so dumb. It's easier to break 'em than to wash 'em . . ."

As his vacant eyes moved across the crowd of amused onlookers, he slowly mirrored their smiles and finally broke into an uncertain grin at the joke which he obviously did not understand.

I felt sick inside as I looked at his dull, vacuous smile, the wide, bright eyes of a child, uncertain but eager to please. They were laughing at him because he was mentally retarded. **P**

Charly, 1967. Selmur Productions. Movie still.

Viewing the photograph: How does the photo show that Charlie has changed?

16. *Mazeltov* or *mazel tov* (mäz′ əl tôf′) is a Hebrew phrase used to express congratulations or best wishes.

Vocabulary

invariably (in vār′ ē ə blē) *adv.* constantly; always

cower (kou′ ər) *v.* to shrink away, as in fear or shame

VIEWING THE PHOTOGRAPH

From the motion picture *Charly*

Viewing Response *Charlie's posture is more assured; his clothes are more business-like; his facial expression shows that he is serious, determined, and absorbed in thought.*

P Literary Elements

CHARACTERIZATION This is a central moment in the plot, in which Charlie has the opportunity to see himself as others once saw him. It gives him a sense of how far he has come, but he also feels a profound sense of identity with the boy and anger at the people in the restaurant. Ask students what they think Charlie feels as he watches the boy respond to the people around him.

Listening and Speaking *Minilesson*

Adjusting to the Audience Note that as much as Charlie wants to communicate with Miss Kinnian, he talks over her head. Perhaps one of the most important characteristics of a good speaker is the ability to adjust to the level of the audience.

Activity Have students select an oral report from their portfolios and rewrite it for a much younger audience. Have them deliver their revised versions in small groups and discuss the kinds of changes they made to adjust to a different audience. **L2** **COLLAB. LEARN.**

Q Critical Thinking

INFERRING Ask students to discuss what Charlie comes to understand from his encounter with the dishwasher. *(Charlie sees both sides; he knows the bewilderment and desire to please felt by the boy; he also now understands the reason people laugh at him. He sees himself as others saw him.)*

R Active Reading Strategies

EVALUATE Ask students what they think of Charlie's decision to work to increase human intelligence. Is this the right choice, given what Charlie has experienced? Should he, rather, teach scientists to leave well enough alone? Ask students to refer to specific examples from the text to support their answer. *(While Charlie's goal seems noble, the story suggests that there are benefits to leaving well enough alone.)*

Teaching Support

And I had been laughing at him too.

Q Suddenly, I was furious at myself and all those who were smirking at him. I jumped up and shouted, "Shut up! Leave him alone! It's not his fault he can't understand! He can't help what he is! But for God's sake . . . he's still a human being!"

The room grew silent. I cursed myself for losing control and creating a scene. I tried not to look at the boy as I paid my check and walked out without touching my food. I felt ashamed for both of us.

How strange it is that people of honest feelings and sensibility, who would not take advantage of a man born without arms or legs or eyes—how such people think nothing of abusing a man born with low intelligence. It infuriated me to think that not too long ago I, like this boy, had foolishly played the clown.

> It infuriated me to think that not too long ago I, like this boy, had foolishly played the clown.

And I had almost forgotten.

I'd hidden the picture of the old Charlie Gordon from myself because now that I was intelligent it was something that had to be pushed out of my mind. But today in looking at that boy, for the first time I saw what I had been. *I was just like him!*

Only a short time ago, I learned that people laughed at me. Now I can see that unknowingly I joined with them in laughing at myself. That hurts most of all.

I have often reread my progress reports and seen the illiteracy, the childish naiveté,[17] the mind of low intelligence peering from a dark room, through the keyhole, at the dazzling light outside. I see that even in my dullness I knew that I was inferior, and that other people had something I lacked—something denied me. In my mental blindness, I thought that it was somehow connected with the ability to read and write, and I was sure that if I could get those skills I would automatically have intelligence too.

Even a feeble-minded man wants to be like other men.

A child may not know how to feed itself, or what to eat, yet it knows of hunger.

This then is what I was like, I never knew. Even with my gift of intellectual awareness, I never really knew.

R This day was good for me. Seeing the past more clearly, I have decided to use my knowledge and skills to work in the field of increasing human intelligence levels. Who is better equipped for this work? Who else has lived in both worlds? These are my people. Let me use my gift to do something for them.

Tomorrow, I will discuss with Dr. Strauss the manner in which I can work in this area. I may be able to help him work out the problems of widespread use of the technique which was used on me. I have several good ideas of my own.

There is so much that might be done with this technique. If I could be made into a genius, what about thousands of others like myself? What fantastic levels

17. Here, *illiteracy* refers to Charlie's earlier inability to read and write well. *Naiveté* (nä ēv′ tā′) is innocence, or lack of worldly knowledge and experience.

MEETING INDIVIDUAL NEEDS — SPECIAL NEEDS

Visually Impaired Legal blindness includes a wide range of impairment, from those who have no vision to those who can see with the aid of strong magnification. Visual impairment need not cut students off from information sources. Web sites, for example, connect the visually impaired to the world of the Internet.

Activity Encourage students to explore, evaluate, and list resources in libraries and on the Internet that they and their visually impaired friends can use for research and enjoyment. *(Books and magazines are available in large print editions and on tape. On the Internet, key in "visual impairment" or "blindness.")*

Additional Resources

Inclusion Strategies

might be achieved by using this technique on normal people? On *geniuses?*

There are so many doors to open. I am impatient to begin.

PROGRESS REPORT 13

S

May 23 It happened today. Algernon bit me. I visited the lab to see him as I do occasionally, and when I took him out of his cage, he snapped at my hand. I put him back and watched him for a while. He was unusually disturbed and vicious.

May 24 Burt, who is in charge of the experimental animals, tells me that Algernon is changing. He is less cooperative; he refuses to run the maze any more; general motivation has decreased. And he hasn't been eating. Everyone is upset about what this may mean.

T

May 25 They've been feeding Algernon, who now refuses to work the shifting-lock problem. Everyone identifies me with Algernon. In a way we're both the first of our kind. They're all pretending that Algernon's behavior is not necessarily significant for me. But it's hard to hide the fact that some of the other animals who were used in this experiment are showing strange behavior.

Dr. Strauss and Dr. Nemur have asked me not to come to the lab any more. I know what they're thinking but I can't accept it. I am going ahead with my plans to carry their research forward. With all due respect to both of these fine scientists, I am well aware of their limitations. If there is an answer, I'll have to find it out for myself. Suddenly, time has become very important to me.

May 29 I have been given a lab of my own and permission to go ahead with the research. I'm on to something. Working day and night. I've had a cot moved into the lab. Most of my writing time is spent on the notes which I keep in a separate folder, but from time to time I feel it necessary to put down my moods and my thoughts out of sheer habit.

I find the *calculus of intelligence* to be a fascinating study. Here is the place for the application of all the knowledge I have acquired. In a sense it's the problem I've been concerned with all my life.

May 31 Dr. Strauss thinks I'm working too hard. Dr. Nemur says I'm trying to cram a lifetime of research and thought into a few weeks. I know I should rest, but I'm driven on by something inside that won't let me stop. I've got to find the reason for the sharp regression[18] in Algernon. I've got to know *if* and *when* it will happen to me.

U

June 4

LETTER TO DR. STRAUSS (*copy*)

Dear Dr. Strauss:

Under separate cover I am sending you a copy of my report entitled, "The Algernon-Gordon Effect: A Study of Structure and Function of Increased Intelligence," which I would like to have you read and have published.

As you see, my experiments are completed. I have included in my report all of my formulae, as well as mathematical analysis in the appendix. Of course, these should be verified.

18. *Regression* is a return to an earlier, less advanced condition or behavior pattern.

S Active Reading Strategies

QUESTION What might it mean that Algernon has suddenly become "disturbed and vicious"? *(Perhaps he is feeling some of the same frustration Charlie felt when he was competing with the mouse.)*

T Literary Elements

FORESHADOWING Ask students to identify the foreshadowing in the journal entry on May 24. *(Algernon's decline is indicative of what will happen to Charlie.)*

Vocabulary Skills

Word Origins By *calculus of intelligence*, Charlie means something like a method of measuring or calculating intelligence. The word *calculus* comes from a Latin word meaning "small stone." Drivers of Roman horse-drawn cabs used small stones to determine (calculate) how far they had driven and how much their passengers owed.

U Literary Elements

FORESHADOWING Point out to students that they should be on the lookout for signs that what happened to Algernon is happening to Charlie.

REAL-WORLD CONNECTION

Experimentation on Laboratory Animals This story directs the reader's attention to a moral question about experimentation on humans. Although the story does not focus on Algernon and other laboratory animals, there may be another moral question to consider—is it moral to experiment on animals?

Activity Have students clip articles about the use of laboratory animals for experimentation from magazines and newspapers. Students should prepare an essay on this issue, including a well-defined thesis, along with evidence and examples to support their positions. **L2**

VIEWING THE PHOTOGRAPH

Diana Ong is known for her ability to combine different mediums and for her playful experimentation with them.

Viewing Response *This work shows someone undergoing a profound change.*

Active Reading Strategies

QUESTION Ask students what they think Charlie means when he says he is sorry that his work "must rest upon the ashes of the work of two men I regard so highly." *(Charlie has proved that what Drs. Nemur and Strauss did cannot be permanent.)*

Because of its importance to both you and Dr. Nemur (and need I say to myself, too?) I have checked and rechecked my results a dozen times in the hope of finding an error. I am sorry to say the results must stand. Yet for the sake of science, I am grateful for the little bit that I here add to the knowledge of the function of the human mind and of the laws governing the artificial increase of human intelligence.

I recall your once saying to me that an experimental *failure* or the *disproving* of a theory was as important to the advancement of learning as a success would be. I know now that this is true. I am sorry, however, that my own contribution to the field must rest upon the ashes of the work of two men I regard so highly.

Yours truly,

Charles Gordon
encl.: rept.

Conversion. Diana Ong. Computer generated.
Viewing the art: In your opinion, how might this face show what is happening to Charlie?

June 5 I must not become emotional. The facts and the results of my experiments are clear, and the more sensational aspects of my own rapid climb cannot obscure the fact that the tripling of intelligence by the surgical technique developed by Drs. Strauss and Nemur must be viewed as having little or no practical applicability (at the present time) to the increase of human intelligence.

As I review the records and data on Algernon, I see that although he is still in his physical infancy, he has regressed mentally. Motor activity is impaired; there is a general reduction of glandular activity; there is an accelerated loss of co-ordination.

Vocabulary
obscure (əb skyoor′) *v.* to hide
impaired (im pārd′) *adj.* lessened in quality; damaged

Teaching Support

Reading *Minilesson*

Paraphrasing As Charlie becomes more objective and scientific, his writing may seem difficult to read and comprehend. Keyes deliberately makes these passages difficult by using complex words and sentence structure. Explain that paraphrasing is a strategy that helps to ensure comprehension. Knowing one must paraphrase gives purpose to reading and helps focus the reader's attention.

Activity To help students with comprehension, have them work in small groups to paraphrase Charlie's entries from June 4 to June 15. Ask some groups to share their paraphrases. Allow time for the class to assess how well each group conveyed the meaning of the text. **L2** COLLAB. LEARN.

Additional Resources

Reading Skills Practice Workbook

There are also strong indications of progressive[19] amnesia.

As will be seen by my report, these and other physical and mental deterioration syndromes[20] can be predicted with statistically significant results by the application of my formula.

The surgical stimulus to which we were both subjected has resulted in an intensification and acceleration of all mental processes. The unforeseen development, which I have taken the liberty of calling the *Algernon-Gordon Effect,* is the logical extension of the entire intelligence speed-up. The hypothesis[21] here proven may be described simply in the following terms: Artificially increased intelligence deteriorates at a rate of time directly proportional to the quantity of the increase.

I feel that this, in itself, is an important discovery.

As long as I am able to write, I will continue to record my thoughts in these progress reports. It is one of my few pleasures. However, by all indications, my own mental deterioration will be very rapid.

I have already begun to notice signs of emotional instability and forgetfulness, the first symptoms of the burnout.

W

June 10 Deterioration progressing. I have become absentminded. Algernon died two days ago. Dissection shows my predictions were right. His brain had decreased in weight and there was a general smoothing out of cerebral convolutions as well as a deepening and broadening of brain fissures.

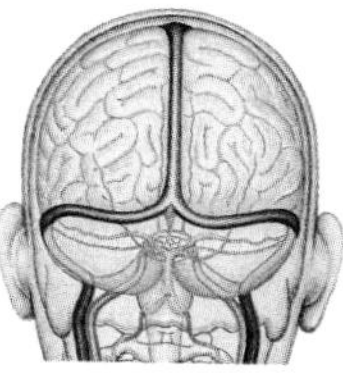

Did You Know?
Charlie cuts up Algernon's brain to study it. A healthy brain surface would have many irregular folds *(convolutions)* and cracks *(fissures)* that are long, narrow, and shallow.

I guess the same thing is or will soon be happening to me. Now that it's definite, I don't want it to happen.

I put Algernon's body in a cheese box and buried him in the back yard. I cried.

June 15 Dr. Strauss came to see me again. I wouldn't open the door and I told him to go away. I want to be left to myself. I have become touchy and irritable. I feel the darkness closing in. It's hard to throw off thoughts of suicide. I keep telling myself how important this introspective[22] journal will be.

X

It's a strange sensation to pick up a book that you've read and enjoyed just a few months ago and discover that you don't remember it. I remembered how great I thought John Milton was, but when I picked up *Paradise Lost* I couldn't understand it at all. I got so angry I threw the book across the room.

I've got to try to hold on to some of it. Some of the things I've learned. Oh, God, please don't take it all away.

Y

June 19 Sometimes, at night, I go out for a walk. Last night I couldn't remember where I lived. A policeman took me

19. In this context, *progressive* means "advancing steadily."
20. *Deterioration* means "a worsening," and a *syndrome* is a group of symptoms that, together, indicate a disease. The combined term refers to diseases that result in a lessening of some ability or strength.
21. A *hypothesis* (hī poth′ ə sis) is an unproven idea or theory.
22. *Introspective* means "looking into or examining one's own thoughts and feelings."

Vocabulary

stimulus (stim′ yə ləs) *n.* something that causes a response

W Active Reading Strategies

REVIEW Ask students to pay particular attention to the tone of Charlie's journal entries as he loses intelligence. What do they notice? *(One obvious change is the return of emotion to Charlie's writing. He has moved away from the objective scientific stance and now feels emotion for Algernon and himself.)*

X Active Reading Strategies

QUESTION Ask why Charlie keeps reminding himself of the importance of the journal. What impact will the journal have? *(Charlie believes his journal will warn others against doing what has been done to him. The journal shows his pain all too clearly.)*

Y Active Reading Strategies

CONNECT Ask students whether they have changed their thinking about what is worse—never having had intelligence or losing it.

MEETING INDIVIDUAL NEEDS — MULTIPLE MODES OF EXPRESSION

Interpersonal Charlie reports on his findings in the entry dated June 5, which he begins with the words, "I must not become emotional." Clearly Charlie is trying to provide an objective analysis of his situation and prognosis, so he suppresses his emotions.

Activity Have groups of students read through the day's entry and discuss what Charlie must have felt while he was doing his experiments and as he was writing his conclusions. Ask: *Why do people sometimes keep important thoughts and feelings to themselves? What are the effects of this behavior? How can talking to another person help?* **L2** COLLAB. LEARN.

Z Literary Elements

AUTHOR'S PURPOSE Point out to students the agony Charlie suffers as he loses what he once knew. Is the author suggesting that Charlie would have been better off without interference? *(Keyes seems to leave little doubt that he thinks Charlie would have been much better off without interference.)*

AA Active Reading Strategies

REVIEW Note that as Charlie's writing style changes, he seems to become several different people. Ask students to identify some of the style changes. *(On June 21, Charlie is angry and determined to fight. On June 22, he seems to have lost his anger; he is confused and passive. On June 30, he is angry again, but he is angry with himself.)*

BB Active Reading Strategies

QUESTION Why is it important to Charlie that someone know what is happening to him? *(He wants to record it to help further medical knowledge.)*

home. I have the strange feeling that this has all happened to me before—a long time ago. I keep telling myself I'm the only person in the world who can describe what's happening to me.

June 21 Why can't I remember? I've got to fight. I lie in bed for days and I don't know who or where I am. Then it all comes back to me in a flash. Fugues of amnesia. Symptoms of senility[23]—second childhood. I can watch them coming on. It's so cruelly logical. I learned so much and so fast. Now my mind is deteriorating rapidly. I won't let it happen. I'll fight it. I can't help thinking of the boy in the restaurant, the blank expression, the silly smile, the people laughing at him. No—please—not that again . . .

June 22 I'm forgetting things that I learned recently. It seems to be following the classic pattern—the last things learned are the first things forgotten. Or is that the pattern? I'd better look it up again . . .

I reread my paper on the *Algernon-Gordon Effect* and I get the strange feeling that it was written by someone else. There are parts I don't even understand.

Motor activity impaired. I keep tripping over things, and it becomes increasingly difficult to type.

June 23 I've given up using the typewriter completely. My coordination is bad. I feel that I'm moving slower and slower. Had a terrible shock today. I picked up a copy of an article I used in my research, Krueger's *Uber psychische Ganzheit,* to see if it would help me understand what I had done. First I thought there was something wrong with my eyes. Then I realized I could no longer read German. I tested myself in other languages. All gone.

June 30 A week since I dared to write again. It's slipping away like sand through my fingers. Most of the books I have are too hard for me now. I get angry with them because I know that I read and understood them just a few weeks ago.

I keep telling myself I must keep writing these reports so that somebody will know what is happening to me. But it gets harder to form the words and remember spellings. I have to look up even simple words in the dictionary now and it makes me impatient with myself.

Dr. Strauss comes around almost every day, but I told him I wouldn't see or speak to anybody. He feels guilty. They all do. But I don't blame anyone. I knew what might happen. But how it hurts.

July 7 I don't know where the week went. Todays Sunday I know because I can see through my window people going

> I keep telling myself I must keep writing these reports so that somebody will know what is happening to me.

23. In psychiatry, a *fugue* (fūg) *of amnesia* is a condition during which a person seems to be aware of his or her actions but can't recall them later. *Senility* (si nil′ ə tē) refers to the loss of physical and mental abilities that can accompany old age.

Teaching Support

Interdisciplinary Connection

Science There is a great deal of discussion now about medical ethics. Just because a scientist *can* do something does not necessarily mean he or she *should* do it.

Activity Have students research the ethical considerations surrounding one of the following questions: *Should we clone animals to increase the food supply? Should animals be used for medical research? Should we tamper with human genes in babies still in the womb? Should we clone humans? Should employers have access to the results of genetic testing paid for by insurance? Should terminal patients be given experimental drugs?* Students should develop three- to five-minute-long oral reports in which they take an ethical stand on one of these issues. **L2**

to church. I think I stayed in bed all week but I remember Mrs. Flynn bringing food to me a few times. I keep saying over and over Ive got to do something but then I forget or maybe its just easier not to do what I say Im going to do.

CC I think of my mother and father a lot these days. I found a picture of them with me taken at a beach. My father has a big ball under his arm and my mother is holding me by the hand. I dont remember them the way they are in the picture. All I remember is my father drunk most of the time and arguing with mom about money.

He never shaved much and he used to scratch my face when he hugged me. My mother said he died but Cousin Miltie said he heard his mom and dad say that my father ran away with another woman. When I asked my mother she slapped my face and said my father was dead. I dont think I ever found out which was true but I don't care much. (He said he was going to take me to see cows on a farm once but he never did. He never kept his promises . . .)

July 10 My landlady Mrs Flynn is very worried about me. She says the way I lay around all day and dont do anything I remind her of her son before she threw him out of the house. She said she doesnt like loafers. If Im sick its one thing, but if Im a loafer thats another thing and she wont have it. I told her I think Im sick.

I try to read a little bit every day, mostly stories, but sometimes I have to read the same thing over and over again because I dont know what it means. And its hard to write. I know I should look up all the words in the dictionary but its so hard and Im so tired all the time.

Then I got the idea that I would only use the easy words instead of the long hard ones. That saves time. I put flowers on Algernons grave about once a week. Mrs Flynn thinks Im crazy to put flowers on a mouses grave but I told her that Algernon was special.

DD ***July 14*** Its sunday again. I dont have anything to do to keep me busy now because my television set is broke and I dont have any money to get it fixed. (I think I lost this months check from the lab. I dont remember)

I get awful headaches and asperin doesnt help me much. Mrs Flynn knows Im really sick and she feels very sorry for me. Shes a wonderful woman whenever someone is sick.

July 22 Mrs Flynn called a strange doctor to see me. She was afraid I was going to die. I told the doctor I wasnt too sick and that I only forget sometimes. He asked me did I have any friends or relatives and I said no I dont have any. I told him I had a friend called Algernon once but he was a mouse and we used to run races together. He looked at me kind of funny like he thought I was crazy.

EE He smiled when I told him I used to be a genius. He talked to me like I was a baby and he winked at Mrs Flynn. I got mad and chased him out because he was making fun of me the way they all used to.

July 24 I have no more money and Mrs Flynn says I got to go to work somewhere and pay the rent because I havent paid for over two months. I dont know any work but the job I used to have at Donnegans Plastic Box Company. I dont want to go back there

CC Literary Elements

FLASHBACK Ask students why they think Keyes introduces these memories of Charlie's parents at this point. How do these memories contribute to our understanding of Charlie's character? *(This flashback shows Charlie as no longer able to solve problems or think things through. He has just given up.)*

DD Active Reading Strategies

REVIEW Ask students what differences they notice between Charlie's July 10 and July 14 entries. *(Charlie isn't reading anymore and he is forgetful. He and Mrs. Flynn are now sure he is sick. He has almost completely reverted to his former self.)*

EE Literary Elements

IRONY Note that Charlie can no longer tolerate treatment from others that he used to accept as friendly.

Life Skills Connection

Keeping a Journal Though Charlie's situation is a radical one, his journal does demonstrate the value of recording one's innermost thoughts and feelings. A journal can provide an interesting record of growing up.

Activity Have each student keep a journal for one month. Students need not turn the journals in, but at the end of the month, each should write a paragraph describing his or her feelings about looking back over the month's writing. **L2**

Critical Thinking

EVALUATING Ask students what they think of Charlie's conclusion about his coworkers. He says "they were once your friends and if they laughed at you that doesnt mean anything because they liked you too." Is Charlie correct, or is this idea just more evidence of his becoming less and less intelligent? *(There is an ironic sense in which Charlie is correct; he felt liked, and he had a place in the social circle at work that was comfortable to him and to his coworkers. On the other hand, it is only his lack of intelligence that allows him to deceive himself.)*

Active Reading Strategies

QUESTION What do Joe and Frank's actions reveal about their characters? *(They obviously were threatened by the genius Charlie, but they actually do seem to have some genuine affection for him now. They probably realize how brave he was.)*

Teaching Support

because they all knew me when I was smart and maybe theyll laugh at me. But I dont know what else to do to get money.

July 25 I was looking at some of my old progress reports and its very funny but I cant read what I wrote. I can make out some of the words but they dont make sense.

Miss Kinnian came to the door but I said go away I dont want to see you. She cried and I cried too but I wouldnt let her in because I didnt want her to laugh at me. I told her I didn't like her any more. I told her I didnt want to be smart any more. Thats not true. I still love her and I still want to be smart but I had to say that so shed go away. She gave Mrs Flynn money to pay the rent. I dont want that. I got to get a job.

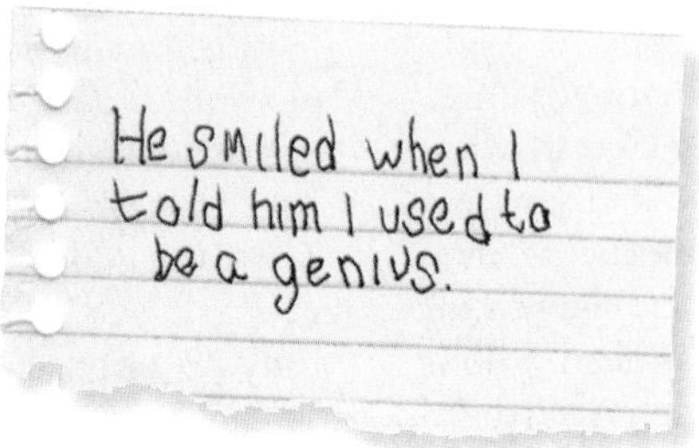

Please . . . please let me not forget how to read and write . . .

July 27 Mr Donnegan was very nice when I came back and asked him for my old job of janitor. First he was very suspicious but I told him what happened to me then he looked very sad and put his hand on my shoulder and said Charlie Gordon you got guts.

Everybody looked at me when I came downstairs and started working in the toilet sweeping it out like I used to. I told myself Charlie if they make fun of you dont get sore because you remember their not so smart as you once thot they were. And besides they were once your friends and if they laughed at you that doesnt mean anything because they liked you too.

One of the new men who came to work there after I went away made a nasty crack he said hey Charlie I hear your a very smart fella a real quiz kid. Say something intelligent. I felt bad but Joe Carp came over and grabbed him by the shirt and said leave him alone you lousy cracker or Ill break your neck. I didnt expect Joe to take my part so I guess hes really my friend.

Later Frank Reilly came over and said Charlie if anybody bothers you or trys to take advantage you call me or Joe and we will set em straight. I said thanks Frank and I got choked up so I had to turn around and go into the supply room so he wouldnt see me cry. Its good to have friends.

July 28 I did a dumb thing today I forgot I wasnt in Miss Kinnians class at the adult center any more like I use to be. I went in and sat down in my old seat in the back of the room and she looked at me funny and she said Charles. I dint remember she ever called me that before only Charlie so I said hello Miss Kinnian Im redy for my lesin today only I lost my reader that we was using. She startid to cry and run out of the room and everybody looked at me and I saw they wasnt the same pepul who used to be in my class.

Then all of a suddin I remembered some things about the operashun and me getting smart and I said holy smoke I reely pulled a Charlie Gordon that time. I went away before she come back to the room.

Thats why Im going away from New York for good. I dont want to do nothing

MEETING INDIVIDUAL NEEDS — SPECIAL NEEDS

Emotional Keyes shows how the people around Charlie respond to his diminishing intelligence. His former boss is nice, his coworkers protect him, and Miss Kinnian cries. Rather than express the complex emotions these characters have, Keyes chooses to suggest their emotions through their actions.

Activity Have students record their responses to what is happening to Charlie. How would they behave if they met him? What would they say about him to one another? What feelings would they have? Then have them work in small groups to share their responses. **L1** **COLLAB. LEARN.**

Additional Resources

Inclusion Strategies

Tulips and an Iris, mid-17th century. Attributed to the Master of the Borders Mughal. Opaque watercolor on paper. Folio 12⅝ x 8 in. (26.4 x 16.1 cm.)

Viewing the painting: Why might this painting of three flowers be a symbol for Charlie's life?

VIEWING THE PAINTING

The Mughals were a people of Central Asia who brought Islamic culture to India. Mughal monarchs were responsible for a cultural renaissance often called the Golden Age of Northern India.

Viewing Response *The small tulip represents Charlie before he grew in intelligence. The tulip in the center of the painting represents Charlie at the height of his intellectual powers. The iris, which is small, represents Charlie at the end of the story when his intelligence has diminished. Just as the iris is different from the tulip, so too is Charlie at the end of the story different from the writer of the first progress report. All three flowers appear delicate, yet strong, perhaps symbolizing Charlie's sensitive nature.*

MEETING INDIVIDUAL NEEDS — MULTIPLE MODES OF EXPRESSION

Bodily-Kinesthetic Some students learn best through movement.

Activity These students may enjoy watching parts of the film *Charly* with the sound turned off. Cliff Robertson does an excellent job of using body language to highlight the changes in Charlie's intelligence level. Have students report to the class on how the actor used body language to develop Charlie's character. **L2**

Critical Thinking

EVALUATE Discuss Charlie's notion that he is actually better off now than before the experiment. Is he? Or has he been permanently damaged? *(Some students may say that Charlie at least has his memories of being brilliant. Others may note that those include the memory of a profound loss. Charlie has forever lost his innocence and his dreams.)*

Active Reading Strategies

QUESTION Ask students what they think is the significance of the title, "Flowers for Algernon." *(Charlie put flowers on Algernon's grave because the mouse "was special." Because everyone identified Charlie with Algernon, the title is also a tribute to Charlie and his struggle. Both were victims of science.)*

Thematic Focus

Lean on Me Ask students how Charlie's story complicates their thinking about dependence and independence.

ASSESSMENT

Quick Checks, p. 11

like that agen. I dont want Miss Kinnian to feel sorry for me. Evry body feels sorry at the factery and I dont want that eather so Im going someplace where nobody knows that Charlie Gordon was once a genus and now he cant even reed a book or rite good.

Im taking a cuple of books along and even if I cant reed them Ill practise hard and maybe I wont forget every thing I lerned. If I try reel hard maybe Ill be a littel bit smarter than I was before the operashun. I got my rabits foot and my luky penny and maybe they will help me.

If you ever reed this Miss Kinnian dont be sorry for me Im glad I got a second chanse to be smart becaus I lerned a lot of things that I never even new were in this world and Im grateful that I saw it all for a littel bit. I dont know why Im dumb agen or what I did wrong maybe its becaus I dint try hard enuff. But if I try and practis very hard maybe Ill get a littl smarter and know what all the words are. I remember a littel bit how nice I had a feeling with the blue book that has the torn cover when I red it. Thats why Im gonna keep trying to get smart so I can have that feeling agen. Its a good feeling to know things and be smart. I wish I had it rite now if I did I would sit down and reed all the time. Anyway I bet Im the first dumb person in the world who ever found out something importent for sience. I remember I did somthing but I dont remember what. So I gess its like I did it for all the dumb pepul like me.

Good-by Miss Kinnian and Dr. Strauss and evreybody. And P.S. please tell Dr Nemur not to be such a grouch when pepul laff at him and he woud have more frends. Its easy to make frends if you let pepul laff at you. Im going to have lots of frends where I go.

P.P.S. Please if you get a chanse put some flowrs on Algernons grave in the bak yard . . .

Teaching Support

Grammar and Language Minilesson

Contractions Write the following phrases from the story on the board: *Im taking a cuple of books along; maybe Ill be a littel bit smarter; I dont know why; its a good feeling.* Ask students which words require apostrophes to be spelled correctly. Point out that an apostrophe takes the place of an omitted letter in a contraction.

Activity Ask students to add apostrophes to all of the words on page 140 that require them. Students should also note which letters the apostrophes stand for. **L2**

Additional Resources

- ***Grammar and Language Transparency 10***
- ***Grammar and Language Workbook,*** p. 269
- ***Grammar and Composition Handbook,*** Lesson 13.7
- ***Writer's Choice,*** Lesson 20.7

Responding to Literature

PERSONAL RESPONSE

- If you could talk with Charlie before he leaves New York City, what would you want to say to him? Explain your answer.
- Think of a time when you felt like avoiding people after a failure. What helped you overcome your feelings?

Brackets connect questions that are paired to develop higher-level thinking skills.

Analyzing Literature

RECALL

1. In the entry dated May 20, what does Charlie realize about "smart" people and himself?
2. What are some of the first things Charlie loses when the experiment starts to fail? What does he fear losing the most?
3. List the people in Charlie's life. Explain briefly what each thinks about Charlie at the beginning of the story and at the end.
4. Why does Charlie decide to leave New York City?

INTERPRET

5. How does the author show Charlie's increasing intelligence? Provide examples from the story.
6. Do you think Charlie's other types of "intelligence" increase or decrease? Give examples to support your answer.
7. **Theme Connection** Charlie feels very cut off from other people. Consider how other people feel about Charlie at the end of the story. Do you think he should feel as lonesome as he does? Why or why not?
8. At the end, does Charlie have a better or worse view of himself? Support your opinion with examples.

EVALUATE AND CONNECT

9. Look back at the **Literary Element** on **irony** on page 124. How does Keyes use irony in the last part of the story? Find several examples.
10. Think of a time when someone you admired let you down. How would you talk about that person now? Explain.

LITERARY ELEMENTS

Foreshadowing

Foreshadowing is the planting of clues to prepare readers for events that will happen later. Daniel Keyes uses foreshadowing when he has Miss Kinnian say to Charlie,

> ". . . I just hope I wasn't wrong to advise you to go into this in the first place."

Foreshadowing can add suspense. For example, it can be used to warn readers that the story may take an unexpected turn.

1. Look over the story and list some of the statements and actions that foreshadow the failure of the experiment.
2. Would the story have been better if the failure had come as a complete surprise? Explain.

● See **Literary Terms Handbook**, p. R4.

Responding to the Selection

PERSONAL RESPONSE

- Some students may say they would want to apologize to Charlie for the way certain individuals treat people with disabilities.
- It helps to overcome embarrassment if one remembers that everyone has failed on occasion.

Analyzing Literature

1. People are often unkind to those with impairments.
2. Charlie loses his memory, coordination, and good humor. He is afraid he will forget how to read and write.
3. Charlie's coworkers make fun of him at first. By the end of the story, they admire his courage. Miss Kinnian admires Charlie's motivation at first but later comes to feel sorry for his loss. The doctors don't seem to regard him as a human being.
4. Charlie leaves because he doesn't want people to feel sorry for him.
5. The author shows Charlie's increasing intelligence by his improved spelling and punctuation, vocabulary, increased understanding and sensitivity to the people around him, and eventual intellectual superiority to the doctors who operated on him.
6. Charlie shows increased sensitivity and imagination. For example, after his operation he does much better on the inkblot tests.
7. Students may say that the people around him care about him. Others may agree with Charlie that pity isn't a substitute for friendship.
8. Some students may say that Charlie's view of himself is worse because he wants to hide from the people who once knew him. He sees only what he lacks and he can no longer see his own good qualities.
9. It is ironic that Charlie uses his genius to find out what his own fate will be and that his former friends can only be kind to him when he has lost his abilities.
10. Students are likely to suggest that they would talk about the person who let them down with a sense of sadness and disappointment.

LITERARY ELEMENTS

1. One hint occurs when Dr. Strauss wants to delay publishing. Another is when Miss Kinnian hopes it wasn't wrong for her to advise Charlie to participate. A third is the change in Algernon.
2. Possible answer: The story would be less interesting without the sense of impending doom.

Additional Resources

Literary Elements Transparency 11

Literature and Writing

Writing About Literature

Students' explanations should

- clearly take a stand as to whether the style helps
- use examples from the story

Creative Writing

Students' letters should

- address all the questions posed in the assignment
- use the correct format for a personal letter

Extending Your Response

Literature Groups Suggest that students consider the power of peer pressure. **COLLAB. LEARN.**

Internet Connection Suggest that students look for information on Dr. Irene Pepperberg, an animal behaviorist, and her parrot Alex.

Art Activity Point out to students that some more recent versions of the Rorschach Test use color.

Literature and Writing

Writing About Literature

Style In the story, Daniel Keyes uses a unique style of punctuation, spelling, and grammar to show the changes in Charlie's personality and mental development. Write a brief explanation of how these style elements work in the story. For example, did they help you understand the main character and the story better or did they interfere with reading? Give examples from the story to support your response.

Creative Writing

Letter Writing Look over your notes from the **Reading Focus** on page 112 about what you would gain and lose by becoming smarter or more talented than your classmates. Write a letter to the "new" you from a best friend or family member. Address these questions: How do people feel about you as you change? What do they see you doing? Do they try to keep up with you? What happens in the end? If you wish, share your work with the class.

Extending Your Response

Literature Groups

Fitting In–at What Price? Charlie's desire to be like everyone else motivates him to have an operation. In a group, discuss these questions: Why did Charlie have to change? Why didn't the other people change? Share your answers with other groups.

interNET CONNECTION

Animals Online How much can animals learn? How much of their behavior is based on instinct? Find out by gathering information on the Internet. Hold a class discussion to talk about your findings.

Art Activity

Seeing Spots Create your own Rorschach ink blot cards, using blank index cards, water color, ink, or acrylics. Dab some ink or paint on the center of a card. Fold the card in half with the ink on the inside. Open the card and let it dry. How many images do you see in each card? List the different images, and share your cards with the class to get more responses.

Reading Further

You might enjoy these works about experiments and the characters involved in them.

Frankenstein by Mary Shelley (Learning Channel's Great Books)

Mrs. Frisby and the Rats of NIMH by Robert O'Brien

Rescue Josh McGuire by Benjamin Mikaelsen

Save your work for your portfolio.

interNET CONNECTION

Brain Twisters Online Some students may enjoy learning more about intelligence tests and trying their hand at some mind-stretching puzzles and problems online. Suggest they search the Internet for sites using the keywords *intelligence tests*.

Skill Minilessons

RETEACH • REVIEW

GRAMMAR AND LANGUAGE • SPELLING

Homophones are words that sound alike but are spelled differently and have different meanings. Examples are *threw* and *through, wrap* and *rap,* and *pier* and *peer.* Homophones are often misused. Notice that Charlie uses some homophones incorrectly in "Flowers for Algernon."

Avoid spelling errors by using the correct homophone.

PRACTICE Substitute the correct word for each boldfaced word.

1. He took **they're** tests and **red** the notes.
2. Dr. Nemur **herd** him come up the **stares.**
3. He said he **wood right** in his journal.
4. They used **plane** paper in **there** book.

- For more about spelling, see **Language Handbook,** pp. R46–R49.

READING AND THINKING • CAUSE AND EFFECT

Many events in stories are connected by cause-and-effect relationships. Each event causes other events to happen.

- For more about cause and effect, see **Reading Handbook,** p. R97.

Cause	→	Effect
Because Charlie has a strong desire to learn,	→	Miss Kinnian recommends him for the operation to increase intelligence.

PRACTICE Copy and complete the following cause-and-effect chart.

Cause	→	Effect
1. Because Charlie's operation is a success,	→	
2.	→	the factory workers demand that Charlie be fired.
3. Because Mr. Donnegan lets Charlie go,	→	

VOCABULARY • ETYMOLOGY

Etymology is the study of word origins. For example, *stimulus* is a Latin word that means "a sharp-pointed stick used to goad animals on." *Stimulus* also was used metaphorically as "something that causes a response," and this is the meaning that made its way into English in the late 1600s. Another example is *intellectual*, which comes from Latin words that mean "choose" and "between." An intellectual person is good at choosing which ideas to keep and which to reject.

PRACTICE Read the following etymologies. For each word, briefly explain how its historical meaning is tied to its current meaning.

obscure: from the Latin word *obscurus,* which means "covered over"

motivation: from the French *motif,* which comes from the Latin *movere,* meaning "to move"

tangible: from the Latin *tangibilis*, which means "to touch"

ASSESSMENT

- ***Quick Checks,*** p. 11
- ***Selection and Theme Assessment,*** pp. 17–20
- ***Performance Assessment,*** pp. 9–10
- ***Testmaker: ExamView Pro***
- ***Interactive Tutor: Self-Assessment***

Skill Minilessons

GRAMMAR AND LANGUAGE
SPELLING PATTERNS

1. their, read
2. heard, stairs
3. would, write
4. plain, their

READING AND THINKING
CAUSE AND EFFECT

Cause	→	Effect
1. Because Charlie's operation is a success,	→	**he gains intelligence.**
2. Because Charlie is smarter than they are,	→	**the factory workers demand that Charlie be fired.**
3. Because Mr. Donnegan lets Charlie go,	→	**Charlie has no income.**

Remind students that the fact that one action happens before another does not necessarily make the first action the cause of the second.

VOCABULARY
ETYMOLOGY

1. Something obscure is hard to see or understand, as if it were covered over, hidden, or veiled.
2. Someone with motivation is moved to do something.
3. Something tangible can be felt.

Additional Resources

- ***Grammar and Language Workbook,*** pp. 291–292
- ***Grammar and Composition Handbook,*** Lesson 15.1
- ***Writer's Choice,*** Lesson 23.6
- ***Reading Skills Practice Workbook,*** pp. 19–20, 21–22
- ***Vocabulary Practice,*** p. 10

Reading and Thinking Skills

Objective

- To make inferences by connecting prior knowledge with presented information

Teaching Strategies

Point out to students that education and experience help readers make more accurate inferences. The more one knows and the more experience one has, the easier it is to make inferences.

Exercise

1. Charlie's head is probably bandaged.
2. They probably look down on Charlie. Experience suggests that teasing often reflects what people really think.

Additional Resources

Reading Skills Practice Workbook

Reading and Thinking Skills

Making Inferences

An **inference** is an educated guess that a reader makes after connecting his or her own knowledge with information presented in a selection. Writers often use facts and events to imply, or hint at, an idea without saying it outright. Good readers can read between the lines and use what they know to figure out what the writer is hinting at. What idea about Charlie does the writer of "Flowers for Algernon" imply in the following passage from one of Charlie's progress reports?

> Dr Strauss says I shud rite down what I think and evrey thing that happins to me from now on. I dont know why but he says its importint so they will see if they will use me.

One of the first things you may notice is that Charlie misspells several words. Your own knowledge of spelling helps you figure out that Charlie has difficulty writing and may not be very smart.

- For more about making inferences, see **Reading Handbook,** pp. R100–R101.

EXERCISE

Read the excerpt below from "Flowers for Algernon." Then answer the questions.

> We had a lot of fun at the factery today. Joe Carp said hey look where Charlie had his operashun what did they do Charlie put some brains in. I was going to tell him but I remembered Dr Strauss said no. Then Frank Reilly said what did you do Charlie forget your key and open your door the hard way. That made me laff. Their really my friends and they like me.

1. What inferences can you make about Charlie's appearance? What clues helped you to make those inferences?
2. What inference can you make about how Joe Carp and Frank Reilly feel about Charlie? How does your own experience help you make this inference?

Teaching Support

MEETING INDIVIDUAL NEEDS — SPECIAL NEEDS

Less-Proficient Readers Explain to students that many actions, observations, and occurrences in a literary work have a purpose. Thus readers must always be on the alert, wondering, asking questions, and speculating. Unless one reads actively, it is easy to miss important details and to become confused.

Activity Paraphrase the paragraphs on page 137 in which Charlie discusses his parents. Ask students what they can infer from Charlie's description. How do their experiences help them understand the significance of what Charlie describes? **L1**

Additional Resources

Inclusion Strategies

Before You Read

The Kid Nobody Could Handle

MEET KURT VONNEGUT

Kurt Vonnegut says that he can't stand to read what he writes. "I make my wife do that, then ask her to keep her opinions to herself," he says. Despite his own criticism, Vonnegut is one of the most popular authors of his generation. He is known for his fantasy and humor, as well as his beliefs in human dignity, hope, and free will. Vonnegut encourages young readers to think locally. "Write poetry for someone you like," he says. "Serve your community and be content with your success within it."

Kurt Vonnegut was born in 1922. This story was published in 1968 in Welcome to the Monkey House.

READING FOCUS

Why do some people give up on a task while others never quit trying?

QuickWrite

List activities, people, or things in your life that take up your time but make you happy. Compare your list with a partner.

Setting a Purpose

Read to discover how one character works to help another find happiness.

BUILDING BACKGROUND

The Time and Place This story is set in a small town and features a character who has just moved from Chicago to live with a relative.

Did You Know? John Philip Sousa is among the most famous names in band music and is appropriately called the March King for the 140 marches he composed in the late 1800s. Sousa is best known for his military music and for his years as leader of the U.S. Marine Band.

VOCABULARY PREVIEW

unnerving (un nurv′ ing) *adj.* causing nervousness or upset; disturbing; p. 147

arrogant (ar′ ə gənt) *adj.* full of self-importance; too proud; p. 147

diversion (di vur′ zhən) *n.* something that draws the attention away; distraction; p. 148

appalled (ə pôld′) *adj.* shocked; horrified; p. 148

quest (kwest) *n.* a search made to achieve a goal; p. 151

furtive (fur′ tiv) *adj.* secret; shifty; sly; p. 152

bravado (brə vä′ dō) *n.* a false show of bravery; pretended courage; p. 152

remorse (ri môrs′) *n.* a deep, painful feeling of guilt or sorrow for wrongdoing; p. 153

futility (fū til′ ə tē) *n.* uselessness; hopelessness; p. 155

Before Reading

Objectives

- To read and analyze a short story
- To analyze dialogue in stories
- To write an essay

Skills

Reading/Thinking: Inferring; Evaluating; Problem and Solution
Writing: Dialogue; Journal Entry
Vocabulary: Antonyms
Grammar/Language: Commas
Listening/Speaking: Debating; Oral Presentation
Life Skills: Job Description
Collaboration: Literature Groups

Motivating STUDENTS

Literature Launchers: "Getting to Know Kurt Vonnegut, Jr."

Videodisc Side A, Segment 6

Also available in VHS.

Selection Focus Transparency 11: Before presenting the quotation, have volunteers share the story of the last time they helped someone.

Reading Focus: As an extension of the Reading Focus, ask students to list one or two accomplishments and discuss them with the class.

RESOURCE MANAGER

Teaching Tools and Resources
- Theme Two Planning Guide, pp. 23–30
- Literature Groups Sourcebook

Essential Lesson Support

Lesson-Specific Instruction
- Selection Focus Transparency 11
- Literary Elements Transparency 12
- Active Reading Guide,* p. 12
- Selection Vocabulary Practice, p. 11
- inTIME magazine, p. 2

Assessment
- Selection Quick Checks,* p. 12
- Sel. and Theme Assmt., pp. 21–22
- Testmaker: ExamView Pro
- Performance Assessment, p. 11

Systematic Language Instruction
- Gr. & Comp. Hbk., Lessons 3.3
- Vocabulary Power, Lesson 7
- Spelling Power, Lesson 6

English Language Learners
- ELL Sourcebook, p. 31
- Spanish Summaries, p. 11
- Audio Library*
- English, Yes!

Spec. Needs/Strat. Interven.
- Interactive Rdg. Sbk., pp. T73–T76
- Interactive Rdg. Wbk., pp. 25–28
- Inclusion Strat. Sbk., pp. 11–12, 23–24
- Audio Library*

* Also available in Spanish

Reading the Selection

SUMMARY

High school band leader George Helmholtz is so enthusiastic about music that he convinces everyone to support his band. His optimism is questioned by Jim Donnini, a hostile, silent boy, empty of hope or ambition. One evening Helmholtz finds Jim destroying the chemistry lab. He stops the boy and gives him a precious trumpet. The next morning, Helmholtz learns that Jim's guardian is prepared to send the boy away. In despair he smashes the trumpet, a gesture that finally touches Jim.

Spanish Summaries, p. 11

A Active Reading Strategies

VISUALIZE Read the first paragraph of the story aloud to students and instruct them to listen with their eyes closed as they visualize the setting and the character. What strikes them most about the description?

VOCABULARY Remind students to use content clues to unlock the meanings of new vocabulary words.

Additional Resources

Active Reading Guide, p. 12
Audio Library
Spanish Audio Library

Teaching Support

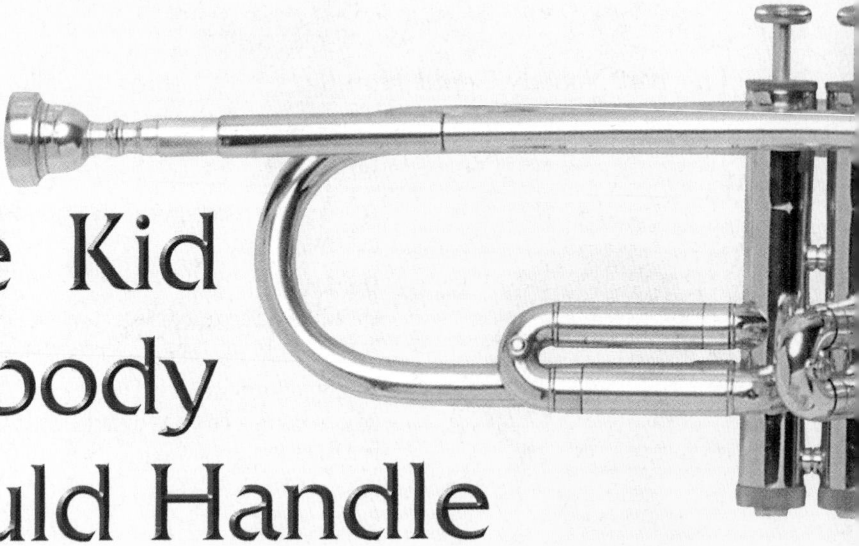

The Kid Nobody Could Handle

Kurt Vonnegut

A It was seven-thirty in the morning. Waddling, clanking, muddy machines were tearing a hill to pieces behind a restaurant, and trucks were hauling the pieces away. Inside the restaurant, dishes rattled on their shelves. Tables quaked, and a very kind fat man with a headful of music looked down at the jiggling yolks of his breakfast eggs. His wife was visiting relatives out of town. He was on his own.

The kind fat man was George M. Helmholtz, a man of forty, head of the music department of Lincoln High School, and director of the band. Life had treated him well. Each year he dreamed the same big dream. He dreamed of leading as fine a band as there was on the face of the earth. And each year the dream came true.

CONNECTING TO OTHER SELECTIONS

COMPARING selections

This selection is paired with "Thank You, M'am" on page 161. A lesson for teaching a comparison of the two selections appears on page 166.

The chart at the right shows three other ways to connect "The Kid Nobody Could Handle" to selections in this book.

For specific teaching strategies, see the ***Theme Two Planning Guide.***

Connection		Title
Life Skills: Teaching and Mentoring	→	"The Treasure of Lemon Brown," p. 5
Thematic: Adjustment	→	"Stop the Sun," p. 607
Literary: Descriptive Language	→	"The Moustache," p. 282

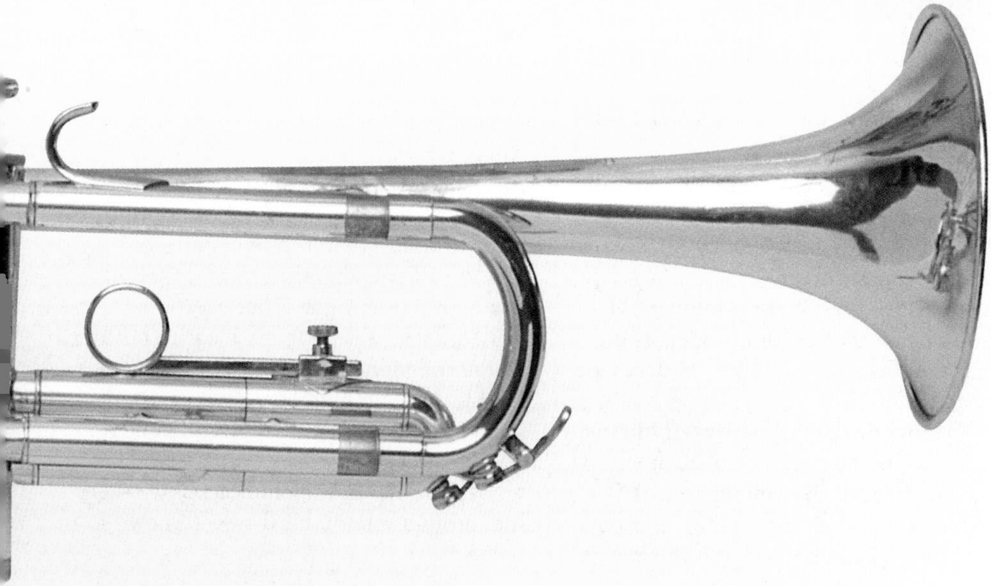

It came true because Helmholtz was sure that a man couldn't have a better dream than his. Faced by this unnerving sureness, Kiwanians, Rotarians, and Lions[1] paid for band uniforms that cost twice as much as their best suits, school administrators let Helmholtz raid the budget for expensive props, and youngsters played their hearts out for him. When youngsters had no talent, Helmholtz made them play on guts alone.

Everything was good about Helmholtz's life save his finances. He was so dazzled by his big dream that he was a child in the marketplace. Ten years before, he had sold the hill behind the restaurant to Bert Quinn, the restaurant owner, for one thousand dollars. It was now apparent, even to Helmholtz, that Helmholtz had been had.[2]

Quinn sat down in the booth with the bandmaster. He was a bachelor, a small, dark, humorless man. He wasn't a well man. He couldn't sleep, he couldn't stop working, he couldn't smile warmly. He had only two moods: one suspicious and self-pitying, the other arrogant and boastful. The first mood applied when he was losing money. The second mood applied when he was making it.

Quinn was in the arrogant and boastful mood when he sat down with Helmholtz.

1. The *Kiwanians, Rotarians, and Lions* are members of the Kiwanis, Rotary, and Lions clubs, groups of business and professional people who work to do good things for a community.

2. The expression *to be had* means "to be cheated or deceived."

Vocabulary

unnerving (un nurv′ ing) *adj.* causing nervousness or upset; disturbing
arrogant (ar′ ə gənt) *adj.* full of self-importance; too proud

B Active Reading Strategies

QUESTION Ask students what kind of person they think Helmholtz is. *(He seems to be a happy, motivated man.)*

C Literary Elements

WORD CHOICE Make sure that students understand what the narrator means when he says Helmholtz is a "child in the marketplace." *(It may be that he is not a practical man, but a dreamer—gullible and easily taken advantage of.)*

Vo•cab•u•lar•y Skills

Synonyms The use of the verb *dazzled* in reference to Helmholtz's dream of leading a top-notch school band is much more specific than the similar action verb *impressed*. All good writers try to use the most specific verb to identify an action. Have students check a thesaurus or a synonym finder for alternatives to the verbs *talk*, *eat*, *break*, and *walk*.

MEETING INDIVIDUAL NEEDS — ENGLISH LANGUAGE LEARNERS

Idioms English language learners may find the idioms in this selection challenging. Write the following idioms from pages 146–147 on the board: *tearing (something) to pieces, played their hearts out.* Invite volunteers to explain what these phrases mean. Discuss the connection between literal and figurative meanings.

Activity Encourage students to try to figure out idiomatic meaning based on context and literal meaning. Later, have students list some of the idioms in the selection in their vocabulary notebooks with paraphrases and drawings or explanations.

Additional Resources

English Language Learners Sourcebook, p. 31

D Literary Elements

DIALOGUE Remind students that dialogue enhances characterization. Ask students how Quinn's dialogue emphasizes the description of his "arrogant and boastful mood." *(In Quinn's speech, he rubs it in that Helmholtz lost money.)*

E Active Reading Strategies

QUESTION How does Vonnegut characterize Jim? What characteristics does he choose to emphasize in describing the boy? *(Jim is clearly someone who cannot risk having much feeling at all. He is like a robot; he mops without thinking, taking care only to protect his boots from the water.)*

F Active Reading Strategies

QUESTION Both Helmholtz and Quinn have "dreams." Ask students to discuss how their dreams differ. *(Quinn focuses on money, whereas Helmholtz focuses on achievement.)*

G Active Reading Strategies

QUESTION Why is Helmholtz "appalled" by Jim's expressionless eyes? *(Helmholtz, being an idealist, is devastated to see a young man so completely destroyed in so short a life.)*

He sucked whistlingly on a toothpick, and talked of vision—his own.

D "I wonder how many eyes saw the hill before I did?" said Quinn. "Thousands and thousands, I'll bet—and not one saw what I saw. How many eyes?"

"Mine, at least," said Helmholtz. All the hill had meant to him was a panting climb, free blackberries, taxes, and a place for band picnics.

"You inherit the hill from your old man, and it's nothing but a pain in the neck to you," said Quinn. "So you figure you'll stick me with it."

"I didn't figure to stick you," Helmholtz protested. "The good Lord knows the price was more than fair."

"You say that now," said Quinn gleefully. "Sure, Helmholtz, you say that now. Now you see the shopping district's got to grow. Now you see what I saw."

"Yes," said Helmholtz. "Too late, too late." He looked around for some diversion, and saw a fifteen-year-old boy coming toward him, mopping the aisle between booths.

E The boy was small but with tough, stringy muscles standing out on his neck and forearms. Childhood lingered in his features, but when he paused to rest, his fingers went hopefully to the silky beginnings of sideburns and a mustache. He mopped like a robot, jerkily, brainlessly, but took pains not to splash suds over the toes of his black boots.

"So what do I do when I get the hill?" said Quinn. "I tear it down, and it's like somebody pulled down a dam. All of a sudden everybody wants to build a store where the hill was."

"Um," said Helmholtz. He smiled genially at the boy. The boy looked through him without a twitch of recognition.

"We all got something," said Quinn. "You got music; I got vision." And he smiled, for it was perfectly clear to both where the money lay. "Think big!" said Quinn. "Dream big! That's what vision is. Keep your eyes wider open than anybody else's." F

"That boy," said Helmholtz, "I've seen him around school, but I never knew his name."

Quinn laughed cheerlessly. "Billy the Kid? The storm trooper? Rudolph Valentino? Flash Gordon?"[3] He called the boy. . . . "Hey, Jim! Come here a minute."

Helmholtz was appalled to see that the boy's eyes were as expressionless as oysters. G

"This is my brother-in-law's kid by another marriage—before he married my sister," said Quinn. "His name's Jim Donnini, and he's from the south side of Chicago, and he's very tough."

Jim Donnini's hands tightened on the mop handle.

"How do you do?" said Helmholtz.

"Hi," said Jim emptily.

"He's living with me now," said Quinn. "He's my baby now."

"You want a lift to school, Jim?"

3. *Billy the Kid* was a legendary Wild West gunslinger. A *storm trooper* was a member of a military organization in Nazi Germany known for its cruelty and savagery. *Rudolph Valentino* played the romantic hero in many early movies, and *Flash Gordon* is a comic book hero.

Vocabulary

diversion (di vur′ zhən) *n.* something that draws the attention away; distraction

appalled (ə pôld′) *adj.* shocked; horrified

Teaching Support

Writing Minilesson

Dialogue Vonnegut reveals a great deal about Quinn and Helmholtz through dialogue—through what they say and how they say it. Quinn whines and boasts when he talks to Helmholtz. Helmholtz's manner of speaking is enthusiastic, upbeat, and positive.

Activity Have each student write out a real or imaginary conversation between two people. Using as little physical description as possible, students should try to reveal who the characters are and how they feel through dialogue. **L2**

Additional Resources

Writer's Choice, Lesson 4.4

Le Modèle Rouge (The Red Model), 1935. René Magritte.
Viewing the painting: How might these boots be a symbol for Jim?

"Not very funny, sometimes," said Helmholtz. He pushed his eggs away.

"Like some whole new race of people coming up," said Quinn wonderingly. "Nothing like the kids we got around here. Those boots, the black jacket—and he won't talk. He won't run around with the other kids. Won't study. I don't think he can even read and write very good."

"Does he like music at all? Or drawing? Or animals?" said Helmholtz. "Does he collect anything?"

"You know what he likes?" said Quinn. "He likes to polish those boots—get off by himself and polish those boots. And when he's really in heaven is when he can get off by himself, spread comic books all around him on the floor, polish his boots, and watch television." He smiled ruefully.[4] "Yeah, he had a collection too. And I took it away from him and threw it in the river."

"Threw it in the river?" said Helmholtz.

"Yeah," said Quinn. "Eight knives—some with blades as long as your hand."

Helmholtz paled. "Oh." A prickling sensation spread over the back of his neck. "This is a new problem at Lincoln High. I hardly know what to think about it." He swept spilled salt together in a neat little pile, just as he would have liked to sweep together his scattered thoughts. "It's a kind

"Yeah, he wants a lift to school," said Quinn. "See what you make of him. He won't talk to me." He turned to Jim. "Go on, kid, wash up and shave."

Robotlike, Jim marched away.

"Where are his parents?"

"His mother's dead. His old man married my sister, walked out on her, and stuck her with him. Then the court didn't like the way she was raising him, and put him in foster homes for a while. Then they decided to get him clear out of Chicago, so they stuck me with him." He shook his head. "Life's a funny thing, Helmholtz."

4. *Ruefully* means "regretfully."

VIEWING THE PAINTING

René Magritte is known for putting unlikely images in juxtaposition. His work is surreal, dreamlike, and often designed to shock.

Viewing Response *Students may suggest that the image could symbolize Jim trying to emerge from his tough exterior.*

H Active Reading Strategies

REVIEW Quinn's summary of Jim's life offers a portrait of what happened to empty Jim so completely of human emotions. Ask students to imagine the life Jim has led up until now.

I Active Reading Strategies

QUESTION Quinn boasts that Helmholtz looked at the hill but didn't see its potential. Ask students if Helmholtz sees potential where Quinn does not. *(Quinn looks at Jim and doesn't see his potential, while Helmholtz does.)*

MEETING INDIVIDUAL NEEDS — MULTIPLE MODES OF EXPRESSION

Interpersonal Students who are particularly attuned to the emotions of others may be interested in considering strategies to reach a person like Jim.

Activity Have students work in small groups to discuss how to work with an adolescent who has been almost completely disillusioned. What advice do they, as adolescents, have to offer adults who work with young people? Ask groups to prepare and present brief oral reports to the class.
L2 **COLLAB. LEARN.**

J Literary Elements

DIALOGUE Ask students how the different personalities of Quinn and Helmholtz are reflected in both their speech and their attitudes toward Jim. *(Quinn speaks in fragments and is not thoughtful about Jim's problems, whereas Helmholtz speaks standard English and considers both Jim and the social problem as a whole. While Quinn sees strict discipline as the solution to his problems with Jim, Helmholtz hopes that music will provide a cure.)*

K Critical Thinking

INFERRING Ask students what they can infer from Helmholtz's driving an old car. *(This is, perhaps, another indication of his indifference to money and possessions.)*

L Active Reading Strategies

CONNECT Ask students what examples of grandiose dreams they see in the story. *(Quinn's dream or vision of a shopping center is one example. So is Helmholtz's dream of reaching Jim.)* What are some of the students' dreams? What do they have in common with the characters' dreams?

of sickness, isn't it? That's the way to look at it?"

"Sick?" said Quinn. He slapped the table. "You can say that again!" He tapped his chest. "And Doctor Quinn is just the man to give him what's good for what ails him."

"What's that?" said Helmholtz.

"No more talk about the poor little sick boy," said Quinn grimly. "That's all he's heard from the social workers and the juvenile court, and God knows who all. From now on, he's the no-good bum of a man. I'll ride his tail till he straightens up and flies right or winds up in the can for life. One way or the other."

"I see," said Helmholtz.

Like listening to music?" said Helmholtz to Jim brightly, as they rode to school in Helmholtz's car.

Jim said nothing. He was stroking his mustache and sideburns, which he had not shaved off.

"Ever drum with the fingers or keep time with your feet?" said Helmholtz. He had noticed that Jim's boots were decorated with chains that had no function but to jingle as he walked.

Jim sighed with ennui.[5]

"Or whistle?" said Helmholtz. "If you do any of those things, it's just like picking up the keys to a whole new world—a world as beautiful as any world can be."

Jim gave a soft Bronx cheer.[6]

"There!" said Helmholtz. "You've illustrated the basic principle of the family of brass wind instruments. The glorious voice of every one of them starts with a buzz on the lips."

The seat springs of Helmholtz's old car creaked under Jim, as Jim shifted his weight. Helmholtz took this as a sign of interest, and he turned to smile in comradely fashion. But Jim had shifted his weight in order to get a cigarette from inside his tight leather jacket.

Helmholtz was too upset to comment at once. It was only at the end of the ride, as he turned into the teachers' parking lot, that he thought of something to say.

"Sometimes," said Helmholtz, "I get so lonely and disgusted, I don't see how I can stand it. I feel like doing all kinds of crazy things, just for the heck of it—things that might even be bad for me."

Jim blew a smoke ring expertly.

"And then!" said Helmholtz. He snapped his fingers and honked his horn. "And then, Jim, I remember I've got at least one tiny corner of the universe I can make just the way I want it! I can go to it and gloat over it until I'm brand-new and happy again."

"Aren't you the lucky one?" said Jim. He yawned.

"I am, for a fact," said Helmholtz. "My corner of the universe happens to be the air around my band. I can fill it with music. Mr. Beeler, in zoology, has his butterflies. Mr. Trottman, in physics, has his pendulum and tuning forks. Making sure everybody has a corner like that is about the biggest job we teachers have. I—"

The car door opened and slammed, and Jim was gone. Helmholtz stamped out Jim's cigarette and buried it under the gravel of the parking lot.

Helmholtz's first class of the morning was C Band, where beginners thumped and wheezed and tooted as best they could, and looked down the long, long, long road

5. *Ennui* (än wē′) means "boredom."
6. A *Bronx cheer* is an expression of scorn or ridicule, not of good will or good wishes.

Teaching Support

MEETING INDIVIDUAL NEEDS — ADVANCED LEARNERS

Music Therapy Psychologists and music therapists use music to assess the mental state of patients and to treat them. Music therapy is particularly effective with children and adolescents who have been abused or who are mentally ill. It is also effective with the elderly, with Alzheimer's patients, and with terminally ill patients. Music therapy is also used by healthy people to reduce stress.

Activity Have groups plan and conduct an Internet search on how music therapy is used. Have students begin by searching for the American Music Therapy Association on the Internet. Assign each group one of these areas: music therapy and mental illness; music therapy and Alzheimer's disease; or music therapy and children with learning disabilities. Have students report their findings to the class. **L3** COLLAB. LEARN.

through B Band to A Band, the Lincoln High School Ten Square Band, the finest band in the world.

Helmholtz stepped onto the podium and raised his baton. "You are better than you think," he said. "A-one, a-two, a-three." Down came the baton.

C Band set out in its quest for beauty—set out like a rusty switch engine, with valves stuck, pipes clogged, unions leaking, bearings dry.

Helmholtz was still smiling at the end of the hour, because he'd heard in his mind the music as it was going to be someday. His throat was raw, for he had been singing with the band for the whole hour. He stepped into the hall for a drink from the fountain.

As he drank, he heard the jingling of chains. He looked up at Jim Donnini. Rivers of students flowed between classrooms, pausing in friendly eddies,[7] flowing on again. Jim was alone. When he paused, it wasn't to greet anyone, but to polish the toes of his boots on his trousers legs. He had the air of a spy in a melodrama, missing nothing, liking nothing, looking forward to the great day when everything would be turned upside down.

He had the air of a spy in a melodrama, missing nothing, liking nothing, looking forward to the great day when everything would be turned upside down.

"Hello, Jim," said Helmholtz. "Say, I was just thinking about you. We've got a lot of clubs and teams that meet after school. And that's a good way to get to know a lot of people."

Jim measured Helmholtz carefully with his eyes. "Maybe I don't want to know a lot of people," he said. "Ever think of that?" He set his feet down hard to make his chains jingle as he walked away.

When Helmholtz returned to the podium for a rehearsal of B Band, there was a note waiting for him, calling him to a special faculty meeting.

The meeting was about vandalism.

Someone had broken into the school and wrecked the office of Mr. Crane, head of the English Department. The poor man's treasures—books, diplomas, snapshots of England, the beginnings of eleven novels—had been ripped and crumpled, mixed, dumped and trampled, and drenched with ink.

Helmholtz was sickened. He couldn't believe it. He couldn't bring himself to think about it. It didn't become real to him until late that night, in a dream. In the dream Helmholtz saw a boy with barracuda teeth, with claws like baling hooks. The monster climbed into a window of the high school and dropped to

7. *Eddies* are circular currents of wind or water. The students were stopping to socialize in small groups and then moving on.

Vocabulary
quest (kwest) *n.* a search made to achieve a goal

M Author's Craft

WORD CHOICE Point out Vonnegut's choice of words to describe the sounds of the C band. Vonnegut compares the band with "a rusty switch engine, with valves stuck, pipes clogged, unions leaking, bearings dry." Vonnegut hammers home how awful the band sounds to underscore how completely unfazed the optimistic Helmholtz is.

N Active Reading Strategies

REVIEW Ask students how they know that Helmholtz's optimism is undiminished, even when he listens to the cacophony of the C band students. *(He "was still smiling at the end of the hour . . .")*

O Literary Elements

DIALOGUE Have a volunteer read Jim's dialogue in this paragraph aloud. Then have students discuss how his attitude is revealed by his words.

MEETING INDIVIDUAL NEEDS — SPECIAL NEEDS

Emotional Helmholtz is a person who inspires others by his faith in them. There is a psychological theory that suggests that a person's performance can be influenced by what persons in authority expect of that person.

Activity Have students discuss this idea in small groups and identify and relate situations in which they did better because a teacher, coach, or other authority figure had faith in them and clearly conveyed positive expectations. Have students develop a list of things authority figures can do to convey positive expectations and help young people succeed. **L1**

Additional Resources
Inclusion Strategies

P Critical Thinking

INFERRING Ask students what they can infer about Helmholtz from the sentence, "There was nothing to do but dress up and go to school." *(He loves the treasures of the band room dearly and is willing to go there in the middle of the night to protect them.)*

Q Literary Elements

DIALOGUE What does the dialogue here say about Helmholtz's emotions? *(He is angry, but more appalled and amazed than anything. Even though he has watched the destruction, he maintains control of his voice and chooses his words carefully.)*

R Literary Elements

DIALOGUE How do Helmholtz's dialogue and Vonnegut's description of Jim's character define the problem of the story? *(Helmholtz explains that what Jim is wrecking is "the best thing" people can do, but Jim is without fear, dreams, or love so he is not affected by Helmholtz's words.)*

the floor of the band rehearsal room. The monster clawed to shreds the heads of the biggest drum in the state. Helmholtz woke up howling. There was nothing to do but dress and go to school.

At two in the morning, Helmholtz caressed the drum heads in the band rehearsal room, with the night watchman looking on. He rolled the drum back and forth on its cart, and he turned the light inside on and off, on and off. The drum was unharmed. The night watchman left to make his rounds.

The band's treasure house was safe. With the contentment of a miser counting his money, Helmholtz fondled the rest of the instruments, one by one. And then he began to polish the sousaphones. As he polished, he could hear the great horns roaring, could see them flashing in the sunlight, with the Stars and Stripes and the banner of Lincoln High going before.

Did You Know?
The *sousaphone* (so͞o′ zə fōn′), a large circular tuba with a wide bell that faces forward, is named for John Philip Sousa.

"Yump-yump, tiddle-tiddle, yump-yump, tiddle-tiddle!" sang Helmholtz happily. "Yump-yump-yump, ra-a-a-a-a, yump-yump, yump-yump—boom!"

As he paused to choose the next number for his imaginary band to play, he heard a furtive noise in the chemistry laboratory next door. Helmholtz sneaked into the hall, jerked open the laboratory door, and flashed on the lights. Jim Donnini had a bottle of acid in either hand. He was splashing acid over the periodic table of the elements, over the blackboards covered with formulas, over the bust of Lavoisier.[8] The scene was the most repulsive thing Helmholtz could have looked upon.

Jim smiled with thin bravado.

"Get out," said Helmholtz.

"What're you gonna do?" said Jim.

"Clean up. Save what I can," said Helmholtz dazedly. He picked up a wad of cotton waste and began wiping up the acid.

"You gonna call the cops?" said Jim.

"I—I don't know," said Helmholtz. "No thoughts come. If I'd caught you hurting the bass drum, I think I would have killed you with a single blow. But I wouldn't have had any intelligent thoughts about what you were—what you thought you were doing."

"It's about time this place got set on its ear," said Jim.

"Is it?" said Helmholtz. "That must be so, if one of our students wants to murder it."

"What good is it?" said Jim.

"Not much good, I guess," said Helmholtz. "It's just the best thing human beings ever managed to do." He was helpless, talking to himself. He had a bag of tricks for making boys behave like men—tricks that played on boyish fears

8. The *periodic table* is a chart showing all known chemical elements. The *bust of Lavoisier* (lä vwä zyā′) is a statue of the 18th-century French scientist known as the founder of modern chemistry, who lived during the 1700s.

Vocabulary
furtive (fur′ tiv) *adj.* secret; shifty; sly
bravado (brə vä′ dō) *n.* a false show of bravery; pretended courage

Teaching Support

INTERDISCIPLINARY CONNECTION

Musical Students may come to a better understanding of Helmholtz's enthusiasm by researching marching music, especially the music of John Philip Sousa.

Activity Have students prepare presentations on the life and work of John Philip Sousa and share their work with the rest of the class. They should also discuss how Helmholtz's behavior exemplifies Sousa's work. **L2**

R

and dreams and loves. But here was a boy without fear, without dreams, without love.

"If you smashed up all the schools," said Helmholtz, "we wouldn't have any hope left."

"What hope?" said Jim.

"The hope that everybody will be glad he's alive," said Helmholtz. "Even you."

"That's a laugh," said Jim. "All I ever got out of this dump was a hard time. So what're you gonna do?"

"I have to do something, don't I?" said Helmholtz.

"I don't care what you do," said Jim.

"I know," said Helmholtz. "I know." He marched Jim into his tiny office off the band rehearsal room. He dialed the telephone number of the principal's home. Numbly, he waited for the bell to get the old man from his bed.

Jim dusted his boots with a rag.

Helmholtz suddenly dropped the telephone into its cradle before the principal could answer. "Isn't there anything you care about but ripping, hacking, bending, rending, smashing, bashing?" he cried. "Anything? Anything but those boots?"

"Go on! Call up whoever you're gonna call," said Jim.

S

Helmholtz opened a locker and took a trumpet from it. He thrust the trumpet into Jim's arms. "There!" he said, puffing with emotion. "There's my treasure. It's the dearest thing I own. I give it to you to smash. I won't move a muscle to stop you. You can have the added pleasure of watching my heart break while you do it."

Jim looked at him oddly. He laid down the trumpet.

"Go on!" said Helmholtz. "If the world has treated you so badly, it deserves to have the trumpet smashed!"

"I—" said Jim. Helmholtz grabbed his belt, put a foot behind him, and dumped him on the floor.

T

Helmholtz pulled Jim's boots off and threw them into a corner. "There!" said Helmholtz savagely. He jerked the boy to his feet again and thrust the trumpet into his arms once more.

Jim Donnini was barefoot now. He had lost his socks with his boots. The boy looked down. The feet that had once seemed big black clubs were narrow as chicken wings now—bony and blue, and not quite clean.

The boy shivered, then quaked. Each quake seemed to shake something loose inside, until, at last, there was no boy left. No boy at all. Jim's head lolled, as though he waited only for death.

U

Helmholtz was overwhelmed by remorse. He threw his arms around the boy. "Jim! Jim—listen to me, boy!"

Jim stopped quaking.

"You know what you've got there—the trumpet?" said Helmholtz. "You know what's special about it?"

Jim only sighed.

"It belonged to John Philip Sousa!" said Helmholtz. He rocked and shook Jim gently, trying to bring him back to life. "I'll trade it to you, Jim—for your boots. It's yours, Jim! John Philip Sousa's trumpet is yours! It's worth hundreds of dollars, Jim—thousands!"

Jim laid his head on Helmholtz's breast.

"It's better than boots, Jim," said Helmholtz. "You can learn to play it.

Vocabulary

remorse (ri môrs′) *n.* a deep, painful feeling of guilt or sorrow for wrongdoing

S Critical Thinking

INFERRING Ask students why they think Helmholtz gives Jim his trumpet and why Jim doesn't smash it. *(Helmholtz is desperate to find something Jim cares about. Perhaps Helmholtz's sacrifice for his sake has touched Jim in some way.)*

T Active Reading Strategies

QUESTION Why does Helmholtz take Jim's boots off, and what effect does the gesture have on the boy? *(Helmholtz realizes that the boots are the only thing Jim cares about; he is childlike and vulnerable without them.)*

U Critical Thinking

EVALUATING Ask students to read the body language of the two participants to evaluate the action. Has Helmholtz touched something in Jim? Or is the boy devastated by his loss? Share the following model.

Model: I think that Helmholtz has affected Jim, because Jim wouldn't let someone be so close. Also, Jim accepts the affection. In my opinion, his asking "dully" for his boots shows that he feels stripped of everything he cares about. I think the immensity of what it means to lose something hits home.

Listening and Speaking *Minilesson*

Debating The discussion between Helmholtz and Jim in the chemistry lab is central to the understanding of the story. It is the only time these two individuals confront one another directly. Helmholtz advocates hope for a better future; Jim laughs at the idea.

Activity Divide the class into two groups: one will take Jim's cynical outlook; the other will present Helmholtz's hopeful view. Have students read through the scene carefully, finding examples of each character's beliefs and motivations so they can prepare arguments and counter-arguments. Then have the groups stage a debate on which viewpoint best reflects society today. **L2** **COLLAB. LEARN.**

Active Reading Strategies

CONNECT Note that Vonnegut began the story with the same imagery. Why does he repeat the image of the "waddling, clanking, muddy machines"? *(This image seems to be associated with Quinn and his destructive approach to life.)*

Active Reading Strategies

QUESTION Ask students why they think Quinn fails to call Jim by his name. *(Quinn doesn't seem to see Jim as a person.)*

You're somebody, Jim. You're the boy with John Philip Sousa's trumpet!"

Helmholtz released Jim slowly, sure the boy would topple. Jim didn't fall. He stood alone. The trumpet was still in his arms.

"I'll take you home, Jim," said Helmholtz. "Be a good boy and I won't say a word about tonight. Polish your trumpet, and learn to be a good boy."

"Can I have my boots?" said Jim dully.

"No," said Helmholtz. "I don't think they're good for you."

He drove Jim home. He opened the car windows and the air seemed to refresh the boy. He let him out at Quinn's restaurant. The soft pats of Jim's bare feet on the sidewalk echoed down the empty street. He climbed through a window, and into his bedroom behind the kitchen. And all was still.

The next morning the waddling, clanking, muddy machines were making the vision of Bert Quinn come true. They were smoothing off the place where the hill had been behind the restaurant. They were making it as level as a billiard table.

Helmholtz sat in a booth again. Quinn joined him again. Jim mopped again. Jim kept his eyes down, refusing to notice Helmholtz. And he didn't seem to care when a surf of suds broke over the toes of his small and narrow brown Oxfords.

"Eating out two mornings in a row?" said Quinn. "Something wrong at home?"

"My wife's still out of town," said Helmholtz.

"While the cat's away—" said Quinn. He winked.

"When the cat's away," said Helmholtz, "this mouse gets lonesome."

Quinn leaned forward. "Is that what got you out of bed in the middle of the night, Helmholtz? Loneliness?" He jerked his head at Jim. "Kid! Go get Mr. Helmholtz his horn."

Jim raised his head, and Helmholtz saw that his eyes were oysterlike again. He marched away to get the trumpet.

Quinn now showed that he was excited and angry. "You take away his boots and give him a horn, and I'm not supposed to get curious?" he said. "I'm not supposed to start asking questions? I'm not supposed to find out you caught him taking the school apart? You'd made a lousy crook, Helmholtz. You'd leave your baton, sheet music, and your driver's license at the scene of the crime."

"I don't think about hiding clues," said Helmholtz. "I just do what I do. I was going to tell you."

John Philip Sousa

Teaching Support

Reading Minilesson

Problem and Solution When Helmholtz catches Jim vandalizing the chemistry lab, Helmholtz faces, perhaps for the first time in his life, a problem he can't solve. He has tried everything to help the boy, and it seems that none of his old strategies work. Review the text to map out the problem he has and his ways of solving it.

Activity Have students work in small groups to fill in the chart at the right. Students should note which proposed solution was effective.
L2 COLLAB. LEARN.

Additional Resources

Reading Skills Practice Workbook

Problem: Jim is emotionally closed off to the world and is bitter and spiteful. He cares about nothing. Helmholtz wants to reach Jim and make him realize there are good things in life.			
Solution 1: *Helmholtz tries to befriend Jim after he offers him a ride to school.*	**Solution 2:** *Helmholtz tries to interest Jim in school clubs.*	**Solution 3:** *Helmholtz gives Jim his trumpet and takes Jim's boots in return.*	**Solution 4:** *Helmholtz destroys his trumpet in a gesture of despair over Jim's life. (Effective)*

Quinn's feet danced and his shoes squeaked like mice. "Yes?" he said. "Well, I've got some news for you too."

"What is that?" said Helmholtz uneasily.

"It's all over with Jim and me," said Quinn. "Last night was the payoff. I'm sending him back where he came from."

"To another string of foster homes?" said Helmholtz weakly.

"Whatever the experts figure out to do with a kid like that." Quinn sat back, exhaled noisily, and went limp with relief.

"You can't," said Helmholtz.

"I can," said Quinn.

"That will be the end of him," said Helmholtz. "He can't stand to be thrown away like that one more time."

"He can't feel anything," said Quinn. "I can't help him; I can't hurt him. Nobody can. There isn't a nerve in him."

"A bundle of scar tissue," said Helmholtz.

"It's all over with Jim and me," said Quinn. "Last night was the payoff."

The bundle of scar tissue returned with the trumpet. Impassively,[9] he laid it on the table in front of Helmholtz.

Helmholtz forced a smile. "It's yours, Jim," he said. "I gave it to you."

"Take it while you got the chance, Helmholtz," said Quinn. "He doesn't want it. All he'll do is swap it for a knife or a pack of cigarettes."

"He doesn't know what it is, yet," said Helmholtz. "It takes a while to find out."

"Is it any good?" said Quinn.

"Any good?" said Helmholtz, not believing his ears. "Any good?" He didn't see how anyone could look at the instrument and not be warmed and dazzled by it. "Any good?" he murmured. "It belonged to John Philip Sousa."

Quinn blinked stupidly. "Who?"

Helmholtz's hands fluttered on the table top like the wings of a dying bird. "Who was John Philip Sousa?" he piped. No more words came. The subject was too big for a tired man to cover. The dying bird expired and lay still.

After a long silence, Helmholtz picked up the trumpet. He kissed the cold mouthpiece and pumped the valves in a dream of a brilliant cadenza.[10] Over the bell of the instrument, Helmholtz saw Jim Donnini's face, seemingly floating in space—all but deaf and blind. Now Helmholtz saw the futility of men and their treasures. He had thought that his greatest treasure, the trumpet, could buy a soul for Jim. The trumpet was worthless.

Deliberately, Helmholtz hammered the trumpet against the table edge. He bent it around a coat tree. He handed the wreck to Quinn.

"Ya busted it," said Quinn, amazed. "Why'dja do that? What's that prove?"

9. To do something *impassively* is to do it without showing any emotion.

10. A *cadenza* is a difficult musical solo near the end of a musical composition.

Vocabulary
futility (fū til′ ə tē) *n.* uselessness; hopelessness

X Critical Thinking

EVALUATING Ask students to decide, from what they have read thus far, with whom they agree: Quinn or Helmholtz. Is Jim hopeless, or does he just need some time and love? Have students support their views with incidents from the story. *(One possible response is that Jim is still young enough to be reached.)*

FINE ART TRANSPARENCY 32

You may want to use ***Fine Art Transparency 32*** to consider the ways in which music affects musicians.

REAL-WORLD CONNECTION

Gangs Jim reacts to his lack of love and close family relationships by developing a hard, intimidating front. Not having a place where they belong often drives similar young men into gangs where they develop a sense of "family." Have students research gangs, looking particularly for what draws young people into gangs. What do they appear to be searching for? Students' presentations should achieve an effective balance between researched information and original ideas. **L2**

Active Reading Strategies

REVIEW Helmholtz's optimism has been destroyed by his encounter with Jim. Just as he hits bottom, Jim begins to feel again, and Quinn sees the change. As Helmholtz loses his optimism, the pessimistic Quinn begins to feel hope. Ask students to locate the point in the story at which this change takes place. *("Jim Donnini's eyes filled with pity and alarm. They came alive." "Quinn looked at Jim, and something like hope flickered for the first time in his bitterly lonely old face.")*

Literary Elements

RESOLUTION Point out to students that the ending of the story is somewhat ambiguous. Is Jim better off? Has Helmholtz saved him? Ask students to support their views by citing specific parts of the story. *(Both characters seem to be better off.)*

Thematic Focus

Lean on Me Helmholtz wants Jim to lean on him (and at one point Jim literally does lean on the older man). What does Helmholtz gain by helping people? *(He confirms his optimistic view of the world and people and reaffirms his place in it.)* In general, what are the paybacks of allowing someone to lean on you? *(You find your inner strength, and you feel needed.)*

ASSESSMENT

Quick Checks, p. 12

Teaching Support

"I—I don't know," said Helmholtz. A terrible blasphemy[11] rumbled deep in him, like the warning of a volcano. And then, irresistibly, out it came. "Life is no damn good," said Helmholtz. His face twisted as he fought back tears and shame.

Helmholtz, the mountain that walked like a man, was falling apart. Jim Donnini's eyes filled with pity and alarm. They came alive. They became human. Helmholtz had got a message through. Quinn looked at Jim, and something like hope flickered for the first time in his bitterly lonely old face.

Drawing Music, 1997. Tam Van Tran. Ink on paper, 4¾ x 3⅝ in. Collection of the artist.

Viewing the art: If you were Jim, what message might this drawing have for you?

Two weeks later, a new semester began at Lincoln High.

In the band rehearsal room, the members of C Band were waiting for their leader—were waiting for their destinies as musicians to unfold.

Helmholtz stepped onto the podium, and rattled his baton against his music stand. "The Voices of Spring," he said. "Everybody hear that? The Voices of Spring?"

There were rustling sounds as the musicians put the music on their stands. In the pregnant silence[12] that followed their readiness, Helmholtz glanced at Jim Donnini, who sat on the last seat of the worst trumpet section of the worst band in school.

His trumpet, John Philip Sousa's trumpet, George M. Helmholtz's trumpet, had been repaired.

"Think of it this way," said Helmholtz. "Our aim is to make the world more beautiful than it was when we came into it. It can be done. You can do it."

A small cry of despair came from Jim Donnini. It was meant to be private, but it pierced every ear with its poignancy.[13]

"How?" said Jim.

"Love yourself," said Helmholtz, "and make your instrument sing about it. A-one, a-two, a-three." Down came his baton.

11. A *blasphemy* is an expression of scorn for something considered sacred.
12. A *pregnant silence* is one filled with importance or meaning.
13. Here, *poignancy* (poin′ yən sē) means "sharply felt emotion or distress."

Grammar and Language *Minilesson*

Commas Point out that long introductory prepositional and participial phrases should be followed by commas. Short prepositional phrases don't require commas. Write the following sentences on the board and point out Vonnegut's use of commas. *With the contentment of a miser counting his money, Helmholtz fondled the rest of the instruments, one by one; Over the bell of the instrument, Helmholtz saw Jim Donnini's face.*

Activity Have students find three sentences that begin with prepositional or participial phrases followed by commas elsewhere in the story. Then have them write three sentences of their own that begin with a prepositional or participial phrase followed by a comma. **L2**

Additional Resources

- ***Grammar and Language Transparency 11***
- ***Grammar and Language Workbook,*** pp. 257–264
- ***Grammar and Composition Handbook,*** Lesson 13.2
- ***Writer's Choice,*** Lesson 20.2

Responding to Literature

PERSONAL RESPONSE

- How did you react to George M. Helmholtz's repeated efforts to get through to Jim?
- What, in your opinion, might Helmholtz have done differently?

Brackets connect questions that are paired to develop higher-level thinking skills.

Analyzing Literature

RECALL

1. What do Helmholtz and Quinn say about their earlier business deal?
2. What is Helmholtz's big dream? When does it come true?
3. Name two or three ways Helmholtz tries to reach Jim.
4. What makes Jim's eyes fill "with pity and alarm"?

INTERPRET

5. What does their discussion of a business deal tell you about Helmholtz and Quinn?
6. What makes Helmholtz a successful teacher?
7. What do you learn about Helmholtz from the way he treats Jim?
8. The author writes that Helmholtz "had got a message through" to Jim. What is the message?

EVALUATE AND CONNECT

9. Does Helmholtz live up to his idea that "our aim is to make the world more beautiful than it was when we came into it"? Explain your answer.
10. Theme Connection Compare Quinn's and Helmholtz's ways of responding to Jim. Explain how each man is important in Jim's life.

LITERARY ELEMENTS

Dialogue

Dialogue is conversation between two or more characters. Dialogue reveals the personality of a character through the spoken words and descriptions of facial expressions and body language. Good dialogue sounds natural, like an overheard conversation. It can contain slang, sentence fragments, and contractions because that's how people talk.

1. What information about Quinn and Helmholtz is presented in their dialogue about the hill at the beginning of the story?
2. Find an example of natural dialogue from Helmholtz, from Quinn, and from Jim. What does each character's way of speaking reveal about his personality?

- See **Literary Terms Handbook**, p. R3.

Responding to the Selection

PERSONAL RESPONSE

Some students may appreciate Helmholtz's repeated attempts to get through to Jim.

Analyzing Literature

1. Quinn boasts about his ability to see the potential in the land, and Helmholtz says that the price he got for it was more than fair.
2. Helmholtz dreams of leading the finest band on the face of the earth. His dream comes true each year.
3. Helmholtz tries to reach Jim by asking about his interests, by suggesting clubs, and by finally giving him his most prized possession—John Philip Sousa's trumpet.
4. Jim's eyes fill with pity and alarm when Helmholtz loses his idealism and smashes his trumpet.
5. Quinn is clever in his financial dealings and has a tendency to gloat. Helmholtz is not clever about money and is focused on his music and his students.
6. Helmholtz is a successful teacher because he is optimistic; he can see the potential in each child, and he is lavish in his praise.
7. Helmholtz's treatment of Jim makes it clear that he is a kind man who looks for the good in everyone.
8. Helmholtz's message for Jim is that he wants him to feel something, to experience emotions, to dream and hope.
9. Helmholtz does live up to his ideal. He could just walk away from Jim but does not. Also, his music makes the world "more beautiful."
10. Quinn is a disciplinarian, demanding that Jim obey. Helmholtz focuses on help and encouragement. Quinn provides a home and stability, and Helmholtz arouses hope.

LITERARY ELEMENTS

1. Quinn tends to boast. Helmholtz demonstrates his peace-loving nature and disinclination to argue.
2. Helmholtz's "I've got at least one tiny corner of the universe . . ." shows idealism. Quinn's "I'll ride his tail . . ." shows a tendency to discipline. Jim's "Aren't you the lucky one?" shows sarcasm.

Additional Resources

Literary Elements Transparency 12

Extending Your Response

Writing About Literature

Students' paragraphs should

- explore Helmholtz's and Quinn's attitudes toward the hill and Jim
- explain how Vonnegut uses Quinn to highlight the kind of person Helmholtz is

Literature Groups Point out to students that a solution need not eradicate a problem to be useful. Complex problems may require multiple solutions. COLLAB. LEARN.

Learning for Life Students who have had musical training may have some ideas they can share with the group about the qualities that make a good music teacher or band leader.

Personal Writing

Students' journal entries should

- explain feelings about a treasured object.
- support their ideas with concrete examples.
- use parallelism to describe contrasting attitudes and characteristics.

Skill Minilesson

VOCABULARY • ANTONYMS

1. open
2. humble
3. encouraging
4. pleased

Additional Resources

Vocabulary Practice, p. 11

Extending Your Response

Writing About Literature

Contrasting Characters Write a paragraph or two in which you contrast Helmholtz and Quinn. What is Quinn's approach to treating a troubled kid? What is Helmholtz's approach? What is the attitude of each toward the hill behind the restaurant? How does the author use Quinn to emphasize the kind of person that Helmholtz is? Emphasize the contrast between characters by using parallelism, similar grammatical structures, in describing the characters' traits.

Literature Groups

Public Problems A writer's job, Vonnegut believes, is to warn society about its problems so that people can work for change. What problems might Vonnegut be addressing in "The Kid Nobody Could Handle"? What solutions does he suggest? Are they, in your opinion, useful solutions? Discuss these questions with your group. Then compare your responses with those of other groups.

Learning for Life

Job Description What does it take to be a band leader? Write a job description that the principal of Helmholtz's school might write to look for a replacement when Helmholtz retires. As you write, think about the music skills a band leader like Helmholtz would need as well as the abilities required to reach different kinds of students.

Personal Writing

Journal Entry Look back at your list of things that make you happy from the **Reading Focus** on page 145. Write a journal entry to explain your feelings about one of these items. Be specific about what makes you happy and why. Support your ideas with details and examples.

Save your work for your portfolio.

RETEACH • REVIEW

Skill Minilesson

VOCABULARY • ANTONYMS

An **antonym** is a word with a meaning that is opposite that of another word. Most words have antonyms, and writers often use antonyms to present contrast, as the example shows.

I used to think Lena was an honest person, but she has proved to me that she is untrustworthy.

PRACTICE Complete each sentence by writing an antonym for the word that is underlined.

1. Not all criminal behavior is furtive; some is quite ____.
2. How can two sisters be so different? One is so ____, the other so arrogant!
3. Dad thought his chatter from the bleachers would be ____; instead, it was unnerving.
4. You thought I'd be ____ by your behavior, but I was appalled.

ASSESSMENT

- ***Quick Checks,*** p. 12
- ***Selection and Theme Assessment,*** pp. 21–22
- ***Performance Assessment,*** p. 11
- ***Testmaker: ExamView Pro***
- ***Interactive Tutor: Self-Assessment***

interNET CONNECTION

Have students search the Internet for instructions and tips on how to play the trumpet or another band instrument. They should teach themselves the basics from reading the instructions and then present a lesson demonstrating the instrument to the class. In preparing the lesson, the students should concentrate on a sequence of activities involved in playing the instrument.

MEDIA Connection

SONG LYRICS

What would you like to be? Loved? Free? Part of a crowd? Cool? Des'ree tells you to be many things!

You Gotta Be

By Des'ree and A. Ingram; Sony Music Entertainment, 1994

from *I Ain't Movin'* by Des'ree

Listen as your day unfolds
challenge what the future holds
Try to keep your head up to the sky
Lovers they may cause you tears
Go ahead release your fears
Stand up and be counted, don't be ashamed to cry
You gotta be

CHORUS:
You gotta be bad
You gotta be bold
You gotta be wiser
You gotta be hard
You gotta be tough
You gotta be stronger
You gotta be cool, you gotta be calm, you gotta stay
together
All I know, all I know, love will save the day

Herald what your mother said
Read the books your father read
Try to solve the puzzle in your own sweet time
Some may have more cash than you
Others take a different view
My oh my, you gotta be

CHORUS

Time asks no questions,
it goes on without
you
Leaving you behind if
you can't stand the
pace
The world keeps on
spinning, can't stop it
if you tried to
The best part is danger
staring you in the
face

Listen as your day
unfolds
challenge what the future holds
Try to keep your head up to the sky
Lovers they may cause you tears
Go ahead release your fears
Stand up and be counted, don't be ashamed to cry
You gotta be

CHORUS

Got to be bad
Got to be bold
Got to be wise
Don't ever be cold
Got to be hard
Not too, too hard
All I know is love will save the day.

Analyzing Media

1. According to the song, what people can help a person face the future?
2. Is everything listed in this song important to you? Which advice is not? Explain.

MEDIA Connection

Objective

- To read and analyze song lyrics

Literature LINK

The Kid Nobody Could Handle
This song connects to "The Kid Nobody Could Handle" (pp. 146–156). In that story, Jim's tough stance is a facade; he is not truly strong because he lacks love.

Analyzing Media

1. Parents can help children meet life's challenges.
2. Many students may find only some of the of the behaviors mentioned in the song relevant to them. Some, for example, may say they choose not to be "hard."

Additional Resources

Media Connections, p. 3

in TIME ***magazine***

Teaching Support

Reading *Minilesson*

Questioning The primary component of active reading is questioning. Asking questions of the work helps readers stay involved and is essential to both comprehension and interpretation.

Activity Ask students to form small groups to develop a series of questions about the song. Encourage groups to come up with as many questions as possible. Then have students try to answer as many of their own questions as they can. Have the entire class discuss any questions that students don't feel they can answer. **L3** **COLLAB. LEARN.**

Additional Resources

Reading Skills Practice Workbook

interNET CONNECTION

Kurt Vonnegut is an idealist much like George Helmholtz, although probably not so optimistic. Have students research Vonnegut's life to look for connections to Helmholtz. **L2**

Before Reading

Objectives

- To read and analyze a short story
- To analyze the elements of characterization in a short story
- To write a paragraph about setting

Skills

Reading/Thinking: Evaluating; Cause and Effect
Writing: Paragraph About Setting
Grammar/Language: End Punctuation and Quotation Marks
Listening/Speaking: Literature Groups
Collaboration: Literature Groups

Motivating STUDENTS

Literature Launchers: "Langston Hughes: Words and Works"

Videodisc Side A, Segment 4

Also available in VHS.

Selection Focus Transparency 12: Before presenting the transparency, have students discuss the qualities that make a person trustworthy.

Reading Focus: As an extension to the Reading Focus, have students discuss what behaviors might lead them *not* to trust a person.

Before You Read

Thank You, M'am

MEET LANGSTON HUGHES

While working as a busboy in Washington, D.C., Langston Hughes showed some of his poems to a famous customer, the poet Vachel Lindsay. That night, Lindsay read the poems to an audience. In time, Hughes became known as the Poet Laureate of Black America. Hughes's subjects, he once said, are "people up today and down tomorrow, working this week and fired the next, beaten and baffled, but determined not to be wholly beaten." Hughes was one of the first African Americans to make a living as a writer and lecturer.

Langston Hughes was born in 1902 and died in 1967. This story was published in 1958.

READING FOCUS

Think of someone you trust. Consider your reasons for trusting that person.

Chart It!
Copy the following chart, and list some qualities that you find in people you trust.

A trustworthy person is	

Setting a Purpose
Read to find out how two characters come to trust each other despite unlikely circumstances.

BUILDING BACKGROUND

The Time and Place The setting of "Thank You, M'am" is a street scene and a rooming house, probably in a large city. The story, however, might take place in any city in the United States and at almost any time.

Did You Know? A rooming house is a place where people rent rooms to live in. Rooming houses are often found in urban areas, providing homes for people who cannot afford an apartment or a house of their own.

VOCABULARY PREVIEW

slung (slung) *adj.* hung or thrown loosely; p. 161
frail (frāl) *adj.* lacking in strength; weak; p. 162
barren (bar′ ən) *adj.* bare; empty; dull or uninteresting; p. 164

RESOURCE MANAGER

Teaching Tools and Resources
- Theme Two Planning Guide
- Literature Groups Sourcebook

Essential Lesson Support
Lesson-Specific Instruction
- Selection Focus Transparency 12
- Literary Elements Transparency 13
- Active Reading Guide,* p. 13
- Selection Vocabulary Practice, p. 12
- *in*TIME magazine, p. 29

Assessment
- Selection Quick Checks,* p. 13
- Sel. and Theme Assmt., p. 23
- Testmaker: ExamView Pro
- Performance Assessment, p. 12

Systematic Language Instruction
- Gr. & Comp. Hbk., L. 3.4

English Language Learners
- ELL Sourcebook, p. 32
- Spanish Summaries, p. 12
- Audio Library*
- English, Yes!

Spec. Needs/Strat. Interven.
- Interactive Rdg. Sbk., pp. T76–T78
- Interactive Rdg. Wbk., pp. 29-30
- Inclusion Strat. Sbk., pp. 39–40
- Audio Library*

* Also available in Spanish

Thank You, M'am

The City from Greenwich Village, 1922. John Sloan. Oil on canvas, 26 x 33¾ in. National Gallery of Art, Washington, DC.

Langston Hughes

She was a large woman with a large purse that had everything in it but hammer and nails. It had a long strap and she carried it slung across her shoulder. It was about eleven o'clock at night, and she was walking alone, when a boy ran up behind her and tried to snatch her purse. The strap broke with the single tug the boy gave it from behind. But the boy's weight, and the weight of the purse combined caused him to lose his balance so, instead of taking off full blast as he had hoped, the boy fell on his back on the sidewalk, and his legs flew up. The large woman simply turned around and kicked him right square in his blue jeaned sitter. Then she reached down, picked the boy up by his shirt front, and shook him until his teeth rattled.

Vocabulary
slung (slung) *adj.* hung or thrown loosely

Reading the Selection

SUMMARY

Mrs. Luella Jones is on her way home when a young boy tries to steal her purse. Mrs. Jones catches the boy and drags him home with her. She makes him wash his face, serves him dinner, and dishes up some homespun wisdom. She also asks him why he tried to steal her purse. When he tells her he wanted blue suede shoes, she gives him money to buy a pair and sends him on his way, telling him to behave himself. The boy wants to say more but ends up saying only, "Thank you, M'am."

Spanish Summaries, p. 12

Active Reading Strategies

PREDICT Ask students to use the title and the first paragraph to predict what they think the story will be about.

VOCABULARY If you haven't previewed the selection vocabulary with students, stop and remind them to use context clues to unlock the meanings of new vocabulary words.

Additional Resources

Active Reading Guide, p. 13
Audio Library
Spanish Audio Library

Teaching Support

CONNECTING TO OTHER SELECTIONS

COMPARING *selections*

This selection can be paired with "The Kid Nobody Could Handle" on page 146. A lesson for teaching a comparison of the two selections appears on page 166.

The chart at the right shows three other ways to connect "Thank You, M'am" to selections in this book.

For specific teaching strategies, see the ***Theme Two Planning Guide***.

Connection	Title
Life Skills: Lifelong Learning	→ "Golden Glass," p. 51
Thematic: Facing Responsibility	→ "The Gettysburg Address," p. 472
Literary: Setting	→ "The Woman in the Snow," p. 856

VIEWING THE PAINTING

John Wesley Hardrick spent his life in Indianapolis, where an elementary school teacher recognized his talent. He studied art and went on to paint landscapes and people, including noteworthy portraits of African Americans. His work played an important role in the Harlem Renaissance. Hardrick died in 1967.

Viewing Response *The writer uses dialogue action and details to reveal Mrs. Jones's character. The painter reveals his subject's character through her posture, facial expression, and clothing.*

B Literary Elements

CHARACTERIZATION Roger says he didn't mean to steal the purse and that he will run away if she lets go. What do these responses say about his character? *(He is nervous and not truthful.)*

C Active Reading Strategies

QUESTION Discuss the probable impact on Mrs. Jones when she learns that the boy has no one at home to tell him to wash his face. *(She is motivated to help the boy—to show him someone cares.)*

D Author's Craft

WORD CHOICE Hughes says a great deal with few words. What image does he convey with the words *frail* and *willow-wild*? *(The boy is both thin and frenetic. Willow branches wave in the wind.)*

Portrait of a Woman, 1932. John Wesley Hardrick. Oil on board, 30 x 24 in. Hampton University Museum, Hampton, VA. Indianapolis Museum of Art in cooperation with Indiana University Press.

Viewing the painting: How does the writer reveal Mrs. Jones's character? How does the painter reveal the character of his subject?

The woman said, "What did you want to do it for?"

The boy said, "I didn't aim to."

She said, "You a lie!"

By that time two or three people passed, stopped, turned to look, and some stood watching.

"If I turn you loose, will you run?" asked the woman.

"Yes'm," said the boy.

"Then I won't turn you loose," said the woman. She did not release him.

"I'm very sorry, lady, I'm sorry," whispered the boy.

"Um-hum! And your face is dirty. I got a great mind to wash your face for you. Ain't you got nobody home to tell you to wash your face?"

"No'm," said the boy.

"Then it will get washed this evening," said the large woman starting up the street, dragging the frightened boy behind her.

After that the woman said, "Pick up my pocketbook, boy, and give it here."

She still held him. But she bent down enough to permit him to stoop and pick up her purse. Then she said, "Now ain't you ashamed of yourself?"

Firmly gripped by his shirt front, the boy said, "Yes'm."

He looked as if he were fourteen or fifteen, frail and willow-wild, in tennis shoes and blue jeans.

The woman said, "You ought to be my son. I would teach you right from wrong. Least I can do right now is to wash your face. Are you hungry?"

Vocabulary
frail (frāl) *adj.* lacking in strength; weak

162 THEME 2

Teaching Support

MEETING INDIVIDUAL NEEDS — ENGLISH LANGUAGE LEARNERS

Pronoun Reference Briefly review subject and object pronouns and possessive pronouns. Have volunteers list the forms on the board and discuss gender and number. Remind students that *it* can be the neutral subject of a sentence about time or weather. Also note that a pronoun usually refers to a noun that preceded it but can also refer to something that follows.

Activity Ask students to identify the noun referents for *She* and *it* in the first sentence on page 161. *(woman and purse)* Continue with the paragraph. Remind students to look back for the noun referents of pronouns if they have trouble following the story line.

Additional Resources

English Language Learners Sourcebook, p. 32

"No'm," said the being-dragged boy. "I just want you to turn me loose."

"Was I bothering *you* when I turned that corner?" asked the woman.

"No'm."

"But you put yourself in contact with *me*," said the woman. "If you think that that contact is not going to last awhile, you got another thought coming. When I get through with you, sir, you are going to remember Mrs. Luella Bates Washington Jones."

Sweat popped out on the boy's face and he began to struggle. Mrs. Jones stopped, jerked him around in front of her, put a half nelson[1] about his neck, and continued to drag him up the street. When she got to her door, she dragged the boy inside, down a hall, and into a large kitchenette-furnished room at the rear of the house. She switched on the light and left the door open. The boy could hear other roomers laughing and talking in the large house. Some of their doors were open, too, so he knew he and the woman were not alone. The woman still had him by the neck in the middle of her room. **E**

She said, "What is your name?"

"Roger," answered the boy.

"Then, Roger, you go to that sink and wash your face," said the woman, whereupon she turned him loose—at last. Roger looked at the door—looked at the woman—looked at the door—*and went to the sink.*

"Let the water run until it gets warm," she said. "Here's a clean towel."

"You gonna take me to jail?" asked the boy, bending over the sink.

"Not with that face, I would not take you nowhere," said the woman. "Here I am trying to get home to cook me a bite to eat and you snatch my pocketbook! Maybe you ain't been to your supper either, late as it be. Have you?"

"There's nobody home at my house," said the boy.

"Then we'll eat," said the woman. "I believe you're hungry—or been hungry—to try to snatch my pocketbook."

"I wanted a pair of blue suede shoes,"[2] said the boy.

"Well, you didn't have to snatch *my* pocketbook to get some suede shoes," said Mrs. Luella Bates Washington Jones. "You could of asked me." **F**

"M'am?"

The water dripping from his face, the boy looked at her. There was a long pause. A very long pause. After he had dried his face and not knowing what else to do dried it again, the boy turned around, wondering what next. The door was open. He could make a dash for it down the hall. He could run, run, run, run, *run*!

The woman was sitting on the daybed.[3] After a while she said, "I were young once and I wanted things I could not get."

There was another long pause. The boy's mouth opened. Then he frowned, but not knowing he frowned.

The woman said, "Um-hum! You thought I was going to say *but*, didn't you? You thought I was going to say, *but I didn't snatch people's pocketbooks*. Well, I wasn't going to say that." Pause. Silence. "I have done things, too, which I would not tell **G**

1. A *half nelson* is a wrestling hold made from behind by hooking one arm under the opponent's arm and pressing the hand across the back of the opponent's neck.

2. *Blue suede shoes* are men's shoes made of velvety soft leather. These shoes became popular for a time in the late 1950s after Elvis Presley recorded a hit song called "Blue Suede Shoes."

3. A *daybed* is a sofa that can be converted into a bed.

E Active Reading Strategies

QUESTION Ask students why Mrs. Jones leaves her door open. Is she showing the boy she trusts him? Or does she want to be able to summon her neighbors easily? *(Given what the reader knows about Mrs. Jones, it is likely that she wants to increase the boy's trustworthiness by acting as if he were trustworthy.)*

F Literary Elements

CHARACTERIZATION Ask students why they think Mrs. Jones tells the boy he should simply have asked for the shoes. What does that statement say about her? What does it say about what she wants to teach him? *(Mrs. Jones doesn't want him to feel so uncared for that he grows up believing he has to steal.)*

G Critical Thinking

EVALUATING Ask students to evaluate the effectiveness of Mrs. Jones's approach to Roger. How important is it that she acknowledges that she has "done things too"?

Model: I think that Mrs. Jones wants to teach Roger a lesson and discourage him from turning to a life of crime. She is aware that scolding him will probably not have much effect. Admitting that she felt as he does, wanted nice things, and even made mistakes demonstrates her understanding of the boy. The boy trusts her because she shares his feelings.

Reading Minilesson

Cause and Effect A key reading and thinking skill is the ability to perceive clearly the relationship between cause and effect. In literature, the relationship is not as clear as it is in pure logic. Often a single effect will have many causes, and the opposite is also true.

Activity Ask students to review the story and try to determine as many possible causes for Roger's attempting to steal Mrs. Jones's purse and for Mrs. Jones's helping him.

Additional Resources

Reading Skills Practice Workbook

H Literary Elements

CHARACTERIZATION What does Mrs. Jones's not asking Roger personal questions tell the reader about her character? Is it important that she calls him "son"? *(She understands what Roger needs and tries to make him feel accepted.)*

I Active Reading Strategies

PREDICT How will Roger behave in the future? Hughes leaves his story open-ended. Is there any reason to conclude that Roger will behave himself differently in the future? *(The boy now has someone who cares about him and believes in him; it is likely such trust will inspire him to live differently.)*

Thematic Focus

Lean on Me Discuss with students how this story connects to the theme. Do they think Mrs. Jones is someone Roger will always remember for the help she gave him?

ASSESSMENT

Quick Checks, p. 13

Teaching Support

Thank You, M'am

you, son—neither tell God, if he didn't already know. So you set down while I fix us something to eat. You might run that comb through your hair so you will look presentable."

> He did not trust the woman *not* to trust him. And he did not want to be mistrusted now.

In another corner of the room behind a screen was a gas plate and an icebox. Mrs. Jones got up and went behind the screen. The woman did not watch the boy to see if he was going to run now, nor did she watch her purse which she left behind her on the daybed. But the boy took care to sit on the far side of the room where he thought she could easily see him out of the corner of her eye, if she wanted to. He did not trust the woman *not* to trust him. And he did not want to be mistrusted now.

"Do you need somebody to go to the store," asked the boy, "maybe to get some milk or something?"

"Don't believe I do," said the woman, "unless you just want sweet milk yourself. I was going to make cocoa out of this canned milk I got here."

"That will be fine," said the boy.

She heated some lima beans and ham she had in the icebox, made the cocoa, and set the table. The woman did not ask the boy anything about where he lived, or his folks, or anything else that would embarrass him. Instead, as they ate, she told him about her job in a hotel beauty shop that stayed open late, what the work was like, and how all kinds of women came in and out, blondes, red-heads, and Spanish. Then she cut him a half of her ten-cent cake.

"Eat some more, son," she said.

When they were finished eating she got up and said, "Now, here, take this ten dollars and buy yourself some blue suede shoes. And next time, do not make the mistake of latching onto *my* pocketbook *nor nobody else's*—because shoes come by devilish like that will burn your feet. I got to get my rest now. But I wish you would behave yourself, son, from here on in."

She led him down the hall to the front door and opened it. "Goodnight! Behave yourself, boy!" she said, looking out into the street.

The boy wanted to say something else other than, "Thank you, m'am," to Mrs. Luella Bates Washington Jones, but he couldn't do so as he turned at the barren stoop and looked back at the large woman in the door. He barely managed to say, "Thank you," before she shut the door. And he never saw her again.

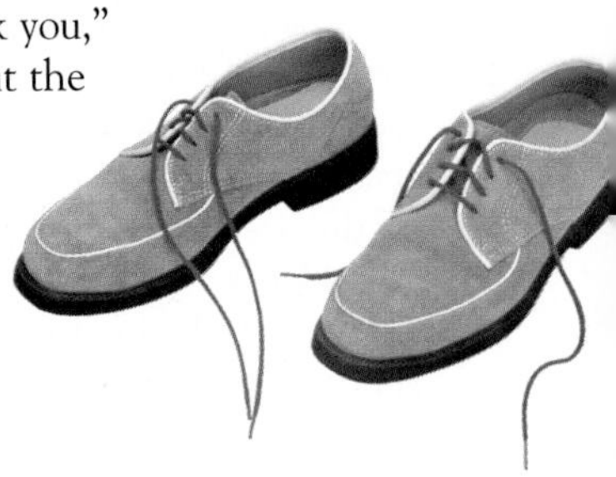

Vocabulary

barren (bar′ ən) *adj.* bare; empty; dull or uninteresting

Grammar and Language *Minilesson*

End Punctuation and Quotation Marks

Write these sentences on the board: *You might run that comb through your hair so you will look presentable. "That will be fine," said the boy. Behave yourself, boy!* Present these rules for end punctuation and quotation marks: Periods and commas always go inside; colons and semicolons never go inside: and question marks and exclamation points go inside if they are part of the question or exclamation.

Activity Ask students to find five direct quotations from the story, copy the final sentences of each quotation, and explain how the end punctuation is handled. **L2**

Additional Resources

- ***Grammar and Language Transparency 12***
- ***Grammar and Language Workbook,*** p. 267
- ***Grammar and Composition Handbook,*** Lessons 13.1, 13.6
- ***Writer's Choice,*** Lesson 20.6

Responding to Literature

PERSONAL RESPONSE

- Were you surprised by the ending of this story? Why or why not?
- Which lines from the story will you remember? Why?

Analyzing Literature

RECALL AND INTERPRET

1. What does Mrs. Jones tell Roger he should have done to get the blue suede shoes he wants? Does Mrs. Jones seem to be a wealthy woman? Give details to support your answer.
2. How does Roger behave when he is in Mrs. Jones's room? Why, in your opinion, does Roger decide to stay there?
3. What does Mrs. Jones tell Roger when he leaves her building? How do you know that she has made an impression on Roger?

EVALUATE AND CONNECT

4. Of the adjectives *honest, generous, gullible,* and *mean,* which describe Mrs. Jones? Defend your choices.
5. After reading the story, would you say that Roger is trustworthy? Why or why not? Support your answer with examples and with information you wrote for the **Reading Focus** on page 160.
6. Do you find the characters in "Thank You, M'am" realistic? Cite examples from the text to explain your answer.

LITERARY ELEMENTS

Characterization

Characterization includes all the methods an author uses to develop a character. In "Thank You, M'am," Langston Hughes provides direct information about the characters. He also lets their words and actions reveal their personalities.

1. What traits does Mrs. Jones demonstrate when she drags Roger up the street?
2. Mrs. Jones says, "I were young once and I wanted things I could not get." What do these words reveal?
3. Find a quotation and an action that shows an important trait in Roger's personality.

● See **Literary Terms Handbook,** p. R2.

Extending Your Response

Literature Groups

Crime and Punishment Did Roger's punishment fit his crime? Debate the issue with your group. As you develop the thesis of your debate, consider these questions: Was Roger punished? If so, how? What did Mrs. Jones hope to accomplish when she brought him home? What effect did her actions have on him? Support your points with evidence from the story.

Writing About Literature

Setting Write a paragraph or two explaining the importance of setting to the story. Think about these questions as you write: What does Mrs. Jones's home reveal about her life? How would the story be different if the events had all taken place on the street? How does the setting affect the mood, tone, and meaning of the story?

Responding to the Selection

PERSONAL RESPONSE

Students should support their responses with examples.

Analyzing Literature

1. She tells him he should have asked. She does not seem wealthy; people who live in rooming houses usually don't have much money.
2. Roger is well behaved. Some students will suggest that he stays in the room because he is fascinated by Mrs. Jones; others may say he is afraid to try to leave.
3. Mrs. Jones tells Roger to behave himself. She has made an impression because he thanks her.
4. Mrs. Jones seems honest and generous; she has little but is still willing to feed the boy and offer him money for shoes.
5. Roger seems eager to earn Mrs. Jones's trust. Students might note that people often live up to the positive expectations of others.
6. The characters seem realistic. Roger in particular seems unsure of how to handle himself in such an unlikely situation.

Extending Your Response

Literature Groups Point out that the question of how to handle crimes committed by young people is part of a national debate. COLLAB. LEARN.

Writing About Literature

Students' responses should

- answer the two questions posed in the assignment
- use specific details and examples to support generalizations

LITERARY ELEMENTS

1. She is strong, determined, and angry.
2. They reveal her empathy for Roger.
3. When Mrs. Jones tells Roger he could have asked her for shoes, he replies, "M'am?" with "water dripping off his face." This shows surprise; he is not accustomed to generosity. His use of "M'am" shows courtesy.

Additional Resources

Literary Elements Transparency 13

ASSESSMENT

- ***Quick Checks,*** p. 13
- ***Selection and Theme Assessment,*** p. 23
- ***Performance Assessment,*** p. 12
- ***Testmaker: ExamView Pro***
- ***Interactive Tutor: Self-Assessment***

COMPARING *selections*

Objective

- To compare two short stories about boys on the verge of serious trouble

COMPARE **SETTINGS**

1. The urban setting is essential to the action of "Thank You, M'am." Purse snatchings happen less frequently in small towns where people know one another. In "The Kid Nobody Could Handle," Jim Donnini would have been one tough kid among many if the story had been set in a city.
2. In a contemporary setting, the adults might hesitate to help the boys; troubled youths today might seem more menacing.

COMPARE **SYMBOLS**

Ask students to include their own experience in the discussion. Do shoes have symbolic value in the lives of some young people now?
COLLAB. LEARN.

Additional Resources

Literature Groups Sourcebook

COMPARE **CHARACTERS**

1. Students' paragraphs should take a clear stand and explain why students think one approach is better than the other.
2. Students' journal entries should focus on the key ideas discussed in the encounter.

Teaching Support

Critical Thinking

COMPARING SELECTIONS

The Kid Nobody Could Handle **and** Thank You, M'am

COMPARE **SETTINGS**

The City from Greenwich Village, 1922 (detail).

"The Kid Nobody Could Handle" and "Thank You, M'am" take place in the mid-1900s.

1. How does the urban setting of "Thank You, M'am" help determine the action of the story? In what ways does the small-town setting of "The Kid Nobody Could Handle" make Jim Donnini stand out to the other characters?
2. How might the settings of both stories be different if they took place in the present? How might the new settings affect the characters and their actions?

COMPARE **SYMBOLS**

In "Thank You, M'am," Roger was willing to steal so that he could buy a pair of blue suede shoes. In "The Kid Nobody Could Handle," Jim's prized possession was a pair of big black boots. With a small group, compare the importance of the shoes in each story. Consider the following questions: What did the shoes mean to each boy? What did they mean to Mrs. Jones and George Helmholtz? What does "walking in another person's shoes" mean for each story?

COMPARE **CHARACTERS**

In both stories the main character faces a similar challenge or conflict—how to help a young person on the verge of serious trouble.

1. Compare the approaches of Mrs. Jones and George Helmholtz. How do you account for the success of each approach? Would you favor one approach over the other? Why? List the pros and cons for each approach. Then write a paragraph explaining which approach you think is more successful.
2. Suppose that George Helmholtz met Mrs. Jones. What might happen at their meeting? What advice or experiences might they share? Write a journal entry by one or the other, describing this encounter.

PORTFOLIO OPTIONS

Select and Reflect Have students reflect on their analyses for the first activity under Compare Characters by asking themselves these questions:

- Does my analysis reflect a thoughtful response to the issues?
- Why do I prefer one approach? What does my preference say about me?

Students should clip their reflections to their analyses and place them in their portfolios. At a later time, they may consider using the comments to revise their analyses as portfolio showcase pieces.

Additional Resources

Writing Assessment and Portfolio Management, pp. 41–47

GRAMMAR LINK

Avoiding Run-on Sentences

A **simple sentence** consists of a main clause–a group of words with both a subject and a verb. A **run-on sentence** can occur when two or more main clauses are combined without correct punctuation.

Problem 1 Two main clauses with no punctuation between them
The boy grabbed the woman's purse the strap broke.

Solution A Separate the main clauses into two sentences.
The boy grabbed the woman's purse. The strap broke.

Solution B Separate the main clauses with a comma and a conjunction.
The boy grabbed the woman's purse, and the strap broke.

Solution C Separate the main clauses with a semicolon.
The boy grabbed the woman's purse; the strap broke.

Problem 2 Main clauses joined by only a comma
Mrs. Jones leaves the door open, Roger doesn't run away.

Solution Add a conjunction after the comma.
Mrs. Jones leaves the door open, but Roger doesn't run away.

Problem 3 Main clauses joined by only a conjunction
Roger wants blue suede shoes and Mrs. Jones seems to understand.

Solution Add a comma before the conjunction.
Roger wants blue suede shoes, and Mrs. Jones seems to understand.

• For more about run-on sentences, see **Language Handbook,** p. R12.

EXERCISE

Write *S* if the sentence is correct. If it is a run-on sentence, rewrite the sentence to correct it. (There is often more than one way to correct a run-on sentence.)

1. Helmholtz is a good-hearted man he tries to be kind to Jim.
2. Jim is unfriendly and rude, Helmholtz is determined to get through to him.
3. Helmholtz finds Jim destroying property and the sight makes him feel sick.
4. Jim's boots seem to represent his attitude; without them, he behaves differently.

GRAMMAR LINK

Objective

- To learn to recognize and correct run-on sentences

Teaching Strategies

Have students identify the subject and predicate in each of the sample sentences so they learn to recognize when two or more main clauses are run together.

Exercise

1. Helmholtz is a good-hearted man; he tries to be kind to Jim.
2. Jim is unfriendly and rude, but Helmholtz is determined to get through to him.
3. Helmholtz finds Jim destroying property, and the sight makes him feel sick.
4. S

Additional Resources

- ***Grammar and Language Workbook,*** pp. 26–27, 57
- ***Grammar and Composition Handbook,*** Lesson 1.6
- ***Writer's Choice,*** Lesson 7.2

Teaching Support

Writing *Minilesson*

Creating a Convincing Character
Sometimes authors describe character traits, but allowing characters reveal themselves through their speech and actions is more effective. Write this sentence on the board: *Mary was a self-pitying person.* Ask students for ideas that would show Mary as a self-pitying person. Give the following example: *Mary dabbed her eyes with a tissue and said with a quivering chin, "No one has any idea how much I have to endure."*

Activity Have each student write a paragraph describing someone through that person's actions and words. Students may read their paragraphs to one another and guess which qualities they tried to reflect. **L2**

Additional Resources

- ***Writer's Choice,*** Lesson 4.5

Before Reading

Objectives

- To read and analyze a story
- To understand how a narrative strategy affects the reader's perception of a story
- To write a paragraph about setting

Skills

Reading/Thinking: Inferring; Sequence of Events; Visualizing
Writing: Paragraph About Setting; Video Dialogue; Letter to the Editor
Vocabulary: The Prefix *co-*
Grammar/Language: Sentence Fragments; Words Ending in *-ly*
Listening/Speaking: Literature Groups
Life Skills: Letter to the Editor
Collaboration: Literature Groups

Motivating STUDENTS

Selection Focus Transparency 13: Before presenting the photographs, discuss how environment affects a person's mood.

Reading Focus: As an extension of the Reading Focus, ask each student to interview an older relative or friend about changes that have occurred since he or she was young. Then students should discuss their findings in small groups.

Before You Read

The Journey

MEET PATRICIA PRECIADO MARTIN

Patricia Preciado Martin (prä sē ä′ dō mär tēn′) says her stories are "a verbal quilt of my mexicana life experiences sewn together with the fragile threads of love . . ." Instead of sewing bits of multicolored fabric, she pieces together her "personal and collective memories, impressions, observations, visions, inspirations, and *milagros* [miracles]." Martin has been a teacher in the Peace Corps, is active in the Mexican American community, and is the mother of two adult children.

Patricia Preciado Martin has been a resident of Tucson, Arizona, all her life. "The Journey" was first published in 1980 in La Confluencia.

READING FOCUS

How do people in your family view the past and changes that have occurred since they were young?

Chart It!

Using a chart like the one below, write names of friends or family members and their ways of looking at the past.

Grandma Brennan	Lives in Florida now, but she loves to tell stories about growing up in a bungalow in Chicago in the time of streetcars.

Setting a Purpose

Read to discover how two different generations see the same city.

BUILDING BACKGROUND

The Time and Place This contemporary story is set in Tucson, which has a large Hispanic population. There are many Spanish words and phrases in this story, and most are followed immediately by their English translations.

Did You Know? In the 1950s, many city residents moved to the suburbs, forcing downtown merchants out of business. Years later, businesses and residents returned to abandoned downtowns, giving these areas a new look. For many people, visiting the places where they grew up means looking at a garage or strip mall where homes once stood.

VOCABULARY PREVIEW

drone (drōn) *v.* to talk in a dull, monotonous tone or make a steady, low, humming sound; p. 170
primly (prim′ lē) *adv.* in a formal, proper way; p. 170
laboriously (lə bôr′ ē əs lē) *adv.* with great effort; p. 171
renovate (ren′ ə vāt′) *v.* to make like new; p. 173
patriarch (pā′ trē ärk′) *n.* the male head of a family; p. 173
laden (lād′ən) *adj.* loaded; weighed down; burdened; p. 173
distinct (dis tingkt′) *adj.* clearly heard, seen, or felt; p. 173

RESOURCE MANAGER

Teaching Tools and Resources
- Theme Two Planning Guide
- Literature Groups Sourcebook

Essential Lesson Support

Lesson-Specific Instruction
- Selection Focus Transparency 13
- Literary Elements Transparency 14
- Active Reading Guide,* p. 14
- Selection Vocabulary Practice, p. 13

Assessment
- Selection Quick Checks,* p. 14
- Sel. and Theme Assmt., p. 24
- Testmaker: ExamView Pro
- Performance Assessment, p. 13

Systematic Language Instruction
- Gr. & Comp. Hbk., L. 3.5

English Language Learners
- ELL Sourcebook, p. 33
- Spanish Summaries, p. 13
- Spanish Translations, pp. 53–56
- Audio Library*
- English, Yes!

Spec. Needs/Strat. Interven.
- Interactive Rdg. Sbk., pp. T78–T81
- Interactive Rdg. Wbk., pp. 31–32
- Audio Library*

* Also available in Spanish

The Journey

Patricia Preciado Martin

In the warm and sun-filled days
I remember in the haze
The happy sounds of children laughing,
The rustle of the cottonwoods.
Now all is old and cold and dark
Underneath Presidio Park.

The bell rings, the bus slows, and finally stops. I get off at the corner of Fifth and Congress. One North Fifth Avenue. The MARTIN LUTHER KING JR. APARTMENTS. LOW COST HOUSING FOR THE ELDERLY. Gray concrete walls five stories high. Honorable Mayor James M. Corbett, Jr. Honorable Councilmen Richard Kennedy, Kirk Storch, Conrad Joyner, Rudy Castro, and John Steiger. *Anno Domini*[1] 1969. [A]

1. The Latin term *Anno Domini* (an′ ō dom′ i nī′), or its abbreviation, A.D., means "year of the Lord," and refers to dates since the birth of Jesus Christ.

Reading the Selection

SUMMARY

A woman takes her elderly aunt on a weekly outing in her hometown of Tucson, Arizona. As they travel their usual route, the younger woman pays particular attention to the sights and sounds of the town. The older woman travels backward in time as she walks, until the journey ends at the place where she grew up, much changed but still full of memories for her.

Spanish Summaries, p. 13

[A] Active Reading Strategies

QUESTION Point out that Martin's style is different from many of the authors students have read thus far. Ask them what they notice about how she writes. *(She repeats, uses sentence fragments, and relates what she sees and thinks moment to moment.)*

VOCABULARY Remind students to use context clues to unlock the meanings of new vocabulary words.

Additional Resources

Active Reading Guide, p. 14

Audio Library

Spanish Audio Library

Teaching Support

CONNECTING TO OTHER SELECTIONS

The chart at the right shows three ways to connect "The Journey" to other selections in this book.

For specific teaching strategies, see the ***Theme Two Planning Guide***.

Connection		Title
Life Skills: Lifelong Learning	→	"The Black Walnut Tree," p. 299
Thematic: Reflections of the Past	→	"The Medicine Bag," p. 78
Literary: Style	→	"Chanclas," p. 71

B Literary Elements

NARRATION Ask students why they think Martin includes such things as the titles of magazine stories and signs outside the elevator. *(Each detail becomes part of the atmosphere of the story—of the place where Tía lives and of the city itself.)*

C Active Reading Strategies

QUESTION What impact does the frequent use of Spanish have on the story? *(The use of Spanish emphasizes the fact that the experiences and memories Martin portrays are deeply influenced by Hispanic culture.)*

D Critical Thinking

INFERRING Martin says, "We begin our walk; our journey." What can you infer from her calling the walk a journey? *(Because a journey is a long trip, the walk may take us farther than we expect.)*

Teaching Support

I go through the double-wide glass doors of the apartment building. (ENTER HERE ONLY.) Electronically operated. The high-ceilinged waiting room is painted bright yellow (to make it seem cheerful). The room is bare except for a few weatherbeaten chairs and scarred coffee tables cluttered with tattered magazines. GOOD HOUSEKEEPING—"Decorate A Bedroom With Sheets." U.S. NEWS AND WORLD REPORT—"The Effect of Arab Oil Prices on Wall Street." COSMOPOLITAN—"How To Tell If Your Husband Is Faithful." The black-and-white TV drones on, addressing no one in particular. The elevator clanks along noisily. (UP: DOWN: PRESS BUTTON ONLY ONCE.) A few viejitos[2] are coming and going with purpose. Some are waiting for the mail. Some are waiting for visitors. Some are just waiting.

And Tía[3] is there, as always. Every Saturday. Summer or winter, spring or fall, for the last two years. Except when the weather is too cold or too wet. It can never be too hot. Her small delicate figure is nearly lost in the big overstuffed chair (Donated by the Cochran Family; In Memory of Our Son, Lawrence, Jr.; Cochran Realty and Investments). Tía is waiting for me. Quietly, primly, regally, her hands folded in her lap. She is wearing a shawl and a small knit hat. A flowered print dress and black stockings and shoes.

"Ah, mihijita, ya llegaste."[4] I take her arm, and she rises to her feet, not without difficulty. On one arm she carries a straw bag, and on the other a worn black umbrella (just in case). We walk slowly out the wide glass doors (EXIT HERE ONLY) into the late morning sunshine.

"Qué bueno que llegaste temprano. Tengo mucho que hacer, y la tienda está lejos. It is good that you arrived early. I have a lot to do, and the store is far away."

We begin our walk; our journey. Every Saturday she insists on taking the same route. Across town. Down Congress Street. Past the Regal Cigar Store (MAGAZINES, CIGARS, NOVELTIES). Past the Discount Clothing City (GANGAS HOY! 60 DAYS TO PAY! SE HABLA ESPAÑOL). Past the empty store windows with the dusty, limbless mannequins.[5] We walk slowly, without talking. We turn on South Sixth Avenue and go south, past the numerous bars and liquor stores. A hippie plays a guitar for quarters in front of the O.K. Bar. We walk past Armory Park. Winter visitors are playing shuffleboard in the sunshine and winos are sleeping in the grass. On Ochoa Street we turn west again and walk toward the

2. In Spanish, *viejitos* (vē′ ə hē′ tōs) means "old people."
3. *Tía* (tē′ ə) is Spanish for "aunt."
4. "My little girl, now you've arrived."
5. The sign reads, "BARGAINS TODAY! . . . SPANISH SPOKEN." *Mannequins* (man′ i kins) are dummies used to display clothes for sale.

Vocabulary
drone (drōn) *v.* to talk in a dull, monotonous tone or make a steady, low, humming sound
primly (prim′ lē) *adv.* in a formal, proper way

MEETING INDIVIDUAL NEEDS — ENGLISH LANGUAGE LEARNERS

Hispanic Heritage This story deals with a time, a place, and people deeply influenced by Hispanic heritage. Point out to students the many elements of Hispanic culture that permeate the story. Religion, language, foods, architecture, and music are all mentioned.

Activity Have students who are native speakers of Spanish discuss with the rest of the class their reading of the story. To what extent does this story reflect their own heritage? Also discuss the use of present tense throughout the selection. **L1**

Additional Resources

English Language Learners Sourcebook, p. 33

gleaming white towers of the Cathedral. San Agustín. The Dove of the Desert.[6] The pigeons flutter over our heads when the noon bells chime. Sr. Enríquez, the old bell chimer, died long ago. He climbed the rickety stairs to the bell tower three times a day for more years than anyone could remember. One day he climbed up and played the Noon Angelus[7] and never climbed down again. They found him with the bell rope still in his hands. Now the Angelus is a recorded announcement.

Tía laboriously climbs the concrete steps to the vestibule[8] of the Cathedral. I open the heavy carved doors for her and she makes her way into the cool darkness. The perfume of the incense from the early morning funeral Mass still lingers in the air.

(Sra. Juanita Mendoza. Born in Tucson of a Pioneer Family, Grandmother Eight Children. Twelve Grandchildren. Seven Great-Grandchildren.)

Down, down, the long corridor Tía walks until she reaches the side chapel of the Virgen de Guadalupe. La Madre de Nosotros. La Reina de Las Américas.[9] She lights a small vigil candle and prays for the souls of husbands and brothers and sons. The ones who have died or lost their souls in Los Angeles. Father Carrillo walks by, intent on something. Cuentas and almas. Bills and souls. El Padre.[10] Son of Barrio Anita. The pride of the people. "Y cómo estás, Doña Luz?"[11] He grasps her hand warmly.

We walk out once more into the brightness. Past an elegant old home that is now a funeral parlor. Down South Meyer and west on Cushing Street. Past a sign that says Barrio Histórico. THIS AREA HAS BEEN OFFICIALLY DESIGNATED AS AN HISTORICAL LANDMARK AND IS OFFICIALLY REGISTERED WITH THE NATIONAL REGISTER OF HISTORICAL PLACES. In bronze. Most of the houses in the Barrio Histórico are owned by Mr. Kelly Rollings, a local automobile dealer and millionaire and amateur anthropologist.[12] He owns the old Robles House. It is now the Cushing Street Bar. "EAT, DRINK AND BE MERRY IN AN AUTHENTIC RESTORED OLD ADOBE."

"That's where the Robles' lived," Tía tells me, in Spanish. "They had a piano. The Señora played beautifully. Everyone would come to listen. People would leave flowers on her doorstep." She continued. "On Sundays we would all walk down for

6. Saint Augustine (the English spelling) is sometimes called "Dove of the Desert" because he was born near the Sahara in northern Africa in A.D. 354.
7. In some churches, a bell is rung at morning, noon, and night to signal the time for saying a special prayer called, in Latin, the *Angelus* (an′ jə ləs).
8. A *vestibule* (ves′ tə būl′) is a small entrance hall.
9. These are names for Mary, the mother of Jesus Christ.
10. The people are proud of their priest (*El Padre*, "the Father") because he is from their neighborhood (*barrio*).
11. *Sr.* and *Sra.* are abbreviations for *Señor* (sen yôr′) and *Señora*, (sen yôr′ ə) like *Mr.* and *Mrs.* in English. *Don* (don) or *Doña* (dōn′ yə) before a person's first name is a title of respect for an acquaintance or employer.
12. An *anthropologist* studies humans and their cultures.

Vocabulary
laboriously (lə bôr′ ē əs lē) *adv.* with great effort

E Active Reading Strategies

REVIEW Ask students who Sra. Juanita Mendoza is. *(She is the person whose funeral has just been solemnized.)*

F Literary Elements

NARRATION The author presents several names for the Virgin Mary. Ask students how this kind of repetition affects the reader. *(The repetition emphasizes the importance of the Virgin Mary in Hispanic culture.)*

G Active Reading Strategies

CONNECT Ask students how Tía's memory of the Robles house contrasts with its current use. *(The home seems almost to represent to Tía the epitome of Hispanic family life—filled with people, music, flowers, and love. Now it is a bar.)*

LITERATURE & HUMANITIES

Using the *National Museum of Women in the Arts* CD, encourage students to examine the photograph "From Generation to Generation," and consider the significance of the title. Then discuss kinds of things that are passed from one generation to the next and how the photographer communicates this idea.

Reading Minilesson

Sequence of Events Some students may be confused by the switch of focus from the present to the past. It may be helpful to them to slow down and pay particular attention to when and how the focus changes.

Activity Have students read through this story and make a two-column list. On the left side they should list the characteristics of Tuscon today; on the right they should list the characteristics of the Tuscon that existed when Tía was young. **L2**

Additional Resources

Reading Skills Practice Workbook

VIEWING THE PAINTING

Emil Bisttram was born in Hungary, but from the time he first visited New Mexico in 1930, he became completely committed to painting the people and scenery of the Southwest.

Viewing Response *The woman seems to be a person of great self-possession and dignity.*

H Active Reading Strategies

QUESTION Ask students why they think Tía keeps repeating "Can you believe that the Santa Cruz had water?!" *(It gives the impression that the women are walking along the banks of what was the river—and that one of the most negative changes over the years is the destruction of the river.)*

the Paseo[13] in the Plaza of the Cathedral. Sometimes we would walk down to the river. (It had water then! G Can you believe that the Santa Cruz had water?!) In the summers we would picnic under the cool shade of the cottonwood trees. Everywhere there was music."

We continue south on Convent Street. Mr. Ortega is sitting on his porch. He pays his rent now to Coldwell and Banker, based in New York. "Buenas Tardes, Doña Luz." "Buenas Tardes, Don Felipe." We walk on slowly. Tía continues. "His father and his grandfather had tierras by the river. Everywhere it was green. They grew flowers and vegetables. And oh! The flowers! The perfume was everywhere in the summer breezes. His father, Don Raimundo, sold vegetables from a cart. All of us children would run after the cart. He gave us free sugar cane. Now the river is dry. The milpas[14] are gone and the people are gone. H (The river had water then! Can you believe that the Santa Cruz had water?!)

13. Here, the *Paseo* (pə sä′ ō) is a stroll that many people took after church services.
14. *"Buenas Tardes"* (bwā′ nəs tär′ des) means "Good afternoon." *Tierras* (tyer′ əs) are gardens or small fields, and *milpas* (mēl′ pəs) are fields, usually of corn.

Comadre Rafaelita, 1934. Emil J. Bisttram. Oil on canvas, 72 x 44 in. The Anschutz Collection, Denver, CO.

Viewing the painting: What do the woman's pose and her setting tell you about her way of life? How does it compare with that of Tía?

Teaching Support

MEETING INDIVIDUAL NEEDS — SPECIAL NEEDS

Learning Disabled The style of this story may be somewhat confusing to some students, since it is nonlinear, structured as a series of impressions held together by the old aunt's journey. A good analogy for this story's style is a collage—a grouping of related pictures and objects that form a single impression. Sometimes it is easier to comprehend a visual collage than a literary one.

Activity Ask students to create collages that represent their homes or neighborhoods. Have them present and explain their collages to the class. Invite classmates to evaluate how the collages communicate information. What impressions might they give to people unfamiliar with the subject? **L1**

Additional Resources

Inclusion Strategies

The Freeway had cut the river from the people. The Freeway blocks the sunshine. The drone of the traffic buzzes like a giant unsleeping bee. A new music in the barrio.

On down South Convent. Past the old Padilla House. THIS HOUSE IS A REGISTERED HISTORICAL LANDMARK. In brass. It is being renovated. The sign has gone up. LOS ARCOS. ANTIQUES, PRIMITIVES,[15] AND COLLECTIBLES.

At last we arrive at our destination. Romero's Convent Street Market. Tía opens the screen door. RAINBOW BREAD IS GOOD. Rafael Romero. Patriarch of the Barrio. Mr. Rollings has offered him a good price. Mr. Romero has no price, but he has no sons either. "Buenas Tardes, Doña Luz." "Buenas Tardes, Don Rafael." Tía fills her bag. The ancient cash register rings and whirs metallically. Queso blanco. Salsa de tomate. Campbell's Chicken Noodle Soup. White bread. Tortillas de maíz. Tortillas de harina. Cheerios. Pan Mexicano. Coffee. Saladitos[16] for me. "Gracias, Doña Luz. Hasta luego."

Then around the corner. Down South Main. I follow unquestioning. I know that the journey is not over. There is always one more destination. Toward the Tucson Community Center Complex. The Pride of Tucson. MUSIC HALL. LITTLE THEATRE, CONVENTION HALL. CONCERT ARENA. URBAN RENEWAL. Honorable Mayor James M. Corbett, Jr. Honorable Councilmen William Ruck, Ramon Castillo, Richard Kennedy, Robert Royal, and Conrad Joyner, *Anno Domini* 1971. Concrete walls, and steps, and fountains. Fountains, fountains, everywhere. (The river had water then! Can you believe that the Santa Cruz had water?!)

The pace of Tía quickens now. I follow her, carrying the straw bag laden with groceries. We walk past the Concert Hall to the vast parking lot of the Community Center Complex. A billboard reads: CONCERT TONIGHT. ALICE COOPER.[17] SOLD OUT. We stop in the middle of the parking lot. The winter sun is warm. The heat rises from the black asphalt. The roar of the Freeway is even more distinct. It is the end of the journey. I know what Tía will say.

"Aquí estaba mi casita. It was my father's house. And his father's house before that. They built it with their own hands with adobes made from the mud of the river. All their children were born here. I was born here. It was a good house, a strong house. When it rained, the adobes smelled like the good clean earth."

15. *Los Arcos*, or The Arches, is the shop name. *Primitives* are folk art, works of art with a simple style.

16. Tía's groceries include white cheese (*queso blanco*), tomato sauce (*salsa*), bread (*pan*), and little salted snacks (*saladitos*).

17. *Alice Cooper* is a rock performer who was very popular in the 1970s.

Vocabulary

renovate (ren′ ə vāt′) *v.* to make like new
patriarch (pā′ trē ärk′) *n.* the male head of a family
laden (lād′ ən) *adj.* loaded; weighed down; burdened
distinct (dis tingkt′) *adj.* clearly heard, seen, or felt

I Critical Thinking

INFERRING Ask students what they can infer about the symbolism of the freeway. Share the following model:

Model: To me, the freeway seems to be a symbol of all the negative changes that have occurred in the barrio. Tía states all of the negative things the freeway has caused.

J Active Reading Strategies

QUESTION Why does the narrator call Tía's father's house "the end of the journey"? *(Clearly Tía takes the same route each time, traveling back in time to her own childhood. It is this long-ago destination that makes Tía's trip a journey.)*

Real-World Connection

Old Buildings Have each student research the history of a local building that is a hundred or more years old. How have the appearance and use of the building changed over the years? Have them gather important dates and, if possible, quotations from a local historian. They should parahrase and summarize their research and present it to the class. **L2**

interNET CONNECTION

Have students explore the FDA's Web site, www.fda.gov. By learning how to read the nutritional information labels on foods, they can compare the foods they buy to see which are the healthiest. **L2**

K Author's Craft

WORD CHOICE Ask students whether they think there might be a double meaning to Tía's statement, "Ya es tarde," which means, "It is late." *(There is a suggestion that it is too late now—that the past is gone and cannot be retrieved.)*

L Literary Elements

THEME Ensure that students understand that Tía's statement is central to the meaning of the story. She is suggesting that beauty can still be found.

Thematic Focus

Lean on Me Discuss with students the interdependence the two characters experience. The old woman depends on her niece for help in her journey. The younger woman depends on her aunt for the nostalgic journey back to the past.

ASSESSMENT

Quick Checks, p. 14

FINE ART TRANSPARENCY 9

You may want to use ***Fine Art Transparency 9*** to discuss sights, smells, sounds, and tastes that trigger students' memories of the past.

She pauses. She sees shadows I cannot see. She hears melodies I cannot hear. "See, here! I had a fig tree growing. In the summer I gave figs to the neighbors and the birds. And there—I hung a clay olla with water to sip from on the hot summer days. We always had a breeze from the river. I had a bougainvillea; it was so beautiful! Brilliant red. And I had roses and a little garden. Right here where I am standing my comadres[18] and I would sit and visit in the evenings. We would watch the children run and play in the streets. There was no traffic then. And there was laughter everywhere."

K "Ah, well," she sighs. "Ya es tarde. It is time to go." I turn to follow her and then turn to look once more to the place where her casita once stood. I look across the parking lot. I look down. "Tía, Tía," I call. "Ven!" She turns and comes toward me. "Look!" I say excitedly. "There is a flower that has pushed its way through the asphalt! It is blooming!"

"Ah, mihijita," she says at last. Her eyes are shining. "You have found out the secret of our journeys."

"What secret, Tía?"

"Que las flores siempre ganan. The flowers always win." L

We turn away from the sun that is beginning to drop in the West. I take her arm again. There is music everywhere.

Refrain

ABUELITA, ABUELITA,
ABUELITA, NO LLORES.
TE TRAIGO, TE TRAIGO,
TE TRAIGO
UNA RAMITA DE FLORES.[19]

18. An *olla* (ō′ yə) is a pot with a handle. *Bougainvillea* (bo͞o′ gən vil′ ē ə) is a shrub or vine with brilliant purple or red flowers. Tía's *comadres* (kō mä′ drāz) were her close women friends.

19. *Abuelita* means "granny" or "old woman." *No llores* is "don't weep." *Te traigo* means "I bring you." And the last line is "A small bouquet of flowers." Pronunciations: *abuelita* (a′ bwə lē′ tə), *no llores* (nō yôr′ ās), *te traigo* (tā trī′ gō), *una ramita de flores* (o͞o′ nə rä mē′ tə dā flō′ rās)

Bougainvillea

Teaching Support

Grammar and Language Minilesson

Sentence Fragments Explain that skilled writers often use sentence fragments for literary effect. Point out that in business correspondence and newsletters, fragments are not considered proper.

Activity As an aid to recognizing and correcting sentence fragments, have students find five examples of fragments in the story and rewrite them to make them complete sentences. **L2**

Additional Resources

- ***Grammar and Language Transparency 13***
- ***Grammar and Language Workbook,*** pp. 24–25
- ***Grammar and Composition Handbook,*** Lesson 1.2
- ***Writer's Choice,*** Lessons 7.1, 8.2

Responding to Literature

PERSONAL RESPONSE

- What thoughts did you have about the narrator, her aunt, and their walk as you read the end of the story? Write a quick note to a classmate explaining why you thought this way.

Brackets connect questions that are paired to develop higher-level thinking skills.

Analyzing Literature

RECALL

1. What does the writer describe in the first four lines of the stanza that introduces "The Journey"? What is described in the last two lines?
2. Where does the narrator go to meet her aunt?
3. What has happened to the home of the Robles family?
4. How has the Santa Cruz River changed?

INTERPRET

5. Why might the writer have chosen to begin the story with a poem?
6. Why, in your opinion, does Tía follow the same route on her walks each week?
7. What is suggested about the ownership of land and buildings in the Barrio Histórico?
8. Why, do you think, does the narrator repeat her thoughts about the river?

EVALUATE AND CONNECT

9. How are the stops Tía makes on her weekly journey similar? How are they different?
10. Examine the references to music and flowers in this story of change. How does the author use this **imagery** to make her point?

Clay olla.

LITERARY ELEMENTS

Narration

Narration is storytelling, and writers use countless techniques to tell their stories. As you read "The Journey," you follow events through the eyes of a first-person narrator whose thoughts seem to leap from one thing to another as she considers every small detail, makes connections, and responds to her aunt's recollections.

1. Identify three or four details the narrator mentions, and tell how they help readers understand Tía's journey.
2. Which details make Tía's journey seem sad? Which add hope to the story?

• See **Literary Terms Handbook,** p. R6.

Responding to the Selection

PERSONAL RESPONSE

This sentimental journey makes the reader nostalgic; one begins to think that the past was a kind of golden age that is now lost.

Analyzing Literature

1. In the first four lines of the poem, the narrator describes the past. In the last two lines, she describes the present.
2. The narrator goes to the Martin Luther King Jr. Apartments to meet her aunt.
3. The Robles family home has become a bar.
4. The river no longer has water; it has been cut off from its source by the freeway.
5. The writer may have begun with a poem because the poem says in a brief and pointed manner what the story says in a more leisurely way.
6. Tia follows the same route so she can remember her past and end up at her childhood home.
7. It is suggested that people who are not of Hispanic heritage own the buildings.
8. The river is symbolic of the destruction of the barrio. The freeway has cut it off from its source.
9. Tía always goes to the same places and frequently says the same things; the people she encounters and what she buys change from trip to trip.
10. The music and flowers, symbolic of the beauty of Hispanic culture, endure despite the destruction of the architecture and the river. The flower, especially, is a strong symbol of the endurance of beauty.

LITERARY ELEMENTS

1. The river shows the contrast between the times. The melodies Tía hears reflect the power of her memories. The flower shows that the past lives on.
2. The converted buildings and the concrete make the journey seem sad. The flowers and music lend hope.

Additional Resources

Literary Elements Transparency 14

Literature and Writing

Writing About Literature

Students' paragraphs should
- explain why the author has chosen this setting
- use specific details from the story

Creative Writing

Students' video dialogues should
- include camera directions and directions for actors
- include dialogue appropriate to both characters

Extending Your Response

Literature Groups Write the word *nostalgia* on the board and invite volunteers to explain what it means. Remind students that nostalgia often blurs the bad times and highlights the good. **COLLAB. LEARN.**

Internet Connection Ask students to plan their research after brainstorming with their classmates for potential sources that might have information about historic preservation. The National Park Service's Web site is one good place to start looking for this type of information.

Learning for Life Suggest that students look over the policies on letters to the editor in their local newspaper for guidelines on length and format.

Literature and Writing

Writing About Literature

Setting Most of the scenes in this story take place on the streets of an old city. Why do you think the author has chosen this setting? Explain your answer in a paragraph. When writing, think about what the neighborhood means to the older woman.

Creative Writing

A Scene with Tía Imagine yourself as the narrator in "The Journey." What would you talk about with your aunt after your shopping trip? Write the dialogue for a short film set in Tía's apartment. Include camera directions and directions for the actors.

Extending Your Response

Literature Groups

Out of the Past Look over your response from the **Reading Focus** on page 168 and compare your chart with the situation in the story. With your group, discuss how characters in the story and in your chart are alike and different in their views of the past. Then summarize your comparisons and present your ideas to the class.

interNET CONNECTION

Use the Internet to research government policies on historic buildings or neighborhoods where you live. Type keywords such as "historic preservation" into a search engine. Share your findings with the class.

Learning for Life

Letter to the Editor Suppose that you are the narrator, and you've discovered that one more old building on Tía's journey is to be razed. Write a letter to the editor of a local Tucson newspaper stating your opinion about tearing down the building. Do you want it to be preserved, or is it a good idea to replace the building with something new? Give reasons for your opinion.

Reading Further

For other stories of how one generation helps another, try these books:

Images and Conversations by Patricia Preciado Martin

After the Dancing Days by Margaret Rostkowski

Something for Joey by Richard E. Peck

A Day No Pigs Would Die by Robert Newton Peck

Save your work for your portfolio.

Skill Minilessons

RETEACH • REVIEW

GRAMMAR AND LANGUAGE • WORDS ENDING IN *-ly*

Many adjectives can be made into adverbs by adding *-ly*.

Tía is quiet, prim, *and* regal.

Tía is waiting for me. Quietly, primly, regally, *her hands are folded in her lap.*

- For more about adding suffixes, see **Language Handbook,** pp. R47–R48.

PRACTICE Write the adverbial form of each adjective listed below. Then use each adverb in a sentence of your own.

1. vigorous
2. reluctant
3. efficient
4. private
5. good-natured

READING AND THINKING • VISUALIZING

You will understand more of a story if you stop occasionally to visualize, or see in your mind, a person or place in the text. For example, it is easy to visualize Tía as she waits for her niece because the writer includes many details. In other scenes, the writer may include fewer details. An efficient reader will imagine the details that bring the story to life.

- For more about visualizing, see **Reading Handbook,** p. R95.

PRACTICE Read through "The Journey" to find a description of a place that interests you. Study the description and imagine you are there. Then sketch the scene. Include as many details as you can.

VOCABULARY • THE PREFIX *co-*

The prefixes *co-, col-, con-,* and *com-* often add the meaning "with" or "together" to a word or root. For example, a *coworker* is "a person who works with another." If you *convoke* a meeting, you call people together, since the root *voke* is from the Latin *voc-,* meaning "call." Notice that many words beginning with *co-* are hyphenated.

PRACTICE Use each word below in a sentence. Then verify the words' meanings by definition or example.

1. costars
2. co-owners
3. cosponsors
4. coanchors
5. coexist
6. connect
7. cooperate
8. commute

Skill Minilessons

GRAMMAR AND LANGUAGE
WORDS ENDLING IN *-LY*

1. vigorously
2. reluctantly
3. efficiently
4. privately
5. good-naturedly

Sentences will vary.

READING AND THINKING
VISUALIZING

Suggest that students sketch the scene they visualize and share their drawings with others in the class. Students should be prepared to cite portions of the text that inspired their drawings.

VOCABULARY
THE PREFIX *CO-*

Students' sentences should use the words properly and should make sense.

Additional Resources

- ***Grammar and Language Workbook,*** p. 129
- ***Grammar and Composition Handbook,*** Lessons 6.1–6.2
- ***Writer's Choice,*** Lesson 12.5
- ***Reading Skills Practice Workbook,*** pp. 27–28
- ***Vocabulary Practice,*** p. 13

ASSESSMENT

- ***Quick Checks,*** p. 14
- ***Selection and Theme Assessment,*** p. 24
- ***Performance Assessment,*** p. 13
- ***Testmaker: ExamView Pro***
- ***Interactive Tutor: Self-Assessment***

Technology Skills

Objectives

- To learn to create and add images to word-processing documents
- To investigate the copyright laws governing the downloading of images
- To produce a document that includes a scanned image

Teaching Options

Have students work in pairs to draw images using the functions taught in the textbook. You may want to assign criteria for the project to ensure students use a variety of options. For example, tell students that the document must contain at least three shapes, three line widths, and six colors. Have pairs of students share their drawings with the class.

Teaching Support

Technology Skills

Word Processing: Working with Images

Pictures, graphs, maps, and charts are powerful communication tools. They can present a lot of information at a glance, and can spark readers' interest in the text that follows. Images work best when they support or enrich the meaning of the written text. They should strengthen your message, not just impress your readers.

In a small group, analyze the images in several magazines. How do the covers capture your attention? What do illustrations add to the meaning of articles? Do photographs look staged or candid? How are images used in ads? Discuss what you discover about how images are used for different purposes and audiences.

Technology Tip

Search the World Wide Web for photos and clip art you can add to your documents. To download an image, click the right mouse button (on the Mac, just click and hold). Select **Save As,** name the file, and save it to a specific location on your computer.

Inserting Pictures

You can add graphics (clip art, photos, graphs, and so on) to your word processing documents. Here's how.

1. Open a new document. Pull down the **Insert** menu and select **Picture.**
2. A window will open asking you to select the folder where picture files are stored. Ask your teacher or lab instructor where to find the appropriate folder.
3. Browse through the picture files. Choose a picture you would like to insert into your document, then double click on it (or single click to select it and click on the **Insert** button). The picture will be copied onto your page.
4. To change the size of the picture, click on it. A border with eight "handles" will appear, as shown on the lower left. Resize the picture by clicking and dragging on the handles. To move the picture, click inside the border and drag it.

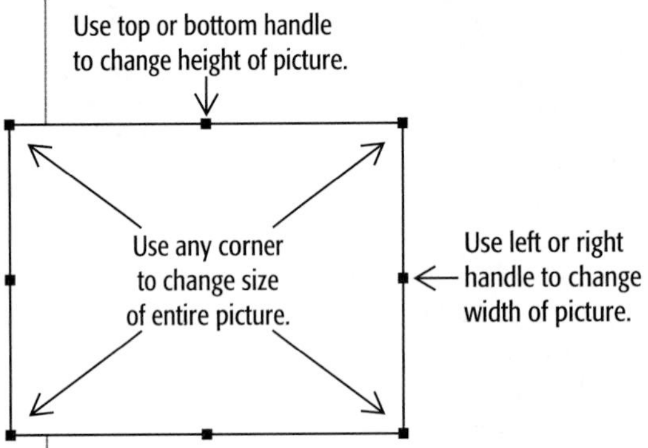

Drawing Tools

Most word processing programs have drawing features that allow you to create your own images. Follow the steps below to explore the drawing tool.

1. Open a new document. Find the **Drawing** icon on the standard toolbar. Click on it to open the drawing toolbar.

2. The drawing toolbar should contain icon buttons for several of the following tools. Click on each one, and try it out in your document. To delete an object you draw, select it and press the delete key.

Meeting Individual Needs: MULTIPLE MODES OF EXPRESSION

Spatial Point out that newspapers and magazines require page setups that include text and images. Explain that the challenge in designing a newpaper or magazine page lies in making the text fit as well as presenting an attractive layout.

Activity Have students design a page of their own. They may use writing from their portfolio as the text. Students should choose images that enhance the presentation of their pieces. Students may scan photographs, insert clip art, or draw charts. When students have completed their page layouts, display the work for the class. **L2**

The Drawing Toolbar

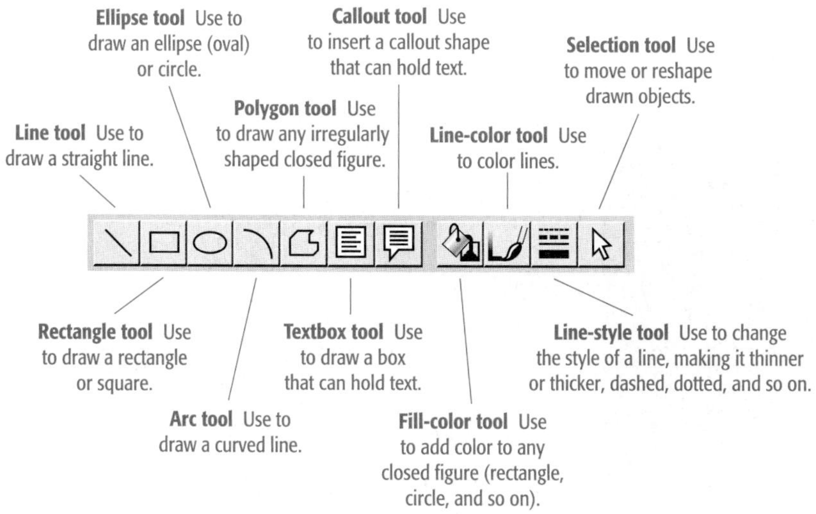

Your word processing software may also contain icon buttons that will allow you to:

- horizontally or vertically flip an object or picture
- group objects so that they will all move together (especially handy when you need to make up a drawing from several different lines and shapes)
- move an object in a many-layered group to the front or back

ACTIVITIES

1. Research the copyright laws relating to the use of images on the Internet. Use *copyright law* along with *images, clip art,* or *photos* as keywords on a search engine. Pay particular attention to the "fair use exemption" clause for schools.
2. If you have access to a scanner, scan pictures to accompany one of the selections in this theme. Import them into a word processing document, along with a summary of the selection. Print the result for your classroom bulletin board.
3. On your word processor, compose a step-by-step explanation of how to scan and import pictures into a document. Use formatting techniques to make your explanation clear. Be prepared to present your explanation orally in class.

Activities

1. Students should share what they learn with the rest of the class. Remind students that they must follow copyright laws for images as well as text.
2. You may wish to allow students to create their own images if they choose.
3. Students should present each step in a logical order that is easy to follow.

TechnoTalk

Imports The term *import,* meaning "an item brought in from the outside," refers to an item that is brought into a document from an outside source. For example, scanned images are imports, as are clip art images.

interNET CONNECTION

Online Publishing If your school has a Web site, find out whether you can publish online students' designed pages from the activity on the left. You may also have students visit other schools' online student newspapers to see examples of design and content. **L2**

Before Reading

Objectives

- To read and analyze two poems
- To identify the mood of each poem

Skills

Reading/Thinking: Inferring
Grammar/Language: Pronouns and Antecedents
Listening/Speaking: Reciting a Poem
Collaboration: Literature Groups; Performance

Motivating STUDENTS

Selection Focus Transparency 14: Before presenting the transparency, discuss with students what *home* means to different people they know or have read about.

Reading Focus: As an extension of the Reading Focus, ask students to identify the sights, sounds, and smells that they associate with the word *home*.

Before You Read

Knoxville, Tennessee* and *Legacies

MEET NIKKI GIOVANNI

Although Nikki Giovanni grew up in Ohio, she spent many summers in Knoxville with her grandmother. Of "Knoxville, Tennessee," she says, "I simply tried to recall and capture . . . the summertime freedom. . . . The poem is fun to me because the experience was fun. And sometimes happiness is a good enough reason to write a poem." Like the child in "Legacies," Giovanni was close to her grandmother, from whom she learned pride and a sense of responsibility to her African American roots.

Nikki Giovanni was born Yolande Cornelia Giovanni in Knoxville in 1943. These poems were first published in 1968 and 1972.

READING FOCUS

What makes your home special for you? Why are some people more important to you than others?

Sharing Ideas
Jot down your answers. Then share them with a partner. Do your partner's answers remind you of reasons you hadn't thought of?

Setting a Purpose
Read one person's thoughts and feelings about home.

BUILDING BACKGROUND

Nikki Giovanni thinks of "Knoxville, Tennessee" as a "fun" poem, but she is known for writing poetry with strong themes of change and revolution. The ideas in her poetry come out of her background. She graduated from Fisk University in Nashville, Tennessee, in 1967, during the Civil Rights movement and became a strong voice in the struggle for equal treatment of African Americans. Since that time, she has published twelve books of poetry and become an English professor at Virginia Polytechnic University in Blacksburg, Virginia. Her poetry has earned her many awards, including the American Library Association commendation in 1973 for *My House,* one of the best books for young adult readers.

RESOURCE MANAGER

Teaching Tools and Resources
- Theme Two Planning Guide
- Literature Groups Sourcebook

Essential Lesson Support

Lesson-Specific Instruction
- Selection Focus Transparency 14
- Literary Elements Transparency 15
- Active Reading Guide,* p. 15
- Selection Vocabulary Practice, p. 7

Assessment
- Selection Quick Checks,* p. 15
- Sel. and Theme Assmt., pp. 25–26
- Testmaker: ExamView Pro
- Performance Assessment, p. 14

Systematic Language Instruction
- Gr. & Comp. Hbk., Lessons 3.6, 3.7
- Vocabulary Power, Lesson 8
- Spelling Power, Lesson 7

English Language Learners
- ELL Sourcebook, p.34
- Spanish Summaries, p. 14
- Audio Library*
- English, Yes!

Spec. Needs/Strat. Interven.
- Interactive Rdg. Sbk., pp. T81–T83
- Interactive Rdg. Wbk., p. 33
- Audio Library*

* Also available in Spanish

A Chat In the Road, 1991. Anna Belle Lee Washington. Oil on canvas, 20 x 30 in.

Knoxville, Tennessee

Nikki Giovanni

I always like summer
best
you can eat fresh corn
from daddy's garden
and okra
and greens
and cabbage
and lots of
barbecue
and buttermilk
and homemade ice-cream
at the church picnic
and listen to
gospel music
outside
at the church
homecoming
and go to the mountains with
your grandmother
and go barefooted
and be warm
all the time
not only when you go to bed
and sleep

Reading the Selection

A Active Reading Strategies

QUESTION Ask students why they think Giovanni lists the specific foods she does. *(One might call these summer foods and comfort foods. They are also ethnic foods—foods that call to mind her specific African American heritage.)*

B Literary Elements

MOOD Ask students what mood or feeling Giovanni conveys by her use of the word *warm*. *(She is talking about something more than temperature. She seems to be referring to a feeling of love and closeness.)*

Additional Resources

- ***Active Reading Guide,*** p. 15
- ***Audio Library***
- ***Spanish Audio Library***

LITERATURE & HUMANITIES

You may wish to use "Cumpleaños de Lala y Tudi," on page 254 of *Introducing Art* and invite students to examine the scene and write a poem from the point of view of any character. Allow students to recite their poems for the class.

Teaching Support

MEETING INDIVIDUAL NEEDS — ENGLISH LANGUAGE LEARNERS

Southern Summer This poem refers to foods, customs, and music that may be unfamiliar to English language learners and many other students in the class. Poll the group: How many have tasted okra, greens, buttermilk, barbecue? How many have been to a church picnic? How many have listened to gospel music?

Activity Group students to allow those who have experience with these foods and customs and with this music to share it with those who do not. Ask students to relate their experiences using details that will bring the customs to life for the other students. Encourage students to bring in samples of the music or foods, if possible. **L1**

Additional Resources

- ***English Language Learners Sourcebook,*** p. 34

CONNECTING TO OTHER SELECTIONS

For a teaching strategy that connects this poem to the selection from *On the Road with Charles Kuralt,* see the ***Theme Six Planning Guide.***

C Active Reading Strategies

QUESTION What do students think the grandmother is proud of? *(She is proud of her recipe and skill and of being able to pass on her heritage to her granddaughter.)*

D Active Reading Strategies

REVIEW Ask students why they think the girl turns down her grandmother's offer. *(The girl seems to feel that knowing how to make the rolls would cut her off from her grandmother, not bind her more closely to her.)*

E Active Reading Strategies

QUESTION What did each of them mean? *(Both the girl and her grandmother are trying to express love.)*

F Critical Thinking

INFERRING Why is it so hard for people to say what they mean? *(Many times we find it difficult to put our deepest feelings into words. Asking for what we need makes us vulnerable because it reveals so much of our inner selves.)*

Thematic Focus

Lean on Me Each poem's speaker leans on her grandmother, but the nature of the reliance is different. Ask students to compare and contrast each speaker's dependence.

ASSESSMENT

Quick Checks, p. 15

Teaching Support

Legacies

Nikki Giovanni

her grandmother called her from the playground
"yes, ma'am"
"i want chu to learn how to make rolls" said the old
woman proudly
but the little girl didn't want
to learn how because she knew
even if she couldn't say it that
that would mean when the old one died she would be less
dependent on her spirit so
she said
"i don't want to know how to make no rolls"
with her lips poked out
and the old woman wiped her hands on
her apron saying "lord
these children"
and neither of them ever
said what they meant
and i guess nobody ever does

Petite Fille, 1982. Loïs Mailou Jones. Watercolor, 30 x 24 in. Courtesy of the artist.

Grammar and Language *Minilesson*

Pronouns and Antecedents Write this sentence from the poem on the board: *her grandmother called her from the playground.* Point out that a pronoun refers to a noun or group of words that usually precede the pronoun and are called the pronoun's antecedent. To what or whom does *her* in this sentence refer? *(the little girl)* Note that, in this case, the noun to which the pronoun refers follows the pronoun.

Activity Have students list all the pronouns in both Giovanni poems. Ask them to write each pronoun's antecedent. **L2**

Additional Resources

- ***Grammar and Language Transparency 14***
- ***Grammar and Language Workbook,*** pp. 109–110
- ***Grammar and Composition Handbook,*** Lesson 4.3
- ***Writer's Choice,*** 11.2

Responding to Literature

PERSONAL RESPONSE

- What reactions do these poems stir in you? Make a web for each poem to record your response.

Analyzing Literature

RECALL AND INTERPRET

1. What is the main idea presented in "Knoxville, Tennessee"? How does the speaker feel about Knoxville? Explain.
2. Summarize what happens in "Legacies." How does the girl feel about her grandmother? What clue does the speaker give?

EVALUATE AND CONNECT

3. In which of the two poems can you place yourself more easily? Explain your reasons.
4. How would each of the young people in these poems define "home"? Which definition is closer to your thoughts about what "home" means?
5. How do the children's feelings about home in these two poems compare with your notes from the **Reading Focus** on page 180?
6. How are the grandmothers in the two poems alike? Cite lines from the poems to support your points.

LITERARY ELEMENTS

Mood

Mood is the emotional effect that a poem or story has on a reader. The author creates a mood through his or her choice of words and details to describe the setting, events, and objects. In "Knoxville, Tennessee," Nikki Giovanni creates a nostalgic mood by sharing her favorite childhood memories.

1. What other emotions describe the mood of "Knoxville, Tennessee"?
2. What mood did you find in "Legacies"? Did a second or third reading change that mood? Explain.

- See **Literary Terms Handbook**, p. R6.

Extending Your Response

Literature Groups

Communication Gap The narrator in "Legacies" says "neither of them ever said / what they meant / and I guess nobody ever does." Do you agree or disagree? Discuss the problems of communication some people find when talking about their feelings to members of a different generation.

Performing

Reciting a Poem With a partner, practice reading "Knoxville, Tennessee" aloud. Show the rush of the speaker's recollections, while keeping your reading clear for your audience.

Responding to the Selection

PERSONAL RESPONSE

"Knoxville" evokes feelings of the joy of summer. "Legacies" leads the reader to infer the words that have gone unsaid.

Analyzing Literature

1. The main idea is that the speaker has wonderful, warm memories of Knoxville, the place she associates with summer.
2. In "Legacies," the grandmother invites her granddaughter to learn to make rolls; she refuses. The girl loves her grandmother.
3. Many students will identify with "Knoxville" because it is a youthful poem.
4. Both girls seem to identify home with their grandmothers. Some students will agree that home is where they feel love.
5. Many students will identify with the feelings of love and warmth.
6. Both grandmothers are associated with food and nurturing. In "Knoxville, Tennessee," the grandmother makes the speaker feel "warm all the time"; she also, presumably, prepares the food the speaker remembers with fondness. In "Legacies," the grandmother is hoping to share her knowledge of cooking with her granddaughter.

Extending Your Response

Literature Groups Suggest students answer the question by considering why students find it easier to talk about feelings with people their own age. COLLAB. LEARN.

Performing Point out that this is a happy poem; urge readers to smile as they read it. COLLAB. LEARN.

LITERARY ELEMENTS

1. Emotions that describe the mood of the poem are happiness and joy.
2. The mood of "Legacies" is sad because of the missed opportunities it represents.

Additional Resources

Literary Elements Transparency 15

ASSESSMENT

- ***Quick Checks,*** p. 15
- ***Selection and Theme Assessment,*** pp. 25–26
- ***Performance Assessment,*** p. 14
- ***Testmaker: ExamView Pro***
- ***Interactive Tutor: Self-Assessment***

LEAN ON ME 183

Before Reading

Objectives

- To read and analyze a short story
- To analyze the effect of a first-person point of view
- To define character traits

Skills

Reading/Thinking: Inferring; Using Text Structures; Evaluating; Understanding Details
Writing: Journal Entry
Vocabulary: Analogies
Grammar/Language: Commas and Compound Sentences; Capitalization
Listening/Speaking: Role-Playing
Life Skills: Researching Community Resources
Collaboration: Literature Groups; Listening and Speaking

Motivating → STUDENTS

Selection Focus Transparency 15: Before presenting the transparency, discuss with students the dangers of basing judgments on first impressions.

Reading Focus: As an extension of the Reading Focus, show students photographs of people and have them write down their impressions. Then sample these. Point out differences and discuss how first impressions are often based on stereotypes.

Before You Read

A Mother in Mannville

MEET MARJORIE KINNAN RAWLINGS

Marjorie Kinnan Rawlings produced her best work after moving in 1928 from New York City to a seventy-two-acre orange grove in Cross Creek, Florida. Rawlings found inspiration for her writing in the local scenery and likable neighbors. The area was the setting for her best-known novel, *The Yearling*, which won the Pulitzer Prize in 1939. "For myself, the Creek satisfies a thing that had gone hungry and unfed since childhood days," she said.

Marjorie Kinnan Rawlings was born in 1896 in Washington, D.C., and died in Florida in 1953. "A Mother in Mannville" was published in 1940.

READING FOCUS

Have you ever thought you knew someone well, only to discover something that changed your impression of him or her?

Journal
Describe your experience in your journal. Is your relationship different now because of what you found out?

Setting a Purpose
Read about one person's impression of another and an important discovery.

BUILDING BACKGROUND

The Time and Place This story takes place in the 1930s in North Carolina near an orphanage.

Did You Know? Orphanages were common in the 1930s. Such institutions cared for and protected children who were abandoned or had no guardian. The Great Depression occurred during this time, and parents sometimes sent children to orphanages because they were too poor to clothe and feed them.

VOCABULARY PREVIEW

suffused (sə fūzd′) *adj.* spread through or over, as with light, color, emotion, or quality; p. 186
integrity (in teg′ rə tē) *n.* moral uprightness; honesty; p. 187
subterfuge (sub′ tər fūj′) *n.* a trick or other method used to escape or conceal something; deception; p. 188
instinctive (in stingk′ tiv) *adj.* rising from an impulse or natural tendency; not learned; p. 189
intimate (in′ tə mit) *adj.* very close and familiar; p. 189
impel (im pel′) *v.* to drive to action; cause; p. 190
savor (sā′ vər) *v.* to take great delight in; p. 191
anomalous (ə nom′ ə ləs) *adj.* not following the usual or regular; abnormal; p. 192

RESOURCE MANAGER

Teaching Tools and Resources
- Theme Two Planning Guide
- Literature Groups Sourcebook

Essential Lesson Support

Lesson-Specific Instruction
- Selection Focus Transparency 15
- Literary Elements Transparency 16
- Active Reading Guide,* p. 16
- Selection Vocabulary Practice, p. 14

Assessment
- Selection Quick Checks,* p. 16
- Sel. and Theme Assmt., pp. 27–28
- Testmaker: ExamView Pro
- Performance Assessment, p. 15

Systematic Language Instruction
- Gr. & Comp. Hbk., Lessons 3.8, 3.9

English Language Learners
- ELL Sourcebook, p.35
- Spanish Summaries, p. 15
- Spanish Translations, pp. 57–62

- Audio Library*
- English, Yes!

Spec. Needs/Strat. Interven.
- Interactive Rdg. Sbk., pp. T84–T86
- Interactive Rdg. Wbk., pp. 34–35
- Inclusion Strat. Sbk., pp. 25–26, 53–54
- Audio Library*

* Also available in Spanish

A Mother in Mannville

Marjorie Kinnan Rawlings

The orphanage is high in the Carolina mountains. Sometimes in winter the snowdrifts are so deep that the institution is cut off from the village below, from all the world. Fog hides the mountain peaks, the snow swirls down the valleys, and a wind blows so bitterly that the orphanage boys who take the milk twice daily to the baby cottage reach the door with fingers stiff in an agony of numbness.

A

"Or when we carry trays from the cookhouse for the ones that are sick," Jerry said, "we get our faces frostbit, because we can't put our hands over them. I have gloves," he added. "Some of the boys don't have any."

He liked the late spring, he said. The rhododendron was in bloom, a carpet of color, across the mountainsides, soft as the May winds that stirred the hemlocks. He called it laurel.

"It's pretty when the laurel blooms," he said. "Some of it's pink and some of it's white."

I was there in the autumn. I wanted quiet, isolation, to do some troublesome writing. I wanted mountain air to blow out the malaria from too long a time in the subtropics. I was homesick, too, for the

Reading the Selection

SUMMARY

A writer working near an orphanage in the Carolina mountains becomes attached to one of the orphan boys. Jerry helps her through the winter by chopping wood and kindling and caring for her dog. As she comes to know the boy, she learns to love and admire him. One evening, the boy tells the narrator that his mother is alive. The narrator is outraged; she cannot imagine what sort of mother would abandon such a child. When the time comes for the writer to leave, she discovers that Jerry has made up the story about his mother.

Spanish Summaries, p. 15

A Active Reading Strategies

VISUALIZE Read the first paragraph aloud, having students visualize the setting. Then ask them to discuss and compare their mental images.

VOCABULARY If you haven't previewed the selection vocabulary with students, stop and remind them to use context clues to unlock the meanings of the new vocabulary words.

Additional Resources

- ***Active Reading Guide,*** p. 16
- ***Audio Library***
- ***Spanish Audio Library***

CONNECTING TO OTHER SELECTIONS

The chart at the right shows three ways to connect "A Mother in Mannville" to other selections in this book.

For specific teaching strategies, see the ***Theme Two Planning Guide.***

Connection		Title
Life Skills: Supporting and Contributing	→	from *Harriet Tubman: Conductor on the Underground Railroad,* p. 480
Thematic: Search for Acceptance	→	"Homeless," p. 39
Literary: Setting	→	"The Drummer Boy of Shiloh," p. 439

B Active Reading Strategies

PREDICT Ask students what kind of person they think the narrator is on the basis of her initial response to Jerry. Have them pay attention to whether their initial impressions of the narrator were accurate as the story progresses.

C Active Reading Strategies

QUESTION What does the woodpile tell the narrator about Jerry's character? *(He works hard and well, and he takes pride in what he does.)*

D Literary Elements

FIRST-PERSON POINT OF VIEW Note that when the narrator looks closely at Jerry for the first time, she presents to the readers a description that makes him seem ethereal. Ask students to cite elements in her description of him that are romanticized. *("hair the color of corn shocks," "eyes very direct and like the sky when rain is pending," "a light came over him . . . suffused glory")*

A Mother in Mannville

Did You Know?
A *shock* is a bundle of corn or wheat set upright in a field.

flaming of maples in October, and for corn shocks and pumpkins and black-walnut trees and the lift of hills. I found them all, living in a cabin that belonged to the orphanage, half a mile beyond the orphanage farm. When I took the cabin, I asked for a boy or man to come and chop wood for the fireplace. The first few days were warm, I found what wood I needed about the cabin, no one came, and I forgot the order.

I looked up from my typewriter one late afternoon, a little startled. A boy stood at the door, and my pointer dog, my companion, was at his side and had not barked to warn me. The boy was probably twelve years old, but undersized. He wore overalls and a torn shirt, and was barefooted.

He said, "I can chop some wood today."

I said, "But I have a boy coming from the orphanage."

"I'm the boy."

"You? But you're small."

"Size don't matter, chopping wood," he said. "Some of the big boys don't chop good. I've been chopping wood at the orphanage a long time."

I visualized mangled and inadequate branches for my fires. I was well into my work and not inclined to conversation. I was a little blunt.

"Very well. There's the ax. Go ahead and see what you can do."

I went back to work, closing the door. At first the sound of the boy dragging brush annoyed me. Then he began to chop. The blows were rhythmic and steady, and shortly I had forgotten him, the sound no more of an interruption than a consistent[1] rain. I suppose an hour and a half passed, for when I stopped and stretched, and heard the boy's steps on the cabin stoop,[2] the sun was dropping behind the farthest mountain, and the valleys were purple with something deeper than the asters.

The boy said, "I have to go to supper now. I can come again tomorrow evening."

I said, "I'll pay you now for what you've done," thinking I should probably have to insist on an older boy. "Ten cents an hour?"

"Anything is all right."

We went together back of the cabin. An astonishing amount of solid wood had been cut. There were cherry logs and heavy roots of rhododendron, and blocks from the waste pine and oak left from the building of the cabin.

"But you've done as much as a man," I said, "This is a splendid pile."

I looked at him, actually, for the first time. His hair was the color of the corn shocks and his eyes, very direct, were like the mountain sky when rain is pending—gray, with a shadowing of that miraculous blue. As I spoke, a light came over him, as though the setting sun had touched him with the same suffused glory with which it touched the mountains. I gave him a quarter.

1. Here, *consistent* means simply "steady."
2. A *stoop* is a small porch, platform, or staircase leading to the entrance of a house or building.

Vocabulary
suffused (sə fūzd′) *adj.* spread through or over, as with light, color, emotion, or quality

Teaching Support

MEETING INDIVIDUAL NEEDS — ENGLISH LANGUAGE LEARNERS

Compound Words Point out that English often combines two simple, often closely associated words into one longer word. The new word often expands the meaning of the original words. Compound words may be open (two words), closed (one word), or hyphenated. Write these words on the board: *typewriter, undersized, overalls, barefooted.*

Activity Have students find five more compound words in the story. Ask them to try to define the words using clues from the text. Have students write the words, their definitions, and a sentence for each in their vocabulary notebooks.

Additional Resources

English Language Learners Sourcebook, p. 35

"You may come tomorrow," I said, "and thank you very much."

He looked at me, and at the coin, and seemed to want to speak, but could not, and turned away.

"I'll split kindling[3] tomorrow," he said over his thin ragged shoulder. "You'll need kindling and medium wood and logs and backlogs."

At daylight I was half wakened by the sound of chopping. Again it was so even in texture that I went back to sleep. When I left my bed in the cool morning, the boy had come and gone, and a stack of kindling was neat against the cabin wall. He came again after school in the afternoon and worked until time to return to the orphanage. His name was Jerry; he was twelve years old, and he had been at the orphanage since he was four. I could picture him at four, with the same grave gray-blue eyes and the same—independence? No, the word that comes to me is "integrity."

The word means something very special to me, and the quality for which I use it is a rare one. My father had it—there is another of whom I am almost sure—but almost no man of my acquaintance possesses it with the clarity, the purity, the simplicity of a mountain stream. But the boy Jerry had it. It is bedded on courage, but it is more than brave. It is honest, but it is more than honesty. The ax handle

Boy Holding Logs, 1873. Winslow Homer. Oil on canvas, 12⅛ x 9¼ in.

Viewing the painting: Study the boy in this painting. What hopes and dreams do you imagine that he and Jerry may share?

3. *Kindling* is material for starting a fire, especially small pieces of dry wood.

Vocabulary
integrity (in teg′ rə tē) *n.* moral uprightness; honesty

Viewing the Painting

Winslow Homer, a realistic painter with a strong sense of color, is best known for his seascapes.

Viewing Response *Both boys may share a desire to be appreciated, loved, and cared for.*

E Critical Thinking

INFERRING Ask students what they can infer from Rawlings's emphasis on the evenness of the sound Jerry makes chopping wood. What does it say about his character? *(He works consistently and steadily.)*

F Literary Elements

FIRST-PERSON POINT OF VIEW The narrator gives a complex definition of *integrity*. Discuss with students what the narrator means when she uses the term. *(Integrity seems to have to do with consistency, honesty, and the courage of one's convictions. A person with integrity does what he or she believes to be right regardless of the consequences—and almost without having to think about it.)*

Fine Art Transparency 6

You may want to use ***Fine Art Transparency 6*** in a discussion of the importance of physical work.

Writing *Minilesson*

Defining a Quality Rawlings provides a good model for defining a quality when she discusses integrity. Note that she begins with an abstract generalization when she describes integrity as more than honesty and more than courage, but the most powerful part of her definition is the example.

Activity Have students write a positive or negative definition of a quality like integrity following Rawlings's example. Have them follow this formula:

1. [This person] has [this quality].
2. Abstract definition of the quality.
3. Example of the person's demonstration of the quality. **L2**

Additional Resources

Writer's Choice, Lesson 5.1

LEAN ON ME 187

VIEWING THE PAINTING

Boston painter Rogert Vonnoh introduced French impressionism to America.

Viewing Response *The beauty of the surroundings in this painting has a calming effect on the viewer, much like the effect of the setting on the reader.*

G Literary Elements

FIRST-PERSON POINT OF VIEW Ask students what features the narrator presents that contribute to her portrait of Jerry's character here. *(She says he takes full and complete responsibility for his actions. He works methodically and conscientiously without supervision but likes company and conversation.)*

H Active Reading Strategies

QUESTION Rawlings says Jerry is "great of heart." What does she mean by that? *(He instinctively looks for ways to do kindnesses.)*

Springtime. Robert Vonnoh (1858–1933). Oil on canvas, 20 x 24 in. Private collection.
Viewing the painting: How does the mood of this painting reflect the mood of the story?

broke one day. Jerry said the woodshop at the orphanage would repair it. I brought money to pay for the job and he refused it.

"I'll pay for it," he said. "I broke it. I brought the ax down careless."

"But no one hits accurately every time," I told him. "The fault was in the wood of the handle. I'll see the man from whom I bought it."

It was only then that he would take the money. He was standing back of his own carelessness. He was a free-will agent and he chose to do careful work, and if he failed, he took the responsibility without subterfuge. G

And he did for me the unnecessary thing, the gracious thing, that we find done only by the great of heart. Things no training can teach, for they are done H

Vocabulary
subterfuge (sub′ tər fūj′) *n.* a trick or other method used to escape or conceal something; deception

Teaching Support

Reading *Minilesson*

Using Text Structures Authors use specific details and examples to capture a reader's attention and illustrate concretely the points they are trying to make. If a generalization seems difficult to grasp, a good strategy is to read the example that follows and then reread the generalization.

Activity Have students carefully reread Rawlings's descriptions of Jerry's integrity and great-heartedness (pages 187–188) and then read the generalizations about him to see how they relate. Have students divide sheets of paper into two columns and label one *Integrity* and the other *Great Heartedness.* Under each word, have them write words and phrases from the story that describe these characteristics. **L2**

Additional Resources

Reading Skills Practice Workbook

on the instant, with no predicated[4] experience. He found a cubbyhole beside the fireplace that I had not noticed. There, of his own accord, he put kindling and "medium" wood, so that I might always have dry fire material ready in case of sudden wet weather. A stone was loose in the rough walk to the cabin. He dug a deeper hole and steadied it, although he came, himself, by a short cut over the bank. I found that when I tried to return his thoughtfulness with such things as candy and apples, he was wordless. "Thank you" was, perhaps, an expression for which he had had no use, for his courtesy was instinctive. He only looked at the gift and at me, and a curtain lifted, so that I saw deep into the clear well of his eyes, and gratitude was there, and affection, soft over the firm granite of his character.

He made simple excuses to come and sit with me. I could no more have turned him away than if he had been physically hungry. I suggested once that the best time for us to visit was just before supper, when I left off my writing. After that, he waited always until my typewriter had been some time quiet. One day I worked until nearly dark. I went outside the cabin, having forgotten him. I saw him going up over the hill in the twilight toward the orphanage. When I sat down on my stoop, a place was warm from his body where he had been sitting.

He became intimate, of course, with my pointer, Pat. There is a strange communion between a boy and a dog. Perhaps they possess the same singleness of spirit, the same kind of wisdom. It is difficult to explain, but it exists. When I went across the state for a weekend, I left the dog in Jerry's charge. I gave him the dog whistle and the key to the cabin, and left sufficient food. He was to come two or three times a day and let out the dog, and feed and exercise him. I should return Sunday night, and Jerry would take out the dog for the last time Sunday afternoon and then leave the key under an agreed hiding place.

My return was belated and fog filled the mountain passes so treacherously that I dared not drive at night. The fog held the next morning, and it was Monday noon before I reached the cabin. The dog had been fed and cared for that morning. Jerry came early in the afternoon, anxious.

"The superintendent said nobody would drive in the fog," he said. "I came just before bedtime last night and you hadn't come. So I brought Pat some of my breakfast this morning. I wouldn't have let anything happen to him."

"I was sure of that. I didn't worry."

"When I heard about the fog, I thought you'd know."

He was needed for work at the orphanage and he had to return at once. I gave him a dollar in payment, and he looked at it and went away. But that night he came in the darkness and knocked at the door.

"Come in, Jerry," I said, "if you're allowed to be away this late."

"I told maybe a story," he said. "I told them I thought you would want to see me."

"That's true," I assured him, and I saw his relief. "I want to hear about how you managed with the dog."

4. Here, *predicated* means "established; basic."

Vocabulary

instinctive (in stingk′ tiv) *adj.* rising from an impulse or natural tendency; not learned

intimate (in′ tə mit) *adj.* very close and familiar

I Author's Craft

FIGURATIVE LANGUAGE Note that Rawlings twice uses the images of granite or bedrock and clear water to describe Jerry's character. She mentions the "clarity . . . of a mountain stream," and says that Jerry's integrity is "bedded on courage." Here she talks about the "clear well of his eyes" and the "firm granite of his character." Ask students what these descriptions say about Jerry's character. *(Rawlings sees him as being completely consistent, honest, hard-working, and morally strong.)*

J Active Reading Strategies

QUESTION The narrator says she "could no more have turned . . . [Jerry] away than if he had been physically hungry," suggesting that he is hungry for something. Ask students what they think that might be. *(Jerry is hungry for family, for someone to love him as a mother would.)*

K Active Reading Strategies

RESPOND Ask students to respond to the narrator's behavior in forgetting about Jerry. How would they feel in his position?

L Active Reading Strategies

QUESTION Ask students to discuss Jerry's behavior in caring for Pat. What do his actions say about the kind of person he is? *(Like his way of wood chopping, Jerry's actions with the dog say volumes about what a fine person he is—kind, caring, and faithful.)*

MEETING INDIVIDUAL NEEDS — MULTIPLE MODES OF EXPRESSION

Interpersonal Rawlings says that Jerry's courtesy is *instinctive*—that it is inborn, not learned.

Activity Invite students in small groups to discuss what courtesy is and what the distinction is between learned and instinctive courtesy. Very young children can be quite rude, but they can also have considerable instinctive courtesy. What might instinctive courtesy be like? **L2** **COLLAB. LEARN.**

VIEWING THE PHOTOGRAPH

Viewing Response *In some parts of the United States, people's activities are strongly affected by seasonal changes. In the story, the coming of winter meant chopping wood and driving in fog. Also, both characters are responsive to their environment.*

M Active Reading Strategies

QUESTION Ask students why the dog finds more comfort from Jerry than from the narrator. What is it about Jerry that the dog loves? *(Given what we know about the narrator, so often preoccupied with her writing, it is probably safe to assume that Jerry pays more undivided attention to the dog.)*

N Critical Thinking

INFERRING Knowing that Jerry lives in the orphanage, what can you infer from his telling the narrator that she looks like his mother? *(This is perhaps Jerry's way of asking the narrator to become his mother or of wishing that she were.)*

O Active Reading Strategies

QUESTION Ask students why the narrator reacts so strongly to the idea that Jerry has a mother. *(She cannot imagine voluntarily giving up such a child.)*

Teaching Support

M He sat by the fire with me, with no other light, and told me of their two days together. The dog lay close to him, and found a comfort there that I did not have for him. And it seemed to me that being with my dog, and caring for him, had brought the boy and me, too, together, so that he felt that he belonged to me as well as to the animal.

"He stayed right with me," he told me, "except when he ran in the laurel. He likes the laurel. I took him up over the hill and we both ran fast. There was a place where the grass was high and I lay down in it and hid. I could hear Pat hunting for me. He found my trail and he barked. When he found me, he acted crazy, and he ran around and around me, in circles."

We watched the flames.

"That's an apple log," he said. "It burns the prettiest of any wood."

We were very close.

He was suddenly impelled to speak of things he had not spoken of before, nor had I cared to ask him.

N "You look a little bit like my mother," he said. "Especially in the dark, by the fire."

"But you were only four, Jerry, when you came here. You have remembered how she looked, all these years?"

"My mother lives in Mannville," he said.

O For a moment, finding that he had a mother shocked me as greatly as anything in my life has ever done, and I did not know why it disturbed me. Then I understood my distress. I was filled with a passionate resentment that any woman should go away and leave her son. A fresh anger added itself. A son like this one—The orphanage was a wholesome place, the executives were kind, good people, the food was more than adequate, the boys were healthy, a ragged shirt was no hardship, nor the doing of clean labor. Granted, perhaps, that the boy felt no lack, what blood fed the bowels of a woman who did not yearn over this child's lean body that had come in parturition[5] out of her own? At four he would have looked the same as now. Nothing, I thought, nothing in life could change those eyes. His quality must be

5. *Parturition* (pär′ tə rish′ ən) is the act of giving birth.

Viewing the photograph: How do you feel when you think of fall and winter? Why are these seasons important in the story?

Vocabulary

impel (im pel′) *v.* to drive to action; cause

MEETING INDIVIDUAL NEEDS: SPECIAL NEEDS

Less-Proficient Readers Less-proficient readers may have trouble with this passage, "Granted, perhaps, that the boy felt no lack, what blood fed the bowels of a woman who did not yearn over this child's lean body that had come in parturition out of her own?" Make sure that students understand all the individual words, then set them to the task of sorting out the meaning. *(Even if the boy doesn't miss having a mother, what kind of person could leave a child born of her own body?)*

Activity Have students work in groups to try to paraphrase this passage. Have each group share its effort with the class. **L1** COLLAB. LEARN.

Additional Resources

Inclusion Strategies

apparent to an idiot, a fool. I burned with questions I could not ask. In any, I was afraid, there would be pain.

"Have you seen her, Jerry—lately?"

"I see her every summer. She sends for me."

I wanted to cry out, "Why are you not with her? How can she let you go away again?"

He said, "She comes up here from Mannville whenever she can. She doesn't have a job now."

His face shone in the firelight.

P "She wanted to give me a puppy, but they can't let any one boy keep a puppy. You remember the suit I had on last Sunday?" He was plainly proud. "She sent me that for Christmas. The Christmas before that"—he drew a long breath, savoring the memory—"she sent me a pair of skates."

"Roller skates?"

My mind was busy, making pictures of her, trying to understand her. She had not, then, entirely deserted or forgotten him. But why, then— I thought, "I must not condemn her without knowing."

"Roller skates. I let the other boys use them. They're always borrowing them. But they're careful of them."

What circumstance other than poverty—

"I'm going to take the dollar you gave me for taking care of Pat," he said, "and buy her a pair of gloves."

I could only say, "That will be nice. Do you know her size?"

"I think it's $8\frac{1}{2}$," he said.

He looked at my hands.

"Do you wear $8\frac{1}{2}$?" he asked.

"No. I wear a smaller size, a 6."

"Oh! Then I guess her hands are bigger than yours."

Q I hated her. Poverty or no, there was other food than bread, and the soul could starve as quickly as the body. He was taking his dollar to buy gloves for her big stupid hands, and she lived away from him, in Mannville, and contented herself with sending him skates.

"She likes white gloves," he said. "Do you think I can get them for a dollar?"

"I think so," I said.

I decided that I should not leave the mountains without seeing her and knowing for myself why she had done this thing.

R The human mind scatters its interests as though made of thistledown, and every wind stirs and moves it. I finished my work. It did not please me, and I gave my thoughts to another field. I should need some Mexican material.

Did You Know?
Thistledown is the soft, fluffy down on the flower head of a thistle.

I made arrangements to close my Florida place. Mexico immediately, and doing the writing there, if conditions were favorable. Then, Alaska with my brother. After that, heaven knew what or where.

I did not take time to go to Mannville to see Jerry's mother, nor even to talk with the orphanage officials about her. I was a trifle abstracted[6] about the boy, because of

6. Here, *abstracted* means "lost in thought"; preoccupied.

Vocabulary
savor (sā′ vər) *v.* to take great delight in

P Active Reading Strategies

QUESTION What impact does Jerry's story have on the relationship between him and the narrator? *(His story leads the narrator to become less concerned about him.)*

Q Author's Craft

ALLUSION The narrator's statement, "there was other food than bread" is an allusion to "Man does not live by bread alone." Ask students to interpret this allusion in light of the story. *(The narrator suggests that even if the mother were poor, the love she felt for her son should have enabled her to keep him.)*

R Critical Thinking

EVALUATING Although the narrator vows to find Jerry's mother, she becomes distracted. Ask students to evaluate her behavior. She suggests that being distracted is typical (human). Is it? Should she have acted differently? Share the following model:

Model: I think the narrator is infuriated with Jerry's mother, yet it seems as though she plans to abandon the boy, as she imagines his mother did. I think the narrator decides that if Jerry actually has a mother, he doesn't need her. So she finds a way to justify leaving. I think Jerry will suffer greatly from the loss of his friend. She says it's only human to change, but I think the effects of her actions on Jerry will be harmful.

Real-World Connection

Adoption Trends Historically it has been difficult to place older children for adoption. Many who choose to adopt prefer infants. Have students do some research into current adoption trends to find out what tends to happen to older children who need adoptive parents. Ask each student to find an article on the subject in a magazine or newspaper and report on it. **L2**

Active Reading Strategies

RESPOND Ask students what they think of the narrator's relief at not having to say good-bye to Jerry. Is her response understandable? Is there a sense in which the narrator is doing exactly what she condemned Jerry's "mother" for? *(Many students may feel that her response is hard to understand—that she is doing precisely what she condemned his mother for doing.)*

Active Reading Strategies

RESPOND Ask students why they think Rawlings ends the story here. Why doesn't she tell the reader what happens next? Do students think the ending is effective?

Thematic Focus

Lean on Me It is clear that the narrator leaned on Jerry for help. How does Jerry lean on the narrator? *(He hopes she will become a source of maternal affection.)*

ASSESSMENT

Quick Checks, p. 16

my work and plans. And after my first fury at her—we did not speak of her again—his having a mother, any sort at all, not far away, in Mannville, relieved me of the ache I had had about him. He did not question the anomalous relation. He was not lonely. It was none of my concern.

He came every day and cut my wood and did small helpful favors and stayed to talk. The days had become cold, and often I let him come inside the cabin. He would lie on the floor in front of the fire, with one arm across the pointer, and they would both doze and wait quietly for me. Other days they ran with a common ecstasy through the laurel, and since the asters were now gone, he brought me back vermilion maple leaves, and chestnut boughs dripping with imperial yellow. I was ready to go.

I said to him, "You have been my good friend, Jerry. I shall often think of you and miss you. Pat will miss you too. I am leaving tomorrow."

He did not answer. When he went away, I remember that a new moon hung over the mountains, and I watched him go in silence up the hill. I expected him the next day, but he did not come. The details of packing my personal belongings, loading my car, arranging the bed over the seat, where the dog would ride, occupied me until late in the day. I closed the cabin and started the car, noticing that the sun was in the west and I should do well to be out of the mountains by nightfall. I stopped by the orphanage and left the cabin key and money for my light bill with Miss Clark.

"And will you call Jerry for me to say good-bye to him?"

"I don't know where he is," she said. "I'm afraid he's not well. He didn't eat his dinner this noon. One of the other boys saw him going over the hill into the laurel. He was supposed to fire the boiler this afternoon. It's not like him; he's unusually reliable."

I was almost relieved, for I knew I should never see him again, and it would be easier not to say good-bye to him.

I said, "I wanted to talk with you about his mother—why he's here—but I'm in more of a hurry than I expected to be. It's out of the question for me to see her now too. But here's some money I'd like to leave with you to buy things for him at Christmas and on his birthday. It will be better than for me to try to send him things. I could so easily duplicate—skates, for instance."

She blinked her honest spinster's[7] eyes.

"There's not much use for skates here," she said.

Her stupidity annoyed me.

"What I mean," I said, "is that I don't want to duplicate things his mother sends him. I might have chosen skates if I didn't know she had already given them to him."

She stared at me.

"I don't understand," she said. "He has no mother. He has no skates."

7. *Spinster* usually refers to an older woman who has never been married.

❖

Vocabulary
anomalous (ə nom′ ə ləs) *adj.* not following the usual or regular; abnormal

Teaching Support

Grammar and Language *Minilesson*

Commas and Compound Sentences
Write these sentences on the board: *The days had become cold, and often I let him come inside the cabin. I expected him the next day, but he did not come. I was almost relieved, for I knew I should never see him again.* Explain that these are all compound sentences—two complete sentences joined by coordinating conjunctions, such as *and, but,* and *for*. Note that a comma precedes the coordinating conjunction.

Activity Have students find five other examples of compound sentences in the story. Then have them write five properly punctuated compound sentences of their own. **L2**

Additional Resources

- ***Grammar and Language Transparency 15***
- ***Grammar and Language Workbook,*** p. 259–260
- ***Grammar and Composition Handbook,*** Lesson 13.3
- ***Writer's Choice,*** Lesson 20.3

Responding to Literature

PERSONAL RESPONSE

- What were your thoughts when you read the last sentence of this story? Write these thoughts in your journal.

Brackets connect questions that are paired to develop higher-level thinking skills.

Analyzing Literature

RECALL

1. How does the narrator's impression of Jerry change?
2. What does Jerry say about his mother?
3. How does the narrator react to what Jerry tells her about his mother?
4. Describe how Jerry spends his days at the narrator's cabin.

INTERPRET

5. What causes the narrator to believe that Jerry has integrity?
6. What does Jerry's description of his mother tell you about him?
7. Why do you think the narrator reacts as she does to Jerry's description of his mother and their relationship?
8. Why, do you think, does Jerry respond as he does to the narrator's news that she is leaving?

EVALUATE AND CONNECT

9. Theme Connection In what ways do Jerry and the narrator find closeness and strength in their relationship? Select details from the story to support your view.
10. Think about your response to the **Reading Focus** on page 184. How was your experience similar to the narrator's? How was it different?

LITERARY ELEMENTS

Narrator

A **narrator** is the person who tells a story. The narrator may be the author of a true story, such as R. A. Sasaki's "A Dictionary of Japanese-American Terms." In fiction, the narrator may be a voice outside the story or a character who participates in the story. A narrator outside the story uses the **third-person point of view.** A narrator who is a character in a story uses the **first-person point of view** to describe his or her experiences.

1. What type of narrator is this storyteller—an outside voice, a character, or the author? Explain.
2. Sometimes a narrator isn't knowledgeable or mature enough to fully explain a story. Suppose that Jerry were the narrator. How might he have told the story? Would he have been more or less reliable than the adult narrator? Explain.

- See **Literary Terms Handbook,** p. R6.

Responding to the Selection

PERSONAL RESPONSE

Many students will feel sorry for Jerry, because he has lost a chance to be close to someone he cares about.

Analyzing Literature

1. At first the narrator hardly notices the boy. Then she comes to love and respect him.
2. Jerry says he visits his mother and that she sends him gifts.
3. The narrator is horrified that Jerry's mother could abandon him.
4. Jerry works, plays with the dog, and sometimes lies by the fire waiting for the narrator to finish her work so they can talk.
5. Jerry's taking responsibility for breaking the ax makes her see him as a person of integrity.
6. Jerry's description of his mother reflects a relationship Jerry wishes he had with someone.
7. The narrator has come to care for Jerry and cannot imagine how someone could leave him.
8. Jerry is wounded when he hears that the narrator is leaving.
9. Jerry begins to feel he has a place of his own at the narrator's cabin. The narrator does not worry about being late because she trusts Jerry to take care of things.
10. Students may say that when their impressions proved to be incorrect, they felt disappointed.

LITERARY ELEMENTS

1. The narrator is a character in the story.
2. The adult point of view is important to this story because Jerry probably can't articulate, and doesn't entirely understand, why he invents a mother.

Additional Resources

Literary Elements Transparency 16

Literature and Writing

Writing About Literature

Students' paragraphs should

- begin with a clear statement of what quality is attributed to the narrator
- include specific examples

Personal Writing

Students' journal entries should

- include precise descriptions
- explain the need filled

Extending Your Response

Literature Groups Encourage students to strive for a balanced perspective, paying attention to both the narrator's kindnesses and her failures. **COLLAB. LEARN.**

Listening and Speaking If time permits, allow a second student to play the role of Jerry to see what differences might emerge. **COLLAB. LEARN.**

Learning for Life Suggest that the class might want to think of a charitable project to help one of the institutions identified.

Always preview films before recommending them.

At the MOVIES

Be sure to preview the following video for appropriateness for your class:

The Prince of Egypt, a 1998 musical retelling of the story of Moses.

Literature and Writing

Writing About Literature

Definition The narrator tells us that the remarkable thing about Jerry is his "integrity." She defines the term and even gives an example (Jerry's wish to pay for the ax handle) to help the reader understand the concept. Write your own definition for a quality that you think the narrator possesses. Give examples or make comparisons to help clarify the word.

Personal Writing

Wanted: The Perfect Relative People sometimes wish for a relative they never had, such as a big brother; a healthy, energetic grandparent; or an aunt to take them to special places or to give them special things. In your journal, write a description of a relative you do not have or never knew, but wish you had. Tell how that person might fill a special need in your own life.

Extending Your Response

Literature Groups

Judging the Narrator Do you think the narrator was sensitive and kind, or was she self-absorbed and distant? What did she do for Jerry? What more might she have done? As a group, search for examples that show her concern for Jerry, as well as opportunities she missed for kindness. Also discuss the limits of her ability to help him. Conclude your discussion by writing a brief statement that rates the narrator's response to the boy. Compare your concluding statement with those of other groups.

Listening and Speaking

Among Friends With a small group, brainstorm some things Jerry might tell his friends about his time with the narrator. Without rehearsing, role-play the conversation they might have. The student playing Jerry should mention specific events and how they made him feel. The other students should ask questions or offer comments about what happened.

Learning for Life

Researching Community Resources "A Mother in Mannville" describes the orphanage where Jerry lives. Is there an institution in your town or city that offers help to needy people? Such institutions might include senior citizen homes or shelters for homeless families. Find out more about the institution through research and interviews, and report your findings to the class.

Reading Further

For stories about ways we rely on others, try these:

The Yearling by Marjorie Kinnan Rawlings

The Red Pony by John Steinbeck

Save your work for your portfolio.

Skill Minilessons

RETEACH • REVIEW

GRAMMAR AND LANGUAGE • CAPITALIZATION

Good writers follow these basic rules for capitalization:

- Capitalize the first word of a direct quotation, a quotation that gives the speaker's exact words.
  I could only say, "That will be nice. Do you know her size?"
- Capitalize proper nouns (specific people, places, and things). Do not capitalize common nouns.
  He became intimate, of course, with my pointer, Pat.

PRACTICE Write each sentence, using capital letters as needed. If the sentence is correct, write *C.*

1. "come in, jerry, if you're allowed to be away this late."
2. "I'll pay for it," he said.
3. He said, "she comes up here from mannville whenever she can."
4. his face shone in the firelight.
5. "oh! then I guess her hands are bigger than yours."

● For more about capitalization, see **Language Handbook,** pp. R35–R37.

READING AND THINKING • UNDERSTANDING DETAILS

Writers use details carefully. When Rawlings begins her story with details about dense fog, bitter winds, and swirling snow and deep drifts, she evokes the hardship and chill of orphanage life.

As you read, look for the details the writer uses to create a picture or to support an idea.

● For more about main idea and details, see **Reading Handbook,** pp. R98–R99.

PRACTICE Briefly explain what each detail tells about the character named in parentheses.

1. At first the sound of the boy dragging brush annoyed me. (the narrator)
2. "I have gloves," he added. "Some of the boys don't have any." (Jerry)
3. The dog lay close to him, and found a comfort there that I did not have for him. (Jerry and the narrator)

VOCABULARY • ANALOGIES

An **analogy** is a type of comparison that is based on relationships between things or ideas.

feathers : bird :: hair : mammal
Feathers cover birds; hair covers mammals.

You read the analogy in this way:

Feathers are to birds as hair is to mammals.

When one term is missing, you can finish an analogy by deciding what relationship exists between the first two things or ideas. Then apply that relationship to another pair of words.

PRACTICE Complete each analogy below.

1. avoid : dodge :: savor :
   a. relish b. taste c. swallow
2. happy : sad :: unusual :
   a. scary b. typical c. joyous
3. spurs : impel :: reins :
   a. halt b. measure c. mount
4. heat : cold :: evil :
   a. virtue b. bravery c. dishonesty
5. kindly : well-meaning :: intimate :
   a. distant b. similar c. familiar

Skill Minilessons

GRAMMAR AND LANGUAGE
CAPITALIZATION

1. "Come in, Jerry, if you're allowed to be away this late."
2. Correct
3. He said, "She comes up here from Mannville whenever she can."
4. His face shone in the firelight.
5. "Oh! Then I guess her hands are bigger than yours."

READING AND THINKING
UNDERSTANDING DETAILS

1. The narrator is easily irritated.
2. Jerry appreciates how lucky he is.
3. The dog prefers to snuggle up with Jerry.

VOCABULARY
ANALOGIES

1. a
2. b
3. a
4. a
5. c

Additional Resources

- ***Grammar and Language Workbook,*** p. 243–250
- ***Grammar and Composition Handbook,*** Lesson 12
- ***Writer's Choice,*** Lesson 19
- ***Reading Skills Practice Workbook,*** pp. 29–30
- ***Vocabulary Practice,*** p. 14

ASSESSMENT

- ***Quick Checks,*** p. 16
- ***Selection and Theme Assessment,*** pp. 27–28
- ***Performance Assessment,*** p. 15
- ***Testmaker: ExamView Pro***
- ***Interactive Tutor: Self-Assessment***

GENRE FOCUS

Objective

- To understand the elements of an autobiography

Teaching Strategies

Telling the story of one's life is like telling any other story—a writer must hold the reader's interest. An autobiographer does this by selecting significant and interesting events to include in his or her writing.

Point of View Skepticism is appropriate when reading autobiography. People may tend, in Charles Dickens's words, to make themselves the heroes of their own lives.

Turning Points An autobiographer looks back on his or her life and often discovers meanings in events previously overlooked.

Description Use of vivid details in an autobiography allows the reader to enter into another person's life.

Interaction Between Characters Autobiography often relies on carefully chosen meetings with other people to reveal the meaning of the writer's life.

GENRE FOCUS

AUTOBIOGRAPHY

An **autobiography** is the story of a person's life, written by that person. It is a type of **nonfiction**—writing that is based on fact, history, or personal opinion. Most autobiographies are **narrative nonfiction,** telling about the writer's life while using a story structure that includes characters, setting, and a conflict or problem. Many autobiographies are book length because they narrate the writer's entire life. However, some focus on one or two events or a brief period in the author's life.

When you read an autobiography, look for the following elements:

POINT OF VIEW An autobiography is always written from the first person point of view and uses the pronoun "I."

TURNING POINTS These are vivid and memorable experiences in the writer's life that affected him or her in some important way. A turning point usually is based on a conflict and its resolution.

DESCRIPTION Writers carefully portray a person, place, thing, or event, using the five senses to help the reader experience the story.

INTERACTION BETWEEN CHARACTERS The action of the narrator with people and other creatures gives the reader insights into the personality of the autobiographer.

MODEL

Helen had brought a lot of things into my life and Sam was one of the most precious; he was a Beagle and her own personal pet. . . . — Turning Point

Sam adopted me on sight. It was as though he had read the Faithful Hound Manual because he was always near me; paws on the dash as he gazed eagerly through the windscreen on my rounds, head resting on my foot in our bed-sitting room, trotting just behind me wherever I moved.

(Labels: Interaction of Characters; Description; First Person Point of View)

– *from* All Things Bright and Beautiful *by James Herriot*

Teaching Support

Technology

Students can use word-processing software to create a table of the major elements of autobiography. Have each student open a new document and insert a four-column table with the following headings: *Point of View, Turning Points, Description,* and *Interaction.*

Point of View	Turning Points	Description	Interaction

For each autobiographical piece, a new row can be added to the table and information about each of the four elements of autobiography keyed in. The completed table will serve as a good tool for study. **L2**

ACTIVE READING MODEL

Active Reading Strategies

Tips for Reading an Autobiography

Active readers talk to themselves as they read. Use the suggestions below to help you read autobiographies and other nonfiction narratives actively.

- For more about reading strategies, see **Reading Handbook,** pp. R93–R106.

PREVIEW

Look for dates and clue words that show sequence of events.

QUESTION

Follow the character's thoughts throughout the story. Ask yourself why the character interacts with other people and responds to events as he or she does. How does the character change? Why?

VISUALIZE

An autobiography involves actual places and events as the author remembers them. Try to see people and places and consider why they were important to the writer.

RESPOND

Did the author want to share an experience, teach a lesson, or entertain? An effective reader will analyze and respond to the writer.

APPLYING THE STRATEGIES

Read the selection from Maya Angelou's autobiography, *I Know Why the Caged Bird Sings.* Use the **Active Reading** notes in the margins as you read. Write your responses on a separate sheet of paper to look over when you have finished reading.

Active Reading Strategies

Objective

- To understand and apply strategies for reading and comprehending an autobiography

Teach the Strategies

Explain that reading an autobiography calls for many of the strategies students use to read fiction.

Preview

An author often provides a chronology of significant dates. A good comprehension strategy is to preview the chronology before reading and then to consult it regularly while reading.

Question

Why is the author revealing this information? This is a particularly good question to ask of an autobiography.

Visualize

Visualizing is so important that an autobiographer often includes photographs of people and places mentioned in the work. As with the chronology, it is helpful to glance through the pictures and read the captions before reading the text.

Respond

An author may write honestly or write to justify or glorify himself or herself. Sharp readers evaluate the author to determine whether he or she is a reliable narrator.

Reading Journal

Visualizing Characters

Point out that in the selection from *I Know Why the Caged Bird Sings,* the author is looking back on her childhood. She remembers Mrs. Flowers, a woman who gave her confidence and instilled in her a love of literature and reading.

Activity Ask students to make notes about Mrs. Flowers and Marguerite (the young Maya Angelou) as they read the selection from Angelou's autobiography. Why does Angelou recall the experience so clearly? What details about each of the characters stand out in your mind or remind you of people you know? **L2**

Before Reading

Objectives

- To read and analyze a chapter from an autobiography
- To understand an author's use of dialect
- To write a paragraph about characterization

Skills

Reading/Thinking: Monitoring Comprehension; Evaluating
Writing: Paragraph; Personal Letter
Vocabulary: Negating Prefixes
Grammar/Language: Parentheses; Subject-Verb Agreement
Listening/Speaking: Oral Presentation; Oral Interpretation
Collaboration: Monitoring Comprehension; Literature Groups; Oral Presentation

Motivating → STUDENTS

Selection Focus Transparency 16: Before presenting the painting, have volunteers share experiences in which they were helped by an adult.

Reading Focus: As an extension of the Reading Focus, discuss with students the possibility that they can return a favor by being a mentor or special friend to a younger person. Ask students to think of ways they may be able to work with younger children at school to make them feel special.

ACTIVE READING MODEL

Before You Read

from *I Know Why the Caged Bird Sings*

MEET MAYA ANGELOU

"I love that there are other things I can put my hand to, but I am a Black American female writer," says Maya Angelou (mī′ yə an′ jə lō). Author of more than a dozen books, Angelou has written for Oprah Winfrey's TV company and read her poetry at President Bill Clinton's inauguration. She also has "put her hand to" acting, singing, and dancing. "I really wanted to be the person my grandmother wanted me to be," Angelou says. "And I'm still trying."

Maya Angelou was born in St. Louis, Missouri, in 1928. This selection is from I Know Why the Caged Bird Sings, *which was first published in 1969.*

READING FOCUS

Think of a time you felt important or exceptional because someone gave you special attention.

QuickWrite
Jot down the details of this event. Describe the person, the setting, and your reaction to the situation.

Setting a Purpose
Read to discover how the right encouragement can help a person grow.

BUILDING BACKGROUND

The Time and Place The story takes place during the 1930s in a small Arkansas town. The narrator has not spoken for a year because of a trauma experienced during a stay in St. Louis.

Did You Know? *A Tale of Two Cities,* a novel by Charles Dickens, is set during the French Revolution. Charles Darnay is in prison, condemned to death. Sidney Carton, a family friend, helps Darnay escape, then takes his place in jail. When Carton must face the guillotine, he says, "It is a far, far better thing that I do, than I have ever done."

VOCABULARY PREVIEW

taut (tôt) *adj.* tense; tight; p. 199
persistently (pər sis′ tənt lē) *adv.* repeatedly; p. 201
refined (ri fīnd′) *adj.* free from coarseness or crudeness; showing good taste and manners; p. 201
competently (kom′ pət ənt lē) *adv.* capably; p. 202
valid (val′ id) *adj.* well-supported by facts; true; p. 204
intolerant (in tol′ ər ənt) *adj.* unwilling to put up with; not accepting; p. 205
illiteracy (i lit′ ər ə sē) *n.* the inability to read or write; p. 205
collective (kə lek′ tiv) *adj.* having to do with a group of persons or things; common; shared; p. 205

RESOURCE MANAGER

Teaching Tools and Resources
- Theme Two Planning Guide
- Literature Groups Sourcebook

Essential Lesson Support

Lesson-Specific Instruction
- Selection Focus Transparency 16
- Literary Elements Transparency 17
- Active Reading Guide,* p. 17
- Selection Vocabulary Practice, p. 15

Assessment
- Selection Quick Checks,* p. 17
- Sel. and Theme Assmt., pp. 29–30
- Testmaker: ExamView Pro
- Performance Assessment, p. 16

Systematic Language Instruction
- Gr. & Comp. Hbk., Lessons 3.10
- Vocabulary Power, Lesson 9
- Spelling Power, Lesson 8

English Language Learners
- ELL Sourcebook, p. 36
- Spanish Summaries, p. 16
- Spanish Translations, pp. 63–68
- Audio Library*
- English, Yes!

Spec. Needs/Strat. Interven.
- Interactive Rdg. Sbk., pp. T87–T89
- Interactive Rdg. Wbk., pp. 36–37
- Inclusion Strat. Sbk., pp. 7–8
- Audio Library*

* Also available in Spanish

from I Know Why the Caged Bird Sings

Maya Angelou

Pared Amarilla con Jaula (Yellow Wall with Birdcage), 1990. Elena Climent. Oil on canvas, 42 x 53 in. Mary-Anne Martin/Fine Art, New York.

ACTIVE READING MODEL

Mrs. Bertha Flowers was the aristocrat of Black Stamps. She had the grace of control to appear warm in the coldest weather, and on the Arkansas summer days it seemed she had a private breeze which swirled around, cooling her. She was thin without the taut look of wiry people, and her printed voile[1] dresses and flowered hats were as right for her as denim overalls for a farmer. She was our side's answer to the richest white woman in town.

Her skin was a rich black that would have peeled like a plum if snagged, but then no one would have thought of getting close enough to Mrs. Flowers to ruffle her dress, let alone snag her skin. She didn't encourage familiarity. She wore gloves too.

VISUALIZE Take a moment to picture Mrs. Flowers in your mind. **A**

1. *Voile* (voil) is a light cotton fabric.

Vocabulary
taut (tôt) *adj.* tense; tight

Reading the Selection

SUMMARY

Maya Angelou (called Marguerite as a girl) recalls a woman who had a profound influence on her, Mrs. Bertha Flowers. One day Mrs. Flowers requests that Marguerite help her home with her groceries. Because of a traumatic experience, Marguerite has not spoken in a year. Mrs. Flowers urges Marguerite to speak; she tells her she knows she is intelligent. Mrs. Flowers reads aloud to Marguerite a passage from *A Tale of Two Cities*. When she finishes reading, Marguerite speaks for the first time. She leaves, inspired by the fact that someone like Mrs. Flowers had singled her out for attention.

Spanish Summaries, p. 16

A Active Reading Strategies

VISUALIZE *(Mrs. Flowers is an elegant lady, self-possessed and calm.)* Does she remind you of anyone you know?

VOCABULARY Remind students to use context clues to unlock the meanings of new vocabulary words.

Additional Resources

Active Reading Guide, p. 17
Audio Library
Spanish Audio Library

Teaching Support

CONNECTING TO OTHER SELECTIONS

The chart at the right shows three ways to connect the excerpt from *I Know Why the Caged Bird Sings* to other selections in this book.

For specific teaching strategies, see the ***Theme Two Planning Guide.***

Connection	Title
Life Skills: Teaching and Mentoring	→ "The People Could Fly," p. 388
Thematic: Acceptance	→ "Americans All," p. 642
Literary: Setting	→ "Sorrow Home," p. 504

VIEWING THE PAINTING

Hyacinth Manning-Carner finds faces "fascinating." In a series of paintings of Jamaica, she views her childhood home through adult eyes.

Viewing Response *The woman in the painting seems cool, dignified, and self-possessed, however, her posture seems more casual than that of Mrs. Flowers.*

B Active Reading Strategies

QUESTION *(A person who models the good characteristics of human kind is "the measure.")* Who is that model in your life?

C Active Reading Strategies

QUESTION What does Angelou mean when she says she hated Momma "with the unbalanced passion of the young"? *(She felt embarrassed by her grandmother's actions.)*

D Active Reading Strategies

QUESTION *(The women seem alike because they share many qualities.)* Do you know someone who is like you?

E Active Reading Strategies

PARAPHRASE What does Angelou mean when she says that Momma and Mrs. Flowers were "as alike as sisters, separated only by formal education"? *(Their values and personal qualities were similar and worthy of the same respect.)*

Teaching Support

ACTIVE READING MODEL

I don't think I ever saw Mrs. Flowers laugh, but she smiled often. A slow widening of her thin black lips to show even, small white teeth, then the slow effortless closing. When she chose to smile on me, I always wanted to thank her. The action was so graceful and inclusively benign.[2]

The End of the Day, 1955. Hyacinth Manning-Carner. Pastel on paper, 29 x 22 in.

Viewing the painting: What characteristics of Mrs. Flowers do you see in the woman in this picture? In what ways is she different?

B **QUESTION** What makes someone "the measure of what a human being can be"?

She was one of the few gentlewomen I have ever known, and has remained throughout my life the measure of what a human being can be.

Momma had a strange relationship with her. Most often when she passed on the road in front of the Store, she spoke to Momma in that soft yet carrying voice, "Good day, Mrs. Henderson." Momma responded with "How you, Sister Flowers?"

D **QUESTION** Why might two unrelated women seem as alike as sisters?

Mrs. Flowers didn't belong to our church, nor was she Momma's familiar. Why on earth did she insist on calling her Sister Flowers? Shame made me want to hide my face. Mrs. Flowers deserved better than to be called Sister. Then, Momma left out the verb. Why not ask, "How *are* you, Mrs. Flowers?" With the unbalanced passion of the young, I hated her for showing her ignorance to Mrs. Flowers. It didn't occur to me for many years that they were as alike as sisters, separated only by formal education.

Although I was upset, neither of the women was in the least shaken by what I thought an unceremonious greeting. Mrs. Flowers would continue her easy gait up the hill to her little bungalow, and

2. *Benign* means "kindly and gentle." *Inclusively* means "in a way that includes everyone and everything."

MEETING INDIVIDUAL NEEDS — ENGLISH LANGUAGE LEARNERS

Dialect Marguerite is ashamed because her grandmother speaks a dialect typical of African Americans living in the South at the time. It includes such features as using a singular verb with a plural subject and omitting a verb. There are also differences in pronunciation, such as "sho'ly" for "surely." English language learners may need help with some of the dialect.

Activity Group English language learners with native speakers. Have them look for dialect in the story. Ask the students to work together to change the dialect into standard English and discuss their translations with the group.

Additional Resources

English Language Learners Sourcebook, p. 36

Momma kept on shelling peas or doing whatever had brought her to the front porch.

Occasionally, though, Mrs. Flowers would drift off the road and down to the Store and Momma would say to me, "Sister, you go on and play." As I left I would hear the beginning of an intimate conversation. Momma persistently using the wrong verb, or none at all.

"Brother and Sister Wilcox is sho'ly the meanest—" "Is," Momma? "Is"? Oh, please, not "is," Momma, for two or more. But they talked, and from the side of the building where I waited for the ground to open up and swallow me, I heard the soft-voiced Mrs. Flowers and the textured voice of my grandmother merging and melting. They were interrupted from time to time by giggles that must have come from Mrs. Flowers (Momma never giggled in her life). Then she was gone.

She appealed to me because she was like people I had never met personally. Like women in English novels who walked the moors (whatever they were) with their loyal dogs racing at a respectful distance. Like the women who sat in front of roaring fireplaces, drinking tea incessantly from silver trays full of scones and crumpets.[3] Women who walked over the "heath" and read morocco-bound books[4] and had two last names divided by a hyphen. It would be safe to say that she made me proud to be Negro, just by being herself.

She acted just as refined as whitefolks in the movies and books and she was more beautiful, for none of them could have come near that warm color without looking gray by comparison.

It was fortunate that I never saw her in the company of powhitefolks. For since they tend to think of their whiteness as an evenizer, I'm certain that I would have had to hear her spoken to commonly as Bertha, and my image of her would have been shattered like the unmendable Humpty-Dumpty.

One summer afternoon, sweet-milk fresh in my memory, she stopped at the Store to buy provisions. Another Negro woman of her health and age would have been expected to carry the paper sacks home in one hand, but Momma said, "Sister Flowers, I'll send Bailey up to your house with these things."

3. A *moor* is a stretch of open, rolling, wild land. *Incessantly* means "constantly." A *scone* is a sweet biscuit, and a *crumpet* is an English muffin.
4. Another word for moor is *heath*. A *morocco-bound book* is bound in leather made from goats raised in Morocco, a country in North Africa.

Vocabulary

persistently (pər sis′ tənt lē) *adv.* repeatedly
refined (ri fīnd′) *adj.* free from coarseness or crudeness; showing good taste and manners

ACTIVE READING MODEL

CONNECT

Does anyone you know make you proud to be who you are?

FYI

"Momma" is actually Angelou's grandmother, Mrs. Henderson. Because Angelou was sent to live with her grandmother at an early age, she and her brother Bailey referred to her as "Momma."

F Literary Elements

ALLUSION Take a moment either to draw the response from the group or explain what kinds of novels Angelou is referring to. *(The works of the Brontë sisters, Thomas Hardy, William M. Thackeray, and George Eliot are certainly candidates.)*

G Active Reading Strategies

CONNECT *(There are certain people whose approval is very powerful.)* What characteristics do these people have in common?

H Active Reading Strategies

QUESTION Explain the word and the concept *powhitefolks.* What does Angelou mean when she says powhitefolks "tend to think of their whiteness as an evenizer"? Why would they have treated Mrs. Flowers badly? *(Believing that all black people were lower than they allowed some poor white people to be content with their position. They often bolstered their own egos by treating African Americans with disdain.)*

Real-World Connection

Maya Angelou Ask students to use a search engine to find out more about the life and work of Maya Angelou. Students can use such search terms as the writer's name or *African American writers.* Have students report briefly to the class on the information they uncovered. **L3**

Literature & Humanities

You may wish to use *Introducing Art,* page 226, to introduce students to visual biography. Discuss the influences represented and have students create visual autobiographies.

I Active Reading Strategies

QUESTION *(They share experiences and values.)* Do teenagers ever exchange “age-group looks”?

J Literary Elements

WORD CHOICE Ask students what Angelou means by “I trusted myself back into the store.” Why does she use the word *trusted?* *(Marguerite is unsure about what to wear; all she can do is “trust” that she has made the right choice. The word conveys her nervousness and hesitation.)*

K Active Reading Strategies

RESPOND *(Mrs. Flowers apparently can afford to buy clothes, so it is not surprising that she doesn’t sew.)* What does her lack of skill have to do with the praise she offers?

L Active Reading Strategies

QUESTION *(Momma enjoys Mrs. Flowers’s attention because she seldom gets to talk about such things.)* Does Mrs. Flowers make Momma proud to be herself, too?

M Active Reading Strategies

RESPOND Ask students how it might feel to be in this situation. How is Angelou’s attitude toward the situation different from Momma’s? *(Marguerite is already embarrassed by Momma’s behavior. Momma responds to the compliment and doesn’t consider Marguerite’s feelings.)*

Teaching Support

ACTIVE READING MODEL

QUESTION

I. Why do Sister Flowers and Momma exchange “age-group looks”?

RESPOND

K. Are you surprised that Mrs. Flowers does not sew?

QUESTION

L. Why does Momma want to explain her sewing techniques to Mrs. Flowers?

She smiled that slow dragging smile, “Thank you, Mrs. Henderson. I’d prefer Marguerite, though.” My name was beautiful when she said it. “I’ve been meaning to talk to her, anyway.” They gave each other age-group looks.

Momma said, “Well, that’s all right then. Sister, go and change your dress. You going to Sister Flowers’s.”

The chifforobe was a maze. What on earth did one put on to go to Mrs. Flowers’ house? I knew I shouldn’t put on a Sunday dress. It might be sacrilegious.[5] Certainly not a house dress, since I was already wearing a fresh one. I chose a school dress, naturally. It was formal without suggesting that going to Mrs. Flowers’ house was equivalent to attending church.

Did You Know?
A *chifforobe* (shif′ə rōb) is a tall piece of furniture that has both drawers and space for hanging clothes.

J I trusted myself back into the Store.

“Now, don’t you look nice.” I had chosen the right thing, for once.

“Mrs. Henderson, you make most of the children’s clothes, don’t you?”

“Yes, ma’am. Sure do. Store-bought clothes ain’t hardly worth the thread it take to stitch them.”

“I’ll say you do a lovely job, though, so neat. That dress looks professional.”

Momma was enjoying the seldom-received compliments. Since everyone we knew (except Mrs. Flowers, of course) could sew competently, praise was rarely handed out for the commonly practiced craft.

“I try, with the help of the Lord, Sister Flowers, to finish the inside just like I does the outside. Come here, Sister.”

I had buttoned up the collar and tied the belt, apronlike, in back. Momma told me to turn around. With one hand she pulled the strings and the belt fell free at both sides of my waist. Then her large hands were at my neck, opening the button loops. I was terrified. What was happening?

“Take it off, Sister.” She had her hands on the hem of the dress.

M “I don’t need to see the inside, Mrs. Henderson, I can tell . . .” But the dress was over my head and my arms were stuck in the sleeves. Momma said, “That’ll do. See here, Sister Flowers, I French-seams around the armholes.” Through the cloth film, I saw the shadow

5. *Sacrilegious* means “showing disrespect for something sacred or cherished.”

Vocabulary
competently (kom′ pət ənt lē) *adv.* capably

MEETING INDIVIDUAL NEEDS — SPECIAL NEEDS

Less-Proficient Readers/Learning Disabled Some students may find it difficult to understand Marguerite’s passivity. Discuss how children were once expected to behave in the presence of adults and the extent to which children might hold adults almost in awe.

Activity Have students work in small groups to talk about what they have heard from their parents and older relatives about “how I was brought up.” Have each group report on at least three differences they perceive between the behavior expected of children then and now. **L1**

Additional Resources
Inclusion Strategies

Kept In, 1889. Edward Lamson Henry. Oil on canvas, 13½ x 18 in. © New York State Historical Association, Cooperstown. N-309.61. Photo by Richard Walker.

Viewing the painting: What about this girl reminds you of Marguerite?

M approach. "That makes it last longer. Children these days would bust out of sheet-metal clothes. They so rough."

"That is a very good job, Mrs. Henderson. You should be proud. You can put your dress back on, Marguerite."

"No ma'am. Pride is a sin. And 'cording to the Good Book, it goeth before a fall."

"That's right. So the Bible says. It's a good thing to keep in mind."

O I wouldn't look at either of them. Momma hadn't thought that taking off my dress in front of Mrs. Flowers would kill me stone dead. If I had refused, she would have thought I was trying to be "womanish" and might have remembered St. Louis. Mrs. Flowers had known that I would be embarrassed and that was even worse. I picked up the groceries and went out to wait in the hot sunshine. It would be fitting if I got a sunstroke and died before they came outside. Just dropped dead on the slanting porch.

There was a little path beside the rocky road, and Mrs. Flowers walked in front swinging her arms and picking her way over the stones.

She said, without turning her head, to me, "I hear you're doing very good school work, Marguerite, but that it's all written. The teachers report

RESPOND N

How would you react to Momma?

VIEWING THE PAINTING

Kept In is one of a series of paintings showing a one-room school district. Henry did the series to commemorate civil rights legislation passed in New York in 1878.

Viewing Response *The words "kept in" suggest a punishment. Like Marguerite, she seems alone and a little sad.*

N Active Reading Strategies

RESPOND *(Many people would feel embarrassed as Marguerite does.)* What precisely might one be afraid of?

FYI

St. Louis In referring to St. Louis, Angelou is alluding to where the family was living when a year before the incidents narrated in this chapter, she was sexually abused by her mother's live-in boyfriend. Angelou was so traumatized by the experience that she did not talk for a year.

O Literary Elements

WORD CHOICE What does Angelou mean when she says her grandmother would have thought her "womanish" if she refused? *(Momma would think Marguerite is acting too grown up.)*

Reading Minilesson

Monitoring Comprehension One way to monitor comprehension is to ask and answer questions while reading. Active readers constantly ask themselves questions as they read because it helps with concentration and comprehension. A question about the passage on these pages, for example, is "Why is it so important to Momma that Mrs. Flowers see her seams?"

Activity Have students work in small groups to write questions about the passage on pages 202–203. Compile a list of all the different questions. Then go around the room asking students to answer each one. **L2** COLLAB. LEARN.

Additional Resources

Reading Skills Practice Workbook

Active Reading Strategies (P)

QUESTION Marguerite says she "hung back in the separate unasked and unanswerable questions." What may she have meant by that? *(Mrs. Flowers does not ask and Marguerite cannot answer the questions "What happened to you?" and "Why don't you talk?")*

Active Reading Strategies (Q)

RESPOND Ask students whether they agree with what Mrs. Flowers says about the human voice. If possible, allow students to listen to Angelou reading her own work. Explain that Angelou not only began to speak again; she developed a sonorous and expressive speaking voice that is instantly recognizable and always laden with "deeper meaning."

Active Reading Strategies (R)

QUESTION *(Mrs. Flowers values reading.)* Does Mrs. Flowers recognize a kindred spirit in Marguerite?

Active Reading Strategies (S)

RESPOND *(Students may say that they would feel special but a little nervous.)* Have students ever been in similar situations?

Teaching Support

ACTIVE READING MODEL

that they have trouble getting you to talk in class." We passed the triangular farm on our left and the path widened to allow us to walk together. I hung back in the separate unasked and unanswerable questions. **P**

"Come and walk along with me, Marguerite." I couldn't have refused even if I wanted to. She pronounced my name so nicely. Or more correctly, she spoke each word with such clarity that I was certain a foreigner who didn't understand English could have understood her.

"Now no one is going to make you talk—possibly no one can. But bear in mind, language is man's way of communicating with his fellow man and it is language alone which separates him from the lower animals." That was a totally new idea to me, and I would need time to think about it.

"Your grandmother says you read a lot. Every chance you get. That's good, but not good enough. Words mean more than what is set down on paper. It takes the human voice to infuse[6] them with the shades of deeper meaning." **Q**

QUESTION **R** What is Mrs. Flowers's attitude toward reading?

I memorized the part about the human voice infusing words. It seemed so <u>valid</u> and poetic.

She said she was going to give me some books and that I not only must read them, I must read them aloud. She suggested that I try to make a sentence sound in as many different ways as possible.

"I'll accept no excuse if you return a book to me that has been badly handled." My imagination boggled at the punishment I would deserve if in fact I did abuse a book of Mrs. Flowers'. Death would be too kind and brief.

The odors in the house surprised me. Somehow I had never connected Mrs. Flowers with food or eating or any other common experience of common people. There must have been an outhouse, too, but my mind never recorded it.

The sweet scent of vanilla had met us as she opened the door.

RESPOND **S** How would you feel in this scene?

"I made tea cookies this morning. You see, I had planned to invite you for cookies and lemonade so we could have this little chat. The lemonade is in the icebox."

It followed that Mrs. Flowers would have ice on an ordinary day, when most families in our town bought ice late on Saturdays only a few times during the summer to be used in the wooden ice-cream freezers.

She took the bags from me and disappeared through the kitchen door. I looked around the room that I had never in my wildest fantasies imagined I would see. Browned photographs leered or threatened from the walls and the white, freshly done curtains pushed

6. *Infuse* means "to fill, as with principles or qualities."

Vocabulary
valid (val′ id) *adj.* well-supported by facts; true

MEETING INDIVIDUAL NEEDS — MULTIPLE MODES OF EXPRESSION

Linguistic Students who have a verbal bent may want to do some further research regarding Mrs. Flowers's statement that language alone separates human beings from the animals.

Activity Have students do some basic research on animal communication and how it differs from human speech. What precisely can human beings do that animals cannot? Have students report on their findings using both direct quotations and summaries of information they find. **L2**

against themselves and against the wind. I wanted to gobble up the room entire and take it to Bailey, who would help me analyze and enjoy it.

"Have a seat, Marguerite. Over there by the table." She carried a platter covered with a tea towel. Although she warned that she hadn't tried her hand at baking sweets for some time, I was certain that like everything else about her the cookies would be perfect.

They were flat round wafers, slightly browned on the edges and butter-yellow in the center. With the cold lemonade they were sufficient for childhood's lifelong diet. Remembering my manners, I took nice little lady-like bites off the edges. She said she had made them expressly for me and that she had a few in the kitchen that I could take home to my brother. So I jammed one whole cake in my mouth and the rough crumbs scratched the insides of my jaws, and if I hadn't had to swallow, it would have been a dream come true.

V As I ate she began the first of what we later called "my lessons in living." She said that I must always be intolerant of ignorance but understanding of illiteracy. That some people unable to go to school were more educated and even more intelligent than college professors. She encouraged me to listen carefully to what country people called mother wit. That in those homely sayings was couched[7] the collective wisdom of generations.

When I finished the cookies she brushed off the table and brought a thick, small book from the bookcase. I had read *A Tale of Two Cities*[8] and found it up to my standards as a romantic novel. She opened the first page and I heard poetry for the first time in my life.

W "It was the best of times and the worst of times . . ." Her voice slid in and curved down through and over the words. She was nearly singing. I wanted to look at the pages. Were they the same that I had read? Or were there notes, music, lined on the pages, as in a hymn book? Her sounds began cascading gently. I knew from listening to a thousand preachers that she was nearing the end of her reading, and I hadn't really heard, heard to understand, a single word.

7. Here, *homely* means "simple; ordinary; everyday," and *couch,* as a verb, means "to express in words."
8. *A Tale of Two Cities,* a novel by Charles Dickens, describes English people who become caught up in the bloody French Revolution.

Vocabulary
intolerant (in tol′ ər ənt) *adj.* unwilling to put up with; not accepting
illiteracy (i lit′ ər ə sē) *n.* the inability to read or write
collective (kə lek′ tiv) *adj.* having to do with a group of persons or things; common; shared

ACTIVE READING MODEL

VISUALIZE
What does Mrs. Flowers's house look like? T

QUESTION
What does Mrs. Flowers teach Marguerite in her first "lesson in living"? U

T Active Reading Strategies

VISUALIZE *(Mrs. Flowers's house is elegant without being showy.)* How does the house affect Marguerite?

U Active Reading Strategies

QUESTION *(Mrs. Flowers teaches Marguerite the importance of education, but she urges Marguerite to be gentle with those who have not received an education.)* What lessons have you received from a mentor?

V Critical Thinking

DRAWING CONCLUSIONS Ask students to paraphrase Mrs. Flowers's wisdom. What does she counsel Marguerite to respect? To reject?

Model: Mrs. Flowers says Marguerite should not tolerate ignorance. She also tells her to be understanding of illiteracy and uneducated people. I think she wants Marguerite to know that education does not equal wisdom, and perhaps more important, she wants Marguerite to respect her own uneducated grandmother.

W Active Reading Strategies

QUESTION Ask students what Angelou means when she says she knew from listening to preachers that Mrs. Flowers was coming to the end of her reading even though Angelou had not been listening to the words. *(Angelou is used to hearing the intonation that suggests the sermon or passage is coming to an end. The voice slows down; words are given greater emphasis.)*

Listening and Speaking *Minilesson*

Oral Presentation Try to recapture some of what Marguerite heard when listening to Mrs. Flowers read aloud.

Activity Have students work in small groups to prepare readings of the first paragraph of *A Tale of Two Cities* or of a selected paragraph from this excerpt from *I Know Why the Caged Bird Sings.* Have some groups share their readings with the entire class. Then analyze the oral interpretations and discuss the effects of each interpretation on the listeners.
L2 COLLAB. LEARN.

ACTIVE READING MODEL

"How do you like that?"

It occurred to me that she expected a response. The sweet vanilla flavor was still on my tongue and her reading was a wonder in my ears. I had to speak.

I said, "Yes, ma'am." It was the least I could do, but it was the most also.

"There's one more thing. Take this book of poems and memorize one for me. Next time you pay me a visit, I want you to recite."

Did You Know?
Wormwood is a sweet-smelling plant, but the word is often used to refer to something unpleasant.

X I have tried often to search behind the sophistication of years for the enchantment I so easily found in those gifts. The essence escapes but its aura[9] remains. To be allowed, no, invited, into the private lives of strangers, and to share their joys and fears, was a chance to exchange the Southern bitter wormwood for a cup of mead with Beowulf or a hot cup of tea and milk with Oliver Twist.[10] When I said aloud, "It is a far, far better thing that I do, than I have ever done . . ." tears of love filled my eyes at my selflessness.

QUESTION
Y Why does Marguerite run down the hill?

On that first day, I ran down the hill and into the road (few cars ever came along it) and had the good sense to stop running before I reached the Store.

I was liked, and what a difference it made. I was respected not as Mrs. Henderson's grandchild or Bailey's sister but for just being Marguerite Johnson.

RESPOND
Z Does it matter *why* you are liked?

Childhood's logic never asks to be proved (all conclusions are absolute). I didn't question why Mrs. Flowers had singled me out for attention, nor did it occur to me that Momma might have asked her to give me a little talking to. All I cared about was that she had made tea cookies for *me* and read to *me* from her favorite book. It was enough to prove that she liked me.

9. The *essence* of a thing is its purest form or most basic nature. Its *aura* is the special feeling or mood that seems to surround it.
10. Beowulf, Oliver Twist, and the speaker of the quotation are all famous characters from literature.

X Active Reading Strategies

RESPOND Ask students to paraphrase this paragraph sentence by sentence. *(Angelou has often tried to recapture the delight she felt at Mrs. Flowers's gift. Even though she cannot recapture the exact feeling, she remembers something of what she felt. She recalls what it was like to read the books that Mrs. Flowers lent her: reading them was like being invited into the private lives of strangers.)*

Y Active Reading Strategies

QUESTION *(Marguerite runs for sheer joy.)* How do you think you might have acted?

Z Active Reading Strategies

RESPOND *(It is worthless to be liked for a superficial trait, such as money or looks.)* What is a good reason to like someone?

Thematic Focus

Lean on Me What kind of support does Mrs. Flowers offer Maya?

ASSESSMENT

Quick Checks, p. 17

FINE ART TRANSPARENCY 3

You may want to use ***Fine Art Transparency 3*** in a discussion of what *beauty* and *elegance* mean to students.

Teaching Support

Grammar and Language *Minilesson*

Parentheses Write this sentence on the board: *On that first day, I ran down the hill and into the road (few cars came along it).* Angelou uses parentheses to set off words that add additional information to the sentence or to explain or define a word in the sentence. Although parentheses can be helpful occasionally, their use should be restricted to content of less importance than the main sentence that nonetheless helps the reader to understand the sentence.

Activity Ask students to go back through the story and copy each parenthetical element in the story. Have them identify how the parentheses function in the sentences—to explain, clarify, or add information. **L2**

Additional Resources

- ***Grammar and Language Transparency 16***
- ***Grammar and Language Workbook,*** pp. 271–272
- ***Grammar and Composition Handbook,*** Lesson 13.8
- ***Writer's Choice,*** Lesson 20.8

ACTIVE READING MODEL

Responding to Literature

PERSONAL RESPONSE

- How would you feel if Mrs. Flowers paid the same attention to you as she did to Marguerite? Why would you react this way?

Brackets connect questions that are paired to develop higher-level thinking skills.

Analyzing Literature

RECALL

1. What term does Marguerite use to summarize her opinion of Mrs. Flowers?
2. What decision must Marguerite make when Mrs. Flowers invites her to visit?
3. How does Momma prove to Mrs. Flowers that she sews her clothes in a professional manner?
4. Marguerite gives a detailed description of Mrs. Flowers's house. Summarize her description in two or three sentences.

INTERPRET

5. What details in the story support Marguerite's opinion of Mrs. Flowers?
6. In your opinion, why is Marguerite concerned about what she should wear?
7. What do you learn about Momma from her conversation with Mrs. Flowers about sewing clothes?
8. How does Marguerite react when she sees Mrs. Flowers's house? Why does she react this way?

EVALUATE AND CONNECT

9. Why does Maya Angelou write that Mrs. Flowers is "the measure of what a human being can be"? What do you think is the measure of what a person can be? Make a list of qualities such a person would have.
10. Theme Connection Why would a person like Mrs. Flowers pay special attention to a person like Marguerite? Is Mrs. Flowers typical of people you know? Explain.

LITERARY ELEMENTS

Dialect

A **dialect** is a way of speaking that is associated with a specific geographical area or a group of people. Authors use dialect to give their writing the flavor of a specific region and to reveal the economic or social class of a character. A dialect may have its own vocabulary, grammar, and system for pronunciation. In the United States, the principal dialect is Standard English, but several regional dialects also exist.

1. Momma uses a local dialect that is spoken by some people in the southeastern United States. Find two examples of this dialect. Marguerite doesn't approve of this dialect. Why not?
2. What lesson about Momma and her dialect does Marguerite learn much later?

- See **Literary Terms Handbook,** p. R3.

Responding to the Selection

PERSONAL RESPONSE

Most students will say they would feel flattered to have such attention from a distinguished adult.

Analyzing Literature

1. Marguerite says that Mrs. Flowers was a "gentlewoman."
2. Marguerite must decide what dress to wear.
3. Momma shows Mrs. Flowers the French seams.
4. Mrs. Flowers's house is decorated with photographs and bright white curtains, and it smells of vanilla.
5. Mrs. Flowers is extremely gracious to Marguerite, treating her as a guest. She empathizes with Marguerite when her grandmother shows off the seams. She knows how to reach and inspire the girl by praising her intelligence and sharing books with her.
6. Marguerite realizes that being invited to visit Mrs. Flowers is an honor, and she wants to dress for the occasion.
7. Momma is pleased to be complimented but, being religious, does not want to feel pride.
8. Marguerite is charmed by the house. She reacts as she does because she identifies the house with the person, whom she considers superior to herself and her family.
9. Some qualities that make a person special are graciousness, dignity, integrity, and kindness.
10. Perhaps Mrs. Flowers saw something special in Marguerite. Students may have mentors among their relatives and neighbors.

LITERARY ELEMENTS

1. Marguerite feels that Momma's dialect shows she is uneducated. She sometimes drops verbs ("How you, Sister Flowers?") or uses a singular verb with a plural subject ("Brother and Sister Wilcox is sho'ly the meanest—").
2. Marguerite learns that Momma is Mrs. Flowers's "sister" in all but formal education.

Additional Resources

Literary Elements Transparency 17

Literature and Writing

Writing About Literature

Students' paragraphs should

- identify Mrs. Flowers's attitude toward Marguerite
- include specific details and examples

Personal Writing

Students' letters should

- say why the attention was important
- include details and images

Extending Your Response

Literature Groups Students may want to imagine a day without words. What would they be unable to convey? COLLAB. LEARN.

Performing Suggest that students record themselves as they rehearse so that they can hear how they sound and what they can improve. After each performance, invite the class to analyze the oral interpretation for effects on the listeners.

Learning for Life Point out that "lessons in living" can include both things to do and things not to do.

Teaching Support

Literature and Writing

Writing About Literature

Characterization Marguerite clearly admires and respects Mrs. Flowers, but what does Mrs. Flowers think about Marguerite? Make a list of at least five things Mrs. Flowers says or does with Marguerite. Then use these examples to write an essay explaining her attitude toward Marguerite.

Personal Writing

Dear Friend Review the details you wrote in the **Reading Focus** on page 198. Write a letter to a friend describing a time when someone paid special attention to you. Be sure to tell your friend why you are writing the letter and why this incident is important to you. Include details and images that will capture your friend's attention. If you wish, read your finished letter to a classmate.

Extending Your Response

Literature Groups

Is Language Power? Mrs. Flowers tells Marguerite that "language is man's way of communicating with his fellow man and it is language alone which separates him from the lower animals." Do you agree? Why or why not? Discuss this statement and come to a group decision. List four or five reasons to support your opinion; then present your ideas to the entire class.

Performing

Literature Out Loud Mrs. Flowers tells Marguerite that literature has "shades of deeper meaning" when it is read aloud. When you read literature aloud, you are giving it an oral interpretation. Choose a passage from one of Angelou's books, and give an oral interpretation of it to your class. You may read from another section of *I Know Why the Caged Bird Sings,* or you may choose from Angelou's poems, speeches, or other works.

Learning for Life

Everyday Lessons Mrs. Flowers gives Marguerite a series of "lessons in living." What are some of these lessons? Discuss Mrs. Flowers's ideas. Do you agree with her ideas? Why or why not? Then make a list of three "lessons in living" of your own, and present them in a chart. You may want to use color, pictures, and graphic art in your design. Share your chart with the class.

Reading Further

If you enjoyed Maya Angelou's autobiographical sketch, try:

Amistad: 'Give Us Free' by Steven Spielberg, Maya Angelou, and Debbie Allen

Audiocassette *And Still I Rise* by Maya Angelou (Maya Angelou reads her poems)

Save your work for your portfolio.

Reading Minilesson

Distinguishing Fact from Opinion Ask students to review the difference between fact and opinion. Remind them that an opinion is a writer's belief about something, while a fact is a statement that can be proved with supporting information. Point out that Maya Angelou uses both in her excerpt from *I Know Why the Caged Bird Sings.* For example, she voices an opinion when she says that Momma had a "strange relationship" with Mrs. Flowers. She cites a fact when she refers to Marguerite's keeping silent in school that year.

Activity Invite small groups of students to review the selection and look for at least one other detail from Angelou's childhood that she presents as a fact and one or more details that are opinions. **L1** COLLAB. LEARN.

208 THEME 2

Skill Minilessons

RETEACH • REVIEW

GRAMMAR AND LANGUAGE • SUBJECT-VERB AGREEMENT

The verb of a sentence must agree with its subject in person (first, second, or third) and number (singular or plural).

first person singular:	I *know.*
first person plural:	We *know.*
second person singular:	You *know.*
second person plural:	You *know.*
third person singular:	He, she, or it *knows.*
third person plural:	They *know.*

PRACTICE Rewrite the following sentences so the subjects and verbs agree in person and number.

1. She know Mrs. Flowers well.
2. They both understands that Marguerite is shy.
3. Marguerite is pleased because she knows someone respect her.
4. The writer hopes that you, the reader, understands the people in the story.
5. We all enjoys stories like this.

- For more about subject-verb agreement, see **Language Handbook,** p. R13.

READING AND THINKING • EVALUATING

Evaluating is making a judgment about the worth of something. Good readers evaluate what they read, judging the ways in which information and ideas are presented.

- For more about evaluating and literary response, see **Reading Handbook,** pp. R106–R108.

PRACTICE Maya Angelou presents Mrs. Flowers and Momma as important figures in Marguerite's life. In your opinion, which character is more memorable—Mrs. Flowers or Momma? Use examples from the story to support your answer.

VOCABULARY • NEGATING PREFIXES

The prefixes *in-, im-, ir-,* and *il-* add a negative meaning to many words. For example, *intolerant* means "not tolerant"; *impatience* means "without patience"; *illiteracy* is the opposite of *literacy;* and something *irresistible* cannot be resisted. However, these prefixes don't always add a negative meaning. (An *intense* person isn't calm. You don't *improve* something by showing it to be false.) When in doubt, look up the word in a dictionary.

PRACTICE Write the words in which *in-, im-, il-,* or *ir-* is a negating prefix.

a. impure	i. inform
b. impulse	j. insincere
c. imitate	k. injustice
d. introduce	l. illogical
e. inconvenient	m. illegal
f. increase	n. iron
g. independent	o. irregular
h. inflate	p. irritate

Skill Minilessons

GRAMMAR AND LANGUAGE
SUBJECT-VERB AGREEMENT

1. She knows Mrs. Flowers well.
2. They both understand that Marguerite is shy.
3. Marguerite is pleased because she knows someone respects her.
4. The writer hopes that you, the reader, understand the people in the story.
5. We all enjoy stories like this.

READING AND THINKING
EVALUATING

Good judgment is based on careful consideration of the options.

VOCABULARY
NEGATING PREFIXES

a. impure
e. inconvenient
g. independent
j. insincere
k. injustice
l. illogical
m. illegal
o. irregular

Additional Resources

- ***Grammar and Language Workbook,*** pp. 187–188
- ***Grammar and Composition Handbook,*** Lesson 10.1
- ***Writer's Choice,*** Lesson 16.1
- ***Reading Skills Practice Workbook***
- ***Vocabulary Practice,*** p. 15

ASSESSMENT

- ***Quick Checks,*** p. 17
- ***Selection and Theme Assessment,*** pp. 29–30
- ***Performance Assessment,*** p. 16
- ***Testmaker: ExamView Pro***
- ***Interactive Tutor: Self-Assessment***

MEDIA Connection

Objective

- To understand and apply strategies for reading an interview

Literature LINK

I Know Why the Caged Bird Sings This article connects to the excerpt from *I Know Why the Caged Bird Sings,* the literature selection that immediately precedes this lesson. It presents the mature and successful Maya Angelou.

Analyzing Media

1. Angelou appears dramatic, positive, and good-humored, but honest and often indignant.
2. Angelou knows that even a "natural" writer must work hard at her craft—a reasonable assumption.

Informational Text

*in*TIME For more examples of informational text, direct students to the articles in the *inTIME* magazine.

Additional Resources

Media Connections, p. 4

MEDIA Connection

NEWSPAPER ARTICLE

What kind of person would you expect Marguerite, the young Maya Angelou, to grow up to be?

Maya's Way: Maya Angelou's Zest for Life Continues to Fuel Her Creative Fire

by Patti Thorn—*Rocky Mountain News*, November 23, 1997

As a child, Maya Angelou knew how she'd carry herself when she was grown up: She'd be "friendly, but never gushing," she wrote in her acclaimed memoir *I Know Why the Caged Bird Sings*, "cool but not frigid or distant, distinguished without the awful stiffness."

Now she is nearly 70. And she has some other ideas about maturity:

"Maturity is seeing a young person and saying, 'Do it. Enjoy yourself. (Life's) about that long. Do it. Leave footprints on the sand and laugh as much as possible.'

"People sometimes look as if they've put airplane glue on the back of their hand." She mocks the melodramatic style of someone with their hand to their forehead in despair. Then she shakes her head. "I just can't bear it. I just can't bear it."

Angelou bursts into laughter, her big bear of a body shakes, and if there's any concern that she might have that awful stiffness she hoped to avoid as a child, that dissolves in an instant. Friendly? Indeed. Frigid or distant? Hardly. Distinguished? Check the resumé, which is only getting started with 32 honorary degrees and a Pulitzer Prize nomination.

Many of the essays in her latest collection, *Even the Stars Look Lonesome*, she notes, were written to help her come to grips with various situations. "If I really want to know how I feel about a thing, I write about it," she says. "I can't lie when I start to write. I can't fudge or hedge."

Thus, there's the story of her mother, hooked to an oxygen tank and fighting cancer, another about a visit to a folk museum, where slave cabins were so sanitized for viewing—wooden chairs, a "colorfully blanketed bed"—they aroused Angelou's ire. While the essays are unadorned and conversational, they didn't come easily, says the author. "Critics say 'Maya Angelou has a new book and of course it's good, she's a natural writer,'" she says. "That's like saying you're a natural open heart surgeon. For one page, it might take me five days, two weeks."

Analyzing Media

1. What impression do you have of Angelou after reading this article? Explain.
2. Do you agree with Angelou's comments about writing? Why or why not?

Teaching Support

interNET CONNECTION

Folk Museums Have students search online for more about folk museums like the one mentioned in this article.

Reading Minilesson

Summarizing Explain to the class that summarizing, or restating what you read in your own words, is a good way to better remember and understand the information in a story or article. A good summary is one that is clearly understandable to someone who has not read the original piece.

Activity Have students summarize either the article or the selection from *I Know Why the Caged Bird Sings.* Tell them to include all the main ideas and the essential supporting details. Then have them exchange summaries with a partner and compare the summaries to the original.

Additional Resources

Reading Skills Practice Workbook

Writing Skills

Describing a Person

What makes you feel that you know a person you've only read about? What makes a character seem as familiar as a friend or the neighbor next door? Good writers use the following techniques to bring their readers into a story.

Gather Details When you describe a person, use details to help your readers see and hear that character. Use the most precise descriptive words you can.

Don't just *tell* readers about your subject. *Show* your readers what you're talking about. That's what Maya Angelou does when she describes Mrs. Flowers in *I Know Why the Caged Bird Sings.*

> She was thin without the taut look of wiry people, and her printed voile dresses and flowered hats were as right for her as denim overalls for a farmer.

Organize the Details Introduce your details in a logical order so that readers can easily picture the information. You can group details by order of importance or order of impression. Either way, the details should support a main idea, as shown in the example below.

> She pronounced my name so nicely. Or more correctly, she spoke each word with such clarity that I was certain a foreigner who didn't understand English could have understood her.

ACTIVITIES

1. Choose a character from this theme who seems real to you. Write a paragraph or two describing why you think the character is realistic, and include specific details.
2. Think of a person you admire. List details about the person's appearance, personality, and actions. Use your list of details to help you write a paragraph describing something about the person.

Writing Skills

Objective

- To write a description of a person

Teaching Strategies

One of the most remarkable characteristics of a good description is the extent to which a writer suggests a great deal by emphasizing only one or two characteristics. Selecting just the right details to mention is a primary factor in a good description.

Gather Details Using the most precise word is important. Share with students this dictum from Mark Twain: "The difference between the right word and the almost right word is like the difference between lightning and a lightning bug."

Organize the Details An easy way to organize a description is to go from head to toe, but a better way is to start with the most striking detail.

Activities

1. Students should include specific details about characters.
2. Students' paragraphs should have a central idea or theme and not merely be a list of details.

Additional Resources

Writer's Choice, Lesson 3.6

Grammar and Language *Minilesson*

Commas with Items in a Series Since it is likely that students may be listing items in their descriptions, remind them of the rule for punctuating items in a series. Write the following sentences on the board. *The woman wore a purple dress, a green hat, and yellow shoes. The lean, mean, and hungry-looking fellow is my cousin. She flitted, fluttered, and danced around the room.* Note that commas are used after all but the last item in the series when more than two items are listed.

Activity Have students check their writing from the activities on this page to be sure that all items in a series are properly punctuated. **L2**

Additional Resources

Grammar and Language Transparency 17

Grammar and Language Workbook, p. 257

Grammar and Composition Handbook, Lesson 13.2

Writer's Choice, Lesson 20.2

Before Reading

Objectives

- To read and analyze a chapter from an autobiography
- To recognize point of view
- To write an evaluative paragraph

Skills

Reading/Thinking: Inferring; Evaluating; Predicting; Avoiding Hasty Generalizations
Writing: Combining Sentences for Variety; Evaluative Paragraph; Journal Entry
Vocabulary: Prefixes and Suffixes
Grammar/Language: Capitalization of Compass Points; Words Ending in *-y*
Listening/Speaking: Describing Sounds
Life Skills: Letter of Recommendation
Collaboration: Describing Sounds; Literature Groups

Motivating STUDENTS

Selection Focus Transparency 17: Before presenting the quotation, discuss ways in which people show courage.

Reading Focus: As an extension of the Reading Focus, point out to students that many people around the world have found homes in places far from their original homes. Ask students whether they know people who have moved from a place very different from where they now live. Discuss difficulties and pleasures they have had.

Before You Read

from *Sound-Shadows of the New World*

MEET VED MEHTA

Ved Mehta (ved mā′ tä) has never let his blindness stand in his way. Even as a child, he was determined to be active. He was miserable when his mother forbade him to play roughly with his cousins. Finally, his father assured Mehta that he had told everyone "to let you do whatever you wished." Thereafter, Mehta had a normal childhood. His persistence led him to the Arkansas School for the Blind, and eventually on to Oxford and Harvard.

Ved Mehta was born in India in 1934. This selection is from his autobiography Sound-Shadows of the New World, *which was first published in 1985.*

READING FOCUS

Is a person who cannot see "disabled"? Think about what this word means to you.

QuickWrite
Make a quick list of personality characteristics that you think would be essential to anyone who faces the unfamiliar.

Setting a Purpose
Read to find out how a young blind man from India gets along on his first day in the United States.

BUILDING BACKGROUND

The Time and Place In the 1940s many nations were unable to properly educate people with disabilities. Some of these people were able to come to the United States to study.

Did You Know?
Ved Mehta's religion, Hinduism, one of the world's oldest, is the major religion of India.

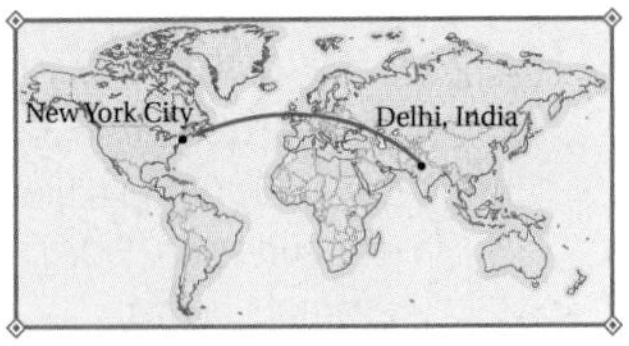

VOCABULARY PREVIEW

encounter (en koun′ tər) *v.* to meet unexpectedly or casually; p. 215
impulse (im′ puls) *n.* an internal force that causes one to act without thinking about it; p. 215
unrestrained (un′ ri strānd′) *adj.* not held in check or under control; p. 216
cringe (krinj) *v.* to draw back, as from fear or dislike; p. 217
servile (sur′ vil) *adj.* like a servant; too humble; p. 218
engulf (en gulf′) *v.* to swallow up; overwhelm; p. 219
resolutely (rez′ ə lo͞ot′ lē) *adv.* determinedly; p. 219
maladjustment (mal′ ə just′ mənt) *n.* poor adjustment to conditions or requirements; p. 220
obligingly (ə blī′ jing lē) *adv.* helpfully; agreeably; p. 220

RESOURCE MANAGER

Teaching Tools and Resources
- Theme Two Planning Guide
- Literature Groups Sourcebook

Essential Lesson Support

Lesson-Specific Instruction
- Selection Focus Transparency 17
- Literary Elements Transparency 18
- Active Reading Guide,* p. 18
- Selection Vocabulary Practice, p. 16

Assessment
- Selection Quick Checks,* p. 18
- Sel. and Theme Assmt., pp. 31-32
- Testmaker: ExamView Pro
- Performance Assessment, p. 17

Systematic Language Instruction
- Gr. & Comp. Hbk., Lessons 3.11, 3.12
- Vocabulary Power, Unit 3 Review/Test
- Spelling Power, Unit 3 Review/Proofreading

English Language Learners
- ELL Sourcebook, pp. 37, 38
- Spanish Summaries, p. 17
- Audio Library*
- English, Yes!

Spec. Needs/Strat. Interven.
- Interactive Rdg. Sbk., pp. T89–T92
- Interactive Rdg. Wbk., pp. 38-39
- Audio Library*

* Also available in Spanish

from Sound-Shadows of the New World

Ved Mehta

At the airport, I was questioned by an immigration official. "You're blind—totally blind—and they gave you a visa?[1] You say it's for your studies, but studies where?"

"At the Arkansas School for the Blind. It is in Little Rock, in Arkansas."

He shuffled through the pages of a book. Sleep was in my eyes. Drops of sweat were running down my back. My shirt and trousers felt dirty.

"Arkansas School is not on our list of approved schools for foreign students."

"I know," I said. "That is why the immigration officials in Delhi gave me only a visitor's visa. They said that when I got to the school I should tell the authorities to apply to be on your list of approved schools, so that I could get a student visa." I showed him a big manila envelope I was carrying; it contained my chest X rays, medical reports, and fingerprint charts, which were necessary for a student visa, and which I'd had prepared in advance.

"Why didn't you apply to an approved school in the first place and come here on a proper student visa?" he asked, looking through the material.

1. A *passport* identifies a traveler as a citizen of a particular country. To enter another country, a traveler must receive a *visa* from that country. Here, the narrator's passport is from India, and U.S. officials in Delhi gave him a visa.

Reading the Selection

SUMMARY

Ved Mehta, a young, blind man from India, describes his first day in the United States. Ved has traveled halfway around the world to attend a school for the blind in the United States. Ved will stay with Muriel di Francesco and her husband, John, who is also blind. Ved learns that John can be independent and self-sufficient because he attended the Perkins School. John promises to help Ved when he applies for admission. Ved learns a great deal about the United States during his first day.

Spanish Summaries, p. 17

A Active Reading Strategies

PREDICT Review the first three paragraphs of the story and have students predict the outcome of Mehta's confrontation with the immigration official. Have students review their predictions after they read further in the story.

VOCABULARY Remind students to use context clues to unlock the meanings of new vocabulary words.

Additional Resources

Active Reading Guide, p. 18

Audio Library

Spanish Audio Library

Teaching Support

CONNECTING TO OTHER SELECTIONS

The chart at the right shows three ways to connect the excerpt from *Sound-Shadows of the New World* to other selections in this book.

For specific teaching strategies, see the ***Theme Two Planning Guide.***

Connection		Title
Life Skills: Lifelong Learning	→	from *Letters from Rifka,* p. 526
Thematic: Facing Obstacles	→	"A Dictionary of Japanese-American Terms," p. 27
Literary: Sensory Detail	→	"O Captain! My Captain!" p. 473

B Active Reading Strategies

QUESTION Ask students how they think Mehta knows that "the official looked up at me, down at his book, and up at me again." *(Mehta may be able to hear or feel the official's movement.)*

FYI

Fight or Flight The fight-or-flight response is a partly psychological, partly physiological response to stress, whether in the form of an obstacle or an attack. Human beings have an internal mechanism that switches on involuntarily when they are threatened. Breathing becomes shallow, the muscles become tense, and adrenaline is released into the body. The body is ready to fight back or run away, whichever is the best choice for survival.

C Active Reading Strategies

CONNECT In India it is highly unusual (even considered an offense or a shame) *not* to stay with friends or relatives, if such accommodation is available. How true is Daddyji's statement that "In the West, people do not, as a rule, stay with relatives and friends"? Ask students whether this observation is true of their own experience. *(Many students will say that it is not true that Americans do not stay with friends and relatives.)*

My knowledge of English was limited. With difficulty, I explained to him that I had applied to some thirty schools but that, because I had been able to get little formal education in India, the Arkansas School was the only one that would accept me; that I had needed a letter of acceptance from an American school to get dollars sanctioned[2] by the Reserve Bank of India; and that now that I was in America I was sure I could change schools if the Arkansas School was not suitable or did not get the necessary approval.

B Muttering to himself, the immigration official looked up at me, down at his book, and up at me again. He finally announced, "I think you'll have to go to Washington and apply to get your visa changed to a student visa before you can go to any school."

I recalled things that Daddyji[3] used to say as we were growing up: "In life, there is only fight or flight. You must always fight," and "America is God's own country. People there are the most hospitable and generous people in the world." I told myself I had nothing to worry about. Then I remembered that Daddyji had mentioned a Mr. and Mrs. Dickens in Washington—they were friends of friends of his—and told me that I could get in touch with them in case of emergency.

"I will do whatever is necessary," I now said to the immigration official. "I will go to Washington."

He hesitated, as if he were thinking something, and then stamped my passport and returned it to me. "We Mehtas carry our luck with us," Daddyji used to say. He is right, I thought.

The immigration official suddenly became helpful, as if he were a friend. "You shouldn't have any trouble with the immigration people in Washington," he said, and asked, "Is anybody meeting you here?"

"Mr. and Mrs. di Francesco," I said.

Mrs. di Francesco was a niece of Manmath Nath Chatterjee, whom Daddyji had known when he himself was a student, in London, in 1920. Daddyji had asked Mr. Chatterjee, who had a Scottish-American wife and was now settled in Yellow Springs, Ohio, if he could suggest anyone with whom I might stay in New York, so that I could get acclimatized[4] to America before proceeding to the Arkansas School, which was not due to open until the eleventh of September. Mr. Chatterjee had written back that, as it happened, his wife's niece was married to John di Francesco, a singer who was totally blind, and that Mr. and Mrs. di Francesco lived in New York, and would be delighted to meet me at the airport and keep me as a paying guest at fifteen dollars a week.

"How greedy of them to ask for money!" I had cried when I learned of the arrangement. "People come and stay with us for months and we never ask for an anna."[5]

C Daddyji had said, "In the West, people do not, as a rule, stay with relatives and friends but put up in hotels, or in houses as paying guests. That is the custom there. Mr. and Mrs. di Francesco are probably a young, struggling couple who could do with a little extra money."

The immigration official now came from behind the counter, led me to an open area,

2. *Sanctioned* means "approved."
3. *[Daddyji]* In India, the suffix *-ji* is added to a name or title to show respect and affection.
4. *Acclimatized* (ə klī′ mə tīzd′) means "adjusted to a new environment or situation."
5. The *anna* is a former coin of India. Sixteen annas equaled one *rupee,* a unit of money still used in India and other countries.

Teaching Support

MEETING INDIVIDUAL NEEDS — ENGLISH LANGUAGE LEARNERS

Immigration Experiences Ask English language learners whether they recall or whether their parents have told stories about their first day in the United States. New people, new language, new sights, sounds, smells—moving to a new continent is a difficult transition.

Activity Have students share their stories of the first day—disasters, triumphs, surprises, mistakes. If other students have lived or traveled abroad, have them share their stories of making their way in a foreign land. COLLAB. LEARN.

Additional Resources

English Language Learners Sourcebook, p. 37

and shouted, with increasing volume, "Francisco! . . . Franchesca! . . . De Franco!" I wasn't sure what the correct pronunciation was, but his shouting sounded really disrespectful. I asked him to call for Mr. and Mrs. di Francesco softly. He bellowed, "Di Fransesco!"

No one came. My mouth went dry. Mr. and Mrs. di Francesco had sent me such a warm invitation. I couldn't imagine why they would have let me down or what I should do next.

Then I heard the footsteps of someone running toward us. "Here I am. You must be Ved. I'm Muriel di Francesco. I'm sorry John couldn't come." I noted that the name was pronounced the way it was spelled, and that hers was a Yankee voice—the kind I had heard when I first encountered Americans at home, during the war[6]—but it had the sweetness of the voices of my sisters.

We shook hands; she had a nice firm grip. I had an impulse to call her Auntie Muriel—at home, an older person was always called by an honorific,[7] like "Auntie" or "Uncle"—but I greeted her as Daddyji had told me that Westerners liked to be greeted: "Mrs. di Francesco, I'm delighted to make your acquaintance."

"You had a terrible trip, you poor boy. What a terrible way to arrive!" Mrs. di Francesco said in the taxi. "Imagine, everything stolen from a bag!"

6. Here, *the war* was World War II, which ended in 1945.

7. An *honorific* is any title of honor or respect, such as "Auntie" or "Mrs."

One bag had contained clothes. The other, a holdall, had contained (in addition to some extra shirts) a number of ivory curios—statues of Lord Krishna, "no evil" monkeys, brooches with a little pattern on them—which Daddyji had bought with the idea that I could sell them at great profit. "You can take the ivory curios to a shop in Little Rock and ask the shop to sell them for you—on commission, of course," he had said. "In America, a lot of people earn and learn. Who knows? Maybe we could start an ivory-export-import business in a year or so, when I retire from government service." He was deputy director general of health services in the Indian government. "I expect there is a great deal of demand over there for hand-carved things." The fact that neither of us had ever sold even a secondhand gramophone didn't stop us from dreaming.

I didn't want Mrs. di Francesco to feel bad, so I made light of the theft. "The other bag is still full," I said.

"The ivory things must have been really valuable," she said. She had helped me fill out the insurance-claim forms. "What a bad introduction to America!"

Did You Know?
Curios are rare or unusual ornamental objects. *Lord Krishna* is one of the most important gods of Hinduism, the main religion in India. A *"no evil" monkey* is a good luck charm, and a *brooch* is a woman's ornamental pin.

Vocabulary

encounter (en koun′ tər) *v.* to meet unexpectedly or casually

impulse (im′ puls) *n.* an internal force that causes one to act without thinking about it

D Author's Craft

SENSORY DETAIL Ask students what Mehta notices about Muriel. *(her footsteps, her voice, and her grip)* On which senses is he relying? *(hearing and touch)* Thus his senses of hearing and touch help him understand and categorize his world.

E Active Reading Strategies

RESPOND Ask students to discuss Daddyji's advice to his son to greet Westerners as they like to be greeted. What do they think of what he taught his son? Is Mehta's greeting too formal, even in the 1940s, for Americans? *(Many will say yes on the basis of current informality.)*

F Active Reading Strategies

EVALUATE Ask what Mehta's making light of his loss so his new friend "won't feel bad" says about him? Is making light of an affront to help another save face "Eastern" as opposed to "Western"? Is it the sort of thing an American visitor might do when traveling in a foreign country? *(Many students may say that anyone who is a visitor will be especially careful not to offend.)*

Writing Minilesson

Combining Sentences for Variety

Write this sentence from the story on the board: *Daddyji had asked Mr. Chatterje, who had a Scottish-American wife and was now settled in Yellow Springs, Ohio, if he could suggest anyone with whom I might stay in New York . . ."* Point out that Mehta has written a sophisticated sentence in which he combines ideas using adjective clauses. Have a volunteer rewrite the sentence as two sentences and show how Mehta combined them.

Activity Have students look through their portfolios for instances in which they could have combined sentences. Ask each student to submit five sentences and their revisions. **L2**

Additional Resources

Writer's Choice, Lesson 14.3

"But it could have happened in Delhi."

She regaled the taxi driver with the story, as if she and I were long-standing friends. "And we had to wait at the airport for two whole hours, filling out insurance forms. And he only knew the prices in rubles."

"Rupees," I said.

"Is that right?" the taxi driver said, from the front seat. "Well, it shouldn't have happened to you, son."

I leaned toward the half-open window and listened for the roar of street crowds, the cries of hawkers, the clatter of tonga wheels, the trot of tonga horses, the crackle of whips, the blasts of Klaxons, the trills of police whistles, the tinkling of bicycle bells—but all I heard was the steady hiss and rush of cars. "In America, you can really travel fast and get places," I said.

Did You Know?
The *hawkers* are people selling things; a *tonga* is a two-wheeled carriage; and *Klaxons* are loud electric horns.

Mrs. di Francesco took both my hands in hers and broke into open, unrestrained laughter. I have never heard a woman laugh quite like that, I thought.

"What are you laughing at?" I asked.

"I'd just noticed that all this time you had your hand in your breast pocket. Are you afraid of having your wallet stolen, too?"

I was embarrassed. I hadn't realized what I had been doing.

The taxi driver took a sharp turn.

"Where are we?" I asked.

"On Broadway," Mrs. di Francesco said.

"Is Broadway a wide road?" I asked.

She laughed. "A very wide avenue—it's the center of the universe."

At home, the center was a circle, but here the center, it seemed, was a straight line. At home, I often felt I was on a merry-go-round, circling activities that I couldn't join in. Here I would travel in taxis amid new friends and have adventures. I tried to voice my thoughts.

"Poor boy, you have difficulty with the language," Mrs. di Francesco said, gently pressing my hand.

"English is difficult," I said, and I tried to make a joke. "When I was small and first learning English, I was always confusing 'chicken' and 'kitchen.'"

"'Chicken' and 'kitchen,'" Mrs. di Francesco repeated, and laughed.

"I have enough trouble speaking English," the taxi driver said. "I could never learn to speak Hindu."[8]

"Hindi," I said, correcting him.

"You see?" the taxi driver said.

Mrs. di Francesco laughed, and the taxi driver joined in.

After a while, the taxi came to a stop. "Here we are at home, on a Hundred and Thirteenth Street between Broadway and Amsterdam," Mrs. di Francesco said.

Though I was carrying a bank draft for eighty dollars, I had only two dollars in cash, which a family friend had given me for good luck. I handed it to Mrs. di Francesco for the taxi.

8. *Hindu* refers to someone who practices Hinduism. *Hindi* is short for *Hindustani,* India's official language.

Vocabulary
unrestrained (un′ ri strānd′) *adj.* not held in check or under control

G Critical Thinking

INFERRING What does Mehta notice about the way Muriel treats the cab driver? He does not say how a woman in India might have behaved in a similar situation, but ask students to make inferences. Discuss how differently they think an Indian woman might have acted. *(An Indian woman would probably have confined her conversation with the cab driver to the bare essentials.)*

H Active Reading Strategies

QUESTION Mehta notices a difference between Muriel and women of his country. Ask students how they think the women Mehta knows laugh. What is the opposite of "unrestrained laughter"? *(The implication is that Indian women laugh quietly, perhaps even muffling the sound with a handkerchief.)*

I Literary Elements

CHARACTERIZATION Emphasize that this is a central statement in the story. In India Mehta feels the center of everything is a circle from which he was excluded. But he hopes that life will be a straight line in the United States—a place where he can learn, a place where he can join in, and a place where he can forge ahead. After the cab ride, in fact, Mehta does stop going around in circles; he begins to move toward his goal and take charge of his life. The realization he has in the cab is a turning point in his life.

Teaching Support

MEETING INDIVIDUAL NEEDS — SPECIAL NEEDS

Learning Disabled Mehta struggles to say what he means and feels in English. Explain to students that sometimes it is difficult to voice one's thoughts because they are too complex or too emotional to express in words.

Activity Ask students to write a journal entry describing a time when they could not quite get something across. What caused the problem? What might have helped to make the situation easier? Ask for volunteers to share their experiences in small groups.
L1 COLLAB. LEARN.

Additional Resources
Inclusion Strategies

"That won't be enough," she said.

"But it is *seven rupees!*" I cried. "At home, one could hire a tonga for a whole day for that."

"This is New York," she said. She clicked open her purse and gave some money to the taxi driver.

The taxi driver put my bags on the curb, shook my hand, and said, "If I go to India, I will remember not to become a tonga driver." He drove away.

We picked up the luggage. Mrs. di Francesco tucked my free hand under her bare arm with a quick motion and started walking. A woman at home would probably have cringed at the touch of a stranger's hand under her arm, I thought, but thinking this did not stop me from making a mental note that the muscle of her arm was well developed.

We went into a house, and walked up to Mr. and Mrs. di Francesco's apartment, on the fourth floor. Mr. di Francesco opened the door and kissed Mrs. di Francesco loudly. Had a bomb exploded, I could not have been more surprised. They'll catch something, I thought. I had never heard any grownups kissing at home—not even in films.

Mr. di Francesco shook my hand. He had a powerful grip and a powerful voice. He took me by the shoulder and almost propelled me to a couch. "This is going to be your bed," he said. "I'm sorry I couldn't come to the airport. Anyway, I knew you wouldn't mind being greeted by a charming

Telephone Booths, 1968. Richard Estes. Oil on canvas, 48 x 69 in. Allan Stone Galleries, New York.

Viewing the painting: How might this painting symbolize Ved's first day in New York City?

Vocabulary

cringe (krinj) *v.* to draw back, as from fear or dislike

VIEWING THE PAINTING

Estes uses photographic realism to portray urban America.

Viewing Response *The reflections blending and merging with the real objects symbolize the confused impressions of Ved's first day.*

Critical Thinking

EVALUATING Discuss the exchange between Mehta and Muriel. Ask students what they think of her bluntness. What do they think of Mehta's naiveté? Is it polite for Muriel to be so blunt since she intends to make up the difference anyway?

Model: Although it might be tempting for Muriel to slip the driver a few dollars to save Mehta from embarrassment, she elects not to. I think she makes this decision because she is married to a blind man, and she undoubtedly knows that such a gesture would be patronizing and insulting. I think she also realizes that part of her job is to teach Mehta about how things really are in the United States.

Active Reading Strategies

QUESTION What picture of Indian society does one get from Mehta's comments? *(Indian society seems to be a strict social hierarchy.)* Which passage conveys this idea? *(Mehta points out a difference between Muriel and the women of his country when he says Indian women would "cringe" at the touch of a stranger.)*

Reading *Minilesson*

Predicting It is important for readers to remain actively involved in a story. Predicting is one way to do that. As students read, ask them to guess who will speak next, what will happen next, or who will be introduced. To do this most efficiently, they should stop periodically and make predictions.

Activity Ask students to make predictions based on what they already know about Muriel and her husband. What kind of man will he be? Why do they think so? When they have finished reading the selection, students should refer to their predictions. **L2**

Additional Resources

Reading Skills Practice Workbook

LEAN ON ME 217

Active Reading Strategies

REVIEW Ask students to list the things about John that amaze Mehta. *(He kisses, he cooks, he is not servile or timid, and he is independent.)*

Active Reading Strategies

QUESTION What modern conveniences is Mehta unfamiliar with? *(Electric stoves, refrigerators, toasters, double beds, and bathtubs.)* What does this tell the reader about the life Mehta led in India? *(People in India have fewer modern conveniences than many Americans have.)*

Critical Thinking

EVALUATING Ask students what they think about Mehta's decision to eat beef even though his religion forbids it. He is following his father's advice to conform to the customs of the country he is in. Do students think he makes the right decision? *(Some students will agree that Mehta did the right thing by going along with American customs. Others may note that eating beef is a religious, not cultural, taboo. These students may feel Mehta should have refused to eat the meat.)*

lady." He doesn't have a trace of the timid, servile manner of music masters and blind people at home, I thought.

"We had a delightful ride from the airport," I said.

Mr. di Francesco wanted to know why we were so late, and Mrs. di Francesco told him about the theft.

"What bad luck!" he said.

"But I got here," I said.

"That's the spirit," he said, laughing.

"John, thank you for starting dinner," Mrs. di Francesco said from what I took to be the kitchen.

"Oh, you cook!" I exclaimed. I had never heard of a blind person who could cook.

"Yes, I help Muriel," he said. "We don't have servants here, as they do in your country. We have labor-saving devices." He then showed me around the apartment, casually tapping and explaining—or putting my hand on—various unfamiliar things: a stove that did not burn coal or give out smoke; an ice chest that stood on end and ran on electricity; a machine that toasted bread; a bed for two people; and a tub in which one could lie down. I was full of questions, and asked how natural gas from the ground was piped into individual apartments, and how people could have so much hot water that they could lie down in it. At home, a husband and wife never slept in one bed, but I didn't say anything about that, because I felt shy.

"Oh, you cook!" I exclaimed. I had never heard of a blind person who could cook.

"Do you eat meat?" Mrs. di Francesco asked me from the kitchen. "Aunt Rita—Mrs. Chatterjee—didn't know."

"Yes, I do eat meat," I called back to her. I started worrying about how I would cut it.

Mrs. di Francesco sighed with relief. "John and I hoped that you weren't a vegetarian. We're having spaghetti and meatballs, which are made of beef. Is that all right?"

I shuddered. As a Hindu, I had never eaten beef,[9] and the mere thought of it was revolting. But I recalled another of Daddyji's sayings, "When in Rome, do as the Romans do," and said, "I promised my father that I would eat anything and everything in America and gain some weight."

Mrs. di Francesco brought out the dinner and served it to us at a small table. "The peas are at twelve and the spaghetti and meatballs at six," she said. I must have looked puzzled, because she added, "John locates his food on a plate by the clock dial. I thought all blind people knew—"

"You forget that India has many primitive conditions," Mr. di Francesco interrupted. "Without a doubt, work for the blind there is very backward."

I bridled.[10] "There is nothing primitive or backward in India."

9. *[never eaten beef]* Hindus don't eat beef because they consider cows to be sacred animals.
10. In this context, to *bridle* means "to show anger or annoyance," as if by throwing back the head the way a horse might when a bridle is put on it.

Vocabulary
servile (sur′ vil) *adj.* like a servant; too humble

Teaching Support

Listening and Speaking *Minilesson*

Describing Sounds Ask students if they are as attentive to the sounds around them as Mehta was.

Activity Have students work in pairs. Each student must plan three sounds (such as rubbing sandpaper on wood, peeling an onion, or biting into an apple) to make for a partner who will be blindfolded. Have each student listen to the three sounds, then report to his or her partner on what he or she heard. The reports should focus on the sound itself rather than on trying to guess what it was. For example, a student might describe a sound as *a wet, crunchy, slurping sound* rather than *biting an apple.* **L2** **COLLAB. LEARN.**

There was a silence, in which I could hear Mr. di Francesco swallowing water. I felt very much alone. I wished I were back home.

"I didn't mean it that way," Mr. di Francesco said.

"I'm sorry," I said, and then, rallying a little, confessed that Braille watches were unheard of in India—that I had first read about them a year or so earlier in a British Braille magazine, and then it had taken me several months to get the foreign exchange[11] and get a Braille pocket watch from Switzerland.

"Then how do blind people there know what time it is—whether it is day or night?" Mr. di Francesco asked.

"They have to ask someone, or learn to tell from the morning and night sounds. I suppose that things *are* a little backward there. That is why I had to leave my family and come here for education."

"The food is getting cold," Mrs. di Francesco said.

I picked up my fork and knife with trembling fingers and aimed for six. I suddenly wanted to cry.

"You look homesick," Mrs. di Francesco said.

I nodded, and tried to eat. A sense of relief engulfed me: we had mutton meatballs at home all the time, and they didn't require a knife. But the relief was short-lived: I had never had spaghetti, and the strands were long and tended to bunch together. They stretched from my mouth to my plate—a sign of my Indian backwardness, I thought. I longed for the kedgeree[12] at home, easily managed with a spoon.

Mrs. di Francesco reached over and showed me how to wrap the spaghetti around my fork, shake it, and pick it up. Even so, I took big bites when I thought that Mrs. di Francesco was not looking—when she was talking to Mr. di Francesco. Later in the meal, it occurred to me that I was eating the food that Daddyji had eaten when he was a student abroad. I resolutely bent my face over the plate and started eating in earnest.

Mrs. di Francesco took away our plates and served us something else, and I reached for my spoon.

"That's eaten with a fork," she said.

I attacked it with a fork. "It is a pudding with a crust!" I cried. "I have never eaten anything like it."

"It's not a pudding—it's apple pie," Mrs. di Francesco said. "By the way, we're having scrambled eggs for breakfast. Is that all right?"

I confessed that I didn't know what they were, and she described them to me.

"Oh, I know—rumble-tumble eggs!" I exclaimed. "I like them very much."

They both laughed. "British-Indian English is really much nicer than American English," Mr. di Francesco said. "You should keep it. In fact, I'll adopt 'rumble-tumble.'"

I felt sad that I had come to America for my studies instead of going to England

11. *Foreign exchange* refers to exchanging one country's money for another's.

12. *Kedgeree* is an Indian dish consisting of fish flakes, boiled rice, and eggs.

Vocabulary

engulf (en gulf′) *v.* to swallow up; overwhelm
resolutely (rez′ ə lo͞ot′ lē) *adv.* determinedly

O Active Reading Strategies

CONNECT Mehta bridles when John says India is "primitive." Then he admits that perhaps things *are* a bit primitive. Why does Mehta "bridle," and why does he change his attitude? *(At first, he wants to defend his homeland against a term that seems extreme; that is a natural reaction. Then he recognizes that John has a point.)* Ask students how they would react if they were in a foreign country and someone criticized the United States for being materialistic or violent, for example. *(Many students may say they would become defensive.)*

P Critical Thinking

INFERRING Although we never meet Daddyji in this excerpt, Mehta refers to him repeatedly. Ask students what kind of person Daddyji seems to be and what they think of the relationship between Mehta and his father. *(Daddyji seems like a loving father and a very wise man. He and his son are close.)*

Q Active Reading Strategies

QUESTION Ask students why they think Mehta wishes he had gone to England instead. *(India, under British rule for many years, was permeated with British culture, and the British brought back to their homeland many foods, words, and other elements of Indian culture. Thus, Mehta would probably have felt more at home in England.)*

REAL-WORLD CONNECTION

Technology for the Visually Impaired Have students conduct research on the devices used today to help the visually impaired. Ask them to read documents from local agencies for the visually impaired and consumer publications. They can also search the Internet and find instruction manuals for certain devices. Have them read one of these manuals and give a brief presentation to the class on how to use the device.

R Active Reading Strategies

RESPOND Ask students how they think Mehta feels about not being fluent in English. How might it feel to want to say something but not be able to express it? *(frustrating)*

S Literary Elements

PLOT Mehta feels as though he were in India—unable to function as others do. Near the end of the selection Mehta discovers a similarity between his life in India and at the di Francescos' and begins to see a way into the center. Ask students if they can identify the point at which Mehta finds a similarity. *(He says he and John linger at the table "much as we might at home.")*

T Literary Elements

PLOT Ask students why they think Mehta chooses to end this segment with John's statement "This is America." *(Mehta has already begun the process of acculturation.)*

Thematic Focus

Lean on Me In this story as well as in some others in this theme, the "leaning" is literal as well as figurative. Mehta leans on Muriel's arm as he leaves the taxi. Ask how Mehta is helped by each of the people mentioned in the story.

ASSESSMENT

Quick Checks, p. 18

first, as Daddyji had done. But no school in England had accepted me.

"We've heard so much about India from Uncle Manmath," Mrs. di Francesco said. "It must be a very exciting place."

"Yes, tell us about India," Mr. di Francesco said.

R I felt confused. I couldn't think of what to say or how to say it.

"You look tired," Mrs. di Francesco said, patting me on the arm.

"I cannot think of the right English words sometimes," I said.

Mrs. di Francesco cleared some things off the table and said, "Don't worry. Now that you're here, your English will improve quickly."

S She went to the kitchen and started washing the plates while Mr. di Francesco and I lingered at the table—much as we might at home.

I asked Mr. di Francesco how he had become self-supporting and independent, with a place of his own.

"You make it sound so romantic, but it's really very simple," he said. He spoke in a matter-of-fact way. "I spent twelve years at the Perkins Institution for the Blind, in Massachusetts. I entered when I was seven, and left when I was nineteen."

"Perkins!" I cried. "I have been trying to go there since I was seven. First, they would not have me because of the war. But after the war they would not have me, either—they said that I would end up a 'cultural misfit.'"

"What does that mean?"

"They said that bringing Eastern people to the West at a young age leads to 'cultural maladjustment'—and they said, 'Blindness is a maladjustment in itself.'"

"But now you're here. I'll call Perkins tomorrow and tell them that the damage is already done, and that your cultural maladjustment would be much worse if you were to end up in Arkansas." He laughed.

I was excited. "Perkins is said to be the best school for the blind anywhere. How did you like it? How was your life there?"

"Life at Perkins? It was probably no different from that of millions of other kids. We played and studied." He added obligingly, "It was a lot of fun."

Fun—so that's what it was, I thought. That is the difference between all the things he did at school and all the things I missed out on by not going to a good school.

"And after Perkins?"

"After Perkins, I studied voice at the New England Conservatory,[13] where Muriel and I met. Then I came to New York, started giving voice lessons, married Muriel, and here I am."

"There must be more to tell."

"There really isn't."

"Did Mrs. di Francesco's parents not object? She is sighted."

"I wasn't asking to marry Muriel's parents. She could do what she pleased. This is America." T

13. Here, the *Conservatory* is a school for instruction in music.

Vocabulary

maladjustment (mal′ ə just′ mənt) *n.* poor adjustment to conditions or requirements

obligingly (ə blī′ jing lē) *adv.* helpfully; agreeably

Teaching Support

Grammar and Language *Minilesson*

Capitalization of Compass Points
Point out that words identifying compass points are sometimes capitalized and sometimes not. Write these sentences on the board: *I used to live south of the border. A north wind blew cold air down my back.* In these instances, the words for the compass points are lowercased.

Activity Have students find instances in the story in which compass points are capitalized: *The West is beautiful; bringing Eastern people to the West.* Ask students to try to articulate the rule for when compass points are capitalized. *(They are capitalized when they refer to a specific part of the country or the world.)* **L2**

Additional Resources

- ***Grammar and Language Transparency 18***
- ***Grammar and Language Workbook,*** pp. 249–250
- ***Grammar and Composition Handbook,*** Lesson 12.4
- ***Writer's Choice,*** Lesson 19.3

Responding to Literature

PERSONAL RESPONSE

- Why might the story of Ved Mehta make a difference in the lives of others? Who else would you like to have read this story? Why?

Brackets connect questions that are paired to develop higher-level thinking skills.

Analyzing Literature

RECALL

1. Describe the problem Ved has with the immigration official.
2. What does the merry-go-round symbolize to Ved?
3. Where does Mr. di Francesco want Ved to attend school?
4. What has Mr. di Francesco achieved?

INTERPRET

5. When Ved is dealing with the immigration official, he recalls his father saying, "In life, there is only fight or flight. You must always fight." Why does Ved remember this?
6. Why does Ved compare his life in India to being on the outside of a merry-go-round?
7. What does Mr. di Francesco mean when he says that the "damage is already done" in regard to Ved's "cultural maladjustment"?
8. Why is Ved so interested in Mr. di Francesco's success?

EVALUATE AND CONNECT

9. Theme Connection The quotes from Daddyji guided Ved. What have people told you to help you live your life?
10. Look back at the list you wrote for the **Reading Focus** on page 212. How do the items on your list compare with the author's personality?

Braillewriter

LITERARY ELEMENTS

Point of View

The selection from *Sound-Shadows of the New World* is a true story told from the **first-person point of view.** This means that the narrator, Ved, tells the story as he experienced it. A first-person narrator can tell about his own feelings. He can also reveal the feelings of other characters through their actions and dialogue.

1. How does the first-person narrator in this selection experience the world around him? Cite several examples.
2. Mehta could have told this story from a **third-person point of view,** using a voice outside the story to describe the characters and events. Do you think this would have been more effective than Mehta's own voice? Why or why not?

● See **Literary Terms Handbook,** p. R7.

Responding to the Selection

PERSONAL RESPONSE

Mehta's story could make a difference in the life of someone who is physically challenged. Students who know someone like this or someone who is foreign born may want that person to read this story for inspiration.

Analyzing Literature

1. Ved does not have the right visa and is not scheduled to attend an approved school.
2. The merry-go-round symbolizes Ved's confusion and sense of being kept outside of the center of life because of his disability.
3. He would like Ved to go to Perkins Institute for the Blind.
4. Mr. di Francesco has achieved independent living.
5. He recalls his father's advice because he is tempted to give up.
6. He felt that he was circling activities that he could not join.
7. Ved is already in the United States; he has already begun to become acclimated.
8. Ved hopes to become as capable and independent as Mr. di Francesco.
9. Answers should include helpful advice.
10. Clearly Mehta's openness to new experiences and ideas is a key to his success.

LITERARY ELEMENTS

1. Ved Mehta is a keen observer, listening to conversations and ambient sounds and reading the tone of voice of people with whom he is dealing.
2. Since this is an autobiography, the voice of the person involved is more immediate and more emotionally involving for readers.

Additional Resources

Literary Elements Transparency 18

Literature and Writing

Writing About Literature

Students' paragraphs should

- take into account how Mehta substitutes perceptions of sound and touch for those of sight
- make a judgment about Mehta's writing style

Creative Writing

Students' journal entries should

- focus on the impressions a sightless person and a stranger in a new land might have
- include specific details and examples

Extending Your Response

Learning for Life Suggest that students refer to what Mehta faced in coming to the United States as evidence of his character and as preparation for independent living.

Internet Connection Have students search the Internet for a radio call-in show or Web site about computers and resources for the blind.

Literature Groups Ask students to consider how Mehta might have behaved if he had not followed his father's advice. COLLAB. LEARN.

Literature and Writing

Writing About Literature

Characterization Look at the descriptions of characters as they appear in this selection. Note that these observations are made by a blind person. Is Mehta, the author, effective in providing a mental image of the di Francescos for his readers? Write a paragraph evaluating how well he describes these two characters.

Creative Writing

Keeping Track Writers often keep journals that help them recall important events and vivid details. Write a journal entry that Ved Mehta might have written about his first day in the United States. Include details about the new things he heard, felt, tasted, and smelled, as well as his impressions of the people and places he encountered.

Extending Your Response

Learning for Life

Seeking Admission Letters of recommendation can occasionally make the difference between acceptance and rejection by a school. Mehta did not get accepted into the Perkins Institution for the Blind because of full enrollment. Write a letter to the school on Mehta's behalf. Ask them to reconsider him for admission. Present examples to support your arguments. Your letter should contain both fact and opinion.

interNET CONNECTION

Resources for the Blind Visit the National Federation of the Blind on the World Wide Web to identify resources Ved Mehta might use today as a blind adult writer. Organize and display information on a chart.

Literature Groups

Culture Shock Ved Mehta was a shy teenager when he came to the United States in 1949. Who were the people he leaned on as a newcomer, and how did they help him? In a small group, discuss how each of the characters in the story helped Mehta adjust to his new surroundings. Consider these questions: How did his father's examples and advice help young Ved? What did Ved learn about sight-impaired people from Mr. and Mrs. di Francesco? What information about U.S. culture did Mehta learn from the other characters?

Reading Further

For other stories of life in India, you might try these:

Portrait of India by Ved Mehta

An Episode of Sparrows by Rumer Goden

Save your work for your portfolio.

Skill Minilessons

RETEACH • REVIEW

GRAMMAR AND LANGUAGE • WORDS ENDING IN *-y*

When you add an ending to a word that ends with *-y,* you may have to change the *y* to *i.* Note the following rules.

CHANGE IT: When the *-y* is preceded by a consonant

happy happier

DON'T CHANGE IT: When the *-y* is preceded by a vowel

enjoy enjoyed

NEVER CHANGE IT: When you add *-ing*

study studying

PRACTICE Add the ending to each word. Write the new word.

1. funny + *-er*
2. cherry + *-es*
3. pray + *-ing*
4. apply + *-ed*
5. monkey + *-s*
6. loyalty + *-es*
7. toy + *-ed*
8. play + *-er*
9. cry + *-ing*
10. stay + *-s*

● For more about suffixes and final *-y*, see **Language Handbook,** p. R48.

READING AND THINKING • AVOIDING HASTY GENERALIZATIONS

A **generalization** is a broad statement that applies to many experiences or people. To make a generalization, you must first observe several specific experiences. If not, you could make a **hasty generalization,** one that is based on too little knowledge. Hasty generalizations may begin with words such as *all, always,* or *never.*

● For more about making generalizations, see **Reading Handbook,** p. R108.

PRACTICE Answer these questions about hasty generalizations from Ved Mehta's autobiography.

1. Explain whether the following statement is a hasty generalization: People in India do not eat spaghetti.
2. Find an example of a hasty generalization that Ved Mehta makes during his first meal with Mr. and Mrs. di Francesco.

VOCABULARY • PREFIXES AND SUFFIXES

The word *maladjustment* may look difficult until you take it apart. It is made from the base word *adjust* with *mal-* as a prefix and *-ment* as a suffix. *Mal-* means "bad or badly," and *-ment* (as in *argument* and *measurement*) is a common suffix. Prefixes and suffixes are often added to familiar words to make new words. When you find unfamiliar words, prefixes, or suffixes, look them up in a dictionary. Also, remember that a final *-e* may drop off a base word when a suffix is attached.

PRACTICE Use what you know about the prefixes, suffixes, and base words that form the numbered words on the left to match each with its meaning on the right.

1. fluidity	a. dissatisfied
2. irreversible	b. free
3. malcontent	c. unable to be undone
4. unenslaved	d. not giving in at all
5. uncompromising	e. the state of being liquid

Skill Minilessons

GRAMMAR AND LANGUAGE
WORDS ENDING IN *-Y*

1. funnier
2. cherries
3. praying
4. applied
5. monkeys
6. loyalties
7. toyed
8. player
9. crying
10. stays

READING AND THINKING
AVOIDING HASTY GENERALIZATIONS

1. Yes. Just because Mehta had never tried spaghetti does not mean that others in India have not tried the dish.
3. When Ved reacts defensively and says there is nothing primitive about India, he makes a hasty generalization.

VOCABULARY
PREFIXES AND SUFFIXES

1. e 2. c 3. a
4. b 5. d

Additional Resources

- ***Grammar and Language Workbook,*** pp. 293–294
- ***Grammar and Composition Handbook,*** Lesson 15.1
- ***Writer's Choice,*** Lesson 23.6
- ***Reading Skills Practice Workbook***
- ***Vocabulary Practice,*** p. 16

ASSESSMENT

- ***Quick Checks,*** p. 18
- ***Selection and Theme Assessment,*** pp. 31–32
- ***Performance Assessment,*** p. 17
- ***Testmaker: ExamView Pro***
- ***Interactive Tutor: Self-Assessment***

Interdisciplinary Connection

Objective

- To learn about emigration to the United States

Teaching Strategies

Point out to students that the United States is a country of immigrants. Except for Native Americans, we or our ancestors all came here from somewhere else within the last five hundred years. We can learn about what made the United States what it is today by studying immigration patterns and the contributions of immigrants to our culture.

Activity

Suggest that each student research his or her own heritage. Reports should include information that is based on answers to the questions listed. Encourage students to create a family tree that shows where different family members came from. Students might also practice delivering their reports before family members and asking for feedback. Then they should revise the report, reorganizing words and sentences if necessary to make their meaning clear.

Teaching Support

Interdisciplinary Connection

SOCIAL STUDIES

Coming to America

When Ved Mehta emigrated from India in 1949, he was seeking an education not available to blind people at home. Alone in a strange country, fifteen-year-old Ved needed someone to lean on. His father's friend contacted a couple who took him in and helped him get acquainted with the United States.

As Ved began his studies in America in the decade following World War II, more than 2.5 million other immigrants came to the United States. Each arrival had a special reason for coming. Each needed support and encouragement. Among these immigrants was the family of young Madeleine Korbel. Her family was looking for freedom from a series of oppressive governments that had for decades controlled her native country of Czechoslovakia. Nearly fifty years later, Madeleine Korbel Albright became the first woman to be named U.S. Secretary of State, a member of the president's cabinet. "All I can offer," she said in an address, "is the benefit of my own experience as someone whose family was driven twice from its home—first by Hitler, then by Stalin—while I was still a girl."

Immigration, 1820–1996:
Top Ten Countries of Last Residence

All countries	**63,140,227**
Germany	7,142,393
Mexico	5,542,625
Italy	5,427,298
United Kingdom	5,225,701
Ireland	4,778,159
Canada	4,423,066
Soviet Union, former	3,752,811
Austria	1,841,068
Hungary	1,673,579
Philippines	1,379,403

Immigration, 1996:
Top Ten Countries of Birth

All countries	**915,900**
Mexico	163,572
Philippines	55,876
India	44,859
Vietnam	42,067
China	41,728
Dominican Republic	39,604
Cuba	26,466
Ukraine	21,079
Russia	19,668
Jamaica	19,089

Source: U.S. Immigration and Naturalization Service

ACTIVITY

Select a country from one of the charts on this page and prepare a report about people moving from that country to the United States. Use a variety of primary and secondary sources and distinguish the value of each as you answer the following questions:

- About how many immigrants come each year?
- Why do they come?
- How do they get here?
- How do they decide where to settle?
- What people or institutions offer support as immigrants learn a new language and new ways?

MEETING INDIVIDUAL NEEDS — MULTIPLE MODES OF EXPRESSION

Spatial Students who have a spatial orientation may learn better through graphic devices. Encourage these students to present their reports graphically through charts, graphs, or pictures.

Activity Have students develop a visual report that displays graphically the impact of immigration on the United States. They may develop a computer presentation, a collage, a video, or even a drama on the subject. **L2**

Vo•cab•u•lar•y *Skills*

Using Familiar Words to Understand New Words

In the selection from *Sound-Shadows of the New World,* Mrs. di Francesco breaks into *unrestrained* laughter. What type of laughter is that?

Hint: What do *restrain* and *un-* mean?

By thinking about words you know, you can guess that Mrs. di Francesco bursts out in laughter that seems to be out of control.

As you read and listen to people speak, you will come across new words. Some of them will look like words you already know. For example, you may read a new word, such as *misinform,* and realize that it contains a familiar word *(inform)* and the prefix *mis-,* which means "not." Other words will have familiar suffixes attached. Still others will remind you of another word you know—perhaps because they share the same root.

EXERCISE

Each underlined word contains a familiar word. Use your knowledge to help you select the correct definition of the underlined word. Check your answers in a dictionary.

1. Mrs. Jones has no intention of being victimized by a purse snatcher.
   The meaning of *victim* indicates that *victimized* means
   a. stopped. **b.** forced to be cruel. **c.** made to suffer.
2. Mrs. Flowers teaches Marguerite to be intolerant of ignorance.
   The meaning of *tolerant* indicates that *intolerant* means
   a. unwilling to endure. **b.** doubtful. **c.** without intelligence.
3. Charlie feels obliged to continue with his journal.
   The meaning of *obligation* indicates that *obliged* means
   a. hardship. **b.** helpful. **c.** required by duty.
4. Roger sees that the door is open, and this emboldens him.
   The meaning of *bold* indicates that *emboldens* means
   a. amuses. **b.** gives courage to. **c.** causes hesitation in.
5. Mrs. Jones's question necessitates a response from Roger.
   The meaning of *necessary* indicates that *necessitates* means
   a. requires. **b.** discourages. **c.** suggests.

Vo•cab•u•lar•y *Skills*

Objective

- To use familiar words to understand new words.

Teaching Strategies

One way to increase vocabulary is to figure out the meanings of words from their roots, prefixes, and suffixes, as well as from context clues. Emphasize that students will retain more knowledge this way rather than by looking up the words because deciphering a word is active learning.

Exercise

1. c
2. a
3. c
4. b
5. a

Additional Resources

Vocabulary Power

MEETING INDIVIDUAL NEEDS — ENGLISH LANGUAGE LEARNERS

Vocabulary Acquisition Students who are not native speakers have already developed many strategies for acquiring vocabulary, whether they realize it or not. Certainly, students sometimes use the dictionary, but they also use many other devices.

Activity Have English language learners work in small groups to talk about how they figure out the meanings of new words in English. You may also want students to develop brief oral reports to deliver to the class on the strategies they use to learn English vocabulary. **L3**

Additional Resource

English Language Learners Sourcebook, p. 38

Objectives

- To write a biographical sketch of approximately 500 to 700 words
- To prewrite, draft, revise, edit, and present a biographical sketch
- To reflect on and assess the sketch

GLENCOE TECHNOLOGY

WRITER'S ASSISTANT CD-ROM

Students can use Glencoe's templates and guidelines software for narrative writing to aid them in working through the steps in the writing process in this lesson.

Teaching Strategies

PREWRITING

Explore Ideas Suggest that students close their eyes and picture the people. Students should include in their freewriting any details they remember.

Research a Subject Point out that it is always better to have too much information than too little. It is easier to cut than to have to strain to think of details to include. Although it's important to keep to a schedule, there's really no such thing as too much research.

Teaching Support

Writing WORKSHOP

Narrative Writing: Biographical Sketch

Whom do you lean on when you are troubled? You may rely on close friends, family members, teachers, or even famous people that you look up to. Whoever they are, these people have helped you through their actions, attitudes, or beliefs. Now you can try to help others by sharing a story about one of these people.

Assignment: Follow the process explained in these pages to develop a biographical sketch: a brief, true story about a person. Write about an episode in the life of this person–an episode that illustrates the theme "Lean on Me."

- As you write your biographical sketch, refer to the **Writing Handbook**, pp. R50–R55.

EVALUATION RUBRIC

By the time you complete this Writing Workshop, you will have

- written a biographical sketch about an episode in someone's life that illustrates the theme "Lean on Me"
- revealed your attitude toward the subject of your sketch
- set a definite tone from the beginning of your biographical sketch
- used realistic dialogue and vivid, specific descriptions to bring your subject to life
- ended with a summary of the subject's life, qualities, or contribution
- presented a sketch that is free of errors in grammar, usage, and mechanics

The Writing Process

PREWRITING

PREWRITING TIP

When you freewrite, pour out all the ideas and details you can think of. Don't stop to read what you've written; keep your pen moving!

Explore Ideas

Spend about ten minutes freewriting about people who come to mind when you think of the words "Lean on Me." Think of people who have given you inspiration, comfort, advice, or a helping hand. Jot down what you remember.

Complete the **Writing Skills** activity on page 211 if you haven't done it already. Then go over your freewriting notes. Choose three people who stand out from the others, and think about what each person means to you. Ask yourself questions like these:

- What qualities does this person have that I admire? How do those qualities come through in the person's appearance, actions, and words?
- What has this person said or done to help me through a hard time? What details do I remember about that experience?

MEETING INDIVIDUAL NEEDS — ENGLISH LANGUAGE LEARNERS

Prewriting in the First Language The complex process of writing can be simplified for less-proficient English language learners by allowing them to complete some steps in their first language.

Activity For this exercise, allow English language learners to prewrite in their first languages if they wish. Then they can look for translations of difficult words before they begin to outline and write their narratives. Also allow students to use words from their first languages to flavor their narratives, much as Martin does in "The Journey."

Additional Resources

English Language Learners Sourcebook

Research a Subject

Which of the three people seems to have affected you most? Select an experience with that person to be the subject of your biographical sketch. How much do you know about your subject? How well do you remember your experience with this person? If you need more information before you write:

- Conduct an interview with someone you can talk to who knows your subject well. Take careful notes, and be sure to include details.
- Visit the library if your subject is a contemporary or historical figure who has inspired you. Look for newspaper articles or books about this person. Did your subject leave a diary or letters that could tell you more about him or her?
- If your subject is someone famous, you may also find useful information about him or her on the Internet. Some search engines are better than others at finding relevant information. Your teacher, a librarian, or other students may be able to suggest ways to make your search effective.

Consider Your Purpose and Audience

Do you want to inspire your readers? Amuse them? Inform them? Set a purpose for your writing. Who will read your finished work? Choose words that they will respond to.

Organize Ideas

Before you start writing, organize your main ideas.

- Organize your writing around the personality traits you admire about your subject. Give examples and describe events to help the reader picture the person.
- Focus on the event or episode that shows why you can lean on your subject. Use a plan like the following:

Introduction:	Introduce the subject and the major event.
Body:	Tell about the major event. Include details about your subject, other people, the action, and the result.
Conclusion:	Summarize the subject's life, qualities, or contribution.

STUDENT MODEL • PREWRITING

Schoolmate, Alexa Johnson. Popular, good at sports. Encouraged me during hike when I sprained my ankle. Trusted me with her secret.

Talked to me about drama club, took my mind off injured ankle. Told me she had diabetes; teachers knew, but she didn't want students to find out and feel sorry for her.

Made me feel special that she trusted me and that I was able to help her out after she'd helped me.

Complete Student Model on p. R120.

Consider Your Purpose and Audience Have each student write his or her purpose and audience on a 3" X 5" card. The student should keep the card nearby while writing. This strategy will help them stay focused on these two important elements.

Organize Ideas Remind students that specific details, examples, and anecdotes are vital to this essay. Review various ways to organize the details.

Once students have decided on the details they plan to include, remind them that the details need to be organized effectively. Simply listing the details is not enough. Have students review ways to organize their details into paragraphs. Then remind them of the importance of providing smooth, effective transitions between their paragraphs. Have them list techniques they have learned for making connections between paragraphs.

Additional Resources

- ***Writing and Proofreading Practice,*** pp. 1–6, 14–20
- ***Writing and Proofreading Transparencies 1–6, 9–10***
- ***Writer's Choice,*** Lesson 4

MEETING INDIVIDUAL NEEDS — MULTIPLE MODES OF EXPRESSION

Spatial Students with strong spatial orientation may choose to prewrite by using a combination of pictures and words.

Activity Have each student sketch the face of the person he or she plans to write about in the center of a sheet of paper and use a combination of words and pictures to add ideas. **L2**

DRAFTING

Drafting Tip
If you have trouble coming up with a good introduction, write the body first. The details may give you a good idea for the beginning.

Dig In to Your First Draft

Start with a strong introduction. You might point out a unique quality of your subject or you might open with a question, a quotation, or an intriguing fact about your subject or the major event.

Keep writing! Don't feel compelled to tell the person's entire life. Stick to the plan you made, describing your main ideas. Include interesting quotations and details to support your ideas.

STUDENT MODEL • DRAFTING

I couldn't believe she knew about my play, which was the next week. It turns out that she's really into drama. She wanted to take drama classes, but because she's so good at sports she felt like she couldn't switch and do something else.

Complete Student Model on p. R120.

REVISING

Revising Tip
While you are working on your revision, think again about your audience. Have you provided all the information readers will need?

Review Your Work

Put your draft aside for a day or two and then reread it. With a partner, go over the **Rubric for Revising** to help you identify gaps in information and places that need improvement. Look for ways you can make your feelings clearer and add specific details that will help your readers understand the subject of your sketch.

RUBRIC FOR REVISING

Your revised essay should have
- a strong introduction
- a consistent point of view
- enough well-chosen details about the person and the event to bring the subject to life
- transitions that help your readers follow your thoughts
- an ending that summarizes your attitude toward the subject

Your revised essay should be free of
- references to people or events that distract readers from your main ideas
- errors in grammar, usage, and mechanics

DRAFTING

Dig In to Your First Draft Suggest that a good way for students to avoid writer's block is to leave a blank line when they can't think of a particular word. Stopping to think while searching for a word can interfere with the flow of ideas.

REVISING

Review Your Work As students revise, remind them that clarity is the key to good writing. Is there anything in what they have written that may be confusing to someone who has not shared their experiences? Have them check their research for details that could make their writing clearer and more effective.

Technology Tip

Using a word processing program will allow students more freedom to revise their work. Encourage students to experiment with the organization of their sketches by moving text.

GLENCOE TECHNOLOGY

Invite students to use the *Revising with Style* CD-ROM, which offers instructions and exercises to help students improve their writing skills.

Teaching Support

Writing *Minilesson*

Sentence Structure The structure of a sentence should accurately reflect the meaning of the sentence. Subordinate ideas should be expressed in subordinate clauses, not strung together with coordinating conjunctions. Write this on the board: *We walked to the store and on the way saw someone trying to grab a lady's shopping bag, and we tried to help her.* Underline the three ideas and ask students to rank them in importance. Then show how the sentence can be rewritten to reflect this ranking. *On our way to the store, we tried to help an old woman who was being robbed.*

Activity Have students examine their writing for opportunities to combine or rewrite sentences. **L2**

Additional Resources

Writer's Choice, Lesson 2.8

EDITING/PROOFREADING

After you have reviewed and revised your biographical sketch, use the **Proofreading Checklist** on the inside back cover to help you catch mistakes in grammar, usage, mechanics, and spelling. If you are unsure about how to punctuate dialogue, review the rules you learned in the **Grammar Link** on page 167.

PROOFREADING TIP
Make sure that dialogue, dates, and the names of cities and states are punctuated properly.

Grammar Hint

When you write a date, use a comma or commas to set off the year that follows the month and the day. Also use a comma or commas to set off the name of a state or country that follows the name of a city or town.

Complete Student Model
For a complete version of the model developed in this Workshop, refer to **Writing Workshop Models**, p. R120.

STUDENT MODEL • EDITING/PROOFREADING

Our camping trip started the morning of april 7 2001 from the Oceanside town of Martinsville California.

Complete Student Model on p. R120.

PUBLISHING/PRESENTING

In what medium will you present your final work? You might read your work aloud, videotape your reading of the biographical sketch, or work with other students to create a bulletin-board display or magazine about "People We Lean On."

PRESENTING TIP
Use photographs, maps, and diagrams or your own artwork to give your work visual impact.

Reflecting

In your journal, describe what you've learned about your relationship with your subject. Then list things you would do differently for your next workshop.

Save your work for your portfolio.

EDITING/PROOFREADING

Suggest that students write their sketches in one color of ink and edit them in another color so that they won't miss their corrections when they rewrite.

PUBLISHING/PRESENTING

Presenting Tip If students choose to read their work aloud, remind them that using appropriate grammar, enunciation, and pace will help ensure that their presentations are understood by their audience and are easy to follow.

Reflecting

Portfolio Encourage students to ask themselves these questions as they review their writing.

Does my narrative essay
- give a clear and detailed portrait of the person?
- explain why this person is important to me?
- include specific details and examples of this person's behavior?

6+1 TRAITS™ OF WRITING
See the annotated **Writing Workshop Models** on pp. R119–R130 for additional help in evaluating student writing and in teaching the **6+1 Traits™ of effective writing.** Annotations and minilessons address and reinforce the **6+1 Traits™:** Ideas, Organization, Voice, Word Choice, Sentence Fluency, Conventions, and Presentation.

ASSESSMENT

Writing Assessment and Portfolio Management
- Writing Assessment, pp. 7–12, 17–19
- Portfolio Management, pp. 40–47

Theme Assessment

Objective

- To give a personal response to the theme "Lean on Me"
- To write a list of questions to ask writers of autobiography
- To complete a self-evaluation, set a goal, and devise a plan for acheiving the goal

Responding to the Theme

1. Students should provide valid reasons and logical explanations for their choices.
2. Accept all reasonable responses.

Analyzing Literature

Students' questions should

- relate to the selection they read.
- reveal at least a basic familiarity with the author's interests and concerns.

Evaluate and Set Goals

Evaluate

Have students list the projects and assignments they completed as a way of reviewing in their own minds what they accomplished. To help students formulate valid reasons for their ratings, you might suggest they develop a class rubric.

Set Goals

In a chart, have students jot down their goals, the steps they will take for achieving them, and checkpoints. Then discuss students' plans in individual conferences.

Theme Assessment

Responding to the Theme

1. Which selection in this theme helped you understand how people "lean" on each other? Explain your answer.
2. What new understanding do you have about the following after completing this theme?
   - the need to belong and fit in with others
   - the effect of self-esteem on relationships
   - the influence of friends and family members
3. Present your theme project to the class.

Analyzing Literature

LOOKING AT AUTOBIOGRAPHERS

This theme contains selections from the autobiographies of Maya Angelou, Ved Mehta, and James Herriot. Which author would you most like to meet? Write a list of questions you would ask about the selection, the theme, or the author's life. Discuss your questions with a partner.

Evaluate and Set Goals

1. Which of the following did you enjoy the most? Which would you like to improve?
   - reading and responding to the selections
   - doing research with a group
   - making presentations
   - doing independent writing
2. How would you assess your work in this theme, using the following scale? Give at least two reasons for your assessment.
   4 = outstanding 2 = fair
   3 = good 1 = weak
3. Based on your assessment, what skill would you like to improve in the next theme?
4. Write down your goal and two or three steps you will take to achieve it.
5. Review the goal and your plan with a partner or your teacher.

Build Your Portfolio

SELECT

Choose two of the best pieces of work you did in this theme, and include them in your portfolio. Use these questions to help you choose:

- ✦ Which did you enjoy doing the most?
- ✦ Which challenged you the most?
- ✦ Which did you learn the most from?
- ✦ Which expressed your ideas the best?

REFLECT

Write some notes to accompany the pieces you selected. Use these questions to guide you:

- ✦ What was the best feature about the piece?
- ✦ What did you learn from creating it?
- ✦ If you did it over again, what would you do differently?

ASSESSMENT

Writing Assessment and Portfolio Management
- Writing Assessment, pp. 1–12
- Portfolio Management, pp. 40–47

Testmaker: ExamView Pro

Interactive Tutor: Self-Assessment

GLENCOE TECHNOLOGY

MINDJOGGER VIDEOQUIZZES
VIDEODISC

Use *MindJogger* to review Theme 2 content.

Theme 2
Side A

Also available in VHS.

Reading on Your Own

If you have enjoyed the literature in this theme, you might also be interested in the following books.

Cezanne Pinto

by Mary Stolz In this fictional memoir, an elderly man tells his story of being born into slavery, escaping to freedom, serving in the Civil War, and becoming a cowboy in Texas. As he nears his ninetieth birthday, Cezanne Pinto remembers his lifelong struggle for freedom and the friends who helped him along the way.

Timothy of the Cay

by Theodore Taylor This follow-up to the acclaimed novel *The Cay* traces the life of Timothy, who goes to sea as a boy and grows up to command a ship. It also tells of Philip, who hopes to regain his sight after being blinded in a shipwreck and rescued by Timothy.

Far North

by Will Hobbs Fifteen-year-old Gabe must rely on another teenager and an elderly Native American hunter after their plane crashes in the frozen Canadian wilderness. As they struggle to survive, Gabe develops a new appreciation for the world of the Far North and its inhabitants.

Walk Two Moons

by Sharon Creech What do you do when you need your mother, and your grandparents need *you?* In this story, thirteen-year-old Sal and her grandparents set out on a long drive to find Sal's missing mother and solve both problems. Along with a serious theme, there is humor in their search.

Reading on Your Own

Tips for Independent Reading

Stress the imprtance of each student's spending at least thirty minutes a day in independent reading and suggest books, such as those shown here, related to this theme.

Reading the Novel As students read novels associated with the theme "Lean on Me," encourage them to pay attention to how the author uses the relationships between characters to tell the story. Explain that how characters react to one another, and what they learn from each other, are often the most important and meaningful aspects of a story.

Practice Present the following discussion questions after students have read a few chapters of their novels: How does the author present the characters and their relationships with one another? How important are these relationships to the story? How do the characters' relationships develop the plot? What can be learned about a character from his or her relationships?

Glencoe Literature Library

WalkingTwo Moons, by Sharon Creech, is available in the *Glencoe Literature Library*. For a complete listing of the titles, see the **Glencoe Resources for Independent Reading** in the front of this book.

At the MOVIES

Be sure to preview the following video for appropriateness for your class:

Babe, a movie in which smart, articulate people and animals show what "Lean on Me" really means.

MEETING INDIVIDUAL NEEDS — SPECIAL NEEDS

You may wish to recommend *Walk Two Moons* to your less-proficient readers. The humor and even pace of this story will draw readers in and keep them involved in the story.

The books listed at the right are rated for average students **(L2)** or for students who need more challenging reading **(L3)**.

- *Far North* by Will Hobbs **L2**
- *Timothy of the Cay* by Theodore Taylor **L3**
- *Cezanne Pinto* by Mary Stolz **L2**

Standardized Test Practice

Answers and Analyses

1. B To answer this question, students must distinguish the features and elements of consumer materials. Students should take note that the flyer presents prices, offers a discount, and otherwise tries to convince people to buy office supplies at Oliver's. These clues indicate that it is an advertisement—the best choice is B.

The Princeton Review TEST-TAKING TIP

Remind students that they do not need to memorize the story or passage; they only need to understand the main idea and the understand the main idea and the general organization of the passage. when students begin to answer the questions, they should look back to the passage and find evidence for their answer. Students are never asked to speculate without adequate evidence; they only need to refer back to the passage and find the clues in the text.

The Princeton Review TEST-TAKING TIP

If students run into an unfamiliar word on the test, they may be able to get an idea of its meaning if they focus on its parts. For instance, words that start with *non-*, *un-*, *a-*, *dis-*, and *in-* generally reverse what the rest of the word means. They may also be able to identify the roots of certain words, such as the common root "dict" (meaning *word*) in dictionary and predict. Students should take whatever clues they can in order to determine the meaning of a word.

The Princeton Review

Standardized Test Practice

Read the following material. Then read each question on page 233. Decide which is the best answer to each question. Mark the letter for that answer on your paper.

Oliver's Office Supplies Central

Everything you need for your office, school, and home!

It's definitely worth your time to come to Oliver's Office Supplies Central today! Located in Las Rosas, Oliver's has the largest selection of office supplies anywhere in the state, and our prices are unbeatable. Come in and compare our prices on these very popular items:

	Brenner's Offices	Supply City	Oliver's Office Supplies
Stargazer Nylon Binder	$11.49	$12.35	$ 7.48
Trails Backpack	10.60	12.21	9.99
Carl's Computer Paper	4.12	3.75	2.44
Super Stapler	3.89	3.99	3.19
Worldly Word Processor (Model 225)	159.40	179.66	132.11
Fabulous 3 Drawer File Cabinet	89.97	91.99	65.00

If you come in this week, Oliver's is offering an additional 10% off the everyday low discount price on these selected items. Come see our reduced prices on a multitude of other items. At Oliver's, you will find many name brands at the lowest prices around. We guarantee that you will be satisfied with what we have to offer. You'll never shop for supplies anywhere else!

Oliver's Supplies Central
83 Route 9
Las Rosas

MEETING INDIVIDUAL NEEDS — ENGLISH LANGUAGE LEARNERS

Informational Advertisements After reading through the passage, ask students what sort of products they might expect to see in an ad for a restaurant supply store. Some examples they may come up with are ovens, silverware, cooking utensils, tables, candles, and so on. When students do not know the English translations for an item in their inventory, have them write the word down in their native language. Then have students describe the item to the class and ask students to guess the English word for the item.

1 The passage is most like —
- A an instruction manual.
- B an advertisement.
- C a warranty.
- D a schedule.

2 The last paragraph in the ad is included in order to convince you that —
- J people who shop at Oliver's have a lot of money to spend.
- K Oliver's has more name brand merchandise than other stores.
- L Oliver's appeals to shoppers looking for great deals.
- M local office managers buy all of their supplies at Oliver's.

3 In the passage, the word multitude means —
- A large number.
- B warehouse.
- C short list.
- D small number.

4 Based on the information in the ad, you can conclude that Supply City —
- J does not carry name brand office supplies.
- K is more convenient than Oliver's.
- L has the highest prices on most supplies.
- M is larger than Brenner's Offices.

5 You can tell from the passage that —
- A Trails Backpacks are more expensive at Brenner's Offices than at Supply City.
- B Super Staplers are cheaper at Supply City than at Oliver's Office Supplies.
- C Items at Supply City are always less expensive than items at Brenner's Offices.
- D Carl's Computer Paper is the least expensive item at Oliver's Office Supply.

STOP

Answers and Analyses

2. L Remind students to carefully reread the final paragraph. Almost every sentence in the paragraph discusses low prices, so the best inference is choice L.
3. A The final paragraph advertises "an additional 10% off these selected items," and "reduced prices on a multitude of other items." Using the context, students can deduce that *multitude* is in opposition to *selected* and therefore means a large number. Students may also recognize the word part *multi-*, which means much or many, from words they are already familiar with, such as *multiply*.
4. L Students can use the process of elimination (POE) to answer this question. The *size, convenience,* and *brands* carried in other stores are never mentioned in the advertisement, eliminating choices J, K, and M. However, the prices of items in the three stores are compared, and in most cases Supply City is the most expensive.
5. D Students need to use their experience reviewing tables to answer this question. The advertisement provides a table comparing the prices of the three stores. For each answer choice, students should find the row listing the item mentioned, then find the columns listing the stores and prices being compared. In examining the table, students may also notice that Oliver's offers the lowest price for each item listed. They can then confirm that choice D is correct.

Tested Objectives

Item	Reading Objective
1, 5	Compare and contrast the features and elements of consumer materials to gain meaning from documents
2	Evaluate the unity, coherence, logic, internal consistency, and structural patterns of text
3	Use word meanings within the appropriate context and be able to verify those meanings by definition, restatement, example, comparison, or contrast
4	Read and understand grade-level-appropriate material. Describe and connect the essential ideas, arguments, and perspectives of text, as they relate to text structure, organization, and purpose

MORE PRACTICE

For additional practice, assign pages from one of the following standardized test resources available as part of Glencoe Literature.

Additional Resources
ITBS Preparation and Practice
SAT-9 Preparation and Practice
TerraNova Preparation and Practice

Theme 3 At a Glance
Which Way to Go?

THEME OPENING

Theme 3: WHICH WAY TO GO?

SELECTIONS

SKILL FEATURES

WRITING WORKSHOP

THEME ASSESSMENT

- **Responding to the Theme, Analyzing Literature, Evaluate and Set Goals** (p. 328)
- **Build Your Portfolio** (p. 328)
- **Reading on Your Own** (p. 329)

  Shabanu: Daughter of the Wind by Suzanne Fisher Staples

  The Rain Catchers by Jean Thesman

  American Dragons: Twenty-Five Asian American Voices edited by Laurence Yep

  Banner in the Sky by James Ramsey Ullman
- **Standardized Test Practice** (pp. 330–331)

KEYS TO LITERARY CONNECTIONS

Comparing Selections

The **Comparing Selections** feature in this theme provides opportunities for addressing diverse aspects of the reading and literature curriculum.

For example, in **Comparing Selections** on page 256, students compare "In the Middle of a Pitch," a short story by Bill Meissner, with "Casey at the Bat." Through this comparison students' gain exposure to various forms of sports writing, as well as insights into the authors' purposes for writing.

World Literature

The Student Edition contains a variety of literature that represents cultures from around the world. World literature selections are highlighted with the icon above.

TEACHING SUPPORT

The Teaching Support offers a wealth of interactive instructional support:

Meeting Individual Needs
- Special Needs
- English Language Learners
- Multiple Modes of Expression
- Advanced Learners

Internet Connection

Assessment

Portfolio Options

Minilessons
- Grammar and Language
- Reading
- Writing
- Listening and Speaking

Connecting to Other Selections

Real-World Connection

Interdisciplinary Connection

Life Skills Connection

Family and Community Activity

Key to Ability Levels

The activities throughout this theme have been coded for students of various abilities.

L1 BASIC activities for all students

L2 AVERAGE activities for average to above-average students

L3 ADVANCED LEARNERS activities for above-average students

Teaching Today

The Glencoe *Teaching Today* professional development Web site at www.teachingtoday.glencoe.com features daily teaching tips, free downloads, annotated Web resources, educational news, and a wealth of information on a wide range of topics.

Theme 3 At a Glance (continued)

Which Way to Go?

Reading Skills in this theme

Variety of Texts

In addition to short stories and a series of poems, this theme includes the following:

- cartoon
- comic strip
- folktales
- newspaper article

Comprehension Skills

The following instructional support for comprehension skills appears in this theme of the Student Edition:

- **Active Reading Strategies and Model** (pp. 296–301)
- **Monitoring Comprehension** (p. 280)
- **Reading and Thinking Minilessons** (pp. 249, 279, 293, 313, 321)

See also the **Reading Minilessons** throughout the theme in this Teacher Wraparound Edition.

For strategies for reading longer works, such as novels and novellas, see "Tips for Independent Reading" on page 329.

Reading Resources

Active Reading Guide The ***Active Reading Guide*** provides graphic organizers and study guide questions to support students' reading of each selection (***Active Reading Guide***, pp. 19–27).

Interactive Reading Sourcebook and **Interactive Reading Workbook** The ***Interactive Reading Sourcebook*** and ***Interactive Reading Workbook*** offer focused comprehension strategies and lessons on critical thinking skills as well as fluency practice and activities to teach and support phonics, decoding, spelling, and vocabulary development.

Vocabulary Power The ***Vocabulary Power*** workbook (Lessons 10–14) provides systematic teaching, practice, and assessment of vocabulary for better reading comprehension.

Audio Library Available on audiocassette and on CD, the ***Audio Library*** provides valuable comprehension support.

Glencoe Literature Library Each title in the ***Glencoe Literature Library*** includes a full-length work plus related readings. A separate Study Guide is available for each title.

Five-Star Stories These anthologies of familiar short stories adapted and abridged for a variety of reading levels include exercises to help increase students' vocabulary and improve their reading comprehension.

The Contemporary Readers ***The Contemporary Readers*** are nonfiction books linked to various themes and designed for developing readers from a wide range of backgrounds.

Literature Classics CD-ROM The selections on this CD-ROM can be searched by author, theme, or genre.

inTIME and **Humanities Across TIME** Coproductions of Glencoe and Time, Inc., these resources include a wealth of high-interest nonfiction related to the selections in this theme.

Assessment in this theme

Glencoe's Assessment Advantage

Assessment Options in the Student Edition

This program offers a number of diverse ways to evaluate student understanding and skill proficiency. In the Student Edition, use the following:

- **Responding to Literature**
  Following each selection, students are asked to recall facts, interpret ideas, and evaluate concepts as they answer a variety of questions and complete activities to extend their understanding.
- **Theme Assessment (pp. 328–329)**
  Here students respond to the selections on personal and analytical levels. They also assume ownership of their learning by setting and evaluating goals and by selecting work for their portfolios.

See also the many **Assessment Resources** listed on the facing page.

The Princeton Review

Standardized Test Practice

The Princeton Review has developed the Standardized Test Practice pages found at the end of this thematic unit (pp. 330–331). For additional practice, direct students to the following resources:

- ITBS Preparation and Practice
- SAT-9 Preparation and Practice
- TerraNova Preparation and Practice

Writing Skills in this theme

Writing Skills

The Student Edition of Theme 3 offers strong instructional support for writing skills:

In **Extending Your Response,** which follows each selection:

- **Writing About Literature**
- **Personal/Creative Writing**

See also the **Writing Minilessons** throughout the theme in this Teacher Wraparound Edition.

Writing Workshops

Theme 3 concludes with a **Writing Workshop** that guides students through the process for writing an evaluation (pp. 324–327).

Writing Resources

Writer's Assistant CD-ROM Each **Writing Workshop** is supplemented by an interactive writing guide on the ***Writer's Assistant*** CD-ROM. This easy-to-use writing guide provides prompts, templates, and other tools that lead students through the writing process.

Grammar and Composition Handbook The ***Grammar and Composition Handbook*** (Lessons 4.1–6.2) provides systematic instruction in English language conventions.

Spelling Power The ***Spelling Power*** workbook (Lessons 9–12) provides systematic teaching, practice, and assessment of spelling to help students become better spellers and thus enhance their writing.

Writing and Proofreading Practice Blackline masters present in-depth instruction and practice on a specific step in the writing process and proofreading (pp. 1–7, 21–27).

Writing and Proofreading Transparencies Transparencies provide graphic organizers and proofreading exercises for whole-class instruction (pp. 1–6, 11–12, 29–30).

Research and Report Writing Guide This resource provides extensive tips and activities to guide students in their writing projects in the literature classroom as well as in classes across the curriculum.

Style and Documentation Sourcebook for Writers This sourcebook is a combination reference and workbook, giving students the most up-to-date information and guidance regarding traditional as well as technological research strategies and documentation.

Revising with Style This resource offers instruction and exercises focusing on the revision process and covering topics from proofreading and correcting common grammatical errors to sentence combining and reordering.

Assessment Resources

Selection Quick Checks For each selection, a **Quick Check** of three to five short-answer questions measures students' literal comprehension.

Selection and Theme Assessment The ***Selection and Theme Assessment*** instrument tests students' abilities to recall, interpret, and evaluate what they've read. The tests consist of multiple-choice, short answer, and essay questions.

Performance Assessment Alternative assessment instruments and rubrics for Theme 3 are found in the ***Performance Assessment*** ancillary.

Writing Assessment and Portfolio Management These notes and strategies, student models, and assessment tools assist with the task of measuring students' progress as writers and as monitors of their own writing.

Testmaker: ExamView Pro Teachers can customize selection and Theme 3 tests by accessing the ***Testmaker*** database.

Interactive Tutor: Self-Assessment The ***Interactive Tutor: Self-Assessment*** software provides multiple-choice tests with immediate feedback to help students evaluate their knowledge and understanding of each literature selection.

MindJogger Videoquizzes Using a popular game show format, ***MindJogger Videoquizzes*** on videocassettes enable teachers to evaluate student understanding of Theme 3 in a quick and fun manner.

Theme 3 Skills Scope and Sequence

Lessons	Literary Elements	Reading and Thinking	Writing
In the Middle of a Pitch	Conflict, SE p. 247 *Conflict, TWE pp. 240, 241* *Foreshadowing, TWE p. 240* *Imagery, TWE p. 243* *Irony, TWE p. 245*	Creative Thinking, SE p. 249 *Infer, TWE pp. 240, 244* *Drawing Conclusions, TWE pp. 241, 242* SN *Learning Disabled, TWE p. 242*	Rich Language, SE p. 248 From Prose to Poetry, SE p. 248
Casey at the Bat	Narrative Poetry, SE p. 255 *Narrative Poetry, TWE pp. 253, 254* *Rhyme Scheme, TWE p. 254*	Comic Strip, SE p. 250 Comparing Selections, SE p. 250 *Author's Purpose, TWE p. 250* *Infer, TWE p. 252* *Adjusting Reading Rate, TWE p. 254*	Poetry, SE p. 255
The Wise Old Woman	Climax, SE p. 264 *Climax, TWE pp. 260, 263* *Characterization, TWE p. 262*	*Infer, TWE p. 263* *Author's Purpose, TWE p. 263*	Compare Folktales, SE p. 265 Short Story, SE p. 265
Bagged Wolf	Rising Action, SE p. 277 *Characterization, TWE pp. 270, 273* *Rising Action, TWE pp. 271, 272, 274, 275* *Symbolism, TWE p. 274*	Summarizing, SE p. 279 Monitoring Comprehension, SE p. 280 *Drawing Conclusions, TWE pp. 271, 275* *Main Idea and Supporting Details, TWE p. 271* *Synthesize, TWE p. 275*	Symbolism, SE p. 278 Scene from a Short Story, SE p. 278 *Symbolism, TWE p. 275* SN *Learning Disabled, TWE p. 280*
The Moustache	Characterization, SE p. 291 *Characterization, TWE pp.283, 284, 287, 289, 290* *Imagery, TWE p. 284* *Figurative Language, TWE p. 286* *Plot, TWE p. 288* *Climax, TWE p. 289*	Clarifying, SE p. 293 *Main Idea and Supporting Details, TWE p. 284* *Drawing Conclusions, TWE p. 287* *Make Critical Judgments, TWE p. 289*	Comparison, SE p. 292 Dialogue, SE p. 292
The Black Walnut Tree	Poetry, SE p. 294 Symbol, SE p. 300	Poetry, SE p. 296	Story Structure, SE p. 301 Nature Poem, SE p. 301
A Time to Talk Fire and Ice and Dust of Snow	Lyric Poetry, SE p. 306 *Meter, TWE p. 303* *Lyric Poetry, TWE pp. 303, 304, 305* *Alliteration, TWE p. 304* *Rhyme Scheme, TWE p. 305*	Author's Purpose, SE p. 313 *Generalize, TWE p. 303* *Compare and Contrast, TWE p. 305*	Poem to Poem, SE p. 307 Metaphor, SE p. 307
Between What I See and What I Say…	Free Verse, SE p. 312 *Free Verse, TWE p. 310*	Author's Purpose, SE p. 313 ELL *Read Along, TWE p. 315*	Reading Between the Lines, SE p. 313 Essay, SE p. 313 *Editing, TWE p. 314*
Identity and the lesson of the moth	Theme, SE p. 320 *Theme, TWE pp. 317, 319* *Imagery, TWE pp. 317, 319*	Compare and Contrast, SE p. 321 Newspaper Article, SE p. 322 *Compare and Contrast, TWE p. 319* *Distinguish Fact from Opinion, TWE p. 322*	Style, SE p. 321
Writing WORKSHOP Expository Writing: Writing an Evaluation			ELL *Organizing, TWE p. 324*

Key: Student material is in roman. Teacher material is in italic. Technology ELL English Language Learners

Vocabulary and Spelling	Grammar and Language	Listening, Speaking, and Viewing	Life Skills; Study and Research; Technology
Connotation, SE p. 249 ELL *Multiple Meaning Words,* TWE p. 240	Participles, SE p. 249 *Verbs,* TWE p. 246 SN *Less-Proficient Readers,* TWE p. 248	Literature Groups, SE p 248	Music Research, SE p. 248 Comparing Ideas, SE p. 248 *Interviewing,* TWE p. 245
Specialized Terms, TWE p. 253 ELL *Vocabulary,* TWE p. 253		Literature Groups, SE p. 255	Social Studies, SE p. 257 *Video,* TWE p. 254
Synonyms, SE p. 265 *Connotation,* TWE p. 260	*Adverbs,* TWE p. 262 ELL *Verb Tenses,* TWE p. 260	Literature Groups, SE p. 265	Social Studies Research, SE p. 265 Multimedia: Adding Sound and Video to Presentations, SE p. 266 SN *Learning Disabled,* TWE p. 266
Latin Roots, SE p. 279 ELL *-ing Forms,* TWE p. 270 *Dictionaries,* TWE p. 276	Punctuating Compound Sentences, SE p. 279 *Punctuating Dialogue,* TWE p. 276	Literature Groups, SE p. 278 Storytelling, SE p. 278	Internet Connection, SE p. 278 Science Report, SE p. 278 *Science Research,* TWE p. 273 *Cartoon Research,* TWE p. 274
Roots, SE p. 293 *Connotation and Denotation,* TWE p. 284 *Multiple-Meaning Words,* TWE p. 285	Adverb Phrases, SE p. 293 *Capitalization of Proper Nouns,* TWE p. 290	Literature Groups, SE p. 292 Performing on the Road, SE p. 292 ELL *Cultural References,* TWE p. 283 SN *Emotional,* TWE p. 285	Health Research, SE p. 292 *Collaborating,* TWE p. 287 *Health Research,* TWE pp. 286, 289 *Internet Connection,* TWE p. 289
	Concrete and Abstract Nouns, SE p. 301	Literature Groups, SE p. 301 Oral Reading, SE p. 301	
Dictionary Skills–Pronunciation, SE p. 309 ELL *Personalized Pronunciation Keys,* TWE p. 308	Action Verbs, SE p. 307 ELL *Unfamiliar Meanings,* TWE p. 303 *Commas,* TWE p. 304	Literature Groups, SE p. 307	
Roots, TWE p. 311	Subject-Verb Agreement, SE p. 314 *Subject-Verb Agreement,* TWE p. 311	Literature Groups, SE p. 313 Effective Listening Techniques, SE p. 315	You as Critic, SE p. 313
ELL *Contractions,* TWE p. 317	*Adjective Phrases,* TWE p. 318	Literature Groups, SE p. 321	

SN **Special Needs/Strategic Intervention**

Theme 3 RESOURCE MANAGER

Lessons	Essential Resources	English Language Learners
In the Middle of a Pitch Bill Meissner Pacing: 2 Days	**Lesson-Specific Instruction** Selection Focus Transp. 18 * Active Reading Guide, p. 19 Literary Elements Transp. 19 Vocabulary Practice, p. 17 * Quick Checks, p. 19 Selection and Theme Assessment, p. 33 Testmaker: ExamView Pro Performance Assessment, p. 18 **Systematic Language Instruction** Grammar and Comp. Hbk., L. 4.1 Vocabulary Power, Lesson 10 Spelling Power, Lesson 9	English Language Learners Sourcebook, p. 39 Spanish Summaries, p. 18 * Audio Library English, Yes!
Casey at the Bat Earnest Lawrence Thayer Pacing: 2 Days	**Lesson-Specific Instruction** Selection Focus Transp. 19 * Active Reading Guide, p. 20 Literary Elements Transparency 20 * Quick Checks, p. 20 Selection and Theme Assessment, p. 34 Testmaker: ExamView Pro Performance Assessment, p. 19 **Systematic Language Instruction** Grammar and Comp. Hbk., L. 4.2–4.3	English Language Learners Sourcebook, p. 40 Spanish Summaries, p. 19 Spanish Translations, pp. 69–70 * Audio Library English, Yes!
The Wise Old Woman Yoshiko Uchida Pacing: 2 Days	**Lesson-Specific Instruction** Selection Focus Transp. 20 * Active Reading Guide, p. 21 Literary Elements Transp. 21 Vocabulary Practice, p. 18 * Quick Checks, p. 21 Selection and Theme Assessment, pp. 35–36 Testmaker: ExamView Pro Performance Assessment, p. 20 **Systematic Language Instruction** Grammar and Comp. Hbk., L. 4.4–4.5 Vocabulary Power, Lesson 11 Spelling Power, Lesson 10	English Language Learners Sourcebook, p. 41 Spanish Summaries, p. 20 * Audio Library English, Yes!
Bagged Wolf Carol Kendall and Yao-wen Li Pacing: 2 Days	**Lesson-Specific Instruction** Selection Focus Transp. 21 * Active Reading Guide, p. 22 Literary Elements Transp. 22 Vocabulary Practice, p. 19 * Quick Checks, p. 22 Selection and Theme Assessment, pp. 37–38 Testmaker: ExamView Pro Performance Assessment, p. 21 **Systematic Language Instruction** Grammar and Comp. Hbk., L. 4.6–4.7	English Language Learners Sourcebook, p. 42 Spanish Summaries, p. 21 * Audio Library English, Yes!
The Moustache Robert Cormier Pacing: 2 Days	**Lesson-Specific Instruction** Selection Focus Transp. 22 * Active Reading Guide, p. 23 Literary Elements Transp. 23 Vocabulary Practice, p. 20 * Quick Checks, p. 23 Selection and Theme Assessment, pp. 39–40 Testmaker: ExamView Pro Performance Assessment, p. 22 **Systematic Language Instruction** Grammar and Comp. Hbk., L. 5.1 Vocabulary Power, Lesson 12	English Language Learners Sourcebook, p. 43 Spanish Summaries, p. 22 Spanish Translations, pp. 71–77 * Audio Library English, Yes!

Key: Workbook — Blackline Masters — Textbook — Transparency — CD-ROM — Videodisk (also available in videocassette)

Special Needs/ Strategic Intervention	Reteaching and Enrichment
Interactive Reading Sourcebook, pp. T93–T95 Interactive Reading Workbook, pp. 40–41 Inclusion Strategies Sourcebook, pp. 17–18 Theme Three Planning Guide, p. 8 * Audio Library	Fine Art Transparency 29 Reading Skills Practice Workbook pp. 35–36 Grammar and Language Transp. 19 Gr. and Lang. Wkbk., pp. 75–76, 171–172 Grammar and Comp. Hbk., L. 3.1 TIME *Humanities Across TIME*, Cover 19 Interactive Tutor: Self-Assessment Vocabulary PuzzleMaker Web Site (lit.glencoe.com)
Interactive Reading Sourcebook, pp. T96–T98 Interactive Reading Workbook, pp. 42–43 Inclusion Strategies Sourcebook, pp. 79–80 Theme Three Planning Guide, p. 16 * Audio Library	Literature Launchers, Side A, Segment 9 Media Connection Activities, p. 5 TIME *Humanities Across TIME*, Cover 19 Interactive Tutor: Self-Assessment Vocabulary PuzzleMaker Web Site (lit.glencoe.com)
Interactive Reading Sourcebook, pp. T98–T101 Interactive Reading Workbook, pp. 44–45 Inclusion Strategies Sourcebook, pp. 19–20, 93–94 Theme Three Planning Guide, p. 23 * Audio Library	Reading Skills Practice Workbook pp. 37–38 Grammar and Language Transp. 20 Gr. and Lang. Wkbk., pp. 129–130 Grammar and Comp. Hbk., L. 6.1 Interactive Tutor: Self-Assessment Vocabulary PuzzleMaker Web Site (lit.glencoe.com)
Interactive Reading Sourcebook, pp. T101–T103 Interactive Reading Workbook, pp. 46–47 Inclusion Strategies Sourcebook, pp. 13–14 Theme Three Planning Guide, p. 31 * Audio Library	Reading Skills Practice Workbook pp. 39–40 Grammar and Language Transp., 21 Gr. and Lang. Wkbk., pp. 265–266, 267–268 Grammar and Comp. Hbk., L. 13.6, 14.1 Interactive Tutor: Self-Assessment Vocabulary PuzzleMaker Web Site (lit.glencoe.com)
Interactive Reading Sourcebook, pp. T103–T105 Interactive Reading Workbook, pp. 48–49 Inclusion Strategies Sourcebook, pp. 53–54 * Audio Library	Reading Skills Practice Workbook, pp. 41–42 Grammar and Language Transp. 22 Gr. and Lang. Wkbk., pp. 145–146, 247–249 Grammar and Comp. Hbk., L. 7.3, 12.2–12.4 Interactive Tutor: Self-Assessment Vocabulary PuzzleMaker Web Site (lit.glencoe.com)

Web   Audiocassette   Diskette   *Also available in Spanish

Independent Reading

Encourage students to spend thirty minutes each day in independent reading. The following Glencoe components and outside resources provide opportunities for reading related to this theme.

The Glencoe Literature Library

You may want to assign one or more of these titles for independent reading. For a complete listing of titles available in the Glencoe Literature Library, see page T94 of this book

- *Shabanu: Daughter of the Wind* by Suzanne Fisher Staples
- *Hatchet* by Gary Paulsen
- *Jacob Have I Loved* by Katherine Paterson
- *Dragonwings* by Lawrence Yep

inTIME Magazine News stories, feature articles, reviews, profiles, and essays in the magazine connect to an author, work, or theme in *the Student Edition.* See the **in*TIME* Teacher's Guide** for specific connections to this theme.

Resources for Less-Proficient Readers

For reading especially created for less-proficient readers, suggest

- *Five-Star Stories*
- *The Contemporary Readers*

Additional Resources for Independent Reading

The following titles are listed with specific reading selections throughout this theme. You may want to suggest that students look for these in your local or school library.

- *Shoeless Joe* by W.P. Kinsella
- *Plain City* by Virginia Hamilton
- *Classic Poems to Read Aloud* edited by James Berry
- *Home on the Range: Cowboy Poetry* by Paul B. Janeczko
- *Come a Stranger* by Cynthia Voigt
- *The Prince and the Pauper* by Mark Twain
- *The Rain Catchers* by Jean Thesman
- *American Dragons: Twenty-Five Asian American Voices* edited by Laurence Yep
- *Banner in the Sky* by James Ramsey Ullman

RESOURCE MANAGER (continued)

Lessons	Essential Resources		English Language Learners
The Black Walnut Tree MARY OLIVER PACING: 1 DAY	**Lesson-Specific Instruction** Selection Focus Transp. 23 * Active Reading Guide, p. 24 Literary Elements Transp. 24 * Quick Checks, p. 24 Selection and Theme Assessment, pp. 41–42 Testmaker: ExamView Pro Performance Assessment, p. 23	**Systematic Language Instruction** Grammar and Comp. Hbk., L. 5.2 Vocabulary Power, Lesson 13 Spelling Power, Lesson 11	Spanish Summaries, p. 23 * Audio Library English, Yes!
A Time to Talk Fire and Ice *and* Dust of Snow ROBERT FROST PACING: 2 DAYS	**Lesson-Specific Instruction** Selection Focus Transp. 24 * Active Reading Guide, p. 25 Literary Elements Transp. 25 * Quick Checks, p. 25 Selection and Theme Assessment, pp. 43–44 Testmaker: ExamView Pro Performance Assessment, p. 24	**Systematic Language Instruction** Grammar and Comp. Hbk., L. 5.3–5.4 Vocabulary Power, Lesson 14 Spelling Power., Lesson 12	English Language Learners Sourcebook, pp. 44, 45 Spanish Summaries, p. 24 * Audio Library English, Yes!
Between What I See and What I Say . . . OCTAVIO PAZ PACING: 1 DAY	**Lesson-Specific Instruction** Selection Focus Transp. 25 * Active Reading Guide, p. 26 Literary Elements Transp. 26 * Quick Checks, p. 26 Selection and Theme Assessment, pp. 45–46 Testmaker: ExamView Pro Performance Assessment, p. 25	**Systematic Language Instruction** Grammar and Comp. Hbk., L. 6.1 Vocabulary Power, Unit 3 Review/Test Spelling Power., Unit 3 Review/Proofreading	English Language Learners Sourcebook, pp. 46, 47 Theme Three Planning Guide, p. 58 Spanish Summaries, p. 25 Spanish Translations, p. 78 * Audio Library English, Yes!
Identity JULIO NABOA POLANCO *and* the lesson of the moth DON MARQUIS PACING: 2 DAYS	**Lesson-Specific Instruction** Selection Focus Transp. 26 * Active Reading Guide, p. 27 Literary Elements Transp. 27 * Quick Checks, p. 27 Selection and Theme Assessment, pp. 47–48	Testmaker: ExamView Pro Performance Assessment, p. 26 TIME *inTIME* magazine p. 24 **Systematic Language Instruction** Grammar and Comp. Hbk., L. 7.3	English Language Learners Sourcebook, p. 48 Spanish Summaries, p. 26 Spanish Translations, pp. 79–80 * Audio Library English, Yes!
Writing WORKSHOP **Expository Writing: Writing an Evaluation** PACING: 2 DAYS	Writing Assessment and Portfolio Management, pp. 1-13, 20-22, 41-48		English Language Learners Sourcebook, p. 9 English, Yes!

Key: Workbook · Blackline Masters · Textbook · Transparency · CD-ROM · Videodisk (also available in videocassette)

Special Needs/ Strategic Intervention	Reteaching and Enrichment
Interactive Reading Sourcebook, pp. T106-T108 Interactive Reading Workbook, p. 50 Inclusion Strategies Sourcebook, pp. 15-16 Theme Three Planning Guide, p. 47 * Audio Library	Fine Art Transparency 5 Reading Skills Practice Workbook, pp. 43-44 Gr. and Lang. Wkbk., pp. 63-64 Grammar and Comp. Hbk., L. 2.1 Interactive Tutor: Self-Assessment Vocabulary PuzzleMaker Web Site (lit.glencoe.com)
Interactive Reading Sourcebook, pp. T108-T110 Interactive Reading Workbook, p. 51 Theme Three Planning Guide, p. 52 * Audio Library	Literature Launchers, Side A, Segment 8 Fine Art Transparency 13 Reading Skills Practice Workbook, pp. 45-46 Grammar and Language Transp. 23 Gr. and Lang. Wkbk., pp. 75-76, 259-260 Grammar and Comp. Hbk., L. 3.1, 13.2 TIME *Humanities Across TIME*, Cover 4 Interactive Tutor: Self-Assessment Vocabulary PuzzleMaker Web Site (lit.glencoe.com)
Interactive Reading Sourcebook, pp. T11-T113 Interactive Reading Workbook, p. 52 Theme Three Planning Guide, p. 58 * Audio Library	Literature Launchers, Side A, Segment 7 Fine Art Transparency 30 Reading Skills Practice Workbook, pp. 47-48 Grammar and Language Transp. 24 Gr. and Lang. Wkbk., pp. 195-196 Grammar and Comp. Hbk., L. 10.5 Interactive Tutor: Self-Assessment
Interactive Reading Sourcebook, pp. T113-T115 Interactive Reading Workbook, p. 53 Inclusion Strategies Sourcebook, pp. 39-40 * Audio Library	Reading Skills Practice Workbook, pp. 49-50 Grammar and Language Transp. 25 Gr. and Lang. Wkbk., pp. 145-146 Grammar and Comp. Hbk., L. 7.3 Media Connection Activities, p. 6 Interactive Tutor: Self-Assessment Vocabulary PuzzleMaker Web Site (lit.glencoe.com)
	Writing and Proofreading Practice, pp. 1-6, 21-27 Writing and Proofreading Transparencies 1-6, 11-12, 29-30 Revising with Style Writer's Assistant

Theme RESOURCES

To explore the theme further, you may want to use these resources:

- Listening and Speaking Activities (pp. 7-9)
- Viewing and Representing Activities (pp. 1-6, 13-15)
- Critical Thinking Skills (pp. 7-8)
- Media Connection Activities, (pp. 5-6)
- Interdisciplinary Activities (pp. 10-13)
- Family and Community Activities (p. 23)
- Selection and Theme Assessment (pp. 33-48, 129-130)
- Performance Assessment (pp. 66, 92)

TIME Humanities Across TIME

See also these additional theme planning resources:

- Theme Three Planning Guide
- Interactive Reading Sourcebook
- Literature Groups Sourcebook
- Interactive Lesson Planner
- Interactive Teacher Edition
- Glencoe Web Site (lit.glencoe.com)

PRESENTATION Plus!

Use Glencoe's ***Presentation Plus!*** This multimedia teaching tool lets you present dynamic lessons that will engage your students. Using Microsoft PowerPoint®, you can customize the presentation to create your own personalized lessons.

Web   Audiocassette   Diskette   *Also available in Spanish

![THEME 3]

Which Way to Go?

Theme Objectives

- To enjoy short stories, folktales, and poems about making decisions
- To analyze the literary elements in short stories, folktales, and poems
- To apply strategies for reading poetry

Teaching Strategies

Have students read and discuss the quotation by Muriel Strode in preparation for the discussion questions below.

VIEWING THE PHOTOGRAPH

Responding to the Photograph

Discussion questions:

- How do roads come to exist? *(Someone has traveled a path initially, and others follow.)*
- How can this photo be interpreted figuratively? *(A person has reached a crossroads and must decide which path to follow in life.)*

Which Way to Go?

“Do not follow where the path may lead. Go instead where there is no path and leave a trail.”

–Muriel Strode

234

TEACHER to TEACHER

EAST FORSYTH HIGH SCHOOL • GREENSBORO, NORTH CAROLINA

As we read the stories, I have students compare and contrast characters to themselves. What similarities do they share? How do they differ? This writing assignment gives students the ability to analyze characters' choices and their own choices, helping them to know which way to go. One writing assignment includes a short dialogue with a character; in another, students assume the guise of the character and, from that perspective, write about themselves as the student; or students can select a passage and rewrite it from another point of view.

—ROB SLATER

THEME 3

THEME CONTENTS

GENRE FOCUS *POETRY*

Introducing Theme 3

Direct your students' attention to the Theme Contents. Ask them to read through the list of selections. Present these questions for discussion:

- What types of literature does this theme include? *(short stories, folktales, poems)*
- Which type interests you the most? Which interests you the least? Why?

LITERATURE & HUMANITIES

Have students listen to ***American Music: Cultural Traditions* (CD set),** Vol. 2, Tracks 28, 29, 30, "Three Places in New England." Ask them to discuss what aspects of the period the music calls to mind.

GLENCOE TECHNOLOGY

LITERATURE CLASSICS CD-ROM

Search for other selections related to the theme of "Which Way to Go?"

RESOURCE MANAGER

See the ***Theme Three Planning Guide*** for additional teaching notes, strategies, and resources for introducing the theme "Which Way to Go?"

Exploring the Theme

Which Way to Go?

Discuss making choices with your students. Have them mention some choices they have had to make recently and some choices their parents or others have had to make. You may want to mention choices you have made. Help students to see that making choices is a part of everyday living and that everyone can grow and learn from them.

Starting Points

Daring to Be Different

Draw attention to Gary Larson's *The Far Side* cartoon. Invite students to explain what is happening in the cartoon. Ask how the cartoon communicates the cartoonist's attitude about "daring to be different." *(The driver wants to know how to get to Point A from Point B, and the person giving directions has no idea. The driver is different from other people the man has encountered.)*

Big Decisions and Lessons Learned

Students' responses should include an explanation of the choice presented in the books, movies, or TV shows. Encourage students to discuss whether they agreed with the decision made and why or why not. Students should explain what they learned about decision making or about a specific decision from the books, movies, or TV shows they have listed.

Exploring the Theme

Which Way to Go?

Choices. Your life is full of them. Should you try out for the basketball team or the track team? Is it better to have a lot of casual friends or a handful of close ones? Some choices are difficult, like deciding to take a risk or selecting a difficult path over an easy one. In this theme, you will discover how the choices people make can help them grow.

Starting Points

DARING TO BE DIFFERENT

Sometimes people make choices based on what they think others expect them to do. They may be afraid to be different, or they may not realize that other options are available. How does Gary Larson show this idea with his cartoon?

BIG DECISIONS AND LESSONS LEARNED

Making difficult choices is a theme that comes up over and over in books, movies, and television shows. With a partner, make a list of books, movies, or TV shows that deal with choices. Try to include those set in different historical periods. What, if anything, did you learn from them?

The Far Side by Gary Larson

"Well, lemme think. ... You've stumped me, son. Most folks only wanna know how to go the other way."

The Far Side, © 1986 FARWORKS INC. All rights reserved.

Family and Community Activity

Decision-Making Log Ask students to keep a daily log of choices they make throughout the theme. Encourage them to try to note each decision they make, no matter how insignificant it may seem, and how they arrived at each decision. Students should also note later whether their earlier choices turned out to be good ones. Toward the end of the theme, have students review their logs to analyze how they made their best decisions and what caused them to make poor ones. Have students write several paragraphs summarizing what they learned about their decision-making skills. **L2**

Additional Resources

Family and Community Activities, p. 23

Theme Projects

Choose one of the projects below to complete as you read the selections in this theme. Work on your own, with a partner, or with a group.

CRITICAL VIEWING
Art Ahead of Its Time

1. Many artists who are famous today were seen as unconventional, or even daring, during their day. Search through art history books for an artist whose work represented a unique approach in his or her day.
2. Find postcards showing some of the artist's work. Write captions explaining why the work was considered different. Be prepared to discuss how the work affected people's opinions about art.
3. Paste the pictures and text onto poster board.

Femme au Beret, 1938. Pablo Picasso. Oil on canvas, 18⅛ x 15 in. Private collection.

LEARNING FOR LIFE
Prepare a Feature Article

1. Interview an adult you respect about his or her life choices. Take a notebook and pen or a tape recorder to the interview. Ask if you can take pictures.
2. Ask questions such as the following:
   - What made you decide to become a . . . ?
   - Was there something else you once wanted to do with your life? Why did your goals change?
   - What was the best decision you've made?
3. Write a feature article about the person, using exact quotations and pictures.

MULTIMEDIA PROJECT
Campaign for Teens

1. Find an issue that faces teens today, such as deciding how to avoid smoking. Gather information and pictures about the possible physical and emotional effects of making that choice.
2. Use a Web publishing program to create and edit text, graphics, and sound.
3. Decide on a message to present to your audience. Choose the information that will best get your point across. Write introductions, headings, and comments.
4. Follow the directions in the software to complete your page.

interNET CONNECTION

For more about the selections in this theme, visit Glencoe's Web site at: lit.glencoe.com.

Theme Projects

Teaching Strategies

The following suggestions may help your students plan and carry out their theme projects.

Critical Viewing

- Suggest that students consider whether they agree with the views at the time of their chosen artist's work or with current views.
- Remind students to write the captions in their own words.
- Have students give a brief report on their posters to the class.

Learning For Life

- Review basic interviewing skills, such as asking *who, what, when, where,* and *why,* and preparing questions in advance.
- Encourage students to listen carefully to the person's answers: these may lead to other interesting questions.
- Stress the importance of using direct quotations and of selecting interesting remarks.

Multimedia Project

- Suggest that students explore similar topics on other Web sites.
- Encourage students to combine media in ways that will maximize the impact of their message.
- Help students identify the message they want to present and to focus the information on their pages to that message.
- Encourage students to use unfamiliar aspects of the program.

Additional Resources

- ***Interdisciplinary Activities,*** pp. 10–13
- ***Viewing and Representing Activities,*** pp. 13–15
- ***Listening and Speaking Activities,*** pp. 7–9
- ***Critical Thinking Skills,*** pp. 7–8
- ***Selection and Theme Assessment,*** pp. 129–130
- ***Performance Assessment,*** p. 66

interNET CONNECTION

Glencoe Literature Web Site
For other ideas related to "Which Way to Go?" suggest that students type *careers* or *jobs* into a search engine.

Before Reading

Objectives

- To read and analyze a short story about a man whose life has changed
- To identify conflict in a short story
- To write an analysis of the author's use of similes

Skills

Reading/Thinking: Drawing Conclusions; Inferring
Writing: Poem
Vocabulary: Word Meanings; Connotation
Grammar/Language: Verbs
Listening/Speaking: Oral Reading
Collaboration: Literature Groups

Motivating → STUDENTS

Selection Focus Transparency 18: Have students view and discuss this 1951 photograph of the frequently injured Mickey Mantle.

Reading Focus: As an extension of the Reading Focus, have students compare their own goals and worries about athletics to the goals and worries of a professional athlete.

Before You Read

In the Middle of a Pitch

MEET BILL MEISSNER

Bill Meissner says, "I know the meaning of the home run. It's the slow circling of the bases, and then the return. I know it well. My father was a traveling salesman with the highway wrapped around his wrist like a gray sweatband." Meissner grew up playing baseball in Iowa and Wisconsin, and he relates the sport to many comings and goings in life. A poet and short story writer, he teaches creative writing in St. Cloud, Minnesota.

Bill Meissner was born in 1948. "In the Middle of a Pitch" was published in 1994 in Hitting Into the Wind.

READING FOCUS

What do you think athletes dream about or hope to achieve? What do you suppose they worry about?

Web It!
Share your ideas with a partner. Then make a web of words that you would use in answering the questions above.

Setting a Purpose
Read to find out how a former athlete deals with unfulfilled dreams.

BUILDING BACKGROUND

The Time and Place This story is set in modern times and ordinary places in the United States.

Did You Know? Four million Americans under the age of fifteen suffer from sprains, strains, deep cuts, and fractures playing sports and other games each year. Even professional players suffer from injuries that can keep them away from the game or even end their careers.

VOCABULARY PREVIEW

elaborate (i lab′ ər it) *adj.* complicated and fancy; p. 240
potential (pə ten′ shəl) *n.* possibility of success; p. 241
gaudily (gô′ də lē) *adv.* in a way that is bright and showy to the point of being in bad taste; p. 241
curt (kurt) *adj.* so brief or short as to seem rude; p. 242
pitch (pich) *n.* an often high-pressure sales presentation; p. 242
aromatic (ar′ ə mat′ ik) *adj.* having a pleasant smell or special, delicate flavor; p. 242
adept (ə dept′) *adj.* highly skilled; masterful; p. 243
subtle (sut′ əl) *adj.* not open or direct; not obvious; p. 243
corroded (kə rōd′ əd) *adj.* eaten away by degrees, by gnawing or chemical action; p. 245
heft (heft) *v.* to lift up; p. 245

RESOURCE MANAGER

Teaching Tools and Resources
- Theme Three Planning Guide
- Literature Groups Sourcebook

Essential Lesson Support
Lesson-Specific Instruction
- Selection Focus Transparency 18
- Literary Elements Transparency 19
- Active Reading Guide,* p. 19
- Selection Vocabulary Practice, p. 17

Assessment
- Selection Quick Checks,* p. 19
- Sel. and Theme Assmt., p. 33
- Testmaker: ExamView Pro
- Performance Assessment, p. 18

Systematic Language Instruction
- Gr. & Comp. Hbk., Lesson 4.1
- Vocabulary Power, Lesson 10
- Spelling Power, Lesson 9

English Language Learners
- ELL Sourcebook, p. 39
- Spanish Summaries, p. 18
- Audio Library*
- English, Yes!

Spec. Needs/Strat. Interven.
- Interactive Rdg. Sbk., pp. T93–T95
- Interactive Rdg. Wbk., pp. 40–41
- Inclusion Strat. Sbk., pp. 17–18
- Audio Library*

* Also available in Spanish

In the Middle of a Pitch

A

Bill Meissner

High and Outside–A Study, 1981. John Dobbs. Watercolor and chalk on paper, 4¾ x 4½ in. Courtesy John Dobbs and ACA Galleries, New York.

Reading the Selection

SUMMARY

The main character, Dusty Sikarsky, is a former professional baseball player, a very successful pitcher in the major leagues until he hurts his arm and cannot play anymore. He becomes a used car salesman, turning his back on baseball, unhappy with his life. Then he changes his life by becoming involved with baseball again and helping children enjoy the game.

Spanish Summaries, p. 18

A Active Reading Strategies

PREDICT Ask students to predict what the plot of the story will be, based on the title of this selection and the art on this page.

VOCABULARY If you haven't previewed the selection vocabulary with students, stop and remind them to use context clues to unlock the meaning of new vocabulary words.

Additional Resources

Active Reading Guide, p. 19
Audio Library
Spanish Audio Library

Teaching Support

CONNECTING TO OTHER SELECTIONS

COMPARING *selections*

This selection is paired with "Casey at the Bat" on pages 252–254. A lesson for teaching a comparison of the two selections appears on page 256.

The chart at the right shows three other ways to connect "In the Middle of a Pitch" to selections in this book.

For specific teaching strategies, see the ***Theme Three Planning Guide.***

Connection		Title
Life Skills: Decision Making	→	"Stop the Sun," p. 607
Thematic: Life's Disappointments	→	"The Battleground," p. 511
Literary: Tone	→	"The Drummer Boy of Shiloh," p. 439

B Critical Thinking

INFER Note the phrase "he feels the old aching." Encourage students to identify what the author means by this phrase. *(He has lived with the pain for a long time.)*

C Literary Elements

CONFLICT Have students evaluate Sikarsky's internal conflict between youth and age. Encourage students to identify the ways the author conveys this conflict in the opening paragraphs. *(The first paragraph stresses the contrast between Sikarsky's glamorous past and his mundane present. Dusty feels like a sports hero but looks old and feels pain.)*

D Active Reading Strategies

VISUALIZE Have students review the third paragraph of the story (beginning "He remembers the rush . . .") Ask them to picture how each of the three scenes depicted looked, felt, or sounded. Call for examples of the author's use of sensory detail to make these scenes vivid. *(flutter of paper, tingling static electricity, click and spark)*

E Literary Elements

FORESHADOWING Ask students to identify this use of foreshadowing. What may be the significance of this slowing down? *(That first fabulous moment in the major leagues is etched forever in his memory. He will find himself living in the shadow of the past.)*

Teaching Support

In the Middle of a Pitch

He wakes before his alarm to the far away song of an umpire calling a third strike. Standing in front of the bathroom mirror, he leans forward, narrowing his eyes at himself as if he were peering at the catcher for his sign. Then he stretches, his hands high, almost touches the plaster ceiling where the spiderweb cracks seem to lengthen a little each week. When he brings his right arm down in an imaginary pitch, a strike, he feels the old aching. Staring at the arm in the mirror, he wonders how the flesh got so flabby. *It didn't look that way yesterday, did it?* he thinks. Yesterday the tendons were taut[1] and ready like some finely tuned musical instrument; yesterday he was sure he could hear every muscle humming. B

Everything happens so fast, he thinks, *everything happens in a day.* One day he's Dusty Sikarsky, starting pitcher for a major league team. The next day he's Dusty Sikarsky, used car salesman, tossing curves at the off-balance customers. C As he dresses for work, his mind spans twenty years to the baseball days. He thinks about how you work your way up through the leagues: First it's town ball, where he pitched his team into the tournaments with his fastball. The photographer for the local paper could hardly catch that pitch with his flashbulb. Next the minor league scouts stood waiting for him after a game, their smiles like piano keys, and everything speeded up, as if someone had tilted the whole world and it started sliding toward him. A minor league coach watched him, chin on his hand, for three months in Class A, then, at midseason, the coach nodded at him once. The next day Dusty was moved up to Triple A, the bleachers bigger and more freshly painted, the fans louder. He kept moving up, faster and quicker. His life seemed to be rushing toward him and flying away from him at the same moment. His arm felt great, and the more he threw, the better it felt. The leather ball loved his fingertips. "The kid's so good he could pitch blindfolded and still strike out the side," a coach once remarked. On the mound, Dusty went through his motion: kicking, reaching way back in the still air with his right arm. Then he whirled down hard, and the ball was nestled in the catcher's mitt long before Dusty's cap, jolted from his head, had a chance to fall to the grass in front of the mound. The ball was like music that passed so fast you never really heard it.

He remembers the rush as he was called to the bigs: the flutter of a paper contract, the tingling static electricity as he slid a major league uniform over his head for the first time in the locker room, the click and spark of spikes on concrete as he jogged down the ramp to the dugout. D

The next thing he knew, the game was starting, and the first batter stepped to the plate. Then, the funniest thing happened—everything slowed down. E It took half an hour to reach up to adjust the bill of his cap. His windup[2] felt like an <u>elaborate</u>

1. *Tendons* are strong cords that attach muscles to bones; the tendons in the man's arm felt tense and tight *(taut).*

2. A pitcher's *windup* is a series of regular and distinctive motions, such as swinging the arms, made before releasing a pitch.

Vocabulary
elaborate (i lab′ ər it) *adj.* complicated and fancy

MEETING INDIVIDUAL NEEDS

ENGLISH LANGUAGE LEARNERS

Multiple-Meaning Words English language learners may have difficulty with words that have more than one meaning. Write the word *pitch* on the board, and point out that in this story it has two meanings. Explain both meanings. Explain that context is important when defining words. Use other terms from this story—such as *plate, strike,* and *start*—as other examples.

Activity After defining the various meanings of these other terms, have students work with partners to write two sentences for each word, each sentence showing a different meaning of the word.

Additional Resources

English Language Learners Sourcebook, p. 39

dance performed underwater. When he threw that first pitch, the ball seemed to take a year to reach home plate, like some kind of satellite aimed for the moon, just rotating over and over slowly in the soft, endless vacuum of space.

Somehow, he made it through the first game and he did all right. He pitched six innings, gave up a couple of hits, but no runs. Not bad for a first outing. The guys patted him on the back after the game. The catcher congratulated him and told him later how his eyes always widened each time he delivered the ball. He had a great year, and the papers called him the Rookie Sensation. The sportswriters always used the word <u>potential</u> when they wrote about him; they predicted he'd be the best in the game.

The sportswriters always used the word *potential* when they wrote about him; they predicted he'd be the best in the game.

The seasons passed. One, two, three of them. He chalked up fifty wins. Then, one night in Chicago, too cool for June, when the bases were loaded in the late innings, he reached as far back as he could
F to fire a fastball and felt something snap in his arm. Not *snap,* exactly—it was more of a *ping,* like the off-key sound of a thin wire or guitar string being plucked. It didn't hurt at first, though he remembers shaking his arm a few times as if it had ants on it.

When he threw his next pitch, and the next, he knew something was wrong. The ball didn't quite go where it was aimed. Just an inch or two off target, but that's all it takes. He lost that game on a double. After that, the batters began hitting his curve, his slider. His fastball lost its jump, no longer appeared to be rising as it reached the batter, but instead drew a straight line to the sweet spot of their bats.

That's when the music slowed down, his career like a record clicked off in the middle of its playing, the needle dragging across the vinyl.

The team put him on the disabled list and he sat it out for a couple weeks. He worked with the trainer in the clubhouse, rotating the arm, wrapping it with heat, kneading the muscle as if it were bread dough about to rise. After he gave up six or seven runs in each of his next three starts, the manager shook his head and said the owners wanted him sent down to the minors.

"How long?" Dusty remembers asking the manager. He felt suddenly short of breath, unable to exhale a full sentence.

The manager stood chewing a toothpick, staring only at Dusty's arm. "Just a while. That's all. A month, maybe. You'll be back, kid."

"Yeah," he responded. "A month."

A month became the rest of the season. He struggled in the minors, too—even the rookies were hitting his best pitches, taking them to the <u>gaudily</u> painted wooden

Vocabulary

potential (pə ten′ shəl) *n.* possibility of success

gaudily (gô′ də lē) *adv.* in a way that is bright and showy to the point of being in bad taste

F Literary Elements

CONFLICT Note the external conflict introduced when Sikarsky hears the sound in his arm. Ask students what Sikarsky has come into conflict with. *(nature, or the limits of his body)*

On The Lighter Side

Sounds We Don't Miss Some students may be unfamiliar with the idiosyncrasies of vinyl record playing. For fun, you may wish to demonstrate the sound of a needle scraping across a record.

FYI

Most major league baseball players play first in the minor leagues. There are three levels of minor league baseball: A, AA (double A), and AAA (triple A). Triple A is the highest level. Minor league baseball is still professional, but the pay is low.

LITERATURE & HUMANITIES

Have students look at the portrait *Night Baseball,* in *Introducing Art,* page 206. Encourage discussion about the elements of the painting and how the artist creates the feeling that a baseball game is an exciting event.

Reading Minilesson

Critical Thinking: Drawing Conclusions This author leaves many details that are important to his story unsaid. The reader must base conclusions about these details on other information in the story. For instance, the author does not state directly what Sikarsky's life has been like since he left baseball, but this information is important to the story. This conclusion can be drawn from the details provided.

Activity Have students discuss what they think Sikarsky has done or not done since he left baseball. They should support their conclusions with specific details the author has provided about Sikarsky. **L2** **COLLAB. LEARN.**

Additional Resources

Reading Skills Practice Workbook

fences advertising CHEER and BRYLCREEM—A LITTLE DAB'LL DO YA, and COLGATE WITH GARDOL.

G The next February, he got a letter from the club. He remembers staring at the outside of the long beige envelope that morning, not certain if he should open it or not. He set it down on the desk. He remembers watching TV for a while. The Colgate ad appeared—an announcer with a mike stood behind an invisible protective Gardol shield as a major league pitcher threw fastballs at him. The pitches bounced off the shield one by one. Dusty clicked the set off. After lunch, he picked the letter up again. As he tore it open, the ripping paper made the sound of crackling ice. The letter told him, in a few curt sentences, that his contract wouldn't be renewed. The last sentences read: *Thank you for your contribution to the club. Best wishes in the future.*

He remembers crumpling the letter in his fist, tossing it into the waste basket, and jogging out to the nearby sandlot field. Though it was cold outside and patches of ice still plastered themselves to the field, Dusty threw fastball after fastball toward the warped[3] black and white plate, none of them strikes. The pain in his arm seemed to make a noise that grew louder and louder, like a scream caught beneath the skin.

The shrill sound of his alarm clock brings him back to his apartment. He jogs into the bedroom, clicks off the ringing alarm. All that was years ago, he thinks as he brushes his teeth, combs his graying slicked-back hair, slides on his snappy brown striped tie and brown suit jacket, then slips out the front door for work. He's got a new career, and he's a different man now—he's Dusty Sikarsky, best damn car salesman in El Dorado, Kansas. He's got his sales pitch down perfect, and he's got plaques on the wall of his office at Edge Motors and citations[4] from the El Dorado Businessmen's Club to prove it. He's got a quick, bright smile on his face and the music in his voice; his boss once said he could sell any car on the lot blindfolded. H

Dusty tastes the first warmth of April air as he walks through the town. It's a taste he's almost forgotten, a taste aromatic and rich that seems to come from deep inside the thawed earth and from deep inside himself at the same moment. By the time he reaches the low, tin-sided building at the car lot, he's puffing. He grins at his coworkers as he lopes toward his dark paneled office. Inside, as he waits for the first customer, he takes a wheezy drag from his cigarette, pours a mug of coffee, and, cupping a powdered sugar donut in his palm, stares beyond the hulls of the cars to the shimmering water mirage[5] beginning to form at the far end of the asphalt lot.

The whole town seems to know about his days in the majors. As he walks down

3. Something that is *warped* is bent or twisted in places where it once was flat.

4. Here, *citations* are awards for outstanding achievement.

5. Here, a *mirage* is an optical effect created by the reflection of light over hot pavement. Sikarsky sees a pool of water that doesn't exist on the asphalt lot.

Vocabulary

curt (kurt) *adj.* so brief or short as to seem rude

pitch (pich) *n.* an often high-pressure sales presentation

aromatic (ar′ ə mat′ ik) *adj.* having a pleasant smell or special, delicate flavor

Cultural Note

Advertising The story makes reference to Brylcreem, a product that may be unfamiliar to students. Explain that Brylcreem is a hair cream once very popular in the forties, fifties, and sixties. Brylcreem's slogan was "A little dab'll do ya."

G Critical Thinking

DRAWING CONCLUSIONS Encourage students to draw a conclusion about why Sikarsky watched TV and why he turned it off. Share the following model to illustrate the process used in drawing conclusions.

Model: I think Sikarsky was afraid the letter was bad news. He turned on his TV set instead of reading the letter to delay thinking about his career's ending. The ad on TV just reminded him of what he could no longer do. I think he turned off the set to avoid these reminders.

H Literary Elements

CONFLICT Ask students whether it is true that Sikarsky is "a different man now," as he states. Encourage students to note the similarities between the description of Sikarksy as a pitcher and Sikarsky as a used-car salesman. *(Students should note that he has changed but not entirely.)*

Teaching Support

Meeting Individual Needs: SPECIAL NEEDS

Learning Disabled Students with learning disabilities may be able to express their reactions to the moods in the story through pictures rather than words.

Activity Invite students to use a computer drawing tool or pen and paper to sketch key scenes that express the mood of the story. Students may also collect and display pictures from newspapers or magazines that convey the same mood. **L1**

Additional Resources

Inclusion Strategies

Untitled, 1993. Bret Willis. Color transparency, 4 x 5 in. Private collection.

Viewing the photograph: Which objects in this collection do you think would mean the most to Dusty Sikarsky? Why?

Main in front of the crumbling two-story brick facades,[6] a little heavier and a little grayer, the kids open their eyes wide as they pass and then whisper behind him: "You know who *that* is? That's Dusty Sikarsky. He pitched in the majors." Some of the older guys at work smile and say, "Hey Dusty, what was it like, pitching in the big leagues?" Dusty usually just shakes his head. He wants to reply, *What's there to say? You just throw a ball at a glove.* But he doesn't want to sound flip[7] so he just says something pat like "Good. It was real good."

He never talks much about the big leagues, never mentions the injury. For years now, he's managed to avoid talking about it, has become adept at a subtle curve of conversation, a change of subject. *Gardol,* he thought once after he dodged a coworker's question about baseball, *an invisible protective shield.* He never goes to the town league baseball games on the weekends, though his buddies sometimes ask him to take in a game. Once in a while, as a gag, he'll ball up an old invoice, go into his windup, pitch it hard through the bright light of the open doorway, and the guys nod at him and know he remembers.

"You should pick up a baseball sometime, Dusty," the boss told him once.

6. A building's front is its *facade* (fə säd′), a word that comes from the Latin word for *face.*

7. *Flip* means "lacking proper respect or seriousness."

Vocabulary

adept (ə dept′) *adj.* highly skilled; masterful

subtle (sut′ əl) *adj.* not open or direct; not obvious

I Author's Craft

IMAGERY Note the author's use of pitching terminology to describe Sikarsky's current situation, such as "curve of conversation." Encourage students to discuss why the author chooses baseball terms to describe Sikarsky's present actions. *(It emphasizes Sikarsky's continuing connection to the game.)*

J Literary Elements

CONFLICT Ask whether the detail here shows that Sikarsky has resolved his internal conflict. Ask students to speculate why Sikarsky avoids talking about baseball. *(It is probably a painful memory for him.)*

VIEWING THE PHOTOGRAPH

Bret Willis (born in 1968) is a New York-based award-winning still-life photographer. Known for combining his perspective with beautiful lighting, his works encourage perceptions about even ordinary objects.

Viewing Response *Sikarsky might prefer the baseballs and the trophy of the hand holding a baseball because he was a pitcher.*

MEETING INDIVIDUAL NEEDS — ADVANCED LEARNERS

Offer Advice Gifted and talented students may want to focus on Sikarsky's internal conflict. Encourage them to consider whether Sikarsky's life has been happy since leaving baseball.

Activity Have these students play the role of therapist by offering advice to Sikarsky on what he can do to make his life happier. Have them jot down their ideas and then share them in a discussion. **L3**

VIEWING THE PAINTING

Edward Hopper (1882–1967) was born and died in New York State, although he spent some time in Europe. He is best known for paintings that, despite their realism, convey an eerie sense of loneliness and isolation.

Viewing Response *The setting is sterile, and the work seems to be lonely and uninteresting. Comparing Sikarsky's job in an office to his career as a pitcher makes his current situation seem even more desperate.*

K Critical Thinking

INFER Ask students to identify the details that tell the reader Sikarsky does not like his job. *(He describes it as monotonous and depressing, "dry," and lifeless to the touch.)*

FINE ART TRANSPARENCY 29

You may want to use ***Fine Art Transparency 29*** to discuss the importance of baseball in the United States.

Office at Night, 1940. Edward Hopper. Oil on canvas, $22\frac{3}{16} \times 25\frac{1}{8}$ in. Collection Walker Art Center, Minneapolis. Gift of the T. B. Walker Foundation, Gilbert N. Walker Fund, 1948.

Viewing the painting: Describe the setting of Hopper's painting. What does Hopper seem to be saying about this type of work? What does the painting add to the description in the story of Sikarsky's life as a salesperson? Explain.

"Ever think of coaching or something?" Dusty just took a slurp of coffee, pretending not to hear. "Cripes, with no wife, no kids," the boss added, "you got all the time in the world."

His arm doesn't hurt like it used to the first couple years after he was cut from the team. It only aches a little once in a while as he lifts a pile of ledgers[8] or when he leans his weight the wrong way on the waxed fender of a Chevy while making a pitch about what a workhorse the V6 engine is, how fast this machine would be on the highway even though it's got a few miles on the ol' speedometer.

This April day passes with its usual blur of stats[9] and sales, printouts and K

8. *Ledgers* are books containing financial records.

9. Here, *stats* (short for *statistics*) are numbers relating to car sales. *Stats* can also refer to baseball statistics.

Teaching Support

REAL-WORLD CONNECTION

Sports for the Fun of It Both the cartoon on page 250 and the story "In the Middle of a Pitch" have something philosophical to say about the game of baseball. Specifically, they both deal with playing the game for the pure joy of it. Have students identify what is intruding on the joy of the game for the narrator in "In the Middle of a Pitch."

Activity Have students discuss the times they have participated in a sport, whether an organized or just a casual game with friends. Ask them to name the times they had the most fun, and the least fun, participating in a sport. They may also describe what they enjoy about watching their favorite sport and what detracts from the fun of watching. After students have shared their experiences, the class should list those things that make playing a sport fun and those that make it less fun. **L2** COLLAB. LEARN.

receipts. Another day passes beneath his fingertips and it feels dry to the touch. In the late afternoon, an ad appears in the *El Dorado Weekly* proclaiming SHINY CLEAN USED CARS FOR SPRING. In the picture, Dusty, pudgy and not quite smiling, poses stiffly beside a Dodge, like he doesn't know what to do with his hands.

After work, on his way home, Dusty takes a detour to the town ball field. Shouldering through the creaking fence gate, he pulls off his wide striped tie, unbuttons the top button of his white shirt. He sits down on the front row of the bleachers, slips off his brown suit jacket, tosses it over a corroded railing. He can hear the whistle of the wind through the high backstop, a rusty music. He sits there a while, gazing at the empty sunlit field from behind the barrier of wires. Rolling up his sleeves, he massages the muscle of his right arm. Then he notices, directly behind the plate, widened gaps in the backstop wires. *A wild pitch could get caught in there easy,* Dusty thinks. *It could get caught for years between the bent wires.*

Another day passes beneath his fingertips and it feels dry to the touch.

Turning his head, Dusty notices two boys biking across the grass. He thinks at first that they're cutting across the field on their way to the video games at the arcade, but they stop in the middle of the infield. One skinny kid who looks about seven keeps trying to pitch from the gravelly mound sixty feet away, but can't quite get his throws to home plate. He hefts the ball like a shotput, and the ball skitters in the dirt a few feet from the plate where another boy, short and chunky, stands with a catcher's mitt that's too big for his hand. The boy who's pitching moves a few steps closer. An idea crosses Dusty's mind that he should go out there and give the kid a few tips. The kid brings his arm down pretty well, but he's bending all wrong at the elbow. *Naw,* he thinks. *Let the kids have their game.* The boy tosses another one, a rounded throw that skips in front of the catcher's mitt, rolls all the way to the backstop.

The skinny kid runs from the mound to retrieve it. By the time the boy reaches the backstop, Dusty is stretching his arm through the bent wires to pick up the baseball, snagging the sleeve of his white shirt on a sharp, loose wire.

"You stuck, mister?" the kid asks.

Dusty smiles up at the boy from his knees.

"Nope," Dusty blurts. "Yeah. I mean, I don't know."

A little embarrassed, Dusty manages a chuckle. Still clutching the baseball, he hears something in the sleeve tear as he pulls his arm back. *It's okay,* he thinks, *you*

Vocabulary

corroded (kə rōd′ əd) *adj.* eaten away by degrees, by gnawing or chemical action
heft (heft) *v.* to lift up

L Literary Elements

SYMBOLISM Ask students to explain the significance of Sikarsky's removing his tie and suit jacket. Encourage students to identify what the clothes symbolize. *(They symbolize the oppressiveness of his job.)*

M Active Reading Strategies

PREDICT Ask students to predict what will happen after Sikarsky sits down in the bleachers and begins watching the boys play baseball.

N Literary Elements

IRONY Point out that the boy asks Sikarsky, "You stuck, mister?" Ask students to consider whether Sikarsky is "stuck." If so, what is he stuck on? Have students consider Sikarsky's response to this question in their responses. *(Sikarsky is figuratively stuck in a job he doesn't enjoy.)*

Life Skills Connection

Interviewing Explain that very often athletes or others whose jobs rely on a physical skill suffer an injury and must do something else with their lives than what they have planned.

Activity Have students interview someone—a relative, a neighbor, a teacher, or a family friend—who had to change career paths as a result of an injury or illness. Encourage them to find out how the person dealt with the change, what made the person choose the career he or she did, and how the person dealt with the failure of his or her original plans. Have students share the results of their interviews to identify any common attitudes among the people they interviewed. **L2**

can replace a shirt. You can put a Band-Aid on a scratched arm.

He stands with the ball, faces the boy through the wires, and grins. The boy cups his hands as if expecting Dusty to toss the ball over, as if expecting a brief spring shower. But Dusty doesn't toss the ball. Instead, he finds himself stepping through a gate in the fence, hears his voice ask, "Wanna learn some pitches?" Instead, Dusty finds himself slipping off his polished shoes and brown dress socks, then climbing the small mountain of the pitcher's mound, all that gravel suddenly tender and welcoming beneath his bare feet.

❖

Triple A - 143, 1979. Gregory Thorp. Cibachrome photograph, 13 x 19½ in. Courtesy Carl Solway Gallery, Cincinnati, OH.

Viewing the photograph: What part of Sikarsky's life might this photograph represent? Explain your answer.

VIEWING THE PHOTOGRAPH

Viewing Response *This photograph could represent Sikarsky's time in the minor leagues—when he moved from A to triple A before moving up to the majors, where sportswriters called him the Rookie Sensation. The photograph captures a time when Sikarsky was first showing his "great potential."*

Thematic Focus

Which Way to Go? Sikarsky makes a decision in this story. Have students identify the two choices Sikarsky faces in his decision. *(Sikarsky must choose whether he will continue to suppress his baseball past or use it to help others.)*

ASSESSMENT

Quick Checks, p. 19

Teaching Support

Grammar and Language *Minilesson*

Verbs Remind students that verbs should be chosen carefully to portray vividly the action in a sentence. Note the author's use of vivid action verbs such as *hefts, skitters, tosses,* and *massages.*

Activity Ask students to find other examples of vivid action verbs in the story. Then have them find examples of other, less-vivid action verbs and substitute more precise verbs to portray the action. **L2**

Additional Resources

- ***Grammar and Language Transparency 19***
- ***Grammar and Language Workbook,*** p. 75
- ***Grammar and Composition Handbook,*** Lesson 3.1
- ***Writer's Choice,*** Lesson 10.1

Responding to Literature

PERSONAL RESPONSE

- Were you surprised by the ending of this story? Why or why not?

Brackets connect questions that are paired to develop higher-level thinking skills.

Analyzing Literature

RECALL

1. Why does Sikarsky remember his baseball career at the beginning of the story?
2. Describe how Sikarsky feels about his years as a pitcher. How did he deal with his injury?
3. What are some similarities and differences in Sikarsky's life as a ballplayer and his life as a salesperson?
4. What brings about a second change in Sikarsky's life?

INTERPRET

5. Why, do you suppose, does Sikarsky still think about his life as a ballplayer after twenty years? Give several reasons.
6. What qualities does Sikarsky show that may have a positive effect on his future? Explain.
7. In your opinion, does Sikarsky think of himself as a failure or as a success? Give examples to support your answer.
8. **Foreshadowing** is the planting of clues to prepare readers for what will happen later in a piece of literature. How does the writer foreshadow the end of the story? Explain.

EVALUATE AND CONNECT

9. Would the story be as effective if Sikarsky had become a famous actor or had recovered from his injury and played ball again? Explain your answer.
10. Theme Connection How do Sikarsky's choices affect his life? Support your answer with examples from the story.

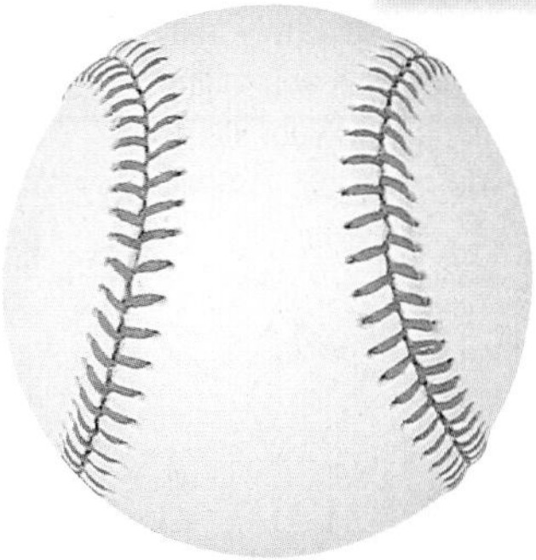

LITERARY ELEMENTS

Conflict

The tension that builds in a story is called **conflict.** The main character in this story has two kinds of conflict: external and internal. An **external conflict** is a struggle between a character and an outside force, such as nature or society. An **internal conflict** is a problem in a character's mind that is solved by the character's making choices among ideas or issues.

1. List an internal and an external conflict in the story.
2. Explain each conflict in the words that Sikarsky might have used if he were being interviewed by a sports reporter. Use examples from the story.

● See **Literary Terms Handbook,** p. R2.

Responding to the Selection

PERSONAL RESPONSE

Students' responses should include specific examples from the story to support their explanations for whether they were surprised.

Analyzing Literature

1. Sikarsky remembers his baseball career because even after twenty years he misses the game and because his pitching arm still aches.
2. Sikarsky is proud of his fast rise as a minor and then major league pitcher. His injury was devastating to him, and since then he has tried to have nothing to do with baseball.
3. Some similarities: "tossing curves" (at batters, then at customers), "sales pitch," Sikarsky's high level of accomplishment (citations and awards), and that he could pitch and sell any car "blindfolded." Some differences: refuses to discuss or play baseball, feels old and achy.
4. Encountering the two boys playing baseball on an April day and wanting to help one improve his throwing technique bring about the second change.
5. Sikarsky misses baseball—the excitement and sense of accomplishment; his arm still aches; selling used cars is not as glamorous as baseball.
6. Sikarsky has a warm smile, is friendly, works hard, and is talented and accomplished.
7. Students' responses should reveal their understanding of Sikarsky's ambivalence about his current condition and give examples from the story supporting their opinions.
8. Students' responses should reveal an understanding that Sikarsky's fond memories of baseball foreshadow his eventual reconnection to the game.
9. Students' responses should reveal their understanding of how important it is for Sikarsky to adjust his altered circumstances in a mature and positive way.
10. Students' responses should explain how Sikarsky's choices suggest that he may be coming to terms with the realities of his situation.

LITERARY ELEMENTS

1. Example of internal conflict: between youth and age or whether Sikarsky should become involved with baseball again. Examples of external conflict: Sikarsky versus his medical problem.
2. Students' responses should be presented in Sikarsky's style and should include examples from the story.

Additional Resources

Literary Elements Transparency 19

Literature and Writing

Writing About Literature

Students' paragraphs should
- include several similes from the story
- explain what they added to the story

Creative Writing

Students' poems should
- include similes
- focus on an aspect of baseball and a feeling they want to convey about that

Extending Your Response

Literature Groups Groups should arrive at a conclusion about why baseball is the national pastime. To support their conclusion they should use references to the text, other works, or personal experience. COLLAB. LEARN.

Interdisciplinary Activity Remind students they can use any type of music, but they must relate their choice to the story.

Learning for Life Suggest that groups start by brainstorming about comparisons.

Literature and Writing

Writing About Literature

Rich Language "In the Middle of a Pitch," contains several **similes**—comparisons using the word *like* or *as.* For example, the narrator says that a baseball thrown by the young Sikarsky was "like music that passed so fast you never really heard it." List other similes from the story. In your opinion, what do the similes add to the story? How do they help you understand or enjoy it more? Write your answer in a paragraph.

Creative Writing

From Prose to Poetry Use the similes you found in the story—or create some of your own—to write a four-to-six stanza poem about baseball. Will it be about your own passion for the sport, or your distaste for it? Will it be about baseball stadiums? the players? the fans? Consider using the words and phrases from your web in the **Reading Focus** on page 238. Recite your poem, enhancing its meaning through expressive use of voice and gestures.

Extending Your Response

Literature Groups

Baseball Forever What is it about baseball players that attracts fans? Do injuries to players change this passion? Why do some fans switch from one hero to another as the players they admire grow too old or become injured? Discuss these questions in your group and come to a consensus about why baseball is considered a national pastime.

Learning for Life

Comparing Ideas Bill Meissner compares his own father's comings and goings with the activity in a baseball game. List three or four ways you might compare a ball game to some part of your life. Then write a sentence in which you make that comparison. Share your ideas with a small group.

Interdisciplinary Activity

Mood Music Imagine that "In the Middle of a Pitch" is being made into a television drama. You are the music director and must show changes in Sikarsky's emotions and attitude. Select two scenes—one from the beginning of the story and one from the end. Choose music that you think would be appropriate and helpful to an audience. Play the music for your class as you read aloud the two parts of the story. Ask for a group evaluation.

Reading Further

If you enjoyed this story, read:
Shoeless Joe by W. P. Kinsella

Save your work for your portfolio.

MEETING INDIVIDUAL NEEDS — SPECIAL NEEDS

Less-Proficient Readers Some students may have trouble distinguishing between the connotative and denotative meanings of words they read. Encourage them to look up these words in the dictionary to find the denotations. Students should then look at the context in which each word appears and then think of any emotional or cultural association that the word might have. This association, or connotation, may be negative or positive.

Activity Pair less-proficient readers with other students to review "In the Middle of a Pitch." Give students at least four words from the story that have positive or negative connotations. Have them look up the definitions, check the context in the story, and then discuss the meanings of the words. Words with positive connotations include *sensation* and *potential.* Words with negative connotations include *off-key* and *curt.* **L2**

Skill Minilessons

RETEACH • REVIEW

GRAMMAR AND LANGUAGE • PARTICIPLES

A **participle** is a verb form that can function as an adjective. A **present participle** ends in *-ing*.

He was famous as the starting pitcher for a major league team.

A **past participle** usually ends in *-ed,* but irregular verbs may have different endings.

The old park once had freshly painted bleachers.

A **participial phrase** is a group of words that includes a participle and acts as an adjective.

Curving smoothly, the ball sped past.

PRACTICE List the participles and participial phrases in the following sentences. Tell if each is a present or a past participle, and if it is part of a participial phrase.

1. His windup was like a dance performed under water.
2. They placed his name on the disabled list.
3. Remembering his days as a pitcher, he watched as the boy threw the ball.
4. Caught in the fence and hidden behind bushes, the ball was not found for months.

• For more about participles, see **Language Handbook,** p. R31.

READING AND THINKING • CREATIVE THINKING

When you use **creative thinking** in your reading, you can look at characters and conflicts in new ways. For example, you might question why a character is involved in a conflict, what he or she is doing about it, and whether there are other ways that the character might handle the situation.

• For more about reading and thinking strategies, see **Reading Handbook,** pp. R84–R96.

PRACTICE Skim "In the Middle of a Pitch." List clues to Dusty Sikarsky's problem, and note the suggestions his friends make to help him solve his problem. Reread the ending, which tells about Dusty's meeting with the boys. Then write one or two paragraphs suggesting whether you think Dusty solved his problem and ways he might have found a solution earlier in the story.

VOCABULARY • CONNOTATION

The definition of a word is its **denotation.** However, a word may sometimes be used in a way that implies a special attitude or emotion. This is its **connotation.** For example, one of the definitions of *pitch* is "sales talk." But *pitch* is sometimes used in a negative way that implies that the speaker is using "pushy" language and may be making dishonest claims.

PRACTICE Write a sentence for each word, using the connotation shown in parentheses.

1. off balance (unpleasantly surprised)
2. nestled (snug and safe)
3. warped (twisted and ugly)
4. minor (unimportant, secondary)
5. facade (false front, a covering for the real surface)

• For more about connotation and denotation, see **Reading Handbook,** p. R92.

Skill Minilessons

GRAMMAR AND LANGUAGE
PARTICIPLES

1. *performed under water:* Past participle; part of participial phrase
2. *disabled:* Past participle.
3. *Remembering his days as a pitcher:* Present participle; part of participial phrase.
4. *Caught in the fence and hidden behind bushes:* Past participles; part of participial phrase.

READING AND THINKING
CREATIVE THINKING

Students' paragraphs should refer to specific examples from the text, such as Dusty's refusal to talk about (or participate in) baseball, and his friends' suggestions he get involved with the game again.

VOCABULARY
CONNOTATION

Students should write one sentence for each word, and it should clearly show that they understand the meaning.

Additional Resources

- ***Grammar and Language Workbook,*** p. 171
- ***Grammar and Composition Handbook,*** Lesson 9.1
- ***Writer's Choice,*** Lesson 15.1
- ***Reading Skills Practice Workbook***
- ***Vocabulary Practice,*** p. 17

ASSESSMENT

- ***Quick Checks,*** p. 19
- ***Selection and Theme Assessment,*** p. 33
- ***Performance Assessment,*** p. 18
- ***Testmaker: ExamView Pro***
- ***Interactive Tutor: Self-Assessment***

MEDIA Connection

Objective

- To understand the use of humor to convey a message

Literature LINK

Casey at the Bat This cartoon connects to "Casey at the Bat" (pp. 252–254). Both the character in the cartoon and the hero of the poem strike out.

Analyzing Media

1. Students may respond that the cartoon suggests that having fun is more important than winning a game.
2. Students may say that while a desire to win is an important part of any game, they primarily play to have fun. Some students may add that when winning becomes the reason for playing, a good deal of the fun is lost.

Informational Text

inTIME For examples of informational text, direct students to the articles in the *inTIME* magazine.

Additional Resources

Media Connections, p. 5

MEDIA Connection

COMIC STRIP

How do you feel about winning or losing a pick-up ball game? Perhaps cartoonist Bill Amend's friends have an attitude that may surprise or amuse you.

by Bill Amend

Fox Trot

Fox Trot, © 1992. Bill Amend. Reprinted with permission of Universal Press Syndicate. All rights reserved.

Analyzing Media

1. What ideas about sportsmanship does this cartoon suggest?
2. In your opinion, is the purpose of a game to have fun or to win? When you're competing, which motive is stronger?

Teaching Support

interNET CONNECTION

Cartoonists Have students use a search engine to find background and interviews about the purposes of cartoons from a cartoonist's perspective. **L2**

Reading Minilesson

Author's Purpose Explain that writers and cartoonists often use exaggeration for comic effect. Ask students to identify at least two ways Amend uses exaggeration in this cartoon and explain his purpose for using exaggeration.

Activity Have students review several cartoons from a newspaper. Students should note which cartoons rely on exaggeration. Ask them to identify the ways the cartoonists have used exaggeration for comic effect and to make a point. **L2**

Additional Resources

Reading Skills Practice Workbook

Before You Read

Casey at the Bat

MEET ERNEST LAWRENCE THAYER

Ernest Lawrence Thayer could have followed in his father's footsteps and run one of his family's woolen mills in Massachusetts. Instead, he surprised his family by taking a job as a humor columnist for the *San Francisco Examiner*. Thayer had a low opinion of his writing ability and once said, "I put out large quantities of nonsense . . . from advertisements to editorials." The ballad "Casey at the Bat" was one of Thayer's last contributions to the *Examiner*.

Ernest Lawrence Thayer was born in 1863 and died in 1940. "Casey at the Bat" was published in the San Francisco Examiner *in 1888.*

READING FOCUS

What is your reaction as you watch an exciting moment in a ball game?

FreeWrite

How might you act if your team were relying on you to win a championship game? Write a brief answer.

Setting a Purpose

Read to enjoy a very tense moment for a group of baseball fans.

BUILDING BACKGROUND

The Time and Place This poem was written about a fictitious baseball player. The action takes place before a hometown crowd of 5,000 spectators.

Did You Know? The national love affair with baseball was well under way when "Casey at the Bat" was first published. Abner Doubleday, a ballplayer from Cooperstown, New York, is often credited with forming the rules of baseball in 1839. Yet it was actually a group of businessmen who instituted the sport as we know it today. These men formed the New York Knickerbocker Base Ball Club in 1845. They changed the rules of a popular game called "town ball," in which the ball was thrown directly at players who ran haphazardly, often colliding. The Knickerbockers established bases and the "three strikes, you're out" rule, among other things.

Before Reading

Objectives

- To read and analyze a poem about a man facing an opportunity
- To identify narrative poetry and its elements
- To write a few verses of narrative poetry

Skills

Reading/Thinking: Inferring; Adjusting Reading Rate
Vocabulary: Context Clues
Collaboration: Literature Groups

Motivating STUDENTS

Literature Launchers: "When All Eyes Are on You"

Videodisc Side A, Segment 9

Also available in VHS.

Selection Focus Transparency 19: Have students respond to the quotation and look for its relevance to the selection.

Reading Focus: As an extension of the Reading Focus, have students practice using specific adjectives and vivid phrases as they discuss their reactions.

RESOURCE MANAGER

Teaching Tools and Resources
- Theme Three Planning Guide
- Literature Groups Sourcebook

Essential Lesson Support

Lesson-Specific Instruction
- Selection Focus Transparency 19
- Literary Elements Transparency 20
- Active Reading Guide,* p. 20

Assessment
- Selection Quick Checks,* p. 20
- Sel. and Theme Assmt., p. 34
- Testmaker: ExamView Pro
- Performance Assessment, p. 19

Systematic Language Instruction
- Gr. & Comp. Hbk., Lessons 4.2, 4.3

English Language Learners
- ELL Sourcebook, p. 40
- Spanish Summaries, p. 19
- Spanish Translations, pp. 69–70
- Audio Library*
- English, Yes!

Spec. Needs/Strat. Interven.
- Interactive Rdg. Sbk., pp. T96–T98
- Interactive Rdg. Wbk., pp. 42–43
- Inclusion Strat. Sbk., pp. 79–80
- Audio Library*

* Also available in Spanish

Reading the Selection

Active Reading Strategies

QUESTION Explain to students that the author's use of the word *died* is not to be taken in a literal sense. Ask students why they think the author chose this word. *(The author uses such a strong word to indicate the feelings of the crowd when seeing a player get an out.)*

Additional Resources

- ***Active Reading Guide,*** p. 20
- ***Audio Library***
- ***Spanish Audio Library***

Critical Thinking

INFER After students read this stanza, ask them to infer what the audience is feeling. Is the majority of the crowd loyal to the Mudville nine?

FYI

In the game of baseball, there are nine players on the field: pitcher, catcher, first baseman, second baseman, shortstop, third baseman, right fielder, center fielder, and left fielder.

Casey at the Bat

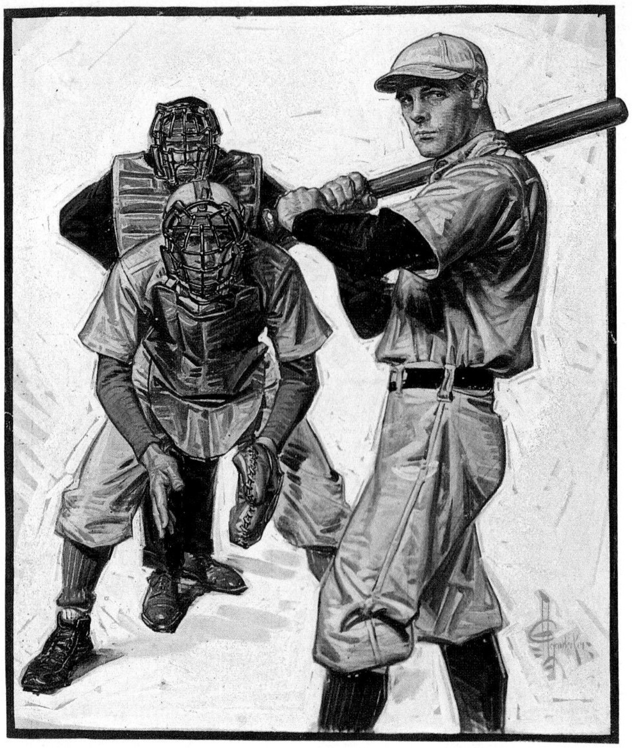

Baseball Scene of Batter, Catcher and Umpire, 1915. Joseph Christian Leyendecker. Oil on canvas, 31 x 22 in. Judy Goffman Fine Art, New York.

Ernest Lawrence Thayer

The outlook wasn't brilliant
  for the Mudville nine that day:
The score stood four to two
  with but one inning more to play.

And then when Cooney died at first,
  and Barrows did the same,
A sickly silence fell
  upon the patrons of the game.

A straggling few got up
  to go in deep despair. The rest
Clung to that hope which springs eternal
  in the human breast;

Teaching Support

CONNECTING TO OTHER SELECTIONS

COMPARING *selections*

This selection is paired with "In the Middle of a Pitch" on page 239. A lesson for teaching a comparison of the two selections appears on page 256.

The chart at the right shows three other ways to connect "Casey at the Bat" to selections in this book.

For specific teaching strategies, see the ***Theme Three Planning Guide***.

Connection	Title
Life Skills: Decision Making	"The Medicine Bag," p. 78
Thematic: Facing Failure	"Mother and Daughter," p. 62
Literary: Suspense	"Paul Revere's Ride," p. 449

They thought if only Casey
could but get a whack at that—
We'd put up even money° now
with Casey at the bat.

But Flynn preceded° Casey,
as did also Jimmy Blake,
And the former° was a lulu
and the latter° was a cake;

So upon that stricken multitude
grim melancholy° sat,
For there seemed but little chance
of Casey's getting to the bat.

But Flynn let drive a single,
to the wonderment of all,
And Blake, the much despis-ed,
tore the cover off the ball;

And when the dust had lifted,
and the men saw what had occurred,
There was Jimmy safe at second
and Flynn a-hugging third.

Then from 5,000 throats and more
there rose a lusty yell;
It rumbled through the valley,
it rattled in the dell;

It knocked upon the mountain
and recoiled upon the flat,
For Casey, mighty Casey,
was advancing to the bat.

There was ease in Casey's manner
as he stepped into his place;
There was pride in Casey's bearing
and a smile on Casey's face.

And when, responding to the cheers,
he lightly doffed his hat,
No stranger in the crowd could doubt
'twas Casey at the bat.

Ten thousand eyes were on him
as he rubbed his hands with dirt;
Five thousand tongues applauded
when he wiped them on his shirt.

Then while the writhing pitcher
ground the ball into his hip,
Defiance gleamed in Casey's eye,
a sneer curled Casey's lip.

And now the leather-covered sphere
came hurtling through the air,
And Casey stood a-watching it
in haughty grandeur there.

Close by the sturdy batsman
the ball unheeded sped—
"That ain't my style," said Casey.
"Strike one," the umpire said.

From the benches, black with people,
there went up a muffled roar,
Like the beating of the storm-waves
on a stern and distant shore.

"Kill him! Kill the umpire!"
shouted someone on the stand;
And it's likely they'd have killed him
had not Casey raised his hand.

8 *Put up even money* means fans recognize that the teams have an even chance of winning.

9 *Preceded* means "came before."

10 *Former* refers to the first one mentioned, and *latter* to the last one mentioned. Both Flynn and Blake seem to be considered poor batters.

11 *Grim melancholy* describes the crowd's mood, which is serious and sadly thoughtful.

Vocabulary Skills

Context Clues Point out that the words *lulu* and *cake* were slang terms that were familiar to readers at the time the poem was written. Ask students to infer the meanings from the context of the previous and next stanzas. Have them check their definitions in a dictionary of slang terms.

C Literary Elements

NARRATIVE POETRY: Description
Narrative poetry, like a story, develops characters, plot, and setting. In this poem, the fans play a major role, but the author never uses the word *fan* or *audience*. Point out that the *stricken multitude* both refers to and describes the fans. There are many other mentions of the audience in the poem. Have students identify them and analyze the author's use of description to develop the character of the audience.

D Active Reading Strategies

EVALUATE Have students evaluate Casey in terms of what type of player he is, what his attitude is, and whether he is nervous about coming up to bat in the last inning with two outs. *(He is very confident about his ability.)*

MEETING INDIVIDUAL NEEDS — ENGLISH LANGUAGE LEARNERS

Vocabulary This poem contains many words with which English language learners may be unfamiliar, such as *whack, dell, doffed,* and *stern.* Have volunteers provide definitions for these words, using a dictionary if needed.

Activity Have students listen to the poem as they follow along in their books. Then have students list unfamiliar terms while reading this poem the second time. Mixed groups should look up the definitions and pronunciations of the words in a dictionary and use each word in a sentence. Students should then reread the poem.

Additional Resources

English Language Learners Sourcebook, p. 40

E Literary Elements

RHYME SCHEME Review how to mark rhyme scheme. Ask students to identify the rhyme scheme of this stanza. *(abcb)*

F Literary Elements

NARRATIVE POETRY: Pace In this poem, the writer uses suspense to develop the plot. Point out that a writer can build suspense by slowing down the action or repeating phrases. Encourage students to contrast the slowing down of the action with the abrupt way the poem ends and to analyze the effect of the contrast.

VIEWING THE ART

Viewing Response *The fans here seem intensely involved—as the Mudville fans must have been. They are on their feet, yelling and gesturing excitedly.*

Thematic Focus

Which Way to Go? Have students consider the choices Casey makes when he steps up to bat. Are these good choices for the team? Why or why not?

ASSESSMENT

Quick Checks, p. 20

Casey at the Bat

With a smile of Christian charity
 great Casey's visage° shone;
He stilled the rising tumult;°
 he bade the game go on;

He signaled to the pitcher, [E]
 and once more the spheroid° flew;
But Casey still ignored it,
 and the umpire said, "Strike two."

"Fraud!" cried the maddened thousands,
 and the echo answered fraud;
But one scornful look from Casey
 and the audience was awed.

They saw his face grow stern and cold,
 they saw his muscles strain,
And they knew that Casey
 wouldn't let that ball go by again.

The sneer is gone from Casey's lips, [F]
 his teeth are clenched in hate;
He pounds with cruel violence
 his bat upon the plate.

And now the pitcher holds the ball,
 and now he lets it go,
And now the air is shattered
 by the force of Casey's blow.

Oh, somewhere in this favored land
 the sun is shining bright;
The band is playing somewhere,
 and somewhere hearts are light,

And somewhere men are laughing,
 and somewhere children shout;
But there is no joy in Mudville—
 mighty Casey has struck out.

37 Casey's *visage* (viz′ ij) is his face.
38 *Tumult* (to͞o′ məlt) means "noisy uproar."
39 A *spheroid* is a round object–in this case, a baseball.

Crowd at the Polo Ground, 1895. Jay Hambidge. Four-color proof, 18⅞ x 14 in. Museum of the City of New York.

Viewing the painting: How do these fans seem to feel about the game they are watching? How does the artist create this impression?

Teaching Support

A&E HOME VIDEO.® *The following videotape program is available from Glencoe. Be sure to preview the video for appropriateness for your class:*

- ***Biography:* "Babe Ruth"***

*Also available in the Glencoe Literature *Video Library.*

Reading Minilesson

Adjusting Reading Rate Narrative poetry grows out of an oral tradition and is often more effective when read aloud. Read several stanzas aloud to the class, then have students take turns reading stanzas aloud. Make sure the reading is fluent and that the suspense of the poem is captured in the readings through students' use of appropriate reading rate.

Activity Have students change the poem to the present tense and read as though they are announcing the game for radio or TV, using a rate of speech appropriate to the listeners' needs and the subject matter. **L2**

Reading Skills Practice Workbook

Responding to Literature

PERSONAL RESPONSE

- What was your reaction when Casey struck out? How might your response compare to the reaction spectators may have

Analyzing Literature

RECALL AND INTERPRET

1. How does Casey behave at the plate during the first two pitches? the third pitch? What does Casey's behavior say about his personality?
2. Describe the action of the game through the third stanza. What would encourage the crowd to "put up even money"?
3. Why, do you think, does the poet have Casey strike out?

EVALUATE AND CONNECT

4. **Suspense** is a feeling of building excitement or uncertainty about what is going to happen next. How effective is the author's use of suspense in this poem? Use examples from the text in your answer.
5. Casey appears at first to be a hero. What other heroes do you know in literature? Think of heroes from different historical eras. Do they ever fail?
6. Does Casey seem true to life? Why or why not?

LITERARY ELEMENTS

Narrative Poetry

Narrative poetry tells a story. A narrative poem has characters, a plot with a conflict, and a setting. Centuries ago, the stories of a tribe or village were passed along by a storyteller. To help people remember the tales, storytellers often used songs or poems. Today, narrative poems are usually printed or recorded.

1. What is the main conflict in "Casey at the Bat"?
2. In which line does the writer bring the story to a climax?
3. Where does the writer show how the conflict is resolved?

- See **Literary Terms Handbook,** p. R6.

Extending Your Response

Literature Groups

Spreading the Word "Casey at the Bat" became famous after actor William De Wolf Hopper recited it thousands of times before enthusiastic crowds and made a recording of it in 1906. How might a modern-day audience differ from one in Hopper's time? Discuss ways to perform the poem that you think would appeal to a modern audience. Give a presentation of one of your ideas to the class, and ask classmates to analyze your delivery.

Writing About Literature

The Return of Mighty Casey In 1906, Grantland Rice, a famous sportswriter, penned a poem he called "Casey's Revenge." It begins, "There were saddened hearts in Mudville for a week or even more; / There were muttered oaths and curses– every fan in town was sore." Provide a few more verses to this sequel. Will Casey strike out again or be a hero?

Responding to the Selection

PERSONAL RESPONSE

Some students may have expected Casey to strike out. Others may have been surprised. They should explain their responses.

Analyzing Literature

1. He watches the first pitch with "haughty grandeur" and greets the second with a "charitable smile." He is angry about the third pitch. His behavior shows arrogance.
2. It's the last inning and the home team is losing. The first two batters are out. Casey is so good that, if he were at bat, the crowd would not bet against his team.
3. Some students may think that the moral of the poem is that a person without humility eventually fails.
4. Student responses should include examples of the author's use of foreshadowing and an explanation of how it adds interest.
5. Some students may believe that fictional heroes never fail, while others will mention specific characters who are heroes despite failure.
6. Some students may believe that when a game is on the line, a real player usually tries hardest.

Extending Your Response

Literature Groups Students should consider the changes in baseball audiences throughout the history of the game. Presentations should respond to the changes students have identified. COLLAB. LEARN.

Writing About Literature

Students' verses should

- retain the meter and the rhyme scheme of the original
- explain what becomes of Casey

LITERARY ELEMENTS

1. Possibilities: Casey against the pitcher or Casey against himself.
2. Line 48 is the climax, when Casey swings the bat.
3. The last line of the poem shows the resolution of the conflict.

Additional Resources

Literary Elements Transparency 20

ASSESSMENT

- ***Quick Checks,*** p. 20
- ***Selection and Theme Assessment,*** p. 34
- ***Performance Assessment,*** p. 19
- ***Testmaker: ExamView Pro***
- ***Interactive Tutor: Self-Assessment***

WHICH WAY TO GO? 255

COMPARING *selections*

Objective

- To compare a short story and a narrative poem about conflict in baseball

COMPARE **STORIES**

1. The main characters face internal conflicts and set goals. Both encounter failure.
2. The outcomes generate interest. Readers want to see whether the characters succeed. The vivid descriptions of setting make both interesting. Both describe the sense of community among fans.
3. Both writers create tension and interest by showing action, not telling what characters think.

COMPARE AUTHORS' **PURPOSES**

1. Thayer's purpose may have been to show that overconfidence results in disappointment.
2. Meissner's purpose may have been to show how athletes cope with injuries and their consequences.

Additional Resources

Literature Groups Sourcebook

COMPARE **FANS**

Students' analyses should

- compare the roles of fans
- compare and contrast the portrayals of fans
- use examples from the text

Students' letters should

- state whether the student supports the person's actions
- support opinions with reasons

Teaching Support

Critical Thinking

COMPARING SELECTIONS

In the Middle of a Pitch and **Casey at the Bat**

COMPARE **STORIES**

Both selections are about baseball, but that's not all they have in common.

1. What, other than playing the game, is an important topic in both "In the Middle of a Pitch" and "Casey at the Bat"?
2. In what ways do both selections appeal to readers who aren't baseball fans? Think of three reasons not related to baseball why readers may enjoy these two works.
3. How do Bill Meissner and Ernest Lawrence Thayer make their selections suspenseful and interesting? What techniques do both writers use?

Baseball Scene of Batter, Catcher and Umpire, 1915 (detail).

COMPARE **AUTHORS' PURPOSES**

Thayer later criticized his poem about Casey and his fans because he didn't think it deserved so much attention.

1. What might Thayer's purpose have been when he wrote the poem?
2. What do you think Meissner's purpose was for writing his story?

Discuss your answers with a small group, and give reasons to support your opinions.

COMPARE **FANS**

Fans are an important part of "Casey at the Bat" and "In the Middle of a Pitch."

- How do Casey's fans affect his behavior? How does the reader know that Sikarsky also has fans, even after his release from the ball club? Write a few paragraphs comparing the attitudes displayed by the fans of each player.
- With a group, discuss why someone may become a fan or supporter of a particular person or activity. What obligations do people and groups have toward their fans? What obligations do fans have toward the groups and people they admire? Write a letter to a fan or to one of the characters in these two selections. Explain why you support or do not support the person. Back up your opinions with reasons and examples from the selection.

PORTFOLIO OPTIONS

Select and Reflect Have students review the assignment to write a few paragraphs comparing the importance of fans in these two selections. Ask them to review their paragraphs to ensure that they compared (showed similarities) rather than contrasted (pointed out differences) the role of fans in the two selections. Encourage students to include examples from each of the selections to support their comparisons. Students should make margin notations on their paragraphs containing ideas for later revision of the work.

Additional Resources

Writing Assessment and Portfolio Management, pp. 42–48

Interdisciplinary Connection SOCIAL STUDIES

The Evolution of America's Game

Picture a baseball game being played in the 1840s. The pitcher sails an underhand ball toward the catcher's thin leather glove. Players chase balls on uneven outfields, and balls bounce on infields strewn with pebbles. The ball, probably lopsided from too many hits with the bat, is changed only two or three times in an entire game. Only one umpire is present, so the players can—and do—trick him.

Today, pitchers fire overhand fastballs to catchers with padded mitts. Baseball fields are impeccably cared for. An average major league game uses between fifty and sixty baseballs, and six umpires govern the field.

Baseball has come a long way from its earlier versions, known as cricket and rounders, played by colonists in New England in the 1700s. The rules, playing fields, and players have changed, but the passion of fans hasn't waned. Jacques Barzun, a modern writer, educator, and baseball fan once said, "Whoever wants to know the heart and mind of America had better learn baseball." He speaks for millions of devoted fans who have been captivated by the sport through all of its changes. Here's a look at some of the major ones.

ACTIVITY

Invent a variation of a game you enjoy, such as kickball, checkers, or a card game. Revise the rules to make the game more fun, then rename the new version and teach your classmates to play.

The Knickerbocker Nine baseball club, 1864.

Early Baseball	Modern Baseball
The number of players on a side, the number of bases and distance between them, and other rules varied from place to place in the 1700s and early 1800s.	Alexander Cartwright, a New York sports enthusiast, laid out the present dimensions of the playing field in 1845 and wrote basic rules of the game.
Baseball was played mostly in New England until the Civil War, when Union soldiers spread its popularity across the country.	By 1903, sixteen teams played for one of two major leagues. Today, baseball is played enthusiastically around the globe, as far away as Japan. Players are stronger and faster than ever before.
African American ballplayers were not allowed to play in the major or minor leagues, so they started their own leagues in the 1920s and 1930s.	Jackie Robinson of the Brooklyn Dodgers became the first African American major league ballplayer in 1947.

Interdisciplinary Connection

Objective

- To understand the history of, and the changes in, baseball

Teaching Strategies

As students work at developing their own games, make sure they test their new rules to ensure that they work.

Activity

Students' responses should reflect well-thought-out rule changes that make the game more interesting and challenging.

Teaching Support

MEETING INDIVIDUAL NEEDS

MULTIPLE MODES OF EXPRESSION

Interpersonal Many students will have difficulty understanding the rules of a new game without an oral explanation or a demonstration. Choose a game with which students are familiar and, as a class, break down the rules in order to teach someone who has never played the game.

Activity Divide students into groups and have each member explain the rules of his or her new game. Then have the student demonstrate with a volunteer how to play. Groups can then spend time practicing the new games. **L2** COLLAB. LEARN.

Before Reading

Objectives

- To read and analyze a folktale about a man learning to deal with power
- To identify the climax of a short story
- To write a comparison of two folktales

Skills

Reading/Thinking: Inferring; Identifying the Author's Purpose
Writing: Folktale
Vocabulary: Connotation; Synonyms
Grammar/Language: Adverbs
Listening/Speaking: Research Presentation
Collaboration: Literature Groups

Motivating STUDENTS

Selection Focus Transparency 20: As students view the transparency, discuss the quotaion and their answers.

Reading Focus: As an extension of the Reading Focus, ask students to share their lists of folktales, discussing similarities and differences.

Before You Read

The Wise Old Woman

MEET YOSHIKO UCHIDA

Yoshiko Uchida (yō shē′ kō ū′ chē dä) was among the many Japanese Americans sent to relocation centers during World War II. Uchida is renowned for her detailed narratives of life in such a center. Many of her other writings, however, are retellings of Japanese folktales. She hoped that the folktales would teach young Americans about Japanese culture and also entertain them. Uchida once expressed the hope that ". . . all children, in whatever country they may live, have the same love of fun and a good story."

Yoshiko Uchida was born in 1921 and died in 1992. This story was published in 1965.

READING FOCUS

The number *three* often appears in folktales. What folktales can you recall that feature three main events, wishes, riddles, or characters?

List It!
With a partner, make a list of folktales in which the number *three* appears. Explain how *three* appears in each tale.

Setting a Purpose
Read to discover how three challenges affect a village.

BUILDING BACKGROUND

The Time and Place This folktale is set in a Japanese village.

Did You Know? Folktales from around the world often follow a similar pattern. They begin with a dreamlike "once upon a time" or "in a land far away" that helps listeners or readers be carried away by the often fantastic events of the story. Characters are quickly introduced, and conflict appears early in the story. The characters are often in direct contrast to each other: one is very, very good and the other is terribly evil. Three events, riddles, or wishes often carry the plot along to the frequent conclusion of "happily ever after."

VOCABULARY PREVIEW

haughtily (hô′ tə lē) *adv.* in a way that shows too much pride in oneself and great scorn for others; p. 259
decree (di krē′) *v.* to set forth an official rule, order, or decision; dictate; p. 259
banish (ban′ ish) *v.* to force a person to leave a country or community; p. 259
bewilderment (bi wil′ dər mənt) *n.* deep confusion; p. 262
commend (kə mend′) *v.* to express approval of; p. 262
summon (sum′ ən) *v.* to send for or request the presence of, especially with authority; p. 263

RESOURCE MANAGER

Teaching Tools and Resources
- Theme Three Planning Guide,
- Literature Groups Sourcebook

Essential Lesson Support

Lesson-Specific Instruction
- Selection Focus Transparency 20
- Literary Elements Transparency 21
- Active Reading Guide,* p. 21
- Selection Vocabulary Practice, p. 18

Assessment
- Selection Quick Checks,* p. 21
- Sel. and Theme Assmt., pp. 35-36
- Testmaker: ExamView Pro
- Performance Assessment, p. 20

Systematic Language Instruction
- Gr. & Comp. Hbk., Lessons 4.4, 4.5
- Vocabulary Power, Lesson 11
- Spelling Power, Lesson 10

English Language Learners
- ELL Sourcebook, p. 41
- Spanish Summaries, p. 20
- Audio Library*
- English, Yes!

Spec. Needs/Strat. Interven.
- Interactive Rdg. Sbk., pp. T98-T101
- Interactive Rdg. Wbk., pp. 44-45
- Inclusion Strat. Sbk., pp. 19-20, 93-94
- Audio Library*

* Also available in Spanish

The Wise Old Woman

Adapted by Yoshiko Uchida

Landscape, Mid-Edo. Ike Gyokuran. Hanging scroll; ink and colors on silk, 44⅛ x 19³⁄₁₆ in. Gift of the Asian Art Foundation of San Francisco, The Avery Brundage Collection. Asian Art Museum of San Francisco. B76 D3.

MANY LONG YEARS AGO, there lived an arrogant and cruel young lord who ruled over a small village in the western hills of Japan. "I have no use for old people in my village," he said haughtily. "They are neither useful nor able to work for a living. I therefore decree that anyone over seventy-one must be banished from the village and left in the mountains to die."

A

Vocabulary

haughtily (hô′ tə lē) *adv.* in a way that shows too much pride in oneself and great scorn for others

decree (di krē′) *v.* to set forth an official rule, order, or decision; dictate

banish (ban′ ish) *v.* to force a person to leave a country or community

Reading the Selection

SUMMARY

This story is set in the distant past in a Japanese village ruled by a cruel lord. The lord orders that everyone over the age of seventy-one must be taken to the mountains and left there, but the main character disobeys and keeps his mother hidden in his house. When another cruel lord tries to take over the village by issuing three difficult challenges, the main character's mother is the only person in the village with the wisdom to answer them and save the village. As a result, the lord revokes his order about the older citizens.

Spanish Summaries, p. 20

A Active Reading Strategies

CONNECT Have students discuss how the beginning of this story resembles the beginning of most folk tales. *(It takes place in the distant past.)*

VOCABULARY Remind students to use context clues to unlock the meanings of new vocabulary words.

Additional Resources

- ***Active Reading Guide,*** p. 21
- ***Audio Library***
- ***Spanish Audio Library***

Teaching Support

CONNECTING TO OTHER SELECTIONS

The chart at the right shows three ways to connect "The Wise Old Woman" to other selections in this book.

For specific teaching strategies, see the ***Theme Three Planning Guide***.

Connection	Title
Life Skills: Problem Solving	→ "The Dinner Party," p. 870
Thematic: Mother-Son Relationships	→ "A Mother in Mannville," p. 185
Literary: Folktale	→ "The People Could Fly," p. 389

B Active Reading Strategies

CONNECT Ask students to imagine having to comply with such a rule. Encourage them to understand why these villagers complied and to imagine whether there were any options open to the villagers.

Vo•cab•u•lar•y Skills

Connotation Point out the author's use of the word *wail* in the second column of this page. Ask students what the connotations of *wail* are that make it a good choice. Encourage students to compare this choice with other words that describe wind (*whistling, rushing,* and others students might suggest).

C Literary Elements

CLIMAX Remind students that, to reach a climax in a story, first the author must provide rising action. Ask students to explain how this paragraph contributes to the climax. *(When the main character finally decides he cannot leave his mother, this sets up the climax, or turning point, of the story.)*

Teaching Support

"What a dreadful decree! What a cruel and unreasonable lord we have," the people of the village murmured. But the lord fearfully punished anyone who disobeyed him, and so villagers who turned seventy-one were tearfully carried into the mountains, never to return.

Gradually there were fewer and fewer old people in the village and soon they disappeared altogether. Then the young lord was pleased.

"What a fine village of young, healthy and hardworking people I have," he bragged. "Soon it will be the finest village in all of Japan."

Now there lived in this village a kind young farmer and his aged mother. They were poor, but the farmer was good to his mother, and the two of them lived happily together. However, as the years went by, the mother grew older, and before long she reached the terrible age of seventy-one.

"If only I could somehow deceive the cruel lord," the farmer thought. But there were records in the village books and everyone knew that his mother had turned seventy-one.

Each day the son put off telling his mother that he must take her into the mountains to die, but the people of the village began to talk. The farmer knew that if he did not take his mother away soon, the lord would send his soldiers and throw them both into a dark dungeon to die a terrible death.

"Mother—" he would begin, as he tried to tell her what he must do, but he could not go on.

Then one day the mother herself spoke of the lord's dread decree. "Well, my son," she said, "the time has come for you to take me to the mountains. We must hurry before the lord sends his soldiers for you." And she did not seem worried at all that she must go to the mountains to die.

"Forgive me, dear mother, for what I must do," the farmer said sadly, and the next morning he lifted his mother to his shoulders and set off on the steep path toward the mountains. Up and up he climbed, until the trees clustered close and the path was gone. There was no longer even the sound of birds, and they heard only the soft wail of the wind in the trees. The son walked slowly, for he could not bear to think of leaving his old mother in the mountains. On and on he climbed, not wanting to stop and leave her behind. Soon, he heard his mother breaking off small twigs from the trees that they passed.

"Mother, what are you doing?" he asked.

"Do not worry, my son," she answered gently. "I am just marking the way so you will not get lost returning to the village."

The son stopped. "Even now you are thinking of me?" he asked, wonderingly.

The mother nodded. "Of course, my son," she replied. "You will always be in my thoughts. How could it be otherwise?"

At that, the young farmer could bear it no longer. "Mother, I cannot leave you in the mountains to die all alone," he said. "We are going home and no matter what the lord does to punish me, I will never desert you again."

So they waited until the sun had set and a lone star crept into the silent sky. Then in the dark shadows of night, the farmer carried his mother down the hill and they returned quietly to their little house. The farmer dug a deep hole in the floor of his kitchen and made a small room where he could hide his mother. From that day, she spent all her time in the secret room and

MEETING INDIVIDUAL NEEDS — ENGLISH LANGUAGE LEARNERS

Verb Tenses This story is told in the past tense, but the dialogue is in the present tense. English language learners may have difficulty switching between tenses. Explain to students that the narration of the story is in the past tense because the events occurred long ago. The dialogue takes place in the time the events occurred.

Activity Have students read the passage on page 261 that begins "The cruel young lord . . ." through ". . . help me now?" Have students identify and list the past-tense verbs. Next to each word, students should write the present-tense form.

Additional Resources

English Language Learners Sourcebook, p. 41

the farmer carried meals to her there. The rest of the time, he was careful to work in the fields and act as though he lived alone. In this way, for almost two years, he kept his mother safely hidden and no one in the village knew that she was there.

Standing Beauty, 1851. Ando Hiroshige. Hanging scroll, ink and color on paper, 91.5 x 27.7 cm. The British Museum, London.

Viewing the painting: Notice the woman's posture and expression. What qualities might she have in common with the old woman in this story?

Then one day there was a terrible commotion among the villagers for Lord Higa of the town beyond the hills threatened to conquer their village and make it his own.

"Only one thing can spare you," Lord Higa announced. "Bring me a box containing one thousand ropes of ash and I will spare your village."

The cruel young lord quickly gathered together all the wise men of his village. "You are men of wisdom," he said. "Surely you can tell me how to meet Lord Higa's demands so our village can be spared."

But the wise men shook their heads. "It is impossible to make even one rope of ash, sire," they answered. "How can we ever make one thousand?"

"Fools!" the lord cried angrily. "What good is your wisdom if you cannot help me now?"

And he posted a notice in the village square offering a great reward of gold to any villager who could help him save their village.

But all the people in the village whispered, "Surely, it is an impossible thing, for ash crumbles at the touch of the finger. How could anyone ever make a rope of ash?" They shook their heads and sighed, "Alas, alas, we must be conquered by yet another cruel lord."

The young farmer, too, supposed that this must be, and he wondered what would happen to his mother if a new lord even more terrible than their own came to rule over them.

When his mother saw the troubled look on his face, she asked, "Why are you so worried, my son?"

So the farmer told her of the impossible demand made by Lord Higa if the village was to be spared, but his mother did

D Active Reading Strategies

PREDICT Ask students to predict what may happen to the young, cruel lord later in the story. Have them provide support for their predictions, including details from the story, other stories they have read, or life experiences they have had.

VIEWING THE PAINTING

Painter and printmaker Ando Hiroshige (1797–1858), although known especially for his landscape art, conveys in his figures too a sense of his period.

Viewing Response *The woman in this painting, perhaps a waitress or tradesman's wife, is alert and attentive. Like the old woman in the story, she seems ready and eager to be of service.*

E Literary Elements

CLIMAX Point out to students that the author uses irony during the climax to highlight an important point of the story. Review the meaning of irony with students. Help them identify the irony in this story, and ask them how it relates to the author's message. *(Lord Higa is doing to the young lord just what the young lord did to the village elders—making arbitrary demands just because he has the power to do so. To meet these demands, the young lord needs the wisdom of the elders he has banished.)*

MEETING INDIVIDUAL NEEDS — MULTIPLE MODES OF EXPRESSION

Logical-Mathematical Students who have logical or mathematical skills will be interested in the challenges the town faced. Encourage them to consider alternative solutions to the challenges issued to the village.

Activity Have students present an alternative solution to one of the village's challenges. Encourage students to produce a model demonstrating their solution. **L2**

Active Reading Strategies

PREDICT Ask students to predict whether the main character's mother will solve the challenge again. Make sure students give support for their predictions.

Author's Craft

CHARACTERIZATION Point out to students that the lord is characterized not only through description *(cruel)*, but also through dialogue. Have students provide examples. *("And again you are stupid fools!")*

Active Reading Strategies

QUESTION Ask students why, in their opinion, the mother finds the challenge so easy. You may wish to share the following model to illustrate the thinking process involved in answering questions about a story.

Model: I think that because the mother has lived longer, she has more experience than anyone else in the town. She has faced more challenges in life to compare to those facing the town. I think her experiences make her wiser and better able to think of solutions to these challenges.

not seem troubled at all. Instead she laughed softly and said, "Why, that is not such an impossible task. All one has to do is soak ordinary rope in salt water and dry it well. When it is burned, it will hold its shape and there is your rope of ash! Tell the villagers to hurry and find one thousand pieces of rope."

The farmer shook his head in amazement. "Mother, you are wonderfully wise," he said, and he rushed to tell the young lord what he must do.

"You are wiser than all the wise men of the village," the lord said when he heard the farmer's solution, and he rewarded him with many pieces of gold. The thousand ropes of ash were quickly made and the village was spared.

In a few days, however, there was another great commotion in the village as Lord Higa sent another threat. This time he sent a log with a small hole that curved and bent seven times through its length, and he demanded that a single piece of silk thread be threaded through the hole. "If you cannot perform this task," the lord threatened, "I shall come to conquer your village."

The young lord hurried once more to his wise men, but they all shook their heads in bewilderment. "A needle cannot bend its way through such curves," they moaned. "Again we are faced with an impossible demand."

"And again you are stupid fools!" the lord said, stamping his foot impatiently. He then posted a second notice in the village square asking the villagers for their help.

Once more the young farmer hurried with the problem to his mother in her secret room.

"Why, that is not so difficult," his mother said with a quick smile. "Put some sugar at one end of the hole. Then, tie an ant to a piece of silk thread and put it in at the other end. He will weave his way in and out of the curves to get to the sugar and he will take the silk thread with him."

"Mother, you are remarkable!" the son cried, and he hurried off to the lord with the solution to the second problem.

Once more the lord commended the young farmer and rewarded him with many pieces of gold. "You are a brilliant man and you have saved our village again," he said gratefully.

But the lord's troubles were not over even then, for a few days later Lord Higa sent still another demand. "This time you will undoubtedly fail and then I shall conquer your village," he threatened. "Bring me a drum that sounds without being beaten."

"But that is not possible," sighed the people of the village. "How can anyone make a drum sound without beating it?"

This time the wise men held their heads in their hands and moaned, "It is hopeless. It is hopeless. This time Lord Higa will conquer us all."

The young farmer hurried home breathlessly. "Mother, Mother, we must solve another terrible problem or Lord Higa will conquer our village!" And he quickly told his mother about the impossible drum.

His mother, however, smiled and answered, "Why, this is the easiest of them

Vocabulary
bewilderment (bi wil′ dər mənt) *n.* deep confusion
commend (kə mend′) *v.* to express approval of

Teaching Support

Grammar and Language *Minilesson*

Adverbs This story uses many adverbs, beginning with the first paragraph. Write the phrases *fearfully punished* and *tearfully carried* on the board and review the use of adverbs. Help students understand their importance in creating vivid writing.

Activity Have students find verbs in the story to make more vivid by adding adverbs. For instance, in the first paragraph, they could select *ruled, decree,* and *banished*. Encourage students to add adverbs that help convey the action in the story, for example, *arrogantly ruled, formally decree, forever banished*. Caution students not to add meaningless adverbs. **L2**

Additional Resources

- ***Grammar and Language Transparency 20***
- ***Grammar and Language Workbook,*** p. 129
- ***Grammar and Composition Handbook,*** Lesson 6.1
- ***Writer's Choice,*** Lesson 10.5

all. Make a drum with sides of paper and put a bumblebee inside. As it tries to escape, it will buzz and beat itself against the paper and you will have a drum that sounds without being beaten."

The young farmer was amazed at his mother's wisdom. "You are far wiser than any of the wise men of the village," he said, and he hurried to tell the young lord how to meet Lord Higa's third demand.

When the lord heard the answer, he was greatly impressed. "Surely a young man like you cannot be wiser than all my wise men," he said. "Tell me honestly, who has helped you solve all these difficult problems?"

The young farmer could not lie. "My lord," he began slowly, "for the past two years I have broken the law of the land. I have kept my aged mother hidden beneath the floor of my house, and it is she who solved each of your problems and saved the village from Lord Higa."

He trembled as he spoke, for he feared the lord's displeasure and rage. Surely now the soldiers would be summoned to throw him into the dark dungeon. But when he glanced fearfully at the lord, he saw that the young ruler was not angry at all. Instead, he was silent and thoughtful, for at last he realized how much wisdom and knowledge old people possess.

"I have been very wrong," he said finally. "And I must ask the forgiveness of your mother and of all my people. Never again will I demand that the old people of our village be sent to the mountains to die. Rather, they will be treated with the respect and honor they deserve and share with us the wisdom of their years."

And so it was. From that day, the villagers were no longer forced to abandon their parents in the mountains, and the village became once more a happy, cheerful place in which to live. The terrible Lord Higa stopped sending his impossible demands and no longer threatened to conquer them, for he too was impressed. "Even in such a small village there is much wisdom," he declared, "and its people should be allowed to live in peace."

And that is exactly what the farmer and his mother and all the people of the village did for all the years thereafter.

知

He trembled as he spoke, for he feared the lord's displeasure and rage.

恵

Vocabulary

summon (sum′ ən) *v.* to send for or request the presence of, especially with authority

I Critical Thinking

INFER Ask students to examine the lord's statement "Surely a young man like you cannot be wiser . . ." Encourage them to identify what the lord is admitting in this statement and to infer the conclusion that results from it. *(The lord admits that with age comes wisdom. If a young man cannot be wise, an older person would be wiser. The lord's statement contradicts his action of expelling the older people because they are useless.)*

J Literary Elements

CLIMAX Explain to students that the climax of the story occurs when the main character risks his own life and his mother's to tell the truth. Everything up to this point has been building proof that the cruel young lord has been wrong.

Thematic Focus

Which Way to Go? The narrator risks his life to save his mother, and the town's lord risks public embarrassment and loss of pride to allow the town's wise elders to remain. Both of these characters make difficult choices. Ask students to draw parallels to their own lives and the lives of other readers by discussing whether they or other readers have based choices on the fear of taking risks.

ASSESSMENT

Quick Checks, p. 21

Reading *Minilesson*

Author's Purpose In folktales, the author's purpose is often to teach a moral lesson. In this story there are many different types of prejudice and bias held by characters in the story. Three of the main characters in this story—the young man, the town's young lord, and Lord Higa—experience growth by overcoming their prejudices.

Activity Have students identify the prejudices of the young man, the young lord, and Lord Higa and discuss why each character makes choices that require him to overlook or eliminate these biases.
L2 **COLLAB. LEARN.**

Additional Resources

Reading Skills Practice Workbook

Responding to the Selection

PERSONAL RESPONSE

Students' examples should include people who abuse power in ways similar to those used by the young lord in the story.

Analyzing Literature

1. The lord decrees that everyone over the age of seventy-one must be taken to the mountains to die, because he thinks old people are "neither useful nor able to work."
2. The farmer hides his mother in a room below his house.
3. *(a)* The townspeople are to make one thousand ropes of ash. They soak ropes in salt water before burning so the ropes will hold their shape. *(b)* They are to thread silk through a twisting hole in a log. They tie the silk to an ant and put sugar at one end of the hole. *(c)* They are to make a drum that sounds without beating it. They make the drum out of paper and put a bee inside.
4. The young lord learns that older people have experience that makes them wise; therefore, they are useful.
5. The villagers obey the decree because the lord will punish them if they don't.
6. The farmer disobeys the order because he cannot bear to leave his mother to die.
7. The author shows that wisdom comes with age. The village wise men are inexperienced.
8. Power can be abused to everyone's detriment.
9. Answers may relate to prejudice, bias, and stereotyping and the need to overcome these; they may also relate to a message of respect for elders and the wisdom that comes with age.
10. Students may give examples of forced retirement, nursing homes, and popular culture's being geared toward the young through marketing, movies, and television.

Active Reading and Critical Thinking

Responding to Literature

PERSONAL RESPONSE

- The lords in the story may remind you of some people in modern society. If so, who are these people? What do you think about such people?

Brackets connect questions that are paired to develop higher-level thinking skills.

Analyzing Literature

RECALL

1. What does the young lord decree? Why does he make this demand?
2. What does the young farmer do when his mother, the wise old woman, turns seventy-one?
3. Name the three demands from Lord Higa and describe the wise old woman's solutions.
4. What does the young lord learn from the wise old woman?

INTERPRET

5. Why do the villagers go along with the lord's decree even though they don't want to?
6. Why does the young farmer disobey the decree?
7. Why does the author show that only the old woman can solve the problems and not the wise men of the village?
8. What point does this folktale make about people who have power over others?

EVALUATE AND CONNECT

9. What is the message, or theme, of the story? How important is this message for people today?
10. What is your impression of how modern American society treats older people? Explain your answer.

LITERARY ELEMENTS

Climax

The **climax** of a story is the turning point, an exciting moment that all the earlier events lead up to. The climax is part of the plot, or story line. Nearly all folktales have a climax because they are built around a problem, puzzle, or conflict to solve.

1. Describe the climax of "The Wise Old Woman."
2. What makes the climax of this tale exciting?

• See **Literary Terms Handbook,** p. R2.

LITERARY ELEMENTS

1. The climax occurs when the son tells the lord that the challenges have been answered by his mother.
2. The suspense of not knowing what the lord might do when he hears that his decree has been disobeyed makes the climax exciting.

Additional Resources

Literary Elements Transparency 21

Extending Your Response

Writing About Literature

Compare Folktales Folktales have appealed to people since early times when they were sung or told by storytellers. Locate or recall a favorite folktale and compare its characters, setting, and plot to those of "The Wise Old Woman." Write a few paragraphs comparing the two folktales.

Creative Writing

Good Versus Evil Write a very short story following the folktale pattern described in the **Reading Focus** and **Building Background** sections on page 258. Begin with a good character and an evil character, a conflict that includes three main events, and a conclusion. Bring your story to life with well-chosen details, dialogue, and description. Will good win over evil in your story?

Literature Groups

Abuse of Power Rulers throughout history have been known to abuse their power, as do the lords in "The Wise Old Woman." Discuss historical examples of people who were mistreated, such as the elderly in this story. What have people done, and what can people today do, to correct abuses of power?

Interdisciplinary Activity

Social Studies Japan has a history of feudal lords and their samurai warriors, shoguns (military governors), and emperors. Research Japanese rulers from ancient times through today. Learn more about several specific rulers, including their governmental power. Prepare a short written or oral presentation of your findings.

Save your work for your portfolio.

Skill Minilesson

RETEACH • REVIEW

VOCABULARY • SYNONYMS

Synonyms are words that have the same or nearly the same meanings. However, there are small but important differences between synonyms. For example, *bewilderment* and *confusion* are synonyms, but *bewilderment* is deep, hopeless confusion. Still, these two words are synonyms because they mean nearly the same thing.

PRACTICE Use your knowledge of the vocabulary words in the left column to match each to its synonym in the right column.

1. summon	a. proudly
2. decree	b. expel
3. haughtily	c. call
4. commend	d. command
5. banish	e. compliment

Extending Your Response

Writing About Literature

Students' comparisons should

- consider characters, setting, and plot
- compare these to "The Wise Old Woman"

Creative Writing

Students' stories should

- include two main characters—one good and one evil
- include three events that lead to a conclusion

Literature Groups Student responses should demonstrate a thoughtful discussion of the ways people have corrected abuses of power in the past, how they have worked, and what methods might work today. COLLAB. LEARN.

Interdisciplinary Activity Student presentations should demonstrate research and some analysis of how the rulers were able to become as powerful as they were.

Skill Minilesson

VOCABULARY • SYNONYMS

1. c	3. a	5. b
2. d	4. e	

Additional Resources

Vocabulary Practice, p. 18

ASSESSMENT

- ***Quick Checks,*** p. 21
- ***Selection and Theme Assessment,*** pp. 35–36
- ***Performance Assessment,*** p. 20
- ***Testmaker: ExamView Pro***
- ***Interactive Tutor: Self-Assessment***

Technology Skills

Objectives

- To investigate and understand "fair use" of multimedia tools on the Internet
- To practice downloading video and audio clips
- To prepare a presentation that includes video and audio clips

Teaching Strategies

To motivate students, present a completed multimedia (audio, video, text) presentation to the class. Students should gain knowledge about the integration of these media from the presentation. After the presentation is finished, invite students to question the procedures used to compile the presentation.

Teaching Support

Technology Skills

Multimedia: Adding Sound and Video to Presentations

Almost any presentation can be improved by adding sound and video. For instance, if you're presenting a report on an actor, what better way to illustrate his style than with movie clips? You can videotape movie scenes on TV or download film clips from the Internet, but is it legal to use them without the studio's permission? A crash course on copyright law will help you find out.

Fair Use and Multimedia

In general, copyright law protects people who create and produce an original work. Consider for a minute how you would feel if you had written a short story just to have someone else publish it and get all the credit. Copyright law exists to protect you from such "piracy."

However, the law recognizes that students and teachers need to be able to access and share information with one another. To accommodate these needs, the 1976 Copyright Law includes a "fair use" clause allowing educators and students to use limited portions of copyrighted materials without permission and without paying a fee.

The box-office hit *Titanic,* released by Paramount in 1997, made actor Leonardo DiCaprio a household name. His character, Jack Dawson, and Rose DeWitt (played by Kate Winslet) fall in love aboard the ill-fated ship.

Get an Update

The 1976 law was passed years before students had access to the powerful multimedia tools of today. Fortunately, legislators have updated the law to include electronic material. To find out the latest on copyright and multimedia presentations, conduct a World Wide Web search for "Fair Use Guidelines for Educational Multimedia." Follow these guidelines when you use copyrighted materials in a multimedia presentation.

Meeting Individual Needs: SPECIAL NEEDS

Learning Disabled Some students may find the assignment daunting because of the need to understand how both the Internet and presentation software function. To heighten the interest of these students, allow them extra time to investigate audio and video clips on the Internet.

Activity Help students find several sites that include audio and video clips. You may suggest they investigate sites that sell CDs and movies to start. Allow students to search for items of interest to them. Then help them download a few of their favorite clips to share with the rest of the class. **L1**

Additional Resources

Inclusion Strategies

Practice

Work with a partner to access sound and movie files on the Internet. Check with your teacher or lab assistant to be sure you have the necessary software to play these files. This software (sometimes in demonstration versions) can usually be downloaded at no cost.

1. Using an Internet search engine, and type in the keywords *.wav + *.mid. The computer will find all sites with files that have *wav* or *mid* extensions. These two file endings indicate sound files.
2. You should be able to find music and other sound bites from movies, television shows, and other sources. Open and play a few files.
3. Select two files to download. Copy them into a folder where you can find them later.
4. Next search for *.avi + *.mov files. These are movie files. You'll find both live-action movies and animation. They may contain sound as well as moving pictures. Select two files that look interesting, and download them to the folder with your sound files. (Movie files can be huge. Select short ones to avoid long download times.)
5. Open your presentation software, and create a few blank slides. Then pull down the **Insert** menu and select **Movies and Sounds/from File.** Insert the sound and movie files from the folder containing your downloaded files.
6. To play your movies and sounds in a slide show, simply click (or double click) on the image or icon with your mouse. To change this default, click on the image, and select **Action Settings** from the **Slide Show** menu to see what other options are available to you.

TECHNOLOGY TIP

Extensions tell your computer what kind of file it's working with. PC extensions always have three letters; Macintosh files can have two, three, or four. The letters may be all lowercase or all capitals. Here are some common extensions that will help you identify files.

Sound files:
.aif, .au, .ram, .mid, .snd, .wav

Picture files:
.gif, .jpg or .jpeg, .tif or .tiff

Movie files:
.avi, .mov, .mpg or .mpeg, .qt

ACTIVITIES

1. Create a multimedia presentation that includes movies and sounds for one of your writing assignments in this theme. Present your work to your classmates.
2. If you have access to a digital video camera, work with a group to create some video files you can use, in addition to downloaded sounds or movies, in a multimedia slide show that relates to a theme or a selection in this book. Present your slide show to your school's PTA group or show it at an open house for parents.

Activities

1. Make sure students understand the process of downloading the clips and importing them into presentation software before they begin.
2. Suggest students include readings by the author of one of the works in this theme.

TechnoTalk

Audio Mixers Explain to students that there are software programs that turn the computer into a mixer. With such a program, students can download clips and modify them, slowing them down, adding sounds, or editing them. These programs also allow the user to input sounds of their own.

Before Reading

Objectives

- To read and analyze a folktale about a man's struggle
- To identify rising action in the plot of a story
- To write an analysis

Skills

Reading/Thinking: Drawing Conclusions; Identifying Main Idea and Supporting Details; Synthesizing; Summarizing
Writing: Short Story Scene
Vocabulary: Dictionaries; Latin Root *Voc*
Grammar/Language: Punctuating Dialogue; Punctuating Compound Sentences
Listening/Speaking: Storytelling Performance
Collaboration: Literature Groups

Motivating → STUDENTS

Selection Focus Transparency 21: Have students view the photo of the griffin-dragon head and discuss its effectiveness as an image of a protector.

Reading Focus: As an extension of the Reading Focus, have students think about people or animals that frighten them. What criteria do they use to evaluate whether to fear something or someone?

Before You Read

Bagged Wolf

MEET CAROL KENDALL

By the fourth grade, Carol Kendall knew she would be a writer. She had already started her first novel. "It was a lurid tale of cruel stepfathers and pickpockets," she recalls. "I ran out of material after nineteen pages." Kendall's first novel was published in 1946. She is well known as a fantasy writer.

MEET YAO-WEN LI

Yao-wen Li (you wen lē) was a scientist, housewife, and mother before she became a writer. Born in Canton, China, she came to the United States in 1947. Years later, she began to write and translate.

This story was published in 1978 in Sweet and Sour: Tales from China.

READING FOCUS

If someone were about to harm you, how might you protect yourself?

QuickWrite
Jot down your response. With a classmate, share responses.

Setting a Purpose
As you read, notice how various characters try to protect themselves.

BUILDING BACKGROUND

The Time and Place This story dates back to the Ming dynasty, which ruled China from 1368 to 1644.

Did You Know? In the following tale, Tung Kuo is a student of the Chinese philosopher Mo-tzu, who lived from 479 to 381 B.C. Mo-tzu taught that it is what people do, not who they are, that makes them worthy of respect. Students of Mo-tzu lived simply, wore distinctive clothes, and followed his teachings of universal love and the consensus of the common good.

VOCABULARY PREVIEW

prowess (prou′ is) *n.* great ability or skill; p. 269
benevolence (bə nev′ ə ləns) *n.* kindliness; generosity; p. 271
loom (lo͞om) *v.* to appear or come into view in a way that seems very large and, often, threatening; p. 271
scavenger (skav′ in jər) *n.* an animal, such as a hyena or vulture, that feeds on dead, decaying plants or animals; p. 272
advocate (ad′ və kit) *n.* one who publicly supports or urges; p. 272
plight (plīt) *n.* an unfortunate or dangerous situation; p. 274
barter (bär′ tər) *v.* to trade goods for goods; p. 274
gravely (grāv′ lē) *adv.* very seriously; p. 275
sagely (sāj′ lē) *adv.* very wisely; p. 276
aghast (ə gast′) *adj.* filled with fear or horror; p. 276

RESOURCE MANAGER

Teaching Tools and Resources
- Theme Three Planning Guide
- Literature Groups Sourcebook

Essential Lesson Support

Lesson-Specific Instruction
- Selection Focus Transparency 21
- Literary Elements Transparency 22
- Active Reading Guide,* p. 22
- Selection Vocabulary Practice, p. 19

Assessment
- Selection Quick Checks,* p. 22
- Sel. and Theme Assmt., pp. 37–38
- Testmaker: ExamView Pro
- Performance Assessment, p. 21

Systematic Language Instruction
- Gr. & Comp. Hbk., Lessons 4.6, 4.7

English Language Learners
- ELL Sourcebook, p. 42
- Spanish Summaries, p. 21
- Audio Library*

- English, Yes!

Spec. Needs/Strat. Interven.
- Interactive Rdg. Sbk., pp. T101–T103
- Interactive Rdg. Wbk., pp. 46–47
- Inclusion Strat. Sbk., pp. 13–14
- Audio Library*

* Also available in Spanish

Bagged Wolf

Retold by Carol Kendall and Yao-wen Li

One hard winter's day a lean, lank wolf was prowling the mountains in search of food. He was weak with hunger and had already missed two kills when suddenly he saw, munching unconcernedly on a patch of grass, the biggest, fattest, tastiest-looking rabbit he had seen all winter. His stomach fairly ached with longing, but he advanced carefully. In one more moment he would be sinking his teeth into the rabbit's soft neck . . . He went rigid at the rumbling sound of galloping horses. Looking over his shoulder, he saw Lord Chao himself bearing down upon him at the head of a hunting party. Lord Chao! Everyone knew of Lord Chao's prowess with bow and arrow. Where Lord Chao aimed, there Lord Chao struck! A

Vocabulary
prowess (prou′ is) *n.* great ability or skill

Reading the Selection

SUMMARY

Tung Kuo is a man who has studied the philosophy of benevolence. Eager to practice it, he saves the life of a wolf running from hunters. When he is safe, the wolf wants to eat Tung Kuo. Tung Kuo seeks the wisdom of an elder who is to decide whether Tung Kuo should allow himself to be eaten so the wolf won't starve. The elder convinces Tung Kuo to kill the wolf.

Spanish Summaries, p. 21

A Active Reading Strategies

RESPOND Ask students to describe their first response to the wolf. Have them determine whether the wolf is to be a sympathetic character, supporting their conclusion with examples from the story. *(Wolves' reputations in folklore and this wolf's thirst for blood may lead most students to feel the wolf will not be a sympathetic character.)*

VOCABULARY Remind students to use context clues to unlock the meanings of new vocabulary words.

Additional Resources

- ***Active Reading Guide,*** p. 22
- ***Audio Library***
- ***Spanish Audio Library***

Teaching Support

CONNECTING TO OTHER SELECTIONS

The chart at the right shows three ways to connect "Bagged Wolf" to other selections in this book.

For specific teaching strategies, see the ***Theme Three Planning Guide.***

Connection	Title
Life Skills: Decision Making	from *Sound-Shadows of the New World* p. 213
Thematic: Weighing Possibilities	"Raymond's Run," p. 553
Literary: Descriptive Language	from *Harriet Tubman: Conductor on the Underground Railroad,* p. 480

B Active Reading Strategies

PREDICT Ask students to predict whether the wolf will be a protagonist or antagonist. *(Students may at first feel sympathy for the wounded wolf.)*

C Author's Craft

CHARACTERIZATION Explain to students that Tung Kuo is introduced as a kind person hoping to help someone or something in need. Ask students whether they think this description makes him seem vulnerable.

VIEWING THE DRAWING

During the Ming Dynasty (1368–1644) the decorative arts (such as cloisonné, enamelware, bronze- and lacquerwork, and furniture) flourished. Paintings and pottery from that period are particularly prized.

Viewing Response *The Mongol archer depicted in the painting might have been Lord Chao himself—whose skill with the bow and arrow while leading his party was famed. The warrior on horseback in the painting has the same air of confidence that we might expect from Lord Chao.*

B Like an arrow himself, the wolf sprang into the air. He was too late; Lord Chao's arrow was already on its way. It caught him in his hind leg. With a yelp of pain the wolf faltered, but there was no time to nurse the wound. He gave himself a strong push with his good hind leg and shot off down the mountain path. Lord Chao raised a fierce cry, and the whole party came thundering after him. B

C At this very time there was on the mountain path a certain Tung Kuo on his way to the capital. With his book bag, which was his sole belonging, he rode on

Mongol Archer on Horseback. Ming dynasty drawing. By courtesy of The Board of Trustees of The Victoria & Albert Museum, London.

Viewing the painting: Notice the man's dress, posture, and horse. What characteristics does he seem to share with Lord Chao?

Teaching Support

MEETING INDIVIDUAL NEEDS — ENGLISH LANGUAGE LEARNERS

-ing Forms English language learners may be confused by the various *-ing* forms. Helping verbs identify words that end in *-ing* as verbs. Point out that *prowling* is part of the past progressive verb form *was prowling;* this tense conveys continuous action in the past. Contrast this use with that of other *-ing* forms in the paragraph. *(munching, tastiest-looking, longing, would be sinking, rumbling, galloping, bearing down, hunting)*

Activity Discuss the basic functions of other *-ing* forms in the selection. Stay with simple distinctions between verb, noun, and adjective.

Additional Resources

English Language Learners Sourcebook

a tired skinny donkey, and love was in his mind—love for every human being under the sun. He belonged to a brotherhood that believed peace and happiness would come to the world if everyone would practice self-denial for the good of his fellow men. Tung Kuo, being a devoted disciple in this belief, positively ached to practice benevolence. When he saw clouds of dust rising from the ground far away, and heard noises like roaring drums, his first thought was that he might even now be put to the test of loving-kindness.

The wolf, an arrow dragging from his hind leg and blood tracing the dust behind him, came plump in front of him.

"O Merciful Sir!" the beast gasped, "please take pity on me. Save me from Lord Chao!" His chest heaved with the effort to get the words out. "Save me, and I shall repay you in my heart as long as I live!"

The sad sight of the suffering wolf would have unlocked a much stonier heart than Tung Kuo's. "Fear nothing, my good friend," he said. "Even though I myself should be killed by Lord Chao, I shall not deliver you into his bloody hands. I am a follower of the great philosopher[1] Mo-tzu and obey his teachings of love for all mankind, er, and wolfkind." He had climbed off his donkey and knelt beside the wolf. "Be patient and bear a little pain, my good fellow. I must first remove the arrow." Gently, he pulled the arrow from the beast's hind leg.

"Hurry! Hurry!" the wolf cried impatiently. "They are coming closer and closer. I must hide!" He looked about him with eyes of desperation, and then stared at the bag on the donkey's back. "There! Empty out that bag and I'll hide in it."

Obligingly Tung Kuo emptied all the books from his bag and, taking hold of the wolf's scruff, started stuffing him head first into the bag. Very shortly he had a bag full of wolf, except for the hind legs. They sprawled stubbornly out of the top. Hauling the wolf out, he stuffed the spindly hind legs in first, but then he ended with a pointed mouth and black nose jutting out. Head first, hind legs hanging out; legs first, nose showing—he tried and tried again, but he couldn't get everything belonging to the wolf inside the bag.

The distant cloud of dust was growing bigger and closer. Desperately, the wolf cried, "Tie my legs together, stupid! Anything! But hurry! Hurry!"

With the rope from round his waist, Tung Kuo tied up the wolf's legs, and tugging and shoving, managed finally to stuff all of him into the bag. Then he picked up the scattered books and crammed them in wherever he could find space—between the wolf's front and hind legs, under his nose, against his flanks, on top of his head. At last he got the bag closed and, with his remaining strength, heaved it up on the donkey's back. He was scarcely able to totter along the path from weakness, and had indeed moved only twenty footfalls when his way was blocked by Lord Chao himself, looming high on his horse.

1. A *philosopher* studies the meaning and purpose of life and the universe.

Vocabulary

benevolence (bə nev′ ə ləns) *n.* kindliness; generosity
loom (lo͞om) *v.* to appear or come into view in a way that seems very large and, often, threatening

D Critical Thinking

DRAWING CONCLUSIONS Ask students whether they think Tung Kuo is eager to help. Encourage students to think about whether they respect this character and to explain the reasons for their opinions. *(He seems to be more eager to please than to help.)*

E Literary Elements

RISING ACTION Explain to students that rising action occurs when "the plot thickens." In this story, as in many fables and folktales, rising action occurs when the nonhuman characters' human characteristics take over.

F Active Reading Strategies

REVIEW Ask students to recall what bag this is *(his sole belonging)* and what Tung Kuo's emptying it so readily tells the reader about his character. *(He is generous and willing to help at almost any cost.)*

Reading Minilesson

Main Idea and Supporting Details
Many folktales use strong visual images as the supporting details to make their point.

Activity Have students identify the vivid supporting details from the story that help define the story's main idea. Discuss with students what they think the main idea of the story is and ask them to identify the supporting details. **L2**

Additional Resources

Reading Skills Practice Workbook

G Active Reading Strategies

EVALUATE Ask students whether they think Tung Kuo has lied to Lord Chao. Encourage them to think about whether his exchange with Lord Chao is consistent with his philosophies.

H Literary Elements

FIGURATIVE LANGUAGE Ask students to explain what is meant by "all melting heart and wet cheeks" as a description of Tung Kuo's "kind." *(Lord Chao obviously doesn't respect the philosophies of Tung Kuo's religion. Lord Chao is a warrior and regards kind-heartedness as weakness.)*

I Literary Elements

RISING ACTION Much of the rising action in this story develops through dialogue. Encourage students to comment on why dialogue can be more effective in developing plot than a narrator's description of events. *(Dialogue allows a character's tone to be presented and allows the reader to identify with him or her.)*

"Have you seen a wolf?" Lord Chao demanded harshly. "A wounded wolf?"

G Tung Kuo tried to keep his voice steady. "A wounded wolf, my Lord? A wolf is a very cunning animal. He would not run on an open way like this. Have you looked into the hidden paths in the woods?"

H Lord Chao scowled down at him. "I know your kind," he said. "All melting heart and wet cheeks." Suddenly drawing his sword from its scabbard,[2] Lord Chao with a fearful stroke whipped it against a nearby sapling, which fell instantly to the ground. Then he pointed the tip of the sword at Tung Kuo's throat. "Such is the fate of anything that earns my displeasure. Should you find this wolf and aid him in any way to escape me, I shall be mightily displeased with you! Do you understand?"

Quaking, Tung Kuo tried to jerk his eyes from the glittering sword. "Oh, yes, my Lord, I understand very well. I should not like to suffer such a fate, you may depend on that!"

No sooner had the pounding of hooves died away than the wolf began a great noise. "Let me out, let me out! Hurry, will you! I am smothering to death!"

In the urgency of freeing the poor wolf, Tung Kuo let his own fear of Lord Chao slip from his mind. The wolf, however, with his feet squarely on the ground once more, looked up into Tung Kuo's face with a wicked grin.

I "Dear Benevolent Sir, thank you for saving my life from Lord Chao. Unfortunately you have not saved it all the way. Not having eaten this entire day, I am perishing of hunger. If I do not have something to eat soon, I shall die and your effort at saving me will have been in vain. As a matter of fact," he went on cunningly, "I would rather be killed by Lord Chao and served on the table of a nobleman than be starved to death on the roadside and devoured by foul scavengers. As you are such a true advocate of universal love, you won't mind giving up your life to save mine!"

Tung Kuo had no time to reason. With mouth wide open and tongue slavering over his polished white teeth, the wolf charged right at him. The scholar leapt behind his donkey, and from that point dodged the wolf's assaults by jumping to the left or to the right as the animal lunged at him.

When the wolf stood still for a moment with lowered head and panting breath, Tung Kuo reproached[3] him. "When you begged me to save you, did you not say that you would be grateful and would repay me? Now you are safe and sound, you try to eat me. What an ungrateful wolf you are!"

"Not ungrateful," said the wolf craftily, "but a wolf, to be sure. Human beings are the natural enemies of wolves and must be eaten at every opportunity."

"I can scarcely agree with you there," said Tung Kuo. He was thinking furiously. The sun was no longer high. When it went down, and the wolves came in packs, he would surely be eaten. He cleared his

2. A *scabbard* is the case for the blade of a sword, bayonet, or similar weapon.

3. When Tung Kuo *reproached* the wolf, he scolded or blamed him for a fault.

Vocabulary

scavenger (skav′ in jər) *n.* an animal, such as a hyena or vulture, that feeds on dead, decaying plants or animals

advocate (ad′ və kit) *n.* one who publicly supports or urges

Teaching Support

MEETING INDIVIDUAL NEEDS — MULTIPLE MODES OF EXPRESSION

Musical Students with musical abilities may benefit from using rhythm, pitch, and tone to express feelings and ideas. Encourage these students to reflect on the three characters and the distinct emotions they convey on page 272. Have students think of appropriate music that might be played in the background of each character's dialogue.

Activity Have students select music to accompany the dialogue of the characters in this story: Tung Kuo, Lord Chao, the wolf, the tree, and the cow. The music selected should accompany a specific section of the dialogue in the story. The music should reflect the student's interpretation of each character's personality or the emotion being conveyed through the dialogue. **L2**

Blue Tree, 1909–1910. Piet Mondrian. Oil on composition board, 22⅜ x 29½ in. Dallas Museum of Art. Foundation for the Arts Collection. Gift of James H. and Lillian Clark Foundation.

Viewing the painting: How is the subject of Mondrian's painting like the tree in this story?

throat. "As we are both rather winded from all this dashing and dodging about, permit me to propose a solution. The old custom in the case of a dispute is to seek the wisdom of three elders. Let us do that. Their judgments will decide whether you should eat me or not. If they all say yes, I shall of course oblige."

"Very well," said the wolf, "and fair enough. I am weary of all this sparring[4] about. Let us go in search of three elders, then."

They trod on peacefully for a while, but the wolf quickly grew restless when they met nobody on the path. He came to a stop in front of an old tree with most of its branches chopped off.

"We'll ask this tree."

"Ask a tree! Whoever heard of—"

"I am HUNGRY," growled the wolf. "Go on and ask before I forget myself."

Tung Kuo hastily bowed to the tree and, from beginning to now, related the whole

4. Here, *sparring* refers to arguing in a cautious, restrained way, as if the two were testing one another's strength.

Viewing the Painting

Piet Mondrian (1872–1944) was born in, and greatly influenced by the artistic tradition of, the Netherlands. His work evolved from traditional realism, through the abstract-art movement known as *de Stijl* ("the Style"), to his own "neoplastic" style—straight lines in primary colors and black and white.

Viewing Response *The tree in the story was once colorful, laden with leaves, flowers, and fruit. Now it is old, bears no more fruit, and has had branches cut off for firewood. The tree in Mondrian's painting could be likened to the great old tree, now beyond its fruit-bearing years but having stood the test of time.*

J Literary Elements

CHARACTERIZATION Remind students that authors often use dialogue to give the reader a picture of their characters. Ask students to describe Tung Kuo on the basis of the way he speaks. Does he seem to be a wise philosopher?

K Active Reading Strategies

PREDICT Given that the wolf is talking to Tung Kuo, ask students to predict whether the tree will answer. *(Most students will expect the tree to answer.)*

Interdisciplinary Connection

Science In this story the wolf is portrayed as a sly animal that eats human beings; however, wolves in real life are frightened by people, and wolf attacks are extremely rare. Have students think about how much they really know about animal wildlife and from where their information comes. Point out that television, movies, stories, and cartoons may give a false impression about the real nature of animals.

Activity Have students do research on a particular animal of their choice. Instruct them to look for sources that include information on the habits, the personalities, and the populations of the animal they have selected. Students should consider all of this information to define a thesis on their subject, and then present their findings to the class in an oral report. **L2**

WHICH WAY TO GO? 273

L **Literary Elements**

SYMBOLISM Explain to students that the tree represents bitter people. Point out that fables often use things or animals to symbolize universal qualities. Ask students to list other symbols from the story and describe how these symbols help them interpret the story. *(The wolf symbolizes narrow self-interest.)*

M **Active Reading Strategies**

QUESTION Ask students why they think the wolf has chosen the old, run-down cow to ask for an opinion. *(Most likely the cow will have a grudge against human beings.)*

N **Literary Elements**

RISING ACTION Encourage students to think about how the stories the tree and the cow tell contribute to the climax of the story. *(The answers of the tree and the cow heighten the sense of menace to Tung Kuo.)*

Teaching Support

incident in all its details. "And so," he asked at the end of the recital, "is it your opinion that the wolf should eat me after all?"

A booming voice issued from the tree, and Tung Kuo stepped hastily back. "Now that you have told me what you think is a piteous tale, let me tell you about *me*. You could hardly guess that I am an apricot tree. The gardener planted me from a seed, and within a year I gave flowers; a few years later I gave fruit. In ten years my trunk was as big as the gardener's arms about me. The gardener sold my fruits, rested in my shade, and made a great profit. But now I am old and dying and can give no more fruit or thick shade. The only time the gardener comes to me is to cut off more of my limbs for firewood. I have repeatedly begged him to pity my old age and spare me the gashes of his axe and hatchet, but he turns a deaf ear. All my good services mean nothing to him! And you ask *me* whether this wolf in his desperate plight of starvation shouldn't eat you? I say yes! Eat, eat! And when he is finished, may he find the gardener and make a hearty meal of him too!"

Saliva drooling from his jaws, the wolf leapt up to attack Tung Kuo on the spot.

"Not just yet!" said Tung Kuo sternly. "You made an agreement, and you must stick by it. We have two more opinions to seek."

Unwillingly, the wolf swallowed back his saliva as best he could, and the two walked on again to the sound of the wolf's rumbling stomach. After a short time they saw a tired old cow leaning against a half-fallen wall.

"Go and ask that good dame," the wolf demanded. "She looks full of age and wisdom."

"But what is a cow's wisdom . . . ?"

The wolf growled threateningly. "I am about to start biting you!"

Tung Kuo hurriedly addressed himself to the old cow, who stared stonily at him, licked her cracked nose, and when the story finished with the apricot tree's verdict, fetched up a sigh that made her skinny flanks quiver. "The tree is certainly right. Listen to *my* story. The farmer bartered an old knife for me when I was but a calf. I soon got my strength and began to earn a living for him. I pulled his hunting cart while he tasted the joys of hunting; when he tilled the soil, I pulled the plow. I gave my strength freely. In those days, you should have seen how poor he was! In his kitchen there was never enough rice at one time to last three days, and his wine jug held only dust most of the year. If it weren't for me, his wife would still be wearing coarse drab clothes instead of silk and brocade and he would not be playing the country squire with his herds of cows and his fine horses. Every thread of silk, every grain of rice came from *my* efforts." She gave her head a weary toss. "Look at me, if you will. I am old and sick and can no longer work, so they send me out to the field where the sun burns me by day and the icy wind cuts into my skin by night. I heard the farmer's wife complain about wasting feed on me. 'There should be no waste in the whole cow,' she said. 'The skin can be turned into leather, the flesh

Vocabulary
plight (plīt) *n.* an unfortunate or dangerous situation
barter (bär′ tər) *v.* to trade goods for goods

Real-World Connection

Animals in Cartoons Have students find cartoons that deal with encounters between people and animals. They may focus on how the encounter changes an attitude toward animals in general or particular species. Have the class share the cartoons. Students should answer such questions as *What is the nature of the encounter? What attitudes change?* **L2**

N sold as meat and the bones and horns sold for bone meal or even for carving!'

"And then," and the cow's voice sank lower, "just last night she came out here with the son and pointed her long finger at me. 'My son,' she said, 'you have been apprenticed to the butcher for three years now. It is time to sharpen your knife and practice your art.' Bought for a knife, and now slaughtered by one! That is my fate."

The cow drew another long breath. "You say the wolf is thankless and ungrateful. What right have you to demand his thanks? Have you given him your whole life as I did to the farmer? The apricot tree is right. The wolf should eat you. And I can think of some other morsels for his next meal."

O With a joyous snarl, the wolf bared his pointed teeth and made to spring upon Tung Kuo, but the scholar stayed him with an upraised hand. "Not yet!" he said with all the sternness he could bring out of his quivering heart. "There is still more advice to seek, and I believe I see an elder approaching us even now. I shall speak to him."

P Tung Kuo ran ahead of the wolf to meet the old man coming towards them. He had silvery white hair and a long silvery beard, and he carried a staff in his hand.

"O my Venerable[5] Sir," Tung Kuo cried out, "how glad I am to see a fellow man! Only a wise elder like yourself can save me."

"That is possible," said the old man gravely. "What is your trouble, my good friend?"

Q "It is like a nightmare," began Tung Kuo. "This morning when I was on my way to the capital I met this wolf who begged me to save him from Lord Chao's arrows and I did. Can you believe that when the wolf came out safe and sound, he demanded a meal of my body! I finally persuaded him to seek the wisdom of three elders before taking the first bite, but O Sir, that has been another nightmare until now. The wolf insisted that we ask an old apricot tree and an old cow. Both of them bear grudges against men, so of course they sided with the wolf. And now at last heaven is beginning to show pity on me. Only your great wisdom can save me from becoming wolf-fodder."[6]

The wise old man shook his head and pointed his staff at the wolf. "Tung Kuo saved your life, did he not? And you want to repay him by eating him up? Miserable creature who fears neither man nor God! Ungrateful and thankless beast! Scamp back to your den lest I kill you with this stick!"

"Oh, no, not yet, Venerable One," the wolf pleaded. "You have heard only half the story. Be fair and listen to my side as well. You see, Tung Kuo *pretended* to save me, but deep in his heart he planned to kill me all along by tying up my legs and crushing me into his bag with his books. To make certain, he closed the bag tight to suffocate me. Further, my stomach was doubled up and my back sprained with having to curve it. It is a surprise that I came out alive at all! Now tell me, wise old gentleman, does he not deserve to be eaten?"

5. A *venerable* (ven′ ər ə bəl) person deserves respect because of age, character, or rank.

6. Usually, *fodder* refers to the dried hay or grass fed to farm animals. Wolves prefer meat.

Vocabulary
gravely (grāv′ lē) *adv.* very seriously

O Literary Elements

RISING ACTION Point out to students that the wolf's behavior after the answer leads to the climax. His eagerness to eat Tung Kuo makes the rising action more alarming.

P Critical Thinking

DRAWING CONCLUSIONS Ask students why they think Tung Kuo is relieved to seek the advice of a human. Do they think that only a human will be fair in judgment? Or do they think that Tung Kuo relies on the fact that he and the man share a common human bond? *(He is focusing on the common bond.)*

Q Critical Thinking

SYNTHESIZE Have students review Tung Kuo's and the wolf's arguments to the elder. Encourage students to rephrase Tung Kuo's argument in light of what the wolf says in his response. Have students consider the following model before they answer:

Model: Tung Kuo tells how he saved the wolf's life, but he leaves out most of the details of how he did this. The wolf's response uses the missing details to make Tung Kuo look bad. I think Tung Kuo's argument should have included the fact that the wolf asked to have his legs tied up and to be put in the bag to avoid being seen.

Writing Minilesson

Symbolism Explain that when writers give human attributes to nonhuman objects, the reader can often see the animal or human problem or condition more clearly than they would otherwise. The cow's and the tree's stories reveal bitter, selfish characters.

Activity Ask students to think of a negative character trait, such as jealousy or greed. Then have them imagine an inanimate object that might symbolize this trait. Have them write a brief story from the object's point of view, demonstrating the trait. Encourage students to use dialogue to present the character's point of view. **L2**

Vo•cab•u•lar•y Skills

Dictionaries Point out to students that sometimes the adjectives or adverbs used to modify words are *redundant* in that they repeat part of the definition of the word; for example, "free gift," and "devil-hearted fiend." Have students look up the meanings of *gift* and *fiend* to identify that the adjectives used to modify these words are redundant.

Thematic Focus

Which Way to Go? Tung Kuo tries to apply the lessons of kindness he has been taught but learns that benevolence must be practiced wisely. Encourage students to explore the idea that performing good deeds may not always be the right thing to do. Students may cite parts of the story or their own personal experiences in their responses.

ASSESSMENT

Quick Checks, p. 22

The old man looked questioningly at Tung Kuo. "If this is the case, then you are also to blame."

Tung Kuo was alarmed by the old man's sudden change of attitude. "But good sir, you must see that the wolf—"

"Please be quiet," the wise man said sternly. "I am really confused and don't know whom to believe. I have got it firmly in mind as far as the wolf's being wounded by Lord Chao and seeking help from Tung Kuo, but after that I begin to get muddled. Would you be so kind as to reenact the scene for me so that I can see the whole thing for myself and make my fair judgment on who was saved or who was suffocated and beaten half to death by books."

Both the wolf and Tung Kuo were eager to oblige. Tung Kuo tied up the wolf's legs and shut him up tightly in the bag while the wise old man nodded his head sagely.

When the wolf was secure, the wise old man bent towards Tung Kuo. "Have you a dagger?" He made a stabbing motion towards the sack.

Tung Kuo stared at him aghast. "You don't mean that I should *kill* him!"

The wise old man gave a scornful snort. "Will you then release him to eat the both of us? No matter what my judgment is, do you think the wolf will let you reach the capital when you are the only meal in sight? Even if you leave him tied up here in your sack, how long before he eats through your precious books and the rope round his legs and is hot-tongued on your trail? Humane[7] you are—there is no question of that—but you are also worse than a fool. You would remove one humane soul from the world and leave in its place a devil-hearted fiend that preys on humanity."

Tung Kuo slowly drew his dagger from its sheath and looked from it to the humpy bookbag, still undecided. Were the years of teaching and learning to end in the thrust of a dagger into a living being's hide, or—and he smiled grimly—in the thrust of sharp claw and pointed fang into his own living hide? His hide and how many others after he had been gulped down? The bookbag stirred. There was a sound as of teeth gnawing on rope . . .

Tung Kuo killed the wolf.

Ming dynasty (1368–1644)

7. A person who is *humane* shows sympathy and kindness toward humans and animals.

Vocabulary

sagely (sāj′ lē) *adv.* very wisely

aghast (ə gast′) *adj.* filled with fear or horror

Teaching Support

Grammar and Language *Minilesson*

Punctuating Dialogue Remind students that end punctuation used with dialogue must be placed inside quotation marks. Write the following sentence on the board: *"Now tell me, wise old gentleman, does he not deserve to be eaten?"* Point out that the question mark at the end of the question is inside the end quotation mark.

Activity Have students identify as many punctuation marks at the end of dialogue as they can find, on this page or any other. They should note that regardless of the type of punctuation mark used for the dialogue, all are placed within the quotation marks. **L2**

Additional Resources

- ***Grammar and Language Transparency 21***
- ***Grammar and Language Workbook,*** p. 267
- ***Grammar and Composition Handbook,*** Lesson 13.6
- ***Writer's Choice,*** Lesson 20.6

Responding to Literature

PERSONAL RESPONSE

- Were you surprised by the ending? Why or why not?

Brackets connect questions that are paired to develop higher-level thinking skills.

Analyzing Literature

RECALL

1. What does Tung Kuo's brotherhood teach?
2. Why, according to the apricot tree and the cow, do the owners turn their backs on them?
3. After Tung Kuo tells the old man his side of the story, what story does the wolf tell?
4. What does Tung Kuo finally do to the wolf?

INTERPRET

5. A **stereotype** is a general statement about a group of people in which the individual differences are overlooked. Lord Chao stereotypes Tung Kuo when he says, "I know your kind. All melting heart and wet cheeks." What type of person does Lord Chao think Tung Kuo is? Why?
6. When Tung Kuo says the wolf is thankless, the cow replies, "What right have you to demand his thanks?" How might the cow answer her own question? Why?
7. After the wolf says Tung Kuo planned his murder, the old man acts confused, even though he is wise. How might you explain this apparent contradiction?
8. At the close, Tung Kuo asks, "Were the years of teaching and learning to end in the thrust of a dagger . . . ?" What might Tung Kuo answer? Why?

EVALUATE AND CONNECT

9. How dedicated is Tung Kuo to his brotherhood? Give three examples to support your answer.
10. Tung Kuo says, "The old custom in the case of a dispute is to seek the wisdom of three elders." Do you agree with this method? Give two reasons.

LITERARY ELEMENTS

Rising Action

Every good plot contains **rising action,** the point at which the action gets complicated and characters come into conflict with each other. Rising action begins with the events that set up a **conflict,** or central problem. As the conflict unfolds, a sense of excitement builds about what will happen next. Rising action leads up to the **climax,** the turning point in the story when the conflict is usually resolved. Review the action in "Bagged Wolf" to find the rising action.

1. When does the rising action begin?
2. When does it end? How do you know?

● See **Literary Terms Handbook,** p. R8.

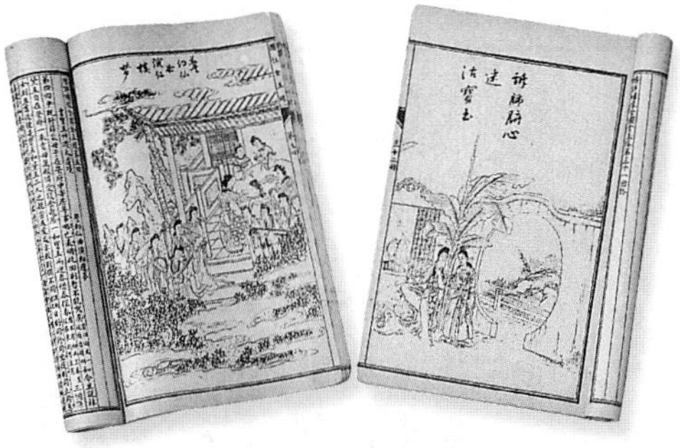

Responding to the Selection

PERSONAL RESPONSE

Some students may have been surprised by the ending. They should relate their reaction to earlier predictions they made about the characters.

Analyzing Literature

1. It teaches kindness and benevolence.
2. They turn their backs on them because human beings are greedy and selfish.
3. The wolf twists the truth to make Tung Kuo look evil.
4. He kills the wolf.
5. Lord Chao thinks Tung Kuo is weak and naïve because he is kind and patient.
6. Tung Kuo has a right to demand the wolf's thanks because he saved the wolf's life.
7. The old man is trying to play a trick on the wolf and needs to convince the wolf that the confusion requires reenactment of the scene.
8. Responses should reflect an understanding that Tung Kuo has learned that there would be no value to society in his sacrificing himself so that the wolf, who will eat others, can live.
9. Tung Kuo's willingness to help the wolf, to use his only possession to save the wolf, and to be eaten by the wolf prove he is dedicated. His bargain to get the opinion of three others and his ultimate stabbing of the wolf are examples that his dedication has limits.
10. Some students may refer to the earlier story about the wise old woman and the lesson the lord learned in that story.

LITERARY ELEMENTS

1. It begins when Tung Kuo meets the wolf on the road.
2. It ends when Tung Kuo kills the wolf. This is when the conflict is resolved.

Additional Resources

Literary Elements Transparency 22

WHICH WAY TO GO? 277

Literature and Writing

Writing About Literature

Students' responses should

- explain the symbolism of the wolf
- examine the wolf's characteristics
- include examples from the story

Creative Writing

Students' scenes should

- include dialogue, narrative description, and intense action
- feature themselves as main characters

Extending Your Response

Literature Groups Students' presentations should state an opinion (whether they agree or disagree with the statement). The opinions should be well thought-out. **COLLAB. LEARN.**

Performance Students' performances should include entertaining storytelling techniques.

Interdisciplinary Activity
Students' reports should demonstrate that they have researched the topic, discuss the behavior of wolves toward human beings, and use details to support their answer to one of the questions asked.

Literature and Writing

Writing About Literature

Symbolism What do you think the wolf symbolizes, or stands for? Intelligence? Weakness? Justice? Examine the wolf's characteristics. Look at what he says and how he treats people. What do other characters think of the wolf? Discuss these questions with a small group. Then, together, write a brief explanation of what the wolf symbolizes. Support your explanation with examples from the story.

Creative Writing

Scene from a Short Story Think about your response in the **Reading Focus** on page 268 and imagine that you are Tung Kuo. What will you do when the wolf informs you that you are about to become his dinner? Rewrite this scene from the story with yourself as the main character. Use dialogue, description, and action to increase reader interest. Read the scene to your classmates.

Extending Your Response

Literature Groups

Worse Than a Fool? The wise old man tells Tung Kuo, "Humane you are–there is no question of that–but you are also worse than a fool." Do you agree with this statement? In your group, discuss reasons this statement about Tung Kuo might be true, then discuss reasons it might not be true. Present your conclusions to the class.

Performing

Wag Your Tale These stories were handed down from generation to generation in the oral tradition. Try your hand at storytelling. Choose a folktale other students might find interesting. Study the story, then tell it to your classmates. Use body gestures, facial expressions, varying tones of voice, and other storytelling techniques to entertain your listeners.

interNET CONNECTION

Investigate wolves throughout the world by keying the words *wolf* or *canid* into a search engine.

Interdisciplinary Activity

Life Science Is the wolf in this Chinese folktale true to life? Prepare a brief report on wolves and their behavior toward humans. Focus on one or two questions like these: Do wolves travel alone? Do they attack humans? Do people hunt wolves? Do wolves ever act sly or play tricks on people? Use the information you find to develop a coherent thesis and make a clear and well-supported conclusion.

Save your work for your portfolio.

Skill Minilessons

RETEACH • REVIEW

GRAMMAR AND LANGUAGE • PUNCTUATING COMPOUND SENTENCES

An **independent clause** has a subject and predicate and can stand alone as a complete sentence. A **compound sentence** contains two or more independent clauses. The clauses usually are joined with a **coordinating conjunction** (*and, but, for, or, nor, so,* and *yet*) and are punctuated with a comma just before the conjunction.

Lord Chao raised a fierce cry, and the whole party came thundering after him.

PRACTICE Rewrite each pair of independent clauses as a compound sentence, using a comma and the coordinating conjunction that makes sense.

1. His stomach fairly ached with longing. He advanced carefully.
2. Save me. I shall repay you in my heart as long as I live!
3. He tried and tried again. He couldn't get everything belonging to the wolf inside the bag.

- For more about punctuation, see **Language Handbook,** pp. R38–R39.

READING AND THINKING • SUMMARIZING

Summarizing is restating what you read in your own words. A summary is a brief description of the main ideas in a longer work. Summarizing can help you better understand and remember the information in a story.

PRACTICE Practice your skill at summarizing with "Bagged Wolf." In one or two paragraphs, summarize the plot of this story. Stick to the major events and use transition words such as *next* and *then* so your reader can follow your ideas easily. Ask a classmate to compare your summary to the original text to see how accurately you have summarized the main ideas and critical details.

- For more about summarizing, see **Reading Handbook,** p. R100.

VOCABULARY • LATIN ROOTS

Many Latin words form roots for English words. For example, *advocate* contains the root *voc.* It comes from the Latin word *vocare,* which means "to call." The Latin prefix *ad-* means "to or toward"; therefore, an *advocate* is someone who is "called to" another person to help his or her cause. Your *advocate* in court is your lawyer. A *consumer advocate* is someone who stands up for consumers and cares about the safety and quality of products.

PRACTICE Use what you know about the root *voc* to answer the questions. (Note: *voc* is sometimes spelled *vok.*) Use a dictionary to check your answer.

1. If you *provoke* laughter in someone, do you make the person start laughing or stop laughing? (Clue: *pro-* means "forth.")
2. If something *evokes* a memory, does it make you remember or make you forget? (Clue: *e-* means "out.")
3. If you *invoke* a law, do you break it, make it, or make use of it? (Clue: *in-* means "on.")

Skill Minilessons

GRAMMAR AND LANGUAGE
PUNCTUATING COMPOUND SENTENCES

1. His stomach fairly ached with longing, but he advanced carefully.
2. Save me, and I shall repay you in my heart as long as I live.
3. He tried and tried again, but he couldn't get everything belonging to the wolf inside the bag.

READING AND THINKING
SUMMARIZING

Responses should be presented in a logical order. Students should include only the major events necessary to understand the story. Summary evaluations should assess accuracy, level of detail, and communication of key ideas.

VOCABULARY
LATIN ROOT *VOC*

1. Start laughing
2. Remember
3. Make use of it

Additional Resources

- ***Grammar and Language Workbook,*** p. 265
- ***Grammar and Composition Handbook,*** Lesson 14.1
- ***Writer's Choice,*** Lesson 8.6
- ***Vocabulary Practice,*** p. 19

ASSESSMENT

- ***Quick Checks,*** p. 22
- ***Selection and Theme Assessment,*** pp. 37–38
- ***Performance Assessment,*** p. 21
- ***Testmaker: ExamView Pro***
- ***Interactive Tutor: Self-Assessment***

Reading and Thinking Skills

Objective

- To learn to monitor comprehension of literature

Teaching Strategies

After reading the strategies for comprehension, ask students to share some of the strategies they use to help them understand what they read. Encourage them to discuss which methods are most and least effective.

Activities

1. Tung Kuo is a poor but loving person. He follows the religious belief that he must sacrifice all for the good of others. He is eager to help others.
2. It suggests Tung Kuo will have the opportunity to help.

Additional Resources

Reading Skills Practice Workbook

Teaching Support

Reading and Thinking Skills

Monitoring Comprehension

Reading is a discussion between you and the writer. To get the most from your reading, you'll need to monitor your comprehension, or check your understanding of the information. Try these strategies as you read:

- Ask questions about things you don't understand. You may find the answers in the next paragraph or two.
- Jot down notes about what you *do* know. It may help you fill in gaps in your understanding.
- Read ahead to look for a main idea or to get an overview of a selection.
- Reread the passage or selection.

For more about monitoring comprehension, see **Reading Handbook,** pp. R93–R106.

ACTIVITY

Read the following passage from "Bagged Wolf," and use one or more of the strategies above to monitor your comprehension. Then answer the questions.

At this very time there was on the mountain path a certain Tung Kuo on his way to the capital. With his book bag, which was his sole belonging, he rode on a tired skinny donkey, and love was in his mind—love for every human being under the sun. He belonged to a brotherhood that believed peace and happiness would come to the world if everyone would practice self-denial for the good of his fellow men. Tung Kuo, being a devoted disciple in this belief, positively ached to practice benevolence. When he saw clouds of dust rising from the ground far away, and heard noises like roaring drums, his first thought was that he might even now be put to the test of loving-kindness.

1. What do you learn about Tung Kuo from this passage?
2. What does the last sentence suggest about what may happen next?

MEETING INDIVIDUAL NEEDS — SPECIAL NEEDS

Learning Disabled Some students may have difficulty identifying and ordering important information in the passage above. Explain that, before rereading a selection, they should review their notes and answer any vocabulary and comprehension questions they can. Then they should construct an outline of the selection. Headings will help order their notes.

Activity Work with students to outline the passage. On the board, write "1. Tung Kuo thinks about love as he travels on a mountain path." Encourage students to supply two additional points. Point out that outlines can help them review material later. **L2**

Additional Resources

Inclusion Strategies

Before You Read

The Moustache

MEET ROBERT CORMIER

"I've aimed for the intelligent reader and have often found that that reader is fourteen years old," said Robert Cormier. He didn't write to make people feel good. He'd rather have readers say of his work, "I don't *like* what happened, but that's the way it *could* happen." Cormier was well known for writing about themes that often appeal to young adults. Some of Cormier's stories focus on ways people respond to abuses of power by institutions.

Robert Cormier was born in 1925 and died in 2000. "The Moustache" was published in 1980 in a collection of short stories called Eight Plus One.

READING FOCUS

Why do you visit, phone, or write to grandparents or other older relatives? Have you visited relatives who live in a nursing home?

Discuss

Ask a partner to define "old." Discuss whether all older people have similar characteristics. Then share your observations with a larger group.

Setting a Purpose

Read to find out about a secret that a grandmother has kept to herself for many years.

BUILDING BACKGROUND

The Time and Place This story takes place in a modern-day nursing home.

Did You Know? Nursing homes are not homes for old people. They are housing for people of any age who require nursing care on a regular or temporary basis.

VOCABULARY PREVIEW

chronic (kron′ ik) *adj.* lasting a long time or returning repeatedly; p. 284

complex (kom′ pleks) *n.* an exaggerated concern or fear; an overwhelming idea or feeling; p. 284

craggy (krag′ ē) *adj.* rugged, uneven, and worn; p. 285

lapse (laps) *v.* to slip, drift, or fall (into); p. 286

lucid (lo͞o′ sid) *adj.* mentally alert; clear-headed; p. 286

conspiratorial (kən spir′ ə tôr′ ē əl) *adj.* joining or acting together, especially to carry out some secret or evil deed or for a hidden or illegal purpose; p. 287

regally (rē′ gəl lē) *adv.* in a grand, dignified manner, as if done by a king or queen; royally; p. 287

pretense (prē′ tens) *n.* a false show or appearance, especially for the purpose of deceiving; falseness; p. 289

serene (sə rēn′) *adj.* calm; peaceful; undisturbed; p. 290

Before Reading

Objectives

- To read and analyze a short story about a young man facing maturity
- To analyze character in a plot
- To write a comparison

Skills

Reading/Thinking: Identifying Main Idea and Supporting Details; Drawing Conclusions; Making Critical Judgments; Clarifying
Writing: Dialogue
Vocabulary: Multiple-Meaning Words; Roots
Grammar/Language: Proper Nouns; Adverb Phrases
Listening/Speaking: Performance
Collaboration: Literature Groups; Performance

Motivating STUDENTS

Selection Focus Transparency 22: Have students view the photograph and discuss what each person brings to the life of the other.

Reading Focus: As an extension of the Reading Focus, have students write a letter to someone real or imagined who is living in a nursing home. After reading the story, groups of students should discuss what to rewrite, add to, or delete from their letters. Ask students to read their revised letters to the class.

RESOURCE MANAGER

Teaching Tools and Resources
- Theme Three Planning Guide
- Literature Groups Sourcebook

Essential Lesson Support

Lesson-Specific Instruction
- Selection Focus Transparency 22
- Literary Elements Transparency 23
- Active Reading Guide,* p. 23
- Selection Vocabulary Practice, p. 20

Assessment
- Selection Quick Checks,* p. 23
- Sel. and Theme Assmt., pp. 39–40
- Testmaker: ExamView Pro
- Performance Assessment, p. 22

Systematic Language Instruction
- Gr. & Comp. Hbk., Lesson 5.1
- Vocabulary Power, Lesson 12

English Language Learners
- ELL Sourcebook, p. 43
- Spanish Summaries, p. 22
- Spanish Translations, pp. 71–77
- Audio Library*
- English, Yes!

Spec. Needs/Strat. Interven.
- Interactive Rdg. Sbk., pp. T103–T105
- Interactive Rdg. Wbk., pp. 48–49
- Inclusion Strat. Sbk., pp. 53–54
- Audio Library*

* Also available in Spanish

Reading the Selection

SUMMARY

Mike is a seventeen-year-old who wears a moustache to signify maturity. He visits his grandmother in a nursing home. Imagining that Mike is her husband, she asks forgiveness for an accusation for which she never apologized. Mike grants forgiveness and realizes his grandmother is a real person. He shaves off his moustache.

Spanish Summaries, p. 22

Active Reading Strategies

REVIEW Have students review the first paragraph and what it tells them about the several characters.

Additional Resources

- ***Active Reading Guide,*** p. 23
- ***Audio Library***
- ***Spanish Audio Library***

VIEWING THE PHOTOGRAPH

This still-life of several tools of the barber's trade focuses on what the refined gentleman of days past encountered when he indulged in a professional shave.

Teaching Support

CONNECTING TO OTHER SELECTIONS

The chart at the right shows three ways to connect "The Moustache" to other selections in this book.

For specific teaching strategies, see the ***Theme Three Planning Guide.***

Connection		Title
Life Skills: Interpersonal: Supporting and Contributing	→	"The Treasure of Lemon Brown," p. 5
Thematic: Understanding Grandparents	→	"The Medicine Bag," p. 78
Literary: Point of View	→	from *I Know Why the Caged Bird Sings,* p. 199

The Moustache

Robert Cormier

At the last minute Annie couldn't go. She was invaded by one of those twenty-four-hour flu bugs that sent her to bed with a fever, moaning about the fact that she'd also have to break her date with Handsome Harry Arnold that night. We call him Handsome Harry because he's actually handsome, but he's also a nice guy, cool, and he doesn't treat me like Annie's kid brother, which I am, but like a regular person. Anyway, I had to go to Lawnrest alone that afternoon. But first of all I had to stand inspection. My mother lined me up against the wall.

She stood there like a one-man firing squad, which is kind of funny because she's not like a man at all, she's very feminine, and we have this great relationship—I mean, I feel as if she really likes me. I realize that sounds strange, but I know guys whose mothers love them and cook special stuff for them and worry about them and all but there's something missing in their relationship.

Anyway. She frowned and started the routine.

"That hair," she said. Then admitted: "Well, at least you combed it."

I sighed. I have discovered that it's better to sigh than argue.

"And that moustache." She shook her head. "I still say a seventeen-year-old has no business wearing a moustache."

"It's an experiment," I said. "I just wanted to see if I could grow one." To tell the truth, I had proved my point about being able to grow a decent moustache, but I also had learned to like it.

"It's costing you money, Mike," she said.

"I know, I know."

The money was a reference to the movies. The Downtown Cinema has a special Friday night offer—half-price admission for high school couples, seventeen or younger. But the woman in the box office took one look at my moustache and charged me full price. Even when I showed her my driver's license. She charged full admission for Cindy's ticket, too, which left me practically broke and unable to take Cindy out for a hamburger with the crowd afterward. That didn't help matters, because Cindy has been getting impatient recently about things like the fact that I don't own my own car and have to concentrate on my studies if I want to win that college scholarship,[1] for instance. Cindy wasn't exactly crazy about the moustache, either.

Now it was my mother's turn to sigh.

"Look," I said, to cheer her up. "I'm thinking about shaving it off." Even though I wasn't. Another discovery: You can build a way of life on postponement.

1. A *scholarship* is money given to help a student continue his or her education. Scholarships are generally awarded for excellent work in high school and may also be based on financial need.

B Literary Elements

CHARACTERIZATION Given the narrator's description of his relationship with his mother, ask students to think about what kind of person the narrator is. *(He seems like a caring person.)*

C Active Reading Strategies

EVALUATE Ask students whether they think Mike is bothered by being mistaken for someone older than seventeen. Encourage students to consider what the moustache symbolizes for Mike. *(While Mike may not like the extra expense caused by his moustache, he seems to like the look of maturity it gives him.)*

LITERATURE & HUMANITIES

Have students examine *Sandia/Watermelon*, in *Introducing Art*, page 114. Then ask them to write an imagined journal entry in which the woman on the swing looks back on her life. What might she value? What might she be able to teach?

MEETING INDIVIDUAL NEEDS — ENGLISH LANGUAGE LEARNERS

Cultural References There are several allusions to American culture in this story. Explain to English language learners that very often a writer's reference to a single holiday memory, such as food, can be a shorthand way to set a mood or express an overall feeling about someone. Write the phrase *turkey dressing* on the board. Explain that turkey is a traditional Thanksgiving or Christmas meal.

Activity Have English language learners share information on holidays native to their countries and the traditional foods served. Help students to compare different traditions, including those mentioned in the story, and the feelings they evoke.

Additional Resources

English Language Learners Sourcebook, p. 43

D Literary Elements

CHARACTERIZATION Ask students what the reader knows, even before Mike's grandmother appears in the story, from Mike's description. *(She was lively and active, cooking and following baseball.)*

E Literary Elements

CHARACTERIZATION Explain that understanding a character's motivation is important to understanding a character's development. Ask students why they think Mike is going to visit his grandmother. *(He is going out of a sense of duty.)*

F Author's Craft

IMAGERY Point out that the author uses *sensory imagery,* appealing to the senses, to convey what the nursing home is like. Call for examples. *(He appeals to the sense of smell with his discussion of the nursing home's "absence of odor.")*

Vo•cab•u•lar•y Skills

Connotation and Denotation Making a connection between *antiseptic* and *impersonal* in the second column of this page can help students grasp the negative connotation of *antiseptic* (unwelcoming, boring) as opposed to its denotation, "free from contamination, bare." Use such contexts as "the empty white walls in the antiseptic room" to help students comprehend shades of meaning.

"Your grandmother probably won't even recognize you," she said. And I saw the shadow fall across her face.

Let me tell you what the visit to Lawnrest was all about. My grandmother is seventy-three years old. She is a resident—which is supposed to be a better word than *patient*—at the Lawnrest Nursing Home. She used to make the greatest turkey dressing in the world and was a nut about baseball and could even quote batting averages, for crying out loud. She always rooted for the losers. D She was in love with the Mets until they started to win. Now she has arteriosclerosis, which the dictionary says is "a chronic disease characterized by abnormal thickening and hardening of the arterial walls." Which really means that she can't live at home anymore or even with us, and her memory has betrayed her as well as her body. She used to wander off and sometimes didn't recognize people. My mother visits her all the time, driving the thirty miles to Lawnrest almost every day. Because Annie was home for a semester break from college, we had decided to make a special Saturday visit. Now Annie was in bed, groaning theatrically[2]—she's a drama major—but I told my mother I'd go, anyway. I hadn't seen my grandmother since she'd been admitted to Lawnrest. Besides, the place is located on the Southwest Turnpike, which meant I could barrel along in my father's new Le Mans. My ambition was to see the speedometer hit seventy-five. Ordinarily, I used the old station wagon, which can barely stagger up to fifty.

Frankly, I wasn't too crazy about visiting a nursing home. They reminded me of hospitals and hospitals turn me off. I mean, the smell of ether makes me nauseous, and I feel faint at the sight of blood. And as I approached Lawnrest—which is a terrible cemetery kind of name, to begin with—I was sorry I hadn't avoided the trip. Then I felt guilty about it. I'm loaded with guilt complexes. Like driving like a madman after promising my father to be careful. Like sitting in the parking lot, looking at the nursing home with dread and thinking how I'd rather be with Cindy. Then I thought of all the Christmas and birthday gifts my grandmother had given me and I got out of the car, guilty, as usual. E

Inside, I was surprised by the lack of hospital smell, although there was another odor or maybe the absence of an odor. The air was antiseptic, sterile. As if there was no atmosphere at all or I'd caught a cold suddenly and couldn't taste or smell. F

A nurse at the reception desk gave me directions—my grandmother was in East Three. I made my way down the tiled corridor and was glad to see that the walls were painted with cheerful colors like yellow and pink. A wheelchair suddenly shot around a corner, self-propelled by an old man, white-haired and toothless, who cackled merrily as he barely missed me. I jumped aside—here I was, almost getting wiped out by a two-mile-an-hour wheelchair after doing seventy-five on the pike. As I walked through the corridor seeking East Three, I couldn't help glancing into the rooms, and it was like some kind of wax museum—all these figures in various

2. When Annie groans *theatrically,* she overdoes her groaning so that it suggests a performance by an actor.

Vocabulary

chronic (kron′ ik) *adj.* lasting a long time or returning repeatedly

complex (kom′ pleks) *n.* an exaggerated concern or fear; an overwhelming idea or feeling

Teaching Support

Reading Minilesson

Identify Main Idea and Supporting Details This is a story of character development. Explain that the first part of the story depicts the main character up to the time of the climax that will cause a change in him. Therefore, to understand the change the character undergoes, it is important to know his initial character according to the details provided by the author.

Activity Have students fill out two charts like the one at the right, thinking of the description of the narrator's character before and after his visit to his grandmother. Then have students list the details that support their characterizations of him. **L2**

Additional Resources

Reading Skills Practice Workbook

Mike's Character Before the Meeting
Supporting Detail
Supporting Detail
Supporting Detail
Supporting Detail

Aunt Fanny (Old Lady in Black), 1920. George Wesley Bellows. Oil on canvas, 44¼ x 34¼ in. Purchased with funds from the Edmundson Art Foundation, Inc. Des Moines Art Center. 1942.1.

Viewing the painting: Mike admires certain features of his grandmother. What features are emphasized in this painting, and what do they suggest about the subject?

stances and attitudes, sitting in beds or chairs, standing at windows, as if they were frozen forever in these postures. To tell the truth, I began to hurry because I was getting depressed. Finally, I saw a beautiful girl approaching, dressed in white, a nurse or an attendant, and I was so happy to see someone young, someone walking and acting normally, that I gave her a wide smile and a big hello and I must have looked like a kind of nut. Anyway, she looked right through me as if I were a window, which is about par for the course[3] whenever I meet beautiful girls.

I finally found the room and saw my grandmother in bed. My grandmother looks like Ethel Barrymore. I never knew who Ethel Barrymore was until I saw a terrific movie, *None But the Lonely Heart,* on TV, starring Ethel Barrymore and Cary Grant.[4] Both my grandmother and Ethel Barrymore have these great craggy faces like the side of a mountain and wonderful voices like syrup being poured. Slowly. She was propped up in bed, pillows puffed behind her. Her hair had been combed out and fell upon her shoulders. For some reason, this flowing hair gave her an almost girlish appearance, despite its whiteness.

She saw me and smiled. Her eyes lit up and her eyebrows arched and she reached out her hands to me in greeting. "Mike, Mike," she said. And I breathed a sigh of relief. This was one of her good days. My

3. This expression means "average; normal." In golf, *par* is the number of strokes set as the standard for skillful play on one hole or all the holes of the course.
4. In this 1944 drama, *Barrymore* played the dying mother of *Grant's* character.

Vocabulary
craggy (krag′ ē) *adj.* rugged, uneven, and worn

VIEWING THE PAINTING

George Wesley Bellows (1882–1925), American painter-lithographer, is noted for his action scenes, seascapes, and portraits. The influence of Robert Henri's American-realism group is apparent in some of Bellows's dark, atmospheric paintings.

Viewing Response *The woman in the painting seems to have acquired serenity through the years. Her large eyes have seen a great deal in her lifetime. The folded hands suggest acceptance.*

Vo·cab·u·lar·y Skills

Multiple-Meaning Words Explain to students that the use of the word *attitude* here means "posture" or "position." Students may be more familiar with the meaning "a feeling or emotion." Explain that these meanings are linked by the fact that both represent positions, physical or mental.

FYI

The Barrymores The Barrymore family has occupied the American stage since 1846, when John Drew, Ethel Barrymore's grandfather, came to America. Ethel began her career as a stage actor and had no problem transferring her talent to movies. Drew Barrymore is from the same family.

MEETING INDIVIDUAL NEEDS — SPECIAL NEEDS

Emotional Learning-disabled students may benefit from a reenactment of the nursing home scene. Have students reread the part from Mike's entering the nursing home to his seeing his grandmother.

Activity Have students act out the scene. Explain that each character—the patients in their rooms, the nurse, the man in the wheelchair, and Mike—has a different perspective on what the nursing home is like. Have each student describe it from his or her character's perspective, and have the students portray the different perspectives in their reenactment. **L1** **COLLAB. LEARN.**

Additional Resources
Inclusion Strategies

G Active Reading Strategies

QUESTION Ask students why they think Mike's grandmother imagines she is bird watching. *(She needs a mental escape from her unhappy surroundings.)*

H Literary Elements

FIGURATIVE LANGUAGE Point out the line "the fog that . . . obscured her mind." Ask students how the word *fog* is used figuratively here. *(It means unclear or confused thoughts.)*

Teaching Support

mother had warned me that she might not know who I was at first.

I took her hands in mine. They were fragile. I could actually feel her bones, and it seemed as if they would break if I pressed too hard. Her skin was smooth, almost slippery, as if the years had worn away all the roughness the way the wind wears away the surfaces of stones.

"Mike, Mike, I didn't think you'd come," she said, so happy, and she was still Ethel Barrymore, that voice like a caress. "I've been waiting all this time." Before I could reply, she looked away, out the window. "See the birds? I've been watching them at the feeder. I love to see them come. Even the blue jays. The blue jays are like hawks—they take the food that the small birds should have. But the small birds, the chickadees, watch the blue jays and at least learn where the feeder is."

She lapsed into silence, and I looked out the window. There was no feeder. No birds. There was only the parking lot and the sun glinting on car windshields.

She turned to me again, eyes bright. Radiant, really. Or was it a medicine brightness? "Ah, Mike. You look so grand, so grand. Is that a new coat?"

"Not really," I said. I'd been wearing my Uncle Jerry's old army-fatigue jacket for months, practically living in it, my mother said. But she insisted that I wear my raincoat for the visit. It was about a year old but looked new because I didn't wear it much. Nobody was wearing raincoats lately.

"You always loved clothes, didn't you, Mike?" she said.

I was beginning to feel uneasy because she regarded me with such intensity. Those bright eyes. I wondered—are old people in places like this so lonesome, so abandoned that they go wild when someone visits? Or was she so happy because she was suddenly lucid and everything was sharp and clear? My mother had described those moments when my grandmother suddenly emerged from the fog that so often obscured her mind. I didn't know the answers, but it felt kind of spooky, getting such an emotional welcome from her.

"I remember the time you bought the new coat—the Chesterfield," she said, looking away again, as if watching the birds that weren't there. "That lovely coat with the velvet collar. Black, it was. Stylish. Remember that, Mike? It was hard times, but you could never resist the glitter."

Did You Know?
Named for a British earl, the *Chesterfield* is a type of overcoat with a velvet collar.

I was about to protest—I had never heard of a Chesterfield, for crying out loud. But I stopped. Be patient with her, my mother had said. Humor her. Be gentle.

We were interrupted by an attendant who pushed a wheeled cart into the room. "Time for juices, dear," the woman said.

Vocabulary
lapse (laps) *v.* to slip, drift, or fall (into)
lucid (lo͞o′ sid) *adj.* mentally alert; clear-headed

INTERDISCIPLINARY CONNECTION

Health The narrator's grandmother has arteriosclerosis, which is a thickening of the walls of the arteries that restricts blood flow. Arteries carry oxygenated blood, so a restriction in arterial blood flow results in the carrying of less oxygen to vital organs such as the brain. When this happens, brain dysfunctions, such as delusions, can occur.

Activity Have students research the causes of arteriosclerosis. They may want to use the Internet, consumer or scientific articles, or government publications for their research. Ask students to determine whether and to what extent arteriosclerosis may be prevented through lifestyle choices. Invite them to present their conclusions to the class. **L2**

She was the standard forty- or fifty-year-old woman: glasses, nothing hair, plump cheeks. Her manner was cheerful but a businesslike kind of cheerfulness. I'd hate to be called "dear" by someone getting paid to do it. "Orange or grape or cranberry, dear? Cranberry is good for the bones, you know."

My grandmother ignored the interruption. She didn't even bother to answer, having turned away at the woman's arrival, as if angry about her appearance.

The woman looked at me and winked. A conspiratorial kind of wink. It was kind of horrible. I didn't think people winked like that anymore. In fact, I hadn't seen a wink in years.

"She doesn't care much for juices," the woman said, talking to me as if my grandmother weren't even there. "But she loves her coffee. With lots of cream and two lumps of sugar. But this is juice time, not coffee time." Addressing my grandmother again, she said, "Orange or grape or cranberry, dear?"

"Tell her I want no juices, Mike," my grandmother commanded regally, her eyes still watching invisible birds.

The woman smiled, patience like a label on her face. "That's all right, dear. I'll just leave some cranberry for you. Drink it at your leisure. It's good for the bones."

She wheeled herself out of the room. My grandmother was still absorbed in the view. Somewhere a toilet flushed. A wheelchair passed the doorway—probably that same old driver fleeing a hit-run accident. A television set exploded with sound somewhere, soap-opera voices filling the air. You can always tell soap-opera voices.

I turned back to find my grandmother staring at me. Her hands cupped her face, her index fingers curled around her cheeks like parenthesis marks.

"But you know, Mike, looking back, I think you were right," she said, continuing our conversation as if there had been no interruption. "You always said, 'It's the things of the spirit that count, Meg.' The spirit! And so you bought the baby-grand piano—a baby grand in the middle of the Depression.[5] A knock came on the door and it was the deliveryman. It took five of them to get it into the house." She leaned back, closing her eyes. "How I loved that piano, Mike. I was never that fine a player, but you loved to sit there in the parlor, on Sunday evenings, Ellie on your lap, listening to me play and sing." She hummed a bit, a fragment of melody I didn't recognize. Then she drifted into silence. Maybe she'd fallen asleep. My mother's name is Ellen, but everyone always calls her Ellie. "Take my hand, Mike," my grandmother said suddenly. Then I remembered—my grandfather's name was Michael. I had been named for him.

"Ah, Mike," she said, pressing my hands with all her feeble strength. "I thought I'd lost you forever. And here you are, back with me again. . . ."

5. Here, *Depression* refers to the period from 1929 to 1939, when the economy was extremely bad and many Americans lived in poverty or suffered severe hardships.

Vocabulary

conspiratorial (kən spir′ ə tôr′ ē əl) *adj.* joining or acting together, especially to carry out some secret or evil deed or for a hidden or illegal purpose

regally (rē′ gəl lē) *adv.* in a grand, dignified manner, as if done by a king or queen; royally

I Critical Thinking

DRAWING CONCLUSIONS Ask students to draw conclusions about how the nurse's treatment makes Mike's grandmother feel. Share the following model to illustrate the conclusion-drawing process:

Model: I think Mike's grandmother knows that she is at the mercy of the nursing home's staff and schedule because she counts on them for everything. Because of this dependence, she seems to feel helpless and annoyed with the way the nurse ignores her, so in turn she ignores the nurse.

J Literary Elements

CHARACTERIZATION Ask students to consider the description the author uses when referring to Mike's grandmother's demeanor. How does the author convey her proud nature to the reader? *(Both her words ["Tell her I want no juices, Mike"] and the author's description ["grandmother commanded regally"] point to her proud nature.)*

Life Skills Connection

Collaborating Students can benefit from sharing reactions to a story with others. Exchanging ideas often helps a person consider something about the story he or she hadn't thought of before. In this story, different readers may react differently to the two main characters.

Activity Have students work with partners to conduct joint reviews of the story in the style of movie reviewers Roger Ebert and Richard Roeper. Encourage students to analyze the characters' strengths and weaknesses and to include their reactions to the characters. Students should conclude with their opinion—thumbs-up or thumbs-down—of the story.
L2 **COLLAB. LEARN.**

VIEWING THE PAINTING

Viewing Response *The view through the open window reminds us of the grandmother's visualizing the birds outside. The lace curtain can represent her life in an earlier period, the breeze, what transports her back in time.*

K Literary Elements

PLOT: Rising Action Students should note that the author is building to the climax of the story by focusing on the grandmother's dialogue and the reader's desire to know about what Mike will do.

L Active Reading Strategies

QUESTION Ask students what the grandmother might mean when she says, "Have you ever really forgiven me for that night?" *(She is probably referring to a fight she had with Mike or some pain she caused him.)*

Open Window, 1993. Linda Fennimore. Colored pencil, 13¼ x 13¼ in. Artist's collection.

Viewing the art: How might this window and the view outside reflect the grandmother's state of mind?

Her expression scared me. I don't mean scared as if I were in danger but scared because of what could happen to her when she realized the mistake she had made. My mother always said I favored her side of the family. Thinking back to the pictures in the old family albums, I recalled my grandfather as tall and thin. Like me. But the resemblance ended there. He was thirty-five when he died, almost forty years ago. And he wore a moustache. I brought my hand to my face. I also wore a moustache now, of course.

K "I sit here these days, Mike," she said, her voice a lullaby, her hand still holding mine, "and I drift and dream. The days are fuzzy sometimes, merging together. Sometimes it's like I'm not here at all but somewhere else altogether. And I always think of you. Those years we had. Not enough years, Mike, not enough. . . ." K

Her voice was so sad, so mournful that I made sounds of sympathy, not words exactly but kind of soothings that mothers murmur to their children when they awaken from bad dreams.

"And I think of that terrible night, Mike, that terrible night. Have you ever really forgiven me for that night?" L

"Listen . . ." I began. I wanted to say: "Nana, this is Mike your grandson, not Mike your husband."

Teaching Support

MEETING INDIVIDUAL NEEDS: MULTIPLE MODES OF EXPRESSION

Spatial The story makes good use of visual imagery. Students with spatial abilities may benefit from expressing these images artistically, using different media to present a unified representation of Mike's experience.

Activity Have students make a collage reflecting either Mike's or his grandmother's point of view. Students may select pictures, objects, and/or quotations to represent images from the story associated with either of the characters. Have students present their finished collages to the class for discussion. **L2**

"Sh . . . sh . . ." she whispered, placing a finger as long and cold as a candle against my lips. "Don't say anything. I've waited so long for this moment. To be here. With you. I wondered what I would say if suddenly you walked in that door like other people have done. I've thought and thought about it. And I finally made up my mind—I'd ask you to forgive me. I was too proud to ask before." Her fingers tried to mask her face. "But I'm not proud anymore, Mike." That great voice quivered and then grew strong again. "I hate you to see me this way—you always said I was beautiful. I didn't believe it. The Charity Ball when we led the grand march and you said I was the most beautiful girl there . . ."

"Nana," I said. I couldn't keep up the pretense any longer, adding one more burden to my load of guilt, leading her on this way, playing a pathetic game of make-believe with an old woman clinging to memories. She didn't seem to hear me.

M "But that other night, Mike. The terrible one. The terrible accusations I made. Even Ellie woke up and began to cry. I went to her and rocked her in my arms and you came into the room and said I was wrong. You were whispering, an awful whisper, not wanting to upset little Ellie but wanting to make me see the truth. And I didn't answer you, Mike. I was too proud. I've even forgotten the name of the girl. I sit here, wondering now—was it Laura or Evelyn? I can't remember. Later, I learned that you were telling the truth all the time, Mike. That I'd been wrong . . ." Her eyes were brighter than ever as she looked at me now, but tear-bright, the tears gathering. "It was never the same after that night, was it, Mike? The glitter was gone. From you. From us. And then the accident . . . and I never had the chance to ask you to forgive me . . ." M

My grandmother. My poor, poor grandmother. Old people aren't supposed to have those kinds of memories. You see their pictures in the family albums and that's what they are: pictures. They're not supposed to come to life. You drive out in your father's Le Mans doing seventy-five on the pike and all you're doing is visiting an old lady in a nursing home. A duty call. And then you find out that she's a person. She's *somebody*. She's my grandmother, all right, but she's also herself. Like my own mother and father. They exist outside of their relationship to me. I was scared again. I wanted to get out of there.

"Mike, Mike," my grandmother said. "Say it, Mike."

I felt as if my cheeks would crack if I uttered a word.

"Say you forgive me, Mike. I've waited all these years . . ."

I was surprised at how strong her fingers were.

"Say, *'I forgive you, Meg.'*"

I said it. My voice sounded funny, as if I were talking in a huge tunnel. "I forgive you, Meg." N

Her eyes studied me. Her hands pressed mine. For the first time in my life, I saw love at work. Not movie love. Not Cindy's sparkling eyes when I tell her that we're going to the beach on a Sunday afternoon. But love like something alive and tender, O

Vocabulary

pretense (prē′ tens) *n.* a false show or appearance, especially for the purpose of deceiving; falseness

M Literary Elements

CHARACTERIZATION Ask students to consider what has been revealed about the grandmother's character. Do they think her regret is wasted? Students should support their responses with their views of how this memory has affected her life.

N Literary Elements

CLIMAX Mike makes a decision to go along with his grandmother's delusion. Point out that at the climax of the story, Mike has come to several realizations about his grandmother and decides to try to help her as a human being, not as a grandmother. Have students locate earlier passages in which the author created tension about Mike's mood and his feelings toward his trip to see her.

O Critical Thinking

MAKE CRITICAL JUDGMENTS Ask students whether they agree with Mike's decision. They should support their opinion with an analysis of the consequences of the alternative decisions Mike could have made.

Real-World Connection

Nursing Home Care Have students locate a magazine or newspaper article about nursing homes. The article can be about the residents or about the operation of nursing homes. Have small groups discuss their articles. Students should use details from their articles to answer such questions as *Why are people in nursing homes? How are nursing homes alike? How do they differ? What are the experiences of people living in them?* **L2**

interNET CONNECTION

Nursing Homes Have students use a search engine to look for additional information about nursing homes. Suggest they try entering key words such as *nursing home* and *aging.*

P Literary Elements

CHARACTER Ask students how Mike is changed by the visit. *(He matures and sees things from a point of view other than his own.)* Why does he shave his moustache? *(He no longer needs a "mask" of maturity.)*

Thematic Focus

Which Way to Go? Mike made several choices in this story. Ask students to imagine how the story might be different, or how Mike might be different, if he had not made any of the choices he did.

ASSESSMENT

Quick Checks, p. 23

O asking nothing in return. She raised her face, and I knew what she wanted me to do. I bent and brushed my lips against her cheek. Her flesh was like a leaf in autumn, crisp and dry.

She closed her eyes and I stood up. The sun wasn't glinting on the cars any longer. Somebody had turned on another television set, and the voices were the show-off voices of the panel shows. At the same time you could still hear the soap-opera dialogue on the other television set.

I waited awhile. She seemed to be sleeping, her breathing serene and regular. I buttoned my raincoat. Suddenly she opened her eyes again and looked at me. Her eyes were still bright, but they merely stared at me. Without recognition or curiosity. Empty eyes. I smiled at her, but she didn't smile back. She made a kind of moaning sound and turned away on the bed, pulling the blankets around her.

I counted to twenty-five and then to fifty and did it all over again. I cleared my throat and coughed tentatively. She didn't move; she didn't respond. I wanted to say, "Nana, it's me." But I didn't. I thought of saying, "Meg, it's me." But I couldn't.

Finally I left. Just like that. I didn't say goodbye or anything. I stalked through the corridors, looking neither to the right nor the left, not caring whether that wild old man with the wheelchair ran me down or not.

On the Southwest Turnpike I did seventy-five—no, eighty—most of the way. I turned the radio up as loud as it could go. Rock music—anything to fill the air. When I got home, my mother was vacuuming the living room rug. She shut off the cleaner, and the silence was deafening. "Well, how was your grandmother?" she asked. P

I told her she was fine. I told her a lot of things. How great Nana looked and how she seemed happy and had called me Mike. I wanted to ask her—hey, Mom, you and Dad really love each other, don't you? I mean—there's nothing to forgive between you, is there? But I didn't.

Instead I went upstairs and took out the electric razor Annie had given me for Christmas and shaved off my moustache.

Vocabulary

serene (sə rēn′) *adj.* calm; peaceful; undisturbed

Teaching Support

Grammar and Language *Minilesson*

Capitalization of Proper Nouns Write the following on the board: *Downtown Cinema, Lawnrest Nursing Home, Southwest Turnpike.* Point out that each of these proper nouns is capitalized. Capitalization often depends on usage, so a word may be capitalized sometimes and not at other times. For example, *cinema, nursing home,* and *turnpike* are capitalized only as part of a proper name.

Activity Read the following list of terms to students: *arcade, golf course, Third Street Arcade, library, Pine Hills Golf Course, Chicago Public Library.* Have students write the terms as you read them, deciding as they write which words should be capitalized. **L2**

Additional Resources

- ***Grammar and Language Transparency 22***
- ***Grammar and Language Workbook,*** pp. 247–249
- ***Grammar and Composition Handbook,*** Lessons 12.2–12.4
- ***Writer's Choice,*** Lessons 19.2–19.4

Responding to Literature

PERSONAL RESPONSE

- What was your reaction to the end of the story?
- What thoughts did you have about any elderly people you know while reading this short story?

Brackets connect questions that are paired to develop higher-level thinking skills.

Analyzing Literature

RECALL

1. Describe the medical condition of Mike's grandmother.
2. When talking to Mike, what does his grandmother reveal about her marriage?
3. What does Mike do when he realizes that his grandmother thinks he is someone else?
4. What does Mike do when he gets home?

INTERPRET

5. Why does the grandmother mistake Mike for his grandfather?
6. What does Mike mean when he says, "Old people aren't supposed to have those kinds of memories"?
7. After Mike kisses his grandmother's cheek, he sees "love at work." What does he mean? What has he learned from his grandmother?
8. Why doesn't Mike tell his mother everything that happened with his grandmother? Why does he shave off his moustache?

EVALUATE AND CONNECT

9. **Theme Connection** Mike makes decisions throughout this story. Do you agree with his decision not to tell his grandmother who he really is? Why does he make this choice?
10. Why is Mike's moustache so important to this story that the author uses it as the title?

LITERARY ELEMENTS

Characterization

Characterization is the way an author reveals information about characters through action, dialogue, and description. Robert Cormier does this by carefully choosing what Mike and his grandmother do, say, and think. Readers learn about the characters' appearance as well as their personalities.

1. Describe what you know about Mike's thoughts.
2. What conclusions can you draw about Mike's feelings? Cite the clues you found in the text.
3. Find dialogue that reveals the personality of Mike's grandmother.

- See **Literary Terms Handbook,** p. R2.

Responding to the Selection

PERSONAL RESPONSE

Responses should include a specific description of the reaction to the end of the story. Students should relate their thoughts about an elderly person to the story.

Analyzing Literature

1. She has arteriosclerosis, a hardening and thickening of the artery walls that restricts blood flow.
2. She reveals that they had some kind of disagreement that made their relationship different.
3. He is scared of what will happen when she finds out she was wrong, but he goes along with her delusion.
4. He shaves off his moustache.
5. She makes the mistake because her memory is failing and he looks like his grandfather.
6. He means that old people don't seem real, as if they were never young or never had problems or sadness—or that old people should be at peace, having come to terms with bad memories.
7. He means that his grandmother loved his grandfather with a much deeper love than he has ever experienced. He learns that he has many things to experience before achieving maturity.
8. Some students may feel that it was too difficult for him to explain. Others may feel Mike wanted to protect his mother from knowing his grandmother was having one of her bad days. The moustache, to Mike, made him seem older. Mike has learned that it takes more than a moustache to be mature.
9. Some students may feel that Mike was right not to spoil his grandmother's fantasy. Others may feel he didn't help her by pretending or that it is always wrong to deceive others.
10. The moustache starts as a symbol of maturity to Mike, but Mike learns there is much more to being an adult than having a moustache. It becomes a symbol of how little he understood about growing older.

LITERARY ELEMENTS

1. *Possible answers:* that he feels guilty; that he cares for his grandmother.
2. *Possible answer:* Mike is scared by his grandmother's behavior. (He refers to her as "spooky.")
3. *Possible answers:* her delight in the birds; her haughty dismissal of the aide; her sorrow and apology.

Additional Resources

Literary Elements Transparency 23

Literature and Writing

Writing About Literature

Students' comparisons should

- analyze the chosen characters' relationship
- explore the type of love the characters share and explain what this love reveals about them

Personal Writing

Students' dialogues should

- include speeches from both characters
- show an awareness that the grandchild may be unfamiliar with what is being described
- use correct punctuation of dialogue

Extending Your Response

Literature Group Group responses should include specific examples from the books, the shows, and the movies cited. COLLAB. LEARN.

Learning for Life Suggest that students present their findings to the class, using graphic aids and photographs to enhance understanding.

Performance Students may want to put on a dress rehearsal for the class before performing in front of a new audience.

Literature and Writing

Writing About Literature

Comparison "The Moustache" is a story about relationships: Mike's relationship with his grandmother, with Cindy, and with his mother; and the relationship between Mike's grandparents. Select one of these relationships. Use well-chosen details to explain the kinds of love each person shows and tell what the relationship reveals about the characters involved.

Personal Writing

Taking on a Role Look back at the observations about visiting a nursing home that you made in the **Reading Focus** on page 281. Now, imagine that you are eighty-five years old and living in a nursing home. Use narrative and descriptive strategies to write a dialogue between yourself and your grandchild as you explain what life was like when you were a teenager.

Extending Your Response

Literature Groups

Reality Checks With your group, discuss books and stories you have read, television shows you have viewed, or movies you enjoyed in which several generations were portrayed. Discuss the various ways teens are shown in these media. Evaluate the ways adults, especially older adults, are depicted. Do these media portray all age groups with accuracy and sensitivity? Share your conclusions with other groups.

Learning for Life

At any age, exercise and diet are important for maintaining health. Use books, Internet sites, and interviews with health professionals to investigate some of the ways teens, adults, and elderly adults can maintain good health.

Performing

On the Road! Student groups often entertain the residents of nursing homes and people who cannot leave their homes. Think of a poem, a story, or a song that others might enjoy. Prepare an act to perform at a hospital, a center for younger children, or a retirement home. In your performance, match your message, vocabulary, voice modulation, and expression to suit your audience and purpose.

Reading Further

For other novels about teens and their elders, try:
Tunes for Bears to Dance To by Robert Cormier
Plain City by Virginia Hamilton

Save your work for your portfolio.

Skill Minilessons

RETEACH • REVIEW

GRAMMAR AND LANGUAGE • ADVERB PHRASES

An **adverb phrase** is a prepositional phrase that describes, or modifies, a verb, an adjective, or another adverb. Like an adverb, an adverb phrase tells *where, when, how, why,* or *to what extent* an action occurs.

Describes a verb	She reached out her hands to me **in greeting.** (this adverb phrase tells *how*)
Describes an adjective	I was surprised **by the lack of hospital smell.** (tells *why*)
Describes an adverb	She looked older **than I remembered.** (tells *to what extent*)

PRACTICE Write each adverb phrase below. Name the word each phrase modifies.

1. Robert Cormier's works can be found in libraries and bookstores.
2. Cormier said that his four children were proud of his success as a writer.
3. Cormier was pleased by the interest teenagers have in his writing.

For more about adverb phrases, see **Language Handbook,** p. R31.

READING AND THINKING • CLARIFYING

Clarifying is stopping to make sure you understand what you've read. Good readers clarify information as they read along. They stop occasionally to review events and descriptions, ask themselves questions, and look for answers to their earlier questions.

PRACTICE Look back at "The Moustache" and find and list at least three points in the story when you had to clarify what was happening or being described.

For more about clarifying, see **Reading Handbook,** pp. R89–R90.

VOCABULARY • GREEK ROOTS

English has developed by borrowing **roots,** or basic word parts, from other languages. The same root may appear in many different English words. For example, *chronos* is a Greek word that means "time." In English, *chron* is a root from which several words are made that have something to do with time. *Chronic* means "constant, lasting a long time," or "returning repeatedly." So, a *chronic* problem keeps occurring; a *chronic* liar lies frequently.

PRACTICE Complete each item below. Verify your answers by looking up each italicized word in the dictionary.

1. List three months in *chronological* order.
2. What do people do when they *synchronize* their watches? (Hint: *syn-* means "together.")
3. Which course usually has a textbook that is a *chronicle*—math, grammar, or history?
4. Which mistake in a carelessly made movie is an *anachronism?*
   a. A brown dog runs after a ball, but a black dog brings it back.
   b. A motorboat passes by the Pilgrims landing at Plymouth Rock.

Skill Minilessons

GRAMMAR AND LANGUAGE
ADVERB PHRASES

1. in libraries and bookstores (modifies *found*)
2. of his success (modifies *proud*)
3. by the interest (modifies *pleased*)

READING AND THINKING
CLARIFYING

Individual students will need to clarify different points in the story. Students should describe why they needed clarification of these points.

VOCABULARY
ROOTS

1. Any three months from earliest in the year to latest are acceptable. The months do not have to be consecutive.
2. They set their watches to the same time.
3. History (It has to do with *time.*)
4. c. (Motorboats are from a different *time.*)

Additional Resources

- ***Grammar and Language Workbook,*** p. 145
- ***Grammar and Composition Handbook,*** Lesson 7.3
- ***Writer's Choice,*** Lesson 13.3
- ***Reading Skills Practice Workbook***
- ***Vocabulary Practice,*** p. 20

ASSESSMENT

- ***Quick Checks,*** p. 23
- ***Selection and Theme Assessment,*** pp. 39–40
- ***Performance Assessment,*** p. 22
- ***Testmaker: ExamView Pro***
- ***Interactive Tutor: Self-Assessment***

Objective

- To understand the elements of poetry

Teaching Strategies

Explain to students that poetry encompasses nursery rhymes and epics such as the *Iliad.* It also includes song lyrics and rap music.

Sound

Encourage students to read poems aloud. Remind them that poets often put much effort into a poem's sound that can be missed if the poem is read silently.

Rhythm and Meter Have students read the model poem aloud and clap or snap their fingers on the stressed syllables to get a sense of the poem's rhythm and meter.

Alliteration Ask students to think of other alliterative phrases they're familiar with *(whispering winds, roses are red)* or to create their own.

Rhyme Point out that many forms of poetry, such as free verse and blank verse, do not rhyme.

Teaching Support

POETRY

A poem can have a dozen words or several thousand lines. It can leave you laughing or crying. It can rhyme or not. It can be hundreds of years old or a current rap. So how can you tell when a piece of writing is a poem? There are no firm rules, but most poems share two major characteristics: sound and language.

SOUND The sound of the words contributes to the overall effect of a poem. Poetry uses many techniques to create different sounds.

1. **Rhythm** Much like the beat of a song, the **rhythm** of a poem is a sound pattern. This pattern is often created by stressed and unstressed syllables in words. A stressed syllable is a word part that carries emphasis when it is read aloud; an unstressed syllable is read more softly. (Stressed syllables are marked with ´; unstressed syllables are marked with ˘.) Notice the different rhythms in the two lines below.

   bouncing up and down

   far, far from the sun's strong glare

2. **Meter** The rhythm of stressed and unstressed syllables that is repeated throughout a poem is called **meter.** The poem by Emily Dickinson on this page, for example, uses **iambic meter**—almost every unstressed syllable is followed by a stressed one.

3. **Alliteration, Assonance, and Onomatopoeia** The repetition of a sound at the beginning of words is called **alliteration,** as is heard in the rhyme "Peter Piper picked a peck of pickled peppers," and in "wantoned with" in line 4 of Emily Dickinson's poem.

   The repetition of a vowel sound is called **assonance**. The following line from Alfred, Lord Tennyson's poem "The Splendor Falls on Castle Walls" contains an example of assonance: "Our echoes roll from soul to soul."

   The use of a word that imitates the sound of what it describes is called **onomatopoeia**. The words *plop, mumble, trill, bubble,* and *buzz* are all examples of onomatopoeia.

4. **Rhyme** Repetition of ending sounds of words is **rhyme.** An example is "shone" and "Bone" (lines 2 and 4). Poems may use rhyming words within a single line of poetry or at the ends of different lines. Many poems use patterns of rhyme.

MODEL

She dealt her pretty words like
  Blades—
How glittering they shone—
And every One unbared a Nerve
Or wantoned with a Bone—

—*Emily Dickinson*

MEETING INDIVIDUAL NEEDS: ADVANCED LEARNERS

Forms of Poetry Point out that there are different forms of poetry, each with its own purposes and characteristics. For example, a ballad is a short narrative poem that usually tells of an exciting or dramatic episode. Other forms of poetry include lyric, epic, couplet, elegy, ode, and sonnet.

Activity Have students choose one form of poetry and study the relationship between its purpose and characteristics. Ask them to share their findings with the class, using a particular poem as an example.

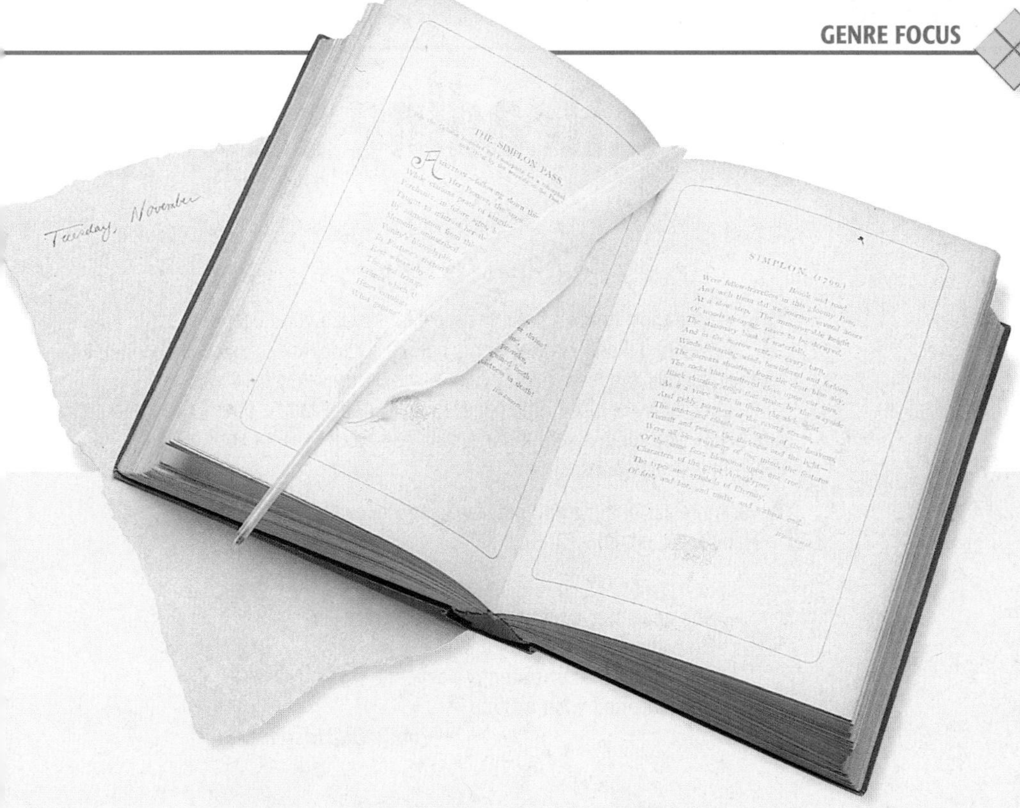

LANGUAGE Many poems have **imagery,** words that appeal to the five senses: touch, taste, smell, sight, and hearing. Nikki Giovanni's poem "Knoxville, Tennessee," on page 181 of this book, contains examples of taste imagery ("eat fresh corn"), hearing imagery ("listen to gospel music"), sight imagery ("go to the mountains"), and touch imagery ("go barefooted").

Poems also use **figures of speech,** language that describes ordinary things in new ways.

1. **Simile or Metaphor** A **simile** is a comparison of two different things using the word *like* or *as.* A simile points out a similarity between the two things. For example, the Dickinson poem uses the simile "words like Blades" to point out that both items can cut. In the poem "The Black Walnut Tree" on page 299, what is the simile in lines 17 and 18?

   A **metaphor** is a comparison of two unlike things without such clue words as *like* or *as.* For example, "words like Blades" is a simile; "words are blades" is a metaphor. In "The Black Walnut Tree," identify and explain the metaphor in lines 34 and 35.

2. **Personification** In **personification,** a writer talks about an object or living thing as if it were a human. The wind, for example, might be described as a person banging on a window.

Language
Remind students that although all writers pay attention to language, poets in particular focus on precise, interesting uses of language. Each word in a poem is chosen for a particular reason.

Simile or Metaphor Remind students that both similes and metaphors are used to compare basically unlike things. Point out that these comparisons help describe something for the reader. Ask students to come up with their own comparisons.

Personification Explain that personification brings a poem to life by assigning human characteristics to nonhuman things. Invite students to share examples of personification that they have encountered in reading.

Technology

Mix and Match

Using a word-processing program, students can have some fun putting together silly poems while thinking about language and similes. Have students set up a page with three columns. In the first column have them list ten plural nouns. In the second have them list ten action verbs that represent human actions. In the third column have them list ten other plural nouns, each preceded by the word *like.* Using the block-and-copy function, have students use one word from each column to form short, one-line, possibly nonsensical poems.

Active Reading Strategies

Objective

- To understand and apply strategies for reading and comprehending poetry

Teach the Strategies

Ask students to read the poem by Emily Dickinson and then to reread it more slowly. Encourage them to think about what the poet is saying. They may wish to think of examples from their own lives that reflect the poem's message.

Question

Encourage students to look for *like* or *as* when they read poetry and to ask how the compared things are similar and different. This attention to the use of similes will give them insight into the poem's meaning.

Listen

Encourage students to read poems aloud, listening to the sounds of the words. Point out that poets often produce a mood by choosing words that make certain sounds.

Teaching Support

ACTIVE READING MODEL

Active Reading Strategies

Active Reading Strategies for Poetry

To get the most out of a poem, readers must put a good deal of themselves into it. Poets choose words not just for their meanings, but also for their sounds, the feelings they call up, the pictures they paint, and even, sometimes, how they look on a page. To really understand a poem, like the one below, you must use your mind, your ears, your eyes–or your mind's eye, and your emotions.

- For more about these and other reading strategies, see **Reading Handbook,** pp. R93–R106.

She dealt her pretty words like Blades—
How glittering they shone—
And every One unbared a Nerve
Or wantoned with a Bone—

—*Emily Dickinson*

QUESTION

If a word has more than one meaning, ask yourself which meaning the poet has in mind. If the poet uses a word in an unusual way, think about possible reasons for that usage. What is the poet getting at?

Say to Yourself . . .

- How can words be like blades? Blades cut. What can words cut? How?
- *Wanton* means "careless." Why is it used as a verb? What does the poet want me to understand about the character in the poem?

LISTEN

Read poems aloud, if possible, or say the words to yourself. Listen for words that call attention to themselves or to particular ideas.

Say to Yourself . . .

- The word *glittering* stands out to me. It's odd to think of words glittering. Why did the poet use this word?

296 THEME 3

Reading Journal

Pros and Cons

Explain to students that the characters in the narrative poem "The Black Walnut Tree" are presented with a decision to make. Have students discuss how they go about making important decisions. Do they find it helpful to write down the pros and cons of their choices? Why?

Activity As students read "The Black Walnut Tree," have them list in their reading journals the pros and cons of the possible choices the characters mention. After reading, students should give their opinions of the choice the characters made. Then ask students to discuss their observations in small groups. **L2**

VISUALIZE

Try to imagine the person or thing or scene described in the words. Build on any details the poet provides.

Say to Yourself . . .

- The word *blades* makes me think of sharp knives. It also makes me think of razor blades. Either way, a cruel scene comes to mind!

CONNECT

Poems invite readers to share feelings and experiences. What connections can you make between the events in Dickinson's poem and your own experiences?

Say to Yourself . . .

- I remember a time when someone's words hurt me deeply. They felt like blades going right through me.

RESPOND

As you read a poem, or immediately afterward, take a moment to answer questions like these: How does the poem make you feel? What message, if any, did you get from the poem? Do you want to share the poem with friends?

Say to Yourself . . .

- The person described in this poem seems frightening. The poem describes a hateful person.

APPLYING THE STRATEGIES

Read the poem that follows, "The Black Walnut Tree." As you read, use the Active Reading Strategies in the margins to help you enjoy the poem.

Visualize

Some students may benefit from being encouraged to draw a picture to represent the poem. Others may benefit from picturing something they have experienced that is similar to that described in the poem.

Connect

Encourage students to look for ways to make connections to the ideas in "The Black Walnut Tree" when they read it. Can they identify with the women in the poem? Can they think of some special item in their own lives that they would not want to see destroyed?

Respond

Encourage students to decide whether they agree or disagree with the message of a poem after they have read it. Evaluating it this way will help them to think about the poem's meaning.

Before Reading

Objectives

- To read and analyze a poem about the possibility of cutting down an old tree
- To identify symbols used in the poem
- To write a description of the story told in the poem

Skills

Writing: Short Poem
Grammar/Language: Concrete and Abstract Nouns
Listening/Speaking: Oral Reading
Collaboration: Literature Groups; Oral Reading

Motivating STUDENTS

Selection Focus Transparency 23: Before presenting the transparency, discuss with students the idea that some things are more important than the money they are worth.

Reading Focus: As an extension of the Reading Focus, ask students to share with a partner the details of the scene or object they have pictured. Invite students to compare what they find impressive in nature.

ACTIVE READING MODEL

Before You Read

The Black Walnut Tree

MEET MARY OLIVER

Even the tables of contents in Mary Oliver's books reveal her love of the natural world. Oliver writes about everything from fish and wild geese to herons, rabbits, and moths. Her poems explore the light and dark sides of nature. Mary Oliver has lived a life away from cities: in Ohio, where she was raised, in Provincetown, Massachusetts, and in rural Virginia. She has received many awards for her poetry, including the Pulitzer Prize in 1984.

Mary Oliver was born in 1935. This poem was first published in 1979.

READING FOCUS

Picture a beautiful or interesting scene or object that has impressed you. What shape, color, size, or other quality captured your attention?

FreeWrite
Jot down descriptive details or ideas that come to mind when you think of that object. How does it connect with your life?

Setting a Purpose
As you read, think about why a river, a tree, or a garden may be of special importance.

BUILDING BACKGROUND

Mary Oliver carries on the American tradition of writing about our connections with nature that Henry David Thoreau started more than 100 years ago. A native of Concord, Massachusetts, Thoreau is the author of *Walden,* a description of his life near the pond during one span of seasons in the mid-1800s. New England poet Robert Frost continued in this tradition, describing the beauties and mysteries he experienced on his farm during the early 1900s.

The Great Heron, published in *The Birds of North America,* 1827–1838. John James Audubon. Aquatint plate, 973 x 635 mm.

RESOURCE MANAGER

Teaching Tools and Resources
- Theme Three Planning Guide
- Literature Groups Sourcebook

Essential Lesson Support
Lesson-Specific Instruction
- Selection Focus Transparency 23
- Literary Elements Transparency 24
- Active Reading Guide,* p. 24

Assessment
- Selection Quick Checks,* p. 24
- Sel. and Theme Assmt., pp. 41–42
- Testmaker: ExamView Pro
- Performance Assessment, p. 23

Systematic Language Instruction
- Gr. & Comp. Hbk., Lesson 5.2
- Vocabulary Power, Lesson 13
- Spelling Power, Lesson 11

English Language Learners
- Spanish Summaries, p. 23
- Audio Library*
- English, Yes!

Spec. Needs/Strat. Interven.
- Interactive Rdg. Sbk., pp. T106–T108
- Interactive Rdg. Wbk., p. 50
- Inclusion Strat. Sbk., pp. 15–16
- Audio Library*

* Also available in Spanish

The Black Walnut Tree

Mary Oliver

My mother and I debate:
we could sell
the black walnut tree
to the lumberman,
and pay off the mortgage.
Likely some storm anyway
will churn down its dark boughs,
smashing the house. We talk
slowly, two women trying
in a difficult time to be wise.
Roots in the cellar drains,
I say, and she replies
that the leaves are getting heavier
every year, and the fruit
harder to gather away.
But something brighter than money
moves in our blood—an edge
sharp and quick as a trowel
that wants us to dig and sow.
So we talk, but we don't do
anything. That night I dream
of my fathers out of Bohemia
filling the blue fields
of fresh and generous Ohio
with leaves and vines and orchards.
What my mother and I both know
is that we'd crawl with shame
in the emptiness we'd made
in our own and our fathers' backyard.
So the black walnut tree
swings through another year
of sun and leaping winds,
of leaves and bounding fruit,
and, month after month, the whip-
crack of the mortgage.

ACTIVE READING MODEL

QUESTION — A: What issue is being debated? What are the two choices the characters face?

QUESTION — B: What is this thing that is brighter than money?

PREDICT — C: Will they have the tree cut down?

LISTEN — D: What is usually meant by the crack of a whip? Why is it a good metaphor for the mortgage?

Reading the Selection

A Active Reading Strategies

QUESTION *(The women debate whether to chop down a tree and sell the wood to help pay the mortgage.)*

B Active Reading Strategies

QUESTION *(Responses may include sentimentality, history, honor, respect for nature, or similar terms.)*

C Active Reading Strategies

PREDICT *(Students should predict that they will not cut the tree down on the basis of lines 16–19, 26–29.)*

D Active Reading Strategies

LISTEN Encourage students to recall the image of a cruel overseer forcing laborers to work.

Thematic Focus

Which Way to Go? The mother and daughter in this poem are faced with two choices. Ask students whether they think the characters are making the right decision.

ASSESSMENT

Quick Checks, p. 24

Teaching Support

CONNECTING TO OTHER SELECTIONS

For a teaching strategy that connects this selection to "Paul Revere's Ride," see the ***Theme Five Planning Guide***.

Additional Resources

- ***Active Reading Guide,*** p. 24
- ***Audio Library***
- ***Spanish Audio Library***

Responding to the Selection

PERSONAL RESPONSE

All responses should be supported by reasons that relate to information and details provided in the poem.

Active Reading Strategies

Ask students to share the strategies they used in reading the poem.

Analyzing Literature

1. The tree is impractical and would pay the mortgage if it could be sold for lumber, so they debate whether to dispose of it.
2. Its roots are growing into the drains, there are too many leaves to rake, and the "fruit" (walnuts) is hard to gather.
3. The narrator pictures her ancestors coming to the New World and planting the rich soil of Ohio with vines and fruit trees.
4. The conflict is internal; each character is deciding whether to get rid of the tree. The decision involves choosing between practicality and sentimentality. They choose sentimentality and keep the tree.
5. Some students may feel they don't believe money is a strong enough reason to get rid of the tree.
6. The honor and respect for the ancestors' hard work is the reason they would "crawl with shame" if they got rid of the tree.
7. Students should refer to specific language from the poem to support the conclusion that mother and daughter are actually in agreement and are not debating.
8. Answers should reflect an understanding that the poet respects and appreciates nature and values it above money or practicality.
9. Responses should reflect students' understanding of the essential similarities between the two and be supported by specifics from the poem.
10. Students should support their responses with specific examples, either from experience or conjecture, of how people make decisions.

ACTIVE READING MODEL

Responding to Literature

PERSONAL RESPONSE

- What do you think about the decision that the mother and daughter make?

Active Reading Response

- Which strategies described on pages 296 and 297 did you use as you read this poem? Explain how the strategies helped you get more out of the poem.

Brackets connect questions that are paired to develop higher-level thinking skills.

Analyzing Literature

RECALL

1. Why are the mother and daughter debating?
2. What reasons do they have to justify selling the black walnut tree?
3. Describe the narrator's dream.

INTERPRET

4. What is the **conflict** in "The Black Walnut Tree?" How is this conflict resolved?
5. Why do the mother and daughter seem to need to justify selling the tree?
6. Explain the connection between the daughter's dream and her debate with her mother.

EVALUATE AND CONNECT

7. In your opinion, is the opening line of the poem **ironic?** (See page R5.) Are the mother and daughter really having a debate? Explain.
8. What attitude toward nature does the poem reflect?
9. What do you learn about the relationship between the mother and daughter in this poem? In what way are they alike? Are they different in any way? Explain.
10. Do you think dreams can affect a person's decisions or actions? Use details from the text and from your own experience to explain.

LITERARY ELEMENTS

Symbol

A **symbol** is an object, person, place, or event that stands for something else. The debate between the mother and daughter in "The Black Walnut Tree," for example, might be seen as a symbol of the conflict between commercial development and the preservation of nature.

1. What other symbol of conflict do you find in the poem?
2. Which two images imply a type of cutting? How are these symbols different?
3. How do these symbols help you understand the poem's message?

- See **Literary Terms Handbook,** p. R10.

LITERARY ELEMENTS

1. Some students may suggest the mortgage as a symbol of reality, practicality, or economic need, and the tree as a symbol of impracticality or beauty.
2. Students may suggest the lumberman (he will cut the tree), the trowel, or the whip. Students should compare the sides of the conflict that they symbolize.
3. Students may suggest that the symbols emphasize how hard the decision is to make between severing a tie with one's past and dealing with the hard reality of economic problems.

Additional Resources

Literary Elements Transparency 24

Extending Your Response

Writing About Literature

Story Structure "The Black Walnut Tree" is a narrative poem; that is, it has the structure of a story. It has characters, setting, theme, and plot. Write a paragraph or two describing the story told in the poem. How is the conflict resolved?

Literature Groups

Exploring Personal Connections The narrator of the poem describes important connections she has with nature, family, past generations, and home. What are those connections? How are they related to and different from the connections in your life? Compare and contrast the narrator's ideas with the ideas and experiences of others in your discussion group.

Creative Writing

Nature Poem Reread your notes from the **Reading Focus** on page 298. Use the notes to help you write a four-stanza poem about your connection with nature. Recite your poem, using voice, tone, and gestures expressively to enhance the meaning.

Performing

Oral Reading Work with a partner to present an oral reading of "The Black Walnut Tree" or your own poem about nature. Divide the poem in some meaningful way, for example, by alternating stanzas or by reading some lines together to help show character development.

Reading Further

If the connection between people and places interests you, try these other books:
Lessons from the Wolverine by Barry Lopez
Walking Up a Rainbow by Theodore Taylor

Save your work for your portfolio.

Skill Minilesson

RETEACH • REVIEW

GRAMMAR AND LANGUAGE • CONCRETE AND ABSTRACT NOUNS

A **concrete noun** names a person, place, or real thing, such as *mother, Ohio,* or *fruit.* An **abstract noun** names an idea, feeling, or quality, such as *happiness, conservation,* or *goodness.* "The Black Walnut Tree" has many concrete nouns, but only a few abstract nouns.

- For more about nouns, see **Language Handbook,** p. R30.

PRACTICE Complete each item.

1. List five concrete nouns in the poem that identify an element of nature.
2. List four concrete nouns that identify people in this poem.
3. Find two abstract nouns that help readers recognize emotions important to the poem.

ASSESSMENT

- ***Quick Checks,*** p. 24
- ***Selection and Theme Assessment,*** pp. 41–42
- ***Performance Assessment,*** p. 23
- ***Testmaker: ExamView Pro***
- ***Interactive Tutor: Self-Assessment***

Extending Your Response

Writing About Literature

Students' paragraphs should

- describe the plot of the poem's story
- refer to specific examples in the poem

Creative Writing

Students' poems should

- focus on an element of nature
- convey the students' feelings about that element

Literature Groups Students should focus on how their own experiences are similar to and different from the narrator's experience. COLLAB. LEARN.

Performing Students may include an explanation of why the division of reading was selected.

Skill Minilesson

GRAMMAR AND LANGUAGE • CONCRETE AND ABSTRACT NOUNS

1. *Possible choices:* tree, storm, boughs, roots, leaves, fruit, blood, fields, leaves, vines, orchards, backyard, sun, winds.
2. Answers include *mother, lumberman, women, fathers.*
3. Answers include *shame* and *emptiness.*

Additional Resources

- ***Grammar and Language Workbook,*** p. 63
- ***Grammar and Composition Handbook,*** Lesson 2.1
- ***Writer's Choice,*** Lesson 9.1

FINE ART TRANSPARENCY 5

You may want to use ***Fine Art Transparency 5*** in a discussion of ways people may look at and appreciate trees.

WHICH WAY TO GO? 301

Before Reading

Objectives

- To read and analyze three poems by Robert Frost about nature and friendship
- To identify the elements of lyric poetry
- To write a list of poetic elements

Skills

Reading/Thinking: Comparing and Contrasting; Generalizing
Writing: Letter
Grammar/Language: Commas; Action Verbs
Listening/Speaking: Discussion
Collaboration: Literature Groups

Motivating STUDENTS

Literature Launchers: "Robert Frost: An Introduction"

Videodisc Side A, Segment 8

Also available in VHS.

Selection Focus Transparency 24: Before presenting the transparency, have students discuss the importance of spending time in nature.

Reading Focus: As an extension of the Reading Focus, invite students to share the ways they protect their solitude.

CONNECTING TO OTHER SELECTIONS

For a teaching strategy that connects "A Time to Talk" to *All Things Bright and Beautiful*, see the ***Theme Two Planning Guide***.

Before You Read

A Time to Talk, Fire and Ice, and *Dust of Snow*

MEET ROBERT FROST

Robert Frost is one of America's best-loved poets. He wrote simply and directly about nature, including human nature. Frost once explained, "You learn first to know what you see and to put fresh words to it." Frost's poetry about the things he loved won him four Pulitzer Prizes.

Frost was born in San Francisco in 1874, but spent most of his life in New England, where he died in 1963.

READING FOCUS

Do you prefer to be alone occasionally, or would you generally rather be with friends?

QuickWrite

Make two quick lists. First, list how you protect your solitude; then list how you reach out to others who may want your company.

Setting a Purpose

Read to explore Robert Frost's thoughts about nature and friendship.

BUILDING BACKGROUND

Over his fifty-year career, Frost wrote about daily events and the out-of-doors. Many of his poems contain simple language, yet touch on complex themes, such as conflicting forces in life and human nature.

Robert Frost standing in front of his hen house, circa 1938.

RESOURCE MANAGER

Teaching Tools and Resources
- Theme Three Planning Guidew
- Literature Groups Sourcebook

Essential Lesson Support

Lesson-Specific Instruction
- Selection Focus Transparency 24
- Literary Elements Transparency 25
- Active Reading Guide,* p. 25

Assessment
- Selection Quick Checks,* p. 25
- Sel. and Theme Assmt., pp. 43–44
- Testmaker: ExamView Pro
- Performance Assessment, p. 24

Systematic Language Instruction
- Gr. & Comp. Hbk., Lessons 5.3, 5.4
- Vocabulary Power, Lesson 14
- Spelling Power, Lesson 12

English Language Learners
- ELL Sourcebook, pp. 44–45
- Spanish Summaries, p. 24
- Audio Library*
- English, Yes!

Spec. Needs/Strat. Interven.
- Interactive Rdg. Sbk., pp. T108–T110
- Interactive Rdg. Wbk., p. 51
- Audio Library*

* Also available in Spanish

The Sweep, 1967. Andrew Wyeth. Tempera, 23¾ x 35 in. Flint Institute of Art, Flint, MI.

A Time to Talk

Robert Frost

When a friend calls to me from the road
And slows his horse to a meaning walk,°
I don't stand still and look around
On all the hills I haven't hoed,
And shout from where I am, What is it?
No, not as there is a time to talk.
I thrust my hoe in the mellow ground,
Blade-end up and five feet tall,
And plod:° I go up to the stone wall
For a friendly visit.

2 Here, the *meaning walk* is a "meaningful or purposeful pace," with the friend slowing down to show that he wishes to talk with the speaker of the poem.
9 To *plod* is to trudge or walk along slowly and heavily.

Reading the Selection

A Active Reading Strategies

QUESTION Ask students what they think the speaker values. *(He values his friends.)*

Additional Resources

- ***Active Reading Guide,*** p. 00
- ***Audio Library***
- ***Spanish Audio Library***

B Literary Elements

LYRIC POETRY Explain to students that lyric poetry expresses an idea or an emotion through vivid detail. Ask them to discuss the poem's message and how Frost conveys it through his use of detail.

C Literary Elements

METER Point out that the author's use of one-syllable words reinforces the idea of plodding. Ask a volunteer to read the poem aloud to demonstrate.

D Critical Thinking

GENERALIZE Have students generalize about the idea the author expresses in this poem. *(Students might suggest, for example, that friends are more important than work.)*

Teaching Support

MEETING INDIVIDUAL NEEDS — ENGLISH LANGUAGE LEARNERS

Unfamiliar Meanings Some English language learners may have difficulty with a technique that is common in poetry, the use of familiar words in unfamiliar settings. Point out to students the use of the words *meaning* in "A Time to Talk" and *dust* in "Dust of Snow." Make sure students understand that the former is similar to *meaningful* and *dust* describes the quality of the snow.

Activity Have students explain the ordinary meaning of *dust* and then relate that meaning to the snow. Then have students discuss what might be meant by *mellow ground* in the first poem and *tasted desire* in the second.

Additional Resources

- ***English Language Learners Sourcebook,*** p. 44

E Author's Craft

ALLITERATION Explain to students that using similar sounds throughout a poem is called alliteration. Have students identify the sounds repeated throughout this poem *(s and f)*. Note that these sounds are similar in that they are quiet, hissing sounds that produce the same effect. Ask students to discuss the effect.

F Literary Elements

LYRIC POETRY The purpose of this lyric poem is to express thoughts about the end of the world. One way the poet does this is through the use of symbolism. Ask students whether they think fire is a good symbol for desire and ice is a good symbol for hate. Make sure they support their opinions. *(Students may agree, given the speaker's examples. Others may see hate as fiery too.)*

G Active Reading Strategies

REVIEW Encourage students to think about the statement the author is making about people and the state of the world. *(He seems to think that excessive passion can be damaging, but that icy hatred can be just as destructive.)*

A New England Winter. George Henry Durrie (1820–1863). Oil on board, 7 ft ¾ in x 12 ft ⅜ in. Santa Barbara Museum of Art.

Fire and Ice

Robert Frost

E Some say the world will end in fire,
Some say in ice.
F From what I've tasted of desire
I hold with those who favor fire.
But if it had to perish twice,
G I think I know enough of hate
To say that for destruction ice
Is also great
And would suffice.°

9 *Suffice* means "be enough."

Teaching Support

Grammar and Language *Minilesson*

Commas The poem "Dust of Snow" provides a good opportunity to evaluate the need for commas in sentences. Point out that the poem is a sentence. Warn students not to place commas in a sentence simply because it is long but to apply them only as rules require.

Activity Have students write the poem out as a sentence. Discuss with students that commas are placed between the subject and verb only if required by a rule, such as to set off an appositive *(no comma after "hemlock tree")* and that no comma is placed before the conjunction *and* unless it is followed by a clause (a group of words containing a subject and a verb). *(No comma after "mood" since there is no subject in the following phrase.)* **L2**

Additional Resources

- ***Grammar and Language Transparency 23***
- ***Grammar and Language Workbook,*** p. 259
- ***Grammar and Composition Handbook,*** Lesson 13.2
- ***Writer's Choice,*** Lesson 20.2

Dust of Snow

Robert Frost

The way a crow
Shook down on me
The dust of snow
From a hemlock° tree

Has given my heart
A change of mood
And saved some part
Of a day I had rued.°

4 The *hemlock* is a kind of evergreen tree in the pine family.
8 To *rue* is to regret or be sorry for.

H Literary Elements

RHYME SCHEME Have students identify the rhyme scheme of this poem. *(ABABCDCD)* Ask students how the rhythm of this rhyme scheme supports the poem's message. *(The rhyme scheme propels the reader along, almost as if skipping, supporting the poem's optimistic message.)*

I Literary Elements

LYRIC POETRY Ask students to identify the role of nature in this poem. *(This poem expresses how nature—in the form of the crow, the snow, and the tree—has changed the speaker's mood.)*

Thematic Focus

Which Way to Go? Ask students to review all three poems by Frost and to identify how they relate to the theme "Which Way to Go?" *(In each poem, the narrator takes a human concern—such as work, how the world will end, or personal problems—and makes it more comprehensible by comparing it to the wonder and simplicity of nature and friendship.)*

ASSESSMENT

Quick Checks, p. 25

CONNECTING TO OTHER SELECTIONS

For a teaching strategy that connects "Fire and Ice" to "The Legend of Sleepy Hollow," see the ***Theme Eight Planning Guide.***

Reading Minilesson

Compare and Contrast The poem "Fire and Ice" compares and contrasts fire and ice, which are used as symbols for ways humanity might be destroyed. Discuss the author's connection between passion and fire and between hatred and ice. Ask how fire and passion, and hatred and ice, are similar. Remind students that comparisons show how two things are alike, and contrast shows how they are different.

Activity Have students compare and contrast the real elements of fire and ice. They may then use these comparisons and contrasts to examine why the poet used these terms as symbols in his poem. **L2**

Additional Resources

Reading Skills Practice Workbook

Responding to the Selection

PERSONAL RESPONSE

Students should support their choice with specifics from the poems they choose.

Analyzing Literature

1. The stone wall stands between them.
2. "Dust of Snow" focuses on the narrator's response to nature.
3. The wall separates the men and prevents the friend from coming to the narrator. The wall keeps others out and must be overcome.
4. The crow's act of shaking snow on him as if it were a prank reminds him that nature is always present, on good days and bad.
5. Students may suggest that people get so caught up in work schedules, deadlines, and personal problems that they fail to make time for friendship. Frost's message is that people should adjust their priorities.
6. Responses should reflect an understanding of the narrator's views of desire and hate.
7. Students should be able to recognize Frost's respect for simplicity.
8. Student responses should relate specifically to an aspect of the selected poem.
9. Responses may include identification of each poem's conflict: between complexity and simplicity, humanity and nature, and self-absorption and a worldview.
10. "Dust of Snow" and "A Time to Talk" are both plausible responses because these simple poems express important messages. Students should support their choice with specific examples from the selected poem.

Active Reading and Critical Thinking

Responding to Literature

PERSONAL RESPONSE

- Which of the poems impressed you most? Why?

Brackets connect questions that are paired to develop higher-level thinking skills.

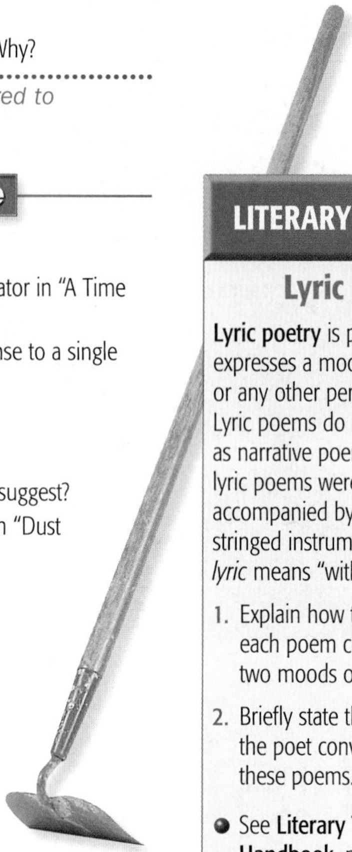

Analyzing Literature

RECALL

1. What stands between the friend and the narrator in "A Time to Talk"?
2. Which poem focuses on the narrator's response to a single scene in nature?

INTERPRET

3. What does the stone wall in "A Time to Talk" suggest?
4. What causes the narrator's mood to change in "Dust of Snow"?

EVALUATE AND CONNECT

5. What message about modern life might Frost be expressing in "A Time to Talk"?
6. How do you respond to the narrator in "Fire and Ice"? Do you agree or disagree with him? Why?
7. Why do you think Frost selected ordinary scenes as he examined human behavior?
8. Which poem speaks to your experiences most directly? Why? Cite the line that applies to you most.
9. **Theme Connection** What types of choices does the narrator of each poem make? What values are reflected in the choices? How does each of the three poems relate to the theme "Which Way to Go"?
10. Frost once said he wrote poems that "begin in delight and end in wisdom." In your opinion, which of the poems follows this form?

LITERARY ELEMENTS

Lyric Poetry

Lyric poetry is poetry that expresses a mood, feeling, idea, or any other personal thought. Lyric poems do not tell stories, as narrative poems do. Originally, lyric poems were sung while accompanied by a lyre, a small stringed instrument. The word *lyric* means "with a lyre."

1. Explain how the narrator of each poem chooses between two moods or situations.
2. Briefly state the single thought the poet conveys in each of these poems.

• See **Literary Terms Handbook**, p. R5.

LITERARY ELEMENTS

1. The first narrator chooses between completing work and making time for a friend. The second narrator chooses which is more devastating: passion or hate. The third narrator's mood is changed by an act of nature.
2. Students may note that each poem emphasizes the significance of simple things.

Additional Resources

Literary Elements Transparency 25

LITERATURE & HUMANITIES

Have students look at *Monolith*, the face of Half Dome, Yosemite National Park in *American History and Culture*, page 481. Ask students to write a short poem, in the style of Frost, that celebrates this scene in nature.

306 THEME 3

Extending Your Response

Writing About Literature

Poem to Poem Frost once wrote: "A poem is best read in the light of all the other poems ever written." List what you know about Frost's poetry that will help you read and understand other poems.

Creative Writing

Country Life Robert Frost spent several years as a farmer. Think about ways that working outdoors might have affected his poetry. Write a letter to a friend in which you use images from Frost's poems to convince the friend to give up city life and move to the country.

Interdisciplinary Activity

Art Robert Frost is known for writing directly and simply, using vivid imagery and symbolism. How could you illustrate one of his poems in a corresponding way? With a partner, create an illustration of one of the poems.

Literature Groups

Poetry Is Metaphor Robert Frost once said, "Education by poetry is education by metaphor." He defines metaphor as "saying one thing and meaning another." Each of the three poems is a metaphor about change and decisions about which way to go. Discuss the metaphor in each poem. What does each poem say, and what is the meaning behind each metaphor? What new ideas or meanings can you find in reading the poems? Discuss your answers with your group.

Reading Further

If you enjoyed Robert Frost's poems, try these other books by well-known poets:

Everywhere Faces Everywhere by James Berry
Classic Poems to Read Aloud edited by James Berry
Home on the Range: Cowboy Poetry by Paul B. Janeczko

Save your work for your portfolio.

Skill Minilesson

RETEACH • REVIEW

GRAMMAR AND LANGUAGE • ACTION VERBS

Words that express action and tell what a subject does are called **action verbs.** These verbs may describe physical actions, such as plowing, or mental actions, such as memorizing. Poets choose specific action verbs for the way they sound and for the images they paint in readers' minds.

PRACTICE Find at least four physical action verbs and four mental action verbs in the Frost poems. Then replace them with other verbs that have similar meanings. Reread the poems. How do the new verbs change the sound of the poems? How do they change the images in your mind?

- For more about using action verbs, see **Language Handbook**, p. R33.

Extending Your Response

Writing About Literature

Students' lists should

- relate the poet's ideas to their own experience and feelings
- refer to symbols used in the poem
- include examples from the poems

Creative Writing

Students' letters should include

- specific images from the poems
- persuasive techniques to incline the reader to favor country living

Literature Groups Discussions should include specifics from each poem and reflect an understanding of the use of metaphor. **COLLAB. LEARN.**

Interdisciplinary Activity
Students' art should focus on one image that symbolizes something about the poem—an event in the action or a mood.

Skill Minilesson

GRAMMAR AND LANGUAGE • ACTION VERBS

There are many action verbs to choose from: *calls, hoed, shout, thrust, plod, perish, shook,* and *saved.* The mental action verbs are *favor, know, tasted,* and *rued.*

Additional Resources

- ***Grammar and Language Workbook,*** p. 75
- ***Grammar and Composition Handbook,*** Lesson 3.1
- ***Writer's Choice,*** Lesson 0.1

ASSESSMENT

- ***Quick Checks,*** p. 25
- ***Selection and Theme Assessment,*** pp. 43–44
- ***Performance Assessment,*** p. 24
- ***Testmaker: ExamView Pro***
- ***Interactive Tutor: Self-Assessment***

FINE ART TRANSPARENCY 13

As a part of the **Literature Groups** activity, you may want to use *Fine Art Transparency 13* in a discussion of how metaphor can be used to describe a scene.

Vo•cab•u•lar•y Skills

Objective

- To identify and understand pronunciation symbols in a dictionary

Teaching Strategies

After students study the chart on page 308, show them where these symbols appear in the dictionary. Most dictionaries give a brief symbol guide on each page and a more lengthy explanation in the front pages. Help students become comfortable with using the dictionary for learning pronunciation by pointing out that each page gives the reader a common word as an example of the symbols used.

Activities

1.a. *Aghast* rhymes with *fast*. (No symbol indicates short *a* sound.)
 b. *Psyche* rhymes with *spikey*. (Straight-line symbol indicates a long *i* sound.)
 c. *Scav* rhymes with *have*. (No symbol indicates a short *a* sound.)

2.a. *angel* (long *a* and soft *g*)
 b. *bucket* (first syllable stressed, short *u*)
 c. *posse's* (first syllable stressed, long *e*)

Additional Resources

Vocabulary Power

Teaching Support

Vo•cab•u•lar•y Skills

Dictionary Skills–Pronunciation

Does *gauge* sound like *page* or like *garage?* Pronouncing an unfamiliar word can be tricky, because vowels and some consonants, like *g* and *c,* have more than one pronunciation. When in doubt, check a dictionary for the correct pronunciation shown with letters and symbols. *Gauge* appears like this: gāj. The first *g* has the "hard" *g* sound; the second one has the "soft" *g* sound–the same sound that *j* has. In between, there is the sound of a long *a*. So *gauge* rhymes with *page.*

In a dictionary pronunciation, a vowel without a symbol has a "short" sound, like the vowels in *pat, pet, pit, hot,* and *hut.* Other vowel sounds are shown by symbols, such as a straight line above the vowel to show that it is a long vowel.

SYMBOL	MEANING	SYMBOL	MEANING
ä	an **ah** sound, as in **father**	ə	the unaccented vowel sound heard at the end of **pencil, lemon, taken**
ô	an **aw** sound, as in **coffee** and **law**	hw	**wh** as in **white**
oo	the vowel sound you hear in **wood**	th	**th** as in **thin**
o͞o	the vowel sound you hear in **fool**	t͟h	**th** as in **this**
oi	the vowel sound you hear in **toy**	zh	the sound heard in the middle of **treasure** or at the end of **garage**
ou	an **ow** sound, as in **cow** and **out**		

An **accent mark** points to the syllable you should stress. Stressing the correct syllable is extremely important in pronunciation. For example, the only difference in the sounds of *dessert* and *desert* is which syllable is stressed.

ACTIVITIES

1. Use the pronunciation given for each word to answer the question that follows it.
   a. *aghast* (ə gast′) Does this word rhyme with *fast* or *waste?*
   b. *psyche* (sī′ kē) Does this word rhyme with *like, spikey, itchy,* or *rich?*
   c. *scavenger* (skav′ in jər) Does the first syllable of this word rhyme with *have* or *save?*
2. Decide which word is represented by each dictionary pronunciation.
   a. ān′ jəl Is this word *angle* (corner) or *angel* (heavenly being)?
   b. buk′ it Is this word *bucket* or *bouquet?*
   c. pos′ ēz Is this word *possess* or *posse's?*

MEETING INDIVIDUAL NEEDS

ENGLISH LANGUAGE LEARNERS

Personalized Pronunciation Keys Most English language learners have difficulty distinguishing among English vowel sounds. Make sure English language learners understand all words referred to on page 308 and the dictionary pronunciation key. Suggest alternatives for unfamiliar words: Instead of *pat* for the short *a* sound and *treasure* for the *zh* sound, you might suggest *cat* and *measure.*

Activity Help students make personalized pronunciation keys for their vocabulary notebooks to consult as they learn new words. Encourage them to consult a dictionary or the glossary in the back of their textbook for pronunciations of new words.

Additional Resources

English Language Learners Sourcebook, p. 45

Before You Read

Between What I See and What I Say . . . /
Entre Lo Que Veo y Digo . . .

MEET
OCTAVIO PAZ

New isn't necessarily better, according to Mexican poet Octavio Paz (ok täv′ yō päz). In fact, he worried that his country was losing its rich literary heritage and culture to a modern society filled with action films, magazines, and "television but not vision." In his writing, Paz attempted to reach across cultural differences to speak from the human soul. Those efforts earned him the Nobel Prize in Literature in 1990.

Octavio Paz was born in 1914 and died in 1998. This poem was published in a collection of Paz's poems entitled A Tree Within.

READING FOCUS

Do you find it difficult to express some emotions and ideas in words? How do poetry and the other arts encourage self-expression?

Define It!

Work with a partner to write a definition of poetry. Then share your definition with another pair of students.

Setting a Purpose

Read to explore the poet's definition of poetry.

BUILDING BACKGROUND

This poem was written in 1982 for a memorial to Roman Jakobson, a Russian-born professor at Harvard University. Jakobson shared with Paz a love of language.

Throughout his writings, Paz posed questions and problems for the reader to ponder. His work appeals to young people because he understood the questions and problems of adolescents. Countries, he said, do the same. "Much the same thing happens to nations and peoples at a certain critical moment in their development. They ask themselves: 'What are we, and how can we fulfill our obligations to ourselves as we are?'"

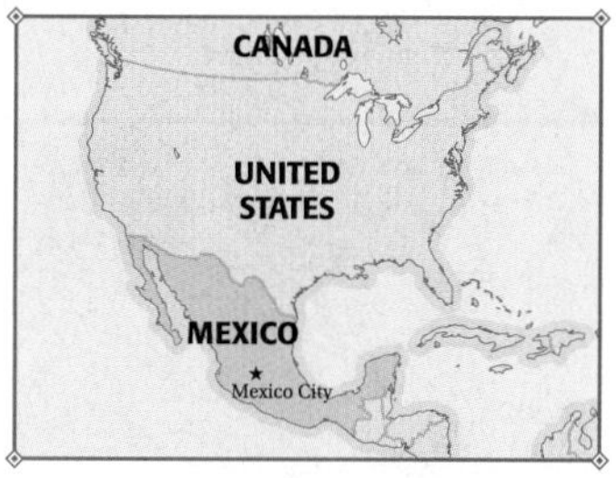

Before Reading

Objectives

- To read and analyze a poem about poetry
- To identify free verse
- To write a paragraph explaining the visual effects of a poem

Skills

Reading/Thinking: Recognizing the Author's Purpose
Writing: Essay
Vocabulary: Roots
Grammar/Language: Subject-Verb Agreement
Life Skills: Decision Making
Collaboration: Literature Groups

Motivating STUDENTS

Literature Launchers: "The World of Octavio Paz"

Videodisc Side A, Segment 7

Also available in VHS.

Selection Focus Transparency 25: Before presenting the quotation, ask students to discuss how important observation is to writing.

Reading Focus: As an extension of the Reading Focus, have students put their definitions of poetry on the board. Encourage students to combine responses to come up with one very detailed definition.

RESOURCE MANAGER

Teaching Tools and Resources
- Theme Three Planning Guide
- Literature Groups Sourcebook

Essential Lesson Support

Lesson-Specific Instruction
- Selection Focus Transparency 25
- Literary Elements Transparency 26
- Active Reading Guide,* p. 26

Assessment
- Selection Quick Checks,* p. 26
- Sel. and Theme Assmt., pp. 45–46
- Testmaker: ExamView Pro
- Performance Assessment, p. 25

Systematic Language Instruction
- Gr. & Comp. Hbk., Lesson 6.1
- Vocabulary Power, Unit 3 Review/Proofreading

English Language Learners
- ELL Sourcebook, pp. 46, 47
- Spanish Summaries, p. 25
- Spanish Translations, p. 78
- Audio Library*
- English, Yes!

Spec. Needs/Strat. Interven.
- Interactive Rdg. Sbk., pp. T111–T113
- Interactive Rdg. Wkbk., p. 52
- Audio Library*

* Also available in Spanish

Reading the Selection

A Active Reading Strategies

EVALUATE Encourage students to consider the difficulty a writer faces in trying to convey abstract ideas, such as emotions, with words. Ask students what technique this poet has used to describe the abstract idea of poetry. *(The poet attempts to describe the abstract idea of poetry by making it seem like a living thing.)*

B Literary Elements

FREE VERSE Free verse can convey meaning through its visual design. Note that the poet talks about poetry "weaving." Have students find examples of weaving and reflection in the structure of the poem. *(In the physical design of the poem, each line begins at the space where the previous one ended, mimicking the weaving process.)*

Additional Resources

Active Reading Guides, p. 26

Audio Library

Spanish Audio Library

Between What I See and What I Say . . .

Octavio Paz

Translated by Eliot Weinberger

for Roman Jakobson

1

Between what I see and what I say,
between what I say and what I keep
silent,
between what I keep silent and what
I dream,
between what I dream and what I
forget:
poetry.
It slips
between yes and no,
says
what I keep silent,
keeps silent
what I say,
dreams
what I forget.
It is not speech:
it is an act.
It is an act
of speech.
Poetry
speaks and listens:
it is real.
And as soon as I say
it is real,
it vanishes.
Is it then more real?

2

Tangible° idea,
intangible
word:
poetry
comes and goes
between what is
and what is not.
It weaves
and unweaves reflections.
Poetry
scatters eyes on a page,
scatters words on our eyes.
Eyes speak,
words look,
looks think.
To hear
thoughts,
see
what we say,
touch
the body of an idea.
Eyes close,
the words open.

25 A *tangible* idea is one that can be perceived, or almost perceived, by the senses, especially by the sense of touch.

Teaching Support

CONNECTING TO OTHER SELECTIONS

For a teaching strategy that connects this selection to "Americans All," see the ***Theme Six Planning Guide.***

FINE ART TRANSPARENCY 30

You may want to use ***Fine Art Transparency 30*** to discuss ways in which books can lead to ambitions and to dreams.

Entre Lo Que Veo y Digo . . .

A Roman Jakobson

Octavio Paz

1

Entre lo que veo y digo,
entre lo que digo y callo,
entre lo que callo y sueño,
entre lo que sueño y olvido,
la poesía.
Se desliza
entre el sí y el no:
dice
lo que callo,
calla
lo que digo,
sueña
lo que olvido.
No es un decir:
es un hacer.
Es un hacer
que es un decir.
La poesía
se dice y se oye:
es real.
Y apenas digo
es real,
se disipa.
¿Así es más real?

2

Idea palpable,
palabra
impalpable:
la poesía
va y viene
entre lo que es
y lo que no es.
Teje reflejos
y los desteje.
La poesía
siembra ojos en la página,
siembra palabras en los ojos.
Los ojos hablan,
las palabras miran,
las miradas piensan.
Oír
los pensamientos,
ver
los que decimos,
tocar
el cuerpo de la idea.
Los ojos
se cierran,
las palabras se abren.

Presence of the Past, 1953 (details). Gunther Gerszo. Oil on Masonite. Museum of Fine Arts, Houston, TX.

Vo•cab•u•lar•y Skills

Roots Use the Spanish version of the poem to point out the similarities between the languages. Explain that Spanish is a Latin language, meaning that its words derive from Latin words. Explain that many English words also derive from Latin words. Encourage students to look for words in the Spanish version that are similar or even identical to the English words *(poesia, no, real, palpable, reflejos, idea)*. Point out that many of the words have Latin roots similar to other English words. (*Disipa*, translated as *vanishes*, shares the same root as *dissipate*; *dice*, translated as *says*, shares the same root as *dictate* and *diction*; *cuerpo*, translated as *body*, shares the same root as *corpse*.

Thematic Focus

Which Way to Go? In this poem, the poet tries to define poetry but acknowledges that each time he thinks he has explained it, it is actually something else.

ASSESSMENT

Quick Checks, p. 26

Grammar and Language *Minilesson*

Subject-Verb Agreement The English version of this poem provides a good review of verbs, as it relies heavily on them. Explain to students that the predicate of a sentence can be compound. Remind students that all the verbs in a sentence must agree with their subjects; if there is only one subject, all the verbs must agree with it.

Activity Have students identify the subject and the predicates in lines 6–13. Have students contrast this sentence with the one in lines 37–39, which has multiple subjects and verbs. For practice, ask students to write three sentences following the single-subject, multiple-predicate construction and three sentences following the multiple-subject, multiple-predicate construction used in lines 37–39. **L2**

Additional Resources

- ***Grammar and Language Transparency 24***
- ***Grammar and Language Workbook,*** p. 195
- ***Grammar and Composition Handbook,*** Lesson 10.5
- ***Writer's Choice,*** Lesson 16.5

Responding to the Selection

PERSONAL RESPONSE

Students' responses should be supported with explanations.

Analyzing Literature

1. Poetry lies between them.
2. He uses the image of weaving.
3. The words "open"; that is, their meaning becomes clear.
4. Answers should reflect an understanding that the author finds the concept of poetry elusive and difficult to grasp or define.
5. As weaving creates something useful or artistic out of separate strands, the author believes poetry makes sense out of random thoughts or occurrences.
6. Students should notice the connection between "eyes" and "see" and between "say" and "words."
7. Students' responses should use specific examples of wording or technique to support their choices.
8. Students should identify some impact, such as reflecting their mood, changing their mood, changing their opinion, or expanding their perspectives.
9. Students should be specific in their explanations of the results of rereading poetry.
10. Responses should reflect thoughtfulness in choice and specific references to the poem as support.

Active Reading and Critical Thinking

Responding to Literature

PERSONAL RESPONSE

- Does Paz's poem make you want to write a poem or read

Brackets connect questions that are paired to develop higher-level thinking skills.

Analyzing Literature

RECALL

1. What lies between the things the narrator sees and the things he says?
2. What image does Paz use to show that poetry puts things together to make something beautiful?
3. According to the poem, what happens when you close your eyes and think about a poem?

INTERPRET

4. Why does Paz describe poetry by telling what it is between, rather than what it is?
5. Why does Paz compare a poem to material that is woven?
6. How do the last two lines of the poem relate to the first line?

EVALUATE AND CONNECT

7. Does Paz's description of poetry emphasize the mystery of poetry or the rules of poetry? Explain your answer.
8. How does poetry affect your life? (Remember that the lyrics of songs are poems.)
9. What happens when you reread a poem many times? Does your interpretation change? Explain.
10. To whom would you recommend this poem? Give reasons for your answer.

LITERARY ELEMENTS

Free Verse

Free verse is poetry that doesn't have a regular pattern of rhythm or rhyme. Free verse sounds like spoken language and contains modern words and phrases. The irregular line lengths and breaks of "Between What I See and What I Say" are characteristics of free verse. Read part of the poem aloud. Lines in free verse are often grouped to show meaning or create images.

1. Look at the form of the poem. How is the beginning different from the remaining lines?
2. How does this poem imitate conversation?

• See **Literary Terms Handbook,** p. R4.

Presence of the Past, 1953. Gunther Gerszo. Oil on Masonite. Museum of Fine Arts, Houston, TX.

LITERARY ELEMENTS

1. The beginning of the poem is more structured and is written as a stanza.
2. Students may suggest that the visual effect of breaking up the lines suggests two people in conversation or that the two sections may represent two speakers.

Additional Resources

Literary Elements Transparency 26

Extending Your Response

Writing About Literature

Reading Between the Lines This poem is about going beyond sight to find meaning. However, the poet has presented the poem in a visual format, breaking up sentences and putting fragments on single lines. Why might the author have written the poem in this way? What effect does this format achieve? How does it affect the way the poem is read? Write a paragraph to explain your thoughts.

Literature Groups

Poetry: Real or Unreal? In the poem, the narrator asks whether poetry is real. He writes: "And as soon as I say / *it is real,* / it vanishes." What makes words and ideas real to you? What poems or other forms of writing can you think of that seemed real or powerful when you read them? If possible, share these selections with your group and discuss your reasons for choosing them.

Personal Writing

You Are What You Write Paz's work was affected by his background, his Mexican nationality, and by his years of living in Asia as Mexico's ambassador to India, Pakistan, Nepal, and Ceylon (now Sri Lanka). Write an essay that explains how your writing is affected by your heritage, by where you live, and by your interests and activities.

Learning for Life

You As a Critic Think about Paz's concern for "television but not vision." Do you agree that our cultural and literacy heritage is at risk because of television? If you do, write to your local newspaper. Share your concern and suggest ways to work against the negative effects of TV. If you think there is "vision" in the television shows you watch, write a letter explaining why you think as you do. Use examples from programs you consider worthwhile. Be sure to include a clear and well-supported conclusion.

Reading Further

If you'd like to read more about choices and discoveries, try these novels:
Come a Stranger by Cynthia Voigt
Park's Quest by Katharine Paterson

Save your work for your portfolio.

Skill Minilesson

RETEACH • REVIEW

READING AND THINKING • AUTHOR'S PURPOSE

Poets have a **purpose,** or goal, for what they write, just as other writers do. Sometimes the purpose is to persuade, to inform, to entertain, or perhaps simply to express an idea or a feeling.

To better understand what you read, try to identify the author's purpose.

PRACTICE Reread the poem. What, do you think, was Paz's purpose for composing this poem for a memorial service to Roman Jakobson, a linguist? Explain your answer.

- For more about author's purpose, see **Reading Handbook,** p. R107.

Extending Your Response

Writing About Literature

Students' paragraphs should

- explain the author's purpose for the visual format of the poem
- explain the effect of the format
- analyze the impact of the format on the pace of the poem

Personal Writing

Students' essays should

- state the effect of their personal experiences on their writing
- demonstrate the effect with specific examples
- analyze how their experiences have had an impact on their writing

Literature Groups Responses should draw conclusions about what is "real" from the works chosen. COLLAB. LEARN.

Learning for Life Suggest that students use a graphic organizer or chart to present their opinions.

Skill Minilesson

READING AND THINKING • AUTHOR'S PURPOSE

Students' responses should reflect an understanding of the term *linguist* (one with an interest in words). Responses may suggest that a linguist would be interested in poetry or may recognize an irony that, according to the poem, poetry is found between words.

Additional Resources

Reading Skills Practice Workbook

ASSESSMENT

- ***Quick Checks,*** p. 26
- ***Selection and Theme Assessment,*** pp. 45–46
- ***Performance Assessment,*** p. 25
- ***Testmaker: ExamView Pro***
- ***Interactive Tutor: Self-Assessment***

GRAMMAR LINK

Objective

- To identify singular and plural subjects and make corresponding verbs agree in number

Teaching Strategies

Remind students that, although they may not be near each other in the sentence, the subject and the verb work together to make the point of the sentence. Caution students not to become distracted by intervening words. In the first example ask students whether the backpack is heavy. Encourage students to recognize that because the *backpack* is the subject of the sentence and is a singular noun, the verb should also be singular.

Exercise

1. are
2. write
3. is
4. have

Additional Resources

Grammar and Language Workbook, p. 195

Grammar and Composition Handbook, Lesson 10.1

Writer's Choice, Lesson 16.1

Teaching Support

GRAMMAR LINK

Subject-Verb Agreement

A **subject** tells who or what is doing something. A **verb** tells what the subject is doing. A singular subject needs a singular verb, and a plural subject needs a plural verb. Making a subject agree with its verb is tricky sometimes, but the following problems and solutions can help you.

Problem 1 *My backpack, filled with poetry books, are heavy.*

Solution Make the verb agree with its subject, not with the closest noun.

My backpack, filled with poetry books, is heavy.

Problem 2 *Each of the poems contain similes.*

Few in the world is as observant as a poet.

Some of Paz's poetry focus on nature.

Solution If the subject is an indefinite pronoun, study the chart below to determine whether it is singular or plural. A few indefinite pronouns can be either singular or plural, depending on the object of the preposition that follows in the sentence.

Indefinite Pronouns		
Singular	**Plural**	**Either**
another, each, either, everybody, everything, much, neither, somebody, something	both, few, many, others, several	all, any, most, none, some

Each of the poems contains similes.

Few in the world are as observant as a poet.

Some of Paz's poetry focuses on nature.

EXERCISE

For each sentence, write the correct form of the verb in parentheses.

1. Some poems, such as "Casey at the Bat," (is, are) humorous.
2. Many poets (write, writes) poems in response to art.
3. Much of Frost's work (is, are) available on-line.
4. All of the local book stores (has, have) a section devoted to poetry.

Writing Minilesson

Editing Point out that one difficulty in subject-verb agreement occurs with the use of intervening phrases. Because the object of the preposition is closer than the subject to the verb, students may tend to make the verb agree with the object rather than the subject of the sentence. This is something that students should look for when they revise and edit their writing.

Activity Have students write a five-sentence paragraph in which each sentence contains an intervening prepositional phrase. Students should exchange their paragraphs and edit one another's sentences for subject-verb agreement. Have students, while they are editing, mark each subject with an S. **L2**

Additional Resources

Writer's Choice, Lessons 2.9, 16.2

Listening, Speaking, and Viewing

Effective Listening Techniques

How can you get the most out of conversations, speeches, instructions, and everything you hear each day? Pay attention to more than words. Octavio Paz tells readers that listening involves eyes and minds, as well as ears:

. . . To hear
thoughts,
see
what we say,
touch
the body of an idea. . . .

Listening Tips

- **Focus** on the speaker's words. Paraphrase, or restate, the speaker's main points. Are the main points supported by details and facts?
- **Watch** the speaker's posture, gestures, and facial expressions. What do they show about how the speaker feels?
- **Think** about ways the speaker's message relates to you. Will it help you learn? Understand? Enjoy?

The Listening Tips can help you answer questions like the following.

Questions for Effective Listening

1. What is the speaker's purpose? (To inform? To persuade? To share feelings?)
2. What are the speaker's main points?
3. What questions do I have after listening to this speaker?
4. What (if any) hidden messages or biases do I detect?

ACTIVITIES

1. With a partner, practice your listening skills. Take turns preparing and presenting a reading or speech. Then write your responses to the first two **Questions for Effective Listening.** Check your responses with your partner.
2. Listen to a short speech. It may be live, or it may be part of a film, a documentary, or a news broadcast. Write your responses to the **Questions for Effective Listening.** Discuss your responses with classmates.

Listening, Speaking, and Viewing

Objective

- To identify and practice effective listening techniques

Teaching Strategies

After reviewing the Listening Tips, ask students to identify barriers to effective listening. They may suggest noise; distractions produced by the speaker, such as fidgeting; preoccupation of the listener; or lack of interest in the subject. Write each barrier on the board. Then go through the list and solicit ideas from students on how to overcome each barrier.

Activities

1. Student responses to question 1 should complete the thought prompted by the question. *(To inform about. . . , to persuade that. . . , to share feelings of. . . .)*
2. Students may wish to jot down their responses as they listen.

Teaching Support

Meeting Individual Needs: English Language Learners

Read Along English language learners may find it difficult to follow a speech if the speaker talks quickly. One way students less familiar with the language can practice their listening skills is to read along as someone reads aloud. This way, students can see and hear the words at the same time. This will help them recognize unfamiliar words when they hear them.

Activity Pair English language learners with English speakers, who will read a passage aloud as the English language learners follow along. Encourage the student reading aloud to speak at a normal pace and with normal intonation rather than reading each word slowly.

Additional Resources

English Language Learners Sourcebook, p. 47

Before Reading

Objectives

- To read and analyze two poems about philosophies of living
- To identify the theme of a poem
- To rewrite two stanzas of a poem

Skills

Reading/Thinking: Comparing and Contrasting; Evaluating
Writing: Comic-Strip Development
Grammar/Language: Adjectives
Listening/Speaking: Role-Playing
Collaboration: Literature Groups

Motivating STUDENTS

Selection Focus Transparency 26: Before presenting the photograph, have students write in their journals about times when they have "pushed the limit."

Reading Focus: As an extension of the Reading Focus, ask students to compare the qualities they have chosen by finding similarities among the qualities, though the plants or insects selected may differ.

Before You Read

Identity and *the lesson of the moth*

MEET JULIO NOBOA POLANCO

Julio Noboa Polanco (ho͞o lē′ ō nä bō′ ä pō lōn′ kō) was in the eighth grade when he wrote the poem "Identity." He got the idea for the poem during a long walk near his West Side home in Chicago after he and his girlfriend had broken up. Noboa now lives in San Antonio, Texas, where he writes a biweekly column for the *San Antonio Express-News* and works in the field of education.

MEET DON MARQUIS

Don Marquis (mär kē′) worked many years as a columnist with the *Evening Sun*, a New York newspaper. In his columns, Marquis created the characters of archy, a poetic cockroach, and his friend, mehitabel the cat. Marquis died in 1937, but his characters live on in poems such as "the lesson of the moth."

READING FOCUS

Imagine that you could be a plant or an animal for just a day. What would you choose to be? A rose? A bear? What qualities would you possess?

Web It!

Use a word web to develop your ideas. Circle the word that states your choice and surround it with details and reasons supporting your choice.

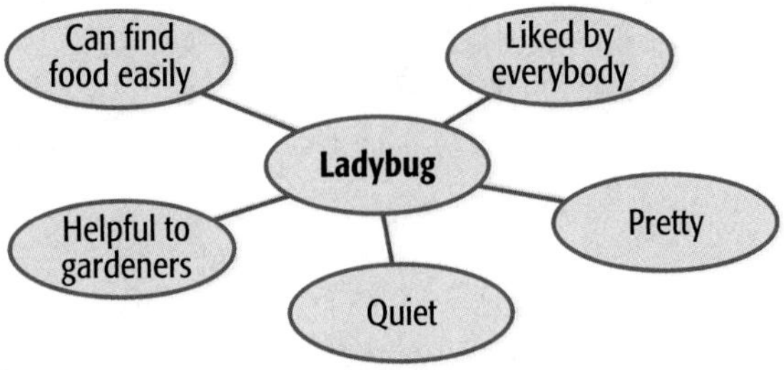

Setting a Purpose

Read to discover the comparisons in these poems.

BUILDING BACKGROUND

Don Marquis's archy liked to write poetry. According to Marquis, archy composed poems like "the lesson of the moth" on a manual typewriter by hurling himself at each typewriter key. "After about an hour of this frightfully difficult literary labor he fell to the floor exhausted," Marquis said. Because archy couldn't reach the shift key, his writing (including his name) didn't include capitalization or punctuation.

RESOURCE MANAGER

Teaching Tools and Resources
- Theme Three Planning Guide
- Literature Groups Sourcebook

Essential Lesson Support

Lesson-Specific Instruction
- Selection Focus Transparency 26
- Literary Elements Transparency 27
- Active Reading Guide,* p. 27
- inTIME *magazine*, p. 24

Assessment
- Selection Quick Checks,* p. 27
- Sel. and Theme Assmt., pp. 47–48
- Testmaker: ExamView Pro
- Performance Assessment, p. 26

Systematic Language Instruction
- Gr. & Comp. Hbk., L. 6.2

English Language Learners
- ELL Sourcebook, p. 48
- Spanish Summaries, p. 26
- Spanish Translations, pp. 79–80
- Audio Library*
- English, Yes!

Spec. Needs/Strat. Interven.
- Interactive Rdg. Sbk., pp. T113–T115
- Interactive Rdg. Wkbk., p. 53
- Inclusion Strat. Sbk., pp. 39–40
- Audio Library*

* Also available in Spanish

Identity

Julio Noboa Polanco

Let them be as flowers,
always watered, fed, guarded, admired,
but harnessed to a pot of dirt.

I'd rather be a tall, ugly weed,
clinging on cliffs, like an eagle
wind-wavering above high, jagged rocks.

To have broken through the surface of stone
to live, to feel exposed to the madness
of the vast, eternal sky.
To be swayed by the breezes of an ancient sea,
carrying my soul, my seed beyond the mountains of time
or into the abyss° of the bizarre.°

I'd rather be unseen, and if,

then shunned° by everyone
than to be a pleasant-smelling flower,
growing in clusters in the fertile valley
where they're praised, handled, and plucked
by greedy, human hands.

I'd rather smell of musty, green stench
than of sweet, fragrant lilac.
If I could stand alone, strong and free,
I'd rather be a tall, ugly weed.

12 An *abyss* is an immeasurably deep hole or a vast emptiness. The *bizarre* (bi zär′) is something that is extremely strange.

14 A person who is being *shunned* is being avoided.

Reading the Selection

A Active Reading Strategies

CONNECT Ask students whether they feel the same way the author does about life. Have them explain their answers.

Additional Resources

- ***Active Reading Guide,*** p. 27
- ***Audio Library***
- ***Spanish Audio Library***

B Literary Elements

THEME Have students think about the theme of this poem. Encourage them to see that the weed and the flower symbolize life-style options.

C Literary Elements

IMAGERY Have students identify the vivid words used by the author to produce an image. Encourage students to contrast these with other words that have similar meanings but do not create such a vivid image.

Teaching Support

Meeting Individual Needs: ENGLISH LANGUAGE LEARNERS

Contractions Students not fluent in English may have difficulty understanding the use of contractions. Explain that contractions are normally used as substitutions for only a few words: *am, are, is, will, not, would, have, has, had.* Because the contractions for *would* and *had* are both *'d*, and the contractions for *is* and *has* are both *'s*, these can be especially confusing.

Activity Write the following sentence on the board: *As you have heard, I had already learned that he did not go.* Have students rewrite this sentence, using contractions. Have the students read their sentences aloud to practice using contractions in speech.

Additional Resources

- ***English Language Learners Sourcebook,*** p. 48

On The Lighter Side

A Weed by Any Other Name

Students may have fun, after reading "Identity," discussing whether they would consider themselves a weed or a flower, and if so what kind of weed or flower. You may first want to talk about some different types of weeds and flowers and their characteristics.

FYI

Insects Both moths and cockroaches are nocturnal, sleeping or hiding during the day and becoming active at night. Whereas cockroaches are truly nocturnal and only come out of hiding when it is dark, moths are actually crepuscular, meaning they emerge at twilight when there is still some light left. Not all cockroaches can fly, but the American cockroach can.

the lesson of the moth

Don Marquis

Teaching Support

Grammar and Language *Minilesson*

Adjective Phrases Reiterate that modifiers make writing vivid and interesting. Remind students that adjectives modify nouns and can be single words placed before the noun or phrases placed elsewhere. Explain that phrasal adjectives often take the form of prepositional phrases. Use the poem "Identity" to demonstrate the use of adjective phrases.

Activity Encourage students to find the adjective phrases in "Identity." (*Of stone, of an ancient sea,* and *of the bizarre* are a few.) Then have students rewrite the lines by changing the placement of the adjectives. (*stone surface,* etc.) Encourage the students also to rewrite some of the poem's single-word adjectives, changing them into phrases. **L2**

Additional Resources

- ***Grammar and Language Transparency 25***
- ***Grammar and Language Workbook,*** p. 145
- ***Grammar and Composition Handbook,*** Lesson 7.3
- ***Writer's Choice,*** Lesson 13.3

i was talking to a moth
the other evening
he was trying to break into
an electric light bulb
and fry himself on the wires

why do you fellows
pull this stunt i asked him
because it is the conventional°
thing for moths or why
if that had been an uncovered
candle instead of an electric
light bulb you would
now be a small unsightly cinder
have you no sense

plenty of it he answered
but at times we get tired
of using it
we get bored with the routine
and crave beauty
and excitement
fire is beautiful
and we know that if we get
too close it will kill us
but what does that matter
it is better to be happy
for a moment
and be burned up with beauty
than to live a long time
and be bored all the while
so we wad all our life up
into one little roll
and then we shoot the roll
that is what life is for
it is better to be a part of beauty
for one instant and then cease to
exist than to exist forever
and never be a part of beauty
our attitude toward life
is come easy go easy
we are like human beings
used to be before they became
too civilized to enjoy themselves

and before i could argue him
out of his philosophy°
he went and immolated° himself
on a patent cigar lighter
i do not agree with him
myself i would rather have
half the happiness and twice
the longevity°

but at the same time i wish
there was something i wanted
as badly as he wanted to fry himself

archy

8 *Conventional* describes what is usual, customary, or traditional.

44 Here, *philosophy* refers to the personal beliefs and principles that guide one's life.

45 The most common meaning of *immolate* is "to destroy by fire," but it can also mean "to offer in sacrifice."

50 *Longevity* (lon jev′ ə tē) means "long life."

D Literary Elements

THEME Ask students to consider whether the lack of capitalization or punctuation contributes to the theme, or message, the poet is trying to convey. Point out that this stlyle emphasizes the monotonous life that the cockroach, the speaker in the poem, has chosen.

E Critical Thinking

EVALUATE Ask students to evaluate the moth's arguments and state whether they agree or disagree with his philosophy. Ask them to identify drawbacks and advantages to the moth's philosophy, using examples from the poem or from personal experience.

Thematic Focus

Which Way to Go? "Identity" and "the lesson of the moth" each offer two philosophies of life. Ask students to describe how both poems explore the positives and negatives of each lifestyle choice.

ASSESSMENT

Quick Checks, p. 27

Reading *Minilesson*

Comparison and Contrast The poet's choice of words helps to convey the message of a poem. For example, in "Identity" the weed is described in the present tense and the flower in the past tense.

Activity Ask students to contrast the tenses of the verbs used to describe the flower's existence and the weed's existence *(fed, guarded, harnessed* versus *clinging, wind-wavering, carrying my soul)*. Have students find other contrasts in word choices used to describe the weed and the flower. Encourage students to explain the effect of these contrasts and how they contribute to the message of the poem. **L2**

Additional Resources

Reading Skills Practice Workbook

CONNECTING TO OTHER SELECTIONS
For a teaching strategy that connects this selection to "Chanclas," see the ***Theme One Planning Guide.***

Responding to the Selection

PERSONAL RESPONSE

Responses should include specific examples from the poem that explain the students' choices.

Analyzing Literature

1. He chooses to be a weed because weeds grow wild and free.
2. The moth explains its philosophy of life to archy the cockroach and then lives its philosophy by flying into a lighter flame.
3. Responses should suggest freedom so may include "like an eagle," "to live," "to be swayed by the breezes," "if I could stand alone," and "strong and free."
4. Archy's attitude toward life is cautious, but slightly regretful. He says he "would rather have half the happiness but twice the longevity," but he's envious of the moth's passion.
5. The comparison appears in the first line. Flowers are like certain types of people—beautiful to look at ("admired," "pleasant-smelling") and popular ("growing in clusters," "praised," "handled").
6. Some images may include the following: lines 3–5, 13, 30–31, and 45–46.
7. Responses should address whether people have become "too civilized to enjoy themselves" and what this statement means.
8. Both the speaker and the moth have a zest for life and want to embrace it at full speed, and both will take risks to do so. (The weed risks being an outcast; the moth risks its life.) Both archy and the flower seek security and safety. They live longer but with more restrictions and less excitement.
9. Students may suggest encouraging archy to take risks.
10. Responses should contain specific examples from the poems that reflect similarities to the student's views. You may want students to identify the character they most admire also.

Active Reading and Critical Thinking

Responding to Literature

PERSONAL RESPONSE

- Which stands out most in your mind: the flower, the weed, the moth, or archy? Why?

Brackets connect questions that are paired to develop higher-level thinking skills.

Analyzing Literature

RECALL

1. What does the speaker in "Identity" choose to be? What are the reasons for the choice?
2. Summarize what happens in "the lesson of the moth."

INTERPRET

3. In your opinion, what kind of life does the weed in "Identity" live? Give three examples to support your claim.
4. What is archy's attitude toward life? Support your answer with examples from the poem.

EVALUATE AND CONNECT

5. Noboa uses a **simile,** which compares two things using *like* or *as.* In what ways might he think flowers are like people? What words or phrases in the poem show this idea?
6. Marquis uses **imagery** to create pictures that reinforce the ideas in the poem. List two images that show the type of life the moth leads.
7. According to lines 40–42 in "the lesson of the moth," what might the moth think about human beings? Do you agree? Why or why not?
8. In what ways might the speaker in "Identity" be like the moth? How is the flower like archy?
9. Describe archy's conflict in lines 48–53. What advice would you give archy to resolve this conflict?
10. Which image do you identify with the most: the flower, the weed, the moth, or archy? Why?

LITERARY ELEMENTS

Theme

The **theme,** or message, of a poem can often be stated in a simple sentence like "Live an honest life," or "Trust your instincts." Sometimes, the theme is not stated, and the reader must infer by looking at the thoughts and actions in the poem. Other times, a character or speaker states the theme directly.

1. State the theme of "Identity." What does the speaker say to reveal this theme?
2. Write a sentence that states the theme of "the lesson of the moth." What does the moth say that gives away the theme?

- See **Literary Terms Handbook,** p. R10.

LITERARY ELEMENTS

1. The theme might be stated as "The price for security (or popularity or belonging) is too high." The line "harnessed to a pot of dirt" reveals this theme. "Be your own person" also captures the theme stated in lines 4–5.
2. Lines 25–29 state the theme. Students should state it in their own words.

Additional Resources

Literary Elements Transparency 27

Extending Your Response

Writing About Literature

Style In his stories of archy and mehitabel, Marquis writes without capitalization and punctuation. Working with a partner, rewrite the first two stanzas of the poem, using standard punctuation and capitalization. Then discuss what is gained and what is lost by using standard conventions of punctuation and capitalization. Does lack of mechanics encourage you to read more about archy? Does it discourage you?

Literature Groups

Friends Camp Out Imagine that a flower, a weed, a moth, and archy are on a camping trip. The moth suggests they go rock climbing. Assign the roles of each character to members of your group, and role-play a conversation. Then discuss the ideas that came out of the role-playing.

Interdisciplinary Activity

Art With a small group, construct a comic strip to show two advantages and two disadvantages of living as either a flower, a weed, a moth, or a cockroach. Before you draw the strip, consider the opinions of the authors and the ideas of each group member. Present the finished strip to the class.

Learning for Life

In Memory A **eulogy** is a speech given to honor a person who has died. Write a eulogy for the moth, flower, weed, or archy. Tell why the character was special and why he or she will be missed and mourned. Include an anecdote, a brief story that can be humorous or meaningful, to give insight into the character. Present your eulogy to the class.

Reading Further

For fiction about choosing a place in life, read:
The Prince and the Pauper by Mark Twain
The Call of the Wild by Jack London

Save your work for your portfolio.

Skill Minilesson

RETEACH • REVIEW

READING AND THINKING • COMPARE AND CONTRAST

When you **compare** two selections, you look at how they are similar. When you **contrast**, you study how two things are different. "Identity" and "the lesson of the moth" are good poems to compare because they are both about making life choices.

- For more about comparing and contrasting, see **Reading Handbook**, p. R101.

PRACTICE Compare and contrast the two poems by answering the following questions.

1. Compare the titles. What information does each give about the poem?
2. Compare the themes of the poems. How do they relate to the theme "Which Way to Go?"

Extending Your Response

Writing About Literature
Students' stanzas should
- contain proper use of quotation marks, punctuation, and capitalization
- include an explanation of their reaction to the lack of mechanics

Literature Groups Suggest that one student in each group take notes, covering the important ideas discussed. COLLAB. LEARN.

Interdisciplinary Activity Make sure students understand that their representations should be humorous.

Learning for Life Suggest that students brainstorm for some basic ideas about the character they chose before they begin writing. Students should deliver their eulogies as though they were at a memorial service for the character, using an appropriately respectful tone.

Skill Minilesson

READING AND THINKING • COMPARE AND CONTRAST

1. *Possible answers:* The title "Identity" conveys what the narrator believes the weed achieves. "the lesson of the moth" suggests that archy may have some admiration for the moth.
2. Each poem represents two ways of approaching life and the choices we make about how to live our lives.

Additional Resources
Reading Skills Practice Workbook

ASSESSMENT

- ***Quick Checks,*** p. 27
- ***Selection and Theme Assessment,*** pp. 47–48
- ***Performance Assessment,*** p. 26
- ***Testmaker: ExamView Pro***
- ***Interactive Tutor: Self-Assessment***

MEDIA Connection

Objective

- To understand and apply strategies for reading a newspaper article

Literature LINK

the lesson of the moth Help students realize that both this newspaper article and the poem "the lesson of the moth" present the same views on choice of lifestyle. Encourage students to find quotations in the article that are similar to statements made by either archy or the moth in the poem.

Informational Text

inTIME For more examples of informational text, direct students to the articles in the *inTIME* magazine.

Teaching Support

MEDIA Connection

NEWSPAPER ARTICLE

For some athletes, baseball, soccer, and basketball aren't exciting enough. Such people have chosen to play new—and often dangerous—types of extreme sports.

Going to the EXTREME: Young daredevils zip into mainstream

by Karen Thomas—*USA Today*, August 13, 1997

EGG HARBOR TOWNSHIP, New Jersey— The skating-themed balloons are perfectly tethered. Happy Birthday streamers are strung. The guests have arrived.

We have a problem!

Matt Hunter, who's set to blow out the fourteen candles on the in-line skating cake, marches over to the piñata that his mother has just hung from a tree. It, too, is shaped like a skate, but it's not quite right.

Matt rips off the papier-mâché brake built into the heel and tosses it into the trash. His broad, self-assured smile says it all: He's hosting the perfect aggressive-skating birthday party. And aggressive means no brakes.

Aggressive or *extreme* sports—trick skating, skateboarding, and biking—are no longer exclusive to the progressive California dude. Driveways across the USA have become the breeding ground for youths as young as six and seven who are using two-, four-, and eight-wheeled toys to attempt flips, spins, jumps, and an array of airborne stunts.

The trend has transformed the curbs, stairways, and railings in communities into battlegrounds pitting pedestrians against daredevils with their wheeled weaponry while the medical community scurries to deal with potential injuries.

With extreme sports still in their infancy, it's too early for specific medical statistics. Unspecified in-line skating injuries treated in hospital emergency rooms have nearly tripled since 1993—from 36,986 to 102,819 last year—according to the Consumer Product Safety Commission. Participation in in-line skating among youths six to seventeen, though, has quadrupled.

Some experts will say at least the kids are moving. As youth participation in every traditional sport declines, in-line skating is the fastest-growing sport among youngsters. The Sporting Goods Manufacturers Association (SGMA) reports 7.9 million participants ages six to seventeen in 1996. Another study by Teenage Research Unlimited shows boys aged twelve to fifteen are more interested in extreme sports than professional basketball.

"You get a good workout, and it's a challenge," says in-line skater Matt Kreutzer, thirteen. He and Hunter are members of a neighborhood skating club, the 609 sk8 crew (609 is Egg Harbor's area code). "You have to have challenges in your life," he says, "or you'll get bored."

While participants, experts, and parents don't concur on safety measures, they do all agree that extreme sports are not a passing phase, and as the practice continues to grow among younger and

Reading *Minilesson*

Distinguishing Fact from Opinion

Point out that the purpose of most newspaper articles is to inform. Explain that often a newspaper article informs the reader not only of facts but of the differing opinions on the subject of the article.

Activity Have students reread the article. Ask them to write down each fact presented in the article as they read. Then have students read their facts for the rest of the class. Encourage students to discuss whether any of the facts identified by students are actually opinion. Help students brainstorm about strategies for distinguishing between a statement of fact and a statement of opinion. **L2**

Additional Resources

Reading Skills Practice Workbook

Analyzing Media

1. Some students may say that people are bored without challenges such as extreme sports provide. Others may say that people participate in extreme sports to be "hip."
2. Responses should be supported with evidence, examples, and reasoning.

Additional Resources

Media Connections, p. 6

younger children, it needs immediate attention.

"There's a valid reason for concern. The (extreme) formula has all the ingredients for a high injury rate," says Dr. Steven Anderson, who chairs the American Academy of Pediatrics' task force on sports medicine. The topic was first brought up at the group's May meeting when it received its first letter from a pediatrician asking what advice to give to parents. "We're going to have to formally look at it, so the academy may have some official position about whether this is a safe and reasonable activity for children," he says. "I'm trying to imagine a scenario where the benefits outweigh the risks."

"I doubt there has been a sport that has rivaled this ever," says the SGMA's Mike May, who says even basketball, traditionally the sport most played by kids, never reached skating's high mark. It's "surprising," he says, that raw data from 1996 shows a decline in kids' participation in nine of the top ten sports. Only in-line skating registered an increase. Extreme is for "your typically normal kid that likes to be on the

edge," says Gary Ream, president of Camp Woodward, a camp in Woodward, Pennsylvania, devoted to extreme sports and gymnastics. "I don't think they're any different than we were as kids."

The image: Another problem.

"People always think these are kids who smoke and do drugs and drop out of school," says Brenda Hunter at her son's birthday party. Matt and his brother, Jake, fifteen, attend Christian school and maintain high grades, she says. The 609 sk8 crew are all "good boys," she says, who come from good families.

But their clothes are over-sized (to fit pads underneath). Wallets dangle from chains attached at the belt (so you don't lose your money on aerial tricks). Some have spray painted their skates and helmets.

That image scares parents, Ream says. And the look is evolving in the early elementary years. "They're hip at nine in the '90s," says Kevin Thatcher, publisher of *Thrasher* magazine, devoted to skateboarding.

"It's the stereotype that skateboarding is so inherently dangerous," Thatcher says. "We're going to be in trouble if we don't give back to the youth by building skate parks."

Parents of his readers call for advice. He tells them, "Take them to the skate spot. Watch them. Listen." But don't stay so long as to embarrass your child. "Disappear when it's uncool."

Analyzing Media

1. Why do some people choose extreme sports over safer activities?
2. What is your opinion of these sports?

interNET CONNECTION

Safety Have students use a search engine to look for articles that address the dangers of intensely challenging sports and how these dangers can be avoided.

REAL-WORLD CONNECTION

Equipment Ask students who practice any extreme sports to bring in their safety equipment and the documentation that came with it. If not enough students have any of this equipment, they can search the Internet for information. Have them compare the instructions and warranties from different manufacturers. For example, how are two helmets from different companies similar? How are they different? What do the warranties promise? What would make the students buy one helmet over the other? Have the students who are less familiar with the equipment read the instructions and teach themselves how to wear and use it. Encourage students to remember what they learned about these products when they are buying safety equipment for themselves.

Objectives

- To write an evaluation of a decision (approximately 500 to 700 words)
- To plan, draft, revise, edit, and present an evaluative essay
- To reflect on and assess one's essay

GLENCOE TECHNOLOGY

WRITER'S ASSISTANT CD-ROM

Students can use Glencoe's templates and guidelines software for expository writing to aid them in working through the steps in the writing process in this lesson.

Teaching Strategies

PREWRITING

Find a Topic Help students choose a decision they feel strongly about. They may want to consider decisions made by parents, teachers, or coaches that affected them. Encourage students to freewrite about such decisions. Then have them examine the list to determine which decision they would be most interested in discussing.

Teaching Support

Writing WORKSHOP

Expository Writing: Writing an Evaluation

What's the hardest decision you've made this year? Were you happy with the decision you made? Do you still have doubts? Evaluating a decision takes a lot of thought, and writing about your thoughts is a good way to sort them out.

Assignment: For this workshop, write an essay evaluating a decision. Follow the process shown on these pages.

- As you write your evaluation, refer to the **Writing Handbook**, pp. R50–R67.

EVALUATION RUBRIC

By the time you complete this Writing Workshop, you will have
- explained the decision that you will evaluate
- set standards, or criteria, for judging your decision and explained how your decision meets your criteria
- provided detailed evidence, examples, and reasons to support the arguments for the decision
- provided relevant background about the decision
- written a conclusion that summarizes the decision
- presented an essay that is free of errors in grammar, usage, and mechanics

The Writing Process

PREWRITING

PREWRITING TIP

Freewrite for fifteen minutes at a time. You might start by completing an idea such as "I surprised myself when I decided to . . ." or "A decision I regret is . . ."

Find a Topic

You may want to evaluate a real-life decision that you or someone else has made. You could also evaluate a decision made by a character in this theme. To find ideas, try freewriting about decisions that have meant something to you. Another strategy is to make an idea tree for the word *decisions.* For a strong essay, choose a decision that you have strong feelings about.

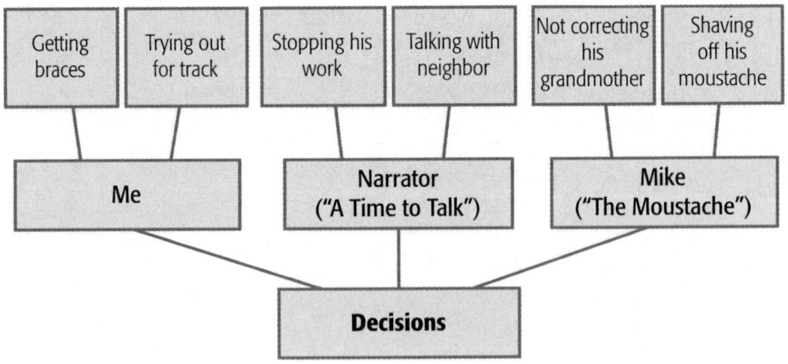

MEETING INDIVIDUAL NEEDS — ENGLISH LANGUAGE LEARNERS

Organizing Students learning English may have a hard time with prewriting and organizing their essays, as they may be more concerned than they need to be at this stage about grammar and vocabulary. Explain that in the early stages of prewriting an essay, their focus should be only on the topic of the essay and the ideas the essay will contain.

Activity Students may wish to jot down their initial ideas about the topic of their essay in their native language. Have them translate this prewriting effort into English before drafting the essay. They should use the English version to draft the essay.

Additional Resources

English Language Learners Sourcebook

Set Your Standards

To evaluate, you need **criteria**—standards for judging. Your criteria reflect what's important to you. You might consider:

- personal happiness
- effects on others
- expense
- ethics

List your own criteria for evaluating the decision you have chosen. You might list them by order of importance, moving from least to most important.

Least important criterion: pride	
Details:	I'm no star, but I do OK. In meets, I've placed second and third.
Second most important criterion: physical fitness	
Details:	Hate to run laps, but getting faster. New personal best: 7.9 sec. for 50 meters.
Most important criterion: pleasure	
Details:	When I run well, I'm happy. Feel like I'm flying. It's happening more often.

Consider Audience and Purpose

Will you write mainly for yourself, exploring a decision in your life? If so, you might plan a personal essay. Will you evaluate the decision of a literary character? If so, you might plan your essay as a letter to that character or as a more formal response to literature.

Get Organized

Your opinion of the decision is the **thesis**—the main idea—of your essay. Write your thesis now, as a sentence. It can be as simple as "I wish I hadn't joined the track team" or "I'm glad I joined the track team." You'll explain your thesis in the body of your essay.

Set Your Standards Remind students that they are writing an *evaluation* of the decision they have chosen. They will need to set standards for evaluating the decision. Have them list the reasons that the decision was good or bad. This list will provide the standards by which the students can judge decisions.

Consider Audience and Purpose Once students have selected an audience, have them think about the reader's point of view. Students should think about how to present their evaluation so the reader will understand it.

Get Organized After students write their opinion statements, suggest that they list their standards for evaluation of the decision. Have students number the evaluation criteria, representing the order in which they will be presented in the evaluation.

Additional Resources

- ***Writing and Proofreading Practice,*** pp. 1–7, 21–27
- ***Writing and Proofreading Transparencies 1–6, 11–12, 29–30***
- ***Writer's Choice,*** Lessons 2.3–2.4

MEETING INDIVIDUAL NEEDS — ADVANCED LEARNERS

Journalism Gifted students may enjoy the challenge of practicing journalism by styling their essays after the newspaper article presented in the Media Connection. They will need to focus on audience and purpose determined earlier and should also ensure that their articles are well organized.

Activity Have students review the article presented in the Media Connection, focusing on its organizational structure. They should determine the purpose of the article and make an outline of it, noting the types of detail included in each section. Students should follow this format to compose their own articles. **L2**

WHICH WAY TO GO? 325

Teaching Strategies

DRAFTING

Explain the Basics Encourage students to consider the audience when determining how much background information to include. Then ask students to think about where the background information should be placed. Tell students the background does not have to be first but should precede the analysis of the decision.

Draft Your Essay Have students freewrite the paragraphs. Remind them that each paragraph should have a transition from the preceding paragraph, a topic sentence, and a conclusion.

REVISING

Improve Your Essay Have students think about a logical order as they reread their essays. They should consider whether their conclusions are successfully supported by details. Encourage students to trade drafts with partners.

GLENCOE TECHNOLOGY

REVISING WITH STYLE CD-ROM

Invite students to use the *Revising with Style* CD-ROM which offers instruction and exercises to help students improve their writing skills.

Teaching Support

DRAFTING

DRAFTING TIP

You can state your thesis in your introduction, or you can build up to it, stating it in your conclusion.

TECHNOLOGY TIP

Use a computer's split screen or clipboard function to keep your prewriting notes handy as you draft.

Explain the Basics

You might "hook" your readers by opening with a question or with an action image. Then explain the decision that you will evaluate. For a decision in a literary selection, include the name of the author, the selection, and the character.

Draft Your Essay

For each criterion, write at least one paragraph showing how the decision measures up. Transitional phrases, such as *for one thing, more important,* and *most important,* will help readers follow your essay. To conclude, sum up your evaluation.

STUDENT MODEL • DRAFTING

Second, joining the track team has made me more physically fit. I used to hate running laps and doing crunches. After a while, though, I started to see the results of doing my exercises. When I found my strength and speed improving I was really encouraged.

Complete Student Model on p. R121.

REVISING

REVISING TIP

Perhaps your thesis is clearer to you now. If so, reword your thesis statement to reflect your new insights.

Improve Your Essay

Set your draft aside and take a break for at least a few minutes—longer, if possible. Then use the **Rubric for Revising** as you go over your draft. You might work with a partner to plan revisions. Make changes that will strengthen your draft.

RUBRIC FOR REVISING

Your revised essay should have
- all the background information your intended audience will need
- a clear statement and discussion of your decision criteria
- effective transitions between paragraphs, passages, and ideas
- a conclusion that provides a clear and well-supported summary of your evaluation
- a consistent pattern of organization

Your revised essay should be free of
- gaps in logic or reasoning
- unnecessary details that make your essay confusing or hard to follow
- errors in grammar, usage, and mechanics

MEETING INDIVIDUAL NEEDS

MULTIPLE MODES OF EXPRESSION

Spatial Students with spatial learning styles may find it easier to organize and draft their essays through the use of diagrams or pictures. Explain to students that films are developed by a technique called "storyboarding," in which the initial organization of the film is mapped out with pictures and captions.

Activity Encourage students to "storyboard" their essays. They can draw sketches that illustrate key scenes or events they want to include. If each sketch appears on a different sheet of paper, they can shuffle the drawings around until they achieve a logical organization for their essays. These drawings can be used as the outline for their essays. **L2**

EDITING/PROOFREADING

Before making a final copy of your essay, use the **Proofreading Checklist** on the inside back cover to help you find and correct errors in grammar and mechanics. The **Grammar Link** on page 314 can help you check your subject-verb agreement.

EDITING TIP

Does your essay use time order to present a series of events? Reread your essay to make sure that the verb tenses are correct.

Grammar Hint

In a complex sentence, you can use *however* to join two clauses. Put a semicolon before it and a comma after it.
Squeaky is the best runner at her school; however, I am happy just doing my best.

Complete Student Model

For a complete version of the model developed in this workshop, refer to **Writing Workshop Models**, p. R121.

STUDENT MODEL • EDITING/PROOFREADING

I thought competition might spoil the fun;
however, my fears faded away once the practices
and meets began in earnest.

Complete Student Model on p. R121.

PUBLISHING/PRESENTING

Your essay can become a springboard for discussion. In a small group, read one another's essays. Then discuss the ideas in each essay. How would others in the group have evaluated the decision? Why? Explore one another's views and criteria.

PRESENTING TIP

If your topic is a literary character's decision, ask classmates to play the role of the character and respond to your essay.

Reflecting

Write your thoughts about the following questions.

- What new ideas about the decision occurred to you as you worked on your essay?
- Which was easier for you: evaluating the decision, or writing about your evaluation? Why?

Save your work for your portfolio.

Teaching Strategies

EDITING/PROOFREADING

Editing Tip Encourage students to read their drafts aloud slowly, pointing at each word as they read it. This will help them to hear exactly what words they have written. Students should correct verb tenses or other problems.

PUBLISHING/PRESENTING

Presenting Tip Have the class work together to produce a group collage representing the various decisions discussed in the essays. Each decision can be written on the collage and accompanied by representative pictures chosen by the students. Decisions made by characters in the theme's stories and poems can also be included. This collage can be displayed in the classroom as a summary of the project.

Reflecting

Portfolio Encourage students to ask themselves these questions as they review their writing:

What have I learned
- about decisions from the other students?
- about viewing my own decisions differently?

6+1 TRAITS™ OF WRITING
See the annotated **Writing Workshop Models** on pp. R119–R130 for additional help in evaluating student writing and in teaching the **6+1 Traits™ of effective writing.** Annotations and minilessons address and reinforce the **6+1 Traits™:** Ideas, Organization, Voice, Word Choice, Sentence Fluency, Conventions, and Presentation.

ASSESSMENT

Writing Assessment and Portfolio Management
- Writing Assessment, pp. 1–12, 20–22
- Portfolio Management, pp. 42–48

Theme Assessment

Objectives

- To give a personal response about the stories, poems, discussions, and activities in this unit
- To write a comparison of two poems
- To complete a self-evaluation, set a goal, and devise a plan for achieving the goal

Responding to the Theme

1. Students should use examples from the relevant story or poem to explain why the character's choice was selected.
2. They should provide an example from a story or a poem to support their response to each question.
3. Theme projects should be presented to the class with a brief explanation.

Analyzing Literature

Student selections must use examples to illustrate the attitudes they are comparing and contrasting.

Evaluate and Set Goals

Evaluate

Encourage students to think of their work as a whole in this theme while making their assessment.

Set Goals

Have students construct a chart that identifies their main goal and lists three steps to achieving it. Students may want to include deadlines for each step. They can check off the steps as they are achieved.

Theme Assessment

Responding to the Theme

1. Which of the choices made by the characters in this theme do you identify with the most? Why?
2. What new ideas do you have about each of the following statements as a result of reading the selections in this theme?
   - Sometimes, decisions have surprising results.
   - Choosing a more difficult path can help us in the long run.
   - Making no decision is worse than making the wrong decision.
3. Present your theme project to the class.

Analyzing Literature

In "Identity" and "the lesson of the moth," the speakers express their beliefs about choices and destiny. Reread these two poems, or choose two similar pieces from the theme. Compare and contrast attitudes toward making difficult choices.

Evaluate and Set Goals

1. Which of the activities below did you enjoy most? Which was the most difficult?
   - reading and thinking about the selections
   - writing independently
   - analyzing and discussing the selections
   - presenting ideas and projects
   - researching topics
2. How would you assess your work in this theme, using the following scale? Give at least two reasons for your assessment.
   4 = outstanding   2 = fair
   3 = good   1 = weak
3. Based on what you found difficult in this theme, choose a goal to work toward in the next theme.
   - Write down your goal and three steps you will take to help you reach it.
   - Meet with your teacher to review your goal and your plan for achieving it.

Build Your Portfolio

SELECT

Choose two of your favorite pieces of work from this theme to include in your portfolio. The following questions can help you choose.

- ✦ Which do you consider your best work?
- ✦ Which turned out to be more challenging than you thought?
- ✦ Which piece did you learn the most from?
- ✦ Which was the most interesting?

REFLECT

Write some notes to accompany the pieces you selected. Use these questions to guide you.

- ✦ What do you like best about the piece?
- ✦ What did you learn from creating it?
- ✦ What might you do differently if you were beginning this piece again?

ASSESSMENT

Writing Assessment and Portfolio Management
- Writing Assessment, pp. 1–12,
- Portfolio Management, pp. 42–48

GLENCOE TECHNOLOGY

MINDJOGGER VIDEOQUIZZES VIDEODISC

Use *MindJogger* to review the Theme 3 content.

Theme 3
Side A

Also available in VHS.

Reading on Your Own

If you have enjoyed reading the selections about making choices and trusting your instincts, try these books.

Shabanu: Daughter of the Wind

by Suzanne Fisher Staples Shabanu is part of a family of nomads in Pakistan. She loves her life, but when she is faced with marriage to a man chosen for her, she tries to run away. The difficult life of the herders in a barren land is depicted realistically.

The Rain Catchers

by Jean Thesman Growing up in house of strong, funny, creative women, fourteen-year-old Grayling discovers the power of telling stories. She also learns how to make decisions of her own.

American Dragons: Twenty-Five Asian American Voices

edited by Laurence Yep The stories in this collection are grouped by such themes as the relationships between generations, experiences of World War II, and the need to question who we are and where we go from here.

Banner in the Sky

by James Ramsey Ullman When Rudi's father dies in his attempt to scale a mountain in the Alps, Rudi decides that he must conquer the peak that killed his father. The author, an experienced climber, adds detailed information to a tense tale of courage and determination.

Reading on Your Own

Tips for Independent Reading

Stress the importance of each student's spending at least thirty minutes a day in independent reading and suggest books, such as those shown here, related to this theme.

Reading the Novel Review with students the five parts of the plot in fiction: exposition, rising action, climax, falling action, and resolution. Encourage them to identify each step of the plot in the novels they read so that they can follow twists in the story line and feel involved as the plot progresses.

Practice Suggest that students keep track of events as they read novels by creating a story map or a plot diagram. Encourage them to share the information in their diagrams with the class.

Glencoe Literature Library

Shabanu: Daughter of the Wind by Suzanne Fisher Staples is available in the *Glencoe Literature Library*. For a complete listing of the titles, see the **Glencoe Resources for Independent Reading** in the front of this book.

The *Glencoe Literature Library Study Guide* provides instructional support and student activities for all works in the *Glencoe Literature Library*.

At the MOVIES

Preview the following video for appropriateness for your class:

In "Field of Dreams," an Iowa farmer hears and heeds a mysterious voice saying, "If you build it, he will come," and legendary ball players come to play on the diamond in the cornfield.

MEETING INDIVIDUAL NEEDS — SPECIAL NEEDS

Your less-proficient readers may enjoy *American Dragons* because the short stories give the satisfaction of reading a novel without overwhelming students with the length.

The following books are rated for average readers **(L2)** or for students who need more challenging reading material **(L3)**.

- *Banner in the Sky* by James Ramsey Ullman **L2**
- *Shabanu: Daughter of the Wind* by Suzanne Fisher Staples **L2**
- *The Rain Catchers* by Jean Thesman **L3**

Standardized Test Practice

Answers and Analyses

1. **A** Warn students to be on the lookout for homophones. In this case, they should recognize the correct spelling for choice A as *bale*, not *bail*.
2. **L** The correct spelling is *canvas*, not *canvass*.
3. **A** Encourage students to look for the word root in order to detect spelling errors.
4. **L** The correct spelling of this homophone is *claws*, not *clause*.
5. **D** The correct spelling is *recommendation*, not *recomendation*.
6. **J** The correct spelling of this homophone is *colonel*, not *kernel*.
7. **C** The correct spelling is *laundry* not *lawndry*.
8. **M** The correct spelling of this homophone is *slay*, not *sleigh*.

The Princeton Review — TEST-TAKING TIP

One of the best ways students can prepare for a verbal test is to read, read, read. Encourage them to first use the context to guess at the meaning of an unfamiliar word and then look it up in the dictionary. Ask them to make an index card for each new word, writing its correct spelling on one side and its definition on the reverse.

The Princeton Review — TEST-TAKING TIP

Remind students that it is extremely important to read the test instructions and questions carefully, looking out for words like NOT and EXCEPT. If they read too quickly or overlook important words, they may know the correct answer, but choose the wrong answer choice anyway.

The Princeton Review

Standardized Test Practice

Read the phrase in each numbered item. Choose the phrase in which the italicized word is NOT spelled correctly.

1
- A a *bail* of hay
- B *bass* guitar
- C *sell* merchandise
- D 14 *carat* gold

2
- J wear a *sweater*
- K go to the *station*
- L paint the *canvass*
- M *simplify* the process

3
- A *aplying* for a job
- B good *insulation* in the attic
- C taking out the *garbage*
- D holding on to the *railing*

4
- J a bowl of *cereal*
- K a closet full of *clothes*
- L the bear's sharp *clause*
- M *chews* the gum

5
- A *millions* of people
- B a *terrific* sport
- C *snuggle* up on the sofa
- D a good *recomendation*

6
- J a *kernel* in the army
- K uses *flour* to bake a cake
- L *kneading* the dough
- M getting up in the *morning*

7
- A a *pleasant* evening
- B *exchange* this blouse
- C a load of *lawndry*
- D passed the *examination*

8
- J the seat on the *aisle*
- K the doctor's *patients*
- L bicycle *pedals*
- M *sleigh* the dragon

MEETING INDIVIDUAL NEEDS

ENGLISH LANGUAGE LEARNERS

Spelling and Pronunciation Spelling and pronunciation go hand in hand. Read through each example individually with your class. Ask students if they are able to identify which word is spelled incorrectly. Once the misspelled word has been determined, ask a volunteer to attempt to write the correct spelling on the board. In the case of homonyms, ask students to define the meaning or meanings of each word.

9
A the apple *cellar* on the corner
B cobwebs on the *ceiling*
C *principal* at my school
D a *tract* of land

10
J *camoflage* pants
K a *flammable* material
L *transmit* a message
M a *sergeant* in the army

11
A a loud *argument*
B a *manicure* for her fingernails
C an *antibiotic* to cure the cold
D an *extravagent* party

12
J the milk's *expirasion* date
K *allergic* to dust
L good *nutrition*
M on a *mission*

13
A the *anchor* in the water
B *tasle* on her graduation cap
C cold, *arctic* weather
D a *barrette* for her hair

14
J *conserving* energy
K a *compound* word
L dug up an *artafact*
M *suspended* from school

15
A an *extrordinary* idea
B *misplace* your keys
C going to *rehearsal*
D the *giraffe* at the zoo

16
J *alowed* to go to the party
K *finally* at the end of the test
L will *probably* join the team
M an intelligent *scientist*

STOP

Answers and Analyses

9. **A** The correct spelling of this homophone is *seller*, not *cellar*. Students should use contextual clues to determine the correct word here. A *cellar* would not be *on the corner*.
10. **J** The correct spelling is *camouflage,* not *camoflage*. Encourage students to use word recognition to eliminate incorrectly spelled words.
11. **D** The correct spelling is *extravagant*, not *extravagent*. This one is difficult–students should use the process of elimination to narrow down their choices.
12. **J** The correct spelling is *expiration*, not *expirasion*.
13. **B** The correct spelling is *tassel*, not *tasle*.
14. **L** The correct spelling is *artifact*, not *artafact*.
15. **A** The correct spelling is *extraordinary*, not *extrordinary*. Students should be familiar with compound words.
16. **A** The correct spelling is *allowed*, not *alowed*.

Item	Language Objective
1–16	Use correct spelling conventions

MORE PRACTICE

For additional practice, assign pages from one of the following standardized test resources available as part of Glencoe Literature.

Additional Resources
ITBS Preparation and Practice
SAT-9 Preparation and Practice
Terra Nova Preparation and Practice

Theme 4 At a Glance
Fantastic Capers and Mischief Makers

THEME OPENING

- Introducing the Theme (p. 333)
- Exploring the Theme (p. 334)
- Theme Projects (p. 335)

Theme 4: FANTASTIC CAPERS AND MISCHIEF MAKERS

SELECTIONS

Media Connection: Calvin and Hobbes (p. 336)

The Ransom of Red Chief (p. 337)

John Henry (p. 350)

***from* The People, Yes** (p. 350)

Active Reading Model: Sally Ann Thunder Ann Whirlwind (p. 360)

Lazy Peter and His Three-Cornered Hat (p. 370)

M'su Carencro and Mangeur de Poulet (p. 377)

Talk (p. 382)

The People Could Fly (p. 388)

The Souls in Purgatory (p. 398)

Spotted Eagle and Black Crow (p. 408)

The Siege of Courthouse Rock (p. 408)

Chicoria (p. 418)

Coyote and Wasichu (p. 418)

Media Connection: Plucky Poodle Returns Alive after Dog-Napping by Coyotes (p. 425)

SKILL FEATURES

Genre Focus: Folktale (p. 358)

Active Reading Strategies (p. 359)

Grammar Link (p. 369)

Listening, Speaking, and Viewing (p. 376)

Vocabulary Skills (p. 387)

Reading and Thinking Skills (p. 395)

Technology Skills (pp. 396–397)

Interdisciplinary Connection (p. 407)

WRITING WORKSHOP

Narrative Writing: Trickster Tale (pp. 426–429)

THEME ASSESSMENT

- **Responding to the Theme, Analyzing Literature, Evaluate and Set Goals** (p. 430)
- **Build Your Portfolio** (p. 430)
- **Reading on Your Own** (p. 431)
  When the Legends Die by Hal Borland
  A String in the Harp by Nancy Bond
  Nothing But the Truth: A Documentary Novel by Avi
  The Thirteen Clocks by James Thurber
- **Standardized Test Practice** (pp. 432–433)

KEYS TO LITERARY CONNECTIONS

Comparing Selections

The **Comparing Selections** feature in this theme provides opportunities for addressing diverse aspects of the reading and literature curriculum.

For example, in **Comparing Selections** on page 386, students compare the characters and the themes in the folktales "M'su Carencro and Mangeur de Poulet" and "Talk." Through this comparison, students expand their understanding of folklore and its role in different cultures.

World Literature

The Student Edition contains a variety of literature that represents cultures from around the world. World literature selections are highlighted with the icon above.

TEACHING SUPPORT

The Teaching Support offers a wealth of interactive instructional support:

Meeting Individual Needs
- Special Needs
- English Language Learners
- Multiple Modes of Expression
- Advanced Learners

Internet Connection

Assessment

Portfolio Options

Minilessons
- Grammar and Language
- Reading
- Writing
- Listening and Speaking

Connecting to Other Selections

Real-World Connection

Interdisciplinary Connection

Life Skills Connection

Family and Community Activity

Key to Ability Levels

The activities throughout this theme have been coded for students of various abilities.

L1 BASIC activities for all students

L2 AVERAGE activities for average to above-average students

L3 ADVANCED LEARNERS activities for above-average students

Teaching Today

The Glencoe *Teaching Today* professional development Web site at www.teachingtoday.glencoe.com features daily teaching tips, free downloads, annotated Web resources, educational news, and a wealth of information on a wide range of topics.

Reading Skills in this theme

Variety of Texts

In addition to folktales and short stories, this theme includes the following:

- comic strips
- ballad
- poetry
- legends
- newspaper article

Comprehension Skills

The following instructional support for comprehension skills appears in this theme of the Student Edition:

- **Active Reading Strategies and Model** (pp. 359–365)
- **Reading and Thinking Minilessons** (pp. 349, 368, 381, 394, 406, 424)

See also the **Reading Minilessons** throughout the theme in this Teacher Wraparound Edition.

For strategies for reading longer works, such as novels and novellas, see "Tips for Independent Reading" on page 431.

Reading Resources

Active Reading Guide The ***Active Reading Guide*** provides graphic organizers and study guide questions to support students' reading of each selection (***Active Reading Guide***, pp. 28–37).

Interactive Reading Sourcebook and **Interactive Reading Workbook** The ***Interactive Reading Sourcebook*** and ***Interactive Reading Workbook*** offer focused comprehension strategies and lessons on critical thinking skills as well as fluency practice and activities to teach and support phonics, decoding, spelling, and vocabulary development.

Vocabulary Power The ***Vocabulary Power*** workbook (Lessons 15–18) provides systematic teaching, practice, and assessment of vocabulary for better reading comprehension.

Audio Library Available on audiocassette and on CD, the ***Audio Library*** provides valuable comprehension support.

Glencoe Literature Library Each title in the ***Glencoe Literature Library*** includes a full-length work plus related readings. A separate Study Guide is available for each title.

Five-Star Stories These anthologies of familiar short stories adapted and abridged for a variety of reading levels include exercises to help increase students' vocabulary and improve their reading comprehension.

The Contemporary Readers ***The Contemporary Readers*** are nonfiction books linked to various themes and designed for developing readers from a wide range of backgrounds.

Literature Classics CD-ROM The selections on this CD-ROM can be searched by author, theme, or genre.

inTIME and **Humanities Across TIME** Coproductions of Glencoe and Time, Inc., these resources include a wealth of high-interest nonfiction related to the selections in this theme.

Assessment in this theme

Glencoe's Assessment Advantage

Assessment Options in the Student Edition

This program offers a number of diverse ways to evaluate student understanding and skill proficiency. In the Student Edition, use the following:

- **Responding to Literature**
  Following each selection, students are asked to recall facts, interpret ideas, and evaluate concepts as they answer a variety of questions and complete activities to extend their understanding.
- **Theme Assessment (pp. 430–431)**
  Here students respond to the selections on personal and analytical levels. They also assume ownership of their learning by setting and evaluating goals and by selecting work for their portfolios.

See also the many **Assessment Resources** listed on the facing page.

The Princeton Review

Standardized Test Practice

The Princeton Review has developed the Standardized Test Practice pages found at the end of this thematic unit (pp. 432–433). For additional practice, direct students to the following resources:

- ITBS Preparation and Practice
- SAT-9 Preparation and Practice
- TerraNova Preparation and Practice

Writing Skills in this theme

Writing Skills

The Student Edition of Theme 4 offers strong instructional support for writing skills:

In **Extending Your Response**, which follows each selection:

- **Writing About Literature**
- **Personal/Creative Writing**

See also the **Writing Minilessons** throughout the theme in this Teacher Wraparound Edition.

Writing Workshops

Theme 4 concludes with a **Writing Workshop** that guides students through the process for writing a trickster tale using narrative writing (pp. 426–429).

Writing Resources

Writer's Assistant CD-ROM Each **Writing Workshop** is supplemented by an interactive writing guide on the ***Writer's Assistant*** CD-ROM. This easy-to-use writing guide provides prompts, templates, and other tools that lead students through the writing process.

Grammar and Composition Handbook The ***Grammar and Composition Handbook*** (Lessons 6.3–8.6) provides systematic instruction in English language conventions.

Spelling Power The ***Spelling Power*** workbook (Lessons 13–16) provides systematic teaching, practice, and assessment of spelling to help students become better spellers and thus enhance their writing.

Writing and Proofreading Practice Blackline masters present in-depth instruction and practice on a specific step in the writing process and proofreading (pp. 1–6, 28–34).

Writing and Proofreading Transparencies Transparencies provide graphic organizers and proofreading exercises for whole-class instruction (pp. 1–6, 13–14).

Research and Report Writing Guide This resource provides extensive tips and activities to guide students in their writing projects in the literature classroom as well as in classes across the curriculum.

Style and Documentation Sourcebook for Writers This sourcebook is a combination reference and workbook, giving students the most up-to-date information and guidance regarding traditional as well as technological research strategies and documentation.

Revising with Style This resource offers instruction and exercises focusing on the revision process and covering topics from proofreading and correcting common grammatical errors to sentence combining and reordering.

Assessment Resources

Selection Quick Checks For each selection, a **Quick Check** of three to five short-answer questions measures students' literal comprehension.

Selection and Theme Assessment The ***Selection and Theme Assessment*** instrument tests students' abilities to recall, interpret, and evaluate what they've read. The tests consist of multiple-choice, short answer, and essay questions.

Performance Assessment Alternative assessment instruments and rubrics for Theme 4 are found in the ***Performance Assessment*** ancillary.

Writing Assessment and Portfolio Management These notes and strategies, student models, and assessment tools assist with the task of measuring students' progress as writers and as monitors of their own writing.

Testmaker: ExamView Pro Teachers can customize selection and Theme 4 tests by accessing the ***Testmaker*** database.

Interactive Tutor: Self-Assessment The ***Interactive Tutor: Self-Assessment*** software provides multiple-choice tests with immediate feedback to help students evaluate their knowledge and understanding of each literature selection.

MindJogger Videoquizzes Using a popular game show format, ***MindJogger Videoquizzes*** on videocassettes enable teachers to evaluate student understanding of Theme 4 in a quick and fun manner.

Theme 4 Skills Scope and Sequence

Lessons	Literary Elements	Reading and Thinking	Writing
The Ransom of Red Chief O. Henry DRP: 53 Lexile: 850	Suspense, SE p. 347 *Characterization, TWE p. 340* *Point of View, TWE p. 342* *Word Choice, TWE p. 344*	Comic Strip, SE p. 336 Verifying Predictions, SE p. 349 *Use Text Structures, TWE p. 336* *Inferring, TWE p. 339* ELL *Games, TWE p. 339* SN *Less-Proficient Readers, TWE p. 344*	Humor in Writing, SE p. 348 Surprise Ending, SE p. 348 *Monologue, TWE p. 340*
John Henry Anonymous and from The People, Yes Carl Sandburg	Ballad, SE p. 356; *TWE pp. 351, 352* *Rhyme Scheme, TWE p. 352* *Exaggeration, TWE p. 354* *Theme, TWE p. 355*	*Monitoring Comprehension, TWE p. 352* *Evaluating, TWE p. 354* SN *Learning Disabled, TWE p. 355*	Describing the Plot, SE p. 357 Telling Your Story, SE p. 357
Sally Ann Thunder Ann Whirlwind Mary Pope Osborne DRP: 55 Lexile: 900	Folktale, SE p. 358 Tall Tale, SE p. 366 *Tall Tale, TWE pp. 362, 363, 364*	Folktale, SE p. 359 Chronological Order, SE p. 368 *Visualize, TWE p. 362* *Predict, TWE p. 363* *Reflect, TWE pp. 364, 365*	Setting, SE p. 367 Tall Tale Letter, SE p. 367 *Using Strong Verbs, TWE p. 369*
Lazy Peter and His Three-Cornered Hat Ricardo E. Alegria DRP: 54 Lexile: 930	Plot, SE p. 375 *Plot, TWE pp. 373, 374*	*Drawing Conclusions, TWE p. 372* *Using Text Structures, TWE p. 373*	Theme, SE p. 375
M'su Carencro and Mangeur de Poulet J. J. Reneaux DRP: 51 Lexile: 790	Title, SE p. 380 *Title, TWE p. 379*	Setting a Purpose for Reading, SE p. 381	Describing Dialect, SE p. 381 Comparing Characters, SE p. 381
Talk Harold Courlander and George Herzog DRP: 47 Lexile: 520	Repetition, SE p. 385 *Repetition, TWE p. 384*	Comparing Selections, SE p. 386 *Connecting, TWE p. 384*	Personification, SE p. 385
The People Could Fly Virginia Hamilton DRP: 46 Lexile: 400	Simile and Metaphor, SE p. 393 *Comparison, TWE p. 390* *Word Choice, TWE p. 392*	Questioning, SE p. 394 Setting a Purpose for Reading, SE p. 395 *Evaluating, TWE p. 390* *Comparison and Contrast, TWE p. 391* SN *Learning Disabled, TWE p. 395*	Style, SE p. 394 First-Person Account, SE p. 394
The Souls in Purgatory Guadalupe Baca-Vaughn DRP: 54 Lexile: 880	Climax and Falling Action, SE p. 404 *Word Choice, TWE p. 401* *Irony, TWE p. 402* *Climax, TWE p. 403*	Summarizing, SE p. 406 *Evaluating, TWE p. 400* *Inferring, TWE p. 400* *Comparison and Contrast, TWE p. 401*	Analyze an Epigraph, SE p. 208 A Character's Journal, SE p. 208
Spotted Eagle and Black Crow Jenny Leading Cloud DRP: 53 Lexile: 760 and The Siege of Courthouse Rock DRP: 54 Lexile: 780	Legend, SE p. 416 *Legend, TWE pp. 411, 412, 413, 415* *Characterization, TWE p. 415*	*Predicting, TWE p. 410* *Evaluating, TWE pp. 412, 413* SN *Less-Proficient Readers, TWE p. 412* *Inferring, TWE p. 414*	Setting, SE p. 417 Write a Tale, SE p. 417
Chicoria Rudolfo A. Anaya DRP: 54 Lexile: 830 and Coyote and Wasichu Sioux Legend	Hero, SE p. 422 *Hero, TWE pp. 420, 421*	Finding Clues, SE p. 424 Newspaper Article, SE p. 425 *Establishing Criteria, TWE p. 420* *Predict, TWE p. 421* *Monitor Comprehension, TWE p. 425*	Dialogue and Narration, SE p. 423 Trickster Story, SE p. 423
Writing Workshop Narrative Writing: Trickster Tale			ELL *Planning a Trickster Tale, TWE p. 426* *Strong Verbs, TWE p. 428*

Key: Student material is in roman. *Teacher material is in italic.* Technology ELL English Language Learners

Vocabulary and Spelling	Grammar and Language	Listening, Speaking, and Viewing	Life Skills; Study and Research; Technology
Dictionary Skills: Definitions, SE p. 349 *Word Meaning,* TWE p. 340 SN *Less-Proficient Readers* TWE p. 348	Colorful Words, SE p. 349 *Writing Numbers,* TWE p. 346	Literature Groups, SE p. 348	Plan a Production, SE p. 348 Internet Connection, SE p. 348; TWE pp. 336, 345 *Video,* TWE p. 343, 348 *Research Lindbergh Kidnapping,* TWE p. 345
Proper Nouns, SE p. 357	Proper Nouns, SE p. 357 *Action Verbs,* TWE p. 354	Song Presentation, SE p. 357 Literature Groups, E p. 357 ELL *Multicultural Songs,* TWE p. 351	
Synonyms, SE p. 368 ELL *The Prefix Out-,* TWE p. 362 *Dialect,* TWE p. 363	Compound Predicates, SE p. 368 Using Irregular Verbs, SE p. 369 ELL *Regionalism and Slang,* TWE p. 358 *Transitive and Intransitive Verbs,* TWE p. 364	Literature Groups, SE p. 367 Dramatization, SE p. 367	Social Studies Research, SE p. 367 SN *Emotional,* TWE p. 363
ELL *The Prefix Un-,* TWE p. 372	*Compound Predicates,* TWE p. 374	Literature Groups, SE p. 375 Storytelling, SE p. 376 ELL *Storytelling in Two Languages,* TWE p. 376	
	Coordinating Conjunctions, TWE p. 379	Literature Groups, SE p. 381 Act It Out, SE p. 381	Social Studies Research, SE p. 381 *Video,* TWE p. 380
Using Roots, SE p. 387 ELL *Extending Roots,* TWE p. 387		Literature Groups, SE p. 385	
	Sentence Fragments, TWE p. 392	Literature Groups, SE p. 394 ELL *Storytelling Techniques,* TWE p. 390	Storyboard, SE p. 394 Photography: The Basics of Picture Taking, SE p. 396
The Prefix *inter-,* SE p. 406 *Word Meaning,* TWE p. 400	Active and Passive Voice, SE p. 406 ELL *Idiomatic Expressions,* TWE p. 400 *Demonstrative Adjectives and Pronouns,* TWE p. 402	Literature Groups, SE p. 405 Design a Picture Book, SE p. 405 SN *Learning Disabled* TWE p. 403	Social Studies Research, SE p. 405 Art and Culture, SE p. 407 *Video,* TWE p. 403
Multiple-Meaning Words, SE p. 417 ELL *Native American Cultures,* TWE p. 409	*Prepositional Phrases,* TWE p. 414	Literature Groups, SE p. 417 *Discussion,* TWE p. 411	Social Studies Research, SE p. 417 *Code of Conduct,* TWE p. 413 *Internet Connection,* TWE p. 415 *Media Legends,* TWE p. 415
The Prefix re-, SE p. 424	Verb Tenses, SE p. 424 ELL *Pronoun Reference,* TWE p. 419 *Proper Adjectives,* TWE p. 420	Literature Groups, SE p. 423	Problem Solving, SE p. 423 Science Research, SE p. 423

SN Special Needs/Strategic Intervention

RESOURCE MANAGER

Lessons	Essential Resources	English Language Learners
The Ransom of Red Chief O. Henry Pacing: 2 Days	**Lesson-Specific Instruction** Selection Focus Transp. 27 * Active Reading Guide, p. 28 Literary Elements Transp. 28 Vocabulary Practice, p. 21 * Quick Checks, p. 28 Selection and Theme Assessment, pp. 49–50 Testmaker: ExamView Pro Performance Assessment, p. 27 **Systematic Language Instruction** Grammar and Comp. Hbk., L. 6.3–6.4 Vocabulary Power, Lesson 15 Spelling Power, Lesson 13	English Language Learners Sourcebook, p. 49 Spanish Summaries, p. 27 * Audio Library English, Yes!
John Henry Anonymous *and* *from* The People, Yes Carl Sandburg Pacing: 2 Days	**Lesson-Specific Instruction** Selection Focus Transp. 28 * Active Reading Guide, p. 29 Literary Elements Transparency 29 * Quick Checks, p. 29 Selection and Theme Assessment, pp. 51-52 Testmaker: ExamView Pro Performance Assessment, p. 28 **Systematic Language Instruction** Grammar and Comp. Hbk., L. 6.5	English Language Learners Sourcebook, p. 50 Spanish Summaries, p. 28 * Audio Library English, Yes!
Sally Ann Thunder Ann Whirlwind Mary Pope Osborne Pacing: 2 Days	**Lesson-Specific Instruction** Selection Focus Transp. 29 * Active Reading Guide, p. 30 Literary Elements Transp. 30 Vocabulary Practice, p. 22 * Quick Checks, p. 30 Selection and Theme Assessment, pp. 53-54 Testmaker: ExamView Pro Performance Assessment, p. 29 TIME *inTIME* magazine, pp. 30–31 **Systematic Language Instruction** Grammar and Comp. Hbk., L. 7.1–7.2 Vocabulary Power, Lesson 16 Spelling Power, Lesson 14	English Language Learners Sourcebook, p. 51 Spanish Summaries, p. 29 * Audio Library English, Yes!
Lazy Peter and His Three-Cornered Hat Ricardo E. Alegria Pacing: 1 Day	**Lesson-Specific Instruction** Selection Focus Transp. 30 * Active Reading Guide, p. 31 Literary Elements Transp. 31 Vocabulary Practice, p. 23 * Quick Checks, p. 31 Selection and Theme Assessment, pp. 55–56 Testmaker: ExamView Pro Performance Assessment, p. 30 **Systematic Language Instruction** Grammar and Comp. Hbk., L. 7.3 Vocabulary Power, Lesson 17 Spelling Power, Lesson 15	English Language Learners Sourcebook, pp. 52–53 Spanish Summaries, p. 30 Spanish Translations, pp. 81–84 * Audio Library English, Yes!
M'su Carencro and Mangeur de Poulet J. J. Reneaux Pacing: 1 Day	**Lesson-Specific Instruction** Selection Focus Transp. 31 * Active Reading Guide, p. 32 Literary Elements Transp. 32 * Quick Checks, p. 32 Selection and Theme Assessment, pp. 57–58 Testmaker: ExamView Pro Performance Assessment, p. 31 **Systematic Language Instruction** Grammar and Comp. Hbk., L. 7.4	Theme Four Planning Guide, p. 36 Spanish Summaries, p. 31 * Audio Library English, Yes!

Key: Workbook · Blackline Masters · Textbook · Transparency · CD-ROM · Videodisk (also available in videocassette)

Special Needs/ Strategic Intervention	Reteaching and Enrichment
Interactive Reading Sourcebook, pp. T116–T118 Interactive Reading Workbook, pp. 54–55 Inclusion Strategies Sourcebook, pp. 29–30 Theme Four Planning Guide, p. 6 * Audio Library	Reading Skills Practice Workbook pp. 51–52 Grammar and Language Transp. 26 Gr. and Lang. Wkbk., pp. 275–276 Grammar and Comp. Hbk., L. 13.10 Media Connection Activities, p. 7 Interactive Tutor: Self-Assessment Vocabulary PuzzleMaker Web Site (lit.glencoe.com)
Interactive Reading Sourcebook, pp. T119–T121 Interactive Reading Workbook, pp. 56 Theme Four Planning Guide, p. 14 * Audio Library	Fine Art Transparency 26 Reading Skills Practice Workbook pp. 53–54 Grammar and Language Transp. 27 Gr. and Lang. Wkbk., pp. 61–62, 75–76 Grammar and Comp. Hbk., L. 3.1 Interactive Tutor: Self-Assessment Vocabulary PuzzleMaker Web Site (lit.glencoe.com)
Interactive Reading Sourcebook, pp. T121–T123 Interactive Reading Workbook, pp. 57–58 Inclusion Strategies Sourcebook, pp. 35–36 * Audio Library	Fine Art Transparency 25 Reading Skills Practice Workbook pp. 55–56 Grammar and Language Transp. 28 Gr. and Lang. Wkbk., pp. 55–56, 77–78, 99–100 Grammar and Comp. Hbk., L. 1.5, 3.2, 3.11 TIME *Humanities Across TIME*, Cover 12 Interactive Tutor: Self-Assessment Vocabulary PuzzleMaker Web Site (lit.glencoe.com)
Interactive Reading Sourcebook, pp. T124–T126 Interactive Reading Workbook, pp. 59–60 Inclusion Strategies Sourcebook, pp. 81–82 Theme Four Planning Guide, p. 28 * Audio Library	Reading Skills Practice Workbook pp. 57–58 Grammar and Language Transp., 29 Gr. and Lang. Wkbk., pp. 55–56 Grammar and Comp. Hbk., L. 1.5 Interactive Tutor: Self-Assessment Vocabulary PuzzleMaker Web Site (lit.glencoe.com)
Interactive Reading Sourcebook, pp. T126–T128 Interactive Reading Workbook, p. 61 Theme Four Planning Guide, p. 36 * Audio Library	Literature Launchers, Side A, Segment 11 Reading Skills Practice Workbook, pp. 59–60 Grammar and Language Transp. 30 Gr. and Lang. Wkbk., pp. 147–148 Grammar and Comp. Hbk., L. 7.5 Interactive Tutor: Self-Assessment Vocabulary PuzzleMaker Web Site (lit.glencoe.com)

Web   Audiocassette   Diskette   *Also available in Spanish

Independent Reading

Encourage students to spend thirty minutes each day in independent reading. The following Glencoe components and outside resources provide opportunities for reading related to this theme.

The Glencoe Literature Library

You may want to assign one or more of these titles for independent reading. For a complete listing of titles available in the Glencoe Literature Library, see page T94 of this book

- *The Adventures of Tom Sawyer* by Mark Twain
- *The Pigman* by Paul Zindel
- *High Elk's Treasure* by Virginia Driving Hawk Sneve
- *Treasure Island* by Robert Louis Stevenson

inTIME Magazine News stories, feature articles, reviews, profiles, and essays in the magazine connect to an author, work, or theme in the Student Edition. See the **in*TIME* Teacher's Guide** for specific connections to this theme.

Resources for Less-Proficient Readers

For reading especially created for less-proficient readers, suggest

- *Five-Star Stories*
- *The Contemporary Readers*

Additional Resources for Independent Reading

The following titles are listed with specific reading selections throughout this theme. You may want to suggest that students look for these in your local or school library.

- *Crow and Weasel* by Barry Holston Lopez
- *The Story Catcher* by Mari Sandoz
- *The Perilous Gard* by Elizabeth Pope
- *Justice and Her Brothers* by Virginia Hamilton
- *A Girl Named Disaster* by Nancy Farmer
- *These Were the Sioux* by Mari Sandoz
- *The Westing Game* by Ellen Raskin
- *When the Legends Die* Hal Borland
- *A String in the Harp* by Nancy Bond
- *Nothing But the Truth: A Documentary Novel* by Avi
- *The Thirteen Clocks* by James Thurber

Theme 4 RESOURCE MANAGER (continued)

Lessons	Essential Resources		English Language Learners
Talk HAROLD COURLANDER AND GEORGE HERZOG PACING: 1 DAY	**Lesson-Specific Instruction** Selection Focus Transp. 32 * Active Reading Guide, p. 33 Literary Elements Transp. 33 Vocabulary Practice, p. 24 * Quick Checks, p. 33	Selection and Theme Assessment, pp. 57–58 Testmaker: ExamView Pro Performance Assessment, p. 31 **Systematic Language Instruction** Grammar and Comp. Hbk., L. 7.5–7.7	English Language Learners Sourcebook, p. 54 Theme Four Planning Guide, p. 44 Spanish Summaries, p. 32 * Audio Library English, Yes!
The People Could Fly VIRGINIA HAMILTON PACING: 2 DAYS	**Lesson-Specific Instruction** Selection Focus Transp. 33 * Active Reading Guide, p. 34 Literary Elements Transp. 34 * Quick Checks, p. 34 Selection and Theme Assessment, pp. 59–60	Testmaker: ExamView Pro Performance Assessment, p. 32 **Systematic Language Instruction** Grammar and Comp. Hbk., L. 8.1–8.2 Vocabulary Power, Lesson 18 Spelling Power., Lesson 16	English Language Learners Sourcebook, p. 55 Spanish Summaries, p. 33 Spanish Translations, pp. 85–87 * Audio Library English, Yes!
The Souls in Purgatory GUADALUPE BACA-VAUGHN PACING: 2 DAYS	**Lesson-Specific Instruction** Selection Focus Transp. 34 * Active Reading Guide, p. 35 Literary Elements Transp. 35 Vocabulary Practice, p. 25 * Quick Checks, p. 35	Selection and Theme Assessment, pp. 61–62 Testmaker: ExamView Pro Performance Assessment, p. 33 **Systematic Language Instruction** Grammar and Comp. Hbk., L. 8.3	English Language Learners Sourcebook, p. 56 Spanish Summaries, p. 34 Spanish Translations, pp. 88–91 * Audio Library English, Yes!
Spotted Eagle and Black Crow *and* **The Siege of Courthouse Rock** JENNY LEADING CLOUD PACING: 2 DAYS	**Lesson-Specific Instruction** Selection Focus Transp. 35 * Active Reading Guide, p. 36 Literary Elements Transp. 36 Vocabulary Practice, p. 26 * Quick Checks, p. 36 Selection and Theme Assessment, pp. 63–64	Testmaker: ExamView Pro Performance Assessment, p. 34 **Systematic Language Instruction** Grammar and Comp. Hbk., L. 8.4–8.5 Vocabulary Power, Unit 4 Review/Test Spelling Power., Unit 4 Review/Proofreading	English Language Learners Sourcebook, p. 57 Spanish Summaries, p. 35 * Audio Library English, Yes!
Chicoria RUDOLFO A. ANAYA *and* **Coyote and Wasichu** SIOUX LEGEND PACING: 2 DAYS	**Lesson-Specific Instruction** Selection Focus Transp. 36 * Active Reading Guide, p. 37 Literary Elements Transp. 37 * Quick Checks, p. 37 Selection and Theme Assessment, pp. 65–66	Testmaker: ExamView Pro Performance Assessment, p. 35 **Systematic Language Instruction** Grammar and Comp. Hbk., L. 8.6	English Language Learners Sourcebook, p. 58 Spanish Summaries, p. 36 Spanish Translations, pp. 92–94 * Audio Library English, Yes!
Writing WORKSHOP Narrative Writing: Trickster Tale PACING: 2 DAYS	Writing Assessment and Portfolio Management, pp. 1–13, 23–25, 41–48		English Language Learners Sourcebook, p. 9 English, Yes!

Key: Workbook · Blackline Masters · Textbook · Transparency · CD-ROM · Videodisk (also available in videocassette)

Special Needs/ Strategic Intervention	Reteaching and Enrichment
Interactive Reading Sourcebook, pp. T129–T131 Interactive Reading Workbook, pp. 62–63 Inclusion Strategies Sourcebook, pp. 59–60 * Audio Library	Reading Skills Practice Workbook, pp. 61-62 Interactive Tutor: Self-Assessment Vocabulary PuzzleMaker Web Site (lit.glencoe.com)
Interactive Reading Sourcebook, pp. T132–T134 Interactive Reading Workbook, pp. 64–65 Theme Four Planning Guide, p. 51 * Audio Library	Literature Launchers, Side A, Segment 12 Reading Skills Practice Workbook, pp. 63-64 Grammar and Language Transp. 31 Gr. and Lang. Wkbk., pp. 51-52 Grammar and Comp. Hbk., L. 1.2 Interactive Tutor: Self-Assessment Vocabulary PuzzleMaker Web Site (lit.glencoe.com)
Interactive Reading Sourcebook, pp. T134–T136 Interactive Reading Workbook, pp. 66–67 Inclusion Strategies Sourcebook, pp. 21–22 * Audio Library	Literature Launchers, Side A, Segment 10 Reading Skills Practice Workbook, pp. 65-66 Grammar and Language Transp. 32 Gr. and Lang. Wkbk., pp. 97-98, 117-118, 127-128 Grammar and Comp. Hbk., L. 3.10, 4.7, 5.2 Interactive Tutor: Self-Assessment Vocabulary PuzzleMaker Web Site (lit.glencoe.com)
Interactive Reading Sourcebook, pp. T137–T139 Interactive Reading Workbook, pp. 68–69 Inclusion Strategies Sourcebook, pp. 43–44 Theme Four Planning Guide, p. 67 * Audio Library	Fine Art Transparency 31 Reading Skills Practice Workbook, pp. 67-68 Grammar and Language Transp. 33 Gr. and Lang. Wkbk., pp. 141-142 Grammar and Comp. Hbk., L. 7.1 TIME *Humanities Across TIME*, Cover 8 Interactive Tutor: Self-Assessment Vocabulary PuzzleMaker Web Site (lit.glencoe.com)
Interactive Reading Sourcebook, pp. T140–T142 Interactive Reading Workbook, pp. 70–71 Theme Four Planning Guide, p. 73 * Audio Library	Fine Art Transparencies 18, 24 Reading Skills Practice Workbook, pp. 69-70 Grammar and Language Transp. 34 Gr. and Lang. Wkbk., pp. 85-96, 123-124 Grammar and Comp. Hbk., L. 3.9, 5.1 Media Connection Activities, p. 8 TIME *Humanities Across TIME*, Cover 8 Interactive Tutor: Self-Assessment Vocabulary PuzzleMaker Web Site (lit.glencoe.com)
Inclusion Strategies Sourcebook, pp. 73–74	Writing and Proofreading Practice, pp. 1-6, 28-34 Writing and Proofreading Transparencies 1-6, 13-14, 31-32 Revising with Style Writer's Assistant

Web Audiocassette Diskette *Also available in Spanish

Theme RESOURCES

To explore the theme further, you may want to use these resources:

- Listening and Speaking Activities (pp. 10-12)
- Viewing and Representing Activities (pp. 16-18)
- Critical Thinking Skills (pp. 9-11)
- Media Connection Activities, (pp. 7-8)
- Interdisciplinary Activities (pp. 14-17)
- Family and Community Activities (p. 24
- Selection and Theme Assessment (pp. 49-66, 131-132)
- Performance Assessment (pp. 67, 92)

TIME Humanities Across TIME

See also these additional theme planning resources:

- Theme Four Planning Guide
- Interactive Reading Sourcebook
- Literature Groups Sourcebook
- Interactive Lesson Planner
- Interactive Teacher Edition
- Glencoe Web Site (lit.glencoe.com)

PRESENTATION *Plus!*

Use Glencoe's ***Presentation Plus!*** This multimedia teaching tool lets you present dynamic lessons that will engage your students. Using Microsoft PowerPoint®, you can customize the presentation to create your own personalized lessons.

THEME 4

Fantastic Capers and Mischief Makers

Theme Objectives

- To enjoy reading about fantastic events and mischievous characters
- To analyze the literary elements in stories, poems, and folktales
- To apply strategies for reading folktales

Teaching Strategies

Have students read the quotation in preparation for the discussion questions below.

VIEWING THE PAINTING

Responding to the Painting

Discussion questions:

- How do the figures in this painting differ from those on regular playing cards? *(Typical face card images remain the same when inverted.)*
- What makes the characters seem mischievous? *(Their expressions, postures, and gestures suggest trickery.)*
- What tricks might these characters know? *(They may perform magic stunts, or they may tell captivating stories.)*

Fantastic Capers and Mischief Makers

"I know a trick worth two of that."

—William Shakespeare

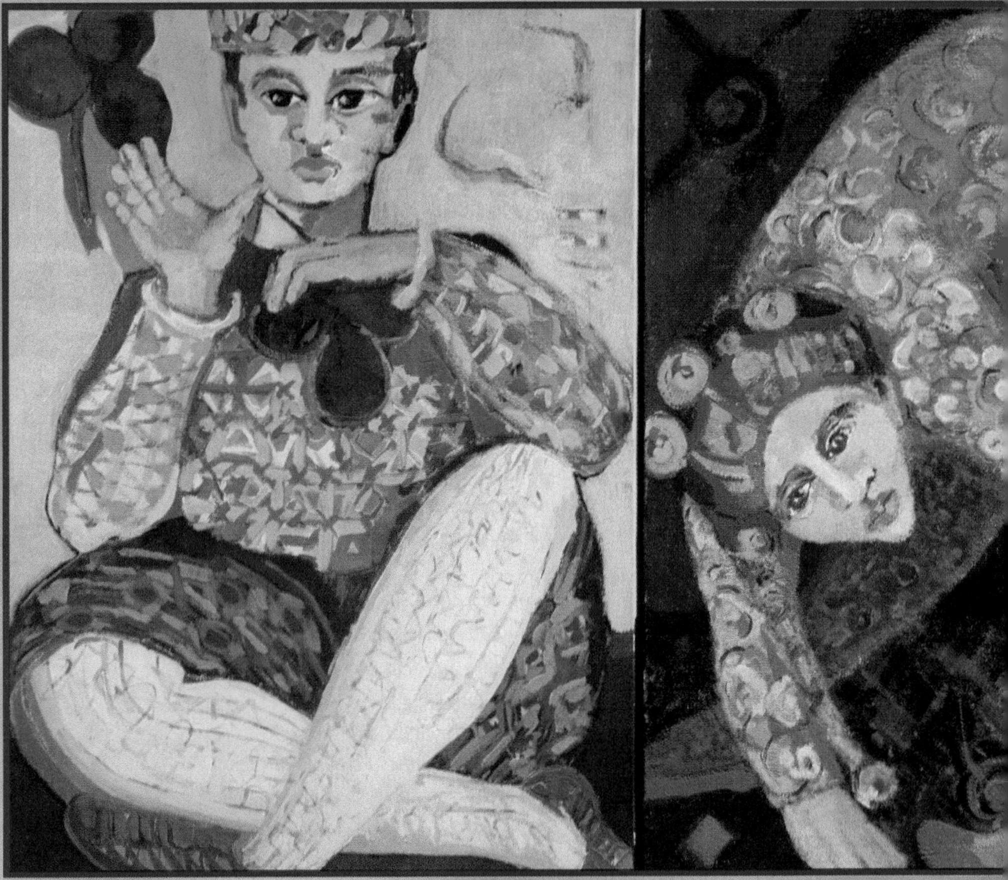

Two of Clover Face Ace of Hearts, 1994 (detail). Maria Angelica Ruiz-Tagle. Oil on canvas, 76 x 46 cm. Private collection.

TEACHER to TEACHER

EAGLE PASS HIGH SCHOOL • EAGLE PASS, TEXAS

I tie in the literature with current events and students' lives, backgrounds, and cultures. In cooperative learning group discussion, students may look at real-life stories of tricksters and adventurers in the media and compare and contrast them with the literature. In addition, I ask them to answer this question: What message or lesson about life does this selection have for readers today? After students have read and discussed all of the selections, I invite them to write their own imaginative tale with a message or moral embedded in the plot. I encourage them to draw on the personalities of the characters in the literature, as well as their own knowledge and experiences, in shaping their stories. Then we hold a storytelling festival in which students perform the tales they have written for the class.

—JOSÉ LOPEZ

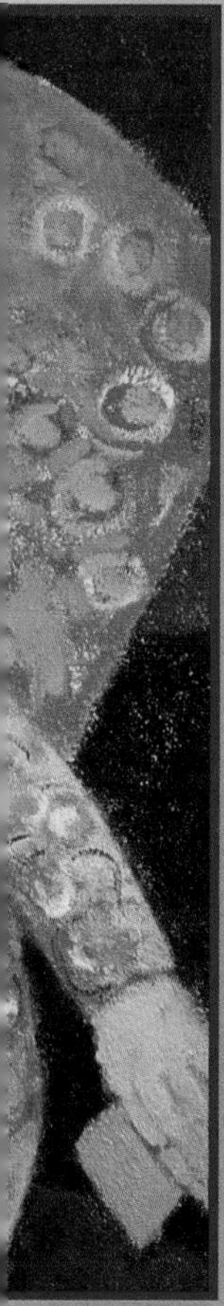

THEME 4

THEME CONTENTS

Introducing Theme 4

Direct your students' attention to the **Theme Contents.** Ask them to read through the list of selections. Present these questions for discussion:

- Point out that "The Ransom of Red Chief" is *by* O. Henry but that "Talk" is *told by* Harold Courlander and George Herzog. Ask students why this distinction is made. *(Folktales are frequently oral legends handed down from generation to generation. Thus, the person who records the tale in writing is not the author but the reteller.)*
- Ask students to consider the meaning of *folk* in folktale. *(Folktales come from the people, from ordinary folks, unlike literary works by those people considered artists.)*
- Which selection listed interests you the most? Which selection interests you the least? Why?

LITERATURE & HUMANITIES

Have students view and discuss "Lake Spirit" from the *National Museum of Women in the Arts*.

GLENCOE TECHNOLOGY

LITERATURE CLASSICS CD-ROM

Search for other selections related to the theme of "Fantastic Capers and Mischief Makers."

RESOURCE MANAGER

See the ***Theme Four Planning Guide*** for additional teaching notes, strategies, and resources for introducing the theme "Fantastic Capers and Mischief Makers."

Exploring the Theme

Fantastic Capers and Mischief Makers

- Students may say that tales of mischief and misfortune teach what not to do. They also exert a liberating influence as we imagine what it would be like to turn the world upside down.
- Students may note that tales of mischief and misfortune often reward the good and punish the bad and, as such, confirm that all is right with the world.

Starting Points

Memories of Mischief

Point out to students that the second *Garfield* cartoon may serve as a good model for theirs. The first panel shows the "setup," the second shows the trick itself, and the third shows the aftermath.

The Trick's on You

Point out that the victim's perspective on mischief may be a function of how long ago the trick was played. Immediately afterward, it may not seem funny at all; years later, the victim may have a different view of the situation.

Exploring the Theme

Fantastic Capers and Mischief Makers

What can readers learn from tales of mischief, misfortune, and magical power? The selections in this theme will give you the opportunity to discuss and answer these questions. Try one of the following options to start your thinking about the theme.

Starting Points

Garfield © 1997 by PAWS, Incorporated. Universal Press Syndicate. Reprinted with permission. All rights reserved.

MEMORIES OF MISCHIEF

Garfield the cat spends a lot of time causing mischief—whether he's persuading his owner to feed him cookies or tricking a bird into being his next meal. Have you or someone you know ever been tricked? Draw a cartoon showing how the incident turned out.

THE TRICK'S ON YOU

Think about a time you played a harmless trick on someone or made mischief of some kind. Put yourself in the place of the person on whom you played the trick or the person your mischief affected. Write a few notes about how you would have felt if you were the victim of the mischief.

Family and Community Activity

Topographic Legends Have students study the geographic features of their community. Is the land flat or mountainous? Are there distinctive bodies of water? Is the land lush and green or desertlike? Then have students select a local topographical feature and use well-chosen details to develop a legend that explains how it came to be. Have students present their stories orally to the class. **L2**

Additional Resources

Family and Community Activities, p. 24

Theme Projects

Complete one of the projects below as you read the selections in "Fantastic Capers and Mischief Makers." Work on your own, with a partner, or with a group.

CRITICAL VIEWING

Modern-Day Folk Heroes

1. Read comic books or watch television shows and films that feature the deeds of a superhero, such as Superman or Wonder Woman.
2. Choose one character to study. What are his or her attributes? What amazing deeds does he or she perform? What message, if any, does his or her story convey?
3. Reflect on what you learned about folk heroes in this theme. What do these folk heroes have in common with modern-day superheroes?
4. Prepare an oral presentation that supports your main points with details from the sources and images of superheroes and folk heroes in action.

MULTIMEDIA PROJECT

Create a Cyber Folk Hero

1. Gather information about a character featured in this theme or a character you discovered or created on your own. Use HyperStudio or similar software to create a multimedia presentation about the character.
2. Create visuals such as cartoons and drawings to show the amazing feats the character performed.
3. Write an introduction for the character, captions for the images, and a conclusion that wraps up your ideas.

LEARNING FOR LIFE

Legends Close to Home

1. Legends may be created when an ordinary person performs a heroic deed, overcomes a huge obstacle, or changes his or her family's fate. Ask your friends and relatives to recount stories of well-known or unusual people in their lives.
2. Choose one story to tell. If possible, plan to interview the subject of the story. Or, interview people who remember the story.
3. During the interview, gather as many details as possible about the story.
4. Put the story down on paper, organizing the events from start to finish.

interNET CONNECTION

For more about "Fantastic Capers and Mischief Makers," visit lit.glencoe.com. You also might search the Internet for hoaxes and urban legends—outrageous stories about events that supposedly happened. Create a collection of your favorite stories.

Theme Projects

Teaching Strategies

The following suggestions may help your students plan and carry out their theme projects.

Critical Viewing

- As students begin their searches, suggest that they ask their parents and grandparents about the superheroes of their youth. Students may wish to research some of these heroes of yesteryear (such as Buck Rogers or the Green Hornet).
- Suggest that students try to find information about how the superhero acquired his or her powers.
- Ask students to think about why there are so many stories of superheroes. Every culture has its legends, and every era has heroes. Why? What need do they fill?
- Almost every superhero has a weakness. Encourage each student to present their hero's weakness along with his or her strengths.

Learning For Life

- Suggest that students ask questions, such as *Who is the most extraordinary person you have ever known?* Or *Have you ever known someone you would consider heroic?* Or *Who in your family will be remembered a hundred years from now?*
- Many folktales and legends have more than one version, changing as they are handed down from generation to generation and retold by writers. Suggest that students try to find more than one version of the story they choose to tell.
- Remind students of the reporter's essential questions: *who? what? when? where? why?* and *how?*

Multimedia Project

- Encourage students to develop a storyboard of their presentations. Have them write out their ideas on 3" X 5" inch cards, one to a card. Then they can rearrange the cards until they have the organization they want.
- Suggest that students build to a climax by starting out with minor feats and ending with the most spectacular.
- Students may want to borrow ideas from comic books by adding color and captions.

Additional Resources

- ***Interdisciplinary Activities,*** pp. 14–17
- ***Viewing and Representing Activities,*** pp. 16–18
- ***Listening and Speaking Activities,*** pp. 10–12
- ***Critical Thinking Skills,*** pp. 9–11
- ***Selection and Theme Assessment,*** pp. 131–132
- ***Performance Assessment,*** p. 67

interNET CONNECTION

Glencoe Literature Web Site

For more information about "Fantastic Capers and Mischief Makers," type the keywords *trickster tale, folktale,* or *tall tale* into a search engine.

MEDIA Connection

Objective

- To read and understand a comic strip

Literature LINK

The Ransom of Red Chief This comic strip connects to "The Ransom of Red Chief" (pp. 338–346). Point out to students that Calvin's ability to inflict mischief on adults is similar to Red Chief's.

Analyzing Media

1. Calvin's description of his question as "conjectural, moral" is precise and accurate, as is his use of "hypothetically."
2. Calvin plans to use Spanish when he runs away to Mexico.

Additional Resources

Media Connections, p. 7

in TIME ***magazine***

interNET CONNECTION

Encourage students to learn more about comic strips by searching the Web for words like *comics, cartooning,* and *animation.* They can also enter the names of individual strips or artists.

Teaching Support

MEDIA Connection

COMIC STRIP

Wouldn't you like to have a friend who could solve every problem? Cartoonist Bill Watterson gives young Calvin a perfect problem-solver.

Calvin & Hobbes © 1986 Watterson Dist. by Universal Press Syndicate. Reprinted with permission. All rights reserved.

Analyzing Media

1. Find two examples in which Calvin uses the English language with great accuracy.
2. What other language does Calvin plan to use? Why might he need a second language?

Reading Minilesson

Use Text Structures Discuss with students the various conventions with which they must be familiar in order to understand comic strips. Mention a few obvious conventions and provide examples. Find an instance of a character thinking to show how that is represented in comics.

Activity Have students bring in the comics section of a local paper. Ask them to evaluate the structure of various comic strips. Have groups make lists of what a reader needs to know in order to understand a comic strip. Have groups present their ideas to the class as a whole.
L2 COLLAB. LEARN.

Additional Resources

Reading Skills Practice Workbook

Before You Read

The Ransom of Red Chief

MEET
O. HENRY

The stories of O. Henry are as colorful as the man who wrote them: William Sydney Porter. He was a writer, a bank teller, and a convicted felon who spent three years in prison. While in jail, Porter adopted the name O. Henry and began a successful writing career. "I'll give you the whole secret of short-story writing," he wrote to his daughter. "Rule 1: Write stories that please yourself. There is no Rule 2."

William Sydney Porter (O. Henry) lived from 1862 to 1910. This story was published in 1918 in The Ransom of Red Chief and Other O. Henry Stories for Boys.

READING FOCUS

Picture a nine- or ten-year-old boy you know. What does he look like? How does he speak and act?

QuickWrite
List some characteristics of a boy this age.

Setting a Purpose
Read to discover what happens when two "con men" and a mischievous young boy get together.

BUILDING BACKGROUND

The Time and Place This story is set in Summit, Alabama, probably in the late 1800s.

Did You Know? O. Henry had firsthand knowledge of being on the wrong side of the law. He was convicted of embezzlement as a young bank teller when a $5,000 deposit was either unrecorded or stolen. He fled the country, only to return when his wife became ill. Friends wondered if he was covering up for a bank official, but the truth about his guilt or innocence was never revealed.

VOCABULARY PREVIEW

prominent (prom′ ə nənt) *adj.* widely known; p. 338
emit (i mit′) *v.* to utter; send forth or give out, as a sound; p. 341
dote (dōt) *v.* to show extreme affection; p. 341
peremptory (pə remp′ tər ē) *adj.* allowing no refusal; p. 342
decry (di krī′) *v.* to criticize openly; p. 343
comply (kəm plī′) *v.* to obey or go along with a request; p. 343
renegade (ren′ ə gād′) *n.* one who abandons or turns against a group, cause, or allegiance; traitor; p. 344
palatable (pal′ ə tə bəl) *adj.* agreeable to the taste, mind, or feelings; acceptable; p. 345
impudent (im′ pyə dənt) *adj.* boldly discourteous; p. 346

Before Reading

Objectives

- To read and analyze a humorous short story
- To examine how writers use suspense
- To write an explanation of humor

Skills

Reading/Thinking: Inferring; Paraphrasing; Evaluating; Verifying Predictions
Writing: Alternate Ending; Monologue
Vocabulary: Word Meaning; Definitions
Grammar/Language: Writing Numbers; Using Colorful Words
Collaboration: Literature Groups

Motivating STUDENTS

Selection Focus Transparency 27: Before presenting the painting, ask students to discuss ways in which mischief is manifested.

Reading Focus: As an extension of the Reading Focus, have students underline the characteristics that applied to them at age nine or ten.

RESOURCE MANAGER

Teaching Tools and Resources
- Theme Four Planning Guide
- Literature Groups Sourcebook

Essential Lesson Support

Lesson-Specific Instruction
- Selection Focus Transparency 27
- Literary Elements Transparency 28
- Active Reading Guide,* p. 28
- Selection Vocabulary Practice, p. 21

Assessment
- Selection Quick Checks,* p. 28
- Sel. and Theme Assmt., pp. 49–50
- Testmaker: ExamView Pro
- Performance Assessment, p. 27

Systematic Language Instruction
- Gr. & Comp. Hbk., L. 6.3, 6.4
- Vocabulary Power, Lesson 15
- Spelling Power, Lesson 13

English Language Learners
- ELL Sourcebook, p. 49
- Spanish Summaries, p. 27
- Audio Library*
- English, Yes!

Spec. Needs/Strat. Interven.
- Interactive Rdg. Sbk., pp. T116–T118
- Interactive Rdg. Wkbk., pp. 54–55
- Inclusion Strat. Sbk., pp. 29–30
- Audio Library*

* Also available in Spanish

Reading the Selection

SUMMARY

Two partners kidnap young Johnny Dorset and hold him for ransom. Surprisingly, Johnny, calling himself Red Chief and wearing turkey feathers in his hair, enjoys the adventure and doesn't particularly want to be returned home. Red Chief is a rambunctious child who talks incessantly and torments one of the kidnappers nearly beyond endurance. The boy's father, Ebenezer Dorset, responds to the ransom note by demanding payment to take the boy back. The kidnappers, demoralized and exhausted, eventually comply with the demand.

Spanish Summaries, p. 27

A Active Reading Strategies

QUESTION Why does the narrator say that the town, "flat as a flannel cake," is "called Summit, of course"? *(One possibility: He may be commenting on the naïveté of the townsfolk; they may have idealized their town, believing it to be on a rise.)*

VOCABULARY If you haven't previewed the selection vocabulary with students, stop and remind them to use context clues to unlock the meanings of new vocabulary words.

Additional Resources

Active Reading Guide, p. 28

Audio Library

Spanish Audio Library

THE RANSOM

It looked like a good thing: but wait till I tell you. We were down South, in Alabama—Bill Driscoll and myself—when this kidnapping idea struck us. It was, as Bill afterward expressed it, "during a moment of temporary mental apparition";[1] but we didn't find that out till later.

A There was a town down there, as flat as a flannel cake, and called Summit, of course. It contained inhabitants of as undeleterious[2] and self-satisfied a class of peasantry as ever clustered around a maypole.

Bill and me had a joint capital of about six hundred dollars, and we needed just two thousand dollars more to pull off a fraudulent town-lot scheme in Western Illinois. We talked it over on the front steps of the hotel. Philoprogenitiveness,[3] says we, is strong in semi-rural communities; therefore, and for other reasons, a kidnapping project ought to do better there than in the radius of newspapers that send reporters out in plain clothes to stir up talk about such things. We knew that Summit couldn't get after us with anything stronger than constables and, maybe, some lackadaisical bloodhounds and a diatribe[4] or two in the *Weekly Farmers' Budget*. So, it looked good.

We selected for our victim the only child of a prominent citizen named Ebenezer Dorset. The father was respectable and tight, a mortgage fancier[5] and a stern, upright collection-plate passer and forecloser. The kid was a boy of ten, with bas-relief[6] freckles, and hair the color of the cover of the magazine you buy at the newsstand when you want to catch a train. Bill and me figured that Ebenezer would melt down for a ransom of two thousand dollars to a cent. But wait till I tell you.

About two miles from Summit was a little mountain, covered with a dense cedar

1. Sam (the narrator) and Bill seem to enjoy using big words, but they don't always choose the right ones. What Bill means here is *aberration* ("a slight mental weakness or disease"), not *apparition* ("a ghost or ghostly vision").
2. *Deleterious* means "causing harm or injury" and usually refers to one's health or well-being. Here, Sam is saying that the townspeople are harmless.
3. *Philoprogenitiveness* is an old, rarely used word meaning "love of one's children."
4. *Lackadaisical* means "showing little energy or interest." *Diatribes* are angry criticisms.
5. A *fancier* is one who has a fondness for a particular thing. Sam means to say that Dorset is a mortgage *financier* (fin′ ən sēr′)—one who arranges mortgages.
6. *Bas-relief* (bä′ ri lēf′) is sculpture in which raised figures are carved on a flat background.

Vocabulary
prominent (prom′ ə nənt) *adj.* widely known

CONNECTING TO OTHER SELECTIONS

The chart at the right shows three ways to connect "The Ransom of Red Chief" to other selections in this book.

For specific teaching strategies, see the ***Theme Four Planning Guide***.

Connection	Title
Life Skills: Problem Solving	from *All Things Bright and Beautiful,* p. 103
Thematic: Troubled Children	"The Kid Nobody Could Handle," p. 146
Literary: Setting	from *On the Road with Charles Kuralt,* p. 635

# of Red Chief

O. Henry

brake. On the rear elevation of this mountain was a cave. There we stored provisions.

B One evening after sundown, we drove in a buggy past old Dorset's house. The kid was in the street, throwing rocks at a kitten on the opposite fence.

"Hey, little boy!" says Bill, "would you like to have a bag of candy and a nice ride?"

The boy catches Bill neatly in the eye with a piece of brick.

"That will cost the old man an extra five hundred dollars," says Bill, climbing over the wheel.

That boy put up a fight like a welterweight cinnamon bear; but, at last, we got him down in the bottom of the buggy and drove away. We took him up to the cave, and I hitched the horse in the cedar brake. After dark I drove the buggy to the little village, three miles away, where we had hired it, and walked back to the mountain.

Bill was pasting court-plaster[7] over the scratches and bruises on his features. There was a fire burning behind the big rock at the entrance of the cave, and the boy was watching a pot of boiling coffee, with two buzzard tail-feathers stuck in his red hair. He points a stick at me when I come up, and says:

"Ha! cursed paleface, do you dare to enter the camp of Red Chief, the terror of the plains?"

"He's all right now," says Bill, rolling up his trousers and examining some bruises on his shins. "We're playing Indian. We're making Buffalo Bill's show look like magic-lantern views of Palestine in the town hall.[8] I'm Old Hank, the Trapper, Red Chief's captive, and I'm to be scalped at daybreak. By Geronimo! that kid can kick hard."

C Yes, sir, that boy seemed to be having the time of his life. The fun of camping out in a cave had made him forget that he was a captive himself. He immediately christened me Snake-eye, the Spy, and announced that, when his braves returned from the warpath, I was to be broiled at the stake at the rising of the sun.

Then we had supper; and he filled his mouth full of bacon and bread and gravy, and began to talk. He made a during-dinner speech something like this:

"I like this fine. I never camped out before; but I had a pet 'possum once, and

7. Like a modern adhesive bandage, *court-plaster* is cloth coated with a sticky substance and used to protect minor wounds.

8. Bill thinks the boy's rough role-playing makes a Wild West frontier show seem as tame and boring as a slide show about a foreign land.

B Critical Thinking

INFERRING Ask students what they can infer about the "kid" from his "throwing rocks at a kitten." *(The boy is likely to be a troublemaker.)*

FYI

Buffalo Bill Buffalo Bill portrayed himself in his Wild West Show, starting in 1872. Before he became an actor, he spent his life as a bullwhacker (driver of a team of oxen), a trapper, a prospector, a buffalo hunter, and a scout in the Civil War.

C Active Reading Strategies

PREDICT Ask students what they think will happen with the boy, given his treatment of Bill and his enjoyment of the camping adventure.

MEETING INDIVIDUAL NEEDS — ENGLISH LANGUAGE LEARNERS

Games of Cowboys and Indians
English language learners may have difficulty identifying the boy's game and the action of the kidnappers. Invite the class to discuss the game and how it was played.

Activity Have English language learners read the story with English-speaking partners. Partners can create a story map identifying what is part of the kidnapping and what is part of the game. Suggest that students note language relating to the game. **COLLAB. LEARN.**

Additional Resources

English Language Learners Sourcebook, p. 49

VIEWING THE PAINTING

Viewing Response *The boy looks as if he might enjoy baseball and mischief. He has an impish air about him.*

D Literary Elements

CHARACTERIZATION Ask students to analyze Red Chief's long monologue on page 340. What does O. Henry convey about his character through what he says and how he says it? *(Red Chief talks constantly, rambles from one topic to the next, and asks hundreds of questions impossible to answer. In short, he's a complete nuisance to the kidnappers.)*

E Literary Elements

SUSPENSE Ask students to describe the effect on the reader of Sam's statement, "That boy had Bill terrorized from the start." *("From the start" implies that the terrorizing will continue and even get worse. As the reader anticipates what will come, the suspense is enhanced.)*

Vo•cab•u•lar•y Skills

Word Meaning *Hist* is an old word used to get someone's attention. It is equivalent to *psst!*

Teaching Support

I was nine last birthday. I hate to go to school. Rats ate up sixteen of Jimmy Talbot's aunt's speckled hen's eggs. Are there any real Indians in these woods? I want some more gravy. Does the trees moving make the wind blow? We had five puppies. What makes your nose so red, Hank? My father has lots of money. Are the stars hot? I whipped Ed Walker twice, Saturday. I don't like girls. You dassent catch toads unless with a string. Do oxen make any noise? Why are oranges round? Have you got beds to sleep on in this cave? Amos Murray has got six toes. A parrot can talk, but a monkey or a fish can't. How many does it take to make twelve?"

Every few minutes he would remember that he was a pesky redskin, and pick up his stick rifle and tiptoe to the mouth of the cave to rubber[9] for the scouts of the hated paleface. Now and then he would let out a war-whoop that made Old Hank the Trapper shiver. That boy had Bill terrorized from the start.

"Red Chief," says I to the kid, "would you like to go home?"

"Aw, what for?" says he. "I don't have any fun at home. I hate to go to school. I like to camp out. You won't take me back home again, Snake-eye, will you?"

"Not right away," says I. "We'll stay here in the cave a while."

"All right!" says he. "That'll be fine. I never had such fun in all my life."

Part of the Game. Karl Witkowski (1860–1910). Oil on canvas, 24 x 20 in. Private collection.

Viewing the painting: Do you think the boy in this painting would get along with Red Chief? Why or why not?

We went to bed about eleven o'clock. We spread down some wide blankets and quilts and put Red Chief between us. We weren't afraid he'd run away. He kept us awake for three hours, jumping up and reaching for his rifle and screeching: "Hist! pard," in mine and Bill's ears, as the fancied crackle of a twig or the rustle of a leaf revealed to his young imagination the stealthy approach of the outlaw band. At last, I fell into a troubled sleep, and dreamed that I had been kidnapped and chained to a tree by a ferocious pirate with red hair.

Just at daybreak, I was awakened by a series of awful screams from Bill. They

9. *Rubber* is short for *rubberneck,* which means "to look with exaggerated curiosity."

Writing Minilesson

Monologue O. Henry has Red Chief ramble on in a monologue that reveals character. It is clear that he is full of curiosity and mischief. Explain that writers of monologues carefully choose words to reveal aspects of character.

Activity Have students create a character and then write a one-paragraph monologue that reveals something about that character. Students should begin by writing the name of the character on paper and then should list the qualities to be revealed through the monologue. Students should read their monologues aloud in groups. Ask group members to identify the qualities revealed in each monologue. **L2** COLLAB. LEARN.

Additional Resources

Writer's Choice, Lesson 4.4

weren't yells, or howls, or shouts, or whoops, or yawps, such as you'd expect from a manly set of vocal organs—they were simply indecent, terrifying, humiliating screams, such as women emit when they see ghosts or caterpillars. It's an awful thing to hear a strong, desperate, fat man scream incontinently[10] in a cave at daybreak.

I jumped up to see what the matter was. Red Chief was sitting on Bill's chest, with one hand twined in Bill's hair. In the other he had the sharp case-knife we used for slicing bacon; and he was industriously and realistically trying to take Bill's scalp, according to the sentence that had been pronounced upon him the evening before.

I got the knife away from the kid and made him lie down again. But, from that moment, Bill's spirit was broken. He laid down on his side of the bed, but he never closed an eye again in sleep as long as that boy was with us. I dozed off for a while, but along toward sun-up I remembered that Red Chief had said I was to be burned at the stake at the rising of the sun. I wasn't nervous or afraid; but I sat up and lit my pipe and leaned against a rock.

"What you getting up so soon for, Sam?" asked Bill.

"Me?" says I. "Oh, I got a kind of a pain in my shoulder. I thought sitting up would rest it."

"You're a liar!" says Bill. "You're afraid. You was to be burned at sunrise, and you was afraid he'd do it. And he would, too, if he could find a match. Ain't it awful, Sam? Do you think anybody will pay out money to get a little imp like that back home?"

"Sure," said I. "A rowdy kid like that is just the kind that parents dote on. Now, you and the Chief get up and cook breakfast, while I go up on the top of this mountain and reconnoitre."

I went up on the peak of the little mountain and ran my eye over the contiguous vicinity. Over toward Summit I expected to see the sturdy yeomanry of the village armed with scythes and pitchforks beating the countryside for the dastardly[11] kidnappers. But what I saw was a peaceful landscape dotted with one man ploughing with a dun mule. Nobody was dragging the creek; no couriers dashed hither and yon, bringing tidings of no news to the distracted parents. There was a sylvan attitude of somnolent sleepiness pervading[12] that section of the external outward surface of Alabama that lay exposed to my view. "Perhaps," says I to myself, "it has not yet been discovered that the wolves have borne away the tender lambkin from the fold. Heaven help the wolves!" says I, and I went down the mountain to breakfast.

When I got to the cave I found Bill backed up against the side of it, breathing hard, and the boy threatening to smash him with a rock half as big as a coconut.

10. *Incontinently* means "uncontrollably."

11. When Sam *reconnoiters* the *contiguous vicinity,* he surveys the area. He expects to see farmers *(yeomanry)* pursuing the mean, sneaky, cowardly *(dastardly)* kidnappers.

12. What Sam sees are peaceful woods. *Sylvan* means "in or among trees." *Somnolent* means "sleepy," and *pervading* means "spreading throughout."

Vocabulary

emit (i mit′) *v.* to utter; send forth or give out, as a sound

dote (dōt) *v.* to show extreme affection

F Active Reading Strategies

QUESTION Ask students why they think Sam goes to such lengths to describe Bill's scream. *(He's trying to impress readers with the extraordinary quality of the sound—and, of course, the description is so exaggerated that it becomes funny.)*

G Active Reading Strategies

PREDICT Ask students to predict the result of Bill's having had his spirit broken. What impact do they think this will have on the rest of the story?

H Active Reading Strategies

QUESTION Why does Sam say he has a pain in his shoulder? *(He doesn't want to admit to Bill that the boy has scared him as well.)*

I Active Reading Strategies

CONNECT Ask students what they think of Sam's idea that parents particularly dote on rowdy children. Is this true, from their experience? *(Students may express the view that parents who dote on their children may allow them more freedom than appropriate—which, in turn, may then lead to rowdy behavior.)*

Reading Minilesson

Paraphrase Sam's description of the landscape surrounding Summit is deliberately complicated by exaggerated and antique language, which O. Henry uses for humorous effect. Including so many difficult words can make the passage hard to read; however, paraphrasing lofty-sounding passages may help students.

Activity Have students work in small groups to paraphrase the paragraph on page 341 that begins "I went up on the peak." They should use context and word roots to help them decode unfamiliar words before looking them up in the dictionary. Ask groups to share their paraphrases and check them for accuracy. **L2** COLLAB. LEARN.

Additional Resources

Reading Skills Practice Workbook

J Author's Craft

POINT OF VIEW Discuss the effect of having Sam, as opposed to Bill, narrate the story. *(If Bill were to tell the sad tale of all his injuries, the story would probably not be so funny. Sam, however, is able to distance himself from the events, and this objectivity allows the reader to laugh at Bill's plight.)*

K Literary Elements

SUSPENSE Ask students how Bill's plea that Sam not leave him alone with the kid adds suspense to the story. *(Obviously, Sam will have to leave Bill alone with him again. His plea adds suspense by making the reader wonder what will happen to Bill next.)*

L Active Reading Strategies

PREDICT Ask students for their reaction to Red Chief's request to "play the Black Scout." Sam doesn't pay much attention to the boy. Is that a mistake? *(By now, students are probably sure that something awful will happen as a result of the new game; the suspense lies in trying to figure out what, exactly, the boy will do.)*

Teaching Support

"He put a red-hot boiled potato down my back," explained Bill, "and then mashed it with his foot; and I boxed his ears. Have you got a gun about you, Sam?"

I took the rock away from the boy and kind of patched up the argument. "I'll fix you," says the kid to Bill. "No man ever yet struck the Red Chief but what he got paid for it. You better beware!"

After breakfast the kid takes a piece of leather with strings wrapped around it out of his pocket and goes outside the cave unwinding it.

"What's he up to now?" says Bill, anxiously. "You don't think he'll run away, do you, Sam?"

"No fear of it," says I. "He don't seem to be much of a homebody. But we've got to fix up some plan about the ransom. There don't seem to be much excitement around Summit on account of his disappearance; but maybe they haven't realized yet that he's gone. His folks may think he's spending the night with Aunt Jane or one of the neighbors. Anyhow, he'll be missed today. Tonight we must get a message to his father demanding the two thousand dollars for his return."

Just then we heard a kind of war whoop, such as David might have emitted when he knocked out the champion Goliath.[13] It was a sling that Red Chief had pulled out of his pocket, and he was whirling it around his head.

J I dodged, and heard a heavy thud and a kind of a sigh from Bill, like a horse gives when you take his saddle off. A rock the size of an egg had caught Bill just behind his left ear. He loosened himself all over and fell in the fire across the frying pan of hot water for washing the dishes. I dragged him out and poured cold water on his head for half an hour. J

By and by, Bill sits up and feels behind his ear and says: "Sam, do you know who my favorite Biblical character is?"

"Take it easy," says I. "You'll come to your senses presently."

"King Herod,"[14] says he. "You won't go away and leave me here alone, will you, Sam?" K

I went out and caught that boy and shook him until his freckles rattled.

"If you don't behave," says I, "I'll take you straight home. Now, are you going to be good, or not?"

"I was only funning," says he sullenly. "I didn't mean to hurt Old Hank. But what did he hit me for? I'll behave, Snake-eye, if you won't send me home, and if you'll let me play the Black Scout today." L

"I don't know the game," says I. "That's for you and Mr. Bill to decide. He's your playmate for the day. I'm going away for a while, on business. Now, you come in and make friends with him and say you are sorry for hurting him, or home you go, at once."

I made him and Bill shake hands, and then I took Bill aside and told him I was going to Poplar Cove, a little village three miles from the cave, and find out what I could about how the kidnapping had been regarded in Summit. Also, I thought it best to send a peremptory letter to old

13. In the Bible story, the boy *David* kills the giant *Goliath* with a stone shot from a sling.

14. In this Bible story, *King Herod* orders the murder of all Hebrew male infants in an effort to kill the child Jesus.

Vocabulary
peremptory (pə remp′ tər ē) *adj.* allowing no refusal

MEETING INDIVIDUAL NEEDS: MULTIPLE MODES OF EXPRESSION

Linguistic Students with linguistic learning styles typically learn well by reading. These students and others may benefit from learning about the dime novels of O. Henry's day. O. Henry is spoofing these novels in the antics and language of the kidnappers as well as in the games of Red Chief.

Activity Have students research dime novels of the period and report to the class on what they learn. What kinds of stories were usually told in dime novels? What relevance do the novels have to the story? **L2**

man Dorset that day, demanding the ransom and dictating how it should be paid.

M "You know, Sam," says Bill, "I've stood by you without batting an eye in earthquakes, fire and flood—in poker games, dynamite outrages, police raids, train robberies, and cyclones. I never lost my nerve yet till we kidnapped that two-legged skyrocket of a kid. He's got me going. You won't leave me long with him, will you, Sam?"

"I'll be back some time this afternoon," says I. "You must keep the boy amused and quiet till I return. And now we'll write the letter to old Dorset."

N Bill and I got paper and pencil and worked on the letter while Red Chief, with a blanket wrapped around him, strutted up and down, guarding the mouth of the cave. Bill begged me tearfully to make the ransom fifteen hundred dollars instead of two thousand. "I ain't attempting," says he, "to decry the celebrated moral aspect of parental affection, but we're dealing with humans, and it ain't human for anybody to give up two thousand dollars for that forty-pound chunk of freckled wildcat. I'm willing to take a chance at fifteen hundred dollars. You can charge the difference up to me."

So, to relieve Bill, I acceded, and we collaborated a letter that ran this way:

O

Ebenezer Dorset, Esq.:[15]

We have your boy concealed in a place far from Summit. It is useless for you or the most skillful detectives to attempt to find him. Absolutely, the only terms on which you can have him restored to you are these: We demand fifteen hundred dollars in large bills for his return; the money to be left at midnight tonight at the same spot and in the same box as your reply—as hereinafter described. If you agree to these terms, send your answer in writing by a solitary messenger tonight at half past eight o'clock. After crossing Owl Creek, on the road to Poplar Cove, there are three large trees about a hundred yards apart, close to the fence of the wheat field on the right-hand side. At the bottom of the fence post, opposite the third tree, will be found a small pasteboard box.

The messenger will place the answer in this box and return immediately to Summit.

If you attempt any treachery or fail to comply with our demand as stated, you will never see your boy again.

If you pay the money as demanded, he will be returned to you safe and well within three hours. These terms are final, and if you do not accede to them no further communication will be attempted.

Two Desperate Men.

I addressed this letter to Dorset, and put it in my pocket. As I was about to start, the kid comes up to me and says:

"Aw, Snake-eye, you said I could play the Black Scout while you was gone."

15. To *accede* (ak sēd′) is to yield and agree to. To *collaborate* (kə lab′ ə rāt′) is to work with another or others. The abbreviation *Esq.* is short for *esquire,* a title of respect or courtesy for a man.

Vocabulary
decry (di krī′) *v.* to criticize openly
comply (kəm plī′) *v.* to obey or go along with a request

M Active Reading Strategies

REVIEW Ask students how O. Henry conveys Bill's feelings about Red Chief. *(He uses exaggeration; Bill says he would endure cyclones and earthquakes rather than stay with the boy.)*

N Active Reading Strategies

QUESTION Ask students why they think Bill wants Sam to ask for fifteen hundred dollars instead of two thousand. Present the following model as an example of the thinking process used:

Model: I think Bill is beginning to figure out why Red Chief's father hasn't tried to find the boy. From Bill's own experience, he knows what a terror Red Chief can be, and he assumes his family might feel the same way. I think he suggests Sam ask for the fifteen hundred dollars rather than two thousand in the hope that they can be rid of the boy more quickly.

O Literary Elements

SUSPENSE How does the ransom note increase the suspense in the story? Ask students to list what kind of response they think the note will elicit. *(Students may say that the father will pay the ransom. They may also suggest that the father may contact the authorities. Some may be able to predict that Ebenezer will turn the tables on the kidnappers.)*

Teaching Support

Meeting Individual Needs: ADVANCED LEARNERS

Literature into Film This story was made into a video by the Learning Corporation of America in 1977 and was remade in 1978. Point out to students that transforming literature into film is a process that requires directors to omit some material from the original and to add other material. How the director makes those choices will determine how successfully the video captures the spirit of the original work.

Activity Have students watch the video and write an analysis of the differences between the video and the story. Students should speculate about why the director chose to make each change. **L3**

P Literary Elements

SUSPENSE Ask students for their reactions to Sam's idea that Red Chief's playing the Black Scout "sounds harmless." What do they assume will happen? *(This is another instance in which Sam appears to be oblivious to how mischievous Red Chief can be; the reader knows that every time Sam leaves Bill alone with Red Chief, something awful happens.)*

Q Author's Craft

WORD CHOICE Point out that much of the story's humor comes from the way Sam and Bill speak—in a mixture of contrived, long words, such as *philoprogenitiveness*, and Western slang such as *whiskerando.*

R Active Reading Strategies

QUESTION Why does Sam go to Poplar Cove? *(He wants to be sure Red Chief is missed before he sends the ransom note; he also wants to mail the letter from someplace other than Summit so that it cannot be traced back to him.)*

Teaching Support

"Play it, of course," says I. "Mr. Bill will play with you. What kind of a game is it?"

"I'm the Black Scout," says Red Chief, "and I have to ride to the stockade to warn the settlers that the Indians are coming. I'm tired of playing Indian myself. I want to be the Black Scout."

P "All right," says I. "It sounds harmless to me. I guess Mr. Bill will help you foil the pesky savages."

"What am I to do?" asks Bill, looking at the kid suspiciously.

"You are the hoss," says Black Scout. "Get down on your hands and knees. How can I ride to the stockade without a hoss?"

"You'd better keep him interested," said I, "till we get the scheme going. Loosen up."

Bill gets down on his all fours, and a look comes in his eye like a rabbit's when you catch it in a trap.

"How far is it to the stockade, kid?" he asks, in a husky manner of voice.

"Ninety miles," says the Black Scout. "And you have to hump yourself to get there on time. Whoa, now!"

The Black Scout jumps on Bill's back and digs his heels in his side.

"For Heaven's sake," says Bill, "hurry back, Sam, as soon as you can. I wish we hadn't made the ransom more than a thousand. Say, you quit kicking me or I'll get up and warm you good."

R I walked over to Poplar Cove and sat around the post office and store, talking with the chawbacons that came in to trade. One whiskerando[16] says that he hears Summit is all upset on account of Elder Ebenezer Dorset's boy having been lost or stolen. That was all I wanted to know. I bought some smoking tobacco, referred casually to the price of black-eyed peas, posted my letter surreptitiously and came away. The postmaster said the mail carrier would come by in an hour to take the mail on to Summit.

When I got back to the cave Bill and the boy were not to be found. I explored the vicinity of the cave, and risked a yodel or two, but there was no response.

So I lighted my pipe and sat down on a mossy bank to await developments.

In about half an hour I heard the bushes rustle, and Bill wabbled out into the little glade in front of the cave. Behind him was the kid, stepping softly like a scout, with a broad grin on his face. Bill stopped, took off his hat and wiped his face with a red handkerchief. The kid stopped about eight feet behind him.

Q "Sam," says Bill, "I suppose you'll think I'm a renegade, but I couldn't help it. I'm a grown person with masculine proclivities and habits of self-defense, but there is a time when all systems of egotism and predominance[17] fail. The boy is gone. I have sent him home. All is off. There was martyrs in old times," goes on Bill, "that suffered death rather than give up the particular graft they enjoyed. None of 'em ever was subjugated to such supernatural tortures as I have

16. *Chawbacons* are the men sitting around chewing tobacco. A *whiskerando* is an old-timer, especially one with whiskers.

17. Bill really shows off his vocabulary here. *Proclivities* are tendencies. *Egotism* is an exaggerated sense of self-importance. *Predominance* is using one's superior power or influence to control others.

Vocabulary

renegade (ren′ ə gād′) *n.* one who abandons or turns against a group, cause, or allegiance; traitor

MEETING INDIVIDUAL NEEDS — SPECIAL NEEDS

Less-Proficient Readers Thinking ahead and using text structures can help less-proficient readers predict what will happen next and stay connected to the story. This skill increases attention, which in turn heightens the suspense in a story such as this one.

Activity Ask students to predict what could happen when the kidnappers go to pick up the ransom money. Brainstorm a list of possibilities together. Then vote on which one is most likely to happen. *(Since nothing goes the way the kidnappers expect it is possible to predict that the ransom money won't be there.)* **L1**

Additional Resources

Inclusion Strategies

been. I tried to be faithful to our articles of depredation;[18] but there came a limit."

"What's the trouble, Bill?" I asks him.

"I was rode," says Bill, "the ninety miles to the stockade, not barring an inch. Then, when the settlers was rescued, I was given oats. Sand ain't a palatable substitute. And then, for an hour I had to try to explain to him why there was nothin' in holes, how a road can run both ways, and what makes the grass green. I tell you, Sam, a human can only stand so much. I takes him by the neck of his clothes and drags him down the mountain. On the way he kicks my legs black-and-blue from the knees down; and I've got to have two or three bites on my thumb and hand cauterized.

"But he's gone"—continues Bill—"gone home. I showed him the road to Summit and kicked him about eight feet nearer there at one kick. I'm sorry we lose the ransom; but it was either that or Bill Driscoll to the madhouse."

Bill is puffing and blowing, but there is a look of ineffable[19] peace and growing content on his rose-pink features.

"Bill," says I, "there isn't any heart disease in your family, is there?"

"No," says Bill, "nothing chronic except malaria and accidents. Why?"

"Then you might turn around," says I, "and have a look behind you."

Bill turns and sees the boy, and loses his complexion and sits down plump on the ground and begins to pluck aimlessly at grass and little sticks. For an hour I was afraid of his mind. And then I told him that my scheme was to put the whole job through immediately and that we would get the ransom and be off with it by midnight if old Dorset fell in with our proposition. So Bill braced up enough to give the kid a weak sort of a smile and a promise to play the Russian in a Japanese war[20] with him as soon as he felt a little better.

I had a scheme for collecting that ransom without danger of being caught by counterplots that ought to commend itself to professional kidnappers. The tree under which the answer was to be left—and the money later on—was close to the road fence with big, bare fields on all sides. If a gang of constables should be watching for any one to come for the note they could see him a long way off crossing the fields or in the road. But no, sirree! At half past eight I was up in that tree as well hidden as a tree toad, waiting for the messenger to arrive.

Exactly on time, a half-grown boy rides up the road on a bicycle, locates the pasteboard box at the foot of the fence post, slips a folded piece of paper into it and pedals away again back toward Summit.

I waited an hour and then concluded the thing was square. I slid down the tree, got the note, slipped along the fence till I struck the woods, and was back at the cave in another half an hour. I opened the note, got near the lantern and read it to Bill. It was written with a pen in a crabbed hand, and the sum and substance of it was this:

18. *Martyrs* are those who suffer or die for a cause. *Graft*, here, refers to money gained dishonestly. *Subjugated* means "forced to undergo an unpleasant experience." *Articles of depredation* are Sam and Bill's rules for robbing people.
19. *Ineffable* means "indescribable" or "unspeakable."

20. In 1905 mighty Russia suffered a humiliating defeat by the less-powerful Japan.

Vocabulary
palatable (pal′ ə tə bəl) *adj.* agreeable to the taste, mind, or feelings; acceptable

S Active Reading Strategies

REVIEW Ask students what Bill means when he says, "Sand ain't a palatable substitute." *(Red Chief's fed him sand, pretending it was oats.)*

T Active Reading Strategies

CONNECT Ask students who have younger brothers or sisters if they have ever experienced an emotion similar to what Bill feels in trying to explain why there is nothing in holes and why the grass is green. Can they describe the feeling? *(One feels both frustrated and ignorant. One wants to reply, "Just because"; but one is also aware that there is a scientific explanation, and it's hard to admit ignorance to a child.)*

U Active Reading Strategies

VISUALIZE Ask students to draw images of the moment before Bill turns around to see Red Chief standing behind him. What facial expressions do they imagine for each of the three characters?

Teaching Support

Real-World Connection

Crime in the Media It is clear that this story could not take place today. The thought of kidnapping is frightening, so making something comic out if it would be difficult.

Activity Have students conduct some research on the events surrounding the kidnapping in 1932 of the infant son of Charles and Anne Lindbergh. Then discuss in class the impact on the world's attitude toward kidnapping.
L2 **COLLAB. LEARN.**

interNET CONNECTION

Students can find information about the Lindbergh case on the Internet, including a long-lost comic strip version of the news story.

Active Reading Strategies

QUESTION Ask students what they think Bill means when he says "I think Mr. Dorset is a spendthrift for making us such a liberal offer." *(Bill thinks paying Mr. Dorset even more to take his son back would be a bargain.)*

Critical Thinking

EVALUATING Ask students what they think of Sam's choice of words as he agrees to pay Mr. Dorset. *(Clearly Sam is pretending that he isn't bothered by the boy, but his agreeing to pay proves that he is. His exaggeratedly casual language betrays his true feelings.)*

Thematic Focus

Fantastic Capers and Mischief Makers Ask students to decide who in this story are the "mischief makers."

ASSESSMENT

Quick Checks, p. 28

Two Desperate Men.

Gentlemen: I received your letter today by post, in regard to the ransom you ask for the return of my son. I think you are a little high in your demands, and I hereby make you a counter-proposition, which I am inclined to believe you will accept. You bring Johnny home and pay me two hundred and fifty dollars in cash, and I agree to take him off your hands. You had better come at night, for the neighbors believe he is lost, and I couldn't be responsible for what they would do to anybody they saw bringing him back. Very respectfully,

EBENEZER DORSET.

"Great pirates of Penzance!"[21] says I; "of all the impudent——"

But I glanced at Bill, and hesitated. He had the most appealing look in his eyes I ever saw on the face of a dumb or a talking brute.

"Sam," says he, "what's two hundred and fifty dollars, after all? We've got the money. One more night of this kid will send me to a bed in Bedlam. Besides being a thorough gentleman, I think Mr. Dorset is a spendthrift[22] for making us such a liberal offer. You ain't going to let the chance go, are you?"

"Tell you the truth, Bill," says I, "this little he ewe lamb has somewhat got on my nerves too. We'll take him home, pay the ransom, and make our getaway."

We took him home that night. We got him to go by telling him that his father had bought a silver-mounted rifle and a pair of moccasins for him, and we were going to hunt bears the next day.

It was just twelve o'clock when we knocked at Ebenezer's front door. Just at the moment when I should have been abstracting[23] the fifteen hundred dollars from the box under the tree, according to the original proposition, Bill was counting out two hundred and fifty dollars into Dorset's hand.

When the kid found out we were going to leave him at home he started up a howl like a calliope and fastened himself as tight as a leech to Bill's leg. His father peeled him away gradually, like a porous plaster.

"How long can you hold him?" asks Bill.

"I'm not as strong as I used to be," says old Dorset, "but I think I can promise you ten minutes."

"Enough," says Bill. "In ten minutes I shall cross the Central, Southern, and Middle Western States, and be legging it trippingly for the Canadian border."

And, as dark as it was, and as fat as Bill was, and as good a runner as I am, he was a good mile and a half out of Summit before I could catch up with him.

21. *The Pirates of Penzance* is an 1879 comic opera in which the pirates have a difficult and silly time trying to carry out a kidnapping.

22. *Bedlam* was an English hospital for the mentally ill. A *spendthrift* is one who spends money either generously or wastefully.

23. Here, *abstracting* means "removing or taking away secretly."

Vocabulary

impudent (im′ pyə dənt) *adj.* boldly discourteous

Teaching Support

Grammar and Language *Minilesson*

Writing Numbers Write the following on the board: "two hundred and fifty dollars," "twelve o'clock," "ten minutes." Point out that O. Henry's spelling out all numbers is different from usage today. Present these rules: Spell out numbers that begin a sentence or that can be written in one or two words. Spell out ordinal numbers and the time of day except to indicate the exact time. Use figures for numbers of more than two words and for dates, house and street numbers, amounts of money of more than two words, percentages, and designations following a noun. Ask students which of the numbers on the board should change according to these rules. *(250)*

Activity Ask students to find five other instances of numbers used in the story. Have students apply the current rules. **L2**

Additional Resources

- ***Grammar and Language Transparency 26***
- ***Grammar and Language Workbook,*** p. 275
- ***Grammar and Composition Handbook,*** Lesson 13.10
- ***Writer's Choice,*** Lesson 20.10

Responding to Literature

PERSONAL RESPONSE

- How did your impression of the boy change from the beginning of the story to the end? Compare the boy with the list of characteristics you made in the **Reading Focus** on page 337.

Brackets connect questions that are paired to develop higher-level thinking skills.

Analyzing Literature

RECALL

1. Why do Bill and Sam decide to stage a kidnapping? Why do they choose Summit for their caper?
2. Describe the kidnapped boy.
3. When does Bill give up on the kidnapping plan? Why does he want to ask for less ransom money?
4. How does the boy's father respond to the ransom letter?

INTERPRET

5. Why does Bill say that the kidnapping plan struck them at a moment when they weren't thinking clearly?
6. Why don't the kidnappers worry that the boy might run away?
7. Why does the **narrator** say "Heaven help the wolves" after seeing no signs of anyone looking for the kidnapped boy?
8. Why do the men sign their ransom letter "Two Desperate Men"?

EVALUATE AND CONNECT

9. Theme Connection How many mischief makers are in this story? Which person do you think is the most mischievous? Explain.
10. How does O. Henry portray the crime of kidnapping in this story? What makes this treatment different from real-life kidnappings you know of or have read about?

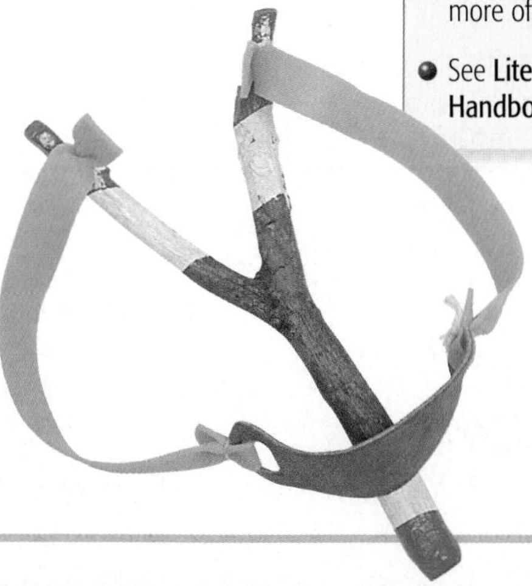

LITERARY ELEMENTS

Suspense

Suspense is the growing anxiety and excitement that a reader feels as the plot of a story unfolds. Suspense draws readers toward the ending of a story. O. Henry uses suspense in an unusual way: he leads his readers to a likely climax, then presents them with a surprise outcome. O. Henry's fans read to see *how* the writer will use suspense to twist the ending, not *whether* he will come through with a surprise.

1. Find some examples of suspense in "The Ransom of Red Chief." How does O. Henry build interest in the upcoming events?
2. How does O. Henry use suspense to make his ending more of a surprise?

- See **Literary Terms Handbook**, p. R10.

347

Responding to the Selection

PERSONAL RESPONSE

At the beginning of the story, Red Chief seems like an ordinarily mischievous nine-year-old; but by the end of the story, he reaches nearly epic proportions as he torments poor Bill.

Analyzing Literature

1. Sam and Bill need money for another dishonest scheme. They choose Summit because they think they can outwit the unsophisticated people of such a small town.
2. Red Chief is a talkative, curious, rambunctious boy, with a substantial streak of mischief.
3. Bill gives up on the kidnapping plan when he sends Red Chief home. He wants to ask for less ransom money because he's afraid no one will pay two thousand dollars to ransom such a wild child.
4. He demands that the kidnappers pay him to take the boy back.
5. He is telling the story after the fact, and he knows why the scheme failed.
6. They don't worry because Red Chief has made it clear that he is having a good time.
7. He says, "Heaven help the wolves" because the victim in this case is more dangerous than the kidnappers.
8. They sign the letter "Two Desperate Men" to make Red Chief's father believe they might harm the boy. The signature is ironic, however, in that the kidnappers eventually become desperate to be rid of the boy.
9. All the major characters are mischief makers, but Red Chief makes the most mischief.
10. It is fun to see the bad guys pay, and the unexpected ending is effective.

LITERARY ELEMENTS

1. O. Henry begins by telling the reader that things will not work out as planned. Suspense is heightened when Sam notices that no one is looking for the boy.
2. By the time Red Chief is returned, the reader has begun to wonder whether Mr. Dorset will really take the boy back.

Additional Resources

Literary Elements Transparency 28

Literature and Writing

Writing About Literature

Students' paragraphs should

- mention three episodes
- explain the source of humor in each

Creative Writing

Students' alternative endings should

- include an explanation of needed changes
- be surprising

Extending Your Response

Learning for Life Mention that one effective way to modernize the story would be to change the games the boy wants to play and to e-mail the ransom request.

Internet Connection Have students share the Web addresses of any good sites they discover while online.

Literature Groups Suggest that students focus on the differences in how Bill and Sam speak so that they can characterize each man individually. COLLAB. LEARN.

At the MOVIES

Be sure to preview the following video for appropriateness for your class:
Waking Ned Divine, the story of two elderly mischief makers who try their luck in a small town in Ireland

Literature and Writing

Writing About Literature

What's Funny? Find three humorous excerpts in "The Ransom of Red Chief," and write a short paragraph for each to explain the humor. Is the description of the event funny? Is the event itself humorous? Which words, dialogue, or sentence structures tickle your funny bone?

Creative Writing

Surprise! Choose another short story, a fairy tale, or a young children's book that has a predictable ending. Compose an alternate ending that readers would find surprising. Include a notation of what might need to be added or changed in the first part of the story to make the new ending reasonable.

Extending Your Response

Learning for Life

Play Time! Many of O. Henry's stories were later produced as plays or movies. Plan a modern production of "The Ransom of Red Chief." Describe the setting and characters, and select actors to play each of the main roles.

interNET CONNECTION

To visit the O. Henry Museum, type "O. Henry Home and Museum" into a search engine. What interesting facts about O. Henry do you discover on the Internet? Compare the information you find with that of your classmates.

Literature Groups

What People Say O. Henry uses **dialogue** to characterize Bill and Sam. For example, Bill often confuses one big word for another, which makes him seem funny and somewhat foolish. Choose about ten lines of dialogue from the story to read aloud in your group. Discuss the word choices and the tone O. Henry uses to show what kind of characters Bill and Sam are. Then, take turns role-playing a conversation that might take place between Bill and Sam after the boy goes home. Imitate the tone and types of word choices the men use.

O'Henry's Full House. Twentieth Century Fox. Movie still.

Reading Further

For other stories of unusual situations, read:
Kidnapped by Robert Louis Stevenson
Crow and Weasel by Barry Holstun Lopez

Save your work for your portfolio.

MEETING INDIVIDUAL NEEDS — SPECIAL NEEDS

Less-Proficient Readers When readers run into unfamiliar or unusual words, such as the vocabulary Bill uses, they may turn to a dictionary to clarify the meanings and usage. Another resource is a thesaurus or a synonym finder. Explain that a thesaurus such as *Roget's* may group related words into topical categories with numbered subdivisions and an alphabetical index. A synonym finder, on the other hand, arranges word entries alphabetically with a list of synonyms for each word.

Activity Pair less-proficient readers with other students and give them access to thesauruses and synonym finders. Have them look up synonyms for the following words and discuss their meanings: *fraudulent, industrious, vicinity, subjugate, surreptitiously*, and *cauterize*. **L1**

Skill Minilessons

RETEACH • REVIEW

GRAMMAR AND LANGUAGE • COLORFUL WORDS

O. Henry's ability to surprise the reader with just the right word—sometimes one he makes up—is unrivaled. This element of surprise is one technique the writer uses to create humor. In "The Ransom of Red Chief," the characters often use unusual adjectives and nouns—dialect the reader would not expect ordinary people to use.

PRACTICE Find the following words or phrases in the story, and explain their meaning. Suggest a more common word or phrase that might have been used.

1. "respectable and tight" (p. 338)
2. "dassent catch toads" (p. 340)
3. "imp like that" (p. 341)
4. "boxed his ears" (p. 342)

READING AND THINKING • VERIFYING PREDICTIONS

Readers often predict the subject and mood of a story based on the title, illustrations, or ideas they already have about a type of character. Readers also make predictions as they read, using clues in the story.

- For more about verifying predictions, see **Reading Handbook,** p. R94.

PRACTICE Look at the notes you made in the **Reading Focus** on page 337. Identify five places in "The Ransom of Red Chief" where you think the boy's appearance and behavior match the child you described. Then explain how the character differed from your idea of a nine- or ten-year-old.

VOCABULARY • DICTIONARY SKILLS: DEFINITIONS

If a word is unfamiliar to you, you can look it up in a dictionary. However, most words have several meanings, and the first definition in the dictionary may not be the one you need. Look for the meaning that relates to how the word was used in what you read or heard. Here is a typical set of meanings for the word *prominent.*

prom·i·nent *adj.* **1.** well-known or important: *a prominent politician.* **2.** very noticeable; obvious: *The tower is a prominent feature of the town.* **3.** sticking out or standing out from a surface: *a prominent chin.*

PRACTICE Decide which of the meanings of *prominent* is used in each sentence below, and write the number of the meaning.

1. Elvis Presley was a *prominent* musician.
2. Many prehistoric humans had *prominent* foreheads.
3. Uncle Fred is a *prominent* member of the golf club.
4. The picture was hung in a *prominent* place in the living room.
5. A tiger's stripes are less *prominent* than a zebra's.

Skill Minilessons

GRAMMAR AND LANGUAGE
USING COLORFUL WORDS

1. proper and careful with money
2. dare not, or should not try to, catch toads
3. mischief maker like the boy
4. slapped him on the side of the head

READING AND THINKING
VERIFYING PREDICTIONS

Students' responses should cite specific behaviors.

VOCABULARY
DICTIONARY SKILLS: DEFINITIONS

1. 1
2. 3
3. 1
4. 2
5. 2

Additional Resources

- ***Grammar and Composition Handbook***
- ***Grammar and Language Workbook***
- ***Writer's Choice,*** Lesson 23.4
- ***Reading Skills Practice Workbook***
- ***Vocabulary Practice,*** p. 21

ASSESSMENT

- ***Quick Checks,*** p. 28
- ***Selection and Theme Assessment,*** pp. 49–50
- ***Performance Assessment,*** p. 27
- ***Testmaker: ExamView Pro***
- ***Interactive Tutor: Self-Assessment***

Before Reading

Objectives

- To read and analyze a ballad and a poem
- To recognize and analyze a ballad
- To write a paragraph on plot

Skills

Reading/Thinking: Monitoring Comprehension; Evaluating
Writing: Story
Grammar/Language: Action Verbs; Proper Nouns
Listening/Speaking: Performance
Collaboration: Literature Groups

Motivating STUDENTS

Selection Focus Transparency 28: Before presenting the painting, have students name people they consider extraordinary and explain why they think so.

Reading Focus: As an extension of the Reading Focus, ask students to consider themselves and family members, too, when they try to think of someone who has triumphed in spite of difficulties.

Before You Read

John Henry and from *The People, Yes*

MEET CARL SANDBURG

Imagine a great American writer standing before an audience and singing folk songs. The writer, Carl Sandburg, was better known for his stories, biographies, and poems, but he also collected and sang folk music. His long poem "The People, Yes" celebrates the power of ordinary people to move forward in spite of hard times, just as folk heroes like John Henry did. Sandburg once said that all he wanted was "to eat regular, . . . to get what I write printed, . . . a little love at home . . . [and] to sing every day."

Carl Sandburg was born in 1878 and died in 1967. "The People, Yes" was first published in 1936.

READING FOCUS

Think of a story you have heard about a person who accomplished something in spite of difficulties.

Plan It!
Jot down details from one or two of the stories you recall.

Setting a Purpose
Read to discover some colorful characters and stories that are part of American culture.

BUILDING BACKGROUND

The Time and Place Many stories about the United States date back to the 1800s, when large numbers of Europeans and Americans from the East Coast began moving westward. Construction of railroads during this century brought new opportunities for some and the destruction of a way of life for others.

Did You Know? Many stories have been told about the crews that laid railroad tracks across the western United States. These workers, many of whom drove the steel spikes that held together the rails and ties, accomplished an amazing task. In the 1850s, track mileage in the United States increased by more than 20,000 miles. John Henry is the name of a hero said to be the greatest steel driver of all.

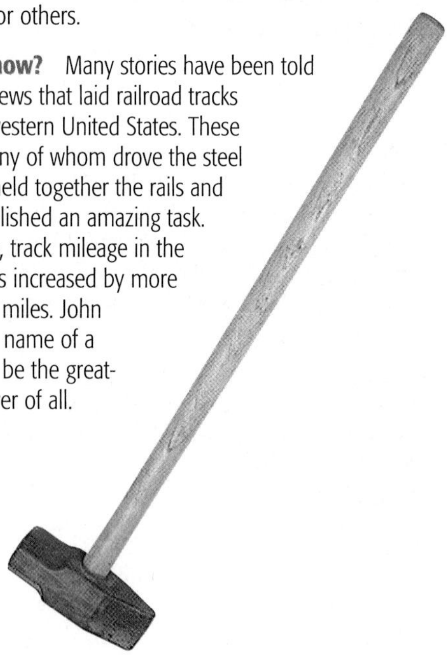

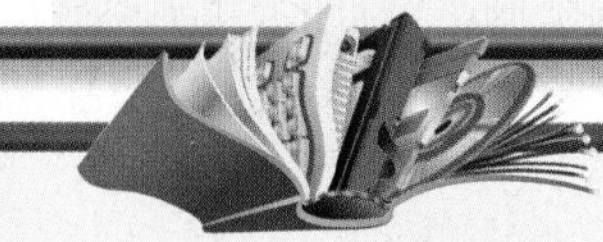

RESOURCE MANAGER

Teaching Tools and Resources
- Theme Four Planning Guide
- Literature Groups Sourcebook

Essential Lesson Support

Lesson-Specific Instruction
- Selection Focus Transparency 28
- Literary Elements Transparency 29
- Active Reading Guide,* p. 29

Assessment
- Selection Quick Checks,* p. 29
- Sel. and Theme Assmt., pp. 51–52
- Testmaker: ExamView Pro
- Performance Assessment, p. 28

Systematic Language Instruction
- Gr. & Comp. Hbk., L. 6.5

English Language Learners
- ELL Sourcebook, p. 50
- Spanish Summaries, p. 28
- Audio Library*
- English, Yes!

Spec. Needs/Strat. Interven.
- Interactive Rdg. Sbk., pp. T119–T121
- Interactive Rdg. Wkbk., p. 56
- Audio Library*

* Also available in Spanish

JOHN HENRY

Anonymous

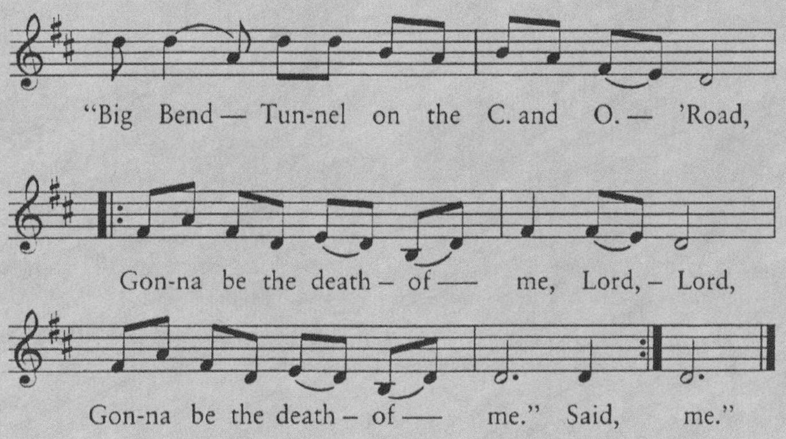

When John Henry was a little baby,
Settin' on his mammy's knee,
Said, "Big Bend Tunnel on the C. and O. 'Road,°
Gonna be the death of me, Lord, Lord,
Gonna be the death of me."

Now John Henry had a little woman,
Her name was Polly Ann,
When John Henry took sick and had to go to bed,
Polly Ann drove steel° like a man, Lord, Lord,
Polly Ann drove steel like a man!

The captain said to John Henry,
"I'm gonna bring that steel drill 'round,
I'm gonna bring that steel drill out on the job,
Gonna whop that steel on down, Lord, Lord,
Gonna whop that steel on down."

3 *C. and O. 'Road* is short for "Chesapeake and Ohio Railroad."
9 When John Henry and Polly Ann *drove steel,* they used a ten-pound hammer to pound a steel stake, called a drill, into rock to make holes for explosives.

Reading the Selection

A Active Reading Strategies

QUESTION John Henry predicts his own demise in the first stanza. How does that prediction set the mood of this ballad? *(The mood is heroic and mournful at the same time.)*

Additional Resources

- ***Active Reading Guide,*** p. 29
- ***Audio Library***
- ***Spanish Audio Library***

B Literary Elements

BALLAD Draw students' attention to the repetition. The use of repetition helped those who originally sang ballads remember them as they were probably not written down.

On The Lighter Side

The Smothers Brothers, a comic duo popular in the late 1960s and 70s, recorded a parody of this ballad.

Teaching Support

MEETING INDIVIDUAL NEEDS — ENGLISH LANGUAGE LEARNERS

Multicultural Songs Every culture has songs about heroes who have triumphed over seemingly impossible odds. Students from different cultures can help in the study of the form by sharing songs from their cultures.

Activity Have English language learners make a list of heroic songs from their native lands. Ask each student to present one song to the class. They may present lyrics only, sing the song, or bring in a recording. Then have each student explain why the story told in the song is important to his or her native culture.

Additional Resources

- ***English Language Learners Sourcebook,*** p. 50

C Literary Elements

RHYME SCHEME Ask students to identify the rhyme scheme in the first stanza. Then ask them to check whether it is regular throughout the song. *(If one eliminates "Lord, Lord," from consideration, the rhyme scheme [a, b, c, b, b] continues throughout the poem. "Fire" and "died" in stanza 9 are instances of assonance. "In" and "wind" and "hand" and "man" rhyme imperfectly; usually the "d" is dropped in the song.)*

D Active Reading Strategies

QUESTION Why will the shaker die if John Henry misses? *(He will probably be killed by the blow of the huge hammer.)*

E Literary Elements

BALLAD Ballads are often songs by and of the people. Ask students what is being celebrated in this ballad. *(The song portrays the fears people may have had that industrialization would put people out of work. John Henry celebrates the strength and determination of the individual.)*

Well, John Henry said to his captain,
"Lord, a man ain't nothin' but
a man,
But before I let your steam drill beat
me down,
I'll die with a hammer in my hand,
Lord, Lord,
I'll die with a hammer in my hand."

John Henry said to his shaker,°
"Shaker, you'd better pray,
If my hammer misses that little piece
of steel,
Tomorrow'll be your buryin' day,
Lord, Lord,
Tomorrow'll be your buryin' day."

Now the captain said to John Henry,
"I believe this mountain's sinkin' in."
John Henry just laughed at his
captain and he said,
"Ain't nothin' but my hammer
suckin' wind, Lord, Lord,
Ain't nothin' but my hammer suckin'
wind."

John Henry said to his shaker,
"Shaker, why don't you sing?
I'm throwin' twenty pounds from my
hips on down,
Just listen to that cold steel ring,
Lord, Lord,
Just listen to that cold steel ring."

Now the man that invented the
steam drill,
He thought he was mighty fine,
But John Henry drove fourteen feet,
And the steam drill only made nine,
Lord, Lord,
And the steam drill only made nine.

John Henry hammered on the
mountain,
And his hammer was striking fire,
But he drove so hard that he broke
his poor heart,
And he laid down his hammer and he
died, Lord, Lord,
He laid down his hammer and he
died.

John Henry had a little baby,
He could hold him in the palm of his
hand,
And the last words I heard that poor
boy say,
"My daddy was a steel-drivin' man,
Lord, Lord,
My daddy was a steel-drivin' man."

Well, they took John Henry to the
tunnel,
And they buried him in the sand,
Every locomotive comes rollin' by
Says, "There lies a steel-drivin' man,
Lord, Lord,
There lies a steel-drivin' man."

So every Monday morning,
When the bluebirds begin to sing,
You can hear those hammers a mile
or more,
You can hear John Henry's hammer
ring, Lord, Lord,
You can hear John Henry's hammer
ring.

21 A *shaker* held the steel drill steady while the steel driver hammered it and then shook the drill to free it from the rock.

Teaching Support

Literature & Humanities

John Henry

Introducing Art, page 157.
Have students compare the images evoked by the poem with those used by the artist.

Reading Minilesson

Monitoring Comprehension Explain that reading is an active process to which the reader brings knowledge, attention, questions, and information. It is crucial to test and verify comprehension while reading by asking questions and rereading passages that seem unclear at first.

Activity Have students work in small groups to develop a series of questions that readers of this ballad should be able to answer. Each group should pass its questions to another group to answer. Exchanges may be made more than once if time permits. **L2** COLLAB. LEARN.

Additional Resources

Reading Skills Practice Workbook

Untitled, 1994. Illustration by Terry Small. From *The Legend of John Henry.*
Viewing the art: How does this image show John Henry's strength and endurance?

F Active Reading Strategies

QUESTION How does the hammering break John Henry's heart? *(Despite his strength and courage, John Henry is defeated by the machine. He wins the battle but loses the war. His heart breaks from effort and from his vision of the end of an era.)*

VIEWING THE ILLUSTRAION

Viewing Response *The art suggests continuous motion, and the man's physique implies strength.*

MEETING INDIVIDUAL NEEDS — MULTIPLE MODES OF EXPRESSION

Musical This theme deals in part with ballads as literature and discusses characteristics that the lyrics have in common, such as simple rhyme scheme, repetition, and a narrative focus. Students who learn musically may benefit from playing or hearing the music itself.

Activity Have students play or listen to a number of ballads and determine which characteristics the melodies have in common. Students should report to the class on their findings. **L2**

H Active Reading Strategies

QUESTION Who is "they"? *(the American people)*

I Critical Thinking

EVALUATING Ask students to describe the structure of the poem. *(Each line finishes the first sentence "They have yarns . . .")*

J Author's Craft

EXAGGERATION Ask students what the yarns to which Sandburg refers have in common. *(They are all exaggerations.)*

K Active Reading Strategies

VISUALIZE Ask students to sketch a picture of the image of the train in lines 12 and 13. *(The curve is so extreme that at one point the engine and caboose are right next to each other.)*

from

The People, Yes

Carl Sandburg

They have yarns
Of a skyscraper so tall they had to put hinges
On the two top stories so to let the moon go by,
Of one corn crop in Missouri when the roots
Went so deep and drew off so much water
The Mississippi riverbed that year was dry,
Of pancakes so thin they had only one side,
Of "a fog so thick we shingled the barn and six feet out on the fog,"
Of Pecos Pete straddling a cyclone in Texas and riding it to the west coast where "it rained out under him,"
Of the man who drove a swarm of bees across the Rocky Mountains and the Desert "and didn't lose a bee,"
Of a mountain railroad curve where the engineer in his cab can touch the caboose and spit in the conductor's eye,
Of the boy who climbed a cornstalk growing so fast he would have starved to death if they hadn't shot biscuits up to him,
Of the old man's whiskers: "When the wind was with him his whiskers arrived a day before he did,"
Of the hen laying a square egg and cackling, "Ouch!" and of hens laying eggs with the dates printed on them,
Of the ship captain's shadow: it froze to the deck one cold winter night,
Of mutineers° on that same ship put to chipping rust with rubber hammers,

16 The *mutineers* are sailors who have openly rebelled against their commanding officers. Their punishment is a nearly impossible task, something like being forced to remove all the paint from the side of a house, using only a sponge.

Teaching Support

Grammar and Language *Minilesson*

Action Verbs Write this phrase from the poem on the board: "of fog so thick we shingled the barn and six feet out on the fog." Point out that *shingled* is an action verb—one that expresses physical or mental actions. Remind students that *have, has,* and *had* are action verbs when they name what the subject owns or holds.

Activity Have students identify as many action verbs as they can find in the poem. What does the number of action verbs say about the style of the poem? **L2**

Additional Resources

- ***Grammar and Language Transparency 27***
- ***Grammar and Language Workbook,*** p. 75
- ***Grammar and Composition Handbook,*** Lesson 3.1
- ***Writer's Choice,*** Lesson 10.1

Of the sheep counter who was fast and accurate: "I just count their feet and divide by four,"
Of the man so tall he must climb a ladder to shave himself,
Of the runt so teeny-weeny it takes two men and a boy to see him,
Of mosquitoes: one can kill a dog, two of them a man,
Of a cyclone that sucked cookstoves out of the kitchen, up the chimney flue, and on to the next town,
Of the same cyclone picking up wagon-tracks in Nebraska and dropping them over in the Dakotas,
Of the hook-and-eye snake unlocking itself into forty pieces, each piece two inches long, then in nine seconds flat snapping itself together again,
Of the watch swallowed by the cow—when they butchered her a year later the watch was running and had the correct time,
Of horned snakes, hoop snakes that roll themselves where they want to go, and rattlesnakes carrying bells instead of rattles on their tails,
Of the herd of cattle in California getting lost in a giant redwood tree that had hollowed out,
Of the man who killed a snake by putting its tail in its mouth so it swallowed itself,
Of railroad trains whizzing along so fast they reach the station before the whistle,
Of pigs so thin the farmer had to tie knots in their tails to keep them from crawling through the cracks in their pens,
Of Paul Bunyan's big blue ox, Babe, measuring between the eyes forty-two ax-handles and a plug of Star tobacco exactly,
Of John Henry's hammer and the curve of its swing and his singing of it as "a rainbow round my shoulder."

L Active Reading Strategies

QUESTION Why does counting the sheep by their feet make the sheep counter special? *(The feet are more numerous, hard to see, and constantly moving, making the task almost impossible.)*

M Literary Elements

THEME What image of America emerges from Sandburg's collection of yarns? *(In Sandburg's America, everything is bigger, smaller, better, more fantastic, taller, or faster growing.)*

N Active Reading Strategies

QUESTION Sandburg refers to John Henry's swinging as "a rainbow round my shoulder," but this line does not appear in the previous poem. What may be a reason for that? *(There are several different versions of the story of John Henry.)*

Thematic Focus

Fantastic Capers and Mischief Makers Do these poems deal more with fantastic capers or mischief makers? Students should defend their responses. *(Although there are some mischief makers, the poems deal primarily with fantastic capers.)*

ASSESSMENT

Quick Checks, p. 29

MEETING INDIVIDUAL NEEDS — SPECIAL NEEDS

Learning Disabled Understanding this poem requires that the reader visualize the images Sandburg produces with words. Learning-disabled students may benefit from being actively involved in visually representing this poem.

Activity Have students draw a mural that represents the entire poem. Assign parts of the poem to individual students or groups of students. Have each person or group draw its section of the poem on a large sheet of paper. Then combine the drawings by taping them together. Each drawing should be accompanied by the lines it illustrates. **L1** **COLLAB. LEARN.**

Additional Resources

Inclusion Strategies

CONNECTING TO OTHER SELECTIONS

For a teaching strategy that connects this selection with "Finding America," see the ***Theme Six Planning Guide.***

Responding to the Selection

PERSONAL RESPONSE

"John Henry" is primarily serious, whereas "The People, Yes" is primarily funny.

Analyzing Literature

1. John Henry was a steel driver on a railroad. The poem tells that, as a baby, he predicted his own death; that he married and had a son; that he defeated the steam drill and died of a broken heart. Eventually he was buried exactly where he predicted, at the Big Bend Tunnel on the C. and O. Railroad.
2. Sandburg tells tall tales of the land and its people.
3. John Henry's challenge is to drive steel faster than the steam drill. He pits himself against the machine in order to demonstrate the strength and value of the individual.
4. Sandburg's repetition of one yarn after the other creates a vivid, lively portrait of American energy and imagination.
5. The arc of John Henry's swing is as big as a rainbow.
6. All three are larger than life. Their exploits and the parts of the country that they have come to represent differ.
7. Life for those who laid track across the wilderness was difficult.
8. Sandburg would probably have enjoyed singing "John Henry." He mentions the railroad and John Henry in his poem: he must regard this story as powerful.
9. The United States is full of extraordinary people and fantastic events.
10. The author says that as a baby John Henry says "Big Bend Tunnel on the C. and O. 'Road,/Gonna be the death of me."

Active Reading and Critical Thinking

Responding to Literature

PERSONAL RESPONSE

- Did you find these poems funny, serious, or both? Explain.

Brackets connect questions that are paired to develop higher-level thinking skills.

Analyzing Literature

RECALL

1. Who was John Henry? What details in the poem tell about his life and death?
2. What kinds of yarns does Carl Sandburg tell in this excerpt from "The People, Yes"?

INTERPRET

3. What is the conflict, or challenge, that John Henry faces? Why does he choose to deal with the conflict in the way that he does?
4. What effect does Sandburg create by repeating one yarn after another?

EVALUATE AND CONNECT

5. Based on your reading of "John Henry," what might the "rainbow round my shoulder" from Sandburg's poem mean?
6. What do Pecos Pete, Paul Bunyan, and John Henry have in common? How are they different?
7. What, if anything, do you learn from "John Henry" about the life of frontier people who laid track in the wilderness?
8. Might Carl Sandburg, in your opinion, have enjoyed singing the ballad "John Henry"? Support your opinion with excerpts from Sandburg's poem.
9. How would you describe the picture Carl Sandburg creates of the United States?
10. How does the author of "John Henry" **foreshadow**, or give clues to the reader, that John Henry will die in the end?

LITERARY ELEMENTS

Ballad

A **ballad** is a narrative song, a song that tells a story. It may describe an important event or a hero. Ballads are passed from one generation to another, often in musical form. Because people learned the stories by listening to singers, ballads often are divided into short stanzas to make them easy to memorize. Many use repeated words and phrases and a regular rhyme scheme, or pattern. For example, in many ballads, the first and third lines rhyme, and the second and last lines rhyme.

1. Look at the first and final stanzas of "John Henry." Describe the rhyme scheme.
2. In "The People, Yes," Carl Sandburg refers to events and people who might appear in older ballads. List five such references.

- See **Literary Terms Handbook,** p. R1–R2.

LITERARY ELEMENTS

1. The rhyme scheme is a, b, c, b, b if one sets aside "Lord, Lord." Otherwise it is a, b, c, d, b.
2. Sandburg refers to Pecos Pete, Paul Bunyan, John Henry, the boy who climbed a cornstalk, and the mutineers.

Additional Resources

Literary Elements Transparency 29

FINE ART TRANSPARENCY 26

You may want to use ***Fine Art Transparency 26*** to discuss activities peculiar to regions in the United States.

Extending Your Response

Writing About Literature

Describing the Plot Because a ballad tells a story, it must have a **plot,** or sequence of events. Write a paragraph or two summarizing the plot of "John Henry." Be sure to introduce the characters, the setting, and the conflict. Then describe the events. Explain how the conflict is resolved, and note what happens at the end of the story.

Creative Writing

Telling Your Story Carl Sandburg's ideas for "The People, Yes" came from observing and talking to people across the United States. Use your notes from the **Reading Focus** on page 350 to write several lines that Sandburg might have added to "The People, Yes" if he had spoken with you.

Literature Groups

Silly or Serious? The Sandburg poem has been characterized as "a series of one liners"–short, funny jokes–and as "a serious panorama of America." Which description do you think is more accurate? Discuss your opinion and reasons. Share your conclusions with the class.

Performing

Song of a Hero The story of John Henry is told as a ballad. Listen to other ballads by such musicians as Woody or Arlo Guthrie, Pete Seeger, Joan Baez, Burl Ives, Mary Chapin Carpenter, or Michael Doucet. With a partner, choose a song which has been performed by at least two artists. Give a brief presentation about the song–its theme, place of origin, and the musicians who have presented it. Play two different recordings and gather your classmates' responses to each interpretation of the song.

Reading Further

For another view of storytelling, try:
The Story Catcher by Mari Sandoz

Save your work for your portfolio.

Skill Minilesson

RETEACH • REVIEW

GRAMMAR AND LANGUAGE • PROPER NOUNS

A **proper noun** is the name of a person, place, thing, or idea. Proper nouns always begin with a capital letter. The Sandburg poem contains many proper nouns, such as the names of states in the United States. The proper nouns in the poem help to establish it as an "all-American" work.

PRACTICE There are twelve proper nouns in the Sandburg poem. Find them, and identify the proper nouns as people, places, things, or ideas.

- For more about proper nouns, see **Language Handbook,** p. R30.

Extending Your Response

Writing About Literature

Students' paragraphs should

- cover all the elements mentioned in the assignment
- describe the plot in terms of conflict and resolution

Creative Writing

Students' stories should

- use simple and concrete language
- follow the form of Sandburg's line

Literature Groups Remind students that there are no right answers to questions such as this one. Students should support their opinions. COLLAB. LEARN.

Performance Encourage students to seek out strikingly different variations of their songs.

Skill Minilesson

GRAMMAR AND LANGUAGE • PROPER NOUNS

1. Missouri—place
2. Mississippi—place
3. Pecos Pete—person
4. Texas—place
5. Rocky Mountains—place
6. Nebraska—place
7. Dakotas—place
8. California—place
9. Paul Bunyan—person
10. Babe—thing (animal)
11. Star—thing (brand name)
12. John Henry—person

Additional Resources

- ***Grammar and Language Workbook,*** p. 61
- ***Grammar and Composition Handbook,*** Lesson 3.1
- ***Writer's Choice,*** Lesson 9.1

ASSESSMENT

- ***Quick Checks,*** p. 29
- ***Selection and Theme Assessment,*** pp. 51–52
- ***Performance Assessment,*** p. 28
- ***Testmaker: ExamView Pro***
- ***Interactive Tutor: Self-Assessment***

GENRE FOCUS

Objective

- To understand folktales

Teaching Strategies

Point out to students that folktales often follow a familiar format, making it easy for the reader to anticipate the structure and sequence of events. This predictability allows the reader to focus on how the tale is told and on the moral.

Setting Although setting is frequently unimportant, it sometimes becomes a character in a folktale, as it does in many Native American tales.

Theme The theme of a folktale is often a simple truth, but the tale adds an emotional element that anchors the truth to reality.

Style Regional tales often use amusing similes and metaphors. Some authors use dialect to tie a tale to a particular part of the country.

Characters and Conflict Characters in folktales are usually somewhat cartoonlike or "flat." They tend to represent a kind of person or personality trait and are not well-rounded psychological portraits of the sort usually found in novels and short stories.

Teaching Support

GENRE FOCUS

FOLKTALE

Long before caped crusaders and animated troublemakers began entertaining audiences in the movies and on TV, people amused themselves by telling stories. They passed along **folktales,** anonymous stories meant to entertain listeners and to keep ideas and customs alive from generation to generation. Today you can find old tales and songs from many cultures retold in books, in the movies, and on television. Myths, tall tales, legends, fables, and fairy tales are kinds of folktales. In all of these you will find some of the following elements.

SETTING The setting, if it is mentioned at all, is described quickly and without much detail. You learn only what you need to know to go on with the story. (In this excerpt from a folktale, there is a fast, wide river with a market on one side and a town on the other.)

THEME The theme of a folktale is usually a lesson about human nature that all people can appreciate. Such a lesson is called a *moral.* (In the model, Rabbit wants to cross the river and tricks Fox into helping him. Later, Rabbit cannot get back because Fox won't be taken in twice. The moral: if you use others, you may not always get what you want.)

MODEL: from "Fox, Alligator, and Rabbit"

Once there was a fast, wide river. On one side stood a market and on the other a town. So to get to the market from the town, you had to cross the river. But—and this was a mighty big "but"—in the middle of the river was Alligator. Now, alligators have their own special way of letting you know they're around—they try and eat you. One day Fox and Rabbit wanted to cross the river to the market. Rabbit was working on some kind of a plan. "Say, Fox," he says, "Is it true you foxes are known for being just about the smartest, cleverest creatures around?"

"Yep," says Fox.

"Then hows about you taking me across the river?"

STYLE The words and phrases in some folktales reflect the speaking style of the teller. The style, or manner of expression, is often conversational and informal. (This folktale has a breezy, informal style, reflecting how a good-natured storyteller would have told it.)

CHARACTERS AND CONFLICT Characters in folktales may be people or talking animals. They are usually simple folk with everyday problems or conflicts. (In the model, Rabbit needs help to get across a river.) Sometimes, however, they have exaggerated abilities or personality traits.

MEETING INDIVIDUAL NEEDS

ENGLISH LANGUAGE LEARNERS

Regionalism and Slang English language learners may find that regional usage and slang get in the way of their understanding some folktales. "Then hows about you" in the example on page 358 may itself pose difficulties.

Activity For this unit, have students work with English-speaking partners or in small mixed groups. English speakers can help English language learners paraphrase or translate the terms into standard English, and then discuss the differences in connotation between the original and the translations.

COLLAB. LEARN.

Additional Resources

English Language Learners Sourcebook

ACTIVE READING MODEL

Active Reading Strategies

Tips for Reading Folktales

Each kind of reading requires slightly different skills. For example, when you read a bus schedule, you need to scan for data. With poetry, you need to listen to the sounds of the poem and take time to visualize the images. When you read a folktale, the following techniques will make you a better reader.

- For more about reading strategies, see **Reading Handbook**, pp. R93–R108.

QUESTION

As you read, focus on what you don't understand and what you want to know more about.

Ask Yourself . . . Do I understand what is happening so far? Why don't I trust this character?

PREDICT

Use clues to guess what might happen next.

Ask Yourself . . . Based on the style in the first paragraph, will this tale be humorous or serious? What will the character do to overcome this problem? Then check your predictions.

CONNECT

Folktales stay popular because readers see themselves in the stories.

Ask Yourself . . . Would I react as the character does? Keep track of your thoughts and feelings as you read.

Ask Yourself . . . Which characters do I like best? least? Do I agree with the message of this tale?

APPLYING THE STRATEGIES

Read the following selection, "Sally Ann Thunder Ann Whirlwind." Use the **Active Reading Model** notes in the margins to help you understand and enjoy the selection.

Active Reading Strategies

Objective

- To understand and apply strategies for reading folktales

Teach the Strategies

A good strategy for reading folktales is to recognize and predict patterns. In a story that begins with three sisters, a reader can be fairly sure that one will come out ahead. Ask students to note patterns they detect in the tales.

Question

Remind students that *why* is often the best question to ask of a story.

Predict

One reason folktales are so popular is that their endings are easy to predict. Part of the enjoyment in reading a folktale is discovering variations in the familiar pattern.

Connect

Other good questions students can ask themselves are *What is the author's purpose? How does the theme apply to me? What does the tale tell about the values of the people who first told it?*

Teaching Support

Reading Journal

Focus on Setting

Explain to students that most folktales have strong ties to a particular place and time. "Sally Ann Thunder Ann Whirlwind" is set on the American frontier in the early years of the nineteenth century. Many details and much of the language of the story are clearly located in this place and time. These elements give the story its particular American "flavor."

Activity As they read, ask students to list in their reading journals the details that "locate" this story in a particular place and time. After reading, students may discuss their lists and discuss how much of the story relies on these local color details. **L2**

Before Reading

Objectives

- To read and analyze a tall tale
- To identify the characteristics of a tall tale
- To write a paragraph on setting

Skills

Reading/Thinking: Chronological Order
Writing: Tall-Tale Letter
Vocabulary: Synonyms
Grammar/Language: Compound Predicates; Transitive and Intransitive Verbs
Listening/Speaking: Performing
Collaboration: Literature Groups

Motivating STUDENTS

Selection Focus Transparency 29: Have students view the transparency and then discuss the questions provided.

Reading Focus: As an extension of the Reading Focus, ask students to list some similes that characterize their accomplishment. If they won a race, for example, they might list some exaggerated ways to complete the sentence, "I ran as fast as . . ."

ACTIVE READING MODEL

Before You Read

Sally Ann Thunder Ann Whirlwind

MEET MARY POPE OSBORNE

Mary Pope Osborne spent most of her childhood on army posts in the southern United States. Today she acknowledges many influences on her work, including "my southern military background, my family, my editor, my work with runaway teenagers, and my interests in philosophy and mythology." Osborne began writing seriously in 1976, during a theater tour with her actor husband. Since then, she has published several novels, biographies, and collections of myths, fairy tales, and tall tales.

Mary Pope Osborne was born in 1949. This selection was first published in 1991 in American Tall Tales.

READING FOCUS

Recall a time when you accomplished something you were really proud of.

Share It!
Make notes about your accomplishment. Share them with a partner.

Setting a Purpose
Read to learn about the accomplishments of a legendary person on the American frontier.

BUILDING BACKGROUND

The Time and Place This story takes place on the frontier of Tennessee or Kentucky, probably in the early 1800s.

Did You Know? From 1835 to 1856, the *Davy Crockett Almanacks* helped spread the legends of women and men on the frontier. Their heroic exploits, real or imagined, were widely admired during that period. The most famous of these figures was Davy Crockett, a legendary American politician and frontiersman, known for bragging and spinning colorful yarns. Although an almanac is a book of interesting facts and statistics, the *Davy Crockett Almanacks* are probably not as factual as most. Crockett was born in 1786 in Tennessee and died in 1836 at the battle of the Alamo in San Antonio, Texas.

VOCABULARY PREVIEW

obliged (ə blījd′) *adj.* forced, bound, or required; p. 361
forage (fôr′ ij) *v.* to hunt or search about for food or needed supplies; p. 364

RESOURCE MANAGER

Teaching Tools and Resources
- Theme Four Planning Guide
- Literature Groups Sourcebook

Essential Lesson Support

Lesson-Specific Instruction
- Selection Focus Transparency 29
- Literary Elements Transparency 30
- Active Reading Guide,* p. 30
- Selection Vocabulary Practice, p. 22

Assessment
- Selection Quick Checks,* p. 30
- Sel. and Theme Assmt., pp. 53–54
- Testmaker: ExamView Pro
- Performance Assessment, p. 29
- inTIME magazine, pp. 30–31

Systematic Language Instruction
- Gr. & Comp. Hbk., L. 7.1, 7.2
- Vocabulary Power, Lesson 16
- Spelling Power, Lesson 14

English Language Learners
- ELL Sourcebook, p. 51
- Spanish Summaries, p. 29
- Audio Library*
- English, Yes!

Spec. Needs/Strat. Interven.
- Interactive Rdg. Sbk., pp. T121–T123
- Interactive Rdg. Wkbk., pp. 57–58
- Inclusion Strat. Sbk., pp. 35–36
- Audio Library*

* Also available in Spanish

Sally Ann Thunder Ann Whirlwind

Mary Pope Osborne

ACTIVE READING MODEL

One early spring day, when the leaves of the white oaks were about as big as a mouse's ear, Davy Crockett set out alone through the forest to do some bear hunting. Suddenly it started raining real hard, and he felt obliged to stop for shelter under a tree. **A** As he shook the rain out of his coonskin cap, he got sleepy, so he laid back into the crotch of the tree, and pretty soon he was snoring.

Vocabulary
obliged (ə blījd′) *adj.* forced, bound, or required

Reading the Selection

SUMMARY

Sally Ann Thunder Ann Whirlwind is a pioneer woman who can perform amazing feats of cleverness and strength. She wins the heart of Davy Crockett, gets a bear to churn her butter, and is the only person ever to knock Mike Fink unconscious. Davy is so smitten with her that he proposes. She accepts and they marry.

Spanish Summaries, p. 29

A Active Reading Strategies

QUESTION Ask students how big a leaf is if it is the size of a mouse ear. Ask them also why they think Osborne uses this particular comparison. *(The leaves are tiny, suggesting that it is early spring. The comparison with mouse ears is in keeping with the rest of the imagery in the story, most of which is taken from nature.)*

VOCABULARY If you haven't previewed the selection vocabulary with students, stop and remind them to use context clues to unlock the meanings of new vocabulary words.

Additional Resources

Active Reading Guide, p. 30
Audio Library
Spanish Audio Library

Teaching Support

CONNECTING TO OTHER SELECTIONS

The chart at the right shows three ways to connect "Sally Ann Thunder Ann Whirlwind" to other selections in this book.

For specific teaching strategies, see the ***Theme Four Planning Guide***.

Connection		Title
Life Skills: Lifelong Learning	→	from *Letters from Rifka,* p. 527
Thematic: Facing Opponents	→	"Barbara Frietchie," p. 459
Literary: Folktale	→	"The Wise Old Woman," p. 259

Historical Note

Davy Crockett was a well-known hero to children of the 1950s and 1960s thanks to a popular television series starring Fess Parker.

B Active Reading Strategies

VISUALIZE *(Davy looks completely ridiculous with his head caught in a tree; he's not only in a foolish position, but he is red in the face with anger and embarrassment.)* How does he feel when he realizes that he will have to be rescued by a girl? *(Davy feels embarrassed.)*

C Active Reading Strategies

QUESTION *(Sally is tall, very strong, and supremely self-confident.)* How does Sally compare with other legendary characters from American folklore? *(She is self-reliant and larger than life, and possesses a pioneer spirit.)*

D Literary Elements

TALL TALE Point out to students that one of the defining elements of this tale is exaggeration. Even Sally's name is bigger, longer, and more repetitious than anyone else's.

E Active Reading Strategies

QUESTION Ask students why they think Sally calls Davy "Sweetie." *(She is emphasizing her equality by calling him the same name he called her.)*

Teaching Support

ACTIVE READING MODEL

VISUALIZE

B Picture Davy trying to get out of this situation.

QUESTION

C How would you characterize Sally Ann so far?

Davy slept so hard, he didn't wake up until nearly sundown. And when he did, he discovered that somehow or another in all that sleeping his head had gotten stuck in the crotch of the tree, and he couldn't get it out.

Well, Davy roared loud enough to make the tree lose all its little mouse-ear leaves. He twisted and turned and carried on for over an hour, but still that tree wouldn't let go. Just as he was about to give himself up for a goner, he heard a girl say, "What's the matter, stranger?"

Even from his awkward position, he could see that she was extraordinary—tall as a hickory sapling, with arms as big as a keelboat tiller's.[1]

"My head's stuck, sweetie," he said. "And if you help me get it free, I'll give you a pretty little comb."

"Don't call me sweetie," she said. "And don't worry about giving me no pretty little comb, neither. I'll free your old coconut, but just because I want to."

D Then this extraordinary girl did something that made Davy's hair stand on end. She reached in a bag and took out a bunch of rattlesnakes. She tied all the wriggly critters together to make a long rope, and as she tied, she kept talking. "I'm not a shy little colt," she said. "And I'm not a little singing nightingale, neither. I can tote a steamboat on my back, outscream a panther, and jump over my own shadow. I can double up crocodiles any day, and I like to wear a hornets' nest for my Sunday bonnet."

E As the girl looped the ends of her snake rope to the top of the branch that was trapping Davy, she kept bragging: "I'm a streak of lightning set up edgeways and buttered with quicksilver.[2] I can outgrin, outsnort, outrun, outlift, outsneeze, outsleep, outlie any varmint[3] from Maine to Louisiana. Furthermore, *sweetie,* I can blow out the moonlight and sing a wolf to sleep." Then she pulled on the other end of the snake rope so hard, it seemed as if she might tear the world apart.

The right-hand fork of that big tree bent just about double. Then Davy slid his head out as easy as you please. For a minute he was so dizzy, he couldn't tell up from down. But when he got everything going straight again, he took a good look at that girl. "What's your name, ma'am?"

"Sally Ann Thunder Ann Whirlwind," she said. "But if you mind your manners, you can call me Sally."

1. The lever used to steer a boat is the *tiller.* Here, a person who uses the tiller is referred to as a *tiller*.
2. *Quicksilver* is a name for mercury, a silver-colored metal that is liquid at room temperature. An old meaning of *quick* is "alive," and liquid mercury moves about as if it were alive.
3. A *varmint* is an informal word for *vermin,* which refers to insects, animals, or people that are troublesome, harmful, or destructive.

Literature & Humanities

I Want You for the U.S. Army

U.S. History and Art, Transparency 20.

Have students view and discuss the elements of exaggeration in this painting.

Meeting Individual Needs: English Language Learners

The Prefix *Out-* Explain to English language learners that English uses the prefix *out-* in a variety of ways. *Out-* can be used in compounds meaning "away from" *(outcast)* or "end" *(outcome).* It can also be used as Sally uses it, inserting the prefix before transitive verbs to mean "to surpass" the action indicated.

Activity Have students consult an unabridged dictionary for a list of verbs combined with *out-* to mean "go beyond or surpass." Have students select five unfamiliar verbs, look up their meanings, then write the meaning with the prefix *out-* and sample sentences. Have students share their choices.

Additional Resources

English Language Learners Sourcebook, p. 51

From then on Davy Crockett was crazy in love with Sally Ann Thunder Ann Whirlwind. He asked everyone he knew about her, and everything he heard caused another one of Cupid's arrows to jab him in the gizzard.

G "Oh, I know Sally!" the preacher said. "She can dance a rock to pieces and ride a panther bareback!"

"Sally's a good ole friend of mine," the blacksmith said. "Once I seen her crack a walnut with her front teeth."

"Sally's so very special," said the schoolmarm. "She likes to whip across the Salt River, using her apron for a sail and her left leg for a rudder!"

Sally Ann Thunder Ann Whirlwind had a reputation for being funny, too. Her best friend, Lucy, told Davy, "Sally can laugh the bark off a pine tree. She likes to whistle out one side of her mouth while she eats with the other side and grins with the middle!"

According to her friends, Sally could tame about anything in the world, too. They all told Davy about the time she was churning butter and heard something scratching outside. Suddenly the door swung open, and in walked the Great King Bear of the Mud Forest. He'd come to steal one of her smoked hams. Well, before the King Bear could say boo, Sally grabbed a warm dumpling from the pot and stuffed it in his mouth.

The dumpling tasted so good, the King Bear's eyes winked with tears. But then he started to think that Sally might taste pretty good, too. So opening and closing his big old mouth, he backed her right into a corner.

Sally was plenty scared, with her knees a-knocking and her heart a-hammering. But just as the King Bear blew his hot breath in her face, she gathered the courage to say, "Would you like to dance?"

As everybody knows, no bear can resist an invitation to a square dance, so of course the old fellow forgot all about eating Sally and said, "Love to."

Then he bowed real pretty, and the two got to kicking and whooping and swinging each other through the air, as Sally sang:

We are on our way to Baltimore,
With two behind, and two before:
Around, around, around we go,
Where oats, peas, beans, and barley grow!

And while she was singing, Sally tied a string from the bear's ankle to her butter churn, so that all the time the old feller was kicking up his legs and dancing around the room, he was also churning her butter!

QUESTION F

What is ironic, or unexpected, about someone like Davy falling for a person like Sally?

PREDICT H

From what you know about Sally, what do you think she will do to the bear?

F Active Reading Strategies

QUESTION *(Davy doesn't seem like the romantic sort. He's a fighter, not a lover.)* Why does Davy fall for Sally? *(He's never met any woman who is his match. Sally is, and he can't resist her.)*

G Literary Elements

TALL TALE What is the effect of having the preacher, the blacksmith, and the schoolmarm boast about Sally's strength and exploits? *(These "objective" confirmations signal to the reader that Sally lives up to her boasts; other people confirm that she's extraordinary.)*

H Active Reading Strategies

PREDICT *(There is no doubt Sally will outwrestle or outsmart the bear.)* What is surprising about the bear's reaction to Sally? *(The bear initially seems charmed by her—not a reaction one would expect from a wild animal.)*

Vocabulary Skills

Dialect Note that throughout the story Osborne uses the dialectical prefix *a-* before the present participle, as in *knees a-knocking* and *heart a-hammering.* What effect does this create?

MEETING INDIVIDUAL NEEDS — SPECIAL NEEDS

Emotional Explain to students that most heroes of myth and legend have weaknesses that balance their strengths. In this story, all of the central characters have limitations—even Sally is afraid of the bear.

Activity Assign groups of students a different hero to research. Ask them to discover the hero's primary weakness and to report to the class on what they find. Then conduct a discussion about why storytellers so often include a weakness in their description of heroes. *(The weakness is what allows readers to identify with the hero.)* **L1**

Additional Resources

Inclusion Strategies

Active Reading Strategies (I)

QUESTION *(Sally is a formidable opponent when she's angry. She also reveals that she is slow to anger, but quick to react when she is angry.)* What exactly does Mike do to anger Sally? *(He tries to hug her.)*

Literary Elements (J)

TALL TALE In many myths and legends, battles between great heroes are depicted. Ask students for examples of such encounters. *(Hector and Achilles in* The Iliad; *Beowulf and Grendel in* Beowulf.*)* Explain that Sally's battle with Mike is a parody of such epic battles.

Active Reading Strategies (K)

REFLECT *(Davy smiles because he knows that Mike was knocked for a loop not by a wild creature but by Sally.)* How does this event influence Davy's feelings for Sally? *(Davy becomes even more infatuated.)*

Active Reading Strategies (L)

QUESTION Why does Osborne have Davy start shouting three miles from Sally's cabin? Present the following model as an example of the thinking process involved:

Model: I think Osborne wants to show that Davy is a good match for Sally and that Sally is impressed with Davy's prowess. When Sally hears his shouting and sees the effect in the wind and trees, she falls in love with him.

Teaching Support

ACTIVE READING MODEL

And folks loved to tell the story about Sally's encounter with another stinky varmint—only this one was a *human* varmint. It seems that Mike Fink, the riverboat man, decided to scare the toenails off Sally because he was sick and tired of hearing Davy Crockett talk about how great she was.

One evening Mike crept into an old alligator skin and met Sally just as she was taking off to forage in the woods for berries. He spread open his gigantic mouth and made such a howl that he nearly scared himself to death. But Sally paid no more attention to that fool than she would have to a barking puppy dog.

QUESTION (I) What does Sally reveal about herself when she gets angry with Mike?

However, when Mike put out his claws to embrace her, her anger rose higher than a Mississippi flood. She threw a flash of eye lightning at him, turning the dark to daylight. Then she pulled out a little toothpick and with a single swing sent the alligator head flying fifty feet! And then to finish him off good, she rolled up her sleeves and knocked Mike Fink clear across the woods and into a muddy swamp. (J)

When the fool came to, Davy Crockett was standing over him. "What in the world happened to you, Mikey?" he asked.

"Well, I—I think I must-a been hit by some kind of wild alligator!" Mike stammered, rubbing his sore head.

REFLECT (K) Why does Davy smile when he knows Sally caused Mike's misfortune?

Davy smiled, knowing full well it was Sally Ann Thunder Ann Whirlwind just finished giving Mike Fink the only punishment he'd ever known.

That incident caused Cupid's final arrow to jab Davy's gizzard. "Sally's the whole steamboat," he said, meaning she was something great. The next day he put on his best raccoon hat and sallied forth[4] to see her.

(L) When he got within three miles of her cabin, he began to holler her name. His voice was so loud, it whirled through the woods like a hurricane.

Sally looked out and saw the wind a-blowing and the trees a-bending. She heard her name a-thundering through the woods, and her heart began to thump. By now she'd begun to feel that Davy Crockett was the whole steamboat, too. So she put on her best hat—an eagle's nest with a wildcat's tail for a feather—and ran outside.

Just as she stepped out the door, Davy Crockett burst from the woods and jumped onto her porch as fast as a frog. "Sally, darlin'!" he cried. "I think my heart is bustin'! Want to be my wife?"

4. When Davy *sallied forth,* he went out briskly or energetically.

Vocabulary
forage (fôr′ ij) *v.* to hunt or search about for food or needed supplies

Grammar and Language *Minilesson*

Transitive and Intransitive Verbs
Explain to students that when an action verb conveys action to a direct object, it is transitive. When an action verb has no direct object, it is intransitive. Then write these sentences from the story on the board and have students identify the underlined verbs as transitive or intransitive:

She threw a flash of eye lightning at him.

Davy smiled. (threw: transitive; smiled: intransitive)

Activity Have students find three more examples of each kind of verb in the story. For each transitive verb, ask them to identify its direct object. **L2**

Additional Resources

- ***Grammar and Language Transparency 28***
- ***Grammar and Language Workbook,*** p. 77
- ***Grammar and Composition Handbook,*** Lesson 3.2
- ***Writer's Choice,*** Lesson 10.2

Untitled, 1991. Michael McCurdy. Wood engraving. From *American Tall Tales.*
Viewing the art: What does the wood engraving of Sally Ann add to your impression of her?

"Oh, my stars and possum dogs, why not?" she said.

From that day on, Davy Crockett had a hard time acting tough around Sally Ann Thunder Ann Whirlwind. His fightin' and hollerin' had no more effect on her than dropping feathers on a barn floor. At least that's what *she'd* tell you. *He* might say something else.

❖

REFLECT

Think about why Sally and Davy might have different opinions about how Davy acts around Sally.

M

VIEWING THE PAINTING

Michael McCurdy grew up in New York and in Massachusetts, where he now lives. His woodcuts appear in his own books as well as in books by other leading American and European writers. McCurdy has a Web page of his own.

Viewing Response *Sally Ann's size and power contrast with her girlish pigtail and her feminine clothing.*

M Active Reading Strategies

REFLECT *(Both Davy and Sally like to boast, and both like to control. Thus neither will be willing to admit to acting less tough around the other.)* Will this couple live happily ever after? Why or why not? *(They are stubborn and willful and larger than life. Their marriage is likely to be a stormy one.)*

Thematic Focus

Fantastic Capers and Mischief Makers Of all of Sally's fantastic capers, ask students to pick their favorite and describe why they like it.

ASSESSMENT

Quick Checks, p. 30

FINE ART TRANSPARENCY 25

You may want to use ***Fine Art Transparency 25*** to discuss the qualities needed to survive in rural areas without plumbing or electricity.

INTERDISCIPLINARY CONNECTION

History Tall tales often invest heroes with the traits that are valuable to the culture from which they originate. Sally is able to tame large animals, make dumplings, sing, swim across rivers, and make rope out of rattlesnakes. Many of her skills were clearly important to have on the American frontier, but they might not be particularly valuable in another setting.

Activity Ask students to work in small groups to discuss the way tales reflect the societies from which they originate. Then have groups answer these questions: *What traits are valued in modern society? What skills and abilities would a modern tall tale attribute to its heroes?*
L2 COLLAB. LEARN.

Responding to the Selection

PERSONAL RESPONSE

The episode with the bear may be a favorite for many students because it is more detailed than some of Sally's other escapades.

Active Reading Response

One way this story connects to real life is exhibited in the fact that, after Davy falls in love with Sally, he can't stop talking about her.

Analyzing Literature

1. Davy's head is caught in the crotch of a tree; Sally rescues him.
2. Davy hears that Sally loves to dance and can ride a panther. He finds out that she can crack a walnut with her front teeth and cross the Salt River using her apron for a sail and her leg for a rudder. She also has a great sense of humor.
3. Sally feeds the bear a dumpling; but then he decides that Sally will taste good and comes after her again. Sally asks him to dance, and the bear agrees. While they are dancing, Sally ties the bear's leg to a butter churn and gets her butter made.
4. Mike Fink is tired of hearing Davy talk about Sally. She knocks him into the swamp.
5. Davy at first treats Sally condescendingly but eventually grows to respect and then love her. He changes because he is impressed with her strength and courage.
6. The stories Davy hears about Sally make him admire her more.
7. Sally's encounter with the bear reveals that she is a great cook, a good dancer, and a clever person.
8. Mike Fink gets what he deserves; she has never done anything to provoke him. Because the encounter leads Davy to love Sally even more, she also gets what she deserves.
9. This selection reflects the need to hunt, the fact that people churn their own butter, the importance of steamboats, and the danger that wild animals pose.
10. Sally's name is as full of fun and hyperbole as she is.

ACTIVE READING MODEL

Responding to Literature

PERSONAL RESPONSE

- Which of Sally's escapades did you think was the most entertaining?

Active Reading Response

Find two or more ways to connect your life with the characters in this selection. If you need help, review the **Active Reading Strategies** on page 359.

Brackets connect questions that are paired to develop higher-level thinking skills.

Analyzing Literature

RECALL

1. Describe how Davy Crockett and Sally Ann Thunder Ann Whirlwind meet.
2. What stories does Davy Crockett hear about Sally from her friends?
3. Summarize what happens when Sally encounters the Great King Bear of the Mud Forest.
4. Why does Mike Fink want "to scare the toenails off Sally"? What happens when he tries to do this?

INTERPRET

5. How does Davy Crockett's attitude toward Sally change during their first meeting? Why does it change?
6. What effect do the stories Davy Crockett hears about Sally have on him? Explain.
7. What does Sally's encounter with the bear reveal about her?

EVALUATE AND CONNECT

8. In your opinion, does Mike Fink get what he deserves for trying to scare Sally? Does Sally get what she deserves? Explain.
9. Think about how people lived in the American wilderness during the 1800s. What true-to-life features of pioneer life does this selection reflect?
10. Do you think Sally's full name is a good one for her? Why or why not?

LITERARY ELEMENTS

Tall Tale

A **tall tale** is a story in which the exploits of a character are exaggerated extravagantly. When you read a tall tale, you expect to find ridiculous and unlikely situations narrated seriously, as if the events in the story were true. Tall tales rely on certain elements to be effective: a hero readers will like, deeds that are unbelievable, and character traits that are wildly exaggerated. For example, Sally Ann Thunder Ann Whirlwind ties rattlesnakes together to make a rope.

1. What, in your opinion, is Sally's most outstanding trait? Give one example of how that trait is exaggerated in the tall tale.
2. Why do you think Sally is an enjoyable heroine?

- See **Literary Terms Handbook**, p. R10.

LITERARY ELEMENTS

1. Sally's most outstanding trait is her courage; she demonstrates this by tying together rattlesnakes.
2. Sally is an enjoyable hero because she has so much determination and self-confidence.

Additional Resources

Literary Elements Transparency 30

Literature and Writing

Writing About Literature

Frontier Setting How important is the **setting** in this tall tale? Write your answer in a paragraph or two, and consider these questions: What details help the reader visualize the old frontier? How would the story be different if it happened in another time or place?

Creative Writing

Tall-Tale Wedding Suppose you were a guest at the wedding of Sally Ann Thunder Ann Whirlwind and Davy Crockett. Write a "tall tale" letter to relatives "back East" about this event. Include details about the setting and the characters. Try to follow the writing style the author uses in the tall tale.

Extending Your Response

Literature Groups

Sally Superhero How would Sally stack up against Superman, Batman, or another modern superhero? Compare her powers and abilities with those of contemporary male and female superheroes. What advantages and disadvantages does Sally have? Discuss them all, then come to an agreement in your group.

Interdisciplinary Activity

Social Studies Work with a partner to research the real story of the Alamo in San Antonio, Texas. Look for first-person accounts of the event, as well as information from secondary sources. Carefully evaluate each source, then use your research to explain how the conflict over Texas arose and how it was resolved. Prepare a brief oral, written, or visual report to share with the class.

Performing

Accomplishments on Stage How do Sally's accomplishments compare with those of real people? Look back at the notes about your own accomplishment from the **Reading Focus** on page 360. Dramatize your story, using the help of one or more students if you need additional actors. Use dialogue, action, and background description to tell your story. Present your dramatization to the class.

Reading Further

If you enjoyed this story, try:
Jackaroo by Cynthia Voigt
The Perilous Gard by Elizabeth Pope

Save your work for your portfolio.

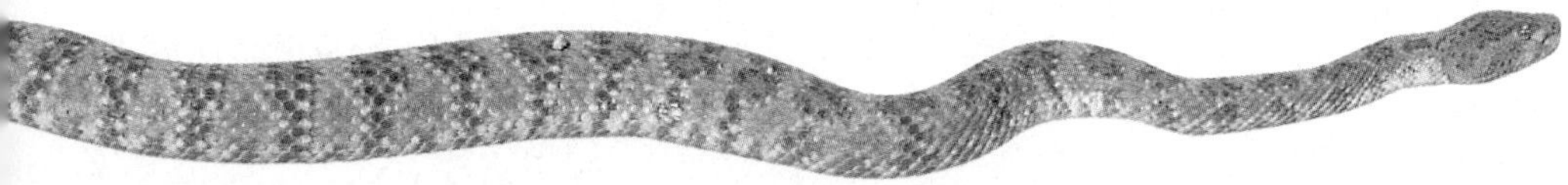

Literature and Writing

Writing About Literature

Students' paragraphs should
- include specific details from the story
- state specifically how the story would change if it were set elsewhere

Creative Writing

Students' letters should
- include specific details from the story
- use the proper format for a personal letter
- follow the writing style used in the tall tale

Extending Your Response

Literature Groups Ask students to consider the impact of advanced technology on the evolution of superheroes. COLLAB. LEARN.

Interdisciplinary Activity Suggest that students include information about the real-life Davy Crockett in their reports.

Performing Students may tend to think of their accomplishments as a single activity rather than as a process, which may make dramatizing seem difficult to them. Explain that the events that led to the situation may be dramatized as well.

Skill Minilessons

GRAMMAR AND LANGUAGE
COMPOUND PREDICATES

1. *subject*–Sally; *compound predicate*–danced *and* rode
2. *subject*–Sally; *compound predicate*–pulled [out] *and* sent
3. *subject*–Sally; *compound predicate*–rolled [up] *and* knocked
4. *subject*–Mike Fink; *compound predicate*–put [on] *and* followed

READING AND THINKING
CHRONOLOGICAL ORDER

c a d b

VOCABULARY
SYNONYMS

1. a 2. a

Additional Resources

Grammar and Composition Handbook, Lesson 1.5

Grammar and Language Workbook, p. 55

Writer's Choice, Lesson 8.5

Reading Skills Practice Workbook Vocabulary Practice, p. 22

RETEACH • REVIEW

Skill Minilessons

GRAMMAR AND LANGUAGE • COMPOUND PREDICATES

A **compound predicate** is two or more verbs or verb phrases that have the same subject. The compound predicates are underlined in the sentences below.

Davy twisted and turned and carried on for over an hour.

Sally reached in a bag and took out a bunch of rattlesnakes.

- For more about predicates, see **Language Handbook,** p. R31.

PRACTICE Write the subject and the compound predicate in each of the following sentences.

1. Sally danced a rock to pieces and rode a panther bareback.
2. Sally pulled out a toothpick and sent the alligator's head flying.
3. Sally rolled up her sleeves and knocked Mike Fink across the woods.
4. Mike Fink put on an alligator skin and followed Sally.

READING AND THINKING • CHRONOLOGICAL ORDER

Chronological order is the grouping of events according to when they occurred. For example, the first and earliest event in Davy and Sally's romance is when Sally pulls Davy's head out of the tree.

- For more about text structures, see **Reading Handbook,** p. R97.

PRACTICE List the following events in chronological order.

a. Davy learns about many of Sally's amazing adventures.
b. Davy asks Sally to be his wife.
c. Sally helps Davy to get out of the tree.
d. Mike Fink tries to scare Sally.

VOCABULARY • SYNONYMS

Using vivid **synonyms** can keep your writing from becoming repetitive and boring. However, you should choose synonyms carefully. Most words have more than one meaning, and one synonym cannot always be substituted for another. A thesaurus is a useful reference book if you understand what each listed synonym means and suggests. For example, Sally is a *rugged* frontier woman. Good synonyms for *rugged* are *strong* and *sturdy.* However, *strong* coffee is neither *sturdy* nor *rugged.*

PRACTICE Choose the correct answer for each question. Check your answers in a dictionary.

1. In which sentence could *forage* be substituted for *search?*
   a. I will *search* through the pantry for a snack.
   b. I must *search* through the crowd for my friend.
2. In which sentence could *oblige* be substituted for *force?*
   a. Good manners *force* one to respond to invitations.
   b. Use a hammer to *force* the nail into the board.

ASSESSMENT

Quick Checks, p. 30

Selection and Theme Assessment, pp. 53–54

Performance Assessment, p. 29

Testmaker: ExamView Pro

Interactive Tutor: Self-Assessment

GRAMMAR LINK

Using Irregular Verbs Correctly

Most verbs have a past form that is made by adding *-ed* to the base form. The past participle form is usually the same as the past form and is always used with another verb, such as a form of *is, have,* or *did.*

Base form: ski; **Past form: skied**; **Past participle form:** has **skied**
Two common kinds of **irregular verbs** do not follow this pattern.

1. A single vowel changes to form the past and the past participle.
   Base form: K. C. and Marta **swim** almost every day.
   Past form: They **swam** yesterday afternoon.
   Past participle form: The girls have **swum** together on the team.

2. The present form changes significantly to form the past and past participle.
   Base form: Don't **bring** anything extra.
   Past form: We **brought** a good map.
   Past participle form: We have **brought** too much to carry.

Problem 1 an improperly formed irregular verb
*Did you bring lunch? Yes, we **brang** enough for everybody.*

Solution Yes, we **brought** enough for everybody.

Problem 2 misuse of the past and past participle forms
*I thought he had **sang** that song before.*

Solution I thought he had **sung** that song before.

• For more about verbs, see **Language Handbook,** pp. R33–R34.

EXERCISE

Rewrite the sentences. In each blank, use the correct form of the underlined verb.

1. I know that Davy Crockett ______ many famous people.
2. Do you understand that problem? I ______ not understand it at first.
3. The bears sleep now, just as they ______ through last winter's terrible cold.
4. She will buy more food than you would have ______.

GRAMMAR LINK

Objective

• To use irregular verbs correctly

Teaching Strategies

Have students work in small groups to list as many examples as they can of the two kinds of irregular formations taught here. Then have them write their lists on the board. Congratulate the group with the greatest number of correct examples.

Exercises

1. knew
2. did
3. slept
4. bought

Additional Resources

- ***Grammar and Language Workbook,*** pp. 99–101
- ***Grammar and Composition Handbook,*** Lesson 3.11
- ***Writer's Choice,*** Lessons 10.11, 10.12

Teaching Support

Writing *Minilesson*

Using Strong Verbs Point out to students that strong, active verbs are an important element of interesting writing. Good sports writers and reporters, for example, are always on the lookout for descriptive verbs to replace the word *beat.* They may say that the Steelers *crushed* Dallas or that Green Bay *mauled* New Orleans. Writing can also be enlivened by replacing adverbs, adjectives, and phrases with strong verbs. Write these sentences on the board as examples: *The tall man with a limp came into the room. The tall man limped into the room.*

Activity Ask each student to choose a portfolio piece that would benefit from stronger verbs and revise it. **L2**

Additional Resources

- ***Writer's Choice,*** Lesson 10.1

Before Reading

Objectives

- To read and analyze a folktale
- To analyze the plot of a folktale
- To write a paragraph on theme

Skills

Reading/Thinking: Drawing Conclusions; Evaluating; Using Text Structures; Inferring
Writing: Paragraph
Grammar/Language: Compound Predicates
Collaboration: Literature Groups

Motivating STUDENTS

Selection Focus Transparency 30: Before presenting the quotations, call for a class definition of *lazy*.

Reading Focus: As an extension of the Reading Focus, have students consider what kinds of people might be most easily tricked.

Before You Read

Lazy Peter and His Three-Cornered Hat

MEET RICARDO E. ALEGRIA

Ricardo E. Alegria's (rē kär′ dō ä′ lā grē′ ə) life is proof of his interest in the folktales and customs of his native land of Puerto Rico. He is an anthropologist and historian, professions for people who study and preserve what they learn of the past. He has been director of an archaeological museum in Puerto Rico and a university professor. Alegria is the author of a book on the sculptures of the Tainos, a group of native people on the island, and he has collected folktales from the region.

Ricardo E. Alegria was born in Puerto Rico in 1921. This story was published in The Three Wishes *in 1968.*

READING FOCUS

Think about different ways to earn a living. Could a person earn a living by tricking others? If so, how?

Journal

Would a person who makes a career out of tricking others be respected in your community? Why or why not? Write your answers in a journal entry.

Setting a Purpose

Read to discover what Lazy Peter, a Puerto Rican trickster, has up his sleeve.

BUILDING BACKGROUND

The Time and Place

The story is set in a Puerto Rican village.

Did You Know? Lazy Peter lives in Puerto Rico, an island in the Caribbean. The Tainos and other Indian groups lived on the island when Spain established a colony there in 1508. Fewer than 100 years later, most of the native peoples were gone, either killed by the European explorers or exiled to other islands. The island became a commonwealth of the United States in 1917.

VOCABULARY PREVIEW

unsound (un sound′) *adj.* not accurate or sensible; p. 372
haggle (hag′ əl) *v.* to bargain, especially about price or the terms of an agreement; p. 373
revive (ri vīv′) *v.* to come back to consciousness; show new life, strength, or freshness; p. 373
priceless (prīs′ lis) *adj.* of greater value than can be measured; p. 373

RESOURCE MANAGER

Teaching Tools and Resources
- Theme Four Planning Guide
- Literature Groups Sourcebook

Essential Lesson Support

Lesson-Specific Instruction
- Selection Focus Transparency 30
- Literary Elements Transparency 31
- Active Reading Guide,* p. 31
- Selection Vocabulary Practice, p. 23

Assessment
- Selection Quick Checks,* p. 31
- Sel. and Theme Assmt., pp. 55–56

- Testmaker: ExamView Pro
- Performance Assessment, p. 30

Systematic Language Instruction
- Gr. & Comp. Hbk., Lesson 7.3
- Vocabulary Power, Lesson 17
- Spelling Power, Lesson 15

English Language Learners
- ELL Sourcebook, p. 52, 53
- Spanish Summaries, p. 30
- Spanish Translations, pp. 81–84
- Audio Library*

- English, Yes!

Spec. Needs/Strat. Interven.
- Interactive Rdg. Sbk., pp. T124–T126
- Interactive Rdg. Wbk., pp. 59–60
- Inclusion Strat. Sbk., pp. 81–82
- Audio Library*

* Also available in Spanish

Lazy Peter and His Three-Cornered Hat

(Pedro Animala y Su Sombrero de Tres Picos)

Adapted by Ricardo E. Alegria

Translated by Elizabeth Culbert

This is the story of Lazy Peter, a shameless rascal of a fellow who went from village to village making mischief.

One day Lazy Peter learned that a fair was being held in a certain village. He knew that a large crowd of country people would be there selling horses, cows, and other farm animals and that a large amount of money would change hands. Peter, as usual, needed money, but it was not his custom to work for it. So he set out for the village, wearing a red three-cornered hat. A

The first thing he did was to stop at a stand and leave a big bag of money with the owner, asking him to keep it safely until he returned for it. Peter told the man that when he returned for the bag of money, one corner of his hat would be turned down, and that was how the owner of the stand would know him. The man promised to do this, and Peter thanked him. Then he went to the drugstore in the village and gave the druggist another bag of money, asking him to keep it until he returned with one corner of his hat turned up. The druggist agreed, and Peter left. He went to the church and asked the priest to keep another bag of money and to return it to him only when he came back with one corner of his hat twisted to the side. The priest said fine, that he would do this.

Reading the Selection

SUMMARY

Lazy Peter tricks a greedy farmer into believing that he has a magic hat. He leaves money with three townspeople. They are to return the money to him when he shows up wearing his tri-cornered hat in a certain way. After witnessing each of the three hand Peter money, the farmer is convinced. He trades Peter ten thousand pesos and his horse for the hat. When the farmer tries to use the hat as Peter did, he discovers that he has been duped.

Spanish Summaries, p. 30

A Active Reading Strategies

QUESTION What does the author mean when he says it is not Peter's "custom" to work for money? *(He means that Peter is not accustomed to having to work to earn money.)*

VOCABULARY If you haven't previewed the selection vocabulary with students, stop and remind them to use context clues to unlock the meanings of new vocabulary words.

Additional Resources

- ***Active Reading Guide,*** p. 31
- ***Audio Library***
- ***Spanish Audiotape Library***

Teaching Support

CONNECTING TO OTHER SELECTIONS

The chart at the right shows three ways to connect "Lazy Peter and His Three-Cornered Hat" to other selections in this book.

For specific teaching strategies, see the ***Theme Four Planning Guide***.

Connection	Title
Life Skills: Implementing and Performing →	"The Tell-Tale Heart," p. 835
Thematic: Realizations →	"Raymond's Run," p. 553
Literary: Moral →	"Bagged Wolf," p. 269

B Active Reading Strategies

EVALUATE Ask students to list the farmer's two most important characteristics. *(He is rich and greedy.)*

C Critical Thinking

DRAWING CONCLUSIONS Ask students why the farmer is intrigued when Peter protects his hat from the rain. Share the following model to demonstrate the process involved in drawing conclusions:

Model: I think the farmer believes that most people use hats to protect themselves from rain. When Peter protects his hat from the rain, the farmer wonders why. I think he decides that the hat must be special in some way and is thus taken in by Peter's trickery.

D Critical Thinking

EVALUATING It is often said that only greedy or dishonest people can be fooled by dishonest tricks. Ask students whether they think that is the case with the farmer. *(Students may point out that the farmer is greedy. Someone less greedy might not believe Peter.)*

Teaching Support

Having disposed of[1] three bags of money, Peter went to the edge of the village where the farmers were buying and selling horses and cattle. He stood and watched for a while until he decided that one of the farmers must be very rich indeed, for he had sold all of his horses and cows. Moreover, the man seemed to be a miser who was never satisfied but wanted always more and more money. This was Peter's man! He stopped beside him. It was raining; and instead of keeping his hat on to protect his head, he took it off and wrapped it carefully in his cape, as though it were very valuable. It puzzled the farmer to see Peter stand there with the rain falling on his head and his hat wrapped in his cape.

After a while he asked, "Why do you take better care of your hat than of your head?"

Peter saw that the farmer had swallowed the bait, and smiling to himself, he said that the hat was the most valuable thing in all the world and that was why he took care to protect it from the rain. The farmer's curiosity increased at this reply, and he asked Peter what was so valuable about a red three-cornered hat. Peter told him that the hat worked for him; thanks to it, he never had to work for a living because, whenever he put the hat on with one of the corners turned over, people just handed him any money he asked for.

The farmer was amazed and very interested in what Peter said. As money-getting was his greatest ambition, he told Peter that he couldn't believe a word of it until he saw the hat work with his own eyes. Peter assured him that he could do this, for he, Peter, was hungry, and the hat was about to start working since he had no money with which to buy food.

With this, Peter took out his three-cornered hat, turned one corner down, put it on his head, and told the farmer to come along and watch the hat work. Peter took the farmer to the stand. The minute the owner looked up, he handed over the bag of money Peter had left with him. The farmer stood with his mouth open in astonishment. He didn't know what to make of it. But of one thing he was sure—he had to have that hat!

Peter smiled and asked if he was satisfied, and the farmer said, yes, he was. Then he asked Peter if he would sell the hat. This was just what Lazy Peter wanted, but he said no, that he was not interested in selling the hat because, with it, he never had to work and he always had money. The farmer said he thought that was unsound reasoning because thieves could easily steal a hat, and wouldn't it be safer to invest in a farm with cattle? So they talked, and Peter pretended to be impressed with the farmer's arguments. Finally he said yes, that he saw the point, and if the farmer would make him a good offer, he would sell the hat. The farmer, who had made up his mind to have the hat at any price, offered a thousand pesos. Peter laughed aloud and said he could make as much as that by just putting his hat on two or three times.

1. The phrase *disposed of* means "dealt with; taken care of."

Vocabulary
unsound (un sound′) *adj.* not accurate or sensible

MEETING INDIVIDUAL NEEDS: ENGLISH LANGUAGE LEARNERS

The Prefix *Un-* Write this sentence on the board: "The farmer said he thought that was unsound reasoning." Point out to English language learners that the prefix *un-* gives negative force to adjectives and to their derivative nouns and adverbs *(unfair, unrest, unfairly)*. Thus a good decision is *fair;* a bad decision is *unfair.*

Activity Have students identify five English adjectives they think can take the prefix *un-*. Ask them to use each of these words in a sentence. Then ask them to check their ideas in the dictionary. Have students share their words, definitions, and sample sentences with the class.

Additional Resources

English Language Learners Sourcebook, p. 52

interNET CONNECTION

The Art of Deception One form of deception that is more socially acceptable than Lazy Peter's is magic. Have students get online and look for sites that teach simple magic tricks that they can learn and perform for the class.

As they continued haggling over the price, the farmer grew more and more determined to have that hat until, finally, he offered all he had realized from the sale of his horses and cows—ten thousand pesos in gold. Peter still pretended not to be interested, but he chuckled to himself, thinking of the trick he was about to play on the farmer. All right, he said, it was a deal. Then the farmer grew cautious and told Peter that, before he handed over the ten thousand pesos, he would like to see the hat work again. Peter said that was fair enough. He put on the hat with one of the corners turned up and went with the farmer to the drugstore. The moment the druggist saw the turned-up corner, he handed over the money Peter had left with him. At this the farmer was convinced and very eager to set the hat to work for himself. He took out a bag containing ten thousand pesos in gold and was about to hand it to Peter when he had a change of heart and thought better of it. He asked Peter please to excuse him, but he had to see the hat work just once more before he could part with his gold. Peter said that that was fair enough, but now he would have to ask the farmer to give him the fine horse he was riding as well as the ten thousand pesos in gold. The farmer's interest in the hat revived, and he said it was a bargain!

Lazy Peter put on his hat again, doubled over one of the corners, and told the farmer that, since he still seemed to have doubts, this time he could watch the hat work in the church. The farmer was delighted with this, his doubts were stilled, and he fairly beamed thinking of all the money he was going to make once that hat was his.

They entered the church. The priest was hearing confession, but when he saw Peter with his hat, he said, "Wait here, my son," and he went to the sacristy[2] and returned with the bag of money Peter had left with him. Peter thanked the priest, then knelt and asked for a blessing before he left. The farmer had seen everything and was fully convinced of the hat's magic powers. As soon as they left the church, he gave Peter the ten thousand pesos in gold and told him to take the horse, also. Peter tied the bag of pesos to the saddle, gave the hat to the farmer, begging him to take good care of it, spurred his horse, and galloped out of town.

As soon as he was alone, the farmer burst out laughing at the thought of the trick he had played on Lazy Peter. A hat such as this was priceless! He couldn't wait to try it. He put it on with one corner turned up and entered the butcher shop. The butcher looked at the hat, which was very handsome, indeed, but said nothing. The farmer turned around, then walked up and down until the butcher asked him what he wanted. The farmer said he was waiting for the bag of money. The butcher laughed aloud and asked if he was crazy. The farmer thought that there must be something wrong with the way he had folded the hat. He took it off and doubled another corner down. But this had no effect on the butcher. So he

2. The *sacristy* is the room in a church where robes or objects used in ceremonies are kept.

Vocabulary

haggle (hag′ əl) *v.* to bargain, especially about price or the terms of an agreement
revive (ri vīv′) *v.* to come back to consciousness; show new life, strength, or freshness
priceless (prīs′ lis) *adj.* of greater value than can be measured

E Active Reading Strategies

PREDICT Point out that many fairy and folktales portray events, actions, and people in threes (three wishes, three pigs, three bears). By leaving three bags of money, Peter has set up an expectation that he will have to go back for them three times. Ask students to predict what will happen the two remaining times.

F Critical Thinking

INFERRING Ask students to infer why the farmer's interest revives when Peter asks him for his horse also. *(The more Peter demands in trade, the more valuable the farmer thinks the hat is.)*

G Literary Elements

PLOT How does Peter's getting the last bag from the priest advance the plot? *(This third demonstration is made more powerful by the church's seeming to approve when the priest hands the money over and gives Peter his blessing.)*

Reading Minilesson

Using Text Structures This story has a structure based on sets of three. The ability to recognize structural patterns can help students predict what will happen and improve their comprehension.

Activity Have students work in pairs to list all the sets of three they can find in the story. Pairs should explain how this structure helps them predict the coming events. *(Peter takes three bags of money to three people; when he brings the farmer to the stand, it is easy to predict that they will visit the druggist and the priest. When the farmer fails to get money from the butcher, it is easy to predict that he will make two more tries. And, finally, the hat has three corners.)*
L2 COLLAB. LEARN.

Additional Resources

Reading Skills Practice Workbook

VIEWING THE PAINTING

Mari Mater O'Neil lives and works in San Juan, Puerto Rico. She is well-known in the Latin American art community for her use of vivid color and intricate patterns in her energy-filled paintings. O'Neil is also an accomplished writer and critic.

Viewing Response *Brilliant color and unrealistic, perspective-free patterns give a feeling of a cheerful and bountiful island.*

H Literary Elements

PLOT Point out that the farmer follows the pattern set by Peter in that he tries three times to make the hat work. Note that his first two tries are with the butcher and the Mayor. Why does the farmer turn to the druggist for his third try? *(He thinks it is a sure thing: if the hat worked once with the druggist, he reasons, it will work again.)*

Thematic Focus

Fantastic Capers and Mischief Makers Ask students whether the red three-cornered hat (or hat with three horns) plays a symbolic role in the story. Do they think the color and the horns connect Peter with the devil—the ultimate mischief maker?

ASSESSMENT

Quick Checks, p. 31

decided to try it out some other place. He went to the Mayor of the town.

The Mayor, to be sure, looked at the hat but did nothing. The farmer grew desperate and decided to go to the druggist who had given Peter a bag of money. He entered and stood with the hat on. The druggist looked at him but did nothing.

The farmer became very nervous. He began to suspect that there was something very wrong. He shouted at the druggist, "Stop looking at me and hand over the bag of money!"

H The druggist said he owed him nothing, and what bag of money was he talking about, anyway? As the farmer continued to shout about a bag of money and a magic hat, the druggist called the police. When they arrived, he told them that the farmer had gone out of his mind and kept demanding a bag of money. The police questioned the farmer, and he told them about the magic hat he had bought from Lazy Peter. When he heard the story, the druggist explained that Peter had left a bag of money, asking that it be returned when he appeared with a corner of his hat turned up. The owner of the stand and the priest told the same story. And I am telling you the farmer was so angry that he tore the hat to shreds and walked home.

The Little Cemetery of Culebra, 1991. Mari Mater O'Neil. Oil on canvas, 48 x 60 in. Collection Ileana Font, Mirama, Puerto Rico.

Viewing the painting: How does the artist use colors, shapes, and objects in this painting to create an impression of Puerto Rico? What does the painting suggest about the setting of this story?

Teaching Support

Grammar and Language *Minilesson*

Compound Predicates Write this sentence from the story on the board: "The Mayor, to be sure, looked at the hat but did nothing." Explain that this sentence contains a compound predicate—two or more simple predicates, or verbs, that have the same subject. Make sure to explain the difference between a compound predicate and a compound sentence. Write this sentence from the story on the board to demonstrate: "The druggist said he owed him nothing, and what bag of money was he talking about anyway?"

Activity Have students identify five compound predicates in the story. **L2**

Additional Resources

- ***Grammar and Language Transparency 29***
- ***Grammar and Language Workbook,*** p. 55
- ***Grammar and Composition Handbook,*** Lesson 1.5
- ***Writer's Choice,*** Lesson 8.5

Responding to Literature

PERSONAL RESPONSE

- If you were the farmer, what would you do after realizing that Peter tricked you?

Analyzing Literature

RECALL AND INTERPRET

1. What does Peter do for a living? How does he select people to trick?
2. When it rains, what does Peter do with his hat? Why?
3. What reason does Peter give the farmer for refusing to sell his hat? What is the true reason?

EVALUATE AND CONNECT

4. Peter tells the farmer that the three-cornered hat is "the most valuable thing in all the world." Evaluate this statement. How is it true and untrue?
5. An **idiom** is an expression that cannot be understood if taken literally, but that makes sense to most people who use the language. Alegria uses an idiom when he says the farmer "swallowed the bait." Looking at context clues, what might this idiom mean? How clear is its meaning?
6. Why does Peter choose a merchant, a druggist, and a priest to hold his money?

LITERARY ELEMENTS

Plot

To understand the **plot**, or action, of a story, readers must first recognize the traits of the main characters. In many stories, the struggle involves a central character, or **protagonist**, who usually has good traits. Opposing the protagonist is a person or force called an **antagonist**, who usually has bad traits.

1. State the plot of this folktale in one or two sentences, and identify the protagonist and the antagonist.
2. What characteristics do you see in Peter and the farmer that help you understand why they struggle?

- See **Literary Terms Handbook**, pp. R1, R7, and R8.

Extending Your Response

RETEACH • REVIEW

Writing About Literature

Theme A story's main message, called the **theme**, can often be stated in one sentence. For example, "Health is a valuable possession" and "Defend yourself against ignorance" could be themes. With a partner, identify the theme of this story. Write a paragraph supporting your statement.

Literature Groups

Is Peter a Liar? Did Peter lie to the farmer? Reexamine the story, looking at everything Peter said. Find three statements Peter made. Discuss whether the statements prove that Peter is a liar.

Responding to the Selection

PERSONAL RESPONSE

Some students may say that they would try to punish Peter. Others may say that they would change their own attitudes toward money.

Analyzing Literature

1. Peter tricks people for a living. He evaluates their faults, looking for greedy people.
2. Peter wraps his hat in his cape to suggest that the hat is valuable.
3. Peter says his hat is too valuable. He wants the farmer to covet the hat.
4. Peter's statement is true for him: it brings him wealth. It is false for the farmer: for him the hat is worthless.
5. *Swallowing the bait* in this context means believing the story Peter tells. The term comes from fishing and indicates the moment that the fish is tricked into believing that the bait is a real worm. The meaning of the term is quite clear.
6. The merchant, druggist, and priest are all respected members of the community.

Extending Your Response

Writing About Literature

Students' paragraphs should

- clearly state the theme
- support their conclusions with specific details from the story

Literature Groups Suggest students begin by agreeing on a definition of a liar. COLLAB. LEARN.

LITERARY ELEMENTS

1. A schemer fools a greedy farmer into believing the trickster's hat can work magic. Lazy Peter is the protagonist. The farmer is the antagonist.
2. They are both greedy; each thinks he is more clever than the other.

Additional Resources

Literary Elements Transparency 31

ASSESSMENT

- ***Quick Checks,*** p. 31
- ***Selection and Theme Assessment,*** pp. 55–56
- ***Performance Assessment,*** p. 30
- ***Testmaker: ExamView Pro***
- ***Interactive Tutor: Self-Assessment***

FANTASTIC CAPERS AND MISCHIEF MAKERS 375

LISTENING, SPEAKING, and VIEWING

Objective

- To develop storytelling skills

Teaching Strategies

Point out to students that storytellers, like comedians, must have an excellent sense of timing. Good storytellers build to suspenseful moments, they wait for laughs, and they pause before punch lines. Suggest that students mark their stories for pauses as they might for a dramatic performance. If students have chosen to tell about a real-life event, encourage them to use precise language—strong nouns, action verbs in the active rather than the passive voice, colorful and appropriate modifiers—to make their presentations more interesting.

Activity

Suggest that listeners take notes on paper with a line drawn down the middle and the words *Keep* and *Improve* written at the top of each column. This will help them give more effective comments. Encourage storytellers to modify their presentations in response to audience feedback. Then provide an opportunity for another storytelling session.

Teaching Support

LISTENING, SPEAKING, and VIEWING

Storytelling

There's more to storytelling than simply repeating the words. Imagine Sam, the narrator of O. Henry's story, shaking his head over "The Ransom of Red Chief" or a jokester chuckling at "Lazy Peter and His Three-Cornered Hat." Skilled storytellers, like skilled moviemakers, blend sound, sight, and motion. They might mimic voices and actions; they might use props. Gifted storytellers also practice a story until they get the words and gestures just right.

Choose an episode from a short story or a real-life event. Practice telling it in front of a mirror, or ask a friend to listen, watch, and give you suggestions. The following guidelines can strengthen your storytelling skills:

- **Use your eyes.** Make eye contact. Don't look over your listeners' heads or at their feet. Move your eyes from one face to the next. Watch for listeners' reactions. When they meet your eyes, you have their attention. That's what you want!
- **Use your voice.** Make it loud or soft, fast or slow, depending on the action in your story. Change pitch and speaking style to fit your characters. If listeners whisper or fidget, it may be because they can't hear. Raise your voice.
- **Use your body.** Think about your posture. Your voice carries best when you stand tall. Changing your posture helps you "become" a character. Gestures work too: a character might "talk with his hands," shrug shyly, or peer sneakily about.
- **Use silence.** A well-timed pause is powerful. When your story's action peaks, pause for a beat. Let your listeners feel the suspense.

ACTIVITY

With a small group of listeners, use the guidelines to tell a story you have written. Use precise language, action verbs, sensory details, colorful modifiers, and active voice to enliven your story. Ask each listener to comment, using these questions as guides: Which of your techniques are especially effective? What is one change that might improve your storytelling?

MEETING INDIVIDUAL NEEDS

ENGLISH LANGUAGE LEARNERS

Storytelling in Two Languages
English language learners may have to concentrate to such an extent on English in storytelling that they lose the animation and expression they have in their native language.

Activity Have students videotape themselves telling their stories in their native languages and in English. Have students watch themselves and note pauses or altered intonation, gestures, and use of body language in their native languages. Then have them try to incorporate these natural gestures into their stories in English.

Additional Resources

English Language Learners Sourcebook, p. 53

Before You Read

M'su Carencro and Mangeur de Poulet

MEET
J. J. RENEAUX

As J. J. Reneaux (re nō′) was growing up in southeastern Texas and southern Louisiana, she listened to the Cajun stories told by her friends and family. Reneaux says that each folktale she retells today "contains a part of me—the beliefs, experiences, and people who have shaped my life." She hopes that "readers and listeners will discover the beauty and spirit of the Cajun people and—perhaps more importantly—of their own lives as well."

J. J. Reneaux was born in 1955. This story was first published in Cajun Folktales *in 1992.*

READING FOCUS

How well do you know yourself? Why do you think it is important to know yourself?

Create It!
Create a banner, poster, or other display to tell about "the real you."

Setting a Purpose
As you read, discover what the characters seem to understand—or seem not to understand—about themselves.

BUILDING BACKGROUND

The Time and Place This traditional tale is from the Cajun people of Louisiana. It is told partly in Cajun dialect, a speech based on French.

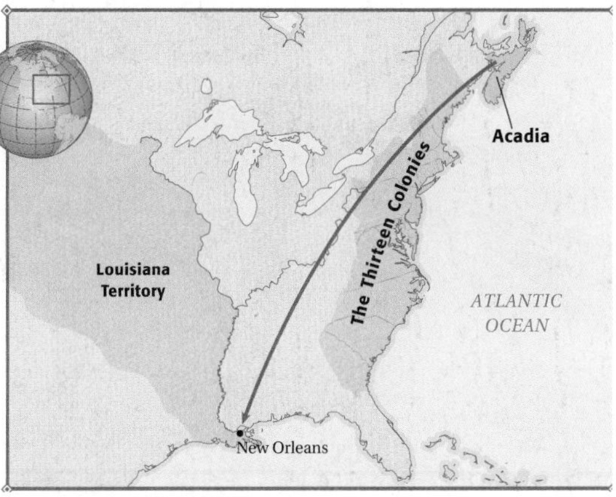

Did You Know? The word *Cajun* comes from *Acadian,* the name of French-speaking Canadians from the colony of Acadia, now Nova Scotia. British settlers captured the French colony in the mid-1700s, forcing the Acadians to move south. They eventually settled in Louisiana, where their French culture lives on today. Their painful experiences of being exiled and looked down upon can be found in Cajun literature.

Before Reading

Objectives

- To read and analyze a folktale
- To understand the significance of a title
- To write a paragraph about dialect

Skills

Reading/Thinking: Setting a Purpose for Reading
Writing: Comparison
Grammar/Language: Coordinating Conjunctions
Listening/Speaking: Acting
Collaboration: Literature Groups

Motivating STUDENTS

Literature Launchers: "The Cajun Storytelling of J.J. Reneaux"

Videodisc Side A, Segment 11

Also available in VHS.

Selection Focus Transparency 31: Before presenting the quotation, have students discuss what "knowing one's self" means.

Reading Focus: As an extension of the Reading Focus, ask students to discuss what it means to know oneself and what may happen to people who don't know themselves.

RESOURCE MANAGER

Teaching Tools and Resources
- Theme Four Planning Guide
- Literature Groups Sourcebook

Essential Lesson Support

Lesson-Specific Instruction
- Selection Focus Transparency 31
- Literary Elements Transparency 32
- Active Reading Guide,* p. 32

Assessment
- Selection Quick Checks,* p. 32
- Sel. and Theme Assmt., pp. 57–58
- Testmaker: ExamView Pro
- Performance Assessment, p. 31

Systematic Language Instruction
- Gr. & Comp. Hbk., L. 7.4

English Language Learners
- Spanish Summaries, p. 31
- Audio Library*
- English, Yes!

Spec. Needs/Strat. Interven.
- Interactive Rdg. Sbk., pp. T126–T128
- Interactive Rdg. Wkbk., p. 61
- Audio Library*

* Also available in Spanish

Reading the Selection

SUMMARY

A chicken hawk tries to convince a buzzard to hunt for his food instead of waiting until something dies. The buzzard insists he is doing his job and acting the way he was made to act, but the chicken hawk disagrees. He begins to show the buzzard how to hunt—but, because he is showing off, he makes a crash landing and dies. The buzzard has the last word, "Suppertime."

Spanish Summaries, p. 31

Active Reading Strategies

TITLE Ask students what the names of the characters suggest. *(Stories that feature animals may remind students of Aesop's fables.)*

Additional Resources

Active Reading Guide, p. 32

Audio Library

Spanish Audio Library

M'su Carencro and Mangeur de Poulet

Retold by J. J. Reneaux

Crow on wire and papier mâché. Saulo Moreno. Height: 8⅝ in. Collection of the artist.

Teaching Support

CONNECTING TO OTHER SELECTIONS

COMPARING selections

This selection is paired with "Talk" on pages 382–384. A lesson for teaching a comparison of the two selections appears on page 386.

The chart at the right shows three other ways to connect "M'su Carencro and Mangeur de Poulet" to selections in this book.

For specific teaching strategies, see the ***Theme Four Planning Guide***.

Connection	Title
Life Skills: Lifelong Learning	"A Dictionary of Japanese-American Terms," p. 27
Thematic: Taking Care of Yourself	"The Legend of Sleepy Hollow," p. 816
Literary: Personification	"The Lesson of the Moth," p. 318

A One day M'su Carencro,[1] the buzzard, was sitting on a fence post real patient-like, just waiting for something to drop dead so he could have his supper, when who should come flapping up but ol' Mangeur de Poulet,[2] the chicken hawk. Mangeur de Poulet calls out, "Hey, *ça va, mon padnat?*"[3]

B M'su Carencro shook his head and sighed, "*Ça va mal!*[4] Not good at all! I am so hungry. I been waitin' for days for somethin' to drop dead so I can have my supper."

C "What you talkin' 'bout?" says know-it-all Chicken Hawk. "If you're so hungry, why don'tcha get out there and hunt you some good fresh meat? You got eyes, you got wings, you got a beak. Go for it! You got to look out for Number One in this world, *mon ami.*"[5]

"*Non, non, non,*" says Buzzard, "you don't understand. I'm s'posed to wait for somethin' to drop dead before I eat it. It's my job. That's just the way *le Bon Dieu*[6] made me."

"*Le Bon Dieu?* Aw, *non!* Don't waste your breath talkin' 'bout the Good God," says Chicken Hawk. "Besides, *mon ami,* even if there is a God, what makes you think he cares whether you get your supper? You gotta do like me, look out fo' yourself. Here, let ol' Chicken Hawk show you how to do that thang."

With that, Mangeur de Poulet leaped into the air and started wildly flapping about in daring loop-the-loops and crazy figure eights, showing off like you've never seen. All of a sudden, he spied a juicy little rabbit right down there next to Buzzard's fence post.

"Aw, this'll show Buzzard," he thought. Chicken Hawk took dead aim and down he zoomed after that rabbit, faster and faster. But Rabbit was smart-smart. She saw Chicken Hawk's shadow closing in on her, and she jumped down her hole just as the big show-off came zooming in. By this time, Chicken Hawk was speeding so fast that his brakes couldn't save him and he slammed smack dab into that fence post! And down he dropped—thunk!—deader than the post itself, right at Buzzard's feet.

D Buzzard looked down at that dead chicken hawk. Then he looked up to heaven. He grins real big and says, "*Merci beaucoup, mon Grand Bon Dieu!*[7] Good God Almighty, thank you!" Then he jumps down off the fence post, smacks his lips, and says, "Suppertime!"

1. *M'su Carencro* (mə syo͞o′ kä ran′ krô) means "Mr. Buzzard." (*M'su* is a short form of *Monsieur,* or "Mister.")
2. *Mangeur de Poulet* (män zhur′ də po͞o lā′) means "Chicken Eater," but Chicken Hawk makes a nicer-sounding name, doesn't it?
3. *Ça va, mon padnat?* (sä vä′ môn päd nä′): How's it going, partner?
4. *Ça va mal!* (sä vä′ mäl′)
5. *Mon ami* (mô nä mē′) means "my friend."
6. *Le Bon Dieu* (lə bôn dyœ′) is "the Good God."
7. *Merci beaucoup, mon Grand Bon Dieu!* (mer sē′ bō ko͞o′ môn gräɴ bôn dyœ′): Thank you very much, my Great Good God!

❖

B Active Reading Strategies

QUESTION What kind of creature is the buzzard that he must wait for something to drop dead so he can eat? *(The buzzard is a carrion eater, like a hyena or a vulture. These creatures often are not highly regarded, but they perform an important service.)*

C Active Reading Strategies

EVALUATE What kind of creature is the chicken hawk? What are his most important traits? *(Chicken Hawk is brash and overconfident.)*

D Literary Elements

TITLE Ask students to propose an alternative title that reflects the theme or moral of the tale. *(Some possibilities might be "Be Yourself," "Don't Show Off," "He Who Waits Gets Supper.")*

Thematic Focus

Fantastic Capers and Mischief Makers Who is the mischief maker in this fable? How does he pay for the mischief?

ASSESSMENT

Quick Checks, p. 32

Grammar and Language Minilesson

Coordinating Conjunctions A coordinating conjunction connects grammatically equal sentence parts or main clauses. Have students identify the elements connected by a conjuction in this sentence: "Mangeur de Poulet leaped into the air and started wildly flapping about." *(leaped/started [verbs])*

Activity Have students find three additional coordinating conjunctions in the story and indicate the elements joined. **L2**

Additional Resources

- ***Grammar and Language Transparency 30***
- ***Grammar and Language Workbook,*** p. 147
- ***Grammar and Composition Handbook,*** Lesson 7.5
- ***Writer's Choice,*** Lesson 13.4

Responding to the Selection

PERSONAL RESPONSE

Some students may feel Chicken Hawk deserved his fate. Others may feel that his punishment was too harsh.

Analyzing Literature

1. It is Buzzard's nature to eat dead creatures.
2. Chicken Hawk looks out for himself by hunting for food.
3. Chicken Hawk shows off by flying in daring loops and crazy figure eights. He crashes and dies.
4. Buzzard smacks his lips and declares, "Suppertime."
5. Buzzard thinks he is what he was meant to be. He seems satisfied.
6. Chicken Hawk's motto is "Look out for Number One." The storyteller has him die by this motto, presumably, because she does not think his is a good philosophy.
7. Chicken Hawk taunts Buzzard because he thinks his way of doing things is better.
8. Buzzard does not show sadness at Chicken Hawk's death because it is not in his nature to do so. Others' deaths mean life to him.
9. Some students may suggest that looking out for number one is by definition a competitive strategy that makes collaboration or looking out for others difficult.
10. Some students may know someone who is overly satisfied with him- or herself. Others may know someone who constantly shows off.

Active Reading and Critical Thinking

Responding to Literature

PERSONAL RESPONSE

◆ Do you feel sorry for Chicken Hawk? Why or why not?

Brackets connect questions that are paired to develop higher-level thinking skills.

Analyzing Literature

RECALL

1. Why is Buzzard waiting around? Why won't Buzzard kill something to eat?
2. How does Chicken Hawk look out for himself—whom he calls "Number One"?
3. How does Chicken Hawk show off? What happens to him?
4. What does Buzzard do when Chicken Hawk falls to the ground?

INTERPRET

5. What, in your opinion, does Buzzard think about who he is? Does he seem satisfied?
6. What is Chicken Hawk's motto? Why do you think the storyteller has Chicken Hawk die by this motto?
7. Why does Chicken Hawk taunt Buzzard?
8. Why doesn't Buzzard show sadness at Chicken Hawk's death?

EVALUATE AND CONNECT

9. How do you "look out for Number One"? Can you look out for yourself without harming others? Consider your answers to the **Reading Focus** on page 377 as you explain.
10. What characteristics do these two **characters** have that remind you of someone you know?

LITERARY ELEMENTS

Title

The words used to identify a literary work are called the **title.** The title an author chooses gives readers clues about what to expect in the story. Take "M'su Carencro and Mangeur de Poulet," for example. A reader who knows that folktales and fables often have animal characters might guess from this title that the story is a folktale or fable. A knowledgeable reader may also assume that the tale has a moral, as many folktales and fables do. In this story, the use of a French title is also a clue that the setting and characters probably speak French.

1. What is the first thing the reader must know to gain information from this title?
2. What clues does this selection title give about the characters or the story?

● See **Literary Terms Handbook,** p. R10.

LITERARY ELEMENTS

1. The reader must know French.
2. They are both birds. The title may remind readers of Aesop's fables.

Additional Resources

Literary Elements Transparency 32

A&E HOME VIDEO® *The following videotape program is available from Glencoe.* Be sure to preview the video for appropriateness for your class:

- A Little Cajun Flavor

Literature and Writing

Writing About Literature

Talk the Talk Traditional folktales often tell about the way people in a culture think or act. J. J. Reneaux retold this tale using the Cajun dialect. Write a few sentences to describe how this dialect made the story interesting.

Personal Writing

Personal Best Compare yourself to Buzzard and Chicken Hawk. Which character are you most like? What situation could you explain that shows how your personality matches one of theirs? Write your comparison in two or three paragraphs.

Extending Your Response

Literature Groups

Wisdom Through Stories According to Reneaux, stories can be "as old as the hills, yet as new as each sunrise. When adults swap stories with children, new links are forged in a timeless chain of humanity." Discuss these questions about storytelling: What stories have been passed down in your family or community? What wisdom do these tales provide?

Listening and Speaking

Act It Out Although this Cajun tale is in written form, it is meant to be told aloud. With a partner, act out "M'su Carencro and Mangeur de Poulet," with each of you taking the role of one character.

Interdisciplinary Activity

Social Studies Research the history of the Cajun people, including why they were evicted from Acadia and how they lead their lives now. What challenges did their new homes present? Include information on the Cajun language, and discuss why the special style of Cajun cooking was developed and how it has had an impact on American cooking. Support your conclusions with analogies, paraphrases, quotations, and opinions.

Save your work for your portfolio.

Skill Minilesson

RETEACH • REVIEW

READING AND THINKING • SETTING A PURPOSE FOR READING

Having a purpose for reading even a short selection can help you get more out of what you read. For example, when you know the origin of a folktale, you can read to learn something about the culture of the people who told the tale.

PRACTICE Reread "M'su Carencro and Mangeur de Poulet." Your purpose is to analyze how the tale reflects the heritage, traditions, attitudes, and beliefs of the author.

- For more about setting a purpose for reading, see **Reading Handbook**, p. R94.

Literature and Writing

Writing About Literature

Students' paragraphs should

- refer to specific examples of dialect in the story
- explain how the use of dialect affects the story

Creative Writing

Students' comparisons should

- state clearly which character they most resemble
- relate a specific situation that illustrates the similarity

Extending Your Response

Literature Groups Point out that although family stories often focus on humorous events, it is still possible to learn from these stories. COLLAB. LEARN.

Listening and Speaking Suggest that students listen to a recording of Cajun dialect before acting out the story.

Interdisciplinary Activity Suggest that students listen to the Cajun dance music known as *zydeco.*

Skill Minilesson

READING AND THINKING • SETTING A PURPOSE FOR READING

Point out that the actions and dialogue of the characters, as well as the outcome of the story, all present aspects of the theme.

Additional Resources

Reading Skills Practice Workbook

ASSESSMENT

- ***Quick Checks,*** p. 32
- ***Selection and Theme Assessment,*** pp. 57–58
- ***Performance Assessment,*** p. 31
- ***Testmaker: ExamView Pro***
- ***Interactive Tutor: Self-Assessment***

Before Reading

Objectives

- To read and analyze a folktale
- To learn about how authors use repetition
- To write a paragraph about personification

Skills

Reading/Thinking: Connecting
Writing: Paragraph
Collaboration: Literature Groups

Motivating STUDENTS

Selection Focus Transparency 32: Have students view the transparency and then answer the question provided.

Reading Focus: As an extension of the Reading Focus, ask students to tell one another about the objects they have chosen and what they think the objects will say.

Before You Read

Talk

MEET HAROLD COURLANDER

Harold Courlander traveled the world, collecting and editing folktales for forty years. He saw folktales as oral literature that contained information about human values and cultural heritage.

Harold Courlander was born in 1908 and died in 1996. "Talk" was first published in 1947 in The Cow-Tail Switch and Other West African Stories.

MEET GEORGE HERZOG

George Herzog was perhaps the world's first *ethnomusicologist*—a person who studies the relationship between music and culture. He recorded primitive and folk music from many cultures.

George Herzog was born in Hungary in 1901 and died in Indiana in 1983.

READING FOCUS

Imagine that one day your breakfast cereal makes a comment (other than its normal crunch).

Note It!
What might your cereal or any other object say about you if it could? Write a brief note explaining your answer.

Setting a Purpose
Read this folktale to find out what happens when inanimate objects come to life.

BUILDING BACKGROUND

The Time and Place
This tale is set in a small village near the city of Accra, the capital of Ghana.

Did You Know?
Ghana is an African country of grasslands and forests on the Gulf of Guinea.

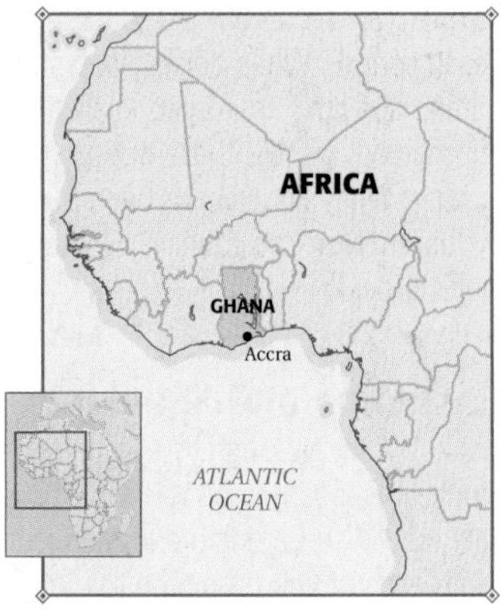

VOCABULARY PREVIEW

ford (fôrd) *n.* a shallow place where a river or stream may be crossed on foot; p. 384

refrain (ri frān′) *v.* to hold oneself back; restrain oneself; p. 384

scowling (skou′ ling) *n.* a facial expression of anger or disapproval; angry frown; p. 384

RESOURCE MANAGER

Teaching Tools and Resources
- Theme Four Planning Guide
- Literature Groups Sourcebook

Essential Lesson Support

Lesson-Specific Instruction
- Selection Focus Transparency 32
- Literary Elements Transparency 33
- Active Reading Guide,* p. 33
- Selection Vocabulary Practice, p. 24

Assessment
- Selection Quick Checks,* p. 33
- Sel. and Theme Assmt., pp. 57–58
- Testmaker: ExamView Pro
- Performance Assessment, p. 31

Systematic Language Instruction
- Gr. & Comp. Hbk., L. 7.5, 7.6, 7.7

English Language Learners
- ELL Sourcebook, p. 54
- Spanish Summaries, p. 32
- Audio Library*
- English, Yes!

Spec. Needs/Strat. Interven.
- Interactive Rdg. Sbk., pp. T129–T131
- Interactive Rdg. Wkbk., pp. 62–63
- Inclusion Strat. Sbk., pp. 59–60
- Audio Library*

* Also available in Spanish

Told by Harold Courlander
and George Herzog

Talk

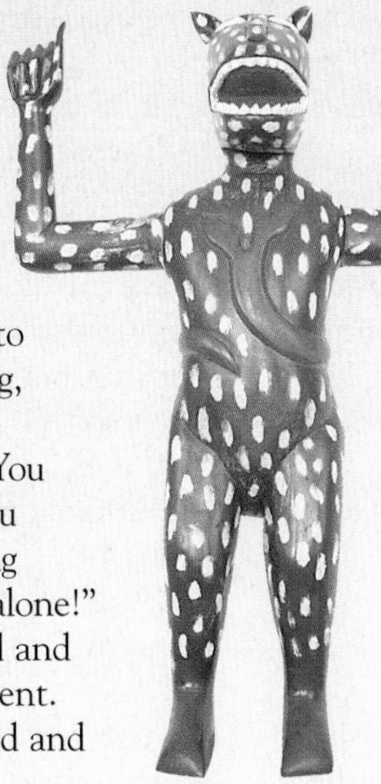

Untitled, 1990. Agbagli Kossi. Painted wood, 37 x 12⅝ x 13⅜ in. Collection of Jean Pigozzi.

Once, not far from the city of Accra on the Gulf of Guinea, a country man went out to his garden to dig up some yams to take to market. While he was digging, one of the yams said to him:

"Well, at last you're here. You never weeded me, but now you come around with your digging stick. Go away and leave me alone!"

The farmer turned around and looked at his cow in amazement. The cow was chewing her cud and looking at him.

"Did you say something?" he asked.

The cow kept on chewing and said nothing, but the man's dog spoke up.

"It wasn't the cow who spoke to you," the dog said. "It was the yam. The yam says leave him alone."

The man became angry, because his dog had never talked before, and he didn't like his tone besides. So he took his knife and cut a branch from a palm tree to whip his dog. Just then the palm tree said:

"Put that branch down!"

The man was getting very upset about the way things were going, and he started to throw the palm branch away, but the palm branch said:

"Man, put me down softly!"

He put the branch down gently on a stone, and the stone said:

"Hey, take that thing off me!"

This was enough, and the frightened farmer started to run for his village. On the way he met a fisherman going the other way with a fish trap on his head.

"What's the hurry?" the fisherman asked.

"My yam said, 'Leave me alone!' Then the dog said, 'Listen to what the yam says!' When I went to whip the dog with a palm branch the tree said, 'Put that branch down!' Then the palm branch said, 'Do it softly!' Then the stone said, 'Take that thing off me!'"

"Is that all?" the man with the fish trap asked. "Is that so frightening?"

"Well," the man's fish trap said, "did he take it off the stone?"

"Wah!" the fisherman shouted. He threw the fish trap on the ground and began to run with the farmer, and on the trail they met a weaver with a bundle of cloth on his head.

Reading the Selection

SUMMARY

Suddenly animals and inanimate objects begin to complain about how they're treated at the hands of humankind—and the people don't like it one bit.

Spanish Summaries, p. 32

Active Reading Strategies

CONNECT Ask students how they would feel if everything around them started talking. Would they react in the same way as the farmer? *(Students may note that they, too, would be surprised.)*

VOCABULARY If you haven't previewed the selection vocabulary with students, stop and remind them to use context clues to unlock the meanings of new vocabulary words.

Additional Resources

- ***Active Reading Guide,*** p. 33
- ***Audio Library***
- ***Spanish Audio Library***

Teaching Support

CONNECTING TO OTHER SELECTIONS

COMPARING *selections*

This selection is paired with "M'su Carencro and Mangeur de Poulet" on pages 377–379. A lesson for teaching a comparison of the two selections appears on page 386.

The chart at the right shows three other ways to connect "Talk" to selections in this book.

For specific teaching strategies, see the ***Theme Four Planning Guide***.

Connection	Title
Life Skills: Lifelong Learning	"If I Forget Thee, O Earth . . .," p. 591
Thematic: Respect of Nature	"The Black Walnut Tree," p. 299
Literary: Repetition	"The Raven," p. 847

B Active Reading Strategies

QUESTION What do the objects and animals that talk have in common? *(They all are used in some way by people, and all are unappreciated.)*

C Literary Elements

REPETITION Most of the dialogue is repeated. Ask students whether this story reminds them of other stories. *(One possibility: "The House That Jack Built.")*

D Literary Elements

REPETITION Because the reader is expecting repetition, the last line of the story is particularly humorous. How is it different from what is expected? *(The stool reverses the pattern by commenting on how impossible it is for a yam to talk.)*

Cultural Note

In many African stories people are urged to give thanks to plants and animals for their help in sustaining life. This story presents the same message from a different point of view.

Thematic Focus

Fantastic Capers and Mischief Makers Who are the mischief makers in this story?

ASSESSMENT

Quick Checks, p. 33

"Where are you going in such a rush?" he asked them.

B "My yam said, 'Leave me alone!'" the farmer said. "The dog said, 'Listen to what the yam says!' The tree said, 'Put that branch down!' The branch said, 'Do it softly!' And the stone said, 'Take that thing off me!'"

"And then," the fisherman continued, "the fish trap said, 'Did he take it off?'"

"That's nothing to get excited about," the weaver said, "no reason at all."

"Oh yes it is," his bundle of cloth said. "If it happened to you you'd run too!"

"Wah!" the weaver shouted. He threw his bundle on the trail and started running with the other men.

They came panting to the ford in the river and found a man bathing.

"Are you chasing a gazelle?"[1] he asked them.

C The first man said breathlessly:

"My yam talked at me, and it said, 'Leave me alone!' And my dog said, 'Listen to your yam!' And when I cut myself a branch the tree said, 'Put that branch down!' And the branch said, 'Do it softly!' And the stone said, 'Take that thing off me!'"

The fisherman panted:

"And my trap said, 'Did he?'"

The weaver wheezed:

"And my bundle of cloth said, 'You'd run too!'"

"Is that why you're running?" the man in the river asked.

"Well, wouldn't you run if you were in their position?" the river said.

The man jumped out of the water and began to run with the others. They ran down the main street of the village to the house of the chief. The chief's servants brought his stool out, and he came and sat on it to listen to their complaints. The men began to recite their troubles.

"I went out to my garden to dig yams," the farmer said, waving his arms. "Then everything began to talk! My yam said, 'Leave me alone!' My dog said, 'Pay attention to your yam!' The tree said, 'Put that branch down!' The branch said, 'Do it softly!' And the stone said, 'Take it off me!'"

"And my fish trap said, 'Well, did he take it off?'" the fisherman said.

"And my cloth said, 'You'd run too!'" the weaver said.

"And the river said the same," the bather said hoarsely, his eyes bulging.

The chief listened to them patiently, but he couldn't refrain from scowling.

"Now this is really a wild story," he said at last. "You'd better all go back to your work before I punish you for disturbing the peace."

So the men went away, and the chief shook his head and mumbled to himself, "Nonsense like that upsets the community."

"Fantastic, isn't it?" his stool said. "Imagine, a talking yam!" D

1. The *gazelle* is a kind of antelope native to hot, dry regions of Africa and Asia.

❖

Vocabulary
ford (fôrd) *n.* a shallow place where a river or stream may be crossed on foot
refrain (ri frān′) *v.* to hold oneself back; restrain oneself
scowling (skou′ ling) *n.* a facial expression of anger or disapproval; angry frown

Teaching Support

Reading Minilesson

Connecting Although most students are unlikely to be familiar with "M'su Carencro and Mangeur de Poulet" or "Talk," each student can probably think of a more familiar tale that has similar characters, plot, or theme.

Activity Ask students to work in small groups to connect "M'su Carencro and Mangeur de Poulet" and "Talk" to stories they already know. For example, they could connect "M'su Carencro and Mangeur de Poulet" to stories about two birds, to stories about a wise character and a confident but unwise character, or to stories in which two creatures compete for food. They can connect "Talk" with stories in which the dialogue is repeated many times with one addition, with stories in which objects and animals speak, or with stories in which unjust treatment is punished. Conduct a discussion on the subject of common themes and situations that run though folktales from many cultures and eras. **L2** COLLAB. LEARN.

Additional Resources

Reading Skills Practice Workbook

Responding to Literature

PERSONAL RESPONSE

- Which character or characters have your sympathy? Why?

Analyzing Literature

RECALL AND INTERPRET

1. Which objects talk to the farmer? How are the comments of the objects alike?
2. How do the fisherman, the weaver, and the man in the river first react to the farmer's news? Why do they join him in his flight?
3. What does the chief say to the three men? What happens that may change the chief's mind about the incidents?

EVALUATE AND CONNECT

4. **Irony** occurs in a story when something happens contrary to what you expect. What is ironic about the ending of this story? What is the effect of this irony?
5. If you were the chief, how would you have responded to the men? Why?
6. In your opinion, is there an important message or theme in this story? Explain your answer.

A storyteller engages her audience.

LITERARY ELEMENTS

Repetition

When storytellers repeat sounds, words, phrases, and sentences, they are using **repetition.** This literary technique emphasizes events, ideas, and feelings by continually reminding readers of the author's point. Repetition also makes stories easier to remember and so is an important aspect of folklore because the stories are retold from memory. In "Talk," the men repeatedly explain their experience with the talking objects.

1. What do you think is the purpose of this story?
2. How does repetition help the storyteller achieve this purpose?

- See **Literary Terms Handbook**, p. R8.

Extending Your Response

Literature Groups

A Conversation Imagine what the objects from "Talk" might say to each other if they were the ones to tell this tale. What conversation might have been heard in the farmer's garden after he ran from his land? As you talk about the objects, also consider why the folktale ended as it did.

Writing About Literature

Personification Giving human characteristics to nonhuman objects is called **anthropomorphism.** This technique is often used in folktales. Write a brief explanation of the human attitudes attributed to each of the nonhuman characters in the story. What effect does this technique have?

Responding to the Selection

PERSONAL RESPONSE

Many students may feel sympathy for the objects and animals that assert their rights against the people who don't appreciate them.

Analyzing Literature

1. The yam, dog, tree, branch, and stone talk to the farmer. Each asks to be treated better.
2. At first they don't take the farmer's concern seriously; but when they hear objects speak, they become frightened.
3. The chief tells the men that they have concocted a wild story and are disturbing the peace; but after his stool speaks, he may change his mind.
4. The irony at the end of the story is that the stool doesn't complain as do the other objects but pretends to be as shocked as the people are that a yam can talk.
5. Many students will say they would have responded as the chief did because they would not have believed in a talking tuber any more than the chief did.
6. The theme stresses the importance of showing respect for nature.

Extending Your Response

Literature Groups Suggest that students act out their ideas of what the objects would say. COLLAB. LEARN.

Writing About Literature

Students' paragraphs should

- describe the human attitudes attributed to each object
- explain how the technique of giving inanimate objects human characteristics affects their reaction to the story

LITERARY ELEMENTS

1. The purpose of the story is to remind people to care for the objects and animals around them.
2. The repetition amplifies the theme by having all the objects support one another.

Additional Resources

Literary Elements Transparency 33

ASSESSMENT

- ***Quick Checks,*** p. 33
- ***Selection and Theme Assessment,*** pp. 57–58
- ***Performance Assessment,*** p. 31
- ***Testmaker: ExamView Pro***
- ***Interactive Tutor: Self-Assessment***

COMPARING selections

Objective

- To compare two folktales that teach a moral about life

COMPARE THEMES

- The theme of "M'su Carencro and Mangeur de Poulet" is to know one's limitations and to respect those of others. The theme of "Talk" has to do with respecting things on which we depend.
- Both themes are important today. Humankind must understand its limitations and respect its interdependence.
- *Freaky Friday* is a book and a movie about a mother and daughter who switch places. Each learns something about the other, and each learns to accept herself the way she is.

COMPARE CHARACTERS

- The farmer and Chicken Hawk both have an inflated sense of their own importance. Each could benefit from greater humility.
- The yam, the tree, the stone, and the dog feel they are entitled to respect. M'su Carencro feels he is entitled to live the way he was fated to live.

Additional Resources

Literature Groups Sourcebook

COMPARE ANIMAL TALES

- Talking animals and objects can make a story more interesting when they focus the reader's attention on a simple trait or idea.
- Sometimes talking creatures—such as the Berenstein Bears—could seem juvenile.
- Some students will say that they liked M'su Carencro because he had the courage to be himself.

Critical Thinking

COMPARING SELECTIONS

M'su Carencro and Mangeur de Poulet and Talk

COMPARE THEMES

Crow on wire and papier mâché.

What, in your opinion, is the universal message, or **theme,** of "Talk"? Of "M'su Carencro and Mangeur de Poulet"?

- A universal theme is one that applies to people all around the world and in all periods of history. Which of the themes do you think is most important for people today to hear? Why?
- Think of a book, movie, or television program that had a message about being yourself woven into a funny story. Write a brief review in which you compare the message of the book, movie, or program with the message of one of these folktales.

COMPARE CHARACTERS

In both selections, the dialogue and action tell what the animal, person, or object thinks about its place in the world. Discuss the following questions about the characters.

- Compare the farmer with the chicken hawk. What view of the world might they share? How could they have avoided conflict with other characters?
- What do the yam, the tree, the stone, and the dog feel they are entitled to? What does M'su Carencro feel that he is entitled to?

COMPARE ANIMAL TALES

Although animals and objects cannot speak in real life, both of these folktales allow creatures to speak for themselves. Write a brief reaction to the presence of talking animals or objects in these tales. The following questions will help you organize your ideas.

- When can talking animals and objects make a story more interesting?
- Could the presence of talking creatures in a story ever mean you would not want to read it? Explain.
- Which characters in the two selections did you find most enjoyable? Why?

PORTFOLIO OPTIONS

Select and Reflect Have students reflect on their paragraphs for the activity above by asking themselves these questions:

- What differentiates talking animals in children's stories from talking animals in folktales and fables?
- Why do writers use talking animals rather than people to make their points?

Students should clip their written reflections to their paragraphs and place them in their portfolios. At a later time, they may consider using the comments to revise their paragraphs as portfolio showcase pieces. **L2**

Additional Resources

Writing Assessment and Portfolio Management, pp. 42–48

Vo•cab•u•lar•y *Skills*

Using Roots

A word's **root** is its basic part. It carries the meaning of the word and can usually be used to make other words. For example, the root of *careless* is *care*. Prefixes and suffixes can be added to *care* to get *careful, uncaring*, and *carefree*.

Some roots come from Anglo-Saxon, or Old English—for example, *amaze, dear, drink, knob, spell, spin,* and *tease*. Even with prefixes and suffixes added to them, you can usually recognize and understand words with these roots. Some words with Greek or Latin roots, however, may be more difficult to interpret. For example, the Latin root *vers*, meaning "to turn," is the basis of the words *reverse* and *versatile*.

If you know the meaning of a root, you may notice it in an unfamiliar word and be able to get some idea of the word's meaning. The chart below shows some common roots.

Root	Meaning	Example	Root	Meaning	Example
anim	life	animal	**aud**	hear	auditorium
belli	war	rebellion	**cogn**	know	recognize
cred	believe	credit	**dom**	house	domestic

EXERCISE

Use the chart above as well as your own knowledge to complete each sentence.

1. If the man is not cognizant of the yam, he does not
   a. know about it.
   b. fear it.
   c. feel annoyed by it.
2. If a stone is audible, it can be
   a. seen.
   b. felt.
   c. heard.
3. Stones are inanimate objects, so they must be
   a. hard.
   b. not alive.
   c. not valuable.
4. If a man runs away from his domicile, he leaves his
   a. field.
   b. home.
   c. helpers.
5. If he tells his story to a credulous listener, the listener is
   a. dishonest.
   b. funny.
   c. believing.
6. If other objects rebel, they will
   a. celebrate.
   b. fight back.
   c. follow a different leader.

Vo•cab•u•lar•y *Skills*

Objective

- To expand vocabulary by identifying root words

Teaching Strategies

Point out to students that learning Latin and Greek roots along with prefixes and suffixes is an excellent way to expand their vocabulary. Challenge pairs of students to find at least two other words that use each root listed. Encourage them to use resources such as a dictionary and the glossary in this textbook. Allow students to use various forms of the same word, such as *cognition* and *cognitive.*

Exercises

1. a
2. c
3. b
4. b
5. c
6. b

Additional Resources

Vocabulary Power

Teaching Support

MEETING INDIVIDUAL NEEDS — ENGLISH LANGUAGE LEARNERS

Extending Roots Learning root words, especially those borrowed from Latin and Greek, can be of great value to English language learners. Have students extend the exercise on this page by learning more words based on the root words listed.

Activity Ask students to use a dictionary to look up words beginning with each of the roots on page 387 and find two additional words and the definitions for each root. Have students write sample sentences and definitions in their vocabulary notebooks.

Additional Resources

English Language Learners Sourcebook, p. 54

Before Reading

Objectives

- To read and analyze a folktale about the ability to fly from slavery
- To learn how writers use similes and metaphors to heighten the impact of descriptions
- To write a paragraph about a writer's style

Skills

Reading/Thinking: Evaluating; Comparing and Contrasting; Questioning
Writing: First-Person Account
Grammar/Language: Sentence Fragments
Collaboration: Literature Groups

Motivating STUDENTS

Literature Launchers: "Virginia Hamilton: Slave Narrative and Fantasy"

Videodisc Side A, Segment 12

Also available in VHS.

Selection Focus Transparency 33: Have students view the transparency and then discuss the questions provided.

Reading Focus: As an extension of the Reading Focus, ask students to add mental methods of escape to their list. Provide examples (such as day dreaming) to get them started. Lead the group to the idea that reading can be an escape.

Before You Read

The People Could Fly

MEET VIRGINIA HAMILTON

Many of Virginia Hamilton's award-winning books celebrate her African American ancestry and culture. "In the background of much of my writing is the dream of freedom tantalizingly out of reach," she says. This dream and her lifelong interest in African folklore are the source of many folktales like "The People Could Fly." The tale, which grew out of hope in the midst of enslavement, had been told orally for two hundred years before Hamilton crafted it into a written story.

Virginia Hamilton was born in Ohio in 1936. The People Could Fly: American Black Folktales *was published in 1985.*

READING FOCUS

Where does someone who is treated with great injustice turn for help?

FreeWrite
Spend a few minutes writing down ways people escape a bad situation.

Setting a Purpose
Read to discover how some people deal with injustice.

BUILDING BACKGROUND

The Time and Place This story takes place on a plantation in North America during the 1700s. Folktales are not specific about time and place because their themes are universal.

Did You Know? When Europeans were struggling through the Dark Ages (A.D. 476 to 1000), Africa boasted civilizations of wealthy kingdoms and talented artists. Then, in 1619, the practice of kidnapping Africans and bringing them to North America for slave labor began. Slavery was allowed to continue in parts of the United States until the end of the Civil War in 1865, when all enslaved people were freed.

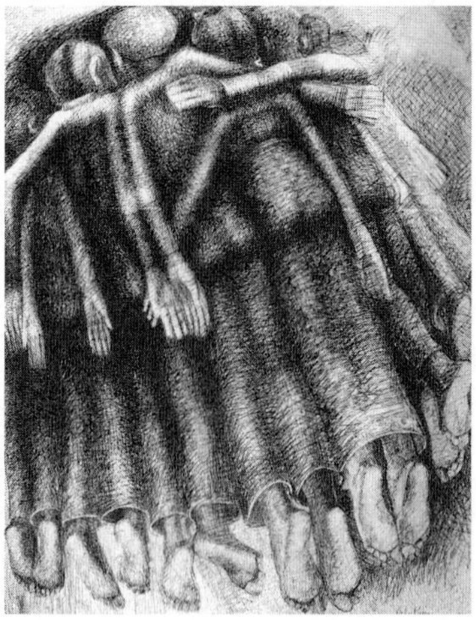

Give Me 2 Wings to Fly Away, 1970s. John Biggers.

RESOURCE MANAGER

Teaching Tools and Resources
- Theme Four Planning Guide
- Literature Groups Sourcebook

Essential Lesson Support

Lesson-Specific Instruction
- Selection Focus Transparency 33
- Literary Elements Transparency 34
- Active Reading Guide,* p. 34

Assessment
- Selection Quick Checks,* p. 34
- Sel. and Theme Assmt., pp. 59–60
- Testmaker: ExamView Pro
- Performance Assessment, p. 32

Systematic Language Instruction
- Gr. & Comp. Hbk., L. 8.1, 8.2
- Vocabulary Power, Lesson 18
- Spelling Power, Lesson 16

English Language Learners
- ELL Sourcebook, p. 55
- Spanish Summaries, p. 33
- Spanish Translations, pp. 85–87
- Audio Library*
- English, Yes!

Spec. Needs/Strat. Interven.
- Interactive Rdg. Sbk., pp. T132–T134
- Interactive Rdg. Wkbk., pp. 64–65
- Audio Library*

* Also available in Spanish

The People Could Fly, 1985. Leo & Diana Dillon. Pastel and watercolor. Private collection.

The People Could Fly

Told by Virginia Hamilton

They say the people could fly. Say that long ago in Africa, some of the people knew magic. And they would walk up on the air like climbin up on a gate. And they flew like blackbirds over the fields. Black, shiny wings flappin against the blue up there. A

Then, many of the people were captured for Slavery. The ones that could fly shed their wings. They couldn't take their wings across the water on the slave ships. Too crowded, don't you know.

The folks were full of misery, then. Got sick with the up and down of the sea. So they forgot about flyin when they could no longer breathe the sweet scent of Africa.

Say the people who could fly kept their power, although they shed their wings. They kept their secret magic in the land of slavery. They looked the same as the other people from Africa who had been coming over, who had dark skin. Say you couldn't tell anymore one who could fly from one who couldn't.

Reading the Selection

SUMMARY

According to this folktale, African people could once fly, but when they were enslaved, many lost their wings. A few, like Toby, kept the power even without wings. Toby saves a young mother and baby from a beating by helping them fly away. Soon others who knew how flew away. Slaves who could not fly were eventually freed, but they told their children about the people who could fly.

Spanish Summaries, p. 33

A Active Reading Strategies

QUESTION Who are "they"—those who say the people could fly? *(They are the storytellers who hand down the story from generation to generation.)*

Additional Resources

Active Reading Guide, p. 34

Audio Library

Spanish Audio Library

Teaching Support

CONNECTING TO OTHER SELECTIONS

The chart at the right shows three ways to connect "The People Could Fly" to other selections in this book.

For specific teaching strategies, see the ***Theme Four Planning Guides***.

Connection	Title
Life Skills: Implementing and Performing	from *Harriet Tubman: Conductor on the Underground Railroad,* p. 480
Thematic: Connecting to Heritage	"The Medicine Bag," p. 78
Literary: Style	"Chanclas," p. 71

B Literary Elements

SIMILE AND METAPHOR Review the difference in structure between a simile and a metaphor and then ask students to identify four metaphors in this paragraph. *(hard lump of clay; hard, glinty coal; hard rock pile; slice-open cut of pain)* Discuss the difference in effect between the two structures. *(A metaphor can be more powerful because it transforms the object compared into the description. The whip isn't like a cut; it becomes a cut.)*

C Critical Thinking

EVALUATING Ask students to evaluate the actions of the overseer as he whips the mother and baby. What do they think of this behavior?

D Literary Elements

COMPARISON Ask students to discuss the effect Hamilton achieves when she describes the baby's cry. The baby doesn't cry like a wounded bird: It cries *like any hurt child.* *(Hamilton is saying, "This child is like you or your child, reader.")*

One such who could was an old man, call him Toby. And standin tall, yet afraid, was a young woman who once had wings. Call her Sarah. Now Sarah carried a babe tied to her back. She trembled to be so hard worked and scorned.

The slaves labored in the fields from sunup to sundown. The owner of the slaves callin himself their Master. Say he was a hard lump of clay. A hard, glinty coal. A hard rock pile, wouldn't be moved. His Overseer[1] on horseback pointed out the slaves who were slowin down. So the one called Driver cracked his whip over the slow ones to make them move faster. That whip was a slice-open cut of pain. So they did move faster. Had to.

Sarah hoed and chopped the row as the babe on her back slept.

Say the child grew hungry. That babe started up bawling too loud. Sarah couldn't stop to feed it. Couldn't stop to soothe and quiet it down. She let it cry. She didn't want to. She had no heart to croon[2] to it.

"Keep that thing quiet," called the Overseer. He pointed his finger at the babe. The woman scrunched low. The Driver cracked his whip across the babe anyhow. The babe hollered like any hurt child, and the woman fell to the earth.

The old man that was there, Toby, came and helped her to her feet.

"I must go soon," she told him.

"Soon," he said.

Sarah couldn't stand up straight any longer. She was too weak. The sun burned her face. The babe cried and cried, "Pity me, oh, pity me," say it sounded like. Sarah was so sad and starvin, she sat down in the row.

"Get up, you black cow," called the Overseer. He pointed his hand, and the Driver's whip snarled around Sarah's legs. Her sack dress tore into rags. Her legs bled onto the earth. She couldn't get up.

Toby was there where there was no one to help her and the babe.

"Now, before it's too late," panted Sarah. "Now, Father!"

"Yes, Daughter, the time is come," Toby answered. "Go, as you know how to go!"

He raised his arms, holding them out to her. *"Kum . . . yali, kum buba tambe,"* and more magic words, said so quickly, they sounded like whispers and sighs.

The young woman lifted one foot on the air. Then the other. She flew clumsily at first, with the child now held tightly in her arms. Then she felt the magic, the African mystery. Say she rose just as free as a bird. As light as a feather.

The Overseer rode after her, hollerin. Sarah flew over the fences. She flew over the woods. Tall trees could not snag her. Nor could the Overseer. She flew like an eagle now, until she was gone from sight. No one dared speak about it. Couldn't believe it. But it was, because they that was there saw that it was.

Say the next day was dead hot in the fields. A young man slave fell from the heat. The Driver come and whipped him. Toby come over and spoke words to the fallen one. The words of ancient Africa once heard are never remembered completely. The young man forgot them as soon as he heard them. They went way inside him. He got up and rolled over on the air. He rode it awhile. And he flew away.

1. An *overseer* is the person who watches over and directs the work of laborers.
2. To sing or hum in a soft, low tone is to *croon.*

Teaching Support

Literature & Humanities

"Nobody Knows the Trouble I've Seen"
Glencoe World of Music, CD 1, Track 27.
Introduce students to the music of the time by playing this selection.

Meeting Individual Needs: English Language Learners

Storytelling Techniques Remind English language learners that most folktales were originally relayed orally. Point out that a storyteller often uses incomplete sentences and abbreviated words. When a story is written down, the writer will often follow this same pattern.

Activity Read the first paragraph aloud in storytelling style. Direct students' attention to the words *climbin* and *flappin.* Talk about the feeling of spoken language that these give. Suggest students replace any incomplete words or sentences with complete forms when they are having difficulty understanding.

Additional Resources

English Language Learners Sourcebook, p. 55

Alexander Chandler, 1955. Andrew Wyeth. Drybrush, 21¼ x 14½ in. Private collection. Photograph courtesy of the Wyeth Collection. © Andrew Wyeth.

Viewing the painting: Study the expression and pose of the man in this painting. What personal qualities might he have in common with Toby?

VIEWING THE PAINTING

Andrew Wyeth, born in 1917, is a well-known American realist. Wyeth's paintings often feature an individual, suggesting a profound loneliness.

Viewing Response *The man's face and posture suggest someone who has endured a great deal with dignity and strength. He is a man who has lived a hard but full life.*

E Active Reading Strategies

QUESTION Hamilton does not explain why the people who could still fly wait until now to do so. Discuss some possible reasons for waiting. *(Students may mention that any exodus needs a leader. Students may also mention that the action of the overseer may have motivated Toby to use his powers.)*

F Active Reading Strategies

QUESTION Ask students to interpret this passage: "The words of ancient Africa once heard are never remembered completely. The young man forgot them as soon as he heard them. They went way inside him." Present the following model to demonstrate the thinking process involved in questioning:

Model: I think Hamilton suggests that Toby has a magic that others cannot duplicate. One kind of magic allows the people to fly; another kind allows Toby to help them fly. Still, the words become a part of the people, and this is what allows them to fly.

Reading Minilesson

Comparison and Contrast Point out that this story is built on contrasts; the people enslaved are contrasted with the people before slavery; the slaves are contrasted with the slave owners and overseers; and the people who remember how to fly are contrasted with those who do not.

Activity Have small groups evaluate these contrasts more fully. Have them divide three sheets of paper into two columns each. The first page should be titled *Before Slavery/After Slavery;* the second page *Slaves/Slave Owners;* the third *Those Who Fly/Those Who Cannot Fly.* Students should list the descriptive words and specific concepts Hamilton uses to describe each. **L2** COLLAB. LEARN.

Additional Resources

Reading Skills Practice Workbook

Active Reading Strategies

VISUALIZE Ask students to describe how they picture the slaves' rising above the overseer and the driver. How do they think the flying people feel? *(exhilarated, relieved, triumphant)*

Author's Craft

WORD CHOICE Ask students why they think Hamilton calls Toby's chant "a dark promise." *(Hamilton gives the chant a sense of ritual and mystery. She suggests that there was a promise made to her people that when suffering became too great, there would be a way out.)*

Thematic Focus

Fantastic Capers and Mischief Makers Ask students to describe how the word *fantastic* applies to this story. Ask them to look it up in the dictionary and to determine which definition of the word fits this story.

ASSESSMENT

Quick Checks, p. 34

Teaching Support

Another and another fell from the heat. Toby was there. He cried out to the fallen and reached his arms out to them. "*Kum kunka yali, kum . . . tambe!*" Whispers and sighs. And they too rose on the air. They rode the hot breezes. The ones flyin were black and shinin sticks, wheelin above the head of the Overseer. They crossed the rows, the fields, the fences, the streams, and were away.

"Seize the old man!" cried the Overseer. "I heard him say the magic *words*. Seize him!"

The one callin himself Master come runnin. The Driver got his whip ready to curl around old Toby and tie him up. The slaveowner took his hip gun from its place. He meant to kill old, black Toby.

But Toby just laughed. Say he threw back his head and said, "Hee, hee! Don't you know who I am? Don't you know some of us in this field?" He said it to their faces. "We are ones who fly!"

And he sighed the ancient words that were a dark promise. He said them all around to the others in the field under the whip, ". . . *buba yali . . . buba tambe. . . .*"

There was a great outcryin. The bent backs straighted up. Old and young who were called slaves and could fly joined hands. Say like they would ring-sing. But they didn't shuffle in a circle. They didn't sing. They rose on the air. They flew in a flock that was black against the heavenly blue. Black crows or black shadows. It didn't matter, they went so high. Way above the plantation, way over the slavery land. Say they flew away to *Free-dom*.

And the old man, old Toby, flew behind them, takin care of them. He wasn't cryin. He wasn't laughin. He was the seer. His gaze fell on the plantation where the slaves who could not fly waited.

"*Take us with you!*" Their looks spoke it but they were afraid to shout it. Toby couldn't take them with him. Hadn't the time to teach them to fly. They must wait for a chance to run.

"Goodie-bye!" The old man called Toby spoke to them, poor souls! And he was flyin gone.

So they say. The Overseer told it. The one called Master said it was a lie, a trick of the light. The Driver kept his mouth shut.

The slaves who could not fly told about the people who could fly to their children. When they were free. When they sat close before the fire in the free land, they told it. They did so love firelight and *Free-dom*, and tellin.

They say that the children of the ones who could not fly told their children. And now, me, I have told it to you.

Grammar and Language *Minilesson*

Sentence Fragments Part of Hamilton's style is to use sentence fragments to imitate people's natural speech. Write this fragment on the board: "When they were free." Explain that this particular fragment is a dependent clause punctuated as a sentence. Show students that one way to correct it would be to move it to the beginning of the paragraph and to join it to the independent clause: *When they were free, the slaves who could not fly told about the people who could fly to their children.*

Activity Have students copy five additional sentence fragments from the story and revise each one to make it a complete sentence. **L2**

Additional Resources

- ***Grammar and Language Transparency 31***
- ***Grammar and Language Workbook,*** p. 51
- ***Grammar and Composition Handbook,*** Lesson 1.2
- ***Writer's Choice,*** Lesson 8.2

Responding to Literature

PERSONAL RESPONSE

- With whom would you like to share this story? Why?
- Look back at your freewriting from the **Reading Focus** on page 388. Would your methods of escape work for any of the characters in this tale?

Brackets connect questions that are paired to develop higher-level thinking skills.

Analyzing Literature

RECALL

1. Why can't the people who were captured fly away from the ships?
2. What happens to the words of ancient Africa once they are heard?
3. How do those who cannot fly react to the amazing flight of their companions?
4. How has the story been passed down?

INTERPRET

5. What other sickness besides seasickness might the captured people have felt? Why?
6. Why does Toby choose to speak the magic words when he does?
7. When Toby speaks the words of Africa, the words go "way inside" a young enslaved man. What does this phrase mean?
8. What messages does this tale hold for people in the days of slavery and for people today?

EVALUATE AND CONNECT

9. In your opinion, does this story succeed in showing the evils of slavery? Explain.
10. Do you agree with Toby's decision not to speak the magic words earlier in the story? Explain your reasoning.

LITERARY ELEMENTS

Simile and Metaphor

The lively descriptions Virginia Hamilton uses in her writing are strengthened by a kind of figurative language in which she compares unlike things. A **simile** makes a comparison by using the words *as* or *like:* "They flew like blackbirds over the fields." Another type of comparison, a **metaphor,** does not use the words *as* or *like:* "He was a hard lump of clay." Figures of speech such as these help readers picture the characters, the action, or the setting of a story.

1. Why did the people who watched Sarah begin to fly think of her as "free as a bird, as light as a feather"?
2. List one additional simile and metaphor from "The People Could Fly." Explain what each adds to a reader's understanding of the characters, setting, or action.

See **Literary Terms Handbook,** pp. R9 and R6.

Responding to the Selection

PERSONAL RESPONSE

Students may feel this story could be shared with anyone who is suffering; it is about the ability of the human spirit to transcend suffering.

Analyzing Literature

1. The people couldn't take their wings on the ships.
2. The words are never remembered completely.
3. They are afraid to shout, although they would like to beg to be taken along. Instead, they must wait for the opportunity to run away.
4. The story has been passed down orally from parents to their children.
5. The captured people might have been homesick because they were taken from their homeland.
6. Toby says the words when the people can no longer endure the suffering.
7. The phrase means that the words become a part of the young man.
8. The story suggests that hope never dies, that every person carries his or her heritage inside, and that victory can be achieved miraculously.
9. The story effectively portrays the utter inhumanity of slavery.
10. Many students will not agree with Toby's decision to wait because the suffering seems so terrible, but some may feel that the ultimate glory may be worth waiting for.

LITERARY ELEMENTS

1. She was no longer tethered to the earth.
2. "They would walk up on the air like climbin up on a gate" is a simile that makes clear how easy flying was. "A hard rock pile, wouldn't be moved" allows the reader to picture how stony cold and unfeeling the master was.

Additional Resources

Literary Elements Transparency 34

Extending Your Response

Writing About Literature

Students' paragraphs should

- clearly state the students' opinions
- cite specific examples from the story

Creative Writing

Students' accounts should

- describe what they see
- tell how they feel

Learning for Life Remind students that a movie depends much more on showing than telling. Students should think primarily in terms of visual images.

Literature Groups Remind students that authors frequently leave some questions unanswered to get readers to think, so students should speculate rather than try to find the "right" answers to these questions.

COLLAB. LEARN.

Skill Minilesson

READING AND THINKING • QUESTIONING

Some questions may include *Why does Hamilton capitalize* Slavery *in the second paragraph of the story? Why does Sarah call Toby "Father"? Why does Hamilton refer to "ancient Africa"?*

Additional Resources

Reading Skills Practice Workbook

Extending Your Response

Writing About Literature

Style In "The People Could Fly," the narrator breaks some rules for writing formal English. For example, she uses sentence fragments. Does this style bother you? Does it make you feel as if you are hearing the story instead of reading it? Write a paragraph to express your opinion. Support it with examples from the story.

Learning for Life

Lights, Camera, Action! Imagine that you have been hired to make a movie of "The People Could Fly." Choose one scene and make a storyboard (a series of drawings that show what happens). If you can put together a cast of actors, you may make a photostory board. Present your plan to the class.

Creative Writing

First-person Account Imagine that you are present when Toby and the others fly. Write a short description of the event and of your reactions to it. How does it make you feel to watch them? What exactly do you see? What do you do next? What advice would you have for those left behind? Why do you think people may or may not believe your story?

Literature Groups

Why Not? Virginia Hamilton raises some questions that she doesn't answer. Why don't the captured people escape sooner? Why doesn't Toby fly away by himself? Why doesn't the Master believe what he sees with his own eyes? Discuss your responses to these and other unanswered questions that are raised in the story. Be prepared to share your ideas with the whole class.

Reading Further

For more by Virginia Hamilton, try these:

Justice and Her Brothers

Arilla Sun Down

Save your work for your portfolio.

Skill Minilesson

RETEACH • REVIEW

READING AND THINKING • QUESTIONING

"The People Could Fly" begins with the words, "They say." Perhaps you have questions about this story introduction. Who are "they" and what do they say? Other phrases and descriptions in the story may have caused you to stop and question how you should interpret their meanings.

PRACTICE Write three or four other questions that the language in this selection raises in your mind. Discuss the questions with classmates. See if you can come up with the answers.

- For more about reading strategies, see **Reading Handbook,** pp. R93–R108.

ASSESSMENT

- ***Quick Checks,*** p. 34
- ***Selection and Theme Assessment,*** pp. 59–60
- ***Performance Assessment,*** p. 32
- ***Testmaker: ExamView Pro***
- ***Interactive Tutor: Self-Assessment***

Reading and Thinking Skills

Setting a Purpose for Reading

When you sit down to read an assignment, what is the first thing you do? Skillful readers take the time to preview the material and then **set a purpose for reading.** They look over the first few paragraphs and ask questions like the following:

- Is the selection fiction, poetry, or nonfiction?
- Do the title and opening images (pictures, charts, or graphs) give clues about the content of the selection?
- Is there dialogue in the selection? Are there clues to the setting?

Scan the opening paragraph from "Spotted Eagle and Black Crow." What purpose can you think of for reading the entire story?

> This is a story of two warriors, of jealousy, and of eagles. This legend is supposed to have been a favorite of the great *Mahpiya Luta*—Chief Red Cloud of the Oglalas.

The selection is a narrative, a Native American legend from the Oglala people. Your purpose for reading on may be to identify the other story elements–plot, theme, and setting. Because legends are written to entertain as well as to inform, you also may read to enjoy the story. You may want to read to find out what life was like then for these Native Americans.

● For more about setting a purpose, see **Reading Handbook,** p. R94.

ACTIVITY

Choose a selection from this book that you have already read, or select a chapter from a history or science book. Determine your purpose for reading by answering the bulleted questions above as well as the following ones.

1. Does this selection contain material that I need to know?
2. What in the selection will interest or entertain me?
3. What is my purpose for reading this selection?

Reading and Thinking Skills

Objective

- To improve reading comprehension by setting a purpose for reading

Teaching Strategies

Reading without a purpose is a lot like going to the grocery store without a list. You may come home with some interesting items, but you'll probably forget the bread.

Activity

Ask students to talk about how setting a purpose and answering the questions influenced their understanding of what they read.

Additional Resources

Reading Skills Practice Workbook

Teaching Support

Meeting Individual Needs: SPECIAL NEEDS

Learning Disabled Demonstrate to students the importance of setting a purpose by giving them a specific purpose for reading.

Activity Have students read or watch something comic (such as a comic strip or cartoon) with a serious purpose. For example, show a cartoon depicting violence and ask students to evaluate whether it might provoke young children to violence. Discuss how reading or watching with a different purpose affected their perception. L1 COLLAB. LEARN.

Additional Resources

Inclusion Strategies

Technology Skills

Objectives

- To learn the basic principles of taking good photographs using modern, automatic-focus cameras.
- To take photographs that help illustrate literature or writing assignments.

Teaching Strategies

Provide students with a sampling of photographs that have been used to supplement and enhance the written word. Magazines such as *Life, National Geographic,* and *Smithsonian* are known for their fine photography, which is used to supplement nonfiction articles. A book of children's poetry, *Reflections on a Gift of Watermelon Pickle,* does a particularly fine job of using photographs to illustrate poetry. Lois Duncan uses her father's photographs of circus performers to illustrate *The Circus Comes Home: When the Greatest Show on Earth Rode the Rails.* Be sure that students also have a chance to look at the work of well-known photographers such as Ansel Adams, Margaret Bourke-White, Alfred Stieglitz, and Alfred Eisenstaedt so they can envision possibilities beyond the photo-album shots they may be used to seeing.

Technology Skills

Photography: The Basics of Picture Taking

Today's technology has created cameras that do most of the work for you. Instead of worrying about shutter speeds and lens openings, you can concentrate on setting up shots or taking candid pictures that say what you want them to. The pictures you take can be scanned and inserted into word processing or Web documents to complement the text and make your work more visually interesting.

Steps to Taking Better Pictures

Try to remember the following points when you take photos.

STEP	REASON
Get close!	If your subject is the Grand Canyon, you'll want a distant shot, but if you're photographing people, get close. Failing to get close enough to a subject is a major reason for ineffective photographs. Focus on the key elements. For instance, if you're taking a head-and-shoulders shot, make sure you can see your subject's eyes.
Keep it simple.	Try to focus on only one or two subjects per photograph. A cluttered background detracts from the overall picture.
Keep it steady!	If you're getting fuzzy pictures, you might be shaking the camera. Try tilting your head forward a bit to balance the camera against your forehead, or use a tripod.
Go off-center.	Put the subject of your picture a little to the left or right of the frame to add variety and a sense of movement.
Experiment!	Try taking pictures from a variety of angles. If you take a photograph from above, the subject is minimized. If you take it from below, it is emphasized. Tilting the camera so your shots are on an angle lends a sense of unease.
Pose with action.	Most posed photographs feature a subject staring at the camera, arms hanging down awkwardly. Try to capture your subjects doing something that expresses who they are, whether it's playing a saxophone or shooting a basketball.
Extreme close-up!	Try the extreme close-up to focus on a specific element. For instance, if you're looking for a shot to accompany a love poem, you can take a picture of two people holding hands, or you can take an extreme close-up of just their hands.

Teaching Support

MEETING INDIVIDUAL NEEDS

MULTIPLE MODES OF EXPRESSION

Spatial Some students may be particularly strong at composing photographs and may be able to help other students capture people and objects in a pleasing way or crop photos in a manner that helps to focus the eye on the most important elements.

Activity Have students look for paintings similar to those that they want to photograph. Using simple shapes and stick figures, have them sketch the basic composition of the painting. These sketches need include no more than the basic shapes in the painting, just enough to be able to see clearly the spatial relationships and arrangements of the people and objects. Then have students attempt to duplicate the arrangement they have identified in the paintings in their photographs. **L2**

Getting Started with Photography

1. The first thing to do is familiarize yourself with your camera. Different cameras have different features. You can get acquainted with them by reading the manual or looking through the photography section at your local library.
2. Study the work of the pros. You can find books of photos by great photographers at the library. The World Wide Web is another good source. Try the Library of Congress site (http://lcweb.loc.gov). Use a search engine and the keywords *photography* and *museums* to find other sources. As you examine an image, ask yourself, What makes this a great photograph? What techniques did the photographer use to convey information or create an impression?
3. Next, go out and take pictures. Take them at night, outdoors, indoors, of groups, of individuals, with flash, and without flash. Experiment. If you have an instant camera, you can view your work immediately and adjust accordingly.
4. Don't be afraid of black and white. Most of the greatest photographers of the past worked with black-and-white film and so do many of today's photographers. You can do things with light and shadow in black and white that color cannot duplicate.
5. The most important aspect of photography is fun. With a little skill and a lot of practice, you can create real art.

TECHNOLOGY TIP

More and more photographers are turning to digital cameras. With a digital camera, a memory card replaces film. You can see your pictures almost instantly on the camera's small screen. If you don't like a picture, you can delete it from memory and try again. The digital picture files can be transferred directly into your computer, where you can use them in word processing documents or put them into an e-mail message.

ACTIVITIES

1. Choose one or two selections from this theme and take photographs that relate to the literature selections. For instance, your photos could illustrate the plot of a story or capture a personal quality of one of the characters.
2. Include photographs with your next written assignment by scanning them into your computer and inserting them into your word processed document.
3. Volunteer to take pictures for a school publication.
4. If you've never used a camera before, follow the instructions that accompany the camera. Once you've taught yourself how to use it, demonstrate what you've learned to a classmate.

This classic photo of a migrant mother was taken by Dorothea Lange in 1936. It has been reprinted and exhibited countless times since then. What do you think makes it a great photo?

Activities

Before sending students off with cameras, have them work in small groups to share ideas about what to photograph. What, for example, might serve as an illustration of "mischief making"? How about a dog with a brand-new shoe in his mouth? A child with a hand in a cookie jar and chocolate on her face? A close-up of a person grinning and winking into the camera? Encourage students to think beyond the obvious and to plan and pose their photographs.

Students' photographs should
- relate to the theme or one of the stories
- clearly enhance the written word

TechnoTalk

Film Speed There are a great many kinds and brands of film to choose from, and it is important to know how to choose the right film for the conditions under which the pictures will be taken. Films are identified by the kind of film (print or slide, black and white or color) and the film speed, indicated on the package by a number. The more light there is, the lower the film speed can be. Most films are labeled by speed from 100 (for bright sunlight) to 800 (which can be used in almost any light condition).

interNET CONNECTION

Film Manufacturers Several major film manufacturers have comprehensive Web sites that include excellent ideas and tips for photographers from professionals to beginners. Students can simply enter the name of the manufacturer.

Before Reading

Objectives

- To read and analyze a tale
- To learn about climax and falling action in stories
- To write a paragraph analyzing the story's epigraph

Skills

Reading/Thinking: Evaluating; Inferring; Comparing and Contrasting; Summarizing
Writing: Journal Entry
Vocabulary: Word Meaning; The Prefix *Inter-*
Grammar/Language: Demonstrative Pronouns and Adjectives; Active and Passive Voice
Collaboration: Idiomatic Expressions; Comparing and Contrasting; Literature Groups

Motivating → STUDENTS

Literature Launchers: "Day of the Dead"

Videodisc Side A, Segment 10

Also available in VHS.

Selection Focus Transparency 34: Have students view the transparency and then discuss the questions provided.

Reading Focus: As an extension of the Reading Focus, have students discuss what can happen when you pretend to be something you are not just to impress another.

Before You Read

The Souls in Purgatory

MEET GUADALUPE BACA-VAUGHN

Guadalupe Baca-Vaughn (gwä dä lo͞o′ pä bä′ kä vôn) has been interested in storytelling since she was a little girl in New Mexico, where her aunt told her stories from old Mexico. Baca-Vaughn later became a teacher, and she shared her love of stories with others. Setting aside Fridays as storytelling time, Baca-Vaughn told stories and invited students to tell their stories. Among the children's favorites, she remembers, were tales of the supernatural, including "The Souls in Purgatory."

Guadalupe Baca-Vaughn was born in 1905. This story was published in 1987 in Voces: An Anthology of Nuevo Mexicano Writers.

READING FOCUS

Have you ever exaggerated your abilities or performed a difficult task to impress another person? What was the result?

Journal
In your journal, list some times you think impressing someone may be important and times when it is not a good idea to try.

Setting a Purpose
Read to find out what happens when a young woman is expected to perform impossible feats.

BUILDING BACKGROUND

The Time and Place Like most folktales, this story does not have a specific setting. It probably originated in Mexico or New Mexico.

Did You Know? The Roman Catholic Church has taught that the souls of those who die without sin go directly to heaven. The souls of those who die having committed mortal—very serious—sins go to hell. However, the souls of those who die having committed less serious sins enter a state of purgatory. In purgatory, these souls wait to be purified from sin in order to enter heaven. The living can help purify these souls by praying and doing good deeds on the souls' behalf.

VOCABULARY PREVIEW

intercession (in′ tər sesh′ ən) *n.* a request, appeal, or prayer in the interest of another or others; p. 400
dumbfounded (dum′ found′ əd) *adj.* made speechless with amazement; astonished; p. 400
reproach (ri prōch′) *v.* to scold or blame; p. 401
vibrant (vī′ brənt) *adj.* full of life and energy; p. 402

RESOURCE MANAGER

Teaching Tools and Resources
- Theme Four Planning Guide
- Literature Groups Sourcebook

Essential Lesson Support

Lesson-Specific Instruction
- Selection Focus Transparency 34
- Literary Elements Transparency 35
- Active Reading Guide,* p. 35
- Selection Vocabulary Practice, p. 25

Assessment
- Selection Quick Checks,* p. 35
- Sel. and Theme Assmt., pp. 61–62
- Testmaker: ExamView Pro
- Performance Assessment, p. 33

Systematic Language Instruction
- Gr. & Comp. Hbk., Lesson 8.3

English Language Learners
- ELL Sourcebook, p. 56
- Spanish Summaries, p. 34
- Spanish Translations, pp. 88–91
- Audio Library*
- English, Yes!

Spec. Needs/Strat. Interven.
- Interactive Rdg. Sbk., pp. T134–T136
- Interactive Rdg. Wbk., pp. 66–67
- Inclusion Strat. Sbk., pp. 21–22
- Audio Library*

* Also available in Spanish

The Souls in Purgatory

Retold by
Guadalupe Baca-Vaughn

Tejedora (Weaver), 1936. Diego Rivera. Watercolor on rice paper, 22½ x 20⅝. Private collection.

Si es verdad, allá va,
Si es mentira, queda urdida.

(If it be true, so it is.
If it be false, so be it.)

There was once an old lady who had raised a niece since she was a tiny baby. She had taught the girl to be good, obedient, and industrious, but the girl was very shy and timid, and spent much time praying, especially to the Souls in Purgatory.

Reading the Selection

SUMMARY

An aunt finds a prospective husband for her niece, but she lies about the girl's ability to sew. The girl is distraught until her aunt reminds her that she has always prayed to the Souls in Purgatory and that they will help her now. The Souls help the girl, asking only that they be invited to the wedding. At the wedding, the Souls tell the new husband that they are old and bent from sewing, whereupon he tells his wife never to sew again so as to preserve her beauty.

Spanish Summaries, p. 34

A Active Reading Strategies

QUESTION Ask students what they think the meaning of the epigraph is. *(The author is saying that she will tell the story whether it is true or not—implying that it has a kind of truth that goes beyond the literal.)*

VOCABULARY If you haven't previewed the selection vocabulary with students, stop and remind them to use context clues to unlock the meanings of new vocabulary words.

Additional Resources

Active Reading Guide, p. 35
Audio Library
Spanish Audio Library

Teaching Support

CONNECTING TO OTHER SELECTIONS

The chart at the right shows three ways to connect "The Souls in Purgatory" to other selections in this book.

For specific teaching strategies, see the ***Theme Four Planning Guide.***

Connection	Title
Life Skills: Problem Solving	→ "The Woman in the Snow," p. 857
Thematic: Unexpected Outcome	→ "The Dinner Party," p. 870
Literary: Characterization	→ "A Mother in Mannville," p. 185

B Active Reading Strategies

REVIEW What kind of person is the niece? Why is the aunt worried about her? *(The niece is so religious and innocent, the aunt fears she may not attract a man.)*

C Critical Thinking

EVALUATING Ask students what they think about the qualities the merchant is looking for in a wife. *(Some students may feel the merchant's expectations are selfish. He wants someone only to serve him.)*

D Critical Thinking

INFERRING Ask students to describe the aunt's character. What can students infer about her? *(The aunt seems spirited, resourceful, and imaginative, possessed of an almost magical quality.)*

Vocabulary Skills

Word Meaning A *hank* is a definite length of thread or yarn; for example, a hank of cotton yarn measures 840 yards.

Teaching Support

The Souls in Purgatory

B As the girl grew older and very beautiful, the old woman began to worry that when she died her niece would be left all alone in the world, a world which her niece saw only through innocent eyes. The old lady prayed daily to all the saints in heaven for their intercession to Our Lord that He might send some good man who would fall in love with her niece and marry her . . . then she could die in peace.

C As it happens, the old woman did chores for a *comadre*[1] who had a rooming house. Among her tenants there was a seemingly rich merchant who one day said that he would like to get married if he could find a nice quiet girl who knew how to keep house, and be a good wife and mother to his children when they came.

D The old lady opened her ears and began to smile and scheme in her mind, for she could imagine her niece married to the nice gentleman. She told the merchant that he could find all that he was looking for in her niece, who was a jewel, a piece of gold, and so gifted that she could even catch birds while they were flying!

The gentleman became interested and said that he would like to meet the girl, and would go to her house the next day.

The old woman ran home as fast as she could, she appeared to be flying. When she got home all out of breath, she called her niece and told her to straighten up the house and get herself ready for the next day, as there was a gentleman who would be calling. She told her to be sure to wash her hair and brush it until it shone like the sun, and to put on her best dress, for in this meeting her future was at stake.

The poor timid girl was dumbfounded. She went to her room and knelt before her favorite *retablo* of the Souls in Purgatory. "Please," she prayed, "don't let my aunt do something rash to embarrass us both."

Did You Know?
A *retablo* (rə tä′ blō) is a wooden panel painted or carved with a religious picture.

The next day she obediently prepared herself for the meeting. When the merchant arrived, he asked her if she could spin. "Spin?" answered the old woman, while the poor embarrassed girl stood by with bowed head. "Spin! The hanks[2] disappear so fast you would think she was drinking them like water."

The merchant left three hanks of linen to be spun by the following day. "What have you done Tía?"[3] the poor girl asked. "You know I can't spin!" "Don't sell yourself short," the old lady replied with twinkling eyes. "Where is your faith in God, the Souls in Purgatory? You pray to them every day. They will help you. Just wait and see!" Sobbing, the girl ran to her room and knelt down beside her bed and began to pray,

1. The Spanish word *comadre* (kō mä′ drā) may refer to a godmother or to any female friend.
2. Here, the *hanks* are bundles of fibers that are spun into yarn or thread.
3. *Tía* (tē′ ə) means "aunt."

Vocabulary

intercession (in′ tər sesh′ ən) *n.* a request, appeal, or prayer in the interest of another or others

dumbfounded (dum′ found′ əd) *adj.* made speechless with amazement; astonished

Meeting Individual Needs: ENGLISH LANGUAGE LEARNERS

Idiomatic Expressions Write these phrases on the board: *the old woman opened her ears; don't sell yourself short.* Point out that with many idiomatic and metaphorical expressions, knowing how to translate each word does not guarantee understanding. Sometimes individual words are used metaphorically.

Activity Have students work in groups to list several idiomatic expressions and try to infer their meanings. English language learners should include expressions from their first languages. Have each group share its list. COLLAB. LEARN.

Additional Resources

English Language Learners Sourcebook, p. 56

E often raising her head to the *retablo* of the Souls in Purgatory which hung on the wall beside her bed. After she quieted down, she thought she heard a soft sound behind her. She turned and saw three beautiful ghosts dressed in white, smiling at her. "Do not be concerned," they said, "we will help you in gratitude for all the good you have done for us." Saying this, each one took a hank of linen and in a wink spun the linen into thread as fine as hair.

F The following day when the merchant came, he was astonished to see the beautiful linen, and was very pleased. "Didn't I tell you, Sir?" said the old lady with pride and joy. The gentleman asked the girl if she could sew. Before the surprised girl could answer, the old aunt cried. "Sew? Of course she can sew. Her sewing is like ripe cherries in the mouth of a dragon." The merchant then left a piece of the finest linen to be made into three shirts. The poor girl cried bitterly, but her aunt told her not to worry, that her devotion to the Poor Souls would get her out of this one too, as they had shown how much they loved her on the previous day.

The three ghosts were waiting for the girl beside her bed when she went into her room, crying miserably. "Don't cry, little girl," they said. "We will help you again, for we know your aunt, and she knows what she is doing and why."

The ghosts went to work cutting and snipping and sewing. In a flash they had three beautiful shirts finished with the finest stitches and the tiniest seams.

The next morning when the gentleman came to see if the girl had finished the shirts, he could not believe his eyes. "They are lovely, they seem to have been made in heaven," he said.

G This time the merchant left a vest of rare satin to be embroidered. He thought he would try this girl for the third and last time. The girl cried desperately, and could not even reproach her aunt. She had decided that she would not ask any more favors of the Souls. She went to her room and lay across the bed and cried and cried. When she finally sat up and dried her tears, she saw the three ghosts smiling at her. "We will help you again, but this time we have a condition, and that is that you will invite us to your wedding." "Wedding? Am I going to get married?" she asked in surprise. "Yes," they said, "and very soon."

Vocabulary
reproach (ri prōch′) *v.* to scold or blame

E Active Reading Strategies

PREDICT Ask students to predict the structure of the story based on what they know about such tales. How many times will the girl ask the spirits to help her? What may be different at their last visit? *(They will probably visit three times and will ask for some sort of payment the last time.)*

F Author's Craft

WORD CHOICE What does Baca-Vaughn mean when she says the girl's sewing is "like ripe cherries in the mouth of a dragon"? *(Perhaps it means that her sewing is quickly finished, because ripe cherries would be quickly gone in the hot dragon's mouth.)*

G Active Reading Strategies

PREDICT Ask students to predict what the souls will do when they come to the wedding. Will they be helpful or hurtful? On what do the students base their predictions?

Reading *Minilesson*

Comparison and Contrast Readers often develop understanding by comparing and contrasting works they have read with new works. This story is similar in some ways to "Rumpelstiltskin," but it is different in many ways as well.

Activity Review the story of Rumpelstiltskin with students. Then have students work in small groups to list the ways this story is similar to and different from "Rumpelstiltskin." Ask them to pinpoint what they see as the most important differences. **L2** **COLLAB. LEARN.**

Additional Resources

Reading Skills Practice Workbook

VIEWING THE PAINTING

José Clemente Orozco (1883–1949) is known as a painter of the Mexican vanguard. He is famous for his murals.

Viewing Response *They seem to have a supernatural or nonhuman air about them.*

H Literary Elements

IRONY Ask students what words the suitor uses to describe the shirts and vest. How are those words ironic? *(Without realizing it, the suitor correctly attributes the sewing to otherworldly forces.)*

I Active Reading Strategies

PREDICT Three times the aunt has predicted that the Souls will help the girl. Ask students whether they now tend to believe the aunt. Present the following model to demonstrate the thinking process involved in predicting:

Model: I've noticed that the aunt seems to be extremely clever; everything she said so far has proved to be true. So it seems sensible for me to assume that everything will turn out well for the girl.

Mujeres, La Cama Azul, 1910–1913. José Clemente Orozco. Oil. Private collection.
Viewing the painting: How do the figures in this painting compare with the descriptions of the souls in this story?

The next day a very happy gentleman came for his vest, for he was sure that the lovely girl would have it ready for him. But he was not prepared for the beauty of the vest. The colors were vibrant and beautifully matched. The embroidery looked like a painting. It took his breath away. Without hesitation, he asked the old lady for her niece's hand in marriage. "For," he said, "this vest looks as if it was not touched by human hands, but by angels!"

The old woman danced with joy, and could hardly contain her happiness. She gave her consent at once. The merchant left to arrange for the wedding. Wringing her hands, the poor girl cried, "But Tía, what am I going to do when he finds out that I can't do any of those things?" "Don't worry, my *Palomita,*[4] the Blessed Souls will get you out of this trouble too. You wait and see!"

Almost at once the old woman went to her *comadre* to tell her the good news, and to ask her to help get ready for the wedding. Soon everything was ready.

4. Used here as an affectionate term, *Palomita* (päl′ ō mē′ tə) means "little dove."

Vocabulary
vibrant (vī′ brənt) *adj.* full of life and energy

Teaching Support

Grammar and Language *Minilesson*

Demonstrative Adjectives and Pronouns Write these words on the board: *this, that, these, those.* Explain to students that these words can be used as demonstrative adjectives or pronouns. When they modify a noun, they are adjectives, as in *This story is funny.* When they substitute for a noun, they are pronouns, as in *This is my favorite story.* Write this sentence from the story on the board and have students identify the function of the underlined word: "<u>This</u> vest looks as if it was not touched by human hands, but by angels!" *(demonstrative adjective)*

Activity Have students find at least one example of each of these words in the story and copy the sentence in which the word appears. Label the word as either a pronoun or an adjective. **L2**

Additional Resources

- ***Grammar and Language Transparency 32***
- ***Grammar and Language Workbook,*** pp. 117, 127
- ***Grammar and Composition Handbook,*** Lessons 4.7, 5.2
- ***Writer's Choice,*** Lesson 12.4

The poor girl did not know how to invite the Souls to her wedding. She timidly went and stood beside her bed and asked the *retablo* to come to her wedding.

The great day finally arrived. The girl looked beautiful in the gown which the merchant had brought as part of her *donas*.[5] Everyone in the village had been invited to the wedding.

During the fiesta when everyone was drinking *brindes* to the bride and groom, and the music was playing, three ugly hags came to the *sala*[6] and stood waiting for the groom to come and welcome them in. One of the hags had an arm that reached to the floor and dragged; the other arm was short. The second hag was bent almost double, and had to turn her head sideways to look up. The third hag had bulging, bloodshot eyes like a lobster. "Jesús María," cried the groom. "Who are those ugly creatures?" "They are aunts of my father, whom I invited to my wedding," answered the bride, knowing quite well who they might be. The groom, being well bred, went at once to greet the ugly hags. He took them to their seats and brought them refreshments. Very casually, he asked the first hag, "Tell me, Señora,[7] why is one of your arms so long and the other one short?" "My son," she answered, "my arms are like that because I spin so much."

The groom went to his wife and said, "Go at once and tell the servants to burn your spinning wheel, and never let me see a spinning wheel in my house, never let me see you spinning ever!"

The groom went to the second hag and asked her why she was so humped over. "My son," she replied, "I am that way from embroidering on a frame so much." The groom went to his wife and whispered, "Burn your embroidery frame at once, and never let me see you embroider another thing."

Next, the groom went to the third hag and asked, "Why are your eyes so bloodshot and bulging?" "My son, it is because I sew so much and bend over while sewing." She had hardly finished speaking when the groom went to his wife and said, "Take your needles and thread and bury them. I never want to see you sewing, never! If I see you sewing, I will divorce you and send you far away, for the wise man learns from others' painful experiences."

Well . . . so the Souls, in spite of being holy, can also be rascals.

Colorín, colorado,
ya mi cuento se ha acabado.
(Scarlet or ruby red,
my story has been said.)

5. The gifts a groom gives to his bride upon their marriage are called *donas* (dō′ nəs).
6. *Brindes* (brēn′ dās) are toasts—drinks in honor of a person or thing. A *sala* (sä′ lə) is a parlor or other large room used for entertaining.
7. *Señora* (sen yôr′ ə) can mean either "Mrs." or, as here, "Madam."

J Literary Elements

CLIMAX Note that the high point of the story comes when the three hags arrive at the wedding. Their arrival heightens the suspense and ties up loose ends in the story.

K Active Reading Strategies

REVIEW Ask students to explain exactly how the Souls help the girl. Is this a satisfying ending to the story? *(The Souls scare her husband into believing that she will become as ugly as they are if she sews. It is an especially satisfying ending because the husband, who wanted only a wife to work for him, now is in the position of ordering her not to work.)*

Thematic Focus

Fantastic Capers and Mischief Makers To whom are the Souls holy? *(The aunt and the girl.)* To whom are they rascals? *(The new husband.)*

ASSESSMENT

Quick Checks, p. 35

A&E HOME VIDEO.® *The following videotape program is available from Glencoe.* Be sure to preview the video for appropriateness for your class.

- *Day of the Dead**

*Also available in the Glencoe Literature *Video Library*.

MEETING INDIVIDUAL NEEDS — SPECIAL NEEDS

Learning Disabled This story may serve as a basis for a discussion about judging people by their appearances. One might say that the merchant is a nice but superficial man. He orders his wife to refrain from sewing because he doesn't want her to lose her beauty.

Activity Ask students to think back on other stories in this theme. How many characters made incorrect judgments based on appearances? Ask students to describe a time when they or someone they know made a similar mistake.

L1 COLLAB. LEARN.

Additional Resources

Inclusion Strategies

Responding to the Selection

PERSONAL RESPONSE

Many students will say they were not sure until near the end that the story would take a humorous twist.

Analyzing Literature

1. The aunt seems bold and outgoing, whereas the girl is timid and shy. Both seem devout.
2. The merchant wants the girl to spin cloth, to sew shirts, and to embroider a vest. She passes the tests with help from the Souls.
3. The girl tells him the Souls are aunts of her father.
4. The Souls make her husband believe that sewing will make her ugly.
5. The Souls suggest that the girl's aunt is doing the right thing. They also suggest that the aunt has supernatural knowledge.
6. The merchant's use of "heavenly" words to describe the clothes is humorous because he is unknowingly correct about who made them.
7. The girl seems more confident. The timid girl at the beginning of the tale would not have been able to concoct an identity for the Souls.
8. The Souls help the girl but trick the merchant.
9. The merchant likes his wife's beauty and dislikes the ugliness of the Souls. He focuses too much on appearance.
10. This story is similar to "Rumpelstiltskin." As the elf helps the princess, the Souls help the girl. The major difference seems to be that the girl earns her help by praying, so the Souls are more benevolent than the elf in "Rumpelstiltskin."

Active Reading and Critical Thinking

Responding to Literature

PERSONAL RESPONSE

- Did you find this story humorous? Why or why not?
- If you were in a challenging situation, would you want the Souls to help you? Explain.

Brackets connect questions that are paired to develop higher-level thinking skills.

Analyzing Literature

RECALL

1. Briefly describe the girl and her aunt. How are they alike and different?
2. List the three tests that the merchant wants the girl to perform. How does she pass each test?
3. What does the girl say when the merchant questions the presence of the Souls at the fiesta?
4. How do the Souls solve the girl's problem?

INTERPRET

5. The Souls tell the girl: "We know your aunt, and she knows what she is doing and why." What do you think the Souls mean by this statement?
6. The merchant says how much he likes his new garments. How does this **dialogue** add to the humor of the story?
7. Is the girl less shy by the end of the story? Explain.
8. "The Souls, in spite of being holy, can also be rascals." Why is this a suitable line to end the story?

EVALUATE AND CONNECT

9. What qualities does the merchant appreciate in his bride? What qualities does he dislike in the Souls? How does the storyteller use this information to **characterize** the merchant?
10. In what ways does this story remind you of other folktales you know? In what ways is it different?

Mexican Shawl (Rebozo), c. 1790. Silk fabric, silver and gold thread, 28½ x 87 in. Parham Park, West Sussex, Great Britain.

LITERARY ELEMENTS

Climax and Falling Action

The **climax** is the turning point of a story. The climax in "The Souls in Purgatory" occurs when the three hags come to the wedding. Readers wait in suspense to see if their arrival will cause a good or bad outcome for the girl. The falling action of a story follows the climax and leads to the resolution of the problem or plot. In this story, the **falling action** occurs when the groom greets the hags and asks each one to explain her appearance.

1. What positive or negative outcomes could result from the climax of "The Souls in Purgatory"?
2. At what point in the falling action is it clear that the hags will solve the girl's problem?
3. Look back at one other folktale from this theme and identify its climax.

● See **Literary Terms Handbook,** pp. R2 and R3.

LITERARY ELEMENTS

1. The Souls could demand an outrageous payment from the girl. They could punish the merchant for his expectations.
2. It is clear that the hags will help the girl when the husband demands that the spinning wheel be destroyed.
3. The climax of "M'su Carencro" occurs when the chicken hawk dies.

Additional Resources

Literary Elements Transparency 35

Literature and Writing

Writing About Literature

Analyze an Epigraph An **epigraph** is a quotation at the beginning of a story that gives a clue about the writer's intention. Read the epigraph at the beginning of "The Souls in Purgatory." What does it tell you about the writer's intention? Is it an effective way to begin the story? Why or why not?

Creative Writing

A Character's Journal Read over your journal entry from the **Reading Focus** on page 398. Imagine that you are the girl in "The Souls in Purgatory." Write a journal entry describing the wedding day. How does she feel when the Souls appear? How does she feel at the end of the story?

Extending Your Response

Literature Groups

Talk About the Three Souls Read over the information about purgatory on page 398. Discuss these questions: Why are the three Souls in purgatory in the first place? Is it surprising that they behave as "rascals" in the story? Why or why not? Finally, discuss possible ways the story would be different if, in the folktale, three angels came to the girl's aid instead of three Souls.

Art Activity

Design a Picture Book Plan a children's picture book to illustrate "The Souls in Purgatory." Reread the folktale and identify the most important images from the story. Be sure to include the different appearances of the Souls, both as ghosts and as hags, in your plan. Make rough sketches of the illustrations and write captions to go with them.

Interdisciplinary Activity

Social Studies What do people around the world believe about life after death? With a partner, research two or three major world religions and compare their views of the afterlife with the view suggested in this story. Conduct your research on the Internet and in encyclopedias and other books. Share your findings with the class.

Reading Further

For stories about girls who had to rely on their wits to escape unwanted suitors, try these novels:
A Girl Named Disaster by Nancy Farmer
Catherine, Called Birdy by Karen Cushman

Save your work for your portfolio.

Literature and Writing

Writing About Literature

Students' paragraphs should
- identify the writer's intention in using the epigraph
- evaluate the effectiveness of the epigraph as a way to begin the story

Creative Writing

Students' journal entries should
- describe the wedding day
- describe the girl's feelings

Extending Your Response

Literature Groups Suggest to students that it might be fun to give the Souls names and histories.
COLLAB. LEARN.

Art Activity Illustrators add to or interpret the text. Drawings can influence readers' perceptions.

FANTASTIC CAPERS AND MISCHIEF MAKERS 405

Skill Minilessons

GRAMMAR AND LANGUAGE
ACTIVE AND PASSIVE VOICE

1. active
2. passive
3. active
4. passive

READING AND THINKING
SUMMARIZING

An old woman finds a potential husband for her niece and challenges him to test her niece's sewing skills. The niece, who cannot sew, is worried until her aunt reminds her that she prays devoutly to the Souls in Purgatory, who will surely help her. The Souls spin and weave for the girl, and the potential husband is convinced that he should marry the girl. When the Souls arrive at the wedding reception, they are ugly and deformed, and they tell the new husband that they lost their looks to sewing and weaving. The husband orders his new wife to preserve her beauty; she is never to sew or spin again.

VOCABULARY
THE PREFIX *INTER-*

1. interlock
2. intercollegiate
3. interstate
4. intertwine
5. interdependence
6. interplanetary

Additional Resources

- ***Grammar and Language Workbook,*** p. 97
- ***Grammar and Composition Handbook,*** Lesson 3.10
- ***Writer's Choice,*** Lesson 10.10
- ***Reading Skills Practice Workbook,*** pp. 65–66
- ***Vocabulary Practice,*** p. 25

RETEACH • REVIEW

Skill Minilessons

GRAMMAR AND LANGUAGE • ACTIVE AND PASSIVE VOICE

A verb is in the **active voice** when the subject performs the action of the verb. A verb is in the **passive voice** when the subject receives the action of the verb.

. . . the old woman began to worry. . . .

The verb *began* is active because the woman (the subject of the clause) is performing the action.

. . . her niece would be left all alone. . . .

The verb phrase *would be left* is passive because the niece (the subject of the clause) receives the action of the verb.

PRACTICE Tell if the underlined verb or verb phrase is in the active or passive voice.

1. The old lady opened her ears.
2. This vest looks as if it was not touched by human hands.
3. Bury your needles and thread.
4. My story has been said.

- For more about active and passive voice, see **Language Handbook,** p. R34.

READING AND THINKING • SUMMARIZING

A **summary** is a short statement that tells the important events and ideas in a story. Summarizing can help you understand and remember a story. It is also a good way to share the story's plot.

- For more about summarizing, see **Reading Handbook,** p. R100.

PRACTICE Summarize "The Souls in Purgatory." Be sure to include the most important events, in the correct order, as well as the important details about characters and setting. However, be sure to select only important elements as you share the story. Ask a partner to compare your summary to the text for accuracy of ideas, inclusion of critical details, and the way it captures the main idea.

VOCABULARY • THE PREFIX *inter-*

Intercession combines the prefix *inter-,* meaning "between" or "among," with the root *cede,* which means "to go." If you try to help one person by making a request of another, you intercede, or "go between" the two people. The request or effort you make is an *intercession.* Sometimes, the prefix *inter-* is attached to a whole word instead of to a root.

PRACTICE Choose the word that fits each phrase.

intercollegiate	interplanetary
interdependence	interstate
interlock	intertwine

1. what the pieces of a jigsaw puzzle do
2. a game between two universities
3. a highway between Ohio and Iowa
4. what vines do when they twist
5. people's need for each other
6. type of travel between Earth and Mars

ASSESSMENT

- ***Quick Checks,*** p. 35
- ***Selection and Theme Assessment,*** pp. 61–62
- ***Performance Assessment,*** p. 33
- ***Testmaker: ExamView Pro***
- ***Interactive Tutor: Self-Assessment***

Interdisciplinary Connection

Art and CULTURE

Celebrating Life and Death, Mexican Style

People often think of death as a sad part of life, but once a year in Mexico, it is cause for celebration. *El Día de los Muertos* (the Day of the Dead) is a uniquely Mexican holiday in which families try to tempt dead loved ones back to earth for a visit. Food, flowers, music, and dancing are all part of this three-day fiesta, which begins on October 31.

At the heart of this celebration are *ofrendas,* or offerings, for deceased relatives. Families often create an altar in their homes to prepare for the arrival of their dead loved ones. Around the altar, they carefully spread out their *ofrenda.* This offering may contain the deceased's favorite foods—such as hot chocolate, tamales, and *mole* (a spicy chocolate-based sauce served over meat)—as well as loaves of *pan de muertos* (bread of the dead), flowers, candles, and old photographs. You might even see some favorite belongings, such as a pair of cowboy boots. Outdoors, orange and yellow flowers line gravestones and pathways to illuminate the way home for the dead.

Candy skulls

Meanwhile, the living take special care to enjoy life. Children exchange candy skulls with friends. Families visit each other and share food left over from the altars. All-night picnics with dancing and singing take place in the cemeteries. In some regions, people even write special poems and songs or perform skits that often focus on humorous memories. One type of poem, the *calavera,* is a humorous obituary for a well-known person who is still alive.

The Day of the Dead fiesta originated hundreds of years ago when Spanish and Aztec cultures integrated in Mexico. (The Spanish, like many of their American neighbors to the north, celebrated All Hallows' Eve on October 31 and All Saints' Day on November 1.) Today, many Mexican American communities blend Halloween with traditional activities for Día de los Muertos.

Young people say the celebration helps them feel close to the memory of their grandparents and other relatives by bringing the spirits of their loved ones back to life with stories and art. By nightfall on November 2, the living and the dead part ways again, at peace with one another.

ACTIVITY

Choose a famous person who is no longer alive and whose life you would like to celebrate with an *ofrenda.* You might want to write a *calavera* (a rhyming poem written in the form of an obituary) for the person too. Make the *ofrenda* a colorful, artistic symbol of the good qualities you remember about that person.

Interdisciplinary Connection

Objective

- To learn about the Mexican tradition of the Day of the Dead

Teaching Strategies

Sandra Cisneros has written a piece titled "An Offering to the Power of Language" in memory of her father in which she celebrates his memory and the tradition of the Day of the Dead. Students may understand the tradition better as a result of reading this piece.

Activity

Have each student present his or her *ofrenda* to the class, explaining its significance. Ask students in the class who are of Mexican heritage to bring in types of objects associated with the Day of the Dead. Many will have objects to share.

Teaching Support

MEETING INDIVIDUAL NEEDS — MULTIPLE MODES OF EXPRESSION

Bodily-Kinesthetic Students who have a bodily-kinesthetic orientation may help the class by researching Mexican folk dancing, especially those dances that might be done as part of the Day of the Dead celebration.

Activity Have students conduct research on Mexican folk dancing and then teach the class one or two simple examples that might be performed as part of the Day of the Dead celebration. **L2**

Before Reading

Objectives

- To read and analyze two Native American legends
- To learn about the nature and transmission of legends
- To write a paragraph identifying modern details in the legends

Skills

Reading/Thinking: Predicting; Evaluating; Inferring
Writing: Folktale
Vocabulary: Multiple-Meaning Words
Grammar/Language: Prepositional Phrases
Listening/Speaking: Discussion
Collaboration: Literature Groups

Motivating STUDENTS

Selection Focus Transparency 35: Have students view the transparency and then discuss the questions provided.

Reading Focus: As an extension of the Reading Focus, have students discuss these two statements about revenge: "An eye for an eye" and "Turn the other cheek." Which advice do they think is better? Why?

Before You Read

Spotted Eagle and Black Crow and *The Siege of Courthouse Rock*

MEET JENNY LEADING CLOUD

Storyteller Jenny Leading Cloud recounted many legends from her Sioux heritage to artist and writer Richard Erdoes in the late 1960s. Erdoes transcribed the stories and published them in his collections of Native American tales. In describing the storyteller, Erdoes said, "She was a very bright, very active, very in-your-face lady. . . . She liked to tell stories." Leading Cloud spent her life in White River, a town on the Rosebud Reservation in South Dakota.

Jenny Leading Cloud was born in South Dakota in the late 1800s and died sometime around 1980.

READING FOCUS

Why do people seek revenge? Think of several reasons.

Share and Write

With a classmate, discuss reasons why people get revenge and how they go about getting revenge. Then write a definition for revenge. Share your definition with the entire class.

Setting a Purpose

As you read, discover how the characters take revenge on their enemies.

BUILDING BACKGROUND

The Time and Place These legends, told from the Sioux point of view, focus on centuries-old competition between the Sioux and the Pahani, or Pawnee, who lived in modern-day Nebraska. The Sioux lived and hunted in what are now Nebraska, Minnesota, Montana, and North and South Dakota.

Did You Know? In Sioux tradition, most young men belonged to a warrior society. They were invited to join or were sponsored by an older warrior. Warriors gained honor and prestige by performing brave acts during battle.

VOCABULARY PREVIEW

sheer (shēr) *adj.* very steep; straight up or down; p. 410
abyss (ə bis′) *n.* an extremely deep hole; p. 411
enmity (en′ mə tē) *n.* the bitter hatred between enemies; ill will; p. 412
alight (ə līt′) *v.* to come down after flight; land; p. 413
pact (pakt) *n.* an agreement; deal; pledge; p. 413
summit (sum′ it) *n.* the highest point or part; peak; p. 415
jut (jut) *v.* to extend outward or upward from a surface; bulge; p. 415

RESOURCE MANAGER

Teaching Tools and Resources
- Theme Four Planning Guide
- Literature Groups Sourcebook

Essential Lesson Support

Lesson-Specific Instruction
- Selection Focus Transparency 35
- Literary Elements Transparency 36
- Active Reading Guide,* p. 36
- Selection Vocabulary Practice, p. 26

Assessment
- Selection Quick Checks,* p. 36
- Sel. and Theme Assmt., pp. 63–64
- Testmaker: ExamView Pro
- Performance Assessment, p. 34

Systematic Language Instruction
- Gr. & Comp. Hbk., Lessons 8.4, 8.5
- Vocabulary Power, Unit 4 Review/Test
- Spelling Power, Unit 4 Review/Proofreading

English Language Learners
- ELL Sourcebook, p. 57
- Spanish Summaries, p. 35
- Audio Library*
- English, Yes!

Spec. Needs/Strat. Interven.
- Interactive Rdg. Sbk., pp. T137–T139
- Interactive Rdg. Wbk., pp. 68–69
- Inclusion Strat. Sbk., pp. 43–44
- Audio Library*

* Also available in Spanish

When the Eagle Spoke to Me, 1979. Jerry Ingram. Watercolor on paper, 18 x 24 in. Collection of the artist.

Spotted Eagle and Black Crow

Told by Jenny Leading Cloud

This is a story of two warriors, of jealousy, and of eagles. This legend is supposed to have been a favorite of the great *Mahpiya Luta*—Chief Red Cloud of the Oglalas.[1] [A]

1. The *Oglalas* (ō glä′ ləs) are a Teton (tē′ ton), or Western Sioux, people. Red Cloud was a chief during the 1860s, when Sioux hunting grounds were overrun by white settlers.

Reading the Selection

SUMMARY

This Native American legend centers on two friends who love the same woman, Red Bird. Out of jealousy, the less-favored Black Crow leaves his friend Spotted Eagle for dead on a war-party excursion. Black Crow tells everyone in the village that Spotted Eagle died in battle, and he marries Red Bird. Spotted Eagle, kept alive by respecting and living among eagles, later returns to the village but tells no one of Black Crow's cruel trick. Later, when their village is attacked, Spotted Eagle gives Black Crow a chance to redeem his honor. Black Crow dies honorably in battle, and Spotted Eagle marries Red Bird.

Spanish Summaries, p. 35

[A] Active Reading Strategies

QUESTION Ask students why they think the story begins as it does. How does this sentence help them understand the story? *(The first sentence summarizes the theme of the story; it is about the strength and courage of warriors, the destructiveness of jealousy, and the magic of eagles.)*

VOCABULARY If you haven't previewed the selection vocabulary with students, stop and remind them to use context clues to unlock the meanings of new vocabulary words.

Additional Resources

- ***Active Reading Guide,*** p. 36
- ***Audio Library***
- ***Spanish Audio Library***

MEETING INDIVIDUAL NEEDS — ENGLISH LANGUAGE LEARNERS

Native American Cultures English language learners may be unfamiliar with many of the cultural elements in this story. Point out that this story involves two Oglala Sioux warriors and their battles with their enemies, the Pahani. The warriors may be legend, but the Sioux are real and Chief Red Cloud was real.

Activity As students read, ask them to look for words that are unfamiliar. Then have small mixed groups identify these words and their significance. Students can create a collage with drawings of the things and captions identifying their significance.

Additional Resources

- ***English Language Learners Sourcebook,*** p. 57

CONNECTING TO OTHER SELECTIONS
For a teaching strategy that connects this selection to "The Medicine Bag," see the ***Theme One Planning Guide.***

B Active Reading Strategies

CONNECT Ask students what they think about the two friends' deciding to steal some ponies just as we might decide to go bowling. Are there activities in modern American society that are equivalent to what the two young men decide to do? *(In general modern culture does not encourage this sort of behavior on the part of adolescents.)*

C Active Reading Strategies

REVIEW Ask students what impact the ritual purification and war medicine have on their evaluation of what Spotted Eagle and Black Crow are about to do. Does it change their interpretation of it? *(It is important for students to understand that what the friends are doing is culturally sanctioned and quite acceptable behavior for young men. It is not the Native American equivalent of juvenile delinquency.)*

Language Note

The word *lariat* comes from the Spanish *la reata*. *Reata* means "to retie."

D Active Reading Strategies

CONNECT Ask students how they think Spotted Eagle feels when he realizes his friend has abandoned him. *(Spotted Eagle seems shocked and devastated by his friend's betrayal.)*

Teaching Support

Many lifetimes ago, there lived two brave warriors. One was named *Wanblee Gleska*—Spotted Eagle. The other's name was *Kangi Sapa*—Black Crow. They were friends but, as it happened, they both loved the same girl, *Zintkala Luta Win*—Red Bird. She was beautiful, a fine tanner and quill-worker,[2] and she liked Spotted Eagle best, which made Black Crow very jealous. Black Crow went to his friend and said, "Let us, you and I, go on a war party against the Pahani. Let us get ourselves some fine horses and earn eagle feathers." Spotted Eagle thought this a good idea. The two young men purified themselves in a sweat bath. They got out their war medicine[3] and their war shields. They painted their faces. They did all that warriors should do before a raid. Then they went against the Pahani.

Their raid was not a success. The Pahani were watchful. The young warriors got nowhere near the Pahani horse herd. Not only did they capture no ponies, but they even lost their own mounts, because while they were trying to creep up to their enemies' herd, the Pahani found their horses. The two young men had a hard time getting away on foot because the enemy were searching for them everywhere. At one time they had to hide themselves in a lake, under the water, breathing through long, hollow reeds which were sticking up above the surface. They were so clever at hiding themselves that the Pahani finally gave up searching for them.

The young men had to travel home on foot. It was a long way. Their moccasins were tattered, their feet bleeding. At last they came to a high cliff. "Let us go up there," said Black Crow, "and see whether the enemy is following us." They climbed up. They could see no one following them; but on a ledge far below them, halfway up the cliff, they spied a nest with two young eagles in it. "Let us at least get those eagles," Black Crow proposed. There was no way one could climb down the sheer rock wall, but Black Crow took his rawhide lariat, made a loop in it, put the rope around Spotted Eagle's chest under his armpits, and lowered him down. When his friend was on the ledge with the nest, Black Crow said to himself, "I will leave him there to die. I will come home alone and then Red Bird will marry me." And he threw his end of the rawhide thong down and left without looking back and without listening to Spotted Eagle's cries of what had happened to the lariat and to Black Crow.

Spotted Eagle cried in vain. He got no answer, only silence. At last it dawned

2. As a *tanner,* Red Bird made animal skins into leather. As a *quill-worker,* she made decorations using porcupine quills.
3. In reward for acts of bravery, warriors were given *eagle feathers* to wear in their headdresses. Among Native Americans, *medicine* refers to objects or ceremonies thought to have special powers.

Vocabulary
sheer (shēr) *adj.* very steep; straight up or down

Reading Minilesson

Predicting Point out that in most works of literature, a character's actions are understandable and consistent. A sweet, good-natured fellow in the first act of a play usually doesn't turn into a despicable villain in the second half with no motivation and no explanation. If a character's actions surprise us, we should be able at least to find some hints or clues that motivate behavior.

Activity Ask small groups to discuss Black Crow's sudden decision to leave his friend. To what extent is the reader prepared for this action? What hints does the reader have that Black Crow may betray his friend? **L2** COLLAB. LEARN.

Additional Resources

Reading Skills Practice Workbook

Concordia University
Library Technology Center
275 Syndicate Street North
St. Paul, MN 55104

"Spotted Eagle died a warrior's death," he told the people. "The Pahani killed him." There was loud wailing throughout the village because everybody had liked Spotted Eagle. Red Bird grieved more than the others. She slashed her arms with a sharp knife and cut her hair to make plain her sorrow to all. But in the end she became Black Crow's wife, because life must go on.

But Spotted Eagle did not die on his lonely ledge. The eagles got used to him. The old eagles brought plenty of food—rabbits, prairie dogs, or sage hens—and Spotted Eagle shared this raw meat with the two chicks. Maybe it was the eagle medicine in his bundle which he carried on his chest that made the eagles accept him. Still, he had a very hard time on that ledge. It was so narrow that, when he wanted to rest, he had to tie himself with the rawhide thong to a little rock sticking out of the cliff, for fear of falling off the ledge in his sleep. In this way he spent a few very uncomfortable weeks; after all, he was a human being and not a bird to whom such a crack in the rock face is home.

At last the young eagles were big enough to practice flying. "What will become of me now?" thought the young warrior. "Once these fledglings[4] have flown the nest for good, the old birds won't be bringing any more food up here." Then he had an inspiration. "Perhaps I will die. Very likely I will die. But I will try it. I will not just sit here and give up." He took his little pipe out of the medicine bundle and lifted it to the sky and prayed, "*Wakan Tanka, onshimala ye.* Great Spirit, pity me. You have created man and his cousin, the eagle. You have given me the eagle's name. I have decided to try to let the eagles carry me to the ground. Let the eagles help me, let me succeed."

He smoked and felt a surge of confidence. He grabbed hold of the legs of the two young eagles. "Brothers," he told them, "you have accepted me as one of your own. Now we will live together, or die together.

4. *Fledglings* are young birds that haven't yet grown the feathers needed to fly.

Vocabulary
abyss (ə bis′) *n.* an extremely deep hole

E Active Reading Strategies

CONNECT How does Red Bird's response to Spotted Eagle's death differ from the possible reaction of a twenty-first-century woman? *(Her initial reaction is much more physical and violent than that which is expected and accepted in modern society.)*

F Literary Elements

LEGEND Ask students at what point they feel "Spotted Eagle and Black Crow" begins to seem like a genuine legend. *(Many students will say that the story takes on the quality of a legend when Spotted Eagle begins to be cared for by the eagle.)*

G Active Reading Strategies

QUESTION Ask students how they interpret Spotted Eagle's "inspiration." Is this just an idea or thought? Or is it possible to think that an outside force, such as the "Ones Above," spoke to Spotted Eagle? *(The story has a strong spiritual dimension, and there is a suggestion that someone or something is looking out for Spotted Eagle.)*

Listening and Speaking *Minilesson*

Discussion The two young men in the story are good friends until jealousy intervenes. Yet the story demonstrates many of the most important principles of friendship—especially trust and respect.

Activity Divide students into groups and have each student write down his or her definition of friendship. One group member should collect the group cards and read them aloud. Have each group establish a group definition of friendship by combining the ideas of individual members. Each member must be given the opportunity to explain his or her definition, and all other members must practice good active listening. Then ask each group to present its definition to the class. **L2** COLLAB. LEARN.

H Literary Elements

LEGEND Ask students to find an example of Spotted Eagle's story taking on the dimensions of a legend. *(He takes on some of the characteristics of an eagle. He even "flies.")*

I Critical Thinking

EVALUATING Ask students to evaluate Spotted Eagle's decision to bear Black Crow's treachery in silence in order not to "set one family against the other." What does this decision say about Spotted Eagle's values? *(This decision demonstrates the importance of tribal life. The whole group is more important than any individual.)*

J Active Reading Strategies

QUESTION What does Black Crow's showing as much courage as Spotted Eagle in defending the village from the Pahani say about Black Crow? *(He is basically a good, courageous man who committed one great crime against friendship—and he atones with his life.)*

K Critical Thinking

EVALUATING Ask students to evaluate Spotted Eagle's response to Black Crow's asking for forgiveness. What does Spotted Eagle's answer say about what is valued in his culture? *(The culture sets high standards for what constitutes forgiveness. It is not enough for Black Crow to say he is sorry; he must demonstrate his remorse by risking his own life as he once risked his friend's.)*

Teaching Support

Great Spirit, pity me. You have created man and his cousin, the eagle. You have given me the eagle's name. I have decided to try to let the eagles carry me to the ground. Let the eagles help me, let me succeed."

H He smoked and felt a surge of confidence. He grabbed hold of the legs of the two young eagles. "Brothers," he told them, "you have accepted me as one of your own. Now we will live together, or die together. *Hokahay.*" And he jumped off the ledge. He expected to be shattered on the ground below, but with a mighty flapping of wings the two young eagles broke his fall and all landed safely. Spotted Eagle said a prayer of thanks to the Ones Above. He thanked the eagles, telling them that one day he would be back with gifts and have a giveaway in their honor.

I Spotted Eagle returned to his village. The excitement was great. He had been dead and had come back to life. Everybody asked him how it happened that he was not dead, but he would not tell them. "I escaped," he said, "and that is all." He saw his love married to his treacherous friend, but bore it in silence. He was not one to bring enmity to his people, to set one family against the other. Besides, what happened could not be changed. Thus he accepted his fate.

A year or so later, a great war party of Pahani attacked his village. The enemy outnumbered them tenfold, and there was no chance of victory for Spotted Eagle's band. All the warriors could do was to fight a slow rear-guard action, which would give the helpless ones—the women, children, and old folks—a chance to escape across the river. Guarding their people this way, the few warriors at hand fought bravely, charging the enemy again and again, making them halt and regroup. Each time, the warriors retreated a little, taking up a new position on a hill, or across a gully. In this way they could save their families.

J Showing the greatest courage, exposing their bodies freely, were Spotted Eagle and Black Crow. In the end they alone faced the enemy. Then, suddenly, Black Crow's horse was hit by several arrows in succession and collapsed under him. "Brother, forgive me for what I have done," he cried to Spotted Eagle. "Let me jump up on your horse behind you."

K Spotted Eagle answered, "You are a Fox. Pin yourself and fight. Then, if you survive, I will forgive you; and if you die, I will forgive you also."

What Spotted Eagle meant was this: Black Crow was a member of the Fox Warrior Society. The braves who belong to it sing this song:

I am a Fox.
If there is anything daring,
If there is anything dangerous to do,
That is a task for me to perform.
Let it be done by me.

Foxes wear a long, trailing sash, decorated with quillwork, which reaches all the way to the ground even when the warrior is on horseback. In the midst of battle, a Fox will sometimes defy death by pinning his sash to the earth with a special wooden pin, or with a knife or arrow. This means: I will stay here, rooted to this spot, facing my foes, until someone comes to release

Vocabulary
enmity (en′ mə tē) *n.* the bitter hatred between enemies; ill will

MEETING INDIVIDUAL NEEDS — SPECIAL NEEDS

Less-Proficient Readers Point out that this story is told in simple language but that it suggests some complicated values that form the basis for some Native American cultures. To understand the story completely, students must read actively and ask questions.

Activity Have small groups write questions about the story. They should focus on any elements in the story that seem strange to them. For example, they may ask such questions as *Why does Spotted Eagle smoke? What is a "giveaway"?* Have groups share their questions and provide answers.
L1 COLLAB. LEARN.

Additional Resources
Inclusion Strategies

the pin, or until the enemies flee, or until I die.

Black Crow pinned his sash to the ground. There was no one to release him, and the enemy did not flee. Black Crow sang his death song. He was hit by lances and arrows and died a warrior's death. Many Pahani died with him.

L Spotted Eagle had been the only one to see this. He finally joined his people, safe across the river. The Pahani had lost all taste to follow them there. "Your husband died well," Spotted Eagle told Red Bird. After some time had passed, Spotted Eagle married Red Bird. And much, much later he told his parents, and no one else, how Black Crow had betrayed him. "I forgive him now," he said, "because once he was my friend, and because he died like a warrior should, fighting for his people, and also because Red Bird and I are happy now."

After a long winter, when spring came again, Spotted Eagle told his wife, "I must go away for a few days to fulfill a promise. I must go alone." He rode off by himself to that cliff. Again he stood at its foot, below the ledge where the eagles' nest had been. He pointed his sacred pipe to the four directions, down to Grandmother Earth and up to the Grandfather, letting the smoke ascend to the sky, calling out: "*Wanblee, misunkala*. Little eagle brothers, hear me."

M High above him in the clouds appeared two black dots, circling. These were the eagles who had saved his life. They came at his call, their huge wings spread majestically, uttering a shrill cry of joy and recognition. Swooping down, they alighted at his feet. He stroked them with a feather fan, and thanked them many times, and fed them choice morsels of buffalo meat, and fastened small medicine bundles around their legs as a sign of friendship, and spread M sacred tobacco offerings around the foot of the cliff. Thus he made a pact of friendship and brotherhood between *Wanblee Oyate*—the Eagle Nation—and his own people. After he had done all this, the stately birds soared up again into the sky, circling motionless, carried by the wind, disappearing into the clouds. Spotted Eagle turned his horse's head homeward, going happily back to Red Bird. N

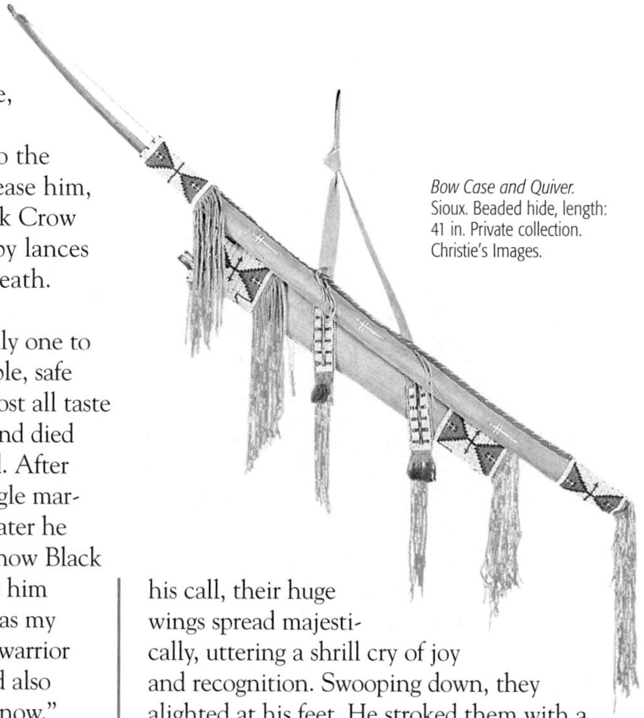

Bow Case and Quiver. Sioux. Beaded hide, length: 41 in. Private collection. Christie's Images.

❖

Vocabulary

alight (ə līt′) *v.* to come down after flight; land

pact (pakt) *n.* an agreement; deal; pledge

L Critical Thinking

EVALUATING Ask students what they think of Spotted Eagle's behavior after Black Crow's death. Why does he preserve his friend's memory so carefully and tell only his parents what happened? *(It is better for the group that Black Crow's bravery be celebrated and his treachery forgotten.)*

M Active Reading Strategies

QUESTION Why does Spotted Eagle honor the eagles? Is it merely because they saved his life, or are there other reasons? Present the following model to demonstrate the process involved in questioning:

Model: I think the eagles symbolize loyalty. They not only help Spotted Eagle, but also come back to him when he calls, unlike Black Crow. Although the crow is a clever bird, eagles are (as the storyteller notes) "majestic," and I think Spotted Eagle wants to share in the qualities they possess.

N Literary Elements

LEGEND This story became a legend in Oglala culture, meaning that it was based on fact, but told and retold, and was perhaps made larger than life and more magical than the original story. Ask students why they think the story was so popular and why they think it was a favorite of Chief Red Cloud's. *(The story became a legend because it touched on feelings and actions that the people valued.)*

Life Skills Connection

Code of Conduct This is a story about revenge and forgiveness in Native American culture. Careful analysis of the story can reveal a code of conduct for a person to follow. For example, one clear principle is that one does not take action in a way that involves more people in the community in the problem—does not "bring enmity to . . . [the] people."

Activity Ask students to work in small groups to write a code of conduct based on the values and acceptable behaviors they see in the story. Have each group report to the class. Discuss how such a code of conduct may apply to modern life. **L2 COLLAB. LEARN.**

SUMMARY

During one of the several battles between the Sioux and the Pahani over land space, the Sioux chase the Pahani up Courthouse Rock, a very steep rock formation. Since Courthouse Rock is accessible only on one side, the Sioux assume that they have won the battle. However, the clever leader of the Pahani whittles a groove in a rock on one of the steep sides of the formation's face and lowers his people to safety with a rope.

Spanish Summaries, p. 35

Active Reading Strategies

REVIEW What characteristics of setting does the narrator choose to highlight? How does the setting contribute to the meaning of the story? *(The area where this event took place is settled land that no longer belongs to Native Americans; it is flat farmland that doesn't even appear to be part of the West. The "wild rocks," then, symbolize the native peoples and the land long ago, before it was settled.)*

Critical Thinking

INFERRING Why does the storyteller mention that "the whites had pushed nations like ours . . . westward onto the prairie"? *(The narrator is writing in praise of both the Oglala Sioux and the Pahani and is suggesting that the two tribes would not have fought had they not been forced to compete for scarce resources.)*

The Siege of Courthouse Rock

Told by Jenny Leading Cloud

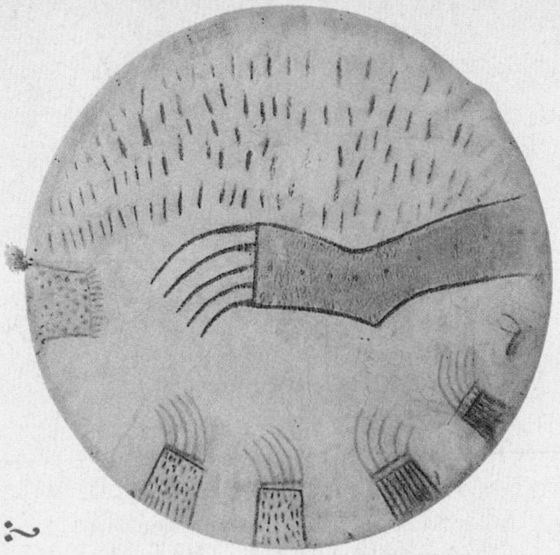

Shield Cover, c. 1820. Upper Missouri. Smithsonian Institution.

Nebraska is green and flat, a part of the vast corn belt. There are farms everywhere, and silos, and the land does not look like the West at all. But as you travel on toward the setting sun, you find three great, wild rocks which rise out of the plains. First you come to Chimney Rock, towering like a giant needle on the prairie. It was a famous landmark for the settlers in their covered wagons as they traveled west on the Oregon trail or took the more southerly route to the Colorado goldfields.

Did You Know?
Yucca (yuk' ə) *plants* have woody stems and clusters of white, bell-shaped, drooping flowers. They grow mainly in desert areas of western and southwestern North America.

Then you come to the twins—Courthouse Rock and Jailhouse Rock. Formed of yellowish stone, they are covered with yucca plants and sagebrush. Mud swallows nest in the rock faces. If you climb one of the twins, there is a wonderful view of the plains all around. And westward beyond the plains rise the chalk cliffs and the sandhills of Nebraska, home of many western Sioux.

A long time ago a Sioux war party surprised a war party of Pahani near Courthouse Rock. We Sioux had been fighting many battles with the Pahani. The whites had pushed nations like ours, whose homeland was further east near the Great Lakes, westward into the prairie and the hunting grounds of other tribes. Maybe the Pahani were there before us; who knows? At any rate, now we were hunting the same herds in the same place, and naturally we fought.

I guess there must have been more of us than of the Pahani, and they retreated to the top of Courthouse Rock to save themselves. Three sides of Courthouse Rock go straight up and down like the sides of a skyscraper. No one can climb them. Only the fourth side had a path to the top, and it could be easily defended by a few brave men.

Thus the Pahani were on the top and the Sioux at the foot of Courthouse Rock. The Sioux chief told his warriors: "It's no

Teaching Support

Grammar and Language Minilesson

Prepositional Phrases Remind students that a prepositional phrase consists of an introductory preposition and the object of that preposition. Prepositional phrases allow writers to show the relationships among ideas, people, and places. Write the following sentence on the board and have volunteers identify the prepositional phrases: *It was a famous landmark for the settlers in their covered wagons as they traveled west on the Oregon trail or took the more southerly route to the Colorado goldfields.*

Activity Have students list five prepositional phrases from the story, each using a different preposition. Have students identify each preposition and its object. Then ask students to construct five original sentences using the same prepositions. **L2**

Additional Resources

- ***Grammar and Language Transparency 33***
- ***Grammar and Language Workbook,*** p. 141
- ***Grammar and Composition Handbook,*** Lesson 7.1
- ***Writer's Choice,*** Lesson 13.1

use trying to storm it. Only three or four men can go up that path abreast,[1] so even women and children could defend it. But the Pahani have no water, and soon they'll run out of food. They can stay up there and starve or die of thirst, or they can come and fight us on the plain. When they climb down, we can kill them and count many coups[2] on them." The Sioux settled down to wait at the foot of the rock.

Q On the summit, as the Sioux chief expected, the Pahani suffered from hunger and thirst. They grew weak. Though there was little hope for them, they had a brave leader who could use his head. He knew that three sides of the rock were unguarded but that one would have to be a bird to climb down them. On one of the three steep sides, however, there was a round bulge jutting out from the rock face. "If we could fasten a rope to it, we could let ourselves down," he thought. But the outcropping was too smooth, round, and wide to hold a lasso.

Then the Pahani leader tried his knife on the rock bulge. He found that the stone was soft enough for the knife to bite easily into, and he began patiently whittling a groove around the bulge. He and his men worked only at night so that the Sioux wouldn't see what they were up to. After two nights they had carved the groove deep enough. When they tied all their rawhide ropes together, they found that the line would reach to the ground.

On the third night the Pahani leader tied one end of the rope around the bulge in the rock. He himself tested it by climbing all the way down and then up again, which took most of the night.

On the next and fourth night, he told his men: "Now we do it. Let the youngest go first." The Pahani climbed down one by one, the youngest and least accomplished first, so that a large group could belay[3] them, and the older and more experienced warriors later. The leader came down last. The Sioux did not notice them at all, and the whole party stole away.

R The Sioux stayed at the foot of the rock for many days. They themselves grew hungry, because they had hunted out all the game. At last a young, brave warrior said: "They must be all dead up there. I'm fed up with waiting; I'll go up and see." He climbed the path to the top and shouted down that nobody was up there.

S That time the joke was on us Sioux. It's always good to tell a story honoring a brave enemy, especially when the story is true. Are there any Pahani listening?

1. *Abreast* means "side by side."
2. Among some Native American peoples, to *count coups* (ko͞oz) meant touching a live enemy and then getting away safely—an act that required skill and courage. This phrase can also refer to telling the stories of such deeds.
3. In mountain climbing, to *belay* is to connect the climbers to one another with a rope. Here, each person probably loops the rope under his arms and around his back for security as he climbs down. The more experienced men stay at the top to hold the rope steady for less skilled climbers.

Vocabulary

summit (sum′ it) *n.* the highest point or part; peak
jut (jut) *v.* to extend outward or upward from a surface; bulge

Q Literary Elements

CHARACTERIZATION What qualities in the Pahani leader allow him to save his people? *(He possesses both courage and ingenuity. Note that he tests the line before he asks his people to use it.)*

R Active Reading Strategies

CONNECT How are the young Sioux warrior and the Pahani leader alike? *(Both show courage and a willingness to go first. Both act courageously on the basis of having thought logically.)*

S Literary Elements

LEGEND Ask students why they think this story became a legend. What cultural values does the story honor? *(The story supports courage and cleverness, along with respect for a brave enemy.)*

Thematic Focus

Fantastic Capers and Mischief Makers Who are the mischief makers in these stories? Explain.

ASSESSMENT

Quick Checks, p. 36

Real-World Connection

Media Legends Ask students to clip stories from current newspapers and magazines that seem to have the qualities on which legends are based. The stories should relate a surprising or extraordinary event that warrants retelling and that might be exaggerated to become more magical or larger than life. The stories should also convey something of what modern society values. **L2**

interNET CONNECTION

Students can discover Courthouse Rock and the area in which this story is set (including Jenny Leading Cloud's home) on several internet sites.

Responding to the Selection

PERSONAL RESPONSE

Many students will say they took the side of the Sioux over the Pahani in "Spotted Eagle and Black Crow" because the story focuses on the Sioux. Students may side with the Pahani in "The Siege of Courthouse Rock" because their actions were so clever.

Analyzing Literature

1. Red Bird is overcome with grief, but she accepts that life must go on.
2. The young eagles save his life.
3. Spotted Eagle forgives Black Crow because Black Crow redeems himself through acts of courage.
4. The Pahani climb down a rope fastened to an outcropping on a ledge.
5. The fact that Red Bird accepts her fate helps Spotted Eagle to hold his tongue.
6. The last paragraph increases the significance of the story by suggesting a special relationship between the Oglala Sioux and the majestic eagle.
7. Spotted Eagle forgives Black Crow because he admires courage; he puts the welfare of the tribe before the welfare the individual; and he loves Red Bird.
8. The narrator admires cleverness.
9. Black Crow and Spotted Eagle are both courageous. The Sioux and Pahani are both courageous and clever.
10. Many students will point out that it is always appropriate to repay a kindness.

Active Reading and Critical Thinking

Responding to Literature

PERSONAL RESPONSE

- Whose side did you take in each of these stories?

Brackets connect questions that are paired to develop higher-level thinking skills.

Analyzing Literature

RECALL

1. How does Red Bird react to word of Spotted Eagle's death?
2. What happens when Spotted Eagle trusts the young eagles to help him?
3. Why does Spotted Eagle finally forgive Black Crow?
4. How do the Pahani escape the Sioux in "The Siege of Courthouse Rock"?

INTERPRET

5. How does Red Bird's reaction affect the events that follow?
6. How might the last paragraph in "Spotted Eagle and Black Crow" increase the significance of the story?
7. What three values does Spotted Eagle possess that allow him to forgive Black Crow?
8. What does the **narrator** of "The Siege of Courthouse Rock" admire more than success in battle?

EVALUATE AND CONNECT

9. A quality held or displayed by a person is a **character trait.** What character traits do Spotted Eagle and Black Crow display? What traits do the Sioux and the Pahani show in "The Siege of Courthouse Rock"?
10. Do you think Spotted Eagle's behavior at the end of the story was appropriate? Explain.

LITERARY ELEMENTS

Legend

A **legend** is a story handed down in a society from several generations. Legends are generally considered to be based loosely on a historical event, but are so old that they cannot be proven true or false. In a legend, a character performs deeds that the society values.

1. Why do you think the story of Spotted Eagle and Black Crow became a legend? Explain your answer.
2. What deed, in your opinion, turned the story of Courthouse Rock into a legend?

- See **Literary Terms Handbook,** p. R5.

Courthouse Rock, c. 1860. Albert Bierstadt. Oil on board, 13 x 18$^{15}/_{16}$ in. University of Nebraska, Lincoln, NE. Great Plains Art Collection.

LITERARY ELEMENTS

1. The story supports many traits valued by the Sioux, including bravery and loyalty.
2. The story became a legend because the Sioux were able to laugh at a joke on themselves.

Additional Resources

Literary Elements Transparency 36

Extending Your Response

Writing About Literature

Setting The events in "The Siege of Courthouse Rock" occurred long ago. What details indicate that Jenny Leading Cloud's version of the story occurred in modern times? Write a paragraph that lists details and explains why you chose those details.

Creative Writing

A Pahani Tale Write a tale from the point of view of a Pahani woman who was with the people besieged on Courthouse Rock. Include the response of your group to the clever trick that freed the Pahani from the Sioux.

Literature Groups

Tales of Honor Behaving in an honorable way is an important element in "Spotted Eagle and Black Crow." With a group, analyze the actions of both warriors. Which actions were honorable? Which ones were not, and why? Consider your ideas from the **Reading Focus** on page 408 as you discuss your answers. Share your responses with the class.

Interdisciplinary Activity

Social Studies Use the Internet, the library, or other appropriate primary and secondary sources to research a topic related to these two selections. For example, you might focus on Chief Red Cloud, the Sioux, the history of South Dakota, or contemporary Native American writers. Evaluate each source, then use the most interesting and reliable information to prepare a brief report for your class. If you wish, include drawings, pictures, or audiotapes.

Reading Further

For information about native peoples of the Midwest, try:

These Were the Sioux by Mari Sandoz

The Life and Death of Crazy Horse by Russell Freedman, with photographs by Amos Bad Heart Bull

Save your work for your portfolio.

Skill Minilesson

RETEACH • REVIEW

VOCABULARY • MULTIPLE-MEANING WORDS

Most words have more than one meaning. These meanings are often related, but sometimes they are very different. For example, the rock wall behind Spotted Eagle's ledge is *sheer,* or very steep. However, *sheer* can also mean "very thin and fine," as in *sheer fabric.* And it can mean "complete or absolute," as in *sheer boredom.* There is yet another *sheer* that comes from a different root altogether and means "to swerve."

PRACTICE For each pair of phrases, write two sentences using the word, one with each meaning. Use a dictionary as needed.

1. a. a rude remark
   b. a rude cabin
2. a. dinner reservations
   b. reservations about cheating
3. a. a copy of the picture
   b. the copy in the ad

ASSESSMENT

- ***Quick Checks,*** p. 36
- ***Selection and Theme Assessment,*** pp. 63–64
- ***Performance Assessment,*** p. 34
- ***Testmaker: ExamView Pro***
- ***Interactive Tutor: Self-Assessment***

Extending Your Response

Writing About Literature

Students' paragraphs should

- list all the details that indicate that Jenny Leading Cloud's version is modern
- explain why those details were chosen

Creative Writing

Students' tales should

- reflect the Pahani view of events
- include the group's response to the trick that freed the Pahani

Literature Groups Suggest that students develop a collaborative definition of honor before they try to decide which actions were honorable. COLLAB. LEARN.

Interdisciplinary Activity Suggest that students choose different topics to cover as broad a range of information as possible. Remind students that the fluency with which they read their reports will help their listeners to follow and understand.

Skill Minilesson

VOCABULARY • MULTIPLE-MEANING WORDS

Possible answers

1. a. Mary was extremely rude to her hostess.
   b. He lived in a rude hut on a lonely mountainside.
2. a. Do they take reservations at Chez Vin?
   b. She had serious reservations about accepting the job offer.
3. a. Do you have another copy of your essay?
   b. Sue wrote the copy for the commercial.

Additional Resources

Vocabulary Practice, p. 26

Before Reading

Objectives

- To read and analyze two modern folktales
- To identify and analyze the traits possessed by heroes
- To write an analysis of narrative and dialogue

Skills

Reading/Thinking: Establishing Criteria; Finding Clues
Writing: Short Story or Play
Vocabulary: The Prefix *Re-*
Grammar/Language: Proper Adjectives; Verb Tenses
Life Skills: Lifelong Learning
Collaboration: Literature Groups

Motivating STUDENTS

Selection Focus Transparency 36: If you have a Spanish speaker in your class, invite that person to read the Mexican proverb to the class in Spanish and in English.

Reading Focus: As an extension of the Reading Focus, ask students why they think people enjoy reading stories about getting even.

Before You Read

Chicoria and *Coyote and Wasichu*

MEET JOSÉ GRIEGO Y MAESTAS

José Griego y Maestas (hō zā′ grē ā′ gō ē mī es′ täs) included "Chicoria" in a collection of stories that represent the culture and history of the Hispanic southwest. He is director of the Guadalupe Historic Foundation in Santa Fe, New Mexico.

José Griego y Maestas was born in 1949. "Chicoria" was first published in Cuentos: Tales from the Hispanic Southwest *in 1980.*

MEET RUDOLFO A. ANAYA

Rudolfo Anaya (rōō dôl′ fō ä nī′ yä), who retells "Chicoria" in English, uses folk stories and myths in his novels about modern life in the Southwest.

Rudolfo Anaya was born in New Mexico in 1937. He is a professor of languages and literature at the University of New Mexico.

READING FOCUS

Is getting even the same thing as seeking revenge? Think about your answer.

Think/Pair/Share

When is getting even dangerous? When is it just a harmless trick? Write a sentence explaining your reactions to these questions. With a partner, discuss your answers, and examine where you agree and disagree. Then share your questions and explanations with a larger group.

Setting a Purpose

Read the next two folktales to discover how different characters use their wits to suit their purposes.

BUILDING BACKGROUND

The Time and Place Both of these tales of mischief come from the recent past. Look for clues that tell the reader these stories are not ancient ones.

Did You Know?

A coyote is more than just an animal in the stories of many civilizations. In Native American literature, the coyote is a trickster. He can appear as a hunter, a thief, or a friend—and he usually gets away with his mischief. Even today, wily coyotes defy the efforts of those who try to destroy them.

Coyote Song, 1997. Mindy Dwyer. Watercolor and colored pencil, 10½ x 8⅝ in. Private collection.

418 THEME 4

RESOURCE MANAGER

Teaching Tools and Resources
- Theme Four Planning Guide
- Literature Groups Sourcebook

Essential Lesson Support

Lesson-Specific Instruction
- Selection Focus Transparency 36
- Literary Elements Transparency 37
- Active Reading Guide,* p. 37

Assessment
- Selection Quick Checks,* p. 37
- Sel. and Theme Assmt., pp. 65–66
- Testmaker: ExamView Pro
- Performance Assessment, p. 35

Systematic Language Instruction
- Gr. & Comp. Hbk., Lessons 8.6, 8.7

English Language Learners
- ELL Sourcebook, p .58
- Spanish Summaries, p. 36
- Spanish Translations, pp. 92–94
- Audio Library*
- English, Yes!

Spec. Needs/Strat. Interven.
- Interactive Rdg. Sbk., pp. T140–T142
- Interactive Rdg. Wbk., pp. 70–71
- Audio Library*

* Also available in Spanish

The World of Don Francisco, 1934. Theoden Van Soelen. Oil on canvas.

Chicoria

Adapted in Spanish
by José Griego y Maestas
Retold in English by Rudolfo A. Anaya

There were once many big ranches in California, and many New Mexicans went to work there. One day one of the big ranch owners asked his workers if there were any poets in New Mexico.

"Of course, we have many fine poets," they replied. "We have old Vilmas, Chicoria, Cinfuegos, to say nothing of the poets of Cebolleta[1] and the Black Poet."

"Well, when you return next season, why don't you bring one of your poets to compete with Gracia[2]—here none can compare with him!"

When the harvest was done the New Mexicans returned home. The following season when they returned to California they took with them

1. *Cebolleta* is the name of a town. Pronunciations: *Vilmas* (vēl′ mäs), *Chicoria* (chē′ kō rē′ ä), *Cinfuegos* (sēn fwā′ gōs), *Cebolleta* (sā′ bō yā′ tä)
2. *Gracia* (grä′ syä)

Reading the Selection

SUMMARY

Chicoria, a New Mexican poet, is invited to California to compete in a poetry contest. Using his wit, one of the trademarks of a fine poet, Chicoria teaches his host, a haughty rancher, a lesson. He bets his friend that the Californian rancher will invite him to eat dinner with him. When the rancher doesn't, Chicoria uses a metaphor to make the rancher understand that he is being very rude. When the rancher realizes his lack of grace, he invites Chicoria to dine with him. Of course, Chicoria wins the poetry contest as well, presumably using the same quick thinking that he used in winning the bet.

Spanish Summaries, p. 36

A Active Reading Strategies

CONNECT Many states have rivalries, especially in towns near borders. Ask students whether they are aware of any rivalries involving their home state or their school with another school.

Additional Resources

Active Reading Guide, p. 37

Audio Library

Spanish Audio Library

Teaching Support

MEETING INDIVIDUAL NEEDS — ENGLISH LANGUAGE LEARNERS

Pronoun Reference English language learners who have not fully internalized pronouns may have some difficulty following the story line. Briefly review subject and object pronouns and possessives. Make sure students understand which are singular, which are plural, and the gender differences.

Activity Direct students' attention to the sentence that begins at the end of page 419 and continues on page 420. Remind students to look for the noun referent for a pronoun if they do not understand. (New Mexicans *is the referent for* they, they, *and* them; Chicoria *is the referent for* him.)

Additional Resources

English Language Learners Sourcebook, p. 58

CONNECTING TO OTHER SELECTIONS

For a teaching strategy that connects this selection to "Barbara Frietchie" and "The Legend of Sleepy Hollow," see the ***Theme Five Planning Guide*** and the ***Theme Eight Planning Guide.***

B Literary Elements

HERO Clearly, Chicoria is to be the hero of this tale. What characteristics does he possess that make him special? *(He is a good poet, a quick wit, a cordial and polite man who never begs but who is able to put others in their place using his wit.)*

C Critical Thinking

ESTABLISHING CRITERIA This tale was published in 1980. Ask students when they think the events described occurred. What clues can they identify to help them answer this question? *(The story appears to have occurred at least a hundred years ago. The behavior of the rancher; his being called "master" by servants; and his asking about customs in New Mexico all point to an era long past.)*

FINE ART TRANSPARENCY 24

You may want to use ***Fine Art Transparency 24*** to discuss the workings of a large ranch.

B the poet Chicoria, knowing well that in spinning a rhyme or in weaving wit there was no *Californio*[3] who could beat him.

As soon as the rancher found out that the workers had brought Chicoria with them, he sent his servant to invite his good neighbor and friend to come and hear the new poet. Meanwhile, the cooks set about preparing a big meal. When the maids began to dish up the plates of food, Chicoria turned to one of the servers and said, "Ah, my friends, it looks like they are going to feed us well tonight!"

The servant was surprised. "No, my friend," he explained, "the food is for *them*. We don't eat at the master's table. It is not permitted. We eat in the kitchen."

"Well, I'll bet I can sit down and eat with them," Chicoria boasted.

"If you beg or if you ask, perhaps, but if you don't ask they won't invite you," replied the servant.

"I never beg," the New Mexican answered. "The master will invite me of his own accord,[4] and I'll bet you twenty dollars he will!"

So they made a twenty dollar bet and they instructed the serving maid to watch if this self-confident New Mexican had to ask the master for a place at the table. Then the maid took Chicoria into the dining room. Chicoria greeted the rancher cordially, but the rancher appeared haughty and did not invite Chicoria to sit with him and his guest at the table. Instead, he asked that a chair be brought and placed by the wall where Chicoria was to sit. The rich ranchers began to eat without inviting Chicoria.

So it is just as the servant predicted, Chicoria thought. The poor are not invited to share the rich man's food!

Then the master spoke: "Tell us about the country where you live. What are some of the customs of New Mexico?" C

"Well, in New Mexico when a family sits down to eat each member uses one spoon for each biteful of food," Chicoria said with a twinkle in his eyes.

The ranchers were amazed that the New Mexicans ate in that manner, but what Chicoria hadn't told them was that each spoon was a piece of tortilla: one fold and it became a spoon with which to scoop up the meal.

"Furthermore," he continued, "our goats are not like yours."

"How are they different?" the rancher asked.

"Here your nannies give birth to two kids, in New Mexico they give birth to three!"

"What a strange thing!" the master said. "But tell us, how can the female nurse three kids?"

"Well, they do it exactly as you're doing it now: While two of them are eating the third one looks on."

The rancher then realized his lack of manners and took Chicoria's hint. He apologized and invited his New Mexican guest to dine at the table. After dinner, Chicoria sang and recited his poetry, putting Gracia to shame. And he won his bet as well.

3. Someone who lives in or is from California is called, in Spanish, a *Californio* (ka lē for′ nyō).
4. The phrase *of his own accord* means "voluntarily; without being asked."

Teaching Support

Grammar and Language *Minilesson*

Proper Adjectives Remind students that proper adjectives are formed from proper nouns. Note that proper adjectives are often different in form from the noun on which they are based. Some common endings are *-an,* as in Puerto Ric*an* man; *-ese,* as in Chin*ese* restaurant; *-ian,* as in Canad*ian* bacon; and *-ish,* as in Turk*ish* bath. Write this sentence on the board: *He apologized and invited his New Mexican guest to dine at the table.* Point out to students that *New Mexican* is a proper adjective, formed from the proper noun *New Mexico.*

Activity Have students find at least three proper adjectives in this theme. They should record the noun from which it springs, the sentence in which the adjective occurs, and the page number on which the sentence appears. **L2**

Additional Resources

- ***Grammar and Language Transparency 34***
- ***Grammar and Language Workbook,*** p. 123
- ***Grammar and Composition Handbook,*** Lesson 5.1
- ***Writer's Choice,*** Lesson 12.2

Coyote and Wasichu

Cowboy, c. 1930s. Aurelio Flores. Earthenware, gesso, paint and varnish, 5½ x 3 x 5¾ in. San Antonio Museum of Art.

Sioux legend

There was a white man who was such a sharp trader that nobody ever got the better of him. Or so people said, until one day a man told this *wasichu:* "There's somebody who can outcheat you anytime, anywhere."

"That's not possible," said the *wasichu.* "I've had a trading post for many years, and I've cheated all the Indians around here."

"Even so, Coyote can beat you in any deal."

"Let's see whether he can. Where is Coyote?"

"Over there, that tricky-looking guy."

"Okay, all right, I'll try him."

The *wasichu* trader went over to Coyote. "Hey, let's see you outsmart me."

"I'm sorry," said Coyote, "I'd like to help you out, but I can't do it without my cheating medicine."

"Cheating medicine, hah! Go get it."

"I live miles from here and I'm on foot. But if you'd lend me your fast horse?"

"Well, all right, you can borrow it. Go on home and get your cheating medicine!"

"Well, friend, I'm a poor rider. Your horse is afraid of me, and I'm afraid of him. Lend me your clothes; then your horse will think that I am you."

"Well, all right. Here are my clothes; now you can ride him. Go get that medicine. I'm sure I can beat it!"

So Coyote rode off with the *wasichu's* fast horse and his fine clothes, while the *wasichu* stood there bare.

Sioux legend told at Grass Mountain,
Rosebud Indian Reservation,
South Dakota, 1974.

SUMMARY

In this Sioux legend, Wasichu (the white man), who has repeatedly cheated Native Americans in trading, finally gets tricked himself. After a challenge from Wasichu, Coyote explains that he can't cheat anyone without his cheating medicine. Coyote says that the horse is afraid of him and that he should borrow Wasichu's clothes to trick the horse, Wasichu gives coyote his clothes. Coyote rides off, leaving Wasichu without clothes or a horse.

Spanish Summaries, p. 36

D Active Reading Strategies

PREDICT Ask students to predict what will happen when the *wasichu* tries to outtrade Coyote.

E Active Reading Strategies

QUESTION Ask students what clues in the story suggest that Coyote is Native American. *(His use of the phrase "cheating medicine" suggests that he is a Native American; also the* wasichu *says he has "cheated all the Indians around here.")*

F Literary Elements

HERO Who is the hero of this story, and what makes him the hero? *(Coyote is the hero because he gets back at the wasichu.)*

Thematic Focus

Fantastic Capers and Mischief Makers The trickster is a popular character in folktales. Ask students why they think this is so.

Real-World Connection

Contemporary Tricksters Have students outline a brief story with a modern setting in which a trickster punishes a real-life modern evil. Help students by providing some examples. Could a trickster outwit a local business that pollutes or a dishonest politician? A schoolyard bully? A lunch thief? A cheater? **L2**

ASSESSMENT

Quick Checks, p. 37

Fine Art TRANSPARENCY 18

You may want to use ***Fine Art Transparency 18*** to discuss how animals inspire storytellers.

CONNECTING TO OTHER SELECTIONS

For a teaching strategy that connects this selection to "The Legend of Sleepy Hollow," see the ***Theme Eight Planning Guide.***

FANTASTIC CAPERS AND MISCHIEF MAKERS 421

Responding to the Selection

PERSONAL RESPONSE

Many students may prefer "Chicoria" because it has a more complex plot.

Analyzing Literature

1. The master suggests the competition, probably because he does not believe the New Mexicans have a chance.
2. Chicoria bets he can get the master to invite him to join him for dinner.
3. The unnamed character tells the *wasichu* that he knows someone who can outcheat him.
4. He says he doesn't have his cheating medicine.
5. Chicoria comes as a poet. He then undertakes the effort to make the master aware of the way he treats his guests and how he looks down on his workers.
6. Chicoria wins respect and twenty dollars.
7. The onlookers hope Coyote will outwit the *wasichu* because he has cheated them.
8. Coyote's original refusal "hooks" the *wasichu* and provides Coyote with a reason to borrow the horse and clothes.
9. In "Chicoria" the New Mexicans win because Chicoria proves their worth. In "Coyote and Wasichu" the onlookers win the chance to see the *wasichu* humiliated.
10. Students may say they have some sympathy for the landowner because he changes and becomes less haughty. They may not have much for the *wasichu* because he does not seem to change.

Active Reading and Critical Thinking

Responding to Literature

PERSONAL RESPONSE

◆ Which story do you find most interesting? Why?

Brackets connect questions that are paired to develop higher-level thinking skills.

Analyzing Literature

RECALL

1. In "Chicoria," who suggests the competition between poets? Why?
2. What is the subject of the bet made between the New Mexicans and Chicoria?
3. In "Coyote and Wasichu," who began the competition between the two main characters?
4. What is the first excuse Coyote offers when he refuses to try to cheat the *wasichu?*

INTERPRET

5. How does the reason for Chicoria's visit change?
6. What does Chicoria win in this tale?
7. Why do you think the onlookers encourage the contest between Coyote and *wasichu?*
8. Why is Coyote's original refusal to cheat important to the story?

EVALUATE AND CONNECT

9. In each of these stories, you find winners other than the **main characters.** Name these other winners and explain what they win.
10. Have you any sympathy for the *wasichu?* for the landowner in "Chicoria"? Explain.

LITERARY ELEMENTS

Hero

The term **hero** is often used in modern literature to refer to the main character in a work of fiction. However, in folktales, legends, and other older forms of writing, a hero often has superhuman abilities, represents the traits most admired by a society, and faces great odds in adventures or battles.

1. Explain why Chicoria may be considered a hero.
2. What characteristics of Coyote are admired by others in the story? Explain why you and your friends would admire these characteristics or would disapprove of them.

● See **Literary Terms Handbook,** p. R4.

LITERARY ELEMENTS

1. In a sense, Chicoria defends the honor of his fellow New Mexicans.
2. Coyote's cleverness and quick wit are admired. It might be fun to have a friend like Coyote because he could trick people who were not behaving. Still deviousness and dishonesty are not admirable qualities.

Additional Resources

Literary Elements Transparency 37

Literature and Writing

Writing About Literature

Dialogue and Narration Skim the two stories and note how the writers use both **dialogue** and **narrative passages** to tell each story. Is the conversation between characters more important in one tale than in the other? Does one story have more narrative paragraphs than the other? Write a brief analysis of each story, explaining how each writer chose to tell the tale.

Creative Writing

Getting Even Even today, some people feel that getting the better of another person is a fun thing to do. Look at the writing you did for the **Reading Focus** on page 418. With a partner, think of a situation in which a trickster must be dealt with. Using interesting and dramatic details, write a short story or play in which one character gets the better of an annoying pest. Read your story or dramatize your play for the class.

Extending Your Response

Literature Groups

Adventure Tales Tales of adventure have been told since storytelling began. Discuss modern stories that rely on adventures for their plots. Why do you think these stories are popular? Brainstorm to come up with a list of reasons with your group, then share them with the class.

Interdisciplinary Activity

Science Much modern fiction relies on science to provide a setting and a plot for exciting adventures. Read a short story or a novel by a well-known writer of science fiction: C. S. Lewis, Jules Verne, Madeleine L'Engle, Ray Bradbury, Robert Heinlein, or Isaac Asimov, for example. Then research one scientific statement or invention that is the basis for the story you chose. Was the adventure scientifically possible? Why or why not? Report on your conclusions.

Learning for Life

Catch a Cheater The people who watch the cheating match between Coyote and the *wasichu* would probably handle the situation differently today. Imagine that you are upset with the man at the trading post who brags about cheating his customers. Decide how to publicize his bad behavior in order to change it. Would you notify an investigative reporter at a television station? Tell your friends and classmates? Suggest the newspaper send a reporter? In a small group, discuss the best modern method for getting justice. Record your suggestion and share it with the class.

Reading Further

For modern tales of trickery, try:
The Maestro by Tim Wynne-Jones
The Westing Game by Ellen Raskin

Save your work for your portfolio.

Literature and Writing

Writing About Literature

Students' paragraphs should

- compare and contrast the stories' use of dialogue and narration

Creative Writing

Students' stories or plays should

- clearly show that the character tricked deserves what happens
- maintain a light-hearted tone

Extending Your Response

Literature Groups Encourage students to include movies as well as books. COLLAB. LEARN.

Interdisciplinary Activity You may point out to students that Jules Verne wrote about many inventions (the submarine, for example) that did not exist when he wrote but do now.

Learning for Life Suggest that students consider a protest march with signs or a Web page on the Internet.

Skill Minilessons

GRAMMAR AND LANGUAGE
USING VERB TENSE

1. There was a white man who was such a sharp trader that nobody ever got the better of him.
2. Every autumn he will go to New Mexico.
3. This is a story of a clever storyteller who uses his wits to win a bet.

READING AND THINKING
FINDING CLUES

Point out that in many tales the group a character belongs to can tell a great deal about why a trick is being played.

VOCABULARY
THE PREFIX *RE-*

1. again
2. back
3. back
4. again

Additional Resources

- ***Grammar and Composition Handbook,*** Lesson 3.9
- ***Grammar and Language Workbook,*** pp. 85–95
- ***Writer's Choice,*** Lesson 10.9
- ***Reading Skills Practice Workbook***

RETEACH • REVIEW

Skill Minilessons

GRAMMAR AND LANGUAGE • VERB TENSES

You know that the **present tense** of a verb names an action that is taking place at the time of the narrative. The **past tense** names an action that is finished. The **future tense** names an action not yet occurring. A good storyteller uses verb tenses carefully to help listeners keep track of the time in which actions take place.

- For more about verb tense, see **Language Handbook,** p. R34.

PRACTICE Rewrite the following sentences by substituting the tense shown in brackets for each verb in the sentence. Be sure the completed sentence will be clear to a reader.

1. [past] There is a white man who is such a sharp trader that nobody will ever get the better of him.
2. [future] Every autumn he goes to New Mexico.
3. [present] This was a story of a clever storyteller who used his wits to win a bet.

READING AND THINKING • FINDING CLUES

A folktale is usually brief, with little room for explanation of why characters behave as they do. As you read these stories, you may wonder why characters are trying to trick one another. There are clues to help you understand their actions. Descriptions, dialogue, and background information may contain clues, but you must read carefully to find them.

PRACTICE With a partner, select one of the two folktales you just finished reading. Look for words and phrases that explain the behavior of the trickster character. Examine what motivates the person against whom the trick is directed. Finally, read to see how the narrator tells you whose side other characters in the story are supporting and why.

- For more about reading strategies, see **Reading Handbook,** pp. R93–R108.

VOCABULARY • THE PREFIX *re-*

When the prefix *re-* is added to a word or root, it changes the meaning in one of two ways. *Re-* can mean either "again" or "back." If you *reread* a book, you read it again, but if you *repay* a loan, you pay it back, not again. Many words join the prefix *re-* to a root rather than to a whole word. In *refrain, re-,* meaning "back," is joined to a Latin root meaning "rein." So, if you *refrain* from an action, you keep yourself from doing it. In a sense, you pull back on the reins. There is also another meaning for *refrain*—a part of a song that is repeated. Here, *re-* has the "again" meaning.

PRACTICE Use your familiarity with the underlined words and the context clues to decide whether the prefix *re-* in each sentence means "again" or "back." Check your answers in a dictionary.

1. When the harvest was done the New Mexicans returned home.
2. The *wasichu* did not recover his clothes or his horse from the clever coyote.
3. The rancher reclined in a comfortable chair and listened to Chicoria's stories.
4. After the *wasichu* reviewed what happened, he knew that he had been tricked.

ASSESSMENT

- ***Quick Checks,*** p. 37
- ***Selection and Theme Assessment,*** pp. 65–66
- ***Performance Assessment,*** p. 35
- ***Testmaker: ExamView Pro***
- ***Interactive Tutor: Self-Assessment***

MEDIA Connection

NEWSPAPER ARTICLE

Are coyotes mischief makers, or are they dangerous creatures? Some people fear this cunning relative of the wolf.

Plucky Poodle Returns Alive After Dog-Napping by Coyotes

by Guy Kelly—*The Rocky Mountain News*, November 24, 1997

If only Henri could talk, what a tale he could tell. Henri, a 13-year-old toy poodle, was carried away last week by a pack of coyotes at Cherry Creek State Recreation Area.

John Turner says he was running in the park Wednesday morning when a half-dozen coyotes attacked Henri and dragged the poodle to what seemed a certain death. But Thursday afternoon, when Susan Turner pulled into the driveway of their Piney Creek home about three miles from the park, there was Henri, bloodied but unbowed.

"It's such a miracle this little dog could escape," Susan Turner said Sunday. "We were absolutely amazed he was able to get away and that he managed to find his way home, because he was really chewed up."

The Turners raced Henri to the Parker Center Animal Clinic, where the 13-pound, 8-ounce dog underwent surgery for three hours, emerging with 40 stitches, nine tubes sticking out of him to drain toxins, and a badly mangled coiffure.

But by Saturday, Henri was well enough to have some chow, and Sunday the petite but proud poodle seemed to have regained his attitude. He strutted about, his tiny torso criss-crossed with black stitches.

Henri probably will go home today, much to the relief of the Turners' two daughters, Freyja and Malaina, who have grown up with the dog.

"This is really one of those times when you wish the dog could talk," said veterinarian Kimberly Roberts. "He's a lucky dog." And plucky.

"He's always been around big dogs and he gets a lot of exercise," John Turner said. "He thinks he's a big dog. He's got an attitude."

Turner said he was running in the southeast corner of the park with Henri and his other two dogs—a Weimaraner and a Labrador retriever-Weimaraner mix—just before dawn Wednesday when the jogger behind him started yelling. One of about six coyotes had snatched Henri.

"We gave chase, but it wasn't quite light and they just went away so quickly all we could hear was the howls as they disappeared," Turner said.

The Turners, who moved to Colorado from Scotland two years ago, returned to the park several times Wednesday and Thursday, hoping to find some sign of Henri.

It's not unusual to see coyotes in the vast open spaces that make up much of the 3,900-acre park, Ranger Jason Trujillo said.

Analyzing Media

1. Why do you think Henri was able to come home alive?
2. How does this article relate to "Coyote and Wasichu"?

MEDIA Connection

Objective

- To learn strategies for reading a newspaper article

Literature LINK

Coyote and Wasichu Point out that the coyote in the story is able to defeat a richer, more powerful man, just as Henri is able to survive his contact with coyotes.

Analyzing Media

1. Henri has an arrogant attitude; he thinks he's a big dog.
2. The "underdog" wins.

Informational Text

*in*TIME For more examples of informational text, direct students to the articles in the *inTIME* magazine.

Additional Resources

Media Connections, p. 8

*inter*NET CONNECTION

Wildlife Encounters Have students use a search engine to look for other wildlife encounters. Suggest such key words as *Yellowstone National Park* or *Doug Peacock* (who studies grizzly bears).

Teaching Support

Reading *Minilesson*

Monitor Comprehension Good readers ask many questions of a newspaper article, and good writers answer them.

Activity Have students read this article paragraph by paragraph. Ask them to write one question that comes to mind at the end of each paragraph. When they have gone through the article this way, have them go back to see whether all their questions were answered somewhere in the article. **L2**

Additional Resources

Reading Skills Practice Workbook

Objectives

- To write a trickster tale of approximately 500 to 700 words
- To plan, draft, revise, edit, and present a trickster tale
- To reflect on and assess the tale

GLENCOE TECHNOLOGY

WRITER'S ASSISTANT CD-ROM

Students can use Glencoe's templates and guidelines software for writing fiction to help them work through the steps in the writing process in this lesson.

Teaching Strategies

PREWRITING

Sketch Your Trickster Suggest that students gather ideas by looking through picture books. Also suggest that they name their character. This will help them create a character who seems real.

Get Set Some students may wish to use a familiar setting. Others may prefer to either research an unknown place or use an imaginary place. Remind students that regardless of the setting, their stories will be more interesting if they include clear, consistent details.

Teaching Support

Writing WORKSHOP

Narrative Writing: Trickster Tale

Look out! You never know what might happen when a trickster is around. Now that you have met such characters as Lazy Peter and Coyote, try your hand at creating a trickster of your own.

Assignment: Follow the process in this Workshop to write an original trickster tale.

- As you write your trickster tale, refer to the **Writing Handbook**, pp. R50–R55.

EVALUATION RUBRIC

By the time you complete this Writing Workshop, you will have

- created a plot that includes a conflict, rising action, a climax, and a resolution
- used dialogue and specific actions to bring the characters to life
- used clear descriptions to develop the characters and setting
- used effective transitions to indicate changes in time or location
- presented a story that is free of errors in grammar, usage, and mechanics

The Writing Process

PREWRITING

PREWRITING TIP

For more ideas, read or listen to tales about such classic tricksters as Brer Rabbit, Grandmother Spider, Anansi, or Tortoise.

Sketch Your Trickster

Your trickster might be a relative of a character you have read about, or your unique creation. Sketching can help you find ideas. You might also try freewriting or brainstorming with friends. Think about your trickster's personality and appearance (human? animal? robot? computer?).

Get Set

Every tale needs a setting–a specific time and place for the action. You might set your tale in the past, present, or future; in your school, a nearby town, a faraway country, or an imaginary galaxy. A chart will help you plan your setting in detail.

Time: 1700s	Place: Gambia River, West Africa			
sights	sounds	smells	feelings	tastes
green, lush jungle murky river mud-colored cave walls trader's greedy eyes	river running mosquito whining	campfire smoke musty river smell	humid heat itchy mosquito bites	

MEETING INDIVIDUAL NEEDS

ENGLISH LANGUAGE LEARNERS

Planning a Trickster Tale English language learners who have lived in or visited other countries may find it easier to establish a setting if they use elements of some of those real places for their new tales. Students may also find it easier to write if they start with characteristics of some tricksters from their own cultures in the new tales.

Activity Allow English language learners to plan and prewrite in their first language. They can then work with partners who also speak the same language but are more proficient in English to translate their ideas. COLLAB. LEARN.

Additional Resources

English Language Learners Sourcebook

Plan Your Audience and Purpose

Will you write for people your own age, for people of all ages, or perhaps for young children? Will your goal be simply to entertain, or will your tale also teach a lesson? Plan how to reach your audience and achieve your purpose. Young children need simple words and sentences; older people might not understand current slang. Fast action and humor will help you entertain readers. If your story is meant to teach a lesson, you might add a moral at the end.

Devise a Plot

All good trickster tales involve a problem. Lazy Peter wants easy money. Coyote wants to get even with an arrogant person. Think of a problem that your trickster might solve. The problem and its outcome will form the plot of your tale. Put together your characters, setting, and plot to create a framework for drafting.

framework for drafting

Characters
Mosquito—trickster
Trader—greedy
Villagers—Mosquito's friends
Setting
Gambia River, 1700s, jungle and cave near the villagers' home
Plot
First: Trader plans to ambush villagers. Mosquito tells trader that villagers will hide in cave.
Next: Trader leads troops into cave. Many are lost in twisting passages.
Last: Villagers, hiding in jungle, escape.

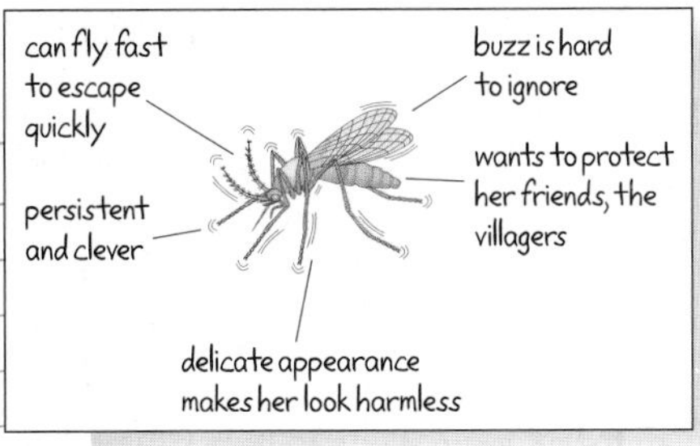

Plan Your Audience and Purpose Suggest that students write a word or two describing their audience and purpose at the top of a sheet of paper. Then have them list important points to consider in reaching the audience and achieving the purpose.

Devise a Plot Remind students that all plots are based on conflict and change. Usually the resolution of the conflict produces a change in the person, the situation, or the place. In addition, have students review techniques for advancing the plot. Remind them that narrative techniques can serve more than one purpose. Dialogue can both move the plot along and define a tale's characters. Clear descriptions of the characters and the scenery can make a tale more vivid and also help to explain why and how things happen.

Additional Resources

- ***Writing and Proofreading Practice,*** pp. 1–6, 28–34
- ***Writing and Proofreading Transparencies 1–6, 13–14, 31–32***
- ***Writer's Choice,*** Lessons 4.2, 4.4

MEETING INDIVIDUAL NEEDS — ADVANCED LEARNERS

Tricks and Morality Point out to students that the best trickster tales are those that have two important elements: The trickster is punishing someone for an immoral action, and the intended target is usually being drawn into the trick by his or her own immoral nature. A moral person would probably not be drawn into the trick. Remind them of the old saying "You can't cheat an honest man."

Activity Ask students who are more gifted writers to add a moral dimension to their tales. **L3**

DRAFTING

Use Time Order Suggest that students consider restricting their tale to a time frame of one day; it will be easier to keep track of events if the time covered is not too long.

Work with Dialogue Working with dialogue is easier if the writer knows some synonyms for *said.* Have students work in groups to brainstorm for as many words as they can think of to replace *said.* Suggest that they also check a synonym finder or a thesaurus for additional words.

REVISING

Once students have put down their basic story in first-draft form, have them explore ways to make the story more appealing to readers. Have them try combining, splitting, and otherwise rewriting sentences. A variety of sentence types keeps a story from seeming humdrum or flat.

GLENCOE TECHNOLOGY

REVISING WITH STYLE CD-ROM

Invite students to use the **Revising With Style** CD-ROM, which offers instruction and exercises to help students improve their writing skills.

Teaching Support

DRAFTING

DRAFTING TIP

Possible openers for your tale: an intriguing line of dialogue, a tense or funny scene, or a classic phrase, such as "Once upon a time" or "Long ago and far away."

Use Time Order

Write what happens first, next, and last in your tale. Include details from your prewriting notes so that readers can picture what you mean. Start a new paragraph whenever the time or place of the action changes. Transitions such as *after an hour, in the morning, near the river,* and so on, will keep your tale on track.

Work with Dialogue

Dialogue reveals characters' traits through their own words. It also keeps your writing from getting bogged down in explanations. For example, if you have your trickster shout, "Slow down! Look out for water snakes!" you can give clues about the setting and the action, as well as your character, through dialogue.

STUDENT MODEL • DRAFTING

"Say, Trader, would you like to make some more money?" whined a voice in the dark. Trader woke with a start. "Lie still!" warned the voice. "Just listen. You know the cave by the river?" Trader nodded as his eyes darted about. "It's full of passages," the voice hummed. "Villagers hide there."

Complete Student Model on p. R122.

REVISING

REVISING TIP

In dialogue don't overuse the vague word *said.* Use a thesaurus to find synonyms richer in sensory detail, such as *whispered, thundered, mumbled,* or *croaked.*

Look Again at Your Tale

After taking a break, reread your draft. Use the **Rubric for Revising** to plan changes that will improve your tale. Working with a partner can make revising easier.

You might jot your changes in the margins of your first draft. Or you might put aside your first draft, write a completely new second draft, and then compare the two.

RUBRIC FOR REVISING

Your revised tale should have
- a plot in which a trickster figure solves a problem
- dialogue that helps to define the characters and describe the action
- transitions that make it clear when the time or location of the story shifts
- well-chosen details and language to help readers picture the setting and characters

Your revised tale should be free of
- switches in the order of events
- errors in grammar, usage, and mechanics

Writing Minilesson

Strong Verbs Point out the importance of using strong verbs—rather than relying primarily on adjectives and adverbs—to make writing vivid. Write this example on the board. *The man walked with a limp, and his shaking hands could hardly hold his cane.* Then ask students how this sentence could be rewritten using stronger verbs. *The man hobbled along, and his hand trembled as he struggled to retain a grip on his cane.*

Activity Have students go through their drafts looking for opportunities to condense and strengthen their writing by using strong verbs and concrete details. **L2**

Additional Resources

Writer's Choice, Lesson 10.1

EDITING/PROOFREADING

Go over your revised tale once more to correct errors in grammar, usage, and mechanics. The **Grammar Link** on page 369 can help you make sure you are using irregular verbs correctly. When you proofread, use the **Proofreading Checklist** on the inside back cover of this book to look for one kind of error at a time.

PROOFREADING TIP
Scan your trickster tale to make sure that punctuation marks—especially quotation marks and commas for dialogue—are in the right places.

TECHNOLOGY TIP
Check your spelling by scrolling backwards on your computer so that reading your tale doesn't distract you.

Grammar Hint

To make sure you have used an irregular verb correctly, ask yourself which tense is needed in the sentence. Then look up the present tense of the verb in the dictionary. It will list all irregular tenses, as shown in the example below.

take (tāk) took, taken, taking

STUDENT MODEL • EDITING/PROOFREADING

Trader ~~taken~~ [took] the mosquito's advice and ~~goed~~ [went] to the cave.

Complete Student Model on p. R122.

Complete Student Model
For a complete version of the model developed in this Workshop, refer to **Writing Workshop Models**, p. R122.

PUBLISHING/PRESENTING

If possible, read your trickster tale aloud to your intended audience. Practice several times first, so that you know your tale almost by heart. Use the storytelling guidelines in the **Listening, Speaking, and Viewing** feature on page 376. After reading your story aloud, ask the audience for their reactions to help you identify ways to improve your story. Their feedback may lead you to reorganize your story to make it more effective, or to add or change words or sentences to make the story clearer.

PRESENTING TIP
Simple props can help you tell your tale. A square of cloth or a stick could represent several objects from your story.

Reflecting

Think about the following questions, and then write responses.

- How did you come up with the idea for your character?
- How is your tale like other trickster tales? How is it unique?

Save your work for your portfolio.

TECHNOLOGY TIP

A word processor allows students to revise their work by moving text. Students can also save several versions of a story by using the "save as" function available on most word-processing software. Suggest that students save multiple versions of their stories so they can see how their changes have improved their work.

EDITING/PROOFREADING

Have students exchange papers for proofreading. Often someone else will spot errors that the writer misses.

PRESENTING

If possible, videotape the presentations so students can review their presentations. Have them analyze their pace, tone, and enunciation so they can see how these elements affect the presentation.

Reflecting

Portfolio Encourage students to ask themselves these questions as they review their writing.

Does my tale
- capture and hold the reader's interest?
- have a clear beginning, middle, and end?
- use dialogue to reveal character?

6+1 TRAITS™ OF WRITING
See the annotated **Writing Workshop Models** on pp. R119–R130 for additional help in evaluating student writing and in teaching the **6+1 Traits™ of effective writing.** Annotations and minilessons address and reinforce the **6+1 Traits™**: Ideas, Organization, Voice, Word Choice, Sentence Fluency, Conventions, and Presentation.

ASSESSMENT

Writing Assessment and Portfolio Management
- Writing Assessment, pp. 1–12, 23–25
- Portfolio Management, pp. 42–48

Theme Assessment

Objectives
- To give a personal response to the stories, poems, folktales, and activities in this theme
- To compare and contrast the author's purpose in two folktales
- To complete a self-evaluation, set a goal, and devise a plan for achieving this goal

Responding to the Theme
1. Students should provide valid reasons for their choices
2. Students should use the ideas in the selection as stimulus for their own ideas
3. Students' presentations should help the audience understand more about folk heroes

Analyzing Literature
Students' writing should
- compare and contrast authors' purposes
- include quotations from the selections

Evaluate and Set Goals

Evaluate

Have students write a brief description of what they found most enjoyable and most difficult in this theme.

To help students formulate valid reasons for their ratings, you may wish to suggest that they develop a class rubric.

Set Goals

In a chart have students jot down their goals, the steps they will take for achieving them, and checkpoints. Discuss students' plans in individual conferences.

Theme Assessment

Responding to the Theme

1. Which story, poem, or folktale in this theme most helped you understand the meaning of "Fantastic Capers and Mischief Makers"?
2. What new thoughts do you have about the following ideas as a result of your reading this theme?
   - Folktales about fantastic creatures or mythical powers can motivate and inspire as well as entertain.
   - Greed can put people at the mercy of dishonest people.
   - Sometimes pranks can backfire.
3. Present your theme project to the class.

Analyzing Literature

CONSIDER THE AUTHOR'S PURPOSE

Some folktales teach lessons about human behavior. Others reveal the values of the society in which they originated; still others simply entertain. Choose two folktales from this theme. Compare and contrast the author's purpose for each.

Evaluate and Set Goals

1. Which of the following activities did you enjoy the most? Which did you find the most difficult?
   - reading and thinking about the selections
   - writing independently
   - analyzing and discussing the selections
   - presenting ideas and projects
   - researching topics
2. How would you assess your work in this theme, using the following scale? Give at least two reasons for your assessment.

   4 = outstanding   2 = fair
   3 = good   1 = weak
3. Based on what you found difficult in this theme, choose a goal to work toward in the next theme.
   - Write down your goal and three steps you will take to help you reach it.
   - Meet with your teacher to review your goal and your plan for achieving it.

Build Your Portfolio

SELECT

Choose two favorite pieces of work from this theme to include in your portfolio. The following questions can help you choose.
- Which turned out to be more challenging than you expected?
- Which did you learn the most from?

REFLECT

Write notes to accompany the pieces you selected. Use these questions to guide you.
- What do you like best about the piece?
- What did you learn from creating it?
- What might you do differently if you were beginning this piece again?

ASSESSMENT

Writing Assessment and Portfolio Management
- Writing Assessment, pp. 1–12
- Portfolio Management, pp. 42–48

GLENCOE TECHNOLOGY

MINDJOGGER VIDEOQUIZZES VIDEODISC

Use *MindJogger* to review the Theme 4 content.

Theme 4
Side A

Also available in VHS.

Reading on Your Own

If you enjoy tales of mischief and fantasy, you will also enjoy the following books.

When the Legends Die

by Hal Borland Left alone in the wilderness when his parents die, Thomas Black Bull uses the survival skills his mother has taught him. He eventually learns how to make his way in the world, facing mischief as well as suffering.

A String in the Harp

by Nancy Bond When Peter Morgan finds an ancient harp key, he enters a frightening world, moving between two historical periods and between the practical and the magical. Peter and his sisters must find the source of the mischief as they are threatened by the key, the past, and modern laws.

Nothing but the Truth: A Documentary Novel

by Avi Philip Malloy discovers how a single act of mischief can change his life and the lives of innocent people. Told through written announcements, journal entries, and newspaper articles—the story shows how lies and mistakes can pile up until few really know the truth.

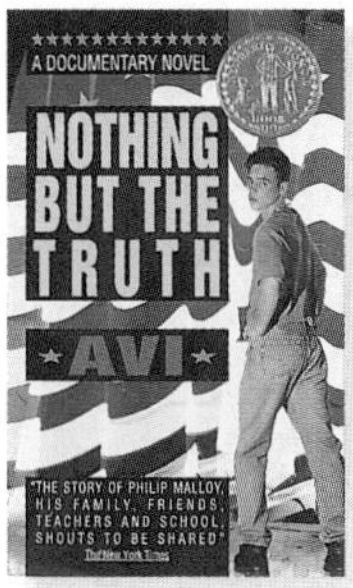

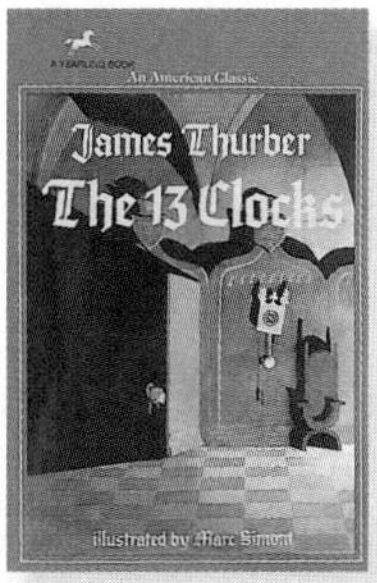

The Thirteen Clocks

by James Thurber This funny tale of mischief combines unusual language, a fantastic plot, and an intriguing cast of characters, including a princess and an evil duke.

MEETING INDIVIDUAL NEEDS — SPECIAL NEEDS

You may wish to recommend Avi's *Nothing but the Truth* to advanced readers. This fast-paced novel appears in short segments in various styles and requires a higher level of sophistication.

The books at the right are rated for average **(L2)** or less-proficient readers **(L1)**.

- *When the Legends Die* by Hal Borland **L2**
- *A String in the Harp* by Nancy Bond **L2**
- *The Thirteen Clocks* by James Thurber **L1**

Reading on Your Own

Tips for Independent Reading

Stress the importance of each student's spending at least a half-hour a day in independent reading and supply a list of readings related to the theme being studied. Review with students the strategy of recognizing and predicting a pattern in a folk story or a story involving mischief or magic. Help students to appreciate the clever variations in patterns that they can discover in the literature they read.

Practice Suggest that students keep brief notes on the familiar elements they discover as they read folktales, legends, and stories involving magic. Have them ask themselves why magic and fantasy are important elements in folk literature. They might also try to explain if and why they enjoyed this genre of literature. Provide opportunities for students to share their discoveries with the class.

Glencoe Literature Library

Nothing But the Truth by Avi is available in the *Glencoe Literature Library*. For a complete listing of the titles, see the **Glencoe Resources for Independent Reading** in the front of this book. The *Glencoe Literature Library Study Guide* provides instructional support and student activities for all titles in the *Glencoe Literature Library*.

At the MOVIES

Be sure to preview the following video for appropriateness for your class:

Aladdin, an animated film, is about a famous caper.

Standardized Test Practice

Answers and Analyses

1. C Students can eliminate choices A and D because there is nothing in the passage to support them. While choice B is a fact in the passage, encourage students to reread the relevant part of the text. They will see that just before Mr. C's comment, Mark is called into the office. The best choice, therefore, is C. Mr. C knew Mark was going to be punished, and this is the direct cause for wishing him luck.

2. K Remind students that they can often determine the meaning of figurative language by understanding its context. In paragraph ten, the narrator lists what he expects will happen to him as punishment because he has been punished similarly before. Therefore, students can infer that choice K is the best answer.

The Princeton Review TEST-TAKING TIP

Advise students to adapt their reading to the passage. If it is a story, they should try to predict what is going to happen as they're reading. If it is scientific or historical writing, students should look for facts. If it is a persuasive passage, students should try to discern what the author is trying to convince the reader to think or to do.

The Princeton Review TEST-TAKING TIP

Remind students that making mistakes during test-taking practice is actually helpful. Mistakes are good indications of what can be improved, and every mistake students make in class is one they can avoid on the actual test!

The Princeton Review

Standardized Test Practice

Read the following passage. Then read each question on page 433. Decide which is the best answer to each question. Mark the letter for that answer on your paper.

Anything But That

I knew from my first hour in school that this would not be one of my best days. But I had no idea how bad it would be. To begin with, I was embarrassed in history class when Ms. Samek called on me. Of course I didn't know the answer. I'd forgotten to read the assignment.

After class, she warned me. "Mark, you are not doing well this quarter and your progress report will reflect that. You aren't even doing enough to pass this class. Think about it and let's discuss the problem." She left me standing there, seriously worried.

Then, of course, I was thirty seconds late for English class. Mr. Parker glared. That was the third time in a week he had given me his famous "look." Could I help it if I had been late a few times?

"Robinson, get out!" he barked, and I headed for the office.

I settled into a chair to wait for Mr. Stolt, the assistant principal. As I sat there, Mr. C, the basketball coach, came in and gave me a small smile. I smiled back and tried to look as though I were in there for a great and noble reason, like winning a geography prize or something.

"What did you do?" he asked.

"Nothing!" I answered. He smiled again.

"Well, make sure you're rested for tomorrow night's game. We're counting on you for big points."

Just then, I was summoned into Mr. Stolt's office. "Good luck," said Mr. C.

I'd been in this room before, so I knew the drill. Mr. Stolt would make me go and apologize to Mr. Parker after school. I'd take a zero on any work I missed. I'd be given after-school detention. I'd promise that this would never happen again. Then I'd be on my way.

But it didn't go that way! "Mark, your grades have been slipping," were Mr. Stolt's first words. "Your careless attitude is affecting your school performance. I'm not going to give you a detention this time. But I'm going to forbid you to play in the last two regular-season basketball games. You've been warned and you need to learn that your actions have consequences."

I wanted to say that I was needed at the games. That these games would determine whether or not we would go to the playoffs. That I'd take any other punishment. But I couldn't get a word out.

"You may go back to class now," Mr. Stolt told me while I was still hunting for words that would make him change his mind. I left the office and stood in the hall, stunned. This was definitely not one of my best days.

MEETING INDIVIDUAL NEEDS — ENGLISH LANGUAGE LEARNERS

Journal English language learners can better relate to what is happening in the reading passage by reflecting on their own experiences at school. Ask these students to write a journal entry describing a typical day at their school. Have students write about all elements of their daily lives at school: friends, teachers, favorite subjects, and the physical surroundings of the building.

1 Why did Mr. C, the basketball coach, wish Mark luck?

A Mark was studying for a big test the next day.

B The team had a big game the next day.

C He knew Mark was about to see the assistant principal for punishment.

D Mr. C was a nice person and he wished everyone he saw good luck.

2 What does the author mean by "I knew the drill" in the tenth paragraph?

J "I knew the principal."

K "I knew what was going to happen."

L "I knew that I was in big trouble."

M "I knew I was sorry."

3 You can tell from this passage that the punishment Mr. Stolt assigned —

A was exactly what Mark expected.

B was worse than Mark expected.

C gave Mark a choice between a detention and not playing basketball.

D left Mark feeling lucky that he had a harsh, yet friendly assistant principal.

4 What is a FACT in the passage?

J During sixth period, Mark was dismissed from the office.

K Ms. Samek teaches history.

L Mark is an excellent student.

M Mark is the most important player on the basketball team.

5 What literary device does the author use to show Mark and Mr. Stoltz's interactions?

A Flashback

B Humor

C Repetition

D Dialogue

6 What is the main idea of the passage?

J A student who doesn't do all of his work will be rewarded.

K Mark is a good example of how a poor student can turn into a star athlete.

L A student learns a lesson about consequences.

M A coach figures out how to motivate a team to make it to the playoffs.

7 What feelings did Mark experience throughout the day?

A happiness and disappointment

B embarrassment and excitement

C disappointment and excitement

D embarrassment and disappointment

STOP

Answers and Analyses

3. B There are many clues in the story to suggest that Mark was expecting a different punishment than he received. He lists what he expects his punishment to be and then states, "But it didn't go that way!" Students can therefore discard choice A. There is nothing in the passage to support choices C or D. Choice B remains, and students should conclude that it is the best one.
4. K The correct answer is choice K, which is supported by evidence in the first paragraph. The other answer choices are unfounded.
5. D Through the process of elimination, students should be able to discard choices B and C. Choice A may be tempting, but even though Mark refers to past experiences in Mr. Stolt's office, there is no actual flashback. The use of dialogue is the primary literary device used to show interactions between characters.
6. L It is important that students be able to infer the underlying meaning of a text. They should look for a lesson or moral to point them toward that meaning. Choice K may be a tempting possibility, but the story is mostly about Mark's punishment, not his life as a star athlete. Furthermore, Mr. Stoltz tells Mark, "you need to learn that your actions have consequences." Choice L restates this lesson.
7. D At the beginning of the story, Mark says he felt "embarrassed" in history class. At the end of the story, he feels disappointed that he received a worse punishment than he expected. Therefore, the most reasonable inference is choice D.

Tested Objectives

Item	Reading Objective
1, 3, 4, 5, 7	Read and understand grade-level-appropriate material; describe and connect the essential ideas, arguments, and perspectives of text, as they relate to text structure, organization, and purpose; identify facts; and identify significant literary devices that define a writer's style
2	Use idioms, analogies, metaphors, and similes to infer the literal and figurative meanings of phrases
6	Compare original text to a summary for accuracy of the main ideas, inclusion of critical details, and the extent to which it conveys the underlying meaning of the original text

MORE PRACTICE

For additional practice, assign pages from one of the following standardized test resources available as part of Glencoe Literature.

Additional Resources

ITBS Preparation and Practice

SAT-9 Preparation and Practice

TerraNova Preparation and Practice

Theme 5 At a Glance

Free to Be

THEME OPENING

Theme 5: FREE TO BE

SELECTIONS

SKILL FEATURES

WRITING WORKSHOP

THEME ASSESSMENT

- **Responding to the Theme, Analyzing Literature, Evaluate and Set Goals** (p. 54)
- **Build Your Portfolio** (p. 544)
- **Reading on Your Own** (p. 545)
  Across Five Aprils by Irene Hunt
  Out of the Dust by Karen Hesse
  Laborers for Liberty: American Women 1865–1890 by Harriet Sigerman
  I Thought My Soul Would Rise and Fly: The Diary of Patsy, a Freed Girl by Joyce Hansen
- **Standardized Test Practice** (pp. 546–547)

KEYS TO LITERARY CONNECTIONS

Comparing Selections

The **Comparing Selections** feature in this theme provides opportunities for addressing diverse aspects of the reading and literature curriculum.

For example, in Comparing Selections on page 463, students examine characters and symbols in the poems "Paul Revere's Ride" and "Barbara Frietchie." Through this comparison, students can gain insight into the ways legendary characters enhance a country's patriotism.

World Literature

The Student Edition contains a variety of literature that represents cultures from around the world. World literature selections are highlighted with the icon above.

TEACHING SUPPORT

The Teaching Support offers a wealth of interactive instructional support:

Meeting Individual Needs
- Special Needs
- English Language Learners
- Multiple Modes of Expression
- Advanced Learners

Internet Connection

Assessment

Portfolio Options

Minilessons
- Grammar and Language
- Reading
- Writing
- Listening and Speaking

Connecting to Other Selections

Real-World Connection

Interdisciplinary Connection

Life Skills Connection

Family and Community Activity

Key to Ability Levels

The activities throughout this theme have been coded for students of various abilities.

L1 BASIC activities for all students

L2 AVERAGE activities for average to above-average students

L3 ADVANCED LEARNERS activities for above-average students

Teaching Today

The Glencoe *Teaching Today* professional development Web site at www.teachingtoday.glencoe.com features daily teaching tips, free downloads, annotated Web resources, educational news, and a wealth of information on a wide range of topics.

Reading Skills in this theme

Variety of Texts

In addition to short stories and historical fiction, this theme includes the following:

- comic strip
- radio transcript
- poetry
- speeches
- biography
- magazine article

Comprehension Skills

The following instructional support for comprehension skills appears in this theme of the Student Edition:

- **Active Reading Strategies and Model** (pp. 509–524)
- **Identifying Persuasive Techniques** (p. 525)
- **Reading and Thinking Minilessons** (pp. 446, 471, 491, 501, 507, 524, 538)

See also the **Reading Minilessons** throughout the theme in this Teacher Wraparound Edition.

For strategies for reading longer works, such as novels and novellas, see "Tips for Independent Reading" on page 545.

Reading Resources

Active Reading Guide The ***Active Reading Guide*** provides graphic organizers and study guide questions to support students' reading of each selection (***Active Reading Guide***, pp. 38–47).

Interactive Reading Sourcebook and **Interactive Reading Workbook** The ***Interactive Reading Sourcebook*** and ***Interactive Reading Workbook*** offer focused comprehension strategies and lessons on critical thinking skills as well as fluency practice and activities to teach and support phonics, decoding, spelling, and vocabulary development.

Vocabulary Power The ***Vocabulary Power*** workbook (Lessons 19–23) provides systematic teaching, practice, and assessment of vocabulary for better reading comprehension.

Audio Library Available on audiocassette and on CD, the ***Audio Library*** provides valuable comprehension support.

Glencoe Literature Library Each title in the ***Glencoe Literature Library*** includes a full-length work plus related readings. A separate Study Guide is available for each title.

Five–Star Stories These anthologies of familiar short stories adapted and abridged for a variety of reading levels include exercises to help increase students' vocabulary and improve their reading comprehension.

The Contemporary Readers ***The Contemporary Readers*** are nonfiction books linked to various themes and designed for developing readers from a wide range of backgrounds.

Literature Classics CD-ROM The selections on this CD-ROM can be searched by author, theme, or genre.

inTIME and **Humanities Across TIME** Coproductions of Glencoe and Time, Inc., these resources include a wealth of high-interest nonfiction related to the selections in this theme.

Assessment in this theme

Glencoe's Assessment Advantage

Assessment Options in the Student Edition

This program offers a number of diverse ways to evaluate student understanding and skill proficiency. In the Student Edition, use the following:

- **Responding to Literature**
  Following each selection, students are asked to recall facts, interpret ideas, and evaluate concepts as they answer a variety of questions and complete activities to extend their understanding.
- **Theme Assessment (pp. 544–545)**
  Here students respond to the selections on personal and analytical levels. They also assume ownership of their learning by setting and evaluating goals and by selecting work for their portfolios.

See also the many **Assessment Resources** listed on the facing page.

The Princeton Review

Standardized Test Practice

The Princeton Review has developed the Standardized Test Practice pages found at the end of this thematic unit (pp. 546–547). For additional practice, direct students to the following resources:

- ITBS Preparation and Practice
- SAT-9 Preparation and Practice
- TerraNova Preparation and Practice

Writing Skills in this theme

Writing Skills

The Student Edition of Theme 5 offers strong instructional support for writing skills:

In **Extending Your Response,** which follows each selection:

- **Writing About Literature**
- **Personal/Creative Writing**

See also the **Writing Minilessons** throughout the theme in this Teacher Wraparound Edition.

Writing Workshops

Theme 5 concludes with a Writing Workshop that guides students through the process for writing a speech (pp. 540–543).

Writing Resources

Writer's Assistant CD-ROM Each **Writing Workshop** is supplemented by an interactive writing guide on the ***Writer's Assistant*** CD-ROM. This easy-to-use writing guide provides prompts, templates, and other tools that lead students through the writing process.

Grammar and Composition Handbook The ***Grammar and Composition Handbook*** (Lessons 9.1–11.4) provides systematic instruction in English language conventions.

Spelling Power The ***Spelling Power*** workbook (Lessons 17–20) provides systematic teaching, practice, and assessment of spelling to help students become better spellers and thus enhance their writing.

Writing and Proofreading Practice Blackline masters present in-depth instruction and practice on a specific step in the writing process and proofreading (pp. 1–6, 15–16).

Writing and Proofreading Transparencies Transparencies provide graphic organizers and proofreading exercises for whole-class instruction (pp. 1–6, 15–16).

Research and Report Writing Guide This resource provides extensive tips and activities to guide students in their writing projects in the literature classroom as well as in classes across the curriculum.

Style and Documentation Sourcebook for Writers This sourcebook is a combination reference and workbook, giving students the most up-to-date information and guidance regarding traditional as well as technological research strategies and documentation.

Revising with Style This resource offers instruction and exercises focusing on the revision process and covering topics from proofreading and correcting common grammatical errors to sentence combining and reordering.

Assessment Resources

Selection Quick Checks For each selection, a **Quick Check** of three to five short-answer questions measures students' literal comprehension.

Selection and Theme Assessment The ***Selection and Theme Assessment*** instrument tests students' abilities to recall, interpret, and evaluate what they've read. The tests consist of multiple-choice, short answer, and essay questions.

Performance Assessment Alternative assessment instruments and rubrics for Theme 5 are found in the ***Performance Assessment*** ancillary.

Writing Assessment and Portfolio Management These notes and strategies, student models, and assessment tools assist with the task of measuring students' progress as writers and as monitors of their own writing.

Testmaker: ExamView Pro Teachers can customize selection and Theme 5 tests by accessing the ***Testmaker*** database.

Interactive Tutor: Self-Assessment The ***Interactive Tutor: Self-Assessment*** software provides multiple-choice tests with immediate feedback to help students evaluate their knowledge and understanding of each literature selection.

MindJogger Videoquizzes Using a popular game show format, ***MindJogger Videoquizzes*** on videocassettes enable teachers to evaluate student understanding of Theme 5 in a quick and fun manner.

Theme 5 SKILLS SCOPE AND SEQUENCE

Lessons	Literary Elements	Reading and Thinking	Writing
The Drummer Boy of Shiloh Ray Bradbury DRP: 52 Lexile: 780	Description, SE p. 444 *Description, TWE p. 440* *Mood, TWE p. 442*	Visualizing, SE p. 446 *Visualize, TWE p. 441* *Analyze Arguments, TWE p. 443*	Paragraph, SE p. 445 Friendly Letter, SE p. 445
Paul Revere's Ride Henry Wadsworth Longfellow	Meter, SE p. 455 *Meter, TWE pp. 450, 451, 453* *Imagery, TWE p. 450* *Alliteration, TWE p. 452*	Radio Transcript, SE p. 457 *Identify Author's Purpose, TWE p. 451* *Evaluate, TWE p. 454* *Activate Prior Knowledge, TWE p. 457*	Setting, SE p. 456 Children's Book, SE p. 456
Barbara Frietchie John Greenleaf Whittier	Rhyme, SE p. 462 *Rhymed Couplets, TWE p. 460* *Dialogue, TWE p. 461* *True Rhyme, TWE p. 461*	Comparing Selections, SE p. 463 *Evaluate, TWE p. 461* *Compare and Contrast, TWE p. 461*	Poem, SE p. 462
The Pinta, the Nina and the Santa Maria; and many other cargoes of Light John Tagliabue *and* **The Other Pioneers** Roberto Félix Salazar	Speaker, SE p. 470 *Speaker, TWE p. 467* *Characterization, TWE p. 468*	Elaboration, SE p. 471 *Evaluate, TWE p. 467* *Chronological Order, TWE p. 469*	Paragraph, SE p. 471 Poem, SE p. 471
The Gettysburg Address Abraham Lincoln DRP: 62 Lexile: 1320 *and* **O Captain! My Captain!** Walt Whitman	Author's Purpose, SE p. 476 *Author's Purpose, TWE pp. 473, 474, 475* *Allusion, TWE p. 473* *Metaphor, TWE p. 475*	*Evaluate, TWE p. 474* *Connecting, TWE p. 475*	Paragraph, SE p. 477 Description, SE p. 477
from **Harriet Tubman** Ann Petry DRP: 57 Lexile: 890	Point of View, SE p. 489 *Point of View, TWE pp. 481, 483, 484* *Motivation, TWE p. 485* *Repetition, TWE p. 485*	Magazine Article, SE p. 478 Using a Time Line, SE p. 491 *Evaluate, TWE p. 478* *Questioning, TWE p. 482* *Infer, TWE pp. 483, 487*	Paragraph, SE p. 490 Dialogue, SE p. 490 *Exposition, TWE p. 487*
I Have a Dream Martin Luther King Jr. DRP: 65 Lexile: 1010	Repetition, SE p. 499 *Repetition, TWE pp. 495, 496, 498* *Diction, TWE p. 498* *Allusion, TWE p. 498*	Analyzing Arguments, SE p. 501 *Use Text Structures, TWE p. 496*	Summary of a Speech, SE p. 500 Extension of a Speech, SE p. 500
Sorrow Home *and* **Sit-ins** Margaret Walker	Assonance, Consonance, and Alliteration, SE p. 506 *Contrast, TWE p. 504* *Assonance, TWE p. 504*	Questioning, SE p. 507 *Infer, TWE p. 505*	Paragraph, SE p. 507 Journal Entry, SE p. 507
The Battleground Elsie Singmaster DRP: 63 Lexile: 890	Historical Fiction, SE p. 508 Exposition, SE p. 522 *Personification, TWE p. 515* *Characterization, TWE p. 519*	Historical Fiction, SE p. 509 Activating Prior Knowledge, SE p. 524 Persuasive Techniques, SE p. 525 *Infer, TWE pp. 513, 515* *Predict, TWE p. 513* SN *Less-Proficient Readers, TWE p. 525*	Fiction Based on Historical Fact, SE p. 523 Journal Entries, SE p. 523 *Kinds of Writing, TWE p. 515*
from **Letters from Rifka** Karen Hesse DRP: 46 Lexile: 450	Narration, SE p. 536 *Narration, TWE pp. 529, 530, 531, 534* *Symbolism, TWE p. 530*	Paraphrasing, SE p. 538 *Comparison and Contrast, TWE p. 530* *Evaluate, TWE pp. 532, 533, 534*	Paragraph, SE p. 537 Narrative, SE p. 537 *Paraphrase, TWE p. 533* *Narrative Writing, TWE p. 539*
Writing Workshop Persuasive Writing: Speech			ELL *Speaking Before Writing, TWE p. 540* *Speech Writing, TWE p. 542*

Key: Student material is in roman. Teacher material is in italic. Technology ELL English Language Learners

Vocabulary and Spelling	Grammar and Language	Listening, Speaking, and Viewing	Life Skills; Study and Research; Technology
The Suffix *-ity*, SE p. 446 Using Homophones, SE p. 447	Adjectives, SE p. 446 ELL *Multiple-Meaning Words, TWE p. 440* *Pronouns as Objects of Prepositions, TWE p. 442*	Literature Groups, SE p. 445 News Broadcast, SE p. 445	History Research, SE p. 445 News Broadcast, SE p. 445 *Media Research, TWE p. 443*
	Capital Letters in Poetry, SE p. 456 ELL *Syntax, TWE p. 450* *Semicolons and Conjunctive Adverbs, TWE p. 454*	Literature Groups, SE p. 456	Internet Connection, SE p. 456 *Video, TWE p. 454* *Historic Timeline, TWE p. 456*
Multiple-Meaning Words, TWE p. 460	*Pronouns, TWE p. 460*	Literature Groups, SE p. 462	Database: Organizing and Grouping Data, SE p. 464
	ELL *Completing Sentences, TWE p. 467* *Irregular Verbs, TWE p. 468*	Literature Groups, SE p. 471	*Video, TWE p. 469*
The Latin Root *tract*, SE p. 477	ELL *Paraphrasing, TWE p. 473* *Noun Clauses, TWE p. 474*	Literature Groups, SE p. 477	*Video, TWE p. 475*
Multiple-Meaning Words, SE p. 491 ELL *Noun Suffixes* -ment *and* -ness, *TWE p. 481*	Proper and Common Nouns, SE p. 491 *Adverbs, TWE p. 488* ELL *Connotation and Denotation, TWE p. 490*	Literature Groups, SE p. 490 Weather Report, SE p. 490	Weather Report, SE p. 490 *Leading and Organizing, TWE p. 483* *Media Research, TWE p. 486*
Antonyms, SE p. 501 ELL *Root Words, TWE p. 495*	Punctuating Quotations, SE p. 501 *Future Tense of Verbs, TWE p. 498*	Literature Groups, SE p. 500 Reaching Your Audience, SE p. 502 ELL *Public Speaking Practice, TWE p. 502*	Social Studies, SE p. 492 Internet Connection, SE p. 500 Music Research, SE p. 500 *Social Studies Research, TWE p. 497*
	Prepositional Phrases, TWE p. 505	Literature Groups, SE p. 507 Poetry Reading, SE p. 507	
Base Words, SE p. 524 ELL *Prefixes, TWE p. 512* ELL *Linguistic, TWE p. 514* *Word Origins, TWE p. 515*	Numbers, SE p. 524 *Using Apostrophes, TWE p. 520*	Literature Groups, SE p. 523 ELL *Historical Fiction, TWE p. 508* *Reenactment, TWE p. 518* SN *Emotional/Learning Disabled, TWE p. 519*	Newspaper Page, SE p. 523 *Social Studies Research, TWE p. 516* *Social Studies Research, TWE pp. 517, 521*
Word Parts that Express Size, SE p. 538	Using Apostrophes, SE p. 538 Using Pronouns Correctly, SE p. 539 *Direct Objects, TWE p. 534*	Literature Groups, SE p. 537 ELL *Social Adjustment, TWE p. 528* SN *Emotional, TWE p. 529*	Plan a Trip, SE p. 537 Internet Connection, SE p. 537 *Social Studies Research, TWE pp. 531, 535*
		ELL *Speaking Before Writing, TWE pp. 540, 541*	

SN Special Needs/Strategic Intervention

Theme 5 RESOURCE MANAGER

Lessons	Essential Resources		English Language Learners
The Drummer Boy of Shiloh RAY BRADBURY PACING: 2 DAYS	**Lesson-Specific Instruction** Selection Focus Transp. 37 * Active Reading Guide, p. 38 Literary Elements Transp. 38 Vocabulary Practice, p. 27 * Quick Checks, p. 38 Selection and Theme Assessment, pp. 67–68	Testmaker: ExamView Pro Performance Assessment, p. 36 **Systematic Language Instruction** Grammar and Comp. Hbk., L. 9.1 Vocabulary Power, Lesson 19 Spelling Power, Lesson 17	English Language Learners Sourcebook, pp. 59–60 Theme Five Planning Guide, p. 6 Spanish Summaries, p. 37 Spanish Translations, pp. 95–99 * Audio Library English, Yes!
Paul Revere's Ride HENRY WADSWORTH LONGFELLOW PACING: 2 DAYS	**Lesson-Specific Instruction** Selection Focus Transp. 38 * Active Reading Guide, p. 39 Literary Elements Transp. 39 * Quick Checks, p. 39 Selection and Theme Assessment, pp. 69–70	Testmaker: ExamView Pro Performance Assessment, p. 37 **Systematic Language Instruction** Grammar and Comp. Hbk., L. 9.2	English Language Learners Sourcebook, p. 61 Spanish Summaries, p. 38 * Audio Library English, Yes!
Barbara Frietchie JOHN GREENLEAF WHITTIER PACING: 2 DAYS	**Lesson-Specific Instruction** Selection Focus Transp. 39 * Active Reading Guide, p. 40 Literary Elements Transp. 40 * Quick Checks, p. 40 Selection and Theme Assessment, pp. 69–70	Testmaker: ExamView Pro Performance Assessment, p. 37 **Systematic Language Instruction** Grammar and Comp. Hbk., L. 9.3	Theme Five Planning Guide, p. 22 Spanish Summaries, p. 39 * Audio Library English, Yes!
The Pinta, the Nina and the Santa Maria; and many other cargoes of Light JOHN TAGLIABUE *and* **The Other Pioneers** ROBERTO FÉLIX SALAZAR PACING: 1 DAY	**Lesson-Specific Instruction** Selection Focus Transp. 40 * Active Reading Guide, p. 41 Literary Elements Transp. 41 * Quick Checks, p. 41 Selection and Theme Assessment, pp. 71–72	Testmaker: ExamView Pro Performance Assessment, p. 38 **Systematic Language Instruction** Grammar and Comp. Hbk., L. 10.1–10.2 Vocabulary Power, Lesson 20 Spelling Power, Lesson 18	English Language Learners Sourcebook, p. 62 Theme Five Planning Guide, p. 29 Spanish Summaries, p. 40 * Audio Library English, Yes!
The Gettysburg Address ABRAHAM LINCOLN *and* **O Captain! My Captain!** WALT WHITMAN PACING: 1 DAY	**Lesson-Specific Instruction** Selection Focus Transp. 41 * Active Reading Guide, p. 42 Literary Elements Transp. 42 Vocabulary Practice, p. 28 * Quick Checks, p. 42 Selection and Theme Assessment, pp. 73–74	Testmaker: ExamView Pro Performance Assessment, p. 39 **Systematic Language Instruction** Grammar and Comp. Hbk., L. 10.3–10.4	English Language Learners Sourcebook, p. 63 Spanish Summaries, p. 41 Spanish Translations, pp. 100–101 * Audio Library English, Yes!

Key: Workbook   Blackline Masters   Textbook   Transparency   CD-ROM   Videodisk (also available in videocassette)

Special Needs/ Strategic Intervention	Reteaching and Enrichment
Interactive Reading Sourcebook, pp. T143–T145 Interactive Reading Workbook, pp. 72–73 Inclusion Strategies Sourcebook, pp. 31–32 Theme Five Planning Guide, p. 6 * Audio Library	Literature Launchers, Side B, Segment 13 Reading Skills Practice Workbook pp. 71–72 Grammar and Language Transp. 35 Gr. and Lang. Wkbk., pp. 121–122, 143–144 Grammar and Comp. Hbk., L. 4.2, 5.1 Interactive Tutor: Self-Assessment Vocabulary PuzzleMaker Web Site (lit.glencoe.com)
Interactive Reading Sourcebook, pp. T146–T148 Interactive Reading Workbook, pp. 74–75 Theme Five Planning Guide, p. 14 * Audio Library	Literature Launchers, Side B, Segment 15 Fine Art Transparency 31 Reading Skills Practice Workbook pp. 73–74 Grammar and Language Transp. 36 Gr. and Lang. Wkbk., p. 265 Grammar and Comp. Hbk., L. 7.6, 13.5 Media Connection Activities, p. 9 Interactive Tutor: Self-Assessment Vocabulary PuzzleMaker Web Site (lit.glencoe.com)
Interactive Reading Sourcebook, pp. T149–T151 Interactive Reading Workbook, pp. 76–77 Inclusion Strategies Sourcebook, pp. 77–78 Theme Five Planning Guide, p. 22 * Audio Library	Reading Skills Practice Workbook pp. 75–76 Grammar and Language Transp. 37 Gr. and Lang. Wkbk., pp. 107–108, 113–114 Grammar and Comp. Hbk., L. 4.1, 4.4 Interactive Tutor: Self-Assessment Vocabulary PuzzleMaker Web Site (lit.glencoe.com)
Interactive Reading Sourcebook, pp. T151–T154 Interactive Reading Workbook, p. 78 * Audio Library	Reading Skills Practice Workbook pp. 77–78 Grammar and Language Transp. 38 Gr. and Lang. Wkbk., pp. 99–104 Grammar and Comp. Hbk., L. 3.11 Interactive Tutor: Self-Assessment Vocabulary PuzzleMaker Web Site (lit.glencoe.com)
Interactive Reading Sourcebook, pp. T154–T157 Interactive Reading Workbook, pp. 79–80 Inclusion Strategies Sourcebook, pp. 45–46, 77–78 Theme Five Planning Guide, p. 35 * Audio Library	Reading Skills Practice Workbook pp. 79–80 Grammar and Language Transp. 39 Gr. and Lang. Wkbk., pp. 165–166 Grammar and Comp. Hbk., L. 8.6 TIME *Humanities Across TIME*, Cover 6 Interactive Tutor: Self-Assessment Vocabulary PuzzleMaker Web Site (lit.glencoe.com)

Web   Audiocassette   Diskette   *Also available in Spanish

INDEPENDENT READING

Encourage students to spend thirty minutes each day in independent reading. The following Glencoe components and outside resources provide opportunities for reading related to this theme.

The Glencoe Literature Library

You may want to assign one or more of these titles for independent reading. For a complete listing of titles available in the Glencoe Literature Library, see page T94 of this book.

- *Johnny Tremain* by Esther Forbes
- *The Slave Dancer* by Paula Fox
- *Sounder* by William H. Armstrong
- *Across Five Aprils* by Irene Hunt
- *Letters from Rifka* by Karen Hesse

inTIME Magazine News stories, feature articles, reviews, profiles, and essays in the magazine connect to an author, work, or theme in the Student Edition. See the ***inTIME* Teacher's Guide** for specific connections to this theme.

Resources for Less-Proficient Readers

For reading especially created for less-proficient readers, suggest

- *Five-Star Stories*
- *The Contemporary Readers*

Additional Resources for Independent Reading

The following titles are listed with specific reading selections throughout this theme. You may want to suggest that students look for these in your local or school library.

- *The Forty-Third War* by Louise Moeri
- *The Courtship of Miles Standish* by Henry Wadsworth Longfellow
- *Till Victory Is Won* by Zak Mettger
- *Grand Mothers* edited by Nikki Giovanni
- *They Had a Dream* by Jules Archer
- *Mine Eyes Have Seen the Glory* by Ann Rinaldi
- *Migrant Workers: Temporary People* by Linda Altman
- *Out of the Dust* by Karen Hesse
- *Laborers for Liberty: American Women 1865–1890* by Harriet Sigerman
- *I Thought My Soul Would Rise and Fly: The Diary of Patsy, a Freed Girl* by Joyce Hansen

RESOURCE MANAGER (continued)

Lessons	Essential Resources		English Language Learners
from **Harriet Tubman** Ann Petry Pacing: 2 Days	**Lesson-Specific Instruction** Selection Focus Transp. 42 * Active Reading Guide, p. 43 Literary Elements Transp. 43 Vocabulary Practice, p. 29 * Quick Checks, p. 43 Selection and Theme Assessment, pp. 75–76	Testmaker: ExamView Pro Performance Assessment, p. 40 **Systematic Language Instruction** Grammar and Comp. Hbk., L. 10.5 Vocabulary Power, Lesson 21 Spelling Power, Lesson 19	English Language Learners Sourcebook, p. 64 Spanish Summaries, p. 42 Spanish Translations, pp. 102–108 * Audio Library English, Yes!
I Have a Dream Martin Luther King Jr. Pacing: 2 Days	**Lesson-Specific Instruction** Selection Focus Transp. 43 * Active Reading Guide, p. 44 Literary Elements Transp. 44 Vocabulary Practice, p. 30 * Quick Checks, p. 44 Selection and Theme Assessment, pp. 77–78	Testmaker: ExamView Pro Performance Assessment, p. 41 **Systematic Language Instruction** Grammar and Comp. Hbk., L. 11.1 Vocabulary Power, Lesson 22 Spelling Power, Lesson 20	English Language Learners Sourcebook, pp. 65, 66 Spanish Summaries, p. 43 Spanish Translations, pp. 109–112 * Audio Library English, Yes!
Sorrow Home *and* **Sit-ins** Margaret Walker Pacing: 1 Day	**Lesson-Specific Instruction** Selection Focus Transp. 44 * Active Reading Guide, p. 45 Literary Elements Transp. 45 * Quick Checks, p. 45 Selection and Theme Assessment, pp. 79–80	Testmaker: ExamView Pro Performance Assessment, p. 42 **Systematic Language Instruction** Grammar and Comp. Hbk., L. 11.2 Vocabulary Power, Lesson 23	English Language Learners Sourcebook, p. 67 Spanish Summaries, p. 44 * Audio Library English, Yes!
The Battleground Elsie Singmaster Pacing: 3 Days	**Lesson-Specific Instruction** Selection Focus Transp. 45 * Active Reading Guide, p. 46 Literary Elements Transp. 46 Vocabulary Practice, p. 31 * Quick Checks, p. 46 Selection and Theme Assessment, pp. 81–82	Testmaker: ExamView Pro Performance Assessment, p. 43 **Systematic Language Instruction** Grammar and Comp. Hbk., L. 11.3	English Language Learners Sourcebook, p. 68 Spanish Summaries, p. 45 * Audio Library English, Yes!
from **Letters from Rifka** Karen Hesse Pacing: 3 Days	**Lesson-Specific Instruction** Selection Focus Transp. 45 * Active Reading Guide, p. 46 Literary Elements Transp. 46 Vocabulary Practice, p. 31 * Quick Checks, p. 46 Selection and Theme Assessment, pp. 81–82	Testmaker: ExamView Pro Performance Assessment, p. 43 **Systematic Language Instruction** Grammar and Comp. Hbk., L. 11.3	English Language Learners Sourcebook, p. 68 Spanish Summaries, p. 45 * Audio Library English, Yes!
Writing Workshop Persuasive Writing: Speech Pacing: 2 Days	Writing Assessment and Portfolio Management, pp. 1–13, 26–28, 41–48		English Language Learners Sourcebook, p. 9 English, Yes!

Key: Workbook · Blackline Masters · Textbook · Transparency · CD-ROM · Videodisk (also available in videocassette)

Special Needs/ Strategic Intervention	Reteaching and Enrichment
Interactive Reading Sourcebook, pp. T157–T159 Interactive Reading Workbook, pp. 81–82 Inclusion Strategies Sourcebook, pp. 63–64 Theme Five Planning Guide, p. 41 * Audio Library	Literature Launchers, Side B, Segment 14 Reading Skills Practice Workbook, pp. 81-82 Grammar and Language Transp. 40 Gr. and Lang. Wkbk., pp. 61–62, 129–133 Grammar and Comp. Hbk., L. 2.1, 6.1–6.3 Media Connection Activities, p. 10 TIME *Humanities Across TIME*, Covers 6, 11 Interactive Tutor: Self-Assessment Vocabulary PuzzleMaker Web Site (lit.glencoe.com)
Interactive Reading Sourcebook, pp. T160–T162 Interactive Reading Workbook, pp. 83–84 Inclusion Strategies Sourcebook, pp. 65–66 Theme Five Planning Guide, p. 49 * Audio Library	Reading Skills Practice Workbook, pp. 83-84 Grammar and Language Transp. 41 Gr. and Lang. Wkbk., pp. 95–96, 267–268 Grammar and Comp. Hbk., L. 3.9, 13.6 TIME *Humanities Across TIME*, Cover 5 Interactive Tutor: Self-Assessment Vocabulary PuzzleMaker Web Site (lit.glencoe.com)
Interactive Reading Sourcebook, pp. T163–T164 Interactive Reading Workbook, p. 85 Theme Five Planning Guide, p. 57 * Audio Library	Grammar and Language Transp. 42 Gr. and Lang. Wkbk., pp. 141–142 Grammar and Comp. Hbk., L. 7.1 TIME *Humanities Across TIME*, Cover 2 Interactive Tutor: Self-Assessment Vocabulary PuzzleMaker Web Site (lit.glencoe.com)
Interactive Reading Sourcebook, pp. T165–T167 Interactive Reading Workbook, pp. 86–87 Theme Five Planning Guide, p. 63 * Audio Library	Reading Skills Practice Workbook, pp. 85-86 Grammar and Language Transp. 43 Gr. and Lang. Wkbk., pp. 269–270, 275–276 Grammar and Comp. Hbk., L. 13.7, 13.10 TIME *Humanities Across TIME*, Cover 8 Interactive Tutor: Self-Assessment Vocabulary PuzzleMaker Web Site (lit.glencoe.com)
Interactive Reading Sourcebook, pp. T167–T169 Interactive Reading Workbook, pp. 86–87 Theme Five Planning Guide, p. 71 * Audio Library	Reading Skills Practice Workbook, pp. 87-88 Grammar and Language Transp. 44 Gr. and Lang. Wkbk., pp. 77–78, 269–270 Grammar and Comp. Hbk., L. 3.2, 13.7 TIME *Humanities Across TIME*, Cover 15 Interactive Tutor: Self-Assessment Vocabulary PuzzleMaker Web Site (lit.glencoe.com)
	Writing and Proofreading Practice, pp. 1-6, 35-41 Writing and Proofreading Transparencies 1-6, 15-16, 33-34 Revising with Style Writer's Assistant

Theme RESOURCES

To explore the theme further, you may want to use these resources:

- Listening and Speaking Activities (pp. 13–15
- Viewing and Representing Activities (pp. 1–6, 19–21)
- Critical Thinking Skills (pp. 12–14)
- Media Connection Activities, (pp. 9–10)
- Interdisciplinary Activities (pp. 18–21)
- Family and Community Activities (p. 25)
- Selection and Theme Assessment (pp. 67–84, 133–134)
- Performance Assessment (pp. 68, 93)

TIME Humanities Across TIME

See also these additional theme planning resources:

- Theme Five Planning Guide
- Interactive Reading Sourcebook
- Literature Groups Sourcebook
- Interactive Lesson Planner
- Interactive Teacher Edition
- Glencoe Web Site (lit.glencoe.com)

PRESENTATION Plus!

Use Glencoe's ***Presentation Plus!*** This multimedia teaching tool lets you present dynamic lessons that will engage your students. Using Microsoft PowerPoint®, you can customize the presentation to create your own personalized lessons.

Web Audiocassette Diskette *Also available in Spanish

THEME 5

Free to Be

Theme Objectives

- To enjoy reading about what freedom has meant to Americans over the centuries
- To analyze the literary elements in fiction, poetry, and speeches
- To apply strategies for reading historical fiction, poetry, and speeches

Teaching Strategies

Have students read the quotation from *Harriet Tubman: Conductor on the Underground Railroad* in preparation for the discussion questions below.

Viewing the Painting

Dane Tilghman's work has celebrated African American history, has been exhibited at the Afro-American Historical and Cultural Museum in Philadelphia, has appeared on "The Cosby Show," and has been featured in newspapers and magazines.

Responding to the Art Discussion questions:

- Why do you suppose this painting is titled *We the People*? *(The faces reflect the diversity of Americans, and the flag is patriotic, like the words* we the people, *which are taken from the Declaration of Independence.)*
- Is dust valuable? *(Discuss the fact that dirt would be a meaningful symbol for many of Harriet Tubman's people who spent their lives working in agricultural jobs—working in dirt that belonged to someone else.)*

Free to Be

"Freedom's not bought with dust."

–Ann Petry, from *Harriet Tubman: Conductor on the Underground Railroad*

We the People, 1986. Dane Tilghman. Watercolor and pencil, 30 x 60 in. Courtesy of the artist.

TEACHER *to* TEACHER

Hettinger High School • Hettinger, North Dakota

On a large sheet of butcher paper, I write the words *FREE TO BE* vertically. I use this vertical set of letters to create a poem horizontally. For each letter, students add a word that to them represents the theme. We end up with a poem the whole class wrote that expresses what the students feel it means to be free. In addition, we cut out words from newspapers and magazines that represent the theme "Free to Be." We then create a collage with the words and display it with the poem.

—Bonnie Mae Smith

THEME 5

THEME CONTENTS

GENRE FOCUS *HISTORICAL FICTION*

Introducing Theme 5

Direct your students' attention to the **Theme Contents.** Ask them to read through the list of selections. Present these questions for discussion:

- On the basis of the titles and what you know about some of the people whose names are mentioned in the titles or as authors, what do many of the selections seem to have in common? *(Students may say that many of the selections deal with events in American history.)*
- What differences do you see among the selections? *(Students may note that different literary genres, different periods in American history, different sexes, and different ethnic backgrounds are represented.)*
- Which selection listed interests you the most? Which selection interests you the least? Why?

LITERATURE & HUMANITIES

American Music: Play "British Grenadiers," Vol. 1, Track 6, to introduce students to the music of the times.

GLENCOE TECHNOLOGY

LITERATURE CLASSICS CD-ROM

Search for other selections related to the theme "Free to Be."

RESOURCE MANAGER

See the ***Theme Five Planning Guide*** for additional teaching notes, strategies, and resources for introducing the theme of "Free to Be."

Exploring the Theme

Free to Be

- Students may tend to focus on individual freedom rather than the freedom of nations because they have come to take political freedom for granted in the modern world.
- Students may also note that freedom is never complete. Along with freedom comes responsibility—and infringing on the rights of others is not tolerated even if that means limiting some rights.

Oliver Wendell Holmes said that we are free to say what we want, but we aren't free to yell fire in a crowded theater because we would cause a dangerous panic. Share this explanation of the limitations on freedom of speech as a way of illustrating the scope of personal freedom in a democratic society.

Starting Points

One Person's Freedom

Call attention to Calvin's statement in the comic strip and ask students what aspect of the statement might impress a teacher. *(He is able to cite excellent references to support his claim to freedom.)*

- Suggest that students tell how they would explain to Calvin why the freedom he is seeking is denied him.
- Encourage students to describe other situations in which freedom was denied, demanded, and won.

Independence Day

Emphasize that students should illustrate both feelings (independence and responsibility) in their art.

Exploring the Theme

Free to Be

The pursuit of freedom can be a source of conflict and satisfaction. It may involve groups of people, such as American colonists fighting for independence from England. It also can be personal, as in the freedom to pursue one's dreams. The selections in "Free to Be" touch on both aspects of freedom. Choose an activity below to begin thinking about what freedom means to different people in different situations.

Starting Points

ONE PERSON'S FREEDOM . . .

In the comic strip "Calvin and Hobbes," Calvin thinks that his "rights" will free him from doing schoolwork. Sometimes, one person's pursuit of freedom may conflict with rules of society or the rights of others.

- Think of a time when the pursuit of freedom by one person or a group of people caused problems for others. Describe the situation.

INDEPENDENCE DAY

Recall a time when you achieved some independence, such as the first time you were allowed to buy your own clothes.

- Was your feeling of independence accompanied by a feeling of responsibility? Create a piece of art that expresses your feelings about the experience.

CALVIN AND HOBBES ©1992Watterson. Reprinted with permission of UNIVERSAL PRESS SYNDICATE. All rights reserved.

Family and Community Activity

"Meaning of Freedom" Interview Ask students to interview a broad spectrum of people about their concept of freedom. What is it? Why is it important? Some possible interview subjects include local politicians, parents, grandparents, military veterans, teachers, and peers. Encourage creativity in the presentation of the interview information: students may use charts and graphs, pictures, or any other method they choose. **L2**

Additional Resources

Family and Community Activities, p. 25

Theme Projects

Choose one of the projects below and complete it as you read the selections in this theme. Work on your own, with a partner, or with a group.

CRITICAL VIEWING

Signs of the Times

1. Gather books and newspaper articles about a war or other conflict involving the United States.
2. Find images, such as posters, political cartoons, and signs, that express support for–or objection to–the conflict.
3. Discuss these questions: Can both sides of a conflict seek or represent freedom? How did the opposing groups in the conflict use ideas about freedom to appeal to their audience?
4. Plan a presentation that describes the conflict and the ideas that both sides had about freedom.

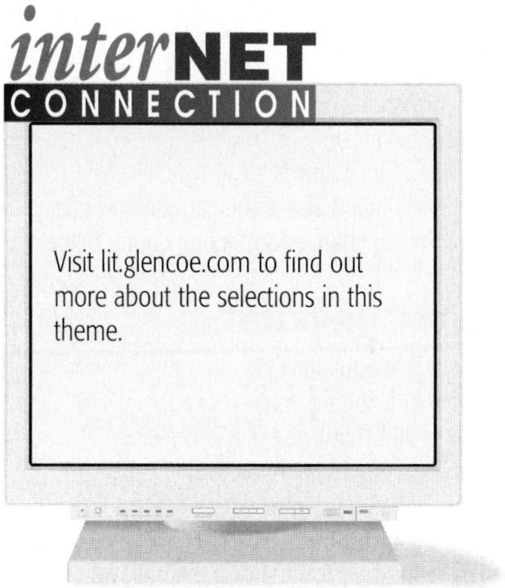

LEARNING FOR LIFE

A Right or a Privilege?

1. Discuss the difference between a right and a privilege. Then, with a group, list some of the rights that U.S. teenagers enjoy. Divide your list into various topics, such as education, recreation, and employment.
2. Now make a list of privileges that young people in the United States enjoy.
3. Research another country, such as Russia or China. What rights and privileges do teenagers from this country have?
4. Share your conclusions with the class. Include visuals, such as a chart that compares and contrasts rights for teenagers in both countries.

MULTIMEDIA PROJECT

A Case for the First Amendment

1. With a group, read the First Amendment to the U.S. Constitution from a social studies book. Discuss the wording of this law, which grants citizens the freedom of speech and expression.
2. Gather video clips, audiotapes, and photos that show people exercising their right of free speech in an inoffensive way.
3. For each item you gather, write a few sentences explaining its importance and why it shows the need for the First Amendment.
4. Organize your work, and then use HyperStudio or similar software to create a multimedia presentation.

Theme Projects

Teaching Strategies

The following suggestions may help your students plan and carry out their theme projects.

Critical Viewing

- Tell students that Web Sites provide information about most conflicts.
- Emphasize that few people willingly fight *for* oppression. Conflicts stem generally from different definitions of, or disagreements about how to achieve, freedom.

Learning for Life

- You may mention that teenage driving is a privilege, not a right. Recent court cases have upheld teenagers' rights to free speech and freedom from unreasonable search and seizure.
- Note that a privilege can be revoked. A right cannot be revoked but may be limited.
- Encourage students to keep an open mind about other countries. A limitation of one privilege may strengthen another.
- Ensure that charts distinguish between rights and privileges.

Multimedia Project

- Point out that the First Amendment articulates a right whose precise meaning continues to evolve.
- Note that what is offensive to one person may not be to another.
- Before they write, ask students why freedom of speech is protected.
- Point out that presentations may be organized chronologically, by theme, or by comparison and contrast.

interNET CONNECTION

Glencoe Literature Web Site

For other ideas related to the theme "Free to Be," students can type such keywords as *freedom* or *Bill of Rights* into a search engine.

Additional Resources

- ***Interdisciplinary Activities,*** pp. 18–21
- ***Viewing and Representing Activities,*** pp. 1–5, 19–21
- ***Listening and Speaking Activities,*** pp. 13–15
- ***Critical Thinking Skills,*** pp. 12–14
- ***Selection and Theme Assessment,*** pp. 67–84, 133–134
- ***Performance Assessment,*** pp. 36–44, 68

Before Reading

Objectives

- To read and analyze a short story about a Civil War drummer boy awaiting his first battle
- To learn how writers use descriptive language to help readers experience the events of a story
- To write an analytical essay

Skills

Reading/Thinking: Analyzing Arguments; Visualizing
Writing: Personal Letter
Vocabulary: The Suffix *-ity*
Grammar/Language: Adjectives; Pronouns as Objects of Prepositions
Collaboration: Literature Groups

Motivating → STUDENTS

Literature Launchers: "A Visit to Shiloh"

Videodisc Side B, Segment 13

Also available in VHS.

Selection Focus Transparency 37: After viewing the painting, have students discuss the differences between war today and in the 1800s.

Reading Focus: As an extension of the Reading Focus, have pairs of students share their coping strategies in small groups.

Before You Read

The Drummer Boy of Shiloh

MEET RAY BRADBURY

Ray Bradbury is often referred to as the greatest living science fiction writer, but he has written about all sorts of subjects—most of which express his flair for revealing human nature. Whether writing about the past or the future, Bradbury says, "Everything's play. If you work at it, it turns into rocks and dust. Everything must be approached happily, for having a lot of fun—even the most serious thing."

Ray Bradbury was born in 1920. "The Drummer Boy of Shiloh" was first published in the Saturday Evening Post *in 1960.*

READING FOCUS

What feelings do you think a soldier may experience before a battle?

QuickWrite

Think of a time when you were afraid of a coming event or awaited an event with great impatience. Write about how you coped with your feelings as you waited.

Setting a Purpose

Read to discover how two very different soldiers deal with fear.

BUILDING BACKGROUND

The Time and Place A significant battle of the U.S. Civil War took place in April of 1862 near Shiloh, Tennessee, a town on the Tennessee River. The Union Army, led by General Ulysses S. Grant, won the encounter, but at the cost of thousands of lives. This battle is recorded as one of the fiercest battles in history, and with it began the legend of a drummer boy.

Did You Know? Most drummers in the Civil War were boys, some as young as twelve. The beat of drums and the blare of bugles, heard above the cannon and rifle booms, alerted soldiers to change formations during battle.

VOCABULARY PREVIEW

solemn (sol′ əm) *adj.* serious; p. 439
askew (ə skū′) *adv.* in a twisted way; crookedly; p. 439
benediction (ben′ ə dik′ shən) *n.* a divine blessing or the condition of being blessed; p. 440
immortality (im′ ôr tal′ ə tē) *n.* the state of living or lasting forever; p. 440
legitimately (li jit′ ə mit lē) *adv.* in a way that follows the rules; legally; p. 441
mutely (mūt′ lē) *adv.* without speaking; silently; p. 443

RESOURCE MANAGER

Teaching Tools and Resources
- Theme Five Planning Guide
- Literature Groups Sourcebook

Essential Lesson Support

Lesson-Specific Instruction
- Selection Focus Transparency 37
- Literary Elements Transparency 38
- Active Reading Guide,* p. 38
- Selection Vocabulary Practice, p. 27

Assessment
- Selection Quick Checks,* p. 38
- Sel. and Theme Assmt., pp. 67–68
- Testmaker: ExamView Pro
- Performance Assessment, p. 36

Systematic Language Instruction
- Gr. & Comp. Hbk., L. 9.1
- Vocabulary Power, Lesson 19
- Spelling Power, Lesson 17

English Language Learners
- ELL Sourcebook, pp. 59, 60
- Spanish Summaries, p. 37
- Spanish Translations, pp. 95–99
- Audio Library*
- English, Yes!

Spec. Needs/Strat. Interven.
- Interactive Rdg. Sbk., pp. T143–T145
- Interactive Rdg. Wkbk., pp. 72–73
- Inclusion Strat. Sbk., pp. 31–32
- Audio Library*

* Also available in Spanish

The Drummer Boy of Shiloh

Ray Bradbury

Union drummer boy at Shiloh.

A In the April night, more than once, blossoms fell from the orchard trees and lit with rustling taps on the drumskin. At midnight a peach stone left miraculously on a branch through winter, flicked by a bird, fell swift and unseen, struck once, like panic, which jerked the boy upright. In silence he listened to his own heart ruffle away, away, at last gone from his ears and back in his chest again.

After that, he turned the drum on its side, where its great lunar face peered at him whenever he opened his eyes.

His face, alert or at rest, was solemn. It was indeed a solemn time and a solemn night for a boy just turned fourteen in the peach field near the Owl Creek not far from the church at Shiloh.

". . . thirty-one, thirty-two, thirty-three . . ."

Unable to see, he stopped counting.

Beyond the thirty-three familiar shadows, forty thousand men, exhausted by nervous expectation, unable to sleep for romantic dreams of battles yet unfought, lay crazily askew in their uniforms. A mile yet farther on, another army was strewn helter-skelter,[1] turning slow, basting

1. Both armies were scattered *(strewn)* in a disorganized way *(helter-skelter)*.

Vocabulary

solemn (sol′ əm) *adj.* serious

askew (ə skū′) *adv.* in a twisted way; crookedly

Reading the Selection

SUMMARY

During the night before the battle of Shiloh, a fourteen-year-old drummer boy cannot sleep because of his fears. The commanding general shares his own feelings of anticipation and concern about what the day will bring. He explains how important the boy's role in the battle will be: the drum is the heart of the army. This revelation brings a measure of peace to the boy as he waits for the battle to begin.

Spanish Summaries, p. 37

A Active Reading Strategies

QUESTION Ask students why they think Bradbury begins the story with the peach blossoms falling on the drum. *(He is setting up the ironic connection that runs throughout the story. The flower symbolizes the beginning of life; the drum symbolizes war and the boy's ultimate death.)*

VOCABULARY Remind students to use context clues to unlock the meanings of new vocabulary words.

Additional Resources

Active Reading Guide, p. 38

Audio Library

Spanish Audio Library

Teaching Support

CONNECTING TO OTHER SELECTIONS

The chart at the right shows three ways to connect "The Drummer Boy of Shiloh" to other selections in this book.

For specific teaching strategies, see the ***Theme Five Planning Guide.***

Connection	Title
Life Skills: Teaching and Mentoring	"The Treasure of Lemon Brown," p. 5
Thematic: Coming of Age	"The Medicine Bag," p. 78
Literary: Legend	"The Legend of Sleepy Hollow," p. 816

Historical Note

Bradbury may expect his readers to recognize the phrase "the drummer boy of Shiloh" from the Confederate song of the same title—or one of many similar songs and poems. Bradbury's original readers would have known that the boy was fated to die.

B Literary Elements

DESCRIPTION Point out to students the emphasis placed on sound in this description. Note that the boy hears the whispering of the men as a "vast wind" that is "arisen from south or north." Ask students to what they think this metaphor refers. *(The armies of the Union and the Confederacy.)*

C Literary Elements

DESCRIPTION Explain to students that the author uses imagery to make his description come to life. Note that Bradbury compares the bones of the boys with "steel bones," or rifles. Human bones are mortal: the metal of the rifles and their bayonets are "eternal." Ask students what Bradbury emphasizes by using this imagery. *(He emphasizes the vulnerability of the soldiers.)*

themselves with the thought of what they would do when the time came: a leap, a yell, a blind plunge their strategy, raw youth their protection and benediction.

B Now and again the boy heard a vast wind come up, that gently stirred the air. But he knew what it was, the army here, the army there, whispering to itself in the dark. Some men talking to others, others murmuring to themselves, and all so quiet it was like a natural element arisen from south or north with the motion of the earth toward dawn.

What the men whispered the boy could only guess, and he guessed that it was: Me, I'm the one, I'm the one of all the rest won't die. I'll live through it. I'll go home. The band will play. And I'll be there to hear it.

Yes, thought the boy, that's all very well for them, they can give as good as they get!

C For with the careless bones of the young men harvested by night and bindled[2] around campfires were the similarly strewn steel bones of their rifles, with bayonets fixed like eternal lightning lost in the orchard grass.

Me, thought the boy, I got only a drum, two sticks to beat it, and no shield.

There wasn't a man-boy on this ground tonight did not have a shield[3] he cast, riveted or carved himself on his way to his first attack, compounded of remote but nonetheless firm and fiery family devotion, flag-blown patriotism and cocksure immortality strengthened by the touchstone of very real gunpowder, ramrod, minnieball and flint.[4] But without these last the boy felt his family move yet farther off away in the dark, as if one of those great prairie-burning trains had chanted them away never to return, leaving him with this drum which was worse than a toy in the game to be played tomorrow or some day much too soon.

The boy turned on his side. A moth brushed his face, but it was peach blossom. A peach blossom flicked him, but it was a moth. Nothing stayed put. Nothing had a name. Nothing was as it once was.

If he lay very still, when the dawn came up and the soldiers put on their bravery with their caps, perhaps they might go away, the war with them, and not notice him lying small here, no more than a toy himself.

"Well, by God, now," said a voice.

The boy shut up his eyes, to hide inside himself, but it was too late. Someone, walking by in the night, stood over him.

"Well," said the voice quietly, "here's a soldier crying *before* the fight. Good. Get it over. Won't be time once it all starts."

And the voice was about to move on when the boy, startled, touched the drum at his elbow. The man above, hearing this, stopped. The boy could feel his eyes,

2. *Bindled* means "bedded" or "bundled." A *bindle* is a bed roll.
3. Civil War soldiers didn't carry *shields* of armor. The narrator is referring to ways the men prepared themselves for battle mentally and emotionally.
4. A *touchstone* is anything used to test for quality or genuineness. In the mid-1800s, a rifle had to be loaded for each shot. The *ramrod* forced gunpowder down the rifle barrel. The *minnieball* was a kind of bullet. *Flint* ignited the powder that shot the bullet.

Vocabulary

benediction (ben′ ə dik′ shən) *n.* a divine blessing or the condition of being blessed
immortality (im′ ôr tal′ ə tē) *n.* the state of living or lasting forever

Teaching Support

MEETING INDIVIDUAL NEEDS

ENGLISH LANGUAGE LEARNERS

Multiple-Meaning Words English language learners may find imagery and multiple-meaning words challenging. Write *raw* on the board. Ask a volunteer to explain what the word usually means. *(uncooked)* Then ask what students think the word means on page 440.

Activity Have students read with more proficient English speakers, to identify the following multiple-meaning words: *stone, face, stirred, brushed,* and *cracked.* Discuss troublesome images, such as "There's your cheek, fell right off the tree overhead."

Additional Resources

English Language Learners Sourcebook, p. 59

sense him slowly bending near. A hand must have come down out of the night, for there was a little rat-tat as the fingernails brushed and the man's breath fanned his face.

"Why, it's the drummer boy, isn't it?"

The boy nodded, not knowing if his nod was seen. "Sir, is that *you*?" he said.

"I assume it is." The man's knees cracked as he bent still closer.

D He smelled as all fathers should smell, of salt sweat, ginger tobacco, horse and boot leather, and the earth he walked upon. He had many eyes. No, not eyes, brass buttons that watched the boy.

He could only be, and was, the General.

"What's your name, boy?" he asked.

"Joby," whispered the boy, starting to sit up.

"All right, Joby, don't stir." A hand pressed his chest gently, and the boy relaxed. "How long you been with us, Joby?"

"Three weeks, sir."

"Run off from home or joined legitimately, boy?"

Silence.

"Fool question," said the General. "Do you shave yet, boy? Even more of a fool. There's your cheek, fell right off the tree overhead. And the others here not much older. Raw, raw, the lot of you. You ready for tomorrow or the next day, Joby?"

"I think so, sir."

E "You want to cry some more, go on ahead. I did the same last night."

"*You*, sir?"

"God's truth. Thinking of everything ahead. Both sides figuring the other side will just give up, and soon, and the war done in weeks, and us all home. Well, that's not how it's going to be. And maybe that's why I cried."

"Yes, sir," said Joby.

The General must have taken out a cigar now, for the dark was suddenly filled with the Indian smell of tobacco unlit as yet, but chewed as the man thought what next to say.

"It's going to be a crazy time," said the General. "Counting both sides, there's a hundred thousand men, give or take a few thousand out there tonight, not one as can spit a sparrow off a tree, or knows a horse clod from a minnieball. Stand up, bare the breast, ask to be a target, thank them and sit down, that's us, that's them. We should turn tail and train four months, they should do the

Eagle drum from the 27th Massachusetts Infantry.

Vocabulary
legitimately (li jit′ ə mit lē) *adv.* in a way that follows the rules; legally

FYI

Soldiers' Mortality
During the Battle of Shiloh, more soldiers were killed than had been killed in *all* previous U.S. wars to date.

D Literary Elements

DESCRIPTION Discuss with students the concrete images Bradbury uses to describe the General. Note that this description also relays some of the drummer boy's feelings to the reader.

E Active Reading Strategies

QUESTION For whom do students think the boy is crying? *(himself)* For whom do they think the General is crying? *(all of the young men on both sides)*

Reading Minilesson

Visualize Having a vivid mental picture of a scene can help students gain a more thorough comprehension of what they are reading.

Activity Have students work in small groups to prepare to perform a scene from the meeting between the General and the boy. (Assign each group specific scenes.) Have groups experiment with the positioning of the characters. Where is the General? Does he stand or sit? Where is the boy? What is his posture? Where is the tree? Where is the drum? How does the arrangement of characters and objects affect the mood of the scene? Have each group perform its scene for the class.
L2 COLLAB. LEARN.

Additional Resources
Reading Skills Practice Workbook

F Literary Elements

DESCRIPTION Note that Bradbury highlights the horror of war by contrasting it with concrete examples of everyday life. Have students list examples. *(The boys have spring fever, but they mistake it for blood lust. The same boys who were swimming in the creek yesterday will be floating there dead tomorrow.)*

G Author's Craft

MOOD Point out that Bradbury uses word choice and rhythm in the General's speech to the boy, which natually speeds up and becomes louder. (Read the passage aloud or have a student do so.) He stirs the boy's heart with the rhythm of his words, just as the boy will stir the men with his drum.

same. But here we are, taken with spring fever and thinking it blood lust, taking our sulphur[5] with cannons instead of with molasses as it should be, going to be a hero, going to live forever. And I can see all of them over there nodding agreement, save the other way around. It's F wrong, boy, it's wrong as a head put on hind side front and a man marching backward through life. It will be a double massacre if one of their itchy generals decides to picnic his lads on our grass. More innocents will get shot out of pure Cherokee enthusiasm than ever got shot before. Owl Creek was full of boys splashing around in the noonday sun just a few hours ago. I fear it will be full of boys again, just floating, at sundown tomorrow, not caring where the tide takes them."

The General stopped and made a little pile of winter leaves and twigs in the darkness, as if he might at any moment strike fire to them to see his way through the coming days when the sun might not show its face because of what was happening here and just beyond.

The boy watched the hand stirring the leaves and opened his lips to say something, but did not say it. The General heard the boy's breath and spoke himself.

"Why am I telling you this? That's what you want to ask, eh? Well, when you got a bunch of wild horses on a loose rein somewhere, somehow you got to

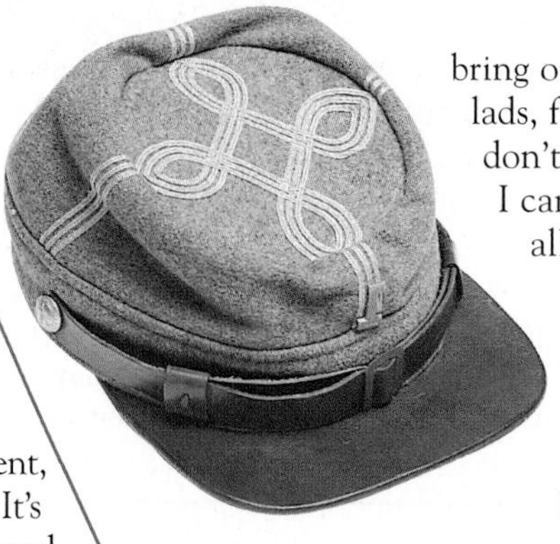

Confederate soldier's hat.

bring order, rein them in. These lads, fresh out of the milkshed, don't know what I know, and I can't tell them: men actually die, in war. So each is his own army. I got to make *one* army of them. And for that, boy, I need you."

"Me!" The boy's lips barely twitched.

"Now, boy," said the General quietly, "you are the heart of the army. Think of that. You're the heart of the army. Listen, now."

And, lying there, Joby listened.

And the General spoke on.

G If he, Joby, beat slow tomorrow, the heart would beat slow in the men. They would lag by the wayside. They would drowse in the fields on their muskets. They would sleep forever, after that, in those same fields, their hearts slowed by a drummer boy and stopped by enemy lead.

But if he beat a sure, steady, ever faster rhythm, then, then their knees would come up in a long line down over that hill, one knee after the other, like a wave on the ocean shore! Had he seen the ocean ever? Seen the waves rolling in like a well-ordered cavalry charge to the sand? Well, that was it, that's what he wanted, that's what was needed! Joby was his right hand and his left. He gave the orders, but Joby set the pace!

So bring the right knee up and the right foot out and the left knee up and the left foot out. One following the other in good time, in brisk time. Move the blood up the body and make the head proud and the spine stiff and the jaw resolute. Focus the eye and set the teeth, flare the nostrils H and tighten the hands, put steel armor all

5. *Blood lust* means "a desire for bloodshed." *Sulphur* (now usually spelled *sulfur*) is a chemical once used as an ingredient of gunpowder; also, when combined with molasses, it was drunk as a medicine.

Teaching Support

Grammar and Language *Minilesson*

Pronouns as Objects of Prepositions Write this sentence from the story on the board: "And I can see all <u>of them</u> over there nodding agreement, save the other way around." Point out to students that a pronoun that is the object of a preposition must be in the objective case *(me, him, her, us, them).*

Activity Have students find three other pronouns that are objects of prepositions in the story. Ask them to read the sentences to the class and identify the object pronouns. Suggest that students test compound objects by "trying out" the components (*him* and *me*) individually to reinforce the sound of the correct choices. **L2**

Additional Resources

- ***Grammar and Language Transparency 35***
- ***Grammar and Language Workbook,*** p. 143
- ***Grammar and Composition Handbook,*** Lesson 4.2
- ***Writer's Choice,*** Lesson 13.2

over the men, for blood moving fast in them does indeed make men feel as if they'd put on steel. He must keep at it, at it! Long and steady, steady and long! Then, even though shot or torn, those wounds got in hot blood—in blood he'd helped stir—would feel less pain. If their blood was cold, it would be more than slaughter, it would be murderous nightmare and pain best not told and no one to guess.

Union soldier's hat.

The General spoke and stopped, letting his breath slack off. Then, after a moment, he said, "So there you are, that's it. Will you do that, boy? Do you know now you're general of the army when the General's left behind?"

The boy nodded mutely.

"You'll run them through for me then, boy?"

"Yes, sir."

"Good. And, God willing, many nights from tonight, many years from now, when you're as old or far much older than me, when they ask you what you did in this awful time, you will tell them—one part humble and one part proud—'I was the drummer boy at the battle of Owl Creek,' or the Tennessee River, or maybe they'll just name it after the church there. 'I was the drummer boy at Shiloh.' Good grief, that has a beat and sound to it fitting for Mr. Longfellow.[6] 'I was the drummer boy at Shiloh.' Who will ever hear those words and not know you, boy, or what you thought this night, or what you'll think tomorrow or the next day when we must get up on our legs and *move!*"

The general stood up. "Well, then. God bless you, boy. Good night."

"Good night, sir."

And, tobacco, brass, boot polish, salt sweat and leather, the man moved away through the grass.

Joby lay for a moment, staring but unable to see where the man had gone.

He swallowed. He wiped his eyes. He cleared his throat. He settled himself. Then, at last, very slowly and firmly, he turned the drum so that it faced up toward the sky.

He lay next to it, his arm around it, feeling the tremor, the touch, the muted thunder as, all the rest of the April night in the year 1862, near the Tennessee River, not far from the Owl Creek, very close to the church named Shiloh, the peach blossoms fell on the drum.

6. Henry Wadsworth *Longfellow* (1807–1882), an American poet, was very popular and highly respected during his lifetime.

Vocabulary

mutely (mūt′ lē) *adv.* without speaking; silently

H Active Reading Strategies

CONNECT The General says that the drumming will inspire the soldiers and become a kind of armor. Help students connect this idea with the boy's earlier thought that he was without "a shield" because he didn't have a weapon. The General is emphasizing that heart and spirit are more important than steel weapons.

I Critical Thinking

ANALYZE ARGUMENTS Ask students to analyze the General's inspirational speech to the boy. Have students consider that he has just predicted that many thousands will die. Share the following model to demonstrate the process involved in analyzing arguments:

Model: The General seems to be upset, at the beginning, about the loss of young life. I think he realizes that he is scaring the boy with his talk of death, so he tries to comfort him by pointing out how important the drummer's job is. From his argument, I think, he wishes there were no wars to fight.

Thematic Focus

Free to Be Ask students how they think this story relates to the theme "Free to Be."

ASSESSMENT

Quick Checks, p. 38

Real-World Connection

Children in War Zones All over the world today, young people are facing the harsh consequences of war.

Activity Have students research the impact of a current conflict on the children of that region. They should present a brief oral report summarizing their discoveries. **L2**

Responding to the Selection

PERSONAL RESPONSE

There is no one correct response to the question. Students' responses will reflect their personalities and experience.

Analyzing Literature

1. The boy is lying under a peach tree, as he awaits the next day's battle.
2. His only defense is his drum, which, he says, is no more than a toy.
3. The General is a wise and experienced soldier. He tells Joby that the beat of the boy's drum will inspire the soldiers to their best effort; he says that Joby is the heart of the army.
4. He turns it so the top of the drum faces the sky.
5. The drummer boy is frightened, lonely, and vulnerable. He considers staying behind because he fears for his life.
6. Both Joby and the General are fearful, and both have shed tears over the prospect of the next day's battle.
7. The importance that the General attaches to the boy's role is unexpected. The General suggests that the boy is the "heart" of the army in that his drumming will inspire the troops.
8. Joby turns his drum face up because he has accepted his role.
9. The General is doing for the boy what he wants the boy to do for the soldiers—he is trying to inspire him. Students will have differing opinions on the wisdom of the General's speaking frankly.
10. Joby may have enlisted because he longed to do something heroic—to fight for freedom. Many people today enlist for the same reason.

Responding to Literature

PERSONAL RESPONSE

- Would you have been encouraged or more fearful after listening to the General's words? As you think about your answer, consider what you wrote for the **Reading Focus** on page 438.

Analyzing Literature

RECALL

1. Where is the drummer boy when the story begins? What is he waiting for?
2. According to the boy, what is his only defense?
3. Describe the General. What does he say to help the drummer boy, Joby, understand his own importance?
4. What does Joby do to his drum at the end of the story?

INTERPRET

5. How does the drummer boy feel about his situation? Why does he consider remaining behind when the fighting begins?
6. How are Joby and the General alike?
7. What is **ironic,** or unexpected, in the dialogue between the General and the drummer boy? How is the boy the "heart of the army"?
8. Why do you think Joby turns his drum to face the sky?

EVALUATE AND CONNECT

9. Why, in your opinion, does the General say what he does to the drummer boy? Do you think it was wise for the General to speak so frankly to the boy?
10. Theme Connection Joby is fourteen years old. Why do you think he and other soldiers enlisted to fight in the Civil War? Why do people enlist in the armed services today?

Brackets connect questions that are paired to develop higher-level thinking skills.

LITERARY ELEMENTS

Description

Description is language that creates a vivid picture of a person, situation, or mood. It brings a reader into the story. In historical fiction, as in "The Drummer Boy of Shiloh," clear description can help readers experience the past.

1. How does the description of the April night in the first three paragraphs set the mood for the story? Explain.
2. What information about setting does the reader get from the descriptions in the next three paragraphs?

- See **Literary Terms Handbook,** pp. R2–R3.

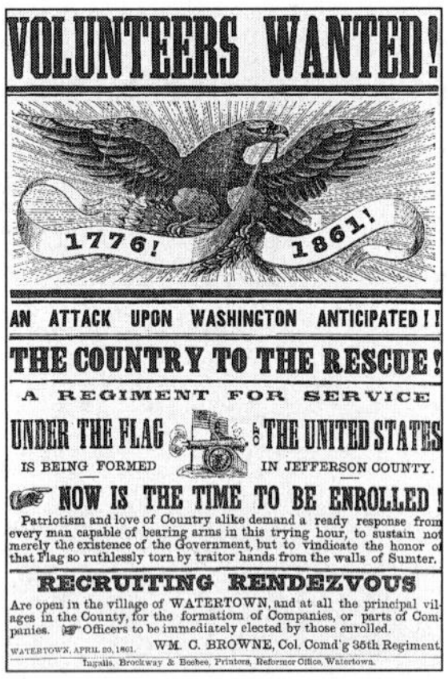

Union recruitment poster.

LITERARY ELEMENTS

1. The night is beautiful, and the whole world is coming to life in the spring. The description contrasts with the boy's brief panic and his solemn face.
2. The next three paragraphs specifically pinpoint the boy's situation—surrounded by the army of men who are asleep or trying to sleep. He hears the whispers of wind and men.

Additional Resources

Literary Elements Transparency 38

Literature and Writing

Writing About Literature

Legend Has It! A play about the legendary drummer boy of Shiloh, written in 1870 by Samuel Muscroft, was popular in the North for nearly forty years after the Civil War. What might have been Muscroft's purpose for writing this play? How might you account for the popularity of this legend, especially in the 1870s? Explain your answers in one or two paragraphs.

Personal Writing

Letter Home Suppose that you are a fourteen-year-old in 1862. Write a letter to a friend who is considering running away to join one of the armies. Explain why you cannot join him or her and why your friend should stay home.

Extending Your Response

Literature Groups

Plot Study There is little action in this story—and no battle action—but a strong plot exists. What is the primary problem and solution in the story? What surprises do you find as the plot unfolds? Answer these questions, and then discuss the following in your group: Does the plot have a satisfying ending? What changes, if any, would make the story more interesting for you? Summarize your group's opinions and share them with the class.

Interdisciplinary Activity

History With a group, research one of the following Civil War topics: the Union forces, the Confederate forces, the issues that sparked the war, or the effects of the war on the North and the South. Present your findings in a report accompanied by visuals, such as a map of battles or a mural of major events. If you wish, you might write a story set during the Civil War and read it or act it out for the class.

Learning for Life

News Broadcast With a partner, research the Battle of Shiloh to find out how long it lasted, what weapons and tactics were used, and how many soldiers died, among other information. Prepare a detailed news report about the battle, as if it just happened. Include charts, maps, profiles of the generals, or photographs, if available. Include quotations from imaginary interviews with fictitious soldiers. Present the news report to your class.

Reading Further

For more stories about young people and war, try these books:

The Bomb by Theodore Taylor
The Forty-Third War by Louise Moeri

Save your work for your portfolio.

Literature and Writing

Writing About Literature

Students' paragraphs should

- respond to both parts of the assignment, suggesting the possible purpose of the play and conjecturing on the popularity of the legend
- back up opinions with clear reasoning

Personal Writing

Students' letters should

- use well-reasoned arguments to persuade
- be in the form of personal correspondence

Extending Your Response

Literature Groups Remind students that conflict in literature is often internal. COLLAB. LEARN.

Interdisciplinary Activity Mention to students that dozens of excellent Internet sites focus on the Civil War.

Learning for Life If possible, have students watch documentaries that show TV news coverage of the Vietnam War or the Gulf War to get a sense of how television has covered wars in the past.

LITERATURE & HUMANITIES

Display Transparency 11, "A Rainy Day in Camp," in *United States History and Art* and have students examine and discuss the mood of the painting. Which is prevalent, patriotism or sorrow? Is the Civil War more often celebrated or mourned in our history?

Skill Minilessons

GRAMMAR AND LANGUAGE
ADJECTIVES

1. lunar
2. flag-blown
3. horse and boot
4. itchy
5. well-ordered

READING AND THINKING
VISUALIZING

Allow students who have artistic ability to draw the scene.

VOCABULARY
THE SUFFIX *-ity*

1. d
2. a
3. f
4. e
5. b
6. g
7. c

Additional Resources

- ***Grammar and Language Workbook,*** p. 121
- ***Grammar and Composition Handbook,*** Lesson 5.1
- ***Writer's Choice,*** Lesson 12.1
- ***Reading Skills Practice Workbook***
- ***Vocabulary Practice,*** p. 27

RETEACH • REVIEW

Skill Minilessons

GRAMMAR AND LANGUAGE • ADJECTIVES

Writers strengthen descriptions with adjectives–words that describe people, places, things, or ideas. When Ray Bradbury writes of "the **careless** bones of young men" and the "**steel** bones of their rifles," he chooses the adjectives *careless* and *steel* to make his description easier for readers to imagine.

- For more about using adjectives, see **Language Handbook**, p. R27.

PRACTICE Look back at "The Drummer Boy of Shiloh" to find one or more adjectives that describe each of the following people, places, things, or ideas.

1. face of the drum
2. patriotism
3. leather
4. generals
5. cavalry charge

READING AND THINKING • VISUALIZING

When you **visualize** a person, place, object, or event, you see it in your mind. Bradbury uses details effectively to help his readers visualize what is happening during a brief episode in the Civil War.

- For more about visualizing, see **Reading Handbook**, p. R95.

PRACTICE Choose a passage from the story. Think about how the scene would look if you were to draw it or stage it. What backdrop, or background scenery, can you imagine? Who is present? Are they standing or sitting? What is the weather like? Write a paragraph describing your view of the scene.

VOCABULARY • THE SUFFIX *-ity*

The suffix *-ity* means "state or condition." It is similar to the suffix *-ness.* Before the Battle of Shiloh, the soldiers have a feeling of *immortality,* the condition of being *immortal.* Something that is *solid* is in a state of *solidity;* something that is *acid* has *acidity.* Attaching a suffix, especially one that begins with a vowel, may change the spelling of a base word. For example, *possible* becomes *possibility* and *fragile* becomes *fragility*.

PRACTICE Use your knowledge of vocabulary to match each word ending in *–ity* with its synonym.

1. authenticity	a. politeness
2. civility	b. phoniness
3. essentiality	c. cruelty
4. durability	d. genuineness
5. artificiality	e. permanence
6. totality	f. importance
7. inhumanity	g. completeness

ASSESSMENT

- ***Quick Checks,*** p. 38
- ***Selection and Theme Assessment,*** pp. 67–68
- ***Performance Assessment,*** p. 36
- ***Testmaker: ExamView Pro***
- ***Interactive Tutor: Self-Assessment***

Vo•cab•u•lar•y Skills

Using Homophones

The word *homophone* comes from *homo,* meaning "same," and *phone,* meaning "sound." Therefore, **homophones** are words that sound the same. However, homophones have different meanings and spellings. For example, to *pedal* a bike is to ride it; to *peddle* a bike is to try to sell it. Not recognizing a homophone can result in spelling errors. Even a computer can't fix your mistake if you wrote *flower* when you should have written *flour,* because both of those words are spelled correctly.

The English language includes many homophones. Those who have watched a short play have *seen* a *scene.* A baby antelope is a *new gnu.* If only one thing is borrowed, it is a *lone loan.* Some homophones are only slightly different in meaning, such as *who's* and *whose,* and you might have to give some thought to choose the correct one. Usually, however, using the wrong homophone is simply a result of being careless.

EXERCISES

1. If the underlined word in the selection below is the correct homophone, write *Correct.* If it is the wrong word, write the correct form.

   The soldiers were not week (1); they were only young and inexperienced. Death awaited many at the break (2) of day, soon after the sun (3) rows (4) in the sky. The general knew (5) that training could lesson (6) the hardships his men would (7) face, but their (8) was no time for that. All he could due (9) was to (10) walk among them, stop, hear (11), and speak to those he found awake. He new (12) that many young hearts were to be stopped by led (13). How heavily his responsibilities must have wade (14) upon him.

2. Complete each sentence by using two homophones. An example is provided.
   Example: The cake baked by a female servant is a cake that the maid made.
   a. If you form your letters correctly, you ______.
   b. I blistered the back of my foot, but new shoes helped my ______.
   c. A just, honest, and proper price for a taxi ride is a ______.
   d. We called the sixty minutes we spent together ______.
   e. Our team lost fourteen out of fifteen games; we only ______.

Vo•cab•u•lar•y Skills

Objective

- To avoid spelling errors by learning to recognize homophones

Teaching Strategies

Divide students into small groups and challenge them to see which group can come up with the longest list of homophones. If they are unsure of the spelling of a homophone, encourage them to look it up in a dictionary.

Exercises

1.
1. weak
2. correct
3. correct
4. rose
5. correct
6. lessen
7. correct
8. there
9. do
10. correct
11. correct
12. knew
13. lead
14. weighed

2.
a. write right
b. heel heal
c. fair fare
d. our hour
e. won one

Additional Resources

Vocabulary Power

Teaching Support

MEETING INDIVIDUAL NEEDS — ADVANCED LEARNERS

Homophones Point out that homophones are often the source of jokes, puns, limericks, and advertising slogans. A pen company, for example, might show its product silhouetted against the moon with the slogan, "We've got the write stuff."

Activity Have students work in small groups to compile a list of homophones. Encourage them to use a dictionary or a thesaurus as they compile their lists. Once they have completed their lists, the group should work together to develop a poem, a cartoon, a joke, or a slogan that uses one or more homophones for humorous effect. Have groups share their work with the rest of the class. **L2** COLLAB. LEARN.

Before Reading

Objectives

- To read and analyze a poem about Paul Revere's ride
- To learn how poets use meter to heighten the effect of the words
- To write a retelling of the poem

Skills

Reading/Thinking: Identifying Author's Purpose; Evaluating
Writing: Children's Book
Grammar/Language: Semicolons and Conjunctive Adverbs; Capital Letters in Poetry
Collaboration: Literature Groups

Motivating STUDENTS

Literature Launchers: "Riding Into History"

Videodisc Side B, Segment 15

Also available in VHS.

Selection Focus Transparency 38: Before presenting the map, have students consider the differences between mass transportation and horseback riding.

Reading Focus: As an extension to the Reading Focus, have students form two groups based on their answer to the question, *Is war a good solution when freedom is denied?* Have them plan and conduct a formal debate.

Before You Read

Paul Revere's Ride

MEET HENRY WADSWORTH LONGFELLOW

Henry Wadsworth Longfellow's father wanted his son to become a lawyer, but the young Longfellow had other ideas. In 1824 he wrote to his father from college: "If I can ever rise in the world, it must be by the exercise of my talent in the wide field of literature." A popular author during his time, Longfellow was known for poems that were gentle, sweet, simple, and romantic. His best-known works include *The Song of Hiawatha*, *Evangeline*, and "Paul Revere's Ride."

Henry Wadsworth Longfellow was born in 1807 and died in 1882. "Paul Revere's Ride" was first published in 1863 in Tales of a Wayside Inn.

READING FOCUS

Imagine that you are an American colonist during 1775. You pay heavy taxes to England, but you are denied a voice in its government. Your neighbors are talking about fighting for independence from England. Weigh the pros and cons of a revolution. What might you contribute to this struggle?

Share It!

Is war a good solution when freedom is denied? Discuss your response with a partner. Then share with the class the points on which you and your partner agree.

Setting a Purpose

Read the story of one person whose contribution to freedom became a legend.

BUILDING BACKGROUND

The Time and Place This poem celebrates the historic ride of Paul Revere, one of the men who rode from Boston to Lexington, Massachusetts, just before the American Revolution. Revere's mission was to warn Samuel Adams and John Hancock, two prominent rebel colonists, that British troops had arrived in Boston and were marching to arrest the two men.

Did You Know? Before and after the ride that made him famous, Paul Revere was well known as a craftsman. He cast musket balls and cannons during the war and church bells after the war. He also made beautiful silverware and copper goods.

Sons of Liberty Bowl, 1768. Paul Revere. Silver, height: 5½ in., lip diameter: 11 in. Gift by Subscription and Francis Bartlett Fund. Courtesy Boston Museum of Fine Arts.

RESOURCE MANAGER

Teaching Tools and Resources
- Theme Five Planning Guide
- Literature Groups Sourcebook

Essential Lesson Support

Lesson-Specific Instruction
- Selection Focus Transparency 38
- Literary Elements Transparency 39
- Active Reading Guide,* p. 39

Assessment
- Selection Quick Checks,* p. 39
- Sel. and Theme Assmt., pp. 69–70
- Testmaker: ExamView Pro
- Performance Assessment, p. 37

Systematic Language Instruction
- Gr. & Comp. Hbk., L. 9.2

English Language Learners
- ELL Sourcebook, p. 61
- Spanish Summaries, p. 38
- Audio Library*
- English, Yes!

Spec. Needs/Strat. Interven.
- Interactive Rdg. Sbk., pp. T146–T148
- Interactive Rdg. Wkbk., pp. 74–75
- Inclusion Strat. Sbk., pp. 31–32
- Audio Library*

* Also available in Spanish

Midnight Ride of Paul Revere, 1931. Grant Wood. Oil on composition board, 30 x 40 in. The Metropolitan Museum of Art, NY.

Paul Revere's Ride

Henry Wadsworth Longfellow

Listen, my children, and you shall hear
Of the midnight ride of Paul Revere,
On the eighteenth of April, in Seventy-five;
Hardly a man is now alive
Who remembers that famous day and year.

Reading the Selection

A Active Reading Strategies

QUESTION Ask students what effect Longfellow was trying to achieve by addressing the readers directly. *(He makes it seem as if the speaker is telling a story to the reader.)*

Additional Resources

- ***Active Reading Guide,*** p. 39
- ***Audio Library***
- ***Spanish Audio Library***

Vo•cab•u•lar•y Skills

Letter-Sound Cues—Before they begin reading, ask students to scan the poem for unfamiliar words, such as *moorings* or *grenadiers.* Suggest that they look at a letter or a group of letters at the beginning, middle, and end of each word. What is the beginning sound or syllable? Does the middle or end of the new word contain words that students already know? Encourage students to ask themselves these questions and then try pronouncing the whole world.

Teaching Support

CONNECTING TO OTHER SELECTIONS

Comparing selections

This selection is compared with "Barbara Frietchie" on pages 459–461. A lesson for teaching a comparison of the two selections appears on page 463.

The chart at the right shows three other ways to connect "Paul Revere's Ride" to selections in this book.

For specific teaching strategies, see the ***Theme Five Planning Guide.***

Connection	Title
Life Skills: Implementing	→ "Golden Glass," p. 51
Thematic: Heroism	→ "The Wise Old Woman," p. 259
Literary: Narrative Poetry	→ "The Black Walnut Tree," p. 299

FYI

Revere's friend who hung the lantern was John Pulling. Of the many colonists who rode out to warn the people in the countryside, only one (Dr. Samuel Prescott) actually made it to Concord. Revere was caught at midnight and arrested.

B Literary Elements

METER Explain to students that the poem is written with usually four stressed syllables to the line. Rhyme scheme and stanza length are irregular. The meter imitates a galloping horse, with the four beats sounding like the four hooves of the horse. Have students read the second stanza aloud, paying attention to the rhythm.

C Author's Craft

IMAGERY Point out to students the picture Longfellow paints of the British ship. The comparison to a prison reflects Longfellow's view of the cause of the Revolution (that Americans were "imprisoned" by the British). Ask the students what they think the reference to the size of the ship suggests. *(the magnitude of the task involved in a tiny group of colonists' taking on mighty Britain)*

He said to his friend, "If the British march
By land or sea from the town to-night,
Hang a lantern aloft in the belfry° arch
Of the North Church tower as a signal light,—
One, if by land, and two, if by sea;
And I on the opposite shore will be,
Ready to ride and spread the alarm
Through every Middlesex° village and farm,
For the country folk to be up and to arm."

Then he said, "Good night!" and with muffled oar
Silently rowed to the Charlestown shore,
Just as the moon rose over the bay,
Where swinging wide at her moorings° lay
The Somerset, British man-of-war;°
A phantom ship, with each mast and spar°
Across the moon like a prison bar,
And a huge black hulk, that was magnified
By its own reflection in the tide.

Meanwhile, his friend, through alley and street,
Wanders and watches with eager ears,
Till in the silence around him he hears
The muster of men at the barrack door,
The sound of arms, and the tramp of feet,
And the measured tread° of the grenadiers,°
Marching down to their boats on the shore.

Then he climbed the tower of the Old North Church,
By the wooden stairs, with stealthy tread,°

8 A *belfry* (bel′ frē) is the bell tower of a church or another building.
13 The county of *Middlesex,* Massachusetts, includes the town of Concord, where the first shots of the Revolutionary War were fired on April 19, 1775.
18 The place where a ship is docked is called its *moorings.*
19 A *man-of-war* is a warship.
20 On a sailing ship, a *spar* is any of the poles used to fasten or support the sails.
29 The *measured tread* is a steady march or walk. In the British army, *grenadiers* (gren′ ə dērz′) were foot soldiers.
32 The *stealthy tread* is the man's secret or sneaky steps.

Teaching Support

Meeting Individual Needs: ENGLISH LANGUAGE LEARNERS

Syntax For those whose native language is not English, the syntax of the poem may pose some difficulties. On the board write "And I on the opposite shore will be." Then write, "And I will be on the opposite shore." Explain that poets often change sentence structure to fit the meter and rhyme scheme.

Activity Have students work in groups that include proficient English speakers to rewrite a stanza of the poem in more straightforward English. Discuss the kinds of changes students made in order to translate the poem into standard syntax. **COLLAB. LEARN.**

Additional Resources

English Language Learners Sourcebook, p. 61

To the belfry-chamber overhead,
And startled the pigeons from their perch
On the somber° rafters, that round him made
Masses and moving shapes of shade,—
By the trembling ladder, steep and tall,
To the highest window in the wall,
Where he paused to listen and look down
A moment on the roofs of the town,
And the moonlight flowing over all.

Beneath, in the churchyard, lay the dead,
In their night-encampment on the hill,
Wrapped in silence so deep and still
That he could hear, like a sentinel's° tread,
The watchful night-wind, as it went
Creeping along from tent to tent,
And seeming to whisper, "All is well!"
A moment only he feels the spell
Of the place and the hour, and the secret dread
Of the lonely belfry and the dead;
For suddenly all his thoughts are bent
On a shadowy something far away,
Where the river widens to meet the bay,—
A line of black that bends and floats
On the rising tide, like a bridge of boats.

Meanwhile, impatient to mount and ride,
Booted and spurred, with a heavy stride
On the opposite shore walked Paul Revere.
Now he patted his horse's side,
Now gazed at the landscape far and near,
Then, impetuous,° stamped the earth,
And turned and tightened his saddlegirth;
But mostly he watched with eager search

---

35 *Somber* means "dark and gloomy."
45 A *sentinel* is a guard.
62 Here, *impetuous* means "acting suddenly."

D Active Reading Strategies

EVALUATE Ask students to list the words and phrases Longfellow uses in lines 31–41 to heighten suspense and the sense of danger. *("Stealthy tread," "somber rafters," "startled," "shapes of shade," "trembling," "steep and tall")* Do they think he effectively emphasizes the risks the patriots are taking with his tone?

E Active Reading Strategies

QUESTION Ask students what they think "the shadowy something" is that Revere's friend sees. *(He sees the "bridge of boats" indicating that the attack by sea has begun.)*

F Literary Elements

METER Read lines 57–65 aloud to the class, emphasizing the meter of the poem. Have students discuss how the meter reflects Revere's eagerness to ride.

Reading Minilesson

Identify Author's Purpose In a poem that is full of action and movement, including a rhythm that mimics the galloping of a horse, Longfellow slows the poem in the fifth stanza. This change in tempo does not advance the action of the poem but adds details to the setting.

Activity Have students work in pairs to read through this stanza carefully. Why do they think Longfellow elected to add these details? Ask each pair to share its conclusion with the class. **L2** COLLAB. LEARN.

Additional Resources

Reading Skills Practice Workbook

VIEWING THE PAINTING

Viewing Response *The horse, barely pausing, stops in mid-stride. The citizen comes to his window in his nightshirt. The night is dark, and the distant places unclear.*

G Literary Elements

ALLITERATION Point out to students the repetition of the soft consonant s in the middle of this stanza, especially "spectral, somber, and still." Then, as the light shines, Longfellow uses harder consonants *(b, g, d)* to emphasize Revere's feeling as he mounts his horse.

H Active Reading Strategies

REVIEW Check with students to be sure they remember what "the second lamp" signifies—that the attack will be "by sea."

Paul Revere's Midnight Ride. Artist unknown.
Viewing the painting: In what ways does this painting capture the drama of Revere's late-night ride?

G
The belfry-tower of the Old North Church,
As it rose above the graves on the hill,
Lonely and spectral° and somber and still.
And lo! as he looks, on the belfry's height
A glimmer, and then a gleam of light!
He springs to the saddle, the bridle he turns,
But lingers and gazes, till full on his sight
A second lamp in the belfry burns! H

67 Something *spectral* is ghost-like.

Teaching Support

MEETING INDIVIDUAL NEEDS: MULTIPLE MODES OF EXPRESSION

Spatial Students with a strong spatial orientation may enjoy tracing Revere's route on a map as they read the poem.

Activity Obtain a modern map of the Lexington-Concord area and help a group of students highlight all the places mentioned in the poem as they trace Revere's route. Have students present their highlighted map to the rest of the class and discuss the differences in travel between then and now.
L2 COLLAB. LEARN.

A hurry of hoofs in a village street,
A shape in the moonlight, a bulk in the dark,
And beneath, from the pebbles, in passing, a spark
Struck out by a steed flying fearless and fleet:°
That was all! And yet, through the gloom and the light,
The fate of a nation was riding that night;
And the spark struck out by that steed, in his flight,
Kindled the land into flame with its heat.

He has left the village and mounted the steep,°
And beneath him, tranquil and broad and deep,
Is the Mystic,° meeting the ocean tides;
And under the alders° that skirt its edge,
Now soft on the sand, now loud on the ledge,
Is heard the tramp of his steed as he rides.

It was twelve by the village clock,
When he crossed the bridge into Medford town.
He heard the crowing of the cock,
And the barking of the farmer's dog,
And felt the damp of the river fog,
That rises after the sun goes down.

It was one by the village clock,
When he galloped into Lexington.
He saw the gilded° weathercock
Swim in the moonlight as he passed,
And the meeting-house windows, blank and bare,
Gaze at him with a spectral glare,
As if they already stood aghast
At the bloody work they would look upon.

76 Here, *fleet* means "very fast."
81 As a noun, *steep* means "a steep slope."
83 The *Mystic* is a short river that flows into Boston Harbor.
84 *Alders* are trees in the birch family.
95 A *gilded* object has, or seems to have, a thin coating of gold.

I Literary Elements

METER Point out to students that Longfellow uses meter to mimic the sounds of the ride as he describes the ride itself.

J Active Reading Strategies

QUESTION Ask students why they think Longfellow chooses to emphasize the passing of time by beginning with the time. *(The emphasis on time makes the scope and distance of Revere's journey seem even more heroic. The fact that the action takes place in the middle of the night makes Revere seem alone in a great expanse of land.)*

Historical Note

In Longfellow's view Lexington, Massachusetts, was the location of the first battle of the American Revolution. It was fought the day after Revere's ride, April 19, 1775. "The bloody work" referred to in this stanza is the result of that battle.

Real-World Connection

Communication Paul Revere's task would have been quite different if he had to perform it today. He would have his choice of many methods of communicating his message.

Activity Have students form small groups and develop brief skits showing Revere phoning, faxing, or e-mailing his message. **L2**

Fine Art
TRANSPARENCY 31

You may want to use ***Fine Art Transparency 31*** to discuss the role of horses in the Revolutionary War.

Critical Thinking

EVALUATE Discuss Longfellow's characterization of the British soldiers and the American farmers. Present the following model to demonstrate the process involved in evaluating:

Model: I think Longfellow is obviously taking sides in this poem. The colonists are the good guys—brave, energetic, courageous—and the British are the bad guys—menacing figures floating on prison ships. But I don't think Longfellow cares about being objective. He is telling the story of an American hero, not writing a history book.

Thematic Focus

Free to Be Ask students what Revere's ride symbolized to Longfellow. What does it mean to Americans today?

ASSESSMENT

Quick Checks, p. 39

A&E HOME VIDEO.® *The following videotape is available from Glencoe.*

Be sure to preview the video for appropriateness for your class:

- **Biography—"Paul Revere: The Midnight Rider"***

*Also available in the Glencoe Literature *Video Library*.

It was two by the village clock,
When he came to the bridge in Concord town.
He heard the bleating of the flock,
And the twitter of birds among the trees,
And felt the breath of the morning breeze
Blowing over the meadows brown.
And one was safe and asleep in his bed
Who at the bridge would be first to fall,
Who that day would be lying dead,
Pierced by a British musket-ball.

You know the rest. In the books you have read,
How the British Regulars° fired and fled,—
How the farmers gave them ball for ball,
From behind each fence and farm-yard wall,
Chasing the red-coats down the lane,
Then crossing the fields to emerge° again
Under the trees at the turn of the road,
And only pausing to fire and load.

So through the night rode Paul Revere;
And so through the night went his cry of alarm
To every Middlesex village and farm,—
A cry of defiance and not of fear,
A voice in the darkness, a knock at the door,
And a word that shall echo forevermore!
For, borne on the night-wind of the Past,
Through all our history, to the last,
In the hour of darkness and peril° and need,
The people will waken and listen to hear
The hurrying hoof-beats of that steed,
And the midnight message of Paul Revere.

112 *Regulars* are soldiers and officers belonging to a permanent, professional army. *Irregulars* are those who are drafted for a short time.
116 To *emerge* is to come out.
127 *Peril* means "danger."

Teaching Support

Grammar and Language *Minilesson*

Semicolons and Conjunctive Adverbs Point out that Longfellow uses semicolons somewhat differently from the way modern writers typically do. A primary use today is between independent clauses when they are linked by a conjunctive adverb. Write these conjunctive adverbs on the board: *therefore, however, moreover, furthermore, nevertheless, consequently.* Explain that when two or more sentences are joined by a conjunctive adverb, the adverb is usually preceded by a semicolon and followed by a comma. Write the following example on the board: *Paul Revere's task was urgent; therefore, he rode as fast as his horse would go.*

Activity Have students write one compound sentence using each of the conjunctive adverbs you have listed. Ask volunteers to share their examples. **L2**

Additional Resources

- ***Grammar and Language Transparency 36***
- ***Grammar and Language Workbook,*** p. 265
- ***Grammar and Composition Handbook,*** Lessons 7.6, 13.5
- ***Writer's Choice,*** Lesson 20.5

Responding to Literature

PERSONAL RESPONSE

- How does this poem make you feel about the United States and the people who helped found it? Explain.

Brackets connect questions that are paired to develop higher-level thinking skills.

Analyzing Literature

RECALL

1. How will the friend signal Revere when the British march?
2. What methods of transportation do the British troops use?
3. Summarize the events in lines 87–106.
4. What happens when the British and the farmers meet?

INTERPRET

5. How might the friend feel waiting in the church? Why?
6. How does Revere seem to feel waiting for the signal? What actions reveal his feelings?
7. The meeting-house windows look at Paul Revere "as if they already stood aghast / At the bloody work they would look upon." What might "the bloody work" refer to?

EVALUATE AND CONNECT

8. **Theme Connection** What types of people make up the American militia? What do you learn from this poem about their desire for freedom? Support your answers with details from the poem.
9. **Imagery** is the use of words and phrases to create images in the minds of readers. What words and phrases does Longfellow use to describe the British ship *Somerset?* Why, do you think, would Longfellow want to create these images of the ship?
10. Where might a situation like the one in the poem occur in the world today? How would you like the problem to be resolved? For ideas, look at what you wrote for the **Reading Focus** on page 448.

LITERARY ELEMENTS

Meter

Meter is a regular pattern, or beat, of stressed and unstressed syllables in a line of poetry. If you read a poem aloud, you can hear the pattern. For example, the meter in "Paul Revere's Ride" sounds like the hoof beats of a galloping horse. To show the meter, mark each stressed syllable with the symbol ´, like this:

Lísten my chíldren and yóu
shall héar

1. Copy the first stanza of the poem, and mark the four stressed syllables in each line.
2. Choose another poem or nursery rhyme. Mark the stressed syllables in the first few lines.

- See **Literary Terms Handbook**, p. R6.

The Old North Church, Boston.

Responding to the Selection

PERSONAL RESPONSE

There is no one correct response. Students' responses should refer to specific elements in the poem.

Analyzing Literature

1. He will hang one lantern in the belfry arch if the British approach by land and two if by sea.
2. The British troops may arrive on foot or by boat.
3. Revere rides through several towns on his way to Concord.
4. The British fire and retreat; the farmers chase them.
5. The friend probably feels anxious because so much depends on the information he must convey.
6. Revere paces anxiously.
7. The bloody work refers to the next day's battle.
8. They are brave farmers defending their right to be free. They are good, rapid shots, and they are persistent.
9. Longfellow uses words that relate the ship to a prison. He also emphasizes how large the ship is. He suggests that the British are imprisoning Americans. He also suggests that the new, young nation is taking on a formidable enemy.
10. Students may suggest that there are countries around the globe in which certain groups are deprived of civil rights. Solutions to situations will vary.

LITERARY ELEMENTS

1. Lísten, my chíldren, and yóu shall héar
   Of the mídnight ríde of Pául Revére,
   On the eíghteenth of Ápril, in Séventy-fíve;
   Hárdly a mán is nów alíve
   Who remémbers that fámous dáy and yéar.
2. Have students share their poems.

Additional Resources

Literary Elements Transparency 39

Extending Your Response

Writing About Literature

Students' retellings should

- deal realistically with the impact of a modern setting on the action of the poem

Creative Writing

Students' books should

- use simple and concrete, but vivid and detailed, language
- make ample use of illustration

Literature Groups Remind students that Longfellow set out to produce an American mythology. Students may identify several moods, such as anticipation, anxiety, or, perhaps, pride. COLLAB. LEARN.

interNET CONNECTION

A helpful time line covering April 18–19, 1775, can be found on the Internet.

Skill Minilesson

GRAMMAR AND LANGUAGE • USING CAPITAL LETTERS IN POETRY

1. Jackson
2. Mississippi
3. In

Extending Your Response

Writing About Literature

Setting Suppose that Paul Revere's ride took place in your neighborhood in the year 2010. With a partner, retell a few stanzas of the poem, using this new setting. How will the different setting affect the action?

Creative Writing

Children's Book Write and illustrate a children's book based on Paul Revere. Include details, dialogue, and vivid language that young readers can understand. Illustrate your storybook, then share it with a child, a family member, or a classmate.

Literature Groups

What's the Mood? Longfellow sets a **mood** (a general feeling or atmosphere) when he says: "And yet, through the gloom and the light, / The fate of a nation was riding that night." What mood do these words help to create? What other phrases or lines from the poem strengthen this mood? In your group, discuss several possibilities, and come up with ten examples from the poem that fit this mood.

interNET CONNECTION

Use the Internet to learn more about Paul Revere's ride, his life, and other events in the American Revolution. Type keywords into a search engine. Use the information you find to write a report you can share with your class.

Reading Further

If you enjoyed "Paul Revere's Ride," try these other poems that Longfellow wrote about historical events:

The Courtship of Miles Standish
The Song of Hiawatha

Save your work for your portfolio.

Skill Minilesson

RETEACH • REVIEW

GRAMMAR AND LANGUAGE • USING CAPITAL LETTERS IN POETRY

A capital letter usually begins a new line of a poem. Poetry written in the twentieth century doesn't always follow this rule. Capital letters also are used for proper nouns–including specific names of people, places, and things–and for proper adjectives.

PRACTICE Find three mistakes in capitalization.

Listen, my classmates, until I am done
With the tale of a patriot's ride to jackson.
He had traveled the black-tarred roads of mississippi,
in a white sports car that was quite zippy.

- For more about capitalization, see **Language Handbook,** pp. R35–R37.

ASSESSMENT

- ***Quick Checks,*** p. 39
- ***Selection and Theme Assessment,*** pp. 69–70
- ***Performance Assessment,*** p. 37
- ***Testmaker: ExamView Pro***
- ***Interactive Tutor: Self-Assessment***

MEDIA Connection

RADIO TRANSCRIPT

Is everything you read about a hero true? Can a person still be a hero if you discover that person's story was used by others to get a point across?

Author Says Revere's Midnight Ride Not a Solitary One

from *All Things Considered*, National Public Radio, April 18, 1994

Robert Siegel, Host: On April 18, in 1775, a fabled event occurred in the American Revolution. The version that came down to most of us was the poem by Henry Wadsworth Longfellow, the one that begins, "Listen my children and you shall hear of the midnight ride of Paul Revere." Revere emerges from a new book by historian David Hackett Fischer as a far more complex and interesting figure. Fischer says the most famous rendering of Revere's story, the Longfellow poem, was crafted for a purpose.

Fischer: Longfellow published the poem in 1861, and it was meant to be a contribution to the Union war effort. Paul Revere becomes a historical loner who does almost everything by himself. The point was that one man, acting alone, could turn the course of history, and this was an appeal to individuals in the North to do it again in another crisis.

Siegel: The ride that emerged from your history is, above all, not a solitary act.

Fischer: No, quite the reverse. We found something like sixty other riders who were out that same night while he was on the road, and all of this doesn't in any way take away from Paul Revere. He, more than anybody, set those other people in motion. Joseph Warren, who was the other major leader, caught wind of it as well and had a secret informer whose identity he never revealed.

The circumstantial evidence is very strong to suggest that it was probably General Gage's American wife, who was deeply divided, who once said that she hoped her husband would never be the instrument of punishing her own people.

Siegel: Why wouldn't Revere tell how many people were involved and how it had all been planned?

Fischer: They wanted to present the idea that they were the innocent victims of British tyranny, and they were very careful to play down any sort of active role on their own part. Paul Revere was asked to write two depositions just after the battle as part of a campaign to prove that the British fired first. What he did was also to tell the story of the midnight ride, and these depositions were both suppressed and remained unpublished for more than a hundred years.

Siegel: Historian David Hackett Fischer of Brandeis University is the author of *Paul Revere's Ride*, published in April 1994 by Oxford University Press.

Analyzing Media

1. Why do you think Paul Revere's statements about April 18 were unpublished for more than a hundred years?
2. If Mrs. Gage *was* the secret informer, was she a hero?

MEDIA Connection

Objective

- To understand and apply strategies for reading a transcript of a radio interview

Literature LINK

Paul Revere's Ride This interview connects to "Paul Revere's Ride," the literature selection that immediately precedes this lesson. Point out the connection by saying that the interview reveals the history behind the legend Longfellow presents in his poem.

Analyzing Media

1. Students may suggest that Revere's deposition was suppressed because it indicated that the British did not fire first. (Actually, Revere was in jail and did not witness the battle.)
2. Some students may feel that Mrs. Gage was a hero. Others may question whether betraying a husband or wife is heroic.

Informational Text

inTIME For more examples of informational text, direct students to the articles in the *inTIME* Magazine.

Additional Resources

Media Connections, p. 9

Teaching Support

Reading Minilesson

Activate Prior Knowledge Students should be relatively familiar with the history of the nation's beginnings.

Activity Have students discuss what they already know about Paul Revere's ride and about the battle that was fought with the English the next day. As students discuss their historical knowledge, make sure their information is factual. Explain the importance of learning the facts, not fictionalized accounts of events.

L2 COLLAB. LEARN.

Additional Resources

Reading Skills Practice Workbook

interNET CONNECTION

American History Have students use a popular search engine to investigate the founding of the United States. Suggest such keywords as *Boston Tea Party, Declaration of Independence,* and *Colonial America.*

Before Reading

Objectives

- To read and analyze a poem about an elderly woman's heroic act
- To identify rhyme scheme in poetry
- To write a poem

Skills

Reading/Thinking: Evaluating; Comparing and Contrasting
Writing: Poem
Vocabulary: Multiple-Meaning Words
Grammar/Language: Pronouns
Collaboration: Literature Groups

Motivating STUDENTS

Selection Focus Transparency 39: Before presenting the photograph, ask students to discuss what they know about the role of women in the Civil War.

Reading Focus: As an extension of the Reading Focus, ask students to share the characteristics they listed. Which did the class as a whole choose most often?

Before You Read

Barbara Frietchie

MEET JOHN GREENLEAF WHITTIER

John Greenleaf Whittier was eighteen years old when his sister secretly sent one of his poems to a local paper in Newburyport, Massachusetts. Not only did the editor of the paper print the poem, but he also encouraged the shy farmer's son to educate himself and develop his talent. After two terms of high school, Whittier went on to work as a journalist, writer, and opponent of slavery. He published more than eight volumes of poetry, numerous articles and reviews, and one novel. He wrote for forty years before achieving financial success with his poetry.

John Greenleaf Whittier was born in Haverhill, Massachusetts, in 1807 and died in 1892. "Barbara Frietchie" was first published in 1863.

READING FOCUS

What makes some people more courageous than others?

Web It!
What characteristics do most brave people share? Make a word web to explore your ideas.

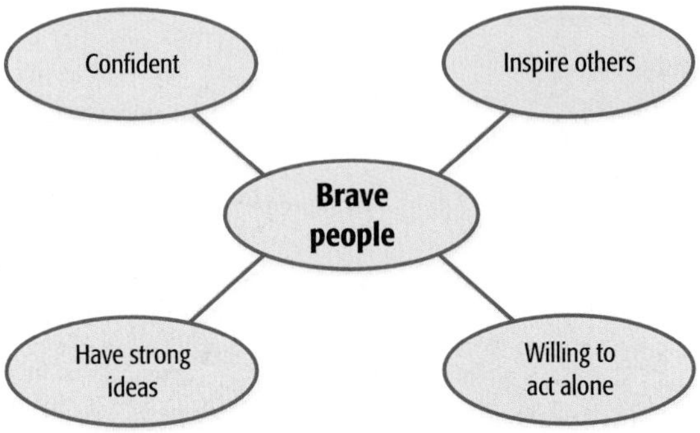

Setting a Purpose
Read to discover how one woman's act of courage became a legend.

BUILDING BACKGROUND

The Time and Place It is September 6, 1862, in Frederick, Maryland. The United States is involved in the Civil War.

Did You Know? The poem you are about to read celebrates the courage of Barbara Frietchie, an elderly woman who reportedly stood up to the Confederate soldiers as they marched through her town. The poem turned Frietchie into a legend. However, like most legends, the story is part truth and part fiction. Many people think that John Greenleaf Whittier gave credit to the wrong woman. It may be that Mary S. Quantrill is the person who waved flags at the Confederates as they marched through Frederick.

RESOURCE MANAGER

Teaching Tools and Resources
- Theme Five Planning Guide
- Literature Groups Sourcebook

Essential Lesson Support

Lesson-Specific Instruction
- Selection Focus Transparency 39
- Literary Elements Transparency 40
- Active Reading Guide,* p. 40

Assessment
- Selection Quick Checks,* p. 40
- Sel. and Theme Assmt., pp. 69–70
- Testmaker: ExamView Pro
- Performance Assessment, p. 37

Systematic Language Instruction
- Gr. & Comp. Hbk., L. 9.3

English Language Learners
- Spanish Summaries, p. 39
- Audio Library*
- English, Yes!

Spec. Needs/Strat. Interven.
- Interactive Rdg. Sbk., pp. T149–T151
- Interactive Rdg. Wkbk., pp. 76–77
- Inclusion Strat. Sbk., pp. 77–78
- Audio Library*

* Also available in Spanish

458 THEME 5

Barbara Frietchie

John Greenleaf Whittier

Barbara Frietchie, 1876.
Dennis Malone Carter.
Oil on canvas, 36¼ x 46¼.
Kirby Collection of Historical Painting, Lafayette College, Easton, PA.

Up from the meadows rich with corn,
Clear in the cool September morn,

The clustered spires of Frederick stand
Green-walled by the hills of Maryland.

Round about them orchards sweep,
Apple and peach tree fruited deep,

Fair as the garden of the Lord
To the eyes of the famished rebel horde,°

On that pleasant morn of the early fall
When Lee marched over the mountain wall;

8 A *horde* is a large group.

Reading the Selection

A Active Reading Strategies

VISUALIZE Emphasize the beautiful setting at the beginning of the poem by asking a volunteer to read the first eight lines aloud. Explain that Frederick, Maryland, almost seems to represent a paradise and stands as a symbol of the United States.

Additional Resources

- ***Active Reading Guide,*** p. 40
- ***Audio Library***
- ***Spanish Audio Library***

Teaching Support

CONNECTING TO OTHER SELECTIONS

COMPARING *selections*

This selection is paired with "Paul Revere's Ride" on pages 449–454. A lesson for teaching a comparison of the two selections appears on page 463.

The chart at the right shows three ways to connect "Barbara Frietchie" to other selections in this book.

For specific teaching strategies, see the ***Theme Five Planning Guide.***

Connection	Title
Life Skills: Lifelong Learning	"The Lesson of the Moth," p. 318
Thematic: Patriotism	"A Dictionary of Japanese-American Terms," p. 27
Literary: Character	"Chicoria," p. 419

B Literary Elements

RHYMED COUPLETS Point out to students that the poem is presented in two-line stanzas, called couplets. Also, point out that, as is usual in this poetic structure, the last words of the lines in each couplet rhyme.

C Active Reading Strategies

QUESTION Ask students which flags are flying—U.S. or Confederate? *(Make sure that they realize that "silver stars" and "crimson bars" signify the U.S. flag.)*

Vo•cab•u•lar•y Skills

Multiple-Meaning Words Point out that here *rent* is the past tense of the verb *rend,* which means "to tear," not the noun with which we are more familiar. *Seam* can also have two meanings: "fabric stitched together" and "crack" or "fissure."

Over the mountains winding down,
Horse and foot, into Frederick town.

Forty flags with their silver stars,
Forty flags with their crimson bars,

Flapped in the morning wind: the sun
Of noon looked down, and saw not one.

Up rose old Barbara Frietchie then,
Bowed with her fourscore° years and ten;

Bravest of all in Frederick town,
She took up the flag the men hauled down

In her attic window the staff she set,
To show that one heart was loyal yet.

Up the street came the rebel tread,
Stonewall° Jackson riding ahead.

Under his slouched hat left and right
He glanced; the old flag met his sight.

"Halt!"—the dust-brown ranks stood fast.
"Fire!"—out blazed the rifle-blast.

It shivered the window, pane and sash;
It rent the banner with seam and gash.

Quick, as it fell, from the broken staff
Dame° Barbara snatched the silken scarf.

She leaned far out on the window-sill,
And shook it forth with a royal will.

---

18 One *score* is twenty, so *fourscore* is eighty.
24 Confederate General Thomas J. Jackson got this nickname after the Battle of Bull Run in 1861. Another general urged his troops to follow the example of Jackson and his men, exclaiming, "They stand like a *stone wall.*"
32 *Dame* is a title formerly used for the woman in charge of a household.

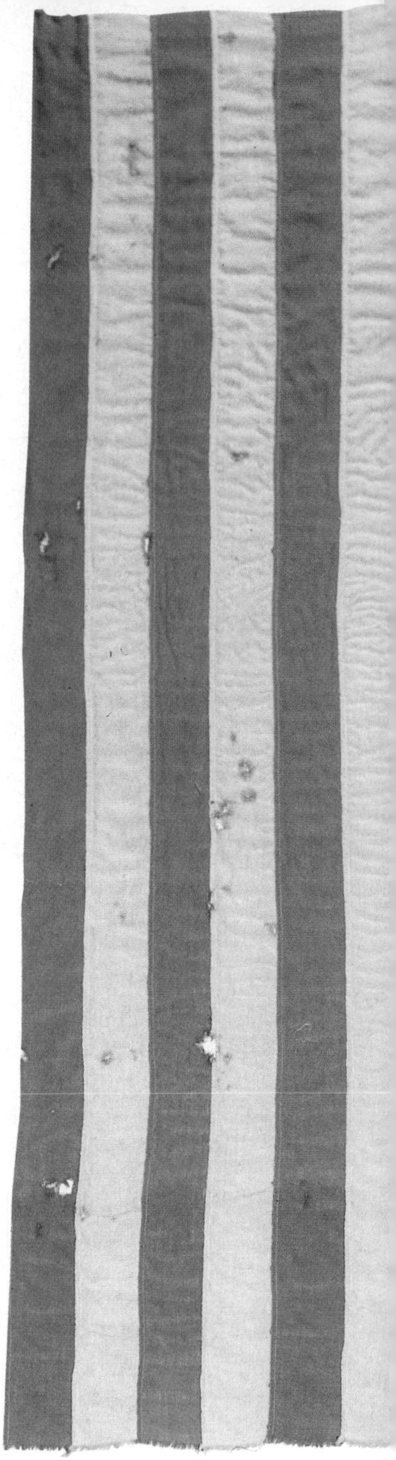

First Maryland Infantry battle flag.

Teaching Support

Grammar and Language *Minilesson*

Pronouns Write these words from page 460 on the board:

her	lines 18, 21
she	lines 20, 21, 33
his	lines 25, 26
it	lines 29, 30, 31, 34

Ask students what part of speech these words are. Define *pronoun* as a word used in place of a noun.

Activity For each of the references, have students identify the noun that the pronoun replaces. They should also label each pronoun as personal or possessive. **L2**

Additional Resources

- ***Grammar and Language Transparency 37***
- ***Grammar and Language Workbook,*** pp. 107, 113
- ***Grammar and Composition Handbook,*** Lessons 4.1, 4.4
- ***Writer's Choice,*** Lessons 11.1, 11.4

"Shoot, if you must, this old gray head,
But spare your country's flag," she said.

A shade of sadness, a blush of shame,
Over the face of the leader came;

The nobler nature within him stirred
To life at that woman's deed and word;

"Who touches a hair of yon gray head
Dies like a dog! March on!" he said.

All day long through Frederick street
Sounded the tread of marching feet:

All day long that free flag tost°
Over the heads of the rebel host.°

Ever its torn folds rose and fell
On the loyal winds that loved it well;

And through the hill-gaps sunset light
Shone over it with a warm good-night.

Barbara Frietchie's work is o'er,
And the Rebel rides on his raids no more.

Honor to her! and let a tear
Fall, for her sake, on Stonewall's bier.°

Over Barbara Frietchie's grave,
Flag of Freedom and Union, wave!

Peace and order and beauty draw
Round thy symbol of light and law;

And ever the stars above look down
On thy stars below in Frederick town!

---

45 *Tost* is an old spelling of *tossed.*
46 *Host,* here, has the old meaning of "army."
54 A *bier* (bēr) is a stand on which a coffin is placed before burial.

D Author's Craft

DIALOGUE Note that this is one of Whittier's most famous lines. Frietchie's use of *your* is the key to the impact that her words have on Jackson. It is, she suggests, his flag as much as hers.

E Critical Thinking

EVALUATE Ask students to evaluate Jackson's reaction. Whittier says that he blushed with shame, and then ordered his men to leave Frietchie alone. Encourage the students to debate the plausibility of a Confederate general's feeling shame at Frietchie's words, and of a brave man's honoring Frietchie's courage.

F Literary Elements

TRUE RHYME Explain to students that Whittier uses true rhyme in these couplets. Tell students that true rhyme means the final consonants are identical.

Thematic Focus

Free to Be Whittier portrays Frietchie as someone who is willing to risk a great deal to preserve her personal idea of freedom. Ask students to discuss the idea that freedom may have a price.

ASSESSMENT

Quick Checks, p. 40

Reading Minilesson

Compare and Contrast Point out that except for being on different sides in the Civil War, Stonewall Jackson and Barbara Frietchie have a great deal in common; in fact, one of the structural devices Whittier uses in this poem emphasizes the essential similarities between the antagonists.

Activity Have students work in groups to create Venn diagrams to show the similarities and differences between Jackson and Frietchie. Have groups share their diagrams with the class, and ask them why they think Whittier emphasizes the characters' similarities. **L2** **COLLAB. LEARN.**

Additional Resources

Reading Skills Practice Workbook

FREE TO BE 461

Responding to the Selection

PERSONAL RESPONSE

Students may note that Frietchie displays courage in facing the enemy alone and integrity in standing up for what she believes.

Analyzing Literature

1. In this ordinary small town, the men have taken down their flags as Jackson draws near. Any person raising a flag will now stand out as heroic.
2. Jackson is shown as feeling shame when Frietchie admonishes him and the narrator says Jackson has a noble nature. Whittier asks the nation to "let a tear fall . . . on his bier."
3. Jackson feels shame and orders his men to leave Frietchie alone. He seems to be a man who recognizes and respects courage, even in the enemy.
4. Whittier suggests that the townspeople are lacking in courage and sees their behavior as disloyal.
5. Most students will say the troops should leave Frietchie alone. Others may think that a single person should not be allowed to determine the course of a campaign.
6. The poem is about a battle of wills.

Extending Your Response

Literature Groups Remind students to consider the beginning, middle, and end of the poem in their answer. COLLAB. LEARN.

Writing About Literature

Students' poems should

- rhyme
- include vivid images

Active Reading and Critical Thinking

Responding to Literature

PERSONAL RESPONSE

- Which of the qualities from the **Reading Focus** on page 458 does Barbara Frietchie display?

Analyzing Literature

RECALL AND INTERPRET

1. The first sixteen lines of the poem establish the **setting.** (See page R9.) Describe the setting in a few sentences. Why, in your opinion, does Whittier begin the poem in this way?
2. How does the narrator describe Stonewall Jackson, the leader of the troops who invaded Frederick? Does the narrator condemn Jackson? Cite lines from the poem to support your answer.
3. How does Jackson react when Barbara Frietchie tells him to spare the flag? What does Jackson's reaction tell you about his character? Explain.

EVALUATE AND CONNECT

4. In lines 20–22 of the poem, what is the speaker's attitude toward all of the townspeople except Barbara Frietchie? Do you agree with the narrator's attitude? Explain.
5. If you were Jackson, how would you have wanted your troops to deal with Frietchie? Explain.
6. Is this poem about a battle? Explain.

LITERARY ELEMENTS

Rhyme

Words that end with the same stressed vowel and consonant pattern are words that **rhyme.** Often, the words at the ends of lines of poetry rhyme. The pattern of end rhyme is called a **rhyme scheme.** In the first stanza of "Paul Revere's Ride," the last words in the first, second, and fifth lines rhyme: *hear, Revere,* and *year.* Call this rhyme *a.* The third and fourth lines also rhyme: *five* and *alive.* Call this rhyme *b.* The rhyme scheme for this stanza is *aabba.*

1. What is the rhyme scheme for the first stanza of "Barbara Frietchie"?
2. Which two stanzas in "Barbara Frietchie" do not have end rhyme?

- See **Literary Terms Handbook,** p. R8.

Extending Your Response

Literature Groups

Turning the Tables John Greenleaf Whittier supported the Union. How might Barbara Frietchie have been portrayed differently if a Confederate soldier had written the poem? Discuss your answers in a group, and then share them with the class.

Writing About Literature

Celebrate Your History Mary S. Quantrill may have been the woman who taunted Jackson. Research her life, and then write a poem as a late tribute to her. Use rhyme and imagery. Present your poem to the class.

LITERARY ELEMENTS

1. *aa*
2. staff/scarf; tost (pronounced *tossed*)/host.

Additional Resources

Literary Elements Transparency 40

ASSESSMENT

- ***Quick Checks,*** p. 40
- ***Selection and Theme Assessment,*** pp. 69–70
- ***Performance Assessment,*** p. 37
- ***Testmaker: ExamView Pro***
- ***Interactive Tutor: Self-Assessment***

COMPARING SELECTIONS

Paul Revere's Ride and Barbara Frietchie

COMPARE CHARACTERS

Both poems are named after famous people from U.S. history. Think about how Paul Revere and Barbara Frietchie are alike and different.

- How are the situations facing the two characters alike? Name at least two important similarities they share.
- What personal traits do Paul Revere and Barbara Frietchie have in common? What personal traits set them apart from each other?
- Fill in a chart like the one below to develop your comparison.

Person	Traits	Date	War	Purpose
Paul Revere				
Barbara Frietchie				

COMPARE LEGENDS

The stories of Paul Revere and Barbara Frietchie are **legends.** They combine historical fact and oral history.

- What single deed is celebrated in each poem?
- What might that deed represent for other people who lived during the historical period?
- Which story do you find more inspiring? Why?

Uncle Sam's hat.

COMPARE SYMBOLS

"Paul Revere's Ride" and "Barbara Frietchie" are poems about freedom and courage. Both poems use symbols to stand for these patriotic ideas.

- Find two symbols in each poem that stand for the ideas of courage, danger, or freedom.
- Sketch the symbols you find in the poems. Then, add symbols for freedom or bravery that come from your own life and times. Create a collection or a collage of these symbols to share with the class. When you present your finished work, be sure to explain what each symbol means to you.

COMPARING selections

Objective

- To compare two poems that deal with events in U.S. history

COMPARE CHARACTERS

- Both Revere and Frietchie are individuals who stand up for their country. Both face great odds.
- Both are courageous and place a high value on honor. Revere is young and active; Frietchie is old and stooped.

COMPARE LEGENDS

- Revere's ride is celebrated in the Longfellow poem. Waving the flag and facing the enemy directly are celebrated in the Whittier poem.
- Their deeds represent active patriotism—the willingness to risk their lives for their beliefs.
- Those who prefer the first may like the clever planning and forethought described. Those who prefer the second may appreciate the simplicity and impact of a single small act.

Additional Resources

Literature Groups Sourcebook

COMPARE SYMBOLS

- In "Paul Revere's Ride" the spark, the flame, and the lantern all symbolize freedom. The tattered flag and the "stars above" symbolize freedom in "Barbara Frietchie."
- Evaluate students' responses on the basis of how they explain the meaning of the symbols.

Teaching Support

PORTFOLIO OPTIONS

Select and Reflect Have students reflect on the symbols they created by asking themselves these questions:

- What qualities of each symbol make me think of freedom or bravery?
- What does my choice of symbols say about what is important to me?

Students should attach their written reflections to their sketches and place them in their portfolios. At a later time they may wish to refer to the comments in revisions of their sketches as portfolio showcase features.

Additional Resources

Writing Assessment and Portfolio Management, pp. 42–48

FREE TO BE 463

Objectives

- To learn how to organize and group data using a database format
- To develop a sample database of sources

Teaching Strategies

Point out that one important element of a database is its ability to sort the records by fields. If, for example, one were to enter a list of names and addresses of the members of a club, one of the fields would be the zip code. When all the addresses are entered, one can sort the records by zip code, grouping all those members who live in the same zip-code area. Because the postal regulations require that bulk mailings be sorted by zip code before they are mailed, the ability to print out address labels by zip code, instead of by name, can be a great time saver for an organization.

Teaching Support

Technology Skills

Database: Organizing and Grouping Data

A database is a handy tool for organizing information. It allows you to sort and group data that you have collected in different ways. Using a database may help you discover relationships between groups of data. Best of all, it's quicker and more accurate than using paper and pencil.

Gather Data

Research a period in U.S. history, such as World War II or the Civil Rights movement. Consult print resources as well as the Internet, then choose a group of about twelve sources that you would recommend to other students. Create categories of information that are common to your sources, such as the title, author, and location of the source.

Using a Database

Database software programs differ, but they all have similar functions. The following table, which contains only a few records, will help you understand some of the terms used in database programs. These terms are defined on the next page.

Fields

Records

Title of Source	Author	Type of Source	Genre	Location
Laborers for Liberty: American Women 1865–1890	Sigerman, Harriet	Book	Nonfiction	School library
Women's Rights National Historic Park, Seneca Falls, NY	National Park Service	Web site	Nonfiction	www.cr.nps.go
"Anthony, Susan Brownell," *Notable American Women,* Vol. 1	Alma Lute	Biographical dictionary	Biography	Public library

MEETING INDIVIDUAL NEEDS

MULTIPLE MODES OF EXPRESSION

Logical-Mathematical The ability to establish logical categories of data and compare and sort correctly may come naturally to some students. However, it may be a challenge to students whose logical thinking skills are not as strong.

Activity Have students work in small groups to choose the categories they will include in their databases. Encourage them to go beyond the categories listed in the text and to include, perhaps, a ranking system to evaluate the sources, as well as other relevant information, such as the length of a book, an article, or a film. Ask each group to establish a logical order in which to display the various fields and records. Ask small groups to share their ideas with the larger group.

L2 COLLAB. LEARN.

Field Each field in a database contains only one kind of information. The top row of a database usually contains the names of the fields.

Field type The most common type of field contains text, as in the table on page 464. You can also define fields to hold numbers, dates, times, yes/no options, and, on some programs, pictures.

Record A record holds information for a single person or item. It includes one piece of information from each of the fields.

Sorting Once your information is in a database, you can sort it in a variety of ways for different purposes. For example, the items in an address book could be sorted alphabetically by persons' names.

Search In the database program's search mode, you can define a search from any field. In the pictured example, for instance, you could use the Type of Source field and ask to see only items from Web sites.

Viewing Options You can see your information in different ways. The table on page 464 shows a layout view. The browse view (below) shows only one record at a time.

TECHNOLOGY TIP
Names of views and other functions differ from one database program to another. The locations of items on menus may also differ. Check with your teacher or lab instructor or use the program's Help button to learn the names and locations in your database program.

Practice

Using your notes on materials about a period in American history, enter the items into a database. If you need help getting started, use your database program's tutorial or Help function or talk to your instructor.

Title of Source	*Laborers for Liberty: American Women 1865–1890*
Author	Sigerman, Harriet
Type of Source	Book
Genre	Nonfiction
Location	School library

1. Begin by defining your fields. You can use or adapt those shown in the example on page 464. Define them as text fields.
2. Enter each item into a record in your database.
3. After you have entered all your records, sort them in at least two different ways.
4. Look at your completed database in both the layout and browse views.
5. Try a few searches—for example, for all the books in your database or all items from Web sites.

ACTIVITIES

1. In your journal, brainstorm to find three ways in which you could use a database, whether for personal or academic reasons.
2. Build a membership database for a school club or team to which you belong.

TechnoTalk

Numbers Versus Text Explain to students that numbers in a database will be entered as text if there is no need to perform calculations on them. Thus, publication dates of books would be entered as text into a database since the user may wish to sort by date but not to add or subtract dates. On the other hand, the price of books would be entered as numbers so the owner could calculate the total value of the inventory.

Activity

1. Encourage students to consider household items that may be in need of categorizing, such as CD's, audio tapes, videotapes, sports card collections, books, and so on.
2. *Students' databases should*
   - be complete; that is, they should contain all the members
   - include any special categories of relevance to the team or club

REAL-WORLD CONNECTION

Databases Have students research how databases are used in offices. Students may interview parents and relatives about databases they use at work, or students may clip articles from magazines and newspapers. Ask each student to report on his or her findings to the entire class. **L2**

Before Reading

Objectives

- To read and analyze two poems that showcase the poets' feelings about their country
- To identify the tone used by the speaker of a poem
- To write a paragraph analyzing symbols

Skills

Reading/Thinking: Evaluating; Chronological Order; Elaborating
Writing: Poem
Grammar/Language: Irregular Verbs
Collaboration: Literature Groups

Motivating STUDENTS

Selection Focus Transparency 40: Before presenting the photograph, have students discuss the treatment of Native Americans when this country was founded.

Reading Focus: As an extension of the Reading Focus, discuss the power of symbols. Ask students why they think people care about symbols, especially national and religious ones.

Before You Read

The Pinta, the Nina and the Santa Maria; and many other cargoes of Light and *The Other Pioneers*

MEET JOHN TAGLIABUE

There's no doubt that John Tagliabue loves poetry: he's been a poet for more than fifty years. "Poetry," he says, "is all a matter of design, play, ritual, decorations, symbolism, and like our life it is always changing."

John Tagliabue was born in Italy in 1923 and lives in Maine. The poem you are about to read was first published in 1963.

MEET ROBERTO FÉLIX SALAZAR

A native of Laredo, Texas, Roberto Félix Salazar (rō ber′ tō fā′ lēs sä lä zär′) wrote "The Other Pioneers" to remind Americans that the first pioneers in the Southwest had Spanish names and that their descendants—American citizens—still do.

Roberto Félix Salazar was born in 1921. "The Other Pioneers" was first published in 1939.

READING FOCUS

What are some symbols of the United States of America? Jot down any symbols that come to mind.

QuickWrite
Share your ideas in a note to a partner.

Setting a Purpose
Read the poems to see how two individuals view their places in U.S. history.

BUILDING BACKGROUND

The Time and Place Two poets, writing in the twentieth century, respond to events from earlier times that built the United States.

Did You Know? Until 1848 present-day Texas, California, Nevada, Utah, most of Arizona and New Mexico, and parts of Colorado and Wyoming were Mexican territory. After a two-year war, the area became part of the United States. Many people from the region had been Mexican citizens and they feared that their freedom to live in a Spanish-speaking culture would be challenged.

Lone Star flag of the Republic of Texas, 1839. Collection of the Star of the Republic Museum, Washington, TX.

RESOURCE MANAGER

Teaching Tools and Resources
- Theme Five Planning Guide
- Literature Groups Sourcebook

Essential Lesson Support

Lesson-Specific Instruction
- Selection Focus Transparency 40
- Literary Elements Transparency 41
- Active Reading Guide,* p. 41

Assessment
- Selection Quick Checks,* p. 41
- Sel. and Theme Assmt., pp. 71–72
- Testmaker: ExamView Pro
- Performance Assessment, p. 38

Systematic Language Instruction
- Gr. & Comp. Hbk., L. 10.1, 10.2
- Vocabulary Power, Lesson 20
- Spelling Power, Lesson 18

English Language Learners
- ELL Sourcebook, p. 62
- Spanish Summaries, p. 40
- Audio Library*
- English, Yes!

Spec. Needs/Strat. Interven.
- Interactive Rdg. Sbk., pp. T151–T154
- Interactive Rdg. Wkbk., p. 78
- Audio Library*

* Also available in Spanish

The Pinta, the Nina and the Santa Maria; and many other cargoes of Light

John Tagliabue

America
I
carry
you
around
with
me
the
way
Buddha°
carried
a
grain
of
sand
the
way
Columbus
carried
a
compass
the
way
Whitman°
carried
a
poem
growing
expanding
like
a
galaxy
the
way
a
firefly
carries
a
galaxy
the
way
Faulkner°
carries
eloquence°
the
way
eloquence
carries
hope,
faith,
and
the
4th
of
July.

Ivory compass, c. 1580. Maker unknown. National Maritime Museum Picture Library.

10 *Buddha* (563?–483? B.C.) was the founder of Buddhism, one of the world's major religions. He believed that all things are connected, so that one might see the world in a grain of sand.
24 Walt *Whitman* (1819–1892) is considered one of America's greatest poets.
42 William *Faulkner* (1897–1962) was an American novelist and short-story writer.
44 *Eloquence* is speech or writing that is effective and stirring.

Reading the Selection

A Active Reading Strategies

QUESTION What does the speaker mean when he says he carries America around with him? *(He feels that he is completely American, that his nationality is part of the bone and fiber of his being.)*

Additional Resources

Active Reading Guide, p. 41
Audio Library
Spanish Audio Library

B Literary Elements

SPEAKER The speaker says that each of the objects mentioned in the poem is like America. Discuss what each of these comparisons might signify about the author's attitude toward America. *(The speaker sees everything in America; it gives him direction, the way a compass does; it is worthy of poetry; it is as expansive as a galaxy; it shines like a firefly; and it inspires eloquence.)*

C Critical Thinking

EVALUATE Review with students the images the author uses to characterize America. Encourage students to discuss his choices. Do they think these images properly represent America? Why?

Teaching Support

MEETING INDIVIDUAL NEEDS — ENGLISH LANGUAGE LEARNERS

Completing Sentences English language learners may find this poem difficult to follow because it separates words and phrases that native speakers will string together automatically.

Activity Have students work in mixed groups to rewrite the poem, filling in the missing words or punctuation. Although the meaning of the poem may become clearer as a result of this exercise, stress to students that the quality of the poem (of a long string of words or stream of light or pathway wherever the poet goes) is lost when words are added.

Additional Resources

English Language Learners Sourcebook, p. 62

D Active Reading Strategies

QUESTION Salazar is writing about the "other" pioneers—other than whom? *(Salazar suggests that most Americans think of pioneers as people from the eastern part of the United States who traveled west in covered wagons; they forget about those who had traveled north from Mexico many years before.)*

E Active Reading Strategies

CONNECT Salazar suggests in the first line that something is driving him to tell the story of these other pioneers. Ask students to think of a time when they felt the need to speak or write to defend someone or themselves.

F Author's Craft

CHARACTERIZATION Ask students what kind of people the other pioneers are. What elements of their character does Salazar stress? *(They are physically strong and have the strength of character to endure hardship. They are devout and brave, and they have a strong family orientation. They are also artistic.)*

D The Other Pioneers

Roberto Félix Salazar

Jose Herrera, 1938. Peter Hurd. Tempera on panel, 48 x 46⅝ in. The Nelson Atkins Museum of Art, Kansas City, MO. Gift of Mr. and Mrs. Robert B. Fizzell through the Friends of Art.

Teaching Support

Grammar and Language *Minilesson*

Irregular Verbs Write these phrases from the poem on the board: "Now I must write . . . They saw the Texas sun rise . . . And they sang the songs . . . And stood the Indian's cruel attacks." Note that the underlined words are all irregular verbs.

Activity Have students write the base form, the past tense, and the past participle for each verb. Then ask them to scan both poems for one other irregular verb and write its base form, past tense, and past participle. **L2**

Additional Resources

- ***Grammar and Language Transparency 38***
- ***Grammar and Language Workbook,*** pp. 99–104
- ***Grammar and Composition Handbook,*** Lesson 3.11
- ***Writer's Choice,*** Lessons 10.11, 10.12

Now I must write
Of those of mine who rode these plains
Long years before the Saxon° and the Irish came.
Of those who plowed the land and built the towns
And gave the towns soft-woven Spanish names.
Of those who moved across the Rio Grande
Toward the hiss of Texas snake and Indian yell.
Of men who from the earth made thick-walled homes
And from the earth raised churches to their God.
And of the wives who bore them sons
And smiled with knowing joy.

They saw the Texas sun rise golden-red with promised wealth
And saw the Texas sun sink golden yet, with wealth unspent.
"Here," they said. "Here to live and here to love."
"Here is the land for our sons and the sons of our sons."
And they sang the songs of ancient Spain
And they made new songs to fit new needs.
They cleared the brush and planted the corn
And saw green stalks turn black from lack of rain.
They roamed the plains behind the herds
And stood the Indian's cruel attacks.
There was dust and there was sweat.
And there were tears and the women prayed.

And the years moved on.
Those who were first placed in graves
Beside the broad mesquite° and the tall nopal.°
Gentle mothers left their graces and their arts
And stalwart° fathers pride and manly strength.
Salinas, de la Garza, Sánchez, García,
Uribe, Gonzálaz, Martinez, de León:
Such were the names of the fathers.
Salinas, de la Garza, Sánchez, García,
Uribe, Gonzálaz, Martinez, de León:
Such are the names of the sons.

---

3 Here, *Saxon* means "English."
26 *Mesquite* (mes kēt′) is a small thorny tree, and *nopal* (nō′ päl) is a kind of cactus. Both plants grow in desert regions of the Americas.
28 To be *stalwart* is to be morally or physically strong.

G Active Reading Strategies

EVALUATE Ask students to list the actions and qualities that Salazar attributes to men and to women. Ask students what they think of his characterizations.

H Active Reading Strategies

QUESTION Ask students why they think Salazar repeats the names of fathers and sons, even though they are identical. *(He repeats the sounds of the names to stress that Hispanic people have been in the United States for generations.)*

Thematic Focus

Free to Be Tagliabue's poem deals explicitly with the idea of freedom, but Salazar's poem does not mention freedom. Ask students what connection they see to the idea of freedom in Salazar's poem.

ASSESSMENT

Quick Checks, p. 41

® *The following videotape program is available from Glencoe.*

Be sure to preview the video for appropriateness for your class:

- **Biography—"Christopher Columbus"***

*Also available in the Glencoe *Literature Video Library*.

Reading Minilesson

Chronological Order Point out that this poem attempts to span the entire history of the Hispanic presence in the United States. Each verse deals with one or more specific time periods. Write these words on the board: *earliest pioneers, taming the land, settling in, today.*

Activity Ask students to write these words along a horizontal time line. Under each phrase, have them write sentences from the poem that relate to the time period described by that phrase. **L3**

Additional Resources

Reading Skills Practice Workbook

FREE TO BE 469

Responding to the Selection

PERSONAL RESPONSE

Students are likely to recall images of the size of the United States and scenes of the Southwest.

Analyzing Literature

1. The speaker in Tagliabue's poem says he carries America with him because it is such an integral part of who he is.
2. The other pioneers are Hispanic people who came from Spain to Mexico to Texas.
3. Each element mentioned contains a whole world and each demands to be explored. Buddha said a grain of sand contains whole worlds; a compass helped Columbus discover new worlds; writing a poem is an act of self-exploration and self-discovery; and galaxies are the next frontier that humankind must explore.
4. They are hard working, brave, and devout. Salazar says "They cleared the brush and planted the corn." He notes that they "stood the Indian's cruel attacks." And he says the women prayed and the men "raised churches."
5. Base evaluation of responses on the reasons that students give: yes, because both speak of Spain; but no, in that only the second speaks of Mexico and of settlers.
6. It shows that Hispanic people have been in the United States for generations.
7. The lack of punctuation in Tagliabue's poem enhances the sense of each element's being connected to the other. Salazar's poem is more formal, as befits a formal monument to his ancestors.
8. Students of Hispanic ancestry may prefer "The Other Pioneers" because it relates directly to their experiences or these of their relatives. Other students may prefer Tagliabue's poem because of the familiar images it contains.
9. Many students will agree that part of the American character includes the need for open spaces, the need to discover new worlds and new ideas, and the need to keep looking for a better life.
10. Salazar probably writes because he feels that not enough attention has been paid to his people. The speaker in Tagliabue's poem might be motivated by his strong feelings about America and about himself as an American.

LITERARY ELEMENTS

1. The tone is serious, imaginative, and proud.
2. The speaker takes pride in and wants others to appreciate his ancestors who crossed the Rio Grande to settle Texas.

Additional Resources

Literary Elements Transparency 41

Active Reading and Critical Thinking

Responding to Literature

PERSONAL RESPONSE

- What images came to mind as you read these poems?

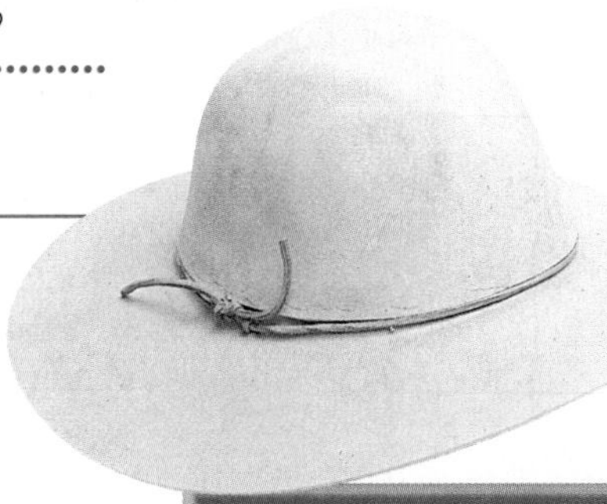

Analyzing Literature

RECALL

1. What does the speaker in Tagliabue's poem do with America? Why?
2. Who are the "other pioneers" in Salazar's poem, and from which country did they come?

INTERPRET

3. What might the sand, compass, poem, and galaxy in Tagliabue's poem all have in common?
4. In your opinion, what is the speaker's opinion of the "other pioneers"? Cite lines from the poem to support your answer.

EVALUATE AND CONNECT

5. Could these two poems exchange titles? Why or why not?
6. Salazar repeats the names of the fathers and sons in the last lines of his poem. What purpose might this **repetition** serve?
7. Salazar uses standard punctuation in his poem, but Tagliabue writes in a **style** (see page R9) that uses very little punctuation. What effect does each style have on the poems?
8. Both poems speak about America. Which poem has more meaning for you? Why?
9. Do you carry a pioneer or an American spirit with you as the people in these poems do? Explain.
10. "The Other Pioneers" opens with "Now I must write . . ." What, do you think, is urging the speaker to write? What might motivate the speaker in Tagliabue's poem?

Brackets connect questions that are paired to develop higher-level thinking skills.

LITERARY ELEMENTS

Speaker

The **speaker** is the voice of a poem. The speaker is either the poet, a fictional person, or even a thing. The speaker's words communicate a particular **tone,** or attitude, toward the subject of the poem. To understand the speaker's feelings, it is important to look at what the speaker says and study how it is said.

1. Describe the tone used by the speaker in "The Pinta, the Nina and the Santa Maria; and many other cargoes of Light."
2. What do you know about the speaker in "The Other Pioneers"?

- See **Literary Terms Handbook,** p. R9.

470 THEME 5

Extending Your Response

Writing About Literature

Symbolism Both poets use symbols in their poems. In "The Other Pioneers," the Texas sun may represent wealth that is to come. What do the symbols in the poems say about each poet's attitude toward the United States? Which symbol do you think is most powerful or effective, and why? What do the symbols you listed in the **Reading Focus** on page 466 say about your view of the United States? Write a paragraph to answer one of these questions.

Creative Writing

Poem Write a poem about how you carry America with you. You might begin with Tagliabue's first nine lines, and then add five or six lines of your own. You also might start with Salazar's first line and tell of what you must write. If you prefer, write the poem using your own style.

Literature Groups

Title A poet usually chooses a title that gives readers a greater understanding of the poem. Discuss the titles of the two poems you have read. In what ways do the titles help you understand the poems?

Interdisciplinary Activity

Social Studies Compare and contrast your family history with that of Salazar's pioneers. Use a Venn diagram like the one below, and list similarities in the area where the circles overlap.

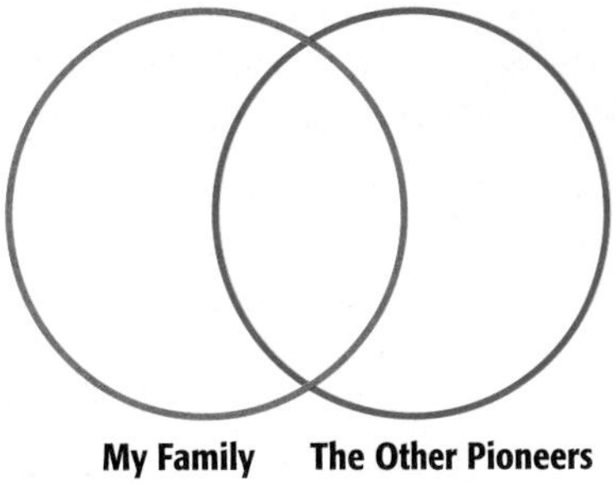

Reading Further

For other stories about Americans, read:
Letters from a Slave Girl by Mary E. Lyons
Dragon's Gate by Laurence Yep

Save your work for your portfolio.

Skill Minilesson

RETEACH • REVIEW

READING AND THINKING • ELABORATION

Elaboration is the use of details to expand on an idea or situation. In the third stanza of "The Other Pioneers," the speaker tells of "those who were first placed in graves." Then the speaker elaborates by identifying those in the graves as "the gentle mothers" and "stalwart fathers," and tells the family names of those buried there.

PRACTICE With a small group, find five or six additional examples of elaboration in the poems. Identify the initial statement and list the elaborating details.

- For more about main idea and details, see **Reading Handbook,** p. R98.

Extending Your Response

Writing About Literature
Students' responses should
- focus on symbols
- compare their effectiveness

Creative Writing
Students' poems should
- contain specific, concrete images
- show evidence of thoughtful analysis

Literature Groups Remind students to listen carefully to the opinions of others. COLLAB. LEARN.

Interdisciplinary Activity Suggest that students interview parents and older relatives for information.

Skill Minilesson

READING AND THINKING • ELABORATION

Tagliabue's poem is elaboration of the word "way" from line 8 to the end. Salazar elaborates as follows:

Statement	Elaborating Details
those	*who plowed the land and built the towns*
men	*who from the earth made thick-walled homes*
the sons	*Salinas, de la Garza, Sánchez, García*

Additional Resources
Reading Skills Practice Workbook

ASSESSMENT

- ***Quick Checks,*** p. 41
- ***Selection and Theme Assessment,*** pp. 71–72
- ***Performance Assessment,*** p. 38
- ***Testmaker: ExamView Pro***
- ***Interactive Tutor: Self-Assessment***

Before Reading

Objectives

- To read and analyze a speech by, and a poem about, Abraham Lincoln
- To recognize and understand an author's purpose
- To write an analytical paragraph about the significance of specific symbols

Skills

Reading/Thinking: Evaluating; Connecting
Writing: Poem or Essay
Vocabulary: The Latin Root *Tract*
Grammar/Language: Noun Clauses
Collaboration: Literature Groups

Motivating STUDENTS

Selection Focus Transparency 41: Before presenting the photograph and quotation, have students discuss what they know about Abraham Lincoln and how they feel about him.

Reading Focus: As an extension of the Reading Focus, ask students to name the first quality they thought of and discuss the similarities and differences in the responses.

Before You Read

The Gettysburg Address and *O Captain! My Captain!*

MEET ABRAHAM LINCOLN

During his public life, Abraham Lincoln became known as an eloquent speaker. His ability to state an important truth in a few memorable words kept his messages alive in the minds of his audiences—and in the minds of readers today.

Abraham Lincoln was born in 1809 and was assassinated in 1865, while he was president.

MEET WALT WHITMAN

Walt Whitman is among the most respected and studied poets in U.S. literature today. Whitman, who attended to wounded and dying soldiers during the Civil War, greatly admired Abraham Lincoln and wrote several poems about him.

Walt Whitman was born in New York in 1819 and died in 1892 in New Jersey.

READING FOCUS

For what is Abraham Lincoln best known?

QuickWrite
Write for three minutes, listing as many qualities as you can to describe Abraham Lincoln.

Setting a Purpose
Read the following selections to increase your understanding of a president who led the nation through the Civil War.

BUILDING BACKGROUND

The Time and Place
More than 40,000 Confederate and Union soldiers were killed or wounded at the Battle of Gettysburg in Pennsylvania in July 1863. In November of that year, the National Cemetery was dedicated at Gettysburg, and President Lincoln gave the now-famous Gettysburg Address honoring the Union dead.

Gettysburg National Military Park.

Did You Know?
Walt Whitman was greatly affected by the Civil War, in which his brother George was wounded. Lincoln's assassination also deeply saddened him.

VOCABULARY PREVIEW

conceive (kən sēv′) *v.* to form; imagine; p. 473
proposition (prop′ ə zish′ ən) *n.* a suggestion or plan; proposal; p. 473
consecrate (kon′ sə krāt′) *v.* to make, declare, or honor as holy; p. 474
detract (di trakt′) *v.* to take something away; lessen; p. 474

RESOURCE MANAGER

Teaching Tools and Resources
- Theme Five Planning Guide
- Literature Groups Sourcebook

Essential Lesson Support
Lesson-Specific Instruction
- Selection Focus Transparency 41
- Literary Elements Transparency 42
- Active Reading Guide,* p. 42
- Selection Vocabulary Practice, p. 28

Assessment
- Selection Quick Checks,* p. 42
- Sel. and Theme Assmt., pp. 73–74
- Testmaker: ExamView Pro
- Performance Assessment, p. 39

Systematic Language Instruction
- Gr. & Comp. Hbk., L. 10.3, 10.4

English Language Learners
- ELL Sourcebook, p. 63
- Spanish Summaries, p. 41
- Spanish Translations, pp. 100–101
- Audio Library*
- English, Yes!

Spec. Needs/Strat. Interven.
- Interactive Rdg. Sbk., pp. T154–T157
- Interactive Rdg. Wkbk., pp. 79–80
- Inclusion Strat. Sbk., pp. 77–78, 45–46
- Audio Library*

* Also available in Spanish

THE GETTYSBURG ADDRESS

Abraham Lincoln

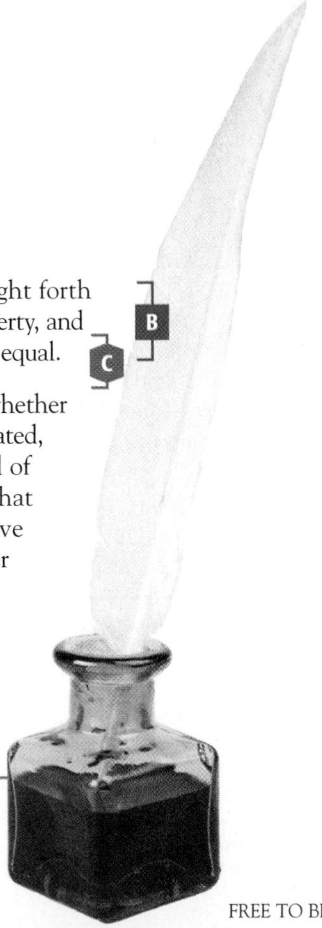

A B C Four score[1] and seven years ago our fathers brought forth on this continent a new nation, conceived in Liberty, and dedicated to the proposition that all men are created equal.

Now we are engaged in a great civil war, testing whether that nation, or any nation so conceived and so dedicated, can long endure. We are met on a great battlefield of that war. We have come to dedicate a portion of that field, as a final resting place for those who here gave their lives that that nation might live. It is altogether fitting and proper that we should do this.

1. A *score* is twenty.

Vocabulary

conceive (kən sēv′) *v.* to form; imagine

proposition (prop′ ə zish′ ən) *n.* a suggestion or plan; proposal

Reading the Selection

A Active Reading Strategies

CONNECT Ask students how they think the relatives of the deceased feel at this moment. Discuss such emotions as honor and loss.

VOCABULARY Remind students to use context clues to unlock the meanings of new vocabulary words.

Additional Resources

- ***Active Reading Guide,*** p. 42
- ***Audio Library***
- ***Spanish Audio Library***

B Literary Elements

AUTHOR'S PURPOSE Despite the fact that his purpose is to dedicate a cemetery, Lincoln begins his speech with an image of birth, not death. Lincoln refers to the birth of our nation. Ask students how they think this affects the tone. *(This reference gives a positive, uplifting, and hopeful tone to his words.)*

C Author's Craft

ALLUSION Point out that Lincoln is referring to the Declaration of Independence when he talks about equality. Why is this reference fitting? *(The deceased soldiers were fighting to abolish slavery.)*

Teaching Support

MEETING INDIVIDUAL NEEDS — ENGLISH LANGUAGE LEARNERS

Paraphrasing English language learners may find nineteenth-century word choice and syntax difficult. Be sure students understand the reverence in which this speech is held. Then, offer several simple paraphrases of the first sentence.

Activity Work with students as a group to paraphrase Lincoln's address, using contemporary language and syntax. Call on students to identify subjects and predicates, to put sentences in subject-verb-object order, and to replace complex clauses.

Additional Resources

- ***English Language Learners Sourcebook,*** p. 63

CONNECTING TO OTHER SELECTIONS

For a teaching strategy that connects this selection to "Thank You, Ma'm," see the *Theme Two Planning Guide.*

VIEWING THE PAINTING

Mort Künstler is an artist whose work is known for both authentic historical detail and a sense of drama.

Viewing Response *The painting portrays "The brave men, living and dead, who struggled here, . . ."*

D Active Reading Strategies

QUESTION Ask students why, in their opinion, Lincoln chooses to emphasize that he cannot really consecrate the cemetery. *(In the next sentence, Lincoln states that "the brave men" who fought there have already made this place holy.)*

E Critical Thinking

EVALUATE Why has Lincoln's speech been so well remembered? *(Lincoln's style and eloquence support his message that this war is about the very fundamental truths on which the nation was founded.)*

F Literary Elements

AUTHOR'S PURPOSE Lincoln delivers this speech to honor the dead, but he is also urging his listeners to support, with their lives if necessary, the task at hand.

The Angle, Gettysburg, Pennsylvania, July 3, 1863, 1988. Mort Künstler. Oil on canvas, 18 x 24 in. Collection of Mr. and Mrs. Robert L. Sharpe.

Viewing the painting: What lines or ideas in the Gettysburg Address does this painting bring to mind? Explain.

D But, in a larger sense, we can not dedicate—we can not consecrate—we can not hallow[2]—this ground. The brave men, living and dead, who struggled here, have consecrated it, far above our poor power to add or detract. E The world will little note, nor long remember what we say here, but it can never forget what they did here. F It is for us the living, rather, to be dedicated here to the unfinished work which they who fought here have thus far so nobly advanced. It is rather for us to be here dedicated to the great task remaining before us—that from these honored dead we take increased devotion to that cause for which they gave the last full measure of devotion—that we here highly resolve that these dead shall not have died in vain[3]—that this nation, under God, shall have a new birth of freedom—and that government of the people, by the people, for the people, shall not perish from the earth.

November 19, 1863

2. *Hallow* is a synonym for *consecrate.*

3. Here, the phrase *in vain* means "for no good purpose; uselessly."

Vocabulary

consecrate (kon′ sə krāt′) *v.* to make, declare, or honor as holy

detract (di trakt′) *v.* to take something away; lessen

Teaching Support

Grammar and Language *Minilesson*

Noun Clauses Explain that noun clauses are subordinate clauses that function as nouns in a sentence. They begin with such words as *how, however, that, what, whatever, where, wherever, which, whichever, who, whoever, whom, whomever, whose, why,* and *when.* They can function as subjects, direct objects, indirect objects, and objects of prepositions. Write the following example on the board, and ask students to identify the functions of the underlined noun clauses.

The world will little note, nor long remember what we say here, but it can never forget what they did here. *(direct objects)*

Activity Have students use the underlined noun clauses as subjects of sentences, using the context in Lincoln's speech.

Additional Resources

- ***Grammar and Language Transparency 39***
- ***Grammar and Language Workbook,*** p. 165–166
- ***Grammar and Composition Handbook,*** Lesson 8.6
- ***Writer's Choice,*** Lesson 14.6

O Captain! My Captain!

Walt Whitman

O Captain! my Captain! our fearful trip is done;
The ship has weather'd every rack,° the prize we sought is won;
The port is near, the bells I hear, the people all exulting,°
While follow eyes the steady keel,° the vessel grim and daring:
But O heart! heart! heart!
O the bleeding drops of red,
Where on the deck my Captain lies,
Fallen cold and dead.

O Captain! my Captain! rise up and hear the bells;
Rise up—for you the flag is flung—for you the bugle trills;
For you bouquets and ribbon'd wreaths—for you the shores
a-crowding;
For you they call, the swaying mass, their eager faces turning:
Here, Captain! dear father!
This arm beneath your head;
It is some dream that on the deck,
You've fallen cold and dead.

My Captain does not answer, his lips are pale and still;
My father does not feel my arm, he has no pulse nor will;
The ship is anchor'd safe and sound, its voyage closed and
done;
From fearful trip, the victor ship comes in with object won:
Exult, O shores, and ring, O bells!
But I, with mournful tread,
Walk the deck my Captain lies,
Fallen cold and dead.

2 Here, *rack* means "storm" or "jolt."
3 People *exulting* are rejoicing greatly.
4 The keel is the main timber that runs the length of a boat's bottom; so, *a steady keel* is a straight, even course.

Flying Cloud, 1852. Currier and Ives. Private collection.

G Literary Elements

METAPHOR Ensure that students recognize that the ship and the captain are metaphors for the country and President Lincoln, who has just been assassinated.

H Literary Elements

AUTHOR'S PURPOSE In the first four lines Whitman's tone and words are joyful and exultant. Then, he switches to a tone of grief. Whitman wants his readers not merely to remember but actually to experience the shock, horror, and irony of the assassination. Ask students why they think the poem is written in the present tense. *(This device conveys a sense of immediacy to the events. It is as though the reader is a part of the action step by step.)*

Thematic Focus

Free to Be Discuss what aspect of freedom Lincoln represents.

ASSESSMENT

Quick Checks, p. 42

A&E HOME VIDEO.® *The following videotape program is available from Glencoe.*

Be sure to preview the video for appropriateness for your class.

- ***Civil War Journals*—"The Gettysburg Civilians"***

*Also available in the Glencoe *Video Library*.

Reading *Minilesson*

Connecting Whitman in his elegy on the death of Lincoln attempts to portray the shock and grief a nation feels when a leader is assassinated. Although no one alive today recalls when Lincoln died, many people can recount where they were and what they felt when John F. Kennedy, Robert Kennedy, or Martin Luther King Jr. was assassinated.

Activity Have students ask relatives or other adults what they remember about the assassination of these individuals. Have students write a paragraph comparing people's feelings at that time with the feelings expressed in Whitman's poem. **L2**

Additional Resources

Reading Skills Practice Workbook

Responding to the Selection

PERSONAL RESPONSE

Students' answers should use specific details from the two selections.

Analyzing Literature

1. Lincoln says that the deeds of the soldiers will be remembered and that his words will be forgotten.
2. The Captain dies at the end of the journey.
3. The irony is that the world does remember his words and may only remember the battle because Lincoln spoke so eloquently about it.
4. The time of Lincoln's death is particularly sad and ironic because the end of the war should have been a time for celebration, not mourning.
5. Death in both selections is seen as both tragic and heroic.
6. Students may find Lincoln's emphasis on doing one's duty and respecting those who have sacrificed for us relevant to their lives.
7. People now might not use the word *captain* to mourn a leader but might still use *father* or *mother,* as those from whom we can learn. Today we speak of a *mentor, role model, hero,* or *teacher* as someone who inspires us.
8. The United States is like a ship in that the country is home to a group of people on a common journey. A country is not like a ship in that a ship's journeys are usually brief. Groups or areas of a country do not always travel together or in the same direction.
9. Many students will say that a leader must communicate with followers and therefore must be an effective speaker. Others may judge on the basis of actions or achievements.
10. Some students may say that both selections make them think of freeing the slaves, since Lincoln is remembered for the Emancipation Proclamation. Others may see the theme more personally. It relates freedom to think as they wish and to say how the country is run.

Active Reading and Critical Thinking

Responding to Literature

PERSONAL RESPONSE

◆ What impression do you have of Lincoln after reading these selections? How does it compare with what you wrote for the **Reading Focus** on page 472?

Brackets connect questions that are paired to develop higher-level thinking skills.

Analyzing Literature

RECALL

1. What does Lincoln say will be most remembered about Gettysburg? What will be forgotten?
2. In Whitman's poem, at what stage in the ship's journey does its captain die?

INTERPRET

3. What irony do you find in Lincoln's comments about what the world will forget and remember?
4. Why does the speaker in the poem find the time of the captain's death to be **ironic** and particularly sad?

Gettysburg grave of unidentified soldiers.

EVALUATE AND CONNECT

5. What feelings about death do these selections convey?
6. What does Lincoln say in his address that you find relevant to your life? Explain.
7. Whitman uses the terms *Captain* and *father* to refer to Lincoln. What terms, in your opinion, might a modern writer use in mourning a great leader? Explain your choices.
8. The term "ship of state" was often used in earlier times to represent a nation. Contrast and compare a ship and the United States. How are they alike? different?
9. Would you care if a leader you respect were a great or a poor speaker? Explain.
10. Theme Connection What have these selections added to your understanding of the theme "Free to Be"?

LITERARY ELEMENTS

Author's Purpose

Historical events may trigger strong emotions. Authors and poets, speechwriters and journalists—many of them attempt to capture the emotion and significance of a world event through words. They might have another purpose for writing, such as to educate the public, build support for a cause, honor a group of people, or simply tell a story. Lincoln and Whitman each based their writing on a very recent historical event about which they felt strongly.

1. In your opinion, for what purpose did Lincoln write the Gettysburg Address? What did he want his words to accomplish?
2. For what reasons might Whitman have been moved by Lincoln's assassination? How does he honor Lincoln in the poem?

● See **Literary Terms Handbook,** p. R1.

LITERARY ELEMENTS

1. Lincoln wanted to pay tribute to the dead and possibly to inspire his listeners to continue the war effort.
2. Whitman admired Lincoln and saw his death as untimely. Whitman honors Lincoln by showing his genuine love and admiration.

Additional Resources

Literary Elements Transparency 42

Extending Your Response

Writing About Literature

Symbols in Poetry What does the captain stand for in the poem "O Captain! My Captain!"? What do the ship and the journey symbolize, or stand for? How do these **symbols** compare with those in the poems on pages 449 and 459? Choose the symbol that you identify with most closely, and write a paragraph explaining what it means to you.

Creative Writing

Honoring a Leader With a group, choose an important historical figure, and write a poem or essay to honor him or her. First, brainstorm to come up with a list of the person's accomplishments. List words to describe that person. Then, as you write, be sure your feelings about the individual come through.

Literature Groups

Pick a Modern-day Patriot Whitman and Lincoln shared an intense love for their country. Discuss other American figures, political or literary, that you consider to be patriotic. How do they express their patriotism? How does their ability to speak or write contribute to their importance?

Reading Further

For more books about Lincoln and his times, try these:
Till Victory Is Won by Zak Mettger
Lincoln, a Photobiography by Russell Freedman

Save your work for your portfolio.

Skill Minilesson

RETEACH • REVIEW

VOCABULARY • THE LATIN ROOT *TRACT*

The word *detract* comes from the Latin prefix *de-*, meaning "down," and the root *tract,* meaning "to drag, draw, or pull." Lincoln said that the soldiers of Gettysburg had accomplished something beyond our powers to *detract*–drag down, or lessen–what they had done.

PRACTICE Match each word with its meaning. Use these prefixes to help you.

ex- "out" *pro-* "forward"
in- "not" *con-* "together"
re- "back"

1. contraction *(n.)*
2. extraction *(n.)*
3. intractable *(adj.)*
4. retraction *(n.)*
5. protracted *(adj.)*

a. long and drawn out
b. something pulled out of something else
c. a withdrawal, as of a promise or statement
d. something shortened or made smaller
e. unable to be guided or led; stubborn

Extending Your Response

Writing About Literature

Students' paragraphs should
- refer to specific examples from the poem
- elaborate on the meaning of each symbol

Creative Writing

Students' poems should
- include vivid descriptions
- show emotion

Literature Groups Remind students that in the United States one can express patriotism by disagreeing with the government. COLLAB. LEARN.

Skill Minilesson

VOCABULARY • THE LATIN ROOT *TRACT*

1. d 2. b 3. e 4. c 5. a

Additional Resources

Vocabulary Practice, p. 28

ASSESSMENT

Quick Checks, p. 42
Selection and Theme Assessment, pp. 73–74
Performance Assessment, p. 39
Testmaker: ExamView Pro
Interactive Tutor: Self-Assessment

MEDIA Connection

Objective

- To understand and apply strategies for reading a magazine article

Literature LINK

Harriet Tubman: Conductor on the Underground Railroad Point out the connection between the article and this selection by emphasizing how very difficult it was for enslaved people to escape.

Analyzing Media

1. Responses may include the fact that Cohen's trip was shorter and he had a phone. In addition, Cohen faced no threat. His journey was voluntary.
2. Brown had a great deal more at stake than Cohen did. For Brown escaping meant a life of freedom.

Informational Text

*in*TIME For more examples of informational text, direct students to the articles in the *inTIME* Magazine.

Additional Resources

Media Connections, p. 10

Teaching Support

MEDIA Connection

MAGAZINE ARTICLE

Anthony Cohen tried to understand what freedom meant to enslaved Henry Brown by following the journey Brown undertook to find freedom in 1848.

Traveling the Long Road to Freedom, One Step at a Time

by Donovan Webster—*Smithsonian,* October 1996

When historian Anthony Cohen set out to retrace a route on the Underground Railroad, he recovered a piece of American history.

In Spencerport, New York, the school cafeteria is packed with kids. Cohen is onstage at the room's far end. He has just started telling the story of Henry (Box) Brown. "He was a slave in Richmond, Virginia, and sometime in 1848 he had himself shipped to freedom in Philadelphia," Cohen says. "He did it in a wooden box measuring three feet by two feet by twenty-six inches. He was in there for twenty-six hours!" The students gasp. "I decided to try the same thing, only I'd ship myself from Philly to New York City."

He sits on the floor, curled tight, knees at his chest. "With the help of a few friends," Cohen says, "we measured around me. My box's dimensions were twenty-four inches by twenty-eight by thirty. We built a trapdoor into one side, so the only person able to open it was me. We drilled one-inch air holes in the box, so I could breathe. Then we figured out that people would be able to see me, so we covered most of the holes over with stickers.

"All I had in the box with me was my telephone, a bottle of water, a small quilt, a pillow, and a pocket-knife," he continues. "The trip was supposed to take two hours, but the train was late. It took more than five hours. Inside the box, the temperature rose to more than 100 degrees. My glasses fogged over. I could see sweat forming on the box's hinges: they were dripping. It was so hot I had to shift around and pull out my pocketknife. I cut the legs off my pants."

I kept thinking: 'Come on, Tony, you can do this; Box Brown did it for twenty-six hours.' Then, when I got to New York, they almost didn't take me off the train. My box had been marked to go farther on, to Long Island, but some friends found me and pulled me off."

Anthony Cohen

Analyzing Media

1. In what ways was Cohen's journey different from that of Box Brown?
2. Cohen suffered greatly. Why, in your opinion, was Brown able to undertake a much longer journey and survive?

Reading Minilesson

Evaluate Students must decide what they think about the article. Were they satisfied with the information they were given? Did they wish the author had told them more about Cohen or Brown?

Activity Ask students to work in small groups to evaluate Webster's article. Have them answer these questions. Then conduct a class discussion to find out the overall reaction of the group. **L2** **COLLAB. LEARN.**

Additional Resources

Reading Skills Practice Workbook

Before You Read

from *Harriet Tubman: Conductor on the Underground Railroad*

MEET ANN PETRY

When Ann Petry was growing up in the early 1900s, textbooks didn't have much to say about the history of slavery. So, she decided to write historical novels that would give an accurate picture of slavery in the United States. Her novel, *The Street,* published in 1946, was the first book by an African American woman to sell more than one million copies. Petry has spent much of her life in Old Saybrook, Connecticut, surrounded by historic sites and antiques that make the past come alive.

Ann Petry was born in 1908. Harriet Tubman: Conductor on the Underground Railroad *was published in 1955.*

READING FOCUS

Would you consider camping outdoors for a month in cold weather? Why or why not?

Journal

In your journal, list reasons someone might have for winter camping and equipment they would need to be comfortable.

Setting a Purpose

Read to understand the hardships that Harriet Tubman—and those she led to freedom—endured during one winter.

BUILDING BACKGROUND

Time and Place The story takes place in December 1851, nine years before the Civil War began. The setting ranges from Maryland to Canada.

Did You Know? Those who used slave labor usually believed that the best way to keep enslaved people powerless was to keep them uneducated. Several states passed laws making it illegal to teach a slave to read or write.

VOCABULARY PREVIEW

incomprehensible (in′ kom prē hen′ sə bəl) *adj.* not understandable; p. 483

incentive (in sen′ tiv) *n.* that which urges to action, especially a promised reward for working harder; p. 483

disheveled (di shev′ əld) *adj.* untidy or rumpled; p. 483

serenity (sə ren′ ə tē) *n.* calmness; peacefulness; p. 485

sullen (sul′ ən) *adj.* stubbornly withdrawn or gloomy because of bad humor; sulky; p. 485

eloquence (el′ ə kwəns) *n.* speech or writing that is expressive, effective, and stirring; p. 485

vain (vān) *adj.* unsuccessful; useless; p. 485

disclose (dis klōz′) *v.* to make known; reveal; p. 486

cajole (kə jōl′) *v.* to persuade, especially by soothing words; coax; p. 486

bleak (blēk) *adj.* cheerless; depressing; p. 488

Before Reading

Objectives

- To read and analyze a chapter from a novel about the life of Harriet Tubman
- To identify the impact of point of view from which a story is told
- To write an analytical essay about the emotional impact of a story

Skills

Reading/Thinking: Questioning; Inferring; Using a Time Line
Writing: Exposition; Dialogue
Vocabulary: Multiple-Meaning Words
Grammar/Language: Adverbs; Proper and Common Nouns
Listening/Speaking: Performing
Life Skills: Leading and Organizing
Collaboration: Literature Groups

Motivating → STUDENTS

Literature Launchers: "The Story of a Remarkable Woman"

Videodisc Side B, Segment 14

Also available in VHS.

Selection Focus Transparency 42: Before presenting the quotation and the painting, ask students to write in their journals about how an enslaved person would feel about freedom.

Reading Focus: Ask students to talk about the greatest physical hardship winter camping would cause if supplies were lacking.

RESOURCE MANAGER

Teaching Tools and Resources
- Theme Five Planning Guide
- Literature Groups Sourcebook

Essential Lesson Support

Lesson-Specific Instruction
- Selection Focus Transparency 42
- Literary Elements Transparency 43
- Active Reading Guide,* p. 43
- Selection Vocabulary Practice, p. 29

Assessment
- Selection Quick Checks,* p. 43
- Sel. and Theme Assmt., pp. 75–76
- Testmaker: ExamView Pro
- Performance Assessment, p. 40

Systematic Language Instruction
- Gr. & Comp. Hbk., L. 10.5
- Vocabulary Power, Lesson 21
- Spelling Power, Lesson 19

English Language Learners
- ELL Sourcebook, p. 64
- Spanish Summaries, p. 42
- Spanish Translations, pp. 102–108
- Audio Library*
- English, Yes!

Spec. Needs/Strat. Interven.
- Interactive Rdg. Sbk., pp. T157–T159
- Interactive Rdg. Wkbk., pp. 81–82
- Inclusion Strat. Sbk., pp. 63–64
- Audio Library*

* Also available in Spanish

Reading the Selection

SUMMARY

This is the tale of one of Harriet Tubman's many trips north on the Underground Railway. Tubman and her eleven companions must walk from Maryland to Canada during the coldest part of winter. Their only respite comes when they stop at the homes that form the Underground Railway. Tubman's leadership skills are sorely tested on this trip, but she inspires the group by telling of others who have made it. The group finally arrives in Canada in December 1851.

Spanish Summaries, p. 42

Harriet Tubman, c. 1945. William H. Johnson. Oil on paperboard, 29⅜ x 23⅜ in. Gift of the Harmon Foundation. National Museum of American Art, Washington, DC.

A Active Reading Strategies

QUESTION Ask students why the slave owners assume the person helping others to escape slavery is a man. *(They probably assume that no woman would undertake such a dangerous task.)*

VOCABULARY Remind students to use context clues to unlock the meanings of new vocabulary words.

Additional Resources

Active Reading Guides, p. 43
Audio Library
Spanish Audio Libary

Teaching Support

CONNECTING TO OTHER SELECTIONS

The chart at the right shows three ways to connect *Harriet Tubman: Conductor on the Underground Railroad* to other selections in this book.

Connection		Title
Life Skills: Leading and Organizing	→	"The People Could Fly," p. 389
Thematic: Overcoming Obstacles	→	"Stop the Sun," p. 607
Literary: Character	→	"My Two Dads," p. 19

For specific teaching strategies, see the ***Theme Five Planning Guide***.

from Harriet Tubman:

Conductor on the Underground Railroad

Ann Petry

A Along the Eastern Shore of Maryland, in Dorchester County, in Caroline County, the masters kept hearing whispers about the man named Moses, who was running off slaves. At first they did not believe in his existence. The stories about him were fantastic, unbelievable. Yet they watched for him. They offered rewards for his capture.

They never saw him. Now and then they heard whispered rumors to the effect that he was in the neighborhood. The woods were searched. The roads were watched. There was never anything to indicate his whereabouts. But a few days afterward, a goodly number of slaves would be gone from the plantation. Neither the master nor the overseer had heard or seen anything unusual in the quarter. Sometimes one or the other would vaguely remember having heard a whippoorwill[1] call somewhere in the woods, close by, late at night. Though it was the wrong season for whippoorwills. B

Sometimes the masters thought they had heard the cry of a hoot owl, repeated, and would remember having thought that the intervals between the low moaning cry were wrong, that it had been repeated four times in succession instead of three. There was never anything more than that to suggest that all was not well in the quarter. Yet when morning came, they invariably discovered that a group of the finest slaves had taken to their heels. C

1. Here, *quarter* refers to the area in which the enslaved people lived. The *whippoorwill,* a North American bird, is active mainly at night; its name imitates the sound of its call.

FYI

Allusion The fact that Harriet Tubman was referred to as Moses alludes to the Old Testament of the Bible. Moses led the slaves out of Egypt, which was under the pharaoh's rule.

B Active Reading Strategies

QUESTION Ask students why they think no one betrayed "Moses." What does this silence say about the slaves? *(They were united in trying to help people escape.)*

C Literary Elements

POINT OF VIEW Students should note that the narrator both describes the situation and gives insight into the thoughts of the masters.

MEETING INDIVIDUAL NEEDS: ENGLISH LANGUAGE LEARNERS

Noun Suffixes *-ment* and *-ness*
Direct English language learners' attention to the words *contentment* and *cleanliness* on page 485. Have students repeat the words after you. Ask what words they recognize in these two. Have students tell you the part of speech the suffixes *-ment* and *-ness* indicate.

Activity As students read the story, ask them to list other words ending in these suffixes *(movements, astonishment, foolishness, darkness, statement, mellowness).* Have students compare lists, discuss definitions, and add the words to vocabulary notebooks.

Additional Resources

English Language Learners Sourcebook, p. 64

D Active Reading Strategies

EVALUATE Ask students why the slave catchers don't immediately follow the runaways. Ask them to evaluate the reason given. *(Ensure that students notice the hypocrisy involved in claiming to follow the tenets of Christianity while enslaving human beings.)*

FYI

"Follow the Drinking Gourd" People escaping slavery used the North Star and the Big Dipper to help them navigate their way north. The folk song "Follow the Drinking Gourd" comes from this period, as the escapees kept their eyes on the Big Dipper to find their way to freedom.

E Active Reading Strategies

QUESTION Ask students why they think Tubman selected the people she would take. *(She was probably careful to select healthy, strong people who could endure the physical and emotional hardships of the trip.)*

VIEWING THE PHOTOGRAPH

Viewing Response *The group is familiar with the hardships of slavery and the danger and discomfort involved in escaping to freedom.*

Harriet Tubman (left) poses with a group of unidentified people she helped to escape from slavery.

Viewing the photograph: What may these people have in common with the eleven people Harriet Tubman conducted to freedom in this selection?

Unfortunately, the discovery was almost always made on a Sunday. Thus a whole day was lost before the machinery of pursuit could be set in motion. The posters offering rewards for the fugitives could not be printed until Monday. The men who made a living hunting for runaway slaves were out of reach, off in the woods with their dogs and their guns, in pursuit of four-footed game, or they were in camp meetings[2] saying their prayers with their wives and families beside them.

Harriet Tubman could have told them that there was far more involved in this matter of running off slaves than signaling the would-be runaways by imitating the call of a whippoorwill, or a hoot owl, far more involved than a matter of waiting for a clear night when the North Star was visible.

In December, 1851, when she started out with the band of fugitives that she planned to take to Canada, she had been in the vicinity of the plantation for days, planning the trip, carefully selecting the slaves that she would take with her.

She had announced her arrival in the quarter by singing the forbidden spiritual—"Go down, Moses, 'way down to Egypt Land"[3]—singing it softly outside the door of a slave cabin, late at night. The husky voice was beautiful even when it was barely more than a murmur borne[4] on the wind.

Once she had made her presence known, word of her coming spread from cabin to cabin. The slaves whispered to each other, ear to mouth, mouth to ear, "Moses is here." "Moses has come." "Get ready. Moses is back again." The ones who had agreed to go North with her put ashcake[5] and salt herring in an old bandanna, hastily tied it into a bundle, and then waited patiently for the signal that meant it was time to start.

There were eleven in this party, including one of her brothers and his wife. It was the largest group that she had ever conducted, but she was determined that more and more slaves should know what freedom was like.

She had to take them all the way to Canada. The Fugitive Slave Law[6] was no

2. *Camp meetings* are religious services held in a tent or outdoors.
3. *["Go down . . . Egypt Land"]* is a line from an African American folk song based on a Bible story about Moses leading the Israelites out of slavery in Egypt. Certain songs were forbidden for fear that they might inspire enslaved people to escape or rebel.
4. *Borne* is the past participle of *to bear* and, here, means "carried; transported."
5. *Ashcake* is a cornmeal bread that's baked among the ashes at the back of a fireplace.
6. The 1850 *Fugitive Slave Law* allowed owners of escaped enslaved people to get those people back, even if the people fleeing slavery had reached free states.

Teaching Support

LITERATURE & HUMANITIES

Display "Forward," Transparency 30 in *United States History and Art*, and have small groups discuss the complex moral choices Tubman made in her work.

Reading Minilesson

Questioning Point out to students that there are a number of questions about this story that an active reader might ask. For example, *If all the enslaved people know that Harriet is around the compound for several days before the escape, why does no one turn her in? Why does Harriet worry about guiding a large group? Why would a large group be more problematic than a small one?*

Activity Have students work in small groups to create five substantive questions that will lead to interesting discussions. Have each group share and then discuss its questions with the rest of the class. Ask students to what extent these discussions broadened their understanding of the work. **L2** **COLLAB. LEARN.**

Additional Resources

Reading Skills Practice Workbook

F longer a great many incomprehensible words written down on the country's lawbooks. The new law had become a reality. It was Thomas Sims, a boy, picked up on the streets of Boston at night and shipped back to Georgia. It was Jerry and Shadrach, arrested and jailed with no warning.

She had never been in Canada. The route beyond Philadelphia was strange to her. But she could not let the runaways who accompanied her know this. As they walked along she told them stories of her own first flight, she kept painting vivid word pictures of what it would be like to be free.

But there were so many of them this time. She knew moments of doubt when she was half-afraid, and kept looking back over her shoulder, imagining that she heard the sound of pursuit. They would certainly be pursued. Eleven of them. Eleven thousand dollars' worth of flesh and bone and muscle that belonged to Maryland planters. If they were caught, the eleven runaways would be whipped and sold South, but she—she would probably be hanged.

They tried to sleep during the day but they never could wholly relax into sleep. She could tell by the positions they assumed, by their restless movements. And they walked at night. Their progress was slow. It took them three nights of walking to reach the first stop. She had told them about the place where they would stay, promising warmth and good food, holding these things out to them as an incentive to keep going.

When she knocked on the door of a farmhouse, a place where she and her parties of runaways had always been welcome, always been given shelter and plenty to eat, there was no answer. She knocked again, softly. A voice from within said, "Who is it?" There was fear in the voice.

She knew instantly from the sound of the voice that there was something wrong. She said, "A friend with friends," the password on the Underground Railroad.

The door opened, slowly. The man who stood in the doorway looked at her coldly, looked with unconcealed astonishment and fear at the eleven disheveled runaways who were standing near her. Then he shouted, "Too many, too many. It's not safe. My place was searched last week. It's not safe!" and slammed the door in her face.

G She turned away from the house, frowning. She had promised her passengers food and rest and warmth, and instead of that, there would be hunger and cold and more walking over the frozen ground. Somehow she would have to instill[7] courage into these eleven people, most of them strangers, would have to feed them on hope and bright dreams of freedom instead of the fried pork and corn bread and milk she had promised them.

They stumbled along behind her, half-dead for sleep, and she urged them on, though she was as tired and as discouraged as they were. She had never been in Canada but she kept painting wondrous

7. To *instill* something is to put it in gradually, little by little.

Vocabulary

incomprehensible (in′ kom prē hen′ sə bəl) *adj.* not understandable

incentive (in sen′ tiv) *n.* that which urges to action, especially a promised reward for working harder

disheveled (di shev′ əld) *adj.* untidy or rumpled

F Critical Thinking

INFER Ask students to infer from this description how drastically the Fugitive Slave Law affected Tubman and other people who had escaped from slavery. Have students review the following model:

Model: I know that the new law meant that enslaved people who had escaped to the North could now be returned to their owners in the South. Now Tubman had to make sure her group reached Canada before they were safe. This would be more difficult than just getting to the North, because they walked most of the way. Also, formerly enslaved people were probably nervous that someone would come after them in their new homes in the North.

Historical Note

In 1851 the average annual salary in the United States was less than $700; thus $11,000 would be equivalent to nearly 15 years' salary.

G Literary Elements

POINT OF VIEW Remind students that the narrator gives readers the thoughts and feelings of Tubman, but describes the events from a third-person point of view.

Life Skills Connection

Leading and Organizing Tubman knew how to inspire and motivate people. Some of her skills were peculiar to her situation, but many of her leadership skills could be used in any situation.

Activity Divide students into small groups and ask each group to list the methods and skills Tubman uses to keep up morale. Which of these are most effective? Have each group share their conclusions with the class. *(Suggested answers: Tubman models the behavior she wants from the group, puts the needs of the group ahead of those of individuals, inspires with well-chosen words; she withholds negative information that might discourage the group.)* **L2** COLLAB. LEARN.

H Literary Elements

POINT OF VIEW Ask students what kind of narration is used in this story. Why do they think Petry chooses this particular narrative stance? *(The third-person omniscient narrator is important to this story because it allows Petry to show the thoughts of the slave owners, Tubman, and others involved in the escape. The third-person narrator lends a work the illusion of objectivity and universality.)*

I Active Reading Strategies

QUESTION Why don't Tubman's companions believe her story about Thomas Garrett? *(They have not encountered much kindness or humanity from white people. They cannot believe in simple generosity or that there are white people who care about their freedom.)*

J Active Reading Strategies

CONNECT Ask students how they would have felt at the moment when the German man said, "Good, bring them in."

word pictures of what it would be like. She managed to dispel[8] their fear of pursuit, so that they would not become hysterical, panic-stricken. Then she had to bring some of the fear back, so that they would stay awake and keep walking though they drooped with sleep.

H Yet during the day, when they lay down deep in a thicket, they never really slept, because if a twig snapped or the wind sighed in the branches of a pine tree, they jumped to their feet, afraid of their own shadows, shivering and shaking. It was very cold, but they dared not make fires because someone would see the smoke and wonder about it.

She kept thinking, eleven of them. Eleven thousand dollars' worth of slaves. And she had to take them all the way to Canada. Sometimes she told them about Thomas Garrett, in Wilmington. She said he was their friend even though he did not know them. He was the friend of all fugitives. He called them God's poor. He was a Quaker and his speech was a little different from that of other people. His clothing was different, too. He wore the wide-brimmed hat that the Quakers wear.

She said that he had thick white hair, soft, almost like a baby's, and the kindest eyes she had ever seen. He was a big man and strong, but he had never used his strength to harm anyone, always to help people. He would give all of them a new pair of shoes. Everybody. He always did. Once they reached his house in Wilmington, they would be safe. He would see to it that they were.

She described the house where he lived, told them about the store where he sold shoes. She said he kept a pail of milk and a loaf of bread in the drawer of his desk so that he would have food ready at hand for any of God's poor who should suddenly appear before him, fainting with hunger. There was a hidden room in the store. A whole wall swung open, and behind it was a room where he could hide fugitives. On the wall there were shelves filled with small boxes—boxes of shoes—so that you would never guess that the wall actually opened.

While she talked, she kept watching them. They did not believe her. She could tell by their expressions. They were thinking, New shoes, Thomas Garrett, Quaker, Wilmington—what foolishness was this? Who knew if she told the truth? Where was she taking them anyway? I

That night they reached the next stop—a farm that belonged to a German. She made the runaways take shelter behind trees at the edge of the fields before she knocked at the door. She hesitated before she approached the door, thinking, suppose that he, too, should refuse shelter, suppose— Then she thought, Lord, I'm going to hold steady on to You and You've got to see me through—and knocked softly.

She heard the familiar guttural[9] voice say, "Who's there?"

She answered quickly, "A friend with friends."

He opened the door and greeted her warmly. "How many this time?" he asked.

"Eleven," she said and waited, doubting, wondering.

He said, "Good. Bring them in." J

He and his wife fed them in the lamplit kitchen, their faces glowing, as they offered food and more food, urging them to eat, saying there was plenty for everybody,

8. To *dispel* something is to make it go away or disappear.

9. A *guttural* voice has a rough, harsh sound.

Teaching Support

interNET CONNECTION

Underground Railroad Have students use a search engine to look for information about runaway enslaved people. Suggest they try entering keywords such as *Harriet Tubman, underground railway,* or *slavery museum.*

MEETING INDIVIDUAL NEEDS: ADVANCED LEARNERS

Persuasion Point out to students that Tubman uses three kinds of stories to persuade her passengers to continue with her. First, she assures them that others will help; then she tells them that others like them have succeeded; finally, she focuses on the consequences of failure.

Activity Have students deliver a persuasive speech on a topic of their choice that follows the same basic pattern of persuasion that Tubman uses. Encourage students to use examples and stories to bring their speeches to life. Students should deliver their speeches to the entire class. **L3**

have more milk, have more bread, have more meat.

They spent the night in the warm kitchen. They really slept, all that night and until dusk the next day. When they left, it was with reluctance. They had all been warm and safe and well-fed. It was hard to exchange the security offered by that clean warm kitchen for the darkness and the cold of a December night.

Harriet had found it hard to leave the warmth and friendliness, too. But she urged them on. For a while, as they walked, they seemed to carry in them a measure of contentment; some of the serenity and the cleanliness of that big warm kitchen lingered on inside them. But as they walked farther and farther away from the warmth and the light, the cold and the darkness entered into them. They fell silent, sullen, suspicious. She waited for the moment when some one of them would turn mutinous.[10] It did not happen that night.

Two nights later she was aware that the feet behind her were moving slower and slower. She heard the irritability in their voices, knew that soon someone would refuse to go on.

K She started talking about William Still and the Philadelphia Vigilance Committee.[11] No one commented. No one asked any questions. She told them the story of William and Ellen Craft and how they escaped from Georgia. Ellen was so fair that she looked as though she were white, and so she dressed up in a man's clothing and she looked like a wealthy young planter. Her husband, William, who was dark, played the role of her slave. Thus they traveled from Macon, Georgia, to Philadelphia, riding on the trains, staying at the finest hotels. Ellen pretended to be very ill—her right arm was in a sling, and her right hand was bandaged, because she was supposed to have rheumatism. Thus she avoided having to sign the register at the hotels for she could not read or write. They finally arrived safely in Philadelphia, and then went on to Boston.

L No one said anything. Not one of them seemed to have heard her.

She told them about Frederick Douglass, the most famous of the escaped slaves, of his eloquence, of his magnificent appearance. Then she told them of her own first vain effort at running away, evoking[12] the memory of that miserable life she had led as a child, reliving it for a moment in the telling.

M But they had been tired too long, hungry too long, afraid too long, footsore too long. One of them suddenly cried out in despair, "Let me go back. It is better to be a slave than to suffer like this in order to be free."

She carried a gun with her on these trips. She had never used it—except as a threat. Now as she aimed it, she experienced a feeling of guilt, remembering that

10. To turn *mutinous* (mūt′ ən əs) is to become openly rebellious.

11. Before the Civil War, this organization raised money to help escaping slaves. *Vigilance* means "the state of being watchful and alert to danger or trouble."

12. Harriet is calling up *(evoking)* this memory.

Vocabulary

serenity (sə ren′ ə tē) *n.* calmness; peacefulness
sullen (sul′ ən) *adj.* stubbornly withdrawn or gloomy because of bad humor; sulky
eloquence (el′ ə kwəns) *n.* speech or writing that is expressive, effective, and stirring
vain (vān) *adj.* unsuccessful; useless

K Literary Elements

MOTIVATION Point out that as the group becomes more downhearted, Tubman tells a different kind of story. She no longer concentrates on stories of the people who will help them. Ask what kind of stories she tells now. For what reasons? *(Now she begins to tell stories of enslaved people who made it to freedom. She no longer speaks of help that comes from others; now she tries to empower them to find help within themselves, from their own innate intelligence, resourcefulness, and courage.)*

L Active Reading Strategies

CONNECT Ask students what effect the silence of the group has on Tubman and on the reader. What does the silence say about the feelings of Tubman's passengers? *(The silence suggests that the group doesn't believe Tubman. It also vividly portrays how completely discouraged and worn out they must have been.)*

M Author's Craft

REPETITION Point out that just before one of the group members loses courage completely, Petry repeats "too long" four times. What do students think the repetitions suggest? *(They emphasize how hard the task of escape has been.)*

MEETING INDIVIDUAL NEEDS — MULTIPLE MODES OF EXPRESSION

Spatial Spatial learners may better understand the hardships Tubman and her companions underwent by tracing Tubman's route.

Activity Using the place names mentioned in the story and maps, have students trace a possible route that the group may have followed. Have them figure out approximately how many miles Tubman and her companions walked. **L2**

Active Reading Strategies

QUESTION Ask students to speculate on how the overseer might force an enslaved person to turn traitor. *(The overseer might threaten loved ones or whip the returned escapee until he or she betrayed information.)*

Active Reading Strategies

CONNECT Ask students what modern phrase they might substitute for "Freedom is not bought with dust." *(Now people might say, "Freedom doesn't come cheap.")*

Historical Note

Tubman's seizures were probably caused by an incident that occurred when she was about fifteen or sixteen years old. When she tried to protect a fellow enslaved person from a beating, her master struck her in the head with a rock. The impact nearly killed her; for the rest of her life, she experienced seizures and blackouts.

Teaching Support

time, years ago, when she had prayed for the death of Edward Brodas, the Master, and then not too long afterward had heard that great wailing cry that came from the throats of the field hands, and knew from the sound that the Master was dead.

One of the runaways said, again, "Let me go back. Let me go back," and stood still, and then turned around and said, over his shoulder, "I am going back."

She lifted the gun, aimed it at the despairing slave. She said, "Go on with us or die." The husky low-pitched voice was grim.

He hesitated for a moment and then he joined the others. They started walking again. She tried to explain to them why none of them could go back to the plantation. If a runaway returned, he would turn traitor, the master and the overseer would force him to turn traitor. The returned slave would disclose the stopping places, the hiding places, the cornstacks they had used with the full knowledge of the owner of the farm, the name of the German farmer who had fed them and sheltered them. These people who had risked their own security to help runaways would be ruined, fined, imprisoned.

She said, "We got to go free or die. And freedom's not bought with dust."

This time she told them about the long agony of the Middle Passage[13] on the old slave ships, about the black horror of the holds, about the chains and the whips. They too knew these stories. But she wanted to remind them of the long hard way they had come, about the long hard way they had yet to go. She told them about Thomas Sims, the boy picked up on the streets of Boston and sent back to Georgia. She said when they got him back to Savannah, got him in prison there, they whipped him until a doctor who was standing by watching said, "You will kill him if you strike him again!" His master said, "Let him die!"

Thus she forced them to go on. Sometimes she thought she had become nothing but a voice speaking in the darkness, cajoling, urging, threatening. Sometimes she told them things to make them laugh, sometimes she sang to them, and heard the eleven voices behind her blending softly with hers, and then she knew that for the moment all was well with them.

She gave the impression of being a short, muscular, indomitable[14] woman who could never be defeated. Yet at any moment she was liable to be seized by one of those curious fits of sleep,[15] which might last for a few minutes or for hours.

Even on this trip, she suddenly fell asleep in the woods. The runaways, ragged, dirty, hungry, cold, did not steal the gun as they might have, and set off by themselves, or turn back. They sat on the ground near her and waited patiently until she awakened. They had come to trust her implicitly,[16] totally. They, too, had come to believe her repeated statement, "We got to go

13. The *Middle Passage* was the sea route followed by slave traders between Africa and the Americas.

14. *Indomitable* (in dom′ ə tə bəl) means "that cannot be conquered; unbeatable."
15. Harriet's *curious fits of sleep* were occasional unexplained spells of dizziness or unconsciousness.
16. To trust *implicitly* (im plis′ it lē) is to have complete faith—no questions, doubts, or hesitations.

Vocabulary
disclose (dis klōz′) *v.* to make known; reveal
cajole (kə jōl′) *v.* to persuade, especially by soothing words; coax

Real-World Connection

Making a Difference Point out to students that there are many different ways to work for a cause one believes in. One can contribute money, one can make speeches, or one can act. Ask them to identify people today (locally, nationally, or internationally) who act on their beliefs by working alongside the people they help.

Activity Have students look in magazines and newspapers for information about a cause that interests them. If possible encourage students to work on a charitable project that involves direct action on their part. **L2**

free or die." She was leading them into freedom, and so they waited until she was ready to go on.

Finally, they reached Thomas Garrett's house in Wilmington, Delaware. Just as Harriet had promised, Garret gave them all new shoes, and provided carriages to take them on to the next stop.

By slow stages they reached Philadelphia, where William Still hastily recorded their names, and the plantations whence they had come, and something of the life they had led in slavery. Then he carefully hid what he had written, for fear it might be discovered. In 1872 he published this record in book form and called it *The Underground Railroad.* In the foreword to his book he said: "While I knew the danger of keeping strict records, and while I did not then dream that in my day slavery would be blotted out, or that the time would come when I could publish these records, it used to afford me great satisfaction to take them down, fresh from the lips of fugitives on the way to freedom, and to preserve them as they had given them."

William Still, who was familiar with all the station stops on the Underground Railroad, supplied Harriet with money and sent her and her eleven fugitives on to Burlington, New Jersey.

Harriet felt safer now, though there were danger spots ahead. But the biggest part of her job was over. As they went farther and farther north, it grew colder; she was aware of the wind on the Jersey ferry and aware of the cold damp in New York. From New York they went on to Syracuse, where the temperature was even lower.

In Syracuse she met the Reverend J. W. Loguen, known as "Jarm" Loguen. This was the beginning of a lifelong friendship. Both Harriet and Jarm Loguen were to become friends and supporters of Old John Brown.

Did You Know?
John Brown was a leader of the American antislavery movement. In 1859 he led an unsuccessful raid of a federal weapons storehouse in Virginia, hoping to inspire a slave rebellion.

From Syracuse they went north again, into a colder, snowier city—Rochester. Here they almost certainly stayed with Frederick Douglass, for he wrote in his autobiography:

Q "On one occasion I had eleven fugitives at the same time under my roof, and it was necessary for them to remain with me until I could collect sufficient money to get them to Canada. It was the largest number I ever had at any one time, and I had some difficulty in providing so many with food and shelter, but, as may well be imagined, they were not very fastidious[17] in either direction, and were well content with very plain food, and a strip of carpet on the floor for a bed, or a place on the straw in the barnloft."

Late in December, 1851, Harriet arrived in St. Catharines, Canada West (now Ontario), with the eleven fugitives. It had taken almost a month to complete this journey; most of the time had been spent getting out of Maryland.

R That first winter in St. Catharines was a terrible one. Canada was a strange frozen land, snow everywhere, ice everywhere, and a bone-biting cold the like of which none of them had ever experienced before. Harriet rented a small frame house in the

17. If they had been *fastidious* (fas tid′ ē əs), they would have been difficult to please or satisfy.

P Critical Thinking

INFER Ask students why they think Tubman feels safer in New Jersey. *(The farther north the group travels, the less likelihood there is of betrayal or recapture.)*

Q Active Reading Strategies

QUESTION Why aren't the runaways "fastidious" about food or shelter? *(As both enslaved people and runaways, they have had little and expect little.)*

R Active Reading Strategies

RESPOND Ask students how they think the runaways feel after reaching Canada.

Writing Minilesson

Exposition Point out to students that Petry provides several paragraphs of exposition at the beginning of this story. When writing about a situation or event the reader knows little about, the writer must establish the context carefully and clearly.

Activity Have students plan their autobiographies. Before they can write about their own birth, however, they must set the scene by explaining something about the place where they were born and their family. Have them write two or more paragraphs of exposition that would precede the words, "On the day I was born . . ." **L2**

Additional Resources

Writer's Choice, Lesson 5.1

VIEWING THE PAINTING

William H. Johnson was one of the African American artists who were part of a movement in the 1920s and 1930s that came to be known as the Harlem Renaissance. Johnson often uses brilliant colors and simplified forms. This brightly colored painting is reminiscent of a quilt in its regularly arranged forms.

Viewing Response *The variety of people and the vocations and skills in the painting suggest the importance of the work done by those who helped in the Underground Railroad.*

Active Reading Strategies

QUESTION What does Petry mean when she says the climate in Maryland "made for ease of living"? Ask students to list the specific things that are easier in a warm climate.

Thematic Focus

Free to Be Point out to students the great risks the people in this story took to gain freedom. Also point out that Tubman's definition of freedom not only encompassed freedom for herself but freedom for all.

ASSESSMENT

Quick Checks, p. 43

Underground Railroad, c. 1945. William H. Johnson. Oil on paperboard, 33⅜ x 36⅜ in. National Museum of American Art, Washington, DC.

Viewing the painting: In what ways does this painting reflect the concept of the Underground Railroad?

town and set to work to make a home. The fugitives boarded with her. They worked in the forests, felling trees, and so did she. Sometimes she took other jobs, cooking or cleaning house for people in the town. She cheered on these newly arrived fugitives, working herself, finding work for them, finding food for them, praying for them, sometimes begging for them.

Often she found herself thinking of the beauty of Maryland, the mellowness of the soil, the richness of the plant life there. The climate itself made for an ease of living that could never be duplicated in this bleak, barren countryside.

In spite of the severe cold, the hard work, she came to love St. Catharines, and the other towns and cities in Canada where black men lived. She discovered that freedom meant more than the right to change jobs at will, more than the right to keep the money that one earned. It was the right to vote and to sit on juries. It was the right to be elected to office. In Canada there were black men who were county officials and members of school boards. St. Catharines had a large colony of ex-slaves, and they owned their own homes, kept them neat and clean and in good repair. They lived in whatever part of town they chose and sent their children to the schools.

When spring came she decided that she would make this small Canadian city her home—as much as any place could be said to be home to a woman who traveled from Canada to the Eastern Shore of Maryland as often as she did.

In the spring of 1852, she went back to Cape May, New Jersey. She spent the summer there, cooking in a hotel. That fall she returned, as usual, to Dorchester County, and brought out nine more slaves, conducting them all the way to St. Catharines, in Canada West, to the bone-biting cold, the snow-covered forests—and freedom.

She continued to live in this fashion, spending the winter in Canada, and the spring and summer working in Cape May, New Jersey, or in Philadelphia. She made two trips a year into slave territory, one in the fall and another in the spring. She now had a definite crystallized[18] purpose, and in carrying it out, her life fell into a pattern which remained unchanged for the next six years.

18. Here, *crystallized* means "having a clear, specific form."

Vocabulary
bleak (blēk) *adj.* cheerless; depressing

Teaching Support

Grammar and Language Minilesson

Adverbs Write these words on the board: *implicitly, totally, finally, hastily, carefully, certainly.* Explain that these words are adverbs, words that modify verbs, adjectives, or adverbs and often answer the question *When? Where? How?* or *To what extent?* Many adverbs are formed by adding *-ly* to adjectives. Note that not all adverbs end in *-ly*.

Activity Have students find as many adverbs ending in *-ly* as they can in the story. They should write the word that each adverb modifies, identify what part of speech the modified word is, and write down the question the adverb answers. *(Example, from page 486:* suddenly fell. Fell *is a verb;* suddenly *answers the question* How did she fall asleep?*)* **L2**

Additional Resources

- ***Grammar and Language Transparency 40***
- ***Grammar and Language Workbook,*** pp. 129–133
- ***Grammar and Composition Handbook,*** Lessons 6.1–6.3
- ***Writer's Choice,*** Lesson 12.5

Responding to Literature

PERSONAL RESPONSE

- Could you have completed a journey like the one Tubman and the fugitives endured? As you think about your answer, review your journal entry from the **Reading Focus** on page 479.

Brackets connect questions that are paired to develop higher-level thinking skills.

Analyzing Literature

RECALL

1. What was the Fugitive Slave Law?
2. What does Harriet Tubman tell the fugitives about Garrett?
3. How does Harriet use her gun?
4. What is life like for the formerly enslaved people who make it to Canada?

INTERPRET

5. Why does Harriet take her group all the way to Canada?
6. How does Harriet use words to keep the runaways going?
7. Why does Harriet refuse to let any of the fugitives return to their former homes?
8. What does Harriet learn about freedom in Canada?

EVALUATE AND CONNECT

9. **Situational irony** exists when the actual outcome of a situation is the opposite of what is expected. What is ironic about the reason many of the fugitive-slave hunters are not available on Sundays?
10. **Theme Connection** Harriet says, "We got to go free or die." Do you think she is right? Is freedom more important than food or shelter or safety? Give reasons for your opinion.

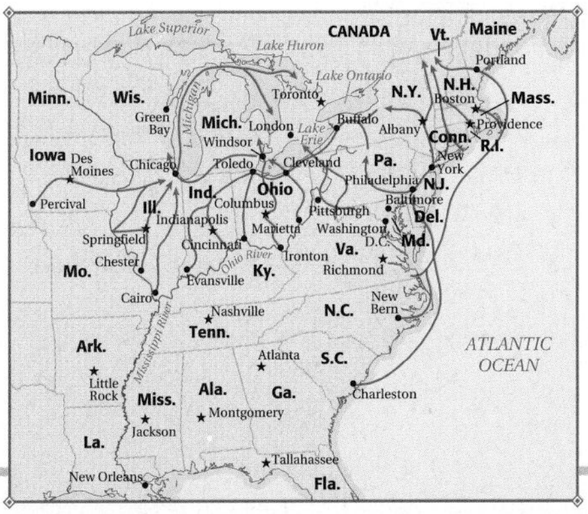

Underground Railroad routes traveled by people escaping slavery during the 1800s.

LITERARY ELEMENTS

Point of View

Point of view is the relationship of the narrator, or storyteller, to the story. In this selection, Petry uses an **omniscient third-person point of view.** The narrator is outside of the story and reveals the thoughts of several characters. We learn not only what Harriet Tubman, the main character, is thinking, but also what various other characters think–slave masters, fugitives, and some of the people who assist them.

1. Look over the story and list some of the things the slave masters think.
2. Would the story have been more interesting told in the first person–that is, as if Tubman were telling her story? Why or why not?

- See **Literary Terms Handbook,** pp. R7–R8.

Responding to the Selection

PERSONAL RESPONSE

Many students will admit that they probably could not have completed a journey like Tubman's. It takes tremendous motivation to go so far with so little real promise of success.

Analyzing Literature

1. The Fugitive Slave Law required runaways in free states to be returned to their owners.
2. Tubman tells them that Garrett is strong but gentle, that he is a Quaker, and that he will give each of them a new pair of shoes.
3. Harriet uses her gun to threaten those who lose courage and want to return to slavery.
4. When the formerly enslaved people reach Canada, they find life hard. But they eventually come to discover that they have a great many important freedoms there, including the freedom to vote, to serve on juries, and to be elected to office.
5. The group has to go to Canada because the Fugitive Slave Law has made running to a free state risky.
6. Harriet uses stories, promises, and threats to keep the runaways going.
7. The runaways cannot return to their former homes because they would be tortured until they gave away the secrets of the Underground Railroad.
8. Harriet learns that freedom is more than changing jobs and keeping one's own money. It is also voting, serving on juries, and running for office.
9. The slave hunters observe Sunday by attending church services as Christians are supposed to do, yet they help to enslave other human beings.
10. **Theme Connection** Some students may feel that freedom is more important than life because a life without choice is not worth living.

LITERARY ELEMENTS

1. The slave masters wonder if Moses really exists. They wonder about the odd bird calls they hear. They wonder how their slaves disappear without a trace.
2. Evaluate responses based on the reasons given.

Additional Resources

Literary Elements Transparency 43

Literature and Writing

Writing About Literature

Students' paragraphs should

- use specific examples from the story
- evaluate the effectiveness of the emotional appeal of each example

Creative Writing

Students' dialogues should

- use words and sentence structures that reflect how people really talk
- use quotation marks correctly

Extending Your Response

Literature Groups Remind students that issues of racism and sexism evoke strong feelings in people, making it especially important in this exercise to listen well and respectfully to others. COLLAB. LEARN.

Interdisciplinary Activity Suggest that students pay attention to public service announcements on radio and television to get a sense of how long they are and how they typically sound.

Performing Suggest that students pick a particular city in southern Canada and a particular city in the South, as data will be easier to find by city than by region. Remind students to use appropriate grammar and word choice and careful enunciation in their presentations.

Literature and Writing

Writing About Literature

Analyzing Emotional Appeal Ann Petry's goal is to make readers understand the situation faced by people escaping slavery. She wants readers to feel the injustice, fear, hunger, cold, and ultimately, the hope of freedom that kept the fugitives going. Write a paragraph analyzing whether, in your opinion, Petry succeeds in her goal. Give examples from the story and describe your emotional response.

Creative Writing

Dialogue Reread the last part of the selection that begins: "Late in December, 1851, Harriet arrived in St. Catharines. . . ." Tubman and the escaped enslaved people have made it to Canada. They are free but homesick in this harsh, cold environment. With a partner, write dialogue for a scene between Tubman and two fugitives discussing their new lives. You could make one character sorry she came north, while the other has decided to run for county office.

Extending Your Response

Literature Groups

Harriet or Moses After escaping slavery herself, Tubman returned to the South nineteen times to rescue three hundred people. In your group, discuss these questions about Tubman: Why was Tubman widely known as "Moses"? If Tubman were alive today, would she suffer from the effects of racism? Would she suffer from the effects of sexism? Which *ism,* in your opinion, might cause her the most trouble?

Interdisciplinary Activity

Communication Imagine that it is 1851 and that radio and social service agencies exist in this time. You work for one such agency in St. Catharines. Tubman arrives with eleven refugees. How will you help them? Prepare a public service announcement asking for support from the community. Rehearse your one-minute speech with a tape recorder. Then deliver it to the class.

Performing

Weather Report The men and women who escaped to Canada were shocked by the bitter weather there. They were used to mild winters in the South. In pairs, research the winter weather in the southern United States and southern Canada. Locate helpful photographs and meteorological data from which you can create charts, graphs, and posters that compare and contrast the two environments. Present your information to the class.

Reading Further

For a view of other strong women, try these books:

Grand Mothers edited by Nikki Giovanni

Eleanor Roosevelt by Russell Freedman

Save your work for your portfolio.

MEETING INDIVIDUAL NEEDS — ENGLISH LANGUAGE LEARNERS

Connotation and Denotation English language learners may need help in identifying words with positive or negative connotations. Write *runaway* on the board and invite students to offer definitions, or give examples using the word. Explain that the dictionary definition of a word is called a denotation, but many words also have a connotation—an emotional or cultural association. Discuss the negative connotation that *runaway* may have (a person who avoids a duty or abandons a family).

Activity Pair English language learners with proficient English speakers to look for words with negative connotations in this selection. Students can discuss the meanings and list the words in their vocabulary notebooks. **L2** COLLAB. LEARN.

Skill Minilessons

RETEACH • REVIEW

GRAMMAR AND LANGUAGE • PROPER AND COMMON NOUNS

A **noun** is a word that names a person, place, thing, or idea. A **proper noun** names a specific person, place, or thing and is capitalized. A **common noun** is not capitalized.

PRACTICE Correct the errors in capitalization.

1. harriet tubman smuggled 300 Fugitives to freedom, leading her people from maryland to Canada.
2. During the civil war, harriet commanded a raid that freed more than 750 Slaves.
3. Her military Campaign was the first in united states history to be led by a Woman.

- For more about proper and common nouns, see **Language Handbook**, p. R30.

READING AND THINKING • USING A TIME LINE

A **time line** is a graphic aid that shows events over a given period of time. A time line may show a few years or a few thousand years, and it may include captions and images.

Enslaved People in Virginia

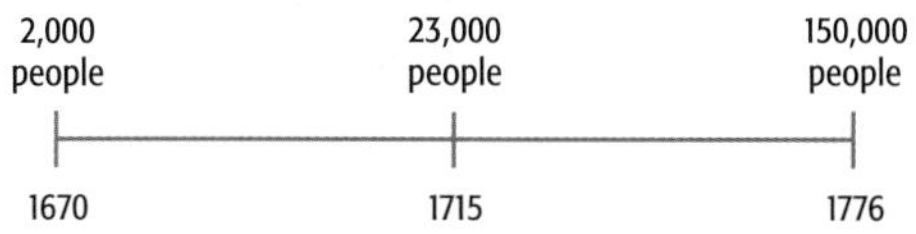

PRACTICE List five or six important events in the story of Harriet Tubman. Construct a time line to show these events. Illustrate your time line. For example, draw a whippoorwill at the start, and a symbol of Canada at the end.

- For more about graphic organizers, see **Reading Handbook**, p. R96.

VOCABULARY • MULTIPLE-MEANING WORDS

Multiple-meaning words can be confusing, especially if a familiar word has another meaning that you don't know. If you read about a nation *forging* a Bill of Rights, you might think the document is a fake. However, *forging* also means "shaping, forming, or creating." In the selection from *Harriet Tubman, vain* means "useless." However, it can also mean "conceited." When you come across a word you know, but that does not make sense in the sentence, look up the word in a dictionary. It may have a second meaning.

PRACTICE Choose the underlined word whose meaning is *different from* the definition given.

1. *corner: the area within an angle*
   He sat in the corner (a) planning how to get a corner (b) on the wheat market.
2. *hard: firm to the touch; resistant to pressure*
   We need hard (a) facts about how hard (b) the metal is.
3. *minute: very tiny*
   Her minute (a) cassette tape held a two-minute (b) account of the events.
4. *prone: having a natural tendency*
   I am prone (a) to fall asleep while prone (b).

Skill Minilessons

GRAMMAR AND LANGUAGE
PROPER AND COMMON NOUNS

1. Harriet Tubman smuggled 300 fugitives to freedom, leading her people from Maryland to Canada.
2. During the Civil War, Harriet commanded a raid that freed more than 750 slaves.
3. Her military campaign was the first in United States history to be led by a woman.

READING AND THINKING
USING A TIME LINE

Because the events in the story all take place during the month of December 1851, students may wish to organize their time lines by the week. Allow them to estimate dates on which events occurred.

VOCABULARY
MULTIPLE-MEANING WORDS

1. b
2. a
3. b
4. b

Additional Resources

- ***Grammar and Language Workbook,*** p. 61–62
- ***Grammar and Composition Handbook,*** Lesson 2.1
- ***Writer's Choice,*** Lesson 9.1
- ***Reading Skills Practice Workbook***
- ***Vocabulary Practice,*** p. 29

ASSESSMENT

- ***Quick Checks,*** p. 43
- ***Selection and Theme Assessment,*** pp. 75–76
- ***Performance Assessment,*** p. 40
- ***Testmaker: ExamView Pro***
- ***Interactive Tutor: Self-Assessment***

Interdisciplinary Connection

Objective

- To understand the basic concept of nonviolent civil disobedience

Teaching Strategies

After students have read about Frances Foster, ask them to think about why nonviolent protests eventually had such a powerful impact. Ask them to list some possible negative outcomes of a violent protest. *(People may be injured on both sides. Those who are undecided may be repelled by violence.)* Ask students why nonviolent protest requires courage.

Activities

1. Students' reports should focus on those aspects of Gandhi's teaching that relate to nonviolent protest.
2. Students' time lines should include captions and visuals for each item.

Teaching Support

Interdisciplinary Connection

SOCIAL STUDIES

The Fight for Civil Rights

Frances Foster was barely fourteen years old when she walked into a store one day in Birmingham, Alabama, knowing that she might be arrested. It was the late 1950s, when segregation was still common in much of the country. African Americans, especially in the South, were familiar with signs reading "No Coloreds" and sometimes couldn't check out books from the public library.

However, African American leaders, such as Birmingham minister Dr. Martin Luther King Jr., gave powerful speeches that inspired people to fight legal segregation. With the help of Dr. King and others, students learned how to organize nonviolent protests, such as sit-ins, marches, and boycotts.

Frances Foster

Frances Foster knew that because she was African American, no one would wait on her at the store's luncheonette that afternoon. But each time Frances was told to leave, she politely requested the same service white patrons received. A television news crew arrived to film her sit-in. The police eventually took Frances to a juvenile detention center, where she watched herself on the evening news.

In 1964 Dr. King won the Nobel Peace Prize for his work. The same year, President Lyndon Johnson signed the Civil Rights Act, making public segregation illegal.

Before 1960 was over, more than 50,000 people had participated in sit-ins at segregated movie theaters, parks, swimming pools, beaches, churches, and hotels. The protesters were arrested, attacked, and sometimes even killed, but support for Civil Rights kept growing. In 1963 Dr. King gave one of the most inspirational speeches of the Civil Rights movement, "I Have a Dream," to 250,000 people at the March on Washington.

Today, the law supports Frances Foster's right to eat at any restaurant she chooses. "I feel that the movement carries on with me today," she says. "I can do anything I want to do."

ACTIVITIES

1. Mahatma Gandhi led a fight against discrimination in India beginning in the 1920s. Dr. King and other civil rights leaders studied Gandhi's ideas to help them organize the Civil Rights movement in the United States. Research Ghandi's work, and prepare a short report on his teachings.
2. Research key events in the Civil Rights movement to make a time line of the movement. Write captions and include visuals for each item on the time line.

MEETING INDIVIDUAL NEEDS

MULTIPLE MODES OF EXPRESSION

Leading and Organizing Point out to students that not every participant in the civil rights movement was as committed to nonviolence as Frances Foster and Martin Luther King Jr. were. There is no doubt that there must have been arguments and discussions about the best methods to use to protest discrimination during the period.

Activity Have students work in groups to develop skits in which the characters argue about how best to protest an unjust situation. Some members of each group should portray people angry and frustrated with how slowly they are reaching their goal. Have each group present its skit to the rest of the class. **L2** COLLAB. LEARN.

Before You Read

I Have a Dream

MEET MARTIN LUTHER KING JR.

Growing up in the segregated South during the Great Depression of the 1930s, Dr. Martin Luther King Jr. saw the effects of prejudice and recognized the need to combat it. "Nonviolence is a powerful and just weapon," said Dr. King, who became a Baptist minister. "It . . . cuts without wounding and ennobles the man who wields it." Dr. King won the Nobel Peace Prize in 1964. He was assassinated when he was only thirty-nine years old.

Martin Luther King Jr. was born in 1929 and was killed in 1968.

READING FOCUS

What dreams and plans do you have for the future? Could anything interfere with those dreams?

FreeWrite

Jot down your thoughts, hopes, or dreams for the future.

Setting a Purpose

Read to learn more about the dream that one man had for himself and the entire nation.

Nobel Peace Prize medal.

BUILDING BACKGROUND

The Time and Place This most famous of Dr. King's speeches was delivered at a Civil Rights rally in Washington, D.C., on August 28, 1963.

Did You Know? After the U.S. Civil War, African Americans were allowed to own land and hold political office. Then laws were passed that made discrimination legal. There were separate schools, separate jobs, even separate water fountains for black and white people. Not until 1954 did the U.S. Supreme Court say that separate but equal treatment was in fact *unequal*—and illegal.

VOCABULARY PREVIEW

discrimination (dis krim′ ə nā′ shən) *n.* unfair treatment, especially as a result of policies directed against minority groups; p. 495

default (di fôlt′) *v.* to fail to do as required; p. 495

desolate (des′ ə lit) *adj.* without comfort; p. 495

inextricably (in eks′ tri kə blē) *adv.* in a way that cannot be separated; p. 496

tribulation (trib′ yə lā′ shən) *n.* great misery or distress; p. 496

wallow (wol′ ō) *v.* to become or remain helpless; p. 497

exalt (ig zôlt′) *v.* to raise in status, dignity, power; glorify; p. 498

discord (dis′ kôrd) *n.* disagreement; conflict; p. 498

prodigious (prə dij′ əs) *adj.* enormous; p. 498

Before Reading

Objectives

- To read and analyze a speech
- To learn about how speakers use repetition for rhetorical effect
- To write a summary

Skills

Reading/Thinking: Evaluating; Identifying Assumptions; Using Text Structures; Inferring; Analyzing Arguments

Writing: Speech Addendum

Vocabulary: Antonyms

Grammar/Language: Future Tense of Verbs; Punctuating Quotations

Collaboration: Literature Groups

Motivating STUDENTS

Selection Focus Transparency 43: Before presenting the photograph, ask students to discuss the Civil Rights movement of the 1960s and how it has affected the lives of many people.

Reading Focus: As an extension of the Reading Focus, ask students to work in groups to imagine the ideal American society a century from now. How will racial differences be handled? Have one person from each group present the group's ideas to the class.

RESOURCE MANAGER

Teaching Tools and Resources

- Theme Five Planning Guide
- Literature Groups Sourcebook

Essential Lesson Support

Lesson-Specific Instruction

- Selection Focus Transparency 43
- Literary Elements Transparency 44
- Active Reading Guide,* p. 44
- Selection Vocabulary Practice, p. 30

Assessment

- Selection Quick Checks,* p. 44
- Sel. and Theme Assmt., pp. 77–78
- Testmaker: ExamView Pro
- Performance Assessment, p. 41

Systematic Language Instruction

- Gr. & Comp. Hbk., L. 11.1
- Vocabulary Power, Lesson 22
- Spelling Power, Lesson 20

English Language Learners

- ELL Sourcebook, pp. 65, 66
- Spanish Summaries, p. 43
- Spanish Translations, pp. 109–112
- Audio Library*
- English, Yes!

Spec. Needs/Strat. Interven.

- Interactive Rdg. Sbk., pp. T160–T162
- Interactive Rdg. Wkbk., pp. 83–84
- Inclusion Strat. Sbk., pp. 65–66
- Audio Library*

* Also available in Spanish

FREE TO BE 493

Reading the Selection

SUMMARY

Dr. King relates in his speech a brief history of the struggle for equality and civil rights in the United States from the Emancipation Proclamation forward. He urges a nonviolent approach to achieving civil rights for all.

Spanish Summaries, p. 43

Active Reading Strategies

QUESTION King uses two images of light *(beacon light of hope* and *joyous daybreak)* in the second paragraph. What other image does he contrast with the images of light? *(the long night of their captivity)*

VOCABULARY If you haven't pre-viewed the selection vocabulary with students, stop and remind them to use context clues to unlock the meanings of new vocabulary words.

Additional Resources

Active Reading Guide, p. 44

Audio Library

Spanish Audio Library

King Mural, 1986. Don Miller. District of Columbia Public Library.

I HAVE A DREAM

Martin Luther King Jr.

Teaching Support

CONNECTING TO OTHER SELECTIONS

The chart at the right shows three ways to connect "I Have a Dream" to other selections in this book.

For specific teaching strategies, see the ***Theme Five Planning Guide.***

Connection		Title
Life Skills: Teaching and Mentoring	→	"The Kid Nobody Could Handle," p. 146
Thematic: Overcoming Discrimination	→	"The Woman in the Snow," p. 857
Literary: Persuasion	→	"Homeless," p. 39

I am happy to join with you today in what will go down in history as the greatest demonstration for freedom in the history of our nation.

A B Fivescore years ago, a great American, in whose symbolic shadow we stand today, signed the Emancipation Proclamation. This momentous[1] decree came as a great beacon light of hope to millions of Negro slaves who had been seared in the flames of withering injustice. It came as a joyous daybreak to end the long night of their captivity.

C But one hundred years later, the Negro still is not free; one hundred years later, the life of the Negro is still sadly crippled by the manacles[2] of segregation and the chains of discrimination; one hundred years later, the Negro lives on a lonely island of poverty in the midst of a vast ocean of material prosperity; one hundred years later, the Negro is still languished[3] in the corners of American society and finds himself in exile in his own land.

D So we've come here today to dramatize a shameful condition. In a sense we've come to our nation's capital to cash a check. When the architects of our republic wrote the magnificent words of the Constitution and the Declaration of Independence, they were signing a promissory note[4] to which every American was to fall heir. This note was the promise that all men, yes, black men as well as white men, would be guaranteed the unalienable[5] rights of life, liberty, and the pursuit of happiness.

It is obvious today that America has defaulted on this promissory note in so far as her citizens of color are concerned. Instead of honoring this sacred obligation, America has given the Negro people a bad check; a check which has come back marked "insufficient funds." We refuse to believe that there are insufficient funds in the great vaults of opportunity of this nation. And so we've come to cash this check, a check that will give us upon demand the riches of freedom and the security of justice.

We have also come to this hallowed spot to remind America of the fierce urgency of now. This is no time to engage in the luxury of cooling off or to take the tranquilizing drug of gradualism.[6] Now is the time to make real the promises of democracy; now is the time to rise from the dark and desolate valley of segregation to the sunlit path of racial justice; now is the time to lift our nation from the quicksands of racial injustice to the solid rock of brotherhood; now is the time to make justice a reality for all God's children. It would be fatal for the nation

1. *Momentous* (mō men′ təs) means "very important."
2. Handcuffs and other physical restraints are *manacles* (man′ ə kəlz).
3. Here, *languished* refers to living under distressing conditions.
4. A *promissory note* is a written promise to pay a certain sum of money to someone at a future date.
5. *Unalienable* rights, according to the Declaration of Independence, are rights that may not be taken away.
6. Dr. King was speaking at the Lincoln Memorial, a place many people consider holy *(hallowed)*. *Gradualism* is trying to bring about social or political change gradually or slowly.

Vocabulary

discrimination (dis krim′ ə nā′ shən) *n.* unfair treatment, especially as a result of policies directed against minority groups

default (di fôlt′) *v.* to fail to do as required

desolate (des′ ə lit) *adj.* without comfort

B Active Reading Strategies

CONNECT Ensure that students recognize the multiple allusions to Abraham Lincoln. "Fivescore" echoes Lincoln's "Fourscore and seven." King is standing at the Lincoln Memorial. And Lincoln signed the Emancipation Proclamation.

C Literary Elements

REPETITION Ask students why Dr. King repeats the phrase "one hundred years later." *(He may wish to emphasize the idea that even though slavery has been abolished for one hundred years, discrimination is still prevalent.)*

D Critical Thinking

EVALUATE Ask students to discuss the image of a check or promissory note for justice and freedom. What impact does this particular metaphor have? *(Clearly King wants to suggest that freedom is not a gift that the country can choose to give or withhold; it is a debt, an obligation, a promise.)*

MEETING INDIVIDUAL NEEDS — ENGLISH LANGUAGE LEARNERS

Root Words Write *emancipation* and *manacles* on the board. Point out that both words share the Latin root *man,* which means "hand" or "by hand." *Manacles* are objects that bind the hands. To *emancipate* means to free the hands. Other words that use this root are ***man**ual,* ***man**ufacture,* ***man**uscript,* and ***man**umission,* which also means to free from slavery.

Activity Have students look up words beginning with *man-* and write down as many as they can find that come from the Latin word meaning "hand." Have students write the words in their vocabulary notebooks.

Additional Resources

English Language Learners Sourcebook, p. 65

E Active Reading Strategies

CONNECT Point out that King's phrase "the sweltering summer of . . . discontent" is a reference to both Shakespeare and John Steinbeck. The original phrase, "the winter of our discontent," comes from *Richard III*. Steinbeck later used the phrase as the title of one of his novels.

F Critical Thinking

IDENTIFYING ASSUMPTIONS Ask students why King says that the freedom of whites is "inextricably bound" to the freedom of blacks. If this assumption is true, what is King's idea of freedom? *(Those who deny freedom to others are victims of their own ignorance and prejudice.)*

G Literary Elements

REPETITION Emphasize that King uses repetition effectively in this speech. Here he repeats "We can never be satisfied" and "We cannot be satisfied" in a rising crescendo that ends with "we will not be satisfied until justice rolls down like waters and righteousness like a mighty stream."

Teaching Support

to overlook the urgency of the moment. This sweltering summer of the Negro's legitimate discontent will not pass until there is an invigorating[7] autumn of freedom and equality.

Nineteen sixty-three is not an end, but a beginning. And those who hope that the Negro needed to blow off steam and will now be content, will have a rude awakening if the nation returns to business as usual. There will be neither rest nor tranquility in America until the Negro is granted his citizenship rights. The whirlwinds of the revolt will continue to shake the foundations of our nation until the bright day of justice emerges.

But there is something that I must say to my people, who stand on the warm threshold which leads into the palace of justice. In the process of gaining our rightful place, we must not be guilty of wrongful deeds. Let us not seek to satisfy our thirst for freedom by drinking from the cup of bitterness and hatred. We must forever conduct our struggle on the high plain of dignity and discipline. We must not allow our creative protest to generate into physical violence. Again and again we must rise to the majestic heights of meeting physical force with soul force; and the marvelous new militancy,[8] which has engulfed the Negro community, must not lead us to a distrust of all white people. For many of our white brothers, as evidenced by their presence here today, have come to realize that their destiny is tied up with our destiny. And they have come to realize that their freedom is inextricably bound to our freedom. We cannot walk alone. And as we talk, we must make the pledge that we shall always march ahead. We cannot turn back.

There are those who are asking the devotees of Civil Rights, "When will you be satisfied?" We can never be satisfied as long as the Negro is the victim of the unspeakable horrors of police brutality; we can never be satisfied as long as our bodies, heavy with the fatigue of travel, cannot gain lodging in the motels of the highways and the hotels of the cities; we cannot be satisfied as long as the Negro's basic mobility is from a smaller ghetto to a larger one; we can never be satisfied as long as our children are stripped of their selfhood and robbed of their dignity by signs stating "For Whites Only"; we cannot be satisfied as long as the Negro in Mississippi cannot vote and a Negro in New York believes he has nothing for which to vote. No! no, we are not satisfied, and we will not be satisfied until "justice rolls down like waters and righteousness like a mighty stream."[9]

I am not unmindful that some of you have come here out of great trials and tribulations. Some of you have come fresh from narrow jail cells. Some of you have come from areas where your quest for freedom left you battered by the storms of persecution and staggered by the winds of police

7. *Sweltering* means "very hot and humid," and *invigorating* means "bringing new life and energy." However, Dr. King is talking about more than just seasonal changes.
8. Dr. King uses *generate into* to mean "produce or cause." *Militancy* is a readiness to fight for a cause.
9. This line is from the Old Testament's Book of Amos.

Vocabulary
inextricably (in eks′ tri kə blē) *adv.* in a way that cannot be separated
tribulation (trib′ yə lā′ shən) *n.* great misery or distress

Reading Minilesson

Use Text Structures Point out that King's speech is carefully organized. He has provided readers and listeners with clear guideposts to make his speech easy to follow. In almost every paragraph the first sentence or two contains the main idea, with the rest of the paragraph providing elaboration.

Activity Have students scan several paragraphs and then copy the sentence in each paragraph that contains the main idea. Point out that students can get the gist of the speech through reading just these sentences. Have one or two students do exactly that to prove the point. **L2**

Additional Resources
Reading Skills Practice Workbook

brutality. You have been the veterans of creative suffering. Continue to work with the faith that unearned suffering is redemptive.[10] Go back to Mississippi. Go back to Alabama. Go back to South Carolina. Go back to Georgia. Go back to Louisiana. Go back to the slums and ghettos of our Northern cities, knowing that somehow this situation can and will be changed. Let us not wallow in the valley of despair.

I say to you today, my friends, so even though we face the difficulties of today and tomorrow, I still have a dream. It is a dream deeply rooted in the American dream. I have a dream that one day this nation will rise up and live out the true meaning of its creed, "We hold these truths to be self-evident, that all men are created equal." I have a dream that one day on the red hills of Georgia, sons of former slaves and the sons of former slave owners will be able to sit down together at the table of brotherhood. I have a dream that one day even the state of Mississippi, a state sweltering with the heat of injustice, sweltering with the heat of oppression, will be transformed into an oasis of freedom and justice. I have a dream that my four little children will one day live in a nation where they will not be judged by the color of their skin, but by the content of their character.

Crowd at Lincoln Memorial listening to King's "I Have a Dream" speech.

I have a dream today!

I have a dream that one day down in Alabama—with its vicious racists, with its Governor having his lips dripping with the

10. If something is *redemptive,* it brings rescue or freedom. Christians believe that Jesus Christ's suffering and death brought *redemption* from sin and punishment.

Vocabulary

wallow (wol′ ō) *v.* to become or remain helpless

H Literary Elements

REPETITION The repetition of "I have a dream" is the most famous portion of the speech. Elicit from students how the repetition of this particular phrase gives hope to and sets a goal for the American people.

I Active Reading Strategies

EVALUATE Ask students to look closely at the elements of King's dream. What exactly does he dream? How realistic are his dreams?

J Critical Thinking

INFER In this speech, King emphasizes his hopes for his own children and the children of others. Ask students what they can infer from his placing the hopes on the future generation. Present to students the following model:

Model: Since Dr. King began his speech by emphasizing how long African Americans have endured discrimination, I think he is well aware that change will not come about immediately. He knows that even if his work brings about significant change, it will not bring about the dream that he has hoped for immediately, so he places his hopes in future generations.

Real-World Connection

Civil Rights Movement The influence of the tactics of the Civil Rights movement has been pervasive. Today, when people disagree with policies or practices, it is quite common to see marches, sit-ins, and vigils.

Activity Have students perform an Internet search and report on a local or national use of these tactics that occurred during the past year or two. **L2**

K Author's Craft

DICTION Note that King says the words of "My Country 'Tis of Thee" must *become* true if the United States is to achieve greatness. Ask students why they think he chose the word *become.* *(He alludes to it not being true yet even though one of our most familiar national hymns has been asserting this for generations.)*

L Literary Elements

ALLUSION Emphasize that King begins his speech with references to the Constitution and the Declaration of Independence. He says that equality is the basis for the American dream. He ends his speech with biblical references. Why, as a minister, does he do this? *(His suggestion is that discrimination is also against God's law.)*

Thematic Focus

Free to Be Ask students what they feel King's definition of freedom is, on the basis of this speech.

ASSESSMENT

Quick Checks, p. 44

words of interposition and nullification[11]—one day right there in Alabama, little black boys and black girls will be able to join hands with little white boys and white girls as sisters and brothers.

I have a dream today!

I have a dream that one day "every valley shall be exalted and every hill and mountain shall be made low. The rough places will be made plain and the crooked places will be made straight, and the glory of the Lord shall be revealed, and all flesh shall see it together."[12]

This is our hope. This is the faith that I go back to the South with. With this faith we shall be able to transform the jangling discords of our nation into a beautiful symphony of brotherhood. With this faith we will be able to work together, to pray together, to struggle together, to go to jail together, to stand up for freedom together, knowing that we will be free one day. And [K] this will be the day. This will be the day when all of God's children will be able to sing with new meaning, "My country 'tis of thee, sweet land of liberty, of thee I sing. Land where my fathers died, land of the pilgrim's pride, from every mountain side, let freedom ring." And if America is to be a great nation, this must become true.

So let freedom ring from the prodigious hilltops of New Hampshire; let freedom ring from the mighty mountains of New York; let freedom ring from the heightening Alleghenies of Pennsylvania; let freedom ring from the snowcapped Rockies of Colorado; let freedom ring from the curvaceous slopes of California. But not only that. Let freedom ring from Stone Mountain of Georgia; let freedom ring from Lookout Mountain of Tennessee; let freedom ring from every hill and molehill of Mississippi. From every mountainside, let freedom ring.

[L] And when this happens, and when we allow freedom to ring, when we let it ring from every village and every hamlet, from every state and every city; we will be able to speed up that day when all God's children, black men and white men, Jews and gentiles,[13] Protestants and Catholics, will be able to join hands and sing in the words of the old Negro spiritual: "Free at last. Free at last. Thank God Almighty, we are free at last."

11. George Wallace, Alabama's then-*Governor,* opposed all efforts to end official segregation in his state. *Interposition* and *nullification* are legal arguments that have to do with a state's right to reject and refuse to enforce federal laws.
12. This passage comes from the Old Testament's Book of Isaiah.
13. People who are not Jews are *gentiles.* (The original Latin root word means "clan.")

Vocabulary
exalt (ig zôlt′) *v.* to raise in status, dignity, power; glorify
discord (dis′ kôrd) *n.* disagreement; conflict
prodigious (prə dij′ əs) *adj.* enormous

Teaching Support

Grammar and Language *Minilesson*

Future Tense of Verbs On the board, write this phrase from the speech: "With this faith, we will be able to work together . . ." Point out that King is using the future tense of the verb, which is formed by using the helping verb *will* before the main verb. The helping verb *shall* is sometimes used when the subject is *I* or *we*. Another way of writing about the future is by using the future perfect tense, which is used to name an action that will be completed before another future event begins. This tense is formed by adding *will have* or *shall have* before the past participle of the verb.

Future	*Future Perfect*
I will/shall go	will/shall have gone
you will eat	will have eaten
he/she/it will stop	will have stopped

Activity Have students work in groups. Assign each group a portion of the speech. Have students find all the sentences that refer to the future. Which of these sentences are in the future tense, and which are in the future perfect tense? **L2**

Additional Resources

- ***Grammar and Language Transparency 41***
- ***Grammar and Language Workbook,*** p. 95–96
- ***Grammar and Composition Handbook,*** Lesson 3.9
- ***Writer's Choice,*** Lesson 10.9

Responding to Literature

PERSONAL RESPONSE

- How does Dr. King's dream compare with the hopes and dreams you wrote about in the **Reading Focus** on page 493?

Brackets connect questions that are paired to develop higher-level thinking skills.

In CONGRESS, July 4, 1776.
A DECLARATION
By the REPRESENTATIVES of the
UNITED STATES OF AMERICA,
In GENERAL CONGRESS ASSEMBLED.

Analyzing Literature

RECALL

1. What document in the United States guarantees the rights of life, liberty, and the pursuit of happiness?
2. How does Dr. King respond to those who "hope that the Negro needed to blow off steam and will now be content"?
3. How does Dr. King feel about the use of violence against white people? Explain.
4. What does Dr. King want his children to be judged by?

INTERPRET

5. Why does Dr. King quote from the Declaration of Independence?
6. To whom is Dr. King talking when he says "this is no time to engage in the luxury of cooling off"? How do you know?
7. Why does Dr. King caution against distrusting all white people?
8. Is Dr. King's dream the American dream? Why or why not?

EVALUATE AND CONNECT

9. **Figurative language** (see page R3) often states a truth beyond the literal meaning. What do you understand by such phrases as "the sunlit path of racial justice" and "a beautiful symphony of brotherhood"?
10. Theme Connection What does *equality* mean? Is equality necessary for you to have a happy life? Is it the most important thing?

LITERARY ELEMENTS

Repetition

Repetition is the recurrence of sounds, words, phrases, or lines. Repetition in a speech may strengthen the message by reminding the audience over and over again of the theme. Repetition can also build a speech to a climax that raises emotions or moves the audience to action.

1. Find three examples of repetition in Dr. King's speech.
2. What effects do you think Dr. King aims for with the repetition of "let freedom ring"?
3. Think of a song you like that uses repetition. What phrase is repeated? What effect does it have?

- See **Literary Terms Handbook**, p. R8.

Responding to the Selection

PERSONAL RESPONSE

Evaluate student responses on the basis of the evidence of their grasp of Dr. King's dream.

Analyzing Literature

1. The Declaration of Independence names the rights of life, liberty, and the pursuit of happiness. These are guaranteed by the Constitution.
2. King says there will be no rest until African Americans are granted their citizenship rights.
3. King is opposed to violence, and he points out that many white people support the cause of civil rights.
4. King wants children to be judged by the content of their character, not the color of their skin.
5. King quotes from the Declaration of Independence because he believes that it identifies the rights he is asking for, and because most citizens, black or white, would subscribe to it as the foundation of our nation.
6. King is probably addressing those politicians of the time who advised against protests and felt that working within the current legal system was preferable to civil disobedience.
7. He says that the freedom of blacks is "inextricably bound" with that of whites.
8. Most students may say that King's dream is the American dream because both are based on individual freedom. Others may say that those who favor separation have their own dream for America.
9. Some students may say that King believes that racial equality and justice are beautiful and uplifting and that the current state of affairs is ugly.
10. **Theme Connection** Equality under the law means that all citizens have the same rights and responsibilities. Some students may feel that equality is the most important thing. Others will regard personal relationships and other things as equally important.

LITERARY ELEMENTS

1. *Possible answers:* "We come here today," "We cannot be satisfied," and "I have a dream."
2. He wants to convince his audience that freedom is not achieved for anyone until it is achieved for all.
3. One effect of repetition is to make a song easy to remember. "Old McDonald Had a Farm" is one example.

Additional Resources

Literary Elements Transparency 44

Literature and Writing

Writing About Literature

Students' summaries should
- cover all the main ideas of the speech
- give a sense of the emotional intensity of the speech

Personal Writing

Students' speeches should
- address all the questions in the assignment
- elaborate on each point using a specific example

Extending Your Response

Literature Groups If possible, play a recording of Dr. King's speech. **COLLAB. LEARN.**

Interdisciplinary Activity The local library may have collections of protest songs that may be checked out. Students should also ask older relatives whether they would share records that contain these songs.

Literature and Writing

Writing About Literature

Summary of a Speech Imagine that you have been assigned to write a summary of Dr. King's speech for a special issue of your school newspaper celebrating Black History Month. Start by listing the main ideas from Dr. King's speech. Then write a summary in one or two paragraphs.

Personal Writing

Getting Along After Dr. King's Time How far do you think we have come in the struggle for racial equality? Write an addition to Dr. King's speech that might be read to people today. Your writing should address these questions: Are Dr. King's words true for people of all races? How big of a problem is racism today? Who are the victims of this racism? Can racism be fought without violence?

Extending Your Response

Literature Groups

Group Reactions Dr. King's speech is both emotional and patriotic. What overall effect does his speech have on you? Which points have the most impact on you? What, if anything, does the speech make you want to do? Share your responses with those in your group. Then make a large word web to record your group's responses and share your word web with the class.

interNET CONNECTION

Use the Internet to find out more about Dr. King's life, work, or family. Type Dr. King's name into a search engine. Gather images, articles, and other data for a brief presentation to the class. Compile this information and write an introduction to the different aspects of Dr. King's life.

Interdisciplinary Activity

Music Many protesters in the Civil Rights movement sang songs about their determination to become free. These freedom songs were based on spirituals, hymns, rhythm and blues, and even football chants. Research freedom songs such as "We Shall Overcome" to create a booklet of song lyrics. Or, gather recordings of the songs and create a collection of music.

Reading Further

If you would like to read more about civil rights, try:
They Had a Dream by Jules Archer

Save your work for your portfolio.

Skill Minilessons

RETEACH • REVIEW

GRAMMAR AND LANGUAGE • PUNCTUATING QUOTATIONS

Direct quotes, or the exact words of a speaker, are enclosed in quotation marks. For example, Martin Luther King said, "So we've come here today to dramatize a shameful condition." Note that the quote is preceded by a comma. If the quote were divided, both parts would be set off with commas and enclosed in quotation marks: "So we've come here today," Dr. King said, "to dramatize a shameful condition." The period and first comma are inside the closing quotation marks.

PRACTICE Rewrite each sentence using the proper punctuation for each quote.

1. Dr. King said Now is the time to make real the promises of democracy.
2. In the process of gaining our rightful place, he warned we must not be guilty of wrongful deeds.
3. I have a dream today! he said.
4. This is our hope said Dr. King. This is the faith that I go back to the South with.

For more about punctuating quotations, see **Language Handbook,** p. R41.

READING AND THINKING • ANALYZING ARGUMENTS

Persuasive writing argues for a certain point of view, aiming to make someone feel a certain way or do something. Persuasive arguments often slant the facts and appeal to readers' emotions. Advertising, editorials, and political speeches, like Dr. King's, are all forms of persuasive writing.

PRACTICE Analyze the argument in Dr. King's speech, asking yourself these questions: Is Dr. King's position clear? Does he present enough evidence? Can the facts he cites be proven? Which statements are opinions rather than facts? What emotions does he appeal to?

For more about analyzing reasonings, see **Reading Handbook,** p. R108.

VOCABULARY • ANTONYMS

One technique that Dr. Martin Luther King Jr. used to communicate strongly and clearly was the presentation of contrasts. Dr. King used antonyms to contrast two situations, ideas, or things. He pointed out that "Nineteen sixty-three is not an *end,* but a *beginning.*" He dreamed that we would "transform the jangling *discords* of our nation into a beautiful *symphony* of brotherhood."

PRACTICE Fill in the blank with an antonym for the underlined word.

1. Everyone has the right to be treated with ___, but many people face discrimination instead.
2. When you face a difficult situation, do your best qualities emerge, or do they ___?
3. Do you say, "What can I, only one ___ person, do against the prodigious forces against me?"
4. The failure to try can never exalt us; instead it will only ___ us.

Skill Minilessons

GRAMMAR AND LANGUAGE
PUNCTUATING QUOTATIONS

1. Dr. King said, "Now is the time to make real the promises of democracy."
2. "In the process of gaining our rightful place," he warned, "we must not be guilty of wrongful deeds."
3. "I have a dream today!" he said.
4. "This is our hope," said Dr. King. "This is the faith that I go back to the South with."

READING AND THINKING
ANALYZING ARGUMENTS

Remind students that there is nothing wrong with emotional appeals, unless the appeals are to our baser emotions.

VOCABULARY
ANTONYMS

Possible answers:

1. fairness, equality
2. hide, disappear
3. small, insignificant
4. diminish, lower

Additional Resources

- ***Grammar and Language Workbook,*** p. 267–268
- ***Grammar and Composition Handbook,*** Lesson 13.6
- ***Writer's Choice,*** Lesson 20.6
- ***Reading Skills Practice Workbook***
- ***Vocabulary Practice,*** p. 30

ASSESSMENT

- ***Quick Checks,*** p. 44
- ***Selection and Theme Assessment,*** pp. 77–78
- ***Performance Assessment,*** p. 41
- ***Testmaker: ExamView Pro***
- ***Interactive Tutor: Self-Assessment***

LISTENING, SPEAKING, and VIEWING

Objective

- To learn techniques of public speaking

Teaching Strategies

Point out to students that examples are an important element in a good speech. Encourage the students to use examples

- to hold the audience's attention
- to make generalizations real

Note that speakers who use examples from their own experience usually remember the example without notes.

Activity

If a video camera is available, tape speeches and have students prepare a written evaluation of their own performance.

Teaching Support

LISTENING, SPEAKING, and VIEWING

Reaching Your Audience

A good speaker captures the attention of the audience. The speaker takes a stand on an issue, aiming to make listeners respond intellectually, emotionally, or through action. To get this response, the speaker must give details, examples, and reasons that will persuade listeners. In addition, a successful speaker will hold the attention of listeners, encourage their interest, and convince them with strong evidence.

Many people have read the moving "I Have a Dream" speech delivered by Dr. Martin Luther King Jr. His use of words, strong feelings, and examples of injustice have impressed readers of the speech. However, only those who have heard Dr. King deliver his speech will understand his message fully. Martin Luther King was a powerful, persuasive speaker.

Guidelines for Public Speaking

Here are some techniques that powerful speakers use. Think about how you can incorporate them into your own speaking style when you give a speech.

- To engage your listeners from the outset, meet their eyes. Eye contact is an unbeatable way to reach people.
- Aim your voice at the last row of your audience. Look often to be sure people in that row are paying attention.
- After each important point, pause. A brief pause calls attention to your words, giving them a chance to sink in. Remember that your words must encourage your audience to feel, think, or act in a certain way.
- Shift position from time to time, as you normally would. If you stand stiffly, your voice can stiffen too.

ACTIVITY

1. Plan to deliver a speech that is about four or five minutes long. You may choose a speech that you have written or one that you have read—a passage from "I Have a Dream" or "The Gettysburg Address," for example.
2. With a partner, take turns practicing your speech. Give each other feedback and suggestions for improvement.
3. Use the feedback to modify the speech's structure and word order. Then present the speech to the class.

MEETING INDIVIDUAL NEEDS — ENGLISH LANGUAGE LEARNERS

Public Speaking Practice English language learners may feel intimidated by speaking in public in English. Also, speaking techniques—eye contact, gestures, volume—vary among cultures. Students will benefit from seeing videos of effective speechmaking in English.

Activity Have students use guidelines on this page to evaluate taped speakers. Suggest they present a segment of a speech they have read. In this way they can concentrate on presentation rather than writing. Videotaping will allow students to analyze their presentations.

Additional Resources

English Language Learners Sourcebook, p. 66

Before You Read

Sorrow Home and *Sit-ins*

MEET MARGARET WALKER

"I have lived most of my life in the segregated South," said Margaret Walker, who grew up in New Orleans and became a legend in African American literature. "My adjustment . . . to this South—whether real or imagined, violent or nonviolent—is the subject and source of all my poetry." Walker experienced the Civil Rights movement firsthand and knew most of the movement's leaders. She also served as head of the Black Studies Program at Jackson State College in Jackson, Mississippi.

Margaret Walker was born in 1915 in Alabama and died in 1998. "Sorrow Home" and "Sit-ins" are from her collection of poetry This Is My Century, *published in 1989.*

READING FOCUS

Where would you like to live when you are an adult? For example, would you prefer a city, a rural area, or a small town?

List It!

Make a list of influences that may help determine where you live throughout your life.

Setting a Purpose

Read the poems to understand the speaker's love of a particular place.

BUILDING BACKGROUND

The Time and Place In "Sorrow Home," the speaker reflects on the South she knew as a child. "Sit-ins" is also set in the South, but later, in the 1960s.

Did You Know? Until the 1960s, a policy of segregation separated African Americans from other people in schools, restaurants, and other public places. On February 1, 1960, four African American college freshmen sat down at a Woolworth's lunch counter in Greensboro, North Carolina, and ordered coffee. The waitress refused to serve them. They stayed. Word spread, and daily sit-ins followed at stores in fifteen cities. Protesters were arrested by the carloads, but others took their places. Today, prejudice may still exist in some places, but segregation is against the law.

Two protestors carry a banner during a Civil Rights march.

Before Reading

Objectives

- To read and analyze two poems about segregation
- To learn about the functions of assonance, consonance, and alliteration in poetry
- To write an essay about poetic imagery

Skills

Reading/Thinking: Inferring; Questioning
Writing: Journal Entry
Grammar/Language: Prepositional Phrases
Listening/Speaking: Poetry Reading
Collaboration: Literature Groups

Motivating STUDENTS

Selection Focus Transparency 44: Before presenting the photograph, ask students how they feel about nonviolent protests.

Reading Focus: As an extension of the Reading Focus, have students draw or write a description of their ideal place to live and then share their descriptions or drawings with the class.

RESOURCE MANAGER

Teaching Tools and Resources
- Theme Five Planning Guide
- Literature Groups Sourcebook

Essential Lesson Support

Lesson-Specific Instruction
- Selection Focus Transparency 44
- Literary Elements Transparency 45
- Active Reading Guide,* p. 45

Assessment
- Selection Quick Checks,* p. 45
- Sel. and Theme Assmt., pp. 79–80
- Testmaker: ExamView Pro
- Performance Assessment, p. 42

Systematic Language Instruction
- Gr. & Comp. Hbk., L. 11.2
- Vocabulary Power, Lesson 23

English Language Learners
- ELL Sourcebook, p. 67
- Spanish Summaries, p. 44
- Audio Library*
- English, Yes!

Spec. Needs/Strat. Interven.
- Interactive Rdg. Sbk., pp. T163–T164
- Interactive Rdg. Wkbk., p. 85
- Audio Library*

* Also available in Spanish

Reading the Selection

A Active Reading Strategies

QUESTION How does Walker stress the depth of her roots? *(Although she left the South because of discrimination, she loves the climate and the land and feels at home there—perhaps more, even, than did the heroes mentioned.)*

Additional Resources

- ***Active Reading Guide,*** p. 45
- ***Audio Library***
- ***Spanish Audio Library***

B Author's Craft

CONTRAST Point out the contrast Walker makes between the North and the South. She portrays the South as warm, tropical, and rural; she portrays the North as cold, urban, and cut off from nature. When she speaks of the South, she paints a picture of home.

C Literary Elements

ASSONANCE The last three lines of the poem use assonance particularly effectively. Note the repeated *o* sounds which give the sense of someone moaning or mourning. *(O, sorrow, home, bone, own.)*

Sorrow Home

Margaret Walker

My roots are deep in southern life; deeper than John Brown°
or Nat Turner° or Robert Lee.° I was sired and weaned°
in a tropic world. The palm tree and banana leaf,
mango and coconut, breadfruit and rubber trees know
me.

Warm skies and gulf blue streams are in my blood. I belong
with the smell of fresh pine, with the trail of coon, and
the spring growth of wild onion.

I am no hothouse bulb° to be reared in steam-heated flats
with the music of El and subway in my ears, walled in
by steel and wood and brick far from the sky.

I want the cotton fields, tobacco and the cane. I want to
walk along with sacks of seed to drop in fallow° ground.
Restless music is in my heart and I am eager to be
gone.

O Southland, sorrow home, melody beating in my bone and
blood! How long will the Klan° of hate, the hounds and
the chain gangs° keep me from my own?

1–2 *John Brown* raided a federal weapons storehouse. *Nat Turner* led an unsuccessful slave rebellion. General *Robert E. Lee* led the Confederate forces during the Civil War. *Sired and weaned* means "born and raised."
9 A *hothouse bulb* is a plant grown in a greenhouse.
13 *Fallow* ground is left unseeded for one season to improve it agriculturally.
17 The Ku Klux *Klan* opposes the influence of certain minority groups.
18 A *chain gang* is a group of convicts, chained together and forced to do hard labor.

Teaching Support

CONNECTING TO OTHER SELECTIONS
For a teaching strategy that connects this selection to *I Know Why the Caged Bird Sings,* see the ***Theme Two Planning Guide.***

Sit-ins

Margaret Walker

Greensboro, North Carolina, in the Spring of 1960

You were our first brave ones to defy their dissonance° of hate
With your silence
With your willingness to suffer
Without violence
Those first bright young to fling your names across pages
Of new southern history
With courage and faith, convictions, and intelligence
The first to blaze a flaming path for justice
And awaken consciences
Of these stony ones.

Come, Lord Jesus, Bold Young Galilean°
Sit Beside this Counter,° Lord, with Me!

1 *Dissonance* can mean both "harsh, unpleasant sounds" and "sharp disagreement."
11 *Jesus* grew up in Galilee, a region of what is now Israel.
12 This sit-in took place at a lunch *counter.*

A sit-in at Woolworth's lunch counter in Greensboro, North Carolina.

D Critical Thinking

INFER Ask students what they can infer about "our first brave ones," from the description given. *(The title suggests they were the people who took part in sit-ins in Greensboro in 1960. Later in the poem the writer suggests they were young people.)*

E Active Reading Strategies

QUESTION Who are "these stony ones"? *(segregationists)*

Thematic Focus

Free to Be Walker's definition of freedom seems closely linked to the idea of place. She wants to be free to live where she chooses and sit where she pleases. Ask students why they think the freedom to be *here* is so important to Walker.

ASSESSMENT

Quick Checks, p. 45

Grammar and Language *Minilesson*

Prepositional Phrases Explain that a preposition relates a noun or pronoun to another word in the sentence. Note that this poem is primarily constructed of prepositional phrases. Write the following on the board, underlining the prepositions: *with your silence, without violence, of new Southern history, of these stony ones, Beside this counter.*

Activity Have students identify the rest of the prepositions in "Sit-ins." Check to be sure they have not included infinitive verb forms. **L2**

Additional Resources

- ***Grammar and Language Transparency 42***
- ***Grammar and Language Workbook,*** pp. 141–142
- ***Grammar and Composition Handbook,*** Lesson 7.1
- ***Writer's Choice,*** Lesson 13.1

Responding to the Selection

PERSONAL RESPONSE

Many students may feel sorrow, just as the speaker does in "Sorrow Home." "Sit-ins" may inspire feelings of respect for those with the courage to stand up for what is right.

Analyzing Literature

1. The narrator is speaking to the South personified.
2. Walker is addressing those who participated in sit-ins.
3. She contrasts the warm, rural South with the walled-in, urban North.
4. Students are likely to suggest that they awaken consciences through their "courage and faith, convictions and intelligence."
5. Students are likely to suggest that the denial of the right to eat or use facilities—let alone the Ku Klux Klan, chain gangs, and bloodhounds—provides sufficient reason.
6. Many students will agree that it must have taken courage to defy the law.
7. The sensory images underscore the author's love of the place and her sorrow at not being able to live there.
8. Some students may note that both poems show that African Americans were not free to be in places or engage in activities to which all Americans had a right.
9. Students may feel that the courage of the protesters should be honored. Students may hope that, even in the face of dogs and fire hoses, they would have continued to be nonviolent.
10. Students may prefer "Sorrow Home" because many will have experienced feelings of homesickness. Those who prefer "Sit-ins" may say that the poem inspires them to take action, to try to make a difference.

Active Reading and Critical Thinking

Responding to Literature

PERSONAL RESPONSE

- How did reading each poem make you feel? Jot down your reactions.

Brackets connect questions that are paired to develop higher-level thinking skills.

Analyzing Literature

RECALL

1. In the final stanza of "Sorrow Home," to whom is the narrator speaking?
2. In "Sit-ins," Margaret Walker addresses a person or persons using the words "you" and "your." Whom is she addressing?

INTERPRET

3. How does the narrator use contrast to describe the South in "Sorrow Home"?
4. In "Sit-ins," how might the people that Walker is speaking to "awaken consciences"?

EVALUATE AND CONNECT

5. In your opinion, does the narrator of "Sorrow Home" have enough reasons to feel such deep sorrow? Explain.
6. Do you agree with the speaker that the young participants at the sit-in show "courage and faith, convictions, and intelligence"? Support your answer.
7. What do the sensory images in "Sorrow Home" add to the poem? Explain.
8. **Theme Connection** Why do you think these two poems are in the theme "Free to Be"? In your opinion, are they good choices for this theme? Explain.
9. "Sit-ins" celebrates nonviolent resistance. Do you agree that the students should be honored? If you had been at the lunch counter with the men, how might you have behaved?
10. Which of the two poems do you find more appealing? Why?

LITERARY ELEMENTS

Assonance, Consonance, and Alliteration

Writers use several techniques to create interesting sound patterns in poetry. **Assonance** is the repetition of vowel sounds in stressed syllables: ***Awe** was the **au**tomatic response of us **all**.* (It is the sound, not the spelling, that creates assonance.) **Consonance** is the repetition of a single consonant sound: *Dee**p** o**p**en s**p**aces s**p**read far.* If the repeated consonant sound comes at the beginning of each word, the element is called **alliteration:** *The **t**errible, **t**reeless **t**undra faced us.*

1. Find one example of consonance and one of alliteration in "Sorrow Home."
2. Where in "Sorrow Home" does the poet use assonance?

- See **Literary Terms Handbook,** pp. R1 and R2.

LITERARY ELEMENTS

1. *Possible Answers:* Walled in by steel. Sacks of seed, of hate, the hounds
2. Sorrow, home, bone; a steam-heated; smell of fresh pine.

Additional Resources

Literary Elements Transparency 45

Extending Your Response

Writing About Literature

Sensory Images A poet uses images as if they cost money—every image must be useful and support the message or theme of the poem. For example, Margaret Walker says that the men at the sit-ins are the first ones to "blaze a flaming path." Readers can see the light of the blaze and feel its heat. Find another image in either of Walker's poems that you think is very effective. Explain in a paragraph why you selected that image.

Personal Writing

Remembering The poet William Wordsworth said poetry is "emotion recollected in tranquillity." Readers can sense the emotions of the speaker who recalls past sights and events in "Sorrow Home." What place or event in your past matters that much to you? In your journal, jot down words that describe the object or event. Next to the words, write the emotions that you felt at the time. If you prefer, refer to your notes from the **Reading Focus** on page 503 and describe your feelings about the place where you want to live as an adult.

Literature Groups

Scenes from a Poem Imagine that you are planning a book that will contain these two poems. How will you illustrate each poem? What images communicate the main message of each poem? Support the images you suggest by referring to specific lines from the poems. When you agree on two or three possible images for each poem, share your ideas with the class.

Listening and Speaking

Poetry Reading Find a poem you like that fits the theme "Free to Be." Take turns reading or reciting poems aloud. Pay attention to others as they read, and offer feedback. When it is your turn, read your poem slowly, clearly, and with emotion.

Reading Further

For a view of home fought for in another land, read: *O Jerusalem!* by Jane Yolen

Save your work for your portfolio.

Skill Minilesson

RETEACH • REVIEW

READING AND THINKING • QUESTIONING

The words a writer chooses can tell you something about his or her attitude about a subject. To understand and respond to a selection, you must ask yourself questions about the words used and the attitudes they may reveal.

- For more about related comprehension strategies, see **Reading Handbook,** pp. R93–R108.

PRACTICE For each group of words, identify one of the following attitudes that the words may reveal.

approval, fear, suspicion, celebration, pride

1. triumph, joy, remembering
2. kindness, honor, courage
3. masked, vague, watchful
4. power, hate, bias
5. achievement, work, triumph

Extending Your Response

Writing About Literature

Students' paragraphs should

- select a vivid image
- give reasons for selecting the image

Personal Writing

Students' journal entries should

- refer to facts, places, events, and emotions
- be private unless a student wishes to share an entry

Literature Groups Suggest that groups agree on the main message of each poem before brainstorming for images. COLLAB. LEARN.

Listening and Speaking Encourage students to explain their reasons for choosing the poems they did.

Skill Minilesson

READING AND THINKING • QUESTIONING

1. celebration
2. approval
3. suspicion
4. fear
5. pride

Additional Resources

Reading Skills Practice Workbook

ASSESSMENT

- ***Quick Checks,*** p. 45
- ***Selection and Theme Assessment,*** pp. 79–80
- ***Performance Assessment,*** p. 42
- ***Testmaker: ExamView Pro***
- ***Interactive Tutor: Self-Assessment***

FREE TO BE 507

Objective

- To understand the special features of historical fiction

Teaching Strategies

Explain that reading historical fiction can be a pleasurable means of learning a great deal of history, especially details of everyday life. Ask each student to write down something he or she has learned from the historical fiction the class has read this year. Discuss the responses.

Accurate Setting Write the word *anachronism* on the board. Show that the word is made of up two Greek roots: *ana* ("backward") and *chronos* ("time"). An anachronism in literature is an event or object that is out of place in the time portrayed—such as George Washington's wearing sneakers.

Attitudes of Characters More than objects or events, characters' attitudes are modernized in much historical fiction. It is sometimes hard to identify with historical attitudes that are regarded as prejudiced or cruel.

The Era and the Plot Ask students to imagine a story about the United States today written a hundred years from now. What attitudes and events would capture this era?

Teaching Support

GENRE FOCUS

HISTORICAL FICTION

Some types of fiction are so realistic that it's hard to believe they aren't true. In **historical fiction,** a story is set in the past—often in a real place—and the action revolves around an actual event or historical period. The story may deal with real historical characters, fictional characters, or a mixture of both. Here are some special features of historical fiction.

Civil War drummer boy.

ACCURATE SETTING Each item or action described in historical fiction must belong in the life of the period–every chair, shoe, meal, game, or tool. Although the writer may invent some characters, their lives must be like those of the people of the time.

ATTITUDES OF CHARACTERS The attitudes and beliefs of people change over time. Characters in a story set many years ago probably will have some attitudes and beliefs different from ours.

MODEL

Having little boys serve as drummers was common during the Civil War. So, in "The Drummer Boy of Shiloh," the general is not surprised to see a boy in the camp. His approving attitude, so wrong today, was judged to be right in 1862.

THE ERA AND THE PLOT In historical fiction, the problems that characters face, and their reactions to the problems, are affected by the attitudes and events of their time. If the events of a story could happen any time, the story is simply fiction.

MODEL

The drummer boy's fear of battle is a problem of any era. However, the Civil War marked the last time that young American boys served in a war. The general, sad but determined, is most likely patterned after Ulysses Grant, the Union commander at Shiloh. The events of the story could occur only during the Civil War.

MEETING INDIVIDUAL NEEDS

ENGLISH LANGUAGE LEARNERS

Historical Fiction Point out that to understand historical fiction, the reader must make allowances for differences in attitude. Explain that students whose native language is not English already have considerable practice in learning to accept attitudes that are different from their own. Then help them extend this ability to understand the historical context of the story.

Activity Ask students to discuss attitudes in the United States that differ from those in their native lands. Given King's speech, Walker's poems, and American history, have students discuss how they think racial attitudes in the 1950s and 1960s differ from attitudes today.

Additional Resources

English Language Learners Sourcebook

ACTIVE READING MODEL

Active Reading Strategies

Tips for Reading Historical Fiction

In historical fiction, you can't count on characters to live, think, or act as people do today. To understand the story, you must build bridges between the present and the past. Here are some strategies that will help.

- For more about reading strategies, see **Reading Handbook,** pp. R93–R108.

CONNECT

As you read, compare and contrast the lives of the characters with your own life. Ask yourself how the times affected the events about which you are reading.

INFER

The writer may not always explain conditions fully. Instead, small clues can lead readers to facts that are important in the story. What inferences can you find in the story that help you understand it better?

VISUALIZE

In historical fiction, trying to imagine the homes, the towns, even the clothing of the period can give you a feeling of being part of the story. Pay special attention to the descriptions of the setting and characters.

RESPOND

What do you think is the writer's purpose in creating this story? What is your response to that purpose?

APPLYING THE STRATEGIES

The next selection is an example of historical fiction. As you read "The Battleground," use the strategies in the margins to help you enjoy the short story.

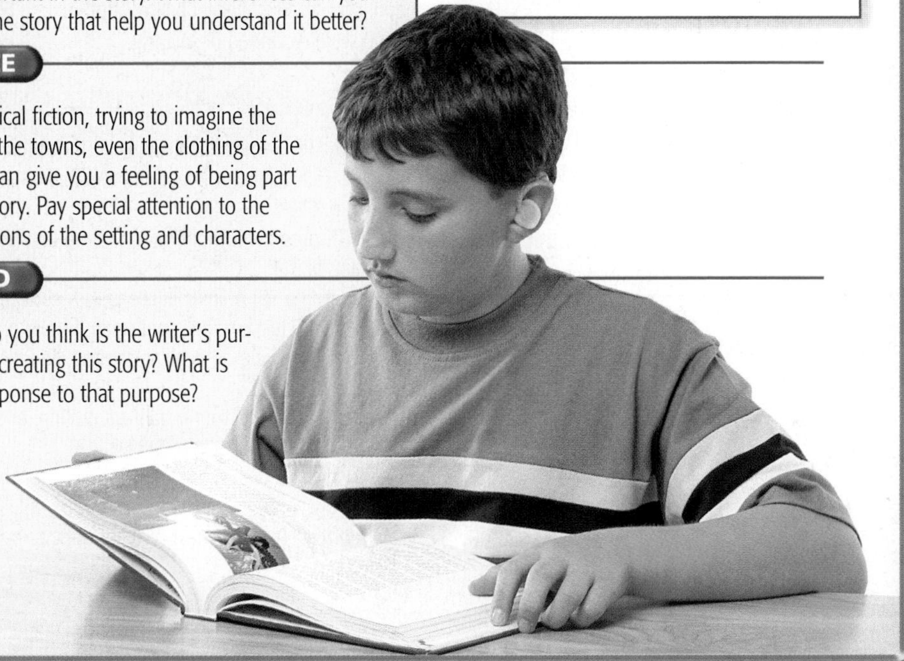

Active Reading Strategies

Objective

- To apply active reading strategies to understand historical fiction

Teach the Strategies

Ask students to imagine that they are suddenly transported into a strange world. How will they use what they know about their own society to help them understand the customs, rules, rituals, and people?

Question

Tell students that it's a good idea to look for similarities before differences. The similarities can serve as stepping stones to the differences.

Infer

The best inferences come from asking questions about the work. *Why is he doing that? What's the problem? Whom is she concerned about?* If the author doesn't provide the answer, the reader needs to infer it.

Visualize

If students have trouble picturing the events in historical fiction, they can consult reference books to look at photographs of the era.

Respond

It's not enough to ask *How would I feel if that happened to me?* That's the second question. The first question is *How would I be different if I had lived back then?*

Teaching Support

Reading Journal

Keeping Track

Encourage students to continue using their reading journals to record ideas and responses to their reading. They should also note questions and reactions to their independent reading.

Activity Remind students that they can set aside a portion of their notebooks as a journal of independent reading, if they have not already done so. Share the following suggestions with students:

- Use the **Reading Further** suggestions to list books you have read or tried to read. Enter comments in your journal.
- List books you have read that are listed in **Reading On Your Own** at the end of each Theme. Comment on each. List additional titles you think would be interesting.
- List and comment on your personal reading from other sources.

Before Reading

Objectives

- To read and analyze a story about the grief of a young Civil War widow
- To learn about the function of exposition in setting the scene for a story
- To write an essay distinguishing fiction from fact

Skills

Reading/Thinking: Inferring; Predicting; Activating Prior Knowledge
Writing: Letter; Journal Entries
Vocabulary: Word Origins; Base Words
Listening/Speaking: Reenactment
Grammar/Language: Using Apostrophes; Numbers
Collaboration: Literature Groups

Motivating → STUDENTS

Selection Focus Transparency 45: Before presenting the quotation, have students consider and discuss the feelings of a president ordering his country's people to battle.

Reading Focus: As an extension of the Reading Focus, have students research first-person civilian accounts of the Civil War and report their findings to the class.

ACTIVE READING MODEL

Before You Read

The Battleground

MEET ELSIE SINGMASTER

Elsie Singmaster was born in Gettysburg, Pennsylvania, grew up not far from there, and moved back after her young husband died. Singmaster spent the rest of her life writing historical fiction, short stories, and novels for children and young adults. The setting for most of her writing was the region around Gettysburg. The local color of the town inspired her early writing. In Gettysburg, Singmaster was surrounded by reminders of the Civil War, which also influenced her work.

Elsie Singmaster was born in 1879 and died in 1958. "The Battleground" was published in 1930 in her book Gettysburg.

READING FOCUS

How do you think the Civil War may have affected civilians?

Brainstorm
In a small group, brainstorm to imagine details of how the Civil War was fought. Share your information with the class.

Setting a Purpose
Read to discover how one young mother responds to events in the Civil War.

BUILDING BACKGROUND

The Time and Place This selection is set in Gettysburg, Pennsylvania, on the day Lincoln delivered the Gettysburg Address.

Did You Know? The Battle of Gettysburg was the turning point in the Civil War. The Union forces led by General George Meade defeated General Robert E. Lee's Confederate army in July of 1863. More than 6,000 soldiers died in battle; another 40,000 were wounded or missing.

General George Meade

VOCABULARY PREVIEW

covet (kuv′ it) *v.* to desire strongly; wish for longingly; p. 513
diligence (dil′ ə jəns) *n.* great attention, care, and effort; p. 513
repress (ri pres′) *v.* to hold back or keep under control; restrain; p. 514
lunacy (lo͞o′ nə sē) *n.* insanity; senseless conduct; folly; p. 514
doggedly (dô′ gid lē) *adv.* stubbornly; firmly; p. 514
wan (won) *adj.* pale or weak, indicating illness or weariness; p. 515
interminable (in tur′ mi nə bəl) *adj.* lasting, or seeming to last, forever; endless; p. 518
righteousness (rī′ chəs nəs) *n.* the condition of being right, moral, just, or legal; p. 519
wretchedness (rech′ id nəs) *n.* great unhappiness or deep distress; p. 521

RESOURCE MANAGER

Teaching Tools and Resources
- Theme Five Planning Guide
- Literature Groups Sourcebook

Essential Lesson Support

Lesson-Specific Instruction
- Selection Focus Transparency 45
- Literary Elements Transparency 46
- Active Reading Guide,* p. 46
- Selection Vocabulary Practice, p. 31

Assessment
- Selection Quick Checks,* p. 46
- Sel. and Theme Assmt., pp. 81–82
- Testmaker: ExamView Pro
- Performance Assessment, p. 43

Systematic Language Instruction
- Gr. & Comp. Hbk., L. 11.3

English Language Learners
- ELL Sourcebook, p. 68
- Spanish Summaries, p. 45
- Audio Library*
- English, Yes!

Spec. Needs/Strat. Interven.
- Interactive Rdg. Sbk., pp. T165–T167
- Interactive Rdg. Wkbk., pp. 86–87
- Audio Library*

* Also available in Spanish

The Battleground

Elsie Singmaster

The Leister farmhouse in Gettysburg, PA, on July 6, 1863, three days after the Battle of Gettysburg ended. Photograph by Alexander Gardner.

Mercifully, Mary Bowman, a widow, whose husband had been missing since the battle of Gettysburg,[1] had been warned, together with other citizens of Gettysburg, that on Thursday the nineteenth of November, 1863, she would be awakened from sleep by a bugler's reveillé,[2] and that during that great day she would hear again the dread sound of cannon.

Nevertheless, hearing again the reveillé, she sat up in bed with a scream and put her hands over her ears. Then, gasping, groping about in her confusion and terror, she rose and began to dress. She put on a dress which had been once a bright plaid, but which now, having lost both its color and the stiff, outstanding quality of the skirts of '63, hung about her in straight and dingy folds. It was clean, but it had upon it certain ineradicable[3] brown stains on which soap and water seemed to have no effect. She was thin and pale, and her eyes had a set look, as though they saw other sights than those directly about her.

ACTIVE READING MODEL

QUESTION (A)

What happened at Gettysburg in the summer of 1863?

RESPOND (B)

What state of mind would you be in if you had lived through the battle?

1. The *Battle of Gettysburg* was fought from July 1 through July 3, 1863.
2. *Reveillé* (rev′ ə lē) is the signal used each morning to call soldiers to roll-call formation.
3. Stains that are *ineradicable* (in′ i rad′ i kə bəl) cannot be removed completely.

Reading the Selection

SUMMARY

Mary Bowman, a war widow, lives near the site of the battle of Gettysburg, where she and the other women tend the wounded. She wanders the battlefield in search of her husband, who is missing but presumed dead. On the day Lincoln comes to deliver the Gettysburg address, Mary is persuaded to attend. Something about Lincoln touches Mary and allows her to recover from her grief.

Spanish Summaries, p. 45

A Active Reading Strategies

QUESTION *(The Battle of Gettysburg was fought in the summer of 1863.)* What kind of story might take place in the aftermath of a battle?

VOCABULARY Remind students to use context clues to unlock the meanings of new vocabulary words.

Additional Resources

- ***Active Reading Guide,*** p. 46
- ***Audio Library***
- ***Spanish Audio Library***

B Active Reading Strategies

RESPOND *(If I'd lived through the battle, I would be in a state of shock.)* Would it be worse to witness the battle as a civilian or to take part in it?

Teaching Support

CONNECTING TO OTHER SELECTIONS

The chart at the right shows three ways to connect "The Battleground" to other selections in this book.

For specific teaching strategies, see the ***Theme Five Planning Guide.***

Connection	Title
Life Skills: Lifelong Learning	from *All But My Life,* p. 663
Thematic: Awakenings	"Raymond's Run," p. 553
Literary: Descriptive Language	"If I Forget Thee, Oh Earth . . . ," p. 591

C Literary Elements

EXPOSITION Singmaster describes Mary as not really looking at things, seeming to look elsewhere. What is Mary seeing? *(Perhaps she is imagining the battle where her husband was killed or the gruesome temporary graves she dug up.)*

D Active Reading Strategies

CONNECT *(Mary's house is much less well cared for than others. Her home reflects her state of shock.)* Why might an author use a house to symbolize a woman's feelings?

E Active Reading Strategies

CONNECT Be sure that students understand that bullets from the battle of Gettysburg made the holes and rents in the shutters and walls of Mary's house.

VIEWING THE PAINTING

Viewing Response *The nurse's daily contact with suffering and death might contribute to great sadness and depression like that experienced by Mary Bowman.*

Teaching Support

The Battleground

ACTIVE READING MODEL

In the bed from which she had risen lay her little daughter; in a trundle bed nearby, her two sons, one about ten years old, the other about four. They slept heavily, lying deep in their beds, as though they would never move. Their mother looked at them with her strange, absent gaze; then she barred a little more closely the broken shutters, and went down the stairs. The shutters were broken in a curious fashion. Here and there they were pierced by round holes, and one hung from a single hinge. The window frames were without glass, the floor was without carpet, the bed without pillows. C

In her kitchen Mary Bowman looked about her as though still seeing other sights. Here, too, the floor was carpetless. Above the stove a patch of fresh plaster on the wall showed where a great rent had been filled in; in the doors were the same little round holes as in the shutters of the room above. But there was food and fuel, which was more than one might have expected from the aspect[4] of the house and its mistress. She opened the shattered door of the cupboard, and, having made the fire, began to prepare breakfast. E

QUESTION

D How does the description of Mary's house help you understand her situation?

Outside the house there was already, at six o'clock, noise and confusion. Last evening a train from Washington had brought to the village Abraham Lincoln; for several days other trains had been bringing less

4. Here, the *rent* is a hole. An *aspect* is how a person or thing looks.

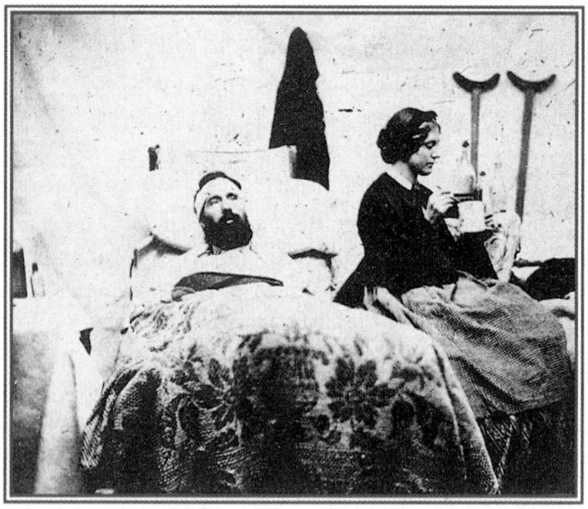

A nurse tends to a wounded soldier at a federal hospital in Nashville, TN, during the Civil War.

Viewing the photograph: In what ways might this woman's experiences as a nurse be similar to Mary Bowman's?

MEETING INDIVIDUAL NEEDS

ENGLISH LANGUAGE LEARNERS

Prefixes Write *exhumation* on the board. Underline *ex* and explain that the prefix in this instance means "out" or "of." To *exhume* means "to take out of the ground." The prefix *ex* can also mean "utterly" or "completely" (as in *exasperate*) or "former" (as in *ex-wife*).

Activity Have students look up words beginning with *ex* in the dictionary. Find five words in which the prefix means "out of" or "from." Write the definition of each word.

Additional Resources

English Language Learners Sourcebook, p. 68

distinguished guests, until thousands thronged[5] the little town. This morning the tract of land between Mary Bowman's house and the village cemetery was to be dedicated for the burial of the Union dead, who were to be laid there in sweeping semicircles round a center on which a great monument was to rise.

ACTIVE READING MODEL

G But of the dedication, of the President of the United States, of his distinguished associates, of the great crowds, of the soldiers, of the crape-banded banners, Mary Bowman and her children would see nothing. Mary Bowman would sit in her little wrecked kitchen with her children. For to her the President of the United States and others in high places who prosecuted war or who tolerated war, who called for young men to fight, were hateful. To Mary Bowman the crowds of curious persons who coveted a sight of the great battlefields were ghouls; their eyes wished to gloat upon ruin, upon fragments of the weapons of war, upon torn bits of the habiliments[6] of soldiers; their feet longed to sink into the loose ground of hastily made graves; the discovery of a partially covered body was precious to them. H

REVIEW F

Think about Mary's reasons for not wanting to take her children to hear President Lincoln speak.

Mary Bowman knew that field! From Culp's Hill to the McPherson farm, from Big Round Top to the poorhouse, she had traveled it, searching, searching, with frantic, insane disregard of positions or of possibility. Her husband could not have fallen here among the Eleventh Corps, he could not lie here among the unburied dead of the Louisiana Tigers! If he was in the battle at all, it was at the Angle that he fell.

She had not been able to begin her search immediately after the battle because there were forty wounded men in her little house; she could not prosecute it with diligence even later, when the soldiers had been carried to the hospitals, in the Presbyterian Church, the Catholic Church, the two Lutheran churches, the Seminary, the College, the Courthouse, and the great tented hospital on the York road. Nurses were here, Sisters of Mercy[7] were here, compassionate women were here by the score; but still she was needed, with all the other women of the village, to nurse, to bandage, to comfort, to pray with those who must die. Little Mary Bowman had assisted at the amputation of limbs, she had helped to control strong I

5. To *throng* is to gather in large numbers; a *throng* is a large crowd.
6. *Crape,* also spelled *crepe* (krāp), is a light, crinkled cloth; black crepe is a traditional symbol of mourning. Those who *prosecuted* war actively supported it, while those who *tolerated* war accepted or put up with it. *Ghouls* are people who enjoy things that disgust and upset most people. *Habiliments* are garments.
7. A *seminary* is a school that trains ministers or priests. The *Sisters of Mercy* are Catholic nuns.

Vocabulary

covet (kuv′ it) *v.* to desire strongly; wish for longingly

diligence (dil′ ə jəns) *n.* great attention, care, and effort

F Active Reading Strategies

REVIEW *(Mary hates those who declared and continued the war and called upon young men to sacrifice their lives. She hates the curious who want to visit the battlefield.)* What kind of speech does Mary believe Lincoln will make?

G Literary Elements

EXPOSITION The author spends a great deal of time setting up the events that precede Lincoln's speech. One element of exposition is Mary's harsh and negative view of people coming to visit the battlefield. Ask students for an alternative explanation of the desire of tourists to visit battlefields. *(Visitors may want to honor the dead.)*

H Literary Elements

EXPOSITION Note that the conflict of the story—the question of whether to hear the president—occurs almost three pages into the story. Ask students why so much detailed exposition is necessary to this story. *(The point of the story is the impact of the past on the present. Without all the exposition, it would be hard for the reader to understand Mary's pain or the depth of her feelings.)*

I Critical Thinking

INFER Why does Singmaster refer to Mary as "Little Mary Bowman"? *(She probably wants to emphasize Mary's fragility, both physical and mental, as well as the enormity of the tasks she had to perform.)*

Reading Minilesson

Predict One way to stay involved in one's reading is to try to predict what will happen next based on what one already knows about the story, how people typically act, and the conventions of the genre or type of writing.

Activity The second paragraph on page 513 makes a specific prediction: Mary will not go to hear Lincoln's speech. Ask students to evaluate this prediction and make a prediction of their own. Then have them write out their reasons for thinking as they do. On what do they base that prediction? Mary's character? Their knowledge of short stories? Their knowledge of history? A combination of factors? **L2**

Additional Resources

Reading Skills Practice Workbook

J Literary Elements

EXPOSITION In the expostion to the story, Mary is contrasted with Hannah Casey in her reaction to the work the women perform and to the war in general. Ask students to compare and contrast the two women. What do they think of Hannah's reaction? *(Be sure that students realize that the descriptions of Hannah's behavior are given from Mary's perspective. Hannah may simply be a strong woman, making the best of a bad situation.)* Why does the author establish this contrast early in the story? *(It is important to establish that Mary's state of mind is exaggerated.)*

K Active Reading Strategies

RESPOND *(No. A real battle would be much more terrifying.)* To what extent would the fear of dying play a part in one's response to a battle?

L Active Reading Strategies

QUESTION *(Hannah acted with energy and courage, as did Molly Pitcher and Barbara Frietchie.)* Is Hannah's comparison valid?

M Active Reading Strategies

EVALUATE *(The narrator believes that the generation after the Civil War would find it difficult to understand the horror of what Mary experienced.)* Can our generation understand?

Teaching Support

ACTIVE READING MODEL

RESPOND

K Do you think that seeing movies or news reports about war would prepare you to experience a real battle?

QUESTION

L Why is Hannah comparing herself to Barbara Frietchie and Molly Pitcher?

EVALUATE

M What do you make of the narrator's comment on people of "this generation"?

men torn by the frenzy of delirium,[8] she had tended poor bodies which had almost lost all semblance to humanity. Neither she nor any of the other women of the villages counted themselves especially heroic; the delicate wife of the judge, the petted daughter of the doctor, the gently bred wife of the preacher forgot that fainting at the sight of blood was one of the distinguishing qualities of their sex; they turned back their sleeves and repressed their tears, and shoulder to shoulder with Mary Bowman and her Irish neighbor, Hannah Casey, they fed the hungry and healed the sick and clothed the naked. If Mary Bowman had been herself, she might have laughed at the sight of her dresses cobbled into trousers, her skirts wrapped round the shoulders of sick men. But neither then nor ever after did Mary laugh at any incident of that summer. J

Hannah Casey laughed, and by and by she began to boast. Meade, Hancock, Slocum, were noncombatants beside her. She had fought whole companies of Confederates, she had wielded bayonets, she had assisted at the spiking of a gun, she was Barbara Frietchie and Molly Pitcher[9] combined. But all her lunacy could not make Mary Bowman smile.

Of John Bowman no trace could be found. No one could tell her anything about him, to her frantic letters no one responded. Her old friend, the village judge, wrote letters also, but could get no reply. Her husband was missing; it was probable that he lay somewhere upon this field, the field upon which they had wandered as lovers.

In midsummer a few trenches were opened, and Mary, unknown to her friends, saw them opened. At the uncovering of the first great pit, she actually helped with her own hands. For those of this generation who know nothing of war, that fact may be written down, to be passed over lightly. The soldiers, having been on other battlefields, accepted her presence without comment. She did not cry, she only helped doggedly, and looked at what they found. That, too, may be written down for a generation which has not known war.

Immediately, an order went forth that no graves, large or small, were to be opened before cold weather. The citizens were panic-stricken with fear

8. Men in a *frenzy of delirium* would be greatly disturbed and upset.
9. *Meade, Hancock,* and *Slocum* commanded Union troops at Gettysburg. *Noncombatants* are people who do not fight. The gun mentioned here would have been a Confederate cannon; *spiking* was a way of disabling a cannon. If you aren't familiar with *Barbara Frietchie,* see page 459. During the Revolutionary War, *Molly Pitcher* fired her wounded husband's cannon until the end of a battle.

Vocabulary

repress (ri pres′) *v.* to hold back or keep under control; restrain
lunacy (lo͞o′ nə sē) *n.* insanity; senseless conduct; folly
doggedly (dô′ gid lē) *adv.* stubbornly; firmly

MEETING INDIVIDUAL NEEDS

MULTIPLE MODES OF EXPRESSION

Linguistic Write these words from page 514 on the board: *frenzy, delirium, panic, lunacy.* All these words can be used to describe distraught mental states. While they have similar meanings, their connotations differ.

Activity Have students look up the definition and derivation of each word in a dictionary, being particularly careful to notice distinctions among the words. Have them use each word in a sentence. **L2**

A crowd of people in Gettysburg watch President Abraham Lincoln on his way to dedicate the National Cemetery, where he gave the Gettysburg Address on November 19, 1863.

of an epidemic; already there were many cases of dysentery and typhoid. Now that the necessity for daily work for the wounded was past, the village became nervous, excited, irritable. Several men and boys were killed while trying to open unexploded shells; their deaths added to the general horror. There were constant visitors who sought husbands, brothers, sweethearts; with these the Gettysburg women were still able to weep, for them they were still able to care; but the constant demand for entertainment for the curious annoyed those who wished to be left alone to recover from the shock of battle. Gettysburg was prostrate, bereft[10] of many of its worldly possessions, drained to the bottom of its well of sympathy. Its schools must be opened, its poor must be helped. Cold weather was coming and there were many, like Mary Bowman, who owned no longer any quilts or blankets, who had given away their clothes, their linen, even the precious sheets which their grandmothers had spun. Gettysburg grudged nothing, wished nothing back, it asked only to be left in peace. **N**

When the order was given to postpone the opening of graves till fall, Mary began to go about the battlefield searching alone. Her good, obedient children stayed at home in the house or in the little field. They were beginning to grow thin and wan, they were shivering in the hot August weather, but their mother did not see. She gave them a great deal more to eat than she had herself, and they had far better clothes than her bloodstained motley.[11] **P**

CONNECT

Consider how the people of Gettysburg changed after the battle. **O**

10. Here, *prostrate* means "made weak and helpless," and *bereft* means "robbed of."
11. Mary's mismatched clothing is her *motley.*

Vocabulary

wan (won) *adj.* pale or weak, indicating illness or weariness

N Literary Elements

PERSONIFICATION Note that Singmaster describes the town as if it were an individual. She describes it as being "nervous," "irritable," "prostrate, bereft," asking only "to be left in peace." This description also fits Mary Bowman.

O Active Reading Strategies

CONNECT *(As with any disaster, many people were without the basic necessities of life, a situation that was to only get worse with the onset of winter. In addition, many residents lost sons, husbands, or brothers in the fighting.)* What are some methods towns today use to rebuild after a disaster?

P Critical Thinking

INFER What does Singmaster's description of Mary's children tell the reader about Mary? *(She has clearly been too distracted to do much more than feed her children. She has certainly been unable to offer them any nurturing or comfort.)*

Vo•cab•u•lar•y Skills

Word Origins *Grudged* is an old form of *begrudged.* The word is from the French and means "to grumble or murmur." The town of Gettysburg does not wish to have the clothes, linen, and sheets given to the wounded soldiers returned—it doesn't hold the soldiers' needs against them.

Writing Minilesson

Kinds of Writing Ask students to imagine that they were related to Mary and had heard from Hannah Casey about her behavior. Have them imagine that they live too far away to visit.

Activity Have students write Mary a letter in which they express their condolences and give her advice about how to get on with her life. Direct students to read their letters over to themselves carefully, so that they will be prepared to read them aloud fluently and expressively. Then invite volunteers to share their letters with the class. **L2**

Additional Resources

Writer's Choice

Q Active Reading Strategies

RESPOND *(Many people would react as Mary did. Shock is sometimes the only reaction one can have to overwhelming situations.)* Can shock protect a person from having to deal with too much at once?

R Active Reading Strategies

As she walks about the battlefield, what is Mary looking for? *(She hopes to find something that her husband carried with him—her picture or a letter. An artifact, she hopes, will bring resignation or acceptance.)*

S Literary Elements

EXPOSITION A clue that the author is still using description to set up the story is the unmended rent in the wall. Earlier in the story, Singmaster mentions the new plaster used to repair this tear.

T Active Reading Strategies

CONNECT *(A close friend may play a similar role.)* In what important ways does the judge help Mary?

Historical Note

The Battle of Gettysburg was fought in July, and Lincoln delivered his address in November. Thus the judge visits Mary one month after the battle and three months before the opening scene of the story.

Teaching Support

The Battleground

An unidentified woman from the 1860s.

RESPOND

Q How might you have felt after wandering the battlefields? Would you cry, or would you respond the way that Mary did?

R She went about the battlefield with her eyes on the ground, her feet treading gently, anticipating loose soil or some sudden obstacle. Sometimes she stooped suddenly. To fragments of shells, to bits of blue or gray cloth, to cartridge belts or broken muskets, she paid no heed; at sight of pitiful bits of human bodies she shuddered. But there lay also upon that field little pocket Testaments, letters, trinkets, photographs. John had had her photograph and the children's, and surely he must have had some of the letters she had written!

But poor Mary found nothing.

One morning, late in August, she sat beside her kitchen table with her head on her arm. The first of the scarlet gum leaves had begun to drift down from the shattered trees; it would not be long before the ground would be covered, and those depressed[12] spots, those tiny wooden headstones, those fragments of blue and gray be hidden. The thought smothered her. She did not cry, she had not cried at all. Her soul seemed hardened, stiff, like the terrible wounds for which she had helped to care.

Suddenly, hearing a sound, Mary had looked up. The judge stood in the doorway; he had known all about her since she was a little girl; something in his face told her that he knew also of her terrible search. She could not ask him to sit down, she said nothing at all. She had been a loquacious[13] person, she had become an abnormally silent one. Speech hurt her.

The judge looked round the little kitchen. The rent in the wall was still unmended, the chairs were broken; there was nothing else to be seen but the table and the rusty stove and the thin, friendless-looking children standing by the door. It was the house not only of poverty and woe, but of neglect. S

"Mary," said the judge, "how do you mean to live?"

Mary's thin, sunburned hand stirred a little as it lay on the table.

"I do not know."

CONNECT

T Who in your life might play a role similar to the one played by the judge in Mary's life?

"You have these children to feed and clothe and you must furnish your house again. Mary—" The judge hesitated for a moment. John Bowman had been a schoolteacher, a thrifty, ambitious soul, who would have thought it a disgrace for his wife to earn her living. The judge laid his hand on the thin hand beside him. "Your children must have food, Mary. Come down to my house, and my wife will give you work. Come now."

12. The *depressed* spots are the tops of graves that have sunk slightly.
13. A *loquacious* person is a talkative one.

INTERDISCIPLINARY CONNECTION

Social Studies John Bowman, the judge thinks, would not have liked the idea of his wife working.

Activity Have students work in groups to research the status of working women in the 1860s. Assign each group a question or series of questions to answer. What kinds of women worked? What kinds of jobs were available? How might women's and men's wages differ? What was the status of many unmarried women in the United States before the Civil War? Have each group report its findings and conclusions based on information gathered from multiple sources, including the internet. **L2** COLLAB. LEARN.

Slowly Mary had risen from her chair, and smoothed down her dress and obeyed him. Down the street they went together, seeing fences still prone, seeing walls torn by shells, past the houses where the shock of battle had hastened the deaths of old persons and little children, and had disappointed the hearts of those who longed for a child, to the judge's house in the square. There wagons stood about, loaded with wheels of cannon, fragments of burst caissons, or with long, narrow pine boxes, brought from the railroad, to be stored against the day of exhumation.[14] Men were laughing and shouting to one another, the driver of the wagon on which the long boxes were piled cracked his whip as he urged his horses.

Hannah Casey congratulated her neighbor heartily upon her finding work.

"That'll fix you up," she assured her.

She visited Mary constantly, she reported to her the news of the war, she talked at length of the coming of the President.

"I'm going to see him," she announced. "I'm going to shake him by the hand. I'm going to say, 'Hello, Abe, you old rail splitter, God bless you!' Then the bands'll play, and the people will march, and the Johnny Rebs[15] will hear 'em in their graves."

Mary Bowman put her hands over her ears.

"I believe in my soul you'd let 'em all rise from the dead!"

"I would!" said Mary Bowman hoarsely. "I would!"

"Well, not so Hannah Casey! Look at me garden tore to bits! Look at me beds, stripped to the ropes!"

And Hannah Casey departed to her house.

Details of the coming celebration penetrated to the ears of Mary Bowman whether she wished it or not, and the gathering crowds made themselves known. They stood upon her porch, they examined the broken shutters, they wished to question her. But Mary Bowman would answer no questions, would not let herself be seen. To her the thing was horrible. She saw the battling hosts,[16] she heard once more the roar of artillery, she smelled the smoke of battle, she was torn by its confusion. Besides, she seemed to feel in the ground beneath her a feebly stirring, suffering, ghastly host. They had begun again to open the trenches, and she looked into them.

V

14. *Caissons* were two-wheeled wagons for hauling ammunition. *Exhumation* (eks′ hū mā′ shən) is the digging up of a corpse. After the battle, the dead were buried quickly to prevent the spread of disease. Later, the bodies would be reburied in coffins in the newly dedicated cemetery.
15. *Johnny Rebs* were Confederate soldiers.
16. Here, *hosts* means "armies."

ACTIVE READING MODEL

CONNECT

Read Mary and Hannah's dialogue. Whose reactions are more similar to what your own might be? U

U Active Reading Strategies

RESPOND *(Many students may feel they would respond as Hannah does; she is ready to go on with life.)* Why do some people cope better than others?

Historical Note

Point out to students that today there are a variety of methods for the identification of bodies. In earlier times many soldiers were never identified. Mary's desire to have her husband's body identified, which would allow her to resume normal living, may never be satisfied.

V Active Reading Strategies

CONNECT Point out that Mary is remembering both the battle and her search for information about what happened to her husband.

MEETING INDIVIDUAL NEEDS — ADVANCED LEARNERS

Trauma and Shock After World War I, many soldiers experienced "shell shock," a condition that included exhaustion, inability to concentrate, irritability, and bouts of hysteria. After Vietnam, many soldiers suffered from post-traumatic stress disorder, a condition that included feelings of disorientation, inability to focus attention, impaired memory, irritability, and intense crying.

Activity Ask students to use the library or the Internet to research both of these conditions. Have them develop lists of symptoms for both disorders. Ask them to compare their lists to Mary's symptoms. Students should then report on what they have learned to the class. **L3**

W Literary Elements

EXPOSITION Point out to students that the word *now* informs readers that the story has returned to the present. Except for the first few paragraphs, the rest of the story up to this point has been presented as flashback.

X Active Reading Strategies

QUESTION *(Mary responds strongly to the judge's suggestion because he is suggesting that she must do something that alarms her.)* What about the judge's answer persuades Mary to go?

Teaching Support

The Battleground

ACTIVE READING MODEL

W

Now, on the morning of Thursday, the nineteenth of November, her children dressed themselves and came down the steps. They had begun to have a little plumpness and color, but the dreadful light in their mother's eyes was still reflected in theirs. On the lower step they hesitated, looking at the door. Outside stood the judge, who had found time in the multiplicity of his cares, to come to the little house.

He spoke with kind but firm command.

"Mary," said he, "you must take these children to hear President Lincoln."

"What!" cried Mary.

"You must take these children to the exercises."

"I cannot!" cried Mary. "I cannot! I cannot!"

QUESTION

X Why does Mary respond so strongly to the judge's suggestion?

"You must!" The judge came into the room. "Let me hear no more of this going about. You are a Christian, your husband was a Christian. Do you want your children to think it is a wicked thing to die for their country? Do as I tell you, Mary."

Mary got up from her chair, and put on her children all the clothes they had, and wrapped about her own shoulders a little black coat which the judge's wife had given her. Then, as one who steps into an unfriendly sea, she started out with them into the great crowd. Once more, poor Mary said to herself, she would obey. She had seen the platform; by going round through the citizen's cemetery she could get close to it.

The November day was bright and warm, but Mary and her children shivered. Slowly she made her way close to the platform, patiently she stood and waited. Sometimes she stood with shut eyes, swaying a little. On the moonlit night of the third day of battle she had ventured from her house down toward the square to try to find some brandy for the dying men about her, and as in a dream she had seen a tall general, mounted upon a white horse with muffled hoofs, ride down the street. Bending from his saddle he had spoken, apparently to the empty air.

"Up, boys, up!"

There had risen at his command thousands of men lying asleep on pavement and street, and quietly, in an interminable line, they had stolen out like dead men toward the Seminary, to join their comrades and begin the long, long march to Hagerstown.[17] It seemed to her that

17. At the battle's end, Confederate General Robert E. Lee had led his defeated troops back to Virginia by way of *Hagerstown,* Maryland, about thirty miles southeast of Gettysburg.

Vocabulary

interminable (in tur′ mi nə bəl) *adj.* lasting, or seeming to last, forever; endless

Listening and Speaking *Minilesson*

Reenactment The painting on page 520 shows one view of Lincoln and the audience at Gettysburg. Ask students how they think the crowd looked from Lincoln's point of view. Did he see the grief in the young widow's face, and the fear and confusion in her children's eyes? What other emotions might he have seen in others in the crowd? *(Possible answers: excitement at seeing the president, joy in the victory, sadness, boredom with all of the speeches)*

Activity Have students work in small groups to practice a reenactment of Lincoln's address and the crowd's reactions. Students should portray such characters as Mary, Hannah, the judge, and Mary's children. Have students perform their reenactment for the class. **L2**

all about her dead men might rise now to look with reproach upon these strangers who disturbed their rest.

The procession was late, the orator of the day was delayed, but still Mary waited, swaying a little in her place. Presently the great guns roared forth a welcome, the bands played, the procession approached. On horseback, erect, gauntleted,[18] the President of the United States drew rein beside the platform, and, with the orator and the other famous men, dismounted. There were great cheers, there were deep silences, there were fresh volleys of artillery, there was new music.

Of it all, Mary Bowman heard but little. Remembering the judge, whom she saw now near the President, she tried to obey the spirit as well as the letter of his command; she directed her children to look, she turned their heads toward the platform.

Men spoke and prayed and sang, and Mary stood still in her place. The orator of the day described the battle, he eulogized[19] the dead, he proved the righteousness of this great war; his words fell upon Mary's ears unheard. If she had been asked who he was, she might have said vaguely that he was Mr. Lincoln. When he ended, she was ready to go home. There was singing; now she could slip away, through the gaps in the cemetery fence. She had done as the judge commanded and now she would go back to her house.

With her arms about her children, she started away. Then someone who stood near by took her by the hand.

"Madam," said he, "the President is going to speak!"

Z Half turning, Mary looked back. The thunder of applause made her shiver, made her even scream, it was so like that other thunderous sound which she would hear forever. She leaned upon her little children heavily, trying to get her breath, gasping, trying to keep her consciousness. She fixed her eyes upon the rising figure before her, she clung to the sight of him as a drowning swimmer in deep waters, she struggled to fix her thoughts upon him. Exhaustion, grief, misery threatened to engulf her, she hung upon him in desperation.

AA Slowly, as one who is old or tired or sick at heart, he rose to his feet, the President of the United States, the Commander in Chief of the Army and Navy, the hope of his country. Then he stood waiting. In great waves of sound the applause rose and died and rose again. He

ACTIVE READING MODEL

CONNECT

Y Think of a time you did something because another person thought it would be good for you to do.

18. An *orator* is a speaker. When President Lincoln arrives, he is sitting upright *(erect)* and wearing long, formal gloves *(gauntlets)*.
19. To *eulogize* (ū′ lə jīz′) the dead is to make a speech praising and honoring them.

Vocabulary
righteousness (rī′ chəs nəs) *n.* the condition of being right, moral, just, or legal

Y Active Reading Strategies

CONNECT *(Students should have a fund of memories about times they did what teachers and parents told them would be good for them.)* Who has given the best advice?

Z Active Reading Strategies

CONNECT Ask students why the applause frightens Mary. What is the "other thunderous sound"? *(Mary is remembering the sound of cannons.)*

AA Author's Craft

CHARACTERIZATION Why does Singmaster describe how Lincoln looks as he stands up? She says he rises "as one who is old or tired or sick at heart." *(Perhaps Lincoln's demeanor itself touches Mary's heart. He too seems grief stricken by the carnage.)*

MEETING INDIVIDUAL NEEDS — SPECIAL NEEDS

Emotional/Learning Disabled
Students with learning disabilities may feel left out—cut off from what is going on—much as Mary feels alienated from what is happening around her.

Activity Ask students to write a brief journal entry describing a time when they felt left out, or alienated. What might help someone in such a situation begin to reconnect with other people? After reading this story, what additional thoughts do students have about working through this type of situation?
L2 COLLAB. LEARN.

VIEWING THE PAINTING

Mort Künstler is an artist whose work is known for both authentic historical detail and a sense of drama.

Viewing Response *The words "old, tired, and sick at heart" are appropriate descriptions of the man in the painting.*

The Gettysburg Address, 1987. Mort Künstler. Oil on canvas, 30 x 30 in. Private collection.

Viewing the painting: How does this painting of Lincoln compare with the narrator's description of him as he rises to give the address?

Teaching Support

Grammar and Language *Minilesson*

Using Apostrophes Write this clause from the story on the board: "Mary Bowman's soul seemed to smooth itself out like a scroll. . . ." For singular nouns, form the possessive by adding *'s (Mary's)*. For plural nouns that end in s add just an apostrophe *(girls')*. Use an apostrophe and an s to form the possessive of an indefinite pronoun *(one's own home)*.

Activity Have students find five instances in the story where the apostrophe is used to form the possessive. **L2**

Additional Resources

- ***Grammar and Language Transparency 43***
- ***Grammar and Language Workbook,*** pp. 269–270
- ***Grammar and Composition Handbook,*** Lesson 13.7
- ***Writer's Choice,*** Lesson 20.7

waited quietly. The winner of debate, the great champion of a great cause, the veteran in argument, the master of men, he looked down upon the throng. The clear, simple things he had to say were ready in his mind, he had thought them out, written out a first draft of them in Washington, copied it here in Gettysburg. It is probable that now, as he waited to speak, his mind traveled to other things, to the misery, the wretchedness, the slaughter of this field, to the tears of mothers, the grief of widows, the orphaning of little children.

Slowly, in his clear voice, he said what little he had to say. To the weary crowd, settling itself into position once more, the speech seemed short; to the cultivated[20] who had been listening to the elaborate periods of great oratory, it seemed commonplace, it seemed a speech which anyone might have made. But it was not so with Mary Bowman, nor with many other unlearned persons. Mary Bowman's soul seemed to smooth itself out like a scroll, her hands lightened their clutch on her children, the beating of her heart slackened, she gasped no more.

She could not have told exactly what he said, though later she read it and learned it and taught it to her children and her children's children. She only saw him, felt him, breathed him in, this great, common, kindly man. His gaze seemed to rest upon her; it was not impossible, it was even probable, that during the hours that passed he had singled out that little group so near him, that desolate woman in her motley dress, with her children clinging about her. He said that the world would not forget this field, these martyrs;[21] he said it in words which Mary Bowman could understand, he pointed to a future for which there was a new task.

"Daughter!" he seemed to say to her from the depths of trouble, of responsibility, of care greater than her own. "Daughter, be of good comfort!"

Unhindered[22] now, amid the cheers, across ground which seemed no longer to stir beneath her feet, Mary Bowman went back to her house. There, opening the shutters, she bent and solemnly kissed her little children, saying to herself that henceforth they must have more than food and raiment;[23] they must be given some joy in life.

20. Here, the *cultivated* are those who are (or think they are) better educated and more refined than most other people.
21. Those who suffer or die for a cause are *martyrs* (mär′ tərz).
22. To *hinder* is to hold back; so, *unhindered* means "not held back."
23. *Raiment* (rā′ mənt) means "clothing."

ACTIVE READING MODEL

QUESTION

How does Lincoln's speech compare with that of the person who spoke before him? BB

CONNECT

Have you ever felt a speaker who was addressing a large group was actually speaking directly to you? Why did you feel that way? CC

Vocabulary

wretchedness (rech′ id nəs) *n.* great unhappiness or deep distress

BB Active Reading Strategies

QUESTION *(To some, the speech seemed brief and commonplace. To Mary, however, the speech brought tremendous comfort.)* Why did some listeners not notice the greatness of the speech?

CC Active Reading Strategies

CONNECT *(Some speakers connect by knowing what is important to the audience.)* How do speakers determine what is important to the audience?

Thematic Focus

Free to Be Ask students to discuss the relationship of this story to the idea of freedom. Is Mary enslaved by her grief? Does Lincoln "emancipate" her?

ASSESSMENT

Quick Checks, p. 46

Real-World Connection

Supporting One Another Throughout the world, people like Mary and her neighbors face illness, tragedy, and poverty.

Activity Divide the class into groups and have them use the Internet to research school, community, church, and other groups whose focus is to offer support and assistance to people in need. Each group should prepare a brief oral report for the class. **L2** COLLAB. LEARN.

Responding to the Selection

PERSONAL RESPONSE

Students may indicate they have felt grief at the loss of life.

Active Reading Response

Students may have used the questioning as a strategy at several turning points in the story, particularly at times when Mary is given advice.

Analyzing Literature

1. Mary is dressed in old, worn-out clothes. She seems not to be paying attention to what's happening around her. Her house is nearly empty of furnishings, and bullet holes are everywhere.
2. The story begins four months after the battle. Mary has searched the battlefields for something that may have belonged to her husband.
3. Mary is repulsed and annoyed by the plans for Lincoln's visit. She finds the curiosity of visitors ghoulish.
4. Mary is deeply touched by the president's speech. She begins to envision the possibility of a future again.
5. Mary is depressed and has no source of income.
6. Beginning to work helps Mary, as does hearing Lincoln's speech.
7. Mary doesn't have much will of her own left, so she simply does what the judge tells her.
8. Mary memorizes Lincoln's speech because it has touched her so deeply.
9. Students should consider their answers to the Reading Focus in preparing their responses.
10. They all show patriotism.

ACTIVE READING MODEL

Responding to Literature

PERSONAL RESPONSE

- What emotions about war do you share with Mary Bowman?

Active Reading Response

- Review the strategy for questioning described on page 509. Identify two or three places in the story where questioning helped you to understand a character, place, or event.

Brackets connect questions that are paired to develop higher-level thinking skills.

Analyzing Literature

RECALL

1. In your own words, describe Mary Bowman and her house as both are described in the first four paragraphs of the story.
2. How long after the Battle of Gettysburg does the story begin? What search has Mary undertaken in that time?
3. How does Mary feel about Lincoln's upcoming visit and the dedication ceremonies?
4. How does Mary Bowman respond to the president's speech?

INTERPRET

5. Why is Mary unable to refurbish her household and care for her children as others in Gettysburg have done?
6. What events or actions, in your opinion, contribute to the slow change in Mary Bowman?
7. Given Mary's determination to avoid the ceremony, why does she take her children to hear Lincoln's speech? Explain.
8. Why, do you think, does Mary memorize Lincoln's speech and teach it to her children?

EVALUATE AND CONNECT

9. Do you identify more with Mary Bowman's reactions to the battle or with Hannah Casey's? Explain, using your response to the **Reading Focus** on page 510 to help you.
10. What attitudes toward their country do Mary Bowman, the people caring for the wounded and dead, and President Lincoln share?

LITERARY ELEMENTS

Exposition

Exposition is the part of a story plot in which the writer presents the information readers will need to follow the story. In "The Battleground," the results of the terrible fighting in and near a small town are described for readers. This information helps readers to understand the characters and the action.

1. How does learning about Mary's connection with the fighting affect the way you respond to her character?
2. Explain how having a battle fought around them may have contributed to townspeople's appreciation of Lincoln's words.

- See **Literary Terms Handbook**, p. R3.

LITERARY ELEMENTS

1. Mary's connection with the fighting makes her behavior comprehensible.
2. More than most, the townspeople of Gettysburg understood the sacrifices that were made to win the battle. They would appreciate Lincoln's hope that the sacrifices were not made in vain.

Additional Resources

Literary Elements Transparency 46

Literature and Writing

Writing About Literature

Fiction from Facts "The Battleground" is fiction, but it is based on historical events. List important characters, events, and places in the story. Which, in your opinion, are fictional? Which are historical facts? How can you tell?

Creative Writing

You Are There This story was written from the third-person point of view. How would it be different if it were a first-person narrative? As Mary Bowman, write three journal entries: one written during the battle, one after searching for your husband, and one after hearing Lincoln's dedication speech.

Extending Your Response

Literature Groups

Building Character Where in the story does Elsie Singmaster use actions and description to reveal Mary's character? Choose a scene from the story to read aloud. With your group, identify the emotions Mary feels at that point. Why, do you think, did Singmaster use so little dialogue to reveal Mary's character?

Learning for Life

Read All About It! Work in a group to create a newspaper front page that might have been published just after the Battle of Gettysburg or just before the dedication ceremony for the Gettysburg National Cemetery. Include a feature story, an interview, and a personal profile of a fictional character of the times.

Interdisciplinary Activity

Art There are many memorials throughout the United States to honor those who fought in Civil War battles. Sketch or design plans for a memorial that would commemorate the contributions of civilians like Mary Bowman.

New York State Memorial at Gettysburg National Cemetery.

Reading Further

For more stories about the effects of the Civil War, try these books:

The Dreams of Mairhe Mehan by Jennifer Armstrong

Mine Eyes Have Seen the Glory by Ann Rinaldi

Save your work for your portfolio.

Literature and Writing

Writing About Literature

Students' lists should

- include all three elements—characters, places, and events
- give reasons for their choices

Creative Writing

Students' journal entries should

- refer to three different days
- reflect Mary's viewpoint

Extending Your Response

Literature Groups Remind students that authors choose details very carefully. Make sure students look at all the details that refer to Mary. COLLAB. LEARN.

Learning For Life Suggest that students collect samples of the three kinds of stories (feature, interview, and personal profile) from their local paper so they understand the basic format of each.

Interdisciplinary Activity For students who aren't artistic, suggest a verbal description.

Skill Minilesson

NUMBERS

Fifty people moved from our town in 1866, the first year after the war. For one hundred miles around, the land had been ruined. I was fourteen years old that year on May 30.

ACTIVATING PRIOR KNOWLEDGE

Point out that knowledge has a "snowball effect." The more you know, the more you learn.
Answers: Students may note that knowing about the Gettysburg Address helped them understand what would happen in the story. Knowing about Lincoln himself might allow one to predict the impact his demeanor would have on Mary. Knowing something about depression helps one understand what is happening to Mary.

BASE WORDS

1. a
2. c
3. c

Additional Resources

- ***Grammar and Language Workbook,*** p. 275–276
- ***Grammar and Composition Handbook,*** Lesson 13.10
- ***Writer's Choice,*** Lesson 20.10
- ***Reading Skills Practice Workbook***
- ***Vocabulary Practice,*** p. 31

RETEACH • REVIEW

Skill Minilessons

GRAMMAR AND LANGUAGE • NUMBERS

When writing about history, you use numbers to present data, the sequence of events, and dates. Some numbers should be represented by words; others should be written as numerals.

1. Spell out numbers that you can write in one or two words *(twenty-two)*.
2. Use numerals for numbers of more than two words *(220)*.
3. Spell ordinal numbers *(first, second, third)*.
4. Spell out any number that begins a sentence, or reword the sentence.
5. Always use numerals to express dates *(June 1)*.

PRACTICE Copy the following paragraph, writing all numbers correctly.

50 people moved from our town in eighteen sixty-six, the 1st year after the war. For 100 miles around, the land had been ruined. I was 14 years old that year on May thirtieth.

- For more about numbers, see **Language Handbook,** p. R45.

READING AND THINKING • ACTIVATING PRIOR KNOWLEDGE

The beginning of "The Battleground" does not state that the setting is the Civil War. Readers must use information they already have, their **prior knowledge,** to connect Gettysburg with the Civil War. To activate prior knowledge, notice clues that jog your memory. Then ask yourself questions to relate those clues with what you already know about a setting or a person.

PRACTICE List four or five clues that you noticed or questions that you asked yourself when you read "The Battleground." Explain how your prior knowledge helped you understand the clues and answer your questions.

- For more about activating prior knowledge, see **Reading Handbook,** p. R94.

VOCABULARY • BASE WORDS

An unfamiliar word is sometimes just a familiar base word with a suffix or prefix (or both) attached to it. You can often get a good idea of what the new word means by looking for a base word within it. For example, Gettysburg's women *repressed* tears while nursing wounded soldiers, and Mary Bowman knew that leaves would hide the *depressed* spots that marked graves. Both *repressed* and *depressed* contain the base word *press. Re-* adds the meaning of "back," so to *repress* tears is to press, or steadily push, them back. *De-* adds the meaning of "down."

PRACTICE Use your knowledge of base words to answer the questions.

1. The cautionary advice that the judge gives Mary about her children is meant to
   a. warn her. b. encourage her. c. inform her.
2. What Mary presupposes is what she
   a. sees and hears. b. remembers. c. assumes beforehand.
3. To say that Mary becomes uncustomarily silent means that her silence is
   a. rude. b. forced on her. c. unusual for her.

ASSESSMENT

- ***Quick Checks,*** p. 46
- ***Selection and Theme Assessment,*** pp. 81–82
- ***Performance Assessment,*** p. 43
- ***Testmaker: ExamView Pro***
- ***Interactive Tutor: Self-Assessment***

Reading and Thinking Skills

Identifying Persuasive Techniques

Writers often write with a single purpose: to convince their readers to think, feel, or act in a certain way. This type of writing is called **persuasive writing.** Persuasive writing may be about unimportant things, such as which toothpaste you should use or which jeans will look best on you. However, many writers also speak out about important topics, such as those that prevent people from feeling "free to be."

Most writers of persuasive articles or speeches do the following:

- take a stand on a topic
- support that stand with examples, details, or background information

A skillful reader must be able to understand what the writer is doing and decide whether to think, feel, or behave in the way the writer suggests. The reader can do these things by asking questions like these:

1. Is the writer's stand clear?
2. Does the writer know enough about the topic to make decisions about it?
3. Do I know why the writer believes as he or she does?
4. Does the writer give enough information to show that the stand he or she has taken is a reasonable one?
5. Do I know enough about the topic to make a decision?

● For more about author's purpose, see **Reading Handbook,** p. R107.

ACTIVITY

Read the following example of persuasive writing. Then, using the questions above to organize your ideas, write three or four paragraphs explaining whether the writer influenced the way you may act, feel, or think about the topic.

> Women have always struggled with their men-folk for the abolition of slavery, the liberation of countries from colonialism, the dismantling of apartheid and the attainment of peace. It is now the turn of men to join women in their struggle for equality.
>
> —*Gertrude Mongella of Tanzania*
> *Secretary General of U.S. Fourth Conference*
> *on the World's Women, 1995*

Reading & Thinking Skills

Objective

- To learn to identify persuasive techniques

Teaching Strategies

Point out that the effectiveness of persuasive writing depends on both the writer and the reader. A writer's ability to persuade depends a great deal on his or her credibility. The knowledge base of the reader, however, is also important. A reader who knows little about the subject should reserve judgment until learning more. It is easy to be persuaded by a credible writer if one knows nothing.

Activity

Students' paragraphs should

- use the questions to organize ideas
- clearly present a position

Additional Resources

Reading Skills Practice Workbook

Teaching Support

MEETING INDIVIDUAL NEEDS — SPECIAL NEEDS

Less-Proficient Readers To identify persuasive techniques, one must learn to identify the author's purpose in general. Encourage students to ask themselves, "Why did the author write this?" Explain that some common purposes are to inform, to persuade, to educate, to entertain, and to describe.

Activity Ask students to clip three articles from the features page of their local newspaper, to read the articles, then to identify the authors' primary purposes in writing them. **L2**

Additional Resources

Inclusion Strategies

Before Reading

Objectives

- To read and analyze a chapter from a novel about a Russian girl who emigrates to the United States
- To learn about narration in fiction
- To write a paragraph about conflict

Skills

Reading/Thinking: Inferring; Comparing and Contrasting; Evaluating; Paraphrasing
Writing: Narrative; Paraphrase
Vocabulary: Word Parts That Express Size
Grammar/Language: Direct Objects; Using Apostrophes
Life Skills: Planning
Listening/Speaking: Interviewing
Collaboration: Literature Group

Motivating STUDENTS

Selection Focus Transparency 46: Before presenting the poem, discuss with students how they might feel if they were emigrating to the United States.

Reading Focus: As an extension of the Reading Focus, ask students to discuss their reactions to characters who face problems similar to theirs.

Before You Read

from *Letters from Rifka*

MEET KAREN HESSE

Karen Hesse (hes) was a lonely child growing up in Baltimore, Maryland. Then, when she was about eleven years old, she read a book on Hiroshima that affected her strongly. "If more books for children had existed at that time with real issues . . . I don't think I would have felt so lonely, so isolated," she says. Now she writes for children to show them that they are not alone in the world. "My hope is to help [young people] through hard times, to present characters who survive ordeals and grow as a result of them," she says.

Karen Hesse was born in 1952. Letters from Rifka *was published in 1992. The book won several awards and was named an American Library Association Best Book for Young Adults.*

READING FOCUS

Do you agree with Karen Hesse that reading helps people feel less isolated?

List It!

With a partner, list five books that you think do a good job of telling young people about others who share their concerns and problems. Include the title, author, and a one-sentence statement of the main conflict.

Setting a Purpose

Read to discover how the ability to read gives one young boy a special kind of freedom.

BUILDING BACKGROUND

The Time and Place Between 1892 and 1943, millions of people emigrated to the United States. The first stop for most European immigrants at that time was Ellis Island in the harbor of New York City, within sight of the Statue of Liberty. Here the immigrants remained until they had received a clean bill of health and official permission to enter the United States.

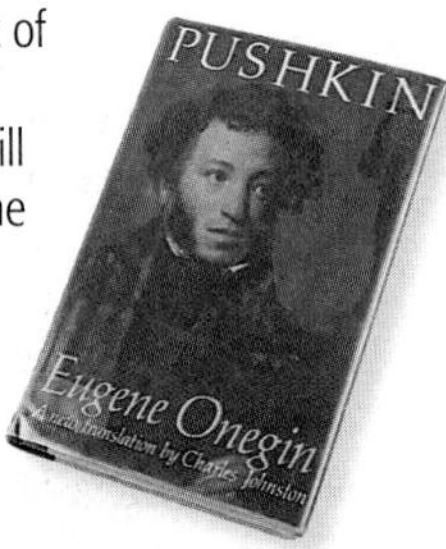

Did You Know? Immigrants brought with them a knowledge and love of writing, music, and art from their countries of origin. The immigrants in the story you are about to read enjoy the work of Alexander Pushkin (1799–1837), one of Russia's greatest poets. Pushkin often earned the disapproval of his government for writing from the point of view of those who fought oppression.

VOCABULARY PREVIEW

minimal (min′ ə məl) *adj.* smallest or least possible; very small; p. 529

tempest (tem′ pist) *n.* a violent windstorm, usually accompanied by rain, hail, snow, or thunder; p. 530

modest (mod′ ist) *adj.* tending to avoid praise or credit; humble; bashful; p. 532

RESOURCE MANAGER

Teaching Tools and Resources
- Theme Five Planning Guide
- Literature Groups Sourcebook

Essential Lesson Support

Lesson-Specific Instruction
- Selection Focus Transparency 46
- Literary Elements Transparency 47
- Active Reading Guide,* p. 47
- Selection Vocabulary Practice, p. 32

Assessment
- Selection Quick Checks,* p. 47
- Sel. and Theme Assmt., pp. 83–84
- Testmaker: ExamView Pro
- Performance Assessment, p. 44

Systematic Language Instruction
- Gr. & Comp. Hbk., L. 11.4
- Vocabulary Power, Unit 5 Review/Test
- Spelling Power, Unit 5 Review/Proofreading

English Language Learners
- ELL Sourcebook, p. 69
- Spanish Summaries, p. 46
- Spanish Translations, pp. 113–120
- Audio Library*
- English, Yes!

Spec. Needs/Strat. Interven.
- Interactive Rdg. Sbk., pp. T167–T169
- Interactive Rdg. Wkbk., pp. 88–89
- Inclusion Strat. Sbk., pp. 69–70
- Audio Library*

* Also available in Spanish

from

Letters from Rifka

Karen Hesse

> . . . The heavy-hanging chains will fall,
> The walls will crumble at a word;
> And Freedom greet you in the light,
> And brothers give you back the sword.
>
> —*Pushkin*

October 22, 1920
Ellis Island

Dear Tovah,

A This is the last letter I will ever write you from Ellis Island. It is almost impossible to believe what has happened today. I don't know where to start.

I woke up feeling like a lump of wool had caught in my throat. I let Ilya sleep in bed beside me last night. I knew it was probably our last night together, whatever happened.

We whispered for a long time in the dark. I told him not to be afraid of America. That he would make friends here. That his uncle would love him and take care of him.

Reading the Selection

SUMMARY

Rifka and Ilya, having recently emigrated from Russia, are waiting at Ellis Island to be allowed into the United States. They must pass the entrance exam to be admitted. While their family watches, the two must prove they can make a contribution to their new country.

Spanish Summaries, p. 46

A Active Reading Strategies

PREDICT Ask students to speculate on the meaning of the first sentence. Why do they think this is Rifka's last letter from Ellis Island? Where is she going?

VOCABULARY If you haven't previewed the selection vocabulary with students, stop and remind them to use context clues to unlock the meanings of new vocabulary words.

Additional Resources

Active Reading Guide, p. 47
Audio Library
Spanish Audio Library

Teaching Support

CONNECTING TO OTHER SELECTIONS

The chart at the right shows three ways to connect *Letters from Rifka* to other selections in this book.

For specific teaching strategies, see the ***Theme Five Planning Guide***.

Connection		Title
Life Skills: Problem Solving	→	from *The Diary of Anne Frank,* p. 697
Thematic: Facing Foreign Experience	→	"My Two Dads," p. 19
Literary: First-Person Narrator	→	"Thank You in Arabic," p. 574

Cultural Note

Before the serfs were emancipated in 1861, there was little social mobility in Russia. Serfs were treated much like slaves. They were bound to the land where they worked.

B Active Reading Strategies

QUESTION Ask students why they think Rifka is worried about not being allowed into the United States. *(Immigration officials could refuse entry to people who were ill, disabled, or unable to work.)*

C Active Reading Strategies

CONNECT Ask students how they think they might feel in Ilya's place. At the age of seven, he has lost his entire family and has been shipped to a country where he doesn't speak the language to live with an uncle he's never met.

VIEWING THE PHOTO

Responding to the Photo *Subjects in this photo show little emotion other than a sober stare. Rifka was assertive and determined, loving toward her family, and firm with Ilya.*

An immigrant family waits at Ellis Island.

Viewing the photograph: Do the people in the photograph seem to share Rifka's attitude toward Ellis Island? Explain.

I told him that in Russia, he would always be a peasant. That would never change. He would die young just as his father had and maybe leave a little boy just as his father had left him. I told him in America, he could grow up to be anything he wanted. He could have a wife and children and live to be an old man and see his grandchildren born.

He said he would stay, if he could marry me.

That made me smile. I'm glad it was dark so he couldn't see. I didn't want him to think I was making fun.

I have learned so much about America in these three weeks. It is hard to believe I got so upset over Ilya and the toilet paper just a few days ago. I laugh about it now. I understand so much more.

B Yet as I woke this morning, with Ilya curled up beside me, I wondered what good would come from my understanding. What chance did I have of staying? Not only did I have no hair, but the ringworm[1] had returned. Every second I had to remind myself not to scratch at the ringworm.

Ilya had America within his grasp, but me, I held nothing. I held only Russia.

Mr. Fargate, the man who makes these decisions, came into the little office beside the ward. He called Ilya in first.

C Ilya gripped my hand and pulled me into the office with him. Mr. Fargate and Doctor Askin discussed Ilya, examined him. Mr. Fargate noticed that Ilya had gained weight.

Ilya's uncle sat in a chair nearby. He was such a little man, with thin blond hair and stormy eyes, just like Ilya's.

1. *Ringworm* is a skin disease that is caused by a tiny fungus (not a worm).

Teaching Support

MEETING INDIVIDUAL NEEDS: ENGLISH LANGUAGE LEARNERS

Social Adjustment Coming to a new country is a major change. It is especially hard on children, who must learn a new language and new customs and make new friends.

Activity In mixed groups, have students who were born outside of the United States discuss with classmates some of their experiences in coming to the United States. If classmates have traveled to a foreign country, even if only for a visit, have them share some things they learned from the experience.

Additional Resources

English Language Learners Sourcebook, p. 69

My family, my whole beautiful family, Papa and Mama and Saul, and Nathan and Asher and Reuben, and Isaac and Sadie and the little baby, Aaron, they were all there too. How I longed to be with them. I looked at each of them, memorizing their faces. My brothers Reuben and Asher and Isaac, I would have known them anywhere. Isaac and Asher look just like Papa, and Reuben, he looks like me. When they first arrived, I hugged and kissed them all.

I whispered to Saul, "Did you get the candlesticks?"

He said, "Yes, Rifka. But I have not given them to Mama yet."

"What are you waiting for?" I asked.

Saul shrugged.

Now I could only look at my family from a distance. Ilya needed me.

Ilya's uncle cowered under the giant shadow of my family. When Nurse Bowen passed him, his hair lifted off his high forehead in the little breeze that she made. He held his hat in his hand, his fingers inching around the brim over and over again, his shoulders hunched. It looked to me like he needed Ilya as much as Ilya needed him.

Mr. Fargate said, "This boy shows minimal intelligence. He doesn't feed himself, he doesn't speak. Has there been any change since his last review, Doctor Askin?"

The doctor said many things, but the more he talked the more clear it became he didn't know Ilya at all.

He believed Ilya *was* a simpleton.

Ilya could read Pushkin. He was smart enough to figure out if he starved himself, he'd get shipped back home. That's not a simpleton. They couldn't send him back for being a simpleton.

Mr. Fargate pushed his glasses up on his nose and leaned over his desk to peer at Ilya.

"Can you speak?" he asked in English.

Ilya stared straight into Mr. Fargate's eyes, but he said nothing.

"He doesn't understand English," Nurse Bowen said.

Mr. Fargate nodded. "Find someone who can translate."

"I can," I offered.

Mr. Fargate looked over his glasses at me. "Ask the boy if he can talk," said Mr. Fargate.

"Talk," I told Ilya in Russian.

Ilya glared at me.

"Ilya, talk!"

Ilya slowly shook his head.

"Go get my Pushkin," I told Ilya.

He looked up at me and brushed his blond hair out of his eyes. His uncle looked up at me too, startled.

"Go on, get the book," I repeated.

Ilya was being as stubborn as ever. He stood in his place and refused to move.

"Ilya," I commanded. "Go over there and get the book of Pushkin. Now!"

I pointed toward my cot.

Ilya stared at me with those stormy green eyes. Then he lowered his chin, brushed past his uncle, and got the book.

"Ilya is a smart boy," I told Mr. Fargate in English.

I looked down at Ilya. "Read to them," I ordered in Russian. "Show them that you are smart enough to live in America. I

Vocabulary

minimal (min′ ə məl) *adj.* smallest or least possible; very small

D Critical Thinking

INFER Ask students what they can infer about Rifka's thoughts from the statement "I looked at each of them, memorizing their faces." *(She doesn't expect to be permitted to stay.)*

E Literary Elements

NARRATION Point out that an important part of narration is characterization. The narrator, Rifka, brings the uncle to life with her comparison of him and Ilya.

F Active Reading Strategies

QUESTION Ask students why they think Ilya refuses to talk when he knows it is so important to pass the entrance exam. *(He is afraid that his uncle doesn't want him and of the unknown new country.)*

MEETING INDIVIDUAL NEEDS — SPECIAL NEEDS

Emotional Ilya's refusal to speak almost keeps him from entering the United States. Explain that Ilya is confronting a dilemma—a situation in which neither choice seems good.

Activity Have students form small groups to discuss Ilya's dilemma and complete a chart with the pros and cons of speaking or not speaking. What other options are open to Ilya? Ask groups to vote on the best choice for Ilya, and have them defend their choices with reasons. **L1** COLLAB. LEARN.

Additional Resources

Inclusion Strategies

G Literary Elements

NARRATION Explain to students that plot is often an element in narration. Ask students to identify a major turning point in the plot. *(The moment at which Ilya's uncle speaks is a major turning point in the plot. The uncle dispels the boy's fears, so Ilya now knows he's wanted and, therefore, is willing to read.)*

H Author's Craft

SYMBOLISM Emphasize that the passages Hesse cites from Alexander Pushkin are themselves symbolic. The first passage seems to represent Ilya's fear—and his stormy disposition. Ask students what the second passage suggests. *(It suggests a happy and peaceful ending to the story.)*

I Literary Elements

NARRATION Remind students that, in this story, the narration includes rising action. Ilya's acceptance into the country is one conflict overcome. Ask students whether they think Rifka will be accepted.

know how clever you are, Ilya. But Mr. Fargate needs to know. Your uncle needs to know too."

I looked back to where the uncle sat with his hat in his lap. The man's eyes never left Ilya. He drank in the sight of his nephew the way a thirsty man pulls at a dipper of water.

Still, Ilya remained silent.

Mr. Fargate lifted the stamp, the deportation[2] stamp.

"Please," I begged Ilya's uncle in Russian. "You are losing him. He must prove to them that he is not a simpleton or they will send him away."

I tried to get the uncle to understand.

"He is afraid of you. He thinks you don't want him."

G "He is my sister's son," Ilya's uncle said in Russian. "Of course I want him. He is my flesh and blood. I sent for him to give him a better life here in America. I work day and night so he can have a good life."

"Do you hear, Ilya?" I said. "Do you hear?"

Ilya turned his eyes for the first time on his uncle.

"Doctor Askin," I said in English. "Ilya is not a simpleton. I know he won't talk to you. But he *can* talk. He can read, too. He is only seven years, but he can read."

I gave Ilya the book. "Now read," I commanded in Russian.

Ilya's uncle got up out of his seat and came over. He put his hat down on the edge of Mr. Fargate's desk and knelt before his nephew. "Please, Ilya," he said. "Do what your friend says."

Ilya brushed the blond hair up onto his forehead. Then he began to read.

> *"Storm-clouds dim the sky; the tempest*
> *Weaves the snow in patterns wild . . ."* H

Ilya's voice shook, but he was reading.

> *"Like a beast the gale is howling,*
> *And now wailing like a child . . ."* H

Tears filled the eyes of Ilya's uncle.

"Is he reading?" Mr. Fargate asked. "Is that Russian?"

Ilya's uncle nodded. "Pushkin."

"Let me see the book a moment," Mr. Fargate said. He reached for the Pushkin. Ilya pulled it back, clasping the book to his chest.

"Show Mr. Fargate the book," I said in Russian. "Go on, Ilya."

Ilya's hands trembled as he handed the book to Mr. Fargate. Mr. Fargate opened our Pushkin to another page. "Read this."

> *". . . I like the grapes whose clusters ripen*
> *Upon the hillside in the sun . . ."* H

Ilya's finger dragged across the page as he read the words.

I smiled. Doctor Askin smiled. Nurse Bowen smiled too.

"He understands this?" Mr. Fargate said. "At the age of seven?"

"Yes, sir," I said. "He understands."

Mr. Fargate lifted the stamp that permitted Ilya to enter the country and thumped it down on Ilya's papers. Ilya was going to stay in America. I

2. *Deportation* is the act of forcing a noncitizen to leave a country because the person is considered undesirable for some reason.

Vocabulary

tempest (tem′ pist) *n.* a violent windstorm, usually accompanied by rain, hail, snow, or thunder

Teaching Support

Reading *Minilesson*

Comparison and Contrast The selection from *Letters from Rifka* has a two-part structure. In the first part of the story, it appears that Ilya will not be allowed to stay, but with Rifka's help he overcomes the obstacle and is welcomed to the United States. In the second part of the story, the sequence is repeated for Rifka.

Activity Have students list all the similarities between the two parts of the story they can remember. Then ask the students to list the differences between Rifka's story and Ilya's. **L2**

Additional Resources

Reading Skills Practice Workbook

"Did I do it right, Rifka?" he asked in Russian.

"Yes, Ilya," I said. "You did it just right."

J Ilya's uncle still knelt on the floor beside us. His arms opened up to take Ilya in. Oh, Tovah. You should have seen the way Ilya and his uncle embraced. In all the times he clung to me, Ilya never held me in such a way. Never.

Ilya had attracted a lot of attention on the ward. No one but myself had ever heard his voice. Now there he was, reading Pushkin. Other nurses and doctors came over. They stood around in wonder at Ilya, now jabbering in Russian as he led his uncle back to his cot.

I could not listen to what they were saying. The time had come for my review. My family waited tensely, some sitting, some standing, waiting for a decision about me. If only I could melt into their tight strong circle, but now, as I had so often over the last year, I stood alone.

K Mr. Fargate was talking with Doctor Askin about me. He wanted to know about the ringworm.

"She arrived fully cured," Doctor Askin said. "They made sure she was clean in Belgium before they sent her."

Please, I prayed. Don't let them check for the ringworm now.

They hadn't checked in over a week. I'd shown no sign of being infectious for so long, they believed the ringworm was gone.

I bit the insides of my cheeks to keep from scratching my itchy scalp. In my head, I repeated Sister Mary Katherine's prayer; I repeated a few Hebrew prayers too.

Mr. Fargate turned to Doctor Askin. "What about her hair? Is there any sign of growth?"

I slipped my hand up to my kerchief and gave a quick scratch. I tried not to, but I couldn't keep my hand away from it. It itched so badly. It had been itching all morning.

"Here, Rifka," Doctor Askin said kindly, starting to unknot my kerchief. "Let me look once more to see if there is any sign of hair."

I pulled away.

Oh, Tovah, if ever I needed to be clever, it was now. L

An Ellis Island doctor checks the health of immigrants.

J Literary Elements

NARRATION Point out to students that the author makes her particular type of narration apparent by having the main character address the person to whom she is sending the letter. What effect does this have on the reader?

K Active Reading Strategies

QUESTION Ask students why Rifka thinks the ringworm has returned. *(Her scalp itches.)* Be sure also that they understand that Rifka won't be allowed into the United States if she has ringworm.

L Active Reading Strategies

QUESTION Why does Rifka say she has to be clever? *(She thinks that if the doctor looks at her scalp, he'll find ringworm. She feels that she must distract the examiners, impressing them with her intellect and ability so that they forget about checking her scalp.)*

Interdisciplinary Connection

Social Studies Rifka is one of a large number of Eastern Europeans who immigrated to the United States in the early 1900s. In fact, each era of American history has been influenced by one or more immigrant groups that left their homelands in "waves." Usually there is a reason a wave of people leaves home.

Activity Have students form small groups to research the historical events that have resulted in great waves of immigration to the United States. Assign each team a national group and a specific period (such as the Irish in the mid-nineteenth century or the Vietnamese in the 1970s.) Ask each group to prepare an oral report on the factors that motivated immigration. **L2** COLLAB. LEARN.

Ⓜ Critical Thinking

EVALUATE Ask students what they think of Rifka's strategy to draw Mr. Fargate's attention from her hair. *(Many students might find her strategy to be clever. Some may consider the ruse deceptive.)*

N Active Reading Strategies

QUESTION What do we learn about Rifka's character as she tries to convince her listeners that hair doesn't matter? *(She is intelligent, resourceful, and logical. Also, she has nerve!)*

O Active Reading Strategies

QUESTION Why does Mama gasp and say "Oy, Rifka"? How does she regard Rifka's answer? What does Mama's reaction reveal about Mama? *(Mama is worried that Rifka is too forward and outspoken. Her reaction may reveal that she is less outspoken than her daughter.)*

"You know," I said. "What does it matter if my hair grows? A girl can not depend on her looks. It is better to be clever. I learned to speak English in three weeks, you know." Ⓜ

"Yes, I know," Mr. Fargate replied.

N "I help here too," I said. "I am a good worker."

Mr. Fargate's eyeglasses slid down to the tip of his nose and he stared over them at me. "Not very modest, is she?"

They all laughed.

"It is true!" I cried. "I *am* a good worker!"

"You are, Rifka," Doctor Askin agreed. He turned to Mr. Fargate. "With the right opportunity, the girl could study medicine. She has skill and talent."

"In your opinion, then," Mr. Fargate said, "she would not end up a ward of the state?"[3]

"Who can tell?" said the doctor. "But the opposite is more likely. I have seen her care for the patients. Compassion is a part of medicine you can't teach, Mr. Fargate. Compassion is a quality I have often seen in Rifka. Look what she did for the boy."

"I still worry about her hair," Mr. Fargate said.

I looked Mr. Fargate right in the eye. "I do not need hair to get a good life," I said.

"Maybe right now you don't," Mr. Fargate answered. "But what about when you wish to marry?"

"If I wish to marry, Mr. Fargate," I said—can you believe I spoke like this to an American official, Tovah?— "if I wish to marry, I will do so with hair or without hair."

I heard Mama gasp. This much English she understood.

Mr. Fargate leaned forward to study me. He stared at me through the glasses balanced at the bottom of his nose.

"You have plenty to say, young lady," Mr. Fargate said.

"Yes," I agreed, "I do." O

"Oy, Rifka," Mama whispered.

I turned toward Mama. What I saw, though, was my brother Saul kneeling beside Ilya. Ilya and Saul were looking at the book of Pushkin together. Then Saul stood and took Ilya's hand and they approached Mr. Fargate.

"Yes?" Mr. Fargate asked.

Ilya looked up at me. "Read to them," he commanded in Russian.

"Ilya, that will not work for me," I told him in his own language. "They already know I can read. My case is not the same as yours."

"Read to them your poetry," Saul said. "The words you have written in the back of this book."

I looked hard at Ilya. "You had no right to show that to anyone," I said. "Those are my words."

---

3. For Rifka to become a *ward of the state,* a judge would have to decide that she cannot take care of herself. A guardian would be appointed to look after her.

Vocabulary
modest (mod′ ist) *adj.* tending to avoid praise or credit; humble; bashful

Teaching Support

Literature & Humanities

Provide opportunities for students to examine the photograph "Steerage" on page 470 in the book *American Art History and Culture*. Have them write a letter from a steerage passenger, describing conditions on the boat and his or her feelings about coming to America.

Meeting Individual Needs: ADVANCED LEARNERS

Stereotypes Some people may incorrectly believe that immigrants from other countries are unintelligent if they cannot communicate fluently in English. However, as people adjust to speaking English, they may use subtle variations of standard English. For example, Saul tells Rifka, "Read to them your poetry," instead of saying "Read your poetry to them." Variations like this may reinforce an unfair stereotype for some people. However, Rifka and Ilya are in fact quite bright and literate.

Activity Have students work in small groups to find examples from the text that indicate Rifka's and Ilya's talent, intelligence, or cleverness. Have groups share their findings with the class.
L3 COLLAB. LEARN.

"They are good words, Rifka," Saul said.

"They are nothing," I answered. "Simple little poems. They don't even rhyme. What good would it do to read such things aloud? Leave it be."

Ilya would not leave it.

He took the Pushkin and elbowed in front of me to stand under the stern eye of Mr. Fargate.

"This," he said, speaking English with a very thick accent. "This Rifka write."

I'd never heard him speak anything but Russian before.

He took a deep breath and let it out. He swallowed once, hard. Then he began reciting my latest poem in English. How I had struggled with the words. Ilya had made me repeat them to him each time I stopped or changed something. Now he remembered it perfectly. He didn't look at the book. He just held it in front of him and said the poem from memory.

"I leave to you the low and leaning room,
where once we drank the honey-sweetened tea,
and bowed our heads in prayer and waited there,
for cossacks[4] with their boots and bayonets."

P They were all listening, even Ilya's uncle.

"I leave behind my cousins, young and dear;
They'll never know the freedom I have known,
Or learn as I have learned, that kindness dwells,
In hearts that have no fear."

4. In the 1800s (when Pushkin wrote), the *cossacks* were members of special military units. Their cruel treatment of Jews, other minorities, and peasants made the cossacks greatly feared and hated.

"You wrote these words?" Mr. Fargate asked.

I nodded, embarrassed.

"Rifka Nebrot," Mr. Fargate said. "This is a very nice poem."

"You think?" I asked. "That is just one poem." I took the book from Ilya and started turning pages. "I have more, Mr. Fargate, many more. I can read to you. Do you have time? Here is one you will like, I think . . ." Q

Mr. Fargate looked at his watch. Then he looked at Doctor Askin. "No wonder the boy never talked. She talks enough for both of them."

Now, I thought, it would be clever to keep quiet.

"Well, Miss Nebrot," Mr. Fargate said. "After giving the matter some consideration, I think you are correct. Whether you wish to marry or not is no business of mine." He turned to Doctor Askin. "Heaven help the man she does marry." R

Turning back to me, he said, "I have no doubt that if you wish to marry, you will manage to do so, whether you have hair or not."

Then he looked over to Mama and Papa. "Mr. and Mrs. Nebrot. These are your daughter's papers. With this stamp I give permission for her to enter the United States of America."

My heart thundered in my chest.

Mr. Fargate stamped my entrance papers and handed them to me. "Here, Rifka Nebrot," he said. "Welcome to America."

The nurses and doctors swept over me. Ilya, too. Best of all my family, my beloved family, Saul, Nathan, Reuben, Asher, Isaac, Mama, Papa, Sadie, and little Aaron. There was such a commotion

P Critical Thinking

EVALUATE Ask students what they think of Rifka's poem. Have them think about how the U.S. officials may view the poem. Have students review the following model:

Model: I am impressed that someone so young could write this poem. I think the officials will be impressed, too. Not only does Rifka make her statement eloquently, but she also exemplifies the American dream.

Q Active Reading Strategies

CONNECT Point out that Rifka is opposed to Ilya's reading her poem aloud at first. After everyone likes it, however, she is prepared to share all of her poems. What does this say about her character? *(She needs acceptance.)* Would you react in the same way?

R Active Reading Strategies

QUESTION Why does Mr. Fargate say "Heaven help the man she does marry"? *(He thinks Rifka is willful and stubborn.)*

Writing Minilesson

Paraphrase Being able to summarize a story in one's own words is an important skill. It is especially useful when one is writing research papers, an activity that calls for paraphrasing factual information. A good paraphrase avoids using the author's original words but at the same time gives an accurate and complete sense of what was has been said.

Activity Have students write a brief paraphrase of what Rifka says about not having hair. Have several students read their paraphrases aloud to the class. Discuss whether the paraphrases met the dual criteria of accuracy and comprehensiveness. **L2**

Additional Resources

Writer's Choice

with all the kissing and the hugging I could hardly breathe.

Then I felt something that made me stiffen with fear. In all the kissing and hugging, someone had loosened the kerchief covering my head. I felt it slipping off.

I tried to get my hand up to hold on to it, but Doctor Askin held my arms. He enfolded me in a crushing hug, and I felt the kerchief sliding down, inching away from the sores it covered, to betray me. The kerchief, as Doctor Askin let go, dropped around my neck, settling on my shoulders like a heavy weight. **S**

With my head exposed to the air, it itched worse than ever.

Quickly my hands flew up to replace the kerchief. I swept it back up in a matter of seconds, trying to cover my head before anyone had a chance to see my scalp.

I wasn't fast enough. Towering over me as he did, Saul had seen it. Doctor Askin had seen it too. They stared down at me.

"Rifka, your head," Saul said.

I pulled the kerchief tightly over my scalp.

Not now, I prayed. They've stamped the papers. Don't let them find out now.

"But Rifka," Saul said. "There's something on your head."

"Take off your kerchief," Doctor Askin ordered.

"Please," I begged in a whisper. "Don't make me take it off."

"Take it off, Rifka," Doctor Askin insisted.

Everyone stared at me, at my trembling hands, at my disloyal kerchief.

My hands shook as I lifted them to the knot under my chin. I had difficulty untying it. Everyone stared at me, at my trembling hands, at my disloyal kerchief. **T**

"Whatever it is," I said, trying to talk my way out of it, "I'm certain it will go away."

I could delay no longer. The kerchief dropped to my shoulders.

"This isn't going away," said Nurse Bowen. "Here, feel for yourself."

She took my hand and guided it up to the top of my head. I stretched my hand out, expecting to feel the ringworm sores under my fingertips.

But I didn't feel ringworm.

I felt hair!

Not very much. But it was hair. My hair! And it was growing. **U**

* * *

Mama and Papa are sitting beside me on a bench at Ellis Island. We are waiting for my brother Isaac. I am writing on the paper Nurse Bowen gave to me.

Saul says at home there is a notebook full of paper, a whole empty notebook for me to write in. He bought it for me himself, with his own money. And at home is a pair of brass candlesticks, he said. A pair just like the ones Mama used to own. Tonight, Saul said, tonight I would give them to her. **V**

On my head is the black velvet hat with the shirring[5] and the light blue lining. My head still itches, but Nurse

5. Here, the *shirring* is a stitched gathering of the velvet.

S Active Reading Strategies

QUESTION Why does Rifka's kerchief feel "like a heavy weight" when it slips off her head? *(She is afraid it will be the cause of her not being allowed to join her family.)*

T Active Reading Strategies

QUESTION Why does Rifka label her kerchief "disloyal"? *(It has betrayed her secret.)*

U Critical Thinking

EVALUATE Before she discovers that her hair is growing, Rifka said her hair doesn't matter. Is she completely sincere? What can one tell from her reaction? *(Many students will say she is not completely sincere; Rifka really does want her hair to grow back. Others may say that she is trying to convince herself that looks are not important.)*

V Literary Elements

NARRATION What does the reader conclude about Rifka when she says "a whole empty notebook for me to write in"? *(Clearly to have new, clean paper is a tremendous luxury. Also, she has been using book margins to write in.)*

Teaching Support

Grammar and Language *Minilesson*

Direct Objects Write this sentence from page 534 on the board: *I pulled the kerchief tightly over my scalp.* Point out that you have underlined the action verb and its direct object. A direct object receives the action of an action verb.

Activity Ask students to find five additional sentences in the story that have direct objects. They should copy the sentences and underline both the verb and the direct object. **L2**

Additional Resources

- ***Grammar and Language Transparency 44***
- ***Grammar and Language Workbook,*** p. 77
- ***Grammar and Composition Handbook,*** Lesson 3.2
- ***Writer's Choice,*** Lesson 10.2

Italian Girl at Ellis Island Finds Her First Penny, 1926. Lewis Hine. The New York Public Library. Gift of the Russell Sage Foundation Library.

Viewing the photograph: What qualities do you think the girl in this photograph may share with Rifka?

Bowen said that is normal. That often the scalp prickles when new hair grows in.

Mama's gold locket lies softly between her breasts again, where it belongs. Around my neck is a small Star of David on a silver chain, a gift from Mama and Papa.

"Saul said this is what you would like the most," Mama had said when she gave it to me.

"Saul was right," I said, and I kissed Mama and Papa on their hands, first one and then the other.

My brother Isaac has gone home to Borough Park to bring his car. He said, "Never mind the trouble, my sister Rifka is going to enter America in style."

A clever girl like me, Tovah, how else should I enter America?

I will write you tonight a real letter, a letter I can send. I will wrap up our precious book and send it to you too, so you will know of my journey. I hope you can read all the tiny words squeezed onto the worn pages. I hope they bring to you the comfort they have brought to me. I send you my love, Tovah. At last I send you my love from America.

Shalom,[6] *my dear cousin,*
Rifka

6. Used both as a greeting and a farewell, *shalom* (shə lōm′) is a Hebrew word meaning "peace."

Viewing the Photograph

Lewis Hine recorded the destruction of Europe during World War I, but is best known for his portraits of immigrants. He broke ground as one of the first photographers to document social conditions.

Viewing Response *The alert, interested look may remind viewers of Rifka.*

Active Reading Strategies

QUESTION Ask students why they think Rifka mentions her Star of David. *(She has not been free to practice her religion in Russia.)*

Thematic Focus

Free to Be Even in the early twentieth century, people still came to the United States for religious and societal freedom. Ask students what they think freedom will mean to Rifka and Ilya.

Assessment

Quick Checks, p. 47

Real-World Connection

Emigration People are still immigrating to the United States in pursuit of freedom.

Activity Assign students to small groups, each group to research emigration from a particular geographic area—East Asia, Latin America, Southeast Asia, Eastern Europe. What difficulties do these individuals face when they come to the United States? What opportunities do they seek? **L2**

Responding to the Selection

PERSONAL RESPONSE

Students' responses will indicate what aspects of the story have made the greatest impression on them.

Analyzing Literature

1. Mr. Fargate thinks Ilya is a simpleton.
2. Rifka demonstrates her effective use of English, telling the doctor that not having hair won't make any difference in her finding work or a husband if she wants one.
3. Ilya helps Rifka pass inspection by showing the doctor and Mr. Fargate her poetry.
4. Rifka receives a notebook and a necklace with a Star of David pendant on it.
5. Ilya must show his uncle that he's not a simpleton because his uncle does not know him, and Rifka wants the uncle to be proud of Ilya. Also, he cannot stay in America if he is a simpleton.
6. Some students may say that Rifka is frightened and that she shows fear particularly when her scarf falls off. Others may cite her courage to speak up to the examining officer.
7. Rifka's poem is well written and intelligent.
8. Rifka says Hebrew prayers and asks for a Star of David.
9. Rifka is compassionate; the doctor says she has shown a real talent for taking care of people. Rifka is talkative; as Mr. Fargate says, she has "plenty to say." Rifka is also smart; she has learned a great deal of English in just three weeks.
10. It is a nerve-wracking experience to wait for the approval of another person. One feels worried and tense, and in such a situation it is easy to make mistakes.

Responding to Literature

PERSONAL RESPONSE

- What three words do you think best describe this story?

Brackets connect questions that are paired to develop higher-level thinking skills.

Analyzing Literature

RECALL

1. What is Mr. Fargate's impression of Ilya?
2. How does Rifka distract the doctor from examining her head?
3. What does Ilya do to help Rifka pass inspection?
4. What gifts do Rifka's family members give her when she finally receives permission to enter the country?

INTERPRET

5. Why does Rifka tell Ilya that he must show his uncle that he is not a simpleton?
6. Do you think Rifka is frightened? Support your answer with examples from the story.
7. Why does Rifka's poem impress the American officials?
8. How do you know that Rifka is Jewish? Give several reasons.

EVALUATE AND CONNECT

9. **Characterization** is the method a writer uses to develop a character's personality. How does the author let you know what kind of person Rifka is? List three adjectives that fit Rifka, and then list details from the story that support those adjectives.
10. Have you ever had to wait for someone's approval the way Rifka waits to have her papers stamped? How was your experience like or different from Rifka's?

LITERARY ELEMENTS

Narration

Narration is the telling of a story. The author of *Letters from Rifka* chose to tell this story through a series of letters written by the main character. Rifka is the narrator, and everything that happens is told from her perspective.

1. What are some advantages of telling a story in the form of letters?
2. What effect does telling the story through Rifka's eyes have on the ringworm episode?
3. How does Rifka tailor, or put together, her story so that her cousin Tovah will know what is important and will understand an unfamiliar situation? How does the author tailor the story for her audience, you?

● See **Literary Terms Handbook,** p. R6.

LITERARY ELEMENTS

1. A story told in the form of letters can reveal emotions as well as thoughts.
2. Telling the story from Rifka's viewpoint heightens the suspense of the ringworm episode. It also makes the reader imagine how the experience feels.
3. Rifka provides details and considerable explanation. Hesse does the same.

Additional Resources

Literary Elements Transparency 47

Literature and Writing

Writing About Literature

Conflict There are several conflicts in this story, both **external** (a character's struggle against some outside force) and **internal** (a struggle within a character's own mind). Write a paragraph identifying and analyzing one conflict of each type. To identify conflicts, begin by asking yourself what the character wants. Look over your list from the **Reading Focus** on page 526. Which of those conflicts are similar to the ones in this story?

Personal Writing

Your Heritage If you know how a member of your family or an acquaintance came to America, write a piece of historical fiction about the experience. Use your imagination to elaborate on the details provided by your parents, grandparents, or elderly friends. Bring your story to life by adding imaginary but possible dialogue. (For help with historical fiction, see the **Genre Focus** on page 508.)

Extending Your Response

Literature Groups

Jump-Start Memories With a group, brainstorm to come up with a list of questions you can ask family members or older friends to help them think about their past. Use your list to start a conversation about adjusting to a new culture or place.

interNET CONNECTION

Today, technology has made communication easier than it was for Rifka. Gather the e-mail addresses of friends or relatives who use the Internet. Begin a correspondence with one person, sending one e-mail per week for a month.

Learning for Life

Plan a Trip Working in a small group, choose one student's country of origin, and plan a trip there. Research the country's history, tourist attractions, and climate. You might visit an on-line travel agent's Web site to help you create a budget and itinerary for your trip. Share your information with the whole class, including a map and pictures of some of the sites you would like to visit.

Reading Further

For more stories about people seeking homes, try:

Migrant Workers: Temporary People by Linda Altman

Save your work for your portfolio.

Literature and Writing

Writing about Literature

Students' paragraphs should

- discuss both internal and external conflict
- describe how the conflicts are resolved

Personal Writing

Students' narratives should

- use description and dialogue
- hold the reader's interest

Extending Your Response

Literature Groups Two good questions for students to ask are *Where did you live when you were my age?* and *What did you enjoy doing when you were my age?* COLLAB. LEARN.

Learning for Life Suggest that students find out whether there is a "best time" to visit the place they have chosen.

Internet Connection Point out to students that dialogue and description made Rifka's letters readable. Suggest they follow her lead when corresponding by e-mail.

Skill Minilessons

GRAMMAR AND LANGUAGE
USING APOSTROPHES

1. Rifka's
2. men's; Ilya's
3. It's; anyone's
4. correct
5. "There's; you're

READING AND THINKING
PARAPHRASING

Students' paraphrases should include the main idea of the conversation.

VOCABULARY
WORD PARTS THAT EXPRESS SIZE

1. An owlet is a baby owl.
2. A megalith is a large stone.
3. Microbiology is the study of tiny things.
4. One would most likely find a statuette on a shelf.
5. Drops will fill a pail first.

Additional Resources

- ***Grammar and Language Workbook,*** p. 269–270
- ***Grammar and Composition Handbook,*** Lesson 13.7
- ***Writer's Choice,*** Lesson 20.7
- ***Reading Skills Practice Workbook***
- ***Vocabulary Practice,*** p. 32

RETEACH • REVIEW

Skill Minilessons

GRAMMAR AND LANGUAGE • USING APOSTROPHES

An **apostrophe** may indicate missing letters in a contraction (as in *cannot* → *can't*). An apostrophe plus *s* forms the possessive of the following items:

- a singular noun *(Rifka's)*
- a plural noun that doesn't end in *s (women's)*
- an indefinite pronoun *(somebody's).*

Use an apostrophe alone to form the possessive of a plural noun that ends in *s (ships').*

For more about using apostrophes, see **Language Handbook,** p. R42.

PRACTICE Rewrite each underlined plural, possessive, or contraction, adding apostrophes if they are needed. (*Note:* One of the underlined words is correct.)

1. Rifkas family was waiting for her.
2. The mens concern was with Ilyas intelligence.
3. Its anyones guess whether Rifka will keep writing poetry.
4. Pushkin was a favorite author of hers.
5. "Theres a lot youre going to have to learn," Mr. Fargate said.

READING AND THINKING • PARAPHRASING

Paraphrasing means restating a text, passage, or conversation. You often paraphrase when you summarize or when you need to simplify an idea for someone. Paraphrasing usually involves changing direct quotes to indirect quotes or making a passage clearer, perhaps by replacing large words with smaller ones and eliminating trivial details.

PRACTICE In a few sentences, paraphrase the conversation between Rifka, Dr. Askin, and Mr. Fargate about Rifka's hair.

For more about paraphrasing, see **Reading Handbook,** p. R99.

VOCABULARY • WORD PARTS THAT EXPRESS SIZE

Some word parts are used to express size. Mr. Fargate says that Ilya has *minimal* intelligence, the least possible intelligence. The word part *mini-* carries the meaning of "small." *Maxi-* has the opposite meaning, so *maximal* intelligence would be the greatest possible intelligence.

Here are some examples of common word parts that express size:

micro-	small	*-et*	small
-let	small	*macro-*	large, enlarged
mega-	large, powerful	*-ette*	small

PRACTICE Use the list of word parts at the left to figure out what the underlined words mean, and then answer the questions.

1. Is an owlet a baby owl or an old owl?
2. Why would it be difficult to lift a stone that was a megalith?
3. Which is a field of science that studies tiny living things–macrobiotics or microbiology?
4. Where would you be likely to find a statuette–on a shelf or on a huge pedestal?
5. Which will fill a pail first–a ceiling that is leaking droplets or a ceiling that is leaking drops?

ASSESSMENT

- ***Quick Checks,*** p. 47
- ***Selection and Theme Assessment,*** pp. 83–84
- ***Performance Assessment,*** p. 44
- ***Testmaker: ExamView Pro***
- ***Interactive Tutor: Self-Assessment***

GRAMMAR LINK

Using Pronouns Correctly

Pronouns are substitutes for nouns. Sentences without pronouns would be clumsy.

Rifka told Rifka's brother that Rifka's poetry was private to Rifka.

Rifka told *her* brother that *her* poetry was private to *her.*

A pronoun refers to a noun or another pronoun, called its **antecedent.** It must be clear *which* antecedent a pronoun refers to, and the correct pronoun must be used.

Problem 1 A pronoun with an unclear antecedent

While Mr. Fargate was dealing with Ilya, he said nothing. [*He* could refer to *Mr. Fargate* or to *Ilya.*]

Solution *While Mr. Fargate was dealing with Ilya, the boy said nothing.* [Use a noun instead of the pronoun.]

Problem 2 Using an object pronoun as a subject

Rifka and him both faced problems during their interviews.

Solution *Rifka and he both faced problems during their interviews.* [In the subject part of a sentence, use a subject pronoun.]

Problem 3 Using a subject pronoun as an object

Rifka's determination helped both Ilya and she.

Solution *Rifka's determination helped both Ilya and her.* [Use an object pronoun as the object of a verb or a preposition.]

- For more about pronoun use, see **Language Handbook,** p. R16.

EXERCISES

1. Revise each sentence to make it clear.
   a. Mr. Fargate wanted to talk with Ilya, but he didn't say a word.
   b. Rifka told Tovah that she had become a more understanding person.
   c. The officials' experience with Rifka and Ilya showed that they did not understand.
   d. Ilya's uncle told Ilya that he could live to be an old man.
2. Choose the correct pronoun.
   a. Emma and (I, me) were the last students to finish.
   b. The teacher asked (she, her) and (I, me) what took us so long.
   c. It turned out that the same thing was true for both Emma and (I, me).
   d. Both (she, her) and (I, me) had been so interested in Rifka's poem that we had read it over and over again.

GRAMMAR LINK

Objective

- To learn to use pronouns correctly

Teaching Strategies

Show students that mistakes in using object pronouns as subjects and subject pronouns as objects most often occur with compound subjects and objects. For example, in the sentence *Rifka and him both faced problems during their interviews,* tell students to cover up the words *Rifka, and,* and *both.* Students will immediately see that *him* is incorrect. Do the same with *Rifka's determination helped both Ilya and she.* Cover up *both Ilya and.*

Exercises

1. a. Mr. Fargate wanted to talk with Ilya, but the boy didn't say a word.
   b. Rifka told Tovah, "I have become a more understanding person."
   c. The officials' experience with Rifka and Ilya showed that the officials did not understand.
   d. Ilya's uncle told Ilya that the boy could live to be an old man.
2. a. I c. me
   b. her, me d. she, I

Teaching Support

Writing Minilesson

Narrative Writing Explain to students that narrative writing tells a story, which may be fictional or factual. To hold readers' interest a writer must present the story in a vivid and clear manner, using logical order, precise words, and proper grammar.

Activity Have students write a one-page narrative about a topic of their choosing. When they have finished, have students trade papers and review each other's work for grammatical errors, sense, and interest level. "Editors" should make written suggestions on the page.

Additional Resources

Writer's Choice, Lesson 4.1

Writing WORKSHOP

Objectives

- To write a persuasive speech of approximately 500 to 700 words
- To plan a persuasive speech by considering one's own views and those of the audience
- To plan, draft, revise, edit, and present a persuasive speech
- To reflect on and assess the persuasive speech

GLENCOE TECHNOLOGY

WRITER'S ASSISTANT CD-ROM

Students can use the templates and guidelines software for persuasive writing to aid them in the writing process.

Teaching Strategies

PREWRITING

Choose a topic Suggest that students brainstorm to list as many topics as possible before narrowing their choices.

Examine your views Point out to students that their views are based partly on their experiences. As they freewrite, encourage them to include specific events and people who have influenced what they think.

Teaching Support

Writing WORKSHOP

Persuasive Writing: Speech

Which freedoms mean the most to you? What controversies concern you? By speaking out, you can rally people behind ideas and issues that you care about. Speaking out involves **persuasion**–the art of convincing others. The language of persuasion is powerful. With it, you can inspire people to see things in a new light and you can motivate them to take action.

Assignment: Follow the process in this workshop to write a persuasive speech that will inspire and motivate your listeners.

- As you write your persuasive speech, see **Writing Handbook**, pp. R50–R60.

EVALUATION RUBRIC

By the time you complete this Writing Workshop, you will have

- created a thesis that states your position clearly and reflects a knowledgeable judgment
- presented detailed evidence, examples, and a reason to support your thesis
- organized main points and reasons in a logical manner
- concluded with a summary of your argument and a call to action
- presented a speech that is free of errors in grammar, usage, and mechanics

The Writing Process

PREWRITING

PREWRITING TIP

For more topic ideas, check the Internet. Many newspapers have Web sites with in-depth looks at current issues. Add new topics to your list.

TECHNOLOGY TIP

To freewrite on a computer, darken the screen on your monitor. Then type, letting your thoughts flow without visual distractions.

Choose a Topic

List selections you have read recently that remind you of freedoms you cherish or situations you'd like to change. Check newspapers and television news programs for issues and ideas that affect your world. Jot down one or two topics that you feel strongly about.

Examine Your Views

Freewrite about each of your topics, one at a time. Explore the reasons each topic is important to you. Examine how the topic touches your life and the lives of those you care about. Then read your freewriting. Underline key ideas and circle well-worded statements or phrases that you could use in your speech. Finally, select the topic you want to pursue.

Consider Your Purpose and Audience

Will you take a straightforward approach? Should you use humor, statistics, or anecdotes to persuade? Your answers depend on your subject and your audience. Match your message, vocabulary, and tone to your intended audience. Also consider the background information your audience will need to understand your topic.

MEETING INDIVIDUAL NEEDS ENGLISH LANGUAGE LEARNERS

Speaking Before Writing Have students form groups with proficient English speakers to discuss topics. Encourage students to listen carefully to various opinions and to incorporate those opinions into plans for their speeches. COLLAB. LEARN.

Additional Resources

English Language Learners Sourcebook

Build Your Framework

When outlining your speech, focus on a single important idea–your **position statement**. This will probably be one of the key ideas from your freewriting activity. Then list several **reasons** that support your position statement. To persuade an audience, you need strong, reliable evidence for each reason. Gather facts, examples, quotations, or statistics, depending on your subject. Be sure your reasoning makes sense. Arrange your information effectively and anticipate and answer the concerns and counter arguments of your audience.

Position Statement: Recycling is an effective way to help relieve the growing problem of garbage.

Reason 1 Too much garbage means more and more space is needed for garbage dumps.

Evidence Newspaper article: "garbage barge" couldn't find a place to deposit the garbage

Survey: local people's attitudes toward new landfill proposal

Reason 2 Burning isn't a good solution either; it creates smells, smoke, and pollution.

Evidence Encyclopedia yearbook: the effects of burning garbage on health and quality of life

Reason 3 Recycling is easy and efficient, and it's something every-one can do.

Evidence Flyer from State Department of the Environment: setting up a local recycling program

Web sites: advice about recycling

Consider your purpose and audience For persuasive writing, knowledge of the audience is particularly important. Ask students how they would persuade their friends that it would be a good idea to have fewer homework assignments. Ask them how they would change their speech if the audience were parents or teachers.

Build your framework Emphasize that the framework a student builds into a speech can be compared to the framework for a house. If poor quality materials (sources) are used, the house will be defective and eventually fall. Point out that students must seek out reliable sources for their information. Explain that although the Internet has some excellent information, it also has a lot of unsubstantiated opinion. If a student is unsure of the validity of a source, it is a good idea to check with an adult or to look for additional sources.

Additional Resources

Writing and Proofreading Practice, pp. 1–6, 35–41

Writing and Proofreading Transparencies 1–6, 15–16

Listening and Speaking *Minilesson*

Speaking Before Writing When planning a speech, a student may find it helpful to discuss the main idea with a friend. The friend may ask questions or make comments that will help the speaker in developing and articulating his or her position.

Activity Pair students whose topics are different and have one student walk through the basic ideas of his or her speech while the other listens. The point is not to give the speech but to talk about what one plans to say. The listener is to take notes and provide constructive criticism, questions, and feedback to the speaker. After about ten minutes, have the students switch roles. **L2**

DRAFTING

Make a strong start A strong start not only captures an audience's interest, it also helps to keep the writer on track. A strong speech comes full circle and ties up all loose ends. In the conclusion, it usually is a good idea to refer to the beginning of the speech.

Follow your thoughts Tell students to be sure to distinguish facts from opinions. It is important for a speechwriter to express his or her opinions, but listeners can be alienated if those opinions are presented as indisputable facts. Remind students to support their arguments with factual evidence and sound reasoning. Suggest that they underline anything they present as a fact and then check to see that each fact is adequately supported.

REVISING

Point out the relationship between a good speech and poetry—both emphasize sound, rhythm, and repetition of key phrases. Such devices can make certain lines memorable. Jesse Jackson used rhyme *(from slave ship to championship; from outhouse to White House).* Winston Churchill used assonance and consonance *(blood, toil, tears, and sweat).*

DRAFTING

DRAFTING TIP

Your word choices affect listeners' emotions. Are listeners more likely to accept an *old* theory or a *proven* theory? a *cheap* plan or a *reasonably priced* plan?

Make a Strong Start

Capture your listeners' attention with your first words. Try using a surprising fact, an intriguing question, a meaningful quotation, or a brief story to lead into your position statement. Make your views clear from the beginning.

Follow Your Thoughts

Write about each of your reasons, citing relevant, convincing evidence and building toward your conclusion. Include effective wording from your freewriting. Transitions such as *one important reason, another reason, the most important reason, finally,* and *because of this* will keep the links between your ideas clear. Conclude with a strong restatement of your position and a call for awareness or for action.

STUDENT MODEL • DRAFTING

Our planet is turning into one big garbage dump. Of course, it's a big planet, but if we don't do something now about the amount of garbage we produce, there won't be much of a planet left in the future for us, or for our kids.

Complete Student Model on p. R124.

REVISING

REVISING TIP

The revising stage is a good place to tighten up your writing. Precise language, active verbs, and sensory details will help you keep your listeners' attention.

Look and Listen

Don't just look over your speech; *listen* to it too. Read it aloud to yourself or to a partner. Listen for meaning and use the **Rubric for Revising.** Then listen again for sound and rhythm. Try repeating one key phrase. Rhythm and repetition will help your listeners remember your words.

RUBRIC FOR REVISING

Your revised speech should have
- an attention-getting opening
- an organization that leads effectively to the conclusion
- relevant and reliable details, statistics, facts, and other specific support for your reasons
- transitions to help listeners follow the flow of ideas
- vivid language to hold the listeners' attention
- a conclusion that restates your position and calls on your audience to take action

Your revised speech should be free of
- arguments that do not support your position
- errors in grammar, usage, and mechanics

Teaching Support

Writing Minilesson

Speech Writing When writing a speech, students should remember they need to help their listeners by repeating "guideposts" and transition words as they go along. Each paragraph of the speech should begin with a transition and a topic sentence. The topic sentence should be followed by reasons or examples, and the paragraph should end with a brief restatement of the topic.

Activity Have students write a practice paragraph using this strict format: topic sentence, three reasons or examples, restatement of the topic. **L2**

Additional Resources

Writer's Choice, Lesson 2.7

EDITING/PROOFREADING

Go over your revised draft, using the **Proofreading Checklist** on the right as a guide. Correct errors in grammar, usage, and mechanics. Be sure that you use pronouns correctly, as shown in the **Grammar Link** on page 539.

Grammar Hint

Sure is an adjective used to modify nouns only. To modify verbs, adjectives, or other adverbs, use the adverb *surely*.

As a volunteer, you will ***surely*** *be doing your community a favor.*

PROOFREADING CHECKLIST

- ☑ Modifiers are correctly used (double-check *sure* and *surely*).
- ☑ Sentences are complete; there are no sentence fragments or run-ons.
- ☑ All verbs agree with their subjects.
- ☑ Pronouns are in the proper forms and agree with their antecedents.
- ☑ Spelling, punctuation, and capitalization are correct.

STUDENT MODEL • EDITING/PROOFREADING

Garbage is a real problem, and it ~~sure~~ surely won't go away by itself.

Complete Student Model on p. R124.

Complete Student Model

For a complete version of the model developed in this Workshop, refer to **Writing Workshop Models**, p. R124.

PUBLISHING/PRESENTING

Record your speech on note cards and then present it to a small group, to your class, or to a larger group at school or in the community. As you speak, watch your audience. Use their verbal and nonverbal feedback to adjust your presentation so that you can get your message across most effectively. For more tips on public speaking, see the **Listening, Speaking, and Viewing** feature on page 502.

PRESENTING TIP

Record your speech word for word or in outline form on note cards. Use double spacing—it will be easier on your eyes as you deliver the speech.

Reflecting

Think about the following questions and then write responses.

- Which part(s) of your speech do you consider strongest? Why?
- Write one suggestion that could help another student write a persuasive speech. Explain the benefits of your advice.

Save your work for your portfolio.

GLENCOE TECHNOLOGY

REVISING WITH STYLE CD-ROM

Invite students to use the Revising with Style CD-ROM, which offers instruction and exercises to help students improve their writing skills.

EDITING/PROOFREADING

Have students exchange papers for proofreading. Often someone else will spot errors that the writer misses. Suggest that students look for punctuation errors, spelling errors, and run-on sentences.

PUBLISHING/PRESENTING

Videotape or audiotape the speeches and allow students to critique themselves.

Reflecting

Portfolio Encourage students to ask themselves these questions as they review their writing.

Does my persuasive speech
- clearly state my position with a well-defined thesis?
- provide facts and examples to convince my listeners?
- use rhythm and sound to emphasize my point?

6+1 TRAITS™ OF WRITING

See the annotated **Writing Workshop Models** on pp. R119–R130 for additional help in evaluating student writing and in teaching the **6+1 Traits™ of effective writing.** Annotations and minilessons address and reinforce the **6+1 Traits™:** Ideas, Organization, Voice, Word Choice, Sentence Fluency, Conventions, and Presentation.

ASSESSMENT

Writing Assessment and Portfolio Management
- Writing Assessment, pp. 1–12, 26–28
- Portfolio Management, pp. 42–48

Theme Assessment

Objectives

- To give a personal response to the stories, poems, discussions, and activities in this theme
- To write an analysis of two works that express the theme Free to Be
- To complete a self-evaluation, set a goal, and devise a plan for achieving this goal

Responding to the Theme

1. Students should provide valid reasons for their choices.
2. Accept all reasonable responses.
3. *Students' presentations should*
   - illustrate First Amendment rights
   - include explanations of why the First Amendment is important

Analyzing Literature

Students' writing should

- clearly show how the selections discussed relate to their feelings about the theme
- include quotations from the selections

Evaluate and Set Goals

Evaluate

Have students write a brief description of what they found most enjoyable and most difficult in this theme.

To help students formulate valid reasons for their ratings, you might suggest that they develop a class rubric.

Set Goals

Have students make charts showing their goals, the steps they will take for achieving them, and checkpoints. Then discuss students' plans in individual conferences.

Theme Assessment

Responding to the Theme

1. Which selection most helped you to understand the theme "Free to Be"?
2. What new thoughts do you have about the following ideas as a result of reading the literature in this theme?
   - Many people in the past made great sacrifices for the freedoms we enjoy today.
   - Religious or political freedom does not come easily.
   - The struggle for freedom continues today.
3. Present your theme project to the class.

Analyzing Literature

ANALYZE THE THEME

Many of the selections in this theme express the dangers and joys that come with the struggle for freedom. Choose two poems or other pieces from this theme that express how you feel about "Free to Be." Write a few paragraphs explaining your ideas. Include quotations from the selections.

Evaluate and Set Goals

1. Which of the following activities did you enjoy the most? Which did you find most difficult?
   - reading and thinking about the selections
   - writing on your own
   - analyzing and discussing the selections
   - presenting ideas and projects
   - researching topics
2. How would you assess your work in this theme, using the scale below? Give at least two reasons for your assessment.
   4 = outstanding   2 = fair
   3 = good   1 = weak
3. Based on what you found challenging in this theme, choose a goal to work toward in the next theme.
   - In your notebook, record your goal and three steps you will take to help you reach it.
   - Meet with your teacher to review your goal and your plan for achieving it.

Build Your Portfolio

SELECT

Choose two of your favorite pieces of work from this theme to include in your portfolio. The following questions can help you choose.

- ✦ Which do you consider your best work?
- ✦ Which turned out to be more challenging than you thought? Why?
- ✦ Which was the most interesting?

REFLECT

Write some notes to accompany the pieces you selected. Use these questions to guide you.

- ✦ What do you like best about the piece?
- ✦ What did you learn from creating it?
- ✦ What might you do differently if you were beginning this piece again?

ASSESSMENT

Writing Assessment and Portfolio Management

- Writing Assessment, pp. 1–12
- Portfolio Management, pp. 42–48

GLENCOE TECHNOLOGY

MINDJOGGER VIDEOQUIZZES VIDEODISC

Use *MindJogger* to review the Theme 5 content.

Theme 5
Side B

Also available in VHS.

Reading on Your Own

If you have enjoyed the literature in this theme, you might also be interested in the following books.

Across Five Aprils
by Irene Hunt Jethrow Creighton fights for freedom in his own way as he is left with the responsibility of maintaining his family's farm when the men and older boys join the army.

Out of the Dust
by Karen Hesse
Fourteen-year-old Billie Jo lost her mother in an accident for which Billie Jo blames her father and herself. In her journal, she records her life in the Oklahoma dust bowl during the Great Depression.

Laborers for Liberty: American Women 1865–1890
by Harriet Sigerman This is the story of American women from New England to New Mexico as they meet new freedoms and challenges, new work opportunities and falling barriers.

I Thought My Soul Would Rise and Fly: The Diary of Patsy, a Freed Girl
by Joyce Hansen In this fictional account, Patsy keeps a diary of her life during the important year of 1865, as slavery ends and the South adjusts to new circumstances.

Reading on Your Own

Tips for Independent Reading

Stress the importance of each student's spending at least thirty minutes a day in independent reading and suggest books, such as those shown here, related to the theme.

Reading the Novel Remind students of the characteristics of historical fiction. Encourage them to think about how the times affect characters and events in the stories they read.

Practice Suggest that students compare their lives and surroundings with those of characters in the story and ask themselves how they might act in similar circumstances.

Glencoe Literature Library

Across Five Aprils by Irene Hunt is available in the *Glencoe Literature Library*. For a complete listing of titles, see the **Glencoe Resources for Independent Reading** in the front of this book.

The *Glencoe Literature Library Study Guide* provides instructional support and student activities for all titles in the *Glencoe Literature Library*.

At the MOVIES

Be sure to review the following video for appropriateness for your class:

In *Prince of Egypt*, Moses leads his followers to a life of freedom. [G]

MEETING INDIVIDUAL NEEDS — SPECIAL NEEDS

You may wish to recommend *I Thought My Soul Would Rise and Fly* by Joyce Hansen to your less-proficient readers. The direct, personal style makes this book appropriate for these students. **L1**

The books listed at the right are rated for average readers **(L2)** or for students who need more challenging reading **(L3)**:

- *Laborers for Liberty: American Women 1865–1890* by Harriet Sigerman **L3**
- *Out of the Dust* by Karen Hesse **L2**
- *Across Five Aprils* by Irene Hunt **L2**

Standardized Test Practice

Answers and Analyses

1. **B** Students should recognize the sequence of *smart, nice,* and *talented* as a compound series of predicate adjectives modifying the pronoun *he*. All sentences should have parallel structure.
2. **J** Choice J uses the correct form of the appositive, a noun or phrase which identifies or adds information to the noun right next to it.
3. **C** Choices A and D contain sentence fragments, and can therefore be eliminated. The wording in choice B, *spend time usually* incorrectly places the adverb *usually,* and thus it, too, can be eliminated. This leaves choice C, which is the correct answer.
4. **J** While choice M is grammatically correct, choice J has the simplest and clearest expression, and is thus the best answer.
5. **D** *Intelligently* is an adverb with no verb to modify, eliminating choice A. Choice B has awkward sentence structure, and the verb does not agree with its subject. Choice C would be correct if *also has* were eliminated. Choice D has the correct form of the compound predicate adjectives *intelligent and well-spoken.*
6. **K** Tell students that *either* is singular; either one person or another performs an action, not both people. Choices L and M have illogical structure. Only choice K uses the *either . . .or* structure correctly.

The Princeton Review TEST-TAKING TIP

If the standardized test allows for it, students should make notes in their test booklet to help themselves answer questions. Encourage them to cross out answer choices they know are wrong.

The Princeton Review

Standardized Test Practice

Read the sentences in each numbered item. Choose the sentence that DOES NOT have a mistake in sentence structure.

1 A I like Eric because he is smart, nice, and that he is talented.
B I like Eric because he is smart, nice, and talented.
C I like Eric because of his smartness, he's nice, and talented.
D I like Eric because he's being smart, nice, and he's talented.

2 J My neighbor, Mrs. Ramirez, likes to work in her garden.
K My neighbor, being Mrs. Ramirez, likes working in the garden.
L Liking to work in the garden is my neighbor Mrs. Ramirez.
M In the garden, Mrs. Ramirez, my neighbor, likes to work.

3 A I usually spend time outdoors after school. Unless it is raining.
B Unless it is raining I spend time usually outdoors after school.
C I usually spend time outdoors after school, unless it is raining.
D I usually spend time outdoors. After school unless it is raining.

4 J After Marcus watched TV, he went upstairs to read a novel.
K After Marcus watched TV, upstairs he went to read a novel.
L Upstairs Marcus went to read a novel, after watching TV.
M Marcus watched TV, and after he went upstairs to read a novel.

5 A The professor is intelligently and well-spoken.
B Intelligent and well-spoken are the professor.
C The professor is intelligent and also has well-spoken.
D The professor is intelligent and well-spoken.

6 J Either Jennifer and I will race in the competition.
K Either Jennifer or I will race in the competition.
L Jennifer or I, either of us will race in the competition.
M Jennifer and I, either or, will race in the competition.

546 THEME 5

MEETING INDIVIDUAL NEEDS

ENGLISH LANGUAGE LEARNERS

Sentence Structure Add-Ins Explain to students that learning sentence structure requires a great amount of practice. Write some simple sentences on the board with space in between words where the sentences can be expanded. For example: "The ____ airplane ______ in the ______." This sentence can be expanded to "The fast airplane flies in the sky." Have students write their own "sentence add-ins" in their notebooks and read them aloud. Some other examples of sentences might be:

- Janice ________ her _________ every weekend.
- _________ is my favorite _________.
- When I am _________ I would like to _________ and __________.

Standardized Test Practice

Read the sentences in each numbered item and look at the underlined words. The underlined words may contain a mistake in word usage. Find the sentence in which the underlined words have CORRECT word usage.

7 A I can't never make it to practice on time.
B I cannot never make it to practice on time.
C I can't ever make it to practice on time.
D I can't not ever make it to practice on time.

8 J Some of my friends walk to school.
K Some of my friend's walk to school.
L Some of my friends walks to school.
M Some of my friend walk to school.

9 A Head throbbing, Joleen quickly taking some aspirin to take away her headache.
B Head throbbing, Joleen quickly took some aspirin to take away her headache.
C Head throbbing, Joleen quick took some aspirin to take away her headache.
D Head throbbing, Joleen most quickly took some aspirin to take away her headache.

10 J Some of the children are waving its hands at the parade marchers.
K Some of the children are waving their hand at the parade marchers.
L Some of the children are waving their hands at the parade marchers.
M Some of the children are wave their hands at the parade marchers.

11 A Duke and his grandfather likes traveling together.
B Duke and his grandfather liking traveling together.
C Duke and his grandfather like to traveling together.
D Duke and his grandfather like traveling together.

12 J In the olden days, people are using horses to get around.
K In the olden days, people used horses to get around.
L In the olden days, people use horses to get around.
M In the olden days, people will use horses to get around.

STOP

Answers and Analyses

7. C Based on students' familiarity and knowledge of contractions, they should conclude that choice C is the best possible answer.
8. J Remind students to eliminate the choices in which the subject and verb do not agree in number, as in incorrect choices L and M. Choice K uses an improper possessive, leaving choice J as the best possible answer.
9. B Choice D uses the superlative *most*, incorrectly suggesting a comparison between Joleen and someone else. Only choice B uses the correct adverb-verb combination with the appropriate verb tense.
10. L Students should be familiar with collective nouns, such as *children.* Since some children are being referred to, the noun is plural and thus the verb should be *their*, eliminating choice J. Choice M can also be eliminated because it contains an incorrect verb form. Only choice L has an object that agrees in number with the possessive pronoun *their.*
11. D Of the four choices, only C and D use the correct verb form, *like.* Because choice C contains *to* unnecessarily, it can be eliminated. Choice D is therefore the correct answer.
12. K Only choice K uses the past tense *used*. Choice K is therefore the correct answer.

The Princeton Review TEST-TAKING TIP

Remind students to make sure they understand the intended meaning of a sentence before attempting to determine the accuracy of its grammar and structure.

Tested Objectives

Item	Language Objective
1, 5	Identify and use parallel structure in all written discourse, including similar grammatical forms to present items in a series, complements, and items juxtaposed for emphasis
2, 3, 4, 6	Use subordination, coordination, apposition, and other devices to indicate the relationship between ideas clearly
7–12	Edit written material to reflect proper grammar

MORE PRACTICE

For additional practice, assign pages from one of the following standardized test resources available as part of Glencoe Literature.

Additional Resources
ITBS Preparation and Practice
SAT-9 Preparation and Practice
TerraNova Preparation and Practice

Theme 6 At a Glance
Flashes of Insight

THEME OPENING

- **Introducing the Theme** (p. 549)
- **Exploring the Theme** (p. 550)
- **Theme Projects** (p. 551)

Theme 6: FLASHES OF INSIGHT

SELECTIONS

Raymond's Run (p. 552)

Media Connection: Fast Finisher (p. 564)

Forgotten Language (p. 566)

New World (p. 566)

Thank You in Arabic (p. 573)

Media Connection: *EarthView* Poll Highlights (p. 589)

"If I Forget Thee, Oh Earth . . ." (p. 590)

I like to see it lap the miles (p. 598)

Southbound on the Freeway (p. 598)

Stop the Sun (p. 606)

The Summer of Vietnam (p. 622)

Finding America (p. 628)

***from* On the Road with Charles Kuralt** (p. 634)

Americans All (p. 642)

SKILL FEATURES

Reading and Thinking Skills (p. 565)

Grammar Link (p. 572)

Interdisciplinary Connection (p. 604)

Vocabulary Skills (p. 605)

Genre Focus: Personal Essay (pp. 618–619)

Active Reading Strategies (pp. 620–621)

Writing Skills (p. 641)

Technology Skills (pp. 648–649)

WRITING WORKSHOP

Technical Writing: Bylaws of an Organization (pp. 650–653)

THEME ASSESSMENT

- **Responding to the Theme, Analyzing Literature, Evaluate and Set Goals** (p. 654)
- **Build Your Portfolio** (p. 654)
- **Reading on Your Own** (p. 655)
  - *The Glory Field* by Walter Dean Myers
  - *SOS Titanic* by Eve Bunting
  - *Parrot in the Oven:* **mi vida** by Victor Martinez
  - *Lupita Mañana* by Patricia Beatty
- **Standardized Test Practice** (pp. 656–657)

KEYS TO LITERARY CONNECTIONS

Comparing Selections

The **Comparing Selections** feature in this theme provides opportunities for addressing diverse aspects of the reading and literature curriculum.

For example, in Comparing Selections on page 597, students examine settings and situations in "Thank You in Arabic" and "If I Forget Thee, Oh Earth. . . ." Through this comparison, students can gain "flashes of insight" as they explore the meanings of home and exile.

World Literature

The Student Edition contains a variety of literature that represents cultures from around the world. World literature selections are highlighted with the icon above.

TEACHING SUPPORT

The Teaching Support offers a wealth of interactive instructional support:

Meeting Individual Needs
- Special Needs
- English Language Learners
- Multiple Modes of Expression
- Advanced Learners

Internet Connection

Assessment

Portfolio Options

Minilessons
- Grammar and Language
- Reading
- Writing
- Listening and Speaking

Connecting to Other Selections

Real-World Connection

Interdisciplinary Connection

Life Skills Connection

Family and Community Activity

Key to Ability Levels

The activities throughout this theme have been coded for students of various abilities.

L1 BASIC activities for all students

L2 AVERAGE activities for average to above-average students

L3 ADVANCED LEARNERS activities for above-average students

Teaching Today

The Glencoe *Teaching Today* professional development Web site at www.teachingtoday.glencoe.com features daily teaching tips, free downloads, annotated Web resources, educational news, and a wealth of information on a wide range of topics.

Reading Skills in this theme

Variety of Texts

In addition to personal essays, this theme includes the following:

- cartoon
- short stories
- magazine article
- opinion poll
- poetry

Comprehension Skills

The following instructional support for comprehension skills appears in this theme of the Student Edition:

- **Active Reading Strategies and Model** (pp. 620–627)
- **Identifying Main Ideas and Supporting Details** (p. 565)
- **Reading and Thinking Minilessons** (pp. 563, 571, 588, 617)

See also the **Reading Minilessons** throughout the theme in this Teacher Wraparound Edition.

For strategies for reading longer works, such as novels and novellas, see "Tips for Independent Reading" on page 655.

Reading Resources

Active Reading Guide The ***Active Reading Guide*** provides graphic organizers and study guide questions to support students' reading of each selection (***Active Reading Guide***, pp. 48–57).

Interactive Reading Sourcebook and **Interactive Reading Workbook** The ***Interactive Reading Sourcebook*** and ***Interactive Reading Workbook*** offer focused comprehension strategies and lessons on critical thinking skills as well as fluency practice and activities to teach and support phonics, decoding, spelling, and vocabulary development.

Vocabulary Power The ***Vocabulary Power*** workbook (Lessons 24–28) provides systematic teaching, practice, and assessment of vocabulary for better reading comprehension.

Audio Library Available on audiocassette and on CD, the ***Audio Library*** provides valuable comprehension support.

Glencoe Literature Library Each title in the ***Glencoe Literature Library*** includes a full-length work plus related readings. A separate Study Guide is available for each title.

Five-Star Stories These anthologies of familiar short stories adapted and abridged for a variety of reading levels include exercises to help increase students' vocabulary and improve their reading comprehension.

The Contemporary Readers ***The Contemporary Readers*** are nonfiction books linked to various themes and designed for developing readers from a wide range of backgrounds.

Literature Classics CD-ROM The selections on this CD-ROM can be searched by author, theme, or genre.

inTIME and Humanities Across TIME Coproductions of Glencoe and Time, Inc., these resources include a wealth of high-interest nonfiction related to the selections in this theme.

Assessment in this theme

Glencoe's Assessment Advantage

Assessment Options in the Student Edition

This program offers a number of diverse ways to evaluate student understanding and skill proficiency. In the Student Edition, use the following:

- **Responding to Literature**
  Following each selection, students are asked to recall facts, interpret ideas, and evaluate concepts as they answer a variety of questions and complete activities to extend their understanding.
- **Theme Assessment (pp. 654–655)**
  Here students respond to the selections on personal and analytical levels. They also assume ownership of their learning by setting and evaluating goals and by selecting work for their portfolios.

See also the many **Assessment Resources** listed on the facing page.

The Princeton Review

Standardized Test Practice

The Princeton Review has developed the Standardized Test Practice pages found at the end of this thematic unit (pp. 656–657). For additional practice, direct students to the following resources:

- ITBS Preparation and Practice
- SAT-9 Preparation and Practice
- TerraNova Preparation and Practice

Writing Skills in this theme

Writing Skills

The Student Edition of Theme 6 offers strong instructional support for writing skills:

In **Extending Your Response,** which follows each selection:
- **Writing About Literature**
- **Personal/Creative Writing**

In **Writing Skills** Lessons:
- **Writing an Effective Introduction** (p. 641)

See also the **Writing Minilessons** throughout the theme in this Teacher Wraparound Edition.

Writing Workshops

Theme 6 concludes with a **Writing Workshop** that guides students through the process for writing bylaws of an organization (pp. 650–653).

Writing Resources

Writer's Assistant CD-ROM Each **Writing Workshop** is supplemented by an interactive writing guide on the ***Writer's Assistant*** CD-ROM. This easy-to-use writing guide provides prompts, templates, and other tools that lead students through the writing process.

Grammar and Composition Handbook The ***Grammar and Composition Handbook*** (Lessons 11.5–13.3) provides systematic instruction in English language conventions.

Spelling Power The ***Spelling Power*** workbook (Lessons 21–24) provides systematic teaching, practice, and assessment of spelling to help students become better spellers and thus enhance their writing.

Writing and Proofreading Practice Blackline masters present in-depth instruction and practice on a specific step in the writing process and proofreading (pp. 1–6, 42–48).

Writing and Proofreading Transparencies Transparencies provide graphic organizers and proofreading exercises for whole-class instruction (pp. 1–6, 35–36).

Research and Report Writing Guide This resource provides extensive tips and activities to guide students in their writing projects in the literature classroom as well as in classes across the curriculum.

Style and Documentation Sourcebook for Writers This sourcebook is a combination reference and workbook, giving students the most up-to-date information and guidance regarding traditional as well as technological research strategies and documentation.

Revising with Style This resource offers instruction and exercises focusing on the revision process and covering topics from proofreading and correcting common grammatical errors to sentence combining and reordering.

Assessment Resources

Selection Quick Checks For each selection, a **Quick Check** of three to five short-answer questions measures students' literal comprehension.

Selection and Theme Assessment The ***Selection and Theme Assessment*** instrument tests students' abilities to recall, interpret, and evaluate what they've read. The tests consist of multiple-choice, short answer, and essay questions.

Performance Assessment Alternative assessment instruments and rubrics for Theme 6 are found in the ***Performance Assessment*** ancillary.

Writing Assessment and Portfolio Management These notes and strategies, student models, and assessment tools assist with the task of measuring students' progress as writers and as monitors of their own writing.

Testmaker: ExamView Pro Teachers can customize selection and Theme 6 tests by accessing the ***Testmaker*** database.

Interactive Tutor: Self-Assessment The ***Interactive Tutor: Self-Assessment*** software provides multiple-choice tests with immediate feedback to help students evaluate their knowledge and understanding of each literature selection.

MindJogger Videoquizzes Using a popular game show format, ***MindJogger Videoquizzes*** on videocassettes enable teachers to evaluate student understanding of Theme 6 in a quick and fun manner.

Theme 6 Skills Scope and Sequence

Lessons	Literary Elements	Reading and Thinking	Writing
Raymond's Run Toni Cade Bambara DRP: 62 Lexile: 1120	External Conflict, SE p. 561 *Interior Monologue, TWE p. 554* *Internal Conflict, TWE p. 557* *Foreshadowing, TWE p. 559*	Predicting, SE p. 563 Magazine Article, SE p. 564 Main Idea and Supporting Details, SE p. 565 *Comparison and Contrast, TWE p. 555* *Drawing Conclusions, TWE pp. 556, 557* *Author's Purpose, TWE p. 564* SN *Less-Proficient Readers, TWE p. 565*	Description (Tone), SE p. 562 Dialogue, SE p. 562 *Personal Response (Tone), TWE p. 557*
Forgotten Language Shel Silverstein and **New World** N. Scott Momaday	Stanza, SE p. 570 *Stanza, TWE pp. 567, 569* *Repetition, TWE p. 567* *Speaker, TWE p. 568*	Previewing, SE p. 571 ELL *Visualizing, TWE p. 567* *Evaluate, TWE p. 569* *Identify Author's Purpose, TWE p. 569*	Comparison, SE p. 571 Poem, SE p. 571 *Description, TWE p. 572*
Thank You in Arabic Naomi Shihab Nye DRP: 55 Lexile: 930	Setting, SE p. 586 *Character, TWE p. 582* *Descriptive Language, TWE p. 583*	Problem and Solution, SE p. 588 *Inferring, TWE pp. 575, 582* *Comparison and Contrast, TWE p. 577* *Analyzing Arguments, TWE p. 578* SN *Less-Proficient Readers, TWE p. 587*	Description (Personal Insight), SE p. 587 Analysis, SE p. 587 *Definition, TWE p. 581*
"If I Forget Thee, Oh Earth . . ." Arthur C. Clarke DRP: 62 Lexile: 1050	Science Fiction, SE p. 596 *Descriptive Language, TWE p. 594* *Climax, TWE p. 595*	Opinion Poll, SE p. 589 Comparing Selections, SE p. 597 *Central Idea, TWE p. 589* SN *Learning Disabled, TWE p. 593* *Drawing Conclusions, TWE p. 595* *Cause and Effect, TWE p. 595*	
I like to see it lap the miles and Emily Dickinson ***Southbound on the Freeway*** May Swenson	Metaphor, SE p. 602 *Descriptive Language, TWE p. 599* *Metaphor, TWE pp. 599, 600*	*Elaborating, TWE p. 601* *Comparison and Contrast, TWE p. 601*	Description (Metaphor), SE p. 603 Interview, SE p. 603
Stop the Sun Gary Paulsen DRP: 50 Lexile: 570	Climax, SE p. 615 *Internal Conflict, TWE p. 608* *Rising Action, TWE p. 610* *Descriptive Language, TWE p. 613*	Cause and Effect, SE p. 617 ELL *Identifying with the Character, TWE p. 608* *Inferring, TWE pp. 609, 611* *Author's Purpose, TWE p. 613*	Explanation, SE p. 616 Scene, SE p. 616 *Describing Feelings, TWE p. 611*
The Summer of Vietnam Barbara Renaud González DRP: 49 Lexile: 560	Personal Essay, SE p. 618 Irony, SE p. 626 *Imagery, TWE p. 624*	Personal Essay, SE p. 620	Explanation (Point of View), SE p. 627 Poem, SE p. 627
Finding America A. C. Greene DRP: 60 Lexile: 910	Speaker, SE p. 632 *Speaker, TWE p. 630* *Setting, TWE p. 631*	*Drawing Conclusions, TWE p. 630* *Paraphrasing, TWE p. 631*	List (Setting's Effects), SE p. 633 Friendly Letter, SE p. 633
from **On the Road with Charles Kuralt** Charles Kuralt DRP: 57 Lexile: 860	Style, SE p. 639 *Style, TWE p. 636* *Language, TWE p. 637* *Direct Address, TWE p. 638*	*Main Idea and Supporting Details, TWE p. 637* *Activating Prior Knowledge, TWE p. 637*	Analyze Style, SE p. 640 Essay, SE p. 640 Writing an Effective Introduction, SE p. 641
Americans All Michael Dorris DRP: 65 Lexile: 1110	Author's Purpose, SE p. 646 *Author's Purpose, TWE p. 644* *Language, TWE p. 644*	*Drawing Conclusions, TWE p. 644* *Comprehension, TWE p. 645*	Letter to the Editor, SE p. 647 Idioms, SE p. 647
Writing Workshop Technical Writing: Bylaws of an Organization			*Plain Language, TWE p. 652*

Key: Student material is in roman. Teacher material is in italic. Technology ELL English Language Learners

Vocabulary and Spelling	Grammar and Language	Listening, Speaking, and Viewing	Life Skills; Study and Research; Technology
Analogies, SE p. 563 *Word History, TWE p. 556*	Troublesome Words, SE p. 563 ELL *Colloquial English, TWE p. 554* *Verb Tense, TWE p. 560*	Literature Groups, SE p. 562 Role-Play and Interview, SE p. 562 SN *Less-Proficient Readers, TWE p. 565*	Learning for Life: Advertisements, SE p. 562
	Using Adjectives Correctly, SE p. 572 *Capitalizing Sentences, TWE p. 568*	Literature Groups, SE p. 571 Reading Poetry Aloud, SE p. 571	
Connotation, SE p. 588 *Suffixes, TWE p. 580* *Word Meaning, TWE p. 581*	Punctuation in Compound Sentences, SE p. 588 ELL *Sharing Languages, TWE p. 575* ELL *Idioms, TWE p. 583* *Prepositional Phrases, TWE p. 584*	Literature Groups, SE p. 587 *Oral Presentation, TWE p. 576* SN *Learning Disabled, TWE p. 582*	History of Middle East, SE p. 587 Social Rules, SE p. 587 *Interviewing, TWE p. 578* *Art and Architecture, TWE p. 579*
Word Meaning, TWE p. 592	*Participles, TWE p. 594*	Literature Groups, SE p. 596 *Political Speech, TWE p. 596*	ELL *Listening and Note-Taking, TWE p. 592*
ELL *Vocabulary, TWE p. 599*	Sentence Patterns, SE p. 603 *Action Verbs, TWE p. 600*	Literature Groups, SE p. 603	
Using Idioms, SE p. 605 Multiple-Meaning Words, SE p. 617 ELL *Idioms, TWE p. 605*	Subject-Verb Agreement, SE p. 617 *Agreement with Collective Nouns, TWE p. 614*	Literature Groups, SE p. 616 SN *Emotional, TWE p. 610*	History, SE p. 604 Research: War, SE p. 616, *TWE p. 612* Internet Connection, SE p. 616
The Suffix *-ize,* SE p. 627	ELL *Borrowed Words, TWE p. 624* *Verb Mood, TWE p. 625*	Literature Groups, SE p. 627 *Reading Aloud, TWE p. 618*	Research: Vietnam, SE p. 627
Analogies, SE p. 633	*Active Voice, TWE p. 630*	Literature Groups, SE p. 633	
Multiple-Meaning Words, SE p. 640 *Word History, TWE p. 637*	ELL *Place Names, TWE p. 636* *Plurals and Possessives of Proper Nouns, TWE p. 638* *Exclamation Points, TWE p. 641*	Literature Groups, SE p. 640	Research: U. S. History, SE p. 640 *Video, TWE p. 638*
Unlocking Meaning, SE p. 647	*Infinitives, TWE p. 644*	Literature Groups, SE p. 647	Cultural Evaluation, SE p. 647 Evaluating On-line Sources, SE p. 648

SN **Special Needs/Strategic Intervention**

Theme 6 RESOURCE MANAGER

Lessons	Essential Resources		English Language Learners
Raymond's Run Toni Cade Bambara Pacing: 2 Days	**Lesson-Specific Instruction** Selection Focus Transp. 47 * Active Reading Guide, p. 48 Literary Elements Transp. 48 Vocabulary Practice, p. 33 * Quick Checks, p. 48 Selection and Theme Assessment, pp. 85–86	Testmaker: ExamView Pro Performance Assessment, p. 45 **Systematic Language Instruction** Grammar and Comp. Hbk., L. 11.5 Vocabulary Power, Lesson 24 Spelling Power, Lesson 21	English Language Learners Sourcebook, p. 70 Spanish Summaries, p. 47 * Audio Library English, Yes!
Forgotten Language Shel Silverstein *and* New World N. Scott Momaday Pacing: 1 Day	**Lesson-Specific Instruction** Selection Focus Transp. 48 * Active Reading Guide, p. 49 Literary Elements Transp. 49 * Quick Checks, p. 49 Selection and Theme Assessment, pp. 87–88	Testmaker: ExamView Pro Performance Assessment, p. 46 **Systematic Language Instruction** Grammar and Comp. Hbk., L. 11.6	English Language Learners Sourcebook, p. 71 Spanish Summaries, p. 48 * Audio Library English, Yes!
Thank You in Arabic Naomi Shihab Nye Pacing: 3 Days	**Lesson-Specific Instruction** Selection Focus Transp. 49 * Active Reading Guide, p. 50 Literary Elements Transp. 50 Vocabulary Practice, p. 34 * Quick Checks, p. 50 Selection and Theme Assessment, pp. 89–90	Testmaker: ExamView Pro Performance Assessment, p. 47 TIME *inTIME* magazine, pp. 14–15 **Systematic Language Instruction** Grammar and Comp. Hbk., L. 11.7	English Language Learners Sourcebook, p. 72, 73 Spanish Summaries, p. 49 Spanish Translations, pp. 121–131 * Audio Library English, Yes!
"If I Forget Thee, Oh Earth..." Arthur C. Clarke Pacing: 2 Days	**Lesson-Specific Instruction** Selection Focus Transp. 50 * Active Reading Guide, p. 51 Literary Elements Transp. 51 Vocabulary Practice, p. 35 * Quick Checks, p. 51 Selection and Theme Assessment, pp. 91–92	Testmaker: ExamView Pro Performance Assessment, p. 48 TIME *inTIME* magazine, pp. 3–5 **Systematic Language Instruction** Grammar and Comp. Hbk., L. 11.8 Vocabulary Power, Lesson 25 Spelling Power, Lesson 22	English Language Learners Sourcebook, p. 74 Spanish Summaries, p. 50 Spanish Translations, pp. 132–135 * Audio Library English, Yes!
I like to see it lap the miles Emily Dickenson *and* *Southbound on the Freeway* May Swenson Pacing: 1 Day	**Lesson-Specific Instruction** Selection Focus Transp. 51 * Active Reading Guide, p. 52 Literary Elements Transp. 52 * Quick Checks, p. 52 Selection and Theme Assessment, pp. 93–94	Testmaker: ExamView Pro Performance Assessment, p. 49 **Systematic Language Instruction** Grammar and Comp. Hbk., L. 11.9	English Language Learners Sourcebook, p. 75 Spanish Summaries, p. 51 * Audio Library English, Yes!

Key: Workbook · Blackline Masters · Textbook · Transparency · CD-ROM · Videodisk (also available in videocassette)

Special Needs/ Strategic Intervention	Reteaching and Enrichment
Interactive Reading Sourcebook, pp. T170–T172 Interactive Reading Workbook, pp. 90–91 Inclusion Strategies Sourcebook, pp. 51–52 Theme Six Planning Guide, p. 6 * Audio Library	Fine Art Transparency 1 Reading Skills Practice Workbook pp. 89–90 Grammar and Language Transp. 45 Gr. and Lang. Wkbk., pp. 65–66, 85–86 Grammar and Comp. Hbk., L. 3.5, 15.1 Media Connection Activities, p. 11 Interactive Tutor: Self-Assessment Vocabulary PuzzleMaker Web Site (lit.glencoe.com)
Interactive Reading Sourcebook, pp. T172–T174 Interactive Reading Workbook, p. 92 Theme Six Planning Guide, p. 14 * Audio Library	Fine Art Transparency 23 Reading Skills Practice Workbook p. 81 Grammar and Language Transp. 46 Gr. and Lang. Wkbk., pp. 243–244 Grammar and Comp. Hbk., L. 12.1 Interactive Tutor: Self-Assessment Vocabulary PuzzleMaker Web Site (lit.glencoe.com)
Interactive Reading Sourcebook, pp. T175–T177 Interactive Reading Workbook, pp. 93–94 Inclusion Strategies Sourcebook, pp. 57–58 Theme Six Planning Guide, p. 20 * Audio Library	Literature Launchers, Side B, Segment 16 Reading Skills Practice Workbook pp. 91–92 Grammar and Language Transp. 47 Gr. and Lang. Wkbk., pp. 141–142, 259–260, 265–266 Grammar and Comp. Hbk., L. 7.1, 14.1 Interactive Tutor: Self-Assessment Vocabulary PuzzleMaker Web Site (lit.glencoe.com)
Interactive Reading Sourcebook, pp. T177–T179 Interactive Reading Workbook, p. 95–96 Inclusion Strategies Sourcebook, pp. 49–50 * Audio Library	Fine Art Transparency 18 Reading Skills Practice Workbook pp. 93–94 Grammar and Language Transp. 48 Gr. and Lang. Wkbk., pp. 171–172 Grammar and Comp. Hbk., L. 9.1 Media Connection Activities, p. 12 TIME *inTIME* magazine, pp. 18–19, 20–21 TIME *Humanities Across TIME*, Cover 7 Interactive Tutor: Self-Assessment Vocabulary PuzzleMaker Web Site (lit.glencoe.com)
Interactive Reading Sourcebook, pp. T180–T182 Interactive Reading Workbook, p. 97 Theme Six Planning Guide, p. 36 * Audio Library	Grammar and Language Transp. 49 Gr. and Lang. Wkbk., pp. 75–76, 133–134 Grammar and Comp. Hbk., L. 3.1, 5.1 Interactive Tutor: Self-Assessment Vocabulary PuzzleMaker Web Site (lit.glencoe.com)

Web Audiocassette Diskette *Also available in Spanish

INDEPENDENT READING

Encourage students to spend thirty minutes each day in independent reading. The following Glencoe components and outside resources provide opportunities for reading related to this theme.

The Glencoe Literature Library

You may want to assign one or more of these titles for independent reading. For a complete listing of titles available in the Glencoe Literature Library, see page T94 of this book.

- *Lupita Mañana* by Patricia Beatty
- *The Glory Field* by Walter Dean Myers
- *Dogsong* by Gary Paulsen
- *The True Confessions of Charlotte Doyle* by Avi
- *I, Juan de Pareja* by Elizabeth Borton de Treviño

inTIME Magazine News stories, News stories, feature articles, reviews, profiles, and essays in the magazine connect to an author, work, or theme in the Student Edition. See the ***inTIME* Teacher's Guide** for specific connections to this theme.

Resources for Less-Proficient Readers

For reading especially created for less-proficient readers, suggest

- *Five-Star Stories*
- *The Contemporary Readers*

Additional Resources for Independent Reading

The following titles are listed with specific reading selections throughout this theme. You may want to suggest that students look for these in your local or school library.

- *Flour Babies* by Anne Fine
- *Madeleine L'Engle's Time Quartet* by Madeleine L'Engle
- *The Complete Poems to Solve* by May Swenson
- *Paper Quake* by Kathryn Reiss
- *The Car* by Gary Paulsen
- *Eleanor Roosevelt: A Life of Discovery* by Russell Freedman
- *SOS Titanic* by Eve Bunting
- *Parrot in the Oven: mi vida* by Victor Martinez

Theme 6 RESOURCE MANAGER (continued)

Lessons	Essential Resources		English Language Learners
STOP THE SUN Gary Paulsen Pacing: 2 Days	**Lesson-Specific Instruction** Selection Focus Transp. 52 * Active Reading Guide, p. 53 Literary Elements Transp. 53 Vocabulary Practice, p. 36 * Quick Checks, p. 53 Selection and Theme Assessment, pp. 95–96	Testmaker: ExamView Pro Performance Assessment, p. 50 **Systematic Language Instruction** Grammar and Comp. Hbk., L. 12.1 Vocabulary Power, Lesson 26 Spelling Power, Lesson 23	English Language Learners Sourcebook, pp. 76, 77 Spanish Summaries, p. 52 Spanish Translations, pp. 136–141 * Audio Library English, Yes!
The Summer of Vietnam Barbara Renaud González Pacing: 2 Days	**Lesson-Specific Instruction** Selection Focus Transp. 53 * Active Reading Guide, p. 54 Literary Elements Transp. 54 Vocabulary Practice, p. 37 * Quick Checks, p. 54 Selection and Theme Assessment, pp. 97–98	Testmaker: ExamView Pro Performance Assessment, p. 51 **Systematic Language Instruction** Grammar and Comp. Hbk., L. 12.2	English Language Learners Sourcebook, p. 78 Spanish Summaries, p. 53 Spanish Translations, pp. 142–143 * Audio Library English, Yes!
Finding America A. C. Greene Pacing: 1 Day	**Lesson-Specific Instruction** Selection Focus Transp. 54 * Active Reading Guide, p. 55 Literary Elements Transp. 55 Vocabulary Practice, p. 38 * Quick Checks, p. 55 Selection and Theme Assessment, pp. 99–100	Testmaker: ExamView Pro Performance Assessment, p. 52 **Systematic Language Instruction** Grammar and Comp. Hbk., L. 12.3–12.4 Vocabulary Power, Lesson 27 Spelling Power, Lesson 24	English Language Learners Sourcebook, p. 79 Spanish Summaries, p. 54 Spanish Translations, pp. 144–145 * Audio Library English, Yes!
from **On the Road with Charles Kuralt** Charles Kuralt Pacing: 2 Days	**Lesson-Specific Instruction** Selection Focus Transp. 55 * Active Reading Guide, p. 56 Literary Elements Transp. 56 Vocabulary Practice, p. 39 * Quick Checks, p. 56 Selection and Theme Assessment, pp. 101–102	Testmaker: ExamView Pro Performance Assessment, p. 53 TIME *inTIME* magazine, pp. 6–8 **Systematic Language Instruction** Grammar and Comp. Hbk., L. 13.1 Vocabulary Power, Lesson 28	English Language Learners Sourcebook, p. 80 Spanish Summaries, p. 56 * Audio Library English, Yes!
Americans All Michael Dorris Pacing: 2 Days	**Lesson-Specific Instruction** Selection Focus Transp. 56 * Active Reading Guide, p. 57 Literary Elements Transp. 57 Vocabulary Practice, p. 40 * Quick Checks, p. 57 Selection and Theme Assessment, pp. 103–104 Testmaker: ExamView Pro	Performance Assessment, p. 54 TIME *inTIME* magazine, pp. 10–11 **Systematic Language Instruction** Grammar and Comp. Hbk., L. 13.2–13.3 Vocabulary Power, Unit 6 Review/Test Spelling Power, Unit 6 Review/Proofreading	English Language Learners Sourcebook, p. 81 Spanish Summaries, p. 56 Spanish Translations, pp. 146–147 * Audio Library English, Yes!
Writing WORKSHOP Technical Writing: Bylaws of an Organization Pacing: 2 Days	Writing Assessment and Portfolio Management, pp. 1–13, 29–33, 41–48		English Language Learners Sourcebook, p. 9 English, Yes!

Key: Workbook · Blackline Masters · Textbook · Transparency · CD-ROM · Videodisk (also available in videocassette)

Special Needs/ Strategic Intervention	Reteaching and Enrichment
Interactive Reading Sourcebook, pp. T182–T184 Interactive Reading Workbook, pp. 98–99 Inclusion Strategies Sourcebook, pp. 47–48 Theme Six Planning Guide, p. 42 * Audio Library	Literature Launchers, Side B, Segment 17 Reading Skills Practice Workbook, pp. 95-96 Grammar and Language Transp. 50 Gr. and Lang. Wkbk., pp. 187-188, 191-192 Grammar and Comp. Hbk., L. 10.3, 10.5 TIME *Humanities Across TIME*, Cover 9 Interactive Tutor: Self-Assessment Vocabulary PuzzleMaker Web Site (lit.glencoe.com)
Interactive Reading Sourcebook, pp. T184–T186 Interactive Reading Workbook, pp. 100–101 Inclusion Strategies Sourcebook, pp. 29–30, 87–88 Theme Six Planning Guide, p. 50 * Audio Library	Literature Launchers, Side B, Segment 18 Reading Skills Practice Workbook, pp. 97-98 Grammar and Language Transp. 51 Interactive Tutor: Self-Assessment Vocabulary PuzzleMaker Web Site (lit.glencoe.com)
Interactive Reading Sourcebook, pp. T187–T189 Interactive Reading Workbook, pp. 102–103 Inclusion Strategies Sourcebook, pp. 75–76 * Audio Library	Fine Art Transparency 19 Reading Skills Practice Workbook, pp. 99-100 Grammar and Language Transp. 52 Gr. and Lang. Wkbk., pp. 97–98 Grammar and Comp. Hbk., L. 3.10 Interactive Tutor: Self-Assessment Vocabulary PuzzleMaker Web Site (lit.glencoe.com)
Interactive Reading Sourcebook, pp. T189–T191 Interactive Reading Workbook, pp. 104–105 Inclusion Strategies Sourcebook, pp. 41–42 Theme Six Planning Guide, p. 66 * Audio Library	Fine Art Transparency 20 Reading Skills Practice Workbook, pp. 101–102 Grammar and Language Transp. 53 Gr. and Lang. Wkbk., pp. 65–66 Grammar and Comp. Hbk., L. 2.3 TIME *Humanities Across TIME*, Cover 18 Interactive Tutor: Self-Assessment Vocabulary PuzzleMaker Web Site (lit.glencoe.com)
Interactive Reading Sourcebook, pp. T192–T194 Interactive Reading Workbook, pp. 106–107 Inclusion Strategies Sourcebook, pp. 91–92 Theme Six Planning Guide, p. 74 * Audio Library	Reading Skills Practice Workbook, pp. 103–104 Grammar and Language Transp. 55 Gr. and Lang. Wkbk., pp. 179–180 Grammar and Comp. Hbk., L. 9.3 Interactive Tutor: Self-Assessment Vocabulary PuzzleMaker Web Site (lit.glencoe.com)
	Writing and Proofreading Practice, pp. 1-6, 42–48 Writing and Proofreading Transparencies 1-6, 17–18, 35–36 Revising with Style Writer's Assistant

Web Audiocassette Diskette *Also available in Spanish

Theme RESOURCES

To explore the theme further, you may want to use these resources:

- Listening and Speaking Activities (pp. 16–18)
- Viewing and Representing Activities (pp. 22–24)
- Critical Thinking Skills (pp. 15–17)
- Media Connection Activities, (pp. 11–12)
- Interdisciplinary Activities (pp. 22–25)
- Family and Community Activities (p. 26)
- Selection and Theme Assessment (pp. 85–104, 135–136)
- Performance Assessment (pp. 69, 93–94)

TIME Humanities Across TIME

See also these additional theme planning resources:

- Theme Six Planning Guide
- Interactive Reading Sourcebook
- Literature Groups Sourcebook
- Interactive Lesson Planner
- Interactive Teacher Edition
- Glencoe Web Site (lit.glencoe.com)

PRESENTATION Plus!

Use Glencoe's *Presentation Plus!* This multimedia teaching tool lets you present dynamic lessons that will engage your students. Using Microsoft PowerPoint®, you can customize the presentation to create your own personalized lessons.

THEME 6

Flashes of Insight

Theme Objectives

- To enjoy reading about what people learn through flashes of insight
- To analyze the literary elements in short stories, memoirs, poems, and personal essays
- To apply strategies for reading personal essays and poems

Teaching Strategies

Have students read the quotation from Oliver Wendell Holmes Sr. in preparation for the discussion questions below.

VIEWING THE PAINTING

In *Miracle of Life*, Christian Pierre shows her children working in a cheerful, stylized laboratory.

Viewing Response Discussion questions:

- What is most unusual in this painting? *(Butterflies and flowers float through the lab.)*
- How might a science lab provide "flashes of insight"? *(Experiments of all kinds can help us see things in a new way.)*

Flashes of Insight

Miracle of Life, 1996. Christian Pierre. Acrylic on Masonite, 48 x 48 in. Private collection.

548

TEACHER to TEACHER

JACKSON NORTH EAST MIDDLE SCHOOL • JACKSON, TENNESSEE

To introduce this theme, I have students skim the literature that we'll be reading. We then list on the board what they already know about the theme and each individual story and what they need to know. As we read each story, I'll ask students why they think it was included in this theme. I ask students to write about a time when they had a flash of insight about passing into a more grown-up world. I also have students write about the literature from different perspectives. For example, students might write about how a newspaper reporter from another part of the country reports a flash of insight or a poet writes about an insightful moment.

—ELIZABETH WOMACK

“A moment's insight is sometimes worth a life's experience.”

—Oliver Wendell Holmes Sr., *The Professor at the Breakfast Table*

THEME 6

THEME CONTENTS

GENRE FOCUS PERSONAL ESSAY

FLASHES OF INSIGHT 549

Introducing the Theme

Direct your students' attention to the **Theme Contents.** Ask them to read through the list of selections. Then present these questions for discussion:

- On the basis of the titles, what types of selections are included in this theme? *(Students may notice that this theme includes short stories, a memoir, poems, and four personal essays.)*
- What titles seem to suggest that the flashes of insight you will be reading about will be of special interest to you?
- Do any of the authors' names seem familiar? What expectations do you have about reading another work by that author?

GLENCOE TECHNOLOGY

LITERATURE CLASSICS CD-ROM

Search for other selections related to the theme "Flashes of Insight."

RESOURCE MANAGER

See the ***Theme Six Planning Guide*** for additional teaching notes, strategies, and resources for introducing the theme "Flashes of Insight."

Exploring the Theme

Flashes of Insight

- Students may recognize the image of a "lightbulb" as a cartoon feature for a "bright idea."
- Explain that flashes of insight are based on experiences that come together to produce new insight.
- To explore the theme further, suggest that students skim their social studies and science texts for examples of individuals who have advanced knowledge through flashes of insight.

Starting Points

Take a New View

Invite students to explain the cartoon. Ask what makes the cartoon humorous. *(The wordplay on* present *makes the cartoon humorous.)*

- Encourage students to share what they know about Ziggy's attitude toward life and to tell whether they agree with it and why.
- After students think of times when a flash of insight can be useful, ask them how they would share that insight with others. Have them discuss productive ways of explaining a new idea to classmates, family, or friends.

Awakening to People

Students might like to share their experiences with the rest of the class. Suggest that they first make notes on the series of events that led up to their flashes of insight. Then have them refer to their notes as they describe the scene. Encourage students to project the emotion of the moment through the presentation.

Exploring the Theme

Flashes of Insight

The way you look at the world is constantly being shaped by your experiences. Occasionally, you learn something that turns on a lightbulb in your head. In an instant, thoughts come together in a way that changes your understanding. Selections in this theme describe such moments. Choose one of the activities below to start your thinking about "Flashes of Insight."

Starting Points

TAKE A NEW VIEW

Ziggy has a flash of insight! He plays with a word, *present,* and it changes from an ordinary word that means *now* to a word that means *gift.* Ziggy realizes that the time we call *now* is a gift—a chance to enjoy today and tomorrow and all the other tomorrows.

- When you look at a person, an experience, a time, a story, or a word in a new way, you, too, can experience a flash of insight into something you have never understood before. When might such an experience be helpful?

AWAKENING TO PEOPLE

Everyone has moments when they awaken to a new understanding of a familiar person.

- Recall a moment when you suddenly understood something important about a family member, friend, or acquaintance. Think of a title for a story you could write to describe your new understanding.

Ziggy by Tom Wilson

ZIGGY © ZIGGY AND FRIENDS, INC. Reprinted with permission of UNIVERSAL SYNDICATE. All rights reserved.

Family and Community Activity

"Desert-Island Question" Interview

Students can interview family and community members in a variation on the "desert-island question." Explain that interviewers often ask their subjects what books, music, or conveniences they would want to have with them if they were stranded on a desert island. Suggest that students ask their subjects to think of three literary selections that help them understand an important idea, emotion, or event in their lives. Students can develop a written questionnaire and leave it with each person for several days' consideration.

Additional Resources

Family and Community Activities, p. 26

Theme Projects

Choose one of the projects below to work on as you read the selections in "Flashes of Insight." Work with a partner or a small group.

CRITICAL VIEWING

Examining Both Sides

1. Gather books, photographs, and other materials about a conflict—a war or other serious disagreement—involving the United States. Examine arguments for and against the issue.
2. Discuss how learning arguments for both sides of any issue can give you a flash of insight.

Autumn. Giuseppe Arcimboldo, 1530–1593. Brescia, Pinacoteca, Civica.

LEARNING FOR LIFE

Who Thought of That?

1. With a partner or a group, search several books of art to find unexpected ways in which artists view common objects.
2. Select an ordinary classroom object, such as an eraser, a computer mouse, or a student's desk or chair. Draw, sculpt, or describe in writing a new way to use or show the object.

interNET CONNECTION

Visit lit.glencoe.com for ideas and links relating to the selections and authors in this theme.

MULTIMEDIA PROJECT

Why Do They Do That?

1. Select an author from those listed in the **Theme Contents** on page 549, or another writer you like but know little about. Gather information about the author. If possible, include a quotation about why he or she writes.
2. Use HyperStudio or similar software to create a multimedia presentation.

Theme Projects

Teaching Strategies

The following suggestions may help your students plan and carry out their theme projects.

Critical Viewing

- Before students collect their photographs, present a few for discussion. Encourage students to describe their initial reactions to what they see. Do they find themselves forming an opinion on the basis of what they see? Suggest that they keep an open mind until their research is completed.
- As students collect their materials, point out that each conflict may have more than two sides. Suggest that they think of the points of view as being on a continuum, with extremes on either side and more moderate views in between.
- Have students plan a visual display with captions to explain how each element contributes to their knowledge of the conflict.

Learning For Life

- Before students begin, discuss the term *perspective* by considering examples of "unexpected ways" in which artists view common objects. How might a spider's view of an eraser on the floor differ from a human being's view of it?
- Share examples of unusual perspectives taken by artists. Some possible sources might include illustrated science fiction and fantasy books, as well as medical and scientific perspectives of subjects.
- Suggest that two or more students observe an object from different perspectives. Then invite them to display their drawings, sculptures, or descriptions together.

Multimedia Project

- Students may perform this project best in pairs or groups in which individual students are responsible for the medium in which they have the most aptitude.
- Students might consider incorporating interviews of readers and their comments about the author the students are featuring.
- Suggest that students prepare a storyboard for their project. Explain that a storyboard acts as a kind of map of what is to appear on the screen at any time.
- If videotaping is to be one of the media students use, encourage them to use the camcorder to achieve interesting and unusual perspectives.

Additional Resources

- ***Interdisciplinary Activities,*** pp. 22–25
- ***Viewing and Representing Activities,*** pp. 22–24
- ***Listening and Speaking Activities,*** pp. 16–18
- ***Selection and Theme Assessment,*** p. 135
- ***Critical Thinking Skills,*** pp. 15–17
- ***Performance Assessment,*** p. 69

interNET CONNECTION

Glencoe Literature Web Site

For more information about "Flashes of Insight," suggest that students enter such keywords as *recycled art* and *inventions*.

Before Reading

Objectives

- To read and analyze a short story about a young girl who has a flash of insight about herself and others
- To identify the element of external conflict in a short story
- To analyze the narrator's tone

Skills

Reading/Thinking: Comparing and Contrasting; Drawing Conclusions; Inferring; Predicting
Writing: Letter; Speech
Vocabulary: Word History; Analogies
Grammar/Language: Verb Tense; Troublesome Words
Listening/Speaking: Interviewing
Life Skills: Designing a Poster
Collaboration: Literature Groups

Motivating → STUDENTS

Selection Focus Transparency 47: Have students view the transparency and then discuss the questions provided.

Reading Focus: As an extension of the Reading Focus, have pairs of students share how something they succeeded in made them feel and how those feelings affected their future goals.

Before You Read

Raymond's Run

MEET TONI CADE BAMBARA

Toni Cade Bambara (kād bäm bä′ rä) wrote to make a difference in the lives of women and African Americans. "I write because I really think I've got hold of something, that if I share it, [it] might save somebody else some time, might lift someone's spirits, or might enable someone to see more clearly," she said. Bambara's works, which include short stories, a novel, and several films, are known for their rich portrayals of ordinary African American life. Bambara was also a respected professor of English and African American studies and a civil rights activist.

Toni Cade Bambara was born in 1939 and died in 1995. "Raymond's Run" was first published in 1972 in Gorilla, My Love.

READING FOCUS

How do you feel when people recognize you for being good at something?

Cluster

Create a cluster to express these feelings.

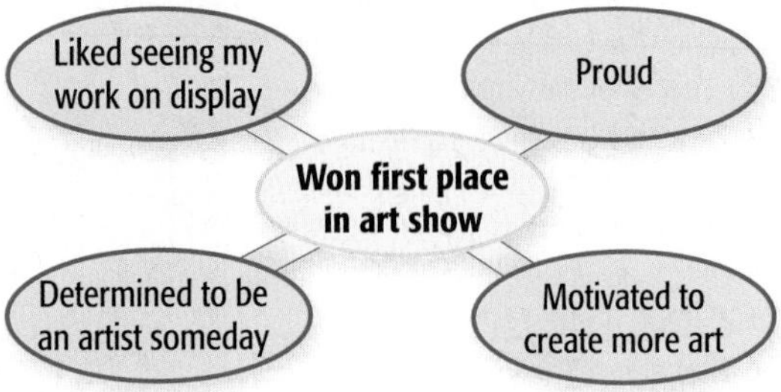

Setting a Purpose

Read to experience a flash of insight that one young person has about her favorite pastime: running.

BUILDING BACKGROUND

The Time and Place This modern story takes place in Harlem, a section of New York City.

Did You Know? A fast runner might earn the nickname "Mercury" after the Roman god who is known for speed. Statues show Mercury with a winged hat and winged sandals.

VOCABULARY PREVIEW

prodigy (prod′ ə jē) *n.* an extraordinarily gifted or talented person, especially a child; p. 555
liable (lī′ ə bəl) *adj.* likely; apt; p. 555
reputation (rep′ yə tā′ shən) *n.* what people generally think about the character of a person or thing; good name; p. 555
crouch (krouch) *v.* to stoop or bend, especially with knees bent; p. 558
obviously (ob′ vē əs lē) *adv.* in a way that is easily seen or understood; clearly; p. 560

RESOURCE MANAGER

Teaching Tools and Resources
- Theme Six Planning Guide
- Literature Groups Sourcebook

Essential Lesson Support

Lesson-Specific Instruction
- Selection Focus Transparency 47
- Literary Elements Transparency 48
- Active Reading Guide,* p. 48
- Selection Vocabulary Practice, p. 33

Assessment
- Selection Quick Checks,* p. 48
- Sel. and Theme Assmt., pp. 85–86
- Testmaker: ExamView Pro
- Performance Assessment, p. 45

Systematic Language Instruction
- Gr. & Comp. Hbk., L. 11.5
- Vocabulary Power, Lesson 24
- Spelling Power, Lesson 21

English Language Learners
- ELL Sourcebook, p. 70
- Spanish Summaries, p. 47
- Audio Library*
- English, Yes!

Spec. Needs/Strat. Interven.
- Interactive Rdg. Sbk., pp. T170–T172
- Interactive Rdg. Wkbk., pp. 90–91
- Inclusion Strat. Sbk., pp. 51–52
- Audio Library*

* Also available in Spanish

Raymond's Run

Toni Cade Bambara

La Miranda 2, 1995. Robin Holder. Monotype with stencils and photo silkscreen, 18 x 14 in. Courtesy of the artist.

I don't have much work to do around the house like some girls. My mother does that. And I don't have to earn my pocket money by hustling; George runs errands for the big boys and sells Christmas cards. And anything else that's got to get done, my father does. All I have to do in life is mind my brother Raymond, which is enough.

Sometimes I slip and say my little brother Raymond. But as any fool can see he's much bigger and he's older too. But a lot of people call him my little brother cause he needs looking after cause he's not quite right. And a lot of smart mouths got lots to say

Reading the Selection

SUMMARY

The two important things in Squeaky's life are running and taking care of her mentally handicapped brother, Raymond. As she concentrates on winning the May Day race, Squeaky becomes aware that Raymond is outside the track, running the race with her. She realizes that, with her help, running will give Raymond his chance to succeed. From this she gains an important insight: Even if she gives up running, she can set other goals.

Spanish Summaries, p. 47

A Active Reading Strategies

PREDICT Ask students to predict the topic of the story, given the title and the information the narrator provides in the first paragraph.

VOCABULARY If you haven't previewed the selection vocabulary with students, stop and remind them to use context clues to unlock the meanings of new vocabulary words.

Additional Resources

Active Reading Guide, p. 48

Audio Library

Spanish Audio Library

Teaching Support

CONNECTING TO OTHER SELECTIONS

The chart at the right shows three ways to connect "Raymond's Run" to other selections in this book.

For specific teaching strategies, see the ***Theme Six Planning Guide.***

Connection		Title
Life Skills: Collaborating	→	from *I Know Why the Caged Bird Sings,* p. 199
Thematic: Confidence in Success	→	"Casey at the Bat," p. 252
Literary: Narrator	→	"Mother and Daughter," p. 62

FYI

Location In New York City, of which Harlem is a part, the longer streets or avenues—such as Lenox Avenue and Amsterdam Avenue—run more or less parallel to each other. Consecutively numbered cross-streets intersect the avenues at right angles. In locating an address, residents usually identify the block; for example, "I'm on Eighty-Sixth Street between Second and Third Avenues."

B Literary Elements

EXTERNAL CONFLICT Ask students how Squeaky deals with conflicts and problems concerning her and her brother. *(She defends Raymond both verbally and physically. If things get rough, she runs.)*

C Author's Craft

INTERIOR MONOLOGUE Point out to students that the author uses interior monologue to make Squeaky seem to be speaking directly to the reader. Have students find an example of how Squeaky, using strong, direct language, reveals her feelings and emotions about events in the narrative. *("There is no track meet that I don't win . . . ," for example)*

about that too, especially when George was minding him. But now, if anybody has anything to say to Raymond, anything to say about his big head,[1] they have to come by me. And I don't play the dozens[2] or believe in standing around with somebody in my face doing a lot of talking. I much rather just knock you down and take my chances even if I am a little girl with skinny arms and a squeaky voice, which is how I got the name Squeaky. And if things get too rough, I run. And as anybody can tell you, I'm the fastest thing on two feet.

B

There is no track meet that I don't win the first place medal. I used to win the twenty-yard dash when I was a little kid in kindergarten. Nowadays, it's the fifty-yard dash. And tomorrow I'm subject to run the quarter-meter relay all by myself and come in first, second, and third. The big kids call me Mercury cause I'm the swiftest thing in the neighborhood. Everybody knows that—except two people who know better, my father and me. He can beat me to Amsterdam Avenue with me having a two fire-hydrant headstart and him running with his hands in his pockets and whistling. But that's private information. Cause can you imagine some thirty-five-year-old man stuffing himself into PAL shorts to race little kids? So as far as everyone's concerned, I'm the fastest and that goes for Gretchen, too, who has put out the tale that she is going to win the first-place medal this year. Ridiculous. In the second place, she's got short legs. In the third place, she's got freckles. In the first place, no one can beat me and that's all there is to it.

C

I'm standing on the corner admiring the weather and about to take a stroll down Broadway so I can practice my breathing exercises, and I've got Raymond walking on the inside close to the buildings, cause he's subject to fits of fantasy and starts thinking he's a circus performer and that the curb is a tightrope strung high in the air. And sometimes after a rain he likes to step down off his tightrope right into the gutter and slosh around getting his shoes and cuffs wet. Then I get hit when I get home. Or sometimes if you don't watch him he'll dash across traffic to the island in the middle of Broadway and give the pigeons a fit. Then I have to go behind him apologizing to all the old people sitting around trying to get some sun and getting all upset with the pigeons fluttering around them, scattering their newspapers and upsetting the waxpaper lunches in their laps. So I keep Raymond on the inside of me, and he plays like he's driving a stage coach which is O.K. by me so long as he doesn't run me over or interrupt my breathing exercises, which I have to do on account of I'm serious about my running, and I don't care who knows it.

Now some people like to act like things come easy to them, won't let on that they practice. Not me. I'll high-prance down 34th Street like a rodeo pony to keep my knees strong even if it does get my mother uptight so that she walks ahead like she's not with me, don't know me, is all by herself on a shopping trip, and I am somebody else's crazy child. Now you take Cynthia Procter for instance. She's just

D

1. Raymond's *big head* may be the result of *hydrocephaly* (hī′ drə sef′ ə lē), a condition in which fluid is trapped around the brain, damaging the brain and enlarging the skull.
2. *Play the dozens* refers to an exchange of insulting remarks.

Teaching Support

MEETING INDIVIDUAL NEEDS

ENGLISH LANGUAGE LEARNERS

Colloquial English On the board, write these expressions taken from the selection. Underline the words in italics.

1. If anyone has something to say about Raymond, they have *to come by me.* *(to say it to me)*
2. Tomorrow I'm *subject* to run the quarter-meter relay. *(scheduled)*
3. She has *put out the tale* that she is going to win. *(told everyone)*

Discuss the meaning of each expression in its context.

Activity Ask partners to look through the story for similar colloquial (informal, conversational) expressions and discuss what each one means in its context.

Additional Resources

English Language Learners Sourcebook, p. 70

D

the opposite. If there's a test tomorrow, she'll say something like, "Oh, I guess I'll play handball this afternoon and watch television tonight," just to let you know she ain't thinking about the test. Or like last week when she won the spelling bee for the millionth time, "A good thing you got 'receive,' Squeaky, cause I would have got it wrong. I completely forgot about the spelling bee." And she'll clutch the lace on her blouse like it was a narrow escape. Oh, brother. But of course when I pass her house on my early morning trots around the block, she is practicing the scales on the piano over and over and over and over. Then in music class she always lets herself get bumped around so she falls accidently on purpose onto the piano stool and is so surprised to find herself sitting there that she decides just for fun to try out the ole keys. And what do you know—Chopin's[3] waltzes just spring out of her fingertips and she's the most surprised thing in the world. A regular prodigy. I could kill people like that. I stay up all night studying the words for the spelling bee. And you can see me any time of day practicing running. I never walk if I can trot, and shame on Raymond if he can't keep up. But of course he does, cause if he hangs back someone's liable to walk up to him and get smart, or take his allowance from him, or ask him where he got that great big pumpkin head. People are so stupid sometimes.

E

So I'm strolling down Broadway breathing out and breathing in on counts of seven, which is my lucky number, and here comes Gretchen and her sidekicks: Mary Louise, who used to be a friend of mine when she first moved to Harlem from Baltimore and got beat up by everybody till I took up for her on account of her mother and my mother used to sing in the same choir when they were young girls, but people ain't grateful, so now she hangs out with the new girl Gretchen, and talks about me like a dog; and Rosie, who is as fat as I am skinny and has a big mouth where Raymond is concerned and is too stupid to know that there is not a big deal of difference between herself and Raymond and that she can't afford to throw stones.[4] So they are steady coming up Broadway and I see right away that it's going to be one of those Dodge City scenes cause the street ain't that big and they're close to the buildings just as we are. First I think I'll step into the candy store and look over the new comics and let them pass. But that's chicken and I've got a reputation to consider. So then I think I'll just walk straight on through them or even over them if necessary. But as they get to me, they slow down. I'm ready to fight, cause like I said I don't feature a whole lot of chit-chat, I much prefer to just

F

3. *Chopin* (shō′ pan) was a nineteenth-century Polish composer famous for his beautiful but difficult piano pieces.

4. The narrator is referring to the saying, "People who live in glass houses shouldn't *throw stones.*" It warns people not to criticize others for something that they themselves might also be criticized for.

Vocabulary

prodigy (prod′ ə jē) *n.* an extraordinarily gifted or talented person, especially a child
liable (lī′ ə bəl) *adj.* likely; apt
reputation (rep′ yə tā′ shən) *n.* what people generally think about the character of a person or thing; good name

D Active Reading Strategies

CONNECT Ask students whether they know people like Cynthia Procter. How do students feel about this kind of person?

E Literary Elements

EXTERNAL CONFLICT Explain to students that even though the conflict the narrator describes affects Raymond, it also affects Squeaky. Ask why. *(because she is responsible for her brother)*

F Literary Elements

EXTERNAL CONFLICT Ask students to point out the different options Squeaky lists to deal with the impending conflict. *(She considers stepping into the candy store and letting the girls pass; walking straight on through them; or staying and fighting.)* Have students consider what her choice says about her character. *(Squeaky does not fight just to fight, but she will defend herself—and Raymond.)*

Reading Minilesson

Comparison and Contrast Squeaky defines herself in contrast to others in the story. Identifying the differences she points out and inferring some comparisons will help students better understand Squeaky's character.

Activity Have students complete the following chart, comparing and contrasting Squeaky with other characters in the story.

SQUEAKY		CYNTHIA		GRETCHEN AND HER SIDEKICKS	
Similarities	Differences	Similarities	Differences	Similarities	Differences

G Critical Thinking

DRAWING CONCLUSIONS What might students conclude from Squeaky's statement about the May Day race? *(She is confident in her ability as a runner and would not back down from any confrontation.)*

H Literary Elements

EXTERNAL CONFLICT Discuss how Squeaky adamantly defends Raymond. Ask students to explain how they think this effectively portrays Squeaky's love for and attachment to Raymond. *(She risks getting into a fight rather than let anyone hurt Raymond.)*

I Active Reading Strategies

EVALUATE Suggest that students imagine they know Squeaky personally and are telling a friend about her. How would they describe Squeaky? *(Don't mess with Squeaky, because she's tough. You're going to want her on your side.)*

Vo•cab•u•lar•y Skills

Word History American pickpockets once called the side pants pockets "side-kicks." They were the hardest pockets to reach because the intended victims' arms were next to them. A wise man kept his wallet in his side pocket, or side-kick. Over time the concept was extended to include any faithful friend.

knock you down right from the jump and save everybody a lotta precious time.

"You signing up for the May Day races?" smiles Mary Louise, only it's not a smile at all. A dumb question like that doesn't deserve an answer. Besides, there's just me and Gretchen standing there really, so no use wasting my breath talking to shadows.

"I don't think you're going to win this time," says Rosie, trying to signify with her hands on her hips all salty,[5] completely forgetting that I have whupped her behind many times for less salt than that.

G "I always win cause I'm the best," I say straight at Gretchen who is, as far as I'm concerned, the only one talking in this ventriloquist-dummy routine. Gretchen smiles, but it's not a smile, and I'm thinking that girls never really smile at each other because they don't know how and don't want to know how and there's probably no one to teach us how, cause grown-up girls don't know either. Then they all look at Raymond who has just brought his mule team to a standstill. And they're about to see what trouble they can get into through him.

H "What grade you in now, Raymond?"

"You got anything to say to my brother, you say it to me, Mary Louise Williams of Raggedy Town, Baltimore."

"What are you, his mother?" sasses Rosie.

"That's right, Fatso. And the next word out of anybody and I'll be *their* mother too." So they just stand there and Gretchen shifts from one leg to the other and so do they. Then Gretchen puts her hands on her hips and is about to say something with her freckle-face self but doesn't. Then she walks around me looking me up and down but keeps walking up Broadway, and her side-kicks follow her. So me and Raymond smile at each other and he says, "Gidyap" to his team and I continue with my breathing exercises, strolling down Broadway toward the ice man on 145th with not a care in the world cause I am Miss Quicksilver[6] herself.

I I take my time getting to the park on May Day because the track meet is the last thing on the program. The biggest thing on the program is the May Pole dancing, which I can do without, thank you, even if my mother thinks it's a shame I don't take part and act like a girl for a change. You'd think my mother'd be grateful not to have to make me a white organdy[7] dress with a big satin sash and buy me new white baby-doll shoes that can't be taken out of the box till the big day. You'd think she'd be glad her daughter ain't out there prancing around a May Pole getting the new clothes all dirty and sweaty and trying to act like a fairy or a flower or whatever you're supposed to be when you should be trying to be yourself, whatever that is, which is, as far as I am concerned, a poor Black girl who really can't afford to buy shoes and a new dress you only wear once a lifetime cause it won't fit next year.

I was once a strawberry in a Hansel and Gretel pageant when I was in nursery school and didn't have no better sense than to dance on tiptoe with my arms in a circle over my head doing umbrella steps and being a perfect fool just so my

5. Here, *signify* is slang for "to stir things up; cause trouble for fun." This is what Rosie is trying to do by being *salty,* or critical and sarcastic.

6. The narrator is comparing herself to Mercury again. Actually, *quicksilver* is another name for the metal mercury, which was named for the swift Roman god. At room temperature, the silver-colored metal is a liquid that flows rapidly.

7. *Organdy* is a lightweight fabric, usually made of cotton.

Teaching Support

MEETING INDIVIDUAL NEEDS — ADVANCED LEARNERS

Research Squeaky is quite successful as a runner within her immediate neighborhood. There are opportunities beyond neighborhood events for boys and girls and men and women to test their racing abilities. Have students share what they know about such events.

Activity Suggest that students use a Web search engine to locate statistics on track and field. They should find and present information about matches all over the world. Suggest that they select two sites with similar events and compare times for similar races, especially the dashes. **L3**

mother and father could come dressed up and clap. You'd think they'd know better than to encourage that kind of nonsense. I am not a strawberry. I do not dance on my toes. I run. That is what I am all about. So I always come late to the May Day program, just in time to get my number pinned on and lay in the grass till they announce the fifty-yard dash.

I put Raymond in the little swings, which is a tight squeeze this year and will be impossible next year. Then I look around for Mr. Pearson, who pins the numbers on. I'm really looking for Gretchen if you want to know the truth, but she's not around. The park is jam-packed. Parents in hats and corsages and breast-pocket handkerchiefs peeking up. Kids in white dresses and light-blue suits. The parkees[8] unfolding chairs and chasing the rowdy kids from Lenox[9] as if they had no right to be there. The big guys with their caps on backwards, leaning against the fence swirling the basketballs on the tips of their fingers, waiting for all these crazy people to clear out the park so they can play. Most of the kids in my class are carrying bass drums and glockenspiels and flutes. You'd think they'd put in a few bongos or something for real like that.

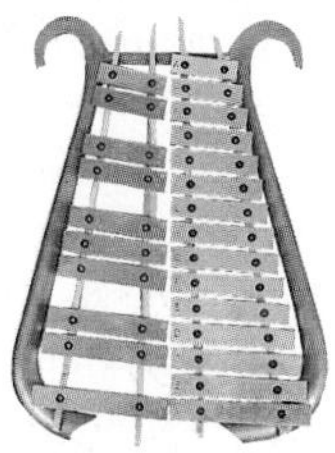

Did You Know?
The *glockenspiel* (glok′ ən spēl′) is a musical instrument that has a series of metal bars mounted in a frame. It is played by striking the bars with two small hammers.

Then here comes Mr. Pearson with his clipboard and his cards and pencils and whistles and safety pins and fifty million other things he's always dropping all over the place with his clumsy self. He sticks out in a crowd because he's on stilts. We used to call him Jack and the Beanstalk to get him mad. But I'm the only one that can outrun him and get away, and I'm too grown for that silliness now.

"Well, Squeaky," he says, checking my name off the list and handing me number seven and two pins. And I'm thinking he's got no right to call me Squeaky, if I can't call him Beanstalk.

"Hazel Elizabeth Deborah Parker," I correct him and tell him to write it down on his board.

"Well, Hazel Elizabeth Deborah Parker, going to give someone else a break this year?" I squint at him real hard to see if he is seriously thinking I should lose the race on purpose just to give someone else a break. "Only six girls running this time," he continues, shaking his head sadly like it's my fault all of New York didn't turn out in sneakers. "That new girl should give you a run for your money." He looks around the park for Gretchen like a periscope in a submarine movie. "Wouldn't it be a nice gesture if you were . . . to ahhh . . ."

I give him such a look he couldn't finish putting that idea into words. Grownups got a lot of nerve sometimes. I pin number seven to myself and stomp away, I'm so burnt. And I go straight for the track and stretch out on the grass while the band winds up with "Oh, the Monkey Wrapped His Tail Around the Flag Pole," which my teacher calls by some other name. The man on the loudspeaker is calling everyone over

8. The city's park employees are the *parkees.*
9. *Lenox* is a street that runs through Harlem.

J Author's Craft

DESCRIPTIVE LANGUAGE Point out to students the vivid details the author uses to describe the May Day festivities. Ask students how these details bring the scene to life.

K Critical Thinking

DRAWING CONCLUSIONS Guide students to draw the same conclusion that Squeaky does: Mr. Pearson wants Squeaky to let someone else win the race. Encourage students to base their conclusions on what Mr. Pearson says and what Squeaky's reaction is. Share the following model:

Model: When Mr. Pearson starts talking about how there are only six runners competing, I think he's implying that not many girls are willing to race against someone who always wins. When he talks about "a nice gesture," Squeaky's reaction makes him stop. I can tell that he's suggesting that Squeaky "throw" the race. That's why I think Squeaky gives him "the look."

L Literary Elements

INTERNAL CONFLICT Ask students to notice the conflicts going on inside Squeaky after her confrontation with Mr. Pearson. *(She is angry about Mr. Pearson's suggestion. At the same time, she is trying to ignore everything that is going on around her, even the fact that she is in the city.)*

Writing Minilesson

Personal Response: Tone Remind students of how indignant Squeaky is at Mr. Pearson's words. Ask students to imagine themselves in Squeaky's position. After the race, they want to share their indignation with a friend. Point out that if Squeaky wrote a letter to someone her own age, she would probably use the conversational tone used in the story.

Activity Suggest that students, in the role of Squeaky, write a letter to an older person (a grandparent or family friend) describing her reaction to Mr. Pearson's comment. Encourage students to be aware of how their language and tone change when they write for a different audience. **L2**

Additional Resources

Writer's Choice, Lesson 4.4

M **Active Reading Strategies**

RESPOND Ask students what they think of Raphael Perez's tactics in the race. Do they think it is fair of him to do what he does? Have students support their answers with reasons. *(Examples: Yes, because "psyching out" other players is OK; professional athletes do it. No, because you should win by being the best runner.)*

N **Active Reading Strategies**

PREDICT Do students think Squeaky's description of Gretchen indicates anything about the outcome of the race? Have them explain their answers. *(Gretchen may give Squeaky the greatest challenge she has had yet. She really seems to know what she's doing.)*

O **Active Reading Strategies**

CONNECT Ask students to relate the race experience to their own lives. Have they ever had the same feeling as Squeaky? In what situation?

Teaching Support

Raymond's Run

to the track and I'm on my back looking at the sky, trying to pretend I'm in the country, but I can't, because even grass in the city feels hard as sidewalk, and there's just no pretending you are anywhere but in a "concrete jungle" as my grandfather says.

The twenty-yard dash takes all of two minutes cause most of the little kids don't know no better than to run off the track or run the wrong way or run smack into the fence and fall down and cry. One little kid, though, has got the good sense to run straight for the white ribbon up ahead so he wins. Then the second-graders line up for the thirty-yard dash and I don't even bother to turn my head to watch cause Raphael Perez always wins. He wins before he even begins by psyching[10] the runners, telling them they're going to trip on their shoelaces and fall on their faces or lose their shorts or something, which he doesn't really have to do since he is very fast, almost as fast as I am. After that is the forty-yard dash which I used to run when I was in first grade. Raymond is hollering from the swings cause he knows I'm about to do my thing cause the man on the loudspeaker has just announced the fifty-yard dash, although he might just as well be giving a recipe for angel food cake cause you can hardly make out what he's sayin for the static. I get up and slip off my sweat pants and then I see Gretchen standing at the starting line, kicking her legs out like a pro. Then as I get into place I see that ole Raymond is on line on the other side of the fence, bending down with his fingers on the ground just like he knew what he was doing. I was going to yell at him but then I didn't. It burns up your energy to holler.

Every time, just before I take off in a race, I always feel like I'm in a dream, the kind of dream you have when you're sick with fever and feel all hot and weightless. I dream I'm flying over a sandy beach in the early morning sun, kissing the leaves of the trees as I fly by. And there's always the smell of apples, just like in the country when I was little and used to think I was a choo-choo train, running through the fields of corn and chugging up the hill to the orchard. And all the time I'm dreaming this, I get lighter and lighter until I'm flying over the beach again, getting blown through the sky like a feather that weighs nothing at all. But once I spread my fingers in the dirt and crouch over the Get on Your Mark, the dream goes and I am solid again and am telling myself, Squeaky you must win, you must win, you are the fastest thing in the world, you can even beat your father up Amsterdam if you really try. And then I feel my weight coming back just behind my knees then down to my feet then into the earth and the pistol shot explodes in my blood and I am off and weightless again, flying past the other runners, my arms pumping up and down and the whole world is quiet except for the crunch as I zoom over the gravel in the track. I glance to my left and there is no one. To the right, a blurred Gretchen, who's got her chin jutting out as if it would win the race all by itself. And on the other side of the fence is Raymond with

10. *Psyching* the runners means scaring or intimidating them.

Vocabulary
crouch (krouch) *v.* to stoop or bend, especially with knees bent

MEETING INDIVIDUAL NEEDS — MULTIPLE MODES OF EXPRESSION

Bodily-Kinesthetic Students with racing experience can share how it feels to get into position for a race and wait for the starting gun. They may also be able to describe how they ready themselves psychologically for a race. Allow students to compare various techniques of preparing for a competition.

Activity Have experienced racers (or a coach) position students for the beginning of a dash (if possible, on an actual track), and then discuss how the imitation of racing affected them emotionally. **L1** COLLAB. LEARN.

Viewing the photograph: Which runner reminds you of Squeaky? Why?

P his arms down to his side and the palms tucked up behind him, running in his very own style, and it's the first time I ever saw that and I almost stop to watch my brother Raymond on his first run. But the white ribbon is bouncing toward me and I tear past it, racing into the distance till my feet with a mind of their own start digging up footfuls of dirt and brake me short. Then all the kids standing on the side pile on me, banging me on the back and slapping my head with their May Day programs, for I have won again and everybody on 151st Street can walk tall for another year.

Q "In the first place . . ." the man on the loudspeaker is clear as a bell now. But then he pauses and the loudspeaker starts to whine. Then static. And I lean down to catch my breath and here comes Gretchen walking back, for she's overshot the finish line too, huffing and puffing with her hands on her hips taking it slow, breathing in

VIEWING THE PHOTOGRAPH

Viewing Response *All three girls show concentration and great determination.*

P Literary Elements

FORESHADOWING Point out that Squeaky is distracted during the race by Raymond's run. Ask students how, given this glimpse of information, they think the story will end.

Q Active Reading Strategies

QUESTION Ask students whether they think Squeaky or Gretchen has won the race and why they think so. *(Students may think Gretchen has won since Squeaky was watching Raymond.)*

FINE ART TRANSPARENCY 1

You may want to use ***Fine Art Transparency 1*** to discuss running as a sport and as a recreational activity.

REAL-WORLD CONNECTION

Athletes in the Media Help students make the connection between what they have read in the story and what happens in the "real" world.

Activity Have students locate a magazine or newspaper article that features an interview with a successful competitor in sports or another field. Have the class break into groups to discuss each article. Students should answer such questions as *Who is the subject of the article? What did he or she accomplish? What was that person's reaction to success? How did he or she speak of his or her competitors? What challenges did that person face? What are his or her goals?*

L2 **COLLAB. LEARN.**

R Critical Thinking

INFERRING Be sure students understand why Squeaky has gained respect for Gretchen and has changed her attitude toward her brother. *(She senses that both have some talent, and she is beginning to think about her own life beyond running.)*

S Active Reading Strategies

COMPARE Ask students to compare what Squeaky knows about herself at the beginning of the story with what she knows about herself at the end. *(She knows that there are things she can do well besides running: She can coach others, she can study harder and do well, and she can make friends with other girls.)*

Thematic Focus

Flashes of Insight Ask students to compare Squeaky to themselves and other young people they know. Are Squeaky's reactions to her new understanding of her brother's talent and her own abilities typical of young people? Have students give examples to support their answers.

ASSESSMENT

Quick Checks, p. 48

steady time like a real pro and I sort of like her a little for the first time. "In first place . . ." and then three or four voices get all mixed up on the loudspeaker and I dig my sneaker into the grass and stare at Gretchen who's staring back, we both wondering just who did win. I can hear old Beanstalk arguing with the man on the loudspeaker and then a few others running their mouths about what the stopwatches say. Then I hear Raymond yanking at the fence to call me and I wave to shush him, but he keeps rattling the fence like a gorilla in a cage like in them gorilla movies, but then like a dancer or something he starts climbing up nice and easy but very fast. And it occurs to me, watching how smoothly he climbs hand over hand and remembering how he looked running with his arms down to his side and with the wind pulling his mouth back and his teeth showing and all, it occurred to me that Raymond would make a very fine runner. Doesn't he always keep up with me on my trots? And he surely knows how to breathe in counts of seven cause he's always doing it at the dinner table, which drives my brother George up the wall. And I'm smiling to beat the band cause if I've lost this race, or if me and Gretchen tied, or even if I've won, I can always retire as a runner and begin a whole new career as a coach with Raymond as my champion. After all, with a little more study I can beat Cynthia and her phony self at the spelling bee. And if I bugged my mother, I could get piano lessons and become a star. And I have a big rep as the baddest thing around. And I've got a roomful of ribbons and medals and awards. But what has Raymond got to call his own?

So I stand there with my new plans, laughing out loud by this time as Raymond jumps down from the fence and runs over with his teeth showing and his arms down to the side, which no one before him has quite mastered as a running style. And by the time he comes over I'm jumping up and down so glad to see him—my brother Raymond, a great runner in the family tradition. But of course everyone thinks I'm jumping up and down because the men on the loudspeaker have finally gotten themselves together and compared notes and are announcing "In first place—Miss Hazel Elizabeth Deborah Parker." (Dig that.) "In second place—Miss Gretchen P. Lewis." And I look over at Gretchen wondering what the "P" stands for. And I smile. Cause she's good, no doubt about it. Maybe she'd like to help me coach Raymond; she obviously is serious about running, as any fool can see. And she nods to congratulate me and then she smiles. And I smile. We stand there with this big smile of respect between us. It's about as real a smile as girls can do for each other, considering we don't practice real smiling every day, you know, cause maybe we too busy being flowers or fairies or strawberries instead of something honest and worthy of respect . . . you know . . . like being people.

❖

Vocabulary
obviously (ob′ vē əs lē) *adv.* in a way that is easily seen or understood; clearly

Teaching Support

Grammar and Language Minilesson

Verb Tense Ask students to note the tense of the majority of the verbs in the story. *(present)* Explain that writers may use the present tense in a story, especially one in the first person, in order to give the story a sense of immediacy. The idea is to give readers the illusion that they are experiencing the events with the characters.

Activity Have students locate a long sentence in which the verbs are in the present tense. Then have them rephrase it in the past. For example:

> So I *stood* there with my new plans, laughing out loud by this time as Raymond *jumped* down from the fence and *ran* over with his teeth showing and his arms down to the side, which no one before him had quite mastered in a running style.

Students may have differing opinions on which style is more effective. **L2**

Additional Resources

- ***Grammar and Language Transparency 45***
- ***Grammar and Language Workbook,*** p. 85
- ***Grammar and Composition Handbook,*** Lesson 3.5
- ***Writer's Choice,*** Lesson 10.5

Responding to Literature

PERSONAL RESPONSE

- Are you satisfied with the ending to this story? In a short note to a classmate, explain why or why not.

Brackets connect questions that are paired to develop higher-level thinking skills.

Analyzing Literature

RECALL

1. Why does Raymond need to be looked after?
2. To which girl—Gretchen, Mary Louise, or Rosie—does Squeaky address her remarks?
3. Describe Raymond's behavior while Squeaky runs the race.
4. After Squeaky wins the race, how does her attitude toward Gretchen change?

INTERPRET

5. How does Squeaky appear to feel about her responsibility for Raymond? Explain.
6. What does Squeaky mean by "this ventriloquist-dummy routine"?
7. Why, in your opinion, did the author name the story after Raymond?
8. How does Squeaky's attitude toward running change at the end of the race? Use details from the story to support your answer.

EVALUATE AND CONNECT

9. Bambara uses a **metaphor** to compare two incidents (see page R6). How is meeting Gretchen and her friends "one of those Dodge City scenes"? In your opinion, is this metaphor appropriate for the story? Why or why not?
10. Recalling your thoughts from the **Reading Focus** on page 552, would you have reacted differently than Squeaky did to winning the race? Explain.

LITERARY ELEMENTS

External Conflict

The **conflict** in a story is a struggle between opposing forces. In an **internal conflict,** a character struggles with his or her emotions or convictions. An **external conflict** is present when the problem or struggle is between characters, or between a character and another force, such as an animal or a storm.

1. Describe two examples in which Squeaky faces an external conflict.
2. Would you enjoy this story if there were no external conflicts? Why or why not?

- See **Literary Terms Handbook,** p. R2.

Responding to the Selection

PERSONAL RESPONSE

Although students may respond differently to the conclusion of the story, the ending is consistent with Squeaky's character, which is direct, honest, and fair.

Analyzing Literature

1. Although Raymond is older than Squeaky, he has the mental age of someone much younger.
2. She speaks to Gretchen because Gretchen is the leader of the group.
3. First he takes a starting position, bending down with his fingers on the ground. When the race starts, he runs it in his own style.
4. Squeaky begins to look upon Gretchen more kindly because she realizes that Gretchen is a serious runner with goals like her own.
5. Squeaky takes the responsibility seriously, defending Raymond against rude remarks and making sure he is safe.
6. She means that although Rosie or Mary Louise may be talking, it is really Gretchen who is feeding them the ideas, using them as a ventriloquist uses a dummy.
7. It is Raymond's running the race that provides the climax to the story, giving Squeaky an insight into her and Raymond's future.
8. She realizes that it is not something she will always do or be good at. She talks of retiring as a runner and beginning a career as Raymond's coach. She also makes plans for studying more.
9. Squeaky is referring to a classic Western scene in which the hero meets the villain in a face-off. It seems to parallel the May Day race because Gretchen has been bragging that she will be the new champion. Like the Western hero, Squeaky has to prove herself.
10. Students may say that athletes generally recognize that the benefits gained from winning a race pay off in many ways: fitness resulting from training, knowledge, and willingness to undertake challenges in other areas.

LITERARY ELEMENTS

1. Squeaky is challenged by Gretchen's desire to beat her. Mr. Pearson's hint that she should let someone else win is another conflict.
2. Students may suggest that the story would not be as interesting without conflicts because Squeaky would not have to overcome any opposition.

Additional Resources

Literary Elements Transparency 48

Literature and Writing

Writing About Literature

Students' explanations should

- use appropriate language to describe the tone
- give examples of the tones they name

Creative Writing

Students' speeches should

- be in the conversational style of speech that Squeaky uses
- reflect her new respect for her competitors

Extending Your Response

Literature Groups Point out to students that, in predicting how Squeaky will act in the future, they should base their ideas on her past behavior. COLLAB. LEARN.

Listening and Speaking Encourage students to watch a televised sports interview to get a feeling for the facial expressions and body language of athletes and their interviewers.

Learning for Life Use this activity as an opportunity to encourage careful organization and presentation of facts.

Literature and Writing

Writing About Literature

Understanding Tone The language used by a writer may reveal an attitude toward characters and events. This way of using language is called **tone.** Write a paragraph describing the tone used by the author of "Raymond's Run." Does it seem mocking? respectful? understanding? Indicate which words and phrases make the author's attitude clear for you.

Creative Writing

Thank-You Speech If Squeaky were to make a few comments upon accepting her award, what might she say? Write a few lines of dialogue, using a tone that Squeaky would use. Consider her new attitude toward running and toward her competitors.

Extending Your Response

Literature Groups

A New Outlook What does Squeaky come to realize about her abilities and the abilities of others at the end of the story? With your group, discuss these new insights. Consider the following questions: How has Squeaky changed? How will these changes affect her relationships with other people? How will Squeaky's realizations make her a better person?

Listening and Speaking

Interview the Winner Imagine that Squeaky's race has just ended and a TV reporter wants the winner's immediate reaction. With a partner, role-play a sportscaster's interview with Squeaky. Perform your interview live before your class. Use the style and attitude you have observed in this type of interview. Ask classmates to evaluate the style of your interview.

Learning for Life

Promote the Race Imagine that you are an artist designing a poster to advertise an annual race or another major event in your school or community. Examine ads for similar events, and list the elements your poster should include. Finally, create the poster. Consider including a short statement about Squeaky and what her participation will mean for the meet.

Reading Further

For other stories about responsibility, try these books:

Flour Babies by Anne Fine

There's a Girl in My Hammerlock by Jerry Spinelli

Save your work for your portfolio.

REAL-WORLD CONNECTION

Running Shoes Squeaky's shoes are obviously an important part of her wardrobe, as they are for any runner. Encourage groups of students to find the Web sites of two or more major running shoe manufacturers. Have them examine the documentation on the sites describing the shoes. What similarities and differences are there between different styles of shoes? How useful do some of the advertised features seem? From what the students read at the Web sites, what shoes do they think would be perfect for helping them win the fifty-yard dash? Have each group give a brief presentation about what they've learned.

Skill Minilessons

RETEACH • REVIEW

GRAMMAR AND LANGUAGE • TROUBLESOME WORDS

Compound words are often troublesome because they can be written several ways—as open compounds, closed compounds, or hyphenated compounds.

For compound modifiers, like *light-blue* and *first-place,* use a hyphen in the following situations:

1. If the compound modifier comes before the noun.
2. When the first word modifies the second word.
3. If a hyphen is needed to make the meaning clearer.

● For more about troublesome words, see **Language Handbook,** pp. R21–R26.

PRACTICE Rewrite the following sentences correctly. If you wish, use a dictionary.

1. I used to win the (twenty-yard, twentyyard, twenty yard) dash when I was a little kid.
2. Tomorrow I will run the (quarter-meter, quartermeter, quarter meter) relay.
3. Oh, I guess I'll play (hand-ball, handball, hand ball) this afternoon.
4. I accidentally pushed the sheet music off the (piano-stool, pianostool, piano stool).
5. The students are in white dresses and (light-blue, lightblue, light blue) suits.

READING AND THINKING • PREDICTING

If you want to get more involved in a story and improve your reading at the same time, try **predicting** while you read. Predicting means making an educated guess about what's going to happen next. To predict well, you must pay attention to details as you read. If you were predicting while reading "Raymond's Run," you probably foresaw the outcome of the race.

PRACTICE Answer these questions about predicting events in "Raymond's Run."

1. In predicting who would win the race, which details or clues would you use from the story?
2. Why, do you think, might predicting make a reader more involved in a story?
3. Does predicting make the story more interesting for you? Why or why not?

● For more about predicting, see **Reading Handbook,** p. R94.

VOCABULARY • ANALOGIES

An **analogy** is a type of comparison that is based on the relationships between things or ideas. Two kinds of analogies deal with synonyms and antonyms.

Synonyms–rapid : quick :: slippery : slick
Antonyms–spend : save :: respond : ignore

To finish an analogy, decide what relationship exists between the first pair of words and apply it to the second pair of words. For example, if the first pair of words are synonyms, the second pair must be synonyms.

PRACTICE Choose the pair of words that best completes each analogy.

1. crouch : bend ::
   a. stoop : stretch
   b. stumble : fall
   c. fear : frighten
   d. leap : jump
   e. race : win
2. obviously : unclearly ::
   a. well : poorly
   b. slightly : mildly
   c. luckily : fortunately
   d. dimly : slowly
   e. quickly : carelessly

● For more about analogies, see **Communications Skills Handbook,** p. R73.

Skill Minilessons

GRAMMAR AND LANGUAGE
TROUBLESOME WORDS

1. twenty-yard
2. quarter-meter
3. handball
4. piano stool
5. light-blue

READING AND THINKING
PREDICTING

1. *Possible answers:* Squeaky's history of winning, her determination, Mr. Pearson's hint about letting someone else win.
2. The reader may be looking forward to a particular development or may just want to see whether he or she is right.
3. Students' answers may suggest their awareness of employing this reading skill or their reasons for trying to use it.

VOCABULARY
ANALOGIES

1. d
2. a

Additional Resources

- ***Grammar and Language Workbook,*** p. 65
- ***Grammar and Composition Handbook,*** Lesson 15.1
- ***Writer's Choice,*** Lesson 9.2
- ***Reading Skills Practice Workbook***
- ***Vocabulary Practice,*** p. 33

ASSESSMENT

- ***Quick Checks,*** p. 48
- ***Selection and Theme Assessment,*** pp. 85–86
- ***Performance Assessment,*** p. 45
- ***Testmaker: ExamView Pro***
- ***Interactive Tutor: Self-Assessment***

MEDIA Connection

Objective

- To read and understand a magazine article

Literature LINK

Raymond's Run Point out the similarities between Leslie and Raymond. Both have similar disabilities, yet both are motivated to succeed in their efforts. In working toward their goals, they receive the encouragement of a caring family.

Analyzing Media

1. She was a late starter in the race, just as she was in life, but she didn't give up. She "made up for lost time" and triumphed.
2. She is healthy now and happy in what she does. She obviously has a loving and caring parent.

Informational Text

*in*TIME For more examples of informational text, direct students to the articles in the *inTIME* magazine.

Additional Resources

Media Connections, p. 11

MEDIA Connection

MAGAZINE ARTICLE

Who are winners in sports events? Who are losers? Joe Henderson knows from personal experience the best answer to these questions.

Fast Finisher

by Joe Henderson—*Runner's World*, October 1996

My daughter Leslie was a slow starter in life. She arrived late, on Labor Day 1982, and was late leaving the hospital because of a blood disorder. In her first six months, Leslie gained only two pounds, then nearly died during heart surgery. Her recovery was complicated by anemia so severe she required several transfusions.

Oh, yes, Leslie also has Down's syndrome and is deaf. She didn't sit up until she was two years old and didn't walk until she was almost four. She'll never talk.

But don't feel sorry for Leslie. She's fourteen and healthy now.

If you picture Down's syndrome kids as slow moving, forget it. If you think of deaf kids as wordless, forget that, too. Neither description fits Leslie.

From the day she stood up and took her first steps, she's been making up for lost time. And for what Leslie lacks in voice, she compensates with sign language.

Leslie Henderson

So, when the opportunity arose, it seemed only natural that Leslie would choose to enter the Special Olympics. We went to a meet this spring.

Leslie lined up, with two other runners, in the eighth heat of the 50 meters. She knew about the starting line and about running in lanes. Some other things, she didn't comprehend so well.

She signed an "8" to me, indicating this was her favorite lane. Fine, but the other two runners were in lanes 1 and 2. This left her all alone on the outside of the track. I had to coax her over to lane 3.

Leslie didn't understand about starts, either. The other two runners took off when signaled. Leslie held her ground. She didn't start after them until they were about ten meters down the track.

Even with the delayed start, Leslie caught one of the others. After finishing, she flopped dramatically onto her back, arms spread wide, eyes closed, tongue hanging out. (She and I like to watch televised track meets together; no doubt she was mimicking the runners she'd seen on TV.)

She knew just what to do on the victory stand. After having the medal draped around her neck, she pumped both arms for ten seconds of triumph.

Analyzing Media

1. Why was Leslie's medal such a triumph for her?
2. Why didn't the writer think you should feel sorry for his daughter? Did this surprise you? Why or why not?

564 THEME 6

Teaching Support

interNET CONNECTION

Special Olympics Have students use a search engine to look for more information on the Special Olympics, using that name as their keyword.

Reading Minilesson

Author's Purpose Point out to students that "Fast Finisher" and "Raymond's Run" share a purpose—to show what challenged children can do in sports. In the story, though, this purpose is secondary to Squeaky's discoveries about herself. Magazine articles can employ a narrative tone, as this one does, telling a story in a way that heightens the reader's interest in its outcome while at the same time providing valuable information.

Activity Suggest that students try retelling this, or another magazine article, as realistic fiction. Point out that they know the outcome, so their task is to create a beginning and a middle that anticipate that ending. **L2**

Additional Resources

Reading Skills Practice Workbook

Reading and Thinking Skills

Strategies for Reading Informational Text

Much of what you read in newspapers, magazines, manuals, textbooks, and guidebooks is informational text. This type of writing is expository; that is, its main purpose is to explain or give instruction on a topic. Here are some suggestions to help you find and understand the most important ideas in informative selections:

- Preview the material by looking at heads and graphic aids that can help you understand the topic. Graphic aids include pictures, diagrams, maps, webs, and time lines.
- As you read, ask yourself questions about what you have read. Asking questions about the material will let you know if you understand what you are reading.
- Look for the way in which the writer has organized information–for example, cause and effect, sequencing, comparison/contrast, and problem and solution.
- Change your reading rate to fit the material. When you're reading about a familiar topic, you can read quickly. When the material is more difficult, you will have to slow down.
- Use context clues to try to determine the meanings of words that are new to you. After you have finished reading, you can look up the exact meanings of these words.
- Look for the main idea of the paragraph. Then find reasons, examples, and details that support the main idea. The following paragraph uses facts and statistics.

> The Special Olympics is an international athletic training and competition program that traces its roots to a summer day camp. In June 1963 Eunice Kennedy Shriver, the sister of President John F. Kennedy, opened her back yard to about 100 local children with developmental disabilities. Shriver offered a variety of recreational activities because she believed that people with mental disabilities were very capable of competing in physical activities. Her idea spread, and in 1968, Shriver and the Joseph P. Kennedy Foundation joined forces with the Chicago Park District to sponsor the first ever Special Olympics. More than 1,000 athletes competed in track and field, swimming, and floor hockey. Today, that number has grown to nearly one million in 140 countries.

For more about reading informational text, see **Reading Handbook**, pp. R87-R88.

ACTIVITY

Find an informational article in a newspaper or magazine about a topic that interests you and presents new information. Use the suggestions given above as you read the article. Test your understanding of what you have read by explaining the main points to a classmate.

Objective

- To develop strategies for reading and understanding informational text

Teaching Strategies

After students read the introduction and the strategies, help them identify examples of informational reading they have done recently. Discuss with students which of the strategies listed they have found most useful. Explain that there is a wide variety of informational text and that in some instances a particular strategy cannot be used. For example, some informational text does not have heads, subheads, or graphic aids. You might want to stress the importance of determining word meaning from context so as not to interrupt the flow of meaning from the passage as a whole.

Activity

Allow time for students to read an informational selection from a source of their choice. Then have students work in pairs to explain to a partner what they have read.

Additional Resources

Reading Skills Practice Workbook

Teaching Support

MEETING INDIVIDUAL NEEDS — SPECIAL NEEDS

Less-Proficient Readers Work with a small group of students to clarify the suggestions given in the lesson for reading informational text. Answer questions students may raise about the strategies suggested. Then have them paraphrase the suggestions and explain whether or not they feel able to implement them.

Activity Duplicate a number of selections from magazines and newspapers at a manageable reading level for less-proficient readers. Pair each less-proficient reader with a peer, have both students read the same article silently, and instruct them to come to an agreement on answers to the following questions:

- How is the article organized?
- What information is the writer trying to get across?
- How would you summarize the article?

L1

Additional Resources

Inclusion Strategies

Before Reading

Objectives

- To read and analyze two poems that express the poets' respective feelings about, and insights into, the natural world
- To identify stanzas in poetry
- To write an explanatory paragraph about what the insights in the poems reveal about nature

Skills

Reading/Thinking: Evaluating; Identifying Author's Purpose; Previewing
Writing: Poetry
Listening/Speaking: Sharing Poems
Grammar/Language: Capitalizing Sentences
Collaboration: Literature Groups

Motivating STUDENTS

Selection Focus Transparency 48: Before presenting the transparency, ask students to write in their journals about their personal relationships with nature.

Reading Focus: As an extension of the Reading Focus, have students share with a partner the story of a lost treasure and how it affected them.

Before You Read

Forgotten Language and *New World*

MEET SHEL SILVERSTEIN

Shel Silverstein wrote and illustrated witty books of children's poetry, but his quirky take on ordinary things appealed to adults as well. He hoped that a person of any age could pick up one of his books and have "a personal sense of discovery."

Shel Silverstein was born in 1932 and died in 1999. "Forgotten Language" was published in Where the Sidewalk Ends.

MEET N. SCOTT MOMADAY

N. Scott Momaday (mō′ mä dā) is a Pulitzer Prize-winning novelist, as well as a poet, painter, playwright, storyteller, and English professor. He won the Native American Prize for Literature in 1990.

N. Scott Momaday was born in 1934. "New World" was published in The Gourd Dancer.

READING FOCUS

Think about something natural that was once important to you but that you haven't thought about lately—the name of something, a dandelion, or a lady bug, for example. Why are things that once were important to you sometimes forgotten?

QuickWrite
Search your memory and list two or three additional things you once treasured.

Setting a Purpose
Read to find out about two lost pleasures.

BUILDING BACKGROUND

Shel Silverstein and N. Scott Momaday, like all good poets, describe the world in ways that make their readers see it in a new light. For example, when Momaday brings his Kiowa background to a story or poem, he helps readers make connections between themselves and nature. In a different way, Silverstein may ask a question that can be answered only after the reader's understanding has changed.

RESOURCE MANAGER

Teaching Tools and Resources
- Theme Six Planning Guide
- Literature Groups Sourcebook

Essential Lesson Support

Lesson-Specific Instruction
- Selection Focus Transparency 48
- Literary Elements Transparency 49
- Active Reading Guide,* p. 49

Assessment
- Selection Quick Checks,* p. 49
- Sel. and Theme Assmt., pp. 87–88
- Testmaker: ExamView Pro
- Performance Assessment, p. 46

Systematic Language Instruction
- Gr. & Comp. Hbk., L. 11.6

English Language Learners
- ELL Sourcebook, p. 71
- Spanish Summaries, p. 48
- Audio Library*

- English, Yes!

Spec. Needs/Strat. Interven.
- Interactive Rdg. Sbk., pp. T172–T174
- Interactive Rdg. Wkbk., p. 92
- Audio Library*

* Also available in Spanish

FORGOTTEN LANGUAGE

Shel Silverstein

Once I spoke the language of the flowers,
Once I understood each word the caterpillar said,
Once I smiled in secret at the gossip of the starlings,
And shared a conversation with the housefly
in my bed.
Once I heard and answered all the questions
of the crickets,
And joined the crying of each falling dying
flake of snow,
Once I spoke the language of the flowers. . . .
How did it go?
How did it go?

Reading the Selection

A Active Reading Strategies

EVALUATE Ask students to evaluate the author's presentation of the idea that the speaker has forgotten his contact with nature. Do they think this approach is effective? Why? *(The poem effectively follows the pattern of someone trying hard to recall a lost thought.)*

B Literary Elements

STANZA Point out to students that this poem is presented as a single stanza. Discuss how this provides a coherent idea of the poem.

Additional Resources

- ***Active Reading Guide,*** p. 49
- ***Audio Library***
- ***Spanish Audio Library***

C Author's Craft

REPETITION Discuss with students the effect of the repetition in the last two lines of the poem. Point out that authors often use this technique to stress an idea. Cite, for example, the last two lines of Robert Frost's poem "Stopping by Woods on a Snowy Evening": "And miles to go before I sleep,/And miles to go before I sleep." What effect does this repetition have? *(It emphasizes the point the author is trying to make.)*

Teaching Support

MEETING INDIVIDUAL NEEDS — ENGLISH LANGUAGE LEARNERS

Visualizing Tell students that to appreciate poetry, they do not have to understand every single word the first time they read or hear a poem. Nor is the poem to be taken literally. (For example, flowers do not talk.) At first, they should listen for the rhythm and spirit of the verse. As they do, they will find that the poetry produces images in their minds.

Activity Suggest that students close their eyes as you read poems. Then ask students to share the images that came to mind. Reread the words that elicited the images. Then discuss the specific words. COLLAB. LEARN.

Additional Resources

- ***English Language Learners Sourcebook,*** p. 71

D Active Reading Strategies

REVIEW Have students quote the lines of the poem that produce images in their minds. Ask students to find any common images from both poems. *(birds, such as starlings and eagles; insects, such as bees and crickets; flowers and trees)*

E Active Reading Strategies

RESPOND Read the poems aloud. Tell students to listen for, and list, words and phrases that stand out for them. Discuss them with the class.

F Literary Elements

SPEAKER Have the students identify the speaker and audience in the poem. *(The speaker is a Native American, like Momaday, who is speaking to the first man who lived on the land—the first Native American.)* What is the speaker's attitude toward nature? *(The speaker respects and reveres nature, which reflects his Native American heritage.)*

Teaching Support

NEW WORLD

N. Scott Momaday

1

First Man,
behold:
the earth
glitters
with leaves;
the sky
glistens
with rain.
Pollen
is borne
on winds
that low
and lean
upon
mountains.
Cedars
blacken
the slopes—
and pines.

2

At dawn
eagles
hie° and
hover°
above
the plain
where light
gathers
in pools.
Grasses
shimmer
and shine.
Shadows
withdraw
and lie
away
like smoke.

3

At noon
turtles
enter
slowly
into
the warm
dark loam.°
Bees hold
the swarm.
Meadows
recede
through planes
of heat
and pure
distance.

4

At dusk
the gray
foxes
stiffen
in cold;
blackbirds
are fixed
in the
branches.
Rivers
follow
the moon,
the long
white track
of the
full moon.

22 To *hie* is to move quickly.
23 To *hover* is to remain as if suspended in the air over a particular spot.

43 *Loam* is a type of soil.

Grammar and Language *Minilesson*

Capitalizing Sentences Remind students that a sentence contains a subject and a predicate that together express a complete thought. The first word of a sentence should be capitalized. This helps signify the break in thought between a sentence and the one before or after it. Explain to students that Momaday has written his poem in complete sentences, which are contained within the stanzas.

Activity Write the first stanza on the board without using capitalization. Have volunteers correct the capitalization on the board. Then have students go through the rest of the poem, noting how many sentences each stanza contains. **L2**

Additional Resources

- ***Grammar and Language Transparency 46***
- ***Grammar and Language Workbook,*** p. 243
- ***Grammar and Composition Handbook,*** Lesson 12.1
- ***Writer's Choice,*** Lesson 19.1

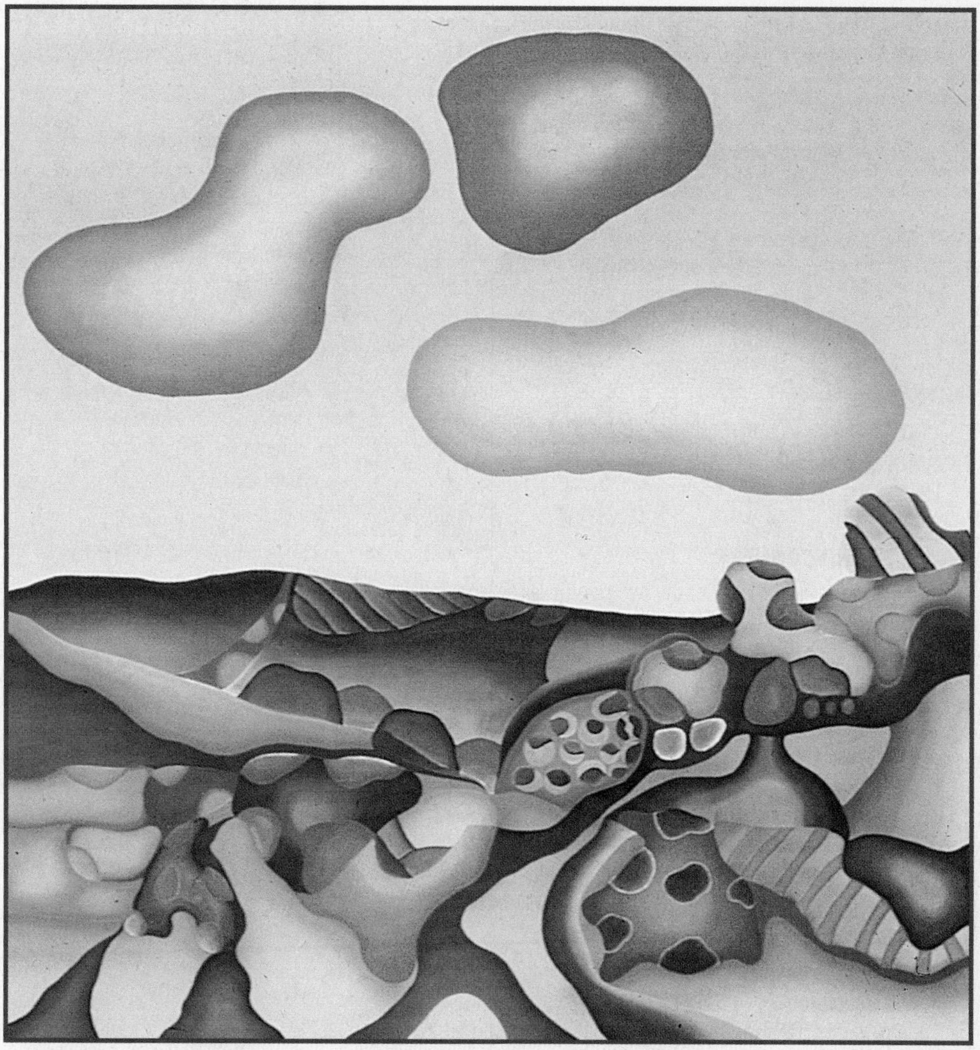

Pink Clouds and Desert, 1970. Linda Lomahaftewa. Oil on canvas, 60 x 60 in. Courtesy of the artist.

G Literary Elements

STANZAS "New World" is a multistanza poem. Have students discuss how authors get their message across in poems of various lengths.

H Critical Thinking

EVALUATE Ask students which images they thought were most effective in this poem. Why?

Thematic Focus

Flashes of Insight The poets put forth different views of people's relationship to nature. The juxtaposition of these two poems should encourage students to gain insights into what humanity's relationship to nature is and how that relates to their everyday lives.

ASSESSMENT

Quick Checks, p. 49

Reading Minilesson

Identify Author's Purpose Explain to students that authors write for different reasons. Some selections are meant to persuade an audience, some to entertain, some to inform, and others to describe—to name a few reasons, or purposes, for writing.

Activity Have students review the two poems and tell what they think were the authors' purposes in writing them. Do students think the authors had the same purpose in mind? Have students explain their answers and give support from the poems. **L2**

Additional Resources

Reading Skills Practice Workbook

Responding to the Selection

PERSONAL RESPONSE

There is no one correct response. Students should support their answers with examples.

Analyzing Literature

1. He no longer has that ability.
2. It takes place when human beings first walked the earth.
3. He has forgotten how to understand nature.
4. They may represent different times of day or different scenes or different periods of life.
5. Both are about human beings and nature. In one poem, a human being has distanced himself so much from nature that he can no longer understand it. In the other the human being is aware and open to the wonders of the land.
6. The poem presents nature from the point of view of a person just discovering something new.
7. In the poet's landscape there are no people, no buildings, no roads. In the future there may be fewer and smaller open spaces because of population growth.
8. Silverstein's poem may be closer to the experience of most people in our society: As we age, we become less attuned to the earth. Other students may relate more to Momaday's view: Each time and age has its own wonders and revelations.
9. Students should cite specific examples of the language that moves them.
10. Students' suggestions should be supported with details from the poems.

Active Reading and Critical Thinking

Responding to Literature

PERSONAL RESPONSE

- What specific words or phrases from these poems remind you to treasure the natural world?

Brackets connect questions that are paired to develop higher-level thinking skills.

Analyzing Literature

RECALL

1. What does the speaker in "Forgotten Language" say about the ability to speak "the language of the flowers"?
2. In what time period is "New World" set?

INTERPRET

3. Why is Silverstein's poem called "Forgotten Language"?
4. Why, do you think, did Momaday divide his poem into four parts?

EVALUATE AND CONNECT

5. How is the subject matter of the two poems alike? How is it different?
6. Theme Connection How does Momaday's poem offer you an opportunity to develop a new insight into the natural world?
7. In your opinion, which element described in "New World" has changed most over time? Which element, do you think, will change the most in the next hundred years?
8. Which of the poems, in your opinion, refers to experiences common to most people? Explain.
9. Briefly describe your thoughts about one of the poems. Explain how the poem's language creates that response in you.
10. Imagine that you are an artist. Reread one of the poems. What colors would you use in a painting to go with the poem? Name details from the poem that suggest these colors.

LITERARY ELEMENTS

Stanza

A **stanza** is a group of lines arranged together in a poem. The lines may be arranged to show a rhyming pattern or to create the form of a poem. You can recognize stanzas by the spaces that divide them.

1. Look at the form created by the stanzas in "New World." How does this form help strengthen the effect of the poem?
2. Why, do you think, did Silverstein write his poem in one stanza?

- See **Literary Terms Handbook**, p. R9.

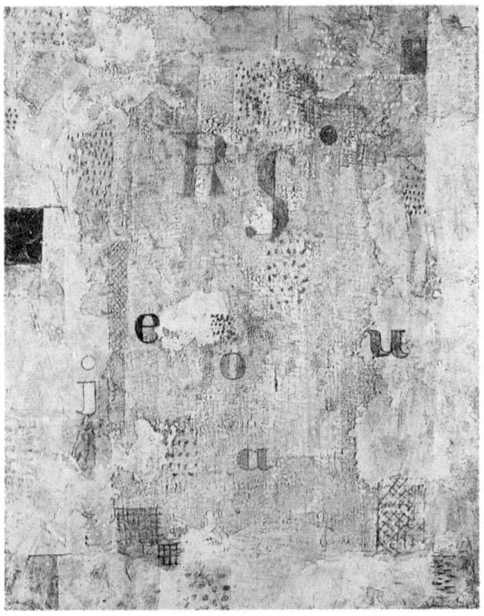

Vocal Fabric of the Singer Rosa Silber (Das Vokaltuch der Kammersangerin Rosa Silber), 1922. Paul Klee. Watercolor and plaster on muslin, mounted on cardboard, 24½ x 20½ in. The Museum of Modern Art, New York.

LITERARY ELEMENTS

1. Students may feel that each stanza is self-contained, picturing a full landscape at different times of day and of life.
2. He is concerned with only one thing: his loss of awareness, as he has aged, of the things around him. His inability to relate to nature as he once did is reinforced by an ending that trails off.

Additional Resources

Literary Elements Transparency 49

Extending Your Response

Writing About Literature

Nature Images Both poems are about nature and how views of nature may change. Write a paragraph comparing the images of nature that each poet uses. Why do some images appear in both poems? Which images do you think are most effective, and why?

Creative Writing

Natural Reflections Write a short poem that expresses your ideas about nature or something you once treasured. You might write a one-stanza poem that rhymes or a three-stanza poem that doesn't rhyme. Use your notes from the **Reading Focus** on page 566 as a starting place.

Listening and Speaking

Sharing Poems When poetry is read aloud, the reader often adds new meaning with gestures and **inflection**–the change in volume of a person's voice. In a group, take turns reading the poems aloud with expression and inflection, emphasizing the words that you think are important. Then discuss each reader's interpretation.

Literature Groups

Remembering the Earth Momaday, who is half Kiowa, often writes to express his respect and love for the earth, as he does in "New World." What can we learn from this attitude? How could it affect your own everyday thoughts and behavior?

Formal Mask, 1989. N. Scott Momaday.

Reading Further

If you enjoyed these poems about nature, try *In a Sacred Manner I Live* edited by Neil Philip.

Save your work for your portfolio.

Skill Minilesson

RETEACH • REVIEW

READING AND THINKING • PREVIEWING

A reader may get an idea of a poem's subject and style by previewing the title and first line. What connections might a reader make when reading the title "New World"? What is a "Forgotten Language"?

PRACTICE Think back to when you were previewing the two poems. Try to recall conclusions you drew. Select one of the poems. What were your expectations of the poem based on the title and first line? Explain why you were or were not surprised by what followed.

- For more about previewing, see **Reading Handbook,** p. R93.

Extending Your Response

Writing About Literature

Students' paragraphs should
- include specific examples from both poems
- give reasons to support their value judgments

Creative Writing

Students' poems should
- use original ideas and language
- show a personal reaction to the subject

Listening and Speaking

Students who have completed their first draft of a poem may benefit from hearing someone else read it. Hearing it read aloud may give them ideas of changes they would like to make.

Literature Groups Suggest that the discussion begin as a roundtable, with each person offering his or her response. Then have a moderator guide the group to find commonalities among the responses. COLLAB. LEARN.

Skill Minilesson

READING AND THINKING • PREVIEWING

Students' responses should
- show that they understand the strategy of active reading
- show that they understand the characteristics of the genre

Additional Resources

Reading Skills Practice Workbook

ASSESSMENT

- ***Quick Checks,*** p. 49
- ***Selection and Theme Assessment,*** pp. 87–88
- ***Performance Assessment,*** p. 46
- ***Testmaker: ExamView Pro***
- ***Interactive Tutor: Self-Assessment***

FLASHES OF INSIGHT 571

GRAMMAR LINK

Objective

- To use adjectives correctly

Teaching Strategies

After students read the two problems, point out that the sense of "more" or "most" is built into words such as *happier* and *happiest*. Adding the word *more* or *most* does not add emphasis to such an adjective. Suggest that if there are single words for the comparative and superlative forms of an adjective, these are the ones to use. Students should use *more* or *most* only when there is no single-word form.

Exercise

1. older
2. more grateful
3. best
4. most ridiculous
5. more honest

Additional Resources

- ***Grammar and Language Workbook,*** p. 133
- ***Grammar and Composition Handbook,*** Lesson 6.3
- ***Writer's Choice,*** Lesson 12.3

Teaching Support

GRAMMAR LINK

Using Adjectives Correctly

When you use an adjective to compare two things, use the **comparative** form of the adjective. Add *-er* to short adjectives and the word *more* to adjectives with at least two syllables.

*We live **longer** than our ancestors did. Are we **more** satisfied with our world?*

To compare more than two things, use the **superlative** form. Add *-est* to short adjectives; add *most* to adjectives with two or more syllables.

*Squeaky is the **fastest** thing on two feet. Raymond seems the **most awkward.***

Some adjectives are irregular and do not follow these patterns.

***Many** teens are on track teams. **More** teens run for fun. **Most** teens enjoy sports.*

Problem 1 *Squeaky is a gooder runner than her friend.*
Her friend is the baddest runner in school.

Solution *Good* and *bad* are irregular adjectives. The comparative form of *good* is *better;* the superlative form is *best.* For the adjective *bad,* the comparative form is *worse;* the superlative form is *worst.*

Squeaky is a better runner than her friend who is the worst runner in school.

Problem 2 *Being herself is more importanter than acting like a girl.*

Solution Never use both *-er* and *more* or *-est* and *most.*

Being herself is more important than acting like a girl.

For more about using adjectives correctly, see **Language Handbook**, p. R17.

EXERCISE

Write the correct comparative or superlative form of the adjective in parentheses.

1. Raymond isn't Squeaky's little brother because he's (old) than she is.
2. Squeaky thinks Mary Louise should be (grateful) to her than she is.
3. Squeaky says she is the (good) runner in the neighborhood.
4. The idea that Gretchen will win is the (ridiculous) thing Squeaky has ever heard.
5. Squeaky is (honest) about needing to practice her skills than Cynthia is.

Writing Minilesson

Writing a Description Have students reread the part of the paragraph on p. 558 in which Squeaky describes how she works herself up to run. Ask students how the writer uses comparative adjectives to show the effect Squeaky's preparations have on her. *("And all the time I'm dreaming this, I get lighter and lighter. . . .")*

Activity Have students write a description of someone trying to change something. It can be a character from "Raymond's Run" or from another story. Suggest that students conclude the description by using comparative and superlative adjectives to describe how the character's efforts succeed or fail. **L2**

Additional Resources

- ***Writer's Choice,*** Lesson 3.1

Before You Read

Thank You in Arabic

MEET
NAOMI SHIHAB NYE

Writing has been an insightful experience for Naomi Shihab Nye (nā ō′ mē shi häb nī). In 1992, soon after the Persian Gulf War, she published *This Same Sky: A Collection of Poetry from Around the World*. Nye, an Arab American, hoped to bring the war to a more human level. "So I found some poems by Iraqi poets and had the kids read them and let them see that these people were no different than we were," she said. "They had the same daily needs, the same inner lives."

Naomi Shihab Nye was born in Missouri in 1952. This memoir was first published in Going Where I'm Coming From *in 1995.*

READING FOCUS

Describe a situation in which you can't make people understand you, or you can't understand others.

Discuss
With a group, discuss why such situations can be upsetting.

Setting a Purpose
Read to find out how a teenage girl deals with situations she doesn't fully understand.

BUILDING BACKGROUND

The Time and Place The author is fourteen years old and is moving to Jerusalem with her family.

Did You Know? Jerusalem is a sacred city to the religions of Judaism, Christianity, and Islam. For centuries, people of these faiths have disputed borders in the Middle East and especially in Jerusalem. When Israel was established in 1948, Jerusalem was divided into an Israeli section and an Arab section. Since 1967, the city has been united under Israeli rule—a source of conflict between Israel and its Arab neighbors.

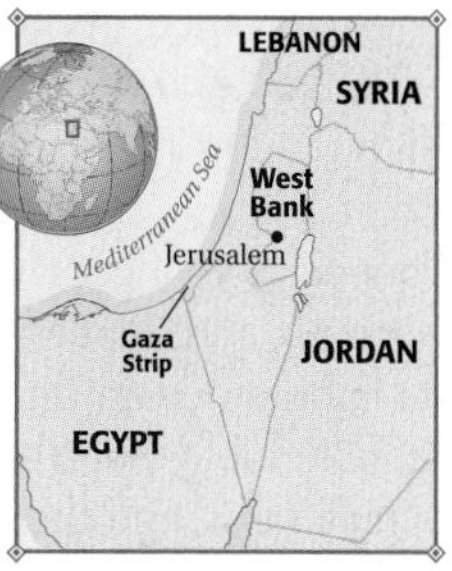

VOCABULARY PREVIEW

crevice (krev′ is) *n.* a narrow crack; p. 574
transition (tran zish′ ən) *n.* passage from one position, condition, or activity to another; change; shift; p. 576
insolence (in′ sə ləns) *n.* deliberate rudeness; disrespect; p. 578
valiant (val′ yənt) *adj.* brave; courageous; p. 582
pious (pī′ əs) *adj.* having either genuine or pretended religious devotion; p. 583
skirmish (skur′ mish) *n.* a brief or minor conflict; p. 583
virtue (vur′ choo͞) *n.* a good quality or admirable trait; p. 584

Before Reading

Objectives

- To read and analyze a memoir
- To identify setting in a literary work
- To write an analysis

Skills

Reading/Thinking: Inferring; Drawing Conclusions; Comparing and Contrasting; Analyzing Arguments; Problem Solving
Writing: Letter; Definition; Paragraphs; Analysis
Vocabulary: Suffixes; Word Meaning; Connotation
Life Skills: Interviewing
Grammar/Language: Prepositional Phrases; Punctuation in Compound Sentences
Listening/Speaking: Oral Presentation
Collaboration: Literature Groups

Motivating STUDENTS

Literature Launchers: "A Conversation with Naomi Nye"

Videodisc Side B, Segment 16

Also available in VHS.

Selection Focus Transparency 49: Have students view the transparency and then discuss the questions.

Reading Focus: As an extension of the Reading Focus, have students communicate a message to other students without using words.

RESOURCE MANAGER

Teaching Tools and Resources
- Theme Six Planning Guide
- Literature Groups Sourcebook

Essential Lesson Support

Lesson-Specific Instruction
- Selection Focus Transparency 49
- Literary Elements Transparency 50
- Active Reading Guide,* p. 50
- Selection Vocabulary Practice, p. 34
- *in*TIME magazine, pp. 14–15

Assessment
- Selection Quick Checks,* p. 50
- Sel. and Theme Assmt., pp. 89–90
- Testmaker: ExamView Pro
- Performance Assessment, p. 47

Systematic Language Instruction
- Gr. & Comp. Hbk., L. 11.7

English Language Learners
- ELL Sourcebook, pp. 72, 73
- Spanish Summaries, pp. 49
- Spanish Translations, pp. 121–131
- Audio Library*
- English, Yes!

Spec. Needs/Strat. Interven.
- Interactive Rdg. Sbk., pp. T175–T177
- Interactive Rdg. Wkbk., pp. 93–94
- Inclusion Strat. Sbk., pp. 57–58
- Audio Library*

* Also available in Spanish

Reading the Selection

SUMMARY

For Naomi, Missouri has been home. As Naomi adjusts to a new life in Jerusalem, she learns Arabic, sees new sights, makes new friends, and eats new foods. But a growing homesickness for the United States and signs of war sadden her. That war sends the family back to the United States, and Naomi realizes that for her the definition of home will include two places.

Spanish Summaries, p. 49

A Active Reading Strategies

REVIEW Ask students to reflect on what information the incident with the vitamins gives about the narrator, her brother, and their relationship with their mother. *(It reveals Naomi's close relationship with her brother. She observes the incident with respect for his composure.)*

VOCABULARY Remind students to use context clues to unlock the meanings of new vocabulary words.

Additional Resources

Active Reading Guide, p. 50

Audio Library

Spanish Audio Library

Thank You in Arabic

Naomi Shihab Nye

Shortly after my mother discovered my brother had been pitching his vitamin C tablets behind the stove for years, we left the country. Her sharp alert, "Now the truth be known!" startled us at the breakfast table as she poked into the dim crevice with the nozzle of her vacuum. We could hear the pills go click, click, up the long tube.

A My brother, an obedient child, a bright-eyed, dark-skinned charmer who scored high on all his tests and trilled a boy's sweet soprano, stared down at his oatmeal. Four years younger than I, he was also the youngest and smallest in his class. Somehow he maintained an intelligence and dignity more notable than those of his older, larger companions, and the pills episode was really a pleasant surprise to me.

Companions in mischief are not to be underestimated, especially when everything else in your life is about to change.

We sold everything we had and left the country. The move had been brewing for months. We took a few suitcases each. My mother cried when the piano went. I wished we could have saved it. My brother and I had sung so many classics over its keyboard— "Look for the Silver Lining" and "Angels We Have Heard on High"—that it would have been nice to return to a year later, when we came straggling back. I sold my life-size doll and my toy sewing machine. I begged my mother to save her red stove for me, so I could have it when I grew up—no one else we knew had a red stove. So my mother asked some friends to save it for me in their barn.

Our parents had closed their imported-gifts stores. Our mother ran a little shop in our neighborhood in St. Louis and our father ran a bigger one in a Sheraton Hotel downtown. For years my brother and I had been sitting with them behind the counters after school, guessing if people who walked through the door would buy something or only browse. We curled up with our library books on Moroccan hassocks and Egyptian camel saddles. I loved the stacks of waiting white paper bags as they lay together, and the reams of new tissue. B
I'd crease the folds as our smooth father in dark suit and daily drench of cologne counted change. Our mother rearranged shelves and penned the perfect tags with calligrapher's ink. My brother and I helped unpack the crates: nested Russian dolls, glossy mother-of-pearl earrings from Bethlehem, a family of sandalwood fans nestled in shredded packaging. Something wonderful was always on its way.

Vocabulary
crevice (krev′ is) *n.* a narrow crack

Teaching Support

CONNECTING TO OTHER SELECTIONS

COMPARING *selections*

This selection is paired with "If I Forget Thee, Oh Earth . . ." on pp. 591–595. A lesson for teaching a comparison of the two selections appears on p. 597.

The chart at the right shows three other ways to connect "Thank You in Arabic" to selections in this book.

For specific teaching strategies, see the ***Theme Six Planning Guide.***

Connection	Title
Life Skills: Lifelong Learning	"A Dictionary of Japanese-American Terms," p. 27
Thematic: Adjustments	"The Moustache," p. 282
Literary: Conflict	"The Medicine Bag," p. 78

But there were problems too. Sometimes whole days passed and nobody came in. It seemed so strange to wait for people to give you money for what you had. But that's what stores did everywhere. Then the stockroom filled with pre-Christmas inventory caught on fire and burned up, right when our father was between insurance policies. We could hear our parents in the living room, worrying and debating after we went to bed at night. Finally they had to give the business up. What seemed like such a good idea in the beginning—presents from around the world—turned into the sad sound of a broom sweeping out an empty space.

Our father had also been attending the Unity School for Christianity for a few years, but decided not to become a minister after all. We were relieved, having felt like imposters the whole time he was enrolled. He wasn't even a Christian, to begin with, but a gently nonpracticing Muslim. He didn't do anything like fasting or getting down on his knees five times a day. Our mother had given up the stern glare of her Lutheran ancestors, raising my brother and me in the Vedanta Society of St. Louis. When anyone asked what we were, I said, "Hindu." We had a swami,[1] and sandalwood incense. It was over our heads, but we liked it and didn't feel very attracted to the idea of churches and collection baskets and chatty parish good will.

Now and then, just to keep things balanced, we attended the Unity Sunday School. My teacher said I was lucky my father came from the same place Jesus came from. It was a passport to notoriety. She invited me to bring artifacts for Show and Tell. I wrapped a red and white *keffiyah* around my friend Jimmy's curly blond head while the girls in lacy socks giggled behind their hands. I told about my father coming to America from Palestine on the boat and throwing his old country clothes overboard before docking at Ellis Island.[2] I felt relieved he'd kept a few things, like the *keffiyah* and its black braided band. Secretly it made me mad to have lost the blue pants from Jericho with the wide cuffs he told us about.

Did You Know?
A *keffiyah* (usually spelled *kaffiyah*) is a type of Arab headdress consisting of folded cloth and a cord.

1. *Vedanta* is a branch of Hinduism, one of the major religions of India. A *swami* is a Hindu religious teacher.

2. *Notoriety* usually refers to being known for something bad, but the author uses it to mean simply "fame." *Artifacts* are objects, such as pots, used in the daily life of an ancient civilization. *Ellis Island,* near New York City, was the main U.S. immigration reception center from 1892 to 1943.

B Literary Elements

SETTING Point out that the author, with descriptive language, creates an exotic atmosphere in the import gift shop. Have students locate and read aloud examples of that language. *(She mentions the countries from which the merchandise comes: Moroccan hassocks, Egyptian camel saddles, Russian dolls, mother-of-pearl earrings from Bethlehem—all distant and exotic places.)*

C Literary Elements

EXTERNAL CONFLICT Explain that external conflict consists of a character's facing an opposing force outside of her- or himself. Discuss what external conflicts the narrator's family faces. *(A fire that destroys uninsured merchandise and slow business lead to money problems.)*

D Critical Thinking

INFERRING Help students infer what type of person the author's father is from her description of his past. *(He is a person who is always ready to try new things. He has moved from country to country, and he has even tried a new religion.)*

MEETING INDIVIDUAL NEEDS — ENGLISH LANGUAGE LEARNERS

Sharing Languages Many English language learners will identify with Naomi. How did they feel in an English-speaking environment for the first time? What were the first English words they learned?

Activity Have learners make a chart listing *thank you* and other words and phrases that visitors to another country might find useful. Involve other students by having class members choose a few words or phrases on the chart to learn with the aid of a partner. **L2**

COLLAB. LEARN.

Additional Resources

English Language Learners Sourcebook, p. 72

E Critical Thinking

DRAWING CONCLUSIONS Discuss with students in what ways the narrator and her brother are growing up ecumenically. *(Their Muslim father, who is married to a Lutheran, takes the children to Hindu services. Their father's involvement in the study of Christianity has exposed them to other religions as well.)*

F Literary Elements

SETTING Encourage students to be aware of how the author uses the senses (sight, hearing, and smell) to re-create the setting of her father's Christmas lectures. For example, when she describes hearing her father speak, she hints at not only the sound of his voice in the background—he is "an excellent speaker"—but also at the sights and smells of the canapés and tarts.

G Literary Elements

SETTING Point out to students the way the speaker describes her new home before even arriving. How do you think she knew what she would find there? *(She tells us that her father has passed on to them the folktales he has learned. He probably has described his home as well.)*

E I liked standing in front of the group, talking about my father's homeland. Stories felt like elastic bands that could stretch and stretch. Big fans purred inside their metal shells. I held up a string of olivewood camels. I didn't tell our teacher about the Vedanta Society. We were growing up ecumenical,[3] though I wouldn't know that word till a long time later in college. One night I heard my father say to my mother in the next room, "Do you think they'll be confused when they grow up?" and knew he was talking about us. My mother, bless her, knew we wouldn't be. She said, "At least we're giving them a choice." I didn't know then that more clearly than all the stories of Jesus, I'd remember the way our Hindu swami said a single word three times, "*Shantih, shantih, shantih*"—peace, peace, peace.

F Our father was an excellent speaker—he stood behind pulpits and podiums easily, delivering gracious lectures on "The Holy Land" and "The Palestinian Question." He was much in demand during the Christmas season. I think that's how he had fallen into the ministerial swoon.[4] While he spoke, my brother and I moved toward the backs of gathering halls, hovering over and eyeing the tables of canapes and tiny tarts, slipping a few into our mouths or pockets.

What next? Our lives were entering a new chapter, but I didn't know its title yet.

G We had never met our Palestinian grandmother, Sitti Khadra, or seen Jerusalem, where our father had grown up, or followed the rocky, narrow alleyways of the Via Dolorosa,[5] or eaten an olive in its own neighborhood. Our mother hadn't either. The Arabic customs we knew had been filtered through the fine net of folktales. We did not speak Arabic, though the lilt of the language was familiar to us—our father's endearments,[6] his musical blessings before meals. But that language had never lived in our mouths.

And that's where we were going, to Jerusalem. We shipped our car, a wide golden Impala, over on a boat. We would meet up with it later.

The first plane flight of my whole life was the night flight out of New York City across the ocean. I was fourteen years old. Every glittering light in every skyscraper looked like a period at the end of the sentence. Good-bye, our lives.

We stopped in Portugal for a few weeks. We were making a gradual transition. We stopped in Spain and Italy and Egypt, where the pyramids shocked me by sitting right on the edge of the giant city of Cairo, not way out in the desert as I had imagined them. While we waited for our baggage to clear customs, I stared at six tall African men in brilliantly patterned dashikis negotiating

Did You Know?
The *dashiki* is a loose, brightly colored African garment.

3. The writer uses *ecumenical* to mean that she was exposed to several different religions.
4. The *ministerial swoon* refers to the narrator's father falling in love with the idea of becoming a minister.
5. The *Via Dolorosa* (vē′ ə dō′ lə rō′ sə), or "Way of Sorrow," is the route by which Jesus was led to his execution.
6. *Endearments* are expressions of affection.

Vocabulary
transition (tran zish′ ən) *n.* passage from one position, condition, or activity to another; change; shift

Teaching Support

Listening and Speaking *Minilesson*

Oral Presentation The author says that she enjoys talking about her father's homeland in front of groups. Suggest that if she enjoys speaking, the audience probably has enjoyed listening, too. Point out that there is always interaction between speakers and their audience. The more positive that interaction, the better the experience for speaker and audience.

Activity Have students work in groups to compose a list of guidelines for making an oral presentation pleasant for both speaker and audience. Their suggestions might include the following:

- Speak on a subject of interest to the audience.
- Look at the audience, making occasional eye contact with people in all parts of the room.
- Speak naturally and vary your voice quality and tone.
- Add meaning to your words with facial expressions and gestures.

Post the lists where students can review the guidelines before making their own oral presentations. **L2** **COLLAB. LEARN.**

with an Egyptian customs agent[7] and realized I did not even know how to say "thank you" in Arabic. How was this possible? The most elemental[8] and important of human phrases in my father's own tongue had evaded me till now. I tugged on his sleeve, but he was busy with visas and passports.[9] "Daddy," I said. "Daddy, I have to know. Daddy, tell me. Daddy, why didn't we ever *learn*?" An African man adjusted his turban. Always thereafter, the word *shookrun*, so simple, with a little roll in the middle, would conjure up[10] the vast African baggage, the brown boxes looped and looped in African twine.

We stayed one or two nights at the old Shepheard's Hotel downtown but couldn't sleep due to the heat and honking traffic beneath our windows. So our father moved us to the famous Mena House Hotel next to the pyramids. We rode camels for the first time, and our mother received a dozen blood-red roses at her hotel room from a rug vendor who apparently liked her pale brown ponytail. The belly dancer at the hotel restaurant twined a gauzy pink scarf around my brother's astonished ten-year-old head as he tapped his knee in time to her music.

Back in our rooms, we laughed until we fell asleep. Later that night, my brother and I both awakened burning with fever and deeply nauseated, though nobody ever threw up. We were so sick that a doctor hung a Quarantine sign in Arabic and English on our hotel room door the next day. Did he know something we didn't know? I kept waiting to hear that we had malaria or typhoid, but no dramatic disease was ever mentioned. We lay in bed for a week. The aged doctor tripped over my suitcase every time he entered to take our temperatures. We smothered our laughter. "*Shookrun*," I would say. But as soon as he left, to my brother, "I feel bad. How do you feel?"

"I feel really, really bad."

"I think I'm dying."

"I think I'm already dead."

At night we heard the sound and lights show from the pyramids drifting across the desert air to our windows. We felt our lives stretching out across a thousand miles. The pharaohs stomped noisily through my head and churning belly. We had eaten spaghetti in the restaurant. I would not be able to eat spaghetti again for years.

Finally, finally, we appeared in the restaurant, thin and weakly smiling, and ordered the famous Mena House *shorraba*, lentil[11] soup, as my brother nervously scanned the room for the belly dancer. Maybe she wouldn't recognize him now.

In those days Jerusalem, which was then a divided city, had an operating airport on the Jordanian side. My brother and I remember flying in upside down, or in a plane dramatically tipped, but it may have been the effect of our medicine. The land reminded us of a dropped canvas, graceful brown hillocks and green patches. Small and provincial,[12] the airport had just two runways, and the first thing I observed as we climbed down slowly from the stuffy plane was all my underwear strewn across

7. A government's *customs agent* inspects imported goods and collects taxes on them.
8. Here, the writer uses *elemental* to mean "basic."
9. Her father's language had escaped her. A *visa* is written permission for a traveler to enter a country, whereas a *passport* identifies the traveler as a citizen of the country that issued it.
10. *Shookrun* is Arabic for "thank you." To *conjure up* something is to call it to mind.
11. The *lentil* is a vegetable related to peas.
12. A *provincial* airport is a local one used for short flights within a region.

H Critical Thinking

INFERRING Ask students to give insights into why the narrator feels it is so necessary to know how to say "thank you" in Arabic. *(Being able to say something as basic as thank you is important to Naomi. Without that ability, she feels separate and distant.)*

I Literary Elements

SETTING Have students discuss Egypt as a setting. Ask them how the setting affects the characters' moods and actions. *(Much of the scenery and many of the people are new to the characters. Trying to take it all in is exhilarating.)*

J Active Reading Strategies

EVALUATE Ask students to evaluate the author's description of her and her brother's illness. How effective is the dialogue in portraying how the children perceived the situation?

Reading Minilesson

Comparison and Contrast Students may better appreciate this memoir if they compare Nye's life in Jerusalem with her life in the United States.

Activity Have students fill in the following chart, as they skim through the selection, listing the similarities and differences of the two places she calls home. **L2**

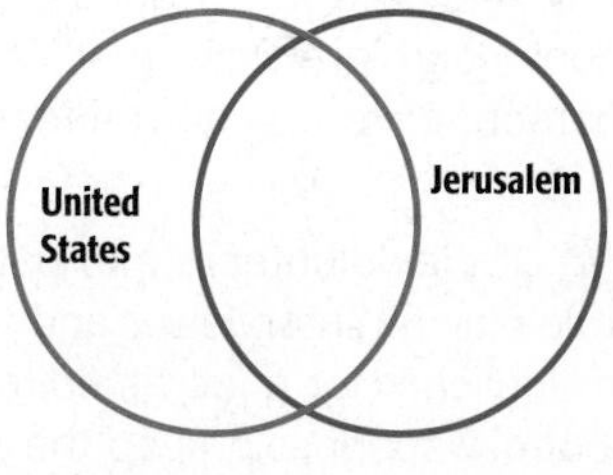

Additional Resources

Reading Skills Practice Workbook

K Literary Elements

SETTING When the narrator and her family reach Jerusalem, she is plunged into a new society and culture. Help students list and discuss the differences between this culture and the one Naomi has been exposed to until now. *(One example: In the United States she would not have been told she could not talk to boys. Nor, if she had politely protested a rule, would she have been expelled from school.)*

L Active Reading Strategies

RESPOND Ask students why they think the rule about speaking to people of the opposite sex was imposed. *(In certain cultures the men and women have distinct roles, and boys and girls learn them early.)*

M Critical Thinking

ANALYZING ARGUMENTS Do students think that the author gives a valid argument for continuing to talk to the boys at her school? Have them support their opinions.

one of them. There were my flowered cotton briefs and my pink panties and my slightly embarrassing raggedy ones and my extra training bra, alive and visible in the breeze. Somehow my suitcase had popped open in the hold and dropped its contents the minute the men pried open the cargo door. So the first thing I did on the home soil of my father was re-collect my underwear, down on my knees, the posture of prayer over that ancient holy land.

Our relatives came to see us at a hotel. Our grandmother was very short. She wore a long, thickly embroidered Palestinian dress, had a musical, high-pitched voice and a low, guttural[13] laugh. She kept touching our heads and faces as if she couldn't believe we were there. I had not yet fallen in love with her. Sometimes you don't fall in love with people immediately, even if they're your own grandmother. Everyone seemed to think we were all too thin.

We moved into a second-story flat in a stone house eight miles north of the city, among fields and white stones and wandering sheep. My brother was enrolled in the Friends Girls School and I was enrolled in the Friends Boys School in the town of Ramallah a few miles farther north—it all was a little confused. But the Girls School offered grades one through eight in English and high school continued at the Boys School. Most local girls went to Arabic-speaking schools after eighth grade.

I was a freshman, one of seven girl students among two hundred boys, which would cause me problems a month later. I was called in from the schoolyard at lunchtime, to the office of our counselor who wore shoes so pointed and tight her feet bulged out pinkly on top.

"You will not be talking to them anymore," she said. She rapped on the desk with a pencil for emphasis.

"To whom?"

"All the boy students at this institution. It is inappropriate behavior. From now on, you will speak only with the girls."

"But there are only six other girls! And I like only one of them!" My friend was Anna, from Italy, whose father ran a small factory that made matches. I'd visited it once with her. It felt risky to walk the aisles among a million filled matchboxes. Later we visited the factory that made olive oil soaps and stacked them in giant pyramids to dry.

"No, thank you," I said. "It's ridiculous to say that girls should only talk to girls. Did I say anything bad to a boy? Did anyone say anything bad to me? They're my friends. They're like my brothers. I won't do it, that's all."

The counselor conferred with the headmaster and they called a taxi. I was sent home with a little paper requesting that I transfer to a different school. The charge: insolence. My mother, startled to see me home early and on my own, stared out the window when I told her.

My brother came home from his school as usual, full of whistling and notebooks. "Did anyone tell you not to talk to girls?" I asked him. He looked at me as if I'd gone goofy. He was too young to know

13. A *guttural* laugh would have a rough, harsh sound.

Vocabulary
insolence (in′ sə ləns) *n.* deliberate rudeness; disrespect

Teaching Support

LIFE SKILLS CONNECTION

Interviewing Explain that when applying for a job or interviewing for admission to a new school, good interviewing skills can help a person make a positive impression.

Activity Divide volunteers into pairs, one to role-play an interviewer and the other an applicant for a job as editor of the school newspaper. To keep the situation realistic, neither person should know what the other is going to say. Give interviewers time to think of questions and interviewees time to consider what they want to say about their qualifications for the job. Ask partners to conduct a five-minute interview before the class while other students take notes on what they think are good interview traits and what should be avoided. Compile a chart of interviewing do's and don'ts from students' notes. **L2** **COLLAB. LEARN.**

the troubles of the world. He couldn't even imagine them.

N "You know what I've been thinking about?" he said. "A piece of cake. That puffy white layered cake with icing like they have at birthday parties in the United States. Wouldn't that taste good right now?" Our mother said she was thinking about mayonnaise. You couldn't get it in Jerusalem. She'd tried to make it and it didn't work. I felt too gloomy to talk about food.

My brother said, "Let's go let Abu Miriam's chickens out." That's what we always did when we felt sad. We let our fussy landlord's red-and-white chickens loose to flap around the yard happily, puffing their wings. Even when Abu Miriam shouted and waggled his cane and his wife waved a dishtowel, we knew the chickens were thanking us.

O My father went with me to the St. Tarkmanchatz Armenian[14] School, a solemnly ancient stone school tucked deep into the Armenian Quarter of the Old City of Jerusalem. It was another world in there. He had already called the school officials on the telephone and

14. *Armenia* is a small country east of Turkey. In the late 1800s and early 1900s, Armenians fled Turkish rule, and some settled in Jerusalem.

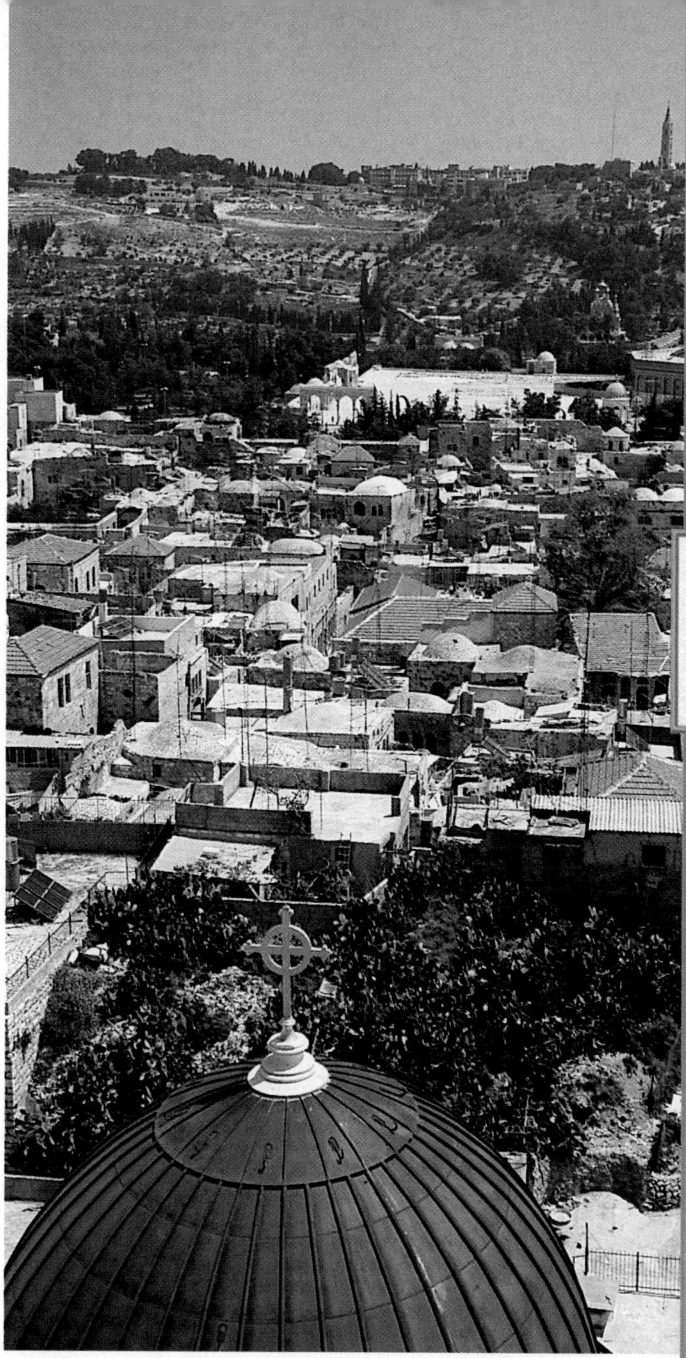

Old City, Jerusalem.

Viewing the photograph: What facts about Jerusalem does this photograph present?

N Literary Elements

SETTING Point out to students that setting includes such things as food. The little things add up to a sense of home.

O Active Reading Strategies

PREDICT Ask students whether they think the author will enjoy her time at the new school, given her first impression of the place. Have them support their opinions.

VIEWING THE PHOTOGRAPH

Viewing Response *Jerusalem is an old and crowded city. Its low-rise profile is in contrast to those of many American cities.*

INTERDISCIPLINARY CONNECTION

Art Explain that over the centuries Jerusalem has been home to people of many cultures and therefore to many art styles.

Activity Have students research the art and architecture of Jerusalem over the centuries and give a brief oral report on one kind, showing photographs from books. If individual students report on different time periods, have them deliver their reports in chronological order. **L2**

Critical Thinking

DRAWING CONCLUSIONS Guide students to conclude that some members of the family have adapted better than others to their new life in Jerusalem. Encourage students to base their thinking on clues in the text. Share the following:

Model: I read that Naomi's father got her into an Armenian school by citing the educational code of the city. This suggests that he is knowledgeable about the culture. Naomi gets angry or gloomy, so I conclude that she is unhappy. After Naomi is expelled from school, her mother merely stares out the window. I interpret this response as meaning that she is somewhat overwhelmed.

Active Reading Strategies

RESPOND Ask students what they think the purpose is of the "hands-and-fingernails check." *(to ensure cleanliness)*

Vo•cab•u•lar•y Skills

Suffixes The suffix *-ian* does end most, though not all, Armenian names. As in many cultures, the names may refer to the place from which the first person to carry that name came. They are similar in that way to such English words as *Bostonian* and *Washingtonian*, except they have become family names.

tried to enroll me, though they didn't want to. Their school was for Armenian students only, kindergarten through twelfth grade. Classes were taught in three languages: Armenian, Arabic and English, which was why I needed to go there. Although most Arab students at other schools were learning English, I needed a school where classes were actually taught in English—otherwise I would have been staring out the windows triple the usual amount.

> I felt I had left my old life entirely.

The head priest wore a long robe and a tall cone-shaped hat. He said, "Excuse me, please, but your daughter, she is not an Armenian, even a small amount?"

"Not at all," said my father. "But in case you didn't know, there is a stipulation[15] in the educational code books of this city that says no student may be rejected solely on the basis of ethnic background, and if you don't accept her, we will alert the proper authorities."

They took me. But the principal wasn't happy about it. The students, however, seemed glad to have a new face to look at. Everyone's name ended in *-ian,* the beautiful, musical Armenian ending—Boghossian, Minassian, Kevorkian, Rostomian. My new classmates started calling me Shihabian. We wore uniforms, navy blue pleated skirts for the girls, white shirts, and navy sweaters. I waited during the lessons for the English to come around, as if it were a channel on television. While other students were on the other channels, I scribbled poems in the margins of my pages, read library books, and wrote a lot of letters filled with exclamation points. All the other students knew all three languages with three entirely different alphabets. How could they carry so much in their heads? I felt humbled by my ignorance. One day I felt so frustrated in our physics class—still another language—that I pitched my book out the open window. The professor made me go collect it. All the pages had let loose at the seams and were flapping free into the gutters along with the white wrappers of sandwiches.

Every week the girls had a hands-and-fingernails check. We had to keep our nails clean and trim, and couldn't wear any rings. Some of my new friends would invite me home for lunch with them, since we had an hour-and-a-half break and I lived too far to go to my own house.

Their houses were a thousand years old, clustered bee-hive-fashion behind ancient walls, stacked and curled and tilting and dark, filled with pictures of unsmiling relatives and small white cloths dangling crocheted edges. We ate spinach pies and white cheese. We dipped our bread in olive oil, as the Arabs did. We ate small sesame cakes, our mouths full of crumbles. They taught me to say "I love you" in Armenian, which sounded like *yes-kay-see-goo-see-rem.* I felt I had left my old life entirely.

Every afternoon I went down to the basement of the school where the kindergarten class was having an Arabic lesson.

15. A *stipulation* is a condition or restriction.

Teaching Support

MEETING INDIVIDUAL NEEDS — MULTIPLE MODES OF EXPRESSION

Linguistic Read aloud this sentence from p. 580: "While other students were on the other channels, I scribbled poems in the margins of my pages, read library books, and wrote a lot of letters filled with exclamation points." Discuss with students why the author may have used so many exclamation points. Students should understand that she was trying to communicate the depth of her emotions. Point out that from this selection it is clear that the author no longer finds it necessary to use exclamation points to express her feelings.

Activity Have students write a letter that the young Naomi might have written, "filled with exclamation points." Then have students locate examples within the selection in which Naomi, as a mature writer, describes the events they wrote about. **L2**

580 THEME 6

Their desks were pint-sized, their full white smocks tied around their necks. I stuffed my fourteen-year-old self in beside them. They had rosy cheeks and shy smiles. They must have thought I was a very slow learner.

More than any of the lessons, I remember the way the teacher rapped the backs of their hands with his ruler when they made a mistake. Their little faces puffed up with quiet tears. This pained me so terribly I forgot all my words. When it was my turn to go to the blackboard and write in Arabic, my hand shook. The kindergarten students whispered hints to me from the front row, but I couldn't understand them. We learned horribly useless phrases: "Please hand me the bellows for my fire." I wanted words simple as tools, simple as *food* and *yesterday* and *dreams*. The teacher never rapped my hand, especially after I wrote a letter to the city newspaper, which my father edited, protesting such harsh treatment of young learners. I wish I had known how to talk to those little ones, but they were just beginning their English studies and didn't speak much yet. They were at the same place in their English that I was in my Arabic.

R From the high windows of St. Tarkmanchatz, we could look out over the Old City, the roofs and flapping laundry and television antennas, the pilgrims and churches and mosques, the olivewood prayer beads and fragrant *falafel*[16] lunch stands, the intricate interweaving of cultures and prayers and songs and holidays.

16. The most ancient section of Jerusalem is called the *Old City.* The *pilgrims* are travelers of all faiths who come to visit, or worship at, the city's holy places. *Mosques* are Muslim places of worship, and *falafel* is an Arab food consisting of ground, spiced vegetables shaped into balls and fried.

We saw the barbed wire separating Jordan from Israel then, the bleak, uninhabited strip of no-man's land reminding me how little education saved us after all. People who had differing ideas still came to blows, imagining fighting could solve things. Staring out over the quiet roofs of afternoon, I thought it so foolish. I asked my friends what they thought about it and they shrugged.

"It doesn't matter what we think about it. It just keeps happening. It happened in Armenia too, you know. Really, really bad in Armenia. And who talks about it in the world news now? It happens everywhere. It happens in *your* country one by one, yes? Murders and guns. What can we do?"

Sometimes after school, my brother and I walked up the road that led past the crowded refugee camp of Palestinians who owned even less than our modest relatives did in the village. The little kids were stacking stones in empty tin cans and shaking them. We waved our hands and they covered their mouths and laughed. We wore our beat-up American tennis shoes and our old sweatshirts and talked about everything we wanted to do and everywhere else we wished we could go.

"I want to go back to Egypt," my brother said. "I sort of feel like I missed it. Spending all that time in bed instead of exploring—what a waste."

"I want to go to Greece," I said. "I want to play a violin in a symphony orchestra in Austria." We made up things. I wanted to go back to the United States most of all. Suddenly I felt like a patriotic citizen. One of my friends, Sylvie Markarian, had just been shipped off to Damascus, Syria, to marry a man who was fifty years old, a widower. Sylvie was exactly my age—we S

Vocabulary Skills

Word Meaning The term *no-man's land* means, as its components suggest, a place where no human being lives. Its origins go back to the fourteenth century. It referred to an area of land outside the north wall of London where criminals were executed. No one wanted to live in such a place. The meaning of *no-man's land* was extended to cover military zones such as the one in Jerusalem—spaces between opposing armies or governments. It is also used figuratively to describe any gray, or indefinite, area.

R Literary Elements

SETTING Ask students to find examples in which the author creates an atmosphere with descriptive language that appeals to the senses of sight, sound, and smell. *(She describes the sights, sounds, and foods of the city, as in the paragraph about the view from the windows of St. Tarkmanchatz.)*

S Active Reading Strategies

RESPOND Have students discuss the fact that the author's friend, at the age of 15, was marrying a 50-year-old man she had never met. How do students feel about the custom of arranging marriages? Have them support their opinions with valid reasons. Suggest that they look for reasons for or against the tradition. *(Example: Parents might be less impressed with superficial attractiveness than with qualities that might endure.)*

Writing Minilesson

Writing a Definition Read to students this line from Robert Frost's poem "Death of a Hired Man": "Home is the place where, when you have to go there, they have to take you in." Have students speculate about whether Naomi Shihab Nye would accept that definition of home and ask them to explain their opinions.

Activity Have students write their own definitions of home. Suggest that they use language that evokes the feelings they have about home. Some students may want to express their feelings in the form of a poem. **L2**

Additional Resources

Writer's Choice, Lesson 5.1

T Literary Elements

CHARACTER Help students understand what the author's reaction to her friend Sylvie's fate reveals about her.

U Critical Thinking

INFERRING Ask students what they can infer from the author's statement "They never seemed to get tired of us." *(The author and her family are endlessly intriguing—a novelty. Just conversing with them is entertainment for the family.)* Point out that although the attention may be flattering, the author is missing America and the home she finds familiar—where she is seen as an ordinary person.

V Active Reading Strategies

QUESTION Ask students to list reasons they think the narrator begins crying without any apparent cause. *(She misses home, she feels uncomfortable in the new culture, and she misses—as well as feels sorry for—her friend.)*

Teaching Support

had turned fifteen two days apart. She had never met her future husband before. I thought this was the most revolting thing I had ever heard of. "Tell your parents no thank you," I urged her. "Tell them you *refuse*."

Sylvie's eyes were liquid, swirling brown. I could not see clearly to the bottom of them.

"You don't understand," she told me. "In United States you say no. We don't say no. We have to follow someone's wishes. This is the wish of my father. Me, I am scared. I never slept away from my mother before. But I have no choice. I am going because they tell me to go." She was sobbing, sobbing on my shoulder. And I was stroking her long, soft hair. After that, I carried two fists inside, one for Sylvie and one for me.

Most weekends my family went to the village to sit with the relatives. We sat and sat and sat. We sat in big rooms and little rooms, in circles, on chairs or on woven mats or brightly covered mattresses piled on the floor. People came in and out to greet my family. Sometimes even donkeys and chickens came in and out. We were like movie stars or dignitaries. They never seemed to get tired of us.

My father translated the more interesting tidbits of conversation, the funny stories my grandmother told. She talked about angels and food and money and people and politics and gossip and old memories from my father's childhood, before he emigrated away from her. She wanted to make sure we were going to stick around forever, which made me feel very nervous. We ate from mountains of rice and eggplant on large silver trays—they gave us little plates of our own since it was not our custom to eat from the same plate as other people. We ripped the giant wheels of bread into triangles. Shepherds passed through town with their flocks of sheep and goats, their long canes and cloaks, straight out of the Bible. My brother and I trailed them to the edge of the village, past the lentil fields to the green meadows studded with stones, while the shepherds pretended we weren't there. I think they liked to be alone, unnoticed. The sheep had differently colored dyed bottoms, so shepherds could tell their flocks apart.

During these long, slow, smoke-stained weekends—the men still smoked cigarettes a lot in those days, and the old *taboon,* my family's mounded bread-oven, puffed billowy clouds outside the door—my crying jags began. I cried without any warning, even in the middle of a meal. My crying was usually noiseless but dramatically wet—streams of tears pouring down my cheeks, onto my collar or the back of my hand.

Everything grew quiet.

Someone always asked in Arabic, "What is wrong? Are you sick? Do you wish to lie down?"

My father made valiant excuses in the beginning. "She's overtired," he said. "She has a headache. She is missing her friend who moved to Syria. She is homesick just now."

My brother stared at me as if I had just landed from Planet X.

Vocabulary
valiant (val′ yənt) *adj.* brave; courageous

MEETING INDIVIDUAL NEEDS: SPECIAL NEEDS

Learning Disabled Learning-disabled students may be able to identify with the narrator's frustration at being mistaken for a "slow learner."

Activity Have students discuss the following scenes:

- the classroom scene in which instructions are given in three languages (p. 580)
- the classroom scene in the basement with the narrator and the kindergartners (p. 581)

Discuss how students might feel in these situations. **L1** COLLAB. LEARN.

Additional Resources

Inclusion Strategies

W

Worst of all was our drive to school every morning, when our car came over the rise in the highway and all Jerusalem lay sprawled before us in its golden, stony splendor pockmarked with olive trees and automobiles. Even the air above the city had a thick, religious texture, as if it were a shining brocade[17] filled with broody incense. I cried hardest then. All those hours tied up in school lay just ahead. My father pulled over and talked to me. He sighed. He kept his hands on the steering wheel even when the car was stopped and said, "Someday, I promise you, you will look back on this period in your life and have no idea what made you so unhappy here."

"I want to go home." It became my anthem. "This place depresses me. It weighs too much. I hate all these old stones that everybody keeps kissing. I'm sick of pilgrims. They act so pious and pure. And I hate the way people stare at me here." Already I'd been involved in two street skirmishes with boys who stared a little too hard and long. I'd socked one in the jaw and he socked me back. I hit the other one straight in the face with my purse.

"You could be happy here if you tried just a little harder," my father said. "Don't compare it to the United States all the time. Don't pretend the United States is perfect. And look at your brother—he's not having any problems!"

"My brother is eleven years old."

I had crossed the boundary from uncomplicated childhood when happiness was a good ball and a hoard[18] of candy-coated Jordan almonds.

One problem was that I had fallen in love with four different boys who all played in the same band. Two of them were even twins. I never quite described it to my parents, but I wrote reams and reams of notes about it on loose-leaf paper that I kept under my sweaters in my closet.

Such new energy made me feel reckless. I gave things away. I gave away my necklace and a whole box of shortbread cookies that my mother had been saving. I gave my extra shoes away to the gypsies. One night when the gypsies camped in a field down the road from our house, I thought about their mounds of white goat cheese lined up on skins in front of their tents, and the wild *oud*[19] music they played deep into the black belly of the night, and I wanted to go sit around their fire. Maybe they could use some shoes.

X

I packed a sack of old loafers that I rarely wore and walked with my family down the road. The gypsy mothers stared into my shoes curiously. They took them into their tent. Maybe they would use them as vases or drawers. We sat with small glasses of hot, sweet tea until a girl bellowed from deep in her throat, threw back her head, and began dancing. A long bow thrummed across the strings. The girl circled the fire, tapping and clicking, trilling a long musical wail from deep in her throat. My brother looked

17. *Brocade* is a heavy cloth woven with raised designs.

18. A *hoard* is a quantity of something stored up for future use.

19. The *oud* (o͞od) is a stringed instrument of southwest Asia and northern Africa.

Vocabulary

pious (pī′ əs) *adj.* having either genuine or pretended religious devotion

skirmish (skur′ mish) *n.* a brief or minor conflict

W Literary Elements

SETTING Point out how the author's description of the setting changes when her attitude toward the setting changes. For example, She says the place depresses her because it weighs too much. "I hate all these old stones . . . I'm sick of pilgrims."

FYI

Gypsies Gypsies are members of a culture that may have originated in northern India and who were originally known for their nomadic lifestyle. The term *gypsy,* when not capitalized, refers to any person who lives his or her life traveling in the same way many Gypsies do.

X Author's Craft

DESCRIPTIVE LANGUAGE Ask students how the author brings her experience with the Gypsies to life by using descriptive details. *(She describes the mounds of goat cheese, the wild music and singing, and the "black belly of the night.")*

MEETING INDIVIDUAL NEEDS — ENGLISH LANGUAGE LEARNERS

Idioms Write the following sentences from the selection on the board, underlining the idioms:

1. *My father translated the more interesting tidbits of conversation.*
2. *My brother stared at me as if I had just landed from Planet X.*

Explain that knowing one sense of a word may help students figure out the meaning of an expression. For example: (1) a *tidbit* is a tasty bit of food or, in this case, an interesting bit of information; (2) *X* can stand for the unknown, so *Planet X* is any unknown place.

Activity Have students find other idioms and discuss their meanings in small groups. **COLLAB. LEARN.**

Additional Resources

English Language Learners Sourcebook, p. 73

Historical Note

The Six Day War of 1967 was, in part, a result of the Cold War between the Soviet Union and the United States. It began with Syrian guerrilla raids on Israel, to which Israel retaliated. The Soviet Union reported that Israel was planning an all-out attack on Syria. In May, Egypt forced United Nations troops to withdraw from the buffer zone between Egypt and Israel. Then Egypt closed the Gulf of Aqaba to Israeli shipping. Jordan and Iraq allied with Egypt. On June 6, the Israelis, with military aid from the United States, struck. The war was over in six days, and all of Jerusalem was under Israel's control.

Y Active Reading Strategies

RESPOND Ask students to imagine how they would feel if they left family behind in a war-torn land. *(Worry about relatives and one's own inability to protect them.)*

Z Active Reading Strategies

QUESTION Ask students why they think the author's parents decided not to return to Missouri. *(They probably have some bad memories there, because their store burned down and they had been in financial trouble.)*

Teaching Support

nervous. He was remembering the belly dancer in Egypt, and her scarf. I felt invisible. I was pretending to be a gypsy. My father stared at me. Didn't I recognize the exquisite oddity of my own life when I sat right in the middle of it? Didn't I feel lucky to be here? Well, yes I did. But sometimes it was hard to be lucky.

In the barbed-wire no-man's land visible from the windows of our house, guns cracked loudly in the middle of the night.

When we left Jerusalem, we left quickly. Left our beds in our rooms and our car in the driveway. Left in a plane, not sure where we were going. The rumbles of fighting with Israel had been growing louder and louder. In the barbed-wire no-man's land visible from the windows of our house, guns cracked loudly in the middle of the night. We lived right near the edge. My father heard disturbing rumors at the newspaper that would soon grow into the infamous Six Day War[20] of 1967. We were in England by then, drinking tea from thin china cups and scanning the newspapers. Bombs were blowing up in Jerusalem. We worried about the village. We worried about my grandmother's dreams, which had been getting worse and worse, she'd told us. We worried about the house we'd left, and the chickens, and the children at the refugee camp. But there was nothing we could do except keep talking about it all.

My parents didn't want to go back to Missouri because they'd already said goodbye to everyone there. They thought we might try a different part of the country. They weighed the virtues of different states. Texas was big and warm. After a chilly year crowded around the small gas heaters we used in Jerusalem, a warm place sounded appealing. In roomy Texas, my parents bought the first house they looked at. My father walked into the city newspaper and said, "Any jobs open around here?"

I burst out crying when I entered a grocery store—so many different kinds of bread.

A letter on thin blue airmail paper reached me months later, written by my classmate, the bass player in my favorite Jerusalem band. "Since you left," he said, "your empty desk reminds me of a snake ready to strike. I am afraid to look at it. I hope you are having a better time than we are."

Of course I was, and I wasn't. *Home* had grown different forever. *Home* had doubled. Back *home* again in my own country, it seemed impossible to forget the place we had just left: the piercing call of the *muezzin*[21] from the mosque at

20. *Infamous* means "having a reputation for evil or criminal acts." The *Six Day War* between Israel and the Arab countries of Egypt, Syria, and Jordan resulted in Israel expanding its boundaries and taking control of Jerusalem.

21. The *muezzin* (mo͞o′ zən), or crier, calls the time for Muslims to pray five times daily.

Vocabulary
virtue (vur′ cho͞o) *n.* a good quality or admirable trait

Grammar and Language *Minilesson*

Prepositional Phrases Write the following phrases on the board: *on thin blue airmail paper, by my classmate, of a snake, in my own country.* Remind students that each underlined word is a preposition, a word that shows the relationship between a noun or pronoun and some other word in a sentence.

Activity Ask students to locate other prepositional phrases from the story. Add these to the list on the board, underlining the preposition in each one. Or list just the prepositions on the board, which should include *for, during, at, over, from,* and *with.* Ask students first to think of a phrase that begins with each preposition. Then have them choose five of the phrases and use them in sentences. **L2**

Additional Resources

- ***Grammar and Language Transparency 47***
- ***Grammar and Language Workbook,*** p. 141
- ***Grammar and Composition Handbook,*** Lesson 7.1
- ***Writer's Choice,*** Lesson 13.1

Untitled. Illustration by Nancy Carpenter. From *Sitta's Secret.*
Viewing the painting: Imagine this meeting. What may be happening?

prayer time, the dusky green tint of the olive groves, the sharp, cold air that smelled as deep and old as my grandmother's white sheets flapping from the line on her roof. What story hadn't she finished?

Our father used to tell us that when he was little, the sky over Jerusalem crackled with meteors and shooting stars almost every night. They streaked and flashed, igniting the dark. Some had long golden tails. For a few seconds, you could see their whole swooping trail lit up. Our father and his brothers slept on the roof to watch the sky. "There were so many of them, we didn't even call out every time we saw one."

During our year in Jerusalem, my brother and I kept our eyes cast upwards whenever we were outside at night, but the stars were different since our father was a boy. Now the sky seemed too orderly, stuck in place. The stars had learned where they belonged. Only people on the ground kept changing.

Viewing the Illustration

Viewing Response Have students explore the painting through questions.

- Is power being transferred?
- Is the woman consoling or supporting the girl?
- Whose is the "flash of insight"?

Active Reading Strategies

RESPOND Discuss with students how the author's idea of home has changed since the beginning of the story. *(Now, she says, her sense of home has doubled. It has elements of Jerusalem as well as of the United States.)*

Thematic Focus

Flashes of Insight Be sure students understand what the narrator means about home. Explain that she realizes that both her American and her Arabic ancestries are important to her concept of home. She will carry aspects of both with her to wherever she lives and calls home.

Assessment

Quick Checks, p. 50

Real-World Connection

Music Ask students to think of song lyrics that express feelings similar to those of the young Naomi. Have students form groups in which they share the lines that seem to capture those emotions. Students should be able to answer such questions as *What is each lyric about? How are the experiences they describe the same? How are they different?* and *Which song might Naomi have especially appreciated at the time?* **L1**

Responding to the Selection

PERSONAL RESPONSE

Students should cite specific examples from the text.

Analyzing Literature

1. Money problems—brought on by a lack of business and the fire that destroyed uninsured inventory—force the Shihabs to close their business.
2. *Shookrun* means "thank you."
3. It makes her think that getting an education was not enough to stop people from believing that fighting would solve anything.
4. He's only eleven years old.
5. She seems uncertain of the future. She is also fearful that she's left her past life behind forever.
6. She may feel that lacking this "most elemental and important of human phrases" shuts her off from the simplest communication with most of the people around her.
7. She is worried and feels powerless to do anything but talk about it.
8. Part of it is being an adolescent and dealing with the new sensations of a maturing body. Another part is her feeling that she just doesn't fit in there.
9. She understands that her Arab heritage is as much a part of her sense of home as her American heritage.
10. She may look beyond her experiences in the United States for her view of what "normal" everyday life is, and perhaps she will be more adventurous in making friends and choosing new experiences.

Active Reading and Critical Thinking

Responding to Literature

PERSONAL RESPONSE

- Which incidents or images from this selection stay in your mind? Jot them down in your journal and tell why they affected you.

Brackets connect questions that are paired to develop higher-level thinking skills.

Analyzing Literature

RECALL

1. Why do the Shihabs close their business and move to Jerusalem?
2. How do you say *thank you* in Arabic?
3. What does the barbed wire separating Jordan from Israel make young Naomi think about?
4. What reason does Naomi give for her brother's not being homesick?

INTERPRET

5. In your opinion, how does the narrator feel about her parents' decision to move?
6. Why is Naomi upset about not being able to say *thank you* in Arabic?
7. How does Naomi feel about the prospect of her father's people going to war with Israel?
8. Why, in your opinion, does Naomi cry so much while she is in Jerusalem?

EVALUATE AND CONNECT

9. Theme Connection What insight does Naomi gain from her experience in Jerusalem?
10. In your opinion, how might Naomi's year in Jerusalem have affected her life after she returned to the United States? Explain.

LITERARY ELEMENTS

Setting

The time and place in which the events of a story occur are its **setting.** In "Thank You in Arabic," Nye uses sensory images to portray her home near Jerusalem. For example, on the drive to school, "all Jerusalem lay sprawled before us in its golden, stony splendor pockmarked with olive trees and automobiles. Even the air above the city had a thick, religious texture, as if it were a shining brocade filled with broody incense."

1. Why is the time an important element in the setting of this selection?
2. In your opinion, which place was most important in the narrator's life? How did the writer show this? Explain your choice.

- See **Literary Terms Handbook**, p. R9.

LITERARY ELEMENTS

1. Jerusalem is facing war, which affects her family's choice of homes. Also, her age is an important factor.
2. Students may feel that the United States is more important. The narrative begins and ends there. But the point of the selection is how this first visit to Jerusalem broadened Naomi's thinking.

Additional Resources

Literary Elements Transparency 50

Literature and Writing

Personal Writing

Your Own Awakening Think back to your discussion from the **Reading Focus** on page 573. What situation have you experienced that led to some sort of an awakening, or flash of insight? It might be a new way of understanding your family or geographic heritage. In a few paragraphs, describe the experience, including your thoughts and reactions.

Writing About Literature

Close Characters In this memoir, Naomi Shihab Nye describes her childhood experiences in her father's homeland. What do you learn about the relationship between Naomi and her father from this memoir? Look at descriptions of Naomi and her father, as well as their actions and dialogue. Write a brief analysis of her changing relationship with her father.

Extending Your Response

Literature Groups

Friendly Advice When Naomi's friend Sylvie learns that her parents want her to marry a man she has never met, Naomi urges her to refuse. What would you advise Sylvie to do? What would you do if you were in her position? Discuss possible solutions to Sylvie's situation.

Interdisciplinary Activity

Social Studies With a partner, research the history of the Middle East since 1948 (when the present state of Israel was founded). Draw maps of the changing borders at four points in time: 1949, 1968, 1991, and the present.

Learning for Life

Rules of Conduct Naomi gets into trouble in the Friends Boys School because she talks to the boys. What are some of the rules of your school or group of friends—written rules or generally accepted ways to behave—that someone from another place might not know? Write a list of these rules so that a newcomer might fit in. Discuss with the class how the newcomer might view your rules.

Reading Further

To discover places important to other people, read

Madeleine L'Engle's Time Quartet by Madeleine L'Engle

Dandelion Wine by Ray Bradbury

Save your work for your portfolio.

Literature and Writing

Personal Writing

Students' paragraphs should

- clearly describe a personal awakening
- describe the student's thoughts and reactions to the experience

Writing About Literature

Students' analyses should

- include the students' perceptions of that relationship
- be supported by examples and interpretations of incidents from the selection

Extending Your Response

Literature Groups Point out that any advice students might give Sylvie would depend on her being able and willing to carry it out. COLLAB. LEARN.

Interdisciplinary Activity Encourage students to use various sources in their research, such as periodicals, history books, and the Internet.

Learning for Life Invite students to suggest additional rules that they think should be enforced.

Teaching Support

MEETING INDIVIDUAL NEEDS — SPECIAL NEEDS

Less-Proficient Readers Some students may need help distinguishing fact from opinion in a nonfiction selection. Remind them that sentences that begin with "I think/thought" or "I feel/felt" state the author's opinions. Descriptive words, such as *excellent* and *beautiful*, usually indicate opinions. On the other hand, statistics and figures are usually based on fact, although the facts may sometimes be incorrect.

Activity Pair less-proficient readers with more skilled readers and have them review the selection, looking for examples of facts and opinions. Discuss their findings with the class. **L1** COLLAB. LEARN.

Skill Minilessons

GRAMMAR AND LANGUAGE
PUNCTION IN COMPOUND SENTENCES

1. We worried about the children at the refugee camp; however, there was . . .
2. I wish I had known how to talk to those little ones, but they were . . .
3. They took me; however, the . . .
4. Our father had also been attending the Unity School for Christianity for a few years, but he . . .
5. Something wonderful was always on its way, but there were . . .

READING AND THINKING
PROBLEM AND SOLUTION

Students' analyses should recognize that Naomi's solutions were not always appropriate to the society in which she was living, which was one reason she felt out of place there.

VOCABULARY
CONNOTATION

1. unpleasant
2. pleasant
3. none
4. unpleasant
5. unpleasant

Additional Resources

- ***Grammar and Language Workbook,*** pp. 259, 265
- ***Grammar and Composition Handbook,*** Lesson 14.1
- ***Writer's Choice,*** Lessons 20.3, 20.5
- ***Reading Skills Practice Workbook,*** pp. 91–92
- ***Vocabulary Practice,*** p. 34

RETEACH • REVIEW

Skill Minilessons

GRAMMAR AND LANGUAGE • PUNCTUATION IN COMPOUND SENTENCES

Follow these rules when punctuating compound sentences.

- When the clauses of a compound sentence are joined by a conjunction, use a comma before the conjunction.
- When there is no conjunction joining two clauses of a compound sentence, use a semicolon before, and a comma after, the conjunctive adverb that joins the clauses. Some common conjunctive adverbs are *therefore, however, then, nevertheless, consequently,* and *besides.*

For more about punctuation in a compound sentence, see **Language Handbook,** p. R12.

PRACTICE Punctuate the following sentences.

1. We worried about the children at the refugee camp however there was nothing we could do except keep talking about it.
2. I wish I had known how to talk to those little ones but they were just beginning their English studies and didn't speak much yet.
3. They took me however, the principal wasn't happy about it.
4. Our father had also been attending the Unity School for Christianity for a few years but he decided not to become a minister after all.
5. Something wonderful was always on its way but there were problems too.

READING AND THINKING • PROBLEM AND SOLUTION

Most stories revolve around a main character facing a **problem** and attempting to find a **solution** for the problem. During Naomi's year-long stay in Jerusalem, she faces many problems, from finding a suitable school to dealing with what she considers harsh treatment of students.

PRACTICE Reread the memoir to see how Nye has organized the text using problems and solutions. Create a chart showing several examples.

For more about problems and solutions, see **Reading Handbook,** pp. R106–R107.

VOCABULARY • CONNOTATION

When you want to create a mood or influence your readers' attitude, you can sometimes use words in a way that adds to their meaning. This added meaning is the word's **connotation.** For example, Nye uses three descriptive synonyms–*bulge, puff,* and *stuff.* Nye uses the words in contexts that give them connotations that influence the reader's attitude or mood.

PRACTICE Tell if each underlined word has no connotation, a pleasant connotation, or an unpleasant connotation.

1. I was called in from the schoolyard at lunchtime, to the office of our counselor who wore shoes so pointed and tight her feet <u>bulged</u> out pinkly on top.
2. That <u>puffy</u> white layered cake with icing like they <u>have</u> at birthday parties in the United States.
3. We let our fussy landlord's red-and-white chickens loose to flap around the yard happily, <u>puffing</u> their wings.
4. Their little faces <u>puffed</u> up with quiet tears.
5. I <u>stuffed</u> my fourteen-year-old self in beside them.

For more about connotation, see **Reading Handbook,** p. R92.

ASSESSMENT

- ***Quick Checks,*** p. 50
- ***Selection and Theme Assessment,*** pp. 89–90
- ***Performance Assessment,*** p. 47
- ***Testmaker: ExamView Pro***
- ***Interactive Tutor: Self-Assessment***

MEDIA Connection

OPINION POLL

Who are more concerned about the environment–teens or their parents? A poll offers some insights.

EarthView Poll Highlights

In March 1998, a thousand teenagers and a thousand "baby boomers" (adults then forty to fifty-five years old) took part in a national poll about the environment. Below are some highlights of the survey, sponsored by the National 4-H Council and Honda.

Future of the Environment

1. Boomers and teens agree that we are running out of time to save the world's environment from permanent damage.
   - Teens: 77%
   - Boomers: 67%

Sources of Environmental Damage

2. Greatest barriers to improving environmental conditions in the United States:
   - "Lack of individual concern": teens: 45%, boomers: 32%
   - Corporations: teens: 20%, boomers: 32%
   - Government leaders: teens: 19%, boomers: 22%

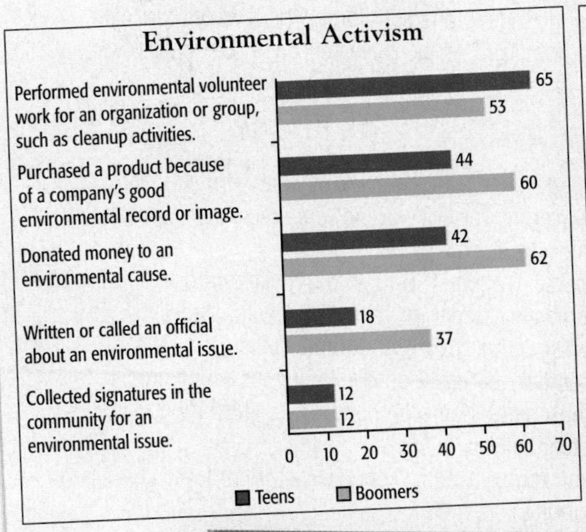

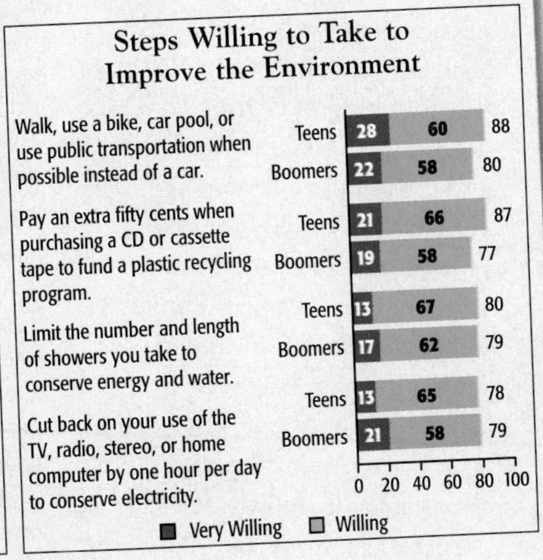

Analyzing Media

1. With a group, summarize the information on each graph. What do these graphs tell you about the concerns of teens and parents for the environment?
2. What programs or ideas to protect the environment do you think are most effective?

MEDIA Connection

Objective

- To read a survey report and understand the insights offered by polls

Literature LINK

If I Forget Thee, O Earth . . .
Explain that in the next selection—a science fiction story—students will get an unusual view of Earth. Science fiction often projects futuristic scenarios of conditions that are possible if current trends continue. Suggest that students keep the results of the poll in mind as they read "If I Forget Thee, O Earth . . ."

Analyzing Media

1. Responses should be supported by data.
2. Responses should be personal and supported by sound reasoning.

Informational Text

*in*TIME For more examples of informational text, direct students to the articles in the *inTIME* magazine.

Additional Resources

Media Connections, p. 12

Teaching Support

Reading *Minilesson*

Central Idea Tell students that an oft-quoted saying of the environmental movement came out of the mouth of a fictional character. The late Walt Kelley's creation was an opossum named Pogo, who lived in the Okefenokee Swamp (a real place). Speaking of an endangered environment, Pogo says, "We have met the enemy, and he is us."

Activity Write the quotation on the board and have students in small groups discuss their understanding of it. Then have them reread the selection to identify which populations support it and which seem opposed. **L2**

Additional Resources

Reading Skills Practice Workbook

interNET CONNECTION

Online Allies Students concerned with preserving the environment may locate Internet sites sponsored by environmental activists.

Before Reading

Objectives

- To read and analyze a science fiction story
- To identify the difference between science fiction and fantasy

Skills

Reading/Thinking: Drawing Conclusions; Cause and Effect
Writing: Speech
Vocabulary: Word Meaning
Grammar/Language: Participles
Listening/Speaking: Political Speech
Collaboration: Literature Groups

Motivating STUDENTS

Selection Focus Transparency 50: Have students view the transparency and then discuss the questions provided.

Reading Focus: As an extension of the Reading Focus, have students share their predictions with a partner.

Before You Read

"If I Forget Thee, Oh Earth . . ."

MEET ARTHUR C. CLARKE

Arthur C. Clarke has been a fan of futuristic fiction since he was twelve years old. "Science fiction is virtually the only kind of writing that's dealing with real problems and possibilities; it's a concerned fiction," Clarke says. He was a successful author when he moved to Sri Lanka in 1956 to set up an underwater exploration business. Clarke is a native of England who has written more than fifty books, including *2001: A Space Odyssey.*

Arthur C. Clarke was born in 1917. He wrote "If I Forget Thee, Oh Earth . . ." in 1950.

READING FOCUS

Where do you think the human race will be in 500 years?

Freewrite
Take a few moments to write your prediction of life in the distant future.

Setting a Purpose
Read to discover the connection between a distant past and a fictional future.

BUILDING BACKGROUND

The Time and Place The story takes place somewhere in our solar system in the distant future.

Did You Know? The title of this story is taken from the Book of Psalms in the Bible. The original psalm begins "If I forget thee, O Jerusalem" and was sung by the Jewish captives in Egypt during the pharaohs' time. The Jews felt torn away from their homeland, as the characters are in Clarke's story.

VOCABULARY PREVIEW

purged (purjd) *adj.* cleansed of whatever is unclean; p. 591
unwavering (un wā′ vər ing) *adj.* unchanging; not shifting or moving; steady; p. 592
disperse (dis purs′) *v.* to go off in different directions; p. 592
steadfastly (sted′ fast′ lē) *adv.* faithfully; steadily; p. 593
anguish (ang′ gwish) *n.* extreme suffering; p. 594
perennial (pə ren′ ē əl) *adj.* lasting for a long time; p. 595
comprehend (kom′ pri hend′) *v.* to grasp mentally; understand fully; p. 595
scour (skour) *v.* to rub energetically in order to clean, wash, or brighten; p. 595
insight (in′ sīt) *n.* an understanding of the inner character or hidden nature of something; p. 595

RESOURCE MANAGER

Teaching Tools and Resources
- Theme Six Planning Guide
- Literature Groups Sourcebook

Essential Lesson Support
Lesson-Specific Instruction
- Selection Focus Transparency 50
- Literary Elements Transparency 51
- Active Reading Guide,* p. 51
- Selection Vocabulary Practice, p. 35
- *in*TIME magazine, pp. 3–5

Assessment
- Selection Quick Checks,* p. 51
- Sel. and Theme Assmt., pp. 91–92
- Testmaker: ExamView Pro
- Performance Assessment, p. 48

Systematic Language Instruction
- Gr. & Comp. Hbk., L. 11.8
- Vocabulary Power, Lesson 25
- Spelling Power, Lesson 22

English Language Learners
- ELL Sourcebook, p. 74
- Spanish Summaries, p. 50
- Spanish Translations, pp. 132–135
- Audio Library*
- English, Yes!

Spec. Needs/Strat. Interven.
- Interactive Rdg. Sbk., pp. T177–T179
- Interactive Rdg. Wkbk., pp. 95–96
- Inclusion Strat. Sbk., pp. 49–50
- Audio Library*

* Also available in Spanish

"IF I FORGET THEE, OH EARTH..."

Arthur C. Clarke

When Marvin was ten years old, his father took him through the long, echoing corridors that led up through Administration and Power, until at last they came to the uppermost levels of all and were among the swiftly growing vegetation of the Farmlands. Marvin liked it here: it was fun watching the great, slender plants creeping with almost visible eagerness toward the sunlight as it filtered down through the plastic domes to meet them. The smell of life was everywhere, awakening inexpressible longings in his heart: no longer was he breathing the dry, cool air of the residential levels, purged of all smells but the faint tang of ozone.[1] He wished he could stay here for a little while, but Father would not let him. They went onward until they had reached the entrance to the Observatory, which he had never visited: but they did not stop, and Marvin knew with a sense of rising excitement that there could be only one goal left. For the first time in his life, he was going Outside.

1. *Ozone* is a gas that has a sharp odor and is sometimes used as a disinfectant. Ozone is present in the earth's atmosphere.

Vocabulary
purged (purjd) *adj.* cleansed of whatever is unclean

Reading the Selection

SUMMARY

When Marvin is ten years old, his father takes him to the outer reaches of their colony in space. The experience is intended to give him an insight into the past and future of his people. All that is left of the past on Earth is a radioactive ruin from an atomic Armageddon. The hope for the future is that someday the poisons will clear away so that the Colony's descendants will be able to reclaim Earth.

Spanish Summaries, p. 50

A Active Reading Strategies

QUESTION Ask students why they think the writer opens with a description of the different environments through which Marvin and his father pass. *(This immediately introduces the reader to the setting of the story and establishes it as a futuristic environment.)*

VOCABULARY Remind students to use context clues to unlock the meanings of new vocabulary words.

Additional Resources

Active Reading Guide, p. 51

Audio Library

Spanish Audio Library

Teaching Support

CONNECTING TO OTHER SELECTIONS

COMPARING *selections*

This selection is paired with "Thank You in Arabic" on pp. 574–586. A lesson for teaching a comparison of the two selections appears on p. 597.

The chart at the right shows three ways to connect "If I Forget Thee, Oh Earth . . ." to other selections in this book.

For specific teaching strategies, see the ***Theme Six Planning Guide.***

Connection	Title
Life Skills: Planning and Designing	*The Diary of Anne Frank,* p. 697
Thematic: Future Generations	"Legacies," p. 182
Literary: Mood	from *Anne Frank: The Diary of a Young Girl*, p. 675

B Active Reading Strategies

VISUALIZE To help students form mental pictures of Marvin and his father on board their vehicle, read aloud the paragraph beginning "There were a dozen . . ." as students close their eyes to visualize the images. Call for volunteers to describe what they see.

C Literary Elements

SCIENCE FICTION Explain to students that one of the most important elements of science fiction is the setting. How do students know immediately that this is science fiction? *(Clarke provides a futuristic world with his description of the stars and the landscape, which is typical of science fiction.)*

Vocabulary Skills

Word Meaning After students have read the definition of *unscintillating*, ask them which term they would prefer to have describe their conversations: *scintillating* or *unscintillating*. Explain that the verb *scintillate* emerged around 1623 to describe an action that threw off sparks. The adjective *scintillating* came to describe a "live and witty conversation."

Teaching Support

B There were a dozen of the surface vehicles, with their wide balloon tires and pressurized cabins, in the great servicing chamber. His father must have been expected, for they were led at once to the little scout car waiting by the huge circular door of the airlock. Tense with expectancy, Marvin settled himself down in the cramped cabin while his father started the motor and checked the controls. The inner door of the lock slid open and then closed behind them: he heard the roar of the great air pumps fade slowly away as the pressure dropped to zero. Then the "Vacuum" sign flashed on, the outer door parted, and before Marvin lay the land which he had never yet entered.

C He had seen it in photographs, of course: he had watched it imaged on television screens a hundred times. But now it was lying all around him, burning beneath the fierce sun that crawled so slowly across the jet-black sky. He stared into the west, away from the blinding splendor of the sun—and there were the stars, as he had been told but had never quite believed. He gazed at them for a long time, marveling that anything could be so bright and yet so tiny. They were intense unscintillating[2] points, and suddenly he remembered a rhyme he had once read in one of his father's books:

Twinkle, twinkle, little star,
How I wonder what you are.

Well, *he* knew what the stars were. Whoever asked that question must have been very stupid. And what did they mean by "twinkle"? You could see at a glance that all the stars shone with the same steady, unwavering light. He abandoned the puzzle and turned his attention to the landscape around him.

They were racing across a level plain at almost a hundred miles an hour, the great balloon tires sending up little spurts of dust behind them. There was no sign of the Colony: in the few minutes while he had been gazing at the stars, its domes and radio towers had fallen below the horizon. Yet there were other indications of man's presence, for about a mile ahead Marvin could see the curiously shaped structures clustering round the head of a mine. Now and then a puff of vapor would emerge from a squat smokestack and would instantly disperse.

They were past the mine in a moment: Father was driving with a reckless and exhilarating[3] skill as if—it was a strange thought to come into a child's mind—he were trying to escape from something. In a few minutes they had reached the edge of the plateau on which the Colony had been built. The ground fell sharply away beneath them in a dizzying slope whose lower stretches were lost in shadow. Ahead, as far as the eye could reach, was a jumbled wasteland of craters, mountain ranges, and ravines. The crests of the mountains, catching the low sun, burned like islands

2. Stars seem to be twinkling, *scintillating* (sint′ əl ā′ ting), when seen through Earth's atmosphere. These stars are *unscintillating;* they do not twinkle.

3. Father drives with skill, but the recklessness makes the ride exciting, or *exhilarating* (ig zil′ ə rāt ing).

Vocabulary
unwavering (un wā′ vər ing) *adj.* unchanging; not shifting or moving; steady
disperse (dis purs′) *v.* to go off in different directions

MEETING INDIVIDUAL NEEDS — ENGLISH LANGUAGE LEARNERS

Listening and Note-Taking Have all students discuss the selection thus far. They might answer such questions as *Where does the story take place?* and *Why do you think they are there?* Model good listening and note-taking skills for English language learners. Also, encourage all speakers to speak slowly and clearly so that everyone can follow their answers.

Activity Ask English language learners to review their notes and sum up what other students have said during the discussion. Then encourage them to add their own ideas.

Additional Resources
English Language Learners Sourcebook, p. 74

of fire in a sea of darkness: and above them the stars still shone as steadfastly as ever.

There could be no way forward—yet there was. Marvin clenched his fists as the car edged over the slope and started the long descent. Then he saw the barely visible track leading down the mountainside, and relaxed a little. Other men, it seemed, had gone this way before.

Night fell with a shocking abruptness as they crossed the shadow line and the sun dropped below the crest of the plateau. The twin searchlights sprang into life, casting blue-white bands on the rocks ahead, so that there was scarcely need to check their speed. For hours they drove through valleys and past the foot of mountains whose peaks seemed to comb the stars, and sometimes they emerged for a moment into the sunlight as they climbed over higher ground.

And now on the right was a wrinkled, dusty plain, and on the left, its ramparts and terraces[4] rising mile after mile into the sky, was a wall of mountains that marched into the distance until its peaks sank from sight below the rim of the world. There was no sign that men had ever explored this land, but once they passed the skeleton of a crashed rocket, and beside it a stone cairn surmounted[5] by a metal cross.

It seemed to Marvin that the mountains stretched on forever: but at last, many hours later, the range ended in a towering, precipitous[6] headland that rose steeply from a cluster of little hills. They drove down into a shallow valley that curved in a great arc toward the far side of the mountains: and as they did so, Marvin slowly realized that something very strange was happening in the land ahead.

The sun was now low behind the hills on the right: the valley before them should be in total darkness. Yet it was awash with a cold white radiance that came spilling over the crags beneath which they were driving. Then, suddenly, they were out in the open plain, and the source of the light lay before them in all its glory.

It was very quiet in the little cabin now that the motors had stopped. The only sound was the faint whisper of the oxygen

6. *Precipitous* means "very steep."

NASA photograph of the moon.

Viewing the photograph: In what ways is this vehicle like the one Marvin and his father travel in? In what ways is it different?

4. Here, the *ramparts* are high, steep banks or cliffs, and *terraces* are level strips of land.

5. A *cairn* is a mound of stones piled up as a memorial. This one is topped, or *surmounted,* with a cross.

Vocabulary

steadfastly (sted′ fast′ lē) *adv.* faithfully; steadily

D Active Reading Strategies

RESPOND Ask students how the atmosphere the writer creates makes them feel. *(gloomy, fearful)*

E Literary Elements

SCIENCE FICTION One element that is common to most science fiction is suspense. Ask how the author produces suspense during the long ride. *(The author makes the journey seem eerie and dangerous as the vehicle speeds through nearly complete darkness. Suddenly the darkness is replaced by a "cold white radiance.")* Point out that the suspense is not yet resolved; the reader doesn't yet know what the source of the light is.

F Active Reading Strategies

QUESTION Ask students what they think Marvin is thinking as the motor stops and he looks on the scene in silence. *(He may be expecting that something important is about to happen.)*

VIEWING THE PHOTOGRAPH

Viewing Response *Students should make a point-by-point comparison, involving size, structure, and mobility.*

MEETING INDIVIDUAL NEEDS — SPECIAL NEEDS

Learning Disabled Tell students that this story takes place in the future. Have them think about any movies, novels, or television programs they have seen or read that take place in the future. How did the people dress? Were the buildings they lived in like ours? How were they different?

Activity Have students draw a picture of what they think the Colony in this story looks like. Encourage them to share and explain their drawings. **L1**

Additional Resources

Inclusion Strategies

Active Reading Strategies

PREDICT Marvin knows the outside world through books and photographs but not firsthand. Ask students to predict what he will learn about what has changed the world. Encourage students to base their predictions on what they have read in this story and what they know about science fiction. Share the following model:

Model: Based on what I've read, I assume that Marvin will learn that he and the others are on another planet because something terrible happened on Earth. Knowing the possibilities of nuclear destruction today, I think that he will learn that Earth was destroyed by a nuclear bomb or meltdown.

Author's Craft

DESCRIPTIVE LANGUAGE Without ever referring directly to the specific time or place, the author uses descriptive language to produce two contrasting worlds that affect Marvin. Help students make a list of words and phrases that affected them most.

VIEWING THE PHOTOGRAPH

Viewing Response *(The moon appears to be arid, rocky, and hilly or mountainous.)*

feed and an occasional metallic crepitation[7] as the outer walls of the vehicle radiated away their heat. For no warmth at all came from the great silver crescent that floated low above the far horizon and flooded all this land with pearly light. It was so brilliant that minutes passed before Marvin could accept its challenge and look steadfastly into its glare, but at last he could discern the outlines of continents, the hazy border of the atmosphere, and the white islands of cloud. And even at this distance, he could see the glitter of sunlight on the polar ice.

The moon.
Viewing the photograph: What scientific statement does the photo make?

It was beautiful, and it called to his heart across the abyss of space. There in that shining crescent were all the wonders that he had never known—the hues of sunset skies, the moaning of the sea on pebbled shores, the patter of falling rain, the unhurried benison[8] of snow. These and a thousand others should have been his rightful heritage, but he knew them only from the books and ancient records, and the thought filled him with the anguish of exile.

Why could they not return? It seemed so peaceful beneath those lines of marching cloud. Then Marvin, his eyes no longer blinded by the glare, saw that the portion of the disk that should have been in darkness was gleaming faintly with an evil phosphorescence: and he remembered. He was looking upon the funeral pyre of a world—upon the radioactive aftermath of Armageddon.[9] Across a quarter of a million miles of space, the glow of dying

7. A series of repeated crackles, rattles, or similar sounds is called *crepitation.*
8. *Benison* means "a blessing."
9. The *phosphorescence* (fos′ fə res′ əns) is a glow; a *pyre* (pīr) is a pile of wood used for burning a dead body; and *Armageddon* (är′ mə ged′ ən), here, refers to nuclear war. A Bible prophecy connects Armageddon, a place in Israel, with the world's great and final battle between good and evil.

Vocabulary
anguish (ang′ gwish) *n.* extreme suffering

Teaching Support

Grammar and Language *Minilesson*

Participles Write the following phrases on the board, asking students to identify the function of the underlined words:

shining crescent
marching cloud
falling rain

Remind students that present participles, or *-ing* verb forms, can also function as adjectives, or descriptive words. On this page the author uses them effectively to accentuate the contrast between the lonely outpost of the Colony and life as it was when Earth was alive and habitable.

Activity Have students look through the last two pages of the selection to find other phrases with highly visual participles used as adjectives. Add them to the list on the board. **L2**

Additional Resources

- ***Grammar and Language Transparency 48***
- ***Grammar and Language Workbook,*** p. 171
- ***Grammar and Composition Handbook,*** Lesson 9.1
- ***Writer's Choice,*** Lesson 13.1

atoms was still visible, a perennial reminder of the ruinous past. It would be centuries yet before that deadly glow died from the rocks and life could return again to fill that silent, empty world.

And now Father began to speak, telling Marvin the story which until this moment had meant no more to him than the fairy tales he had once been told. There were many things he could not understand: it was impossible for him to picture the glowing, multicolored pattern of life on the planet he had never seen. Nor could he comprehend the forces that had destroyed it in the end, leaving the Colony, preserved by its isolation, as the sole survivor. Yet he could share the agony of those final days, when the Colony had learned at last that never again would the supply ships come flaming down through the stars with gifts from home. One by one the radio stations had ceased to call: on the shadowed globe the lights of the cities had dimmed and died, and they were alone at last, as no men had ever been alone before, carrying in their hands the future of the race.

Then had followed the years of despair, and the long-drawn battle for survival in this fierce and hostile world. That battle had been won, though barely: this little oasis of life was safe against the worst that Nature could do. But unless there was a goal, a future toward which it could work, the Colony would lose the will to live, and neither machines nor skill nor science could save it then.

So, at last, Marvin understood the purpose of this pilgrimage. He would never walk beside the rivers of that lost and legendary world, or listen to the thunder raging above its softly rounded hills. Yet one day—how far ahead?—his children's children would return to claim their heritage. The winds and the rains would scour the poisons from the burning lands and carry them to the sea, and in the depths of the sea they would waste their venom[10] until they could harm no living things. Then the great ships that were still waiting here on the silent, dusty plains could lift once more into space, along the road that led to home.

That was the dream: and one day, Marvin knew with a sudden flash of insight, he would pass it on to his own son, here at this same spot with the mountains behind him and the silver light from the sky streaming into his face.

He did not look back as they began the homeward journey. He could not bear to see the cold glory of the crescent Earth fade from the rocks around him, as he went to rejoin his people in their long exile.

10. *Venom* is the poison released by some animals, but here the word refers to deadly, radioactive pollution.

❖

Vocabulary
perennial (pə ren′ ē əl) *adj.* lasting for a long time
comprehend (kom′ pri hend′) *v.* to grasp mentally; understand fully
scour (skour) *v.* to rub energetically in order to clean, wash, or brighten
insight (in′ sīt) *n.* an understanding of the inner character or hidden nature of something

I Critical Thinking

DRAWING CONCLUSIONS Why does Marvin's father take him on the journey? *(He thinks Marvin is old enough now to be able to understand what happened on Earth and to deal with the consequences of that disaster. He wants Marvin to be impressed enough so that he will prepare his children's children to return to Earth.)*

J Literary Elements

CLIMAX A flash of insight comes to Marvin about why his father has brought him there: His father is handing over a legacy, which is both the past and the still-living hope for the future. Help students to understand what this says about the characters' relationship. *(It is clear that Marvin and his father have a close relationship. The father understands that, after he tells his son about Earth's horrible past, the boy will know what he must do in the future.)*

Thematic Focus

Flashes of Insight The lesson that Marvin learns about the world he has grown up in and the world his father left behind gives him insight into his future and the hope for generations to come.

ASSESSMENT
Quick Checks, p. 51

Reading Minilesson

Cause and Effect Explain to students that plots often contain a chain of events that starts with a cause that produces an effect, which in turn produces another effect. Sometimes one cause produces several effects. Point out that the main cause in this story is the destruction of Earth and that the main effect is the Colony's exile.

Activity Have students make assumptions about the cause of the destruction of Earth. They may list several causes or even a chain of events that led to the destruction. Students may present their assumptions in a graphic organizer. **L2**

Additional Resources
Reading Skills Practice Workbook, p. 59

FINE ART TRANSPARENCY 18

You may want to use ***Fine Art Transparency 18*** to discuss aspects of Earth that seem like Eden and ways to preserve the planet.

Responding to the Selection

PERSONAL RESPONSE

Students should recognize that as dark as this story is, Clarke leaves us with the hope that Earth can be restored.

Analyzing Literature

1. It was a scout car with wide balloon tires and a pressurized cabin. This description helps the reader understand that the landscape is rugged and that the atmosphere does not support human life.
2. He sees Earth. He knows his people's history and what they had and lost on that shining planet.
3. Marvin sees the radioactive aftermath of Earth, poisoned by nuclear war. He cannot visit because that glow means death to every living thing.
4. The description of the routine Marvin and his father must go through to leave the controlled atmosphere of the Colony makes clear that the events are not taking place on Earth. The effect is deliberate.
5. Clarke probably intended the story as a warning of what we can lose if we use nuclear weapons. There has been a continued increase of countries capable of building nuclear weapons.
6. Students may hope that government officials all over the world will read the selection and heed its message.

Extending Your Response

Literature Groups Have students keep in mind that Clarke has Marvin make certain assumptions about what the quality of life on Earth was like in our day, which may or may not agree with students' views. Students should nonetheless recognize how important it is to take care of the environment. COLLAB. LEARN.

Listening and Speaking Students' speeches should include practical suggestions, including a time frame for that return.

Responding to Literature

PERSONAL RESPONSE

- Do you think Clarke's story is hopeful or discouraging about the future? How does his prediction compare with your own from the **Reading Focus** on page 590? Explain.

Analyzing Literature

RECALL AND INTERPRET

1. Describe the vehicle that Marvin's father uses. How does this description help you to understand the setting of the story?
2. When the vehicle stops, what does Marvin see "low above the far horizon"? Why, in your opinion, has it "called to his heart across the abyss of space"?
3. What does Marvin see that prevents him from visiting the disk? What is the name of this disk, and what, do you think, is the reason for what he sees?

EVALUATE AND CONNECT

4. How does the author's description of technology affect your understanding of the story? Give examples. Do you think this effect is intentional?
5. What message might Clarke be sending to readers? What things are happening on our planet today that may have inspired him to write this story?
6. Who else would you like to have read this selection? Explain.

LITERARY ELEMENTS

Science Fiction

Science fiction is a type of literature in which the events and situations are scientifically plausible. Critics debate the difference between science fiction and **fantasy.** Some say science fiction must follow the laws of science, while fantasy may contain unexplainable events. Others lump the two together and call the literature **speculative fiction.**

1. How does the author use facts as he describes life in the Colony? List three examples.
2. If this story were fantasy, how might the description of the Colony change? If you could break the laws of science, how would you change the ending?

- See **Literary Terms Handbook,** p. R9.

Extending Your Response

Literature Groups

Images from Earth Focus on Clarke's descriptions of Earth. What ideas or impressions do these images give you? How might they change your thinking about Earth? Discuss how these images add to your understanding of the story.

Listening and Speaking

Politics of the Future Should residents spend resources to improve life in the Colony or prepare for a return to Earth? Write and deliver a speech to persuade others to agree with your position.

LITERARY ELEMENTS

1. He describes what it is like to live without an atmosphere, travel in a pressurized vehicle, and live in a controlled environment.
2. The situation would not follow scientific laws and would not make sense in the natural world. In a fantasy a radioactive cleanup could occur.

Additional Resources

Literary Elements Transparency 51

ASSESSMENT

- ***Quick Checks,*** p. 51
- ***Selection and Theme Assessment,*** pp. 91–92
- ***Performance Assessment,*** p. 48
- ***Testmaker: ExamView Pro***
- ***Interactive Tutor: Self-Assessment***

COMPARING SELECTIONS

Thank You in Arabic and "If I Forget Thee, Oh Earth . . ."

COMPARE SETTINGS

Both Naomi and Marvin find themselves in settings that awaken them to the meaning of the word "home." Arthur C. Clarke and Naomi Shihab Nye use precise details to show these settings. Reread descriptions of the Colony and of Jerusalem. Briefly explain which of the two places is most real to you, and give examples from the story to support your choice.

Tire tracks on the moon.

COMPARE SITUATIONS

Naomi journeys to a foreign land, learns about herself and others, and returns home. Marvin journeys to a barren landscape and experiences a new feeling about the place that should have been his home. Think of some experiences of exile or homecoming that you know about personally or have learned about.

1. List these situations, noting the details.
2. Describe one of these situations to a small group.
3. Answer any questions the group may have.
4. Practice telling the story again and then share it with the class.

COMPARE ATTITUDES

Both of these stories raise questions about war. Naomi Shihab Nye expresses her opinions on the fighting in the Middle East, but the results of war are only implied in Arthur C. Clarke's story. Make a Venn diagram comparing and contrasting how the stories treat war.

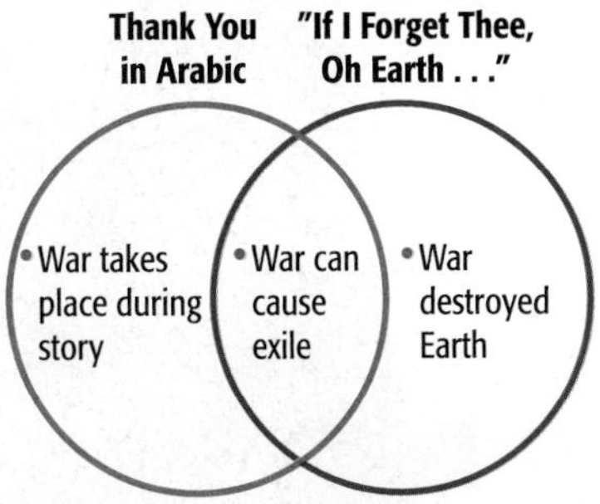

COMPARING selections

Objective

- To compare two selections that deal with the theme of "Flashes of Insight"

COMPARE SETTINGS

Students' comparisons should

- address the definition of home in each selection
- cite specific examples from the selections that support their reactions

COMPARE SITUATIONS

Students' presentations should

- correspond to the ideas of exile or homecoming
- include convincing details
- incorporate answers to questions from the smaller group

Additional Resources

Literature Groups Sourcebook

COMPARE ATTITUDES

Students' diagrams should

- compare the effects of war on people's sense of home
- contrast the choices available to the main characters in the face of war
- include both specific statements and inferences

Teaching Support

PORTFOLIO OPTIONS

Select and Reflect Have students reflect on their analyses for the activity by asking themselves these questions:

- Does my analysis include details?
- Are my comparisons based on parallel situations?

Students should clip their reflections to their analyses and place them in their portfolios. At a later time, they may consider using the comments to revise their analyses as portfolio showcase pieces. **L2**

Additional Resources

Writing Assessment and Portfolio Management, pp. 41–48

Before Reading

Objectives

- To read and analyze two poems
- To identify the use of an extended metaphor in poetry
- To use metaphors in a description

Skills

Reading/Thinking: Elaborating; Comparing and Contrasting
Writing: Interview
Grammar/Language: Action Verbs; Sentence Patterns
Collaboration: Literature Groups

Motivating STUDENTS

Selection Focus Transparency 51: Before presenting the photograph, have students list and discuss technological advances that have occurred in their lifetimes.

Reading Focus: As an extension of the Reading Focus, have partners think of any machine or equipment (such as a bicycle) that they have given a name to and explain why.

Before You Read

I like to see it lap the miles* and *Southbound on the Freeway

MEET EMILY DICKINSON

Emily Dickinson did well in school, went to parties, and was considered clever, but she eventually withdrew from the world around her. As a writer, she is known for her passion and wit. "If I read a book and it makes my whole body so cold that no fire can ever warm me, I know *that* is poetry," she said.

Emily Dickinson lived from 1830 to 1886.

MEET MAY SWENSON

May Swenson worked as a journalist, secretary, and editor, but above all she was a poet. She said that her poetry came from "a craving to get through the curtains of things as they *appear*, to things as they *are*, and then into the larger, wilder space of things as they *are becoming*."

May Swenson was born in 1913 and died in 1989.

READING FOCUS

Are people and machines alike in any way? How are they different?

Diagram It!
Use a Venn diagram to show your answers to the questions above. Include ideas about action, appearance, and function.

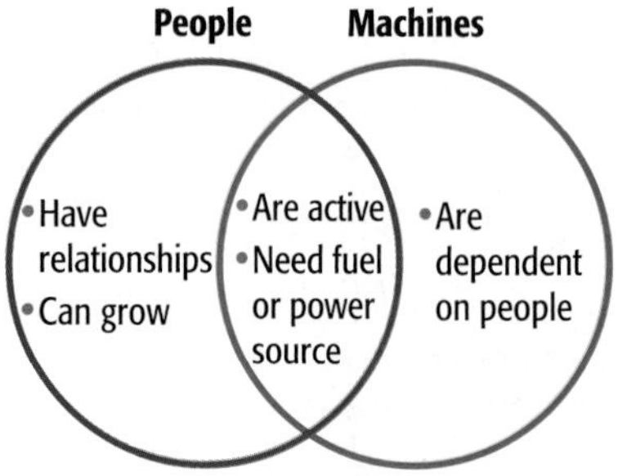

Setting a Purpose
Read to discover the unusual ways in which two poets look at certain objects.

BUILDING BACKGROUND

Emily Dickinson wrote "I like to see it lap the miles" in response to seeing a steam locomotive for the first time. Steam-powered trains were introduced in 1830 and earned the nickname "iron horses" because they replaced horse-drawn cars.

RESOURCE MANAGER

Teaching Tools and Resources
- Theme Six Planning Guide
- Literature Groups Sourcebook

Essential Lesson Support

Lesson-Specific Instruction
- Selection Focus Transparency 51
- Literary Elements Transparency 52
- Active Reading Guide,* p. 52

Assessment
- Selection Quick Checks,* p. 52
- Sel. and Theme Assmt., pp. 93–94
- Testmaker: ExamView Pro
- Performance Assessment, p. 49

Systematic Language Instruction
- Gr. & Comp. Hbk., L. 11.9

English Language Learners
- ELL Sourcebook, p. 75
- Spanish Summaries, p. 51
- Audio Library*
- English, Yes!

Spec. Needs/Strat. Interven.
- Interactive Rdg. Sbk., pp. T180–T182
- Interactive Rdg. Wkbk., p. 97
- Audio Library*

* Also available in Spanish

I like to see it lap the miles

Emily Dickinson

I like to see it lap the miles,
And lick the valleys up,
And stop to feed itself at tanks;
And then, prodigious,° step

Around a pile of mountains,
And, supercilious,° peer
In shanties° by the sides of roads;
And then a quarry° pare°

To fit its sides, and crawl between,
Complaining all the while
In horrid, hooting stanza;°
Then chase itself down hill

And neigh like Boanerges;°
Then, punctual as a star,
Stop—docile and omnipotent°—
At its own stable door.

4 *Prodigious,* here, means "enormous."
6 *Supercilious* means "having excessive pride or scorn."
7 *Shanties* are crude huts or cabins.
8 A *quarry* is a pit from which stone is cut or blasted. To *pare* is to shave off the outer layer.

11 A *stanza* is a group of lines; this poem has four stanzas.
13 In the Bible, Jesus calls two of his followers *Boanerges,* or "sons of thunder," because of their fiery tempers.
15 *Omnipotent* means "having unlimited power."

Through to the Pacific, 1870. Currier and Ives. 12 x 15¼ in. Museum of the City of New York.

Reading the Selection

A Author's Craft

DESCRIPTIVE LANGUAGE Dickinson begins the poem with "I like to see." Have students list at least ten things she likes to see the train do. *(lap, lick, stop, feed, step, peer, pare, crawl, complain, chase, neigh, and stop)* Explain that all these verbs suggest motion.

FYI

Biblical Reference The New Testament reference to Boanerges appears in Mark 3:17: "And James, the son of Zebedee and John, the brother of James: and he surnamed them Boanerges, which is, sons of thunder."

B Literary Elements

METAPHOR Explain to students that the entire poem compares a train to a horse, assigning the characteristics of a horse to a train. This is an extended metaphor. Have students cite especially colorful examples.

Teaching Support

MEETING INDIVIDUAL NEEDS — ENGLISH LANGUAGE LEARNERS

Vocabulary English language learners may find the vocabulary in Dickinson's poem especially difficult. Have students listen as you read the poem aloud or play the audio. Then have students follow along in their books as you read it again.

Activity Add more meaning to the difficult words—both those that are defined and any you believe will be difficult for students—by using them in sentences that give more meaning. Help students look up words that remain problematic and use them in sentences of their own.

Additional Resources

English Language Learners Sourcebook, p. 75

C Active Reading Strategies

CONNECT Read aloud Swenson's poem. Help students pick out descriptive words that give a picture of "the creature." Read aloud Dickinson's poem and have students compare the poets' choices of verbs and adjectives. *(Dickinson uses action verbs such as* lap, lick, stop, feed, *and* step. *Many of Swenson's verbs are forms of* to be, *though she also uses some action verbs:* turning, passes, winding, hiss. *Many of Dickinson's adjectives are precise but scholarly—*prodigious, supercilious, punctual, docile, omnipotent*—though she does not hesitate to describe a "horrid, hooting stanza." Swenson uses fewer and more everyday adjectives:* round, dark, red, soft, shadowy, hard.*)*

D Literary Elements

METAPHOR Review the definition of *metaphor* and *extended metaphor* with students. Then discuss the extended metaphor in each poem. Have students demonstrate their recognition of the concept by citing examples from Swenson's poem.

Southbound on

May Swenson

A tourist came in from Orbitville,
parked in the air, and said:

The creatures of this star
are made of metal and glass.

Through the transparent parts
you can see their guts.

Their feet are round and roll
on diagrams or long

measuring tapes, dark
with white lines.

They have four eyes.
The two in the back are red.

Sometimes you can see a five-eyed
one, with a red eye turning

on the top of his head.
He must be special—

the others respect him
and go slow

when he passes, winding
among them from behind.

They all hiss as they glide,
like inches, down the marked

tapes. Those soft shapes,
shadowy inside

the hard bodies—are they
their guts or their brains?

Teaching Support

Grammar and Language *Minilesson*

Action Verbs Explain to students that an action verb is a word that names an action as opposed to merely establishing a state of being or a condition. *(to be, to seem, to become)* Remind students that actions can be both mental and physical. Write the following on the board and have volunteers identify the action verbs.

I like to see it lap the miles,
And lick the valleys up,
And stop to feed itself at tanks;
And then, prodigious, step
Around a pile of mountains.

(like, to see, lap, lick, stop, to feed, step)

Activity Have students identify the rest of the action verbs in the poem. Point out that after the first line, Dickinson uses only action verbs. Discuss how this affects the message of the poem. **L2**

Additional Resources

- ***Grammar and Language Transparency 49***
- ***Grammar and Language Workbook,*** p. 75
- ***Grammar and Composition Handbook,*** Lesson 3.1
- ***Writer's Choice,*** Lesson 10.1

the Freeway

Landscape in Forward Motion, 1989. Stephen Fox. Oil on linen, 42 x 58 in. O.K. Harris Works of Art, New York.

E Critical Thinking

ELABORATING Explain to students that an extended metaphor elaborates on a comparison. Ask students to take the metaphor even further in the poem. They may continue discussing the human beings where Swenson leaves off, or they may describe different types of automobiles.

F Active Reading Strategies

EVALUATE Have students consider this photograph after reading the poem by Swenson. How accurate is her description?

Thematic Focus

Flashes of Insight Train and car travel are both everyday occurrences today, but the poets' insights give us a different perspective. As students read the poems, encourage them to think of other things they might look at with a poet's viewpoint.

ASSESSMENT

Quick Checks, p. 52

Reading Minilesson

Comparison and Contrast Students may better understand the message of the poems if they visualize how the poets came to the comparisons, or metaphors, on which they based the poems.

Activity Have students choose one of the poems to analyze. Have them use a graphic organizer to present their comparison and contrast. As they read, they should list the subject in one column and the thing that it is being compared to in another. Then they should list ways the two are alike and ways they are different. After students have finished their charts, they can share them with the class. **L2**

Additional Resources

Reading Skills Practice Workbook

CONNECTING TO OTHER SELECTIONS

For a teaching strategy that connects this selection to "The Tell-Tale Heart," see the ***Theme Eight Planning Guide.***

Responding to the Selection

PERSONAL RESPONSE

Students may find the new perspective strange at first but should also be able to recognize the wit.

Analyzing Literature

1. Some details are those related to valleys, mountains, roads, a quarry, and hills, which are the settings.
2. The speaker comes from Orbitville.
3. A horse and a train are compared. She uses such phrases as "feed itself" and "stable door," yet she is obviously writing about a train.
4. The tourist is looking at cars on the highway—the "creatures of this star." They are made of metal and glass, have round, rolling feet, and headlights (eyes).
5. Students' answers should reflect an understanding of Dickinson's formality and Swenson's more casual style.
6. A likely answer might be that everyday speech is not rhymed, and cars are a part of everyday life.
7. Students' answers should reflect an understanding that the poet's description was meant to give readers a different perspective on an everyday phenomenon.
8. Students may find that both titles accurately reflect the tone of the poems.
9. A possible choice might be the Dickinson poem as being the poem whose extended metaphor is most fully developed. Those who choose the Swenson poem may like the science fiction element of cars as "creatures of this star."
10. Students will be more familiar with the experience of freeways and may therefore choose Swenson's poem as the one that gives them a new understanding of a common object.

Active Reading and Critical Thinking

Responding to Literature

PERSONAL RESPONSE

- Describe your reactions to the poems. Did you find them humorous? strange? both?

Brackets connect questions that are paired to develop higher-level thinking skills.

Analyzing Literature

RECALL

1. What settings are identified in Emily Dickinson's poem?
2. Where does the tourist in May Swenson's poem come from?

INTERPRET

3. What two things are compared in Dickinson's poem? How do you know?
4. What is the tourist in "Southbound on the Freeway" looking at? Who are "the creatures of this star"? How do you know?

EVALUATE AND CONNECT

5. How might Dickinson write about a car? How might Swenson describe a train? Think of details and examples each poet might use.
6. In "Southbound on the Freeway," Swenson uses **free verse.** The sentences have the rhythm of everyday speech. Why, in your opinion, might she have chosen free verse?
7. In your opinion, how accurate is the tourist in describing the creatures? Consider your response to the **Reading Focus** on page 598 as you answer this question.
8. Why, in your opinion, is the title of each poem appropriate–or inappropriate?
9. Which poem, in your opinion, made the most intriguing comparison? Why do you think so?
10. Theme Connection Which poem do you think is most likely to give readers a flash of insight–a new understanding of a common object? Explain.

LITERARY ELEMENTS

Metaphor

A **metaphor** is a comparison that doesn't use the words *like* or *as.* The two things being compared are usually not similar. For example, a train and an animal are different, but the poet sees some similarities between them. Since the comparison in Dickinson's poem is used throughout the entire poem, it is an **extended metaphor.**

1. What characteristics of a train might be noted in a comparison with an animal?
2. What is the metaphor in Swenson's poem? What other metaphor might be used to describe the creatures on the highway?

- See **Literary Terms Handbook,** p. R6.

Ladder to Success, 1994. John Holcroft. Oil on canvas, 420 x 295 mm. Private collection.

LITERARY ELEMENTS

1. Strength, speed, fuel or food, ability to cover distances, and "hooting" are shared characteristics.
2. The automobile is compared to the principal life species. Another metaphor might be to see it as part of a giant machine.

Additional Resources

Literary Elements Transparency 52

Extending Your Response

Writing About Literature

Making Metaphors May Swenson's tourist sees strange creatures rolling along a measuring tape. Imagine you are one of the "soft shapes" inside the creatures. What do you see when you view the tourist from Orbitville parked in the air? Write a brief description in which you use a metaphor to compare the tourist with something familiar.

Creative Writing

Interview With a partner, present an interview for a local TV station. The subject of your interview can be a visitor from Orbitville or an artist who illustrates books about transportation. Assign the roles of reporter and interviewee. Be prepared with thoughtful questions and answers that give insights into the future of transportation.

Literature Groups

Guts or Brains? The speaker of "Southbound on the Freeway" asks if the soft bodies are "their guts or their brains." Discuss this question among yourselves. List reasons why the bodies might be the guts. Then list reasons why they might be the brains. Present your group's ideas to the class.

Art Activity

Visual Metaphors Create a drawing or collage using images that work like metaphors; for example, a train with hooves and a tail, or a row of cars with eyes and mouths. Create a display of class images.

Reading Further

If you enjoyed these poems, you might want to try the following collections:

The Complete Poems to Solve by May Swenson

I Wouldn't Thank You for a Valentine: Poems for Young Feminists by Carol Ann Duffy

Save your work for your portfolio.

Skill Minilesson

RETEACH • REVIEW

GRAMMAR AND LANGUAGE • SENTENCE PATTERNS

Poets often use unusual sentence patterns. Dickinson separates the adjective *prodigious* from the pronoun it modifies:

I like to see it *lap the miles . . .*
And then, prodigious, *step*
Around a pile of mountains

- For more about sentences, see **Language Handbook**, pp. R32–R33.

Swenson places the adjective *dark* after the noun it modifies:

Their feet are round and roll
on diagrams or long
measuring tapes, dark
with white lines.

PRACTICE Write two sentences imitating each of the patterns shown above.

Extending Your Response

Writing About Literature

Students' descriptions should
- relate to a familiar object or animal
- include a metaphor

Creative Writing

Students' interviews should
- contain thoughtful questions that require detailed answers
- give insight into the future of transportation

Literature Groups Encourage students to respond with the same restrained wit that the poet uses. COLLAB. LEARN.

Art Activity You may use the artistic metaphors to inspire writers to produce corresponding poems.

Skill Minilesson

GRAMMAR AND LANGUAGE • SENTENCE PATTERNS

Students' sentences should be clearly patterned on the examples.

Additional Resources

- ***Grammar and Language Workbook,*** p. 133
- ***Grammar and Composition Handbook,*** Lesson 5.1
- ***Writer's Choice,*** Lesson 12.7

ASSESSMENT

- ***Quick Checks,*** p. 52
- ***Selection and Theme Assessment,*** pp. 93–94
- ***Performance Assessment,*** p. 49
- ***Testmaker: ExamView Pro***
- ***Interactive Tutor: Self-Assessment***

Interdisciplinary Connection

Objective

- To understand the historical implications of the Vietnam War

Teaching Strategies

Suggest that students locate Vietnam in relation to the equator as a way of understanding why its climate is hot and wet.

Activities

1. Students' reports on that country today should include information about Vietnam's economy and its political system. A report about recognition of service in Vietnam might include mention of the Vietnam Veterans Memorial in Washington, D.C.
2. Students should note that America's peak of involvement came in 1968 and that American military support waned after 1969.

Interdisciplinary Connection — HISTORY

The Vietnam War

It was a war that pitted U.S. soldiers against a Communist army called the Vietcong. It was a country little known to the Americans who went to battle on beaches, in jungles, and in rice paddies. It was the longest war the United States ever fought—and the only one it never won. It was the Vietnam War.

In the 1950s the Vietcong of North Vietnam attempted to invade South Vietnam and create a Communist country. The United States came to the aid of South Vietnam, sending more than 2.5 million U.S. military personnel from the mid-1950s until 1975.

As American soldiers marched with heavy equipment through thick, dark jungles, they knew one wrong step could set off a Vietcong land mine. The relentless enemy attacks and the constant heat, rain, and insects left the U.S. soldiers miserable. They struggled to cope with discomfort, illness, fear, and the deaths that took place every day, including massacres of Vietnamese civilians.

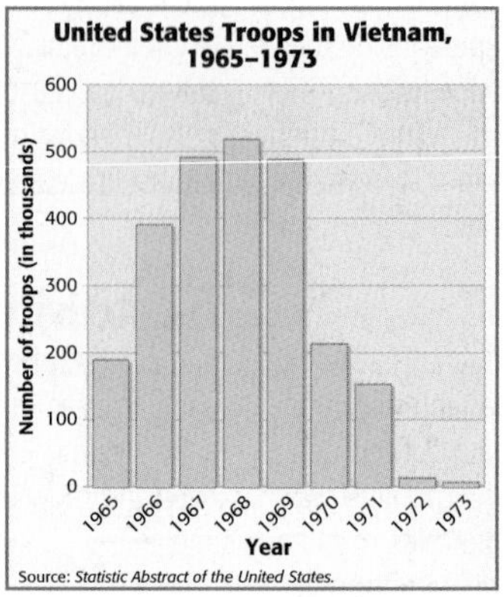

When the United States withdrew from Vietnam in 1975, some 58,000 Americans had been declared killed or missing. More than 300,000 others had been injured.

The war never had complete public support in the United States. As a result, returning soldiers felt that few understood what it had been like to serve in Vietnam. The war left many Vietnam veterans at odds with themselves and with their country.

"... all of a sudden, you're back on this airplane, with ... people who are laughing and happy—and you're coming out of this freaky atmosphere, and you land back in the United States of America. And nobody cares, and nobody wants you to be in uniform. You get in a taxi and off you go! You try to go home."

—John Kerry, U.S. senator from Massachusetts who served in Vietnam in the U.S. Navy

ACTIVITIES

1. What is life like for the people of Vietnam today? How has the United States recognized its citizens who served in the war? Research answers to one or more questions you have about Vietnam. Prepare a brief report.
2. Study the chart showing the number of troops sent to Vietnam each year. What story does the chart tell? Write a paragraph describing the information and any patterns you see in the chart.

Teaching Support

MEETING INDIVIDUAL NEEDS — MULTIPLE MODES OF EXPRESSION

Logical-Mathematical Explain that one of the troubling issues in the aftermath of the Vietnam War was how statistics were used. To show that the United States and its ally South Vietnam were winning the war, U.S. military commanders purportedly inflated the number of enemy casualties. Critics charged that these "body counts" may have lengthened the duration of the war.

Activity Have students work in small groups to research the annual casualty statistics of the Vietnam War for both sides. Suggest that they present them in graphs and charts. Encourage a discussion on how these statistics might be interpreted by those who were for and those who were against the war.
L3 COLLAB. LEARN.

Vo•cab•u•lar•y Skills

Using Idioms

A word or phrase that has a meaning other than its literal meaning is an **idiom.** Saying that a *dog* is tied up in the backyard probably means that the dog is literally tied up. But saying that a *person* is tied up in the backyard probably means that the person is busy there. Some idioms, such as "Get off my back," and "Cut it out!" are familiar. Unfamiliar idioms, however, can cause confusion.

- One way to figure out the meaning of an unfamiliar idiom is to think about what the ordinary meanings of the words suggest.

  Naomi and her brother attended a talk by a swami about the use of incense. The talk was over their heads, but they liked it.

  If something were literally over their heads, it would be above them and, therefore, hard to reach. In this case, the talk was beyond the reach of their understanding. The idiom means "beyond their understanding."

- Context clues are also useful in dealing with unfamiliar idioms.

  Although she is famous today, Emily Dickinson chose to live a private life, and published little of her poetry. As a result, Dickinson never saw her star rise.

  Context clues suggest that being private and publishing few poems kept Dickinson from "seeing her star rise." They contrast her current fame with her situation during her lifetime. These clues suggest that when a person's "star rises," he or she is becoming famous.

For more about idioms, see **Reading Handbook,** p. R90.

EXERCISE

Use the ordinary meanings of the underlined words and context clues to figure out the meaning of each underlined idiom. Then write a short definition of the idiom.

1. There was nothing stale or ordinary about Emily Dickinson's poetry. Her work broke new ground with originality and skill.
2. For most of her life, she refused to leave her home to go shopping or to attend social gatherings, choosing to remain out of the mainstream.
3. She withdrew from social relationships. On the other hand, she wrote letters constantly to her friends.
4. Dickinson buried herself in her work, completing hundreds of brilliant poems before her death at the age of fifty-six.

Vo•cab•u•lar•y Skills

Objective

- To recognize and understand idioms

Teaching Strategies

After students have read the first part of the page, encourage them to visualize the literal meaning of each idiom, which will help them understand it. For example, if something is "over your head," you will find it beyond your mind. Never "seeing your star rise" suggests the failure of something that is climbing to be recognized at its greatest height.

Exercise

1. was different from what had been done before
2. apart from what everyone else was doing
3. in contrast
4. busied herself without seeing what else was going on around her

Additional Resources

Vocabulary Power

Teaching Support

MEETING INDIVIDUAL NEEDS — ENGLISH LANGUAGE LEARNERS

Idioms Students may be familiar with some idioms in their first language. Suggest that they share and translate them. Have them think about how new speakers of that language might learn the idioms.

Activity Have students figure out the following common idioms, using the suggestions on this page.

- Max got up on the wrong side of the bed this morning. *(feeling cranky)*
- Boy, you really know how to take the wind out of someone's sails with your criticisms. *(deflate someone's spirit)*
- Toby put her nose to the grindstone to finish the job. *(worked hard)*

Additional Resources

English Language Learners Sourcebook, p. 76

Before Reading

Objectives

- To read and analyze a short story about a boy's struggle to understand his father
- To identify the climax of a short story
- To write an analysis of how the author develops character

Skills

Reading/Thinking: Inferring; Identifying Author's Purpose; Recognizing Cause and Effect
Writing: Description; Scene
Vocabulary: Multiple-Meaning Words
Grammar/Language: Agreement with Collective Nouns; Subject-Verb Agreement
Collaboration: Literature Groups

Motivating STUDENTS

Literature Launchers: "Haunted by the Past"

Videodisc Side B, Segment 17

Also available in VHS.

Selection Focus Transparency 52: Have students view the transparency and then discuss the questions provided.

Reading Focus: As an extension of the Reading Focus, have partners team up with another pair and compare lists for common problems and possible solutions.

Before You Read

Stop the Sun

MEET GARY PAULSEN

Gary Paulsen, an award-winning author of survival stories, has an unlikely hero: a librarian. "There's nothing that has happened to me that would have happened if she hadn't got me to read," he says. That's quite a statement from a former dog sledder who ran his dogs in the Iditarod race, rode a motorcycle to Alaska, and ate raw turtle eggs as research for a book. Paulsen writes and reads from 5:30 A.M. until he goes to bed at midnight. "You really have to be able to read to learn things," he says. "You try to learn to grow to be more."

Gary Paulsen was born in 1939. "Stop the Sun" was first published in Boy's Life *in 1986.*

READING FOCUS

When might someone your age have trouble communicating with a family member?

List It!
With a partner, make a list of problems that can cause poor communication among family members. Next to each problem, list your advice for trying to solve each problem.

Setting a Purpose
Read to find out what happens when a teenage boy digs into his father's battle-scarred past.

BUILDING BACKGROUND

The Time and Place
This story takes place in an American city sometime in the 1980s.

Did You Know?
From 1965 to 1973, U.S. troops fought alongside the South Vietnamese in their struggle against Communist North Vietnam.

Chopper Pickup (detail), 1969. Brian H. Clark. Acrylic, 40 x 40 in. United States Army Center of Military History, Washington, DC.

VOCABULARY PREVIEW

syndrome (sin′ drōm′) *n.* a group of symptoms that, together, indicate a certain disease; p. 608
dry (drī) *adj.* not interesting; dull; boring; p. 608
specific (spi sif′ ik) *adj.* entirely clear and definite; p. 608
founder (foun′ dər) *v.* to break down, collapse, or fail; p. 611
inert (i nurt′) *adj.* without power to move or act; lifeless; p. 613

RESOURCE MANAGER

Teaching Tools and Resources
- Theme Six Planning Guide
- Literature Groups Sourcebook

Essential Lesson Support

Lesson-Specific Instruction
- Selection Focus Transparency 52
- Literary Elements Transparency 53
- Active Reading Guide,* p. 53
- Selection Vocabulary Practice, p. 36

Assessment
- Selection Quick Checks,* p. 53
- Sel. and Theme Assmt., pp. 95–96
- Testmaker: ExamView Pro
- Performance Assessment, p. 50

Systematic Language Instruction
- Gr. & Comp. Hbk., L. 12.1
- Vocabulary Power, Lesson 26
- Spelling Power, Lesson 23

English Language Learners
- ELL Sourcebook, pp. 76–77
- Spanish Summaries, p. 52
- Spanish Translations, pp. 136–141
- Audio Library*
- English, Yes!

Spec. Needs/Strat. Interven.
- Interactive Rdg. Sbk., pp. T182–T184
- Interactive Rdg. Wkbk., pp. 98–99
- Inclusion Strat. Sbk., pp. 47–48
- Audio Library*

* Also available in Spanish

Reading the Selection

STOP THE SUN

Gary Paulsen

Con Thien Run, 1967. H. Avery Chenowith. Acrylic, 3½ x 2½ ft. United States Marine Corps Art Collection, Washington, DC.

Terry Erickson was a tall boy, 13, starting to fill out with muscle but still a little awkward. He was on the edge of being a good athlete, which meant a lot to him. He felt it coming too slowly, though, and that bothered him.

But what bothered him even more was when his father's eyes went away.

SUMMARY

Terry Erickson is troubled by his father's strange behavior. At times he seems to go "away," and all Terry knows is that it relates to his father's experience in Vietnam. However, no one actually talks about it. Probing, Terry presses his father after an excruciating public episode of his father's post-traumatic stress syndrome. Terry learns what happened. As a result, he realizes that he can never really understand his father's fear but can accept his father for who he is.

Spanish Summaries, p. 52

A Active Reading Strategies

QUESTION Ask students what they can conclude about Terry from the opening paragraph of the story. *(He wants to be a good athlete but feels he is not developing fast enough. This may suggest that Terry is not usually patient about waiting for things to happen.)*

VOCABULARY Remind students to use context clues to unlock the meanings of new vocabulary words.

Additional Resources

- ***Active Reading Guide,*** p. 53
- ***Audio Library***
- ***Spanish Audio Library***

Teaching Support

CONNECTING TO OTHER SELECTIONS

The chart at the right shows three ways to connect "Stop the Sun" to other selections in this book.

For specific teaching strategies, see the ***Theme Six Planning Guide.***

Connection	Title
Life Skills: Supporting and Contributing	"Flowers for Algernon," p. 113
Thematic: Acceptance	"The Kid Nobody Could Handle," p. 146
Literary: Flashback	"Golden Glass," p. 51

B Active Reading Strategies

PREDICT Ask students whether they think Terry's father's episodes will "go away" or get worse as the story progresses. *(Some students may suggest that they will go away now that he is talking to a therapist. Others may decide that they will continue because it is not a simple problem.)*

C Literary Elements

INTERNAL CONFLICT Ask students if they understand why Terry is pursuing the issue. *(Not knowing exactly what's wrong or what will happen is what troubles Terry the most.)*

D Active Reading Strategies

QUESTION Ask students why Terry did not want Mr. Carlson to know his father was in the war. *(He may feel embarrassed about describing his father's behavior.)*

Teaching Support

Usually it happened when it didn't cause any particular trouble. Sometimes during a meal his father's fork would stop halfway to his mouth, just stop, and there would be a long pause while the eyes went away, far away.

After several minutes his mother would reach over and take the fork and put it gently down on his plate, and they would go back to eating—or try to go back to eating—normally.

They knew what caused it. When it first started, Terry had asked his mother in private what it was, what was causing the strange behavior.

"It's from the war," his mother had said. "The doctors at the veterans' hospital call it the Vietnam syndrome."[1]

B

"Will it go away?"

"They don't know. Sometimes it goes away. Sometimes it doesn't. They are trying to help him."

"But what happened? What actually caused it?"

"I told you. Vietnam."

"But there had to be something," Terry persisted. "Something made him like that. Not just Vietnam. Billy's father was there, and he doesn't act that way."

"That's enough questions," his mother said sternly. "He doesn't talk about it, and I don't ask. Neither will you. Do you understand?"

"But, Mom."

"That's enough."

And he stopped pushing it. But it bothered him whenever it happened. When something bothered him, he liked to stay with it until he understood it, and he understood no part of this. C

Words. His father had trouble, and they gave him words like Vietnam syndrome. He knew almost nothing of the war, and when he tried to find out about it, he kept hitting walls. Once he went to the school library and asked for anything they might have that could help him understand the war and how it affected his father. They gave him a dry history that described French involvement, Communist involvement, American involvement. But it told him nothing of the war. It was all numbers, cold numbers, and nothing of what had *happened*. There just didn't seem to be anything that could help him.

Another time he stayed after class and tried to talk to Mr. Carlson, who taught history. But some part of Terry was embarrassed. He didn't want to say why he wanted to know about Vietnam, so he couldn't be specific.

"What do you want to know about Vietnam, Terry?" Mr. Carlson had asked. "It was a big war."

Terry had looked at him, and something had started up in his mind, but he didn't let it out. He shrugged. "I just want to know what it was like. I know somebody who was in it." D

"A friend?"

"Yessir. A good friend."

1. *Vietnam syndrome* refers to the lasting psychological problems suffered by many Vietnam veterans. Some of the symptoms are anger, nervousness, and nightmares.

Vocabulary

syndrome (sin′ drōm′) *n.* a group of symptoms that, together, indicate a certain disease

dry (drī) *adj.* not interesting; dull; boring

specific (spi sif′ ik) *adj.* entirely clear and definite

MEETING INDIVIDUAL NEEDS

ENGLISH LANGUAGE LEARNERS

Identifying with the Character
Explain that in a short story such as this, readers may figure out the meaning of difficult passages if they try to identify with the character and understand his or her conflict.

Activity Invite students to isolate any phrases or expressions that describe Terry's character and his conflict. Have students restate these passages in their own words.

Additional Resources

English Language Learners Sourcebook, p. 77

Mr. Carlson had studied him, looking into his eyes, but didn't ask any other questions. Instead he mentioned a couple of books Terry had not seen. They turned out to be pretty good. They told about how it felt to be in combat. Still, he couldn't make his father be one of the men he read about.

And it may have gone on and on like that, with Terry never really knowing any more about it except that his father's eyes started going away more and more often. It might have just gone the rest of his life that way except for the shopping mall.

It was easily the most embarrassing thing that ever happened to him.

It started as a normal shopping trip. His father had to go to the hardware store, and he asked Terry to go along.

When they got to the mall they split up. His father went to the hardware store, Terry to a record store to look at albums.

War & Peace, 1990. Tsing-Fang Chen. Acrylic on canvas, 66 x 96 in. Lucia Gallery, New York.
Viewing the painting: How does the artist reflect opposite ideas—war and peace—in this painting?

E Active Reading Strategies

EVALUATE Help students evaluate the ways Terry goes about finding out what is wrong with his father. *(Students may decide that going to the library to find out more about the Vietnam War makes sense. Others may believe that talking to a sympathetic person might be more direct. Turning to Mr. Carlson was a good idea, especially as the teacher seems to have understood what Terry needed.)*

F Critical Thinking

INFERRING Terry keeps trying to find out what Vietnam syndrome is. Have students infer what this tells the reader about his character and his feeling for his dad. *(He is persistent about achieving a goal once he's set his mind on it. Some of Terry's concern about his father is fear that his father's behavior will somehow lead to trouble for him. But mostly he cares about his dad and wants to help him heal.)*

VIEWING THE PAINTING

Dr. Tsing-Fang Chen was born in Taiwan and studied art in Paris. Today Chen is known as an influential artist. His work incorporates such themes as Eastern versus Western cultures, humanity, and liberty.

Viewing Response *Soldiers are armed and in camouflage, but sitting quietly in a lush, fertile field.*

MEETING INDIVIDUAL NEEDS — ADVANCED LEARNERS

Research Explain that combat photographers first appeared during the Civil War. Before that, the public at home had to depend on artists who sketched scenes on site. Those people who photographed wars over the years were often in as much danger as the men doing the fighting.

Activity Suggest that students research combat photography and learn more about the men and women who took the pictures. Some students may prefer to do a review of combat photography over the years. Others may prefer to focus on a single conflict, such as World War II or the Vietnam War. Have them share what they learn in either an oral or a written report. Suggest that they include samples of the photography in their reports. **L3**

G Active Reading Strategies

PREDICT Ask students to predict what is happening as Terry waits for his father. Tell them that they should base their predictions on Terry's previous description of the scene at the shopping mall.

H Literary Elements

RISING ACTION Ask students how the incident in the hardware store intensifies Terry's need to understand his father and thus advances the plot. *(At first he is so embarrassed that he wants to walk away. But this feeling is not as strong as his concern for his father. He realizes that he must learn what is wrong and, if possible, help his father.)*

I Literary Elements

CLIMAX Point out to students that this paragraph indicates what the climax will be: the confrontation between Terry and his father. Have students predict how the climax will lead to the resolution of the plot.

Teaching Support

Terry browsed so long that he was late meeting his father at the mall's front door. But his father wasn't there, and Terry looked out to the car to make sure it was still in the parking lot. It was, and he supposed his father had just gotten busy, so he waited.

Still his father didn't come, and he was about to go to the hardware store to find him when he noticed the commotion. Or not a commotion so much as a sudden movement of people.

Later, he thought of it and couldn't remember when the feeling first came to him that there was something wrong. The people were moving toward the hardware store and that might have been what made Terry suspicious.

There was a crowd blocking the entry to the store, and he couldn't see what they were looking at. Some of them were laughing small, nervous laughs that made no sense.

Terry squeezed through the crowd until he got near the front. At first he saw nothing unusual. There were still some people in front of him, so he pushed a crack between them. Then he saw it: His father was squirming along the floor on his stomach. He was crying, looking terrified, his breath coming in short, hot pants like some kind of hurt animal.

It burned into Terry's mind, the picture of his father down on the floor. It burned in and in, and he wanted to walk away, but something made his feet move forward. He knelt next to his father and helped the owner of the store get him up on his feet. His father didn't speak at all but continued to make little whimpering sounds, and they led him back into the owner's office and put him in a chair. Then Terry called his mother and she came in a taxi to take them home.

He couldn't remember when the feeling first came to him that there was something wrong.

Waiting, Terry sat in a chair next to his father, looking at the floor, wanting only for the earth to open and let him drop in a deep hole. He wanted to disappear.

Words. They gave him words like Vietnam syndrome, and his father was crawling through a hardware store on his stomach.

When the embarrassment became so bad that he would cross the street when he saw his father coming, when it ate into him as he went to sleep, Terry realized he had to do something. He had to know this thing, had to understand what was wrong with his father.

When it came, it was simple enough at the start. It had taken some courage, more than Terry thought he could find. His father was sitting in the kitchen at the table and his mother had gone shopping. Terry wanted it that way; he wanted his father alone. His mother seemed to try to protect him, as if his father could break.

Terry got a soda out of the refrigerator and popped it open. As an afterthought,

610 THEME 6

MEETING INDIVIDUAL NEEDS — SPECIAL NEEDS

Emotional Ask small groups of students to think of a mall with a store like the one Terry and his father visited. Discuss the surroundings. What kind of people shop there? How do you think they would behave if they saw Terry's father? What would you do if you were there?

Activity Invite groups of students to create one-page character logs for Terry and his father that describe how each character appears to others and how each person really feels. **L1** **COLLAB. LEARN.**

Additional Resources

Inclusion Strategies

he handed it to his father and got another for himself. Then he sat at the table.

J His father smiled. "You look serious."

"Well . . ."

It went nowhere for a moment, and Terry was just about to drop it altogether. It may be the wrong time, he thought, but there might never be a better one. He tightened his back, took a sip of pop.

"I was wondering if we could talk about something, Dad," Terry said.

His father shrugged. "We already did the bit about girls. Some time ago, as I remember it."

"No. Not that." It was a standing joke[2] between them. When his father finally got around to explaining things to him, they'd already covered it in school. "It's something else."

"Something pretty heavy, judging by your face."

"Yes."

"Well?"

I still can't do it, Terry thought. Things are bad, but maybe not as bad as they could get. I can still drop this thing.

K "Vietnam," Terry blurted out. And he thought, there, it's out. It's out and gone.

"No!" his father said sharply. It was as if he had been struck a blow. A body blow.

"But, Dad."

"No. That's another part of my life. A bad part. A rotten part. It was before I met your mother, long before you. It has nothing to do with this family, nothing. No."

So, Terry thought, so I tried. But it wasn't over yet. It wasn't started yet.

"It just seems to bother you so much," Terry said, "and I thought if I could help or maybe understand it better. . . ." His words ran until he foundered, until he could say no more. He looked at the table, then out the window. It was all wrong to bring it up, he thought. I blew it. I blew it all up. "I'm sorry."

But now his father didn't hear him. Now his father's eyes were gone again, and a shaft of something horrible went through Terry's heart as he thought he had done this thing to this father, caused his eyes to go away.

"You can't know," his father said after a time. "You can't know this thing."

Terry said nothing. He felt he had said too much.

"This thing that you want to know—there is so much of it that you cannot know it all, and to know only a part is . . . is too awful. I can't tell you. I can't tell anybody what it was really like."

L It was more than he'd ever said about Vietnam, and his voice was breaking. Terry hated himself and felt he would hate himself until he was an old man. In one second he had caused such ruin. And all because he had been embarrassed. What difference did it make? Now he had done this, and he wanted to hide, to leave. But he sat, waiting, knowing that it wasn't done.

His father looked to him, through him, somewhere into and out of Terry. He wasn't in the kitchen anymore. He wasn't in the house. He was back in the green places, back in the hot places, the wet-hot places.

2. A *standing joke* is one that continues to be told or shared over time.

Vocabulary
founder (foun′ dər) *v.* to break down, collapse, or fail

J Critical Thinking

INFERRING Ask students what the "standing joke" reveals about the relationship between father and son. *(The two have had private conversations before, suggesting that they are close and generally feel comfortable in each other's presence.)*

K Literary Elements

CLIMAX Explain that the climax of a story is the part to which all of the action has been leading. Ask students where the climax begins and why they think so. *(Terry's confrontation with his father is the beginning of the climax because it is where all the action—Terry's search for answers—has been leading.)*

L Literary Elements

CLIMAX Have students discuss what this insight reveals about what has gone on before, and what is likely to come after this encounter. *(Terry has apparently learned some factual things about Vietnam ["the wet-hot places"], but they haven't helped him understand his father's experience. Terry realizes that his father's pain is deeper than he knew.)*

Writing Minilesson

Describing Feelings Point out to students that, in describing a character's emotions, the author often describes that person's physical reaction as well. For example, before Terry confronted his father, "he tightened his back, took a sip of pop." As he watched his father's eyes go away again, "a shaft of something horrible went through Terry's heart." Explain that this sequence, in a way, parallels what happened to his father in the hardware store. He responded to the memory with not only his emotions, but his body as well.

Activity Suggest that students write a description of a person's reaction to a strong emotion and incorporate in it how that character reacts physically. **L2**

Additional Resources

Writer's Choice, Lesson 3.2

"You think that because I act strange, that we can talk and it will be all right," his father said. "That we can talk and it will just go away. That's what you think, isn't it?"

Terry started to shake his head, but he knew it wasn't expected.

"That's what the shrinks say," his father continued. "The psychiatrists tell me that if I talk about it, the whole thing will go away. But they don't know. They weren't there. You weren't there. Nobody was there but me and some other dead people, and they can't talk because they couldn't stop the morning."

Terry pushed his soda can back and forth, looking down, frightened at what was happening. *The other dead people,* he'd said, as if he were dead as well. *Couldn't stop the morning.*

"I don't understand, Dad."

"No. You don't." His voice hardened, then softened again, and broke at the edges. "But see, see how it was. . . ." He

Rice Paddies–Vietnam, 1966. Augustine Acuna. Watercolor, 18 x 28 in. United States Army Center of Military History, Washington, DC.

Viewing the painting: How does this scene call forth a response from the viewer?

Historical Note

Students' understanding of this story may be aided by knowing the effects of the Vietnam War on American society. Explain that Americans were so deeply divided about the war that protests for and against the war sometimes turned violent. Many felt that the United States should never have gotten involved. Others felt that it was important to stop the spread of communism. Even when the war was over, returning veterans felt that their sacrifices were not appreciated. It took many years before the divisions began to heal.

VIEWING THE PAINTING

Viewing Response *The drab colors, the marshy setting, and the dark, anonymous figures all suggest the artist's view of the war.*

Teaching Support

REAL-WORLD CONNECTION

Gulf War Syndrome Have students locate a magazine or a newspaper article that deals with Gulf War syndrome. Since there is as yet no medical consensus on this ailment, students should be alert for articles that reveal new information and that show different biases. Have students discuss the different points of view. They should answer such questions as *What are the different viewpoints? What groups represent those viewpoints? How is the issue being resolved, or is it?* **L2**

COLLAB. LEARN.

trailed off, and Terry thought he was done. His father looked back down to the table, at the can of soda he hadn't touched, at the tablecloth, at his hands, which were folded, inert on the table.

"We were crossing a rice paddy in the dark," he said, and suddenly his voice flowed like a river breaking loose. "We were crossing the paddy, and it was dark, still dark, so black you couldn't see the end of your nose. There was a light rain, a mist, and I was thinking that during the next break I would whisper and tell Petey Kressler how nice the rain felt, but of course I didn't know there wouldn't be a Petey Kressler."

He took a deep, ragged breath. At that moment Terry felt his brain swirl, a kind of whirlpool pulling, and he felt the darkness and the light rain because it was in his father's eyes, in his voice.

"So we were crossing the paddy, and it was a straight sweep, and then we caught it. We began taking fire from three sides, automatic weapons, and everybody went down and tried to get low, but we couldn't. We couldn't get low enough. We could never get low enough, and you could hear the rounds hitting people. It was just a short time before they brought in the mortars[3] and we should have moved, should have run, but nobody got up, and after a time nobody *could* get up. The fire just kept coming and coming, and then incoming mortars, and I heard screams as they hit, but there was nothing to do. Nothing to do."

"Dad?" Terry said. He thought, maybe I can stop him. Maybe I can stop him before . . . before it gets to be too much. Before he breaks.

"Mortars," his father went on, "I hated mortars. You just heard them *wump* as they fired, and you didn't know where they would hit, and you always felt like they would hit your back. They swept back and forth with the mortars, and the automatic weapons kept coming in, and there was no radio, no way to call for artillery. Just the dark to hide in. So I crawled to the side and found Jackson, only he wasn't there, just part of his body, the top part, and I hid under it and waited, and waited, and waited.

"Finally the firing quit. But see, see how it was in the dark with nobody alive but me? I yelled once, but that brought fire again, so I shut up and there was nothing, not even the screams."

His father cried, and Terry tried to understand, and he thought he could feel part of it. But it was so much, so much and so strange to him.

"You cannot know this," his father repeated. It was almost a chant. "You cannot know the fear. It was almost dark, and I was the only one left alive out of 54 men, all dead but me, and I knew that the Vietcong were just waiting for light. When the dawn came, 'Charley'[4] would come out and finish everybody off, the way they always did. And I thought if I could stop the dawn, just stop the sun from coming up, I could make it."

3. *Mortars* are small, portable cannons that fire explosive shells, also sometimes called mortars.

4. The *Vietcong* were the Communist forces whom American soldiers often referred to as *Charley.*

Vocabulary
inert (i nurt′) *adj.* without power to move or act; lifeless

FYI

Rice Paddies To grow rice, planters set young shoots of rice in flooded terraced fields called paddies. A rice paddy may be submerged in two to four inches of water.

M Author's Craft

DESCRIPTIVE LANGUAGE Ask students to examine how the author uses sensory details to re-create the battle scene and Mr. Erickson's feelings. *(One recurring detail is the heat and wetness; another is the darkness. His father also describes the sounds: the thud of the mortars, the screaming, and then the silence. Every detail contributed to Mr. Erickson's terror at the time, which is why he recalls them so vividly.)*

N Active Reading Strategies

QUESTION Examine why Terry wants his father to stop in the middle of the story. *(Terry is afraid his father will break under the strain of reliving that experience. At the same time, he may fear learning more than he himself can bear, because it is clear to him that the experience was horrible.)*

Reading Minilesson

Author's Purpose Explain to students that authors have a purpose for their writing, whether it be to entertain, to inform, or to describe. Often selections have several purposes. For example, in the story "If I Forget Thee, Oh Earth . . ." the author both entertains his readers and warns them about the dangers of nuclear proliferation.

Activity Have students review the selection, looking for the different purposes Paulsen may have had for writing this story. Students should take into consideration the fact that the author covers historical events and the effects of these events. **L2**

Additional Resources

Reading Skills Practice Workbook

Active Reading Strategies

RESPOND Read aloud the father's speech about stopping the sun in a way that will help students understand what he felt. You may wish to share the following model to illustrate an interpretation.

Model: Based on what I have read, I know that Mr. Erickson was the only survivor and really thought he was next to death. His only hope for survival, he thought, was for darkness to continue. I believe it's a miracle he lived. He must know that he cannot communicate all his fear to his son, but I think he probably wouldn't want to.

Active Reading Strategies

QUESTION Terry now understands some things about his father, but some things he cannot. What insight has he gained? *(He realizes that some things he can never understand because he did not share the experience. He hopes that trying to understand will be enough to help.)*

Thematic Focus

Flashes of Insight As Terry gains insight about his father's ordeal and also about Vietnam, he comes to understand his father—and history—better.

ASSESSMENT

Quick Checks, p. 53

Terry felt the fear, and he also felt the tears coming down his cheeks. His hand went out across the table, and he took his father's hand and held it. It was shaking.

"I mean I actually thought that if I could stop the sun from coming up, I could live. I made my brain work on that because it was all I had. Through the rest of the night in the rain in the paddy, I thought I could do it. I could stop the dawn." He took a deep breath. "But you can't, you know. You can't stop it from coming, and when I saw the gray light, I knew I was dead. It would just be minutes, and the light would be full, and I just settled under Jackson's body, and hid."

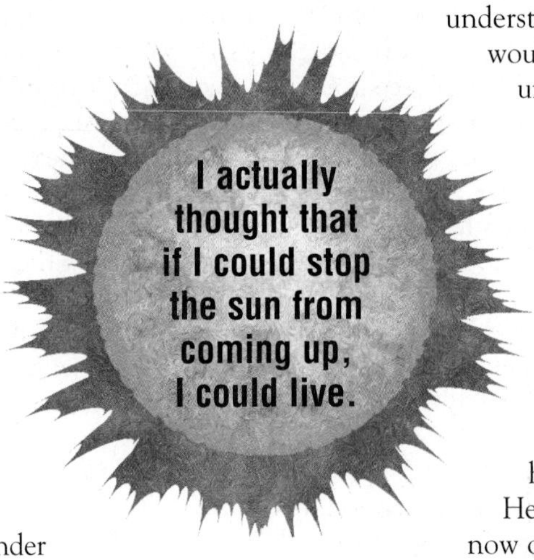

He stopped, and his face came down into his hands. Terry stood and went around the table to stand in back of him, his hands on his shoulders, rubbing gently.

"They didn't shoot me. They came, one of them poked Jackson's body and went on and they left me. But I was dead. I'm still dead, don't you see? I died because I couldn't stop the sun. I died. Inside where I am—I died."

Terry was still in back of him, and he nodded, but he didn't see. Not that. He understood only that he didn't understand, and that he would probably never understand what had truly happened. And maybe his father would never be truly normal. But Terry also knew that it didn't matter. He would try to understand, and the trying would have to be enough. He would try hard from now on, and he would not be embarrassed when his father's eyes went away. He would not be embarrassed no matter what his father did. Terry had knowledge now. Maybe not enough and maybe not all that he would need.

But it was a start.

Teaching Support

Grammar and Language *Minilesson*

Agreement with Collective Nouns

Write the following on the board:

My family is at home.

My family are always going off alone.

Collective nouns name a group: *staff, faculty, team, family.* They take a plural form of the verb only when they refer to the *individuals* in the group. Otherwise, they take a singular verb form. When collective nouns themselves are plural—*staffs, faculties, families*—they take a plural verb form.

Activity Ask for the correct verb form for each sentence.

1. The jury still (disagrees, disagree). about the defendant's guilt. *(disagree)*
2. The team (was, were) divided in their tastes in food. *(were)*
3. The flock of sheep (was, were) guided by the shepherd. *(was)* **L2**

Additional Resources

- ***Grammar and Language Transparency 50***
- ***Grammar and Language Workbook,*** p. 191
- ***Grammar and Composition Handbook,*** Lesson 10.3
- ***Writer's Choice,*** Lessons 9.5, 16.3

Responding to Literature

PERSONAL RESPONSE

- What images in this story are most vivid for you? Why?

Brackets connect questions that are paired to develop higher-level thinking skills.

Analyzing Literature

RECALL

1. When do Terry's father's eyes "go away"?
2. Why is Terry interested in the Vietnam War?
3. What causes Terry's father to crawl on the floor of the hardware store?
4. What reason does Terry's father have for wanting to "stop the sun"?

INTERPRET

5. What might Terry's father's eyes **symbolize** in this story?
6. In your opinion, why does Terry's father insist that Vietnam has "nothing to do with this family"?
7. Why is Terry so bothered by his father's behavior?
8. Theme Connection What does Terry understand, and not understand, about his father by the end of the story?

EVALUATE AND CONNECT

9. How might knowing about a family member's past affect how others feel about that person?
10. Theme Connection What have you learned about the ways in which world events can affect ordinary families?

LITERARY ELEMENTS

Climax

The **climax** of a story is the highest point of action in the plot. All of the earlier events in the story build up to the climax. The ending of the story depends on what happens at the climax.

1. At what point in "Stop the Sun" does the climax occur?
2. How does the action of the characters at the climax affect the outcome of the story?

- See **Literary Terms Handbook**, p. R2.

Responding to the Selection

PERSONAL RESPONSE

Students may choose the vivid war scenes, but they may also find the interaction between father and son closer to their own experience.

Analyzing Literature

1. His eyes go "away" when he thinks of Vietnam.
2. It is the only clue he has to what's wrong with his father.
3. He is reliving an experience from Vietnam, triggered by something he has seen or heard.
4. He knew that darkness was his only protection.
5. They may stand for his feeling that he died with the other men or for what he has seen: the horrors of war.
6. It is partly because he cannot bear to share it with them and partly because he wants to protect them from the horror of the experience.
7. Terry doesn't know what to expect and hopes he won't be embarrassed by his father's behavior.
8. He doesn't truly understand what really happened, but he does understand that it continues to cause his father great pain.
9. It might help them to understand and even forgive that person's actions.
10. Students' answers should show that they recognize that the great events of history affect ordinary people, not just the big names in the history books.

LITERARY ELEMENTS

1. It comes when Terry's father finishes his explanation and Terry feels some of his father's fear.
2. Terry can now think beyond his own concerns and really take care of his father.

Additional Resources

Literary Elements Transparency 53

FLASHES OF INSIGHT 615

Literature and Writing

Writing About Literature

Students' explanations should

- describe Terry's changing feelings
- use specific examples from the selections

Creative Writing

Students' scenes should

- evoke the mood the music creates
- describe both the trigger and the original event

Extending Your Response

Literature Groups Ask students to share only ideas that do not invade their family's privacy.

COLLAB. LEARN.

Interdisciplinary Activity
Remind students that a time line will not show the relative size of the conflicts. These statistics would best be represented on a graph.

LITERATURE & HUMANITIES

World History and Art Transparency 51, "Vietnam War Memorial." Have students discuss Maya Ying Lin's choice of materials for this monument.

Literature and Writing

Writing About Literature

Characterization Gary Paulsen develops characters by sharing their thoughts and feelings with the reader. In a paragraph, explain how Paulsen shows the changes in Terry's feelings for his father. Use examples from Terry's thoughts and his words.

Creative Writing

Flashback A **flashback** is a jump back to an earlier point in time, triggered by something in the present. In "Stop the Sun," Terry's questions lead to his father's detailed flashback of a night in Vietnam. In a few paragraphs, create a scene in which a piece of music triggers a flashback to a pleasant memory. Describe both the trigger and the original event.

Extending Your Response

Literature Groups

Communication Gap Look back at your list from the **Reading Focus** on page 606, and add new ideas that you have after reading "Stop the Sun." Share lists in your group and identify similarities. Discuss ways to avoid or solve breakdowns in communication within a family or another group.

*inter*NET CONNECTION

Use the World Wide Web to find examples of songs about war sung during the Vietnam War. An example is Pete Seeger's circular song, "Where Have All the Flowers Gone." Discuss the lyrics with a group.

Interdisciplinary Activity

Social Studies: History What types of international conflicts has the United States been involved in since 1950? What forces or events led up to these tensions, and what were the results? Use reference materials to help you create a time line of U.S. military involvement overseas. If you wish, work with a group to build a time line that you can post in the classroom.

Reading Further

For more Newbery Honor Books by Gary Paulsen, try these:
Dogsong
Canyons

Save your work for your portfolio.

Skill Minilessons

RETEACH • REVIEW

GRAMMAR AND LANGUAGE • SUBJECT-VERB AGREEMENT

A verb must agree with its subject in person and number, even when words or phrases separate the subject from the verb.

*Terry, after hearing about his father's experiences, **knows** more about him.*

The subject, *Terry,* is a third-person, singular noun. The third-person, singular form of the verb is *knows.*

- For more about subject-verb agreement, see **Language Handbook,** pp. R13–R14.

PRACTICE Copy and complete each sentence, choosing the correct verb in parentheses.

1. Terry and his father (were, was) planning to meet at the front door of the mall.
2. The troops in the night patrol (crosses, cross) the jungle together.
3. The enemy soldiers, the Vietcong, expectantly (await, awaits) dawn.
4. Terry's father, when his eyes go away, (seem, seems) to be in Vietnam.

READING AND THINKING • CAUSE AND EFFECT

Authors may connect ideas by showing a cause-and-effect relationship. In "Stop the Sun," Terry worries that he might be causing his father's illness until he learns that war experiences are the real cause.

- For more about cause and effect, see **Reading Handbook,** p. R97.

PRACTICE Use each pair of words in a sentence that shows a cause-and-effect relationship.

1. war, fear
2. joke, laughter
3. conversation, awakening

VOCABULARY • MULTIPLE-MEANING WORDS

Many words have more than one meaning. For example, the noun *founder* means "a person who founds, or establishes." William Penn was the *founder* of Pennsylvania. The verb *founder* means "to break down, collapse, or fail." Terry *foundered* when he ran out of words. Context clues usually help when a familiar word looks strange. When they fail, use a dictionary.

- For more about multiple-meaning words, see **Reading Handbook,** pp. R89–R90.

PRACTICE Write an original sentence for each underlined word. Pay careful attention to the contexts. Consult a dictionary as needed.

1. a tale with <u>humor</u>
   <u>humor</u> your guest
2. <u>pitch</u> the ball
   the <u>pitch</u> of the slope
3. a doe and <u>fawn</u>
   <u>fawn</u> over the child
4. a <u>loud</u> noise
   a <u>loud</u> tie
5. <u>master</u> a skill
   <u>master</u> of the house

Skill Minilessons

GRAMMAR AND LANGUAGE
SUBJECT-VERB AGREEMENT

1. were
2. cross
3. await
4. seems

READING AND THINKING
CAUSE AND EFFECT

Students' sentences should show true cause-and-effect relationships.

VOCABULARY
MULTIPLE-MEANING WORDS

Students' sentences should show that they understand the meaning of both uses of each word.

Additional Resources

- ***Grammar and Language Workbook,*** p. 187
- ***Grammar and Composition Handbook,*** Lesson 10.5
- ***Writer's Choice,*** Lesson 16.1
- ***Reading Skills Practice Workbook***
- ***Vocabulary Practice,*** p. 36

ASSESSMENT

- ***Quick Checks,*** p. 53
- ***Selection and Theme Assessment,*** pp. 95–96
- ***Performance Assessment,*** p. 50
- ***Testmaker: ExamView Pro***
- ***Interactive Tutor: Self-Assessment***

GENRE FOCUS

Objective

- To understand the elements of a personal essay

Teaching Strategies

Explain that a personal essay usually grows out of the writer's strong feelings about a particular topic. Unlike news reports, essays express the writer's opinions. Ask students to think about topics on which they would like to express their personal opinions.

Personal Opinions and Experience Point out that to be convincing, an essayist must back up his or her opinions with facts and personal experiences.

Informal Language Explain that one reason for the use of informal language is to make the reader feel as though the essayist is speaking directly to him or her. Another might be to make the writing more accessible.

Teaching Support

GENRE FOCUS

PERSONAL ESSAY

Many types of nonfiction are meant to inform or to relate experiences based on fact. For example, biographies, textbooks, and news articles are packed with factual information. One type of nonfiction, the **personal essay,** is meant to let the writer express himself or herself.

Most personal essays share the characteristics explained and illustrated on these two pages.

1 PERSONAL OPINIONS AND EXPERIENCE
In a personal essay, the writer shares his or her own beliefs and experiences. Even when pointing out a universal truth, the essayist builds up to it by sharing personal experiences.

2 INFORMAL LANGUAGE
The author of a personal essay writes as he or she might speak in normal conversation, using familiar words, even slang. The writing may include fragments and run-on sentences that ramble on, jumping from idea to idea in a loose, conversational way.

3 TONE The writer of a personal essay often speaks to readers as directly as friends speak to each other. This direct informal approach can make it easy to identify the author's tone, or attitude, about a topic. Another way to identify tone is to look at the author's specific word choices. The words an author chooses may communicate a particular attitude.

4 IMAGERY Like a poet, an essayist wants to share with readers his or her view of things and reactions to them. To do so, the writer uses sensory details that combine ideas forcefully.

Listening and Speaking *Minilesson*

Reading Aloud Explain that another meaning of the word *reflections* is "thoughts." The author started with an interior thought process and then shaped his thoughts into a written form.

Activity Ask students how they would read aloud a personal essay. Record their ideas on the board. Students' responses might include the following ideas:

- I would follow the tone of the piece.
- I would try to sound as though I were thinking aloud.
- I would speak directly to my audience and watch for their responses.
- I would try to use my voice to convince the audience of my point of view.

Have volunteers apply their suggestions by reading aloud the excerpt on page 619. **L2** COLLAB. LEARN.

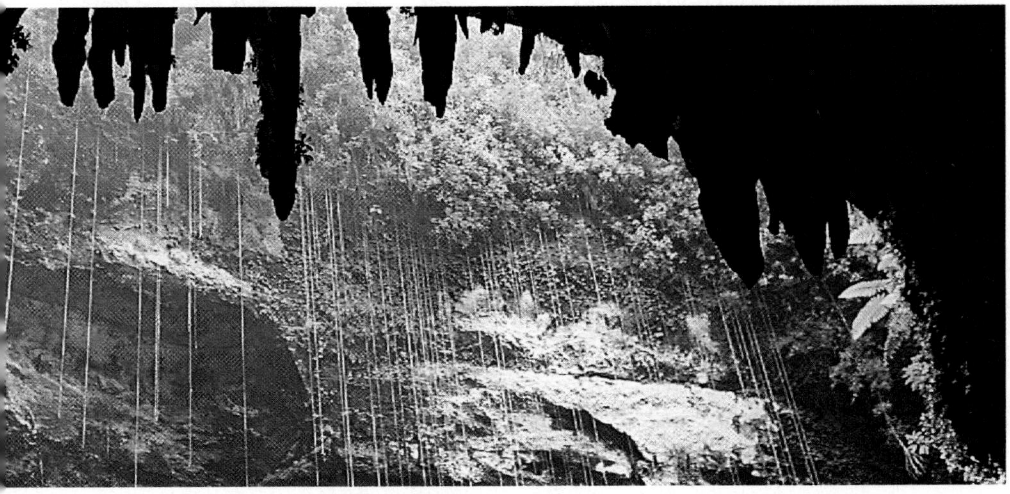

MODEL

Inside the mountains are old creeks that run in circles over the floors of low-ceilinged caves. The fish in these waters are white and translucent; you can see a pink haze of organs beneath the skin. Where there should be eyes there are bulges that do not move. On the walls are white spiders like grey tight buttons of surgical cotton suspended on long hairy legs. There are white beetles, too, scurrying through the hills of black bat dung.

I have always been suspicious of these caves because walls crumble easily under your fingertips; there is no moisture in the air and it smells like balloons. The water smells like oranges but has no taste. Nothing you do here makes any sound.

—Barry Holstun Lopez, from *Desert Notes: Reflections in the Eye of the Raven*

1 PERSONAL OPINIONS AND EXPERIENCE
In this passage, the writer describes his experience in a deep mountain cave. To do this, he shares what he sees, smells, and touches.

2 INFORMAL LANGUAGE
Lopez's casual observation is startling in its contrasts. Notice how he contrasts light and dark.

3 TONE
While Lopez seems to marvel at what he finds in the caves, their otherworldly nature fosters in him a sense of distrust, which he shares with the reader.

4 IMAGERY
Lopez uses sensory details to make the reader feel as if he or she is in the cave with him.

Tone Be sure students understand that the tone of a personal essay may be angry, even sarcastic. An essay that is light or humorous, though, can still make a point.

Imagery Point out that the use of imagery is another way the essay draws the reader into a sense of a one-on-one conversation. The more the reader can sense the writer's point of view, the more he or she can relate to the message.

Technology

Electronic Notebooks

Encourage students to start a file of topics on which they have strong feelings. Have them enter brief notes along with their ideas. As these topics accumulate, they will find that they can eliminate some that are no longer as important as they once seemed to be. The ideas that remain can be used as the bases for personal essays. **L2**

Active Reading Strategies

Objective

- To understand and apply strategies for reading and comprehending personal essays

Teaching Strategies

Ask students to think about their abilities as listeners. Can they put themselves in the speaker's shoes so that they understand his or her experiences? Are they able to separate fact from opinion? Can they critically evaluate the speaker's arguments? Point out that these qualities are important in reading personal essays.

Preview

Students need to recognize that if the topic is one about which they have strong opinions, they should be cautious about rejecting or accepting the author's arguments without reading further.

Clarify

Explain to students that in well thought out personal essays, writers make a series of points, which they then connect to make their argument.

Teaching Support

ACTIVE READING MODEL

Active Reading Strategies

Tips for Reading a Personal Essay

Reading a personal essay can be a lot like listening to a friend talk. However, in a personal essay, organized thoughts and carefully worded choices can make the message more powerful than normal conversation.

- For more about comprehension and sustained silent reading, see **Reading Handbook,** pp. R87–R106.

PREVIEW

As you read the first few paragraphs, identify the general topic and listen for the writer's tone, or attitude. Is the writer amused or angered by the subject? Does he or she expect you to laugh, cry, or listen thoughtfully?

Ask Yourself . . .

- What do the writer's style and word choices tell me about this essay?
- Why might a friend start a conversation this way? What would he or she expect from me?

CLARIFY

Does the writer make thoughts and ideas clear? Do examples, descriptions, and anecdotes elaborate ideas effectively?

Ask Yourself . . .

- Do I understand the main points the author is trying to make?
- Is the writer making a more important point in this paragraph than in other paragraphs? Can I state the main point in my own words?

Reading Journal

Students have been using their reading journals to record ideas and responses to their reading. Encourage them to continue this practice as they respond in personal essays. Suggest that students share their responses with others in the class.

Activity Point out that personal essays, because they express a writer's viewpoints, frequently elicit personal responses from readers. Suggest that as students respond to a personal essay they use their Reading Journal to note the new information they have learned from the essay.

QUESTION

Put yourself in the place of the writer. Ask yourself if you can understand his or her feelings and ideas. If you don't understand, you may want to go back and reread. You may also decide to read ahead at a slower pace. Sometimes reading ahead will answer your questions.

Ask Yourself . . .

- Do I understand the point the writer is trying to make?
- What details provide clues to the purpose of this essay?

EVALUATE

As you read, think about your reaction to the writer's words. Have your opinions and understanding of the topic changed? Were thoughts presented logically, or was the reasoning biased or faulty?

Ask Yourself . . .

- What is my opinion about this writer's thoughts and ideas?
- Were the writer's opinions adequately supported?
- Does the writer succeed in his or her purpose?

APPLYING THE STRATEGIES

Read the following personal essay, "The Summer of Vietnam." Use the **Active Reading Model** notes in the margins as you read. Write your responses on a separate piece of paper, and review them when you have finished reading.

Question

Explain that the writer of a personal essay may have had experiences that are new to readers. Students can make the connection to the experiences, however, by thinking of similar feelings they have had.

Evaluate

Encourage students to value their own judgment of a personal essay if they have applied the active reading strategies they just learned.

FLASHES OF INSIGHT 621

Before Reading

Objectives

- To read and analyze a personal essay
- To identify the literary elements in the personal essay, such as the use of irony to set the tone
- To write an analysis of the author's use of the first-person point of view

Skills

Grammar/Language: Verb Mood
Writing: Paragraph; Poem
Vocabulary: The Suffix *-ize*
Collaboration: Literature Groups

Motivating STUDENTS

Literature Launchers: "Paying Tribute to Fallen Soldiers"

Videodisc Side B, Segment 18

Also available in VHS.

Selection Focus Transparency 53: Have students view the transparency and then discuss the questions provided.

Reading Focus: As an extension of the Reading Focus, have students in small groups share the experiences they jotted down along with their reactions to them.

ACTIVE READING MODEL

Before You Read

The Summer of Vietnam

MEET BARBARA RENAUD GONZÁLEZ

Barbara Renaud González describes herself this way: "I am the daughter of an illegal immigrant. My mother is a Mexican. . . . I am visibly Mexican and an invisible American." González grew up in Texas and graduated from college with a degree in social work. She is a regular contributor to the *Dallas Morning News* and a local public radio station.

Barbara Renaud González was born in 1953. "The Summer of Vietnam" was published in 1992 in New Chicana/Chicano Writing.

READING FOCUS

You have read about Vietnam. Have you ever talked about this war with someone who experienced it in some way?

Journal

Using what you know from what people have said or written, jot down some thoughts about war in general or about Vietnam.

Setting a Purpose

Read to experience the thoughts and feelings of a writer who saw many people go to Vietnam—and never come back.

BUILDING BACKGROUND

The Time and Place Barbara Renaud González wrote the following essay in the 1990s, more than twenty years after the Vietnam War.

Did You Know? The Medal of Honor, the Distinguished Service Cross, and the Bronze Star are awarded by the U.S. government to men and women who risk their lives or perform extraordinary, heroic actions during battle. The Purple Heart may be awarded to those wounded or killed in action.

Purple Heart

VOCABULARY PREVIEW

adolescence (ad′ əl es′ əns) *n.* the period or process of growing from youth to adulthood; teenage years; p. 624

extinguish (iks ting′ gwish) *v.* to put out; end; destroy; p. 624

constitute (kon′ stə to͞ot′) *v.* to form; make up; compose; p. 625

prestigious (pre sti′ jəs) *adj.* having widely recognized importance and influence; impressive; p. 625

agonize (ag′ ə nīz′) *v.* to suffer greatly; struggle painfully; p. 625

redeemed (ri dēmd′) *adj.* gotten or won back; recovered; p. 625

RESOURCE MANAGER

Teaching Tools and Resources
- Theme Six Planning Guide
- Literature Groups Sourcebook

Essential Lesson Support

Lesson-Specific Instruction
- Selection Focus Transparency 53
- Literary Elements Transparency 54
- Active Reading Guide,* p. 54
- Selection Vocabulary Practice, p. 37

Assessment
- Selection Quick Checks,* p. 54
- Sel. and Theme Assmt., pp. 97–98
- Testmaker: ExamView Pro
- Performance Assessment, p. 51

Systematic Language Instruction
- Gr. & Comp. Hbk., L. 12.2

English Language Learners
- ELL Sourcebook, p. 78
- Spanish Summaries, p. 53
- Spanish Translations, pp. 142–143
- Audio Library*
- English, Yes!

Spec. Needs/Strat. Interven.
- Interactive Rdg. Sbk., pp. T184–T186
- Interactive Rdg. Wkbk., pp. 100–101
- Inclusion Strat. Sbk., pp. 29–30, 87–88
- Audio Library*

* Also available in Spanish

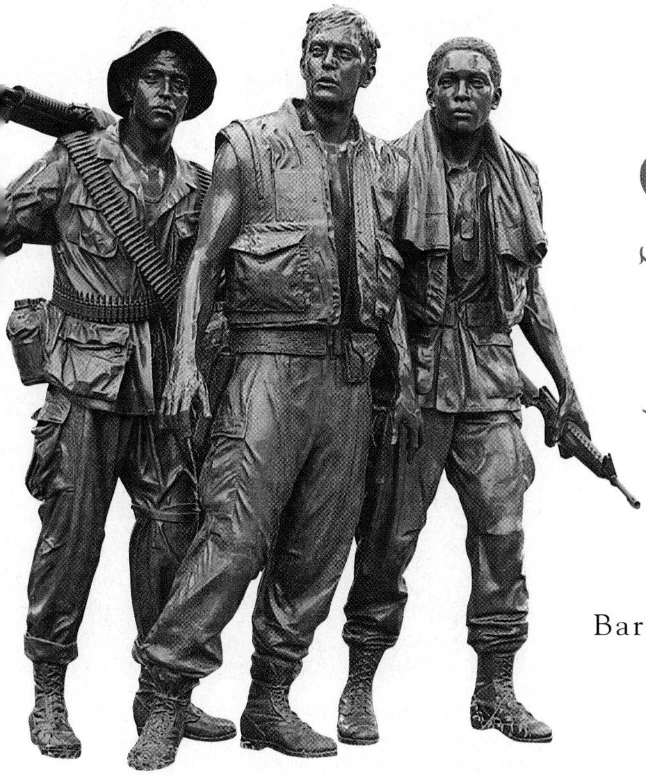

The Summer of Vietnam

Barbara Renaud González

Three Servicemen, 1984. Frederick Hart. Cast bronze, height: 7 ft. National Park Service, Washington, DC.

ACTIVE READING MODEL

So, what are you writing about? I ask Bill Broyles, the former *Newsweek Magazine* goldenboy.[1] He's the Texas man who can write *anything* and get it published. Unlike me.

"Vietnam," he says. The worst answer. The only answer that can make me cry.

Instead, at night I remember.

Ernesto Sánchez is Vietnam to me. Born July 9, 1947. In a place called Kennedy, Texas. Died in the summer of 1967, somewhere in Vietnam. Somewhere in my 13th summer.

This is my Vietnam.

PREDICT

Can you guess from the first two paragraphs what the writer's attitude about Vietnam might be?

A

1. Anyone referred to as a *goldenboy* (or *goldengirl*) is seen as having a promising future.

Reading the Selection

SUMMARY

Barbara Renaud González was a girl at the time of the Vietnam War, fully confident that the personable young Latino men in uniforms who occupied her daydreams would return safely. Many did not, and her ongoing pain at this loss is twofold. She mourns the individuals but also is angry at the lack of recognition the Latino community has received for its disproportionate sacrifices.

Spanish Summaries, p. 53

A Active Reading Strategies

PREDICT *(The author is obviously affected by the subject.)* Ask students to predict from other clues what the essay is about. *(The names Ernesto Sánchez and Kennedy, Texas, are clues to the topic of this essay.)*

VOCABULARY If you haven't previewed the selection vocabulary with students, stop and remind them to use context clues to unlock the meanings of new vocabulary words.

Additional Resources

- ***Active Reading Guide,*** p. 54
- ***Audio Library***
- ***Spanish Audio Library***

Teaching Support

CONNECTING TO OTHER SELECTIONS

The chart at the right shows three ways to connect "The Summer of Vietnam" to other selections in this book.

For specific teaching strategies, see the ***Theme Six Planning Guide.***

Connection	Title
Life Skills: Leading and Organizing →	"I Have a Dream," p. 494
Thematic: War →	"Paul Revere's Ride," p. 449
Literary: Narrator →	"The Journey," p. 169

B Literary Elements

IMAGERY What feeling is the author trying to convey with the use of such images as "Ken dolls" and "marine boys"? *(She is sharing with us the innocence of a girl who in her day-dreams equated as romantic figures Ken dolls with real, live Marines.)*

VIEWING THE PHOTOGRAPH

Viewing Response *The seemingly endless list of casualties evokes emotional responses from visitors to the wall. Perhaps the fact that so many Americans opposed the war adds to the impact of the art—a testimonial to those who died.*

C Active Reading Strategies

CONNECT *(Latinos were well represented in the ranks, in a higher percentage than they were represented in the population. Another large group was made up of African Americans.)* Have students calculate what the numbers represent. What is 22 percent of 3,427? What is 12 percent? *(754 and 411, which added together equal one-third of the total)*

ACTIVE READING MODEL

B

I sang love songs to them. Made up Ken dolls after them. Imagined kissing them. I still do. Marine-boys. Boys in dress green with stiff brass buttons that would catch your breaking heart when they gave you the biggest *abrazo*[2] of your life. Then they died in Vietnam.

Always teasing me. "This last dance is for you, Barbara," they'd say. Taught me to dance those skip-steps of adolescence. Told me they'd wait for me. And they never came back from Vietnam to see how I'd grown up for them.

Vietnam Veterans Memorial, 1982. Maya Lin. Washington, DC.

Viewing the photograph: Why, in your view, has this memorial wall become such a powerful monument?

CONNECT

C What do I know about the people who died in Vietnam and those who survived?

I knew they would not die. Heroes don't die in the movies, after all. The good guys always win. Who would dare extinguish the crooked smile football hands and Aqua Velva[3] faces I knew so well? My brothers-at-war.

Of the 3,427 Texas men who died in Vietnam, 22 percent were Latinos. And another 12 percent of the dead were African-American. The minorities were *not* a minority in the platoons, but a majority of the frightened faces. And one-third of the body bags.[4]

2. An *abrazo* (ə brä′ zō) is a hug or embrace.
3. *Aqua Velva* is the brand name of a popular after-shave lotion.
4. In the U.S. Army, a *platoon* consists of four squads having ten soldiers each. *Body bags* are zippered bags, usually made of rubber, for transporting human corpses.

Vocabulary

adolescence (ad′ əl es′ əns) *n.* the period or process of growing from youth to adulthood; teenage years

extinguish (iks ting′ gwish) *v.* to put out; end; destroy

Teaching Support

MEETING INDIVIDUAL NEEDS — ENGLISH LANGUAGE LEARNERS

Borrowed Words Ask students to think of words in their first language for which they do not know an exact English equivalent. Explain that this is often the way such words work their way into English, as *machismo* did from Spanish. If a language lacks a word, speakers borrow one from another.

Activity Have students make a "pitch" for lending words from their first language to English. Have each student write, pronounce, and then offer several reasons to "buy" the word. Ask students to "sell" their message as radio or television ads might.

Additional Resources

English Language Learners Sourcebook, p. 78

This at a time when Latinos constituted 12 percent of the population.

But the machismo goes a long way in war. We Latinos received more medals, thirteen of the prestigious Medal of Honor,[5] than any other group.

We can count soldiers in the American Revolution (as Spaniards), the Roosevelt Rough Riders,[6] both sides of the Civil War, and plenty of fathers and abuelitos[7] in the world wars. Soldiering doesn't require U.S. citizenship, and no one cares how you crossed the border if you're willing to fight on our side.

We lost our best men in Vietnam. Isaac Camacho died first in 1963. Everett Alvarez was the first American pilot shot down, spending eight-and-a-half years as a POW.[8] Juan Valdez was in the last helicopter leaving Vietnam. First in, and last out. They didn't go to Canada or Mexico.[9] They went directly to Vietnam.

But from Oliver Stone, you would think that all our boys looked like Tom Cruise. Or agonized at China Beach.[10] No. They were my brothers, uncles, cousins, my heroes.

Sometimes it looks as if they died for nothing. Impossible. It cannot be. Blood lost is blood redeemed, they say. What is the boy worth? If he died for all of us, then we must gain in proportion to the sacrifice. A Medal of Honor for the neighborhood school. Some Distinguished Service Crosses for family housing. Maybe the Bronze Stars for the judge or councilman. Flying Crosses for a good job. And a Purple Heart for a mother who still cries in Spanish.

5. *Machismo* (mä chēz′ mō) is the idea that males are (or should be) masculine and superior to females. (Men who are seen as having these qualities are described as being *macho.*) The *Medal of Honor* is the highest U.S. military decoration.
6. The *Rough Riders* were members of a cavalry unit, led by Theodore *Roosevelt*, that fought in Cuba during the Spanish-American War.
7. *Abuelitos* (ä′ bwə lē′ tōs) are grandfathers or old men.
8. Alvarez was a prisoner of war, or *POW.*
9. Some young men fled to *Canada* or *Mexico* to avoid military service in Vietnam.
10. Oliver Stone directed the 1989 movie *Born on the Fourth of July,* starring Tom Cruise. *China Beach* was a 1980s television drama about Vietnam.

❖

Vocabulary

constitute (kon′ stə to͞ot′) *v.* to form; make up; compose

prestigious (pre sti′ jəs) *adj.* having widely recognized importance and influence; impressive

agonize (ag′ ə nīz′) *v.* to suffer greatly; struggle painfully

redeemed (ri dēmd′) *adj.* gotten or won back; recovered

EVALUATE

D What information is based on fact, and what is the author's opinion?

CLARIFY

E What does González mean by "no one cares how you crossed the border" and "they didn't go to Canada or Mexico"?

QUESTION

F How does the author seem to feel about the recognition of Latino soldiers in Vietnam?

EVALUATE

G Does it serve the writer's purpose to end the essay with a listing of military awards?

D Active Reading Strategies

EVALUATE *(The statistics are facts. The author's opinion is in her tone, which suggests that these facts are not well enough known.)*

E Active Reading Strategies

CLARIFY *(The author is suggesting that even illegal aliens have served this country well and bravely.)*

F Active Reading Strategies

QUESTION *(The author is angry that movies and television programs do not show the extent of Latino representation in the ranks.)*

G Active Reading Strategies

EVALUATE *(The author is proud of the awards but suggests that it would be more useful to the Latino community if its sacrifices were compensated for with such necessities of life as schools and housing.)*

Thematic Focus

Flashes of Insight The author was a young girl at the time of the war. Have students discuss whether their gender would determine how they felt about the war. Are there some insights they could gain about Vietnam from their mothers or grandmothers or other women who were alive during the war?

ASSESSMENT

Quick Checks, p. 54

Grammar and Language *Minilesson*

Verb Mood Write the following sentences on the board:

If I were you, I'd pay attention to the signs.
If the earth were flat, we'd sail off the edge.

Explain that the subjunctive form of the verb is often introduced by the word *if* followed by an imaginary situation. The use of *were* often indicates the subjunctive, even when a subject is singular.

The examples are not in the subjunctive mood. They refer to actual or possible situations.

If she was ill, why did she work?
If he likes chocolate, he'll love these.

Activity Have students tell which sentences are in the subjunctive mood.

1. If I'm late, don't lock me out.
2. If Sam were running for class president, I'd vote for him. *(subjunctive)*
3. If the walls were thicker, we wouldn't have heard anything. *(subjunctive)*

Additional Resources

Grammar and Language Transparency 51

Responding to the Selection

PERSONAL RESPONSE

Students may say that the war goes beyond what they have seen in movies and television shows.

Analyzing Literature

1. The Vietnam War is his subject.
2. They were friendly, self-confident, and fond of teasing the young girl, who so clearly idolized them.
3. Latinos constituted 12 percent of the population. However, 22 percent of Texas men who died in Vietnam were Latinos.
4. Sometimes it looks as if they died for nothing, the war was lost, but blood lost is blood redeemed. (The sacrifice of their lives resulted in the saving of many other lives.) If he died for all of us, then we must gain in proportion to the sacrifice. (One man's sacrifice for his country should result in benefits for all—better housing, schools, and jobs, for example.)
5. She may be somewhat jealous of his status and ability to get anything published, but she apparently is moved by his subject to write of her own feelings about Vietnam in the form of this essay.
6. She does not seem to be afraid that they might not return. Her naive attitude has been shaped by movies with happy endings.
7. She means that her personal experience of Vietnam is associated with the memories of young men she knew, which the name of the country always arouses.
8. She says that the idea of their having died for nothing is "impossible. It cannot be." She says that their deaths must not have been in vain. Our memorial to each boy should be as great as his sacrifice. Let us do more than give medals. Let us build a nation that they would have been proud to die for, as we can be proud of them, even as we mourn them.
9. At first she was naively supportive of her patriotic friends and neighbors. Later she is just as admiring of them but wonders whether their sacrifice was worth it, since nothing good, beyond some medals, seems to have come of it for the people left behind.
10. Students may gain insight into how divisive the war was in American society. One issue was the disproportionate representation of minorities in the services.

LITERARY ELEMENTS

1. She says, "No one cares how you crossed the border if you're willing to fight on our side." (Supporters of the war set aside their disapproval of illegal immigration for the aliens' support.)
2. The author says that those with medals need good schools, jobs, housing, and political representation.

Additional Resources

Literary Elements Transparency 54

Active Reading and Critical Thinking

ACTIVE READING MODEL

Responding to Literature

PERSONAL RESPONSE

- How has this essay changed or affected your attitude toward war?

Active Reading Response

- Which of the **Active Reading Strategies** on pages 620–621 did you find most useful in reading this essay?

Brackets connect questions that are paired to develop higher-level thinking skills.

Analyzing Literature

RECALL

1. What is the subject of the article Bill Broyles is writing?
2. Describe the boys González admired when she was thirteen.
3. What percentage of the U.S. population was Hispanic during the Vietnam War? What percentage of the soldiers from Texas who died were Hispanic?
4. What kinds of comments are made by people who think the fighting in Vietnam was worth the sacrifice?

INTERPRET

5. What seems to be the writer's attitude toward Broyles? toward Broyles's subject?
6. How does González feel about the danger to her friends as they leave for Vietnam? Why, do you think, does she have this attitude?
7. What does González mean by "this is my Vietnam"?
8. In your opinion, does González agree with those who think the men in Vietnam died for nothing? Does she side with those who believe "that we must gain in proportion to the sacrifice"? Explain.

EVALUATE AND CONNECT

9. What stand do you think González takes on the war? Do you agree with her position? Support your answers with examples. Look at your response in the **Reading Focus** on page 622.
10. Theme Connection What new insight might readers of this essay gain? Why?

LITERARY ELEMENTS

Irony

Irony is the use of language to show the contrast between what things may seem to be and what they really are. For example, thirteen-year-old Barbara admires the young Marines, their uniforms, and their stiff brass buttons. She knows from the movies that they will win and will not die. The irony is that these uniforms and brass buttons put them in a place where they may, in fact, die.

1. How does the writer use irony to contrast attitudes toward illegal aliens and attitudes toward those who enlist in the military?
2. Find and explain another example of irony in the essay.

- See **Literary Terms Handbook,** p. R5.

Extending Your Response

Writing About Literature

Point of View In this essay, González recalls childhood memories and retells them from a **first-person point of view,** using the pronouns *I* and *me.* Write a paragraph or two explaining how González's use of a personal experience strengthens or weakens the effect of her essay.

Creative Writing

Celebrate Your Heritage González is a Mexican American who writes about Mexican Americans. Write a poem in which you celebrate your own heritage and the contributions that Americans of your ethnic background have made to the country. If possible, include imagery–language that describes what you see, hear, feel, smell, or taste–in your poem.

Literature Groups

Hollywood vs. the Real World González writes that "from [the movie director] Oliver Stone, you would think that all our boys looked like Tom Cruise." With a group, discuss various movies and television programs that succeed or fail in showing realistic views of life in the United States. Be prepared to summarize your group's ideas for the class.

Interdisciplinary Activity

Math Numbers tell a story. With a partner, research the number of U.S. soldiers from various ethnic backgrounds who died in Vietnam. Create a chart that shows which ethnic group lost the highest percentage of soldiers. With your class, discuss and explain your reactions to these numbers. What story do they seem to tell?

Reading Further

For a girl's experience of a different war, read *Summer of My German Soldier* by Bette Greene.

Save your work for your portfolio.

Skill Minilesson

RETEACH • REVIEW

VOCABULARY • THE SUFFIX *-ize*

A **suffix** is a word part added to the end of a word. Suffixes change the meaning of a word, but only slightly. For example, the suffix *-ize* means "to cause to be or become." Adding this suffix to the noun *fertile* simply changes the noun into a verb, *fertilize.* Think of *capitalize.* When you *capitalize* a letter, you cause it to become a capital. When you *agonize,* you cause yourself to be in agony.

- For more about suffixes, see **Language Handbook,** pp. R47–R48.

PRACTICE Match each word in the left column with its meaning. Use what you know about the suffix *-ize* to help you.

1. humanize	a. able to get along well with others
2. socialize	b. thrifty, not wasteful
3. economize	c. clearly intended for a particular individual
4. localize	d. like a person instead of an animal
5. personalize	e. limited or confined to a particular place

Extending Your Response

Writing About Literature

Students' paragraphs should
- cite examples to support their thinking
- be based on the effect the point of view has on their reading

Creative Writing

Students' poems should
- include vivid imagery
- employ a rhythm that reflects the celebratory tone

Literature Groups Point out to students that their summaries should reflect the major points of view within the group. COLLAB. LEARN.

Interdisciplinary Activity Remind students that statistics are just numbers. Their interpretation and the emotions they call forth, however, go beyond mere numbers and symbols.

Skill Minilesson

VOCABULARY • THE SUFFIX *-ize*

1. d 2. a 3. b
4. e 5. c

Additional Resources

Vocabulary Practice, p. 37

LITERATURE & HUMANITIES

Have students examine the lyrics of the anti-war song "Waist Deep in Big Muddy," from American Music: Cultural Traditions, Volume 2 Track 20.

ASSESSMENT

- ***Quick Checks,*** p. 54
- ***Selection and Theme Assessment,*** pp. 97–98
- ***Performance Assessment,*** p. 51
- ***Testmaker: ExamView Pro***
- ***Interactive Tutor: Self-Assessment***

Before Reading

Objectives

- To read and analyze a personal essay
- To recognize the role of the speaker in a personal essay
- To list and discuss elements of setting in the personal essay

Skills

Reading/Thinking: Drawing Conclusions; Paraphrasing
Writing: Letter
Grammar/Language: Active Voice
Vocabulary: Analogies
Collaboration: Literature Groups

Motivating STUDENTS

Selection Focus Transparency 54: Before presenting the transparency, ask students to recall their first introductions to the Declaration of Independence.

Reading Focus: As an extension of the Reading Focus, suggest that students in small groups role-play the act of signing the Declaration of Independence, then discuss their feelings about it.

LITERATURE & HUMANITIES

Have students view *United States History and Art* Transparency 4, "The Declaration of Independence" and discuss their thoughts on the Declaration of Independence.

Before You Read

Finding America

MEET A. C. GREENE

When A. C. Greene sits down to write, he asks himself what he can say that readers will care about. As a journalist and university instructor, he has developed this philosophy: "You have to think that you're saying something or revealing one little point in life that never has quite been revealed in quite this fashion about quite this type of situation. And then you write."

Alvin Carl Greene was born in 1923 in Abilene, Texas. This selection was taken from a transcript of the MacNeil/Lehrer NewsHour *on June 30, 1986.*

READING FOCUS

Imagine that you are watching leaders in the American colonies as they walk up to sign the Declaration of Independence.

Quickwrite

In a few sentences, describe your feelings at this historic moment.

Setting a Purpose

Read to find out how a World War II soldier discovers the meaning of the Fourth of July.

BUILDING BACKGROUND

The Time and Place The following selection is set in Philadelphia, Pennsylvania, during World War II.

Did You Know? Most Americans today think of the founding fathers as heroes, but many people of their time saw them as traitors to England. Treason was punishable by death; yet the patriots showed great courage. John Hancock signed his name to the Declaration of Independence in large letters so that England's King George could see it easily. Benjamin Franklin said, "We must all hang together, or assuredly we shall all hang separately."

VOCABULARY PREVIEW

diverse (di vurs′) *adj.* noticeably different; varied; p. 630
compelling (kəm pel′ ing) *adj.* impressive and forceful; p. 630
paramount (par′ ə mount′) *adj.* above all others in influence or importance; supreme; p. 630
lurk (lurk) *v.* to lie hidden or move about in a sneaky way; p. 631
resolve (ri zolv′) *n.* steady determination; firmness of purpose; p. 631

RESOURCE MANAGER

Teaching Tools and Resources
- Theme Six Planning Guide
- Literature Groups Sourcebook

Essential Lesson Support

Lesson-Specific Instruction
- Selection Focus Transparency 54
- Literary Elements Transparency 55
- Active Reading Guide,* p. 55
- Selection Vocabulary Practice, p. 38

Assessment
- Selection Quick Checks,* p. 55
- Sel. and Theme Assmt., pp. 99-100
- Testmaker: ExamView Pro
- Performance Assessment, p. 52

Systematic Language Instruction
- Gr. & Comp. Hbk., L. 12.3, 12.4
- Vocabulary Power, Lesson 27
- Spelling Power, Lesson 24

English Language Learners
- ELL Sourcebook, p. 79
- Spanish Summaries, p. 54
- Spanish Translations, pp. 144-145
- Audio Library*
- English, Yes!

Spec. Needs/Strat. Interven.
- Interactive Rdg. Sbk., pp. T187-T189
- Interactive Rdg. Wkbk., pp. 102-103
- Inclusion Strat. Sbk., pp. 75-76
- Audio Library*

* Also available in Spanish

Finding America

A. C. Greene

One summer evening in the middle of World War II, I found myself wandering the streets of Philadelphia—a little lost, and more than a little lonesome. I had arrived in town only a few days before—a sailor from Texas who had never been any further east than Chicago.

The Fourth of July, 1917. Childe Hassam. Oil on canvas, 36 x 26 in. Private collection.

Reading the Selection

SUMMARY

The author recalls how, as a young sailor facing combat in World War II, he found himself at Independence Hall in Philadelphia, where the Declaration of Independence was signed. Standing at that spot, he feels the power of that history, and it gives new meaning to his own experiences.

Spanish Summaries, p. 54

A Active Reading Strategies

PREDICT Ask students to use words and phrases on the first page to establish time and place. How do these give clues to the topic of the essay? *(World War II, streets of Philadelphia. Since he is a sailor, one would assume he is going East to fight in the war.)*

VOCABULARY If you haven't previewed the selection vocabulary with students, stop and remind them to use context clues to unlock the meanings of new vocabulary words.

Additional Resources

- ***Active Reading Guide,*** p. 55
- ***Audio Library***
- ***Spanish Audio Library***

Teaching Support

CONNECTING TO OTHER SELECTIONS

The chart at the right shows three ways to connect "Finding America" to other selections in this book.

For specific teaching strategies, see the ***Theme Six Planning Guide.***

Connection		Title
Life Skills: Lifelong Learning	→	"Homeless," p. 39
Thematic: America's History	→	"The People, Yes," p. 354
Literary: Tone	→	"The Treasure of Lemon Brown," p. 5

B Literary Elements

SPEAKER Point out to students how the speaker felt at the beginning of the narrative. Have students locate and read aloud the phrases and sentences that convey that feeling. *(Possible answers: a little lost and lonesome; alone without a plan or a phone number.)*

C Active Reading Strategies

QUESTION What does the author mean when he says, "I put my foot in the Fourth of July"? *(He felt as though he had stepped back in time and could sense the power that the events of the Fourth of July, 1776, had on people then.)*

D Critical Thinking

DRAWING CONCLUSIONS Does the author expect the reader to recognize this quotation from the Declaration of Independence? *(The author is assuming the reader will recognize them, since he places them in the text before he tells where they came from.)*

It was my first liberty[1] in the city of brotherly love. I left the naval station alone without a plan or a phone number to my name and rode the Broad Street subway to Center Square where city hall towered over downtown, with William Penn at its tiptop, hands outstretched, blessing his city. I passed some wonderfully attractive restaurants with red roses on snowy tables, but when I looked at the menu posted in the window, the prices took away my hunger. My navy salary was $64 a month. I settled for a bowl of clam chowder at the Reading Terminal Oyster Bar.

B Emerging at dusk, I walked down Market Street feeling even more lonesome—the least important sailor in the U.S. Navy. Turning into a side street and walking a few more blocks, I realized I had no idea where I was. The sidewalks were empty. I stopped and looked around, glancing at the doorway of the red brick building where I had halted. A plaque was mounted there, and the words brought me to tears as I read them. "The Birthplace of the United States of America." Looking upward, following the lines of the familiar spire, I recognized this was Independence Hall, where the Declaration of Independence was signed July 4, 1776. It happened here. That diverse group of heroes gathered on this very spot to make that final, awesome decision. Thomas Jefferson, who wrote the document; Benjamin Franklin, age 70; John Adams, who would one day be President of the United States; Francis Hopkinson, author and songwriter; Benjamin Rush, physician. They touched these bricks that morning, taking those decisive steps, turning their back on the safety of concession. Cautiously, with a sort of metaphysical[2] expectation, I placed my foot in that stone footprint. I put my foot in the Fourth of July. C

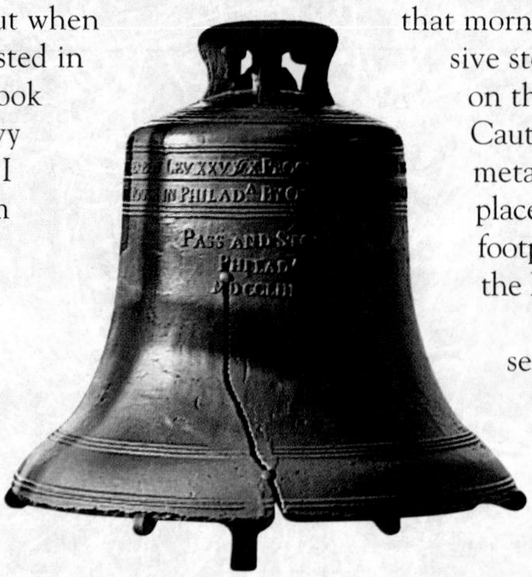

The Liberty Bell. Philadelphia, PA.

Suddenly, the bold sentences thundered through me with new and immediate power. "We hold these truths to be self-evident: that all men are created equal, that they are endowed by their Creator with certain unalienable[3] rights, and among these rights are life, liberty and the pursuit of happiness." D It was, it is the most compelling document in American history, paramount in its importance. Because without it, the other

1. In the navy, *liberty* is time off granted to a sailor to go ashore.

2. *Concession,* here, is an act of giving something up. These men chose to stand up for their beliefs rather than to keep giving in to the British. *Metaphysical* refers to what is beyond the limits of the physical world. Walking where these men walked carries the author, in mind and spirit, into their presence.

3. Rights given *(endowed)* by God may not be taken away *(are unalienable).*

Vocabulary

diverse (di vurs′) *adj.* noticeably different; varied
compelling (kəm pel′ ing) *adj.* impressive and forceful
paramount (par′ ə mount′) *adj.* above all others in influence or importance; supreme

Teaching Support

Grammar and Language *Minilesson*

Active Voice Write the following sentences on the board:

1. *A plaque was mounted there.*
2. *That heroic group gathered on this spot to make that awesome decision.*

Explain that a sentence is in the active voice when the subject *performs* the action of the verb, as in sentence 2. A sentence is in the passive voice when the subject *receives* the action, as in sentence 1. The active voice is usually a strong, direct way to express an idea. The passive voice is useful when the writer does not know who performed the action.

Activity Have students identify the voice in the following sentences:

1. The jet was hit by gunfire. *(passive)*
2. A helicopter rescued the crew. *(active)*
3. All three men were lifted to safety. *(passive)*

Additional Resources

- ***Grammar and Language Transparency 52***
- ***Grammar and Language Workbook,*** p. 97
- ***Grammar and Composition Handbook,*** Lesson 3.10
- ***Writer's Choice,*** Lesson 10.10

documents and amendments remain locked in the hearts and minds of those who conceived them.

These men who put their names to that declaration put their lives on the line—the firing line or the lines to the gallows.[4] If the colonies lost the revolution, there was no place for them to hide, no shelter from the wrath of King George, no Bill of Rights to call on for protection. Their names were on this treasonable paper. There was no denial.

I could hear voices. John Hancock, president of Congress and first in line, penning that now familiar signature and exclaiming, we are told, "King George will have no trouble reading that." None of them acknowledging the fear that must have lurked beneath the consciousness of them all. They were not just signing a petition; they were demanding the noose.

And yet there was surely an even stronger fear lurking: would it work? Even if the battles and political struggles were successful, what terrible creature might they be loosing on mankind? What price independence at a time in history when it had never before been defined? Even the taste for human freedom was uncertain. They were writing the original recipe. That to secure these rights governments were instituted among men deriving[5] their just powers from the consent of the governed.

And there I was that darkening evening in Philadelphia, waiting to be sent into a war which, in a sense, was being fought because of what they did here on that long before July 4—a war from which I had no assurance of returning. A war that would cost me years of time and the death of friends and take me where I, like millions of others, would ask, "What am I doing here?" **E**

But where might I have been had they hesitated, had they divided and lacked resolve? With all the flaws and failings of the creature they created, where would the world be? Would I have chosen otherwise? Of course not. No, all these thoughts didn't find me that one night. Over the years I have believed, then changed my mind; have taken stands, then deserted them; have raged and wondered and prayed. But no matter what I've discovered about my country or myself, I've not forgotten that evening more than 40 years ago when I put my foot in the Fourth of July.

4. *Gallows* refers to the frame from which condemned criminals were hanged.

5. To *derive* is to get from a source.

❖

Vocabulary
lurk (lurk) *v.* to lie hidden or move about in a sneaky way
resolve (ri zolv′) *n.* steady determination; firmness of purpose

E Author's Craft

SETTING The author has a purpose in tying together the atmosphere and feelings of the country during World War II with that of the time of the American Revolution. How does he draw a parallel between the two times? *(The men who signed the document were frightened of what might happen to them because of that. He, too, was frightened, but he, as they did before him, would not choose otherwise.)*

Thematic Focus

Flashes of Insight The author uses his personal revelation about the meaning of the Declaration to help him through a crucial time in his life. Ask students to think about something that people take for granted and how they can gain some new insight about it.

ASSESSMENT

Quick Checks, p. 55

FINE ART TRANSPARENCY 19

You may want to use ***Fine Art Transparency 19*** to discuss ways in which stories of historical events help you understand your country.

Reading Minilesson

Paraphrasing Some of the language of the essay parallels the language of the Declaration of Independence and is difficult to comprehend. By putting the language into their own words, or paraphrasing, students will be better able to understand.

Activity Read aloud the portions of the Declaration of Independence that are paralleled here. After each portion ask students to use their own words to explain what they heard. Help them to put it in the language of today. For example, "We hold these truths to be self-evident: that all men are created equal . . .": We believe that it goes without saying that everyone is equal. **L2**

Additional Resources

Reading Skills Practice Workbook

FLASHES OF INSIGHT 631

Responding to the Selection

PERSONAL RESPONSE

Some students may choose to do a "word sketch," jotting down descriptive words and phrases inspired by the essay.

Analyzing Literature

1. He feels lonely and lost.
2. Independence Hall. The Declaration of Independence was signed there.
3. They feared that they might be hanged for treason and that the newly independent nation might fail.
4. He makes a connection between what he faces and what the signers did; and he realizes that his experience is a direct result of what they did. The fact that the signers went ahead despite their fears gives him the resolve to face his future.
5. The words of the Declaration of Independence have new meaning for him. He believes in what they and his country represent.
6. He is referring to the Constitution of the United States, whose articles and amendments are the blueprints for this country's government and law. Without the Declaration of Independence to establish America's freedom, the Constitution would never have been written.
7. He is talking about the new United States, an experiment in democracy that might have failed instead and have been taken over by tyrants.
8. If the democracy had not been founded by these men, the United States might never have chosen to stand up against the oppressors of Europe and Asia.
9. The writer suggests, in his last paragraph, that there have been times when he was not so certain about his beliefs as he is now. Then, however, he recalls that evening when he discovered the true ideals of the United States as they were on July 4, 1776.
10. Students' answers may point out that the Declaration did not abolish all inequities, such as those based on servitude and sex discrimination or racial inequality.

Responding to Literature

PERSONAL RESPONSE

- Visualize the many scenes from this story. Quickly sketch the one you found most vivid.

Brackets connect questions that are paired to develop higher-level thinking skills.

Analyzing Literature

RECALL

1. At first, how does the speaker feel in Philadelphia?
2. What is the red brick building that the speaker calls "The Birthplace of the United States of America"? What once occurred there?
3. What two fears do the signers of the Declaration have?
4. What feelings and observations does the speaker express as he considers being sent into war?

INTERPRET

5. In your opinion, why have the speaker's feelings changed by the end of the story?
6. What might the speaker mean when he says that without the Declaration, "the other documents and amendments remain locked in the hearts and minds of those who conceived them"?
7. What might the "terrible creature" be that the signers were "loosing on mankind"? Why might it be terrible?
8. What might the speaker mean when he says the war (World War II) "was being fought because of what they did here"?

EVALUATE AND CONNECT

9. The **title** of a selection often gives important information about people and their ideas. Why might this story be called "Finding America"?
10. Do you think the Declaration and the freedom it created have "flaws and failings," as the writer suggests? Explain.

LITERARY ELEMENTS

Speaker

The **speaker** is the voice in a poem. In nonfiction and fiction, this term can also refer to the **narrator,** the person or character who tells a story. A speaker may reveal his or her own attitudes and opinions. For example, the speaker of "Finding America" shares his deepest thoughts with readers.

1. How would you tell this true story differently if you were the speaker?
2. How might a person who lost a loved one in World War II tell this story differently? Explain.
3. How might the speaker react to a student who didn't know the history of the Declaration of Independence?

• See **Literary Terms Handbook,** p. R9.

LITERARY ELEMENTS

1. Students' answers should be highly personal.
2. He or she might explore whether the cause was worth the loved one's life.
3. The speaker would be troubled by such ignorance of our country's founding document.

Additional Resources

Literary Elements Transparency 55

Extending Your Response

Writing About Literature

Setting In "Finding America," A. C. Greene shares a flash of insight that he experienced during World War II. Join with a small group of students, and list the effects that the setting–both time and place–might have had on Greene's attitude. You may find it helpful to reread parts of the selection and try to visualize the setting as Greene saw it.

Creative Writing

Letter from Philadelphia Imagine that you are seeing Independence Hall for the first time. Describe your thoughts and feelings in a letter to a friend back home. If you need help getting started, review what you wrote for the **Reading Focus** on page 628. Consider using a narrative form, including setting, dialogue, and quotations.

Literature Groups

What If? A. C. Greene asks, "But where might I have been had they hesitated, had they divided and lacked resolve?" In a small group, discuss possible answers to this question. Then agree on the two most likely ones. Be prepared to share your responses with the class.

Interdisciplinary Activity

Art Draw, sketch, or paint a picture to accompany Greene's story. If you prefer, find a photograph or painting that captures the thoughts and emotions of the speaker. Remember that the setting you choose will create an atmosphere for the story.

Reading Further

For other ways to find America, read *Paperquake: A Puzzle* by Kathryn Reiss

Save your work for your portfolio.

Skill Minilesson

RETEACH • REVIEW

VOCABULARY • ANALOGIES

An **analogy** is a type of comparison that is based on the relationships between things or ideas.

stomp : walk :: shout : talk

To *stomp* is to *walk* loudly; to *shout* is to *talk* loudly.

If an analogy uses words with similar meanings, try to make up a sentence that uses both words plus a descriptive word. For example, "to *slurp* is to *drink* noisily." Then see if the same descriptive word can also be used to describe the relationship between another pair of words.

PRACTICE Choose the pair of words that best completes each analogy.

1. lurk : wait ::
   a. spy : watch
   b. study : cheat
   c. skip : run
   d. gulp : drink
   e. tease : criticize
2. diverse : similar ::
   a. small : heavy
   b. sad : cheerful
   c. familiar : dangerous
   d. important : serious
   e. thankful : apologetic

For more about analogies, see **Communications Skills Handbook**, p. R73.

Extending Your Response

Writing About Literature

Students' lists should

- recognize the historic and emotional atmosphere of the setting
- explain how the atmosphere may have affected the speaker

Creative Writing

Students' letters should

- be personal and not a reflection of the selection
- show a feeling for and an understanding of the significance of the site

Literature Groups Point out that students, in suggesting scenarios, can refer to the history of other nations whose experiments with independence have been less successful. COLLAB. LEARN.

Interdisciplinary Activity Encourage students to use color and motion to capture the thoughts and emotions of the writer.

Skill Minilesson

VOCABULARY • ANALOGIES

1. a
2. b

Additional Resources

Vocabulary Practice, p. 38

ASSESSMENT

- ***Quick Checks,*** p. 55
- ***Selection and Theme Assessment,*** pp. 99–100
- ***Performance Assessment,*** p. 52
- ***Testmaker: ExamView Pro***
- ***Interactive Tutor: Self-Assessment***

Before Reading

Objectives

- To read and analyze a personal essay
- To identify the elements of style in a personal essay
- To write an analysis of the author's use of informal language to produce a personal style

Skills

Reading/Thinking: Identifying Main Idea and Supporting Details; Activating Prior Knowledge
Writing: Essay
Vocabulary: Word History; Multiple-Meaning Words
Grammar/Language: Plurals and Possessives of Proper Nouns
Collaboration: Literature Groups

Motivating STUDENTS

Selection Focus Transparency 55: Before presenting the poem, ask students to share some of their favorite place names.

Reading Focus: As an extension of the Reading Focus, have students share the names they have thought of for the places they live and vote for their favorites.

Before You Read

from *On the Road with Charles Kuralt*

MEET CHARLES KURALT

Charles Kuralt was already entertaining crowds at thirteen, when he recited "Casey at the Bat" for fans at a Charlotte Hornets minor-league baseball game. He continued for the rest of his life to share his interest in ordinary people with extraordinary stories to tell—as a newspaper journalist, a television personality, and a writer.

Charles Kuralt was born in 1934 and died in 1997. On the Road with Charles Kuralt *was first published in 1985.*

READING FOCUS

How did your city or town get its name?

Brainstorm

Think of other names that would suit the place you live, and discuss why you think these names would be appropriate.

Setting a Purpose

Read to discover some of the stories behind the unusual names of towns across the United States.

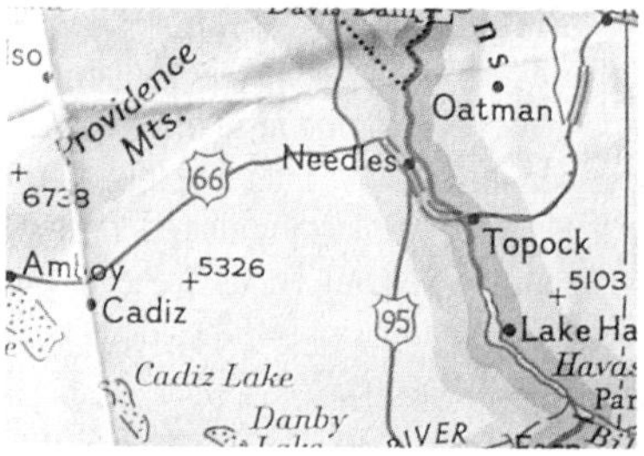

BUILDING BACKGROUND

The Time and Place From 1967 to 1980, author and journalist Charles Kuralt traveled across the United States with a three-person television crew, looking for the "unimportant and irrelevant and insignificant." His reports profiling uncelebrated people in often obscure places were broadcast during CBS news programs.

Did You Know? During the years Kuralt traveled around the United States, he received twelve Emmy awards for outstanding work in television.

VOCABULARY PREVIEW

vain (vān) *adj.* overly concerned with or proud of one's appearance, abilities, or accomplishments; conceited; p. 636

pauper (pô′ pər) *n.* a very poor person, especially one supported by public charity; p. 638

quaint (kwānt) *adj.* charming in an old-fashioned way; pleasingly unusual or odd; p. 638

RESOURCE MANAGER

Teaching Tools and Resources
- Theme Six Planning Guide
- Literature Groups Sourcebook

Essential Lesson Support

Lesson-Specific Instruction
- Selection Focus Transparency 55
- Literary Elements Transparency 56
- Active Reading Guide,* p. 56
- Selection Vocabulary Practice, p. 39
- inTIME magazine, pp. 6–8

Assessment
- Selection Quick Checks,* p. 56
- Sel. and Theme Assmt., pp. 101–102
- Testmaker: ExamView Pro
- Performance Assessment, p. 53

Systematic Language Instruction
- Gr. & Comp. Hbk., L. 13.1
- Vocabulary Power, Lesson 28

English Language Learners
- ELL Sourcebook, p. 80
- Spanish Summaries, p. 56
- Audio Library*
- English, Yes!

Spec. Needs/Strat. Interven.
- Interactive Rdg. Sbk., pp. T189–T191
- Interactive Rdg. Wkbk., pp. 104–105
- Inclusion Strat. Sbk., pp. 41–42
- Audio Library*

* Also available in Spanish

from On the Road with Charles Kuralt

Charles Kuralt

Reading the Selection

SUMMARY

Charles Kuralt lovingly recites the names of American towns and cities and tells the stories behind the names. On the road, Kuralt reads the history of America's westward expansion in the milestones and wonders how long it will be before these markers disappear.

Spanish Summaries, p. 55

Active Reading Strategies

RESPOND Ask students for their personal reactions to the picture of a road stretching out before them. Tell them to remember what they felt and compare it to how they feel after reading the author's own thoughts on traveling.

VOCABULARY If you haven't previewed the selection vocabulary with students, stop and remind them to use context clues to unlock the meanings of new vocabulary words.

Additional Resources

- ***Active Reading Guide,*** p. 56
- ***Audio Library***
- ***Spanish Audio Library***

Teaching Support

CONNECTING TO OTHER SELECTIONS

The chart at the right shows three ways to connect "On the Road with Charles Kuralt" to other selections in this book.

For specific teaching strategies, see the ***Theme Six Planning Guide.***

Connection	Title
Life Skills: Teaching and Mentoring →	"The Wise Old Woman," p. 259
Thematic: Remembrances →	"Knoxville, Tennessee," p. 181
Literary: Descriptive Language →	"The Battleground," p. 511

B Active Reading Strategies

QUESTION Who is the "we" Kuralt begins his essay with? *(He's talking about his TV crew, though he might as well be talking about any Americans who travel.)*

C Literary Elements

STYLE Ask students to point out examples of how Kuralt conveys his feelings for his subject. *(He speaks of being "in love with American names"; he quotes Stephen Vincent Benét, who said, "I have fallen in love with American names"; and he lists the names of places as though they were poetry.)*

D Literary Elements

STYLE Stephen Vincent Benét is addressed as if he were there as well. Ask students why they think he does this. *(Kuralt's style includes his personal reactions to writings, and he gives immediacy to the mood.)*

FINE ART TRANSPARENCY 20

You may want to use ***Fine Art Transparency 20*** to encourage students to make a connection to the theme.

B We spend a lot of time in bus stations. When every place else in town is closed, you can still get a cup of coffee in a bus station. I don't know how long it's been since you've been in a bus station, but if you are in love with American names, you could be happy just sitting here all day and listening.

BUS ANNOUNCER: This will be the first call for the eastbound bus for Junction City, Harrisburg, Halsey, Brownsville, Crawfordsville, Holley, Sweet Home, Hoodoo, Sisters, Bend,—

Did you hear what that man said? Sweet Home, Hoodoo, Sisters, and Bend? I suppose the names of Paris and London and Rome make some people's hearts beat faster. As for me, give me Sweet Home, Hoodoo, Sisters, and Bend.

BUS ANNOUNCER: Cheyenne, Denver, Dallas, Oklahoma City, Wichita, Kansas City, St. Louis.

"I have fallen in love with American names," Stephen Vincent Benét[1] wrote. "The sharp names that never get fat. The snakeskin titles of mining claims. The plumed war bonnet of Medicine Hat, Tucson and Deadwood and Lost Mule Flat." D Oh, we know what you mean, Mr. Benét, we have been there too, to Bug Tussle and Granny's Neck and Hell-for-Certain, and we have learned that America's names tell stories if you will listen to them. Stories of hard times on the frontier.

Times couldn't have been very easy in Gnaw Bone, Indiana. Life must have been a little chancy in Cut and Shoot, Texas. And probably not much better for the settlers who named Hardscrabble Creek in Oregon. But more common are the satisfied names like Humansville or New Deal or Fair Play or Enough. Or outright Chamber of Commerce names like Frostproof, Florida, which of course isn't really. Likewise, we found little competition in Competition, Missouri. And no excessive opportunity in Opportunity, Washington. But their founders *hoped* there'd be, you see. The Chamber of Commerce instinct is strong, but sometimes vain. One night we passed through what must be the smallest town in America, about three families, and named, of course, Jumbo.

Americans have always loved the names of faraway places. I mean, why name a town Stony Lonesome when you can name it Valparaiso? It's a safe bet that the namers of Palestine and Warsaw had never been to either place; they just thought those names sounded nice. E And if those folks in Ohio who named their towns for Cairo and Lima had ever been there, they wouldn't call them "Cay-ro" and "Lie-ma." The same goes

1. *Benét* (bə nā′) was an American who wrote poems, novels, and short stories in the first part of the twentieth century.

Vocabulary
vain (vān) *adj.* overly concerned with or proud of one's appearance, abilities, or accomplishments; conceited

Teaching Support

MEETING INDIVIDUAL NEEDS — ENGLISH LANGUAGE LEARNERS

Place Names Explain that American place names come from many different sources. They may come from other languages—such as Native American (Massachusetts) or French (Baton Rouge), settlers' names (Pennsylvania), and cities and towns in other states or countries (New London). Sometimes they are descriptive (Vermont comes from "green mountain" in French), or they may tell a story (Hardscrabble Creek).

Activity Using a local map or bus schedule, have students role-play a bus announcer calling out the names of nearby towns and cities. Help students find out how these places got their names. **COLLAB. LEARN.**

Additional Resources
English Language Learners Sourcebook, p. 80

for "CAL-lus," Maine, and "MAD-rid," Iowa, and "Vi-EE-na," Georgia. Faraway places with strange sounding names, which sound even stranger coming out of American mouths. And if Odysseus, that old Greek traveler, could have come as we did to this intersection in North Carolina [*sign pointing in different directions to Carthage and Troy,*[2] N.C.], which way would he turn?

E On we drove to Grubville, Missouri, where a traveler could always get a little grub. We had a Pepsi and a pack of Nabs there ourselves. And on to Limberlost Landing, Indiana, where limber Jim McDowell got lost in the swamps one day.

Some town names are just obviously the result of indecision or desperation. When they were trying to think of a name for one pleasant North Carolina community, somebody suggested why not call it this? Somebody else, why not call it that? Until one wise man said, why not call it Whynot? And indeed, why not?

"I have fallen in love with American names." So have we, Mr. Benét. All those places named out of patriotism, some of them, or convenience, or humor, or hope; all those places, all those lovely names. Sweet Home and Hoodoo and Sisters and Bend.

F People travel far too fast to read milestones nowadays. And whenever you find one, you can be sure it's a very unimportant road. But when one particular milestone was planted 150 years ago, it was on the most important road in America. The road started one mile back in Cumberland, Maryland. And it went—west.

The road was a dream of Washington and Jefferson's; and John C. Calhoun made a great speech in favor of it. He said, "Let us conquer space." The space he meant was not from here to the moon. But in 1817, it might as well have been. It was from Cumberland, Maryland, clear to the Illinois frontier. And they built it with mattocks and axes and paving stones. They actually built the thing west to the river

Did You Know?
The *mattock* is a tool consisting of a handle and a two-bladed head, used for loosening soil and cutting roots.

2. The adventures of *Odysseus* (ō dis' ē əs) are described in two works written around 800 B.C. The original *Carthage* was founded around 700 B.C. in northern Africa, and *Troy* was first built more than 4,000 years ago in what is now western Turkey.

E Literary Elements

LANGUAGE Read aloud the names Kuralt selected and ask why students think he chose these names. *(Lead students to see how Kuralt selects names that are humorous, ironic, and characteristically American.)*

Vocabulary Skills

Word History The term *milestone* referred, originally (ca. 1746), to informational stones that gave the distance from or to a given point. Later it came to mean any important point in someone's life. An example from students' lives might be graduation. New words have also entered English from other languages. Have students look up the following words and cite their origin.

1. chocolate
2. banjo
3. banana
4. raccoon

F Critical Thinking

IDENTIFYING MAIN IDEA AND SUPPORTING DETAILS Guide students to see that this paragraph contains the main idea of the essay. Have students explain how all the other paragraphs and ideas lead up to this. Use the following model:

Model: It seems to me that so far in the essay, Kuralt has deliberately selected names of seemingly insignificant places. He speaks of these places with humor and fondness, as if he were persuading me to agree. I think the point of his description is to make the reader see that it is important to slow down and take time to enjoy the history of the United States.

Reading Minilesson

Activating Prior Knowledge Explain to students that one purpose Kuralt has for writing is to make readers aware of what they are missing in America. He lists the names of cities and gives histories of the names. He also gives descriptions of the cities or towns. As Kuralt points out, "People travel too far too fast. . . ." Often we carry knowledge about our history without even taking time to reflect on it.

Activity Have students recall information about the community or the school's history. Ask small groups to compile their information. Once they have devised a structure of the history, have them present it. **L2** COLLAB. LEARN.

Additional Resources

Reading Skills Practice Workbook

town of Wheeling, and west to Zanesville, and west to the prairie village of Columbus, Ohio, and west across the Wabash. It was the longest, straightest road in history and a marvel of the world. They called it the National Road.

We stumbled upon a few miles of the old roadbed in Ohio; a few cobblestones, a few massive old abandoned bridges. And we thought we better show you these things now, because before long there might be nothing left to show you.

Already the road is a nearly forgotten part of the American romance. This incredible road, which carried so many peddlers and paupers and preachers and politicians west to the new America; and carried so many poor families in battered wagons from worn-out farms west to a second chance. Ideas went west, mail and newspapers; and in fancy stagecoaches, Jenny Lind and P. T. Barnum;[3] and in groaning Conestoga freight wagons, calico and iron and whiskey and gunpowder—all the things it took to build a country. The National Road brought Henry Clay east from Kentucky and Abraham Lincoln from Illinois.

You mustn't imagine that it was just a road. It was an Appian Way,[4] sixty-six feet wide for six hundred miles. "A finer road," an English traveler said, "than the highway from London to Bath." It must have been impossible for travelers on this highroad through the wilderness to imagine that anything would ever take its place. In places, the route of the National Road is now called U.S. 40. In places, it is called Interstate 70, our new National Road, on which the thunder of the big diesels drowns out the creaking echo of the Conestoga wagons.

But in quieter places, the vacant windows of shuttered general stores still reflect the pathway of the original road. A handful of the fine old taverns—which once watered the horses and brandied the gentlemen—still stand. The one on Mount Washington in Pennsylvania is remembered as unusual: its landlady was civil and her husband was sober.

Nobody reads the mileposts anymore; great green signs have taken their place. And the traffic roars up the hills past the old tollhouses with their quaint list of charges: "For every chariot, coach, coachee, stage, phaeton or chaise[5] with two horses and four wheels, 12 cents." Today's chariots pass without reading or paying.

We just wanted to show you this much before it's too late. If you go slow enough and look hard enough, you can still find traces in the weeds, the last faint traces of the road that made us a nation.

3. *Lind* was a Swedish opera singer. *Barnum,* an American showman, brought Lind to the United States and managed her very successful nationwide concert tour in the 1850s.
4. The *Appian Way* was the first and best of the great roadways built by the ancient Romans. Construction began in 312 B.C., eventually extending the road to 366 miles. The road is still in use today.
5. The *coachee* is a carriage shaped like a coach, but longer and open in the front. The *phaeton* (fā′ ət ən) is a light, low, open four-wheeled carriage. And the *chaise* is a light two-wheeled carriage, often with a hood or folding top.

Vocabulary

pauper (pô′ pər) *n.* a very poor person, especially one supported by public charity
quaint (kwānt) *adj.* charming in an old-fashioned way; pleasingly unusual or odd

G Active Reading Strategies

CONNECT Ask students whether reading the essay has stirred their interest in learning more about the roads mentioned and discuss sources for locating that information.

H Author's Craft

DIRECT ADDRESS Kuralt speaks directly to his readers in order to convey his enthusiasm and to stimulate theirs. Remind students of their reactions to the picture of the road on page 635. How do they feel now that they have shared Kuralt's enthusiasm?

Thematic Focus

Flashes of Insight The author has personal insight and in sharing it hopes to enlighten the reader.

ASSESSMENT

Quick Checks, p. 56

A&E HOME VIDEO.® *The following videotape program is available from Glencoe.* Be sure to preview the video for appropriateness for your class:

- **Biography: Charles Kuralt—A Life on the Road***

*Also available in the Glencoe Literature *Video Library*.

Teaching Support

Grammar and Language *Minilesson*

Plurals and Possessives of Proper Nouns Explain that to make a proper noun plural, one must add -s or -es—even if the name ends in the consonant y or s. Write these examples on the board:

Grant	Henry
the Grants	the Henrys

Explain that the possessive form of proper nouns is similar to that of common nouns: -'s for the singular form, -s' for the plural.

Activity Have students choose the right form of the proper noun in each phrase:

Ms. [González's/Gonzálezes] article *(González's)*

the [Frost's/Frosts] from Iowa *(Frosts)*

the [Henrys/Henry's] from Florida *(Henrys)* **L2**

Additional Resources

- ***Grammar and Language Transparency 53***
- ***Grammar and Language Workbook,*** p. 65
- ***Grammar and Composition Handbook,*** Lesson 2.3
- ***Writer's Choice,*** Lessons 9.3, 20.7

Active Reading and Critical Thinking

Responding to Literature

PERSONAL RESPONSE

- What do you think Charles Kuralt might have said about the region in which you live?

Brackets connect questions that are paired to develop higher-level thinking skills.

Analyzing Literature

RECALL

1. Who, in Kuralt's opinion, should spend some time in a bus station?
2. What are some of the "faraway places" Americans have used as names for their towns?
3. What was the National Road?
4. What is a *milestone?*

INTERPRET

5. What are some of the reasons, in your opinion, that Kuralt enjoys place names?
6. Why, do you think, might settlers name a town Lima or Warsaw?
7. Why, do you think, does Kuralt want readers to know about the National Road?
8. Why does America have lots of "great green signs"?

EVALUATE AND CONNECT

9. Theme Connection In your view, what can give Americans new insights about their country's value besides visiting places with interesting names?
10. Would you enjoy traveling with someone like Charles Kuralt? Explain why or why not.

Charles Kuralt (far right) and his traveling crew.

LITERARY ELEMENTS

Style

Some authors write in such a distinctive way that readers can guess who they are by reading a short paragraph. **Style** is the distinctive way in which a writer uses words, constructs sentences, and creates meaning. Charles Kuralt developed a style of writing in which he used a conversational tone and often addressed the reader directly.

1. List some questions Kuralt liked to ask the reader.
2. Point out places where it seems as though Kuralt could be speaking directly to you.

● See **Literary Terms Handbook**, p. R9.

FLASHES OF INSIGHT 639

Responding to the Selection

PERSONAL RESPONSE

Students should try to look at their region through the eyes of a traveler.

Analyzing Literature

1. Everyone who is in love with American names should spend time there.
2. Valparaiso (Chile), Palestine, Warsaw (Poland), Cairo (Egypt), Lima (Peru), Madrid (Spain), Calais (France), Vienna (Austria), Carthage (ancient city in North Africa), Troy (ancient city in Asia Minor)
3. The road built to connect the East to the West was the National Road.
4. A milestone is a stone that gives the distance from or to a given point.
5. He likes the stories they tell, their humor, and how they sound.
6. They may simply have liked the sound of them or had a dream of visiting them one day.
7. He wants to call people's attention to its historical landmarks and in this way help prevent their total disappearance from the landscape.
8. National standards for roads require that signs be easy to read, so they usually have white letters on a green background.
9. Possibilities may include reading history and biography as well as watching TV programs and videos about different communities in America.
10. Students should give reasons for answering as they do.

LITERARY ELEMENTS

1. "Did you hear what that man said?" "I mean, why name a town Stony Lonesome when you can name it Valparaiso?"
2. "I don't know how long it's been since you've been in a bus station." "Did you hear what that man said?" "You mustn't imagine that it was just a road."

Additional Resources

Literary Elements Transparency 56

Extending Your Response

Writing About Literature

Students' analyses should

- answer the question of why Kuralt chose this quotation
- cite examples of how Kuralt supported Benét's idea

Personal Writing

Students' essays should

- include an attributed quote
- use informal language
- reflect personal opinions
- have a direct, personal tone

Literature Groups Students may have observed the ways people talk in films about different times and places. Encourage them to act this out. COLLAB. LEARN.

Interdisciplinary Activity Encourage students to research the most common modes of travel in the time period they choose. After students have had time to write and review their ideas, call on volunteers to share their thoughts with the class.

Skill Minilesson

VOCABULARY • MULTIPLE-MEANING WORDS

1. b   2. c   3. a

Additional Resources

Vocabulary Practice, p. 39

Extending Your Response

Writing About Literature

Names, American Style Kuralt based "American Names" on poet Stephen Vincent Benét's remark, "I have fallen in love with American names." Reread Benét's words carefully. Then, analyze why Kuralt may have chosen this quote, and explain how well he supported Benét's idea.

Interdisciplinary Activity

History Charles Kuralt was interested in finding out about the lives of ordinary people. Conduct your own investigation of a specific time period and location in the United States. Find out, for example, what life was like for a formerly enslaved person during the Reconstruction of the South after the Civil War, or what a woman might have experienced as a settler in the West in the mid-1800s. Then, write a description from the point of view of one of those people. Include the most interesting details from your research.

Personal Writing

"Quote Me!" Use a book of quotations, Internet sources, or periodicals to find a quote that expresses an idea you would like to share. Write a short essay based on and including the quote. You might use it in the title of the essay to emphasize your point.

Literature Groups

Hurry Up! Discuss why many people in the United States seem to be in such a hurry. Name stories, poems, songs, movies, or television programs that show this characteristic of many Americans at different periods in U.S. history.

Reading Further

If you enjoy traveling in books, read *The Car* by Gary Paulsen

Save your work for your portfolio.

Skill Minilesson

RETEACH • REVIEW

VOCABULARY • MULTIPLE-MEANING WORDS

Many multiple-meaning words, such as the *bark* of a dog and the *bark* of a tree, are different parts of speech and have different meanings. However, some words, such as *vain,* have different meanings for the same part of speech, which can be confusing.

Vain can mean "conceited" or "worthless" or "having little or no effect." By paying attention to context clues, you can tell which meaning is correct in a sentence.

PRACTICE Use context clues to help you decide which would be the best synonym for *vain* in each example.

1. She is untrustworthy and makes vain promises.
   a. conceited   b. worthless   c. unsuccessful
2. I made a vain effort to eat my soup with a fork.
   a. conceited   b. worthless   c. unsuccessful
3. His vain comments showed how high an opinion he had of himself.
   a. conceited   b. worthless   c. unsuccessful

• For more about multiple-meaning words, see **Reading Handbook**, pp. R89–R90.

ASSESSMENT

- ***Quick Checks,*** p. 56
- ***Selection and Theme Assessment,*** pp. 101–102
- ***Performance Assessment,*** p. 53
- ***Testmaker: ExamView Pro***
- ***Interactive Tutor: Self-Assessment***

Writing Skills

Writing an Effective Introduction

You and your remote control are exploring the possibilities as a new hour of television is starting. What makes you stop clicking that button and stay with a show? An interesting beginning! In the same way, a good introduction can make you sit up and pay close attention in school when someone begins to speak. Good writers and good speakers know that a strong introduction will attract and hold an audience.

Off to a Good Start! Whether you are planning an essay or a speech, you want to focus on a strong beginning. One way to do this is by surprising your reader. Consider the first sentence of the selection from *On the Road with Charles Kuralt:* "We spend a lot of time in bus stations." This statement is unusual and helps Kuralt catch the reader's attention. Then he moves right into the main idea of his essay by telling his readers why he is in bus stations.

> We spend a lot of time in bus stations. When every place else in town is closed, you can still get a cup of coffee in a bus station. I don't know how long it's been since you've been in a bus station, but if you are in love with American names, you could be happy just sitting here all day and listening.

Statement of Purpose Always plan to introduce a topic in an interesting way. Then use your introduction to lead your audience to the main idea of your essay or speech. You may want to be serious or funny, entertaining or persuasive, but you always want to be interesting. The list below may help you think of other introductory techniques that will guarantee an attentive audience for your ideas.

- Begin with a vivid story, a joke, or a funny story.
- Let your first sentence be an unexpected, interesting statement or question.

● For more about the writing process, see **Writing Handbook,** pp. R50–R53.

ACTIVITIES

1. Choose a selection you have read that has a strong introduction. Write a paragraph or two giving reasons and examples to support your choice.
2. Think of an awakening that you have experienced or that someone has told you about. List details that you might include in an introduction to an essay about the experience. Explain how each detail would help you write a strong introduction.

Writing Skills

Objective

- To write an effective introduction

Teaching Strategies

After students have read the first part of page 641, tell them that writing a strong opening is not necessarily something even accomplished writers manage to do immediately. They are more likely to follow the writing process by putting down their ideas as fast as they can and then strengthening the opening during the revision stage.

Activities

1. Students may cite examples from the text or from other sources.
2. Encourage students to follow through on their ideas and write the introduction to the essay.

Additional Resources

- ***Writer's Choice,*** Lesson 4.1

Teaching Support

Grammar and Language *Minilesson*

Exclamation Points Explain that students should use exclamation points sparingly. Have them refer to the selection with a strong introduction to see how words alone provide strength and emphasis.

Activity Have partners scan newspapers for exclamation points. They can suggest other ways for the writer to show strong emotion. **L1**

Additional Resources

- ***Grammar and Language Transparency 54***
- ***Grammar and Language Workbook,*** p. 255
- ***Grammar and Composition Handbook,*** Lesson 2.3
- ***Writer's Choice,*** Lesson 20.1

Before Reading

Objectives

- To read and analyze a personal essay
- To identify the author's purpose in a personal essay
- To write a list of idioms commonly used in America

Skills

Reading/Thinking: Drawing Conclusions; Monitoring Comprehension
Writing: Letter
Vocabulary: Unlocking Meaning
Grammar/Language: Infinitives
Life Skills: Examining Popular Culture
Collaboration: Literature Groups

Motivating STUDENTS

Selection Focus Transparency 56: Before presenting the quotation, encourage students to discuss the things they have in common as a class.

Reading Focus: As an extension of the Reading Focus, have the group create a master list of the objects and beliefs they think most American share, removing duplications.

Before You Read

Americans All

MEET MICHAEL DORRIS

Michael Dorris's life changed when a neighbor repaid him for some yard work by giving him a book. He recalled, "I was stunned by the undiluted power a novel could contain." Reading helped lead him to a career as an anthropologist—a scientist who studies the development of human cultures—and as a professor of Native American studies at Dartmouth College. Dorris, who was Irish, French, and Modoc, also gained fame as a writer of poetry, essays, and novels.

Michael Dorris was born in 1945 and died in 1997. "Americans All" was first printed by Newsday *in 1992.*

READING FOCUS

Do all Americans share the same music? language? values? Is there anything that all Americans have in common?

List It!
With a partner, list objects and beliefs that you think most Americans share.

Setting a Purpose
Read to find out how one writer describes his fellow Americans.

BUILDING BACKGROUND

The Time and Place In this essay, Michael Dorris shares some thoughts about the people of the United States in modern times.

VOCABULARY PREVIEW

emphatically (em fat′ i kəl ē) *adv.* very definitely; clearly; p. 643
proximity (prok sim′ ə tē) *n.* closeness in space, time, order, or degree; nearness; p. 644
manifest (man′ ə fest′) *adj.* obvious; clear; plain; evident; p. 644
incompatible (in′ kəm pat′ ə bəl) *adj.* not capable of existing or working together in harmony; conflicting; p. 644
disembark (dis′ im bärk′) *v.* to get off of a train, airplane, ship, or other vehicle; p. 644
revel (rev′ əl) *v.* to take great pleasure; p. 644

RESOURCE MANAGER

Teaching Tools and Resources
- Theme Six Planning Guide
- Literature Groups Sourcebook

Essential Lesson Support

Lesson-Specific Instruction
- Selection Focus Transparency 56
- Literary Elements Transparency 57
- Active Reading Guide,* p. 57
- Selection Vocabulary Practice, p. 40
- inTIME magazine, PP. 10–11

Assessment
- Selection Quick Checks,* p. 57
- Sel. and Theme Assmt., pp. 103–104
- Testmaker: ExamView Pro
- Performance Assessment, p. 54

Systematic Language Instruction
- Gr. & Comp. Hbk., L. 13.2, 13.3
- Vocabulary Power, Unit 6 Review/Test
- Spelling Power, Unit 6 Review/Proofreading

English Language Learners
- ELL Sourcebook, p. 81
- Spanish Summaries, p. 56
- Spanish Translations, pp. 146–147
- Audio Library*
- English, Yes!

Spec. Needs/Strat. Interven.
- Interactive Rdg. Sbk., pp. T192–T194
- Interactive Rdg. Wkbk., pp. 106–107
- Inclusion Strat. Sbk., pp. 91–92
- Audio Library*

* Also available in Spanish

Americans All

Ferry Boat Trip (detail), c. 1943–1944. William H. Johnson. Oil on paperboard, 33⅝ x 28½ in. National Museum of American Art, Washington, DC.

Michael Dorris

I recognize them instantly abroad: on the street, in crowded rooms, on airplanes, at restaurants—but how? It's emphatically not skin color, not clothing, not little red-white-and-blues stitched to their breast pockets. They don't have to say anything, to show a passport, or to sing the "Star Spangled Banner," but nevertheless they're unmistakable in any foreign setting. A

Americans. We come in all varieties of size, age, and style. We travel singly and in groups. We're alternately loud and disapproving or humble and apologetic. We seek each other out or self-consciously avoid each other's company. We pack our gear in Gucci bags or stuff it into Patagonia backpacks, travel first class or on Eurorail passes, stay in youth hostels[1] or in luxury hotels, but none of that matters.

1. *Eurorail passes* are inexpensive train tickets that allow purchasers to travel throughout Europe within a limited period of time. *Hostels* are inexpensive lodging places.

Vocabulary
emphatically (em fat′ i kəl ē) *adv.* very definitely; clearly

Reading the Selection

SUMMARY

Michael Dorris has observed that when Americans see each other overseas, they recognize each other as Americans. Sometimes that brings the travelers together in a way that would never happen at home. Dorris poses a question: Why don't all Americans recognize and relish the diversity of their country's people when they are at home? As different as we are, we have much in common.

Spanish Summaries, p. 56

A Active Reading Strategies

PREDICT Encourage students to examine the beginning of the essay to discover what the essay might be about. *(The key word, Americans, stands by itself, followed by this sentence. "We come in all varieties. . . ." This clue, along with the title, suggests that the essay is about many different kinds of Americans.)*

VOCABULARY If you haven't previewed the selection vocabulary with students, stop and remind them to use context clues to unlock the meanings of new vocabulary words.

Additional Resources

- ***Active Reading Guide,*** p. 57
- ***Audio Library***
- ***Spanish Audio Library***

Teaching Support

CONNECTING TO OTHER SELECTIONS

The chart at the right shows three ways to connect "Americans All" to other selections in this book.

For specific teaching strategies, see the ***Theme Six Planning Guide.***

Connection	Title
Life Skills: Lifelong Learning →	"My Two Dads," p. 19
Thematic: Discoveries →	"Between What I See and What I Say," p. 310
Literary: Author's Purpose →	"The Lesson of the Moth," p. 318

FLASHES OF INSIGHT 643

B Literary Elements

AUTHOR'S PURPOSE By describing his personal experience with Americans both at home and abroad, what point does the author make? *(All Americans have things in common.)*

C Author's Craft

LANGUAGE Dorris makes a shift from the first-person singular to the first-person plural. Discuss with students how this change affects the meaning of the essay. *(He wants to include the reader in his designation "Americans all.")*

D Literary Elements

AUTHOR'S PURPOSE The author says, "To be Americans means to be not the clone of the people next door." What do students think the author means by this? *(He means that in an open society, people can dare to be different, and he wants to persuade readers to agree.)*

E Critical Thinking

DRAWING CONCLUSIONS What does the author believe is the strength of American society? *(its diversity)*

It's as though we're individually implanted with some invisible beeper, some national homing device, that's activated by the proximity of similar equipment.

B This common denominator is manifest in shared knowledge (we all know who Mary Tyler Moore[2] is), topics of mutual interest or dispute (guns, the environment, choice), and popular culture (do we or do we not deserve a thousand-calorie break today?). In other words, we take the same things seriously or not seriously, are capable of speaking, when we choose to, not merely a common language but a common idiom,[3] and know the melodies, if not all the words, to many of the same songs.

C Why, then, doesn't any of this count when we're *not* overseas? Why, at home, do we seem so different from each other, so mutually incompatible, so strange and forbidding? Do we have to recognize each other in Tokyo or Cairo in order to see through the distinctions and into the commonalities?[4] How does that "we," so obvious anywhere else in the world, get split into "us" and "them" when we're stuck within our own borders?

D The answer is clear: to be Americans means to be not the clone of the people next door. E I fly back from any homogeneous country, from a place where every person I see is blond, or black, or belongs to only one religion, and then disembark at JFK. I revel in the cadence[5] of many accents, catch a ride to the city with a Nigerian-American or Russian-American cab driver. Eat Thai food at a Greek restaurant next to a table of Chinese-American conventioneers[6] from Alabama. Get directions from an Iranian-American cop and drink a cup of Turkish coffee served by a Navajo student at Fordham who's majoring in Japanese literature. Argue with everybody about everything. I'm home.

from *Newsday*
October 1992

2. *Mary Tyler Moore* is an actress who had a popular television show during the 1970s.
3. *Common idiom* refers to the way words are put together to express thoughts so that most people with the same background understand them. An *idiom* is an expression whose meaning cannot always be determined from the literal meaning of its words.
4. *Distinctions* are differences, and *commonalities* are similarities.
5. A *clone* is an exact copy, and *homogeneous* (hō′ mə jē′ nē əs) means "having a similar character or similar parts throughout." *JFK* refers to the New York City airport named for President John F. Kennedy. The rhythmic flow, or rising and falling sound, of speech is its *cadence*.
6. *Conventioneers* are people who attend conventions, large meetings of state or national organizations.

Vocabulary

proximity (prok sim′ ə tē) *n.* closeness in space, time, order, or degree; nearness
manifest (man′ ə fest′) *adj.* obvious; clear; plain; evident
incompatible (in′ kəm pat′ ə bəl) *adj.* not capable of existing or working together in harmony; conflicting
disembark (dis′ im bärk′) *v.* to get off of a train, airplane, ship, or other vehicle
revel (rev′ əl) *v.* to take great pleasure

Teaching Support

Grammar and Language *Minilesson*

Infinitives Write this sentence on the board, underlining the infinitive forms: *They don't have to say anything, to show a passport, or to sing . . .* Explain that the underlined words are infinitive verb forms. Here they are part of the predicate. They can also be the subject: *To overeat is dangerous.* The infinitive is the basic form of a verb, from which all other forms (past, present, singular, and plural) derive.

Activity Have students find other examples of the author's use of the infinitive form to identify the sentence part in which it is used. Make sure students do not confuse prepositional phrases beginning with *to* with infinitives. *"To be Americans means to be . . . next door."* [subject and predicate] **L2**

Additional Resources

- ***Grammar and Language Transparency 55***
- ***Grammar and Language Workbook,*** p. 179
- ***Grammar and Composition Handbook,*** Lesson 9.3
- ***Writer's Choice,*** Lesson 15.3

Ferry Boat Trip, c. 1943–1944.
Viewing the painting: Would you, like Michael Dorris, "recognize them instantly abroad"? Why or why not?

VIEWING THE PAINTING

The *Ferry Boat Trip* is among many paintings Johnson has done of people in New York City. In this painting of children, the Brooklyn Bridge is shown on the left and a tugboat on the right.

Viewing Response *These young people might be recognizable as Americans for their casual posture and apparent friendliness.*

Thematic Focus

Flashes of Insight The author tries to persuade us that Americans have their diversity in common. Have students share what insights they had about the issue of diversity. Discuss, for example, how well diversity is tolerated among teenagers.

ASSESSMENT

Quick Checks, p. 57

Reading Minilesson

Comprehension Explain that using a graphic aid may help students understand essays in which the author makes many points, as in "Americans All."

Activity On the board, make the following chart and ask students to complete it by listing the similarities and differences described by the author.

How Americans Are . . .

Alike	Different

(Americans are alike in having shared knowledge and popular culture. They are different in race, religion, and appearance.) **L2**

Additional Resources

Reading Skills Practice Workbook

Responding to the Selection

PERSONAL RESPONSE

Students should support their responses with thoughtful reasoning.

Analyzing Literature

1. It refers to Americans traveling abroad.
2. They have their knowledge of popular culture in common.
3. When they are at home, they seem not to count.
4. No. He says, "To be Americans means to be not the clone of the people next door."
5. We recognize brands of clothing and ways of talking and behaving as familiar.
6. They are all aspects of popular culture that most Americans are likely to know.
7. He is probably suggesting that, when we are abroad, we concentrate less on the differences that divide us and more on what we share.
8. He enjoys the diversity of American life, especially in a big city.
9. Students should base their responses on their personal reactions.
10. Students will probably answer no. Their reasons should support their response.

Responding to Literature

PERSONAL RESPONSE

◆ If you were in a foreign country, do you think you would recognize other Americans? Why or why not?

Brackets connect questions that are paired to develop higher-level thinking skills.

Analyzing Literature

RECALL

1. To whom does the pronoun "them" refer in the opening sentence?
2. What, according to Dorris, do Americans have in common?
3. When do the things Americans have in common seem not to count?
4. Does Dorris think that all Americans should try to be alike? Explain.

INTERPRET

5. What, in your opinion, does Dorris mean when he says, "We're individually implanted with some invisible beeper . . . activated by the proximity of similar equipment"?
6. How do the references to Mary Tyler Moore, a thousand-calorie break, and the environment support Dorris's main idea?
7. What might Dorris want readers to consider when he asks, "How does that 'we' . . . get split into 'us' and 'them' when we're stuck within our own borders?"
8. Why does the writer "revel" in what he experiences when he arrives home after foreign travel?

EVALUATE AND CONNECT

9. In the second paragraph, Dorris repeatedly begins a sentence with "we" to drive his point home. Does his use of **repetition** convince you to believe him? Why or why not?
10. Are you a "clone of the people next door"? Give three reasons why or why not.

LITERARY ELEMENTS

Author's Purpose

The **author's purpose** is the reason a piece of literature was written: to entertain, inform, persuade, or explain. The main purpose of an essay like "Americans All" is to persuade readers to see a situation the way the writer sees it.

1. State briefly the situation described by Michael Dorris.
2. How does Dorris show his attitude toward the situation? Give examples to support your answer.
3. In your opinion, how successful is Michael Dorris in persuading Americans to see themselves as he does?

● See **Literary Terms Handbook,** p. R1.

LITERARY ELEMENTS

1. Americans abroad seem to recognize shared experience. At home, we concentrate on differences.
2. He wonders why we behave this way and concludes by celebrating the diversity of this country.
3. By using supporting details, he succeeds in his purpose.

Additional Resources

Literary Elements Transparency 57

Extending Your Response

Personal Writing

Dear Editor Write a letter to the editor of your newspaper. State one of Dorris's ideas, and explain why you agree or disagree with him. Give examples based on personal experience to back up your opinion. Look at your response to the **Reading Focus** on page 642.

Literature Groups

Why? Dorris asks four questions in his fourth paragraph. Join with your group and answer his four questions. Give two reasons or examples to support each answer.

Learning for Life

Examining Popular Culture Dorris wrote, "We all know who Mary Tyler Moore is," referring to the power of television to spread popular culture. Imagine that you are a person from another country seeing a popular U.S. show for the first time. Write an evaluation of the show, drawing conclusions about American culture from it.

Writing About Literature

Idioms When Dorris says Americans speak a common idiom, he means we understand the same buzz words, slang, and jargon. An **idiom** is a word or phrase that has a meaning other than that shown by its parts. For example, if a coach tells a runner, "You're wasting time! Here's where I draw the line," the runner doesn't expect the coach to draw a line on the floor. With a partner, list some idioms common to you and your classmates.

Reading Further

If you enjoyed this essay, try these books about Americans who are like and unlike others:

Eleanor Roosevelt: A Life of Discovery by Russell Freedman

And One for All by Theresa Nelson

Save your work for your portfolio.

Skill Minilesson

RETEACH • REVIEW

VOCABULARY • UNLOCKING MEANING

You can often unlock the meaning of a word by analyzing parts of the word that are familiar. For example, if you know that *emphatically* means "very definitely" or "clearly," you may be able to guess that *emphasis* means "a special stress or importance given to something."

- For more on unlocking word meanings, see **Reading Handbook,** pp. R89–R90.

PRACTICE Use your knowledge of the vocabulary words from this selection to write a definition for each underlined word.

1. Their laughter was a manifestation of their shared memory.
2. The revelry continued all day.
3. Every traveler found a compatible partner.
4. The cities are approximately forty miles apart.

Extending Your Response

Personal Writing

Students' letters should

- include a clearly stated position.
- give examples based on personal experience to back up opinions.

Writing About Literature

Students' lists should

- include the idioms that are truly common.

Literature Groups Suggest that students end their discussion by summarizing their conclusions. COLLAB. LEARN.

Learning for Life Suggest that students share their evaluations with a partner and discuss them.

Skill Minilesson

VOCABULARY • UNLOCKING MEANING

1. showing
2. celebration
3. well matched
4. about

Additional Resources

Vocabulary Practice, p. 40

ASSESSMENT

- ***Quick Checks,*** p. 57
- ***Selection and Theme Assessment,*** pp. 103–104
- ***Performance Assessment,*** p. 54
- ***Testmaker: ExamView Pro***
- ***Interactive Tutor: Self-Assessment***

Technology Skills

Objectives

- To evaluate on-line sources by identifying and analyzing points of view
- To recognize, analyze, and compare points of view from diverse sources

Teaching Strategies

A good motivational introduction to this feature would be to follow through on the Technology Tip for checking the credentials of Internet writers. Actually performing a check will assure students that such information is public and accessible. Other possibilities for verification include searching the catalogue of a local library and logging on to a book distributor or publisher's list to corroborate a bibliography.

Technology Skills

Internet: Evaluating Online Sources

"The number of UFO sightings worldwide proves that extraterrestrial beings are visiting Earth regularly."
"UFOs are a sign that the end of the world is at hand. We cannot identify these objects; they are beyond our understanding."
"UFOs are simply unidentified flying objects. They could be balloons or airplanes or even meteors. The existence of UFOs does not prove that life exists on other planets."

Each statement above presents a different point of view on the subject of UFOs. As you explore the Internet, you will find that many topics can be interpreted in a number of ways. Because the Net provides a voice to so many people on such a variety of topics, you will need to sort through the information to determine for yourself what you can believe and which point of view you can accept.

Before You Get Started

Take a few minutes and consider how you form your own opinions. What influences your thinking? How, exactly, do you determine what you believe? Do you consider all the facts? Do you go with a gut feeling or a hunch? Do you ask for the opinions of others and then weigh the strengths of their arguments? Jot down in your journal several sentences that sum up how you arrive at your own conclusions.

TECHNOLOGY TIP

You can often use the Internet to check on a person's reliability as a source of information. If a writer claims to teach at a university, check the list of faculty names at the university's Web site. The American Medical Association may be able to help you find out whether the person offering medical opinions is a licensed physician. Most professions have organizations that keep records of their members, and these organizations usually have Web sites. A search engine will help you find these sites.

Point of View: How Can You Tell?

A statement that represents only one point of view often includes context clues to let the reader know that the assertion is just an opinion. Such hints include: *in my opinion, I submit, I assert, I believe, we feel, I surmise, we infer that,* and *the speculation is.* A reader who is alert to such clues will not be led into thinking that a point of view is a statement of fact.

You may have more trouble when the person does not use such hints. The above statements about UFOs, for example, simply state opinions as though they were facts. When you come across such statements–as you are likely to do often on the Internet–you will need to analyze what the writers say.

- Is the evidence from a reliable source? Anyone can operate a Web site. Doing so does not necessarily make the person an authority on a topic.

Teaching Support

interNET CONNECTION

Narrowing the Search Students may be able to find Web sites with direct links to other sites. Depending on the search engine they use, students should find information on the home page that indicates whether there are such links. Museums, national organizations, special interest groups, and local clubs often coordinate sources this way.

MEETING INDIVIDUAL NEEDS — MULTIPLE MODES OF EXPRESSION

Interpersonal Forming groups that include students with strong technical abilities and others who have strong analytical skills should encourage a good interchange of ideas and analysis as they search the Internet and evaluate sites.

Activity Begin by having partners choose the tasks they are most comfortable with, then encourage them to explain what they are doing. Once partners have developed a strategy for searching and verifying, have them exchange roles at least briefly. **L2** COLLAB. LEARN.

- Is the source someone commonly known and accepted as an expert in the field under discussion? For example, a professor who teaches American literature at a major university is probably a more reliable source of information about Mark Twain than a television personality or a surgeon would be.
- Has the source convincingly argued his or her case?
- What evidence does the source offer to support her or his arguments?
- Can information presented as factual be confirmed by other sources?
- Are there other points of view that present equally convincing arguments?

Practice

With a partner, decide on a topic that interests both of you. Try to choose a topic on which people are likely to have different points of view.

1. Log on to the World Wide Web. Open a search engine, and type in keywords that describe the topic you are researching. For example, if you were searching for sites about UFOs, *UFO* and *theories* might be useful keywords.
2. Browse through the hits to locate examples of differing points of view. For each opinion you come across, record the name and URL (Web address) of the site on which it is found and a brief summary of the point of view. When you have found and documented at least two different points of view, log off.
3. Together, determine the criteria by which you will evaluate these points of view. On what will you base the credibility of the opinions? Factual evidence? Strength of persuasive arguments? Attractiveness of Web site? Your personal opinions?
4. Cooperatively, write a brief report in which you:
   a. compare and contrast the points of view expressed.
   b. evaluate the opinions and explain the criteria you used in your evaluation.
   c. decide which point of view, if any, you and your partner agree with.
5. Share your report with your class.

ACTIVITIES

1. Do a World Wide Web search on an issue in the news, such as pollution or the destruction of the world's rain forests. Find at least two different points of view on the subject. In your journal, compare your own opinion with those you find on the Net.
2. Create a site on your school's Intranet where students can argue their points of view on particular topics of interest to your community.

Activities

1. Review the Practice directions with the class to be sure everyone understands how to check their sources. Give students adequate time to follow the steps listed under Practice as they perform the activity. Encourage a follow-up discussion in which students share information on strategies that worked and those that did not.
2. *Students' projects should:*
- demonstrate an ability to use the available technology to search the Internet for relevant sites
- show a recognition that not all such sites have equal validity
- indicate an understanding that there may be more than one valid point of view on any one topic

TechnoTalk

Old Terms for New Concepts

Students may be familiar with the term "the Information Superhighway," which refers to the Internet. Explain that this metaphor has often been extended to include such metaphors as *exploring, addresses, gateways, on-ramps,* and *search engines.* Ask students to list other terminology they are familiar with, differentiating between those that stretch the travel metaphor, are borrowed from other fields, or were coined specifically for this technology *(such as modem).*

Objectives

- To create the bylaws of an organization (approximately 500 to 700 words)
- To plan, draft, revise, edit, and present the bylaws of an organization
- To reflect on and revise the bylaws of an organization

GLENCOE TECHNOLOGY

WRITER'S ASSISTANT CD-ROM
Students can use Glencoe's templates and guidelines software for expository writing to aid them in working through the steps of the writing process in this lesson.

Teaching Strategies

PREWRITING

Brainstorm and Gather Ideas Since the articles of the bylaws will probably span a range of topics, students may wish to divide into a number of groups. Each group can focus on one article. Be sure groups communicate with one another to ensure that all relevant topics are covered and duplication is avoided.

Teaching Support

Writing WORKSHOP

Technical Writing: Bylaws of an Organization

The year is 1787. Delegates meet at a convention in Philadelphia to design a new system of government. They work together to draft the Constitution of the United States—a written plan that explains how the government of a new nation will operate. For this workshop, you will play a role similar to the role played by the delegates at the Constitutional Conventional. You will write the bylaws of an organization, a set of rules and guidelines (resembling a constitution) that describes how your student government or other school-sponsored organization should operate.

Assignment: Follow the process on these pages to write your own bylaws for the student council or a club at your school.

- As you write your bylaws, refer to the **Writing Handbook**, pp. R50-R55.

EVALUATION RUBRIC

By the time you complete this Writing Workshop, you will have

- written a clear and concise document stating the bylaws of an organization
- considered the various topics that are often included in bylaws
- created a format for the document that easily guides your readers through the sequence of articles and sections
- used design elements (such as headings, subheadings, and boldface type) to help readers focus their attention on the main points
- presented a document that is free of errors in grammar, usage, and mechanics

The Writing Process

PREWRITING

PREWRITING TIP
Many middle school student councils post their constitutions and bylaws on the Internet. Download some of these documents to help you gather ideas for your own set of bylaws. Pay close attention to the content, organization, and format.

Brainstorm and Gather Ideas
Choose a school-sponsored organization you have joined or would like to join. Then brainstorm to create a list of questions that relate to how that organization functions. Here are some examples:

- What are the goals?
- Who are the members?
- Why and when do the members hold meetings?
- How many leaders are there? What are their duties?
- How should the leaders be chosen?

Thinking about the answers to these questions is a great warm-up exercise for writing the bylaws of the organization you have chosen. Another source of ideas is the United States Constitution. You might read the Constitution in your social studies book and notice how it is written and what topics are covered.

LIFE SKILLS CONNECTION

Student Organizations Most schools are home to a variety of student organizations, from the student council to small special-interest clubs. Most of these organizations have a constitution, bylaws, or both. Note that a constitution is usually a statement of an organization's basic principles. The bylaws state the rules by which the organization operates—how officers are elected, how new members are admitted, and how decisions are made.

Activity Have students search for examples of student organization constitutions or bylaws. They may ask club secretaries in their own school as well as do research on the Internet. A number of national organizations such as the 4-H Clubs have posted models on their sites. Have students discuss what they learned from their searches. **L2** COLLAB. LEARN.

Know Your Audience and Purpose

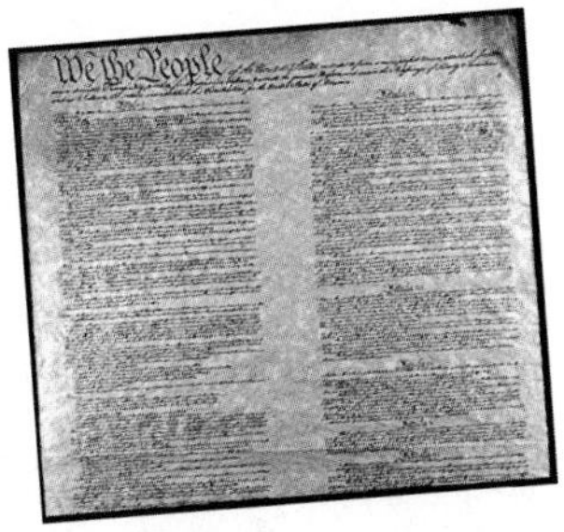

Your audience will be the members and prospective members of the organization. The main purpose for writing bylaws is to provide clear, easy-to-follow rules about the operation of the organization. Well-written bylaws can help prevent conflicts over such issues as the goals of the organization, how an election should be held, or which officer is responsible for a certain task.

The writers of the United States Constitution successfully addressed these questions in planning their framework for government. The Preamble introduces the Constitution to Americans and states its purpose.

> We, the people of the United States, in order to form a more perfect union, establish justice, insure domestic tranquility, provide for the common defense, promote the general welfare, and secure the blessing of liberty to ourselves and our posterity, do ordain and establish this Constitution for the United States of America.

The student council at Beckwith Middle School in Massachusetts decided to imitate the content and sentence structure of the Preamble in their own bylaws.

STUDENT MODEL

We, the students of Beckwith Middle School, in order to form a more perfect union; establish good school relations; and promote school spirit, scholarship, and traditions, do ordain and establish this Constitution for the Student Council of Beckwith Middle School.

Complete Student Model on p. R124.

As you plan your bylaws, include a statement of purpose directed to your audience.

Create a Format

Arrange your bylaws in an easy-to-follow format structured like a detailed outline. The main topics, called **articles**, might include membership, officers and their duties, elections, meetings, and committees. Each article is further divided into subtopics, called **sections**, which explain aspects of the main topics in more detail. Decide what topics and subtopics you wish to include in your bylaws. Then create an outline to use as a guide when you write your draft. Use Roman numerals to number the articles.

STUDENT MODEL • PREWRITING

STUDENT COUNCIL BYLAWS

Preamble: Purpose

Article I: Name

Article II: General Membership

Section 1: Homeroom Representatives

Section 2: Nomination and election

Article III: Officers

Section 1: Duties

Section 2: Election

Article IV: Meetings

Section 1: Place and Time

Section 2: Attendance Policy

Article VI: Committees

Section 1: School Activities Committee

Section 2: Community Service Committee

Article VII: Amendments

Complete Student Model on p. R124.

Know Your Audience and Purpose Suggest that students write a profile of the audience—that is, the group belonging to the organization.

Create a Format A set of bylaws can be a complicated document. Since the bylaws are meant to be a tool to make it easier to run an organization, the document should be easy to use. Identifying and distinguishing the various sections are important aspects of creating the bylaws. People using the bylaws should be able to locate information easily.

There are several ways students can accomplish this. They can use different fonts and different type sizes for different kinds of headings. Extra spacing between sections can also help distinguish areas that deal with different topics. Students should use such elements in a consistent way. If students need more ideas, remind them of the bylaws they looked at during prewriting. If students are divided into groups, all groups need to use the same format.

Additional Resources

- ***Writing and Proofreading Practice,*** pp. 1–6, 42–48
- ***Writing and Proofreading Transparencies 1–6, 17–18, 35–36***
- ***Writers Choice,*** Lesson 5.1

MEETING INDIVIDUAL NEEDS — MULTIPLE MODES OF EXPRESSION

Bodily-Kinesthetic Encourage students to discuss ways to make the bylaws clearer. Is the format helpful? Would visual aids—such as organizational diagrams—help? Are the articles easy to understand when they are read aloud?

Activity Suggest that teams role-play to help develop the bylaws. For example, one student could portray a student who wants to join the organization. What questions would he or she ask? Have other students read answers from the bylaws. Are all the student's questions covered? Were the answers easy to find? **L2** COLLAB. LEARN.

FLASHES OF INSIGHT 651

DRAFTING

Begin with a Clear Focus Suggest that students get together to determine the main topics they want to cover. Then have them arrange these topics in a logical order that is easy to follow. Have them draw up an outline showing the topics they will cover and the order in which the topics will be discussed.

Elaborate on Your Outline Whether students are working in groups or as a class, have them go through the outline, filling in the information that is appropriate for each article. Remind them that they want to accomplish two things: The bylaws should be comprehensive, and they should be clear.

TECHNOLOGY TIP

Use a drawing program that allows text to be moved around and enables students to try out a variety of ideas. Encourage students to save ideas under different names, for example, BYLAWS1 and BYLAWS2.

REVISING

Relax and Reconsider Emphasize the importance of a cooling-off period at this stage of writing. Point out that distancing oneself from one's work allows one to return to it with a fresh, critical eye. This step in the process should be built into any schedule that sets up a writing deadline.

Teaching Support

DRAFTING

DRAFTING TIP
Use various fonts (regular, *italic*, and **boldface**) and type sizes to draw the reader's eye to the main points in the bylaws. Use extra spacing between headings and subheadings.

Begin with a Clear Focus

Try opening your bylaws with a striking sentence that states the purpose of your document. Like the students at Beckwith Middle School, you might try imitating the distinctive style of the Preamble of the Constitution of the United States. Reread the examples on page 651 as you write your own preamble.

Elaborate on Your Outline

Using the outline of your bylaws as a road map, elaborate on the numbered articles and sections you listed. Provide specific details that explain each topic and subtopic.

STUDENT MODEL • DRAFTING

ARTICLE II

GENERAL MEMBERSHIP

Section 1. Homeroom Representatives The Student Council shall be made up of students who are in the sixth, seventh, and eighth grades. Each homeroom will have two Student Council representatives.

Complete Student Model on p. R124.

REVISING

REVISING TIP
Listen as a partner reads your draft aloud. Catch confusing or unclear sentences and straighten them out.

TECHNOLOGY TIP Check your school computer lab for software to help you format your bylaws.

Relax and Reconsider

If you can, take a break from your draft. Then return to it, and use the **Rubric for Revising** to plan changes that will improve your message.

RUBRIC FOR REVISING

Your revised bylaws should have

- an introduction that clearly states the purpose of a school-sponsored organization or club
- a description of how the organization should operate
- well-developed articles and sections
- a consistent and logical organization
- a format that helps readers quickly see the arrangement of ideas
- design elements that draw attention to main topics and subtopics
- no errors in grammar, usage, and mechanics

Writing *Minilesson*

Plain Language As students revise their bylaws, have them focus on the explanations they have written. It is easy to start writing long complicated sentences that are difficult to understand. Have them try to break up such sentences into smaller, more manageable parts. Also, have them check to make sure they haven't used terminology that would be unfamiliar to readers. These are easy traps to fall into when writing such a document. Remind students to keep the bylaws simple and easy to understand.

Activity Have students who have worked on one part of the bylaws read through the text of another part. They may find sections that are unclear or repetitious. **L2** **COLLAB. LEARN.**

Additional Resources

- ***Writer's Choice,*** Lesson 24.3

EDITING/PROOFREADING

When your bylaws read exactly the way you want them to, it's time to proofread for errors in grammar, usage, and mechanics. The **Proofreading Checklist** at the right can help.

Grammar Hint

Items in a run-on list should be written in parallel form.

The student council is responsible for meeting the following goals: encouraging school pride among students, helping to solve school problems, and promoting better relationships between teachers and students.

PROOFREADING CHECKLIST

- Items in a list are correctly written in parallel structure.
- Sentences are complete; there are no fragments or run-ons.
- Verbs agree with subjects.
- Pronouns are in the correct forms and agree with their antecedents.
- Spelling, capitalization, and punctuation are correct.

STUDENT MODEL • EDITING/PROOFREADING

The Secretary will take notes at all Council meetings, writes letters and other communications for the Council, and gives the school administration information about Council activities.

Complete Student Model

For a complete version of the model developed in this Workshop, refer to **Writing Workshop Models**, p. R124.

Complete Student Model on p. R124.

PUBLISHING/PRESENTING

Bylaws are an important document for any organization. To emphasize the importance of your bylaws, print out a copy of your document on good quality paper and bind the pages together in a folder. Share your bylaws with the members of the organization or with a small group of classmates.

PRESENTING TIP

For easy reference, use index tabs to identify the topic of each article of the bylaws.

Reflecting

Write your thoughts about this project in your journal.

- What was most challenging about writing these bylaws? Why?
- How might you use your skill in writing bylaws in the future? Explain.

Save your work for your portfolio.

GLENCOE TECHNOLOGY

REVISING WITH STYLE CD-ROM

Invite students to use the *Revising with Style* CD-ROM, which offers instruction and exercises to help students improve their writing skills.

EDITING/PROOFREADING

Have students use the **Proofreading Checklist** in the *Grammar and Composition Handbook.*

Have students be especially careful in checking the formatting elements. These should be used in a consistent way throughout the bylaws.

Additional Resources

Grammar and Composition Handbook, Lesson 5.3

PRESENTING/PUBLISHING

The class may wish to present the bound copy of their bylaws to the school library or to an appropriate school organization.

Reflecting

Portfolio Encourage students to ask themselves these questions as they review their work:

- Do the bylaws cover all the necessary topics?
- Are the bylaws clearly written and easy to use?
- Did working on the bylaws help in learning how to express ideas clearly?

6+1 TRAITS™ OF WRITING

See the annotated **Writing Workshop Models** on pp. R119–R130 for additional help in evaluating student writing ad in teaching the **6+1 Traits™ of effective writing.** Annotations and minilessons address and reinforce the **6+1 Traits™**: Ideas, Organization, Voice, Word Choice, Sentence Fluency, Conventions, and Presentation.

ASSESSMENT

Writing Assessment and Portfolio Management

- Writing Assessment, pp. 1–12, 29–33
- Portfolio Management, pp. 42–48

Theme Assessment

Objectives

- To respond to the stories, discussions, and activities in this theme
- To identify a foil in one selection from the theme
- To complete a self-evaluation, set a goal, and devise a plan for achieving the goal

Responding to the Theme

1. Students should provide examples to support their responses.
2. Responses should be based on sound reasons and be supported by examples from the selection.
3. Encourage students to evaluate their own theme projects.

Analyzing Literature

Students' writing should

- have an introductory paragraph that identifies the two stories and the characters being compared
- include details from the two stories to support students' conclusions

Evaluate and Set Goals

Evaluate

Have students list the projects and assignments they completed in the theme. Suggest that they add other contributions they made as well, such as helping a classmate use a drawing program.

To help students formulate valid reasons for their ratings, you might suggest they develop a class rubric.

Set Goals

Have students use a chart to organize their goals, the steps they will take for achieving them, and checkpoints. Then discuss students' plans in individual conferences.

Theme Assessment

Responding to the Theme

1. Based on your reading in this theme, explain the following statements about "Flashes of Insight."
   - Reading about a new way of looking at the world can lead to personal growth.
   - Understanding an event may change the way a reader thinks.
2. Which selection in the theme helped you to gain a new insight? Explain.
3. Present your theme project to the class.

Analyzing Literature

FIND THE FOIL

A **foil** is a character who draws attention to traits of a main character by showing contrasting traits. For example, a very selfish character will contrast with the generosity of the main character. Identify a foil somewhere in this theme, and describe how the foil helps you understand the main character.

Evaluate and Set Goals

1. Which of the following activities did you enjoy the most in this theme? Which was most difficult?
   - reading and understanding the selections
   - writing on your own
   - analyzing and discussing the selections
   - presenting ideas and projects
   - researching topics
2. How would you assess your work in this theme, using the following scale? Give at least two reasons for your assessment.

   4 = outstanding   2 = fair
   3 = good   1 = weak
3. Think about what you found challenging in this theme and choose a goal to work toward in the next theme.
   - Record your goal and three steps you will take to help you reach it.
   - Meet with your teacher to review your plan for achieving your goal.

Build Your Portfolio

SELECT

Choose two of your favorite pieces of work from this theme to include in your portfolio. The following questions can help you choose.

- ◆ Which did you learn the most from?
- ◆ Which was more challenging than you expected?
- ◆ Which was the most interesting to others?

REFLECT

Write some notes to accompany the pieces you selected. Use these questions to guide you.

- ◆ What do you like best about the piece?
- ◆ What did others like best?
- ◆ What did you learn from creating it?

ASSESSMENT

Writing Assessment and Portfolio Management
- Writing Assessment, pp. 1–12
- Portfolio Management, pp. 41–48

GLENCOE TECHNOLOGY

MINDJOGGER VIDEOQUIZZES
VIDEODISC

Use *MindJogger* to review the Theme 6 content.

Theme 6
Side B

Also available in VHS.

Reading on Your Own

If you enjoyed the literature in this theme, you might also be interested in the following books.

The Glory Field

by Walter Dean Myers This is a story of the Lewis family, beginning in their African homeland and ending in contemporary America. Throughout the decades, they manage to maintain continuous ownership of a piece of land, the Glory Field. The author focuses on a strong teenage character in each generation as he tells their story.

SOS Titanic

by Eve Bunting
As the *Titanic* sinks, Irish immigrants trapped in cabins below deck awaken to new values and extend help to old enemies, as well as to family members.

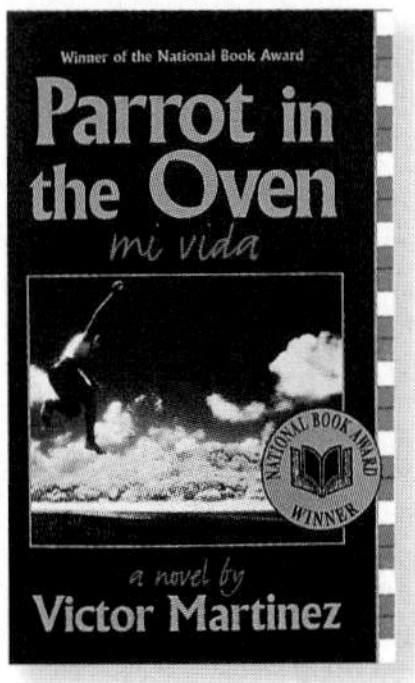

Parrot in the Oven: *mi vida*

by Victor Martinez Manny Hernandez is fourteen, and his father has him convinced that he is "just a penny"—not worth much. One way to be worth a lot is to be part of a gang, and Manny must decide.

Lupita Mañana

by Patricia Beatty Lupita Torres is thirteen when she and her older brother enter the United States to find work and support their widowed mother and younger siblings. The two must weigh the need to find jobs with the dangers and difficulties of crossing a border illegally.

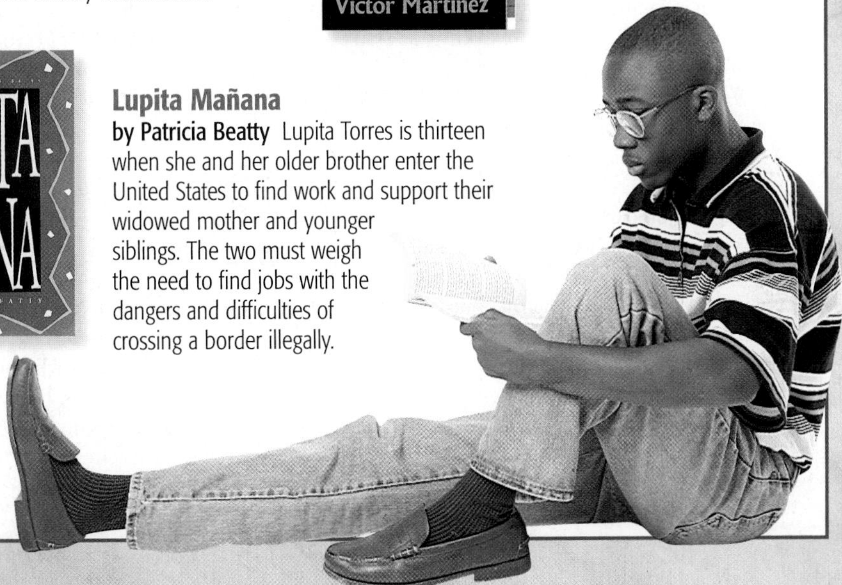

Reading on Your Own

Tips for Independent Reading

Stress the importance of each student's spending at least a half-hour a day in independent reading and supply a list of readings related to the theme under study. Explain that the opening pages of a novel often contain information about the main character(s) that alerts careful readers to major plot developments or themes. Students should think about the main concerns of the characters and look for examples of physical description, dialogue, thoughts, actions, and judgements by other characters, the narrator, or the author.

Practice Ask students to read the first few pages of their novel and then stop to reflect on the characters. As they continue reading, encourage them to consider how the initial concerns of the characters are being played out. When students finish reading, have them review the opening pages and discuss how the central themes of the novels are communicated through the characters.

Glencoe Literature Library

The Glory Field by Walter Dean Myers is available in the *Glencoe Literature Library*. For a complete listing of the titles, see the **Glencoe Resources for Independent Reading** in the front of this book.

The *Glencoe Literature Library Study Guide* provides instructional support for works in the *Glencoe Literature Library*.

At the MOVIES

Be sure to preview the following videos for appropriateness for your class.

Films that deal with "Flashes of Insight"—new ways of looking at reality—include *Old Yeller*, *Antz*, and *Seal Morning*.

MEETING INDIVIDUAL NEEDS — SPECIAL NEEDS

You may wish to recommend *The Glory Field* by Walter Dean Myers to your less-proficient readers. The accessible subject matter and writing style make this book particularly appropriate for these students. **L1**

The books listed at the right are rated for average readers **(L2)** or for students who need more challenging reading material **(L3)**:

- *Lupita Mañana* by Patricia Beatty **L2**
- *SOS Titanic* by Eve Bunting **L2**
- *Parrot in the Oven: mi vida* by Victor Martinez **L3**

Standardized Test Practice

The Princeton Review **TEST-TAKING TIP**

Students should look for clues about the author's purpose. Is the author making an argument? Raising a question? Describing a historical event?

Students should also look for clues about the author's attitude or tone. Is the author's tone objective and scientific, or opinionated and argumentative?

Make sure that students are not trying to memorize the passage. Remind them that they can always refer to it if needed.

The Princeton Review **TEST-TAKING TIP**

Ask the class to finish this sentence: "Gee, Ron! That's a great haircut, and—." The word "and" is used to continue a thought or trend, so the sentence will probably end positively. Now take the same sentence and change only one word: "Gee, Ron! That's a great haircut, but—." Ask the class what will follow. How did they know it would be something bad? Words like "but" tell us that something different will follow.

Answers and Analyses

1. B The opening sentence of the passage states that Hughes was "one of the most influential poets," and the first line of the concluding paragraph states that he "continued to break new ground." Therefore, choice B is the most reasonable answer.

The Princeton Review

Standardized Test Practice

Read the following passage. Then read each question on page 657. Decide which is the best answer to each question. Mark the letter for that answer on your paper.

Langston Hughes: A Poet's Journey

Langston Hughes was one of the most influential poets in a movement known as the Harlem Renaissance. Hughes was born on February 1, 1902, in Joplin, Missouri. In 1914, he moved to Illinois to live with his father and stepmother. While in grade school in Illinois, Hughes developed an interest in poetry, and before he had finished high school, he had read the works of many famous thinkers and poets.

In 1919, Hughes moved to Mexico, where his father had become a prosperous businessman. However, Hughes did not agree with his father's plans for him to attend college and study engineering. He returned to New York, where he studied for a year at Columbia University. He then began two years of travel, working at odd jobs in several countries.

When Hughes returned to the United States, he rejoined his mother in Washington, D.C., and took a job as a hotel busboy. In the restaurant, he saw Vachel Lindsay, a noted poet. Hughes was too shy to approach and introduce himself, but while Lindsay dined, Hughes managed to slide several of his own poems under Lindsay's plate. As he read the poems, Lindsay noticed that Hughes was using structural qualities he himself aimed for. That night he read Hughes's poems to an audience of selected guests, and overnight Hughes became a respected local figure.

With Lindsay's guidance, Hughes submitted several of his pieces to magazines for publication. One poem, "The Weary Blues," won a prize from *Opportunity*, a leading periodical that featured African American writing. This poem became the title piece for Hughes's first volume of verse, published in 1926.

Hughes received his college degree in 1929. That same year, he completed his first novel, *Not Without Laughter*. His career skyrocketed from this point, and Hughes suddenly found himself to be a writer of national fame. He was particularly well known for his readings of his own pieces.

Until his death in 1967, Hughes continued to break new ground in poetry by creating verse that dealt with life as an African American man. He created several fictitious characters, such as Jesse Simple, a wise and humorous black laborer. With Simple, he explored America through the eyes of a minority figure. In addition, Hughes contributed a weekly column to the *New York Post* that began to express to a growing nation the experiences of its African American citizens. With his writing, Hughes helped to bridge the gap between people of different ethnic backgrounds.

MEETING INDIVIDUAL NEEDS **ENGLISH LANGUAGE LEARNERS**

Crossword Puzzle Have students create a crossword puzzle based on the life of Langston Hughes. Ask students to choose about fifteen words from the passage that incorporate some element of Hughes's life. This will assist students in learning key vocabulary words. Some words they may choose are *Renaissance, stepmother, businessman, college, engineering, university, busboy, opportunity, minority, poetry, ethnic, background.*

1 The author of the passage seems to believe that Langston Hughes was —

A unlucky.

B talented.

C impatient.

D quiet

2 What does "break new ground" mean in the last paragraph of the passage?

J write new poetry

K write new poetry

L accomplish new feats

M explore new places

3 What structural pattern does the author use in this passage?

A order of importance

B chronological order

C reverse chronological order

D order of preference

4 Which is the best summary of the passage?

J Travel is good for aspiring young poets.

K Langston Hughes's background influenced his career as a writer.

L Hughes held many different jobs during his life.

M Hughes never got along well with his father, and they had particularly bad times in 1919.

5 Why did Vachel Lindsay find Hughes's poems impressive?

A He liked reading poems with his dinner.

B He, too, had traveled and understood Hughes's work.

C He thought Hughes was very motivated.

D The poems had a structure similar to that in his own work.

6 This passage is most like—

J a newspaper editorial.

K a scientific article.

L an advertisement.

M an encyclopedia article.

STOP

Answers and Analyses

2. **L** Students should use the immediate context of the specific expression to help them arrive at the best choice. This sentence states that Hughes created "verse that dealt with life as an African American man." Hughes's creation of new poetry and new characters implies that he accomplished new feats, making choice L the best answer.
3. **B** Students can discover the structural pattern of the passage by reviewing a few of the opening sentences of each paragraph. Clues such as dates and time markers will help students to conclude that the passage describes important events in Hughes's life chronologically.
4. **K** Students can use the process of elimination (POE) to narrow down the possibilities for this question. The title indicates that the passage is specifically about Hughes, making choice J too broad. There is nothing in the passage to suggest choice L, and choice M is only a small detail in the passage, not a summary. The remaining and best answer is choice K.
5. **D** Upon reviewing the part of the passage directly concerning Vachel Lindsay, students will see that Lindsay "noticed that Hughes was using structural qualities he himself aimed for." Choice D roughly paraphrases this sentence and is thus the best answer.
6. **M** Since there is no science in this passage and since nothing is being sold, students can eliminate choices K and L. A newspaper editorial makes an attempt to persuade the reader, rather than to simply inform, so choice J can also be eliminated. Choice M is the best answer.

Tested Objectives

Item	Language Objective
1, 5	Read and understand grade-level appropriate material. Describe and connect the essential ideas, arguments, and perspectives of text, as they relate to text structure, organization, and purpose.
2	Use idioms, analogies, metaphors, and similes to infer the literal and figurative meanings of phrases
3, 6	Evaluate the unity, coherence, logic, internal consistency, and structural patterns of text
4	Compare original text to a summary for accuracy of the main ideas, inclusion of critical details, and the extent to which it conveys the underlying meaning of the original text

MORE PRACTICE

For additional practice, assign pages from one of the following standardized test resources available as part of Glencoe Literature.

Additional Resources

ITBS Preparation and Practice

SAT-9 Preparation and Practice

TerraNova Preparation and Practice

Theme 7 At a Glance

Faces of Dignity

THEME OPENING

- **Introducing the Theme** (p. 659)
- **Exploring the Theme** (p. 660)
- **Theme Projects** (p. 661)

Theme 7: FACES OF DIGNITY

SELECTIONS

from **All but My Life** (p. 662)

from **Anne Frank: The Diary of a Young Girl** (p. 674)

Media Connection: The Anne Frank House Web Site (p. 684)

The Anne Frank House: Amsterdam (p. 686)

Active Reading Model: The Diary of Anne Frank (p. 696)

Media Connection: I Think Myself Out (p. 776)

SKILL FEATURES

Interdisciplinary Connection (p. 672)

Reading and Thinking Skills (p. 673)

Grammar Link (p. 690)

Writing Skills (p. 691)

Genre Focus: Drama (pp. 692–693)

Active Reading Strategies (pp. 694–695)

Vocabulary Skills (p. 777)

WRITING WORKSHOP

Expository Writing: Historical Research Report (pp. 778–781)

THEME ASSESSMENT

- **Responding to the Theme, Analyzing Literature, Evaluate and Set Goals** (p. 782)
- **Build Your Portfolio** (p. 782)
- **Reading on Your Own** (p. 783)
  Number the Stars by Lois Lowry
  After the War by Carol Matas
  The Island on Bird Street by Uri Orlev
  I Am Fifteen—and I Don't Want to Die by Christine Arnothy
- **Standardized Test Practice** (pp. 784–785)

KEYS TO LITERARY CONNECTIONS

Comparing Selections

The **Comparing Selections** feature in this theme provides opportunities for addressing diverse aspects of the reading and literature curriculum.

For example, in Comparing Selections on page 689, students examine the content of and experiences in the excerpt from *Anne Frank: The Diary of a Young Girl* and "The Anne Frank House: Amsterdam." Through this comparison, students can better appreciate the dignity of a young girl dealing with the Holocaust.

World Literature

The Student Edition contains a variety of literature that represents cultures from around the world. World literature selections are highlighted with the icon above.

TEACHING SUPPORT

The Teaching Support offers a wealth of interactive instructional support:

Meeting Individual Needs
- Special Needs
- English Language Learners
- Multiple Modes of Expression
- Advanced Learners

Internet Connection

Assessment

Portfolio Options

Minilessons
- Grammar and Language
- Reading
- Writing
- Listening and Speaking

Connecting to Other Selections

Real-World Connection

Interdisciplinary Connection

Life Skills Connection

Family and Community Activity

Key to Ability Levels

The activities throughout this theme have been coded for students of various abilities.

L1 BASIC activities for all students

L2 AVERAGE activities for average to above-average students

L3 ADVANCED LEARNERS activities for above-average students

Teaching Today

The Glencoe *Teaching Today* professional development Web site at www.teachingtoday.glencoe.com features daily teaching tips, free downloads, annotated Web resources, educational news, and a wealth of information on a wide range of topics.

Reading Skills in this theme

Variety of Texts

In addition to drama, this theme includes the following:

- memoir
- diary
- Web site
- poem
- song lyrics

Comprehension Skills

The following instructional support for comprehension skills appears in this theme of the Student Edition:

- **Active Reading Strategies and Model** (pp. 694–710)
- **Activating Prior Knowledge** (p. 673)
- **Reading and Thinking Minilessons** (pp. 671, 775)

See also the **Reading Minilessons** throughout the theme in this Teacher Wraparound Edition.

For strategies for reading longer works, such as novels and novellas, see "Tips for Independent Reading" on page 783.

Reading Resources

Active Reading Guide The ***Active Reading Guide*** provides graphic organizers and study guide questions to support students' reading of each selection (***Active Reading Guide***, pp. 58–65).

Interactive Reading Sourcebook and **Interactive Reading Workbook** The ***Interactive Reading Sourcebook*** and ***Interactive Reading Workbook*** offer focused comprehension strategies and lessons on critical thinking skills as well as fluency practice and activities to teach and support phonics, decoding, spelling, and vocabulary development.

Vocabulary Power The ***Vocabulary Power*** workbook (Lessons 29–32) provides systematic teaching, practice, and assessment of vocabulary for better reading comprehension.

Audio Library Available on audiocassette and on CD, the ***Audio Library*** provides valuable comprehension support.

Glencoe Literature Library Each title in the ***Glencoe Literature Library*** includes a full-length work plus related readings. A separate Study Guide is available for each title.

Five-Star Stories These anthologies of familiar short stories adapted and abridged for a variety of reading levels include exercises to help increase students' vocabulary and improve their reading comprehension.

The Contemporary Readers ***The Contemporary Readers*** are nonfiction books linked to various themes and designed for developing readers from a wide range of backgrounds.

Literature Classics CD-ROM The selections on this CD-ROM can be searched by author, theme, or genre.

inTIME and **Humanities Across TIME** Coproductions of Glencoe and Time, Inc., these resources include a wealth of high-interest nonfiction related to the selections in this theme.

Assessment in this theme

GLENCOE'S ASSESSMENT ADVANTAGE

Assessment Options in the Student Edition

This program offers a number of diverse ways to evaluate student understanding and skill proficiency. In the Student Edition, use the following:

- **Responding to Literature**
  Following each selection, students are asked to recall facts, interpret ideas, and evaluate concepts as they answer a variety of questions and complete activities to extend their understanding.
- **Theme Assessment (pp. 782–783)**
  Here students respond to the selections on personal and analytical levels. They also assume ownership of their learning by setting and evaluating goals and by selecting work for their portfolios.

See also the many **Assessment Resources** listed on the facing page.

The Princeton Review

Standardized Test Practice

The Princeton Review has developed the Standardized Test Practice pages found at the end of this thematic unit (pp. 784–785). For additional practice, direct students to the following resources:

- ITBS Preparation and Practice
- SAT-9 Preparation and Practice
- TerraNova Preparation and Practice

Writing Skills in this theme

Writing Skills

The Student Edition of Theme 7 offers strong instructional support for writing skills:

In **Extending Your Response,** which follows each selection:
- **Writing About Literature**
- **Personal/Creative Writing**

In **Writing Skills** Lessons:
- **Using Transitions in Cause-Effect Relationships** (p. 691)

See also the **Writing Minilessons** throughout the theme in this Teacher Wraparound Edition.

Writing Workshops

Theme 7 concludes with a **Writing Workshop** that guides students through the process for writing a historical research report (pp. 778–781).

Writing Resources

Writer's Assistant CD-ROM Each **Writing Workshop** is supplemented by an interactive writing guide on the ***Writer's Assistant*** CD-ROM. This easy-to-use writing guide provides prompts, templates, and other tools that lead students through the writing process.

Grammar and Composition Handbook The ***Grammar and Composition Handbook*** (Lessons 13.4–13.7) provides systematic instruction in English language conventions.

Spelling Power The ***Spelling Power*** workbook (Lessons 25–28) provides systematic teaching, practice, and assessment of spelling to help students become better spellers and thus enhance their writing.

Writing and Proofreading Practice Blackline masters present in-depth instruction and practice on a specific step in the writing process and proofreading (pp. 1–6, 49–57).

Writing and Proofreading Transparencies Transparencies provide graphic organizers and proofreading exercises for whole-class instruction (pp. 1–6, 37–38).

Research and Report Writing Guide This resource provides extensive tips and activities to guide students in their writing projects in the literature classroom as well as in classes across the curriculum.

Style and Documentation Sourcebook for Writers This sourcebook is a combination reference and workbook, giving students the most up-to-date information and guidance regarding traditional as well as technological research strategies and documentation.

Revising with Style This resource offers instruction and exercises focusing on the revision process and covering topics from proofreading and correcting common grammatical errors to sentence combining and reordering.

Assessment Resources

Selection Quick Checks For each selection, a **Quick Check** of three to five short-answer questions measures students' literal comprehension.

Selection and Theme Assessment The ***Selection and Theme Assessment*** instrument tests students' abilities to recall, interpret, and evaluate what they've read. The tests consist of multiple-choice, short answer, and essay questions.

Performance Assessment Alternative assessment instruments and rubrics for Theme 7 are found in the ***Performance Assessment*** ancillary.

Writing Assessment and Portfolio Management These notes and strategies, student models, and assessment tools assist with the task of measuring students' progress as writers and as monitors of their own writing.

Testmaker: ExamView Pro Teachers can customize selection and Theme 7 tests by accessing the ***Testmaker*** database.

Interactive Tutor: Self-Assessment The ***Interactive Tutor: Self-Assessment*** software provides multiple-choice tests with immediate feedback to help students evaluate their knowledge and understanding of each literature selection.

MindJogger Videoquizzes Using a popular game show format, ***MindJogger Videoquizzes*** on videocassettes enable teachers to evaluate student understanding of Theme 7 in a quick and fun manner.

Theme 7 SKILLS SCOPE AND SEQUENCE

Lessons	Literary Elements	Reading and Thinking	Writing
from **All but My Life** GERDA WEISSMANN KLEIN DRP: 49 Lexile: 680	Memoir, SE p. 669 *Memoir, TWE pp. 664, 666, 667, 668* *Irony, TWE p. 665*	Identifying Assumptions, SE p. 671 *Infer, TWE p. 664* *Drawing Conclusions, TWE pp. 666, 668* *Elaborate, TWE p. 666* *Main Idea and Supporting Details, TWE p. 666* SN *Less-Proficient Readers, TWE p. 670*	Title, SE p. 670 Letter, SE p. 670
from **Anne Frank: The Diary of a Young Girl** ANNE FRANK DRP: 49 Lexile: 1100	Journal, SE p. 682 *Irony, TWE p. 676* *Journal, TWE pp. 676, 680* *Tone, TWE p. 677*	Activating Prior Knowledge, SE p. 673 Website, SE p. 684 SN *Less-Proficient Readers, TWE p. 673* *Make Critical Judgments, TWE p. 679* *Skimming, TWE p. 679* *Identify Bias, TWE p. 681* *Synthesizing, TWE p. 684*	Characterization, SE p. 683 Reflection, SE p. 683 *Interpretation, TWE p. 681*
The Anne Frank House: Amsterdam JOAN LABOMBARD	Rhythm, SE p. 688	Comparing Selections, SE p. 689 *Drawing Conclusions, TWE p. 687*	Paragraph, SE p. 688 Using Transitions in Cause-Effect Relationships, SE p. 691 *Factual Descriptions, TWE p. 690*
The Diary of Anne Frank FRANCES GOODRICH AND ALBERT HACKETT	Drama, SE p. 692 Acts and Scenes, SE p. 710 Dialogue, SE p. 728 Stage Directions, SE p. 742 Dramatic Monologue, SE p. 761 Tragedy, SE p. 773 ELL *Drama Across Cultures, TWE p. 692* *Dialogue, TWE pp.* ELL *698, 714, 717, 726, 756, 758* *Acts and Scenes, TWE pp. 701, 711, 772* *Flashback, TWE p. 701* *Irony, TWE pp. 703, 713, 733, 740, 748, 766* *Characterization, TWE pp. 706, 730, 757, 763* *Symbolism, TWE pp. 706, 719* *Stage Directions, TWE pp. 709, 729, 736, 738, 739, 747, 764* *Conflict, TWE pp. 711, 737, 740, 758* *Author's Purpose, TWE p. 716* *Metaphor, TWE p. 720* *Suspense, TWE p. 729* *Plot, TWE pp. 739, 760* *Comedy, TWE p. 747* *Dramatic Monologue, TWE pp. 751, 752* *Simile, TWE p. 753* *Foreshadowing, TWE pp. 766, 769* *Mood, TWE p. 767* *Imagery, TWE p. 768* *Tragedy, TWE pp. 769, 772*	Drama, SE p. 694 Focusing on a Question, SE p. 775 Song Lyrics, SE p. 776 *Infer, TWE pp. 701, 702, 711, 715, 720, 732, 734, 746, 748, 755, 765* *Verify Predictions, TWE pp. 703, 721* *Summarize, TWE pp. 703, 721* *Drawing Conclusions, TWE pp. 704, 724, 729, 733, 736, 751, 760* SN *Visually Impaired, TWE p. 704* *Evaluate, TWE pp. 705, 719, 731* *Set a Purpose for Reading, TWE p. 705* *Synthesize, TWE pp. 707, 714, 749* *Analyze Arguments, TWE p. 713* *Judge the Credibility of a Source, TWE p. 719* *Make Critical Judgments, TWE pp. 722, 756, 763* *Generalize, TWE p. 734* *Paraphrase, TWE p. 737* *Elaborate, TWE p. 746* *Distinguish Fact from Opinion, TWE p. 749* SN *Less-Proficient Readers, TWE p. 752* SN *Less-Proficient Readers, TWE p. 763* *Author's Purpose, TWE p. 776*	Journal Entry, SE pp. 710, 728, 742 Letter, SE p. 761 Explanation, SE p. 774 Character Sketch, SE p. 774 *Descriptive Writing, TWE pp. 709, 747* *Persuasion, TWE p. 714* *Outlining, TWE p. 722* *Dialogue, TWE p. 735* SN *Learning Disabled, TWE p. 739* *Prewriting, TWE p. 758* *Introductions and Conclusions, TWE p. 770*
Writing WORKSHOP Expository Writing: Historical Research Report			ELL *Historical Research Alternatives, TWE p. 778* SN *Learning Disabled, TWE p. 779* *Sequencing, TWE p. 780*

Key: Student material is in roman. Teacher material is in italic. Technology ELL English Language Learners

Vocabulary and Spelling	Grammar and Language	Listening, Speaking, and Viewing	Life Skills; Study and Research; Technology
The Latin Root *vert,* SE p. 671 ELL *Vocabulary: Connotation,* *TWE p. 664*	Writing Dates, SE p. 671 *Adjectives, TWE p. 668*	Literature Groups, SE p. 670 *Oral Reading, TWE p. 667*	Internet Connection, SE p. 670 Geography Research, SE p. 670 Europe: Fifty Years of Change SE p. 672 *Video, TWE p. 663* *History Research, TWE p. 665*
Antonyms, SE p. 683 *Context Clues, TWE p. 676* *Multiple-Meaning Words, TWE p. 679*	ELL *Articles, TWE p. 676* *Colons, TWE p. 680*	Literature Groups, SE p. 683	Interview, SE p. 683 *Present Day Persecution, TWE p. 677* SN *Learning Disabled, TWE p. 678*
	Using Commas Correctly, SE p. 690 *Correct Pronoun Use, TWE p. 687* *Avoiding Run-on Sentences, TWE p. 691*	Literature Groups, SE p. 688	
Synonyms, SE p. 743 Etymology, SE p. 775 Analyzing Words, SE p. 777 *Homophones, TWE p. 704* ELL *Directional Words, TWE p. 712* *Context Clues, TWE p. 715* *Etymology, TWE p. 724* *Roots, TWE p. 753* ELL *Homophones, TWE p. 762* ELL *Latin Word Parts, TWE p. 777*	Italics and Quotation Marks, SE p. 775 *Troublesome Pairs, TWE p. 708* *Adjectives and Adverbs, TWE p. 726* ELL *Understanding Print Conventions, TWE p. 730* *Less or Fewer, TWE p. 740* ELL *Prepositions, TWE p. 744* *Indefinite Pronouns, TWE p. 760* *Punctuating Dates, TWE p. 772*	Literature Groups, SE pp. 710, 728, 742, 761, 774 Readers Theater, SE p. 774 ELL *Dialogue, TWE p. 698* *Radio Drama, TWE p. 707* *Effective Listening Techniques, TWE p. 715* *Oral Reading, TWE pp. 725, 764* SN *Emotional, TWE pp. 727, 733* *Debate, TWE p. 741* SN *Learning Disabled, TWE p. 746* *Public Speaking, TWE p. 751* SN *Learning Disabled, TWE p. 755*	History Research, SE p. 774 *History Research, TWE pp. 699, 700, 702, 720, 736, 753, 765* *Creating and Producing, TWE p. 701* *Health Research, TWE p. 717* *Planning, TWE pp. 718, 734* *Internet Connection, TWE pp. 719, 768* *Internet Research, TWE p. 723* *Art Research, TWE p. 729* *Interview, TWE p. 731* *Psychology Research, TWE p. 732* *Video, TWE p. 748* *Time Management, TWE p. 757* *Leading and Organizing, TWE p. 771*

SN Special Needs/Strategic Intervention

Theme 7 RESOURCE MANAGER

Lessons	Essential Resources		English Language Learners
from **All but My Life** Gerda Weissmann Klein Pacing: 2 Days	**Lesson-Specific Instruction** Selection Focus Transp. 57 * Active Reading Guide, p. 58 Literary Elements Transp. 58 Vocabulary Practice, p. 41 * Quick Checks, p. 58 Selection and Theme Assessment, pp. 105–106	Testmaker: ExamView Pro Performance Assessment, p. 55 TIME *inTIME* magazine, p. 17 **Systematic Language Instruction** Grammar and Comp. Hbk., L. 13.4 Vocabulary Power, Lesson 29 Spelling Power, Lesson 25	English Language Learners Sourcebook, p. 82 Spanish Summaries, p. 57 * Audio Library English, Yes!
from **Anne Frank: The Diary of a Young Girl** Anne Frank Pacing: 2 Day	**Lesson-Specific Instruction** Selection Focus Transp. 58 * Active Reading Guide, p. 59 Literary Elements Transp. 59 Vocabulary Practice, p. 42 * Quick Checks, p. 59 Selection and Theme Assessment, pp. 107–108	Testmaker: ExamView Pro Performance Assessment, p. 56 **Systematic Language Instruction** Grammar and Comp. Hbk., L. 14.5 Vocabulary Power, Lesson 30	English Language Learners Sourcebook, p. 83 Spanish Summaries, p. 58 Spanish Translations, pp. 148–152 * Audio Library English, Yes!
The Anne Frank House: Amsterdam Joan LaBombard Pacing: 2 Days	**Lesson-Specific Instruction** Selection Focus Transp. 59 * Active Reading Guide, p. 60 Literary Elements Transp. 60 Vocabulary Practice, p. 689 * Quick Checks, p. 60 Selection and Theme Assessment, pp. 107–108	Testmaker: ExamView Pro Performance Assessment, p. 56 **Systematic Language Instruction** Grammar and Comp. Hbk., L. 13.6 Vocabulary Power, Lesson 31 Spelling Power, Lesson 27	Spanish Summaries, p. 59 Spanish Translations, p. 153 * Audio Library English, Yes!
The Diary of Anne Frank Act 1, Scenes 1–2 Frances Goodrich and Albert Hackett Pacing: 3 Days	**Lesson-Specific Instruction** Selection Focus Transp. 60 * Active Reading Guide, p. 61 Literary Elements Transp. 61 Vocabulary Practice, p. 43 * Quick Checks, p. 61	**Systematic Language Instruction** Grammar and Comp. Hbk., L. 13.7	English Language Learners Sourcebook, p. 84 Spanish Summaries, p. 60 Spanish Translations, pp. 154–164 * Audio Library English, Yes!
The Diary of Anne Frank Act 1, Scene 3 Pacing: 3 Days	**Lesson-Specific Instruction** * Active Reading Guide, p. 62 Literary Elements Transp. 62 Vocabulary Practice, p. 43 * Quick Checks, p. 62	**Systematic Language Instruction** Vocabulary Power, Lesson 32	English Language Learners Sourcebook, p. 85 Spanish Translations, pp. 165–181 Spanish Audio Library English, Yes!

Key: Workbook Blackline Masters Textbook Transparency CD-ROM Videodisk (also available in videocassette)

Special Needs/ Strategic Intervention	Reteaching and Enrichment
Interactive Reading Sourcebook, pp. T195–T197 Interactive Reading Workbook, pp. 108–109 * Audio Library	Fine Art Transparency 8 Reading Skills Practice Workbook pp. 105–106 Grammar and Language Transp. 56 Gr. and Lang. Wkbk., pp. 121–123 Grammar and Comp. Hbk., L. 5.1 Interactive Tutor: Self-Assessment Vocabulary PuzzleMaker Web Site (lit.glencoe.com)
Interactive Reading Sourcebook, pp. T198–T200 Interactive Reading Workbook, pp. 110–112 Inclusion Strategies Sourcebook, pp. 97–98 * Audio Library	Fine Art Transparency 8 Reading Skills Practice Workbook pp. 107–108 Grammar and Language Transp. 57 Gr. and Lang. Wkbk., pp. 265–266 Grammar and Comp. Hbk., L. 13.5 Media Connection Activities, p. 13 Interactive Tutor: Self-Assessment Vocabulary PuzzleMaker Web Site (lit.glencoe.com)
Interactive Reading Sourcebook, pp. T200–T203 Interactive Reading Workbook, p. 112 Theme Seven Planning Guide, p. 22 * Audio Library	Fine Art Transparency 4 Grammar and Language Transp. 58 Gr. and Lang. Wkbk., pp. 53–54, 111–112, 161–162 Grammar and Comp. Hbk., L. 4.1, 13.3, 14.1, 14.4 Interactive Tutor: Self-Assessment Vocabulary PuzzleMaker Web Site (lit.glencoe.com)
Interactive Reading Sourcebook, pp. T203–T208 Interactive Reading Workbook, p. 113–120 Inclusion Strategies Sourcebook, pp. 71–72 Theme Seven Planning Guide, p. 31 * Audio Library	Literature Launchers, Side B, Segment 20 Reading Skills Practice Workbook pp. 111–112 Grammar and Language Transp. 60 Gr. and Lang. Wkbk., p. 113 Grammar and Comp. Hbk., L. 13.7 Interactive Tutor: Self-Assessment Vocabulary PuzzleMaker Web Site (lit.glencoe.com)
Interactive Reading Sourcebook, pp. T203–T208	Grammar and Language Transp. 61 Gr. and Lang. Wkbk., p. 121 Grammar and Comp. Hbk., L. 5.1, 6.1 Interactive Tutor: Self-Assessment Vocabulary PuzzleMaker Web Site (lit.glencoe.com)

Web   Audiocassette   Diskette   *Also available in Spanish

Independent Reading

Encourage students to spend thirty minutes each day in independent reading. The following Glencoe components and outside resources provide opportunities for reading related to this theme.

The Glencoe Literature Library

You may want to assign one or more of these titles for independent reading. For a complete listing of titles available in the Glencoe Literature Library, see page T94 of this book.

- *Anne Frank Remembered: The Story of the Woman Who Helped to Hide the Frank Family* by Miep Gies and Alison Leslie Gold
- *Number the Stars* by Lois Lowry
- *Letters from Rifka* by Karen Hesse
- *The Clay Marble* by Minfong Ho
- *Journey to Jo'burg* by Beverly Naidoo

inTIME Magazine News stories, feature articles, reviews, profiles, and essays in the magazine connect to an author, work, or theme in the Student Edition. See the **in*TIME* Teacher's Guide** for specific connections to this theme.

Resources for Less-Proficient Readers

For reading especially created for less-proficient readers, suggest

- *Five-Star Stories*
- *The Contemporary Readers*

Additional Resources for Independent Reading

The following titles are listed with specific reading selections throughout this theme. You may want to suggest that students look for these in your local or school library.

- *Farewell to Manzanar* by Jeanne Wakatsuki Houston
- *The Devil in Vienna* by Doris Orgel
- *Anne Frank: The Diary of a Young Girl* by Anne Frank
- *The Last Seven Months of Anne Frank* by Willy Lindwer
- *After the War* by Carol Matas
- *The Island on Bird Street* by Uri Orlev
- *I Am Fifteen—and I Don't Want to Die* by Christine Arnothy

RESOURCE MANAGER (continued)

Lessons	Essential Resources		English Language Learners
The Diary of Anne Frank Act 1, Scenes 4–5 Pacing: 2 Days	**Lesson-Specific Instruction** * Active Reading Guide, p. 63 Literary Elements Transp. 63 Vocabulary Practice, p. 43 * Quick Checks, p. 63 Selection and Theme Assessment, pp. 109–110	Testmaker: ExamView Pro **Systematic Language Instruction** Spelling Power, Lesson 28	English Language Learners Sourcebook, p. 86 Spanish Translations, pp. 182–195 * Audio Library English, Yes!
The Diary of Anne Frank Act 2, Scenes 1–2 Pacing: 2 Days	**Lesson-Specific Instruction** * Active Reading Guide, p. 64 Literary Elements Transp. 64 Vocabulary Practice, p. 44 * Quick Checks, p. 64	**Systematic Language Instruction** Vocabulary Power, Unit 7 Review/Test	English Language Learners Sourcebook, p. 87 Spanish Translations, pp. 196–211 Spanish Audio Library English, Yes!
The Diary of Anne Frank Act 2, Scenes 3–5 Pacing: 4 Days	**Lesson-Specific Instruction** * Active Reading Guide, p. 65 Literary Elements Transp. 65 Vocabulary Practice, p. 44 * Quick Checks, p. 65 Selection and Theme Assessment, pp. 111–112	Testmaker: ExamView Pro Performance Assessment, p. 57 **Systematic Language Instruction** Spelling Power, Unit 7 Review/ Proofreading	English Language Learners Sourcebook, pp. 88, 89 Spanish Translations, pp. 211–221 * Audio Library English, Yes!
Writing WORKSHOP Expository Writing: Historical Research Report Pacing: 2 Days	Writing Assessment and Portfolio Management, pp. 1–13, 34–37, 41–48		English Language Learners Sourcebook, p. 9 English, Yes!

Key: Workbook · Blackline Masters · Textbook · Transparency · CD-ROM · Videodisk (also available in videocassette)

Special Needs/ Strategic Intervention	Reteaching and Enrichment
Interactive Reading Sourcebook, pp. T203–T208 * Audio Library	Grammar and Language Transp. 62 Gr. and Lang. Wkbk., p. 229 Interactive Tutor: Self-Assessment Vocabulary PuzzleMaker Web Site (lit.glencoe.com)
Interactive Reading Sourcebook, pp. T203–T208 Inclusion Strategies Sourcebook, pp. 83–84	Fine Art Transparency 17 Grammar and Language Transp. 63 Gr. and Lang. Wkbk., p. 261 Grammar and Comp. Hbk., L. 4.5 Interactive Tutor: Self-Assessment Vocabulary PuzzleMaker Web Site (lit.glencoe.com)
Interactive Reading Sourcebook, pp. T203–T208 * Audio Library	Fine Art Transparency 23 Grammar and Language Transp. 64 Gr. and Lang. Wkbk., pp. 261–262, 267 Grammar and Comp. Hbk., L. 13.2–13.4, 13.6 Media Connection Activities, p. 14 Interactive Tutor: Self-Assessment Vocabulary PuzzleMaker Web Site (lit.glencoe.com)
Inclusion Strategies Sourcebook, pp. 75–76	Writing and Proofreading Practice, pp. 1–6, 49–57 Writing and Proofreading Transparencies 1–6, 19–20, 21–22, 37–38 Revising with Style Writer's Assistant

Web Audiocassette Diskette *Also available in Spanish

Theme RESOURCES

To explore the theme further, you may want to use these resources:

- Listening and Speaking Activities (pp. 19–21)
- Viewing and Representing Activities (pp. 25–27)
- Critical Thinking Skills (pp. 18–20)
- Media Connection Activities, (pp. 13–14)
- Interdisciplinary Activities (pp. 26–29)
- Family and Community Activities (p. 27)
- Selection and Theme Assessment (pp. 105–112, 137–138
- Performance Assessment (pp. 70, 94)

TIME Humanities Across TIME

See also these additional theme planning resources:

- Theme Seven Planning Guide
- Interactive Reading Sourcebook
- Literature Groups Sourcebook
- Interactive Lesson Planner
- Interactive Teacher Edition
- Glencoe Web Site (lit.glencoe.com)

PRESENTATION Plus!

Use Glencoe's *Presentation Plus!* This multimedia teaching tool lets you present dynamic lessons that will engage your students. Using Microsoft PowerPoint®, you can customize the presentation to create your own personalized lessons.

THEME 7

Faces of Dignity

Theme Objectives

- To enjoy learning about people who keep their dignity in the face of great hardship
- To analyze the literary elements in memoir, diary, poetry, and drama selections
- To apply strategies for reading drama

Teaching Strategies

Have students read the quotation from *Anne Frank: The Diary of a Young Girl* in preparation for the discussion questions below.

VIEWING THE ART

This sculpture, located in Jerusalem, is named for Janusz Korczak, a Jewish doctor who ran a Jewish orphanage in Warsaw in the 1930s.

Responding to the Art

Discussion questions:

- How does this sculpture support Anne Frank's belief that beauty is "around you"? *(Korczak's face shows determination to help the children he cares for.)*
- How does the sculpture contradict her words? *(The children's faces reflect suffering.)*

Korczak and the Children of the Ghetto. Boris Saktsier.

658

TEACHER *to* TEACHER

SCHOARBAR MIDDLE SCHOOL • KELCHIHAN, ALASKA

I do in-depth historical lessons as well as literature lessons when teaching this theme. I use audiotapes of music from the 1930s and 1940s, and I show excerpts from *Schindler's List* and from videos that show the Japanese experience. At other times I have brought in speakers from the Jewish community or shown clips of Hitler giving speeches. I also show World War II footage and bring in *Life* magazine photographs, newspaper clippings, and posters. I want students to see many aspects of World War II and to see the power of courage, faith, and strength. Students are required to conduct a library and Internet search on World War II and how World War I contributed to World War II. We discuss the move of the Frank family, then read the play and books. As a special project, students build a scale-model of the house where the Frank family hid from the Nazis.

—SHEILA BLANKENSHIP

THEME 7

THEME CONTENTS

Introducing Theme 7

Direct your students' attention to the **Theme Contents.** Ask them to read through the list of selections. Present these questions for discussion:

- What do you already know about Anne Frank and the Holocaust?
- How do you think these selections will fit the theme "Faces of Dignity?" *(Students may note the great hardships people endured during the Holocaust.)*
- Which selection interests you most? Why?

LITERATURE & HUMANITIES

American Music: Cultural Traditions, CD volume 2, track 12. You might want to play the song "Boogie Woogie Bugle Boy" to introduce students to the music of World War II.

GLENCOE TECHNOLOGY

LITERATURE CLASSICS CD-ROM

Search for other selections related to the theme "Faces of Dignity."

RESOURCE MANAGER

See the ***Theme Seven Planning Guide*** for additional teaching notes, strategies, and resources for introducing the theme "Faces of Dignity."

Exploring the Theme

Faces of Dignity

- Students may mention that people remain strong for the sake of family or for the love of their country.
- Students may mention that people find in religious faith the strength to overcome their fears.

Introduce the word *dignity* to students and discuss its meaning. (Dignity *refers to the self-respect a person shows in his or her manner or appearance.)* Ask students to give examples of dignified behavior. Students may propose ideas for dignified responses to situations that arise at school or among peers.

Starting Points

Meeting with Dignity

Draw your students' attention to the photograph. Point out its details—the barracks, the fence, the shaved heads, the youthfulness of the prisoners.

- Remind students that the imprisonment and mistreatment of women and children by the Nazis was unprecedented and that a U.S. soldier confronted with this scene would have had no prior experience with people who had endured such suffering.
- Encourage students to think about a soldier's feelings at seeing these prisoners. *(Possibilities include sadness, anger, despair at the inhumanity of others, triumph because good has finally won.)*
- Encourage students to consider the prisoners' feelings when they saw the soldiers arrive. *(Possibilities include joy, admiration for the soldiers, relief, confusion, and uncertainty about the future.)*

Dignified Moments

Students may also want to consider an act of heroism or compassion by someone they know. Encourage them to express why they admire the act.

Exploring the Theme

Faces of Dignity

What is it that helps a person to endure a crisis with immense courage and dignity? Some people cope with difficult situations by focusing on a guiding principle, such as religious faith or a belief in the goodness of people. Others focus on whatever beauty and goodness they can find in a situation. In this theme, you will learn about people who endured the Holocaust with inner strength and self-respect.

Starting Points

MEETING WITH DIGNITY

The people in the photograph are about to regain the freedom long denied them by the Nazis in World War II. Put yourself in the place of one of the American soldiers who has just arrived to free those who were imprisoned. What will you say to the first person you meet? How will you respond to these survivors who have lost everything except their lives and their dignity?

Young and old survivors of the Dachau concentration camp in Germany cheer approaching U.S. troops in 1945. Courtesy of U.S. Holocaust Memorial Museum.

DIGNIFIED MOMENTS

Difficult times often bring out the best in people. Volunteers work to help flood victims, or a neighbor takes food to someone who has lost a loved one.

- In the newspaper or on TV, find an example of a person who has shown heroism or compassion in an emergency. Write a note to that person expressing your admiration for their act.

Family and Community Activity

Our Town's *Faces of Dignity* Have students compile information, as a class project, into a book titled *[name of your town]'s Faces of Dignity.* Have students interview local people who have faced crises. Students may want to call local veterans' organizations, cancer survivors' support groups, or similar groups for names of people to interview. Students should be assigned tasks in a specific area of book development—research, interviewing and writing, photography, production, and publication. The book can be created on desktop-publishing software and should include a cover design, a table of contents, an introduction, and a list of the students' contributions. L2 COLLAB. LEARN.

Additional Resources

Family and Community Activities, p. 27

Theme Projects

Choose one of the projects below to work on as you read the selections in "Faces of Dignity." Work on your own, with a partner, or with a group.

CRITICAL VIEWING
Gallery of Hope

1. Look through photography books, newspapers and magazines, and history books for images of people enduring crises or difficult times with dignity. You might focus on an historical period–such as the Depression or World War II–or on a contemporary topic.
2. Create a collage, computer slide show, or photo album using the images you've found.
3. Write a caption or paragraph describing the significance of each image and why you think it shows dignity.

interNET CONNECTION

For more about this theme, visit Glencoe's Web site at lit.glencoe.com.

To learn more about the Holocaust, type *Holocaust* or *Anne Frank* into a search engine.

LEARNING FOR LIFE
Change Makers

1. Research a contemporary problem or crisis that is in the news and is important to you, such as disease, injustice, poverty, hunger, or war.
2. Find one person–an activist, educator, victim, ordinary citizen, or professional–who has worked to help the victims of this crisis.
3. Write a poem or an essay about the person you have selected.

MULTIMEDIA PROJECT
Exhibit of Heroes

1. Create an exhibit about people who have faced crises with dignity. Subjects might include Rosa Parks, Mahatma Gandhi, Dolores Huerta, a friend, a relative, or a neighbor.
2. Find or create pictures of the people and write brief biographies that show the qualities that allowed the person to behave as he or she did.
3. Include quotes or speeches by the people in your exhibit.

Theme Projects

Teaching Strategies

The following suggestions may help your students plan and carry out their theme projects.

Critical Viewing

- Encourage students to focus on photographs that convey the dignity of suffering people.
- Suggest that students focus on a theme to unite their presentation, such as people enduring similar hardships.
- Encourage students to consider why they chose a particular image and to capture that reason in their paragraphs.

Learning For Life

- Before students select a problem for study, suggest that they focus on a narrow issue—a particular disease or a particular war, for example.
- Remind students of the variety of research materials available, including video documentaries, biographies, Web sites, brochures, and pamphlets that deal with specific problems.
- Encourage students to consider the theme of dignity when writing about the person they have chosen. How has the person demonstrated dignity or treated victims with dignity?

interNET CONNECTION

Glencoe Literature Web Site
For more information about "Faces of Dignity," visit the United States Holocaust Museum online.

Multimedia Project

- Encourage students to select someone they admire and whom they find interesting.
- Encourage students to analyze the material they have gathered to find the qualities that allowed these people to behave with dignity.
- Suggest that students find quotations that show the beliefs, principles, or memories that helped people face their crises.

Additional Resources

- ***Interdisciplinary Activities,*** pp. 26–29
- ***Viewing and Representing Activities,*** pp. 25–27
- ***Listening and Speaking Activities,*** pp. 19–21
- ***Critical Thinking Skills,*** pp. 18–20
- ***Selection and Theme Assessment,*** pp. 137–138
- ***Performance Assessment,*** p. 70

FACES OF DIGNITY 661

Before Reading

Objectives

- To read, analyze, and identify the literary elements of a memoir
- To write a paragraph analyzing the title of the memoir

Skills

Reading/Thinking: Inferring; Elaborating; Identifying Main Idea and Supporting Details; Drawing Conclusions; Identifying Assumptions
Writing: Letter
Vocabulary: The Latin Root *vert*
Grammar/Language: Adjectives; Writing Dates
Listening/Speaking: Oral Reading
Collaboration: Oral Reading; Literature Groups

Motivating → STUDENTS

Literature Launchers: "The Horror of the Holocaust"

Videodisc Side B, Segment 19

Also available in VHS.

Selection Focus Transparency 57: Before presenting the quotation, discuss with students how suffering changes a person.

Reading Focus: Ask students to consider how they and their loved ones would deal with a crisis.

Before You Read

from *All but My Life*

MEET GERDA WEISSMANN KLEIN

Gerda Weissmann was just eighteen when the Nazis sent her to the first of a series of labor camps in Poland and Germany. Three years later, in early 1945, she was forced on a freezing three-hundred-mile march into the former Czechoslovakia. American soldiers freed Gerda in May of that year, and she eventually married one of the soldiers, Kurt Klein. Her story was the focus of the film *One Survivor Remembers*, which won an Academy Award in 1996.

Gerda Weissmann Klein was born in Poland in 1924. This selection is from her memoir All but My Life*, published in 1957 and updated in 1995.*

READING FOCUS

In your experience, how do people respond to the suffering of others? to their own suffering?

Journal
Write your ideas in your journal.

Setting a Purpose
Read to find out how the author responds to both her suffering and her new-found freedom.

BUILDING BACKGROUND

The Time and Place
It is May 1945 in Volary, Czechoslovakia. American soldiers have just freed the author and her fellow prisoners.

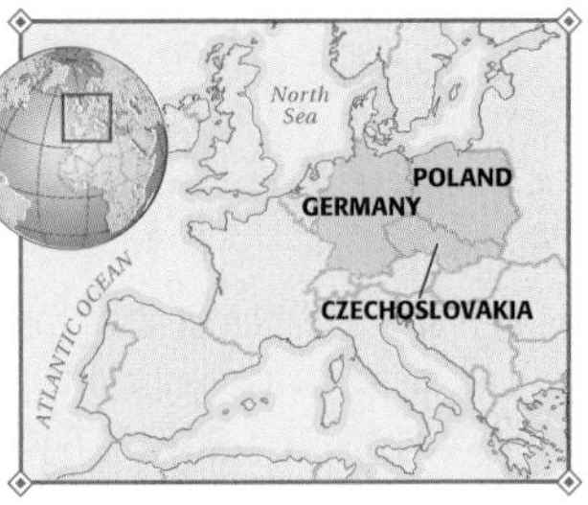

VOCABULARY PREVIEW

grimace (grim′ əs) *n.* a twisting of the face, as in pain or displeasure; p. 664
embodiment (em bod′ ē mənt) *n.* the bodily form of an idea or quality; visible form; p. 664
demean (di mēn′) *v.* to degrade; disgrace; p. 664
invigorating (in vig′ ə rāt ing) *adj.* energizing; refreshing; p. 665
capitulate (kə pich′ ə lāt′) *v.* to stop resisting; surrender; p. 666
bedraggled (bi drag′ əld) *adj.* wet, dirty, and rumpled; untidy; p. 666
inevitably (i nev′ ə tə blē) *adv.* in a way that cannot be avoided or prevented; p. 667
revert (ri vurt′) *v.* to return to an earlier condition, behavior, or belief; p. 667

RESOURCE MANAGER

Teaching Tools and Resources
- Theme Seven Planning Guide
- Literature Groups Sourcebook

Essential Lesson Support

Lesson-Specific Instruction
- Selection Focus Transparency 57
- Literary Elements Transparency 58
- Active Reading Guide,* p. 58
- Selection Vocabulary Practice, p. 41
- inTIME magazine, p. 17

Assessment
- Selection Quick Checks,* p. 58
- Sel. and Theme Assmt., pp. 105–106
- Testmaker: ExamView Pro
- Performance Assessment, p. 55

Systematic Language Instruction
- Gr. & Comp. Hbk., L. 13.4
- Vocabulary Power, Lesson 29
- Spelling Power, Lesson 25

English Language Learners
- ELL Sourcebook, p. 82
- Spanish Summaries, p. 57
- Audio Library*
- English, Yes!

Spec. Needs/Strat. Interven.
- Interactive Rdg. Sbk., pp. T195–T197
- Interactive Rdg. Wkbk., pp. 108–109
- Audio Library*

* Also available in Spanish

from All but My Life

Gerda Weissmann Klein

As I look back now, trying to recall my feelings during those first hours, I actually think that there were none. My mind was so dull, my nerves so worn from waiting, that only an emotionless vacuum remained. Like many of the other girls I just sat and waited for whatever would happen next.

In the afternoon a strange vehicle drove up. In it were two soldiers in strange uniforms, one of whom spoke German.

The German mayor of the town was with them. He was trying to tell the two soldiers that he really was not anti-Semitic.[1] The soldiers were Americans; I knew as soon as I heard them speak to one another. Arthur[2] had spoken their language a little. A

Tears welled from my eyes as they approached us. The German-speaking soldier patted me with his clean hand. "Don't cry, my child," he said with compassion, "it is all over now."

"We must return to headquarters," said the other one in German. "Can you girls wait until morning? We shall return."

I remember nothing else happening that day. The next thing I remember was waking up, wrapped snugly and warm in a coat which the SS[3] had B

1. To be *anti-Semitic* (an′ tē sə mit′ ik) is to be anti-Jewish.
2. *Arthur* was the author's brother.
3. The *SS* were the German soldiers in charge of killing prisoners in countries conquered by Germany during World War II.

Reading the Selection

SUMMARY

In this excerpt from her memoir, Gerda Weissman Klein describes her liberation by American soldiers in Czechoslovakia at the end of World War II. She reflects on the suffering she endured at the hands of the Nazis and how it affected her and her friends and family. She also describes returning to Czechoslovakia years later with her husband and children.

Spanish Summaries, p. 57

A Active Reading Strategies

REVIEW Have students identify the people who arrived in the vehicle and explain what the mayor was doing. *(The two soldiers are Americans, who have come to take the Jewish prisoners to a hospital. The mayor appears to be trying to defend himself against charges that he is anti-Semitic.)*

VOCABULARY Remind students to use context clues to unlock the meanings of new vocabulary words.

Additional Resources

Active Reading Guide, p. 58

Audio Library

Teaching Support

CONNECTING TO OTHER SELECTIONS

The chart at the right shows three ways to connect *All but My Life* to other selections in this book.

For specific teaching strategies, see the ***Theme Seven Planning Guide.***

Connection		Title
Life Skills: Lifelong Learning	→	"A Dictionary of Japanese-American Terms," p. 27
Thematic: Atrocities of War	→	"Stop the Sun," p. 607
Literary: Character Traits	→	from *Sound-Shadows of the New World,* p. 213

A&E HOME VIDEO.® *The following videotape program is available from Glencoe.* Be sure to preview the video for appropriateness for your class:

- **The Lost Children of Berlin***

*Also available in the Glencoe Literature *Video Library*.

B Critical Thinking

INFER Point out the phrase "in my pitifully thin face." Ask students what this description tells the reader about Klein's condition. What can one infer from this detail about her time in captivity? *(She did not have enough food, and she lived under difficult conditions.)*

C Literary Elements

MEMOIR The author describes herself as being ashamed. Point out that a memoir is not only a description of past events but an analysis of them. Ask students whether this line is the author's description of what she knew at the time or something she realized later. *(Students might suggest she realized this later given the wording of the sentence.)*

D Active Reading Strategies

QUESTION The author has made several references to cleanliness. Ask students to find the earlier references. Why does the author contrast the cleanliness of the soldier with the dirt of the prisoners? *(The contrast underlines the horrible conditions in which the prisoners lived.)*

LITERATURE & HUMANITIES

Encourage students to share their responses to the painting on page 545 of *American Art History and Culture*.

Teaching Support

left behind, waking up with what I thought was a smile, which must have seemed more like a grimace in my pitifully thin face.

The austere[4] hall was bathed in sunshine, and I woke up with the knowledge that I was free. I was eager to go outside, to move about freely. Perhaps I would meet the Americans again. I swayed as I started to walk. My skin was hot and dry. As I reached the door, the first thing I saw was that strange vehicle bouncing toward us through the brilliant May sunshine. I was overcome with joy.

I called to the other girls that some Americans were coming. The soldier on the left made a motion to the driver who stopped the vehicle across the yard from where I was standing. The soldier jumped out and walked toward me. He wasn't the one who had come the day before. Shaking my head, I stared at this man who was to me the embodiment of all heroism and liberty. He greeted me. I must tell him from the start, I resolved, so that he has no illusions[5] about us. Perhaps I had acquired a feeling of shame. After all, for six long years the Nazis had tried to demean us.

"May I see the other ladies?" he asked.

"Ladies!" my brain repeated. He probably doesn't know, I thought. I must tell him.

"We are Jews," I said in a small voice.

"So am I," he answered. Was there a catch[6] in his voice, or did I imagine it?

I could have embraced him but I was aware how dirty and repulsive I must be.

"Won't you come with me?" he asked. He held the door open. I didn't understand at first. I looked at him questioningly but not a muscle in his face moved. He wanted me to feel that he had not seen the dirt or the lice. He saw a lady and I shall be forever grateful to him for his graciousness.

"I want you to see a friend of mine," I remember telling the American, and we started to walk toward Liesel.[7] On the dirty, straw-littered floor Lilli was lying, covered with rags. As we tried to reach Liesel, she looked up, her eyes enormous, burning in their sockets. She looked at my companion and her face lit up with a strange fire. I heard her say something in English, and saw how the American bent down closer and answered her. Her hands were shaking as she gently, unbelievingly touched the sleeve of his jacket. In the exchange that followed, I made out the word "happy." I understood that word. Then she sighed, released his hand and, looking at him, shook her head and whispered, "Too late."

We moved on to Liesel. Liesel just smiled, and said nothing. She didn't seem to care much. I looked back at Lilli; her eyes were fixed on the American, a solitary tear ran down her cheek. An ant was crawling over her chin. Shortly afterward, Lilli died.

I heard the American give commands in English. He seemed furious that things weren't moving fast enough. He explained

4. *Austere* means "plain" and "lacking in luxuries."
5. Here, *illusions* means "false ideas."
6. Here, a *catch* is a break, or shakiness, resulting from emotion.
7. *Liesel* (lē′ sel)

Vocabulary

grimace (grim′ əs) *n.* a twisting of the face, as in pain or displeasure
embodiment (em bod′ ē mənt) *n.* the bodily form of an idea or quality; visible form
demean (di mēn′) *v.* to degrade; disgrace

MEETING INDIVIDUAL NEEDS — ENGLISH LANGUAGE LEARNERS

Vocabulary: Connotation To understand the impact of the soldier's reference to the prisoners as ladies, students need to appreciate the connotation of *lady.* Students learning English may only understand the term to mean an adult woman (a common misuse of the term). Explain that the term actually connotes dignity.

Activity Have students suggest famous women or relatives who they believe fit the connotation of *lady.* Ask students to explain why the person they have suggested could be described not only as a woman but also as a lady.

Additional Resources

English Language Learners Sourcebook, p. 82

to me in German that a hospital was being set up for us. Then he asked me:

"Is there anything I can do for you in particular?"

"Yes, there is," I said. "If you would be kind enough, and could find the time. You see, I have an uncle in Turkey. Could you write to him, let him know that I am alive, and that I hope he has news from my parents and my brother?"

He took out a notebook, and removed the sunglasses he had been wearing. I saw tears in his eyes. He wore battle gear with a net over his helmet. And as he wrote, I looked at him and couldn't absorb enough of the wonder that he had fought for my freedom.

He snapped his book shut.

"I would like to ask you a question," he said softly. "But please don't answer if you don't want to. We are aware of what has happened. Tell me, were you girls sterilized?"[8]

I did not answer at once. I was too full of emotion. Why should he, of all people, who looked to me like a young god, inquire about the deepest treasure that I, who must have looked like an animal to him, carried still within me?

"We were spared," I managed to say.

A few moments later, joined by his companion and the mayor, he drove off. Before I had even asked his name—he vanished!

Within an hour, Red Cross trucks arrived. Litter[9] bearers gently but swiftly loaded the ill. Other soldiers carried girls in their arms like babies, speaking to them soothingly in words the girls did not understand. But the gestures of warmth and help were unmistakable. In a trance I walked to a truck and got in. On the soldiers' sleeves was a red diamond, the insignia of the Fifth U.S. Infantry Division. Their uniforms, their language, their kindness and concern made it true: we were finally free!

The hospital we were taken to was a converted school. Wounded German soldiers had been moved to the third floor so that we could be installed in the first two floors. How strange—in a matter of one day, the world had changed: Germans were put out to make room for us.

We were taken to a room where huge caldrons of water were being heated on a stove. Round wooden tubs stood steaming on the floor.

A woman in a white coat motioned me to undress.

Doing so, I stepped into one of the tubs. The warm water, reaching to my neck, felt strange: it had been at least three years since last I sat in a tub. Bidding me stand, the nurse soaped my body with quick, invigorating pressure. It was pleasantly painful to sit back in the tub again and let the warm water engulf me.

A young peasant girl came in, her cheeks rosy and shining, her colorful peasant skirt

Did You Know?
Military *insignia* (in sig′ nē ə) are the badges sewn or pinned to uniforms to show rank, division, assignment, and so on.

8. When a woman is *sterilized,* an operation is performed that makes her unable to reproduce.
9. A *litter* is a stretcher for carrying a sick or injured person.

Vocabulary
invigorating (in vig′ ə rāt ing) *adj.* energizing; refreshing

E Literary Elements

IRONY Remind students that one form of irony, sometimes called *situational irony,* occurs when a situation turns out surprisingly different from what has been expected. Ask students what is ironic about Lilli's uttering the word *happy*.

F Active Reading Strategies

EVALUATE Ask students whether they believe the writer's view of her appearance is accurate, and have them explain their opinions.

Historical Note

Before indoor plumbing was common, people took baths in metal or wooden tubs. Water was heated over a fire or on a stove and then was poured into tubs, with cooler water, for the bath. Afterwards, the tub was emptied and hung on a wall. In Eastern Europe, even in the 1940s, many buildings were not equipped with hot-and-cold running water.

Interdisciplinary Connection

History The Red Cross is an international organization formed in 1864 at the Geneva Convention, an international meeting that established guidelines for the humane treatment of war victims. Since then the Red Cross has worked to prevent and relieve human suffering during wars and natural disasters around the world. During World War II, the Red Cross assisted more than 75 million people in 40 countries. The organization was instrumental in helping Jews find their families after being separated in the war.

Activity Have students review recent newspapers or news magazines for references to how the Red Cross is currently helping disaster or war victims. Suggest that students present their findings in a written report. **L2**

G Critical Thinking

DRAWING CONCLUSIONS Ask students to explain why the writer purchased poison. Why didn't she use it? Share the following model to demonstrate the process involved in drawing conclusions:

Model: When Gerda was taken prisoner, she was separated from her family, not fed or bathed, and was forced on a long march in winter. I think she probably bought the poison because she thought death would be the only way out of her situation. She never used it, so I conclude that she never gave up hope that things would get better.

H Critical Thinking

ELABORATE Note that the author does not state how this made her feel. Ask students to imagine what it would be like to have nothing at all, not even a shirt. Explain how this situation would make a person feel. *(Students may say one would feel lost or hopeless.)*

I Literary Elements

MEMOIR Note that the author recalls in detail how the two groups of soldiers looked. Why does she remember these details so clearly? *(She probably remembers the vivid details because it was one of the most important events in her life.)*

Teaching Support

reaching to her ankles, her deep-cut blouse revealing her full bosom. I felt slight and thin. When I saw the girl gather up my clothes in a basket, I looked at the nurse with a questioning glance.

"They will be burned," she said.

Only one thought remained. With my wet hand I reached for my ski boots, took the left one and reached under the lining. There was the dirty shapeless package containing the pictures I wanted to save. I pulled the pictures out and laid them on the dry towel beside the tub. And the other packet—the poison I had bought in Grünberg[10]—I gratefully let go to the fire. G

I stepped out of the tub; the nurse dried my body and hair. As I stood, before a clean blue and white checkered man's shirt was put on me, I realized abruptly that I possessed nothing, not even a stitch of clothing that I could call my own. I owned only the pictures of Papa, Mama, Arthur, and Abek that I had carried for three years. H

A blanket was thrown over my shoulders as I was led to a bunk. The sheets were fresh and white. A nurse brought me a drink of milk. Milk!—I hadn't had any in three years. As I drank it something tremendous and uncontrollable broke loose within me. My body shook convulsively.[11] I wanted to stop it but I couldn't. I heard my voice and could do nothing about it.

A nurse hurried up; then a doctor. I heard him say, "No, let her cry it out."

Long pent-up[12] emotions finally burst out. I cried for Ilse, for Suse,[13] for other friends, and finally for my family too. Deep in my heart I had known they were dead, but dreams about happy reunions with them had kept me going.

When I opened my eyes a night had passed. A nurse was approaching with a breakfast tray. This is the life of a fairy princess, I thought.

As I lay daydreaming after breakfast there was a sudden commotion. Nurses hurried in.

"Germany has capitulated!" they told us. "The war in Europe is over!"

For me, the war had ended with my liberation. I had not realized that the fighting had continued after that.

I looked out the window. Coming down the hilly, winding road was a company of unarmed and bedraggled German soldiers. As they passed my window, I could see their unshaven faces and hollow cheeks. Proud, handsome American soldiers guarded them. I

A doctor and a nurse came in. They stopped at each bed. After asking my name and birthplace, the doctor asked for my date of birth.

"May 8, 1924."

"May 8!" the doctor exclaimed. "Why, today is the eighth."

"Happy birthday!" the nurse chanted.

After they left, I repeated to myself, "It's my birthday, my twenty-first birthday, and Germany capitulated!"

10. *Grünberg* (grōōn′ burg) was, at the time, a city in eastern Germany. (In 1950 it became part of Poland and was given a Polish name.)
11. *Convulsively* means "suddenly and violently."
12. *Pent-up* emotions have been held in and not expressed or released.
13. *Ilse* (il′ sə), *Suse* (sōō′ sə)

Vocabulary
capitulate (kə pich′ ə lāt′) *v.* to stop resisting; surrender
bedraggled (bi drag′ əld) *adj.* wet, dirty, and rumpled; untidy

Reading Minilesson

Identifying Main Idea and Supporting Details Remind students that this theme is about dignity. Discuss with them how the main idea of this work fits into the theme. This excerpt provides many examples of human dignity in the face of suffering and hardship. Encourage students to think about the main idea whenever they read by looking for scenes or details that are similar.

Activity Have students review the selection to find examples of human dignity, and ask students to list these scenes or details. In a group discussion, students should summarize the main idea and the examples that support it. **L2** COLLAB. LEARN.

Additional Resources

Reading Skills Practice Workbook

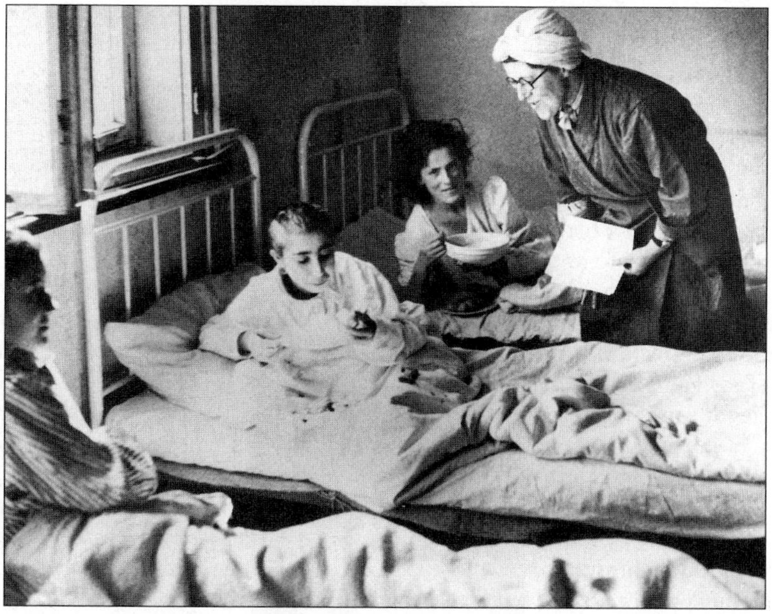

A French Relief Service worker tends to survivors of the Bergen-Belsen concentration camp. May 2, 1945.

Viewing the photograph: Bergen-Belsen was one of several former Nazi concentration camps that were converted into refugee camps and hospitals for victims of the Holocaust. How does this photo compare with the hospital Gerda describes?

I thought of Tusia,[14] who had so desperately wanted my assurance that we would both be free on this day. I remembered her lying dead in the snow. Why am I here? I wondered. I am no better.

As I lay back on my white clean pillow, lost in thought, I heard someone approach. It was the doctor again. He put something in my hand.

"For your birthday," he said, smiling.

It was a piece of chocolate.

Inevitably, we all revert to the core of our existence in moments of crisis and look for our lodestar.[15] I have tried to follow mine ever since I left my parents and my childhood home. I know full well what saw me through those unspeakable years. It was the powerful memory of an evening at home. The living room of my childhood. My father smoking his pipe and reading the evening paper; my mother working on her needlepoint; my brother and I doing our homework; the lamps throwing a soft glow around the room as my cat, stretched out on the green-patterned carpet, purred softly. An evening at home. How many

14. *Tusia* (tōō′ sē ə)

15. A *lodestar* is a star that guides. Here, it is the beliefs that guide one through life.

Vocabulary

inevitably (i nev′ ə tə blē) *adv.* in a way that cannot be avoided or prevented

revert (ri vurt′) *v.* to return to an earlier condition, behavior, or belief

VIEWING THE PHOTOGRAPH

In this photograph, an English volunteer, Joyce Parkinson, works with the French Relief Service to aid people freed from concentration camps.

Viewing Response *The photo depicts a setting and an experience similar to Gerda's.*

J Active Reading Strategies

REVIEW Point out that often the name of a person, a place, or an event is given without explanation. Remind students to use context clues to help them understand the reference. Ask them to identify Tusia, given the information that is provided. *(Tusia was a fellow prisoner and a friend of the author's.)*

K Literary Elements

MEMOIR Ask students to explain the words "I am no better." How do these words help characterize Gerda? *(Students may conclude that the author is comparing her past with that of her friend. This shows her as compassionate and humble.)*

FYI

Chocolate was scarce during the war, as were all products that had to be imported. Ships could not risk attacks by the enemy except for essential shipping, carrying military personnel and materials.

Listening and Speaking *Minilesson*

Oral Reading Point out that writing dialogue can be challenging because an author is trying to capture the sound of speech in writing. Explain to students that a writer's choice of words can help the reader "hear" the dialogue and thereby make a discussion more realistic.

Activity Have students review the passage beginning "A doctor and a nurse came in" on page 666 and ending with "It was a piece of chocolate" on page 667. Ask them to identify the words that provide clues to how the dialogue was spoken. *(exclaimed, changed, repeated, he said, smiling)* Working in small groups, students should read the passage aloud, speaking the dialogue as suggested by the author's choice of verbs.

L2 **COLLAB. LEARN.**

L Critical Thinking

DRAWING CONCLUSIONS Ask students to explain what the author means when she says, "I am home again." *(The author has been able to re-create the peace and warmth of her childhood home.)*

M Literary Elements

MEMOIR Note that Klein always remained haunted by why she lived and others died. Ask students to consider how Klein's memoir helps to answer that question. *(Klein seems to feel that her "life's work" explains why she survived and others did not.)* Encourage them to think about the benefits of a memoir like this one. *(Memoirs help writers understand themselves and their experiences, find meaning in the events of their lives, and communicate to others the meaning of past experiences.)*

Thematic Focus

Faces of Dignity Several people demonstrate dignity during hardship in this memoir. Have students name people who demonstrate dignity and ways that is shown in the memoir.

ASSESSMENT

Quick Checks, p. 58

times I saw that picture—from my bunk in the camps, looking down on the barbed wire, during the bitterness of bone-chilling nights during the death march. Those evenings at home that I had thought dull and boring! The desire to know them once more became a driving force leading to survival. I never saw my childhood home again nor any member of my family. But their images at times merge into those of my husband, and are recreated in my children. I am home again. (L)

Gerda Weissmann Klein

After nearly a half century, the opportunity presented itself for my return to the scene of the last chapter of that dark past. My husband, my children, and my friends made a pilgrimage[16] to Volary, Czechoslovakia, the place where I was liberated—the site where the curtain closed on the tragedy, where the stirring of love and hope blossomed again in the springtime of my life.

We went back in the autumn and, for Kurt and me, in the autumn of our lives. Although everything had changed for me, nothing there seemed to have changed. As if frozen in time and memory, I stood again in the doorway of the abandoned factory where I first greeted the freedom I had dreamed about for so many years. I paused at the graves of my beloved friends who were never privileged to know the joy of freedom, the security of a loaf of bread, or the supreme happiness of holding a child in their arms. I listened to the gentle wind in the trees, to the screech of a bird, and I looked at the flickering memorial candles on the headstones of their graves. It brought up the unanswerable question that has haunted me ever since the day I left them there: Why? (M)

I lingered at the window of what used to be the American field hospital, now a furniture factory, where I lay in critical condition for many months. It was the window next to my double-decker bunk, in which I awoke on my first day of freedom to ask myself, "Why am I here? . . . I am no better!"

Standing there, I prayed, in the hope that perhaps through my life's work I might have provided a fragment of the answer and given back a small part of what I have received.

Gerda Weissmann Klein
Arizona, August 1994

16. A *pilgrimage* is a long journey, especially to a holy place or for a religious purpose.

Teaching Support

Grammar and Language *Minilesson*

Adjectives Review with students that adjectives modify nouns and that using them creates mental images that make writing more vivid. Point out to students the paragraph beginning "I looked out the window," on page 666 and the use of adjectives in it.

Activity Have students identify the adjectives in the paragraph and the words they modify. Ask students to rewrite the paragraph without the adjectives. Encourage students to note how the scene is more difficult to imagine without the adjectives. **L2**

Additional Resources

- ***Grammar and Language Transparency 56***
- ***Grammar and Language Workbook,*** pp. 121–123
- ***Grammar and Composition Handbook,*** Lesson 5.1
- ***Writer's Choice,*** Lesson 12.1

Responding to Literature

PERSONAL RESPONSE

- What moment in this memoir do you think is most powerful? Why?

Brackets connect questions that are paired to develop higher-level thinking skills.

Analyzing Literature

RECALL

1. Who accompanies the U.S. soldiers when they first visit Gerda and the other survivors?
2. What are Gerda's feelings when the U.S. soldiers first arrive?
3. When an American soldier comes back to help the freed prisoners, what questions does he ask Gerda? How does she answer?
4. What is the "unanswerable question" that has haunted the author? How does she deal with the question?

INTERPRET

5. Why, in your opinion, does the mayor tell the soldiers that he "really was not anti-Semitic"?
6. On the first day of her liberation, why do you think Gerda just waits for "whatever would happen next"?
7. What do the soldier's questions and Gerda's responses reveal about the suffering she has endured?
8. How might the writing of this memoir represent one answer to the author's "unanswerable question"?

EVALUATE AND CONNECT

9. When the first soldier arrives, the author feels that she must reveal that she is a Jew. Are you surprised by this action? Explain.
10. What new ideas do you have about the ways in which people respond to suffering? How do your new ideas compare with those you wrote for the **Reading Focus** on page 662?

LITERARY ELEMENTS

Memoir

A **memoir** is a type of writing that tells about a significant time or event in a writer's life. Memoirs are told in the first person, from the narrator's point of view. A memoir can be very personal and revealing, much like a journal. Sometimes the journals of people are published as memoirs.

1. What significant time in the writer's life is presented in this selection from Klein's memoir?
2. To what other time periods does the memoir refer? Why are these other times significant?

- See **Literary Terms Handbook,** p. R6.

Responding to the Selection

PERSONAL RESPONSE

Students' responses should include an explanation of why the moment they have selected is the most powerful.

Analyzing Literature

1. The German mayor accompanies them.
2. She was devoid of feelings.
3. "May I see the other ladies?" "Is there anything I can do for you?" and "Were you girls sterilized?" Gerda responds that they are Jews, that she would like the soldier to notify her family, and that they were spared sterilization.
4. It is why she lived when others died. She believes that her life's work may be part of the answer.
5. Students may suggest that the mayor was ashamed or was afraid of punishment.
6. Students may mention her feelings of powerlessness, her weak condition, or her feeling that as long as she has been saved, nothing else matters.
7. They reveal that the prisoners have been made to feel ashamed, that some prisoners have been sterilized, and that she has been separated from her family.
8. The memoir tells about the Holocaust, and awareness may help prevent it from happening again.
9. Students should refer to details from the selection that support their responses.
10. Students' responses should reflect what they learned about people's responses to suffering.

LITERARY ELEMENTS

1. Klein's liberation at the end of World War II is presented.
2. The memoir refers to the author's return to Czechoslovakia and to her life there before she was taken prisoner—significant because of their normalcy and happiness.

Additional Resources

Literary Elements Transparency 58

Literature and Writing

Writing About Literature

Students' paragraphs should

- include an analysis of how the title reflects the main ideas of the memoir
- include an alternative title

Creative Writing

Students' letters should

- include a description of the events in the hospital and in Europe
- take the form of a personal letter

Extending Your Response

Literature Groups Group summaries should explain, using examples from the memoir, how survival was both a privilege and a burden. **COLLAB. LEARN.**

Interdisciplinary Activity Students should locate both Grünberg and Volary.

Literature and Writing

Writing About Literature

Title Write a paragraph or two explaining the meaning of the title that Klein chose for her memoir: *All but My Life.* Think about these questions as you write: What did the author lose during the war? How was she able to keep her dignity? How does the title relate to her unanswerable question, "Why am I here?" What alternative title might you suggest? Be prepared to explain your choice.

Creative Writing

Letter Home Imagine that you are the doctor who gave Gerda Weissmann Klein a piece of chocolate for her birthday. As the doctor, write a letter home, describing the events in the hospital and in Europe. If you wish, read about World War II, the Nazis, and their concentration camps so that you can include additional facts and details in your letter.

Extending Your Response

Literature Groups

Survival Tale Klein writes that "survival is both an exalted privilege and a painful burden." Discuss the ways in which surviving the Holocaust has been a privilege and a burden for Klein. Summarize the thoughts of your group in a few sentences to share with the class.

*inter*NET CONNECTION

The Nazis mistreated and killed millions of civilians who opposed them or of whom they did not approve. Among them were handicapped people, political opponents, and Gypsies. Use the Internet to search for information about such a group.

Interdisciplinary Activity

Geography On a map, find the Grünberg concentration camp in western Poland where Gerda Weissmann Klein was forced to work. Then locate the town of Volary, in what is now the southwestern part of the Czech Republic, where the Americans freed Gerda and the other women in the labor camp.

Reading Further

If you would like to read other accounts of young people during the war, try these books:

Farewell to Manzanar by Jeanne Wakatsuki Houston

The Devil in Vienna by Doris Orgel

Save your work for your portfolio.

Teaching Support

MEETING INDIVIDUAL NEEDS — SPECIAL NEEDS

Less-Proficient Readers Remind less-proficient readers of the difference between fact and opinion. Explain that an opinion is a belief that cannot be proven, while a fact is known to be true. In writing about an experience, authors often insert their own opinions. This is true for Gerda Weissmann Klein, as she describes her thoughts and feelings on her first day of liberation from the Nazis.

Activity Ask less-proficient readers to work together to identify opinions and facts in the memoir by Klein. *(Facts: American soldiers liberated Klein and the other enslaved women. Germany surrendered on Klein's birthday, May 8. Opinions: Klein thinks the American soldier looks like a young god. On the day of her freedom, Klein believes that she looks like an animal.)* **L1** **COLLAB. LEARN.**

Skill Minilessons

RETEACH • REVIEW

GRAMMAR AND LANGUAGE • WRITING DATES

When you write dates, keep these rules in mind:

- You can write a century or a decade in one of two ways: *twentieth century* or *20th century.*
- Write the name of a decade in numerals and add *-s: 1940s* or *40s.* You also can spell out the decade: *the forties.*
- Dates usually begin with the month (spelled out with the first letter capitalized), the day (numeral and comma), and the year (numeral): *January 2, 1944.* However, European writers reverse the day and month, and eliminate the comma: *2 January 1944.*

PRACTICE Rewrite the three sentences in which dates have been written incorrectly.

1. The Dutch boy's diary was dated May second 1942.
2. What will the thirtieth century be like?
3. Trouble began in the early 19 thirties.
4. They came to the United States Aug, 3, 1939.

● For more about commas, see **Language Handbook,** pp. R38–R40.

READING AND THINKING • IDENTIFYING ASSUMPTIONS

An **assumption** is a belief, taken for granted, based on opinion or experience; it may or may not be true. Identifying the assumptions characters make can help you better understand their behavior. In *All but My Life,* Gerda Weissmann Klein doesn't understand that the soldier is holding the door *for her;* she assumes that she is not worthy of such courtesy. This false assumption shows how worthless the Nazis must have made her feel.

PRACTICE Identify three other assumptions made by characters in *All but My Life* and describe the beliefs on which they are based. Write a few sentences for each assumption, telling whether it is true or false. Explain what you learn about the author or the situation by identifying the assumption.

VOCABULARY • THE LATIN ROOT *vert*

Revert comes from two word parts: the prefix *re-,* meaning "back," and the root *vert,* meaning "to turn." Someone who *reverts* "turns back" to an earlier way of behaving. Words containing the root *vert* have to do with turning. To *invert* something is to turn it upside down. An *advertisement* turns people's attention toward a product. The root may drop the *t,* as in *reverse,* which means "turned backwards."

PRACTICE Use the prefixes below to match each word with its meaning.

di-	"aside"	*extra-*	"outside"
con-	"together"	*contra-*	"against"

1. divert
2. converge
3. extrovert
4. controversy

a. to move toward each other
b. one whose personality is unreserved and outgoing
c. to change the direction of
d. a quarrel or debate

Skill Minilessons

GRAMMAR AND LANGUAGE
WRITING DATES

1. The Dutch boy's diary was dated May 2, 1942.
2. Correct.
3. Trouble began in the early 1930s.
4. They came to the United States August 3, 1939.

READING AND THINKING
IDENTIFYING ASSUMPTIONS

Students' responses should include what each assumption is and who is making it, and should explain what the assumption reveals about the person or the situation.

VOCABULARY
LATIN ROOT *VERT*

1. c
2. a
3. b
4. d

Additional Resources

- ***Grammar and Language Workbook,*** pp. 261–262
- ***Writer's Choice,*** Lesson 12.1
- ***Reading Skills Practice Workbook***
- ***Vocabulary Practice,*** p. 41

ASSESSMENT

- ***Quick Checks,*** p. 58
- ***Selection and Theme Assessment,*** pp. 105–106
- ***Performance Assessment,*** p. 55
- ***Testmaker: ExamView Pro***
- ***Interactive Tutor: Self-Assessment***

Interdisciplinary Connection

Objective

- To identify the boundary changes of European nations since the end of World War II

Teaching Strategies

As students compare the two maps, encourage them to determine which nations on the earlier map have undergone the most changes since World War II.

Activity

Estonia, Latvia, Lithuania, Russia, Belarus, Ukraine, and Moldova (formerly Soviet Union); Malta (formerly Italy); Bosnia and Herzegovina, Slovenia, Croatia, and Macedonia (formerly Yugoslavia); Slovakia and Czech Republic (formerly Czechoslovakia)

Interdisciplinary Connection GEOGRAPHY

Europe: Fifty Years of Change

Germany had an unstoppable war machine from 1939 to 1942. The German army invaded nation after nation across Europe, bringing much of the continent under its control. Finally, in 1945, the Nazi government surrendered to the combined forces of England, France, the Soviet Union, and the United States.

Following the war, Germany was reduced in size and divided. First, it was divided into four parts, with each part occupied and governed by England, France, the United States, or the Soviet Union. The Soviet zone eventually became East Germany, a communist country. The other zones joined to form West Germany.

In the fifty years following World War II, the boundaries and governments of many European nations changed. The two parts of Germany were reunified in 1990. The Soviet Union was disbanded in 1991.

ACTIVITY

With a group, compare the two maps. List the nations on the 1997 map that are not shown on the earlier map. Where were they in the 1940s? Describe the changes that you see.

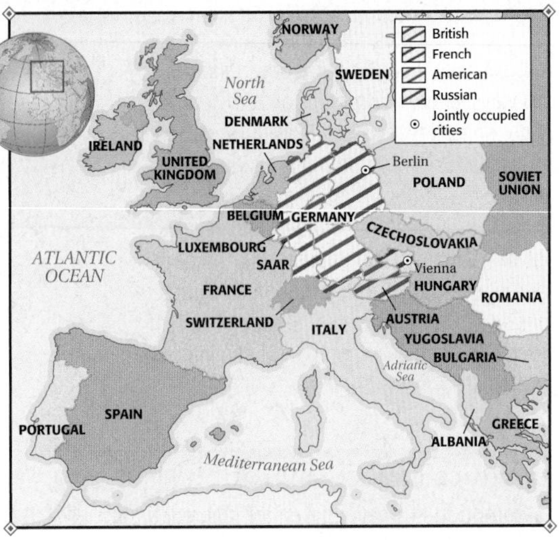

Europe After World War II

Europe in 1997

Teaching Support

MEETING INDIVIDUAL NEEDS — MULTIPLE MODES OF EXPRESSION

Logical and Mathematical Explain that the boundary changes in individual countries would have a tremendous impact on the citizens living in them. Students with logical and mathematical learning styles may understand this better by further exploring the relationship between the two maps.

Activity Have students work in groups to produce a map of one nation or a group of nations once united in some way. They should outline the boundaries as they were when they were unified and then subdivide each outlined area to show the new nations.

L2 **COLLAB. LEARN.**

Reading and Thinking Skills

Activating Prior Knowledge

What you already know about any topic you are preparing to study or read is called *prior knowledge.* Besides facts, prior knowledge includes personal experiences that can be related to your reading. Activating, or tapping into, your prior knowledge helps you understand what is happening in a piece of writing. It also can help you identify questions to ask as you read.

Reread the following passage from *All but My Life.* Think about what readers might already know that will help them understand this scene.

> In the afternoon a strange vehicle drove up. In it were two soldiers in strange uniforms, one of whom spoke German.
>
> The German mayor of the town was with them. He was trying to tell the two soldiers that he really was not anti-Semitic. The soldiers were Americans; I knew as soon as I heard them speak to one another.

The scene takes place in Czechoslovakia in 1945. What do you know about the events in Europe at this time? Why is it significant that a soldier speaks German? What does *anti-Semitic* mean? Why do you suppose the mayor is claiming that he is not anti-Semitic?

- For more about activating prior knowledge, see **Reading Handbook,** p. R94.

ACTIVITY

Before you read the next selection, from *Anne Frank: The Diary of a Young Girl,* list what you already know about the times, places, and attitudes that were important to World War II. If you already know details about Anne Frank's life, include them in your list. Then share your prior knowledge in a discussion with your class.

Reading and Thinking Skills

Objective

- To learn techniques for activating prior knowledge when reading

Teaching Strategies

As students think about a reader's prior knowledge when reading the excerpt, remind them to consider that prior knowledge also includes the definitions of words.

Activity

Students' lists should reflect specific facts the students already know relative to time, places, and attitudes.

Additional Resource

Reading Skills Practice Workbook

Teaching Support

MEETING INDIVIDUAL NEEDS — SPECIAL NEEDS

Less-Proficient Readers Remind students that a book often provides a reader with information that can become "prior knowledge" for their reading. Explain that the material on book covers and introductory pages gives readers information that can help them as they read. Provide students with a selection of books to demonstrate these aids.

Activity Have students look through the books and list the ways they provide information, including the author's biography, a time line, or drawings. Have students explain how these devices improve comprehension. **L1**

Additional Resources

Inclusion Strategies

Before Reading

Objectives

- To read and analyze a diary excerpt showing the dignity of a girl suffering persecution
- To identify the literary elements of a journal
- To write a character sketch

Skills

Reading/Thinking: Making Critical Judgments; Skimming; Drawing Conclusions; Identifying Bias
Writing: Reflective Paragraph; Diary Entry
Vocabulary: Context Clues; Multiple-Meaning Words; Antonyms
Life Skills: Interviewing
Grammar/Language: Colons
Collaboration: Literature Groups

Motivating STUDENTS

Selection Focus Transparency 58: Have the class view and discuss Bacon's self-portrait. Suggest that as they read the selection they consider ways in which people view themselves.

Reading Focus: As an extension of the Reading Focus, have students share their own experiences with diaries, such as whether they have kept one and why they started or stopped making entries.

Before You Read

from *Anne Frank: The Diary of a Young Girl*

MEET ANNE FRANK

Anne Frank's world changed in 1940, when the Nazis began persecuting Jewish people in the Netherlands. Two years later, the teenager's family went into hiding on the top floor of the warehouse where her father had run his business. Despite her confinement, Anne had many hopes and dreams for herself and a strong desire to be a writer. She kept a diary, and in it she wrote: "I want to be useful or bring enjoyment to all people, even those I've never met. I want to go on living even after my death!"

Anne Frank was born in 1929 and died in early 1945. Anne Frank: The Diary of a Young Girl *was first published in Dutch in 1947.*

READING FOCUS

Why do you think many teenagers keep diaries?

Quick List
Make a list of people, ideas, or thoughts you might write about in a private diary.

Setting a Purpose
Read to explore the hopes and dreams of one teenager.

BUILDING BACKGROUND

The Time and Place Anne Frank recorded her daily life in a diary from June 1942 to July 1944. This selection contains two passages from her diary—one from before she went into hiding, and another just one month before the Nazis found her family.

Did You Know? During the Holocaust, two million Jewish children died. Both Anne and her sister Margot died of typhoid fever in the Bergen-Belsen concentration camp.

Statue of Anne Frank. Mari Andriessen. Westermarkt, Amsterdam.

VOCABULARY PREVIEW

melancholy (mel′ ən kol′ ē) *adj.* sadly thoughtful; p. 676
enhance (en hans′) *v.* to make greater; p. 676
ban (ban) *v.* to forbid; outlaw; prohibit; p. 677
superficial (so͞o′ pər fish′ əl) *adj.* lacking deep meaning; shallow; unimportant or unnecessary; p. 677
prejudice (prej′ ə dis) *n.* an opinion formed without considering all sides of a question; p. 679
perturb (pər turb′) *v.* to disturb greatly; p. 680
ponder (pon′ dər) *v.* to think over carefully; p. 680
waver (wā′ vər) *v.* to become uncertain; falter; p. 681
tranquillity (trang kwil′ ə tē) *n.* the state or quality of being calm and free from disturbance; quietness; p. 681

RESOURCE MANAGER

Teaching Tools and Resources
- Theme Seven Planning Guide
- Literature Groups Sourcebook

Essential Lesson Support
Lesson-Specific Instruction
- Selection Focus Transparency 58
- Literary Elements Transparency 59
- Active Reading Guide,* p. 59
- Selection Vocabulary Practice, p. 42

Assessment
- Selection Quick Checks,* p. 59
- Sel. and Theme Assmt., pp. 107–108
- Testmaker: ExamView Pro
- Performance Assessment, p. 56

Systematic Language Instruction
- Gr. & Comp. Hbk., L. 14.5
- Vocabulary Power, Lesson 30
- Spelling Power, Lesson 26

English Language Learners
- ELL Sourcebook, p. 83
- Spanish Summaries, p. 58
- Spanish Translations, pp. 148–152
- Audio Library*
- English, Yes!

Spec. Needs/Strat. Interven.
- Interactive Rdg. Sbk., pp. T198–T200
- Interactive Rdg. Wkbk., pp. 110–112
- Inclusion Strat. Sbk., pp. 97–98
- Audio Library*

* Also available in Spanish

from

Anne Frank: The Diary of a Young Girl

Anne Frank

Portion of a page from Anne Frank's diary dated October 10, 1942.

Saturday, 20 June, 1942

I haven't written for a few days, because I wanted first of all to think about my diary. It's an odd idea for someone like me to keep a diary; not only because I have never done so before, but because it seems to me that neither I—nor for that matter anyone else—will be interested in the unbosomings[1] of a thirteen-year-old schoolgirl. Still, what does that matter? I want to write, but more than that, I want to bring out all kinds of things that lie buried deep in my heart. **A**

1. *Unbosomings* are Anne's expressions, in her diary, of her most personal thoughts and feelings; in these writings, she "gets things off her chest."

Reading the Selection

SUMMARY

In the first of two entries taken from her diary, Anne is thirteen years old. She gives a brief biographical sketch of herself and her family and provides background about the plight of Jews in Europe at the time. Her family is not yet in hiding. The second entry in this selection is two years later. In it Anne describes her conflicting feelings about her father and Peter Van Daan, whose family is in hiding with the Franks. Anne also describes some of her theories about human nature and her dreams and fears about the future.

Spanish Summaries, p. 58

A Active Reading Strategies

QUESTION Ask students to think about why Anne says she would not be interested in reading the thoughts of a thirteen-year-old schoolgirl. Have students contrast their reactions with their perceptions of Anne after they have read the second entry.

VOCABULARY Remind students to use context clues to unlock the meanings of new vocabulary words.

Additional Resources

- ***Active Reading Guide,*** p. 59
- ***Audio Library***
- ***Spanish Audio Library***

Teaching Support

CONNECTING TO OTHER SELECTIONS

COMPARING *selections*

This selection is paired with "The Anne Frank House: Amsterdam" on page 687. A lesson for teaching a comparison of the two selections appears on page 689.

The chart at the right shows three other ways to connect *Anne Frank: The Diary of a Young Girl* to selections in this book.

For specific teaching strategies, see the ***Theme Seven Planning Guide.***

Connection	Title
Life Skills: Collaborating	"The People Could Fly," p. 389
Thematic: Children and War	"The Drummer Boy of Shiloh," p. 439
Literary: First-Person Point of View	from *I Know Why the Caged Bird Sings,* p. 199

B Literary Elements

IRONY Irony can arise when later events make statements written in a diary turn out to be untrue. Point out Anne's remark that "probably nobody cares" about her diary. Ask students to explain why this is ironic. *(Her diary has become one of the most memorable pieces of Holocaust writing.)*

C Literary Elements

JOURNAL Review with students that journals can be kept for a variety of purposes—to keep a strictly factual record of events or to interpret events, for example. Ask students to identify what Anne's purpose is in keeping her diary. What is her purpose in giving it a name? *(Its name makes the diary seem more like a friend to Anne.)*

Vo·cab·u·lar·y Skills

Context Clues Note the phrase "common round." Point out that each culture has its own idioms. Encourage students to define the phrase based on the information in the preceding sentences.

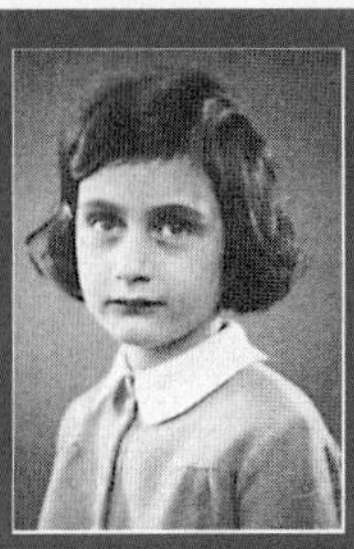

Anne in 1935.

There is a saying that "paper is more patient than man"; it came back to me on one of my slightly melancholy days, while I sat chin in hand, feeling too bored and limp even to make up my mind whether to go out or stay at home. Yes, there is no doubt that paper is patient and as I don't intend to show this cardboard-covered notebook, bearing the proud name of "diary," to anyone, unless I find a real friend, boy or girl, probably nobody cares. And now I come to the root of the matter, the reason for my starting a diary: it is that I have no such real friend.

Let me put it more clearly, since no one will believe that a girl of thirteen feels herself quite alone in the world, nor is it so. I have darling parents and a sister of sixteen. I know about thirty people whom one might call friends—I have strings of boy friends, anxious to catch a glimpse of me and who, failing that, peep at me through mirrors in class. I have relations, aunts and uncles, who are darlings too, a good home, no—I don't seem to lack anything. But it's the same with all my friends, just fun and joking, nothing more. I can never bring myself to talk of anything outside the common round. We don't seem to be able to get any closer, that is the root of the trouble. Perhaps I lack confidence, but anyway, there it is, a stubborn fact and I don't seem to be able to do anything about it.

Hence, this diary. In order to enhance in my mind's eye the picture of the friend for whom I have waited so long, I don't want to set down a series of bald facts in a diary like most people do, but I want this diary itself to be my friend, and I shall call my friend Kitty. No one will grasp what I'm talking about if I begin my letters to Kitty just out of the blue, so, albeit[2] unwillingly, I will start by sketching in brief the story of my life.

My father was thirty-six when he married my mother, who was then twenty-five. My sister Margot was born in 1926 in Frankfort-on-Main, I followed on June 12, 1929, and, as we are Jewish, we emigrated to Holland in 1933, where my father was appointed Managing Director of Travies N.V. This firm is in close relationship with the firm of Kolen & Co. in the same building, of which my father is a partner.

The rest of our family, however, felt the full impact of Hitler's anti-Jewish laws,[3] so life was filled with anxiety. In 1938 after the pogroms,[4] my two uncles (my mother's brothers) escaped to the U.S.A.

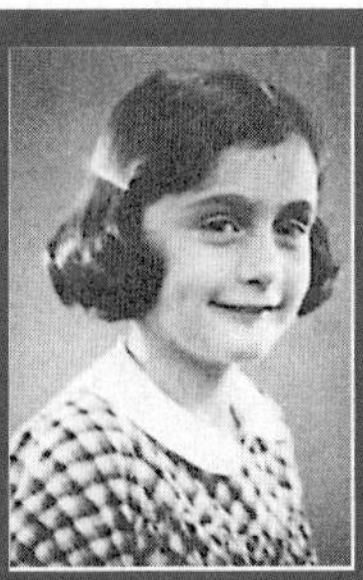

Anne in December 1935.

2. *Albeit* is another way of saying "although" or "even if."
3. An *impact* is a strong effect. Anti-Jewish feelings increased sharply in Germany during the early 1930s, and many Jews left the country after Hitler came to power in 1933.
4. *Pogroms* (pō gromz′) were organized efforts to persecute and kill Jews. The Netherlands tried to stay neutral early in the war, but Germany invaded the nation.

Vocabulary

melancholy (mel′ ən kol′ ē) *adj.* sadly thoughtful

enhance (en hans′) *v.* to make greater

Teaching Support

MEETING INDIVIDUAL NEEDS — ENGLISH LANGUAGE LEARNERS

Articles Students learning English often have difficulty choosing between *a, an,* and *the.* Write the phrase "the reason I started a diary" on the board. Explain that *the* often refers to something specific that has already been named or something of which only one exists. *A* and *an* refer to one of many things or to something that has not yet been identified.

Activity Have students provide the correct articles for the following: "____ diary is mine." "____ White House is in Washington." "____ car you bought is ____ beauty." Students should explain why they selected the articles they did.

Additional Resources

English Language Learners Sourcebook, p. 83

My old grandmother came to us, she was then seventy-three. After May 1940 good times rapidly fled: first the war, then the capitulation,[5] followed by the arrival of the Germans, which is when the sufferings of us Jews really began. Anti-Jewish decrees followed each other in quick succession. Jews must wear a yellow star, Jews must hand in their bicycles, Jews are banned from trams and are forbidden to drive. Jews are only allowed to do their shopping between three and five o'clock and then only in shops which bear the placard "Jewish shop." Jews must be indoors by eight o'clock and cannot even sit in their own gardens after that hour. Jews are forbidden to visit theaters, cinemas, and other places of entertainment. Jews may not take part in public sports. Swimming baths, tennis courts, hockey fields, and other sports grounds are all prohibited to them. Jews may not visit Christians. Jews must go to Jewish schools, and many more restrictions of a similar kind.

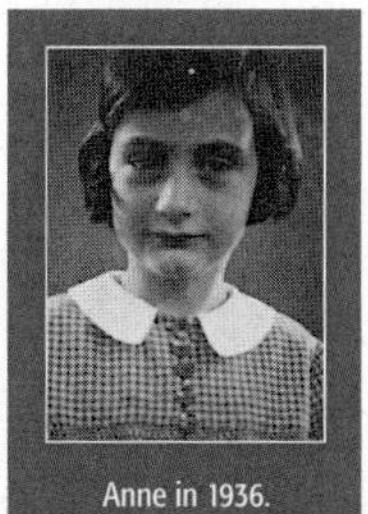
Anne in 1936.

So we could not do this and were forbidden to do that. But life went on in spite of it all. Jopie[6] used to say to me, "You're scared to do anything, because it may be forbidden." Our freedom was strictly limited. Yet things were still bearable.

Granny died in January 1942; no one will ever know how much she is present in my thoughts and how much I love her still.

In 1934 I went to school at the Montessori[7] Kindergarten and continued there. It was at the end of the school year, I was in form 6B, when I had to say good-bye to Mrs. K. We both wept, it was very sad. In 1941 I went, with my sister Margot, to the Jewish Secondary School, she into the fourth form and I into the first.

So far everything is all right with the four of us and here I come to the present day.

Saturday, 15 July, 1944

Dear Kitty,

We have had a book from the library with the challenging title of: *What Do You Think of the Modern Young Girl?* I want to talk about this subject today.

The author of this book criticizes "the youth of today" from top to toe, without, however, condemning the whole of the young brigade as "incapable of anything good." On the contrary, she is rather of the opinion that if young people wished, they have it in their hands to make a bigger, more beautiful and better world, but that they occupy themselves with superficial things, without giving a thought to real beauty.

Anne in 1937.

5. The surrender, or *capitulation* (kə pich′ ə lā′ shən), of the Dutch army came on May 14, 1940.
6. Anne's best friend was *Jopie* deWaal (yo′ pē də väl′).
7. A *Montessori* (mon′ tə sôr′ ē) school is a type of private school that encourages students to act, think, and speak freely.

Vocabulary
ban (ban) *v.* to forbid; outlaw; prohibit
superficial (so͞o′ pər fish′ əl) *adj.* lacking deep meaning; shallow; unimportant or unnecessary

D Author's Craft

TONE Point out that a writer sets the tone of the selection by choosing the manner in which to describe events. Ask students to consider the tone of Anne's description of the life of Jews. Encourage them to contrast Anne's description with some other ways their lives could have been described. *(She takes a positive attitude, whereas other descriptions could focus on the negative.)*

E Active Reading Strategies

CONNECT Ask students to identify the statements in this passage that support the theme of "Faces of Dignity."

Cultural Note

In European schools, students are not in "grades" but, particularly in England, are instead in "forms." The forms are roughly equivalent to American schools' grades, except that the numbering system begins again when the student moves on to each higher-level school. Secondary school begins with the equivalent of approximately seventh grade.

F Active Reading Strategies

REVIEW Note that the second entry is two years later. Ask students how old Anne is now and what they think she has been doing since the earlier entry.

Real-World Connection

Present Day Persecution Point out that dictatorships and the persecution of minorities did not end with World War II. Many news organizations have Web sites that provide in-depth reporting on worldwide events of this nature.

Activity Have students conduct research on world news Web sites to learn more about countries in which the government persecutes some minorities. Remind students that persecution may be in the form of violence rather than restrictions. Have them locate the country and identify its leader, the group being persecuted, and the form of persecution. They may wish to work in pairs or groups. Students should share their findings with the class in a group discussion.

L2 **COLLAB. LEARN.**

FYI

Anne's Life The Frank family originally lived in Germany, but in 1933 they moved to the Netherlands to escape Nazi persecution. However, the Germans occupied the Netherlands, and the Frank family went into hiding when Anne was thirteen. They remained there for two years but were discovered and sent to concentration camps, where they all died except Anne's father. Anne's diary was published posthumously in 1947.

Margot and Anne Frank

Teaching Support

MEETING INDIVIDUAL NEEDS

SPECIAL NEEDS

Learning Disabled Students with learning disabilities may benefit from organizing the historical information and time frames mentioned in the diary to make its setting clearer.

Activity Have students make a time line of events in Anne's life, beginning with her birth and ending with her death. Suggest they use information from the Before You Read page, as well as the diary, to organize the time line. **L1**

Additional Resources

Inclusion Strategies

In some passages the writer gave me very much the feeling she was directing her criticism at me, and that's why I want to lay myself completely bare to you for once and defend myself against this attack.

I have one outstanding trait in my character, which must strike anyone who knows me for any length of time, and that is my knowledge of myself. I can watch myself and my actions, just like an outsider. The Anne of every day I can face entirely without prejudice, without making excuses for her, and watch what's good and what's bad about her. This "self-consciousness" haunts me, and every time I open my mouth I know as soon as I've spoken whether "that ought to have been different" or "that was right as it was." There are so many things about myself that I condemn; I couldn't begin to name them all. I understand more and more how true Daddy's words were when he said: "All children must look after their own upbringing." Parents can only give good advice or put them on the right paths, but the final forming of a person's character lies in their own hands.

In addition to this, I have lots of courage, I always feel so strong and as if I can bear a great deal, I feel so free and so young! I was glad when I first realized it, because I don't think I shall easily bow down before the blows that inevitably come to everyone.

Anne in 1938.

But I've talked about these things so often before. Now I want to come to the chapter of "Daddy and Mummy don't understand me." Daddy and Mummy have always thoroughly spoiled me, were sweet to me, defended me, and have done all that parents could do. And yet I've felt so terribly lonely for a long time, so left out, neglected, and misunderstood. Daddy tried all he could to check my rebellious spirit, but it was no use, I have cured myself, by seeing for myself what was wrong in my behavior and keeping it before my eyes.

Anne in 1939.

How is it that Daddy was never any support to me in my struggle, why did he completely miss the mark when he wanted to offer me a helping hand? Daddy tried the wrong methods, he always talked to me as a child who was going through difficult phases. It sounds crazy, because Daddy's the only one who has always taken me into his confidence, and no one but Daddy has given me the feeling that I'm sensible. But there's one thing he's omitted: you see, he hasn't realized that for me the fight to get on top was more important than all else. I didn't want to hear about "symptoms of your age," or "other girls," or "it wears off by itself"; I didn't want to be treated as a girl-like-all-others, but as Anne-on-her-own-merits. Pim[8] didn't understand that. For that matter, I can't confide in anyone, unless they tell me a lot about themselves, and as I know very little about Pim, I don't feel that I can tread upon more intimate ground with him. Pim **G**

8. *Pim* was a nickname Anne gave her father.

Vocabulary
prejudice (prej′ ə dis) *n.* an opinion formed without considering all sides of a question

G Critical Thinking

MAKE CRITICAL JUDGMENTS Ask students whether they agree that it is difficult to confide in someone who has not confided in them. Encourage them to consider whether adults generally confide in children.

Model: Anne says that she has trouble confiding in her father because he does not confide in her. I think she feels that confiding should be an equal exchange. After you confide in someone, that person knows more about you than before. If you confide in someone who does not confide in you, that person knows more about you than you know about the other person. Eventually, you may not feel equal to the other person.

Vo·cab·u·lar·y Skills

Multiple-Meaning Words Explain to students that *outstanding* can mean "excellent" or simply "noticeable." Ask them to consider which meaning applies in the first line of the second paragraph of column 1, in light of what they know about Anne.

Reading *Minilesson*

Skimming Review with students the importance of skimming to make reading more efficient. Explain that reading every word can be inefficient when a reader is looking for something specific—in addition to wasting time, reading every word can distract a reader from his or her purpose.

Activity Anne Frank quotes and reflects on philosophical statements. Have students skim the entries to find three such statements. Ask students to identify Anne's reaction to each. Encourage students to skim, looking for clues to help them find the statements. **L2**

Additional Resources

Reading Skills Practice Workbook

H Literary Elements

JOURNAL Note that *anyone* refers to human beings, not things. What does Anne's use of this term reveal about her attitude toward her diary? *(She truly views "Kitty" as a friend.)*

I Critical Thinking

DRAWING CONCLUSIONS Anne refers to her "half-completed task." Ask students to conclude what task she refers to. Why is it only half completed? *(One possibility is that Anne's half-completed task is growing up, especially building her "repose and self-confidence.")*

J Active Reading Strategies

REVIEW Note that Anne refers to her disappointment. Have students identify what has disappointed Anne and how her discussions of her father and Peter support her conclusions. *(Anne is disappointed by her inability to form a close, equal relationship with her father and to create a bond with Peter based on mutual understanding.)*

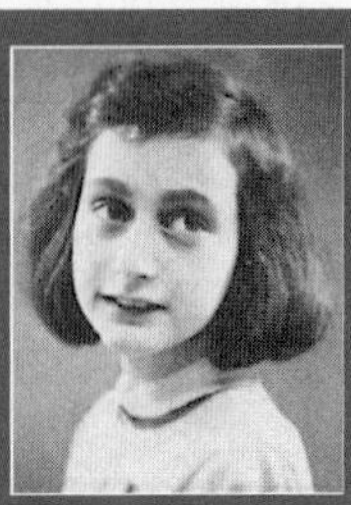
Anne in 1940.

always takes up the older, fatherly attitude, tells me that he too has had similar passing tendencies. But still he's not able to feel with me like a friend, however hard he tries. These things have made me never mention my views on life nor my well-considered theories to anyone but my diary and, occasionally, to Margot. I concealed from Daddy everything that perturbed me; I never shared my ideals[9] with him. I was aware of the fact that I was pushing him away from me.

I couldn't do anything else. I have acted entirely according to my feelings, but I have acted in the way that was best for my peace of mind. Because I should completely lose my repose[10] and self-confidence, which I have built up so shakily, if, at this stage, I were to accept criticisms of my half-completed task. And I can't do that even from Pim, although it sounds very hard, for not only have I not shared my secret thoughts with Pim but I have often pushed him even further from me, by my irritability.

This is a point that I think a lot about: why is it that Pim annoys me? So much so that I can hardly bear him teaching me, that his affectionate ways strike me as being put on, that I want to be left in peace and would really prefer it if he dropped me a bit, until I felt more certain in my attitude towards him. Because I still have a gnawing feeling of guilt over that horrible letter that I dared to write him when I was so wound up. Oh, how hard it is to be really strong and brave in every way!

Yet this was not my greatest disappointment; no, I ponder far more over Peter[11] than Daddy. I know very well that I conquered him instead of he conquering me. I created an image of him in my mind, pictured him as a quiet, sensitive, lovable boy, who needed affection and friendship. I needed a living person to whom I could pour out my heart; I wanted a friend who'd help to put me on the right road. I achieved what I wanted, and slowly but surely, I drew him towards me. Finally, when I had made him feel friendly, it automatically developed into an intimacy which, on second thought, I don't think I ought to have allowed.

Anne in 1941.

We talked about the most private things, and yet up till now we have never touched on those things that filled, and still fill, my heart and soul. I still don't know quite what to make of Peter, is he superficial, or does he still feel shy, even of me? But dropping that, I committed one error in my desire to make a real friendship: I switched over and tried to get at him by developing it into a more intimate relation, whereas I should have explored all

9. People's *ideals* involve what they believe to be standards of excellence or perfection.
10. Anne's *repose* was her calm, relaxed manner.
11. *Peter* Van Daan (fän dän) and his parents lived in hiding with the Franks. Peter and Margot were closer in age, but Peter and Anne became closer friends.

Vocabulary
perturb (pər turb′) *v.* to disturb greatly
ponder (pon′ dər) *v.* to think over carefully

Teaching Support

Grammar and Language *Minilesson*

Colons Review the use of colons within sentences and remind students that a colon can be a signal to introduce an example or to introduce a definition. A colon used in such a way must follow an independent clause.

Activity Have students find the two examples of colon use on this page and identify how each is being used. Then have students rewrite the following two passages, using colons: page 677, "Anti-Jewish decrees . . . forbidden to drive," and page 679, "I have one outstanding . . . knowledge of myself." **L2**

Additional Resources

- ***Grammar and Language Transparency 57***
- ***Grammar and Language Workbook,*** pp. 265–266
- ***Grammar and Composition Handbook,*** Lesson 13.5
- ***Writer's Choice,*** Lesson 20.5

other possibilities. He longs to be loved and I can see that he's beginning to be more and more in love with me. He gets satisfaction out of our meetings, whereas they just have the effect of making me want to try it out with him again. And yet I don't seem able to touch on the subjects that I'm so longing to bring out into the daylight. I drew Peter towards me, far more than he realizes. Now he clings to me, and for the time being, I don't see any way of shaking him off and putting him on his own feet. When I realized that he could not be a friend for my understanding, I thought I would at least try to lift him up out of his narrow-mindedness and make him do something with his youth.

Anne in 1942.

"For in its innermost depths youth is lonelier than old age." I read this saying in some book and I've always remembered it, and found it to be true. Is it true then that grown-ups have a more difficult time here than we do? No. I know it isn't. Older people have formed their opinions about everything, and don't waver before they act. It's twice as hard for us young ones to hold our ground, and maintain our opinions, in a time when all ideals are being shattered and destroyed, when people are showing their worst side, and do not know whether to believe in truth and right and God.

K

Anyone who claims that the older ones have a more difficult time here certainly doesn't realize to what extent our problems weigh down on us, problems for which we are probably much too young, but which thrust themselves upon us continually, until, after a long time, we think we've found a solution, but the solution doesn't seem able to resist the facts which reduce it to nothing again. That's the difficulty in these times: ideals, dreams, and cherished hopes rise within us, only to meet the horrible truth and be shattered.

It's really a wonder that I haven't dropped all my ideals, because they seem so absurd[12] and impossible to carry out. Yet I keep them, because in spite of everything I still believe that people are really good at heart. I simply can't build up my hopes on a foundation consisting of confusion, misery, and death. I see the world gradually being turned into a wilderness, I hear the ever approaching thunder, which will destroy us too, I can feel the sufferings of millions and yet, if I look up into the heavens, I think that it will all come right, that this cruelty too will end, and that peace and tranquillity will return again.

In the meantime, I must uphold my ideals, for perhaps the time will come when I shall be able to carry them out.

Yours, Anne

12. *Absurd* means "silly" or "ridiculous."

Vocabulary

waver (wā′ vər) *v.* to become uncertain; falter

tranquillity (trang kwil′ ə tē) *n.* the state or quality of being calm and free from disturbance; quietness

K Critical Thinking

IDENTIFY BIAS Note Anne's statement that "older people have formed their opinions about everything." Encourage students to consider whether they agree with this statement. They should note that the statement reflects a bias about older people. How did Anne form this bias? *(She has drawn her conclusions from how they talk to her alone.)*

Thematic Focus

Faces of Dignity Note that Anne's line, "Yet I keep them, because in spite of everything I still believe that people are really good at heart," has become perhaps the most famous and most poignant in Anne's diary. Ask students how this statement supports the theme. *(The statement shows that a person can maintain hope in the face of the most horrible circumstances.)*

ASSESSMENT

Quick Checks, p. 59

FINE ART TRANSPARENCY 8

You may want to use ***Fine Art Transparency 8*** to discuss the importance of interaction among peers.

Writing Minilesson

Interpretation Students may gain additional insight into Anne's life and the lives of those around her by imagining what a diary from someone else hiding with Anne would have said.

Activity Have students write a diary entry from either Mr. Frank's or Peter's point of view. Encourage students to use the style Anne used—writing a letter to a "real friend." Students should focus on the passages from Anne's diary about the person whose point of view they have chosen. **L2**

Additional Resources

Writer's Choice, Lesson 1.2

FACES OF DIGNITY 681

Responding to the Selection

PERSONAL RESPONSE

Students' responses should compare their experiences with Anne's.

Analyzing Literature

1. Anne keeps a diary as a substitute for a friend in whom she can confide.
2. Anne claims she knows herself.
3. It is lonelier because young people have not formed opinions, so it is more difficult for them to decide how to act.
4. They are shattered when they meet the "horrible truth."
5. Students' responses may include that she keeps her word; she doesn't give up; or that she never stops needing someone in whom to confide.
6. Students' responses should include examples from the text.
7. Factors include that she is trapped; she is isolated from her peers; and she cannot confide in the people around her.
8. Students' responses should include examples from the text.
9. Students' responses should contrast the elements of a factual account with the elements of a fictional account and the emotional response to an actual victim of the Holocaust.
10. Students should cite passages from the text that affected them differently because they knew her fate.

Active Reading and Critical Thinking

Responding to Literature

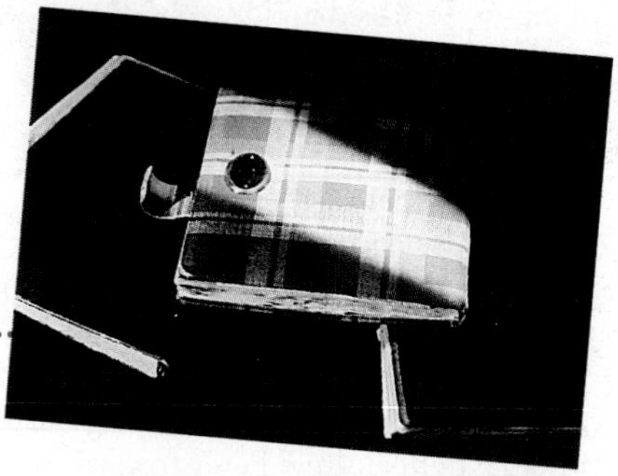

PERSONAL RESPONSE

◆ How do Anne's relationship with her parents, her view of freedom, and her ideas about friendship compare with your own? Look back at your notes from the **Reading Focus** on page 674 as you answer this question.

Brackets connect questions that are paired to develop higher-level thinking skills.

Analyzing Literature

RECALL

1. Why does Anne plan to keep a diary?
2. What outstanding character trait does Anne claim to have?
3. Why is youth lonelier than old age, according to Anne?
4. What does Anne believe happens to the ideals, dreams, and hopes of young people?

INTERPRET

5. What does Anne's faithfulness to her decision to keep a diary tell you about her?
6. Why, in your opinion, does Anne say that "There are so many things about myself that I condemn"?
7. What factors in her life probably influence Anne's belief that youth is a lonely time?
8. What, in your opinion, gives Anne the ability to hope regarding her plans and dreams?

EVALUATE AND CONNECT

9. How is reading Anne's diary different from reading a short story about a girl like her?
10. How does your knowledge of Anne's death affect your experience of reading her diary?

LITERARY ELEMENTS

Journal

A **journal,** or **diary,** is an account of day-to-day events or a record of experiences, thoughts, or ideas. Journals are updated regularly and are usually only for private use, although some are made public, usually after the death of the writer. Journal writing is a type of nonfiction because it records actual events.

1. What historical events are recorded in this selection from *Anne Frank: The Diary of a Young Girl*?
2. Anne wrote for herself. What benefit have we received from Anne's diary being made public?

● See **Literary Terms Handbook,** p. R5.

LITERARY ELEMENTS

1. The recorded events include the Nazi rule of Germany and occupation of Holland and the Nazis' treatment of Jews in occupied countries.
2. Students' responses should contain specific reasons that support their conclusions.

Additional Resources

Literary Elements Transparency 59

Extending Your Response

Writing About Literature

Characterization Anne writes about the people who share the small living space above the factory. Describe one of these people and your attitude toward him or her. Give details about the person's appearance, self-image, and opinions of the other occupants. Explain which of Anne's words and descriptions help to shape your attitude.

Personal Writing

Reflections on Prejudice Imagine that you are a non-Jewish student in Europe during the Nazi regime. What are your reactions as you see restrictions placed on Jewish friends or acquaintances? Knowing that the Nazis kill or jail their opponents, will you protest? Why or why not? Explain your answers in a few paragraphs.

Learning for Life

Interview with Anne Write three questions that you would like to ask Anne if she were alive today. Exchange questions with a partner and write answers you think Anne might give, keeping in mind what you know about her. Discuss the questions and answers with your partner.

Literature Groups

Age-old Questions Do you agree that "youth is lonelier than old age"? How would you define "lonely"? How do circumstances influence a person's sense of loneliness? Debate the question.

Reading Further

To know more about Anne Frank, read the rest of *Anne Frank: The Diary of a Young Girl.*

Save your work for your portfolio.

Skill Minilesson

RETEACH • REVIEW

VOCABULARY • ANTONYMS

Antonyms are words with opposite meanings. *Whisper* and *scream* are antonyms because their meanings are opposite.

Not all words have antonyms, but some words have several. *Whisper,* for example, has many: *scream, yell, holler, bellow, whoop,* and *howl* are a few. When choosing an antonym for a word, read all of the choices and choose the word that expresses your exact meaning.

PRACTICE Choose the antonym for each word.

1. ban
   a. cause b. require c. discourage
2. perturb
   a. soothe b. excite c. annoy
3. melancholy
   a. joyful b. interested c. determined
4. tranquillity
   a. ugliness b. happiness c. excitement
5. enhance
   a. conquer b. injure c. decrease

Extending Your Response

Writing About Literature

Students' character sketches should

- arise out of specific details from the text
- contain their opinions of the person

Personal Writing

Students' paragraphs should

- describe their reactions
- explain why they would or would not protest

Learning for Life Students should be able to explain why they chose the three questions they would ask if Anne were alive. Answers should be supported by the information provided about her.

Literature Groups Groups should discuss both sides of the question. COLLAB. LEARN.

Skill Minilesson

VOCABULARY • ANTONYMS

1. b 2. a 3. a 4. c 5. c

Additional Resources

Vocabulary Practice, p. 42

ASSESSMENT

- ***Quick Checks,*** p. 59
- ***Selection and Theme Assessment,*** pp. 107–108
- ***Performance Assessment,*** p. 56
- ***Testmaker: ExamView Pro***
- ***Interactive Tutor: Self-Assessment***

MEDIA Connection

Objective

- To read and understand a Web site

Literature LINK

Anne Frank: The Diary of a Young Girl This Web site connects to *Anne Frank: The Diary of a Young Girl* (pp. 674–681). The Web site contains background information on how the diary was found and how it came to be published.

LITERATURE & HUMANITIES

Have students view "The Farewell" on *The National Museum of Women in the Arts* CD. Discuss Kathe Kollwitz's depiction of separation.

MEDIA Connection

WEB SITE

Some people who keep diaries imagine that their writings may be widely read someday. This portion of a Web site describes how Anne Frank's diary made her one of the most famous teenagers and well-known writers in the world.

from the Anne Frank House Web site

Address: www.annefrank.nl

The Story Behind the Diary

While in hiding Anne Frank keeps a diary. In more than two years she fills several notebooks.

Anne would have liked to correspond with someone from the outside world, but that would have been far too dangerous. Therefore, she makes up imaginary friends to whom she writes the letters in her diary. After about a year Anne singles out one of these imaginary friends to address the letters in her diary to; this friend is called Kitty.

Anne tries to describe daily life in the Annex and the news from the outside world, too. Sometimes there are exciting events to report, for example a bombing or a break-in in the middle of the night. In her pursuit Anne Frank succeeds in describing the ups and downs of those living in hiding in an honest and also, at times, comic way.

On a Dutch Free Radio Oranje broadcast from England in March of 1944, there is a call-up for ordinary citizens to provide their diaries for collection after the war for historical purposes. It is then that Anne realizes that her diary could actually be of interest to others. She makes a plan to rework her diary into a real book.

In the ten weeks from May 20th until August 4, 1944, Anne rewrites a big portion of her diary. Especially the beginning is greatly improved. In the meantime she continues writing her daily entries. Her rewrite is still not completed when the Secret Annex is raided by police on August 4, 1944. Anne is taken away; the diary is left behind. By then Anne has filled 321 pages with her words.

After the arrest of those in hiding, Miep Gies and Bep Voskuijl, the company secretaries, remain behind.

Teaching Support

Reading *Minilesson*

Synthesizing Explain that often the introduction of new facts requires us to rethink our earlier assumptions and conclusions. The Web site introduces the fact that Anne was aware her diary might be collected and read by others for historical purposes. Students need to place this new information in context and to consider whether it changes any of their earlier responses to the diary.

Activity Have students engage in a class discussion. They should consider the question of how the knowledge that her diary might be read by others may have affected Anne's purpose in writing. Encourage them to consider how the content of her entries may have been affected. **L2** COLLAB. LEARN.

Additional Resources

Reading Skills Practice Workbook

684 THEME 7

from the Anne Frank House Web site

Address: www.annefrank.nl

Together they discover Anne's notebooks lying scattered on the floor of the empty hiding place. Miep saves the diaries with the hope that she will see Anne again. After the war has ended, when she learns that Anne has died, she gives the notebooks and loose pages to Otto Frank, recently returned from the concentration camp, with the words: "Here is your daughter Anne's legacy to you."

Through the urging of friends, Otto Frank decides to publish his daughter's work. He compiles one book made up of the original diary and Anne's rewritten version. Anne Frank had already chosen the title "The Secret Annex" herself, and in June 1947 the book is published in the Netherlands.

After the initial release of 1,500 copies, *The Secret Annex* is translated and published in more than fifty-five languages. The diary of Anne Frank is one of the most widely read books in the world.

"It took a very long time to read it and I must say I was very surprised about the deep thoughts Anne had, her seriousness, especially her self-criticism. It was quite a different girl than I had known as my daughter. She never showed these kind of inner feelings."

—*Otto Frank*

Analyzing Media

1. What new facts about Anne's diary did you learn from this Web site?
2. How do you think Anne might react to her diary's popularity?

Analyzing Media

1. Students' responses should refer to specific facts given in the Web site.
2. Students' responses should be based on what they learn about Anne from reading the diary entries.

Additional Resources

Media Connections, p. 13

Informational Text

inTIME For more examples of informational text, direct students to the articles in *inTIME* magazine.

interNET CONNECTION

Anne Frank House This media connection is from the Anne Frank House Web site. Have students review other material at this Web site and list other topics covered on the site.

MEETING INDIVIDUAL NEEDS: MULTIPLE MODES OF EXPRESSION

Linguistic The quotation from Otto Frank provided on the Web site is well chosen and interesting. In a couple of sentences, it teaches the reader something about Anne and about her father.

Activity Have students obtain magazine, videotape, or documentary interviews with Miep Gies and select three or four quotations from her that teach the reader something new about Anne's life, the lives of those around her, or the world situation. Students should share their selections with the class and explain their choices. **L2**

Before Reading

Objectives

- To read and analyze a poem
- To identify rhythm in a poem
- To write a theoretical conversation

Skills

Reading/Thinking: Drawing Conclusions
Grammar/Language: Correct Pronoun Use
Collaboration: Literature Groups

Motivating STUDENTS

Selection Focus Transparency 59: Before presenting the transparency, ask volunteers to share places they find important and to explain why they find them so.

Reading Focus: As an extension of the Reading Focus, have students discuss other memory triggers, such as smells and tastes, that remind them of a special person or place.

Before You Read

The Anne Frank House: Amsterdam

MEET JOAN LABOMBARD

Poet Joan LaBombard (lä bōm′ bärd) was on a trip to Europe with her husband when she visited the Anne Frank house—the place Anne lived in hiding from the Germans. LaBombard was surprised by the small size of the Franks' living quarters and by how little privacy the family would have had. When LaBombard left, she started to cry. "I felt her [Anne's] presence really strongly," she says. Later, back at her home in Los Angeles, she was inspired to write this poem, "The Anne Frank House."

Joan LaBombard was born in 1920. Her poem "The Anne Frank House: Amsterdam," first appeared in Yankee *magazine in 1988.*

READING FOCUS

Why do certain places, sounds, or items remind you of other people?

QuickWrite

List five places or things that remind you of a special person.

Setting a Purpose

Read to explore the thoughts and feelings that one poet had after visiting the hiding place of Anne Frank.

BUILDING BACKGROUND

The Time and Place This poem is set in Amsterdam, the Netherlands, in and near the restored building where Anne and her family were once in hiding.

Did You Know? Since the Anne Frank House opened to the public in 1960, about 600,000 people have visited it each year. The visitors can see Anne's diary and the rooms where she and the others lived in hiding. Anne's photos of movie stars remain on the walls. The building also has exhibits on hate crimes and on the history of the Nazis and the Netherlands during World War II.

Front view of the former warehouse now known as the Anne Frank House.

RESOURCE MANAGER

Teaching Tools and Resources
- Theme Seven Planning Guide
- Literature Groups Sourcebook

Essential Lesson Support

Lesson-Specific Instruction
- Selection Focus Transparency 59
- Literary Elements Transparency 60
- Active Reading Guide,* p. 60

Assessment
- Selection Quick Checks,* p. 60
- Sel. and Theme Assmt., pp. 107–108
- Testmaker: ExamView Pro
- Performance Assessment, p. 56

Systematic Language Instruction
- Gr. & Comp. Hbk., L. 13.6
- Vocabulary Power, Lesson 31
- Spelling Power, Lesson 27

English Language Learners
- Spanish Summaries, p. 59
- Spanish Translations, p. 153
- Audio Library*
- English, Yes!

Spec. Needs/Strat. Interven.
- Interactive Rdg. Sbk., pp. T200–T203
- Interactive Rdg. Wkbk., p. 112
- Audio Library*

* Also available in Spanish

686 THEME 7

The Anne Frank House: Amsterdam

Joan LaBombard

Wasn't that you in the Flower Market
holding the fresh-cut blooms,
dahlias, yellow chrysanthemums
like suns that would never fade?
Were you the one who hovered°
by the fruit stalls
A and the trays of slithery eels
in Albert Cuypstraat° market,
your arms thin in the raveled sweater?
I think I passed you on Mozes en Aåronstraat°
teaching yourself the faces, the faces
to the next generation.
Anne, each day, strangers file
soberly through your room.
Your schoolgirl pictures are still there
pasted to the raw wall—
the postcard of Venice, Norma Shearer.°
The window you dared not peer from
looks out on a yard overgrown
with leggy geraniums.
Guinea hens scratch in the dirt.
When I came from your house,
I swear I saw you framed
in the sunset's red apocalypse,°
the sun roaring down behind you
and the sky in flames,
through which you walked, most womanly,
into the pages of your testament°
B and did not burn.

5 Here, *hovered* means "lingered or remained nearby."

8–10 The market is on a street, or *straat* (strät), named for an eighteenth-century Dutch painter, Aelbert Cuyp (ko͞op). Line 10 refers to a street, *Mozes en Aåronstraat* (mō′ zəs en är′ ôn strät′), named for two early Jewish leaders.

17 *Venice* (ven′ is) is the Italian city that has canals for streets. *Shearer* was a popular movie star of the 1930s and 1940s.

24 An *apocalypse* (ə pok′ ə lips′) can be either a remarkable revelation or terrible doom and destruction.

28 Here, Anne's diary is the *testament,* a statement of beliefs or opinions offered as evidence of the truth.

Reading the Selection

A Active Reading Strategies

EVALUATE Have students consider what the author's purpose is in selecting this image of the market. *(A homely image draws attention to Anne's ordinary life.)*

Additional Resources

- ***Active Reading Guide,*** p. 60
- ***Audio Library***
- ***Spanish Audio Library***

B Critical Thinking

DRAWING CONCLUSIONS Ask students to explain what the last line of the poem means. *(Anne Frank survives in her writing even today.)*

Thematic Focus

Faces of Dignity "The Anne Frank House: Amsterdam" is an expression of Anne Frank's dignity. The poet contrasts Anne's dignity with the mundane events of life around the house in which she lived, conveying that human dignity transcends all that is ordinary.

ASSESSMENT

- ***Quick Checks,*** p. 60

Teaching Support

Grammar and Language Minilesson

Correct Pronoun Use A relative pronoun introduces a clause that modifies a noun or pronoun: "Were you the one *who* went?" *Who, whom,* and *whose* refer to people; *which* and *that* refer to objects.

Activity Have students fill in the correct relative pronoun.

Anne Frank was a girl (*who, whom)* wrote a diary.

LaBombard visited the house (*that, which)* Anne occupied.

Additional Resources

- ***Grammar and Language Transparency 58***
- ***Grammar and Language Workbook,*** pp. 111–112
- ***Grammar and Composition Handbook,*** Lesson 4.1
- ***Writer's Choice,*** Lesson 11.1

COMPARING selections

This selection is paired with the excerpt from *Anne Frank: The Diary of a Young Girl* on page 674. A lesson for teaching a comparison of the two selections appears on page 689.

Responding to the Selection

PERSONAL RESPONSE

Students' responses should make specific reference to the poem.

Analyzing Literature

1. The narrator pictures Anne in the flower market, the marketplace, the street, her room, and in the sunset. Students should explain the significance of these places.
2. The narrator tells Anne that strangers come to her room, her postcards are still there, and the yard is untended. Students should consider whether Anne would be interested in the impact her diary has had on the world.
3. Students should consider the actions of the Nazis and the condition of wartime Europe.
4. Students may compare the style of the poem to the style of the diary.
5. Students may discuss the nature of the diary and the confidences it reveals.
6. Students should consider all the meanings of *testament.*

Extending Your Response

Writing About Literature

Students' responses should

- explain why they selected the places they might "see" Anne.

Literature Groups Groups should consider the effects on the reader of various types of poems and the author's purpose in this poem. COLLAB. LEARN.

FINE ART TRANSPARENCY 4

You may want to use ***Fine Art Transparency 4*** to discuss the significance of flowers in this self-portrait.

Active Reading and Critical Thinking

Responding to Literature

PERSONAL RESPONSE

- What impressions do you have about Anne Frank after reading this poem?

Analyzing Literature

RECALL AND INTERPRET

1. In what settings besides the Anne Frank House does the narrator picture Anne? Why, in your opinion, does she select these places?
2. What information does the narrator share with Anne about the house as it is now? Why, do you think, might she want to tell Anne about these things?
3. What do lines 22–29 mean? Why are the apocalypse, flames, and burning appropriate images?

EVALUATE AND CONNECT

4. The narrator addresses Anne as if she were an old friend. What effect might that have on a reader?
5. Why might the narrator feel that she knows Anne like an old friend? Do you feel that way? Explain.
6. *Testament* has several meanings. Which one, do you think, does the poet have in mind in line 28? Why?

LITERARY ELEMENTS

Rhythm

Rhythm is the pattern of stressed and unstressed syllables in a poem. The pattern gives each line a kind of beat. In the first line of "The Anne Frank House," you might read the pattern of beats like this, using the symbol (´) to indicate a stressed syllable:

Wásn't that yóu
in the Flówer Márket

1. Choose another line from the poem and show the pattern of stressed syllables.
2. Do all lines have the same rhythm? How does the pattern of stress give this poem a conversational tone?

- See **Literary Terms Handbook**, p. R8.

Extending Your Response

Writing About Literature

Seeing Anne Frank Where might you connect with or "see" Anne Frank, as the poet did when she visited Anne's hiding place? What might you say to Anne? Refer to your notes from the **Reading Focus** on page 686 to help you write your answer.

Literature Groups

Stanzas The poem is written in one stanza. Discuss other ways the poem might have been presented—as a rhyming poem or a narrative poem, for example. Consider different settings and themes. Why might the poet have chosen to write a single stanza?

LITERARY ELEMENTS

1. Students' markings should reflect the way the line would be spoken.
2. They do not have the same rhythm. Students' responses should contrast the irregular rhythm of conversation with the more formal stress pattern of some poems.

Additional Resources

Literary Elements Transparency 60

ASSESSMENT

- ***Quick Checks,*** p. 60
- ***Selection and Theme Assessment,*** pp. 107–108
- ***Performance Assessment,*** p. 56
- ***Testmaker: ExamView Pro***
- ***Interactive Tutor: Self-Assessment***

Critical Thinking

COMPARING SELECTIONS

from Anne Frank: The Diary of a Young Girl **and** The Anne Frank House: Amsterdam

COMPARE **CONTENT**

A reader often needs background information to fully understand a literature selection.

1. How much would you understand about Anne's situation if you had read the poem before learning anything else about her life?
2. Does Anne's diary include enough background information for readers today to understand what is happening to her without additional reading? Explain how, and why, Anne provides information about her situation.
3. How does reading Anne's diary affect your understanding of the poem?
4. How does reading the poem add to your appreciation of Anne's diary?

COMPARE **EXPERIENCES**

Think about your experiences with some of the elements that make up the story of Anne Frank. You, or people you know or have read about, have experienced fear, prejudice, injustice, loneliness, hatred, and all of the normal problems faced by young people as they grow.

- Jot down some common experiences that help you understand the tragedy of Anne's life.
- List phrases from Anne's diary and from LaBombard's poem that help you understand the tragedy.
- Share your notes with a small group.

COMPARE **RESPONSES**

Both selections focus the reader's thoughts on Anne Frank's life. As she talks to her diary, Anne shares her feelings about her own life. In the poem, the writer speaks to Anne and expresses her feelings about Anne's life. Compare the Anne of Joan LaBombard's poem with the Anne who wrote the diary.

1. Which selection brought you closer to Anne Frank? Explain your answer.
2. Which selection best brings out the theme "Faces of Dignity"?
3. Which selection do you think you will remember longer? Why?

COMPARING *selections*

Objective

- To compare a poem and a diary that express the theme of dignity

COMPARE **CONTENT**

1. Possible responses: she was optimistic; she lived during a war.
2. The first entry describes how Jews fared during Nazi occupation. She includes this so that her "friend," Kitty, will understand Anne's life.
3. The diary clarifies references to optimism, her "testament," or the significance of strangers in her room.
4. The poem may help students see the impact of the diary on the world's perceptions.

COMPARE **EXPERIENCES**

Students' notes should

- explain the links between their experiences and Anne's
- include quotations from the diary and the poem that help them understand the tragedy

Additional Resources

Literature Groups Sourcebook

COMPARE **RESPONSES**

1. Students' responses should refer to specific examples from the selection(s).
2. Students should explain how the selection they chose best demonstrates the theme.
3. Students may refer to specific phrases, images, or a personal response the selection evoked when explaining their choices.

PORTFOLIO OPTIONS

Review and Expand Have students review the phrases they selected from the diary and the poem and expand on them as follows:

- Write an explanation of how the phrases selected help them understand Anne's tragedy.
- Explain how one selected phrase brought them closer to Anne's life.

Students should keep their lists and explanations in their portfolios. They may want to use these as the basis for an essay about the impact of the Holocaust. **L2**

Additional Resources

Writing Assessment and Portfolio Management, pp. 41–48

GRAMMAR LINK

Objective

- To understand the use of commas with nonessential appositives and adjective clauses

Teaching Strategies

When students read the examples and problems aloud, have them omit the underlined material from the sentences. To help them determine whether the missing portion is essential, encourage them to consider whether the sentence as they have read it conveys enough information to stand alone.

Exercise

1. Correct
2. The hiding place, which was in a warehouse, was very crowded.
3. The Van Daan family, who also feared the Nazis, hid with the Franks.
4. Anne, a thirteen-year-old, kept a detailed record of her experiences in hiding.

Additional Resources

- ***Grammar and Language Workbook,*** pp. 161–162
- ***Grammar and Composition Handbook,*** Lessons 13.3, 14.4
- ***Writer's Choice,*** Lesson 20.2

Teaching Support

GRAMMAR LINK

Using Commas Correctly

Some rules about using commas require more thought than others. Two examples are the rules about using commas with appositives and with adjective clauses. An **appositive** is a noun or pronoun (and its modifiers, if any) that renames or explains another noun or pronoun. An **adjective clause** is a clause used as an adjective.

If the clause or appositive is **essential,** or necessary, to the meaning of the sentence, no commas are used to set it off. If it is **nonessential,** not necessary to the meaning, it *is* set off by commas. An easy way to decide if information is essential or if it is "extra" is to think about whether it could be omitted.

Essential appositive: *The writer Anne Frank lives on through her work.*
Nonessential appositive: *Margot Frank, Anne's older sister, was close to her.*

Essential adjective clause: *People who hid the Jews showed courage.*
Nonessential adjective clause: *Margot, who hid with Anne, was a sweet girl.*

Problem 1 Missing commas with a nonessential appositive
Anne Frank a young victim of the Nazis kept a diary.

Solution Set off a nonessential appositive with commas.
Anne Frank, a young victim of the Nazis, kept a diary.

Problem 2 Missing commas with a nonessential adjective clause
Anne's father who survived the Holocaust later published her diary.

Solution Set off a nonessential adjective clause with commas.
Anne's father, who survived the Holocaust, later published her diary.

- For more about commas, see **Language Handbook,** pp. R38–R40.

EXERCISE

Rewrite each sentence, adding necessary commas. If the sentence is correct as written, write *Correct.*

1. The Nazis treated people who were Jewish very badly.
2. The hiding place which was in a warehouse was very crowded.
3. The Van Daan family who also feared the Nazis hid with the Franks.
4. Anne a thirteen-year-old kept a detailed record of her experiences in hiding.

Writing Minilesson

Factual Descriptions Explain to students that using appositives and adjective clauses is a good way to present factual information in a few words. Ask students to review Anne's brief sketch of her life in the last two paragraphs of page 676. Have students record some facts about their own lives after reading Anne's biographical sketch.

Activity Ask students to compose a paragraph similar to Anne's that gives a brief story of their backgrounds. Each paragraph should contain three appositives and three adjective clauses. Review students' work to check punctuation. **L2**

Additional Resources

- ***Writer's Choice,*** Lesson 3.1

Writing Skills

Using Transitions in Cause-Effect Relationships

Anne Frank muses about why she is keeping a diary: "I want to write, but more than that, I want to bring out all kinds of things that lie buried deep in my heart. . . . And now I come to the root of the matter, the reason for my starting a diary: it is that I have no such real friend."

Her musings show that several reasons, or **causes,** can lead to one event. In the same way, several results, or **effects,** can arise from one cause. When you write, choose appropriate transitions to make cause-and-effect relationships clear.

Transitions for Cause and Effect				
since for	so therefore	if hence	that's why as a result	because then

Anne Frank's thoughts often explore causes and effects. In the quotations from her diary, below, notice the underlined transitions that show cause and effect.

"Let me put it more clearly, <u>since</u> no one will believe that a girl of thirteen feels herself quite alone in the world. . . ."

"The rest of our family, however, felt the full impact of Hitler's anti-Jewish laws, <u>so</u> life was filled with anxiety."

". . . the writer gave me very much the feeling that she was directing her criticism at me, and <u>that's why</u> I want to lay myself completely bare to you for once and defend myself against this attack."

"It's really a wonder that I haven't dropped all my ideals, <u>because</u> they seem so absurd and impossible to carry out."

"I must uphold my ideals, <u>for</u> perhaps the time will come when I shall be able to carry them out."

ACTIVITIES

1. Write three sentences giving reasons why you follow a particular holiday tradition. In each sentence, correctly use a different transition from the boxed list.
2. Write a paragraph explaining the causes or effects of an historical event. Use transitions from the boxed list to make the cause-effect relationships clear.

Writing Skills

Objective

- To understand the use of transitions to make cause-and-effect relationships clear

Teaching Strategies

To help students identify cause-and-effect relationships, have them rephrase the first three examples—giving the effect first, using the transition *because,* and then stating the cause.

Activities

1. Students' sentences should use a transition word from the list provided and should be punctuated correctly.
2. Students' paragraphs should use transitions effectively to help the reader understand the cause-and-effect relationship.

Additional Resources

Writer's Choice, Lesson 2.7

Teaching Support

Grammar and Language Minilesson

Avoiding Run-on Sentences Point out that transitions for cause and effect often connect independent clauses. Remind students that such clauses must be joined with a comma and a coordinating conjunction or with a semicolon. Review the boxed terms, explaining that *therefore, then, hence, that's why,* and *as a result* must be preceded by a comma and a conjunction, when they introduce a clause, or by a semicolon to avoid a run-on sentence.

Activity Have students write four compound sentences using the transition terms above and punctuating the sentences correctly. **L2**

Additional Resources

Grammar and Language Transparency 59

Grammar and Language Workbook, pp. 53–54

Grammar and Composition Handbook, Lesson 14.1

Writer's Choice, Lesson 7.2

GENRE FOCUS

Objective

- To understand the elements of drama

Teaching Strategies

Explain that drama is storytelling and therefore contains many of the same elements as stories—such as characters, plot, and climax—but that in drama these elements are communicated to an audience through sight and sound rather than through writing. Ask students to consider the methods a playwright, a stage manager, or the actors might use to produce a mood in a drama.

Setting and Mood Encourage students to visualize the stage when they read the setting of a scene. Ask them to imagine sitting in the audience and viewing the scene described. Explain that the term *at rise* means "at the rising of the curtain," or the way the stage looks when the lights go down and the play begins.

GENRE FOCUS

DRAMA

The first time you acted out a scene from your favorite TV show or imitated a conversation to make someone laugh, you were creating a drama. A **drama,** or play, is a story performed for an audience. It is a type of entertainment that people have been performing and viewing since ancient times. Understanding the elements of drama will help you appreciate plays.

The main character in Washington Irving's story *Rip Van Winkle* falls asleep one day and doesn't wake up for eighteen years. This scene is from the beginning of a play based on the story.

- For more about drama, see **Literary Terms Handbook,** p. R3.

1 SETTING AND MOOD Dramas usually begin by describing the time and place of the action and giving information about the opening scene. The names of the characters are included here, as are the sounds and sights that the audience will experience when the curtain rises. This information helps actors develop their roles, and it allows readers to get into the mood, or atmosphere, of the play.

MODEL: "Rip Van Winkle"

SCENE 1

TIME: *Early autumn, a few years before the Revolutionary War.*

SETTING: *A village in the Catskill Mountains. At left, there is an inn with a sign, King George Tavern, and a picture of King George III. A British Union Jack hangs on flagpole. At right are a tree and a well.*

AT RISE: *NICHOLAS VEDDER, DERRICK VAN BUMMEL, BROM DUTCHER, and PETER VANDERDONK are seated outside the tavern. VEDDER is sprawled back in his chair. DUTCHER and VANDERDONK are at table, playing checkers. VAN BUMMEL is reading aloud from paper. From time to time, a rumble of thunder can be heard in the distance. . . .*

Teaching Support

MEETING INDIVIDUAL NEEDS

ENGLISH LANGUAGE LEARNERS

Drama Across Cultures Some English language learners may not be familiar with American stage plays. The manner in which drama is presented follows different customs in different cultures. In some societies, for instance, all the roles are played by men. In others, costumes and movements are highly ritualized.

Activity Ask students to share their knowledge of drama in their cultures. Ask students to describe some techniques used in presentation, such as the use of costumes or sets. **COLLAB. LEARN.**

Additional Resources

English Language Learners Sourcebook

Rip Van Winkle awakens to peculiar surroundings in Seattle Children's Theater's 1989 production of *Rip Van Winkle and the Legend of Sleepy Hollow: A Tribute to Washington Irving.*

2 PLAY FORMAT
In a play, each character's name is printed in the center or on the left-hand side of the page, followed by his or her words, or lines. The name appears in capital letters, boldface type, or some other special way to set it off from the character's words. In this way, actors reading the script can easily see where each speaker's lines begin.

3 STAGE DIRECTIONS
Stage directions describe the appearance of the stage; the sounds to be heard; and the clothing, movements, and expressions of the actors. Without stage directions, it would be difficult for directors and actors to understand what the playwright had in mind. People who are reading the play instead of watching it use stage directions to visualize the action.

4 DIALOGUE AND CHARACTERIZATION
A play's action moves forward because of the words of the characters. **Dialogue,** the words spoken in a play, tells the story while revealing the personalities of its characters. What does the dialogue between Rip and Dame Van Winkle tell the audience about these two characters?

VEDDER. [*Pointing off right as a merry whistle is heard.*] Well, here comes one man who is not troubled by these problems—Rip Van Winkle. [*RIP VAN WINKLE enters, holding bucket and gun. He props gun against tree at right, then crosses to men.*] . . .

VEDDER. Sit down, Rip. Derrick is reading us the news.

VANDERDONK. How about a game of checkers, Rip?

RIP. [*Hesitating.*] I don't know. Dame Van Winkle sent me for a bucket of water, but—maybe *one* game. [*Sets down bucket and draws stool up to table. Suddenly DAME VAN WINKLE's voice is heard.*]

DAME VAN WINKLE. [*Calling from off right.*] Rip! R-i-p! Rip Van Winkle!

RIP. Oh, my galligaskins! It's my wife! [*DAME VAN WINKLE enters with a broom and crosses directly to RIP.*]

DAME VAN WINKLE. So this is how you draw water from the well! Sitting around with a lot of lazy, good-for-nothing loafers. [*Tries to hit RIP with broom.*] Pick up that bucket, you dawdling Dutchman, and fill it with water!

Play Format Have students identify the different characters who have lines in the example shown.

Stage Directions Remind students that a drama is developed both visually and through dialogue. Explain that a playwright must describe the visuals as well as write the dialogue.

Dialogue and Characterization Encourage students, when responding to the question, to discuss what the dialogue reveals about each character and the characters' relationships to one another.

Technology

Character Log

Students can use word processing software to record notes on the characters in the play *The Diary of Anne Frank.* They can record what they learn about the characters in a multi-column chart with the following headings:

Biographical Fact	Personality Trait	Quotation	Page Number

When a fact about or a personal characteristic of a character is revealed, have students record that information under the appropriate heading, including interesting quotations they want to remember. This information will be helpful as they organize a character sketch or compare and contrast characters. **L2**

Active Reading Strategies

Objective

- To understand and apply strategies for reading and comprehending drama

Teach the Strategies

Encourage students to skim the cast list before reading the scene in order to help them visualize who will be involved in the action.

Visualize

Suggest that students read a scene's opening stage directions carefully and that they begin reading the dialogue only when they have a good mental picture of the scene. Encourage them to recall what they have learned previously about the setting—the time of year, the time of day, or any other facts that will help them place the scene in context.

Predict

Point out that often the audience of a play has more information than any of the individual characters. Encourage students to be aware of plot developments that are not revealed to all characters and to predict how these may affect the development of the story.

Teaching Support

ACTIVE READING MODEL

Active Reading Strategies

Tips for Reading Drama

Playwrights usually plan their work for people in a theater audience. Active readers, however, can also enjoy drama.

- For more strategies for reading fluently, see **Reading Handbook,** pp. R84–R86.

VISUALIZE

As you read, take time to understand stage directions. The details you find in these directions will help you visualize the setting and imagine the actors as if they were performing the play in front of you.

Ask Yourself . . .

- Which characters are onstage now? Where are they standing?
- What does this character look like? How is he or she dressed? What is the expression on his or her face?
- What should I remember about the setting of the scene? How does this setting affect or reveal the plot?

PREDICT

In a drama, events occur in logical sequence. As you read, try to predict what will happen next in the play. Base your prediction on what has happened so far and what the characters have revealed about their personalities.

Ask Yourself . . .

- Has the playwright included hints of what might happen next?
- What do I hope will happen to these characters? Are those events likely?
- How will this character react to good or bad news?
- Will the play end happily or unhappily?

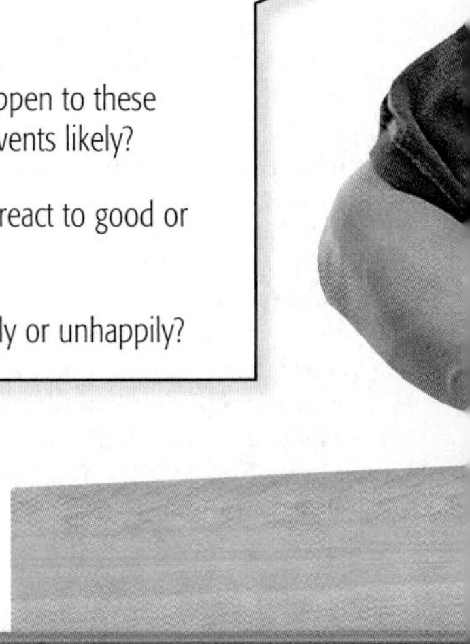

Reading Journal

Suggest that students respond to the text in their reading journals. Tell them that questions, observations, opinions, predictions, and strong reactions are all valid entries.

Activity For "Faces of Dignity," students may use their journals to do the following:
- Record what they already know about the topic of the selection
- Record reactions to segments of the selection that stir them
- List descriptive words that help them picture a situation
- Make a time line showing the order of events
- Comment on what they learned about the Holocaust that they did not know before reading

QUESTION

As you read a play, ask yourself questions about the dialogue, action, and the setting to check your understanding.

Ask Yourself . . .

- Do I follow what is happening in this scene?
- What details about the setting help me understand this play?
- What behavior can I expect from this character?

RESPOND

As a reader or a member of the audience, you will respond to the characters and the situations they face. Getting involved with the characters and their problems will help you get more out of the drama and determine its **theme,** or main message.

Ask Yourself . . .

- What are my feelings about each of the characters?
- Why am I interested in what will happen to them?
- With which of the characters do I feel a particular connection? Do these characters and their problems remind me of anyone I know?

APPLYING THE STRATEGIES

Read the play that follows, *The Diary of Anne Frank.* As you read, use the **Active Reading Model** in the margins of act 1, scene 1, to help you enjoy the play.

Question

Encourage students to imagine themselves in the time and the place of a play's setting. This will help them to understand the actions of the characters, who may be typical of a time when standards of speech and behavior differed from today's.

Respond

Remind students that the purpose of drama is often to reveal something about human nature. Encourage students to consider which aspects of human nature are being explored in a drama. This will help them focus on the play's message.

FACES OF DIGNITY 695

Before Reading

Objectives

- To read and analyze a play
- To identify acts and scenes, dialogue, and stage directions in a play
- To write journal-entry responses

Skills

Reading/Thinking: Inferring; Predicting; Verifying Predictions; Summarizing; Drawing Conclusions; Evaluating; Setting a Purpose for Reading; Elaborating; Synthesizing; Analyzing Arguments; Making Critical Judgments; Generalizing; Paraphrasing

Writing: Journal Entry; Description; Outlining; Persuasion; Dialogue

Vocabulary: Homophones; Context Clues; Etymology; Synonyms

Grammar/Language: Troublesome Pairs; Adjectives and Adverbs; Less/Fewer

Listening/Speaking: Radio Drama; Listening Techniques; Oral Reading; Debate

Life Skills: Creating and Producing; Planning; Interviewing

Collaboration: Literature Groups; Performing; Interdisciplinary Activity

Motivating STUDENTS

Literature Launchers: "A Struggle to Survive"
Videodisc
Side B,
Segment 20
Also available in VHS.

Selection Focus Transparency 60: Have students discuss Zlata's diary and other forms a diary might take today.

Reading Focus: As an extension of the Reading Focus, discuss how students would deal with interacting with others in a crowded space.

ACTIVE READING MODEL

Before You Read

The Diary of Anne Frank, Act 1

MEET FRANCES GOODRICH AND ALBERT HACKETT

"Think of this thirteen-year-old child writing this diary. The vitality of it is amazing," Frances Goodrich has said. Inspired by *Anne Frank: The Diary of a Young Girl*, the authors, a husband-and-wife team, spent two years writing a play about Anne. They met with Anne's father, Otto Frank, the only family member to survive the war, and also visited the building in which the Franks had hidden. The play, *The Diary of Anne Frank*, has won many awards, including the Pulitzer Prize.

The Diary of Anne Frank *was first published in 1956.*

READING FOCUS

Imagine sharing a small living space with several people. What are some of the difficulties you might face in getting along?

Journal

Jot down your ideas about why some people desire more time alone than others do.

Setting a Purpose

Read to find out how several people cope when they are forced to live in a crowded, and very dangerous, situation.

BUILDING BACKGROUND

The Time and Place It is July of 1942 in German-controlled Holland. World War II has been going on for three years.

Did You Know?

During World War II, Jews in Europe were forced into hiding to avoid German labor and death camps. Most hideouts were tiny and uncomfortable: a barn, an attic, a basement, or even the space under a floorboard.

VOCABULARY PREVIEW

conspicuous (kən spik′ ū əs) *adj.* easily seen; apparent; p. 701
unabashed (un′ ə basht′) *adj.* not ashamed or self-conscious; bold; p. 706
loathe (lōth) *v.* to regard with extreme disgust; hate; p. 709
vile (vīl) *adj.* very bad; unpleasant; foul; p. 715
indignantly (in dig′ nənt lē) *adv.* with dignified anger in response to an insult or injustice; p. 718
aggravating (ag′ rə vāt′ ing) *adj.* irritating; annoying; p. 718
subdued (səb dōōd′) *adj.* quiet and downcast; p. 725
jubilation (jōō′ bə lā′ shən) *n.* great joy and excitement; p. 736

696 THEME 7: FACES OF DIGNITY

RESOURCE MANAGER

Teaching Tools and Resources
- Theme Seven Planning Guide
- Literature Groups Sourcebook

Essential Lesson Support

Lesson-Specific Instruction
- Selection Focus Transp. 60
- Lit. Elements Transp. 61–65
- Active Reading Guide,* pp. 61–65
- Sel. Vocab. Practice, pp. 43–44

Assessment
- Selection Quick Checks,* p. 61
- Sel. and Theme Assmt., pp. 109–112
- Testmaker: ExamView Pro
- Performance Assessment, p. 57

Systematic Language Instruction
- Gr. & Comp. Hbk., L. 13.7
- Vocabulary Power, Lesson 32, Unit 7 Review/Test
- Spelling Power, Lesson 28, Unit 7 Review/Proofreading

English Language Learners
- ELL Sourcebook, pp. 84–89
- Spanish Summaries, p. 60
- Spanish Translations, pp. 154–221
- Audio Library*
- English, Yes!

Spec. Needs/Strat. Interven.
- Interactive Rdg. Sbk., pp. T203–T208
- Interactive Rdg. Wkbk., pp. 113–120
- Inclusion Strat. Sbk., pp. 71–72, 83–84
- Audio Library*

* Also available in Spanish

The Diary of Anne Frank

Frances Goodrich and Albert Hackett

The Diary of Anne Frank, 1959. 20th Century Fox. Movie still.

CHARACTERS

MR. FRANK	PETER VAN DAAN	ANNE FRANK
MIEP	MRS. FRANK	MR. KRALER
MRS. VAN DAAN	MARGOT FRANK	MR. DUSSEL
MR. VAN DAAN		

Reading the Selection

SUMMARY

Act 1, Scenes 1–2
After World War II, Otto Frank returns to the attic where he hid with his family and the Van Daans during the Nazi occupation of Amsterdam, Netherlands. Among the items is his daughter Anne's diary. When he begins to read it, the memories transport him back to 1942 and the day that the two families go into hiding in the attic. The families must follow strict rules to ensure they are not discovered. Mr. Kraler and Miep are non-Jewish friends who risk their lives to bring the families food and news of the war.

Spanish Summaries, p. 60

Active Reading Strategies

PREDICT Ask students to predict the relationships between the characters from their position and demeanor in the still photograph of the cast.

VOCABULARY Remind students to use context clues to unlock the meanings of new vocabulary words.

Additional Resources

- ***Active Reading Guide,*** pp. 61–65
- ***Audio Library***
- ***Spanish Audio Library***

Teaching Support

CONNECTING TO OTHER SELECTIONS

The chart at the right shows three ways to connect *The Diary of Anne Frank* to other selections in this book.

For specific teaching strategies, see the ***Theme Seven Planning Guide.***

Connection		Title
Life Skills: Implementing and Performing	→	from *Harriet Tubman: Conductor on the Underground Railroad,* p. 480
Thematic: Heroic Attitudes	→	"The Kid Nobody Could Handle," p. 146
Literary: Character Traits	→	"Thank You in Arabic," p. 574

Active Reading Strategies

VISUALIZE *(Students may note that the stage as described would look like a sparsely furnished, dimly lit attic.)* Point out the directional clues—such as *left, right, center,* and *under*—in the opening stage directions. Encourage students to focus on these directional words to place the scene clearly in their minds.

ACTIVE READING MODEL

ACT 1

SCENE 1

[*The scene remains the same throughout the play. It is the top floor of a warehouse and office building in Amsterdam, Holland. The sharply peaked roof of the building is outlined against a sea of other rooftops, stretching away into the distance. Nearby is the belfry of a church tower, the Westertoren, whose carillon*[1] *rings out the hours. Occasionally faint sounds float up from below: the voices of children playing in the street, the tramp of marching feet, a boat whistle from the canal.*

VISUALIZE

B What would the stage look like if you were part of an audience for this drama?

The three rooms of the top floor and a small attic space above are exposed to our view. The largest of the rooms is in the center, with two small rooms, slightly raised, on either side. On the right is a bathroom, out of sight. A narrow steep flight of stairs at the back leads up to the attic. The rooms are sparsely furnished with a few chairs, cots, a table or two. The windows are painted over, or covered with makeshift blackout curtains.[2] *In the main room there is a sink, a gas ring for cooking and a wood-burning stove for warmth.*

The room on the left is hardly more than a closet. There is a skylight in the sloping ceiling. Directly under this room is a small steep stairwell, with steps leading down to a door. This is the only entrance from the building below. When the door is opened we see that it has been concealed on the outer side by a bookcase attached to it.

The curtain rises on an empty stage. It is late afternoon, November, 1945.

The rooms are dusty, the curtains in rags. Chairs and tables are overturned.

The door at the foot of the small stairwell swings open. MR. FRANK *comes up the steps into view. He is a gentle, cultured European in his middle years. There is still a trace of a German accent in his speech.*

He stands looking slowly around, making a supreme effort at self-control. He is weak, ill. His clothes are threadbare.

After a second he drops his rucksack on the couch and moves slowly about. He opens the door to one of the smaller rooms, and then abruptly closes it again, turning away. He goes to the window at the back, looking off at the Westertoren as its carillon strikes the hour of six, then he moves restlessly on.

From the street below we hear the sound of a barrel organ and children's voices at play. There is a many-colored scarf hanging from a nail. MR. FRANK *takes*

1. The *carillon* (kar′ ə lon′) is a set of bells sounded by machinery, rather than rung manually.
2. *Blackout curtains* were used to hide room lights from enemy bombers.

Teaching Support

MEETING INDIVIDUAL NEEDS — ENGLISH LANGUAGE LEARNERS

Dialogue English language learners may have some difficulty with the sentence fragments in dialogue. Explain that ellipses in the dialogue indicate both pauses and interruptions in speech: an ellipsis in the middle of a line of dialogue indicates a pause, and an ellipsis at the end of a line indicates that the character is interrupted or that his or her voice trails off.

Activity Have two students read aloud the exchange between Mr. Frank and Miep on page 699. The actors should read fluently and pause where indicated by the ellipses. **COLLAB. LEARN.**

Additional Resources

English Language Learners Sourcebook, p. 84

it, putting it around his neck. As he starts back for his rucksack, his eye is caught by something lying on the floor. It is a woman's white glove. He holds it in his hand and suddenly all of his self-control is gone. He breaks down, crying.

We hear footsteps on the stairs. MIEP GIES[3] *comes up, looking for* MR. FRANK. MIEP *is a Dutch girl of about twenty-two. She wears a coat and hat, ready to go home. She is pregnant. Her attitude toward* MR. FRANK *is protective, compassionate.*]

MIEP. Are you all right, Mr. Frank?

MR. FRANK. [*Quickly controlling himself.*] Yes, Miep, yes.

MIEP. Everyone in the office has gone home . . . It's after six. [*Then pleading.*] Don't stay up here, Mr. Frank. What's the use of torturing yourself like this?

MR. FRANK. I've come to say good-bye . . . I'm leaving here, Miep.

MIEP. What do you mean? Where are you going? Where?

MR. FRANK. I don't know yet. I haven't decided.

MIEP. Mr. Frank, you can't leave here! This is your home! Amsterdam is your home. Your business is here, waiting for you . . . You're needed here . . . Now that the war is over, there are things that . . .

MR. FRANK. I can't stay in Amsterdam, Miep. It has too many memories for me. Everywhere there's something . . . the house we lived in . . . the school . . . that street organ playing out there . . . I'm not the person you used to know, Miep. I'm a bitter old man. [*Breaking off.*] Forgive me. I shouldn't speak to you like this . . . after all that you did for us . . . the suffering . . .

MIEP. No. No. It wasn't suffering. You can't say we suffered.

[*As she speaks, she straightens a chair which is overturned.*]

MR. FRANK. I know what you went through, you and Mr. Kraler.[4] I'll remember it as long as I live. [*He gives one last look around.*] Come, Miep.

[*He starts for the steps, then remembers his rucksack, going back to get it.*]

MIEP. [*Hurrying up to a cupboard.*] Mr. Frank, did you see? There are some of your papers here. [*She brings a bundle of papers to him.*] We found them in a heap of rubbish on the floor after . . . after you left.

MR. FRANK. Burn them.

[*He opens his rucksack to put the glove in it.*]

MIEP. But, Mr. Frank, there are letters, notes . . .

RESPOND (C)
How does this opening scene make you feel about Mr. Frank?

QUESTION (D)
What do you think Mr. Frank might be referring to when he says "after all that you did for us"?

QUESTION (E)
Why does Mr. Frank want to burn the bundle of papers that Miep shows him?

3. *Miep Gies* (mēp gēs)
4. *Kraler* (krä′ lər)

C Active Reading Strategies

RESPOND *(Mr. Frank evokes empathy by his actions and demeanor.)*

D Active Reading Strategies

QUESTION *(Miep probably helped his family in the past.)* Ask students to recall the time in which the opening scene is set, and point out Miep's statement beginning, "Now that the war is over."

E Active Reading Strategies

QUESTION *(The papers remind Mr. Frank of a time he wants to forget.)* Encourage students to consider what motivates a character to make certain statements or to take certain actions by imagining themselves as the character and how they would react to the situation portrayed.

INTERDISCIPLINARY CONNECTION

History Adolf Hitler's rise to power as head of the Nazi party and chancellor of Germany is still puzzling to many people. After World War I, which the Germans lost, Germany was virtually bankrupted by the enormous sums of money it was forced to pay to the victorious Allied forces. Just as Germany resolved these problems, a worldwide depression hit, damaging Germany's economy as much as those of other nations. In addition, the Germans were humiliated by their loss of standing and power in the European community. Hitler's forceful, pro-German speeches appealed to the people in their time of economic difficulty.

Activity Have students research Web sites, old newspaper articles, or books about Hitler to find interesting quotations from Hitler's speeches. Students should discuss their findings in class. **L2**

F **Active Reading Strategies**

QUESTION *(The events of the past begin to unfold as Otto reads Anne's diary, and her voice takes the action back in time.)* Ask students what Anne's offstage voice lends to a dramatic production.

G **Active Reading Strategies**

PREDICT *(Anne's diary will reveal her experiences during hiding.)* Encourage students to consider how the rules about Jews may have affected the Franks and Van Daans during their time in hiding. *(The rules made life more dangerous for people such as Miep, who were trying to help the Jews.)* Have students list words that might describe the emotional state of people living under such rules.

H **Active Reading Strategies**

RESPOND Point out to students the absence of any complaints by Anne in her opening statements. Why, do students think, doesn't she talk about being frightened, sad, or confused? *(At the beginning, going into hiding may have seemed like a fun game.)*

Teaching Support

ACTIVE READING MODEL

MR. FRANK. Burn them. All of them.

MIEP. Burn *this?*

[*She hands him a paperbound notebook.*]

MR. FRANK. [*Quietly.*] Anne's diary. [*He opens the diary and begins to read.*] "Monday, the sixth of July, nineteen forty-two." [*To* MIEP.] Nineteen forty-two. Is it possible, Miep? . . . Only three years ago. [*As he continues his reading, he sits down on the couch.*] "Dear Diary, since you and I are going to be great friends, I will start by telling you about myself. My name is Anne Frank. I am thirteen years old. I was born in Germany the twelfth of June, nineteen twenty-nine. As my family is Jewish, we emigrated to Holland when Hitler[5] came to power."

[*As* MR. FRANK *reads on, another voice joins his, as if coming from the air. It is* ANNE'S VOICE.]

F QUESTION: Why does Anne's voice begin to read along with Mr. Frank?

MR. FRANK AND ANNE. "My father started a business, importing spice and herbs. Things went well for us until nineteen forty. Then the war came, and the Dutch capitulation,[6] followed by the arrival of the Germans. Then things got very bad for the Jews."

[MR. FRANK'S VOICE *dies out.* ANNE'S VOICE *continues alone. The lights dim slowly to darkness. The curtain falls on the scene.*]

G PREDICT: What do you think Anne's diary will reveal?

ANNE'S VOICE. You could not do this and you could not do that. They forced Father out of his business. We had to wear yellow stars.[7] I had to turn in my bike. I couldn't go to a Dutch school any more. I couldn't go to the movies, or ride in an automobile, or even on a streetcar, and a million other things. But somehow we children still managed to have fun. Yesterday Father told me we were going into hiding. Where, he wouldn't say. At five o'clock this morning Mother woke me and told me to hurry and get dressed. I was to put on as many clothes as I could. It would look too suspicious if we walked along carrying suitcases. It wasn't until we were on our way that I learned where we were going. Our hiding place was to be upstairs in the building where Father used to have his business. Three other people were coming in with us . . . the Van Daans and their son Peter . . . Father knew the Van Daans but we had never met them . . .

H RESPOND: What is your first impression of *this* Anne Frank?

[*During the last lines the curtain rises on the scene. The lights dim on.* ANNE'S VOICE *fades out.*]

5. Thousands of German Jews left the country after *Hitler* became the head of the government in 1933.
6. Germany began its invasion of the Netherlands on May 10, 1940, and forced the surrender, or *capitulation* (kə pich′ ə lā′ shən), of the Dutch army a few days later.
7. The Nazis ordered Jews to wear *yellow stars* at all times for easy identification. The six-pointed Star of David is a religious symbol of the Jewish people.

MEETING INDIVIDUAL NEEDS

ADVANCED LEARNERS

History Throughout Europe, including the Netherlands, many citizens resisted Hitler's anti-Semitic laws. Many people went into hiding in the Netherlands, and many were helped by the Dutch to escape the occupied country.

Activity Have students research the Dutch resistance movement. Encourage them to find other stories of Dutch people who helped Jews hide or escape. Have students present their findings to the class. **L3**

SCENE 2

[It is early morning, July, 1942. The rooms are bare, as before, but they are now clean and orderly.

MR. VAN DAAN, a tall, portly man in his late forties, is in the main room, pacing up and down, nervously smoking a cigarette. His clothes and overcoat are expensive and well cut.

MRS. VAN DAAN sits on the couch, clutching her possessions, a hatbox, bags, etc. She is a pretty woman in her early forties. She wears a fur coat over her other clothes.

PETER VAN DAAN is standing at the window of the room on the right, looking down at the street below. He is a shy, awkward boy of sixteen. He wears a cap, a raincoat, and long Dutch trousers,[8] like "plus fours." At his feet is a black case, a carrier for his cat. The yellow Star of David is conspicuous on all of their clothes.]

MRS. VAN DAAN. *[Rising, nervous, excited.]* Something's happened to them! I know it!

MR. VAN DAAN. Now, Kerli!

MRS. VAN DAAN. Mr. Frank said they'd be here at seven o'clock. He said . . .

MR. VAN DAAN. They have two miles to walk. You can't expect . . .

MRS. VAN DAAN. They've been picked up. That's what's happened. They've been taken . . .

[MR. VAN DAAN indicates that he hears someone coming.]

MR. VAN DAAN. You see?

[PETER takes up his carrier and his schoolbag, etc., and goes into the main room as MR. FRANK comes up the stairwell from below. MR. FRANK looks much younger now. His movements are brisk, his manner confident. He wears an overcoat and carries his hat and a small cardboard box. He crosses to the VAN DAANS, shaking hands with each of them.]

MR. FRANK. Mrs. Van Daan, Mr. Van Daan, Peter. *[Then, in explanation of their lateness.]* There were too many of the Green Police[9] on the streets . . . we had to take the long way around.

[Up the steps come MARGOT FRANK, MRS. FRANK, MIEP (not pregnant now), and MR. KRALER. All of them carry bags, packages, and so forth. The Star of David is conspicuous on all of the FRANKS' clothing. MARGOT is eighteen, beautiful, quiet, shy. MRS. FRANK is a young mother, gently bred, reserved. She, like MR. FRANK, has a slight German accent. MR. KRALER is a Dutchman, dependable, kindly.

As MR. KRALER and MIEP go upstage[10] to put down their parcels, MRS. FRANK turns back to call ANNE.]

MRS. FRANK. Anne?

[ANNE comes running up the stairs. She is thirteen, quick in her movements, interested

8. *Dutch trousers* are loose pants gathered a few inches below the knees.

9. One branch of the Nazi police force was called the *Green Police* because its members wore green uniforms.

10. *Upstage* refers to the back of the stage; *downstage* is the front, near the audience.

Vocabulary

conspicuous (kən spik′ ū əs) *adj.* easily seen; apparent

I Literary Elements

ACTS AND SCENES Point out to students that this part of the the play is still act 1, but this is now scene 2. Explain that a new scene usually signals the passage of time or a change in location. Have students contrast the time and location of this scene with those of scene 1. *(Scene 1 is set after the war, as Otto is reading Anne's diary. Scene 2 returns to the past and re-creates events as they actually happened.)*

J Literary Elements

FLASHBACK Explain that a flashback is a device used for telling what happened previously that places the audience, or reader, in an earlier time. Ask students what event triggers this flashback. *(Mr. Frank's reading Anne's diary triggers it.)*

K Critical Thinking

INFER Ask students what they can infer from Mrs. Van Daan's dialogue. *(She is obviously anxious and afraid.)*

LIFE SKILLS CONNECTION

Creating and Producing The stage directions for a drama provide information about how the stage should look to the audience. From these instructions the set designer takes his or her cues about how to construct a set. Details are left to the imagination of the individual set designer.

Activity Have students draw the stage set on the basis of the directions provided in scene 1. Remind them that at a minimum they must include whatever the playwrights have included but that they may add other details appropriate to the setting if they wish. Students should display their drawings in the classroom as an aid to other students reading the play. **L2**

VIEWING THE PHOTOGRAPH

The movie from which this photograph is taken is based on the play of the same title, *The Diary of Anne Frank*, by Frances Goodrich and Albert Hackett.

Viewing Response *Anne looks apprehensive as she climbs the stairs.*

Active Reading Strategies

PREDICT Ask students to explain who Mr. Kraler is. Remind them to consider what they already know about who stayed in hiding.

Critical Thinking

INFER Ask students what Miep's statement tells the audience about the families' going into hiding. Was this something they did on the spur of the moment? *(From Miep's statement students should understand that much preparation was made before going into hiding.)*

The Diary of Anne Frank, 1959. 20th Century Fox. Movie still.

Viewing the photograph: What mood, or emotional atmosphere, does this scene suggest to you?

in everything, mercurial[11] in her emotions. She wears a cape, long wool socks and carries a schoolbag.]

MR. FRANK. [*Introducing them.*] My wife, Edith. Mr. and Mrs. Van Daan [*MRS. FRANK hurries over, shaking hands with them.*] . . . their son, Peter . . . my daughters, Margot and Anne.

[*ANNE gives a polite little curtsy as she shakes MR. VAN DAAN's hand. Then she immediately starts off on a tour of investigation of her new home, going upstairs to the attic room.*
MIEP and MR. KRALER are putting the various things they have brought on the shelves.]

MR. KRALER. I'm sorry there is still so much confusion.

MR. FRANK. Please. Don't think of it. After all, we'll have plenty of leisure to arrange everything ourselves.

MIEP. [*To MRS. FRANK.*] We put the stores of food you sent in here. Your drugs are here . . . soap, linen here.

MRS. FRANK. Thank you, Miep.

MIEP. I made up the beds . . . the way Mr. Frank and Mr. Kraler said. [*She starts out.*] Forgive me. I have to hurry. I've got to go to the other side of town to get some ration books[12] for you.

MRS. VAN DAAN. Ration books? If they see our names on ration books, they'll know we're here.

11. Anne is *mercurial* (mər kyoor′ ē əl) in that her emotions change quickly and unpredictably.
12. *Ration books* contain coupons that people use to buy a limited amount of food and supplies.

Teaching Support

REAL-WORLD CONNECTION

Symbols of the Holocaust Explain to students that in the countries Germany occupied during the war, Jews had to wear a Star of David on their clothing at all times. Explain also that Jews who were sent to concentration camps were tattooed with an identification number.

Activity Have students read magazine articles or books containing interviews with Holocaust survivors to learn more about how these symbols affected the people who were forced to wear them. Encourage students to draw conclusions from the information they gathered from multiple sources and present their findings in an oral report. **L2**

MR. KRALER. There isn't anything . . . } *Together*

MIEP. Don't worry. Your names won't be on them. [*As she hurries out.*] I'll be up later. } *Together*

MR. FRANK. Thank you, Miep.

N **MRS. FRANK.** [*To* MR. KRALER.] It's illegal, then, the ration books? We've never done anything illegal.

MR. FRANK. We won't be living here exactly according to regulations.

[*As* MR. KRALER *reassures* MRS. FRANK, *he takes various small things, such as matches, soap, etc., from his pockets, handing them to her.*]

MR. KRALER. This isn't the black market, Mrs. Frank. This is what we call the white market[13] . . . helping all of the hundreds and hundreds who are hiding out in Amsterdam.

[*The carillon is heard playing the quarter-hour before eight.* MR. KRALER *looks at his watch.* ANNE *stops at the window as she comes down the stairs.*]

O **ANNE.** It's the Westertoren!

P **MR. KRALER.** I must go. I must be out of here and downstairs in the office before the workmen get here. [*He starts for the stairs leading out.*] Miep or I, or both of us, will be up each day to bring you food and news and find out what your needs are. Tomorrow I'll get you a better bolt for the door at the foot of the stairs. It needs a bolt that you can throw yourself and open only at our signal. [*To* MR. FRANK.] Oh . . . You'll tell them about the noise?

MR. FRANK. I'll tell them.

MR. KRALER. Good-bye then for the moment. I'll come up again, after the workmen leave.

MR. FRANK. Good-bye, Mr. Kraler.

MRS. FRANK. [*Shaking his hand.*] How can we thank you?

[*The others murmur their good-byes.*]

MR. KRALER. I never thought I'd live to see the day when a man like Mr. Frank would have to go into hiding. When you think—

[*He breaks off, going out.* MR. FRANK *follows him down the steps, bolting the door after him. In the interval before he returns,* PETER *goes over to* MARGOT, *shaking hands with her. As* MR. FRANK *comes back up the steps,* MRS. FRANK *questions him anxiously.*]

MRS. FRANK. What did he mean, about the noise?

MR. FRANK. First let us take off some of these clothes.

[*They all start to take off garment after garment. On each of their coats, sweaters, blouses, suits, dresses, is another yellow Star of David.* MR. *and* MRS. FRANK *are underdressed quite simply. The others wear several things, sweaters, extra dresses, bathrobes, aprons, nightgowns, etc.*]

MR. VAN DAAN. It's a wonder we weren't arrested, walking along the streets . . . Petronella with a fur coat in July . . . and that cat of Peter's crying all the way.

ANNE. [*As she is removing a pair of panties.*] A cat?

MRS. FRANK. [*Shocked.*] Anne, please!

ANNE. It's all right. I've got on three more.

13. In the *black market,* goods were sold illegally, usually at very high prices. In the *white market,* which also violated Nazi laws, goods were donated by people who wanted to help the Jews.

N Literary Elements

IRONY Remind students that irony occurs when a situation or statement is different from what is expected under the circumstances. What is ironic about Mrs. Frank's concern about doing anything illegal? *(They are living illegally by hiding.)*

O Active Reading Strategies

RESPOND Ask students to describe Anne's reaction to the carillon. Have them give possible reasons for her reaction. *(She seems excited and pleased by the familiar sound.)*

P Critical Thinking

VERIFY PREDICTIONS Note that in this dialogue we learn who Mr. Kraler is and what his role will be. Ask students to verify whether this information matches their predictions about Mr. Kraler.

Reading Minilesson

Summarize Remind students that often the beginning of a play or a story gives information about the characters and the setting. Suggest to students that it is a good practice to stop and review what they have learned so far, from time to time, so they can recall various characters as the action progresses.

Activity After reading page 703, have students write a brief summary of facts they have learned thus far about the characters' situation and a brief list of the personality traits of the characters that have been introduced. Invite students to share their summaries in small groups. **L2** **COLLAB. LEARN.**

Additional Resources

Reading Skills Practice Workbook

Q Critical Thinking

DRAWING CONCLUSIONS Note that Mr. Frank resumes his instructions without mentioning the marching soldiers or anyone's fear. Why doesn't he mention it? Have students discuss various reasons he may have for simply resuming his instructions.

[She pulls off two more. Finally, as they have all removed their surplus clothes, they look to MR. FRANK, *waiting for him to speak.]*

MR. FRANK. Now. About the noise. While the men are in the building below, we must have complete quiet. Every sound can be heard down there, not only in the workrooms, but in the offices too. The men come at about eight-thirty, and leave at about five-thirty. So, to be perfectly safe, from eight in the morning until six in the evening we must move only when it is necessary, and then in stockinged feet. We must not speak above a whisper. We must not run any water. We cannot use the sink, or even, forgive me, the w.c.[14] The pipes go down through the workrooms. It would be heard. No trash . . . [MR. FRANK *stops abruptly as he hears the sound of marching feet from the street below. Everyone is motionless, paralyzed with fear.* MR. FRANK *goes quietly into the room on the right to look down out of the window.* ANNE *runs after him, peering out with him. The tramping feet pass without stopping. The tension is relieved.* MR. FRANK, *followed by* ANNE, *returns to the main room and resumes his instructions to the group.*] . . . No trash must ever be thrown out which might reveal that someone is living up here . . . not even a potato paring. We must burn everything in the stove at night. This is the way we must live until it is over, if we are to survive.

Q

[There is silence for a second.]

MRS. FRANK. Until it is over.

MR. FRANK. *[Reassuringly.]* After six we can move about . . . we can talk and laugh and have our supper and read and play games . . . just as we would at home. *[He looks at his watch.]* And now I think it would be wise if we all went to our rooms, and were settled before eight o'clock. Mrs. Van Daan, you and your husband will be upstairs. I regret that there's no place up there for Peter. But he will be here, near us. This will be our common room, where we'll meet to talk and eat and read, like one family.

MR. VAN DAAN. And where do you and Mrs. Frank sleep?

MR. FRANK. This room is also our bedroom.

MRS. VAN DAAN. That isn't right. We'll sleep here and you take the room upstairs.

MR. VAN DAAN. It's your place.

Together

MR. FRANK. Please. I've thought this out for weeks. It's the best arrangement. The only arrangement.

MRS. VAN DAAN. *[To* MR. FRANK.*]* Never, never can we thank you. *[Then to* MRS. FRANK.*]* I don't know what would have happened to us, if it hadn't been for Mr. Frank.

MR. FRANK. You don't know how your husband helped me when I came to this country . . . knowing no one . . . not able to speak the language. I can never repay him for that. *[Going to* VAN DAAN.*]* May I help you with your things?

MR. VAN DAAN. No. No. *[To* MRS. VAN DAAN.*]* Come along, *liefje*.[15]

MRS. VAN DAAN. You'll be all right, Peter? You're not afraid?

PETER. *[Embarrassed.]* Please, Mother.

14. Short for "water closet," the *w.c.* is a bathroom.

15. *Liefje* (lēf′ hyə) or (lēf yə) is Dutch for "darling."

Vo·cab·u·lar·y Skills

Homophones Remind students that homophones are words that sound alike but are spelled differently and have different meanings. Have students identify and define the homophone of *paring*. *(Answer: pairing—grouping with others in pairs.)*

Teaching Support

MEETING INDIVIDUAL NEEDS — SPECIAL NEEDS

Visually Impaired Visually impaired students may find it difficult to recognize different typefaces. For some students, the boldfaced capital letters that indicate who is speaking and italics that indicate stage directions may not be easily distinguishable from the regular typeface used for dialogue.

Activity Help students use other clues. Point out that the stage directions are in brackets and the character names are capitalized. Using page 704, have students highlight the character names and the stage directions. They should then recognize that the remaining words are dialogue. **L1**

Additional Resources

Inclusion Strategies

The Diary of Anne Frank, 1959. 20th Century Fox. Movie still.
Viewing the photograph: What do the expressions on Anne's and Peter's faces reveal about their attitudes toward each other?

[They start up the stairs to the attic room above. MR. FRANK *turns to* MRS. FRANK.*]*

R

MR. FRANK. You too must have some rest, Edith. You didn't close your eyes last night. Nor you, Margot.

ANNE. I slept, Father. Wasn't that funny? I knew it was the last night in my own bed, and yet I slept soundly.

MR. FRANK. I'm glad, Anne. Now you'll be able to help me straighten things in here. [*To* MRS. FRANK *and* MARGOT.] Come with me . . . You and Margot rest in this room for the time being.

[He picks up their clothes, starting for the room on the right.]

MRS. FRANK. You're sure . . . ? I could help . . . And Anne hasn't had her milk . . .

MR. FRANK. I'll give it to her. [*To* ANNE *and* PETER.] Anne, Peter . . . it's best that you take off your shoes now, before you forget.

[He leads the way to the room, followed by MARGOT.*]*

MRS. FRANK. You're sure you're not tired, Anne?

ANNE. I feel fine. I'm going to help Father.

MRS. FRANK. Peter, I'm glad you are to be with us.

PETER. Yes, Mrs. Frank.

*[*MRS. FRANK *goes to join* MR. FRANK *and* MARGOT.

During the following scene MR. FRANK *helps* MARGOT *and* MRS. FRANK *to hang up their clothes. Then he persuades them both to lie down and rest. The* VAN DAANS *in their room above settle themselves. In the main room* ANNE *and* PETER *remove their shoes.* PETER *takes his cat out of the carrier.]*

ANNE. What's your cat's name?

PETER. Mouschi.[16]

ANNE. Mouschi! Mouschi! Mouschi! [*She picks up the cat, walking away with it. To* PETER.] I love cats. I have one . . . a darling little cat. But they made me leave her behind. I left some food and a note for the neighbors to take care of her . . . I'm going to miss her terribly. What is yours? A him or a her?

S

PETER. He's a tom. He doesn't like strangers.

[He takes the cat from her, putting it back in its carrier.]

16. ***Mouschi*** (mōōs′ kē)

VIEWING THE PHOTOGRAPH

Viewing Response *Anne is open and cheerful, but Peter is more reserved.*

R Active Reading Strategies

QUESTION Note the contrast between Anne's reaction to her last night at home and the reactions shown by Margot and Mrs. Frank. What does this tell the audience about each of these characters? *(Margot and Mrs. Frank did not sleep because they were fearful, but Anne did sleep, suggesting her optimism.)*

S Critical Thinking

EVALUATE Ask students to consider whether Peter's statement that his cat doesn't like strangers is true. Why may Peter say this? *(He may want his cat's affection for himself. Being shy and awkward, he may be using this excuse to close off communication.)*

Reading Minilesson

Set a Purpose for Reading When students read for a specific purpose, reading rate and comprehension improve. Explain that focusing on a question can help them organize and better understand any material they read. Share with students that reading for the purpose of teaching, or helping others understand the material, is a good way to learn more about the materials themselves.

Activity Have students select a page from the play and compose four questions to teach the material. They should write two questions that review the action and two about character development, irony, foreshadowing, or symbolism. Use the questions for discussion. **L2**

Additional Resources

Reading Skills Practice Workbook

T **Literary Elements**

CHARACTERIZATION Ask students what Peter's and Anne's exchange reveals about their personalities. *(Anne is very personable, whereas Peter is reserved and shy.)*

U **Literary Elements**

SYMBOLISM Have students consider the symbolic meaning that the star can still be seen after it has been removed; in effect, it cannot be removed. What is it that the star symbolizes that cannot be removed? *(The Nazis' feelings toward and treatment of the Jews cannot be removed; also Anne's religion is always with her.)*

ANNE. [*Unabashed.*] Then I'll have to stop being a stranger, won't I? Is he fixed?

PETER. [*Startled.*] Huh?

ANNE. Did you have him fixed?

PETER. No.

ANNE. Oh, you ought to have him fixed—to keep him from—you know, fighting. Where did you go to school?

PETER. Jewish Secondary.

ANNE. But that's where Margot and I go! I never saw you around.

PETER. I used to see you . . . sometimes . . .

ANNE. You did?

PETER. . . . in the school yard. You were always in the middle of a bunch of kids.

[*He takes a penknife from his pocket.*]

ANNE. Why didn't you ever come over?

PETER. I'm sort of a lone wolf.

[*He starts to rip off his Star of David.*]

ANNE. What are you doing?

PETER. Taking it off.

ANNE. But you can't do that. They'll arrest you if you go out without your star.

[*He tosses his knife on the table.*]

PETER. Who's going out?

ANNE. Why, of course! You're right! Of course we don't need them any more. [*She picks up his knife and starts to take her star off.*] I wonder what our friends will think when we don't show up today?

PETER. I didn't have any dates with anyone.

ANNE. Oh, I did. I had a date with Jopie to go and play ping-pong at her house. Do you know Jopie de Waal?

PETER. No.

ANNE. Jopie's my best friend. I wonder what she'll think when she telephones and there's no answer? . . . Probably she'll go over to the house . . . I wonder what she'll think . . . we left everything as if we'd suddenly been called away . . . breakfast dishes in the sink . . . beds not made . . . [*As she pulls off her star, the cloth underneath shows clearly the color and form of the star.*] Look! It's still there! [*PETER goes over to the stove with his star.*] What're you going to do with yours?

PETER. Burn it.

ANNE. [*She starts to throw hers in, and cannot.*] It's funny, I can't throw mine away. I don't know why.

PETER. You can't throw . . . ? Something they branded you with . . . ? That they made you wear so they could spit on you?

ANNE. I know. I know. But after all, it *is* the Star of David, isn't it?

[*In the bedroom, right, MARGOT and MRS. FRANK are lying down. MR. FRANK starts quietly out.*]

PETER. Maybe it's different for a girl.

[*MR. FRANK comes into the main room.*]

MR. FRANK. Forgive me, Peter. Now let me see. We must find a bed for your cat. [*He goes to a cupboard.*] I'm glad you brought your cat. Anne was feeling so badly about hers. [*Getting a used small washtub.*] Here we are. Will it be comfortable in that?

PETER. [*Gathering up his things.*] Thanks.

MR. FRANK. [*Opening the door of the room on the left.*] And here is your room. But I warn you, Peter, you can't grow any more. Not an inch, or you'll have to sleep with

Vocabulary
unabashed (un′ ə basht′) *adj.* not ashamed or self-conscious; bold

Teaching Support

MEETING INDIVIDUAL NEEDS

MULTIPLE MODES OF EXPRESSION

Spatial Students with spatial learning styles will benefit from making something that helps them understand the story. Explain that the families' cramped quarters are an important part of the story.

Activity Have these students build a model stage set based on the playwrights' description of the scene. They may want to work in pairs on this project. Display the models in the classroom for students' reference while they are reading the play. **L2** COLLAB. LEARN.

your feet out of the skylight. Are you hungry?

PETER. No.

MR. FRANK. We have some bread and butter.

PETER. No, thank you.

MR. FRANK. You can have it for luncheon then. And tonight we will have a real supper . . . our first supper together.

PETER. Thanks. Thanks.

[*He goes into his room. During the following scene he arranges his possessions in his new room.*]

MR. FRANK. That's a nice boy, Peter.

ANNE. He's awfully shy, isn't he?

MR. FRANK. You'll like him, I know.

ANNE. I certainly hope so, since he's the only boy I'm likely to see for months and months.

[*MR. FRANK sits down, taking off his shoes.*]

MR. FRANK. Annele,[17] there's a box there. Will you open it?

[*He indicates a carton on the couch. ANNE brings it to the center table. In the street below there is the sound of children playing.*]

ANNE. [*As she opens the carton.*] You know the way I'm going to think of it here? I'm going to think of it as a boarding house. A very peculiar summer boarding house, like the one that we—[*She breaks off as she pulls out some photographs.*] Father! My movie stars! I was wondering where they were! I was looking for them this morning . . . and Queen Wilhelmina![18] How wonderful!

17. Both *Annele* (än′ ə lə) and *Anneke,* which is used later, are terms of affection.

18. *Wilhelmina* (wil′ hel mē′ nə) was queen of the Netherlands from 1890 to 1948. She and her family escaped to England at the time of the German invasion.

MR. FRANK. There's something more. Go on. Look further.

[*He goes over to the sink, pouring a glass of milk from a thermos bottle.*]

ANNE. [*Pulling out a pasteboard-bound book.*] A diary! [*She throws her arms around her father.*] I've never had a diary. And I've always longed for one. [*She looks around the room.*] Pencil, pencil, pencil, pencil. [*She starts down the stairs.*] I'm going down to the office to get a pencil.

MR. FRANK. Anne! No!

[*He goes after her, catching her by the arm and pulling her back.*]

ANNE. [*Startled.*] But there's no one in the building now.

MR. FRANK. It doesn't matter. I don't want you ever to go beyond that door.

ANNE. [*Sobered.*] Never . . . ? Not even at nighttime, when everyone is gone? Or on Sundays? Can't I go down to listen to the radio?

MR. FRANK. Never. I am sorry, Anneke. It isn't safe. No, you must never go beyond that door.

[*For the first time ANNE realizes what "going into hiding" means.*]

ANNE. I see.

MR. FRANK. It'll be hard, I know. But always remember this, Anneke. There are no walls, there are no bolts, no locks that anyone can put on your mind. Miep will bring us books. We will read history, poetry, mythology. [*He gives her the glass of milk.*] Here's your milk. [*With his arm about her, they go over to the couch, sitting down side by side.*] As a matter of fact, between us, Anne, being here has certain advantages for you. For instance, you remember the battle you had with your

V Active Reading Strategies

REVIEW Ask students to identify the contents of the box. Why is Anne so happy to have these things? *(The pictures are her prized possessions; they remind her of home. A diary is something she has always wanted.)*

W Critical Thinking

SYNTHESIZE Ask students to describe Mr. Frank's relationship with Anne. Have them refer to specific examples from the text that support their description. *(Mr. Frank and Anne are close and seem to communicate well. Examples include when Mr. Frank asks Anne to help him straighten up while the others rest and when they talk about Peter.)*

X Active Reading Strategies

EVALUATE Ask students what this statement means. Have them refer to examples from the text that suggest Anne has not fully realized what hiding means before this. *(Examples include the fact that Anne slept soundly the night before, her excitement at being near the Westeroren, her running to the window when the soldiers march by, and her running down to get a pencil.)*

Listening and Speaking Minilesson

Radio Drama Explain to students that before television, dramas were presented on the radio. Point out that radio actors had to compensate for the lack of visual clues by describing scenes and objects in their speech.

Activity Have students perform a scene from the play as a radio drama. Suggest they consider how they can express the appropriate emotion through their interpretation of the dialogue. Ask a student volunteer to make sound effects to help set the mood. Have audience members face away from the performance to help them focus on the dialogue. **L2** COLLAB. LEARN.

VIEWING THE PHOTOGRAPH

Viewing Response *Anne and her father appear to be close. He appears to care a great deal for her.*

The Diary of Anne Frank, 1959. 20th Century Fox. Movie still.

Viewing the photograph: What does this scene tell you about the relationship between Anne and her father?

Teaching Support

Grammar and Language *Minilesson*

Troublesome Pairs Review with students that *it's* is a contraction of *it is*. Have students reread the statements on page 706: "It's funny, I can't throw mine away" and "Maybe it's different for a girl." Have students reread both statements, replacing *it's* with *it is* to understand that the statement still makes sense. Explain to students that the possessive form of *it* takes no apostrophe. *(its)*

Activity Read the following sentence to students: "It's time to take the car to the shop to replace its tires." Have students identify both uses in the sentence. Encourage them to try replacing *its* with *it is* to determine whether the apostrophe is needed. Ask students to write two sentences using *it's* and two using *its* to practice using these words correctly. **L1**

Additional Resources

- ***Grammar and Language Transparency 60***
- ***Grammar and Language Workbook,*** p. 113
- ***Grammar and Composition Handbook,*** Lesson 13.7
- ***Writer's Choice,*** Lesson 17.2

Y mother the other day on the subject of overshoes? You said you'd rather die than wear overshoes? But in the end you had to wear them? Well now, you see, for as long as we are here you will never have to wear overshoes! Isn't that good? And the coat that you inherited from Margot, you won't have to wear that any more. And the piano! You won't have to practice on the piano. I tell you, this is going to be a fine life for you!

[ANNE's panic is gone. PETER appears in the doorway of his room, with a saucer in his hand. He is carrying his cat.]

Z **PETER.** I . . . I . . . I thought I'd better get some water for Mouschi before . . .

MR. FRANK. Of course.

[As he starts toward the sink the carillon begins to chime the hour of eight. He tiptoes to the window at the back and looks down at the street below. He turns to PETER, indicating in pantomime that it is too late. PETER starts back for his room. He steps on a creaking board. The three of them are frozen for a minute in fear. AA *As PETER starts away again, ANNE tiptoes over to him and pours some of the milk from her glass into the saucer for the cat. PETER squats on the floor, putting the milk before the cat. MR. FRANK gives ANNE his fountain pen, and then goes into the room at the right. For a second ANNE watches the cat, then she goes over to the center table, and opens her diary.*

In the room at the right, MRS. FRANK has sat up quickly at the sound of the carillon. MR. FRANK comes in and sits down beside her on the settee, his arm comfortingly around her.

Upstairs, in the attic room, MR. and MRS. VAN DAAN have hung their clothes in the closet and are now seated on the iron bed. MRS. VAN DAAN leans back exhausted. MR. VAN DAAN fans her with a newspaper. ANNE starts to write in her diary. The lights dim out, the curtain falls. BB

In the darkness ANNE'S VOICE comes to us again, faintly at first, and then with growing strength.]

ANNE'S VOICE. I expect I should be describing what it feels like to go into hiding. But I really don't know yet myself. I only know it's funny never to be able to go outdoors . . . never to breathe fresh air . . . never to run and shout and jump. It's the silence in the nights that frightens me most. Every time I hear a creak in the house, or a step on the street outside, I'm sure they're coming for us. The days aren't so bad. At least we know that Miep and Mr. Kraler are down there below us in the office. Our protectors, we call them. I asked Father what would happen to them if the Nazis found out they were hiding us. Pim said that they would suffer the same fate that we would . . . Imagine! They know this, and yet when they come up here, they're always cheerful and gay as if there were nothing in the world to bother them . . . Friday, the twenty-first of August, nineteen forty-two. Today I'm going to tell you our general news. Mother is unbearable. She insists on treating me like a baby, which I loathe. Otherwise things are going better. The weather is . . .

[As ANNE'S VOICE is fading out, the curtain rises on the scene.]

Vocabulary

loathe (lōth) *v.* to regard with extreme disgust or hatred; hate

Y Active Reading Strategies

QUESTION Ask students why they think Mr. Frank lists all of these "good" things for Anne. *(He does not want her to become disheartened.)*

Z Active Reading Strategies

REVIEW Ask students to explain what Peter means by "before." *(He means before they have to be quiet.)* Have them recall the rules spelled out earlier and what time of day it is now. *(They cannot run water after the workers arrive at 8:00.)*

AA Author's Craft

STAGE DIRECTIONS Note how much the playwright reveals to the audience about the characters without dialogue. Have students describe what they learn about each character through these actions. *(Anne is generous; Peter cares for the cat; Mrs. Frank is nervous; Mr. Frank takes care of her.)*

BB Active Reading Strategies

PREDICT Ask students to predict which characters will have the most and least trouble with their experience in hiding. Have them support their predictions with examples.

Thematic Focus

Faces of Dignity Ask students which character shows the most dignity.

ASSESSMENT

Quick Checks, p. 61

Writing *Minilesson*

Descriptive Writing News writing requires the ability to describe events so that the reader can understand what has happened. Explain that a good news story does this by beginning with a descriptive sentence that summarizes the story. An opening description should also be interesting enough to make the reader want to read more.

Activity Have students imagine that the war ends while the Franks are still in hiding and that the students are reporters who discover them. Ask students to write the first line of a news story about the Franks. What would make the reader want to read the rest of the story? **L2**

Additional Resources

Writer's Choice, Lesson 3.1

Responding to the Selection

PERSONAL RESPONSE

Students' responses should refer to specific examples from the text to support their explanations.

Active Reading Response

Students should give explanations for their choices.

Analyzing Literature

1. He is saying good-bye because he is leaving. Miep shows him Anne's diary. Students may suggest the play opens with this scene to explain that the story comes from Anne's diary or to inform the audience that Mr. Frank is the only survivor.
2. Mrs. Van Daan is afraid that the Franks have been captured because she recognizes how serious the situation is.
3. He is grateful to Mr. Van Daan for helping him when he first arrived in Holland. Mr. Frank makes sacrifices for others.
4. Students' responses should refer to specific examples from the text.
5. Possible responses include that some people will want more privacy than others and that they have different reactions to their circumstances.
6. Possible responses: Anne feels closer to her father. She wants to be treated as an adult.

Extending Your Response

Literature Groups Groups may want to discuss whether they agree with the statement. COLLAB. LEARN.

Personal Writing

Students' journal entries should

- address the students' own reactions to living under similar circumstances

Responding to Literature

PERSONAL RESPONSE

- Which two characters do you find most interesting so far? Why?

Active Reading Response

- Which Active Reading notes did you find most helpful? Why?

Analyzing Literature

RECALL AND INTERPRET

1. Why is Mr. Frank in the warehouse in scene 1, and what occurs that he does not expect? Why do you think the play opens with this scene?
2. What is worrying Mrs. Van Daan as scene 2 begins? Does she understand the seriousness of the situation? Explain.
3. Why is Mr. Frank grateful to Mr. Van Daan? What do Mr. Frank's actions toward the Van Daans reveal about him?

EVALUATE AND CONNECT

4. Compare the attitudes of Anne and Peter toward their yellow stars as they remove them from their clothes. Which character behaves the way you might have acted? Explain.
5. How does the first conversation between Anne and Peter introduce the problems in store for the people in the annex?
6. Compare Anne's talk with her father and her diary entry about her mother. How might these events indicate future problems in the annex? Review what you wrote for the **Focus Activity** on page 696 to help you answer this question.

LITERARY ELEMENTS

Acts and Scenes

In a play, an **act** covers a significant part of the plot. Acts are divided into **scenes,** which are comparable to the chapters of a book. A change in scene often indicates a change in time or place. Act 1, scene 1 of *The Diary of Anne Frank* takes place in the Secret Annex in November of 1945.

1. Where and when does act 1, scene 2 take place?
2. What changes take place between scene 1 and scene 2?

- See **Literary Terms Handbook,** pp. R1 and R9.

Extending Your Response

Literature Groups

Words of Comfort Mr. Frank tells Anne: "There are no walls, there are no bolts, no locks that anyone can put on your mind." Do you agree that it is a reassuring concept? Discuss your thoughts.

Personal Writing

Reflections on a Diary How is Anne adjusting as scene 2 ends? What frustrations would you share with her if you were living under similar circumstances? Respond in a journal entry of your own.

LITERARY ELEMENTS

1. Act 1, scene 2, takes place in the annex in July 1942.
2. The setting for scene 2 is three years earlier.

Additional Resources

Literary Elements Transparency 61

ASSESSMENT

- ***Quick Checks,*** p. 61
- ***Selection and Theme Assessment,*** pp. 109–112
- ***Performance Assessment,*** p. 57
- ***Testmaker: ExamView Pro***
- ***Interactive Tutor: Self-Assessment***

SCENE 3

A [It is a little after six o'clock in the evening, two months later.

B MARGOT is in the bedroom at the right, studying. MR. VAN DAAN is lying down in the attic room above.

The rest of the "family" is in the main room. ANNE and PETER sit opposite each other at the center table, where they have been doing their lessons. MRS. FRANK is on the couch. MRS. VAN DAAN is seated with her fur coat, on which she has been sewing, in her lap. None of them are wearing their shoes.

Their eyes are on MR. FRANK, waiting for him to give them the signal which will release them from their day-long quiet. MR. FRANK, his shoes in his hand, stands looking down out of the window at the back, watching to be sure that all of the workmen have left the building below.

After a few seconds of motionless silence, MR. FRANK turns from the window.]

MR. FRANK. [*Quietly, to the group.*] It's safe now. The last workman has left.

[There is an immediate stir of relief.]

ANNE. [*Her pent-up energy explodes.*] WHEE!

MRS. FRANK. [*Startled, amused.*] Anne!

MRS. VAN DAAN. I'm first for the w.c.

[She hurries off to the bathroom. MRS. FRANK puts on her shoes and starts up to the sink to prepare supper. ANNE sneaks PETER's shoes from under the table and hides them behind her back. MR. FRANK goes into MARGOT's room.]

MR. FRANK. [*To MARGOT.*] Six o'clock. School's over.

[MARGOT gets up, stretching. MR. FRANK sits down to put on his shoes. In the main room PETER tries to find his.]

PETER. [*To ANNE.*] Have you seen my shoes?

ANNE. [*Innocently.*] Your shoes?

PETER. You've taken them, haven't you?

ANNE. I don't know what you're talking about.

PETER. You're going to be sorry!

ANNE. Am I?

[PETER goes after her. ANNE, with his shoes in her hand, runs from him, dodging behind her mother.]

MRS. FRANK. [*Protesting.*] Anne, dear!

PETER. Wait till I get you!

C **ANNE.** I'm waiting! [*PETER makes a lunge for her. They both fall to the floor. PETER pins her down, wrestling with her to get the shoes.*] Don't! Don't! Peter, stop it. Ouch!

MRS. FRANK. Anne! . . . Peter!

[Suddenly PETER becomes self-conscious. He grabs his shoes roughly and starts for his room.]

ANNE. [*Following him.*] Peter, where are you going? Come dance with me.

PETER. I tell you I don't know how.

ANNE. I'll teach you.

PETER. I'm going to give Mouschi his dinner.

ANNE. Can I watch?

PETER. He doesn't like people around while he eats.

Reading the Selection

SUMMARY

Act 1, Scene 3

Life is getting tense for the occupants of the Secret Annex. The Franks and Van Daans have been in the attic for two months, and the signs of confinement are beginning to show. Anne, still a child, is rambunctious and curious. Mr. Dussel, a cranky, fussy dentist, moves in with the two families. He brings horrible news that counters Mr. Kraler's reports that things are improving.

Spanish Summaries, p. 60

A Literary Elements

ACTS AND SCENES Have students identify the change that marks a new scene here. *(Two months have passed.)*

B Critical Thinking

INFER Have students speculate on how each of the people in the annex has been spending his or her days, on the basis of information in the stage directions.

C Literary Elements

CONFLICT Review the element of internal conflict, or conflict within a character. Ask students to explain Peter's internal conflict. *(Peter enjoys Anne's company, but he wants to give the impression of being a loner.)*

Teaching Support

MEETING INDIVIDUAL NEEDS: MULTIPLE MODES OF EXPRESSION

Logical and Mathematical Students with logical and mathematical learning abilities may understand the action of this drama by using a chart to represent graphically the actions of the characters. Explain that much of what occurs in this play takes the form of cause and effect. One character does something that leads to a result, or effect.

Activity Have students make a chart of the causes and effects in two scenes from the play. Charts should have three columns, labeled *Character, Cause,* and *Effect*. An example might be

Peter	Feeding cat	Floor squeaks

L2

VIEWING THE PHOTOGRAPH

Viewing Response *Mr. Frank has the closest relationship to Anne. Mr. Van Daan doesn't seem to be amused by her. Mrs. Frank enjoys seeing Anne in a happy mood.*

The Diary of Anne Frank, 1959. 20th Century Fox. Movie still.

Viewing the photograph: Notice the facial expressions of the adults in this scene. How does each person seem to respond to Anne?

Teaching Support

MEETING INDIVIDUAL NEEDS

ENGLISH LANGUAGE LEARNERS

Directional Words Students learning English may have difficulty understanding the spatial relationships signaled by directional words used to describe a setting. Review the terms *in front of, behind, next to, beside, above*, and *below*. Also explain that the directions *left* and *right* are from the point of view of the actors, not the audience.

Activity Bring in a picture of a room from a magazine. Have students describe the location of various objects in the room using each of the terms above.

Additional Resources

English Language Learners Sourcebook, p. 85

ANNE. Peter, please.

PETER. No!

[*He goes into his room.* ANNE *slams his door after him.*]

MRS. FRANK. Anne, dear, I think you shouldn't play like that with Peter. It's not dignified.

ANNE. Who cares if it's dignified? I don't want to be dignified.

[MR. FRANK *and* MARGOT *come from the room on the right.* MARGOT *goes to help her mother.* MR. FRANK *starts for the center table to correct* MARGOT*'s school papers.*]

D **MRS. FRANK.** [*To* ANNE.] You complain that I don't treat you like a grown-up. But when I do, you resent it.

ANNE. I only want some fun . . . someone to laugh and clown with . . . After you've sat still all day and hardly moved, you've got to have some fun. I don't know what's the matter with that boy.

MR. FRANK. He isn't used to girls. Give him a little time.

ANNE. Time? Isn't two months time? I could cry. [*Catching hold of* MARGOT.] Come on, Margot . . . dance with me. Come on, please.

MARGOT. I have to help with supper.

E **ANNE.** You know we're going to forget how to dance . . . When we get out we won't remember a thing.

[*She starts to sing and dance by herself.* MR. FRANK *takes her in his arms, waltzing with her.* MRS. VAN DAAN *comes in from the bathroom.*]

MRS. VAN DAAN. Next? [*She looks around as she starts putting on her shoes.*] Where's Peter?

ANNE. [*As they are dancing.*] Where would he be!

MRS. VAN DAAN. He hasn't finished his lessons, has he? His father'll kill him if he catches him in there with that cat and his work not done. [MR. FRANK *and* ANNE *finish their dance. They bow to each other with extravagant formality.*] Anne, get him out of there, will you?

ANNE. [*At* PETER*'s door.*] Peter? Peter?

PETER. [*Opening the door a crack.*] What is it?

ANNE. Your mother says to come out.

PETER. I'm giving Mouschi his dinner.

MRS. VAN DAAN. You know what your father says.

[*She sits on the couch, sewing on the lining of her fur coat.*]

PETER. For heaven's sake, I haven't even looked at him since lunch.

MRS. VAN DAAN. I'm just telling you, that's all.

ANNE. I'll feed him.

PETER. I don't want you in there.

MRS. VAN DAAN. Peter!

PETER. [*To* ANNE.] Then give him his dinner and come right out, you hear?

[*He comes back to the table.* ANNE *shuts the door of* PETER*'s room after her and disappears behind the curtain covering his closet.*]

MRS. VAN DAAN. [*To* PETER.] Now is that any way to talk to your little girlfriend?

PETER. Mother . . . for heaven's sake . . . will you please stop saying that?

MRS. VAN DAAN. Look at him blush! Look at him! F

PETER. Please! I'm not . . . anyway . . . let me alone, will you?

D Critical Thinking

ANALYZE ARGUMENTS Ask students to consider Mrs. Frank's statement. Does she make a good point? Is she treating Anne like a grown-up? Is Anne behaving like one? Have students support their answers.

E Literary Elements

IRONY Note the irony in Anne's remark about getting out. Encourage students to note other examples of such irony as they read the play.

F Active Reading Strategies

RESPOND Ask students to describe their reaction to Mrs. Van Daan and to Peter's relationship with her. Are students sympathetic to Peter? *(Most students will sympathize with Peter.)*

MEETING INDIVIDUAL NEEDS — MULTIPLE MODES OF EXPRESSION

Musical Explain to students that background music is often used in drama productions to help set the mood. The music used in a theatrical production or a movie is called a *score.*

Activity Have students identify the points in scenes where they would add music. Ask them to describe the type of music they would select and how it would help set the mood. **L2**

G Literary Elements

DIALOGUE Ask students to describe the tone of the dialogue in this section. What tone do the playwrights want to get across with this dialogue? *(The dialogue has a comic tone. Anne and Peter are teasing each other, showing they are behaving like normal children despite their circumstances.)*

H Critical Thinking

SYNTHESIZE Invite students to describe what life is like for the two families on the basis of the dialogue and stage directions on this page. What difficulties are they facing? *(The families are crowded and having difficulty finding any privacy.)*

MRS. VAN DAAN. He acts like it was something to be ashamed of. It's nothing to be ashamed of, to have a little girlfriend.

PETER. You're crazy. She's only thirteen.

MRS. VAN DAAN. So what? And you're sixteen. Just perfect. Your father's ten years older than I am. [*To* MR. FRANK.] I warn you, Mr. Frank, if this war lasts much longer, we're going to be related and then . . .

MR. FRANK. *Mazeltov!*[19]

MRS. FRANK. [*Deliberately changing the conversation.*] I wonder where Miep is. She's usually so prompt.

G

[*Suddenly everything else is forgotten as they hear the sound of an automobile coming to a screeching stop in the street below. They are tense, motionless in their terror. The car starts away. A wave of relief sweeps over them. They pick up their occupations again.* ANNE *flings open the door of* PETER'*s room, making a dramatic entrance. She is dressed in* PETER'*s clothes.* PETER *looks at her in fury. The others are amused.*]

ANNE. Good evening, everyone. Forgive me if I don't stay. [*She jumps up on a chair.*] I have a friend waiting for me in there. My friend Tom. Tom Cat. Some people say that we look alike. But Tom has the most beautiful whiskers, and I have only a little fuzz. I am hoping . . . in time . . .

PETER. All right, Mrs. Quack Quack!

ANNE. [*Outraged—jumping down.*] Peter!

PETER. I heard about you . . . How you talked so much in class they called you Mrs. Quack Quack. How Mr. Smitter made you write a composition . . . "'Quack, quack,' said Mrs. Quack Quack."

ANNE. Well, go on. Tell them the rest. How it was so good he read it out loud to the class and then read it to all his other classes!

PETER. Quack! Quack! Quack . . . Quack . . . Quack . . .

[ANNE *pulls off the coat and trousers.*]

ANNE. You are the most intolerable, insufferable[20] boy I've ever met!

[*She throws the clothes down the stairwell.* PETER *goes down after them.*]

PETER. Quack, quack, quack!

MRS. VAN DAAN. [*To* ANNE.] That's right, Anneke! Give it to him!

ANNE. With all the boys in the world . . . Why I had to get locked up with one like you! . . .

PETER. Quack, quack, quack, and from now on stay out of my room!

[*As* PETER *passes her,* ANNE *puts out her foot, tripping him. He picks himself up, and goes on into his room.*]

MRS. FRANK. [*Quietly.*] Anne, dear . . . your hair. [*She feels* ANNE'*s forehead.*] You're warm. Are you feeling all right?

ANNE. Please, Mother.

[*She goes over to the center table, slipping into her shoes.*]

MRS. FRANK. [*Following her.*] You haven't a fever, have you?

ANNE. [*Pulling away.*] No. No.

MRS. FRANK. You know we can't call a doctor here, ever. There's only one thing to do . . . watch carefully. Prevent an illness before it comes. Let me see your tongue.

ANNE. Mother, this is perfectly absurd.

MRS. FRANK. Anne, dear, don't be such a baby. Let me see your tongue. [*As* ANNE

19. *Mazeltov* (mä′ zəl tof) or (mä zəl tōv′) is a Hebrew word used to express congratulations or best wishes.

20. Both *intolerable* and *insufferable* mean "unbearable."

Teaching Support

Writing Minilesson

Persuasion Explain to students that persuasion is written for the specific purpose of convincing the reader to agree with an opinion. Point out that good persuasive writing includes examples that help the reader come to the same conclusion about a topic as the writer.

Activity Ask students to select a character from the play that completes one of these sentences: "____ would be a good friend," or "____ would not be a good friend." Have students write three to four paragraphs, persuading the reader to agree by using examples of the character's behavior. **L2**

Additional Resources

Writer's Choice, Lesson 6.1

refuses, MRS. FRANK *appeals to* MR. FRANK.] Otto . . . ?

MR. FRANK. You hear your mother, Anne.

[ANNE *flicks out her tongue for a second, then turns away.*]

MRS. FRANK. Come on—open up! [*As* ANNE *opens her mouth very wide.*] You seem all right . . . but perhaps an aspirin . . .

MRS. VAN DAAN. For heaven's sake, don't give that child any pills. I waited for fifteen minutes this morning for her to come out of the w.c.

ANNE. I was washing my hair!

MR. FRANK. I think there's nothing the matter with our Anne that a ride on her bike, or a visit with her friend Jopie de Waal wouldn't cure. Isn't that so, Anne?

[MR. VAN DAAN *comes down into the room. From outside we hear faint sounds of bombers going over and a burst of ack-ack.*][21]

MR. VAN DAAN. Miep not come yet?

MRS. VAN DAAN. The workmen just left, a little while ago.

MR. VAN DAAN. What's for dinner tonight?

MRS. VAN DAAN. Beans.

MR. VAN DAAN. Not again!

MRS. VAN DAAN. Poor Putti! I know. But what can we do? That's all that Miep brought us.

[MR. VAN DAAN *starts to pace, his hands behind his back.* ANNE *follows behind him, imitating him.*]

ANNE. We are now in what is known as the "bean cycle." Beans boiled, beans *en casserole,* beans with strings, beans without strings . . .

[PETER *has come out of his room. He slides into his place at the table, becoming immediately absorbed in his studies.*]

MR. VAN DAAN. [*To* PETER.] I saw you . . . in there, playing with your cat.

MRS. VAN DAAN. He just went in for a second, putting his coat away. He's been out here all the time, doing his lessons.

MR. FRANK. [*Looking up from the papers.*] Anne, you got an excellent in your history paper today . . . and very good in Latin.

ANNE. [*Sitting beside him.*] How about algebra?

MR. FRANK. I'll have to make a confession. Up until now I've managed to stay ahead of you in algebra. Today you caught up with me. We'll leave it to Margot to correct.

ANNE. Isn't algebra vile, Pim!

MR. FRANK. Vile!

MARGOT. [*To* MR. FRANK.] How did I do?

ANNE. [*Getting up.*] Excellent, excellent, excellent, excellent!

MR. FRANK. [*To* MARGOT.] You should have used the subjunctive[22] here . . .

MARGOT. Should I? . . . I thought . . . look here . . . I didn't use it here . . .

[*The two become absorbed in the papers.*]

ANNE. Mrs. Van Daan, may I try on your coat?

MRS. FRANK. No, Anne.

21. *Ack-ack* was the slang name for antiaircraft gunfire. It was the Allies who were bombing Nazi-controlled Netherlands.

22. The *subjunctive* is a verb form used to express wishes, possibilities, or things that are opposed to fact. In the sentence, "If I were you, I wouldn't go," *were* is the subjunctive.

Vocabulary
vile (vīl) *adj.* very bad; unpleasant; foul

Active Reading Strategies

INFER Ask students what Mr. Frank thinks is wrong with Anne. Does he believe she is ill? *(He does not believe she is ill but thinks she needs to play like she used to.)*

Vo•cab•u•lar•y Skills

Context Clues Remind students that words or phrases that do not appear in the dictionary are sometimes used in writing, especially dialogue. Mrs. Van Daan uses the term *Putti* in the left column of this page. Ask students what this word means. Encourage them to rely on the context to figure out its meaning.

Listening and Speaking *Minilesson*

Effective Listening Techniques Point out to students that listening to or watching a drama makes demands on an audience. The audience must listen actively and remember events so they can follow the story. Explain that one active listening technique is to think of questions about what is being said.

Activity Have students volunteer to take parts and read a page of dialogue from the play. Advise the rest of the class to close their books so they can focus on listening. Ask students to think of two questions about the dialogue as they listen. When the page has been read, students should write down their questions. These can be used for class discussion.
L2 **COLLAB. LEARN.**

Active Reading Strategies

REVIEW Have students review where everyone is onstage during this scene. What are Margot and Mr. Frank doing? Encourage students to consider the impact on the characters of living in such close quarters.

Active Reading Strategies

QUESTION Ask students how the personalities of Mrs. Frank and Mrs. Van Daan are different. *(Mrs. Van Daan is very excitable and melodramatic and draws attention to herself. Mrs. Frank is more reserved and dignified.)*

Literary Elements

AUTHOR'S PURPOSE Note the activity in this scene. Ask students what the author's purpose is in providing the details of the various characters' actions. Encourage the students to consider why all the characters are ignoring what the others are doing.

Teaching Support

MRS. VAN DAAN. [*Giving it to* ANNE.] It's all right . . . but careful with it. [ANNE *puts it on and struts with it*.] My father gave me that the year before he died. He always bought the best that money could buy.

ANNE. Mrs. Van Daan, did you have a lot of boyfriends before you were married?

MRS. FRANK. Anne, that's a personal question. It's not courteous to ask personal questions.

MRS. VAN DAAN. Oh I don't mind. [*To* ANNE.] Our house was always swarming with boys. When I was a girl we had . . .

MR. VAN DAAN. Oh, God. Not again!

MRS. VAN DAAN. [*Good-humored*.] Shut up! [*Without a pause, to* ANNE. MR. VAN DAAN *mimics* MRS. VAN DAAN, *speaking the first few words in unison with her*.] One summer we had a big house in Hilversum. The boys came buzzing round like bees around a jam pot. And when I was sixteen! . . . We were wearing our skirts very short those days and I had good-looking legs. [*She pulls up her skirt, going to* MR. FRANK.] I still have 'em. I may not be as pretty as I used to be, but I still have my legs. How about it, Mr. Frank?

MR. VAN DAAN. All right. All right. We see them.

MRS. VAN DAAN. I'm not asking you. I'm asking Mr. Frank.

PETER. Mother, for heaven's sake.

MRS. VAN DAAN. Oh, I embarrass you, do I? Well, I just hope the girl you marry has as good. [*Then to* ANNE.] My father used to worry about me, with so many boys hanging round. He told me, if any of them gets fresh, you say to him . . . "Remember, Mr. So-and-So, remember I'm a lady."

ANNE. "Remember, Mr. So-and-So, remember I'm a lady."

[*She gives* MRS. VAN DAAN *her coat*.]

MR. VAN DAAN. Look at you, talking that way in front of her! Don't you know she puts it all down in that diary?

MRS. VAN DAAN. So, if she does? I'm only telling the truth!

[ANNE *stretches out, putting her ear to the floor, listening to what is going on below. The sound of the bombers fades away*.]

MRS. FRANK. [*Setting the table*.] Would you mind, Peter, if I moved you over to the couch?

ANNE. [*Listening*.] Miep must have the radio on.

[PETER *picks up his papers, going over to the couch beside* MRS. VAN DAAN.]

MR. VAN DAAN. [*Accusingly, to* PETER.] Haven't you finished yet?

PETER. No.

MR. VAN DAAN. You ought to be ashamed of yourself.

PETER. All right. All right. I'm a dunce. I'm a hopeless case. Why do I go on?

MRS. VAN DAAN. You're not hopeless. Don't talk that way. It's just that you haven't anyone to help you, like the girls have. [*To* MR. FRANK.] Maybe you could help him, Mr. Frank?

MR. FRANK. I'm sure that his father . . . ?

MR. VAN DAAN. Not me. I can't do anything with him. He won't listen to me. You go ahead . . . if you want.

MR. FRANK. [*Going to* PETER.] What about it, Peter? Shall we make our school coeducational?[23]

MRS. VAN DAAN. [*Kissing* MR. FRANK.] You're an angel, Mr. Frank. An angel. I don't know

23. A *coeducational* school has both male and female students.

MEETING INDIVIDUAL NEEDS

ADVANCED LEARNERS

Read More About It Advanced learners may benefit from reading more about Anne Frank. Explain that the play is an adaptation, or the playwrights' elaboration, of Anne's diary.

Activity Have these students obtain the complete diary from the library. Encourage them to read Anne's diary entries that correspond to some of the scenes in the play. Ask them to compare the playwrights' version of events with the diary entries. **L3**

The Diary of Anne Frank, 1959. 20th Century Fox. Movie still.
Viewing the photograph: How does this scene illustrate a typical day in hiding for the Franks?

why I didn't meet you before I met that one there. Here, sit down, Mr. Frank . . . [*She forces him down on the couch beside* PETER.] Now, Peter, you listen to Mr. Frank.

MR. FRANK. It might be better for us to go into Peter's room.

M [*PETER jumps up eagerly, leading the way.*]

MRS. VAN DAAN. That's right. You go in there, Peter. You listen to Mr. Frank. Mr. Frank is a highly educated man.

[*As* MR. FRANK *is about to follow* PETER *into his room,* MRS. FRANK *stops him and wipes the lipstick from his lips. Then she closes the door after them.*]

ANNE. [*On the floor, listening.*] Shh! I can hear a man's voice talking.

N **MR. VAN DAAN.** [*To* ANNE.] Isn't it bad enough here without your sprawling all over the place?

[*ANNE sits up.*]

MRS. VAN DAAN. [*To* MR. VAN DAAN.] If you didn't smoke so much, you wouldn't be so bad-tempered.

MR. VAN DAAN. Am I smoking? Do you see me smoking?

MRS. VAN DAAN. Don't tell me you've used up all those cigarettes.

MR. VAN DAAN. One package. Miep only brought me one package.

MRS. VAN DAAN. It's a filthy habit anyway. It's a good time to break yourself. O

MR. VAN DAAN. Oh, stop it, please.

MRS. VAN DAAN. You're smoking up all our money. You know that, don't you?

MR. VAN DAAN. Will you shut up? [*During this,* MRS. FRANK *and* MARGOT *have studiously kept their eyes down. But* ANNE, *seated on the floor, has been following the discussion interestedly.* MR. VAN DAAN *turns to see her staring up at him.*] And what are you staring at?

VIEWING THE PHOTOGRAPH

Viewing Response *The scene shows Anne's father helping her with her studies and Anne's mother sewing, which were typical of their daily activities.*

M Active Reading Strategies

QUESTION Ask students what has caused Peter to "jump up eagerly" to go to his room. *(He finally has an excuse to escape the uncomfortable situation.)*

N Active Reading Strategies

REVIEW Have students identify the events that have made Mr. Van Daan irritable. Is he really angry with Anne? Explain.

O Literary Elements

DIALOGUE Contrast the bickering in the dialogue on this page with the bickering in the dialogue on the previous page. Have students consider how the dialogue on each page conveys a different mood. *(The bickering on the previous page was lighthearted, but on this page it is more serious and hurtful.)*

INTERDISCIPLINARY CONNECTION

Health The conditions under which the people in the annex were living would likely have caused them to be in poor health. People who are isolated indoors under stressful conditions with a poor diet can suffer serious health consequences. The human body takes some nutrients that it needs to stay healthy, such as vitamin D, from sunshine. In addition, human beings benefit from eating a wide variety of foods, especially fresh fruits and vegetables, that each provide different important vitamins and minerals necessary to the body. Prolonged exposure to stressful conditions can also cause serious physical effects.

Activity Have students research, in Web sites or magazine articles, the types of physical problems associated with stress. **L2**

Active Reading Strategies

EVALUATE Have students consider Mrs. Frank's role in the group. Encourage them to support their conclusions with specific examples.

Active Reading Strategies

CONNECT Note Anne's reaction to Mr. Van Daan. Have students compare how they might react to his remarks.

Active Reading Strategies

QUESTION Ask students to speculate why Mr. Van Daan is angry. Encourage them to contrast what his life was like before with how it is now. *(Mr. Van Daan used to be the head of his household and a businessman with authority. Now Mr. Frank is in charge and Mr. Van Daan may be frustrated at not having a clearly defined role in the group.)*

ANNE. I never heard grown-ups quarrel before. I thought only children quarreled.

MR. VAN DAAN. This isn't a quarrel! It's a discussion. And I never heard children so rude before.

ANNE. [*Rising, indignantly.*] *I,* rude!

MR. VAN DAAN. Yes!

P MRS. FRANK. [*Quickly.*] Anne, will you get me my knitting? [*ANNE goes to get it.*] I must remember, when Miep comes, to ask her to bring me some more wool.

MARGOT. [*Going to her room.*] I need some hairpins and some soap. I made a list.

[*She goes into her bedroom to get the list.*]

MRS. FRANK. [*To ANNE.*] Have you some library books for Miep when she comes?

ANNE. It's a wonder that Miep has a life of her own, the way we make her run errands for us. Please, Miep, get me some starch. Please take my hair out and have it cut. Tell me all the latest news, Miep. [*She goes over, kneeling on the couch beside MRS. VAN DAAN.*] Did you know she was engaged? His name is Dirk, and Miep's afraid the Nazis will ship him off to Germany to work in one of their war plants. That's what they're doing with some of the young Dutchmen . . . they pick them up off the streets—

MR. VAN DAAN. [*Interrupting.*] Don't you ever get tired of talking? Suppose you try keeping still for five minutes. Just five minutes.

Q [*He starts to pace again. Again ANNE follows him, mimicking him. MRS. FRANK jumps up and takes her by the arm up to the sink, and gives her a glass of milk.*]

MRS. FRANK. Come here, Anne. It's time for your glass of milk.

MR. VAN DAAN. Talk, talk, talk. I never heard such a child. Where is my . . . ? Every evening it's the same, talk, talk, talk. [*He looks around.*] Where is my . . . ?

MRS. VAN DAAN. What're you looking for?

MR. VAN DAAN. My pipe. Have you seen my pipe?

MRS. VAN DAAN. What good's a pipe? You haven't got any tobacco.

MR. VAN DAAN. At least I'll have something to hold in my mouth! [*Opening MARGOT's bedroom door.*] Margot, have you seen my pipe?

MARGOT. It was on the table last night.

[*ANNE puts her glass of milk on the table and picks up his pipe, hiding it behind her back.*]

MR. VAN DAAN. I know. I know. Anne, did you see my pipe? . . . Anne!

MRS. FRANK. Anne, Mr. Van Daan is speaking to you.

ANNE. Am I allowed to talk now?

R MR. VAN DAAN. You're the most aggravating . . . The trouble with you is, you've been spoiled. What you need is a good old-fashioned spanking.

ANNE. [*Mimicking MRS. VAN DAAN.*] "Remember, Mr. So-and-So, remember I'm a lady."

[*She thrusts the pipe into his mouth, then picks up her glass of milk.*]

Vocabulary

indignantly (in dig′ nənt lē) *adv.* with dignified anger in response to an insult or injustice

aggravating (ag′ rə vāt ing) *adj.* irritating; annoying

Teaching Support

Life Skills Connection

Planning Explain to students that before going into hiding, Mr. Frank and others had to plan carefully. They had to consider what supplies they would need, how to avoid being discovered, how to get to their hideout, and contingency plans in case anything went wrong.

Activity Ask students to imagine they are going on a thirty-day hike through the woods alone. Have them plan what they will take with them. They should make a list and explain why each item is included. **L2**

S

MR. VAN DAAN. [*Restraining himself with difficulty.*] Why aren't you nice and quiet like your sister Margot? Why do you have to show off all the time? Let me give you a little advice, young lady. Men don't like that kind of thing in a girl. You know that? A man likes a girl who'll listen to him once in a while . . . a domestic girl, who'll keep her house shining for her husband . . . who loves to cook and sew and . . .

ANNE. I'd cut my throat first! I'd open my veins! I'm going to be remarkable! I'm going to Paris . . .

MR. VAN DAAN. [*Scoffingly.*] Paris!

ANNE. . . . to study music and art.

MR. VAN DAAN. Yeah! Yeah!

ANNE. I'm going to be a famous dancer or singer . . . or something wonderful.

[*She makes a wide gesture, spilling the glass of milk on the fur coat in* MRS. VAN DAAN's *lap.* MARGOT *rushes quickly over with a towel.* ANNE *tries to brush the milk off with her skirt.*]

T

MRS. VAN DAAN. Now look what you've done . . . you clumsy little fool! My beautiful fur coat my father gave me . . .

ANNE. I'm so sorry.

MRS. VAN DAAN. What do you care? It isn't yours . . . So go on, ruin it! Do you know what that coat cost? Do you? And now look at it! Look at it!

ANNE. I'm very, very sorry.

MRS. VAN DAAN. I could kill you for this. I could just kill you!

[MRS. VAN DAAN *goes up the stairs, clutching the coat.* MR. VAN DAAN *starts after her.*]

MR. VAN DAAN. Petronella . . . *liefje! Liefje!* . . . Come back . . . the supper . . . come back!

MRS. FRANK. Anne, you must not behave in that way.

ANNE. It was an accident. Anyone can have an accident.

MRS. FRANK. I don't mean that. I mean the answering back. You must not answer back. They are our guests. We must always show the greatest courtesy to them. We're all living under terrible tension. [*She stops as* MARGOT *indicates that* VAN DAAN *can hear. When he is gone, she continues.*] That's why we must control ourselves . . . You don't hear Margot getting into arguments with them, do you? Watch Margot. She's always courteous with them. Never familiar. She keeps her distance. And they respect her for it. Try to be like Margot.

ANNE. And have them walk all over me, the way they do her? No, thanks!

MRS. FRANK. I'm not afraid that anyone is going to walk all over you, Anne. I'm afraid for other people, that you'll walk on them. I don't know what happens to you, Anne. You are wild, self-willed. If I had ever talked to my mother as you talk to me . . .

ANNE. Things have changed. People aren't like that any more. "Yes, Mother." "No, Mother." "Anything you say, Mother." I've got to fight things out for myself! Make something of myself!

MRS. FRANK. It isn't necessary to fight to do it. Margot doesn't fight, and isn't she . . . ?

U

ANNE. [*Violently rebellious.*] Margot! Margot! Margot! That's all I hear from everyone . . . how wonderful Margot is . . . "Why aren't you like Margot?"

MARGOT. [*Protesting.*] Oh, come on, Anne, don't be so . . .

ANNE. [*Paying no attention.*] Everything she does is right, and everything I do is wrong!

S Critical Thinking

EVALUATING Ask students to analyze Mr. Van Daan's statements in light of his relationship with his wife. Are his remarks believable? *(Earlier Mrs. Van Daan was showing off, and Mr. Van Daan was amused; Mrs. Van Daan often does not listen to Mr. Van Daan and is not a quiet person.)*

T Literary Elements

SYMBOLISM Ask students why the coat is so important to Mrs. Van Daan. What does the coat symbolize for her? *(It symbolizes a better time—namely, the time before the war.)*

U Active Reading Strategies

CONNECT Have students discuss whether they have ever felt inadequate compared to someone else. How were their reactions similar to Anne's?

interNET CONNECTION

Have students research Holocaust museums or memorials in the United States and in other countries. **L2**

V Literary Elements

METAPHOR Review with students that a metaphor compares two things without using the words *like* or *as.* Have students identify the metaphor in this line and ask them to explain it. *(Anne says, "I am the goat" rather than saying she is like a goat. She means that she is blamed for the faults of others, like the scapegoat in the Bible.)*

W Critical Thinking

INFER Have students describe what Miep's visits mean to those in hiding. Encourage them to refer to specific examples from the text to support their conclusions.

Teaching Support

V I'm the goat[24] around here! . . . You're all against me! . . . And you worst of all!

[*She rushes off into her room and throws herself down on the settee, stifling her sobs.* MRS. FRANK *sighs and starts toward the stove.*]

MRS. FRANK. [*To* MARGOT.] Let's put the soup on the stove . . . if there's anyone who cares to eat. Margot, will you take the bread out? [MARGOT *gets the bread from the cupboard.*] I don't know how we can go on living this way . . . I can't say a word to Anne . . . she flies at me . . .

MARGOT. You know Anne. In half an hour she'll be out here, laughing and joking.

MRS. FRANK. And . . . [*She makes a motion upwards, indicating the* VAN DAANS.] . . . I told your father it wouldn't work . . . but no . . . no . . . he had to ask them, he said . . . he owed it to him, he said. Well, he knows now that I was right! These quarrels! . . . This bickering!

MARGOT. [*With a warning look.*] Shush. Shush.

[*The buzzer for the door sounds.* MRS. FRANK *gasps, startled.*]

MRS. FRANK. Every time I hear that sound, my heart stops!

MARGOT. [*Starting for* PETER*'s door.*] It's Miep. [*She knocks at the door.*] Father?

[MR. FRANK *comes quickly from* PETER*'s room.*]

MR. FRANK. Thank you, Margot. [*As he goes down the steps to open the outer door.*] Has everyone his list?

MARGOT. I'll get my books. [*Giving her mother a list.*] Here's your list. [MARGOT *goes into her and* ANNE*'s bedroom on the right.* ANNE *sits up, hiding her tears, as* MARGOT *comes in.*] Miep's here.

[MARGOT *picks up her books and goes back.* ANNE *hurries over to the mirror, smoothing her hair.*] W

MR. VAN DAAN. [*Coming down the stairs.*] Is it Miep?

MARGOT. Yes. Father's gone down to let her in.

MR. VAN DAAN. At last I'll have some cigarettes!

MRS. FRANK. [*To* MR. VAN DAAN.] I can't tell you how unhappy I am about Mrs. Van Daan's coat. Anne should never have touched it.

MR. VAN DAAN. She'll be all right.

MRS. FRANK. Is there anything I can do?

MR. VAN DAAN. Don't worry.

[*He turns to meet* MIEP. *But it is not* MIEP *who comes up the steps. It is* MR. KRALER, *followed by* MR. FRANK. *Their faces are grave.* ANNE *comes from the bedroom.* PETER *comes from his room.*]

MRS. FRANK. Mr. Kraler!

MR. VAN DAAN. How are you, Mr. Kraler?

MARGOT. This is a surprise.

MRS. FRANK. When Mr. Kraler comes, the sun begins to shine.

MR. VAN DAAN. Miep is coming?

MR. KRALER. Not tonight.

[KRALER *goes to* MARGOT *and* MRS. FRANK *and* ANNE, *shaking hands with them.*]

MRS. FRANK. Wouldn't you like a cup of coffee? . . . Or, better still, will you have supper with us?

24. A *goat* or *scapegoat* is one who is blamed or punished for other people's mistakes. In the Bible, the high priest Aaron symbolically placed the Jews' sins on the head of a goat that was then driven into the wilderness.

MEETING INDIVIDUAL NEEDS

ADVANCED LEARNERS

European Resistance Students who are advanced learners may benefit from further research about the European resistance to the Nazis. Point out to students that many non-Jews in Europe tried to help Jews escape. These people were seen as heroes by many after the war as a result of the sacrifices they made to resist Nazi persecution.

Activity Have students research the life of Miep Gies. How did her experiences during World War II affect the rest of her life? **L3**

MR. FRANK. Mr. Kraler has something to talk over with us. Something has happened, he says, which demands an immediate decision.

MRS. FRANK. [*Fearful.*] What is it?

X [*MR. KRALER sits down on the couch. As he talks he takes bread, cabbages, milk, etc., from his briefcase, giving them to MARGOT and ANNE to put away.*]

MR. KRALER. Usually, when I come up here, I try to bring you some bit of good news. What's the use of telling you the bad news when there's nothing that you can do about it? But today something has happened . . . Dirk . . . Miep's Dirk, you know, came to me just now. He tells me that he has a Jewish friend living near him. A dentist. He says he's in trouble. He begged me, could I do anything for this man? Could I find him a hiding place? . . . So I've come to you . . . I know it's a terrible thing to ask of you, living as you are, but would you take him in with you?

MR. FRANK. Of course we will.

MR. KRALER. [*Rising.*] It'll be just for a night or two . . . until I find some other place. This happened so suddenly that I didn't know where to turn.

MR. FRANK. Where is he?

MR. KRALER. Downstairs in the office.

MR. FRANK. Good. Bring him up.

MR. KRALER. His name is Dussel . . . Jan Dussel.[25]

MR. FRANK. Dussel . . . I think I know him.

MR. KRALER. I'll get him.

[*He goes quickly down the steps and out. MR. FRANK suddenly becomes conscious of the others.*]

MR. FRANK. Forgive me. I spoke without consulting you. But I knew you'd feel as I do.

MR. VAN DAAN. There's no reason for you to consult anyone. This is your place. You have a right to do exactly as you please. The only thing I feel . . . there's so little food as it is . . . and to take in another person . . . Y

[*PETER turns away, ashamed of his father.*]

MR. FRANK. We can stretch the food a little. It's only for a few days.

MR. VAN DAAN. You want to make a bet?

MRS. FRANK. I think it's fine to have him. But, Otto, where are you going to put him? Where?

PETER. He can have my bed. I can sleep on the floor. I wouldn't mind.

MR. FRANK. That's good of you, Peter. But your room's too small . . . even for *you.*

ANNE. I have a much better idea. I'll come in here with you and Mother, and Margot can take Peter's room and Peter can go in our room with Mr. Dussel.

MARGOT. That's right. We could do that.

MR. FRANK. No, Margot. You mustn't sleep in that room . . . neither you nor Anne. Mouschi has caught some rats in there. Peter's brave. He doesn't mind. Z

ANNE. Then how about *this?* I'll come in here with you and Mother, and Mr. Dussel can have my bed.

MRS. FRANK. No. No. *No!* Margot will come in here with us and he can have her bed. It's the only way. Margot, bring your things in here. Help her, Anne.

[*MARGOT hurries into her room to get her things.*]

ANNE. [*To her mother.*] Why Margot? Why can't I come in here?

25. *Jan Dussel* (yän doos′ əl)

X Active Reading Strategies

REVIEW Ask students to explain why Mr. Kraler is carrying food in his briefcase. *(No one can know he is taking food to the warehouse, or those in hiding might be discovered.)*

Y Critical Thinking

VERIFY PREDICTIONS Ask students to recall their earlier analysis of why Mr. Van Daan is irritable. Does this statement verify or change their previous conclusions?

Z Active Reading Strategies

REVIEW Have students relate this statement to Peter's earlier offer to sleep on the floor. What does this say about Peter? *(He is a generous, humane person.)*

Reading Minilesson

Summarizing When students read longer works, their comprehension improves if they pause to summarize what they have read. Point out to students that summarizing requires recalling and organizing and can be useful later for studying. Explain that a summary should be written in their own words and should include only main points.

Activity Have students write a brief summary of the story thus far. Ask them to review their summaries in a group to determine whether they have included the most important details. **L2**

Additional Resources

Reading Skills Practice Workbook

AA **Critical Thinking**

MAKE CRITICAL JUDGMENTS Have students explain why Mr. Frank wants to use the cognac now. Do they agree with his decision? *(He wants the others to know that he appreciates their willingness to welcome another person in to the Secret Annex. He also wants to welcome Mr. Dussel into the "family." He may also hope that the cognac will help the adults to relax and adjust to the idea of having another person live in their cramped space.)*

VIEWING THE PHOTOGRAPH

Viewing Response *Anne looks defiant, while Margot appears to be listening to her mother.*

MRS. FRANK. Because it wouldn't be proper for Margot to sleep with a . . . Please, Anne. Don't argue. Please.

[*ANNE starts slowly away.*]

MR. FRANK. [*To ANNE.*] You don't mind sharing your room with Mr. Dussel, do you, Anne?

ANNE. No. No, of course not.

MR. FRANK. Good. [*ANNE goes off into her bedroom, helping MARGOT. MR. FRANK starts to search in the cupboards.*] Where's the cognac?[26]

MRS. FRANK. It's there. But, Otto, I was saving it in case of illness.

MR. FRANK. I think we couldn't find a better time to use it. Peter, will you get five glasses for me? AA

[*PETER goes for the glasses. MARGOT comes out of her bedroom, carrying her possessions, which she hangs behind a curtain in the main room. MR. FRANK finds the cognac and pours it into the five glasses that PETER brings him. MR. VAN DAAN stands looking on sourly. MRS. VAN DAAN comes downstairs and looks around at all the bustle.*]

MRS. VAN DAAN. What's happening? What's going on?

MR. VAN DAAN. Someone's moving in with us.

MRS. VAN DAAN. In here? You're joking.

26. *Cognac* (kōn′ yak) is a brandy.

The Diary of Anne Frank, 1959. 20th Century Fox. Movie still.

Viewing the photograph: Notice how Anne and Margot interact with their mother. What does this scene tell you about the personality of each girl?

Teaching Support

Writing *Minilesson*

Outlining Review with students the importance of outlining a topic before beginning to write. Remind students that an outline is a sketch of the major points to be covered with a brief reference to the details that are to support the points.

Activity Have students produce an outline for a speech on the topic "Life in hiding was difficult." Encourage students to consider the main topics that would support that statement and the details from the play that support the main topics. **L2**

Additional Resources

- ***Writer's Choice,*** Lesson 24.7

MARGOT. It's only for a night or two . . . until Mr. Kraler finds him another place.

MR. VAN DAAN. Yeah! Yeah!

[*MR. FRANK hurries over as MR. KRALER and DUSSEL come up. DUSSEL is a man in his late fifties, meticulous, finicky . . . bewildered now. He wears a raincoat. He carries a briefcase, stuffed full, and a small medicine case.*]

MR. FRANK. Come in, Mr. Dussel.

MR. KRALER. This is Mr. Frank.

DUSSEL. Mr. Otto Frank?

MR. FRANK. Yes. Let me take your things. [*He takes the hat and briefcase, but DUSSEL clings to his medicine case.*] This is my wife Edith . . . Mr. and Mrs. Van Daan . . . their son, Peter . . . and my daughters, Margot and Anne.

[*DUSSEL shakes hands with everyone.*]

MR. KRALER. Thank you, Mr. Frank. Thank you all. Mr. Dussel, I leave you in good hands. Oh . . . Dirk's coat.

BB

[*DUSSEL hurriedly takes off the raincoat, giving it to MR. KRALER. Underneath is his white dentist's jacket, with a yellow Star of David on it.*]

DUSSEL. [*To MR. KRALER.*] What can I say to thank you . . . ?

MRS. FRANK. [*To DUSSEL.*] Mr. Kraler and Miep . . . They're our life line. Without them we couldn't live.

CC

MR. KRALER. Please. Please. You make us seem very heroic. It isn't that at all. We simply don't like the Nazis. [*To MR. FRANK, who offers him a drink.*] No, thanks. [*Then going on.*] We don't like their methods. We don't like . . .

MR. FRANK. [*Smiling.*] I know. I know. "No one's going to tell us Dutchmen what to do with our damn Jews!"

MR. KRALER. [*To DUSSEL.*] Pay no attention to Mr. Frank. I'll be up tomorrow to see that they're treating you right. [*To MR. FRANK.*] Don't trouble to come down again. Peter will bolt the door after me, won't you, Peter?

PETER. Yes, sir.

MR. FRANK. Thank you, Peter. I'll do it.

MR. KRALER. Good night. Good night.

GROUP. Good night, Mr. Kraler.

We'll see you tomorrow, *etc., etc.*

[*MR. KRALER goes out with MR. FRANK. MRS. FRANK gives each one of the "grown-ups" a glass of cognac.*]

MRS. FRANK. Please, Mr. Dussel, sit down.

[*MR. DUSSEL sinks into a chair. MRS. FRANK gives him a glass of cognac.*]

DUSSEL. I'm dreaming. I know it. I can't believe my eyes. Mr. Otto Frank here! [*To MRS. FRANK.*] You're not in Switzerland then? A woman told me . . . She said she'd gone to your house . . . the door was open, everything was in disorder, dishes in the sink. She said she found a piece of paper in the wastebasket with an address scribbled on it . . . an address in Zurich.[27] She said you must have escaped to Zurich.

ANNE. Father put that there purposely . . . just so people would think that very thing!

DUSSEL. And you've been *here* all the time?

MRS. FRANK. All the time . . . ever since July.

[*ANNE speaks to her father as he comes back.*]

ANNE. It worked, Pim . . . the address you left! Mr. Dussel says that people believe we escaped to Switzerland.

27. ***Zurich*** (zoor′ ik)

BB Active Reading Strategies

QUESTION Ask students why Mr. Dussel is wearing Dirk's coat. *(Wearing it prevents his being identified as a Jew by the Star of David on his own coat.)*

CC Active Reading Strategies

REVIEW Note that Mr. Kraler protests that he and Miep are not heroic. Have students recall what Mr. Frank said earlier about the fate of Dutch people caught helping Jews. Ask students to consider how Mr. Kraler's statement expresses the theme "Faces of Dignity." *(They are risking their lives by helping, and they are too dignified to accept praise for helping human beings.)*

FYI

The play *The Diary of Anne Frank* was first presented in Amsterdam on November 27, 1956, approximately a year after it opened in America. Queen Juliana of the Netherlands attended. During the play people in the audience sobbed out loud and cried out at the end when the Nazis discovered the families.

Real-World Connection

Internet Research Dussel mentions that he thought the Franks had gone to Zurich. Explain to students that Switzerland played an important role in World War II but remained neutral.

Activity First, have students locate Zurich on a map. Then have students research Web sites about World War II to locate those that discuss Switzerland's role. Have students share the search terms and Web sites they discovered that most successfully led them to the information. **L2**

Active Reading Strategies

EVALUATE Ask students to explain why Peter is humiliated. *(His father's selfishness, particularly where food is concerned, embarasses him.)* Have them characterize his relationship with his father, referring specifically to examples from the text to support their responses.

Critical Thinking

DRAWING CONCLUSIONS Ask students why Mr. Frank does not want to continue the conversation. *(He wants to spare the feelings of the others.)*

Vocabulary Skills

Etymology Remind students that English contains a great many foreign words. *Rucksack* is a German term that, like many German nouns, is a compound word formed of two or more other words—in this case *ruck,* meaning "back," and *sack,* which has the same meaning as in English.

Teaching Support

MR. FRANK. I'm glad. . . . And now let's have a little drink to welcome Mr. Dussel. [*Before they can drink,* MR. DUSSEL *bolts his drink.* MR. FRANK *smiles and raises his glass.*] To Mr. Dussel. Welcome. We're very honored to have you with us.

MRS. FRANK. To Mr. Dussel, welcome.

[*The* VAN DAANS *murmur a welcome. The "grown-ups" drink.*]

MRS. VAN DAAN. Um. That was good.

MR. VAN DAAN. Did Mr. Kraler warn you that you won't get much to eat here? You can imagine . . . three ration books among the seven of us . . . and now you make eight.

[PETER *walks away, humiliated. Outside a street organ is heard dimly.*]

DUSSEL. [*Rising.*] Mr. Van Daan, you don't realize what is happening outside that you should warn me of a thing like that. You don't realize what's going on . . . [*As* MR. VAN DAAN *starts his characteristic pacing,* DUSSEL *turns to speak to the others.*] Right here in Amsterdam every day hundreds of Jews disappear . . . They surround a block and search house by house. Children come home from school to find their parents gone. Hundreds are being deported . . . people that you and I know . . . the Hallensteins . . . the Wessels . . .

MRS. FRANK. [*In tears.*] Oh, no. No!

DUSSEL. They get their call-up notice . . . come to the Jewish theater on such and such a day and hour . . . bring only what you can carry in a rucksack. And if you refuse the call-up notice, then they come and drag you from your home and ship you off to Mauthausen.[28] The death camp!

MRS. FRANK. We didn't know that things had got so much worse.

DUSSEL. Forgive me for speaking so.

ANNE. [*Coming to* DUSSEL.] Do you know the de Waals? . . . What's become of them? Their daughter Jopie and I are in the same class. Jopie's my best friend.

DUSSEL. They are gone.

ANNE. Gone?

DUSSEL. With all the others.

ANNE. Oh, no. Not Jopie!

[*She turns away, in tears.* MRS. FRANK *motions to* MARGOT *to comfort her.* MARGOT *goes to* ANNE, *putting her arms comfortingly around her.*]

MRS. VAN DAAN. There were some people called Wagner. They lived near us . . . ?

MR. FRANK. [*Interrupting, with a glance at* ANNE.] I think we should put this off until later. We all have many questions we want to ask . . . But I'm sure that Mr. Dussel would like to get settled before supper.

DUSSEL. Thank you. I would. I brought very little with me.

MR. FRANK. [*Giving him his hat and briefcase.*] I'm sorry we can't give you a room alone. But I hope you won't be too uncomfortable. We've had to make strict rules here . . . a schedule of hours . . . We'll tell you after supper. Anne, would you like to take Mr. Dussel to his room?

ANNE. [*Controlling her tears.*] If you'll come with me, Mr. Dussel?

[*She starts for her room.*]

DUSSEL. [*Shaking hands with each in turn.*] Forgive me if I haven't really expressed my gratitude to all of you. This has been such

28. Located in Austria, *Mauthausen* (mout′ hou′ zən) was a Nazi concentration camp.

Meeting Individual Needs: MULTIPLE MODES OF EXPRESSION

Interpersonal Students with interpersonal learning styles can benefit from group discussions of their reactions to the play. Point out that throughout the play Anne displays more interest in the outside world than any of the other characters.

Activity Have students work in groups to find examples in the play of this contrast between Anne and the other characters. Then have students discuss possible reasons that the others would have for not showing interest and reasons that Anne does. **L2** COLLAB. LEARN.

a shock to me. I'd always thought of myself as Dutch. I was born in Holland. My father was born in Holland, and my grandfather. And now . . . after all these years . . . [*He breaks off.*] If you'll excuse me.

[*DUSSEL gives a little bow and hurries off after ANNE. MR. FRANK and the others are subdued.*]

ANNE. [*Turning on the light.*] Well, here we are.

[*DUSSEL looks around the room. In the main room MARGOT speaks to her mother.*]

MARGOT. The news sounds pretty bad, doesn't it? It's so different from what Mr. Kraler tells us. Mr. Kraler says things are improving.

FF **MR. VAN DAAN.** I like it better the way Kraler tells it.

[*They resume their occupations, quietly. PETER goes off into his room. In ANNE's room, ANNE turns to DUSSEL.*]

ANNE. You're going to share the room with me.

GG **DUSSEL.** I'm a man who's always lived alone. I haven't had to adjust myself to others. I hope you'll bear with me until I learn.

ANNE. Let me help you. [*She takes his briefcase.*] Do you always live all alone? Have you no family at all?

DUSSEL. No one.

[*He opens his medicine case and spreads his bottles on the dressing table.*]

ANNE. How dreadful. You must be terribly lonely.

DUSSEL. I'm used to it.

ANNE. I don't think I could ever get used to it. Didn't you even have a pet? A cat, or a dog?

DUSSEL. I have an allergy for fur-bearing animals. They give me asthma.

ANNE. Oh, dear. Peter has a cat.

DUSSEL. Here? He has it here?

ANNE. Yes. But we hardly ever see it. He keeps it in his room all the time. I'm sure it will be all right.

DUSSEL. Let us hope so.

[*He takes some pills to fortify himself.*]

ANNE. That's Margot's bed, where you're going to sleep. I sleep on the sofa there. [*Indicating the clothes hooks on the wall.*] We cleared these off for your things. [*She goes over to the window.*] The best part about this room . . . you can look down and see a bit of the street and the canal. There's a houseboat . . . you can see the end of it . . . a bargeman lives there with his family . . . They have a baby and he's just beginning to walk and I'm so afraid he's going to fall into the canal some day. I watch him. . . .

DUSSEL. [*Interrupting.*] Your father spoke of a schedule.

ANNE. [*Coming away from the window.*] Oh, yes. It's mostly about the times we have to be quiet. And times for the w.c. You can use it now if you like.

DUSSEL. [*Stiffly.*] No, thank you.

ANNE. I suppose you think it's awful, my talking about a thing like that. But you don't know how important it can get to be, especially when you're frightened . . . About this room, the way Margot and I did

Vocabulary
subdued (səb do͞od′) *adj.* quiet and downcast

FF Active Reading Strategies

QUESTION Ask students why Mr. Kraler's news is different from Mr. Dussel's. What reasons would Kraler have for saying things are improving? *(He wants to reassure them to keep their hope alive.)*

GG Active Reading Strategies

QUESTION Ask students to conclude whether Mr. Dussel is glad to be in the attic. Have them list reasons he might be glad and reasons he might not be glad. Ask students to support their views with quotations from the text. *(He may be glad to be there instead of in a concentration camp. He might not be glad because so many people are in such a small space.)*

Listening and Speaking *Minilesson*

Oral Reading A play is, of course, meant to be read aloud. Encourage students to think of the play as a script for the actors. Point out that the playwrights' use of punctuation marks, such as ellipses, dashes, and exclamation points, all give the actors an idea of how the lines should be read.

Activity Select students to take parts in a scene. Have them scan the scene to find their characters' lines and review those lines for punctuation that will give clues to how the line should sound. Then have students read the scene aloud. They should speak the lines according to the punctuation clues given. **L2** **COLLAB. LEARN.**

HH Literary Elements

DIALOGUE Ask students to identify one or two personality traits of Mr. Dussel, referring to specific dialogue to support their conclusions. *(fussiness, inability to adapt well, asthmatic reaction to cats, negative attitude)*

II Active Reading Strategies

RESPOND Ask students to describe their reaction to Anne's difficulties in getting along with Mr. Dussel.

JJ Active Reading Strategies

RESPOND Ask students to consider how many adults—other than her parents—live with Anne. *(three)* Have them discuss how they might respond if they lived under these circumstances.

Teaching Support

. . . she had it to herself in the afternoons for studying, reading . . . lessons, you know . . . and I took the mornings. Would that be all right with you?

HH

DUSSEL. I'm not at my best in the morning.

ANNE. You stay here in the mornings then. I'll take the room in the afternoons.

DUSSEL. Tell me, when you're in here, what happens to me? Where am I spending my time? In there, with all the people?

ANNE. Yes.

DUSSEL. I see. I see.

ANNE. We have supper at half past six.

DUSSEL. [*Going over to the sofa.*] Then, if you don't mind . . . I like to lie down quietly for ten minutes before eating. I find it helps the digestion.

ANNE. Of course. I hope I'm not going to be too much of a bother to you. I seem to be able to get everyone's back up.

[*DUSSEL lies down on the sofa, curled up, his back to her.*]

DUSSEL. I always get along very well with children. My patients all bring their children to me, because they know I get on well with them. So don't you worry about that.

[*ANNE leans over him, taking his hand and shaking it gratefully.*]

ANNE. Thank you. Thank you, Mr. Dussel.

[*The lights dim to darkness. The curtain falls on the scene. ANNE'S VOICE comes to us faintly at first, and then with increasing power.*]

ANNE'S VOICE. . . . And yesterday I finished Cissy Van Marxvelt's latest book. I think she is a first-class writer. I shall definitely let my children read her. Monday the twenty-first of September, nineteen forty-two. Mr. Dussel and I had another battle yesterday. Yes, Mr. Dussel! According to him, nothing, I repeat . . . nothing, is right about me . . . my appearance, my character, my manners. While he was going on at me I thought . . . sometime I'll give you such a smack that you'll fly right up to the ceiling! (II) Why is it that every grown-up thinks he knows the way to bring up children? Particularly the grown-ups that never had any. (JJ) I keep wishing that Peter was a girl instead of a boy. Then I would have someone to talk to. Margot's a darling, but she takes everything too seriously. To pause for a moment on the subject of Mrs. Van Daan. I must tell you that her attempts to flirt with father are getting her nowhere. Pim, thank goodness, won't play.

[*As she is saying the last lines, the curtain rises on the darkened scene. ANNE'S VOICE fades out.*]

Grammar and Language *Minilesson*

Adjectives and Adverbs Review with students that adjectives modify nouns, and adverbs modify verbs, adjectives, and other adverbs. Remind students that adjectives and adverbs don't necessarily modify the word that follows them in a sentence and for interest are often placed elsewhere in the sentence.

Activity Have students identify the adjectives and adverbs in the passage at the top of column 2 on page 726, "ANNE'S VOICE comes to us . . . my children read her." Students should identify the word that each adjective and adverb modifies. **L2**

Additional Resources

- ***Grammar and Language Transparency 61***
- ***Grammar and Language Workbook,*** pp. 121–122
- ***Grammar and Composition Handbook,*** Lessons 5.1, 6.1
- ***Writer's Choice,*** Lessons 12.1, 12.5

The Diary of Anne Frank, 1959. 20th Century Fox. Movie still.

Viewing the photograph: What might Anne and Mr. Dussel be discussing in this scene?

VIEWING THE PHOTOGRAPH

Viewing Response *They might be discussing their arrangements for sharing the room or arguing over the use of the bathroom.*

Thematic Focus

Faces of Dignity How do the characters' actions in this part of the play display their faces of dignity?

ASSESSMENT

Quick Checks, p. 62

MEETING INDIVIDUAL NEEDS — SPECIAL NEEDS

Emotional Students may benefit from group discussions that allow them to hear and respond to the opinions of other students in the class.

Activity As a class, discuss the concept of persecution and record students' ideas on the board. Ask them to think about the persecution of Jews in Nazi-occupied Europe and consider that persecution of peoples still occurs. Encourage them to consider examples of some form of persecution that they have seen in the media.

L1 COLLAB. LEARN.

Additional Resources

Inclusion Strategies

Responding to the Selection

PERSONAL RESPONSE

Students may reflect on and explain their response to the question.

Analyzing Literature

1. Anne. Anne and Peter have become more comfortable with each other.
2. The young people are studying history, Latin, and algebra. The parents are hopeful about the future; education is important to them; and they need to keep busy.
3. Mr. Kraler needs to know whether Dussel can stay with them. The Franks are generous, and Mr. Frank has taken the role of leader and decision maker; the Van Daans are selfish and careful about supplies.
4. Students should support their explanations with examples from the story or from their own experience.
5. Anne's relationship with her mother is more tense than with her father. Students should give examples to support their conclusions.
6. Students' responses should explain whether they believe the statement.

Extending Your Response

Literature Groups Groups should consider the different types of families when arriving at a definition. COLLAB. LEARN.

Creative Writing Students' journals should reflect a characterization of Mr. Dussel that can be supported by references in the play.

Active Reading and Critical Thinking

Responding to Literature

PERSONAL RESPONSE

- Have your first impressions of the members of the Secret Annex changed? Why or why not?

Analyzing Literature

RECALL AND INTERPRET

1. Who is Mrs. Quack Quack? What does the audience learn about Anne and Peter from their teasing each other?
2. What are the young people studying? What does their parents' insistence that they study tell you about the parents?
3. Why does Mr. Kraler arrive unexpectedly? What do the responses of the Van Daans and the Franks show about each character?

EVALUATE AND CONNECT

4. In your opinion, is Mr. and Mrs. Van Daan's criticism of Anne justified? Is their attitude unusual for adults? Explain.
5. What is Anne's relationship with her mother? with her father? How does her attitude toward her parents seem different from, or typical of, the ways young people today relate to their parents?
6. Mr. Kraler tells the group, "You make us seem very heroic. It isn't that at all. We simply don't like the Nazis." Do you believe this statement is the complete truth? Why or why not?

LITERARY ELEMENTS

Dialogue

Dialogue is conversation between characters. In a play, the words of each character are *not* set off in quotes as they would be in a narrative. Instead, the name of the character is printed in front of the words that he or she speaks. Notice that, in some cases, a brief description follows the name of the person speaking.

MR. KRALER. Good-bye then for the moment. I'll come up again, after the workmen leave.
MR. FRANK. Good-bye, Mr. Kraler.
MRS. FRANK. [*Shaking his hand.*] How can we thank you?

1. Who are the three characters in the example above?
2. Which character speaks first?

- See **Literary Terms Handbook,** p. R3.

Extending Your Response

Literature Groups

Anne's "Family" The characters in the annex are frequently referred to as a "family." In your opinion, is this an accurate term? How would you define *family?* Share your group's thoughts with the rest of the class.

Creative Writing

A New Hiding Place Suppose Mr. Dussel were keeping a journal. Write an entry for his first night at the Secret Annex. Keep in mind that he is aware of the brutality going on outside. How would this knowledge affect his impression of the people and the place?

LITERARY ELEMENTS

1. Mr. Kraler, Mr. Frank, Mrs. Frank.
2. Mr. Kraler speaks first.

Additional Resources

Literary Elements Transparency 62

ASSESSMENT

- ***Quick Checks,*** p. 62
- ***Selection and Theme Assessment,*** pp. 109–112
- ***Testmaker: ExamView Pro***
- ***Interactive Tutor: Self-Assessment***

The Diary of Anne Frank (Continued)

SCENE 4

[It is the middle of the night, several months later. The stage is dark except for a little light which comes through the skylight in PETER*'s room.*

Everyone is in bed. MR. *and* MRS. FRANK *lie on the couch in the main room, which has been pulled out to serve as a makeshift double bed.* MARGOT *is sleeping on a mattress on the floor in the main room, behind a curtain stretched across for privacy. The others are all in their accustomed rooms.*

A *From outside we hear two drunken soldiers singing "Lili Marlene." A girl's high giggle is heard. The sound of running feet is heard coming closer and then fading in the distance. Throughout the scene there is the distant sound of airplanes passing overhead.*

B *A match suddenly flares up in the attic. We dimly see* MR. VAN DAAN. *He is getting his bearings.*[29] *He comes quickly down the stairs, and goes to the cupboard where the food is stored. Again the match flares up, and is as quickly blown out. The dim figure is seen to steal back up the stairs.*

There is quiet for a second or two, broken only by the sound of airplanes, and running feet on the street below.

Suddenly, out of the silence and the dark, we hear ANNE *scream.]*

ANNE. *[Screaming.]* No! No! Don't . . . don't take me!

[She moans, tossing and crying in her sleep. The other people wake, terrified. DUSSEL *sits up in bed, furious.]*

DUSSEL. Shush! Anne! Anne, for God's sake, shush!

ANNE. *[Still in her nightmare.]* Save me! Save me!

[She screams and screams. DUSSEL *gets out of bed, going over to her, trying to wake her.]*

DUSSEL. For God's sake! Quiet! Quiet! You want someone to hear?

[In the main room MRS. FRANK *grabs a shawl and pulls it around her. She rushes in to* ANNE*, taking her in her arms.* MR. FRANK *hurriedly gets up, putting on his overcoat.* MARGOT *sits up, terrified.* PETER*'s light goes on in his room.]*

MRS. FRANK. *[To* ANNE*, in her room.]* Hush, darling, hush. It's all right. It's all right. *[Over her shoulder to* DUSSEL*.]* Will you be kind enough to turn on the light, Mr. Dussel? *[Back to* ANNE*.]* It's nothing, my darling. It was just a dream.

*[*DUSSEL *turns on the light in the bedroom.* C MRS. FRANK *holds* ANNE *in her arms. Gradually* ANNE *comes out of her nightmare, still trembling with horror.* MR. FRANK *comes into the room, and goes quickly to the window, looking out to be sure that no one outside has heard* ANNE*'s screams.* MRS. FRANK *holds* ANNE*, talking softly to her. In the main room* MARGOT *stands on a chair, turning on the center hanging lamp. A light goes on in the* VAN DAANS' *room overhead.* PETER *puts his robe on, coming out of his room.]*

29. When Mr. Van Daan is *getting his bearings,* he is figuring out his position in the dimly lit room and deciding where to go.

Reading the Selection

SUMMARY

Act 1, Scenes 4–5

Anne's nightmares foreshadow trouble to come. After celebrating the first night of Hanukkah, they hear a noise below. Mr. Frank goes downstairs and concludes that a thief has been there. Dussel and the Van Daans are sure that the Green Police will discover them now, but the Franks choose to remain hopeful about their future.

Spanish Summaries, p. 60

A Literary Elements

STAGE DIRECTIONS Note the stage directions for offstage sounds. Ask students why the playwright has included this detail. How do these sounds contribute to the play? *(They help build the tension and provide a foil for the group's situation in light of the horrors outside.)*

B Critical Thinking

DRAWING CONCLUSIONS Ask students to conclude what Mr. Van Daan is doing here. *(stealing food)*

C Author's Craft

SUSPENSE Point out that a playwright can create a suspenseful mood through the staging of a play. Have students identify the details that contribute to the suspense of the opening of the scene.

Teaching Support

INTERDISCIPLINARY CONNECTION

Art At the end of the war, many photographs were taken of the surviving prisoners in Nazi concentration camps in the environment in which they lived. For many people, seeing these pictures brought about a full realization of the horrors of the Holocaust. The photographs also conveyed the dignity of the prisoners in a way that words never could.

Activity Have students conduct research in books, magazines, and Web sites to find photographs of concentration camps and Holocaust survivors like the image on page 660. Students should discuss what they learn from the photographs that they have not learned from their reading about the Holocaust. **L2**

D Literary Elements

CHARACTERIZATION Ask students what this dialogue reveals about Mr. Dussel. Encourage them to consider what they know about his past to explain why he might be having a difficult time. *(He is not a patient man. He has always lived alone and finds it hard coping with so many people in such close quarters.)*

E Active Reading Strategies

QUESTION Note that this is the first time the characters have spoken German, although it is likely that is the language the families would have actually been speaking. Why do the playwrights present this dialogue in German? *(It helps to indicate this is a private conversation between Mr. and Mrs. Frank.)*

DUSSEL. [*To* MRS. FRANK, *blowing his nose.*] Something must be done about that child, Mrs. Frank. Yelling like that! Who knows but there's somebody on the streets? She's endangering all our lives.

MRS. FRANK. Anne, darling.

DUSSEL. Every night she twists and turns. I don't sleep. I spend half my night shushing her. And now it's nightmares!

[MARGOT *comes to the door of* ANNE'S *room, followed by* PETER. MR. FRANK *goes to them, indicating that everything is all right.* PETER *takes* MARGOT *back.*]

MRS. FRANK. [*To* ANNE.] You're here, safe, you see? Nothing has happened. [*To* DUSSEL.] Please, Mr. Dussel, go back to bed. She'll be herself in a minute or two. Won't you, Anne?

DUSSEL. [*Picking up a book and a pillow.*] Thank you, but I'm going to the w.c. The one place where there's peace!

[*He stalks out.* MR. VAN DAAN, *in underwear and trousers, comes down the stairs.*]

MR. VAN DAAN. [*To* DUSSEL.] What is it? What happened?

DUSSEL. A nightmare. She was having a nightmare!

MR. VAN DAAN. I thought someone was murdering her.

DUSSEL. Unfortunately, no.

[*He goes into the bathroom.* MR. VAN DAAN *goes back up the stairs.* MR. FRANK, *in the main room, sends* PETER *back to his own bedroom.*]

MR. FRANK. Thank you, Peter. Go back to bed.

[PETER *goes back to his room.* MR. FRANK *follows him, turning out the light and looking out the window. Then he goes back to the main room, and gets up on a chair, turning out the center hanging lamp.*]

MRS. FRANK. [*To* ANNE.] Would you like some water? [ANNE *shakes her head.*] Was it a very bad dream? Perhaps if you told me . . . ?

ANNE. I'd rather not talk about it.

MRS. FRANK. Poor darling. Try to sleep then. I'll sit right here beside you until you fall asleep.

[*She brings a stool over, sitting there.*]

ANNE. You don't have to.

MRS. FRANK. But I'd like to stay with you . . . very much. Really.

ANNE. I'd rather you didn't.

MRS. FRANK. Good night, then. [*She leans down to kiss* ANNE. ANNE *throws her arm up over her face, turning away.* MRS. FRANK, *hiding her hurt, kisses* ANNE'S *arm.*] You'll be all right? There's nothing that you want?

ANNE. Will you please ask Father to come.

MRS. FRANK. [*After a second.*] Of course, Anne dear. [*She hurries out into the other room.* MR. FRANK *comes to her as she comes in.*] *Sie verlangt nach Dir!*

MR. FRANK. [*Sensing her hurt.*] Edith, *Liebe, schau . . .*

MRS. FRANK. *Es macht nichts! Ich danke dem lieben Herrgott, dass sie sich wenigstens an Dich wendet, wenn sie Trost braucht! Geh hinein, Otto, sie ist ganz hysterisch vor Angst.* [*As* MR. FRANK *hesitates.*] *Geh zu ihr.*[30] [*He looks at her for a second and then goes to get a cup of water for* ANNE. MRS. FRANK *sinks down on the bed,*

30. The Franks' conversation in German beginning *"Sie verlangt . . ."* translates as follows: MRS. FRANK. "She wants to see you." MR. FRANK. "Edith, dear, look . . ." MRS. FRANK. "It's all right. Thank God that at least she turns to you when she is in need of comfort. Go in, Otto, she is hysterical with fear. Go to her."

Teaching Support

Meeting Individual Needs: ENGLISH LANGUAGE LEARNERS

Understanding Print Conventions Direct English language learners' attention to the text in German. Ask students to compare these lines to the other lines in the play. Discuss the effect that having this text in German has. If there are any German speakers in the class, invite them to read the lines aloud.

Activity Have students look through the text for examples of print conventions. In addition to italics for non-English words, these include all capital letters to identify characters, square brackets and italics for stage directions, and the use of ellipses in dialogue.

Additional Resources

English Language Learners Sourcebook, p. 86

her face in her hands, trying to keep from sobbing aloud. MARGOT *comes over to her, putting her arms around her.*] She wants nothing of me. She pulled away when I leaned down to kiss her.

F

MARGOT. It's a phase . . . You heard Father . . . Most girls go through it . . . they turn to their fathers at this age . . . they give all their love to their fathers.

MRS. FRANK. You weren't like this. You didn't shut me out.

MARGOT. She'll get over it . . .

[*She smooths the bed for* MRS. FRANK *and sits beside her a moment as* MRS. FRANK *lies down. In* ANNE*'s room* MR. FRANK *comes in, sitting down by* ANNE. ANNE *flings her arms around him, clinging to him. In the distance we hear the sound of ack-ack.*]

G

ANNE. Oh, Pim. I dreamed that they came to get us! The Green Police! They broke down the door and grabbed me and started to drag me out the way they did Jopie.

MR. FRANK. I want you to take this pill.

ANNE. What is it?

MR. FRANK. Something to quiet you.

[*She takes it and drinks the water. In the main room* MARGOT *turns out the light and goes back to her bed.*]

MR. FRANK. [*To* ANNE.] Do you want me to read to you for a while?

ANNE. No. Just sit with me for a minute. Was I awful? Did I yell terribly loud? Do you think anyone outside could have heard?

MR. FRANK. No. No. Lie quietly now. Try to sleep.

H

ANNE. I'm a terrible coward. I'm so disappointed in myself. I think I've conquered my fear . . . I think I'm really grown-up . . . and then something happens . . . and I run to you like a baby . . . I love you, Father. I don't love anyone but you.

MR. FRANK. [*Reproachfully.*] Annele!

ANNE. It's true. I've been thinking about it for a long time. You're the only one I love.

MR. FRANK. It's fine to hear you tell me that you love me. But I'd be happier if you said you loved your mother as well . . . She needs your help so much . . . your love . . .

I

ANNE. We have nothing in common. She doesn't understand me. Whenever I try to explain my views on life to her she asks me if I'm constipated.

MR. FRANK. You hurt her very much just now. She's crying. She's in there crying.

ANNE. I can't help it. I only told the truth. I didn't want her here . . . [*Then, with sudden change.*] Oh, Pim, I was horrible, wasn't I? And the worst of it is, I can stand off and look at myself doing it and know it's cruel and yet I can't stop doing it. What's the matter with me? Tell me. Don't say it's just a phase! Help me.

MR. FRANK. There is so little that we parents can do to help our children. We can only try to set a good example . . . point the way. The rest you must do yourself. You must build your own character.

ANNE. I'm trying. Really I am. Every night I think back over all of the things I did that day that were wrong . . . like putting the wet mop in Mr. Dussel's bed . . . and this thing now with Mother. I say to myself, that was wrong. I make up my mind, I'm never going to do that again. Never! Of course I may do something worse . . . but at least I'll never do *that* again! . . . I have a nicer side, Father . . . a sweeter, nicer side. But I'm

F Critical Thinking

EVALUATE Note that until this point there has not been much dialogue from Margot. What do we learn about her here? *(She is a caring person, and she tries to make her mother feel better.)*

G Active Reading Strategies

REVIEW Have students recall and describe who the Green Police are. *(They are Nazis.)*

H Active Reading Strategies

RESPOND Why does Anne say she is "a terrible coward"? Ask students whether they agree with this statement. *(She has nightmares. Most students will not think her actions are cowardly but rather normal under the conditions.)*

I Active Reading Strategies

RESPOND Have students compare and contrast Mrs. Frank to Anne's descriptions of her. *(Mrs. Frank is concerned about her daughter, but Anne describes her as "unbearable" and believes her mother treats her like a baby.)*

Life Skills Connection

Interview Mr. Frank says that all parents can do is set an example, but that children "must build [their] own character." Encourage students to consider whether they agree with this statement and also whether they think other adults whom they know would agree with Mr. Frank's statement.

Activity Have students interview an adult, such as a parent or grandparent, to get reactions to Mr. Frank's statement. Remind students to take notes during the interview so they can accurately recall the person's statements. Ask them to compare the person's response with their predictions. Students can present their findings to the class. **L2** **COLLAB. LEARN.**

J Critical Thinking

INFER Ask students to speculate what Anne would say to complete the sentence. What prevents her from keeping "the good Anne outside"?

K Active Reading Strategies

QUESTION Note the footnote defining a fatalist. Why does Anne think it is strange that a fatalist would be the most frightened? *(Fatalists believe everything is predestined, so it makes sense that a fatalist would accept situations, not fear them.)*

VIEWING THE PHOTOGRAPH

Viewing Response *They seem to be watching something frightening, given the expressions on their faces. They may be watching an air raid, possibly one that broke the window. Some members of the group look awed and hopeful as they look out from the Secret Annex.*

Teaching Support

scared to show it. I'm afraid that people are going to laugh at me if I'm serious. So the mean Anne comes to the outside and the good Anne stays on the inside, and I keep on trying to switch them around and have the good Anne outside and the bad Anne inside and be what I'd like to be . . . and might be . . . if only . . . only . . .

[She is asleep. MR. FRANK *watches her for a moment and then turns off the light, and starts out. The lights dim out. The curtain falls on the scene.* ANNE'S VOICE *is heard dimly at first, and then with growing strength.]*

ANNE'S VOICE. . . . The air raids are getting worse. They come over day and night. The noise is terrifying. Pim says it should be music to our ears. The more planes, the sooner will come the end of the war. Mrs. Van Daan pretends to be a fatalist.[31] What will be, will be. But when the planes come over, who is the most frightened? No one else but Petronella! . . . Monday, the ninth of November, nineteen forty-two. Wonderful news! The Allies have landed in Africa. Pim says that we can look for an early finish to the war. Just for fun he asked each of us what was the first thing we wanted to do when we got out of here. Mrs. Van Daan longs to be home with her own things, her needle-point chairs, the Beckstein piano her father gave her . . .

31. A *fatalist* is someone who believes that fate controls everything that happens.

The Diary of Anne Frank, 1959. 20th Century Fox. Movie still.
Viewing the photograph: Why is the group standing by the window? In your opinion, is this scene frightening or hopeful?

MEETING INDIVIDUAL NEEDS: ADVANCED LEARNERS

Group Psychology Students may be interested in exploring further the reasons the people in the annex were having trouble getting along. Explain that there are studies showing how the lack of sunlight and being housebound affects people's moods.

Activity Have students research this topic to learn more about the problems caused by the difficult conditions under which the group was living. Students may write a short paper or present an oral report to the class. **L3**

the best that money could buy. Peter would like to go to a movie. Mr. Dussel wants to get back to his dentist's drill. He's afraid he is losing his touch. For myself, there are so many things . . . to ride a bike again . . . to laugh till my belly aches . . . to have new clothes from the skin out . . . to have a hot tub filled to overflowing and wallow in it for hours . . . to be back in school with my friends . . .

[As the last lines are being said, the curtain rises on the scene. The lights dim on as ANNE'S VOICE *fades away.]*

SCENE 5

[It is the first night of the Hanukkah[32] *celebration.* MR. FRANK *is standing at the head of the table on which is the Menorah. He lights the Shamos, or servant candle,*[33] *and holds it as he says the blessing. Seated listening is all of the "family," dressed in their best. The men wear hats,* PETER *wears his cap.]*

MR. FRANK. *[Reading from a prayer book.]* "Praised be Thou, oh Lord our God, Ruler of the universe, who has sanctified us with Thy commandments and bidden us kindle the Hanukkah lights. Praised be Thou, oh Lord our God, Ruler of the universe, who has wrought wondrous deliverances for our fathers in days of old. Praised be Thou, oh Lord our God, Ruler of the universe, that Thou has given us life and sustenance[34] and brought us to this happy season." *[*MR. FRANK *lights the one candle of the Menorah as he continues.]* "We kindle this Hanukkah light to celebrate the great and wonderful deeds wrought through the zeal with which God filled the hearts of the heroic Maccabees, two thousand years ago. They fought against indifference, against tyranny and oppression,[35] and they restored our Temple to us. May these lights remind us that we should ever look to God, whence cometh our help." Amen. [Pronounced O-mayn.]

ALL. Amen.

*[*MR. FRANK *hands* MRS. FRANK *the prayer book.]*

MRS. FRANK. *[Reading.]* "I lift up mine eyes unto the mountains, from whence cometh my help. My help cometh from the Lord who made heaven and earth. He will not suffer thy foot to be moved. He that keepeth thee will not slumber. He that keepeth Israel doth neither slumber nor sleep. The Lord is thy keeper. The Lord is thy shade upon thy right hand. The sun shall not smite thee by day, nor the moon by night. The Lord shall keep thee from all evil. He shall keep thy soul. The Lord shall guard thy going out and thy coming in, from this time forth and forevermore." Amen.

ALL. Amen.

*[*MRS. FRANK *puts down the prayer book and goes to get the food and wine.* MARGOT

32. The eight-day Jewish holiday *Hanukkah* (hä′ nə kə) is celebrated in December. It honors a victory in 165 B.C. over Syrian enemies.
33. The *Menorah* (mə nôr′ ə) is a candlestick with nine branches. On the first day of Hanukkah, one candle is lit, and an additional candle is lit on each of the following days. The *Shamos* (shäm′ əs) or (shä′ mäs), *or servant candle,* is used to light the others.
34. Here, *sanctified* means "set apart as holy." *Wrought* is an old form of the word *worked. Sustenance* is food and other necessities of life.
35. *Zeal* means "great devotion." It was the *Maccabees,* a family of Jewish patriots, who led the Jews to victory. They fought the Syrians' cruel and unjust use of power (*tyranny* and *oppression*).

L Active Reading Strategies

RESPOND Ask students what the first thing is that they would want to do if they were in Anne's position.

M Critical Thinking

DRAWING CONCLUSIONS Ask students to consider why the playwrights included the Hanukkah scene. Have them consider the significance of the ceremony in praising "this happy season."

N Literary Elements

IRONY Have students explain the irony in the prayer reference to the heroic Maccabees fighting tyranny and oppression. Encourage them to compare the statement about the Maccabees to the situation facing the Jews in hiding.

MEETING INDIVIDUAL NEEDS: SPECIAL NEEDS

Emotional Students with special needs will benefit from being able to participate in a class activity that requires teamwork and cooperation. Discuss with students the elements involved in staging a drama, such as lights, props, sound effects, and costumes in addition to the presentation of the dialogue.

Activity Have students work together to perform a scene from the play. Groups should work together on the lighting, props, sound effects, and performing the parts. Have the groups analyze and evaluate each other's performances. **L1** COLLAB. LEARN.

Additional Resources

Inclusion Strategies

O Critical Thinking

INFER Ask students to determine Mr. Dussel's religious knowledge from this exchange. Does he practice his religion? Ask students whether they are surprised by this. *(Perhaps they shouldn't be. He said at the outset [p. 725], "I always thought of myself as Dutch.")*

P Critical Thinking

GENERALIZE Ask students to consider what "kind of Jews" the Nazis were persecuting from the fact that Mr. Dussel is in hiding with the others. *(Both religious Jews and ethnic Jews.)*

Q Literary Elements

CHARACTERIZATION Ask students to speculate about why Anne brought presents. What does it say about Anne that she is the only one who has presents? *(As sharp-tongued and independent as she may be, she is nonetheless goodhearted.)*

Teaching Support

helps her. MR. FRANK *takes the men's hats and puts them aside.*]

DUSSEL. [*Rising.*] That was very moving.

ANNE. [*Pulling him back.*] It isn't over yet!

MRS. VAN DAAN. Sit down! Sit down!

ANNE. There's a lot more, songs and presents.

DUSSEL. Presents?

MRS. FRANK. Not this year, unfortunately.

MRS. VAN DAAN. But always on Hanukkah everyone gives presents . . . everyone!

DUSSEL. Like our St. Nicholas'[36] Day.

[*There is a chorus of "no's" from the group.*]

MRS. VAN DAAN. No! Not like St. Nicholas! What kind of a Jew are you that you don't know Hanukkah?

MRS. FRANK. [*As she brings the food.*] I remember particularly the candles . . . First one, as we have tonight. Then the second night you light two candles, the next night three . . . and so on until you have eight candles burning. When there are eight candles it is truly beautiful.

MRS. VAN DAAN. And the potato pancakes.

MR. VAN DAAN. Don't talk about them!

MRS. VAN DAAN. I make the best *latkes*[37] you ever tasted!

MRS. FRANK. Invite us all next year . . . in your own home.

MR. FRANK. God willing!

MRS. VAN DAAN. God willing.

MARGOT. What I remember best is the presents we used to get when we were little . . . eight days of presents . . . and each day they got better and better.

MRS. FRANK. [*Sitting down.*] We are all here, alive. That is present enough.

ANNE. No, it isn't. I've got something . . . [*She rushes into her room, hurriedly puts on a little hat improvised from the lamp shade, grabs a satchel bulging with parcels and comes running back.*]

MRS. FRANK. What is it?

ANNE. Presents!

MRS. VAN DAAN. Presents!

DUSSEL. Look!

MR. VAN DAAN. What's she got on her head?

PETER. A lamp shade!

ANNE. [*She picks out one at random.*] This is for Margot. [*She hands it to* MARGOT, *pulling her to her feet.*] Read it out loud.

MARGOT. [*Reading.*]

"You have never lost your temper.
You never will, I fear,
You are so good.
But if you should,
Put all your cross words here."

[*She tears open the package.*] A new crossword puzzle book! Where did you get it?

ANNE. It isn't new. It's one that you've done. But I rubbed it all out, and if you wait a little and forget, you can do it all over again.

MARGOT. [*Sitting.*] It's wonderful, Anne. Thank you. You'd never know it wasn't new.

[*From outside we hear the sound of a streetcar passing.*]

ANNE. [*With another gift.*] Mrs. Van Daan.

MRS. VAN DAAN. [*Taking it.*] This is awful . . . I haven't anything for anyone . . . I never thought . . .

36. In the Netherlands, Christian children receive gifts from *St. Nicholas* on December 6.

37. *Latkes* (lät′ kəz) are potato pancakes.

Life Skills Connection

Planning Mr. Frank made careful plans for his family and the Van Daans to go into hiding. *The Diary of Anne Frank* explores the conflicts that arise once the families are living in close quarters. Point out that each character learns something about himself or herself and about the others during their long time together.

Activity Working in groups, have students develop an instruction manual for going into hiding. Encourage students to think about how the situation in the annex might have been different if the extended "family" had known at the beginning the things learned while in hiding. Have students make a list of things to do and things to avoid. **L2** COLLAB. LEARN.

MR. FRANK. This is all Anne's idea.

MRS. VAN DAAN. [*Holding up a bottle.*] What is it?

ANNE. It's hair shampoo. I took all the odds and ends of soap and mixed them with the last of my toilet water.

MRS. VAN DAAN. Oh, Anneke!

ANNE. I wanted to write a poem for all of them, but I didn't have time. [*Offering a large box to* MR. VAN DAAN.] Yours, Mr. Van Daan, is *really* something . . . something you want more than anything. [*As she waits for him to open it.*] Look! Cigarettes!

MR. VAN DAAN. Cigarettes!

ANNE. Two of them! Pim found some old pipe tobacco in the pocket lining of his coat . . . and we made them . . . or rather, Pim did.

MRS. VAN DAAN. Let me see . . . Well, look at that! Light it, Putti! Light it.

[MR. VAN DAAN *hesitates.*]

ANNE. It's tobacco, really it is! There's a little fluff in it, but not much.

[*Everyone watches intently as* MR. VAN DAAN *cautiously lights it. The cigarette flares up. Everyone laughs.*]

PETER. It works!

MRS. VAN DAAN. Look at him.

MR. VAN DAAN. [*Spluttering.*] Thank you, Anne. Thank you.

[ANNE *rushes back to her satchel for another present.*]

ANNE. [*Handing her mother a piece of paper.*] For Mother, Hanukkah greeting.

[*She pulls her mother to her feet.*]

MRS. FRANK. [*She reads.*] "Here's an I.O.U. that I promise to pay. Ten hours of doing whatever you say. Signed, Anne Frank."

[MRS. FRANK, *touched, takes* ANNE *in her arms, holding her close.*]

DUSSEL. [*To* ANNE.] Ten hours of doing what you're told? *Anything* you're told?

ANNE. That's right.

DUSSEL. You wouldn't want to sell that, Mrs. Frank?

MRS. FRANK. Never! This is the most precious gift I've ever had!

[*She sits, showing her present to the others.* ANNE *hurries back to the satchel and pulls out a scarf, the scarf that* MR. FRANK *found in the first scene.*]

ANNE. [*Offering it to her father.*] For Pim.

MR. FRANK. Anneke . . . I wasn't supposed to have a present!

[*He takes it, unfolding it and showing it to the others.*]

ANNE. It's a muffler . . . to put round your neck . . . like an ascot, you know. I made it myself out of odds and ends . . . I knitted it in the dark each night, after I'd gone to bed. I'm afraid it looks better in the dark!

MR. FRANK. [*Putting it on.*] It's fine. It fits me perfectly. Thank you, Annele.

[ANNE *hands* PETER *a ball of paper, with a string attached to it.*]

ANNE. That's for Mouschi.

PETER. [*Rising to bow.*] On behalf of Mouschi, I thank you.

ANNE. [*Hesitant, handing him a gift.*] And . . . this is yours . . . from Mrs. Quack Quack. [*As he holds it gingerly in his hands.*] Well . . . open it . . . Aren't you going to open it?

PETER. I'm scared to. I know something's going to jump out and hit me.

ANNE. No. It's nothing like that, really.

R Active Reading Strategies

EVALUATE Ask students to consider how Anne's giving of presents unites the "family" members.

S Active Reading Strategies

PREDICT Have students describe how Anne's gifts have made the others feel about her. Encourage students to predict whether the others' attitudes toward Anne will change.

Writing Minilesson

Dialogue Point out that writing dialogue is different from other writing because people must be made to speak in a variety of ways for dialogue to be realistic. It must reflect the way each particular character would sound when speaking. For example, Anne speaks a great deal because she is outgoing, and she speaks quickly. Peter, who is shy, speaks less and in shorter sentences.

Activity Have students write a dialogue that might occur between an elderly woman and a teenager. Encourage students to consider the words and manner of speech each character would use. **L2**

Additional Resources

Writer's Choice, Lesson 4.4

Active Reading Strategies

REVIEW Have students recall an earlier scene from the play to explain why Anne gives Peter a razor. *(In act 1, scene 3, Anne teased Peter about having "only a little fuzz" instead of whiskers.)*

Critical Thinking

DRAWING CONCLUSIONS Ask students why Mr. Van Daan is disgusted about the cat. *(He seems to be jealous of the attention Peter gives the cat. He may also resent having to share food with the animal.)*

Literary Elements

STAGE DIRECTIONS Ask students why they think the playwrights have included this detail. Why is the dog barking persistently? *(The dog's barking might signal danger.)* What effect might this have on the audience?

MRS. VAN DAAN. [*As he is opening it.*] What is it, Peter? Go on. Show it.

ANNE. [*Excitedly.*] It's a safety razor!

DUSSEL. A what?

ANNE. A razor!

MRS. VAN DAAN. [*Looking at it.*] You didn't make that out of odds and ends.

ANNE. [*To* PETER.] Miep got it for me. It's not new. It's second-hand. But you really do need a razor now.

DUSSEL. For what?

ANNE. Look on his upper lip . . . you can see the beginning of a mustache.

DUSSEL. He wants to get rid of that? Put a little milk on it and let the cat lick it off.

PETER. [*Starting for his room.*] Think you're funny, don't you?

DUSSEL. Look! He can't wait! He's going in to try it!

PETER. I'm going to give Mouschi his present!

[*He goes into his room, slamming the door behind him.*]

MR. VAN DAAN. [*Disgustedly.*] Mouschi, Mouschi, Mouschi.

[*In the distance we hear a dog persistently barking.* ANNE *brings a gift to* DUSSEL.]

ANNE. And last but never least, my roommate, Mr. Dussel.

DUSSEL. For me? You have something for me?

[*He opens the small box she gives him.*]

ANNE. I made them myself.

DUSSEL. [*Puzzled.*] Capsules! Two capsules!

ANNE. They're ear-plugs!

DUSSEL. Ear-plugs?

ANNE. To put in your ears so you won't hear me when I thrash around at night. I saw them advertised in a magazine. They're not real ones . . . I made them out of cotton and candle wax. Try them . . . See if they don't work . . . see if you can hear me talk . . .

DUSSEL. [*Putting them in his ears.*] Wait now until I get them in . . . so.

ANNE. Are you ready?

DUSSEL. Huh?

ANNE. Are you ready?

DUSSEL. Good God! They've gone inside! I can't get them out! [*They laugh as* MR. DUSSEL *jumps about, trying to shake the plugs out of his ears. Finally he gets them out. Putting them away.*] Thank you, Anne! Thank you!

MR. VAN DAAN. A real Hanukkah!

MRS. VAN DAAN. Wasn't it cute of her?

MRS. FRANK. I don't know when she did it.

MARGOT. I love my present.

} *Together*

ANNE. [*Sitting at the table.*] And now let's have the song, Father . . . please . . . [*To* DUSSEL.] Have you heard the Hanukkah song, Mr. Dussel? The song is the whole thing! [*She sings.*] "Oh, Hanukkah! Oh Hanukkah! The sweet celebration . . ."

MR. FRANK. [*Quieting her.*] I'm afraid, Anne, we shouldn't sing that song tonight. [*To* DUSSEL.] It's a song of jubilation, of rejoicing. One is apt to become too enthusiastic.

Vocabulary

jubilation (jo͞o′ bə lā′ shən) *n.* great joy and excitement

Teaching Support

MEETING INDIVIDUAL NEEDS: MULTIPLE MODES OF EXPRESSION

Logical and Mathematical Students with logical and mathematical learning abilities may be interested in exploring statistics from the Holocaust. Point out that the Nazis ran many concentration camps and death camps where they sent not only Jews and other ethnic groups but also people who violated their strict regulations—those who helped Jews, and those who spoke against the Nazis.

Activity Have students research information on the Nazi camps and make a map showing their locations. Students can include on the map statistics about each camp, such as how long it existed, how many prisoners it held, and other statistics. **L2**

ANNE. Oh, please, please. Let's sing the song. I promise not to shout!

MR. FRANK. Very well. But quietly now . . . I'll keep an eye on you and when . . .

[As ANNE starts to sing, she is interrupted by DUSSEL, who is snorting and wheezing.]

W

DUSSEL. *[Pointing to PETER.]* You . . . You! *[PETER is coming from his bedroom, ostentatiously[38] holding a bulge in his coat as if he were holding his cat, and dangling ANNE's present before it.]* How many times . . . I told you . . . Out! Out!

MR. VAN DAAN. *[Going to PETER.]* What's the matter with you? Haven't you any sense? Get that cat out of here.

PETER. *[Innocently.]* Cat?

MR. VAN DAAN. You heard me. Get it out of here!

PETER. I have no cat.

[Delighted with his joke, he opens his coat and pulls out a bath towel. The group at the table laugh, enjoying the joke.]

DUSSEL. *[Still wheezing.]* It doesn't need to be the cat . . . his clothes are enough . . . when he comes out of that room . . .

MR. VAN DAAN. Don't worry. You won't be bothered any more. We're getting rid of it.

DUSSEL. At last you listen to me.

[He goes off into his bedroom.]

MR. VAN DAAN. *[Calling after him.]* I'm not doing it for you. That's all in your mind . . . all of it! *[He starts back to his place at the table.]* I'm doing it because I'm sick of seeing that cat eat all our food.

PETER. That's not true! I only give him bones . . . scraps . . .

X

MR. VAN DAAN. Don't tell me! He gets fatter every day! Damn cat looks better than any of us. Out he goes tonight!

PETER. No! No!

ANNE. Mr. Van Daan, you can't do that! That's Peter's cat. Peter loves that cat.

MRS. FRANK. *[Quietly.]* Anne.

PETER. *[To MR. VAN DAAN.]* If he goes, I go.

MR. VAN DAAN. Go! Go!

MRS. VAN DAAN. You're not going and the cat's not going! Now please . . . this is Hanukkah . . . Hanukkah . . . this is the time to celebrate . . . What's the matter with all of you? Come on, Anne. Let's have the song.

ANNE. *[Singing.]* "Oh, Hanukkah! Oh, Hanukkah! The sweet celebration."

MR. FRANK. *[Rising.]* I think we should first blow out the candle . . . then we'll have something for tomorrow night.

MARGOT. But, Father, you're supposed to let it burn itself out.

MR. FRANK. I'm sure that God understands shortages. *[Before blowing it out.]* "Praised be Thou, oh Lord our God, who hast sustained us and permitted us to celebrate this joyous festival."

[He is about to blow out the candle when suddenly there is a crash of something falling below. They all freeze in horror, motionless. For a few seconds there is complete silence. MR. FRANK slips off his shoes. The others noiselessly follow his example. MR. FRANK turns out a light near him. He motions to PETER to turn off the center lamp. PETER tries to reach it, realizes he cannot and gets up on a chair. Just as he is touching the lamp he loses his balance. The chair goes out from under him. He falls. The iron lamp

38. Peter holds the bulge in a showy way that is meant to attract notice *(ostentatiously)*.

W Active Reading Strategies

REVIEW Ask students why Peter seems to delight in teasing Mr. Dussel. *(Because he is so critical of everything the children do.)*

X Literary Elements

CONFLICT Note that the mood earlier in this scene was one of togetherness. Have students explain what occurred to produce the conflict in this part of the scene.

Reading Minilesson

Paraphrase Remind students that paraphrasing is restating a piece of writing to convey the same meaning. Explain to students that paraphrasing is a good way to make sure they understand the material they have read.

Activity Have students write a paraphrase of the stage directions on pages 737–738 describing Peter's fall. Remind students to use their own words to express the details of the stage directions. **L2**

Additional Resources

Reading Skills Practice Workbook

VIEWING THE PHOTOGRAPH

Viewing Response *A noise would make them fear that they had been discovered. They would likely respond by remaining still and keeping quiet.*

Y Literary Elements

STAGE DIRECTIONS Note that the dog barks again. Have students review their earlier discussion of why the detail of the dog barking was included in the stage directions. Have students explain the significance of the dog barking here. *(The dog has heard the prowler, too.)*

Z Active Reading Strategies

RESPOND Ask students if they are surprised that Anne faints here. Why does she faint? *(She faints from fear.)*

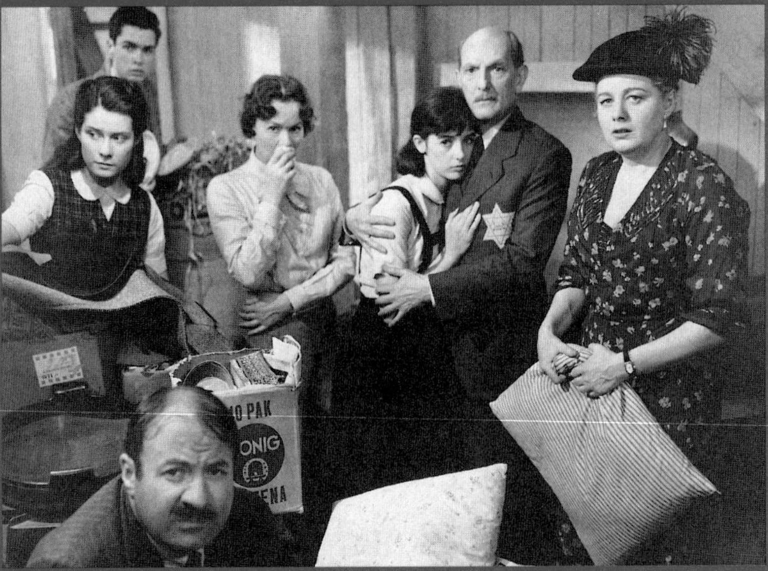

The Diary of Anne Frank, 1959. 20th Century Fox. Movie still.

Viewing the photograph: Why might a noise under the Secret Annex alarm the occupants? How do you think they will respond to the noise?

shade crashes to the floor. There is a sound of feet below, running down the stairs.]

MR. VAN DAAN. [*Under his breath.*] God Almighty! [*The only light left comes from the Hanukkah candle.* DUSSEL *comes from his room.* MR. FRANK *creeps over to the stairwell and stands listening. The dog is heard barking excitedly.*] Do you hear anything? Y

MR. FRANK. [*In a whisper.*] No. I think they've gone.

MRS. VAN DAAN. It's the Green Police. They've found us.

MR. FRANK. If they had, they wouldn't have left. They'd be up here by now.

MRS. VAN DAAN. I know it's the Green Police. They've gone to get help. That's all. They'll be back!

MR. VAN DAAN. Or it may have been the Gestapo,[39] looking for papers . . .

MR. FRANK. [*Interrupting.*] Or a thief, looking for money.

MRS. VAN DAAN. We've got to do something . . . Quick! Quick! Before they come back.

MR. VAN DAAN. There isn't anything to do. Just wait.

[MR. FRANK *holds up his hand for them to be quiet. He is listening intently. There is complete silence as they all strain to hear any sound from below. Suddenly* ANNE *begins to sway. With a low cry she falls to the floor in a faint.* MRS. FRANK *goes to her quickly, sitting beside her on the floor and taking her in her arms.*] Z

MRS. FRANK. Get some water, please! Get some water!

[MARGOT *starts for the sink.*]

MR. VAN DAAN. [*Grabbing* MARGOT.] No! No! No one's going to run water!

MR. FRANK. If they've found us, they've found us. Get the water. [MARGOT *starts*

39. The *Gestapo* (gə stä′ pō) were the Nazi secret police.

Teaching Support

MEETING INDIVIDUAL NEEDS — MULTIPLE MODES OF EXPRESSION

Linguistic Explain to students that plays, like films, are reviewed by critics. There were rave reviews for *The Diary of Anne Frank* when it opened.

Activity Have students write a review of the play. They should read other movie or play reviews to get ideas. Encourage them to take a position on whether they would recommend the play to others, explaining and supporting their views with examples from the play. **L2**

again for the sink. MR. FRANK, getting a flashlight.] I'm going down.

[MARGOT rushes to him, clinging to him. ANNE struggles to consciousness.]

MARGOT. No, Father, no! There may be someone there, waiting . . . It may be a trap!

MR. FRANK. This is Saturday. There is no way for us to know what has happened until Miep or Mr. Kraler comes on Monday morning. We cannot live with this uncertainty.

MARGOT. Don't go, Father!

MRS. FRANK. Hush, darling, hush. [MR. FRANK slips quietly out, down the steps, and out through the door below.] Margot! Stay close to me.

[MARGOT goes to her mother.]

MR. VAN DAAN. Shush! Shush!

AA

[MRS. FRANK whispers to MARGOT to get the water. MARGOT goes for it.]

MRS. VAN DAAN. Putti, where's our money? Get our money. I hear you can buy the Green Police off, so much a head. Go upstairs quick! Get the money!

MR. VAN DAAN. Keep still!

MRS. VAN DAAN. [Kneeling before him, pleading.] Do you want to be dragged off to a concentration camp? Are you going to stand there and wait for them to come up and get you? Do something, I tell you!

MR. VAN DAAN. [Pushing her aside.] Will you keep still!

[He goes over to the stairwell to listen. PETER goes to his mother, helping her up onto the sofa. There is a second of silence, then ANNE can stand it no longer.]

ANNE. Someone go after Father! Make Father come back!

PETER. [Starting for the door.] I'll go.

MR. VAN DAAN. Haven't you done enough?

[He pushes PETER roughly away. In his anger against his father PETER grabs a chair as if to hit him with it, then puts it down, burying his face in his hands. MRS. FRANK begins to pray softly.]

ANNE. Please, please, Mr. Van Daan. Get Father.

MR. VAN DAAN. Quiet! Quiet!

[ANNE is shocked into silence. MRS. FRANK pulls her closer, holding her protectively in her arms.]

MRS. FRANK. [Softly, praying.] "I lift up mine eyes unto the mountains, from whence cometh my help. My help cometh from the Lord who made heaven and earth. He will not suffer thy foot to be moved . . . He that keepeth thee will not slumber . . ."

BB

[She stops as she hears someone coming. They all watch the door tensely. MR. FRANK comes quietly in. ANNE rushes to him, holding him tight.]

MR. FRANK. It was a thief. That noise must have scared him away.

MRS. VAN DAAN. Thank God.

MR. FRANK. He took the cash box. And the radio. He ran away in such a hurry that he didn't stop to shut the street door. It was swinging wide open. [A breath of relief sweeps over them.] I think it would be good to have some light.

MARGOT. Are you sure it's all right?

MR. FRANK. The danger has passed. [MARGOT goes to light the small lamp.] Don't be so terrified, Anne. We're safe.

DUSSEL. Who says the danger has passed? Don't you realize we are in greater danger than ever?

MR. FRANK. Mr. Dussel, will you be still!

AA Literary Elements

PLOT Note that the presence of the burglar is an example of rising action in the plot. How does this event add to the suspense? *(The characters realize that someone now knows of their presence.)*

BB Literary Elements

STAGE DIRECTIONS Encourage students to consider how the playwrights have created suspense in this scene. What stage directions contribute to the suspense? *(The directions include moments of silence while the characters listen and stare at the door, waiting for someone to burst through.)*

MEETING INDIVIDUAL NEEDS — SPECIAL NEEDS

Learning Disabled Students with learning disabilities may have difficulty reading drama because it is not written in paragraph form with topic sentences. Some students may have a difficult time organizing and recalling information. Explain that writing their own summaries of what has happened in each scene will help them identify the main topics of the scene.

Activity Have students write a brief summary of the events that occur in the Hanukkah scene. Students should trade papers with a partner to see whether their summaries include main ideas and details. Encourage students to summarize each scene they read. **L1**

Additional Resources

Inclusion Strategies

CC Literary Elements

CONFLICT This scene contributes to the development of the plot by highlighting the conflicts among the characters. Have students identify the characters in conflict in this scene. *(Mr. Dussel and Mrs. Van Daan.)*

FYI

Who Betrayed the Franks? It was later determined that the person who ultimately betrayed the Franks was probably an employee in the warehouse. He would have been paid the equivalent of $1.40 for each person found in hiding.

DD Author's Craft

IRONY Note that the words of the Hanukkah song contribute to the irony in this play. Have students explain how the lines of the song are ironic. *(The song says it is the "happiest of seasons," but the residents of the annex are miserable.)*

[*MR. FRANK takes ANNE back to the table, making her sit down with him, trying to calm her.*]

CC

DUSSEL. [*Pointing to PETER.*] Thanks to this clumsy fool, there's someone now who knows we're up here! Someone now knows we're up here, hiding!

MRS. VAN DAAN. [*Going to DUSSEL.*] Someone knows we're here, yes. But who is the someone? A thief! A thief! You think a thief is going to go to the Green Police and say . . . I was robbing a place the other night and I heard a noise up over my head? You think a thief is going to do that?

DUSSEL. Yes. I think he will.

MRS. VAN DAAN. [*Hysterically.*] You're crazy!

[*She stumbles back to her seat at the table. PETER follows protectively, pushing DUSSEL aside.*]

DUSSEL. I think some day he'll be caught and then he'll make a bargain with the Green Police . . . if they'll let him off, he'll tell them where some Jews are hiding!

[*He goes off into the bedroom. There is a second of appalled silence.*]

MR. VAN DAAN. He's right.

ANNE. Father, let's get out of here! We can't stay here now . . . Let's go . . .

MR. VAN DAAN. Go! Where?

MRS. FRANK. [*Sinking into her chair at the table.*] Yes. Where?

MR. FRANK. [*Rising, to them all.*] Have we lost all faith? All courage? A moment ago we thought that they'd come for us. We were sure it was the end. But it wasn't the end. We're alive, safe. [*MR. VAN DAAN goes to the table and sits. MR. FRANK prays.*] "We thank Thee, oh Lord our God, that in Thy infinite mercy Thou hast again seen fit to spare us." [*He blows out the candle, then turns to ANNE.*] Come on, Anne. The song! Let's have the song! [*He starts to sing. ANNE finally starts falteringly to sing, as MR. FRANK urges her on. Her voice is hardly audible at first.*]

DD

ANNE. [*Singing.*]

"Oh, Hanukkah! Oh, Hanukkah!
The sweet . . . celebration . . ."

[*As she goes on singing, the others gradually join in, their voices still shaking with fear. MRS. VAN DAAN sobs as she sings.*]

GROUP. "Around the feast . . . we . . . gather
In complete . . . jubilation . . .
Happiest of sea . . . sons
Now is here.
Many are the reasons for good cheer."

[*DUSSEL comes from the bedroom. He comes over to the table, standing beside MARGOT, listening to them as they sing.*]

"Together
We'll weather
Whatever tomorrow may bring."

[*As they sing on with growing courage, the lights start to dim.*]

"So hear us rejoicing
And merrily voicing
The Hanukkah song that we sing.
Hoy!"

[*The lights are out. The curtain starts slowly to fall.*]

"Hear us rejoicing
And merrily voicing
The Hanukkah song that we sing."

[*They are still singing, as the curtain falls.*]

Curtain

Teaching Support

Grammar and Language *Minilesson*

Less *or* Fewer Many students avoid using the word *fewer* and as a result misuse the word *less*. Review with students that *fewer* is the correct term to use when referring to individual items and *less* is correct when referring to concepts or categories of items. Use the following example: *Because they had less food, the Franks ate fewer meals.*

Activity Have students identify the correct term to use with the following words: *trouble, children, money, dollars, sickness, diseases.* Encourage them to suggest their own examples. **L2**

Additional Resources

- ***Grammar and Language Transparency 62***
- ***Grammar and Language Workbook,*** pp. 229–230
- ***Writer's Choice,*** Lesson 17.2

The Diary of Anne Frank, 1959. 20th Century Fox. Movie still.
Viewing the photograph: What contrast is shown in this scene with Margot, Mrs. Frank, and Anne?

VIEWING THE PHOTOGRAPH

Viewing Response *Their expressions, reflecting fear and sadness, contrast with the celebration of Hanukkah.*

Thematic Focus

Faces of Dignity Discuss the difficulties of remaining dignified under such harsh circumstances as presented in the play.

ASSESSMENT

Quick Checks, p. 63

Listening and Speaking *Minilesson*

Debate Arguing a controversial point requires that students speak to persuade others and that they listen to understand opposing points of view. Explain that to persuade successfully, one must stay focused on the subject, use examples, and explain why the opposing point of view is wrong.

Activity Have students debate the question of whether the families should have left the annex after the burglary incident. Divide the class into two groups: one in favor and one against leaving. Have them discuss the points to be raised in their arguments. **L2** COLLAB. LEARN.

Responding to the Selection

PERSONAL RESPONSE

Students' responses should explain their reactions to the suspense in scenes 4 and 5.

Analyzing Literature

1. Anne dreams that she is being captured. We learn that Dussel does not like Anne.
2. Anne plans to give everyone presents, showing she cares about the others and trying to make the best of things. Mrs. Frank is moved because the gift shows that Anne cares about her.
3. It takes the joy out of the celebration. It reminds them of their present danger.
4. The families are being oppressed just as Jews were in the time of the Maccabees.
5. Answers should include specific references to the play and each character's reaction.
6. Students may refer to the group members' inability or unwillingness to understand and respect the differences in others.

Extending Your Response

Literature Groups Groups should discuss specific examples from the play that illustrate suspense. COLLAB. LEARN.

Personal Writing Students' journal entries should describe various circumstances that cause people to show a good side and a bad side.

Active Reading and Critical Thinking

Responding to Literature

PERSONAL RESPONSE

- How did you respond to the scares in scenes 4 and 5? What were your first thoughts when Anne screamed?

Analyzing Literature

RECALL AND INTERPRET

1. What nightmare wakes Anne? What do you learn about Dussel and Anne from this episode?
2. What surprise does Anne plan for Hanukkah, and what does the surprise show about her? Why do you think Mrs. Frank is moved by Anne's actions?
3. What effect does the noise downstairs have on the celebration? Of what is it a reminder?

EVALUATE AND CONNECT

4. Hanukkah is a Jewish celebration of freedom from oppression. How does this add to the meaning of the play?
5. What do you learn about the family members from their reactions to the intruder downstairs? Were the various reactions surprising to you? Explain.
6. How are the crises that arise between group members similar, in a small way, to the crisis in Europe?

LITERARY ELEMENTS

Stage Directions

Stage directions are instructions in a play that give important information about characters and setting. Stage directions may give details about a character's appearance or actions. These directions are meant to help an actress or an actor to understand how to play a role, or to help a director set up the stage, but they are also useful for readers.

- Choose eight or ten lines of dialogue that do not have specific stage directions. Visualize the scene. Then write directions for the actors to follow as they speak.

See **Literary Terms Handbook,** p. R9.

Extending Your Response

Literature Groups

Holes in the Story The audiences for *The Diary of Anne Frank* know how the play will end. What may they not know as they watch the play? Discuss how dramatizing Anne's nightmare at this point in the story strengthens the suspense for the audience. What other events in the play add to the suspense?

Personal Writing

Looking at Both Sides Anne talks to her father about the two sides of herself: the good Anne and the mean Anne. Does everyone have a good side and a mean side? Under what circumstances might people show a good side? a bad side? Write your ideas in your journal.

Skill Minilesson

VOCABULARY • SYNONYMS

1. furiously
2. subdued
3. jubilation

Additional Resources

Vocabulary Practice, p. 43

LITERARY ELEMENTS

- Students' stage directions should be consistent with the characters' actions in the scene.

Additional Resources

Literary Elements Transparency 63

ASSESSMENT

- ***Quick Checks,*** p. 63
- ***Selection and Theme Assessment,*** pp. 109–112
- ***Performance Assessment,*** p. 57
- ***Testmaker: ExamView Pro***
- ***Interactive Tutor: Self-Assessment***

Skill Minilesson

RETEACH • REVIEW

VOCABULARY • SYNONYMS

Some words, such as *happiness,* have many levels of meaning. For instance, *happiness* can mean "mild contentment" or "intense joy." To make clear a particular level of happiness, a writer may choose a synonym that is more precise. *Jubilation,* for example, means "great, joyful happiness."

PRACTICE Choose a synonym to answer each question.

1. Is a person who screams over a disappointment behaving indignantly or furiously?
2. Are the voices of people discussing a tragedy calm or subdued?
3. Does the winning side in a championship game show delight or jubilation?

Before You Read

The Diary of Anne Frank, Act 2

BUILDING BACKGROUND

The Time and Place More than one year has passed since the end of act 1.

Did You Know? During Anne's first year in hiding, the Germans continued their conquest of Europe and North Africa. At the same time, Hitler crafted a plan to kill all Jewish people in German-controlled Europe.

By 1944, when act 2 of the play begins, the war has taken a turn in favor of the Allied forces–the United States, Great Britain, and the Soviet Union. In 1943 Soviet troops attacked German forces from the east, pushing them out of the Soviet Union. Meanwhile, American, British, and Canadian troops approached from the south, driving the Germans out of North Africa and eventually invading Southern Europe. By the summer of 1944, Italy (an ally of Germany) and France were free from Nazi rule.

VOCABULARY PREVIEW

disgruntled (dis grunt′ əld) *adj.* displeased; p. 744

onslaught (ôn′ slôt′) *n.* a forceful or destructive attack; assault; p. 747

foreboding (fôr bō′ ding) *n.* a feeling that something evil is going to happen; p. 748

apprehension (ap′ ri hen′ shən) *n.* fear of what may happen; dread; p. 749

intuition (in′ to͞o ish′ ən) *n.* an ability to know things without having to reason them out; p. 755

poise (poiz) *n.* relaxed and self-controlled dignity in manner; p. 760

stealthily (stel′ thə lē) *adv.* in a secret or sneaky manner; p. 762

frenzy (fren′ zē) *n.* a state of great excitement or deep disturbance; p. 762

pandemonium (pan′ də mō′ nē əm) *n.* wild disorder and uproar; p. 765

Before Reading

Objectives

- To read and analyze a play
- To identify dramatic monologue and tragedy in a drama
- To write a letter and a character analysis

Skills

Reading/Thinking: Inferring; Elaborating; Synthesizing; Distinguishing Fact and Opinion; Drawing Conclusions; Making Critical Judgments; Focusing on a Question

Writing: Description; Prewriting; Letter; Introductions and Conclusions; Character Sketches

Vocabulary: Roots; Etymology

Grammar/Language: Indefinite Pronouns; Punctuating Dates; Italics and Quotation Marks

Listening/Speaking: Public Speaking; Readers Theater; Oral Reading

Life Skills: Time Management; Leading and Organizing

Collaboration: Literature Groups; Readers Theater

MEETING INDIVIDUAL NEEDS — ADVANCED LEARNERS

Political Personalities Some historians have said that the World War II era saw the greatest collection of strong, charismatic, powerful political and military leaders ever. Review with students that Winston Churchill, Franklin Roosevelt, Adolf Hitler, Benito Mussolini, Field Marshal Rommel, Field Marshal Montgomery, Joseph Stalin, and General Patton were all important figures in World War II and they all had powerful leadership skills.

Activity Have students select one or two of these historic figures to study in more detail. Have them present their findings to the class, focusing on how the person(s) they have chosen interacted with the other leaders. **L3**

Reading the Selection

SUMMARY

Act 2, Scenes 1–2

About a year and a half has passed since the first day in the attic, and Anne has matured into a young woman. Tensions continue in the attic since food is scarcer now than it was before. In addition, one of Mr. Kraler's workers has begun to ask a lot of questions that indicate he knows the families are in the attic. Probably due to stress, Mr. Kraler is in the hospital with ulcers. As time goes on, Anne and Peter develop a close friendship, which increases the tension between the adults and children, as well as between the two families.

Spanish Summaries, p. 60

A Active Reading Strategies

REVIEW Have students review the facts the audience learns from Anne's diary entry that opens act 2.

VOCABULARY If you haven't previewed the selection vocabulary with students, stop and remind them to use context clues to unlock the meanings of new vocabulary words.

The Diary of Anne Frank (Continued)

ACT 2

SCENE 1

A [*In the darkness we hear* ANNE'S VOICE, *again reading from the diary.*]

ANNE'S VOICE. Saturday, the first of January, nineteen forty-four. Another new year has begun and we find ourselves still in our hiding place. We have been here now for one year, five months, and twenty-five days. It seems that our life is at a standstill.

[*The curtain rises on the scene. It is late afternoon. Everyone is bundled up against the cold. In the main room* MRS. FRANK *is taking down the laundry which is hung across the back.* MR. FRANK *sits in the chair down left, reading.* MARGOT *is lying on the couch with a blanket over her and the many-colored knitted scarf around her throat.* ANNE *is seated at the center table, writing in her diary.* PETER, MR. *and* MRS. VAN DAAN, *and* DUSSEL *are all in their own rooms, reading or lying down.*
As the lights dim on, ANNE'S VOICE *continues, without a break.*]

ANNE'S VOICE. We are all a little thinner. The Van Daans' "discussions" are as violent as ever. Mother still does not understand me. But then I don't understand her either. There is one great change, however. A change in myself. I read somewhere that girls of my age don't feel quite certain of themselves. That they become quiet within and begin to think of the miracle that is taking place in their bodies. I think that what is happening to me is so wonderful . . . not only what can be seen, but what is taking place inside. Each time it has happened I have a feeling that I have a sweet secret. [*We hear the chimes and then a hymn being played on the carillon outside.*] And in spite of any pain, I long for the time when I shall feel that secret within me again.

[*The buzzer of the door below suddenly sounds. Everyone is startled,* MR. FRANK *tiptoes cautiously to the top of the steps and listens. Again the buzzer sounds, in* MIEP'S *V-for-Victory*[40] *signal.*]

MR. FRANK. It's Miep!

[*He goes quickly down the steps to unbolt the door.* MRS. FRANK *calls upstairs to the* VAN DAANS *and then to* PETER.]

MRS. FRANK. Wake up, everyone! Miep is here! [ANNE *quickly puts her diary away.* MARGOT *sits up, pulling the blanket around her shoulders.* MR. DUSSEL *sits on the edge of his bed, listening, disgruntled.* MIEP *comes up the steps, followed by* MR. KRALER. *They bring flowers, books, newspapers, etc.* ANNE *rushes to* MIEP, *throwing her arms affectionately around her.*] Miep . . . and Mr. Kraler . . . What a delightful surprise!

40. *V-for-Victory* was three short buzzes followed by a long one, based on Morse Code for the letter *v.*

Vocabulary
disgruntled (dis grunt′ əld) *adj.* displeased

Teaching Support

FINE ART TRANSPARENCY 17

You may want to use ***Fine Art Transparency 17*** to discuss reasons that people tell their stories.

MEETING INDIVIDUAL NEEDS — ENGLISH LANGUAGE LEARNERS

Prepositions English language learners sometimes have difficulty selecting the appropriate preposition to accompany particular verbs. With practice, students can learn the correct English constructions. Use examples to demonstrate standard prepositional usage, such as "Anne is *seated at* the center table," "Mr. Dussel *sits on* the edge of the bed," (page 744) "*goes directly to* the stove" (page 746). Explain the difference between *seated at* and *seated on* and *goes to* and *goes with.*

Activity Have students write one sentence using each of the constructions.

Additional Resources

English Language Learners Sourcebook, p. 87

The Diary of Anne Frank, 1959. 20th Century Fox. Movie still.

Viewing the photograph: What effect do Miep's visits have on Anne and the other occupants of the Secret Annex?

Language Note

Morse Code Morse code (named after Samuel Morse, who developed it) is a method of communication used when voice transmission is not possible. It was originally used for telegraph messages. In Morse code, each letter in the alphabet and the numbers 0–9 are represented by a combination of dots and dashes, or short and long sounds that can be tapped out to form a message. Until 1999, ships at sea used Morse code as well as motion electronic communication systems. Morse code for the letters SOS (··· --- ···) is an international distress signal.

VIEWING THE PHOTOGRAPH

Viewing Response *She cheers them with news of the outside world, food, and other items.*

MEETING INDIVIDUAL NEEDS — MULTIPLE MODES OF EXPRESSION

Bodily-Kinesthetic Students who enjoy physical activity and manipulating objects may be interested in learning how to use Morse code. Point out that the letter-by-letter code can be found on the Internet, in any comprehensive dictionary, or in an encyclopedia.

Activity Have students obtain a copy of the Morse code alphabet and prepare a two- or three-word message that one of the play's characters might have sent. Have students present their Morse code message to the class, tapping it out or using a flashlight. **L2**

B Active Reading Strategies

CONNECT Ask students what Anne means when she says she can smell the wind and cold. Ask them whether they have ever had this experience.

C Critical Thinking

INFER Have students explain what information is implied from Peter's question. *(His cat has disappeared.)*

D Critical Thinking

ELABORATE Ask students what the audience learns from Mrs. Van Daan's remarks about the cake. *(They learn that another year has passed without peace.)*

MR. KRALER. We came to bring you New Year's greetings.

MRS. FRANK. You shouldn't . . . you should have at least one day to yourselves.

[She goes quickly to the stove and brings down teacups and tea for all of them.]

ANNE. Don't say that, it's so wonderful to see them! [*Sniffing at MIEP's coat.*] I can smell the wind and the cold on your clothes. B

MIEP. [*Giving her the flowers.*] There you are. [*Then to MARGOT, feeling her forehead.*] How are you, Margot? . . . Feeling any better?

MARGOT. I'm all right.

ANNE. We filled her full of every kind of pill so she won't cough and make a noise.

[She runs into her room to put the flowers in water. MR. and MRS. VAN DAAN come from upstairs. Outside there is the sound of a band playing.]

MRS. VAN DAAN. Well, hello, Miep. Mr. Kraler.

MR. KRALER. [*Giving a bouquet of flowers to MRS. VAN DAAN.*] With my hope for peace in the New Year.

C PETER. [*Anxiously.*] Miep, have you seen Mouschi? Have you seen him anywhere around?

MIEP. I'm sorry, Peter. I asked everyone in the neighborhood had they seen a gray cat. But they said no.

[MRS. FRANK gives MIEP a cup of tea. MR. FRANK comes up the steps, carrying a small cake on a plate.]

MR. FRANK. Look what Miep's brought for us!

MRS. FRANK. [*Taking it.*] A cake!

MR. VAN DAAN. A cake! [*He pinches MIEP's cheeks gaily and hurries up to the cupboard.*] I'll get some plates.

[DUSSEL, in his room, hastily puts a coat on and starts out to join the others.]

MRS. FRANK. Thank you, Miepia. You shouldn't have done it. You must have used all of your sugar ration for weeks. [*Giving it to MRS. VAN DAAN.*] It's beautiful, isn't it?

MRS. VAN DAAN. It's been ages since I even saw a cake. Not since you brought us one last year. [*Without looking at the cake, to MIEP.*] Remember? Don't you remember, you gave us one on New Year's Day? Just this time last year? I'll never forget it because you had "Peace in nineteen forty-three" on it. [*She looks at the cake and reads.*] "Peace in nineteen forty-four!" D

MIEP. Well, it has to come sometime, you know. [*As DUSSEL comes from his room.*] Hello, Mr. Dussel.

MR. KRALER. How are you?

MR. VAN DAAN. [*Bringing plates and a knife.*] Here's the knife, *liefje*. Now, how many of us are there?

MIEP. None for me, thank you.

MR. FRANK. Oh, please. You must.

MIEP. I couldn't.

MR. VAN DAAN. Good! That leaves one . . . two . . . three . . . seven of us.

DUSSEL. Eight! Eight! It's the same number as it always is!

MR. VAN DAAN. I left Margot out. I take it for granted Margot won't eat any.

ANNE. Why wouldn't she!

MRS. FRANK. I think it won't harm her.

MR. VAN DAAN. All right! All right! I just didn't want her to start coughing again, that's all.

DUSSEL. And please, Mrs. Frank should cut the cake.

Teaching Support

MEETING INDIVIDUAL NEEDS — SPECIAL NEEDS

Learning Disabled Learning-disabled students may be able to visualize and remember the action of the play better by studying the pictures provided with the selection. Review with students the group picture provided at the beginning of the play and identify each character.

Activity Working in groups, students should discuss what is happening in each picture from the play and relate it to the corresponding scene. Encourage students to describe what happened before and after the events depicted. **L1** COLLAB. LEARN.

Additional Resources

Inclusion Strategies

MR. VAN DAAN. What's the difference?

MRS. VAN DAAN. It's not Mrs. Frank's cake, is it, Miep? It's for all of us.

Together

DUSSEL. Mrs. Frank divides things better.

MRS. VAN DAAN. [*Going to* DUSSEL.] What are you trying to say?

MR. VAN DAAN. Oh, come on! Stop wasting time!

Together

MRS. VAN DAAN. [*To* DUSSEL.] Don't I always give everybody exactly the same? Don't I?

MR. VAN DAAN. Forget it, Kerli.

MRS. VAN DAAN. No. I want an answer! Don't I?

DUSSEL. Yes. Yes. Everybody gets exactly the same . . . except Mr. Van Daan always gets a little bit more.

[*VAN DAAN advances on DUSSEL, the knife still in his hand.*]

MR. VAN DAAN. That's a lie!

[*DUSSEL retreats before the onslaught of the VAN DAANS.*]

MR. FRANK. Please, please! [*Then to* MIEP.] You see what a little sugar cake does to us? It goes right to our heads!

MR. VAN DAAN. [*Handing* MRS. FRANK *the knife.*] Here you are, Mrs. Frank.

MRS. FRANK. Thank you. [*Then to* MIEP *as she goes to the table to cut the cake.*] Are you sure you won't have some?

MIEP. [*Drinking her tea.*] No, really, I have to go in a minute.

[*The sound of the band fades out in the distance.*]

PETER. [*To* MIEP.] Maybe Mouschi went back to our house . . . they say that cats . . . Do you ever get over there . . . ? I mean . . . do you suppose you could . . . ?

MIEP. I'll try, Peter. The first minute I get I'll try. But I'm afraid, with him gone a week . . .

DUSSEL. Make up your mind, already someone has had a nice big dinner from that cat!

[*PETER is furious, inarticulate.*[41] *He starts toward DUSSEL as if to hit him.* MR. FRANK *stops him.* MRS. FRANK *speaks quickly to ease the situation.*]

MRS. FRANK. [*To* MIEP.] This is delicious, Miep!

MRS. VAN DAAN. [*Eating hers.*] Delicious!

MR. VAN DAAN. [*Finishing it in one gulp.*] Dirk's in luck to get a girl who can bake like this!

MIEP. [*Putting down her empty teacup.*] I have to run. Dirk's taking me to a party tonight.

ANNE. How heavenly! Remember now what everyone is wearing, and what you have to eat and everything, so you can tell us tomorrow.

MIEP. I'll give you a full report! Good-bye, everyone!

MR. VAN DAAN. [*To* MIEP.] Just a minute. There's something I'd like you to do for me.

[*He hurries off up the stairs to his room.*]

41. Peter is so angry that he becomes unable to speak (*inarticulate*).

Vocabulary
onslaught (ôn′ slôt′) *n.* a forceful or destructive attack; assault

E Author's Craft

COMEDY Point out that serious drama often contains moments of comedy, known as comic relief, to provide contrast to a play's overall serious tone. Encourage students to find the humor in this scene.

F Literary Elements

STAGE DIRECTIONS Note the stage directions for the sound of a band outside. What purpose do the playwrights have in including the sound of a band playing? *(The band emphasizes the fact that life goes on outside the annex. The fading music accentuates the decline of the New Year's celebration.)*

G Active Reading Strategies

QUESTION Note that several characters have items that are important to them. Ask students why Peter's cat was important to him. *(Peter has given most of his affection to the cat; Mouschi has been his best friend.)*

Writing Minilesson

Description Point out that Anne's diary is a description of events that she has witnessed. Anne does two things that are important to a good description: She describes the people and the surroundings in enough detail that the reader can visualize them, and she interprets the action by adding her own reactions and insight so that the action has meaning for the reader.

Activity Have students write a brief description of the cake-cutting scene (pages 746–747) as if they have witnessed it. They should write their description for a reader who was not there. Encourage students to set the scene so that the reader can visualize it and to interpret it for the reader. **L2**

Additional Resources

Writer's Choice, Lesson 3.2

H Literary Elements

CHARACTERIZATION Note Peter's threats to Mr. Dussel. Have students recall other examples of Peter's threats of violence. What do these events tell us about Peter's character? *(He has a temper and, although reserved, feels intensely and is loyal to those he loves.)*

I Literary Elements

IRONY Note the irony of Mr. Van Daan's use of the term *selfish* to describe his wife. Ask students to predict what Mr. Van Daan will use the money for. *(Most students will predict that he will buy cigarettes.)*

J Critical Thinking

INFER Point out that Mr. Kraler's statements give some clues as to the conditions in Amsterdam at this time.

Teaching Support

MRS. VAN DAAN. [*Sharply.*] Putti, where are you going? [*She rushes up the stairs after him, calling hysterically.*] What do you want? Putti, what are you going to do?

MIEP. [*To* PETER.] What's wrong?

PETER. [*His sympathy is with his mother.*] Father says he's going to sell her fur coat. She's crazy about that old fur coat.

DUSSEL. Is it possible? Is it possible that anyone is so silly as to worry about a fur coat in times like this?

H PETER. It's none of your darn business . . . and if you say one more thing . . . I'll, I'll take you and I'll . . . I mean it . . . I'll . . .

[*There is a piercing scream from* MRS. VAN DAAN *above. She grabs at the fur coat as* MR. VAN DAAN *is starting downstairs with it.*]

MRS. VAN DAAN. No! No! No! Don't you dare take that! You hear? It's mine! [*Downstairs* PETER *turns away, embarrassed, miserable.*] My father gave me that! You didn't give it to me. You have no right. Let go of it . . . you hear?

[MR. VAN DAAN *pulls the coat from her hands and hurries downstairs.* MRS. VAN DAAN *sinks to the floor, sobbing. As* MR. VAN DAAN *comes into the main room the others look away, embarrassed for him.*]

MR. VAN DAAN. [*To* MR. KRALER.] Just a little—discussion over the advisability[42] I of selling this coat. As I have often reminded Mrs. Van Daan, it's very selfish of her to keep it when people outside are in such desperate need of clothing . . . [*He gives the coat to* MIEP.] So if you will please to sell it for us? It should fetch a good price. And by the way, will you get me cigarettes. I don't care what kind they are . . . get all you can.

MIEP. It's terribly difficult to get them, Mr. Van Daan. But I'll try. Good-bye.

[*She goes.* MR. FRANK *follows her down the steps to bolt the door after her.* MRS. FRANK *gives* MR. KRALER *a cup of tea.*]

MRS. FRANK. Are you sure you won't have some cake, Mr. Kraler?

MR. KRALER. I'd better not.

MR. VAN DAAN. You're still feeling badly? What does your doctor say?

MR. KRALER. I haven't been to him.

MRS. FRANK. Now, Mr. Kraler! . . .

MR. KRALER. [*Sitting at the table.*] Oh, I tried. But you can't get near a doctor these days . . . they're so busy. After weeks I finally managed to get one on the telephone. I told him I'd like an appointment . . . I wasn't feeling very well. J You know what he answers . . . over the telephone . . . Stick out your tongue! [*They laugh. He turns to* MR. FRANK *as* MR. FRANK *comes back.*] I have some contracts here . . . I wonder if you'd look over them with me . . .

MR. FRANK. [*Putting out his hand.*] Of course.

MR. KRALER. [*He rises.*] If we could go downstairs . . . [MR. FRANK *starts ahead,* MR. KRALER *speaks to the others.*] Will you forgive us? I won't keep him but a minute.

[*He starts to follow* MR. FRANK *down the steps.*]

MARGOT. [*With sudden foreboding.*] What's happened? Something's happened! Hasn't it, Mr. Kraler?

42. *Advisability* means "suitability" or "the quality of being wise, fitting, or proper."

Vocabulary

foreboding (fôr bō′ ding) *n.* a feeling that something evil is going to happen

REAL-WORLD CONNECTION

Historic Video Many movies have been made about World War II and the Holocaust and their impact on families and loved ones.

Activity Borrow such a video from the library and have students watch it in class. Ask each student to write a brief summary of the film and his or her reaction to it. **L2**

[MR. KRALER stops and comes back, trying to reassure MARGOT with a pretense of casualness.]

MR. KRALER. No, really. I want your father's advice . . .

MARGOT. Something's gone wrong! I know it!

MR. FRANK. *[Coming back, to MR. KRALER.]* If it's something that concerns us here, it's better that we all hear it.

MR. KRALER. *[Turning to him, quietly.]* But . . . the children . . . ?

K **MR. FRANK.** What they'd imagine would be worse than any reality.

[As MR. KRALER speaks, they all listen with intense apprehension. MRS. VAN DAAN comes down the stairs and sits on the bottom step.]

MR. KRALER. It's a man in the storeroom . . . I don't know whether or not you remember him . . . Carl, about fifty, heavy-set, near-sighted . . . He came with us just before you left.

MR. FRANK. He was from Utrecht?[43]

MR. KRALER. That's the man. A couple of weeks ago, when I was in the storeroom, he closed the door and asked me . . . how's Mr. Frank? What do you hear from Mr. Frank? I told him I only knew there was a rumor that you were in Switzerland. He said he'd heard that rumor too, but he thought I might know something more. I didn't pay any attention to it . . . but then a thing happened yesterday . . . He'd brought some invoices to the office for me to sign. As I was going through them, I looked up. He was standing staring at the bookcase . . . your bookcase. He said he thought he remembered a door there . . . Wasn't there a door that used to go up to the loft? Then he told me he wanted more money. Twenty guilders[44] more a week.

MR. VAN DAAN. Blackmail! L

MR. FRANK. Twenty guilders? Very modest blackmail.

MR. VAN DAAN. That's just the beginning.

DUSSEL. *[Coming to MR. FRANK.]* You know what I think? He was the thief who was down there that night. That's how he knows we're here.

MR. FRANK. *[To MR. KRALER.]* How was it left? What did you tell him?

MR. KRALER. I said I had to think about it. What shall I do? Pay him the money? . . . Take a chance on firing him . . . or what? I don't know.

DUSSEL. *[Frantic.]* For God's sake don't fire him! Pay him what he asks . . . keep him here where you can have your eye on him. M

MR. FRANK. Is it so much that he's asking? What are they paying nowadays?

MR. KRALER. He could get it in a war plant. But this isn't a war plant. Mind you, I don't know if he really knows . . . or if he doesn't know.

MR. FRANK. Offer him half. Then we'll soon find out if it's blackmail or not.

DUSSEL. And if it is? We've got to pay it, haven't we? Anything he asks we've got to pay!

43. *Utrecht* (ū′ trekt) is a city in the central Netherlands.

44. The *guilder* is the basic monetary unit of the Netherlands. Twenty guilders is about ten dollars in American money.

Vocabulary
apprehension (ap′ ri hen′ shən) *n.* fear of what may happen; dread

K Active Reading Strategies

EVALUATE Ask students to explain Mr. Frank's statement. Why doesn't Mr. Kraler want to speak in front of everyone? *(He doesn't want everyone to worry more.)*

L Critical Thinking

SYNTHESIZE Review with students the meaning of *blackmail.* Have them explain what has led to Mr. Van Daan's conclusion that they are being blackmailed.

M Active Reading Strategies

REVIEW Have students identify the problem facing the group. What are the possible solutions? Why doesn't Mr. Dussel think firing Carl is a good solution?

Reading Minilesson

Distinguish Fact from Opinion
Throughout the play, one of the conflicts among the characters is disagreement over how to interpret facts. Remind students that a fact is provable, and an opinion is a conclusion based on what one believes or feels. Point out that Peter's cat is missing is a fact, whereas the statement that it has been eaten is an opinion.

Activity Have students review the exchange with Mr. Kraler on page 749 and identify those statements that are fact and those that are opinion. Have students make a chart with two columns labeled *Fact* and *Opinion* to list their selections under. **L2**

Additional Resources
Reading Skills Practice Workbook

VIEWING THE PHOTOGRAPH

Viewing Response *The characters seem older and much more serious in this scene.*

LITERATURE & HUMANITIES

Have students examine "Empty Pods" on *The National Museum of Women in the Arts* CD. Discuss how the Israeli artist conveys both hope and hopelessness.

The Diary of Anne Frank, 1959. 20th Century Fox. Movie still.

Viewing the photograph: Compare this image with the one on page 705. How have both characters changed since they came to the Secret Annex?

Teaching Support

INTERDISCIPLINARY CONNECTION

The Arts Bring newspaper or magazine advertisements for movies and plays to demonstrate advertising techniques to students. Encourage students to comment on the types of information, pictures, and visual techniques used in the advertisements to attract attention.

Activity Have students work in groups to design an advertisement to attract theatergoers to *The Diary of Anne Frank*. Students may want to use a computer graphics program, or they may want to hand paint the advertisement. Encourage them to consider including information that will pique viewers' curiosity and using interesting lettering and design to attract attention. **L2** COLLAB. LEARN.

MR. FRANK. Let's decide that when the time comes.

MR. KRALER. This may be all my imagination. You get to a point, these days, where you suspect everyone and everything. Again and again . . . on some simple look or word, I've found myself . . .

[*The telephone rings in the office below.*]

MRS. VAN DAAN. [*Hurrying to* MR. KRALER.] There's the telephone! What does that mean, the telephone ringing on a holiday?

MR. KRALER. That's my wife. I told her I had to go over some papers in my office . . . to call me there when she got out of church. [*He starts out.*] I'll offer him half then. Good-bye . . . we'll hope for the best!

[*The group call their good-bye's half-heartedly.* MR. FRANK *follows* MR. KRALER, *to bolt the door below. During the following scene,* MR. FRANK *comes back up and stands listening, disturbed.*]

N

DUSSEL. [*To* MR. VAN DAAN.] You can thank your son for this . . . smashing the light! I tell you, it's just a question of time now.

[*He goes to the window at the back and stands looking out.*]

MARGOT. Sometimes I wish the end would come . . . whatever it is.

MRS. FRANK. [*Shocked.*] Margot!

[ANNE *goes to* MARGOT, *sitting beside her on the couch with her arms around her.*]

MARGOT. Then at least we'd know where we were.

MRS. FRANK. You should be ashamed of yourself! Talking that way! Think how lucky we are! Think of the thousands dying in the war, every day. Think of the people in concentration camps.

ANNE. [*Interrupting.*] What's the good of that? What's the good of thinking of misery when you're already miserable? That's stupid!

MRS. FRANK. Anne!

[*As* ANNE *goes on raging at her mother,* MRS. FRANK *tries to break in, in an effort to quiet her.*]

O

ANNE. We're young, Margot and Peter and I! You grown-ups have had your chance! But look at us . . . If we begin thinking of all the horror in the world, we're lost! We're trying to hold onto some kind of ideals . . . when everything . . . ideals, hopes . . . everything, are being destroyed! It isn't our fault that the world is in such a mess! We weren't around when all this started! So don't try to take it out on us!

[*She rushes off to her room, slamming the door after her. She picks up a brush from the chest and hurls it to the floor. Then she sits on the settee, trying to control her anger.*]

MR. VAN DAAN. She talks as if we started the war! Did we start the war?

[*He spots* ANNE*'s cake. As he starts to take it,* PETER *anticipates him.*]

P

PETER. She left her cake. [*He starts for* ANNE*'s room with the cake. There is silence in the main room.* MRS. VAN DAAN *goes up to her room, followed by* MR. VAN DAAN. DUSSEL *stays looking out the window.* MR. FRANK *brings* MRS. FRANK *her cake. She eats it slowly, without relish.* MR. FRANK *takes his cake to* MARGOT *and sits quietly on the sofa beside her.* PETER *stands in the doorway of* ANNE*'s darkened room, looking at her, then makes a little movement to let her know he is there.* ANNE *sits up, quickly, trying to hide the signs of her tears.* PETER *holds out the cake to her.*] You left this.

ANNE. [*Dully.*] Thanks.

N Active Reading Strategies

REVIEW Have students review the dates for the settings of act 2 and the final scene of act 1. On the basis of these, have them consider whether they agree with Dussel's conclusions.

O Literary Elements

DRAMATIC MONOLOGUE Note that Anne's monologue is derived from the diary entry presented earlier in the theme. What do students think Anne means by saying that the adults are taking it out on them?

P Critical Thinking

DRAWING CONCLUSIONS Ask students why no one responds to Anne's remarks. Encourage them to consider whether this failure to respond supports her comments.

Listening and Speaking Minilesson

Public Speaking One purpose of public speaking is to inform others. An example of this is broadcasting, which informs the listener or viewer of events they did not witness and about which they may have little knowledge. A good broadcasting report provides the audience with enough detail to understand the event.

Activity Have students prepare a news broadcast report based on information from act 2, scene 1. Suggest that the audience already knows that groups of people have been in hiding for some time. Reports might begin, "The government today admitted that their attempt to . . ." Ask volunteers to present their completed news reports to the class. **L2**

Q **Literary Elements**

DRAMATIC MONOLOGUE Have students contrast Peter's monologue with Anne's. What do the differences in the way they are delivered say about the characters? *(Anne is more confident than Peter, and Peter is unused to expressing his feelings.)*

R **Active Reading Strategies**

QUESTION Ask students to whom "his lordship" refers. Why does she use this term? *(Mr. Dussel—He acts as if he deserves special treatment, and he is very demanding.)*

S **Active Reading Strategies**

REVIEW Have students compare and contrast Anne's attitude in act 2 with her attitude in act 1. *(Anne was more playful and childlike in act 1.)* Ask students to consider what has caused the differences. *(In act 2 she is older; she has spent a long time living in hiding and is more introspective.)*

Teaching Support

[*PETER starts to go out, then comes back.*]

PETER. I thought you were fine just now. You know just how to talk to them. You know just how to say it. I'm no good . . . I never can think . . . especially when I'm mad . . . That Dussel . . . when he said that about Mouschi . . . someone eating him . . . all I could think is . . . I wanted to hit him. I wanted to give him such a . . . a . . . that he'd . . . That's what I used to do when there was an argument at school . . . That's the way I . . . but here . . . And an old man like that . . . it wouldn't be so good.

ANNE. You're making a big mistake about me. I do it all wrong. I say too much. I go too far. I hurt people's feelings . . .

[*DUSSEL leaves the window, going to his room.*]

PETER. I think you're just fine . . . What I want to say . . . if it wasn't for you around here, I don't know. What I mean . . .

[*PETER is interrupted by DUSSEL's turning on the light. DUSSEL stands in the doorway, startled to see PETER. PETER advances toward him forbiddingly. DUSSEL backs out of the room. PETER closes the door on him.*]

ANNE. Do you mean it, Peter? Do you really mean it?

PETER. I said it, didn't I?

ANNE. Thank you, Peter!

[*In the main room MR. and MRS. FRANK collect the dishes and take them to the sink, washing them. MARGOT lies down again on the couch. DUSSEL, lost, wanders into PETER's room and takes up a book, starting to read.*]

PETER. [*Looking at the photographs on the wall.*] You've got quite a collection.

ANNE. Wouldn't you like some in your room? I could give you some. Heaven knows you spend enough time in there . . . doing heaven knows what . . .

PETER. It's easier. A fight starts, or an argument . . . I duck in there.

ANNE. You're lucky, having a room to go to. His lordship is always here . . . I hardly ever get a minute alone. When they start in on me, I can't duck away. I have to stand there and take it.

PETER. You gave some of it back just now.

ANNE. I get so mad. They've formed their opinions . . . about everything . . . but we . . . we're still trying to find out . . . We have problems here that no other people our age have ever had. And just as you think you've solved them, something comes along and bang! You have to start all over again.

PETER. At least you've got someone you can talk to.

ANNE. Not really. Mother . . . I never discuss anything serious with her. She doesn't understand. Father's all right. We can talk about everything . . . everything but one thing. Mother. He simply won't talk about her. I don't think you can be really intimate with anyone if he holds something back, do you?

PETER. I think your father's fine.

ANNE. Oh, he is, Peter! He is! He's the only one who's ever given me the feeling that I have any sense. But anyway, nothing can take the place of school and play and friends of your own age . . . or near your age . . . can it?

PETER. I suppose you miss your friends and all.

ANNE. It isn't just . . . [*She breaks off, staring up at him for a second.*] Isn't it

MEETING INDIVIDUAL NEEDS

SPECIAL NEEDS

Less-Proficient Readers Less-proficient readers may have a habit of pausing to reread words. This interrupts the flow of reading, creating a barrier to understanding. Some of this can be avoided by prereading.

Activity Have students skim a page of the play to learn which characters are in the scene. Then ask them to read the page. Encourage students to continue reading when they reach an unfamiliar word and sound out the word, using their knowledge of sound-letter correspondences. They may recognize the spoken word, or they may use context clues to identify and define the word. **L1**

Additional Resources

Inclusion Strategies

funny, you and I? Here we've been seeing each other every minute for almost a year and a half, and this is the first time we've ever really talked. It helps a lot to have someone to talk to, don't you think? It helps you to let off steam.

PETER. [*Going to the door.*] Well, any time you want to let off steam, you can come into my room.

ANNE. [*Following him.*] I can get up an awful lot of steam. You'll have to be careful how you say that.

PETER. It's all right with me.

ANNE. Do you mean it?

PETER. I said it, didn't I?

[*He goes out. ANNE stands in her doorway looking after him. As PETER gets to his door he stands for a minute looking back at her. Then he goes into his room. DUSSEL rises as he comes in, and quickly passes him, going out. He starts across for his room. ANNE sees him coming, and pulls her door shut. DUSSEL turns back toward PETER's room. PETER pulls his door shut. DUSSEL stands there, bewildered, forlorn.*
The scene slowly dims out. The curtain falls on the scene. ANNE'S VOICE comes over in the darkness . . . faintly at first, and then with growing strength.]

ANNE'S VOICE. We've had bad news. The people from whom Miep got our ration books have been arrested. So we have had to cut down on our food. Our stomachs are so empty that they rumble and make strange noises, all in different keys. Mr. Van Daan's is deep and low, like a bass fiddle. Mine is high, whistling like a flute. As we all sit around waiting for supper, it's like an orchestra tuning up. It only needs Toscanini to raise his baton and we'd be off in the Ride of the Valkyries. Monday, the sixth of March, nineteen forty-four. Mr. Kraler is in the hospital. It seems he has ulcers.[45] Pim says we are his ulcers. Miep has to run the business and us too. The Americans have landed on the southern tip of Italy. Father looks for a quick finish to the war. Mr. Dussel is waiting every day for the warehouse man to demand more money. Have I been skipping too much from one subject to another? I can't help it. I feel that spring is coming. I feel it in my whole body and soul. I feel utterly confused. I am longing . . . so longing . . . for everything . . . for friends . . . for someone to talk to . . . someone who understands . . . someone young, who feels as I do . . .

[*As these last lines are being said, the curtain rises on the scene. The lights dim on. ANNE'S VOICE fades out.*]

SCENE 2

[*It is evening, after supper. From outside we hear the sound of children playing. The "grownups," with the exception of MR. VAN DAAN, are all in the main room. MRS. FRANK is doing some mending, MRS. VAN DAAN is reading a fashion magazine. MR. FRANK is going over business accounts. DUSSEL, in his dentist's jacket, is pacing up and down, impatient to get into his bedroom. MR. VAN DAAN is upstairs working on a piece of embroidery in an embroidery frame. In his room PETER is sitting before the mirror, smoothing his hair. As the scene goes on, he*

45. Arturo *Toscanini* (täs′ kə nē′ nē) was an Italian orchestra conductor. *Ride of the Valkyries* is a passage from an opera by Richard Wagner, a German composer. Mr. Kraler's *ulcers* are sores on the lining of his stomach.

T Active Reading Strategies

CONNECT Ask students whether they have ever had the experience of "knowing" someone for a long time before "getting to know" that person. Ask them why they think this happens.

U Author's Craft

SIMILE Note the simile Anne uses in her description. Ask students to identify the two things Anne is comparing. Point out that this simile is effective because it appears to the readers' auditory sense.

Vocabulary Skills

Roots The root word *lorn,* which appears in *forlorn* in the left column, comes from an old English word meaning "to lose." Have students use the root word to explain what it means to look forlorn or to be lovelorn.

MEETING INDIVIDUAL NEEDS — ADVANCED LEARNERS

History of Setting Students may be interested in learning more about the play's setting. Discuss with students some examples from the play of the different life styles and social standards that existed during the time in which the play is set.

Activity Have students research magazines and newspapers from the 1940s to learn more about the daily lives of people at that time. Encourage students to consider social activities, work habits, leisure activities, and family life as subjects for further research. **L3**

VIEWING THE PHOTOGRAPH

Viewing Response *Putting up pictures of movie stars reflects Anne's childish fascination with them and may indicate her aspiration to lead an extraordinary life.*

Anne Frank Remembered, 1996. Sony Pictures Classics. Movie still.

Viewing the photograph: Anne covered her bedroom wall with photos of various movie stars and the young English princesses Elizabeth and Margaret. In what ways does this wall reflect Anne's childhood interests? How might it show her aspirations as a young adult?

puts on his tie, brushes his coat and puts it on, preparing himself meticulously for a visit from ANNE. *On his wall are now hung some of* ANNE*'s motion picture stars.*

In her room ANNE *too is getting dressed. She stands before the mirror in her slip, trying various ways of dressing her hair.* MARGOT *is seated on the sofa, hemming a skirt for* ANNE *to wear.*

In the main room DUSSEL *can stand it no longer. He comes over, rapping sharply on the door of his and* ANNE*'s bedroom.*]

ANNE. [*Calling to him.*] No, no, Mr. Dussel! I am not dressed yet. [DUSSEL *walks away, furious, sitting down and burying his head in his hands.* ANNE *turns to* MARGOT.] How is that? How does that look?

MARGOT. [*Glancing at her briefly.*] Fine.

ANNE. You didn't even look.

MARGOT. Of course I did. It's fine.

ANNE. Margot, tell me, am I terribly ugly?

MARGOT. Oh, stop fishing.

Teaching Support

MEETING INDIVIDUAL NEEDS: MULTIPLE MODES OF EXPRESSION

Spatial Students who can draw may best express their reactions to the play through illustrations. Point out that artwork helps add visual interest to writing and that many books are prized as much for their illustrations as for their stories.

Activity Have students select two or three pages from the play that do not already have art on them. Ask students to sketch or draw an illustration to accompany each page they've selected. Encourage them to consider drawing not only a representation of the scene but an object important to the scene or something that evokes the same mood as the scene. **L2**

ANNE. No. No. Tell me.

MARGOT. Of course you're not. You've got nice eyes . . . and a lot of animation,[46] and . . .

ANNE. A little vague, aren't you?

[She reaches over and takes a brassière out of MARGOT's sewing basket. She holds it up to herself, studying the effect in the mirror. Outside, MRS. FRANK, feeling sorry for DUSSEL, comes over, knocking at the girls' door.]

MRS. FRANK. [*Outside.*] May I come in?

MARGOT. Come in, Mother.

MRS. FRANK. [*Shutting the door behind her.*] Mr. Dussel's impatient to get in here.

ANNE. [*Still with the brassière.*] Heavens, he takes the room for himself the entire day.

MRS. FRANK. [*Gently.*] Anne, dear, you're not going in again tonight to see Peter?

V **ANNE.** [*Dignified.*] That is my intention.

MRS. FRANK. But you've already spent a great deal of time in there today.

ANNE. I was in there exactly twice. Once to get the dictionary, and then three-quarters of an hour before supper.

MRS. FRANK. Aren't you afraid you're disturbing him?

ANNE. Mother, I have some intuition.

MRS. FRANK. Then may I ask you this much, Anne. Please don't shut the door when you go in.

ANNE. You sound like Mrs. Van Daan!

[She throws the brassière back in MARGOT's sewing basket and picks up her blouse, putting it on.]

MRS. FRANK. No. No. I don't mean to suggest anything wrong. I only wish that you wouldn't expose yourself to criticism . . . that you wouldn't give Mrs. Van Daan the opportunity to be unpleasant.

ANNE. Mrs. Van Daan doesn't need an opportunity to be unpleasant!

MRS. FRANK. Everyone's on edge, worried about Mr. Kraler. This is one more thing . . . W

ANNE. I'm sorry, Mother. I'm going to Peter's room. I'm not going to let Petronella Van Daan spoil our friendship.

[MRS. FRANK hesitates for a second, then goes out, closing the door after her. She gets a pack of playing cards and sits at the center table, playing solitaire. In ANNE's room MARGOT hands the finished skirt to ANNE. As ANNE is putting it on, MARGOT takes off her high-heeled shoes and stuffs paper in the toes so that ANNE can wear them.]

MARGOT. [*To ANNE.*] Why don't you two talk in the main room? It'd save a lot of trouble. It's hard on Mother, having to listen to those remarks from Mrs. Van Daan and not say a word. X

ANNE. Why doesn't she say a word? I think it's ridiculous to take it and take it.

MARGOT. You don't understand Mother at all, do you? She can't talk back. She's not like you. It's just not in her nature to fight back.

ANNE. Anyway . . . the only one I worry about is you. I feel awfully guilty about you.

46. Here, *animation* means "liveliness; spiritedness."

Vocabulary

intuition (in′ to͞o ish′ ən) *n.* an ability to know things without having to reason them out

V Critical Thinking

INFER Ask students to speculate on how much time has passed between scenes 1 and 2. Have students infer what has happened during the time between the scenes.

W Active Reading Strategies

QUESTION Have students recall why everyone is worried about Mr. Kraler. Why would Mr. Kraler's illness put everyone "on edge"?

X Active Reading Strategies

PREDICT Ask students why Peter and Anne would not want to talk in the main room. Encourage them to predict what Anne and Peter might talk about that would prevent them from meeting in the main room.

MEETING INDIVIDUAL NEEDS — SPECIAL NEEDS

Learning Disabled Learning-disabled students may benefit from hearing other interpretations of events in the play.

Activity Ask groups to discuss the plot developments in the play. Ask each group to review the main plot and the subplot and identify four events that advance the main plot and two events that advance the subplot. *(The main plot concerns the group's life in hiding. Events include the arrival of Mr. Dussel, the Hanukkah celebration, Peter knocking over the lamp, and the arrival of the intruder. The subplot is Anne's relationship with Peter. Events include Anne teasing Peter and Peter and Anne meeting privately.)* **L1** COLLAB. LEARN.

Additional Resources

Inclusion Strategies

Y Critical Thinking

MAKE CRITICAL JUDGMENTS Ask students to consider what Margot's statement means. What do we learn about the hardships of being in hiding from this statement? *(Her statement suggests the boredom and lack of purpose that they live with every day.)*

Z Literary Elements

DIALOGUE Review the meaning of *sarcasm* with students. Several people in this scene take a sarcastic tone. Ask students to identify other examples on this page. *(Anne: "Dear, dear Mr. Dussel"; Mrs. Van Daan: "I don't know what good it is to have a son," "Do you mind?" and "I didn't know I had anything to say about it.")*

[*She sits on the stool near* MARGOT, *putting on* MARGOT'*s high-heeled shoes*.]

MARGOT. What about?

ANNE. I mean, every time I go into Peter's room, I have a feeling I may be hurting you. [MARGOT *shakes her head*.] I know if it were me, I'd be wild. I'd be desperately jealous, if it were me.

MARGOT. Well, I'm not.

ANNE. You don't feel badly? Really? Truly? You're not jealous?

Y **MARGOT.** Of course I'm jealous . . . jealous that you've got something to get up in the morning for . . . But jealous of you and Peter? No.

[ANNE *goes back to the mirror*.]

ANNE. Maybe there's nothing to be jealous of. Maybe he doesn't really like me. Maybe I'm just taking the place of his cat . . . [*She picks up a pair of short white gloves, putting them on*.] Wouldn't you like to come in with us?

MARGOT. I have a book.

[*The sound of the children playing outside fades out. In the main room* DUSSEL *can stand it no longer. He jumps up, going to the bedroom door and knocking sharply*.]

DUSSEL. Will you please let me in my room!

ANNE. Just a minute, dear, dear Mr. Dussel. [*She picks up her Mother's pink stole and adjusts it elegantly over her shoulders, then gives a last look in the mirror*.] Well, here I go . . . to run the gauntlet.[47]

[*She starts out, followed by* MARGOT.]

Z **DUSSEL.** [*As she appears—sarcastic*.] Thank you so much.

[DUSSEL *goes into his room.* ANNE *goes toward* PETER'*s room, passing* MRS. VAN DAAN *and her parents at the center table*.]

MRS. VAN DAAN. My God, look at her! [ANNE *pays no attention. She knocks at* PETER'*s door*.] I don't know what good it is to have a son. I never see him. He wouldn't care if I killed myself. [PETER *opens the door and stands aside for* ANNE *to come in*.] Just a minute, Anne. [*She goes to them at the door*.] I'd like to say a few words to my son. Do you mind? [PETER *and* ANNE *stand waiting*.] Peter, I don't want you staying up till all hours tonight. You've got to have your sleep. You're a growing boy. You hear?

MRS. FRANK. Anne won't stay late. She's going to bed promptly at nine. Aren't you, Anne?

ANNE. Yes, Mother . . . [*To* MRS. VAN DAAN.] May we go now?

MRS. VAN DAAN. Are you asking me? I didn't know I had anything to say about it.

MRS. FRANK. Listen for the chimes, Anne dear.

[*The two young people go off into* PETER'*s room, shutting the door after them*.]

MRS. VAN DAAN. [*To* MRS. FRANK.] In my day it was the boys who called on the girls. Not the girls on the boys.

MRS. FRANK. You know how young people like to feel that they have secrets. Peter's room is the only place where they can talk.

MRS. VAN DAAN. Talk! That's not what they called it when I was young.

[MRS. VAN DAAN *goes off to the bathroom.* MARGOT *settles down to read her book.* MR. FRANK *puts his papers away and brings a chess game to the center table. He and* MRS. FRANK *start to play. In*

47. To *run the gauntlet* is to endure opposition or difficulties.

Teaching Support

MEETING INDIVIDUAL NEEDS

MULTIPLE MODES OF EXPRESSION

Interpersonal Students with interpersonal learning styles can benefit from working with others to develop their understanding of the characters. Point out that some of the characters in this play have very distinctive personality traits.

Activity Have students work in pairs to present an interview of either Mr. Dussel or Mr. Van Daan. Suggest that this be an imaginary interview that might have taken place had the group been rescued. Encourage students to consider what questions they would want to ask the character they've chosen and how that particular character would respond. **L2** COLLAB. LEARN.

PETER's room, ANNE speaks to PETER, indignant, humiliated.]

ANNE. Aren't they awful? Aren't they impossible? Treating us as if we were still in the nursery.

[She sits on the cot. PETER gets a bottle of pop and two glasses.]

PETER. Don't let it bother you. It doesn't bother me.

AA **ANNE.** I suppose you can't really blame them . . . they think back to what *they* were like at our age. They don't realize how much more advanced we are . . . When you think what wonderful discussions we've had! . . . Oh, I forgot. I was going to bring you some more pictures.

PETER. Oh, these are fine, thanks.

ANNE. Don't you want some more? Miep just brought me some new ones.

PETER. Maybe later.

[He gives her a glass of pop and, taking some for himself, sits down facing her.]

BB **ANNE.** *[Looking up at one of the photographs.]* I remember when I got that . . . I won it. I bet Jopie that I could eat five ice-cream cones. We'd all been playing ping-pong . . . We used to have heavenly times . . . we'd finish up with ice cream at the Delphi, or the Oasis, where Jews were allowed . . . there'd always be a lot of boys . . . we'd laugh and joke . . . I'd like to go back to it for a few days or a week. But after that I know I'd be bored to death. I think more seriously about life now. I want to be a journalist . . . or something. I love to write. What do you want to do?

PETER. I thought I might go off some place . . . work on a farm or something . . . some job that doesn't take much brains.

ANNE. You shouldn't talk that way. You've got the most awful inferiority complex.

PETER. I know I'm not smart.

ANNE. That isn't true. You're much better than I am in dozens of things . . . arithmetic and algebra and . . . well, you're a million times better than I am in algebra. *[With sudden directness.]* You like Margot, don't you? Right from the start you liked her, liked her much better than me.

PETER. *[Uncomfortably.]* Oh, I don't know.

[In the main room MRS. VAN DAAN comes from the bathroom and goes over to the sink, polishing a coffee pot.]

ANNE. It's all right. Everyone feels that way. Margot's so good. She's sweet and bright and beautiful and I'm not.

PETER. I wouldn't say that.

ANNE. Oh, no, I'm not. I know that. I know quite well that I'm not a beauty. I never have been and never shall be.

PETER. I don't agree at all. I think you're pretty.

ANNE. That's not true!

PETER. And another thing. You've changed . . . from at first, I mean. CC

ANNE. I have?

PETER. I used to think you were awful noisy.

ANNE. And what do you think now, Peter? How have I changed?

PETER. Well . . . er . . . you're . . . quieter.

[In his room DUSSEL takes his pajamas and toilet articles and goes into the bathroom to change.]

ANNE. I'm glad you don't just hate me.

PETER. I never said that.

ANNE. I bet when you get out of here you'll never think of me again.

AA Active Reading Strategies

EVALUATE Ask students to consider in what ways Anne and Peter might be "more advanced" than their parents were at that age. *(Growing up with the persecution and restrictions of the Nazi occupation, having to flee Germany, the world being at war, rationing, and facing imminent death have matured them well beyond their years.)*

BB Literary Elements

CHARACTERIZATION Have students discuss what insight is gained into Anne's life from this speech. Note that her childhood came to an abrupt end and cannot be regained.

CC Literary Elements

CHARACTERIZATION Note Peter's assertion that Anne has changed. In what ways has Anne changed? How has Peter changed? *(Anne is more serious and mature. Peter is more willing to talk to others and to express his feelings.)*

Life Skills Connection

Time Management Point out to students that the families in hiding had a great deal of time on their hands, and so they would have needed to stay busy to prevent boredom.

Activity Have students list what they would do under these circumstances by making a daily schedule to describe how they would spend each hour of the day. Encourage them to consider what activities they would have available to them and the restrictions on noise that were present. **L2**

DD Author's Craft

DIALOGUE Ask students how the playwrights' use of dialogue helps reveal the characters' emotions. Why is Anne talking so much? *(The diary expresses her feelings; she is naturally talkative.)*

EE Literary Elements

CONFLICT Ask students to identify the conflict between the characters in this scene. *(They are both afraid to reveal their feelings to each other.)* What is Anne's internal conflict? *(She wants Peter to kiss her, but she is afraid.)*

PETER. That's crazy.

ANNE. When you get back with all of your friends, you're going to say . . . now what did I ever see in that Mrs. Quack Quack.

PETER. I haven't got any friends.

ANNE. Oh, Peter, of course you have. Everyone has friends.

PETER. Not me. I don't want any. I get along all right without them.

ANNE. Does that mean you can get along without me? I think of myself as your friend.

PETER. No. If they were all like you, it'd be different.

[*He takes the glasses and the bottle and puts them away. There is a second's silence and then* ANNE *speaks, hesitantly, shyly.*]

ANNE. Peter, did you ever kiss a girl?

DD

PETER. Yes. Once.

ANNE. [*To cover her feelings.*] That picture's crooked. [PETER *goes over, straightening the photograph.*] Was she pretty?

PETER. Huh?

ANNE. The girl that you kissed.

PETER. I don't know. I was blindfolded. [*He comes back and sits down again.*] It was at a party. One of those kissing games.

ANNE. [*Relieved.*] Oh. I don't suppose that really counts, does it?

PETER. It didn't with me.

ANNE. I've been kissed twice. Once a man I'd never seen before kissed me on the cheek when he picked me up off the ice and I was crying. And the other was Mr. Koophuis,[48] a friend of Father's who kissed my hand. You wouldn't say those counted, would you?

PETER. I wouldn't say so.

ANNE. I know almost for certain that Margot would never kiss anyone unless she was engaged to them. And I'm sure too that Mother never touched a man before Pim. But I don't know . . . things are so different now . . . What do you think? Do you think a girl shouldn't kiss anyone except if she's engaged or something? It's so hard to try to think what to do, when here we are with the whole world falling around our ears and you think . . . well . . . you don't know what's going to happen tomorrow and . . . What do you think?

EE

PETER. I suppose it'd depend on the girl. Some girls, anything they do's wrong. But others . . . well . . . it wouldn't necessarily be wrong with them. [*The carillon starts to strike nine o'clock.*] I've always thought that when two people . . .

ANNE. Nine o'clock. I have to go.

PETER. That's right.

ANNE. [*Without moving.*] Good night.

[*There is a second's pause, then* PETER *gets up and moves toward the door.*]

PETER. You won't let them stop you coming?

ANNE. No. [*She rises and starts for the door.*] Sometime I might bring my diary. There are so many things in it that I want to talk over with you. There's a lot about you.

PETER. What kind of things?

ANNE. I wouldn't want you to see some of it. I thought you were a nothing, just the way you thought about me.

PETER. Did you change your mind, the way I changed my mind about you?

48. *Koophuis* (koip′ hœs)

Teaching Support

Writing Minilesson

Prewriting Once students have a topic for writing, they need to jot down ideas for developing the topic. Explain to students that prewriting helps focus on what will be included in a piece of writing. Prewriting should include any ideas they have on a topic; some ideas can be eliminated later if they do not fit well as the draft is developed.

Activity Have students imagine that they are going to write a play with Miep Gies as the heroine. Have them jot down their ideas for what to include in such a play. Who would the characters be? What events would occur in act 1? act 2? What time periods would the play cover? **L2**

Additional Resources

Writer's Choice, Lesson 2.3

The Diary of Anne Frank, 1959. 20th Century Fox. Movie still.
Viewing the photograph: How do you think Anne might feel at this moment?

VIEWING THE PHOTOGRAPH

Viewing Response *Anne probably feels a combination of emotions—apprehension, curiosity, and happiness.*

MEETING INDIVIDUAL NEEDS — MULTIPLE MODES OF EXPRESSION

Linguistic Note that Anne says, "We all know each other so well now we could finish each other's sentences." (page 760) Discuss with students whether, as the play progresses, readers also begin to feel they know the characters well.

Activity Have students list the names of all the characters in the play. Then have them select from the play one quotation from each character that illustrates his or her personality. Students should be prepared to explain what each quotation says about the character and why it has been chosen. **L2**

FF Critical Thinking

DRAWING CONCLUSIONS Why does Anne suddenly go over to Mrs. Van Daan and kiss her cheeks? *(Perhaps she is expressing her happiness or is glad that Mrs. Van Daan brought Peter into the world.)*

GG Active Reading Strategies

REVIEW Ask students to review how long the group has been in hiding. *(Students should recall that they went into hiding in July 1942, so they have been there nearly two years.)*

HH Literary Elements

PLOT Have students identify the main plot and the subplot in this play. *(The main plot concerns the interaction of the group and the question of whether they will be found; the subplot involves the relationships between the characters.)* Review with students what events occurred in act 2 so far to advance the main plot. *(The incident with the cake, the blackmail by the employee.)* What questions remain unanswered? *(Whether the employee will turn them in.)*

Thematic Focus

Faces of Dignity Have students discuss the hardship of remaining dignified in such a situation.

ASSESSMENT

Quick Checks, p. 64

ANNE. Well . . . You'll see . . .

[For a second ANNE stands looking up at PETER, longing for him to kiss her. As he makes no move she turns away. Then suddenly PETER grabs her awkwardly in his arms, kissing her on the cheek. ANNE walks out dazed. She stands for a minute, her back to the people in the main room. As she regains her poise she goes to her mother and father and MARGOT, silently kissing them. They murmur their good nights to her. As she is about to open her bedroom door, she catches sight of MRS. VAN DAAN. She goes quickly to her, taking her face in her hands and kissing her first on one cheek and then on the other. Then she hurries off into her room. MRS. VAN DAAN looks after her, and then looks over at PETER's room. Her suspicions are confirmed.]

MRS. VAN DAAN. *[She knows.]* Ah hah!

[The lights dim out. The curtain falls on the scene. In the darkness ANNE'S VOICE comes faintly at first and then with growing strength.]

ANNE'S VOICE. By this time we all know each other so well that if anyone starts to tell a story, the rest can finish it for him. We're having to cut down still further on our meals. What makes it worse, the rats have been at work again. They've carried off some of our precious food. Even Mr. Dussel wishes now that Mouschi was here. Thursday, the twentieth of April, nineteen forty-four. Invasion fever[49] is mounting every day. Miep tells us that people outside talk of nothing else. For myself, life has become much more pleasant. I often go to Peter's room after supper. Oh, don't think I'm in love, because I'm not. But it does make life more bearable to have someone with whom you can exchange views. No more tonight. P.S. . . . I must be honest. I must confess that I actually live for the next meeting. Is there anything lovelier than to sit under the skylight and feel the sun on your cheeks and have a darling boy in your arms? I admit now that I'm glad the Van Daans had a son and not a daughter. I've outgrown another dress. That's the third. I'm having to wear Margot's clothes after all. I'm working hard on my French and am now reading *La Belle Nivernaise*.[50]

[As she is saying the last lines—the curtain rises on the scene. The lights dim on, as ANNE'S VOICE fades out.]

49. *Invasion fever* refers to the widely held expectation that the Allies would soon invade areas of Europe occupied by German forces.
50. *La Belle Nivernaise* (lä bel′ nē′ ver nāz′) was a work by a nineteenth-century French novelist.

Vocabulary
poise (poiz) *n.* relaxed and self-controlled dignity in manner

Teaching Support

Grammar and Language Minilesson

Indefinite Pronouns Note that Anne's diary entry says, "If *anyone starts* to tell a story . . ." Remind students that *anyone* is a singular indefinite pronoun, so it takes a singular verb, in this case *starts*. Review with students other singular indefinite pronouns, such as *everybody, somebody, each, either,* and *one.*

Activity Have students write sentences about the play using each of the pronouns listed. Discuss the use of the singular verb with *each, either,* and *one,* and make sure students use the words as pronouns, not modifiers. **L2**

Additional Resources

- ***Grammar and Language Transparency 63***
- ***Grammar and Language Workbook,*** p. 113
- ***Grammar and Composition Handbook,*** Lesson 4.5
- ***Writer's Choice,*** Lesson 11.5

Responding to Literature

PERSONAL RESPONSE

- How did you react to the change in Anne's relationship with Peter? Does the change surprise you? Explain.

Analyzing Literature

RECALL AND INTERPRET

1. As a new year begins, Anne recognizes that she has changed. How does she describe those changes, and how does she feel about them? What other changes in Anne do her Hanukkah gifts (from the end of act 1) show?
2. How does each family member react to Miep's gift of a cake? What do these reactions reveal about each person? about their situation?
3. Why is Anne dressing up? How do the family members feel about this? Why?

EVALUATE AND CONNECT

4. What does Anne mean when she says, "We have problems that no other people our age have ever had"? Does Anne fully understand the problems she has? Explain.
5. How is Mr. Kraler's news of the blackmail a kind of turning point for the members of the Secret Annex? What does it mean for them?
6. What two sides of life in the Secret Annex are shown in act 2, scene 1 and scene 2? Is one side more important than the other? Explain.

LITERARY ELEMENTS

Monologue

A **monologue** is a long, uninterrupted speech by one character in a play. A monologue may provide important information about character and plot. In the opening of act 2, for example, Anne reads from her diary, describing the situation at the start of 1944.

- Identify and describe two other monologues in the play. For each example, explain what you learn about the character who is speaking or about the plot.

See **Literary Terms Handbook,** p. R6.

Extending Your Response

Literature Groups

A Precious Object Mrs. Van Daan's fur coat appears in the story several times. How does its importance change? Why might it have such deep meaning for Mrs. Van Daan? for Mr. Van Daan? for other members of the Secret Annex?

Creative Writing

Pen Pals Anne and Margot sometimes wrote letters to each other during their stay in the Secret Annex. Write a letter from Margot to Anne about Anne's growing friendship with Peter. As you write, keep in mind what she says to Anne in the play.

Responding to the Selection

PERSONAL RESPONSE

Students should explain their reactions to the change in Anne and Peter's relationship.

Analyzing Literature

1. Students should refer to the fact that Anne is approaching womanhood and that she is pleased with the changes.
2. Most are grateful. Their reactions reveal that they are hungry, that they are not getting along, that their hopes for peace in 1943 were not realized, and that they have remained in hiding longer than anticipated.
3. She dresses up to meet with Peter. Students' responses should refer to various family members and their reactions.
4. Students should discuss the frightening world situation and should use specific examples from the play to support how well Anne understands the problems.
5. The family realizes that someone might betray them.
6. Act 2, scene 1 shows how relationships in the annex and the situation outside have deteriorated. Scene 2 demonstrates Anne's growing maturity. Students should support their conclusion with specific examples.

Extending Your Response

Literature Groups Students should refer to what the coat symbolizes for Mrs. Van Daan. Responses regarding Mr. Van Daan should refer to his shame over what has become of his family and the way they must live. COLLAB. LEARN.

Creative Writing Students' letters should reflect Margot's character as described in the play.

LITERARY ELEMENTS

Students should explain how the monologue advances the characterization.

Additional Resources

- ***Literary Elements Transparency 64***

ASSESSMENT

- ***Quick Checks,*** p. 64
- ***Selection and Theme Assessment,*** pp. 109–112
- ***Performance Assessment,*** p. 57
- ***Testmaker: ExamView Pro***
- ***Interactive Tutor: Self-Assessment***

Reading the Selection

SUMMARY

Act 2, Scenes 3–5
The desperation and anxiety in the attic finally come to a head. Miep arrives in the midst of a heated argument with news that the invasion has begun; the group is so happy that they forget their present situation. Weeks pass and the mood is tense once again. Three days go by without a visit from Miep. Everyone knows something is wrong. In the middle of a monologue in which Anne explains the importance of faith to Peter, the Green Police burst in, cutting off Anne's voice. In the final scene of the play, Mr. Frank finishes reading the diary and explains that Anne, Margot, and Mrs. Frank all died at Bergen-Belsen.

Spanish Summaries, p. 60

A Active Reading Strategies

REVIEW Note that these stage directions repeat a scene earlier in the play.

B Active Reading Strategies

REVIEW Ask students to contrast this argument with the polite dialogue between the characters when they first went into hiding.

The Diary of Anne Frank (Continued)

SCENE 3

[It is night, a few weeks later. Everyone is in bed. There is complete quiet. In the VAN DAANS' *room a match flares up for a moment and then is quickly put out.* MR. VAN DAAN, *in bare feet, dressed in underwear and trousers, is dimly seen coming stealthily down the stairs and into the main room, where* MR. *and* MRS. FRANK *and* MARGOT *are sleeping. He goes to the food safe and again lights a match. Then he cautiously opens the safe, taking out a half-loaf of bread. As he closes the safe, it creaks. He stands rigid.* MRS. FRANK *sits up in bed. She sees him.]*

MRS. FRANK. *[Screaming.]* Otto! Otto! *Komme schnell!*

[The rest of the people wake, hurriedly getting up.]

MR. FRANK. *Was ist los? Was ist passiert?*

*[*DUSSEL, *followed by* ANNE, *comes from his room.]*

MRS. FRANK. *[As she rushes over to* MR. VAN DAAN.*] Er stiehlt das Essen!*[51]

DUSSEL. *[Grabbing* MR. VAN DAAN.*]* You! You! Give me that.

MRS. VAN DAAN. *[Coming down the stairs.]* Putti . . . Putti . . . what is it?

DUSSEL. *[His hands on* VAN DAAN'S *neck.]* You dirty thief . . . stealing food . . . you good-for-nothing . . .

MR. FRANK. Mr. Dussel! For God's sake! Help me, Peter!

*[*PETER *comes over, trying, with* MR. FRANK, *to separate the two struggling men.]*

PETER. Let him go! Let go!

*[*DUSSEL *drops* MR. VAN DAAN, *pushing him away. He shows them the end of a loaf of bread that he has taken from* VAN DAAN.*]*

DUSSEL. You greedy, selfish . . . !

*[*MARGOT *turns on the lights.]*

MRS. VAN DAAN. Putti . . . what is it?

[All of MRS. FRANK'S *gentleness, her self-control, is gone. She is outraged, in a frenzy of indignation.]*

MRS. FRANK. The bread! He was stealing the bread!

DUSSEL. It was you, and all the time we thought it was the rats!

MR. FRANK. Mr. Van Daan, how could you!

MR. VAN DAAN. I'm hungry.

MRS. FRANK. We're all of us hungry! I see the children getting thinner and thinner. Your own son Peter . . . I've heard him moan in his sleep, he's so hungry. And you come in the night and steal food that should go to them . . . to the children!

MRS. VAN DAAN. *[Going to* MR. VAN DAAN *protectively.]* He needs more food than the rest of us. He's used to more. He's a big man.

51. MRS. FRANK. "Come quickly!" MR. FRANK. "What's the matter? What has happened?" MRS. FRANK. "He is stealing food!"

Vocabulary
stealthily (stel′ thə lē) *adv.* in a secret or sneaky manner
frenzy (fren′ zē) *n.* a state of great excitement or deep disturbance

Teaching Support

MEETING INDIVIDUAL NEEDS — ENGLISH LANGUAGE LEARNERS

Homophones English language learners can be confused by homophones. Point out to students that some words sound alike but have different spellings and different meanings. Often the homophones are also different parts of speech. When such a word is used, the listener must determine which meaning and part of speech best fits the context.

Activity Read aloud the sentences in the opening stage directions containing the words *week, flares, bare, seen, stairs,* and *sees.* Have students identify other spellings and meanings of words that sound the same as these.

Additional Resources
English Language Learners Sourcebook, p. 88

[MR. VAN DAAN breaks away, going over and sitting on the couch.]

MRS. FRANK. *[Turning on MRS. VAN DAAN.]* And you . . . you're worse than he is! You're a mother, and yet you sacrifice your child to this man . . . this . . . this . . .

MR. FRANK. Edith! Edith!

[MARGOT picks up the pink woolen stole, putting it over her mother's shoulders.]

C

MRS. FRANK. *[Paying no attention, going on to MRS. VAN DAAN.]* Don't think I haven't seen you! Always saving the choicest bits for him! I've watched you day after day and I've held my tongue. But not any longer! Not after this! Now I want him to go! I want him to get out of here!

MR. FRANK. Edith!
MR. VAN DAAN. Get out of here?
} *Together*

MRS. VAN DAAN. What do you mean?

MRS. FRANK. Just that! Take your things and get out!

D

MR. FRANK. *[To MRS. FRANK.]* You're speaking in anger. You cannot mean what you are saying.

MRS. FRANK. I mean exactly that!

[MRS. VAN DAAN takes a cover from the FRANKS' bed, pulling it about her.]

MR. FRANK. For two long years we have lived here, side by side. We have respected each other's rights . . . we have managed to live in peace. Are we now going to throw it all away? I know this will never happen again, will it, Mr. Van Daan?

MR. VAN DAAN. No. No.

MRS. FRANK. He steals once! He'll steal again!

[MR. VAN DAAN, holding his stomach, starts for the bathroom. ANNE puts her arms around him, helping him up the step.]

MR. FRANK. Edith, please. Let us be calm. We'll all go to our rooms . . . and afterwards we'll sit down quietly and talk this out . . . we'll find some way . . .

MRS. FRANK. No! No! No more talk! I want them to leave!

MRS. VAN DAAN. You'd put us out, on the streets?

MRS. FRANK. There are other hiding places.

MRS. VAN DAAN. A cellar . . . a closet. I know. And we have no money left even to pay for that.

MRS. FRANK. I'll give you money. Out of my own pocket I'll give it gladly.

[She gets her purse from a shelf and comes back with it.]

MRS. VAN DAAN. Mr. Frank, you told Putti you'd never forget what he'd done for you when you came to Amsterdam. You said you could never repay him, that you . . . E

MRS. FRANK. *[Counting out money.]* If my husband had any obligation to you, he's paid it, over and over.

MR. FRANK. Edith, I've never seen you like this before. I don't know you.

MRS. FRANK. I should have spoken out long ago.

DUSSEL. You can't be nice to some people.

MRS. VAN DAAN. *[Turning on DUSSEL.]* There would have been plenty for all of us, if *you* hadn't come in here!

MR. FRANK. We don't need the Nazis to destroy us. We're destroying ourselves.

[He sits down, with his head in his hands. MRS. FRANK goes to MRS. VAN DAAN.]

Language Note

Language Similarities English, like Dutch and Danish, is a Germanic language. Many English words are derived from the same word origins as German words. On page 762, note the similarities between *komme* and the English translation *come, was ist* and the English translation *what is*, and *stiehlt* and the English translation *stealing*.

C Literary Elements

CHARACTERIZATION Ask students what they learn about Mrs. Frank's character in this scene. *(Mrs. Frank has been very reserved and careful not to offend anyone, but it is revealed that she does not approve of Mr. Van Daan's behavior and has grown to resent his presence.)* Are students surprised by her response? Have students consider why Mrs. Frank has not revealed her feelings before.

D Active Reading Strategies

RESPOND Ask students whether they agree with Mrs. Frank that Mr. Van Daan should leave.

E Critical Thinking

MAKE CRITICAL JUDGMENTS Ask students what Mrs. Van Daan is trying to do here. What technique is she using to persuade the Franks to let them stay? *(Mrs. Van Daan is trying to make Mr. Frank feel guilty by reminding him of past favors Mr. Van Daan did for the Franks.)*

MEETING INDIVIDUAL NEEDS: SPECIAL NEEDS

Less-Proficient Readers Less-proficient readers can have some difficulty understanding lapses or shifts in time in a story. Previewing the text and keeping a chart can help these students understand the passage of time.

Activity Have students skim the opening stage directions for each scene of the play and create a list of acts and scenes. Next to each listing have them write important plot elements. When their lists are complete, ask students to review them and to write, between each entry, how much time has passed between the two scenes. **L1**

Additional Resources

Inclusion Strategies

Active Reading Strategies

REVIEW Have students recall the relationship between Mr. and Mrs. Van Daan throughout the play. Then ask them to consider why Mrs. Van Daan behaves differently toward Mr. Van Daan now. *(She feels bad that Mrs. Frank became angry with him.)*

G Literary Elements

TRAGEDY Review with students that one element of tragedy is the characters' downfall. Ask students to consider how Mr. Dussel's counting of the potatoes is tragic. *(It shows how desperate the relationships between the characters have become and how difficult their circumstances are because they do not have enough food.)*

H Literary Elements

STAGE DIRECTIONS Note the stage directions that have Mr. Dussel continue to count the potatoes while the others talk, despite Margot's pleas. What does this action contribute to the scene? *(It emphasizes the desperation and determination of the characters.)*

MRS. FRANK. [*Giving* MRS. VAN DAAN *some money.*] Give this to Miep. She'll find you a place.

ANNE. Mother, you're not putting *Peter* out. Peter hasn't done anything.

MRS. FRANK. He'll stay, of course. When I say I must protect the children, I mean Peter too.

[*PETER rises from the steps where he has been sitting.*]

PETER. I'd have to go if Father goes.

F [*MR. VAN DAAN comes from the bathroom. MRS. VAN DAAN hurries to him and takes him to the couch. Then she gets water from the sink to bathe his face.*]

MRS. FRANK. [*While this is going on.*] He's no father to you . . . that man! He doesn't know what it is to be a father!

PETER. [*Starting for his room.*] I wouldn't feel right. I couldn't stay.

MRS. FRANK. Very well, then. I'm sorry.

ANNE. [*Rushing over to PETER.*] No, Peter! No! [*PETER goes into his room, closing the door after him. ANNE turns back to her mother, crying.*] I don't care about the food. They can have mine! I don't want it! Only don't send them away. It'll be daylight soon. They'll be caught . . .

MARGOT. [*Putting her arms comfortingly around ANNE.*] Please, Mother!

MRS. FRANK. They're not going now. They'll stay here until Miep finds them a place. [*To MRS. VAN DAAN.*] But one thing I insist on! He must never come down here again! He must never come to this room where the food is stored! We'll divide what we have . . . an equal share for each! [*DUSSEL hurries over to get a sack of potatoes from the food safe. MRS. FRANK goes on, to MRS. VAN DAAN.*] You can cook it here and take it up to him.

[*DUSSEL brings the sack of potatoes back to the center table.*]

MARGOT. Oh, no. No. We haven't sunk so far that we're going to fight over a handful of rotten potatoes.

DUSSEL. [*Dividing the potatoes into piles.*] Mrs. Frank, Mr. Frank, Margot, Anne, Peter, Mrs. Van Daan, Mr. Van Daan, myself . . . Mrs. Frank . . . G

[*The buzzer sounds in MIEP's signal.*]

MR. FRANK. It's Miep!

[*He hurries over, getting his overcoat and putting it on.*]

MARGOT. At this hour?

MRS. FRANK. It is trouble.

MR. FRANK. [*As he starts down to unbolt the door.*] I beg you, don't let her see a thing like this!

MR. DUSSEL. [*Counting without stopping.*] . . . Anne, Peter, Mrs. Van Daan, Mr. Van Daan, myself . . .

MARGOT. [*To DUSSEL.*] Stop it! Stop it!

DUSSEL. . . . Mr. Frank, Margot, Anne, Peter, Mrs. Van Daan, Mr. Van Daan, myself, Mrs. Frank . . . H

MRS. VAN DAAN. You're keeping the big ones for yourself! All the big ones . . . Look at the size of that! . . . And that! . . .

[*DUSSEL continues on with his dividing. PETER, with his shirt and trousers on, comes from his room.*]

MARGOT. Stop it! Stop it!

[*We hear MIEP's excited voice speaking to MR. FRANK below.*]

MIEP. Mr. Frank . . . the most wonderful news! . . . The invasion has begun!

Teaching Support

Listening and Speaking *Minilesson*

Oral Reading Oral reading can sometimes sound unnatural because students do not anticipate what they are reading. Hesitant reading usually occurs because the reader's eye focuses only on the word being read, and this slows down reading. One way to improve reading aloud is to practice letting the eyes move forward to the next word or two while reading.

Activity Have students work in small groups to improve oral reading skills. Taking turns, they should read aloud, concentrating on letting their eyes move ahead to the next word or two while they read. Encourage students to provide feedback to help each other improve their readings. **L2**

MR. FRANK. Go on, tell them! Tell them!

[*MIEP comes running up the steps, ahead of MR. FRANK. She has a man's raincoat on over her nightclothes and a bunch of orange-colored flowers in her hand.*]

MIEP. Did you hear that, everybody? Did you hear what I said? The invasion has begun! The invasion!

[*They all stare at MIEP, unable to grasp what she is telling them. PETER is the first to recover his wits.*]

PETER. Where?

MRS. VAN DAAN. When? When, Miep?

MIEP. It began early this morning . . .

[*As she talks on, the realization of what she has said begins to dawn on them. Everyone goes crazy. A wild demonstration takes place. MRS. FRANK hugs MR. VAN DAAN.*]

MRS. FRANK. Oh, Mr. Van Daan, did you hear that?

[*DUSSEL embraces MRS. VAN DAAN. PETER grabs a frying pan and parades around the room, beating on it, singing the Dutch National Anthem. ANNE and MARGOT follow him, singing, weaving in and out among the excited grown-ups. MARGOT breaks away to take the flowers from MIEP and distribute them to everyone. While this pandemonium is going on MRS. FRANK tries to make herself heard above the excitement.*]

MRS. FRANK. [*To MIEP.*] How do you know?

MIEP. The radio . . . The B.B.C.! They said they landed on the coast of Normandy![52]

PETER. The British?

MIEP. British, Americans, French, Dutch, Poles, Norwegians . . . all of them! More than four thousand ships! Churchill spoke, and General Eisenhower![53] D-Day they call it!

MR. FRANK. Thank God, it's come!

MRS. VAN DAAN. At last!

MIEP. [*Starting out.*] I'm going to tell Mr. Kraler. This'll be better than any blood transfusion.

MR. FRANK. [*Stopping her.*] What part of Normandy did they land, did they say?

MIEP. Normandy . . . that's all I know now . . . I'll be up the minute I hear some more!

[*She goes hurriedly out.*]

MR. FRANK. [*To MRS. FRANK.*] What did I tell you? What did I tell you?

[*MRS. FRANK indicates that he has forgotten to bolt the door after MIEP. He hurries down the steps. MR. VAN DAAN, sitting on the couch, suddenly breaks into a convulsive sob. Everybody looks at him, bewildered.*]

MRS. VAN DAAN. [*Hurrying to him.*] Putti! Putti! What is it? What happened?

MR. VAN DAAN. Please. I'm so ashamed.

[*MR. FRANK comes back up the steps.*]

DUSSEL. Oh, for God's sake!

MRS. VAN DAAN. Don't, Putti.

MARGOT. It doesn't matter now!

MR. FRANK. [*Going to MR. VAN DAAN.*] Didn't you hear what Miep said? The

52. *B.B.C.* stands for "British Broadcasting Corporation." *Normandy* is a region of northwestern France, across the English Channel from the southern coast of England.

53. Winston *Churchill* was the prime minister of England, and Dwight D. *Eisenhower* commanded the Allied forces in Europe.

Vocabulary

pandemonium (pan′ də mō′ nē əm) *n.* wild disorder and uproar

I Active Reading Strategies

QUESTION Note the stage direction that has Mrs. Frank hug Mr. Van Daan. Why does she do this? Ask students to identify what might have really caused Mrs. Frank to be so angry with the Van Daans. *(She may have taken out her anger at being in hiding and the fear of what could happen to them on Mr. Van Daan.)*

J Active Reading Strategies

PREDICT Ask students to predict what effect Miep's news will have on life in the secret annex.

K Critical Thinking

INFER Ask students what Miep's statement tells the audience about Mr. Kraler. *(He is very sick.)*

Interdisciplinary Connection

History D-Day, when the Allied forces invaded France, was June 6, 1944. France had been taken over by Germany earlier in the war. Many countries—America, England, France, and others—united in an effort to defend Europe against Germany. D-Day was a complicated, highly secret operation. Decoy plans about an invasion elsewhere were "leaked" to German military strategists to confuse them. On June 6 the Allied forces crossed the English Channel and stormed the beaches at Normandy to begin the liberation of France. One of the bloodiest and most costly battles of the war, it was successful and ultimately led to the defeat of Germany. **L2**

Activity Have students locate Normandy on a map. Encourage them to identify the possible difficulties the invasion forces faced. **L2**

Active Reading Strategies

REVIEW Ask students to recall what incident Anne refers to with this statement. *(A warehouse employee broke into the warehouse and heard noise upstairs in the Secret Annex.)* How did they resolve their problem? *(Mr. Frank authorized Mr. Kraler to pay the employee for his silence.)*

M Literary Elements

IRONY Ask students to identify the irony in this statement. *(Her diary became one of the best-selling books of all time.)*

N Literary Elements

FORESHADOWING Ask students how this statement foreshadows Anne's future. *(She is known all over the world.)*

invasion has come! We're going to be liberated! This is a time to celebrate!

[*He embraces* MRS. FRANK *and then hurries to the cupboard and gets the cognac and a glass.*]

MR. VAN DAAN. To steal bread from children!

MRS. FRANK. We've all done things that we're ashamed of.

ANNE. Look at me, the way I've treated Mother . . . so mean and horrid to her.

MRS. FRANK. No, Anneke, no.

[ANNE *runs to her mother, putting her arms around her.*]

ANNE. Oh, Mother, I was. I was awful.

MR. VAN DAAN. Not like me. No one is as bad as me!

DUSSEL. [*To* MR. VAN DAAN.] Stop it now! Let's be happy!

MR. FRANK. [*Giving* MR. VAN DAAN *a glass of cognac.*] Here! Here! *Schnapps! Locheim!*[54]

[VAN DAAN *takes the cognac. They all watch him. He gives them a feeble smile.* ANNE *puts up her fingers in a V-for-Victory sign. As* VAN DAAN *gives an answering V-sign, they are startled to hear a loud sob from behind them. It is* MRS. FRANK, *stricken with remorse. She is sitting on the other side of the room.*]

MRS. FRANK. [*Through her sobs.*] When I think of the terrible things I said . . .

[MR. FRANK, ANNE *and* MARGOT *hurry to her, trying to comfort her.* MR. VAN DAAN *brings her his glass of cognac.*]

MR. VAN DAAN. No! No! You were right!

MRS. FRANK. That I should speak that way to you! . . . Our friends! . . . Our guests!

[*She starts to cry again.*]

DUSSEL. Stop it, you're spoiling the whole invasion!

[*As they are comforting her, the lights dim out. The curtain falls.*]

ANNE'S VOICE. [*Faintly at first and then with growing strength.*] We're all in much better spirits these days. There's still excellent news of the invasion. The best part about it is that I have a feeling that friends are coming. Who knows? Maybe I'll be back in school by fall. Ha, ha! The joke is on us! The warehouse man doesn't know a thing and we are paying him all that money! . . . Wednesday, the second of July, nineteen forty-four. The invasion seems temporarily to be bogged down. Mr. Kraler has to have an operation, which looks bad. The Gestapo have found the radio that was stolen. Mr. Dussel says they'll trace it back and back to the thief, and then, it's just a matter of time till they get to us. Everyone is low. Even poor Pim can't raise their spirits. I have often been downcast myself . . . but never in despair. I can shake off everything if I write. But . . . and that is the great question . . . will I ever be able to write well? I want to so much. I want to go on living even after my death. Another birthday has gone by, so now I am fifteen. Already I know what I want. I have a goal, an opinion.

[*As this is being said—the curtain rises on the scene, the lights dim on, and* ANNE'S VOICE *fades out.*]

54. *Schnapps* (schnäps) is the cognac, or brandy. *Locheim!* (lə KHĪ′ əm) or (lə khä′ yim) means "To Life!"

Teaching Support

MEETING INDIVIDUAL NEEDS: ADVANCED LEARNERS

Journal Writing Students may benefit from further reflection on the impact the events depicted in the play had on the characters.

Activity Have students write a journal entry that any of the characters other than Anne might have written. Suggest that the journal entry be a description of what that character has learned from his or her experiences in hiding. Encourage students to consider what insights that character may have gained about himself or herself and about others. **L3**

SCENE 4

[It is an afternoon a few weeks later . . . Everyone but Margot is in the main room. There is a sense of great tension. Both MRS. FRANK *and* MR. VAN DAAN *are nervously pacing back and forth,* DUSSEL *is standing at the window, looking down fixedly at the street below.* PETER *is at the center table, trying to do his lessons.* ANNE *sits opposite him, writing in her diary.* MRS. VAN DAAN *is seated on the couch, her eyes on* MR. FRANK *as he sits reading. The sound of a telephone ringing comes from the office below. They all are rigid, listening tensely.* MR. DUSSEL *rushes down to* MR. FRANK.*]*

DUSSEL. There it goes again, the telephone! Mr. Frank, do you hear?

MR. FRANK. [*Quietly.*] Yes. I hear.

DUSSEL. [*Pleading, insistent.*] But this is the third time, Mr. Frank! The third time in quick succession! It's a signal! I tell you it's Miep, trying to get us! For some reason she can't come to us and she's trying to warn us of something!

MR. FRANK. Please. Please.

MR. VAN DAAN. [*To* DUSSEL.] You're wasting your breath.

DUSSEL. Something has happened, Mr. Frank. For three days now Miep hasn't been to see us! And today not a man has come to work. There hasn't been a sound in the building!

MRS. FRANK. Perhaps it's Sunday. We may have lost track of the days.

MR. VAN DAAN. [*To* ANNE.] You with the diary there. What day is it?

DUSSEL. [*Going to* MRS. FRANK.] I don't lose track of the days! I know exactly what day it is! It's Friday, the fourth of August. Friday,

The Diary of Anne Frank, 1959. 20th Century Fox. Movie still.
Viewing the photograph: Describe the expression on Mr. Van Daan's face. How do you think he feels about himself and his situation?

O Author's Craft

MOOD Have students identify the mood in the opening of scene 4. How does this mood contrast with the mood in the last scene? *(Scene 4 opens with tension; the previous scene ended with everyone in better spirits.)*

P Active Reading Strategies

RESPOND Remind students that the audience watching this play knows the outcome. What effect might this dialogue have on the audience? *(The audience knows that something bad is going to happen, so this would add to the tension and the tragedy.)* What effect does it have on students?

Q Active Reading Strategies

PREDICT Ask students to predict what the information in Dussel's statement may mean.

VIEWING THE PHOTOGRAPH

Viewing Response *Mr. Van Daan looks worried. He probably fears their being discovered by the Nazis.*

MEETING INDIVIDUAL NEEDS — MULTIPLE MODES OF EXPRESSION

Bodily-Kinesthetic Explain to students that making costumes for a drama is very important because clothes can reveal something about a character. In a play set in another time, costumes also contribute to the authenticity of the play's setting.

Activity Using clues from the play and research about clothing at the time of the play's setting, have students design costumes for two of the play's characters. The costumes should be consistent with the character. **L2**

Active Reading Strategies

PREDICT Ask students to speculate about who is making the telephone call. What would they do in Mr. Frank's position?

Literary Elements

IMAGERY Explain to students that Viennese waltzes were often played at gala balls or other happy occasions. Ask them to consider what effect is achieved by the waltz playing in the background. *(It heightens the desperation of their situation by contrasting it with the gaiety of the outside world.)*

VIEWING THE PHOTOGRAPH

Viewing Response *Peter has kept to himself. His expression suggests he is worried about what will become of them.*

and not a man at work. [*He rushes back to* MR. FRANK, *pleading with him, almost in tears.*] I tell you Mr. Kraler's dead. That's the only explanation. He's dead and they've closed down the building, and Miep's trying to tell us!

MR. FRANK. She'd never telephone us.

DUSSEL. [*Frantic.*] Mr. Frank, answer that! I beg you, answer it!

MR. FRANK. No.

MR. VAN DAAN. Just pick it up and listen. You don't have to speak. Just listen and see if it's Miep.

DUSSEL. [*Speaking at the same time.*] For God's sake . . . I ask you.

MR. FRANK. No. I've told you, no. I'll do nothing that might let anyone know we're in the building.

The Diary of Anne Frank, 1959. 20th Century Fox. Movie still.

Viewing the photograph: How has Peter dealt with being in hiding up to this point? What does his expression suggest about what the future might hold?

PETER. Mr. Frank's right.

MR. VAN DAAN. There's no need to tell us what side you're on.

MR. FRANK. If we wait patiently, quietly, I believe that help will come.

[*There is silence for a minute as they all listen to the telephone ringing.*]

DUSSEL. I'm going down. [*He rushes down the steps.* MR. FRANK *tries ineffectually*[55] *to hold him.* DUSSEL *runs to the lower door, unbolting it. The telephone stops ringing.* DUSSEL *bolts the door and comes slowly back up the steps.*] Too late. [MR. FRANK *goes to* MARGOT *in* ANNE's *bedroom.*]

MR. VAN DAAN. So we just wait here until we die.

MRS. VAN DAAN. [*Hysterically.*] I can't stand it! I'll kill myself! I'll kill myself!

MR. VAN DAAN. For God's sake, stop it!

[*In the distance, a German military band is heard playing a Viennese waltz.*]

MRS. VAN DAAN. I think you'd be glad if I did! I think you want me to die!

MR. VAN DAAN. Whose fault is it we're here? [MRS. VAN DAAN *starts for her room. He follows, talking at her.*] We could've been safe somewhere . . . in America or Switzerland. But no! No! You wouldn't leave when I wanted to. You couldn't

55. *Ineffectually* means "without effect; uselessly."

Teaching Support

interNET CONNECTION

Simon Wiesenthal Foundation This organization was founded by a Holocaust survivor to bring Nazis to justice. Have students visit the Wiesenthal Center's Web site to learn what efforts the group has made in finding and prosecuting Nazi war criminals. **L2**

leave your things. You couldn't leave your precious furniture.

MRS. VAN DAAN. Don't touch me!

[*She hurries up the stairs, followed by* MR. VAN DAAN. PETER, *unable to bear it, goes to his room.* ANNE *looks after him, deeply concerned.* DUSSEL *returns to his post at the window.* MR. FRANK *comes back into the main room and takes a book, trying to read.* MRS. FRANK *sits near the sink, starting to peel some potatoes.* ANNE *quietly goes to* PETER'*s room, closing the door after her.* PETER *is lying face down on the cot.* ANNE *leans over him, holding him in her arms, trying to bring him out of his despair.*]

ANNE. Look, Peter, the sky. [*She looks up through the skylight.*] What a lovely, lovely day! Aren't the clouds beautiful? You know what I do when it seems as if I couldn't stand being cooped up for one more minute? I *think* myself out. I think myself on a walk in the park where I used to go with Pim. Where the jonquils and the crocus and the violets grow down the slopes. You know the most wonderful part about *thinking* yourself out? You can have it any way you like. You can have roses and violets and chrysanthemums all blooming at the same time . . . It's funny . . . I used to take it all for granted . . . and now I've gone crazy about everything to do with nature. Haven't you?

T **PETER.** I've just gone crazy. I think if something doesn't happen soon . . . if we don't get out of here . . . I can't stand much more of it!

U **ANNE.** [*Softly.*] I wish you had a religion, Peter.

PETER. No, thanks! Not me!

ANNE. Oh, I don't mean you have to be Orthodox . . . or believe in heaven and hell and purgatory[56] and things . . . I just mean some religion . . . it doesn't matter what. Just to believe in something! When I think of all that's out there . . . the trees . . . and flowers . . . and seagulls . . . when I think of the dearness of you, Peter . . . and the goodness of the people we know . . . Mr. Kraler, Miep, Dirk, the vegetable man, all risking their lives for us every day . . . When I think of these good things, I'm not afraid any more . . . I find myself, and God, and I . . . V

[PETER *interrupts, getting up and walking away.*]

PETER. That's fine! But when I begin to think, I get mad! Look at us, hiding out for two years. Not able to move! Caught here like . . . waiting for them to come and get us . . . and all for what?

ANNE. We're not the only people that've had to suffer. There've always been people that've had to . . . sometimes one race . . . sometimes another . . . and yet . . .

PETER. That doesn't make me feel any better!

ANNE. [*Going to him.*] I know it's terrible, trying to have any faith . . . when people are doing such horrible . . . But you know what I sometimes think? I think the world may be going through a phase, the way I was with Mother. It'll pass, maybe not for hundreds of years, but someday . . . I still believe, in spite of everything, that people are really good at heart. W

PETER. I want to see something now . . . Not a thousand years from now!

[*He goes over, sitting down again on the cot.*]

56. Jews in the *Orthodox* branch of Judaism are the most traditional, strictly observing the ancient laws and customs. *Purgatory* is the Roman Catholic belief in a place of temporary punishment for the souls of the dead.

T Literary Elements

FORESHADOWING Have students explain how Peter's statements foreshadow what will happen.

U Active Reading Strategies

RESPOND Ask students whether they are surprised by this statement. Have them consider in their responses the reasons the families are in hiding. *(They are in hiding because of their ethnicity.)*

V Literary Elements

TRAGEDY Note Anne's monologue about how she has coped with everything that has happened. How does this revelation contribute to the tragedy of the story?

W Active Reading Strategies

RESPOND Have students respond to this statement, explaining why they agree or disagree with Anne. How does the statement make them feel about Anne and about her story?

MEETING INDIVIDUAL NEEDS — MULTIPLE MODES OF EXPRESSION

Musical Remind students that in the early days of film—through the 1920s—there was no sound, only pictures, and musical accompaniment was provided by instrumentalists in the theater. The music was very important because it had to reflect the mood and emotion that speaking parts would have conveyed.

Activity Have students make a "silent picture" presentation of the major events and moods in the play. They should select pictures and music to accompany them that give the audience a sense of the mood in various scenes of the play. **L2**

Active Reading Strategies

QUESTION Ask students what Mr. Frank's statement means. Why will they no longer live in fear? *(They are facing what they have feared for so long.)*

Active Reading Strategies

PREDICT Ask students what they think Anne might have said to complete this thought. Ask students whether they think any—and, if so, which—of her hopes were fulfilled.

FYI

The Diary of Anne Frank had its German opening in seven cities simultaneously on October 1, 1956. At the end of the play, the audiences sat in shocked silence without applauding. Shortly after, Germans began openly expressing remorse for what had happened; since the end of the war, Germans had not publicly spoken about the Nazi atrocities.

ANNE. But, Peter, if you'd only look at it as part of a great pattern . . . that we're just a little minute in the life . . . [*She breaks off.*] Listen to us, going at each other like a couple of stupid grown-ups! Look at the sky now. Isn't it lovely? [*She holds out her hand to him.* PETER *takes it and rises, standing with her at the window looking out, his arms around her.*] Someday, when we're outside again, I'm going to . . .

[*She breaks off as she hears the sound of a car, its brakes squealing as it comes to a sudden stop. The people in the other rooms also become aware of the sound. They listen tensely. Another car roars up to a screeching stop.* ANNE *and* PETER *come from* PETER's *room.* MR. *and* MRS. VAN DAAN *creep down the stairs.* DUSSEL *comes out from his room. Everyone is listening, hardly breathing. A doorbell clangs again and again in the building below.* MR. FRANK *starts quietly down the steps to the door.* DUSSEL *and* PETER *follow him. The others stand rigid, waiting, terrified. In a few seconds* DUSSEL *comes stumbling back up the steps. He shakes off* PETER's *help and goes to his room.* MR. FRANK *bolts the door below, and comes slowly back up the steps. Their eyes are all on him as he stands there for a minute. They realize that what they feared has happened.* MRS. VAN DAAN *starts to whimper.* MR. VAN DAAN *puts her gently in a chair, and then hurries off up the stairs to their room to collect their things.* PETER *goes to comfort his mother. There is a sound of violent pounding on a door below.*]

MR. FRANK. [*Quietly.*] For the past two years we have lived in fear. Now we can live in hope.

[*The pounding below becomes more insistent. There are muffled sounds of voices, shouting commands.*]

MEN'S VOICES. *Auf machen! Da drinnen! Auf machen! Schnell! Schnell! Schnell!*[57] etc., etc.

[*The street door below is forced open. We hear the heavy tread of footsteps coming up.* MR. FRANK *gets two school bags from the shelves, and gives one to* ANNE *and the other to* MARGOT. *He goes to get a bag for* MRS. FRANK. *The sound of feet coming up grows louder.* PETER *comes to* ANNE, *kissing her good-bye, then he goes to his room to collect his things. The buzzer of their door starts to ring.* MR. FRANK *brings* MRS. FRANK *a bag. They stand together, waiting. We hear the thud of gun butts on the door, trying to break it down.*

ANNE *stands, holding her school satchel, looking over at her father and mother with a soft, reassuring smile. She is no longer a child, but a woman with courage to meet whatever lies ahead.*

The lights dim out. The curtain falls on the scene. We hear a mighty crash as the door is shattered. After a second ANNE'S VOICE *is heard.*]

ANNE'S VOICE. And so it seems our stay here is over. They are waiting for us now. They've allowed us five minutes to get our things. We can each take a bag and whatever it will hold of clothing. Nothing else. So, dear Diary, that means I must leave you behind. Good-bye for a while. P.S. Please, please, Miep, or Mr. Kraler, or anyone else. If you should find this diary, will you please keep it safe for me, because some day I hope . . .

[*Her voice stops abruptly. There is silence. After a second the curtain rises.*]

57. "Open up! Inside there! Open up! Quick! Quick! Quick!" Pronunciation: *Auf machen!* (ouf mäkн' ən) *Da drinnen!* (dä drin' ən) *Schnell!* (shnel)

Teaching Support

Writing Minilesson

Introductions and Conclusions Students sometimes have difficulty writing introductions and conclusions. Explain that an introduction announces to the reader the topic of writing; a conclusion includes some analysis of the material that has been presented.

Activity Have students write an introduction and a conclusion to one of the scenes from the play. Have them review the scene, asking themselves, "What is this scene about?" Each introduction should answer that question without using the words "This scene is about ..." Then, have them think about what they learned from reading the scene to write a concluding sentence.

Additional Resources

Writer's Choice, Lessons 2.4, 5.10

The Diary of Anne Frank, 1959. 20th Century Fox. Movie still.
Viewing the photograph: How does this image illustrate Mr. Frank's closing words about Anne?

VIEWING THE PHOTOGRAPH

Viewing Response *Mr. Frank is reading from Anne's diary and appears to be moved by what he has read.*

FYI

The group discovered in the annex was on the last train to take Jewish prisoners out of the Netherlands before Germany was defeated. Anne died of typhus at Bergen-Belsen concentration camp in March 1945. Her mother and sister were already dead.

FINE ART TRANSPARENCY 23

You may want to use ***Fine Art Transparency 23*** in a discussion of sources of support and healing in tragic or difficult situations.

LIFE SKILLS CONNECTION

Leading and Organizing Point out to students that in the play Mr. Frank takes the role of leader of the group. In a discussion, students should point out examples of things that Mr. Frank did as leader of the group in hiding. Discuss why he took certain actions and what effect they had on the other members of the group.

Activity Have small groups discuss the qualities needed in a leader. They should list at least five qualities and then compare the qualities of Mr. Frank to their lists. **L2**

Z Literary Elements

ACTS AND SCENES Have students recall that the play is a flashback begun with Mr. Frank's revisiting the annex after the war. Ask students to speculate about why the playwrights return to this scene.

AA Literary Elements

TRAGEDY Note that this statement from Anne's diary is repeated at the end of the play. How does it contribute to the tragic nature of the play? *(She died because of the evil deeds of people, although she had thought that people were good.)*

Thematic Focus

Faces of Dignity Have students describe in what way each character in the play represents the theme, using examples from the play to support their responses.

ASSESSMENT

Quick Checks, p. 65

Teaching Support

SCENE

5

Z *[It is again the afternoon in November, 1945. The rooms are as we saw them in the first scene.* MR. KRALER *has joined* MIEP *and* MR. FRANK. *There are coffee cups on the table. We see a great change in* MR. FRANK. *He is calm now. His bitterness is gone. He slowly turns a few pages of the diary. They are blank.]*

MR. FRANK. No more.

[He closes the diary and puts it down on the couch beside him.]

MIEP. I'd gone to the country to find food. When I got back the block was surrounded by police . . .

MR. KRALER. We made it our business to learn how they knew. It was the thief . . . the thief who told them.

*[*MIEP *goes up to the gas burner, bringing back a pot of coffee.]*

MR. FRANK. *[After a pause.]* It seems strange to say this, that anyone could be happy in a concentration camp. But Anne was happy in the camp in Holland where they first took us. After two years of being shut up in these rooms, she could be out . . . out in the sunshine and the fresh air that she loved.

MIEP. *[Offering the coffee to* MR. FRANK.*]* A little more?

MR. FRANK. *[Holding out his cup to her.]* The news of the war was good. The British and Americans were sweeping through France. We felt sure that they would get to us in time. In September we were told that we were to be shipped to Poland . . . The men to one camp. The women to another. I was sent to Auschwitz. They went to Belsen. In January we were freed, the few of us who were left. The war wasn't yet over, so it took us a long time to get home. We'd be sent here and there behind the lines where we'd be safe. Each time our train would stop . . . at a siding, or a crossing . . . we'd all get out and go from group to group . . . Where were you? Were you at Belsen? At Buchenwald?[58] At Mauthausen? Is it possible that you knew my wife? Did you ever see my husband? My son? My daughter? That's how I found out about my wife's death . . . of Margot, the Van Daans . . . Dussel. But Anne . . . I still hoped . . . Yesterday I went to Rotterdam.[59] I'd heard of a woman there . . . She'd been in Belsen with Anne . . . I know now.

[He picks up the diary again, and turns the pages back to find a certain passage. As he finds it we hear ANNE'S VOICE.*]*

ANNE'S VOICE. In spite of everything, I still believe that people are really good at heart. AA

*[*MR. FRANK *slowly closes the diary.]*

MR. FRANK. She puts me to shame.

[They are silent.]

The Curtain Falls

58. ***Auschwitz*** (oush' vits), ***Belsen*** (bel' zən), and ***Buchenwald*** (bo͞o' KHən vält') or (bo͞o' k'n wôld') were the sites of Nazi concentration camps in Poland and Germany that specialized in exterminating prisoners.
59. ***Rotterdam*** is a city in the southwestern Netherlands.

Grammar and Language *Minilesson*

Punctuating Dates Note that dates appear in various forms throughout the play. Review with students that a comma is used in the date only when the month, day, and year are provided, in that order. The year is preceded by a comma and followed by a comma when it does not end the sentence. If only the month and year appear, no comma is needed. Remind students that an apostrophe is used in a date to show omitted digits in a date, but not to make years plural.

Activity Write the following on the board without punctuation and have students punctuate the dates. *It was May 5, 1942, when the soldiers came. We left in August 1943. The war ended in '45. The war was the biggest event of the 1940s.* **L2**

Additional Resources

- ***Grammar and Language Transparency 64***
- ***Grammar and Language Workbook,*** pp. 261–262
- ***Grammar and Composition Handbook,*** Lessons 13.2–4
- ***Writer's Choice,*** Lesson 20.4

Responding to Literature

PERSONAL RESPONSE

- Did the ending of the play surprise you in any way? Why or why not?

Brackets connect questions that are paired to develop higher-level thinking skills.

Analyzing Literature

RECALL

1. How do Mr. and Mrs. Frank react to Mr. Van Daan's stealing the bread? How does his family react?
2. What news does Miep bring?
3. Anne and Peter each view their situation differently. Explain their points of view.
4. What are Mr. Frank's last words of encouragement to the group?

INTERPRET

5. What does the audience learn about each character from the uproar over the stolen bread?
6. What do you learn about the characters from their reactions to Miep's news?
7. How do you account for the difference in the way Peter and Anne view their situation?
8. What does Mr. Frank mean by his final words of encouragement?

EVALUATE AND CONNECT

9. Who, in your opinion, behaves better during the scene with the stolen bread, the young people or the adults? Explain.
10. Why do you think the playwrights end the play with these five words: *She puts me to shame?* Do you agree with Mr. Frank's self-criticism? Is the criticism meant for anyone else? Explain your answer.

LITERARY ELEMENTS

Tragedy

In a **tragedy,** the main character, a dignified or heroic person, suffers a downfall, or death. This downfall may be the result of a personal weakness, such as pride, or it may result from outside forces over which the character has no control. In this play, Anne Frank is the main character.

1. In what ways is Anne heroic?
2. Are there other heroes in the story?
3. What causes Anne's "downfall"?

- See **Literary Terms Handbook,** p. R10.

Responding to the Selection

PERSONAL RESPONSE

Students should explain whether they were surprised by the ending.

Analyzing Literature

1. Mr. and Mrs. Frank are upset; Mrs. Van Daan excuses her husband's behavior; Peter is ashamed.
2. The Allied invasion has begun.
3. Anne is hopeful and optimistic. Peter is not hopeful.
4. Mr. Frank says, "For two years we have lived in fear. Now we can live in hope."
5. Students should refer to an element of each character's nature that is revealed in the scene.
6. Students should refer specifically to examples from the scene to explain what is revealed about the characters.
7. Peter is older, and is not as outgoing. Anne is closer to her family and has a religious belief that Peter does not.
8. The event everyone has most feared has now occurred, so they no longer need to fear it. Instead, they can now hope that the war will end and that they will be spared.
9. Students' opinions should be supported by examples of the behavior of the characters.
10. Students' answers should consider Mr. Frank's mood and statements at the beginning of the play and should explain how the statement could apply to others.

LITERARY ELEMENTS

1. Possible answers include Anne's bravery; Anne's concern for others; or her hopefulness for the future.
2. Students should support their selections with examples from the text and discussion of the elements of heroism.
3. Anne's downfall is caused by outside forces, specifically the Nazi invasion.

Literature and Writing

Writing About Literature

Students' paragraphs should

- take the position that Miep and Kraler are "righteous"
- include examples from the selection

Creative Writing

Students' comparisons should

- focus on Mr. Frank and Mr. Van Daan as parents
- be supported with specific examples from the selection

Extending Your Response

Literature Groups By "in spite of everything," Anne means that the acts of many who are clearly not good have not destroyed her faith in people. Students should judge whether she may have felt the same way at the end of her life by discussing what happened to her. **COLLAB. LEARN.**

Performing Students' presentations should reflect preparation and practice and should be supported by an explanation of why the scene is significant. **COLLAB. LEARN.**

Interdisciplinary Activity Students presentations should demonstrate research and an ability to present relevant facts. **COLLAB. LEARN.**

Literature and Writing

Writing About Literature

Analyzing Characters The Holocaust Museum in Israel honors rescuers like Miep and Kraler as the "Righteous Among Nations of the World." Examine how Miep and Kraler interact with the group hiding in their building–the way they speak to each person, their comments about the dangers to themselves, and the attitude each group member shows to them. Then write a paragraph or two explaining how the playwrights show that Miep and Kraler are righteous.

Creative Writing

Comparing Fathers Think about Mr. Frank's comment that "There is so little that we parents can do to help our children. We can only try to set a good example." Write two brief character sketches in which you compare Mr. Frank and Mr. Van Daan as parents. Include examples of their actions, thoughts, and words.

Extending Your Response

Literature Groups

Anne's Famous Words In her diary, Anne Frank wrote this famous sentence: "In spite of everything, I still believe that people are really good at heart." What does Anne mean by *in spite of everything?* Using examples from the play and your knowledge of what happened to Anne after leaving the annex, discuss her words. Would she, in your opinion, have made the same statement near the end of her life?

Performing

Readers Theater Work with another student or a small group to prepare a readers theater presentation of an episode from the play that you find very significant. As part of your presentation, explain your reasons for choosing that episode. Ask classmates to comment on the effectiveness of your presentation.

Interdisciplinary Activity

History In every European country courageous people risked their lives to rescue Jews from Nazi persecution. With a group, research some of the rescuers, such as Miep Gies, Raoul Wallenberg, Oskar Schindler, and the villagers of Le Chambon-sur-Lignon. Share with the class the motives and the actions of each person or group.

Miep Gies

Reading Further

If you would like to read about Anne Frank from another point of view, try one of these books:

Anne Frank Remembered: The Story of the Woman Who Helped to Hide the Frank Family by Miep Gies and Alison Leslie Gold

The Last Seven Months of Anne Frank by Willy Lindwer

Save your work for your portfolio.

Skill Minilessons

RETEACH • REVIEW

GRAMMAR AND LANGUAGE • ITALICS AND QUOTATION MARKS

The following rules for using type treatments can help you understand materials you are reading.

- Quotation marks set off the title of a short story, essay, song, poem, news or feature article, or chapter from a book. ("The Anne Frank House" is a poem about a building in Amsterdam.)
- Italics or underlining set off the title of a book, play, film, television series, magazine, newspaper, or work of art. (*The Diary of Anne Frank* is a story of hope.)
- Italics or underlining identify a word being defined or being used as a word. Definitions are placed in quotation marks. (The word *diary* comes from a Latin word meaning "daily.")

PRACTICE Rewrite the following sentences and correct the mistakes in type treatments.

1. In 1947 Otto Frank published his daughter's diary under the title "The Diary of a Young Girl."
2. While in hiding, Anne Frank wrote a number of short stories, including *The Best Little Table.*
3. "Mazeltov" is a Hebrew word meaning *congratulations.*
4. The word Holocaust refers to the mass killing of millions of people, especially Jews, during World War II.

For more about italics and quotation marks, see **Language Handbook,** p. R41.

READING AND THINKING • FOCUSING ON A QUESTION

Focusing on a question at the beginning of a story, chapter, act, or scene is a good way to read for meaning. At the beginning of act 1, for example, you could focus on the question *What is Anne's relationship with her father (or mother)?* Look for details that help you to understand Anne's relationships.

PRACTICE Think of questions that will help a friend read the play for the first time. Write one question to be considered before reading each scene in act 2.

For more about questioning strategies, see **Reading Handbook,** p. R94.

VOCABULARY • ETYMOLOGY

The **etymology,** or history, of a word may be quite straightforward. *Onslaught* comes from an Old English word that means "to strike." *Stealthily* comes from an Old English word meaning "to steal." Sometimes, however, a word's history is like a story. *Pandemonium* was made up by John Milton to be the name of the capital of hell in his famous poem *Paradise Lost.* He created the word by combining Greek words meaning "all" and "demons."

PRACTICE Use the information about word histories to answer these questions.

1. *Frenzy* comes from the Greek word *phrenesis,* which means "insanity." Which word do you think probably has the same history–*frantic, friend,* or *French?*
2. *Apprehension* comes from the Latin word *apprehendere,* which means "to take hold of." If a criminal was *apprehended,* was the criminal wounded, arrested, or put on trial?
3. *Foreboding* comes from the Old English *fore,* meaning "before," and *bode,* meaning "messenger." If you *forestall* an action, do you encourage it, prevent it, or react to it?

Skill Minilessons

GRAMMAR AND LANGUAGE
ITALICS AND QUOTATION MARKS

1. In 1947, Otto Frank published his daughter's diary under the title *The Diary of a Young Girl.*
2. While in hiding, Anne Frank wrote a number of short stories, including "The Best Little Table."
3. *Mazeltov* is a Hebrew word meaning "congratulations."
4. The word *Holocaust* refers to the mass killing of millions of people, especially Jews, during World War II.

READING AND THINKING
FOCUSING ON A QUESTION

Students' questions should reflect the main theme, idea, or event presented in the scenes.

VOCABULARY
ETYMOLOGY

1. frantic
2. arrested
3. prevent it

Additional Resources

- ***Grammar and Language Workbook,*** p. 267
- ***Grammar and Composition Handbook,*** Lesson 13.6
- ***Writer's Choice,*** Lesson 20.6
- ***Reading Skills Practice Workbook***
- ***Vocabulary Practice,*** p. 44

ASSESSMENT

- ***Quick Checks,*** p. 65
- ***Selection and Theme Assessment,*** pp. 111–112
- ***Performance Assessment,*** p. 57
- ***Testmaker: ExamView Pro***
- ***Interactive Tutor: Self-Assessment***

interNET CONNECTION

Word Derivations Invite students to go online and use a search engine to locate the *Web of Online Dictionaries.* Students can search the site's etymology dictionaries for information about the derivation of new or unfamiliar words in this selection.

Objective

- To read and understand song lyrics

Literature LINK

The Diary of Anne Frank These song lyrics connect to *The Diary of Anne Frank* (pages 697–772). Point out to students that the theme of the song comes from a line in the play that captures the essence of Anne Frank's approach to dealing with stress.

Analyzing Media

1. The song title comes from a line in the play when Anne is trying to comfort Peter. It also sums up Anne's optimistic nature, her courage in the face of fear, and the way in which her imagination enabled her to cope with her plight.
2. Students' responses should explain the benefits that visualization would have for someone in a difficult situation.

Informational Text

inTIME For more examples of informational text, direct students to the articles in *inTIME* magazine.

Additional Resources

Media Connections, p. 14

Teaching Support

MEDIA Connection

SONG LYRICS

How would you cope with being forced to stay inside for two years? Lyricist Enid Futterman wrote these words to describe how Anne Frank would "think herself out" of the Secret Annex during her period of hiding.

I Think Myself Out

I'm facing the night.
I think myself stars.
I think myself free.
I'm bathing in moonlight.
I'm breathing the sea.

The night faces me
and takes me away
to walk on the wind
to ride on the rain
to come to the day.

It's morning.
It's evening.
It's raining.
It's snowing.
There are roses and lilies
and crocuses growing.
Sunlight is shining.
Breezes are blowing.
I'm running.
I'm leaping.
I'm flying
I'm going,
I'm going outside.

I think myself rain,
rain in my hair
I think myself air,
air on myself.
I think myself out.

from "I Am Anne Frank"
Copyright © 1985 by Enid Futterman and Michael Cohen

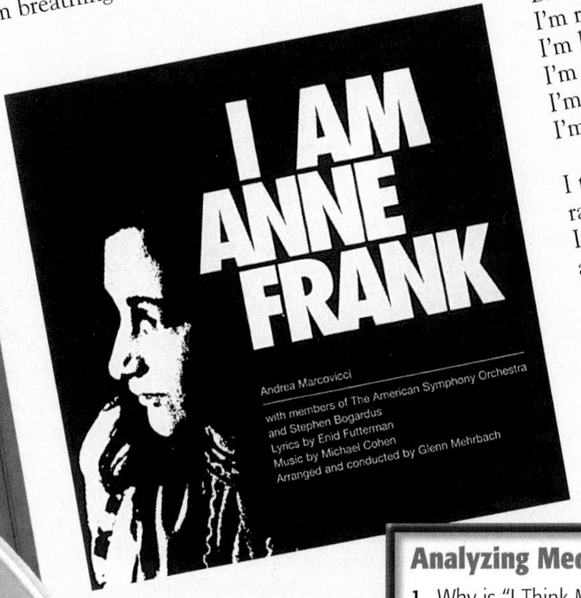

Analyzing Media

1. Why is "I Think Myself Out" an appropriate title for this song?
2. How would visualizing the images in the song help you if you couldn't see them firsthand?

interNET CONNECTION

Visualization Explain that when Anne "thinks herself out," she uses visualization techniques to imagine herself in a more desirable place. Have students search the Internet for more information on visualization strategies, such as those used by athletes.

Reading Minilesson

Identify Author's Purpose Song lyrics are essentially poetry. As with poetry, song lyrics often have a message that the poet wants the listener to consider. Point out to students that there can be more than one message in a poem or in a song. Encourage students to consider the play, which is not only the literal story of the Franks in hiding but is also a story about human nature.

Activity Have students review the song lyrics on this page to identify the two things this song covers. Encourage the students to consider what the song is literally about and what else it might be saying. Ask them which of these is the poet's message. **L2**

Additional Resources

Reading Skills Practice Workbook

Vo•cab•u•lar•y *Skills*

Analyzing Words

Context clues may not always provide the meaning of an unfamiliar word. Before turning to a dictionary, break the word into pieces, and look carefully to see if its parts are familiar.

The harm done to the Franks was irreversible.

This sentence provides no clue to the meaning of *irreversible.* However, the word parts are helpful. The base word *reverse* is familiar. Also, the prefix *ir-* is familiar to anyone who knows other words with the same prefix–*irregular,* for example. It is likely that you know that the suffix *-ible* means "able." Putting the clues together reveals that *irreversible* means "not able to be reversed." In the sentence, the harm done to the Franks cannot be undone.

Another kind of analysis is needed if an unfamiliar word is not built on a base word you know. However, it may have a root you recognize.

It is sad to think about the brevity of Anne Frank's life.

The root *brev* is in the word *abbreviation,* so you may realize that *brevity* has something to do with shortness. In the sentence, it is sad to think that Anne Frank's life was so short.

EXERCISE

Analyze the underlined words on the left and match each one to its meaning on the right.

1. an instinctive reaction	a. remedy
2. a nondescript house	b. deaths
3. a preexisting condition	c. reveal
4. disclose the facts	d. measure
5. count the fatalities	e. stillness
6. to feel rejuvenated	f. already present
7. provide a curative	g. natural; unlearned
8. difficult to quantify	h. made young again
9. a state of quietude	i. make strong or firm
10. solidify her support	j. hard to describe in words

Vo•cab•u•lar•y *Skills*

Objective

- To analyze unfamiliar words by recognizing their parts

Teaching Strategies

Encourage students to assume, when they are reading, that they probably know what the parts of unfamiliar words mean and to find the clue within the word that will help them understand what the word means. You might also suggest that students sound out an unfamiliar word using their knowledge of sound-letter correspondences to see if they recognize the spoken word.

Exercise

1. g
2. j
3. f
4. c
5. b
6. h
7. a
8. d
9. e
10. i

Additional Resources

Vocabulary Power

Teaching Support

MEETING INDIVIDUAL NEEDS — ENGLISH LANGUAGE LEARNERS

Latin Word Parts Students whose first languages are Latin based may recognize many root words that can help them analyze unfamiliar English words. In fact, these students may have a wide vocabulary of root words from which to draw.

Activity Have students review the list of underlined words in the exercises on this page to identify any words in their first language that have the same roots and similar meanings. Have the students share these with the class so that all of the students can better understand the common links among languages. COLLAB. LEARN.

Additional Resources

English Language Learners Sourcebook, p. 89

Objectives

- To write a historical research report of approximately 500 to 700 words
- To plan, draft, revise, edit, and present a historical research report
- To reflect on and assess the report

GLENCOE TECHNOLOGY

WRITER'S ASSISTANT CD-ROM

Students can use Glencoe's templates and guidelines software for expository writing to aid them in working through the steps in the writing process in this lesson.

Teaching Strategies

PREWRITING

Find Ideas Have students brainstorm to research ideas about the World War II era. Encourage them to question the ideas' relationships to the selections in this theme.

Shape Your Topic As students skim through their initial research, encourage them to write down additional questions that come to mind as they are reading; these questions may help them find a good topic.

Teaching Support

Writing WORKSHOP

Expository Writing: Historical Research Report

Important events touch the lives of people for many years, after the events took place. By examining the past, you may improve your understanding of the present. One way to examine history is to write about it.

Assignment: Use the process on these pages to write a report about a historical person or event.

- As you write your research report, refer to **Writing Handbook**, pp. R56–R60.

EVALUATION RUBRIC

By the time you complete this Writing Workshop, you will have

- provided a clear thesis statement about a historical person or event
- gathered information from a variety of sources to provide necessary background and support your thesis statement
- quoted, paraphrased, or summarized the information you gathered
- concluded with a paragraph that clearly and convincingly restates the thesis
- included a list of sources
- presented a report that is free of errors in grammar, usage, and mechanics

The Writing Process

PREWRITING

PREWRITING TIP

Need more ideas? Flip through the pages of your social studies textbook. Pictures, maps, or chapter headings might suggest an interesting topic to you.

TECHNOLOGY TIP

Check your word processing program. It may have an outlining feature to help you plan your report.

Find Ideas

What more would you like to know about events described in the selections in "Faces of Dignity"? On your own or with a partner, choose one or two people or events that you would like to know more about. Then brainstorm a list of questions about the topics you select.

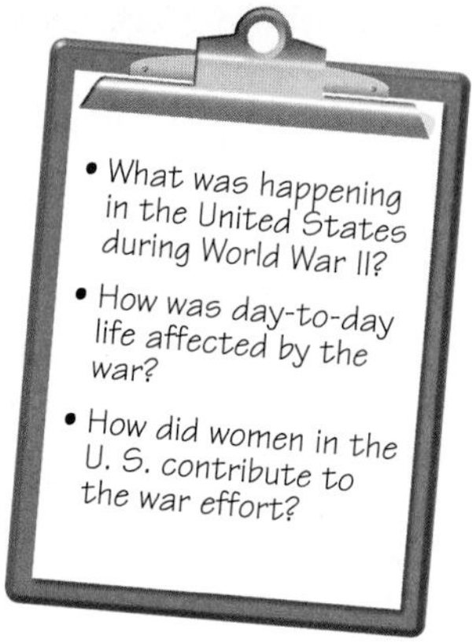

Shape Your Topic

Choose one of the questions you wrote and explore it further, using a general reference book. Narrow your topic until you find a focus that you can cover thoroughly in a short report.

Consider Your Audience and Purpose

The purpose of your report is to present information in an interesting way. Your audience will be your teacher and classmates–and perhaps others. You might make a copy for your family, your library, or your local historical society.

MEETING INDIVIDUAL NEEDS — ENGLISH LANGUAGE LEARNERS

Historical Research Alternatives Students learning English may consider choosing an event, a place, or a person from another country as their topic. Keep in mind that locating print resources may be challenging.

Activity Encourage students to consider a topic that is likely to inform the class of an unfamiliar historical event or person. Have them brainstorm to list modern historical events and figures that they have learned about from their families.

Additional Resources

English Language Learners Sourcebook

Search Out the Facts

Look for information from a variety of sources. Some sources, called **primary sources,** are documents and personal accounts from the time of the event. Primary sources include letters, diaries, government documents, and newspaper stories. They provide a first-hand look at a person or an event.

Other sources, called **secondary sources,** include encyclopedia articles, history books, and biographies. Secondary sources are based on information gathered from other sources. They offer a long-term view of the person or event.

Regardless of the kind of source you use, make sure the information is reliable, up to date, and unbiased.

Source Card

Source number ①

Reader's Digest Association. *Our Glorious Century.* New York: Reader's Digest, 1995.

my own book

Note Card

①

Women begin working in industry

By fall, 1943, nearly 16 million women were working outside their homes.

(Paraphrase) page 218

Take Notes

As you do your research, make **note cards** for the information you may want to include in your report. Paraphrase, summarize, or quote directly the information from your sources. Be sure to keep track of where each idea comes from. Record your sources on **source cards** like the one shown on this page. You will use source cards to prepare a bibliography or list of works cited. For more information on taking notes and creating source cards and a works-cited list, see the **Writing Handbook,** pages R57–R60.

Thesis statement: Rosie the Riveter was an important role model for women as well as a force for social change.

I. Rosie, the Image
- *A. The image was different from the reality.*
- *B. The image of Rosie changed people's attitudes and helped women join the workforce.*

II. Women in the Workforce
- *A. Men left jobs to go to war.*
- *B. Up to then, women had been discouraged from doing "men's" work.*
- *C. Advertisements showing Rosie helped create a positive image of working women.*

III. Rosie's Legacy
- *A. Women learned new skills.*
- *B. Working brought women financial independence.*
- *C. Equal opportunity and equal pay don't seem like strange ideas anymore.*

Write Your Thesis, Outline a Plan

This is the time to choose a focus for your report. Look over your notes and see what main idea they suggest. State this idea in one or two sentences–your **thesis statement.**

Next create an outline to guide you as you draft. List the main points that you will make and the details explaining each point. Plan to show causes and effects. Your outline might look something like the one begun on this page. For more about creating an outline, see the **Writing Handbook,** page R56.

Use Visual Aids

Use visual aids such as maps, charts, and graphs to make your report more appealing and easier to understand. Look at the graph shown here. This visual aid gives readers a quick, easy way to grasp and compare the statistics presented.

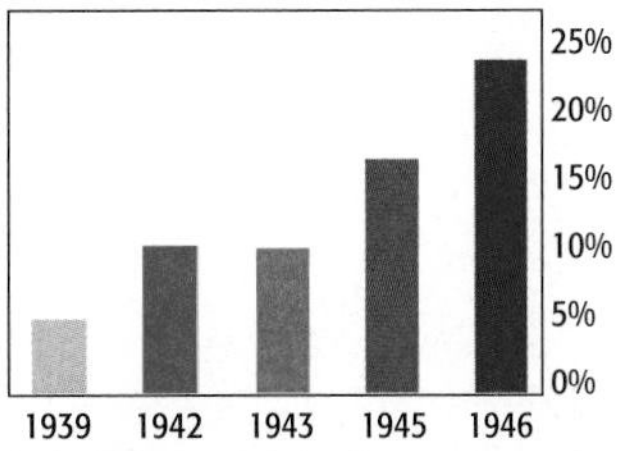

Women in the Iron and Steel Workforce.

Consider Your Audience and Purpose Explain to students that doing research on their topics will make them class experts in their subjects. When writing, they should consider how they can share their expertise with others.

Search out the Facts Encourage students to keep their cards well organized. Explain that their reports will be much easier to write if they have carefully organized their research materials. All the notes they take should indicate the source so they will know where to look if they need more information.

Outline a Plan Remind students that the key to a good report is a good thesis. Everything in a report should contribute to explaining one main idea, or thesis. If any students are unsure of their thesis at this point, have them review their note cards and source cards. Does one issue, idea, or event that they have researched stand out? If so, that should become the focus of the report. The thesis will explain the history or importance of that focus.

Additional Resources

- ***Writing and Proofreading Practice,*** pp. 1–6, 49–57
- ***Writing and Proofreading Transparencies 1–6, 19–20, 37–38***
- ***Writer's Choice,*** Unit 5

MEETING INDIVIDUAL NEEDS — SPECIAL NEEDS

Learning Disabled Some students with learning disabilities may have difficulty organizing their research into an outline. Encourage students to write their thesis in a sentence and then to look at the sentence parts for ideas on how the report should be organized.

Activity Have students review the example on page 779. Ask students to highlight the parts of the outline with the parts of the thesis sentence they describe. When they have done this, have them divide their own thesis statements into the main points they will need to cover. **L1**

Additional Resources

- ***Inclusion Strategies***

DRAFTING

Write a Working Opener Encourage students not to frustrate themselves by trying to begin their drafts with the perfect opening sentence. Suggest that they begin drafting with their thesis and start writing. After they have written several paragraphs, they may review the draft to see whether other sentences they have written would work as the opener. Suggest that students move sentences around during the drafting process.

Write On Remind students to follow their outlines during their drafting. Each point in the outline should be explained in the draft.

REVISING

Consider Changes When their first drafts are complete, encourage students to review their notes, looking for interesting material that did not fit into the outline categories. In particular, have them check their notes for interesting quotations that would make their reports come alive.

GLENCOE TECHNOLOGY

Invite students to use the **Revising with Style** CD-ROM, which offers instruction and exercises to help students improve their writing skills.

Teaching Support

DRAFTING

DRAFTING TIP
One way to show cause-and-effect relationships is to use transitions. For help with transitions, see the **Writing Skills** feature on page 691.

Write a Working Opener

Your first paragraph should not only catch readers' interest but also provide the background information they will need. You might start with an intriguing sentence and then add facts about the people, events, or time period. If you end your opener with your thesis, readers will find your report easy to follow.

STUDENT MODEL • DRAFTING

During World War II, Rosie the Riveter was one of the most famous women in the United States. Pictures of her were everywhere: a typical American woman dressed in work clothes and holding a wrench or a rivet gun in her hand. But she wasn't a real person. She was a symbol of all the women who went to work in factories during the war.

Complete Student Model on pp. R128–R129.

Write On

Develop your main points by using details, quotes, and examples. Make causes and effects clear. Your outline will help you stay organized, but if a new point occurs to you, try it out. Be sure to credit your sources in a style approved by your teacher. You might conclude with a personal reflection about your topic.

REVISING

REVISING TIP
Check your prewriting notes to be sure you have correctly matched information and sources.

Consider Changes

Take a break before you begin revising. You might ask a classmate to help. Using the Rubric for Revising as a guide, plan your changes.

RUBRIC FOR REVISING

Your revised historical research report should have

- an opening with a well-defined thesis
- information from a variety of primary and secondary sources
- appropriate quotations, facts, and other support
- transitions and parallel structures to make your report easy to follow
- a conclusion that clearly restates your thesis
- a correctly formatted works-cited list or bibliography
- properly credited source material
- no errors in grammar, usage, and mechanics

Writing *Minilesson*

Sequencing Students often make very few changes to their drafts during revision, generally staying with their original plan. Encourage students to think of drafting as a process for getting all the information down and revising as the step in which the writing is reorganized. Explain that ideas in a report must be adequately supported. Expert opinions, whether quoted or paraphrased, are an important source of such support.

Activity Have students exchange drafts with at least one other person. While they are reading others' drafts, encourage them to jot down any questions they have. These questions will draw the writer's attention to areas that need reorganization or further explanation.
L2 **COLLAB. LEARN.**

Additional Resources

Writer's Choice, Lesson 5.2

EDITING/PROOFREADING

After revising your report, go over it once more to catch errors in grammar, usage, and mechanics. The **Proofreading Checklist** on the inside back cover offers guidelines. Double-check your use of commas, as shown in the **Grammar Link** on page 690.

Grammar Hint

When you use commas to set off a phrase, don't forget the second comma.

Norman Rockwell, a famous illustrator, created one of the best-known images of Rosie the Riveter.

STUDENT MODEL • EDITING/PROOFREADING

The Ofice of War Information, a Government agency encouraged all citizen's to contribute.

Complete Student Model on pp. R128–R129.

Complete Student Model

For a complete version of the model developed in this workshop, refer to **Writing Workshop Models**, pp. R128–R129.

PUBLISHING/PRESENTING

You can add an extra dimension to your report with photos, charts or other visuals or with relevant audiotaped material. If your report involves people you know, send them a copy. If it is about community figures or events, you might give a copy to your local historical society or library.

PRESENTING TIP

For an oral presentation, try accompanying your report with audiotaped music of the period.

Reflecting

Think about the following questions before writing your responses.

- Which did you find easier, doing your research or writing your report? Explain.
- What are the two most useful pieces of advice you could give to another student who is about to write a research report?

Save your work for your portfolio.

EDITING/PROOFREADING

Encourage students to read through their revised reports, focusing on the words, the spelling, and the punctuation of each sentence. Suggest that they read through once for spelling, once for sentence structure, and once for punctuation. Focusing on one issue at a time will help them avoid errors.

PUBLISHING/PRESENTING

Students should consider providing an oral presentation of the information to the class. Talking to the class about the information will be more natural and interesting than reading the report word for word. Have students make sure that their presentations are appropriate for their audience in vocabulary, pace, and tone. Remind them to use precise language to make their message clear. Have them review their notes for details that could enliven their oral presentation.

Reflecting

Portfolio Encourage students to ask themselves the following questions as they review their writing. Does my research report

- focus on a stated thesis?
- contain enough detail to explain the topic to others?
- explore a topic of interest to me?

ASSESSMENT

Writing Assessment and Portfolio Management

- Writing Assessment, pp. 1–12, 34–37
- Portfolio Management, pp. 41–48

6+1 TRAITS™ OF WRITING

See the annotated **Writing Workshop Models** on pp. R119–R130 for additional help in evaluating student writing and in teaching the **6+1 Traits™ of effective writing.** Annotations and minilessons address and reinforce the **6+1 Traits™:** Ideas, Organization, Voice, Word Choice, Sentence Fluency, Conventions,and Presentation.

Theme Assessment

Objectives

- To give a personal response to the selections in this theme
- To analyze the use of flashback
- To complete a self-evaluation, set a goal, and devise a plan for achieving the goal

Responding to the Theme

1. Students should describe the main experiences of the characters they have selected to support their explanations.
2. Students should refer to selections in the theme that expanded these ideas for them.
3. Projects should relate to the theme.

Analyzing Literature

Students' responses should examine what the flashback technique added to the play and should refer to examples from the play to support their conclusions.

Evaluate and Set Goals

Remind students that *enjoyable* and *challenging* are not mutually exclusive.

Suggest that students think about something that was done well and something that needed improvement when making their assessments.

Set Goals

Have students make a graph with their three goals on one axis and time frames for achieving them on the other. They can plot their progress toward their goal on the graph.

Theme Assessment

Responding to the Theme

1. In which selection were the main character's experiences most moving to you? Why?
2. As a result of your reading this theme, what new thoughts do you have about these ideas?
   - Crises can bring out the best and the worst in people.
   - It is important to seek the good in even the worst situations.
   - Ordinary people can be heroes.
3. Present your theme project to the class.

Analyzing Literature

FLASHBACK

In *The Diary of Anne Frank,* a long flashback is used to show the Frank family's experiences while hiding from the Nazis. Why, do you think, did the author choose to begin and end the play with events that occurred much later than the main narrative? What does the use of flashback in this play accomplish? Explain your answers using examples from the play.

Evaluate and Set Goals

1. Which of the following activities were the most enjoyable? Which were the most challenging?
   - reading and understanding the selections
   - writing on your own
   - analyzing and discussing selections
   - presenting ideas and projects
   - researching topics
2. How would you assess the work you've completed in this theme, using the following scale? Give two or more reasons for your assessment.

   4 = outstanding   2 = fair
   3 = good   1 = weak
3. Think of an aspect of this theme that you found difficult. Choose a goal to work toward in the next theme.
   - Record your goal and three steps you will take to help you reach it.
   - Meet with your teacher to review your plan for achieving your goal.

Build Your Portfolio

SELECT

Choose two of your favorite pieces of work from this theme to include in your portfolio. The following questions can help you choose.

- ◆ Which do you consider your best work?
- ◆ Which did you learn the most from?
- ◆ Which was the most interesting?

REFLECT

Write some notes to accompany the pieces you selected. Use these questions to guide you:

- ◆ What do you like best about the piece?
- ◆ What did you learn from creating it?
- ◆ What might you do differently if you were beginning this piece again?

782 THEME 7

ASSESSMENT

Writing Assessment and Portfolio Management
- Writing Assessment, pp. 1–12
- Portfolio Management, pp. 41–48

GLENCOE TECHNOLOGY

MINDJOGGER VIDEOQUIZZES VIDEODISC

Use *MindJogger* to review the Theme 7 content.

Theme 7
Side B

Also available in VHS.

Reading on Your Own

If you have enjoyed the literature in this theme, you might also be interested in these books, which show the dignity of many kinds of people during a time when the world was at war.

Number the Stars

by Lois Lowry Annemarie Johansen and her best friend Ellen Rosen live in Copenhagen, Denmark, a city of shortages and Nazi soldiers. When the Germans begin to "relocate" Copenhagen's Jews in 1943, Ellen moves in with Annemarie's family. Soon Annemarie must risk her own life to save her friend.

The Island on Bird Street

by Uri Orlev A Jewish boy, left on his own for months during World War II, learns to survive in a ruined house in the Warsaw Ghetto of Poland. He learns how to find food, contact others, and live amid constant danger.

After the War

by Carol Matas Ruth is fifteen when she is freed from a Nazi concentration camp and fears that she is the only surviving member of her family. She joins an underground organization to make a dangerous and illegal journey to Palestine. Along the way, she rediscovers her inner strength and finds reasons for hope.

I Am Fifteen—and I Don't Want to Die

by Christine Arnothy The autobiography of Christine Arnothy focuses on one terrifying year during World War II when the author's family hid in the cellars of Budapest as German and Russian armies battled for control of Hungary.

Reading on Your Own

Tips for Independent Reading

Stress the importance of each student's spending at least thirty minutes a day in independent reading and suggest books, such as those shown here, related to this theme.

Reading the Novel Explain that the suggested readings will explore the theme of facing suffering and trials with dignity. As they read, students might compare the way the main characters in the stories deal with difficult situations to the responses of Anne Frank.

Practice As students do their independent reading, they might ask themselves questions like these: How might I respond to the situations in which the main characters in the stories find themselves? What tests of my stamina and dignity might arise in my own life? How can I prepare myself for challenges I might face in the future?

Glencoe Literature Library

Number the Stars by Lois Lowry is available in the *Glencoe Literature Library*. For a complete listing of titles, see the **Glencoe Resources for Independent Reading** in the front of this book.

The *Glencoe Literature Library Study Guide* provides instructional support and student activities for works in the *Glencoe Literature Library*.

MEETING INDIVIDUAL NEEDS — SPECIAL NEEDS

- You may wish to recommend *The Island on Bird Street* by Uri Orlev to your less-proficient readers. Its subject matter makes it an appropriate choice for these readers. **L1**

The books listed at the right are rated for average readers **(L2)** or for students who need more challenging reading material **(L3)**:

- *Number the Stars* by Lois Lowry **L2**
- *I am Fifteen—and I Don't Want to Die* by Christine Arnothy **L3**
- *After the War* by Carol Matas **L3**

Standardized Test Practice

Answers and Analyses

1. A A comma is used to indicate a pause after an introductory phrase, eliminating choices C and D. In choice B, no comma is necessary after *excited*, because *excited and nervous* is not a series of three or more items. Choice A is therefore the correct answer.
2. M The last name *Roberts* is a proper noun and should be capitalized. Additionally, the title *Colonel* should be capitalized because it comes before a proper name.
3. B Only choice B punctuates the sentence correctly.
4. L Proper adjectives formed from the names of nationalities should be capitalized, as in *French*, but the common noun *food* should not be.
5. A The full names of buildings, bridges, and monuments should be capitalized, as in *Eiffel Tower*. Also, students should know that the indefinite article *an* precedes words starting with vowels, and the article *a* precedes words starting with consonants. This eliminates choice C and leaves choice A, which is the correct answer.
6. K *My classmate* is a noninessential appositive, and thus should be set off by commas, as in choice K.
7. A A colon should be used to introduce a list of items that ends a sentence. Students can therefore eliminate choices B and C. In addition, a series listing three or more items uses a comma after each item in the list, leaving choice A as the correct answer.
8. L *Countryside* should not be capitalized because it does not indicate a specific place. *East* is capitalized, however, because it designates a specific region. However, remind students that when compass points are used to indicate direction, they should not be capitalized.

The Princeton Review

Standardized Test Practice

Read the sentences in each numbered item. Look at the underlined words. Choose the sentence in which the underlined words have CORRECT capitalization and punctuation.

1 A Excited and nervous, Sharon took the stage and began her solo.
B Excited, and nervous, Sharon took the stage and began her solo.
C Excited and nervous Sharon took the stage and began her solo.
D Excited and nervous; Sharon took the stage and began her solo.

2 J I spoke to colonel Roberts on the phone yesterday.
K I spoke to Colonel roberts on the phone yesterday.
L I spoke to colonel roberts on the phone yesterday.
M I spoke to Colonel Roberts on the phone yesterday.

3 A "Welcome to the party" Maxwell said as he greeted each guest.
B "Welcome to the party," Maxwell said as he greeted each guest.
C "Welcome to the party." Maxwell said as he greeted each guest.
D "Welcome to the party, Maxwell said as he greeted each guest.

4 J The french food was delicious.
K The French Food was delicious.
L The French food was delicious.
M The french Food was delicious.

5 A The Eiffel Tower is an amazing architectural feat.
B The Eiffel tower is an amazing architectural feat.
C The Eiffel Tower is a amazing architectural feat.
D The eiffel tower is an amazing architectural feat.

6 J Juan, my classmate is extremely intelligent.
K Juan, my classmate, is extremely intelligent.
L Juan my classmate is extremely intelligent.
M Juan: my classmate, is extremely intelligent.

7 A The menu for the wedding is as follows: chicken, rice, and salad.
B The menu for the wedding is as follows, chicken, rice, and salad.
C The menu for the wedding is as follows; chicken, rice, and salad.
D The menu for the wedding is as follows: chicken rice and salad.

8 J Have you seen the countryside in the east?
K Have you seen the Countryside in the East?
L Have you seen the countryside in the East?
M Have you seen the Countryside in the east!

MEETING INDIVIDUAL NEEDS

ENGLISH LANGUAGE LEARNERS

Capitalization Ask students to imagine that they are writing a letter to a grandparent describing a recent school trip. Have students write down all parts of the letter that have some form of capitalization. Some examples they may use are: the opening, the salutation, the name of the location visited, and activities. This exercise will give students a sense of what words must be capitalized. You might remind students to capitalize names of people and also words that show family relationships when the words are used as titles or as substitutes for names. For example:

- Grandpa Joe is sweet.
- On rainy days, my grandfather does crossword puzzles.
- On rainy days, Grandpa does crossword puzzles.

9 A The park is closed, let's go to my house.
B The park is closed let's go to my house.
C The park is closed: let's go to my house.
D The park is closed; let's go to my house.

10 J Both girl's dresses were pink.
K Both girls' dresses were pink.
L Both girls' dress's were pink.
M Both girls dresses were pink.

11 A I wanted to use my new Walkman, but I didn't have any batteries.
B I wanted to use my new Walkman but I didn't have any batteries.
C I wanted to use my new Walkman, but, I didn't have any batteries.
D I wanted to use my new Walkman; but I didn't have any batteries.

12 J Andrew lives down the street from Walloon lake.
K Andrew lives down the street from walloon lake.
L Andrew lives down the street from Walloon Lake.
M Andrew lives down the street from walloon Lake.

13 A "The play is at 6,30," said Mrs. Hatcher.
B "The play is at 6:30, said Mrs. Hatcher.
C "The play is at 6:30," said Mrs. Hatcher.
D "The play is at 6:30" said Mrs. Hatcher.

14 J Francis speaks german and japanese.
K Francis speaks german and Japanese.
L Francis speaks German and japanese.
M Francis speaks German and Japanese.

15 A I ran into Colleen, my best friend, on my way to the store.
B I ran into Colleen my best friend on my way to the store.
C I ran into Colleen, my best friend on my way to the store.
D I ran into Colleen: my best friend, on my way to the store.

16 J My favorite story as a child was *Jack and The Beanstalk.*
K My favorite story as a child was *Jack And The Beanstalk.*
L My favorite story as a child was *Jack and the Beanstalk.*
M My favorite story as a child was *Jack and the beanstalk.*

STOP

Answers and Analyses

9. D A semicolon joins two independent clauses that are closely connected in meaning. Choices A and B are run-on sentences, and choice C misuses a colon.
10. K The word *both* is plural, which eliminates choice J. *Dresses* should not be possessive, eliminating choice L. It is the *girls* who own the *dresses*, so the plural possessive *girls'*, choice K, is the correct answer.
11. A Because there are two independent clauses within one sentence, students should recognize it to be a compound sentence that must be joined by a comma and the conjunction *but*.
12. L Since the word *lake* is preceded by its specific, proper name, *Walloon*, both words specify the name of the lake and should both be capitalized.
13. C Students should be familiar with the proper punctuation for numerical indications of time, as well as for quotation marks in dialogue.
14. M Names of languages should always be capitalized.
15. A Nonessential appositives should be set off within commas.
16. L All of the important words in story titles should be capitalized. Small words, such as the articles *a* and *the* should be lowercase.

The Princeton Review TEST-TAKING TIP

Remind students to be alert to various instances of unusual capitalization when they take the test. For instance, important historical events, periods of time, and documents should be capitalized. However, articles and prepositions within those names are not capitalized (e.g., the Battle of Hastings).

Tested Objectives

Item	Language Objective
1–16	Use correct punctuation and capitalization

MORE PRACTICE

For additional practice, assign pages from one of the following standardized test resources available as part of Glencoe Literature.

Additional Resources
ITBS Preparation and Practice
SAT-9 Preparation and Practice
TerraNova Preparation and Practice

Theme 8 At a Glance
Hair-Raising Tales

THEME OPENING

Theme 8: HAIR-RAISING TALES

SELECTIONS

SKILL FEATURES

WRITING WORKSHOP

THEME ASSESSMENT

- **Responding to the Theme, Analyzing Literature, Evaluate and Set Goals** (p. 878)
- **Build Your Portfolio** (p. 878)
- **Reading on Your Own** (p. 879)
  The House of Dies Drear by Virginia Hamilton
  Companions of the Night by Vivian Vande Velde
  Redwall by Brian Jacques
  Foundation by Isaac Asimov
- **Standardized Test Practice** (pp. 880–881)

KEYS TO LITERARY CONNECTIONS

Comparing Selections

The **Comparing Selections** feature in this theme provides opportunities for addressing diverse aspects of the reading and literature curriculum.

For example, in Comparing Selections on page 854, students compare "The Tell-Tale Heart" by Edgar Allan Poe with his poem "The Raven." Through this comparison, students gain insights into the way the author uses elements that contribute to the mood of horror.

World Literature

The Student Edition contains a variety of literature that represents cultures from around the world. World literature selections are highlighted with the icon above.

TEACHING SUPPORT

The Teaching Support offers a wealth of interactive instructional support:

Meeting Individual Needs
- Special Needs
- English Language Learners
- Multiple Modes of Expression
- Advanced Learners

Internet Connection

Assessment

Portfolio Options

Minilessons
- Grammar and Language
- Reading
- Writing
- Listening and Speaking

Connecting to Other Selections

Real-World Connection

Interdisciplinary Connection

Life Skills Connection

Family and Community Activity

Key to Ability Levels

The activities throughout this theme have been coded for students of various abilities.

L1 **BASIC** activities for all students

L2 **AVERAGE** activities for average to above-average students

L3 **ADVANCED LEARNERS** activities for above-average students

Teaching Today

The Glencoe *Teaching Today* professional development Web site at www.teachingtoday.glencoe.com features daily teaching tips, free downloads, annotated Web resources, educational news, and a wealth of information on a wide range of topics.

Reading Skills in this theme

Variety of Texts

In addition to drama and short stories, this theme includes the following:

- cartoon
- television transcript
- poetry
- Web site

Comprehension Skills

The following instructional support for comprehension skills appears in this theme of the Student Edition:

- **Active Reading Strategies and Model** (pp. 833–843)
- **Verifying Predictions** (p. 867)
- **Reading and Thinking Minilessons** (pp. 811, 831)

See also the **Reading Minilessons** throughout the theme in this Teacher Wraparound Edition.

For strategies for reading longer works, such as novels and novellas, see "Tips for Independent Reading" on page 879.

Reading Resources

Active Reading Guide The ***Active Reading Guide*** provides graphic organizers and study guide questions to support students' reading of each selection (***Active Reading Guide***, pp. 66–71).

Interactive Reading Sourcebook and **Interactive Reading Workbook** The ***Interactive Reading Sourcebook*** and ***Interactive Reading Workbook*** offer focused comprehension strategies and lessons on critical thinking skills as well as fluency practice and activities to teach and support phonics, decoding, spelling, and vocabulary development.

Vocabulary Power The ***Vocabulary Power*** workbook (Lessons 33–36) provides systematic teaching, practice, and assessment of vocabulary for better reading comprehension.

Audio Library Available on audiocassette and on CD, the ***Audio Library*** provides valuable comprehension support.

Glencoe Literature Library Each title in the ***Glencoe Literature Library*** includes a full-length work plus related readings. A separate Study Guide is available for each title.

Five–Star Stories These anthologies of familiar short stories adapted and abridged for a variety of reading levels include exercises to help increase students' vocabulary and improve their reading comprehension.

The Contemporary Readers ***The Contemporary Readers*** are nonfiction books linked to various themes and designed for developing readers from a wide range of backgrounds.

Literature Classics CD-ROM The selections on this CD-ROM can be searched by author, theme, or genre.

inTIME and Humanities Across TIME Coproductions of Glencoe and Time, Inc., these resources include a wealth of high-interest nonfiction related to the selections in this theme.

Assessment in this theme

Glencoe's Assessment Advantage

Assessment Options in the Student Edition

This program offers a number of diverse ways to evaluate student understanding and skill proficiency. In the Student Edition, use the following:

- **Responding to Literature**
  Following each selection, students are asked to recall facts, interpret ideas, and evaluate concepts as they answer a variety of questions and complete activities to extend their understanding.
- **Theme Assessment (pp. 878–879)**
  Here students respond to the selections on personal and analytical levels. They also assume ownership of their learning by setting and evaluating goals and by selecting work for their portfolios.

See also the many **Assessment Resources** listed on the facing page.

The Princeton Review

Standardized Test Practice

The Princeton Review has developed the Standardized Test Practice pages found at the end of this thematic unit (pp. 880–881). For additional practice, direct students to the following resources:

- ITBS Preparation and Practice
- SAT-9 Preparation and Practice
- TerraNova Preparation and Practice

Writing Skills in this theme

Writing Skills

The Student Edition of Theme 8 offers strong instructional support for writing skills:

In **Extending Your Response,** which follows each selection:

- **Writing About Literature**
- **Personal/Creative Writing**

See also the **Writing Minilessons** throughout the theme in this Teacher Wraparound Edition.

Writing Workshops

Theme 8 concludes with a **Writing Workshop** that guides students through the process for writing a mystery story (pp. 874–877).

Writing Resources

Writer's Assistant CD-ROM Each **Writing Workshop** is supplemented by an interactive writing guide on the ***Writer's Assistant*** CD-ROM. This easy-to-use writing guide provides prompts, templates, and other tools that lead students through the writing process.

Grammar and Composition Handbook The ***Grammar and Composition Handbook*** (Lessons 13.8–14.5) provides systematic instruction in English language conventions.

Spelling Power The ***Spelling Power*** workbook (Lessons 29–32) provides systematic teaching, practice, and assessment of spelling to help students become better spellers and thus enhance their writing.

Writing and Proofreading Practice Blackline masters present in-depth instruction and practice on a specific step in the writing process and proofreading (pp. 1–6, 58–64).

Writing and Proofreading Transparencies Transparencies provide graphic organizers and proofreading exercises for whole-class instruction (pp. 1–6, 39–40).

Research and Report Writing Guide This resource provides extensive tips and activities to guide students in their writing projects in the literature classroom as well as in classes across the curriculum.

Style and Documentation Sourcebook for Writers This sourcebook is a combination reference and workbook, giving students the most up-to-date information and guidance regarding traditional as well as technological research strategies and documentation.

Revising with Style This resource offers instruction and exercises focusing on the revision process and covering topics from proofreading and correcting common grammatical errors to sentence combining and reordering.

Assessment Resources

Selection Quick Checks For each selection, a **Quick Check** of three to five short-answer questions measures students' literal comprehension.

Selection and Theme Assessment The ***Selection and Theme Assessment*** instrument tests students' abilities to recall, interpret, and evaluate what they've read. The tests consist of multiple-choice, short answer, and essay questions.

Performance Assessment Alternative assessment instruments and rubrics for Theme 8 are found in the ***Performance Assessment*** ancillary.

Writing Assessment and Portfolio Management These notes and strategies, student models, and assessment tools assist with the task of measuring students' progress as writers and as monitors of their own writing.

Testmaker: ExamView Pro Teachers can customize selection and Theme 8 tests by accessing the ***Testmaker*** database.

Interactive Tutor: Self-Assessment The ***Interactive Tutor: Self-Assessment*** software provides multiple-choice tests with immediate feedback to help students evaluate their knowledge and understanding of each literature selection.

MindJogger Videoquizzes Using a popular game show format, ***MindJogger Videoquizzes*** on videocassettes enable teachers to evaluate student understanding of Theme 8 in a quick and fun manner.

Theme 8 Skills Scope and Sequence

Lessons	Literary Elements	Reading and Thinking	Writing
Sorry, Right Number Stephen King	Screenplay, SE p. 809 *Setting, TWE pp. 792, 807* *Plot, TWE p. 793* *Character, TWE p. 796* *Humor, TWE p. 798* *Screenplay, TWE pp. 798, 801, 803*	Sequence of Events, SE p. 811 Television Transcripts, SE p. 812 *Inferring, TWE pp. 793, 803* *Evaluating, TWE pp. 794, 797* SN *Less-Proficient Readers, TWE p. 795* SN *Emotional, TWE p. 797* *Predicting, TWE p. 798* *Analyzing Arguments, TWE p. 812*	Evaluation, SE p. 810 Screenplay, SE p. 810 *Filling In, TWE p. 804*
The Legend of Sleepy Hollow Washington Irving DRP: 66 Lexile: 1210	Literary Legend, SE p. 829 *Legend, TWE p. 818* *Description, TWE p. 818* *Character, TWE p. 819* *Point of View, TWE p. 821* *Mood, TWE p. 824* *Climax, TWE p. 825* *Sensory Words, TWE p. 827*	Cause and Effect, SE p. 832 ELL *Visualizing, TWE p. 817* *Evaluating, TWE pp. 821, 822, 826* *Inferring, TWE p. 823* *Predicting, TWE p. 825* SN *Learning Disabled, TWE p. 827*	Point of View, SE p. 830 Urban Legend, SE p. 830 *Following a Model, TWE p. 826*
The Tell-Tale Heart Edgar Allan Poe DRP: 54 Lexile: 750	Suspense Story, SE p. 832 Mood, SE p. 842 *Mood, TWE p. 837* *Italics, TWE p. 841*	Suspense Story, SE p. 833 Web Site, SE p. 844 *Evaluating, TWE p. 836* ELL *Building Background, TWE p. 836* *Author's Purpose, TWE p. 838* *Drawing Conclusions, TWE p. 839* *Infer, TWE p. 841* *Narrating a Movie, TWE p. 844*	Suspenseful Scene, SE p. 843 Police Report, SE p. 843
The Raven Edgar Allan Poe	Allusion, SE p. 853 *Rhyme, TWE p. 848* *Allusion, TWE p. 849* *Style, TWE p. 851*	Comparing Selections, SE p. 854 SN *Less-Proficient Readers, TWE p. 848* *Inferring, TWE pp. 849, 852* *Paraphrasing, TWE p. 849*	Poem, SE p. 853 *Poetry, TWE p. 851*
The Woman in the Snow Patricia C. McKissack DRP: 53 Lexile: 630	Oral Tradition, SE p. 865 *Mood, TWE p. 861* *Character, TWE p. 863* *Oral Tradition, TWE p. 864*	Making and Verifying Predictions, SE p. 867 *Inferring, TWE p. 858* ELL *Understanding Setting, TWE p. 858* *Drawing Conclusions, TWE pp. 858, 859* SN *Less-Proficient Readers, TWE p. 861* SN *Learning Disabled, TWE p. 867*	Chronicling Change, SE p. 866 Your Oral Tradition, SE p. 866 *Personal Response, TWE p. 868*
The Dinner Party Mona Gardner DRP: 53 Lexile: 690	Resolution, SE p. 872 *Character, TWE p. 871* *Plot, TWE p. 871*	*Evaluate, TWE p. 871* *Sequence of Events, TWE p. 871*	Comparing Characters, SE p. 873 Analysis, SE p. 873 *Planning, TWE p. 875*
Writing Workshop Narrative Writing: Mystery Story			*Planning, TWE p. 875* SN *Less-Proficient Readers, TWE p. 876*

Key: Student material is in roman. Teacher material is in italic. Technology ELL English Language Learners

Vocabulary and Spelling	Grammar and Language	Listening, Speaking, and Viewing	Life Skills; Study and Research; Technology
Latin Root: *ject,* SE p. 811 Using Base Words, SE p. 814 *Word History, TWE p. 796* *Word Meaning, TWE p. 804* ELL *Base Words, TWE p. 814*	End Punctuation, SE p. 811 ELL *Print Conventions, TWE p. 792* ELL *Colloquial English, TWE p. 796* *Dashes, TWE p. 808*	Literature Groups, SE p. 810 Critical Viewing, SE p. 813 Acting Up, SE p. 810 *Acting, TWE p. 793* ELL *Understanding Critical Viewing, TWE p. 813*	Music Research, SE p. 810 *Problem Solving, TWE p. 800* *Video, TWE p. 801* *Internet Connection, TWE p. 802* *Health Resource, TWE p. 803* *Architectural Research, TWE p. 805* *The Televised Version, TWE p. 807* *Video, TWE p. 810*
Latin Root: *spec,* SE p. 831 SN *Less-Proficient Readers, TWE p. 818* *Word Meaning, TWE pp. 821, 823* *Glossary, TWE p. 826*	Varying Sentence Structure, SE p. 831 *Complex Sentences, TWE p. 828*	Literature Groups, SE p. 830 *Role-Playing, TWE p. 820* *Real-World Connection, TWE p. 823* *Reading Aloud, TWE p. 832*	Casting Actors, SE p. 830 Internet Connection, SE p. 831 *Science Research, TWE p. 821* *Planning, TWE p. 822* *Television Transcript, TWE p. 823* *Social Studies Research, TWE p. 841*
Analogies, SE p. 843	*Kinds of Sentences, TWE p. 840*	Literature Groups, SE p. 843 SN *Less-Proficient Readers, TWE p. 839*	Presenting an Argument, SE p. 843
ELL *Compound Words, TWE p. 847* *Word Meanings, TWE p. 851*	*Archaic Language, TWE p. 852*	Literature Groups, SE p. 853	Science: The Science of Dreams, SE p. 855 *Video, TWE p. 852*
Prefixes, SE p. 866	Using Apostrophes to Show Possession, SE p. 868 *Punctuating Interior Dialogue, TWE p. 864*	Literature Groups, SE p. 866	Social Studies Research, SE p. 866 *Art Research, TWE p. 860* *History Research, TWE p. 863*
Multiple-Meaning Words, SE p. 873		Literature Groups, SE p. 873	Performance Appraisal, SE p. 873
		ELL *Mysteries from Other Cultures, TWE p. 874*	

SN **Special Needs/Strategic Intervention**

Theme 8 RESOURCE MANAGER

Lessons	Essential Resources		English Language Learners
SORRY, RIGHT NUMBER STEPHEN KING PACING: 4 DAYS	**Lesson-Specific Instruction** Selection Focus Transp. 61 * Active Reading Guide, p. 66 Literary Elements Transp. 66 Vocabulary Practice, p. 45 * Quick Checks, p. 66 Selection and Theme Assessment, pp. 113–114	Testmaker: ExamView Pro Performance Assessment, p. 58 **Systematic Language Instruction** Grammar and Comp. Hbk., L. 13.8 Vocabulary Power, Lesson 33 Spelling Power, Lesson 29	Spanish Summaries, p. 61 Spanish Audio Library English, Yes!
The Legend of Sleepy Hollow WASHINGTON IRVING PACING: 2 DAYS	**Lesson-Specific Instruction** Selection Focus Transp. 62 * Active Reading Guide, p. 67 Literary Elements Transp. 67 Vocabulary Practice, p. 46 * Quick Checks, p. 67 Selection and Theme Assessment, pp. 115–116	Testmaker: ExamView Pro Performance Assessment, p. 59 **Systematic Language Instruction** Grammar and Comp. Hbk., L. 13.9–13.10 Vocabulary Power, Lesson 34 Spelling Power, Lesson 30	English Language Learners Sourcebook, p. 94 Spanish Summaries, p. 62 * Audio Library English, Yes!
The Tell-Tale Heart EDGAR ALLAN POE PACING: 2 DAYS	**Lesson-Specific Instruction** Selection Focus Transp. 63 * Active Reading Guide, p. 68 Literary Elements Transp. 68 Vocabulary Practice, p. 47 * Quick Checks, p. 68 Selection and Theme Assessment, pp. 117–118	Testmaker: ExamView Pro Performance Assessment, p. 60 TIME *inTIME* magazine, pp. 22–23 **Systematic Language Instruction** Grammar and Comp. Hbk., L. 14.1, 14.2	English Language Learners Sourcebook, p. 95 Spanish Summaries, p. 63 Spanish Translations, pp. 222–226 * Audio Library English, Yes!
The Raven EDGAR ALLAN POE PACING: 3 DAYS	**Lesson-Specific Instruction** Selection Focus Transp. 64 * Active Reading Guide, p. 69 Literary Elements Transp. 69 * Quick Checks, p. 69 Selection and Theme Assessment, pp. 119–120	Testmaker: ExamView Pro Performance Assessment, p. 61 **Systematic Language Instruction** Grammar and Comp. Hbk., L. 14.3 Vocabulary Power, Lesson 35 Spelling Power, Lesson 31	English Language Learners Sourcebook, p. 96 Spanish Summaries, p. 64 Spanish Translations, pp. 227–232 * Audio Library English, Yes!
The Woman in the Snow PATRICIA C. MCKISSACK PACING: 2 DAYS	**Lesson-Specific Instruction** Selection Focus Transp. 65 * Active Reading Guide, p. 70 Literary Elements Transp. 70 Vocabulary Practice, p. 48 * Quick Checks, p. 70 Selection and Theme Assessment, pp. 121–122	Testmaker: ExamView Pro Performance Assessment, p. 62 **Systematic Language Instruction** Grammar and Comp. Hbk., L. 14.4 Vocabulary Power, Lesson 36 Spelling Power, Lesson 32	English Language Learners Sourcebook, p. 97 Spanish Summaries, p. 65 Spanish Translations, pp. 233–238 * Audio Library English, Yes!

Key: Workbook · Blackline Masters · Textbook · Transparency · CD-ROM · Videodisk (also available in videocassette)

Special Needs/ Strategic Intervention	Reteaching and Enrichment
Interactive Reading Sourcebook, pp. T209-T212 Interactive Reading Workbook, pp. 121-124 Inclusion Strategies Sourcebook, pp. 99-100 Theme Eight Planning Guide, p. 6 Spanish Audio Library	Literature Launchers, Side B, Segment 23 Reading Skills Practice Workbook pp. 113-114 Grammar and Language Transp. 65 Gr. and Lang. Wkbk., pp. 255-256, 271-272 Grammar and Comp. Hbk., L. 13.1, 13.8 Media Connection Activities, p. 15 Interactive Tutor: Self-Assessment Vocabulary PuzzleMaker Web Site (lit.glencoe.com)
Interactive Reading Sourcebook, pp. T212-T215 Interactive Reading Workbook, pp. 125-128 Inclusion Strategies Sourcebook, pp. 33-34, 85-86 * Audio Library	Literature Launchers, Side B, Segment 21 Fine Art Transparency 15 Reading Skills Practice Workbook pp. 115-116 Grammar and Language Transp. 66 Gr. and Lang. Wkbk., pp. 157-158, 323-324 Grammar and Comp. Hbk., L. 8.2 Interactive Tutor: Self-Assessment Vocabulary PuzzleMaker Web Site (lit.glencoe.com)
Interactive Reading Sourcebook, pp. T215-T218 Interactive Reading Workbook, pp. 139-130 Inclusion Strategies Sourcebook, pp. 41-42 Theme Eight Planning Guide, p. 22 * Audio Library	Literature Launchers, Side B, Segment 22 Reading Skills Practice Workbook pp. 117-118 Grammar and Language Transp. 67 Gr. and Lang. Wkbk., pp. 47-50 Grammar and Comp. Hbk., L. 13.1 Media Connection Activities, p. 16 Interactive Tutor: Self-Assessment Vocabulary PuzzleMaker Web Site (lit.glencoe.com)
Interactive Reading Sourcebook, pp. T218-T220 Interactive Reading Workbook, pp. 131-132 Inclusion Strategies Sourcebook, pp. 45-46 Theme Eight Planning Guide, p. 30 * Audio Library	Fine Art Transparency 11 Reading Skills Practice Workbook pp. 69-70, 119-120 Grammar and Language Transp. 68 Gr. and Lang. Wkbk., pp. 283-284 Grammar and Comp. Hbk., L. 15.3 Interactive Tutor: Self-Assessment Vocabulary PuzzleMaker Web Site (lit.glencoe.com)
Interactive Reading Sourcebook, pp. T221-T224 Interactive Reading Workbook, pp. 133-134 Inclusion Strategies Sourcebook, pp. 49-50 Theme Eight Planning Guide, p. 36 * Audio Library	Fine Art Transparency 28 Reading Skills Practice Workbook pp. 75-76, 121-122 Grammar and Language Transp. 69 Gr. and Lang. Wkbk., pp. 267-268, 269-270 Grammar and Comp. Hbk., L. 13.6, 13.7 Interactive Tutor: Self-Assessment Vocabulary PuzzleMaker Web Site (lit.glencoe.com)

Web Audiocassette Diskette *Also available in Spanish

Independent Reading

Encourage students to spend thirty minutes each day in independent reading. The following Glencoe components and outside resources provide opportunities for reading related to this theme.

The Glencoe Literature Library

You may want to assign one or more of these titles for independent reading. For a complete listing of titles available in the Glencoe Literature Library, see page T96 of this book.

- *A Christmas Carol* by Charles Dickens
- *The House of Dies Drear* by Virginia Hamilton
- *A Wrinkle in Time* by Madeleine L'Engle

inTIME Magazine News stories, feature articles, reviews, profiles, and essays in the magazine connect to an author, work, or theme in the Student Edition. See the ***inTIME* Teacher's Guide** for specific connections to this theme.

Resources for Less-Proficient Readers

For reading especially created for less-proficient readers, suggest

- *Five-Star Stories*
- *The Contemporary Readers*

Additional Resources for Independent Reading

The following titles are listed with specific reading selections throughout this theme. You may want to suggest that students look for these in your local or school library.

- *Tangerine* by Edward Bloor
- *Alien Game* by Catherine Dexter
- *Wings of a Falcon* by Cynthia Voigt
- *Haunted Waters* by Mary Pope Osborne
- *Look for Me by Moonlight* by Mary Downing Hahn
- *Companions of the Night* by Vivian Vande Velde
- *Redwall* by Brian Jacques
- *Foundation* by Isaac Asimov

Theme 8 RESOURCE MANAGER (continued)

Lessons	Essential Resources		English Language Learners
The Dinner Party MONA GARDNER PACING: 2 DAYS	**Lesson-Specific Instruction** Selection Focus Transp. 66 * Active Reading Guide, p. 71 Literary Elements Transp. 71 Vocabulary Practice, p. 49 * Quick Checks, p. 71 Selection and Theme Assessment, pp. 123–124	Testmaker: ExamView Pro Performance Assessment, p. 63 TIME *inTIME* magazine, pp. 12–13 **Systematic Language Instruction** Grammar and Comp. Hbk., L. 14.5 Vocabulary Power, Unit 8 Review/Test Spelling Power, Unit 8 Review/ Proofreading	Theme Eight Planning Guide, p. 44 Spanish Summaries, p. 66 * Audio Library English, Yes!
Writing **WORKSHOP** Narrative Writing: A Mystery Story PACING: 2 DAYS	Writing Assessment and Portfolio Management, pp. 1–13, 38–40, 41–48		English Language Learners Sourcebook, p. 9 English, Yes!

Key: Workbook Blackline Masters Textbook Transparency CD-ROM Videodisk (also available in videocassette)

Special Needs/ Strategic Intervention	Reteaching and Enrichment
Interactive Reading Sourcebook, pp. T Interactive Reading Workbook, p. 135 Inclusion Strategies Sourcebook, pp. 25–26 * Audio Library	Fine Art Transparency 16 Reading Skills Practice Workbook pp. 61–62, 123–124 Interactive Tutor: Self-Assessment Vocabulary PuzzleMaker Web Site (lit.glencoe.com)
Inclusion Strategies Sourcebook, pp. 73–74	Writing and Proofreading Practice, pp. 1–7, 58–64 Writing and Proofreading Transparencies 1–6, 23–24, 39–40 Revising with Style Writer's Assistant

Theme RESOURCES

To explore the theme further, you may want to use these resources:

- Listening and Speaking Activities (pp. 22–24)
- Viewing and Representing Activities (pp. 1–6, 28–30)
- Critical Thinking Skills (pp. 21–22)
- Media Connection Activities, (pp. 15–16)
- Interdisciplinary Activities (pp. 30–33)
- Family and Community Activities (p. 28)
- Selection and Theme Assessment (pp. 113–124, 139–140)
- Performance Assessment (pp. 71, 94)

TIME Humanities Across TIME

See also these additional theme planning resources:

- Theme Eight Planning Guide
- Interactive Reading Sourcebook
- Literature Groups Sourcebook
- Interactive Lesson Planner
- Interactive Teacher Edition
- Glencoe Web Site (lit.glencoe.com)

PRESENTATION Plus!

Use Glencoe's ***Presentation Plus!*** This multimedia teaching tool lets you present dynamic lessons that will engage your students. Using Microsoft PowerPoint®, you can customize the presentation to create your own personalized lessons.

Web Audiocassette Diskette *Also available in Spanish

THEME 8

Hair-Raising Tales

Theme Objectives

- To enjoy reading suspenseful stories
- To analyze the literary elements in plays, short stories, and poems
- To apply strategies for reading suspenseful tales and poems

Teaching Strategies

Have students read the quotation by Stephen King in preparation for the discussion questions below.

VIEWING THE PHOTOGRAPH

Viewing Response Discussion questions:

- What kind of movie do you think the people in this photograph are viewing, given their expressions and body language? *(They are probably viewing a scary movie.)*
- How does 3-D viewing affect your response to a movie? Does it intensify the action for you?

TEACHER *to* TEACHER

WACOOCHEE JUNIOR HIGH SCHOOL • SALEM, ALABAMA

I try to plan my year so that I teach urban legends and campfire tales around the same time as Halloween. I encourage students to learn oral storytelling as we work through selections in this theme. We blank out the windows of the classroom and use flashlights as our campfire. Then I tailor an urban legend and tell students my "own" story. I tell the story in a dramatic way and even add a few screams. As a class, we discuss what makes a good urban legend and how urban legends can become each student's story. Then students go to work and craft their own stories. They can use one of the stories we've read as a model and give it a personal twist, or they can write one based on the class model. Then we go back to the blacked-out windows and flashlight campfire so students can tell their stories.

—BRENDON O'NEILL

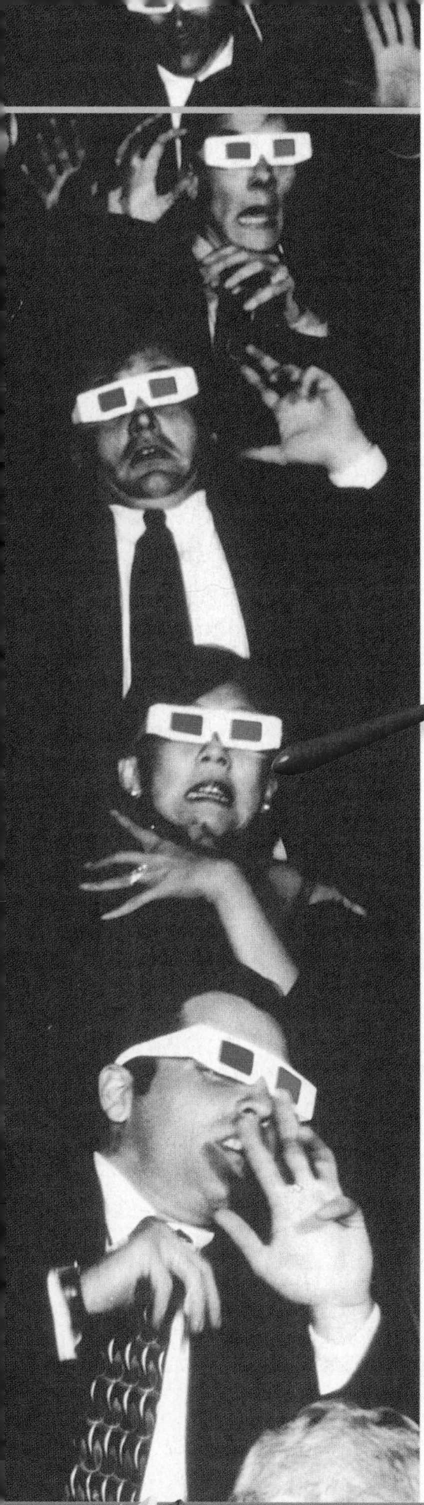

THEME 8

THEME CONTENTS

Introducing Theme 8

Direct students' attention to the **Theme Contents.** Ask them to read through the list of selections. Present these questions for discussion:

- What types of selections are included in this theme? *(Students may notice that this theme has a drama, short stories, and a poem. They may recognize the authors as famous for scary stories.)*
- Which of the titles or authors interest you?
- Have you read other works by these authors? What expectations do you have about reading these selections?

LITERATURE & HUMANITIES

"Manhattan Backwash"
National Museum of Women in the Arts
Have students examine this painting and discuss what elements of the scene would make it an ideal setting for a tale of horror.

GLENCOE TECHNOLOGY

LITERATURE CLASSICS CD-ROM
Search for other selections related to the theme "Hair-Raising Tales."

RESOURCE MANAGER

See the ***Theme Eight Planning Guide*** for additional teaching notes, strategies, and resources for introducing the theme "Hair-Raising Tales."

Exploring the Theme

Hair-Raising Tales

- Students may be familiar with the physical changes that occur when faced with something scary, including a prickling sensation of the scalp. They may also have observed a house pet whose hair stands on end when it is frightened.
- Students may understand that the pleasure of reading a suspense tale or watching a scary movie is knowing that they are safe once they finish.

To explore the theme further, suggest that students investigate folktales and traditional literature to discover how widespread and popular such tales are.

Starting Points

Ghoulish Humor

Draw students' attention to the cartoon, The Quigmans. Invite students to explain what is happening in the cartoon. Ask how the cartoonist makes a scary situation humorous. Make sure that students, especially English language learners, understand that "check out" is a slang expression for "to die." Have them compare death to a check-out counter at the supermarket.

Heart-Stopping Moments

Students may like to share their experiences with the rest of the class. Suggest building up atmosphere by describing the setting and the circumstances that led to their being frightened. Encourage students to include sensory imagery that captures the sounds, sights, and even smells of the setting.

Exploring the Theme

Hair-Raising Tales

It's night. You're alone with a book. The words fill your head with scary music, although the room is silent. Shadows on the wall move each time you turn the page. Your heart pounds. You race, reluctantly, to the end of the story. You are scared and thrilled. Like an intense thriller or tale of horror, the selections in "Hair-Raising Tales" will make your spine tingle and pulse quicken. Choose one of the activities below to begin your thinking about the theme.

Starting Points

GHOULISH HUMOR

Humor and horror may seem to be unlikely partners. However, many scary stories heighten the suspense by putting funny surprises together with frightful moments. Other stories simply poke fun at traditional horror plots.

- Create a comic strip that either turns a scary situation into a funny one or pokes fun at a popular scary story you've read recently.

HEART-STOPPING MOMENTS

Every now and then, our imaginations get the best of us. In the dark, the lamp's shadow on the wall becomes a lunging monster. The rustle of the trees becomes a haunting voice.

- Remember a time when your imagination went into overdrive and scared you silly. Write two or three paragraphs describing the scene that set off your imagination.

"Pine box or plastic?"

Family and Community Activity

Audience Response Form Ask students to invite family and community members to watch their multimedia presentation. Have students observe how each person reacts. Explain that movie directors often have screenings of early versions of their work to observe the audiences' reactions. If they do not react as expected to a specific scene, the director may change that scene. Audience members may also fill out carefully developed response sheets after such a viewing. Encourage students to develop response sheets for their audiences. **L2**

Additional Resources

Family and Community Activities, p. 28

Theme Projects

Choose one of the projects below to work on as you read the selections in this theme. Work on your own, with a partner, or with a group.

LEARNING FOR LIFE

Critic's Corner

1. Read a movie or book review of your favorite horror, thriller, or mystery story.
2. Compare your own thoughts and feelings about the book or film with those in the review. On what do you and the critic agree? On what do you disagree? In your opinion, is the review a fair one? Explain.
3. Write a letter to the critic describing your reactions to the review. Cite reasons and examples to explain why you think the review was on target or unfair.

interNET CONNECTION

For more about "Hair-Raising Tales," visit Glencoe's Web site at lit.glencoe.com

You can learn more about your favorite horror writer online. Many authors have their own Web sites. Check them out, or visit the site of the Biography Channel.

Dracula, starring Bela Lugosi, 1931. Movie still.

CRITICAL VIEWING

Book vs. Movie

1. Find a scary story or novel that has been produced in a movie version. Read the story and then watch the movie.
2. Compare the written story with the film version. How much do they have in common? What elements appear in the film but not in the story, and vice versa? Which version do you prefer, and why?
3. Write a brief report comparing and contrasting the written story with the film. Be sure to explain which form you enjoyed more.

MULTIMEDIA PROJECT

Build a Fright Site

1. Choose four or five of your favorite villains from literature. Write descriptions of their evil deeds and physical appearances, collect or draw pictures of them, and create audio clips of yourself reading the scary dialogue.
2. Use drawing software to create a multimedia presentation that invites people to vote on their favorite villain.
3. Organize and present your work.

Theme Projects

Teaching Strategies

The following suggestions may help your students plan and carry out their theme projects.

Learning For Life

- Before students read reviews, suggest that they write down their own reactions to help them keep their own opinions uninfluenced by reviewers' comments.
- Suggest that students lay their and critic's reactions side by side to find areas of agreement and disagreement.
- Point out to students that the tone of the letter will affect its reception. Students should "respectfully disagree."

Critical Viewing

- Suggest that students make notes on the major characters and plot developments. These, rather than slight differences, are most important in comparing.
- Encourage students to watch the video with partners who share their taste in authors. They will find that each person recalls or notices different things.
- If students choose a contemporary author, suggest that they watch the credits to see whether the author helped develop the script.

interNET CONNECTION

Glencoe Literature Web Site

For more information on "Hair-Raising Tales," suggest that students type the keywords *suspense stories, mysteries,* and *Alfred Hitchcock* into a search engine.

Multimedia Project

- Students may perform this project best in pairs or groups in which individual students are responsible for the medium for which they have the most aptitude.
- Encourage students to incorporate into their presentations scary sound effects, such as squeaky doors, footsteps, or demonic laughter.
- If videotaping is to be one of the media students use, encourage them to use lighting effects to cast menacing shadows.

Additional Resources

- ***Interdisciplinary Activities,*** pp. 30–33
- ***Viewing and Representing Activities,*** pp. 1–6, 28–30
- ***Listening and Speaking Activities,*** pp. 22–24
- ***Critical Thinking Skills,*** pp. 21–22
- ***Selection and Theme Assessment,*** pp. 139–140
- ***Performance Assessment,*** p. 71

Before Reading

Objectives

- To read and analyze the screenplay of a suspense drama
- To identify the elements of a screenplay
- To write an evaluation of the screenplay

Skills

Reading/Thinking: Inferring; Evaluating; Predicting; Sequencing
Writing: Monologue; Scripts
Vocabulary: Word History; Word Meaning; Latin Root *ject*
Grammar/Language: End Punctuation; Dashes
Listening/Speaking: Acting; Performing
Life Skills: Problem Solving
Collaboration: Literature Groups

Motivating STUDENTS

Literature Launchers: "Stephen King: Be Very Afraid"

Videodisc Side B, Segment 23

Also available in VHS.

Selection Focus Transparency 61: Before presenting the painting, ask students to discuss the elements that produce a dark mood in both fine art and writing.

Reading Focus: As an extension of the Reading Focus, have students share what kinds of things scare them.

Before You Read

Sorry, Right Number

MEET STEPHEN KING

Stephen King has this advice for talented writers: "If you work out with weights for fifteen minutes a day over a course of ten years, you're gonna get muscles. If you write for an hour and a half a day for ten years, you're gonna turn into a good writer." King, a writer who seems constantly to have a book on the best-seller list, should know. He has published more than thirty horror novels.

Stephen King was born in Maine in 1947. Sorry, Right Number *was first published in 1993 in* Nightmares and Dreamscapes.

READING FOCUS

What kinds of things scare you? Is it ever fun to be scared?

Web It!
Make a word web to record the kinds of things that frighten you or the things that you enjoy in a scary movie or story.

Setting a Purpose
As you read, consider what you find frightening in this play.

BUILDING BACKGROUND

The Time and Place *Sorry, Right Number* is a modern drama about an ordinary American family. It is written as a screenplay.

Did You Know? Some critics think that horror is popular today because it is *cathartic.* That is, it frightens people but then lets them relax at the end. They project their fears onto the monster and stop worrying about their own problems, which look small by comparison.

Phantom of the Opera, starring Lon Chaney, 1925. Movie still.

VOCABULARY PREVIEW

dejected (di jek′ tid) *adj.* sad; depressed; in low spirits; p. 793
strenuous (stren′ ū əs) *adj.* very active; energetic; p. 800
amiable (ā′ mē ə bəl) *adj.* friendly, good-natured; p. 801
interim (in′ tər im) *n.* the time between events; meantime; p. 804
presumably (pri zōō′ mə blē) *adv.* supposedly; probably; p. 804
impending (im pen′ ding) *adj.* about to occur; p. 805
chasm (kaz′ əm) *n.* a deep hole or crack, as in the earth's surface; p. 807
bland (bland) *adj.* dull and uninteresting; p. 808

RESOURCE MANAGER

Teaching Tools and Resources
- Theme Eight Planning Guide
- Literature Groups Sourcebook

Essential Lesson Support

Lesson-Specific Instruction
- Selection Focus Transparency 61
- Literary Elements Transparency 66
- Active Reading Guide,* p. 66
- Selection Vocabulary Practice, p. 45

Assessment
- Selection Quick Checks,* p. 66
- Sel. and Theme Assmt., pp. 113–114
- Testmaker: ExamView Pro
- Performance Assessment, p. 58

Systematic Language Instruction
- Gr. & Comp. Hbk., L. 13.8
- Vocabulary Power, Lesson 33
- Spelling Power, Lesson 29

English Language Learners
- ELL Sourcebook, pp. 90, 91, 92, 93
- Spanish Summaries, p. 61
- Spanish Translations, pp. 90-91
- Audio Library*
- English, Yes!

Spec. Needs/Strat. Interven.
- Interactive Rdg. Sbk., pp. T209–T212
- Interactive Rdg. Wkbk., pp. 121-124
- Inclusion Strat. Sbk., pp. 99-100
- Audio Library*

* Also available in Spanish

SORRY, RIGHT NUMBER

Stephen King

Reading the Selection

SUMMARY

The character Bill Weiderman is a well-known author of horror stories. His wife Katie has been frightened by a phone call from a sobbing woman who Katie believes is her younger sister Dawn. Terrified because they cannot reach her, the couple races to Dawn's isolated farmhouse, only to find everything normal. During the night, however, Katie awakes to find that her husband has died of a heart attack. Five years later, on the anniversary of his death, Katie tries to place a warning call to her earlier self. In her grief, though, she cannot speak, and once again the call is incomplete.

Spanish Summaries, p. 61

Active Reading Strategies

PREDICT Have students read the "Author's Note" and first screenplay directions. Ask them to discuss the author's tone and voice in these notes and to predict what the notes will contribute to their reading of the play.

Additional Resources

Active Reading Guide, p. 66

Audio Library

Spanish Audio Library

Teaching Support

CONNECTING TO OTHER SELECTIONS

The chart at the right shows three ways to connect *Sorry, Right Number* to other selections in this book.

For specific teaching strategies, see the ***Theme Eight Planning Guide.***

Connection		Title
Life Skills: Implementing and Performing	→	"The Battleground," p. 511
Thematic: Family Ties	→	"Raymond's Run," p. 553
Literary: Dialogue	→	*The Diary of Anne Frank,* p. 697

FYI

Title Source Stephen King's title may be based on a classic suspense film, *Sorry, Wrong Number* (1948), which in turn was based on a play by Lucille Fletcher. The film stars Barbara Stanwyck as a woman who overhears a plot to kill a helpless woman, only to discover—too late—that she is that woman.

B Active Reading Strategies

VISUALIZE Remind students that they can use information the author gives and what they infer from it to help them visualize how the characters look and dress and what their house is like.

C Literary Elements

SETTING Explain that suspense stories often take place in ordinary settings. Ask what effect this may have on the stories. *(This contrast with the unexplainable events may make the events even more horrifying, suggesting that they could occur in the reader's own life.)*

Teaching Support

CHARACTERS

KATIE WEIDERMAN	BILL WEIDERMAN	MINISTER
JEFF WEIDERMAN	POLLY WEIDERMAN	GROUNDSKEEPER
CONNIE WEIDERMAN	OPERATOR	HANK
DENNIS WEIDERMAN	DAWN	

AUTHOR'S NOTE: *Screenplay abbreviations are simple and exist, in this author's opinion, mostly to make those who write screenplays feel like lodge brothers.*[1] *In any case, you should be aware that* CU *means* close-up; ECU *means* extreme close-up; INT. *means* interior; EXT. *means* exterior; B.G. *means* background; POV *means* point of view. *Probably most of you knew all that stuff to begin with, right?*

A

ACT 1

[FADE IN ON: KATIE WEIDERMAN'S MOUTH, ECU.
She's speaking into the telephone. Pretty mouth; in a few seconds we'll see that the rest of her is just as pretty.]

KATIE. Bill? Oh, he says he doesn't feel very well, but he's always like that between books . . . can't sleep, thinks every headache is the first symptom of a brain tumor . . . once he gets going on something new, he'll be fine.

B C

[SOUND, B.G.: THE TELEVISION. THE CAMERA DRAWS BACK. KATIE is sitting in the kitchen phone nook, having a good gab with her sister while she idles through some catalogues. We should notice one not-quite-ordinary thing about the phone she's on: it's the sort with two lines. There are LIGHTED BUTTONS to show which ones are engaged. Right now only one—KATIE's—is. As KATIE CONTINUES HER CONVERSATION, THE CAMERA SWINGS AWAY FROM HER, TRACKS[2] *ACROSS THE KITCHEN, and through the arched doorway that leads into the family room.]*

B C

KATIE. *[Voice, fading.]* Oh, I saw Janie Charlton today . . . yes! Big as a *house!* . . .

[She fades. The TV gets louder. There are three kids: JEFF, eight, CONNIE, ten, and DENNIS, thirteen. Wheel of Fortune *is on, but they're not watching. Instead they're engaged in that great pastime, Fighting About What Comes On Later.]*

JEFF. Come *onnn!* It was his first *book!*

CONNIE. His first *gross* book.

DENNIS. We're gonna watch Cheers and Wings, just like we do every week, Jeff.

[DENNIS speaks with the utter finality[3] *only a big brother can manage. "Wanna talk about it some more and see how much pain I can inflict on your scrawny body, Jeff?" his face says.]*

JEFF. Could we at least tape it?

D

1. *Lodge brothers* are men who belong to the same social club. Lodges sometimes have special ceremonies that seem mysterious to outsiders.
2. When a movie camera *tracks,* it moves smoothly. Often, it's mounted on a little wheeled platform that moves along a set of tracks.
3. Dennis speaks with complete *(utter)* decisiveness *(finality)*.

MEETING INDIVIDUAL NEEDS

ENGLISH LANGUAGE LEARNERS

Print Conventions English language learners may be confused by the different typefaces. Remind students of the various people who work with a script: director, actors, camera operators, sound engineers. Explain that the typeface indicates whose direction is provided. Tell students that italics signifies stage directions, uppercase-boldface indicates who is speaking, and regular type indicates dialogue.

Activity Make an overhead transparency of pages 792–793. Assign each student a "job" in the production of the script. Then call on students to highlight the directions that apply to them.

Additional Resources

English Language Learners Sourcebook, p. 90

CONNIE. We're taping CNN[4] for Mom. She said she might be on the phone with Aunt Lois for quite awhile.

JEFF. How can you tape CNN? It *never stops!*

DENNIS. That's what she likes about it.

[*JEFF gets up, walks to the window, and looks out into the dark. He's really upset. DENNIS and CONNIE, in the grand tradition of older brothers and sisters, are delighted to see it.*]

D

DENNIS. Poor Jeffie.

JEFF. [*Turns to them.*] It was his *first* book! Don't you guys even *care?*

CONNIE. Rent it down at the Video Stop tomorrow, if you want to see it so bad.

JEFF. They don't rent R-rated pictures to little kids and you know it!

CONNIE. [*Dreamily.*] Shut up, it's Vanna! I *love* Vanna!

JEFF. Dennis—

DENNIS. Go ask Dad to tape it on the VCR in his office and quit being such a totally annoying little kid.

[*JEFF crosses the room, poking his tongue out at Vanna White as he goes. THE CAMERA FOLLOWS as he goes into the kitchen.*]

KATIE. . . . so when he asked me if *Polly* had tested strep positive, I had to remind him she's away at prep school . . .[5] and Lois, I miss her . . .

[*JEFF is just passing through, on his way to the stairs.*]

KATIE. Will you kids *please* be quiet?

JEFF. [*Glum.*] They'll be quiet. *Now.*

[*He goes up the stairs, a little dejected. KATIE looks after him for a moment, loving and worried.*]

KATIE. They're squabbling again. Polly used to keep them in line, but now that she's away at school . . . I don't know . . . maybe sending her to Bolton wasn't such a hot idea. Sometimes when she calls home she sounds so *unhappy* . . .

E

[*INT. BELA LUGOSI[6] AS DRACULA, CU. Drac's standing at the door of his Transylvanian castle. Someone has pasted a comic-balloon coming out of his mouth which reads: "Listen! My children of the night! What music they make!" The poster is on a door, but we only see this as JEFF opens it and goes into his father's study. INT. A PHOTOGRAPH OF KATIE, CU. THE CAMERA HOLDS, THEN PANS[7] SLOWLY RIGHT. We pass another photo, this one of POLLY, the daughter away at school. She's a lovely girl of sixteen or so. Past POLLY is DENNIS . . . then CONNIE . . . then JEFF. THE CAMERA CONTINUES TO PAN AND ALSO WIDENS OUT so we can see BILL WEIDERMAN, a man of about forty-four.*]

4. *CNN* stands for Cable News Network.
5. *Strep,* or strep throat infection, is caused by the streptococcus bacteria. A *prep school* is a private high school that prepares students for college; Polly's school, Bolton, is also a boarding school.
6. Following this horrifyingly successful 1931 film, *Bela Lugosi* (bel′ ə lo͞o gō′ sē) went on to play other movie monsters and mad scientists, as well as ordinary people.
7. When a movie camera *pans,* it makes a slow, sweeping movement to capture a series of images that represent one continuous scene.

Vocabulary

dejected (di jek′ tid) *adj.* sad; depressed; in low spirits

D Critical Thinking

INFERRING What are some clues that this play takes place in the present? *(the presence of a telephone, television set, and VCR, as well as the characters' use of current colloquial English)*

E Literary Elements

PLOT Explain that there is a subplot that relates to the overall storyline. Ask students to identify it. *(It revolves around Jeff and his relationship to his father.)* Encourage students to discuss how the subplot develops along with the main plot.

Listening and Speaking Minilesson

Acting Point out that acting in any kind of play requires more than just memorizing and reciting the words correctly. Listening to the other actors is equally important. It helps with timing, ensuring that one actor does not talk over another's lines or leave long pauses between speeches.

Activity Encourage students who have acted in school productions to share what they have learned about listening and speaking in a play. Form groups of students, mixing those with acting experience and others to dramatize several scenes from *Sorry, Right Number.* **L2** **COLLAB. LEARN.**

F Active Reading Strategies

RESPOND Help students understand the position Jeff has in the family. Share the following model to illustrate the thinking process involved in responding.

Model: I know from the stage directions that Jeff is the youngest kid. He wants to watch a movie based on his father's first book, but his older brother and sister pay no attention to his wishes. I think he's feeling left out. Jeff's too young to read his father's books, but he may think that watching the movie will bring him closer to his dad.

G Active Reading Strategies

QUESTION Have students discuss Bill's character. Does he have a sense of humor? *(Yes.)* What does he do for a living? *(He writes horror novels.)* How does his job affect the story? *(It adds to the element of suspense.)* Have students support their answers with examples from the play.

Teaching Support

He looks tired. He's peering into the word-processor on his desk, but his mental crystal ball must be taking the night off, because the screen is blank. On the walls we see framed book-covers. All of them are spooky. One of the titles is Ghost Kiss.

JEFF comes up quietly behind his dad. The carpet muffles his feet. BILL sighs and shuts off the word-cruncher. A moment later JEFF claps his hands on his father's shoulders.]

JEFF. BOOGA-BOOGA!

BILL. Hi, Jeffie.

[*He turns in his chair to look at his son, who is disappointed.*]

JEFF. How come you didn't get scared?

BILL. Scaring is my business. I'm case-hardened.[8] Something wrong?

JEFF. Daddy, can I watch the first hour of *Ghost Kiss* and you tape the rest? Dennis and Connie are hogging *everything.*

[*BILL swivels to look at the book-jacket, bemused.*]

BILL. You sure you want to watch *that,* champ? It's pretty—

JEFF. *Yes!*

[*INT. KATIE, IN THE PHONE NOOK.*

In this shot, we clearly see the stairs leading to her husband's study behind her.]

KATIE. I *really* think Jeff needs the orthodontic[9] work but you know Bill—

[*The other line rings. The other light stutters.*]

KATIE. That's just the other line, Bill will—

[*But now we see BILL and JEFF coming downstairs behind her.*]

BILL. Honey, where're the blank videotapes? I can't find any in the study and—

KATIE. [*To BILL.*] *Wait!* [*To LOIS.*] Gonna put you on hold a sec, Lo.

[*She does. Now both lines are blinking. She pushes the top one, where the new call has just come in.*]

KATIE. Hello, Weiderman residence.

[*SOUND: DESPERATE SOBBING.*]

SOBBING VOICE. [*Filter.*][10] Take . . . please take . . . t-t-

KATIE. Polly? Is that you? What's wrong?

[*SOUND: SOBBING. It's awful, heartbreaking.*]

SOBBING VOICE. [*Filter.*] *Please—quick—*

[*SOUND: SOBBING . . . Then, CLICK! A broken connection.*]

KATIE. Polly, calm down! Whatever it is can't be that b—

[*HUM OF AN OPEN LINE.*

JEFF has wandered toward the TV room, hoping to find a blank tape.]

8. *Case-hardened* means "made callous or insensitive." Bill's business is scaring people through his writing, so he is used to all the scary tricks.
9. *Orthodontic* work refers to a type of dentistry involving irregularities of the teeth. Jeff may need braces to straighten his teeth.
10. An electronic *filter* makes the actor's voice sound as if it is coming over the telephone line. The actor has to do the sobbing.

794 THEME 8

Reading Minilesson

Evaluating Explain that evaluating a text often improves comprehension as well as analytical skills. Ask students to think about which characters in the play are the most believable. Point out that when writers are in the revision stage, they may evaluate each character by isolating his or her speaking parts and reading all of them to see whether the characterization is consistent and believable.

Activity Have students choose one character and read all of his or her speaking parts up to this point. Encourage students to share what they learn about how the author revealed what that character is like. Have them evaluate in a written report how successfully he does it. **L2**

Additional Resources

Reading Skills Practice Workbook

BILL. Who was that?

[Without looking at her husband or answering him, KATIE *slams the lower button in again.]*

H **KATIE.** Lois? Listen, I'll call you back. That was Polly, and she sounded very upset. No . . . she hung up. Yes. I will. Thanks.

[She hangs up.]

BILL. *[Concerned.]* It was Polly?

KATIE. Crying her head off. It sounded like she was trying to say "Please take me home" . . . I knew that school was bumming her out . . . Why I ever let you talk me into it . . .

[She's rummaging frantically on her little phone desk. Catalogues go slithering to the floor around her stool.]

KATIE. *Connie did you take my address book?*

CONNIE. *[Voice.]* No, Mom.

*[*BILL *pulls a battered book out of his back pocket and pages through it.]*

I **BILL.** I got it. Except—

KATIE. I know, that dorm phone is always busy. Give it to me.

BILL. Honey, calm down.

KATIE. I'll calm down after I talk to her. She is sixteen, Bill. Sixteen-year-old girls are prone to depressive interludes.[11] Sometimes they even k . . . just give me the number!

BILL. 617-555-8641.

[As she punches the numbers, THE CAMERA SLIDES IN TO CU.*]*

KATIE. Come on, come on . . . don't be busy . . . just this once . . .

[SOUND: CLICKS. *A pause. Then . . . the phone starts ringing.]*

KATIE. *[Eyes closed.]* Thank You, God.

VOICE. *[Filter.]* Hartshorn Hall, this is Frieda. If you want Christine, she's still in the shower, Arnie.

KATIE. Could you call Polly to the phone? Polly Weiderman? This is Kate Weiderman. Her mother.

VOICE. *[Filter.]* Oh! sorry. I thought—hang on, please, Mrs. Weiderman.

[SOUND: THE PHONE CLUNKS DOWN.]

VOICE. *[Filter, and very faint.]* Polly? Pol? . . . Phone call! . . . It's your mother!

[INT. A WIDER ANGLE ON THE PHONE NOOK, WITH BILL.]

BILL. Well?

KATIE. Somebody's getting her. I hope.

*[*JEFF *comes back in with a tape.]*

JEFF. I found one, Dad. Dennis hid 'em. As usual.

BILL. In a minute, Jeff. Go watch the tube.

JEFF. But—

BILL. I won't forget. Now go *on*.

*[*JEFF *goes.]*

KATIE. Come on, come on, come on . . .

BILL. Calm down, Katie.

KATIE. *[Snaps.]* If you'd heard her, you wouldn't tell me to calm down! She sounded—

POLLY. *[Filter, cheery voice.]* Hi, mom!

KATIE. Pol? Honey? Are you all right?

POLLY. *[Happy, bubbling voice.]* Am I *all right?* I aced my bio exam, got a B on my French Conversational Essay, and Ronnie Hansen asked me to the Harvest Ball. I'm

11. People who are *prone to depressive interludes* get depressed occasionally.

H Active Reading Strategies

PREDICT Students probably know that Stephen King is a writer of horror stories. Have students predict where the horror will come into the plot.

I Active Reading Strategies

EVALUATE Ask why Katie reacts the way she does when she hears the sobbing over the phone. *(She is convinced it is her daughter who is upset, and she feels guilty for sending her to boarding school as it is.)* Would students react the same way?

MEETING INDIVIDUAL NEEDS — SPECIAL NEEDS

Less-Proficient Readers Explain to less-proficient readers that it is important to keep track of the major events in order to understand the plot of a story. Stopping periodically to record events will improve students' comprehension.

Activity Write on the board *What is happening here?* Ask students to work in groups to list, in sequence, what has happened so far in this scene. Have them begin by describing the setting and listing the characters.

L1 COLLAB. LEARN.

Additional Resources

Inclusion Strategies

J Literary Elements

CHARACTER Ask students to contrast the characters of Bill and Katie on the basis of their reactions to the phone call. *(Bill seems to be rational and less concerned than Katie, who is almost hysterical over the phone call.)*

K Active Reading Strategies

EVALUATE Why is Katie so convinced that the caller is someone in her family? *(She recognizes a quality in the voice that is extremely familiar.)* Ask students whether they think her reaction is typical of parents. *(Some students may say yes, while others feel it depends on the individual.)*

Vocabulary Skills

Word History When Polly says "'Kay," she is using a short form of *okay.* This word, which came into the language in 1839, is spelled variously as *O.K., OK, o.k.,* and *okay.* One theory on its origins is that it was an incorrectly spelled abbreviation of *all correct.* Another is that it stood for President Martin Van Buren's nickname: "Old Kinderhook." Van Buren was born in Kinderhook, New York. Some of his supporters formed the Democratic O.K. Club in support of his try for reelection.

Teaching Support

so all right that if one more good thing happens to me today, I'll probably blow up like the *Hindenburg.*[12]

KATIE. You didn't just call me up, crying your head off?

[*We see by* KATIE*'s face that she already knows the answer to this question.*]

POLLY. [*Filter.*] Heck no!

KATIE. I'm glad about your test and your date, honey. I guess it was someone else. I'll call you back, okay?

POLLY. [*Filter.*] 'Kay. Say hi to Dad!

KATIE. I will.

[*INT. THE PHONE NOOK, WIDER.*]

BILL. She okay?

KATIE. Fine. I could have *sworn* it was Polly, but . . . *she's* walking on air.

BILL. So it was a prank. Or someone who was crying so hard she dialed a wrong number . . . "through a shimmering film of tears," as we veteran hacks[13] like to say.

J KATIE. It was not a prank and it was not a wrong number! It was someone in *my family!*

BILL. Honey, you can't know that.

KATIE. No? If Jeffie called up, just crying, would you know it was him?

BILL. [*Struck by this.*] Yeah, maybe. I guess I might.

[*She's not listening. She's punching numbers, fast.*]

BILL. Who you calling?

[*She doesn't answer him.* SOUND: PHONE RINGS TWICE. *Then:*]

OLDER FEMALE VOICE. [*Filter.*] Hello?

KATIE. Mom? Are you . . . [*She pauses.*] Did you call just a few seconds ago?

VOICE. [*Filter.*] No, dear . . . why?

KATIE. Oh . . . you know these phones. I was talking to Lois and I lost the other call.

VOICE. [*Filter.*] Well, it wasn't me. Kate, I saw the *prettiest* dress in La Boutique today, and—

KATIE. We'll talk about it later, Mom, okay?

VOICE. [*Filter.*] Kate, are you all right?

KATIE. I have . . . Mom, I have to go. 'Bye. [*She hangs up. Then, to Bill:*] *I tell you it was someone in my family and she sounded*—oh, you don't understand. I *knew* that voice. K

BILL. But if Polly's okay and your mom's okay . . .

KATIE. [*Positive.*] It's Dawn.

BILL. Come on, hon, a minute ago you were sure it was Polly.

KATIE. It *had* to be Dawn. I was on the phone with Lois and Mom's okay so Dawn's the only other one it *could* have been. She's the youngest . . . I could have mistaken her for Polly . . . and she's out there in that farmhouse alone with the baby!

BILL. [*Startled.*] What do you mean, alone?

KATIE. Jerry's in Burlington! It's Dawn! *Something's happened to Dawn!*

[CONNIE *comes into the kitchen, worried.*]

CONNIE. Mom? Is Aunt Dawn okay?

BILL. So far as we know, she's fine. Take it easy, doll. Bad to buy trouble before you know it's on sale. L

12. In 1937 the airship *Hindenburg* exploded in midair and crashed to the ground.
13. Bill is poking fun at himself. *Hacks* are authors whose books sell well even though the writing is dull and unimaginative, like the overused phrase Bill gives as an example.

MEETING INDIVIDUAL NEEDS — ENGLISH LANGUAGE LEARNERS

Colloquial English Write these expressions on the board, underlining the words in italics: I *aced* my *bio* exam. *(I got a good grade on my biology examination.)* You didn't just *call me up, crying your head off?* *(weeping uncontrollably)* *Bad to buy trouble before you know it's on sale.* *(anticipate trouble needlessly)*

Activity Ask students what each sentence means and discuss how they were able to figure out the meaning. Explain that stage directions indicate what the character is feeling, and these may help them understand what the sentence means.

Additional Resources

English Language Learners Sourcebook, p. 91

[*KATIE punches numbers and listens. SOUND: The DAH-DAH-DAH of a busy signal. KATIE hangs up. BILL looks a question at her with raised eyebrows.*]

KATIE. Busy.

BILL. Katie, are you sure—

KATIE. She's the only one left—it had to be her. Bill, I'm scared. Will you drive me out there?

[*BILL takes the phone from her.*]

BILL. What's her number?

KATIE. 555-6169.

[*BILL dials. Gets a busy. Hangs up and punches 0.*]

OPERATOR. [*Filter.*] Operator.

BILL. I'm trying to reach my sister-in-law, operator. The line is busy. I suspect there may be a problem. Can you break into the call, please?

Housecall, 1995. Diana Ong. Computer graphic. Private collection.

Viewing the art: What might the woman's expression tell the viewer about the topic of this call?

[*INT. THE DOOR TO THE TV ROOM. All three kids are standing there, silent and worried. INT. THE PHONE NOOK, WITH BILL AND KATIE.*]

M

OPERATOR. [*Filter.*] What is your name, sir?

BILL. William Weiderman. My number is—

OPERATOR. [*Filter.*] Not the William Weiderman that wrote *Spider Doom?!*

BILL. Yes, that was mine. If—

OPERATOR. [*Filter.*] Oh, I just *loved* that book! I love *all* your books! I—

BILL. I'm delighted you do. But right now my wife is very worried about her sister. If it's possible for you to—

OPERATOR. [*Filter.*] Yes, I can do that. Please give me your number, Mr. Weiderman, for the records. [*She GIGGLES.*] I *promise* not to give it out.

BILL. It's 555-4408.

M

L Critical Thinking

EVALUATE Point out Bill's comment, "Bad to buy trouble before you know it's on sale." Ask students to judge how appropriate that comment is at this point in the plot. *(Some students may feel that it is generally good advice. However, readers familiar with suspenseful stories will understand that there will be trouble.)*

VIEWING THE ART

Viewing Response *The woman's posture and expression may be viewed as casual and unconcerned, suggesting a casual conversation about everyday events.*

MEETING INDIVIDUAL NEEDS — SPECIAL NEEDS

Emotional Help prepare students emotionally for the suspenseful elements of the story. Remind them that people read scary stories and watch scary movies because they know what they see and hear is not real.

Activity Make two columns on the board headed *Sounds* and *Sights.* Ask students to suggest scary sounds and scary sights they have heard and seen in suspense movies and on spooky television shows. **L1**

Additional Resources

Inclusion Strategies

M Author's Craft

HUMOR Discuss how the appearance of the operator serves a double purpose. Ask students to cite the purposes. *(She offers comic relief in that she is behaving so foolishly in the midst of a crisis. At the same time, she delays the action, thus building further tension as Bill tries unsuccessfully to reach his sister-in-law.)*

N Literary Elements

SCREENPLAY Have students review the stage directions beginning "They stare . . ." Ask students to visualize the camera angles and discuss the effect.

M

OPERATOR. [*Filter.*] And the call number?

BILL. [*Looks at* KATIE.] Uh . . .

KATIE. 555-6169.

BILL. 555-6169.

OPERATOR. [*Filter.*] Just a moment, Mr. Weiderman . . . *Night of the Beast* was also great, by the way. Hold on.

[*SOUND: TELEPHONIC CLICKS AND CLACKS.*]

KATIE. Is she—

BILL. Yes. Just . . .

[*There's one final* CLICK.]

OPERATOR. [*Filter.*] I'm sorry, Mr. Weiderman, but that line is not busy. It's off the hook. I wonder if I sent you my copy of *Spider Doom*—

[*BILL hangs up the phone.*]

KATIE. Why did you hang up?

BILL. She can't break in. Phone's not busy. It's off the hook.

N

[*They stare at each other bleakly.*
EXT. A LOW-SLUNG SPORTS CAR PASSES THE CAMERA. NIGHT.
INT. THE CAR, WITH KATIE AND BILL.
KATIE's scared. BILL, at the wheel, doesn't look exactly calm.]

KATIE. Hey, Bill—tell me she's all right.

BILL. She's all right.

KATIE. Now tell me what you really think.

BILL. Jeff snuck up behind me tonight and put the old booga-booga on me. He was disappointed when I didn't jump. I told him I was case-hardened. [*Pause.*] I lied.

KATIE. Why did Jerry have to move out there when he's gone half the time? Just her and that little tiny baby? *Why?*

BILL. Shh, Kate. We're almost there.

KATIE. Go faster.

[*EXT. THE CAR.*
He does. That car is smokin'.
INT. THE WEIDERMAN TV ROOM.
The tube's still on and the kids are still there, but the horsing around has stopped.]

CONNIE. Dennis, do you think Aunt Dawn's okay?

DENNIS. [*Thinks she's dead, decapitated*[14] *by a maniac.*] Yeah. Sure she is.

[*INT. THE PHONE, POV FROM THE TV ROOM.*
Just sitting there on the wall in the phone nook, lights dark, looking like a snake ready to strike.
FADE OUT.]

ACT 2

[*EXT. AN ISOLATED FARMHOUSE.*
A long driveway leads up to it. There's one light on in the living room. Car lights sweep up the driveway. The WEIDERMAN *car pulls up close to the garage and stops.*
INT. THE CAR, WITH BILL AND KATIE.]

KATIE. I'm scared.

[*BILL bends down, reaches under his seat, and brings out a pistol.*]

BILL. [*Solemnly.*] Booga-booga.

O

KATIE. [*Total surprise.*] How long have you had that?

BILL. Since last year. I didn't want to scare you or the kids. I've got a license to carry. Come on.

[*EXT. BILL AND KATIE.*

14. While he tries to reassure Connie, Dennis actually fears that Dawn has had her head chopped off—that she has been *decapitated*.

Teaching Support

Reading *Minilesson*

Predicting Remind students that one characteristic of hair-raising tales that appeals to readers and viewers is not knowing the ending. However, authors often plant clues in the story. Sometimes those clues are deliberately misleading and are meant to tease the audience.

Activity Have students study the last scene in act 1 for clues to the outcome of act 2. Ask them to write their predictions on a slip of paper, with an explanation of which clues suggested that ending. Collect the predictions and hand them back to students after they complete the play. **L2**

Additional Resources

Reading Skills Practice Workbook

They get out. KATIE stands by the front of the car while BILL goes to the garage and peers in.]

BILL. Her car's here.

[THE CAMERA TRACKS WITH THEM to the front door. Now we can hear the TV, PLAYING LOUD. BILL pushes the doorbell. We hear it inside. They wait. KATIE pushes it. Still no answer. She pushes it again and doesn't take her finger off. BILL looks down at:
EXT. THE LOCK, BILL'S POV.
Big scratches on it.
EXT. BILL AND KATIE.]

BILL. *[Low.]* The lock's been tampered with.

[KATIE looks, and whimpers. BILL tries the door. It opens. The TV is louder.]

BILL. Stay behind me. Be ready to run if something happens. Gosh, I wish I'd left you home, Kate.

[He starts in. KATIE comes after him, terrified, near tears.
INT. DAWN AND JERRY'S LIVING ROOM. From this angle we see only a small section of the room. The TV is much louder. BILL enters the room, gun up. He looks to the right . . . and suddenly all the tension goes out of him. He lowers the gun.]

KATIE. *[Draws up beside him.]* Bill . . . what . . .

[He points.
INT. THE LIVING ROOM, WIDE, BILL AND KATIE'S POV.

Viewing the photograph: What mood in the screenplay does this picture reflect? How do you think the photographer achieved the mood?

O Active Reading Strategies

PREDICT Point out that so far in the play there has not been any violence. Read aloud the exchange, on pp. 798–799, between Bill and Katie as they reach Dawn's home. Then have students predict what Bill and Katie will find when they enter the farmhouse.

VIEWING THE PHOTOGRAPH

Viewing Response *A deserted highway and a dark sky are often symbols of the unknown, even of the threatening. The choice of setting and weather conditions, as well as the camera angle, film exposure, and kind of film, all contribute to the mood.*

MEETING INDIVIDUAL NEEDS — MULTIPLE MODES OF EXPRESSION

Musical Tell students that music has played a role in drama dating back to ancient Greece. Have students discuss movies whose soundtracks heightened their enjoyment of the action on the screen.

Activity Ask students to consider the kind of music they would choose for the soundtrack to *Sorry, Right Number.* Have them suggest titles, describe the music, and, if possible, play an excerpt. Encourage students to think of ways of making their own eerie music, either with instruments or their voices. **L2**

Active Reading Strategies

CONNECT Ask students to notice that the book the baby is nibbling on is the same as the movie being telecast that night. Have students discuss the significance of this coincidence. *(The suggestion may be that readers can expect some ghosts to appear.)*

Active Reading Strategies

REVIEW Have students review the explanations for the events at the farm, comparing them with the details on page 799. Ask students to list any unanswered questions.

Teaching Support

The place looks like a cyclone hit it . . . but it wasn't robbery and murder that caused this mess; only a healthy eighteen-month-old baby. After a strenuous day of trashing the living room, Baby got tired and Mommy got tired and they fell asleep on the couch together. The baby is in DAWN's lap. There is a pair of Walkman earphones on her head. There are toys—tough plastic Sesame Street and PlaySkool stuff, for the most part—scattered all over. The baby has also pulled most of the books out of the bookcase. Had a good munch on one of them, too, by the look. BILL goes over and picks it up. It is Ghost Kiss.]

BILL. I've had people say they just eat my books up, but this is ridiculous.

[*He's amused. KATIE isn't. She walks over to her sister, ready to be mad . . . but she sees how really exhausted DAWN looks and softens.*

INT. DAWN AND THE BABY, KATIE'S POV.

Fast asleep and breathing easily, like a Raphael painting of Madonna and Child.

THE CAMERA PANS DOWN TO: the Walkman. We can hear the faint strains of Huey Lewis and the News.[15] *THE CAMERA PANS A BIT FURTHER TO a Princess telephone on the table by the chair. It's off the cradle. Not much; just enough to break the connection and scare people to death.*

INT. KATIE.

She sighs, bends down, and replaces the phone. Then she pushes the STOP button on the Walkman.

INT. DAWN, BILL, AND KATIE.

DAWN wakes up when the music stops. Looks at BILL and KATIE, puzzled.]

DAWN. [*Fuzzed out.*] Well . . . hi.

[*She realizes she's got the Walkman phones on and removes them.*]

BILL. Hi, Dawn.

DAWN. [*Still half asleep.*] Shoulda called, guys. Place is a mess.

[*She smiles. She's radiant when she smiles.*]

KATIE. We *tried.* The operator told Bill the phone was off the hook. I thought something was wrong. How can you sleep with that music blasting?

DAWN. It's restful. [*Sees the gnawed book BILL's holding.*] Oh, Bill, I'm sorry! Justin's teething and—

BILL. There are critics who'd say he picked just the right thing to teethe on. I don't want to scare you, beautiful, but somebody's been at your front door lock with a screwdriver or something. Whoever it was forced it.

DAWN. Gosh, no! That was Jerry, last week. I locked us out by mistake and he didn't have his key and the spare wasn't over the door like it's supposed to be. So he took the screwdriver to it. It didn't work, either—that's one tough lock.

BILL. If it wasn't forced, how come I could just open the door and walk in?

DAWN. [*Guiltily.*] Well . . . sometimes I forget to lock it.

KATIE. You didn't call me tonight, Dawn?

DAWN. Gee, no! I didn't call *anyone!* I was too busy chasing Justin around! He kept

15. *Raphael's* famous painting shows the infant Jesus on his mother's lap, and *Huey Lewis and the News* was a popular rock band, not a news program.

Vocabulary
strenuous (stren' ū əs) *adj.* very active; energetic

800 THEME 8

LIFE SKILLS CONNECTION

Problem Solving Remind students that in most stories the main characters have a problem that they must solve. In a mystery or suspense story the characters often have to put clues together to explain strange circumstances. Point out that real life often has its own hair-raising circumstances, such as losses or injuries that result from accidents.

Activity Have students work in small groups to discuss situations in which someone has faced a threat of danger. Ask them to examine how they or others solved the problem with as little damage as possible. Then have them compare the situations to find common elements—such as cool-headedness, calling for help, and taking precautions in advance—that enabled them to deal with the situation.
L2 COLLAB. LEARN.

wanting to eat the fabric softener! Then he got sleepy and I sat down here and thought I'd listen to some tunes while I waited for your movie to come on, Bill, and I fell asleep—

[*At the mention of the movie* BILL *starts visibly and looks at the book. Then he glances at his watch.*]

BILL. I promised to tape it for Jeff. Come on, Katie, we've got time to get back.

KATIE. Just a second.

[*She picks up the phone and dials.*]

DAWN. Gee, Bill, do you think Jeffie's old enough to watch something like that?

BILL. It's network. They take out the blood-bags.

DAWN. [*Confused but* amiable.] Oh. That's good.

[*INT. KATIE, CU.*]

DENNIS. [*Filter.*] Hello?

KATIE. Just thought you'd like to know your Aunt Dawn's fine.

DENNIS. [*Filter.*] Oh! Cool. Thanks, Mom.

[*INT. THE PHONE NOOK, WITH DENNIS AND THE OTHERS. He looks very relieved.*]

DENNIS. Aunt Dawn's okay.

[*INT. THE CAR, WITH BILL AND KATIE. They drive in silence for awhile.*]

KATIE. You think I'm a hysterical idiot, don't you?

BILL. [*Genuinely surprised.*] No! I was scared, too.

KATIE. You sure you're not mad?

BILL. I'm too relieved. [*Laughs.*] She's sort of a scatterbrain, old Dawn, but I love her.

KATIE. [*Leans over and kisses him.*] I love *you*. You're a sweet man.

BILL. I'm the *boogeyman!*

KATIE. I am not fooled, sweetheart.

[*EXT. THE CAR. PASSES THE CAMERA and we DISSOLVE*[16] *TO:*

INT. JEFF, IN BED. His room is dark. The covers are pulled up to his chin.]

JEFF. You *promise* to tape the rest?

[*CAMERA WIDENS OUT so we can see BILL, sitting on the bed.*]

BILL. I promise.

JEFF. I especially liked the part where the dead guy ripped off the punk rocker's head.

BILL. Well . . . they *used* to take out all the blood-bags.

JEFF. What, Dad?

BILL. Nothing. I love you, Jeffie.

16. In film, to *dissolve* is to fade out on one scene while the next scene fades in and becomes clearer.

Vocabulary

amiable (ā′ mē ə bəl) *adj.* friendly, good-natured

Literary Elements

SCREENPLAY Discuss with students the liberties a screenplay allows a writer to take. *(quick changes of scene, close-up angles, different audience perspectives)* Ask students how this differs from stage plays. *(Stage plays are performed live, so the author does not get the convenience of changing camera angles and quickly changing scenes.)*

Active Reading Strategies

EVALUATE Bill refers to himself as someone who scares people. Does he himself scare easily? *(He tries to find reasonable explanations for things. It is when he runs out of such explanations that he gets scared.)*

A&E HOME VIDEO.® *The following videotape program is available from Glencoe.*

Be sure to preview the video for appropriateness for your class:

- **Nightmare: Birth of Victorian Horror***

*Also available in the Glencoe Literature *Video Library*.

MEETING INDIVIDUAL NEEDS — MULTIPLE MODES OF EXPRESSION

Linguistic Remind students that as readers they have been aware of hints and clues to plot developments. For example, the title and the scary phone call that opens *Sorry, Right Number* suggests that the telephone will be an important plot device in the play.

Activity Have small groups of students plan opening scenes for plays. Have them brainstorm significant events that might foreshadow the climax of the play: for example, threatening weather forecasts; news bulletins warning of an escaped convict; the arrival of a mysterious, threatening letter. Have students summarize how the climax might prove the ominous hints were real. **L2** COLLAB. LEARN.

HAIR-RAISING TALES 801

BILL. [*Guiltily.*] I'll edit it.

KATIE. 'Night. And thanks again. For everything.

[*She leaves.* BILL *sits in his chair.*
INT. TV, CU.
A couple is necking in a car. Suddenly the passenger door is ripped open by the dead guy and we DISSOLVE TO:
INT. KATIE, IN BED.
It's dark. She's asleep. She wakes up . . . sort of.

KATIE. [*Sleepy.*] Hey, big guy—

[*She feels for him, but his side of the bed is empty, the coverlet still pulled up. She sits up. Looks at:*
INT. A CLOCK ON THE NIGHT-TABLE, KATIE'S POV.
It says 2:03 A.M. *Then it flashes to 2:04.*
INT. KATIE.
Fully awake now. And concerned. She gets up, puts on her robe, and leaves the bedroom.
INT. THE TV SCREEN, CU.
Snow.]

KATIE. [*Voice, approaching.*] Bill? Honey? You okay? Bill? Bi—

[*INT. KATIE, IN BILL'S STUDY.*
She's frozen, wide-eyed with horror.
INT. BILL, IN HIS CHAIR.
He's slumped to one side, eyes closed, hand inside his shirt. DAWN *was sleeping.* BILL *is not.*
EXT. A COFFIN, BEING LOWERED INTO A GRAVE.]

MINISTER. [*Voice.*] And so we commit the earthly remains of William Weiderman to the ground, confident of his spirit and soul. "Be ye not cast down, brethren . . ."

[*EXT. GRAVESIDE.*
All the WEIDERMANS *are ranged here.* KATIE *and* POLLY *wear identical black dresses and veils.* CONNIE *wears a black skirt and white blouse.* DENNIS *and* JEFF *wear black suits.* JEFF *is crying. He has Rambo the Dragon under his arm for a little extra comfort.*
CAMERA MOVES IN ON KATIE. *Tears course slowly down her cheeks. She bends and gets a handful of earth. Tosses it into the grave.*

KATIE. Love you, big guy.

[*EXT. JEFF.*
Weeping.
EXT. LOOKING DOWN INTO THE GRAVE.
Scattered earth on top of the coffin.
DISSOLVE TO:
EXT. THE GRAVE.
A GROUNDSKEEPER *pats the last sod into place.*]

GROUNDSKEEPER. My wife says she wishes you'd written a couple more before you had your heart attack, mister. [*Pause.*] I like Westerns, m'self.

[THE GROUNDSKEEPER *walks away, whistling.*
DISSOLVE TO:
EXT. A CHURCH. DAY.
TITLE CARD: FIVE YEARS LATER.
THE WEDDING MARCH *is playing.* POLLY, *older and radiant with joy, emerges into a pelting shower of rice. She's in a wedding gown, her new husband by her side. Celebrants throwing rice line either side of the path. From behind the bride and groom come others. Among them are* KATIE, DENNIS, CONNIE, *and* JEFF *. . . all five*

U Critical Thinking

INFERRING Remind students that Bill has not been able to start a new book. Ask them why he might want to watch the movie. *(Sometimes when authors face writer's block, they look back over past successes to reassure themselves that they can write and that the block is only temporary.)*

V Literary Elements

SCREENPLAY Scenes from the film *The Ghost Kiss* serve as background for the action of the play. Ask students how they think these scenes relate to the play. *(They suggest that something strange is happening.)*

W Active Reading Strategies

REVIEW Ask students to explain what happened to Bill. *(He had a heart attack and died.)*

Interdisciplinary Connection

Health Explain to students that the purpose of preventive medicine is, as its name suggests, to prevent health problems such as heart disease.

Activity Tell students to use health texts and other reference materials to research preventive medicine aimed at avoiding heart problems. Suggest that they present a one-page written report on how the following approaches can help prevent heart disease: stress reduction, exercise, healthy diet. **L2**

Active Reading Strategies

REVIEW Have students review the stage directions and discuss the changes that have occurred since the previous scene. *(Five years have passed, Polly is getting married, and Katie has a new husband.)* Ask students how they would know this information if they were watching the play on television. *(A title card explains it is five years later. There are also visual clues, such as the exterior of the church and the presence of new characters. Later, the dialogue reveals other information.)*

Vo•cab•u•lar•y Skills

Word Meaning When Polly refers to herself as a "creep," she means she has been an unpleasant and difficult person. This modern-day meaning can be traced in the connotations of other, older meanings: (1) a slow movement; (2) an unpleasant feeling, such as that of something crawling over one's skin (used in the plural: *the creeps*).

Viewing the Photograph

Viewing Response *The wedding bouquet symbolizes a new beginning. It is used by the dramatist to link time and place; as Polly throws the flowers, the scene changes. Flowers are also used in funeral services, so the roses may link the previous scene to this one, five years later.*

years older. With KATIE is another man. This is HANK. In the interim, KATIE has also taken a husband.
POLLY turns and her mother is there.]

POLLY. Thank you, Mom.

KATIE. [*Crying.*] Oh doll, you're so welcome.

[They embrace. After a moment POLLY draws away and looks at HANK. There is a brief moment of tension, and then POLLY embraces HANK, too.]

POLLY. Thank you too, Hank. I'm sorry I was such a creep for so long . . .

HANK. [*Easily.*] You were never a creep, Pol. A girl only has one father.

CONNIE. Throw it! Throw it!

[After a moment, POLLY throws her bouquet.
EXT. THE BOUQUET, CU, SLOW MOTION.
Turning and turning through the air.
DISSOLVES TO:
INT. THE STUDY, WITH KATIE. NIGHT.
The word-processor has been replaced by a wide lamp looming over a stack of blueprints. The book jackets have been replaced by photos of buildings. Ones that have first been built in HANK's mind, presumably. KATIE is looking at the desk, thoughtful and a little sad.]

HANK. [*Voice.*] Coming to bed, Kate?

Vocabulary
interim (in′ tər im) *n.* the time between events; meantime
presumably (pri zo͞o′ mə blē) *adv.* supposedly; probably

Viewing the photograph: Why is a bouquet important in this play? What does it symbolize?

Teaching Support

Writing Minilesson

Filling In Point out that five years have gone by between the last scene and this one. Have students look for clues from the author that tell them what has happened in the interim.

Activity Tell students to choose one character with whom they identify. Have them write a brief monologue in which that character comes to the front of the set and explains what has happened to him or her in those five years. **L2**

Additional Resources

Writer's Choice, Lesson 4.2

[She turns and THE CAMERA WIDENS OUT *to give us* HANK. *He's wearing a robe over pajamas. She comes to him and gives him a little hug, smiling. Maybe we notice a few streaks of gray in her hair; her pretty pony has done its fair share of running*[19] *since* BILL *died.]*

KATIE. In a little while. A woman doesn't see her first one get married every day, you know.

HANK. I know.

*[*THE CAMERA FOLLOWS *as they walk from the work area of the study to the more informal area. This is much the same as it was in the old days, with a coffee table, stereo, TV, couch, and* BILL*'s old easy-chair. She looks at this.]*

HANK. You still miss him, don't you?

KATIE. Some days more than others. You didn't know, and Polly didn't remember.

HANK. *[Gently.]* Remember what, doll?

KATIE. Polly got married on the five-year anniversary of Bill's death.

HANK. *[Hugs her.]* Come on to bed, why don't you?

KATIE. In a little while.

HANK. Okay. Maybe I'll still be awake.

[He kisses her, then leaves, closing the door behind him. KATIE *sits in* BILL*'s old chair. Close by, on the coffee table, is a remote control for the TV and an extension phone.* KATIE *looks at the blank TV, and* THE CAMERA MOVES IN *on her face. One tear rims one eye, sparkling like a sapphire.]*

KATIE. I *do* still miss you, big guy. Lots and lots. Every day. And you know what? It hurts.

[The tear falls. She picks up the TV remote and pushes the ON *button.*

INT. TV, KATIE'S POV.

An ad for Ginsu Knives comes to an end and is replaced by a STAR LOGO.

ANNOUNCER. *[Voice.]* Now back to Channel 63's Thursday night Star Time Movie . . . *Ghost Kiss.*

[The logo DISSOLVES INTO *a guy who looks like he died in a car crash about two weeks ago and has since been subjected to a lot of hot weather. He comes staggering out of the same old crypt.*

INT. KATIE.

Terribly startled—almost horrified. She hits the OFF *button on the remote control. The TV blinks off.*

KATIE*'s face begins to work. She struggles against the impending emotional storm, but the coincidence of the movie is just one thing too many on what must have*

19. *[her pretty . . . running]* The passage of time has left Katie looking and feeling older.

Vocabulary
impending (im pen′ ding) *adj.* about to occur

Active Reading Strategies

CONNECT Explain that anniversaries of major events can stir people's memories so strongly that they feel they are reliving them. Ask students to discuss the emotions Katie must be experiencing. *(She is probably both sad about her late husband and happy for her daughter.)*

INTERDISCIPLINARY CONNECTION

Art Explain to students that the first drawings of a building to be constructed are renderings of what the architect and the client have discussed. Once the final design is chosen, the architect helps develop blueprints that the various contractors will use in constructing the building.

Activity Have students ask administrative personnel for the opportunity to study the school's blueprints. Have students identify such things as rooms, closets, doors, and stairways. Invite an architect or engineer to explain what information is included on the plans and how it is used during construction and later. **L2**

HAIR-RAISING TALES 805

VIEWING THE ART

Viewing Response *Students may see the woman as ready to speak. This is appropriate to Katie's decision to make the phone call that is still a mystery to her.*

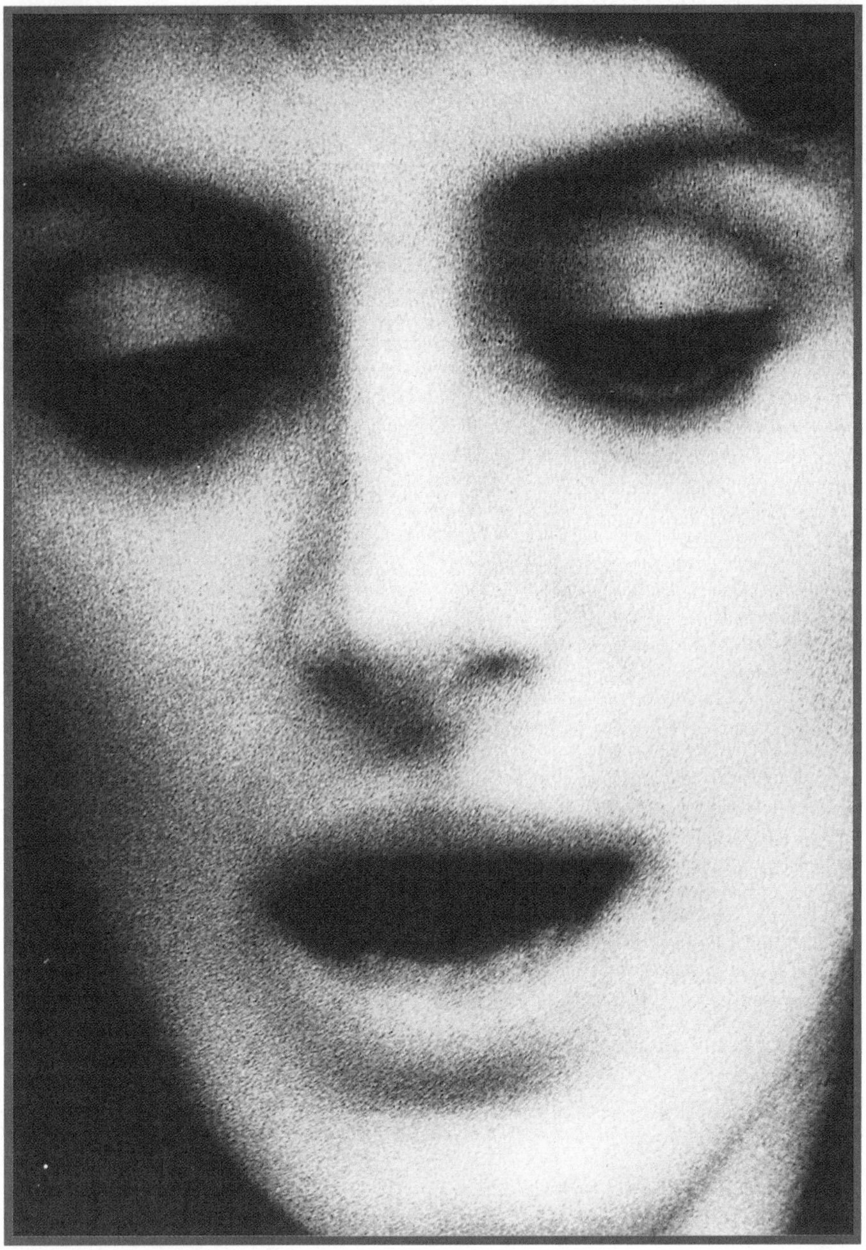

Viewing the photograph: How do the emotions shown in this photograph compare with Katie's feelings and her state of mind?

Teaching Support

MEETING INDIVIDUAL NEEDS

ADVANCED LEARNERS

Warnings Throughout the past there were many occasions when having knowledge about a future event would have changed the course of history. An example would be knowing about a future attack, which would thus have forestalled a war.

Activity Have students think of an event in history that they wish they could change. Have them write messages they would like to have sent to a key person, if they could have. Encourage students to share their messages with the class, explaining how they would have changed history. **L3**

already been one of the most emotionally trying days of her life. The dam breaks and she begins to sob . . . terrible heart-broken sobs. She reaches out for the little table by the chair, meaning to put the remote control on it, and knocks the phone onto the floor.

SOUND: The HUM OF AN OPEN LINE.

Her tear-stained face grows suddenly still as she looks at the telephone. Something begins to fill it . . . an idea? an intuition? Hard to tell. And maybe it doesn't matter.

INT. THE TELEPHONE, KATIE'S POV.

THE CAMERA MOVES IN TO ECU . . . MOVES IN until the dots in the off-the-hook receiver look like chasms.

SOUND OF OPEN-LINE BUZZ UP TO LOUD. WE GO INTO THE BLACK . . . and hear:]

BILL. [*Voice.*] Who are you calling? Who do you *want* to call? Who *would* you call, if it wasn't too late?

[*INT. KATIE.*

There is now a strange hypnotized look on her face. She reaches down, scoops the telephone up, and punches in numbers, seemingly at random.

SOUND: RINGING PHONE.

KATIE continues to look hypnotized. The look holds until the phone is answered . . . and she hears herself *on the other end of the line.*]

KATIE. [*Voice; filter.*] Hello, Weiderman residence.

[*KATIE—our present-day KATIE with the streaks of gray in her hair—goes on sobbing, yet an expression of desperate hope is trying to be born on her face. On some level she understands that the depth of her grief has allowed a kind of telephonic time-travel. She's trying to talk, to force the words out.*]

KATIE. [*Sobbing.*] Take . . . please take . . . t-t-

[*INT. KATIE, IN THE PHONE NOOK, REPRISE.*[20]

It's five years ago. BILL is standing beside her, looking concerned. JEFF is wandering off to look for a blank tape in the other room.]

KATIE. Polly? What's wrong?

[*INT. KATIE, IN THE STUDY.*]

KATIE. [*Sobbing.*] *Please—quick—*

[*SOUND: CLICK OF A BROKEN CONNECTION.*]

KATIE. [*Screaming.*] *Take him to the hospital! If you want him to live, take him to the hospital! He's going to have a heart attack! He—*

[*SOUND: HUM OF AN OPEN LINE.*

Slowly, very slowly, KATIE hangs up the telephone. Then after a moment, she picks it up again. She speaks aloud with no self-consciousness whatever. Probably doesn't even know she's doing it.]

KATIE. I dialed the old number. I dialed—

[*SLAM CUT*[21] *TO:*

INT. BILL, IN THE PHONE NOOK WITH KATIE BESIDE HIM.

He's just taken the phone from KATIE and is speaking to the operator.]

OPERATOR. [*Filter, GIGGLES.*] I *promise* not to give it out.

BILL. It's 555-

[*SLAM CUT TO:*

INT. KATIE, IN BILL' S OLD CHAIR, CU.]

20. The repetition of an earlier scene or part of a scene is a *reprise* (ri prēz′).

21. A *slam cut* is a sudden shift to another scene, with no fade-out or dissolve.

Vocabulary

chasm (kaz′ əm) *n.* a deep hole or crack, as in the earth's surface

Z Active Reading Strategies

EVALUATE Why does Katie react the way she does when she sees what is on television? *(It brings back too many memories of the night of her husband's death.)* What effect does her violent reaction seem to cause? *(It seems to cause a change in the time continuum.)*

AA Literary Elements

SETTING Point out that the telephone is an important element of the setting. A play set in earlier times could not develop in the same way. Have students discuss other present-day elements that may affect the action of a work. *(Students may mention the Internet, VCRs, and cordless phones.)*

Real-World Connection

The Televised Version Discuss with students the connection between a published work and its television presentation.

Activity Have students locate and watch a video of a suspense novel or story and then compare it to the printed version. (An example is Charles Dickens's *A Christmas Carol.*) Have the class work in groups to discuss the adaptation. Students should answer such questions as *How true is the production to the original? Are the characters and setting the way you visualized them as you read the piece? If you had written the script, what information would you have included to help realize the author's ideas? What directions would you have given the director? The actors? The camera operators? Do you think it's hard or easy to adapt a suspense story for television? Why or why not?* **L2**

BB Active Reading Strategies

REVIEW Ask students to explain the ending of the story. Are they surprised? What hints, if any, did they get from story? *(They might note Katie's identification of the voice as familiar.)*

CC Active Reading Strategies

CONNECT Ask students who have read other Stephen King works or seen films based on his writing whether they recognized similar story elements in this play. Discuss whether this knowledge helped them predict the ending.

Thematic Focus

Hair-Raising Tales Point out that many people believe that it is possible to foretell the future or that there are some unexplained mysteries. Ask students if they believe that and how they account for what they believe.

ASSESSMENT

Quick Checks, p. 66

KATIE. [*Finishes.*] -4408.

[*INT. THE PHONE, CU.*
KATIE's trembling finger carefully picks out the number, and we hear the corresponding tones: 555-4408.
INT. KATIE, IN BILL'S OLD CHAIR, CU.
She closes her eyes as the PHONE BEGINS TO RING. Her face is filled with an agonizing mixture of hope and fear. If only she can have one more chance to pass the vital message on, it says . . . just one more chance.]

KATIE. [*Low.*] Please . . . please . . .

RECORDED VOICE. [*Filter.*] You have reached a non-working number. Please hang up and dial again. If you need assistance—

[*KATIE hangs up again. Tears stream down her cheeks. THE CAMERA PANS AWAY AND DOWN to the telephone.*
INT. THE PHONE NOOK, WITH KATIE AND BILL, REPRISE.]

BILL. So it was a prank. Or someone who was crying so hard she dialed a wrong number . . . "through a shimmering film of tears," as we veteran hacks like to say.

KATIE. It was not a prank and it was not a wrong number! It was someone in *my family!*

[*INT. KATIE (PRESENT DAY) IN BILL'S STUDY.*]

KATIE. Yes. Someone in my family. Someone very close. [*Pause.*] Me.

[*She suddenly throws the phone across the room. Then she begins to SOB AGAIN and puts her hands over her face. THE CAMERA HOLDS on her for a moment, then DOLLIES[22] ACROSS TO:*
INT. THE PHONE.
It lies on the carpet, looking both bland and somehow ominous. CAMERA MOVES IN TO ECU—the holes in the receiver once more look like huge dark chasms. We HOLD, then
FADE TO BLACK.]

22. When a movie camera *dollies,* it moves smoothly, either on tracks or wheels.

❖

Vocabulary
bland (bland) *adj.* dull and uninteresting

Teaching Support

Grammar and Language *Minilesson*

Dashes Remind students that dashes are often used to show a sudden break or change in thought of speech. For example, Katie begins to say, "I dialed the old number. I dialed—" The dash shows where she breaks off. The dash also alerts the next actor to the point at which he or she should begin speaking.

Activity Have students skim the selection to find other examples of dashes used this way. Make sure they do not confuse dashes with hyphens (as in *two-digit number*). **L2**

Additional Resources

- ***Grammar and Language Transparency 65***
- ***Grammar and Language Workbook,*** p. 271
- ***Grammar and Composition Handbook,*** Lesson 13.8
- ***Writer's Choice,*** Lesson 20.8

Responding to Literature

PERSONAL RESPONSE

- Did the ending of this play surprise you? Why or why not?

Brackets connect questions that are paired to develop higher-level thinking skills.

Analyzing Literature

RECALL

1. What is Katie saying about Bill as the play begins?
2. Who does Katie think is sobbing at the other end of the phone line?
3. Why do the Weidermans drive to Dawn's house?
4. Why is the date of Polly's wedding important to Katie?

INTERPRET

5. What do the stage directions tell the audience about Katie's attitude toward Bill's headache?
6. Why do you think Katie draws the conclusion she does about the phone call?
7. Why is Bill's gun important in act 2?
8. After Polly's wedding, whom does Katie call, and why is she able to make the phone call?

EVALUATE AND CONNECT

9. Theme Connection Many of Stephen King's stories have normal, everyday settings and characters. Do you think this makes the horror part more or less frightening when it comes?
10. *Sorry, Right Number* is a horror story with very little blood or gore. The character Bill Weiderman writes stories with lots of gore. Which kind of story appeals to you? List several reasons for your answer.

LITERARY ELEMENTS

Screenplay

A **screenplay** is the script of a film, which contains dialogue, stage directions, and instructions about camera shots and angles. A screenplay is very much like the script for a stage play.

Dialogue is preceded by the name of the speaker, just as it is in a stage play script. A screenplay also includes stage directions in brackets and italic type. These directions are written for directors, actors, and camera operators. For example, when Connie asks if Dawn is okay, Dennis replies, "Yeah. Sure she is." However, readers know from the stage direction that he really thinks she's been decapitated by a maniac. An actor must show by expression, tone, and gestures what Dennis really thinks.

1. How do the stage directions that describe Bill's office add to your understanding of the character?
2. Would you prefer to *see* this story as a movie instead of reading the screenplay? Why or why not?

● See **Literary Terms Handbook,** p. R9.

Responding to the Selection

PERSONAL RESPONSE

Students familiar with the genre probably anticipated some kind of twist at the end but were surprised at how the author accomplished it.

Analyzing Literature

1. She is saying that he doesn't feel well and complains of several symptoms.
2. At first she believes it is her older daughter, Polly.
3. Her phone is off the hook, and they are afraid that something has happened to her.
4. It is the anniversary of Bill's death.
5. They say that she's having a "good gab with her sister," which suggests that she is not very worried.
6. She is already concerned about having her oldest child away from home.
7. It adds to the tension of the scene.
8. Katie has apparently called herself, five years earlier, on the night Bill died. She has apparently entered some kind of supernatural time warp.
9. It makes the horror part more frightening when it comes because of the contrast between the ordinary and the eerie.
10. Students should give several reasons for preferring one type over the other.

LITERARY ELEMENTS

1. He is close to his family, has a sense of humor, and writes horror. He works alone but in a family setting.
2. Many students would probably like to see the movie because they would enjoy the special effects. Some students, though, will not have trouble visualizing the events.

Additional Resources

Literary Elements Transparency 66

Literature and Writing

Writing About Literature

Students' evaluations should
- be concise
- make a strong positive or negative argument with supporting statements

Creative Writing

Students' scripts should
- reveal Polly's feelings at the time of the marriage
- show us something about Hank's character in relation to Katie and Polly

Extending Your Response

Interdisciplinary Activity
Students may find it helpful to use film scores that are already available in CD or tape format.

Literature Groups Suggest that students confine the discussion to fictional works or playful situations rather than truly frightening personal experiences. COLLAB. LEARN.

Performing Encourage students to evaluate their own reading and suggest ways they might improve it. Have them then repeat their reading and reevaluate it.

At the MOVIES

Be sure to preview the following video for appropriateness for your class.

In *Rear Window* (1954) suspense builds as a helpless man watches a crime unfold.

Literature and Writing

Writing About Literature

For the Role of the Dead Writer . . . Imagine you work for a film producer. *Sorry, Right Number* is one of a dozen screenplays you're assigned to evaluate. Write a few paragraphs telling the producer your opinion of the story. Would it make a good movie? Should your boss invest several million dollars in it? Why or why not? What actors would you recommend to play the characters?

Creative Writing

Fill in the Blanks The play jumps from Bill's funeral to Polly's wedding five years later. Write a page of a screenplay from Polly's point of view, filling in some of the blanks in those five years. What happens when she learns of her father's death? How does she feel about Hank, her mother's new husband? Use the screenplay format, with dialogue and stage directions.

Extending Your Response

Interdisciplinary Activity

Music Before a movie is released, a composer scores it–adds music to heighten the emotional impact. Look through CDs or tapes and identify music that would enhance *Sorry, Right Number.* Make a list of the titles and musicians, and determine where in the movie they should be played. If you own the CDs, bring them to class and play the tracks you've chosen.

Literature Groups

Boo! Bill spends his career trying to scare his readers. Jeff tries unsuccessfully to scare him. Katie is afraid the movie version of *Ghost Kiss* will scare the kids, but in fact, Jeff's favorite part is the goriest. Review your notes from the **Reading Focus** on page 790. In a group, discuss scaring people: What's the point? Is it better to be the scarer or the scared?

Performing

Acting Up With a group of three students, act out the scene in which Jeff, Connie, and Dennis first appear. Remember to follow the stage directions regarding your voice inflections and movements. Ask your classmates for feedback on your performance.

Reading Further

Other novels that use time shifts and suspense are:
Tangerine by Edward Bloor
Alien Game by Catherine Dexter

Save your work for your portfolio.

810 THEME 8

Skill Minilessons

RETEACH • REVIEW

GRAMMAR AND LANGUAGE • END PUNCTUATION

The three types of punctuation used to end a sentence are the period, the question mark, and the exclamation point. A period ends a declarative statement: "He'll be fine." or a mild imperative: "Then don't call me Jeffie." A question mark ends an interrogative sentence: "Could we at least tape it?" An exclamation point shouts: "It never stops!"

PRACTICE Rewrite each sentence, using correct end punctuation.

1. What's your name
2. I promised to tape the movie for Jeff
3. It was not a wrong number
4. I suspect there may be a problem
5. Are you sure you want to watch that movie

- For more about punctuation, see **Language Handbook,** pp. R38–R43.

READING AND THINKING • TEXT STRUCTURE: SEQUENCE OF EVENTS

Authors organize their writing in different ways depending on their purpose and topic. The pattern of organization that a writer uses is called **text structure.** One important type of text structure is chronological order, which presents events in the sequence in which they occur. In *Sorry, Right Number,* Stephen King uses chronological order and also **flashback,** which interrupts the sequence and moves the action back in time. The end of the play flashes back and forth between the older Katie making the phone call and the younger Katie receiving it. This flashback creates an intense mood and brings the play to its conclusion.

PRACTICE Reread the last few pages of the play. List the places where the time order changes. The first flashback occurs when Katie hears her own voice answer, "Hello, Weiderman residence." Where does the action flash forward again? back again? How do you know? What does the flashback tell you about Katie and her feelings? What do you think was King's purpose in using flashback in this play? Explain.

- For more about text structures and sequencing, see **Reading Handbook,** pp. R97–R99.

VOCABULARY • LATIN ROOT *JECT*

The word *dejected* comes from the Latin prefix *de-,* meaning "down," and the root *ject,* meaning "to throw." A *dejected* person feels "thrown down." If you *reject* something, you "throw" it back. If you *inject* a comment, you "throw" it in. The prefix *ob-,* meaning "against," is used in *object.* When you *object* to an idea, you "throw" something "against" it. Below are some of the prefixes that have been attached to *ject* to create words:

inter-: between   *pro-:* forward   *e-:* out

PRACTICE Use the meaning of *ject* and the prefixes on the left to answer the questions.

1. If someone *interjects* a comment, does the person interrupt, shout, or repeat something?
2. Which of the following is most useful to an *ejected* pilot—a windshield, a parachute, or radar?
3. Which weapon is designed to be used as a *projectile*—an arrow, a sword, or a battering ram?

Skill Minilessons

GRAMMAR AND LANGUAGE
END PUNCTUATION

1. What's your name?
2. I promised to tape the movie for Jeff.
3. It was not a wrong number!
4. I suspect there may be a problem.
5. Are you sure you want to watch that movie?

READING AND THINKING
TEXT STRUCTURE: SEQUENCE OF EVENTS

The future Katie calls the present Katie, trying to warn her of Bill's ill health. All of the events actually take place in the past, with today's Katie trying to reach back from the future. She cannot, so the play ends with the future Katie sobbing.

VOCABULARY
LATIN ROOT *JECT*

1. That person interrupts.
2. A parachute is what the pilot needs.
3. An arrow is a projectile.

Additional Resources

- ***Grammar and Language Workbook,*** p. 255
- ***Grammar and Composition Handbook,*** Lesson 13.1
- ***Writer's Choice,*** Lesson 20.1
- ***Reading Skills Practice Workbook***
- ***Vocabulary Practice,*** p. 45

ASSESSMENT

- ***Quick Checks,*** p. 66
- ***Selection and Theme Assessment,*** pp. 113–114
- ***Performance Assessment,*** p. 58
- ***Testmaker: ExamView Pro***
- ***Interactive Tutor: Self-Assessment***

MEDIA Connection

Objective

- To read and understand a television transcript

Literature LINK

Sorry, Right Number Point out that the author of the play is not only part of the panel but is referred to as one of the major influences on the growing popularity of the suspense genre.

Analyzing Media

1. Possible answer: There is comfort in knowing that after reading, hearing, or seeing a scary story, we will find that everything is all right in the real world.
2. R. L. Stine's *Goosebump* books are similar to old fairy tales in that both give young readers chills and the satisfaction of knowing that the scary things are happening to the characters and not to them.

Informational Text

inTIME For more examples of informational text, direct students to the articles in *inTIME* magazine.

Additional Resources

Media Connections, p. 15

MEDIA Connection

TELEVISION TRANSCRIPT

Do you enjoy horror stories? Reporters Cokie Roberts and Jeff Greenfield lead a discussion of America's "obsession with the dark side."

American Gothic

from ABC *Nightline*, December 10, 1997

COKIE ROBERTS

It's safe to say that kids have always been fascinated by scary stuff—terrifying fairy tales, ghost stories on camping trips, horror movies so popular they have sequels in the double digits, not to mention the delight over slimy substances and artificial bugs and snakes. But now grownups seem to be getting in on the fun, celebrating Halloween in a big way, watching TV shows and movies that can't be called cheery by any description and reading millions and millions of books by authors like Anne Rice and Stephen King. King has sold one book for every American, over 250 million of them.

JEFF GREENFIELD

These are the good times, right? The cold war is over, the economy is booming, unemployment is dropping, inflation is gone, the budget is almost balanced, even the crime rate is falling. So here's something to puzzle over. If the reality is so sunny, why are the stories we're drawn to so dark? If it is morning in America, why is so much of our fact and fiction coming from round midnight?

COKIE ROBERTS

Mr. King, your books have certainly been incredibly popular. You've heard this discussion about all of the meaningfulness in this. Are we reading too much into this or are people just having fun reading your books?

STEPHEN KING

Yeah, I think you probably are reading a little bit too much into it. . . . We like to be scared, we like to pretend, we like to make believe.

COKIE ROBERTS

But haven't children liked to be scared from time out of mind? I mean the Brothers Grimm and Hans Christian Andersen did a pretty good job of scaring them.

STEPHEN KING

Sure, and the inheritors of the Brothers Grimm and Hans Christian Andersen are people like R. L. Stine. . . . Being scared for fun is something that's always appealed to young people. It's not much different than the roller coaster thing or, you know, the loop-de-loop thing, only it's at the movie theater where you can get dark, put your arm around your girlfriend or your boyfriend and enjoy being scared.

Analyzing Media

1. What is your answer to the question "Why are the stories we're drawn to so dark?"
2. How are modern-day horror stories similar to old fairy tales?

Teaching Support

interNET CONNECTION

Authors on the Web Suggest that students use a search engine to discover whether favorite suspense writers are represented on the Internet.

Reading Minilesson

Analyzing Arguments Point out that the panelists are discussing whether the popularity of horror stories is something to be concerned about. Explain, if necessary, that *gothic* in this context refers to stories that are mysterious or violent.

Activity Divide students into three groups, one to analyze each of the arguments of the panelists. Have them answer these questions:

- What position does the panelist take?
- Does he or she support his or her argument with examples or evidence?
- Do you find the argument convincing? Explain. **L2** COLLAB. LEARN.

Additional Resources

Reading Skills Practice Workbook

LISTENING, SPEAKING, and VIEWING

Critical Viewing

"Seeing is believing," people used to say—but that was before the era of special effects. Today, you know that what you see, whether on television, in films, or on the Internet, can't always be taken at face value. A smart viewer is a critical viewer: not necessarily one who finds fault, but one who thinks carefully about what he or she sees. The following questions can help you evaluate what you find on the screen.

Questions for Critical Viewing

What's the purpose?

- Are you viewing something made to entertain, to inform, or to persuade? Purpose affects accuracy. If a film is made to entertain, it may not be accurate in every detail, even when based on real-life events. If an infomercial has two purposes—to inform viewers and to sell a product—it may omit facts that would decrease sales.

Are statements supported by facts?

- Do you detect a bias—a "slant" that reflects personal views? Watch for manipulation of statistics and for opinions presented as facts.

Is the subject presented fairly?

- Are there "loaded" images or words—ones designed to trigger emotions? Appeals to emotion shouldn't lead viewers to ignore the voice of reason.

What's the source?

- Who created the material you're viewing? Is the creator known for artistry, accuracy, or independent thinking—or for sensationalism or bias? (A librarian can help you find out.)

What are the details?

- When, where, and how was the material produced? How might these conditions affect its content?

ACTIVITIES

1. With a partner or on your own, view a televised news show. Use the **Questions for Critical Viewing** to evaluate it, and share your evaluation with your class.
2. Use the **Questions for Critical Viewing** to evaluate a mysterious or chilling event that you've seen on film or on television. Write a paragraph explaining your evaluation.

LISTENING, SPEAKING, and VIEWING

Objective

- To recognize that critical viewers must think about what they see on the Internet, in films, or on television

Teaching Strategies

After students have read the first paragraph, ask them to define in their own words a critical viewer. Point out that the object of this lesson is to change them from passive viewers to active and aware viewers. You may wish to play a video of a commercial or public service announcement and then model using the Questions for Critical Viewing.

Activities

1. Students' evaluations should respond point by point to the Questions for Critical Viewing.
2. Students' explanations should show an increased awareness of the need for active, critical viewing.

Teaching Support

MEETING INDIVIDUAL NEEDS — ENGLISH LANGUAGE LEARNERS

Understanding Critical Viewing
Make sure English language learners understand that critical viewing means thinking about and questioning what one sees. Ask students what they know about how information gets posted on the Internet and why they need to be even more critical of the Internet than of TV and film.

Activity Have pairs or small groups of students discuss the Questions for Critical Viewing. Suggest that students break the bulleted items down into a series of shorter questions and then apply the questions to a program they have seen recently. COLLAB. LEARN.

Additional Resources

English Language Learners Sourcebook, p. 92

Vo•cab•u•lar•y *Skills*

Objective

- To recognize base words and use them to decode longer words

Teaching Strategies

After students have read the first part of the page, call for volunteers to use each pair of examples in two sentences: *presume* and *presumably, applicable* and *inapplicable, suppose,* and *supposition.* Discuss how the meaning of the base word is affected by the addition of an affix. Have students point out any spelling changes to the base word.

Exercises

1. (a) pun; (b) grime; (c) fine; (d) suppose; (e) final; (f) credit; (g) pressure; (h) general; (i) accuse; (j) body
2. (a) upset; (b) the future; (c) unchangeable; (d) cannot be said; (e) guessing who it was

Additional Resources

Vocabulary Power

Vo•cab•u•lar•y *Skills*

Using Base Words

In *Sorry, Right Number,* the stage directions describe the office of Bill Weiderman five years after his death: "The book jackets have been replaced by photos of buildings. Ones that have first been built in Hank's mind, *presumably.*"

If you don't know what *presumably* means, how can you figure it out? The base word, *presume,* may be a familiar word that can help you guess at the meaning. A **base word** can stand alone or it can be the basis of other words. Suffixes or prefixes or both can be attached to a base word to make new words.

Prefixes often change the meaning of a word, as when *applicable* becomes *inapplicable.* Suffixes, on the other hand, often merely change the part of speech, as when *apply* becomes *applicable.* (An exception to this is *-less;* clearly, *hope* and *hopeless* have very different meanings.)

The spelling of the end of a base word often changes when a suffix is added. The *y* in *apply* disappears when *applicable* is formed. The *e* in *suppose* changes to an *i* to make *supposition.* Even so, base words are usually obvious if you look for them.

If you come across an unfamiliar word, look at it carefully to see if it has a base word you know. A familiar base word can help you understand a new word.

• For more about spelling base words, see **Language Handbook,** pp. R46–R49.

EXERCISES

1. Write the base word from which each word below was formed. (Remember, a vowel at the end of a base word may disappear when a suffix is added.)

   a. punster
   b. begrime
   c. finery
   d. presuppose
   e. finality
   f. accredited
   g. pressurized
   h. generalization
   i. accusatory
   j. disembodied

2. Use your knowledge of the base words and familiar prefixes and suffixes in the underlined words to answer each question.

   a. If Katie has a feeling of <u>disquietude</u>, is she relieved, tired, or upset?
   b. Is a <u>prophetic</u> phone call one that tells about danger, the future, or the past?
   c. If an event of the past is <u>irreversible</u>, is it unknown, unchangeable, or unimportant?
   d. If a fear is <u>inexpressible</u>, is it one that cannot be said, explained, or relieved?
   e. If Katie <u>theorizes</u> about who has called, does that mean she is guessing who it was, describing the voice, or becoming frightened?

Teaching Support

MEETING INDIVIDUAL NEEDS

ENGLISH LANGUAGE LEARNERS

Base Words Ask English language learners whether there are base words in their first language to which prefixes and suffixes are added. Encourage them to share examples and explain how the meaning changes when an affix is added.

Activity Help students isolate each base word in the exercises and discuss its meaning. Then discuss how that meaning changes with the addition of an affix. Have students add the base words and new words with sample sentences to thier vocabulary notebooks.

Additional Resources

English Language Learners Sourcebook, p. 93

Before You Read

The Legend of Sleepy Hollow

MEET WASHINGTON IRVING

The Hudson River Valley in New York is the setting of Washington Irving's eerie and popular short story, "The Legend of Sleepy Hollow." Irving lived and traveled in the region. Then, while traveling in Europe, he was encouraged by the famous writer Sir Walter Scott to publish stories and essays based on his travels. As a result, Irving published *The Sketch Book of Geoffrey Crayon, Gent* in 1820. "The Legend of Sleepy Hollow" and "Rip Van Winkle," another tale from *The Sketch Book*, are considered by many to be the first American short stories.

Washington Irving was born in 1783 and died in 1859. "The Legend of Sleepy Hollow" was first published in The Sketch Book *in 1820.*

READING FOCUS

What stories about scary or unexplainable events have you heard in your community?

Share It!

Share a scary story or ghost story with a partner. Use vivid language and active verbs as you tell your story. Then listen to your partner tell you one. What do your two stories have in common?

Setting a Purpose

Read to discover what makes "The Legend of Sleepy Hollow" a scary tale.

BUILDING BACKGROUND

The Time and Place Irving based "The Legend of Sleepy Hollow" on an old German legend. However, he Americanized it, placing it in New York's Hudson River Valley near the village of Tarrytown, sometime in the 1800s. Some of the characters in this story are of Dutch descent. Many Dutch people settled in what is now New York.

VOCABULARY PREVIEW

dominant (dom′ ə nənt) *adj.* having the greatest power or force; controlling; p. 817

apparition (ap′ ə rish′ ən) *n.* ghostly vision; p. 817

conscientious (kon′ shē en′ shəs) *adj.* guided by one's conscience; showing careful attention to what is right and wrong; p. 818

speculation (spek′ yə lā′ shən) *n.* an opinion or conclusion based on guesswork; p. 819

perceive (pər sēv′) *v.* to take in or grasp mentally; notice; p. 820

renown (ri noun′) *n.* widespread reputation; fame; p. 821

wary (wār′ ē) *adj.* cautious; on the alert; p. 822

pensive (pen′ siv) *adj.* thinking deeply, often about something sad; p. 822

aloof (ə lo͞of′) *adj.* emotionally distant; uninvolved; standoffish; p. 826

Before Reading

Objectives

- To read and analyze a literary legend
- To identify a literary legend
- To rewrite a section of the story

Skills

Reading/Thinking: Inferring; Predicting; Evaluating; Distinguishing Cause from Effect

Writing: Opening Scene; Legend; Memo

Vocabulary: Word Meaning; Glossary; Latin Root *spec*

Grammar/Language: Complex Sentences; Varying Sentence Structure

Listening/Speaking: Role-Playing

Life Skills: Planning; Teaching and Mentoring

Collaboration: Literature Groups

Motivating STUDENTS

Literature Launchers: "Where the Legend Lives On"

Videodisc Side B, Segment 21

Also available in VHS.

Selection Focus Transparency 62: Before presenting the photograph, discuss ways in which horror stories might be enhanced in oral readings.

Reading Focus: Ask students to share their scary events.

RESOURCE MANAGER

Teaching Tools and Resources

- Theme Eight Planning Guide
- Literature Groups Sourcebook

Essential Lesson Support

Lesson-Specific Instruction

- Selection Focus Transparency 62
- Literary Elements Transparency 67
- Active Reading Guide,* p. 67
- Selection Vocabulary Practice, p. 46

Assessment

- Selection Quick Checks,* p. 67
- Sel. and Theme Assmt., pp. 115-116
- Testmaker: ExamView Pro
- Performance Assessment, p. 59

Systematic Language Instruction

- Gr. & Comp. Hbk., L. 13.9, 13.10
- Vocabulary Power, Lesson 34
- Spelling Power, Lesson 30

English Language Learners

- ELL Sourcebook, p. 94
- Spanish Summaries, p. 62
- Audio Library*
- English, Yes!

Special Needs/Strat. Interven.

- Interactive Rdg. Sbk., pp. T212-T215
- Interactive Rdg. Wkbk., pp. 125-128
- Inclusion Strat. Sbk., pp. 33-34, 85-86
- Audio Library*

* Also available in Spanish

Reading the Selection

SUMMARY

Ichabod Crane is the gangly, greedy, and generally unappealing schoolmaster in Sleepy Hollow (now Tarrytown, New York). He convinces himself that the lovely Katrina Van Tassel, daughter of a wealthy landowner, welcomes his courtship. Ichabod's main rival is Brom Bones. Telling ghost stories is a favorite pastime in Sleepy Hollow, and everyone is aware that the schoolmaster believes these tales. Taking advantage of this, Brom masquerades as a headless horseman and scares the schoolmaster out of town, never to return.

Spanish Summaries, p. 62

Active Reading Strategies

PREDICT Ask students what the title means. What is a legend? *(a story from the past that often gets exaggerated over time)* Do students know any other legends?

VOCABULARY If you haven't previewed the selection vocabulary with students, stop and remind them to use context clues to unlock the meanings of new vocabulary words.

Additional Resources

Active Reading Guides, p. 67

Audio Library

Teaching Support

Illustration © 1990 by Russ Flint from *The Legend of Sleepy Hollow.*

CONNECTING TO OTHER SELECTIONS

The chart at the right shows three ways to connect "The Legend of Sleepy Hollow" to other selections in this book.

For specific teaching strategies, see the ***Theme Eight Planning Guide.***

Connection	Title
Life Skills: Lifelong Learning	"Fire and Ice," p. 304
Thematic: Doubting Appearances	"Coyote and Wasichu," p. 421
Literary: Legends and Folktales	"Chicoria," p. 419

In the bosom of one of those spacious coves which indent the eastern shore of the Hudson, there lies a small market town, which by some is called Greensburgh, but which is more generally and properly known by the name of Tarrytown. This name was given by the good housewives of the adjacent[1] country, from the tendency of their husbands to linger about the village tavern on market days. Not far from this village, perhaps about two miles, there is a little valley among high hills, which is one of the quietest places in the whole world. A small brook glides through it, with just murmur enough to lull one to repose, and the occasional whistle of a quail, or tapping of a woodpecker, is almost the only sound that ever breaks in upon the uniform tranquility.[2] This glen has long been known by the name of Sleepy Hollow.

A drowsy, dreamy influence seems to hang over the land. The whole neighborhood abounds with local tales, haunted spots, and twilight superstitions. The dominant spirit, however, that haunts this enchanted region is the apparition of a figure on horseback without a head. It is said by some to be the ghost of a Hessian trooper[3] whose head had been carried

1. *Adjacent* (ə jā′ sənt) means "surrounding" or "nearby."
2. *Tranquility* (trang kwil′ ə tē) means "peacefulness."
3. A *Hessian* (hesh′ ən) *trooper* is a German soldier who fought with the British during the American Revolution.

Vocabulary

dominant (dom′ ə nənt) *adj.* having the greatest power or force; controlling

apparition (ap′ ə rish′ ən) *n.* ghostly vision

B Active Reading Strategies

CONNECT Remind students of the play *Sorry, Right Number,* in which eerie and suspenseful events take place against a very ordinary setting. Ask students to compare that setting to the one in "The Legend of Sleepy Hollow." What is ordinary about Sleepy Hollow?

C Active Reading Strategies

CONNECT Have students locate an example of the contrast between the description of a "sleepy" landscape and the report of "the apparition." *("A small brook glides through it, with just murmur enough to lull one to repose" in contrast with "The dominant spirit, however, that haunts this enchanted region is the apparition of a figure on horseback without a head.")*

LITERATURE & HUMANITIES

Invite students to look at the painting *Girl Attacked by a Strange Bird,* in *Introducing Art,* page 266. As they examine the artwork, ask them to consider contrasting ordinary settings with events that are eerie.

MEETING INDIVIDUAL NEEDS: ENGLISH LANGUAGE LEARNERS

Visualizing Ask English language learners to visualize what the Hudson River Valley was like in the early 1800s. Help students locate the area on a map. Invite vounteers to describe what a northern forest looks like and sounds like, both by day and by night.

Activity Depending on class size, you may want to read this selection as a group. Pause at the end of each paragraph to discuss the setting, mood, and characters and how the plot unfolds. Encourage students to listen to the selection on audio as many times as they wish. **COLLAB. LEARN.**

Additional Resources

English Language Learners Sourcebook, p. 94

D Literary Elements

LEGEND What is the legend mentioned in the title? *(the legend of the Headless Horseman)* How did that legend get started? *(It started with an actual event, the death of a Hessian mercenary, and grew from that.)*

E Author's Craft

DESCRIPTION Have students pick out details the author uses to create a feeling of suspense and eeriness in the description of the Headless Horseman. *(The author describes the death of the Hessian soldier, his nightly "haunting" in quest of his head, and the rushing speed with which he passes.)*

F Active Reading Strategies

REVIEW To help students to put the story into factual historic context, tell them to watch for clues that suggest where and when the story takes place. *(An example is the reference to the Revolutionary War.)*

F D away by a cannonball, in some nameless battle during the Revolutionary War. His haunts are not confined to the valley, but extend at times to the adjacent roads, and especially to the vicinity of a church at no great distance. Certain historians of those parts claim that the body of the trooper having been buried in the churchyard, the ghost rides forth to the scene of battle in nightly quest of his head; and that the rushing speed with which he sometimes passes along the Hollow is owing to his being late, and in a hurry to get back to the churchyard before daybreak. The specter[4] is known, at all the country firesides, by the name of the Headless Horseman of Sleepy Hollow.

In this by-place of nature, there abode, some thirty years since, a worthy fellow of the name of Ichabod Crane, who sojourned[5] in Sleepy Hollow for the purpose of instructing the children of the vicinity. The name of Crane was not inapplicable to his person.[6] He was tall, but exceedingly lank, with narrow shoulders, long arms and legs, hands that dangled a mile out of his sleeves, feet that might have served for shovels, and his whole frame most loosely hung together. To see him striding along the profile of a hill on a windy day, with his clothes bagging and fluttering about him, one might have mistaken him for the spirit of famine descending upon the earth, or some scarecrow eloped[7] from a cornfield.

E His schoolhouse was a low building of one large room, rudely constructed of logs. From here the low murmur of his pupils' voices might be heard in a drowsy summer's day, like the hum of a beehive; interrupted now and then by the authoritative voice of the master, in the tone of menace or command; or, perhaps, by the appalling sound of the birch, as he urged some tardy loiterer along the flowery path of knowledge. Truth to say, he was a conscientious man, and ever bore in mind the golden maxim,[8] "Spare the rod and spoil the child."—Ichabod Crane's scholars certainly were not spoiled.

The revenue arising from his school was small, and would have been scarcely sufficient to furnish him with daily bread, for he was a huge feeder. To help out his maintenance, he was, according to country custom in those parts, boarded and lodged at the houses of the farmers whose children he instructed. With these he lived successively a week at a time, thus going the rounds of the neighborhood, with all his worldly effects tied up in a cotton handkerchief. In addition, he was the singing master of the neighborhood, and picked up many bright shillings by instructing the young folks in psalmody.[9] Thus, by various little makeshifts, the worthy pedagogue[10] got on tolerably enough, and was thought, by all who understood nothing of the labor of headwork, to have a wonderfully easy life of it.

4. A *specter* is a ghost.
5. Here, *abode* means "lived." *Ichabod* (ik′ ə bod). Someone who has *sojourned* has traveled.
6. The name *Crane* fit the man because he resembled a long-legged, long-necked bird.
7. Here, *eloped* means "run off" or "escaped."
8. A *maxim* is a saying.
9. *Psalmody* is the singing of hymns.
10. *Makeshifts* are things done in place of the proper or desired things. A *pedagogue* (ped′ ə gog′) is a teacher.

Vocabulary

conscientious (kon′ shē en′ shəs) *adj.* guided by one's conscience; showing careful attention to what is right and wrong

Teaching Support

MEETING INDIVIDUAL NEEDS — SPECIAL NEEDS

Less-Proficient Readers Help students to see that many of the words are familiar or can be figured out with the help of context, footnotes, vocabulary listings, and letter-sound cues.

Activity Read aloud the first paragraph, substituting more familiar language for difficult terms, as in the following example:

> In the *center* of one of those *wide inlets* that cut into the shore of the Hudson, there lies a small market town. . . .

Read other sentences as a fill-in exercise, with students supplying the missing synonyms. **L1**

Additional Resources

Inclusion Strategies

Illustration © 1992 by Michael Garland from *The Legend of Sleepy Hollow.*

Viewing the painting: Which of Ichabod Crane's characteristics are depicted in this painting?

The schoolmaster is generally a man of some importance in the female circle of a rural neighborhood, being considered of vastly superior taste and accomplishments to the rough country swains.[11] Our man was esteemed by the women as a man of great learning, for he had read several books quite through, and was a perfect master of Cotton Mather's[12] *History of New England Witchcraft,* in which, by the way, he most firmly believed. It was often his delight, after his school was dismissed in the afternoon, to stretch himself on the rich bed of clover bordering the little brook that whimpered by his schoolhouse, and there con over old Mather's direful[13] tales.

G

Another of his sources of fearful pleasure was to pass long winter evenings with the old Dutch wives and listen to their marvelous tales of ghosts and goblins, and haunted fields, and haunted brooks, and haunted bridges, and haunted houses, and particularly of the Headless Horseman, or Galloping Hessian of the Hollow, as they sometimes called him. He would delight them equally by his anecdotes of witchcraft, and would frighten them woefully with speculations upon comets and shooting stars, and with the alarming fact that the world did absolutely turn round, and that they were half the time topsy-turvy!

G

But if there was a pleasure in all this, it was dearly purchased by the terrors of his walk homewards later. What fearful shapes

11. *Swains* are young men or suitors.

12. *Cotton Mather* (1663–1728) wrote more than 450 books about religion, history, and medicine.

13. To *con over* is to study. *Direful* means "dreadful."

Vocabulary

speculation (spek′ yə lā′ shən) *n.* an opinion or conclusion based on guesswork

VIEWING THE ART

Michael Garland is a prolific illustrator. Much of his best-known work is in the field of children's literature.

Viewing Response *It gives him the persona of a severe teacher or historian.*

G Literary Elements

CHARACTER Ichabod Crane's person and character are revealed through the author's description of his physical appearance, his actions as a teacher, and what he enjoys. Have students list the characteristics the author gives and speculate on what significance they have to the outcome of the story. *(Answers might include his interest in witchcraft and tales of the supernatural, especially the Headless Horseman.)*

Historical Note

Cotton Mather (1663–1728) was a Boston minister who originally approved of the Salem witchcraft trials and executions (1692–1693) but later concluded that they were unfair. He was a prolific writer, publishing more than four hundred works on a variety of subjects.

MEETING INDIVIDUAL NEEDS — MULTIPLE MODES OF EXPRESSION

Spatial Students who are visual learners may find it helpful to depict the spatial relationships of the setting. A map of Sleepy Hollow will also help students understand where the action of the story takes place.

Activity Have students draw a simple road map of Sleepy Hollow, adding new sites as they encounter them in the text. The map should include the churchyard where the Hessian trooper is buried, the Van Tassel farm, Major André's Tree, Wiley's Swamp, and the bridge over the brook. **L2**

Active Reading Strategies

QUESTION Why does Ichabod find Katrina Van Tassel desirable? *(She is very wealthy and attractive.)*

Active Reading Strategies

VISUALIZE Point out how the author uses Ichabod's active visualizing of his future luxury to help readers "see" both Ichabod's nature and what he wants for himself.

and shadows beset his path amidst the dim and ghastly glare of a snowy night! And how often was he thrown into complete dismay by some rushing blast, howling among the trees, in the idea that it was the Galloping Hessian on one of his nightly scourings![14]

Among the musical disciples who assembled, one evening in each week, to receive his instructions in psalmody was Katrina Van Tassel, the daughter and only child of a prosperous Dutch farmer. She was a blooming lass of fresh eighteen; plump as a partridge; ripe and melting and rosy-cheeked as one of her father's peaches; and universally famed, not merely as a beauty, but as an heiress. She was a little of a coquette,[15] as might be perceived even in her dress, which was a mixture of ancient and modern fashions, as most suited to set off her charms.

Ichabod Crane had a soft and foolish heart, and it is not to be wondered at that so tempting a morsel soon found favor in his eyes, more especially after he had visited her in her paternal mansion.[16] Old Baltus Van Tassel was a perfect picture of a thriving, contented farmer. His stronghold was situated on the banks of the Hudson, in one of those green, sheltered, fertile nooks, in which the Dutch farmers are so fond of nestling. Close by the farmhouse was a vast barn that might have served for a church, every window and crevice of which seemed bursting forth with the treasures of the farm.

The pedagogue's mouth watered as he looked upon this sumptuous[17] promise of luxurious winter fare. In his devouring mind's eye he pictured to himself every roasting-pig running about him with a pudding in his belly, and an apple in his mouth. The pigeons were snugly put to bed in a comfortable pie and tucked in with a coverlet of crust; the geese were swimming in their own gravy. Not a turkey but he beheld daintily trussed up, with its gizzard under its wing, and, perhaps, a necklace of savory sausages.

As the enraptured[18] Ichabod fancied all this and as he rolled his great green eyes over the fat meadowlands, his heart yearned after the damsel who was to inherit these domains.

When he entered the house, the conquest of his heart was complete. It was one of those spacious farmhouses, with high-ridged but lowly sloping roofs, built in the style handed down from the first Dutch settlers, the low projecting eaves forming a piazza[19] along the front. From this piazza the wondering Ichabod entered the hall, which formed the center of the mansion. Here rows of resplendent pewter[20] ranged on a long dresser; a door left ajar gave him a peep into the best parlor, where the claw-footed chairs and dark mahogany tables shone like mirrors; and a corner cupboard, knowingly left open, displayed immense treasures of old silver and well-mended china.

From the moment that Ichabod laid his eyes upon these regions of delight, the peace of his mind was at an end, and his only

14. *Scourings* are searches.
15. A *coquette* (kō ket′) is a flirt.
16. A *morsel* is a small portion. A *paternal mansion* is a house belonging to a person's father.
17. *Sumptuous* means "costly, showy, and magnificent."
18. *Enraptured* means "carried away by intense joy or delight."
19. A *piazza* (pē az′ ə) is a large covered porch.
20. *Resplendent* (ri splen′ dənt) means "splendid" or "gleaming." *Pewter* is a mixture of tin, lead, and copper.

Vocabulary
perceive (pər sēv′) *v.* to take in or grasp mentally; notice

Teaching Support

Listening and Speaking *Minilesson*

Role-Playing In describing Katrina Van Tassel's two suitors, the author establishes that they are very different in appearance and character. Therefore, their conversations should also be distinctive.

Activity Discuss with students the differences between the two men. Encourage students to choose one of the two men into whose character they can project themselves. Have volunteers then role-play each man having a conversation with Katrina. The topic of the conversation should be the town's history. Suggest that students incorporate each character's physical appearance into their portrayals. Ask students to analyze the performances, focusing on language choices and characterizations. **L2** COLLAB. LEARN.

study was how to gain the affections of the peerless[21] daughter of Van Tassel. In this enterprise, however, he had to encounter a host of fearful adversaries[22] of real flesh and blood, the numerous admirers who beset every portal to her heart, keeping a watchful and angry eye upon each other, but ready to fly out in the common cause against any new competitor.

Among these the most formidable was a burly, roaring, roistering blade,[23] of the name of Abraham, or, according to the Dutch abbreviation, Brom Van Brunt. He was broad-shouldered and double-jointed, with short, curly black hair, and a bluff but not unpleasant countenance, having a mingled air of fun and arrogance. From his Herculean[24] frame and great powers of limb, he had received the nickname of "Brom Bones," by which he was universally known. He was famed for great knowledge and skill in horsemanship. He was foremost at all races. He was always ready for either a fight or a frolic, but had more mischief than ill will in his composition; and, with all his overbearing roughness, there was a strong dash of waggish[25] good humor at bottom. He had three or four boon[26] companions, who regarded him as their model, and at the head of whom he scoured the country, attending every scene of feud or merriment for miles round.

This reckless hero had for some time singled out the blooming Katrina for the object of his gallantries, and it was whispered that she did not altogether discourage his hopes. Certain it is, his advances were signals for rival candidates to retire. When his horse was seen tied to Van Tassel's paling,[27] a sure sign that his master was courting within, all other suitors passed by in despair.

Such was the formidable rival with whom Ichabod Crane had to contend, and, considering all things, a stouter[28] man than he would have shrunk from the competition, and a wiser man would have despaired. He had, however, a happy mixture of pliability and perseverance[29] in his nature.

To have taken the field openly against his rivals would have been madness. Ichabod, therefore, made his advances in a quiet and gently insinuating[30] manner. Under cover of his character of singing master, he made frequent visits at the farmhouse.

I profess not to know how women's hearts are wooed and won. To me they have always been matters of riddle and admiration. He who wins a thousand common hearts is entitled to some renown; but he who keeps undisputed sway over the heart of a coquette is indeed a hero. Certain it is, this was not the case with the redoubtable[31] Brom Bones. From the moment Ichabod Crane made his advances, the interests of the former evidently declined. His horse

21. *Peerless* means "without equal; matchless."
22. *A host of fearful adversaries* is a large number of rivals.
23. *Formidable* (for′ mi də bəl) means "causing fear or awe due to size, strength, or power." A *roistering blade* is a lively and attractive young man.
24. *Herculean* (hur′ kyə lē′ ən) means "very strong and muscular," and is taken from the Greek hero *Hercules*.
25. *Waggish* means "humorous" or "friendly."
26. *Boon* means "merry."
27. A *paling* is one of the pickets of a fence.
28. *Stouter* means "braver" or "stronger."
29. *Pliability* is the ability to adjust to changes. *Perseverance* is determination to continue despite difficulty.
30. *Insinuating* means "suggesting indirectly; hinting."
31. Something that is *redoubtable* causes fear or awe and deserves respect.

Vocabulary
renown (ri noun′) *n.* widespread reputation; fame

Vocabulary Skills

Word Meaning The word *retire* has more than one meaning, although all meanings suggest a withdrawal from involvement. As used here (. . . his advances were signals for rival candidates to retire), it means "to retreat or withdraw." It can also mean "to go to bed" and "to leave one's occupation or position." In baseball *to retire the side* means to keep the three scheduled batters in an inning from getting on base.

J Critical Thinking

EVALUATE What sort of person does Brom Bones seem to be? How does the author give readers clues to his character? *(He describes Bones's "Herculean" physique and his practical jokes, always emphasizing that Bones is basically good natured: "[He] had more mischief than ill will in his composition.")*

K Literary Elements

POINT OF VIEW Ask students who is telling the story. Is the storyteller a character in the story? From whose point of view does the reader see the events unfold? *(The story is told in the third person by someone familiar with most of the details.)*

INTERDISCIPLINARY CONNECTION

Science Point out that the characters in this story depend on written and oral tales for their "proof" that supernatural beings exist. Remind students that scientists require objective tests to prove or disprove a phenomenon.

Activity Have students work in small groups to plan an objective test to test whether the Headless Horseman exists. They should refer to science texts as they describe in writing how they would test this phenomenon. COLLAB. LEARN.

L Critical Thinking

EVALUATE Have students compare the two suitors (Brom Bones and Ichabod Crane). Who do you think has the better chance of winning Katrina's heart? Why? *(Students may cite the following characteristics of the suitors: Although Ichabod has the status of a man of education, Brom has physical strength, daring, and a sense of humor.)*

Historical Note

Quilting frolics were neighborhood gatherings at which quilters worked together to put the final touches on a quilt that one woman had designed and sewn together. They were often called *quilting bees*. In nature, bees are social beings that keep busy and cooperate to perform their tasks. An American term (first used about 1769), *bee* was used with many other words such as *spinning*, *candy*, *logging*, and *shucking*. The *spelling bee* may be the last survivor of this type of gathering.

K was no longer seen tied at the palings on Sunday nights, and a deadly feud gradually arose between him and the schoolmaster of Sleepy Hollow.

L Brom, who had a degree of rough chivalry in his nature, would have carried matters to open warfare, and have settled their pretensions to the lady according to the mode of the knights-errant of yore[32]—by single combat; but Ichabod was too conscious of the superior might of his adversary to enter the lists[33] against him. He had overheard a boast of Bones, that he would "double the schoolmaster up, and lay him on a shelf of his own schoolhouse"; and he was too wary to give him an opportunity. There was something extremely provoking in this obstinately pacific system; it left Brom no alternative but to play boorish[34] practical jokes upon his rival. Ichabod became the object of whimsical persecution to Bones and his gang of rough-riders. They harried his hitherto peaceful domains;[35] smoked out his singing school, by stopping up the chimney; broke into the schoolhouse at night and turned everything topsy-turvy; so that the poor schoolmaster began to think all the witches in the country held their meetings there.

In this way matters went on for some time, without producing any material effect on the relative situation of the rivals. On a fine autumn afternoon, Ichabod, in pensive mood, sat enthroned on the lofty stool whence he usually watched all the concerns of his little literary realm. His scholars were all busily intent upon their books, or slyly whispering behind them with one eye kept upon the master; and a kind of buzzing stillness reigned throughout the schoolroom. It was suddenly interrupted by the appearance of a man who came clattering up to the school door with an invitation to Ichabod to attend a merry-making, or "quilting frolic," to be held that evening at Mynheer[36] Van Tassel's.

All was now bustle and hubbub in the late quiet schoolroom. The scholars were hurried through their lessons; books were flung aside without being put away on the shelves; inkstands were overturned, benches thrown down; and the whole school was turned loose an hour before the usual time.

M The gallant Ichabod now spent at least an extra half-hour brushing up his best and indeed only suit of rusty black, and arranging his locks by a bit of broken looking glass that hung up in the schoolhouse. That he might make his appearance before his mistress in the true style of a cavalier,[37] he borrowed a horse from the farmer with whom he was living and issued forth, like a knight-errant in quest of adventures. But

32. *Chivalry* (shiv′ əl rē) refers to the qualities of a knight, such as honor, courage, skill in battle, and respect for women. Here, *pretensions* are claims. *Knights-errant of yore* are wandering knights of long ago.
33. To *enter the lists* is to compete in a tournament.
34. The *obstinately pacific system* refers to Ichabod's stubborn refusal to compete openly with Brom. *Boorish* means "crude; bad-mannered."
35. Brom and his friends raided the schoolhouse—the one territory that Ichabod controlled *(his domains)* and that had been peaceful up to this time *(hitherto)*.
36. *Mynheer* (mīn hār′) is Dutch for *Mr.* or *Sir.* (The word is sometimes shortened to *Heer.*)
37. A *cavalier* is a gallant knight.

Vocabulary
wary (wār′ ē) *adj.* cautious; on the alert
pensive (pen′ siv) *adj.* thinking deeply, often about something sad

Teaching Support

Life Skills Connection

Planning Ask students whether "The Legend of Sleepy Hollow" would make a good movie for television. Have students support their answers.

Activity Have students work in small groups to discuss a live-action (as opposed to animated) movie. Tell them to list the characters and beside them to write the names of actors they would cast in each role. Suggest that students support each suggestion by listing other parts those actors have had that would recommend them for this production.
L2 **COLLAB. LEARN.**

it is proper that I should, in the true spirit of romantic story, give some account of the looks and equipment of my hero and his steed. The animal he bestrode was a broken-down plow horse that had outlived almost everything but his viciousness. He was gaunt[38] and shaggy, with a thin neck and a head like a hammer; his rusty mane and tail were tangled and knotted with burrs. Still, he must have had fire in his day, if we may judge from the name he bore of Gunpowder.

Ichabod was a suitable figure for such a steed. He rode with short stirrups, which brought his knees nearly up to the pommel[39] of the saddle; his sharp elbows stuck out like grasshoppers'. He carried his whip perpendicularly in his hand, and, as his horse jogged on, the motion of his arms was not unlike the flapping of a pair of wings.

It was toward evening that Ichabod arrived at the castle of the Heer Van Tassel, which he found thronged[40] with the pride and flower of the adjacent country. Brom Bones, however, was a hero of the scene, having come to the gathering on his favorite steed, Daredevil, a creature, like himself, full of mettle[41] and mischief, which no one but himself could manage.

I pause to dwell upon the world of charms that burst upon the enraptured gaze of my hero as he entered the state parlor of Van Tassel's mansion. Not those of the lasses, but the ample charms of a genuine Dutch country tea table. There was the doughty doughnut, the tenderer olykoek, and the crisp and crumbling cruller;[42] sweet cakes and shortcakes, ginger cakes and honey cakes, and the whole family of cakes. And then there were apple pies and peach pies and pumpkin pies, besides slices of ham and smoked beef; not to mention broiled shad[43] and roasted chickens.

I want breath and time to discuss this banquet as it deserves, and am too eager to get on with my story. Happily, Ichabod Crane was not in so great a hurry as his historian, but did ample justice to every dainty.

He could not help, too, rolling his large eyes round him as he ate, and chuckling with the possibility that he might one day be lord of all this scene of almost unimaginable luxury and splendor. Then, he thought, how soon he'd turn his back upon the old schoolhouse and kick any itinerant[44] pedagogue out-of-doors that should dare to call him comrade!

And now the sound of the music from the common room, or hall, summoned to the dance. How could the flogger of urchins[45] be otherwise than animated and joyous? The lady of his heart was his partner in the dance, and smiling graciously in reply to all his amorous looks, while Brom Bones, sorely smitten with[46] love and jealousy, sat brooding by himself in one corner.

When the dance was at an end, Ichabod was attracted to a knot of the sager[47] folks, who, with old Van Tassel, sat smoking at one end of the piazza, gossiping over former

38. *Gaunt* means "looking like skin and bones."
39. The *pommel* of a saddle is the part that juts out at the front and top.
40. *Thronged* means "crowded."
41. *Mettle* is spirit and courage.
42. The *doughty* (dō′ tē), *olykoek* (ol′ i kook′), and *cruller* (krul′ ər) are three types of pastries.
43. *Shad* is a kind of fish.
44. *Itinerant* (ī tin′ ər ənt) means "traveling from place to place."
45. A *flogger of urchins* is one who whips children.
46. *Amorous* (am′ ər əs) means "loving; romantic." *Sorely smitten with* means "extremely affected by."
47. *Sager* (sāj′ ər) means "wiser" or "better educated."

M Active Reading Strategies

REVIEW How does the author create a comical picture of Ichabod Crane? *(He describes his awkward physique and some of the foolish activities in which the schoolmaster engages.)*

Vocabulary Skills

Word Meaning In the sentence "I want breath and time to discuss this banquet . . . ," the word *want* means "lack."

N Critical Thinking

INFERRING Ask students to which they think Ichabod is more attracted, Katrina or her wealth. Have them find support for their answers in the text.

Real-World Connection

Television Transcript Help students conduct their own television discussion and make an audio- and/or videorecording of it. Explain that the printed version of the discussion is the transcript.

Activity Ask students to picture themselves on a panel that recommends scripts for made-for-television movies. Have the class break into groups to discuss adapting "The Legend of Sleepy Hollow" for television. Students should answer such questions as *What qualities do you look for in a suspense movie? What does this story have that meets those criteria? What does it lack? Where would you film this story? What kind of special effects would you use? What audience would you target? Why? Why do you think modern audiences would be interested in a story more than 150 years old?* **L2** **COLLAB. LEARN.**

Active Reading Strategies (O)

EVALUATE What do the ghost stories have to do with the rest of the plot? How do they affect Ichabod? *(They set the mood of the story and reveal Ichabod's superstitious nature.)*

Literary Elements (P)

MOOD How does the author's having the characters exchange ghost stories affect the mood of the story? *(It builds up a sense that something frightening will happen.)*

Active Reading Strategies (Q)

RESPOND Ask students how they feel about Ichabod. Why does Katrina change her mind about him? *(Possible answer: She may respect him as a teacher but is not interested in him romantically.)*

Historical Note

John André (1750–1780) was the British officer assigned to negotiate with American general Benedict Arnold, who was ready to betray West Point to the British. André was captured by American forces as he returned to his post. Because he was in civilian clothes and carried incriminating papers (in his boots), he was tried and hanged as a spy.

Teaching Support

times, and drawing out long stories about the war. But all these were nothing to the tales of ghosts and apparitions that succeeded.[48] Many dismal tales were told about funeral trains and mourning cries and wailings heard and seen about the great tree where the unfortunate Major André was taken, and which stood in the neighborhood. The chief part of the stories, however, turned upon the favorite specter of Sleepy Hollow, the Headless Horseman, who had been heard several times of late, patrolling the country, and, it was said, tethered his horse nightly among the graves in the churchyard.

The tale was told of old Brouwer, a disbeliever in ghosts, how he met the horseman returning from his foray into Sleepy Hollow, and was obliged to get up behind him; how they galloped over bush and brake, over hill and swamp, until they reached the bridge, when the horseman suddenly turned into a skeleton, threw old Brouwer into a brook, and sprang away over the treetops with a clap of thunder.

This story was immediately matched by a thrice-marvelous adventure of Brom Bones, who made light of the Galloping Hessian as an arrant jockey. He affirmed[49] that, on returning one night from the neighboring village of Sing Sing, he had been overtaken by this midnight trooper; that he had offered to race with him for a bowl of punch, and should have won it, too, for Daredevil beat the goblin horse all hollow, but, just as they came to the church bridge, the Hessian bolted, and vanished in a flash of fire.

All these tales sank deep in the mind of Ichabod. He repaid them in kind with large extracts[50] from his invaluable author, Cotton Mather, and added many fearful sights which he had seen in his nightly walks about Sleepy Hollow.

The revel now gradually broke up. Ichabod only lingered behind, according to the custom of country lovers, to have a tête-à-tête[51] with the heiress, fully convinced that he was now on the high road to success. What passed at this interview I will not pretend to say, for in fact I do not know. Something, however, must have gone wrong, for he certainly sallied forth, after no very great interval, with an air quite desolate and chopfallen.[52] Without looking to the right or left to notice the scene of rural wealth on which he had so often gloated, he went straight to the stable, and with several hearty cuffs and kicks, roused his steed most uncourteously from the comfortable quarters.

It was the very witching time of night that Ichabod, heavy-hearted and crestfallen, pursued his travel homewards.

All the stories of ghosts and goblins that he had heard in the afternoon now came crowding upon his recollection. He had never felt so lonely and dismal. He was, moreover, approaching the very place where many of the scenes of the ghost stories had been laid. In the center of the road stood an enormous tulip tree. It was connected with the tragical story of the unfortunate André, who had been taken prisoner close by, and was universally known by the name of Major André's Tree.

48. Here, *succeeded* means "followed; came after."
49. *Made light of* means "joked about." *Arrant* (ar′ ənt) means "outright." *Affirmed* means "stated firmly and positively."
50. *Extracts* are passages or images from a book.
51. A *tête-à-tête* (tet′ ə tet′) is a private conversation between two people.
52. *Sallied forth* means "went out briskly." Someone who is *chopfallen* is discouraged or downhearted.

Meeting Individual Needs: ADVANCED LEARNERS

Filling in the Blanks Point out that all we know of Ichabod's interview with Katrina is that she rejected him. The author does not know why, he says, but that does not mean that readers cannot imagine the scene and conjecture.

Activity Suggest that students, working in pairs, imagine the scene and write a description of it through the eyes of various people as they might have recorded it in a journal: Katrina, her mother and father, Ichabod, and Bones. Have students share their versions. **L3** **COLLAB. LEARN.**

About two hundred yards from the tree a small brook crossed the road, and ran into a marshy and thickly wooded glen, known by the name of Wiley's Swamp. A few rough logs, laid side by side, served for a bridge over this stream. To pass this bridge was the severest trial. It was at this identical spot that the unfortunate André was captured. This has ever since been considered a haunted stream, and fearful are the feelings of the schoolboy who has to pass it alone after dark.

Illustration © 1992 by Michael Garland from *The Legend of Sleepy Hollow.*
Viewing the painting: How could you explain this picture if you hadn't read the story?

R As he approached the stream his heart began to thump. He summoned up, however, all his resolution, gave his horse half a score of kicks in the ribs, and attempted to dash briskly across the bridge. But instead of starting forward, the perverse old animal made a lateral[53] movement, and ran broadside against the fence. Ichabod, whose fears increased with the delay, jerked the reins on the other side and kicked lustily with the opposite foot. It was all in vain. His steed started, it is true, but it was only to plunge to the opposite side of the road into a thicket of brambles and alder bushes. Just at this moment a splashing step by the side of the bridge caught the sensitive ear of Ichabod. In the dark shadow of the grove, on the margin of the brook, he beheld something huge, misshapen, black, and

53. *Perverse* means "stubbornly determined to go against what is expected or desired." *Lateral* means "sideways."

VIEWING THE ART

Viewing Response *Students may suggest a legend of their own.*

R Literary Elements

CLIMAX Ask students to describe how the author builds to the climax. *(He creates a sense of terror by letting readers feel Ichabod's fear.)*

Reading Minilesson

Predicting Point out to students that the author has prepared his readers for Ichabod Crane's scary ride home by telling of the schoolmaster's interest in, and fear of, ghosts.

Activity Ask students to use the author's hints and clues to predict what will happen to Ichabod Crane on his late-night ride. Have them write their predictions down and check them when they finish the story. **L2**

Additional Resources

Reading Skills Practice Workbook

Vo•cab•u•lar•y Skills

A Glossary of Horror Point out to students that this story employs words used in many suspense stories. Share with them this glossary of horror:

apparition—a ghostly figure

demon—evil spirit

ghost—the soul of a dead person

goblin—evil or mischievous sprite

specter—disembodied spirit

spirit—supernatural being

supernatural—beyond the normal universe; ghostly

witch—a woman with evil supernatural powers

S Critical Thinking

EVALUATE Ask students what they think of how Ichabod behaves when faced with the thing he fears most. Is his behavior as they expected, or does Ichabod surprise them? Use the following model to illustrate the thinking process in evaluating.

Model: Ichabod Crane must be terrified, because he believes in ghosts. I know I would be. But it seems to me that he shows some real self-control despite his terror. He keeps thinking of ways to escape, such as trying to reach the bridge to escape the horseman. I think, yes, that's what I'd do in the same situation. This surprises me, because I sort of expect him to be more cowardly.

towering. It stirred not, but seemed gathered up in the gloom, like some gigantic monster ready to spring upon the traveler.

The hair of the affrighted pedagogue rose upon his head with terror. What was to be done? To turn and fly was now too late; and besides, what chance was there of escaping ghost or goblin, if such it was, which could ride upon the wings of the wind? Summoning up, therefore, a show of courage, he demanded in stammering accents, "Who are you?" He received no reply. He repeated his demand in a still more agitated voice. Still there was no answer. Just then the shadowy object of alarm put itself in motion, and, with a scramble and a bound, stood at once in the middle of the road. Though the night was dark and dismal, yet the form of the unknown might now in some degree be made out. He appeared to be a horseman of large dimensions, and mounted on a black horse of powerful frame. He made no offer of harm or sociability, but kept aloof on one side of the road, jogging along on the blind side of old Gunpowder, who had now got over his fright and waywardness.

S Ichabod, who had no relish[54] for this strange midnight companion, and bethought himself of the adventure of Brom Bones with the Galloping Hessian, now quickened his steed, in hopes of leaving him behind. The stranger, however, quickened his horse to an equal pace. Ichabod pulled up and fell into a walk, thinking to lag behind—the other did the same. There was something in the moody and dogged silence of this persistent companion that was mysterious and appalling. It was soon fearfully accounted for. On mounting a rising ground, which brought the figure of his fellow traveler in relief against the sky, gigantic in height, and muffled in a cloak, Ichabod was horror-struck on perceiving that he was headless—but his horror was still more increased on observing that the head, which should have rested on his shoulders, was carried before him on the pommel of the saddle. His terror rose to desperation. He rained a shower of kicks and blows upon Gunpowder, hoping, by a sudden movement, to give his companion the slip—but the specter started full jump with him.

They had now reached the road which turns off to Sleepy Hollow; but Gunpowder, who seemed possessed with a demon, instead of keeping on it, made an opposite turn, and plunged headlong downhill to the left. This road leads through a sandy hollow, and just beyond swells the green knoll on which stands the whitewashed church.

As yet the panic of the steed had given his unskillful rider an apparent advantage in the chase; but just as he had got halfway through the hollow the girths[55] of the saddle gave way, and he felt it slipping from under him. He seized it by the pommel, and endeavored to hold it firm, but in vain; and he had just time to save himself by clasping old Gunpowder round the neck, when the saddle fell to the earth, and he heard it trampled underfoot by his pursuer. The goblin was hard on his

54. *Relish for* means "enjoyment of" or "interest in."

55. *Girths* are straps passed under the horse's belly to hold the saddle on.

Vocabulary
aloof (ə lo͞of′) *adj.* emotionally distant; uninvolved; standoffish

Teaching Support

Writing Minilesson

Following a Model Point out that, after more than 150 years, this early suspense story is still a good example of the genre. Ask students to consider using it as a model for a suspense story they may write.

Activity Have students list the elements of this story that make it a good model for a modern-day suspense story. *(The list may include the following: an eerie setting, a superstitious main character, a conflict between two opposite kinds of characters, rumors of ghosts, events that could be explained as being supernatural.)* Encourage students to write the opening scene for a story, incorporating one or more of these elements. **L2**

Additional Resources

Writer's Choice, Lesson 3.2

haunches; and (unskillful rider that he was!) he had much ado to maintain his seat, sometimes slipping on one side, sometimes on another, and sometimes jolted on the high ridge of his horse's backbone, with a violence that he feared would cleave him asunder.[56]

T An opening in the trees now cheered him with the hopes that the church bridge was at hand. He recollected the place where Brom Bones's ghostly competitor had disappeared. "If I can but reach that bridge," thought Ichabod, "I am safe." Just then he heard the black steed panting and blowing close behind him; he even fancied that he felt his hot breath. Another convulsive kick in the ribs, and old Gunpowder sprang upon the bridge; he thundered over the resounding planks; he gained the opposite side; and now Ichabod cast a look behind to see if his pursuer would vanish, according to the rule, in a flash of fire and brimstone.[57] Just then he saw the goblin rising in his stirrups, and in the very act of hurling his head at him. U Ichabod endeavored to dodge the horrible missile, but too late. It encountered his cranium with a tremendous crash—he was tumbled headlong into the dust, and Gunpowder, the black steed, and the goblin rider passed by like a whirlwind.

The next morning the old horse was found without his saddle, and with the bridle under his feet, soberly cropping the grass at his master's gate. Ichabod did not make his appearance at breakfast—dinner hour came, but no Ichabod. The boys assembled at the schoolhouse, and strolled idly about the banks of the brook, but no schoolmaster. An inquiry was set on foot, and after diligent investigation they came upon his traces. In one part of the road leading to the church was found the saddle trampled in the dirt. The tracks of horses' hoofs deeply dented in the road, and evidently at furious speed, were traced to the bridge, beyond which, on the bank of a broad part of the brook, where the water ran deep and black, was found the hat of the unfortunate Ichabod, and close beside it a shattered pumpkin.

The brook was searched, but the body of the schoolmaster was not to be discovered. The mysterious event caused much speculation at the church on the following Sunday. Knots of gazers and gossips were collected in the churchyard, at the bridge, and at the spot where the hat and pumpkin had been found. The stories of Brouwer, of Bones, and a whole store of others, were called to mind; and when they had diligently considered them all, and compared them with the symptoms of the present case, they shook their heads, and came to the conclusion that Ichabod had been carried off by the Galloping Hessian. As he was a bachelor, and in nobody's debt, nobody troubled his head any more about him. The school was removed to a different quarter of the Hollow, and another pedagogue reigned in his stead.

It is true, an old farmer, who had been down to New York on a visit several years after, and from whom this account of the ghostly adventure was received, brought home word that Ichabod Crane was still alive; that he had left the neighborhood, partly through fear of the goblin and

56. *Much ado* is great difficulty. To *cleave him asunder* means "to tear him to pieces."

57. *Brimstone* is smelly, yellow smoke. The "flash" would show that the goblin was from hell, which is said to burn with fire and brimstone.

T Active Reading Strategies

VISUALIZE Read aloud the first full paragraph on page 827. Ask students how they visualize what is described in this paragraph. *(Some students might guess it is Brom who is following Ichabod.)*

U Author's Craft

SENSORY WORDS Have students pick out sensory words that add power to the climactic chase. That is, what sounds do they hear? What do they see? Feel? *(They hear the black steed panting and blowing, and they feel his breath; they hear the horses thundering over the bridge; they see the pursuer rise in his stirrups and hurl his head; they hear and feel the missile hit Ichabod's head and sense his falling to the ground as the goblin rider passes by in a whirlwind.)*

Meeting Individual Needs: SPECIAL NEEDS

Learning Disabled Learning-disabled students may have difficulty visualizing what Ichabod Crane experienced on his wild ride.

Activity To help students understand the events, draw the following chart on the board and help students complete it as they reread the narrative of the ride. **L1**

What he saw	What he did
pp. 825–26: He saw something huge.	He asked, "Who's there?"
p. 825: He saw a large shadow in the road.	

Additional Resources

Inclusion Strategies

Active Reading Strategies

EVALUATE Is it clear that something supernatural happened? Ask students whether another explanation is possible. *(No. Bones probably put a cloak over his head and carried a pumpkin in his hand. He wanted to scare away the man he thought was his rival for Katrina's affections.)*

VIEWING THE ART

Russ Flint's illustrations are most often seen in books for young children.

Viewing Response *Students should note that the bridge is obviously old.*

Thematic Focus

Hair-Raising Tales Ask students whether the term *hair-raising tales* is appropriate for this genre. Why? Point out the first sentence of the first full paragraph on page 826: "The hair of the affrighted pedagogue rose upon his head with terror." Call on volunteers to recount similar experiences that they have had.

ASSESSMENT

Quick Checks, p. 67

FINE ART TRANSPARENCY 15

You may want to use ***Fine Art Transparency 15*** to discuss rural life in the 1800s.

partly in mortification[58] at having been suddenly dismissed by the heiress. Brom Bones, too, who shortly after his rival's disappearance conducted the blooming Katrina in triumph to the altar, was observed to look exceedingly knowing whenever the story of Ichabod was related, and always burst into a hearty laugh at the mention of the pumpkin, which led some to suspect that he knew more about the matter than he chose to tell.

The old country wives, however, who are the best judges of these matters, maintain to this day that Ichabod was spirited away by supernatural means.[59] The bridge became more than ever an object of superstitious awe; the schoolhouse, being deserted, soon fell to decay, and was reported to be haunted by the ghost of the unfortunate pedagogue; and the plowboy, loitering homeward of a still summer evening, has often fancied his voice at a distance, chanting a melancholy psalm tune among the tranquil solitudes[60] of Sleepy Hollow.

58. *Mortification* is great shame or embarrassment.

59. The country wives blamed Crane's disappearance on ghosts or some other unnatural, unearthly methods.

60. *Solitudes* are lonely, isolated places.

Illustration © 1990 by Russ Flint from *The Legend of Sleepy Hollow.*

Viewing the painting: Could this be a modern scene? Why or why not?

Teaching Support

Grammar and Language *Minilesson*

Complex Sentences Remind students of the following points: A complex sentence has a main clause and one or more subordinate clauses. A subordinate clause is a group of words that has a subject and a predicate but does not express a complete thought and cannot stand alone as a sentence.

Write the following sentence on the board, without underlining, and have students identify the subordinate clause (1 line) and the main clause (2 lines).

He recollected the place where Brom Bones's ghostly competitor had disappeared.

Activity Have each student write three complex sentences about the story. Then have pairs trade sentences to identify the main and subordinate clauses.

L2 COLLAB. LEARN.

Additional Resources

Grammar and Language Transparency 66

Grammar and Language Workbook, p. 157

Grammar and Composition Handbook, Lesson 8.2

Writer's Choice, Lesson 14.2

Active Reading and Critical Thinking

Responding to Literature

PERSONAL RESPONSE

◆ What would you do if you thought you were being chased by a ghostly figure? Jot down a few words of advice for Ichabod Crane.

Brackets connect questions that are paired to develop higher-level thinking skills.

Analyzing Literature

RECALL

1. What does Ichabod Crane look like? Cite details from the story.
2. How does Crane spend his afternoons and evenings?
3. Why does Crane become rivals with Brom Bones?
4. According to the townspeople, what happened to Crane?

INTERPRET

5. Why is Ichabod Crane's physical appearance important in this story?
6. What does Crane's fascination with the supernatural tell us about his character?
7. Why is Crane interested in Katrina? Why might Crane think Katrina would be interested in him? Give several reasons for your answers.
8. What do you suppose really happened to Crane? What in the story supports your answer?

EVALUATE AND CONNECT

9. Think back to the ghostly stories you discussed in the **Reading Focus** on page 815. What elements do they have in common with "The Legend of Sleepy Hollow"? Why do you think writers of scary stories often use so many of the same elements?
10. In your opinion, did Ichabod Crane deserve the fate that befell him? Why or why not?

LITERARY ELEMENTS

Literary Legend

A **legend** is a type of folktale—a story believed to be based on a historical event. Legends often exaggerate the truth. For example, many legends give characters extraordinary abilities that they did not possess in real life. Many legends were originally oral tales, but most have now been written down. A legend becomes a **literary legend** when a published version of the story is the form that is familiar to most people.

1. What aspects of "The Legend of Sleepy Hollow" might be based in fact?
2. How might the publication of a legend affect the original (oral) story?
3. What other literary legends can you name?

● See **Literary Terms Handbook,** p. R5.

Responding to the Selection

PERSONAL RESPONSE

Most students will say they would try to escape.

Analyzing Literature

1. He is tall and thin. His frame is loose, with narrow shoulders, long arms and legs, hands that dangle out of his sleeves, and big feet.
2. He spends his afternoons and evenings reading and discussing tales of witchcraft, ghosts, and goblins.
3. Crane becomes a rival of Brom Bones when both are courting Katrina Van Tassel.
4. The townspeople conclude that Crane has been carried off by the galloping Hessian.
5. Crane's appearance is important to the story because, as the author suggests, it seems somewhat threatening. The author compares it to the spirit of famine or a scarecrow. It also gives the story a comic touch.
6. It tells us that if someone pretends to be a ghost, Crane will likely believe this to be true.
7. Crane is interested mainly in the money Katrina—and her future husband—will inherit. The young women of the town respect the schoolmaster's apparent learning. Crane also has a high opinion of himself. At first, Katrina seems to encourage his attention.
8. Crane probably ran away and found a place in another town. The story refers to the farmer, who supposedly has told this tale to the author and says that he "brought home word that Ichabod Crane was still alive."
9. Students' answers may include such elements as eerie setting, scary characters, unexplained sights and sounds, and strange events.
10. Yes, because he was a foolish and not particularly nice person. No, because there were nicer ways that Brom Bones might have competed with his rival, especially since Katrina rejected him.

LITERARY ELEMENTS

1. The setting is real. Cotton Mather and Major André were real. Hessians did fight with the British army.
2. It might establish one version of the story as authoritative.
3. Casey Jones, John Henry, and Johnny Appleseed are literary legends.

Additional Resources

Literary Elements Transparency 67

HAIR-RAISING TALES 829

Literature and Writing

Writing About Literature

Students' stories should

- reveal something new about the story
- be consistent with the events of the original story

Creative Writing

Students' legends should

- explain something that could happen where they live
- provide an explanation that is consistent with the events they describe

If some students are reluctant to read their legends aloud, suggest that they practice privately to insure that their delivery will be fluent.

Extending Your Response

Learning for Life Encourage students to write their memos in the tone of someone who is used to getting what she or he wants.

Literature Groups Suggest that students sum up their findings by using a graphic device such as a chart or Venn diagram. COLLAB. LEARN.

Literature and Writing

Writing About Literature

Point of View "The Legend of Sleepy Hollow" is told from a **third-person point of view,** that is, by a narrator who is not a character in the story. How might this story be different if told from a character's point of view? Imagine you are Katrina or Ichabod or any other character, and rewrite a section of the story from that point of view.

Creative Writing

Urban Legends Have you heard that alligators live in the sewers of New York City? This story is an **urban legend,** a contemporary tale based on events that seem possible, but probably did not occur. With a partner, write an urban legend. Begin with something scary or strange that could happen where you live. Brainstorm ways to exaggerate your tale. Share your legend with the class.

Extending Your Response

Learning for Life

Casting Actors Imagine you are directing a movie version of "The Legend of Sleepy Hollow." Write a **memo** to a casting agent describing the actor you want for each major character. Include specific talents and characteristics you require of each.

interNET CONNECTION

"Legend" on the Web Pay a virtual visit to Sleepy Hollow and Tarrytown. Type the names of these places into a search engine, and visit Web sites to learn more about the region, the legend, and Washington Irving.

Literature Groups

Compare American Legends How does "The Legend of Sleepy Hollow" compare with other American legends, such as those about Johnny Appleseed and Davy Crockett? Brainstorm a list of American legends that includes Irving's story. Discuss how the tales are similar and different. Present your conclusions to the class.

Johnny Appleseed

Reading Further

For strange tales from other places, try:

Wings of a Falcon by Cynthia Voigt

Haunted Waters by Mary Pope Osborne

Save your work for your portfolio.

Skill Minilessons

RETEACH • REVIEW

GRAMMAR AND LANGUAGE • VARYING SENTENCE STRUCTURE

Many sentences follow a set pattern:
subject + verb + direct object or predicate noun
(A **direct object** receives the action of the verb. A **predicate noun** follows a linking verb and renames the subject.)
Ichabod Crane [subject] *had* [verb] *a soft and foolish heart* [direct object].
However, you can add rhythm to your writing by rearranging the order of sentence elements so that you don't always start with the subject.
A soft and foolish heart [direct object] *had* [verb] *Ichabod Crane* [subject].

- For more about sentence structure, see **Language Handbook,** pp. R32–R33.

PRACTICE Rewrite the following sentences by changing the order of sentence elements.

1. The schoolhouse was a low building with one large room.
2. Ichabod Crane was a schoolmaster to remember.
3. A dreamy atmosphere hung over the valley where Ichabod Crane lived.
4. Brom Bones brooded, worried by his love.
5. The sad animal Crane rode was a broken-down plow horse.

READING AND THINKING • CAUSE AND EFFECT

In "The Legend of Sleepy Hollow," Washington Irving uses a string of cause-and-effect relationships. For example, Crane's fearful imagination causes him to believe in the story of the Headless Horseman.

PRACTICE Complete each sentence to show the effect of the cause. Then explain in writing how the three effects you named caused the final event in the story.

1. Because Ichabod admires the rich property of Baltus Van Tassel, he ______ .
2. Because Brom Bones loves Katrina, he ______ .
3. Because Ichabod believed in the story of the Headless Horseman, he ______ .

- For more about text structures and cause and effect, see **Reading Handbook,** p. R97.

VOCABULARY • THE LATIN ROOT *SPEC*

The word *speculation* comes from the Latin root *spec,* which means "to see or look at." This root is found in many words, often with a prefix that modifies its meaning. For example, if you *suspect* someone or something, you "look under" the surface. The prefix *sus-* is the same as *sub-* and means "under." The following prefixes have been attached to *spec:*

intro-: inside *circum-:* around
retro-: back *pro-:* forward

PRACTICE Use the meaning of *spec* and the prefixes listed to complete each statement.

1. If you are a *circumspect* person, you are
   a. clumsy c. fast
   b. careful d. humorous
2. *Introspective* people pay attention to
   a. neighbors c. feelings
   b. clothing d. classmates
3. To look at something in *retrospect* is to look
   a. afterwards c. through a telescope
   b. with regret d. beforehand

ASSESSMENT

- ***Quick Checks,*** p. 67
- ***Selection and Theme Assessment,*** pp. 115–116
- ***Performance Assessment,*** p. 59
- ***Testmaker: ExamView Pro***
- ***Interactive Tutor: Self-Assessment***

Skill Minilessons

GRAMMAR AND LANGUAGE
VARYING SENTENCE STRUCTURE

1. A low building with one large room was the schoolhouse.
2. A schoolmaster to remember was Ichabod Crane.
3. Over the valley where Ichabod Crane lived hung a dreamy atmosphere.
4. Worried by his love, Brom Bones brooded.
5. A broken-down plow horse was the sad animal Crane rode.

READING AND THINKING
CAUSE AND EFFECT

1. . . . courts Tassel's daughter, Katrina.
2. . . . frightens Crane away from her.
3. . . . was terrified by the figure he saw.

Crane's courting of Katrina sets in motion the chain of events that leads to the climax of the story, when the supposed apparition so terrifies Crane that he runs away, never to return.

VOCABULARY
LATIN ROOT *SPEC*

1. b
2. c
3. a

Additional Resources

- ***Grammar and Language Workbook,*** p. 323
- ***Grammar and Composition Handbook,*** Lesson 8.2
- ***Writer's Choice,*** Lesson 14.1
- ***Reading Skils Practice Workbook***
- ***Vocabulary Practice,*** p. 46

GENRE FOCUS

Objective

- To understand the elements of a suspense story

Teaching Strategies

Explain that writers of suspense stories use all elements of a story—characters, setting, conflict, and climax—to intensify the excitement and suspense. Tell students to think about a suspense story they would like to write so they can apply what they learn to their own work.

Characters Remind students that Ichabod Crane is a rather foolish man. The author establishes Crane's weaknesses early so readers will understand why he does the things he does when confronted with a supposed ghost.

Setting Point out that the setting of "The Legend of Sleepy Hollow" is especially suited to a suspense story because of historical events that occurred in Sleepy Hollow.

Conflict and Climax Ask students to notice how crisp and direct the author's narrative is in his description of the scariest moment in the story.

Teaching Support

GENRE FOCUS

SUSPENSE STORY

What keeps your eyes glued to the pages of a mystery, a horror story, or a spooky tale? Writers of these stories are experts in the art of suspense—the building excitement and anxiety that pulls readers into a story and keeps them hooked until the end. To create this tension and arouse curiosity, writers give special attention to the elements described below.

MODEL: "The Legend of Sleepy Hollow"

CHARACTERS The main characters are full-bodied. They are described in detail, so that readers learn about their appearance, actions, and thoughts–including their fears. For example, in "The Legend of Sleepy Hollow," readers see that Ichabod Crane's imagination often gets the better of him, especially after a night spent telling ghost stories.

> What fearful shapes and shadows beset his path amidst the dim and ghastly glare of a snowy night! And how often was he thrown into complete dismay by some rushing blast, howling among the trees, in the idea that it was the Galloping Hessian on one of his nightly scourings!

SETTING Every detail about the setting contributes to the feeling of tension, and sometimes, of foreboding. This tension can be achieved by making the setting obviously mysterious and frightening, as illustrated in the model on the right. However it can also be achieved more subtly by making the setting unnaturally ordinary or perfect and leaving the reader feeling uneasy.

> . . . a small brook crossed the road, and ran into a marshy and thickly wooded glen, known by the name of Wiley's Swamp. A few rough logs, laid side by side, served for a bridge over this stream. . . .This has . . . been considered a haunted stream, and fearful are the feelings of the schoolboy who has to pass it alone after dark.

CONFLICT AND CLIMAX The conflicts, or problems, that the characters experience lead to the moment of most intense excitement, called the *climax.* In the resolution of a suspense story, the source of the conflict or problem is usually revealed, but the problem may or may not be solved.

> Just then [Ichabod] saw the goblin rising in his stirrups, and in the very act of hurling his head at him.

Listening and Speaking *Minilesson*

Reading Aloud Remind students that many suspense stories were first passed on orally. For the story to be effective, the storyteller had to use not only the words of the story but his or her voice to convey the tension that such stories evoke.

Activity Ask for volunteers to read aloud the three models on this page. After hearing everyone read, encourage them to assess their own readings and offer ideas on how to add to the tension. Suggestions may include stressing certain words, varying the pace, changing pitch, and exaggerating facial expressions and posture. **L2** COLLAB. LEARN.

ACTIVE READING MODEL

Active Reading Strategies

Tips for Reading a Suspense Story

Suspense stories can keep you reading for hours if you are an active reader. You'll get more out of the story if you talk to yourself as it unfolds. Use the following strategies to help you enjoy the suspense stories in this theme.

- For more about reading strategies, see **Reading Handbook,** pp. R81–R118.

QUESTION

As the plot twists and turns, you may feel like racing ahead in the story to find out what happens. However, be sure you understand details.

Ask Yourself . . . What does this conversation tell about the characters? Why is this background information in the story? What will it tell me that I need to know?

PREDICT

Look for clues that suggest what might happen next, and then make predictions about the story's outcome. Later, as you continue to read, verify or adjust your predictions.

Ask Yourself . . . What are the possible outcomes? Which one is most likely? Is this character clever enough or brave enough to find a way out of this dilemma?

CONNECT

Let yourself be carried away by the tension and excitement.

Ask Yourself . . . What would I do in this situation? What advice would I give these characters?

APPLYING THE STRATEGIES

Read the next selection, "The Tell-Tale Heart." As you read, use the **Active Reading Model** notes in the margins to help you enjoy the selection.

Active Reading Strategies

Objective

- To understand and apply strategies for reading and comprehending suspense stories

Teaching Strategies

Point out that in a suspense story, looking ahead may relieve some of the nearly unbearable tension; but reading more slowly gives readers time to question, predict, and respond. These techniques allow readers to appreciate more fully the development of characters and action.

Question

Students need to recognize that questioning need not interrupt the flow of reading. Their questioning may be merely a response or moment of curiosity about the introduction of an idea or clue.

Predict

Predicting the outcome of a suspense story is a way of participating in the dilemmas of the characters.

Connect

Ask students to recall their reaction to what Ichabod Crane saw. If they found themselves thinking about running as fast as they could as if they were there, they were responding just as the author wanted them to.

Teaching Support

Reading Journal

Encourage students to use their reading journals to record ideas and responses as they read.

Activity Ask students if they have ever had the impulse, when watching a suspense film, to warn the characters of impending danger. Suggest that they write down their warning in their journals as they read "The Tell-Tale Heart." They might answer any of the following questions:

- How could I change the tragic outcome of this story?
- What kind of ending would I like to see instead?
- If I were a character in this drama, how could I bring about that change?

Before students begin reading "The Tell-Tale Heart" on page 835, share with them the examples of reading journal entries in the front part of this Teacher's Wraparound Edition.

Before Reading

Objectives

- To read and analyze a short story that explores how terror and fear affect an unbalanced person
- To identify mood in a short story
- To write an analysis of a scary scene

Skills

Reading/Thinking: Evaluating; Identifying Author's Purpose; Drawing Conclusions; Inferring
Writing: Report
Vocabulary: Analogies
Grammar/Language: Kinds of Sentences
Listening/Speaking: Role-Playing
Life Skills: Presenting an Argument
Collaboration: Literature Groups

Motivating STUDENTS

Literature Launchers: "The Master of the Macabre"

Videodisc Side B, Segment 22

Also available in VHS.

Selection Focus Transparency 63: Before presenting the painting, ask students how artists might represent their ideas about themselves in a self-portrait.

Reading Focus: Discuss students' answers to the question *Do we see ourselves as others see us?*

ACTIVE READING MODEL

Before You Read

The Tell-Tale Heart

MEET EDGAR ALLAN POE

"I was never *really* insane, except on occasions where my heart was touched," Edgar Allan Poe once wrote to his mother-in-law. During his life, Poe was known for writing about mysterious forces, wicked crimes, and death. Unfortunately, his life was as sad as those of most of his characters. He was poor for most of his life. His mother died when he was two, and he was disowned by his foster father. In addition, Poe's wife died when she was only twenty-four.

Edgar Allan Poe was born in 1809 and died in 1849. "The Tell-Tale Heart" was first published in Pioneer *magazine in January 1843.*

READING FOCUS

Do we see ourselves as others see us?

FreeWrite
How is the way people view themselves different from the way others view them? Freewrite your answer.

Setting a Purpose
Read this short story to find out what the narrator thinks about himself and the acts he has committed.

BUILDING BACKGROUND

Did You Know? Poe spent most of his life writing poetry, beginning as a teenager and sacrificing material comforts for twenty years so that he could concentrate on his art. The success he finally found with his poem "The Raven" didn't improve his financial status. The poem was reprinted and parodied everywhere, and Poe was invited to tour the country lecturing and reading his work. However, he was paid less than $15 for the poem, and lecturing paid barely enough to support him. Three years after "The Raven" came out, Poe still could not afford to keep his house warm during his wife's final battle with tuberculosis.

VOCABULARY PREVIEW

acute (ə kūt′) *adj.* sharp and strong or intense; p. 835
vex (veks) *v.* to disturb, annoy, or anger, especially by some small, repeated action; p. 836
stifled (stī′ fəld) *adj.* held back; smothered; p. 837
wane (wān) *v.* to draw to a close; approach an end; p. 839
audacity (ô das′ ə tē) *n.* reckless boldness; daring; p. 840
singularly (sing′ gyə lər lē) *adv.* unusually or remarkably; extraordinarily; p. 841
vehemently (vē′ ə mənt lē) *adv.* strongly; intensely; passionately; p. 841
hypocritical (hip′ ə krit′ i kəl) *adj.* pretending to be what one is not; fake; insincere; p. 841

RESOURCE MANAGER

Teaching Tools and Resources
- Theme Eight Planning Guide
- Literature Groups Sourcebook

Essential Lesson Support
Lesson-Specific Instruction
- Selection Focus Transparency 63
- Literary Elements Transparency 68
- Active Reading Guide,* p. 68
- Selection Vocabulary Practice, p. 47
- inTIME magazine, pp. 22-23

Assessment
- Selection Quick Checks,* p. 68
- Sel. and Theme Assmt., pp. 117–118
- Testmaker: ExamView Pro
- Performance Assessment, p. 60

Systematic Language Instruction
- Gr. & Comp. Hbk., L. 14.1, 14.2

English Language Learners
- ELL Sourcebook, p. 95
- Spanish Summaries, p. 63
- Spanish Translations, pp. 222-226
- Audio Library*
- English, Yes!

Special Needs/Strat. Interven.
- Interactive Rdg. Sbk., pp. T215–T218
- Interactive Rdg. Wkbk., pp. 129–130
- Inclusion Strat. Sbk., pp. 41–42
- Audio Library*

* Also available in Spanish

The Tell-Tale Heart

Edgar Allan Poe

ACTIVE READING MODEL

E!—NERVOUS—VERY, VERY DREADFULLY NERVOUS been and am; but why *will* you say that I am mad? The dis- had sharpened my senses—not destroyed—not dulled them. e all was the sense of hearing acute. I heard all things in the n and in the earth. I heard many things in hell. How, then, am ? Hearken! and observe how healthily—how calmly I can tell e whole story.

ADJUST SPEED

What is unusual about the punctuation? What does it suggest about the narrator? **A**

Vocabulary

acute (ə kūt′) *adj.* sharp and strong or intense

Reading the Selection

SUMMARY

A murderer takes hours to enter his victim's room. As the terrified victim, an old man, waits, the beating of his heart seems to fill the room. Finally, with a loud yell, the murderer leaps on the old man and kills him. He dismembers the body and buries it beneath the floorboards. Shortly after, the police arrive to investigate the cry. The murderer calmly convinces the police that the shriek was the result of a bad dream. Even as he talks, though, he begins to hear a sound. In his horrified imagination, the murderer believes it is the old man's heart, and screams out his confession.

Spanish Summaries, p. 63

A Active Reading Strategies

ADJUST SPEED *(The many dashes as well as exclamation points suggest the narrator's frantic state of mind.)* Ask students how this affects their reading of the story. *(They may find that it slows them down, which was the author's intent.)*

Additional Resources

- ***Active Reading Guides,*** p. 68
- ***Audio Library***
- ***Spanish Audio Library***

Teaching Support

CONNECTING TO OTHER SELECTIONS

COMPARING *selections*

This selection is paired with "The Raven" on pages 847–852. A lesson for teaching a comparison of the two selections appears on page 854.

The chart at the right shows three other ways to connect "The Tell-Tale Heart" to selections in this book.

For specific teaching strategies, see the ***Theme Eight Planning Guide.***

Connection	Title
Life Skills: Planning and Designing	from *Harriet Tubman: Conductor on the Underground Railroad,* p. 480
Thematic: Creative Viewpoints	"Southbound on the Freeway," p. 600
Literary: First-Person Narrator	from *On the Road with Charles Kuralt,* p. 635

B Active Reading Strategies

CLARIFY *(Students are likely to suggest that the narrator is trying to tell his audience that he killed the old man and to put the blame on his victim's staring eye.)* Ask students why the narrator compares the old man's eye to that of a vulture. *(The narrator is, as he says, a very nervous person, and he imagines he is in danger.)*

C Active Reading Strategies

VISUALIZE *(To help students imagine the movements of the narrator as he enters the old man's room, have volunteers act them out.)*

D Critical Thinking

EVALUATING Ask students from what point of view the story is being told. *(first person)* What are the advantages and disadvantages of telling this kind of story this way? *(Advantage: The readers "get into" the mind of the character, and the first-person voice helps them to do this. Disadvantage: Readers have only the narrator's point of view of the events.)*

LITERATURE & HUMANITIES

"Romeo and Juliet", Glencoe World of Music CD5, Tracks 1, 2, 3

Play the CD as students read. Discuss the music's effect on the mood of the tale.

Teaching Support

The Tell-Tale Heart

CLARIFY (B)
What is the narrator trying to tell you?

It is impossible to say how first the idea entered my brain; but once conceived, it haunted me day and night. Object there was none. Passion there was none. I loved the old man. He had never wronged me. He had never given me insult. For his gold I had no desire. I think it was his eye! yes, it was this! One of his eyes resembled that of a vulture—a pale blue eye, with a film over it. Whenever it fell upon me, my blood ran cold; and so by degrees—very gradually—I made up my mind to take the life of the old man, and thus rid myself of the eye for ever.

VISUALIZE (C)
Try to picture the movements of this man as he enters the room.

Now this is the point. You fancy me mad. Madmen know nothing. But you should have seen *me*. You should have seen how wisely I proceeded—with what caution—with what foresight—with what dissimulation[1] I went to work! I was never kinder to the old man than during the whole week before I killed him. And every night, about midnight, I turned the latch of his door and opened it—oh, so gently! And then, when I had made an opening sufficient for my head, I put in a dark lantern, all closed, closed, so that no light shone out, and then I thrust in my head. Oh, you would have laughed to see how cunningly I thrust it in! I moved it slowly—very, very slowly, so that I might not disturb the old man's sleep. It took me an hour to place my whole head within the opening so far that I could see him as he lay upon his bed. Ha!—would a madman have been so wise as this? (D) And then, when my head was well in the room, I undid the lantern cautiously—oh, so cautiously—cautiously (for the hinges creaked)—I undid it just so much that a single thin ray fell upon the vulture eye. And this I did for seven long nights—every night just at midnight—but I found the eye always closed; and so it was impossible to do the work; for it was not the old man who vexed me, but his Evil Eye. And every morning, when the day broke, I went boldly into the chamber, and spoke courageously to him, calling him by name in a hearty tone, and inquiring how he had passed the night. So you see he would have been a very profound[2] old man, indeed, to suspect that every night, just at twelve, I looked in upon him while he slept.

Upon the eighth night I was more than usually cautious in opening the door. A watch's minute hand moves more quickly than did mine. Never before that night, had I *felt* the extent of my own powers—of my sagacity.[3] I could scarcely contain my feelings of triumph. To think

1. *Dissimulation* means "the hiding or disguising of one's true feelings and intentions."
2. Here, *profound* means "very thoughtful and wise."
3. *Sagacity* (sə gas′ ə tē) is wisdom and good judgment.

Vocabulary
vex (veks) *v.* to disturb, annoy, or anger, especially by some small, repeated action

MEETING INDIVIDUAL NEEDS — ENGLISH LANGUAGE LEARNERS

Building Background Ask students what they know about vultures. If necessary, explain that vultures are large birds of prey. They are related to hawks, eagles, and falcons; but vultures live mainly off carrion—that is, dead animals. Point out that the word *vulture* is also used to describe persons who prey on others, waiting until people are weakened, and then coming in for the "kill."

Activity Have students skim page 836 to find out how the narrator uses the term *vulture*. *(One of his eyes resembled that of a vulture.)* Ask students how that eye made the narrator feel. *(as if the old man would attack him)*

Additional Resources

English Language Learners Sourcebook, p. 95

that there I was, opening the door, little by little, and he not even to dream of my secret deeds or thoughts. I fairly chuckled at the idea; and perhaps he heard me; for he moved on the bed suddenly, as if startled. Now you may think that I drew back—but no. His room was as black as pitch with the thick darkness, (for the shutters were close fastened, through fear of robbers,) and so I knew that he could not see the opening of the door, and I kept pushing it on steadily, steadily.

I had my head in, and was about to open the lantern, when my thumb slipped upon the tin fastening, and the old man sprang up in the bed, crying out—"Who's there?"

I kept quite still and said nothing. For a whole hour I did not move a muscle, and in the mean time I did not hear him lie down. He was still sitting up in the bed, listening;—just as I have done, night after night, hearkening to the death watches[4] in the wall.

F Presently I heard a slight groan, and I knew it was the groan of mortal terror. It was not a groan of pain or of grief—oh, no!—it was the low stifled sound that arises from the bottom of the soul when overcharged with awe. I knew the sound well. Many a night, just at midnight, when all the world slept, it has welled up from my own bosom, deepening, with its dreadful echo, the terrors that distracted me. I say I knew it well. I knew what the old man felt, and pitied him, although I chuckled at heart. I knew that he had been lying awake ever since the first slight noise, when he had turned in the bed. His fears had been ever since growing upon him. He had been trying to fancy them causeless, but could not. He had been saying to himself—"It is nothing but the wind in the chimney—it is only a mouse crossing the floor," or "it is merely a cricket which has made a single chirp." Yes, he has been trying to comfort himself with these suppositions:[5] but he had found all in vain. *All in vain;* because Death, in approaching him, had stalked with his black shadow before him, and enveloped the victim. And it was the mournful influence of the unperceived shadow that caused him to feel—although he neither saw nor heard—to *feel* the presence of my head within the room. G

When I had waited a long time, very patiently, without hearing him lie down, I resolved to open a little—a very, very little crevice[6]

ACTIVE READING MODEL

VISUALIZE E

Imagine a movie scene showing the narrator's entry into the old man's room.

RESPOND H

What effect does this very slow action have on you?

4. *Death watches* are beetles that bore into wood, especially of old houses and furniture. Some superstitious people believe that these insects' ticking sounds foretell death.
5. *Suppositions* are things one assumes, or supposes, to be true.
6. A *crevice* (krev′ is) is a crack in or through something.

Vocabulary

stifled (stī′ fəld) *adj.* held back; smothered

E Active Reading Strategies

VISUALIZE *(Students may suggest that the narrator gives a detailed description of his plan and actions, which an actor could use to interpret the role.)* Have volunteers read aloud selected passages as other students visualize the movie's action.

F Literary Elements

MOOD The slow action conveys the intensity of the old man's fear, stimulating in the audience the same feeling. Have students discuss their emotional reactions to the scene.

G Literary Elements

MOOD Discuss with students how the author uses the sense of hearing to intensify the sense of terror and anxiety. *(He describes a silence so intense that he can hear bugs moving in the wall. The old man's groan is the only sound.)*

H Active Reading Strategies

RESPOND *(Students may recognize that the slow action makes readers concentrate on every detail, letting their sense of fear and terror increase.)* Ask students how long they think "a long time" is, in this case.

MEETING INDIVIDUAL NEEDS: MULTIPLE MODES OF EXPRESSION

Bodily-Kinesthetic The narrator describes how he waited hours before entering the old man's room. Ask students to give examples of the slowest movements they can think of in the real world. *(An example might be an artist's adding the finishing touch to a painting. Students may also cite slow-motion in films.)*

Activity Have students, working individually or in pairs, present a slow-motion version of a common activity. These might include tying shoelaces, eating a sandwich, or brushing one's hair. After all students have performed, have them discuss how it felt to move that slowly. **L2** COLLAB. LEARN.

VIEWING THE ART

The scene is from the 1963 film *Hidden Room of 1,000 Horrors* based on "The Tell-Tale Heart."

Viewing Response *The enactment of the mad narrator's description emphasizes his cruelty and the helplessness of the victim.*

I Active Reading Strategies

PREDICT *(Students may suggest that the reader is not sure whether the heartbeat is that of the narrator or the old man. The title suggests that the sound of the heart is a device the author will use again.)* Ask students how they interpret the term *tell-tale* and what that word suggests about the end of the story. *(*Tell-tale *means "revealing." Perhaps the loudly beating heart will reveal the old man's murderer.)*

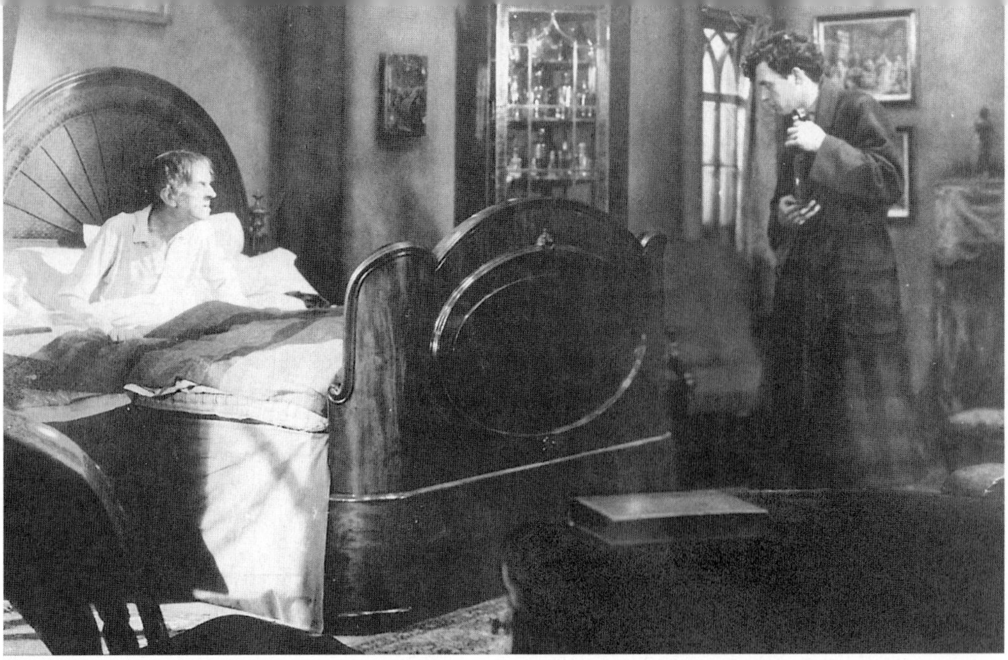

Hidden Room of 1,000 Horrors (The Tell-Tale Heart), 1963. Movie still.

Viewing the photograph: How does this photograph add to the horror of the story?

in the lantern. So I opened it—you cannot imagine how stealthily, stealthily—until, at length, a single dim ray, like the thread of the spider, shot from out the crevice and fell upon the vulture eye.

It was open—wide, wide open—and I grew furious as I gazed upon it. I saw it with perfect distinctness—all a dull blue, with a hideous veil over it that chilled the very marrow in my bones; but I could see nothing else of the old man's face or person: for I had directed the ray as if by instinct, precisely upon the damned spot.

PREDICT

I Based on the vivid description of the heartbeat, what do you think will happen?

And now have I not told you that what you mistake for madness is but over acuteness of the senses?—now, I say, there came to my ears a low, dull, quick sound, such as a watch makes when enveloped in cotton. I knew *that* sound well, too. It was the beating of the old man's heart. It increased my fury, as the beating of a drum stimulates the soldier into courage.

But even yet I refrained and kept still. I scarcely breathed. I held the lantern motionless. I tried how steadily I could maintain the ray upon the eye. Meantime the hellish tattoo[7] of the heart increased. It grew quicker and quicker, and louder and louder every instant. The old

7. The heart was making a drumming or rapping sound. (This *tattoo* comes from a Dutch word; the other *tattoo,* a design on the skin, comes from the language of Tahiti, a Pacific island.)

Teaching Support

Reading Minilesson

Author's Purpose Ask students what the author's purpose is in writing a suspense story. *(to entertain; to scare readers)* Point out that readers who choose this genre do so because they *want* to be scared. Explain that readers who are familiar with the genre share with the author an understanding of what certain situations and symbols mean.

Activity Have students read through the story and find examples of such situations and symbols. *(Possible examples: the darkness, references to an Evil Eye, midnight as the time of the murder, the murderer's stalking the victim, the cry in the night, the mad narrator.)* **L2**

Additional Resources

Reading Skills Practice Workbook

man's terror *must* have been extreme! It grew louder, I say, louder every moment!—do you mark me well? I have told you that I am nervous: so I am. And now at the dead hour of the night, amid the dreadful silence of that old house, so strange a noise as this excited me to uncontrollable terror. Yet, for some minutes longer I refrained and stood still. But the beating grew louder, louder! I thought the heart must burst. And now a new anxiety seized me—the sound would be heard by a neighbor! The old man's hour had come! With a loud yell, I threw open the lantern and leaped into the room. He shrieked once—once only. In an instant I dragged him to the floor, and pulled the heavy bed over him. I then smiled gaily, to find the deed so far done. But, for many minutes, the heart beat on with a muffled sound. This, however, did not vex me; it would not be heard through the wall. At length it ceased. The old man was dead. I removed the bed and examined the corpse. Yes, he was stone, stone dead. I placed my hand upon the heart and held it there many minutes. There was no pulsation. He was stone dead. His eye would trouble me no more.

ACTIVE READING MODEL

ADJUST SPEED J

How might you vary your reading rate in this passage? Why?

If still you think me mad, you will think so no longer when I describe the wise precautions I took for the concealment of the body. The night waned, and I worked hastily, but in silence. First of all I dismembered the corpse. I cut off the head and the arms and the legs.

I then took up three planks from the flooring of the chamber, and deposited all between the scantlings.[8] I then replaced the boards so cleverly, so cunningly, that no human eye—not even *his*—could have detected any thing wrong. There was nothing to wash out—no stain of any kind—no blood-spot whatever. I had been too wary for that. A tub had caught all—ha! ha!

K When I had made an end of these labors, it was four o'clock—still dark as midnight. As the bell sounded the hour, there came a knocking at the street door. I went down to open it with a light heart—for what had I *now* to fear? L There entered three men, who introduced themselves, with perfect suavity, as officers of the police. A shriek had been heard by a neighbor during the night; suspicion of foul play had been aroused; information had been lodged at the police office, and they (the officers) had been deputed[9] to search the premises.

8. The *scantlings* (more commonly called joists) are the boards that hold up the floor planks.
9. *Suavity* (swäv′ ə tē) is a smooth, polite, gracious manner. The officers were appointed, or *deputed* (di pū′ tid), by a superior officer. (This makes them deputies, in effect, although they probably have other official titles.)

Vocabulary
wane (wān) *v.* to draw to a close; approach an end

J Active Reading Strategies

ADJUST SPEED *(Students will probably read this part faster, as was the author's intention.)* Ask them to point out where the action slows again. *(It slows down after the old man is dead.)*

K Critical Thinking

DRAWING CONCLUSIONS How long does the scene in the bedroom take? *(The narrator always started at midnight and it is over at 4:00 A.M., so it took four hours.)*

L Active Reading Strategies

PREDICT Ask students who they think is at the door. Why do they think so? Share the following model to illustrate the thinking process involved in predicting.

Model: The narrator seems sure about not being caught, but I don't think he's going to get away with his crime. When I read about someone knocking on the door, I immediately thought that it has to be the police. Besides, the story sounds like a confession, probably to the police.

MEETING INDIVIDUAL NEEDS — SPECIAL NEEDS

Less-Proficient Readers To help students understand how long the narrator took to enter the old man's room, adapt the action in the story to the capabilities of the students.

Activity Have students play the narrator and stand (or sit) completely still for one or two minutes. Ask the actors how long the period felt. Did it seem like a long time? Then ask the same questions of the students watching. How do you think the character managed to do that for hours? *(Students may suggest that the murderer was intent on committing the crime, so he was willing to wait.)* **L1**

Additional Resources
Inclusion Strategies

VIEWING THE PHOTOGRAPH

The image is from the 1963 film *Hidden Room of 1,000 Horrors*, based on Poe's "The Tell-Tale Heart."

Viewing Response *The movie still shows a man alone, apparently suffering an inner torment. A comparison of the effects of the two images should include reasons for their effectiveness.*

Active Reading Strategies

PREDICT *(Students may understand that the police officers sit down because they are satisfied with the man's explanation of events.)* What is the narrator trying to prove to himself by sitting down over the dead man's hiding place? *(He wants to round out his "perfect triumph" by demonstrating his confidence.)*

A&E HOME VIDEO.® *The following videotape program is available from Glencoe.*

Be sure to preview the video for appropriateness for your class:

- **Biography: Edgar Allan Poe***

*Also available in the Glencoe Literature *Video Library*.

ACTIVE READING MODEL

Hidden Room of 1,000 Horrors (The Tell-Tale Heart), 1963. Movie still.

Viewing the photograph: What seems to be tormenting the man in this picture? Compare this realistic image with the illustration of the eye on page 835. Which image best helps you to visualize the story? Why?

PREDICT

What do you think may be indicated when the officers sit down?

I smiled—for *what* had I to fear? I bade the gentlemen welcome. The shriek, I said, was my own in a dream. The old man, I mentioned, was absent in the country. I took my visitors all over the house. I bade them search—search *well*. I led them, at length, to *his* chamber. I showed them his treasures, secure, undisturbed. In the enthusiasm of my confidence, I brought chairs into the room, and desired them *here* to rest from their fatigues, while I myself, in the wild audacity of my perfect triumph, placed my own seat upon the very spot beneath which reposed[10] the corpse of the victim.

The officers were satisfied. My *manner* had convinced them. I was singularly at ease. They sat, and while I answered cheerily, they chatted

10. Here, *reposed* means "lay dead."

Vocabulary

audacity (ô das′ ə tē) *n.* reckless boldness; daring

singularly (sing′ gyə lər lē) *adv.* unusually or remarkably; extraordinarily

Teaching Support

Grammar and Language *Minilesson*

Kinds of Sentences Write the following sentences on the board:

1. I smiled—for what had I to fear?
2. The officers were satisfied.
3. I could bear those hypocritical smiles no longer!
4. "Villains!" I shrieked, "dissemble no more!"
5. Was it possible they heard not?

Remind students that different kinds of sentences serve different purposes. A sentence can make a statement, ask a question, give a command, or express strong feeling.

Activity Have students identify the purpose of each sentence. *((1) to ask a question; (2) to make a statement; (3) to express strong feeling; (4) to give a command; (5) to ask a question)* **L2**

Additional Resources

- ***Grammar and Language Transparency 67***
- ***Grammar and Language Workbook,*** pp. 47–49
- ***Grammar and Composition Handbook,*** Lesson 13.1
- ***Writer's Choice,*** Lesson 8.1

of familiar things. But, ere long, I felt myself getting pale and wished them gone. My head ached, and I fancied a ringing in my ears: but still they sat and still chatted. The ringing became more distinct—it continued and became more distinct: I talked more freely to get rid of the feeling: but it continued and gained definitiveness—until, at length, I found that the noise was *not* within my ears.

No doubt I now grew *very* pale—but I talked more fluently,[11] and with a heightened voice. Yet the sound increased—and what could I do? It was *a low, dull, quick sound—much such a sound as a watch makes when enveloped in cotton*. I gasped for breath—and yet the officers heard it not. I talked more quickly—more vehemently; but the noise steadily increased. I arose and argued about trifles, in a high key and with violent gesticulations;[12] but the noise steadily increased. Why *would* they not be gone? I paced the floor to and fro with heavy strides, as if excited to fury by the observations of the men—but the noise steadily increased. Oh God! what *could* I do? I foamed—I raved—I swore! I swung the chair upon which I had been sitting, and grated it upon the boards, but the noise arose over all and continually increased. It grew louder—louder—*louder!* And still the men chatted pleasantly, and smiled. Was it possible they heard not? Almighty God!—no, no! They heard!—they suspected!—they *knew!*—they were making a mockery of my horror!—this I thought, and this I think. But anything was better than this agony! Anything was more tolerable than this derision![13] I could bear those hypocritical smiles no longer! I felt that I must scream or die!—and now—again!—hark! louder! louder! louder! *louder!*—

"Villains!" I shrieked, "dissemble[14] no more! I admit the deed!—tear up the planks!—here, here!—it is the beating of his hideous heart!"

11. To speak *fluently* is to do so smoothly and effortlessly.
12. *Trifles* are unimportant things. Bold, expressive gestures are *gesticulations*.
13. *Derision* is scornful mockery or ridicule.
14. Here, *dissemble* means "to disguise one's true thoughts or feelings; act in an insincere way."

Vocabulary

vehemently (vē′ ə mənt lē) *adv.* strongly; intensely; passionately

hypocritical (hip′ ə krit′ i kəl) *adj.* pretending to be what one is not; fake; insincere

ACTIVE READING MODEL

RESPOND

Imagine this scene being enacted as a movie. How might an audience respond?

N Critical Thinking

INFER How does the narrator's mental state change once he thinks he hears something? *(He becomes more and more agitated, talking fast and loudly.)*

O Author's Craft

ITALICS Why do you think the author italicizes this sentence? "It was a low, dull, quick sound—much such a sound as a watch makes when enveloped in cotton." *(He may be suggesting another explanation for the sound the murderer hears. He may be hearing the watch, which his guilty conscience imagines is the murdered man's heart.)*

P Active Reading Strategies

RESPOND *(Students may say an audience would be relieved that the murderer was discovered.)* Ask students how they felt.

Thematic Focus

Hair-Raising Tales The author gives the readers a glimpse into the terror of a disturbed mind. Have students compare their reactions to this story with those they have had to scary movies, TV shows, or other fictional presentations. Ask them how their reactions differ depending on where they are, the time of day, their state of mind, and whether they are alone.

ASSESSMENT

Quick Checks, p. 68

Real-World Connection

Violence on TV Help students make the connection between what they have read and the real world.

Activity Tell students you would like them to compare the murder described in this story with the violence currently on television. Have the class break into groups to discuss whether this type of story is suitable for television. Students should answer such questions as *If you were adapting this story for television, would you show the murder or simply have the narrator describe it? Why? Does "The Tell-Tale Heart" remind you of any suspense dramas you've seen on TV? How did those stories affect you? Does the fact that Poe's story is considered literature make it more acceptable?* **L2** COLLAB. LEARN.

Active Reading and Critical Thinking

ACTIVE READING MODEL

Responding to Literature

PERSONAL RESPONSE

- Can you hear the beating of the dead man's heart as you finish the story? What incidents from the story stay in your mind?

Active Reading Response

- Which prediction did you make that was supported by evidence later in the story?

Brackets connect questions that are paired to develop higher-level thinking skills.

Analyzing Literature

RECALL

1. What reason does the narrator give for committing the murder?
2. What does the old man do when he hears the narrator at his bedroom door?
3. Why do the police come to the door?
4. What does the narrator hear while talking to the police officers in the victim's bedroom?

INTERPRET

5. What does the narrator want his audience to understand about him as he talks about his murder plans? Explain.
6. How does the narrator feel about frightening the old man? Support your answer with examples from the story.
7. How does the narrator react when the police first arrive? Why does he behave this way?
8. Why does the narrator confess to his crime?

EVALUATE AND CONNECT

9. Theme Connection How does the author make the narrator a convincing character? Is any of his behavior normal? Explain.
10. Who has the "tell-tale" heart in this story—the narrator or the old man? Defend your choice.

LITERARY ELEMENTS

Mood

The **mood** of a story is the emotional effect it has on a reader. The overall mood of "The Tell-Tale Heart" is one of anxiety and fear. One way Poe achieves this mood is through the rhythm of his language, which mimics a fast, irregular heartbeat. Poe's use of exclamation marks and dashes conveys agitation, as does the narrator's repetition of the word "nervous."

1. Find three other passages in the story in which punctuation and repetition help project a mood.
2. Find a description of the victim that supports the story's overall mood of anxiety and fear.

• See **Literary Terms Handbook,** p. R6.

Responding to the Selection

PERSONAL RESPONSE

Students may have different reactions to the story, based on their personal feelings about this genre.

Active Reading Response

Have students review their predictions to verify them.

Analyzing Literature

1. He says that he had to get rid of the old man's eye, which reminded him of a vulture.
2. He springs up and calls out, "Who's there?"
3. A neighbor calls them after hearing a shriek.
4. He believes he hears the old man's heart beating. He may, however, be hearing the victim's watch ticking or his own heart.
5. He tries to convince his audience that he is sane. His claim is that a madman would not have been as clever and careful as he was in planning and executing this murder.
6. He both pities and laughs at him. Knowing that the old man is terrified seems to confirm the narrator's belief in his own cleverness.
7. He tells the reader that he opened the door with "a light heart." He believes he has left no evidence of his guilt.
8. He thinks the officers hear the same sound as he does, and he wants to get away from the sound, so he confesses.
9. The author makes the narrator sound as if he is really telling a story and the readers are his audience. From the beginning of the story we see that none of the narrator's thoughts or actions are normal.
10. The tell-tale heart can refer to the old man's heart if the story is interpreted as describing a supernatural event. It can also be the narrator's heart. He may finally have been so overcome with guilt and fear, and so frightened, that his own heart impelled him to give himself away.

LITERARY ELEMENTS

1. The author's interruption of the flow by using dashes. The narrator's description of his reaction to the old man's fear and the final line of the story are other examples.
2. "I knew that he had been lying awake . . . but he had found all in vain."

Additional Resources

Literary Elements Transparency 68

Extending Your Response

Literature Groups

Unanswered Questions What questions do you still have about this story? With your group, discuss questions such as these: Is the narrator of the story insane, or is he just evil? How do you explain the power that the old man's eye and heartbeat had over the narrator? Why did the narrator continue to hear the old man's heartbeat after he was dead? Share your answers with the rest of the class.

Learning for Life

Presenting an Argument Imagine you are the narrator's defense attorney. Write an argument for why he should not be convicted of murder. As you write, anticipate and respond to counterarguments from people who may believe he is guilty. Deliver your argument to your classmates.

Writing About Literature

Suspenseful Scene Which scene from this story did you find most gripping or scary? Why did it affect you this way? Write a paragraph or two explaining your answer. Include details and examples from the story to support your answer.

Creative Writing

Police Report Imagine that you are one of the police officers called to the house after a neighbor heard a scream. What facts do you uncover? Write a police report about this case.

Reading Further

If you enjoyed this story, try
Look for Me by Moonlight by Mary Downing Hahn

Save your work for your portfolio.

Skill Minilesson

RETEACH • REVIEW

VOCABULARY • ANALOGIES

An **analogy** is a type of comparison that is based on the relationships between things or ideas. Analogies are often used on tests to measure how well you can figure things out and how good your vocabulary is. A test will not tell you what kind of relationship is shown by the first pair of words. You'll have to figure that out. Then you'll need to find another pair of words that could be used to illustrate the same relationship.

- For more about analogies, see **Communications Skills Handbook,** pp. R72–R73.

PRACTICE Complete each analogy.

1. cramp : sharp :: ache :
   a. brief c. sudden
   b. dull d. slight
2. loud : quiet :: stifled :
   a. soft c. released
   b. ignored d. touched
3. knock : pound :: vex :
   a. soothe c. scold
   b. torture d. comfort
4. taunt : scorn :: praise :
   a. approval c. disgust
   b. complaint d. care

Extending Your Response

Literature Groups Have students think about the questions before they come together as a group. After they have concluded their discussion, ask how their opinions on these questions have changed since they heard other people's ideas. COLLAB. LEARN.

Learning for Life Have students role-play as the narrator's defense attorney in a style they think is authentic.

Writing About Literature

Students' analyses should

- include convincing details and examples from the story

Creative Writing

Students' reports should

- include the questions asked and the word-for-word answers of the person being questioned
- include an impartial summary of the interview

Skill Minilesson

VOCABULARY • ANALOGIES

1. b 3. b
2. c 4. a

Additional Resources

Vocabulary Practice, p. 47

ASSESSMENT

- ***Quick Checks,*** p. 68
- ***Selection and Theme Assessment,*** pp. 117–118
- ***Performance Assessment,*** p. 60
- ***Testmaker: ExamView Pro***
- ***Interactive Tutor: Self-Assessment***

HAIR-RAISING TALES 843

Media Connection

Objective

- To read and understand a Web site

Literature LINK

The Tell-Tale Heart Point out the similarities between the unexplained horror in this script, that of "The Tell-Tale Heart," and *Sorry, Right Number*. In each case the action takes place in an everyday setting. In such ordinariness, though, lurks unexpected danger.

interNET CONNECTION

Winning Prizes Students can use a search engine to locate other prize-winning books in a variety of genres.

Media Connection

WEB SITE

The word "mystery" probably conjures images of Sherlock Holmes and the board game *Clue* instead of Greek tragedies. See how these elements fit together to give us the mysteries that we enjoy today.

The History of the Mystery

Address: http://www.mysterynet.com/history/

From Poe to the Present

Mystery and crime stories are among the most popular forms of fiction today, and the popularity of the genre is no mystery to millions of readers worldwide.

The fascination with mystery and crime can be traced back to Ancient Greece, where playwrights like Sophocles and Euripides enthralled the local citizenry with their plays combining mystery and drama. In first-century B.C. Rome, Cicero argued passionately in court in defense of accused criminals, captivating Romans with his speeches.

Each April in New York City, the Mystery Writers of America hosts the annual Edgar Allan Poe awards to honor outstanding mystery writers. Their top honor, the Edgar, is shown here.

Mystery and crime stories as we know them today did not emerge until the mid-nineteenth century when Edgar Allan Poe introduced mystery fiction's first fictional detective, Auguste C. Dupin, in his 1841 story, "The Murders in the Rue Morgue." The acknowledged father of the mystery story, Poe continued Dupin's exploits in stories such as "The Mystery of Marie Roget" (1842) and "The Purloined Letter" (1845).

"The Murders in the Rue Morgue" is the most famous example of a mystery style known as the "locked room," in which "a murder victim is found inside an apparently sealed enclosure and the detective's challenge is to discover the murderer's modus operandi" (Crime Classics).

Poe was one of the first to shift the focus of mystery stories from the description of shocking events and eerie setting to a "study of the criminal's mind" (Crime Classics).

As important as his contributions were to the genre, Poe was influenced greatly by the early work of Charles Dickens who,

Teaching Support

Reading Minilesson

Narrating a Movie Ask students to think of a mystery story or novel that was adapted for film, explaining that many popular movies come from novels. Explain that the narrative parts of the novels—that is, those without dialogue—are sometimes read aloud by a narrator in the movie adaptation. To be effective, the narrator must read well enough to be understood but not distract from the action on the screen.

Activity Have students select a section of a novel they think would make a good movie. Have them choose a part that a narrator might read as a voice-over for the action on the screen. Challenge students to read the parts aloud, using appropriate pace and enunciation to make the scene exciting.

Additional Resource

Reading Skills Practice Workbook

The History of the Mystery

Address: http://www.mysterynet.com/history/

with his contemporary, Wilkie Collins, made major contributions to the genre as well. The rising literacy rates combined with more leisure time contributed greatly to the popularity of novels in general and mysteries in particular.

In 1878, with the publication of "The Leavenworth Case," Katherine Anne Greene became the first woman to write a detective novel. This novel introduced elements of detection later used to great effect by writers of the English-country-house-murder school, a style that focuses on "members of a closed group, often in a country house or village, who become suspects in a generally bloodless and neat murder solved by a great-detective kind of investigator" (Crime Classics).

Sherlock Holmes, Sir Arthur Conan Doyle's brilliant detective, arrived on the mystery scene in the late nineteenth century in "A Study in Scarlet" (1887). Holmes possessed a singular style unlike any detective seen before. With his distinctive style and his flair for deducing clues, Holmes, with his ever-reliable sidekick, Dr. Watson, quickly became indispensable to mystery readers everywhere.

The 1920s ushered in the Golden Age of mystery fiction. A time of growing prosperity in both England and America, the popularity of mystery fiction was at an all-time high.

During the height of Golden Age fiction's popularity, London publisher Allen Lane came up with an idea that further helped to expand the availability of mysteries to the public. Along with his two brothers, he obtained limited rights to hardcover books written by Dorothy L. Sayers and other mystery writers. Their new paperback line was issued in 1935 with only ten titles and quickly expanded to seventy titles within a year. Penguins, as they were called, were easily accessible to the public due to their much lower cost and availability in department stores, where most of the public shopped at the time. These paperbacks helped to bring mysteries, along with other types of fiction as well, to the public.

Another type of crime fiction, the "police procedural," surfaced in the 1940s, and its style coincided perfectly with the advent of television. As its name implies, it differed from other styles of crime writing because of its realistic portrayal of police methods. The stories were always presented from the point of view of the police, usually in a gritty, realistic style.

Mystery in all its forms will undoubtedly continue to capture the public's imagination, regardless of the medium, well into the future.

Analyzing Media

1. How has the mystery story developed since its origins in Ancient Greece? In what ways has the genre stayed the same?
2. What types of mysteries do you enjoy? Jot down the names of your favorite mystery writers, book titles, television shows, and movies.

Analyzing Media

1. Today's mystery may be one of several sub-genres—crime, detective, or horror, for example.
2. Suggest that students share their favorites.

Informational Text

inTIME For more examples of informational text, direct students to the articles in *inTIME* magazine.

Additional Resources

Media Connections, p. 16

interNET CONNECTION

Alfred Hitchcock, who directed a number of classic mystery movies, has become a legend in film history. Suggest that students search the Internet for sites that deal with his work. Have them select several addresses that interest them. You may wish to explore them before allowing students access.

Before Reading

Objectives

- To read and analyze a poem with elements of a suspense tale
- To identify allusions in the poem

Skills

Reading/Thinking: Inferring; Paraphrasing
Writing: Poetry
Vocabulary: Word Meanings
Grammar/Language: Archaic Language
Listening/Speaking: Reading Aloud
Collaboration: Literature Groups

Motivating STUDENTS

Selection Focus Transparency 64: Have students view the transparency and discuss the questions provided.

Reading Focus: As an extension of the Reading Focus, have students discuss their answers to the question *Is it easy to forget, even briefly, a time of sorrow?*

Before You Read

The Raven

READING FOCUS

Is it easy to forget, even briefly, a time of sorrow?

Journal

Write a few things you might say to help a friend who is mourning the loss of a loved one.

Setting a Purpose

Read to find out whether the narrator is trying to forget something or someone, or if he is trying to remember.

BUILDING BACKGROUND

The Time and Place "The Raven" may be based on incidents from Edgar Allan Poe's own experiences during his days as a student at the University of Virginia. The setting is the room of a man who is reading an old academic book on a stormy night.

Did You Know? Poe's most famous poem was "The Raven." After its publication in 1845, the poem gained the kind of popularity that a hit song enjoys today. Unlike popular modern songwriters, however, the writer didn't become wealthy.

Poe's death has been as haunted by misfortune as his life was. His family couldn't afford a tombstone for his grave. Years after his death, a tombstone purchased by a distant relative was ready for delivery when it was struck by a train and destroyed. The people of Baltimore raised money for a monument to Poe, who had lived there, but the clay model was destroyed by fire before it could be cast in bronze. A second model was demolished in an earthquake. Finally, in 1875, the bronze sculpture shown on the right was erected in Poe's honor.

Edgar Allan Poe Monument, Baltimore, MD.

RESOURCE MANAGER

Teaching Tools and Resources
- Theme Eight Planning Guide
- Literature Groups Sourcebook

Essential Lesson Support

Lesson-Specific Instruction
- Selection Focus Transparency 64
- Literary Elements Transparency 69
- Active Reading Guide,* p. 69

Assessment
- Selection Quick Checks,* p. 69
- Sel. and Theme Assmt., pp. 119–120
- Testmaker: ExamView Pro
- Performance Assessment, p. 61

Systematic Language Instruction
- Gr. & Comp. Hbk., L. 14.3
- Vocabulary Power, Lesson 35
- Spelling Power, Lesson 31

English Language Learners
- ELL Sourcebook, p. 96
- Spanish Summaries, p. 64
- Spanish Translations, pp. 227–232
- Audio Library*
- English, Yes!

Special Needs/Strat. Interven.
- Interactive Rdg. Sbk., pp. T218–T220
- Interactive Rdg. Wkbk., pp. 131–132
- Inclusion Strat. Sbk., pp. 45–46
- Audio Library*

* Also available in Spanish

The Raven

Edgar Allan Poe

A

Once upon a midnight dreary, while I pondered, weak and weary,
Over many a quaint and curious volume of forgotten lore°—
While I nodded, nearly napping, suddenly there came a tapping,
As of some one gently rapping, rapping at my chamber door.
"'Tis some visitor," I muttered, "tapping at my chamber door—
Only this and nothing more."

Ah, distinctly I remember it was in the bleak December;
And each separate dying ember° wrought° its ghost upon the floor.
Eagerly I wished the morrow;—vainly I had sought to borrow
From my books surcease° of sorrow—sorrow for the lost Lenore—
For the rare and radiant maiden whom the angels name Lenore—
Nameless *here* for evermore.

---

2 *Lore* means "learning."
8 An *ember* is a glowing fragment of wood in the ashes of a fire. *Wrought* means "worked."
10 *Surcease* means "an end."

Reading the Selection

SUMMARY

The narrator is in his study late one night when he hears a rapping. Saddened by the recent death of his beloved, Lenore, he summons his courage to open the door, only to find no one there. Finally he realizes the rapping comes from the window. When he opens it, a large raven enters. To every question the man asks, the raven answers, "Nevermore." The man wants to know whether he will ever see his darling again, and the raven deepens his despair by answering again, "Nevermore."

Spanish Summaries, p. 64

A Active Reading Strategies

CONNECT Alert students to the first stanza of the poem. Have students note the opening words. Where else have they seen these words? *(Many traditional tales begin with the words* Once upon a time.*)*

Additional Resources

Active Reading Guides, p. 69
Audio Library

Teaching Support

MEETING INDIVIDUAL NEEDS: ENGLISH LANGUAGE LEARNERS

Compound Words Students have learned that they can often figure out new words by looking for familiar word parts. Explain that compound words usually have at least one part that should be familiar to students. Knowing this should help them figure out the meaning of the whole word.

Activity Ask students to identify the two words in each compound word and define the compound.

- "Nameless here for evermore." *(ever and more; forever)*
- "Quoth the Raven, 'Nevermore'." *(never and more; never again)*

Additional Resources

English Language Learners Sourcebook, p. 96

COMPARING selections

This selection is paired with "The Tell-Tale Heart" on pages 835–841. A lesson for teaching a comparison of the two selections appears on page 854.

For a teaching strategy that connects this selection to "Talk," see the ***Theme Four Planning Guide.***

HAIR-RAISING TALES 847

B Active Reading Strategies

PREDICT Ask students to predict who or what is tapping. How do they know? *(The raven of the title is tapping.)*

C Literary Elements

RHYME Remind students that some poems have rhyme that appears at the end of the line and has a definite pattern. Ask them how this poem differs. *(This poem employs internal rhymes as in these examples: "Eagerly I wished the morrow;—vainly I had sought to borrow/From my books surcease of sorrow.")*

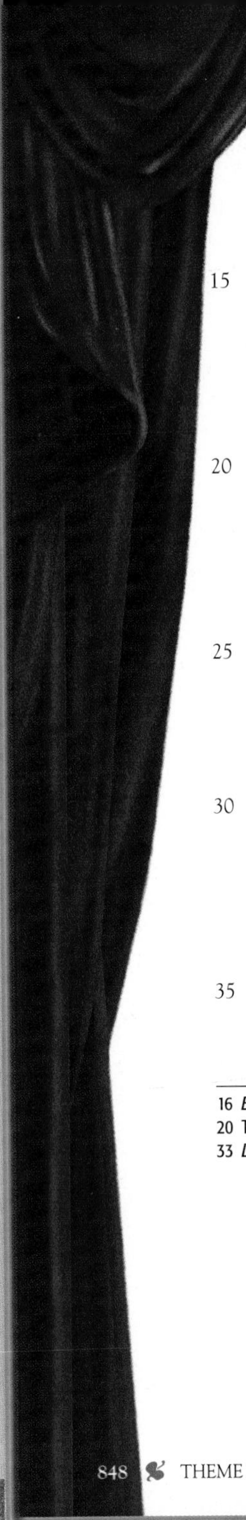

And the silken, sad, uncertain rustling of each purple curtain
Thrilled me—filled me with fantastic terrors never felt before;
So that now, to still the beating of my heart, I stood repeating
"'Tis some visitor entreating° entrance at my chamber door—
Some late visitor entreating entrance at my chamber door;—
    This it is and nothing more."

Presently my soul grew stronger; hesitating then no longer,
"Sir," said I, "or Madam, truly your forgiveness I implore;°
But the fact is I was napping, and so gently you came rapping,
And so faintly you came tapping, tapping at my chamber door,
That I scarce was sure I heard you"—here I opened wide the door;—
    Darkness there and nothing more.

Deep into that darkness peering, long I stood there wondering, fearing,
Doubting, dreaming dreams no mortal ever dared to dream before;
But the silence was unbroken, and the stillness gave no token,
And the only word there spoken was the whispered word, "Lenore!"
This I whispered, and an echo murmured back the word "Lenore!"
    Merely this and nothing more.

Back into the chamber turning, all my soul within me burning,
Soon again I heard a tapping somewhat louder than before.
"Surely," said I, "surely that is something at my window lattice;°
Let me see, then, what thereat is, and this mystery explore—
Let my heart be still a moment and this mystery explore;—
    'Tis the wind and nothing more!"

---

16 *Entreating* is pleading.
20 To *implore* is to ask earnestly.
33 *Lattice* refers to strips of wood or metal overlapped in a crisscross pattern.

Teaching Support

MEETING INDIVIDUAL NEEDS — SPECIAL NEEDS

Less-Proficient Readers Explain to students that questioning a text will help them better understand. Write the five *W*'s and an *H* questions on the board. Answering such questions will also promote involvement in the story.

Activity Have students answer the following questions: Who is telling the story? *(a man)* Why is the narrator sad? *(His beloved has died.)* Where does the story take place? *(in the man's study)* When does it take place? *(late at night in December)* What happens? *(A raven raps on the man's window and comes inside.)* How does the raven respond to the man's questions? *("Nevermore.")* **L1**

Additional Resources

Inclusion Strategies

Open here I flung the shutter, when, with many a flirt and flutter
In there stepped a stately Raven of the saintly days of yore.°
Not the least obeisance° made he; not a minute stopped or stayed he;
But, with mien° of lord or lady, perched above my chamber door—
Perched upon a bust° of Pallas° just above my chamber door—
Perched, and sat, and nothing more.

Then this ebony bird beguiling° my sad fancy into smiling,
By the grave and stern decorum° of the countenance° it wore,
"Though thy crest be shorn and shaven, thou," I said, "art sure no craven,°
Ghastly grim and ancient Raven wandering from the Nightly shore—
Tell me what thy lordly name is on the Night's Plutonian shore!"°
Quoth the Raven, "Nevermore."

Much I marvelled this ungainly° fowl to hear discourse° so plainly,
Though its answer little meaning—little relevancy bore;
For we cannot help agreeing that no living human being
Ever yet was blessed with seeing bird above his chamber door—
Bird or beast upon the sculptured bust above his chamber door,
With such name as "Nevermore."

But the Raven, sitting lonely on the placid° bust, spoke only
That one word, as if his soul in that one word he did outpour.
Nothing farther then he uttered—not a feather then he fluttered—
Till I scarcely more than muttered "Other friends have flown before—
On the morrow *he* will leave me, as my hopes have flown before."
Then the bird said "Nevermore."

38 *Saintly days of yore* are sacred days of long ago. This refers to the Bible story in which ravens bring food to the prophet Elijah in the wilderness.
39 *Obeisance* (ō bā′ səns) is a polite gesture of respect, such as a bow or curtsy.
40 *Mien* (mēn) means "a way of carrying oneself" or "manner."
41 A *bust* is a statue of the head and shoulders. *Pallas* is another name for Athena, the Greek goddess of wisdom.
43 Someone who is *beguiling* uses charm to influence.
44 *Decorum* (di kôr′ əm) is dignity. *Countenance* is a facial expression.
45 A *craven* is an extremely cowardly person.
47 A *Plutonian shore* refers to darkness, like the edge of death. In Roman mythology, Pluto was god of the dead, whose land of darkness was separated from the land of the living by rivers.
49 *Ungainly* means "awkward-looking." *Discourse* means "to speak or converse."
55 *Placid* means "peaceful."

D Literary Elements

ALLUSION Have students discuss whether they think the raven's entrance is threatening. Is there any significance in its perching on the bust of Pallas? *(The bird's entrance seems heavy with symbolism rather than threat. The poet alludes to biblical ravens that were compassionate and compares the bird to lordly people. Its landing on the bust of the goddess of wisdom suggests that it will bring the narrator some wisdom, perhaps from beyond the grave.)*

E Critical Thinking

INFERRING What effect does the Raven's repetition of the word *nevermore* have on the narrator at first? *(The narrator seems to think it is a coincidence that the bird answers that way.)*

FINE ART TRANSPARENCY 11

You may want to use ***Fine Art Transparency 11*** to discuss ways in which ordinary objects can create a mood.

Reading Minilesson

Paraphrasing Students should understand the overall mood of "The Raven." If they have difficulty with certain passages, suggest that they ask themselves what the narrator is feeling and thinking.

Activity Assess students' understanding of the poetry by asking them to paraphrase the following stanzas on page 849: lines 49–54 *(I could hardly believe that the raven said anything, and what it said didn't mean anything anyway.)* lines 55–60 *(That seemed to be the only word the raven could speak. However, when I muttered, "I've lost all my other friends," the raven answered.)* Ask pairs of students to compare their paraphrases to see it they have accurately conveyed the poem's meaning. **L2**

Additional Resources

Reading Skills Practice Workbook

VIEWING THE PAINTING

Gustave Doré illustrated books by such major writers as Dante and Byron. His work was a commercial success, but not always admired by critics.

Viewing Response *The mood in the painting reflects the despondency of the speaker of the poem.*

FYI

Despite the early problems with Poe's memorials (see Background on page 846), his native city has recently found a way to celebrate his work. When the Cleveland Browns' franchise in the National Football League was moved to Baltimore in 1996, the team was renamed the Ravens after Poe's famous creation.

The Raven. Gustave Doré (1832–1883). Engraving.

Viewing the art: In what ways does this picture match the mood of "The Raven"? Explain.

Teaching Support

MEETING INDIVIDUAL NEEDS — MULTIPLE MODES OF EXPRESSION

Intrapersonal Remind students that, for a long time after the poem was written, it was as popular as a hit song is today. Discuss what kind of personal appeal the poem must have had.

Activity Ask students to think about how this poem makes them feel and then to think of a song, contemporary or other kind, that has the same effect on them. Encourage students to use that selection as background music as they read aloud the poem. **L2**

Startled at the stillness broken by reply so aptly° spoken,
"Doubtless," said I, "what it utters is its only stock and store
Caught from some unhappy master whom unmerciful Disaster
Followed fast and followed faster till his songs one burden bore—
Till the dirges° of his Hope that melancholy burden bore
Of 'Never—nevermore.'"

But the Raven still beguiling all my fancy into smiling,
Straight I wheeled a cushioned seat in front of bird, and bust and door;
Then, upon the velvet sinking, I betook myself to linking
Fancy unto fancy, thinking what this ominous bird of yore—
What this grim, ungainly, ghastly, gaunt, and ominous bird of yore
Meant in croaking "Nevermore."

This I sat engaged in guessing, but no syllable expressing
To the fowl whose fiery eyes now burned into my bosom's core;
This and more I sat divining,° with my head at ease reclining
On the cushion's velvet lining that the lamp-light gloated o'er,
But whose velvet violet lining with the lamp-light gloating o'er,
She shall press, ah, nevermore!

Then, methought, the air grew denser, perfumed from an unseen censer°
Swung by Seraphim° whose foot-falls tinkled on the tufted° floor.
"Wretch," I cried, "thy God hath lent thee—by these angels he hath sent thee
Respite—respite° and nepenthe° from thy memories of Lenore;
Quaff,° oh quaff this kind nepenthe and forget this lost Lenore!"
Quoth the Raven "Nevermore."

---

61 *Aptly* means "appropriately."
65 *Dirges* are slow, mournful songs, often funeral hymns.
75 *Divining* means "guessing."
79 A *censer* is a container for burning incense.
80 *Seraphim* are angels of the highest rank, said to have three pairs of wings. *Tufted* means "carpeted."
82 *Respite* (res′ pit) is a brief period of relief from pain or labor. *Nepenthe* (ni pen′ thē) is a sleeping drug or anything that eases pain or sorrow by bringing forgetfulness.
83 To *quaff* is to drink deeply.

F Active Reading Strategies

QUESTION Who is the narrator and what has happened to put him in such a dejected mood? *(The narrator is a scholar or student whose love, Lenore, has died.)* How do the narrator's feelings about the raven change as the bird continues to repeat the word *nevermore*? Have students give examples to support their answers. *(At first he thinks that the bird learned the word from another person as sad as he is now. Then he begins to think of the raven not as lordly but as "grim, ungainly, ghastly, gaunt, and ominous.")*

G Author's Craft

STYLE The poet makes several connections to images of death and sorrow. Have students find them and explain the connection. *(He imagines the bird's master as someone overwhelmed by disaster, refers to funeral dirges, and reminds us that Lenore, now dead, once sat on the chair into which he sinks. These thoughts reinforce the narrator's feeling that the bird is a link to death and sorrow.)*

Vo•cab•u•lar•y Skills

Word Meanings Explain that the words *methinks* and *methought* mean "it seems (seemed) to me."

Writing Minilesson

Poetry Ask students whether, based on what they know about Edgar Allan Poe, they think he usually wrote in this same mood. *(Students may think that is true, on the basis of "The Raven" and "The Tell-Tale Heart.")*

Activity Suggest that students "answer" Poe's dark poem by writing a poem of consolation. Encourage them to use Poe's form, if they wish, but to turn the message around to one of comfort. For example, the repeated word can be *evermore* in response to a positive idea. Students' poems need not be as long as the original. **L3**

Additional Resources

Writer's Choice, Lesson 3.2

HAIR-RAISING TALES 851

Active Reading Strategies

EVALUATE What does the narrator think the raven is? *(He thinks the bird is a prophet of evil but that it tells the truth, and that truth is not comforting.)*

Critical Thinking

INFER How does the raven intensify the narrator's sorrow? *(In answer to the question of whether he will ever be reunited with Lenore, the raven answers, "Nevermore.")*

Thematic Focus

Hair-Raising Tales Point out that the narrator of the poem is in a mournful mood and that, for the depressed, the world seems to echo dark feelings. Ask students to consider the possibility that the call of the bird is just that, a call; but to the grieving man, it becomes a confirmation that happiness will exist nevermore.

ASSESSMENT

Quick Checks, p. 69

At the MOVIES

Be sure to preview the following video for appropriateness for your class:

Seven Crows a Secret, from the National Film Board of Canada, explores the significance of crows in history, literature, art, and science.

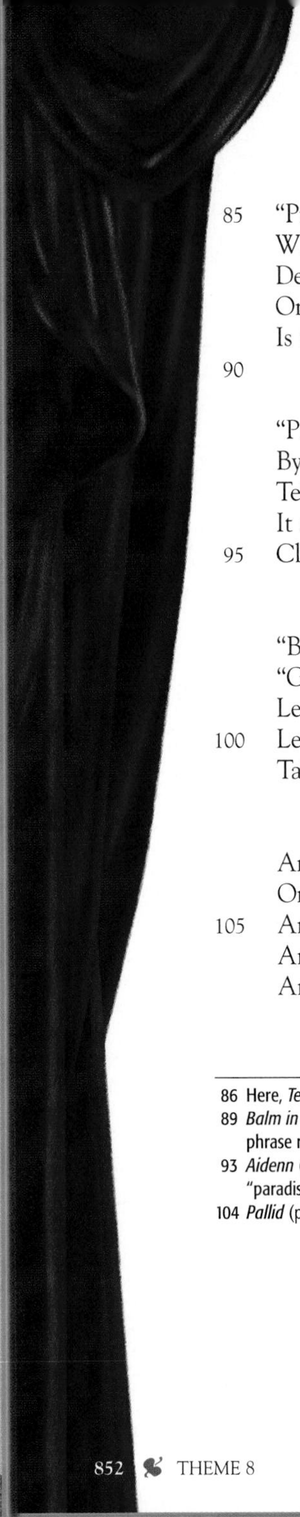

"Prophet!" said I, "thing of evil!—prophet still, if bird or devil!—
Whether Tempter° sent, or whether tempest° tossed thee here ashore,
Desolate yet all undaunted, on this desert land enchanted—
On this home by Horror haunted—tell me truly, I implore—
Is there—*is* there balm in Gilead?°—tell me—tell me, I implore!"
Quoth the Raven "Nevermore."

"Prophet!" said I, "thing of evil!—prophet still, if bird or devil!
By that Heaven that bends above us—by that God we both adore—
Tell this soul with sorrow laden if, within the distant Aidenn,°
It shall clasp a sainted maiden whom the angels name Lenore—
Clasp a rare and radiant maiden whom the angels name Lenore."
Quoth the Raven "Nevermore."

"Be that word our sign of parting, bird or fiend!" I shrieked, upstarting—
"Get thee back into the tempest and the Night's Plutonian shore!
Leave no black plume as a token of that lie thy soul hath spoken!
Leave my loneliness unbroken!—quit the bust above my door!
Take thy beak from out my heart, and take thy form from off my door!"
Quoth the Raven "Nevermore."

And the Raven, never flitting, still is sitting, *still* is sitting
On the pallid° bust of Pallas just above my chamber door;
And his eyes have all the seeming of a demon's that is dreaming,
And the lamp-light o'er him streaming throws his shadow on the floor;
And my soul from out that shadow that lies floating on the floor
Shall be lifted—nevermore!

86 Here, *Tempter* is the Devil. A *tempest* is a violent storm.
89 *Balm in Gilead* (gil′ ē əd) means "relief from pain and suffering." In the Bible, the phrase refers to a healing ointment made from a tree in a region of Palestine.
93 *Aidenn* (ā′ den) comes from an Arabic form of *Eden* and means "heaven" or "paradise."
104 *Pallid* (pal′ id) means "pale."

Teaching Support

Grammar and Language *Minilesson*

Archaic Language Point out to students that, in the past, poetry often included archaic language, language no longer commonly used. For example, in this poem Poe uses the contractions *'tis* and *o'er* and the pronouns *thee* and *thy,* although such words had long since ceased to be used in everyday speech.

Activity Have students look through the poem and locate other examples of archaic language and figure out what they mean. *(thereat, meaning "there"; thou, meaning "you"; quoth, meaning "said"; betook, meaning "caused himself to"; methought, meaning "it seemed to me"; hath, meaning "has")* **L2**

Additional Resources

- ***Grammar and Language Transparency 68***
- ***Grammar and Language Workbook,*** p. 283
- ***Grammar and Composition Handbook,*** Lesson 15.3
- ***Writer's Choice,*** Lesson 23.2

Responding to Literature

PERSONAL RESPONSE

- What questions would you like to ask the speaker? What would you ask the raven?

Analyzing Literature

RECALL AND INTERPRET

1. What is the speaker's mood at the beginning of the poem? Why does he feel this way? Explain.
2. When the speaker hears tapping at his door, who does he think it is at first? How does he feel when it turns out to be something else? Include details from the poem in your answers.
3. What is the speaker's first reaction to the raven's presence? What is his reaction by the poem's end? What happens to change his mind?

EVALUATE AND CONNECT

4. What effect might the **repetition** of "Nevermore" have on a reader? Find three other examples of repetition in the poem.
5. Poe said that he broke the mood of "The Raven" at the halfway point, the end of line 54. What effect might this change have on a reader? Support your answer with examples.
6. Do you think the raven knows what it is saying? Or is the speaker projecting his own thoughts onto it? Explain your answer.

LITERARY ELEMENTS

Allusion

An **allusion** is a reference to a character, place, or situation from another work of art or literature, or from history. For example, the raven in Poe's poem may be an allusion to the bird that served as a messenger for Apollo, the Greek sun god. Also, *ravenous,* meaning "extremely hungry," comes from the word *raven.* That meaning is echoed in the line "Take thy beak from out my heart."

1. What other animal could Poe have used in place of the raven in this poem?
2. Find three other allusions in the poem and research their meanings.

- See **Literary Terms Handbook,** p. R1.

Extending Your Response

Creative Writing

A Poet Speaks Write a short poem inspired by either the mood or the rhyme scheme and rhythm of "The Raven." (For more on **rhyme scheme,** see **Literary Terms Handbook,** page R8.) Rehearse your poem with a partner, and then recite it for the class.

Literature Groups

Nevermore? Reexamine the poem. As a group, identify lines that show how the speaker's attitude toward the dead Lenore changes throughout the poem. Share your conclusions with the class.

Save your work for your portfolio.

Responding to the Selection

PERSONAL RESPONSE

Encourage students to write questions that avoid the answer "Nevermore."

Analyzing Literature

1. He is "weak and weary" because he is mourning his lost love.
2. He thinks it may be Lenore's spirit. The disappointment renews the pain.
3. At first he thinks the raven will distract him. Then he thinks the bird has been sent by God. Finally, he thinks the bird is a fiend sent to torture him.
4. The repetition of *nevermore* strikes the reader like a bell tolling a death. Examples of repetition: "rapping"; "and nothing more"; "and this mystery explore"; "tell me."
5. Until that point the reader is distracted from the story of Lenore. Then the poet turns the raven's single answer into a comment on all the narrator's lost hopes.
6. The narrator phrases his questions so that he cannot draw any hope from the bird's answer.

Extending Your Response

Creative Writing

Students' poems should

- reflect the mood or the rhyme scheme and rhythm of the original
- be clear and expressive

Literature Groups Suggest that students isolate all reference to Lenore and read them aloud to begin. COLLAB. LEARN.

LITERARY ELEMENTS

1. Sample answer: He might have used an owl that constantly repeated "who."
2. The ravens of the Bible that fed Elijah; Pallas, the Greek goddess of wisdom; Pluto, the Roman god of the dead; balm in Gilead, in the Bible a place of refuge; and Aidenn, another spelling of the biblical Eden are alluded to.

Additional Resources

Literary Elements Transparency 69

ASSESSMENT

- ***Quick Checks,*** p. 69
- ***Selection and Theme Assessment,*** pp. 119–120
- ***Performance Assessment,*** p. 61
- ***Testmaker: ExamView Pro***
- ***Interactive Tutor: Self-Assessment***

COMPARING selections

Objective

- To compare two selections

COMPARE SETTINGS

Students' comparisons should

- address the use of doors as a plot device in each selection
- explain how the author uses darkness to enhance the mood of each piece
- contrast the presence or absence of sound in both settings

COMPARE TECHNIQUES

Students' responses should

- give specific examples of elements that contribute to the mood of horror
- cite the specific or implied suggestion of the supernatural
- compare the mental state of each narrator

COMPARE EXPERIENCES

Students' comparisons should

- reflect students' understanding that Poe's work greatly influenced later writers of suspense in this country and abroad
- discuss the subject matter, the main character, and the details as they appear in different eras
- include students' own reactions to both narratives

Additional Resources

Literature Groups Sourcebook

Teaching Support

Critical Thinking

COMPARING SELECTIONS

The Tell-Tale Heart and The Raven

COMPARE SETTINGS

The settings of "The Tell-Tale Heart" and "The Raven" are important parts of these stories.

1. Compare Poe's use of doors in advancing the plot of the two selections.
2. Why, do you think, is darkness important in each selection?
3. Contrast the presence or absence of sound in the two settings.

COMPARE TECHNIQUES

Both "The Tell-Tale Heart" and "The Raven" are stories that rely on horror and fear of the supernatural to capture an audience.

1. What elements in each story create the mood of horror?
2. How is the supernatural used in each story?
3. How is the personality of the narrator in each story important in creating the mood?

COMPARE EXPERIENCES

Think about your experience of modern horror stories and films. How are contemporary stories of fear and the supernatural like these tales by Poe? How are they different? With a group, choose a modern story of horror or the supernatural—from a book or a film—and compare it with one of Poe's works. In your comparison, discuss the subject matter, the main character, and the details that create horror or fear for the audience. Share comparisons with another group.

The Raven. Gustave Doré (1832–1883). Engraving.

854 THEME 8

PORTFOLIO OPTIONS

Response Analysis Have students analyze one of their responses for an activity above by asking themselves these questions:

- Does my response include specific details?
- Are my comparisons based on parallel situations?
- What changes should I include when I do my revision?

Students should clip their reflections to their analyses and place them in their portfolios. At a later time, they may consider using the comments to revise their analyses as portfolio showcase pieces. **L2**

Additional Resources

Writing Assessment and Portfolio Management, pp. 41–48

Interdisciplinary Connection — SCIENCE

The Science of Dreams

While you are sleeping, your mind is working. It is making up stories–often strange and unreal tales–called *dreams.* You dream of being chased through your house by a bear. Or, you are soaring high on the back of a bird, with clouds brushing past you. Some dreams of events or people seem so real that you must remind yourself that you were just dreaming. Perhaps that is what really happened to the narrator of "The Raven" when he saw a raven mysteriously appear in his study.

Scientists have made many discoveries about the way people dream. You probably dream four or five times a night. During dreams, your eyes move back and forth beneath your eyelids, as if you are reading quickly or watching something that is moving back and forth. This is "rapid eye movement," or *REM.* During REM sleep, you also may breathe faster, and certain parts of your body may twitch. Normally, however, most of your muscles are at rest. This is your body's way of keeping you from acting out your dreams.

In the story *Alice in Wonderland,* Lewis Carroll writes a bizarre adventure about Alice, who dreams that she follows a white rabbit down a rabbit hole.

Examining Your Dreams

Researchers believe you are most likely to dream about the day's experiences, but dreams also may reflect wishes and fears. Despite years of study, researchers disagree about the purpose of dreams. Do they merely entertain you during sleep? Do they improve learning? No one knows for sure. Like well-written stories, dreams convey sights, sounds, smells, tastes, and textures that seem real even when you know they are not. Chances are good that if you wake up suddenly–because of a ringing alarm clock or other loud noise–you will recall at least a few details from your dreams. Some writers keep journals of their dreams to help them create stories and reflect on life. It is believed that Edgar Allan Poe used this technique.

ACTIVITY

For a week, keep a journal of some of the more vivid images you remember from your dreams. Write them down as soon as you wake up. Then, choose some images you wouldn't mind sharing and use them to help create a story or poem. If you have difficulty remembering dreams, choose a real event and describe it as if it had been a dream.

Interdisciplinary Connection

Objective

- To understand that dreams can provide inspiration for stories

Teaching Strategies

Suggest that students, in order to help them recall their dreams, lie still with their eyes closed for several moments after they wake up from one. They should write down what they remember as soon as they can because the memory of dreams tends to fade quickly.

Activity

Students' journals should

- include only images that students are willing to share
- provide a basis for further elaboration rather than reconstruct a complete dream

Teaching Support

MEETING INDIVIDUAL NEEDS — MULTIPLE MODES OF EXPRESSION

Spatial Explain to students that surrealism is a style of painting that is considered dreamlike or nightmarish because of its strange imagery.

Activity Suggest that students conduct research about artists who painted in this style and report back to the class on what they learn. Encourage them to share reproductions of at least one artist's work that they feel typifies the dreamlike quality of surrealism. **L2**

Before Reading

Objectives

- To read and analyze a short story that combines elements of history with the unexplained and the supernatural
- To identify the oral tradition as a part of storytelling
- To write an evaluation of the story

Skills

Reading/Thinking: Inferring; Drawing Conclusions
Writing: Historical Analysis
Vocabulary: Prefixes
Grammar/Language: Punctuating Interior Dialogue
Collaboration: Literature Groups

Motivating STUDENTS

Selection Focus Transparency 65: Have students view the transparency and then discuss the questions provided.

Reading Focus: As an extension of the Reading Focus, have students discuss why some people believe in supernatural beings.

Before You Read

The Woman in the Snow

MEET PATRICIA C. McKISSACK

Patricia C. McKissack's life was shaped by the Civil Rights movement of the 1960s. "That was the period in which African Americans were really looking up . . . and doors were opening—ever so slightly, but still opening." McKissack and her husband, Fred, have cowritten nearly one hundred books, many dealing with African American history. The story "The Woman in the Snow" touches upon changing attitudes toward racial segregation between the 1930s and 1960s.

Patricia C. McKissack was born in Nashville, Tennessee, in 1944. She has also published under her birth name, L'Ann Carwell.

READING FOCUS

Do you like stories about supernatural beings? Why might a person believe in any of these beings?

Discuss
Are stories of supernatural beings always scary stories?

Setting a Purpose
Read to experience a story about the supernatural and the changing attitudes on race in the United States.

BUILDING BACKGROUND

The Time and Place The story takes place in an unnamed town in the American South. The first part after the introduction is set in 1935, during the Depression, when millions of workers were jobless. Then the story changes to 1960.

Did You Know? In 1955 Montgomery, Alabama, like many southern towns, was racially segregated. Although seventy-five percent of the city's bus riders were African American, they had to give up their seats to white riders. When Rosa Parks refused to get up after a long day's work and give her seat to a white man, she was arrested. The Women's Political Caucus swung into action, distributing 35,000 leaflets around the city calling for a bus boycott. The majority of black residents carpooled and walked for an entire year until the U.S. Supreme Court forced the city to integrate the buses.

VOCABULARY PREVIEW

pivotal (piv′ ət əl) *adj.* of central importance; p. 857
plummet (plum′ it) *v.* to fall downward; p. 858
petite (pə tēt′) *adj.* small and slender; little; p. 859
recoil (ri koil′) *v.* to draw back, as in fear; p. 859
pathetically (pə thet′ i kəl ē) *adv.* pitifully; p. 861
careening (kä rēn′ ing) *adj.* tilting or swaying while moving, as if out of control; p. 861
substance (sub′ stəns) *n.* basic material; solid quality; p. 862
console (kən sōl′) *v.* to comfort or cheer someone who is sad or disappointed; p. 863

RESOURCE MANAGER

Teaching Tools and Resources
- Theme Eight Planning Guide
- Literature Groups Sourcebook

Essential Lesson Support

Lesson-Specific Instruction
- Selection Focus Transparency 65
- Literary Elements Transparency 70
- Active Reading Guide,* p. 70
- Selection Vocabulary Practice, p. 48

Assessment
- Selection Quick Checks,* p. 70
- Sel. and Theme Assmt., pp. 121–122
- Testmaker: ExamView Pro
- Performance Assessment, p. 62

Systematic Language Instruction
- Gr. & Comp. Hbk., L. 14.4
- Vocabulary Power, Lesson 36
- Spelling Power, Lesson 32

English Language Learners
- ELL Sourcebook, p. 97
- Spanish Summaries, p. 65
- Spanish Translations, pp. 233–238
- Audio Library*
- English, Yes!

Special Needs/Strat. Interven.
- Interactive Rdg. Sbk., pp. T221–T224
- Interactive Rdg. Wkbk., pp. 133–134
- Inclusion Strat. Sbk., pp. 49–50
- Audio Library*

* Also available in Spanish

The Woman in the Snow

Bus in a Snowstorm. John Wesley Hardrick (1891–1968). Oil on board, 20 x 24 in. Indianapolis Museum of Art.

Retold by Patricia C. McKissack

The year-long Montgomery, Alabama, bus boycott in 1955–56 was a pivotal event in the American civil rights movement. Blacks refused to ride the buses until their demand of fair and equal treatment for all fare-paying passengers was met. Today the right to sit anywhere on a public bus may seem a small victory over racism and discrimination.

Vocabulary
pivotal (piv′ ət əl) *adj.* of central importance

Reading the Selection

SUMMARY

On a snowy night in 1935, Grady Bishop, a bigoted white bus driver in Montgomery, Alabama, refuses to take a young black woman and her sick baby to the hospital because she lacks the fare. The next morning the papers report that the woman and her baby were found frozen to death in the snow. On the first anniversary of her death, Grady relives the experience. Swerving to avoid the ghosts of the woman and her baby, he crashes and dies. Twenty-five years later to the day, Ray Hammond, the first African American bus driver in the city, encounters the mother and her baby. As Ray takes them to the hospital, he tells the mother of the changes the Civil Rights movement has brought. Now she can rest; she is never seen again.

Spanish Summaries, p. 65

A Active Reading Strategies

QUESTION Ask students to notice the byline of the story. What is its significance? *(This story has been passed orally from one person to another, and she has recorded it.)*

VOCABULARY Remind students to use context clues to unlock the meanings of new vocabulary words.

Additional Resources

Active Reading Guide, p. 70
Audio Library
Spanish Audio Library

CONNECTING TO OTHER SELECTIONS

The chart at the right shows three ways to connect "The Woman in the Snow" to other selections in this book.

For specific teaching strategies, see the ***Theme Eight Planning Guide.***

Connection		Title
Life Skills: Collaborating	→	"Stop the Sun," p. 607
Thematic: Equal Rights	→	"I Have a Dream," p. 494
Literary: Character Traits	→	"Americans All," p. 643

B Active Reading Strategies

CONNECT The author talks about the changes brought about by the boycott. Ask students to share what they already know about that time.

C Active Reading Strategies

EVALUATE Have students evaluate the first paragraph on page 858. Ask them how the tone of the story shifts. *(The paragraph is informational. The narrative starts with the words "Many cities had. . .")*

D Critical Thinking

INFERRING Point out to students that the author gives information about Grady's character but doesn't specify his race. Why not? How can you tell his race? *(On the basis of what the author has told us, we know that there were no African American bus drivers, so Grady has to be white.)*

E Critical Thinking

DRAW CONCLUSIONS Why does Grady call the Hall Street Express "The Blackbird Express"? Does the route manager share his attitude? How can you tell? You may wish to share the following model to illustrate the thinking process involved in drawing conclusions.

Model: Billy, the route manager, corrects Grady for using that demeaning expression. The author also says that Billy "walks away in disgust." These clues suggest to me that Billy does not share Grady's attitude.

Teaching Support

B But that single issue changed the lives of African Americans everywhere. After the successful boycott in Montgomery, blacks in other cities challenged bus companies, demanding not only the right to sit wherever they chose but also employment opportunities for black bus drivers. C Many cities had their own "bus" stories. Some are in history books, but this story is best enjoyed by the fireplace on the night of the first snowfall.

D Grady Bishop had just been hired as a driver for Metro Bus Service in 1935. When he put on the gray uniform and boarded his bus, nothing mattered, not his obesity,[1] not his poor education, not growing up the eleventh child of the town drunk. Driving gave him power. And power mattered.

E One cold November afternoon Grady clocked in for the three-to-eleven shift. "You've got Hall tonight," Billy, the route manager, said matter-of-factly.[2]

"The Blackbird Express." Grady didn't care who knew about his nickname for the route. "Not again." He turned around, slapping his hat against his leg.

"Try the *Hall Street Express*," Billy corrected Grady, then hurried on, cutting their conversation short. "Snow's predicted. Try to keep on schedule, but if it gets too bad out there, forget it. Come on in."

Grady popped a fresh stick of gum into his mouth. "You're the boss. But tell me. How am I s'posed to stay on schedule? What do those people care about time?"

Most Metro drivers didn't like the Hall Street assignment in the best weather, because the road twisted and turned back on itself like a retreating snake. When slick with ice and snow, it was even more hazardous. But Grady had his own reason for hating the route. The Hall Street Express serviced black domestics[3] who rode out to the fashionable west end in the mornings and back down to the lower east side in the evenings.

"You know I can't stand being a chauffeur for a bunch of colored maids and cooks," he groused.

"Take it or leave it," Billy said, walking away in disgust.

Grady started to say something but thought better of it. He was still on probation,[4] lucky even to have a job, especially during such hard times.

F Snow had already begun to fall when Grady pulled out of the garage at 3:01. It fell steadily all afternoon, creating a frosted wonderland on the manicured lawns that lined West Hall. But by nightfall the winding, twisting, and bending street was a driver's nightmare.

The temperature plummeted, too, adding a new challenge to the mounting snow. "Hurry up! Hurry up! I can't wait all day," Grady snapped at the boarding passengers. "Get to the back of the bus," he hustled them on impatiently. "You people know the rules."

The regulars recognized Grady, but except for a few muffled groans they paid

1. *Obesity* (ō bē′ sə tē) is the condition of being extremely overweight.
2. When Billy spoke *matter-of-factly,* he was businesslike, showing little or no emotion.
3. Household workers are often called *domestics.*
4. Here, *on probation* refers to Grady's working for a trial period before being given a permanent job—or let go.

Vocabulary
plummet (plum′ it) *v.* to fall downward

MEETING INDIVIDUAL NEEDS — ENGLISH LANGUAGE LEARNERS

Understanding Setting Write the following sentences on the board and discuss with students the meaning of each: "The year-long Montgomery, Alabama, bus boycott in 1955–56 was pivotal to the American Civil Rights movement." *(African Americans' refusal to ride the buses in 1955–1956 marked a turning point in the fight for equal rights.)* "The winding, twisting, and bending street was a driver's nightmare." *(Bus drivers were afraid of what might happen on the dangerous street.)*

Activity Encourage students to describe the setting of the story, including the physical and social environments.

Additional Resources

English Language Learners Sourcebook, p. 97

their fares and rode in sullen silence out to the east side loop.

"Auntie! Now, just why are you taking your own good time getting off this bus?" Grady grumbled at the last passenger.

The woman struggled down the wet, slippery steps. At the bottom she looked over her shoulder. Her dark face held no clue of any emotion. "Auntie? Did you really call me *Auntie?*" she said, laughing sarcastically. "Well, well, well! I never knew my brother had a white son." And she hurried away, chuckling.

Grady's face flushed with surprise and anger. He shouted out the door, "Don't get uppity with me! Y'all know *Auntie* is what we call all you old colored women." Furious, he slammed the door against the bitter cold. He shook his head in disgust. "It's a waste of time trying to be nice," he told himself.

But one look out the window made Grady refocus his attention to a more immediate problem. The weather had worsened. He checked his watch. It was a little past nine. Remarkably, he was still on schedule, but that didn't matter. He had decided to close down the route and take the bus in.

That's when his headlights picked up the figure of a woman running in the snow, without a hat, gloves, or boots. Although she'd pulled a shawl over the lightweight jacket and flimsy dress she was wearing, her clothing offered very little protection against the elements.[5] As she pressed forward against the driving snow and wind, Grady saw that the woman was very young, no more than twenty. And she was clutching something close to her body. What was it? Then Grady saw the baby, a small bundle wrapped in a faded pink blanket.

"These people," Grady sighed, opening the door. The woman stumbled up the steps, escaping the wind that mercilessly ripped at her petite frame.

"Look here. I've closed down the route. I'm taking the bus in."

In big gulping sobs the woman laid her story before him. "I need help, please. My husband's gone to Memphis looking for work. Our baby's sick, real sick. She needs to get to the hospital. I know she'll die if I don't get help."

"Well, I got to go by the hospital on the way back to the garage. You can ride that far." Grady nodded for her to pay. The woman looked at the floor. "Well? Pay up and get on to the back of the bus so I can get out of here."

"I—I don't have the fare," she said, quickly adding, "but if you let me ride, I promise to bring it to you in the morning."

"Give an inch, y'all want a mile. You know the rules. No money, no ride!"

"Oh, please!" the young woman cried. "Feel her little head. It's so hot." She held out the baby to him. Grady recoiled.

Desperately the woman looked for something to bargain with. "Here," she said, taking off her wedding ring. "Take this. It's gold. But please don't make me get off this bus."

He opened the door. The winds howled savagely.

"Please," the woman begged.

5. Here, *elements* means "the forces of nature; weather."

Vocabulary

petite (pə tēt′) *adj.* small and slender; little
recoil (ri koil′) *v.* to draw back, as in fear

F Active Reading Strategies

EVALUATE What is the weather like? What decision does Grady make? Do you think this has anything to do with his treatment of the passengers? *(It is snowing heavily, making it dangerous to drive. In his haste to get back safely, he is probably even ruder than usual.)*

G Active Reading Strategies

EVALUATE Ask students whether they think Grady's action toward the woman and her baby are in keeping with his character. Have students support their views by referring to the text.

Reading Minilesson

Drawing Conclusions Remind students that authors may not tell their readers everything about a character. Instead, they may give their readers hints from which the readers can draw conclusions.

Activity Draw students' attention to the description of Grady Bishop's background: "When he put on the gray uniform . . . And power mattered." Then discuss the following questions: What kind of power did Grady have? *(He had the power to make life easy or difficult for his passengers.)* Why does the author mention Grady's weight and lack of education? *(She is suggesting that there may have been better-qualified African Americans who could have done the job.)* **L2**

Additional Resources

Reading Skills Practice Workbook

VIEWING THE PHOTOGRAPH

Viewing Response *The setting—a snow storm—is emphasized here.*

Old Trinity in Winter. Guy Wiggins (1883–1962). Oil on canvas, 24 x 20 in. Private collection.
Viewing the painting: What literary element in the story does this painting emphasize?

Teaching Support

MEETING INDIVIDUAL NEEDS: MULTIPLE MODES OF EXPRESSION

Spatial Explain to students that artists who are interested in social causes can choose how they present the case for what they believe in. For example, they could make a statement about civil rights by painting a realistic scene of the Montgomery bus boycott. Or, they could choose to show just one person—such as Rosa Parks—who defied the bus company as a symbol of the entire black community.

Activity Have students research the works of one of the following artists and report on how the artist has dealt with social issues: Jacob Lawrence, Ben Shahn, Faith Ringgold. Ask each student to present his or her findings in an oral report accompanied by examples of the artist's work. **L2**

"Go on home, now. You young gals get hysterical over a little fever. Nothing. It'll be fine in the morning." As he shut the door the last sounds he heard were the mother's sobs, the baby's wail, and the moaning wind.

H Grady dismissed the incident until the next morning, when he read that it had been a record snowfall. His eyes were drawn to a small article about a colored woman and child found frozen to death on Hall Street. No one seemed to know where the woman was going or why. No one but Grady.

"That gal should have done like I told her and gone on home," he said, turning to the comics.

It was exactly one year later, on the anniversary of the record snowstorm, that Grady was assigned the Hall Street Express again. Just as before, a storm heaped several inches of snow onto the city in a matter of hours, making driving extremely hazardous.

I By nightfall Grady decided to close the route. But just as he was making the turnaround at the east side loop, his headlight picked up a woman running in the snow—the same woman he'd seen the previous year. Death hadn't altered her desperation. Still holding on to the blanketed baby, the small-framed woman pathetically struggled to reach the bus.

Grady closed his eyes but couldn't keep them shut. She was still coming, but from where? The answer was too horrible to consider, so he chose to let his mind find a more reasonable explanation. From some dark corner of his childhood he heard his father's voice, slurred by alcohol, mocking him. *It ain't the same woman, dummy. You know how they all look alike!*

Grady remembered his father with bitterness and swore at the thought of him. This *was* the same woman, Grady argued with his father's memory, taking no comfort in being right. Grady watched the woman's movements breathlessly as she stepped out of the headlight beam and approached the door. She stood outside the door waiting . . . waiting.

J The gray coldness of Fear slipped into the driver's seat. Grady sucked air into his lungs in big gulps, feeling out of control. Fear moved his foot to the gas pedal, careening the bus out into oncoming traffic. Headlights. A truck. Fear made Grady hit the brakes. The back of the bus went into a sliding spin, slamming into a tree. Grady's stomach crushed against the steering wheel, rupturing his liver and spleen.[6] *You've really done it now, lunkhead.* As he drifted into the final darkness, he heard a woman's sobs, a baby wailing—or was it just the wind?

K Twenty-five years later, Ray Hammond, a war hero with two years of college, became the first black driver Metro hired. A lot of things had happened during those two and a half decades to pave the way for Ray's new job. The military had integrated its forces

6. To *rupture* is to break or burst open. The *liver* and *spleen,* both located near the stomach, are important internal organs.

Vocabulary

pathetically (pə thet′ i kəl ē) *adv.* pitifully

careening (kä rēn′ ing) *adj.* tilting or swaying while moving, as if out of control

H Active Reading Strategies

RESPOND Have students respond to what happens to the woman and to Grady's reaction to it. How do they feel about his character now? *(Most students will be disgusted by his lack of compassion.)*

I Active Reading Strategies

EVALUATE Ask students to describe what Grady sees one year later. What are some possible explanations for the apparition? *(It may be that Grady, reminded by the weather of what happened to the woman and her baby, imagines her coming back to haunt him; or he may see the woman's ghost.)*

J Author's Craft

MOOD How does the author create a sense of fear? Why is Grady afraid? *(She re-creates the circumstances of the year before. Also, she describes Grady's terrified reaction. He may be afraid partly because of feelings of guilt.)*

K Active Reading Strategies

REVIEW Ray Hammond is another bus driver. What does his being hired say about the times? *(Things are beginning to change.)*

MEETING INDIVIDUAL NEEDS: SPECIAL NEEDS

Less-Proficient Readers Less-proficient readers may need help following the action in the scene in which Grady sees the apparition and crashes.

Activity Guide students through each paragraph by asking these questions:

1. How much time has passed since the last scene? *(one year)*
2. What does the third sentence mean? *(The woman's ghost acted as she had in life.)*
3. Who is speaking the words in italics? *(Grady remembers what his father said to him.)*
5. Who is speaking the words in italics? *(Grady imagines his father saying them.)* **L2**

Additional Resources

Inclusion Strategies

Active Reading Strategies

QUESTION Have students discuss why Ray is afraid. *(The anniversary and the similar weather conditions make him think he might see the woman's ghost.)*

Historical Note

Martin Luther King (1929–1968), an ordained Baptist minister, was an advocate of nonviolence and racial brotherhood. The Montgomery bus boycott was Dr. King's first experience in leading a major protest. He went on to lead others. In 1963 he helped organize the March on Washington, at which he delivered his "I Have a Dream" speech. In 1964 he received the Nobel Peace Prize for his work toward a peaceful adoption of integration.

Literature & Humanities

To provide background for the Civil Rights movement, use *The World of Music* CD 1, Track 23, "We Shall Overcome."

during the Korean War. In 1954 the Supreme Court had ruled that segregated[7] schools were unequal. And one by one, unfair laws were being challenged by civil rights groups all over the South. Ray had watched the Montgomery bus boycott with interest, especially the boycott's leader, Dr. Martin Luther King, Jr.

Ray soon found out that progress on the day-to-day level can be painfully slow. Ray was given the Hall Street Express.

"The white drivers call my route the Blackbird Express," Ray told his wife. "I'm the first driver to be given that route as a permanent assignment. The others wouldn't take it."

"What more did you expect?" his wife answered, tying his bow tie. "Just do your best so it'll be easier for the ones who come behind you."

In November, Ray worked the three-to-eleven shift. "Snow's predicted," the route manager barked one afternoon. "Close it down if it gets bad out there, Ray."

The last shift on the Hall Street Express.

Since he was a boy, Ray had heard the story of the haunting of that bus route. Every first snowfall passengers and drivers testified that they'd seen the ghost of Eula Mae Daniels clutching her baby as she ran through the snow.

"Good luck with Eula Mae tonight," one of the drivers said, snickering.

"I didn't know white folk believed in haints,"[8] Ray shot back.

But parked at the east side loop, staring into the swirling snow mixed with ice, Ray felt tingly, as if he were dangerously close to an electrical charge. He'd just made up his mind to close down the route and head back to the garage when he saw her. Every hair on his head stood on end.

He wished her away, but she kept coming. He tried to think, but his thoughts were jumbled and confused. He wanted to look away, but curiosity fixed his gaze on the advancing horror.

Just as the old porch stories had described her, Eula Mae Daniels was a small-framed woman frozen forever in youth. "So young," Ray whispered. "Could be my Carolyn in a few more years." He watched as the ghost came around to the doors. She was out there, waiting in the cold. Ray heard the baby crying. "There but for the grace of God goes one of mine," he said, compassion overruling his fear. "Nobody deserves to be left out in this weather. Ghost or not, she deserves better." And he swung open the doors.

The woman had form but no substance. Ray could see the snow falling *through* her. He pushed fear aside. "Come on, honey, get out of the cold," Ray said, waving her on board.

Eula Mae stood stony still, looking up at Ray with dark, questioning eyes. The driver understood. He'd seen that look before, not from a dead woman but from plenty of his passengers. "It's okay. I'm for

7. In general terms, *integrate* means "to bring parts (or people) together," and *segregate* means the opposite. Military service had long been open to all races, but African Americans were usually trained separately and often assigned to all-black units. In southern states, segregation laws had required that blacks and whites use "separate but equal" public facilities.

8. *Haints* is Ray's way of saying *haunts,* meaning "ghosts."

Vocabulary

substance (sub′ stəns) *n.* basic material; solid quality

Teaching Support

Real-World Connection

The TV Version Point out that a director of a television version of this story might choose to make this a real ghost story or might leave the viewer uncertain as to whether there was really a ghost.

Activity Have students work in small groups to discuss whether the television version would be more effective as a real ghost story or should be left to the viewer's interpretation. Students should answer such questions as *What message is the story trying to send about Civil Rights? Which approach would convey that message better? Why? If you wanted to leave it up to viewers to decide whether there was really a ghost, how would you do that? If you handled it as a straight ghost story, how would you present it?*

L2 COLLAB. LEARN.

Viewing the photograph: This photograph was taken in Montgomery, Alabama, in April 1956. The "EASE THAT SQUEEZE" sign refers to traffic problems, not seating on the bus. What information about the bus boycott does this photo reveal?

real. Ray Hammond, the first Negro to drive for Metro. Come on, now, get on," he coaxed her gently.

Eula Mae moved soundlessly up the steps. She held the infant to her body. Ray couldn't remember ever feeling so cold, not even the Christmas he'd spent in a Korean foxhole.[9] He'd seen so much death, but never anything like this.

The ghost mother consoled her crying baby. Then with her head bowed she told her story in quick bursts of sorrow, just as she had twenty-five years earlier. "My husband is in Memphis looking for work. Our baby is sick. She'll die if I don't get help."

"First off," said Ray. "Hold your head up. You got no cause for shame."

"I don't have any money," she said. "But if you let me ride, I promise to bring it to you tomorrow. I promise."

Ray sighed deeply. "The rule book says no money, no ride. But the book doesn't say a word about a personal loan." He took a handful of change out of his pocket, fished around for a dime, and dropped it into the pay box. "You're all paid up. Now, go sit yourself down while I try to get this bus back to town."

9. A *foxhole* is a pit that soldiers usually dig quickly for cover from enemy fire.

Vocabulary
console (kən sōl′) *v.* to comfort or cheer someone who is sad or disappointed

M Active Reading Strategies

EVALUATE How are Ray's actions different from Grady's? Why? *(He is fearful but because he is sympathetic to what Eula Mae has suffered, he chooses to right the wrong.)*

N Active Reading Strategies

EVALUATE Point out to students that Eula Mae is more surprised by Ray than he is by her. Why? What is the significance of her puzzlement? *(In her lifetime she never saw an African American bus driver. The significance of the story is that Eula Mae is reliving events set in an earlier time.)*

Viewing the Photograph

Viewing Response *The Associated Press photo is a testimony to the boycott's effectiveness; only the driver is on the bus.*

O Literary Elements

CHARACTER Discuss what Ray's exchange with Eula Mae shows about his character. *(Students may suggest that he is kind and dedicated to Civil Rights.)*

Fine Art Transparency 28

You may want to use ***Fine Art Transparency 28*** to discuss kinds of modern transportation and our dependence on them.

Interdisciplinary Connection

History Explain that fictional works—stories, movies, and television plays—may have historical facts embedded in them. Point out that even though historical events and people may be part of the setting, authors may take some freedom in changing facts to suit the dramatic nature of the presentation.

Activity Have students isolate those sections of the selection that they believe are fact. Then have them check those facts against historical records of the events in Montgomery, Alabama, in 1955 and the years covered in this story. **L2**

Literary Elements

ORAL TRADITION Point out to students that the author shares some historical information as background. Why do you think it is important to the oral tradition? *(It is the way to share a people's history.)*

Active Reading Strategies

RESPOND What do you think was the significance of Eula Mae's ghost? Why did she never appear again? *(Eula Mae's ghost is a symbol for past mistreatment of African Americans. Putting that "ghost" to rest is part of the process of ending racism.)*

Historical Note

The bus driver had Rosa Parks arrested, which brought on the bus boycott. For 381 days, more than 50,000 African Americans walked, car-pooled, used jitneys, and even rode mules to work rather than use the buses.

Thematic Focus

Hair-Raising Tales This story includes some factual events within a ghost story. Have students discuss whether this makes the story more believable or less believable. Does it take away from or add to the scary qualities?

ASSESSMENT

Quick Checks, p. 70

Teaching Support

Eula Mae started to the back of the bus.

"No you don't," Ray stopped her. "You don't have to sit in the back anymore. You can sit right up front."

The ghost woman moved to a seat closer, but still not too close up front. The baby fretted. The young mother comforted her as best she could.

They rode in silence for a while. Ray checked in the rearview mirror every now and then. She gave no reflection, but when he looked over his shoulder, she was there, all right. "Nobody will ever believe this," he mumbled. "*I* don't believe it.

"Things have gotten much better since you've been . . . away," he said, wishing immediately that he hadn't opened his mouth. Still he couldn't—or wouldn't—stop talking.

"I owe this job to a little woman just about your size named Mrs. Rosa Parks. Down in Montgomery, Alabama, one day, Mrs. Parks refused to give up a seat she'd paid for just because she was a colored woman."

Eula Mae sat motionless. There was no way of telling if she had heard or not. Ray kept talking. "Well, they arrested her. So the colored people decided to boycott the buses. Nobody rode for over a year. Walked everywhere, formed car pools, or just didn't go, rather than ride a bus. The man who led the boycott was named Reverend King. Smart man. We're sure to hear more about him in the future. . . . You still with me?" Ray looked around. Yes, she was there. The baby had quieted. It was much warmer on the bus now.

Slowly Ray inched along on the icy road, holding the bus steady, trying to keep the back wheels from racing out of control. "Where was I?" he continued. "Oh yeah, things changed after that Montgomery bus boycott. This job opened up. More changes are on the way. Get this: They got an Irish Catholic[10] running for President. Now, what do you think of that?"

About that time Ray pulled the bus over at Seventeenth Street. The lights at Gale Hospital sent a welcome message to those in need on such a frosty night. "This is it."

Eula Mae raised her head. "You're a kind man," she said. "Thank you."

Ray opened the door. The night air gusted up the steps and nipped at his ankles. Soundlessly, Eula Mae stepped off the bus with her baby.

"Excuse me," Ray called politely. "About the bus fare. No need for you to make a special trip . . . back. Consider it a gift."

He thought he saw Eula Mae Daniels smile as she vanished into the swirling snow, never to be seen again.

10. John F. Kennedy's election made him the first Catholic president, as well as the first president born in the 1900s and the youngest president.

Grammar and Language *Minilesson*

Punctuating Interior Dialogue Have students turn to page 861 and locate the sentences Grady hears in his head. Explain that when a writer wishes to show what someone is thinking, he or she may not use quotation marks. In this case, the writer used italics to let readers know that this is what Grady was thinking.

Activity Write the following sentences on the board without punctuation. Have students decide which words require quotation marks around them and which should be italicized.

1. Ray Hammond was worried. *What will I do if I see Eula Mae and her baby?*
2. Ray told his wife, "I don't think anyone will see Eula Mae again." **L2**

Additional Resources

- ***Grammar and Language Transparency 68***
- ***Grammar and Language Workbook,*** p. 267
- ***Grammar and Composition Handbook,*** Lesson 13.6
- ***Writer's Choice,*** Lesson 20.6

Responding to Literature

PERSONAL RESPONSE

- Think about what you discussed for the **Reading Focus** on page 856. Was this story scary? Why or why not?

Brackets connect questions that are paired to develop higher-level thinking skills.

Analyzing Literature

RECALL

1. What is presented as Grady Bishop's main personality trait?
2. What happens to Grady a year later when he again sees the woman with the baby?
3. What enables Ray Hammond to get a job driving buses?
4. What does Ray do for the woman and baby?

INTERPRET

5. Why, in your opinion, is Grady such an angry person?
6. Why does Grady fear the woman the second time he sees her?
7. What qualities that make Ray a good bus driver also make him the person the ghost has been waiting for?
8. Why, in your opinion, does the woman appear to ride the bus one more time?

EVALUATE AND CONNECT

9. Is it fair to say Grady represents the bad old days and Ray the dawn of equality? Why or why not?
10. What, do you think, would happen if a parent with a sick child tried to board a bus today, but could not afford the fare?

Untitled (513/3), 1982. Gerhard Richter. Oil on canvas, 69.8 x 54.6 cm. Private collection.

LITERARY ELEMENTS

Oral Tradition

Long before people invented writing, they told stories. Stories passed down in this way are part of the **oral tradition** of a society. Since most people long ago spent the daylight hours finding and preparing food, storytelling often took place after dark, around the fire. The flames and shadows made it easy for listeners to believe in the "haints," ghosts, and other beings whose presence could not be explained.

1. The author of "The Woman in the Snow" says, "This story is best enjoyed by the fireplace on the night of the first snowfall." Do you think that sounds engaging? Why or why not?
2. Think back on scary stories you've been told. List three stories you've heard. Was it scarier to hear them than it would be to read them?

- See **Literary Terms Handbook,** p. R7.

Responding to the Selection

PERSONAL RESPONSE

Some students may feel that dying on his bus was an appropriate end, whereas others may wish he had had a chance to see his world change and, ideally, to repent for what he did.

Analyzing Literature

1. He is presented as an angry, bigoted man.
2. He is so terrified that he crashes the bus and dies.
3. His skill and training, supported by court rulings and the Civil Rights movement, enable Ray Hammond to get a job driving a bus.
4. He helps her complete the journey she started by taking her and her baby to the hospital.
5. His father made him feel as though he was worthless.
6. He is afraid of ghosts, and he remembers his role in her death.
7. Ray is caring and positive, and he is African American.
8. She is trying to complete the journey she started in life, to get her child to the hospital.
9. It is not completely fair; although things have improved, they are not perfect. For example, only Ray is assigned to the Hall Street Express route.
10. Some students may think that other passengers or the bus driver would take care of the fare. Others may feel that the driver would suggest the parent call 911 for help.

LITERARY ELEMENTS

1. Students may feel that sitting by the fireplace is a good way to share a suspense story. Others may feel that they would rather have the lights on so as not to be too scared.
2. Students may prefer hearing the stories because the reader adds an extra element of drama.

Additional Resources

Literary Elements Transparency 70

Extending Your Response

Personal Writing

Students' responses should

- give examples of ways things have changed for better or for worse
- make comparisons with past events or circumstances

Writing About Literature

Students' recommendations should

- explain the scary elements of the story
- evaluate the characterizations and the ending

Interdisciplinary Activity Suggest that where possible students use reference materials to bring each person's life up to date.

Literature Groups Follow the debate by encouraging questions from listeners. COLLAB. LEARN.

Skill Minilesson

VOCABULARY • PREFIXES

1. e 3. c 5. b
2. a 4. d

Additional Resources

Vocabulary Practice, p. 48

Extending Your Response

Personal Writing

A Change for the Better? Ray tells the woman in the snow how much things have improved since she "went away." For example, buses and jobs have been integrated. Do you think the world has improved in your lifetime? Write a couple of paragraphs about how some things have changed in recent times, for either better or worse. You might ask your parents about the changes they've seen in their lifetimes and write a paragraph about those changes.

Interdisciplinary Activity

Social Studies Research the history of the boycotts, sit-ins, and laws of the 1950s and 1960s that helped end segregation. Make a chart listing the people who helped during these difficult times. After each name, write a brief summary statement explaining the person's contribution. Include dates and place names when possible. Share your findings with your class.

Writing About Literature

Your Oral Tradition You're on the committee searching for stories to read aloud at a library Scare-a-thon. In a paragraph or two, explain why "The Woman in the Snow" is suitable for your reading. Consider whether it is scary enough, if the characters are convincing, and whether or not its ending is effective.

Literature Groups

Compare Drivers There are many differences between the two bus drivers in this story. Divide your group in two to discuss the following statements:

- Each driver gives to others what he has gained from his own life.
- Each driver gets back from life what he gives out to others.

Cite passages from the story to support your opinion.

Save your work for your portfolio.

Skill Minilesson

RETEACH • REVIEW

VOCABULARY • PREFIXES

Eula Mae Daniels tries to *console* her baby. *Console* comes from the Latin prefix *com-,* which means "together," and the Latin word *solari,* which means "to calm or soothe." Ray Hammond has watched her with *compassion. Passion* originally meant "to suffer," so *compassion* is the feeling of "suffering with" another person.

Co-, com-, con-, cor-, and *col-* are different spellings of the same prefix. The spelling differs depending on what letter follows the prefix.

PRACTICE Look for word parts that you recognize in each word on the left. Then use what you know about prefixes and other word parts to match each word to its definition.

1. correlate a. to blend
2. commix b. to work together
3. constrain c. to hold in or back by force
4. correspond d. to write letters or notes back and forth
5. collaborate e. to show a connection between

ASSESSMENT

- ***Quick Checks,*** p. 70
- ***Selection and Theme Assessment,*** pp. 121–122
- ***Performance Assessment,*** p. 62
- ***Testmaker: ExamView Pro***
- ***Interactive Tutor: Self-Assessment***

Reading and Thinking Skills

Making and Verifying Predictions

As a skillful reader, you become involved in the action of a story and in the behavior of the characters. You wonder what will happen next. How will this character behave when faced with a problem? To make useful predictions, you use your prior knowledge of the situation and details from the story. For example, what did you think Grady would do when you first read the following passage from "The Woman in the Snow"? What did you know that helped you predict his behavior?

> "I—I don't have the fare," she said, quickly adding, "but if you let me ride, I promise to bring it to you in the morning."

As you continue reading, you check to see if your predictions were correct. You are **verifying predictions.** Did you use your prior knowledge of segregation and racial attitudes? Did you consider Grady's personality and his attitudes?

- For more about making and verifying predictions, see **Reading Handbook,** p. R94.

ACTIVITY

Choose a selection from this book that you would enjoy rereading, or a novel or short story you are reading for pleasure. As you begin to read, watch for clues about the characters, the setting, and the plot. Call on your prior knowledge–your reading or personal experiences that fit into the subject of the story. Then write down your prediction as the plot unfolds. Do this five or six times, and then verify your predictions. Consider these questions:

1. How did you choose when to make your predictions? Did you choose to make a prediction when the action was exciting or when a character needed to make a decision?
2. Were your predictions usually correct?
3. Why were some predictions incorrect? Had you read too quickly? Did you have enough prior knowledge to predict correctly? Did you have a clear understanding of the character's motivations?
4. How did making and verifying predictions improve your reading comprehension?

Reading and Thinking Skills

Objective

- To understand how to make and verify predictions

Teaching Strategies

Point out to students that the actions of well-developed characters are usually predictable. Explain that when someone acts "out of character" in a story, it may be because the writer wants to surprise the reader or suggest that characters can be irrational or inconsistent.

Activity

Have students write their answers to each question and compare them with a partner's responses. Discuss question 4 as a class.

Additional Resources

Reading Skills Practice Workbook

Teaching Support

MEETING INDIVIDUAL NEEDS — SPECIAL NEEDS

Learning Disabled Students with disabilities will benefit from an oral review of the skill taught on this page.

Activity Work through other examples from "The Woman in the Snow." Model for students how you were able to predict that Ray would see the ghosts: *When I read that Ray Hammond was going to drive the Hall Street Express Route, I immediately thought of that story.* (p. 862) Then ask students to predict how Ray will behave when he does see Eula Mae's ghost. (pp. 862–863) Have them write down the clues on which they base their predictions. **L1** COLLAB. LEARN.

Additional Resources

Inclusion Strategies

GRAMMAR LINK

Objective

- To use apostrophes correctly

Teaching Strategies

If, after practice, students still have difficulty in placing the apostrophe, make two columns on the board. In one write singular forms of common and proper nouns. In the other write the plural form of each noun. Remind students that the possessive form of a singular noun is formed by adding an apostrophe and an -s. The possessive case of a plural noun is formed by adding only an apostrophe if the word ends in s. Have students add the apostrophe or the apostrophe and -s for the possessive form of each noun. Allow space on the board for nouns that form their plurals irregularly—for example, *children, women, men, teeth,* and *mice.* The plural possessives of such exceptions add an apostrophe and -s.

Exercise

1. (a) baby's; (b) folk's; (c) driver's; (d) piles'; (e) yours; (f) buses'; (g) watch's; (h) address's; (i) brakes'; (j) children's

Additional Resources

- ***Grammar and Language Workbook,*** p. 269
- ***Grammar and Composition Handbook,*** Lesson 13.7
- ***Writer's Choice,*** Lessons 7.8, 9.3, 20.7

Teaching Support

GRAMMAR LINK

Using Apostrophes to Show Possession

The apostrophe is used to show possession. Sometimes it is used alone; sometimes it is combined with the letter *s.*

Problem 1 Singular possessive nouns

Grady Bishops job is driving a bus.

One snowy night, the bus brakes don't work.

Solution Use an apostrophe and an *s* to make a singular noun possessive, even if the noun ends in *-s.*

Grady Bishop's job is driving a bus.

One snowy night, the bus's brakes don't work.

Problem 2 Plural nouns ending in *-s*

The passengers groans are muffled when they recognize Grady.

Solution Add an apostrophe to make the plural noun possessive.

The passengers' groans are muffled when they recognize Grady.

Problem 3 Plural nouns not ending in *-s*

Grady doesn't care at all about peoples needs or difficulties.

Solution If a plural noun does not end in *-s,* add an apostrophe and an *s.*

Grady doesn't care at all about people's needs or difficulties.

Problem 4 Possessive personal pronouns

If a woman needs help, it's not Grady's problem, it's her's.

Solution Omit apostrophes in possessive pronouns, such as *hers.*

If a woman needs help, it's not Grady's problem, it's hers.

● For more about apostrophes, see **Language Handbook,** p. R42.

EXERCISE

Write the possessive form of each word.

a. baby	**c.** driver	**e.** yours	**g.** watch	**i.** brakes
b. folk	**d.** piles	**f.** buses	**h.** address	**j.** children

868 THEME 8

Writing Minilesson

Writing a Personal Response Students have now read works of several authors in the genre of suspense stories and poems. Ask them to consider which author's works they would like to read more of.

Activity Have students complete the statement *I would like to read more of [author]'s work because . . .* and support their statement with at least three reasons. **L2**

Additional Resources

- ***Writer's Choice,*** Lesson 2.4

Before You Read

The Dinner Party

MEET MONA GARDNER

When Mona Gardner wrote a story set in India, she knew her setting well. She lived in India, as well as in Japan, China, Hong Kong, and Bali. In the late 1930s, she traveled all over the Far East as a correspondent for an American newspaper syndicate, reporting on the turmoil that would lead to World War II.

Mona Gardner (1900–1982?) was born in Seattle, Washington. This story first appeared in the Saturday Review of Literature *in 1942.*

READING FOCUS

Do men and women handle crises differently? Does one gender react better than the other?

Journal

Describe a time when someone prejudged your ability to handle a tough situation on the basis of your gender.

Setting a Purpose

As you read this story, consider the feelings of the women and men at the dinner party.

BUILDING BACKGROUND

The Time and Place The time is the early 1900s. The place is India when it was a British colony.

Did You Know? Most societies once had firmly established roles for the men and women of that society. These roles depended largely on tradition, and also on the fact that women, because they bore children, were more likely than men to perform tasks that allowed them to care for children. Because many roles were based on gender, some societies developed beliefs that these roles were only suitable for one gender. In modern times, these beliefs have changed in many cultures. Both men and women have been freed to do work and to pursue hobbies based on their abilities and preferences.

VOCABULARY PREVIEW

naturalist (nach′ ər ə list) *n.* one who studies living things, especially plants or animals, by observing them directly; p. 871

arresting (ə res′ ting) *adj.* demanding the attention; striking; p. 871

sober (sō′ bər) *v.* to make or become serious and quiet; p. 871

forfeit (fôr′ fit) *v.* to lose as a penalty for some error or failure; p. 871

Before Reading

Objectives

- To read and analyze a suspense story with a surprise ending
- To identify the unexpected resolution of the plot
- To write a comparison of two characters

Skills

Reading/Thinking: Evaluating; Sequence of Events
Writing: Essay
Vocabulary: Multiple-Meaning Words
Collaboration: Literature Groups

Motivating STUDENTS

Selection Focus Transparency 66: Have students view the transparency and then discuss the questions provided.

Reading Focus: As an extension of the Reading Focus, discuss whether men and women handle crises differently.

RESOURCE MANAGER

Teaching Tools and Resources
- Theme Eight Planning Guide
- Literature Groups Sourcebook

Essential Lesson Support

Lesson-Specific Instruction
- Selection Focus Transparency 66
- Literary Elements Transparency 71
- Active Reading Guide,* p. 71
- Selection Vocabulary Practice, p. 49
- inTIME magazine, pp. 12-13

Assessment
- Selection Quick Checks,* p. 71
- Sel. and Theme Assmt., pp. 123-124
- Testmaker: ExamView Pro
- Performance Assessment, p. 63

Systematic Language Instruction
- Gr. & Comp. Hbk., L. 14.5
- Vocabulary Power, Unit 8 Review/Test
- Spelling Power, Unit 8 Review/Proofreading

English Language Learners
- Spanish Summaries, p. 66
- Audio Library*
- English, Yes!

Special Needs/Strat. Interven.
- Interactive Rdg. Sbk., pp. T224-T226
- Interactive Rdg. Wkbk., p. 135
- Inclusion Strat. Sbk., pp. 25-26
- Audio Library*

* Also available in Spanish

HAIR-RAISING TALES 869

Reading the Selection

SUMMARY

A dinner party in colonial India is the scene of a friendly but spirited argument over whether women have the nerves to handle a crisis. Only an American scientist notices the expression that crosses the hostess's face. When she orders a servant to set a plate of milk on the verandah, he realizes that it is bait for a cobra. To keep everyone from startling the snake into attacking, he proposes a forfeit for anyone who moves. When the cobra exits the room, there is screaming. It seems that the men have won the argument. Then the scientist asks the hostess how she knew the snake was there. "Because," she answers, "it was crawling across my foot."

Spanish Summaries, p. 66

Active Reading Strategies

PREDICT Have students read the first two paragraphs and predict what the major conflict is. *(The "spirited discussion" about differences between the sexes suggests that the conflict is about assumptions made about each sex.)*

Additional Resources

Active Reading Guide, p. 71

Audio Library

The Dinner Party

Mona Gardner

An Elegant Dinner Party. Jean Beraud (1849–1936). Pencil and watercolor heightened with white, 10 x 13 in. Private collection. Christie's Images.

Teaching Support

FINE ART TRANSPARENCY 16

You may want to use ***Fine Art Transparency 16*** to discuss reasons some animals evoke fear or dislike in many people.

CONNECTING TO OTHER SELECTIONS

The chart at the right shows three ways to connect "The Dinner Party" to other selections in this book.

For specific teaching strategies, see the ***Theme Eight Planning Guide.***

Connection		Title
Life Skills: Implementing and Performing	→	"Thank You, M'am," p. 161
Thematic: Breaking Stereotypes	→	from *The Diary of a Young Girl,* p. 675
Literary: Plot	→	"Chanclas," p. 71

The country is India. A large dinner party is being given by a colonial official and his wife. The guests are army officers and government attachés[1] and their wives, and an American naturalist.

A

At one side of the long table a spirited discussion springs up between a young woman and a colonel. The woman insists women have long outgrown the jumping-on-a-chair-at-sight-of-a-mouse era. The colonel says that women haven't the nerve control of men. Several men at the table agree with him.

"A woman's unfailing reaction in any crisis," the colonel says, "is to scream. And while a man may feel like it, yet he has that ounce more of control than a woman has. And that last ounce is what counts!"

The American scientist does not join in the argument, but sits watching the other guests. As he looks, he sees a strange expression come over the face of the hostess. She is staring straight ahead, the muscles of her face contracting slightly. With a small gesture she summons the native boy standing behind her chair. She whispers to him. The boy's eyes widen; he turns quickly and leaves the room. No one else sees this, nor the boy when he puts a bowl of milk on the verandah[2] outside the glass doors.

B

The American comes to with a start. In India, milk in a bowl means only one thing. It is bait for a snake. He realizes there is a cobra in the room.

He looks up at the rafters—the likeliest place—and sees they are bare. Three corners of the room, which he can see by shifting only slightly, are empty. In the fourth corner a group of servants stand, waiting until the next course can be served. The American realizes there is only one place left—under the table.

His first impulse is to jump back and warn the others. But he knows the commotion will frighten the cobra and it will strike. He speaks quickly, the quality of his voice so arresting that it sobers everyone.

"I want to know just what control everyone at this table has. I will count three hundred, and not one of you is to move a single muscle. The persons who move will forfeit 50 rupees.[3] Now! Ready!"

The people sit like stone images while he counts. He is saying ". . . two-hundred and eighty . . ." when, out of the corner of his eye, he sees the cobra emerge and make for the bowl of milk. Screams ring out as he jumps to slam shut the verandah doors.

C

"You were right, Colonel!" the host says. "A man has just shown us an example of real control."

D

"Just a minute," the American says, turning to his hostess, "there's one thing I'd like to know. Mrs. Wynnes, how did you know that cobra was in the room?"

A faint smile lights up the woman's face as she replies: "Because it was crawling across my foot."

1. *Attachés* (at′ ə shāz′) are assistants to an ambassador or other high official.
2. A *verandah* is a long porch, usually with a roof, along one or more sides of a house.
3. *Rupees* (ro͞o pēz′) are units of money used in India.

Vocabulary

naturalist (nach′ ər ə list) *n.* one who studies living things, especially plants or animals, by observing them directly
arresting (ə res′ ting) *adj.* demanding the attention; striking
sober (sō′ bər) *v.* to make or become serious and quiet
forfeit (fôr′ fit) *v.* to lose as a penalty for some error or failure

B Author's Craft

CHARACTER Remind students that the author has made one character a naturalist. How does that fact affect the outcome of the story? *(The scientist is by profession an observer; it is he who notices the change in the hostess's expression and her order to set out bait for a cobra.)*

C Literary Elements

PLOT: *Resolution* Why does it appear at first that the colonel has won the argument? *(The American naturalist, a man, obviously knew the cobra was in the room yet remained calm.)*

D Critical Thinking

EVALUATE Who is ultimately the winner in the discussion? Why? Ask students if they were surprised by the ending. Why or why not? *(The winner appears to be the young woman who has insisted that women would not scream in response to a crisis. The hostess proves that by her actions.)*

Thematic Focus

Hair-Raising Tales This is a very short story that seems to have almost no action, yet much is happening under the surface. Ask students whether that fact makes it scarier and more suspenseful. Have students give examples to support their answers.

ASSESSMENT

Quick Checks, p. 71

Reading Minilesson

Sequence of Events Point out that this story is told from the point of view of the American scientist, not exactly as things happened.

Activity Ask students to list the events of the story as they actually happened. *(1. A young woman and a colonel engage in an argument about the differences between the sexes. 2. A cobra crawls across the foot of the hostess. 3. The American naturalist notices the hostess's change of expression. 4. The hostess summons a servant and gives him orders. 5. The servant puts a bowl of milk on the verandah. 6. The naturalist challenges the guests to remain still. 7. The cobra emerges. 8. The naturalist reveals the hostess's courage.)* **L2**

Additional Resources

Reading Skills Practice Workbook

Responding to the Selection

PERSONAL RESPONSE

Students may agree and also point out that both he and the hostess prevented a potentially dangerous panic among the guests.

Analyzing Literature

1. They argue over whether women can remain as calm as men in a crisis.
2. He sees a strange expression come over the hostess's face.
3. He tries to keep everyone calm and safe by challenging the guests to remain absolutely still or forfeit fifty rupees.
4. The hostess has the most control, although it can be argued that the scientist is equally controlled.
5. She makes a generalization about all women.
6. She tells him to put a bowl of milk on the verandah.
7. Yes, he shows control by keeping the guests still.
8. The story shows readers how generalizations about people and groups are frequently incorrect.
9. No, we do not know the characters as individuals but by type. The author tells us just enough about the characters to set up and resolve the conflict.
10. Students may be able to answer from their own experience how such an argument would be made today. They may also expect the argument to be challenged, citing examples of courage in women and cowardice in men.

Active Reading and Critical Thinking

Responding to Literature

PERSONAL RESPONSE

- What was your reaction to the host's praise of the American scientist? Do you agree that he was "an example of real control"?

Brackets connect questions that are paired to develop higher-level thinking skills.

Analyzing Literature

RECALL

1. What do the young woman and the colonel argue about?
2. When does the American first realize something is wrong?
3. What does the American do when he sees the snake bait being put on the verandah?
4. Who turns out to have the most control in this story?

INTERPRET

5. How does the young woman show that she is not free from prejudice?
6. What does the hostess whisper to the servant?
7. Does the American show "that last ounce of control"? Support your answer.
8. What, in your opinion, is the purpose of this story?

EVALUATE AND CONNECT

9. Are any of the characters in this very short story developed fully by the writer? What effect does this kind of characterization have on the story?
10. Review your notes from the **Reading Focus** on page 869. Do you think the colonel's argument could be made today? If so, what response would he be likely to get? What facts would you give to prove or disprove his claim?

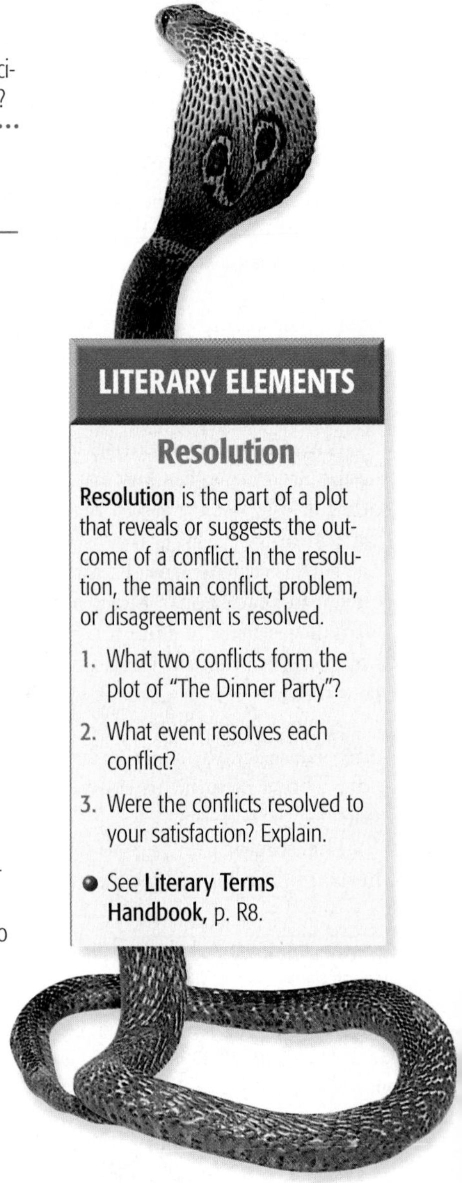

LITERARY ELEMENTS

Resolution

Resolution is the part of a plot that reveals or suggests the outcome of a conflict. In the resolution, the main conflict, problem, or disagreement is resolved.

1. What two conflicts form the plot of "The Dinner Party"?
2. What event resolves each conflict?
3. Were the conflicts resolved to your satisfaction? Explain.

- See **Literary Terms Handbook**, p. R8.

LITERARY ELEMENTS

1. One conflict is the argument about differences between the sexes. The other is how to remove the cobra safely.
2. The exit of the cobra resolves both conflicts.
3. Students might note that the author successfully made her point in the resolution.

Additional Resources

Literary Elements Transparency 71

Extending Your Response

Writing About Literature

Comparing Characters With a partner, reread the story and make notes on the characteristics shown by the British colonel and the American naturalist. Write a brief comparison of the two.

Learning for Life

Performance Appraisal You are a supervisor at NASA, evaluating applicants for a training program for future astronauts. Evaluate the four main characters in the story: the colonel, the hostess, the young woman, and the American naturalist. In two or three paragraphs, explain why you would or would not consider each person for the program.

Personal Writing

Attitudes and Arguments Why, in your opinion, does the hostess in the story have so little dialogue? If you had been the hostess, would you have responded to the claims made at the start of the story that men had more control of their emotions than women had of theirs? What might you have said after the cobra had been shut out?

Literature Groups

In Our Nature Even the young woman who argues with the colonel agrees that women used to jump on chairs at the sight of a mouse. Is she right? Were women more timid a few generations back? Have they outgrown that? Is it likely that all British military men would share the colonel's ideas? Would all American scientists have the wits to keep everyone sitting quietly? Is it fair to generalize about any group? Discuss these questions within your group.

Save your work for your portfolio.

Skill Minilesson

RETEACH • REVIEW

VOCABULARY • MULTIPLE-MEANING WORDS

Knowing one meaning of a word can sometimes help you figure out another meaning. For example, if a suspected criminal is *arrested,* the person is stopped. An *arresting* sight is one that stops you by demanding your attention.

PRACTICE Use your knowledge to match each underlined word with its definition.

1. a cutting remark
2. a pocket of ignorance
3. a command of French
4. on the scent of the thief
5. a spotty record of attendance

a. mastery
b. inconsistent
c. small area
d. meant to hurt
e. trail of clues

Extending Your Response

Writing About Literature

Students' comparisons should
- be based on the what the characters reveal in the story

Personal Writing

Students' responses should
- answer all the questions posed
- be supported by strong arguments

Learning for Life Suggest that students begin by listing what they believe are the ideal character traits for an astronaut.

Literature Groups Challenge students to answer the questions without making further generalizations. COLLAB. LEARN.

Skill Minilesson

VOCABULARY • MULTIPLE-MEANING WORDS

1. d
2. c
3. a
4. e
5. b

Additional Resources

Vocabulary Practice, p. 49

ASSESSMENT

- ***Quick Checks,*** p. 71
- ***Selection and Theme Assessment,*** pp. 123–124
- ***Performance Assessment,*** p. 63
- ***Testmaker: ExamView Pro***
- ***Interactive Tutor: Self-Assessment***

Writing WORKSHOP

Objectives

- To write a mystery story of approximately 500 to 700 words
- To plan, draft, revise, edit, and present a mystery story
- To reflect on and revise the mystery story

GLENCOE TECHNOLOGY

WRITER'S ASSISTANT CD-ROM

Students can use Glencoe's templates and guidelines software for narrative writing to aid them in working through the steps in the writing process in this lesson.

Teaching Strategies

PREWRITING

Choose a Tale Tell students to take sufficient time to think through this step. Remind them of the criteria for writing this piece:

- The story should be one they have heard, read, or seen on film or TV.
- They must be able to explain the mystery rationally.

Examine the Facts Point out to students that if they cannot complete this step, they might consider looking for another mystery.

Teaching Support

Writing WORKSHOP

Narrative Writing: Mystery Story

Mysteries, spine-tingling stories–who can resist them? Whether it's a suspenseful television show, an urban legend, or a real-life experience, a mystery story can be fun to read, hear, or tell. We love to shiver through a chilling tale, and we feel relieved when there is a logical explanation for a mysterious event.

Assignment: Follow the process described on these pages to develop your own mystery story that includes a logical explanation of a puzzling event.

- As you write your story, refer to **Writing Handbook**, pp. R50–R55.

EVALUATION RUBRIC

By the time you complete this Writing Workshop, you will have

- written an opening that captures your reader's attention
- developed a plot through the stages of exposition, rising action, climax, falling action, and resolution
- used realistic dialogue, specific action, and description to develop characters, create a setting, and add suspense
- revealed a logical explanation for the mysterious event
- expressed your reaction to the incidents in the story
- presented a mystery story that is free of errors in grammar, usage, and mechanics

The Writing Process

PREWRITING

PREWRITING TIP

To get ideas for ways to tell your mystery story, make a list of your favorites from stories you have read in Theme 8. For each story, write one or more things that make it especially effective.

Choose a Tale

Take a moment to recall mysteries that you've heard, read, or seen on film or TV. How is the air of mystery created? How are mysterious events explained? Now think of a mysterious event that you have experienced or heard of and use it as the basis for your mystery story.

Story:
One night when I was eight years old, my little sister and I thought a ghost was outside our bedroom window.

Details:
** we'd been telling ghost stories*
** mysterious bright lights*
** rattling sounds at window*
** cold, windy weather*
** many businesses nearby*

Explanation:
We'd been seeing the searchlights used by a local business to advertise a big sale.

MEETING INDIVIDUAL NEEDS — **ENGLISH LANGUAGE LEARNERS**

Mysteries from Other Cultures Encourage English language learners to write a story based on a mysterious event from their own cultures. Discuss with students what constitutes a fact as opposed to an unsupported opinion or belief.

Activity Suggest that students ask family members about mysteries that relate to people or places in their cultures, whether in the United States or in their native countries. Remind students that they can flavor their writing with real cultural elements, familiar characters from their cultures, and plausible settings. **COLLAB. LEARN.**

Additional Resources

English Language Learners Sourcebook

Examine the Facts

In a sentence or two, summarize your plot. Then list the details of the story and decide on a reasonable explanation for the mysterious event.

Consider Your Purpose and Audience

Plan your draft with your purpose and audience in mind. When writing a mystery story, your purpose is to entertain and even to scare your audience a little. How you do that will depend on your audience. Your audience for this story will be your teacher and classmates so try to include special effects that will increase the suspense for them.

Map Out the Plot

Map out the events of your plot that build to the climax–the moment of greatest suspense or most intense excitement for your audience. Then add narrative and descriptive details that will make the events clearer and more intriguing. For example, you might include a moment of dialogue, a decisive action, a personal observation, or a vivid image. What logical explanation can you offer to account for these mysterious events? What conclusion can you draw about the experience?

Events	*Supporting Details*
My little sister and I lay wide awake.	We were frozen with fear and too scared to move.
We saw something weird.	A spooky white light flickered outside the window.
We heard a terrifying sound.	The window rattled noisily for a few minutes.
We jumped toward the window to scare the ghost away.	The ghost flashed by the window again just as we jumped.
We screamed and ran to the kitchen.	"Mom! Dad! We just saw a ghost!"

Explanation: *We were seeing a local car dealer's search light, not a ghost.*

Conclusion: *We scared ourselves. The stories we'd been telling made us imagine a ghost was outside.*

Consider Your Purpose and Audience Suggest that students keep in mind that their audience will be made up of people with various attitudes and preconceptions. For example, some may be skeptical about supernatural occurrences, while others may believe wholeheartedly in them. Explain that students should do their best to write a mystery that is intriguing and has believable characters to keep their audience involved.

Map Out the Plot Point out that effective techniques for advancing the plot include dialogue, descriptions of specific actions, and descriptions of the ways various characters react. Ask students to use these techniques, as well as simply to recount the sequence of events. You might encourage them to plant clues that will help readers guess the outcome of the mystery. Students can also include "red herrings" to throw readers off track. Stress that the ending should provide a solution to the mystery. Encourage students to think through their plot carefully and end their story with a dramatic twist if possible.

Additional Resources

- ***Writing and Proofreading Practice,*** pp. 1–6, 58–64
- ***Writing and Proofreading Transparencies*** 1–6, 39–40
- ***Writer's Choice,*** Lessons 5.1.–5.10

Writing *Minilesson*

Planning Point out that careful planning and research are important parts of crafting an effective mystery story. So is maintaining a critical eye by distancing oneself from the story when you are in the later stages of the writing process.

Activity Encourage students to give every stage of their writing a cooling-off period. For example, if they complete one step in the afternoon, they should set aside their work until the next day. Select volunteers to follow this course of action and to keep a journal on how it helped their writing.

Additional Resources

- ***Writer's Choice,*** Lesson 5.7

DRAFTING

Open with Suspense Students may find ideas for good opening sentences by looking at reviews of suspense movies or television dramas.

Unravel the Mystery Remind students to make the first-person voice as engaging and immediate as if they had just encountered the mystery.

REVISING

Rework or Rewrite Remind students of the importance of a cooling-off period at this stage of writing. Point out that distancing oneself from one's work allows one to return to it with a fresh, critical eye. When students revise their drafts, they should make sure that the events and clues provided early in the mystery support the ending.

GLENCOE TECHNOLOGY

REVISING WITH STYLE CD-ROM

Invite students to use the *Revising with Style* CD-ROM, which offers instruction and exercises to help students improve their writing skills.

Teaching Support

Writing **WORKSHOP**

DRAFTING

DRAFTING TIP
Consider various ways to create suspense at the beginning of your mystery story. For example, describe an eerie setting, a superstitious character, or a supernatural event.

Open with Suspense

Start with background information about the chilling tale. Don't provide your explanation right away. Instead, create suspense to capture readers' attention. Weave clues into your opening but don't add them up for readers yet.

Unravel the Mystery

Writing the explanation for a mysterious event is similar to playing the role of detective. Show how the clues you presented in the plot lead to the real meaning of what happened. Refer to your prewriting notes and make your reasoning clear.

STUDENT MODEL • DRAFTING

The car dealer sometimes used searchlights when he was having a sale. The lights were so bright they shone for miles and miles, and they waved back and forth in the sky. That night the lights just happened to swing in the direction of our house. And what about the rattling at the window? "It's just the wind," said my father.

Complete Student Model on p. R130.

REVISING

REVISING TIP
Does your partner find your explanation of the mystery hard to follow? Try adding transitions such as *thus, this shows that, since, because, therefore,* or *so.*

Rework or Rewrite

After a break, return to your draft to map out changes. Use the **Rubric for Revising** as a guide. If you have a partner, ask him or her to point out strong points as well as weak points. You might either rework your original or write another draft from scratch.

RUBRIC FOR REVISING

Your revised mystery story should have
- an opening that engages the reader's attention and builds suspense
- a well-organized plot
- narrative and descriptive details that help the reader visualize the story
- a clear and logical explanation of a mysterious event
- a conclusion that reflects on the meaning of the event

Your revised story should be free of
- events and details that do not advance the plot
- unclear or confusing transitions
- errors in grammar, usage, and mechanics

MEETING INDIVIDUAL NEEDS — SPECIAL NEEDS

Less-Proficient Readers Less-proficient readers may lack the self-confidence to offer helpful criticism to their peers. Work with students to create a peer-editing checklist that includes the following items: intriguing puzzle, believable sleuth, helpful clues, and a conclusion that wraps up the story or offers a surprise ending.

Activity Pair readers of varied reading abilities. Have them read their mysteries aloud and then edit their partner's story using their checklist.
L2 **COLLAB. LEARN.**

Additional Resources

Inclusion Strategies

EDITING/PROOFREADING

Before making a final copy, check your grammar and mechanics, making needed corrections. Look for each point mentioned on the **Proofreading Checklist.** Pay special attention to the use of apostrophes, as shown in the **Grammar Link** on page 868.

Grammar Hint

Never use an apostrophe in *its*, the possessive pronoun meaning "belonging to it." *It's*, with an apostrophe, is the contraction of *it is*.

It's only the wind. The wind howled its way down the street.

PROOFREADING CHECKLIST

- Punctuation, including apostrophes, is correct. (Be sure no apostrophes are used with personal pronouns such as *theirs, yours,* and *its.*)
- Sentences are complete; there are no fragments or run-ons.
- All verbs agree with their subjects.
- Spelling and capitalization are correct.

STUDENT MODEL • EDITING/PROOFREADING

A strange white shape apeared and then vanished. "Its so spooky" I told my sister.

Complete Student Model on p. R130.

Complete Student Model

For a complete version of the model developed in this Workshop, refer to **Writing Workshop Models**, p. R130.

PUBLISHING/PRESENTING

Team up with a partner to perform a dramatic reading of your story for your class. Use your voice, facial expressions, and gestures to dramatize moments of suspense in your story. As you read, your partner can create sound effects to heighten exciting moments in the plot.

PRESENTING TIP

The audience's reaction to your story may help you see where your story could be reorganized so it is easier to follow.

Reflecting

Think about the following questions. Write detailed responses in your journal.

- On which part of this assignment did you work hardest? Explain.
- What part of your story would you like to go back and rework? Why?

Save your work for your portfolio.

EDITING/PROOFREADING

Students can use the Proofreading Checklist in the *Grammar and Composition Handbook* as they review their work.

Having students read their work aloud is a good way to catch typographical errors and incorrect usage.

PUBLISHING/PRESENTING

Students who present their writing orally should take adequate time to rehearse and improve their deliveries.

Reflecting

Portfolio Encourage students to ask themselves these questions as they review their work:

- How did my audience react when they read or heard my mystery story?
- Does this reaction suggest that some portions of the work require further clarification?
- Which parts of the story work well enough to serve as a model for further revision?

ASSESSMENT

Writing Assessment and Portfolio Management

- Writing Assessment, pp. 1–12, 38–40
- Portfolio Management, pp. 41–48

6+1 TRAITS™ OF WRITING

See the annotated **Writing Workshop Models** on pp. R119–R130 for additional help in evaluating student writing and in teaching the **6+1 Traits™ of effective writing.** Annotations and minilessons address and reinforce the **6+1 Traits™:** Ideas, Organization, Voice, Word Choice, Sentence Fluency, Conventions, and Presentation.

HAIR-RAISING TALES 877

Theme Assessment

Objectives

- To respond to the stories, discussions, and activities in this theme
- To write a comparison of two stories
- To complete a self-evaluation, set a goal, and devise a plan for achieving the goal

Responding to the Theme

1. Students should explain their criteria and support their choices with reference to the selections.
2. Students' responses should be based on sound reasons and be supported by examples from selections in this theme.
3. Encourage students to evaluate their own theme projects.

Analyzing Literature

Students' writing should

- have an introductory paragraph that identifies the two stories and the characters being compared
- include details from the two stories to support students' conclusions

Evaluate and Set Goals

Evaluate

Have students list the projects they found most rewarding and those they felt were less challenging. Suggest that when they set goals for themselves, they keep these lists in mind.

To help students formulate valid reasons for their ratings, you may suggest that they develop a class rubric.

Set Goals

Encourage students to refer to their lists of projects that they found difficult and to include improvement in at least one of them in their lists of goals. When you hold individual conferences, discuss ways to achieve these goals.

Theme Assessment

Responding to the Theme

1. Which selection did you find the scariest? Why?
2. What new thoughts do you have about the following ideas as a result of reading this theme?
   - Our own imaginations can be scarier than fiction.
   - An overactive imagination can cause big trouble for its owner.
   - Some stories reflect our worst fears.
3. Present your theme project to the class.

Analyzing Literature

SUSPENSE

Writers create suspense by making readers wonder what might happen next. Choose two suspenseful scenes from the theme. Explain how each writer creates suspense in the selection.

Evaluate and Set Goals

1. Of the following activities, which did you enjoy the most? Which did you find the most difficult?
   - reading and understanding the selections
   - writing your own pieces
   - analyzing and discussing the selections
   - presenting ideas and projects
   - researching topics
2. How would you assess your work in this theme, using the following scale? Give at least two reasons for your assessment.

   4 = outstanding 2 = fair
   3 = good 1 = weak
3. Think about what you found challenging in this theme, and choose a goal to work toward in the future.
   - Record your goal and three steps you will take to try to reach it.
   - Meet with your teacher to review your plan for achieving your goal.

Build Your Portfolio

SELECT

Choose two pieces of work from this theme for your portfolio. Write a note to accompany each choice. Use these questions as a guide.

- ✦ Which do you consider your best work? Why?
- ✦ Which turned out to be most challenging? What did you learn from creating it?

REFLECT

Take some time to review all of the work you have selected for your portfolio. Organize the pieces–by theme or by order of preference, for example. Then prepare a table of contents and an introductory note for your completed portfolio.

ASSESSMENT

Writing Assessment, pp. 1–12.
Portfolio Management, pp. 41–48

GLENCOE TECHNOLOGY

MINDJOGGER VIDEOQUIZZES VIDEODISC

Use *MindJogger* to review the Theme 8 content.

Theme 8
Side B

Also available in VHS.

Reading on Your Own

If you have enjoyed the literature in this theme, you might also be interested in the following books.

The House of Dies Drear

by Virginia Hamilton The house is old, huge, and guarded by a cross caretaker. In addition, there are supposed to be a buried treasure and a ghost. Thomas and his family discover the history of the house and of their own ancestors as they explore the building's connection with the Underground Railroad.

Companions of the Night

by Vivian Vande Velde Sixteen-year-old Kerry is always sensitive to her little brother Ian's tears. As a result, she agrees to make a scary late-night trip to the laundromat to recover Ian's stuffed bear. At the laundromat, Kerry's scary adventure begins.

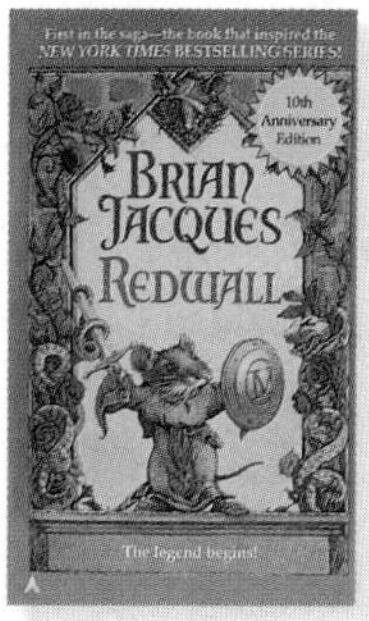

Redwall

by Brian Jacques The creatures living at Redwall Abbey are a peaceful group until the king of vermin declares war against them. Matthias, an apprentice mouse, sets out to find a magic sword that can save Redwall. This is the first book in a series of more than ten tales of quests and fights between good and evil.

Foundation

by Isaac Asimov This book is the first in a series of books that combine science and technology with human strengths and weaknesses. Characters must struggle to achieve their dreams in this classic science fiction novel.

Reading on Your Own

Tips for Independent Reading

Stress the importance of each student's spending at least a half-hour a day in independent reading and supply a list of readings related to the theme under study. Advise students that questioning as they read suspense stories will help them get the most enjoyment from their reading. If they succeed in figuring out the clues that the writer has provided in the descriptions of character and setting, the climax of the story will be even more satisfying.

Practice As students read, have them jot down short responses to questions like the following: What does the setting suggest about the nature of the story? How will this character respond to events in the story? In what ways is the main character like you? How might you react in similar circumstances?

Glencoe Literature Library

The House of Dies Drear by Virginia Hamilton is one of seventy books available in the *Glencoe Library*. For a complete listing, see the **Glencoe Resources for Independent Reading** in the front of this book. *The Study Guides for Glencoe Literature* provide instructional support and student activities for works in the *Glencoe Library*.

MEETING INDIVIDUAL NEEDS — SPECIAL NEEDS

You may wish to recommend *The House of Dies Drear* by Virginia Hamilton to your less-proficient readers. The accessible subject matter and writing style make this book particularly appropriate for these students. **L1**

The books listed below are rated for average readers **(L2)** or for students who need more challenging reading **(L3).**

- *Redwall* by Brian Jacques **L2**
- *Companions of the Night* by Vivian Vande Velde **L2**
- *Foundation* by Isaac Asimov **L3**

Standardized Test Practice

The Princeton Review TEST-TAKING TIP

Students should attempt to answer each question with complete focus. They should not allow previously troublesome questions to distract them from the question they are answering at the present moment. Once students have read a question, considered the answer choices, and chosen an answer, they should put that question behind them and move on to the next one using the same systematic approach.

The Princeton Review TEST-TAKING TIP

Explain the importance of not acting on impulse, even if students feel they know the best answer right away. Students should never answer reading comprehension questions without first referring back to the passage and then considering every answer choice before selecting their answer.

The Princeton Review

Standardized Test Practice

Read the following passage. Then read each question on page 881. Decide which is the best answer to each question. Mark the letter for that answer on your paper.

Operating Your New Air Conditioner

Once your air conditioner is installed, you can escape the uncomfortable heat and enjoy some wonderful cool air. Read the operating instructions below to learn how to use your new air conditioner.

Control Panel Functions

There are two knobs on the control panel. These control the functions of the air conditioning unit.

Selector Knob

Fan:	The fan will circulate the air, but it won't cool the air. It runs at medium speed.
Low Cool:	Circulates cold air at a slow speed.
Medium Cool:	Circulates cold air at a medium speed.
High Cool:	Circulates cold air at a high speed.

Thermostat Knob

This knob allows you to adjust the temperature of the air. Set the thermostat at the highest number (10) to get the coldest air temperature.

Energy Saving Tips

- Avoid placing the air conditioner in a window that gets direct sunlight.
- Lower the thermostat temperature if the outside temperature drops during the evening hours.
- Keep the filter clean.
- Keep windows and outside doors closed to keep warm air out and cold air in.
- Turn off the air conditioner when you are not at home.

MEETING INDIVIDUAL NEEDS — ENGLISH LANGUAGE LEARNERS

Household Appliance Identification Read the passage to your class. Pass around index cards with the names of specific household appliances on them to groups of two or three students. Ask students to draw pictures of a human interacting with each appliance. Some examples you may want to use are: *hair dryer, refrigerator, dishwasher, lamp,* and *garden hose*.

1 You can tell from this passage that—

A a thermostat setting of six is colder than a thermostat setting of ten.

B a thermostat setting of six is warmer than a thermostat setting of ten.

C the air conditioner doesn't work if placed in a window with direct sunlight.

D the air conditioner works best when placed in a window with direct sunlight.

2 The selector knob is used to determine—

J whether or not to circulate cold air and what speed to use.

K how long the air conditioning unit has been running.

L the amount of energy used to run the air conditioner.

M the temperature of the air that is circulated.

3 Which of the following is an OPINION in the passage?

A Keeping the filter clean saves energy.

B Cool air is wonderful.

C The unit operates at three speeds.

D Ten is the highest thermostat setting.

4 The thermostat knob is used to—

J choose a desired function.

K stop the air conditioner.

L pick a temperature.

M start the machine.

5 This passage is most like—

A a newspaper advertisement.

B a schedule.

C an instruction manual.

D a political flyer.

STOP

Answers and Analyses

1. B The passage states that the highest thermostat setting is 10, and that 10 is the coldest temperature. Students can then deduce that 6 cannot be any colder than 10. Using this logic, students will know that 6 must be warmer than 10, making choice B the best answer.
2. J Advise students to reread the "Selector Knob" section. Students should conclude that the selector knob is used for setting the fan or the speed of cold air to be circulated. The section says nothing about how long the unit has been running, the amount of energy it uses, or the temperature of the air that is circulated. Choice J is therefore the best answer.
3. B Have students carefully read through each answer choice and ask themselves if the statement sounds like a fact or an opinion. Encourage them to look for qualitative adjectives like *wonderful* or *terrible* to identify an opinion as opposed to a fact. Remind them that the opinion must be stated in the passage. Choice B is the best answer.
4. L As in question 2, remind students to refer back to the relevant part of the passage. The first sentence in the "Thermostat Knob" section says that the knob "allows you to adjust the temperature of the air." Therefore, choice L is the only appropriate answer.
5. C Ask students to review elements of each of the passage types listed as answer choices. From the passage's title, they should then deduce that the information within the selection is a set of instructions on operating an air conditioner, making choice C the best answer.

Tested Objectives

Item	Language Objective
1, 5	Compare and contrast the features and elements of consumer materials to gain meaning from documents (e.g., warranties, contracts, product information, and instructional manuals)
1, 5	Read and understand grade-level-appropriate material; describe and connect the essential ideas, arguments, and perspectives of the text by using their knowledge of text structure, organization, and purpose

MORE PRACTICE

For additional practice, assign pages from one of the following standardized test resources available as part of Glencoe Literature.

Additional Resources

ITBS Preparation and Practice

SAT-9 Preparation and Practice

TerraNova Preparation and Practice

Reference Section

Literary Terms Handbook

A

Act A major division of a play. A play may be subdivided into several acts. Most modern plays have one, two, or three acts. *The Diary of Anne Frank,* for example, has two acts. Acts are usually composed of one or more scenes.

See page 710.
See also SCENE.

Alliteration The repetition of consonant sounds, most often at the beginnings of words and syllables. Edgar Allan Poe uses alliteration in the following line from "The Raven":

Doubting, dreaming dreams no mortal ever
dared to dream before. . . .

See pages 294–295, and 506.

Allusion A reference in a work of literature to a well-known character, place, or situation in history or from another work of literature, music, or art. For example, O. Henry's "The Ransom of Red Chief" contains an allusion to the biblical story of David and Goliath, a tale in which a small and apparently powerless hero overcomes a feared and powerful giant.

See page 853.

Antagonist A person or force that opposes the **protagonist,** or central character, in fiction. The reader is generally meant not to sympathize with the antagonist. In "The Treasure of Lemon Brown," there are several antagonists—for example, the thugs who attack Greg and Lemon Brown and the problems of age and loneliness that afflict the elderly musician.

See also CONFLICT, PROTAGONIST.

Anthropomorphism Attributing human characteristics to an animal or object. For example, in the folktale "Talk," the farmer's crops and animals speak to the farmer and to one another.

Assonance The repetition of vowel sounds, especially in a line of poetry. For example, the sound of long *e* is repeated in Margaret Walker's "Sorrow Home."

. . . reared in steam-heated flats

See page 506.
See also ALLITERATION, CONSONANCE.

Author's purpose The intention of the writer—for example, to explain, to tell a story, to persuade, to amuse, or to inform. An author may have more than one purpose. In "The Gettysburg Address," one of Lincoln's purposes was to honor a group of people.

See pages 476 and 646.

Autobiography The story of a person's life written by that person.

See page 196.
See also BIOGRAPHY, MEMOIR.

B

Ballad A short narrative song or poem. Folk ballads, which usually tell of an exciting or dramatic episode, were passed on by word of mouth for generations before being written down. The story of John Henry was passed down primarily in musical form. Literary ballads, which usually have

LITERARY TERMS HANDBOOK R1

known authors, are written in imitation of folk ballads.

See page 356.
See also NARRATIVE POETRY, ORAL TRADITION.

Biography The account of a person's life written by someone other than the subject. Biographies can be short or book-length.

See also AUTOBIOGRAPHY, MEMOIR.

C

Character A person or other creature in a literary work. A **dynamic character** is one who changes during the story, as does Jim in Kurt Vonnegut's "The Kid Nobody Could Handle." A **static character** remains the same throughout the story, like the crazed narrator of Edgar Allan Poe's "The Tell-Tale Heart."

See pages 23, 46–47, 358, 508, and 832.
See also CHARACTERIZATION.

Characterization The methods a writer uses to develop the personality of a character. In **direct characterization,** the story's narrator makes statements about a character's personality. In **indirect characterization,** a character's personality is revealed through his or her words and actions and through what others think and say about him or her. These techniques are often combined, as in the characterization of the father in Gary Paulsen's "Stop the Sun."

See pages 165, 291, and 692–693.
See also CHARACTER.

Climax The point of greatest interest or suspense in a narrative. Usually the climax comes at the turning point in a story or drama. In "Raymond's Run," by Toni Cade Bambara, the climax occurs as Squeaky races against Gretchen and notices Raymond running on the other side of the fence.

See pages 264, 404, 615, and 832.
See also FALLING ACTION, PLOT, RISING ACTION.

Comedy A type of drama that is humorous and has a happy ending.

See also DRAMA, TRAGEDY.

Conflict The central struggle between opposing forces in a story or play. An **external conflict** is the struggle of a character against an outside force, such as fate, nature, society, or another person. In Yoshiko Uchida's tale "The Wise Old Woman," a man and his mother struggle against the ruler's demands. An **internal conflict** exists within the mind of a character. The man in Uchida's story is torn between loyalty to the ruler and love for his mother.

See pages 247, 358, 561, and 832.
See also ANTAGONIST, PLOT, PROTAGONIST.

Consonance The repetition of identical or similar end or intermediate consonant sounds. The vowel sounds that accompany these repeated consonants usually differ. Shel Silverstein uses consonance in the following line from "Forgotten Language":

Once I understood each word the caterpillar said, . . .

See page 506.
See also ALLITERATION, ASSONANCE, RHYME, SOUND DEVICES.

Couplet Two successive lines of verse that form a unit and usually rhyme. John Greenleaf Whittier's poem "Barbara Frietchie" is composed entirely of rhyming couplets, including the following example:

Over Barbara Frietchie's grave,
Flag of Freedom and Union, wave!

D

Description Writing that creates an impression of a setting, a person, an animal, an object, or

R2 LITERARY TERMS HANDBOOK

an event by appealing to one or more of the five senses. In the excerpt from James Herriot's *All Things Bright and Beautiful,* the veterinarian provides a vivid description of his work with a large patient.

See pages 196 and 444.

Dialect A variation of language spoken by a particular group or by many people within a geographic region. Dialects differ from standard language. They may contain different structures, sounds, forms, or word meanings. An example of dialect appears in *I Know Why the Caged Bird Sings,* by Maya Angelou.

Momma responded with "How you, Sister Flowers?"

See page 207.

Dialogue Conversation between characters in a literary work. These lines from "Golden Glass," by Alma Luz Villanueva, are an example of dialogue in a work of fiction:

"Jason already said he'd bring my food and stuff."

"Where do you plan to shower and go to the bathroom?" Vida wondered.

"With the hose when it's hot and I'll dig holes behind the barn," Ted said so quietly as to seem unspoken.

See pages 157, 692–693, and 728.
See also MONOLOGUE.

Drama A work of literature intended to be performed for an audience. *The Diary of Anne Frank,* by Frances Goodrich and Albert Hackett, is an example of modern drama.

See pages 692–693.
See also STAGE DIRECTIONS.

E

Elegy A mournful or melancholy poem that honors someone who is dead. Some elegies are written in rhyming couplets that follow a strict metric pattern.

Epic A long narrative poem, written in a dignified style, that celebrates the adventures and achievements of one or more heroic figures of legend, history, or religion.

See also NARRATIVE POETRY.

Essay A short piece of nonfiction writing on a single topic. The purpose of the essay is to communicate an idea or opinion. A **formal essay** is serious and impersonal. An **informal essay** may be written in a more conversational style. Anna Quindlen's "Homeless" is an informal essay.

See page 618.

Exaggeration. See HYPERBOLE.

Exposition The author's introduction to the characters, setting, and situation of a story. In the opening paragraphs of "The Battleground," Elsie Singmaster uses exposition to introduce the reader to the background of the story.

See page 522.
See also PLOT.

F

Fable A short, simple tale that teaches a moral and sometimes uses animal characters. Often, the moral is directly stated at the end of the fable. Sometimes, however, the moral is understood by the reader but not directly stated.

See also THEME.

Falling action In a play or story, the action that follows the climax.

See page 404.
See also PLOT, RISING ACTION.

Fiction Literature in which situations and characters are invented by the writer. Two types of fiction are short stories and novels.

See pages 508–509.
See also NONFICTION, NOVEL, SHORT STORY.

LITERARY TERMS HANDBOOK

Figurative language Language that communicates ideas beyond the literal meanings of words. Figurative language includes elaborate expressions or figures of speech, as opposed to literal language. Although it appears in all kinds of writing, figurative language is especially prominent in poetry.

See also METAPHOR, PERSONIFICATION, SIMILE, SYMBOL.

Figure of speech An expression used to compare one person or thing to another person or thing that is familiar to the reader. Simile, metaphor, and personification are examples of figures of speech. In "The Treasure of Lemon Brown," Walter Dean Myers uses a figure of speech by calling Lemon Brown's memories his "treasure."

See also METAPHOR, PERSONIFICATION, SIMILE.

Flashback An interruption in a chronological narrative. A flashback presents readers with scenes from events that happened before that point in the story or before the story began.

Folklore The traditional beliefs, customs, stories, songs, and dances of a culture. Folklore is an oral tradition and is based on the lives of common people.

See also FOLKTALE, LEGEND, MYTH, ORAL TRADITION.

Folktale A traditional story passed down orally long before being written down. The author of a folktale is generally anonymous. Folktales include animal stories, trickster tales, fairy tales, myths, legends, and tall tales. "M'su Carencro and Mangeur de Poulet" is a Cajun folktale retold by J. J. Reneaux.

See page 358.
See also LEGEND, MYTH, ORAL TRADITION, TALL TALE.

Foreshadowing The use of clues by an author to prepare readers for events that will happen in a narrative, as in "The Summer of Vietnam," by Barbara Renaud González.

> "Vietnam," he says. The worst answer. The only answer that can make me cry.
> Instead, at night I remember.

See page 141.
See also PLOT, RISING ACTION, SUSPENSE.

Frame story The telling of a story within a story. The frame is the outer story, which usually comes before and follows the inner–and more important–story.

Free verse Poetry that has no fixed pattern of meter, rhyme, line length, or stanza arrangement. "The Pinta, the Nina and the Santa Maria; and many other cargoes of Light," by John Tagliabue, is an example of free verse.

See page 312.
See also METER, RHYME, RHYTHM.

G

Genre An artistic or literary category. Fiction, nonfiction, poetry, and drama are the main literary genres.

H

Haiku Originally a Japanese form of poetry that has three lines and seventeen syllables. The first and third lines have five syllables each; the middle line has seven.

Hero The main character of a literary work, usually a person with admirable qualities. Sally Ann Thunder Ann Whirlwind is the hero of the story by Mary Pope Osborne.

See page 422.
See also PROTAGONIST, TALL TALE.

Historical fiction A novel, play, short story, or narrative poem that sets fictional characters in an earlier historical period and contains accurate details about that time. "The Drummer Boy of Shiloh," by Ray Bradbury, is set during the Civil War.

See page 508.
See also GENRE.

Hyperbole (hī pur′ bə lē) A figure of speech that uses exaggeration to express strong emotion, make a point, or create humor. The following sentence from Langston Hughes's "Thank You, M'am" contains an example of hyperbole:

She was a large woman with a large purse that had everything in it but hammer and nails.

See also FIGURE OF SPEECH.

I

Imagery Language that emphasizes sense impressions to help the reader see, hear, feel, smell, and taste things described in the work. Margaret Walker uses imagery in this passage from "Sorrow Home":

Warm skies and gulf blue streams are in my blood. I belong / with the smell of fresh pine, with the trail of coon, and / the spring growth of wild onion.

See page 109.
See also FIGURATIVE LANGUAGE.

Irony A contrast between what is said or done and what is expected. **Situational irony** occurs when the outcome of a situation is the opposite of what was expected. **Verbal irony** occurs when a person says one thing and means another–for example, saying "Nice guy!" about someone you dislike.

See pages 124 and 626.

J

Journal An account of day-to-day events or a record of experiences, ideas, or thoughts. A journal may also be called a **diary.** *Anne Frank: The Diary of a Young Girl* is Anne Frank's account of a short period in her life.

See page 682.
See also NONFICTION.

L

Legend A traditional story handed down orally and believed to be based on actual people or events. "The Siege of Courthouse Rock" is a Sioux legend retold by Jenny Leading Cloud.

See pages 416 and 829.
See also FABLE, FOLKLORE, FOLKTALE, MYTH, ORAL TRADITION, TALL TALE.

Limerick A light humorous poem with a regular rhythm pattern and a rhyme scheme of *aabba.*

See also METER, RHYME.

Local color The portrayal of a region's natural and human environment, including the speech and behavior of the inhabitants, usually as a way of adding a realistic flavor to a story. Washington Irving's "The Legend of Sleepy Hollow" uses local color to enhance the tale.

Lyric A verse or poem that can be sung. The words to "I Think Myself Out," by Enid Futterman, are song lyrics.

See also RHYME SCHEME.

Lyric poetry Poems that express thoughts or emotions about a subject. Many of Robert Frost's poems, such as "Fire and Ice," are lyric poems.

See page 306.
See also FIGURATIVE LANGUAGE, IMAGERY, METER, RHYME.

LITERARY TERMS HANDBOOK R5

M

Memoir A narrative emphasizing the narrator's personal experience during a period or at an event. The selection from *All But My Life,* by Gerda Weissmann Klein, is a memoir.

See page 669.
See also AUTOBIOGRAPHY, BIOGRAPHY.

Metaphor A figure of speech that compares seemingly unlike things. Unlike a **simile,** a metaphor does not use the clue *like* or *as.* There are many metaphors in the "I Have a Dream" speech by Martin Luther King:

Now is the time to rise from the dark and desolate valley of segregation to the sunlit path of racial justice; now is the time to lift our nation from the quicksands of racial injustice....

See pages 295, 393, and 602.
See also FIGURE OF SPEECH, IMAGERY, SIMILE.

Meter A regular pattern of stressed and unstressed syllables that gives a line of poetry a predictable rhythm. For example, the meter is marked in the following lines from Walt Whitman's poem "O Captain! My Captain!":

The ship has weather'd every rack, the prize we
sought is won:
The port is near, the bells I hear, the people all
exulting.

See pages 294 and 455.
See also RHYTHM.

Monologue A long speech by a character in a play.

See page 761.

Mood The emotional quality or atmosphere of the story or poem. In "If I Forget Thee Oh Earth . . . ," Arthur C. Clarke establishes a nostalgic mood that extends throughout the story.

See pages 183, 692–693, and 842.
See also SETTING.

Myth A traditional story of unknown origin that explains the beliefs and practices of a people. Myths may tell of extraordinary events from earlier times and may deal with gods, heroes, and supernatural events.

See also FOLKLORE, FOLKTALE, HERO, LEGEND, ORAL TRADITION, TALL TALE.

N

Narration The telling of a sequence of events. "A Mother in Mannville," by Marjorie Kinnan Rawlings, relies heavily on narration to develop the plot.

See pages 175 and 536.
See also NARRATIVE POETRY.

Narrative poetry Verse that tells a story. "The Raven," by Edgar Allan Poe, is a narrative poem.

See page 255.
See also NARRATION.

Narrator The person who tells a story. In fiction, the narrator may be a character in the story. Squeaky, for example, narrates the story in "Raymond's Run," by Toni Cade Bambara.

See pages 35 and 183.
See also POINT OF VIEW.

Nonfiction Writing based on fact, not on imagination. Among the categories of nonfiction are biographies, autobiographies, and essays. For example, *On the Road with Charles Kuralt* is nonfiction.

See also AUTOBIOGRAPHY, BIOGRAPHY, ESSAY, FICTION, JOURNAL.

Novel A book-length fictional narrative. The novel has more space than a short story to develop its plot, characters, setting, and theme.

See also FICTION, SHORT STORY.

O

Ode A lyric poem, usually rhymed, often in the form of an address and usually dignified or lofty in subject.

See also LYRIC.

Onomatopoeia The use of a word or a phrase that actually imitates or suggests the sound of what it describes. The following line from Emily Dickinson's "I like to see it lap the miles" contains this example of onomatopoeia:

In horrid, hooting stanza . . .

See also SOUND DEVICES.

Oral tradition Stories, knowledge, customs, and beliefs passed by word of mouth from one generation to the next. "Coyote and Wasichu," as edited and retold by Richard Erdoes and Alfonso Ortiz, is an example of a story passed down through the oral tradition.

See page 865.
See also FOLKLORE, FOLKTALE, LEGEND, MYTH.

P

Parallelism The use of a series of words, phrases, or sentences that have similar grammatical form. Parallelism emphasizes the items that are arranged in the similar structures. Note the following example from Robert Cormier's "The Moustache":

"Nana, this is Mike your grandson,
not Mike your husband."

See also REPETITION.

Personification A figure of speech in which a human quality is given to an animal, object, or idea. The plants of the tropics are personified in Margaret Walker's poem "Sorrow Home":

. . . The palm tree and banana leaf, mango and
coconut, breadfruit and rubber trees know me.

See pages 295 and 385.
See also FIGURATIVE LANGUAGE, FIGURE OF SPEECH, METAPHOR.

Plot The sequence of events in narrative works such as stories, novels, plays, and some nonfiction. The plot begins with **exposition,** which introduces the story's characters, setting, and situation. The **rising action** adds complications to the story's **conflicts,** or problems, leading to the **climax,** or point of greatest interest or suspense. The **falling action** is the logical result of the climax, and the **resolution** presents the final outcome.

See pages 46–47, 375, and 508.
See also CONFLICT, FALLING ACTION, RISING ACTION.

Poetry A type of literature in which language, images, sound, and rhythm are combined to create an emotional effect. Poetry is a compact form of writing that often, but not always, uses rhyme, meter, and figurative language. Other characteristics of some poems are the use of metaphor and simile and the division of the work into stanzas.

See pages 294–295.
See also FIGURATIVE LANGUAGE, METAPHOR, METER, RHYME, SIMILE.

Point of view The relationship of the narrator to the story. A story using **first-person point of view** is told by one of the characters, as in "The Raven," by Edgar Allan Poe. The reader sees everything through that character's eyes. In a story with a **limited third-person point of view,** the narrator is outside the story and reveals the thoughts of only one character, but refers to that character as *he* or *she.* In "Stop the Sun," Gary Paulsen uses this point of view. In a story with an **omniscient point of view,** such as "Bagged Wolf," by Carol Kendall and Yao-wen Li, the narrator is also outside the story, but can reveal events, thoughts, and actions of the characters as

well as background information important to the story.

See pages 196, 221, and 489.
See also AUTHOR'S PURPOSE.

Props Theater slang (a shortened form of *properties*) for objects and elements of the scenery of a stage play or movie set.

Protagonist The central character in a story, drama, or dramatic poem. Usually the action revolves around the protagonist, who is involved in the main conflict. For example, Grady is the protagonist of Patricia C. McKissack's "The Woman in the Snow."

See ANTAGONIST, CONFLICT.

Pun A humorous play on two or more meanings of the same word. Puns often appear in advertising headlines and slogans—for example, "Our hotel rooms give you suite feelings."

R

Refrain A line or lines repeated regularly, usually in a poem or song.

Repetition The recurrence of sounds, words, phrases, lines, or stanzas in a speech or piece of writing. When a line or stanza is repeated in a poem, it is called a refrain. Martin Luther King's speech is famous for his powerful repetition of two phrases:

"I have a dream that . . ."
"I have a dream today!"

See pages 385 and 499.
See also PARALLELISM, REFRAIN.

Resolution The part of a plot that comes after the falling action. The resolution reveals or suggests the outcome of the conflict.

See page 872.
See also CONFLICT, PLOT.

Rhyme The repetition of identical or similar sounds at the ends of words that appear close to one another in a poem. **End rhyme** occurs at the ends of lines, as in Edgar Allan Poe's "The Raven." **Slant rhyme** occurs when words include sounds that are similar but not identical. Slant rhyme usually involves some variation of **consonance** (the repetition of consonant sounds) or **assonance** (the repetition of vowel sounds). An example of slant rhyme is these lines from May Swenson's "Southbound on the Freeway":

". . . when he passes, winding
among them from behind."

See pages 294 and 462.
See also ASSONANCE, CONSONANCE, REPETITION, RHYME SCHEME.

Rhyme scheme The pattern formed by the end rhyme in a poem. The rhyme scheme is shown by the use of a different letter of the alphabet to name each new rhyme. The famous opening stanza of Henry Wadsworth Longfellow's poem "Paul Revere's Ride" has a rhyme scheme of *aabba.*

Listen, my children, and you shall hear *a*
Of the midnight ride of Paul Revere, *a*
On the eighteenth of April, in Seventy-five; *b*
Hardly a man is now alive *b*
Who remembers that famous day and year. *a*

See also RHYME.

Rhythm The pattern created by the arrangement of stressed and unstressed syllables, especially in poetry. Rhythm gives poetry a musical quality. Rhythm can be regular (with a predictable pattern or meter) or irregular.

See pages 294 and 688.
See also METER.

Rising action The part of a plot that adds complications to the problems in the story and increases reader interest. In Edgar Allen Poe's "The Tell-Tale Heart," the suspense increases as the narrator's plans are related.

See page 277.
See also FALLING ACTION, PLOT.

S

Scene A subdivision of an act in a play. A change in scene often indicates a change in time or place.

See page 710.
See also ACT.

Science fiction Fiction dealing with the impact of science on societies of the past, present, or future. "If I Forget Thee, Oh Earth . . . ," by Arthur C. Clarke, is science fiction.

See page 596.

Screenplay The script of a film, containing dialogue, stage directions, and detailed instructions about camera shots and angles.

See page 809.
See also DRAMA, STAGE DIRECTIONS.

Setting The time and place in which the events of a short story, novel, or drama occur. The setting often helps create an atmosphere, or mood.

See pages 46–47, 56, 165, 586, 692–693, and 832.
See also PLOT.

Short story A brief fictional narrative in prose. Elements of the short story include plot, character, setting, point of view, and theme. "The Moustache," by Robert Cormier, is a short story.

See pages 46–47 and 832.
See also CHARACTER, PLOT, POINT OF VIEW, SETTING, THEME.

Simile A figure of speech using *like* or *as* to compare seemingly unlike things. This example of a simile comes from N. Scott Momaday's "New World":

Shadows / withdraw / and lie / away / like smoke.

See pages 295 and 393.
See also FIGURE OF SPEECH.

Sonnet A poem containing fourteen lines, usually written in iambic pentameter. Sonnets have strict patterns of rhyme and usually deal with a single theme, idea, or sentiment.

Sound devices Techniques used to create a sense of rhythm or to emphasize particular sounds. Sound devices include onomatopoeia, alliteration, consonance, assonance, and rhyme.

See also ALLITERATION, ASSONANCE, CONSONANCE, ONOMATOPOEIA, RHYTHM.

Speaker The voice in a poem, similar to the narrator in a work of fiction. The speaker's tone may communicate an attitude toward the subject of the poem. For example, the speaker of Henry Wadsworth Longfellow's "Paul Revere's Ride" adopts the tone of a public speaker addressing an audience:

Listen, my children, and you shall hear
Of the midnight ride of Paul Revere . . .

See pages 470 and 632.
See also TONE.

Stage directions In a drama, instructions that describe the appearance and actions of characters, as well as sets, costumes, and lighting. Examples of stage directions can be found in *The Diary of Anne Frank,* by Frances Goodrich and Albert Hackett.

See pages 692–693 and 742.

Stanza A group of lines forming a unit in a poem. Stanzas are, in effect, the paragraphs of a poem.

See page 570.

Stereotype A character who is not developed as an individual but who shows traits and mannerisms supposedly shared by all members of a group.

See page 42.

Style The author's choice and arrangement of words and sentences in a literary work. Style can reveal an author's purpose in writing and attitude toward his or her subject and audience. In "The Dinner Party," the author uses an unexciting,

matter-of-fact style to support the calm attitude of the story's hero.

See pages 73, 358, and 639.
See also AUTHOR'S PURPOSE, GENRE.

Suspense A feeling of curiosity, uncertainty, or even dread about what is going to happen next. Writers increase the level of suspense in a story by giving readers clues to what may happen. In "The Tell-Tale Heart," Edgar Allan Poe builds suspense by gradually revealing the narrator's insanity.

See pages 347 and 832.
See also PLOT, RISING ACTION.

Symbol Any object, person, place, or experience that means more than what it is. In "The Black Walnut Tree," by Mary Oliver, the tree is a symbol of a family's success in overcoming hard times.

See pages 87 and 300.

T

Tall tale An imaginative tale of adventures or amazing feats of folk heroes. The tales take place in realistic local settings. Carl Sandburg's *The People, Yes* identifies the heroes of various tall tales.

See page 366.
See also FOLKLORE, FOLKTALE, HERO, LEGEND, MYTH, ORAL TRADITION.

Theme The main idea of a story, poem, novel, or play. Some works have a stated theme. More frequently works have a theme that is not stated but is revealed gradually through other elements such as plot, character, setting, point of view, symbol, and irony.

See pages 14, 46–47, 320, and 358.

Title The name of a literary work.

See page 380.

Tone The attitude of the narrator toward a subject. The tone may be eerie, threatening, serious, or light, for example. In "Mother and Daughter," by Gary Soto, the tone is humorous.

See page 68.

Tragedy A play in which a main character suffers a downfall. The tone of a tragedy is serious, and the ending is usually an unhappy one. In plays written before the nineteenth century, the main character is often a person of dignified or heroic stature. The character's downfall may result from outside forces or from a weakness within the character, which is known as a **tragic flaw.**

See page 773.

U

Understatement Language that makes something seem less important than it really is. In *On the Road with Charles Kuralt,* the writer observes: "Times couldn't have been very easy in Gnaw Bone, Indiana." The reader realizes things must have been extremely difficult if citizens had to gnaw on bones to survive.

V

Voice An author's distinctive style or the particular speech patterns of a character in a story. The voice of the narrator in *On the Road with Charles Kuralt* is the voice of a person who observes and enjoys words and places.

See also AUTHOR'S PURPOSE, STYLE, TONE.

Language Handbook

Troubleshooter

Use the Troubleshooter to help you recognize and correct common writing errors.

Sentence Fragment

A sentence fragment does not express a complete thought. It might be missing a subject, a predicate, or both.

Problem: A fragment that lacks a subject

David was hungry. Hadn't eaten all day. *frag*

Solution: Add a subject to the fragment to make a complete sentence.

David was hungry. He hadn't eaten all day.

Problem: A fragment that lacks a predicate

Someone had taken her seat. A tall man. *frag*

Solution: Add a predicate to make the sentence complete.

Someone had taken her seat. A tall man was sitting there.

Problem: A fragment that lacks both a subject and a predicate

We found the kitten. In the garage. *frag*

Solution: Combine the fragment with another sentence.

We found the kitten in the garage.

Rule of Thumb

You can use fragments when talking with friends or writing personal letters. Some writers use fragments to produce special effects in stories or dialogue. Use complete sentences, however, in writing for school or business.

Troubleshooter

Exercise

Have the students identify the following as sentences or fragments. Then have them add elements to the fragments to make them complete sentences.

1. The cherry trees in full blossom.
2. Reflected in the waters of the tidal basin.
3. Washington, D. C., is beautiful in the spring.
4. Having balmy weather and striking architecture.
5. Many tourists from all over the world.
6. Visited government buildings and took numerous pictures.
7. Security checks occur often.
8. Lindbergh's *Spirit of Saint Louis* in the Air and Space Museum.
9. Often arrive to lobby for important causes.
10. On the streets around the Capitol.

Answers

1. F; In spring the cherry trees are in full blossom.
2. F; The flowers are reflected in the waters of the tidal basin.
3. Sentence
4. F; The city, having balmy weather and striking architecture, attracts tourists.
5. F; Many tourists from all over the world visit Washington.
6. F; Our school group visited government buildings and took numerous pictures.
7. Sentence
8. F; Lindbergh's *Spirit of Saint Louis* hangs in the National Air and Space Museum.
9. F; Citizen groups often arrive to lobby for important causes.
10. F; They gather on the streets around the Capitol.

Exercise

Direct the students to correct the run-on sentences below. They may use any of the methods illustrated on the student page.

1. The students were disappointed, they did not have time to visit the Statue of Liberty.
2. Matt ordered several new mysteries but the bookstore's supply had not arrived.
3. The hockey team wore their new uniforms they had worked hard to earn them.
4. Oxygen is odorless and tasteless so is hydrogen.
5. The birdwatchers spotted a large flock of geese the birds were headed south for the winter.
6. Snow fell all night many schools were closed the next day.
7. Raw carrots and celery are healthy snacks keep some in your lunchbox.
8. The accident occurred in front of our house we called 911 for help.
9. An earthquake leveled the village many people lost friends and family members.
10. Our school sponsored a parade float students volunteered to decorate it.

Answers

1. The students were disappointed. They did not have time to visit the Statue of Liberty.
2. Matt ordered several new mysteries, but the bookstore's supply had not arrived.
3. The hockey team wore their new uniforms. They had worked hard to earn them.
4. Oxygen is odorless and tasteless; so is hydrogen.
5. The birdwatchers spotted a large flock of geese. The birds were headed south for the winter.
6. Snow fell all night. Many schools were closed the next day.
7. Raw carrots and celery are healthy snacks. Keep some in your lunchbox.
8. The accident occurred in front of our house; we called 911 for help.
9. An earthquake leveled the village. Many people lost friends and family members.
10. Our school sponsored a parade float, and students volunteered to decorate it.

Run-on Sentence

A run-on sentence is two or more sentences incorrectly written as one sentence.

Problem: Two main clauses separated only by a comma

They put up the tent in a hurry, night was falling. *run-on*

Solution A: Replace the comma with a period or other end mark and begin the new sentence with a capital letter.

They put up the tent in a hurry. Night was falling.

Solution B: Place a semicolon between the main clauses.

They put up the tent in a hurry; night was falling.

Problem: Two main clauses with no punctuation between them

I loved the movie my sister hated it. *run-on*

Solution A: Separate the main clauses with a period or other end mark and begin the second sentence with a capital letter.

I loved the movie. My sister hated it.

Solution B: Add a comma and a coordinating conjunction between the main clauses.

I loved the movie, but my sister hated it.

Problem: Two main clauses with no comma before the coordinating conjunction

Kristie was moving and her classmates would miss her. *run-on*

Solution: Add a comma before the coordinating conjunction.

Kristie was moving, and her classmates would miss her.

Lack of Subject-Verb Agreement

A singular subject calls for a singular form of the verb. A plural subject calls for a plural form of the verb.

Problem: A subject that is separated from the verb by an intervening prepositional phrase

A bowl of cherries (are) on the table. *agr*

Solution: Ignore a prepositional phrase that comes between a subject and a verb. Make sure that the verb agrees with the subject of the sentence. The object of the preposition is never the subject.

A bowl of cherries is on the table.

Problem: A sentence that begins with *here* or *there*

There (goes) my brothers. *agr*

Here (is) Andy and Fatima. *agr*

Solution: The subject is never *here* or *there.* In sentences that begin with *here* or *there,* look for the subject *after* the verb. The verb must agree with the subject.

There go my brothers.

Here are Andy and Fatima.

Problem: An indefinite pronoun as the subject

Either of the sisters (walk) the dog at night. *agr*

Some of the clothing (are) too small. *agr*

Some of the clothes (is) too small. *agr*

Solution: Some indefinite pronouns are singular, some are plural, and some can be either singular or plural, depending upon the noun they refer to. Determine whether the indefinite pronoun is singular or plural and make sure that the verb agrees with it.

Either of the sisters walks the dog.

Some of the clothing is too small.

Some of the clothes are too small.

Exercise

Have students correct subject-verb agreement in the following sentences. Some sentences are correct.

1. A kettle of crabs were cooking on the stove.
2. Here comes the hungry picnickers.
3. Neither of the boys want any seafood.
4. Some of the food was shared with neighbors.
5. A bunch of bananas are hanging in the produce section.
6. Each of the campers select a piece of fruit.
7. There drifts the ashes from the campfire.
8. Most of the firewood was wet.
9. Each of the students know the answer.
10. A pack of matches litter the floor.

Answers

1. kettle was
2. picnickers come
3. Neither wants
4. Correct
5. bunch is hanging
6. Each selects
7. ashes drift
8. correct
9. Each knows
10. pack litters

Exercise

Direct students to choose the correct verb from the parentheses in the following sentences.

1. An apple and an orange (provide, provides) natural sugar at lunch.
2. The violin and the cello (are, is) featured in this musical selection.
3. A book or a DVD (make, makes) a welcome birthday gift.
4. Roger, the store's owner and manager, (hire, hires) the clerks and baggers.
5. High winds or rain (cause, causes) hazardous driving conditions.
6. A horse and buggy (carry, carries) the couple to the church.
7. The best man and the maid of honor (offer, offers) toasts to the bride and groom.
8. Either a letter or an e-mail (get, gets) a prompt response from the company.
9. The painter and decorator (has, have) more business than she can handle.
10. Corned beef and cabbage (are, is) a hearty meal.

Answers

1. provide
2. are
3. makes
4. hires
5. causes
6. carries
7. offer
8. gets
9. has
10. is

Problem: A compound subject that is joined by *and*

Joe and Eric shares a room. *agr*

The author and illustrator are Virginia Clay. *agr*

Solution A: If the parts of the compound subject refer to different people or things, use a plural verb.

Joe and Eric share a room.

Solution B: If the parts of the compound subject name one unit or if both parts refer to the same person or thing, use a singular verb.

The author and illustrator is Virginia Clay.

Rule of Thumb

If the subject can be replaced by *he, she,* or *it,* use a singular verb. If *they* can replace the subject, use a plural verb.

Problem: A compound subject that is joined by *or* or *nor*

Either a skunk or two raccoons visits our porch each night. *agr*

Neither the stars nor the moon are visible. *agr*

Solution: Make the verb agree with the subject that is closer to it.

Either a skunk or two raccoons visit our porch each night.

Neither the stars nor the moon is visible.

Incorrect Verb Tense or Form

A verb has various tenses to indicate when the action takes place.

Problem: An incorrect or missing verb ending

I (ask) you the same question yesterday. *tense*

We have never (hike) this far before. *tense*

Solution: Add *-ed* or *-d* to a regular verb to form the past tense and the past participle.

I asked you the same question yesterday.

We have never hiked this far before.

Problem: An improperly formed irregular verb

He (payed) for the groceries. *tense*

The vine had (creeped) up the wall. *tense*

Solution: Use the correct past or past-participle form of an irregular verb. These forms vary; memorize them or look them up.

He paid for the groceries.

The vine had crept up the wall.

Problem: Confusion between the past form and the past participle

She has (swam) half a mile. *tense*

I (seen) that movie last week. *tense*

Solution A: Use the past-participle form of an irregular verb, not the past form, when you use the auxiliary verb *have.*

She has swum half a mile.

Solution B: When you do not use the auxiliary verb *have,* use the past form, not the past participle.

I saw that movie last week.

LANGUAGE HANDBOOK

LANGUAGE HANDBOOK

Exercise

Have the students choose the correct verb from the parentheses in each of the following sentences.

1. Yesterday Myra (plant, planted) flowers in the front yard.
2. The bell has (sound, sounded) for recess.
3. The children's chorus (singed, sang) at the convention.
4. Mrs. Brent (buyed, bought) all the ingredients for the cake.
5. The girl (standed, stood) on tiptoe to reach the highest shelf.
6. Deirdre has (written, wrote) her pen pal a letter.
7. The puppies (ate, eaten) all their food.
8. My sister (teached, taught) me to do origami.
9. The fans have (broke, broken) down the goalie's cage.
10. The senator (spoke, spoken) quietly to his aide.

Answers

1. planted
2. sounded
3. sang
4. bought
5. stood
6. written
7. ate
8. taught
9. broken
10. spoke

Exercise

Direct the students to correct the pronoun use in the following sentences.

1. Mary asked Kim if she had written the right answer.
2. Juan and Sergio brought the groceries to his house.
3. Alana and her sang a duet at the Thanksgiving concert.
4. Leo and me built a workbench in our shop class.
5. Them and us have always been good friends.
6. The teacher praised Greg and I for our art work.
7. The trouble with Jay and she is that they think they're always right.
8. Mr. Levy helped we and our friends finish our projects.
9. Katie told Dee that she was late.
10. The community center had activities for my friends and I.

Answers

1. Mary asked if Kim had written the right answer.
2. Juan and Sergio brought the groceries to Juan's house.
3. Alana and she sang a duet at the Thanksgiving concert.
4. Leo and I built a workbench in our shop class.
5. They and we have always been good friends.
6. The teacher praised Greg and me for our artwork.
7. The trouble with Jay and her is that they think they're always right.
8. Mr. Levy helped us and our friends finish our projects.
9. Katie told Dee that Dee was late.
10. The community center had activities for my friends and me.

Incorrect Use of Pronouns

The noun that a pronoun refers to is called its antecedent. A pronoun must refer to its antecedent clearly. A subject pronoun refers to the subject in a sentence. An object pronoun refers to the object in a sentence.

Problem: A pronoun that can refer to more than one antecedent

Kenny went to see Tom because he was lonely. *ant*

Solution: Rewrite the sentence, substituting a noun for the pronoun.

Kenny went to see Tom because Tom was lonely.

Problem: A personal pronoun as a subject

Hassan and him are good friends. *pro*

Us and our teacher planned the project. *pro*

Solution: Use a subject pronoun as the subject part of a sentence.

Hassan and he are good friends.

We and our teacher planned the project.

Problem: A personal pronoun as an object

Mom sent Lanny and I a postcard. *pro*

I'm going swimming with he and his cousin. *pro*

Solution: Use an object pronoun as the object of a verb or preposition.

Mom sent Lanny and me a postcard.

I'm going swimming with him and his cousin.

Rule of Thumb

People often choose the wrong form of a pronoun when the pronoun is part of a compound subject or object. Saying the sentence with only the pronoun as the subject or object will often make the correct choice clear. For example, change *Mom sent Lanny and I a postcard* to *Mom sent I a postcard.* The pronoun *I* sounds wrong and should be changed to *me.*

Incorrect Use of Adjectives

Some adjectives have irregular forms: comparative forms for comparing two things and superlative forms for comparing more than two things.

Problem: Incorrect use of *good, better, best*

He's (more good) at music than art. *adj*

They're the (goodest) athletes in the school. *adj*

Solution: The comparative and superlative forms of *good* are *better* and *best.* Do not use *more* or *most* or the endings *-er* or *-est* with *good.*

He's better at music than art.

They're the best athletes in the school.

Problem: Incorrect use of *bad, worse, worst*

Of everyone who lost, she felt the (most bad.) *adj*

The news was (badder) than we'd expected. *adj*

Solution: Do not use *more* or *most* or the endings *-er* or *-est* with *bad.*

Of everyone who lost, she felt the worst.

The news was worse than we'd expected.

Problem: Incorrect use of comparative adjectives

In spring the days grow (more) warmer. *adj*

Solution: Do not use both *-er* and *more* at the same time.

In spring the days grow warmer.

Problem: Incorrect use of superlative adjectives

Today Ted ran (most fastest.) *adj*

Solution: Do not use both *-est* and *most* at the same time.

Today Ted ran fastest.

Exercise

Direct the students to choose the correct adjective from the parentheses.

1. Keisha does (gooder, better) work than Amanda.
2. Pearl turned in the (goodest, best) history project in the class.
3. The (baddest, worst) time for planting some flower bulbs is summer.
4. My sore ankle hurts (badder, worse) during the night.
5. Bev is (shorter, more shorter) than her sister.
6. The tall girl was wearing the (prettiest, most prettiest) dress I have ever seen.
7. That book must be the (longest, most longest) one in the library.
8. The trail guide carried the (heaviest, most heaviest) load.
9. Velma said she was the (happiest, most happiest) girl in the world.
10. No one could be (luckier, more luckier) than Drew.

Answers

1. better
2. best
3. worst
4. worse
5. shorter
6. prettiest
7. longest
8. heaviest
9. happiest
10. luckier

Exercise

Direct the students to add commas to the following sentences where needed.

1. My father a licensed plumber works every day but Sunday.
2. Carol bought lettuce tomatoes and radishes for the salad.
3. "I've decided" said Diego "to become a farmer."
4. Ms. Burns who teaches foreign languages has traveled around the world.
5. We searched in the kitchen in the living room and in the garden for the missing keys.
6. The waiter announced "There is a gray sedan with its lights on in the parking lot."
7. We all applauded Jerry who won the award for being most helpful.
8. Karen my older sister is becoming as good a cook as my mother.
9. The carpet was covered with small round dark pellets.
10. When the game was over the crowd went home.

Answers

1. My father, a licensed plumber, works every day but Sunday.
2. Carol bought lettuce, tomatoes, and radishes for the salad.
3. "I've decided," said Diego, "to become a farmer."
4. Ms. Burns, who teaches foreign languages, has traveled around the world.
5. We searched in the kitchen, in the living room, and in the garden for the missing keys.
6. The waiter announced, "There is a gray sedan with its lights on in the parking lot."
7. We all applauded Jerry, who won the award for being most helpful.
8. Karen, my older sister, is becoming as good a cook as my mother.
9. The carpet was covered with small, round, dark pellets.
10. When the game was over, the crowd went home.

Incorrect Use of Commas

Commas signal a pause between parts of a sentence and help to clarify meaning.

Problem: Missing commas in a series of three or more items

Kathryn drew a monkey‸ a snake‸ and a parrot. *com*

He ran down the sidewalk‸ up the front steps‸ and into the building. *com*

Solution: When there are three or more items in a series, use a comma after each one, including the item that precedes the conjunction.

Kathryn drew a monkey, a snake, and a parrot.

He ran down the sidewalk, up the front steps, and into the building.

Problem: Missing commas with direct quotations

"Remember‸" said Mr. Hu‸ "to bring some ideas to class." *com*

Solution: The first part of an interrupted quotation ends with a comma followed by quotation marks. The interrupting words are also followed by a comma.

"Remember," said Mr. Hu, "to bring some ideas to class."

Problem: Missing commas with nonessential appositives

Chantelle Peron‸ an eighth grader‸ will speak at the assembly. *com*

Solution: Determine whether the appositive is important to the meaning of the sentence. If it is not essential, set off the appositive with commas.

Chantelle Peron, an eighth grader, will speak at the assembly.

Problem: Missing commas with nonessential adjective clauses

This story‸ which I enjoyed very much‸ is about a flood. *com*

Solution: Determine whether the clause is essential to the meaning of the sentence. If it is not essential, set off the clause with commas.

This story, which I enjoyed very much, is about a flood.

Problem: Missing comma with an introductory adverb clause

Although Jean-Paul felt shy, he tried to be friendly. *com*

Solution: Place a comma after an introductory adverb clause.

Although Jean-Paul felt shy, he tried to be friendly.

Incorrect Use of Apostrophes

An apostrophe shows possession. It can also indicate the missing letters in a contraction.

Problem: A singular possessive noun

James sweatshirt is in the hall. *poss*

The cats cry woke me up. *poss*

Solution: Use an apostrophe and an *s* to form the possessive of a singular noun, even one that ends in *s.*

James's sweatshirt is in the hall.

The cat's cry woke me up.

Problem: A plural possessive noun ending in *s*

The birds tails help them control their flight. *poss*

Solution: Use an apostrophe alone to form the possessive of a plural noun that ends in *s.*

The birds' tails help them control their flight.

Problem: A plural possessive noun not ending in *s*

The mens gym needs new equipment. *poss*

Solution: Use an apostrophe and an *s* to form the possessive of a plural noun that does not end in *s.*

The men's gym needs new equipment.

Exercise

Direct the students to write the singular possessive, the plural, and the plural possessive of the following nouns.

1. girl
2. woman
3. child
4. bird
5. James
6. sister-in-law
7. commander in chief
8. sheep
9. month
10. bride
11. man
12. calf
13. trio
14. prince
15. governor

Answers

1. girl's	girls	girls'
2. woman's	women	women's
3. child's	children	children's
4. bird's	birds	birds'
5. James's	Jameses	Jameses'
6. sister-in-law's	sisters-in-law	sisters-in-law's
7. commander in chief's	commanders in chief	commanders in chief's
8. sheep's	sheep	sheep's
9. month's	months	months'
10. bride's	brides	brides'
11. man's	men	men's
12. calf's	calves	calves'
13. trio's	trios	trios'
14. prince's	princes	princes'
15. governor's	governors	governors'

Exercise
Direct students to identify the errors in the following sentences.

1. This locker is your's.
2. You can't judge a book by it's cover.
3. Annette is learning to speak japanese.
4. Brad asked, "who owns this sweater?"
5. I think its raining too hard to go out.
6. Dolores agreed that the mistake was her's.
7. The restaurant specialized in german dishes.
8. The official language of Brazil is portuguese.
9. The teacher wore her hair in a french twist.
10. The small green car is our's.

Answers
1. yours
2. its
3. Japanese
4. Who
5. it's
6. hers
7. German
8. Portuguese
9. French
10. ours

Problem: A possessive personal pronoun

That ball is your's; this one is our's. *poss*

Solution: Do not use an apostrophe with a possessive personal pronoun.

That ball is yours; this one is ours.

Problem: Confusion between *its* and *it's*

That plant is losing it's leaves, and its brand new! *poss*

Solution: Do not use an apostrophe to form the possessive of *it.* Use an apostrophe to form the contraction of *it is.*

That plant is losing its leaves, and it's brand new!

Incorrect Capitalization

The first word of a sentence as well as proper nouns and proper adjectives should always begin with a capital letter.

Problem: Words referring to ethnic groups, nationalities, and languages

The menu at the brazilian restaurant was written in the portuguese language. *cap*

Solution: Capitalize proper nouns and adjectives that refer to ethnic groups, nationalities, and languages.

The menu at the Brazilian restaurant was written in the Portuguese language.

Problem: The first word of a direct quotation

She said, "we have a surprise for you." *cap*

Solution: Capitalize the first word in a direct quotation that is a complete sentence. A direct quotation gives the speaker's exact words.

She said, "We have a surprise for you."

Troublesome Words

Use this section to learn the correct use of easily confused or misused words and expressions.

accept, except

Accept means "to receive." *Except* means "other than."

He would not **accept** the money.

Everyone **except** Alisha is here.

affect, effect

Affect is a verb meaning "to cause a change in" or "to influence." *Effect* as a noun means "result." As a verb, *effect* means "to bring about or accomplish."

A rainy day can **affect** your mood.

Praise has a good **effect** on most people.

Advances in medicine will **effect** a healthier society.

a lot

A lot is two words. It means "a large amount or number," but its meaning is vague; avoid using it in formal writing.

I collected **a lot** of shells. [vague]

I collected dozens of shells. [more precise]

all ready, already

All ready means "completely prepared." *Already* means "before" or "by this time."

She is **all ready** for the big day.

I've **already** seen that movie.

all together, altogether

All together means "in a group." *Altogether* means "completely."

The books cost $9.98 **all together.**

Soon the sun disappeared **altogether.**

amount, number

Use *amount* with nouns that cannot be counted. Use *number* with nouns that can be counted.

There was a small **amount** of milk in the carton.

We found a large **number** of coins in the jar.

Exercise

Direct students to choose the correct word from the parentheses.

1. Do not (accept, except) a damaged package.
2. How do tides (affect, effect) coastlines?
3. The tourists were (all ready, already) to start sightseeing.
4. Margo used (all together, altogether) too much sugar in the cake.
5. Everyone (accept, except) Keith attended the game.
6. Mr. Rossi has (all ready, already) finished his report.
7. The game can be played by any (amount, number) of people.
8. The training sessions had no (affect, effect) on the dog's behavior.
9. Ken has nothing to donate to the cause (accept, except) his services.
10. A large (amount, number) of rain fell last night.

Answers

1. accept
2. affect
3. all ready
4. altogether
5. except
6. already
7. number
8. effect
9. except
10. amount

Exercise
Direct students to choose the correct word from the parentheses.

1. Alma sat (beside, besides) her mother on the porch swing.
2. The weather was too (bad, badly) for the camping trip.
3. Sonia asked, "(Can, May) I help with the decorations?"
4. Today Renaldo ran (farther, further) than yesterday.
5. The twins divided the work (among, between) them.
6. Pat (doesn't, don't) know the answer to the third problem.
7. The captain of the Meteors (choose, chose) his team first.
8. (Beside, Besides) Steve, Maya and Bette will represent the school.
9. Mother asked me to (bring, take) a casserole to Mrs. Green.
10. "(Can, May) I (bring, take) a friend home for dinner?" I asked.

Answers
1. beside
2. bad
3. May
4. farther
5. between
6. doesn't
7. chose
8. Besides
9. take
10. May, bring

bad, badly *Bad* is sometimes used as a predicate adjective after a linking verb. *Badly* is an adverb; it modifies an action verb.	I feel **bad.** I did **badly** on the test.
beside, besides *Beside* means "next to." *Besides* means "in addition to."	Sit here **beside** me. **Besides** skating, baseball is my favorite sport.
between, among Use *between* for two people or things. Use *among* when talking about groups of three or more.	The debate was **between** Sheila and Todd. The bread was shared **among** five people.
bring, take *Bring* means "to carry from a distant place to a closer place." *Take* means "to carry from a nearby place to a more distant one."	Please **bring** me a towel. **Take** this note to your parents.
can, may *Can* indicates ability. *May* expresses permission or possibility.	I **can** swim twenty laps. When the work is done, you **may** rest.
choose, chose *Choose* means "to select." *Chose* means "selected."	Everyone must **choose** a partner. Nadine **chose** yesterday's menu.
doesn't, don't The subject of the contraction **doesn't** (*does not*) is the third-person singular (*he* or *she*). The subject of the contraction **don't** (*do not*) is *I, you, we,* or *they*.	He **doesn't** understand. They **don't** understand.
farther, further *Farther* refers to physical distance. *Further* refers to time or degree.	Tyler ran **farther** than Nadia. Snow usually begins **further** into the winter. I'll need to think about this **further.**

fewer, less

Use *fewer* in comparisons with nouns that can be counted. Use *less* in comparisons with nouns that cannot be counted.

Fewer students are absent today than yesterday.

There was **less** rain last summer than this one.

formally, formerly

Formally is the adverb form of *formal.* *Formerly* means "in times past."

He bowed **formally.**

The teacher was **formerly** a dancer.

good, well

Good is often used as an adjective meaning "pleasing" or "able." *Well* may be used as an adverb telling how ably something is done or as an adjective meaning "in good health."

Cara is a **good** skater.

She skates **well.**

Because he had a cold, he did not feel **well.**

in, into

In means "inside." *Into* indicates movement from outside to a point within.

The sweater is **in** the drawer.

Put the coin **into** the slot.

its, it's

Its is the possessive form of *it.* *It's* is the contraction of *it is.*

The Earth turns on **its** axis.

Ecologists believe **it's** important to recycle.

lay, lie

Lay means "to put" or "to place." *Lie* means "to recline" or "to be positioned."

Please **lay** the blanket on the grass.

I'll **lie** here in the shade.

Rule of Thumb

Be careful not to confuse the present-tense and past-tense forms of *lie* and *lay.* The past-tense form of *lie* is *lay.* The past-tense form of *lay* is *laid.*

Then I **lay** in the shade.
I **laid** the blanket on the grass.

Exercise

Direct students to choose the correct word from the parentheses.

1. On Sunday (fewer, less) people than expected attended the performance.
2. The new principal was (formally, formerly) introduced at the school assembly.
3. Belle could sing very (good, well).
4. Everyone stopped talking when the princess walked (in, into) the room.
5. (Lay, Lie) your books on the kitchen table when you come home.
6. Esther and her sister both swim (good, well).
7. The teacher, (formally, formerly) known as Miss Jackson, is now called Mrs. Cox.
8. Bob paced up and down (in, into) the small room.
9. Tell the dog to (lay, lie) on the blanket.
10. The book has lost (its, it's) cover.

Answers

1. fewer
2. formally
3. well
4. into
5. Lay
6. well
7. formerly
8. in
9. lie
10. its

Exercise
Direct students to choose the correct word from the parentheses.

1. Who (learned, taught) you to swim?
2. Please (leave, let) me come with you to the concert.
3. Donald never likes to (loose, lose) at games.
4. I saw (many, much) of my friends in the audience.
5. Mardi Gras is a celebration that (precedes, proceeds) Lent.
6. I cleaned up after I had eaten, (as, like) I had been taught.
7. The coat was made (of, off) imported wool.
8. The motorcade will (precede, proceed) down Pennsylvania Avenue.
9. The girl's dress hung (loose, lose) from the shoulders.
10. The clerk won't (leave, let) more than two students at a time enter the store.

Answers
1. taught
2. let
3. lose
4. many
5. precedes
6. as
7. of
8. proceed
9. loose
10. let

learn, teach

Learn means "to gain knowledge." *Teach* means "to give knowledge."

Children **learn** foreign languages easily.

I can **teach** you how to skate.

leave, let

Leave means "to go away." *Let* means "to allow."

They will **leave** at noon.

Let her go where she wishes.

like, as

Use *like,* a preposition, to introduce a prepositional phrase. Use *as,* a subordinating conjunction, to introduce a subordinate clause. Many authorities believe that *like* should not be used to introduce a clause.

The kite soared **like** a bird.

He won first prize, **as** we expected.

Rule of Thumb

As can be a preposition in some cases—for example, *He worked as a carpenter.*

loose, lose

Loose means "not firmly attached." *Lose* means "to misplace" or "to fail to win."

One of her teeth was **loose.**

Don't **lose** this key.

We can't **lose** this game.

many, much

Use *many* with nouns that can be counted. Use *much* with nouns that cannot be counted.

Many flowers were in bloom.

Much applause greeted the band.

of, off

Of is a preposition used to indicate direction, origin, or material. *Off* is the opposite of "on."

The bank is south **of** the park.

Have you read the poems **of** Emily Dickinson?

Please turn **off** the light.

precede, proceed

Precede means "to go or come before." *Proceed* means "to continue."

January **precedes** February.

Finish one task and **proceed** to the next.

quiet, quite

Quiet means "silent" or "motionless." *Quite* means "completely" or "entirely."

At night the street is **quiet.**

The sneakers didn't **quite** fit.

raise, rise

Raise means "to cause to move upward." *Rise* means "to move upward."

They **raise** the flag each morning.

The sun is starting to **rise.**

reason . . . is that, because

Both terms are used to state a reason. Do not use them together in a sentence.

The **reason** I can't go **is that** I have to babysit.

I can't go **because** I have to babysit.

set, sit

Set means "to place" or "to put." *Sit* means "to place oneself in a seated position."

Set the box on the table.

Sit here and rest.

than, then

Than introduces the second part of a comparison. *Then* means "at that time."

Oranges are sweeter **than** grapefruit.

I ate lunch, and **then** I read.

their, they're, there

Their is the possessive form of *they. They're* is the contraction of *they are. There* means "at" or "in that place."

They look like **their** mother.

The winners are tired, but **they're** happy.

Stay **there** until I call you.

theirs, there's

Theirs means "that or those belonging to them." *There's* is the contraction of *there is.*

Our cat is black, and **theirs** is gray.

There's a storm coming.

to, too, two

To means "in the direction of." *Too* means "also" or "excessively." *Two* is the number after one.

Pass the ball **to** Mario.

We were **too** excited to sleep.

She scored **two** points.

LANGUAGE HANDBOOK

Exercise

Direct students to choose the correct word from the parentheses.

1. Everyone seemed (quiet, quite) satisfied with the results.
2. Two members of the patrol (raise, rise) the flag each morning.
3. (Set, Sit) the books on the top shelf.
4. The children knew that the gifts were (theirs, there's).
5. Preheat the oven; (than, then) place the frozen pizza on the middle rack.
6. No one eats at that restaurant; (the reason is because, the reason is that) the service is so slow.
7. Grandma likes to (set, sit) in her rocker on the porch.
8. I have three cousins; (there, they're) all about my age.
9. The chair is (to, too) wobbly to sit on.
10. Marla is more excited (than, then) I am about the trip.

Answers

1. quite
2. raise
3. Set
4. theirs
5. then
6. the reason is that
7. sit
8. they're
9. too
10. than

Exercise
Direct students to choose the correct word from the parentheses.

1. To (who, whom) was the question directed?
2. (Who's, Whose) coat is hanging in the hall?
3. (Who, Whom) do you expect to arrive first?
4. May I borrow (your, you're) umbrella?
5. I don't know (who's, whose) books have been left here.
6. Have you heard (who's, whose) the guest speaker at the assembly?
7. (Your, You're) scheduled to make the next report.
8. Be sure to study (your, you're) lines for the play.
9. (Who, Whom) knows the quickest route to the theater?
10. (Who's, Whose) speech was the most persuasive?

Answers
1. whom
2. Whose
3. Whom
4. your
5. whose
6. who's
7. You're
8. your
9. Who
10. Whose

where at

Do not use *at* after *where* to ask *at what place?*

Where is the bus stop? [not *Where is the bus stop at?*]

who, whom

Use *who* for subjects. Use *whom* for objects.

Who got the highest grade?

Whom did you see? [direct obj.]

To **whom** should I address this letter? [obj. of a prep.]

Rule of Thumb

When speaking informally, people often use *who* instead of *whom* in sentences like *Who did you see?* In writing and formal speech, distinguish between *who* and *whom.*

who's, whose

Who's is the contraction of *who is. Whose* is the possessive form of *who.*

Who's hungry?

I don't know **whose** hat this is.

your, you're

Your is the possessive form of *you. You're* is the contraction of *you are.*

Tell us about **your** trip.

You're older than he is.

Grammar Glossary

This glossary will help you quickly locate information on parts of speech and sentence structure.

A

Abstract noun. *See* Noun.

Action verb. *See* Verb.

Active voice. *See* Voice.

Adjective A word that modifies a noun or pronoun. An adjective can provide information about size, shape, color, texture, feeling, sound, smell, number, or condition. Adjectives appear in various positions in a sentence. (We hoped for *cool, sunny* weather. The weather was *cool* and *sunny.*)

Many adjectives have different forms to indicate **degree of comparison.** *(light, lighter, lightest)*

The **comparative degree** compares two persons or things. *(bigger, lovelier, more important)*

The **superlative degree** compares more than two persons or things. *(biggest, loveliest, most important)*

A **possessive noun** (such as poet's, classes', or Emerson's) or a **possessive pronoun** (my, your, his, its, our, their) functions as an adjective. It answers the question *which one?*

A **demonstrative adjective** is a pronoun that answers the question *Which one?* (*This* story is exaggerated.)

A **predicate adjective** follows a linking verb and describes the subject by telling what it is like. (That tree looks *old.*)

A **proper adjective** is formed from a proper noun and begins with a capital letter. Proper adjectives are often created by using the following suffixes: *-an, -ian, -n, -ese,* and *-ish.* (Ital*ian)*

Adjective clause. *See* Clause.

Adverb A word that modifies, or describes, a verb, an adjective, or another adverb by making its meaning more specific. Adverbs answer the questions *How? When? Where?* and *To what extent?* When modifying a verb, an adverb may appear in various positions in a sentence. (Ann spoke *gently* to Claude. *Quickly* she told him the news.)

When modifying an adjective or another adverb, an adverb appears directly before the modified word. (We were *very* excited about the discovery.) The negatives *no, not,* and the contraction *-n't* are adverbs. (I could wait *no* longer.) Other negative words, such as *nowhere* and *never,* can function as adverbs of time, place, and degree. (She has *never* visited us.)

Some adverbs have different forms to indicate **degree of comparison.** *(loud, louder, loudest, sweetly, more sweetly, most sweetly)* The **comparative** form of an adverb compares two actions. The **superlative** form compares three or more actions. Some adverbs do not form the comparative and superlative in the regular manner. *(badly, worse, worst)*

Adverb clause. *See* Clause.

Antecedent. *See* Pronoun.

Appositive A noun or a pronoun that is placed next to another noun or pronoun to identify it or add information about it. (Her sister *Beth* is in ninth grade.)

Appositive phrase. *See* Phrase.

Grammar Minilesson

Sentence Openings You can help to achieve a lively style in writing by varying sentence openings. Regular word order in English occurs when the subject is followed by the predicate. One way to change this pattern is to begin a sentence with an adverb or an adverb clause.

Example

Mimi opened the door cautiously.
Cautiously, Mimi opened the door.
When no one was looking, Mimi opened the door.

Activity Have the students write three sentences having regular word order. Then direct them to write two variations of each original sentence, one beginning with an adverb and the other beginning with an adverb clause.

Exercise
Direct the students to combine each pair of simple sentences into a complex sentence containing a subordinate clause.

1. The bell rang noisily.
   Sarah jumped up to answer it.
2. Most people preferred to ride the free ferry.
   The walk across the bridge was short and scenic.
3. The clock struck midnight.
   Cinderella fled from the ball.
4. The landowner treated his tenants fairly.
   The landowner's holdings were extensive.
5. Pick up your free sample now.
   Our supply will soon run out.

Possible Answers
1. When the bell rang noisily, Sarah jumped up to answer it.
2. Although the walk across the bridge was short and scenic, most people preferred to ride the free ferry.
3. Cinderella fled from the ball as the clock struck midnight.
4. The landowner, whose holdings were extensive, treated his tenants fairly.
5. Pick up your free sample now because our supply will soon run out.

Article The adjective *a, an,* or *the.*

A and *an* are **indefinite articles,** which refer to one of a general group of persons, places, things, or ideas. (He bought *a* book.)

The is a **definite article,** which identifies a specific person, place, thing, or idea. (He found *the* book helpful.)

B

Base form. *See* Verb tense.

C

Clause A group of words that has a subject and a predicate and that is used as part of a sentence. Clauses fall into two categories: *main clauses* and *subordinate clauses.*

A **main clause** has a subject and a predicate and can stand alone as a sentence. There must be at least one main clause in every sentence. (Samantha turned on the radio, and everyone began to dance.)

A **subordinate clause** has a subject and a predicate, but it cannot stand alone as a sentence. A subordinate clause makes sense only when attached to a main clause. Many subordinate clauses begin with subordinating conjunctions or relative pronouns. (He hadn't seen them *since he was a baby.*) The chart on this page shows the types of subordinate clauses.

Collective noun. *See* Noun.

Common noun. *See* Noun.

Comparative degree. *See* Adjective; Adverb.

Complement A word or a phrase that completes the meaning of a verb. Three kinds of complements are *direct objects, indirect objects,* and *subject complements.*

A **direct object** answers the question *What?* or *Whom?* after an action verb. (She threw the *ball.* He saw *Sarah.*)

An **indirect object** answers the question *To whom? For whom? To what?* or *For what?* after an action verb. (He gave *Sarah* a mitt.)

A **subject complement** follows a subject and a linking verb. It identifies or describes a subject. The two kinds of subject complements are *predicate nouns* and *predicate adjectives.*

A **predicate noun** (also called a **predicate nominative**) is a noun that follows a linking verb and defines the

Types of Subordinate Clauses

Clause	Function	Example	Begins with . . .
Adjective clause	Modifies a noun or pronoun in the main clause	I'm reading a book *that I can't put down.*	A relative pronoun, such as *that, which, who, whom,* or *whose*
Adverb clause	Modifies the verb in the main clause	I didn't see him *until I turned around.*	A subordinating conjunction, such as *after, although, because, if, since,* or *until*
Noun clause	Acts as a subject, an object, or a predicate nominative in another clause	*Whoever scores the most points* wins.	Words such as *how, that, what, whatever, when, where, which, who, whom, whoever, whose,* and *why*

subject by telling what it is. (The flowers were *roses.*)

A **predicate adjective** is an adjective that follows a linking verb and describes the subject by telling what it is like. (The roses were *beautiful.* They smelled *sweet.*)

Complete predicate. *See* Predicate.

Complete subject. *See* Subject.

Complex sentence. *See* Sentence.

Compound noun. *See* Noun.

Compound predicate. *See* Predicate.

Compound preposition. *See* Preposition.

Compound sentence. *See* Sentence.

Compound subject. *See* Subject.

Concrete noun. *See* Noun.

Conjunction A word that joins single words or groups of words.

A **coordinating conjunction** *(and, but, or, nor, for, yet)* joins words or groups of words that are equal in grammatical importance. (I needed some milk, *but* the store was closed.)

Correlative conjunctions *(both . . . and, just as . . . so, not only . . . but also, either . . . or, neither . . . nor)* work in pairs to join words or phrases of equal importance. (I was at home *both* Saturday *and* Sunday.)

A **subordinating conjunction** *(after, although, because, before, if, in order that, since, than, though, until, when, while)* joins a subordinate idea or clause to a main clause. (She arrived *after* the show had begun.)

A **conjunctive adverb** is used to clarify the relationship between main clauses in a sentence. Conjunctive adverbs can replace *and (also, besides, furthermore, moreover)* or *but (however, nevertheless, still),* state a result *(consequently, therefore, so, thus),* or state equality *(equally, likewise, similarly).* (March is a cold month; *however,* some mild days do occur.)

Coordinating conjunction. *See* Conjunction.

Correlative conjunction. *See* Conjunction.

D

Declarative sentence. *See* Sentence.

Definite article. *See* Article.

Demonstrative adjective. *See* Adjective.

Demonstrative pronoun. *See* Pronoun.

Direct object. *See* Complement.

E F G

Exclamatory sentence. *See* Sentence.

Future perfect tense. *See* Verb tense.

Future tense. *See* Verb tense.

Gerund A verb form that ends in *-ing* and is used as a noun. A gerund may function as a subject, an object of a verb, or an object of a preposition. (*Singing* always made Keisha happy. No one could keep her from *singing.*)

Gerund phrase. *See* Phrase.

H

Helping verb A verb that helps the main verb tell about an action or make a statement. (They *had been* sleeping.) The forms of *be* and *have* are the most common helping, or **auxiliary,** verbs. *(am, is, are, was, were, being, been; has, have, had, having)* Other helping verbs are *can, could; do, does, did; may, might; must; shall, should; will, would.*

I

Imperative sentence. *See* Sentence.

Indefinite article. *See* Article.

Exercise

Direct the students to use coordinating or correlative conjunctions or conjunctive adverbs to combine the following sentence pairs.

1. Trains and buses were once the most popular means of cross-country travel. Today air travel is preferred.
2. Books on tape and film versions of the classics are generally available. They have not replaced traditional print versions.
3. Tourism is the major industry of Hawaii. It is also an important source of revenue in Mexico.
4. Many patent medicines claim to relieve common illnesses. Bed rest is often the cheapest and most effective cure.
5. That restaurant serves homemade soup daily. It is a great favorite with regular patrons.

Possible Answers

1. Trains and buses were once the most popular means of cross-country travel; however, today air travel is preferred.
2. Books on tape and film versions of the classics are generally available, but they have not replaced traditional print versions.
3. Tourism is the major industry of Hawaii, and it is also an important source of revenue in Mexico.
4. Many patent medicines claim to relieve common illnesses, but bed rest is often the cheapest and most effective cure.
5. That restaurant serves homemade soup daily, for it is a great favorite with regular patrons.

Exercise
Direct students to tell whether the following sentences are in regular or inverted word order.

1. Who has the key to the front door?
2. Down the grassy slope tumbled the laughing children.
3. Several interesting books lay on the table.
4. On a brass pedestal stood the huge statue.
5. Here come the school band in their new uniforms.
6. Confetti and tickertape littered the street.
7. On the reverse side of the coin was stamped a Latin motto.
8. The aroma of freshly baked bread filled the air.
9. Around a bend in the road thundered the huge locomotive.
10. There was no solution to the problem.

Answers
1. regular
2. inverted
3. regular
4. inverted
5. inverted
6. regular
7. inverted
8. regular
9. inverted
10. inverted

Indefinite pronoun. *See* Pronoun.

Indirect object. *See* Complement.

Infinitive A verb form that begins with the word *to* and functions as a noun, an adjective, or an adverb. (David wanted *to swim.*)

Infinitive phrase. *See* Phrase.

Intensive pronoun. *See* Pronoun.

Interjection A word or phrase that expresses strong feeling. An interjection has no grammatical connection to other words in a sentence. Commas follow mild ones; exclamation points follow stronger ones. (*Well,* here we are. *Aha!* I found it.)

Interrogative pronoun. *See* Pronoun.

Interrogative sentence. *See* Sentence.

Intransitive verb. *See* Verb.

Inverted order In a sentence written in inverted order, the predicate comes before the subject. Some sentences are written in inverted order for emphasis. (Back and forth *swung the hammock.*) The subject generally follows the predicate in a sentence that begins with *there* or *here.* (*There* is a new girl in the class. *Here* stands the monument.) Questions, or interrogative sentences, are generally written in inverted order. Questions that begin with *who* or *what* follow normal word order.

Irregular verb. *See* Verb tense.

L M N

Linking verb. *See* Verb.

Main clause. *See* Clause.

Noun A word that names a person, a place, a thing, or an idea. The chart on this page shows the main types of nouns.

Noun clause. *See* Clause.

Number A noun, pronoun, or verb is **singular** in number if it refers to one, **plural** if it refers to more than one.

O

Objective pronoun. *See* Pronoun.

Order of subject and predicate. *See* Inverted order.

P

Participial phrase. *See* Phrase.

Types of Nouns

Noun	Function	Examples
Abstract	Names an idea, a quality, or a characteristic	honesty, fear
Collective	Names a group of things or people	audience, set
Common	Names a general type of person, place, thing, or idea	pilot, kitchen, cabinet, suspense
Compound	Is made up of two or more words	shoelace, home run
Concrete	Names things that you can see or touch	book, house, lamp
Possessive	Shows possession, ownership, or the relationship between two nouns	*Don's* notebook
Predicate	Follows a linking verb and gives information about the subject	Sondra became the class *president.*
Proper	Names a particular person, place, thing, or idea	Michael Jordan, Sugar Bowl, Stanley Cup, Communism

Participle A verb form that can function as an adjective. Present participles always end in *-ing.* (The *burning* sand hurt her feet.) Although past participles often end in *-ed,* they can take other forms as well. (He tried to repair the *broken* table.)

Passive voice. *See* Voice.

Past perfect tense. *See* Verb tense.

Past tense. *See* Verb tense.

Personal pronoun. *See* Pronoun.

Phrase A group of words that acts in a sentence as a single part of speech.

An appositive phrase is an appositive along with any modifiers. If not essential to the meaning of the sentence, an appositive phrase is set off by commas. (He brought her a gift, *a bouquet of wildflowers,* on her birthday.)

A gerund phrase includes a gerund and any complements and modifiers needed to complete its meaning. (*Climbing steep hills* builds strong muscles.)

An infinitive phrase includes the infinitive and any complements and modifiers. (In the evening, I like *to curl up with a book.*)

A participial phrase contains a participle and any modifiers necessary to complete its meaning. (*Gliding over the frozen pond,* the skater felt at peace with the world.)

A prepositional phrase begins with a preposition and ends with a noun or a pronoun called the object of the preposition. A prepositional phrase can function as an adjective, modifying a noun or a pronoun. (We found an album *of old photographs.*) A prepositional phrase may also function as an adverb when it modifies a verb, an adverb, or an adjective. (Donny plays *in a band.*)

A verb phrase consists of one or more auxiliary verbs followed by a main verb. (The campers *should have followed* the trail more closely.)

Possessive noun. *See* Noun.

Possessive pronoun. *See* Pronoun.

Predicate The verb or verb phrase and any modifiers that tell what the subject of a sentence does, has, is, or is like.

A simple predicate is a verb or verb phrase that tells something about the subject. (Snowflakes *melted.*)

A complete predicate includes the simple predicate and any words that modify or complete it. (Melting snowflakes *formed a puddle on the windowsill.*)

A compound predicate has two or more verbs or verb phrases that are joined by a conjunction and share the same subject. (James *heard* but *misunderstood* the question.)

Predicate adjective. *See* Adjective; Complement.

Predicate noun. *See* Complement; Noun.

Preposition A word that shows the relationship of a noun or pronoun to some other word in the sentence. Prepositions include *about, above, across, among, as, behind, below, beyond, but, by, down, during, except, for, from, into, like, near, of, on, outside, over, since, through, to, under, until, with.* (We walked *along* the river.)

A compound preposition is made up of more than one word. Compound prepositions include *according to, across from, ahead of, as to, because of, by means of, in addition to, in spite of,* and *on account of.* (They sat *across from* each other.)

Prepositional phrase. *See* Phrase.

Present perfect tense. *See* Verb tense.

Present tense. *See* Verb tense.

Progressive form. *See* Verb tense.

Pronoun A word that takes the place of one or more nouns and the words that describe those nouns.

Exercise

Direct the students to combine the following sentence pairs by using appositives and verbal phrases.

1. The deer stood perfectly still in the middle of the road.
   The deer had been frightened by the headlights.
2. The tree was silhouetted against the sky.
   The tree had lost the last of its leaves.
3. Jerry asked for attention.
   Jerry was the class president.
4. Martha began a new project.
   She carved figurines from soap.
5. The skier lost her balance.
   The skier leaned too far forward.

Possible Answers

1. Having been frightened by the headlights, the deer stood perfectly still in the middle of the road.
2. The tree, which had lost the last of its leaves, was silhouetted against the sky.
3. Jerry, the class president, asked for attention.
4. Martha began to carve figurines from soap.
5. Leaning too far forward, the skier lost her balance.

Activity Students should develop an effective writing style by varying the types and structures of their sentences. Direct the students to write a short account of an interesting or frightening experience. When they revise their accounts, they should strive for variety in their sentences. You might want to supply a model like the following.

Example

What a way to begin a school day! I had forgotten to set my alarm, and, as a result, I woke up a half-hour later than usual. Besides my regular morning routine, I had part of a report to finish before class. How could I make up the time?

I quickly washed and scrambled into my clothes, taking as many shortcuts as I could think of. Skipping breakfast, I sat down at the computer and got to work on my report. Just as I was finishing, my mother looked in on me. "You can go back to bed if you want to," she said. "I just heard on the radio that classes have been canceled because a water main burst."

The word or group of words that a pronoun refers to is called its **antecedent.** (In the following sentence, *Carla* is the antecedent of *she. Carla went shopping because she needed new sneakers.*)

A **demonstrative pronoun** points out specific persons, places, things, or ideas. *(this, that, these, those)*

An **indefinite pronoun** refers to persons, places, or things in a more general way than a noun does. *(all, another, any, both, each, either, everything, few, many, most, much, neither, nobody, none, one, several, some)*

An **intensive pronoun** adds emphasis to another noun or pronoun. If an intensive pronoun is omitted, the meaning of the sentence will be the same. (I *myself* would rather stay home.)

An **interrogative pronoun** is used to form questions. *(who, whom, whose, what, which)*

A **personal pronoun** refers to a specific person or thing. Personal pronouns have three cases called nominative, possessive, and objective. The case depends on the function of the pronoun in the sentence. The chart on this page shows the case forms of the various personal pronouns.

A **reflexive pronoun** reflects back to a noun or pronoun used earlier in the sentence, indicating that the same person or thing is involved. (Louise taught *herself* to play the piano.)

A **relative pronoun** is used to begin a subordinate clause. *(who, whose, whomever, that, what, whom, whoever)*

Proper adjective. *See* Adjective.

Proper noun. *See* Noun.

R

Reflexive pronoun. *See* Pronoun.

Regular verb. *See* Verb tense.

Relative pronoun. *See* Pronoun.

S

Sentence A group of words expressing a complete thought. Every sentence has a subject and a predicate. Sentences can be classified by function or by structure. The chart on the next page shows the categories by function; the following subentries describe the categories by structure. *See also* Clause; Predicate; Subject.

A **simple sentence** has only one main clause and no subordinate clauses. (Wendy hiked.) A simple sentence may contain a compound subject, a compound

Personal Pronouns

Case	Singular Pronouns	Plural Pronouns	Function in Sentence
Nominative	I, you, she, he, it	we, you, they	subject or predicate nominative
Objective	me, you, her, him, it	us, you, them	direct object, indirect object, or object of a preposition
Possessive	my, mine, your, yours, her, hers, his, its	our, ours, your, yours, their, theirs	replacement for the possessive form of a noun

Types of Sentences			
Sentence Type	**Function**	**Ends with . . .**	**Examples**
Declarative sentence	Makes a statement	A period	The village postponed the fireworks.
Exclamatory sentence	Expresses strong emotion	An exclamation point	Don't stop for anything!
Imperative sentence	Gives a command or makes a request	A period or an exclamation point	Be sure to attend the concert.
Interrogative sentence	Asks a question	A question mark	Has everyone eaten lunch?

predicate, or both. (Wendy and Jane hiked. Wendy swam and hiked. Wendy and Jane swam and hiked.) The subject and the predicate can be expanded with adjectives, adverbs, prepositional phrases, appositives, and verbal phrases. As long as the sentence has only one main clause, however, it remains a simple sentence. (Joseph and Fabienne, my new neighbors, recently moved to the United States from Haiti and plan to settle here.)

A **compound sentence** has two or more main clauses. Each main clause of a compound sentence has its own subject and predicate, and these main clauses are usually joined by a comma and a coordinating conjunction. (The day was warm and muggy, but the breeze was refreshing.) Semicolons may also be used to join the main clauses in a compound sentence. (Water poured from the sky; the drought was over.)

A **complex sentence** has one main clause and one or more subordinate clauses. (He laughed when he saw them.)

Simple predicate. *See* Predicate.

Simple sentence. *See* Sentence.

Simple subject. *See* Subject.

Subject The part of a sentence that tells whom or what the sentence is about.

A **simple subject** is the main noun or pronoun. (*Snowflakes* drifted down.)

A **complete subject** includes the simple subject and any words that modify it. (*Big fluffy snowflakes* drifted down.)

A **compound subject** has two or more subjects that are joined by a conjunction. The subjects share the same verb. (Either *Tatiana* or *Sean* usually scores highest.)

Subordinate clause. *See* Clause.

Subordinating conjunction. *See* Conjunction.

Superlative degree. *See* Adjective; Adverb.

T

Tense. *See* Verb tense.

Transitive verb. *See* Verb.

V

Verb A word that expresses an action or a state of being and is necessary to make a statement. *(move, feels, said)*

An **action verb** tells what someone or something does. Action verbs can express either physical or mental action. (We *walked* through the park. I *had forgotten* his name.)

Exercise

Have students identify the complete subject in each of the following sentences and tell whether it is simple or compound.

1. The weather report sounded ominous.
2. Heavy snow and gale-force winds continued throughout the day.
3. In a few minutes, the car disappeared beneath a pile of snow.
4. Wind and rain cause erosion.
5. Several anxious parents brought their children home.
6. Without a court order, the officers could not enter the premises.
7. Heaps of sandbags kept the floodwaters from damaging homes near the river.
8. Both the kitchen table and the chairs were piled high with newspapers.
9. Someone sent me an anonymous letter.
10. Either a teacher or an administrator must remain at school until 4 P.M.

Answers

1. The weather report, simple
2. Heavy snow and gale-force winds, compound
3. the car, simple
4. Wind and rain, compound
5. Several anxious parents, simple
6. the officers, simple
7. Heaps of sandbags, simple
8. Both the kitchen table and the chairs, compound
9. Someone, simple
10. Either a teacher or an administrator, compound

Exercise

Direct the students to identify the verbs in the following sentences as transitive, intransitive, or linking.

1. A small raft drifted along the river.
2. The riverbanks were homes for a variety of birds and small animals.
3. Sunlight shining through the trees made shadows on the ground.
4. A gentle breeze stirred the leaves on the trees.
5. Occasionally, a fish leaped out of the water.
6. People were fishing along the bank.
7. Time passed quickly and quietly.
8. Jim helped himself to a sandwich from the lunch basket.
9. In this place, no one bothered him.
10. The riverbank was a perfect place for relaxation.

Answers

1. intransitive
2. linking
3. transitive
4. transitive
5. intransitive
6. intransitive
7. intransitive
8. transitive
9. transitive
10. linking

A **transitive verb** is an action verb that is followed by a direct object–a word or words that answer the question *What?* or *Whom?* (She *ate* the bread.)

An **intransitive verb** is an action verb that is *not* followed by a direct object. (She *ate* quickly.) A dictionary will indicate whether a verb is transitive or intransitive.

A **linking verb** links, or joins, the subject of a sentence with a word or expression that identifies or describes the subject. (He *is* the winner.) A linking verb does not show action. The most commonly used linking verb is *be* in all its forms. *(am, is, are, was, were, will be, been, being)* Other linking verbs are *appear, become, feel, grow, look, remain, seem, sound, smell, stay,* and *taste.*

Verb phrase. *See* Phrase.

Verb tense The tense of a verb indicates when the action or state of being occurs. All verb tenses are formed from the four principal parts of a verb: a base form *(drive)*; a present participle *(driving)*; a simple past form *(drove)*; and a past participle *(driven)*.

A **regular verb** forms its simple past and past participle by adding *-ed* to the base form. *(open, opened, opened)*

An **irregular verb** forms its past and past participle in some other way. *(speak, spoke, spoken)*

In addition to present, past, and future tenses, there are three perfect tenses.

The **present perfect tense** expresses an action or condition that occurred at some indefinite time in the past. This tense also shows an action or condition that began in the past and continues into the present. (Edward *has presented* his report. I *have lived* here for four years.)

The **past perfect tense** indicates that one past action or condition began *and* ended before another past action started. (They *had pitched* their tents before the rain started.)

The **future perfect tense** indicates that one future action or condition will begin *and* end before another future event starts. Use *will have* or *shall have* with the past participle of a verb. (By tomorrow you *will have finished* that book.)

Each of the six tenses has a **progressive form** that expresses a continuing action. To make the progressive forms, use the appropriate tense of the verb *be* with the present participle of the main verb. (Rita *is listening.*)

Verbal. *See* Gerund; Infinitive; Participle.

Voice The voice of a verb shows whether the subject performs the action or receives the action of a verb.

The verb is in the **active voice** when the subject of the sentence performs the action. (Erica *painted* that picture.)

The verb is in the **passive voice** when the subject receives the action of the verb. (That picture *was painted* by Erica.)

Mechanics

This section will help you use correct capitalization, punctuation, and abbreviations in your writing.

Capitalization

Capitalizing Sentences, Quotations, and Salutations

Rule	Example
A capital letter appears at the beginning of a sentence.	**W**e had won. **E**veryone screamed and yelled.
Capitalize the first word when quoting the exact words of a speaker.	Justin said, "**W**e're safe for now."
When a quoted sentence is interrupted by explanatory words, such as *she said,* do not begin the second part of the sentence with a capital letter.	"We're safe," Justin said, "**f**or now."
When the second part of a quotation is a new sentence, put a period after the explanatory words and begin the new part with a capital letter.	"We're safe for now," Justin said. "**L**et's get some sleep."
Do not capitalize an indirect quotation.	Justin said that **w**e were safe for now.
Capitalize the first word in the salutation and the closing of a letter. Capitalize the title and the name of the person addressed.	**D**ear **M**r. **A**lfonso: **V**ery truly yours,

Capitalizing Names and Titles of People

Rule	Example
Capitalize the names of people and the initials that stand for their names.	**A**nthony **C**ruz **G. J. B**uchard
Capitalize a title or an abbreviation of a title when it comes before a person's name or when it is used in direct address.	**P**resident Lincoln "We need better housing for the poor, **G**overnor."

Exercise

Direct the students to correct the capitalization errors in the following items.

1. The clock struck twelve. a masked stranger entered the room.
2. The stranger explained that He was an invited guest.
3. "Did you notice," whispered Diane, "How everyone stopped and stared?"
4. "I stared too," said Fields. "he doesn't belong here, I'm sure."
5. Just then e. g. fleming, the host, entered the room.
6. Approaching the stranger, he said, "Good evening, governor."
7. The stranger laughed, "You spoiled my fun, mr. Fleming. I had everyone guessing my identity."
8. Mr. Fleming addressed the guests, "enjoy yourselves. There are more surprises in store."
9. Those who had questioned the stranger's presence were embarrassed. you would be too.
10. The next stranger might be mayor Giuliani!

Answers

1. twelve. A
2. he
3. how
4. He
5. E. G. Fleming
6. Governor
7. Mr.
8. Enjoy
9. You
10. Mayor

Exercise

Have the students explain why each of the following items is or is not capitalized. They should refer to the rules for capitalization on page R36.

1. the mayor of the town
2. Mayor Powell
3. Kankakee
4. Mount Whitney
5. Michigan
6. Lake Champlain
7. my aunt's house
8. Aunt Teresa
9. New England
10. the West

Answers

1. Do not capitalize a title that is a substitute for a person's name.
2. Capitalize a title that precedes a person's name.
3. Capitalize the names of cities.
4. Capitalize the names of geographic features.
5. Capitalize the names of states.
6. Capitalize the names of geographic features.
7. Do not capitalize the names of family relationships when they follow a possessive pronoun.
8. Capitalize words that show family relationships when used as titles.
9. Capitalize the names of sections of the country.
10. Capitalize compass points when they refer to a specific section of the country.

Rule	Example
Do not capitalize a title that follows or is a substitute for a person's name.	Margaret Reilly was elected **m**ayor. He asked to speak to the **m**ayor.
Capitalize the names and the abbreviations of academic degrees that follow a person's name. Capitalize *Jr.* and *Sr.*	Donna Teshima, **M.D.** Lawrence Palmer **J**r.
Capitalize words that show family relationships when used as titles or as substitutes for a person's name.	We visited **A**unt Anne. He gave **G**randpa a ride.
Do not capitalize words that show family relationships when they follow a possessive noun or pronoun.	We visited Diego's **a**unt. He gave my **g**randpa a ride.
Always capitalize the pronoun *I*.	After **I** eat, **I**'m going for a bike ride.

Capitalizing Names of Places

Rule	Example
Rule of Thumb Do not capitalize articles and prepositions in proper nouns. Gulf **of** Mexico Lake **of** the Woods	
Capitalize the names of cities, counties, states, countries, and continents.	**M**inneapolis **F**airfield **C**ounty **A**laska **P**eople's **R**epublic of **C**hina
Capitalize the names of bodies of water and other geographical features.	**I**ndian **O**cean **C**ape **F**ear **M**ount **E**verest
Capitalize the names of sections of a country and regions of the world.	the **M**idwest the **M**iddle **E**ast
Capitalize compass points when they refer to a specific section of a country.	the **N**orthwest the **S**outh

Rule	Example
Do not capitalize compass points when they indicate direction.	New Mexico is **s**outh of Colorado.
Do not capitalize adjectives made from words indicating direction.	**n**orthern Montana
Capitalize the names of streets and highways.	**S**oldier's **F**ield **R**oad
Capitalize the names of buildings, bridges, monuments, and other structures.	**P**eachtree **C**enter **B**uilding **B**ear **M**ountain **B**ridge

Capitalizing Other Proper Nouns and Adjectives	
Rule	**Example**
Capitalize the names of clubs, organizations, businesses, institutions, and political parties.	**I**deal **C**omputer **S**ervices **C**itizens for **C**lean **A**ir
Capitalize brand names but not the nouns following them.	**E**agle bicycles
Capitalize the names of days of the week, months, and holidays.	**M**onday **F**ebruary **I**ndependence **D**ay
Do not capitalize the names of seasons.	**w**inter, **s**pring, **s**ummer, **f**all
Capitalize the first word, the last word, and all important words in the title of a book, play, short story, poem, essay, article, film, television series, song, magazine, newspaper, and chapter of a book.	***T**he **D**iary of **A**nne **F**rank* "**H**ow to **P**aint with **W**atercolors"
Capitalize the names of ethnic groups, nationalities, and languages.	**P**eruvian **A**rab **S**wahili
Capitalize proper adjectives that are formed from the names of ethnic groups and nationalities.	**E**nglish sheepdog **V**ietnamese restaurant

Exercise

Direct the students to correct errors in capitalization in the following sentences. You might opt to dictate the sentences, having students decide which words to capitalize.

1. Louisiana is located East of Texas.
2. Mineral deposits were discovered in Central New Mexico.
3. The bank will be closed on memorial day.
4. After a long, cold Winter, everyone welcomes Spring.
5. My dog really likes Barkly Biscuits.
6. Who wrote the short story "The night the bed fell"?
7. The streets in this area were paved by wpa workers in the 1930s.
8. My uncle translates greek and russian stories.
9. Have you ever gone to the top of the Empire State building?
10. Wendell lives on Greene avenue and Bleeker street.

Answers

1. Louisiana is located east of Texas.
2. Mineral deposits were discovered in central New Mexico.
3. The bank will be closed on Memorial Day.
4. After a long, cold winter, everyone welcomes spring.
5. My dog really likes Barkly biscuits.
6. Who wrote the short story "The Night the Bed Fell"?
7. The streets in this area were paved by WPA workers in the 1930s.
8. My uncle translates Greek and Russian stories.
9. Have you ever gone to the top of the Empire State Building?
10. Wendell lives on Greene Avenue and Bleeker Street.

Exercise
Direct the students to supply commas and end marks in the following sentences.

1. What a fun-filled day we had
2. Everyone enjoyed the rides and the picnic lunch
3. How many people were expected to attend the auction
4. Count them as they take their seats
5. The mayor expressed his gratitude to the chairman to the committee members and to all the voters
6. Cheering loudly the spectators encouraged the racers
7. Do you agree Max that everyone had a wonderful time
8. How my mother would have loved the excitement
9. The smallest boys played games ate popcorn and exhausted themselves
10. In the middle of the afternoon someone organized a softball game

Answers
1. What a fun-filled day we had!
2. Everyone enjoyed the rides and the picnic lunch.
3. How many people were expected to attend the auction?
4. Count them as they take their seats.
5. The mayor expressed his gratitude to the chairman, to the committee members, and to all the voters.
6. Cheering loudly, the spectators encouraged the racers.
7. Do you agree, Max, that everyone had a wonderful time?
8. How my mother would have loved the excitement!
9. The smallest boys played games, ate popcorn, and exhausted themselves.
10. In the middle of the afternoon, someone organized a softball game.

Punctuation

Using the Period and Other End Marks

Rule	Example
Use a period at the end of a declarative sentence.	Tim was reading a magazine.
Use a period at the end of an imperative sentence that does not express strong feeling.	Please pass the juice.
Use a question mark at the end of an interrogative sentence.	What time is it**?**
Use an exclamation point at the end of an exclamatory sentence or a strong imperative.	What a great idea**!** Call an ambulance**!**
Use an exclamation point at the end of an interjection that expresses strong emotion.	Ouch**!** This bush has thorns.

Using Commas

Rule	Example
Use commas to separate three or more items in a series.	She got dressed**,** ate breakfast**,** and ran to catch the bus.
Use a comma to show a pause after an introductory word and to set off names used in direct address.	No**,** I don't agree with you. Tell me**,** Derek**,** how do you feel?
Use a comma after two or more introductory prepositional phrases or when the comma is needed to make the meaning clear. A comma is not needed after a single short prepositional phrase, but it is acceptable to use one.	By the end of the next century**,** this town will be a big city. From the strong**,** people count on leadership. (comma needed to prevent misreading) After the rain the air smelled clean. (no comma needed)
Use a comma after an introductory participle and an introductory participial phrase.	Splashing and shrieking**,** the children played in the pool.

Rule	Example
Use commas to set off words that interrupt the flow of thought in a sentence.	Kevin, unlike his brother, enjoys arts and crafts.
Use a comma after conjunctive adverbs such as *however, moreover, furthermore, nevertheless,* and *therefore.*	The governor has increased employment; furthermore, he has reduced taxes.
Use commas to set off an appositive if it is not essential to the meaning of a sentence.	My dog, a large collie, always sleeps on my bed.
Use a comma before a conjunction (*and, or, but, nor, so, for, yet*) that joins main clauses.	Rebecca searched for the trail, but night was falling.
Use a comma after an introductory adverb clause.	Because the snow was so deep, school was canceled.
In most cases, do not use a comma with an adverb clause that comes at the end of a sentence.	School was canceled because the snow was so deep.
Use a comma or a pair of commas to set off an adjective clause that is not essential to the meaning of a sentence.	Nadia, who is thirteen years old, created a documentary video.
Do not use a comma or pair of commas to set off an essential clause from the rest of the sentence.	Students **who are thirteen or older** can join the video club.
Use commas before and after the year when it is used with both the month and the day. If only the month and the year are given, do not use a comma.	July 4, 1776, is an important day in U.S. history. In November 1998 they moved to Canada.
Use commas before and after the name of a state or a country when it is used with the name of a city. Do not use a comma after the state if it is used with a ZIP code.	She flew to Dallas, Texas, last week. The address is 25 Porter Street, Largo, FL 34640.
Use commas or a pair of commas to set off an abbreviated title or degree following a person's name.	Joy Isaac, Ph.D., will speak on the future of genetics.
Use a pair of commas to set off *too* in the middle of a sentence when *too* means "also."	The birds, too, were enjoying the sunshine.

Exercise

Direct the students to supply commas where they are needed in the following sentences. One sentence is correct.

1. Grapefruit like oranges can be used to make marmalade.
2. Mother was busy in the kitchen and soon tempting aromas filled the house.
3. My uncle a talented carpenter built a shelving unit for my room.
4. My teacher went to Cincinnati Ohio for an English convention.
5. The man who lives upstairs repairs watches and fine jewelry.
6. When the fire alarm sounded the students quietly left the building.
7. My aunt loves animals; however pets are not permitted in her apartment building.
8. Joseph Mann M. D. is a general practitioner.
9. I called your house last night but no one answered the phone.
10. On April 9 1865 Lee surrendered to Grant.

Answers

1. Grapefruit, like oranges, can be used to make marmalade.
2. Mother was busy in the kitchen, and soon tempting aromas filled the house.
3. My uncle, a talented carpenter, built a shelving unit for my room.
4. My teacher went to Cincinnati, Ohio, for an English convention.
5. correct
6. When the fire alarm sounded, the students quietly left the building.
7. My aunt loves animals; however, pets are not permitted in her apartment building.
8. Joseph Mann, M. D., is a general practitioner.
9. I called your house last night, but no one answered the phone.
10. On April 9, 1865, Lee surrendered to Grant.

Exercise

Direct the students to supply the appropriate punctuation in the following sentences.

1. The conference will begin at 8 30 A.M.
2. The campsite had water, electricity, and a supply of firewood campers had to bring food, sleeping bags, and clothing.
3. The students needed the following pencils, paper, and art supplies.
4. The meeting should begin at 7 30 therefore, the officers must arrive early.
5. "Those who know the answer" said the teacher "should raise their hands."
6. I'll bring napkins paper cups and a tablecloth.
7. In heavy snow boots are a necessity.
8. The room was dark my friend couldn't find the light switch.
9. The film will be shown at 1 30 2 30 and 3 30.
10. I gave the letter to Ms. Aubrey my science teacher.

Answers

1. The conference will begin at 8:30 A.M.
2. The campsite had water, electricity, and a supply of firewood; campers had to bring food, sleeping bags, and clothing.
3. The students needed the following: pencils, paper, and art supplies.
4. The meeting should begin at 7:30; therefore, the officers must arrive early.
5. "Those who know the answer," said the teacher, "should raise their hands."
6. I'll bring napkins, paper cups, and a tablecloth.
7. In heavy snow, boots are a necessity.
8. The room was dark; my friend couldn't find the light switch.
9. The film will be shown at 1:30, 2:30, and 3:30.
10. I gave the letter to Ms. Aubrey, my science teacher.

Rule	Example
Use a comma or commas to set off a direct quotation.	He said, "Call me if you need some help." "Call me," he said, "if you need some help."
Use a comma after the salutation of a friendly letter and after the closing of both a friendly letter and a business letter.	Dear Grandpa, Love, Truly yours,
Use a comma when necessary to prevent misreading of a sentence.	After the spring, rain is unusual here.

Using Semicolons and Colons

Rule	Example
Use a semicolon to join the parts of a compound sentence when a coordinating conjunction, such as *and, or, nor,* or *but,* is not used.	I looked in the drawer; it was empty.
Use a semicolon to join parts of a compound sentence when the main clauses are long and are subdivided by commas. Use a semicolon even if these clauses are already joined by a coordinating conjunction.	Ashley leaped, grabbed a branch, and hoisted herself up; but the water, gray and swirling, was rising rapidly.
Use a semicolon to separate main clauses joined by a conjunctive adverb. Be sure to use a comma after the conjunctive adverb.	His work had been outstanding; therefore, he was given a raise.
Use a colon to introduce a list of items that ends a sentence. Use words such as *these, the following,* or *as follows* to signal that a list is coming.	Be sure to bring the following: a swimsuit, a towel, sunscreen, and sunglasses.
Do not use a colon to introduce a list preceded by a verb or preposition.	Be sure to bring a swimsuit, a towel, sunscreen, and sunglasses. (No colon is used after *bring.*)
Use a colon to separate the hour and the minutes when you write the time of day.	Meet me at 12:30.
Use a colon after the salutation of a business letter.	Dear Ms. Kendall:

Using Quotation Marks and Italics	
Rule	**Example**
Use quotation marks before and after a direct quotation.	**"**He's wearing a green tee shirt,**"** I said.
Use quotation marks with both parts of a divided quotation.	**"**I knew his name,**"** I said, **"**but I've forgotten it.**"**
Use a comma or commas to separate a phrase such as *she said* from the quotation itself. Place the comma that precedes the phrase inside the closing quotation marks.	"Let's get pizza**,**" she said**,** "and then rent a movie."
Place a period that ends a quotation inside the closing quotation marks.	He said, "Mom is at work**.**"
Place a question mark or an exclamation point inside the quotation marks when it is part of the quotation.	Julie asked, "What causes the colors of the sunset**?**"
Place a question mark or an exclamation point outside the quotation marks when it is part of the entire sentence.	How nice of him to say "You go first"**!**
Use quotation marks for the title of a short story, essay, poem, song, magazine or newspaper article, or book chapter.	short story: **"**Thank You, M'am**"** poem: **"**Thirteen Ways of Looking at a Blackbird**"** article: **"**Kids Clean Up the City**"**
Use italics or underlining for the title of a book, play, film, television series, magazine, newspaper, or work of art.	book: *All Things Bright and Beautiful* magazine: *People* painting: *The Starry Night*
Use italics or underlining for the names of ships, trains, airplanes, and spacecraft.	ship: *Titanic* train: *Orient Express* spacecraft: *Challenger*

Exercise

Direct the students to correct the use of quotation marks and italics (underlining) in the following sentences.

1. The teacher announced, "You have ten more minutes to finish the test".
2. We read The Medicine Bag, a short story.
3. "Come to my house", invited Beth, "so we can work together."
4. Little Men, a book by Louisa May Alcott, is a sequel to Little Women.
5. Katie asked, "How much longer do we have to wait"?
6. How exciting it was to hear Mr. Santucci quietly say, "Yes, you can come with us to the game!"
7. "Only my mom knows," said Meg, how hard it is for me to give a speech.
8. Did you hear Art say, "I'm dropping out of the club?"
9. My parents subscribe to Newsweek magazine.
10. Is the Broadway Limited still running?

Answers

1. The teacher announced, "You have ten more minutes to finish the test."
2. We read "The Medicine Bag," a short story.
3. "Come to my house," invited Beth, "so we can work together."
4. *Little Men,* a book by Louisa May Alcott, is a sequel to *Little Women.*
5. Katie asked, "How much longer do we have to wait?"
6. How exciting it was to hear Mr. Santucci quietly say, "Yes, you can come with us to the game"!
7. "Only my mom knows," said Meg, "how hard it is for me to give a speech."
8. Did you hear Art say, "I'm dropping out of the club"?
9. My parents subscribe to *Newsweek* magazine.
10. Is the *Broadway Limited* still running?

Exercise
Direct the students to insert apostrophes in the following sentences. One sentence is correct as is.

1. Who will win the prize is anyones guess.
2. Three boys bicycles were in the stand outside the school door.
3. There are two cs and two ms in *accommodate.*
4. My brother will graduate in the class of 08.
5. Now its too dark to take a walk outside.
6. My sisters coat is too long for me.
7. Is the hot chocolate on the table yours or mine?
8. In a written assignment, you should spell out the *ands.*
9. The visiting team will use the womens locker room.
10. After youve spoken, wait for a response.

Answers
1. Who will win the prize is anyone's guess.
2. Three boys' bicycles were in the stand outside the school door.
3. There are two *c's* and two *m's* in *accommodate.*
4. My brother will graduate in the class of '08.
5. Now it's too dark to take a walk outside.
6. My sister's coat is too long for me.
7. correct
8. In a written assignment, you should spell out the *and's.*
9. The visiting team will use the women's locker room.
10. After you've spoken, wait for a response.

Using Apostrophes

Rule	Example
Use an apostrophe and an *s ('s)* to form the possessive of a singular noun.	my father**'s** car Charles**'s** helmet
Use an apostrophe and an *s ('s)* to form the possessive of a plural noun that does not end in *s.*	the geese**'s** wings the children**'s** room
Use an apostrophe alone to form the possessive of a plural noun that ends in *s.*	three boy**s'** seats the Miller**s'** apartment
Use an apostrophe and an *s ('s)* to form the possessive of an indefinite pronoun.	someone**'s** jacket anyone**'s** name
Do not use an apostrophe in a possessive pronoun.	The cat cleaned **its** paws. My home is **yours.** The computer is **hers.**
Use an apostrophe to replace letters that have been omitted in a contraction.	it + is = it**'s** can + not = ca**n't** I + have = I**'ve**
Use an apostrophe to form the plural of a letter, a figure, or a word that is used as itself.	Write three *7***'s.** The word is spelled with two *m***'s.** The sentence contains three *and***'s.**
Use an apostrophe to show missing numbers in a year.	the fall of **'02**

Rule of Thumb

If a thing is jointly owned by two or more individuals, only the last name should show possession: *Rob and Sarah's dog.* If the ownership is not joint, each name should show possession: *Amanda's and Bernadette's mothers.*

Using Hyphens, Dashes, and Parentheses	
Rule	**Example**
Use a hyphen to show the division of a word at the end of a line. Always divide the word between its syllables. **Rule of Thumb** One-letter divisions (for example, *e-lectric*) are not permissible. Avoid dividing personal names if possible.	Consult a dictionary for correct di- vision of syllables.
Use a hyphen in a number written as a compound word.	forty-five
Use a hyphen in a fraction.	We expect a one-third increase in enrollment. Add about one-third of the flour.
Use a hyphen or hyphens in certain compound nouns.	merry-go-round great-grandmother
Hyphenate a compound modifier only when it precedes the word it modifies.	I enjoy a well-written story. The story was well written.
Use a hyphen after the prefixes *all-*, *ex-*, and *self-* when they are joined to a noun or an adjective.	all-star ex-president self-conscious
Use a hyphen to separate a prefix from a word that begins with a capital letter.	un-American mid-December
Use a dash or dashes to show a sudden break or change in thought or speech.	I found my old skates—they didn't fit me anymore—and donated them to the thrift shop.
Use parentheses to set off words that define or helpfully explain a word in a sentence.	The puma **(**also known as the mountain lion or cougar**)** is one of the big cats of the Americas.

LANGUAGE HANDBOOK

Exercise

Direct the students to explain why hyphens, dashes, and parentheses are used in the following sentences.

1. The small dog barked loudly when strangers approached.
2. My grandfather is seventy-six years old.
3. The musical tribute to Broadway had an all-star cast.
4. The koala (it looks like a teddy bear) is native to Australia.
5. Ms. Benjamin complimented me on my well-planned project.
6. The school held a pre-Thanksgiving Day party.
7. The new poll shows that Governor Johnson has suffered a one-fourth decrease in popularity since the beginning of this year.
8. The pillowcase was embroidered with tiny forget-me-nots.
9. My objection to the plan–you asked me for it–is that it's too complicated.
10. One third of the sailors became violently seasick.

Answers

1. Use a hyphen to show the division of a word at the end of a line.
2. Use a hyphen in compound numbers.
3. Use a hyphen after the prefix *all-*.
4. Use parentheses to set off words that explain a word in a sentence.
5. Hyphenate a compound modifier when it precedes the noun it modifies.
6. Use a hyphen to separate a prefix from a word that begins with a capital letter.
7. Use a hyphen in a fraction used as a modifier.
8. Use hyphens in certain compound nouns.
9. Use dashes to show a sudden change in thought or speech.
10. Do not hyphenate a fraction used as a noun.

Exercise

Direct students to answer the following questions about abbreviations.

1. When units of measure are abbreviated, which units are followed by periods, English or metric?
2. When you write exact times, what abbreviations do you use for morning and afternoon?
3. When do you abbreviate the names of days and months?
4. When are street names and state names spelled out? When are they abbreviated?
5. How do you write abbreviations that are pronounced as words or letter by letter?

Answers

1. Abbreviations of English measures are followed by periods.
2. A.M. is the abbreviation used for morning hours; P.M. is used for afternoon.
3. Abbreviate days and months only in charts and lists.
4. Street names and state names are spelled out in general text and abbreviated only on envelopes.
5. Use capital letters and no periods for abbreviations that are pronounced as words or letter by letter.

Abbreviations

Rule	Example
Abbreviate the titles *Mr., Mrs., Ms.,* and *Dr.* before a person's name. Also abbreviate a professional or academic degree that follows a name. The titles *Jr.* and *Sr.* are *not* preceded by a comma.	George Ryan **Sr.** Raquel Sanchez, **Ph.D.**
Use capital letters and no periods with abbreviations that are pronounced letter by letter or as words. Exceptions are *U.S.* and *Washington, D.C.,* which do use periods.	**NOW** National Organization for Women **AHL** American Hockey League
With exact times, use *A.M.* (ante meridiem, "before noon") and *P.M.* (post meridiem, "after noon"). For years, use *B.C.* (before Christ) and, sometimes, *A.D.* (anno Domini, "in the year of the Lord," after Christ).	9:30 **A.M.** 1:55 **P.M.** 2000 **B.C.** **A.D.** 350
Abbreviate days and months only in charts and lists.	Project Deadlines Outline **Sept.** 30 First draft **Oct.** 30 Final report **Nov.** 15
In scientific writing, abbreviate units of measure. Use periods with English units but not with metric units.	inch(es) **in.** yard(s) **yd.** meter(s) **m** milliliter(s) **ml**
On envelopes only, abbreviate street names and state names. In general text, spell out street names and state names.	Ms. Denise Pitkin 29 Gould **St.** Lake Oswego, **OR** 97034 Denise lives on Gould **Street** in Lake Oswego, **Oregon.**

Writing Numbers	
Rule	**Example**
In charts and tables, always write numbers as numerals. Other rules apply to numbers not in charts or tables.	Student Test Scores Student / Test **1** / Test **2** / Test **3** Lai, W. / **82** / **89** / **94** Ostos, A. / **88** / **90** / **87**
Spell out a number that is expressed in one or two words.	This year I will turn **fourteen,** and my mom will turn **forty-two.**
Use a numeral for a number of more than two words.	The necklace had **136** beads.
Spell out a number that begins a sentence or reword the sentence so that it does not begin with a number.	**Three hundred twenty** people signed the petition. The petition was signed by **320** people.
Write a very large number as a numeral followed by the word *million* or *billion.*	The sun is about **93 million** miles from Earth.
Related numbers should be written the same way. If one number must be written as a numeral, use numerals for all the numbers.	There were **249** students in the school, and only **7** were absent.
Spell out an ordinal number (*first, second*).	He was the **eighth** winner of the annual award.
Use words to express the time of day unless you are writing the exact time or using the abbreviation *A.M.* or *P.M.*	Be at my house by **two o'clock.** The movie begins at **4:40.** He exercises at about **8:00 A.M.**
Use numerals to express dates, house and street numbers, apartment and room numbers, telephone numbers, page numbers, amounts of money of more than two words, and percentages. Write out the word *percent.*	November **11, 1952** page **7** **60** percent **one** dollar **ten** cents **$1.10**

Exercise

Direct students to write sentences containing the following numbers or groups of numbers as they should appear.

1. ninety-three million
2. forty-five percent
3. 2nd time
4. twenty minutes after three in the afternoon
5. 13 years old
6. 586 (at the beginning of a sentence)
7. 586 (within a sentence)
8. four dollars and fifty-five cents
9. seven hundred fifty *and* forty
10. today's date

Sample answers

1. The town's population was 93 million.
2. Only 45 percent of the students did well on the test.
3. Some students watched the movie a second time.
4. The last bell rings at 3:20 P.M.
5. The twins are thirteen years old.
6. Five hundred eighty-six pieces of mail were delivered in a half-hour.
7. In one day 586 tons of food was delivered to the starving villagers.
8. The scarf cost $4.55.
9. Of the 750 people enrolled in the math program, only 40 opted to continue for the second year.
10. The package arrived on December 10, 2002.

Exercise

Dictate the following sentences and ask the students to spell the underlined word.

1. The bride's <u>veil</u> was fingertip length.
2. If you work hard, you can <u>exceed</u> your parents' expectations.
3. The wheat <u>field</u> was destroyed by grasshoppers.
4. How much does that huge pumpkin <u>weigh?</u>
5. A deliberate attempt to <u>deceive</u> is a lie.
6. Did the mountain climber <u>succeed</u> in breaking a record?
7. The woman will <u>intercede</u> with the authorities for her husband's release.
8. The only <u>occupant</u> of the canoe was a frightened boy.
9. Deliveries should be made using the <u>freight</u> elevator.
10. I do not like <u>either</u> of the dresses.

Spelling

The following basic rules, examples, and exceptions will help you master the spellings of many words.

ie and *ei*

Many writers find the rules for certain combinations of letters, like *ie* and *ei,* difficult to remember. One helpful learning strategy is to develop a rhyme to remember a rule. Look at the following rhyme for the *ie* and *ei* rule.

Rule	Examples
Put *i* before *e,*	piece, field, relief
except after *c*	perceive, deceit, conceive
or when sounded like *a,*	eighty, veil, freight
as in *neighbor* and *weigh.*	

Exceptions The words *seize, leisure, weird, height, either, foreign, protein,* and *species* do not follow the rule.

-cede, -ceed, and *-sede*

Because various combinations of letters in English are sometimes pronounced the same way, it is often easy to make slight spelling errors. With the exceptions below, spell the *sēd* sounds at the end of words as *-cede:* precede, accede, intercede.

Exceptions One word uses *-sede* to spell the final *sēd* sounds: supersede.

Three words use *-ceed* to spell the final *sēd* sounds: proceed, exceed, succeed.

Unstressed vowels

Notice the vowel sound in the second syllable of the word *his-to-ry.* This is the unstressed vowel sound; dictionary respellings use the schwa symbol (ə) to indicate it. Because any vowel can be used to spell this sound, you might find yourself uncertain about which vowel to use. To spell words with unstressed vowels, try thinking of a related word in which the syllable containing the vowel sound is stressed.

Unknown Spelling	Related Word	Correct Spelling
hist_ry	hist**o**ric	history
occup_nt	occup**a**tion	occupant
pot_nt	pot**e**ntial	potent
or_gin	or**i**ginal	origin

Adding prefixes

When adding a prefix to a word, keep the original spelling of the word. If the prefix forms a double letter, keep both letters.

inter + national = international
un + necessary = unnecessary
re + elect = reelect

Suffixes and the silent *e*

Many English words end in a silent letter *e*. Sometimes the *e* is dropped when a suffix is added. When adding a suffix that begins with a consonant to a word that ends in silent *e*, keep the *e*.

excite + ment = excitement
shame + ful = shameful

Common Exceptions awe + ful = awful; judge + ment = judgment

When adding the suffix *y* or a suffix that begins with another vowel to a word that ends in silent *e*, usually drop the *e*.

scare + y = scary
complete + ion = completion

Common Exception mile + age = mileage

When adding a suffix that begins with *a* or *o* to a word that ends in *ce* or *ge*, keep the *e* so the word will retain the soft *c* or *g* sound.

notice + able = noticeable
courage + ous = courageous

When adding a suffix that begins with a vowel other than *e* to a word that ends in *ee* or *oe*, keep the *e*.

canoe + able = canoeable
agree + ing = agreeing

Exercise

Dictate the following sentences and ask the students to spell the underlined word.

1. The child's hurtful remark was unintentional.
2. The school is replacing the broken desks.
3. Keep the group small so it will be manageable.
4. The dinner preparations will take less time if you help.
5. The summer day was peaceful and calm.
6. The communications officer radioed for help.
7. Kevin is thin but wiry.
8. The boy chose an outrageous color scheme for his room.
9. Have you bought a replacement for your lost textbook?
10. The bread is so hard that it isn't sliceable.

Exercise

Direct the students to combine each word with the suffix that follows it.

1. actual + ly
2. skillful + ly
3. spin + ing
4. advise + ing
5. replay + ed
6. defer + ed
7. refer + ence
8. plain + ness
9. pad + ing
10. side + walk

Answers

1. actually
2. skillfully
3. spinning
4. advising
5. replayed
6. deferred
7. reference
8. plainness
9. padding
10. sidewalk

Suffixes and the final *y*

When adding a suffix to a word that ends in a consonant + *y*, change the *y* to *i* unless the suffix begins with *i*. Keep the *y* in a word that ends in a vowel + *y*.

apply + ed = applied	apply + ing = applying
destroy + ed = destroyed	destroy+ ing = destroying

Doubling the final consonant

Double the final consonant in a one-syllable word that ends in a single consonant preceded by a single vowel. Double the final consonant if the word has an accent on the last syllable and the accent stays there after the suffix is added or if it is a word made up of a prefix and a one-syllable word.

grin + ing = grinning	plan + er = planner
refer + al = referral	repel + ent = repellent
remop + ed = remopped	unplug + ing = unplugging

Do not double the final consonant if the accent is not on the last syllable or if the accent shifts when the suffix is added. Also do not double the final consonant if it is preceded by two vowels or by another consonant. If the word ends in a consonant and the suffix begins with a consonant, do not double the final consonant.

counsel + ing = counseling	melt + ed = melted
prefer + ence = preference	treat + ing = treating
commit + ment = commitment	travel + ing = traveling

Adding *-ly* and *-ness*

When adding *-ly* to a word that ends in a single *l*, keep the *l*, but when the word ends in a double *l*, drop one *l*. When adding *-ness* to a word that ends in *n*, keep the *n*.

ideal + ly = ideally	real + ly = really
full + ly = fully	dull + ly = dully
thin + ness = thinness	open + ness = openness

Forming compound words

When forming a compound word, keep the original spelling of both words.

air + plane = airplane	ball + park = ballpark
post + card = postcard	pea + nut = peanut

Forming plurals

English words form plurals in many ways. Most nouns simply add *-s.* The following chart shows other ways of forming plural nouns and some common exceptions to the pattern.

GENERAL RULES FOR FORMING PLURALS		
If a word ends in	**Rule**	**Example**
ch, s, sh, x, z	add *-es*	watch, watches
a consonant + *y*	change *y* to *i* and add *-es*	berry, berries
a vowel + *y* or *o*	add *-s*	monkey, monkeys video, videos
a consonant + *o* common exceptions	generally add *-es* but sometimes add *-s*	potato, potatoes solo, solos
f or *ff* common exceptions	add *-s* change *f* to *v* and add *-es*	cuff, cuffs loaf, loaves
lf	change *f* to *v* and add *-es*	elf, elves
fe	change *f* to *v* and add *-s*	wife, wives

A few plurals are exceptions to the rules in the previous chart, but they are easy to remember. The following chart lists these plurals and some examples.

SPECIAL RULES FOR FORMING PLURALS	
Rule	**Example**
To form the plural of proper names and one-word compound nouns, follow the general rules for plurals.	Marino, Marinos Burch, Burches wristwatch, wristwatches
To form the plural of hyphenated compound nouns or compound nouns of more than one word, make the most important word plural.	sister-in-law, sisters-in-law half-moon, half-moons maid of honor, maids of honor
Some nouns have unusual plural forms.	foot, feet mouse, mice child, children
Some nouns have the same singular and plural forms.	moose, moose deer, deer scissors, scissors

Exercise

Direct the students to write the plurals of the following words.

1. ferry
2. calf
3. life
4. radio
5. pulley
6. pocket watch
7. dairy
8. tomato
9. solo
10. Walsh
11. mouse
12. sandwich
13. mother-in-law
14. crash
15. woman

Answers

1. ferries
2. calves
3. lives
4. radios
5. pulleys
6. pocket watches
7. dairies
8. tomatoes
9. solos
10. Walshes
11. mice
12. sandwiches
13. mothers-in-law
14. crashes
15. women

Writing Handbook

The Writing Process

The writing process consists of five stages, from choosing a topic to presenting a finished piece of writing. These stages are prewriting, drafting, revising, editing/proofreading, and publishing/presenting. You do not need to follow them in a strict order but can move back and forth between stages as your ideas develop. For example, before revising your first draft, you might present it to a friend for feedback, or you might go back to prewriting and gather more information about your topic.

The Writing Process

Prewriting

In the prewriting stage, you explore topic ideas, choose a topic, gather information, and begin to organize your material.

Exploring ideas

Ask yourself the following questions before you begin:

- What is my general purpose—an assignment, a personal reason?
- What audience do I have in mind—classmates, the general public?
- What do my purpose and audience determine about the length of my paper? The kinds of topics that are appropriate? The tone and language of my writing (formal or informal; serious or light; objective or personal)?

Once you have given some thought to these questions, the following techniques can help you find a topic to write about.

- Scan your memory for interesting, funny, or moving personal experiences.
- Flip through a variety of magazines and newspapers.
- Browse through a library catalog.
- Brainstorm for topics with a group of classmates.

R50 WRITING HANDBOOK

Choosing a topic

When you have several possible topics in mind, ask yourself these questions about each one:

- Does it fulfill my assignment or my own purpose for writing?
- Is it appropriate for the length of paper I plan to write? Would I need to narrow or broaden this topic?
- Do I know enough about this topic, or can I find enough information?

Gathering information

How you gather your information will depend upon the kind of paper you are writing.

If you are writing a personal essay, try one or both of the following techniques.

Freewriting Set a time limit of ten minutes and write down everything that comes to mind on your topic. You might want to list your thoughts and images under general headings or make a cluster diagram.

Discussion Talk about your topic with other people. Take notes on your ideas as they come to you.

If you are writing a report or a persuasive essay, you will probably need to locate pertinent factual information and take notes.

Use library resources, such as books, magazines, newspapers, documentary and informational videos, and the Internet.

Interview people knowledgeable about your topic, such as teachers and other professionals, members of organizations, hobbyists, people from a pertinent country or culture, or people who lived through an era important to your topic.

Organizing your material

Determine the main points, subtopics, or events you will be writing about and the general order in which to present them.

Sometimes the best order will be obvious. For example, a biography usually calls for chronological order; a persuasive essay often begins or ends with the most important point; a description of a place may lend itself to spatial order, such as from near to far or from low to high. For other kinds of writing, such as science reports, you will need to experiment to find the best order.

After deciding on the general order, make a rough outline. It can be a simple list or an outline with headings and subheadings.

Drafting

In the drafting stage, use your notes and outline to write a rough version of your paper. Drafting is an opportunity to explore and develop your ideas.

Tips for drafting

- You might want to write your draft quickly, capturing the rapid flow of your ideas, or you might wish to work slowly, rethinking and revising as you write. Choose the approach that works best for you.
- Whether you work quickly or slowly, don't focus too much on details. Concentrate on developing the main ideas. At this stage, just list the supporting points that you will develop later.
- Keep your purpose in mind and use your outline as a guide. If part of your outline doesn't work, omit it. If better ideas occur to you as you write, feel free to change your direction.

Revising

In the revising stage, evaluate your draft and look for ways to improve and refine it. Before you revise, put your draft aside for a while; then reread it carefully. At this point, you might benefit from a peer review of your writing.

Peer review

Discuss your writing with one or more students, called peer reviewers. You may want to direct the responses of your peer reviewers in specific ways:

- Have readers summarize your paper in their own words. If you do not hear your ideas restated, you should revise for clarity.
- Ask readers to tell you what parts of your writing they liked best and why. You may want to expand those elements when you revise.
- Discuss the ideas in your writing with your readers. Have them share their own ideas about the topic. Include any new insights you gain in your revision.

Tips for revising

Ask yourself the following questions:

- Does my writing have an introduction, a body, and a conclusion?
- Is my writing appropriate for my audience?
- Is the organization of my information and ideas logical and effective?
- Have I developed my ideas clearly and with enough detail?

R52 WRITING HANDBOOK

- Do all of my details support my main idea? Are any of them irrelevant or confusing?
- Is my information accurate?
- Have I chosen the best, most precise words?
- Have I achieved my purpose?

Editing/Proofreading

The editing stage is the time to polish your revised draft, proofread it for errors in grammar and spelling, and make a clean copy of it. Use the checklist below and the proofreading checklist found on the inside back cover of this book.

Editing for style

Use the following checklist:

- ☑ Is the tone of my writing appropriate to my purpose?
- ☑ Have I made clear connections between ideas?
- ☑ Have I used effective transitions between sentences and paragraphs?
- ☑ Have I used a variety of sentence types?
- ☑ Have I used precise words?

Publishing/Presenting

There are many opportunities for presenting school writing projects or your independent writing to an audience. Consider some of the following suggestions:

- Give or send your writing to a friend or relative.
- Present it orally to your class.
- Submit it to a local newspaper.
- Submit it to the newsletter of an appropriate organization.
- Submit it to a magazine that accepts writing by young people.
- Send it to an appropriate group of people via e-mail.
- Post it on an electronic bulletin board.
- Join or form a writers' group at your school, library, or youth center. Such groups can provide useful feedback to their members.

WRITING HANDBOOK R53

Writing Modes

Writing is often identified as being one of four types, or modes: expository, descriptive, narrative, or persuasive.

Expository Writing

Expository writing informs and explains. The most familiar form of expository writing is the essay. Other examples of expository writing include instructions, newspaper or magazine articles, and textbooks. The chart below lists four types of expository writing. Whatever type of writing you are doing, the checklist here can help you write more effectively.

- ☑ Does my opening contain attention-getting details or questions to hook the reader?
- ☑ Have I presented information in a logical order?
- ☑ Are my explanations complete, clear, and accurate?
- ☑ Have I included interesting examples? Facts? Statistics? Quotations from experts?
- ☑ Have I defined any unfamiliar terms?
- ☑ Have I made any comparisons clear and logical?
- ☑ Does my conclusion bring my writing to a satisfactory close?

Type	Introduction	Body	Sample Questions
Definition	Identify the item you are defining and clearly state your purpose for writing.	Supply details to give readers a clear understanding of the item you are defining.	What is the Internet?
Compare and contrast	Identify the objects you are comparing and your purpose for making the comparison.	List the similarities and differences between the subjects. Organize by subject or feature.	How is the government of Canada similar to that of the United States? Different from?
Process	State the process you are explaining and its importance.	Describe the process step-by-step.	How are animated cartoons made?
Cause and effect	Write a topic sentence that makes the cause-and-effect relationship clear.	Use a pattern of cause-to-effect or effect-to-cause. Use transition words like *as a result, therefore,* and *because.*	Why did the *Titanic* sink?

R54 WRITING HANDBOOK

WRITING HANDBOOK

Descriptive Writing

When you write a description, your goal is to communicate a vivid impression of a person, place, or thing. You will need to observe, remember, or imagine your subject carefully. Then select details and organize your ideas. Descriptive writing is found in travel brochures, in advertisements, and often in combination with narrative writing. The checklist here can help you improve your descriptive writing.

- ☑ Have I organized details in a logical way?
- ☑ Are my transitions smooth and clear?
- ☑ Have I used sensory details that capture the mood or feeling of the subject being described?
- ☑ Have I used vivid and precise language?
- ☑ Have I shown a scene rather than told about it?
- ☑ Have I included appropriate metaphors, similes, and other figures of speech?
- ☑ Have I chosen words with the appropriate connotation as well as denotation?

Narrative Writing

When you write a narrative, you are telling a story. If the story recounts true events that happened to real people, it is nonfiction. If it springs from your imagination, it is fiction. Fiction and nonfiction narratives share the same basic elements: setting, characters, and action. Check your narrative writing with the list here.

- ☑ Have I introduced the characters and the setting in sufficient detail?
- ☑ Have I presented a conflict or sequence of events?
- ☑ Have I told the story from a consistent point of view?
- ☑ If the order of events is not chronological, can the reader follow the order easily?
- ☑ Is there a satisfactory conclusion?

Persuasive Writing

The purpose of persuasive writing is to convince an audience to think or act in a particular way. Effective persuasive writing presents an opinion and backs it up with sound reasons. Use the checklist at the right to improve your persuasive writing.

- ☑ Have I stated my position clearly?
- ☑ Have I arranged my arguments from strongest to weakest or from weakest to strongest?
- ☑ Have I backed up my position with facts, statistics, and examples?
- ☑ Have I taken into account the values and interests of my audience?
- ☑ Have I avoided highly emotional language?
- ☑ Have I concluded with a summary of my argument, a strong appeal, or a call to action?

WRITING HANDBOOK R55

WRITING HANDBOOK

Research Report Writing

When you write a research report, you explore a topic by gathering factual information from several sources. Through your research, you develop a point of view or draw a conclusion, which becomes the thesis statement of your report.

Selecting a Topic

Because a research report usually takes several weeks to research and write, your choice of topic is especially important. Follow these guidelines:

- Brainstorm a list of questions about a general subject you would like to explore. Choose a question that is neither too narrow nor too broad for the length of your paper. Use that question as your topic.
- Be sure your topic genuinely interests you.
- Be sure you can find information from several sources on your topic.

Doing Research

Start by reading a general reference source such as an encyclopedia. This will give you a broad overview of your topic. Then go on to other sources. The catalog in a library can tell you what books are available on your topic. Online databases such as the *Readers' Guide to Periodical Literature* can help you find magazine and newspaper articles on your topic. Electronic sources such as CD-ROMs or the Internet are especially useful for topics related to current events and research. If you need help in finding or using any of these resources, ask the librarian.

As you gather information, make sure each source you use is reliable. Check publication dates of books and articles to see how up-to-date the information is. If you interview someone for information, be sure that person is an expert in the field or has firsthand knowledge. Be aware that anyone can post material on the Internet, so make sure that any online information you find comes from a reputable source.

Evaluating Sources

There are two kinds of sources: primary and secondary.

A **primary source** is a firsthand account of an event—that is, an account written by someone who actually experienced or witnessed the event.

I Know Why the Caged Bird Sings, in which Maya Angelou tells her life story, is an example of a primary source.

A **secondary source** is one written on the basis of research and interpretation; the writer has not personally seen or experienced the event.

Whether your sources are primary or secondary, make sure they are
- authoritative–written by recognized experts on the topic
- reliable–published in reputable books, periodicals, or Web sites
- up-to-date–based on the most current research in the field
- appropriate–closely related to the topic of your report

Making Source Cards

In a research report, you must document the sources of your information. To keep track of your sources, write the author, title, publication information, and location of each source on a separate index card. Give each source card a number and write that number in the upper right-hand corner. These cards will be useful for preparing your documentation.

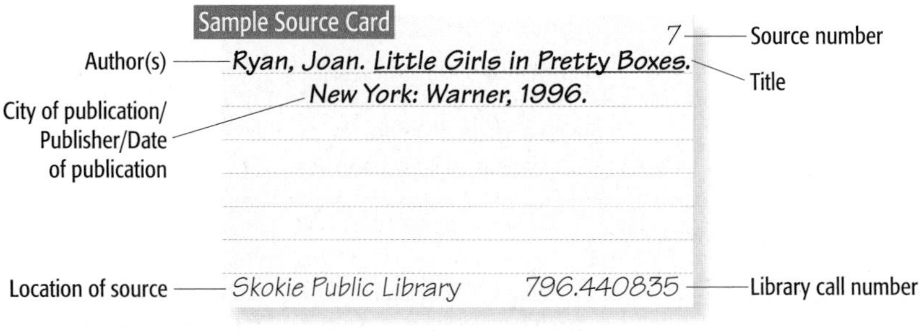

Compiling Note Cards

As you find material on your topic, record each important piece of information on a separate note card. The following suggestions will help you take notes efficiently and avoid plagiarizing, that is, presenting someone else's words or ideas as your own.

- If the passage is lengthy, write the main points and summarize the details.
- If the information is presented in only a sentence or two, paraphrase, or restate it in your own words.
- If the author's wording is especially effective, you might want to use the passage as a quotation. Copy the exact words and put them in quotation marks.

Your note cards should include the information shown in the sample note card shown on the following page.

WRITING HANDBOOK R57

WRITING HANDBOOK

Sample Note Card

Write a key word or phrase that tells you what the information is about.

7 — Write the source number from your source card.

Physical problems
Some former gymnasts, now in their twenties, have the bone density of 90-year-olds. p. 26

Write the number of the page or pages on which you found the information.

Developing Your Thesis

As you begin researching and learning about your topic, stay focused on the overall point you want to make. Write down a thesis statement and keep it in mind as you continue your research to determine what information is and is not relevant. However, be prepared to change your thesis if the information you find does not support it.

Writing an Outline

When you have gathered information from several sources, use your note cards to write an outline. First, group together note cards that contain related information. Use the topic of each group as a main heading in your outline. Under each main heading, write subheadings that show the kinds of information you will provide. Write your thesis statement at the beginning of your outline.

Sample Outline

The price of success for female Olympic gymnasts is quite high and may not be worth the sacrifices needed to make it to the top.

I. Changes in gymnastics since 1972
   A. Effect of Olga Korbut
   B. Age of athletes
   C. Need to be small and thin
II. Injuries
   A. Daily strain on the body
   B. Accidents
III. Emotional pressure
   A. Time spent training
   B. Pressures from parents and coach
   C. Rigid scoring system

The thesis statement identifies your topic and the overall point you will make.

Label main headings with Roman numerals.

Label subheadings with capital letters.

R58 WRITING HANDBOOK

Documenting Your Information

To avoid plagiarism, or the presentation of someone else's words or ideas as if they were your own, you must document the sources of all the information you use in your report. Document, or credit, the source of each quotation, paraphrase, or summary. You do not need to credit a source for information that is considered common knowledge. There are two common ways to document information.

Footnotes To document with footnotes, place a number directly after each item that you are documenting. This number should be slightly above the base line of your text, and it should come after any punctuation (see the example below). The full documentation information goes at the bottom of the page, with a matching number.

> The declaration was read in public for the first time on July 6, 1776.[1]
>
> [1]John Smith, The Declaration of Independence (New York: DI, 2001) 221.

Parenthetical Documentation In this method, a reference to the source appears in parentheses at the end of the sentence containing information from that source. Provide enough information for your readers to identify the source in your works-cited list at the end of your report. Here are the basic rules to follow.

- Cite the author's name and the number of the page where you found the information.

  The declaration was first read in public by militia colonel John Nixon (Smith 222).
- If you mention the author's name in the sentence, you do not need to repeat it.

  Smith says that the reading was greeted with wild applause (224).
- If your source does not identify a particular author, as in a newspaper or encyclopedia article, give the first word or two of the title of the piece.

  The two-hundredth anniversary of the reading was commemorated by a parade and fireworks ("Reading Celebrated").

WRITING HANDBOOK R59

WRITING HANDBOOK

Bibliography or Works Cited

The final page of your research report should be a list of all the sources that you used to prepare your report. Arrange entries alphabetically by the author's last name (or by title when no author is mentioned), as shown below. Label your list *Works Cited*. The term *bibliography* can also be used. The chart below gives examples of entries for the most common types of sources. Use these examples and models when you compile your own list of works cited.

Type of Source	Format Example
Article in an encyclopedia	"Honeybee." *The New Encyclopedia Britannica*. 1998.
Article in a magazine	Johnson, Sally A. "A Beekeeper's Year." *Apiculture* (Sept. 1999): 40–44.
Article in a newspaper	Bertram, Jeffrey. "African Bees: Fact or Myth?" *Orlando Sentinel* 18 Aug. 1999: D2.
Audiocassette	*Easy Beekeeping*. University of North Carolina Extension Office. Audiocassette. 1998.
Book with one author	Stelley, Diane G. *Beekeeping: An Illustrated Handbook.* Blue Ridge Summit, PA: Tab, 1993.
Book with two authors	Markham, Ron, and Cheryl Courson. *The Handbook of Beekeeping*. Ithaca, NY: Cornell UP, 1996.
Book with three or more authors	Sammataro, Diana, et al. *The Beekeeper's Handbook*. Ithaca, NY: Cornell UP, 1998.
CD-ROM	"Bee Flight." *Flights of Fancy*. CD-ROM. Baltimore, MD: Learning Incorporated, 1999.
Interview	Seidler, Harold. Personal interview. 25 March 2001.
Videocassettte	*Beekeeping*. University of North Carolina Extension Office. Videocassette. 1998.
Web site	Sanford, Malcolm T. "Small Hive Beetle." *Bee Culture* (Feb. 1999). 13 Feb. 2001 <http://www.bee.airoot.com/beeculture/99feb/99feb4.html>.

R60 WRITING HANDBOOK

Business and Technical Writing

Business Writing

In the business world, good writing means clear and concise writing. Examples of business writing include documents such as letters, memos, job applications, and proposals. The format and tone of business writing depend on audience and purpose.

Business Letters

Business letters are more formal than social letters you might write to friends or relatives. Business letters are written to a specific reader, sometimes to a person you have never met. Business letters are a direct and effective way to inform, to persuade, or to obtain something.

Types of Business Letters

Business letters serve many purposes and can help you with your career development. For example, you might write a letter requesting an interview or information about a career that interests you. When you are old enough to work, you might write a letter applying for a job. The following chart summarizes a few types of business letters that you might use for finding a job, exploring career opportunities, or handling personal matters.

Type	Purpose	Example
Letter of Inquiry	To request an interview or ask for information	You are interested in a future career as a newspaper reporter. You write to ask the managing editor of a local newspaper for an interview.
Application Letter	To apply for a job or a volunteer program	Your middle school encourages students to spend time doing community service. You write to a nursing home director and apply for the position of volunteer worker.
Complaint Letter	To complain about a situation or a product	You have had your new computer repaired twice in six months. You write to the manufacturer to express your disappointment with the product.
Opinion Letter	To state your view about a situation or an issue	The city council member for your district has proposed building a new youth center. You write to her to express your support.

WRITING HANDBOOK R61

Format of Business Letters

PRACTICE

Evaluation Rubric

Your revised letter of inquiry should have
- a heading, an inside address, a greeting, and a closing
- a beginning paragraph that states your purpose for writing and focuses on your reader
- a clear and concise message
- well-organized paragraphs
- no errors in grammar, usage, or mechanics

Format of Business Letters

Two standard formats for business letters are block style and modified block style. In **block style**, all the letter parts line up at the left margin. In **modified block style**, the heading and closing begin just right of center, and the paragraphs are indented.

The following business letter uses modified block style. You might follow this format for the business letters you write.

46 Brendan Street
Kingwood, TX 77345
March 11, 20__

Heading
Writer's address and the date on separate lines

Ms. Carolyn Vincenti
Town Center Building, Suite 7B
1 Cross Boulevard
Kingwood, TX 77345

Inside Address
Reader's name and address on separate lines

Dear Ms. Vincenti:

Salutation or Greeting
The word *Dear* and the reader's name followed by a colon

In my social studies class at Haley Middle School, we are doing projects on careers, and I have chosen newspaper reporting as my topic. I have read many of your articles in the *Kingwood Monitor* and would be very interested in talking with you about your job.

Introduction
Purpose for writing the letter–request for an interview

Would it be possible for me to meet with you for a brief interview sometime in the next two weeks? I could come to the Town Center building any weekday after three o'clock. You can reach me at the address above or call me at 555-8947.

Body Paragraph
Details concerning the writer's request

I look forward to hearing from you. Learning about your work as a reporter would be very valuable to me and my classmates. Thank you for your time and interest.

Conclusion
Restatement of the writer's request and an expression of appreciation

Sincerely,
James Yuan
James Yuan

Closing
Final word such as *Sincerely* followed by a comma and the writer's signature and typed name

PRACTICE

Choose a career that interests you. Write a letter of inquiry to someone who can provide you with helpful information about that career. Ask him or her for an interview. Remember to follow correct business letter format.

Memos

A memorandum, or memo, is a brief business note that gives the reader important information on a topic. Unlike business letters, memos are usually written to people you know or work with.

Types of Memos

Memos communicate a variety of messages. You might write a memo to make an announcement, to answer a question, to give a reminder, or to provide instructions.

Format of Memos

Memos are written in the block style. Each heading and paragraph starts at the left margin. The headings of a memo are printed in capital letters followed by a colon. A memo has no formal closing. Memos may include bulleted or numbered lists to highlight important information.

TO: Hiking Club members
FROM: Mike Nguyen
SUBJECT: Saturday outing
DATE: October 5, 20__

If you plan to participate in our next outing, please be at the front entrance of the school on Saturday, October 10, at 10:00 A.M. Wear or bring the following:

- sturdy rubber-soled shoes
- long pants
- sweater or sweatshirt
- notebook and pencil
- lunch, including a beverage

Headings
Group of readers, writer's name, subject and date on separate lines

Message
Details explaining writer's purpose–to give instructions

Bulleted List
Formatting technique for aiding comprehension

PRACTICE

Write a memo that gives quick, brief instructions about a club activity–either real or imaginary. Your readers are fellow club members. Remember to follow correct memo style and to use formatting techniques that help your readers easily understand your message.

Format of Memos

PRACTICE

Evaluation Rubric

Your memo should have

- the headings TO, FROM, SUBJECT, and DATE
- colons after each heading
- clear and concise information
- bulleted lists or other formatting techniques to aid comprehension
- no errors in grammar, usage, or mechanics

Business Forms

PRACTICE

Evaluation Rubric

Your filled-out application should have

- clear, accurate answers to each question
- correctly placed information
- neat and legible handwriting or printing
- bulleted lists or other formatting techniques to aid comprehension
- no errors in grammar, usage, or mechanics

Business Forms

Business forms are documents designed for gathering and organizing information. Knowing how to fill out a job application form is especially important for your career development. Study the following job application.

Volunteer Application Form

Thank you for considering volunteer work at the Muir Library.

Name: Martha Alvarez Date June 1, 20__

Address: 3532 11th Avenue North

City: Mill Valley State: CA Zip: 94941

Phone: 415-555-1212 Fax: 415-555-5510

DOB: 11/29/88 SSN: 123-45-6789

Best times to reach you: After 3:30 p.m. weekdays

Education *(circle highest level completed)*:

7 (8) 9 10 11 12

Is this experience for school credit? Yes (No)

School name and address: Mill Valley Middle School

Why do you want to volunteer?

I have good organization skills and I know I would be a help to the library staff. In addition, I am already familiar with the layout of the library because I spend a lot of time there. I enjoy reading aloud to my little sister; I would especially like to be a volunteer reader during the story hour.

Signature: Martha Alvarez

Note that the form is filled out neatly in ink.

Abbreviations commonly used on applications include DOB (date of birth) and SSN or SS# (social security number).

Include hyphens in your social security number.

PRACTICE

Fill out an application form to do community service. For example, you might apply to a library, an animal shelter, or a nursing home. Work with a partner to evaluate each other's work.

R64 WRITING HANDBOOK

WRITING HANDBOOK

Technical Writing

Technical writing presents information about a topic related to industry, science, or technology. The facts must be accurate, and the ideas clearly explained. Every piece of technical writing is designed to accomplish a specific purpose–to inform, to instruct, or to persuade a specific audience. Technical documents, such as reports and proposals, are tightly structured and generally follow a specific format.

Formatting Techniques

The visual appearance of technical documents is important. Use formatting techniques, such as those shown in the chart below, to help focus your readers' attention and to highlight key points.

Formatting Technique	Purpose	Example
Headings and Subheadings	Leads readers through sequence of main ideas	How to Operate a Bicycle Pump Step 1
Numbered and Bulleted Lists	Emphasizes a sequence of steps or a series of related points	Goals of the Student Council • To help solve school problems • To organize school activities • To promote school spirit
Fonts and Typefaces	Adds visual appeal to the document	Helvetica Font and Times Font **Boldface** and *Italics*

Types of Technical Writing

Technical writing covers a wide range of categories, such as lab reports for your science class or work procedures for a project at your school. Other examples of technical documents include instructions for operating a tool, sets of activities for designing a system, or procedures for explaining the bylaws of an organization (see Writing Workshop, Theme 6, pages 650–653).

Operating a Tool To write instructions for operating a tool, list numbered steps arranged in correct sequence, or chronological order. Begin the sentence for each step with an action verb, such as *look, adjust,* or *focus*. Focus your readers' attention on the main steps and the parts of the tool by using headings and other formatting techniques such as boldfaced type. Include pictures or diagrams if they will help your readers better understand the instructions and visualize the tool. Study the example that follows.

WRITING HANDBOOK R65

Types of Technical Writing: Operating a Tool

PRACTICE

Evaluation Rubric

Your instructions for operating a tool should have

- clear and concise information
- easy-to-understand steps arranged in proper sequence
- design elements and graphics, such as a sketch showing basic parts of the tool, to aid comprehension
- no errors in grammar, usage, or mechanics

OPERATING A MICROSCOPE

The purpose of a microscope is to magnify specimens so that small details become visible. By learning how to operate a microscope, you can imagine you're a biologist on the brink of an incredible discovery. Just follow these steps.

Step 1

Place the microscope on a flat surface that is clear of objects. Face the **arm** of the microscope toward you.

Step 2

Look through the **eyepiece**. Adjust the **diaphragm** so that the light comes through the opening in the **stage**.

Step 3

Place a slide on the stage so that the specimen is in the field of view. Use the **stage clips** to hold the slide firmly in place.

Step 4

Focus first with the **coarse adjustment** and the **low-power objective** lens. Once the specimen is in focus on low power, turn the **revolving nosepiece** until the **high-power objective** is in place. Use **the fine adjustment focus** ONLY with this lens.

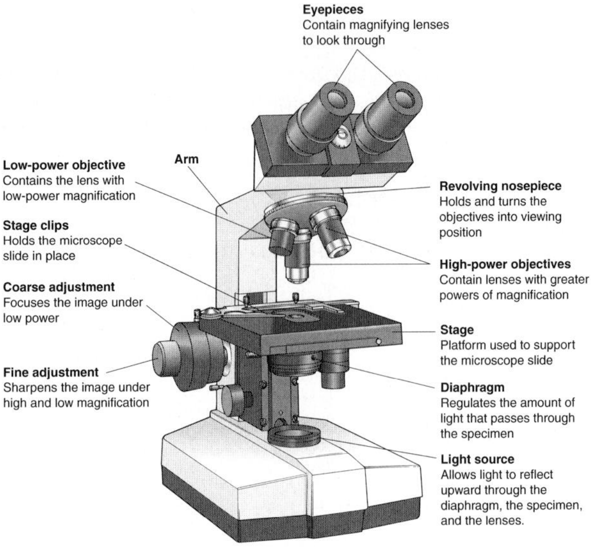

PRACTICE

Write a technical document that identifies the sequence of activities needed to operate a basic tool you know how to use. For example, you might choose a bicycle pump or a can opener. If possible, include a sketch of the tool with labeled parts.

Designing a System A system is made up of a series of parts or a set of objects that work together for a common purpose. For example, a multimedia presentation is a system that combines various forms of media, such as visuals and sound, to provide an audience with information on a topic. To write about designing a system like a multimedia presentation, describe the parts and how they work together. Study the following example.

DESIGNING MULTIMEDIA PRESENTATIONS

You want to present a research report to your classmates. How can you hold their attention? Your presentation can be exciting if you use various media. Knowing how to design a multimedia presentation may also help you in your future careers.

Audience and purpose for writing

Learning the Basics

A multimedia presentation involves using several types of media. Here are a variety of elements you can combine in creative ways:

- slides
- cassette or CD recordings
- charts and graphs
- photographs
- videotapes
- food samples

Bulleted list highlighting various parts of the system

For example, to discuss life in the Philippines, you could show photographs of the country. You could also play a recording of the country's language and music and present a video about the Filipino people.

Example of how parts of the system work together

Adding Computer Technology

To design multimedia productions or presentations on a computer, you need to have certain tools. These include computer graphic software and drawing programs. Animation programs make still images move, while authoring systems tie all the parts of your multimedia presentation together. Your computer manual will tell you which of these tools your computer can support.

PRACTICE

Write a technical document that identifies the sequence of activities needed to design a system, such as work procedures for a project at your school. For example, to design a recycling program, you would describe the jobs that needed to be done and then explain how people would work together to complete the project.

Types of Technical Writing: Designing a System

PRACTICE

Evaluation Rubric

Your technical document on designing a system should have

- an introduction that explains your topic and focuses on your reader
- formatting features, such as headings, subheadings, and boldface type, to help guide your readers through the sequence of ideas
- an explanation of how the basic parts of a system work together
- clear and concise information
- no errors in grammar, usage, or mechanics

Using a Computer for Writing

Using a computer with a word processing program to write offers advantages at every stage of the writing process.

Prewriting

A computer can help you gather and organize ideas and information.

Brainstorming

While brainstorming for topics or details, you can dim the computer screen and do "invisible writing." Some writers find that this technique allows their ideas to flow more freely.

Researching

CD-ROMs are disks that store large amounts of text, graphics, and sounds. If your computer has a CD-ROM player, you can use a CD-ROM encyclopedia to find not only text and pictures, but also sound, animated cartoons or graphics, and live-action video clips.

If you have a modem and are connected with an online service, you can access material from an online encyclopedia or magazine.

Outlining

Some word processing programs offer an outlining feature that automatically indents headings and uses various type styles for main headings and subheadings.

Drafting/Revising

Most word processing programs make it easy to do the following:

- *insert* new text at any point in your document
- *delete* or *copy* text
- *move* text from one position to another
- *undo* a change you just made
- *save* each draft or revision of your document
- *print* copies of your work-in-progress for others to read

Editing/Proofreading

You can edit and proofread directly on the computer. If you prefer, you can mark your changes on a printout, or hard copy, of your document and then input the changes on screen. Either way, the following word processing features are helpful.

- **Grammar checker** The computer finds possible errors in grammar and suggests revisions.
- **Spelling checker** The computer finds misspellings and suggests corrections.
- **Thesaurus** If you want to replace an inappropriate or overused word, you can highlight the word and the computer will suggest synonyms.
- **Search and replace** If you want to change or correct something that occurs several times in your document, the computer can instantly make the change throughout the document.

Rule of Thumb: The grammar checker, spelling checker, and thesaurus cannot replace your own careful reading and judgment. Because English grammar is so complex, the suggestions that the grammar checker makes may not be appropriate. Spelling is easier for a computer to monitor, but the spelling checker will not tell you that you have typed *brake* when you meant *break,* for example, because both are valid words. The thesaurus may offer you several synonyms for a word, but you need to consider the connotations of each before deciding which synonym fits your context.

Presenting

The computer allows you to enhance the readability, attractiveness, and visual interest of your document in many ways.

Formatting your text

The computer gives you a variety of options for the layout and appearance of your text. You can easily add or change the following elements.

- margin width and number of columns
- type size and style
- page numbering
- header or footer (information such as a title that appears at the top or bottom of every page)

Visual aids

Some word processing programs have graphic functions that allow you to create graphs, charts, and diagrams.

COMMUNICATIONS SKILLS HANDBOOK R69

Study and Test-Taking Skills

Study Skills

Use this section to learn skills for studying effectively.

Taking notes in class

The notes you take while listening in class will help you understand and remember what you hear. Follow these guidelines:

- Take down only the main ideas and key details.
- Listen for transitions and signal words.
- Use numerals, abbreviations, and symbols for speed.

Using study time effectively

Follow these guidelines:

- Review your assignments and due dates. Write the due dates in a calendar.
- Break down your long-term goals into smaller tasks.
- Study at the same time and in the same place each day.
- Begin study time with your most difficult assignment.
- Take a short break after reaching each goal.
- Try a variety of study methods, including reading, summarizing, developing your own graphic aids (such as clusters), and discussing material with a study partner.

Taking Classroom Tests

Use this section to learn strategies for taking classroom tests.

Preparing for a test

Use these tips to prepare for a test:

- Find out what information the test will cover.
- Make a study schedule. Include time for reviewing your class notes, homework, quizzes, and textbook.
- As you study, jot down questions that might be on the test.
- If you have difficulty answering them, look up the information.
- Once you know the material fairly well, study with another student or group of students. Pool your study questions and take turns answering them.

R70 COMMUNICATIONS SKILLS HANDBOOK

COMMUNICATIONS SKILLS HANDBOOK

Taking objective tests

An objective test is a test of factual information. The answers to the questions will be either right or wrong; you will not be asked to give your own ideas. At the beginning of an objective test, scan the number of items. Then budget your time.

Multiple-choice items Multiple-choice items include an incomplete sentence or a question and three or four responses. Use these tips for answering multiple-choice questions.

- Read each item carefully to know what information you are looking for.
- Read all choices before answering. Sometimes an answer may seem correct, but a choice that follows it may be better.
- Be careful about choosing answers that contain absolute words, such as *always, never, all,* or *none.* Since most statements have exceptions, absolute statements are often incorrect.

Example:

Which of the following statements is true of mammals and only of mammals?
a. They have four limbs.
b. They drink their mother's milk.
c. They are warm-blooded.
d. They have backbones.

Not *all* mammals have four limbs; not *only* mammals are warm-blooded or have backbones. All mammals and only mammals drink their mother's milk. The correct answer is *b.*

Answering essay questions

Essay questions usually require an answer of at least one paragraph. Use the following guidelines:

- Read the question carefully. If permitted, underline key words.
- Plan your time to allow for revision.
- Jot down key ideas to include in your answer.
- Develop a thesis statement and a rough outline.
- Provide several supporting details for each main idea.
- In your conclusion, summarize what you have shown.

COMMUNICATIONS SKILLS HANDBOOK R71

Key Verbs in Essay Questions	
Argue	Give your opinion and reasons that support your opinion.
Compare and contrast	Discuss likenesses and differences.
Define	Give details that show exactly what something is like.
Demonstrate (also illustrate, show)	Give examples to support a point.
Describe	Present a picture with words.
Discuss	Show detailed information on a particular subject.
Explain	Give reasons.
Identify	Give specific characteristics.
List (also outline, trace)	Give details, give steps in order, give a time sequence.
Summarize	Give a short overview of the most important ideas or events.

Taking Standardized Tests

Standardized tests are given to large groups of students. Use this section to learn strategies for taking standardized tests.

Tips for taking standardized tests

Use the following tips for taking standardized tests.

- Most standardized tests are graded electronically. Make sure you understand how to mark your answer sheet and be careful to avoid stray marks that might be misread.
- If points are not subtracted for incorrect answers, try to give an answer for every item, even if you are only guessing.
- If you can't answer a question quickly, move on to the next item. You can go back to the unanswered questions later if you have time.

Reading comprehension A reading-comprehension item includes a written passage and questions about the passage. The questions will ask you to identify the main idea or draw conclusions from the information.

Vocabulary Vocabulary items may ask you to choose a word that best completes a sentence, or they may ask you to select a definition of a word in a sentence. Using what you know about context clues, root words, and prefixes will help you make the right choice.

R72 COMMUNICATIONS SKILLS HANDBOOK

COMMUNICATIONS SKILLS HANDBOOK

Analogies Analogy items test your understanding of the relationships between things or ideas. On standardized tests, analogies are written in an abbreviated format, as shown below.

man : woman :: buck : doe

The symbol *:* means "is to"; the symbol *::* means "as."

This chart shows some word relationships you may find in analogy tests.

Relationship	Definition	Example
Synonyms	Two words have a similar meaning.	huge : gigantic :: scared : afraid
Antonyms	Two words have opposite meanings.	bright : dull :: far : near
Use	Words name a user and something used.	farmer : tractor :: writer : pen
Cause-effect	Words name a cause and its effect.	tickle : laugh :: polish : shine
Category	Words name a category and an item in it.	fish : tuna :: building : house
Description	Words name an item and a characteristic of it.	knife : sharp :: joke : funny

Grammar, usage, and mechanics Standardized tests measure your understanding of correct grammar, usage, and mechanics, usually by asking you to identify the section of a sentence that contains an error. Look for errors in grammar, usage, spelling, capitalization, and punctuation.

COMMUNICATIONS SKILLS HANDBOOK R73

Listening, Speaking, and Viewing Skills

Listening Effectively

By improving your listening skills, you can increase your ability to understand and remember what you hear.

Tips for effective listening

Use these tips to sharpen your listening skills.

- Clear your mind of distractions and concentrate on the speaker's words. Identify the main points or ideas. If you will need to use the information later, take notes.
- If you don't understand something, ask a question. Asking questions right away helps avoid confusion later on.
- If the information is important and you are the only listener, repeat the information back to the speaker to make sure you have understood correctly.
- If you have taken notes, review them as soon as possible after the speaker has finished; fill in information you may have left out.

Listening critically

As you listen, it is important to evaluate what you are hearing. Ask yourself these questions:

- Is the information accurate? What experience or education does the speaker have? What are his or her sources of information?
- Are the ideas logical and reasonable? Does the speaker back them up with sound facts, reasons, and examples?
- Is the speaker biased? Does he or she want something from me, such as my money or my vote? If so, could the information be exaggerated, distorted, or incomplete?

Interpreting nonverbal clues

Understanding nonverbal clues is part of effective listening. Nonverbal clues are everything you may notice about a speaker *except* what the speaker says. As you listen, ask yourself these questions:

- Where and how is the speaker standing?
- Are some words spoken more loudly than others?

R74 COMMUNICATIONS SKILLS HANDBOOK

- Does the speaker make eye contact?
- Does he or she smile or look angry?
- What message is sent by the speaker's gestures and facial expression?

Analyzing oral interpretations of literature

As you listen to oral interpretations of literature, ask yourself the following questions both to increase your appreciation of oral presentations of literature and to analyze the effectiveness of such presentations.

- Is this presentation interesting to me? Why or why not?
- Has the speaker provided enough background information to help me understand the selection?
- What feelings, thoughts, and attitudes does the speaker communicate?
- Does the speaker convey the theme, conflict, and characters clearly?
- What gestures, movements, and facial expressions does the speaker use to aid my understanding of the selection? How does the speaker's posture affect the presentation?
- Does the speaker pronounce words clearly and correctly? How does he or she use vocal techniques such as pitch, rate, and volume to help interpret the selection?

PRACTICE

Encourage your teacher to hold a poetry appreciation day in class. Each student should select a short poem to present orally. Use the bulleted questions above to help you evaluate each presentation. You can create an evaluation form using the questions as entries on the form. For each question, rate the speaker's performance as S–superior, E–excellent, G–good, or F–fair.

Speaking Effectively

Use this section to improve your speaking skills in both formal and informal situations.

Speaking informally

Most of your communication is informal. When you speak with your friends, family, and neighbors, you use informal speech. Human relationships depend on this effective form of communication.

- Be courteous. Listen until the other person has finished speaking. Do not interrupt.
- Speak in a relaxed and spontaneous manner.
- Make eye contact with your listeners.

Analyzing oral interpretations of literature

PRACTICE

Rubric

Help students create forms to use when evaluating the presentations. Encourage positive feedback and helpful criticism after each presentation.

- Do not monopolize a conversation. Let others have a chance to speak.
- When telling a story, show enthusiasm. Act out the parts and draw in your audience.
- When giving an announcement or directions, speak clearly and slowly. Check that your listeners understand the information.

Giving a formal speech

Unlike informal speaking, giving a formal speech involves considerable thought and planning. Delivering a speech in front of a live audience is the last stage of a five-stage process that is similar to the writing process. Like an essay or report, a formal speech has an introduction, a thesis statement, supporting facts and details, and a conclusion. The success of your speech will depend as much on the way you present it as on its content. Keep the following tips in mind as you practice and present your speech:

- Speak clearly and at a normal pace.
- Vary the volume and pitch of your voice according to what you are saying, as you do in normal speech.
- Pause after making an important point or after giving your audience a lot of information.
- Use hand gestures to emphasize important points and to help convey information. Be sure the gestures you use feel natural to you.
- Make eye contact with people in different parts of the audience.
- Pay attention to the reactions of your audience and use audience feedback to improve your presentation.

Giving an oral interpretation of literature

Like a formal speech, oral interpretations of literature involve thoughtful planning and preparation. When you select performance material, you should take into consideration the following factors: the quality of the literature, its audience appeal, the oral possibilities of the literature, and your feelings for the selection. Whether you select a poem, a famous speech, or an excerpt from a play, you can use the following tips to help make your presentation successful.

- Study your selection, paying close attention to setting, plot, mood, conflict, theme, and characters. These are the elements you will want to communicate clearly to your listeners.
- Create an introduction that will capture your audience's attention, provide necessary background information, and set the scene.
- Prepare a performance script, marking words that you will emphasize and places where you will gesture, pause, or change pace.

- Rehearse vigorously. Read the selection silently several times. Then read it aloud several times, practicing gestures, movements, and vocal variations. Practice looking up at the audience periodically.
- In performance, pronounce the words clearly and correctly, vary your vocal expression, establish and maintain eye contact with your audience, and share your enthusiasm for the selection.

PRACTICE

Select a short poem from your textbook to present orally. Use the bulleted tips above to help you plan, prepare, and present this poem. You may enjoy working with a partner before presenting your poem to the class. After each of you has had time to study and rehearse, take turns presenting your poems to each other. Use the questions on page R75 to help critique each other's performances.

Giving an oral response to literature

Often in class you may be asked to give an oral book report, analyze a poem, or offer your reactions to a short story you have read. To help you prepare an effective oral response in such situations, ask yourself the following questions:

- What is the main purpose of the selection? (Does it describe a scene or a moment in time? Tell a story? Present an argument?)
- If the selection is nonfiction (essay, biography, or informational article, for example), what main ideas are presented? What details in the selection support those main ideas? What is my response to these ideas?
- If the selection is fiction (poetry, short story, novel, novella, or play), what major theme is presented? What important details in the selection help reveal this theme? What effect does the theme have on me?
- How would I describe the author's style? What examples of word choice, sentence structure, plot development, characterization, and literary devices can I find that illustrate the author's style? What effect does the author's style have on the mood and tone of the selection? What do I like or dislike about this style?
- What is my overall response to the selection? How did the author succeed or not succeed in entertaining and enlightening me?

COMMUNICATIONS SKILLS HANDBOOK

Giving an oral interpretation of literature

PRACTICE

Rubric

Students' oral interpretations should include an introduction that gives any necessary background information and sets the scene for the audience. Students should speak clearly and make proper eye contact during their performances. Remind them that the use of gestures, voice, and facial expressions will help communicate the meaning of the poem to the audience.

Giving an oral response to literature

PRACTICE

Rubric

Students' oral responses to literature should

- offer as much summary of the selection as the audience will need to understand the presentation
- include examples from the selection that strongly support the student's ideas
- explain the student's overall reaction and response to the selection

Giving a persuasive speech

PRACTICE

Rubric

In their persuasive speeches, students should

- state their positions clearly in their introductions
- support their positions and refute opposing positions with authoritative evidence
- use both fact and opinion, distinguishing between the two
- end with a well-supported conclusion

PRACTICE

Choose a selection from your textbook that you particularly enjoyed. Prepare an oral response to give to your class. Use the questions above to help you plan what you will say. After you have gathered material for your talk, go through your ideas and select only the most important points to present. Then select examples from the selection that strongly support those points. Discard weak examples. Be sure to include your own reaction to the selection and provide solid reasons for your response.

Giving a persuasive speech

Preparing and delivering a persuasive speech involves hard work, good research skills, and the ability to organize your arguments clearly and logically. Use the following tips to help you present a persuasive speech convincingly to your audience:

- Choose a topic you feel strongly about and focus on a single important point–your position statement.
- State your position clearly.
- Support your position with authoritative evidence. (You can gather evidence from library resources, the Internet, and interviews with experts.)
- Use both facts and opinions to support your position but be sure to distinguish the facts from the opinions.
- Identify and acknowledge arguments opposing your position. Then use authoritative evidence to refute those opposing arguments.
- End your speech with a clear and well-supported conclusion.

PRACTICE

Choose a statement below about which you have a strong opinion. State your position on the issue and support it with sound reasons. Acknowledge opposing opinions and refute them with sound reasons. You may need to do a little research to complete this activity. You could interview teachers, students, and family members and search the Internet for information about the issue you have chosen. Organize your arguments on paper. Be prepared to present your arguments orally.

1. Students who own computers should be allowed to "attend class" online from home.
2. The movie-rating system should be changed so that young people have an easier time getting into the movies they want to see.
3. Students should go to school year-round.
4. All students should be required to take one music course and one art course and to participate in one team sport before graduating from eighth grade.

Working in Groups

Use this section to learn how to work cooperatively with people in a group.

Roles in groups

Groups accomplish their goals most efficiently by assigning different roles to their members. The chart below shows three basic roles and the responsibilities of each.

Group Member	Responsibilities
Chairperson	Announces each discussion topic; keeps the discussion focused; moves the group toward a decision
Recorder	Writes down all ideas; reads ideas to be reviewed; records final decisions
Participants	Contribute and defend ideas; voice constructive criticism; vote on decisions

Group procedures

Once roles have been assigned, the group works toward its goal in an orderly way.

- The group sets an agenda, a list of things to be done or discussed.
- The chairperson announces the topic at hand.
- Participants contribute ideas and discuss the pros and cons of each.
- After sufficient discussion, the chairperson may ask the recorder to read the suggestions.
- The chairperson gives each participant a last chance to present his or her ideas.
- The chairperson calls for a vote and announces the decision.
- The recorder writes down the decision.

Sometimes the group needs more time to generate ideas and think about them. In this case, the meeting might end without a decision but with everyone clearly understanding his or her responsibilities for the next meeting.

COMMUNICATIONS SKILLS HANDBOOK R79

Viewing Effectively

Information is as likely to be transmitted through visual images as through the spoken or written word. Sharpening your visual perceptions can help you understand and analyze movies, videos, television programs, and advertisements.

Viewing to understand

Images that are prominent in a film may be symbols of a theme or an idea the director wants to convey. Images from nature such as a river, a snake, or a storm are often used as symbols. So are colors, such as yellow for warmth or green for growth.

Facial expressions, gestures, posture, and clothing can be clues to the feelings and motives of characters in a drama. Clothing and hairstyles are also clues to the historical setting.

Viewing critically

Critical viewing means thinking about what you see while watching a TV program, newscast, film, or video. It requires paying attention to what you hear and see and deciding whether information is true, false, or exaggerated. If the information *seems* to be true, try to determine whether it is based on a fact or an opinion.

Fact versus opinion A fact is something that can be proved or disproved. An opinion is what someone *believes* is true. Opinions are based on feelings and experiences and cannot be proved.

Television commercials, political speeches, and even the evening news contain both facts and opinions. They use emotional words and actions to persuade the viewer to agree with a particular point of view. They may also use faulty reasoning, such as linking an effect with the wrong cause. Think through what is being said. The speaker may seem sincere, but do his or her reasons make sense? Are the reasons based on facts or on unfair generalizations?

Commercials contain both obvious and hidden messages. The obvious message is the spoken words of the commercial. The hidden message comes across in *how* the message is presented. Look carefully at commercials to see whether a product is really worth buying.

R80 COMMUNICATIONS SKILLS HANDBOOK

Reading Handbook

The Reading Process

As reading materials get more difficult, you'll need to use a variety of active reading strategies to understand texts. This handbook is designed to help you find and use the tools you'll need before, during, and after reading.

Word Identification

Word identification skills are necessary building blocks for understanding what you read. They prepare you to deal with unknown words you'll encounter.

Look before, at, and after a new word. Use the other words and sentences around an unknown word to help you make an educated guess about what that word might be. Think about the following questions as you try to read new words.

- Can I sound this new word out?
- Can I figure out this new word from its place in the sentence?
- What other word would make sense in this sentence?

Using letter-sound cues

One way to figure out a new word is to try to sound it out. Use the following tips when sounding out new words:

- Look at the beginning of the word. What letter or group of letters makes up the beginning sound or syllable of the word?

  Example: In the word *magnificent, mag* rhymes with *bag.*

- Look at the end of the word. What letter or group of letters makes up the ending sound or syllable?

  Example: In the word *magnificent, cent* is a word you know.

- Look at the middle of the word. Is there a word you already know inside the new word? What vowel or vowel pattern is represented in each syllable?

  Example: In the word *magnificent,* the syllables *ni* and *fi* have the same vowel sound as the word *it.*

Now try pronouncing the whole word: *mag ni fi cent.*

READING HANDBOOK R81

READING HANDBOOK

Using language structure cues

Word order, or **syntax,** helps you make sense of a sentence, so looking at the position of a new word in a sentence can help you identify a word. For instance, look at the following nonsense sentence:

The drazzy lurds miffled the bonkee blams.

Your experience with English sentence patterns and parts of speech tells you that the action word, or verb, in this sentence is *miffled.* Who did the *miffling?*–the *lurds.* What kind of *lurds* were they?–*drazzy.* Whom did they *miffle?*–the *blams.* What kind of blams were they?–*bonkee.* Even though you do not know word meanings in the nonsense sentence, you can make some sense of the entire sentence by using syntax.

Use the order of words in a sentence to help you figure out parts of speech. Then use that knowledge to identify new words and their meanings.

Using context clues

When you read on your own, you can often figure out the meaning of a new word by looking at its **context,** the words and sentences that surround it. For instance, look at the following example:

Mr. Hargrove was very upset at first. However, my offer to pay for his broken window seemed to ***mollify*** *him.*

You can guess from the first sentence that *mollify* is a word that means something different than being upset. If you guessed that it means to "calm someone down," you have successfully used context clues to find meaning.

Tips for Using Context

- Look before, at, and after the unknown word for
  - –a synonym or definition of the unknown word in a sentence
    The ***flotilla,*** *a* ***small group of ships,*** *could be seen in the harbor.*
  - –a clue to what the word is like or not like
    Unlike *her* ***punctual*** *sister, Susan was always* ***late.***
  - –a general topic associated with the word
    The ***cooking*** *teacher discussed the best way to* ***poach*** *the fish.*
  - –a description or action associated with the word
    He used the ***mulching*** *tool to* ***dig*** *up the garden.*
- Connect what you know with what the author has written.
- Predict a possible meaning and apply the meaning in the sentence.
- Try again if your guess does not make sense.

R82 READING HANDBOOK

READING HANDBOOK

Using word parts to read new words

Noticing word parts can help you sound out and understand unknown words. Look at the following word parts:

- **Roots** The base part of a word is called its root. If you know the root within a new word, start from there to sound out the rest of the word. (*Insecurity* comes from the root *secure.*)
- **Plurals** Many times nouns are changed from singular to plural by adding *-s*, *-es,* or *-ies. (dogs, buses, babies)*
- **Comparative endings** Used for adjectives and adverbs, *-er* or *-est* added to a word forms a comparison. *(stronger, strongest)*
- **Inflectional endings** Other endings, such as *-ing* or *-ed,* can be important parts of both the meaning and pronunciation of a word *(walk, walked, walking)*.
- **Prefixes** These syllables, added to the beginning of words, change the meaning of the words. For example, *un-* means "not," so *unnecessary* means "not necessary."
- **Suffixes** Added to the end of a word, a suffix may change the word's meaning. For example, *-less* means "without" or "lacking," so *useless* means "without use."

Using reference materials

When looking at or around an unknown word does not help you identify it, dictionaries, glossaries, thesauruses, and other reference sources can be useful tools. References provide derivations and spellings as well as pronunciations.

A **dictionary** provides the pronunciation and literal meaning or meanings of a word. It also gives other forms of the word, its part of speech, alternative spellings, examples, synonyms, origins, and other useful information. Look at the dictionary entry below to see what valuable information it provides.

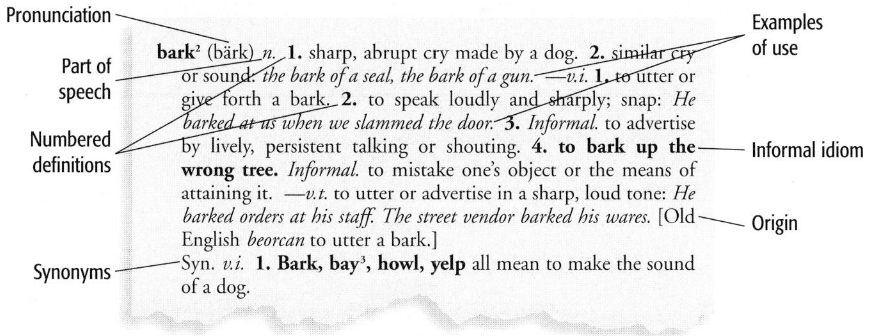

bark[2] (bärk) *n.* **1.** sharp, abrupt cry made by a dog. **2.** similar cry or sound: *the bark of a seal, the bark of a gun.* —*v.i.* **1.** to utter or give forth a bark. **2.** to speak loudly and sharply; snap: *He barked at us when we slammed the door.* **3.** *Informal.* to advertise by lively, persistent talking or shouting. **4. to bark up the wrong tree.** *Informal.* to mistake one's object or the means of attaining it. —*v.t.* to utter or advertise in a sharp, loud tone: *He barked orders at his staff. The street vendor barked his wares.* [Old English *beorcan* to utter a bark.]
Syn. *v.i.* **1. Bark, bay**[3]**, howl, yelp** all mean to make the sound of a dog.

READING HANDBOOK R83

A **glossary** is a condensed dictionary within a specific text. It provides an alphabetical listing of words used within that text, together with their definitions and other information necessary to understand the words as they appear in the text. Look at the example below.

A

abash [ə bash′] *v.* to make embarrassed and ashamed.
abet [ə bet′] *v.* to approve of, encourage, or help.
– **abettor,** *n.*
abject [ab′jekt, ab jekt′] *adj.* having lost one's spirit and self-respect; wretched.
abrasion [ə brā′zhən] *n.* a scraping.
abscond [ab skond′] *v.* to run off quickly and secretly.
absolve [ab zolv′, -solv′] *v.* to set free from responsibility or blame.
abut [ə but′] *v.* to be next to; border on.
abyss [ə bis′] *n.* a bottomless depth.

A **thesaurus** is a dictionary of synonyms. It can be especially useful for choosing precise, descriptive language. Some thesauruses are available on CD-ROM and on the Internet.

Reading Fluency

Becoming an accomplished reader is like learning a sports skill or a musical instrument: the more you practice, the better you'll be. The more you read aloud, the less attention you will need to pay to sounding words out and the more attention you can give to understanding the meaning in a selection.

Tips for Becoming a Fluent Reader

- Develop a good sight vocabulary.
- Practice reading out loud on independent level materials.
- Begin with a short interesting passage.
- Reread the same passage out loud at least three times.
- As your reading sounds smoother, move on to a longer or slightly more difficult passage.

R84 READING HANDBOOK

Reading in appropriate level materials

How do you decide if something is too easy, too hard, or just right for you to read? If you want to develop into a smooth, fluent reader, it is important to read regularly in materials that are easy for you. However, it is also important to grow as a strategic reader. To do that, you will want to read materials that are challenging but manageable.

To decide what level of reading material is right for each reading task, look at the following chart:

Reading Level	Definition/Criteria	When/Why to Use
Independent level	No more than 5 difficult words per 100 words read	On your own, anytime To practice smooth reading
Instructional level	No more than 10 difficult words per 100 words read	With support from teacher, parent, or other more experienced reader To challenge yourself
Beyond instructional level	More than 10 difficult words per 100 words read	As material read to you by someone else To develop new vocabulary through listening

Adjusting reading rate—skimming, scanning, and careful reading

Adjust your reading speed to suit your purposes and the task you face. When you read something for enjoyment, you might read quickly. If you want to refresh your memory of a passage or get a quick impression of new material, skim the selection. **Skimming** is reading quickly over a piece of writing to find its main idea or to get a general overview of it. When you need to find a particular piece or type of information, scan the selection. In **scanning,** you run your eyes quickly over the material, looking only for key words or phrases that have to do with the information you seek.

When you read a chapter of a textbook filled with new concepts, when you follow complex written directions, or when you study for a test, read slowly, take notes, make a graphic organizer, and even reread passages in order to remember them later.

Look at the models on the next page.

The sun was almost down as Stacy climbed the steps of the sagging old porch. She had to push aside some cobwebs to get to the doorbell. As her hand went up, the door mysteriously opened slowly and with an ominous creaking sound. Stacy poked her head inside to see if anyone was there. A candle was burning on a table in the corner. Suddenly she saw a gray figure glide up the staircase. Maybe the kids were right about this old house!

Green plants make food by a process called photosynthesis. In this process, energy from light is combined with water and carbon dioxide to make food. Light is absorbed by a green substance in leaves called chlorophyll. This substance is stored in bodies called chloroplasts. In each chloroplast, the light causes carbon dioxide to mix with the hydrogen atoms in water to make sugar. From this sugar, plants make food.

Which paragraph could you read more quickly? Why? What would you do to be sure you remembered the information in each paragraph?

Reading aloud

There are various reasons for reading out loud. Oral reading can make any writer's work come to life. A readers theater, a dialogue or monologue, and other enactments allow you to convey meaning with your voice and can be enjoyable ways of sharing a memorable selection. Reading a complicated paragraph aloud can also be a powerful aid to understanding. Here are some suggestions for reading aloud:

- First read the selection silently a number of times.
- Think about the best way to make the main ideas understandable to your listeners.
- Use pauses to separate complete thoughts and be sure you observe all punctuation marks.
- Read carefully and clearly. Vary your speed and volume to reflect the important ideas in a passage.
- Use a lively voice. Emphasize important words and phrases to make the meaning clear.
- Practice difficult words and phrases until you've mastered them.
- Practice in front of another person, if possible, or use a tape recorder to hear how you sound.

Reading silently

When you read silently for any length of time, be sure to avoid distractions or interruptions.

Tips for Sustained Silent Reading

- Be sure you're comfortable but not too comfortable.
- Check your concentration regularly by asking yourself questions about the selection.
- Summarize what you've read from time to time.
- Use a study guide or story map (see page R104) to help you keep focused through difficult passages.
- Make a graphic organizer, if necessary, to understand and remember important concepts or a sequence of events.
- Take regular breaks when you need them.

PRACTICE

With a partner, choose a selection from your text and look it over. Read the selection silently, adjusting your speed to the difficulty of the text. When both of you have finished, take turns asking questions to check your comprehension. Finally, choose a small section of the passage and take turns reading it aloud. Exchange suggestions about your oral reading.

Reading a Variety of Texts

Whether you read for education or entertainment, reading a variety of texts will improve your skills as a strategic reader. Throughout this textbook, you can read examples of both classic and contemporary writing. From "The Tell-Tale Heart" to "On the Road with Charles Kuralt," you will see how a wide variety of selections broadens your knowledge and deepens your appreciation of people and cultures.

Reading varied sources

Strategic readers take advantage of a variety of sources for information and for entertainment. For instance, to create a detailed and interesting portrait of a famous person from your hometown or state, you might refer to sources like those listed below:

- **Encyclopedias** provide a basic foundation of information.
- **Letters, memos, speeches, newspapers,** and **magazines** add personal perspectives not available in other sources.
- **Databases, library indexes,** and **Internet sites** often supply or lead you to interesting information.

READING HANDBOOK

Reading silently

PRACTICE

Encourage students not to rush when reading silently. Remind them that it is more important to comprehend what they read than to read quickly. As they finish reading a portion of the selection, have students paraphrase what they read to test their comprehension.

READING HANDBOOK R87

Reading for various purposes

PRACTICE

Rubric

In their presentations, students should comment on the various reading strategies they used depending on their purpose for reading. Remind students to maintain eye contact with the audience during their presentations and to speak clearly and slowly.

- **Novels, poems, plays,** and **anthologies** (collections of literature) provide excellent opportunities to read for pleasure as well as to explore the ideas of a writer in a particular time.

Reading for various purposes

Active reading begins with thinking about a reason for reading. You may find that you have more than one purpose or that your purposes overlap. For instance, you might read to enjoy an intense and thrilling mystery for entertainment and, at the same time, discover how police detectives work. The reading strategies you use to guide you through a text will depend on your purposes.

When your purpose for reading is

- **to be informed,** read slowly, take notes, construct a graphic organizer, reread, and review difficult sections.
- **to be entertained,** read at a faster rate.
- **to appreciate a writer's craft,** read at a rate appropriate to the language to enjoy how well others write.
- **to discover models for your own writing,** look at other writers' works to help stimulate your own ideas.
- **to take action,** be sure you understand all facts, directions, and instructions.

PRACTICE

Choose a topic that interests you and read about it in at least three sources. Decide on an action to take as a result of your reading. You may write a short report, give a speech, demonstrate how something works, or try to persuade your classmates to believe or do something. Make a short presentation to your class, explaining your purpose for reading and the value of each of your sources.

Vocabulary Development

Having a good vocabulary means more than just knowing the meanings of isolated words. It means knowing the larger concepts that surround those words. The best way to build a good vocabulary is to read widely, listen carefully, and participate actively in discussions where new words and concepts are used.

Listening

Books that may be just a little too hard for you to read on your own are often excellent choices as selections to be read aloud to you. They provide a good way to learn new vocabulary. "Read alouds" also give you a model for your own future oral reading. As you hear new words,

try to pay attention to their context, or the words and thoughts surrounding the unknown words. Try to guess what meaning would make sense for new words. Many times you will guess accurately if you pay careful attention.

Using experience and prior knowledge

Because of your life experiences, you know certain things and understand the meanings of certain words and ideas. Those experiences, called **prior knowledge,** help you determine word meanings. For instance, if you have had experience using computers, you'll understand the following sentence:

She needed to clean her mouse to make her cursor move more smoothly.

Sometimes you'll need to look beyond the exact meaning of words in a selection.

- Idioms An expression that has a meaning apart from the literal meaning of the words is called an idiom. If someone has *pulled the wool over your eyes,* he or she has fooled you. When someone is *pulling your leg,* he or she is joking with you. In each case, combine the words with prior knowledge to interpret what the expression means.
- Multiple meanings Words can have more than one meaning, so check the context to be sure the meaning you have chosen makes sense.
  We may have to ***fire*** *that crew if they can't put out the* ***fire.***
  Will you ***check*** *to see if my* ***check*** *is in the mail?*
- Figurative language Writers sometimes make comparisons by using figurative language, such as similes and metaphors. A **simile** uses *like* or *as* to compare two unlike things, while a **metaphor** compares two unlike things without using *like* or *as.*
  Simile: *Sleep covered him* ***like*** *a soft, heavy blanket.*
  Metaphor: *Her mood was a dark cloud that shadowed the room.*
- Analogies A comparison based on the relationship between two things or ideas is called an analogy. Analogies sometimes are written like this: *fish : gills :: human : lungs.* To understand the analogy, try turning it into short identical sentences. For instance, *A fish breathes with gills. A human breathes with lungs.*

Clarifying meanings with reference aids

Sometimes meanings of words and phrases can remain unclear even after using context clues, drawing on your personal background, and listening carefully. In that case, look to other reference aids to help clarify the meanings and usage of difficult terms.

- **Thesauruses** and books of synonyms can clarify a word by listing other words that have similar meanings. Be sure to notice what part of speech a word is so you can determine how to use it in a sentence.
- **Dictionaries** will often be able to clear up word meanings because they provide a variety of definitions for a word and examples of each definition in a sentence. You can often find the meaning of idioms by looking in a dictionary under the main word in the phrase. Look at the idioms listed under the entry word *fire.*

between two fires. under physical or verbal attack from both sides.
on fire. a. burning; ignited. **b.** inflamed or overwhelmed with intense emotional feeling; eager; zealous; passionate.
to catch fire. to become ignited; begin to burn.
to go through fire and water. to experience or endure great danger, hardships, or trials.
to hang fire. a. to fail or be slow to discharge: *The artillery hung fire, and the enemy got through the line.* **b.** to be slow in acting; hesitate. **c.** to be delayed: *The deal hung fire for several weeks.*
to lay a fire. to arrange material so that it may be burned.
to open fire. a. to begin to shoot: *They opened fire on the enemy.* **b.** to begin; commence.
to play with fire. to do or meddle with something dangerous or risky.
to set fire to. to cause to burn; ignite.

- **Computer software** will often include reference materials that can clarify meanings and usage for difficult words.

Using word parts and origins to determine meaning

Another way to determine the meaning of a word is to take the word itself apart. If you understand the meaning of the **base,** or **root** part, of a word and also know the meanings of key syllables added to the beginning or end of the base, you can often figure out what a word means.

Word Part	Definition	Example
Root or base	the most basic part of a word	*ced* means "go"
Prefix	a syllable used before a root word to add to or change its meaning	*pre-* means "before" *precede* means "go before"
Suffix	a syllable used after a root word to change its meaning or its use	*-ous* means "full of" *joyous* means "full of joy"

Word origins English contains many words based on roots from ancient languages like Greek and Latin. Having some knowledge of word derivations in either of these languages can help you determine meanings, pronunciations, and spellings in English.

Root	Meaning	Example
astro (Greek)	star	astronaut, astronomy, asterisk
ped (Latin)	foot	pedal, pedestrian
vid (Latin)	see	video, evidence
hydr (Greek)	water	hydrant, dehydrate

Affixes These syllables are added either to the beginning or end of a word. For example, the word *unusually* is made up of the root *usual* and the affixes *un-* and *-ly*. The prefix *un-* means "not." The suffix *-ly* means "in a particular manner." If you put them together, *unusually* means "not in the usual manner."

PRACTICE

Look up each of the following word parts in a dictionary:

-able -meter -tion tri- inter- ortho- trans- circum-

Write down the meaning of each word part and its language of origin. Then, for each word part, write down two or more words that include that word part. For example, the prefix *extra-* means "outside" or "beyond." It comes from the Latin word *extra*. *Extraordinary, extra-terrestrial, extravagant,* and *extracurricular* are examples of words that include the prefix *extra-*.

Using word meanings across subjects

Have you ever learned a new word and then noticed it in many places and across many subjects? The word may not mean exactly the same thing in each place, but you can often use what you know about a word's meaning to help you interpret its meaning in a different context. Look at the following example from two subjects:

Social studies: *One major **product** manufactured in the South is cotton cloth.*

Math: *After you multiply those two numbers, explain how you arrived at the **product**.*

You may know that a product is something manufactured by a company. In math, a product is a number that results from multiplying two other numbers together. In both situations, a product is the result of something.

Using word parts and origins to determine meaning

PRACTICE

Answers

-able: capable of, fit for; French
Possible examples: collectable, breakable

-meter: instrument or means of measuring; French
Possible examples: thermometer, speedometer

-tion: act or process, result of an act or process, state or condition; Middle English
Possible examples: multiplication, dehydration

tri-: three; Middle English
Possible examples: tripod, trilogy

inter-: between, among; Middle English
Possible examples: interface, interplanetary

ortho-: straight, corrective; Latin
Possible examples: orthodontics, orthopedics

trans-: across, beyond; Latin
Possible examples: transform, transaction

circum-: around; Old French
Possible examples: circumnavigate, circumstance

Using word meanings across subjects

PRACTICE

Suggest to students that they make a chart to help them keep track of their understanding of new vocabulary words. In one column, have them list the new vocabulary words from the beginning of the chapter they have selected. In the next column, have them write what they predict the words might mean before they read the chapter, based on their prior knowledge. In the last column, have them write their refined definition of the words based on syntax and context.

Listening to news stories and current events is a good way to increase your vocabulary. Actively discuss ideas as well as new vocabulary that you hear in news reports. Friends, teachers, and parents will have their own ideas about the subtle meanings of words, so careful listening will add to your vocabulary development. Look at the model on the next page. Can you figure out the meaning of the italicized word in the first sentence of the following news report?

> The U.S. Customs Department announced today that its agents *confiscated* dozens of stolen computers near the U.S.-Canadian border. The computers were found in a large unmarked truck that had initially been stopped for speeding. Agents hope to use the computers as evidence in the case.

What strategies did you use to determine that *confiscated* means "seized"? How could you use the word in another context?

PRACTICE

Find a science or social studies textbook that includes a list of key vocabulary at the beginning of a chapter. Use prior knowledge or word parts to predict what the words might mean. Then read the passages in which the words are located and use syntax or context to check or further refine the meanings you predicted.

Determining denotation and connotation

Determining special meanings of words is an important aid to understanding. Look at these two examples of ways to distinguish between word meanings:

- **Denotation** A denotation expresses the literal, or dictionary, meaning of a word. A word may have more than one denotation, but all of its denotations will be listed in the dictionary.
- **Connotation** When a word has an emotion or an underlying value that accompanies its dictionary meaning, it has a connotation. You may say that flowers have a *fragrance* but that garbage has a *stench.* Both words mean "smell," but the connotation of *fragrance* is pleasant, while the word *stench* connotes something unpleasant.

Understanding historical influences on words

In addition to giving you word spellings, pronunciations, and meanings, a dictionary will give you the historical background of a word. Many

English words have Greek, Latin, or Anglo-Saxon origins. The Earl of Sandwich used to enjoy eating meat between two pieces of bread. Can you guess how we have used that historical influence to add to our English vocabulary? It's also easy to see why Janus, the Roman god of beginnings, gave his name to the first month of the year.

PRACTICE

If you are interested in learning more about the history of the English language, you might enjoy doing some research in your school library or on the Internet to find the answers to the following questions. Be prepared to share what you learn with the class.

1. Who were the earliest settlers of Britain? What language did they speak? What modern languages have descended from this language?
2. Who invaded Britain in A.D. 499? What do we call the language they imposed on Britain?
3. Who conquered England in 1066? What influence did they have on the language of England?
4. Modern English began with the "Great Vowel Shift." What was the "Great Vowel Shift," and when did it occur?
5. English continues to grow and change. Every day we add new words to our language. What new words can you think of that have entered our language recently? Which ones have come from technology, science, or business? Which ones have been borrowed from other countries?

Comprehension

The main job in reading is to comprehend, or understand, what you have read. Using the best strategies at the right times will help you improve your comprehension and make your reading interesting and fun.

Previewing

Before you begin to read, it's helpful to **preview** a selection.

- **Look** at the title and the illustrations that are included.
- **Read** the headings, subheadings, and anything in bold letters.
- **Skim** the passage; that is, take a quick look at the whole thing.
- **Decide** what the author's purpose might be for writing.
- **Predict** what the selection will be about.
- **Set a purpose** for your own reading.

Understanding historical influences on words

PRACTICE

Sample Answers

1. Some of the earliest settlers of England were Celtic people, who spoke a non-Germanic language, from which Welsh, Irish, and Scots Gaelic have descended.
2. The Angles, Saxons, and Jutes, which were Germanic tribes, invaded Britain in A.D. 499. Their language became Old English.
3. The French-speaking Normans conquered England in 1066, bringing many French words into English and marking the beginning of the Middle English period.
4. Between 1500 and 1800, the sounds of English vowels changed for some unknown reason to the pronunciations we use today.
5. Possible new words:
   Internet, aficionado, modem, laser, cloning, email, Ebonics.

READING HANDBOOK

Using knowledge and experience to understand

When you use your own knowledge and experience and combine it with the words on a page, you create meaning in a selection. Drawing on this personal background is called **activating prior knowledge.** Ask yourself questions like these as you start to read:

- What do I know about this topic?
- Have I been to places similar to the setting described by this writer?
- What experiences have I had that compare with what I am reading?
- What characters from life or literature remind me of the characters or narrator in the selection?

Establishing and adjusting purposes for reading

Think about these possible purposes that you might have for reading:

- to find out something
- to understand a process or an idea
- to interpret a writer's work and create meaning in a passage
- to enjoy a selection or be entertained by a story
- to solve problems or to perform a task

Each purpose allows for different active reading strategies. To find information for a report, you might skim an entire passage until you find the section you're looking for and then read more slowly. To understand new information, you might read slowly from beginning to end or even reread passages that are unclear. To simply enjoy a piece of good writing, you may allow yourself to read quickly or slow yourself down to appreciate something beautifully written.

Whatever your purposes are as you move through a selection, it's important to be able to adjust those purposes as well as your strategies to get the most out of your reading.

Making and verifying predictions

As you read, take educated guesses about story events and outcomes. **Make predictions** before and during your reading. Using your prior knowledge and the information you have gathered in your preview, predict what you will learn or what might happen in a selection. Whether your original prediction is precisely accurate does not matter, but careful predictions and later **verifications** or **adjustments** based on your reading may increase your understanding of a selection.

Monitoring and modifying reading strategies

No matter what your purposes for reading, your most important task is to understand what you have read. Ask yourself questions as you

R94 READING HANDBOOK

move through a passage. Monitor or check your understanding using the following strategies:

- **Summarize** what you read by answering who, what, where, why, and when.
- **Clarify** what you don't understand by careful rereading.
- **Question** important ideas and story elements.
- **Predict** what will happen next.
- **Evaluate** what you have read so far.

Tips for Monitoring Understanding

- **Reread.** If silently rereading a passage several times does not help to clear it up, try reading it aloud.
- **Map out the main thoughts or ideas.** A graphic organizer can help get your thoughts on track. (See pages R96 and R103.)
- **Look for context clues.** Often a writer will include an example or a definition of a difficult word in the surrounding sentences.
- **Ask questions.** Teachers, parents, and other classmates can shed light on difficult passages.
- **Write comments** as well as questions on another piece of paper for later review or discussion.
- **Use reference aids.** Dictionaries, glossaries, thesauruses, and encyclopedias–electronic or print–provide easy access to most information.

Visualizing

Creating pictures in your mind as you read is a powerful aid to understanding. According to your imagination and the text, what do characters look like? What does the setting look like? Can you picture the steps in a process when you read nonfiction? If you can visualize what you read, selections will be more vivid, and you'll recall them better later on. Be sure, though, that what you picture is accurately based on information from the text.

PRACTICE

During a time when your teacher is reading aloud to you, either from a piece of fiction or nonfiction, try sketching what you're hearing. If the selection is fiction, draw a character, setting, or action from the text description. If the selection is nonfiction, see if you can draw the steps in a process or make a small diagram of a place or thing described. Compare your sketch with a partner's and talk about similarities and differences. Ask your teacher or a friend to read the text aloud again so that you can adjust or verify your information.

Visualizing

PRACTICE

You may want to post students' pictures on a bulletin board to compare the different ways in which students visualized what they heard.

READING HANDBOOK

Constructing graphic organizers

Graphic organizers help you draw a picture of what you're reading so you can sort ideas out, clear up difficult passages, and remember important ideas in a selection. Look at the following examples of good graphic organizers and notice how they are used.

Web You can show a main idea and supporting details by using a web. Put the main idea in the middle circle and the supporting details in the surrounding circles. Notice how you might include other circles branching off from the detail circles. Use those for further information about your details.

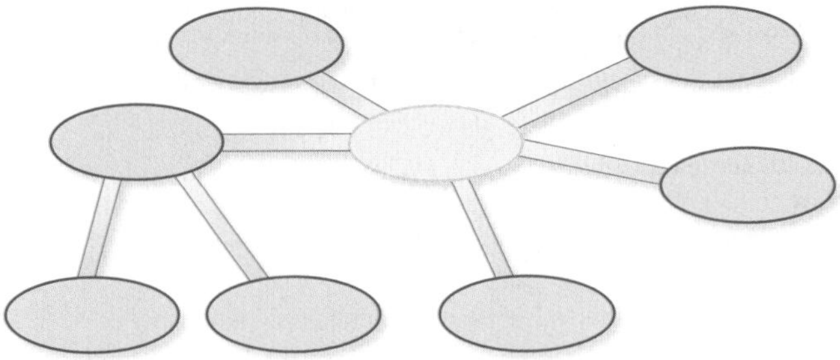

Flowchart When you want to keep track of events in a time order or show a cause-and-effect relationship between events, use a flowchart. Arrange your ideas or events in the boxes, putting them in their logical order. Then draw arrows between the boxes to show how one idea or event flows into another.

Venn diagram To look at the similarities and differences between two ideas, characters, or events, use a Venn diagram. The outer portions of each circle will show how two items contrast, or are different. Use the overlapping portion of the circles to show how they are the same.

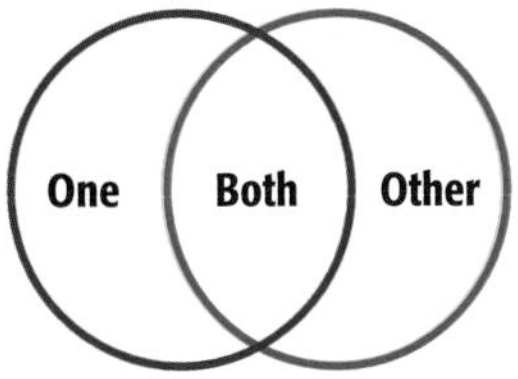

R96 READING HANDBOOK

READING HANDBOOK

Using text structures

Writers organize their ideas in a variety of ways, depending on their topic and their purpose for writing. When you find that pattern of organization or **text structure** within a selection, it's easier to locate and recall a writer's ideas. Here are four examples of ways that writers structure or organize text:

Kind of Organization	Purpose	Clues
Comparison and contrast	To determine similarities and differences	Words and phrases such as *similarly, on the other hand, in contrast to, but, however*
Cause and effect	To explore the reasons for something and to examine the results of events or actions	Words and phrases such as *so, because, as a result*
Chronological order	To present events in time order	Words and phrases such as *first, next, then, later, finally*
Problem/Solution	To examine how conflicts or obstacles are overcome	Words and phrases such as *need, attempt, help, obstruction*

To find the text structure of a passage, look for **signal words and phrases** that contain clues about how the writer has organized ideas. Read the model below and the one on the next page.

In order to organize his science project, Jamie **first** needed to determine how many specimens he would use in his control group and again in his test group. **Then** he would have to order some cockroaches, arrange for the delivery of the glass cases where the little critters would live for two months, and find out how much and what they would eat. **After he did that,** Jamie sat down with his plans for the project to determine what he intended to prove.

Signal words and phrases

READING HANDBOOK R97

Jon listened carefully as the woman interviewed on the nightly news telecast explained how that particular day had been the best and the worst day of her life. **On the one hand,** the tornado that tore through her tiny community left her nothing but a concrete slab to call home. Everything her family had worked for was gone. **On the other hand,** she and her husband and their daughter were safe. The young mother's face was full of tiny cuts and bruises, **but** she smiled continuously at the little girl who played on her lap. **In contrast to** the reporter's worried expression and concerned questions, both husband and wife expressed how lucky they felt. As the interview ended, Jon knew he had found a wonderful subject for his Thanksgiving narrative essay.

Signal words and phrases

What is the basic text structure of the first model? What is the structure of the second model? Explain how you determined your answers.

Determining main ideas and supporting details

The most important idea in a paragraph or passage is called the **main idea.** The examples or ideas that further explain the main idea are called **supporting details.** Some main ideas are clearly stated in sentences within a passage. Other times, without directly stating a main idea, an author will suggest it by providing a variety of clues.

Many times the main idea will be the first sentence of a paragraph, but not always. A main idea might be anywhere, even in the last sentence in a passage.

A selection can have a number of main ideas in it. Each paragraph can contain a main idea, as in most nonfiction, or entire passages can have a main idea, as in both fiction and nonfiction.

When you need to find the main idea, ask yourself these questions:

- What is each sentence about?
- Is there one sentence that tells about the whole passage or that is more important than the others?
- If the main idea is not directly stated, what main idea do the supporting details point out?

R98 READING HANDBOOK

READING HANDBOOK

Finding the main ideas will help you understand a selection. Look at the following model.

Main idea — **Many of the animals that live on the ocean floor have found a way to cope with the darkness—they are luminous.** Some species of fish are hosts to bacteria that glow in the dark. When they eat the bacteria, the hosts' bodies glow from the bacteria inside them. One species of fish in the Indian Ocean has these bacteria in spots under each eye. The fish's eyes seem to glow in the dark. However, when the fish is threatened, it can raise black folds of skin that hide the light. The bathysphere fish seems to have lights in its teeth to attract food, while the hatchet fish glows with lights that only look like teeth. These lights seem to scare away other fish.

Supporting details

Sequencing

The order in which thoughts are arranged is called **sequence.** A good sequence is one that is logical, given the ideas in a selection. Here are three common forms of sequencing:

- Chronological order–time order
- Spatial order–the order in which things would be arranged within a certain space
- Order of importance–going from most important to least important or the other way around

Recognizing the sequence of something is important when you have to follow directions. If you fail to follow steps in a certain order, you may not be able to accomplish your task.

Paraphrasing

Retelling something using your own words is **paraphrasing.** You might paraphrase just the main ideas of a selection, or you might retell an entire story in your own words. Paraphrasing is a useful strategy for reviewing and for checking comprehension.

Original text: *The Four Corners area of Colorado, Utah, New Mexico, and Arizona is home to a multitude of ancient dwellings.*

Paraphrase: *In the area where Colorado, Utah, New Mexico, and Arizona meet, you can find many very old homes.*

READING HANDBOOK R99

Paraphrasing

PRACTICE

Rubric

Students' paraphrases should be accurate retellings of the selection, including the main points and important details. From the paraphrases, it should be clear that each student comprehends the meaning of the selection.

Summarizing

PRACTICE

Rubric

Students' summaries of "I Have a Dream" should include such main ideas as the continuing struggle for equality, and a nonviolent approach to achieving civil rights.

PRACTICE

Read "Plucky Poodle Returns Alive After Dog-Napping by Coyotes" on page 425 of this book. Then, on a separate sheet of paper, paraphrase the first three paragraphs of this selection. When you have finished, trade paraphrases with a partner. Evaluate each other's work. Is the paraphrase an accurate retelling? Are any important details missing? How can the paraphrase be improved? After receiving feedback from your partner, revise your paraphrase and share it with the class.

Summarizing

When you **summarize,** you relate the main ideas of a selection in a logical sequence and in your own words. To create a good summary, include all the main ideas and only essential supporting details.

A good summary can be easily understood by someone who has not read the whole text or selection. Look at the following model and summary.

> The Dead Sea is not dead. It is not a sea either. Even though the water of the Dead Sea is too salty for fish and other animals to live there, some microscopic organisms that use the sun to photosynthesize, and others from which petroleum can be made make the waters of the Dead Sea their home. This body of water is not a sea but is instead a salt lake. It has the lowest elevation of any place on Earth. The water contains more salt and other minerals than any other body of water.
>
> **Summary:** The Dead Sea, a salt lake, is the saltiest body of water in the world and is also the lowest place on Earth. Even though fish and other animals cannot live there, microscopic plants call the Dead Sea home.

PRACTICE

Read "I Have a Dream" on page 494 of this book. On a separate sheet of paper, list the main ideas in the selection. Under each main idea, list the supporting details that explain it. Use this information to write a one-paragraph summary of what you have read.

Drawing and supporting inferences

Writers don't always directly state what they want you to understand in a selection. By providing clues and interesting details, they suggest certain

information. Whenever you combine those clues with your own background and knowledge, you are drawing an inference. An **inference** involves using your reason and experience to come up with an idea based on what an author implies or suggests. The following active reading behaviors are examples of drawing an inference:

- **Predicting** When you guess what a story will be about or what will happen next, you are predicting.
- **Drawing conclusions** A conclusion is a general statement you can make and explain with reasoning or with supporting details from a selection.
- **Generalizing** When you draw an inference that can apply to more than one item or group, you are making a generalization.
- **Classifying** When you recognize something as fitting into a category, you classify it.

Finding similarities and differences across texts

As your reading takes you across a variety of sources, compare and contrast the things you've read. When you look for similarities and differences in your reading selections, you'll gain a better understanding of all the material you've read. Ask yourself in what ways sources might be alike or different. What is included in one selection that might be left out of another? Why might that be?

Here are some of the ways you can compare and contrast writers' works:

- **Scope** Take a broad look at each entire selection. How would you compare the time periods covered? How much information is given in each nonfiction selection? How many characters and settings are involved in fiction pieces?
- **Treatment** Look at how each writer presents important ideas. Who tells the story? Is the narrator's attitude serious or funny? How would you compare the writers' purposes and styles?
- **Organization** Compare selections in terms of how writers arrange their thoughts. Is a writer using **chronological order? Comparison and contrast? Cause and effect? Problem and solution?**

When you look for similarities and differences in what you've read, you'll learn to read more critically and get more out of each selection.

Distinguishing fact from opinion

When deciding whether to believe what a writer has written, you need to distinguish between fact and opinion. A **fact** is a statement that can be proved with supporting information. An **opinion,** on the other hand, is what a writer believes on the basis of his or her personal viewpoint.

READING HANDBOOK R101

Writers can support their opinions with facts, but an opinion is something that cannot be proved. Look at the following examples of fact and opinion.

Fact: *Two students in our school scored higher on national tests than any other students in our district.*
Opinion: *Everyone knows that our school has the smartest students in the district.*

When interpreting something you read, be sure that you distinguish between statements of fact and statements of opinion.

Answering questions

How do you decide where to look for answers to questions about selections you've read? Look at the chart below to help you decide.

Type of Question	What Is It?	Example	How to Find the Answer
Literal	Has a definite answer	What color was Snow White's hair?	Look for direct statement in text.
Interpretive	Answer based on text and prior knowledge	Why was Snow White a threat to the queen?	Use text information and/or prior knowledge.
Open-ended	No right or wrong answer	Is Snow White a role model for today's children?	Use personal background and feelings.

You may find various types of questions on a test.

Tips for Answering Test Questions

- **True-or-false questions** If any part of a true or false question is false, the correct answer is "false."
- **Short answer** Use complete sentences so your responses will be clear. Try to put your thoughts in logical sequence.
- **Multiple choice** First read all the responses. Eliminate the answers you know are incorrect. Choose the best answer from the remaining responses.

Representing text information

After reading various sources, you may want to reproduce what you have learned in a visual way, perhaps to present it to your class or to show the teacher that you have understood it.

- Outlines An outline is helpful if you are organizing information to present a report. Roman numerals, together with uppercase and lowercase letters, show the basic structure of the report. Look at this sample model of a topic outline.

Each main topic is one of the big ideas of your subject. Suppose that your subject is surfing. The first main topic could be the history of surfing.

I. Main topic
  A. First subtopic
    1. Division of a subtopic
    2. Division of a subtopic
  B. Second subtopic

If you wish to divide a subtopic, you must have at least two divisions. Each division must relate to the subtopic above it.

If you have subtopics under a main topic, there must be at least two. They must relate directly to the main topic.

- Time lines A time line shows the chronological order of events over a period of time. Look at the example below.

The title shows the subject of the time line. It also may include the dates covered.

Space between events shows the amount of time that passed between them. Which two events came closest together?

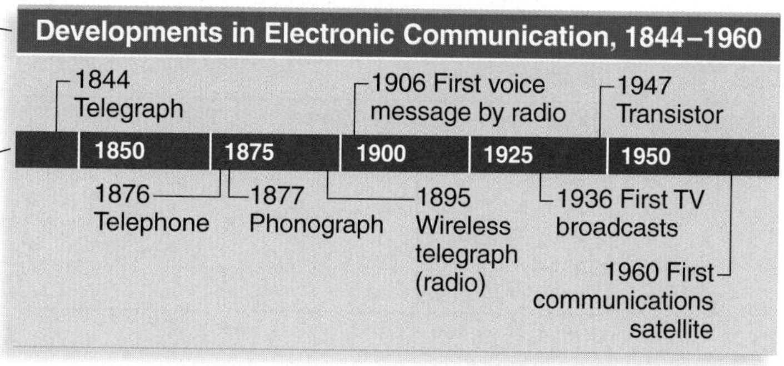

- Graphic organizers Word webs, flow charts, Venn diagrams, and other kinds of graphic organizers can help you present information in a visual way.

Using study strategies

If you're preparing for a quiz or test or getting ready for a class presentation, you'll want to use a study strategy that helps you organize and remember the material you've read. Here are some useful strategies.

- Using story maps A story map can help you sort out important literary elements in works of fiction. Look at the model on the next page to see how a story map works as a tool for review.

READING HANDBOOK R103

READING HANDBOOK

STORY MAP

Characters Bob, Sylvia, Mr. DuPree	**Setting** Small town in Maine
Plot Conflict (problem): Sylvia loses Bob's pet dog.	**Plot** Resolution (solution): Mr. DuPree finds the dog.

- **Using KWL** KWL is a good way to keep track of what you are learning when you read informational text. Make three columns on a page. Label the first column *What I **K**now,* the second column *What I **W**ant to Know,* and the third column *What I **L**earned.* Before you begin reading, list the things you already know about a topic in the first column. List your questions in the second column. When you've finished reading, record what you've learned in the third column. You can add more columns to record places where you found information and places to look for more.

KWL

What I Know	What I Want to Know	What I Learned	Where I Got Information
			Where I Can Get More

- **Using SQ3R** A useful study strategy for studying subject areas like science or social studies is SQ3R. It stands for **s**urvey, **q**uestion, **r**ead, **r**ecord, and **r**eview. Here's how it works.
  1. **Survey** Take a quick look over the entire selection you need to study. Notice anything boldfaced. Look at headings, subheadings, or pictures.
  2. **Question** Think of a number of questions you'll want to answer as you read.
  3. **Read** Read the selection carefully. Vary your reading rate as you encounter easy or difficult passages.
  4. **Record** Take notes about important ideas. Record your comments and additional questions that come up as you read.
  5. **Review** When you've finished reading, go back over the text once again to be sure you've understood important ideas.

R104 READING HANDBOOK

- Creating and using study guides Your teacher may provide you with a guide to focus your attention on important vocabulary and ideas. You can also create your own guide by using end-of-chapter questions to focus your reading.

PRACTICE

Select a chapter from your social studies or science text. Use SQ3R as you read the material. Have a classmate quiz you by using end-of-chapter questions to see how well you remember what you studied.

Evaluating what you read

In many of your classes, you are asked to evaluate the text materials that you read. This is especially true of expository writing–such as persuasive essays, informational articles, and political editorials. When evaluating expository writing, critical readers take into consideration the following factors: unity, coherence, logic, internal consistency, and structural patterns. Ask yourself these questions:

Unity
- What is the subject? Does the author stay focused on the subject?
- Are there ideas that should be deleted because they don't relate to the topic or don't add anything to the topic? What are they?

Coherence
- Do I understand clearly the point made? What is that point?
- Does anything in the text confuse me? Why? How could it be fixed?

Logic
- Does the text make sense? Why or why not?
- Does the author use sound reasoning to support his or her ideas? What examples of sound reasoning and weak reasoning can I find?

Internal consistency
- Is the main idea (or ideas) followed by supporting details? Can I identify those supporting details?
- Has the author provided what he or she promised? (For example, if the author promises to support an argument with three sound reasons, are three reasons supplied? If an author is explaining how to do something, are all the necessary steps provided?)
- Has the author maintained a consistent point of view? Explain?

Structural patterns
- What text structure is used to organize the ideas? (for example, comparison/contrast, steps in a process, cause/effect, topical, spatial, or problem/solution)
- Is the text structure appropriate for the material? Why or why not?

READING HANDBOOK

Using study strategies

PRACTICE

After students have finished quizzing each other on the chapter, have them make a list of unanswered questions they still have and other sources that may offer more information.

Evaluating what you read

PRACTICE

Rubric

Students' evaluations should show that careful thought has gone into answering the questions listed under each of the five factors. Remind students that even answers that are based on one's own opinion should be supported by evidence from the selection.

PRACTICE

Choose a piece of expository writing to evaluate. You may select a favorite editorial or opinion column from your school or community newspaper or an informational article from a popular magazine. Evaluate the article on the basis of the five factors listed above. Prepare answers to the questions listed under each factor. Be prepared to present your evaluation orally to the class or in written form.

Literary Response

Whenever you share your thoughts and feelings about something you've read, you are responding to a text. You have your own learning style, so you will want to respond in ways that are comfortable for you. Some students learn best when speaking and writing, while others enjoy moving around or creating something artistic.

Tips for Responding to and Interpreting Literature

- **Discuss** what you have read and share your views in active classroom discussions or at home.
- **Keep a journal** about what you read. Record your thoughts and feelings as well as questions you might have about a selection.
- **Take part in dramatizations, oral interpretations,** and **readers theater.** These activities can allow you to present characters through actions and dialogue and allow you to use your voice, facial expressions, and body language to convey meaning.
- **Tape record or videotape** your oral readings or dramatizations.

Supporting responses and interpretations

Whether you respond with your mind or with your emotions, you need to support your responses by going back to the text itself. Make sure you provide details from the author's work to back up your thoughts and feelings. It is not enough to say, "I really liked the main character." You must show what you liked about him or her. Look for specific descriptions and information. Ask yourself questions like these:

- What is interesting about this story's setting?
- What do I like or dislike about this character?
- How is the overall theme or idea expressed?
- What specific details account for my views about this selection?
- How have my own experiences and prior knowledge influenced my feelings in this selection?

Identifying the purpose of a text

Authors have a variety of reasons for writing. They may simply want to **entertain** you. They may want to **inform** you about a topic. They may feel the need to **express** thoughts and emotions through a narrative or biographical essay. They also may want to **influence** your thinking and **persuade** you to believe something or to act in a certain way. How can you tell what a writer's purpose is? To identify the purposes of different types of texts, use the following tips.

Tips for Identifying the Purpose of a Text

- **Look at word choices.** Authors select words according to the words' connotations, which carry emotional or implied meanings, as well as their denotations, or dictionary meanings.
- **Consider the intended audience.** Most selections are written with an audience in mind. A speech at a pep rally might have a different purpose than one given before student council members.
- **Look at the structure of the text.** Figuring out whether a writer has used chronological order, comparison-and-contrast structure, or cause-and-effect structure can help you determine his or her purpose.

Comparing elements across genres

Have you ever seen a movie or a television program that was based on a book you read? How were they similar? How were they different? Sometimes scenes are left out of the movie in order to make the story fit into a particular time frame. Some characters in movies are not represented precisely as they are described in books. As you look to see how the same story may vary across cultures or genres, look at similarities and differences in the following story elements:

- Characters Are all characters represented? Are some characters combined?
- Settings Is the setting presented similarly in each work? What differences affect the story as a whole?
- Plot How is the plot adjusted to fit the strengths and limitations of the genre?
- Themes or ideas Are important ideas well developed?
- Author's point of view Does the author's attitude affect how the story is told?
- Author's purpose Why is the author telling this story?
- Author's style What format and word choices are used?

READING HANDBOOK

Analyzing inductive and deductive reasoning

As you think about works you've read, ask yourself whether the reasoning behind an author's ideas is logical. Here are two kinds of logical reasoning writers use.

Inductive reasoning When you consider a certain number of examples a writer gives you or see a particular number of cases to illustrate a point or an idea, you may be able to arrive at a **generalization**–a conclusion or general statement–by using **inductive reasoning.** For example, if the tulips your class planted on the north side of your school building did not grow, there is never grass on that side of the building, and a tree planted there last year still has no leaves, you can inductively reason that the north side of the building may not be the best place to plant things. This logic moves from the specific to the general.

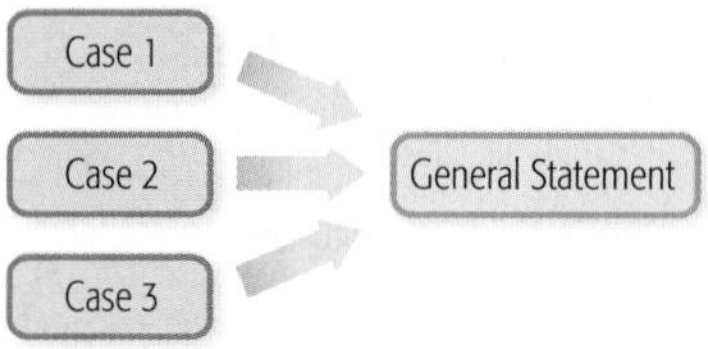

Deductive reasoning When you take a general statement and apply it through reasoning to a number of specific situations, you are using **deductive reasoning.** For example, you know that many kinds of plants do not grow well in shady areas. Therefore, you can deductively reason that it might not be wise to plant tulips or expect grass or trees to grow on the shady side of the building. This logic moves from the general to the specific.

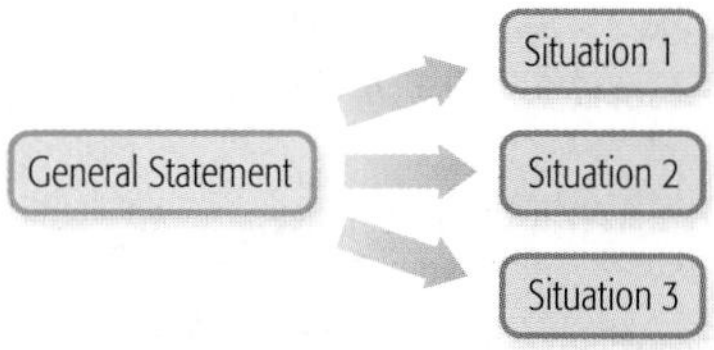

Inquiry and Research

Asking and answering questions is at the heart of being an active reader. As you read in a variety of sources, you will think of new questions or revise your original questions to take into account new information. When you ask important questions and carefully research thorough answers, you will draw conclusions about your topic. The process may lead you to other interesting questions and areas for further study.

R108 READING HANDBOOK

READING HANDBOOK

Forming and revising questions

Finding an interesting and relevant question or topic is an important first step in doing research and deserves your careful attention.

Tips for Asking Research Questions

- Think of a question or topic that interests you.
- Choose a question that helps you focus your investigation on one main idea.
- Be sure the question is not too broad or too narrow.
  Too broad: *How can people preserve the environment?*
  Better: *What changes in waste management law have been made in my state within the last five years?*

Using text organizers

Once you've found an interesting question to investigate, the next step is to locate information and then to organize it. Textbooks, references, magazines, and other sources use a variety of ways to help you find what you need quickly and efficiently.

- **Tables of contents** Look at a table of contents first to see whether a resource offers information you need.
- **Indexes** An index is an alphabetical listing of significant topics covered in a book. It is found in the back of a book.
- **Headings and subheadings** Headings often identify the information that follows.
- **Graphic features** Photos, diagrams, maps, charts, graphs, and other graphic features can convey a large amount of information at a glance.

Using multiple sources for research

The research you do will be more interesting and balanced when you include various types of sources. Each source will provide a different slant to your topic. To find the most recent information, it may be necessary to use sources other than books. The following are some helpful resources for conducting research:

- **Print resources:** textbooks, magazines, reference books, and other specialized references
- **Nonprint information:** films, videos, and recorded interviews
- **Electronic texts:** CD-ROM encyclopedias and the Internet
- **Experts:** people who are specialists on the topic you've chosen

READING HANDBOOK R109

Interpreting graphic aids

When you're researching a topic, be sure to read and interpret the graphic aids included. **Graphic aids** let you see information at a glance.

Reading a map Maps are flat representations of land. A **compass rose** allows you to determine direction. A **legend** explains the map's symbols, and a **scale** shows you how the size of the map relates to the actual distances covered. Look at the map below.

Reading a graph A graph shows you how two or more things relate. Graphs can use circles, dots, bars, or lines. Look at the title and the labels on the bar graph below. Can you interpret the information?

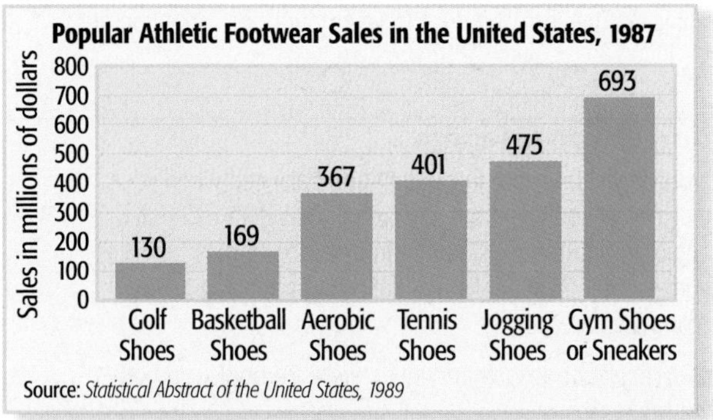

Reading a table A table allows you to group numbers or facts and to put them into categories so you can compare what is in each category. Look at the table on the next page. Read the title first. You are looking at populations of the largest U.S. cities. Now read the labels at the top of each column. The information in the first two columns shows you the cities compared and their rank by size. You can read across rows to find

R110 READING HANDBOOK

information about one city, or you can compare the five largest cities with one another in any given year. What other information can you gather from this table?

Population of Largest U.S. Cities

Rank	City	1950	1960	1970	1980	1990
1	New York City	7,891,984	7,781,984	7,895,563	7,071,639	7,322,564
2	Los Angeles	1,970,358	2,479,015	2,811,801	2,966,850	3,485,398
3	Chicago	3,620,962	3,550,404	3,369,357	3,005,072	2,783,726
4	Houston	596,163	938,219	1,233,535	1,595,138	1,630,553
5	Philadelphia	2,071,605	2,002,512	1,949,996	1,688,210	1,585,577

Source: *U.S. Bureau of the Census*

PRACTICE

Look in a current newspaper or newsmagazine to find an example of a chart, graph, or table. Explain the graphic aid to the class and briefly analyze the information presented.

Organizing information

Now that you've read about your research topic in a variety of sources, how will you put it all together? Here are some suggestions:

- **Record** information on note cards. Use a new card for each main idea or important piece of information.
- **Summarize** information before you write it on a card. That way you'll have the main ideas in your own words.
- **Outline ideas** by putting your note cards in order and creating a written outline so you can see how subtopics and supporting information will fit under the main ideas.
- **Make a table or graph** to compare items or categories of information.

Tips for Charting Information

- Decide what information you want your audience to see at a glance.
- Decide what kind of table or graph will best show the information.
- Choose a title for your graphic aid and label the categories horizontally and vertically.
- Check the accuracy of your information; plot it out carefully.
- Use various colors, if possible, to distinguish between items.

READING HANDBOOK

Interpreting graphic aids

PRACTICE

Students' presentations should cover the main features of the graphic aids being used and clearly analyze the information presented.

READING HANDBOOK

Producing projects and reports

How should you present the information you've gathered? Before you decide, think about these questions:

- How can I briefly and clearly convey important information? What would best capture the attention of my audience?
- What graphic aids can I use to illustrate my main ideas?
- What pattern of organization would suit this information? Chronological order? Comparison and contrast? Cause and effect?
- Would an illustration or a cartoon help to make a certain point?

When considering a format to use for your report, you might consider a **written** or an **oral report,** a **debate,** an **interview,** or a **dramatic** or **video presentation.**

Drawing conclusions and asking further questions

You will certainly form opinions about your topic after you've finished your research. A **conclusion** is a general statement that you'll make about what you have learned. Remember that you started your research with an important question, so your answer to that question may help to form your conclusion. In the best situations, a conclusion will lead you to other interesting questions and areas for further reading.

Read the following excerpts and the conclusion that follows. Then look at the question for further research.

> *Project Mercury*, initiated in 1958 and completed in 1963, was the United States' first human-in-space program. It was designed to further knowledge about humanity's capabilities in space. . . . The *Gemini* spacecraft, twice as large as the *Mercury* capsule, accommodated two astronauts. *Apollo* was the designation for the United States' effort to land a person on the Moon and return that person safely to Earth. The goal was successfully accomplished with *Apollo 11* on July 20, 1969, culminating eight years of rehearsal and centuries of dreaming. . . . *Project Skylab* was designed to demonstrate that humans can work and live in space for prolonged periods without ill effects.

R112 READING HANDBOOK

In a historic moment, Mission Commander Robert Cabana and Russian Cosmonaut/Mission Specialist Sergei Krikalev swung open the hatch between the *Endeavour* and the First Element of the International Space Station at 1:15 CST, Thursday, December 10, 1998. . . . International Space Station flight controllers at Mission Control, Houston, and at the Russian Mission Control Center in Korolev, outside Moscow, will spend the next five months monitoring the station's systems. . . . The International Space Station continues the largest scientific cooperative program in history, drawing on the resources and scientific expertise of 16 nations.

Conclusion: Space exploration has become more advanced in the past thirty years, involving the scientific cooperation of a number of countries around the world.

Question for further research: What advances in space exploration does NASA hope to accomplish in the next thirty years?

Tips for Drawing Conclusions

- Don't try to twist the facts to support your ideas.
- Don't make statements that go beyond the facts you've gathered.
- Recognize that your conclusions may be different than you originally thought they might be.
- Be sure to record accurately where you got your information.
- Never present someone else's ideas as if they were your own.

Reading Consumer, Workplace, and Public Documents

Every day you come into contact with a wide variety of important reading materials that affect your life. Long after you leave school, you will need to understand, interpret, and make use of written materials to function effectively in the world. Here are some tips for dealing successfully with consumer, workplace, and public documents.

Following technical directions

Whether you are assembling a model airplane, installing a software program on your computer, or learning about the latest dance moves, you should be aware of ways to improve your efficiency in following written directions.

- Read all of the directions before proceeding with the project. Reading the directions completely through will give you an idea of the scope and complexity of the task.

READING HANDBOOK R113

Following technical directions

PRACTICE

Rubric

Students' demonstrations should

- include all steps that are necessary to the completion of the task
- present each step in its proper order
- use transition words to make the order of the steps clear to the audience
- show that the student fully understands the task he or she is demonstrating

- Start with step 1 and do all the steps in the order in which they are presented. Do not skip a step in order to save time.
- Pay attention to the cues that tell you the order in which to complete the steps. This is easy where the steps are labeled. However, when steps are not labeled, look for transition words such as *first, next, then,* and *finally* to help you.
- If the directions include diagrams, use the diagrams to help you interpret the written instructions. Compare the view shown in the diagram with your view of the item you are assembling, installing, or operating. (For example, if you are looking at a diagram that shows how to connect cables from a VCR to a television set, line up the VCR and the television set so that you are looking at the same view that appears on the diagram.)
- If you have trouble understanding how to do a particular step, look at the next step. It may provide a clue to what to do. (A diagram, for example, may show what the previous step should look like when completed.)
- If you still have trouble or if the instructions include technical terms that you don't understand, check another source. Some instructional manuals include a glossary of technical terms. Others include diagrams of the item with all the parts labeled. Most include telephone numbers, fax numbers, or e-mail addresses that you can use to contact an expert for advice.

PRACTICE

Select a task that requires following a set of directions (for example, assembling a toy or cutting and pasting a document on your computer). You can choose a task that you already have mastered or one that you need to learn. Practice the task until you are thoroughly comfortable doing it. Then demonstrate your understanding of the task in front of the class. Explain each step in its proper order.

Interpreting product information

Educated consumers have learned to read product information carefully and, in particular, to be wary of extravagant claims made by the manufacturer. Here are some tips to help you choose wisely when buying products.

- **Note the exact wording of product descriptions.** The federal government has established strict guidelines for describing certain products. For example, pancake syrup cannot be labeled maple syrup unless it contains a specific minimum amount of real maple syrup. Companies that don't meet this requirement use a label such as "maple-flavored" syrup. The same is true of chocolate, cheese, and juice products. Watch out for words such as "choco-

R114 READING HANDBOOK

latey," "chocolate-flavored," "cheesy," or "cheese-like." The products they describe may contain no real chocolate or cheese at all. Another example is orange juice. Check juice labels carefully. Does the container say "orange drink" or "orange juice"? If it says "orange juice," does it say "100% orange juice," "freshly squeezed," or "made from frozen concentrate"?

- **Read the ingredients.** The best way to find out if a "chocolate-flavored" product actually contains any real chocolate is to read the ingredients label. It is usually printed in small type on the side or back of a product. The federal government requires companies to list ingredients in the order of their weight, starting with the ingredient that makes up the largest part of the product. The remaining ingredients are then listed in descending order. Reading ingredients lists can be revealing. For example, how much fruit might you expect to find in a blueberry pancake mix that lists "blueberry pieces" last? What opinion would you have of a breakfast cereal that is advertised as being healthful but lists sugar as its second main ingredient?
- **Check out warning labels.** The federal government requires companies to provide warning labels for all products containing elements that might pose a risk to consumers. Both over-the-counter and prescription drugs contain descriptions of potential side effects. Children's toys include age-appropriate labels as well as warnings about choking hazards. Many restaurant menus now include warnings about ordering undercooked ground beef or egg items because of potential food poisoning. Before buying or using a product, read any "Warning" or "Caution" to help you stay safe.
- **Be wary of product claims.** You should make a point of carefully evaluating all product claims you read. If a product contains a splashy label that says "New, Improved," try to find out how the product has been improved or if the change even is an improvement at all. If a product is advertised as the top-selling one in its field, ask yourself if it is the top-selling one because it is truly better or simply because it has name recognition. Be wary of products that claim they contain "more than ever" (more than what?) or are "Doctor Recommended" (which doctor or doctors?) or meet "Government Safety Standards." (Are the government safety standards strong enough?) Can you think of other examples?
- **Be aware of the limitations on product warranties and service contracts.** Warranties are a special category of product information. A *warranty* is a written guarantee of the integrity of a product and of the maker's responsibility for repairing or replacing defective parts. The warranty document is usually included with the instructional manual or other product information that accompanies household appliances, electronic equipment, bicycles, and other products. *Service contracts* are warranties you can purchase that

Interpreting product information

PRACTICE

Rubric

Students' presentations should demonstrate consideration of all the guidelines mentioned for interpreting product information. Students should come to a conclusion about the honesty, usefulness, and purpose of the written materials they interpret.

provide additional coverage not included in a warranty. If you receive a warranty (or purchase a service contract) for a product you buy, you should read the entire document carefully so that you know exactly what the terms are. After studying it, you should be able to answer the following questions:

- Is the warranty (or service contract) "limited" or "lifetime"?
- Is the warranty in effect for 90 days, one year, longer than one year, or for as long as I own the product?
- Does the warranty cover both labor and parts, only parts, or only selected parts?
- What specific items are not covered by the warranty?
- Am I responsible for sending the product to a service facility at my expense?
- Are there any other restrictions or conditions specified in the warranty?
- Whom do I contact to request warranty service or to ask questions about my warranty, and how do I contact them?

PRACTICE

Select a packaged food product that you have at home. Read and evaluate all the print material on the package. What claims, if any, are presented? Can you verify or dispute any of the claims? What are the main ingredients of the product? What warnings, if any, are printed on the package? Share what you learned with your classmates.

Using workplace documents

Whether you are looking for a part-time job, sending or receiving a business letter, or trying to communicate more effectively in a workplace setting, here are some tips to help you deal with the world of business.

Job application forms In the near future, you will be old enough to secure a work permit, and you may give serious thought to looking for part-time work. At that time, you will need to fill out a job application form. How you fill it out is important because the application represents your first contact with your potential employer and therefore your first opportunity to make a good impression. When filling out an application form, you might find it helpful to keep the following directions in mind:

- Read all instructions carefully before filling in any blanks.
- Pay attention to details. For example, if the instructions ask you to list first the most recent job you have held, do it. Not doing so may send the employer the wrong message about your ability to follow directions.

  - In general, you should try to fill out the form as completely as possible so that the employer can give your application full consideration. Because employers are not allowed to discriminate on the basis of race, color, gender, religion, national origin, age, or disability, they cannot require you to answer questions about those subjects; however, some employers ask questions about those topics in a Voluntary Self-Identification Record section on their application forms. Read such sections carefully. They will specify that you can choose not to answer those questions if you wish.
  - Always be honest. Do not make up information. If you have no special skills, school honors, or past jobs to list, leave those sections blank.
  - If you do not understand a question on the form, ask a parent, guardian, or teacher for help.

- **Business Letters and Memos** It is not too early to start learning the skills you'll need to read and interpret business letters and memos as well as to create your own.
  - A good business letter should begin with the sender's address, the date, and the receiver's name and address followed by a respectful greeting. The body of the letter should include a brief introduction stating the purpose of the letter, a clear description of the purpose, and a closing paragraph thanking the receiver for any help he or she can provide. Finally, the letter should include a respectful closing followed by the sender's signature and typed name. You can find more information about business letters and a sample letter on pages R61 and R62 of the Writing Handbook in this book.
  - Business memos are used within a company as a way for employees to communicate with one another. Memos can be written on paper or typed electronically on computers and sent as e-mail messages. Either way, a good memo should always supply the following information: the receiver's name, the sender's name, a subject title, the date, and a clear description of the subject. If the purpose of the memo is to provide information only, it may begin with the acronym FYI, which means "For Your Information." This tells the reader that no specific action or response is required. If the memo requires a response (for example, an analysis of the information, an opinion, or an answer to a question), the sender should indicate clearly that he or she wants a response. You can find a sample memo on page R63 of the Writing Handbook in this book.

READING HANDBOOK R117

Using public documents

PRACTICE

Ask students to comment on how they evaluated the Web sites they found and what kinds of documents these sites provided.

Using public documents

You probably already know that the Internet can be an extremely valuable source of information when you need to do research for a paper, report, or project. However, you also need to be aware that the information you find on the Internet is not always reliable. Anyone can create a Web site. Before accepting and using information you find on the Internet, ask yourself these questions: Is the Web site source credible? Is the author of the material an accepted authority? Has the information on the Web site been updated recently? Can I verify the information on other Web sites or in other reliable sources?

Nonprofit, government, and educational organizations are the most reliable sources of information on the Internet. Their Internet addresses end in *.org, .gov,* and *.edu.* Web sites operated by the federal government are especially reliable and provide a wealth of public documents that offer helpful information on a wide variety of consumer- and civic-related topics. Web sites that originate outside the United States include country abbreviations such as *.UK* (United Kingdom) in their addresses.

PRACTICE

Search the Internet for a nonprofit, government, or educational Web site that provides helpful consumer information. After selecting a site, find a topic at that site that interests you. Gather information about that topic to present in a short written paper (one or two pages) or oral report (five minutes) to the class. Include documentation that identifies the source of the information you've gathered. If you have trouble finding a suitable Web site, visit the Web site of the Federal Consumer Information Center at *www.pueblo.gsa.gov.*

Writing Workshop Models

The following Writing Workshop Models are complete versions of the student models developed in the Writing Workshops at the end of each theme in this book. Use these models as examples of how one student might have responded to the assignments in the Writing Workshops.

Theme 1, pages 90–93

Descriptive Writing: Personal Essay

Me and Tig

A When I look at my cat Tig, I can see myself. Like Tig, I am athletic and focused, but also lazy and easily distracted. Like Tig, I am independent, but I also like to be with people. These contradictions make me who I am.

B Tig and I are both medium-sized, and we're both growing. We're also both pretty strong and muscular. I'm not good at team sports like soccer, but I like to run and swim and dance. Dancing involves a lot of stretching, and sometimes after my dance class, I'll just stretch out in a patch of sunlight in my room and rest. I like the feel of the warm sun on my tired muscles. Once I start resting, I get really lazy. I just want to lie there. Sometimes my cat will come join me. I like to watch the sun play on her black fur, and I try to imagine what it would be like to be covered with fur like that.

C Tig's fur requires a lot of attention, and she spends a lot of time licking herself to keep clean. She always seems like she is concentrating hard on her bath, not paying attention to anything else. When I read or study, I try to be the same way and focus like Tig. Sometimes my mom has to stand in front of me and wave her hands to get me to look up from my book! While I'm often able to focus on a project, I can also be easily distracted. Sticking with one thing can be hard when my sisters are making noise or the TV is on or I feel like going to the kitchen for a snack.

Another great quality about Tig is that she is very loving. Tig hops in my lap every chance she gets and curls up on my pillow to go to sleep at night. But at other times, she seems perfectly happy by herself. She can stretch out on the windowsill and just watch people go by for hours. I like to do things by myself too. I like to read and go on bike rides by myself. Sometimes I just want to be left alone to do these things. But I like to be with my friends too. I have three best friends whom I go to the movies with almost every week. D If we don't go to the movies, we just hang out and listen to music. Sometimes we sleep over at each other's houses. I wouldn't want to be without them, even though I like to be alone at times.

I am sometimes confused when I think about who I am and what I like and dislike. I don't understand how I can be interested in so many things at once. For instance, how can I want to do well in school but goof off at the same time? But then I look at Tig, who bounds around the house one minute and is curled up sound asleep the next, and it makes sense that lots of qualities can exist in one person. I hope that in twenty years I will still be able to do a bunch of different things, because I think variety makes me a happier and more interesting person.

Teaching the Writing Workshop Models

Use the annotated writing models on pages R119–R130 as teaching tools to show how students might apply the **6+1 Traits™ of Writing:** Ideas, Organization, Voice, Word Choice, Sentence Fluency, Conventions, and Presentation.

Invite students to comment on the essay using the criteria in the Writing Workshop rubrics on pages 90 and 92

A Ideas and Content

Thesis Statement This thesis sentence neatly sums up the personal qualities the writer touches upon in this paragraph.

B Organization

Comparisons The second paragraph explores the first contradiction shared by the writer and the cat. The reader will note that the essay has been organized by feature (contradictions), not by subject (writer and cat).

C Literary Elements

Point of View Although neither of these sentences contains a first-person personal pronoun, the essay as a whole is written in first person. Remind students that even in a personal essay, too many *I's* and *we's* may tire the reader.

D Voice

Tone This sentence, like others throughout this essay, helps to establish the essay's informal and conversational tone.

Writing Minilesson

Focus on Sentence Style and Variety
Like most descriptive essays, this one consists primarily of declarative sentences. The writer, however, makes sparing but effective use of exclamatory and interrogative sentences. Point out to students that the writer's use of various kinds of sentences helps to express the writer's personality or style.

Activity Have students locate the exclamatory and interrogative sentences in the essay. Then ask them to discuss how making other sentences exclamatory or interrogative may increase or detract from the essay's overall effectiveness.

WRITING WORKSHOP MODELS

Invite students to comment on the biographical sketch using the criteria in the Writing Workshop rubrics on pages 226 and 228.

A Ideas and Content

Introduction The writer gives just enough background information in the introduction to help readers feel the same surprise the writer felt upon hearing Alexa's revelations. Remind students that the information they include in their own introductions should further their narratives.

B Literary Elements

Puns The writer makes a pun on two meanings of the phrase *by accident:* (1) by chance and (2) from an unexpected event that resulted in loss or injury. Ask students to look for another pun in the essay. *(Possible answer: The title has both literal and figurative meanings.)*

C Sentence Style and Variety

Indirect Quotation Although this dialogue between the writer and Alexa is only implicit, it nonetheless flows smoothly and naturally. Have students rewrite the indirect quotations in the passage as direct quotations. Then have them discuss which form of dialogue is more effective.

D Ideas and Content

Details The writer's use of precise details, such as Alexa's being "diabetic" and needing a "shot of insulin," lends authenticity to the writing.

Teaching Support

Theme 2, pages 226–229

Narrative Writing: Biographical Sketch

Leaning on Each Other

A I've gone to school with Alexa Johnson for four years, but we never really knew each other that well. This year she was the best basketball player in school, boys and girls included. She was also really popular and was always busy after school with her friends, if she wasn't at basketball practice. I always hung out with my friends from drama class after school, and I didn't know many jocks. B But a few months ago my class went on a field trip to the beach, and by accident I got to know Alexa a lot better.

We were on a camping trip for two days with about twenty other kids. It started the morning of April 7, 2001, from the oceanside town of Martinsville, California. It was fun for a while, but after a few hours, I tripped on a rock and twisted my ankle. One of our teachers, Mr. Lewis, helped me put an ice pack on it. It felt better after a while, but still not great. I couldn't walk very fast, so when we hiked, I stayed at the end of the group. Mr. Lewis kept making everyone stop and wait for me, and I felt bad that I was holding everyone back.

Earlier Alexa had been at the front of the trail with her friends, but now all of a sudden she was walking back where I was. She was walking slowly C and looking around, so I said, "Hi." She asked me how my ankle was doing, and I said it was okay but still sore. She smiled and said that was too bad because I had a play to do soon. I couldn't believe she knew about my play, which was the next week. It turns out that she's really into drama. She wanted to take drama classes, but because she's so good at sports, she felt she couldn't switch and do something else. She is an only child and has lived with her mom since her parents were divorced. She said her mom really loves to watch her play. She felt like she would let her mom down if she quit.

While we were talking, the rest of the class had gotten way ahead of us. But it was okay because I wasn't by myself anymore. When Alexa noticed that everyone was gone, she asked me if I would do her a favor. D It turned out that the reason she had come to the back of the group was she was diabetic and had to give herself a shot of insulin. She wanted me to be her lookout and make sure nobody else saw. Mr. Lewis knew she was diabetic, but she hadn't told any of her friends. She didn't want them to think she was sick. We went behind a big rock, and she gave herself a shot while I watched to see if anybody was coming back to look for us. Then we kept on hiking. She helped me over rocks in the patch, and eventually we caught up with everyone else again.

I felt really special that Alexa trusted me with her secret. I promised her that I wouldn't tell, but I also said that I thought it wasn't such a big deal. Her friends would probably understand. They wouldn't think she was weird. She said she'd think about telling them. The next week Alexa came to see me in the play. She brought her mom. Afterwards I saw them both talking to Ms. Fuentes, the drama teacher.

I hope Alexa does drama next year. If she does, maybe I'll try out for intramural sports. I'd feel better about trying sports if she was around. On the beach trip, we really had to lean on each other. Since then, I think we're both a little stronger and more able to try new things.

Writing Minilesson

Focus on Voice The writer's engaging tone helps readers share the writer's evident interest in the subject. The writer engages the reader with wit and surprise and shows interest through revelatory details such as Alexa's relationship with her mother.

Activity Have students exchange drafts of their own biographical sketches with a partner and have partners check for places in the drafts where their interest increased or flagged. Ask the partners to write down questions as they read. Answers to those questions may make the narrative more interesting.

Theme 3, pages 324–327

Expository Writing: Writing an Evaluation

Reasons to Run

In Tony Cade Bambara's short story "Raymond's Run," Squeaky tells the readers, "I run. That is what I am all about." She decided to enter the May Day race and ended up the winner in the fifty-yard dash. This year I also made a decision about running. I am glad to say that I joined the track team at Du Sable Middle School.

How do I know that I made the right decision? I listed three criteria, from least important to most important, and jotted them down as questions. **A** Did becoming a member of the track team give me a sense of pride? Did I improve my physical fitness? Do I find running enjoyable? Here are my answers.

B First, I am proud of my performance at track meets. Unlike Squeaky, I'm not a star or a champion. In "Raymond's Run," she said,"I always win cause I'm the best." I know I am not the fastest runner. Although I rarely win, competing in races still fills me with pride. I usually place second or third in races. For me, doing my best is just as good as being the best.

Second, joining the track team has made me more physically fit. I used to hate running laps and doing crunches. After a while, though, I started to see the results of doing my exercises. When I found my strength and speed improving, I was really encouraged. Reading about Squeaky taught me the value of training for a race. In "Raymond's Run," she said, "Now some people like to act like things come easy to them, won't let on that they practice. Not me. I'll high-prance down 34th Street like a rodeo pony to keep my knees strong." She also stated, "And you can see me any time of day practicing running. I never walk if I can trot." My decision to join the track team has made me want to work to become an athlete in top condition.

C Above all, I know I made a wise decision by joining the track team because I now enjoy running more than I ever could have imagined. I can't believe how happy I am. Just like Squeaky, whenever I am running fast, I feel as though I am flying. In "Raymond's Run," Squeaky described this sensation so vividly. As she started the May Day race, she said, "I am off and weightless again, flying past the other runners, my arms pumping up and down and the whole world is quiet except for the crunch as I zoom over the gravel in the track."

D After I made the decision to join the track team, I was filled with doubts. I was afraid my pride would be hurt if I didn't come in first place. I was worried that I'd hate the practices. I thought competition might spoil the fun; however, my fears faded away once the practice and track meets began in earnest. I took pride in my performance, regardless of the outcome of each race. I didn't mind the practice because I became so physically fit. Most important, I discovered that running was a great joy.

WRITING WORKSHOP MODELS

Invite students to comment on the essay by using the criteria in the Writing Workshop rubrics on pages 324 and 326.

A Sentence Style and Variety

Parallelism The sentences listing the writer's three criteria are parallel in structure. Point this out to students and then ask them to describe ways in which the sentences are parallel. *(Possible answers: the sentences are all questions, the questions are all rhetorical, the questions all begin with a form of the verb* do*)*

B Conventions

Paragraphing The writer devotes a single paragraph to each of the three criteria listed in the second paragraph. Students should check their own essays to be sure that new paragraphs begin whenever a new criterion is considered.

C Organization

Transitions The transition in this sentence tells the reader that a new idea has begun and that this idea is more important than the previous ideas. Ask students to suggest other transitions that would work in place of "above all." *(Possible answers: most important, third, last)*

D Voice

Risk-taking In the conclusion, the writer admits having doubts and bravely lists them. Encourage students to take similar risks in their own evaluative essays.

Writing Minilesson

Focus on Ideas and Content

Throughout this essay, the writer uses Tony Cade Bambara's short story "Raymond's Run" as a basis for judgment. For example, the writer includes relevant quotations from the short story to elaborate on how each criterion was met. Explain to students, however, that it is not always necessary or desirable to use quotations. Often a paraphrase of an idea works just as well.

Activity Have students paraphrase each quotation in the model essay and share their paraphrases with partners. Have partners discuss whether the ideas that were borrowed from "Raymond's Run" work better as paraphrases or as quotations.

Invite students to comment on the trickster tale using the criteria in the Writing Workshop rubrics on pages 426 and 428.

A Literary Elements

Setting The trickster tale opens with a clear, concise description of the setting—the time and place of the story. Encourage students to discuss how the first sentence sets the stage for the events that will occur in the tale.

B Sentence Style and Variety

Parallelism These two sentences, having the same grammatical form and some of the same words, add a distinctive rhythm to the tale. Read the sentences aloud and have students listen to the repetition and the sound of the word patterns. Ask students if they can find other kinds of repetition in the paragraph. *(Possible answer: the repeated verb "buzzed")*

C Conventions

Punctuation Correctly punctuated lines of dialogue help readers understand what a character is saying. The character's spoken words are enclosed in quotation marks and the speaker tag is set off with a comma. Have students proofread the dialogue in their own trickster tales for errors in punctuation.

Teaching Support

Theme 4, pages 426–429

Narrative Writing: Trickster Tale

Mosquito and Trader

A Some three hundred years ago, Mosquito lived in the murky swamps along the Gambia River in West Africa. Though she was a tiny, delicate creature, she was clever and kind. Mosquito was a friend to all the surrounding villagers, and they knew they could always depend on her.

One day, as Mosquito was flying high above the Gambia River, she observed a horrible scene. Trader had attacked a small village and kidnapped many of its people. Trader made the captured villagers form a line and chained their ankles so they wouldn't escape. Then Trader forced the villagers to march for miles on a rugged, narrow trail along the banks of the Gambia River. When the exhausted people finally reached the Atlantic Ocean, Trader loaded them on a ship headed to the distant shores of the Caribbean, where they would be bought and sold again. The merchant of the ship gave Trader bags bulging with gold and silver coins in exchange for the villagers. Trader's greedy eyes bulged. "I will become richer than a king," said Trader, who loved money more than anything else in the world. "Tomorrow, with the help of my troops, I'll ambush the largest village along the Gambia."

B Never before had Mosquito witnessed such an evil deed. Never before had Mosquito overheard such a wicked plan. "I must stop this wicked person from capturing any more villagers and selling them into slavery," Mosquito said. She buzzed and buzzed around her swamp until she thought of a scheme.

She flew to the largest village along the Gambia River. She told the leader there, "Beware! Trader is gathering his troops to raid this place and to kidnap the men, women, and children. Flee as fast as you can! Find a place in the jungle where you will be safe. I am on my way to tell Trader that you and the other villagers are hiding in a cave."

C The leader replied, "Thank you for your warning, Mosquito." At night all the people crept quietly into the lush green jungle. All the creatures in the jungle helped the villagers find hiding spots. That same evening Mosquito flew into Trader's hut. Trader was asleep on his cot, dreaming about money. Suddenly, Mosquito interrupted his dream. "Say, Trader, would you like to make some more money?" whispered a voice in the dark. Trader woke with a start. "Lie still!" warned the voice. "Just listen. You know the cave by the river?" Trader nodded as his eyes darted about. "It's full of passages," the voice hummed. "Villagers hide there. You will find more people in those caves than in the village you are planning to ambush tomorrow. A great fortune awaits you if you capture the people in the cave."

Trader's greedy eyes bulged. His love for money made him easy to fool. He believed every word that Mosquito told him. Then Trader fell back asleep and dreamed of all the money he could gain from his evil business.

The next morning was hot and humid. Trader led his troops along the Gambia River. As they drew nearer to the cave, Trader said to his troops, "Do you smell the campfire smoke? People probably stopped here on their way to the cave." Feeling confident, Trader and his troops trudged onward until they finally reached the great cave by the river.

Once inside the cave, Trader and his troops lit torches and began their search for the villagers.

Writing Minilesson

Focus on Organization

Point out to students that the incidents described in "Mosquito and Trader" are arranged in *sequence*. The chain of events is logically connected and clearly organized. The tale closes with a sense of resolution, tying up loose ends. The reader is left with something to think about.

Activity Have students create a flowchart listing the sequence of events in "Mosquito and Trader." When students retell the trickster tale orally, they should use their flowcharts as a guide.

D The cave was a giant maze, full of twisting passages. Mosquito, flying high above, observed the entire scene. She heard the voices of Trader and his troops echoing from the entrance to the cave. They were screaming, "Help! Help! We are lost!" Then the voices became fainter and fainter until Mosquito could no longer hear them.

Later that night, the villagers who had escaped Trader and his troops left their hiding places in the jungle and gathered together. They celebrated their freedom and praised Mosquito for her cleverness. As they joined hands and formed a circle, the villagers sang, "Mosquito is the greatest trickster! Mosquito is the greatest trickster!"

WRITING WORKSHOP MODELS

D Word Choice

Sensory Details Well-chosen sensory details, such as the ones in this sentence, help readers picture the scene. Have students identify other words and phrases in this paragraph that vividly describe the sights and sounds. *(Possible answers: "flying high above," "his troops echoing from the entrance to the cave," "the voices became fainter and fainter")*

Invite students to comment on the speech using the criteria in the Writing Workshop rubrics on pages 540 and 542.

A Literary Elements

Metaphors The writer begins the speech with a metaphor—a figure of speech comparing unlike things—to warn readers of the need to reduce garbage. Have students discuss the following: Is the imagery of the metaphor striking? Does the metaphor have a persuasive effect?

B Organization

Logical Sequence The writer presents an argument that moves logically from problems to solutions. Encourage students to organize their own speeches in problem-solution order and remind them that ending a speech with solutions helps persuade listeners that the solutions are sound.

C Voice

Awareness of Audience and Purpose In this paragraph, the writer addresses the audience in the second person for a specific purpose. Have students identify the audience and state the purpose of this paragraph.

D Organization

Transition Sentences This sentence makes a clear transition from the discussion of one type of recycling to another. Have students point to other transition sentences in the speech.

Teaching Support

Theme 5, pages 540–543

Persuasive Writing: Speech

Garbage Is Everywhere

A Our planet is turning into one big garbage dump. Of course, it's a big planet, but if we don't do something now about the amount of garbage we produce, in the future there won't be much of a planet left for us or for our kids. Recycling is one very important way that we kids can help create less garbage.

B There are several reasons why it's important to reduce the amount of garbage we produce. First of all, garbage in landfills takes a very long time to decompose. We fill up landfills faster than the garbage gets absorbed into the earth, so we are running out of room. Several years ago a barge full of garbage floated up and down the Atlantic coast, looking for a place to dump its cargo. But no state would take it. They all had too much garbage already.

An alternative to dumping trash in big piles is to burn it. But garbage that is burned in incinerators causes air pollution. We already have a severe air pollution problem due to the number of cars on the planet. We don't need to be making more pollution! This is the second reason we should try to reduce waste. The third reason is very simple. Garbage is ugly and smells bad. This seems silly, but when you are walking in a park and see litter all over the ground or have to hold your breath when you drive past a landfill (the way people on Staten Island do when they pass the gigantic Fresh Kills landfill) you realize that it is not so silly after all.

How can we help solve this problem? The most important thing you can do is recycle and make sure everybody else in your family does too.

C Recycling basically means re-using. You can recycle many kinds of things. An aluminum soda can, for example, can be melted down at a recycling plant and re-used to make a new can. You can also recycle glass, newspapers, and lots of kinds of plastic. Most cities have programs set up that help make recycling easy. Some have curbside recycling. You put your bottles and newspapers out on the curb once a week in a special bin, and a truck comes by and picks them up. Other cities have "blue bag" recycling. With this system, you put your recyclables in a blue plastic bag and put it in the dumpster with the rest of your garbage. Everything is picked up and sorted out later on.

D This kind of home recycling is the most obvious kind, but there are other things you can do too. One good way to cut down on garbage is to re-use things yourself. Some stores sell food and other things, like shampoo, in bulk. If you bring your own container, you will save some plastic. In addition, bulk items are usually less expensive.

In short, recycling is at your fingertips. Garbage is a real problem, and it surely won't go away by itself. If you want the planet to be healthy and beautiful when you grow up and stay that way for your kids and other people in the future, it's up to you to do something about it now. Recycling is easy. It's good for you, and it's good for the Earth. There's no good reason why you can't start today.

Writing Minilesson

Focus on Ideas and Content The persuasive effect of the speech is due in large part to the writer's frequent use of elaboration—the addition of relevant and compelling information. To persuade listeners that recycling is important, the writer bolsters the arguments of the speech with helpful details, examples, facts, and anecdotes.

Activity Have students review the drafts of their own speeches to see whether they have included enough relevant information to persuade their listeners that their arguments are valid. Have them revise their drafts to include relevant, accurate, and up-to-date information wherever their speeches are not fully elaborated.

Theme 6, pages 650–653

Technical Writing: Bylaws of an Organization

Student Council Bylaws

PREAMBLE

We the students of Du Sable Middle School, in order to form a more perfect school environment, achieve good school relations, promote school spirit, and encourage excellence in the classroom and in the community, do establish these Bylaws for the Student Council of Du Sable Middle School.

ARTICLE I NAME

The name of the organization will be the Du Sable Middle School Student Council.

ARTICLE II GENERAL MEMBERSHIP

Section 1. *Homeroom Representatives*
Students in the sixth, seventh, or eighth grade will serve on the Student Council. Each homeroom will have two Student Council representatives.

Section 2. *Nomination and Election*
Elections for membership in the Student Council take place each fall during the third week of school. All students running for Student Council must be approved by the principal.

2.1 Each student who wishes to be a homeroom representative must collect at least ten signatures from students in his or her homeroom and at least one signature from a teacher familiar with his or her work.

2.2 The names of all nominees for homeroom representative will appear on a ballot for each homeroom. Students in each homeroom will vote by secret ballot. The two nominees receiving the highest number of votes will become homeroom representatives.

Section 3. *Expectations and Duties*
Homeroom representatives are expected to be good citizens of the school, hard working and dedicated students, and leaders in encouraging school spirit and good relationships between students, teachers, the administration, and the community. Members of the Student Council are also expected to attend meetings and follow the rules of the Student Council.

ARTICLE III OFFICERS

The officers of the Student Council will include the President, Vice President, Secretary, and Treasurer.

Section 1. *Nomination and Election*
Elections of Student Council officers will take place each fall during the third week of school. All students running for office on the Student Council must be approved by the school principal.

1.1 Each student running for Student Council President or Vice President must collect at least twenty signatures from students in the school and signatures from at least two teachers who are familiar with his or her work.

1.2 Each student running for Student Council Secretary or Treasurer must collect at least fifteen signatures from students in the school and signatures from at least two teachers who are familiar with his or her work. For students running for Secretary, one of those teachers must be a language arts teacher. For students running for Treasurer, at least one of those teachers must be a math teacher.

1.3 Students running for the positions of President, Vice President, Secretary, or Treasurer may only run for one office during each election. Any student who tries to run for more than one office will be disqualified and will lose his or her nomination.

1.4 All students running for the positions of President, Vice President, Secretary, or

WRITING WORKSHOP MODELS

Invite students to comment using the criteria in the Writing Workshop rubrics on pages 650 and 652.

A Literary Elements

Allusion The preamble of the bylaws contains an allusion—an indirect reference to a well-known person, event, or text. In phrases such as "we the" and "in order to form a more perfect," the preamble of the bylaws echoes the Preamble of the U. S. Constitution. Suggest to students that this allusion lends a seriousness of purpose to the bylaws.

B Organization

Awareness of Audience and Purpose
The writer has broken down the bylaws into articles, sections, and subsections for a specific audience and purpose. Ask students to identify the audience and to suggest how the organization of the bylaws might serve that audience. *(Possible answer: audience: any student who is or wishes to become a member of the student council or who wishes to account for the council's actions; purpose: to make citing specific bylaws easier)*

C Conventions

Superlative Adjectives In this sentence, the writer correctly uses a superlative adjective *(most)*—an adjective comparing more than two things. Point out to students that using the comparative degree here *(more)* would show a lack of foresight because elections for an office may not always be limited to two candidates.

D Word Choice

Precise Language The writer uses unambiguous language such as "deciding vote" and "equally divided." Tell students that the bylaws' precise language helps to ensure that the student council will be able to follow its bylaws without dispute. Have them identify other instances of precise language in the bylaws. *(Possible answers: "each student," "all nominees," "must give a speech")*

Treasurer must give a speech to the student body explaining why they are running for office and what they will do to help the Student Council.

C **1.5** The student who receives the most votes for President, Vice President, Secretary, or Treasurer is elected to that position. He or she will serve in that position for the rest of the school year.

Section 2. *Officers' Duties and Responsibilities*

D **2.1** *President* The President will manage discussion at meetings of the Council, lead the Student Council Executive Board, and cast the deciding vote on a question when the votes of the Council are equally divided.

2.2 *Vice-President* The Vice President will manage discussion at meetings of the Council when the President is absent, serve as a member of the Student Council Executive Board, take the roll at meetings, and send written warnings to members who do not observe the attendance policy.

2.3 *Secretary* The Secretary will take notes, or minutes, at all Council meetings; serve as a member of the Student Council Executive Board; write letters, memos and other communications for the Council; and give the school administration information about Council activities.

2.4 *Treasurer* The Treasurer will keep records of how much money the Student Council collects and how that money is spent, make regular reports at each Student Council meeting, serve as a member of the Student Council Executive Board, and manage the school store and all Student Council fund-raising events.

ARTICLE IV MEETINGS

Section 1. *Place and Time* The Student Council will meet in room 208 according to the following schedule:

1.1 The first meeting of the Student Council will be held each fall in the week after the election.

1.2 The Student Council will meet after school on the first Tuesday of each month that school is in session. More meetings may be scheduled by the Executive Board if necessary due to Student Council activities.

Section 2. *Attendance Policy* All members of the Student Council must follow the rules for attendance:

2.1 Members must attend all meetings of the Student Council.

2.2 If a student must miss a meeting for medical reasons, he or she may bring a note from a doctor or the school nurse to the following meeting. If the student is able to provide a note, the absence will be excused.

2.3 Any student with more than two unexcused absences or more than three excused absences may be asked to leave the Student Council.

ARTICLE V COMMITTEES

Section 1. *Selection of Committees* There will be two standing committees, the School Activities Committee and Community Service Committee, whose members will be appointed by the Student Council. Other committees may be appointed as necessary.

Section 2. *School Activities Committee* The School Activities Committee will perform the following duties:

2.1 Organize Student Council fund-raisers, such as the October bake sale and the April car wash

Teaching Support

Writing Minilesson

Focus on Conventions The paragraphing and punctuation conventions of bylaws are different from those of other types of writing. Articles, sections, and subsections must be clearly and consistently labeled and set apart for ease of reference. Special punctuation, such as periods after section heads, may be necessary too.

Activity Have students write three amendments to the Student Council Bylaws, following the paragraphing and punctuation conventions established in the document. Have students ask their peers to check the amendments for paragraphing or punctuation errors.

2.2 Represent the Student Council at school activities, including the Thanksgiving Float Competition, School Spirit Pep Rallies, the Spring Dance, and other student activities during the school year

Section 3. *Community Service Committee*
The Community Service Committee will perform the following duties:

3.1 Organize an annual walk for a worthy cause, such as curing a disease

3.2 Organize student volunteers at the Du Sable Township Animal Shelter

3.3 Organize the annual Thanksgiving dinner for the homeless

ARTICLE VI AMENDMENTS
Amendments to the Student Council Bylaws must be presented in written form at a Student Council meeting. If the suggested amendment is approved by two-thirds of the Council members, that amendment will become a part of the Student Council Bylaws.

WRITING WORKSHOP MODELS R127

Invite students to comment on the report using the criteria in The Writing Workshop rubrics on pages 780 and 778.

A Ideas and Content

Thesis Statement The report includes a focused thesis statement. Tell students that a good thesis statement makes clear what ideas the writer will develop in the rest of a report or essay. Then ask students to use the thesis statement to try to determine what the report will demonstrate.
(Possible answer: The report will demonstrate the importance of Rosie the Riveter's part in the war effort.)

B Conventions

Citing Sources The writer avoids plagiarism by correctly citing the source for this idea both here and in the works-cited list at the end of the report. Plagiarism is the presentation of someone else's idea as one's own. Encourage students to review correct citation styles before drafting their own reports.

Teaching Support

Theme 7, pages 778–781

Expository Writing: Historical Research Report

Rosie the Riveter

During World War II, Rosie the Riveter was one of the most famous women in the United States. Pictures of her were everywhere: a typical young American woman, dressed in work clothes with a wrench or a rivet gun in her hand. The name "Rosie" may have come from Rosie Bonavita, part of a two-woman crew that set more than three thousand rivets in a record six hours (Our 218). But Rosie was more than a real person. She was a symbol of all the women who went to work in factories during the war. Even though she wasn't real, Rosie the Riveter played an important part in the war effort by being a role model for other women, encouraging them to go out and work at jobs they'd never done before. **A**

During World War II, millions of men left their jobs to enter the armed forces. Somebody had to fill their jobs to keep the country going. There were normal peacetime jobs to be done, like driving buses and running trains. And there were also special wartime jobs to do, like building bombers or making ammunition in the factories. Women had worked in factories before in our nation's history, but their jobs were usually concentrated in certain areas, such as the garment industry (Appleby et al. 308–309). In the 1940s, there was still a clear division between "men's jobs" and "women's jobs." That's where Rosie came in. **B**

Rosie the Riveter was created by a team of advertisement designers working in the Office of War Information. The OWI, a government agency, encouraged all citizens to contribute to the war effort. This organization was dedicated to explaining why America was in the war and what ordinary people could do to help their country win (War). The OWI commissioned famous American painters to design posters and advertisements featuring "Rosie," a typical American woman doing her part to help her country. The main point of the posters was to convince people that women could, and should, go outside their traditional roles to help in the war effort.

The advertising worked, as the graph here shows.

Women in the Iron and Steel Workforce

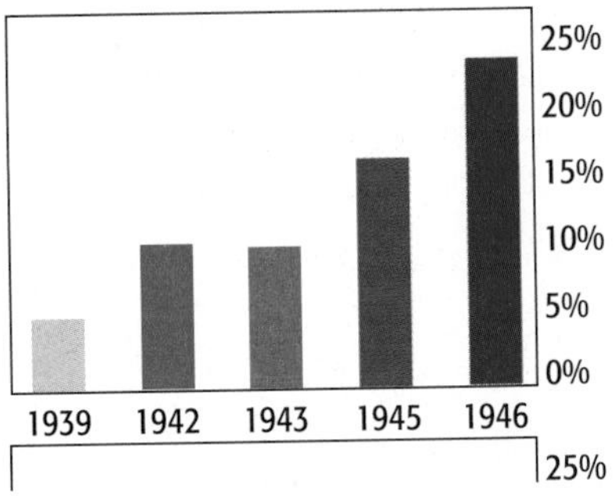

During the war, more than six million women went to work in jobs that had traditionally been done by men. Women learned many new skills, such as welding, hammering, and of course, riveting. Being part of the work force during the war changed many women's lives. **C** Jane Ward Mayta says, "I learned a lot in those years. . . . I learned to look for a job. I learned to get along with and mingle with people from totally different backgrounds. We were all in little pockets before then" (Wise and Wise 12).

In 1945 the war ended. Of course, when men returned from the war, they expected their jobs back. Many women had to leave their factory jobs. But the experience of working during the war inspired women to look for new challenges and

opportunities in the years that followed. Women became more independent and sure of their own skills. They also became used to making more money. As the Web page for the American Airpower Heritage Museum (AAHM) says, "Lasting social changes were brought about by the fact that women began working outside the home."

D Today, many years later, some of the social changes inspired by Rosie the Riveter are not unusual to us. It is normal to assume that women and men should be paid the same if they do the same work. And the idea that a woman shouldn't work in a particular field simply because she's a woman is no longer acceptable. We have Rosie the Riveter to thank for some of these changes. She was a real inspiration for generations of women. D

Works Cited

Appleby, Joyce, et al. *The American Journey*. New York: Glencoe/McGraw-Hill, 1998.

Our Glorious Century: Key Events, Pictures, Places, Personalities, Milestones, Memories, Lifestyles, Traditions, Insights. New York: Reader's Digest, 1995.

"Rosie the Riveter: Women Join the Industrial Workforce." 4 Dec. 1999 American Airpower Heritage Museum. 1 Feb. 2001 <http://www.airpowermuseum.org/ trrosier.html>.

United States. Dept. of Labor. *Women in Factories.* Estimated number of women production workers employed in manufacturing industries Oct. 1939-May 1947. Washington: GPO, 1947.

War Aims Through Art: The U.S. Office of War Information. Office of Exhibits Central, Smithsonian Institution. 22 Jan. 2001 <http://www.americanhistory.si.edu/victory/victory5.htm>.

Wise, Nancy Baker, and Christy Wise. *A Mouthful of Rivets: Women at Work in World War II.* San Francisco: Jossey-Bass, 1994.

WRITING WORKSHOP MODELS

C Ideas and Content

Accurate Details The writer supports the topic sentence of this paragraph on page R128 ("The advertising worked . . .") with verifiable facts. Have students point out other verifiable facts presented in the report.

(Possible answers: "During World War II, millions of men left their jobs to enter the armed forces"; "In 1945 the war ended")

D Organization

Conclusion The conclusion extends the chronological sequence of the report to the present day. Even so, the conclusion keeps its focus on themes introduced in the first paragraph (Rosie as inspiration to women and as force for social change). Have students compare the final paragraphs of their reports with their introductions to see that their reports maintain focus.

Writing Minilesson

Focus on Publishing/Presenting

Among the many forms of elaboration presented in the report, the writer includes a bar graph. Graphs present information in visual form. Point out to students that this graph allows the writer to avoid having to include a string of repetitive sentences containing many numbers.

Activity Have students discuss other ways of visually presenting the information shown in the bar graph (in a line graph, for example). Then, to illustrate the effectiveness of graphs at presenting statistical information, have students write a paragraph that presents the same information provided in the bar graph.

Invite students to comment on the story using the criteria in the Writing Workshop rubrics on pages 874 and 876.

A Literary Elements

Mood The mood of this story is quickly established as suspenseful. Have students discuss what makes the introduction suspenseful. *(Possible answer: descriptive words and phrases such as "frozen in our beds" and "too scared to move.")*

B Ideas and Content

Background Information The writer provides necessary background information in this paragraph. Without this information, the solution to the mystery would seem less credible. Ask students to identify this information. *(Answer: the day was "windy," and there were car dealerships nearby)*

C Sentence Style and Variety

Sentence Rhythm The sentences in this paragraph flow smoothly from one to another. Have students discuss the rhythm of the sentences.

D Organization

Sequence of Events The writer presents most of the events of this narrative in chronological order. Suggest to students that chronological order can be an effective narrative tool for creating suspense.

Teaching Support

Theme 8, pages 874–877

Narrative Writing: Mystery Story

The Ghost at the Window

A My little sister and I were frozen in our beds, too scared to move. The ghost flashed by our window one more time. We looked at each other and we knew it wasn't going to leave us alone. We had to either confront it or run away. Either way, we were going to have to get out of bed. I was a very frightened eight-year-old.

B It had been a cold, windy day, but it was snug and warm indoors. Our beds faced each other so that we slept toe to toe under the long window on the east wall of the room. We could hear traffic noises from the freeway just a block away, but we were used to them. We lived near the university district, which had a lot of traffic even late at night. Besides the university, there were lots of convenience stores and restaurants, plus many larger businesses like car dealerships and mattress stores.

We usually went to bed at eight o'clock. Because we shared a room and liked to chat, it was hard to go right to sleep. That night we had been telling each other scary stories. That's when we saw the ghost.

A strange white shape appeared and then vanished outside our window. We both saw it at the same time and screamed. Then we waited to see what would happen. It disappeared, but then came back a few moments later. The window rattled, but the white light just hung there for a second and then went away again. We lay in bed and watched, terrified. "It's so spooky," I told my sister.

C After a while, we realized we had to do something. We got on top of the covers and counted to three. On three we both jumped towards the window, to see if we could scare the ghost away. Right when we got there, the ghost appeared again. We screamed again and ran out of the room. We ran downstairs to the kitchen. Our parents were still awake. "Mom and Dad, we just saw a ghost!" We both talked at once, trying to explain what we had seen. Our parents made us slow down and explain it one bit at a time.

D When we were done they looked at us and smiled. They said they would go upstairs and take a look at this ghost. While they went upstairs, my sister and I stayed in the kitchen where it was safe.

Our parents came back a minute later. They were laughing. They sat down and asked if we remembered the big search lights we had seen outside the car dealership that was only a few blocks away. The car dealer sometimes used them at night when he was having a sale. The lights were so bright that they shone for miles and miles, and they waved back and forth in the sky. That night they just happened to be pointed right at our house.

I felt really dumb. "But what about the rattling window?" I asked.

"It's just the wind," said my father.

My sister and I went back upstairs. When we crawled into our beds, the light flashed past the window again, and the glass rattled a little bit. We looked at each other and reminded ourselves that it was definitely not a ghost. We weren't going to tell each other scary stories at bedtime for a while!

Writing Minilesson

Focus on Word Choice The writer's use of vivid verbs and adjectives such as "frozen," "flickered," "spooky," and "snug" not only helps to establish a mood but supplies the reader with the necessary sensory detail to "see" the events of the narrative.

Activity Have students look over the drafts of their own mysteries for opportunities to add vivid verbs and adjectives. Encourage them to make a two-column chart. In the first column, students should list lackluster verbs and adjectives they find in their stories; in the second column, vivid substitutes for the lackluster words.

Glossary

This glossary lists the vocabulary words found in the selections in this book. The definition given is for the word as it is used in the selection; you may wish to consult a dictionary for other meanings of these words. The key below is a guide to the pronunciation symbols used in each entry.

a	at	**ō**	hope	**ng**	sing
ā	ape	**ô**	fork, all	**th**	thin
ä	father	**oo**	wood, put	**th** (underlined)	this
e	end	**o͞o**	fool	**zh**	treasure
ē	me	**oi**	oil	**ə**	ago, taken, pencil, lemon, circus
i	it	**ou**	out	**′**	indicates primary stress
ī	ice	**u**	up	**ʹ**	indicates secondary stress
o	hot	**ū**	use		

A

abyss (ə bisʹ) *n.* an extremely deep hole; p. 411

acute (ə kūt′) *adj.* sharp and strong or intense; p. 835

adept (ə dept′) *adj.* highly skilled; masterful; p. 243

adolescence (adʹ əl es′ əns) *n.* the period or process of growing from youth to adulthood; teenage years; p. 624

advocate (ad′ və kit) *n.* one who publicly supports or urges; p. 272

aggravating (ag′ rə vāt ing) *adj.* irritating; annoying; p. 718

aggression (ə gresh′ ən) *n.* the habit or practice of launching attacks; p. 21

aghast (ə gast′) *adj.* filled with fear or horror; p. 276

agonize (ag′ ə nīzʹ) *v.* to suffer greatly; struggle painfully; p. 625

alight (ə līt′) *v.* to come down after flight; land; p. 413

aloof (ə lo͞of′) *adj.* emotionally distant; uninvolved; standoffish; p. 823

alternative (ôl tur′ nə tiv) *n.* another choice; p. 106

amiable (ā′ mē ə bəl) *adj.* friendly, good-natured; p. 801

anguish (ang′ gwish) *n.* extreme suffering; p. 594

angular (ang′ gyə lər) *adj.* bony and lean; p. 51

anomalous (ə nom′ ə ləs) *adj.* not following the usual or regular; abnormal; p. 192

anonymous (ə non′ ə məs) *adj.* having no known name or origin; lacking qualities that make one different; p. 40

appalled (ə pôld′) *adj.* shocked; horrified; p. 148

apparition (apʹ ə rish′ ən) *n.* ghostly vision; p. 817

apprehension (apʹ ri hen′ shən) *n.* fear of what may happen; dread; p. 749

aromatic (ar′ ə matʹ ik) *adj.* having a pleasant smell or special, delicate flavor; p. 242

arresting (ə res′ ting) *adj.* demanding the attention; striking; p. 871

GLOSSARY R131

arrogant (ar′ ə gənt) *adj.* full of self-importance; too proud; p. 147
askew (ə skū′) *adv.* in a twisted way; crookedly; p. 439
audacity (ô das′ ə tē) *n.* reckless boldness; daring; p. 840
awed (ôd) *adj.* filled with wonder combined with respect; p. 84

B

ban (ban) *v.* to forbid; outlaw; prohibit; p. 677
banish (ban′ ish) *v.* to force a person to leave a country or community; p. 259
baptism (bap′ tiz′ əm) *n.* a ceremony in which a person is cleansed of sin and becomes a member of a Christian religion; p. 71
barren (bar′ ən) *adj.* bare; empty; dull or uninteresting; p. 164
barter (bär′ tər) *v.* to trade goods for goods; p. 274
bedraggled (bi drag′ əld) *adj.* wet, dirty, and rumpled; untidy; p. 666
benediction (ben′ ə dik′ shən) *n.* a divine blessing or the condition of being blessed; p. 440
benevolence (bə nev′ ə ləns) *n.* kindliness; generosity; p. 271
bewilderment (bi wil′ dər mənt) *n.* deep confusion; p. 262
bland (bland) *adj.* dull and uninteresting; p. 808
bleak (blēk) *adj.* cheerless; depressing; p. 488
blithely (blīth′ lē) *adv.* in a lighthearted way; cheerfully; p. 20
bravado (brə vä′ dō) *n.* a false show of bravery; pretended courage; p. 152
brazenly (brā′ zən lē) *adv.* in a boldly rude manner; p. 21

C

cajole (kə jōl′) *v.* to persuade, especially by soothing words; coax; p. 486
capitulate (kə pich′ ə lāt′) *v.* to stop resisting; surrender; p. 666
careening (kä rēn′ ing) *adj.* tilting or swaying while moving, as if out of control; p. 861
catastrophic (kat′ əs trof′ ik) *adj.* disastrous; p. 104
chasm (kaz′ əm) *n.* a deep hole or crack, as in the earth's surface; p. 807
chronic (kron′ ik) *adj.* lasting a long time or returning repeatedly; p. 284
collective (kə lek′ tiv) *adj.* having to do with a group of persons or things; common; shared; p. 205
commence (kə mens′) *v.* to begin; start; p. 9
commend (kə mend′) *v.* to express approval of; p. 262
communion (kə mūn′ yən) *n.* closeness to, and sympathy with, another through sharing feelings or thoughts; p. 52
compelling (kəm pel′ ing) *adj.* impressive and forceful; p. 630
competently (kom′ pət ənt lē) *adv.* capably; p. 202
complex (kom′ pleks) *n.* an exaggerated concern or fear; an overwhelming idea or feeling; p. 284
comply (kəm plī′) *v.* to obey or go along with a request; p. 343
comprehend (kom′ pri hend′) *v.* to grasp mentally; understand fully; p. 596
conceive (kən sēv′) *v.* to form; imagine; p. 473
concoct (kon kokt′) *v.* to make or put together, using skill and intelligence; p. 53
conscientious (kon′ shē en′ shəs) *adj.* guided by one's conscience; showing careful attention to what is right and wrong; p. 818
consecrate (kon′ sə krāt′) *v.* to make, declare, or honor as holy; p. 474
console (kən sōl′) *v.* to comfort or cheer someone who is sad or disappointed; p. 863
conspicuous (kən spik′ ū əs) *adj.* easily seen; apparent; p. 701
conspiratorial (kən spir′ ə tôr′ ē əl) *adj.* joining or acting together, especially to carry out some secret or evil deed or for a hidden or illegal purpose; p. 287
constitute (kon′ stə to͞ot′) *v.* to form; make up; compose; p. 625

R132 GLOSSARY

convey (kən vā′) *v.* to express; communicate; p. 30
corroded (kə rōd′ əd) *adj.* eaten away by degrees, by gnawing or chemical action; p. 245
covet (kuv′ it) *v.* to desire strongly; wish for longingly; p. 513
cower (kou′ ər) *v.* to shrink away as in fear or shame; p. 131
craggy (krag′ ē) *adj.* rugged, uneven, and worn; p. 285
crevice (krev′ is) *n.* a narrow crack; p. 574
cringe (krinj) *v.* to draw back, as from fear or dislike; p. 217
crouch (krouch) *v.* to stoop or bend, especially with knees bent; p. 558
crux (kruks) *n.* the most important point or part; p. 41
curt (kurt) *adj.* so brief or short as to seem rude; p. 242

D

decree (di krē′) *v.* to set forth an official rule, order, or decision; dictate; p. 259
decry (di krī′) *v.* to criticize openly; p. 343
default (di fôlt′) *v.* to fail to do as required; p. 495
dejected (di jek′ tid) *adj.* sad; depressed; in low spirits; p. 793
demean (di mēn′) *v.* to degrade; disgrace; p. 664
desolate (des′ ə lit) *adj.* without comfort; p. 495
detract (di trakt′) *v.* to take something away; lessen; p. 474
diligence (dil′ ə jəns) *n.* great attention, care, and effort; p. 513
discern (di surn′) *v.* to detect or recognize; identify; p. 21
disclose (dis klōz′) *v.* to make known; reveal; p. 486
discord (dis′ kôrd) *n.* disagreement; conflict; p. 498
discrimination (dis krim′ ə nā′ shən) *n.* unfair treatment, especially as a result of policies directed against minority groups; p. 495
disembark (dis′ im bärk′) *v.* to get off of a train, airplane, ship, or other vehicle; p. 644
disgruntled (dis grunt′ əld) *adj.* displeased; p. 744
disheveled (di shev′ əld) *adj.* untidy or rumpled; p. 483
disperse (dis purs′) *v.* to go off in different directions; p. 592
distinct (dis tingkt′) *adj.* clearly heard, seen, or felt; p. 174
diverse (di vurs′) *adj.* noticeably different; varied; p. 630
diversion (di vur′ zhən) *n.* something that draws the attention away; distraction; p. 148
docile (dos′ əl) *adj.* easily managed, trained, or taught; p. 103
doggedly (dô′ gid lē) *adv.* stubbornly; firmly; p. 514
dominant (dom′ ə nənt) *adj.* having the greatest power or force; controlling; p. 817
dote (dōt) *v.* to show extreme affection; p. 341
drone (drōn) *v.* to talk in a dull, monotonous tone or make a steady, low, humming sound; p. 170
dry (drī) *adj.* not interesting; dull; boring; p. 608
dumbfounded (dum′ found′ əd) *adj.* made speechless with amazement; astonished; p. 400

E

eerie (ēr′ ē) *adj.* weird, especially in a frightening way; p. 10
elaborate (i lab′ ər it) *adj.* complicated and fancy; p. 240
eloquence (el′ ə kwəns) *n.* speech or writing that is expressive, effective, and stirring; p. 485
embodiment (em bod′ ē mənt) *n.* the bodily form of an idea or quality; visible form; p. 664
emit (i mit′) *v.* to utter; send forth, or give out, as a sound; p. 341
emphatically (em fat′ i kəl ē) *adv.* very definitely; clearly; p. 643
emulate (em′ yə lāt′) *v.* to imitate; p. 28

GLOSSARY R133

encounter (en koun′ tər) *v.* to meet unexpectedly or casually; p. 215

enfeebled (en fē′ bəld) *adj.* lacking force, strength, or effectiveness; weakened; p. 40

engulf (en gulf′) *v.* to swallow up; overwhelm; p. 219

enhance (en hans′) *v.* to make greater; p. 676

enmity (en′ mə tē) *n.* the bitter hatred between enemies; ill will; p. 412

exalt (ig zôlt′) *v.* to raise in status, dignity, power; glorify; p. 498

extinguish (iks ting′ gwish) *v.* to put out; end; destroy; p. 624

F

forage (fôr′ ij) *v.* to hunt or search about for food or needed supplies; p. 364

ford (fôrd) *n.* a shallow place where a river or stream may be crossed on foot; p. 384

foreboding (fôr bō′ ding) *n.* a feeling that something evil is going to happen; p. 748

forfeit (fôr′ fit) *v.* to lose as a penalty for some error or failure; p. 871

founder (foun′ dər) *v.* to break down, collapse, or fail; p. 611

frail (frāl) *adj.* lacking in strength; weak; p. 162

frenzy (fren′ zē) *n.* a state of great excitement or deep disturbance; p. 762

frustration (frus trā′ shən) *n.* disappointment or irritation at being kept from doing or achieving something; p. 107

furtive (fur′ tiv) *adj.* secret; shifty; sly; p. 152

futility (fū til′ ə tē) *n.* uselessness; hopelessness; p. 155

G

gaudily (gô′ də lē) *adv.* in a way that is bright and showy to the point of being in bad taste; p. 241

gloat (glōt) *v.* to feel or express pleasure or satisfaction in one's own success or achievement, especially in a triumphant or slightly nasty way; p. 63

gravely (grāv′ lē) *adv.* very seriously; p. 275

grimace (grim′ əs) *n.* a twisting of the face, as in pain or displeasure; p. 664

H

haggle (hag′ əl) *v.* to bargain, especially about price or the terms of an agreement; p. 373

haughtily (hô′ tə lē) *adv.* in a way that shows too much pride in oneself and great scorn for others; p. 259

heft (heft) *v.* to lift up; p. 245

humility (hū mil′ ə tē) *n.* the quality of being humble or modest; p. 32

hypocritical (hip′ ə krit′ i kəl) *adj.* pretending to be what one is not; fake; insincere; p. 841

hysteria (his ter′ ē ə) *n.* great, uncontrollable terror, panic, or other strong emotion; p. 54

I

illiteracy (i lit′ ər ə sē) *n.* the inability to read or write; p. 205

immortality (im′ ôr tal′ ə tē) *n.* the state of living or lasting forever; p. 440

impaired (im pārd′) *adj.* lessened in quality; damaged; p. 135

impel (im pel′) *v.* to drive to action; cause; p. 190

impending (im pen′ ding) *adj.* about to occur; p. 806

impromptu (im promp′ to͞o) *adj.* made or done on the spur of the moment, without preparation; p. 6

impudent (im′ pyə dənt) *adj.* boldly discourteous; p. 346

impulse (im′ puls) *n.* an internal force that causes one to act without thinking about it; p. 215

incentive (in sen′ tiv) *n.* that which urges to action, especially a promised reward for working harder; p. 483

incompatible (in′ kəm pat′ ə bəl) *adj.* not capable of existing or working together in harmony; conflicting; p. 644

incomprehensible (in′ kom prē hen′ sə bəl) *adj.* not understandable; p. 483
incur (in kur′) *v.* to acquire (something undesirable); bring upon oneself; p. 31
indifference (in dif′ ər əns) *n.* a lack of feeling, concern, or care; p. 20
indignantly (in dig′ nənt lē) *adv.* with dignified anger in response to an insult or injustice; p. 718
inert (i nurt′) *adj.* without power to move or act; lifeless; p. 613
inevitably (i nev′ ə tə blē) *adv.* in a way that cannot be avoided or prevented; p. 667
inextricably (in eks′ tri kə blē) *adv.* in a way that cannot be separated; p. 496
infinite (in′ fə nit) *adj.* boundless; limitless; extremely great; p. 105
inflict (in flikt′) *v.* to force (something unwelcome) on someone; p. 33
inhibition (in′ hə bish′ ən) *n.* a restraint on one's urges; p. 105
insight (in′ sīt) *n.* an understanding of the inner character or hidden nature of something; p. 598
insolence (in′ sə ləns) *n.* deliberate rudeness; disrespect; p. 578
instinctive (in stingk′ tiv) *adj.* rising from an impulse or natural tendency; not learned; p. 189
integrity (in teg′ rə tē) *n.* moral uprightness; honesty; p. 187
intellectual (int′ əl ek′ cho̅o̅ əl) *adj.* appealing to or involving intelligence or mental ability; p. 130
intently (in tent′ lē) *adv.* in a firmly focused way; with concentration; p. 8
intercession (in′ tər sesh′ ən) *n.* a request, appeal, or prayer in the interest of another or others; p. 400
interim (in′ tər im) *n.* the time between events; meantime; p. 804
interminable (in tur′ mi nə bəl) *adj.* lasting, or seeming to last, forever; endless; p. 518
intimate (in′ tə mit) *adj.* closely associated; p. 189
intolerant (in tol′ ər ənt) *adj.* unwilling to put up with; not accepting; p. 205
intricate (in′ tri kit) *adj.* full of complicated detail; p. 31
intuition (in′ to̅o̅ ish′ ən) *n.* an ability to know things without having to reason them out; p. 755
invariably (in vār′ ē ə blē) *adv.* constantly; always; p. 131
invigorating (in vig′ ə rāt ing) *adj.* energizing; refreshing; p. 666
involuntary (in vol′ ən ter′ ē) *adj.* not done willingly; p. 8

J

joviality (jō′ vē al′ ə tē) *n.* hearty, good-natured humor; p. 21
jubilation (jo̅o̅′ bə lā′ shən) *n.* great joy and excitement; p. 736
jut (jut) *v.* to extend outward or upward from a surface; bulge; p. 415

L

laboriously (lə bôr′ ē əs lē) *adv.* with great effort; p. 171
laden (lād′ ən) *adj.* loaded; weighed down; burdened; p. 173
lapse (laps) *v.* to slip, drift, or fall (into); p. 286
legacy (leg′ ə sē) *n.* anything handed down from an ancestor or from the past; p. 40
legitimately (li jit′ ə mit lē) *adv.* in a way that follows the rules; legally; p. 441
liable (lī′ ə bəl) *adj.* likely; apt; p. 555
loathe (lōth) *v.* to regard with extreme disgust; hate; p. 709
loom (lo̅o̅m) *v.* to appear or come into view in a way that seems very large and, often, threatening; p. 271
lucid (lo̅o̅′ sid) *adj.* mentally alert; clear-headed; p. 286
lunacy (lo̅o̅′ nə sē) *n.* insanity; senseless conduct; folly; p. 514

GLOSSARY R135

lurch (lurch) *v.* to move suddenly in a jerky and uneven manner; p. 67

lurk (lurk) *v.* to lie hidden or move about in a sneaky way; p. 631

M

maladjustment (mal′ ə just′ mənt) *n.* poor adjustment to conditions or requirements; p. 220

malice (mal′ is) *n.* a desire to harm another; ill will; p. 104

manifest (man′ ə fest′) *adj.* obvious; clear; plain; evident; p. 644

meager (mē′ gər) *adj.* not enough in amount or quantity; insufficient; p. 64

melancholy (mel′ ən kol′ ē) *adj.* sadly thoughtful; p. 676

meticulous (mi tik′ yə ləs) *adj.* showing great concern about details; p. 55

minimal (min′ ə məl) *adj.* smallest or least possible; very small; p. 529

modest (mod′ ist) *adj.* tending to avoid praise or credit; humble; bashful; p. 532

mutely (mūt′ lē) *adv.* without speaking; silently; p. 443

N

naive (nä ēv′) *adj.* innocent to the ways of the world; p. 32

naturalist (nach′ ər ə list) *n.* one who studies living things, especially plants or animals, by observing them directly; p. 871

O

obliged (ə blījd′) *adj.* forced, bound, or required; p. 361

obligingly (ə blī′ jing lē) *adv.* helpfully; agreeably; p. 220

obscure (əb skyoor′) *v.* to hide; p. 134

obviously (ob′ vē əs lē) *adv.* in a way that is easily seen or understood; clearly; p. 560

ominous (om′ ə nəs) *adj.* threatening harm or evil; p. 11

onslaught (ôn′ slôt′) *n.* a forceful or destructive attack; assault; p. 747

opportunist (op′ ər tōō′ nist) *n.* one who takes advantage of every opportunity, regardless of consequences; p. 127

P

pact (pakt) *n.* an agreement; deal; pledge; p. 413

painstakingly (pānz′ tā′ king lē) *adv.* in a way requiring close, careful labor or attention; p. 30

palatable (pal′ ə tə bəl) *adj.* agreeable to the taste, mind, or feelings; acceptable; p. 345

pandemonium (pan′ də mō′ nē əm) *n.* wild disorder and uproar; p. 765

paramount (par′ ə mount′) *adj.* above all others in influence or importance; supreme; p. 630

pathetically (pə thet′ i kəl ē) *adv.* pitifully; p. 861

patriarch (pā′ trē ärk′) *n.* the male head of a family; p. 173

pauper (pô′ pər) *n.* a very poor person, especially one supported by public charity; p. 638

pensive (pen′ siv) *adj.* thinking deeply, often about something sad; p. 822

perceive (pər sēv′) *v.* to take in or grasp mentally; notice; p. 820

peremptory (pə remp′ tər ē) *adj.* allowing no refusal; p. 342

perennial (pə ren′ ē əl) *adj.* lasting for a long time; p. 595

persistently (pər sis′ tənt lē) *adv.* repeatedly; p. 200

perturb (pər turb′) *v.* to disturb greatly; p. 680

petite (pə tēt′) *adj.* small and slender; little; p. 859

pious (pī′ əs) *adj.* having either genuine or pretended religious devotion; p. 583

pitch (pich) *n.* an often high-pressure sales presentation; p. 242

pivotal (piv′ ət əl) *adj.* of central importance; p. 857

placid (plas′ id) *adj.* calm or peaceful; p. 106
plight (plīt) *n.* an unfortunate or dangerous situation; p. 274
plummet (plum′ it) *v.* to fall downward; p. 858
poise (poiz) *n.* relaxed and self-controlled dignity in manner; p. 760
ponder (pon′ dər) *v.* to think over carefully; p. 680
potential (pə ten′ shəl) *n.* possibility of success; p. 241
prejudice (prej′ ə dis) *n.* an opinion formed without considering all sides of a question; p. 679
prestigious (pre sti′ jəs) *adj.* having widely recognized importance and influence; impressive; p. 625
presumably (pri zo͞o′ mə blē) *adv.* supposedly; probably; p. 805
pretense (prē′ tens) *n.* a false show or appearance, especially for the purpose of deceiving; falseness; p. 289
priceless (prīs′ lis) *adj.* of greater value than can be measured; p. 373
primly (prim′ lē) *adv.* in a formal, proper way; p. 170
prodigious (prə dij′ əs) *adj.* enormous; p. 498
prodigy (prod′ ə jē) *n.* an extraordinarily gifted or talented person, especially a child; p. 555
prominent (prom′ ə nənt) *adj.* widely known; p. 338
proposition (prop′ ə zish′ ən) *n.* a suggestion or plan; proposal; p. 473
prowess (prou′ is) *n.* great ability or skill; p. 269
proximity (prok sim′ ə tē) *n.* closeness in space, time, order, or degree; nearness; p. 644
purged (purjd) *adj.* cleansed of whatever is unclean; p. 591

Q

quaint (kwānt) *adj.* charming in an old-fashioned way; pleasingly unusual or odd; p. 638
quest (kwest) *n.* a search made to achieve a goal; p. 151

R

recoil (ri koil′) *v.* to draw back, as in fear; p. 859
redeemed (ri dēmd′) *adj.* gotten or won back; recovered; p. 625
refined (ri fīnd′) *adj.* free from coarseness or crudeness; showing good taste and manners; p. 201
refrain (ri frān′) *v.* to hold oneself back; restrain oneself; p. 384
regally (rē′ gəl lē) *adv.* in a grand, dignified manner, as if done by a king or queen; royally; p. 287
remorse (ri môrs′) *n.* a deep, painful feeling of guilt or sorrow for wrongdoing; p. 153
renegade (ren′ ə gād′) *n.* one who abandons or turns against a group, cause, or allegiance; traitor; p. 344
renovate (ren′ ə vāt′) *v.* to make like new; p. 173
renown (ri noun′) *n.* widespread reputation; fame; p. 821
repress (ri pres′) *v.* to hold back or keep under control; restrain; p. 514
reproach (ri prōch′) *v.* to scold or blame; p. 401
reputation (rep′ yə tā′ shən) *n.* what people generally think about the character of a person or thing; good name; p. 555
resolutely (rez′ ə lo͞ot′ lē) *adv.* determinedly; p. 219
resolve (ri zolv′) *n.* steady determination; firmness of purpose; p. 631
revel (rev′ əl) *v.* to take great pleasure; p. 644
revert (ri vurt′) *v.* to return to an earlier condition, behavior, or belief; p. 667
revive (ri vīv′) *v.* to come back to consciousness; show new life, strength, or freshness; p. 373
righteousness (rī′ chəs nəs) *n.* the condition of being right, moral, just, or legal; p. 519

S

sacred (sā′ krid) *adj.* holy; deserving of great respect; p. 85
sagely (sāj′ lē) *adv.* very wisely; p. 276

GLOSSARY
GLOSSARY R137

GLOSSARY

savor (sā′ vər) *v.* to take great delight in; p. 191

scavenger (skav′ in jər) *n.* an animal, such as a hyena or vulture, that feeds on dead, decaying plants or animals; p. 272

scour (skour) *v.* to rub energetically in order to clean, wash, or brighten; p. 597

scowling (skou′ ling) *n.* a facial expression of anger or disapproval; angry frown; p. 384

serene (sə rēn′) *adj.* calm; peaceful; undisturbed; p. 290

serenity (sə ren′ ə tē) *n.* calmness; peacefulness; p. 485

servile (sur′ vil) *adj.* like a servant; too humble; p. 218

sheathe (shēth) *v.* to enclose in a case or covering; p. 54

sheepishly (shē′ pish lē) *adv.* in an awkwardly embarrassed way; bashfully; p. 81

sheer (shēr) *adj.* very steep; straight up or down; p. 410

simultaneously (sī′ məl tā′ nē əs lē) *adv.* at the same time; p. 20

singularly (sing′ gyə lər lē) *adv.* unusually or remarkably; extraordinarily; p. 841

skirmish (skur′ mish) *n.* a brief or minor conflict; p. 583

slither (slith′ ər) *v.* to move along with a sliding or gliding motion, as a snake; p. 52

slung (slung) *adj.* hung or thrown loosely; p. 161

smug (smug) *adj.* overly pleased with oneself; too self-satisfied; p. 20

sober (sō′ bər) *v.* to make or become serious and quiet; p. 871

solemn (sol′ əm) *adj.* serious; p. 439

sophisticated (sə fis′ tə kā′ tid) *adj.* having or showing knowledge or experience of the world; p. 65

specific (spi sif′ ik) *adj.* entirely clear and definite; p. 603

speculation (spek′ yə lā′ shən) *n.* an opinion or conclusion based on guesswork; p. 819

stately (stāt′ lē) *adv.* noble; dignified; majestic; p. 79

steadfastly (sted′ fast′ lē) *adv.* faithfully; steadily; p. 593

stealthily (stel′ thə lē) *adv.* in a secret or sneaky manner; p. 762

stifled (stī′ fəld) *adj.* held back; smothered; p. 837

stimulus (stim′ yə ləs) *n.* something that causes a response; p. 135

strenuous (stren′ ū əs) *adj.* very active; energetic; p. 800

subdued (səb dōōd′) *adj.* quiet and downcast; p. 725

subsequently (sub′ sə kwənt lē) *adv.* at a later time; p. 21

substance (sub′ stəns) *n.* basic material; solid quality; p. 862

subterfuge (sub′ tər fūj′) *n.* a trick or other method used to escape or conceal something; deception; p. 188

subtle (sut′ əl) *adj.* not open or direct; not obvious; p. 243

suffused (sə fūzd′) *adj.* spread through or over, as with light, color, emotion, or quality; p. 186

sullen (sul′ ən) *adj.* stubbornly withdrawn or gloomy because of bad humor; sulky; p. 485

summit (sum′ it) *n.* the highest point or part; peak; p. 415

summon (sum′ ən) *v.* to send for or request the presence of, especially with authority; p. 263

superficial (sōō′ pər fish′ əl) *adj.* lacking deep meaning; shallow; unimportant or unnecessary; p. 677

syndrome (sin′ drōm′) *n.* a group of symptoms that, together, indicate a certain disease; p. 608

T

tamale (tə mä′ lē) *n.* cornmeal, meat, and red peppers in corn husks, cooked by steaming or roasting; p. 71

tangible (tan′ jə bəl) *adj.* able to be seen, touched, or felt; real; p. 129

taunt (tônt) *v.* to make fun of in a scornful, insulting way; p. 64

taut (tôt) *adj.* tense; tight; p. 199

R138 GLOSSARY

tempest (tem′ pist) *n.* a violent windstorm, usually accompanied by rain, hail, snow, or thunder; p. 530
tentatively (ten′ tə tiv lē) *adv.* hesitantly; uncertainly; p. 6
tirade (tī rād′) *n.* a long angry or scolding speech; p. 67
tranquillity (trang kwil′ ə tē) *n.* the state or quality of being calm and free from disturbance; quietness; p. 681
transition (tran zish′ ən) *n.* passage from one position, condition, or activity to another; change; shift; p. 576
tremor (trem′ ər) *n.* a shaking or trembling movement; p. 8
tribulation (trib′ yə lā′ shən) *n.* great misery or distress; p. 496

U

unabashed (un′ ə basht′) *adj.* not ashamed or self-conscious; bold; p. 706
uncomprehendingly (un kom′ pri hend′ ing lē) *adv.* without understanding; p. 106
unnerving (un nurv′ ing) *adj.* causing nervousness or upset; disturbing; p. 147
unrestrained (un′ ri strānd′) *adj.* not held in check or under control; p. 216
unseemly (un sēm′ lē) *adj.* not proper to the time or place; not in good taste; p. 80
unsound (un sound′) *adj.* not accurate or sensible; p. 372
unwavering (un wā′ vər ing) *adj.* unchanging; not shifting or moving; steady; p. 592

V

vain (vān) *adj.* 1. unsuccessful; useless; p. 485 2. overly concerned with or proud of one's appearance, abilities, or accomplishments; conceited; p. 636
valiant (val′ yənt) *adj.* brave; courageous; p. 582
valid (val′ id) *adj.* well-supported by facts; true; p. 204
vehemently (vē′ ə mənt lē) *adv.* strongly; intensely; passionately; p. 841
vex (veks) *v.* to disturb, annoy, or anger, especially by some small, repeated action; p. 836
vibrant (vī′ brənt) *adj.* full of life and energy; p. 402
vile (vīl) *adj.* very bad; unpleasant; foul; p. 715
virtue (vur′ cho͞o) *n.* a good quality or admirable trait; p. 584
vividly (viv′ id lē) *adv.* clearly; intensely; p. 52

W

wallow (wol′ ō) *v.* to become or remain helpless; p. 497
wan (won) *adj.* pale or weak, indicating illness or weariness; p. 515
wane (wān) *v.* to draw to a close; approach an end; p. 839
wary (wār′ ē) *adj.* cautious; on the alert; p. 822
waver (wā′ vər) *v.* to become uncertain; falter; p. 681
wretchedness (rech′ id nəs) *n.* great unhappiness or deep distress; p. 521

GLOSSARY R139

Spanish Glossary

A

abyss/abismo *s.* hueco muy profundo; p. 411
acute/agudo *adj.* fuerte o intenso; p. 835
adept/versado *adj.* experto; muy capacitado; p. 243
adolescence/adolescencia *s.* período o proceso de crecimiento de la juventud a la edad adulta; pubertad; p. 624
advocate/defensor *s.* el que apoya públicamente una causa; p. 272
aggravating/exasperante *adj.* irritante; molesto; p. 718
aggression/agresión *s.* acción de atacar; p. 21
aghast/espantado *adj.* lleno de miedo o terror; p. 276
agonize/agonizar *v.* sufrir mucho; pensar en algo con gran dolor o preocupación; p. 625
alight/aterrizar *v.* tocar tierra después de un vuelo; p. 413
aloof/retraído *adj.* emocionalmente distante; reservado; p. 823
alternative/alternativa *s.* otra posibilidad; p. 106
amiable/amigable *adj.* amistoso; amable; cordial; p. 801
anguish/angustia *s.* gran sufrimiento; p. 594
angular/angular *adj.* huesudo y flaco; p. 51
anomalous/anómalo *adj.* que no es usual ni regular; anormal; p. 192
anonymous/anónimo *adj.* que no tiene nombre u origen; que carece de cualidades que lo distinguen; p. 40
appalled/pasmado *adj.* horrorizado; sobresaltado; impresionado; p. 148
apparition/aparición *s.* visión fantasmal; p. 817
apprehension/aprensión *s.* miedo de lo que pueda ocurrir; temor; p. 749
aromatic/aromático *adj.* que tiene un olor agradable o un sabor especial y delicado; p. 242
arresting/llamativo *adj.* que llama la atención; impresionante; p. 871
arrogant/arrogante *adj.* lleno de vanidad; presumido; p. 147
askew/oblicuamente *adv.* de modo torcido; p. 439
audacity/audacia *s.* osadía; atrevimiento; p. 840
awed/admirado *adj.* que siente asombro y respeto a la vez; p. 84

B

ban/censurar *v.* prohibir; desaprobar; p. 677
banish/desterrar *v.* obligar a una persona a abandonar su país o comunidad; deportar; p. 259
baptism/bautismo *s.* ceremonia en la que se limpia de pecado a una persona e ingresa a la religión cristiana; p. 71
barren/árido *adj.* vacío; tedioso o falto de interés; p. 164
barter/trocar *v.* intercambiar objetos; canjear; p. 274
bedraggled/mugriento *adj.* mojado, sucio y arrugado; desgreñado; p. 666
benediction/bendición *s.* gracia divina o acto de ser bendecido; p. 440
benevolence/benevolencia *s.* amabilidad; generosidad; p. 271
bewilderment/estupefacción *s.* gran confusión; p. 262
bland/insulso *adj.* soso; insípido; aburridor; p. 808
bleak/desolado *adj.* triste; deprimente; p. 488
blithely/despreocupadamente *adv.* de un modo tranquilo y alegre; p. 20
bravado/bravuconería *s.* falsa demostración de valentía; coraje fingido; p. 152

R140 SPANISH GLOSSARY

brazenly/descaradamente *adv.* de un modo atrevido y rudo; p. 21

C

cajole/persuadir *v.* convencer con promesas o palabras amables; halagar; p. 486
capitulate/capitular *v.* rendirse; dejar de resistirse; p. 666
careening/tambaleante *adj.* que se inclina o se ladea mientras se mueve, como si estuviera fuera de control; p. 861
catastrophic/catastrófico *adj.* desastroso; p. 104
chasm/grieta *s.* hueco o abertura profunda, como en la superficie terrestre; p. 807
chronic/crónico *adj.* que dura mucho tiempo o que se repite continuamente; p. 284
collective/colectivo *adj.* que tiene que ver con un grupo de personas o cosas; común; compartido; p. 205
commence/comenzar *v.* empezar; iniciar; p. 9
commend/ensalzar *v.* aprobar; alabar; p. 262
communion/comunión *s.* cercanía y entendimiento entre dos personas; p. 52
compelling/irresistible *adj.* importante; impresionante y convincente; p. 630
competently/competentemente *adv.* capazmente; hábilmente; p. 202
complex/complejo *s.* preocupación o miedo exagerado; idea o sentimiento obsesivo; perturbación; p. 284
comply/acatar *v.* obedecer o cumplir una solicitud; p. 343
comprehend/comprender *v.* captar mentalmente; entender por completo; p. 596
conceive/concebir *v.* formar; imaginar; p. 473
concoct/confeccionar *v.* hacer o fabricar con habilidad e ingenio; p. 53
conscientious/concienzudo *adj.* que actúa guiado por la conciencia; que se interesa por lo que es bueno y malo; p. 818
consecrate/consagrar *v.* declarar o tratar como sagrado; p. 474
console/consolar *v.* calmar o animar a alguien que está triste o desilusionado; p. 863
conspicuous/conspicuo *adj.* sobresaliente; aparente; p. 701
conspiratorial/de conspirador *adj.* que obra en conjunto, especialmente para llevar a cabo un acto secreto, incorrecto o ilegal; p. 287
constitute/constituir *v.* formar; crear; p. 625
convey/transmitir *v.* expresar; comunicar; p. 30
corroded/corroído *adj.* carcomido o consumido mediante una acción química; p. 245
covet/codiciar *v.* desear con fuerza; anhelar; p. 513
cower/encogerse *v.* agacharse, como cuando se tiene miedo o vergüenza; p. 131
craggy/escabroso *adj.* abrupto, áspero y desgastado; p. 285
crevice/grieta *s.* hendedura estrecha; p. 217
cringe/contraerse *v.* encogerse o retirarse, como cuando se siente miedo o desagrado; p. 217
crouch/acuclillarse *v.* agacharse o encogerse, especialmente con las rodillas dobladas; p. 558
crux/punto crucial *s.* punto o parte más importante; p. 41
curt/lacónico *adj.* tan corto o breve que parece descortés; p. 242

D

decree/decretar *v.* dar una regla, orden o decisión oficial; dictaminar; p. 259
decry/desaprobar *v.* criticar abiertamente; p. 343
default/incumplir *v.* fallar; dejar de hacer algo solicitado; p. 495
dejected/abatido *adj.* triste; deprimido; desanimado; p. 793
demean/degradar *v.* rebajar; deshonrar; p. 664
desolate/desolado *adj.* que no se puede consolar; p. 495
detract/quitar *v.* reducir mérito o valor; desvirtuar; p. 474
diligence/diligencia *s.* gran atención, cuidado y esfuerzo; p. 513
discern/discernir *v.* detectar o reconocer; identificar; p. 21

SPANISH GLOSSARY

SPANISH GLOSSARY R141

SPANISH GLOSSARY

disclose/divulgar *v.* revelar; dar a conocer; publicar; p. 486
discord/discordia *s.* desacuerdo; conflicto; p. 498
discrimination/discriminación *s.* trato injusto, especialmente como resultado de políticas contra grupos minoritarios; p. 495
disembark/desembarcar *v.* bajarse de un tren, avión, barco u otro vehículo; p. 644
disgruntled/descontento *adj.* malhumorado; p. 744
disheveled/desaliñado *adj.* desarreglado; p. 483
disperse/dispersar *v.* ir en diferentes direcciones; p. 592
distinct/claro *adj.* que se puede escuchar, ver o sentir claramente; p. 174
diverse/diverso *adj.* patentemente diferente; variado; p. 630
diversion/distracción *s.* algo que distrae o aparta la atención; p. 148
docile/dócil *adj.* fácil de manejar, entrenar o enseñar; p. 103
doggedly/tenazmente *adv.* tercamente; firmemente; p. 514
dominant/dominante *adj.* que tiene el mayor poder o fuerza; aquél que controla; p. 817
dote/adorar *v.* demostrar inmenso afecto; p. 341
drone/hablar monótonamente *v.* hablar con tono soso; hacer un sonido bajo y constante, como un zumbido; p. 170
dry/árido *adj.* que no es interesante; aburridor; p. 608
dumbfounded/sin habla *adj.* que queda mudo por el asombro; pasmado; p. 400

E

eerie/misterioso *adj.* raro, especialmente de un modo que causa miedo; p. 10
elaborate/elaborado *adj.* complicado; hecho con mucho esmero; p. 240
eloquence/elocuencia *s.* acto de hablar o escribir de modo expresivo, efectivo y conmovedor; p. 485
embodiment/encarnación *s.* representación de una idea o cualidad; forma visible; p. 664
emit/emitir *v.* pronunciar; enviar o hacer un sonido; p. 341
emphatically/enfáticamente *adv.* muy definidamente; claramente; p. 643
emulate/emular *v.* imitar; p. 28
encounter/encontrarse *v.* tener una reunión inesperada; ver a alguien casualmente; p. 215
enfeebled/debilitado *adj.* que carece de fuerza, vigor o efectividad; p. 40
engulf/absorber *v.* tragar; sumir; p. 219
enhance/realzar *v.* aumentar; intensificar; p. 676
enmity/enemistad *s.* odio entre enemigos; hostilidad; p. 412
exalt/exaltar *v.* elevar en condición, dignidad o poder; glorificar; p. 498
extinguish/extinguir *v.* apagar; terminar; destruir; p. 624

F

forage/forrajear *v.* cazar o buscar alimento o suministros; p. 364
ford/vado *s.* lugar poco profundo de un río o quebrada que se puede atravesar a pie; p. 384
foreboding/presentimiento *s.* sensación de que algo malo está por ocurrir; p. 748
forfeit/perder *v.* dejar de tener una cosa o derecho como castigo; confiscar; p. 871
founder/fallar *v.* desbaratarse; caer; irse a pique; p. 611
frail/frágil *adj.* que no tiene fuerza; débil; p. 162
frenzy/frenesí *s.* estado de gran emoción o profunda alteración; p. 762
frustration/frustración *s.* desilusión o irritación por no poder hacer o alcanzar algo; p. 107
furtive/furtivo *adj.* secreto; engañoso; p. 152
futility/futilidad *s.* insignificancia; algo que es inútil o no vale la pena; p. 155

R142 SPANISH GLOSSARY

G

gaudily/ostentosamente *adv.* de un modo muy llamativo, al punto de ser de mal gusto; p. 241
gloat/vanagloriarse *v.* sentir o expresar placer o satisfacción por un éxito o logro, particularmente de un modo triunfante o malicioso; p. 63
gravely/gravemente *adv.* muy seriamente; p. 275
grimace/mueca *s.* gesto de la cara, como cuando se siente dolor o fastidio; p. 664

H

haggle/regatear *v.* pedir rebaja de un precio o discutir los términos de un acuerdo; p. 373
haughtily/altivamente *adv.* de un modo que muestra demasiado orgullo propio y desprecio por otros; p. 259
heft/levantar *v.* alzar; p. 245
humility/humildad *s.* cualidad de ser humilde o modesto; p. 32
hypocritical/hipócrita *adj.* que aparenta ser lo que no es; solapado; falso; p. 841
hysteria/histeria *s.* gran terror, furia u otra emoción muy fuerte e incontrolable; p. 54

I

illiteracy/analfabetismo *s.* no saber leer ni escribir; p. 205
immortality/inmortalidad *s.* capacidad de vivir o durar por siempre; p. 440
impaired/deteriorado *adj.* rebajado en calidad; dañado; p. 135
impel/impeler *v.* impulsar; motivar; causar; p. 190
impending/inminente *adj.* que está por ocurrir; p. 806
impromptu/impremeditado *adj.* que se hace de manera espontánea y sin preparación; p. 6
impudent/impudente *adj.* descarado; atrevido; p. 346
impulse/impulso *s.* fuerza interna que nos hace actuar sin pensarlo; p. 215
incentive/incentivo *s.* algo que motiva una acción, especialmente la recompensa que se promete por un esfuerzo o trabajo; p. 483
incompatible/incompatible *adj.* que no es capaz de existir o actuar conjuntamente y en armonía; contrario; p. 644
incomprehensible/incomprensible *adj.* imposible de entender; p. 483
incur/incurrir *v.* adquirir una obligación o algo indeseable; contraer una deuda; p. 31
indifference/indiferencia *s.* falta de sentimiento, preocupación o interés; p. 20
indignantly/indignadamente *adv.* de modo que demuestra rabia debido a un insulto o injusticia; p. 718
inert/inerte *adj.* que no se puede mover o actuar; sin vida; p. 613
inevitably/inevitablemente *adv.* que no se puede evitar o prevenir; p. 667
inextricably/inextricablemente *adv.* de un modo que no se puede separar; p. 496
infinite/infinito *adj.* sin límites; extremadamente grande; p. 105
inflict/infligir *v.* imponer algo que no se desea; p. 33
inhibition/inhibición *s.* acto de contener un impulso o deseo; p. 105
insight/perspicacia *s.* comprensión de la condición o naturaleza oculta de algo; visión; p. 598
insolence/insolencia *s.* atrevimiento; descortesía; p. 578
instinctive/instintivo *adj.* que surge de un impulso o tendencia natural; que no se ha aprendido; p. 189
integrity/integridad *s.* rectitud moral; honestidad; p. 187
intellectual/intelectual *adj.* referente a la inteligencia o habilidad mental; p. 130
intently/resueltamente *adv.* con concentración y firmeza; p. 8
intercession/intercesión *s.* solicitud, llamado u oración en bien de otros; p. 400

SPANISH GLOSSARY
SPANISH GLOSSARY R143

interim/ínterin *s.* tiempo entre dos sucesos; mientras tanto; p. 804
interminable/interminable *adj.* que dura o parece durar por siempre; eterno; p. 518
intimate/íntimo *adj.* muy cercano; allegado; p. 189
intolerant/intolerante *adj.* que no acepta o cede; p. 205
intricate/intrincado *adj.* con muchos detalles complicados; p. 31
intuition/intuición *s.* habilidad de saber algo sin tener que razonarlo; p. 755
invariably/invariablemente *adv.* de modo constante; siempre; p. 131
invigorating/vigorizador *adj.* tonificante; fortalecedor; refrescante; p. 666
involuntary/involuntariamente *adj.* sin intención o voluntad; p. 8

J

joviality/jovialidad *s.* buen humor; alegría; p. 21
jubilation/júbilo *s.* gran alegría y emoción; p. 736
jut/sobresalir *v.* proyectar fuera de una superficie; p. 415

L

laboriously/laboriosamente *adv.* con gran esfuerzo; p. 171
laden/cargado *adj.* repleto; atiborrado; p. 173
lapse/deslizarse *v.* caer o resbalarse; p. 286
legacy/legado *s.* algo que se recibe de un antepasado o del pasado; p. 40
legitimately/legítimamente *adv.* de un modo que sigue las reglas; legalmente; p. 441
liable/propenso *adj.* que tiene tendencia a; predispuesto; p. 555
loathe/abominar *v.* odiar; detestar; p. 709
loom/vislumbrarse *v.* asomarse o hacerse presente de un modo que parece muy grande y a menudo amenazador; p. 271
lucid/lúcido *adj.* mentalmente alerta; sagaz; p. 286
lunacy/disparate *s.* locura; conducta absurda; p. 514
lurch/tambalearse *v.* moverse repentinamente de modo abrupto y sin equilibrio; dar tumbos; p. 67
lurk/acechar *v.* ocultarse o moverse furtivamente; estar latente; p. 631

M

maladjustment/inadaptación *s.* que no se ajusta bien a las condiciones o los requisitos; p. 220
malice/malicia *s.* deseo de lastimar u ofender a alguien; p. 104
manifest/manifiesto *adj.* obvio; claro; preciso; evidente; p. 644
meager/exiguo *adj.* que no es suficiente en cantidad o volumen; insuficiente; p. 64
melancholy/melancólico *adj.* nostálgico; pensativo y triste; p. 676
meticulous/meticuloso *adj.* que se preocupa mucho por los detalles; p. 55
minimal/mínimo *adj.* lo más pequeño o lo menos posible; muy pequeño; p. 529
modest/modesto *adj.* que no desea elogios; humilde; sencillo; p. 532
mutely/mudamente *adv.* sin hablar; silenciosamente; p. 443

N

naive/ingenuo *adj.* inocente de las realidades de la vida; p. 32
naturalist/naturalista *s.* quien estudia los seres vivos, especialmente plantas y animales, mediante observación directa; p. 871

O

obliged/obligado *adj.* forzado, comprometido o impulsado a hacer algo; p. 36

R144 SPANISH GLOSSARY

obligingly/servicialmente *adv.* que muestra deseos de ser útil o servir; cortésmente; p. 220
obscure/ocultar *v.* esconder; disimular; p. 134
obviously/obviamente *adv.* de un modo que se puede ver o entender fácilmente; claramente; p. 560
ominous/ominoso *adj.* siniestro; nefasto; amenazador; p. 11
onslaught/embestida *s.* ataque furioso o destructivo; asalto; p. 747
opportunist/oportunista *s.* alguien que se aprovecha de cualquier oportunidad sin importarle las consecuencias; p. 127

P

pact/pacto *s.* acuerdo; convenio; p. 413
painstakingly/esmeradamente *adv.* de un modo que requiere gran cuidado o atención; p. 30
palatable/apetecible *adj.* agradable al gusto, la mente o los sentimientos; apetitoso; p. 345
pandemonium/pandemonio *s.* gran desorden o disturbio; p. 765
paramount/supremo *adj.* por encima de todos los demás en influencia o importancia; superior; p. 630
pathetically/patéticamente *adv.* trágicamente; conmovedoramente; p. 861
patriarch/patriarca *s.* líder masculino de una familia; anciano respetable; p. 173
pauper/indigente *s.* persona muy pobre que suele vivir de la caridad pública; p. 638
pensive/pensativo *adj.* que está callado y dedicado a pensar, a menudo cosas tristes; p. 822
perceive/percibir *v.* captar mentalmente; notar; p. 820
peremptory/perentorio *adj.* que no permite negativa; urgente; p. 342
perennial/perenne *adj.* que dura por largo tiempo; p. 595
persistently/persistentemente *adv.* repetidamente; p. 200
perturb/perturbar *v.* molestar; inquietar; turbar; p. 680
petite/menudo *adj.* de estatura baja y delgado; pequeño; p. 859
pious/piadoso *adj.* que demuestra devoción religiosa real o fingida; p. 583
pitch/plática de propaganda *s.* presentación de ventas con presión; p. 242
pivotal/fundamental *adj.* de importancia central; p. 857
placid/plácido *adj.* calmado o pacífico; p. 106
plight/aprieto *s.* situación difícil o peligrosa; p. 274
plummet/desplomarse *v.* caer verticalmente; p. 858
poise/aplomo *s.* actitud serena y controlada; p. 760
ponder/ponderar *v.* pensar algo cuidadosamente; p. 680
potential/potencial *s.* posibilidad de éxito; p. 241
prejudice/prejuicio *s.* opinión que se tiene de algo sin considerar todos los aspectos; p. 679
prestigious/prestigioso *adj.* que goza de importancia e influencia; notable; p. 625
presumably/presumiblemente *adv.* supuestamente; probablemente; p. 805
pretense/simulación *s.* demostración o apariencia falsa, especialmente con el propósito de engañar; falsedad; p. 289
priceless/incalculable *adj.* de tanto valor que no se puede calcular; p. 170
primly/remilgadamente *adv.* de un modo muy formal; p. 170
prodigious/prodigioso *adj.* enorme; vasto; p. 498
prodigy/prodigio *s.* persona extraordinariamente talentosa o inteligente, en particular un niño; p. 555
prominent/prominente *adj.* ampliamente conocido; p. 338
proposition/proposición *s.* sugerencia o plan; propuesta; p. 473
prowess/habilidad *s.* gran pericia o destreza; p. 269

SPANISH GLOSSARY R145

proximity/proximidad *s.* cercanía en espacio, tiempo, orden o grado; p. 644
purged/purgado *adj.* limpio o purificado de cualquier suciedad; p. 591

Q

quaint/pintoresco *adj.* con un encanto antiguo; raro o peculiar de modo placentero; p. 638
quest/búsqueda *s.* intento de alcanzar una meta; p. 151

R

recoil/recular *v.* retroceder, como cuando se siente miedo; p. 859
redeemed/redimido *adj.* rescatado; recuperado; p. 625
refined/refinado *adj.* libre de aspereza; que muestra buen gusto y educación; p. 201
refrain/refrenarse *v.* abstenerse de hacer algo; restringirse; p. 384
regally/fastuosamente *adv.* de un modo grandioso; digno de un rey o una reina; majestuosamente; p. 287
remorse/remordimiento *s.* sentimiento de culpa o arrepentimiento; p. 153
renegade/renegado *s.* el que abandona o le da la espalda a un grupo, causa o alianza; traidor; p. 344
renovate/renovar *v.* modernizar; volver como nuevo; p. 173
renown/renombre *s.* amplia reputación; fama; p. 821
repress/reprimir *v.* mantener bajo control; oprimir; p. 514
reproach/reprochar *v.* regañar o culpar; p. 401
reputation/reputación *s.* opinión general sobre la condición de una persona o cosa; buen nombre; p. 555
resolutely/resueltamente *adv.* con determinación; p. 219
resolve/resolución *s.* determinación fija; firmeza al actuar; p. 631
revel/deleitarse *v.* recrearse; hacer algo con placer; p. 644
revert/revertir *v.* volver a una condición, comportamiento o creencia anterior; p. 667
revive/revivir *v.* recuperar la conciencia; mostrar nueva vida, fuerza o frescura; p. 373
righteousness/rectitud *s.* comportamiento recto, justo o legal; p. 519

S

sacred/sagrado *adj.* bendito; que merece gran respeto; p. 85
sagely/sabiamente *adv.* muy sensatamente; p. 276
savor/saborear *v.* deleitarse con algo; p. 191
scavenger/carroñero *s.* animal que se alimenta de carroña, como por ejemplo las hienas o buitres que se alimentan de plantas o animales muertos y en descomposición; p. 272
scour/frotar *v.* restregar con fuerza para limpiar, lavar o brillar; p. 597
scowling/ceño fruncido *s.* expresión facial de rabia o desacuerdo; p. 384
serene/sereno *adj.* calmado; pacífico; tranquilo; p. 290
serenity/serenidad *s.* calma; tranquilidad; p. 485
servile/servil *adj.* que sirve humildemente; p. 218
sheathe/enfundar *v.* meter en un forro o cubierta; p. 54
sheepishly/tímidamente *adv.* de modo que demuestra timidez o vergüenza; p. 81
sheer/escarpado *adj.* muy empinado; perpendicular; p. 410
simultaneously/simultáneamente *adv.* al mismo tiempo; p. 20
singularly/singularmente *adv.* de modo único o especial; extraordinariamente; p. 841
skirmish/pleito *s.* conflicto leve o de poca duración; escaramuza; p. 538
slither/culebrear *v.* deslizarse o escurrirse por el suelo como una serpiente; p. 52

slung/tirar *v.* lanzar o arrojar; p. 161
smug/presumido *adj.* demasiado vanidoso; p. 20
sober/calmarse *v.* adquirir una actitud seria y callada; p. 871
solemn/solemne *adj.* serio; p. 439
sophisticated/sofisticado *adj.* que tiene o demuestra conocimiento o experiencia del mundo; p. 65
specific/específico *adj.* muy claro y definido; p. 603
speculation/especulación *s.* opinión o conclusión basada en una suposición; p. 819
stately/solemnemente *adv.* de modo noble, digno o majestuoso; p. 79
steadfastly/constantemente *adv.* resueltamente; con determinación; p. 593
stealthily/clandestinamente *adv.* de un modo secreto o furtivo; p. 762
stifled/reprimido *adj.* frenado; oprimido; p. 837
stimulus/estímulo *s.* algo que causa una respuesta; p. 135
strenuous/vigoroso *adj.* muy activo; lleno de energía; p. 800
subdued/sometido *adj.* callado y abatido; p. 725
subsequently/posteriormente *adv.* después; más adelante; p. 21
substance/sustancia *s.* material básico; solidez; p. 862
subterfuge/subterfugio *s.* truco o método usado para escapar o esconder algo; evasiva; p. 188
subtle/sutil *adj.* que no es abierto o directo; que no es obvio; p. 243
suffused/bañado *adj.* cubierto de luz, color, emoción o cualidad; p. 186
sullen/malhumorado *adj.* retraído o taciturno debido al mal humor; hosco; p. 485
summit/cumbre *s.* punto o parte más alta; cima; p. 425
summon/convocar *v.* solicitar la presencia de alguien, a menudo con autoridad; p. 263
superficial/superficial *adj.* sin un significado profundo; vacío; que no tiene importancia o no es necesario; p. 677
syndrome/síndrome *s.* grupo de síntomas que, en conjunto, definen cierta enfermedad; p. 608

T

tamale/tamal *s.* mezcla de diversos ingredientes envueltos en hojas de maíz que se cocina al vapor o a la brasa; p. 71
tangible/tangible *adj.* que se puede ver, tocar o sentir; real; p. 129
taunt/mofarse *v.* burlarse de modo despreciable o insultante; p. 129
taut/tirante *adj.* tenso; estirado; p. 199
tempest/tempestad *s.* fuerte ventarrón, por lo común acompañado de lluvia, granizo, nieve o truenos; p. 530
tentatively/tentativamente *adv.* que no es definitivo; inciertamente; p. 6
tirade/diatriba *s.* discurso largo, furioso o lleno de críticas; p. 67
tranquillity/tranquilidad *s.* estado o cualidad de mantener la calma; quietud; p. 681
transition/transición *s.* paso de una posición, condición o actividad a otra; cambio; p. 576
tremor/temblor *s.* estremecimiento o sacudida; p. 8
tribulation/tribulación *s.* gran problema o pena; p. 496

U

unabashed/desenvuelto *adj.* que no demuestra timidez; atrevido; p. 706
uncomprehendingly/incomprensiblemente *adv.* de modo que no se entiende; p. 106
unnerving/inquietante *adj.* que causa inquietud o molestia; angustioso; p. 147
unrestrained/desenfrenado *adj.* que no se controla; p. 216
unseemly/impropio *adj.* que no es apropiado para el momento o lugar; que no es de buen gusto; p. 80
unsound/falso *adj.* que no es correcto o preciso; p. 372

SPANISH GLOSSARY

unwavering/firme *adj.* constante; que no cambia ni se mueve; p. 592

V

vain/vano *adj.* inútil; ineficaz; p. 485
valiant/valiente *adj.* que demuestra valor; p. 582
valid/válido *adj.* respaldado por los hechos; verdadero; p. 204
vehemently/vehementemente *adv.* intensamente; apasionadamente; p. 841
vex/fastidiar *v.* molestar o enfurecer, especialmente mediante una acción repetitiva y tonta; p. 836
vibrant/vibrante *adj.* lleno de vida y energía; p. 402
vile/vil *adj.* muy malo; abominable; perverso; p. 715
virtue/virtud *s.* buena cualidad o rasgo admirable; p. 584
vividly/vívidamente *adv.* claramente; intensamente; p. 52

W

wallow/quedar desvalido *v.* quedar indefenso; p. 497
wan/lánguido *adj.* pálido o débil, como resultado de una enfermedad o gran cansancio; p. 515
wane/declinar *v.* llegar al fin; menguar; p. 839
wary/cauteloso *adj.* cuidadoso; alerta; p. 822
waver/vacilar *v.* dudar; p. 681
wretchedness/desdicha *s.* gran tristeza o profunda pena; p. 521

R148 SPANISH GLOSSARY

Index of Skills

References beginning with R refer to handbook pages.

Literary Concepts

INDEX OF SKILLS R149

R150 INDEX OF SKILLS

Reading and Thinking

INDEX OF SKILLS R151

R152 INDEX OF SKILLS

Grammar and Language

INDEX OF SKILLS R153

INDEX OF SKILLS R155

Vocabulary

Writing

R156 INDEX OF SKILLS

INDEX OF SKILLS R157

Listening, Speaking, and Viewing

R158 INDEX OF SKILLS

Research and Study Skills

INDEX OF SKILLS R159

R160 INDEX OF SKILLS

Media and Technology

Life Skills

Interdisciplinary Studies

INDEX OF SKILLS R161

Index of Authors and Titles

R162 INDEX OF AUTHORS AND TITLES

INDEX OF AUTHORS AND TITLES R163

R164 INDEX OF AUTHORS AND TITLES

Index of Art and Artists

INDEX OF ART AND ARTISTS R165

R166 INDEX OF ART AND ARTISTS

Acknowledgments

(Continued from page iv)

Literature

Theme 1

"The Treasure of Lemon Brown" by Walter Dean Myers. © 1983, Walter Dean Myers. Originally appeared in *Boys' Life.* Reprinted by permission of the author.

"My Two Dads" by Marie G. Lee, reprinted by permission of the author. "My Two Dads" first appeared in the *Brown Alumni Monthly.*

"A Dictionary of Japanese-American Terms" by R. A. Sasaki, from *Into the Fire,* copyright © 1996 by The Greenfield Review Press. Reprinted by permission of the author.

"Homeless" from *Living Out Loud* by Anna Quindlan. Copyright © 1987 by Anna Quindlan. Reprinted by permission of Random House, Inc.

"Homeless Children Write Book About Homelessness" Copyright © NPR® 1993. The news report by NPR's Howard Berkes was originally broadcast on National Public Radio's "Weekend Edition® Saturday" on December 25, 1993, and is used with the permission of National Public Radio, Inc. Any unauthorized duplication is strictly prohibited.

"The Farmer and His Sons" from *Anno's Aesop* by Mitsumasa Anno. Copyright © 1989 by Mitsumasa Anno. Reprinted by permission of Orchard Books, New York.

"Golden Glass" by Alma Luz Villanueva. Reprinted by permission of the author.

"Mother and Daughter" from *Baseball in April and Other Stories,* copyright © 1990 by Gary Soto, reprinted by permission of Harcourt Brace & Company.

"Chanclas" from *The House on Mango Street.* Copyright © 1984 by Sandra Cisneros. Published by Vintage Books, a division of Random House, Inc., and in hardcover by Alfred A. Knopf, Inc., a division of Random House, Inc. Reprinted by permission of Susan Bergholz Literary Services, New York. All rights reserved.

"Real Indians Eat Jell-O" by Laurie Carlson. Reprinted by permission of the author.

"The Medicine Bag" by Virginia Driving Hawk Sneve, from *Boys' Life,* March 1975. Reprinted by permission of the author.

Theme 2

"All in a Day's Work" Copyright © 1973, 1974 by James Herriot, from *All Things Bright and Beautiful* by James Herriot. Reprinted by permission of Harold Ober Associates Incorporated. Copyright © 1973, 1974 by James Herriot, from *All Things Bright and Beautiful* by James Herriot. Reprinted by permission of St. Martin's Press Incorporated.

"Flowers for Algernon" by Daniel Keyes. Copyright © 1959, 1987 by Daniel Keyes. Reprinted by permission of the author.

"The Kid Nobody Could Handle," from *Welcome to the Monkey House* by Kurt Vonnegut Jr. Copyright © 1961 by Kurt Vonnegut Jr. Used by permission of Delacorte Press/Seymour Lawrence, a division of Bantam Doubleday Dell Publishing Group, Inc., a division of Random House, Inc.

"You Gotta Be" Words and Music by Des'ree, Additional Music by Ashley Ingram. Copyright © 1994 Sony Music Publishing, U.K. and Careers-BMG Music Publishing Inc. All rights on behalf of Sony Music Publishing U.K. administered by Sony/ATV Music Publishing, 8 Music Square West, Nashville, TN 37203. All rights reserved. Used by permission.

"Thank You Ma'am" by Langston Hughes. Copyright © 1958 by Langston Hughes. Copyright renewed 1986 by George Houston Bass. Reprinted by permission of Harold Ober Associates Incorporated.

"The Journey" from *Days of Plenty, Days of Want* by Patricia Preciado Martin. (University of Arizona Press, 1999). Originally published in *La Confluencia,* 1980. Reprinted by permission of the author.

"Knoxville, Tennessee" from *Black Feeling, Black Talk, Black Judgment* by Nikki Giovanni. Copyright © 1968, 1970 by Nikki Giovanni. By permission of HarperCollins Publishers.

"Legacies" from *My House* by Nikki Giovanni. Copyright © 1972 by Nikki Giovanni. By permission of HarperCollins Publishers.

"A Mother in Mannville" reprinted with the permission of Scribner, a division of Simon & Schuster from *When the Whippoorwill* by Marjorie Kinnan Rawlings. Copyright 1936, 1940 by Marjorie Kinnan Rawlings; copyrights renewed © 1964, 1968 by Norton Baskin.

Excerpt from *I Know Why the Caged Bird Sings* by Maya Angelou. Copyright © 1969 by Maya Angelou. Reprinted by permission of Random House, Inc.

Excerpt from "Maya's Way: Maya Angelou's Zest for Life Continues to Fuel Her Creative Fire" by Patti Thorn. Reprinted with permission from the Rocky Mountain News.

Theme 3

"In the Middle of a Pitch" by Bill Meissner. From *Hitting Into the Wind,* Random House, 1994, Southern Methodist University paperback, 1997. Reprinted by permission of the author.

"The Wise Old Woman" from *Sea of Gold,* copyright © 1965 by Yoshiko Uchida. Courtesy of the Bancroft Library, University of California, Berkeley.

"Bagged Wolf" from *Sweet and Sour: Tales From China.* Copyright © 1980 by Carol Kendall and Yao-wen Li. Reprinted by permission of Bodley Head.
"Bagged Wolf" from *Sweet and Sour: Tales From China.* Copyright © 1980 by Carol Kendall and Yao-wen Li. Reprinted by permission of Clarion Books/Houghton Mifflin Co. All rights reserved.

"The Moustache" from *Eight Plus One: Stories by Robert Cormier* by Robert Cormier. Copyright © 1975 by Robert Cormier. Reprinted by permission of Pantheon Books, a division of Random House, Inc.

"The Black Walnut Tree" from *Twelve Moons* by Mary Oliver. Copyright © 1978 by Mary Oliver. First appeared in *The Ohio Review.* By permission of Little, Brown & Company.

"Fire and Ice" and "Dust of Snow" from *The Poetry of Robert Frost,* edited by Edward Connery Lathem, copyright 1951 by Robert Frost, copyright 1923, © 1969 by Henry Holt and Company, Inc. Reprinted by permission of Henry Holt and Company, Inc.

"Between What I See and What I Say . . ./Entre Lo Que Veo y Digo . . ." by Octavio Paz, from *Collected Poems 1957–1987.* Copyright © 1986 by Octavio Paz and Eliot Weinberger. Reprinted by permission of New Directions Publishing Corp.

"Identity" by Julio Noboa Polanco. Reprinted by permission of the author.

"the lesson of the moth," from *Archy and Mehitabel* by Don Marquis. Copyright 1927 by Doubleday, a division of Bantam Doubleday Dell Publishing Group, Inc. Used by permission of Doubleday, a division of Bantam Doubleday Dell Publishing Group, Inc., a division of Random House, Inc.

"Going to the EXTREME: Young daredevils zip into mainstream" by Karen Thomas. Copyright © 1997, USA Today. Reprinted with permission.

Theme 4

"John Henry" from *A Natural Man: The True Story of John Henry* by Steve Sanfield. Reprinted by permission of David R. Godine, Publisher, Inc. Copyright © 1986 by Steve Sanfield.

Excerpt from *The People, Yes* by Carl Sandburg, copyright © 1936 by Harcourt Brace & Company and renewed 1964 by Carl Sandburg, reprinted by permission of the publisher.

"Sally Ann Thunder Ann Whirlwind" from *American Tall Tales* by Mary Pope Osborne. Text copyright © 1991 by Mary Pope Osborne. Reprinted by permission of Alfred A. Knopf, Inc., a division of Random House, Inc.

"Lazy Peter and His Three-Cornered Hat" from *The Three Wishes: A Collection of Puerto Rican Folktales,* copyright © 1969 by Ricardo E. Alegria. Reprinted by permission of the author.

"M'su Carencro and Mangeur de Poulet" from *Cajun Folktales* by J. J. Reneaux (August House, 1992). Copyright © 1992 by J. J. Reneaux. Reprinted by permission of August House, Inc.

"Talk" from *The Cow-Tail Switch and Other West African Stories* by Harold Courlander and George Herzog, copyright © 1947 by Henry Holt and Company, Inc., © 1975 by Harold Courlander. Reprinted by permission of Henry Holt and Company, Inc.

"The People Could Fly" from *The People Could Fly* by Virginia Hamilton. Text copyright © 1985 by Virginia Hamilton. Reprinted by permission of Alfred A. Knopf, Inc., a division of Random House, Inc.

"The Souls in Purgatory" by Guadalupe Baca-Vaughn. Reprinted by permission of the author.

"Spotted Eagle & Black Crow" from *The Sound of Flutes* by Richard Erdoes. Copyright © 1976 by Richard Erdoes. Reprinted by permission of Pantheon Books, a division of Random House, Inc.

"The Siege of Courthouse Rock" from *American Indian Myths and Legends* by Richard Erdoes and Alfonso Ortiz, editors. Copyright © 1984 by Richard Erdoes and Alfonso Ortiz, editors. Reprinted by permission of Pantheon Books, a division of Random House, Inc.

"Chicoria" from *Cuentos: Tales from the Hispanic Southwest* retold in English by Rudolfo A. Anaya. Copyright © 1980 by The Museum of New Mexico Press. Reprinted by permission of the publisher.

"Coyote and Wasichu" from *American Indian Myths and Legends* by Richard Erdoes and Alfonso Ortiz, editors. Copyright © 1984 by Richard Erdoes and Alfonso Ortiz. Reprinted by permission of Pantheon Books, a division of Random House, Inc.

"Pet survives trip on the wild side: plucky poodle returns alive after dog-napping by coyotes" by Guy Kelly. Reprinted with the permission of the Rocky Mountain News.

Theme 5

"The Drummer Boy of Shiloh" by Ray Bradbury. Reprinted by permission of Don Congdon Associates, Inc. Copyright © 1960 by the Curtis Publishing Co., renewed 1988 by Ray Bradbury.

"Author Says Paul Revere's Midnight Ride Not a Solitary One" Copyright © NPR® 1994. The news report by NPR's Robert Siegel was originally broadcast on National Public Radio's "All Things Considered®" on April 18, 1994, and is used with the permission of National Public Radio, Inc. Any unauthorized duplication is strictly prohibited.

"The Pinta, the Nina, and the Santa Maria and many other cargoes of light" by John Tagliabue, reprinted from *Prairie Schooner* by permission of the University of Nebraska Press. Copyright © 1963 University of Nebraska Press. Copyright © renewed 1991 University of Nebraska Press.

"The Other Pioneers" by Roberto Felix Salazar. *The LULAC National,* July 1939. Reprinted by permission of the League of United Latin American Citizens.

"Traveling the Long Road to Freedom, One Step at a Time" by Donovan Webster, from *Smithsonian* October 1996. Reprinted by permission of the author.

Excerpt from *Harriet Tubman: Conductor on the Underground Railroad* by Ann Petry. Reprinted by permission of Russell & Volkening as agents for the author. Copyright © 1955 by Ann Petry, renewed in 1983 by Ann Petry.

"I Have a Dream" reprinted by arrangement with The Heirs to the Estate of Martin Luther King, Jr., c/o Writers House, Inc. as agent for the proprietor. Copyright © 1968 by the Estate of Martin Luther King.

"Sorrow Home" from *This Is My Century: New and Collected Poems.* Copyright © 1989 by Margaret Walker Alexander. Reprinted by permission of the University of Georgia Press.

"Sit-Ins" from *This Is My Century: New and Collected Poems.* Copyright © 1989 by Margaret Walker Alexander. Reprinted by permission of the University of Georgia Press.

"Almost in America" from *Letters from Rifka* by Karen Hesse, © 1992 by Karen Hesse. Reprinted by permission of Henry Holt and Company, Inc.

Theme 6

"Raymond's Run" from *Gorilla, My Love* by Toni Cade Bambara Copyright © 1970 by Toni Cade Bambara. Reprinted by permission of Random House, Inc.

Excerpt from "Fast Finisher" by Joe Henderson, reprinted by permission of Runner's World Magazine. Copyrighted 1996, Rodale Press, Inc. All rights reserved.

"Forgotten Language" from *Where the Sidewalk Ends* by Shel Silverstein. Copyright © 1974 by Evil Eye Music, Inc. Used by permissions of HarperCollins Publishers.

"New World" copyright © N. Scott Momaday, from *In the Presence of the Sun,* St. Martin's Press, 1992. Reprinted by permission of the author.

"Thank You in Arabic" from *Going Where I'm Coming From.* Copyright © 1995 by Naomi Shihab Nye. Reprinted by permission of the author.

Excerpts from EarthView Survey, Copyright © 1998 National 4-H Council. Reprinted by permission.

"If I Forget Thee, Oh Earth" by Sir Arthur C. Clarke. Reprinted by permission of the author and the author's agents, Scovil Chichak Galen Literary Agency, Inc.

Poem #585 reprinted by permission of the publishers and the trustees of Amherst College from *The Poems of Emily Dickinson,* Thomas H. Johnson, ed., Cambridge, Mass.: The Belknap Press of Harvard University Press, Copyright © 1951, 1955, 1979, 1983 by the President and Fellows of Harvard College.

"Southbound on the Freeway" reprinted with the permission of Simon & Schuster Books for Young Readers, an imprint of Simon & Schuster Children's Publishing Division from *The Complete Poems to Solve* by May Swenson. Copyright © 1993 The Literary Estate of May Swenson. First appeared in the *New Yorker,* 2/16/63.

"Stop the Sun" copyright © 1986 by Gary Paulsen, from *Boys' Life,* January 1986. Reprinted by permission.

"The Summer of Vietnam" copyright © 1992 by Barbara Renaud Gonzalez. First published in *New Chicana/Chicano Writing,* University of Arizona Press. Reprinted by permission of Susan Bergholz Literary Services, New York. All rights reserved.

"Americans All" from *Paper Trail* by Michael Dorris. Copyright © 1994 by Michael Dorris. Reprinted by permission of HarperCollins Publishers, Inc.

Excerpt from "Beckwith Middle School Student Council Constitution" users.massed.net/~kellytp/. Reprinted by permission of the school.

Theme 7

Excerpts from *All But My Life* by Gerda Klein. Copyright © 1957 and copyright renewed 1995 by Gerda Weissmann Klein. Reprinted by permission of Hill & Wang, a division of Farrar, Straus & Giroux, Inc.

Excerpt from *Anne Frank: The Diary of a Young Girl* by Anne Frank. Copyright © 1952 by Otto H. Frank. Used by permission of Doubleday, a division of Bantam Doubleday Dell Publishing Group, Inc., a division of Random House, Inc.

Excerpt from the Anne Frank House Web site (www.annefrank.nl/), reprinted by permission of the Anne Frank Center, New York.

"The Anne Frank House: Amsterdam" by Joan LaBombard from *The Counting of Grains,* 1990, San Diego Poets Press. This poem first appeared in *Yankee* magazine, September 1988. Reprinted by permission of the author.

The Diary of Anne Frank by Frances Goodrich and Albert Hackett. Copyright © 1954, 1956 as an unpublished work. Copyright © 1956 by Albert Hackett, Frances Goodrich Hackett and Otto Frank. Reprinted by permission of Random House, Inc.

Lyric excerpts of "I Think Myself Out." Lyrics by Enid Futterman, Music by Michael Cohen. Copyright © 1985 by Enid Futterman and Michael Cohen. The arrangement copyright © 1996 by Enid Futterman and Michael Cohen. Jem Associates and Williamson Music owners of publication and allied rights throughout the world (all rights administered by Williamson Music). International Copyright Secured. All Rights Reserved. Used by Permission.

Theme 8

"Sorry, Right Number" by Stephen King. Reprinted by permission of Stephen King, c/o Arthur B. Green & Co.

Excerpt from "American Gothic," *ABC Nightline,* December 10, 1997. Special thanks to ABC News Nightline for permission to reprint.

"The Woman in the Snow" from *The Dark Thirty* by Patricia McKissack. Text copyright © 1992 by Patricia McKissack. Reprinted by permission of Alfred A. Knopf, Inc., a division of Random House, Inc.

"The Dinner Party" by Mona Gardner, copyright © 1942, 1970 by *Saturday Review,* reprinted by permission of Bill Berger Associates, Inc.

Excerpt from "The History of the Mystery" MysteryNet.com, copyright © 1996, 1999 Newfront Productions. Reprinted by permission.

Maps

Ortelius Design, Inc.

Photography

Abbreviation key: **AH**=Aaron Haupt; **AR**=Art Resource, New York; **BAL**=Bridgeman Art Library, London/New York; **CB**=Corbis-Bettmann; **CI**=Christie's Images; **FMWPC**= Frank & Marie-Therese Wood Print Collection, Alexandria VA; **LPBC/AH**=book provided by Little Professor Book Company. Photo by AH; **LOC**=Library of Congress; **PR**=Photo Researchers; **SIS**=Stock Illustration Source; **SS**=SuperStock; **TSI**=Tony Stone Images; **TSM**=The Stock Market.

Cover (baseball mitt)Geoff Butler, (painting)*Strike,* 1949. Jacob Lawrence. Tempera on Masonite, 20 x 24 in. The Howard University Gallery of Art, Washington DC; **vii** (t to b)CI, Anna Belle Lee Washington/SS, Daniel Cox/Natural Exposures, CI, AR, NASA, Anne Frank House & Museum, Amsterdam, Christopher Johnson/Stock Boston; **viii** (t)Peter Menzel/MATERIAL WORLD, (b)Amanita Pictures; **ix** SS; **x** Amanita Pictures; **xi** (t, bl)Corbis, (br)China Pictorial Photo Service; **xii** Daniel J. Cox/Natural Exposures; **xiii** Kactus Foto, Santiago, Chile/SS; **xiv** (t)First Image, (b)Movie Still Archives; **xv** Dane Tilghman; **xvi** (l)Amanita Pictures, (r)Private collection/Christian Pierre/SS; **xvii** Jeffrey Hall; **xviii** Dave G. Houser/Corbis; **xix** (t)Francisco Cruz/SS, (b)The Kobal Collection; **xx** Illustrated by Russ Flint; **xxi** (l)courtesy Mystery Writers of America, (r)First Image; **xxii** Illustrated by Gustave Dore; **xxx–1** Peter Menzel/MATERIAL WORLD; **2** Universal Press Syndicate; **3** Amanita Pictures; **4** courtesy Harper Collins Publishers; **5** Lee MARhall/FPG; **7** National Museum of American Art, Washington DC/AR (1967.59.748); **11** Private collection/Gil Mayers/SS; **13** Amanita Pictures; **14** First Image; **15** CI/SS; **17** ©1998 Separate Cinema Archive; **18** Courtesy Karl Jacoby; **19** Courtesy Katie Butler; **20–21** Matt Meadows; **22** (t)Matt Meadows, (b)D.J. Ball/TSI; **23** Alain Evrard/PR; **26** Rob Leri; **27** David and Jeanne Carlson, from *American Scene Painting, California 1930s and 1940s* by R.L. Westphal; **29** Courtesy Allen Say; **31** Doug Martin; **32** David Forbert/SS; **33** The E. Gene Crain Collection; **36** Tom Tracy/TSI; **38** (t)courtesy Random House, (c)Joyce Ravid, (b)Doug Martin; **39** Amanita Pictures, (inset)Doug Martin; **40** First Image; **42** Charles Gupton/Stock Boston; **46** Amanita Pictures; **49** Geoff Butler; **50** (l)courtesy Alma Luz Villanueva, (r)Geoff Butler; **51** Suzanne Murphy/FPG; **53** Private collection/David Nevins/SS; **56** H. Armstrong Roberts; **59** AH; **61** (t)courtesy Carolyn Soto, (b)First Image; **62** Courtesy Yreina D. Cervantez; **66** Courtesy El Museo del Barrio, gift of Joanne Blanco; **68** Amanita

Pictures; **70** (t)AP/Wide World Photo, (b)Amanita Pictures; **71** (t)AH, (b)Matt Meadows; **72** AH; **74** Courtesy El Museo del Barrio, gift of Joann Blanco; **76** Amanita Pictures; **77** Courtesy Virginia Driving Hawk Sneve; **79** Kam Mak/SIS; **80** Doug Martin; **82** CI; **84** AR/Werner Forman Archive/British Museum, London; **85** David Schultz/TSI; **87** Amanita Pictures; **88** From the David T. Vernon Collection of Native American Indian Center, Colter Bay Indian Arts Museum, Grand Teton National Park WY. Photographers John Oldenkamp and Cynthia Sabransky; **95** (t)AH, (b)Geoff Butler; **98–99** SS; **100** Universal Press Syndicate; **101** Matt Meadows; **102** AP/Wide World Photos; **103** CI; **104** Mark Torso; **106** Rob Talbot/TSI; **107** Amanita Pictures; **108** AH; **109** USDA; **110** AH; **112** Courtesy Daniel Keys; **115** Bob Daemmrich/Stock Boston; **116** Movie Still Archives; **119, 121** Archive Photo; **122 through 125** Amanita Pictures; **128** Doug Martin; **129** Amanita Pictures; **131** PhotoFest; **134** Diana Ong/SS; **135** ©Kodansha Ltd. 1986; **139** Collection of Prince Sadruddin Aga Khan, Geneva; **141** Matt Meadows; **145** Les Stone/Sygma; **146–147** AH; **149** Giraudon/AR; **152** Doug Martin; **154** CB; **156** Courtesy Tam Van Tran; **157** Amanita Pictures; **158** AH; **159** Ron Davis/Shooting Star; **160** (t)Schomburg Center for Research in Black Culture, The New York Public Library, Astor, Lenox and Tilden Foundation, (b)Amanita Pictures; **161** Gift of Helen Farr Sloan, ©1998 Board of Trustees, National Gallery of Art, Washington DC; **162** Hampton University Museum, Hampton VA; **164** Amanita Pictures; **166** National Gallery of Art, Washington DC; **168** Courtesy Patricia P. Martin; **169, 170–171** Chuck Place; **172** Photograph: James O. Milmoe. Courtesy The Anschutz Collection; **173** Chuck Place; **174** (t)Chuck Place, (b)Jeffrey Dunn/Stock Boston; **175, 176, 177** Geoff Butler; **180** Judie Burstein/Globe Photos; **181** Anna Belle Lee Washington/SS; **182** Courtesy Loïs Mailou Jones; **184** Archive Photos; **185** (t)W. Cody/Corbis Los Angeles, (b)Amanita Pictures; **186** Keith Turpie; **187–188** CI; **189** Amanita Pictures; **190** William J. Weber; **191** Thomas R. Fletcher/Stock Boston; **192** Amanita Pictures; **193** Lambert/Archive Photos; **197** Geoff Butler; **198** Yoham Kahana/Shooting Star; **199** Courtesy Mary-Anne Martin/Fine Art, New York; **200** Hyacinth Manning-Carner/SS; **202** Amanita Pictures; **203** NY State Historical Association, Cooperstown, photo by Richard Walker; **206** John Kaprielian/PR; **207** Amanita Pictures; **209** Doug Martin; **210** Paul Fetters/Matrix; **212** AP/Wide World Photo; **213** Amanita Pictures; **215** AH; **216** Ganjay M. Marathe/Dinodia Picture Agency; **217** ©1998 Richard Estes/licensed by VAGA, New York, NY/courtesy of the Marlborough Galleries, New York.; **221** First Image; **224** Amanita Pictures; **227** Bob Daemmrich/Stock Boston; **231** (br)Geoff Butler, (others)LPBC/AH; **234–235** Corbis Media; **237** CI/SS; **238** Jim Altobell; **239** Courtesy ACA Galleries, New York and John Dobbs; **243** Bret Wills; **244** Collection Walker Art Center, Minneapolis. Gift of the T. B. Walker Foundation, Gilbert M. Walker Fund, 1948; **246** Gregory Thorp; **247** Glencoe photo; **251** (t)Glencoe photo, (b)Doug Martin; **252** Photo courtesy the Archives of the American Illustrators Gallery, New York. ©by Asap of Holderness NH 03245 USA; **254** Museum of the City of New York; **256** Photo courtesy the Archives of the American Illustrators Gallery, New York. ©by Asap of Holderness NH 03245 USA; **257** National Baseball Library, Cooperstown NY; **258** Glencoe photo; **259** Asian Art Museum of San Francisco, The Avery Brundage Collection (B76 D3); **261** ©The British Art Museum; **264** Doug Martin; **266** Photofest; **268** Courtesy of Chu-tsing Li; **269** Daniel J. Cox/Natural Exposures; **270** By courtesy of The Board of Trustees of The Victoria & Albert Museum, London/BAL/SS; **273** Dallas Museum of Art, Foundation for the Arts Collection, gift of James H. and Lillian Clark Foundation. Mondrian/Holtzman Trust; **276** CI; **277** China Pictorial Photo Service; **281** (l)Beth Bergman, (r)AH; **282** AH; **285** *Aunt Fanny*, 1920. George Wesley Bellows. Oil on canvas, 44 1/4 x 34 1/4in. Des Moines Art Center Permanent Collections; Purchased with funds fromthe Edmundson Art Foundation, Inc., 1942.1. Photo credit: Michael Tropea, Chicago; **286** Doug Martin; **288** SIS; **291** Doug Martin; **292** Stephen Rose/TSI; **295** First Image; **297** Geoff Butler; **298** (t)Barbara Savage Cheresh, (b)CI; **299** Amanita Pictures; **300** Doug Martin; **301** First Image; **302** (t)CB, (b)Alden Blackington, courtesy Dartmouth College Library; **303** Flint Institute of Arts. Gift of the Viola E. Bray Charitable Trust (67.29); **304–305** CI; **306** Doug Martin; **307** A & F Michler/Peter Arnold, Inc.; **309** CB; **310, 311, 312** CI; **316** (t)Clem Spalding, (bl)Paul Thompson/FPG, (br)Ed Frascino, courtesy University Press of New England; **317** SS; **318** Jack Novak/SS; **320** Roger K. Burnard; **323** Rudi VonBriel; **325** Bob Daemmrich/Stock Boston; **329** (br)Geoff Butler, (others) LPBC/AH; **332** Kactus Foto, Santiago, Chile/SS; **334** Universal Press Syndicate; **335** First Image; **336** Universal Press Syndicate; **337** CB; **338–339** AH; **340** CI; **347** Geoff Butler; **348** Everett Collection; **350** (l)CB, (r)Amanita Pictures; **351** Matt Meadows; **353** From *The Legend of John Henry* by Terry Small. Copyright ©1994 by Terry Small. Used by permission of Bantam Doubleday Dell Books for Young Readers; **357** Doug Martin; **359** Geoff Butler; **360** Paul Conklin; **365** Michael McCurdy, courtesy Alfred A. Knopf; **366–367** S. Michael Bisceglie/Animals Animals; **370** Glencoe photo; **371** AH; **374** Collection of Ileana Font, Mirama, Puerto Rico; **375** Amanita Pictures; **377** Courtesy J.J. Reneaux; **378** Courtesy Saulo Moreno; **380** Roger K. Burnard; **382** (t)Herbert Cohen, (b)courtesy IN University; **383** Photo: Claude Postel/©C.A.A.C.–The Pigozzi Collection, Geneva; **384** AH; **385** Geoff Butler; **386** Saulo Moreno; **388** (t)Ron Rovtar, (b)Photo by Earlie Hudnell, Jr./Artcetera; **389** Courtesy Leo & Diana Dillon; **391** Photo courtesy the Wyeth Collection; **394** Chase Swift/Corbis Los Angeles; **397** CB; **398** (l)courtesy Carlos G. Vaughn, (r)Richard B. Levine; **399** CI; **400** Chuck Place; **401** AH; **402** Instituto Nacional de Bellas Artes Direccion de Asuntos Juridicon; **404** Nicolas Sapieha/AR; **407** Photo by Christopher G. Knight; **408** Richard Erdoes; **409** Courtesy Jerry Ingram; **411** Mark Newman/SS; **413** CI; **414** (t)Natural History Museum, Smithsonian Institution, (b)Grant Heilman; **416** University of NE Lincoln, Christlieb Collection. Photograph by Roger Bruhn; **418** (t)Glencoe photo, (bl)Glencoe photo, (br)courtesy Mindy Dwyer; **419** Museum of TX Tech University, Lubbock TX; **421** Courtesy the San Antonio Museum of Art; **422** AH; **423** Movie Still Archive; **430** (br)Geoff Butler, (others)LPBC/AH; **434–435** Dane Tilghman; **436** Universal Press Syndicate; **438** Ralph Merlino/Shooting Star; **439** LOC; **441** Larry Sherer/High Impact; **442–443** First Image; **444** NY Historical Society; **448** (t)CB, (b)Museum of Fine Art, Boston. Gift by subscription and Francis Bartlett Fund.; **449** Arthur Hoppock Hearn Fund, 1950, The Metropolitan Museum of Art, New York (50.117); **452** SS; **454** Doug Martin; **455** Tom Brass/Stock Boston; **458** FPG; **459** Photo by Thomas Kosa; **460–461** Larry Sherer/High Impact; **463** FMWPC; **466** (t)Phyllis Graber Jensen, (b)Photo by Frank Lerner, ©1975 Time-Life Books. Courtesy The Showers-Brown Collection, The Star of The Republic Museum TX; **467** National Maritime Museum; **468** The Nelson-Atkins Museum of Art, Kansas City MO. Gift of Mr. and Mrs. Robert B. Fizzell through the Friends of Art; **470** Panhandle-Plains Historical Museum; **472** (t)LOC, (c)David Noble/FPG, (b)FPG; **473** Amanita Pictures; **474** Collection of Mr. & Mrs. Robert L. Sharpe; **475** AR; **476** Lance Nelson/TSM; **478** Wayne Sorce; **479** (l)AP/Wide World Photos, (r)Amanita Pictures; **480** National Museum of American Art, Washington DC/AR; **482** CB; **487** National Portrait Gallery, Smithsonian Institution/AR; **488** National Museum of American Art, Washington DC/AR; **492** (l)Corbis, (r)courtesy Frances Foster, (border)AH; **493** (l)Bob Adelman/Magnum Photos, (r)Corbis; **494** *The King Mural* by Don Miller ©District of Columbia Public Library; **497** FPG; **499** FMWPC; **500** AH; **503** (t)Nancy Crampton, (b)UPI/CB; **504** Grant Heilman; **505** AP/Wide World Photos; **506** Matt Meadows; **508** National Archives; **509** Geoff Butler; **510** (l)Adams County Historical Society, Gettysburg, Pennsylvania; (r)LOC; **511** LOC; **512** US Army Military Historical Institute; **515** National Archives (#111-B-357); **516** AH; **520** From the original painting by Mort Kunstler, *The Gettysburg Address* ©1987 Mort Kunstler, Inc.; **523** Randy O'Rouke/TSM; **526** (l)courtesy Scholastic, Inc., (r)Amanita Pictures; **527** Tim Courlas; **528** North Wind Picture Archives; **531** LOC; **532** Amanita Pictures; **535** Photography Collection, Miriam and Ira D. Wallach Division of Art, Prints and Photographs, The New York Public Library.

Editing/Proofreading Checklist

Use this proofreading checklist to help you check for errors in your writing, and use the proofreading symbols in the chart below to mark places that need corrections.

- ☑ Have I avoided run-on sentences and sentence fragments and punctuated sentences correctly?
- ☑ Have I used every word correctly, including plurals, possessives, and frequently confused words?
- ☑ Do verbs and subjects agree? Are verb tenses correct?
- ☑ Do pronouns refer clearly to their antecedents and agree with them in person, number, and gender?
- ☑ Have I used adverb and adjective forms and modifying phrases correctly?
- ☑ Have I spelled every word correctly and checked the unfamiliar ones in a dictionary?

Proofreading Symbols		
⊙	Lieut Brown	Insert a period.
∧	No one came the party.	Insert a letter or a word.
≡	I enjoyed paris.	Capitalize a letter.
/	The Class ran a bake sale.	Make a capital letter lowercase.
⁀ ‿	The campers are home sick.	Close up a space.
(sp)	They visited N.Y.	Spell out.
∧ ∧;	Sue please come I need your help.	Insert a comma or a semicolon.
∿	He enjoyed feild day.	Transpose the position of letters or words.
#	alltogether	Insert a space.
ℊ	We went to to Boston.	Delete letters or words.
∨ ∨ ∨	She asked, Whos coming?	Insert quotation marks or an apostrophe.
/ = /	mid January	Insert a hyphen.
¶	"Where?" asked Karl. "Over there," said Ray.	Begin a new paragraph.

Concordia University
Library Technology Center
275 Syndicate Street North
St. Paul, MN 55104